CONTINUUM ENCYCLOPEDIA OF
POPULAR MUSIC
OF THE WORLD

VOLUME I:
MEDIA, INDUSTRY AND SOCIETY

Editorial Board

www.continuumpopmusic.com

CONTINUUM ENCYCLOPEDIA OF
POPULAR MUSIC
OF THE WORLD

VOLUME I:
MEDIA, INDUSTRY AND SOCIETY

EDITED BY
JOHN SHEPHERD, DAVID HORN,
DAVE LAING, PAUL OLIVER AND PETER WICKE

continuum
LONDON • NEW YORK

First published 2003 by
Continuum
The Tower Building, 11 York Road, London SE1 7NX
370 Lexington Avenue, New York, NY 10017–6503

British Library Cataloguing-in-Publication Data
A catalogue record for this book is available from the
British Library
ISBN 0–8264–6321 5

Typeset by Wyvern 21 Ltd, Bristol
Printed and bound in Great Britain by Bath Press Ltd, Bath

Contents

Introduction

The *Continuum Encyclopedia of Popular Music of the World* had its genesis in the International Association for the Study of Popular Music (IASPM) in the mid-1980s.

IASPM was established in the early 1980s as a response to the increasing number of scholars publishing in the field of popular music. These scholars needed an organization through which to share and comment on their work, through which to advocate the legitimacy and desirability of work on popular music, and through which to advocate the inclusion of popular music studies in the academy.

Early in the life of IASPM, there was a recognition of the need for a comprehensive and reliable reference work on popular music that would serve the needs of scholars, researchers, students, and information and media professionals, as well as the general public.

The *Continuum Encyclopedia of Popular Music of the World* was planned as a response to that need. The first volume to be produced from the *Encyclopedia* project was *Popular Music Studies: A Select International Bibliography*, published in 1997.

The title of this, the first volume of the *Encyclopedia* proper, is *Media, Industry and Society*. It will be followed by volumes on Performance and Production, Locations, Genres and Personalities.

Because no model existed for this kind of comprehensive, scholarly reference work on popular music, extensive research was undertaken to develop a systematic, subject-based taxonomy for such a new field of study. It is for this reason that, rather than alphabetically, the entries in these volumes are organized in terms of sections and subsections that reflect the logic of this taxonomy. Subject areas that, in an alphabetical sequence, would have been scattered arbitrarily throughout the volumes are in this way brought together and organized

coherently to constitute an unprecedented body of knowledge. Because the volumes are organized in this way, it is important for the reader to consult both the Table of Contents and the pages setting out the Arrangement of the Material at the beginning of each volume. However, each volume has its own index that makes it easy to locate discussions of specific terms within a range of entries.

It is in part the subject-based character of these volumes that makes them distinctive among popular music reference works. The scholarly character of these volumes is apparent also in the comprehensive end matter that is provided for most entries: bibliographies, discographies, sheet music listings, filmographies, and listings of visual recordings. The volumes draw on the expertise of the world's leading popular music scholars, and are additionally distinctive in covering the popular music of the whole world rather than specific regions of it.

This volume contains two major sections of the *Continuum Encyclopedia of Popular Music of the World*: 'Social and Cultural Dimensions' and 'The Industry.' The section on 'Social and Cultural Dimensions' contains many entries on social phenomena of relevance to the practise of popular music: entries such as Class, Deviance, Fashion, Gender and Sexuality, Love and Courtship, Politics, Religion and Spirituality, and Youth. Additionally, 'Social and Cultural Dimensions' includes entries on three other sets of phenomena that provide contexts for the practise and use of popular music: institutions and practises that document popular music; the study of popular music; and stylistic and textual practises that are not themselves musical in character. The section on 'Social and Cultural Dimensions' thus contains subsections on 'Documentation,' 'Popular Music Studies' and 'Stylistic and Textual Dimensions,' together with the subsections on 'Social Phenomena' and 'Venues.' The subsection on 'Popular Music Studies' contains entries on academic disciplines and intellectual trajectories (for example, poststructuralism) that have contributed to research and publications on popular music. The aim has been to give an account of and assess not only the contribution of the particular discipline or intellectual trajectory to the study of popular music, but also the way in which the discipline or intellectual trajectory has itself been affected by popular music studies.

One observation needs to be made on the section on 'The Industry.' This section contains numerous entries on recording studios and record labels, many of which are of historical importance. For reasons of historical documentation, the sheet music listings, discographical references and discographies for these entries contain the first publication details of songs and recordings. However, to assist readers in hearing this music where possible, reference is also frequently made to reissues of older recordings on compact disc. The reissues listed are those that were available at the time the entry was signed off for publication. The period during which entries for this volume were signed off stretched from August 1997 to November 2001. Reissues listed in the discographical references and discographies of these entries may as a consequence no longer be available. However, the likelihood is that these particular recordings have been reissued elsewhere since that time. This principle regarding the listing of reissues is one that extends to many other entries in the volume.

The distinction between discographical references and discographies is an important one. If a particular piece of music is referred to in an entry, there will also be a reference to it in the entry's end matter, either in the sheet music listing or in the discographical references (and sometimes both). Discographies, on the other hand, provide a list of representative recordings of relevance to the entry in general. It must be stressed that these discographies are solely representative, and are not intended to be comprehensive. A distinction is drawn in discographical references and discographies between dates of recording and dates of issue where these differ. Dates of recording are in roman type; dates of issue are italicized.

Details of all films and visual recordings (videos) referred to in an entry are provided in a filmography or visual recordings listing at the end of the entry. Items in filmographies contain references to those responsible for the films' music.

The definition of popular music is an issue that continues to be debated and is of clear importance to the scope of these volumes. The Editorial Board has resisted the temptation to offer a precise definition of the term 'popular music' in its instructions to contributors, recognizing that the terms 'popular,' 'classical' and 'folk' are discursive in character, and changing products of historical, social, political and cultural forces rather than terms that designate easily distinguishable musics. The question of where 'the popular' ends and 'the folk' begins has proved particularly difficult. The advice given to contributors has been that music created and disseminated in rural situations in an exclusively oral-aural fashion with little currency outside its location of origin does *not* constitute a prime focus for these volumes. However, it does not follow from this that such music should not be discussed if it is commonly accepted as 'popular,' or if it forms an important source for later styles or genres commonly accepted as 'popular.' While the principal emphasis of the *Encyclopedia* is on the urban, the commodified and the mass disseminated rather than on the rural, the oral-aural and the restrictedly local, therefore, this emphasis is far from exclusive. The principal test for including music as 'popular' has been whether it has been so regarded by communities of practitioners or users. The tendency has therefore been to be inclusive rather than exclusive. As a consequence, 'classical' music is included if its use has been popular in character.

The *Encyclopedia* will be global in scope. However, it is important to emphasize that this volume on its own is not comprehensively global, although the intention of the Editorial Board has been to include internationally important material on a world basis. Information relating to the music industries and social and cultural dimensions that is, by contrast, of purely or mainly national, regional or local importance will be included in subsequent volumes on Locations, whose coverage is, indeed, comprehensively global.

Ottawa, Canada
March 2002

Acknowledgments

The Editorial Board's first debt of gratitude is to Philip Tagg, Reader in Music in the Institute of Popular Music at the University of Liverpool, who, over a two-year period in the early 1990s, developed a detailed taxonomy of popular music, its practise and its study. This taxonomy served as a basic model for developing the structure of the *Encyclopedia* as well as its major sections and headword lists. Thanks are also due to the University of Göteborg (Sweden) for agreeing to second Philip from its Department of Musicology to the Institute of Popular Music at the University of Liverpool during the first of these two years.

A special word of thanks is due to Alyn Shipton, whose vision and dedication in the formative period of the *Encyclopedia* were vital to the development and long-term viability of an ambitious publishing project.

Thanks are also due to the University of Liverpool, the University of Exeter, the University of Göteborg (Sweden), and especially Carleton University (Ottawa), all of which have made significant financial contributions, as well as contributions in kind, in support of this project. In this context, special thanks go to Professor Graeme Davis, Vice-Chancellor of the University of Liverpool when the project began; Dr. John ApSimon, Dean of Graduate Studies and Research (1991–96) and subsequently Acting Vice-President (Academic) (1996–97) and Vice-President (Research and External) (1997–2000), Carleton University; Professor Janice Yalden, Dean of Arts (1988–92), Carleton University; Dr. Stuart Adam, Dean of Arts (1992–97) and subsequently Vice-President (Academic) and Provost, Carleton University; Dr. Roger Blockley, Dean of Graduate Studies and Research, Carleton University; Dr. Aviva Freedman, Dean of Arts and Social Sciences, Carleton University; and Dr. Feridun Hamdullahpur, Vice-President (Research), Carleton University. In addition, thanks are due to Ocean Group, plc, to BMI and to the British Academy for their financial assistance in the earlier stages of the project's development at the University of Liverpool.

So many individuals have made important contributions to the development of the *Encyclopedia* since work on it began 12 years ago. Regrettably, it is impossible to mention them all. However, the Editorial Board is especially grateful to Carole Pegg, who at Exeter conducted an important initial study on the feasibility of developing an encyclopedia on world popular music; and to Jean-Pierre Sévigny at Carleton for his extensive work on the *Encyclopedia*'s headword lists and lists of contributors. The Editorial Board is grateful also to Mick Gidley at the University of Exeter and to Paul Wells, Director of the Center for Popular Music at Middle Tennessee State University, both of whom contributed significantly to the early development of the *Encyclopedia*; to Paul Hansen, who lent administrative assistance to the project at the University of Liverpool; to Andy Linehan, Curator of Popular Music, British Library National Sound Archive, for his invaluable assistance with discographical information; and to Steve Cork at the British Library for his enormous help with sheet music information. Thanks are also due to Mona-Lynn Courteau, Janet Hilts, Megan Jerome and Sundar Subramanian, senior students in Carleton's B.Mus. program, and Joy Gugelar, a master's student in Carleton's School of Journalism and Communication, for their excellent work as research assistants. Many of the contributors to this volume of the *Encyclopedia* also often gave willingly of their time and expertise in addition to writing their entries, and the Editorial Board would like to extend thanks to them.

The Editorial Board wishes to thank Janet Joyce and

Veronica Higgs at the Continuum International Publishing Group in London for their unwavering support through the long and sometimes difficult process that led to the completion of this volume of the *Encyclopedia*. Veronica's expertise and calm guidance have been very much appreciated by both the Editorial Board and the editorial team at Carleton. Without Janet's conviction and determination, this project would never have come to fruition.

Finally, the Editorial Board wishes to place on record its sincere appreciation for the work undertaken at Carleton University by the editorial team: Jennifer Wilson (chief editor), Jennie Strickland (project manager), Jennifer Rae-Brown, Karen Barber, Janet Shorten and Emily Wilson. Very special thanks are due to Jennifer Wilson, who has been with the project since 1996. The very high editorial standards evidenced in the entries that follow are due entirely to her professionalism, patience and total commitment to the project, as well as to her wonderful ability to lead the work of her colleagues.

List of Contributors

Charles R. Acland is Assistant Professor, Department of Communication Studies, Concordia University, Canada.

Francesco Adinolfi is senior editor at *Il manifesto*, Italy.

Rob Allingham is Archive Manager for Gallo Africa (Ltd.), South Africa.

Gwen Ansell is Executive Director of the Institute for the Advancement of Journalism, Johannesburg, South Africa.

Julio Arce teaches in the Department of Art (III), Faculty of Geography and History, Complutense University of Madrid, Spain.

Chris Atton is Lecturer in Journalism and Media, Napier University, Edinburgh.

Dagfinn Bach coordinates contacts among arts organizations within Artspages International AS in Norway.

William Barlow is Professor of Radio, Television and Film, School of Communications, Howard University, Washington, DC.

Stephen Barnard is a freelance writer based in Hatfield, UK.

Giusy Basile teaches cinematographic studies at the University of Lille 3, France.

Vanessa Bastian is a music industry researcher and analyst based in London.

Ian Biddle is Lecturer, Department of Music, University of Newcastle Upon Tyne, UK.

John Borwick is an audio writer and consultant in the United Kingdom.

Anna Botelho lives in Niteroi, RJ, Brazil.

Rob Bowman is Associate Professor, Department of Music, York University, Canada.

David Brackett is Assistant Professor of Music, State University of New York at Binghamton.

Barbara Bradby is Senior Lecturer in Sociology, Trinity College, Dublin, Ireland.

Mike Brocken is a broadcaster for the BBC and managing director of Mayfield Records, UK.

David Buckley works as a freelance writer in Munich, Germany.

Robert Burnett is Professor of Media and Communication, Karlstad University, Sweden.

Isabelle Canno lives and writes in Paris.

Jon Caramanica is a writer living in New York.

Michael Chanan is Principal Lecturer, Cultural and Media Studies, University of the West of England.

Robert Clarida is a partner at the New York law firm of Cowan, Liebowitz & Latman, P.C.

Martin Cloonan is Senior Lecturer in Adult Education, University of Glasgow.

Sara Cohen is Senior Lecturer, Institute of Popular Music, University of Liverpool.

John Collins is Associate Professor of Music, School of Performing Arts, University of Ghana.

Susan C. Cook is Professor of Music and Women's Studies, University of Wisconsin-Madison.

Alfredo Cruz is a veteran jazz broadcaster and public radio producer in Long Beach, California.

Don Cusic is Professor of Music Business, Belmont University, Nashville, Tennessee.

Jim Dawson is a writer in Hollywood.

Tia DeNora is Reader in Sociology, University of Exeter.

Veit Erlmann is Professor of Ethnomusicology and Anthropology, University of Texas at Austin.

Graeme Ewens is a freelance journalist and editor living in London.

Franco Fabbri is a musician and musicologist working for RAI-Radio Tre, Italy.

Jerry Fabris is Curator of Sound Recordings at Edison National Historic Site, West Orange, New Jersey.

Jan Fairley is a Fellow, Institute of Popular Music, University of Liverpool.

Colin Fallows is Professor of Sound and Visual Arts, John Moores University, Liverpool.

Kai Fikentscher is Professor of Music, School of Contemporary Arts, Ramapo College of New Jersey.

Jon Fitzgerald is Associate Professor of Popular Music Theory and History, Contemporary Music Program, Southern Cross University, Lismore, Australia.

Jay Flemma is an associate at the New York law firm of Ronald S. Bienstock & Associates, P.C.

Ken Garner is Senior Lecturer in Media and Journalism, Glasgow Caledonian University.

Reebee Garofalo is Professor of American Studies, College of Public and Community Service, University of Massachusetts at Boston.

Peter Goddard researches media history and institutions at the University of Liverpool.

Juan Pablo González is Professor of Music, Music Institute of the Pontificia Universidad Católica de Chile, Chile.

Lucy Green is Reader, Institute of Education, University of London.

Steve Greenfield is a senior academic, Centre for the Study of Law, Society and Popular Culture, University of Westminster, London.

Günter Gretz is a collector and producer of African music living in Germany.

Pekka Gronow is manager of radio archives with the Finnish Broadcasting Company.

Gestur Guðmundsson researches youth culture, rock, and the sociology of education and work in Denmark.

Donna Halper teaches journalism, media history and media criticism at Emerson College, Boston.

Flemming Harrev is a freelance journalist working in Denmark.

David Harris is owner and chief engineer of Studio B Mastering in Charlotte, North Carolina.

David Hesmondhalgh is Lecturer in Sociology, Faculty of Social Sciences, the Open University, UK.

Markus Heuger is Head of Studio, Akustische Kunst, Westdeutscher Rundfunk, Köln, Germany.

Janet Hilts is a senior student in the B.Mus. program, Carleton University, Canada.

Ken Hirschkop is Senior Lecturer in English, University of Manchester.

David Horn is Director, Institute of Popular Music, University of Liverpool.

Shuhei Hosokawa is Associate Professor of Humanities and Social Sciences, Tokyo Institute of Technology.

Bruce Johnson is Associate Professor of English, University of New South Wales, Australia.

Mike Jones is Course Director for the University of Liverpool's MBA (Music Industries) degree.

Steve Jones is Professor of Communication, University of Illinois at Chicago.

Olivier Julien is chargé de cours and researcher (with l'Observatoire Musical Français), Department of Musicology, University of Paris-Sorbonne.

Isaac Kalumbu is Assistant Professor of Ethnomusicology, School of Music, Michigan State University.

Keir Keightley is Assistant Professor, Faculty of Information and Media Studies, University of Western Ontario, Canada.

M. William Krasilovsky is an attorney specializing in music copyright in New York.

Holly Kruse is Visiting Assistant Professor, Department of Communication, University of Tulsa.

Dave Laing is Reader, Centre for Communication and Information Studies, School of Communication and Creative Industries, University of Westminster, London.

Marion Leonard is Lecturer, Institute of Popular Music, University of Liverpool.

Claire Levy is Associate Professor of Musicology, Institute of Art Studies, Bulgarian Academy of Sciences.

Andrew Leyshon is Professor of Economic and Social Geography, University of Nottingham.

Ulf Lindberg is Lecturer in Swedish, Department of Scandinavian Studies, University of Aarhus, Denmark.

Andrew Linehan is Curator of Popular Music, British Library National Sound Archive.

Brian Longhurst is Professor of Sociology, University of Salford, UK.

Karen Lury is Lecturer, Department of Theatre, Film and Television Studies, University of Glasgow.

Tara McCall has an M.A. in Communications from McGill University, Canada.

Tom McCourt is Assistant Professor of Communication, University of Illinois at Springfield.

Peter McLuskie is a freelance lecturer and Education and Training Coordinator, Light House Media Centre, Wolverhampton, UK.

Stephen Mamula is a Ph.D. candidate in ethnomusicology at Columbia University, New York.

Peter Manuel is Professor of Ethnomusicology, CUNY Graduate Center and John Jay College, New York.

Robert J. Marlowe is a writer and record collector based in New York.

Kathryn Marsh is Lecturer in Music Education, Sydney Conservatorium of Music, University of Sydney, Australia.

Peter Martin is Dean of Undergraduate Studies, Faculty of Social Sciences and Law, University of Manchester.

Portia K. Maultsby is Professor of Ethnomusicology, Indiana University at Bloomington.

Louise Meintjes is Assistant Professor, Departments of Music and Cultural Anthropology, Duke University, North Carolina.

Morten Michelsen is Assistant Professor, Department of Musicology, University of Copenhagen, Denmark.

Richard Middleton is Professor of Music, University of Newcastle Upon Tyne, UK.

Andre Millard is Professor of History and Director of American Studies, University of Alabama at Birmingham.

Takuo Morikawa is a member of the Japanese Association for the Study of Popular Music.

Christian Mörken is A&R/Marketing Manager for OK Visions Entertainment/TRU NOTE Records, Germany.

Mark Anthony Neal is Assistant Professor of English, State University of New York at Albany.

Keith Negus is Senior Lecturer, Department of Media and Communications, Goldsmiths College, University of London.

Paul Oliver is Director of the International Centre for Vernacular Architecture, Oxford Brookes University.

Aleš Opekar is head of the Jazz and Popular Music Department, Czech Radio 3 – Vltava, Czech Republic.

Guy Osborn is Senior Lecturer in Law and Co-Director of the Centre for the Study of Law, Society and Popular Culture, University of Westminster, London.

Berndt Ostendorf is Professor of American Cultural History, Amerika Institut, Ludwig Maximilian Universität, Munich, Germany.

Cilene Peres is founding owner of the Mix House label, Brazil.

Richard Peterson is Professor of Sociology, Vanderbilt University, Nashville, Tennessee.

Aymeric Pichevin is a music journalist living in Paris.

Paolo Prato is Program Director of Blu Sat 2000, the satellite radio of the Italian Episcopal Conference, Rome, Italy.

Robert Pruter is Government Documents Librarian, Lewis University, Romeoville, Illinois.

Corey D. Ramey is the owner of CD-RAMEY.com and lives in Tennessee.

Motti Regev is Senior Lecturer, Department of Sociology, Political Science and Communication, The Open University of Israel.

Suzel Ana Reily is Senior Lecturer, School of Anthropological Studies, Queen's University, Belfast, Northern Ireland.

Eric W. Rothenbuhler is Director of Graduate Media Studies, New School University, New York.

Catherine Rudent teaches musicology at the University of Paris IV-Sorbonne.

John W. Rumble is Historian, Country Music Hall of Fame, Nashville, Tennessee.

Tony Russell is a music historian living in London.

Paul Rutten is Professor of Cultural Industries, Arts and History Faculty, Erasmus University, Rotterdam, The Netherlands.

Jennifer Rycenga is Associate Professor of Comparative Religious Studies, San José State University, San José, California.

Howard Rye is an independent scholar based in London.

David Sanjek is Director, BMI Archives, New York.

David Schwarz is an adjunct in the Media Studies Faculty, New School University, New York.

T.M. Scruggs is Assistant Professor of Ethnomusicology, University of Iowa.

John Shepherd is Professor of Music and Sociology, Carleton University, Canada.

Alyn Shipton is a freelance writer and broadcaster living in Oxford.

Roy Shuker is Associate Professor and Media Studies Program Coordinator, School of English and Media Studies, Massey University, New Zealand.

Mark Slobin is Professor of Music, Wesleyan University, Connecticut.

Jeff Smith is Assistant Professor, Film and Media Studies Program, Washington University, St. Louis, Missouri.

Warrick Sony is manager and co-owner of Shifty Studio, Cape Town, South Africa.

Alan Stanbridge is Assistant Professor of Visual and Performing Arts, University of Toronto, Canada.

Chris Stapleton is a journalist working in London.

Martin Stokes is Associate Professor of Music, University of Chicago.

Robert Strachan is Visiting Lecturer, Institute of Popular Music, University of Liverpool.

Will Straw is Associate Professor, Department of Art History and Communications Studies, McGill University, Montréal, Canada.

John Street is Reader in Politics, University of East Anglia, UK.

Tamás Szőnyei is a journalist and an editor at *Magyar Narancs*, Budapest, Hungary.

Joseph Tarsia is the Founder and Principal, Sigma Sound Studios, Philadelphia.

Paul Théberge holds the Canada Research Chair in Music, Carleton University, Canada.

Jeff Todd Titon is Professor of Music and Director of the Ph.D. Program in Ethnomusicology, Brown University, Providence, Rhode Island.

Jason Toynbee is Senior Lecturer in Communication, Culture and Media, Coventry University, UK.

Martha Tupinambá de Ulhôa is Professor of Musicology, Universidade do Rio de Janeiro, Brazil.

Peter Wade is Professor of Social Anthropology, University of Manchester.

Deena Weinstein is Professor of Sociology, DePaul University, Chicago.

Hans Weisethaunet is Associate Professor of Ethnomusicology, University of Bergen, Norway.

Paul F. Wells is Director of the Center for Popular Music and Associate Professor of Music, Middle Tennessee State University.

Cliff White is a freelance journalist working in London.

Peter Wicke is Director of the Center for Popular Music Research, The Humboldt University, Berlin, Germany.

Ralph W. Willett is Senior Fellow, University of Hull, UK.

Robert Witmer is Associate Professor of Music, York University, Canada.

Masahiro Yasuda is a Ph.D. candidate with the Centre for Mass Communication Research, Leicester University, UK.

José Roberto Zan teaches Sociology of Culture and Art at the Institute of Arts, University of Campinas, São Paulo, Brazil.

Abbreviations

A&R	artist and repertoire
AACM	Association for the Advancement of Creative Musicians
ABA	American Bandmasters Association
ABC	American Broadcasting Company
ABC	Audit Bureau of Circulations (UK)
ABC	Australian Broadcasting Corporation
ACB	Association of Concert Bands
ACTRA	Alliance of Canadian Cinema, Television and Radio Artists
A/D	analog/digital
ADAMI	Société civile pour l'administration des droits des artists et musiciens interprètes
ADC	analog-to-digital converter
ADR	alternative dispute resolution
ADT	artificial double tracking
AES	Audio Engineering Society
AFM	American Federation of Musicians
AFN	American Forces Network
AFRS	Armed Forces Radio Service
AFRTS	Armed Forces Radio and Television Service
AFTRA	American Federation of Television and Radio Artists
AGVA	American Guild of Variety Artists
AIR	All India Radio
AKM	Staatlich Genehmigte Gesellschaft der Autoren, Komponisten und Musikverlager (Austria)
AM	amplitude modulation
AMC	American Music Conference
amp	amplifier
AOL	America Online
AOR	album-oriented rock
APRA	Australian Performing Right Association
ARC	American Record Company
ARIA	Australian Record Industry Association

ARSC	Association for Recorded Sound Collections
ARTISJUS	Bureau Hongrois pour la Protection des Droits d'Auteur
ASBDA	American School Band Directors Association
ASCAP	American Society of Composers, Authors and Publishers
AT&T	American Telephone and Telegraph Company
ATBB	alto, tenor, bass, bass
ATV	Associated Television Ltd.
AV	audiovisual
BAPMAF	Bokoor African Popular Music Archives Foundation
BARD	British Association of Record Dealers
BASBWE	British Association of Symphonic Bands and Wind Ensembles
BBC	British Broadcasting Corporation
BDS	Broadcast Data Systems
BECTU	Broadcasting, Entertainment, Cinematograph and Theatre Union (UK)
BESLA	Black Entertainment and Sports Lawyers Association
BET	Black Entertainment Television
BIB	Board for International Broadcasting
BID	Berlin Independents Days
BIEM	International Bureau of Societies Administering the Rights of Mechanical Recording and Reproduction [Bureau International des Sociétés gerant les Droits d'Enregistrement et de Reproduction Mécanique]
BIPE	Bureau d'aide à l'Insertion Professionnelle des Étudiants
BMG	Bertelsmann Music Group/Bertelsmann Musik Gesellschaft
BMI	Broadcast Music Inc.
BMRB	British Market Research Bureau
BPI	British Phonographic Industry
BPM	beats per minute
BUMA	Het Bureau voor Muziek-Auteursrecht (The Netherlands)
BVMG	Buena Vista Music Group
CAA	Creative Artists' Association
CASH	Composers and Authors Society of Hong Kong
CB	citizens' band
CBC	Canadian Broadcasting Corporation
CBDNA	College Band Directors National Association
CBS	Columbia Broadcasting System
CCM	Contemporary Christian music
CD	compact disc
CDC	Carnival Development Committee (Trinidad and Tobago)
CD-R	CD-Recordable
CD-ROM	compact disc read-only memory
CEA	Centre Européen d'Achats
CEDDI	Centre Européen de Distribution International
CEO	chief executive officer
CHA	Copyright Holders' Association (Chinese Taipei)
CHR	Contemporary Hit Radio
CIA	Central Intelligence Agency
CIEM	Confédération Internationale des Editeurs de Musique
CIMI	Comité International pour la Musique Instrumentale

CINARS	Commerce international des arts de la scène/International Exchange for the Performing Arts
CIRPA	Canadian Independent Record Production Association
CISAC	Confédération Internationale des Sociétés d'Auteurs et Compositeurs
CMA	Chinese Musicians' Association
CMA	Country Music Association
CMEA	Council for Mutual Economic Assistance
CMF	Country Music Foundation
CND	Campaign for Nuclear Disarmament
COMPASS	Composers and Authors Society of Singapore
CPA	Concert Promoters Association (UK)
CPU	central processing unit
D/A	digital/analog
DAB	digital audio broadcasting
DAC	digital-to-analog converter
DAT	digital audio tape
dB	decibel
DCC	digital compact cassette
demo	demonstration
DEMS	Development Education Media Services Foundation (the Philippines)
DGG	Deutsche Grammophon Gesellschaft
DIN	Deutsche Industrie Normen
DJ	disc jockey
DLT	digital linear tape
DSP	digital signal processing
DTP	desktop publishing
DVD	digital versatile disc/digital video disc
ECAD	Escritório Central de Arrecadação e Distribuição
EMI	Electric and Musical Industries Ltd.
EP	extended play
EPROM	electrically programmable read-only memory
EQ	equalizer
FACTOR	Foundation to Assist Canadian Talent on Records
FBI	Federal Bureau of Investigation
FCC	Federal Communications Commission (US)
FEN	Far East Network
FFRR	full frequency range recording
FIA	International Federation of Actors
FIM	International Federation of Musicians
FLADEM	Federation of Latin American Publishers
FM	frequency modulation
fps	frames per second
FRC	Federal Radio Commission
FSK	frequency shift keying
FSLN	Frente Sandinista de Liberación Nacional
G&W	Gulf & Western
GATT	General Agreement on Tariffs and Trade

GDM	Gesamtverband Deutscher Musikfachgeschäfte/Association of German Retailers
GDR	German Democratic Republic
GEMA	Gesellschaft für Musikälische Aufführungs- und Mechanische Vervielfältigungsrechte (Germany)
GESAC	Groupement Européen des Sociétés d'Auteurs et Compositeurs
GMA	Gospel Music Association
GTL	Gramophone and Typewriter Ltd.
hi-fi	high fidelity
HMV	His Master's Voice
Hz	hertz
IAEL	International Association of Entertainment Lawyers
IASA	International Association of Sound and Audiovisual Archives
IASPM	International Association for the Study of Popular Music
IATSE	International Alliance of Theatrical Stage Employees
IBB	International Broadcasting Bureau
IBOC	in-band on-channel
IC	integrated circuit
ICAMD	International Centre for African Music and Dance
ICM	International Creative Management
IFPI	International Federation of the Phonographic Industry
IGEB	Die Internationale Gesellschaft zur Erforschung und Förderung der Blasmusik [The International Society for the Promotion and Investigation of Band Music]
IJF	International Jazz Federation
ILMC	International Live Music Conference
ILO	International Labour Organization
IMF	International Managers Forum
IMMS	International Military Music Society
INS	Immigration and Naturalization Service (US)
IPR	Intellectual Property Rights
ips	inches per second
IRA	Irish Republican Army
ISP	Internet service provider
ITB	International Talent Booking
JASPM	Japanese Association for the Study of Popular Music
JASRAC	Japanese Society for Rights of Authors, Composers and Publishers
JFM	Jamaica Federation of Musicians & Affiliated Artistes
KCI	Yayasan Karya Cipta Indonesia
kHz	kilohertz
LD	laser disc
LFE	low-frequency effects
LP	long-playing record
MBI	Music Business International
MC	Master of Ceremonies (rapping)
MCA	Music Corporation of America
MCPS	Mechanical Copyright Protection Society
MD	minidisc

MGM	Metro-Goldwyn-Mayer
MIA	Music Industries Association (UK)
MIAC	Music Industry Advisory Council (Australia)
MIDEM	Marché d'Industrie de Disque et d'Editions Musicale
MIDI	musical instrument digital interface
MMF	Music Managers Forum
MNW	Music NetWork
MoD	music on demand
MOR	middle-of-the-road [music]
MP3	MPEG Layer III
MPB	música popular brasileira
MPEG	Moving Picture Experts Group
MPGA	Music Producers Guild of the Americas
MTC	MIDI time code
MTV	Music Television
MU	Musicians Union (UK)
MUJ	Musicians' Union of Japan
NAB	National Association of Broadcasters (US)
NACPA	North American Concert Promoters Association
NACWPI	National Association of College Wind and Percussion Instructors
NAIRD	National Association of Independent Record Distributors and Manufacturers
NAMM	National Association of Music Merchants (US)
NARAS	National Academy of Recording Arts and Sciences
NARD	National Association of Rudimental Drummers
NARM	National Association of Recording Merchandisers (US)
NAS	National Academy of Songwriters (US)
NBA	National Band Association
NBC	National Broadcasting Company
NCBA	National Catholic Bandmasters' Association
NVGD	Nederlandse Vereniging van Grammofoonplaten Detailhandelaren (The Netherlands)
OWI	Office of War Information
PANAFEST	Pan African Festival
PAs	personal appearances
PAS	Percussive Arts Society
PC	personal computer
PCM	pulse code modulation
PMRC	Parents Music Resource Center
PPD	published price to dealer
PPI	Philips Phonographische Industrie
PPL	Phonographic Performance Ltd.
ppq	pulses per quarter-note
PRS	Performing Right Society
PVC	polyvinyl chloride
R&B	rhythm and blues
R&D	research and development
RAM	random access memory
RAO	Russian Authors Organization

RCA	Radio Corporation of America
R-DAT	rotary head-DAT
RFE	Radio Free Europe
RIAA	Recording Industry Association of America
RIAJ	Recording Industry Association of Japan
RKO	Radio-Keith-Orpheum
RL	Radio Liberty
rpm	revolutions per minute
SABAM	Société Belge des Auteurs, Compositeurs et Editeurs
SACEM	Société des Auteurs, Compositeurs et Editeurs de Musique
SACM	Sociedad de Autores y Compositores de Música (Mexico)
SADAIC	Sociedad Argentina de Autores y Compositores de Música
SAG	Screen Actors Guild (US)
SAMRO	South African Music Rights Organisation
SCD	Sociedad Chilena del Derecho de Autor
SCMS	Serial Copy Management System
SCSI	small computer systems interface
SDMI	Secure Digital Music Initiative
SESAC	Society of European Stage Authors and Composers
SGAE	Sociedad General de Autores y Editores (Spain)
SIAE	Società Italiana degli Autori ed Editori
SME	Sony Music Entertainment
SMEJ	Sony Music Entertainment Japan
SMPA	Swiss Music Promoters Association
SMPTE	Society of Motion Picture and Television Engineers
SNAM	Syndicat National des Artistes Musiciens de France
SNCC	Student Non-Violent Co-ordinating Committee
SNEP	Syndicat National de l'Edition Phonographique (France)
SPARS	Society of Professional Audio Recording Services
SPEBSQSA	Society for the Preservation and Encouragement of Barber Shop Quartet Singing in America, Inc.
SPEDIDAM	Société de perception et de distribution des droits des artist-interprètes
SPN	Stichting Popmuziek Nederland
STEED	send tape echo echo delay
STIM	Svenska Tonsättares Internationella Musikbyra (Sweden)
TOBA	Theater Owners Booking Agency
TRO	The Richmond Organization
U&I	Utilities and Industries Corporation
UA	United Artists
UMG	Universal Music Group
UNESCO	United Nations Educational, Scientific and Cultural Organization
USIA	United States Information Agency
VAAP	Vsesojuznoje Agentstvo po Avtorskim Pravam
VCR	video cassette recorder
VDU	visual display unit
VHF	very high frequency
VJ	video jockey
VOA	Voice of America

VPL	Video Performance Ltd.
VTR	videotape recorder
VUT	Verband Unabhängiger Tonträgerprodzenten
WASBE	World Association for Symphonic Bands and Ensembles
WBDNA	Women Band Directors National Association
WCI	Warner Classics International
WEA	Warner-Elektra-Atlantic
WIPO	World Intellectual Property Organization
WMG	Warner Music Group
WMI	Warner Music International
WOMAD	World of Music, Arts and Dance
WOMEX	Worldwide Music Expo
WPA	Work Projects Administration
WTO	World Trade Organization
ZAIKS	Stowarzyszenie Autorow (Poland)

Arrangement of the Material

Part I
Social and Cultural Dimensions

1. Documentation

Archives

The term 'archive' refers to a collection of popular music artifacts, sound recordings, documents, sheet music, memorabilia or ephemera, or a place, organization or part of an organization where such materials are kept. Archives may be used for the documentation, study and practise of popular music, or as resource centers for musicians and journalists. Archival materials contain information relating to various aspects within the study of popular music, ranging from biography, history and chronology to performance practise, ethnography and textual analysis.

Archives tend not to cover the general subject area of popular music but, instead, concentrate on specific aspects of popular music, such as a particular genre, music within a given location or specific temporal limit, or popular music associated with specific ethnic groups, such as archives relating to African-American musics. Very few of these collections actually call themselves archives of 'popular music.' Even an exception such as the Center for Popular Music at Middle Tennessee State University in Murfreesboro is a cross-genre collection that concentrates on US music, with a specific focus on the southern states. Indeed, general archives that do not have specific parameters, such as the Klaus-Kuhnke Archive of Popular Music in Bremen, Germany, are rare in the field. Accordingly, there is a wide variety of institutions and private collections that can be categorized under the broad heading of 'popular music archives.' Because of this diversity, the conditions of archives vary, and there is a lack of uniformity in the area. Archives may range from the meticulously cataloged to the unsorted, uncounted or uninventoried.

Many archives and collections are linked to, or incorporated within, larger institutions. For instance, national and regional libraries, such as the Centre Georges Pompidou in Paris and the National Sound Archive in London, hold popular music archives within their larger collections. Other archives are affiliated with, and administered by, universities. Archives may also be contained within radio stations like the Voice of Kenya, which holds around 200,000 microgroove recordings, 30,000 tapes and 10,000 discs relating to Kenyan and African popular music. There are also a number of privately run collections, which are generally individually owned and curated, and are accessible to interested parties. The British Institute of Jazz Studies, for example, is a large private collection kept in an individual's house. Because of the personal nature of these collections, it is difficult to calculate exactly how many exist. Moreover, as archival policies are not governed by institutional guidelines in these instances, the archiving techniques and criteria for inclusion are often diverse and idiosyncratic, with little regulation or uniformity in how the collections are kept, cataloged and maintained. Neither is there much conformity in the content of these collections, as the materials contained within archives generated by an individual are ultimately a reflection of the specific circumstances, interests and events that led to their collection.

It is common for the private archives of individuals to become incorporated within the collections of public or commercial bodies. For example, the personal archive of folk music critic and Bob Dylan biographer Robert Shelton has been housed between the Experience Music Project in Seattle, Washington and the Institute of Popular Music at the University of Liverpool in the United Kingdom. Many large, institutionally administered archives have actually developed from private collections. Originally called the British Institute of Recorded Sound, the

UK National Sound Archive was set up as a private initiative by the collector Patrick Saul, and was later incorporated into the national library system as an archive that holds over half a million items. However, the patchwork nature of the archival field naturally means that there is a certain disparity in many areas of archiving, such as how particular organizations are funded, specific agreements and even ownership of materials (some archives are established on the basis of donation or purchase, while others operate on a permanent loan basis). There are also few standard procedures relating to how archives are augmented. Donations of materials may be the result of ad hoc arrangements that are often based on the reputation and prominence of a particular institution in the field or on personal relationships between the donor and archivist, whereas the active seeking out of new materials is more likely to be undertaken by larger organizations that have the necessary funds and staffing capabilities.

The collection and development of archives can be categorized as being either passive or active. Within these defining criteria, a 'passive' archive is one that is solely concerned with the collection, documentation and preservation of existing materials. Alternatively, the archivist may be 'active' in the actual acquisition of materials through, for example, the collection of field recordings, interviews and photographs. The latter approach is exemplified by the proactive approach of John and Alan Lomax who, from the 1920s onward, traveled throughout the United States recording materials for the Library of Congress's Archive of American Folk Song. Their efforts led to the preservation of materials that would not otherwise have been collected. Archivists may also have an effect on the way in which hitherto marginal musics are more widely disseminated and heard. For example, Fairley (1989) points to the influence of Lucy Duran, an ethnomusicologist and archivist at the National Sound Archive, on the increased popularity of Gambian *kora* music in the United Kingdom. Fairley credits Duran with introducing the music to various key disc jockeys, thus stimulating interest among a 'non-specialist, concert-going audience' (101).

The collection and preservation of popular music artifacts are in themselves fairly new phenomena: there were no non-art music archives prior to the twentieth century. This has meant that there is generally a lack of archives containing materials from before the 1920s, as, although sound archives existed before this time, their focus was on materials other than popular music. For example, one of the earliest sound archives, the Phonogrammarchiv, established at the Österreichische Akademie der Wissenschaften in Vienna in 1899, was set up specifically to collect ethnographic sound recordings rather than music. Furthermore, there has been a problem in terms of the availability of actual existing material relating to early forms of popular music, as musicians' 'working lives were directed at the present, and few if any of their activities were undertaken with one eye on posterity. Consequently ... potential archival materials [apart from printed music] are permanently in short supply' (Horn 1982, 315).

In the late nineteenth century, US copyright legislation required the deposit of sheet music to the federal Library of Congress. This led to the collection of a wealth of materials that are stored in the American Sheet Music Collection at the institution in Washington, DC. Indeed, US legislation was a central factor in the early development of popular music archives; the fact that statutory copyright could be obtained by the deposit of materials to the Library of Congress facilitated the establishment of such archives. However, the deposit of sound recording materials was not mandatory until 1972, when an amendment to US copyright statutes on recorded sound made it obligatory to deposit recordings to the institution. The Library's Recorded Sound Reference Center collections began in the 1920s, when record companies gave the Library samples of their records. The Library's audio collections have come to rank among the largest in the world, and include sound technology ranging from the first wax cylinders through LPs and audiotapes to compact audio discs and the latest sound-carrying formats. The Library of Congress was one of the first institutions to recognize sound recordings as a valuable archival source and to value them in terms of their contribution to the national culture. It was also the first of a growing number of archives established under the mandate of preserving musical history and tradition within a particular locality. The Hogan Archive of New Orleans Jazz is another example of an early archive that brings together jazz and the city, valuing and contextualizing music within its specific geographical locality.

The lack of early official curating of popular music materials may be linked to a general hostility to its perceived ephemeral nature. Indeed, the development of archives can be linked to a series of processes through which popular music has been recognized as an important form and therefore worthy of curating. For instance, the collection of folk music materials can be linked to the politics and aesthetics of the folk revival of the 1920s and 1930s. Here, the archivist's project is specifically legitimized by ideas of worth inherent in folk's politics, as the protection and collection of the music and culture 'of the people' are central to the movement's raison d'être. The most significant early collection in this field was the Library of Congress's Archive of American Folk

Song, set up in 1928 by Robert Winslow Gordon. The archive was significant in the subsequent direction that the folk movement took, as its collection of field recordings contributed to the creation of a canon for the revivals in North American folk. As folk musics have gradually been accepted and valued as important to the history and heritage of individual countries, a multitude of archives concerned with the preservation of national identity and folk traditions has become established throughout the world. Examples of such archives include the collection of Bulgarian folklore and traditional music at the Institute of Art Studies within the Bulgarian Academy of Sciences, and the Irish Traditional Music Archive in Dublin.

Throughout the twentieth century, the study of non-Western and popular musics in the academy led to university departments reacting to a perceived need for an accessible body of artifacts for study. A direct link can be traced between the rise of ethnomusicology as an academic discipline and the establishment of non-Western art music archives. Indeed, by the very nature of its methodologies (the collation of field recordings and primary research), ethnomusicology necessitated the founding of archives in the area. For instance, the ethnomusicologist George Herzog worked at the Berlin Phonogramm-Archiv until he emigrated to the United States where, in the late 1940s, he established Indiana University's Archives of Traditional Music, which cover indigenous American Indian musics, as well as African and European folk musics.

Many university archives have evolved as a result of the personal research interests of individual academics. For example, collections of materials originally used in specific musicological, ethnomusicological or anthropological research projects are being used as resources for general scholarly work. The Robert Pring-Mill Collection at the Institute of Popular Music at the University of Liverpool was a result of the scholar's long-term interest in Latin American music and culture. Other archives housed in educational institutions have been established in response to a particular area being understudied or undervalued in terms of academic research. For instance, the African Music Archive at Johannes Gutenberg-University in Mainz, Germany, a collection of sound recordings and written materials relating to modern African pop music, was specifically created to redress the balance of existing African music collections.

Likewise, as jazz began to be regarded as a 'serious' form, various collections and archives were created, such as the Institute of Jazz Studies at Rutgers University, New Jersey, set up by Marshall Stearns in 1952. The gradual appropriation of jazz as art music through its critical acceptance and incorporation into academic study and discourse has meant that collections relating to the genre are proportionally high when judged against popular music archives as a whole. A worldwide network of jazz archives has developed, including such institutions as the Jazz-Institut Darmstadt (Germany), which covers domestic and international jazz styles. Indeed, it can be pointed out that the emergence of jazz archives is not merely a reflection of this process, but can be seen as an active part of the process whereby jazz began to be perceived as separate from other types of popular music through its critical elevation into the realms of 'serious' music.

Similarly, developments in the styles and ideologies of rock and pop music in the 1960s were important to the emergence of archives of these genres. As rock became infused with values more aesthetically in tune with high art, it was taken more seriously by critics and enthusiasts, and thus the collection of related materials became increasingly legitimized. Since the late 1960s, rock music archives have taken a variety of forms, from educational archives attached to academic institutions, such as the Music Library and Sound Recordings Archives at Bowling Green State University in Ohio, established in 1967, to multimillion-dollar commercial investments, such as the Experience Music Project in Seattle.

There have been instances where the premise of preservation has been steeped in a particular political or ideological agenda – for instance, the Libri Prohibiti in Prague, which was set up in 1991 to collect and preserve books, magazines and sound recordings from the Czech underground reflecting the Communist era (1948–89). Here, the archive is infused with political significance, as it is intended to document the legacy of resistance within underground popular culture in the country. Australian archives, such as the Central Australia Aboriginal Media Association and the Australian Institute of Aboriginal and Torres Strait Islander Studies, include collections of traditional and contemporary indigenous Aboriginal musics related to the reclamation of a cultural heritage suppressed and denied under colonialism. The archival collation of such materials can be related to central issues connected with the study of noncanonical musics, such as protectionism. Feld (1994) points out that, although the academic study of non-Western musics may be advantageous to those cultures, notions of 'endangered music' and 'endangered culture' within ethnomusicology can be problematic, as 'preservationist agendas often have very conservative political slants, and invoking the notion of endangerment may dredge up fears of control, of desires to freeze time and place' (287).

There are sound archives whose objective is the collation of material without specific generic parameters or particular aesthetically loaded agendas. The National Sound Archive, for example, attempts to collect all recordings issued in Britain, including the output of all major record labels, along with tapes of all the major broadcast channels from the national broadcasting company, the BBC. However, the multifarious nature of soundcarrier productions means that there are inherent problems in any archive that aims to be totally comprehensive. The multitude of companies working at a minimal level in the recording industry, for instance, makes the task of creating a fully comprehensive sound archive collection almost impossible. Also, the donation of sound recordings to archives such as the National Sound Archive is often maintained under voluntary agreements, which means that there may be inconsistencies in the collection.

Despite the multitude of different archives, the level of resources, funding and priority allocated to the cataloging and curating of popular music falls some way behind that afforded more traditionally valued art forms. For example, although the British Library has cataloged classical sheet music, it has not cataloged popular song, as this has not been viewed as a priority. Also, collections of popular music materials have continued to suffer from the low status accorded to sound recordings. In the United Kingdom, for instance, sound recordings are generally not kept in public libraries for long periods and are not viewed as an archival priority. Rather, they are regarded as having a limited shelf life and are often sold off after a period of time. Hence, what is and what is not preserved is often refracted through the ideologies of selection. Indeed, the primacy of the written word in libraries and archives as a whole can be seen to affect the perceived value of particular archival materials. Sheet music may be historically favored, with descending value given to recorded sound, audiotape, shellac and other associated materials (posters, concert programs, eight-track recordings, correspondence between companies, and fanzines). As a result of the situation of popular music (and, similarly, film and television) archives within the larger field of general archival endeavor, sound and audiovisual archivists have been careful to apply non-value-laden terminology to their materials. A report on audiovisual archives for the United Nations Educational, Scientific and Cultural Organization (UNESCO) points out that archivists should 'avoid phrases like "non-book," "non-text" or "special materials" . . . The implication is that one type of material is "normal" or "standard," while everything else, by being defined in reference to it, is of lesser status' (Edmondson 1998, 2.7).

Certain negative implications surround the term 'archive' itself, relating to the perceived inaccessibility and the content of archives. As Edmondson (1998) points out, in popular use the term commonly has 'wide and non-specific connotations as a place where "old" or noncurrent materials are kept. With its popular connotations of dust, cobwebs and decay, of material forgotten, locked away and remote from ordinary access, the word is often a public relations liability' (3.4.2). Despite these perceptions, the popular music archive has been quick to utilize technological developments. The evolution of new technologies has seen many existing archives tapping into new ways of utilizing and disseminating their materials. Archives such as the Library of Congress and the Rodgers and Hammerstein Archives of Recorded Sound at the New York Public Library have made copies of selected materials available via the Internet. CD-ROMs have also become common in the cataloging of archives. The British Library, for example, has published a series of CD-ROMs that allow efficient access to information about hundreds of thousands of published musical works. Also, archivists in the field have attempted to group together to share information and develop a coherent project in terms of practical criteria and rules for the profession. There are a number of associations specifically or partly concerned with sound archiving. Bodies such as the International Association of Sound and Audiovisual Archives (IASA) and the Association for Recorded Sound Collections (ARSC) have acted as forums for the dissemination of archival issues and have attempted to formulate ground rules and ethical codes for the practise. The IASA, for example, has drawn up Cataloguing Rules for Audiovisual Media, aiming to outline and unify cataloging problems, and to develop solutions relating to sound recordings and film among its members. Included in the document are standards for the cataloging of recorded materials, outlines toward a uniform method of logging discographical information and clarification of copyright issues. It is clear, then, that archives have continued to reflect changes in their environment, with archivists utilizing newly developed archival methods and attempting new solutions to problems in the field.

Bibliography

Edmondson, Ray. 1998. *A Philosophy of Audiovisual Archiving*.
http://www.unesco.org/webworld/en/highlights/audiovisual_archiving/philo3.htm

Fairley, Jan. 1989. 'Out of the Archive and into the World of Music.' *Popular Music* 8(1) (January): 101–106.

Feld, Steven. 1994. 'From Schizophonia to Schismogenesis: On the Discourses and Commodification Practices of "World Music" and "World Beat."' In Charles Keil and Steven Feld, *Music Grooves: Essays and Dialogues*. Chicago and London: University of Chicago Press, 257–89.

Horn, David. 1982. 'Review of *Resources of American Music History: A Directory of Source Materials from Colonial Times to World War II*, by D.W. Krummel, Jean Geil, Doris J. Dyen and Deane L. Root.' *Popular Music* 2: 314–16.

ROBERT STRACHAN and MARION LEONARD

Bibliographies

Reference bibliographies of popular music (systematic listings providing access to information) – as opposed to 'descriptive bibliography,' which is the study of the physical characteristics of printed texts – may be grouped into two categories: works that provide information about the existence of individual pieces of popular music; and works that list literature on popular music.

Bibliographies of Popular Music

Music as a whole is served by a range of bibliographic tools whose main tasks are to identify particular pieces of music and, in varying degrees, provide details about factors such as composer, exact title, date (typically of publication; sometimes also of composition), publisher and number of pages. Included in this range are: catalogs of major music libraries; systematic listings of individual composers' works (including thematic catalogs); catalogs of manuscripts and early printed music, with library locations; lists of music for performance on particular instruments and by instrumental and vocal groups; and regularly published lists of recently published music (either published separately as a national music list, or included in a country's national bibliography, along with other publications).

The provision of this range of bibliographic tools grew up around classical music and is designed to serve it. The printing and publishing of a score constitute the principal event – however long ago it occurred – that triggers the bibliographic process. The score is perceived in two ways: as the expression of the individual composer's ideas; and as an indispensable step in the process of enabling performance to take place. The two dominant organizational principles follow from this: by individual composer and/or by performance medium. Insofar as it fits within this approach, popular music can expect to be included in such general bibliographic works, and, indeed, a bibliography listing current music, such as *The British Catalogue of Music* (1957–), regularly lists many recently published performance editions of popular music, usually in the form of arrangements, for solo or ensemble performance. However, expectation and reality in this instance are commonly found to be far apart. *The Catalogue of Printed Music in the British Library to 1980*

(Baillie 1981–87), containing several million entries in its 62 volumes, includes an entry for just one published song by Burt Bacharach. *The New Grove Dictionary of American Music* (Hitchcock and Sadie 1986) contains a systematic catalog of the works of George Gershwin (by Wayne Schneider), but opts for highly selective listings for his contemporaries Irving Berlin, Jerome Kern and Cole Porter.

In terms of works that have accepted the established choice of possible formats and their accompanying principles and that have dedicated themselves to a subject area of popular music, the United States has been better provided for than any other country – although it is noticeable in this case that most attention has been paid to the period predating the rapid growth of commercially published popular music. Bibliographies of colonial North American popular music include: two inventories of eighteenth-century secular manuscripts (including bugle calls and theater music), with library locations (Fuld and Davidson 1980; Keller 1981); a bibliography of songsters printed before 1821 (Lowens 1976); and a 'national tune index' to almost 40,000 items of eighteenth-century secular music, with music *incipits* (Rabson and Keller 1980). This last example is also interesting, however, in that, although it is based on printed sources and incorporates and builds on the thematic catalog approach, it moves the entire enterprise away from a composer focus in order to deal with its material.

Bibliographies of twentieth-century popular music that have also followed established formats and procedures are comparatively few in number. Two quite different examples are: a guide to locating musical scores used for silent films (Anderson 1988); and – perhaps surprisingly, given the importance of improvisation in the genre's aesthetics – a catalog of jazz music in print (Voigt 1982). One particular format with a quite minor role in classical music bibliography, the song index organized by title, has played a much more prominent role in the bibliography of twentieth-century popular music. Many song indexes are designed to guide users to published music. Havlice's *Popular Song Index* (1978–) and Gargan's and Sharma's *Find That Tune* (1984–88), for example, following a model set by Sears's *Song Index* (1926) for classical song, are indexes to songs in published anthologies. But, in other indexes, the provision of publication information has been one undertaking among several. The most extensive index of US popular song, comprising Cohen-Stratyner (1988) and Shapiro and Pollock (1985, with annual supplements), provides details of composer and lyricist, publication and key performances on record, on stage and in films in equal measure.

For many compilers and users of bibliographic

information on popular music, the functional alphabetical song title list, although clearly useful, fails to reflect the fascination that lies in diversity of detail, and different emphases in listing have been developed. Two in particular stand out: the chronological listing, as demonstrated by Lowe's *Directory of Popular Music, 1900–1965* (1975), which organizes British publications by date of copyright deposit; and the listing by song type or theme, such as Dichter's and Shapiro's labor of love, *Early American Sheet Music: Its Lure and Its Lore, 1768–1889* (1941), and the more utilitarian *The Stecheson Classified Song Directory* (Stecheson and Stecheson 1961–78), which groups over 100,000 songs under 400 subject headings.

Areas of the music industry, such as retailing, have made use of volumes such as those of the Stechesons, but one particular type of index had its source in the industry itself; not only that, it reflected changing economic realities there. Performance indexes compiled by performing rights organizations were an offshoot of those organizations' need to collect and compile such data for the economic advantage of their members. Although these types of index are song indexes, they have been generated according to a set of priorities different from those of conventional bibliographies. ASCAP's *Index of Performed Compositions* (1952–78) and BMI's *Performindex* (1945–64), both containing enormous lists (ASCAP's 1963 volumes include over 200,000 titles), reflect actual performance, live and/or broadcast.

Although the prominence of the popular song index in its various guises has meant that popular music bibliography can be said to occupy a distinctive area within bibliographic practise, a more major distinction involving popular music lies elsewhere. In all those areas of popular music where the primary material is not the published score but the recording, bibliographies have conceded primacy of place as an identifying medium to their close relative, discographies. In some genres, published score and recorded performance are both important sources, but for many, especially from the 1950s onward, listings of recordings have become the major tool.

Bibliographies of Popular Music Literature

As with virtually any subject area, books on popular music appear in the various general bibliographic resources, such as the printed and on-line catalogs of major libraries and national bibliographies. In their printed form, these catalogs have tended to provide only limited access by subject (as opposed to author), but on-line keyword searching has made them much more responsive to such an approach. For popular music literature in periodical form, general indexes rarely do more than scratch the surface – inevitably, perhaps, given the

vast number of articles – although the regularity with which articles on popular music subjects appear both in non-specialist sources and in specialist journals serving other disciplines (for example, sociology, psychology) has meant that non-music indexes have an important part to play in mapping the field. One type of general periodical index that came into existence in the 1970s, the 'citation index,' offers a particularly rich and versatile source of information. Both the *Arts and Humanities Citation Index* (1976–) and the *Social Sciences Citation Index* (1957–) provide access by indexed author, keywords and – the feature that most distinguishes these works and is responsible for their size – by cited references (author and keyword) in the indexed articles.

As with bibliographies of music, the majority of general bibliographies of music literature are oriented toward classical music, but two types stand out as including sufficient coverage of popular music to make them useful tools for popular music research: the cumulative index and the area bibliography (which covers music in a specific geographic area). Coverage of popular music in *The Music Index* (1949–), the major indexing tool for periodical articles, increased steadily during the 1980s and 1990s and, although a great many periodicals devoted to popular musics have continued to be omitted, publication of the index in CD-ROM form has made it a powerful search tool. Its closest rival, the *International Index to Music Periodicals*, has full indexing only back to 1996, although it does offer 'fulltext' access to some current journals. Popular music coverage has also increased strikingly in the classified abstracting-and-indexing service for music, the *Répertoire International de Littérature Musicale* (*RILM*), since its inception in 1967. Its 1995 volume contains over 900 entries for 'jazz, pop and rock,' in many languages. Most useful for periodical articles, the *RILM* listing also includes books, parts of books and Ph.D. theses, the majority with abstracts of their contents.

Among area bibliographies, those covering the United States were among the first to recognize the need not only to represent popular music on an equal footing, but to integrate it into their coverage. Jackson (1973), Horn (1977), Horn and Jackson (1988) and Marco (1996) for the country as a whole and Skowronski (1981) and Floyd and Reisser (1983) for African-American music all in their way take for granted that earlier tendencies to ignore or underrepresent popular idioms were inappropriate. The desire to represent the music of a region as a whole can also be seen to underpin the works of McLean (1977) for Oceania and Crisp (1982) for Australia, while De Lerma (1981–84) extends the holistic idea to a globally conceived bibliography of black music, including Africa and the Caribbean. Outside a geocultural context dominated by classical music, most area works tend to emphasize 'traditional' music, but Gray (1991) departs from that tendency in giving attention to what his book's subtitle describes as the 'traditional, popular, art and liturgical musics of sub-Saharan Africa.'

The first bibliographies devoted entirely to an aspect of popular music appeared on the genre of jazz (Merriam 1954; Reisner 1959; Carl Gregor, Duke of Mecklenburg 1969), and the genre-centered bibliography has been the principal approach ever since. Significant works have appeared, for example, in book and article form, on blues (Hart, Eagles and Howorth 1989; Ford 1999), music hall (Senelick, Cheshire and Schneider 1981), rap (McCoy 1992), rock (Hoffmann 1981; Hoffmann and Cooper 1986–94) and rockabilly (Cooper and Haney 1990), while jazz has continued to feature strongly, most notably in the internationally conceived works of Hefele (1981), and Carl Gregor, Duke of Mecklenburg and Ruecker (1983–88). The first major on-line bibliography (Rodman's and Coates's *Everyday I Write the Book*) was conceived, broadly, along generic lines, in this case embracing rock and pop.

Periodical indexes devoted exclusively to literature on popular music have had a checkered career, illustrating the magnitude of the task. The most ambitious, *POMPI* (Clark and Linehan 1988–91), completed five annual listings of English-language material, the last of which included 10,000 entries from 90 journal titles, organized in a subject list that indicated the wide range of the project's coverage. Hefele's single-handed attempt to list German-language articles on jazz, rock and pop (1991) resulted in 17,000 entries for one year's coverage (1988–89).

Separately published area bibliographies devoted exclusively to popular music are comparative rarities, notable examples being the compilations of Fairley (1985) for Latin America, especially Chile, and Perrone (1986) for Brazil. The area approach has been covered better in those historical studies of particular regions or countries that include good bibliographies, such as Kotek's history of Czech popular music (1994–95), which provides detailed bibliographies for every chapter. Musical practise and the social and cultural contexts of popular musical activity have been even rarer candidates for in-depth bibliographic treatment, although exceptions are provided by works on brass instruments (Fasman 1990), education (Maas and Schmidt-Brunner 1988) and gender (Bowers and Bareis 1991).

As with other reference books, bibliographic works that declare an intention to represent the fullness and diversity of popular music often turn out to have more limited aims. Useful though they are, the books by Iwaschkin (1986; over 5,000 unannotated entries for

books) and Taylor (1985; an annotated guide) are limited to Anglo-American music. The first work to attempt to break away from both this domination and that of the English language was Tagg's *DOPMUS* (1989), in which slightly under half of the 2,309 entries are in languages other than English. Tagg's bibliography contains no entries for works on individuals, giving space instead to locations, major genres, sociocultural topics and theoretical perspectives. Tagg's work both inspired and laid the foundation for Shepherd et al. (1997), which, in line with its role as a precursor of the *Continuum Encyclopedia of Popular Music of the World*, prioritizes its concerns as being 'with the study of popular music on a world basis' and one of its key aims as 'to rectify the Anglo-American bias of most other reference works' (xxvii).

Bibliography

American Society of Composers, Authors and Publishers (ASCAP). 1952–78. *ASCAP Index of Performed Compositions*. 6 vols. New York: ASCAP.

Anderson, Gillian B. 1988. *Music for Silent Films, 1894–1929: A Guide*. Washington, DC: Library of Congress.

Arts and Humanities Citation Index. 1976–. Philadelphia: Institute for Scientific Information.

Baillie, Laureen, ed. 1981–87. *The Catalogue of Printed Music in the British Library to 1980*. 62 vols. London: Saur.

Bowers, Jane, and Bareis, Urba. 1991. 'Bibliography on Music and Gender.' *The World of Music* 33(2): 65–103.

The British Catalogue of Music. 1957–.

Broadcast Music Inc. (BMI). 1945–64 . *BMI Performindex*. New York: BMI.

Carl Gregor, Duke of Mecklenburg. 1969. *International Jazz Bibliography: Jazz Books from 1919 to 1968*. Strasbourg: Heitz.

Carl Gregor, Duke of Mecklenburg, and Ruecker, Norbert. 1983–88. *International Bibliography of Jazz Books. Vol. 1: 1921–1949*. Baden-Baden: Koerner.

Clark, Chris, and Linehan, Andy. 1988–91. *POMPI: Popular Music Periodicals Index (1984–9)*. 5 vols. in 3. London: British Library.

Cohen-Stratyner, Barbara. 1988. *Popular Music, 1900–1919*. Detroit, MI: Gale Research.

Cooper, B. Lee, and Haney, Wayne S. 1990. *Rockabilly: A Bibliographic Resource Guide*. Metuchen, NJ: Scarecrow Press.

Crisp, Deborah. 1982. *Bibliography of Australian Music: An Index to Monographs, Journal Articles and Theses*. Armidale: Australian Music Studies Project.

De Lerma, Dominique-René. 1981–84. *Bibliography of Black Music*. 4 vols. Westport, CT: Greenwood Press.

Dichter, Harry, and Shapiro, Elliott. 1941. *Early American*

Sheet Music: Its Lure and Its Lore, 1768–1889. New York: Bowker.

Fairley, Jan. 1985. 'Annotated Bibliography of Latin-American Popular Music with Particular Reference to Chile and Nueva Canción.' *Popular Music* 5: 305–56.

Fasman, Mark J. 1990. *Brass Bibliography: Sources on the History, Literature, Pedagogy, Performance and Acoustics of Brass Instruments*. Bloomington, IN: Indiana University Press.

Floyd, Samuel A., and Reisser, Marsha J. 1983. *Black Music in the United States: An Annotated Bibliography of Selected Reference and Research Materials*. New York: Kraus.

Ford, Robert. 1999. *A Blues Bibliography: The International Literature of an Afro-American Music Genre*. Bromley, Kent: Paul Pelletier.

Fuld, James J., and Davidson, Mary Wallace. 1980. *18th-Century American Secular Music Manuscripts: An Inventory*. Philadelphia: Music Library Association.

Gargan, William, and Sharma, Sue. 1984–88. *Find That Tune: An Index to Rock, Folk-Rock, Disco and Soul in Collections*. 2 vols. New York: Neal-Shumann.

Gray, John. 1991. *African Music: A Bibliographical Guide to the Traditional, Popular, Art and Liturgical Musics of Sub-Saharan Africa*. Westport, CT: Greenwood Press.

Hart, Mary L., Eagles, Brenda M., and Howorth, Lisa N. 1989. *The Blues: A Bibliographical Guide*. New York: Garland.

Havlice, Patricia Pate. 1978–. *Popular Song Index*. Metuchen, NJ: Scarecrow Press.

Hefele, Bernhard. 1981. *Jazz-Bibliography/Jazz-Bibliographie: International Literature on Jazz, Blues, Spirituals, Gospel and Religious Music*. Munich: Saur.

Hefele, Bernhard. 1991. *Jazz-Rock-Pop: Eine Bibliographie der deutschsprachigen Literatur von 1988 bis 1989* [Jazz-Rock-Pop: A Bibliography of German-Language Literature]. Munich: Saur.

Hitchcock, H. Wiley, and Sadie, Stanley, eds. 1986. *The New Grove Dictionary of American Music*. 4 vols. London: Macmillan.

Hoffmann, Frank. 1981. *The Literature of Rock, 1954–1978*. Metuchen, NJ: Scarecrow Press.

Hoffmann, Frank, and Cooper, B. Lee. 1986–94. *The Literature of Rock II-III (1979–1990)*. 2 vols. Metuchen, NJ: Scarecrow Press.

Horn, David. 1977. *The Literature of American Music in Books and Folk Music Collections: A Fully Annotated Bibliography*. Metuchen, NJ: Scarecrow Press.

Horn, David, and Jackson, Richard. 1988. *The Literature of American Music in Books and Folk Music Collections: A Fully Annotated Bibliography. First Supplement*. Metuchen, NJ: Scarecrow Press.

International Index to Music Periodicals. 1996–. Alexandria, VA: Chadwycj-Healey Inc.

Iwaschkin, Roman. 1986. *Popular Music: A Reference Guide*. New York: Garland.

Jackson, Richard. 1973. *United States Music: Sources of Bibliography and Collective Biography*. Brooklyn, NY: Institute for Studies in American Music.

Keller, Kate Van Winkle. 1981. *Popular Secular Music in America Through 1800: A Preliminary Checklist of Manuscripts in North American Collections*. Philadelphia: Music Library Association.

Kotek, Josef. 1994–95. *Dejiny ceske popularni hudby a zpevu* [The History of Czech Popular Music and Singing]. 2 vols. Praha: Academia.

Lowe, Leslie. 1975. *Directory of Popular Music, 1900–1965*. Droitwich: Peterson.

Lowens, Irving. 1976. *A Bibliography of Songsters Printed in America Before 1821*. Worcester, MA: American Antiquarian Society.

Maas, Georg, and Schmidt-Brunner, Wolfgang. 1988. *Pop/Rock im Unterricht: Eine kommentierte Bibliographie* [Pop/Rock in Education: An Annotated Bibliography]. Mainz: Schott.

Marco, Guy. 1996. *The Literature of American Music III*. 2 vols. (Vol. 2 is a cumulative index to Horn 1977, Horn and Jackson 1988 and Marco 1996). Lanham, MD: Scarecrow Press.

McCoy, Judy. 1992. *Rap Music in the 1980s: A Reference Guide*. Metuchen, NJ: Scarecrow Press.

McLean, M. 1977. *An Annotated Bibliography of Oceanic Music and Dance*. Wellington, NZ: The Polynesian Society.

Merriam, Alan. 1954. *A Bibliography of Jazz*. Philadelphia: American Folklore Society.

The Music Index. 1949–. Warren, MI: Harmonie Park Press.

Perrone, Charles. 1986. 'An Annotated Interdisciplinary Bibliography and Discography of Brazilian Popular Music.' *Latin American Music Review* 7(2): 302–40.

Rabson, Carolyn, and Keller, Kate Van Winkle. 1980. *The National Tune Index: 18th Century Secular Music*. 80 microfiches. New York: University Music Editions.

Reisner, Robert G. 1959. *The Literature of Jazz: A Selective Bibliography*. New York: New York Public Library.

Répertoire International de Littérature Musicale/RILM Abstracts. 1967–. New York: RILM.

Rodman, Gilbert B., and Coates, Norma. *Everyday I Write the Book: A Bibliography of (Mostly) Academic Work on Rock and Pop Music*.
http://www.cas.usf.edu/communication/rodman/biblio/biblio-front.html

Sears, Minnie E. 1926. *Song Index: An Index to More Than*

12,000 Songs in 177 Song Collections. New York: Wilson.

Senelick, Laurence, Cheshire, David F., and Schneider, Ulrich. 1981. *British Music Hall, 1840–1923: A Bibliography and Guide to Sources*. Hamden, CT: Archon Books.

Shapiro, Nat, and Pollock, Bruce. 1985–. *Popular Music, 1920–1979: A Revised Cumulation*. 3 vols., with annual supplements by Bruce Pollock. Detroit, MI: Gale Research.

Shepherd, John, et al. 1997. *Popular Music Studies: A Select International Bibliography*. London: Mansell.

Skowronski, JoAnn. 1981. *Black Music in America: A Bibliography*. Metuchen, NJ: Scarecrow Press.

Social Sciences Citation Index. 1957–. Philadelphia: Institute for Scientific Information.

Stecheson, Anthony, and Stecheson, Anne. 1961–78. *The Stecheson Classified Song Directory*. 2 vols. Hollywood, CA: Music Industry Press.

Tagg, Philip. 1989. *DOPMUS: Documentation of Popular Music Studies*. Göteborg: IASPM.

Taylor, Paul. 1985. *Popular Music Since 1955: A Critical Guide to the Literature*. London: Mansell.

Voigt, John. 1982. *Jazz Music in Print and Jazz Books in Print*. 3rd ed. Boston, MA: Hornpipe Music.

DAVID HORN

Biography/Autobiography

A biography is an account of a person's life by someone other than that person, while an autobiography is an account of a person's life by that same person. Popular music biography and autobiography can include the life history of an artist, a music industry professional or an ensemble. Popular music audiences' interest in biographical information means that biographies and autobiographies occur across a multitude of genres and cultures, and their subject matter encompasses a huge range of differing types of musical acts and protagonists.

The widespread popularity of biography from the 1970s onward has led Frith (1983) to describe biographies as the 'dominant source of pop information' (271). Indeed, the demand for popular music biographies has meant that some journalists such as George Tremlett, Dave Marsh, Victor Bockris, Ray Coleman and James Gregory have become akin to 'professional popular music biographers': prolific writers on a variety of differing subjects and performers. For instance, in the mid-1970s Tremlett produced biographies of artists such as Gary Glitter, Slade, Marc Bolan, the Who, the Osmonds, the Rolling Stones and David Bowie. Likewise, in the 1980s and 1990s Dave Marsh wrote numerous works on Elvis Presley, Bruce Springsteen, Michael Jackson and Black Sabbath.

A life story is often considered a comparatively uncomplicated form of narrative and is frequently presented as such. However, popular music biography is a form that is affected by, and reflects, issues in music practise and consumption, from the way in which music is marketed to the ideologies that surround it. Popular music biography has identifiable stylistic and generic conventions, and the type of biography varies considerably, depending on who is being written about. These can be roughly divided according to the ways in which Thornton (1990) outlines historical importance as being ascribed to a popular cultural event: 'sales figures, biographical interest, critical acclaim or amount of media coverage' (87). Five distinct types of biography are discernible according to this model: the cut-and-paste cash-in; the serious historical appraisal; the scandalous exposé; the insider's 'true life' account; and the autobiography. However, there is not always such a clear demarcation between these types, and many biographies evidence significant overlaps between them.

The cut-and-paste cash-in can be concerned with anyone who is popular at a given moment and therefore marketable. The distinctive feature of these biographies is that they generally include very little original research material, consisting primarily of press clippings taken from secondary sources (press releases, magazine clippings, interviews from the music press), and are often padded out with heavy use of photographs. As they do not rely on time-consuming research, these books are quickly produced on a minimal budget. This is often related to the perceived 'shelf life' of their subject. If an artist or act is currently popular but is seen within the music industry as having a short-term span of commercial viability, then any merchandising or related product has to be put on the market quickly. Shuker (1994) describes these works as 'quickie' publications, which read like 'press releases . . . emphasising the pictorial aspect rather than any extended critical commentary,' and are 'often little more than pseudo-publicity' (73). As such, they bear little resemblance to some of the meticulously researched works published on a wide variety of popular music subjects. However, they are useful in terms of how they fit into wider strategies of marketing and promotion, or historically, in tracing 'how star appeal has been defined at different moments' (Frith 1983, 272).

The serious historical appraisal – which first appeared in the 1950s with works on jazz and blues musicians, such as Alan Lomax's study of 'Jelly Roll' Morton (1949) and Paul Oliver's *Bessie Smith* (1959) – has some parallels with critical biographies of literary figures, which have been categorized as 'an account of a writer's life for the purpose of evaluating and explaining' their work (Gray 1984, 33). Both types of account attempt to analyze the work of their subjects by putting it into an historical context, often in order to try to explain its cultural importance or sociological relevance. Savage's (1992) account of the history of the Sex Pistols, for example, traces the lives of the major figures in the group's development, framed within a picture of the social landscape of the United Kingdom in the 1970s and an outline of the political and cultural movements that he cites as influential on the ideologies of punk. There are also a number of biographies of this kind that use various types of textual analysis to explain the aesthetic and cultural significance of their subjects. This can often take the form of relating lyric content to factors in an artist's life, such as spirituality (Turner 1993), political orientation (Wolfe and Lornell 1992) or literary and musical influences (Shelton 1986), but it may also include other forms of commentary on their work. Calt (1994), for example, mixes a biographical narrative of Skip James, which he relates to racial politics within the United States, with lyric analysis and musicological information (such as chord changes and number of beats) relating to individual texts. Likewise, Watson (1996) blends musicological analysis with cultural studies and a history of leftist philosophy in order to explain the life and work of Frank Zappa.

As they set themselves up as being 'serious' and 'critical' evaluations, these accounts are generally written on subjects whose work has a fairly high level of critical cachet over a particular period of time. Thornton (1990) suggests two specific ways in which the past of an individual is 'contained' in writings on popular culture: a biographical strategy, which 'offers glimpses of the past through the lives of their protagonists and histories which are held together by the idiosyncratic voice of their authors,' and the 'art historical' approach, which evaluates the career and importance of their subject on 'political and aesthetic grounds' (87). Serious historical appraisals lie somewhere between these categories, in that they work in the same way as art histories by relating the life and work of their subject to the contexts of their particular cultural and political landscape, but are ultimately dominated by the voice of the author.

As performers are often steeped in myth, fantasy and contrived commercial images, in any 'serious' biography there is a need to authenticate the narrative voice and establish biographical authority. Biographical authority can be established in a number of ways: the biographer may claim to be close to the subject, a close spectator of events, an expert or an analyst. The authorial voice not only narrates and contextualizes, but also controls aesthetic judgments within the text. Indeed, when a par-

ticular artist has been subject to a number of biographies, this becomes all the more apparent. Biographers may set up their narrative authority with reference to other biographies. For instance, Clinton Heylin's *Bob Dylan: Behind the Shades* (1991) goes to great lengths to point out apparent factual inaccuracies and lapses of aesthetic judgment in other biographers' texts.

Another common form of popular music biography is the scandalous exposé. Their aim is to expose the 'real' or secret lives of their subjects. Because they set out to look behind the public persona of or destroy myths about their subjects, they are generally concerned with figures that are deeply rooted within the public consciousness. The most famous writer in this idiom was Albert Goldman, whose biographies of John Lennon and Elvis Presley were controversial in their mix of sensationalist revelations and myth debunking. In terms of research, these works are variable, but can be as widely researched as the critical biography. Goldman, for instance, states that he conducted 1,200 interviews over six years in researching *The Lives of John Lennon*. In terms of intent, they are fairly similar to the critical biography in that, in both categories, the stated aim is to provide 'true' accounts of their subjects. Where they often differ from critical biographies is in their tone (deliberately scandalous as opposed to reverential or critical), and in their general lack of analysis of their subject's work.

Likewise, the insider's 'true life' accounts are generally concerned with subjects who have had commercial longevity, lasting critical acclaim or cult status. They are written (or ghostwritten) by those supposedly close to the subject (Brown and Gaines 1983). Consequently, these types of biography generally consist of anecdotes and fond reminiscences, or are written in the mode of the scandalous exposé. As with all biography, there is a problem here regarding objectivity, as there is a need to establish biographical legitimacy in order to tell a story. As Robert Shelton, the biographer of Bob Dylan, admits, 'there's a great deal of lying that goes on in biography . . . It's technique, manipulation of the reader' (1996, 17).

Popular music autobiographies can also be seen in the light of the relationships between music, mythology and the music industry. Examples are provided by works such as Woody Guthrie's 1943 autobiography *Bound for Glory*, which is steeped in personal and North American mythology, and Marianne Faithfull's early 1990s autobiography, which uses the images and language of 1960s popular culture and mysticism. However, Harlos (1995) sees the proliferation of jazz autobiographies in the 1980s as a 'genuine opportunity (by musicians) to seize narrative authority' (134) from generally white non-playing critics. Hence, the whole trend is seen as a reaction against the way that jazz had previously been classified, historicized and documented. The autobiography can also be influential on popular music practise in the way that a certain genre may be understood, viewed and articulated by subsequent musicians. Instances of this are provided by the way in which Guthrie's writings were influential on notions of authenticity in the folk revival of the late 1950s, and by the way in which the prison journals of Mikis Theodorakis contributed to the politicization of Greek popular music in the 1970s.

In the United Kingdom in the 1990s, an emergent form of popular music autobiography was the 'confessional memoir,' which often documented the experiences of marginalized figures. Books such as Giles Smith's *Lost in Music* (1995), John Otway's *Cor Baby, That's Really Me* (1990) and Ed Jones's *This Is Pop* (1999) present themselves as celebrations of failure. The jacket of Otway's book, for instance, promises the story of 'rock and roll's greatest failure, bad records and rank incompetence.' Although humorous and bathetic in tone, these accounts are generally concerned with addressing and attacking the mythologies surrounding rock music culture from within and the construction of identity through music. They are interesting in the way that they allow marginalized voices to be included in rock history. Giles Smith, for example, writes about his experiences working in a commercially unsuccessful rock band, and recounts his experiences with record companies and life in the industry from a perspective that would go undocumented in the normal subject matter of the rock biography. Ultimately, like all types of popular music biography, these memoirs cannot be separated from the political economies and ideologies of popular music.

The biography, then, makes a considerable contribution to the discourses that attend popular music practise. It works to create, reinforce and also challenge the dominant representations of popular musicians. This reflexivity can be connected to a need to link an individual's creativity with the details of his/her life, especially with forms that have been ascribed 'artistic' connotations, such as blues, jazz, and rock since the mid-1960s. Here, the emotional capacity of an individual's music is often directly related to particular events in his/her life. The biography is active both in the creation of mythologies and authenticities, where it is important that the musician is understood to have 'lived the music,' and in the challenging of established myths surrounding a particular artist. As Frith (1983) points out, 'the problem seems to be that in dealing with rock lives we are dealing with ciphers that signify commercial calculations, audience expectations, vested interests as well as individual experience' (276).

Bibliography

Bockris, Victor. 1995. *Transformer: The Lou Reed Story*. New York: Simon & Schuster.

Bockris, Victor. 1998. *Keith Richards: The Biography*. New York: Da Capo Press.

Bockris, Victor. 1999. *Patti Smith: An Unauthorized Biography*. New York: Simon & Schuster.

Bockris, Victor, and Malanga, Gerard. 1983. *Up-tight: The Story of the Velvet Underground*. London: Omnibus Press.

Brown, Peter, and Gaines, Steven. 1983. *The Love You Make: An Insider's Story of the Beatles*. New York: McGraw-Hill.

Calt, Stephen. 1994. *I'd Rather Be the Devil: Skip James and the Blues*. New York: Da Capo Press.

Faithfull, Marianne, with Dalton, David. 1994. *Faithfull: An Autobiography*. London: Michael Joseph.

Frith, Simon. 1983. 'Rock Biography.' *Popular Music* 3: 271–77.

Goldman, Albert. 1981. *Elvis*. New York: McGraw-Hill.

Goldman, Albert. 1988. *The Lives of John Lennon*. London: Bantham.

Gray, Martin. 1984. *A Dictionary of Literary Terms*. Beirut: York Press.

Guthrie, Woody. 1943. *Bound for Glory*. New York: E.P. Dutton & Co.

Harlos, Christopher. 1995. 'Jazz Autobiography: Theory, Practice, Politics.' In *Representing Jazz*, ed. Kim Gabbard. Durham, NC and London: Duke University Press, 131–68.

Heylin, Clinton. 1991. *Dylan: Behind the Shades*. London: Viking.

Jones, Ed. 1999. *This Is Pop*. London: Canongate.

Lomax, Alan. 1993. *Mister Jelly Roll: The Fortunes of Jelly Roll Morton, New Orleans Creole and 'Inventor of Jazz'*. New York: Pantheon Books. (First published New York: Duell, Sloan and Pearce, 1949.)

Marsh, Dave. 1979. *Born to Run: The Bruce Springsteen Story*. Garden City, NY: Dolphin Books.

Marsh, Dave. 1982. *Elvis*. New York: Times Books.

Marsh, Dave. 1985. *Trapped: Michael Jackson and the Crossover Dream*. New York: Bantam Books.

Marsh, Dave. 1987. *Glory Days: Bruce Springsteen in the 1980s*. New York: Pantheon Books.

Oliver, Paul. 1959. *Bessie Smith*. London: Cassell.

Otway, John. 1990. *Cor Baby, That's Really Me: Rock and Roll's Greatest Failure*. London: Omnibus.

Savage, Jon. 1992. *England's Dreaming: Anarchy, Sex Pistols, Punk Rock, and Beyond*. New York: St. Martin's Press.

Shelton, Robert. 1986. *No Direction Home: The Life and Music of Bob Dylan*. London: Penguin.

Shelton, Robert. 1996. 'Wanted Man' (Interview). *The Telegraph* 54 (Spring).

Shuker, Roy. 1994. *Understanding Popular Music*. London: Routledge.

Smith, Giles. 1995. *Lost in Music: A Pop Odyssey*. London: Picador.

Theodorakis, Mikis. 1973. *Journals of Resistance*. London: Hart, Davies, MacGibbon.

Thornton, Sarah. 1990. 'Strategies for Reconstructing the Popular Past.' *Popular Music* 9(1): 87–95.

Tremlett, George. 1974a. *The Gary Glitter Story*. London: Futura.

Tremlett, George. 1974b. *The Osmond Story*. London: Futura.

Tremlett, George. 1974c. *The Rolling Stones Story*. London: Futura.

Tremlett, George. 1975a. *The Paul McCartney Story*. London: Futura.

Tremlett, George. 1975b. *The Slade Story*. London: Futura.

Tremlett, George. 1976. *The John Lennon Story*. London: Futura.

Turner, Steve. 1993. *Van Morrison: Too Late to Stop Now*. London: Viking.

Watson, Ben. 1996. *Frank Zappa: The Negative Dialectics of Poodle Play*. New York: St. Martin's Griffin.

Wolfe, Charles, and Lornell, Kip. 1992. *The Life and Legend of Leadbelly*. New York: HarperCollins.

ROBERT STRACHAN

Discography

A discography is a systematic catalog of sound recordings. The information given varies according to the type of music cataloged, but typically it will include at least the artist credit under which the recording was made, details of accompanists or other participants, the place and date of recording, the titles of the works performed, and issue details. The discographer may confine the latter to the original issue number, with or without contemporary issues for other territories, or may seek to include all issues of a particular type or from one or more countries, or to give complete coverage of all issues and reissues.

Where recordings from the 78 rpm era are involved, it is usual to quote the matrix number allocated to each direct-cut recording. Numbers appearing on later recordings generally relate to the issue process rather than to the recording session, and are usually listed, if at all, only for 45 rpm singles.

In specialist discographies, a wide range of additional information may be given, including composer credits, names of recording personnel, addresses of recording studios, issue dates of individual records and sales figures. The detail given concerning such matters as variations in the instrumentation occurring within a recording session is likely to vary according to the perceived needs of users, the availability of information and the conscientiousness of the discographer. Minor variations in presentation between different issues may or may not engage the discographer's attention.

While some discographies list only recordings issued or made for issue on commercial records, it is increasingly common practise in specialist discographies and in documentation of the pre-tape era to attempt to catalog all surviving sound documents, including films, transcribed broadcasts and private recordings. Complete comprehensiveness is impractical for the period after the invention of the tape recorder, but is sometimes attempted in studies of major figures such as Duke Ellington.

Discographies draw their information primarily from company files, when available, and from information published in catalogs and in LP sleeves and CD inserts. This often needs to be supplemented by reference to contemporary news sources and oral-history materials. These sources are frequently inadequate and necessitate informed deduction. Some specialist discographies set out and reference conflicting information.

The first use of the word 'discography' recorded by the Oxford English Dictionary (OED) is in an English-language publication from China in 1932, but both the word and the concept as now understood first came into general use among jazz enthusiasts. In view of the premium that lovers of jazz placed on personal expression and spontaneous creativity, it was inevitable that they would soon realize that any useful discussion of the music heard on records depended on establishing who exactly was on them and in what order they had been made. This consideration applies equally to any vernacular music which must be studied in actual performance, rather than by means of scores.

During 1936, two pioneer attempts at documenting recorded jazz were published, both under the auspices of leading enthusiasts' periodicals. First came Hilton Schleman's *Rhythm on Record: Who's Who and Register of Recorded Dance Music, 1906–1936* and then Charles Delaunay's *Hot Discography*. These works adopted rather different approaches, with Schleman's, as the subtitle implies, giving information about a wider spread of popular music, but with much less detail. In contrast, Delaunay's work was, to a degree, selective by quality as well as by musical style.

Delaunay's presentation found the greatest favor with users, and from his pioneering work there developed the system for documenting the minutiae of recording history currently used by jazz and blues discographers and generally copied for the documentation of other vernacular musics. Delaunay himself refined and expanded his work, which culminated in *New Hot Discography: The Standard Directory of Recorded Jazz* (1948). In the meantime, an attempt at a non-selective complete listing of jazz and blues recordings had been made by Orin Blackstone with *Index to Jazz* (1945–48).

The final step to a fully developed system was taken by Dave Carey and Albert McCarthy in *The Directory of Recorded Jazz and Swing Music* (1949–57), generally known by its cover title, *Jazz Directory*. This was the first discography to organize its contents by recording sessions in matrix-number order, and it sought to attain comprehensive coverage of jazz, blues and African-American gospel music using a generally inclusive approach to related areas of popular music. Unfortunately, the project was discontinued at the letter 'L,' overwhelmed by the massive increase in the volume of recordings issued as a consequence of the spread of the LP.

Most subsequent attempts at comprehensive discographies of jazz and blues limit their coverage chronologically in order to make the material manageable. Brian Rust's *Jazz Records* (1983), first published as *Jazz Records, A-Z*, in two volumes covering 1897–1931 and 1932–42, and Robert M.W. Dixon's and John Godrich's *Blues and Gospel Records 1902–1942* (1964; fourth edition published in 1997 as *Blues and Gospel Records 1890–1943*) together cover African-American music and its derivatives up to their closing dates.

For subsequent eras, the various volumes of Jørgen Grunnet Jepsen's *Jazz Records 1942–1962* (1963–70) have been updated by Erik Raben's still-proceeding *Jazz Records, 1942–80*. Mike Leadbitter's and Neil Slaven's *Blues Records: January 1943–December 1966* (1968) has been superseded by volumes variously attributed to Leadbitter, Slaven, Leslie Fancourt and Paul Pelletier, covering 1943–70. African-American gospel music is covered by Cedric J. Hayes's and Robert Laughton's *Gospel Records 1943–1969: A Black Music Discography* (1992).

Largely derivative of these works for the material in common, but extending the coverage chronologically and stylistically, are the discographies of Walter Bruyninckx, whose *70 Years of Recorded Jazz 1917–1987* (1987–97) in fact continues to the date on which each of its loose-leaf sections was prepared for publication. Tom Lord's *The Jazz Discography* (1992–) owes a large debt to Bruyninckx's work.

In addition to these general works, jazz and blues scholarship has spawned numerous specialist discographies of individual artists, including bio-discographies (works combining biographical and discographical information, usually in one sequence), such as

that of Clarence Williams by Tom Lord (1976). Lord's work is unusual in also containing a diagram of the structure of each recorded item. Most periodicals in the field have also concerned themselves with discography, and some have been wholly or mainly devoted to it, notably *The Jazzfinder* (New Orleans, 1948), *The Discophile* (London, 1948–58), *Matrix* (Victoria, Australia, 1954–58; Stoke-on-Trent, later Madeley, UK, 1959–75), *Discographical Forum* (London, 1960–85), *Journal of Jazz Discography* (Newport, Wales, 1975–79) and *Names & Numbers* (Amsterdam, 1985–87; 1998–). Allen (1981) provides a comprehensive guide to this material up to the date of publication.

Outside the field of African-American music and its derivatives, coverage has been more restricted. Brian Rust has concerned himself with popular dance music of the 78 rpm era in both the United States and Britain with his *The American Dance Band Discography, 1917–1942* (1975) and *British Dance Bands on Record, 1911–1945*, with Sandy Forbes (1989). Rust has also concerned himself with other areas of entertainment music, compiling *British Music Hall on Record* (1979), and *London Musical Shows on Record, 1897–1976*, with Rex Bunnett (1977). His inevitably selective but wide-ranging *The Complete Entertainment Discography, from the Mid-1890s to 1942*, with Allen G. Debus (1973), includes 'the minstrel pioneers, the vaudevilleans, the film stars and radio personalities, and the straight actors and actresses – some of whom even lifted their voices in song' (1), and thus finds room for a list including Gracie Fields and Carmen Miranda, Eddie Cantor and Paul Robeson.

Although most discography has been organized around the cataloging of the works of performers in the chosen stylistic area, an alternative approach is the cataloging of the output of a record label, without regard to content. Label lists confined to record numbers, artists and titles are more of a valuable tool for discographers than discographies in themselves, but in recent years many volumes have appeared giving the normal spread of discographical information about all the records on particular labels. The 'Discographies' series published by Greenwood Press has included a number of such studies, many compiled by the French discographer Michel Ruppli. Examples of Ruppli's work include *Atlantic Records: A Discography* (1979) and *The Savoy Label: A Discography* (1980). Max E. Vreede's illustrated discography of the Paramount 12000/13000 'race' series (1971) is a particularly noteworthy achievement in this area.

In the field of ethnic music, Richard Spottswood's *Ethnic Music on Records: A Discography of Ethnic Recordings Produced in the United States, 1893–1942* (1990) is the first work to attempt systematic coverage of any one area. A comprehensive discography of pre-1942 country music has been compiled, but still awaits publication.

Discographical treatment of music from the rock and pop eras has tended to be most evident in the area of individual artist or group discographies. A number of these have introduced new variants into discographical practise, such as the inclusion of album covers (as, for example, in Ron Barry's *The Elvis Presley American Discography* (1976)) and detailed narrative accounts of recording sessions (as in Mark Lewisohn's *Complete Beatles Recording Sessions* (1988) and Ernst Jorgensen's *Elvis Presley: A Life in Music – The Complete Recording Sessions* (1998)). Although many discographies of rock and pop from the mid-1950s on are less systematic when judged by the standards set by their jazz and blues counterparts, there are a number that do follow similar imperatives. Another Presley work, for example, Colin Escott's and Martin Hawkins's *Elvis Presley: An Illustrated Discography* (1981), includes names of all participating musicians.

Nevertheless, it is apparent that many works listing rock and pop records abide by a rather different set of priorities. Recognition of the importance of record label names and issue numbers is common to all forms of discography, but interest in non-headlining musicians and in details such as place of recording is less consistently apparent in rock and pop discographies than interest in headlining musicians and song titles. A significant difference is evident in the tendency of many rock and pop compilations to provide data on year of release in preference to date of recording. This points to the existence of a very different emphasis, one that focuses on the life history of the record as a commercial artifact. This is borne out by – and helps to explain – the prevalence among sources providing information about rock and pop recordings of books devoted to lists of chart success.

Only perhaps a distant cousin of the classic discography, these volumes (as exemplified in the numerous compilations of Joel Whitburn, based on chart lists in *Billboard*; see, for example, Whitburn 2000a, 2000b, 2000c) proliferate in the rock and pop field, far outnumbering other forms of record listing. The many permutations of the chart list, from 'Top 100' to 'Number Ones,' from chronological to alphabetical, all revolve ultimately around an appeal to the idea of competitive commercial success, in which record industry and audience are inseparably involved. More traditional discography, by contrast, has never shown a great deal of interest in the commercial afterlife of the events it so meticulously catalogs. Information regarding release dates, for example, is included infrequently, and figures for numbers of records pressed and sold by companies are similarly inconsistent (Dan Mahony's *The Columbia 13/14000-D Series* (1961) is one example of an exception).

Partly, this is explained by difficulties of access to the files: record companies have not always been willing to release this, more commercial, kind of information. But, partly also, it reflects a value system inherent in much discography: the recording activity by the musicians is the primary focus of attention, and the subsequent fate of the recording in the world is of less concern.

The considerable achievements of discography – and of the international roster of discographers who have compiled them, whether in isolation or in global networks – can be seen to be based on a belief in the importance of detail and of the need for absolute accuracy. In making this principle available, and in pairing it with the assumption that the roles of all participating musicians are worthy of being noted, discography goes considerably beyond pedantry into a way of thinking that sees each recorded event as a unique conjuncture of specific elements and activities.

Discographies

Barry, Ron. 1976. *The Elvis Presley American Discography*. Phillipsburg, NJ: Spectator Service, Maxigraphics.

Blackstone, Orin. 1945–48. *Index to Jazz*. New Orleans: Gordon Gullickson.

Bruyninckx, Walter. 1987–97. *70 Years of Recorded Jazz 1917–1987*. Mechelen, Belgium: The author.

Carey, Dave, and McCarthy, Albert. 1949–57. *The Directory of Recorded Jazz and Swing Music*. Fordingbridge, Hampshire/London: Delphic Press/Cassell.

Delaunay, Charles. 1936. *Hot Discography*. Paris: Jazz Hot.

Delaunay, Charles. 1948. *New Hot Discography: The Standard Directory of Recorded Jazz*. New York: Criterion.

Dixon, Robert M.W., and Godrich, John. 1964. *Blues and Gospel Records 1902–1942*. Hatch End, Middlesex: Brian Rust.

Dixon, Robert M.W., Godrich, John, and Rye, Howard. 1997. *Blues and Gospel Records 1890–1943*. 4th ed. Oxford: Clarendon Press.

Escott, Colin, and Hawkins, Martin. 1981. *Elvis Presley: An Illustrated Discography*. New York: Omnibus.

Hayes, Cedric J., and Laughton, Robert. 1992. *Gospel Records 1943–1969: A Black Music Discography*. London: Record Information Services.

Jepsen, Jørgen Grunnet. 1963–70. *Jazz Records 1942–1962*. Copenhagen: Nordisk Tidskrift and Karl Emil Knudsen.

Jorgensen, Ernst. 1998. *Elvis Presley: A Life in Music – The Complete Recording Sessions*. New York: St. Martin's Press.

Leadbitter, Mike, and Slaven, Neil. 1968. *Blues Records: January 1943–December 1966*. London: Hanover Books.

Leadbitter, Mike, et al. 1987–94. *Blues Records, 1943–1970: A Selective Discography*. London: Record Information Services.

Lewisohn, Mark. 1988. *Complete Beatles Recording Sessions*. New York: Harmony Books.

Lord, Tom. 1976. *Clarence Williams*. Chigwell, Essex: Storyville Publications.

Lord, Tom. 1992–. *The Jazz Discography*. West Vancouver, BC/Redwood, NY: Lord Music Reference/Cadence Jazz Books.

Mahony, Dan. 1961. *The Columbia 13/14000-D Series: A Numerical Listing*. Stanhope, NJ: W.C. Allen.

Raben, Erik. 1989–. *Jazz Records, 1942–80*. Copenhagen: JazzMedia.

Ruppli, Michel. 1979. *Atlantic Records: A Discography*. 4 vols. Westport, CT: Greenwood Press.

Ruppli, Michel. 1980. *The Savoy Label: A Discography*. Westport, CT: Greenwood Press.

Rust, Brian. 1961. *Jazz Records, A-Z, 1897–1931*. Hatch End, Middlesex: The author.

Rust, Brian. 1965. *Jazz Records, A-Z, 1932–1942*. Hatch End, Middlesex: The author.

Rust, Brian. 1975. *The American Dance Band Discography, 1917–1942*. New Rochelle, NY: Arlington House.

Rust, Brian. 1979. *British Music Hall on Record*. Harrow, Middlesex: General Gramophone Publications.

Rust, Brian. 1983. *Jazz Records*. 5th ed. Chigwell, Essex: Storyville Publications.

Rust, Brian, with Bunnett, Rex. 1977. *London Musical Shows on Record, 1897–1976*. Harrow, Middlesex: General Gramophone Publications.

Rust, Brian, with Debus, Allen G. 1973. *The Complete Entertainment Discography, from the Mid-1890s to 1942*. New Rochelle, NY: Arlington House.

Rust, Brian, with Forbes, Sandy. 1989. *British Dance Bands on Record, 1911–1945*. Harrow, Middlesex: General Gramophone Publications.

Schleman, Hilton. 1936. *Rhythm on Record: Who's Who and Register of Recorded Dance Music, 1906–1936*. London: Melody Maker.

Spottswood, Richard. 1990. *Ethnic Music on Records: A Discography of Ethnic Recordings Produced in the United States, 1893–1942*. Urbana, IL: University of Illinois Press.

Strong, Martin C. 1998. *The Great Rock Discography*. New York: Times Books.

Vreede, Max E. 1971. *Paramount 12000/13000 Series*. London: Storyville Publications (illustrated discography).

Whitburn, Joel. 2000a. *Joel Whitburn Presents the Billboard Hot 100 Charts: The Nineties*. Menomonee Falls, WI: Record Research.

Whitburn, Joel. 2000b. *Joel Whitburn Presents Top R&B Singles, 1942–1999: Chart Data Compiled from Billboard's R&B Singles Charts, 1942–1999*. Menomonee Falls, WI: Record Research.

Whitburn, Joel. 2000c. *The Billboard Book of Top 40 Hits*. 7th ed. New York: Billboard Books.

Bibliography

Allen, Daniel, comp. 1981. *Bibliography of Discographies. Vol. 2: Jazz*. New York and London: Bowker.

Bakker, Dick M. 1990. 'Discographies and Discographers.' *Discographical and Micrographical Basics* 4: 28–32.

Bourke, Tony. 1988. *Index of Record Label Listings*. Ongar, Essex: The author.

Cooper, David. 1975. *International Bibliography of Discographies: Classical Music and Jazz & Blues, 1962–1972*. Littleton, CO: Libraries Unlimited.

Foreman, Lewis. 1974. *Systematic Discography*. London: Clive Bingley.

Godrich, John. 1969. 'Discographical Games People Play.' *Storyville* 23: 175–78.

Gronow, Pekka. 1968. 'Discography as a Science.' *Jazz Monthly* 152: 9–12.

Kennington, Donald, and Read, Danny L. 1980 (1970). *The Literature of Jazz: A Critical Guide*. 2nd ed. London: The Library Association.

Kernfeld, Barry, and Rye, Howard. 1994/95. 'Comprehensive Discographies of Jazz, Blues, and Gospel.' *Notes: Quarterly Journal of the Music Library Association* 51(2): 501–47; 51(3): 865–91.

Macleod, Beth, and Ginsberg, David. 1977. 'State of the Art Survey of Reference Sources in Music.' *Reference Services Review* 5(1): 21–29.

Moon, Pete, comp. 1972 (1969). *A Bibliography of Jazz Discographies Published Since 1960*. 3rd ed. South Harrow, Middlesex: British Institute of Jazz Studies.

Patrick, James. 1972. 'The Uses of Jazz Discography.' *Notes: Quarterly Journal of the Music Library Association* 29: 17–23.

Patrick, James. 1973. 'Discography as a Tool for Music Research and Vice-Versa.' *Journal of Jazz Studies* 1(1): 65–81.

Rust, Brian. 1980. *Brian Rust's Guide to Discography*. Westport and London: Greenwood Press.

Sheatsley, Paul. 1964. 'A Quarter Century of Jazz Discography.' *Record Research* 58: 3–6.

HOWARD RYE with DAVID HORN

Electronic Information

The development of the Internet has transformed opportunities for the storage and distribution of information relating to popular music and has greatly increased its quantity and accessibility. It has also introduced unique possibilities for the exchange of information about popular music between individuals and groups regardless of geographic location or cultural boundaries.

Collections of Information

Information on popular music has long been collected for specific purposes among record companies and industry organizations, as well as practitioners and fans of particular musical styles. However, such collections were not readily available to the general public until the mid-1990s. The rise of the personal computer, the development of sophisticated database software and the facility to link computer networks via the Internet to the World Wide Web made information covering almost every aspect of popular music more accessible to computer users throughout the world. Search software (such as the Z39.50 protocol), often located elsewhere on the Internet, enables the fast retrieval of specific information and allows the construction of on-line databases without the need for substantial indexes or bibliographies to be compiled and stored on the local computer system.

CD-ROM offers an alternative delivery system for such collections of information. By the mid-1990s, several popular music databases had been compiled and published on CD-ROM for sale to libraries and institutions (such as Wadleigh 1996). CD-ROM and the World Wide Web both allow vast quantities of information to be stored and sorted electronically, but Web-based databases have the added advantage of enabling the information that they contain to be updated continually.

The collected information relating to popular music on the World Wide Web includes text-based sources as diverse as: new and existing journals and journal indexes; lyrics, tablatures and sheet music; and a plethora of reference sources and sites devoted to the study of artists and performers, instruments, musical genres and composition. The academic sector (for example, at Indiana University, Bloomington, USA, and McGill University, Montréal, Canada) is creating large-scale multimedia projects aimed at delivering a wide range of student music resources on-line (such as audio, video, notation and bibliographic data). Increasingly, the audio- and videoclips are made available for downloading.

Broadly speaking, popular music databases and collections available on the World Wide Web can be classified into three types – commercial, academic and fan-related – although the distinction is not always material to users seeking information. Commercial databases include those maintained by record companies (such as *Sony Music Online*) to track and promote their current catalog, by industry organizations to record the ownership of copyrighted material (*BMI.com Repertoire*) and by retail organizations to catalog material available for sale (*Pepper Music Network*). Academic databases, established

by scholars to collect and share information furthering the study of particular aspects of popular music, range from collections on aspects of musical notation or sound (*SHARC Timbre Database*) through bibliographies (*Everyday I Write the Book*) to text collections (*JazzWeb*). Fan collections can be the most exhaustive, often being the product of an almost obsessive desire to collect and store even the most ephemeral information relating to an artist or genre (such as those linked from the comprehensive *Ultimate Band List* or the *RoJaRo* index to rock and jazz publications).

However, there are drawbacks associated with such a profusion of collected popular music information. Since the information collected derives from a range of variable sources and is often dependent on the preferences of those compiling the information, it is extremely difficult to check its status or reliability. Many fan collections can contain information that is partial, incomplete or impossible to verify. The transience of the World Wide Web poses additional problems because pages and collections can move or change without warning, cease to be updated or disappear altogether. Consequently, users must take care in how they use such information and the status they associate with it.

The issue of copyright on the Internet is a further reason for prudence. With copyright laws in most territories framed to restrict the reproduction of printed material, the status of electronic information and the definition of copying are often unclear. It should be understood that, technically, retrieving and storing information electronically may constitute copying and thus may breach copyright. However, in the United Kingdom a defense of 'fair-dealing' protects legitimate uses (for research or private study, criticism or review, and for reporting current events) where rights-holders' interests are not damaged. Many other territories have laws framed along similar lines. In practise, the issue of copyright is unlikely to be a problem and prosecutions are rare where material is copied for 'legitimate' purposes, its authorship is acknowledged and no part of it is used in a way that violates its author's intentions. In due course, copyright issues are likely to be resolved through the updating of national copyright laws (a process that has already begun in the United States) and through the development of reliable Electronic Copyright Management Systems, which allow users to read, but not to download or print, copyrighted material. For further information on copyright laws as they relate to electronic information, see Oppenheim (1996a, 1996b) and the *United States Copyright Office: The Library of Congress*.

The principal value of such collections to users may be the opportunity to retrieve raw information, such as discographies, catalog numbers, chart positions and bibliographic data. Users will need to take particular care in utilizing analytical or evaluative material from such sources, since it is generally unrefereed and its validity may be in question. It is also good practise to print and retain copies of any information downloaded from the World Wide Web in case it changes, permission to use it must be requested or the information becomes unavailable.

Searching for popular music information on the World Wide Web can be another problem. While conventional 'search engines' can produce useful results for very specific search items, a search for the Beatles can produce over 700,000 results. Search sites devoted to music in general or to particular artists, such as the *MCU Virtual Library: Music* and the *Ultimate Band List*, can help to narrow a search, but pages of hypertext links, often maintained by universities with departments of music or popular music, usually provide the easiest paths to particular types of information.

Exchange of Information

Through electronic mail (E-mail), the Internet has also transformed opportunities for personal communication, enabling correspondents to send messages almost instantaneously to others around the world. E-mail has also facilitated the development of on-line shopping, allowing customers who browse through catalogs or virtual stores on the World Wide Web to place orders and make payments electronically. A growing globalization of the market is one consequence of this for the popular music industry, with recordings and merchandise no longer restricted largely to particular territories. For popular music scholars and fans alike, E-mail has opened up new prospects for exchanging information and forging links with those with similar interests, regardless of location.

In its more sophisticated forms, E-mail can expand the possibilities of electronic communication. Electronic mailing lists, bulletin boards and newsgroups cater to the tastes of almost every popular music enthusiast by enabling the circulation of a single message to many subscribers. Their subject matter ranges from scholarly requests for information (as in the *International Association for the Study of Popular Music* (IASPM) bulletin board) to the unfettered discussions of Usenet newsgroups; Mitchell (1997) describes one such newsgroup based in New Zealand. The quality of these discussion groups is highly variable. Some control quality by limiting access (by subscription, for example, in the case of IASPM) or by having a moderator who acts as gatekeeper (for example, *rec.music.beatles.info*). Unmoderated newsgroups are often dominated by their most persistent or

opinionated subscribers at the expense of people who have more moderate or popular views (see *rec.music.beatles.moderated* and *rec.music.beatles.info*). The chat room, a virtual room where visitors can meet others and share ideas on music and other subjects (for example, at *SonicNet*), is becoming increasingly popular. Once a person joins a chat room, others in the chat room can see everything that is typed in real time.

Illustrating the reach of the Internet and its importance for popular music, Paul McCartney's on-line question-and-answer multimedia 'webcast' in May 1997 from the Cavern in Liverpool attracted more than 3 million viewers (Digital Media Solutions 1997). About 18 months later, Madonna reportedly surpassed Paul McCartney's record for the largest 'webcast' audience with an estimated 9 million viewers (Mariano 2000).

High-speed Internet access provided by broad-band services is poised to usher in a new era in multimedia experiences for home users. Broad-band connections enable the downloading of Web pages, music and multimedia files in seconds instead of minutes. Events emphasizing the audio, video and text capabilities of the Internet, as well as its reach and immediacy, will become increasingly common, eventually offering an important new delivery system for popular music products and merchandise.

The future use of electronic information is not a simple extrapolation of how it is currently used; its vast potential cannot be accurately predicted because it is not fully understood at the moment. Regardless of its inherent unpredictability, electronic information will remain an integral part of popular music as society is transformed by the digital age.

Bibliography

Digital Media Solutions. 1997. *Music Industry Leads the Digital Age: Record-breaking 'Webcast' by Paul McCartney*.
http://www.sun.com/media/pressrel/digitalmusic.html
Mariano, Gwendolyn. 2000. *Madonna Webcast Shows Internet Is Not TV*.
http://news.cnet.com/news/0-1005-200-3890055.html
Mitchell, Tony. 1997. 'New Zealand Music on the Internet: A Study of the NZPOP Mailing List.' *Perfect Beat* 3(2) (January): 77–95.
Oppenheim, Charles. 1996a. 'The Legal Issues Concerning Electronic Copyright Management Systems.' *Ariadne* 2.
http://www.ariadne.ac.uk/issue2/copyright/
Oppenheim, Charles. 1996b. 'Copyright Issues for eLib Project Co-ordinators.' *Ariadne* 3.
http://www.ariadne.ac.uk/issue3/copyright/
Rodman, Gilbert B., and Coates, Norma. *Everyday I Write*

the Book: A Bibliography of (Mostly) Academic Work on Rock and Pop Music. http://www.cas.usf.edu/communication/rodman/biblio/biblio-front.html

Wadleigh, Michael. 1996. *RocknRom: The Ultimate Database of Popular Music*. London: Penguin Electronic (CD-ROM).

World Wide Web Sites

BMI.com   Repertoire.   http://repertoire.bmi.com/titlesrch.asp

International Association for the Study of Popular Music. http://www.iaspm.net/

JazzWeb. http://www.northwestern.edu/jazz/

MCU Virtual Library: Music. http://mcu.edu/library/music.htm

Pepper Music Network. http://www.jwpepper.com

Rec.music.beatles.moderated and *rec.music.beatles.info.* http://www.rmb.simplenet.com/

RoJaRo. http://www.notam.uio.no/rojaro/

SHARC Timbre Database. http://sparky.parmly.luc.edu/sharc/

SonicNet. http://www.sonicnet.com/home/index.jhtml

Sony Music Online. http://www.sonymusic.com/

Ultimate Band List. http://ubl.artistdirect.com/

United States Copyright Office: The Library of Congress. http://www.loc.gov/copyright/

PETER GODDARD and COREY D. RAMEY

Encyclopedias

Introduction

An encyclopedia is a reference book that offers detailed information on a wide variety of subjects, or on a wide variety of topics within a specific subject. In its original Greek use, *enkyklopedia* meant 'a circle of learning,' hence a rounded (liberal) education. By the sixteenth century, the word began to be used to refer to a book that would deliver all-round knowledge, and by 1620, in England, Francis Bacon had made ambitious plans for such a book, one that would embrace all areas of human thought and activity in a systematic, scientific way. Bacon's plans remained unfulfilled, and the general acceptance of both the idea and the word 'encyclopedia' with this meaning dates from the period of the Enlightenment and especially the *Encyclopédie* of Diderot, D'Alembert et al. (1751–65), closely followed by the first edition of the *Encyclopaedia Britannica* (1771).

The history of the encyclopedia contains several smaller, interlocking histories and is marked by numerous debates about issues such as focus, scope, structure, authorship, emphasis and value. Although attempts to compile encyclopedic works in the area of popular music are a comparatively recent development (and, in the case of the present project, a major reference work covering popular music on a global scale, an unprecedented concept), they reflect and frequently respond to these interlocking histories and debates and need to be seen in their light.

The Specialist Encyclopedia

One early development in the history of the form, the specialist encyclopedia, soon became widely accepted as uncontentious. Pioneering works such as Walther's *Musikalisches Lexicon* (1732) established the field of music as appropriate for this treatment (alongside subjects such as chemistry), by virtue of the diversity of its human aspects and the special nature of its technical language (Walther's was the first music reference work to combine biography and terminology in one sequence). The publication of this work set in train a process that culminated in multi-volume modern music encyclopedias such as *The New Grove Dictionary of Music and Musicians* (Sadie 1980) and *Die Musik in Geschichte und Gegenwart* (Blume 1949–86).

When the earliest popular music encyclopedias, such as Feather's *The Encyclopedia of Jazz* (1955), appeared, they were, in one sense, following a lead set by Walther and others over 200 years before. But the lineage was not entirely direct: also influential were reference works that focused on an individual musical genre, such as Kobbé's guide to opera plots, the *Complete Opera Book* (1919). Like them, these early reference works on popular music often display a two-part process: a narrowing of the specialist field (music), typically to that of an individual genre of music; and a separation of this narrower part from the whole. Although in one sense this process challenges the idea, established by the general music reference works, of the need to see music as a whole, it is also part and parcel of the specialist encyclopedia tradition, which can be seen as a set of steps, each offering the possibility of increased depth in the coverage of a narrower field.

Where problems have arisen for popular music within the tradition of specialist encyclopedias is in the treatment it has received as a specialism within a specialism, rather than as a specialism in its own right. Until the appearance of *The New Grove Dictionary of American Music* (Hitchcock 1986), no work purporting to be an encyclopedia covering a wide range of music practises had taken much more than a token interest in popular music. The majority of music encyclopedias focused uniquely or predominantly on the Western art music tradition, enlarging their scope in the second half of the twentieth century to include ethnomusicology. In this respect, it is instructive to compare the aims of

The New Grove Dictionary of Music and Musicians with regard to popular music and non-Western music (ethnomusicology): popular music is covered through major genre entries and entries of 'leading and influential figures' (viii) and no particular claims are made; the subject matter of ethnomusicology has coverage that is claimed to be 'far more extensive and methodical than anything ever attempted before' (ix).

Reasons for the omission, marginalization or at best underrepresentation of popular music in general music encyclopedias can be sought and found in the necessarily complex processes of decision-making that have characterized encyclopedia compilation since the eighteenth century. These processes have involved issues such as the need to impose some form of limitation on scope, the relationship of the text to existing scholarship (in terms of both interest and achievement), level of writing, and readership. But at the same time, neither the processes nor the results can be divorced from a cultural politics which at least until the 1980s saw popular music as an inferior form of culture, undeserving of serious study. Indeed, a key motivating factor behind many popular music projects has been a desire to respond to this negative attitude toward popular music as manifested in many general music reference books. Thus, *The Guinness Encyclopedia of Popular Music*, for example, declares that its 'ultimate intention . . . is once and for all to place popular music shoulder to shoulder with classical and operatic music. It is a legitimate plea for acceptance and tolerance' (Larkin 1992, 14).

If the advent of reference works on popular music can be seen to some degree as an attempt to correct an omission or imbalance, it would be wrong to imply that only encyclopedias dominated by classical music have been hegemonic, either in intent or in effect. Reference works on popular music have themselves often displayed implicit agendas to influence and control that which they set out to map. For example, the same *Guinness Encyclopedia*'s conception of popular music was entirely dominated by that of the Anglo-Saxon world, while the preface to Clarke's *The Penguin Encyclopedia of Popular Music* (1989) makes clear its editor's disgruntlement with regard to contemporary trends.

Similarly, most popular music reference works have tended to assume that biography should play a fundamental role, and indeed it could be argued that, in giving the name 'encyclopedia' to what are primarily biographical dictionaries of performers and composers, popular works such as Shestack's *The Country Music Encyclopedia* (1974) and the *Guinness Encyclopedia* have gone further in implying not just the primacy of the individual, but the primacy of certain areas of individual activity in the popular music field. In this context, Hardy's and Laing's

The Encyclopedia of Rock (1976) is notable for its attempt to redress an imbalance in many popular music reference works in its inclusion, *inter alia*, of entries for producers, business figures and session musicians.

Another, more dramatic way of handling the prevalence of biography – that of omitting biographical entries altogether – has been attempted only rarely in popular music. The most notable achievements have been outside the Anglophone world (and untranslated within it): *Encyklopedie jazzu a moderní populární hudby* (Matzner, Poledák and Wasserberger 1983), and *Rock, Pop, Jazz, Folk: Handbuch der populären Musik* (Wicke and Ziegenrücker 1985). The importance of the subject dictionary ('*Sachwörterbuch*') as a genre of encyclopedia is considerable, for it has proved hard to use such dictionaries without rapidly gaining an increased awareness – to an extent by no means always possible in a compilation dominated by biography – of the depth, diversity and interconnectedness of the area of endeavor in question. The impact that these two pioneering popular music books have had on the English-language world of reference compilation has been slight (not that they are without precedent in that world: *The Harvard Dictionary of Music* (Apel 1969) and *The New Harvard Dictionary of Music* (Randel 1986) operate by the same principle); but their approach is reflected in the design of the *Continuum Encyclopedia of Popular Music of the World* (CEPMOW).

The issues of comprehensiveness and scope have been significant ones for most of the history of both general and specialized reference works. A shift has occurred over time – and especially as a result of the growth of scientific knowledge – from debates over the virtues of the concept of a universal work toward the corollary questions of how and where universality can be limited (or provided with a special focus), while still being claimed. In fashioning a way through this dilemma, two factors have been of prime importance: the expansion and limitations of human scholarship; and a desire to assist with the self-improvement of readers. Acting on this approach, general encyclopedias have customarily seen as unproblematic decisions to omit areas of human activity and experience that are absent from or underrepresented in that scholarship. Knowledge of these areas is, *ipso facto*, less likely to be deemed vital to the self-improvement of readers. One such area has regularly been that of leisure.

Rationale and Status

This debate has inevitably been linked to those that address the issue of the rationale of any particular encyclopedia project, and these in their turn have led into issues of status. Although often viewed as a conservative force because of its tendency, in any area, to reflect both given knowledge and given values, the encyclopedia has also been seen as forward-looking and having radical, even potentially revolutionary, force. This was certainly how the French *encyclopédistes* viewed their humanist project in the context of the intellectual control exercised by the dominant Jesuit culture in France during the earlier part of the eighteenth century when the *encyclopédistes* were active. In the words of one historian of lexicography, the *Encyclopédie* (1751–65) 'did not simply inform; it incited' (McArthur 1986, 106). A more pragmatic but still visionary educational aim informed the Scottish compilers of the *Encyclopaedia Britannica* (1771). Both radical traditions – the cultural-political and the educational – have remained at work, often in tandem and often in an ambiguous, although nonetheless effective, way. When, for example, an encyclopedia includes – or, better, is entirely devoted to – a previously neglected subject, it uses both the conservative image of the encyclopedia as a genre and a range of other consensual factors – its reputation for objectivity, its scientific division of the subject, its apparently overriding interest in 'facts,' its fondness for crisp, no-nonsense language – as a way to confer status on a radical project whose aim is to survey a previously neglected area.

Reference works on popular music are extremely interesting in this context. On the one hand, their attempts to document areas with little status can be seen as radical vis-à-vis the world at large. On the other hand, many tend to be aimed not at that larger world so much as at a captive audience of existing enthusiasts. In this respect, they tend to be less interested in self-improvement than in providing what they judge that audience wants, rather than needs, to know – and will pay to find out. In part, this situation reflects the relative absence of popular music from educational curricula until the later twentieth century; but it is also a reflection of the commercial judgments at play in the field of popular music reference publishing.

It is also the case, however, that reference works on popular music have frequently found it impossible to rely entirely on a given picture of a subject area and a current level of knowledge about it. In his preface to one of the most ambitious, genre-based projects of the late twentieth century, *The New Grove Dictionary of Jazz* (Kernfeld 1988), editor Barry Kernfeld acknowledges the accepted aim of an encyclopedia as being 'to reflect the current understanding of its subject and not to initiate research,' but goes on to note that the project has upheld this tradition in the breach: 'a large amount of information is published for the first time here, and . . . many of the major articles present new thinking on the ways in which jazz may be approached' (vii). CEPMOW has been

conceived in much the same tradition, but with an even greater emphasis on the need to map the subject systematically in a way that has not been attempted hitherto.

One further aspect of rationale and status deserves attention. For many people – practitioners, fans, critics and scholars – a crucial element in the importance of popular music is its fluidity. Encyclopedias, by contrast, may be seen as having a tendency to fix what they describe, more so than other texts, and this is perhaps one reason for the comparative lateness on the encyclopedia scene of major popular music reference projects. Nevertheless, the world of popular music is also rich in and heavily dependent on information, ranging from fixed data (for example, a complete list of the songs of a dead songwriter) to data that change almost daily (for example, chart positions). In this environment, the encyclopedia of popular music is often under pressure to be a superior data source, incorporating under one title all the data available at a particular moment that have been scattered in innumerable smaller works. But the task is an enormous one. The single publication that has come nearest to achieving this goal is Kinkle's four-volume *The Complete Encyclopedia of Popular Music and Jazz, 1900–1950* (1974). Kinkle avoids chart lists, but includes a year-by-year chronology and lists of works and recordings, as well as biographies. Although heavily relied on as a reference source, the publication is inevitably selective. Books dedicated to chart listings are less selective in their approach, but the nature of their data is such that a great many permutations are always possible (number one hits, Top 40 singles, Top 20 albums and so on), and they are fully geared to exploiting this. The way forward for popular music reference works would seem to be to exploit the enormous potential of computerized databases to handle effectively this kind of information. Encyclopedias on popular music could then be designed in such a way as to draw on and be linked to these networks of information, while at the same time placing their contents within explanatory contexts and providing the necessary perspectives on them.

Structure and Organization

Another long-running debate has concerned structure, in particular the choice between a classified and an alphabetical ordering of entries. Although an alphabetical order became the preferred model, most early ideas and attempts were based on a classified structure, which was intended to be a direct embodiment of the thinking behind the enterprise. When the alphabetical approach began to dominate, it did not remove the need for an underpinning classification, which was often regarded as essential. In general encyclopedias, such a classification amounts to a theory of knowledge, and in encyclopedias that provide an outline of the underlying classification, such as the *Encyclopaedia Britannica*, a theory of knowledge is what it is duly called.

Almost without exception, popular music reference works have adopted an alphabetical approach, although typically without explanation of an underpinning system. Some, nevertheless, display some evidence of a systematic approach: Stambler's and Landon's *Encyclopedia of Folk, Country and Western Music* (1969), for example, includes entries for instruments, collectors, institutions and festivals alongside its biographies, and the volume also offers several informal critical essays. Feather's approach in *The Encyclopedia of Jazz* (1955) perhaps comes closest to a classified structure: the biographical dictionary is kept distinct, and there are separate sections for an historical overview, a chronology, a musical analysis, a survey of jazz outside the United States and an assessment. CEPMOW is different both from other musical works and from most other encyclopedias in reverting to the earlier model of an explicit classified structure.

As encyclopedias in electronic form (CD-ROM or DVD-ROM) become more and more common, any residue of the debate over the comparative merits of alphabetical and classified approaches seems likely to disappear. But the great advantages that computer searching has over traditional methods, including the speed at which links between texts can be followed, do not remove the need for an underpinning structure; indeed, they may well make it more necessary than ever.

The prevalence of alphabetical ordering as a general practise is perhaps one reason (apart from modesty) that other terms have come to be used synonymously with 'Encyclopedia': 'Dictionary' and 'Lexicon' have been two popular alternatives, both implying a certain ordering of their information. Adding to the semantic proliferation and possible confusion, but with different implications, have been terms such as 'Companion,' designed to hold on to a sense of authority while suggesting a greater degree of approachability (Gammond 1991; Hardy and Laing 1990).

Authorship

A further debate has concerned single or multiple authorship. Following the *Encyclopédie*'s demonstration of the validity – indeed, the necessity – of multiple authors, general works have tended to proceed along those lines, but the question of whether single authorship is feasible in narrower subjects has continued to be raised, and single authorship characterized many specialized works that described themselves as encyclopedias well into the twentieth century. By the end of the century, the argument seemed very largely settled in favor of multi-authored works in almost all cases where 'true' encyclopedic status was sought, but the historical importance of single authorship was acknowledged. Encyclopedic works on popular music, both those of a general nature and those devoted to individual genres, have regularly been either single-authored or coauthored (Gammond 1991; Herzhaft 1979), although often 'with assistance' (for example, Feather asked overseas contributors to supply his essays on jazz outside the United States). But as the level of documented information has increased, and in the wake of commercial activity and audience interest in the field of world music, the practical and intellectual difficulty of accomplishing the task with one or two authors has been increasingly acknowledged. Even those works for which a lion's share of the credit is given to a single author or a pair of authors, such as Clarke (1989) and Hardy and Laing (1990), acknowledge the help of specialists in certain areas. The exact contributions made by such specialists are not always obvious, as the practise of 'signing' entries (a custom recognized in many subjects as essential) has seldom been adopted in popular music works. Clarke, for example, contents himself with the observation that 'I have largely allowed the judgements of my various contributors to stand,' without feeling compelled to identify where those judgments may be found (1989, ix).

Standard Features

In the area of what should be regarded as the standard features of the encyclopedia – maps, illustrations, regular revisions and so on – a general consensus was apparent by around the end of the nineteenth century. One feature in particular that had come to be regarded as imperative was good bibliographical information. But if, as one writer put it (having surveyed the history of the encyclopedia in enormous detail), 'the saving grace of all good encyclopedias is of course the bibliographies attached to their articles' (Collison 1964, 228), popular music encyclopedias have often been found wanting. Many treat this kind of information in a cursory fashion: primary sources such as sheet music and recordings tend to be very selectively and unsystematically listed and, if a secondary literature of books and articles is included, it is often relegated to an 'all-in' bibliography at the end of the publication (in which the user must search).

In mitigation, two points need to be made. First, popular music has some particularly knotty problems to solve as far as primary sources for individual musicians are concerned: the proliferation of individual pieces of music; the equal proliferation of recordings; and the variable relationship between the two. Second, much bibliographical information comes from relatively ephemeral and nontraditional bibliographical sources, such as album sleeve notes, fanzine interviews and press 'bios.'

In this respect, it has to be noted that the particular bibliographical and discographical problems posed by many sources for popular music scholarship have not been solved by major non-popular music works either. *The New Grove Dictionary of American Music*, for example, is clearly at home with its lengthy bibliographical handling of the notated output of a major figure such as George Gershwin, but fails to acknowledge a single recording of his music – as if recorded interpretation of this songwriter were of minor significance. When it comes to a figure such as Bob Dylan, it lists album titles only.

More open to interpretation than the need for bibliographical information has been that for an index, and in many encyclopedias, across all fields, cross-referencing using a range of typographical means became something of a twentieth-century substitute. Nevertheless, the major international works have maintained highly detailed indexes. In contrast, reference works on popular music have frequently ignored the need for an index. In this, they are at least in good company, for all the *New Grove* dictionaries from 1980 up to the late 1990s omitted one – a fact that engendered considerable criticism. Selective cross-referencing is, however, a reasonably regular feature of popular reference works also.

Conclusion

Encyclopedias have established a place for themselves as works that need to be taken seriously, and, as such, they have often both reflected what their constituency of users considers serious and helped to underpin it. In popular music, the same observation applies, but with the addition that what the constituency of users considers serious may continue to strike non-constituents as the opposite. That part of the encyclopedia's function that – in the tradition of Diderot – looks backward with a new gaze in order to look forward radically is therefore likely still to be of major importance. At the same time, two tendencies threaten to make this progress uneven: the view of the encyclopedia's function as being to fix parameters; and the devoutly retrospective gaze of even those books that find the daily fluidity fascinating.

Bibliography

Apel, Willi, ed. 1969. *The Harvard Dictionary of Music*. 2nd ed. Cambridge, MA: Belknap Press.

Blume, Friedrich, ed. 1949–86. *Die Musik in Geschichte und Gegenwart: allgemeine Enzyklopädie der Musik* [Music in the Past and the Present: A General Encyclopedia of Music]. Kassel: Bärenreiter-Verlag.

Clarke, Donald, ed. 1989. *The Penguin Encyclopedia of Popular Music*. New York: Viking.

Collison, Robert. 1964. *Encyclopaedias: Their History Throughout the Ages*. New York and London: Hafner.

Diderot, Denis, and D'Alembert, Jean, eds. 1751–65. *Encyclopédie, ou dictionnaire raisonné des sciences, des arts et des métiers* [An Encyclopedia, or Rational Dictionary of the Sciences, Arts and Crafts]. Paris: Briasson, David L'aîné, Le Breton.

Encyclopaedia Britannica; or, A Dictionary of Arts and Sciences, Compiled Upon a New Plan. 1771. Edinburgh: A. Bell and C. Macfarquhar.

Feather, Leonard. 1955. *The Encyclopedia of Jazz*. New York: Horizon Press.

Gammond, Peter. 1991. *The Oxford Companion to Popular Music*. Oxford: Oxford University Press.

Hardy, Phil, and Laing, Dave, eds. 1976. *The Encyclopedia of Rock*. St. Alban's: Panther.

Hardy, Phil, and Laing, Dave. 1990. *The Faber Companion to 20th-Century Popular Music*. London: Faber and Faber.

Herzhaft, Gérard. 1979. *Encyclopédie du blues: étude bio-discographique d'une musique populaire négro-américaine* [An Encyclopedia of the Blues: A Bio-Discographical Study of an African-American Popular Music]. Lyon: Fédérop.

Hitchcock, H. Wiley, ed. 1986. *The New Grove Dictionary of American Music*. London: Macmillan.

Kernfeld, Barry, ed. 1988. *The New Grove Dictionary of Jazz*. London: Macmillan.

Kinkle, Roger D. 1974. *The Complete Encyclopedia of Popular Music and Jazz, 1900–1950*. 4 vols. New Rochelle, NY: Arlington House Publishers.

Kobbé, Gustav. 1919. *Complete Opera Book*. New York and London: Putnam.

Larkin, Colin, ed. 1992. *The Guinness Encyclopedia of Popular Music*. Enfield, Middlesex: Guinness.

Matzner, Antonín, Poledák, Ivan, and Wasserberger, Igor, eds. 1983. *Encyklopedie jazzu a moderní populární hudby* [Encyclopedia of Jazz and Modern Popular Music]. Praha: Editio Supraphon, 112.

McArthur, Tom. 1986. *Worlds of Reference: Lexicography, Learning and Language from the Clay Tablet to the Computer*. Cambridge: Cambridge University Press.

Randel, Don, ed. 1986. *The New Harvard Dictionary of Music*. Cambridge, MA: Belknap Press.

Sadie, Stanley, ed. 1980. *The New Grove Dictionary of Music and Musicians*. London: Macmillan.

Shestack, Melvin. 1974. *The Country Music Encyclopedia*. New York: Crowell.

Stambler, Irwin, and Landon, Grelun. 1969. *Encyclopedia of Folk, Country and Western Music*. New York: St. Martin's Press.

Walther, Johann G. 1732. *Musikalisches Lexicon, oder musikalische Bibliothek* [Musical Lexicon, or Musical Library]. Leipzig: Deer.

Wicke, Peter, and Ziegenrücker, Wieland. 1985. *Rock, Pop, Jazz, Folk: Handbuch der populären Musik* [Rock, Pop, Jazz, Folk: A Handbook of Popular Music]. Leipzig: Deutscher Verlag für Musik.

DAVID HORN

Field Recording

Field recordings are recordings made in the normal performance site or locality of the musicians as opposed to in a recording studio. Until the advent of the cylinder machine and subsequent developments in recording, the preservation of songs and music required that they be transcribed and written down by hand. In March 1890, Jesse Walter Fewkes, an anthropologist at Harvard University, recorded songs of the Passamaquoddy Indians in Calais, Maine, and in so doing was the first person in the world to record 'in the field.'

As cylinder equipment became more available in the first decade of the twentieth century, field recording was undertaken in a number of European countries, with the Australian composer Percy Grainger and the Hungarian composer Béla Bartók preserving significant examples of English folk song and Hungarian gypsy music, respectively. Among the most important of early field recordings were those made by Frances Densmore with many nations of Native Americans. She commenced her work for the Bureau of American Ethnology in 1907 and continued into the 1930s. During this time, field recording had become increasingly employed by ethnomusicologists and folk song collectors such as Howard Odum, John A. Lomax and Natalie Curtis Burlin.

At the State University of Iowa, Milton Metfessel developed 'phonophotography,' the simultaneous graphic representation, sound recording and photography of a singer in the field. Unfortunately, the initial experiments made with Howard Odum were not applied later. Nevertheless, the Archive of American Folk Song of the Library of Congress commenced with the cylinder recordings made in Darien, Sea Islands by its first field director, Robert Winslow Gordon, and subsequently by John A. Lomax and his son, Alan Lomax. They were assisted by other field collectors, including the African-American author Zora Neale Hurston, who recorded black music with Alan Lomax in Florida in the late 1930s. Lomax also recorded in the Bahamas and commenced extensive fieldwork outside the United States. After World War II, he resumed this work for his 'Cantometrics' project of comparative studies in singing styles and techniques.

Although the emphasis of field recording was princip-ally ethnomusicological, from the late 1920s commercial record companies such as Columbia, OKeh and Victor began to record in the southern United States with mobile field units, bringing rural traditions, especially 'hillbilly' and 'race' music, to a larger listening audience. In parallel, Hispanic and Acadian ('Cajun') French performers were recorded in the field. With the popularization of the tape recorder in the 1950s, field recording increased dramatically, and the methods of making recordings were accessible to amateurs and professionals alike. So Zoltán Kodály noted that, in the period 1907–51, some 85 gypsy laments and 14 parodies had been recorded in the field, whereas the decade 1952–63 added 503 laments and 183 parodies to the corpus. This he attributed largely to the tape recorder, but also to changes in attitude among gypsy informants. Motivations and intentions in field recording undoubtedly affected the nature of the examples collected, some recordings being made in pursuit of a particular style, instrumentation or even specific song type. In other instances, it was felt necessary to admonish singers whose repertoires did not accord with a prescribed, admissible style.

In the subsequent 20 years, fieldwork was conducted extensively throughout the world, much of the collected material being made available on long-playing records and cassette tapes. Remarkable among these were the recordings made by David Lewiston and issued on Nonesuch Records, his peregrinations taking him from the Amazon to the Himalayas; Lewiston's recordings in Nepal and Kashmir were particularly valued. Others did fieldwork in specific regions and under the auspices of research institutions and universities. Alice Moyle collected songs in the Northern Territory of Australia, for example those issued by the Institute of Aboriginal Studies. Harold Courlander made many recordings of Haitian and Cuban music which were issued in the 1950s by Moses Asch on his Folkways label, one of the first extensive catalogs devoted to ethnic music. Similarly, in South Africa Hugh Tracey made important albums from his fieldwork, which were issued by Decca, one of the first of the major companies to issue such sets. Field recordings were not only disseminated on disc; in the same period, Peter Kennedy, an English folklorist, made records all over the United Kingdom, which formed the basis of his radio series *As I Roved Out*, which was relayed weekly by the BBC for some 15 years in the 1950s and 1960s. In France, the Office de Coopération Radiophonique produced an exceptional series of field recordings on its OCORA label, with excellent standards of production. In the 1960s, the Office de Radiodiffusion-Télévision Française continued this work with important recordings made in Africa by Michael Vuylsteke

(Burundi), Tolia Nikiprowetsky (Niger) and Charles Duvelle (Congo). At the Musée de l'Homme, Guilbert Rouget of the Département d'Ethnomusicologie directed a series of field recordings in association with the Centre National de la Recherche Scientifique in West Africa, Brazil and elsewhere.

In the 1970s, the trend toward coordinated field recording projects was endorsed by UNESCO, under whose auspices a number of exhaustive series was issued. Among these was a 10-volume series of African music edited for the International Institute for Comparative Music Studies and Documentation. Under the general editorship of Paul Collaer, in association with several museums and scholars, these were issued by Bärenreiter-Musicaphon, Kassel, Germany. UNESCO collections became increasingly ambitious, with as many as 30 volumes of *A Musical Anthology of the Orient* being issued, with Alain Daniélou as overseeing editor. He was also editor of the UNESCO *Musical Sources* collection, drawing from national and regional archives, which included studio recordings. Bärenreiter also issued a multi-volume *Anthology of South-East Asian Music* with UNESCO support, but published by the Institute of Musicology of the University of Basel. In Britain, Tangent was one of several companies, including Saydisc and Transatlantic, that issued field records on long-playing discs. Among these was a six-volume set of *Music in the World of Islam*, principally recorded by Jean Jenkins of the Horniman Museum.

This was undoubtedly the great period of field recording, when Alan Lomax was traveling extensively around the world and David Fanshawe was amassing a large collection in the Middle East and the Pacific. Few of the field researchers in non-Western countries were native to the countries in which they recorded or were of non-Western origin. An exception was Deben Bhattacharya from Benares (Varanasi), India, who, however, was a BBC producer before moving to Sweden. Between 1960 and 1975, he produced 75 albums from his field recordings in places from Hungary to Nepal. By now, the ethical problems of field recording and its intrusiveness on culture and custom, the relationship between fieldworker and the traditional musician, the motivations behind recording and the uses to which the results were applied, were the subject of serious concern to researchers such as Bruno Nettl (1964) and Steven Feld (1994). Yet field researchers have not only succeeded in documenting many of the world's indigenous music traditions, but have also illumined the constant elements, as well as the changes in regional musics in the years of increasing globalization. This has been significant in the forms of African-American music, of which some have been lost, others barely survived, while a number with roots in the past that have been at least partially documented have become major influences on popular music.

Bibliography

Cowley, John. 1993. 'Don't Leave Me Here: The Field Trips.' In *Nothing But the Blues: The Music and the Musicians*, ed. Lawrence Cohn et al. New York: Abbeville Press, 265–311.

Feld, Steven. 1994. 'From Schizophonia to Schismogenesis: On the Discourses and Commodification Practices of "World Music" and "World Beat."' In Charles Keil and Steven Feld, *Music Grooves: Essays and Dialogues*. Chicago and London: University of Chicago Press, 257–89.

Kodály, Zoltán. 1972. *Folk Music of Hungary*. Rev. ed. Hungarian National Commission for UNESCO. Budapest: Corvina.

Lomax, Alan. 1993. *The Land Where the Blues Began*. London: Methuen.

Malm, William P. 1967. *Music Cultures of the Pacific, the Near East, and Asia*. Englewood Cliffs, NJ: Prentice-Hall.

Metfessel, Milton. 1928. *Phonophotography in Folk Music: American Negro Songs in New Notation*. Chapel Hill, NC: University of North Carolina Press.

Nettl, Bruno. 1964. *Theory and Method in Ethnomusicology*. New York: Free Press of Glencoe.

Spottswood, Richard, ed. 1982. *Ethnic Recordings in America: A Neglected Heritage*. Washington, DC: American Folklife Center, Library of Congress.

PAUL OLIVER

Film and Television Documentaries

In the context of popular music, a film documentary is a 'factual' film or television program about a popular music artist, act, scene or event. The term 'documentary' was first coined in the mid-1920s by the Scottish filmmaker John Grierson to describe filmmaking that attempts to 'photograph the living scene and the living story' (Grierson 1946, 80). Popular music documentaries generally fall into the categories of 'concert films, tour movies and documentary profiles of living or dead stars' (Wootton 1995, 95), along with social histories of popular music genres and periods, including films that document a particular popular music scene or movement.

The concert film is perhaps the most established genre in the documentary field and has precursors in jazz and big band short performance films of the 1930s. One of the earliest and most influential full-length concert films, *Jazz on a Summer's Day* (1959), recorded the Newport Jazz Festival. This film mixed live performances, seascape shots, talking heads and images from in and around the festival, thus attempting to create 'slice of life' tableaux. The film was taken as a blueprint for many later films, and its influence can be seen clearly in festival documentaries such as *Monterey Pop* (1968), *Woodstock: 3 Days of Peace and Music* (1970) and *Message to Love: The Isle of Wight Festival* (1996). The concert footage in these films introduced the use of visual editing techniques that attempted to capture the feel of musical performance. Methods such as repeated rapid zooming of the camera lens from a wide shot to a closeup, split screens and attempts to match visual images to lyrical phrases became standard characteristics of concert films for the next decade (Tagg 1997).

By the late 1960s, there was a tendency within the narrative of documentary films to assume that the events they presented had a wider cultural significance. The success of earlier concert and festival films helped this idea to become established and contributed to the way in which importance was subsequently attributed to the events that they recorded. For instance, the Woodstock movie employed a narrative that elevated the importance of the event by presenting the festival as the high point of the US counterculture. The film creates a narrative of countercultural life (juxtaposing music with drug use, communal scenes and comment on the Vietnam war), thus attempting to present a coherent composite of late 1960s youth experience. This ideological symbolism, along with the film's lasting commercial success at the box office and on video, served to crystallize the filmmaker's view of the event in the public imagination and enhance the legendary status of Woodstock as the touchstone of the counterculture.

In the 1980s, films such as Jonathan Demme's Talking Heads' concert film *Stop Making Sense* (1984) and the U2 film *Rattle and Hum* (1988) opted for a starker, more naturalistic look, using a formula pioneered by Martin Scorsese in his 1978 film of the Band, *The Last Waltz*. Using less complicated camera angles, black-and-white film, an absence of fast cutting and no audience reaction shots, these concert films aimed to present popular music performance without the distraction of intercut images. Later concert films challenged the conventions of the form through stylized and conceptual representations, such as the Pet Shop Boys' *Performance* (1992), which employs an abstract narrative echoing the visual characteristics of the stage-show footage, or R.E.M.'s *Tourfilm* (1990), which uses different directors and visual style for each song.

The development of popular music documentary has been closely linked to the direct cinema movement of the 1960s, which sought to present the film as a document of real events without the interference of a vocal narrative interpretation. Direct cinema avoided devices such as statement of events, voice-over narration and talking heads, in an attempt to let the subjects of the documentary 'speak for themselves' (Monaco 1980). With its aspirations toward objectivity, the genre was particularly suited to tour movies, which mix live performance with backstage footage and the day-to-day workings of touring. Indeed, the most commercially successful direct cinema films had touring rock musicians in their 'natural habitat' as their subjects. Films such as D.A. Pennebaker's film of Bob Dylan, *Don't Look Back* (1967), and the Rolling Stones' films *Gimme Shelter* (1970) and *Cocksucker Blues* (1972) had an extensive influence on popular music documentaries that followed, establishing many of the conventions of subsequent films in the genre.

Such documentaries supposedly look behind the public persona of the star by offering a glimpse into the 'private world' of the backstage area, where performers are seen 'being themselves.' However, the backstage footage is often as contrived and controlled as actual stage performance, and merely acts to reinforce an artist's public persona rather than stripping away any surrounding mythology. For instance, Romney (1995) argues that all Dylan's actions in *Don't Look Back* are 'laid on for the camera,' and the supposedly natural backstage scenes in the film are a 'repertoire of the techniques used by an artist to repel criticism while maintaining his own mystique' (88). Despite the confessional premise of *In Bed with Madonna* (1991), the artist's explicit awareness of the camera and asides to the crew over what should be recorded make clear Madonna's control over the whole project. Rather than exposing the machinations of the documentary form, the film's self-awareness serves to reiterate Madonna's public image of strength, independence and autonomy.

Likewise, even a film such as the Chet Baker documentary *Let's Get Lost* (1988), which is, supposedly, confessional and uncompromising in nature, taps into wellworn mythologies and stylistic conventions associated with jazz musicians. Indeed, by the 1980s, the conventions of direct cinema had become so synonymous with popular music documentary that they were subject to parody in films such as *This Is Spinal Tap* (1984) and *Fear of a Black Hat* (1994). All film documentaries offer representations of a musical event or act that are colored by directorial choice, degree of access to and control by artist and record company, and stylistic conventions associated with specific musical genres.

The reinforcement of public persona and popular music myth within film and television documentaries has meant that they have often been used as promotional tools for the music industry. Examples of this practise include the television documentaries *The Doors Are Open* and *The Stones in the Park*, made by Granada TV in the late 1960s, which coincided with tours and album releases. The late 1990s saw an increased marketing synergy, with the broadcast of a popular music documentary series often being scheduled to coincide with the release of a tie-in compilation album (such as *John Peel's Sounds of the Suburbs*). VH1's *Behind the Music* series, despite being reliant on the exposure of scurrilous details about rock artists' personal and professional lives, proved so popular that many acts organized comeback tours to coincide with the screening of individual programs. Other programs have stimulated market demand for recordings: for example, the US broadcast of Ken Burns's television documentary series *Jazz* (2001) was watched by 60 million viewers and has been credited with doubling the sales of jazz recordings in the United States.

A number of film documentaries have attempted to document popular musical movements and scenes without concentrating on one particular act or artist. Some of these films attempt to present a rounded picture of their respective scenes by including established and unknown acts. For example, *D.O.A.* (1981) profiles the British punk scene of the late 1970s, and *The Decline of Western Civilization, Parts 1 and 2* (1981, 1988) deal with the Los Angeles punk and heavy metal scenes. Concentrating on events around one place, these films offer a 'sociological' approach by showing the social and political contexts of musical movements. In *D.O.A.*, performances from various punk groups are intercut with interviews, shots of urban decay and scenes from the life of an unemployed youth on a London council estate. Like documentaries that concentrate on 'star' performers, these films are far from value-free, as they often reiterate established connections between musical genres and social relationships.

In addition, documentaries that do not have music as their central subject often use popular music as an integral part of their soundtrack. For instance, *The Rock and Roll Years* was a long-running BBC television documentary series that presented events from British social history by means of a montage of images taken from news footage. The programs featured an on-screen print commentary, which ran along the bottom of the screen while popular music provided the soundtrack. In this instance, music was used to give the on-screen footage historical context or to create a sense of atmosphere, or was employed as a device to match the images to the lyrical theme of a song. In other instances, popular music has been selected for use in documentaries to exploit the sociocultural associations of particular artists or popular music genres.

Bibliography

Grierson, John. 1946. *Grierson on Documentary*, ed. Forsyth Hardy. London: Collins.

Monaco, James. 1980. 'American Documentary Since 1960.' In *Cinema: A Critical Dictionary*, ed. Richard Roud. London: Nationwide Book Services, 50–56.

Romney, Jonathan. 1995. 'Access All Areas: The Real Space of Rock Documentary.' In *Celluloid Jukebox: Popular Music and the Movies Since the 50s*, ed. Jonathan Romney and Adrian Wootton. London: British Film Institute, 82–93.

Tagg, Philip. 1997. *Film and TV Music*. Liverpool. Unpublished.

Wootton, Adrian. 1995. 'The Do's and Don'ts of Rock Documentaries.' In *Celluloid Jukebox: Popular Music and the Movies Since the 50s*, ed. Jonathan Romney and Adrian Wootton. London: British Film Institute, 94–105.

Discographical Reference

John Peel's Sounds of the Suburbs. Shifty/Import 9900/9901. *1999*: UK.

Documentaries

Cocksucker Blues, dir. Robert Frank. 1972. USA. 90 mins.

The Decline of Western Civilization, dir. Penelope Spheeris. 1981. USA. 100 mins.

The Decline of Western Civilization 2: The Metal Years, dir. Penelope Spheeris. 1988. USA. 90 mins.

D.O.A., dir. Lech Kowalski. 1981. USA. 93 mins.

Don't Look Back, dir. D.A. Pennebaker. 1967. USA. 95 mins.

Gimme Shelter, dir. Al Maysles, David Maysles and Charlotte Mitchell Zwerin. 1970. USA. 95 mins.

In Bed with Madonna, dir. Alek Keshishian. 1991. USA. 118 mins.

Jazz on a Summer's Day, dir. Bert Stern. 1959. USA. 85 mins.

The Last Waltz, dir. Martin Scorsese. 1978. USA. 120 mins.

Let's Get Lost, dir. Bruce Weber. 1988. USA. 125 mins.

Message to Love: The Isle of Wight Festival, dir. Murray Lerner. 1996. USA. 128 mins.

Monterey Pop, dir. James Desmond, Barry Feinstein, Richard Leacock, Al Maysles, D.A. Pennebaker and Nicholas Proferes. 1968. USA. 98 mins.

Pet Shop Boys: Performance, dir. David Alden. 1992. UK. 105 mins.

R.E.M.: Tourfilm, dir. Jim McKay. 1990. USA. 85 mins.

Stop Making Sense, dir. Jonathan Demme. 1984. USA. 99 mins.

U2: Rattle and Hum, dir. Phil Joanou. 1988. USA. 90 mins.

Woodstock: 3 Days of Peace and Music, dir. Michael Wadleigh. 1970. USA. 230 mins.

Filmography

Fear of a Black Hat, dir. Rusty Cundieff. 1994. USA. 86 mins. Comedy ('Mockumentary'). Original music by NWH.

This Is Spinal Tap, dir. Rob Reiner. 1984. USA. 82 mins. Comedy ('Mockumentary'). Original music by Christopher Guest, Michael McKean, Rob Reiner, Harry Shearer.

ROBERT STRACHAN and MARION LEONARD

Halls of Fame/Museums

General museums have tended to ignore popular music. Value judgments have obviously played a crucial role in this exclusion; low and popular culture and their attendant artifacts have not, traditionally, been deemed worthy of serious attention in a field dominated for many years by the aesthetics of Western high cultural 'excellence.' In addition, traditional ways of presenting music (via scores and letters, for example) have failed to capture the excitement and significance of the sound medium. Modern technologies have provided alternatives, and the move to interactive museums has also been influential, but there is still little sign of popular music playing a central role in the mainstream of museum culture. However, the emergence of specialist museums and the popularity of one-off exhibitions in traditional establishments indicate that there is a market for popular music and its artifacts.

Examples of successful popular music exhibitions include the 1993 'Twist and Shout' display in Sheffield in the United Kingdom, and the 1991 'Harmonious Relations: Popular Music in Family Life on Merseyside' exhibit, held at the National Museums and Galleries on Merseyside. Specialist museums include the National Centre for Popular Music in Sheffield, the Delta Blues Museum, a division of the Carnegie Library, at Clarksdale, Mississippi, and Rock Circus in London, a venue run by Madame Tussaud's. A central theme of the 'museumification' of popular music history is the high commercial value accorded to its artifacts, with sheet music, musical instruments, previously unheard and unreleased tapes, and various fashion accessories reaching high prices at auction. Many of these pieces of memorabilia find their way into the display cabinet as symbols of rock's fascination not just with its past, but with past personalities.

Another category of musical museum to gain some prominence is the single-performer museum: for example, the Bob Marley Museum in Kingston, Jamaica, the Edith Piaf Museum in Paris and the Liberace Museum in Las Vegas. The latter is also a non-profit-making venture, with donations going to the Liberace Foundation for the Performing and Creative Arts. An interesting twist to the theme of how to commemorate the life of a rock legend was provided in the United Kingdom by the National Trust, which purchased the home that Paul McCartney lived in between 1957 and 1964 in Forthlin Road, Liverpool, the venue for many a Beatles composing and rehearsal session.

The main problem with 'museumification' is how to translate a sound phenomenon with a temporal aspect, such as popular music, into a frozen object in a museum. This problem is in part overcome by the interactive nature of some of the exhibits found in these institutions. The contradiction inherent in objectifying and historicizing a cultural form that has traditionally signified vibrancy, youth and 'nowness' is not helped by the decision of an institution such as Cleveland's Rock and Roll Hall of Fame to completely marginalize such contemporary genres as grunge, rap and techno in its choice of exhibits, thus laying itself even more open to charges of white, baby-boomer nostalgia. 'Museumification,' apart from carrying with it complicating notions of ossification, brings a kind of respectability to a cultural form long associated with the candor of youthful abandon, and plays a part in the canonization of an art form that, apologists have maintained, elides such high/low cultural constructs. The role and function of museums therefore complicate, as well as throw light on, the contradictory forces determining popular music and culture in Western society.

An important development related to the 'museumification' of popular culture has been the development of musical halls of fame. These are organizations that recognize and reward enduring achievements in popular music, and institutionalize and promote specific musical genres. They sprang up largely because traditional museums had been little interested in popular culture. Another reason for their proliferation is that they allow greater specificity, and so they can target their audience. Often, they do this by honoring and commemorating the leading musical figures and icons of popular musics, and thus play unashamedly on people's interest in celebrities, while collating artifacts and memorabilia which have, in some cases, become part of rock legend.

In the twentieth century, in relation to popular culture, the idea of the hall of fame originated as a means of recognizing sporting heroes, particularly in the United States. The Baseball Hall of Fame, the National Football Foundation and College Hall of Fame, the Basketball Hall of Fame and the Pro Football Hall of Fame all predated any musical halls of fame. They recognized the new star/fan nexus of the media age and, indeed, the term 'fan' was first used in connection with the followers of baseball.

With regard to popular music, the Country Music Association (CMA), founded in 1958, made the first significant move toward setting up a hall of fame. The CMA was established to promote the genre of country music in the United States, and was conceived as part of a rigorous commercial counterattack on rock 'n' roll in the late 1950s. The institution of the Country Music Hall of Fame in Nashville, Tennessee on 31 March 1967 was part of the campaign. The building's ultramodern design was modeled on a professional baseball hall of fame in Cooperstown, New York. The Country Music Hall of Fame built up a substantial holding of country music memorabilia and boasted an extensive archive, which was open to the public for research purposes. It also acted as the new center for the CMA. Each year, with the exception of 1963, the Hall of Fame recognized the achievements of country performers through a process of induction. The first honorees, in 1961, were Jimmie Rodgers, Fred Rose and Hank Williams. An important part of the Country Music Hall of Fame's role was to raise the commercial standing of country music and to play a proactive role in defining the genre.

The founding of a similar institution for rock was more bound up with notions of nostalgia and the emergence of a new adult community for rock styles. The Rock and Roll Hall of Fame in Cleveland, Ohio was founded in January 1986, but it was not finally inaugurated until the opening of I.M. Pei's $92 million museum on 2 September 1995. Essentially, the Rock and Roll Hall of Fame is reactive, in the sense that inductees have to have been active recording stars for over 25 years before they can be considered. The lavish, high-profile annual ceremonies at which inductees are asked to perform reactivated the ailing careers of many fifties and sixties rock legends, and thus further helped to discourage the notion of rock and youth as synonymous. Many critics pointed out that the Rock and Roll Hall of Fame was therefore a way of institutionalizing and rationalizing the middle-aged angst of an estranged babyboomer rock audience. An educational and research component was then added almost as an afterthought, but the main function of this institution was to canonize pop's heritage at a time when fifties and sixties pop culture was being recycled and rediscovered in the CD era.

Another important aspect of the Rock and Roll Hall of Fame was the way it revitalized the local Cleveland economy. Indeed, one of the phenomena of the 1980s in Anglo-American culture was the increasing economic importance of 'heritage culture,' as cities such as Liverpool in the United Kingdom, whose traditional economic base as a seaport and as a center for manufacturing industries had been eroded, looked to relaunch themselves, in part, as heritage economies. The 'museumification' of, for example, Liverpool's illustrious popular past (particularly its excellence in music and soccer) became a feature of that city's media profile. Similar strategies were adopted in other cities in the United

Kingdom – for example, Sheffield, with its National Centre for Popular Music, and, of course, London, with institutions such as the British Music Centre, which, at the beginning of the twenty-first century, was still at the planning and fund-raising stage.

In North America by the late 1990s, dozens of halls of fame had been inaugurated with the purpose of championing local musics, helping to define what was distinctive about these music scenes, and reinvigorating the local economy through alliances with business. Examples of such institutions are the North Carolina Music Hall of Fame, the Buffalo Music Hall of Fame, the Alabama Music Hall of Fame and the National Cleveland-Style Polka Hall of Fame.

The Songwriters' Hall of Fame, set up in 1969, is perhaps a slightly different case, its emphasis being more on the archival and historical dimensions of 'museumification.' The country singer Johnny Cash remains the only performer to be inducted into the country, rock 'n' roll and songwriters' halls of fame.

In Australia, numerous such institutions exist: for example, the Australian Jazz Archive, the Australian Folk Trust, the Country Music Association of Australia and the Archives of Maori and Pacific Music. Central to their operation, in addition to any role as information or resource center, is the idea of promoting a sense of civic or state pride through the sponsorship of local initiatives. The success of these institutions in revitalizing local economies highlights the fact that such institutions have an important economic function, in addition to their primary purpose of paying tribute to the lives and works of important musicians.

Many of the halls of fame mentioned above have their own Web sites on the Internet. Yet more 'halls of fame' exist on the Internet only, and serve as forums for debate for fans of specific musical genres – for example, the Internet Jazz Hall of Fame and the SynthPop Hall of Fame. Another example is provided by the Canadian Music Hall of Fame, whose English-Canadian members (from Oscar Peterson in 1978 to David Foster in 1998) are inducted as part of the annual Juno Awards. Indeed, awards ceremonies such as the MTV Music Awards, the MTV Video Music Awards and the Brit Awards garner considerable media attention. The Mercury Music Prize was established in 1992 and can be thought of as the music industry's equivalent of literature's Booker Prize.

In analyzing the different functions of museums, halls of fame, and awards-conferring institutions and ceremonies, one can see distinctive and important shifts of emphasis. At one end of the spectrum is the traditional museum – perhaps rendered high-tech as a result of the subject matter and available technology, but nonetheless an institution whose primary purpose is the preservation and 're-creation' of 'facts' and 'knowledge' – and at the other end is the hall of fame, where perhaps there is no building and the primary purpose – if not the sole purpose – is awards and thus promotion.

Bibliography

Daly, Stephen, and Wice, Nathaniel. 1995. *alt.culture: An A-Z of the 90s Underground and Online*. London: Fourth Estate.

Malone, Bill C. 1985. *Country Music, U.S.A.* Rev. ed. Austin, TX: University of Texas Press.

Moore, Kevin. 1997. *Museums and Popular Culture*. London: Cassell.

Savage, Jon. 1996. *Time Travel: Pop, Media and Sexuality 1976–96*. London: Chatto & Windus.

DAVID BUCKLEY

Histories

Histories of popular music in book form constitute a highly diverse body of writing, but may be categorized as belonging to a number of broad types. Five such types are: books that integrate popular music into a wider musico-historical narrative; broadly conceived histories of popular music; genre histories; histories of industry and technology; and works characterized by regional, temporal and/or thematic focus. Beyond the book, an important contribution has also been made by histories in the form of media (especially television) programs.

Histories Integrating Popular Music

One of the first music scholars to recognize the need for an alternative historiographical approach to one centered uniquely on the art music tradition was Gilbert Chase. Chase's first history, *The Music of Spain* (1941), began to extend the boundaries of historical exploration in search of 'the sum total of musical experience,' in which 'such hybrid manifestations as urban street music and popular theatrical music' were as deserving of inclusion as other 'manifestations of the human instinct' (17). As Crawford shows (1987, xiv), this approach did not merely involve the addition of a previously neglected element; rather, it implied a reconfiguring of attitudes to a nation's musical culture. This Chase achieved in *America's Music* (1955). Influenced by the work and ideas of Oscar Sonneck and Charles Seeger, he abandoned previous views of musical endeavors in the United States as a reflection (albeit an unusual one) of European high culture in favor of an emphasis on the ways in which sociocultural experiences that were distinctly North American had forged distinctly North American music. That music, including folk and popular traditions (which occupied almost half the book's 31 chapters), had to be seen in all its diversity; it also had to be seen holistically.

Thus, the first major example of the integration of popular music into a broader historical narrative occurred in an enterprise whose overarching purpose was not so much to demonstrate a historiographical truth about popular music as to see it as a crucial part of what made a particular nation's music different. Chase's success meant that, at least as far as the historiography of North American music was concerned, a new pattern had been set, albeit one that enabled differing emphases to be introduced. A European view of North American musical distinctiveness and of the key contribution of popular traditions lay behind Mellers's *Music in a New Found Land* (1964), a work that also shifted the historiographical gaze more toward the twentieth century. Hitchcock's concise account (1969) followed Chase in attaching equal importance to what Hitchcock termed the 'cultivated' and the 'vernacular' traditions (43), but identified the growth and spread of a dualistic culture in the nineteenth and twentieth centuries as particularly significant. By the 1990s, although Hitchcock's terms were still in use, diversity rather than dualism was seen as a defining feature of the North American musical experience. *The Cambridge History of American Music* (Nicholls 1998) linked explicit recognition of this with the perception – which had clear echoes of Chase's approach – that 'the many manifestations of music – from simple to complex, popular to recherché, concrete to abstract – are interdependent rather than independent' (xiii). At the same time, *The Cambridge History* parted company with other histories of music in the United States – and aligned itself with a late twentieth-century hesitation before the enormity of the task that had by now been constructed – in abandoning the single-author approach in favor of one that reflected a 'multiplicity of viewpoints' (xiii), assigning to different authors each of the 10 chapters that were either devoted to popular music or relevant to its history.

Although histories of music in Britain were slower than their US counterparts to recognize the importance of popular music and seek ways to integrate it into their historical narratives, the decision to use a multi-author approach, and thus enable popular music specialists to be included, was a characteristic of both Temperley (1981) and, more extensively, Banfield (1995).

The extent to which changes in the historiography of North American music fed into other work can be seen in general histories of twentieth-century music by Austin (1966) and Sternfeld (1973). At the same time, the limitations of this influence were also universally apparent. What drew Austin's attention away from serious music, for example, was jazz, and only jazz; not even jazz merited a mention, however, in the tenth volume of *The New Oxford History of Music* (Cooper 1974).

In one particular type of general history, that of African-American music, the major concern has regularly been not so much to integrate popular music idioms – the scale of the African-American contribution has meant that this has regularly been recognized, most notably in Southern's groundbreaking work (1971) – but, rather, to preserve a notion of African-American musical and cultural distinctiveness across all idioms, including the European Classical tradition, in which the African-American contribution has been significant. The complex cultural politics of this distinctiveness, present though barely discernible in Southern's work, have played an increasingly important role in African-American musical historiography, beginning in the work of Jones (1963) and finding perhaps their most sophisticated statement in Floyd, whose historical explorations enabled him to argue 'for a hermeneutic that is African-American in character and method' (1995, 273). In at least partial contrast, Gilroy's historical and political commentary on the wider black diasporic experience (1993), seen through the metaphor of the 'Black Atlantic' and with a key role for music, expressed equal discomfiture with notions of an historical continuum and an undistinguishing pluralism, while at the same time seeking both to retain the possibility of identity and to acknowledge the reality of mutation by proposing the notion of a 'changing same' (xi, 106, 198).

Broadly Conceived Histories of Popular Music

The twentieth century produced no attempts at a comprehensive international history of popular music. The size of the task was only part of the explanation; the growth of popular music scholarship that took place on an international scale from the late 1970s on was not characterized by a consistent level of interest in historiography, of the kind that might have led to the formation of networks of scholars around a multi-volume project. Instead, the vacant area remained occupied by a small number of populist single-authored histories, almost all of which restricted what they meant by popular music to the Anglo-American world. Most wittily perceptive of these – especially on the interconnections between musical, social and commercial activity – was Whitcomb (1972); most substantial-looking was Clarke (1995). Clarke makes 'no apology for concentrating . . . on the English-speaking world, and especially the USA' (8), nor for the personal views upon which his judgments are often founded (as illustrated both by the title, *The Rise and Fall of Popular Music*, and in the preface: 'It will always be true that the best stuff lasts, but it does

seem as though the music industry today cranks out a higher percentage of inferior product than ever before' (x)). No such reservations influenced the earlier work of Spaeth (1948), whose decade-by-decade approach offered a wealth of information on more minor North American songwriters in particular.

Van der Merwe's *The Origins of the Popular Style* (1989) also devoted considerable space to North American music, but the book distinguished itself clearly from other broadly conceived histories. The subtitle directs attention to the author's main preoccupation: a meticulous scholarly investigation into 'the antecedents of twentieth-century popular music.' Van der Merwe's detective-like search for clues led him to take in a range of European and African music, with a particular focus on the nineteenth-century parlor song. His aim was not an historical overview but, rather, the establishment of musical connections. Neither was there a desire to contextualize: his intent, he admits, is 'solely musicological' (3).

Connections between Europe and the United States also formed a key part of Wicke's *Von Mozart zu Madonna* (1998). In contrast to Van der Merwe, however, Wicke identified the history of popular music as 'a cultural-historical process, whose roots reach back deep into the eighteenth century' (7–8; author's translation).

Genre Histories

Most popular music histories produced during the twentieth century preferred to select one or more specific focus on the subject as a whole. End-of-century hindsight over the range of these histories suggested that historians consistently preferred one focus above all others, for genre histories far outnumbered the others; and, within that category, histories of genres originating in the United States – from minstrelsy (Toll 1974) to hip-hop (Toop 1991) – were easily the most numerous. The genre focus appeared, in the main, to be a reflection of the emergence of generic labels during the century as the principal means of differentiation in both the production and the reception of popular music. The preponderance of genres from the United States given historical treatment was partly, no doubt, a reflection of the major impact of those genres, both in the United States and beyond. Within the United States itself, however, it may also have been a consequence of the growth of confidence in North American vernacular culture that resulted from a series of events: the New Deal, the end of the Depression, the US role in World War II. There was also an element of happy coincidence – by the time a new postwar generation of historians was turning its attention to vernacular culture, the genres in question had been in existence long enough to have histories worthy of book-length studies.

The genre that has consistently received the most thorough historiographical treatment – jazz – was also the first to be given respectful historical attention by knowledgeable enthusiasts. From the outset, the impulse to delve systematically into jazz's history was an international one. It was already apparent in the 1930s in both Europe and the United States, in works of criticism by Goffin (1932) and Panassié (1934), and in collections such as that of Ramsey and Smith (1939), a multi-authored volume that integrated the knowledge of nine writers around four historical themes, incorporating critical assessment of individuals. The first single-authored attempt at an historical overview was Blesh's *Shining Trumpets* (1946), a work that offers a good example of the merits and disadvantages of single authorship in relatively uncharted territory. A passionate and informative advocate for early jazz, Blesh was critical of what he saw as its commercial dilution, and sternly disinclined to regard any music that departed from New Orleans-derived styles as jazz. Blesh's opinions found a willing echo in the first British-produced jazz history – Harris (1952) – a volume that found its way into a great many British jazz lovers' homes in the postwar period. More balanced and wide-ranging accounts followed, both from the United States (notably those of Ulanov (1952) and Stearns (1956)) and from Europe (Dauer 1958; Malson 1967). The pattern of combining historical material with evaluative assessment, suggested by Ramsey and Smith, was developed by Berendt, whose *Das Jazzbuch* (1953) became, in its German original, its numerous translations and its many revised editions, one of the most widely read of all jazz books.

All these approaches to the construction of jazz history followed established practise in allowing the historians themselves to determine narrative priorities. An alternative approach, which recognized the growth of interest in oral history, was found in several volumes, most notably Shapiro and Hentoff (1955) and Taylor (1982). In contrast, the influence of academic musicology was apparent in the two historical works of Schuller (1968, 1989). Each text was devoted to a narrow time period, 'early' jazz and swing, but both were distinguished by three assumptions: that jazz merited serious musicological-historical treatment; that its history could be constructed in terms of musical evolution alone; and that existing methods of musicological analysis (such as analysis of structure) were appropriate tools. In his full use of these methods, Schuller also drew renewed attention to a long-running theme in jazz history: the desire to extricate the music from popular culture.

As the music's own history proceeded and as the volume of academic scholarship began to grow, the historian was presented with an increasingly challenging corpus of both musical and written material. In this context, the narrower focus permitted by the historical study of a specific subgenre attracted increased attention. By the 1990s, in the work of Stowe (1994) and Erenberg (1998) on swing, the narrowing of the time frame was allowing the implications of social and cultural studies approaches to be realized, while the work of DeVeaux on bebop (1997) demonstrated an innovative meeting of those studies with musicology. Each text in its own way aimed to see the music in terms of the social, political and economic particularities of the time, without '[doing] violence to its distinctive qualities' (DeVeaux 1997, 31). Meanwhile, attempts to meet the challenge of an ever-expanding subject in one volume continued to be made, from the 1970s (Collier 1978) to the late 1990s (Gioia 1997).

Among other genres originating in the United States, only blues and rock have received a comparable degree of international historical attention. The British contribution to blues history is evident in such historical overviews as those by Oliver (1969) and Oakley (1976), and that of French historians exemplified by Bas-Rabérin (1973). In sharp contrast to most jazz historians – and in an anticipation of historical thinking that would find a place in popular music scholarship around the late 1980s – Oliver recognized the possibility of a genre having different historical meanings: a glamorous music; a symbol of oppression; a proud tradition; a brand of humiliation; a music of protest; a music of self-pity; a source of jazz; an inspiration to music-making (1969, 6).

The first comprehensive history of rhythm and blues, rock 'n' roll and early rock was also by a European (Gillett 1970). Gillett shared with other European historians of North American genres an approach that, in differing degrees, allotted a crucial role to recordings, which in part reflected the way Europeans had learned the music. But Gillett used the record industry both as a frame for his history, which he recounted 'primarily in terms of hit records as determined by *Billboard*' (1983, ix), and as a key player in what he saw as a primary antithesis between major and independent labels.

Gillett was motivated also by the perception that rising academic attention to popular culture in the late 1960s was marginalizing music. A similar concern lay behind Malone's classic history of country music, *Country Music, U.S.A.* (1968). More than most other genres, country music suffered an enduring academic indifference, reflected both in the United States and abroad. While Malone wrote – successfully – for an international audience, his targets were domestic, and included 'historians of the South' who, as Malone wrote at the time of the revised edition, 'still ignore the music of their region's working people' (1985, xi). In an interesting reflection on changing priorities and agendas, Malone conceded that in his first edition he had 'expended too much energy defending country music as an art form and asserting its folkness,' implying that this was to the detriment of the account of the music as 'southern culture's chief industry' (1985, x, xi).

Issues Raised by Genre Histories

Genre histories have raised numerous issues in popular music historiography. Among these, two deserve particular attention: continuity and change; and the relationship of art and commerce. These will be examined briefly in a comparison of historical studies of jazz and rock.

DeVeaux (1991) showed how fundamental to jazz history has been the notion of an organic relationship uniting all the musics subsumed under the banner of a 'jazz tradition' into one 'seamless continuum' (530). Perhaps paradoxically, the notion was accepted both by conservative historians opposed to change and by proponents of new developments such as bebop. The former saw new developments as a temporary obstacle in the evolutionary path, while 'it proved . . . in the interests of the modernists to have their music legitimated as the latest phase of a (now) long and distinguished tradition' (539). The idea of an underlying organic essence removed any lingering suspicion, in whatever quarter, that what was called 'jazz' was actually rather disjointed, and allowed thoughts to turn to notions of the artistic status that a genre acquires when it can be shown to be an organic entity evolving over time. Definition played an important part here also: a definition of jazz required a theory of overall continuity to underpin it and, in its turn, bestowed validity and status upon it.

In rock and pop history, the claim for continuity, whether between the music and its predecessors or within the music as a whole, has been much more open to dispute. Gillett described audiences since 1956 as forming 'quite different sensibilities from the preceding generations' (1983, xii). Palmer's account (1995) bears the subtitle 'an unruly history,' its author declaring that 'rock and roll history is particularly resistant to neatness and order' (11). Chambers (1985) saw pop music as 'a field of continual novelties,' and focused his main attention on 'moments' or 'irruptions' that occur 'whenever a sound powerful enough to threaten existing arrangements emerges' (xi–xii); others saw change as less whimsical – Peterson (1990), for example, emphasized the need for historians to recognize the importance of structural reorganization within the industrial–technological–legal complex in the emergence of rock 'n' roll.

In an important argument (although not in a history as such) Negus (1996) pointed to the limitations of many existing approaches – 'radical break' theories, hunting for antecedents and claims for 'Darwinian progression' – and, drawing on Lipsitz (1990), proposed in their stead a position based on the concept of ongoing dialogical activity, which recognizes that 'there is not one rock history,' but several, and that genres do not simply emerge, mature and die, but 'arise out of and are actively made through dialogic . . . movements through time [and] space,' during which their 'boundaries are often transformed' (160, 163), and they acquire 'new significance in different situations and as part of other dialogues' (139).

On the second, related theme of art and commerce, jazz history has been dominated by the view that close proximity to the commercial imperatives of the music industry has a potentially destructive effect. In order to claim progress toward becoming an art form, it has to be shown that clear water between jazz and commerce has been both established and maintained. As DeVeaux showed, there is an 'added twist' to this argument, for the argument for art and against commerce is closely tied to the idea of ethnic authenticity: the art form can therefore be shown to enjoy oppositional status, as the 'triumphant reversal . . . of a formerly enslaved people' toward not one but two dominating presences: the European Classical tradition and popular culture (1991, 526).

In rock history, the role of the industry has been painted in negative colors by numerous writers, drawing on arguments of Leavis, Adorno and Marx in varying measure. As with jazz, this encouraged the development of an aesthetic ideology founded on a notion of independence, but in the case of rock that independence was found within the industry, in the creativity of independent labels. Against this, as Frith explained (1981, 47ff.), more optimistic readings, derived in part from the thinking of Benjamin, saw it as characteristic of capitalist mass reproduction that it left space for new opportunities. Whereas writers such as Laing (1969) viewed this in dialectical terms, emphasizing the tensions and contradictions at work, others, influenced in part by postmodernism, favored a more celebratory, pluralist approach.

Histories of Industry and Technology

Histories of the music industry and its associated technologies have broadly favored three approaches: the history of recorded sound and the record industry; the more general history of the music business; and the history of specific institutions (companies, labels, organizations). The two pioneering histories of recorded sound approached the subject with different emphases: Read and Welch (1959) offered a hugely detailed account of technological innovation and change, while Gelatt

(1955) combined technical and economic developments with elements of music history to form an absorbing narrative. More recent histories, such as those of Millard (1995) and Gronow and Saunio (1998), adopted a similar approach to Gelatt's, with the difference that Gronow's and Saunio's history was genuinely international. Alternative approaches were taken by Chanan (1995), one of whose aims was to relate technical and commercial history to shifts in how music has been used and perceived, and by Kenney (1999), who examined the relationship between recording and US popular memory within a specific time frame, 1890–1945.

Few attempts have been made to construct a more broadly based music business history. By far the most notable was Russell Sanjek's meticulously detailed three-volume chronicle of the 'popular music business' in the United States (1988), the third volume of which was subsequently abridged and revised by his son, David (Sanjek and Sanjek 1996). Individual companies – publishers, record companies, manufacturers, promotion and management businesses – and organizations – especially those dealing in rights – feature prominently in historical work on the music industry, as individual musicians do in more music-centered historical accounts, but comparatively few have had their 'biographies' written. Among those that have, record companies have had the most coverage, from Escott's and Hawkins' account of Sun Records (1975) and Gillett's of Atlantic Records (1975), through Kennedy's study of Gennett (1994), to Martland's commemorative history of EMI (1997). Ehrlich's history of the Performing Right Society (1989) was an important, pioneering contribution to the study of the development of rights organizations.

Works Characterized by Regional, Temporal and/or Thematic Focus

A characteristic of the genre-centered approach is that it creates and defines a manageable subject area, while at the same time offering the opportunity to make links to other possible perspectives across the overall field. Dixon and Godrich (1970) centered their study of blues on the historical relationship between the music and the record industry, while Russell (1970) linked blues, early country music and the record industry in a study of racial interaction. McCarthy's account of dance bands from 1910 to 1950 (1971) paid particular attention to the role of radio. A number of histories linked genre to social group, such as those defined by gender (for example, Steward and Garratt on women in pop (1984)) or class (for example, Scott's account of bourgeois song (1989)).

In the case of genres whose reach became national or international, greater specialization has frequently been introduced by elevating one or more alternative perspectives to a controlling role. Thus, the specificities of locality determined jazz histories such as Lange's of Germany (1966) and Starr's of the Soviet Union (1983), soul histories such as Pruter's of Chicago (1991), and rock 'n' roll histories such as Dix's of New Zealand (1988), while both place and politics are central to Ryback's history of rock in Eastern Europe and the Soviet Union (1990). In other histories, centered on a genre whose reach outside its originating locality and culture has been more restricted, locality's role became virtually definitional. Thus, in studies of genres from many different localities around the world, such as *zouk* from Martinique (Guilbault 1993), Cajun music from Louisiana (Savoy 1984), *rembétika* from Greek port cities such as Thessaloníki (Holst 1977) or Dominican *bacháta* (Pacini Hernandez 1995), the history of the genre is inextricably linked to specifics of place and region. In a further refinement, place and genre come together with class in Peña (1985) to define the world of the Texas-Mexican *conjunto*.

Another branch of popular music historiography has dispensed with a generic focus and chosen to concentrate on one or more of these alternative perspectives. Among these histories, a focus on place has been perhaps the most common, albeit controlled by different approaches and sometimes further defined by other factors such as type of location or time span. Hamm's wide-ranging history of popular song styles in the United States (1979) was driven by a musicological imperative, while both Russell's account of popular music in England in a particular period, 1840–1914 (1987), and Coplan's study of urban popular music in South African black townships (1985) were mainly sociocultural in their interests and methodology. In contrast, Manuel's ambitious survey (1988) ranged widely over the 'non-Western world,' combining the two approaches as it did so.

Many specific social, cultural and economic phenomena in the ambit of popular music have received historical treatment, often in a frame marked out by regional or temporal factors – works such as Eberly (1982) on North American music radio, Cloonan (1996) on the censorship of popular music in Britain and Cowley (1996) on carnival in Trinidad.

Issues raised by genre histories can be seen also in many of the histories organized around different perspectives, but the particular filter through which the historian's gaze passes can present these issues in a different light. In histories defined by factors of race, such as Floyd (1995), for example, the issue of continuity is tied to that of African-American social, cultural and political identity, while in Russell (1987) what ties the narrative together is not a sense of – or dispute about – organic evolution in the homes, theaters and public places of Victorian and Edwardian England but, rather, the matter of class.

Media Histories

Writers of serious popular music histories face many practical challenges, most of them common to writers of histories in other subjects: establishing authority; setting limits, temporal or otherwise; organizing and selecting source materials; providing appropriate background information; sustaining interest over a period of time (in two senses: time period covered, and time taken by the reader); achieving narrative momentum; integrating narrative, description and analysis. These challenges are faced also by producers of media histories – histories that most often come in the form of multi-part program series for television or radio, and that have appeared at regular intervals, from Tony Palmer's *All You Need Is Love* (1976) to Ken Burns's *Jazz* (2000).

Some of the challenges are felt even more keenly. The time constraints that govern media broadcasting place limitations on even the most ambitious series; keeping the audience's attention (including that of the casual, non-committed audience) is a stronger commercial imperative; and the scope for analytical discussion is generally much more limited. Media histories also have to confront the very real problem that a subject may not readily lend itself to division into equal-sized portions to fit the requirements of a series. But popular music media histories also have opportunities to explore different methods. Most obviously, they have the advantage over text-based histories of being able to incorporate the sounds that are their subject, and, in the case of film histories, can add moving images of that music in performance. Film histories can also use the convention of setting sound commentary over the top of images (moving or still) to create a situation in which the viewer receives two types of information simultaneously.

While media histories owe a clear debt to the traditions and conventions of text-based histories, they also demonstrate their media lineage. This can be seen in their use of recorded interviews. In media methodology, the interview occupies a virtually unassailable position as a primary technique in the process by which a subject receives media treatment, and this has fed into media histories of popular music in a relatively untroubled way. Issues for discussion revolve around questions of balancing opinions gathered via interview, rather than around the admissibility of the material itself. Text-based histories of popular music have inevitably been affected by uncertainties about oral history that have regularly troubled the discipline of history, and while oral history has often had an important role to play, even to the extent of occasional publication of books constructed entirely out of such material (for example, Shapiro and Hentoff 1955), it does not in general have the same primacy of place as media histories have given it. The imaginative use that can be made of oral history in a single film (as opposed to a series) is seen in Bruce Ricker's *The Last of the Blue Devils* (1980), in which the world of Kansas City big bands and blues is revisited over 40 years later via the reminiscences of the surviving musicians.

Bibliography

Austin, William W. 1966. *Music in the Twentieth Century: From Debussy Through Stravinsky*. New York: Norton.

Banfield, Stephen, ed. 1995. *The Blackwell History of Music in Britain. Vol. 6: The Twentieth Century*. Oxford: Blackwell.

Bas-Rabérin, Philippe. 1973. *Le Blues moderne, 1945–1973* [Modern Blues, 1945–1973]. Paris: Michel.

Berendt, Joachim. 1953. *Das Jazzbuch: Entwicklung und Bedeutung der Jazzmusik* [The Jazz Book: The Development and Meaning of Jazz]. Frankfurt: Fischer.

Blesh, Rudi. 1946. *Shining Trumpets: A History of Jazz*. New York: Knopf.

Chambers, Iain. 1985. *Urban Rhythms: Pop Music and Popular Culture*. London: Macmillan.

Chanan, Michael. 1995. *Repeated Takes: A Short History of Recording and Its Effects on Music*. London: Verso.

Chase, Gilbert. 1941. *The Music of Spain*. New York: Norton.

Chase, Gilbert. 1955. *America's Music: From the Pilgrims to the Present*. New York: McGraw-Hill.

Clarke, Donald. 1995. *The Rise and Fall of Popular Music*. London: Viking.

Cloonan, Martin. 1996. *Banned!: Censorship of Popular Music in Britain, 1967–92*. Aldershot: Arena.

Collier, James Lincoln. 1978. *The Making of Jazz: A Comprehensive History*. Boston, MA: Houghton Mifflin.

Cooper, Martin, ed. 1974. *The New Oxford History of Music. Vol. 10: The Modern Age, 1890–1960*. London: Oxford University Press.

Coplan, David. 1985. *In Township Tonight!: South Africa's Black City Music and Theatre*. Johannesburg: Ravan Press.

Cowley, John. 1996. *Carnival, Canboulay and Calypso: Traditions in the Making*. Cambridge: Cambridge University Press.

Crawford, Richard. 1987. 'Foreword.' In Gilbert Chase, *America's Music: From the Pilgrims to the Present*. 3rd rev. ed. Urbana, IL: University of Illinois Press, xi–xxiv.

Dauer, Alfons M. 1958. *Der Jazz, seine Ursprünge und seine*

Entwicklung [Jazz: Its Origins and Its Development]. Eisenach: Röth.

DeVeaux, Scott. 1991. 'Constructing the Jazz Tradition: Jazz Historiography.' *Black American Literature Forum* 24: 525–60.

DeVeaux, Scott. 1997. *The Birth of Bebop: A Social and Musical History*. Berkeley, CA: University of California Press.

Dix, John. 1988. *Stranded in Paradise: New Zealand Rock 'n' Roll, 1955–1988*. Wellington: Paradise Publications.

Dixon, Robert M.W., and Godrich, John. 1970. *Recording the Blues*. London: Studio Vista.

Eberly, Philip K. 1982. *Music in the Air: America's Changing Tastes in Popular Music, 1920–1980*. New York: Hastings House.

Ehrlich, Cyril. 1989. *Harmonious Alliance: A History of the Performing Right Society*. Oxford: Oxford University Press.

Erenberg, Lewis A. 1998. *Swingin' the Dream: Big Band Jazz and the Rebirth of American Culture*. Chicago: University of Chicago Press.

Escott, Colin, and Hawkins, Martin. 1975. *Catalyst: The Sun Records Story*. London: Aquarius.

Floyd, Samuel A. 1995. *The Power of Black Music: Interpreting Its History from Africa to the United States*. New York: Oxford University Press.

Frith, Simon. 1981. *Sound Effects: Youth, Leisure, and the Politics of Rock 'n' Roll*. New York: Pantheon.

Gelatt, Roland. 1955. *The Fabulous Phonograph, from Tin Foil to High Fidelity*. Philadelphia: Lippincott.

Gillett, Charlie. 1975. *Making Tracks: Atlantic Records and the Growth of a Multi-Billion-Dollar Industry*. New York: Dutton.

Gillett, Charlie. 1983 (1970). *The Sound of the City: The Rise of Rock and Roll*. Rev. ed. London: Souvenir Press. (First published New York: Outerbridge & Dienstfrey, 1970.)

Gilroy, Paul. 1993. *The Black Atlantic: Modernity and Double Consciousness*. London: Verso.

Gioia, Ted. 1997. *A History of Jazz*. New York: Oxford University Press.

Goffin, Robert. 1932. *Aux Frontières du jazz* [At the Frontiers of Jazz]. Paris: Sagittaire.

Gronow, Pekka, and Saunio, Ilpo. 1998. *An International History of the Recording Industry*, trans. Christopher Moseley. London: Cassell.

Guilbault, Jocelyne. 1993. *Zouk: World Music in the West Indies*. Chicago: University of Chicago Press.

Hamm, Charles. 1979. *Yesterdays: Popular Song in America*. New York: Norton.

Harris, Rex. 1952. *Jazz*. Harmondsworth: Penguin.

Hitchcock, H. Wiley. 1969. *Music in the United States: A Historical Introduction*. Englewood Cliffs, NJ: Prentice-Hall.

Holst, Gail. 1977. *Road to Rembetika: Music from a Greek Subculture. Songs of Love, Sorrow and Hashish*. Athens: Anglo-Hellenic Publishing.

Jones, LeRoi (Imamu Amiri Baraka). 1963. *Blues People: Negro Music in White America*. New York: William Morrow & Co.

Kennedy, Rick. 1994. *Jelly Roll, Bix and Hoagy: Gennett Studios and the Birth of Recorded Jazz*. Bloomington, IN: Indiana University Press.

Kenney, William Howard. 1999. *Recorded Music in American Life: The Phonograph and Popular Memory, 1890–1945*. New York: Oxford University Press.

Laing, Dave. 1969. *The Sound of Our Time*. London: Sheed & Ward.

Lange, Horst H. 1966. *Jazz in Deutschland: Die Deutsche Jazz-Chronik 1900–1960* [Jazz in Germany: The Chronicle of German Jazz, 1900–1960]. Berlin: Colloquium.

Lipsitz, George. 1990. *Time Passages: Collective Memory and American Popular Culture*. Minneapolis, MN: University of Minnesota Press.

Malone, Bill C. 1985 (1968). *Country Music, U.S.A.* Rev. ed. Austin, TX: University of Texas Press.

Malson, Lucien. 1967. *Histoire du jazz* [History of Jazz]. Lausanne: Editions Rencontre.

Manuel, Peter. 1988. *Popular Musics of the Non-Western World: An Introductory Survey*. New York: Oxford University Press.

Martland, Peter. 1997. *Since Records Began: EMI, the First 100 Years*. London: Batsford.

McCarthy, Albert. 1971. *The Dance Band Era: The Dancing Decades from Ragtime to Swing, 1910–1950*. London: Studio Vista.

Mellers, Wilfrid. 1964. *Music in a New Found Land: Themes and Developments in the History of American Music*. London: Barrie & Rockliff.

Millard, Andre J. 1995. *America on Record: A History of Recorded Sound*. Cambridge: Cambridge University Press.

Negus, Keith. 1996. 'Histories.' In *Popular Music in Theory: An Introduction*. Cambridge: Polity Press, 136–63.

Nicholls, David, ed. 1998. *The Cambridge History of American Music*. Cambridge: Cambridge University Press.

Oakley, Giles. 1976. *The Devil's Music: A History of the Blues*. London: BBC.

Oliver, Paul. 1969. *The Story of the Blues*. London: Barrie & Rockliff.

Pacini Hernandez, Deborah. 1995. *Bacháta: A Social History of a Dominican Popular Music*. Philadelphia: Temple University Press.

Palmer, Robert. 1995. *Rock & Roll: An Unruly History*. New York: Harmony Books.

Panassié, Hugues. 1934. *Le Jazz hot* [Hot Jazz]. Paris: Correa.

Peña, Manuel. 1985. *The Texas-Mexican Conjunto: History of a Working-Class Music*. Austin, TX: University of Texas Press.

Peterson, Richard. 1990. 'Why 1955?: Explaining the Advent of Rock Music.' *Popular Music* 9(1): 97–116.

Pruter, Robert. 1991. *Chicago Soul*. Urbana, IL: University of Illinois Press.

Ramsey, Frederic, and Smith, Charles Edward, eds. 1939. *Jazzmen*. New York: Harcourt, Brace.

Read, Oliver, and Welch, Walter L. 1959. *From Tin Foil to Stereo: Evolution of the Phonograph*. Indianapolis: Howard W. Sams.

Russell, Dave. 1987. *Popular Music in England, 1840–1914: A Social History*. Manchester: Manchester University Press.

Russell, Tony. 1970. *Blacks, Whites and Blues*. London: Studio Vista.

Ryback, Timothy. 1990. *Rock Around the Bloc: A History of Rock Music in Eastern Europe and the Soviet Union*. New York: Oxford University Press.

Sanjek, Russell. 1988. *American Popular Music and Its Business: The First Four Hundred Years*. 3 vols. New York: Oxford University Press.

Sanjek, Russell, and Sanjek, David. 1996. *Pennies from Heaven: The American Popular Music Business in the Twentieth Century*. New York: Da Capo Press.

Savoy, Ann Allen, ed. 1984. *Cajun Music: A Reflection of a People*. Eunice, LA: Bluebird Press.

Schuller, Gunther. 1968. *Early Jazz: Its Roots and Musical Development*. New York: Oxford University Press.

Schuller, Gunther. 1989. *The Swing Era: The Development of Jazz, 1930–1945*. New York: Oxford University Press.

Scott, Derek B. 1989. *The Singing Bourgeois: Songs of the Victorian Drawing Room and Parlour*. Milton Keynes: Open University Press.

Shapiro, Nat, and Hentoff, Nat. 1955. *Hear Me Talkin' to Ya: The Story of Jazz by the Men Who Made It*. New York: Rinehart.

Southern, Eileen. 1971. *The Music of Black Americans: A History*. New York: Norton.

Spaeth, Sigmund. 1948. *A History of Popular Music in America*. New York: Random House.

Starr, S. Frederick. 1983. *Red and Hot: The Fate of Jazz in the Soviet Union*. New York: Oxford University Press.

Stearns, Marshall W. 1956. *The Story of Jazz*. New York: Oxford University Press.

Sternfeld, F.W., ed. 1973. *A History of Western Music. Vol. 5: Music in the Modern Age*. New York: Praeger.

Steward, Sue, and Garratt, Sheryl. 1984. *Signed, Sealed and Delivered: True Life Stories of Women in Pop*. London: Pluto Press.

Stowe, David W. 1994. *Swing Changes: Big-Band Jazz in New Deal America*. Cambridge, MA: Harvard University Press.

Taylor, Arthur R. 1982. *Notes and Tones: Musician-to-Musician Interviews*. New York: Perigree Books.

Temperley, Nicholas, ed. 1981. *The Athlone History of Music in Britain. Vol. 5: The Romantic Age*. London: Athlone Press.

Toll, Robert C. 1974. *Blacking Up: The Minstrel Show in Nineteenth-Century America*. New York: Oxford University Press.

Toop, David. 1991. *Rap Attack 2: African Rap to Global Hip Hop*. London: Serpent's Tail.

Ulanov, Barry. 1952. *A History of Jazz in America*. New York: Viking.

Van der Merwe, Peter. 1989. *The Origins of the Popular Style: The Antecedents of Twentieth-Century Popular Music*. Oxford: Clarendon Press.

Whitcomb, Ian. 1972. *After the Ball*. London: Allen Lane.

Wicke, Peter. 1998. *Von Mozart zu Madonna: Eine Kulturgeschichte der Popmusik* [From Mozart to Madonna: A Cultural History of Pop Music]. Leipzig: Kiepenheuer.

Filmography

The Last of the Blue Devils, dir. Bruce Ricker. 1980. USA. 90 mins. Documentary.

DAVID HORN

Music Press

The music press – magazines, newspapers or journals primarily concerned with popular music – constitutes an important medium through which information about music and the meanings of popular music are negotiated, created and disseminated. The term 'music press' encompasses a variety of publications that evidence different styles, formats, journalistic strategies and ideologies, as well as various levels of engagement with the subject. However, the music press can be broadly categorized into several distinct types of publications, each catering to different markets: the weekly pop and rock music press (a phenomenon unique to Britain, where these are often referred to as 'inkies'); 'teen-pop' magazines; genre-based magazines; glossy (usually monthly) magazines with a general responsibility for covering popular music; musicians' magazines; trade journals; and fanzines or zines. There are distinct national variations in the structure of the music too.

A number of periodicals concerned with popular music existed as early as the late nineteenth century – for example, the trade magazine *Billboard* (US, 1894), and *The Music Hall* (UK, 1889). However, the roots of the modern music press lie in the jazz age, with publications such as *Melody Maker* (UK). Originally established as a trade paper in 1926, *Melody Maker* evolved into a general magazine aimed at jazz audiences and musicians. Various other titles followed in the next 20 years, including the jazz publications *Down Beat* (US, 1934), *Jazz Hot* (France, 1935), *Jazz Journal* (UK, 1948) and *The Beat* (Australia, 1949). The 1950s and 1960s saw the emergence of pop papers targeted at a predominantly early teenage pop market, including British magazines such as *New Musical Express* (NME) (1952, launched as *Musical Express* in 1946), *Record Mirror* (1953) and *Disc* (1958). The content of all these early examples is reflected in more contemporary teen-pop magazines, including *RTR Countdown* (New Zealand) and *Popcorn* (Bulgaria). The journalistic style and content of these pop publications have tended to be light, with short articles, little assumed knowledge of music history and a strong focus on the 'star' persona or pinup value of featured performers. This type of magazine has been an important marketing tool, as it generally has a much larger circulation than the weekly or monthly rock press. For instance, in 2000–2001 *Smash Hits* (UK) had a circulation of around 270,000, nearly four times that of the UK 'inkies' (ABC 2001).

The emerging split between rock and pop in the latter part of the 1960s saw a repositioning of several titles and the launch of new publications in response to the popularity and journalistic style of the underground press. *Melody Maker* and *NME* moved toward pop interests, while new titles such as *Rock & Folk* (France, 1966), *Crawdaddy!* (US, 1966), *Rolling Stone* (US, 1968), *Creem* (US, 1968) and *Sounds* (UK, 1970) emerged, specifically aimed at the rock market. These publications were produced as either weekly broadsheet-style music papers (*NME*, UK; *Hot Press*, Ireland) or glossy monthly magazines, and were marketed to appeal to a late teenage (and predominantly male) readership. Although these new titles adhered to essentially the same format as the pop and jazz publications that had preceded them, they featured longer, more in-depth articles and reviews, with an increased 'seriousness' in journalistic content, often attempting to place rock music within a specific sociopolitical context. In the early 1970s, a new, increasingly stylized form of journalistic writing developed that reflected the concerns and discourse of rock music culture. In the 1980s and 1990s, a number of new titles using similar layout and journalistic practise were launched in order to reach new markets. Conforming to the 'glossy' format, *Q* (UK) and *Mojo* (UK) have appealed to older CD-buying consumers, while *Les Inrockuptibles* (France) and *Spin* (US) have displayed a bias toward contemporary alternative acts.

Although there is often an editorial policy governing the amount of emphasis put on a particular genre (for example, *Rolling Stone* has concentrated on rock, whereas *Smash Hits* has favored pop), both rock and teen-pop titles have evidenced a fairly wide coverage that includes numerous genres. However, a number of publications have concentrated on particular styles or subgenres. These niche magazines have catered for such specialist areas of taste as heavy metal (*Aardschok*, The Netherlands), hip-hop (*The Source*, US; *RER*, France; *Black Music Review*, Japan), blues (*Living Blues*, US; *Blues Unlimited*, UK) and folk (*Folk Roots*, UK). They have also concentrated specifically on acts in their circulation area: *Oxmox*, for instance, has covered the German alternative and heavy metal scene, while the long-running *Congo Disque* (Zaire) has covered Central African music since 1963.

Despite differences in niche coverage, target audience and journalistic style, much of the music press conforms to a common format. Publications generally start with a news section, which consists of brief reports on the music industry, concert tour and recording news, and personal information about popular artists. There is a features section, which usually contains profiles of and interviews with popular artists, or those deemed 'important' by writers and editors. In addition, most publications include a reviews section that covers concerts and recently released recordings; added to this, there may be a gig guide, with listings of upcoming concerts. In many cases, advertisements can also be thought of as making up a crucial part of a publication's content, adding to the sense of connectedness between music fans and enthusiasts by notifying readers of tour dates, new record releases, job opportunities, and the sale of music equipment, rare records or fanzines.

As well as magazines that concentrate on the promotion and criticism of popular music acts and artists, there is also a longstanding tradition of musicians' magazines. These magazines, which include *Guitars and Claviers* (France), *Canadian Musician* (Canada) and *Making Music* (UK), have concentrated on the technical and mechanical aspects of music-making, and consist of reviews of new musical instruments, hardware and accessories on the market, along with transcriptions or tablature and interviews with musicians. Interviews in these publications are distinct in that they are conducted with a focus on aspects of music-making, such as musical technique, and discussions on musical equipment. As Théberge (1991) points out, the majority of these magazines carry advertising aimed only at musicians, thus attempting to create a sense of community among music practitioners and consumers.

In some countries where there is no specialist music press, the development of popular music has been aided by coverage in publications that are not primarily oriented toward music. In the 1950s, for instance, the South African magazine *Drum*, directed at urban Africans, covered a mixture of politics, shebeen life, labor, crime, fashion, sex, literature and music. The magazine gave important coverage to the African 'Jazz Age' of the cosmopolitan black suburb of Sophiatown, and also set the style for music coverage later emulated by magazines across Africa, and by later South African imitations such as *Bona* and *Pace*.

The music press has been seen as central to the marketing and promotion of popular music. Along with radio and television, it has often been characterized as one of a number of gatekeepers positioned between the music industry and its audience. Hirsch's (1990) organization-set analysis of the music industry presents the music press as an institutional regulator of music industry output that acts as a filter between the recording industry and its audience. He argues that record companies release more products than can feasibly be successful in commercial terms and that, by selecting particular acts for heavy promotion, the music press acts as a regulator, narrowing down the number of 'products' that have an increased chance of gaining commercial success.

It is clear that the industry recognizes the importance of this relationship in terms of promotion and sales, and there are various strategies by which record companies attempt to influence the selection of products for coverage by the music press. Indeed, the relationship between the press and record labels is characterized by regular cajoling, promises of prominent coverage, and the provision of free food, alcohol and travel. Wale (1972) gives the example of a 1971 London press launch for Elektra Records, where £6,000 was spent on 'luxurious foods and . . . vintage wine' (263). Negus (1992) points out that record companies actively court music press interest through their publicity departments, which maintain close personal contact with individual journalists, often 'matchmaking' relationships between particular journalists and acts which are seen to suit each other in terms of genre and taste. Furthermore, publicity departments may 'coach' new artists on what type of questions they may be asked and how they should respond in interviews. This process can occur early in the professional life of a particular act, when record companies and management may try to manipulate the journalistic desire to 'break' new music. Hesmondhalgh (1996, 129) gives the example of the way in which the UK independent record label Creation selected several key journalists to attend rehearsals and socialize with the newly signed British rock band Oasis, thus encouraging a favorable response before taking the risk of booking tour dates or releasing

recordings. Commentators have pointed to other ways in which the economic dependence of music journalists on record companies can operate. Chapple and Garofalo (1977) highlight the practise of journalists reselling 'free product' in order to subsidize their salaries; other critics (Frith 1983; Toynbee 1993; Negus 1992) have commented that many journalists are concurrently employed as A&R and publicity staff by the industry, or may manage acts or be musicians themselves.

This interdependence between the music industry and the music press has been seen as fostering a close relationship that calls into question the critical autonomy of the press. Indeed, the question of autonomy is central to the way in which the music press operates in terms of perceived ideology, content and journalistic style. On the one hand, it has to foster a workable relationship with the record companies and press offices, and, on the other, it has to maintain the image of distance from the industry in order to preserve its critical credibility in the eyes of its readership. Stratton (1982) argues that music magazines mask a capitalist/artistic dichotomy by creating the appearance of critical distance. In turn, this supposed independence legitimates the critical content of the music press. This 'distance' and 'independence' are reflected in the way music is written about in these publications, in that journalists serve to 'distance popular music consumers from the fact that they are essentially purchasing an economic commodity, by stressing the product's cultural significance' (Shuker 1994, 97).

The strategy of placing music within its social context can be viewed as operating in various ways. Frith (1983, 176) argues that the music press has created a 'sociology of rock,' in terms of which the readerships of particular publications identify with specific subcultures, taste cultures or life styles. In a publication such as *NME*, for example, records have been judged by their 'authenticity as a youth cultural product' (Frith 1983, 176): the major aesthetic criterion through which music has been valued has been derived according to the perceived social locations of the publication's readership. However, this approach to criticism does not simply constitute a one-way process in terms of which publications react to their audiences; rather, music magazines have been seen as playing a key role in the creation of a community or as leaders in the formation of taste cultures. Frith (1996) sees the role of the critic as 'creating a knowing (select) community,' which defines itself in opposition to the 'undiscriminating pop consumer' (67). Toynbee (1993) regards the press as dynamic in the creation and marketing of music scenes through the alliance of particular acts with constructed 'movements.' All of the selected acts within a movement are portrayed as socially, politically or aesthetically consistent. He argues that this constitutes a 'periodization,' in which new acts are launched within distinct social time scales. Furthermore, Toynbee argues that the music press fulfills a didactic and corrective purpose, guiding its readership from one period to another through various strategies that invite the readership to identify with the editorial position. In turn, this ascription of 'sociological' meaning by the press has been seen to affect not only the way in which music is interpreted, but also its practise and production. Street (1986) argues that the 'politicisation' of punk was due largely to the ascription of social meaning by the music press, which created political meanings for the music, as it 'forged the link between a three chord rock song and unemployment' (83).

The marketing of popular music journalism to different demographic and 'ethnic' groups demands that the music press address different 'imagined' communities. Frith (1983) points out that *Rolling Stone* has been active in the maintenance of an imaginary youth culture that no longer exists, harking back to the ideals of the US counterculture of the 1960s (the same argument could be applied to magazines such as *Mojo*, *Q* and *Rock & Folk*). Alternatively, Théberge (1991) sees musicians' magazines as central to the formation of a sense of community among musicians. He argues that the technological advancements in the 1980s and the increasingly internationalized and technical context of musical production have meant that local 'musical communities' have come to have less influence over aspiring musicians. In this model, the musicians' magazine has become a forum for the exchange of information and the encouragement of identity as part of a musical community.

As Toynbee (1993) and Shuker (1994) argue, another facet of the music press's role in leading taste is the part it plays in the formation of a popular music 'canon.' This canon constitutes a hegemonic discourse in which a number of artists are deemed 'great,' and are constantly referenced and reiterated as such. This process is articulated in the proliferation of press articles that list versions of the 100 best albums, singles and artists (of a particular year, decade or 'of all time'). Even in publications from non-English-speaking countries (France's *Rock & Folk*, for example), these selections have tended to be Anglo-American, with a heavy emphasis on late-1960s rock music. Indeed, the general content of many international publications (*Rockin' On Japan*, *Rock & Folk*) and the publication of *Rolling Stone* in German- and Japanese-language editions have reflected the global predominance of Anglo-American artists within the multinational record industry.

However, while the music press is undoubtedly an important source of music information and publicity, other promotional avenues and strategies (such as links with radio, the film industry and international music television channels) have demonstrated a clear ability to market music on a global scale. The concentration on marketing through these channels, along with other factors such as the rise of electronic publications and the fragmentation of the rock market, has in some cases led to a drop in circulation figures for established music press publications. In 2000, *Melody Maker* ceased publication after 73 years when its circulation figures dropped to around 30,000 (compared with a high of 250,000 in the 1970s), and the UK monthly magazine *Select* folded in the same year. Publishing companies have responded to this situation by attempting to diversify, often by using the brand profile of existing print publications to move into other media formats. Publishing houses IPC and Emap, for example, have expanded their music titles, such as *Kerrang!*, *Mixmag* and *Smash Hits*, into online publication, e-retail, and television and radio, using the same names to create 'umbrella' brands. This kind of expansion has enabled certain publications to continue as viable concerns. For instance, while its print circulation has been steadily declining (to below 100,000), *NME*'s Web-based portal reached 29 million page impressions per month in 2001. Such developments suggest that the music press must stay in tune with rapidly changing trends in information technology in order to survive. While the demand for music criticism and evaluation will undoubtedly remain, future advances in technology will continue to present fresh challenges to the nature and practises of music journalism.

Bibliography

Audit Bureau of Circulations (ABC). 2001. *Consumer Magazines Circulation Figures*. http://www.abc.org.uk

Chapple, Steve, and Garofalo, Reebee. 1977. *Rock 'n' Roll Is Here to Pay: The History and Politics of the Music Industry*. Chicago: Nelson-Hall.

Draper, Robert. 1990. *The Rolling Stone Story*. Edinburgh: Mainstream.

Flippo, Chet. 1974a. 'The History of *Rolling Stone*: Part I.' *Popular Music & Society* 3: 159–88.

Flippo, Chet. 1974b. 'The History of *Rolling Stone*: Part II.' *Popular Music & Society* 3: 258–80.

Flippo, Chet. 1974c. 'The History of *Rolling Stone*: Part III.' *Popular Music & Society* 3: 281–98.

Frith, Simon. 1983. *Sound Effects: Youth, Leisure and the Politics of Rock 'n' Roll*. New York: Pantheon.

Frith, Simon. 1996. *Performing Rites: On the Value of Popular Music*. Oxford: Oxford University Press.

Hesmondhalgh, David. 1996. *Independent Record Companies and Democratisation in the Popular Music Industry*. Unpublished Ph.D. thesis, Goldsmiths College, London.

Hirsch, Paul M. 1990. 'Processing Fads and Fashions: An Organization-Set Analysis of Cultural Industry Systems.' In *On Record: Rock, Pop, and the Written Word*, ed. Simon Frith and Andrew Goodwin. New York: Pantheon, 127–39. (First published in *American Journal of Sociology* 77 (1972): 639–59.)

Negus, Keith. 1992. *Producing Pop: Culture and Conflict in the Popular Music Industry*. London: Edward Arnold.

Rimmer, Dave. 1985. *Like Punk Never Happened*. London: Faber & Faber.

Shuker, Roy. 1994. *Understanding Popular Music*. London: Routledge.

Stratton, Jon. 1982. 'Between Two Worlds: Art and Commercialism in the Record Industry.' *The Sociological Review* 30: 267–85.

Street, John. 1986. *Rebel Rock: The Politics of Popular Music*. Oxford: Basil Blackwell.

Théberge, Paul. 1991. 'Musicians' Magazines in the 1980s: The Creation of a Community and a Consumer Market.' *Cultural Studies* 5(3): 270–93.

Toynbee, Jason. 1993. 'Policing Bohemia, Pinning Up Grunge: The Music Press and Generic Change in British Pop and Rock.' *Popular Music* 12(3): 289–300.

Wale, Michael. 1972. *Voxpop: Profiles of the Pop Process*. London: Harrap.

MARION LEONARD and ROBERT STRACHAN with GWEN ANSELL (South Africa), STEVE JONES (United States), OLIVIER JULIEN (France), CLAIRE LEVY (Bulgaria), CHRISTIAN MÖRKEN (Germany) and MASAHIRO YASUDA (Japan/France)

Popular Music Journals

The emergence of popular music as a distinct area of academic study since the late 1960s has resulted in the establishment of numerous dedicated journals. These journals can be categorized as academic periodical publications that gather together scholarly research articles, book reviews and information on new developments within the field of popular music studies. These publications are often produced on a quarterly, four-monthly or biannual basis and are generally peer-reviewed by editorial boards made up of specialists within the field. Early examples include the German- and English-language *Jazzforschung/Jazz Research*, first published in 1969 by the Institute for Jazz Research in cooperation with the International Society for Jazz Research, and the US journal *Popular Music and Society*, founded in 1971 by R. Serge Denisoff.

A number of dedicated popular music journals now exist, covering a wide range of methodological approaches and subject matter. Established in 1981, *Popular Music* (UK) has included material that addresses issues relating to a variety of musical styles and genres from throughout the world. No restriction is imposed by editors as to the areas covered within *Popular Music* and therefore articles have ranged from textual analyses to examinations of industrial practise, and from historical accounts to discussions of place and identity. Articles published in this journal offer a variety of perspectives from disciplines including musicology, anthropology, history and cultural geography. Some academic journals are connected to professional associations, such as the *Journal of Popular Music Studies*, which was established as the house journal of the US branch of the International Association for the Study of Popular Music (IASPM), and *Popular Ongaku Kenkyou*, which is connected to the Japanese Association for the Study of Popular Music (JASPM).

Other popular music journals, while including a range of academic approaches, have a more select focus. These have generally concentrated on popular music with regard to particular generic styles or racial and cultural origins, or within a specific geographical area. *Perfect Beat* (Australia), for example, was established in 1992 and is specifically concerned with the study of the popular music and cultures of Australia, New Zealand, Hawaii, Papua New Guinea and the island nations of the South Pacific Forum. In a similar sense, the US publications *The Black Perspective in Music* (which appeared from 1973 to 1990) and the *Black Music Research Journal* (from 1980 onward) have published research relating to the aesthetics, history and criticism of black musics.

The interdisciplinary nature of popular music studies means that academic work in the field is often published in journals related to other disciplines such as sociology, media studies, law and cultural studies. The appearance of popular music articles in these publications can be intermittent, although there are occasional special issues that relate to various aspects of popular music. *Media, Culture & Society* (UK) and *Cultural Studies* (UK), for instance, published special issues on popular music and the music industry in 1986 and 1991, respectively. However, there is evidence of resistance to the inclusion of popular music studies in some traditional musicological journals. In a content analysis of the US journals *Ethnomusicology* and the *Journal of the American Musicological Society*, Wicks (1998) found that, over a 50-year period up to 1996, four articles were concerned with jazz while five dealt with other forms of contemporary popular music, amounting to less than 0.5 percent of the journals' total content. However, important articles dealing with 'world music' issues have appeared in the ethnomusicology journals *The World of Music* and *Yearbook for Traditional Music*. Moreover, some musicological journals have been more receptive to the inclusion of popular music research. For instance, the Italian journal

Musica/Realtà has included articles on popular music since its inception in 1980.

The late 1990s saw the establishment of a number of on-line peer-reviewed journals, such as the *NTAMA Journal of African Music and Popular Culture* (Germany), *Critical Musicology* (UK) and the Dutch publication *Soundscapes*. A number of existing journals also began to offer on-line versions of their print titles. *Popular Music*, for instance, can now be downloaded on payment of a per-article fee. The increasing number of courses related to popular music and the growing interest in popular music research suggest that there is potential for the establishment of new publications through which to present research developments.

Bibliography

Black Music Research Journal. Chicago: Center for Black Music Research, Columbia College.

The Black Perspective in Music. Cambria Heights, NY: Foundation for Research in the Afro-American Creative Arts.

Critical Musicology. http://www.leeds.ac.uk/music/Info/CMJ/cmj.html

Ethnomusicology. Champaign, IL: University of Illinois Press.

Jazzforschung/Jazz Research. Graz: International Society for Jazz Research and Institute for Jazz Research, University of Music and Dramatic Arts.

Journal of the American Musicological Society. Chicago: University of Chicago Press.

Journal of Popular Music Studies. New York: Taylor & Francis.

Musica/Realtà. Milano: Dedalo Libri.

'The Music Industry in a Changing World.' 1991. *Cultural Studies* 5(3) (Special Issue).

NTAMA Journal of African Music and Popular Culture. Mainz: Institut für Ethnologie und Afrika-Studien, Johannes Gutenberg-Universität.

Perfect Beat: The Pacific Journal of Research into Contemporary Music and Popular Culture. Sydney: Centre for Contemporary Music Studies, Macquarie University.

'Popular Music.' 1986. *Media, Culture & Society* 8(3) (Special Issue).

Popular Music. Cambridge: Cambridge University Press.

Popular Music and Society. Bowling Green, OH: Bowling Green State University Popular Press.

Popular Ongaku Kenkyou. Tokyo: Jissen Women's Junior College.

Soundscapes. http://www.icce.rug.nl/~soundscapes/

Wicks, Sammie Ann. 1998. 'America's Popular Music Traditions as "Canon-Fodder."' *Popular Music and Society* 22(1): 55–90.

The World of Music. Bamberg: Department of Ethnomusicology, Otto-Friedrich University.

Yearbook for Traditional Music. Los Angeles: Department of Ethnomusicology, University of California.

ROBERT STRACHAN and MARION LEONARD

Song Collecting

Introduction

Before the introduction of recording equipment in the early twentieth century, the songs of traditional performers and folk singers could be collected only through direct notation from live performance 'in the field.' The process required considerable skill, and often involved the singer giving repeat performances, in whole or in part, so that unfamiliar words and phrases, inflections and elisions, dialects and mannerisms – in addition to melodies and tune variants – could be accurately transcribed. In order that the songs could subsequently be played and compared to other versions in circumstances that might be far removed from the locations where they were collected, the music was often transcribed for piano, although traditional singers rarely, if ever, used such an accompaniment. This practise, also intended to bring folk song to the attention of a larger public and, in particular, to children in schools, has been strenuously criticized (Harker 1985).

As a term, 'song collecting' often refers solely to the finding and documenting of songs from traditional performers, such as was undertaken by the English collector Cecil Sharp in the Appalachian Mountains. However, although many of Sharp's predecessors, such as the US professor Francis James Child, were assiduous collectors of songs, they did not collect in the field, but, rather, drew their material from diverse sources, which ranged from the manuscripts of friends to lyrics quoted in plays or literary texts.

Both the collectors in the field and those whose sources were totally eclectic were intent on publishing the fruits of their work. It is therefore necessary to make a distinction between the means of collecting and between the kinds of song collections that were published. It is also necessary to distinguish between the collecting of songs, by whatever means, and scholarship about collected songs.

Although it may appear paradoxical, the first published collections of traditional songs were drawn from eclectic sources, and were followed later by the results of collecting in the field. The term 'song collection' is therefore used for an anthology of songs from various sources, and 'song collector' for a person who collects and edits such songs for publication. A compilation of songs gathered from 'live' informants and performers in the field is regarded as a volume of 'collected songs,' and the gatherer and compiler of such a collection is referred to as a 'collector of songs.'

However, it should be noted that these categories, although generally applicable, are not totally exclusive, since some collectors, like Walter Scott (later, Sir Walter Scott), are classifiable under both headings. A further complication arises where song collectors have published song collections that have included excursions into ballad form or poetic compositions purporting to be in a traditional idiom, some being written by the collectors themselves. Such was the case with Robert Burns, whose posthumously published *Merry Muses of Caledonia* (ca. 1800) included a number of erotic songs from the tradition often reworked or adapted, although the majority of the songs were his own compositions (Randall 1966).

History

It is likely that the earliest collectors were themselves singers, while the printers of broadsides, ballad sheets, songsters and chapbooks were among the first publishers of traditional songs. Their street literature was certainly known to the earliest song collectors, who sometimes included the simple compositions of such printer–vendors in their song collections as authentic traditional songs. Thomas Percy, later Bishop of Dromore, Ireland, is credited with the first of these song collections; his *Reliques of Ancient English Poetry* (1765) consisted largely of ballads, which he had 'improved.' For this, he was vigorously attacked by the meticulous Joseph Ritson, whose *Collection of Scottish Songs* was published in 1794. Eight years later, the young Walter Scott published his first work, the three-volume *Minstrelsy of the Scottish Border*. Scott drew from literary sources, but also made 'raids' in the Vale of Yarrow and Liddesdale to collect the words (but not the tunes) of traditional songs from local singers (Millgate 1984).

While many Scottish song collections were published in the nineteenth century, John Bell of Northumberland was one of a few regional English song collectors. But it was not until 1843 that a small volume of collected songs was published – *Old English Songs as now Sung by the Peasantry of the Weald of Surrey and Sussex*, by the Rev. John Broadwood. It is generally acknowledged as the first volume of collected songs to have been notated directly from traditional singers. Broadwood was not of the English peasantry of the period, but he was in close contact with its members. A rare early collector who could be said to have been both of peasant stock and a collector in the field was the poet John Clare. Many of his songs were drawn from ballad sheets and chapbooks, some were his own compositions, and fewer than a score in his unpub-

lished manuscripts identified the singer from whom he had obtained a song (Deacon 1983). Believing that folk songs were 'collective compositions,' most collectors of songs were more interested in the words and/or the music of an item than in the identification of the singer from whom it was gained.

During the nineteenth century, a considerable amount of research and classification of ballads was undertaken, not only in Britain but also in Scandinavia and the European countries generally, as well as in the United States. Francis James Child's song collection, *English and Scottish Ballads* (1857–59), reached a broad readership, due, in part, to his eminence and his determination. It was expanded for the third edition and published as *The English and Scottish Popular Ballads* (1882–98); during the appearance of the five volumes its compiler died. It should be noted that Child's collection of some 300 texts, together with variants, exercised a defining but limiting influence on subsequent collections in separating 'ballads' from other forms of folk and popular song.

At the close of the nineteenth century, the most productive and systematic collector of English songs was the 'squarson' (squire and parson), the Rev. Sabine Baring-Gould, an eccentric man of prodigious energy and wide interests. Author of over 200 publications, his collections of songs (collected songs) included the four-volume *Songs of the West* (1889–92) and, shortly after, the eight-volume *English Minstrelsie: A National Monument of English Song* (1895–97). Within a time span of approximately two years (1888–90), Baring-Gould collected some 600 songs from over 50 named 'singing men' (and four women), but bowdlerized them for publication (Dickinson 1970). This editing out of sexual content or connotations also applied to Cecil Sharp's *Folk Songs from Somerset*, which he published in 1905 with his friend and field assistant, the Rev. Charles Marson (Reeves 1958). Although Sharp was more interested in tunes than in texts, and even at this date was given to regarding his 'folk singer' informants as 'peasants,' he was the most influential collector of songs of his day. Others included the scholar Frank Kidson, the composers Vaughan Williams and Percy Grainger, and the members of the Folk Song Society, founded in 1898. Sharp's lesser-known contemporary, Alfred Owen Williams, was a former railroad worker who collected songs from agricultural laborers; he shared Sharp's values, but was more attracted in his collecting to words than to melodies, as is evident in his *Folk-Songs of the Upper Thames* (1923).

Between 1916 and 1918, Cecil Sharp, accompanied by his young assistant Maud Karpeles, garnered nearly 1,600 folk tunes in the Southern Appalachians of the

United States, where British ballads and songs had persisted over some two centuries. Sharp died six years later, leaving a remarkable legacy. In the United States, others were collecting in the field, often pursuing the song traditions of a particular occupation: N. Howard 'Jack' Thorp's *Songs of the Cowboys* (1908) constituted the first collection of songs (collected songs) of this genre (Fife and Fife 1966), closely followed by John Avery Lomax's *Cowboy Songs and Other Frontier Ballads* (1911). Extensive collecting of work songs, sea songs and shanties, Native American music and many other song types, forms and traditions followed, spurred on by the Archive of Folk Music of the Library of Congress and the American Folklore Society, as well as by many regional and state organizations committed to the collecting of folk songs. The work of such organizations was made more effective by the advent of portable recording machines, and collection by transcription declined.

Beyond Britain and the United States, similar collections have been made, with similar successes and problems. Thus, the anthologies of bushwhacker songs from the Australian outback are conventional song collections, although some combine traditional songs with self-conscious poems purporting to be in the same idiom, sometimes differentiated as 'literary bush ballads' (Ward 1964). Many ballads and songs in Australia were circulated by publication in 'songsters,' including G. Chanson's (George Loyau's) *Sydney Songster* (ca. 1869), *The Queenslanders' New Colonial Camp Fire Song Book* (1865) and *The Native Companion Songster* (1889). The earliest collector of bush ballads and songs was Charles Thatcher from Bristol and Brighton, England, who went to Australia to dig for gold. Collecting songs in the 'diggings,' he also performed them and published his *Colonial Songster* in 1865. He died in Shanghai in 1870 at the age of 57. Of the writers who used the bush ballad form, including Will Ogilvie and Henry Lawson, A.B. 'Banjo' Paterson was the best known. He first published the ballads that he collected as *The Old Bush Songs* in 1905, while his own verses were published in an anthology 18 years later and proved to be very influential.

Bibliography

Anderson, Hugh, ed. 1962. *Colonial Ballads*. Melbourne: F.W. Cheshire.

Anderson, Hugh. 1991. *George Loyau: The Man Who Wrote Bush Ballads; Together with the Queenslanders' New Colonial Camp Fire Song Book, and the Sydney Songster*. Ascot Vale, Victoria: Red Rooster.

Baring-Gould, Sabine. 1895–97. *English Minstrelsie: A National Monument of English Song*. 8 vols. Edinburgh: T.C. and E.C. Jack.

Baring-Gould, Sabine, and Sheppard, H. Fleetwood. 1889–92. *Songs of the West*. 4 vols. London: Methuen.

Broadwood, John. 1843. *Old English Songs as now Sung by the Peasantry of the Weald of Surrey and Sussex*. London: Balls and Co.

Burns, Robert. 1979 (ca. 1800). *The Secret Cabinet of Robert Burns: Merry Muses of Caledonia*. Edinburgh: P. Harris.

Child, Francis James, ed. 1962 (1882–98). *The English and Scottish Popular Ballads*. 5 vols. New York: Cooper Square.

Deacon, George. 1983. *John Clare and the Folk Tradition*. London: Sinclair Browne.

Dickinson, Bickford H.C. 1970. *Sabine Baring-Gould: Squarson, Writer and Folklorist, 1834–1924*. Newton Abbot: David and Charles.

Fife, Austin E., and Fife, Alta S. 1966. *Songs of the Cowboys, by N. Howard ('Jack') Thorp: Variants, Commentary, Notes and Lexicon*. New York: C.N. Potter.

Harker, Dave. 1985. *Fakesong: The Manufacture of British 'Folksong,' 1700 to the Present Day*. Milton Keynes: Open University Press.

Karpeles, Maud. 1973. *An Introduction to English Folk Song*. London: Oxford University Press.

Lomax, John Avery. 1938 (1911). *Cowboy Songs and Other Frontier Ballads*. Rev. ed. New York: Macmillan.

Millgate, Jane. 1984. *Walter Scott: The Making of a Novelist*. Toronto: University of Toronto Press.

The Native Companion Songster. 1889. Brisbane: F. Crawford.

Paterson, A.B., ed. 1905. *The Old Bush Songs*. Sydney: Angus and Robertson.

Paterson, A.B. 1923. *The Collected Verse of A.B. Paterson*. Sydney: Angus and Robertson.

Percy, Thomas. 1765. *Reliques of Ancient English Poetry*. 3 vols. London: Dodsley.

Randall, Eric Lemuel. 1966. *The Merry Muses and Other Burnsian Frolics: From the Secret Collection of Robert Burns*. London: Luxor Press.

Reeves, James. 1958. *The Idiom of the People: English Traditional Verse from the MSS of Cecil Sharp*. London: Heinemann.

Ritson, Joseph. 1975 (1794). *Collection of Scottish Songs*. New York: AMS Press.

Scott, Walter. 1806. *Minstrelsy of the Scottish Border*. 3 vols. 3rd ed. Edinburgh: Ballantyne.

Sharp, Cecil J., and Karpeles, Maud. 1960 (1924). *English Folk Songs from the Southern Appalachians*. London: Oxford University Press.

Sharp, Cecil J., and Marson, Charles L. 1905. *Folk Songs from Somerset*. 2nd ed. London: Simpkin, Marshall, Hamilton, Kent.

Stewart, Douglas A., and Keesing, Nancy, eds. 1973. *Australian Bush Ballads*. Sydney: Angus and Robertson.

Thatcher, Charles R. 1865. *Thatcher's Colonial Songster*. Melbourne: Charlwood & Son.

Ward, Russell, ed. 1964. *The Penguin Book of Australian Ballads*. Victoria: Penguin Books.

Williams, Alfred. 1923. *Folk-Songs of the Upper Thames*. London: Duckworth.

PAUL OLIVER

2. Popular Music Studies

African-American Studies

African-American studies, Afro-American studies, Black studies, Africana studies, Pan-African studies and Afro-Caribbean studies are different names for academic units involved in 'the multidisciplinary analysis of the lives and thoughts of people of African ancestry on the African continent and throughout the world' (Harris, Hine and McKay 1990, 7). An outgrowth of the 1960s civil rights and black power movements and student activism, African-American studies became formalized as a discipline during this era. The organizational structure of these units encompasses departments, programs, institutes and centers. Although curricula models vary in design, they share common principles and objectives. For example, the curricula of many units focus on the lives and experiences of African Americans, referencing the history and culture of an African past within this context. Others fully explore this history through the juxtaposition of separate courses on African history and culture and the African-American experience. Still others emphasize the trilateral relationship between Africa, the African Caribbean and the African Americas, but concentrate primarily on African Americans. Regardless of these differences, Carter G. Woodson's *The Mis-Education of the Negro* (1990; first published in 1933), together with the 1920s literary and artistic movement labeled the Harlem Renaissance, provided the framework within which the areas of history, sociology, literature and the arts form the basis of the curricula. Thus, the approach to African-American studies is multidisciplinary, and the field derives its methods and analytical tools primarily from these areas of study (Harris, Hine and McKay 1990, 7; Aldridge and Young 2000).

The Early Literature: Cultural Misrepresentations

In the 1870s, African-American politicians, writers and educators from small, historically black institutions conducted pioneering research on African-American culture and history, in which the issues of race, culture and class surfaced as central themes (see Trotter 1878; G.W. Williams 1882–83). These studies ran counter to the 'negative images and representations of African Americans that were institutionalized within academic and popular cultures' (Banks 1996, 364), images and representations whose source lay in the descriptions of the songs, dances and life styles of African slaves that had appeared in the diaries, journals, reports and memoirs of slave traders, slaveholders, travelers and missionaries in the seventeenth and eighteenth centuries and had become reference points for the negative portrayal of African slaves in North America. Interpreting the cultural expressions of the slaves through the lens of European values and conventions, these observers had characterized the music, dance and playing of instruments as 'barbaric,' 'wild' and 'nonsensical' (see, for a sampling of these works, B. Jackson 1967; Epstein 1977; Southern 1983; Southern and Wright 1990). By the nineteenth century, such representations had become institutionalized in North American popular culture through blackface minstrelsy, a theatrical form that featured white performers in blackened face in caricature of African Americans. In turn, these negative visual images, combined with the negative representations of blacks in the early literature, influenced the assessment of and tone of writing on African-American music in the twentieth century.

The first scholarly studies on African-American music focused on the question of originality (also referred to as the 'origins controversy'). Some scholars argued that Negro spirituals and secular songs represented poor imitations of European traditions. Others contended that they were original, defined by a performance style rooted in African traditions (see Waterman 1963;

Westcott 1977; and Epstein 1983 for a summation of this debate). While both groups of scholars employed comparative and quantitative approaches, they used a different set of research data for analysis.

The proponents of the European origins theory were primarily philosophers, sociologists and literary scholars (see, for example, Wallaschek 1970 (originally published in 1893); White 1928; Johnson 1930; G.P. Jackson 1933, 1944). They based their conclusions on a superficial analysis of melodies and texts published in collections of Euro- and African-American folk music, as well as performances of African-American music by white singers. The limitations of Western notational systems, and the inability of transcribers and non-black performers to convey the aesthetic qualities – slides, bends, timbral changes, rhythmic complexities and so on – central to improvised African-American performance, are noticeable flaws in this methodology. Moreover, these researchers did not consider the textual transformations that occurred during the transfer from one culture to another (Maultsby and Burnim 2001, 576).

Anthropologists and folklorists introduced a different perspective on the origins debate (Herskovits 1958; Waterman 1943, 1971; Lomax 1978). Using ethnographic and quantitative data from extensive field research in Africa and the diaspora, they documented similarities in the construction of form, melody and rhythm, as well as the improvisatory approach to African and African-American music-making. These researchers concluded that the process of syncretism 'forged the unique character of spirituals as a genre grounded in African-derived musical values yet shaped into its distinctiveness as a direct result of the North American socio-cultural experience' (Maultsby and Burnim 2001, 576).

The Quest for Racial Identity

Within the context of the 1920s Harlem Renaissance movement, a group of African-American intellectuals and artists extended the discourse on African-American music and culture by introducing new analytical models for the study of vernacular traditions, as well as new approaches to the creation of works marked by a racial identity. Their studies of vernacular forms examined the cultural values and social practises of black people that shaped the unique character of musical performance. Through their analysis of song texts, they interpreted the meaning and significance of this music in black community life (Ballanta-Taylor 1925; Johnson and Johnson 1989a, 1989b (originally published in 1925 and 1926); Locke 1969 (first published in 1936); Work 1969 (first published in 1915)). In the quest to elevate the status of African-American vernacular expressions and to liberate themselves from the restrictions of European models, these intellectuals and artists debated ways in which to create new modes of expression based on African-American traditions. The greatest challenge was reaching a consensus on how to transform the Negro spiritual into a 'higher' art form to win mainstream recognition. Such debates introduced the issues of race, culture and class into discourses on African-American music, and these remained central themes in subsequent writings on black music (see, for example, Du Bois 1995 (first published in 1903); Lewis 1995; Locke 1969, 1992 (first published in 1936 and 1925, respectively); Hughes 1976 (first published in 1926); Hurston 1976 (first published in 1935); Haas 1972).

In the 1930s, research on African-American music had begun to shift from pre-Civil War folk forms and their postwar manifestations to jazz and blues. Although folklorists had made field recordings of the blues and other vernacular forms since the early 1900s, record labels did not acknowledge the commercial potential of black music until the release of the 'race' record series in 1920. Since they were marketed only in African-American communities, North American society remained largely unaware of blues and jazz until their introduction into the mainstream by white performers. The first publications on these traditions were based primarily on commercial recordings, published reviews and anecdotes. The writers were mainly journalists, record collectors and aficionados from Europe (see, for example, Osgood 1926; Ramsey and Smith 1939; Panassié 1960, 1970 (first published in 1942 and 1936, respectively); Sargeant 1975 (first published in 1938); Hodeir 1979 (first published in 1956); Stearns 1956; Charters 1959). Their works were primarily historical and employed a descriptive approach to discussions about musical evolution, performers and musical features. In many cases, they filtered their interpretation through a Western cultural lens that reinforced many of the racial stereotypes popularized in nineteenth-century literature (for a critique of blues literature, see Titon 1994 and Evans 1982; and of jazz literature, see DeVeaux 1991).

By the end of World War II, the character of North American society had changed. While the country experienced new levels of economic prosperity, race relations began to deteriorate. In the 1950s and through the grass-roots activities that led to the modern civil rights movement, the nation and the world became exposed to the racial inequalities and other conditions that had a negative impact on African Americans and influenced new artistic expressions. These events gradually forged new directions in studies on African-American history and culture, and led to broader interpretations of the blues and jazz traditions. Moving beyond culturally biased descriptive studies, writers began to examine the cultural and social forces that underlay musical creativity (see, for example, Oliver 1960, 1969; Hentoff 1961; Charters and Kunstadt 1962).

Black Empowerment and the Critique of Black Artistic Expression

The black power movement of the late 1960s inspired the founding of university research centers devoted exclusively to the documentation, study and research of African-American history and culture, as well as the formation of ensembles for the performance of all forms of black artistic expression. At Indiana University in 1970, for example, Dominique René de Lerma established the first Black Music Center. Although many universities established jazz ensembles in music departments, the first and only extant black popular music ensemble recognized as constituting a credit course was formed by Portia Maultsby in 1971 at Indiana University; housed in the Department of Afro-American Studies, this ensemble tours the country. Gospel music choirs also became commonplace on US university campuses during this era. By design, they were organized independently of academic units by students who insisted on defining the structure, repertoire and performances of these groups. The same impetus that led to the founding of research centers and performing ensembles inspired the establishment of scholarly journals whose editors encouraged new approaches to the study and interpretation of the African-American experience.

During the 1970s, a new generation of scholars began to reexamine the history and critique the cultural expressions of African Americans, employing an Afrocentric methodology. This approach acknowledged the importance of Africa in shaping the cultural traditions and social relations of African Americans. It also advocated the interpretation of the black experience and the critique of artistic expression by black people themselves. This Afrocentric model borrowed paradigms and integrated methodologies from other disciplines when relevant. This eclectic approach is illustrated in studies on the African musical continuum among African Americans in the United States, which build on approaches established earlier by anthropologists and folklorists (see, for example, Oliver 1970; Nketia 1973, 1981; Wilson 1974, 1981, 1992; Kaufman and Guckin 1979; Maultsby 1990; Brown 1990; Kubik 1999).

The shift toward an Afrocentric interpretation of African-American artistic expression led to a new body of scholarship on jazz and blues. When black jazz and blues musicians introduced a new aesthetic to create bebop and urban blues in the 1940s, music critics responded negatively to these radical changes, retaining their loyalty to the older styles. With the introduction of free jazz by black musicians and the mainstream popularity of third stream or symphonic jazz in the 1960s, the earlier tension between critics and black jazz musicians reached new heights. At the same time, blues revivalists ignored the merit of urban blues, giving preference to rural blues and citing their 'authenticity.' Such responses to new forms of black musical creativity generated a debate among critics and black musicians. The issue became: How should black music be defined and from whose perspective (Maultsby and Burnim 2001, 581–84)?

To address these questions and to reclaim ownership of black music and return it to the black community, LeRoi Jones (now Imamu Amiri Baraka) and other literary critics of the 1960s black arts movement critiqued this tradition using an Afrocentric model. They examined the creation, performance and meaning of blues and jazz against the backdrop of black people's struggle against racism and social injustice (Jones 1963, 1967; Spellman 1970; L. Neal 1989). Jones's influential *Blues People* (1963) and *Black Music* (1967) led to changes in approaches to the study and critique of black music, and they became the models for writers of the following decades (see, for example, Kofsky 1970; Murray 1976; Kelley 1997; M.A. Neal 1999; Smith 1999). These works also provided the foundation for ethnographic studies and narratives derived from oral histories in the study of creative processes, musical structures and meaning (see, for example, Keil 1966; Ferris 1978; Rowe 1979; Evans 1982; Pearson 1987; Peretti 1992; Berliner 1994; Titon 1994; Monson 1996).

Expanding the Musical Canon in African-American Studies

Prior to the 1980s, studies on post-World War II urban musical traditions were scant in the literature on African-American music. This resulted, in part, from commonly held views that gospel and popular musics had little, if any, artistic merit. As gospel music spread beyond the sanctuaries of black churches into the repertoire of symphony orchestras, university choirs, and R&B and hip-hop artists, and featured in television commercials and on film soundtracks, scholars of African-American studies could no longer ignore this tradition. Employing ethnographic data and Afrocentric analytical models, they examined gospel music as part of a continuum of practises associated with African rituals and its interrelatedness with the folk spiritual and blues traditions, as well as its influence on popular music expressions. Gospel also became a metaphor for the portrayal of the impact of class, race and culture on African-American urban life following World War I (see, for example, Boyer 1973; Williams-Jones 1975, 1977;

Burnim 1985, 1988; Lornell 1988; Allen 1991; Harris 1992; Maultsby 1992; Reagon 1992).

Studies on popular music remained on the margins of African-American studies until the 1980s. The first publications on this tradition were descriptive narratives on performers, hit recordings and record labels (see, for example, Larkin 1970; Shaw 1970, 1978; Gillett 1974; Broven 1978) and historical overviews (Gillett 1984). The publication of Phyl Garland's *The Sound of Soul* (1969) established new directions for studies on this tradition. Similar to the works of LeRoi Jones, her examination of soul music established the significance of context in interpreting popular music expression. To determine what she called the ethnic forces that helped shape the character of soul music, Garland traced the emergence of earlier black musical traditions, relating them to historical events and black cultural practises. Moreover, she examined the appropriation of soul music and the practises of the music industry that prevented blacks from becoming 'Kings' and 'Queens' of their own music (Maultsby and Burnim 2001, 584). Garland's approach to the study of black popular music provided the model for ethnographic studies on this tradition (Haralambos 1975). Other noteworthy studies drew primarily on empirical research and interviews with musicians (Hirshey 1984; Guralnick 1986). An important yet controversial study from the 1980s was *The Death of Rhythm & Blues* (1988) by music critic Nelson George, which examined the development of black popular music against the backdrop of an 'integrated' society. This work, which intertwined the issues of class with those of identity, authenticity and the politics of the music industry, revealed changes in African-American culture and the practises of the record industry that took the 'soul' out of the music.

In the 1990s, studies on black popular music became a part of the canon in many academic disciplines. This resulted, in part, from the growing interest in the post-World War II era and the emergence of hip-hop music and culture as a national and global phenomenon. As the sounds of hip-hop blared from car radios, boomboxes and headphones, hip-hop culture spread into all areas of North American life. The pervasive influence of black culture on contemporary North America had begun, however, two decades earlier with the explosion of disco. Hollywood quickly appropriated and exploited black music and culture through the release of the disco film *Saturday Night Fever* (1977) and, in the 1990s, through a plethora of hip-hop films. Through film and appearances on MTV (Music Television) and BET (Black Entertainment Television), hip-hop artists became media stars, appearing in commercials, advertising campaigns and on the covers of mainstream magazines. This level of exposure, combined with the harsh messages and images of gangsta rap, brought a curiosity about and fascination for inner-city life. It also generated much criticism and controversy, which did not go unnoticed by scholars of all academic disciplines.

Throughout the 1990s, hip-hop and other black musical genres became topics for conference presentations, symposia, articles and books. Although many scholars had once ignored black music, they began to use it as a tool to examine various aspects of African-American and the broader North American culture (see, for example, Kelley 1994, 1997; Ward 1998; M.A. Neal 1999; Werner 1999). The publications of African Americanists that had been marginalized in earlier decades became the cornerstone for this research. Moreover, researchers employed many of the theoretical models and analytical tools established in African-American studies. The works of scholars in popular music studies also became central to these studies, providing paradigms, methodological and analytical approaches, and topics for investigation. For example, issues of race, gender, identity, ethnicity, authenticity and media representation explored in the works of British cultural studies scholars such as Stuart Hall (Hall and du Gay 1996; Morley and Chen 1996) and Paul Gilroy (1993a, 1993b) were central to studies on African-American popular music published in the 1990s (see, for example, Dyson 1991, 1996; Berry 1994a, 1994b; Perkins 1996; Guillory and Green 1998; Ward 1998).

Popular music studies has provided African Americanists with paradigms to examine new topics. While de-emphasizing the Marxist interpretation, African-American scholars borrowed theories from the German philosopher Theodor Adorno (1975, 1978, 1990) and British sociologist Simon Frith (1978, 1988) in order to examine industrial issues related to the mass production and marketing of African-American popular music (see, for example, George 1988; Garofalo 1990; Rose 1994; Early 1995; Cashmore 1997). Further influenced by the work of European scholars in popular music studies and the general field of cultural studies, African Americanists have extended their research to embrace the African diaspora. Although some scholars had done so in earlier decades, diasporic studies became more fully integrated into the African-American studies curricula in the 1990s. Largely inspired by the works of Paul Gilroy and Stuart Hall, music specialists have begun to examine the reciprocal influence of black North American music on Africa and its diasporic cultures, and issues of identity, ethnicity and representation are central to these studies (Lipsitz 1994; L.F. Williams 1995; Erlmann 1999; Kalumbu 1999; Monson 2000).

The intertwining of African-American and popular

music studies has produced new approaches for examining post-World War II black culture and for chronicling the events that have an impact on the lives of black people. The study of popular music has provided new tools for African Americanists to use in examining the issues of class, identity, representation and gender, and the multiple and heterophonic voices of black people. It has also extended the field of scholarly inquiry to include issues of commodification and the mass marketing of black culture. African-American studies has contributed to popular music by offering new research methods that employ ethnographic data, including interviews and oral histories. The analytical models from this discipline can also be used to frame music as an expression of culture in order to bring more balanced interpretation to the literature that treats music primarily as a commodity for consumption. Finally, African-American studies offers methods for examining and interpreting the popular music traditions of minority cultures throughout the world. In general, the multi- and interdisciplinary nature of African-American and popular music studies enables these distinct areas to interconnect, because popular music shapes and is shaped by broader social and cultural conditions.

The development of institutions such as the Center for Black Music Research at Columbia College, Chicago, directed by Samuel Floyd, and the Archives of African American Music and Culture at Indiana University, directed by Portia Maultsby, has enhanced the impact of African-American studies on the study of popular music by providing resources and programming relevant to this field of study. As cultural studies becomes an increasingly acceptable academic paradigm and African-American studies continues to be transformed by its impact, African-American studies and the study of popular music are likely to continue to inform each other.

Bibliography

Adorno, Theodor W. 1975 (1967). 'Culture Industry Reconsidered.' *New German Critique* 6: 12–19.

Adorno, Theodor W. 1978 (1938). 'On the Fetish Character of Music and the Regression of Listening.' In *The Essential Frankfurt School Reader*. London: Oxford University Press, 270–99.

Adorno, Theodor W. 1990 (1941). 'On Popular Music.' In *On Record: Rock, Pop, and the Written Word*, ed. Simon Frith and Andrew Goodwin. New York: Pantheon Books, 301–14. (First published in *Studies in Philosophy and Social Science* 9 (1941): 17–48.)

Aldridge, Delores P., and Young, Carlene, eds. 2000. *Out of the Revolution: The Development of Africana Studies*. Lanham, MD: Lexington Books.

Allen, Ray. 1991. *Singing in the Spirit: African-American Sacred Quartets in New York City*. Philadelphia: University of Pennsylvania Press.

Ballanta-Taylor, Nicholas George Julius. 1925. *Saint Helena Island Spirituals*. New York: G. Schirmer.

Banks, James A. 1996. 'Black Studies.' In *Encyclopedia of African-American Culture and History*, Vol. 1, ed. Jack Salzman, David Lionel Smith and Cornel West. New York: Macmillan Library Reference, 364–69.

Berliner, Paul F. 1994. *Thinking in Jazz: The Infinite Art of Improvisation*. Chicago: University of Chicago Press.

Berry, Venise T. 1994a. 'Feminine or Masculine: The Conflicting Nature of Female Images in Rap Music.' In *Cecilia Reclaimed: Feminist Perspectives on Gender and Music*, ed. Susan C. Cook and Judy S. Tsou. Urbana, IL: University of Illinois Press, 163–201.

Berry, Venise T. 1994b. 'Redeeming the Rap Music Experience.' In *Adolescents and Their Music: If It's Too Loud, You're Too Old*, ed. Jonathon S. Epstein. New York: Garland Publishing, 165–87.

Boyer, Horace. 1973. 'Gospel Music Comes of Age.' *Black World* 33: 42–48, 79–86.

Broven, John. 1978 (1974). *Rhythm and Blues in New Orleans*. Gretna, LA: Pelican Publishing. (First published as *Walking to New Orleans: The Story of New Orleans Rhythm & Blues*. Bexhill-on-Sea: Blues Unlimited.)

Brown, Ernest D. 1990. 'Something from Nothing and More from Something: The Making and Playing of Music Instruments in African-American Cultures.' *Selected Reports in Ethnomusicology* 8: 275–91.

Burnim, Mellonee. 1985. 'The Black Gospel Tradition: A Complex of Ideology, Aesthetic, and Behavior.' In *More Than Dancing: Essays on Afro-American Music and Musicians*, ed. Irene V. Jackson. Westport, CT: Greenwood Press, 147–67.

Burnim, Mellonee. 1988. 'Functional Dimensions of Gospel Music Performance.' *Western Journal of Black Studies* 12(2): 52–61.

Cashmore, Ellis. 1997. *The Black Culture Industry*. London and New York: Routledge.

Charters, Samuel B. 1959. *The Country Blues*. New York: Rinehart.

Charters, Samuel B., and Kunstadt, Leonard. 1962. *Jazz: A History of the New York Scene*. Garden City, NY: Doubleday.

DeVeaux, Scott. 1991. 'Constructing the Jazz Tradition: Jazz Historiography.' *Black American Literature Forum* 25 (Fall): 525–60.

Du Bois, W.E.B. 1995 (1903). *The Souls of Black Folk*. New York: Signet/Penguin Books.

Dyson, Michael E. 1991. 'Performance, Protest, and Prophecy in the Culture of Hip-Hop.' *Black Sacred Music: A Journal of Theomusicology* 1 (Spring): 13–24.

Dyson, Michael E. 1996. *Between God and Gangsta Rap:*

Bearing Witness to Black Culture. New York: Oxford University Press.

Early, Gerald Lyn. 1995. *One Nation Under a Groove: Motown and American Culture*. Hopewell, NJ: Ecco Press.

Epstein, Dena J. 1977. *Sinful Tunes and Spirituals: Black Folk Music to the Civil War*. Urbana, IL: University of Illinois Press.

Epstein, Dena J. 1983. 'A White Origin for the Black Spiritual?: An Invalid Theory and How It Grew.' *American Music* 1(2): 53–59.

Erlmann, Veit. 1999. *Music, Modernity, and the Global Imagination: South Africa and the West*. New York: Oxford University Press.

Evans, David. 1982. *Big Road Blues: Tradition and Creativity in the Folk Blues*. Berkeley, CA: University of California Press.

Ferris, William. 1978 (1970). *Blues from the Delta*. New York: Anchor Press.

Frith, Simon. 1978. *The Sociology of Rock*. London: Constable.

Frith, Simon. 1988. *Music for Pleasure: Essays in the Sociology of Pop*. New York: Routledge.

Garland, Phyl. 1969. *The Sound of Soul*. Chicago: H. Regnery Co.

Garofalo, Reebee. 1990. 'Crossing Over: 1939–1989.' In *Split Image: African Americans in the Mass Media*, ed. Jannette L. Dates and William Barlow. Washington, DC: Howard University Press, 57–121.

George, Nelson. 1988. *The Death of Rhythm & Blues*. New York: Pantheon Books.

Gillett, Charlie. 1974. *Making Tracks: Atlantic Records and the Growth of a Multi-Billion-Dollar Industry*. New York: E.P. Dutton.

Gillett, Charlie. 1984 (1970). *The Sound of the City: The Rise of Rock and Roll*. New York: Pantheon Books.

Gilroy, Paul. 1993a. *The Black Atlantic: Modernity and Double Consciousness*. Cambridge, MA: Harvard University Press.

Gilroy, Paul. 1993b. *Small Acts: Thoughts on the Politics of Black Cultures*. London and New York: Serpent's Tail.

Guillory, Monique, and Green, Richard C., eds. 1998. *Soul: Black Power, Politics, and Pleasure*. New York: New York University Press.

Guralnick, Peter. 1986. *Sweet Soul Music: Rhythm and Blues and the Southern Dream of Freedom*. New York: Harper & Row.

Haas, Robert Bartlett, ed. 1972. *William Grant Still and the Fusion of Cultures in American Music*. Los Angeles: Black Sparrow Press.

Hall, Stuart, and du Gay, Paul, eds. 1996. *Questions of Cultural Identity*. Thousand Oaks, CA: Sage.

Haralambos, Michael. 1975. *Right On: From Blues to Soul in Black America*. New York: Drake Publishers.

Harris, Michael W. 1992. *The Rise of Gospel Blues: The Music of Thomas Andrew Dorsey in the Urban Church*. New York: Oxford University Press.

Harris, Robert L., Jr., Hine, Darlene Clark, and McKay, Nellie. 1990. *Black Studies in the United States: Three Essays*. New York: Ford Foundation.

Hentoff, Nat. 1961. *The Jazz Life*. New York: Dial Press.

Herskovits, Melville J. 1958. *The Myth of the Negro Past*. Boston, MA: Beacon Press.

Hirshey, Gerri. 1984. *Nowhere to Run: The Story of Soul Music*. New York: Times Books.

Hodeir, André. 1979 (1956). *Jazz: Its Evolution and Essence*, trans. David Noakes. New York: Grove Press.

Hughes, Langston. 1976 (1926). 'The Negro Artist and the Racial Mountain.' In *Voices from the Harlem Renaissance*, ed. Nathan Huggins. New York: Oxford University Press, 305–307.

Hurston, Zora N. 1976 (1935). 'Spirituals and Neo-Spirituals.' In *Voices from the Harlem Renaissance*, ed. Nathan Huggins. New York: Oxford University Press, 344–47.

Jackson, Bruce, ed. 1967. *The Negro and His Folklore in Nineteenth-Century Periodicals*. Austin, TX: University of Texas Press.

Jackson, George P. 1933. *White Spirituals in the Southern Uplands: The Story of the Fasola Folk, Their Songs, Singings, and 'Buckwheat Notes'*. Chapel Hill, NC: University of North Carolina Press.

Jackson, George P. 1944. *White and Negro Spirituals, Their Life Span and Kinship, Tracing 200 Years of Untrammeled Song Making and Singing Among Our Country Folk, with 116 Songs as Sung by Both Races*. New York: J.J. Augustin.

Johnson, Guy B. 1930. *Folk Culture on St. Helena Island, South Carolina*. Chapel Hill, NC: University of North Carolina Press.

Johnson, James W., and Johnson, J. Rosamond. 1989a (1925). *The Book of American Negro Spirituals*. New York: Da Capo Press.

Johnson, James W., and Johnson, J. Rosamond. 1989b (1926). *The Second Book of American Negro Spirituals*. New York: Da Capo Press.

Jones, LeRoi (Imamu Amiri Baraka). 1963. *Blues People: Negro Music in White America*. New York: William Morrow & Co.

Jones, LeRoi (Imamu Amiri Baraka). 1967. *Black Music*. New York: William Morrow & Co.

Kalumbu, Isaac. 1999. *The Process of Creation and Production of Popular Music in Zimbabwe*. Ph.D. thesis, Indiana University.

Kaufman, Fredrick, and Guckin, John P. 1979. *The*

African Roots of Jazz. Sherman Oaks, CA: Alfred Publishing Co.

Keil, Charles. 1966. *Urban Blues*. Chicago: University of Chicago Press.

Kelley, Robin D.G. 1994. *Race Rebels: Culture, Politics, and the Black Working Class*. New York: Free Press.

Kelley, Robin D.G. 1997. *Yo' Mama's Disfunktional!: Fighting the Culture Wars in Urban America*. Boston, MA: Beacon Press.

Kofsky, Frank. 1970. *Black Nationalism and the Revolution in Music*. New York: Pathfinder Press.

Kubik, Gerhard. 1999. *Africa and the Blues*. Jackson, MS: University Press of Mississippi.

Larkin, Rochelle. 1970. *Soul Music*. New York: Lancer Books.

Lewis, David Levering, ed. 1995. *W.E.B. Du Bois: A Reader*. New York: H. Holt and Co.

Lipsitz, George. 1994. *Dangerous Crossroads: Popular Music, Postmodernism, and the Poetics of Place*. London and New York: Verso.

Locke, Alain. 1969 (1936). *The Negro and His Music*. New York: Arno Press.

Locke, Alain, ed. 1992 (1925). *The New Negro: Voices of the Harlem Renaissance*. New York: Atheneum.

Lomax, Alan. 1978 (1968). *Folk Song Style and Culture*. New Brunswick, NJ: Transaction Books.

Lornell, Kip. 1988. *Happy in the Service of the Lord: Afro-American Gospel Quartets in Memphis*. Urbana, IL: University of Illinois Press.

Maultsby, Portia K. 1990. 'Africanisms in African-American Music.' In *Africanisms in American Culture*, ed. Joseph E. Holloway. Bloomington, IN: Indiana University Press, 185–210.

Maultsby, Portia K. 1992. 'The Impact of Gospel Music on the Secular Music Industry.' In *We'll Understand It Better By and By: Pioneering African American Gospel Composers*, ed. Bernice Johnson Reagon. Washington, DC: Smithsonian Institution Press, 19–33.

Maultsby, Portia K., and Burnim, Mellonee. 2001. 'Overview.' In *The Garland Encyclopedia of World Music*, Vol. 3, ed. Ellen Koskoff. New York: Garland Publishing Co., 572–91.

Monson, Ingrid. 1996. *Saying Something: Jazz Improvisation and Interaction*. Chicago: University of Chicago Press.

Monson, Ingrid, ed. 2000. *The African Diaspora: A Musical Perspective*. New York: Garland.

Morley, David, and Chen, Kuan-Hsing, eds. 1996. *Stuart Hall: Critical Dialogues in Cultural Studies*. London and New York: Routledge.

Murray, Albert. 1976. *Stomping the Blues*. New York: McGraw-Hill.

Neal, Larry. 1989 (1971). 'The Ethos of the Blues.' In *Visions of a Liberated Future: Black Arts Movement Writings*, ed. Michael Schwartz. New York: Thunder's Mouth Press, 107–17.

Neal, Mark Anthony. 1999. *What the Music Said: Black Popular Music and Black Public Culture*. New York: Routledge.

Nketia, J.H. Kwabena. 1973. 'The Study of African and Afro-American Music.' *The Black Perspective in Music* 1: 7–15.

Nketia, J.H. Kwabena. 1981. 'African Roots of Music in the Americas: An African View.' In *Report of the 12th Congress*. London: American Musicological Society, 82–88.

Oliver, Paul. 1960. *Blues Fell This Morning: The Meaning of the Blues*. London: Cassell.

Oliver, Paul. 1969. *The Story of the Blues*. Philadelphia: Chilton Book Co.

Oliver, Paul. 1970. *Savannah Syncopators: African Retentions in the Blues*. New York: Stein and Day.

Osgood, Henry O. 1926. *So This Is Jazz*. Boston, MA: Little, Brown, and Company.

Panassié, Hugues. 1960 (1942). *The Real Jazz*. Rev. ed. New York: Barnes.

Panassié, Hugues. 1970 (1936). *Hot Jazz: The Guide to Swing Music*, trans. Lyle and Eleanor Dowling. Westport, CT: Negro Universities Press.

Pearson, Nathan W., Jr. 1987. *Goin' to Kansas City*. Urbana, IL: University of Illinois Press.

Peretti, Burton W. 1992. *The Creation of Jazz: Music, Race, and Culture in Urban America*. Urbana, IL: University of Illinois Press.

Perkins, William Eric, ed. 1996. *Droppin' Science: Critical Essays on Rap Music and Hip Hop Culture*. Philadelphia: Temple University Press.

Ramsey, Frederic, Jr., and Smith, Charles Edward, eds. 1939. *Jazzmen*. New York: Harcourt, Brace and Company.

Reagon, Bernice Johnson, ed. 1992. *We'll Understand It Better By and By: Pioneering African American Gospel Composers*. Washington, DC: Smithsonian Institution Press.

Rose, Tricia. 1994. *Black Noise: Rap Music and Black Culture in Contemporary America*. Hanover, NH: University Press of New England.

Rowe, Mike. 1979 (1973). *Chicago Breakdown*. New York: Da Capo Press.

Sargeant, Winthrop. 1975 (1938). *Jazz, Hot and Hybrid*. 3rd ed. New York: Da Capo Press.

Shaw, Arnold. 1970. *The World of Soul: Black America's Contribution to the Pop Music Scene*. New York: Cowles Book Co.

Shaw, Arnold. 1978. *Honkers and Shouters: The Golden Years of Rhythm and Blues*. New York: Macmillan.

Smith, Suzanne E. 1999. *Dancing in the Street: Motown and the Cultural Politics of Detroit*. Cambridge, MA: Harvard University Press.

Southern, Eileen, ed. 1983 (1971). *Readings in Black American Music*. 2nd ed. New York: W.W. Norton.

Southern, Eileen, and Wright, Josephine. 1990. *African-American Traditions in Song, Sermon, Tale, and Dance, 1600s–1920: An Annotated Bibliography of Literature, Collections, and Artworks*. New York: Greenwood Press.

Spellman, A.B. 1970 (1966). *Black Music, Four Lives*. New York: Schocken Books. (Originally published as *Four Lives in the Bebop Business*. New York: Pantheon Books.)

Stearns, Marshall W. 1956. *The Story of Jazz*. New York: Oxford University Press.

Titon, Jeff Todd. 1994 (1977). *Early Downhome Blues: A Musical and Cultural Analysis*. 2nd ed. Chapel Hill, NC: University of North Carolina Press.

Trotter, James M. 1878. *Music and Some Highly Musical People*. New York: Charles T. Dillingham.

Wallaschek, Richard. 1970 (1893). *Primitive Music: An Inquiry into the Origin and Development of Music, Songs, Instruments, Dances, and Pantomimes of Savage Races*. New York: Da Capo Press.

Ward, Brian. 1998. *Just My Soul Responding: Rhythm and Blues, Black Consciousness, and Race Relations*. Berkeley, CA: University of California Press.

Waterman, Richard A. 1943. *African Patterns in Trinidad Negro Music*. Ph.D. thesis, Northwestern University.

Waterman, Richard A. 1963. 'On Flogging a Dead Horse: Lessons Learned from the Africanisms Controversy.' *Ethnomusicology* 7(2): 83–87.

Waterman, Richard A. 1971 (1952). 'African Influence on the Music of the Americas.' In *Anthropology and Art: Readings in Cross-Cultural Aesthetics*, ed. Charlotte M. Otten. Garden City, NY: The Natural History Press.

Werner, Craig. 1999. *A Change Is Gonna Come: Music, Race & the Soul of America*. New York: Plume.

Westcott, William. 1977. 'Ideas of Afro-American Musical Acculturation in the U.S.A.: 1900 to the Present.' *Journal of the Steward Anthropological Society* 8(2) (Spring): 107–36.

White, Newman I. 1928. *American Negro Folk-Songs*. Cambridge, MA: Harvard University Press.

Williams, George Washington. 1882–83. *History of the Negro Race in America*, Vols. 1 and 2. New York: G.P. Putnam's Sons.

Williams, Linda Faye. 1995. *The Impact of African-American Music on Jazz in Zimbabwe: An Exploration in Radical Empiricism*. Ph.D. thesis, Indiana University.

Williams-Jones, Pearl. 1975. 'Afro-American Gospel Music: A Crystallization of the Black Aesthetic.' *Ethnomusicology* 19(3): 373–85.

Williams-Jones, Pearl. 1977. 'The Musical Quality of Black Religious Folk Ritual.' *Spirit* 1: 21–30.

Wilson, Olly. 1974. 'The Significance of the Relationship Between Afro-American Music and West Africa.' *The Black Perspective in Music* 2: 3–22.

Wilson, Olly. 1981. 'The Association of Movement and Music as a Manifestation of a Black Conceptual Approach to Music.' In *Report of the 12th Congress*. London: American Musicological Society, 98–105.

Wilson, Olly. 1992. 'The Heterogeneous Sound Ideal in African-American Music.' In *New Perspectives on Music: Essays in Honor of Eileen Southern*, ed. Josephine Wright with Samuel A. Floyd, Jr. Warren, MI: Harmonie Park Press, 327–38.

Woodson, Carter G. 1990 (1933). *The Mis-Education of the Negro*. New York: Africa World Press.

Work, John W. 1969 (1915). *Folk Song of the American Negro*. New York: Negro Universities Press.

Filmography

Saturday Night Fever, dir. John Badham. 1977. USA. 119 mins. Musical Drama. Original music by Barry Gibb, Maurice Gibb, Robin Gibb, Barry Robin, David Shire.

PORTIA K. MAULTSBY and ISAAC KALUMBU

Anthropology

The study of popular music falls within the domain of social or cultural anthropology rather than that of physical anthropology. Social anthropology is a social science discipline still generally associated with the study of relatively distant, isolated and exotic 'others' from non-industrialized and so-called 'non-Western' cultures. As Hannerz (1992) has stated, 'some anthropologists have seen their vocation as a study of "the other" with a preference for the most Other, as different as possible from that anthropologist's self which is most often rooted in an urban, industrial or even post-industrial, capitalist large-scale social order' (5). Nevertheless, many anthropologists have more recently conducted their research at or much nearer to home, although the notion of 'anthropology at home' is still a somewhat contentious issue within the discipline, with some practitioners firmly believing that the process of becoming an anthropologist ought to involve research in less familiar contexts.

Wherever they base their research, social anthropologists typically study people in small groups, such as kinship or peer groups, ethnic groups or lineages, and investigate the cultural worlds that these groups create for themselves, with 'culture' defined as a way of life. There is a range of familiar issues on which these studies typically focus, such as kinship, political or belief systems, and the construction of collective and ethnic identity. Social anthropology is distinguished not only by its interest in such issues and its own distinctive intellectual heritage, but also by its research methodology and approach. Social anthropological research usually involves identifying and traveling to a particular place (the 'field') and conducting 'fieldwork' that involves participation in, and systematic, detailed and intensive observation of, the everyday lives of the groups being studied. The anthropologist then returns home to analyze the data collected, explore emerging issues, construct an argument, and write up a description and interpretation in the form of a text that is referred to as an 'ethnography.'

Music is often a focus or aspect of anthropological research because of the important part it plays in the life of so many groups. Anthropologists have drawn attention to the musical practises, ideas and styles that are popular within such groups, looking at the way in which musical activities are structured and organized socially, economically and politically, and are shaped by various institutions and social conventions, and to the way in which music is valued and made meaningful. They have tended to concentrate on the non-commercial musical and oral traditions of groups based in rural contexts or ethnic groups in urban contexts, and this research has been closely linked to ethnomusicology and informed by the seminal work of scholars such as John Blacking, Alan Merriam and Bruno Nettl. Hence, Hannerz (1992) has pointed out that 'the growth and spread of media have had curiously little impact on the mainstream of anthropological as well as sociological thought' (26).

Increasingly, however, anthropologists are drawing on issues and theories from cultural and media studies in order to study more commercialized popular music within shifting, mass-mediated and industrialized contexts. Some have studied popular music audiences and popular music in domestic life (see, for example, Cavicchi 1998); others have focused on particular musical events, such as festivals or carnivals (see, for example, A. Cohen 1993); and many have studied local scenes from the perspective of particular popular music genres or styles (see, for example, S. Cohen 1991; Waterman 1990; Guilbault 1993; Vestel 1997; Stokes 1992). The following discussion focuses on an example of one of the latter types of study to illustrate in more detail the characteristics of an anthropological approach to the study of popular music.

Ruth Finnegan's book *The Hidden Musicians* (1989) concerns amateur 'grass-roots' music-making and its role and significance in contemporary urban and industrial life. It is based on extensive fieldwork conducted in the English town of Milton Keynes. To determine the range and variety of local music-making, Finnegan conducted a broad survey of all music-making in Milton Keynes using questionnaires and telephone interviews; she also carried out fieldwork involving more qualitative research methods, such as extended interviews and participant observation, which enabled her to focus in more detail on the characteristics of particular musical genres and styles (including jazz, country and rock). She treated them as separate musical 'worlds,' looking at the individuals and groups, activities and relationships, meanings and values involved with them. She described the different approaches of these musical worlds to common activities such as musical learning, composition and performance, thus highlighting the social conventions and collective understandings that distinguished them; she also emphasized overlaps and relationships between the worlds, and common ways in which all local music-making was supported and funded; and she illustrated the way in which local musical worlds were bound into complex relationships with a series of music institutions and patterns outside the town.

Finnegan thus adopted an anthropological approach that emphasized fieldwork conducted over an extended period of time so that she could study music as social and cultural practise. Her approach differed from those that treat music solely as text or depend on secondary source material, and from those that deal with broad processes and structures in a more generalized or abstract fashion. Finnegan studied local musical worlds from the perspective and understanding of those who participated in them in order to highlight alternative ways of behaving and thinking and different approaches to common events. Her work thus reveals a typical anthropological interest in comparison, cultural diversity and indigenous concepts and values. In addition, Finnegan adopted and utilized an anthropological emphasis on social relations, focusing on those between individuals, groups and institutions; those between musical practises and ideas; and those between the social, cultural and economic dimensions of musical worlds. In the process, she examined local music-making in relation to issues such as class, kinship, age, gender and ethnicity.

Finnegan drew on this description of music-making in Milton Keynes to consider more generally the role and significance of music in people's lives. She concluded that people should get involved with music because it provides a context for their activities and relationships and a means through which they can express personal and collective identity and value, and because it allows for the meaningful structuring of their actions in time and space. She made detailed observations of specific groups, situations and contexts in Milton Keynes in order to study fundamental issues, drawing out the broader implications of her encounters and dialogs with music-makers in the town and using them to inform and develop more general theories about music behavior. This integration of theory and description is characteristic of much anthropological analysis; it distinguishes anthropological studies from those that develop theoretical models based on what people are assumed to be doing, without direct communication with them or firsthand observation of what they are doing, and from those that rely on neat generalities and universal laws or models that often 'homogenize' people and obscure life's complexities and contradictions.

Many of its practitioners have perceived social anthropology as a science, involving systematic investigation of a culture and its customs and rites in order to identify underlying social laws or rules. Under the influence of Clifford Geertz and literary criticism, however, anthropologists treated culture as something to be interpreted in order to determine its meaning. More recently, anthropologists have begun to question such accepted principles of ethnographic research. Critical attention has been paid to the practise of ethnography and the power relations involved (see, for example, works by James Clifford, George Marcus, Michael Fischer and Renato Rosaldo), with increasing emphasis placed on fieldwork as an encounter, relationship or dialog between ethnographer and informant. Debates in anthropology have also drawn attention to the production of anthropological texts and the politics and ethics of textual representation – the way in which anthropologists not only study, but also write about, culture – showing how anthropological writing often reveals as much about the anthropologists as the people and events they write about. There have been criticisms of anthropologists who impose their own values and interpretations without adequately representing the diversity and complexity of voices, views and interpretations among the people they are studying. Some anthropologists and ethnomusicologists have consequently experimented with alternative methods of representing musical cultures in textual form, and different ways of positioning themselves within those texts and in relation to their subject. Guilbault (1993), for example, emphasized coauthorship in her book on *zouk* music, commissioning chapters from several specialists and informants and integrating their contrasting perspectives, experiences and interpretations of *zouk* with her own.

Bibliography

Blacking, John. 1976. *How Musical Is Man?* London: Faber.

Cavicchi, Daniel. 1998. *Tramps Like Us: Music and Meaning Among Springsteen Fans*. New York: Oxford University Press.

Clifford, James. 1988. *The Predicament of Culture: Twentieth-Century Ethnography, Literature, and Art*. Cambridge, MA: Harvard University Press.

Clifford, James, and Marcus, George E., eds. 1986. *Writing Culture: The Poetics and Politics of Ethnography*. Berkeley, CA: University of California Press.

Cohen, A. 1993. *Masquerade Politics: Explorations in the Structure of Urban Cultural Movements*. Berkeley and Los Angeles: University of California Press.

Cohen, Sara. 1991. *Rock Culture in Liverpool: Popular Music in the Making*. Oxford: Oxford University Press.

Finnegan, Ruth. 1989. *The Hidden Musicians: Music-Making in an English Town*. Cambridge: Cambridge University Press.

Geertz, Clifford. 1973. *The Interpretation of Cultures*. New York: Basic Books.

Guilbault, Jocelyne. 1993. *Zouk: World Music in the West Indies*. Chicago: University of Chicago Press.

Hannerz, Ulf. 1992. *Cultural Complexity: Studies in the Social Organization of Meaning*. New York: Columbia University Press.

Marcus, George E., and Fischer, Michael M.J. 1986. *Anthropology as Cultural Critique: An Experimental Moment in the Human Sciences*. Chicago: University of Chicago Press.

Merriam, Alan. 1964. *The Anthropology of Music*. Evanston, IL: Northwestern University Press.

Nettl, Bruno. 1964. *Theory and Method in Ethnomusicology*. New York: The Free Press of Glencoe.

Rosaldo, Renato. 1989. *Culture and Truth: The Remaking of Social Analysis*. London: Routledge.

Stokes, Martin. 1992. *The Arabesk Debate: Music and Musicians in Modern Turkey*. Oxford: Clarendon Press.

Vestel, V. 1997. 'Fans, Fear and Phantoms: The Quest for Pleasure and Authenticity in Norwegian Black Metal.' Unpublished paper presented at the 'Music Fan Cultures' conference, University of Copenhagen, 23 October.

Waterman, Christopher A. 1990. *Jújù: A Social History and Ethnography of an African Popular Music*. Chicago: University of Chicago Press.

SARA COHEN

Black Studies

Black studies focuses on the study of black life and culture primarily in Africa and the Americas. In the academy, it has been housed principally in the humanities – the study of black literature, art and history – although, because of the centrality of blacks in debates about race relations, slavery and racism, black studies is prominently featured in the social sciences, particularly sociology. The discipline has often gone hand in hand with political efforts by blacks and others to further the causes of equal protection under the law and the freeing of communities and nations of blacks from colonialism, slavery and Jim Crow segregation. Eric Williams's *Capitalism and Slavery* (1994) is one of the best examples of the kind of political scholarship that found a home in the burgeoning field of black studies. Popular music studies has been engaged in a reciprocal relationship with black studies, contributing to the field by highlighting the ways in which black popular music has both reflected and influenced the political, social, cultural and philosophical terrain of the global black experience, and at the same time revealing the influence of black studies in terms of themes and approaches.

The first major academic study of black life and culture done by an African American was W.E.B. Du Bois' sociological work *The Philadelphia Negro* (1899). The publication in 1933 of Carter G. Woodson's *The Mis-Education of the Negro* was perhaps the foundation for black studies in the United States. Written some 70 years after the Emancipation Proclamation, Woodson's cogent argument for the meticulous and rigorous study of the African past and the African-American present had been forged during a period of tremendous economic and political growth for African Americans. Although the formation of black studies would later play a role in addressing anti-black racism domestically, many of the leading intellectuals and artists were fixated on the impact of what Joseph Holloway (1990) later called 'Africanisms' within North American life and culture. Thus, the work of visual artist Aaron Douglass, best expressed perhaps in his painting *Building Stately Mansions*, referenced African folk art and the duality of African and North American influences on what Cornel West has termed 'New World Africans.' In another example, Du Bois became engrossed in the Pan-African Congress movement, attending his first conference in 1919. As early as the nineteenth century, black thinkers such as Martin Delaney and Henry Highland Garnett had articulated 'African-centered' philosophies, as they openly considered a return to Africa for black slaves and former slaves some years before Marcus Garvey created a mass 'Back to Africa' movement in the 1920s.

Many of the early concepts of Pan-Africanism were powerfully expressed after World War I in the work of Senegalese poet Léopold Senghor, who, along with writers Aimé Césaire and Léon Damas, developed the concept of *négritude* – an aesthetic that reflected a common consciousness among peoples of African descent. In 1960, Senghor became president of Senegal. In the late 1950s and 1960s, Senegal, Ghana, Nigeria, the Belgian Congo and Kenya were among the first independent African states, and the efforts of those peoples to break free of European colonialism paralleled the struggles of African Americans to resist Jim Crow segregation in the United States.

In the post-World War II period, there were many 'Black Atlantic' exchanges between diasporic African peoples that furthered the cultivation of black studies (see Gilroy 1993). Richard Wright's collection of essays, *Black Power*, gave firsthand accounts of the efforts of those in rebellion in colonized African states. Ghanaian president Kwame Nkrumah was trained in US schools. Psychologist and Algerian political activist Frantz Fanon's works *The Wretched of the Earth* and *Black Skin, White Masks* found an audience among the black intelligentsia and young radicals globally. Katherine Dunham's Caribbean-influenced dance theories became the template for contemporary black dance, inspiring figures like Alvin Ailey and Arthur Mitchell, and a wide range of people who found ways to connect to African culture through dance. The music of South African performers such as pianist Dollar Brand (aka Abdullah Ibrahim), trumpeter Hugh Masekela and vocalist Miriam Makeba, and Jamaican reggae, courtesy of the Wailers, the genre's early progenitors, began to have an impact on African-American cultural sensibilities. African Americans and others started to dress in African-style clothing like dashikis and wear their hair in natural (African) styles, and to embrace other forms of African culture expressed in dance, music, fashion, food and language (Swahili). These very public expressions of African-style culture by African Americans and others gave Pan-Africanism a heightened visibility in the late 1960s, coinciding with the creation of black studies departments in North American colleges and universities.

On a strictly symbolic level, the marriage between civil rights/black power leader Stokely Carmichael (Kwame Turé) and Miriam Makeba in 1968 personified the concept of Pan-Africanism. Nigerian-born musician Fela Kuti immigrated to the United States at this time and was profoundly affected by the politics of the black power movement and the music of James Brown. Fela's style of music, which he dubbed Afro-pop, was used as a powerful tool against the repressive forces within his native Nigeria, as he relayed forms of resistance to which he was introduced in the United States via heavily syncopated grooves. More than two decades after the birth of Afro-pop, hip-hop groups in the United States such as the Roots and Common would acknowledge the impact of Fela's music on their own work.

In the aftermath of the civil rights and black power movements, the field of black studies was reenergized by political developments on the African continent, most notably the anti-apartheid movement. In the context of black struggles in Southern Africa, a new generation of students was exposed to African politics through plays such as *Sarafina!* and *Master Harold and the Boys*, Wole Soyinka's dramatic depictions of life in South Africa, the music of Ladysmith Black Mambazo, and films such as *A Dry White Season, Cry Freedom* and the movie version of *Sarafina!*. Issues such as the drought/famine in Ethiopia and the Sudan introduced other aspects of African life into black studies. Lastly, the move toward multicultural education and pluralism in US higher education helped to instigate a focus on global black studies. It was in this context that Nigerian writer Chinua Achebe was able to offer his critical reading of Joseph Conrad's *Heart of Darkness* from the standpoint of the nameless and faceless African natives who populated the Congo region. Achebe's essay, along with the work of a generation of black literary critics such as Hortense Spillers, Houston Baker, Mary Helen Washington and Henry Louis Gates, whose *The Signifying Monkey* was published in 1988, helped to consolidate distinct theories of African-American and African-centered styles of reading and teaching literature.

This new focus on black studies, both domestically and globally, also coincided with the acceptance of 'Afrocentric' philosophical theories among black college students and the black masses. Conceived in large part by scholars such as Molefi Asante and Ron Karenga and Egyptologists like Jacob Carruthers, Afrocentrism attempted to counter legitimately what many of its purveyors viewed as rampant Eurocentrism. In many regards, Afrocentrism became a fault line in black studies, demarcating sharp differences in modes of inquiry by traditional Africanists, African Americanists engaged in traditional social-science and humanities-based research, African-American postmodernists who focused on so-called 'identity politics' and Afrocentrists.

Black Studies and Popular Music

LeRoi Jones's *Blues People* (1963) was the first text to bridge the fields of popular music studies and black studies in a significant way. Arguably, Jones's text single-handedly made the study of black music a credible endeavor within traditional black studies, by forcibly calling attention to the role that music had played, and continued to play, in the everyday life of blacks. *Blues People* acted as a blueprint for the study of black popular music by many later writers. Among the studies that show its imprint, in their different ways, are Nelson George's *The Death of Rhythm & Blues* (1988), Tricia Rose's *Black Noise: Rap Music and Black Culture in Contemporary America* (1994), Craig Werner's *A Change Is Gonna Come: Music, Race & the Soul of America* (1999), Brian Ward's *Just My Soul Responding: Rhythm and Blues, Black Consciousness, and Race Relations* (1998) and Mark Anthony Neal's *What the Music Said: Black Popular Music*

and Black Public Culture (1999). In other examples, texts such as Suzanne Smith's *Dancing in the Street: Motown and the Cultural Politics of Detroit* (1999), Clyde Woods's *Development Arrested: The Cotton and Blues Empire of the Mississippi Delta* (1998) and Paul Gilroy's *The Black Atlantic: Modernity and Double Consciousness* (1993) use popular music as a subtext to examine working-class resistance, labor exploitation and modernity. Such texts have been of value to black studies because they examine black music in the context of traditional historical narratives and thus illuminate those narratives as well as musical expression, often from the perspective of laypeople as opposed to that of the elite figures who have dominated expressions of black life and culture.

Conversely, the acceptance of black studies as a legitimate field of scholarly inquiry and its attendant focus on literature and expressive culture contributed to the acceptance of popular music studies. Texts such as Lawrence Levine's *Black Culture and Black Consciousness* (1977) and Charles Keil's *Urban Blues* (1966), building on the earlier writings of Zora Neale Hurston, Langston Hughes and Sterling Brown, made clear that black folk culture and popular music represent genuine locations for the examination of black political and social sensibilities. With many black scholars, including W.E.B. Du Bois, E. Franklin Frazier and St. Clair Drake, having grounded the emergent field of black studies in the everyday realities of black life, the examination of the role of music and leisure would be a natural extension of that logic. In many regards, the focus on everyday life in black studies contributed to the context for the acceptance of North American cultural studies among black intellectuals, and many black studies programs and departments in North America are currently subsumed under the rubric of cultural studies.

Bibliography

Anderson, Jervis. 1982. *This Was Harlem: A Cultural Portrait, 1900–1950*. New York: Farrar Straus Giroux.

Banks, William M. 1996. *Black Intellectuals: Race and Responsibility in American Life*. New York: W.W. Norton.

Carson, Clayborne. 1995. *In Struggle: SNCC and the Black Awakening of the 1960s*. Cambridge, MA: Harvard University Press.

Cone, James H. 1972. *The Spirituals and the Blues: An Interpretation*. New York: Seabury Press.

Du Bois, W.E.B. 1899. *The Philadelphia Negro: A Social Study*. Philadelphia: Published for the university.

Du Bois, W.E.B. 1995 (1903). *The Souls of Black Folk*. New York: Signet/Penguin Books.

Dyson, Michael E. 1993. *Reflecting Black: African-*

American Cultural Criticism. Minneapolis, MN: University of Minnesota Press.

Ellison, Ralph. 1995. *The Collected Essays of Ralph Ellison*, ed. John F. Callahan. New York: Modern Library.

Fanon, Frantz. 1965. *The Wretched of the Earth*, trans. Constance Farrington. New York: Grove Press.

Fanon, Frantz. 1967. *Black Skin, White Masks*, trans. Charles Lam Markmann. New York: Grove Press.

Floyd, Samuel A., ed. 1990. *Black Music in the Harlem Renaissance: A Collection of Essays*. New York: Greenwood Press.

Gates, Henry Louis. 1988. *The Signifying Monkey: A Theory of Afro-American Literary Criticism*. New York: Oxford University Press.

George, Nelson. 1988. *The Death of Rhythm & Blues*. New York: Pantheon Books.

Gilroy, Paul. 1993. *The Black Atlantic: Modernity and Double Consciousness*. Cambridge, MA: Harvard University Press.

Haymes, Stephen. 1995. *Race, Culture, and the City: A Pedagogy for Black Urban Struggle*. Albany, NY: State University of New York Press.

Holloway, Joseph E., ed. 1990. *Africanisms in American Culture*. Bloomington, IN: Indiana University Press.

Johnson, James Weldon. 1991. *Black Manhattan*. New York: Da Capo Press.

Jones, LeRoi (Imamu Amiri Baraka). 1963. *Blues People: Negro Music in White America*. New York: William Morrow & Co.

Keil, Charles. 1966. *Urban Blues*. Chicago: University of Chicago Press.

Kelley, Robin D.G. 1994. *Race Rebels: Culture, Politics, and the Black Working Class*. New York: Free Press.

Levine, Lawrence W. 1977. *Black Culture and Black Consciousness: Afro-American Folk Thought from Slavery to Freedom*. New York: Oxford University Press.

Lewis, David Levering. 1997. *When Harlem Was in Vogue*. New York: Penguin Books.

Neal, Mark Anthony. 1999. *What the Music Said: Black Popular Music and Black Public Culture*. New York: Routledge.

Rose, Tricia. 1994. *Black Noise: Rap Music and Black Culture in Contemporary America*. Hanover, NH: University Press of New England.

Smith, Suzanne E. 1999. *Dancing in the Street: Motown and the Cultural Politics of Detroit*. Cambridge, MA: Harvard University Press.

Soyinka, Wole. 1973. *Collected Plays*. New York: Oxford University Press.

Wallace, Michele. 1992. *Black Popular Culture: A Project*, ed. Gina Dent. Seattle, WA: Bay Press.

Ward, Brian. 1998. *Just My Soul Responding: Rhythm and Blues, Black Consciousness, and Race Relations*. Berkeley, CA: University of California Press.

Werner, Craig. 1999. *A Change Is Gonna Come: Music, Race & the Soul of America*. New York: Plume.

Williams, Eric. 1994. *Capitalism and Slavery*. Chapel Hill, NC: University of North Carolina Press.

Woods, Clyde. 1998. *Development Arrested: The Cotton and Blues Empire of the Mississippi Delta*. New York: Verso.

Woodson, Carter G. 1990 (1933). *The Mis-Education of the Negro*. New York: Africa World Press.

Wright, Richard. 1954. *Black Power: A Record of Reactions in a Land of Pathos*. New York: Harper.

Filmography

A Dry White Season, dir. Euzhan Palcy. 1989. UK/USA. 105 mins. Drama. Original music by Dave Grusin.

Cry Freedom, dir. Richard Attenborough. 1987. USA/UK. 157 mins. Drama. Original music by George Fenton, Jonas Gwangwa.

Sarafina!, dir. Darrell J. Roodt. 1992. France/UK/South Africa. 98 mins. Musical Drama. Original music by Stanley Myers, Mbongeni Ngema.

MARK ANTHONY NEAL

Communication (Communication Studies)

Introduction

Communication is the academic discipline that studies the phenomenon of communication. In so doing, the discipline of communication considers how communication is constituted, how it occurs, and what the consequences are of particular communicative acts and specific types of communicative practises (Schirato and Yell 1996). It was during the second half of the twentieth century that communication, or communication studies, became a well-established area of academic inquiry, with a rich theoretical tradition (O'Sullivan et al. 1994; McQuail and Windahl 1993).

In very general terms, communication can be thought of as (a) the conveying of information from A to B, with effect, and (b) the production and negotiation of meanings, a practise that occurs within specific social contexts.

A number of definitions and associated models of communication have been proposed. These vary according to the theoretical frames of reference employed, and the emphasis placed on different aspects of the communication process. These transmission-oriented frameworks usually include reference to communication as a process that implies a sender, a channel, a message, a receiver, a relationship between sender and receiver, an effect, a context in which communication occurs, and a range of phenomena to which 'messages' refer. Two additional processes sometimes alluded to are 'encoding' (at the sender's end) and 'decoding' (at the receiver's end). Encoding is the translation of a message into a language or code suitable for both the means of transmission and the intended recipient; decoding refers to the interpretation (or re-translation) of the message to extract meaning.

Communication involves far more than just language or verbal texts. Communication is present in a range of media, written, visual and aural, with music an aspect of all three. Music is a fundamental form of human communication. Along with many other animal species, humans use organized sound to communicate. In the case of humans, music may be thought of as a subset of this organized sound (see, for example, Shepherd and Wicke 1997). That music produces 'sense' and conveys 'meanings' is clear and unquestionable. What need to be considered are 'the attributes of the processes governing musical meaning' (Middleton 1990, 172), and how these operate in particular contexts. Popular music scholars have engaged with communication studies in examining such questions as: What conditions and contexts encourage the use of music rather than another medium? What are the special communicative properties of music? How does popular music 'speak' to its listeners? Why do listeners respond differently to the same musical styles and formats? How does music contribute to and represent culture? As Lull (1992) concludes: 'Music is a passionate sequencing of thoughts and feelings that expresses meaning in a manner that has no parallel in human life' (1).

In approaching these questions, popular music studies has been influenced by two dominant theoretical approaches to the analysis of communication: first, structuralism and semiology, which lead to an emphasis on texts; and, second, those audience-/consumption-oriented schools of sociology (e.g., symbolic interactionism, hermeneutics) that emphasize the social skills and competence that consumers/audiences possess, and the exercise of forms of communicative competence. These approaches are not discrete, and particular popular music studies will sometimes draw on both; for example, the study of music-oriented youth subcultures has utilized semiotics to examine the signifying codes and practises of the elements of style, and symbolic interactionism in relation to the cultural capital (and, frequently, the oppositional stance) associated with the subculture.

Structuralism and Semiology

These have informed the analysis of musical texts, primarily songs but also music videos, record covers and photographs, and readings of subcultural style. Such an approach has been strongly evident within musicology, and includes lyric analysis and the role of genre.

Music as organized sound has traditionally been defined in terms of beat, harmony, melody and, in much popular music, song lyrics. Particular texts of popular music shape audience consciousness through sheer thematic repetition (hooks), and through repeated exposure via radio and the playlists of music video channels. Genre labels (such as 'rock' or 'dance') function as codes, shorthand indicators of the music's characteristics, associated values and major audiences. It seems to have been generally accepted that musicians communicate – 'speak' – directly to individual listeners and to distinct audience constituencies through particular genres. Middleton (1990), Shepherd (1991, 128–85) and Tagg (1979, 1991) have, in their different ways, concentrated on the ability of musical sounds to effect communication.

However, considerable emphasis has, in addition, often been placed on lyrics as a means of understanding the communicative power of popular music (see, for example, Denski 1992). Yet, there has been continued debate over listeners' awareness of lyrics, and the polysemic nature of songs – the manner in which the same lyric content is decoded differently by particular listeners, especially in the case of political messages ('protest songs') and, usually at a more implicit level, ideologies of romance, and personal and social identity (Frith 1988; Longhurst 1995). Some lyrics, especially from rap and heavy metal songs, have been the subject of social debate and legal prosecution, with controversy over their 'effects' and the claimed existence of subliminal messages, particularly in relation to 'rock suicides' (Shuker 1994, 251–81).

As communicative texts, music videos raise questions as to the relative importance of their aural and visual dimensions, and the structural relationship between music and image (Goodwin 1993), especially in relation to power and gender (Lewis 1990).

Audience-/Consumption-Oriented Sociology

Music provides a soundtrack to accompany daily life, and a stimulus to physical activity, notably dancing, but also aerobics, driving and sex. Music also contributes to the context and meaning of other media texts, most notably on film soundtracks and in television advertisements. Different listening experiences and patterns are engendered by these parameters (Frith 1996).

A major concern has been the manner in which listeners identify with particular artists and genres, the shared characteristics of such listening constituencies (see, for example, Lewis 1992) and the listening strategies that they adopt (see, for instance, Moore 1993 on progressive rock).

Dance is a central cultural activity, closely associated with music, ritual, courtship and pleasure. It is a non-verbal form of communication, which nevertheless can express emotion and assert status and gender/ethnic identity (Hanna 1992). Certain forms of dance are identified with particular musical genres (for example, disco, rock 'n' roll and rap).

A significant dimension of such analyses is the role played by social contexts, including technology. A number of scholars have shown how the technological means whereby music is produced and transferred to audiences influences the nature of its reception. The listening experience is mediated differently via phonograph, tape cassette player and the Internet, and is further influenced by factors such as volume (Théberge 1997). These factors are additionally modified by context, with the ways in which music is received, listened to, interpreted and used by listeners in a wide variety of situations the subject of considerable analytical discussion. Individuals and groups interact with popular music physically, emotionally and cognitively. These different modes of engagement can be very personal – a private experience – but it is the social experience of music that is more common.

Grossberg (1992) observes that rock 'n' roll 'is inseparable from its audience. Consequently, every interpretation of the musical texts also interprets their audiences, as well as the relationship among them' (153), a process that is linked to social and political struggles. Analyses of youth subcultures initially emphasized how such subcultures appropriate and innovate musical forms and styles as a basis for their identity, expressing oppositional cultural politics at the symbolic level. Representing the intellectual crosscurrents between cultural and communication studies, such work drew heavily on semiotics (Hebdige 1979). While this perspective has been modified, the value of music as a component of the identity of subcultural groups and local scenes has continued to be widely recognized.

Popular music studies has both borrowed from and informed communication studies. The production and negotiation of meanings through music as text, technology and subcultural practise have established the importance of music as a central communicative form.

Bibliography

Denski, Stan. 1992. 'Music, Musicians and Communication: The Personal Voice in a Common Language.' In *Popular Music and Communication*, ed. James Lull. 2nd ed. Newbury Park, CA: Sage, 33–48.

Frith, Simon. 1988. 'Why Do Songs Have Words?' In *Music for Pleasure: Essays in the Sociology of Pop*. Cambridge: Polity Press, 105–28.

Frith, Simon. 1996. *Performing Rites: On the Value of Popular Music*. Cambridge, MA: Harvard University Press.

Goodwin, Andrew. 1993. *Dancing in the Distraction Factory: Music Television and Popular Culture*. Oxford and Minneapolis: University of Minnesota Press.

Grossberg, Lawrence. 1992. 'Rock and Roll in Search of an Audience.' In *Popular Music and Communication*, ed. James Lull. 2nd ed. Newbury Park, CA: Sage, 152–75.

Hanna, Judith. 1992. 'Identity and Desire in Popular Music and Social Dance.' In *Popular Music and Communication*, ed. James Lull. 2nd ed. Newbury Park, CA: Sage, 176–95.

Hebdige, Dick. 1979. *Subculture: The Meaning of Style*. London: Methuen.

Lewis, George H. 1992. 'The Dimensions of Musical Taste.' In *Popular Music and Communication*, ed. James Lull. 2nd ed. Newbury Park, CA: Sage, 134–51.

Lewis, Lisa. 1990. *Gender Politics and MTV: Voicing the Difference*. Philadelphia: Temple University Press.

Longhurst, Brian. 1995. *Popular Music and Society*. Cambridge: Polity Press.

Lull, James, ed. 1992. *Popular Music and Communication*. 2nd ed. Newbury Park, CA: Sage.

McQuail, Denis, and Windahl, Sven. 1993. *Communication Models for the Study of Mass Communications*. 2nd ed. London: Longman.

Middleton, Richard. 1990. *Studying Popular Music*. Milton Keynes: Open University Press.

Moore, Allan F. 1993. *Rock: The Primary Text. Developing a Musicology of Rock*. Buckingham: Open University Press.

Negus, Keith. 1996. *Popular Music in Theory*. Cambridge: Polity Press.

O'Sullivan, Tim, et al. 1994. *Key Concepts in Communication and Cultural Studies*. London: Methuen.

Schirato, Tony, and Yell, Susan. 1996. *Communication and Cultural Literacy: An Introduction*. St. Leonards, NSW: Allen & Unwin.

Shepherd, John. 1991. *Music as Social Text*. Cambridge: Polity Press.

Shepherd, John, and Wicke, Peter. 1997. *Music and Cultural Theory*. Cambridge: Polity Press.

Shuker, Roy. 1994. *Understanding Popular Music*. London and New York: Routledge.

Tagg, Philip. 1979. *Kojak – 50 Seconds of Television Music: Toward the Analysis of Affect in Popular Music*. Göteborg: Skrifter från Musikvetenskapliga Institutionen, 2.

Tagg, Philip. 1991. *Fernando the Flute: Analysis of Musical Meaning in an Abba Mega-Hit*. Liverpool: Institute of Popular Music, University of Liverpool.

Théberge, Paul. 1997. *Any Sound You Can Imagine:*

Making Music/Consuming Technology. Hanover and London: Wesleyan University Press.

ROY SHUKER

Content Analysis

In social, media and communication studies, content analysis is a widespread method for analyzing verbal, visual or textual material by transforming its content into quantitative data. The method is based on classification strategies to identify items of content which can then be statistically analyzed – for example, how many instances of violence occur during a typical evening of prime-time television viewing, or how many Asian-American women appear in one day of television commercials (see Krippendorff 1980). The method emerged in US communications research during the 1950s with the widespread increase in television viewing (see Berelson 1952), and it quickly rose to prominence as the first step toward more critically oriented media research as compared with the previous behaviorist models of quantitative analyses.

Content analysis falls broadly into four categories: (a) frequency analysis (how often an item of content occurs); (b) valency analysis (how often a given text argues for or against an issue); (c) intensity analysis (how strongly an item of content defends or opposes an issue); and (d) contingency analysis (how certain repeated items of content are related to other items of content). The ability to link items of content on sophisticated computerized models of statistical analysis (see West 2001) led to the widespread application of this method (see Holsti 1969).

Initially, content analysis also gained a certain currency in popular music research (see Carey 1969a, 1969b; Cole 1971; Horton 1990), since song lyrics seemed to provide a firm basis for analysis. The emergence of the videoclip prompted new attempts to apply this method to the textual analysis of music videos (see Altrogge and Amann 1991; Altrogge 2001). However, it soon became apparent that an analysis of popular music based solely on lyrical content would produce unsatisfactory results.

The crucial problem with content analysis lies in the process of transforming unquantified material into quantitative data. The issue of validity embedded in this process often remains hidden within the numeric results of the statistical analysis. But there is always the basic question of what counts as an item of content and how it is connected to the designed scheme of variables. Even in a supposedly straightforward analysis of violence in media content, where content analysis has become the privileged method, the research is based on a highly complex and discursively mediated concept – the concept of violence – which, even if it is broken down into a set of empirical variables, does not take into account matters of framing, shaping, design and artistic form. What is considered a strength of content analysis – the provision of a method for the textual analysis of media content without examining audience reaction – can also be perceived as its main theoretical weak point, because it leaves the definition and identification of content, its classification and validation in theoretical terms, wide open to speculative or subjective interpretation. In other words, the notion of 'content' put forward by content analysis as something fixed, uncontested and unmediated is highly problematic, and not only when applied to popular music or music video.

Bibliography

Altrogge, Michael. 2001. *Tönende Bilder: Interdisziplinäre Studien zu Musik und Bildern in Videoclips und ihrer Bedeutung für Jugendliche* [Sounding Images: Interdisciplinary Studies in Music and Images in Videoclips and Their Importance for Young People]. Berlin: Vistas.

Altrogge, Michael, and Amann, Rolf. 1991. *Videoclips – die geheimen Verführer der Jugend?: Ein Gutachten zur Struktur, Nutzung und Bewertung von Heavy-Metal-Videoclips* [Videoclips – The Hidden Persuaders of Youth?: A Report on the Structure, Use and Evaluation of Heavy Metal Videoclips]. Berlin: Vistas.

Berelson, Bernard. 1952. *Content Analysis in Communication Research*. Glencoe, IL: Free Press.

Carey, J.T. 1969a. 'Changing Courtship Patterns in the Popular Song.' *American Journal of Sociology* 74: 720–31.

Carey, J.T. 1969b. 'The Ideology of Autonomy in Popular Lyrics: A Content Analysis.' *Psychiatry* 32: 150–64.

Carney, Thomas F. 1972. *Content Analysis: A Technique for Systematic Inference from Communications*. Winnipeg: University of Manitoba Press.

Cole, R.R. 1971. 'Top Songs in the Sixties: A Content Analysis of Popular Lyrics.' *American Behavioral Scientist* 14: 389–400.

Holsti, Ole R. 1969. *Content Analysis for the Social Sciences and Humanities*. Reading, MA: Addison-Wesley Pub. Co.

Horton, Donald. 1990 (1957). 'The Dialogue of Courtship in Popular Song.' In *On Record: Rock, Pop, and the Written Word*, ed. Simon Frith and Andrew Goodwin. New York: Pantheon, 14–26.

Krippendorff, Klaus. 1980. *Content Analysis: An Introduction to Its Methodology*. Beverly Hills, CA: Sage Publications.

Riffe, Daniel, Lacy, Stephen, and Fico, Frederick G. 1998. *Analyzing Media Messages: Using Quantitative Content Analysis in Research*. Mahwah, NJ: Erlbaum.

West, Mark D., ed. 2001. *Theory, Method, and Practice in Computer Content Analysis*. Westport, CT: Ablex Pub.

PETER WICKE

Cultural Studies

Introduction

Although there is considerable overlap between popular music studies and cultural studies, the two remain quite distinct traditions. Since it is a particular form of culture, popular music has required a special vocabulary and set of methods. But the division is also a result of the different institutional histories of the fields. This distinction has on occasion resulted in popular music studies diverging from and even challenging dominant trends in cultural studies. However, the major tendency has been for the different orientations and approaches that have characterized the development of cultural studies to influence the study of popular music.

Orientations and Approaches

Two related perspectives have emerged in cultural studies. The tension between them gives this interdisciplinary field a certain (though never very precise) orientation. First, 'culture is ordinary' (Williams 1997), and can be characterized both by its distinction from the realm of art and refined sensibility, and by the fact that it is enacted by ordinary people on an everyday basis. In this approach, then, culture means the shared experiences and practises that constitute a particular mode of behavior or even whole way of life. Examples might include the culture of mods and skinheads (Cohen 1972), working-class teenage girls (McRobbie 1991), black British youth (Gilroy 1987) and so on.

A second approach treats culture as text, that is, as a structured series of signs. Texts are language-based in the first instance, but potentially include all artifacts and practises that have sign value and can therefore be read, from shopping malls (Morris 1993) to dance music (Gilbert and Pearson 1999). Again, there is a political undercurrent, namely, that some readings of texts may be 'resistant' to dominant power relations, and allow an independent 'space' or 'position' for the reader.

These two approaches have retained their distinctiveness, especially in relation to methods: ethnography is preferred in the first case, textual analysis in the second. However, in practise they often merge.

Origins and Intellectual Trajectory

Paradoxically, the hybrid nature of cultural studies has much to do with the importance in its development of a single institution: the Centre for Contemporary Cultural Studies (CCCS) at the University of Birmingham. Here, during the 1970s and early 1980s, under the leadership of Stuart Hall, a group of academics from various disciplines produced a powerfully synthetic form of cultural analysis. The most important component was Marxism, as revised by Althusser and Gramsci. CCCS researchers used the work of these writers to move beyond the orthodox Marxist view that the economic power of capitalism inevitably leads to cultural domination. Instead, the cultural sphere might be conceived after Althusser (1969) as 'relatively autonomous' or, later, from a Gramscian perspective, as 'a force field of relations shaped by . . . contradictory pressures and tendencies' which arise as competing social groups strive to legitimate their power (Bennett 1986, xiii).

Such revisionism was then combined with semiotics, derived principally from Barthes (1967, 1973) and Eco (1972). Semiotics allowed analysis not only of prima facie symbolic forms (films, television, magazines), but also of cultural artifacts considered more broadly – for example, motorbikes (Willis 1978) or punk clothing (Hebdige 1979). Hall's essay of 1974 (1997) on the encoding and decoding of television discourse brought together the new Marxism and semiotics brilliantly. His conclusion that a variety of readings of television is possible, from 'dominant' to 'oppositional,' suggested an open, yet radical, conception of popular culture that has remained influential.

During the 1980s, feminism, along with the rise of the politics of ethnicity and sexuality, displaced Marxism's privileged category, class, in cultural studies. At the same time, poststructuralism challenged the formalist tendency in semiotics and its assumption that subject positions could be 'read off' texts. As attention shifted away from class, the issue of cultural identity, which might be traversed by multiple discourses of race, gender, sexuality and so on, came to the fore. In terms of epistemology, relativism (the work of Foucault and Baudrillard was especially influential here) supplanted the Marxist depth model. Increasingly, culture came to be seen as a single level or plane, rather than a superstructure articulated, albeit in a complex fashion, with a socioeconomic base. Accompanying these intellectual developments was the rapid growth and professionalization of the field of cultural studies across the English-speaking world, and especially in the United States. The widespread establishment of cultural studies departments and courses at the beginning of the twenty-first century suggests that the original conception of the field as an 'intellectual guerrilla movement' is outmoded (McGuigan 1997, 1).

Cultural Studies' Relation to Popular Music Studies

There are clear affinities between cultural studies and popular music studies. The notion of the popular is pivotal in both. Both have oscillated between, on the one hand, affirming 'the people' as active subjects of history and, on the other hand, being duly skeptical of such voluntarism. Both fields are interdisciplinary, drawing on theories and methods from older disciplines, yet attempting to bring them to bear in a coherent fashion on nontraditional objects of study. In practise, however, the flow of ideas between the two fields has tended to be along fairly well-defined channels. In addition, it has been mainly one way, *from* a generalizing cultural studies *to* a specifying popular music studies. Perhaps the most important instance of this has been in the area of popular music and youth subculture.

In the 1970s, the CCCS devoted considerable attention to British youth subcultures (see, for example, Willis 1974, 1978; Cohen 1972; Hall and Jefferson 1976). Several conclusions were drawn from this research, most significantly the idea that subcultural style represents an imaginary relationship with the parent, working-class culture, and that this, in turn, constitutes a form of symbolic resistance to dominant class relations.

Subsequently, the CCCS approach to subculture has been reexamined, and to some extent contradicted, by popular music scholars. As early as 1985, Dave Laing was arguing that the Birmingham researchers had failed to engage with the specificity of music in subcultures. Punk, in particular, represented a special case because a new musical style had been created inside the subculture, rather than being imported as with, say, Teddy boys (rock 'n' roll) or mods (soul music). The case of punk also suggested that relations between subculture and the music industry were complex, and not to be reduced to the 'defusion' or 'incorporation' of an authentic expressive impulse, as Hebdige (1979) had suggested.

Straw (1991) has also challenged CCCS orthodoxy by proposing that a system of music 'scenes,' built out of alliances between different groups (sexualities, ethnicities, classes and so on), has supplanted subcultures. The scene is best exemplified in electronic dance music, with its 'reworking and transformation of styles originating elsewhere' (381). For Straw, a complex interaction between cultural alliances, geographical dispersion and stylistic change is at stake here, rather than unilinear, subcultural expression. In an important sense, then, Straw is working with the grain of contemporary cultural studies, even as he revises the classical CCCS approach to subculture.

Grossberg represents a slightly different case. In an influential early piece (1984), he worked from inside cultural studies as it were, characterizing rock 'n' roll as an 'apparatus' that empowers postwar youth, albeit in a contradictory fashion, and that yields, partly through the resonance of the body with musical rhythms, an oppositional politics. This is an affirmatory cultural studies, with popular music placed right at the center.

Grossberg has continued to develop this approach in more recent work (1991), even accommodating the notion that rock 'n' roll has died (1994).

If these examples suggest at least a working relationship between popular music studies and cultural studies, there has also been marked divergence. In particular, where the latter has focused strongly on cultural consumption (Fiske 1989; Willis 1990), the former has always been more oriented toward production. Frith's work (1983, 1988) has been influential here, with its examination of the relations between music industry structures, musicianship and popular music style. Frith calls on North American sociology of culture – for example, the interactionism of Becker (1982) or the 'production of culture' school (Peterson 1976) – rather than on British cultural studies. His brisk skepticism is also rather at odds with the enthusiasm that (even when extenuated via 'high' theory) tends to mark out cultural studies.

The other main area of divergence between popular music studies and cultural studies has been textual analysis. Cultural studies has developed a rich mix of semiotics and discourse analysis with which to read and interpret texts. In popular music studies, on the other hand, although there has been excellent work on semiotics by Tagg (for example, 1982, 1993), most textual analysis has remained grounded in musicology. That is to say, it is based on production codes, chiefly functional tonality and serialism, originally used to generate 'high' art music. Illuminating though much of this analysis has been, it has had the double effect of restricting textual analysis to trained musicologists, and reducing the opportunities for development of a method proper to popular music's phonographic and oral modalities. Arguably, cultural studies' 'home-grown' methods are better attuned to the forms, textures and rhythms of the texts that it treats, from architecture to the Web page.

Cultural studies has continued to have a wide if diffuse impact on popular music studies. Recent research into local music scenes around the world, for example, has much of the cultural studies ethic and approach, even when it is conducted by avowed sociologists or ethnomusicologists. Nonetheless, the two fields, each eclectic and synthetic in its own way, will continue to develop more or less independently for the foreseeable future.

Bibliography

Althusser, Louis. 1969. *For Marx*. London: Allen Lane. (Originally published as *Pour Marx*. Paris: F. Maspero, 1965.)

Barthes, Roland. 1967. *Elements of Semiology*. London: Jonathon Cape. (First published as *Elements de Semiologie*. Paris: Éditions du Seuil, 1964.)

Barthes, Roland. 1973. *Mythologies*. London: Paladin. (Originally published as *Mythologies*. Paris: Éditions du Seuil, 1957.)

Becker, Howard S. 1982. *Art Worlds*. Berkeley, CA: University of California Press.

Bennett, Tony. 1986. 'Introduction: Popular Culture and "the Turn to Gramsci."' In *Popular Culture and Social Relations*, ed. Tony Bennett, Colin Mercer and Janet Woollacott. Milton Keynes: Open University Press, xi–xix.

Cohen, Phil. 1972. 'Subcultural Conflict and Working Class Community.' In *Working Papers in Cultural Studies*, 2. Birmingham: Centre for Contemporary Cultural Studies, 5–51.

Eco, Umberto. 1972. 'Towards a Semiotic Inquiry into the Television Message.' In *Working Papers in Cultural Studies*, 3. Birmingham: Centre for Contemporary Cultural Studies, 103–21.

Fiske, John. 1989. *Understanding Popular Culture*. Boston, MA: Unwin Hyman.

Frith, Simon. 1983. *Sound Effects: Youth, Leisure and the Politics of Rock 'n' Roll*. London: Constable.

Frith, Simon. 1988. 'The Industrialization of Music.' In *Music for Pleasure: Essays in the Sociology of Pop*. Cambridge: Polity, 11–23.

Gilbert, Jeremy, and Pearson, Ewan. 1999. *Discographies: Dance Music, Culture, and the Politics of Sound*. London: Routledge.

Gilroy, Paul. 1987. *There Ain't No Black in the Union Jack: The Cultural Politics of Race and Nation*. London: Hutchinson.

Grossberg, Lawrence. 1984. 'Another Boring Day in Paradise: Rock and Roll and the Empowerment of Everyday Life.' *Popular Music* 4: 225–58.

Grossberg, Lawrence. 1991. 'Rock, Territorialization and Power.' *Cultural Studies* 5(3): 358–67.

Grossberg, Lawrence. 1994. 'Is Anybody Listening? Does Anybody Care?: On "The State of Rock."' In *Microphone Fiends: Youth Music and Youth Culture*, ed. Andrew Ross and Tricia Rose. London and New York: Routledge, 41–58.

Hall, Stuart. 1997 (1974). 'The Television Discourse – Encoding and Decoding.' In *Studying Culture: An Introductory Reader*, ed. Ann Gray and Jim McGuigan. 2nd ed. London: Arnold, 28–34.

Hall, Stuart, and Jefferson, Tony, eds. 1976. *Resistance Through Rituals: Youth Subcultures in Post-War Britain*. London: Hutchinson.

Hebdige, Dick. 1979. *Subculture: The Meaning of Style*. London: Methuen.

Laing, Dave. 1985. *One Chord Wonders: Power and Meaning in Punk Rock*. Milton Keynes: Open University Press.

McGuigan, Jim. 1997. 'Introduction.' In *Cultural Methodologies*, ed. Jim McGuigan. London: Sage, 1–11.

McRobbie, Angela. 1991. 'The Culture of Working-Class Girls.' In Angela McRobbie, *Feminism and Youth Culture: From 'Jackie' to 'Just Seventeen'*. London: Macmillan, 35–60.

Morris, Meaghan. 1993. 'Things to Do with Shopping Centres.' In *The Cultural Studies Reader*, ed. Simon During. London and New York: Routledge, 295–319.

Peterson, Richard A., ed. 1976. *The Production of Culture*. Beverly Hills, CA: Sage Publications.

Straw, Will. 1991. 'Systems of Articulation, Logics of Change: Communities and Scenes in Popular Music.' *Cultural Studies* 5(3): 368–88.

Tagg, Philip. 1982. 'Analysing Popular Music: Theory, Method and Practice.' *Popular Music* 2: 37–67.

Tagg, Philip. 1993. '"Universal" Music and the Case of Death.' *Critical Quarterly* 35(2): 54–85.

Williams, Raymond. 1997. 'Culture Is Ordinary.' In *Studying Culture: An Introductory Reader*, ed. Ann Gray and Jim McGuigan. 2nd ed. London: Arnold, 5–14.

Willis, Paul. 1974. *Symbolism and Practice: The Social Meaning of Pop Music*. Stencilled Paper No. 13. Birmingham: Centre for Contemporary Cultural Studies.

Willis, Paul. 1978. *Profane Culture*. London: Routledge and Kegan Paul.

Willis, Paul. 1990. *Common Culture: Symbolic Work at Play in the Everyday Cultures of the Young*. Milton Keynes: Open University Press.

JASON TOYNBEE

Dialogics

'Dialogics' is the name given to a trend in the late twentieth-century study of popular music inspired by the work of the Russian philosopher and literary critic Mikhail Bakhtin. It emerged as an alternative to formalist and sociological accounts of popular music, capable of disclosing the social meaning of a particular work in the details of its musical style.

In the 1930s, Bakhtin claimed that the linguistic style of the modern novel was so radically different from everything before it that a new understanding of language was required to comprehend it. Poetics had traditionally assumed that writers drew their language from a system that was complex, but essentially unified. In the novel, however, language appeared as something stratified by its usage, internally divided into competing styles representing different social groups, generations, professions, literary and nonliterary genres and so forth. The words the novelist drew on did not take their bearings from their place in a unified system; instead, 'each word tastes of the context and contexts in which it has lived its socially charged life: all words and forms are populated by intentions' (Bakhtin 1981, 293). Novelists dipped into this social 'heteroglossia' (as Bakhtin called it) and then attempted to reshape this already loaded discourse for their own purposes, using the social intentions embodied in styles to orchestrate their chosen themes. 'The style of a novel,' Bakhtin claimed, 'is to be found in the combination of its styles; the language of a novel is the system of its languages' (1981, 262). In this kind of writing, language was 'double-voiced': its meaning and effect depended both on its use in the original social context from which it was drawn *and* on its role in the 'higher unity' of the novel itself. The novelist did not just reproduce language; he/she had to respond to its already existing social meanings. Writing of this kind was 'dialogical.'

In the 1980s, literary critics in Europe and North America found this account of the relation of language to literature irresistible. For many, it seemed an ideal marriage of the linguistic emphasis characteristic of structuralism and poststructuralism with the larger social perspectives of humanist and political criticism. For, while Bakhtin assumed that intentions and meanings were incarnate in language rather than individual expression, his vision of heteroglossia seemed to bring the social world back into the heart of the system.

Critics and writers interested in popular music have had to confront the same dilemma as their literary counterparts. On the one hand, the formal, technical tools inherited from musical analysis, focused on the elaboration of large-scale pitch structures, seem to miss the point of most popular music; on the other hand, sociological or cultural studies approaches to popular music frequently reduce actual works or performances to the expression of communal identities, evading the technical complexities and interest of popular music altogether. A dialogical approach to music might show, as Bakhtin said of literature, that every work is 'internally, immanently sociological' (1929, 3–4), thus bridging the gap between textual and contextual study.

In fact, members of Bakhtin's own intellectual circle had tried their hand at a dialogical analysis of music in the 1920s and 1930s. I.I. Sollertinsky, a member of this group who was later to become music director of the Leningrad Philharmonic, wrote a series of studies of classical symphony-writing heavily influenced by the ideas of Bakhtin and his circle (1932, 1946). Although in these studies Sollertinsky named Beethoven the dialogical composer par excellence, it is Mahler's symphonies that emerge as the true musical equivalent of the novels identified by Bakhtin. According to Sollertinsky, in Mahler one finds both popular and traditional lyrical material presented in a not-quite-serious, indirect, ironizing mode, creating in the music a 'doubleness' clearly akin to the 'double-voicing' Bakhtin thought typical of novelistic discourse. In Mahler's work, this indirectness or doubleness is a mark of tragedy, for it demonstrates that Mahler – or, rather, his age – could no longer produce the serious heroic symphonies he wished to.

Naturally, dialogism in popular music is interpreted quite differently. The dialogical critic analyzes musical works and performances as complex systems or combinations of previously existing musical materials or styles, whether these are set off as distinctive motifs, rhythms, vocal styles, instrumental combinations, or explicit quotations or samples. As with the novel, the meaning of the musical piece will depend on how it re-articulates its various materials, which may be presented directly as quotation or 'at an angle,' with some level of distance or irony. But in this case dialogism is not tragic. Analyses such as Middleton's study of the Eurythmics (1995) or Rose's account of female rappers (1994) use the idea of dialogism to demonstrate how formally complex popular music can be, disclosing layers of musical reference and meaning that would remain invisible to orthodox harmonic or melodic analysis. Rose shows how the shrewd reusing of earlier materials from Afro-American music and politics allows female rappers to conduct a subtle argument with the sexism characteristic of some male rapping. In a similar vein, Lipsitz (1990) uses the concept of dialogism to show that rock, far from being a mere commercial vulgarization of popular music tradition, re-accents elements taken from US folk and blues in order to articulate a new, more urban style of resistance to the imperatives of the dominant North American order.

In these studies and more generally, the dialogical nature of popular music, which has become ever more obvious in the age of sampling and DJ-led music-making, is celebrated rather than mourned. Popular music's explicit interest in the reframing and interweaving of musical materials which still 'taste of the context and contexts in which [they have] lived' is rightly taken as evidence of its fundamentally social character. In this respect, writers like Tomlinson (1992) have defended artists such as Miles Davis against those who regard the dialogical melding of different musics as an affront to the purity of a particular form. Where others see sellout, the dialogical critic sees evidence of the necessarily impure, hybrid nature of popular music. The dialogical analysis of popular music, like the dialogical analysis of the novel that inspired it, is thus a means of both interpreting and championing its object.

Bibliography

Bakhtin, M.M. 1929. *Problemy tvorchestva Dostoevskogo* [Problems of Dostoevsky's Art]. Leningrad: Priboi.

Bakhtin, M.M. 1981. 'Discourse in the Novel.' In M.M. Bakhtin, *The Dialogic Imagination: Four Essays*, ed. Michael Holquist, trans. Caryl Emerson and Michael Holquist. Austin, TX: University of Texas Press, 259–422. (Originally published as 'Slovo v romane.' In M.M. Bakhtin, *Voprosy literatury i estetiki*. Moscow: Khudozhestvennaia literatura, 1975, 72–233.)

Lipsitz, George. 1990. *Time Passages: Collective Memory and American Popular Culture*. Minneapolis, MN: University of Minnesota Press.

Middleton, Richard. 1995. 'Authorship, Gender and the Construction of Meaning in the Eurythmics' Hit Recordings.' *Cultural Studies* 9: 465–85.

Middleton, Richard. 2000. 'Introduction: Locating the Popular Music Text.' In *Reading Pop: Approaches to Textual Analysis in Popular Music*, ed. Richard Middleton. Oxford: Oxford University Press, 1–19.

Rose, Tricia. 1994. *Black Noise: Rap Music and Black Culture in Contemporary America*. Hanover, NH: University Press of New England.

Sollertinsky, I.I. 1932. *Gustav Mahler*. Leningrad: Gosmuzizdat.

Sollertinsky, I.I. 1946. 'Istoricheskie tipy simfonicheskoi dramaturgii' [Historical Types of Symphonic Dramaturgy]. In *Izbrannye stat'i o muzyke* [Selected Articles on Music]. Leningrad and Moscow: Isskustvo, 301–11.

Tomlinson, Gary. 1992. 'Cultural Dialogics and Jazz: A White Historian Signifies.' In *Disciplining Music: Musicology and Its Canons*, ed. Katherine Bergeron and Philip V. Bohlman. Chicago: University of Chicago Press, 64–94.

Walser, Robert. 1993. *Running with the Devil: Power, Gender and Madness in Heavy Metal Music*. Hanover and London: Wesleyan University Press.

KEN HIRSCHKOP

Discourse Analysis

Discourse analysis is concerned with language as it is used in social actions such as asking questions, giving answers, telling stories or constructing versions of events in texts. As such, it differentiates itself from linguistics or philosophy, both of which work with an *ideal* kind of language, abstracted from actual speech or writing (Potter and Wetherell 1987). The analysis of discourse has been applied in at least three ways to popular music: song lyrics have been analyzed as performed language; discourses on or about music and stars have been examined; and there has been a debate about whether music itself can be analyzed as discourse.

The fact that popular music, as it has come to be understood, is primarily, and distinctively, popular *song* has encouraged attempts to analyze the ways in which language is used in it. The simplest way of doing this, 'content analysis,' assumes that the words of songs can be separated from their musical setting, and then verbal similarities and differences classified. Discourse analysis rejects this separation, seeing the musical setting as a crucial part of what is being 'done' with language in a song. If content analysis (e.g., Horton 1956–57) derives from a positivist vision of the social world, where the quantification of standardized elements tells about reality, discourse analysis is more concerned with how particular versions of the world are socially constructed. For instance, content analysis of early blues lyrics would take them as accounts of agricultural work, railroad travel, drink and sexual relations in the deep South. Discourse analysis would be more concerned with the ironizing of these accounts (Hatch and Millward 1987, 60ff.), or with the social acts of call-and-response achieved by the musical settings of these words.

At its broadest, popular song is always a performance which, while not actual conversation, draws on the resources of everyday language in both words and their delivery to communicate its message or messages. The ways in which the vocal performance differs from a notional, textual version provided the starting point for the first essays in discourse analysis of popular music. Influential here was Roland Barthes' essay 'The Grain of the Voice' (1977), in which he talked of the 'individual thrill' produced by the very materiality of certain singing voices, and the depth of where melody 'works away at' language and its sounds. Barthes wanted to 'displace the fringe of contact between music and language,' and saw the grain of the voice as a form of writing, the 'sung writing of language.' Taylor's and Laing's article 'Disco-Pleasure-Discourse' (1979) drew on Barthes in analyzing the pleasure of popular music as stemming from the performing of language as discourse. However, they shifted the emphasis away from Barthes' unusual concentration on the aural properties of song to an analysis of the visual aspects of performance, using Mulvey's analysis of the gendered spectacle and 'gaze' of cinema (1975).

Bradby's and Torode's 'Pity Peggy Sue' (1984) built on this use of Mulvey's theory of the 'male gaze,' adapting it into a more specific theory of the gendered, triangular relation between singing subject, love object and listening audience. In an attempt to illuminate the sociological theory of 'secondary socialisation' in adolescence through the use of a discourse analysis drawn from Lacanian psychoanalysis, it was argued that teenagers go through a second process of language learning in acquiring the adult language of love. This process parallels and reworks the infant's acquisition of a gendered identity along with its learning of language in the Oedipal phase. The discursive performances of popular song are forms of rehearsal for adolescents of their new gendered positionings in relation to language and the body.

Analyzing the material features of language as actually used in the performance allowed Bradby and Torode to argue that the feminine 'imaginary' or 'semiotic' sphere can be heard as in revolt against the imposition of patriarchal signification in rock. The implications of this theory for female song and women's discursive positionings were taken up by Bradby in an article on sixties girl-group music (1990), which argued that the discourse of the 'girl' articulates a subjectivity divided against itself. This is achieved musically through the setting of a girl's solo voice against the main group singing over her, pitting her affirmative 'do-talk' against a chorus of 'don't-talk' from her older, more sensible, maternal self. This sense of a 'maternal' discourse running through the voices in female performed music was subsequently applied to the relationship between Madonna and men acted out in her musical performance toward her male chorus in 'Material Girl' (Bradby 1992).

Taylor's and Laing's original use of 'discourse' made oblique reference to Michel Foucault. In identifying 'bravura' and 'confessional' modes of singing, they stated that this contrast represented 'two different discourses of sexuality (in Foucault's sense of the term)' (1979, 48). They also referred to the 'constant generation of subject positions' (45) in music, and to the 'proliferating discourses around sexuality' (48). These phrases evoke Foucault's (1981) theory of sexuality as a productive power in itself. Foucault's theory explicitly broke with Freud's 'hydraulic' view of sexuality as a force that could be repressed, perverted or liberated, but that was essentially controlled by a power outside itself (the superego, as the internalization of social norms). Instead, Foucault substituted the idea that sexuality, from the nineteenth century onward, divided and proliferated into multiple sites of power and pleasure. Through these sites, new kinds of power were exercised over bodies, in a more specific way than previously, as new disciplines and institutions (medicine, criminology, psychiatry, prostitution, pornography) redefined pleasures in new discourses that identified individuals into groups (Foucault 1981, 47–49).

Taylor and Laing argued that Frith and McRobbie (1978) had betrayed a residual Freudianism in their talk of sexual 'expression' and 'repression' in rock music. The authors of 'Disco-Pleasure-Discourse' argued, by contrast, that it is 'patriarchal culture,' in the form of the 'all-pervasive, listening equivalent of the male gaze,' that generates the proliferation of discourses identified (48). These discourses 'structurally exclude' (45) female desire, rather than simply repressing women, and they generate

sexualities as power and pleasure, rather than simply controlling or expressing sexuality as a force.

Foucault's critics have argued that, if his theory were correct, there would have been an ever-increasing extension of the network of disciplinary powers, instead of the generally liberalizing tendencies of the twentieth century (Giddens 1992). From this point of view, the place of 'resistance' to discursive power in Foucault's work becomes important. Foucault himself at times drew a parallel between 'the pleasure that comes of exercising a power' and 'the pleasure that kindles at having to evade this power,' and he saw in 'these attractions, these evasions, . . . *perpetual spirals of power and pleasure*' (1981, 47; italics in original). In the play of power, resistance becomes as much a part of the game as is pursuit.

Following this trend, much of the legacy of Foucault's work within popular music studies has focused on notions of resistance and negotiation, thus, effectively, assimilating discourse theory into the British subcultural studies tradition. A sense of popular music as a powerful discursive regime, generating sometimes resistant discourses of sexuality, race and gender, merges in much writing of the 1980s and 1990s with the traditional Marxist opposition of a controlling commercial 'mainstream' to resistant currents elsewhere.

These notions surface, for instance, in Walser's analysis of heavy metal music (1993), which he sees as a resistant discourse developed by white, working-class young men, where real contradictions are resolved in a fantasy of power that is both musical and gendered. Discourse is not mentioned in Stringer's article on the Smiths (1992), where he chooses instead to talk of their 'image' and of the 'star text.' But his analysis of how they contested the dominant meanings of 'whiteness' and 'Englishness' during the 1980s, incorporating a refusal both of the masculinist politics of Thatcherism and of the 'healthy sexuality' of much black popular music (Stringer 1992, 21), owes much to Foucault and could well be described as a form of 'discourse analysis.'

Green also uses a concept of discourse loosely derived from Foucault in her *Music, Gender, Education* (1997, 4), although here there is a move away from the use of discourse analysis as an attempt to decode verbal-musical meaning toward an examination of how discourses on music have shaped the ideas and practise of music and of gender. Green shows how the 'mind/body' split in discourse is mapped onto both the masculine/feminine and the classical/popular divisions. While these patternings are used socially to exclude both women and popular music from 'serious' consideration, they cannot be consistently maintained, and they allow also for the contradictory affirmation of certain musical roles for women, particularly that of singing. The associations of singing with the body and of the body with femaleness and sexuality mean that the discourses veer always dangerously toward the branding of women as sexual beings. In this way, Green gives gender to Barthes' bodily 'grain,' and holds on to the analysis of power that has made Foucault's discourse analysis the academic heir to Marx.

Other writers view 'discourse' differently. Fenster (1990), for instance, invokes Foucault in his article on US country musician Buck Owens's 'struggle for discursive control,' particularly when he analyzes actual texts by and about Owens. Here, the struggle over authenticity is seen as affected by who and where the discourses are emanating from – record company or artist. However, his theoretical concluding section uses a Marxist conception of ideology. It is worth emphasizing the distinctiveness of an approach in terms of discourse, both because it breaks with the theory of ideology as 'false consciousness,' which so easily lends itself to Adorno's condemnation of popular culture, and because discourse analysis has a commitment to the *empirical* tradition derived from its links with linguistics – a grounding that has been lacking in much theoretical deployment of the term 'ideology.'

An analysis of country music by Fox (1992) is situated at the intersection of this theoretical divide – between the Marxist tradition as evidenced in the widespread critical writing on the 'ideology of authenticity' in folk music, rock and other genres (following Frith 1981), and the commitment to the empirical grounding of theory found in much discourse analysis. As the title of one of his examples, 'Hello, I'm a Jukebox,' suggests, Fox argues that the discourse of country music continually 'talks back' to the question 'Is country music for real?,' so creating a constantly spinning ironic discursive space, and resisting both 'authenticity' and 'commodity fetishism' just as it embraces them.

The empirical tradition of black US sociolinguistics informs Brackett's (1992) analysis of James Brown's 'Superbad,' which also uses notions from rhetorical and performance analysis. While Brackett himself makes no reference to discourse, and describes his method as a 'musical and textual analysis,' this underplays the extent to which his is both an analysis of *performed* language, and one that 'displaces the fringe of contact between music and language' as Barthes advocated in his work on 'the grain' of the voice. Neither music nor text can be analyzed in isolation, and Brown's delivery continually strains their boundary. Politically, the effect is of the 'double-voiced utterance,' the term used by Mikhail Bakhtin and applied by Henry Louis Gates (1988) to the way in which African Americans speak at once through the language of the white United States and through black speech codes, applied here by Brackett to Brown's musical-linguistic performance.

Rose uses not dissimilar concepts of 'hidden transcripts' and of 'dialogic exchange' with the dominant white culture to analyze rap music's 'discursive battles' with its portrayal in the media (1994, 99–145). Her analysis of rap lyrics, while it can be criticized for omitting to analyze these words as performed musically, nevertheless brings home the extent to which rap lyrics represent the verbal-musical act of *response* to the accusations and aggressions of white-controlled institutions, rather than the separatist statement they are usually thought to be. Rose also applies these notions of dialogic exchange to the work of women rappers, 'in dialogue with one another, black men, black women, and dominant American culture' (1994, 148). Her committed engagement with both rap in general and women's role in rap is acknowledged in Aparicio's (1998) similarly engaged commitment in her analysis of the lyrics of salsa and other Latin American genres that have been frequently condemned for their sexism.

Because of its focus on language, some writers dispute the relevance of discourse analysis to popular music, seeing it as a kind of linguistic imperialism over a sphere that for them is preeminently about feeling. However, the question posed by McClary and Walser (1990) to rival academic writing, 'Does it kick butt?,' is perhaps only the US, male-vernacular version of Barthes' description of the 'individual thrill.' In *Running with the Devil* (1993), Walser has since gone on to elaborate a theory of discourse, arguing that music itself forms a discourse, but one that is located in the body and feeling. In line with this theory, Walser has developed the metaphor of 'forging' to describe the power enacted by heavy metal musicians. However, Walser's strikingly convincing social defense of heavy metal in his final chapter relies almost entirely on *lyric* analysis.

Shepherd and Wicke (1997, 144–49) have pointed out that Walser was talking about the *language* through which music is understood rather than musical meaning itself. Shepherd's and Wicke's own argument is that music, though a fundamental form of social communication, must not be reduced to language, but must preserve its relative autonomy as a communicative system. For them, music and language are equal, but different. They work in different ways as semiotic systems, but are equal in their ability to encompass society, to be structured by and to structure social interaction.

Leaving aside the question of how or whether music communicates as a system autonomous from language, it is clear that the production and consumption of musical performances are accompanied by vast amounts of talk and writing. These are resources for understanding the social production of meaning around music that have perhaps been underutilized. Discourse analysis provides methods with which to analyze these ordinary social activities of talk and writing about music. As such, it attempts to be both democratic and grounded in what people do socially as fans, critics, players and singers of music.

Bibliography

Aparicio, Frances R. 1998. *Listening to Salsa: Gender, Latin Popular Music, and Puerto Rican Cultures*. Hanover, NH: University Press of New England.

Barthes, Roland. 1977. 'The Grain of the Voice.' In Roland Barthes, *Image, Music, Text,* trans. Stephen Heath. New York: Hill and Wang, 179–89.

Brackett, David. 1992. 'James Brown's "Superbad" and the Double-Voiced Utterance.' *Popular Music* 11(3): 309–24.

Bradby, Barbara. 1990. 'Do-Talk and Don't-Talk: The Division of the Subject in Girl-Group Music.' In *On Record: Rock, Pop and the Written Word*, ed. Simon Frith and Andrew Goodwin. London: Routledge, 341–68.

Bradby, Barbara. 1992. 'Like a Virgin-Mother?: Materialism and Maternalism in the Songs of Madonna.' *Cultural Studies* 6(1): 73–96.

Bradby, Barbara, and Torode, Brian. 1984. 'Pity Peggy Sue.' *Popular Music* 4: 183–205.

Fenster, Mark. 1990. 'Buck Owens, Country Music and the Struggle for Discursive Control.' *Popular Music* 9(3): 275–90.

Foucault, Michel. 1981. *The History of Sexuality, Vol. 1: An Introduction*, trans. Robert Hurley. London: Pelican Books.

Fox, Aaron A. 1992. 'The Jukebox of History: Narratives of Loss and Desire in the Discourse of Country Music.' *Popular Music* 11(1): 53–72.

Frith, Simon. 1981. '"The Magic That Can Set You Free": The Ideology of Folk and the Myth of the Rock Community.' *Popular Music* 1: 159–68.

Frith, Simon, and McRobbie, Angela. 1978. 'Rock and Sexuality.' *Screen Education* 29: 3–19. (Reprinted in *On Record: Rock, Pop and the Written Word*, ed. Simon Frith and Andrew Goodwin. London: Routledge, 371–89.)

Gates, Henry Louis. 1988. *The Signifying Monkey: A Theory of Afro-American Literary Criticism*. New York: Oxford University Press.

Giddens, Anthony. 1992. *The Transformation of Intimacy: Sexuality, Love, and Eroticism in Modern Societies*. Cambridge: Polity Press.

Green, Lucy. 1997. *Music, Gender, Education*. Cambridge: Cambridge University Press.

Hatch, David, and Millward, Stephen. 1987. *From Blues to Rock: An Analytical History of Pop Music*. Manchester: Manchester University Press.

Horton, Donald. 1956–57. 'The Dialogue of Courtship in Popular Song.' *American Journal of Sociology* 62: 569–78. (Reprinted in *On Record: Rock, Pop and the Written Word*, ed. Simon Frith and Andrew Goodwin. London: Routledge, 14–26.)

McClary, Susan, and Walser, Robert. 1990. 'Start Making Sense!: Musicology Wrestles with Rock.' In *On Record: Rock, Pop and the Written Word*, ed. Simon Frith and Andrew Goodwin. London: Routledge, 277–92.

Mulvey, Laura. 1975. 'Visual Pleasure and Narrative Cinema.' *Screen* 16(3): 6–18.

Potter, Jonathan, and Wetherell, Margaret. 1987. *Discourse Analysis and Social Psychology*. London: Sage Publications.

Rose, Tricia. 1994. *Black Noise: Rap Music and Black Culture in Contemporary America*. Hanover, NH: Wesleyan University Press.

Shepherd, John, and Wicke, Peter. 1997. *Music and Cultural Theory*. Cambridge: Polity Press.

Stringer, Julian. 1992. 'The Smiths: Repressed, (But Remarkably Dressed).' *Popular Music* 11(1): 15–26.

Taylor, Jenny, and Laing, Dave. 1979. 'Disco-Pleasure-Discourse: On "Rock and Sexuality."' *Screen Education* 31: 43–48.

Walser, Robert. 1993. *Running with the Devil: Power, Gender and Madness in Heavy Metal Music*. Hanover, NH: Wesleyan University Press.

Sheet Music

Hall, Tom T., comp. and lyr. 1969. 'Hello, I'm a Jukebox.' New York: Unichappell Music Inc./Morris Music Inc.

Discographical References

Brown, James. 'Superbad.' King 6329. *1970*: USA.

Madonna. 'Material Girl.' Sire 29083. *1985*: USA.

BARBARA BRADBY

Economics

Although there are several descriptive accounts of the music industry from an economic point of view (D'Angelo 1989; Burnett 1990; Lange 1986; Vogel 2001), the industry has not been the subject of sustained theoretical study by professional economists. However, aspects of the industry have been analyzed by economists of both the neoclassical and political economy (Marxist) schools.

Neoclassical economists have developed an 'economics of the arts,' typified in the work of Baumol (in Towse 1997), Towse (1993) and Throsby (2001). Baumol's celebrated 'law' claims that, because in live performance the productivity of artistic labor rises only slowly (if at all), production costs increase at a much greater rate than box-office receipts. Dealing only with classical music organizations, Baumol calculates that ticket sales account for under 40 percent of costs, with sponsorship and donations making up the shortfall (Towse 1997). It is arguable that most small- and medium-scale performances in rock and jazz are equally unprofitable, although the 'donors' are generally the musicians, who accept very low rates of pay. Additionally, Baumol recognizes that the possibility of mass audiences for recordings and broadcasts of performances may offset the 'cost disease' (Towse 1997, 191). Elsewhere, Stamm (2000) uses econometric techniques to analyze the recording industry.

From within the political economy school, both Miège (1989) and Garnham (2000) have drawn attention to the specific strategies adopted by record companies in order to control the market, emphasizing their creation of a broad portfolio or catalog of products to counteract the uncertainty of consumer behavior. While the writers on arts economics are focused mainly on the 'high arts,' including classical music, Miège, in a discussion of Marx's comments on the work of the singer, distinguishes between singing, which produces surplus value through sales of records or television appearances, and the unproductive labor of the subsidized music sector (1989, 25). Less sophisticated work on the industry inspired by Marxism can be found in Chapple and Garofalo (1977) and Eliot (1990).

Economists of both persuasions have drawn attention to the importance of intellectual property rights in the musical economy and the implications of these monopolistic rights, defined as a form of 'rent,' for the functioning of a market in music (Taylor and Towse 1998; Andersen et al. 2000). Kozul-Wright and Stanbury (1998) approach this issue from a development economics perspective.

Issues of monopoly and competition have inspired the application of competition economics to the music industry by regulatory bodies such as the European Commission, the UK government's Competition Authority and the US Fair Trade Commission.

The cultural industries in general (including the record industry) are cited by Lash and Urry (1994) in their discussion of the economics of post-Fordist regimes. Following Baudrillard (1981), they define such cultural production as a 'sign economy,' and emphasize the vanguard role of such industries as producers of signs in providing a model mode of production for the economy as a whole. Their argument echoes that of Attali (1985), whose flamboyant and historicized 'political economy of music' has been highly influential, although not among economists.

Bibliography

Andersen, B., et al. 2000. *Copyrights and Competition: Towards Policy Implications for Music Business Development*. Manchester: ESRC Centre for Research on Innovation and Competition, Manchester University.

Attali, Jacques. 1985 (1977). *Noise: The Political Economy of Music*, trans. Brian Massumi. Minneapolis, MN: University of Minnesota Press.

Baudrillard, Jean. 1981. *For a Critique of the Political Economy of the Sign*, trans. Charles Levin. St. Louis, MO: Telos Press.

Burnett, Robert. 1990. *Concentration and Diversity in the International Phonogram Industry*. Göteborg: Department of Journalism and Mass Communication, University of Göteborg.

Chapple, Steve, and Garofalo, Reebee. 1977. *Rock 'n' Roll Is Here to Pay: The History and Politics of the Music Industry*. Chicago: Nelson-Hall.

D'Angelo, Mario. 1989. *La Renaissance du disque: les mutations mondiales d'une industrie culturelle* [The Rebirth of the Record: Global Changes in a Cultural Industry]. Paris: La documentation française.

Eliot, Marc. 1990. *Rockonomics: The Money Behind the Music*. London: Omnibus.

Garnham, Nicholas. 2000. *Emancipation, the Media, and Modernity: Arguments About the Media and Social Theory*. Oxford: Oxford University Press.

Kozul-Wright, Zeljka, and Stanbury, Lloyd. 1998. *Becoming a Globally Competitive Player: The Case of the Music Industry in Jamaica*. Geneva: UN Conference on Trade and Development.

Lange, André. 1986. *Stratégies de la musique* [Strategies of Music]. Brussels: Mardaga.

Lash, Scott, and Urry, John. 1994. *Economies of Signs and Space*. London: Sage.

Miège, Bernard. 1989. *The Capitalization of Cultural Production*. New York: International General.

Stamm, K. Brad. 2000. *Music Industry Economics: A Global Demand Model for Pre-recorded Music*. Lewiston, NY: Edwin Mellen Press.

Taylor, Millie, and Towse, Ruth. 1998. 'The Value of Performers' Rights: An Economic Approach.' *Media, Culture and Society* 20(4): 631–52.

Throsby, David. 2001. *Economics and Culture*. Cambridge: Cambridge University Press.

Towse, Ruth. 1993. *Singers in the Marketplace: The Economics of the Singing Profession*. Oxford: Clarendon Press.

Towse, Ruth, ed. 1997. *Baumol's Cost Disease: The Arts and Other Victims*. Cheltenham, UK: Edward Elgar.

Vogel, Harold L. 2001. *Entertainment Industry Economics:*

A Guide for Financial Analysis. 5th ed. Cambridge and New York: Cambridge University Press.

DAVE LAING

Ethnomusicology

History

Modern ethnomusicology originated in the late nineteenth century as part of a quest for universal psychological principles that might be verified empirically and cross-culturally through careful analysis of data gathered from 'non-Western' peoples, many of them colonial subjects. Intersecting with other discourses such as philology (which became linguistics) and folklore (growing out of romantic nationalism in Europe), ethnomusicology developed three branches: the 'oriental,' concerned with comparative analysis of 'high-culture' European and Asian styles (hence the common term 'comparative musicology'/*vergleichende Musikwissenschaft*); the 'primitive,' dealing with 'nonliterate tribal' peoples (in Africa, Oceania, Asia, North and South America); and the 'folk,' concerned with the internal 'primitives' of Europe and the United States.

Finally dubbed 'ethnomusicology' by Jaap Kunst around 1955 (Kunst 1959), the discipline came of age through institutional grounding in the United States as part of the post-World War II expansion of universities and the invention of an interdisciplinary enterprise called 'area studies.' The North American ethnomusicology scene became the most populous and, eventually, the most influential. In the 1950s and 1960s, discourse there centered on the perceived split between two wings: the anthropological, represented by scholars like Alan Merriam and David McAllester, who were trained in cultural anthropology, and the musicological. The dispute centered on whether ethnomusicology studied 'the music itself,' or whether it was necessary always to view the music 'in context' after fieldwork immersion in a foreign culture. Mantle Hood's 'bimusicality' project, in the pioneering program at the University of California at Los Angeles (UCLA), privileged experiential initiation into unfamiliar music systems through performance.

By the 1970s, this crack had been papered over as scholars moved toward integrating the two approaches. Around this time, it became possible for 'popular music' to be considered a fit object of study, for the following reasons (among others): (a) classic ethnography of isolated groups became politically difficult, owing to postcolonialism and the global position of the United States; (b) the rise of new, heavily urbanizing nation-states meant that there were ever fewer 'untouched' peoples to study; (c) globalization of technologies allowed for the dramatic growth of internal and world markets for mass-mediated musics; and (d) scholars began to legitimize

studying 'one's own' culture, not just those of 'others.' As an example of (d), Mark Slobin undertook fieldwork on isolated folk musics in Afghanistan in the late 1960s but, by the early 1970s, noticed that ignoring 'radio music' skewed the understanding of local styles (Slobin 1976). By the mid-1970s, Slobin was studying music of his own 'heritage' as part of an interest in issues of ethnicity and identity in the United States (Slobin 1982, 1989).

New source materials filtered into research approaches. The work of pioneering folklore-based scholars (for example, Archie Green) demonstrated that early commercial sources – sheet music and, particularly, sound recording – rather than being the detritus of cultural destruction, often represented the benchmark and reservoir of the very local traditions that ethnomusicologists had been seeking all along (Green 1972). Spottswood's pioneering discography, *Ethnic Music on Records* (1990), made more precise research possible. Historical studies by ethnomusicologists on North American subcultural musics began to appear (Slobin 1982; Glasser 1995), as the dictum that 'the past is a foreign country' started to make perfect methodological sense for ethnomusicology, a discipline based on the study of alterity.

In Europe before 1989, East European ethnomusicologists and folklorists engaged in the detailed study of 'folk' traditions as part of state-subsidized nationalism under socialist rule, and they have continued this line of inquiry, generally eschewing the study of popular musics. West European ethnomusicologists have been slow to recognize the 'ethnic' and 'popular' music in their midsts but, by the late 1990s, it had been generally recognized that styles from former colonies, or those from groups of newer immigrants, might form a major area of research, particularly with official recognition in many European Union states that their societies are 'multicultural.' Initially, research began in Sweden, demonstrating the crossover of forms among the various components of the population; Hemetek has edited a volume with a broad view of musical 'diversity' from an Austrian base (1996).

Approaches

In addressing the long and complex interaction of ethnomusicology and popular music studies, the word 'popular' needs careful consideration in approaches to the methodologies and results of research. One perspective that might facilitate an understanding of ethnomusicological inquiry would distinguish the study of the 'popular' understood as the creation and reception of the most broadly accepted musical forms from the study of the 'popular' viewed as a technologically produced and managed commodity, although the two overlap in many respects.

Ethnomusicology and the Broadly Popular

For most of modernity (the mid-eighteenth century on), there has been a cultural practise of plundering the 'popular,' as understood by the intelligentsia and the upper classes of Euro-American societies. This has meant that the educated and the affluent could spend part of their time collecting bits of culture deemed ancient, typical or customary from the lower classes. The term 'popular' was one of the labels applied to such materials, and in some European languages the word retained this meaning, as, for example, in the title of the Musée des arts et traditions populaires in Paris.

The gradual widespread adoption in English of the German-derived terms based on 'folk' supplanted this notion of 'popular,' but ethnomusicologists have continued to study 'what's popular' – meaning not only what's currently fashionable, or produced by the recording industry cartel, but also what people most commonly or passionately choose as a basis for dancing, listening, identifying with and remembering. This analytical attitude can be subdivided into headings: What is broadly popular among given genders, social formations, locations and so on.

Such an approach sidesteps thorny issues raised by the more materialist approach to the popular detailed below; for example, Keil and Keil (1992) have studied 'polka happiness' as a popular musical phenomenon among Polish Americans in a way that includes, but extends beyond, issues of commodification. This perspective holds for numerous studies of popular micromusical systems based on heritage and affinity. It also informs studies of musical forms that move freely between cities and rural areas in many recently urbanized parts of the world (for example, Turino 1993 on Peru), where issues of popular taste spill beyond questions of 'mediaization.' Even in media-based studies, if they are about local, rather than transnational, flow (see Manuel 1993 on India), intense popularity becomes the focus of attention. It is in such ethnographically based work that ethnomusicology remains truest to its roots as the study of small-scale populations and an interest in the older notion of 'the popular.'

Ethnomusicology and the Technologically Popular

Noted above was ethnomusicology's historical shift from studying local musics to researching transnationally produced musics, moving from fieldwork on person-to-person transmission to research on the mediated forms of performing and perceiving, now understood as 'production' and 'consumption.' This meant that the 'cutting-edge' works of ethnomusicology in the 1980s focused on musics that were popular both locally and technologically, as studies based on both the ethnography and the history of popular forms began to emerge, beginning in Africa (Waterman 1990; Erlmann 1991) and the Caribbean (Austerlitz 1997; Guilbault 1993) and broadening through the 1990s to include many other world areas, such as the United States (Walser 1993), Eastern Europe, once the heartland of 'folk' studies (see Slobin's 1996 anthology), and more and more regions of Africa and Asia (Danielson 1997 on Egypt; Jones 1992 on China). Even a broad survey stressing tradition, Yampolsky's massive CD anthology of Indonesia (1991), found it necessary to include a representation of 'classic' popular musics.

There are (at least) two main reasons for this shift: (a) the simple fact that it is impossible to find a world music in which mediated popular music forms do not play a significant role in local commerce and consciousness; and (b) the advent of the megafield called 'cultural studies.' Ethnomusicology has found itself surrounded by a huge interdisciplinary literature and methodology that privilege the popular, principally in terms of a Marxist-derived analysis. Cultural studies, beginning in Britain in the 1960s, has channeled off into multiple streams of inquiry that have a materialist bent and a textual frame of analytical reference, approaches that come naturally to ethnomusicology's concerns. Enhanced by the more traditional ethnographic methods, ethnomusicology has seriously amplified its interdisciplinary voice even as it has tried to avoid the pitfalls and excesses of trendsetting approaches. Institutionally, overlap of membership in organizations like IASPM and the broadening of teaching responsibilities among academic ethnomusicologists to include popular music studies have accelerated the pace of 'popularization' of the discipline.

Bibliography

Austerlitz, Paul. 1997. *Merengue: Dominican Music and Dominican Identity*. Philadelphia: Temple University Press.

Danielson, Virginia. 1997. *The Voice of Egypt: Umm Kulthūm, Arabic Song, and Egyptian Society in the Twentieth Century*. Chicago: University of Chicago Press.

Erlmann, Veit. 1991. *African Stars: Studies in Black South African Performance*. Chicago: University of Chicago Press.

Glasser, Ruth. 1995. *My Music Is My Flag: Puerto Rican Musicians and Their New York Communities, 1917–1940*. Berkeley and Los Angeles: University of California Press.

Green, Archie. 1972. *Only a Miner*. Urbana, IL: University of Illinois Press.

Guilbault, Jocelyne. 1993. *Zouk: World Music in the West Indies*. Chicago: University of Chicago Press.

Hemetek, Ursula, ed. 1996. *Echo der Vielfalt/Echoes of Diversity*. Wien: Böhlau.

Jones, Andrew F. 1992. *Like a Knife: Ideology and Genre in Contemporary Chinese Popular Music*. Ithaca, NY: East Asia Program, Cornell University.

Keil, Charles, and Keil, Angeliki. 1992. *Polka Happiness*. Philadelphia: Temple University Press.

Kunst, Jaap. 1959. *Ethnomusicology: A Study of Its Nature, Its Problems, Methods and Representative Personalities to Which Is Added a Bibliography*. The Hague: Martinus Nijhoff.

Manuel, Peter. 1993. *Cassette Culture: Popular Music and Technology in North India*. Chicago: University of Chicago Press.

Slobin, Mark. 1976. *Music in the Culture of Northern Afghanistan*. Tucson, AZ: University of Arizona Press.

Slobin, Mark. 1982. *Tenement Songs: The Popular Music of the Jewish Immigrants*. Urbana, IL: University of Illinois Press.

Slobin, Mark. 1989. *Chosen Voices: The Story of the American Cantorate*. Urbana, IL: University of Illinois Press.

Slobin, Mark, ed. 1996. *Retuning Culture: Musical Changes in Central and Eastern Europe*. Durham, NC: Duke University Press.

Spottswood, Richard K. 1990. *Ethnic Music on Records: A Discography of Ethnic Recordings Produced in the United States, 1893–1942*. Urbana, IL: University of Illinois Press.

Turino, Thomas. 1993. *Moving Away from Silence: Music of the Peruvian Altiplano and the Experience of Urban Migration*. Chicago: University of Chicago Press.

Walser, Robert. 1993. *Running with the Devil: Power, Gender, and Madness in Heavy Metal Music*. Hanover, NH: Wesleyan University Press/University Press of New England.

Waterman, Christopher. 1990. *Jùjú: A Social History and Ethnography of an African Popular Music*. Chicago: University of Chicago Press.

Yampolsky, Philip. 1991. *Music of Indonesia, Vol. 2: Indonesian Popular Music*. Washington, DC: Smithsonian/Folkways Records (Smithsonian/Folkways SF-40056).

MARK SLOBIN

Feminism

'Feminism' is a term used to refer to a social movement that has encouraged women to claim equality with men, and to challenge practises, ideas and stereotypes that demean women and maintain them in a subordinate position in relation to men. It is problematic to offer exact dates for the emergence of feminism. A number of writers point to stirrings of British feminism in the seventeenth century; however, Humm (1992) notes that '"feminism" as a term for the politics of equal rights for women did not come into English use until the 1890s' (1). The development of feminism is often divided into the 'first wave,' which includes the suffrage movement of the late nineteenth century, and the 'second wave,' from the 1960s onward.

As the women's movement began to fragment during the mid- to late 1970s, many different varieties of feminism emerged. The term 'feminism' thus subsumes a number of distinct strands, or schools of thought, each associated with different theoretical assumptions and political agendas; hence the common references to liberal, Marxist or radical feminism, for example, or to feminist psychoanalysis or postmodern feminism. Feminist critics have also offered critiques of the emerging academic canon of feminist writing, which, initially, often tended to represent the concerns of white, Western, middle-class women rather than focusing on the different contexts of female experience. During the 1990s, writers such as Kamen (1991) and Findlen (1995) discussed the differences that were emerging between the outlook and experience of a younger generation of feminist women and the more established approaches of 'second wave' feminism. These texts presented the concerns and reflections of this younger generation (also referred to as 'third wave' feminism) and emphasized the importance of including the often absent perspectives of women of color and those living on low incomes. Feminism is thus not a monolithic, unchanging or easily defined movement. Indeed, the plurality of opinion and activism signaled by the term has encouraged the use of the word 'feminisms' in preference to the singular 'feminism,' which seems to suggest a cohesive body of thought and purpose. As Bayton (1993) writes: 'Feminism has meant different things to different people at different times. Many more women have been influenced by it and espouse its tenets than would readily call themselves "feminists"' (178).

Feminism has had an impact on both popular music practise and theory. It has, for example, encouraged many women to get involved in popular music-making, and feminist networks have helped to provide the necessary support and material resources that would enable their participation. Petersen (1989) has documented how, during the late 1960s and early 1970s, numerous bands and solo artists began performing women-identified music in the United States. These musicians (including the Chicago Women's Liberation Rock Band, the New Harmony Sisterhood Band and Miss Saffman's Ladies Sewing Circle) often produced music with feminist- or lesbian-identified lyrics. Similarly, during the

1970s feminists in Britain established women-only music groups and workshops, and rehearsal, dance and performance spaces. These initiatives promoted collectivism and cooperation among female musicians and gave women access to musical instruments, technology and training, as well as the confidence to believe that, 'like the boys, they can be music-makers rather than simply music fans' (Bayton 1993, 191). The tradition of offering music 'taster' sessions to women in order to encourage their involvement in music has continued and has developed in recent years to include not only instrumental tuition but also DJ workshops.

The 1970s also saw the establishment of new music businesses run by women, such as Olivia Records (1973) in the United States, 'dedicated to the recording and distribution of music written, recorded, produced, and engineered by women' (Petersen 1989, 208), and the UK specialist mail-order company WRPM (Women's Revolutions Per Minute, 1977). Other feminist initiatives in recent decades have included the promotion of numerous music festivals with the aim of showcasing the work of women musicians. Examples of these events are the annual Chard Festival of Women in Music (UK), promoting folk, classical, jazz and contemporary musicians; the New Zealand Composing Women's Festival, with concerts ranging from jazz to opera to hip-hop; and Ladyfest, a nonprofit, community-based, cultural event that first took place in Olympia, Washington in 2000 and subsequently resulted in the hosting of Ladyfest 2001 events in Bloomington, Indiana, Chicago, Illinois and Glasgow, Scotland.

Popular musicians of both genders have directly or indirectly promoted feminist views or sentiments through their music-making. Some performers, for example, have challenged the masculinity and sexism of rock through their image and performance style. Other performers have produced feminist-inspired lyrics and sounds. In this regard, Davis (1998) has explored how the songs of the blues artists Gertrude 'Ma' Rainey, Bessie Smith and Billie Holiday work within a tradition of feminist consciousness in working-class black communities. The Canadian-born folk/rock singer-songwriter Joni Mitchell provides a further illustration, as during the 1970s she performed songs with lyrics of an autobiographical nature, thus promoting through her music feminism's 'personal as political' message. Some popular musicians have also attempted to create feminist musical sounds and rhythms by deliberately avoiding musical styles and genres perceived as having masculine and/or sexist connotations – for example, rock music or heavy metal, whose musicians have placed particular emphasis on high volume, feedback and screeching vocals and on use of the electric guitar as a phallic symbol. Others, however, have adapted such styles and genres to feminist concerns. During the early 1990s, a feminist network labeled as 'riot grrrl' was promoted by musicians within the underground rock music communities of Olympia, Washington and Washington, DC. The network aimed to empower girls and women, encouraging them to become involved in producing music and to challenge restrictive gender roles (see Leonard 1997). During the 1990s, riot grrrl spread across the United States, Britain and Canada and resulted in the establishment of extensive (print and electronic) zine networks, numerous dedicated 'grrrl' Web sites and the formation of a great many female-centered punk rock bands.

Meanwhile, feminist scholars have critiqued approaches to the study of popular music that ignore, marginalize or stereotype women, and they have promoted not only the study of women in popular music, but also the study of gender (focusing on constructions of masculinity as well as femininity) and of sexuality. Feminist musicologists, for example, have challenged musicology's presentation of a male-dominated canon. McClary (1991) points to the misogynist nature of well-known operatic texts and criticizes musicology for avoiding issues of musical signification. She describes feminist criticism as 'the key to the forbidden door: the door that has prevented me from really being able to understand even that to which I was granted free access' (5), and she sets out the beginnings of a 'feminist criticism of music' (7, 31). She analyzes, for example, the music and music videos of female popular musicians such as Laurie Anderson and Madonna, who 'deliberately problematize their sexual identities within their musical discourses' (32).

Similarly, within sociological and cultural studies feminists have challenged and revised existing male-oriented research in popular music and have highlighted the activities and interests of female musicians and audiences. Wise (1990), for example, has written a personal account of the problems of being both a feminist and an Elvis fan. She suggests that male writers and media presenters have put forward a view of Elvis that promotes a particular version of masculinity and represents a male perspective, and she draws on her own memories and feelings about Elvis in order to promote an alternative perspective. Bayton (1998) has studied how women become rock musicians, highlighting the various obstacles and hurdles that they have to overcome, and circumstances and problems specific to women that affect their participation in rock culture. The work of Bayton and Wise, like that of other feminist writers on popular music, also illustrates the influence of feminist research methods and approaches, particularly the emphasis on self-reflexivity on the part of researchers and on incorporating women's voices and perspectives into academic writing through interviews and quotations.

Bibliography

Bayton, Mavis. 1993. 'Feminist Musical Practice: Problems and Contradictions.' In *Rock and Popular Music: Politics, Policies, Institutions*, ed. Tony Bennett et al. London and New York: Routledge, 177–92.

Bayton, Mavis. 1998. *Frock Rock: Women Performing Popular Music*. Oxford: Oxford University Press.

Davis, Angela Y. 1998. *Blues Legacies and Black Feminism: Gertrude 'Ma' Rainey, Bessie Smith, and Billie Holiday*. New York: Pantheon Books.

Findlen, Barbara, ed. 1995. *Listen Up: Voices from the Next Feminist Generation*. Seattle, WA: Seal Press.

Humm, Maggie, ed. 1992. *Feminisms: A Reader*. Hemel Hempstead: Harvester Wheatsheaf.

Kamen, Paula. 1991. *Feminist Fatale: Voices from the 'Twentysomething' Generation Explore the Future of the 'Women's Movement'*. New York: Donald I. Fine.

Kemp, Sandra, and Squires, Judith, eds. 1997. *Feminisms*. Oxford: Oxford University Press.

Leonard, Marion. 1997. '"Rebel Girl, You Are the Queen of My World": Feminism, "Subculture" and Grrrl Power.' In *Sexing the Groove: Popular Music and Gender*, ed. Sheila Whiteley. London: Routledge, 230–55.

McClary, Susan. 1991. *Feminine Endings: Music, Gender, and Sexuality*. Minneapolis, MN: University of Minnesota Press.

Petersen, Karen E. 1989. 'An Investigation into Women-Identified Music in the United States.' In *Women and Music in Cross-Cultural Perspective*, ed. Ellen Koskoff. Urbana, IL: University of Illinois Press, 203–12.

Wise, Sue. 1990. 'Sexing Elvis.' In *On Record: Rock, Pop, and the Written Word*, ed. Simon Frith and Andrew Goodwin. London: Routledge, 390–98.

SARA COHEN and MARION LEONARD

Folklore

Folklore, clearly, is the 'lore' of the 'folk.' But who the folk are, and what their lore is, is less clear. Are the folk peasants? And if so, how can there be any folklore outside Europe and Asia? Or are the folk just 'ordinary people'? Is their lore best regarded as being encapsulated within cultural artifacts, such as tales, songs and barns, or is it best understood in terms of ideas and processes? And how did, and does, the debate over folklore affect the study of popular music? Folklorists have, paradoxically, both devalued and contributed to the study of popular music. They have devalued it as the debased product of commercial interests, and they have contributed methodologically, calling attention to traditional elements and processes in popular musics.

During the nineteenth century, as the concept of folk-lore gained currency, European intellectuals increasingly believed that peasant traditions, valuable survivals from a preindustrial age, should be collected and preserved before they vanished. But folklorists did not always separate folk and popular forms of cultural expression. Indeed, in England, the term 'folklore' was not coined until 1846, when William Thoms proposed that this word replace the then current term, 'popular antiquities.' The US scholar F.J. Child titled his great collection (1962 (1882–98)) *English and Scottish Popular Ballads*, suggesting that some nineteenth-century folklorists recognized that folklore was not the exclusive province of the rural and illiterate. Rather, as these 'folk' intermingled, usually as servants, with landholders and emerging middle classes, the latter found the 'lore' worth assimilating. The rise of the middle class, and consequent commodification and mass distribution of folklore-based material, such as the broadside ballad, for popular consumption, meant that mass-mediated cultural products, including music, occupied an inferior position. It is North American folklorists who have made the most important contributions to the study of popular music. European and Latin American folklorists have generally avoided it in favor of efforts at preserving musics that they regard as both endangered and authentically 'folk.'

As urbanization, industrialization and literacy increased throughout Europe and North America in the twentieth century, North American folklorists began to reconstruct their subject by distinguishing between folk, popular and 'high' culture. Something 'folk' was said to be old, traditional or customary, and anonymous; its provenance was in the rural areas; it was transmitted orally rather than by means of writing or print; and it was communal, shared by a group of people with a common way of life. 'Popular' was new, or at least not old, and its creators often were known; its provenance was the town and city; it was mass-disseminated by print and, later, by radio, recordings, television, video and computers; it was ephemeral, not traditional; it was created as a product for consumption rather than group participation; and it was sold for profit. 'High' culture shared many of the attributes of 'the popular,' except that its artists were trained in academies and practised within the traditions of the fine arts, not necessarily for money; and although the products were sold, they were not mass-disseminated. The original artwork had great value, but the copy, which was considered popular, did not.

With these distinctions between folk, popular and 'high' culture in mind, folklorists were uneasy with popular music, thinking that, because of its mass appeal and commercial motive, it was supplanting folk music. As a result, folklorists either ignored popular music, while collecting and interpreting folk music, or viewed popular music as a contaminated product, but one in which folk elements could be discerned and rescued. For example, the term 'folk hymn' arose when music scholars like George Pullen Jackson encountered a rural religious song tradition in the southern United States, in which hymnbooks carried printed texts by eighteenth-century English devotional poets like Isaac Watts, but without musical notation. Investigation of the tunes revealed that they circulated orally and descended from the same British and Scots-Irish folk song stock as ballads and instrumental music, and thus folk provenance was established (Jackson 1963). Subsequently, Wilgus and Greenway (1965) directed folklorists' attention to the commercialized, commodified product known as hillbilly music (later country music), and demonstrated that many folk songs were released on hillbilly recordings. The same was the case in other popular music traditions, including blues (Evans 1982).

Folklorists working with these materials were rightly concerned with the interplay of the oral, written and recorded; for, again, the line between folk and popular never was as sharp in practise as in the definitions given above. It turned out that some rural folk singers in the remote areas not only could read, but wrote down their ballads in 'ballit-books,' and that a number of dance fiddlers wrote down music in notation and possessed tunebooks. Distinctions between folk and popular have blurred further since the 1960s, as North American scholars have increasingly researched British-American and African-American musics in the United States using whatever sources – oral, printed, recorded – are available (for example, Bronner 1987; Lornell 1995). But many folklorists felt that Carl Belz, who argued that rock music was folk music because of its preponderance of orality, had gone too far (Belz 1969).

Decades ago, North American academic (that is, university-trained) folklorists gave up the notion that there is a separate group of people, 'the folk,' rural and illiterate, whose survivals from an earlier age must be preserved and studied. At least in Europe and North America, such a class scarcely exists. Instead, since the 1970s, academic folklorists have concentrated on the cultural expression of individuals and small groups within communities, whether rural or urban, oral or written, anonymous or known. Members of the folk group, which may represent any region, class, occupation, level of education and so forth, share context, identity and aesthetic preferences, and the group has some stability over time. Sometimes, the folk group members share ethnicity, gender, class, region and/or age level, and sometimes not.

Just as academic folklorists redefined the folk, so they reinterpreted the nature of the lore. The earlier, item-centered approach conceived of folklore as a series of local products, such as tales, songs, superstitions, material culture such as quilts or barns, and customs that had survived from an earlier age. The spatial diffusion of these anonymous items could be mapped over time. The newer, performance-centered approach conceived of folklore more as a dynamic process, something that emphasized 'artistic communication in small groups,' in Ben-Amos's influential definition of folklore (1972, 13). Folklore-as-performance (which included customs and material culture as well as those aspects of folklore that would be recognized as 'performed') paid particular attention to performer (folk artist or tradition-bearer) and audience, and to the rules (community aesthetics) by which folklore performances proceed.

This new understanding of folklore has enabled folklorists to contribute to the study of popular music forms in the United States, such as blues (Titon 1995), Cajun and zydeco (Ancelet 1988), bluegrass (Rosenberg 1985) and the musics of various ethnic groups (Jabbour 1982; Leary and March 1991; Spottswood 1976; Lornell and Rasmussen 1997). Few folklorists, however, have been attracted to the study of such forms of popular music as rock, soul or hip-hop. Further, folklorists have experienced little success in popularizing their new definition of folklore. As a consequence, there has been little need to confront the problem of the disappearing subject: the folk as peasant.

At the beginning of the twenty-first century, folkloristic study of popular music is drawing closer to approaches from other perspectives, such as ethnomusicology and cultural studies. However, even while the definition of folklore has changed, folklorists have continued to pursue their studies through the time-honored methods of fieldwork, recording, and the study of texts and music. The structuralist considerations of the past, historical and geographical, focused on the 'lore,' have given way to an emphasis on the person, experience, aesthetics, community and communication in performance. Issues of power, ideology, class and gender, which mark cultural studies approaches, have become increasingly attractive to the current generation of folklorists.

Finally, folklorists have had some impact, through institutions that support the arts, on the preservation of traditional expressive culture. In the United States, folklorists have acted as both advocates and arts administrators, directing several million dollars each year to the support of folk artists, apprenticeships, films, recordings and festivals. The criteria of the National Endowment for the Arts and other agencies engaged in this work are somewhat conservative: they emphasize that folklore is the traditional product of families and communities.

However, they have found that popular music often is too, with the result that some of these monies have gone to the support of popular musics that only a few decades ago would have been considered outside the purview of folklore.

Bibliography

Ancelet, Barry Jean. 1988. 'Zydeco/Zarico: Beans, Blues and Beyond.' *Black Music Research Journal* 8(1): 33–49.

Bayard, Samuel P. 1982. *Dance to the Fiddle, March to the Fife: Instrumental Folk Tunes in Pennsylvania*. University Park, PA: Pennsylvania State University Press.

Belz, Carl. 1969. *The Story of Rock*. New York: Oxford University Press.

Ben-Amos, Dan. 1972. 'Toward a Definition of Folklore in Context.' In *Toward New Perspectives in Folklore*, ed. Américo Paredes and Richard Bauman. Austin, TX: University of Texas Press, 3–15.

Bronner, Simon J. 1987. *Old-Time Music Makers of New York State*. Syracuse, NY: Syracuse University Press.

Child, Francis James, ed. 1962 (1882–98). *English and Scottish Popular Ballads*. 5 vols. New York: Cooper Square Publishing.

Evans, David. 1982. *Big Road Blues: Tradition and Creativity in the Folk Blues*. Berkeley, CA: University of California Press.

Jabbour, Alan, ed. 1982. *Ethnic Recordings in America: A Neglected Heritage*. Washington, DC: Library of Congress, American Folklife Center.

Jackson, George Pullen. 1963 (1933). *White Spirituals in the Southern Uplands*. New York: Dover.

Leary, James P., and March, Richard. 1991. 'Dutchman Bands: Genre, Ethnicity, and Pluralism in the Upper Midwest.' In *Creative Ethnicity: Symbols and Strategies of Contemporary Ethnic Life*, ed. Stephen Stern and John Allan Cicala. Logan, UT: Utah State University Press, 21–43.

Lornell, Kip. 1995. *Happy in the Service of the Lord: African-American Sacred Vocal Harmony Quartets in Memphis*. Knoxville, TN: University of Tennessee Press. (First published Urbana, IL: University of Illinois Press, 1988.)

Lornell, Kip, and Rasmussen, Anne K., eds. 1997. *Musics of Multicultural America: A Study of Twelve Musical Communities*. New York: Schirmer Books.

Rosenberg, Neil V. 1985. *Bluegrass: A History*. Urbana, IL: University of Illinois Press.

Spitzer, Nicholas. 1993. 'Romantic Regionalism and Convergent Culture in Central Texas.' In *All That Glitters: Country Music in America*, ed. George H. Lewis. Bowling Green, OH: Bowling Green State University Popular Press, 87–93.

Spottswood, Richard K., ed. 1976. Brochure notes to *Songs of Migration and Immigration* (LP). Washington, DC: Library of Congress Music Division, LBC 6.

Titon, Jeff Todd. 1995. *Early Downhome Blues: A Musical and Cultural Analysis*. 2nd ed. Chapel Hill, NC: University of North Carolina Press. (First published Urbana, IL: University of Illinois Press, 1977.)

Wilgus, D.K., and Greenway, John, eds. 1965. *Journal of American Folklore (Hillbilly Issue)* 78(309) (July-September).

JEFF TODD TITON

Geography

The academic discipline of geography may be broadly defined as 'the study of the Earth's surface as the space within which the human population lives' (Haggett 1993, 220). It is a relatively unusual field of academic inquiry in that it encompasses both social science and physical science approaches, and the discipline as a whole involves the study of the geography of human societies and of the natural world. It is therefore made up of both social scientists and natural scientists, who pursue the fields of human geography and physical geography, respectively.

Despite the significantly different theoretical and methodological approaches they adopt, human and physical geographers are generally seen to be united by their allegiance to what Haggett (1993, 221) describes as the three 'essential characteristics of geographical study': first, a common concern with the spatial variation of phenomena over the Earth's surface; second, a shared ecological focus on the interrelationship between human societies and the environment; and third, an analytical focus on particular places, such as regions, upon which spatial and ecological analyses may be brought to bear.

Geographies of Music

In reality, the conceptual unity between human and physical geography is more written about than practised, and geographical inquiry has tended to evolve on either side of this intradisciplinary divide. Nevertheless, early attempts to write geographies of music were directly influenced by a sub-branch of the discipline known as cultural geography, which did make a concerted effort to straddle the gap between human and physical geography. Appropriately, attempts to approach music from a geographical perspective emerged first in North America, for it was there that cultural geography developed and has been most influential. The field is strongly associated with the work of Carl Sauer and the 'Berkeley School' of cultural geographers that he inspired. From the 1920s onward, Sauer and his colleagues developed an ecological approach to geography, paying attention to the interplay between human societies and the natural environment, and the mutual shaping and modifications that occurred over time within defined regions to create distinctive 'cultural landscapes' (Cosgrove 1993).

To explain the distinctiveness of particular cultural landscapes, cultural geographers utilized the concept of the 'cultural hearth,' which was seen to be a source area of particular cultural practises that are then diffused to contiguous areas. Although Sauer and his colleagues were mostly concerned with agricultural practises, in the late 1960s and early 1970s the concept of the cultural hearth was seized upon by a group of self-styled 'music geographers,' who were interested in the relationship between music, space and place.

According to Carney (1994, 3–4), geographical accounts of music undertaken in the cultural geography tradition have taken one of eight main forms, which have revolved around the investigation of the following phenomena: (a) 'the spatial variation of music'; (b) 'the [co-]evolution of a music style with place'; (c) 'the origin (cultural hearth) and diffusion of music phenomena (e.g., styles, instruments, songs, and musicians)'; (d) 'the psychological and symbolic elements of music pertinent to shaping the character of a place'; (e) 'the effect of music on the cultural landscape (e.g., concert halls, polka ballrooms, and rock festivals)'; (f) 'the spatial organization of music phenomena,' such as record companies, for example; (g) 'the relationship of music to the natural environment (e.g., an outdoor concert at Wolf Trap or the use of wood in the construction of a Native American courting flute)'; and (h) 'the interrelationships of music with other culture traits in a spatial sense (e.g., religion, dialect, politics, foodways, and sports in the American South).'

Of the above, (a) and (b) have been the most common types of analysis, commonly taking the form of descriptions of particular 'music regions,' or the tracking of the diffusion of musical styles out of such regions across space and time. In this sense, therefore, it leaned toward the most humanistic end of the cultural geography tradition (but see (g)). Most of these studies have been restricted to the United States, and have typically focused on the geographies of musical genres such as blues, bluegrass, country and western, jazz, rock 'n' roll and even zydeco (see Carney 1978, 1987, 1994).

This work made little impact in the discipline as a whole. One of the reasons for this was its association with cultural geography, which during the 1960s fell out of favor within the discipline in the face of the so-called 'Quantitative Revolution' in human geography. A concerted effort was made to install a more 'rigorous,' systematic approach to geographical inquiry and to import techniques of theoretical model-building, hypothesis testing and statistical analysis. Cultural geography was criticized for its atheoretical and descriptive approach, and for its focus on the unique, ideographic qualities of place at the expense of broader, nomothetic socio-spatial processes. The position of cultural geography was eroded still further in the 1970s when, partly in response to a growing dissatisfaction with the limitations of the quantitative approach, many human geographers turned toward a broadly Marxist political economy approach to seek an explanation for the uneven distribution of social, economic and political resources over space. Thus, music geographers found themselves doubly castigated: accused of being unscientific by quantitative geographers on the one hand, and of being concerned with frivolous, trivial matters by human geographers interested in political economy on the other. As a subdiscipline out of time and out of favor almost from its inception, the geography of music was fated to remain in the backwaters of human geography for much of its existence.

New Cultural Geographies of Music

During the 1990s, a new literature on the geography of music began to emerge, which sought to move beyond the limitations of the atheoretical and descriptive North American cultural geography tradition. This new work emerged out of the 'new cultural geography' that developed within the discipline from the mid-1980s onward. Motivated in large part by what was seen to be the narrow economism of prevailing political economy approaches in human geography, geographers began to explore the interrelationships between culture, space and place. Whereas in the past cultural geography had revolved around the interplay between the natural environment, human societies and the passing of historical time, the new cultural geography was informed more by social theory and by cultural studies, and focused on issues such as social relations, cultural politics, power, identity and representation (Cosgrove 1993).

Geographers developed new cultural geographies of music as part of a broader interdisciplinary movement (Leyshon, Matless and Revill 1998). Cultural geographers began to explore the interrelationships between music, space and place at the same time as scholars from cultural studies, communications theory and ethnic studies. They in turn discovered the importance of the place of music to the creation of 'difference' and 'cultural hybridity,' and to the possibilities of cultural resistance in a world characterized by time–space compression and the globalization of social relations (for example, see Clifford 1992; Gilroy 1993; Grossberg 1992; Lipsitz 1994; Mitchell 1996; and Taylor 1997). At the same time, anthropological analyses of music were underscoring the importance of place, through accounts of the vernacular production of music within localities as diverse as Liverpool (Cohen 1991), Milton Keynes (Finnegan 1989) and Austin, Texas (Shank 1994).

New geographies of music have sought to draw attention to the following: the ways in which representations of cultural space have tended to be dominated by the textual and the visual at the expense of sonoric landscapes (for example, see Smith 1994, 1998); the role music plays within constructions of local and national identity (see Kong 1995, 1996); and the way in which music is often entangled within processes of capital accumulation, on both local and global scales (see Hudson 1995; Lovering 1998; Sadler 1997).

Above all else, however, what new geographical research on music is concerned to do is draw attention to the mutually constitutive relationship between cultural theory and geography in understanding the ways in which music is produced, distributed and consumed, and the ways in which it is represented and understood. In other words, '[t]o consider the place of music is not to reduce music to its location, to ground it down into some geographical baseline, but to allow a purchase on the rich aesthetic, cultural, economic, and political geographies of musical language' (Leyshon, Matless and Revill 1998, 3).

Bibliography

Carney, George O. 1978. *The Sounds of People and Places: Readings in the Geography of Music*. Washington, DC: University Press of America.

Carney, George O. 1987. *The Sounds of People and Places: Readings in the Geography of American Folk and Popular Music*. 2nd ed. Lanham, MD: University Press of America.

Carney, George O. 1994. *The Sounds of People and Places: A Geography of American Folk and Popular Music*. 3rd ed. Lanham, MD: Rowman & Littlefield.

Clifford, James. 1992. 'Travelling Cultures.' In *Cultural Studies*, ed. Lawrence Grossberg, Cary Nelson and Paula A. Treichler. New York: Routledge, 96–116.

Cohen, Sara. 1991. *Rock Culture in Liverpool: Popular Music in the Making*. Oxford: Oxford University Press.

Cosgrove, Denis. 1993. 'Cultural Geography.' In *The Dictionary of Human Geography*, ed. Ron Johnston, Derek Gregory and David Smith. 3rd ed. Oxford: Blackwell, 111–13.

Finnegan, Ruth. 1989. *The Hidden Musicians: Music-Making in an English Town*. Cambridge: Cambridge University Press.

Gilroy, Paul. 1993. *The Black Atlantic: Modernity and Double Consciousness*. London: Verso.

Grossberg, Lawrence. 1992. *We Gotta Get Out of This Place: Popular Conservatism and Postmodern Culture*. London: Routledge.

Haggett, Paul. 1993. 'Geography.' In *The Dictionary of Human Geography*, ed. Ron Johnston, Derek Gregory and David Smith. 3rd ed. Oxford: Blackwell, 220–23.

Hudson, Ray. 1995. 'Making Music Work.' *Transactions of the Institute of British Geographers* (New Series) 20: 474–85.

Kong, Lily. 1995. 'Popular Music in Geographical Analyses.' *Progress in Human Geography* 19: 183–98.

Kong, Lily. 1996. 'Popular Music in Singapore: Exploring Local Cultures, Global Resources, and Regional Identities.' *Environment and Planning D: Society and Space* 14: 273–92.

Leyshon, Andrew, Matless, David, and Revill, George, eds. 1998. *The Place of Music*. New York and London: Guilford Publications.

Lipsitz, George. 1994. *Dangerous Crossroads: Popular Music, Postmodernism and the Poetics of Place*. London: Verso.

Lovering, John. 1998. 'The Global Music Industry: Contradictions in the Commodification of the Sublime.' In *The Place of Music*, ed. Andrew Leyshon, David Matless and George Revill. New York and London: Guilford Publications, 31–56.

Mitchell, Tony. 1996. *Popular Music and Local Identity: Rock, Pop and Rap in Europe and Oceania*. London: Leicester University Press.

Sadler, David. 1997. 'The Global Music Business as an Information Industry: Reinterpreting Economies.' *Environment and Planning A* 29: 1919–36.

Shank, Barry. 1994. *Dissonant Identities: The Rock'n'Roll Scene in Austin, Texas*. Hanover, NH: University Press of New England.

Smith, Susan. 1994. 'Soundscape.' *Area* 26: 232–40.

Smith, Susan. 1998. 'Beyond Geography's Visual Worlds: The Cultural Production of Sound.' *Progress in Human Geography* 21: 502–29.

Taylor, Timothy. 1997. *Global Pop: World Music, World Markets*. London and New York: Routledge.

ANDREW LEYSHON

History

Since the establishment of history as an academic discipline in mid-nineteenth-century Germany (through the work of the historicists, most notably Leopold von Ranke), historians have been regularly engaged in arguments and struggles over the nature and purpose of their enterprise and the role of the historian. Disputes have been many and varied: between idealists who believe it is necessary to enter into the mental world of the subject(s) studied and positivists who focus on the primacy of collecting facts, in expectation that through these, at some future point, laws will reveal themselves; between proponents of 'history for its own sake' and those who insist on the contemporary relevance of a chosen historical subject; between those who are happy to confer on the historian the mantle of objective searcher for truth and those who (under the particular influence of poststructuralism) deny the possibility of such a role. Whereas such disputes formerly testified to the strength and fascination of the discipline, by the second half of the twentieth century the apparently unresolvable nature of some intellectual dilemmas, coupled with the rise of the social sciences and the image in some quarters of a conservative profession, contributed to the idea that the study of history was 'in decline.' This was complemented by the perception that there had been a shift in public attitudes, away from the twin beliefs that the past could provide guidance and that understanding the essential nature of a thing depended on understanding its origins and history.

Popular culture has been intermittently accused (for example, by politicians concerned at the apparent decline of factual knowledge regarding the activities of their forebears) of fueling this situation by encouraging ahistorical attitudes. Whether or not an enthusiasm for, say, playing computer war games reduces an enthusiasm for knowledge about their historical counterparts is unclear, but a persistently buoyant market, in the late twentieth century, in populist historical accounts of popular culture activities and products themselves suggests that an historical dimension to the ostentatiously contemporary is often a central part of its appeal.

Popular music scholarship, for its part, has not engaged systematically with theoretical issues raised by the academic study of history. The past may be, as Hobsbawm (1998) puts it, 'a permanent dimension of the human consciousness, an inevitable component of the institutions, values and other patterns of human society' (13), but, perhaps because the rise of popular music scholarship coincided with the point at which, in the words of a professional historian, history had become 'a discipline with very little apparent coherence' (Tosh 1991, 230), the centrality suggested by Hobsbawm's statement has not been reproduced in the concerns and directions that have preoccupied most popular music scholars. Any attempt to identify a relationship between the two subjects must certainly recognize that, by the time popular music studies began to come into its own in the late 1970s, the discipline of history had already experimented with many approaches and had been exposed to many debates. Any relationship was likely, therefore, not to reflect the chronology of history's own development, but to be more synchronic in character. It is also the case that parallels

between history and popular music studies may not necessarily indicate influence but, rather, the exposure of both to wider debates, such as those generated as a result of a period of domination by priorities and methods characteristic of the social sciences, or those resulting from the influence of poststructuralism and the study of language (for example, the idea that a source should be regarded as part of the discourse of a particular time, rather than as a repository of factual information). Nevertheless, if the work of only a comparatively small number of scholars (for example, Lipsitz and Middleton) shows a willingness to engage at a theoretical level with historiological issues, popular music scholarship does show the influence of different approaches taken by historians to their task and, therefore, often somewhat indirectly, the impact of theoretical debates.

Aims and Approaches

Fascination with the past, whether theorized or not, almost invariably involves an active relationship between the past and the present within its rationale. Future concerns, while often included, are less frequently explicit. The ways in which this two- and sometimes three-way relationship expresses itself have varied considerably, and with that variety has come a diversity of motivating factors and objectives.

The notion of the past as having an authority over the present, not only speaking to it but guiding it – and, therefore, offering insights into the future also – was substantially broken during the nineteenth century among industrializing cultures, as the often startling differences between present and past attracted more attention. Once established, this sense of disparity – which informed the rise of historicism – led to a variety of emphases. At one extreme lay the study of the past for its own sake. When linked to an interest in accurate historical reconstruction, this approach resulted in many fascinating attempts at 'recovering' the past, but in tending to deny the present's claims for relevance or usefulness it was ultimately branded as conservative.

Little, if any, historical work in popular music has rigorously followed this approach, unless discographies, chart lists and other inventories are considered to have this primary purpose; but its presence is also evident in accounts that are predicated on a desire to preserve or recapture the appeal of such-and-such a past time, style or environment. In these accounts, however – whose varied form ranges widely, from biographies to liner notes, and includes some types of discographical work – another element of 'antiquarian' history is also on display: dissatisfaction with present-day trends. Both nostalgia-driven accounts and charts tend to be conceived against the prevailing fashion and to be posited against a world of endless change as 'a stable reflection, as the *terra firma*, of pop times' (Thornton 1990, 87).

At another extreme, the sense of disparity between past and present has led to a focus on points of disjuncture. The idea that popular music challenges – breaks with – ideas of tradition and continuity, and that it is these breaks that require the historian's attention, has been an important motivating element behind some historical work (for example, Chambers 1985). Some writing on rock 'n' roll and on rock, such as that of Bangs (1991), is fundamentally impatient with historical explanations for the impact of the music and seeks to celebrate disorder as a challenge to the hegemony of cause-and-effect explanations and the culture that sustains them.

A somewhat different approach to the evidence of disjuncture is apparent in work by Middleton. Drawing on Gramsci, Middleton (1990) directs attention to what he terms two levels of profound change in popular music's history: 'conjunctural change,' which displays more 'immediate, ephemeral characteristics,' and 'situational change,' where movement is 'fundamental and relatively permanent, the result of crisis' (12). This approach recognizes the part played by disjuncture in wider historical processes (and continuities). Middleton's aim here is to identify and understand larger processes that are at work in the links between music and socioeconomic structure (16ff.), processes that also have significance for a political understanding of both the past and the present.

Middleton's approach raises awareness of a major influence on history in general, one that has impacted fitfully though significantly on popular music history also. The rise within history itself of an approach that grants primacy to underlying movement in socioeconomic structure and, especially, to systems of relations within it, owed a large debt to Marx. Central to the thought of Marx and his successors was the identification of tensions and contradictions in the socioeconomic system that 'counteract the tendency of the system to maintain itself as a going concern' (Hobsbawm 1998, 196). Understanding this process in the past enabled the historian to offer the tools to analyze the present.

A great many debates followed from the application of Marx's thought to historical work. For music, these included the validity or otherwise of Marx's superstructure metaphor and its implications and, perhaps more important, the issue of whether levels of activity, including those in the superstructure, possessed 'relative autonomy.' But whether strictly Marxist (classical-, vulgar-, post-, neo-, etc.) or not, much popular music scholarship that addresses historiological issues, explicitly or implicitly, has been informed by a conviction that larger underlying, often dialectical, processes of a politically significant nature involving power relations in culture and society need to be identified and analyzed. While there is much variation, some differences of purpose are quite subtle. A principal aim of Chapple's and Garofalo's study of the rock business (1977), for example, is to establish the potential and actual determining power of the industrial system in which the rock business is placed, the better to claim rock, ultimately, as a music of resistance. By comparison, Russell (1987), in his account of popular music in England in the mid-nineteenth and early twentieth centuries, argues (in the words of one reviewer) 'that popular music was playing a part in fashioning the historical processes in the nineteenth century and not merely responding to it' (Herbert 1988, 115).

The issues of agency and autonomy were not, of course, the creation of Marxist or socialist historians; they had preoccupied historians for many generations. But one effect of Marx-influenced approaches was to take agency out of the hands of key individual players and recast it – thus at the same time problematizing autonomy – as the product of tensions and contradictions that are characteristic of the relations between the economic base and other levels of society. Popular music scholars taking up and developing this perception in an historical context have been motivated in part by a need to offer an alternative explanation for historical processes to that offered by more populist accounts, with their reliance on individual agency, but they have also had other targets in mind, such as interpretations influenced by notions of the romantic artist (themselves a likely influence on populist accounts), modernist readings of the potential of individualistic artistic challenge and a musicologically derived focus on great composers.

That it is possible to accept the role of cultural conditioning and dialectical processes in assessing an individual's achievement and come to different conclusions about the role for individual agency is illustrated by three readings of Elvis Presley, by Marcus, Peterson and Middleton. Marcus (1982) sees Presley ultimately as a transcendent figure, escaping 'the limits that could well have given his story a very different ending' (130). Peterson (1990), in contrast, stresses the influence of a conjuncture of social, industrial and technological factors in the rise of rock 'n' roll. Middleton (1990) applies a concept of articulation, in which 'articulating principles' engendered by socioeconomic factors work to combine existing elements into new patterns, set by the intersection of factors such as class, gender, ethnicity and nationality (8–9), and guided by the relative autonomy of cultural fields. While Peterson's approach results in a quite severe constraining of individual agency,

Middleton's allows for it (Presley himself 'rearticulates' existing elements), but insists on the equal ability of other, less sharply defined socioeconomic groups (in business and/or in his audiences) to articulate him to their own purposes.

Oral History

The question of individual agency also arises in the area of oral history, where sources, methods and objectives have combined in fruitful, if often problematic, ways. The problems encountered in popular music historiography by the existence of oral sources are not dissimilar to those encountered elsewhere in historiography: the dangers of relying on memories that may be faulty or partial, or both; the tendency for interviewees to engage in self-validation; the risk that oral reminiscences – which are often collected some time after an event – will be colored by hindsight. But, because for many involved in popular music, as producers or consumers, a written record of their activity has not been a priority, popular music historiography is likely to have a greater need of oral sources than do many other areas.

The incorporation of oral reminiscence into popular music history has links to different schools of history and hence to different, if related, priorities. The desire to elevate the oral record to a position on a par with, or even above, the written record may be no more or less than a pragmatically realistic reassessment of the types of evidence available to anyone wishing to reconstruct the popular music past. Alternatively, the desire to allow voices to speak which traditional historical sources and methods have left inarticulate may be a political statement, one sometimes made more potent by the added insistence that what the oral record shows is that such voices indicate active participation in historical action. As a further, partial alternative, in the casting of the historian as observer-reporter may be seen an alliance with imperatives of sociology and social anthropology.

If popular music history as a body of material has affiliations with these alternative priorities in the use of oral sources, it has formed major alliances with none of them. What the different uses of these sources in popular music history have in common is a recognition of the comparative paucity and partiality of the written record and its tendency to be in the hands of observers rather than participants (although there are some notable exceptions to this general rule, such as jazz trumpeter Louis Armstrong, who left a legacy of published, written but unpublished, and privately recorded reminiscences).

Histories that make use of oral sources tend also to share an underlying conviction that the story those sources tell is somehow closer to reality than the story which ignores them. This may be because, as the author of a book based on recollections of Irish women singers predicts in the case of his own history, via these sources 'the reader will be taken backstage and into the private lives of the . . . performers' (Rowley 1993, 7). At a deeper level, two important books that pioneered the construction of a popular music history around oral reminiscence – one around jazz (Shapiro and Hentoff 1955), the other around blues (Oliver 1965) – use a rich juxtaposition of oral reminiscences from many sources, presented without linking comment, in attempts to re-create the environment, experiences and attitudes that made up the daily lives of the musicians in their own time and place. For Oliver, there were two additional, related points. The 'conversations' with blues musicians that he reproduces are an important antidote in a situation in which, as documentation proliferates in the history of styles, themes and regional characteristics, 'the individual tends to become submerged.' They also allow the minor figures – 'men with small circles of acquaintances, limited aspirations and humble talents' who make up the core of the genre and its world – their rightful place (1965, 5).

Further Issues and Concerns

The consistent presence of an interest in underlying processes and their consequences, over a range of popular music historiography, suggests that much historical work, especially that on music since World War II, would probably accept Tosh's claim that 'the selection of themes for research should be influenced by a sensitivity to those areas of current concern which stand most in need of a historical perspective' (1991, 28). Ward's study (1998) of the relationship between changes in African-American consciousness and rhythm and blues in the 1950s, for example, is at least partially informed by the contribution it can make to understanding 'the ongoing black struggle for justice and equality in America' (15).

At the same time, in the realm of late twentieth-century political history, Mazower (1998) has warned against the dangers of reading the present back into the past, and of assuming, for example, that 'democracy must be deeply rooted in Europe's soil simply because the Cold War turned out the way it did' (xi). In referring approvingly to Hannah Arendt's remark that 'we can no longer afford to take that which was good in the past and simply call it our heritage,' Mazower posits a view of the outcome of twentieth-century political struggles as 'a story of narrow squeaks and unexpected twists, not inevitable victories and forward marches' (xii).

Many popular music historians have taken an ultimately optimistic view of the historical course of their subject, an approach that may bring them within the sphere of Mazower's criticism; others, such as Clarke (1995), have in effect inverted it to support a view of the triumph of the inferior. But, equally, many (including Ward) have taken a more dispassionate view. Much late twentieth-century work on the history of the minstrel show, for example, a subject that could be addressed as the struggle for and ultimate triumph of social decency, focuses instead on the 'tangle of involvement' that it represented (Lott 1993, 92). Some of this work also suggests the validity of a complementary idea to that proposed by Tosh: that historical study may reveal aspects of contemporary concerns that may otherwise not be readily apparent. Work such as Lott's, for example, may encourage the reader to think about the perhaps unsuspected degree to which that form has left an ongoing legacy.

The influence of poststructuralist approaches to history on the purposes of popular music historiography is most clearly seen in work that directs attention away from the very idea of large processes (most typically as a leftover from 'grand narrative' concepts) and the opportunity for political commitment that they may bring, and concentrates on pluralism. Addressing this issue in a review of Durant's *Conditions of Music* (1984), Middleton (1987) draws attention to the value of work that stresses 'historical context, discursive realism, polysemy, and the importance of positioning,' but points also to what he sees as 'the danger of a pluralism in which no articulating memory provides a fulcrum,' asking 'whether the inevitable price for the demystification of the past ... isn't the loss of centre in the present' (101).

A further – and, ultimately, perhaps more profound – late twentieth-century influence on the aims of both history in general and popular music historiography in particular has been that of cultural anthropology, which has enabled historians to draw together elements from a sometimes bewildering variety of legacies (historicism, socialism, 'history from below,' language and communication studies) around an insistence on contextualization and differentiation, in order not merely to validate the everyday, but to embark on the study of how, in the midst of 'thick' history, people have made meaning for themselves. As (classical) musicologist Kerman noted (1985), a good example of an approach wedding complex contextual history to the history of meaning is Austin's 1975 study of the life of Stephen Foster's songs 'from his time to ours' (175ff.).

Historical work by Lipsitz (1990, 1994) on popular music and popular culture within the context of commercialized leisure illustrates how these many lines of thought may interact: a longstanding commitment to

historically grounded labor history with a sympathetic response to poststructuralist insistence on a multiplicity of possible meaning; an anthropological focus on identity and collective memory with an insistence on the role of fundamental underlying tensions within the socioeconomic system – all filtered through the recognition, learned in the classroom, that 'texts from the past' may help us 'gain insight into the complex stories defining our present identities' (1990, xiv) and enable us 'to make informed moral choices about the present' (21). For Lipsitz, one way forward from the impasse that these interactions (and confrontations) may create lies in dialogical criticism, as developed by Bakhtin. Dialogical criticism 'connects affect to agency, and grounds social and ideological choices within the life worlds and collective memories of actual historical subjects. It shows how part of "what popular music is" can be found in "how popular music came to be," but it also eschews the twin pitfalls of formalism and essentialism.' In addressing rock history, for example, the problem that dialogical criticism identifies 'is not whether rock is oppositional or co-optive, but rather how it arbitrates tensions between opposition and co-optation at any given moment' (102).

Bibliography

Austin, William W. 1975. *'Susanna,' 'Jeanie' and 'The Old Folks At Home': The Songs of Stephen C. Foster from His Time to Ours*. Urbana, IL: University of Illinois Press.

Bangs, Lester. 1991. *Psychotic Reactions and Carburetor Dung: Literature as Rock 'n' Roll, Rock 'n' Roll as Literature*. London: Mandarin.

Chambers, Iain. 1985. *Urban Rhythms: Pop Music and Popular Culture*. London: Macmillan.

Chapple, Steve, and Garofalo, Reebee. 1977. *Rock and Roll Is Here to Pay: The History and Politics of the Music Industry*. Chicago: Nelson-Hall.

Clarke, Donald. 1995. *The Rise and Fall of Popular Music*. London: Viking.

Durant, Alan. 1984. *Conditions of Music*. Albany, NY: State University of New York Press.

Herbert, Trevor. 1988. 'Review of *Popular Music in England, 1840–1914*, by Dave Russell.' *Popular Music* 7(1): 114–15.

Hobsbawm, Eric. 1998. *On History*. London: Abacus.

Kerman, Joseph. 1985. *Musicology*. London: Fontana.

Lipsitz, George. 1990. *Time Passages: Collective Memory and American Popular Culture*. Minneapolis, MN: University of Minnesota Press.

Lipsitz, George. 1994. *Dangerous Crossroads: Popular Music, Postmodernism, and the Poetics of Place*. London: Verso.

Lott, Eric. 1993. *Love and Theft: Blackface Minstrelsy and the American Working Class*. New York: Oxford University Press.

Marcus, Greil. 1982. *Mystery Train: Images of America in Rock 'n' Roll Music*. Rev. ed. New York: Dutton.

Mazower, Mark. 1998. *Dark Continent: Europe's Twentieth Century*. London: Allen Lane.

Middleton, Richard. 1987. 'Review of *Conditions of Music*, by Alan Durant.' *Popular Music* 6(1): 99–102.

Middleton, Richard. 1990. *Studying Popular Music*. Buckingham: Open University Press.

Oliver, Paul. 1965. *Conversation with the Blues*. London: Cassell.

Peterson, Richard. 1990. 'Why 1955?: Explaining the Advent of Rock Music.' *Popular Music* 9(1): 97–116.

Rowley, Eddie. 1993. *A Woman's Voice*. Dublin: O'Brien Press.

Russell, Dave. 1987. *Popular Music in England, 1840–1914: A Social History*. Manchester: Manchester University Press.

Shapiro, Nat, and Hentoff, Nat, eds. 1955. *Hear Me Talkin' to Ya: The Story of Jazz by the Men Who Made It*. New York: Rinehart.

Thornton, Sarah. 1990. 'Strategies for Reconstructing the Popular Past.' *Popular Music* 9(1): 87–95.

Tosh, John. 1991. *The Pursuit of History: Aims, Methods and New Directions in the Study of Modern History*. 2nd ed. London: Longman.

Ward, Brian. 1998. *Just My Soul Responding: Rhythm and Blues, Black Consciousness and Race Relations*. London: UCL Press.

DAVID HORN

Literary Criticism

Literary criticism is an academic discipline devoted to the exegesis and evaluation of poetry and prose texts. At various times, literary critics and creative writers have become commentators on popular music, while techniques, concepts and methods originating in literary criticism have been adapted or adopted by popular music scholars.

An early example of the involvement of literary scholars in popular music research was the creation of the canon of traditional 'ballads' from British folk songs by the nineteenth-century editors Francis Child and George Kittredge (Harker 1985). In the heyday of artistic modernism – the early part of the twentieth century – the writers and critics Jean Cocteau and T.S. Eliot praised the music hall performers of Paris and London, and in North America jazz and blues were championed as important artistic productions by both white reviewers such as Carl Van Vechten and Abbe Niles and the black intellectuals of the Harlem Renaissance, Alain Locke and Langston Hughes. In his introduction to *The American Songbag*, Carl Sandburg compared North American folk songs to 'the heights and depths to be found in Shakespeare' (1990, xiii).

In Britain, the influential school of literary criticism associated with F.R. Leavis included the analysis of mass communications in its program of work. This influence is apparent significantly in the discussion by Hoggart (1957) of the religiosity to be found in 1950s popular love songs, and in the work of Hall and Whannel (1964) which discovered positive elements in the songs of the Beatles. A different development of the Leavisite view can be found in the extensive work of Wilfrid Mellers, who imbued his musicological analysis of the Beatles (1973), Bob Dylan (1984) and others with a broader sense of cultural development derived mainly from anthropological notions (see Laing 1994). While these were broadly positive accounts, Bloom (1987), Bayles (1996) and others have applied the 'high art' values of conservative literary criticism negatively to popular music.

A common literary approach to popular music has been to analyze song lyrics as if they were poetry. Examples can be found in the blues scholarship of Charters (1963) and Garon (1975) and in the study of folk songs by Reeves (1958). Literary criticism's emphasis on the study of individual authors has also influenced some popular music criticism that seeks to find thematic unity in an artist's *oeuvre*. This methodology has been applied to singer-songwriters, primarily Bob Dylan, in the critical writings of Williams (1969) and Gray (1972, 2000), and of Ricks (1987), himself a professor of literature.

Such analysis is vulnerable to the accusation that it isolates the semantic level of lyrics from the totality of the performance or recording; and, while it may be a justifiable approach to the work of 'poetic' singer-songwriters, it is less convincing when used to discuss, for example, rap (see Shusterman 1992).

In a broader context, concepts developed in linguistic and literary theory have been adopted by popular music scholars. The Russian critic Bakhtin's notion of the 'carnivalesque' has proved attractive (see, for instance, Watson 1995), as have ideas derived from Saussure's semiotics and initially applied to poetry and fiction by such authors as Kristeva and Barthes. In the study of jazz and rap, Gates's theory of 'signifyin(g)' (1988) has been highly influential. More recently, Jarrett (1999) has proposed 'jazz as a model for writing' through the application of postmodern literary theory.

But probably the most pervasive influence of literary studies on popular music studies is demonstrated in the now widespread tendency to analyze performances or recordings as 'texts,' a tendency that owes as much to the literary version of that concept as to the musicological one (Shepherd 1999). For example, Jarrett has argued that the 'close text-based readings' of the New Criticism associated with John Crowe Ransom, R.P. Blackmur and other academic critics provided 'an analytical language sufficient for the complexities of bebop and successive postwar jazz styles' (1999, 43–44).

Bibliography

Bayles, Martha. 1996. *Hole in Our Soul: The Loss of Beauty and Meaning in American Popular Music*. Chicago: University of Chicago Press.

Bloom, Allan. 1987. *The Closing of the American Mind: How Higher Education Has Failed Democracy and Impoverished the Souls of Today's Students*. New York: Simon & Schuster.

Charters, Samuel B. 1963. *The Poetry of the Blues*. New York: Oak Publications.

Garon, Paul. 1975. *Blues and the Poetic Spirit*. London: Eddison Press.

Gates, Henry Louis, Jr. 1988. *The Signifying Monkey: A Theory of Afro-American Literary Criticism*. New York: Oxford University Press.

Gray, Michael. 1972. *Song and Dance Man: The Art of Bob Dylan*. London: Hart-Davis, MacGibbon.

Gray, Michael. 2000. *Song and Dance Man III: The Art of Bob Dylan*. 3rd rev. ed. London: Cassell.

Hall, Stuart, and Whannel, Paddy. 1964. *The Popular Arts*. London: Hutchinson.

Harker, Dave. 1985. *Fakesong: The Manufacture of British 'Folksong,' 1700 to the Present Day*. Milton Keynes: Open University Press.

Hoggart, Richard. 1957. *The Uses of Literacy: Aspects of Working-Class Life, with Special Reference to Publications and Entertainments*. London: Chatto and Windus.

Jarrett, Michael. 1999. *Drifting on a Read: Jazz as a Model for Writing*. Albany, NY: State University of New York Press.

Laing, Dave. 1994. 'Scrutiny to Subcultures: Notes on Literary Criticism and Popular Music.' *Popular Music* 13(2): 179–90.

Mellers, Wilfrid. 1973. *Twilight of the Gods: The Beatles in Retrospect*. London: Faber & Faber.

Mellers, Wilfrid. 1984. *A Darker Shade of Pale: A Backdrop to Bob Dylan*. London: Faber & Faber.

Reeves, James, ed. 1958. *The Idiom of the People: English Traditional Verse*. London: Heinemann.

Ricks, Christopher. 1987. 'Cliches That Come to Pass.' In *All Across the Telegraph: A Bob Dylan Handbook*, ed. Michael Gray and John Bauldie. London: Sidgwick & Jackson, 22–29.

Sandburg, Carl, comp. 1990 (1927). *The American Songbag*. New York: Harcourt Brace Jovanovich.

Shepherd, John. 1999. 'Text.' In *Key Terms in Popular Music and Culture*, ed. Bruce Horner and Thomas Swiss. Malden, MA: Blackwell, 156–77.

Shusterman, Richard. 1992. *Pragmatist Aesthetics: Living Beauty, Rethinking Art*. Oxford: Blackwell.

Watson, Ben. 1995. *Frank Zappa: The Negative Dialectics of Poodle Play*. New York: St. Martin's Press.

Williams, Paul. 1969. *Outlaw Blues: A Book of Rock Music*. New York: E.P. Dutton.

DAVE LAING

Music Analysis

Generally considered an aspect of music theory, music analysis tends to focus on the study of individual pieces, styles or genres in order to explicate a piece's formal structure. This involves an attempt to understand how a piece of music 'works,' or, in other words, how it creates its effects. Music analysis is distinct from other work in music theory in that it does not explicitly propose either theories for creating music or descriptions of abstract principles embodied in music, although analysis is often used in the service of theory for gathering evidence or for purposes of demonstration.

In the broadest sense, almost all musicians carry out music analysis when they seek to learn from other pieces of music and performers and gain an understanding of how they create their effects. As this broad description implies, music analysis can address the relationship between perception and description. To the extent that it deals with this relationship, scholarly music analysis overlaps with music criticism, and the boundary between the two is indistinct, although it is possible to describe general differences. Music scholars associate music analysis less with presenting the subjective state of a listener (who may or may not be the critic) or persuading the reader of the relevance of a particular interpretation, and more with describing, in as 'neutral' a manner as possible, the constituent elements of a musical work, the relationship between those elements, their relative importance, and the effect of musical context on their function and significance. Music critics, on the other hand, tend to focus more on the temporal experience of hearing the work, and pay more attention to its musical 'surface' (elements of style and rhetoric) and less to its 'deep' structure (see Kerman 1985). Scholarly music analysis is also distinguished from music criticism in that it employs the terms and apparatus of music theory, whereas music criticism may or may not.

As with music theory, scholarly music analysis developed largely as an adjunct to the study of European art music, and consequently tends to derive its information from Western staff notation. This information is embodied in the musical score, which is usually a template of instructions for performance, although it may be a transcription of a performance. This basis in music notation and the score in turn influences notions of what constitutes the musical text, and of the relationship between text and context, with a concomitant belief in the possibility of separating text and context. Reliance on a score as the basis for analysis also produces a specific model of authorship in which the intentions of an historical figure, the 'composer,' are understood to underlie the meaning of the work. Score-based study focuses attention on what can be notated – equal-tempered pitches, arithmetically simple rhythms – and deflects attention from less easily notated elements (particularly those that distinguish particular performances from the score) – microtonal inflections of pitch, complex rhythmic nuances, timbre and articulatory nuances, not to mention visual, olfactory and other environmental aspects of performance.

A belief in the possibility and desirability of 'scientific objectivity' has led music analysis of art music in an increasingly hermetic direction in which its role as a basic pedagogical tool has ceded to justifications that an analysis represents an 'ideal hearing' of a work or, alternatively, that it reveals the 'unconscious reactions' of listeners. Such justifications are usually offered without further support, paradoxically requiring readers to take the resulting statements of 'scientificity' on faith (see Cook 1987). This casual attitude toward explaining the significance of analysis has also had a legitimating function, as it is taken for granted that the object of the analysis is worthy of the effort precisely because this point need not be argued.

While a broad array of analytical techniques has been applied to Western art music, the most influential have been 'Schenkerian analysis,' which analyzes the linear (melodic) motions of a piece in terms of their tonal relationships and connections in a hierarchy of structural levels; and 'set-theoretical analysis,' used largely for post-tonal, twentieth-century music, which parses the pitches of a composition into sets to illustrate their underlying structural relationship to one another. A type of analysis that constitutes a basic element of formal music education is 'Roman numeral analysis,' which labels chords according to their harmonic function. Another common pedagogical and heuristic tool is 'motivic analysis,' which seeks to uncover relationships between different melodic ideas and relate them to one germinating 'cell.' Other techniques include approaches derived from information theory, psychology, phenomenology and semiotics (for useful overviews, see Bent 1987; Cook 1987). The ideal of organicism undergirds most of these approaches, which usually seek to explain the 'unity' or 'coherence' of a given work (Solie 1980).

Whereas the analysis of Western art music is often presented as neutral and contextless (only because that context is taken for granted), the same cannot be said of music analysis in ethnomusicology, which has largely been concerned with the traditional music of non-Western societies, but also occasionally (and increasingly) with popular music produced in mass-mediated, postindustrial contexts. Central issues in ethnomusicological analysis have been: (a) the relationship between music analysis and the terms derived from the cultural traditions of a given repertoire; and (b) the dangers of distortion inherent in transcribing performances in Western staff notation and then using that transcription as a basis for analysis. Important early studies of twentieth-century North American traditional and popular music that brought varying degrees of this sensitivity to the relationship between text and context may be found in Lomax (1968), Seeger (1977, 273–320) and Keil (1966). While Lomax engaged in broad cross-cultural comparisons, and Seeger presented detailed analyses of a single 'folk' tune, Keil, in his own words, relied on 'gross textural characteristics and broad formal criteria rather than exact syntactic analyses' (207) of the sort favored by scholarly music analysts.

The majority of late twentieth-century analytical work on Western popular music can be viewed as lying within a spectrum that includes scientist formalist analysis on the one hand and unapologetically subjective criticism on the other. Work of a highly formalist nature takes as its mission the explication of the 'music itself' and asserts that the analytical tools devised for art music work well for popular music with little or no modification. That is, the analytical techniques are seen as transcending the immediate musical–cultural context in which they were created, and links are rarely essayed between the musical style being analyzed and the analytical technique used to analyze it. This leads to highly formalist analyses of types of popular music that respond best to such analytical techniques. They thus tend to focus on styles of popular music with a high degree of harmonic complexity and/or instrumental virtuosity, such as progressive rock (see Covach 1997), psychedelic rock (see Boone 1997; Brown 1997), blues rock (see Headlam 1995) and the music of the Beatles (Everett 1995; Moore 1997). These analyses (and others collected in Covach and Boone 1997) present a range of approaches that adopt the analytical rhetoric of scholarly music analysis, and include techniques such as Schenkerian analysis, Roman numeral analysis and motivic analysis, all of which are based on transcriptions of recordings (for a critique of the use of transcription in popular music, see Winkler 1997). The strengths of these approaches are much the same as when they are applied to the analysis of art music: they compel the analyst to engage forcefully with the object of study, to learn it thoroughly and to hear it in new ways. Analysts who are effective writers can encourage readers to hear greater detail in songs and help them to understand how their effects are created.

Likewise, the shortcomings of highly formalist approaches to the analysis of popular music duplicate – and amplify – the shortcomings of these approaches when applied to the analysis of art music: they have difficulty in accounting for the effect of difficult-to-notate elements that tend to be important in the experience of musical performance, and they deal with meaning and affect as 'marginal' elements, which are discussed in asides, metaphors and 'digressions' from the avowed purpose of the analysis. In addition to this, popular music that does not respond well to conventional techniques is implicitly marginalized. For example, little work has been done by self-identified music theorists on popular music with a low degree of harmonic complexity and instrumental virtuosity (from the perspective of Western art music), such as 1950s rhythm and blues, 1970s funk, and dance genres in which teleological form is overshadowed by pleasure in repetition (see Middleton 1990, ch. 7).

It must be noted that, for those with formal musical training, there are considerable disciplinary constraints at work if they wish to discuss the details of musical sound: in order to deal with those elements that are difficult to represent in staff notation, analysts must invent new means of graphic representation or devise modifications to existing notation. Innovative means of representation are usually devised with an eye to how the information thus represented is to be analyzed; this in turn produces a methodology that is unavoidably idiosyncratic. Inevitably, there is little institutional or professional encouragement to undertake such ventures. This, however, has not stopped scholars from trying to create new methodologies, and it is at this point that music analysis in popular music studies becomes overtly interdisciplinary, drawing on work from (among others) psychology, linguistics and semiotics. An example of the endeavor to devise methodologies to analyze previously neglected musical elements is the attempt to deal with timbre (that is, the character or quality of sound that distinguishes one instrument or voice from another), which for many seems to offer an opportunity to understand musical sound at its most material. The few attempts to deal with timbre in a sustained fashion diverge considerably, from adjectival description (Shepherd 1991, 152–73) to quasi-scientific sound spectrum analysis (Cogan 1984; Brackett 1995). Neither of these approaches shows signs of being adopted consist-

ently by other scholars, although Shepherd and Wicke (1997) have pursued a more thorough theorization of the relationship between sonic materiality and cultural meaning that may prove to be influential.

Much other musicological work on popular music mixes techniques drawn from music theory with more explicit use of criticism. A work such as Hamm's pioneering survey of the history of US popular music (1979) used music analysis in support of its statements about stylistic change and continuity. Another early example of music analysis used in the service of criticism was the work of Mellers (1973) on the Beatles. Although he was subsequently criticized for his use of terminology derived from the study of art music and for his 'unbridled hermeneutics,' much work followed from his, either overtly or as a result of its general influence. Mellers' concern with musical meaning has been explored by others, who have sought to systematize and theorize musical meaning through recourse to semiotics.

Semiotic methodology in mainstream music analysis can be highly formalist, seeking to discover the ways in which musical elements associate with or exclude each other through rules of distribution. With its focus on the internal relations of syntax, this approach, derived largely from linguistics and phonology, is associated mainly with theorists such as Jean-Jacques Nattiez (1990) and Nicholas Ruwet (1987). In addition to the formal dissection of musical patterns, semiotics also includes the study of connotative signifying processes (see Agawu 1991 for semiotic analyses of both syntactic and connotative levels of Western art music). The internalist approach to semiotics has not been widely applied to examples of popular music, while processes of 'secondary signification' or connotation have been more frequently and fruitfully applied, most notably in the work of Philip Tagg (1979, 1982, 1991), whose systematic exploration of connotation is innovative with respect to mainstream music analysis as well. There are many studies of a single genre that blend attention to connotative meaning with some type of analytical description: for example, the work of Whiteley on psychedelic rock (1992), Walser on heavy metal (1993) and rap (1995), and Moore on progressive rock (1993). There are also studies of a single artist, such as Winkler on Randy Newman (1987), Hawkins on Prince (1992) and Middleton on the Eurythmics (1995), as well as studies that compare styles in order to demonstrate how they signify in relation to one another (Brackett 1994, 1995, ch. 2).

Investigations of musical meaning that look at how the internal structure of musical syntax may create a form of meaning independent of connotative processes have begun examining the link between musical gestures and physical gestures in order to explore the connections between musical meaning and bodily movement. The object of these analyses may range from the physical disposition of performers in relation to one another, to their physical gestures as they perform, to the reactions of audience members, dancers and co-participants (Middleton 1990, 242–43). This approach moves close to an anthropological account of musical meaning and, consequently, it is one that has been explored most often by ethnomusicologists (see Keil 1966, ch. 5). Another approach examines how structures of primary signification may be homologous with internal affective states (Shepherd and Wicke 1997). With the exception of brief studies (such as Middleton 1993), music analysis focused on the signification of bodily gestures has yet to be carried out on individual songs, styles or genres, and, indeed, it is not yet clear what such an analysis would look like. This may be due to the fact that any attempt to execute such an analysis is bound to encounter the same institutional resistance that plagues the other innovative methodologies described earlier.

Bibliography

Agawu, Kofi. 1991. *Playing with Signs: A Semiotic Interpretation of Classic Music*. Princeton, NJ: Princeton University Press.

Bent, Ian. 1987. *Analysis*. New York: W.W. Norton and Co.

Boone, Graeme M. 1997. 'Tonal and Expressive Ambiguity in "Dark Star."' In *Understanding Rock: Essays in Musical Analysis*, ed. John Covach and Graham Boone. New York: Oxford University Press, 171–210.

Brackett, David. 1994. 'The Politics and Practice of "Crossover" in American Popular Music, 1963 to 1965.' *The Musical Quarterly* 78(4) (Winter): 774–97.

Brackett, David. 1995. *Interpreting Popular Music*. Cambridge: Cambridge University Press.

Brown, Matthew. 1997. '"Little Wing": A Study in Musical Cognition.' In *Understanding Rock: Essays in Musical Analysis*, ed. John Covach and Graham Boone. New York: Oxford University Press, 155–69.

Cogan, Robert. 1984. *New Images of Musical Sound*. Cambridge, MA: Harvard University Press.

Cook, Nicholas. 1987. *A Guide to Musical Analysis*. New York: W.W. Norton and Co.

Covach, John. 1997. 'Progressive Rock, "Close to the Edge," and the Boundaries of Style.' In *Understanding Rock: Essays in Musical Analysis*, ed. John Covach and Graham Boone. New York: Oxford University Press, 3–31.

Covach, John, and Boone, Graham, eds. 1997. *Understanding Rock: Essays in Musical Analysis*. New York: Oxford University Press.

Everett, Walter. 1995. 'The Beatles as Composers: The Genesis of *Abbey Road*, Side Two.' In *Concert Music, Rock, and Jazz Since 1945: Essays and Analytical Studies*, ed. Elizabeth West Marvin and Richard Hermann. Rochester, NY: University of Rochester Press, 172–228.

Forte, Allen. 1973. *The Structure of Atonal Music*. New Haven and London: Yale University Press.

Griffiths, Dai. 1988. 'Three Tributaries of "The River."' *Popular Music* 7(1): 27–34.

Hamm, Charles. 1979. *Yesterdays: Popular Song in America*. New York: Norton.

Hawkins, Stan. 1992. 'Prince: Harmonic Analysis of "Anna Stesia."' *Popular Music* 11(3): 325–35.

Headlam, Dave. 1995. 'Does the Song Remain the Same?: Questions of Authorship and Identification in the Music of Led Zeppelin.' In *Concert Music, Rock, and Jazz Since 1945: Essays and Analytical Studies*, ed. Elizabeth West Marvin and Richard Hermann. Rochester, NY: University of Rochester Press, 313–63.

Keil, Charles. 1966. *Urban Blues*. Chicago: University of Chicago Press.

Kerman, Joseph. 1985. *Contemplating Music: Challenges to Musicology*. Cambridge, MA: Harvard University Press.

Lomax, Alan. 1968. *Folk Song Style and Culture*. Washington, DC: American Association for the Advancement of Science.

Mellers, Wilfrid. 1973. *Twilight of the Gods: The Beatles in Retrospect*. London: Faber & Faber.

Middleton, Richard. 1990. *Studying Popular Music*. Milton Keynes and Philadelphia: Open University Press.

Middleton, Richard. 1993. 'Popular Music and Musicology: Bridging the Gap.' *Popular Music* 12(2): 177–90.

Middleton, Richard. 1995. 'Authorship, Gender, and the Construction of Meaning in the Eurythmics' Hit Recordings.' *Cultural Studies* 9(3): 465–85.

Moore, Allan. 1993. *Rock, The Primary Text: Developing a Musicology of Rock*. Milton Keynes and Philadelphia: Open University Press.

Moore, Allan. 1997. *The Beatles: 'Sgt. Pepper's Lonely Hearts Club Band'*. Cambridge: Cambridge University Press.

Nattiez, Jean-Jacques. 1990. *Music and Discourse: Toward a Semiology of Music*, trans. Carolyn Abbate. Princeton, NJ: Princeton University Press.

Ruwet, Nicholas. 1987. 'Methods of Analysis in Musicology.' *Music Analysis* 6: 11–36.

Seeger, Charles. 1977 (1966). 'Versions and Variants of "Barbara Allen" in the Archive of American Song to 1940.' In *Studies in Musicology 1935–1975*. Berkeley, CA: University of California Press, 273–320.

Shepherd, John. 1991. *Music as Social Text*. Cambridge: Polity Press.

Shepherd, John, and Wicke, Peter. 1997. *Music and Cultural Theory*. Cambridge: Polity Press.

Solie, Ruth. 1980. 'The Living Work: Organicism and Musical Analysis.' *Nineteenth-Century Music* 4: 147–56.

Tagg, Philip. 1979. *Kojak – 50 Seconds of Television Music: Toward the Analysis of Affect in Popular Music*. Göteborg: Skrifter från Musikvetenskapliga Institutionen, 2.

Tagg, Philip. 1982. 'Analysing Popular Music: Theory, Method, and Practice.' *Popular Music* 2: 37–68.

Tagg, Philip. 1991. *Fernando the Flute: Analysis of Musical Meaning in an Abba Mega-Hit*. Liverpool: Institute of Popular Music, University of Liverpool.

Walser, Robert. 1993. *Running with the Devil: Power, Gender and Madness in Heavy Metal Music*. Hanover and London: Wesleyan University Press.

Walser, Robert. 1995. 'Rhythm, Rhyme, and Rhetoric in the Music of Public Enemy.' *Ethnomusicology* 39(2): 193–217.

Whiteley, Sheila. 1992. *The Space Between the Notes: Rock and the Counter-Culture*. London: Routledge.

Winkler, Peter. 1987. 'Randy Newman's Americana.' *Popular Music* 7(1): 1–26.

Winkler, Peter. 1997. 'Writing Ghost Notes: The Poetics and Politics of Transcription.' In *Keeping Score: Music, Disciplinarity, Culture*, ed. David Schwarz, Anahid Kassabian and Lawrence Siegel. Charlottesville and London: University Press of Virginia, 169–203.

DAVID BRACKETT

Musicology

The term 'musicology' came into being to refer to the academic study of a particular tradition of music, the canon of European art music. The focal point for musicological studies was the use – within this tradition – of sound in ways regarded as distinctly musical (thus distinguishing such sound from the characteristic use of sound in language).

As musicology's traditional object of study began to expand in the second half of the twentieth century to include other traditions of music, the distinguishing features of musicology became twofold: firstly, a continuing anchoring of musicological studies in the musical use of sound; secondly, the undertaking of musicological research and writing by scholars trained in academic music.

These two features distinguish musicology and its practise from the academic study of music by other kinds of scholars, such as sociologists and scholars of communication. Here, the focus is less often that of the canon of European art music ('classical' music). Further, the traditional preoccupation is with contextual features of musical practise such as the social, the cultural, the economic and the political, rather than with the distinctive use of sound within music.

The predominant features of musicology have caused the discipline to exercise comparatively little influence on popular music studies. This is in contrast to most other disciplines and intellectual trajectories that have featured in the study of popular music. These have more influenced popular music studies than they have been influenced by them. By comparison, musicology has been significantly influenced in *its* development since the late 1970s by the advent of popular music studies. It is in this respect that the relationship between musicology and popular music studies has been quite distinctive.

The Discipline of Musicology

Musicology as an academic discipline first developed in Germany. However, the study of music is very old and goes back beyond the time of the ancient Greeks. Furthermore, the study of music, the writing of scholarly works on music and the giving of music history lectures took place in Europe, and in countries other than Germany, before the foundation of musicology as a discipline. This notwithstanding, the roots of musicology's establishment as an institutionalized academic discipline are to be found in the formation of a German national identity during the nineteenth century (Germany became a nation-state in 1871). Integral to the formation of this identity was the development of a German culture capable of transcending the more parochial political interests of the small, independent and semi-independent principalities and municipalities that constituted the geographical area that was to become Germany at this time. The formal development of musicology, or *Musikwissenschaft*, took place in this context. Indeed, the installation of Carl Breidenstein as the first teaching chair or professor of music in Bonn in 1826 was in response to an expressed need to provide a body of knowledge and a theoretically grounded system of aesthetic values that could guide the writing of music reviews in the press. Out of these activities came the formation of a canon of European music in which German music figured prominently. This canon fulfilled the desire of the bourgeoisie of this part of Europe to establish a common culture that would give them a clear sense of collective identity. The idea of a clear and unbroken tradition of 'German music' from J.S. Bach to Richard Wagner and Johannes Brahms, which did not exist before this time, was a consequence of, rather than a reason for, this canon formation.

The term '*Musikwissenschaft*' was established as the

name of this new discipline through the foundation in 1885 of a journal, *Vierteljahrsschrift für Musikwissenschaft* (Musicology Journal), by Friedrich Chrysander, Philipp Spitta and Guido Adler. It was in the first issue of this journal that Adler published his famous article, 'Umfang, Methode und Ziel der Musikwissenschaft' ('The Scope, Method and Aim of *Musikwissenschaft*'). The article became extremely influential as a summation and projection of the processes of mapping this new field of study which had been going on since the mid-nineteenth century.

Adler's mapping drew a basic distinction between *Historische Musikwissenschaft* (historical musicology) and *Systematische Musikwissenschaft* (systematic musicology). The various approaches to the writing of music history evident in *Musikwissenschaft*'s early days gradually came to be subsumed under the concept of the *Geist*, or spirit, and so of *Geistesgeschiche*: literally, spirit history, or the history of the spirit. It was through this emphasis on *Geist* as opposed to *Körper*, the body, that the essence of a music conceived in the image of an emerging German national identity could over time be distilled from the more general context of European music. The construction of such an historical narrative required that music be conceived as autonomous in its relation to surrounding circumstances. If it could be accepted that music's intrinsic characteristics were essentially unaffected by the circumstances of its creation and appreciation, then the possibility existed for the judgments of historians and scholars to be accepted as just as valid as, if not more so than, those of the composers, entrepreneurs, musicians, music critics and audiences involved with the actual lives of musical works. The authority of these decontextualized judgments was fundamental to the ability to create a canon of German music. Accordingly, Adler's concept of *Systematische Musikwissenschaft* was based on the notion that, in an ahistorical fashion, musical works could be entities unto themselves, capable of being analyzed and understood in almost complete isolation from their surrounding circumstances.

Adler's scheme became extremely influential. It took on the mantle of a canon, and came to be presented as the self-evident and unquestioned way of thinking about and organizing scholarly work on music. It was based on and came to entrench the idea that music as an art form was contained within the parameters of the sounds that embodied it. This concept required a strict differentiation between *music*, whose intrinsic characteristics became the subject matter of *Systematische Musikwissenschaft*, and a 'music' that could only become apparent in *Historische Musikwissenschaft* through biography and the discussion of spiritually encapsulated ideas.

Adler's thinking as reflective of and embodied within German-language musicology came to have a constitutive influence on the development of English-language musicology. In the case of the United States in particular, this was due to the influx of German-language musicologists who emigrated in the 1930s and 1940s in the face of the rise of fascism. Translating within English-language contexts into historical musicology (*Historische Musikwissenschaft*) and music theory and music analysis (*Systematische Musikwissenschaft*), Adler's mapping gave rise to an irreconcilable chasm between *music*, the characteristics of music's sounds, and 'music,' the decontextualized spiritual meanings emanating from such sounds. Crossing this divide to re-integrate these two concepts of music became not only extremely difficult as a consequence of Adler's intellectual mapping, but almost impossible because of the way in which this mapping provided the basis for the organization of musicology in institutional terms. Challenging this mapping came to require not only intellectual imagination, therefore, but also a willingness to contest institutional forms that had behind them the weight of history and the power of social legitimacy. It is in part for these reasons that the logic of Adler's mapping far outlasted the historical circumstances of its creation.

Musicology and Popular Music

The term 'musicology' carries with it a certain ambivalence. It is the nearest translation that has existed in English for the all-encompassing notion of *Musikwissenschaft*. More recently, terms such as 'music studies' have been used to indicate this sense of comprehensiveness. However, within the world of academic music, 'musicology' has more often been used as shorthand for 'historical musicology,' thus excluding the disciplines of music theory and music analysis – disciplines with which historical musicology had only the most distant of relations until the latter years of the twentieth century. Within the world of popular music studies, 'musicology' has generally – if a little imprecisely – been used to signal the increasingly related worlds of historical musicology, music theory and music analysis, but usually without the inclusion of the discipline of ethnomusicology, which itself has exercised an important and distinctive influence on popular music studies since the late 1980s.

Whatever its guise, however, musicology proved intransigently inhospitable to the study of popular music until the latter years of the twentieth century. This was for two related reasons. Firstly, popular music was presumed to be inherently inferior to the music of the canon. Indeed, the term 'popular music' came into being during the nineteenth century as part of the politics of the creation of a high-culture canon of art music with German music at its center. Popular music was contrasted with the presumed authenticity of art music on the one hand and folk music on the other. The terms and ideas of both 'high-culture' (later, 'classical') and 'folk' music were created in part as a reaction to the rise of an increasingly industrialized society and, concomitantly, mass-mediated forms of culture. The presumed 'purity' of the folk – idealized precursors of the industrial age – stood in marked contrast to the perceived threats of that age. However, as Middleton (1990) has observed, 'this "folk" never existed' (129). The supposed purity of folk society together with the presumed authenticity of its music are both myths. 'Culturally,' Middleton writes, 'they originate in the romantic critique of industrial society; politically they derive from the bourgeoisie's attempt to make such critique comfortable, providing an ideologically functioning fantasy which can be used to counter the threat of real workers' culture' (1990, 139). As Middleton concludes, 'The judgement of "authenticity" is always directed at the practice of someone else. Either it removes this practice from its own mode of existence and annexes it to the system of an imperialist cultural morality, or it scapegoats undesirable ("inauthentic") practices and casts them beyond the pale' (1990, 139). Such was the fate of popular music. It could not, by definition, be part of the canon. As such, it could find no place within musicology.

The second reason for the exclusion of popular music was its self-evident social character. Indeed, popular music's social character and importance were, in the view of high-culture critics, the hallmark of its inherent inferiority. However, more was at stake than just the incursion of an inferior cultural form. The social dimensions that popular music could not have helped but bring into the academy would have challenged the very notion of the autonomous art form on which musicology as a discipline was founded. In other words, if musicology could somehow have accommodated intellectually the social character of popular music, it would at the same time have opened the door to a social reading of the canon. This would have made evident the possibility that the music of the canon was no less social than popular music, seriously if not fatally compromising the assumptions on which the presumed superiority of the music of the canon rested. Finally, in leading to a conception of both *music* and 'music' as phenomena that are socially constituted, the study of popular music within musicology could have provided a basis for the reconciliation of historical musicology and music theory. In effecting such a reconciliation, the study of popular music could have led to the collapse of the very

foundations on which musicology as a discipline was built.

It is thus easy to see why the study of popular music was not readily accepted within musicology. However, the situation began to change toward the end of the 1970s, in part because a number of scholars imbued with the musical and cultural experiences of the 1960s obtained positions within the academic world. This occurrence in many ways mirrored the way in which jazz, vilified by moral and cultural guardians in the United States between the 1920s and the 1940s (see, for example, Merriam 1964, 241–42), came to gain acceptance in the academy in the period immediately following World War II, as scholars raised on jazz achieved positions of influence in universities (see Leonard 1962).

The case for the inclusion of popular music as a legitimate object of study for musicology rested in turn on arguments aimed at changing the character of musicology as a discipline (see, for example, Shepherd et al. 1977; Small 1977). The inhospitality of musicology as a home for the study of popular music rested not only on political and institutional considerations, but also on intellectual ones. In a seminal ethnography of bikeboy and hippie cultures that includes a technical (that is to say, musicological) analysis of the preferred musics of these cultures, Willis (1978) makes the observation that 'a really adequate account of the internal parameters of the bikeboys' preferred music and its specific ability to hold and retain particular social meanings must be more technically rigorous than [it] has been.' Willis concludes that 'musicology is the discipline which has the formal resources for this task' (76). Commenting on Willis's assertion, Shepherd (1982) observes that it 'is unfounded in two respects. Firstly ... the analytic tools available from ... musicology are not necessarily appropriate to the task. Second, even if such tools were appropriate, they would not address the central question of how music articulates from within its very structure social and cultural meaning' (148).

The analytic tools available from musicology (more precisely, from music theory and music analysis) are grounded in and developed from a notational encapsulation of the music of the canon. This 'notational centricity,' as Tagg has called it (see Tagg 1979, 28–32), renders these tools unsuitable for the analysis of many forms of popular music. They tend to foreground elements such as those of the relatively fixed pitches symptomatic of melody and harmony in the classical tradition, as well as those of the mathematically simple durational relationships that comprise classical rhythms. Much popular music evidences heavily inflected and 'unstable' pitches, and rhythms that are markedly nuanced, irrational and polyrhythmic in character.

These are musical features for which the traditional analytic tools of music theory are ill suited. Further, these tools have virtually nothing to say about timbres – individualized timbres or 'sounds' being a hallmark of most forms of popular music – or more recently developed recording studio techniques such as reverberation, phasing, wah-wah and fuzz. Add to this musicology's historical inability to conceptualize music as socially constituted, and the intellectual difficulties facing musicologists who might want to study popular music become apparent.

These difficulties are evident in some musicological work on popular music that has nonetheless been extremely important in opening up the discipline of musicology to this new object of study. As Middleton has observed, 'Terminology; methodology; ideology: the effects of these three interlinked aspects of the "musicological problem" run so deep that they can be found even in the work – often very useful work – of scholars sympathetic to, and knowledgeable about, popular music' (1990, 108). In discussing in this vein the work of Wilder (1972), Hamm (1979) and Mellers (1973, 1984), therefore, Middleton's purpose is not 'criticism for criticism's sake,' but to 'try to reveal the ideological underpinnings of the assumptions shared by all those trained in the traditional musicological disciplines' (1990, 114).

It is this musicological legacy that has led Frith (1990) to observe that 'so much musicological analysis of popular music misses the point: its object of study, the discursive text it constructs, is not the text to which anyone listens' (97). McClary and Walser (1990) have made a similar point in a more extended discussion. There has, in other words, been more of a tendency for musicology to construct popular music in its own traditional image than for popular music to effect changes in musicology. This has applied to the world of production as well as to that of consumption. Hennion (1990), for example, has argued that 'a musicological assessment cannot explain why certain songs are successful and why most others fail' (186).

However, this sense that musicology has constructed an object of study to which few people listen has found a wider resonance within musicology itself. It was this sense that 'something was missing' that led McClary (1991) to develop a critical feminist musicology in which popular music has featured prominently. McClary reveals that she 'was drawn to music because it is the most compelling cultural form I know. I wanted evidence that the overwhelming responses I experience with music are not just in my own head, but rather are shared. I entered musicology because I believed that it would be dedicated . . . to explaining how music manages to create such effects' (4). What she found, however, was that

'musicology fastidiously declares issues of musical signification to be off-limits to those engaged in legitimate scholarship.' McClary concludes: '[Musicology] has seized disciplinary control over the study of music and has prohibited the asking of even the most fundamental questions concerning meaning. Something terribly important is being hidden away by the profession, and I have always wanted to know why' (1991, 4).

What has been at stake is something highlighted by popular music, but by no means exclusive to it: the way that people use and relate to music in their everyday lives. As McClary has elsewhere observed (1990), 'Most people care about music because it resonates with experiences that otherwise go unarticulated, whether it is the flood of cathartic release that occurs at the climax of a Tchaikowsky symphony or the groove that causes one's body to dance.' However, she continues, 'our music theories and notational systems do everything possible to mask those dimensions of music that are related to physical human experience and focus instead on the orderly, the rational, the cerebral.' As McClary concludes, 'The fact that the majority of listeners engage with music for more immediate purposes is frowned upon by our institutions' (1990, 14).

It is the importance of the self-evidently social and corporeal to many forms of popular music that has enabled a number of musicologists concerned with popular music to contribute to the development of musicology in ways that transcend the popular as more narrowly conceived. This work has been varied, from Tagg's groundbreaking work in semiology (1979, 1991), to Middleton's magisterial critical assessment of popular music studies (1990), to McClary's incisive feminist intervention (1991), to Walser's combining of cultural theory, music analysis and experience as a performer (1993). It is paradoxical, perhaps, that much, but certainly not all, of the work in this vein has been significantly theoretical and not always easy to access. However, the apparently simple issue of how people use music in their everyday lives can pose many difficult and complex questions.

Popular music studies has certainly not been alone in causing a sea change in the discipline of musicology. Ethnomusicology has been at least as influential, and over a longer period of time. But it has largely been popular music studies that has lent an increasingly critical edge to musicology. As one, younger member of the profession recently observed, 'Theory came to me; I did not come to it. Indeed it was hard to avoid' (McClatchie 2000, 17). This is certainly not a statement that would have been encountered in the discipline much before the end of the twentieth century. However, as the 1990s progressed, the confluence between musicologists, ethnomusicologists and those trained in other disciplines studying popular music became stronger. The writings on popular music of those with an interdisciplinary training as musicologists and ethnomusicologists became more difficult to distinguish from those of scholars trained in other disciplines and intellectual trajectories.

While, in the end, such disciplinary distinctions should not matter in the study of popular music, one distinctly musicological issue can be argued to remain: that of the specific character of sounds recognized as musical within popular music. This, perhaps, is enough to continue to map out for musicology a distinctive, disciplinary role in the essentially interdisciplinary undertaking of popular music studies (see, for example, Shepherd 1999; Shepherd and Wicke 1997; Wicke 1990).

Bibliography

Adler, Guido. 1885. 'Umfang, Methode und Ziel der Musikwissenschaft' [The Scope, Method and Aim of *Musikwissenschaft*]. *Vierteljahrsschaft für Musikwissenschaft* 1: 5–8, 15–20.

Frith, Simon. 1990. 'What Is Good Music?' *Canadian University Music Review/Revue de musique des universités canadiennes* 10(2): 92–102.

Hamm, Charles. 1979. *Yesterdays: Popular Song in America*. New York: W.W. Norton.

Hennion, Antoine. 1990 (1983). 'The Production of Success: An Antimusicology of the Pop Song.' In *On Record: Rock, Pop, and the Written Word*, ed. Simon Frith and Andrew Goodwin. New York: Pantheon Books, 185–206.

Leonard, Neil. 1962. *Jazz and the White Americans: The Acceptance of a New Art Form*. Chicago: University of Chicago Press.

McClary, Susan. 1990. 'Towards a Feminist Criticism of Music.' *Canadian University Music Review/Revue de musique des universités canadiennes* 10(2): 9–18.

McClary, Susan. 1991. *Feminine Endings: Music, Gender, and Sexuality*. Minneapolis, MN: University of Minnesota Press.

McClary, Susan, and Walser, Robert. 1990 (1988). 'Start Making Sense!: Musicology Wrestles with Rock.' In *On Record: Rock, Pop, and the Written Word*, ed. Simon Frith and Andrew Goodwin. New York: Pantheon Books, 277–92.

McClatchie, Stephen. 2000. 'Theory's Children; or, The New Relevance of Musicology.' *Canadian University Music Review/Revue de musique des universités canadiennes* 21(1): 14–27.

Mellers, Wilfrid. 1973. *Twilight of the Gods: The Beatles in Retrospect*. London: Faber & Faber.

Mellers, Wilfrid. 1984. *A Darker Shade of Pale: A Backdrop to Bob Dylan*. New York: Oxford University Press.

Merriam, Alan P. 1964. *The Anthropology of Music*. Evanston, IL: Northwestern University Press.

Middleton, Richard. 1990. *Studying Popular Music*. Milton Keynes and Philadelphia: Open University Press.

Shepherd, John. 1982. 'A Theoretical Model for the Sociomusicological Analysis of Popular Musics.' *Popular Music* 2: 145–77.

Shepherd, John. 1999. 'Text.' In *Key Terms in Popular Music and Culture*, ed. Bruce Horner and Thomas Swiss. Malden, MA: Blackwell Publishers, 156–77.

Shepherd, John, and Wicke, Peter. 1997. *Music and Cultural Theory*. Cambridge: Polity Press.

Shepherd, John, et al. 1977. *Whose Music?: A Sociology of Musical Languages*. London: Latimer New Dimensions.

Small, Christopher. 1977. *Music, Society, Education: A Radical Examination of the Prophetic Function of Music in Western, Eastern and African Cultures with Its Impact on Society and Its Use in Education*. London: John Calder.

Tagg, Philip. 1979. *Kojak – 50 Seconds of Television Music: Toward the Analysis of Affect in Popular Music*. Göteborg: Skrifter från Musikvetenskapliga Institutionen, 2.

Tagg, Philip. 1991. *Fernando the Flute: Analysis of Musical Meaning in an Abba Mega-Hit*. Liverpool: Institute of Popular Music, University of Liverpool.

Walser, Robert. 1993. *Running with the Devil: Power, Gender and Madness in Heavy Metal Music*. Hanover and London: Wesleyan University Press.

Wicke, Peter. 1990. 'Rock Music: Dimensions of a Mass Medium – Meaning Production Through Popular Music.' *Canadian University Music Review/Revue de musique des universités canadiennes* 10(2): 137–56.

Wilder, Alec. 1972. *American Popular Song: The Great Innovators, 1900–1950*. New York: Oxford University Press.

Willis, Paul E. 1978. *Profane Culture*. London: Routledge and Kegan Paul.

JOHN SHEPHERD and PETER WICKE

Music Theory

The term 'music theory' denotes the abstract principles embodied in music and the sounds of which music consists. Virtually all musicians use some sort of abstraction to describe their musical activities and, in this sense, one could argue that all musicians and musics employ a form of music theory. In practise, 'music theory' in the Western context refers to a particular set of abstractions, developed largely to describe and analyze Western art music, that includes the properties of a single sound – pitch, duration, timbre – and those of collections of sounds – acoustics, intervals, scales, modes, melody, harmony, rhythm, form and analysis. The term also refers to the teaching of the fundamentals of music – again, usually as they pertain to Western art music. 'Music analysis' is usually understood as a branch of music theory, and refers to the study of individual pieces, performances and recordings.

According to these understandings of the term 'music theory,' analogous types of music theory exist in the 'high culture' traditions of East Asia, South Asia, Southeast Asia and the Arabic world. Ethnomusicologists studying non-Western musics have either applied theoretical frameworks drawn from Western music, used indigenous theory developed for art music or tried to formulate abstractions based on indigenous musical practises and values. Here, the focus will be on the applications of Western music theory to the study of popular music, because that has been the type of music theory used by the vast majority of scholars working in the field.

Although music theory existed in the West as far back as ancient Greece, music-theoretical writings for the most part either dealt with the raw materials of music or functioned as guidelines for composition until the late eighteenth century, when music theory began to be used to analyze individual works. Initially, the metaphor of music-as-rhetoric figured prominently in analyses, and provided a way of elucidating music as a process produced within a set of socially understood conventions. However, by the second third of the nineteenth century, analyses focused increasingly on musical structure and on the organic relationship of the parts of a piece to the whole. A spatial metaphor such as 'structure' had the effect of de-emphasizing temporal metaphors such as 'rhetoric' and, consequently, of focusing theoretical attention on the notated template for musical performance known as the 'score.' In the score, the representations of sound in musical notation convey information about pitch more accurately than information about rhythm, dynamics, timbre and articulation; notational emphasis thus results from, at the same time as it contributes to, an emphasis on pitch in both compositional pedagogy and analytical study.

Music-theoretical work on popular music has tended to be of the analytical sort, although there have been a few attempts to formulate abstract principles governing music materials that are specific to popular music, as in the work of Moore (1992, 1993, 1995) and Winkler (1978). This analytical work can be divided roughly into two categories: work that accepts the basic aesthetic and methodological assumptions of Western music theory; and work that calls these assumptions into question. The work that uncritically accepts the basic tenets of Western music theory has tended to accommodate popular music to some notion of a canon of masterworks through either 'legitimation' or 'pluralism.' 'Legitimation' works

by selecting music for analysis that contains a type of complexity that responds well to techniques designed for Western art music: musical subjects include jazz, popular song of the 'golden era' of Tin Pan Alley, the Beatles and progressive rock, all subjects containing a relatively high degree of harmonic complexity and, occasionally, of formal complexity as well. Sheet music or transcriptions are typically used to show sophisticated pitch relationships which, it is implied, are every bit as worthy of study as those found in the masterpieces. A 'pluralistic' approach begins by accepting popular music as a legitimate subject of study alongside other musics without interrogating either how conventional musicological techniques automatically make noncanonical musics appear less interesting, or what the social relationships are between the different musics.

Theoretical work that calls musicological assumptions into question tends to begin with a critique of work that does not. These critiques point out that a reliance on musical notation and conventional analytical methodologies produces an emphasis on pitch relations that puts much popular music at a disadvantage. This emphasis misses much of what is important, especially in African-American-derived musics, white 'country' musics, and most North American and British popular music since the mid-1950s. Analytical methods derived from the study of musical scores tend to ignore such elements as microtonal bends and slides, slight rhythmic anticipations and hesitations, personalized and highly varying timbres, heterophonic textures, processual group interaction and the effect of specific performances, arguably all elements as important as pitch relations to both musicians and audiences who participate in popular music. Furthermore, the critique of formalist analyses has extended beyond explicating the inadequacies of specific methodologies to the idea that it is inappropriate either to analyze a popular song (or any piece of music, for that matter) as an autonomous entity or to regard 'meaning' as consisting solely of relationships internal to the piece of music under consideration.

In seeking to develop alternative approaches to traditional analysis, music scholars have adapted concepts and techniques from music theory for their correspondence to musical values that arise in different contexts of production and reception. At the same time, scholars have attempted to consider meaning as part of larger social and historical categories such as genre, style, performer biography and visual image, the role of the music industry, and the role of music in identity formation as it pertains to race, ethnicity, gender and sexuality. This involves moving away from studying musical meaning in a strictly syntactic sense to engaging with meaning in both a semantic and a sociocultural sense. This scholarly work has been overtly interdisciplinary, looking to use music-theoretical methodologies in conjunction with semiotics, psychoanalysis and a wide range of social and political theories. Scholars engaged in this type of work have encountered many of the same difficulties in analyzing musical processes as have ethnomusicologists, who have tended to study art musics outside Western Europe, and traditional or 'folk' musics. Ethnomusicologists have tried to establish the pertinence of their analytical techniques by reference to the cultural context, and to the meaning of the musical practises to participants, including both performers and audience members who are cultural 'insiders.' The situation becomes more complicated in the case of contemporary popular music, in which no simple one-to-one correspondence can be found between a style of music and a self-contained, culturally homogeneous audience (and, indeed, ethnomusicologists are questioning whether such a relationship is possible with any kind of music).

Although it is difficult to gauge the impact of popular music studies on the field of music theory, in general, popular music studies have participated in the rethinking of the field that is under way. This has frequently taken the form of expanding the canon of works to be studied through the processes of 'legitimation' and 'pluralism' noted here, or through an acknowledgment of the importance of contextual issues in establishing the pertinence of techniques used to analyze musical texts.

Bibliography

Bonds, Mark Evan. 1991. *Wordless Rhetoric: Musical Form and the Metaphor of the Oration*. Cambridge, MA: Harvard University Press.

Brackett, David. 1995. *Interpreting Popular Music*. Cambridge: Cambridge University Press.

Bradby, Barbara, and Torode, Brian. 1984. 'Pity Peggy Sue.' *Popular Music* 4: 183–206.

Chester, Andrew. 1990. 'Second Thoughts on a Rock Aesthetic: The Band.' In *On Record: Rock, Pop, and the Written Word*, ed. Simon Frith and Andrew Goodwin. New York: Pantheon Books, 315–19. (First published in *New Left Review* 62 (1970): 75–82.)

Covach, John, and Boone, Graham, eds. 1997. *Understanding Rock: Essays in Musical Analysis*. New York: Oxford University Press.

Cubitt, Sean. 1984. 'Maybellene: Meaning and the Listening Subject.' *Popular Music* 4: 207–24.

Hamm, Charles. 1995 (1988). 'Privileging the Moment of Reception: Music and Radio in South Africa.' In *Putting Popular Music in Its Place*. Cambridge: Cambridge University Press, 249–69.

Keil, Charles. 1994. 'Motion and Feeling Through Music.' In Charles Keil and Steven Feld, *Music Grooves: Essays and Dialogues*. Chicago and London: University of Chicago Press, 53–76. (First published in *Journal of Aesthetics and Art Criticism* 24 (Spring) (1966): 337–49.)

Kerman, Joseph. 1985. *Contemplating Music: Challenges to Musicology*. Cambridge, MA: Harvard University Press.

Marvin, Elizabeth West, and Hermann, Richard, eds. 1995. *Concert Music, Rock, and Jazz Since 1945: Essays and Analytical Studies*. Rochester, NY: University of Rochester Press.

McClary, Susan. 1991. *Feminine Endings: Music, Gender, and Sexuality*. Minneapolis, MN: University of Minnesota Press.

McClary, Susan, and Walser, Robert. 1990 (1988). 'Start Making Sense!: Musicology Wrestles with Rock.' In *On Record: Rock, Pop and the Written Word*, ed. Simon Frith and Andrew Goodwin. New York: Pantheon Books, 277–92.

Mellers, Wilfrid. 1973. *Twilight of the Gods: The Beatles in Retrospect*. London: Faber & Faber.

Middleton, Richard. 1990. *Studying Popular Music*. Milton Keynes and Philadelphia: Open University Press.

Moore, Allan. 1992. 'Patterns of Harmony.' *Popular Music* 11: 73–106.

Moore, Allan. 1993. *Rock, The Primary Text: Developing a Musicology of Rock*. Milton Keynes and Philadelphia: Open University Press.

Moore, Allan. 1995. 'The So-Called "Flattened Seventh" in Rock.' *Popular Music* 14: 185–201.

Shepherd, John. 1982. 'A Theoretical Model for the Sociomusicological Analysis of Popular Musics.' *Popular Music* 2: 145–77.

Tagg, Philip. 1979. *Kojak – 50 Seconds of Television Music: Toward the Analysis of Affect in Popular Music*. Göteborg: Skrifter från Musikvetenskapliga Institutionen, 2.

Tagg, Philip. 1982. 'Analysing Popular Music: Theory, Method, and Practice.' *Popular Music* 2: 37–68.

Walser, Robert. 1993. *Running with the Devil: Power, Gender and Madness in Heavy Metal Music*. Hanover and London: Wesleyan University Press.

Whiteley, Sheila. 1992. *The Space Between the Notes: Rock and the Counter-Culture*. London: Routledge.

Wilder, Alec. 1972. *American Popular Song: The Great Innovators, 1900–1950*. New York: Oxford University Press.

Winkler, Peter. 1978. 'Toward a Theory of Pop Harmony.' *In Theory Only* 4: 3–26.

DAVID BRACKETT

Political Economy

Introduction

The general perspectives present within political economy, together with some of the specific concepts these include, have been a continuing presence within popular music studies, particularly where considerations of the character and influence of the music industry are concerned. In order to situate examples of such work satisfactorily, it is first necessary to briefly sketch the nature and history of political economy and its influence on cultural and media studies in general.

History

In the eighteenth century, 'political economy' was the term used for the field of study that became 'economics' in the late nineteenth century. The field developed in response to the emergence of mercantilism and then capitalism as the dominant economic force in Europe. The growth of markets and the state raised questions about the relationship of the individual to the social order. The theoretical bases of political economy embraced the concepts of social class, the value and division of labor, and such moral dimensions as the nature and operation of self-interest. In his hugely influential book *An Inquiry into the Nature and Causes of the Wealth of Nations* (1776), Adam Smith argued that individuals were usually the best judge of their own interests, and that a freely competitive economic system would result in benefits for the community as a whole.

While advocates of such pluralist economics largely viewed the 'economy' as a separate domain, other political economists argued for its inseparability from society. In part a critical analysis of classical political economy's belief in the power of market forces, Marx's *Critique of Political Economy* emphasized class struggle as the crucial dynamic in capitalist development. Political economy subsequently became associated with particular variants of economics, and was often used as a code word for Marxism. Classical Marxist political economy tended to devalue the significance of culture, seeing it primarily as a reflection of the economic base. With regard to the mass media, this view was given its fullest expression, though in a more sophisticated form, in the work of the Frankfurt School, especially that of Adorno.

Later variants of political economy have aspired to develop 'an integrated field that encompasses the specialised disciplines of politics, economics and international relations' (Gill and Law 1988, xviii; see also Garnham 1990; Jhally 1989). Contemporary political economy has been interested in 'the interplay between economic organisation and political, social and cultural life' (Golding and Murdoch 1997, 18). Such an approach has frequently labeled itself 'critical political economy,' to distinguish and distance itself from what it has considered the 'cruder' formulations of classical (Marxist) political economy.

Both variants of political economy have required analysis of the way in which politics shapes the economy and vice versa. Accordingly, contemporary political economy has explored such issues as: the place of the economy within the larger social system; the importance of market institutions for individual autonomy; private enterprise and capitalism as systems of economic development; poverty and inequality in market economies; global patterns of wealth and inequality; and the limits of the market and the role of government (Levine 1995).

Political Economy of the Media

Political economy has constituted a major dimension of critical communications studies, embodying a skepticism toward business and the state and embracing a commitment to greater social equality and democracy. The application of political economy to the study of the media has had as its starting point the fact that the producers of mass media are industrial institutions, essentially driven by the logic of capitalism – the pursuit of maximum profit. The 'culture industries' are those economic institutions that employ the characteristic modes of production and organization of industrial corporations to produce and disseminate symbols in the form of cultural goods and services, generally, although not exclusively, as commodities (Garnham 1990).

In a synthesis of a series of French studies of cultural production, and taking issue with the earlier arguments of Adorno and Horkheimer, Miège (1989) argues that 'the cultural industries and communication technologies are at the heart of the re-structuration of the management of labor in the Western capitalist societies, and are very related to the current transformation in the exercise of political power' (13). He documents the manner in which new 'social logics' emerge from this process, especially in relation to the valorization of capital and social reproduction.

That these culture industries are owned and controlled by a relatively small number of people, and show a marked tendency toward increased concentration, has been seen as creating a situation involving considerable ideological power – the media as 'consciousness industries.' Schiller (1996) traces the pervasive and increasing inequality in access to information and cultural products as a consequence of the commercialization and privatization of broadcasting, libraries, institutions of higher education and other areas of public discourse. Commenting on the United States, Bagdikian (1997) observes how 'a small number of the country's largest industrial corporations have acquired more public communications power than any private business has ever before possessed in world history,' together creating 'a new communications cartel within the United States' (243). The fact that the music industry has been part of this process of the consolidation of 'imperial corporations' (Barnet and Cavanagh 1994) has raised issues concerning control of the media and in whose interests they operate, and the relationship between diversity and innovation in the market.

Political Economy and Popular Music Studies

Political economy has been a central feature of analyses of the operation of the music industry, especially its sound recording companies. It has also been significant in studies of music and cultural imperialism/globalization, MTV-style television, and state and local government policy toward popular music. It should be noted, however, that many of the authors of these studies are informed by political economy, rather than consciously and fully working within its traditional, more Marxist-oriented, variants.

Studies of the music industry have often fallen into one of two broad categories: those that emphasize corporate power; and those that, critiquing this, emphasize the active role of the consumers of popular music. A 'middle ground' has also emerged, informed by critical political economy, which views the industry as in a state of tension between these two polarities (see Sanjek 1997 for a useful overview of 'divergent approaches to the music industry').

The image of a powerful, corporate, capitalist music industry, able to manipulate and even construct markets and audiences, has its antecedents in the work of the Frankfurt School theorists, who reduced the music industry to the organizational conventions and commercial logic of capitalism (Adorno 1941, 1991). Contemporary variants have made much of how the music business has become an integral part of a global network of leisure and entertainment corporations, typified by a quest for media synergy and profit maximization (see Burnett 1996; Barnet and Cavanagh 1994; Rosselson 1979).

A number of studies from the 1970s and 1980s emphasize the power of the corporate music industry, a view encapsulated in their titles: *Rock 'n' Roll Is Here to Pay* (Chapple and Garofalo 1977); *One for the Money* (Harker 1980); and *Rockonomics* (Eliot 1989). Chapple and Garofalo, for example, argue that the concentration of ownership among the major record companies enables capitalist corporations to 'colonise leisure,' and that the music business is 'firmly part of the American corporate structure' (1977, 300). While these studies focus on mass-produced popular music in largely Western contexts, studies of the production of music in non-Western societies show a similar pattern (Wallis and Malm 1984; Manuel 1995; Robinson, Buck and Cuthbert 1991). However, these writers do allow some limited cul-

tural space for consumer autonomy, the autonomy of the 'local' and the radical potential of popular music. Frith (1988) adopts a more culturally pessimistic view, arguing that the 'relations of cultural production determine the possibilities of cultural consumption' (5). A related but more journalistic body of work has exposed the graft and corruption in the music industry, features viewed as a byproduct of its preoccupation with profit-making (Goodman 1997; Dannen 1990).

Critics of the 'corporate power' position have observed that it can all too easily slip into a form of economic determinism, married to a form of capitalist conspiracy theory – one that sees culture as produced by the economic base and omits any sense of culture's relative autonomy as part of the superstructure. Instead, they have stressed the consumption of popular music as an active, rather than a passive, process (for example, Chambers 1985), and have identified the many instances of oppositional politics in popular music. Most importantly, they have emphasized the tensions and contradictions at work within the music industry. Lash and Urry (1994), for example, postulate that a process of 'vertical disintegration' has occurred, with new, flexible post-Fordist production arrangements emerging in the cultural industries, including music.

At the heart of the debate between the two views has been the issue of the influence and nature of concentration: how does music industry concentration affect the range of opportunities available to musicians and others involved in the production of popular music, and the nature and range of products available to the consumers of popular music? Initial analyses of the relationship between concentration, innovation and diversity in popular music suggested a negative relationship between concentration and diversity in the (Western-dominated) international record industry, relating this to a pattern of market cycles (Peterson and Berger 1975; Rothenbuhler and Dimmick 1982). This view was challenged by Lopes (1992): he argues that a very high level of concentration is accompanied by a high level of diversity, and concludes that innovation and diversity in popular music in a period of high market concentration depend on the system of development and production used by major record companies (see also Burnett 1996).

Subsequent music industry studies have revisited, reworked and revitalized the political economy tradition to develop a 'middle way' between the polarities of corporate power and consumer autonomy. Greater attention has been paid to the filtering processes that are at work before a particular piece of music reaches the charts (Blake 1992; Cusic 1995; Sanjek 1988). For example, Christianen (1995) points to the importance of the number of decision-makers within a firm as a variable in explaining the diversity and innovation generated by a major record company.

Negus has been a key contributor to this approach. In a detailed account of the music industry in the United Kingdom (1992), his central concern is the process of discovery and development of recording artists, which he uses 'as an organising principle to provide a more general account of the recording industry and the production of pop music' (vi). He draws on Bourdieu's (1984) notion of 'cultural intermediaries,' which he sees as more flexible than the traditional concept of 'gate-keepers,' to examine the role of personnel in the music industry in terms of their active role in the production and promotion of particular artists and styles of music.

While Negus stresses the anarchic aspect of many of these industry practises, which he sees as the result of the essential uncertainty endemic to the music business, he also demonstrates how the industry 'has come to favour certain types of music, particular working practices and quite specific ways of acquiring, marketing and promoting artists' (1992, vii). Such established modes of operating work against the employment of new artists and women, and the promotion of styles outside the historically legitimated white rock mainstream. This view is confirmed in studies of the operation of particular record companies, including the 'independents' (Lee 1995; Hesmondhalgh 1997), the marketing of specific genres, notably 'world music' (Garofalo 1993; Mitchell 1996, ch. 2) and North America's black popular music tradition (Garofalo 1994; George 1988; Neal 1997), and artists' engagement with the recording process.

Although Negus is at pains to emphasize 'the cultural worlds being lived and constantly remade, highlighting the webs of relationships and multiple dialogues along and around which the musical and visual identities of pop artists are composed and communicated' (1992, vii; see also Negus 1996, chs. 2 and 3), his work has been subject to strong critique, notably from Harker (1997). Harker argues that Negus 'quietly absorbs the terminology (of the industry and the Harvard Business School) and *its ideological premises and implications* into his discourse' (1997, 47; italics in original). Harker reasserts the value of the classical Marxist critique, with an emphasis on disposable wealth, or the lack of it, and class location, in interpreting 'official' data on trends in the music industry.

Political Economy, MTV and the State

Two other areas of popular music studies informed by political economy have been the operation of MTV and similar cable/satellite music channels, and the state and music policy.

The study of MTV and music video has concentrated primarily on the music video as a form of audiovisual text, largely ignoring the industrial/social context within which they are situated. Instead, studies drawing on political economy have stressed the role of the music video as a promotional device, and the manner in which MTV and similar channels, along with music video programs within 'regular' television schedules, operate as gatekeepers. Banks (1996) concludes that major companies willingly edit videos on a regular basis to conform to MTV's standards, even coercing artists into making changes to song lyrics, while smaller, independent companies usually have difficulty in getting their videos on MTV. Lewis (1990) shows how the industrial practises of MTV operate to construct particular gender discourses and to address male adolescents as a preferred audience.

There have been a number of cases in which state and local government cultural policy has played a significant role in relation to popular music through economically and culturally motivated regulation and intervention. Trade tariffs, industry incentives and suchlike have been used, usually to defend national cultural production against the inflow of foreign media products. State and local governments have increasingly recognized the economic and social potential of popular music. The issues involved have included the defense of national identity, the protection of local markets and the consideration of the music industry as a site for youth employment (see the contributions to Bennett et al. 1993; Malm and Wallis 1992; Breen 1995; McLeay 1998). Several writers have raised the issue of the cultural implications of regional- and city-based music projects and policies (for example, Cohen 1991; Street 1993).

Authors of historical studies of popular music and the state have also necessarily engaged with political economy as an explanatory framework for their analyses. For example, Gaines (1992) examines intellectual property law and the contradictions in legal attempts to accommodate late capitalism. Her study attempts to explain how external changes in material production are reflected within internal structures of law and culture. She rejects Marxist political economy, with its emphasis on the determining role of the economic base, and proposes a more complex view of 'political, social, economic, legal and cultural forms as connected yet disconnected' (1992, 16). Gaines utilizes a dichotomy of the 'circulation-restriction' of cultural commodities to show how the corporate power of monopoly capitalism over signs, images and meanings is in contention with the doctrine of free enterprise within the law.

Kenney's history of the evolution of Chicago jazz (1993) details how a mix of council regulations, licensing law, police practises and moral watchdog organizations influenced the particular form taken by jazz in that city. In a similar project, Chevigny (1991) shows how successive New York City councils applied a network of zoning, fire, building and licensing regulations to control the venues and styles of jazz within the city. Homan (1998) demonstrates the complex relationship between city zoning, licensing and noise regulations in Sydney, Australia, the venues for rock and dance, and the styles of music associated with them.

Conclusion

Political economy has continued to inform popular music studies, but in a more complex fashion than the 'economicism' of many earlier studies. Contemporary approaches have examined popular music by asking of the music industry and of governmental institutions: Who produces the popular music text? For what audience, in what physical contexts and in whose interests? What is privileged, and what is excluded? Such interrogation has necessitated an examination of popular music media institutions in terms of their production practises, financial bases, technology and legislative frameworks, and their construction of audiences.

Bibliography

Adorno, Theodor W., with Simpson, George. 1941. 'On Popular Music.' *Studies in Philosophy and Social Sciences* 9: 17–48.

Adorno, Theodor W., with Simpson, George. 1991. *The Culture Industry: Selected Essays on Mass Culture*, ed. J. Bernstein. London: Routledge.

Bagdikian, B.H. 1997. *The Media Monopoly*. 5th ed. Boston, MA: Beacon Books.

Banks, J. 1996. *Monopoly Television: MTV's Quest to Control the Music*. Boulder, CO: Westview Press.

Barnet, Richard, and Cavanagh, John. 1994. *Global Dreams: Imperial Corporations and the New World Order*. New York: Simon & Schuster.

Bennett, Tony, et al., eds. 1993. *Rock and Popular Music: Politics, Policies, Institutions*. London: Routledge.

Blake, Andrew. 1992. *The Music Business*. London: Batsford.

Bourdieu, Pierre. 1984 (1979). *Distinction: A Social Critique of the Judgement of Taste*. London: Routledge.

Breen, Marcus. 1995. 'The End of the World as We Know It: Popular Music's Cultural Mobility.' *Cultural Studies* 9(3): 486–504.

Burnett, Robert. 1996. *The Global Jukebox: The International Music Industry*. London: Routledge.

Chambers, Iain. 1985. *Urban Rhythms: Pop Music and Popular Culture*. London: Macmillan.

Chapple, Steve, and Garofalo, Reebee. 1977. *Rock 'n' Roll Is Here to Pay: The History and Politics of the Music Industry*. Chicago: Nelson-Hall.

Chevigny, Paul. 1991. *Gigs: Jazz and the Cabaret Laws in New York City*. New York: Routledge.

Christianen, Michael. 1995. 'Cycles in Symbol Production?: A New Model to Explain Concentration, Diversity and Innovation in the Music Industry.' *Popular Music* 14(1): 55–94.

Cohen, Sara. 1991. *Rock Culture in Liverpool: Popular Music in the Making*. Oxford: Oxford University Press.

Cusic, Don. 1995. *Music in the Market*. Bowling Green, OH: Bowling Green University Popular Press.

Dannen, Fredric. 1990. *Hit Men: Power Brokers and Fast Money Inside the Music Business*. New York: Times Books.

De Meyer, Gust. 1996. 'Cultural Globalization and Local Identity: The Case of Belgian Popular Music.' *Popular Music & Society* 20(1) (Spring): 123–34.

Eliot, Marc. 1989. *Rockonomics: The Money Behind the Music*. New York: Franklin Watts.

Fink, Michael. 1989. *Inside the Music Business: Music in Contemporary Life*. New York: Schirmer/Macmillan.

Frith, Simon. 1988. *Music for Pleasure: Essays in the Sociology of Pop*. Cambridge: Polity Press.

Gaines, Jane. 1992. *Contested Culture: The Image, the Voice and the Law*. London: BFI Publishing.

Garnham, Nicholas. 1990. *Capitalism and Communication: Global Culture and the Economics of Information*. London: Sage.

Garofalo, Reebee. 1993. 'Whose World, What Beat: The Transnational Music Industry, Identity and Cultural Imperialism.' *The World of Music* 35(2): 16–32.

Garofalo, Reebee. 1994. 'Culture Versus Commerce: The Marketing of Black Popular Music.' *Public Culture* 7(1): 275–87.

George, Nelson. 1988. *The Death of Rhythm and Blues*. New York: Pantheon.

Gill, Stephen, and Law, David. 1988. *The Global Political Economy: Perspectives, Problems, and Policies*. New York and London: Harvester/Wheatsheaf.

Golding, Peter, and Murdoch, Graham, eds. 1997. *The Political Economy of the Media*, Vol. 1. Cheltenham: Elgar Publishing.

Goodman, Fred. 1997. *The Mansion on the Hill: Dylan, Young, Geffen, Springsteen, and the Head-On Collision of Rock and Commerce*. New York: Times Books.

Harker, Dave. 1980. *One for the Money: Politics and Popular Song*. London: Hutchinson.

Harker, Dave. 1997. 'The Wonderful World of the IFPI: Music Industry Rhetoric, the Critics and the Classical Marxist Critique.' *Popular Music* 16(1): 45–80.

Hayward, Philip. 1995. 'Enterprise on the New Frontier: Music, Industry and the Internet.' *Convergence* 1(2): 29–44.

Hesmondhalgh, David. 1996. 'Flexibility, Post-Fordism

and the Music Industries.' *Media, Culture and Society* 18(3) (July): 469–88.

Hesmondhalgh, David. 1997. 'Post-Punk's Attempt to Democratise the Music Industry: The Success and Failure of Rough Trade.' *Popular Music* 16(3): 255–74.

Homan, Shane. 1998. 'After the Law: Sydney's Phonecian Club, the New South Wales Premier and the Death of Anna Wood.' *Perfect Beat* 4(1) (July): 56–83.

Jhally, Sut. 1989. 'The Political Economy of Culture.' In *Cultural Politics in Contemporary America*, ed. Ian Angus and Sut Jhally. New York: Routledge, 65–81.

Kenney, William. 1993. *Chicago Jazz: A Cultural History, 1904–1930*. New York: Oxford University Press.

Laing, Dave. 1992. '"Sadeness," Scorpions and Single Markets: National and Transnational Trends in European Popular Music.' *Popular Music* 11(2): 127–39.

Lash, Scott, and Urry, John. 1994. *Economies of Signs and Space*. Thousand Oaks, CA: Sage.

Lee, Stephen. 1995. 'Re-examining the Concept of the "Independent" Record Company: The Case of Wax Trax! Records.' *Popular Music* 14(1): 13–23.

Levine, David P. 1995. *Wealth and Freedom: An Introduction to Political Economy*. Cambridge, MA: Cambridge University Press.

Lewis, Lisa. 1990. *Gender Politics and MTV: Voicing the Difference*. Philadelphia: Temple University Press.

Lopes, Paul. 1992. 'Innovation and Diversity in the Popular Music Industry.' *American Sociological Review* 57(1): 56–71.

Malm, Krister, and Wallis, Roger. 1992. *Media Policy and Music Activity*. London and New York: Routledge.

Manuel, Peter, with Bilby, Kenneth, and Largey, Michael. 1995. *Caribbean Currents: Caribbean Music from Rumba to Reggae*. Philadelphia: Temple University Press.

McLeay, Colin. 1998. *The Circuit of Popular Music*. Ph.D. thesis, Human Geography, School of Earth Sciences, Macquarie University, New South Wales, Australia.

Miège, Bernard. 1989. *The Capitalization of Cultural Production*. New York: International General.

Mitchell, Tony. 1996. *Popular Music and Local Identity: Rock, Pop and Rap in Europe and Oceania*. London: Leicester University Press.

Neal, Mark. 1997. 'Sold Out on Soul: The Corporate Annexation of Black Popular Music.' *Popular Music & Society* 21(3): 117–35.

Negus, Keith. 1992. *Producing Pop: Culture and Conflict in the Popular Music Industry*. London: Edward Arnold.

Negus, Keith. 1996. *Popular Music in Theory: An Introduction*. Cambridge: Polity Press.

Peterson, Richard A., and Berger, David G. 1975. 'Cycles in Symbol Production: The Case of Popular Music.' *American Sociological Review* 40: 158–73.

Robinson, Deanna Campbell, Buck, Elizabeth B., and Cuthbert, Marlene. 1991. *Music at the Margins: Popular Music and Global Cultural Diversity*. Newbury Park, CA: Sage Publications.

Rosselson, Leon. 1979. 'Pop Music: Mobiliser or Opiate?' In *Media, Politics and Culture*, ed. C. Gardner. London: Macmillan, 40–50.

Rothenbuhler, Eric, and Dimmick, John. 1982. 'Popular Music: Concentration and Diversity in the Industry, 1974–1980.' *Journal of Communication* 32: 143–49.

Rutten, Paul. 1991. 'Local Popular Music in the National and International Markets.' *Cultural Studies* 5(3) (October): 294–305.

Sanjek, Russell. 1988. *American Popular Music and Its Business: The First Four Hundred Years. Vol. III: From 1900 to 1984*. New York: Oxford University Press.

Sanjek, Russell. 1997. 'Funkentelechy vs. the Stockholm Syndrome: The Place of Industrial Analysis in Popular Music Studies.' *Popular Music & Society* 21(1): 73–92.

Schiller, Herbert. 1996. *Information Inequality: The Deepening Social Crisis in America*. New York: Routledge.

Street, John. 1993. 'Local Differences?: Popular Music and the Local State.' *Popular Music* 12(1): 43–56.

Wallis, Roger, and Malm, Krister. 1984. *Big Sounds from Small Peoples: The Music Industry in Small Countries*. London: Constable.

ROY SHUKER

Political Theory

Political science's contribution to the study of popular music has been smaller than that of the other social sciences, most particularly sociology and social anthropology. One reason for this may lie in the conservative character of the political science community, and its tendency to operate with a relatively narrow definition of 'politics.' Another reason may be the absence of well-established methodological traditions that lend themselves easily to the issues that dominate the study of popular music. This is not to say, however, that political science and political theory have not contributed, and cannot contribute further, to the analysis of popular music, both as the discipline itself adapts (giving more attention to the politics of identity) and as concerns within the study of popular music also change (especially the increasing concern with music policy).

These observations need to be qualified, however, by the acknowledgment that one of the founding figures of politics, Plato, pronounced on the political effects of music. In the *Republic*, Plato goes into considerable detail about the harmonic and rhythmic forms that are, and are not, conducive to proper moral action. For Plato, there is an intimate connection between music and the 'morals and manners' of those who hear it. In Plato's view, political leaders therefore have to be cautious about what music is played, because it may be disruptive of the social order. Hence, Plato draws distinctions between music that, by virtue of its harmonies and rhythms, is acceptable, and music that is unacceptable in the good society (1968, 399–400).

Plato's claim echoes through the endless debate about censorship of music and about the effects of music on its audience. The conservatism of the Platonic legacy is most vividly present in Allan Bloom's *The Closing of the American Mind* (1987), but it has also inhabited organizations like the Parents Music Resource Center in the United States and legislation such as the *Criminal Justice Act* in the United Kingdom. It can be found, too, in the management of music by totalitarian regimes everywhere. But, while Plato's argument has continued to resonate, it has not inspired a tradition of political theorizing about popular music. It is possible to view Greil Marcus's *Mystery Train* as a singular exception to this general rule. This hugely influential book, first published in 1975, traces the expression of the US republican dream in music; and, arguably, all Marcus's subsequent work has been devoted to exploring the ways in which the tensions and aspirations of the US Constitution are revealed within US popular music and culture. But, for the most part, contemporary theorists have, insofar as their arguments engage directly with culture, tended to focus on literature and on film.

Even those political scientists concerned with the representation of politics and its symbols have, for the most part, focused on visual images and the written word. Exploration of the relationship between politics and mass media has typically focused on political satire and on Hollywood's obsession with conspiracy theory. There have been relatively few studies of popular music from within political science (Cloonan 1996; Pratt 1994; Street 1986; Orman 1984).

But where the direct and explicit application of political science has made, until recently, a relatively small contribution to the study of popular music, the tradition of political theorizing associated with Marxism has had a profound influence. In one guise, it has fueled a view of popular music as a form of regulation and control. This position has been most extensively, if not always fairly, attributed to Theodor Adorno (see, for example, Adorno 1941), and has found echoes in leftist criticism of the impact of the music industry on popular music's radical political potential (see Harker 1980; Chapple and Garofalo 1977). In another guise, that of Antonio Gramsci, Marxism has inspired the claims of those who see in the use of popular music the possibility of subversion and resistance (see, for example, Willis 1978). Subsequent writers, concerned to identify music's political significance, have tried to steer a line between these two versions of Marxism, recognizing the limits of both audience interpretation and industry manipulation (see Frith 1981).

Responses to the debates within Marxism, and a questioning of traditional accounts of 'the political,' have cleared new space for the contribution of political study. As the study of politics has focused on political identity and the new social movements, and as the study of popular culture has turned toward questions of policy, particularly within debates over globalization, there has been more dialog. For analysts of social movements, popular music has been recognized as important for its capacity to evoke memories that help forge collective identities (Eyerman and Jamison 1998; Lipsitz 1994). At one level, popular music simply constitutes political identities which then become part of the play of interests within politics. At another level, this ability to give form to a collectivity addresses a fundamental problem in politics, known as 'the logic of collective action.' It asks why rational actors take part in political movements, despite the fact that the costs of participation outweigh the benefits (or, rather, if the movement succeeds they will benefit anyway, and their individual contribution cannot guarantee success). According to the 'logic,' no one joins and nothing changes. That the 'logic' does not always apply can be explained by the way in which collective identities override personal calculations. The role of music and musicians in the collapse of the Berlin Wall provides a dramatic illustration of this counter-logic (Wicke 1992). This is how the study of music informs the study of politics. The relationship also works in reverse.

From within the study of popular music, especially the work being done by social anthropologists and geographers, questions have been raised as to how the distribution of resources, the use of subsidies and the imposition of regulations can give form to local and group musical cultures (Bennett et al. 1993).

It is evident that the study of popular music can contribute to, and benefit from, the study of politics. It is equally apparent that political theory has yet to find its contemporary equivalent of the ancient Greeks' bold pronouncements on music and politics.

Bibliography

Adorno, Theodor W., with Simpson, George. 1941. 'On Popular Music.' *Studies in Philosophy and Social Sciences* 9: 17–48.

Bennett, Tony, et al., eds. 1993. *Rock and Popular Music: Politics, Policies, Institutions*. London: Routledge.

Bloom, Allan. 1987. *The Closing of the American Mind*. New York: Simon & Schuster.

Chapple, Steve, and Garofalo, Reebee. 1977. *Rock 'n' Roll Is Here to Pay: The History and Politics of the Music Industry*. Chicago: Nelson-Hall.

Cloonan, Martin. 1996. *Banned!: Censorship of Popular Music in Britain, 1967–92*. Aldershot: Arena.

Eyerman, Ron, and Jamison, Andrew. 1998. *Music and Social Movements*. Cambridge: Cambridge University Press.

Frith, Simon. 1981. *Sound Effects: Youth, Leisure, and the Politics of Rock 'n' Roll*. New York: Pantheon.

Harker, Dave. 1980. *One for the Money: Politics and Popular Song*. London: Hutchinson.

Lipsitz, George. 1994. *Dangerous Crossroads: Popular Music, Postmodernism and the Poetics of Place*. London: Verso.

Marcus, Greil. 1991 (1975). *Mystery Train: Images of America in Rock 'n' Roll Music*. New York: Penguin.

Orman, John. 1984. *The Politics of Rock Music*. Chicago: Nelson-Hall.

Plato. 1968. *The Republic of Plato*, trans. Allan Bloom. New York: Basic Books.

Pratt, Ray. 1994. *Rhythm and Resistance: The Political Uses of American Popular Music*. Washington, DC: Smithsonian Institution Press.

Street, John. 1986. *Rebel Rock: The Politics of Popular Music*. Oxford: Blackwell.

Wicke, Peter. 1992. '"The Times They Are A-Changin'"': Rock Music and Political Change in East Germany.' In *Rockin' the Boat: Mass Music and Mass Movements*, ed. Reebee Garofalo. Boston, MA: South End Press, 81–92.

Willis, Paul. 1978. *Profane Culture*. London: Routledge.

JOHN STREET

Postcolonialism

On the whole, scholars of popular music have engaged with postcolonial theory somewhat tangentially; a 'First-Worldist' perspective has often predominated, restricting the field of vision to cultural production in Europe and North America. Ethnomusicologists deal more routinely with worlds shaped by a colonial past, but have been committed to modernist methodologies (ethnography, forms of music transcription and analysis) which, some would argue, are too implicated in the colonial process to shed any useful light on their own conditions of existence (Waterman 1991). Postcolonialism has, however, dominated critical thinking in Europe and North America since the publication of Said's *Orientalism* in 1978. Bhabha (1994) introduces a much disputed field with disarming lucidity:

Postcolonial criticism bears witness to the unequal and uneven forces of cultural representation involved in the contest for political and social authority within the modern world order. Postcolonial perspectives emerge from the colonial testimony of Third World countries and the discourses of 'minorities' within the geopolitical divisions of East and West, North and South. They intervene in those ideological discourses of modernity that attempt to give a hegemonic 'normality' to the uneven development and the differential, often disadvantaged, histories of nations, races, communities, peoples. (171)

The work of Said, Bhabha and Spivak has often been taken to define this field, although (collectively viewed) their writings might more usefully be considered as a response to a longer and more diffuse history of inquiry into the cultural conditions of colonialism and its legacy. This would include 'Commonwealth' literature studies (see Ashcroft, Griffith and Tiffin 1989), world systems analysis and the sociology of globalization (see Wallerstein and Gutkind 1976), critical and reflexive movements in late twentieth-century anthropology (see Ardener 1989; Asad 1973; Clifford and Marcus 1986), and the work of *engagé* critics in decolonization struggles, such as Frantz Fanon, C.L.R. James, Chinua Achebe and Ngugi wa Thiong'o.

Said's *Orientalism* forcefully demonstrates a contingent relationship between the colonial process and Western modernity, focusing on the production of forms of knowledge that would sharpen Europe's own sense of cultural destiny and define Europe's colonized 'others' in relation to this. Said's later work emphasizes the continuing force of Orientalist representation in contemporary media, and, more generally, the necessity of reading literary modernism in its colonial context. Said focuses exclusively on the representations of the powerful partners in the colonial relationship, reading these representations for their aporias and exclusions as well as for their more direct depictions of colonized 'others.' Other writers have followed his lead, reading modernist aesthetics in terms of the colonial processes they either metamorphose into abstraction (Jameson 1990) or marginalize and repress (Eagleton 1995). In subsequent work (1991, 1993), Said makes efforts to redeem the modernist canon on the basis of a 'complexity,' which, for some, reintroduces a humanism contradicting his Foucauldian modus operandi (Moore-Gilbert 1997). This work does, however, respond to criticisms of *Orientalism*'s evocation of a totalitarian and somewhat dehistoricized Western episteme, from which there is no escape for either colonizers or colonized. Bhabha and Spivak, by comparison, use various theories of deconstruction, notably those of Lacan and Derrida, to chart a certain ambivalence in colonial practise. Their approach focuses on the unruly dynamics of 'enunciation' (roughly, cultural performance), and the spaces this opens up for resistance. Discussion has focused on the notion of agency that Bhabha's and Spivak's work implies, especially in their critiques of subaltern studies (see Spivak 1996b). Both see postcolonial agency in terms of the spaces opened up by enunciation and the deconstructive energies unleashed in forms of mimicry, 'sly civility' (Bhabha 1994) and 'iterability' (Spivak 1996a). What is repeated, especially as it crosses the colonizer–colonized divide, undermines colonial binarisms in an unstable semiotic 'third space' (Bhabha 1994), and it is the task of critique to recognize and unpack its transformative political potential.

To summarize, the work of Said, Bhabha and Spivak has redirected attention to those on the (post-)colonial margins. It has prompted an ongoing re-theorization of subaltern agency, and it has demanded a global recognition of the material consequences of Europe's enlightenment heritage and its canon of transcendental and 'disinterested' high culture. Its critics, on the other hand (see, for example, Ahmad 1992; Moore-Gilbert 1997), point to stylistic obscurity, a reliance on the authority of First-World theory (in particular that of Foucault, Derrida and Lacan) when the declared purpose of postcolonial critique is precisely to decenter this authority, a tendency inherent in deconstruction to undermine the collective bases of effective political resistance, an insistent privileging of 'reading' in the political struggle, and hence of the reading and writing classes, and a failure to comprehend the 'situatedness' of the critic him-/herself.

Although the impact of postcolonial studies has been marginal in musicology and popular music scholarship, the situation is beginning to change. Social historians of music have begun to look at racial stereotyping in Victorian music hall with explicit reference to postcolonial theory (Pickering 1997), while European popular musical institutions in the colonies (such as brass and military bands) have attracted attention (see Herbert and Sarkissian 1997). Shaking loose a legacy of scholarship devoted to retentions and survivals, writing on the African diaspora has begun to understand music in terms of the creative indeterminacy and evasive strategies of resistance sought by the poststructuralists in literary texts, but encoding them (through call-and-response antiphony, for example) in accessible and democratic participatory forms (Gilroy 1993). For some, this articulates a politics of difference couched in a 'strategic' (following the later Spivak, specifically Spivak 1995) language of alliance with black expressive culture, especially through rap and hip-hop. This is usefully seen as a strategic means of turning 'minorities' in the postcolonial metropolis into a global

majority, and as an effective weapon in the fight against state-sponsored racism and tokenistic liberal multiculturalism (Lipsitz 1994; Gross, McMurray and Swedenburg 1996; Sharma, Hutnyk and Sharma 1996). For others, the importance of musical performance lies in the way it can shape a 'politics of the multiple,' turning exclusive 'either/or' formulations into a more inclusive 'both/and,' restlessly undermining foundationalist identity claims (Back 1995–96). Both arguments are inclined to downplay, if not entirely ignore, the neocolonial political economy of a globalizing music industry, whose extractive use of raw materials, exploitation of cheap labor and cultivation of metropolitan dependency have been extensively discussed by others (Harker 1997; Guilbault 1993); a corollary has been the unabashed reproduction of colonial patterns of representation in world music/world beat discourse (as pointed out by Feld (1994) and Averill (1997)).

Toward the end of the twentieth century, ethnomusicologists began to turn to the history of their discipline with critical vigor. The collusion of anthropological and ethnomusicological research with colonially informed notions of authenticity has been repeatedly noted (Nettl and Bohlman 1991; Blum, Bohlman and Neuman 1991), and the difficulties of disentangling contemporary scholarly aspirations in a postcolonial context from unwanted historical baggage have resulted in exercises in dialogism and other experiments in ethnographic style (see Coplan 1994). Fieldwork has demanded negotiation and accommodation on the part of the fieldworker with national 'invented traditions' in the decolonized world, which has led to a more informed and materially engaged sense of the contradictions inherent in postcolonial culture, both 'at home' and in the diaspora. To take two examples, Averill (1997) demonstrates the ways in which Duvalier's promotion of popular musical genres in Haiti (notably *konpa-dirèk*) drew heavily on a history of bourgeois 'noirisme' in Haiti, itself indebted to Francophone philosophies of negritude; meanwhile, as Austerlitz (1997) shows, on the other side of the island Duvalier's counterpart, Trujillo, promoted a similarly creolized Afro-Caribbean popular genre, merengue, in terms that explicitly denied its 'African' components and valorized its Hispanic roots – an act of interpretative exclusion that was fraught with political consequence for Trujillo's frail but vicious dictatorship and its opponents in the Dominican Republic and elsewhere (see also Pacini Hernandez 1995). Variations on these themes can be found in a valuable ethnomusicological/anthropological literature on popular musics in the Caribbean and Latin America (see Stuempfle 1995; Florine 1998; Manuel 1998; Wade 1998), while the colonial baggage carried by a variety of post-independence popular musics in Africa has been discussed in some detail by Erlmann (1991), Waterman (1990), and Collins and Richards (1989).

Bibliography

Ahmad, Aijaz. 1992. *In Theory: Classes, Nations, Literatures*. London: Verso.

Ardener, Edwin. 1989. 'Social Anthropology and the Decline of Modernism.' In *The Voice of Prophecy and Other Essays*, ed. Malcolm Chapman. Oxford: Blackwell, 191–210.

Asad, Talal, ed. 1973. *Anthropology and the Colonial Encounter*. New York: Humanities Press.

Ashcroft, Bill, Griffith, Gareth, and Tiffin, Helen. 1989. *The Empire Writes Back: Theory and Practice in Post-Colonial Literature*. London: Routledge.

Austerlitz, Paul. 1997. *Merengue: Dominican Music and Dominican Identity*. Philadelphia: Temple University Press.

Averill, Gage. 1997. *A Day for the Hunter, A Day for the Prey: Popular Music and Power in Haiti*. Chicago: University of Chicago Press.

Back, Les. 1995–96. '"X-Amount of Sat Siri Akal!": Apache Indian, Reggae Music and the Cultural Intermezzo.' *New Formations* 27: 128–47.

Bhabha, Homi K. 1994. *The Location of Culture*. London and New York: Routledge.

Blum, Stephen, Bohlman, Philip V., and Neuman, Daniel M., eds. 1991. *Ethnomusicology and Modern Music History*. Urbana, IL: University of Illinois Press.

Clifford, James, and Marcus, George E., eds. 1986. *Writing Culture: The Poetics and Politics of Ethnography*. Berkeley, CA: University of California Press.

Collins, John, and Richards, Paul. 1989. 'Popular Music in West Africa.' In *World Music, Politics, and Social Change*, ed. Simon Frith. Manchester: Manchester University Press, 13–46.

Coplan, David. 1994. *In the Time of Cannibals: Word Music of South Africa's Basotho Migrants*. Chicago: University of Chicago Press.

Eagleton, Terry. 1995. *Heathcliff and the Great Hunger*. London: Verso.

Erlmann, Veit. 1991. *African Stars: Studies in Black South African Performance*. Chicago: University of Chicago Press.

Fanon, Frantz. 1965. *The Wretched of the Earth*, trans. Constance Farrington. London: MacGibbon and Kee.

Feld, Steven. 1994. 'From Schizophonia to Schismogenesis: On the Discourses and Commodification Practices of "World Music" and "World Beat."' In Charles Keil and Steven Feld, *Music Grooves: Essays and Dialogues*. Chicago and London: University of Chicago Press, 257–89.

Florine, Jane. 1998. 'Carlos Jimenez: Reflecting the Power of the People in Argentine Cuarteto Music.' *Popular Music and Society* 22(3): 61–115.

Gilroy, Paul. 1993. *The Black Atlantic: Modernity and Double Consciousness*. London: Verso.

Gross, Joan, McMurray, David, and Swedenburg, Ted. 1996. 'Arab Noise and Ramadan Nights: *Rai*, Rap, and Franco-Maghrebi Identities.' In *Displacement, Diaspora, and Geographies of Identity*, ed. Smadar Lavie and Ted Swedenburg. Durham, NC: Duke University Press, 119–55.

Guilbault, Jocelyne. 1993. *Zouk: World Music in the West Indies*. Chicago: University of Chicago Press.

Harker, Dave. 1997. 'The Wonderful World of the IFPI: Music Industry Rhetoric, the Critics and the Classical Marxist Critique.' *Popular Music* 16(1): 45–80.

Herbert, Trevor, and Sarkissian, Margaret. 1997. 'Victorian Bands and Their Dissemination in the Colonies.' *Popular Music* 16(2): 165–79.

Jameson, Fredric. 1990. 'Modernism and Imperialism.' In *Nationalism, Colonialism, and Literature*, ed. Terry Eagleton, Fredric Jameson and Edward Said. Minneapolis, MN: University of Minnesota Press, 43–66.

Lipsitz, George. 1994. *Dangerous Crossroads: Popular Music, Postmodernism and the Poetics of Place*. London: Verso.

Manuel, Peter. 1998. 'Chutney and Indo-Trinidadian Cultural Identity.' *Popular Music* 17(1): 21–43.

Moore-Gilbert, Bart. 1997. *Postcolonial Theory: Contexts, Practices, Politics*. London: Verso.

Nettl, Bruno, and Bohlman, Philip V., eds. 1991. *Comparative Musicology and Anthropology of Music: Essays on the History of Ethnomusicology*. Chicago: University of Chicago Press.

Pacini Hernandez, Deborah. 1995. *Bacháta: A Social History of a Dominican Popular Music*. Philadelphia: Temple University Press.

Pickering, Michael. 1997. 'John Bull in Blackface.' *Popular Music* 16(2): 181–201.

Said, Edward. 1978. *Orientalism*. London: Penguin.

Said, Edward. 1991. *Musical Elaborations*. London: Chatto and Windus.

Said, Edward. 1993. *Culture and Imperialism*. London: Chatto and Windus.

Sharma, Sanjay, Hutnyk, John, and Sharma, Ashwani, eds. 1996. *Dis-Orienting Rhythms: The Politics of the New Asian Dance Music*. London: Zed Books.

Spivak, Gayatri Chakravorty. 1995. 'Acting Bits/Identity Talk.' In *Identities*, ed. Kwame Anthony Appiah and Henry Louis Gates, Jr. Chicago: University of Chicago Press, 147–80.

Spivak, Gayatri Chakravorty. 1996a. 'Revolutions That As Yet Have No Model.' In *The Spivak Reader*, ed.

Donna Landry and Gerard Maclean. London: Routledge, 75–106.

Spivak, Gayatri Chakravorty. 1996b. 'Subaltern Studies: Deconstructing Historiography.' In *The Spivak Reader*, ed. Donna Landry and Gerard Maclean. London: Routledge, 204–35.

Stuempfle, Stephen. 1995. *The Steelband Movement: The Forging of a National Art in Trinidad and Tobago*. Philadelphia: University of Pennsylvania Press.

Wade, Peter. 1998. 'Music, Blackness, and National Identity: Three Moments in Colombian History.' *Popular Music* 17(1): 1–19.

Wallerstein, Immanuel, and Gutkind, Peter, eds. 1976. *The Political Economy of Contemporary Africa*. Beverly Hills, CA: Sage.

Waterman, Christopher A. 1990. *Jùjú: A Social History and Ethnography of an African Popular Music*. Chicago: University of Chicago Press.

Waterman, Christopher A. 1991. 'The Uneven Development of Africanist Ethnomusicology: Three Issues and a Critique.' In *Comparative Musicology and Anthropology of Music: Essays on the History of Ethnomusicology*, ed. Bruno Nettl and Philip V. Bohlman. Chicago: University of Chicago Press, 169–86.

MARTIN STOKES

Postmodernism

Introduction

Within the literature of popular music studies, the concept of postmodernism has had a relatively high profile. There has been no direct correlation, however, between the ubiquity of the concept and the theoretical clarity with which it has been applied. For some observers (Goodwin 1991, for example), this lack of clarity simply serves to confirm the shortcomings of postmodern theory as an analytical tool. But given the concept's continued prevalence at the end of the twentieth century – and its increased entrenchment in academic orthodoxies – there is a need to clarify the terms of the debates surrounding it. This clarification, together with an assessment of the concept's application within musicological discourse, is undertaken before its use specifically within the field of popular music studies is examined.

Characteristics of Postmodernism

Postmodernism first came to prominence in the fields of literary criticism and architectural theory (for example, Hassan 1971; Jencks 1977), but its influence has been strongly felt throughout the humanities and social sciences. However, despite the fact that the word 'postmodernism' has been in relatively common usage since the 1970s, the concept of postmodernism has continued to be one of the most contested and confusing in

the history of cultural theory. The term itself has remained in a state of constant linguistic flux, being called upon to categorize, define and interpret a bewildering multiplicity of cultural and social phenomena. However, toward the end of the twentieth century, a welcome clarification entered the literature, distinguishing postmodernism, as a primarily cultural and artistic concept, from postmodernity, which addresses new modes of social, political and economic organization.

Notwithstanding their theoretical variance, one common factor has united all conceptualizations of postmodernism: namely, their fundamental relationship to theories of modernism, whether such a relationship is conceived of in terms of a radical break with the modernist tradition (for example, Jameson 1991) or in the light of what are regarded as significant continuities with the modernist impulse (for example, Harvey 1989). Modernism is generally understood as an artistic movement prevalent in the late nineteenth and early twentieth centuries. Among its defining characteristics were: a rejection of Classical and Romantic aesthetic conventions, typified, in the visual arts, by the transition from figurative realism to formal abstraction, and, in music, by the passage from tonality to atonality; an avant-garde experimentalism and theoreticism, with a concomitant antipathy toward popular or mass culture; a didactic rhetorical vanguardism, linked to a fascination with science and technology and encompassing an emancipatory discourse of progress and social change; and an understanding of art – and the artist – as autonomous and independent of social forces.

It is the rejection of these defining characteristics of modernism that has tended to distinguish postmodernism from its modernist precursors. Hence, postmodern artistic practise has repudiated the modernist negation of prior forms, drawing freely and eclectically on a diverse range of stylistic, cultural and historical influences, of which modernism itself may be only one example among many. Furthermore, in contrast to the aesthetic and rhetorical vanguardism of modernism, postmodernism has openly embraced the forms and practises of popular culture, exhibiting a theoretical sensibility that has been both self-reflexive and ironic. Postmodernism has thus incorporated a degree of cultural vernacularism alongside a range of aesthetic techniques previously associated with modernism (for example, collage, fragmentation and juxtaposition) – techniques that, in the context of a postmodern artistic discourse, have been reinterpreted, transformed and intensified. The postmodern reconciliation with popular culture has also suggested a reinstatement of an understanding of the fundamentally social nature of artistic production, which the modernist ideology of aesthetic autonomy had served to obscure. Consequently, if modernism emphasized the formalist autonomy of the avant-garde artwork, postmodernism has stressed social contingency and aesthetic hybridity, plurality and intertextuality.

The radical eclecticism of postmodernism has led some theorists to propose the collapse of the distinction between 'high art' and popular culture as one of the key defining characteristics of the postmodern. Although this claim has been thought to manifest considerable credibility at the level of artistic techniques and practises – which reveal a great deal of cross-fertilization between 'high' and 'low' – it is one that has been difficult to sustain at the level of political economy, much postmodern art having remained resolutely distinct from popular culture in commercial, economic and social terms, thereby confirming the persistence of these categories. A crucial point here has been the acknowledgment that the terms 'high' and 'low' are, themselves, cultural constructs, their emergence – not coincidentally – being broadly contemporaneous with the birth of modernism, a movement that was concerned to assert its aesthetic and social difference from popular or mass culture.

A further defining characteristic of postmodernism has been the employment of parody and pastiche, which, for some theorists, ultimately points toward the essential bankruptcy of postmodern cultural practises (Jameson 1984). For others, however, postmodern parody has been viewed in a considerably more positive light, suggesting a reconsideration and reevaluation of previous cultural forms and codes (for example, Hutcheon 1989; Collins 1989). Resisting a periodizing definition, Eco (1985) has characterized postmodernism as 'a way of operating' (66), suggesting that postmodernism's ironic engagement with the past has been virtually a necessary response to the conceptual and aesthetic limits of high modernism. Thus, postmodernism 'demands, in order to be understood, not the negation of the already said, but its ironic rethinking' (Eco 1985, 68).

Contrary to the cultural authority and aesthetic vanguardism of modernism, the self-reflexive irony, parodic eclecticism and populist intertextuality of postmodern artistic practise have indicated a revisionist approach to traditional cultural hierarchies and value systems. Postmodernism has therefore brought about a theoretical crisis in the assessment of cultural value, the relativism inherent in its defining characteristics and techniques casting doubt on modernist modes of evaluation and judgment.

Indeed, if postmodern theory can be said to have achieved any degree of academic orthodoxy, it has been on the question of the evaluation of postmodern practises, which such orthodoxies have tended to bifurcate.

On the one hand, particularly among Marxist critics such as Fredric Jameson and David Harvey, as well as in the work of Jean-François Lyotard, postmodern eclecticism and relativism have been viewed with suspicion, and have been regarded as a denial and subversion of the aesthetic and sociopolitical sureties of the modernist project; from this essentially neo-modern perspective, postmodern culture has been routinely characterized as depthless, ephemeral and valueless (see, for example, Jameson 1991; Harvey 1989; Eagleton 1985; Lyotard 1982, 1984a, 1984b).

On the other hand, especially for a later generation of cultural studies theorists, such as John Docker and Angela McRobbie, the populist challenge that postmodern relativism has presented to traditional values has heralded a newfound cultural pluralism; here, the diversity and heterogeneity of postmodern culture have been regarded as liberating and empowering, with the analytical focus on a 'micro-politics' of resistance and subversion (see, for example, Docker 1994; McRobbie 1994; Fiske 1994; Kaplan 1987).

Somewhat more dispassionate accounts of postmodernism can be found in the work of those theorists who have made no such claims for either the cultural certainties of modernism or the populist pluralism of postmodernism (for example, Huyssen 1986; Connor 1989; Rose 1991; Best and Kellner 1991, 1997; Bertens 1995).

Postmodernism and Musicological Discourse

In the debate over postmodern musical forms and practises within the discipline of musicology, the tendency has been toward a taxonomic, periodizing conflation of postmodernism with the postwar avant-garde and experimental music traditions (for example, Clarke 1985; Hermand 1991; Boone 1991). Although some commentators have exhibited a more critical, analytical perspective on their object of study (for example, Butler 1980; Hartwell 1993; Chanan 1994; Williams 1997), much of this work has simply reiterated the standard tropes of traditional musicological discourse, in which 'music' – postmodern or otherwise – is defined as music of the Western art tradition, with little or no reference made to contemporary jazz and popular musics. Notable exceptions to this trend include Watkins (1994), Kramer (1995) and McNeilly (1995), although, at the close of the twentieth century, the discipline of musicology still awaited a thoroughly integrated and inclusive study of the music of that century.

Born (1995) offers a theoretical framework for an understanding of musical modernism and postmodernism which suggests that the ambivalence toward popular music is as much a product of the musical forms themselves as it is of musicological discourse. Focusing particularly on postwar serialism, Born characterizes musical modernism in terms of its formalist determinism, scientistic rationalism and vanguardist theoreticism, highlighting its emphasis on institutionally based high technologies, and its teleological, text-centered musical practises. These characteristics, coupled with the modernist negation of tonality, have served to assert the movement's aesthetic difference from popular music.

Citing the experimental music tradition (see Nyman 1974), Born suggests that, in sharp contrast, musical postmodernism has emphasized indeterminism, alternative (often Eastern) philosophies, a performative, politicized attitude toward social relations, an 'artisanal' approach to small-scale technologies, and a minimalist, performance-based approach to music-making. Furthermore, musical postmodernism has made significant reference to, and draws considerable influence from, popular and non-Western musics, whether in terms of musical forms and structures or in relation to performance practises.

Musical postmodernism has thus appeared to effect a rapprochement with popular forms, a tendency apparent not only in the significant precursors of postmodernism – the eclectic neoclassicisms and the jazz- and folk music-influenced works of the early part of the twentieth century – but also in the work of many of the postwar experimentalists and minimalists. Contrary to postmodern claims for the collapse of the distinction between 'high' and 'low' culture, however – and reiterating a point made earlier in the general discussion of postmodernism – Born suggests that this tendency has remained at the level of reference and appropriation, arguing that these forms of musical postmodernism have continued to be 'aesthetically, ideologically, and institutionally distinct from commercial popular music' (1995, 61).

Postmodernism and Popular Music Studies

The field of popular music studies is somewhat loosely constituted, drawing equally on disciplines such as sociology, cultural studies, mass communication and musicology. This disciplinary eclecticism has resulted in an engagement with postmodernism that has been theoretically broad, but lacking in specificity. Reaching their peak in the late 1980s and early 1990s, the complex and often confusing debates between postmodernism and various approaches to the study of popular music have focused on three key issues: the analysis of MTV and music videos; the use of sampling technologies; and the identification of postmodern popular music forms and practises, which has involved the theorizing of the relationship between postmodernism, postmodernity and popular music. In each case, the debates have addressed

not only aesthetic issues, but also questions of consumption, identity and representation. Goodwin's attempt to untangle the various strands of the debates remains a useful, if problematic, guide to the literature (Goodwin 1991; reprinted in Wheale 1995).

By far the most salient and persistent aspect of the debates between postmodernism and various forms of the study of popular music has been the analysis of MTV and music videos. Much of the early work in this field was characterized by a populist theoretical extravagance, a focus on the visual over the musical text and a lack of empirical substantiation, as in the case of Kaplan's claims for the postmodern 'decenteredness' and 'exhilarating . . . heteroglossia' of MTV (Kaplan 1987, 148; see also Fiske 1986; Tetzlaff 1986). Kaplan's study of specific music videos, for example, draws predominantly on psychoanalytically based film theory, eschewing any detailed musical or contextual analysis. More critical – and more contextualist, empirically based – readings of MTV and music videos are to be found in the work of Goodwin (1992, 1993), Straw (1993) and Frith (1988).

Closely related to the work on music videos – and similarly exhibiting both populist and critical orientations – has been the 'Madonna Phenomenon' in late twentieth-century scholarship, in which Madonna's music, videos and public persona became a locus for postmodern and feminist theorizing (see Schwichtenberg 1993b). Enlisting the established cultural studies rhetoric of resistance and subversion, Schwichtenberg characterizes Madonna as a 'postmodern feminist' (1993a), while McClary (1991) suggests that Madonna 'is engaged in rewriting some very fundamental levels of Western thought' (160). In contrast to the subjectivist emphasis on fragmented and multiple identities evident in these perspectives, somewhat less celebratory readings of Madonna's cultural practises highlight the 'sadly continuing social realities of dominance and subordination' (Bordo 1993, 289; see also Freccero 1994).

Debates over the postmodern character of the use of sampling techniques have been similarly contradictory and problematic. Goodwin's adherence to a theoretical orthodoxy rooted in Jameson's notion of 'blank parody' (Jameson 1991), and his consequently pessimistic appraisal of the potential for postmodern creativity and originality, lead him to disavow sampling as an example of postmodern practise (Goodwin 1988, 1991). Théberge (1997) adopts a similar, if somewhat more agnostic, perspective.

Shusterman, drawing on pragmatist philosophy, and emphasizing 'social function, process, and embodied experience' (1992, 212), offers an alternative reading of sampling, arguing for an understanding of rap and its appropriative techniques as characteristically postmodern (1992, 1995). Although not without its own problems – most notably the valorization of autonomous textual examples in terms of traditional aesthetic criteria – Shusterman's reading suggests that 'postmodernism's highlighting of appropriation does not entail the end of originality, only the welcome loss of a certain absolutist conception of it' (1995, 154; see Brennan 1994, 1995 for a critique of Shusterman's position). Focusing on 'vernacular poetics,' black identities and the politics of resistance – and contrary to Rose (1994) – Potter (1995) advances a similarly postmodern reading of rap and hip-hop culture.

Beyond the debates around music videos and sampling techniques, attempts to identify postmodern popular music have been fraught with problems. For example, the search for postmodern popular music forms and practises has been hindered by the familiar rhetoric of the postmodern effacement of cultural hierarchies; often, the only boundaries effaced are those between the musical and socioeconomic specificities of empirical examples (see Jameson 1983, 1984, 1991; Stratton 1989). Furthermore, implicit in any periodizing theory has been the notion that all popular music is 'postmodern' by virtue of belonging to 'the postmodern era.' Such theories have tended to ignore the fact that some aspects of popular music are simply antithetical to postmodernism: for example, rather than illustrating a postmodern eclecticism, the high-culture borrowings of progressive rock have been more accurately read as a neo-modernist claim to cultural legitimacy (Goodwin 1991); similarly, the continued investment, within rock music, in notions of authenticity and the Romantic view of the artist has been at odds with a postmodern reading (Gracyk 1996).

Grossberg (1992) has theorized the links between popular music and the political and socioeconomic characteristics of postmodernity, defining the 'postmodern sensibility' in terms of an 'authentic inauthenticity' (224), and claiming that the purported oppositional stance of rock music has been readily co-opted by the political conservatism of dominant mainstream culture. Reynolds and Press (1995) arrive at similar conclusions. However, their arguments are based on a psychoanalytically decontextualized approach to questions of music and gender.

In sharp contrast – but similarly problematic – have been those populist accounts that privilege the cross-cultural eclecticism and intertextuality of popular music, celebrating its cultural heterogeneity and resistive marginality, although often at the expense of any detailed analysis of political economy (for example, Hebdige 1988; Lipsitz 1990, 1994; McRobbie 1994). In the spirit of these populist accounts, Nehring (1997) takes issue with the postmodern 'cynicism' (48) of theorists such as Grossberg, and Reynolds and Press, drawing on feminist philosophy, and theories of anger and emotion, in a thesis that emphasizes the role of popular music in 'progressive change' (xiii).

Accounts such as those summarized above serve to highlight the lack of clarity and specificity with which the concept of postmodernism has been applied in the field of popular music studies. Notwithstanding this lack of clarity and specificity, however, and despite the fact that the postmodern debate can no longer be counted as a highly active or prominent one, the concept of postmodernism has made a significant contribution to the development of the field of popular music studies. Longhurst's comprehensive study of the field (1995) offers a helpful summary of the intersections between popular music and postmodern theory.

Bibliography

Bertens, Hans. 1995. *The Idea of the Postmodern: A History*. London: Routledge.

Best, Steven, and Kellner, Douglas. 1991. *Postmodern Theory: Critical Interrogations*. New York: Guilford Press.

Best, Steven, and Kellner, Douglas. 1997. *The Postmodern Turn*. New York: Guilford Press.

Boone, Charles. 1991. 'Has Modernist Music Lost Power?' In *Zeitgeist in Babel: The Postmodernist Controversy*, ed. Ingeborg Hoesterey. Bloomington, IN: Indiana University Press, 207–15.

Bordo, Susan. 1993. '"Material Girl": The Effacements of Postmodern Culture.' In *The Madonna Connection: Representational Politics, Subcultural Identities, and Cultural Theory*, ed. Cathy Schwichtenberg. Boulder, CO: Westview Press, 265–90.

Born, Georgina. 1995. *Rationalizing Culture: IRCAM, Boulez, and the Institutionalization of the Musical Avant-Garde*. Berkeley, CA: University of California Press.

Brennan, Tim. 1994. 'Off the Gangsta Tip: A Rap Appreciation, or Forgetting About Los Angeles.' *Critical Inquiry* 20: 663–93.

Brennan, Tim. 1995. 'Rap Redoubt: The Beauty of the Mix.' *Critical Inquiry* 22: 159–61.

Butler, Christopher. 1980. *After the Wake: An Essay on the Contemporary Avant-Garde*. Oxford: Clarendon Press.

Chanan, Michael. 1994. *Musica Practica: The Social Practice of Western Music from Gregorian Chant to Postmodernism*. London: Verso.

Clarke, Garry E. 1985. 'Music.' In *The Postmodern Moment: A Handbook of Contemporary Innovation in the Arts*, ed. Stanley Trachtenberg. Westport, CT: Greenwood Press, 157–76.

Collins, Jim. 1989. *Uncommon Cultures: Popular Culture and Post-Modernism*. London: Routledge.

Connor, Steven. 1989. *Postmodernist Culture: An Introduction to Theories of the Contemporary*. Oxford: Blackwell.

Docker, John. 1994. *Postmodernism and Popular Culture: A Cultural History*. Cambridge: Cambridge University Press.

Eagleton, Terry. 1985. 'Capitalism, Modernism and Postmodernism.' *New Left Review* 152: 60–73.

Eco, Umberto. 1985. 'Postmodernism, Irony, the Enjoyable.' In Umberto Eco, *Reflections on The Name of the Rose*. London: Secker & Warburg, 65–72.

Fiske, John. 1986. 'MTV: Post Structural Post Modern.' *Journal of Communication Inquiry* 10(1): 74–79.

Fiske, John. 1994. *Media Matters: Everyday Culture and Political Change*. Minneapolis, MN: University of Minnesota Press.

Freccero, Carla. 1994. 'Our Lady of MTV: Madonna's "Like a Prayer."' In *Feminism and Postmodernism*, ed. Margaret Ferguson and Jennifer Wicke. Durham, NC: Duke University Press, 179–99.

Frith, Simon. 1988. 'Afterword: Making Sense of Video: Pop into the Nineties.' In Simon Frith, *Music for Pleasure: Essays in the Sociology of Pop*. Cambridge: Polity Press, 205–25.

Goodwin, Andrew. 1988. 'Sample and Hold: Pop Music in the Digital Age of Reproduction.' *Critical Quarterly* 30(3): 34–49.

Goodwin, Andrew. 1991. 'Popular Music and Postmodern Theory.' *Cultural Studies* 5(2): 174–90.

Goodwin, Andrew. 1992. *Dancing in the Distraction Factory: Music Television and Popular Culture*. Minneapolis, MN: University of Minnesota Press.

Goodwin, Andrew. 1993. 'Fatal Distractions: MTV Meets Postmodern Theory.' In *Sound and Vision: The Music Video Reader*, ed. Simon Frith, Andrew Goodwin and Lawrence Grossberg. London: Routledge, 45–66.

Gracyk, Theodore. 1996. *Rhythm and Noise: An Aesthetics of Rock*. Durham, NC: Duke University Press.

Grossberg, Lawrence. 1992. *We Gotta Get Out of This Place: Popular Conservatism and Postmodern Culture*. London: Routledge.

Hartwell, Robin. 1993. 'Postmodernism and Art Music.' In *The Last Post: Music After Modernism*, ed. Simon Miller. Manchester: Manchester University Press, 27–51.

Harvey, David. 1989. *The Condition of Postmodernity: An Enquiry into the Origins of Cultural Change*. Oxford: Blackwell.

Hassan, Ihab. 1971. *The Dismemberment of Orpheus: Toward a Postmodern Literature*. New York: Oxford University Press.

Hebdige, Dick. 1988. *Hiding in the Light: On Images and Things*. London and New York: Routledge.

Hermand, Jost. 1991. 'Avant-Garde, Modern, Postmodern: The Music (Almost) Nobody Wants to Hear.' In *Zeitgeist in Babel: The Postmodernist Controversy*, ed. Ingeborg Hoesterey. Bloomington, IN: Indiana University Press, 192–206.

Hutcheon, Linda. 1989. *The Politics of Postmodernism*. London: Routledge.

Huyssen, Andreas. 1986. *After the Great Divide: Modernism, Mass Culture, Postmodernism*. Bloomington, IN: Indiana University Press.

Jameson, Fredric. 1983. 'Postmodernism and Consumer Society.' In *The Anti-Aesthetic: Essays on Postmodern Culture*, ed. Hal Foster. Seattle, WA: Bay Press, 111–25.

Jameson, Fredric. 1984. 'The Politics of Theory: Ideological Positions in the Postmodernism Debate.' *New German Critique* 33: 53–65.

Jameson, Fredric. 1991. *Postmodernism, or, The Cultural Logic of Late Capitalism*. Durham, NC: Duke University Press.

Jencks, Charles. 1977. *The Language of Post-Modern Architecture*. London: Academy.

Kaplan, E. Ann. 1987. *Rocking Around the Clock: Music Television, Postmodernism, and Consumer Culture*. New York: Methuen.

Kramer, Jonathan D. 1995. 'Beyond Unity: Toward an Understanding of Musical Postmodernism.' In *Concert Music, Rock, and Jazz Since 1945: Essays and Analytical Studies*, ed. Elizabeth West Marvin and Richard Hermann. Rochester, NY: University of Rochester Press, 11–33.

Lipsitz, George. 1990. 'Cruising Around the Historical Bloc: Postmodernism and Popular Music in East Los Angeles.' In George Lipsitz, *Time Passages: Collective Memory and American Popular Culture*. Minneapolis, MN: University of Minnesota Press, 133–60.

Lipsitz, George. 1994. *Dangerous Crossroads: Popular Music, Postmodernism and the Poetics of Place*. London: Verso.

Longhurst, Brian. 1995. *Popular Music and Society*. Cambridge: Polity Press.

Lyotard, Jean-François. 1982. 'Presenting the Unpresentable: The Sublime.' *Artforum* 20(8): 64–69.

Lyotard, Jean-François. 1984a. 'Answering the Question: What Is Postmodernism?' In Jean-François Lyotard, *The Postmodern Condition: A Report on Knowledge*. Minneapolis, MN: University of Minnesota Press, 71–82.

Lyotard, Jean-François. 1984b. 'The Sublime and the Avant-Garde.' *Artforum* 22(8): 36–43.

McClary, Susan. 1991. 'Living to Tell: Madonna's Resurrection of the Fleshly.' In Susan McClary, *Feminine*

Endings: Music, Gender, and Sexuality. Minneapolis, MN: University of Minnesota Press, 148–66.

McNeilly, Kevin. 1995. 'Ugly Beauty: John Zorn and the Politics of Postmodern Music.' *Postmodern Culture* 5(2).

McRobbie, Angela. 1994. *Postmodernism and Popular Culture*. London and New York: Routledge.

Nehring, Neil. 1997. *Popular Music, Gender, and Postmodernism: Anger Is an Energy*. London: Sage.

Nyman, Michael. 1974. *Experimental Music: Cage and Beyond*. New York: Schirmer.

Potter, Russell A. 1995. *Spectacular Vernaculars: Hip-Hop and the Politics of Postmodernism*. New York: State University of New York Press.

Reynolds, Simon, and Press, Joy. 1995. *The Sex Revolts: Gender, Rebellion, and Rock 'n' Roll*. Cambridge, MA: Harvard University Press.

Rose, Margaret. 1991. *The Post-Modern and the Post-Industrial: A Critical Analysis*. Cambridge: Cambridge University Press.

Rose, Tricia. 1994. *Black Noise: Rap Music and Black Culture in Contemporary America*. Hanover, NH: University Press of New England.

Schwichtenberg, Cathy. 1993a. 'Madonna's Postmodern Feminism: Bringing the Margins to the Center.' In *The Madonna Connection: Representational Politics, Subcultural Identities, and Cultural Theory*, ed. Cathy Schwichtenberg. Boulder, CO: Westview Press, 129–45.

Schwichtenberg, Cathy, ed. 1993b. *The Madonna Connection: Representational Politics, Subcultural Identities, and Cultural Theory*. Boulder, CO: Westview Press.

Shusterman, Richard. 1992. 'The Fine Art of Rap.' In Richard Shusterman, *Pragmatist Aesthetics: Living Beauty, Rethinking Art*. Oxford: Blackwell, 150–58.

Shusterman, Richard. 1995. 'Rap Remix: Pragmatism, Postmodernism, and Other Issues in the House.' *Critical Inquiry* 22: 150–58.

Stratton, Jon. 1989. 'Beyond Art: Postmodernism and the Case of Popular Music.' *Theory, Culture & Society* 6(1): 31–57.

Straw, Will. 1993. 'Popular Music and Postmodernism in the 1980s.' In *Sound and Vision: The Music Video Reader*, ed. Simon Frith, Andrew Goodwin and Lawrence Grossberg. London: Routledge, 3–21.

Tetzlaff, David. 1986. 'MTV and the Politics of Postmodern Pop.' *Journal of Communication Inquiry* 10(1): 80–91.

Théberge, Paul. 1997. *Any Sound You Can Imagine: Making Music/Consuming Technology*. Hanover, NH: Wesleyan University Press/University Press of New England.

Watkins, Glenn. 1994. *Pyramids at the Louvre: Music, Culture, and Collage from Stravinsky to the Postmodernists*. Cambridge, MA: The Belknap Press of Harvard University Press.

Wheale, Nigel, ed. 1995. *The Postmodern Arts: An Introductory Reader*. London: Routledge.

Williams, Alastair. 1997. *New Music and the Claims of Modernity*. Aldershot: Ashgate.

ALAN STANBRIDGE

Poststructuralism

'Poststructuralism' refers to a predominantly French-language intellectual tradition that emerged from structuralism. Poststructuralism is at the same time a continuation and a critique of structuralism. Poststructuralism shares with structuralism the idea that it is language and other cultural forms that generate meaning, but it is critical of the structuralist assumption that meanings are ordered or 'centered' within closed linguistic or cultural systems. Like structuralism, post-structuralism has had a direct, but mostly indirect, influence on popular music studies.

The Bases of the Tradition

Poststructuralism can be traced to a paper, 'Structure, Sign, and Play in the Discourse of the Human Sciences,' given by Jacques Derrida at an International Colloquium on Critical Languages and the Sciences of Man at Johns Hopkins University in 1966. Indeed, Elisabeth Roudinesco (1990) has pointed out that the term 'poststructuralism,' 'unknown in France, would even be coined in English to designate what was emerging from the colloquium' (411). Derrida's paper, subsequently published in *Writing and Difference* (1978; first published in 1967 in French), argues against the way in which an excessive familiarity with the concept of 'structure' in Western thought has effectively neutralized its metaphorical character, allowing it, in the words of Michael Payne (1993), to assume a 'fixed origin in language and thought' whose consequence is to 'limit the play [*le jeu*] of structure' (12).

An idea of the fixed character that the concept of 'structure' can assume is to be gained from an explanation provided by Jean Piaget (1971). According to Piaget, a structure: (a) possesses – and functions according to – its own set of intrinsic laws; (b) in terms of – and according to – these laws, processes and eliminates information presented by its environment; and (c) maintains and preserves itself in the face of environmental challenges. In this classic formulation, there appears little opportunity for play or rupture.

However, according to Derrida, structures contain within themselves the potential for rupture. For this reason, language as a structure 'ceases to be a transparent medium of reflection' (Payne 1993, 13). Rather, articulations of reality become discourse, *inhabiting* structures

111

and languages, and are given life through the capacity for play that inheres in structures and languages. While universal concepts of order and authority such as 'God' may be retained, therefore, they are 'unthinkable without rupture, disruption, absence, difference' (Payne 1993, 13).

From the outset, Derrida's work demanded a reinterpretation of the basic semiological scheme associated with French-language structuralism. According to this scheme, a word has meaning through the association of a signifier (the mental imprint of the sound or sight of a word as a material phenomenon) and the signified (the mental concept customarily yet *arbitrarily* associated with the signifier). Thus, in English, the sound of the word 'bird' customarily evokes the mental image of a creature that flies. However, in French, the totally different sound (signifier) 'oiseau' performs much the same function just as successfully. It is through this arbitrary association of signifiers and signifieds that words come to generate meaning. This is accomplished as much, if not more, through the particular location and function of words in the structure of a language as through their relation to external reality.

In questioning the fixed and centered character of structures, Derrida's work and much poststructuralist work that followed challenged this classic understanding of processes of signification. Poststructuralism came to view language as destabilized through the triumph of the signifier – which, by definition, has no meaning – over the signified – which, conventionally, is where established meaning is taken to reside. Accordingly, meanings are no longer as stable, secure and self-evident as they seem. In opposing the rigidity that results from the neutralization of structures' metaphorical character, poststructuralism is not, however, implying that everything is possible, with truth and meaning permanently suspended. Rather than reproducing a concept where meanings are trapped within processes that are permanently centered, poststructuralism celebrates and reflects upon the liberating potential of processes of signification.

Poststructuralism has, however, become something of an umbrella term, and it is incorrect to think that the tradition can be appropriately captured according to a single essence or in terms of one understanding. Various scholars associated with poststructuralism have brought to the tradition their own distinctive contributions. One such contribution is to be found in the work of Jacques Lacan, 20 years Derrida's senior, who argued that it is not subjects who speak language, but language that speaks subjects. In Lacan's scheme, language compensates for absence in the developing world of the child and, in this way, the child comes to be positioned (spoken) by language within the social world in terms of already established subject positions such as those of mother and father. Subjects, in other words, are constituted through language, and thus become an integral part of processes of signification. Subjects are now lost or disappeared in signifying practises in which the signifier is triumphant (in this, subjects come to occupy the position of the signified). To the decentering of language through its capacity for play as a structure is thus added the decentering of the subject and, in terms of subjects being placed within competing or contradictory discourses, the decentering of subjects who are fragmented. This, in turn, means abandoning the notion of unified individuality symptomatic of more traditional, liberal humanist thought. It is through the work of Lacan that the tradition of poststructuralism connects initially with the French-language tradition of psychoanalytic theory.

This notion of the production of the subject has been taken up by other writers in ways that seem to diminish the emphasis placed by Derrida on play and disruption. This tendency is apparent in the way in which Lacan's thinking was taken up by Louis Althusser. One of Althusser's achievements was to synthesize the principles of structuralism with some of those of Marxism. In replacing Lacan's concept of language with his own conception of ideology, Althusser shifted the previous structuralist focus on how language and other symbolic and cultural forms produce meaning to a poststructuralist focus on how *society* produces individuals. As a relatively autonomous realm of social activity, ideology was seen by Althusser as 'hailing' or 'interpellating' individuals within its processes (1971, 173–75). However, while Althusser's work was clearly influenced by that of Lacan, it retained much of the rigidity and sense of oppression associated with structuralism. As a consequence, Althusser must be regarded as a transitional figure in the shift from structuralism to poststructuralism. Yet, it is through Althusser's work that poststructuralism connects initially with critical work in the Marxist tradition.

Althusser's stress on production at the expense of play and disruption is also apparent in the work of Michel Foucault. Foucault's contribution to poststructuralism has been an understanding of the ways in which knowledge systems come to be formed and exercise authority. Central to this understanding has been the concept of 'discourse,' a regulatory linguistic system that orders the statements through which certain forms of knowledge become possible (Foucault 1970, 1972). Discourses involve distinctive ways of categorizing people, places and things. They make distinctive assumptions about what things are, about where they have come from and about what they may lead to. In this way, discourses are taken to order and 'position' subjects within the world through the manner in which they present the world to subjects as 'given.' Indeed, Foucault's later work (1977, 1978) became increasingly concerned with the historical analysis of the relations between knowledge and *power* as discursively constituted. Foucault's work has been highly influential in instigating a 'linguistic turn' in a wide range of disciplines.

In contrast to Althusser and Foucault, other writers have placed a greater stress on play in processes of structure and signification. Notable among these is Julia Kristeva. Language for Kristeva arises as a consequence of the *semiotic* potential of the body and the interpolation of this potential within conventional linguistic practises as fully realized in society. Language, as a consequence, is not unified, but has feminine and masculine aspects, both of which may be taken up equally by men and women. These aspects are, respectively, the *semiotic*, emerging from the semiotized body, and the symbolic order (conventional language as fully realized in society). In a position that resonates with the initial insights of Derrida, Kristeva argues that the *semiotic* has the potential to constantly disrupt the masculine symbolic order. The manner in which the symbolic order can thus be disrupted by the *semiotic* provides crucial insights into texts as critical sites for a politics of gender and subjectivity. In this respect, reports Chris Weedon (1987), Kristeva argues that 'the return of the repressed feminine is manifest, for example, in the "marginal" discourse of the literary avant-garde, such as the poetry of Lautréamont and Mallarmé and the prose of James Joyce' (69–70).

Kristeva's work is of great importance, not only in itself, but in the influence it exerted in Roland Barthes' transition from the more rigid thinking of conventional structuralism and semiotics, as evidenced, for example, in *Mythologies* (1972), to the more playful features of poststructuralism, as represented in later publications such as *The Pleasure of the Text* (1975). It was the emphasis placed on the characters of texts and textuality in this later period that assured Barthes of an international reputation as both a literary and a cultural critic.

Although such generalizations are dangerous, poststructuralism may thus be thought of as an intellectual tradition concerned initially with the destabilization of language as a structure, and with the ways in which this destabilization allows for the insertion of the subject into processes of signification. A consequent shift in emphasis from 'processes of signification' to 'signifying processes' allows for the idea that the processes through which an individual is constituted as a subject are *synonymous* with those of the generation of meaning. There can, as a consequence, be no meaning prior to its con-

struction in a subject as thus constituted. The constitution of subjects is therefore a 'textual' process, and subjects in this way come to be 'positioned' textually. In the words of Richard Middleton (1990), texts are understood, 'not as communicating or expressing a pre-existing meaning but as "positioning subjects" within a *process* of semiosis.' A subject's experience is thus 'constructed *in* the text, in ideology . . . so the problem of the link between "text" and "experience" disappears' (165). This stress on the production of the subject – a fundamental component of poststructuralist thinking – does not always, however, replicate the emphasis placed by some writers on the potential for rupture that inheres in structures.

Poststructuralism and Popular Music

One of the clearest manifestations of poststructuralist thinking in the analysis of popular music as a cultural form is to be found in the highly influential work of Dick Hebdige. The presence of poststructuralist thinking is most noticeable in Hebdige's analysis (1979) of the 1970s punk movement in the United Kingdom. To a considerable degree, Hebdige's analysis invokes the notion of the structural homology. There was, he says, 'a homological relation between the trashy cut-up clothes and spiky hair, the pogo and amphetamines, the spitting, the vomiting, the format of the fanzines, the insurrectionary poses and the "soulless," frantically driven music' of punk subculture (1979, 114). Clothed in chaos, continues Hebdige, the punks 'produced Noise in the calmly orchestrated Crisis of everyday life in the late 1970s – a noise which made (no)sense . . .' If an epitaph were to be written for the punk subculture, concludes Hebdige, one 'could do no better than repeat Poly Styrene's famous dictum: "Oh Bondage, Up Yours!", or somewhat more concisely: the forbidden is permitted, but, by the same token, nothing, not even these forbidden signifiers (bondage, safety pins, chains, hair-dye, etc.), is sacred and fixed' (1979, 114–15).

There was within punk subculture a steadfast refusal to assign meaning, to allow processes of signification to take their 'usual' course. Hebdige elaborates on this process by analyzing the use of the swastika as a symbol relocated within punk subculture. 'Conventionally, as far as the British were concerned,' says Hebdige, 'the swastika signified "enemy."' In punk usage, however, 'the symbol lost its "natural" meaning – fascism. The punks were not generally sympathetic to the parties of the extreme right' (1979, 116). As a consequence, Hebdige is compelled to resort in his analysis of the swastika's significance 'to the most obvious of explanations – that the swastika was worn because it was guaranteed to shock.' Ultimately, concludes Hebdige, 'the symbol was as "dumb" as the rage it provoked. The key to punk style remains elusive. Instead of arriving at the point where we can begin to make sense of the style, we have reached the very place where meaning itself evaporates' (1979, 116–17).

The problem with such a reading, however, is that its implicit claim to a position of privilege belies the same instability of meaning on which it rests. As Dave Laing (1985) indicates, 'This analysis suffers from a very basic fault: it assumes that the meaning of a symbol's use in a particular context is *single* and is determined by the intentions of the "producer" of that symbol-in-context' (96). Laing illustrates this point by reference to an incident in which a member of a punk band, the Wild Boys, was attacked by a Disco-kid for wearing a swastika armband. As Laing points out: 'No doubt the Wild Boy with the arm band "thought" he was exploiting the swastika as an "empty effect," that he was "communicating" absence of "identifiable values."' Unfortunately for him, however, 'the Disco-kid received the communication differently.' For the Disco-kid, concludes Laing, 'the wearing of the swastika armband (common feature of modern fascist bodies as well as the Nazis) signified that the wearer supported the political views signified by that symbol in public discourse' (1985, 96).

Laing thus paints a more complex picture of punk, in which the potential for play at the heart of poststructuralist thinking is put to work in elucidating punk's contradictions: between the desires to undermine discourses and to create alternative ones; between leanings toward 'realist' and 'avant-garde' creative impulses; and between the use of conventional shock (as in swearing) and shock that brings into question the very basis of meaning. It is instructive that, in discussing this last contradiction, Laing draws not only on the work of Kristeva in the form of the distinction she draws between the *semiotic* and the symbolic order, but also on the later work of Barthes – on which Kristeva's work was so influential – in the form of the distinction Barthes drew in his famous essay, 'The Grain of the Voice' (1977), between 'pheno-song' and 'geno-song.' The representational work of 'pheno-song,' according to Laing, is 'not only in the verbal meaning of the lyric but in the signifieds of emotion provided by recognized musical elements.' By contrast, 'the "geno-song" is what, for a particular listener, remains as a signifier with an elusive signified, an obscure object of desire which cannot be pinned down as a feeling or a person' (1985, 129–30).

The distinction drawn by Barthes does, however, point to some problems in applying poststructuralist thinking to *music* in particular, as distinct from cultural forms more generally. In this connection, it is pertinent to bear in mind Richard Middleton's observation on Hebdige's

work: that 'the musical interpretations, brilliant and persuasive as they are, result not so much from any engagement with the specifics of musical practice . . . as from a participant-observer's mediation of contemporary subcultural consensus: nowhere . . . is there sustained discussion of sounds' (2000, 8).

The primacy almost unexceptionally afforded language among symbolic forms within poststructuralism has resulted in a particular view of music that understands its capacity to signify (or act as a 'signifying practise') as being grounded within the realms of the 'pre-symbolic' and the 'pre-linguistic,' if not the 'unconscious.' Because the sounds of music are thought not to be tied to conventional denotative or referential meanings *in the same way* as the sounds of language, it has been argued that they are synonymous with the fundamental bodily awareness of sound which provides the basis in individuals for the development of language. In other words, because the sounds of music are judged to be 'non-referential' and 'non-denotative' in the same way as the pre-linguistic vocalizations of young children, it has been assumed that music is somehow 'prior,' both ontologically and historically, to language. It is understood to belong to the realm of the semiotized body rather than to that of the symbolic order. And because it is assumed that people do not enter society or the realm of the symbolic until they develop the capacity for language, it is concluded that music can be of significance only to subjects as thus constituted socially – and to have meanings that are socially and culturally constituted – by itself being interpolated into language, that is, by tending toward 'pheno-song' and away from 'geno-song.' The 'obscure object of desire which cannot be pinned down as a feeling or a person' – identified by Laing as characterizing 'geno-song' – *is* obscure because it is taken to reside in a state, the 'pre-symbolic,' the 'pre-linguistic' or the 'unconscious,' to which the listener no longer has direct access.

This way of thinking about music is evident in the work of Kristeva. She has argued that:

[W]hile the fundamental function of language is the *communicative* function, and while it transmits a *meaning*, music is a departure from this principle of communication. It does transmit a 'message' between a subject and an addressee, but it is hard to say that it *communicates* a precise *meaning*. It is a combinatory of differential elements, and evokes an algebraic system more than a discourse. If the addressee hears this combinatory as a sentimental, emotive, patriotic, etc., message, that is the result of a subjective interpretation given within the framework of a cultural system rather than the result of a 'meaning' implicit in the 'message.' (1989, 309)

It is this kind of thinking that has allowed music to occupy a somewhat special and paradoxical place within the tradition of poststructuralism. Because music is thought to be 'prior' to language and social awareness, and because, as a consequence, it is thought to lie somewhat outside the influence of ideological processes, it has come to be assigned a 'state of grace' by some scholars, to be thought of as 'pure' and 'innocent' when compared to the 'ideological loading' accompanying other forms of symbolism.

For Barthes, music in this way becomes an ideal 'Other' to the world of conventional, linguistically mediated and ideologically loaded meaning. To talk about music is thus to compromise its 'innocence.' 'As soon as someone speaks about music,' says Barthes, 'or a specific music – as a value *in itself*, or on the contrary – though this is the same thing – as soon as someone speaks about music as a value *for everyone* – i.e., as soon as we are told we must love all music – we feel a kind of ideological cope falling over the most precious substance of evaluation, music: this is "commentary"' (1985a, 279). For Barthes, music therefore lies outside language in making its appeal directly to the body – but not, however, in a manner that would challenge the primacy of language. When the body 'enunciates (musically),' says Barthes, it ' . . . speaks, it declaims, it doubles its voice: *it speaks but says nothing*: for as soon as it is musical, speech – or its instrumental substitute – is no longer linguistic but corporeal; what it says is always and only this: *my body puts itself in a state of speech: quasi parlando*' (1985b, 306).

This line of thinking has had a general influence in popular music studies, particularly in the work of cultural studies scholars such as Lawrence Grossberg. Given the paradoxical position of music in much poststructuralist thinking, Grossberg has been able to argue that the sounds of music empower people in their everyday lives in a particular way. Music in Grossberg's writings is therefore conceived not as a cipher in reflecting the linguistically and socially constituted meanings – or 'subject positions' – within which it is 'interpolated.' It is conceived as an instigator in their production, but an instigator whose sounds seem to be of little or no consequence (apart from their 'brute' presence) to the particular character of the meanings articulated. Grossberg has argued more than once that meanings in rock music cannot be read from the surface of rock's sounds: ' . . . rock and roll cannot be approached by some textual analysis of its message. Rock and roll, whether live or recorded, is a performance whose "significance" cannot be read off the "text"' (1984, 233). Grossberg thus concentrates on questions that are more removed from those of meaning: 'In order to understand the relationship between rock, youth, and fun, I propose to look at the ways in which rock and roll organizes, not the meanings we give to the world, but the ways we are able to invest and locate energy, importance, even ourselves, in those meanings' (1987, 182). By describing it as a formation, argues Grossberg, 'I want to emphasize the fact that the identity and effect of rock depends on more than its sonorial dimension.' Speaking of rock as a formation 'demands that we always locate musical practices in the context of a complex (and always specific) set of relations with other cultural and social practices; hence I will describe it as a cultural rather than as a musical formation' (1994, 41).

The various dimensions of poststructuralist thought are evident in more complex ways in the work of Barbara Bradby. In an article that explicitly acknowledges the psychoanalytic theories of Lacan, and resonates with the textually gendered politics of Kristeva's work, Bradby argues that 'the "girl talk" represented in [girl-group] songs can be analyzed to reveal a structure of *feminine discourse* which offers positions for the speaking female subject' (1990, 343). These positions are created through the play that is possible between the *semiotic* and the symbolic order, between fantasy and reality, between the imaginary – the sphere through which children travel in moving from the *semiotic* to the social – and the symbolic – the realm of conventional language as fully realized in society. Women are thus not just positioned in traditional roles and locations according to masculine discourse. Rather, the exploration of fantasy and romance in girl-group songs becomes 'an exploration of discourse, or the way in which language allows subjects to position themselves in relation to it.' As Bradby concludes, 'if the songs can . . . be analyzed as and through language, the conclusions show that there are more possibilities in language than the patriarchal dominance of symbolic over imaginary proposed as universal by Lacan' (1990, 367).

The debt to Lacanian psychoanalytic theory is evident also in an earlier essay by Bradby and Brian Torode (1984). In analyzing the lyrics of Buddy Holly's 'Peggy Sue,' the authors conclude that the 'song lyrics constantly reiterate a parallel between the infant's situation as a learner of language in early childhood, and the adolescent's situation as a listener to the song, learning the adult language of love' (1984, 204). This analysis does not depend on language alone, however. In a song such as 'Peggy Sue,' claim the authors, 'the role of rhythm in the dramatic representation is crucial.' Its role 'is to intervene in and to transform the meaning of the lyrics.' Yet language remains supreme, for rhythm in itself is 'meaningless: which is why, almost without exception, instrumental rock music is so banal.' Rhythms in this way appear to mediate between the *semiotic* and the symbolic: they 'represent a stylised re-enactment of the life of the child within the domestic scene, a life which the infant is – with intense excitement – preparing to enter, and which the adolescent is – with equal excitement – preparing to leave' (1984, 204–205).

Conclusion

Poststructuralism has thus had a varied yet pervasive influence on the study of popular music. Yet, regardless of how poststructuralist thinking on music has been assimilated and put to use by popular music scholars, it has not been immune to criticism. Poststructuralist thinking on music has in many cases rendered it almost completely amorphous as a symbolic form and, as Middleton observes, has placed it in a situation where virtually any meaning or 'subject position' can be associated with it. In the case of Barthes, says Middleton, the suspicion is 'that "anything goes": that along with meaning, the category of critique itself is abandoned, leaving the field to political quietism, untheorized spontaneism, or apolitical hedonism' (1990, 266–67). Poststructuralist thinking on music was, in the late 1990s, subject to a thoroughgoing critique by Shepherd and Wicke (1997).

Bibliography

Althusser, Louis. 1971. 'Ideology and Ideological State Apparatuses (Notes Towards an Investigation).' In Louis Althusser, *Lenin and Philosophy, and Other Essays*, trans. Ben Brewster. London: New Left Books, 127–86.

Barthes, Roland. 1972. *Mythologies*, trans. Annette Lavers. New York: Hill and Wang. (Originally published as *Mythologies*. Paris: Éditions du Seuil, 1957.)

Barthes, Roland. 1975. *The Pleasure of the Text*, trans. Richard Miller. New York: Hill and Wang. (Originally published as *Le Plaisir du texte*. Paris: Éditions du Seuil, 1973.)

Barthes, Roland. 1977. 'The Grain of the Voice.' In Roland Barthes, *Image, Music, Text*, trans. Stephen Heath. New York: Hill and Wang, 179–89.

Barthes, Roland. 1985a. 'Music, Voice, Language.' In Roland Barthes, *The Responsibility of Forms: Critical Essays on Music, Art, and Representation*, trans. Richard Howard. New York: Hill and Wang, 278–85. (Originally published as *L'Obvie et l'obtus*. Paris: Éditions du Seuil, 1982.)

Barthes, Roland. 1985b. 'Rasch.' In Roland Barthes, *The Responsibility of Forms: Critical Essays on Music, Art, and Representation*, trans. Richard Howard. New York: Hill and Wang, 299–312. (Originally published as *L'Obvie et l'obtus*. Paris: Éditions du Seuil, 1982.)

Bradby, Barbara. 1990. 'Do-Talk and Don't-Talk: The Division of the Subject in Girl-Group Music.' In *On Record: Rock, Pop, and the Written Word*, ed. Simon Frith and Andrew Goodwin. London: Routledge, 341–68.

Bradby, Barbara, and Torode, Brian. 1984. 'Pity Peggy Sue.' *Popular Music* 4: 183–205.

Derrida, Jacques. 1978. 'Structure, Sign, and Play in the Discourse of the Human Sciences.' In Jacques Derrida, *Writing and Difference*, trans. Alan Bass. Chicago: University of Chicago Press, 278–93. (Originally published as *L'Écriture et la différence*. Paris: Éditions du Seuil, 1967.)

Engh, Barbara. 1993. 'Loving It: Music and Criticism in Roland Barthes.' In *Musicology and Difference: Gender and Sexuality in Music Scholarship*, ed. Ruth A. Solie. Berkeley, CA: University of California Press, 66–79.

Foucault, Michel. 1970. *The Order of Things: An Archaeology of the Human Sciences*. London: Tavistock. (Originally published as *Les Mots et les choses: une archéologie des sciences humaines*. Paris: Gallimard, 1966.)

Foucault, Michel. 1972. *The Archaeology of Knowledge*, trans. A.M. Sheridan Smith. New York: Pantheon. (Originally published as *L'Archéologie du savoir*. Paris: Gallimard, 1969.)

Foucault, Michel. 1977. *Discipline and Punish: The Birth of the Prison*, trans. Alan Sheridan. New York: Pantheon. (Originally published as *Surveiller et punir*. Paris: Gallimard, 1975.)

Foucault, Michel. 1978. *The History of Sexuality*, trans. Robert Hurley. New York: Pantheon. (Originally published as *Histoire de la sexualité*. Paris: Gallimard, 1976.)

Grossberg, Lawrence. 1984. 'Another Boring Day in Paradise: Rock and Roll and the Empowerment of Everyday Life.' *Popular Music* 4: 225–58.

Grossberg, Lawrence. 1987. 'Rock and Roll in Search of an Audience.' In *Popular Music and Communication*, ed. James Lull. Newbury Park, CA: Sage, 175–97.

Grossberg, Lawrence. 1994. 'Is Anybody Listening? Does Anybody Care?: On "The State of Rock."' In *Microphone Fiends: Youth Music & Youth Culture*, ed. Andrew Ross and Tricia Rose. New York and London: Routledge, 41–58.

Hebdige, Dick. 1979. *Subculture: The Meaning of Style*. London: Methuen.

Kristeva, Julia. 1989. *Language – the Unknown: An Initiation into Linguistics*, trans. Anne M. Menke. New York: Columbia University Press. (Originally published as *Le Langage, cet inconnu: une initiation à la linguistique*. Paris: Éditions du Seuil, 1981.)

Lacan, Jacques. 1968. *The Language of the Self: The Function of Language in Psychoanalysis*, trans. Anthony Wilden. Baltimore and London: Johns Hopkins University Press. (Originally published as *Fonction et champ de la parole et du langage en psychanalyse*. Paris, 1956.)

Lacan, Jacques. 1977. *Écrits: A Selection*, trans. Alan Sheridan. New York: W.W. Norton. (Originally published as *Écrits*. Paris: Éditions du Seuil, 1966.)

Lacan, Jacques. 1979. *The Four Fundamental Concepts of Psycho-Analysis*, ed. Jacques-Alain Miller, trans. Alan Sheridan. Harmondsworth: Penguin. (*Les Quatre concepts fondamentaux de la psychanalyse*, originally published as Vol. 11 of *Le Séminaire de Jacques Lacan*. Paris: Éditions du Seuil, 1973.)

Lacan, Jacques. 1982. *Feminine Sexuality: Jacques Lacan and the école freudienne*, ed. Juliet Mitchell and Jacqueline Rose, trans. Jacqueline Rose. New York: W.W. Norton.

Laing, Dave. 1985. *One Chord Wonders: Power and Meaning in Punk Rock*. Milton Keynes: Open University Press.

Middleton, Richard. 1990. *Studying Popular Music*. Milton Keynes: Open University Press.

Middleton, Richard. 2000. 'Introduction: Locating the Popular Music Text.' In *Reading Pop: Approaches to Textual Analysis in Popular Music*, ed. Richard Middleton. Oxford: Oxford University Press, 1–19.

Moi, Toril, ed. 1986. *The Kristeva Reader*. Oxford: Basil Blackwell.

Payne, Michael. 1993. *Reading Theory: An Introduction to Lacan, Derrida, and Kristeva*. Oxford: Blackwell.

Piaget, Jean. 1971. *Structuralism*, ed. and trans. Chaninah Maschler. London: Routledge and Kegan Paul. (Originally published as *Le Structuralisme*. Paris: P.U.F., 1968.)

Roudinesco, Elisabeth. 1990. *Jacques Lacan & Co.: A History of Psychoanalysis in France, 1925–1985*, trans. Jeffrey Mehlman. Chicago: University of Chicago Press. (Originally published as Vol. 2 of *La Bataille de cent ans: histoire de la psychanalyse en France*. Paris: Éditions du Seuil, 1986.)

Shepherd, John, and Wicke, Peter. 1997. *Music and Cultural Theory*. Cambridge: Polity Press.

Weedon, Chris. 1987. *Feminist Practice and Poststructuralist Theory*. Oxford: Basil Blackwell.

Discographical Reference

Holly, Buddy. 'Peggy Sue.' Coral 61885. *1957*: USA.

JOHN SHEPHERD

Psychoanalysis

Psychoanalysis is a therapeutic method originated by Sigmund Freud for the treatment of disorders of the personality or behavior. Its principal tool is the 'talking cure,' based on dialog between the trained psychoanalyst and the analysand. During the twentieth century, psychoanalysis was also recognized as a potent theory of human subjectivity and became widely employed in criticism and analysis of artistic practises and products, including music of all kinds. As Gorbman (1987) writes:

'Psychoanalytic theory provides a particularly compelling framework for considering . . . musical emotion and pleasure' (61). Since Freud, various rival schools of psychoanalysis have developed, but the version of the theory most frequently employed in cultural analysis has been that associated with Jacques Lacan, not least because of its 'poststructuralist' emphasis on the role of language in the formation of human subjectivity.

Freudian theory assumes a divided subject, a necessary but impossible construct of forces at perpetual odds in the psyche, between, for example, the affirmations of unconscious drives and the negations of taboos from social spaces. Kohut and Levarie (1957) posit different forms of musical pleasure for the three levels of the mind posited by Freud: 'emotional catharsis for repressed wishes (Id) . . . , mastering of the threats of trauma (Ego) and enjoyable submission to rules (Super-ego)' (406) (see Freud 1953–; for information about Freudian psychoanalysis and other theories of psychoanalysis before Lacan, see Laplanche and Pontalis 1973). For Freud, the structure of the divided subject and its attempts at stability are everywhere in psychic formations and history. His influential theory of *fort-da* suggests that the child makes up for lack of constant attention through play in which active mastery of symbolic distance compensates for his/her passive position in relation to the parent(s) (see Freud 1971, Part II).

The Oedipus complex is another cornerstone of Freudian psychoanalysis in which the child always feels at once comforted and conflicted in the child–mother–father triangle. In a book that randomly employs Freudian ideas to discuss gender roles in rock music, Reynolds and Press (1995) draw on a key feature of the Oedipus complex when they ask rhetorically: 'At its very core, is the meaning of rock incest?' (217).

Lacanian psychoanalysis suggests that the unconscious is structured like a language, splitting experience into fragments that get combined and reassembled like bits of binary code (see Fink 1995). Lacan understands three registers of psychic activity: the Imaginary, the Symbolic and the Real (Lacan 1977, 1978; for introductions to Lacan's work, see Hill 1997; Zizek 1991b, 1992a; Evans 1996). The Imaginary is the experience and the representation of mutually exclusive binary oppositions of plenitude and emptiness, of presence and absence. It is the basis of Lacan's influential 'mirror phase' (Lacan's 'Mirror Phase' (1977, 1–7) is perhaps one of the shortest, most difficult and most highly influential works in psychoanalytic history). In this phase, the infant between the ages of six and 18 months sees him/herself reflected in the ideal image of the mirror (actual mirror, surface of water, face of the mother, face of the other). As the infant gains motor control, he/she 'realizes' in retrospect that the mirror image has always/already been flat, two-dimensional and empty. This revision of early mirror fantasy makes language acquisition possible – the basis of the Lacanian Symbolic Order. While the Imaginary always gives an individual all or nothing, the Symbolic never gives all or nothing but always gives something – linguistic signifiers.

Lacanian psychoanalysis has influenced film theory and cultural studies. Metz (1982) and the contributors to the French journal *Cahiers du cinéma* pioneered this approach, which was in turn developed by the English-language journal *Screen*. More recently, the Slovenian school has been particularly influential in applying Lacan's concepts to popular cultural artifacts. Slavoj Zizek brings together German philosophy, US popular culture and Lacanian psychoanalysis (see Zizek 1989, 1991a, 1992b, 1993, 1994a, 1994b). Other Slovenian writers are working out issues of the relations between musical texts, history and psychoanalysis (see, in particular, Salecl and Zizek 1996).

Lacanian psychoanalysis has had a profound impact on theories of how sound works in early childhood development and in cinema. Researchers working in France have developed a theory of the sonorous envelope – a phase of development in which the newly born infant feels at one with the sound, smell and touch of the mother (see, in particular, Anzieu 1989, 1990a, 1990b; Rosolato 1974). Some writers have taken the sonorous envelope as a fantasy/representation of being enclosed in sound in both physical movie theaters and film soundtracks. Others have shown that the sonorous envelope can be either a positive or a negative fantasy depending on the context.

These writers further suggest that, in the acoustic mirror, the developing child learns to hear the difference between his/her own voice and the voices around him/her – the voices of the mother, the father and others. In this crucial moment, the child hears at once a separating difference between his/her own voice and the voices around him/her and, crucially, a new sense of a communication that this difference paradoxically makes possible (on semiotics and psychoanalysis, see Silverman 1983; on psychoanalysis, feminism and film music, see Silverman 1988; see also Silverman 1992). Later writers have begun to explore the potential of applying the acoustic mirror to musical pieces (see Schwarz 1997).

Historical musicology and psychoanalytic approaches have been combined in the work of Lawrence Kramer, who has applied Lacan's mirror phase to Beethoven's two movement sonata forms (1990), brought music and psychosexual issues together in a study of Schubert (1998), and addressed the relationships between post-modernism, music and psychoanalysis (1995). Bowie

(1993, 93–104) has used a psychoanalytic approach to illuminate the textual transformations of Mozart's and Da Ponte's *Così fan tutte*.

With the exception of Schwarz (1997), the application of Lacanian concepts to popular music has been less than systematic. For example, Gabbard (1996, 139–58) discusses 'phallic' and 'post-phallic' jazz trumpet playing without reference to the conceptual role of the phallus in Lacanian thought, while Waksman (1999) describes Jimi Hendrix's guitar as a 'technophallus' (188). Schwarz employs Lacanian concepts in analyses of such varied musical products as a song by Peter Gabriel, German 'oi' music and a performance by Diamanda Galas. In the Galas chapter, Schwarz makes use of the concept of the 'abject' developed by the post-Lacanian psychoanalyst Julia Kristeva (1982). Other authors have drawn on Kristevan concepts such as the 'abject,' 'jouissance,' 'pheno-text' and 'geno-text' in discussing various forms of popular music, often using Roland Barthes' appropriation of Kristeva's ideas in his influential essay 'The Grain of the Voice' (1977). These authors include Laing (1985), Reynolds (1990), Gilbert and Pearson (1999) and Whiteley (2000). Elsewhere, Shank (1994) claims that 'Lacan's theorisation of desire and the metonymic chain along which it proceeds can provide a basis for understanding the social construction of the possible positions from which a musician or a fan may speak, may sing, may dance, may desire' (129).

To the extent that a piece of music is always/already a product of at once an historical moment and a composer, a performer and a listener, psychoanalysis can provide a vocabulary for bringing these elements together. The relationship between psychoanalysis and history is an uneasy one in any discipline. Scholars who bring psychoanalytic insights into history and historical insights into psychoanalysis often find that one discourse dominates the other. Many wish that there were a third term between them – a term that would mediate the notion that everyone shares certain psychic formations (played out in endless variations from one person to the next) in historical moments that are at once a reflection of such formations and resistant to them. Others, such as Nehring (1997) and Shepherd and Wicke (1997), are more skeptical about the value of the contribution of psychoanalysis to musical metadiscourse.

Bibliography

Anzieu, Didier. 1989. *The Skin Ego*, trans. Chris Turner. New Haven, CT: Yale University Press.

Anzieu, Didier. 1990a. *A Skin for Thought: Interviews with Gilbert Tarrab on Psychology and Psychoanalysis*, trans. Daphne Nash Briggs. London: Karnac Books.

Anzieu, Didier, ed. 1990b. *Psychic Envelopes*, trans. Daphne Nash Briggs. London: Karnac Books.

Barthes, Roland. 1977. 'The Grain of the Voice.' In Roland Barthes, *Image, Music, Text*, trans. Stephen Heath. New York: Hill and Wang, 179–89.

Bowie, Malcolm. 1993. *Psychoanalysis and the Future of Theory*. Oxford: Blackwell.

Evans, Dylan. 1996. *An Introductory Dictionary of Lacanian Psychoanalysis*. London and New York: Routledge.

Fink, Bruce. 1995. *The Lacanian Subject: Between Language and Jouissance*. Princeton, NJ: Princeton University Press.

Freud, Sigmund. 1953–. *The Standard Edition of the Complete Psychological Works of Sigmund Freud*, ed. James Strachey. 24 vols. London: Hogarth Press.

Freud, Sigmund. 1971. *Beyond the Pleasure Principle*. New York and London: W.W. Norton and Company.

Gabbard, Krin. 1996. *Jammin' at the Margins: Jazz and the American Cinema*. Chicago: University of Chicago Press.

Gilbert, Jeremy, and Pearson, Ewan. 1999. *Discographies: Dance Music, Culture, and the Politics of Sound*. London and New York: Routledge.

Gorbman, Claudia. 1987. *Unheard Melodies: Narrative Film Music*. Bloomington, IN: Indiana University Press.

Hill, Philip. 1997. *Lacan for Beginners*. London: Writers and Readers, Ltd.

Kohut, H., and Levarie, S. 1957. 'Observations on the Psychological Functions of Music.' *Journal of the American Psychoanalytic Association* 5: 389–407.

Kramer, Lawrence. 1990. *Music as Cultural Practice, 1800–1900*. Berkeley, CA: University of California Press.

Kramer, Lawrence. 1995. *Classical Music and Postmodern Knowledge*. Berkeley, CA: University of California Press.

Kramer, Lawrence. 1998. *Franz Schubert: Sexuality, Subjectivity, Song*. Cambridge and New York: Cambridge University Press.

Kristeva, Julia. 1982. *Powers of Horror: An Essay on Abjection*, trans. Leon S. Roudiez. New York: Columbia University Press.

Lacan, Jacques. 1977. *Écrits: A Selection*, trans. Alan Sheridan. New York: W.W. Norton and Company.

Lacan, Jacques. 1978. *The Four Fundamental Concepts of Psycho-Analysis*, ed. Jacques-Alain Miller, trans. Alan Sheridan. New York: W.W. Norton and Company.

Laing, Dave. 1985. *One Chord Wonders: Power and Meaning in Punk Rock*. Milton Keynes: Open University Press.

Laplanche, J., and Pontalis, J.-B. 1973. *The Language of Psycho-Analysis*, trans. Donald Nicholson-Smith. New York: W.W. Norton and Company.

Metz, Christian. 1982. *The Imaginary Signifier: Psychoanalysis and the Cinema*, trans. Celia Britton et al. Bloomington, IN: Indiana University Press.

Nehring, Neil. 1997. *Popular Music, Gender, and Postmodernism: Anger Is an Energy*. Thousand Oaks, CA: Sage Publications.

Reynolds, Simon. 1990. *Blissed Out: The Raptures of Rock*. London: Serpent's Tail.

Reynolds, Simon, and Press, Joy. 1995. *The Sex Revolts: Gender, Rebellion and Rock 'n' Roll*. London: Serpent's Tail.

Rosolato, Guy. 1974. 'La voix: entre corps et langage' [The Voice: Between Body and Language]. *Revue française de psychanalyse* 38(1): 75–94.

Salecl, Renata, and Zizek, Slavoj, eds. 1996. *Gaze and Voice as Love Objects*. Durham, NC: Duke University Press.

Schwarz, David. 1997. *Listening Subjects: Music, Psychoanalysis, Culture*. Durham, NC: Duke University Press.

Shank, Barry. 1994. *Dissonant Identities: The Rock 'n' Roll Scene in Austin, Texas*. Hanover, NH: University Press of New England.

Shepherd, John, and Wicke, Peter. 1997. *Music and Cultural Theory*. Cambridge: Polity Press.

Silverman, Kaja. 1983. *The Subject of Semiotics*. New York and Oxford: Oxford University Press.

Silverman, Kaja. 1988. *The Acoustic Mirror: The Female Voice in Psychoanalysis and Cinema*. Bloomington, IN: Indiana University Press.

Silverman, Kaja. 1992. *Male Subjectivity at the Margins*. New York and London: Routledge.

Sullivan, Henry W. 1995. *The Beatles with Lacan: Rock 'n' Roll as Requiem for the Modern Age*. New York: Peter Lang.

Waksman, Steve. 1999. *Instruments of Desire: The Electric Guitar and the Shaping of Musical Experience*. Cambridge, MA: Harvard University Press.

Whiteley, Sheila. 2000. *Women and Popular Music: Sexuality, Identity, and Subjectivity*. London and New York: Routledge.

Zizek, Slavoj. 1989. *The Sublime Object of Ideology*. London and New York: Verso.

Zizek, Slavoj. 1991a. *For They Know Not What They Do: Enjoyment as a Political Factor*. London and New York: Verso.

Zizek, Slavoj. 1991b. *Looking Awry: An Introduction to Jacques Lacan Through Popular Culture*. Cambridge, MA: MIT Press.

Zizek, Slavoj. 1992a. *Enjoy Your Symptom!: Jacques Lacan in Hollywood and Out*. New York and London: Routledge.

Zizek, Slavoj, ed. 1992b. *Everything You Always Wanted to Know About Lacan (But Were Afraid to Ask Hitchcock)*. London and New York: Verso.

Zizek, Slavoj. 1993. *Tarrying with the Negative: Kant, Hegel, and the Critique of Ideology*. Durham, NC: Duke University Press.

Zizek, Slavoj, ed. 1994a. *Mapping Ideology*. London and New York: Verso.

Zizek, Slavoj. 1994b. *The Metastases of Enjoyment: Six Essays on Woman and Causality*. London and New York: Verso.

DAVID SCHWARZ and DAVE LAING

Reception and Consumption Theory

'Reception' denotes the receiving of messages from media sources, while 'consumption' refers to the consuming of media messages. The terms are often used in combination with the concept of audience: an assembly of listeners or hearers. Reception, consumption and the audience have become more important as the study of mass media has brought the realization that social and cultural contexts make a significant contribution to the meanings derived from texts – meanings that may be very different from those the author or producers intend.

The rise of mass-mediated forms of communication in the twentieth century (in particular film and radio and, subsequently, television) led to a number of concerns about the wider effects of these forms on society and individuals. Thus, in its early days, radio was thought to be potentially a tool in the hands of political propagandists (especially in the totalitarian states of the USSR and Nazi Germany). Reception would be determined by political elites, and audiences might be brainwashed. In more democratic societies such as the United States, radio was often linked to the rise of a consumer society or culture and was used to sell particular goods, such as soap powders, in a direct way. From the early days of discussion about reception and audiences, therefore, there has been concern about political manipulation and the wider effects of the control of media messages by those possessing political power and control over economic production.

This sort of approach, which emphasizes notions of manipulation and control, is familiar from commonsense and everyday media discourse. Concern is expressed about the way in which individuals or society are affected by the messages contained in certain media. Particular anxiety is expressed about some vulnerable members of society (especially children or the socially isolated), or about the way in which a society or a culture is degraded by the power of certain media forms. The media are regarded as stimuli that provoke certain reactions on the part of individuals or that lead to social states akin to being drugged. The media are seen to influence or affect through such mechanisms. Many

familiar controversies about the effects of pop or rock music operate in such a domain. For example, the lawsuit over the work of the heavy metal group Judas Priest concerned the extent to which subliminal messages had led to the suicide of two of the group's fans. In a wider context, the arguments for censorship and classification of popular music by the Parents Music Resource Center (PMRC) in the United States reflect a model of the media in which messages are pumped into the minds of vulnerable people, leading to the moral decline of society (Walser 1993).

This concern with effects has been criticized by the uses and gratifications approach to the study of audiences which, as its label suggests, concerns itself with the way in which individuals use the media to gratify certain wants or needs. Much consumer research on, for example, patterns of spending on CDs derives from assumptions about consumers satisfying individual needs through their purchases. Shuker (1998, 63–64; see also Shuker 1994, 229–35) summarizes the main patterns: rock and pop music is mainly consumed by young people (12–25 years old), although those in older age groups have become more important as rock and pop has 'matured' (see also Longhurst 1995, 208); consumption is patterned by age and gender, with younger people, in particular girls, liking pop, and older people liking more rock-based forms; older listeners tend to explore a wider range of genres; some studies show links between the consumption of particular types of music and 'anti-school attitudes'; and 'in ethnically mixed or diverse populations, black adolescents are demonstrably more likely (than their white or Asian counterparts) to favour black music genres' (Shuker 1998, 64).

More radical writers have offered a fundamental critique of approaches that impute individualized effects or wants, or that simply characterize consumption by aggregated individuals (Hall 1980, 1982). In particular, Hall suggests that such paradigms have been unable to understand the complex operation of ideology in contemporary societies. On the basis of a sophisticated Marxism derived in particular from Gramsci and Althusser, Hall argues for a revolution in the study of reception and consumption. In his suggested approach, the audience is considered as structured according to a number of significant social indicators, especially class, gender, race and age. The media message is no longer understood as a stimulus or as a satisfier of wants, but as a complexly structured text, which requires decoding by the analyst using tools derived from semiotics and by members of the audience in accordance with their social status. The media contribute to the way in which an unequal society is reproduced by encouraging dominated groups to accept their domination. The media have a hegemonic role in society. However, cultural forms can also be generated, even from within the capitalist-dominated culture industries, that resist the dominant forms; alternatively, resistance can be derived from the ways in which certain texts are understood or redefined in particular types of use.

This approach has also been used to discuss popular music. On the one hand, pop and rock music can be seen to be part of the ideological constitution of society. As has often been noted, rock music textually constructs certain images of women and gender; these images then contribute to the dominant conceptions of women and to the continued gender oppression and inequality in contemporary society (Reynolds and Press 1995; Whiteley 1997). On the other hand, resistance to such messages and dominant meanings can be found in the use of popular music texts within subcultures and, in particular, within youth subcultures. Music becomes part of a lived subculture that resists dominant meanings (Hall and Jefferson 1976). For example, Willis (1978) shows the centrality of early rock 'n' roll to motorbike boys and of album-based progressive rock to hippies. Other authors have pointed to the way in which pop groups and pop stars are used in gendered subcultures (for example, Garratt 1984). Likewise, certain forms of music, such as punk rock, were sometimes produced in ways that sought to go outside the terrain of the established music industry and to provide alternative or oppositional resources within the punk subculture (Hebdige 1979). The study of popular music as used in youth subcultures has been a continuing theme since the 1960s (see Gelder and Thornton 1997; Thornton 1995).

The consideration of ideological incorporation and resistance has been very influential within the study of reception and consumption. However, its influence and success have led to the identification of some problems. In particular, concern has been expressed about (a) the way in which there is a tendency to view society as somewhat statically divided into a number of antagonistic social groups, which reflect deeper structures; (b) the way in which the complexities of the contemporary media are conceptualized as a number of texts; and (c) the reading of diverse practises and interpretations within a framework of incorporation and resistance. In some respects, many musical practises and phenomena may be interpreted as oppositional when in fact this interpretation may be in the mind of the observer.

As these problems emerged, a new approach began to cohere. In this approach, the emphasis is on how audiences are socially constructed and reconstructed through their interactions with a variety of media. In societies in which a broad variety of media has taken on increased

importance, social life is seen as bound up with interactions fueled by media resources (Willis et al. 1990). Such interactions rely on the ways in which people present themselves or 'perform' in everyday life, which increasingly draw on the 'spectacular' styles, images and modes of behavior offered up by the media. This means that there is a reconceptualization of the media. The media are seen as constituting a mediascape, which is negotiated by the audience in the way that a landscape is. Of particular importance is the way in which media contribute to the development and re-formation of identity and conceptions of self. The picture that emerges from this approach is one of great fluidity and contingency. The way in which music is received and consumed provides much evidence for the ability of this paradigm to explain contemporary social and cultural life.

Popular music is important to the constitution and reconstitution of contemporary identities (Frith 1996). It crosses national boundaries more easily than almost any cultural form and is central to many groups. The development of a number of studies of fans (for example, Aizlewood 1994; Roberts 1994; Lewis 1992) points to the significance of music in this respect. Of particular importance here has been the consideration of the meaning of music and its affective role in social life (Grossberg 1992). Levels of regard and affection for different forms of music may, therefore, be heightened at certain transitional points along life's course – for example, adolescence, parental breakup or relationship breakdown. Music is also part of the mediascape and of contemporary social life and interaction in ways that audience members or consumers find difficult to put into words: 'Music is just part of life, like air. You live with it all the time, so it's tough to judge what it means to you' (Crafts et al. 1993, 109). In this approach, music is a part of everyday life, which is increasingly constituted through media (see also Finnegan 1989).

It can be suggested, therefore, that concern with issues surrounding the reception and consumption of popular music gets to the heart of contemporary social life. There is still scope for the study of 'simple' audiences – people attending a live event such as a rock concert, for instance (Shuker 1994, 198–224). The characteristic modes of social interaction, social patterns and suchlike might be considered. Likewise, the behavior of members of mass audiences listening to mass-mediated and reproduced music can be examined, through studies of the mass circulation of musical commodities and the meanings they generate. Another trend has been the examination of music and music preference as a form of cultural or subcultural capital (see Thornton 1995; Negus 1996, 21–22). However, these processes are increasingly patterned by the interactions of everyday life, or by what can be called the 'diffused' audience (Abercrombie and Longhurst 1998), in which being an audience member is constitutive of everyday life in advanced capitalist societies.

It is certain that debate will continue over the effects of reception and consumption and the constitution of audiences. However, although these issues remain intensely controversial, it is increasingly being recognized that the complexity of global media and cultures problematizes early and continuing understandings of the effect and ideological functions of media. The consideration of the reception and consumption of popular music has been central to these developments and is likely to remain so.

Bibliography

Abercrombie, Nicholas, and Longhurst, Brian. 1998. *Audiences: A Sociological Theory of Performance and Imagination.* London: Sage.

Aizlewood, John, ed. 1994. *Love Is the Drug.* London: Penguin.

Crafts, Susan D., Cavicchi, Daniel, and Keil, Charles. 1993. *My Music.* Hanover, NH: Wesleyan University Press.

Finnegan, Ruth. 1989. *The Hidden Musicians: Music-Making in an English Town.* Cambridge: Cambridge University Press.

Frith, Simon. 1996. 'Music and Identity.' In *Questions of Cultural Identity*, ed. Stuart Hall and Paul du Gay. London: Sage, 108–27.

Garratt, Sheryl. 1984. 'All of Us Love All of You.' In Sue Steward and Sheryl Garratt, *Signed, Sealed and Delivered: True Life Stories of Women in Pop.* London: Pluto, 138–51.

Gelder, Ken, and Thornton, Sarah, eds. 1997. *The Subcultures Reader.* London: Routledge.

Grossberg, Lawrence. 1992. 'Is There a Fan in the House?: The Affective Sensibility of Fandom.' In *The Adoring Audience: Fan Culture and Popular Media*, ed. Lisa A. Lewis. London and New York: Routledge, 5–65.

Hall, Stuart. 1980. 'Encoding/Decoding.' In *Culture, Media, Language: Working Papers in Cultural Studies, 1972–79*, ed. Stuart Hall et al. London: Hutchinson, 128–38.

Hall, Stuart. 1982. 'The Rediscovery of "Ideology": Return of the Repressed in Media Studies.' In *Culture, Society and the Media*, ed. Michael Gurevitch et al. London: Methuen, 56–90.

Hall, Stuart, and Jefferson, Tony, eds. 1976. *Resistance Through Rituals: Youth Subcultures in Post-War Britain.* London: Hutchinson.

Hebdige, Dick. 1979. *Subculture: The Meaning of Style.* London: Methuen.

Lewis, Lisa A., ed. 1992. *The Adoring Audience: Fan Culture and Popular Media.* London and New York: Routledge.

Longhurst, Brian. 1995. *Popular Music and Society.* Cambridge: Polity Press.

Negus, Keith. 1996. *Popular Music in Theory: An Introduction.* Cambridge: Polity Press.

Reynolds, Simon, and Press, Joy. 1995. *The Sex Revolts: Gender, Rebellion, and Rock 'n' Roll.* London: Serpent's Tail.

Roberts, Chris, ed. 1994. *Idle Worship: How Pop Empowers the Weak, Rewards the Faithful and Succours the Needy.* London: Harper Collins.

Shuker, Roy. 1994. *Understanding Popular Music.* London and New York: Routledge.

Shuker, Roy. 1998. *Key Concepts in Popular Music.* London and New York: Routledge.

Thornton, Sarah. 1995. *Club Cultures: Music, Media and Subcultural Capital.* Cambridge: Polity Press.

Walser, Robert. 1993. *Running with the Devil: Power, Gender and Madness in Heavy Metal Music.* Hanover and London: Wesleyan University Press.

Whiteley, Sheila, ed. 1997. *Sexing the Groove: Popular Music and Gender.* London and New York: Routledge.

Willis, Paul. 1978. *Profane Culture.* London: Routledge.

Willis, Paul, et al. 1990. *Common Culture: Symbolic Work at Play in the Everyday Cultures of the Young.* Milton Keynes: Open University Press.

BRIAN LONGHURST

Semiology/Semiotics

Semiology/semiotics (from the Greek *semeion*, meaning 'sign') is the science of signs, as proposed initially by the French linguist Ferdinand de Saussure, who modeled his ideas of semiology on his theories of language (Saussure 1974; first published in 1916), and by his contemporary, the US philosopher Charles Peirce, for whom semiotics – the study of the entire field of patterned communicative processes – was synonymous with logic. A sign is 'something which stands to somebody for something in some respect or capacity' (Peirce, quoted in Hawkes 1977, 126). Peirce distinguishes between various types of sign, notably the *symbol* (where the relationship between sign and object is purely conventional), the *index* (where it is causal) and the *icon* (where it is marked by structural resemblance). Iconic signification has sometimes been considered particularly important in music, and will be discussed below. Indexical signification (where, for instance, a final fade both points to and produces the end of a performance) might be thought to be more important, in such a 'performative' practise as music, than the literature suggests. The mode of symbolic signification dominates the Saussurean system (as it dominates the processes of natural language) and, of the two founding fathers, it is Saussure who had far more influence on the ways in which semiology/semiotics was used within the twentieth-century human sciences, including cultural studies, musicology and popular music studies.

Saussure (one of the progenitors of structuralism) sees language as a self-sustaining, internally coherent system, operating through relations of difference between its constituent units. A huge number of permutations of a small number of available phonemic units generates such distinctions, in sound and hence in meaning, as that between '*dog*' and '*bog*.' Analysis at this level (*synchronic* analysis) reveals what Saussure terms *langue* – the abstract system of the language, access to which produces individual utterances (*parole*). Each significant unit (say, a word) is a *sign*, that is, a two-sided entity holding together a 'sound-image' (or *signifier*) and a 'concept' (or *signified*), and – crucially for Saussure – the relationship between signifier and signified is 'arbitrary': while the sign <dog> brings together the sound-image 'dog' and the concept of a particular sort of animal, nothing in this relationship is 'natural,' and in a different language another signifier (e.g., *chien*) covers the same signified. (Actually, within a given language the relationship is not exactly 'arbitrary' – language-users cannot choose to disregard it – and better terms would be 'conventional' or 'unmotivated.')

Music has often been seen as an internally coherent, autonomous system, relatively detached from 'real life,' and, in this sense, it would seem well placed to benefit from the extension of Saussure's approach, at the hands of Barthes (1967) and others, into a full-fledged theory of semiology. Yet, while the picture of music as a network of signifiers is appealing, on the plane of the signified, the existence in music of denotation (clear, well-bounded semantic reference) seems problematic, or at the very least clearly secondary to connotation (the huge range of associations built on denotations). And this inhibits not only the possibility of a rigorous interpretation of musical signs, but even the possibility of dividing off, segmenting, the signifiers in the first place.

This lacuna has afflicted all attempts at a 'hard' semiology of music – and perhaps helps to explain why, in work on popular music, a focus on a broader, more contextual perspective (a 'softer' approach?) has been more common. Particularly important sources include the 'functionalism' of the Prague School, as mediated especially by Roman Jakobson (1960), which stresses the multidimensionality of the communication process; Barthes' work on the 'mythic' structures of meaning in popular cultural texts (Barthes 1972); theories deriving from the poststructuralism of Lacan, Kristeva and the later Barthes, which break the link between signifier and signified, emphasizing a para-musical fluidity of meaning as it flows along chains of signifiers; and theories of

discourse, which center on larger units of meaning and their formations, as these condition available interpretations. Within work influenced by such approaches, there has been to some extent a tacit agreement to, so to speak, set to one side the question of 'primary signification' in music (Hawkes 1977, 130–34; Middleton 1990, ch. 6). This move has had fruitful results, but, arguably, leaves the consideration of important issues in abeyance.

Semiology and Popular Music Studies

While the typical response to semiology in mainstream music theory has been to pursue its apparent potential for rigorous analysis, anything approaching such a 'hard' approach has been rare in popular music studies. Perhaps parts of the work of Stan Hawkins (e.g., 1992) come closest, and, within a rather different sphere, there have been one or two attempts to apply methods derived from Chomskyan generative theory to 'deep structure,' in ways comparable to the methods of mainstream analytical guru Heinrich Schenker (Perlman and Greenblatt 1981; Steedman 1984; Temperley 1999; and see Middleton 1990, 189–203, 211–14). Far more typical, however, are 'softer' paradigms, often drawing on Barthes and the 'cultural semiology' he inspired, and on applications of semiological theory to visual texts (images, film, clothing). The popularity of this tendency has resulted in a number of rewarding multidimensional, 'situated' studies (Hebdige 1979; Chambers 1985; Laing 1985), which, however, pay only slight attention to *sounds*, and is to be explained partly by reference to the dominance of cultural studies, at least in the Anglophone area, and partly as the product of an understandable skepticism as to whether music really is (as semiological models would generally predict) 'structured like a language.' (The skepticism has a broader provenance; see, for example, Blacking 1976, 21.) In a parallel trajectory, most semiologically oriented analysis of music videos and music in film (e.g., Kaplan 1987; Frith, Goodwin and Grossberg 1993; Goodwin 1993) has drawn on methods developed in film studies, applying them to lyrics, narrative, mise-en-scène and gesture, with only lesser attention to the musical component of the text (but see Gorbman 1987; Cook 1994, 1997; Vernallis 1998; and Tagg, below). Quite separately (and distinctively), work deriving from the formulations of the Italian theorist Umberto Eco has tended to couple an insistence on the broad cultural situating of musical messages with, at the same time, an ultrarigorous modeling of the multileveled network of codes governing the processes of musical semiosis (from minimal unit up to the whole music culture; from sounds through institutional and other mediations to the various discourses that position practise and interpretation alike). Again, exemplars of detailed analysis of specific popular music cases are scarce, but the work of Stefani (1973, 1987a, 1987b) and of Fabbri (1982a, 1982b) on the basic parameters for the understanding of style and genre lay out important potential for future research.

Philip Tagg

Tagg is the best-known and most productive semiologist of popular music (though, perhaps because his methodology is demanding and time-consuming, his influence has been less than might be expected). His classic studies of the *Kojak* television theme tune and of ABBA's 'Fernando' are the only large-scale semiological analyses (Tagg 1979, 1991; for general descriptions of the approach, see Tagg 1982, 1987). Tagg's method assumes that music is made up of 'musemes' (by analogy to the linguistic 'morpheme'). A museme is 'a basic unit of musical expression' (1979, 71) and is distinguished analytically through techniques of 'interobjective comparison' (comparing it to apparently similar units in other pieces in a relevant style), and 'hypothetical substitution' (altering one of the unit's parameters – such as rhythm or modality – to test whether its meaning appears to change). Interobjective comparison, together with 'intersubjective comparison' (testing the responses of competent listeners), also establishes the museme's semantic associations.

The rewards of the method are rich, but its applicability may be limited. It works best where there are extramusical semantic pointers (visual images, dramatic lyrics, strongly suggestive titles) and for genres (such as film and television music) with a programmatic aesthetic and a style linked to nineteenth-century European art music, where hermeneutic codes were well developed. It also works best applied rather loosely to relatively large units (phrases, sections, even complete styles), for, even with Tagg's rigor, complete reliability in musematic segmentation is somewhat speculative. It neglects the level of primary signification, where, arguably, much of music's meaning might lie, and it might be thought to assume a positivistically achieved interpretative consensus rather than building the possibility of negotiation of meaning into its procedures. (For critiques along these lines, see Middleton 1990, 233–36; Walser 1993, 98–99; Shepherd and Wicke 1997, 103–108.)

In some of his later work (Tagg 1992, 1993, 1994a, 1994b), Tagg pursues musical connotations across larger dimensions of musical style, function and genre. Two emergent concepts in particular – 'style indicator' (the 'compositional norms of any given style,' 1992, 378) and 'genre synechdoche' (a reference within a given style to 'certain elements in a "foreign" musical style . . . [thence] to the totality of that style and from that style

to the rest of the culture to which that "foreign" style belongs,' 1992, 376) – expand upon that latent intertextualism which seems always to have suffused Tagg's thinking, and relate it to other tendencies developing in music semiology.

Poststructuralism

One of these tendencies derives from the increasing visibility of the ideas of the Russian theorist Mikhail Bakhtin, whose materialist critique of structuralist semiology insists on the dialogical quality of signifiers – their meaning is always open, a product of the actual historical interchange of usages – and on their socially situated and contested character. Bakhtinian approaches to the intertextuality of musical codes are beginning to appear in work on popular music (Middleton 1995); they also link up, in some ways, with tendencies in poststructuralism.

For poststructuralists, any fixed attachment of a signified to a signifier represents an ideological imposition on the actual fluidity of the semiotic process. Signifieds, it is argued, always turn into signifiers, in an endless chain of deferrals. In this process, then, the subjectivities being constructed by their positioning in the semiotic flow are themselves – far from the stable subjects of structuralist abstraction – in process, pursuing the impossible dream of a plenitude in which both meaning and self are whole. Applying this perspective has produced some fruitful analyses of popular songs (Cubitt 1984; Bradby and Torode 1984), but also, elsewhere, it must be said, a tendency toward analytical passivity and an over-simple valorization of 'audience studies.' More important has been the influence of the later Barthes' project of a 'second semiology.' Barthes, building on Lacanian psychoanalysis and, in particular, on Julia Kristeva's situating of music in a 'pre-symbolic' stage of semiotic process directly in touch with bodily movements and anterior to the structures of 'sense,' proposes that 'below' the level of quasi-linguistic signification in music lies a 'second semiology,' where the text is read as a play of signifiers, their 'voluptuousness' charged with the 'materiality of the body speaking its mother-tongue' (Barthes 1977, 182), and where signification gives way to *signifiance* – the subject is 'lost,' in a state of *jouissance*. Barthes' metaphor of the 'grain of the voice' (for him a preeminent site for *signifiance*) has become celebrated, though examples of its careful application (Laing 1985, 54–56, 129–31) are much fewer than looser, often romanticizing celebrations of popular music's allegedly radical, anti-semantic sensuality.

What the Barthesian 'second semiology' neglects is not only that the 'Other' of meaning is actually a creature of meaning and its structures, but also that the codes which govern this interrelationship – in particular, the institutional and discursive formations that shape their operations and effects – have a 'social history.' Here, attempts to combine poststructuralist trends in semiology with the insights of Michel Foucault on such formations – especially those relating to the gendering of power – have started to pay dividends (McClary 1991; Walser 1993).

The Specificity of Music Semiology

On the whole, work on popular music drawing on semiological perspectives has tended to focus on relatively high levels of analysis (whole songs, styles, techniques), levels more likely to be compatible with interpretation of the extra-musical dimensions of the texts. But this bracketing of the syntax of primary signification has led to a surprising neglect of music's semiological specificity. Saussurean orthodoxy grounds meaning in relations of difference. Yet an insistent stream in music-semiological thought locates 'difference' at one pole of a continuum, with musical semiosis weighted disproportionately toward the other, marked by relations of *equivalence* (Ruwet 1987). The privileging in music of repetition, variation and transformation – of presenting 'difference' as aspects of 'the same' – suggests that here paradigmatic relationships (analogy, metaphor) are at least as important as syntagmatic relationships, or more so. To this extent, music offers a semiology of iconicity. From here, it is a short step, especially through a poststructuralist optic, to following the mechanics of iconicity into some sort of linkage between musical gestures on the one hand and bodily gestures on the other: and not via some romanticization of a presymbolic fullness, but a properly semiotic account of the encultured body's role in the structures of action, feeling and desire.

Such a project (argued in Middleton 1990, 1993; Shepherd and Wicke 1997) has the capacity to overturn the Saussurean model, which fashions all semiologies after the linguistic formula, and replace it with the idea of a deeper-seated yet more varied semiological principle, within which both music and language (and other practises) interrelate and diverge. At the same time, it promises to recast the body/subjectivity problematic, worried over by poststructuralists. Finally, popular music studies may have a particular role to play. Popular music's propensity for repetitive processes, and its frequently close associations with corporeal gesture, make it ideal research material. The way its 'structural iconicity' (Shepherd and Wicke 1997, 114) is often, so to speak, overwritten by a 'choreography of enactment' (sometimes made explicit in performance, always

implicit), such that, following Austin (1962) we might think of coded gestures 'spilling over' into 'music-acts,' outlines an interaction of symbolic, iconic and indexical semioses which is quite specific to music, and, nowadays, most strikingly proffered in popular music practises.

Bibliography

Austin, J.L. 1962. *How to Do Things with Words*. Oxford: Oxford University Press.

Barthes, Roland. 1967. *Elements of Semiology*. London: Jonathon Cape. (First published as *Elements de Semiologie*. Paris: Éditions du Seuil, 1964.)

Barthes, Roland. 1972. *Mythologies*, trans. Annette Lavers. New York: Hill and Wang. (Originally published as *Mythologies*. Paris: Éditions du Seuil, 1957.)

Barthes, Roland. 1977. *Image, Music, Text*, trans. Stephen Heath. New York: Hill and Wang, 179–89.

Blacking, John. 1976. *How Musical Is Man?* London: Faber.

Bradby, Barbara, and Torode, Brian. 1984. 'Pity Peggy Sue.' *Popular Music* 4: 183–205.

Chambers, Iain. 1985. *Urban Rhythms: Pop Music and Popular Culture*. London: Macmillan.

Cook, Nicholas. 1994. 'Music and Meaning in the Commercials.' *Popular Music* 13(1): 27–40.

Cook, Nicholas. 1997. *Analysing Musical Multimedia*. Oxford: Oxford University Press.

Cubitt, Sean. 1984. '"Maybelline": Meaning and the Listening Subject.' *Popular Music* 4: 207–24.

Fabbri, Franco. 1982a. 'A Theory of Musical Genres: Two Applications.' In *Popular Music Perspectives, 1*, ed. David Horn and Philip Tagg. Göteborg and Exeter: IASPM, 52–81.

Fabbri, Franco. 1982b. 'What Kind of Music?' *Popular Music* 2: 131–43.

Frith, Simon, Goodwin, Andrew, and Grossberg, Lawrence, eds. 1993. *Sound and Vision: The Music Video Reader*. London: Routledge.

Goodwin, Andrew. 1993. *Dancing in the Distraction Factory: Music Television and Popular Culture*. London: Routledge.

Gorbman, Claudia. 1987. *Unheard Melodies: Narrative Film Music*. Bloomington, IN: Indiana University Press.

Hawkes, Terence. 1977. *Structuralism and Semiotics*. London: Methuen.

Hawkins, Stan. 1992. 'Prince: Harmonic Analysis of "Anna Stesia."' *Popular Music* 11(3): 325–35.

Hebdige, Dick. 1979. *Subculture: The Meaning of Style*. London: Methuen.

Jakobson, Roman. 1960. 'Closing Statement: Linguistics

and Poetics.' In *Style in Language*, ed. Thomas A. Sebeok. Cambridge, MA: MIT Press, 350–77.

Kaplan, E. Ann. 1987. *Rocking Around the Clock: Music, Postmodernism and Consumer Culture*. London: Methuen.

Laing, Dave. 1985. *One Chord Wonders: Power and Meaning in Punk Rock*. Milton Keynes: Open University Press.

McClary, Susan. 1991. *Feminine Endings: Music, Gender, and Sexuality*. Minneapolis, MN: University of Minnesota Press.

Middleton, Richard. 1990. *Studying Popular Music*. Milton Keynes: Open University Press.

Middleton, Richard. 1993. 'Popular Music Analysis and Musicology: Bridging the Gap.' *Popular Music* 12(2): 177–90.

Middleton, Richard. 1995. 'Authorship, Gender and the Construction of Meaning in the Eurythmics' Hit Recordings.' *Cultural Studies* 9(3): 465–85.

Perlman, Alan M., and Greenblatt, Daniel. 1981. 'Miles Davis Meets Noam Chomsky: Some Observations on Jazz Improvisation and Language Structure.' In *The Sign in Music and Literature*, ed. Wendy Steiner. Austin, TX: University of Texas Press, 169–83.

Ruwet, Nicholas. 1987. 'Methods of Analysis in Musicology.' *Music Analysis* 6(1–2): 11–36. (First published as 'Methodes d'analyse en musicologie.' *Revue Belge de Musicologie* 20 (1966): 65–90.)

Saussure, Ferdinand de. 1974. *Course in General Linguistics*. London: Fontana. (First published as *Cours de Linguistique Générale*. Paris, 1916.)

Shepherd, John, and Wicke, Peter. 1997. *Music and Cultural Theory*. Cambridge: Polity Press.

Steedman, Mark. 1984. 'A Generative Grammar for Jazz Chord Sequences.' *Music Perception* 2(1): 52–77.

Stefani, Gino. 1973. 'Semiotique en musicologie' [Semiotics in Musicology]. *Versus* 5: 20–42.

Stefani, Gino. 1987a. 'A Theory of Musical Competence.' *Semiotica* 66(1–3): 7–22.

Stefani, Gino. 1987b. *Il segno della musica: saggi di semiotica musicale* [The Sign in Music: Studies in Music Semiotics]. Palermo: Sellerio.

Tagg, Philip. 1979. *Kojak – 50 Seconds of Television Music: Toward the Analysis of Affect in Popular Music*. Göteborg: Skrifter från Musikvetenskapliga Institutionen, 2.

Tagg, Philip. 1982. 'Analysing Popular Music: Theory, Method and Practice.' *Popular Music* 2: 37–67.

Tagg, Philip. 1991. *Fernando the Flute: Analysis of Musical Meaning in an Abba Mega-Hit*. Liverpool: Institute of Popular Music, University of Liverpool.

Tagg, Philip. 1992. 'Towards a Sign Typology in Music.' In *Secondo Convegno Europeo di Analisi Musicale, Vol. I* [Second European Convention on Musical Analysis,

Vol. I], ed. Rossana Dalmonte and Mario Baroni. Trento: Università di Trento, 369–78.

Tagg, Philip. 1993. '"Universal" Music and the Case of Death.' *Critical Quarterly* 35(2): 54–85.

Tagg, Philip. 1994a. 'From Refrain to Rave: The Decline of Figure and the Rise of Ground.' *Popular Music* 13(2): 209–22.

Tagg, Philip. 1994b. 'Subjectivity and Soundscape, Motorbikes and Music.' In *Soundscapes: Essays on Vroom and Moo*, ed. Helmi Järviluoma. Tampere: Department of Folk Tradition, 48–66.

Temperley, David. 1999. 'Syncopation in Rock: A Perceptual Perspective.' *Popular Music* 18(1): 19–40.

Vernallis, Carol. 1998. 'The Aesthetics of Music Video: An Analysis of Madonna's "Cherish."' *Popular Music* 17(2): 153–85.

Walser, Robert. 1993. *Running with the Devil: Power, Gender and Madness in Heavy Metal Music*. Hanover, NH: Wesleyan University Press.

Discographical References

ABBA. 'Fernando.' Epic EPC 4036. *1976*: UK.

'*Kojak* (Theme).' *TV Land Crime Stoppers: TV's Greatest Cop Themes*. Rhino 75866. *2000*: USA.

RICHARD MIDDLETON

Sociology

Introduction

Sociology is the discipline concerned with the study of the character and consequences of human relations: that is, with the patterns of social organization found in different societies, with their variety of cultural practises, and the relationships between the two. Sociology shares this general orientation with social anthropology, although in practise sociologists have been primarily concerned with modern, industrialized societies while anthropologists have tended to concentrate on traditional, non-Western ones. Sociology began to develop as an academic discipline – notably in the United States, Germany, France and Britain in the latter years of the nineteenth century – and throughout its development sociologists have been concerned to demonstrate ways in which established patterns of social organization, conceptualized as 'social structures' or recurrent processes, have influenced the ideas and actions of individuals and social groups. In the latter part of the twentieth century, however, there was a renewal of interest in cultural phenomena, in part as a reaction to the influential Marxist contention that patterns of culture were ultimately derived from, and reflections of, fundamental economic structures. It is in this context that interest in the sociological analysis of music – as a cultural product and a cultural practise – has been revived.

Given their basic disciplinary perspective, it is inevitable that, in this more recent period, sociologists should have questioned the assumption, widespread among traditional musicologists, that music – and in particular 'art' music – is autonomous, in the sense that it develops independently of the social circumstances of its production. A sociological perspective on music also calls into question received assumptions concerning the significance of 'serious' music as opposed to 'popular' styles, and the validity of the distinction between them. Indeed, the establishment and maintenance of this distinction may be regarded as the outcome of particular social practises and the pursuit of interests by individuals and groups. As such, it may be viewed from a sociological point of view as socially constructed, and as a topic for investigation in its own right (Martin 2000b). It follows, moreover, in contrast to the traditional assumptions of academic musicology, that sociologists of music are likely to be concerned with 'popular' styles and traditions, precisely because they are the music of the great majority of people, and as such – irrespective of their value to the musicologist – an important element in their cultural experience (Martin 2000a). Some sociological contributions to the analysis of music in contemporary culture are considered below; the distinctive character of contemporary sociological perspectives, however, may best be appreciated through a consideration of their intellectual development.

Background

The word 'sociology' was first used by the French social philosopher Auguste Comte (1789–1857), and is a derivation from Latin *societas* and Greek *logos*. As these terms imply, Comte's project was to establish a distinctive science concerned with the history and constitution of human societies, and rested on two central claims: first, that such societies must be understood as systems of interrelated parts (like biological organisms); and second, that they could be studied using the methods of the natural sciences so as to yield positive knowledge. Thus, the decisive feature of sociological thought is evident even in Comte's embryonic formulation – a concern with the explanation of social life in terms of its *collective* aspects. As such, sociological ideas often ran counter to the strongly individualistic strand in much Enlightenment thought. In their various ways, classical economics, political theories of the 'social contract' and utilitarian philosophy all offered accounts of the social order as the outcome of the qualities or character of individuals (as, for example, in the concept of *homo economicus* in political economy).

Comte's contribution was soon eclipsed, but these central ideas were developed in the work of the French theorist Emile Durkheim (1858–1917), whose fundamental concern was to demonstrate the priority of society over the individual, in the sense that the characteristics of individuals are shaped by their cultural environment, and not vice versa. For Durkheim, like Comte, society is a real entity, sui generis. Through the process of 'socialization,' notably the acquisition of language (although Durkheim said little about this), individuals learn from early infancy to accept the values, beliefs and behavioral patterns that are normal in society. Indeed, through the process of 'internalization,' they become part of their 'selves.' Thus, for Durkheim, the subject matter of sociology is 'social facts,' defined as those collective properties of society that are external to individuals and exert constraint over them.

Like Comte too, Durkheim emphasized the analogy between societies and biological organisms, in which different institutions, like parts of the body, are functionally interdependent: none viable on its own, but together constituting a working system that is greater than the sum of its parts. The ultimate aim of sociological knowledge, then, was to provide the means of social reconstruction – to adapt institutions and individuals so as to ensure the smooth functioning of the whole of society. However, in his critique of Hegel's philosophy, Karl Marx (1818–83) had already dismissed this sort of theory of social order as pseudoscientific and ideological, in the sense that it provided a political legitimation of inequality and exploitation. For Marx, societies are not held together by a common culture and the harmonious integration of their institutions; on the contrary, insofar as a steady state is achieved, it is the outcome of conflict and coercion. In Marx's sociological vision, those who control the economic 'means of production' in a society form a dominant class which is able to subordinate and exploit those who do not. As production technology changes and develops, so too do the 'social relations of production,' so that, as the opening of 'The Communist Manifesto' (1848) puts it: 'The history of all hitherto existing society is the history of class struggles' (Marx and Engels 1977a, 222).

Despite his radically different view of the social order, it is evident that Marx's sociological insight was no less developed than Durkheim's. The dialectic of historical change, he believed, was brought about not by heroic individuals but by the conflict of social classes. He was scornful of the established political economists and their belief that people were naturally self-seeking and acquisitive; these qualities, he argued, were not the cause of competitive capitalism but its consequence. As producers who must confront the natural world in order to live, human beings create patterns of culture, but the products of cultural production – such as religious beliefs, political institutions like the state and economic institutions like the market – appear through the process of 'alienation' as independent entities to which they are subordinate. 'Men make history,' wrote Marx, 'but they do not make it in circumstances of their choosing.' In each case, as with Durkheim, emphasis is on the collective, on the ways in which all individuals are shaped by their social circumstances.

Max Weber (1864–1920) accepted Marx's emphasis on conflict and coercion in understanding the dynamics of social life, but rejected both the view of history as an inexorable dialectic of class conflict, and the rigid economic determinism which at the time had become associated with Marx's thought. History and cultures, Weber argued, are not simply the ultimate outcome of economic processes, but bear the imprint of ideas and beliefs that are not reducible to material factors. Thus, the rise of modern capitalism was neither inevitable nor the result of changes in the 'means of production'; rather, Weber identified a unique configuration of circumstances in late medieval Europe, in which Protestant religious ideology may have had a decisive effect on the pattern of history. Moreover, Weber rejected the Durkheimian idea that collectivities and social 'forces' are supra-individual identities which determine human behavior. 'Societies,' 'classes,' 'social structures' and so on are concepts, not real entities, and to ascribe to them causal powers, or treat them as objects, is to commit the error of reification. For Weber, only real people can act, and the social order is the outcome of individuals and groups pursuing their interests in the light of their beliefs and values.

At the center of Weber's sociology, therefore, is his influential typology of the four basic forms that individual social action may take: traditional (i.e., conforming to custom or precedent); affectual (i.e., arising from feelings or emotions); instrumentally rational (i.e., governed by determination of the most effective means to attain a given end); and value rational (i.e., governed by commitment to a value or ideal) (Hughes, Martin and Sharrock 1995, 105–107). A fundamental opposition may be derived from these forms (crucial, incidentally, for the development of Western tonal music) between traditional societies in which adherence to custom and precedent is of paramount value, and modern societies in which actions are oriented, in ever wider spheres of life, to the rational calculation of effective means–end links; the latter case is best exemplified by the economic system of the modern West, which Weber characterized as 'modern rational capitalism.' Indeed, for Weber, the process by which 'rationalization' inexorably drives out tradition or sentiment as the organizing principle of social action is fundamental to the history of the West

and the emergence of modernity. This important theme in Weber's sociology was echoed during the 1930s and 1940s in the writings of T.W. Adorno (1903–70) and the 'Frankfurt School' of critical social theorists: for them, the 'instrumental reason' that, during the Enlightenment, had liberated humanity from subservience to traditional monarchs and irrational gods had in the modern period become totally oppressive, creating an 'administered,' 'totalitarian' society in which human life was organized only according to the imperatives of technical efficiency and economic rationality. In such a 'mass' society, all forms of culture – including music – are produced industrially, as commodities whose value is not intrinsic but solely monetary – the price they can command on the market.

As the implications of concepts such as rationalization suggest, however, Weber's sociological project did not represent an abandonment of a commitment to the social as the distinctive subject matter of sociology. On the contrary, it seeks to retain this focus while avoiding the pitfalls of determinism and reification, and has provided theoretical resources for a conception of the social world as process, as perpetually constituted and reproduced through the interactions of individuals as they interpret their situations and formulate appropriate courses of action.

This basic orientation is shared by the North American tradition of symbolic interactionism (Blumer 1969) which, drawing on the tradition of pragmatism in philosophy, and in particular the work of G.H. Mead (1863–1931), elaborates a perspective in which social order is seen as the outcome of the activities and interactions of individuals who utilize the fundamental human capacity to 'take the role of the other' – that is, to see themselves reflexively as objects of their own consciousness and thus to formulate appropriate lines of conduct through being able to anticipate the likely reactions of others. It should be emphasized that this view does not entail either a reduction of social life to individual action or a preoccupation with subjectivity, since the overriding concern is with the ways in which 'individual' identities are shaped through the contingencies of the social process. This theoretical tradition was particularly influential in the empirical studies of the 'Chicago School' of sociology from the 1920s on, which focused on such themes as problems of social organization in culturally heterogeneous cities such as Chicago, and (particularly in the work of Everett Hughes) the influence of occupational experiences on the development of personal identity. The interactionist tradition was also a powerful element in the critique of the established structural–functional paradigm that developed in the late 1960s, which led directly to the 'radical' and 'critical' sociologies of the 1970s, and which ultimately had a significant effect on studies in the humanities, including music.

In general, then, symbolic interactionism and Weber's 'interpretive' sociology have been viewed as approaches that understand the emergence of social organization from the 'bottom up' (i.e., through the interactions of individuals), and so have often been contrasted with the 'structural' emphasis of Durkheim (and some readings of Marx), which approaches social order from the 'top down' (through such concepts as social class, social system and so on). Thus, the fundamental task of sociological theory has often been taken to involve the reconciliation of 'structural' aspects of society (such as the obdurate character of institutions, power relations, normative constraints and so on) with the undoubted 'agency' of real people as they create, reproduce (and change) the social order through their ongoing activities.

In sum, modern sociological thought developed out of the early theorists' realization that human life is essentially – and irreducibly – social. However, theoretical perspectives have differed in the extent to which they have (like Durkheim, the functionalist school and the structuralist tradition) emphasized the ways in which real individuals are shaped and constrained by societal structures and processes, or (like Weber and symbolic interactionism) have seen the social order as the outcome of a perpetual process of collaborative interaction. Accordingly, there is a parallel methodological division between those who use quantitative techniques to obtain 'objective' data with a view to explaining the operation of large-scale social processes, and those who employ qualitative methods as they seek an understanding of the dynamics of real-life social settings. Despite these fundamental theoretical and methodological oppositions, however, modern sociology shares with all its founding figures a central concern with understanding the institutions and culture of industrial capitalist societies, and their pattern of development.

The Sociology of Music

As will be evident from the above discussion, sociology is not one of the human sciences, such as economics or political studies, which focus on a particular subset of social activities. It is, rather, concerned with the social processes through which all such activities are realized; thus, there can be a sociology *of* economic activity, *of* politics, and similarly a sociology of music. In fact, several influential contributors to the development of modern social thought – including Herbert Spencer, Georg Simmel, Ernst Bloch, Norbert Elias, Max Weber and Alfred Schutz – wrote on music, and T.W. Adorno

devoted more than half of his extensive writings to the topic (Witkin 1998, 2). Despite this, no very coherent or generally accepted framework for the sociology of music has emerged. This results in part from the heterogeneity of the work that has been done: most of the authors listed above have approached music from the perspective of their own theoretical preoccupations, with little concern for the development of a common discourse, or the use of fundamental sociological concepts to illuminate the field (Martin 1995). But a further important reason for the underdeveloped state of the sociology of music has been the concern of most authors, including those listed above, with the Western art music tradition. Adorno, for example, while making a significant contribution to the analysis of music in the context of social totality, was nevertheless committed to the idea that one particular strand of modernism (initiated by Schoenberg) was the sole representation in music of social truth in the late capitalist era, and was dismissive of all forms of 'popular' music (Adorno 1990). As late as 1987, Supičić, in reviewing the field, deplored the widespread lack of appreciation of 'highly cultured music,' arguing that the role of the sociologist was to help solve the 'problems' this creates for the formulation of 'proper cultural and educational policy' (1987, 231).

Such preconceptions and prior aesthetic commitments have militated against the development of a mature sociology of music, in part because they are so pervasive, and in part because they inhibit the development of a fundamentally sociological perspective. Adorno's adherence to the view that the social analysis of music inevitably involves passing aesthetic judgments cannot be reconciled with the view of those who see sociology as a 'scientific' enterprise which aspires to separate facts from values (Adorno knew this very well, but was concerned to dismiss the pretensions of academic sociology as ideological fantasy). However – and this is of immense significance in the present context – the persistent and widespread acceptance of received notions concerning the aesthetic hierarchy of musical styles in general, and the distinction between 'serious' and 'popular' music in particular, has hindered the acceptance of the idea that the subject matter of the sociology of music is the production and consumption of *all* music in society. Thus, a sociological perspective will not presuppose or take for granted the opposition between 'serious' music (art) and 'popular' music (entertainment), but – without judging the aesthetic value of either – will treat such categories, and their associated discourses, as social constructions (DeNora 1995, 7), and examine the ways in which they are created, applied and challenged. The established hierarchy of musical styles, to take an important example, may then be related to more general patterns of social stratification and culture (for example, Peterson and Simkus 1992), affording social distinction and legitimacy to those who are economically privileged, while sustaining a corresponding devaluation of those who are disadvantaged (Bourdieu 1984). It is also evident that this application of the categories of 'high' and 'low' culture has been widely used to legitimate inequalities in the allocation of resources to musical styles, in terms of public grants, sponsorship, media coverage, educational curricula and so on.

There is currently – and belatedly – increasing acceptance of the idea that the sociology of music must be centrally concerned with 'popular' and other previously marginalized music styles, simply because – by definition – they are the music of most people in most societies. Thus, as suggested in the Introduction, the agenda for the sociology of music differs significantly from that of conventional musicology in that it is not primarily concerned with the decontextualized analysis of musical texts or performances, or with their aesthetic evaluation, but with the use and significance of music in particular social contexts and situations. From this analytical standpoint music is seen as embedded in actual social settings: its 'meaning' cannot be disclosed by an interrogation of the sounds in isolation, but is realized only through the collaborative activities of real people in specific situations.

Music as Collective Action

In recent years, three sociologists in particular have developed general perspectives on music as a social practise: Howard S. Becker and Richard A. Peterson in the United States, and Antoine Hennion in France.

Howard S. Becker: Music as 'Collective Action'

Through the concept of collective action and its application in the analysis of 'art worlds,' and drawing on the US tradition of symbolic interactionism, Howard S. Becker (1974, 1982) has developed an inclusive framework for the sociological analysis of the processes of cultural production and consumption. Thus, the production as well as the reception of music may be understood as occurring within specific contexts of social organization, which may themselves have an effect on the characteristics of the music. As in other areas of artistic production, musicians do not work in social isolation, but locate themselves and channel their creativity in the context of already-existing institutional and aesthetic discourses, each of which is organized around a pattern of established conventions.

Becker's experience as a working musician informs his sociological perspective, which initially located music-making clearly within the sphere of 'work' rather than the more conventional (at least in academic writing) discourse of 'art.' In fact, two of Becker's early essays have been familiar to sociology undergraduates since the 1960s, and as such may well be the best-known writings in the sociology of music (Becker 1963, 79–119). In these essays, Becker explores the problems faced by musicians who aspire to be creative artists (in the jazz field) but who are forced to make a living in low-status 'commercial' work, and the solutions they develop. Among these is the exhibition of 'deviant' activities, as a means of distancing themselves from conventional society and its values, which refuse to grant them the artistic opportunities they consider appropriate. Another solution is to abandon artistic aspirations and pursue a career in commercial music. In his discussion, Becker contrasts the very different 'worlds' of the musicians and the public, whose whims they must pander to in order to survive; from the musicians' perspective, the public has no appreciation of authenticity, importance or progress in music, endlessly demanding only simple, trivial tunes.

These themes are developed in Becker's more general 'art worlds' model (1982), which views all forms of cultural production as collaborative activities organized around established conventions, both practical and aesthetic. Thus, for example, while rock bands, symphony orchestras and country music singers are all engaged in producing 'music,' what distinguishes them sociologically is that each is active within a different musical 'world,' characterized by very different organizational patterns, performance conventions and aesthetic criteria. To be active in such 'worlds,' individuals – whatever the nature of their activities – must orient what they do to the established conventions, the 'taken-for-granted' realities of the 'world' in question. Moreover, these conventions and their associated division of labor are likely to become part of the consciousness of participants (including audiences) – beliefs, that is, about the 'right' or 'proper' ways in which things should be done, or, equally importantly, about how things ideally ought to sound. It is these sorts of criteria, for example, that come into play when the authenticity or validity of any music is in question. Thus, musical styles, from this point of view, are to be understood as particular configurations of conventions, 'internalized' by participants, and having normative authority over what gets done. It should be added that Becker is not claiming that all individuals slavishly adhere to 'conventions': the essential point is that they must take account of them, even if their aim is to reject or subvert them. Indeed, Becker quite explicitly makes the point that artistic success usually depends on some degree of departure from established conventions, though not so much as to make the work incomprehensible to those in the 'art world.'

Becker's 'art worlds' model thus provides a general perspective from which musical practises – including both production and reception – may be understood sociologically. It should be noted, moreover, that this approach transcends, and renders irrelevant, the familiar distinction between 'music' and its 'social context.' As practitioners in any particular style, musicians themselves have 'internalized' the values and conventions of an art world: they know how things ought to sound, or how they would like them to sound, and even in the moment-to-moment unfolding of a performance they will be guided by these considerations in deciding what to do. Becker calls this decision-making the 'editorial moment,' because what is being decided is how things should be done, what to put in and leave out and so on, right down to the most minute details of performance. It is in this way that the artistic aspirations of the individual must be reconciled with the values and conventions of the art world, and that these 'social' elements may be said to enter the musical work itself. Moreover, becoming a recognizably accomplished practitioner in any style involves a process of 'practising' in which such elements normally cease to be matters for conscious reflection, and may be said to be 'embodied' skills (Sudnow 1978; Becker 1982).

As applied to music, then, Becker's 'art worlds' perspective offers a useful example of sociological analysis generally, in that the ideas and actions of individuals are understood in relation to the values and norms of their social context. More specifically, Becker's work builds on G.H. Mead's account of the 'reflexive' nature of human consciousness: art world participants, for example, formulate appropriate courses of action because they are able to imaginatively anticipate the likely reactions of others – audiences, perhaps, or other musicians – to possible actions they might take. While the influence of this perspective has been relatively limited within the sociology of music, its analytic value is particularly evident in two recent musicological studies: DeVeaux's (1997) account of the emergence of 'modern' jazz, and Berliner's (1994) analysis of the lengthy process through which musicians develop the skills to become recognized as capable jazz performers.

Richard A. Peterson: The Production of Culture

Like Becker, Peterson has been concerned to demonstrate the important consequences of the specific ways in which a 'division of labor' emerges and becomes established, or institutionalized, in a particular sphere of cultural production. It is this normal, accepted way of getting things done – a set of conventions, in Becker's terms – which confronts any individual who wishes to participate and to which he/she must adapt. Peterson's emphasis has consistently been on the ways in which

the institutionalized practises of music worlds have an influence on, indeed sometimes determine, the nature of the cultural products that are created. In turn, such practises may themselves be shaped by factors emanating from other, apparently remote, social worlds. One important example concerns the technological developments that made national network television possible from the late 1940s in the United States: one consequence of this was the localization of radio broadcasting, which, in turn, contributed to the emergence of previously marginalized popular music styles (country, blues, jazz and so on), which fueled the explosion of rock 'n' roll in the mid-1950s (Peterson 1990).

Peterson's account of the rise of rock 'n' roll offers a useful example of the 'production of culture' perspective generally. In terms of the existing institutions of the music business at the time, and to many contemporary observers, rock 'n' roll represented the sudden eruption of something both new and threatening, and it was often interpreted in terms of a 'teenage rebellion' against US values. In fact, there was nothing at all new about the music, or the African-American and country styles on which it drew. All had deep historical roots, but had long been marginalized and excluded by a powerful combination of established institutional constraints; not least of these, in the early 1950s, was the domination of the US record business by four major companies aiming for the mainstream, 'middle-of-the-road' market. However, what was new, Peterson argues, was that a number of identifiable factors contributed to the loosening of these constraints by the mid-1950s, so that previously excluded styles could be recorded, broadcast and heard by a mass audience. Chief among these interrelated factors were legal changes, technological innovations, market conditions and the organization of the record business itself. Thus, the rock 'n' roll explosion was not a representation in music of a sudden change in postwar youth values (after all, none of the 'baby-boom' generation had reached their teens by 1955); what it did represent were significant changes in the power structure of the music business, which gave small 'independent' companies, and previously marginalized music styles, a chance to be heard. As Peterson puts it, 'The times were not changing, but the constraints were' (1990, 113).

The 'production of culture' perspective has informed Peterson's research on the composition of the US popular music charts from 1948 to 1975 (Peterson and Berger 1975) and on the development of the country music business (Peterson 1997). In the former case, his argument is that the extent of musical innovation and diversity in the charts (as measured by the number of new artists and new record labels represented) is not a direct reflection of popular tastes, but is to be explained in terms of market concentration (i.e., the extent to which a small number of large companies had control of the industry). When concentration is high, the majors have the power to control what is recorded, marketed and distributed, and consequently what music is available for the public to buy. When concentration is low, and there is more genuine competition (as in the mid-1950s), the balance of power moves toward the smaller companies, the musicians and the consumers. From the 1950s to the early 1970s, Peterson suggests, a cyclical process of industrial concentration and dispersion underlaid the apparent changes of style and taste exhibited by the pop charts: the power of musicians and consumers was inversely related to the degree of concentration in the industry.

Similarly, in his study of the development of country music, Peterson has examined the institutional constraints that in every era have simultaneously shaped the music itself and the business through which it is produced. Unlike the blues or jazz, the musical sources that together became 'country music' have not subsequently been redefined in terms of the aesthetic criteria of art music; on the contrary, country music has remained a widely popular form, legitimated above all by its supposed 'authenticity.' For Peterson, the continuing populism and sense of authenticity attached to country music have to be explained in terms of the ways in which the production and reception of the music were institutionalized in the years between 1923 and 1953, a process he describes as 'the fabrication of authenticity' (1997, 10). Just as historians have examined the 'invention of tradition' (Hobsbawm and Ranger 1983), so Peterson's analysis focuses on the ways in which the commercial development of the music (through concerts, touring, radio, recording and so on) has sought to connect artists and songs to a 'tradition' – by promoting 'new artists who were "authentic" and new songs that were "original"' (Peterson 1997, 209) – and in so doing has constituted that tradition. Peterson shows how the sounds and visual symbols of 'country' music were manipulated so as to lend credibility to songs and their singers, how iconic figures such as Jimmie Rodgers or Hank Williams were identified, and how images such as those of hillbilly territory or the singing cowboy were contrived so as to create, by the 1950s, a recognizable discourse of 'country music.'

Peterson's studies of country music, and of the production of popular music more generally, have thus highlighted the ways in which both artistic expression and entrepreneurial activities are channeled and shaped by the demands and constraints of the institutional arrangements that constitute the commercial realities of the field at any given time. Just as Max Weber emphas-

ized the power of tradition to minimize change in pre-modern cultures, so Peterson demonstrates that, while musical 'culture' is constantly being produced, innovators must find some sort of accommodation with the prevailing institutional constraints, or find that their work is marginalized. Occasionally, though, as in the case of the emergence of rock 'n' roll, the constraints are loosened sufficiently (for reasons that may have little to do with music) to allow a period of change and innovation. It should be evident, then, that Peterson's focus is primarily on the patterns of social organization which have the effect of mediating the expression of any forms of culture; in the present context, an important implication of this perspective is that emergent styles of popular music may not be regarded as the unmediated expression of the values of particular social groups.

Antoine Hennion: Music as Mediation

Both Becker's focus on 'art worlds' and Peterson's concern with the institutional mediation of the 'production of culture' are evident in the work of Hennion, who seeks to overcome the opposition between aesthetic approaches which analyze music as a 'beautiful object' independently of its social context, and reductionist sociological perspectives which see it as a 'social symbol,' neglecting its distinctive qualities (Hennion 1997, 431). Hennion also aims to transcend the opposition between the production and reception of music: his primary focus is thus on the process of 'mediation' – the unique configuration of people (with a variety of aesthetic values) and material objects (instruments, published music, means of recording and amplification, performance locations and so on) which do not so much reproduce styles of music as constitute them in specific settings (1997, 416). Thus, for example, Hennion locates the essence of rock in the large-scale, stage-based high-tech performance, in contrast to the alternative authenticity of street-based rappers, which centers on the immediacy of localized dialog (1997, 431).

Whereas in other areas of cultural production (e.g., literature or painting) the outcome is an art object with a physical reality (books, paintings) which can then be treated as if it were independent of the social circumstances of its production, the fundamental qualities of music – its apparent immateriality, its essentially collaborative nature – make evident its dependence on processes of mediation. Indeed, for Hennion, the ways in which music is realized – the modalities of its mediation – are the key to the development of identifiably different styles and their institutionalization. Thus, for example, in classical music activities are organized in relation to the composition of scores, whereas in jazz it is the activity of the improviser that is fundamental, and in rock it is the creation of large-scale stage perform-ances. Each of these options entails a further array of means by which human activities and material objects are combined in ways that seem appropriate to the aes-thetic values of each style, and that are regarded as 'authentic.' Thus, for Hennion, all cultural production is a process of mediation in which individuals have to collaborate in order to realize, or constitute, the social worlds they inhabit.

Hennion's study of the activities of record producers may serve to illustrate his perspective. He describes his own approach as 'anti-musicology' (Hennion 1990), partly, no doubt, because he is particularly concerned to emphasize the sociological importance of those aspects of the popular song – its commodity status, and its assembly out of unrelated fragments – that Adorno spe-cifically condemned, and partly because he wishes to reject the idea that the song can be treated as a cultural object that may be analyzed or decoded independently of its social context. For Hennion, the producer of pop songs in the studio is not a passive intermediary between singer and audience, but rather an active creator whose skill is to realize, through trial and error, music that sounds right for a possible audience. Thus, the musical arrangement of the song is not incidental to it, but a crucial element in an indivisible process, and similarly the singer will have to generate the sounds that the pro-ducer wants to hear. But these judgments on what 'works' and what does not, made by the producer and other mediators – arrangers, musicians, engineers, sales executives and so on – are all rendered on the basis of some sort of knowledge concerning what a potential audience will want to hear, so that, for Hennion, the audience is not some remote group, but is actually incorporated into the song itself (1989, 413). Similarly, other mediators – radio producers and DJs, journalists, advertisers and so on – all represent and organize music in ways that suit their purposes. In the case of a radio station, for example, appropriate music is selected in accordance with the needs of a programming schedule and its 'time slots,' each intended to attract an audience that advertisers will wish to reach, since 'at the economic level, the product that radio is selling is not the *pro-grammes*, which no one buys, but *listeners'* (Hennion and Meadel 1986, 289–90). But, for Hennion, the so-called 'consumer' also acts as a mediator, using music select-ively for the purposes of establishing particular locales, asserting a sense of identity and so on:

> If we set out to observe its use of music, it is extremely likely that we will never find a public as such, but that we will find only producers: groups of 'youths' (trendies, high school students, suburbanites) caught doing the active, collective work of localis-ation/extension in order to construct for themselves their world on the basis of the world of others. (1989, 418)

It will be clear from these remarks that Hennion's work is rooted in the interpretive, interactionist tradi-tion, and that he exemplifies this tradition's rejection of 'structural' sociology (and its associated 'positivist' methodology); for him, the task of sociology is not the measurement of 'objective' social facts, but the analysis of the processes through which people collaboratively constitute their social worlds. More specifically, by dir-ecting attention to processes of mediation, Hennion's studies are in many respects complementary to those of Becker and Peterson, and to those that analyze music worlds in terms of collaborative processes. In this respect, a notable contribution is Deena Weinstein's study of the culture of heavy metal (2000) as a 'transac-tion' in which three elements – musicians, audiences and mediators – form the interrelated basis of this music world. Clearly, each of these is essential, but none is more fundamental than the others, and Weinstein explores the ways in which the perspectives and interests of people in each of the three groups are significantly different. The subculture of heavy metal, then, emerges as the constantly evolving outcome of the transactions among and within these three groups.

In viewing popular music 'consumers' as themselves active producers of meaning, Hennion (and Weinstein) may be regarded as developing one of the main themes of British cultural studies of the 1970s: the idea of the active appropriation of music in the process of establishing sub-cultural identities (for example, Willis 1978, 1990; Heb-dige 1979). It is also worth noting that Hennion's per-spective directs attention to the range of *uses* to which music may be put. As will become apparent below, these concerns have been increasingly evident in more recent studies: for the purposes of sociological analysis, it is of no consequence that much of popular music may appear, to the academic musicologist, simple or even trivial. For the sociologist, what is important is that such music plays a significant role in the lives of millions of people, consti-tutes an important aspect of contemporary culture (on an increasingly global scale), is the basis of a major industry, and – fundamentally – must be understood as created in and through collaborative social action.

Sociology and Popular Music

As noted above, Adorno was dismissive of popular music and wrote very little about it. Yet, his arguments, which echo both Marx's view of the 'alienated' character of modern life and Weber's pessimism over its increasing rationalization, have had a (perhaps excessively) pervas-ive and continuing influence on much subsequent work in the sociology of popular music. The basis of Adorno's condemnation of popular music is not that it is technically simpler than 'serious' art music (he explicitly denies this), but that under conditions of industrial capitalism it takes the form of a standardized commodity, produced only for the purpose of yielding profit. Since it is standardized, as in the 32-bar AABA format of the 'standard' song, individual pieces cannot achieve the unique integrated totality of a great artwork – despite superficial differences, all such songs are fundamentally the same. As a commodity, it is produced by the 'culture industry' (Horkheimer and Adorno 1979, 120ff.) and shaped by the dictates of the market. It is thus 'objectively untrue and helps to maim the consciousness of those exposed to it' (Adorno 1976, 38), rather than leading to a critical engagement with the established ideology of mass society, as great art is held to do. In Adorno's view, then, popular music, while trivial in itself, is nonetheless significant as one element in the process through which the various media of the 'culture industry' produce and reproduce vast masses of docile consumers, progressively insulated from, and incapable of, radical or oppositional thought.

Similar conclusions, though with contrasting political implications about the operation and effects of mass media, were drawn from many US 'content analysis' studies of the 1940s and 1950s: popular music was regarded as spurious and inconsequential, since it tended overwhelmingly to reflect orthodox values and support dominant cultural patterns. Such studies may be seen to reflect the influential contemporary formulation of sociological functionalism by Talcott Parsons (e.g., 1951), which – echoing Durkheim – interpreted established patterns of culture in terms of their contribution to maintaining the overall equilibrium of the social system. By the 1960s, however, it was clear that the overt content of popular songs was changing: since the advent of rock 'n' roll, 'protest' songs, and references to sex, drugs and political issues were becoming increasingly frequent. As Hirsch (1971) pointed out, this presented a problem for adherents of the theory that popular music reflected prevailing norms: if the music did indeed reflect culture, and in particular the subculture of youth, then that culture must itself be changing, and in ways that might threaten the dominant values of North American society.

Did the change in popular music indicate a more fundamental, and threatening, social transformation? In fact, empirical studies suggested that young people did not 'receive' the subversive 'message' which was supposed to be transmitted by the new wave of songs (Robinson and Hirsch 1972), and, again drawing on symbolic interactionism, Denzin (1970) rejected as simplistic the assumptions underlying the belief that popular music necessarily communicated, or reflected, subversive values. Meanings, he argued, were not inherent in the songs, but rather were defined by people in the specific contexts of their use. The meaning of songs, or any cultural objects, was subject to social processes of interpretation and negotiation – even clearly intended meanings, for example, could be resisted or ignored, often because young people's primary concern was with the *sound* of records, rather than with the 'message' of their lyrics. Similar ideas were developed in later research, which examined ways in which 'youth subcultures' appropriated the sounds and imagery of popular music in the creation of collective or individual identities. Discussion of this issue may serve to crystallize a number of themes that have been developed in subsequent studies in the sociology of popular music.

Youth Cultures and Subcultures

The important role of music in the formation of 'youth cultures' was examined, most notably in the early work of Simon Frith, a sociologist and rock critic whose writings were highly influential in the development of popular music studies. For Frith, the sociological importance of rock music in Britain had much to do with its salience in the development of subcultures based on age rather than class; moreover, he emphasized the growing significance of the distinction between 'pop' – commercial chart-oriented music produced for a mass market (yet nonetheless effective as the basis for the expression of 'teenage' identities) – and 'rock,' also commercially produced but bearing implications of 'sincerity, authenticity, art' and carrying 'a critique of its own means of production' (1983, 11).

Such a distinction, of course, implies that styles of popular music are not inevitably 'affirmative' in Adorno's sense, but may express opposition and resistance, as in the rock 'counterculture' of the late 1960s and early 1970s. As noted above, a series of British studies from the mid-1970s understood successive waves of youth subcultures as critical responses to the powerlessness and alienation engendered by industrial capitalism, and demonstrated the centrality of music to this process of symbolic renunciation, of 'resistance through rituals' (Hall and Jefferson 1976; see also Willis 1978; Hebdige 1979; Chambers 1985; Bradley 1992). The oppositional potential of rock, and of all the musics ultimately derived from African-American styles of the twentieth century, is also an important element in the general theoretical framework developed by John Shepherd. Shepherd's fundamental premise is that the organizational principles and sonic conventions of musical styles are an articulation of the dominant ideology of the social groups that create them: there is thus a 'structural homology' between forms of music and forms of society (1991, 89). Thus, Western tonality, the musical discourse which is hegemonic in industrialized societies, encodes the world-sense of the dominant socioeconomic class, while the music of black Americans, formulated in locations that were remote from the centers of power and wealth both geographically and socially, transforms tonality in ways that express an alternative world-sense – of poverty and powerlessness, exclusion and opposition. Thus, black music styles, from blues and jazz through rap, convey a sense of resistance and of alternative possibilities. An important implication of Shepherd's argument is thus that the increasing influence of African-American styles on popular music through the twentieth century was a result of the growing sense of exclusion and alienation experienced by people, particularly young people, with the advance of industrial capitalism: styles that express resistance and speak of alternatives will resonate with the consciousness of millions who feel trapped and powerless, however distant they are from the origins of black music.

There are echoes of Durkheim in these approaches to understanding the links between the structural location of social groups and the musics they develop, in the sense that cultural particulars are taken as expressions, or indicators, of the state of social totality. To this fundamental premise, however, is added the Marxist emphasis on class divisions and antagonistic power relations: thus, the dominant musical tradition and its organizing principles (functional tonality) are held to be the music not of 'the people' as a whole, but of those (mostly men) who exercise power and control. Although it has been subject to some criticism (e.g., Middleton 1990, 76; Martin 1995, 142ff.), Shepherd's perspective is important in the present context in that it not only provides a general theoretical account of the relationships between musical practises and the structure of industrial societies, but also (in contrast to most of the early theorists) recognizes the sociological significance of popular music in contemporary culture. In addition, it provides a framework for the consideration of a further set of issues that have been troublesome for subcultural approaches to popular music, since in it the dominant ideology is held to prescribe not only class-related values but those based on gender. In this context, influential studies have included McRobbie's (1990) critique of the male-centered assumptions and practise of research into subcultures, McClary's (1991) discussion of music – including popular music – as a 'gendered discourse' and Whiteley's (1997) consideration of the ways in which the so-called 'countercultural' music of the late 1960s

was in fact permeated by the patriarchal values of mainstream society.

Music and Identity

Since the 1980s, efforts to connect youth subcultures and musical styles have largely given way to a more general concern with the role of music in the formation of personal identity. Once again, Frith has been influential in this, pointing to the limitations of approaches that view styles as representing or reflecting the social groups which produce them (the 'homology' idea), and emphasizing instead the ways in which the actual *experience* of music can play a powerful part in the constitution of subjectivity, as well as the attachment to symbolic collectivities. In other words, the social group does not exist prior to the music, or other cultural phenomena, which then express it; rather, the sense of participating in a distinct collectivity is *produced* through such collaborative activities and experiences (Frith 1996a, 111). From this perspective, the sociological importance of music, and popular music in particular, lies in its power to 'construct . . . our sense of identity through the direct experiences it offers of the body, time, and sociability' (1996a, 124). All such experiences are 'obdurately social' (Frith 1996b, 277) in the sense that they involve the establishment of a relationship between 'inner' subjectivity and the 'outer' world of collective cultural practises. In a 'mass' industrial society, music can thus be a strong source of meaning and belonging. In short, it affords 'a way of being in the world' (Frith 1996a, 114), and is a highly salient aspect of the process through which elements of identity – gender, age, ethnicity, class, religion and so on – are established, maintained and changed. Frith's focus on the processes through which the social self is formed thus leads to a distinctively sociological approach to popular music which is not concerned to legitimize it as an object of aesthetic appreciation in the manner of 'high' culture (a project which maintains the separation of 'high' and 'low' cultural realms), but rather to examine the ways in which music is used in the ongoing formulation of identities, and to suggest that in this respect both 'serious' and 'popular' music work in similar ways.

As an example, Walser's study of heavy metal music depicts the genre as a 'discourse shaped by patriarchy' which provides occasions for the accomplishment of male identities (1993, 109). Heavy metal fans are overwhelmingly young men, a group largely excluded from social and economic power in the context of a capitalist and patriarchal society in which such forms of power are accepted as fundamental to the achievement of full male identity. Their consequent insecurities are confronted in heavy metal music, which provides opportunities for the symbolic assertion of masculinity: the 'texts, sounds, images and practices' of heavy metal, says Walser, combine to produce idealized narratives in which masculinity is asserted through the overcoming of resistance. In particular, the threat posed by women is dealt with by the representation of three strategies – misogyny, exscriptation and androgyny – which may be regarded as cultural options for those responding to the music, especially in the theatrical conditions of its performance (1993, 110).

The Music Business

As noted above, it was the view of Adorno and the critical theorists of the Frankfurt School that popular music was to be understood above all as a commodity – trivial in itself but important as a source of ideological mystification – which was produced as part of the 'culture industry' that has developed in modern capitalist societies. Popular culture in all its forms – radio, films, newspapers and magazines, television and so on – is produced and marketed on a mass scale using highly rationalized techniques of industrial production. As a consequence, products such as popular songs are constantly created according to standardized formats (as are their singers), despite the necessary illusion that each is new or original. The immediate aim is the production of profit for the large industrial corporations which, even in the 1940s, were seen to control the music and entertainment industries (Horkheimer and Adorno 1979, 123), but the more general effect is to ensure that the cultural environment of the mass of the population – characterized by trivia, escapism and fantasy – affirms the dominant ideology and marginalizes any alternative perspective. What the 'culture industry' produces is thus 'mass deception' (Horkheimer and Adorno 1979, 120; see also Chapple and Garofalo 1977).

One important implication of the 'culture industry' thesis – that popular music cannot express genuine opposition or dissent – has been considered above. Another is the assumption of passivity among the consumers of popular music seen as a standardized commodity. People are forced to buy from a range of alternatives which are both determined by the industry and similar in all essential respects; moreover, for 'mass deception' to be effective, the ideological messages of popular songs must be accepted by listeners. In contrast to this view, music industry representatives argue that people will not buy what they do not want, and point to the constant unpredictability of record sales. As noted above, Peterson and Berger (1975) attempted to reconcile both industrial efforts to control the market by legal (e.g., marketing) and illegal (e.g., payola) means, and the continuing volatility of consumer demand. In essence, their thesis was that, when industrial concentration is high (i.e., a small number of major companies are responsible for most of the output), the producers – as an oligopoly – can effectively dominate the market. Where concentration is low, however, and many companies are producing successful records, the mechanism of competition ensures both that consumers have a wider range of genuine choice, and that artists have much greater freedom to record what they want. In this situation, power moves away from the companies to both consumers and artists (as in the late 1960s, for example).

Peterson and Berger posited a 'cycle' of concentration and dispersion in the popular music industry, driven by the gradual accumulation of 'unsated demand' during periods of concentration, as the companies' drive for market share leads to increasingly bland (and expensive) products and a neglect of alternative styles, new developments and so on. At crucial periods – notably the emergence of rock 'n' roll in the mid-1950s (Peterson 1990) and the advent of punk in the late 1970s (Laing 1985) – such new sounds, borne by new artists on small independent record labels, are able to break through, and the process of dispersion and re-concentration begins anew. Sociologically, one of the important aspects of the Peterson and Berger thesis is that it treats stylistic changes in popular music not as some sort of 'reflection' of wider changes in society or youth culture, but largely as a consequence of the evolving organizational structure of the music industry.

Critics, however, have questioned the applicability of the notion of 'cycles' of concentration and dispersion: since the 1970s, the evidence has pointed to the occurrence of both increasing industrial concentration *and* a greater range of product diversity (Lopes 1992); the trend has continued with the increasing consolidation of transnational media corporations. What were formerly the 'major' companies in the record business have themselves become the subsidiaries of global media groups. Yet, it has been generally accepted that this intensification of concentration has not resulted in a reduction of consumer choice or the standardization of the musical product: on the contrary, the major companies now distribute a broader range of musics than in any previous era, while at the same time investing heavily in the promotion of mainstream artists who have the potential to sell on a global scale. This situation is the outcome of changes in both industrial organization and technology. As Lopes anticipated, large record companies have developed 'open' management strategies (1992, 57), involving considerable decentralization within the company, together with the contracting out of services, leasing of recordings from independent companies, use of freelance producers and so on. These developments are consistent with the development of 'post-Fordist' production systems in other areas of the economy. Through developments in information technology, too, it has become possible for companies to take advantage of 'flexible specialization' in the production process, in contrast to the standardized mass production of the earlier period (Hesmondhalgh 1996). Advances in recording technology have also enabled greater numbers of musicians to record and produce their own music themselves, further reducing the ability of established companies to control the process. Such companies can still restrict access to the main retail distribution networks, but there is evidence that access to low-cost recording and production has allowed a multiplicity of very small-scale local initiatives to flourish. The production and small-scale marketing of 'alternative' music by local bands in urban areas are significant in that young people can be seen as producers rather than, as in the literature on youth culture, simply consumers; at least equally important, though, is the opportunity for musicians of all styles and traditions to record their own work without recourse to any established record company. Such developments may be seen as evidence of, and as making a major contribution to, the further fragmentation of the popular music market. Moreover, the full implications of the increasing availability of music on the Internet have yet to be realized. The question of how existing copyrights may be protected is already troubling record companies, as is the capacity of musicians to place their own music on a Web site, to be 'downloaded' directly to listeners without reference to orthodox studios, recording companies, wholesale distributors or retailers. Such developments, however, are only the latest stage in the constant process through which, ever since sound recording became commercially viable, technological change has threatened the established interests in the industry. It is a clear demonstration of what Marx described as the tendency for the development of the 'means of production' to constantly subvert the existing 'social relations of production' (Hughes, Martin and Sharrock 1995, 42ff.).

There are, then, somewhat contradictory emphases in sociological perspectives on the music business and its effects. On the one hand are those who, following Adorno, see the high degree of concentration in the industry and its operation on an increasingly global scale as evidence of the power of the 'culture industry' to eliminate genuine choice by dominating its markets, and feeding ideologically loaded 'product' (the term is a good indication of what Adorno called 'the commodification of music') to a mass of docile consumers. Moreover, as recording companies have increasingly become the subsidiaries of multinational corporations, their pro-

duction and marketing strategies are directed more and more by the aim of global exploitation of films, television shows and their associated merchandise. On the other hand, some analysts have taken a contrary stance, echoing Walter Benjamin's (1973) view that even under capitalism technological developments can have empowering and emancipatory potential. The widespread availability of low-cost equipment for sound recording and reproduction, for example, gives people the ability – for the first time – not only to produce and reproduce their own music, but, simply as consumers, to create their own aural environments. All of this can occur without the intervention of the industry which, as in earlier phases of technological innovation, may face serious disruption, intensified by the threat that, through the use of electronic communications, musicians and their audiences may be able to bypass it altogether.

These contrasting interpretations of the role of the popular music business in capitalist societies need not, however, be regarded as incompatible, and may in fact reflect different aspects of the industry's development. Ever since the 1930s, when Adorno and Benjamin debated these matters, what has been taking place is '*both* an immense strengthening of the possibilities of uniformity and control, *and* a broadening and democratisation of opportunities' (Middleton 1990, 67).

Conclusion

While many notable contributors to the development of sociological thought wrote on the subject of music, most accepted (or championed) the received distinction between 'serious' and 'popular' music, and concentrated on the former – despite the fact that the distinction itself was not widely institutionalized until relatively late in the nineteenth century (Weber 1977; DiMaggio 1982). Sociological ideas were influential in the development of popular music studies as a field in the late twentieth century, and in the concurrent emergence of the 'new,' critical musicology, which was explicitly concerned to retrieve the popular musical traditions generally marginalized by academic musicology. These developments undoubtedly stimulated interest in the sociology of music, and are demonstrated in a marked 'turn to the social' in musicological writings. Much of this work, however, reflected a 'cultural studies' orientation, in that its preoccupation was with the interpretation of texts – whether books, films, paintings or music – to reveal their (presumed) social meaning. Such an approach is inconsistent with the social constructionism that has been highly influential in recent sociology, and that is fundamentally concerned with the *constitution* of cultural objects through social practises, and the *uses* to which they may be put in real social situations (in contrast to the deciphering of decontextualized *meanings*). From a sociological perspective, therefore, the often taken-for-granted separation of 'serious' from 'popular' music, and the practises through which it has been constituted and sustained, emerge as topics for investigation in their own right. Thus, Finnegan's (1989) ethnographic account of music-making in an English town was concerned to examine *all* kinds of music, and to document both the extent of musical activities and the ways in which they provided participants with significant involvement in established patterns of social relationships. In this respect, Finnegan's discussion is consistent with Frith's (1996b) emphasis on the ways in which all 'kinds' of music can be particularly effective in affirming individuals' sense of belonging to social groups. It will be apparent that the focus of such studies is on sociological issues arising from the uses of music in contemporary societies rather than on qualities of the music in itself. DeNora's study *Music in Everyday Life* (2000), which examines the use of music in relation to personal identity, embodiment, the creation of social settings and patterns of social organization, may be taken as an indication of the current direction of the sociology of music in general, and of popular music in particular.

Bibliography

Adorno, Theodor W. 1976 (1962). *Introduction to the Sociology of Music*. New York: Seabury Press.

Adorno, Theodor W. 1990 (1941). 'On Popular Music.' In *On Record: Rock, Pop, and the Written Word*, ed. Simon Frith and Andrew Goodwin. New York: Pantheon Books, 301–14.

Becker, Howard S. 1963. *Outsiders: Studies in the Sociology of Deviance*. New York: Free Press of Glencoe.

Becker, Howard S. 1974. 'Art as Collective Action.' *American Sociological Review* 39 (December): 767–76.

Becker, Howard S. 1982. *Art Worlds*. Berkeley, CA: University of California Press.

Benjamin, Walter. 1973. 'The Work of Art in the Age of Mechanical Reproduction.' In *Illuminations*, ed. Hannah Arendt. New York: Schocken Books, 217–51.

Berliner, Paul F. 1994. *Thinking in Jazz: The Infinite Art of Improvisation*. Chicago: University of Chicago Press.

Blumer, Herbert. 1969. *Symbolic Interactionism: Perspective and Method*. Englewood Cliffs, NJ: Prentice-Hall.

Bourdieu, Pierre. 1984 (1979). *Distinction: A Social Critique of the Judgement of Taste*. London: Routledge & Kegan Paul.

Bradley, Dick. 1992. *Understanding Rock 'n' Roll: Popular Music in Britain, 1955–1964*. Milton Keynes and Philadelphia: Open University Press.

Chambers, Iain. 1985. *Urban Rhythms: Pop Music and Popular Culture*. London: Macmillan.

Chapple, Steve, and Garofalo, Reebee. 1977. *Rock 'n' Roll Is Here to Pay: The History and Politics of the Music Industry*. Chicago: Nelson-Hall.

DeNora, Tia. 1995. *Beethoven and the Construction of Genius: Musical Politics in Vienna, 1792–1803*. Berkeley, CA: University of California Press.

DeNora, Tia. 2000. *Music in Everyday Life*. Cambridge and New York: Cambridge University Press.

Denzin, Norman K. 1970. 'Problems in Analyzing Elements of Mass Culture: Notes on the Popular Song and Other Artistic Productions.' *American Journal of Sociology* 75: 1035–38.

DeVeaux, Scott. 1997. *The Birth of Bebop: A Social and Musical History*. Berkeley, CA: University of California Press.

DiMaggio, Paul. 1982. 'Cultural Entrepreneurship in Nineteenth-Century Boston: The Creation of an Organizational Base for High Culture in America.' *Media, Culture and Society* 4: 33–50.

Finnegan, Ruth. 1989. *The Hidden Musicians: Music-Making in an English Town*. Cambridge and New York: Cambridge University Press.

Frith, Simon. 1983. *Sound Effects: Youth, Leisure and the Politics of Rock*. London: Constable.

Frith, Simon. 1996a. 'Music and Identity.' In *Questions of Cultural Identity*, ed. Stuart Hall and Paul du Gay. London: Sage, 108–27.

Frith, Simon. 1996b. *Performing Rites: On the Value of Popular Music*. Oxford: Oxford University Press.

Hall, Stuart, and Jefferson, Tony, eds. 1976. *Resistance Through Rituals: Youth Subcultures in Post-War Britain*. London: Hutchinson.

Hebdige, Dick. 1979. *Subculture: The Meaning of Style*. London: Methuen.

Hennion, Antoine. 1989. 'An Intermediary Between Production and Consumption: The Producer of Popular Music.' *Science, Technology and Human Values* 14(4): 400–24.

Hennion, Antoine. 1990 (1983). 'The Production of Success: An Antimusicology of the Pop Song.' In *On Record: Rock, Pop, and the Written Word*, ed. Simon Frith and Andrew Goodwin. New York: Pantheon Books, 185–206.

Hennion, Antoine. 1997. 'Baroque and Rock: Music, Mediators, and Musical Taste.' *Poetics* 24(6): 415–35.

Hennion, Antoine, and Meadel, Cecile. 1986. 'Programming Music: Radio as Mediator.' *Media, Culture and Society* 8: 281–303.

Hesmondhalgh, David. 1996. 'Post-Fordism, Flexibility and the Music Industries.' *Media, Culture and Society* 18(3): 468–88.

Hirsch, Paul M. 1971. 'Sociological Approaches to the Pop Music Phenomenon.' *American Behavioral Scientist* 14: 371–88.

Hobsbawm, Eric, and Ranger, Terence, eds. 1983. *The Invention of Tradition*. Cambridge and New York: Cambridge University Press.

Horkheimer, Max, and Adorno, Theodor W. 1979 (1944). *Dialectic of Enlightenment*. London: Verso Editions.

Hughes, John A., Martin, Peter J., and Sharrock, W.W. 1995. *Understanding Classical Sociology: Marx, Weber, Durkheim*. London and Thousand Oaks, CA: Sage.

Laing, Dave. 1985. *One Chord Wonders: Power and Meaning in Punk Rock*. Milton Keynes and Philadelphia: Open University Press.

Lopes, Paul D. 1992. 'Innovation and Diversity in the Popular Music Industry, 1969–1990.' *American Sociological Review* 57: 56–71.

Martin, Peter J. 1995. *Sounds and Society: Themes in the Sociology of Music*. Manchester and New York: Manchester University Press.

Martin, Peter J. 2000a. 'Music and Cultural Practices.' In *Musicology and Sister Disciplines*, ed. D.M. Greer. Oxford: Oxford University Press, 331–41.

Martin, Peter J. 2000b. 'Music and the Sociological Gaze.' *Svensk Tidskrift for Musikforskning* (May): 1–16.

Marx, Karl, and Engels, Friedrich. 1977a (1848). 'The Communist Manifesto.' In *Karl Marx: Selected Writings*, ed. David McLellan. New York: Oxford University Press, 221–47.

Marx, Karl, and Engels, Friedrich. 1977b (1846). 'The German Ideology.' In *Karl Marx: Selected Writings*, ed. David McLellan. New York: Oxford University Press, 159–91.

McClary, Susan. 1991. *Feminine Endings: Music, Gender, and Sexuality*. Minneapolis, MN: University of Minnesota Press.

McRobbie, Angela. 1990 (1980). 'Settling Accounts with Subcultures: A Feminist Critique.' In *On Record: Rock, Pop, and the Written Word*, ed. Simon Frith and Andrew Goodwin. New York: Pantheon Books, 66–80.

Middleton, Richard. 1990. *Studying Popular Music*. Milton Keynes and Philadelphia: Open University Press.

Parsons, Talcott. 1951. *The Social System*. Glencoe, IL: Free Press.

Peterson, Richard A. 1990. 'Why 1955?: Explaining the Advent of Rock Music.' *Popular Music* 9(1): 97–116.

Peterson, Richard A. 1997. *Creating Country Music: Fabricating Authenticity*. Chicago: University of Chicago Press.

Peterson, Richard A., and Berger, David G. 1975. 'Cycles in Symbol Production: The Case of Popular Music.' *American Sociological Review* 40(2): 158–73.

Peterson, Richard A., and Simkus, Albert. 1992. 'How Musical Tastes Mark Occupational Status Groups.' In *Cultivating Differences: Symbolic Boundaries and the Making of Inequality*, ed. Michèle Lamont and Marcel Fournier. Chicago: University of Chicago Press, 152–86.

Robinson, John P., and Hirsch, Paul M. 1972. 'Teenage Response to Rock and Roll Protest Songs.' In *The Sounds of Social Change: Studies in Popular Culture*, ed. R. Serge Denisoff and Richard A. Peterson. Chicago: Rand McNally, 222–31.

Shepherd, John. 1991. *Music as Social Text*. Cambridge: Polity Press.

Sudnow, David. 1978. *Ways of the Hand: The Organization of Improvised Conduct*. London: Routledge & Kegan Paul.

Supičić, Ivo. 1987. *Music in Society: A Guide to the Sociology of Music*. Stuyvesant, NY: Pendragon Press.

Walser, Robert. 1993. *Running with the Devil: Power, Gender, and Madness in Heavy Metal Music*. Hanover and London: Wesleyan University Press.

Weber, William. 1977. 'Mass Culture and the Reshaping of European Musical Taste, 1770–1870.' *International Review of the Aesthetics and Sociology of Music* 8: 5–22.

Weinstein, Deena. 2000 (1991). *Heavy Metal: The Music and Its Culture*. Boulder, CO: Da Capo Press.

Whiteley, Sheila, ed. 1997. *Sexing the Groove: Popular Music and Gender*. London and New York: Routledge.

Willis, Paul E. 1978. *Profane Culture*. London and Boston: Routledge & Kegan Paul.

Willis, Paul E. 1990. *Common Culture: Symbolic Work at Play in the Everyday Cultures of the Young*. Milton Keynes: Open University Press.

Witkin, Robert W. 1998. *Adorno on Music*. London and New York: Routledge.

PETER MARTIN

Structural Homology

The 'structural homology' is a concept developed primarily from cultural studies and subcultural theory that has proved useful as an analytical tool for understanding the social and cultural significance of the sounds of music.

The concept of the structural homology was developed by Paul Willis, in part from the early work of Raymond Williams, who argued that it was with the 'discovery of patterns of a characteristic kind that any useful cultural analysis begins' (1965, 63), and in part from the French-language tradition of structuralism. In Willis's words, the structural homology 'is concerned with how far, in their structure and content, particular items [of culture] parallel and reflect the structure, style, typical concerns, attitudes and feelings of the social group' (1978, 191).

The concept has in this way allowed parallels to be drawn between the structures of the 'abstract' or non-denotative use of sounds in music as one cultural form, and the structures of the societies or groups in which particular forms of music have been created and appreciated. Thus, the hierarchical arrangement of notes in functional tonal or 'classical' music, as symbolized by the 'centrality' of the keynote, can be argued to parallel the hierarchical structures of post-Renaissance European societies, with their centralized forms of social, economic and political power (Shepherd 1977). The formalization of this way of thinking about the social significance of music in the concept of the structural homology was prefigured in the work of the ethnomusicologist John Blacking (1973). Another ethnomusicologist, Charles Keil, engaged in this form of musical analysis at the same time as the concept was being developed by subcultural theorists, but independently of them. In his work on the songs of the Tiv of Nigeria, Keil observed that 'what snapped into place was a sense that in trying to describe how songs fit in with "everything else" in a cultural pattern, I was also discovering that "everything else" was as simple as roof structure and compound layout, as basic as everyday conversations and social interactions, as direct and urgent as the struggle for classless society' (1979, 7).

While the concept of the structural homology has been used in the analysis of both 'classical' and 'traditional' or 'folk' musics, its use has been particularly to the fore in the study of popular music because of popular music's indisputably social character (see, for example, Willis 1978 and Shepherd 1982). In this context, Richard Middleton has referred to Shepherd's work as 'the most rigorous attempt at a subcultural homology theory' (2000, 8). However, the concept found a different and much more influential life in the work of Dick Hebdige (1979). In assimilating poststructuralist interpretations of French-language semiology, this work stresses the capacity for the semiotic play of signifiers such as sounds. This notwithstanding, an analysis of music's sounds is missing from Hebdige's work. As Middleton concludes, 'the musical interpretations, brilliant and persuasive as they are, result not so much from any engagement with the specifics of musical practice . . . as from a participant-observer's mediation of contemporary subcultural consensus: nowhere . . . is there sustained discussion of sounds' (2000, 8).

The use of the structural homology has not been without its difficulties and detractors. As Don Michael Randel has observed, 'the difficulty with using such homologies is not that they cannot be produced. It is that they can

always be produced' (1991, 320). Implicit in this observation is the idea that homologies are fictive, the creation of analysts rather than the consequence of music's signifying characteristics. An opposite interpretation, of course, is that homologies can always be produced because they *do* derive from music's signifying characteristics. Regardless of the extreme of these positions, it has been convincingly argued that parallels between musical structures and social structures are too easily drawn, and without sufficiently established theoretical underpinnings; that use of the concept encourages the too easy assumption that music simply reflects society; and that use of the concept allows precious little space for the role of the individual and individual creativity in musical processes. Yet, despite these valid criticisms, the concept has retained some currency. As Middleton has noted, it might be worth 'hang[ing] on to the notion of the homology in a qualified form' (1990, 10). The concept of the structural homology was reinterpreted and put into a new context in the light of these criticisms in the late 1990s by Shepherd and Wicke (1997). This work attempts to steer a path between the two extremes brought into play by Randel's observation.

Bibliography

Blacking, John. 1973. *How Musical Is Man?* Seattle, WA: University of Washington Press.

Hebdige, Dick. 1979. *Subculture: The Meaning of Style*. London: Methuen.

Keil, Charles. 1979. *Tiv Song*. Chicago: University of Chicago Press.

Middleton, Richard. 1990. *Studying Popular Music*. Milton Keynes: Open University Press.

Middleton, Richard, ed. 2000. *Reading Pop: Approaches to Textual Analysis in Popular Music*. Oxford: Oxford University Press.

Randel, Don Michael. 1991. 'Crossing Over with Ruben Blades.' *Journal of the American Musicological Society* 44: 301–23.

Shepherd, John. 1977. 'The Musical Coding of Ideologies.' In John Shepherd et al., *Whose Music?: A Sociology of Musical Languages*. London: Latimer New Dimensions, 69–124. (Reprinted in Shepherd, John. 1991. *Music as Social Text*. Cambridge: Polity Press, 96–127.)

Shepherd, John. 1982. 'A Theoretical Model for the Sociomusicological Analysis of Popular Music.' *Popular Music* 2: 145–77. (Reprinted in Shepherd, John. 1991. *Music as Social Text*. Cambridge: Polity Press, 128–51.)

Shepherd, John. 1992. 'Music as Cultural Text.' In *Companion to Contemporary Musical Thought, Vol. I*, ed. John Paynter et al. London and New York: Routledge, 128–55.

Shepherd, John, and Wicke, Peter. 1997. *Music and Cultural Theory*. Cambridge: Polity Press.

Williams, Raymond. 1965. *The Long Revolution*. Harmondsworth: Penguin.

Willis, Paul. 1978. *Profane Culture*. London: Routledge and Kegan Paul.

JOHN SHEPHERD

Structuralism

'Structuralism' refers principally to a French-language intellectual tradition that began with the work of the Swiss linguist Ferdinand de Saussure in the early part of the twentieth century (Saussure 1959; originally published in 1915). It has been massively influential in fields such as linguistics (Benveniste 1971), cultural anthropology (Lévi-Strauss 1968), psychology (Piaget 1971), literary criticism (Culler 1975), psychoanalysis (Lacan 1968), social and political thought (Althusser 1971), and film studies (Metz 1974). As a major formative influence on Western critical thought of the twentieth century, it has affected directly, but mostly indirectly, certain aspects of the study of popular music.

Saussure's primary concern was with the ways in which language generates meaning. In this, he can be regarded as the founder of the French-language traditions of both structuralism and semiology, traditions that, while closely related, developed their own, largely independent trajectories during the course of the twentieth century. Where the structuralist aspects of his work are concerned, Saussure distanced himself from linguistics' preoccupation with the history of words and their meanings (philology) in arguing that the meanings of words derive more from their placement and role in language than from language's relationships over time with people, societies and external realities. Saussure understood language to be, indeed, a 'structure,' that is, an entity evidencing characteristics of wholeness, transformation and self-regulation (Piaget 1971). Structures – and therefore language – were in this way understood (a) to possess, and function according to, their own set of intrinsic laws; (b) in terms of, and according to, these laws, to be capable of processing and, once having processed, of eliminating information presented by their environment; and (c) through these processes of wholeness and transformation, to be capable of maintaining and preserving themselves in the face of environmental challenges.

Biological organisms evidence these characteristics, as do many systems engineered by people. An important and fundamental implication of language's wholeness and completeness at any moment in history, and of its concomitant ability to maintain itself according to its intrinsic laws, is that meaning is as much produced by language's own structures as it is through language's relationships with its environment of people, societies and external realities. While language certainly has relationships with people, societies and external realities, the independence from them that is guaranteed by its structural characteristics has endowed it with a certain 'relative autonomy.' In this scheme, then, the role of the individual in divining meaning and imparting it to the world through language diminishes considerably. The individual becomes a single factor, and not necessarily the primary one, among many.

The huge influence of structuralism after Saussure has rested largely on the application of these ways of thinking to entire cultural systems (Lévi-Strauss 1968), entire social systems (Althusser 1969, 1971; Althusser and Balibar 1970), and the formation and maintenance of individual consciousness and identity (Lacan 1968).

During the 1970s, structuralism, with its emphasis on the production of meaning through language and other symbolic systems, was understood to offer an alternative to the emphasis on human agency characteristic of the English-language traditions of cultural studies and subcultural theory (see, for instance, Hall 1980). Where the study of popular music is concerned, this alternative trend is evident, for example, in the work of Dave Laing (Taylor and Laing 1979; Laing 1985). The influence of structuralism is evident also in work that explicitly counters traditional musicological approaches to the study of popular music, which locate the source of meanings as presumably contained in and transferred through the structures of songs in the largely unmediated creative abilities of individual musicians. Antoine Hennion (1990, 186), for example, has argued that 'a song's expressive value does not lie in its form . . . a musicological assessment cannot explain why certain songs are successful and why most others fail.' As a result of participant observation in the French music industry, Hennion is able to argue that the success of a song lies in the ability of music industry 'professionals' to sense the needs of the public and, through teamwork in which singers and musicians figure only as members among many others, to craft songs that fulfill those needs. In this way, says Hennion, the 'team shares out the various roles that the single creator once conjoined.' The result, then, 'is a fusion between musical objects and the needs of the public.'

The work of the 'professionals,' continues Hennion (1990, 187), 'goes against the grain of musicological analysis: there is here no such thing as the "structure" of a song' in the sense of there existing a permanent and absolute object; 'each song modifies by degrees the basic model, which does not exist as an absolute.' Equally, the 'professionals' do not simply hand back to the public

141

what the public gives up in having its needs sensed: 'This self-consumption of the public by the public is not without certain effects; what is stated does not take the form of self-contained, indefinite repetition, but is inscribed in the blank spaces within everyday life; it expresses what cannot be said any other way.' It is for this reason that music structures meaning: 'This additional layer of meaning should, in fact, lead us to invert our approach: we ought not to attempt to explain the success of the music through sociology and social relations, but should instead look to the music for revelations about unknown aspects of society.' The influence of structuralism is evident in Hennion's work in the way in which music, in mediated and complex relations with individuals, societies and external realities, is understood to constitute the seat of a specific order of meanings (see also Hennion 1981).

This influence is discernible also in analyses of song lyrics that attempt to understand the ways in which lyrics contribute to the construction of particular versions of the world. These analyses understand lyrics as forming but one aspect of a sonic performance event relying heavily on the use and delivery of the words of everyday conversation, and are therefore in contrast to content analysis, which takes the lyrics of popular songs at their semantic face value, divorced from their musical setting as though they were a form of literately encapsulated poetry. An example of the former kind of approach to understanding lyrics can be found in the work of Laing (1971), who argues that the manner of delivery of the lyrics in Buddy Holly's songs represents a challenge to the traditional sentimentality of the ballad. 'Few notes are held for more than one or two beats in Holly's records,' observes Laing, 'so they avoid the overpowering emotion of the ballads of that period.' Holly's listeners, he continues, 'are not overwhelmed, as they are by a ballad, but continually have their attention redirected by the frequent changes of tone, pitch, and phrasing.' Holly's music, concludes Laing, is therefore 'rarely sentimental' (1971, 68).

A similar line of argument is evident in Laing's earlier analysis (1969) of Buddy Holly's song 'Peggy Sue.' 'The title must be repeated at least thirty times,' says Laing, 'but on each occasion it is sung in a different way from the time before, so as to suggest the infinite variety of his affection for her.' This song, like so many others of Holly's, Laing continues, 'is the song of someone uncertain that his love will be reciprocated.' Laing is able to be even more specific than this in his account of how the delivery of the song's lyrics creates meaning for the listener. Pointing out 'sudden changes of pitch' resembling 'the breaking voice of a young teenager,' Laing concludes that 'the restlessness of the vocal style is the

very incarnation of adolescence' (1969, 101). This approach to lyrical analysis has been both critiqued and developed further by Barbara Bradby within subsequent traditions of psychoanalytic and poststructuralist analysis (Bradby and Torode 1984; Bradby 1990).

It is, however, through its somewhat tenuous relationship to the narrower issue of the generation of meaning or affect through music that structuralism has more directly influenced popular music studies. While the sounds or notes of music often act in conjunction with language (in the form of lyrics, librettos and books) and images (through staging, stage acts, and promotional and marketing material such as record covers and music videos) to evoke meaning or affect, they of themselves seldom evidence clear referential or denotative meaning. It seems to be overwhelmingly through the order of their relatedness to one another that these sounds or notes evoke affect. It might thus be thought that the principles of structuralism would be highly suited to explaining the manner in which individual sounds or notes in music relate to one another to produce affect. While the work of the music theorist Leonard B. Meyer (1956, 1973) has been structuralist in spirit, his has been the exception rather than the rule within musicology, music theory and music analysis, and there is no evidence that he was influenced by structuralism as an identifiable intellectual tradition. Musicology, music theory and music analysis as disciplines have tended to hold the social sciences and the critical intellectual traditions associated with them somewhat at arm's length. The affinity possible between the principles of structuralism and the analysis of music was thus first explicitly identified and explored by the cultural anthropologist Claude Lévi-Strauss (1970).

One way in which Lévi-Strauss analyzed cultures was through the myths or tales by which 'traditional' societies store and reproduce their knowledge systems. Although myths cannot be told without the use of language, Lévi-Strauss understood myths as structures displaying their own internal logic, which endowed them with a relative autonomy in their relations with language. As a consequence, myths displayed a purely 'abstract' dimension as structures quite independent of the structural characteristics of the language used in telling them. Lévi-Strauss perceived in the 'abstract' or non-denotative aspects of music acting structurally a model by which to approach the purely abstract qualities of the mythological systems he was analyzing: 'Music, which is a complete language, not reducible to speech . . . is close to mythology . . . it must be possible to discover in musical discourse some special function that has a particular affinity with myth' (1970, 29). The quality of music that for Lévi-Strauss guaranteed it its own relative autonomy with respect to language, myth, people and societies was its ability to transmute time: 'Music transmutes the segment devoted to listening to it into a synchronic totality, enclosed within itself . . . it immobilizes passing time; it catches it and enfolds it as one catches and enfolds a cloth flapping in the wind' (1970, 16). The insights provided by Lévi-Strauss into the structural principles underlying music as a distinctive form of expression have since been explored further from the perspective of linguistics (Ruwet 1966, 1967), music cognition (Laske 1975a, 1975b) and the study of myth (Tarasti 1979).

To the extent that the study of popular music has been considerably permeated by various forms of cultural theory, structuralism as an intellectual tradition has played a major role in the formation of the theoretical territory that popular music studies has over the years assimilated (see, for example, Middleton 1990, 172–294, and Shepherd and Wicke 1997, 1–94). Often through related intellectual traditions such as that of poststructuralism and those constituted by various strands of psychoanalytic theory, structuralism has provided the foundation for analyses that understand popular music to be significantly instrumental in producing, if not determining, individual and collective senses of identity. It is therefore in terms of the insights that it has to offer the issue of the generation of meaning and affect through music that structuralism as an intellectual tradition has had a more direct impact on popular music studies. This connection is evident in Middleton's work on the importance of repetition in popular music (1990, 269–84), which builds in part on the work of Lévi-Strauss, Ruwet, Laske and Tarasti. Further, through the ways in which it has informed cultural studies and subcultural theory, structuralism has also provided the theoretical components vital to the development of the structural homology as a concept through which popular music's social meanings can be analyzed while the integrity of music is respected as one cultural form among many (Willis 1978; Shepherd 1982).

Bibliography

Althusser, Louis. 1969. *For Marx*. London: Allen Lane.

Althusser, Louis. 1971. *Lenin and Philosophy and Other Essays*. London: New Left Books.

Althusser, Louis, and Balibar, Etienne. 1970. *Reading Capital*. London: New Left Books.

Benveniste, Emile. 1971. *Problems in General Linguistics*. Miami, FL: University of Miami Press. (Originally published as *Problèmes de linguistique générale*. Paris: Gallimard, 1966.)

Bradby, Barbara. 1990. 'Do-Talk and Don't-Talk: The Division of the Subject in Girl-Group Music.' In *On Record: Rock, Pop, and the Written Word*, ed. Simon Frith and Andrew Goodwin. New York: Pantheon, 341–68.

Bradby, Barbara, and Torode, Brian. 1984. 'Pity Peggy Sue.' *Popular Music* 4: 183–205.

Culler, Jonathan. 1975. *Structural Poetics: Structuralism, Linguistics and the Study of Literature*. London: Routledge and Kegan Paul.

Hall, Stuart. 1980. 'Cultural Studies: Two Paradigms.' *Media, Culture and Society* 2(1): 59–72.

Hawkes, Terence. 1977. *Structuralism and Semiotics*. London: Methuen.

Hennion, Antoine. 1981. *Les Professionnels du disque: une sociologie des variétés* [The Recording Professionals: A Sociology of Popular Song]. Paris: A.M. Métailié.

Hennion, Antoine. 1990 (1983). 'The Production of Success: An Antimusicology of the Pop Song.' In *On Record: Rock, Pop, and the Written Word*, ed. Simon Frith and Andrew Goodwin. New York: Pantheon, 185–206.

Lacan, Jacques. 1968. *The Language of the Self: The Function of Language in Psychoanalysis*. Baltimore and London: Johns Hopkins University Press.

Laing, Dave. 1969. *The Sound of Our Time*. London: Sheed and Ward.

Laing, Dave. 1971. *Buddy Holly*. London: Studio Vista.

Laing, Dave. 1985. *One Chord Wonders: Power and Meaning in Punk Rock*. Milton Keynes: Open University Press.

Laske, Otto. 1975a. 'On Psychomusicology.' *International Review of the Aesthetics and Sociology of Music* 6(2): 269–81.

Laske, Otto. 1975b. 'Towards a Theory of Music Cognition.' *Interface* 4: 147–208.

Lévi-Strauss, Claude. 1968. *Structural Anthropology*, trans. Claire Jacobson and Brooke Grundfest Schoepf. London: Allen Lane. (Originally published as *Anthropologie structurale*. Paris: Plon, 1958.)

Lévi-Strauss, Claude. 1970. *The Raw and the Cooked*, trans. John Weightman and Doreen Weightman. London: Jonathan Cape. (Originally published as *Le Cru et la cuit*. Paris: Plon, 1964.)

Metz, Christian. 1974. *Film Language*. London: Oxford University Press.

Meyer, Leonard B. 1956. *Emotion and Meaning in Music*. Chicago: University of Chicago Press.

Meyer, Leonard B. 1973. *Explaining Music*. Los Angeles: University of California Press.

Middleton, Richard. 1990. *Studying Popular Music*. Milton Keynes: Open University Press.

Piaget, Jean. 1971. *Structuralism*, ed. and trans. Chaninah Maschler. London: Routledge and Kegan Paul. (Originally published as *Le Structuralisme*. Paris: P.U.F., 1968.)

Ruwet, N. 1966. 'Méthodes d'analyse en musicologie'

[Methods of Analysis in Musicology]. *Revue Belge de Musicologie* 20: 65–90.

Ruwet, N. 1967. 'Musicologie et linguistique' [Musicology and Linguistics]. *Revue Internationale de Sciences Sociales* 19: 85–93.

Saussure, Ferdinand de. 1959 (1915). *Course in General Linguistics*, trans. Wade Baskin. New York: The Philosophical Library Inc.

Shepherd, John. 1982. 'A Theoretical Model for the Sociomusicological Analysis of Popular Music.' *Popular Music* 2: 145–77. (Reprinted in Shepherd, John. 1991. *Music as Social Text*. Cambridge: Polity Press, 128–51.)

Shepherd, John, and Wicke, Peter. 1997. *Music and Cultural Theory*. Cambridge: Polity Press.

Tarasti, Eero. 1979. *Myth and Music: A Semiotic Approach to the Aesthetics of Myth in Music*. The Hague: Mouton.

Taylor, Jenny, and Laing, Dave. 1979. 'Disco-Pleasure-Discourse: On "Rock and Sexuality."' *Screen Education* 31: 43–48.

Willis, Paul. 1978. *Profane Culture*. London: Routledge and Kegan Paul.

Discographical Reference
Holly, Buddy. 'Peggy Sue.' Coral 61885. *1957*: USA.
JOHN SHEPHERD

Women's Studies

The study of women, gender and popular music has come to encompass research on female music-makers and audiences involved with many different musical genres and styles, as well as research on musical representations of men and women, masculine and feminine, and on conventions and ideas within popular music culture concerning male and female behavior. All of this reflects the influence of women's studies and its general themes, issues and arguments.

Women's Studies as an Academic Tradition

Women's studies is an academic tradition concerned with documenting women's contribution to cultural and intellectual life, reflecting and discussing female experience and engaging with feminist thought. It emerged out of the second wave of feminism in the late 1960s and was first offered as a formal subject in the United States. The subject has developed in adult and higher education, with undergraduate and postgraduate courses taught at hundreds of colleges across the United States and in numerous universities and institutions worldwide, including centers in Canada, Japan, Mexico, Russia and across Europe. The subject has aimed at being interdisciplinary; however, work in the field is often more accurately described as cross- or multidisciplinary.

The form and content of women's studies courses have tended to vary according to the particular academic departments to which they have been linked or within which they have been established. As Allen and Kitch (1998) comment, women's studies is 'disciplined by disciplines, not only for its sources of faculty, but also as a corollary, for its core intellectual frameworks and paradigms' (293).

There has been much debate among feminists about what the focus of women's studies should be, its compatibility with feminism, and, indeed, whether it should even exist. It has, however, had two broad concerns: the study of women whose role and significance in social and cultural life have traditionally been ignored or belittled; and the reexamination of the study of history, society, culture, science and so on from a gendered, female or feminist perspective. During the 1980s and 1990s, a number of gender studies courses developed within academic institutions and, in some cases, departments have chosen to work under the title 'women and gender studies.' However, the case of the Department of Women's Studies at the University of Sydney, which was retitled the Department of Gender Studies in 1998, indicates the shift that has occurred toward the analysis of all constructions of gender and sexuality and away from a concentration on women and women's issues. Some critics have viewed these changes as a depoliticization of women's studies.

To many people, the categories and characteristics of male and female appear to be natural, but one of feminism's main aims has been to question assumptions about the natural basis of sexual differentiation, and to argue that biology does not determine the ways in which women and men act and think. Rather, it has been argued, the ways in which individuals think about themselves and others as men or women are socially constructed. Feminists have thus emphasized gender as opposed to the biological categories of genes and sex, treating it as a social construct and as a relational and political category that produces difference and inequality. These feminist arguments have been central to women's studies, and the emphasis on gender within women's studies has had an impact on popular music studies.

Popular Music and Women's Studies

Differences between men and women are generally perceived to be reflected in popular music culture. Certain styles of rock music, for example, have been described as 'men's music' because they have been perceived as aggressive, rebellious and macho, whereas other forms, such as pop music, have been deemed 'women's music' because they have been associated with romance and perceived as a 'softer' alternative to rock. Often underlying such descriptions is a popular and enduring belief that biological and essential differences between men and women can be linked to particular musical activities and tastes. In addition, the production and industry of rock music have commonly been associated with men, while women have been assigned a more marginal, decorative and less creative role; hence the common stereotypes of glamorous women acting as backup singers for male groups or featuring on their videos and other merchandise, and of girls as undiscerning, passive, adoring fans (in contrast to serious and critical male listeners) who scream at male performers. This reflects a more general tendency within much popular music literature and discourse to present a male version of events and to exclude, marginalize and stereotype women, and to devalue areas of female expertise and creativity.

Within popular music studies, there have been two general responses to such tendencies, stereotypes and assumptions, one of which has been to highlight the issues of gender lying behind them. Thus, some scholars have questioned notions of rock as male culture, and have exposed traditional conventions and ideas concerning male and female behavior that reinforce the subordination of women in popular music and that were previously taken for granted or treated as the norm. However, the focus here is on the second general response, which has been to highlight women's experience within, and their often hidden contribution to, popular music culture. This reflects women's studies' emphasis on writing women back into history and revealing factors that hinder their involvement or recognition, and it accompanies a more critical approach that reinterprets that history from a feminist or gendered perspective.

Wilmer (1977) and Finnegan (1989) have shown how women support, encourage and facilitate music activity within local jazz scenes and in other music scenes. However, women's creative and visible role in music production has also been emphasized. Garratt (1984) and Odintz (1997) discuss the work and experience of women who have founded record labels, managed bands and studios, or produced and engineered albums. Other attempts to document and celebrate women's contribution to popular music have resulted in histories of female performers. Lucy O'Brien (1995), for example, presents a history of female musicians in rock, pop and soul, while Gaar (1992) ambitiously offers a history of women in rock 'n' roll that covers a diverse range of artists, including Willie Mae Thornton and Heart, Goldie and the Gingerbreads and Phranc. Meanwhile, Placksin (1982) and Gourse (1995) focus on the histories of women jazz musicians, and Greig (1989) documents and discusses girl vocal harmony groups. These books offer the reader

details of record releases, band or artist biographies and quoted statements from interviews. Other critics (K. O'Brien 1995; Post 1997; Evans 1994) allow their subjects to speak for themselves by presenting edited transcripts of interviews with female musicians. These are generally prefaced by brief biographical details and are sometimes accompanied by select discographies. In becoming musicians, these women have usually had to overcome obstacles and hurdles that are different from or additional to those faced by men (child-care responsibilities, for example), as Bayton (1998) shows with regard to female rock musicians.

Studies of women in popular music have, however, been influenced by broad debates within feminism and women's studies concerning the categorization of women. The treatment of 'women' as a homogenous category has been criticized, and emphasis has been placed on pluralism, on differences between women and on a multiplicity of male and female identities, a development that has helped to explain the fragmentation of the feminist movement during the early 1980s.

Kearney (1997), for example, points out that 'many journalists who draw straight lines from the female artists of previous periods to today's bands often fail to contextualise the *differences* that exist among these musicians' (214; italics in original). Focusing on the female youth culture known as 'riot grrrl,' which emerged in the early 1990s and was particularly popular in the United States and the United Kingdom, Kearney criticizes the way in which journalists who wrote about that culture emphasized the influence on it of the punk movement of the 1970s. She points instead to other equally important influences on riot grrrl, particularly that of lesbian feminists who sought to establish their own musical alternative to male-dominated rock and developed a separate network of music businesses run by women. Kearney suggests that, by celebrating straight white female musicians such as the members of riot grrrl bands, the media ignore 'many non-white and non-straight performers who continue to revolutionise music [and] are relegated to the margins of mainstream musical discourse . . . the privileging of riot grrrls as the revolutionary musical offspring of punk reaffirms, rather than deconstructs, the popular understanding of rock's heterosexual whiteness' (1997, 217).

In an essay that explores the sexual politics of women's blues in the United States during the 1920s, Carby (1990) highlights the way in which white feminist discourse often works to marginalize non-white women. She argues that the representation of black female sexuality in black women's fiction and in women's blues is quite different from the more general representations of female sexuality within white North American culture or within a (predominantly white) women's culture. Carby uses the work of Bessie Smith, 'Ma' Rainey and Ethel Waters to illustrate the sexual and cultural politics of black women who constructed themselves as sexual subjects in blues songs, and articulated differing interests, opportunities and experiences from those of their black male contemporaries. For example, while in male blues songs the train symbolized independence and mobility, for women it was often seen as a portent of loneliness, as women had fewer opportunities for migration.

Meanwhile, the feminist cultural critic Bell Hooks (1995) has accused Madonna, a white pop star, of expressing an affinity with black culture and style but appropriating it in ways that mock, undermine and exploit it. In her critique of Madonna's controversial 'Like a Prayer' video, Hooks points out that the video is rarely discussed in terms of race and highlights some of the racial imagery featured in it. She discusses, for example, the stereotypes of black people that feature in the video, including the juxtaposition of images of black non-Catholic representations with the image of a black saint which, she suggests, perpetuates the stereotype of Catholicism as a religion with few or no black followers and aligns blacks with Madonna's attack on Catholicism and organized religion. Hooks also discusses the documentary 'Truth or Dare,' in which Madonna chooses as her dance partner a black male with dyed blond hair. She suggests that the dancer was 'positioned as a mirror, into which Madonna and her audience could look and see only a reflection of herself and the worship of "whiteness" she embodies – that white supremacist culture wants everyone to embody' (1995, 324).

Alongside the growing emphasis on difference within the feminist movement, the feminist concern with collective action has tended to give way to a politics of style and to studies of women as active agents engaged in symbolic acts of resistance and empowerment. This trend has been reflected in popular music studies, where female musicians have been shown to manipulate sound and style in order to highlight, challenge or subvert traditional gender ideologies. Studies of Madonna, for example, have focused on the way in which she has experimented with dress and performance style in order to invent a range of masculine and feminine 'selves,' and the way in which she has played on gender-related dichotomies, such as that between virgin and whore, and explored through music a variety of other female stereotypes. Similarly, studies of the riot grrrl movement have described how the musicians involved encouraged the women in their audiences to move to the front of the auditorium and the men to the back, in order to expose and reverse established gender and spatial conventions within rock culture.

Some studies have explored representations of women in popular music lyrics, although there is a flaw in judging lyrics as the primary or central device within a song for communicating a message to the listener. The performance, delivery, tempo, beat, instrumentation, production and style of a song also contribute to the way in which a listener interprets and understands a piece of music. Frith and McRobbie (1990) highlight the complex way in which meanings are produced within popular music by selecting two well-known songs as illustration: Tammy Wynette's 'Stand By Your Man' and Helen Reddy's 'I Am Woman.' The lyrics of Wynette's song appear reactionary, while Reddy's words may be understood as progressive. However, Frith and McRobbie argue that the delivery of these songs challenges such a clear-cut understanding, as 'Tammy Wynette's country strength and confidence seem, musically, more valuable qualities than Helen Reddy's cute, show-biz self-consciousness' (1990, 372).

Popular music scholars have also challenged negative and stereotyped conceptualizations of female fans, who have regularly been presented in news reports and popular literature as passive consumers uncritically supporting mass-produced music, or as swooning teenagers idolizing male pop stars. Studies of female audiences have indicated how active, creative and diverse they are. Rather than simply adoring male 'stars,' for example, some of the much-maligned fans of bands like the Bay City Rollers and Take That have used their idols to create distinctive female cultures and to shape individual and collective female identities. Wise (1990) shows how female fans of Elvis Presley have had their own particular personal and, at the same time, political uses for the performer, rather than simply adoring him, as male rock historians have suggested. Garratt (1990) thus suggests that being a fan is as much, or more, a celebration of girl culture, and a process through which female sexuality and identity are produced, as it is about the male performers involved.

Some female fans of Madonna have copied her style of dress in order to explore the boundaries of acceptable female behavior; a group of k.d. lang fans have produced and distributed a fanzine through which they have made friends and exchanged jokes, information, advice, tapes and so on, on a range of issues directly, but also indirectly, connected with the performer, and, in doing so, have explored their feelings and identities as lesbians; and many female metal fans are, like male metal fans, attracted by the music's symbolic power and rebellion. Kolawole (1995) uses interview material with female fans of gangsta rap to illustrate how they employ particular listening strategies. Her study problematizes the lyrical content of gangsta rap, instances of which may be termed misogynist, and explores how female music enthusiasts negotiate the gendered messages, emphasizing their enjoyment of the music. As Skeggs (1993) notes, some female rappers, such as the US group Bitches With Attitude, have challenged the macho image of this musical genre by using overtly sexual lyrics penned from a female perspective. Similarly, Lewis (1990) focuses on the activities and strategies of resistance deployed by MTV's female musicians and audiences in response to MTV's male address.

Female academics documenting youth and music subcultures have criticized the historical male bias and gender blindness of research in this area. McRobbie (1990) argues that it is vitally important for subcultural studies to explore the ways in which girls and women participate in particular cultures, and to take account of gender, examining how masculinity, femininity and sexuality are represented and articulated. She comments that, unless subcultural theorists address issues of gender, 'our portrayal of girls' culture will remain one-sided and youth culture will continue to "mean" in uncritically masculine terms,' and such issues will be examined only within 'the ghetto of Women's Studies' (68). Gottlieb's and Wald's (1994) work on the riot grrrl movement shows how rock can enable women to actively create distinctive female subcultures. Such examples help to challenge common distinctions between male and female audiences, whereby the former have been associated with alternative and authentic rock, with activity, resistance and empowerment, and with public spaces such as 'the street,' while the latter have been associated with commercial pop, passivity and private domestic spaces.

Conclusion

It has been suggested that there is no longer any need for a specific women's studies since, as with popular music studies, so many academic disciplines and subdisciplines have incorporated research on gender and women. However, such research has been slow to develop in popular music studies. In addition, the study of popular music has so far had little impact on women's studies, although a focus on popular music has been incorporated into some women's studies courses in recognition of its central importance in the construction of gender and sexuality, and because it has allowed women's voices to be heard in ways denied by many other cultural forms. Popular music's emphasis on spectacle and sexuality could perhaps also help to highlight gender as a social construct and element of performance, while the presentation of male popular musicians as sexual objects, their subjection to a female gaze, and their engagement in 'gender-bending' activity, whereby they mix masculine and feminine images in their performance style, may also help to focus the attention of women's studies on men and masculinity, as well as on women.

Bibliography

Allen, Judith A., and Kitch, Sally L. 1998. 'Disciplined by Disciplines?: The Need for an *Interdisciplinary* Research Mission in Women's Studies.' *Feminist Studies* 24(2) (Summer): 275–99.

Bayton, Mavis. 1998. *Frock Rock: Women Performing Popular Music*. Oxford: Oxford University Press.

Carby, Hazel V. 1990. '"It Jus Be's Dat Way Sometime": The Sexual Politics of Women's Blues.' In *Unequal Sisters: A Multicultural Reader in U.S. Women's History*, ed. Ellen Carol DuBois and Vicki L. Ruiz. London: Routledge, 238–49. (First published in *Radical America* 20(4) (1986): 9–24.)

Evans, Liz, ed. 1994. *Women, Sex and Rock 'n' Roll: In Their Own Words*. London: Pandora.

Evans, Mary. 1997. 'In Praise of Theory: The Case of Women's Studies.' In *Feminisms*, ed. Sandra Kemp and Judith Squires. Oxford: Oxford University Press, 17–22.

Finnegan, Ruth. 1989. *The Hidden Musicians: Music-Making in an English Town*. Cambridge: Cambridge University Press.

Frith, Simon, and McRobbie, Angela. 1990. 'Rock and Sexuality.' In *On Record: Rock, Pop, and the Written Word*, ed. Simon Frith and Andrew Goodwin. New York: Pantheon, 371–89.

Gaar, Gillian G. 1992. *She's a Rebel: The History of Women in Rock & Roll*. Seattle, WA: Seal.

Garratt, Sheryl. 1984. 'Crushed by the Wheels of Industry.' In Sue Steward and Sheryl Garratt, *Signed, Sealed and Delivered: True Life Stories of Women in Pop*. London: Pluto Press, 60–81.

Garratt, Sheryl. 1990. 'Teenage Dreams.' In *On Record: Rock, Pop, and the Written Word*, ed. Simon Frith and Andrew Goodwin. New York: Pantheon, 399–409.

Gottlieb, Joanne, and Wald, Gayle. 1994. 'Smells Like Teen Spirit: Riot Grrrls, Revolution and Women in Independent Rock.' In *Microphone Fiends: Youth Music and Youth Culture*, ed. Andrew Ross and Tricia Rose. London: Routledge, 250–74.

Gourse, Leslie. 1995. *Madame Jazz: Contemporary Women Instrumentalists*. Oxford: Oxford University Press.

Greig, Charlotte. 1989. *Will You Still Love Me Tomorrow?: Girl Groups from the 50s On*. London: Virago Press.

Hooks, Bell. 1995. 'Madonna: Plantation Mistress or Soul Sister?' In *Rock She Wrote*, ed. Evelyn McDonnell and Ann Powers. London: Plexus, 318–25.

Kearney, Mary Celeste. 1997. 'The Missing Links: Riot

Grrrl – Feminism – Lesbian Culture.' In *Sexing the Groove: Popular Music and Gender*, ed. Sheila Whiteley. London: Routledge, 207–29.

Kolawole, Helen. 1995. 'Sisters Take the Rap . . . But Talk Back.' In *Girls! Girls! Girls!: Essays on Women and Music*, ed. Sarah Cooper. London: Cassell, 8–19.

Koskoff, Ellen. 1989. *Women and Music in Cross-Cultural Perspective*. Urbana and Chicago: University of Illinois Press.

Lewis, Lisa A. 1990. *Gender Politics and MTV: Voicing the Difference*. Philadelphia: Temple University Press.

McRobbie, Angela. 1990. 'Settling Accounts with Subcultures: A Feminist Critique.' In *On Record: Rock, Pop, and the Written Word*, ed. Simon Frith and Andrew Goodwin. New York: Pantheon, 66–80.

O'Brien, Karen. 1995. *Hymn to Her: Women Musicians Talk*. London: Virago.

O'Brien, Lucy. 1995. *She Bop: The Definitive History of Women in Rock, Pop and Soul*. London: Penguin.

Odintz, Andrea. 1997. 'Technophilia: Women at the Control Board.' In *Trouble Girls: The Rolling Stone Book of Women in Rock*, ed. Barbara O'Dair. New York: Random House, 211–17.

Placksin, Sally. 1982. *Jazzwomen 1900 to the Present: The Words, Lives, and Music*. London: Pluto Press.

Post, Laura. 1997. *Backstage Pass: Interviews with Women in Music*. Norwich, VT: New Victoria Publishers.

Richardson, Diane, and Robinson, Victoria, eds. 1993. *Introducing Women's Studies: Feminist Theory and Practice*. London: Macmillan.

Skeggs, Beverley. 1993. 'Two Minute Brother: Contestation Through Gender, "Race" and Sexuality.' *Innovation* 6(3): 299–322.

Wilmer, Valerie. 1977. *As Serious As Your Life: The Story of the New Jazz*. London: Quartet Books.

Wise, Sue. 1990. 'Sexing Elvis.' In *On Record: Rock, Pop, and the Written Word*, ed. Simon Frith and Andrew Goodwin. New York: Pantheon, 390–98.

Discographical References

Reddy, Helen. 'I Am Woman.' Capitol 3350. *1972*: USA.

Wynette, Tammy. 'Stand By Your Man.' Epic 10398. *1968*: USA.

Visual Recordings

Madonna. 1990. 'Like a Prayer.' *The Immaculate Collection*. Warner Reprise Video 38195-3.

Madonna. 1991. 'Truth or Dare.' International Video Enterprises 68976.

MARION LEONARD and SARA COHEN

3. Social Phenomena

Alcohol

Alcohol and music-making have long been associated with each other in Western cultures. In the Middle Ages and the Early Modern period, the consumption of alcoholic beverages was an integral part of such calendric festivals as May Day, Whitsun and Christmas. Along with the church, the country alehouse was the focal point of the community, and song was an integral part of an evening's entertainment. The coffeehouse and, in the nineteenth century, the pub in Britain and the beer hall in Germany and Central Europe were venues that continued this tradition of entertainment and popular song. Indeed, pub songs became an integral part of working-class culture as the nineteenth century progressed, and they have remained part of the musical vocabulary of working-class culture, particularly in cities with a seafaring tradition such as Dublin and Liverpool. Another important venue in the United Kingdom was the music hall, which doubled as a gin palace for the working- and lower-middle-class patrons. Many of the most popular music hall songs took as their theme drinking and its policing, such as 'Ask a Policeman' ('He'll produce the flowing pot/If the pubs are shut or not').

There has been regular opposition to alcohol during its history, and this has played a major part in its relationship with popular music. Historically, the availability or lack of alcohol has affected the practise of popular music in a number of important ways. Alcohol has been the favorite stimulant for practitioners of certain styles of music, such as the trad jazz revivalists of 1950s Britain. Other genres, such as country music and blues, have at times tended to adopt a highly censorious attitude vis-à-vis the status of alcohol in society, seeing it as a home-breaker and marriage-wrecker. The roots of this

antipathetic stance are, of course, to be found in the various temperance movements of the nineteenth and early twentieth centuries. In the antebellum United States, popular singing troupes such as the Hutchinson Family could find general favor for their temperance songs, such as 'King Alcohol,' whereas their abolitionist songs, for example 'Get Off the Track,' were morally acceptable to an evangelical minority only. Opposition to alcohol grew ever stronger in the United States over the next three generations, resulting in the *Volstead Act*, which introduced Prohibition in January 1920.

Opposition to Prohibition in the 1920s and early 1930s found an outlet in the popular songs of the day, such as Irving Berlin's 'You Cannot Make Your Shimmy Shake on Tea' (1919). Although many musicians were antipathetic to Prohibition, with hillbilly acts such as the Allen Brothers endorsing the practise of 'moonshining' in 'Fruit Jar Blues,' there were also songs that reinforced the government stance, such as 'Drivin' Nails in My Coffin (Every Time I Drink a Bottle of Booze)' and 'I Ain't Going Honky Tonkin' Anymore.'

Although many blues songs of the era told stories of crime and profiteering and depicted the detrimental effects of drinking bootleg liquor on the individual and thus on the family (such as Peetie Wheatstraw's 'Beer Tavern'), the relationship 'alcohol, crime, music' was, in many ways, positive for musicians. Alcohol had kudos – the hard-drinking musician often retained a certain tragic allure for the fan.

Alcohol was central to the lives of many musicians, particularly at one stage to bluesmen, who sometimes equated hard drinking with womanizing. However, incidents of alcohol and/or drug-fueled domestic violence have been just as common, as the case of Ike and Tina Turner evidences. Hard-drinking male performers were far more likely to be tolerated than hard-drinking women singers, whose incapacitation was often thought to be all the more degrading as it undercut traditional female values and the virtues associated with the mother-nurturer stereotype. The career of rhythm and blues singer Janis Joplin, to give just one high-profile example, illustrates this tendency.

Traditionally, alcohol has long been associated with the enjoyment of music for the audience. Indeed, the presence or absence of alcohol has had an important effect on the musical event itself. With certain styles of popular music, such as indie and punk, there is, perhaps, a link between alcohol intake and audience reaction at gigs (for example, the can-throwing at festivals and punk gigs from the 1970s onward) – although, as one gig by the new-wave act the Stranglers in Reykjavik evidenced in 1978, a high intake of alcohol is just as likely to stupefy an audience as to turn it violent (see Buckley 1997). Certain other styles, predominantly those connected with dance music, and, in particular, northern soul and acid house in the United Kingdom, have marginalized alcohol in favor of the use of amphetamines in the former, and Ecstasy in the latter. In fact, at many of the northern soul venues in the 1970s and 1980s, it was impossible to buy alcohol of any sort. In some countries with restrictions on the sale of alcohol – for example, Iceland in the 1970s – alcoholic beverages such as beer were banned, although the sale of hard liquor, with its attendant disorderly effects, was permitted.

In some popular music practises – for example, toasting and karaoke – alcohol consumption has been built into the performance itself to some extent in a ritualized manner. Toasting, long popular in the black ghetto and a direct antecedent of rap, developed through improvisation; the fellowship involved in toasting demanded a bawdy rhymed verse with every drink of spirits (see Lomax 1993, 209). Likewise, karaoke developed out of the Japanese tradition of formalized singing at home or in restaurants. Guests were often 'forced' into performing a turn, either individually or in a group, as part of the evening's entertainment (see Mitsui and Hosokawa 1998).

Alcohol consumption has played an important part in dictating or affecting the life styles of many popular music performers. Some famous performers either have been alcoholics or have died from the effects of alcoholism. The list is a long one, but notable examples are Hank Williams, Jimmy Reed, Edith Piaf and John Bonham. Drink has also been a prime factor in the many cases of outrageous excess witnessed in the international rock field. Jim Morrison's (of the Doors) infamous act of public indecency at a concert in Miami on 1 March 1969, the 'Miami dick flash,' is just one example. In the

1970s, the Eagles' drinking became so notorious that the band members even created a neologism to describe the frantic alcohol-induced binges that accompanied touring: to 'monster.' When drunk, guitarist Eric Clapton took to streaking in public and in 1981 came within minutes of dying of an alcohol-induced perforated ulcer. In the case of performers such as Morrison, alcohol seemed to carry a certain artistic cachet. The examples of Baudelaire, Brendan Behan and Dylan Thomas, all alcoholics, greatly influenced the life style of a romantic rock ideologist like Morrison.

Along with nicotine, alcohol is the most widely available legal drug in the world. Alcohol abuse, or alcoholism, as opposed to excessive or irresponsible drinking, is now commonly identified as a disease in its own right, characterized by an emotional and physical dependence on drink that frequently leads to brain damage, depression, and harm to various internal organs, sometimes resulting in death. Given the ubiquity of alcohol in many societies, it is perhaps no surprise that the entertainment industries, in which emotional and psychological pressures can be high, have witnessed their fair share of alcohol-related casualties. In the field of popular music, the strain of touring, coupled with the constant availability of drink, has led many musicians to become heavy drinkers. This social use of alcohol (to relieve pressure) forms probably the single most important aspect of its history. However, the work of Wills and Cooper (1988) problematizes this assumption by showing, in an empirical survey of British musicians, that a lower percentage of musicians than of the general population are heavy drinkers, despite the fact that musicians suffer from 'above-average levels of psychological anxiety' (82).

Since the advent of stadium rock and huge intercontinental tours by major rock acts, drinks firms such as Molsons, Labatts and Budweiser in North America and Heineken in Europe have sponsored venues or individual tours, thus reinforcing the link in the popular imagination between alcohol and excitement and excess. If the link between stadium rock and big-money sponsorship by drinks firms is a visible one, it should not be forgotten that there has been a centuries-old link between the drinks industry and music-making. Breweries have traditionally sponsored folk and jazz events, although the type of beverage associated with the individual music styles is often revealing of a search for a kind of authenticity. For example, the annual Cropreddy folk festival in the United Kingdom sells 'real ale' to its thirsty punters.

The frequency of references to alcohol in popular music texts is an indication of the link between glamor and heavy drinking. A few examples include 'What

Made Milwaukee Famous,' 'I'm Gonna Hire a Wino to Decorate Our Home,' 'One Bourbon, One Scotch, One Beer,' Dave Bartholomew's 'Who Drank My Beer (While I Was in the Rear)?,' the jazz tune 'Straight, No Chaser' and the English folk song 'John Barleycorn Must Die'; more recent examples include the remake of the traditional Irish song 'Whiskey in the Jar' (1973) by Thin Lizzy, 'Red Red Wine,' written by Neil Diamond in 1967 and recorded by UB40 in 1983, 'When the Hangover Strikes' (1982) by Squeeze, 'Cigarettes and Alcohol' (1994) by Oasis, later covered by Rod Stewart in 1998, and 'Born Slippy' (1995) by Underworld.

Alcohol has been closely linked to popular music in many non-Western cultures. The Ghanaian genre of 'palm-wine music' is said to have got its name 'because it was played and listened to during the afternoon relaxation period in villages when the men would sit under a big tree drinking palm wine, the fermented sap of the palm tree' (Sweeney 1991, 35). In Zimbabwe, specially brewed ritual beer was a central feature of the *bira* spirit possession ceremony for which a mbira ensemble provided musical accompaniment (Berliner 1978, 186–206).

In other places, the association of popular music with alcohol has been a matter of controversy. In Moscow in 1959, the Komsomol (Young Communist League) decided to establish official jazz cafés in order to harness the rising popularity of local jazz groups. The plan foundered on the need to serve alcohol in the cafés, which were subsequently withdrawn from the Komsomol work plan and permitted to operate unofficially (Starr 1994, 268–69).

A different case of official disapproval occurred in the mid-1960s when English-language rock performed in the *cafés cantantes* of Mexico City attracted the attention of the military regime after '[a]lcohol started to be introduced and people began to get really wild, jumping up on stage to dance, throwing things and creating all kinds of chaos' (Zolov 1999, 99).

In some Islamic societies where adherents are forbidden to take alcohol, popular music and musicians have come into conflict with religious orthodoxy. A Muslim musician in Uzbekistan recalled that in the Soviet era he would be required to drink vodka while entertaining Communist Party officials, but that it was sinful: 'The Prophet says the mother of sins is drunkenness' (Levin 1996, 42). In Algeria, *rai* music's celebration of 'alcohol and sexuality' (Schade-Poulsen 1999, 101) made it a target of Islamic militants, and several musicians were murdered because of their disregard of fundamentalist doctrine.

Bibliography

Berliner, Paul. 1978. *The Soul of Mbira: Music and Traditions of the Shona People of Zimbabwe*. Berkeley and Los Angeles: University of California Press.

Buckley, David. 1997. *No Mercy: The Authorized and Uncensored Biography of the Stranglers*. London: Hodder & Stoughton.

Haskins, Jim. 1994 (1977). *The Cotton Club*. New York: Hippocrene Books, Inc.

Herman, Gary. 1994. *Rock 'n' Roll Babylon*. London: Plexus.

Levin, Theodore. 1996. *The Hundred Thousand Fools of God: Musical Travels in Central Asia (and Queens, New York)*. Bloomington and Indianapolis: Indiana University Press.

Lomax, Alan. 1993. *The Land Where the Blues Began*. London: Methuen.

Malone, Bill C. 1985. *Country Music, U.S.A.* Rev. ed. Austin, TX: University of Texas Press.

McKenna, Terence. 1992. *Food of the Gods: The Search for the Original Tree of Knowledge*. New York: Bantam Books.

Melly, George. 1989 (1970). *Revolt into Style: The Pop Arts in the 50s and 60s*. Oxford: Oxford University Press.

Mitsui, Tôru, and Hosokawa, Shuhei, eds. 1998. *Karaoke Around the World: Global Technology, Local Singing*. London and New York: Routledge.

Moseley, Caroline. 1989 (1978). 'The Hutchinson Family: The Function of Their Songs in Ante-Bellum America.' In *American Popular Music, Vol. 1: The Nineteenth Century and Tin Pan Alley*, ed. Timothy E. Scheurer. Bowling Green, OH: Bowling Green University Press, 63–67. (First published in *Journal of American Culture* 1(4) (Winter 1978): 713–23.)

Oliver, Paul. 1990 (1960). *Blues Fell This Morning: Meaning in the Blues*. Cambridge: Cambridge University Press.

Russell, Dave. 1987. *Popular Music in England, 1840–1914: A Social History*. Manchester: Manchester University Press.

Schade-Poulsen, Marc. 1999. *Men and Popular Music in Algeria: The Social Significance of Rai*. Austin, TX: University of Texas Press.

Scheurer, Timothy E. 1989. '"Thou Witty": The Evolution and Triumph of Style and Lyric Writing, 1890–1950.' In *American Popular Music, Vol. 1: The Nineteenth Century and Tin Pan Alley*, ed. Timothy E. Scheurer. Bowling Green, OH: Bowling Green University Press, 104–19.

Shapiro, Harry. 1988. *Waiting for the Man: The Story of Drugs and Popular Music*. London and New York: Quartet.

Starr, S. Frederick. 1994. *Red and Hot: The Fate of Jazz in*

151

the Soviet Union 1917–1991. Rev. ed. New York: Lime-light Editions.

Sweeney, Philip. 1991. *The Virgin Directory of World Music*. London: Virgin.

Wills, Geoff, and Cooper, Cary L. 1988. *Pressure Sensitive: Popular Musicians Under Stress*. London: Sage Publications.

Zolov, Eric. 1999. *Refried Elvis: The Rise of the Mexican Counterculture*. Berkeley and Los Angeles: University of California Press.

Sheet Music

Berlin, Irving, comp. and lyr. 1919. 'You Cannot Make Your Shimmy Shake on Tea.' New York: Irving Berlin, Inc.

Hutchinson, Jesse, Jr., comp. and lyr. 1844. 'Get Off the Track.' Boston, MA: The author.

'King Alcohol.' 1843. Boston, MA: Oliver Ditson.

Monroe, Harry, arr. 1890. 'Ask a Policeman.' New York: Willis Woodward & Co.

Discographical References

Allen Brothers, The. 'Fruit Jar Blues.' *The Chattanooga Boys – Allen Brothers (Austin & Lee Allen): Complete Recorded Works in Chronological Order, Vol. 2 (1930–1932)*. Document Records DOCD-8034. *1998*: Austria.

Bartholomew, Dave. 'Who Drank My Beer (While I Was in the Rear)?' *The Classic New Orleans R&B Sound: The Best of Dave Bartholomew*. Stateside 6036. *1989*: USA.

Oasis. 'Cigarettes and Alcohol.' Creation CRESCD 190. *1994*: UK.

Squeeze. 'When the Hangover Strikes.' *Sweets from a Stranger*. A&M 4899. *1982*: USA.

Stewart, Rod. 'Cigarettes and Alcohol.' *When We Were the New Boys*. Warner Brothers 46792. *1998*: USA.

Thin Lizzy. 'Whiskey in the Jar.' Decca F 13355. *1973*: UK.

UB40. 'Red Red Wine.' DEP International 7 DEP 7. *1983*: UK.

Underworld. 'Born Slippy.' Junior Boy's Own JBO 29CDS. *1995*: UK.

Wheatstraw, Peetie. 'Beer Tavern.' *Complete Works, Vol. 6*. Document 5246. *1995*: Austria.

Discography

Constanten, Tom. 'John Barleycorn Must Die.' *Morning Dew*. Relix RRCD-2063. *1993*: USA.

Davis, Miles. 'Straight, No Chaser.' *At Newport*. Columbia 63417. 1958; *1968*: France.

Frizzell, David, and West, Shelley. 'I'm Gonna Hire a Wino to Decorate Our Home.' *Alone & Together*. K-Tel 3231. *1994*: USA.

Lewis, Jerry Lee. 'What Made Milwaukee Famous.' *Louisiana Piano Rhythms*. Rhino R2-71568. *1994*: USA.

Thorogood, George, and the Destroyers. 'One Bourbon, One Scotch, One Beer.' *George Thorogood and the Destroyers*. Rounder 3013. *1977*: USA.

Tubb, Ernest. 'I Ain't Going Honky Tonkin' Anymore.' *Honky Tonk Classics*. Rounder 14. *1983*: USA.

Tubb, Ernest, and Friends. 'Drivin' Nails in My Coffin (Every Time I Drink a Bottle of Booze).' *The Legendary Ernest Tubb & Friends [Box Set]*. Laserlight 15955. *1993*: USA.

DAVID BUCKLEY with DAVE LAING

Art and Art Schools

The relationships between art and popular music are rich and varied and can be traced at least to the beginning of the twentieth century. In February 1916 in Zurich, Switzerland, Hugo Ball and Emmy Hennings transformed rented premises into the Cabaret Voltaire, 'a combination artists' club, exhibition hall, pub, and cabaret' (Huelsenbeck 1991, 9). Kindred spirits, both artists and writers, converged in Zurich, where they became performers at the cabaret and formed the Dada group. As Dada progenitor Hans Richter puts it, 'The Cabaret Voltaire was a six-piece band. Each played his instrument, i.e. himself, passionately and with all his soul. Each of them, different as he was from all the others, was his own music, his own words, his own rhythm' (Richter 1978, 27). As artists and writers became cabaret performers, a peculiar mix of forms emerged. Richard Huelsenbeck has described some of the song types at the cabaret:

These songs, known only in Central Europe, poke fun at politics, literature, human behaviour, or anything else people will understand. The songs are impudent but never insulting. There is no intention of hurting anyone, only the desire to express an opinion. Sometimes they are erotic . . . The intellectual level is low but not unpleasantly so. Usually, they subsist on refrains and popular music, but Ball made up the melody for every song he wrote. (1991, 10)

Richter notes that 'Huelsenbeck was obsessed with Negro rhythms, with which he and Ball had already experimented in Berlin' (1978, 20), and Ball (1996) writes that Huelsenbeck 'pleads for stronger rhythm (Negro rhythm). He would prefer to drum literature into the ground' (51). Richter comments further on the combination of 'Ball's piano improvisations, Emmy Hennings' thin, unrefined, youthful voice (which was heard alternately in folk-songs and brothel songs)' (1978, 20).

The Dada group also developed sound-poems and simultaneous poetry such as 'L'Amiral cherche une maison à louer.' In his diary, Ball observes that 'All the styles of the last twenty years came together yesterday. Huelsenbeck, Tzara, and Janco took the floor with a "poeme simultan" (simultaneous poem). That is a contrapuntal recitative in which three or more voices speak, sing, whistle etc., at the same time in such a way that the elegiac, humorous, or bizarre content of the piece is brought out by these combinations' (1996, 57).

Chance methodologies in writing were also employed, as outlined by Tzara in 1918 in 'To Make a Dadaist Poem' (1992, 39), which preceded similar cutup and chance methods used by William Burroughs, David Bowie, John Cage and Brian Eno. Dada sound-poems, such as Kurt Schwitters' *Ursonate*, were being performed in Europe during the same period as early jazz scat vocal performances and recordings, such as Louis Armstrong's 'Heebie Jeebies' (1926), were being made.

The Role of Art Schools

Following World War I, the Bauhaus, a revolutionary and hugely influential art school, was founded in Weimar in 1919 and subsequently moved to Dessau in 1925, where it remained until 1928. At the time of the move from Weimar to Dessau, Oskar Schlemmer, head of the stage workshop, described his aspirations for the Bauhaus learning environment:

The artistic climate here cannot support anything that is not the latest, the most modern, up-to-the-minute, Dadaism, circus *variété*, jazz, hectic pace, movies, America, airplane, the automobile. Those are the terms in which people here think. (quoted in Willett 1978, 119)

As with many art schools that would follow, one of the extracurricular activities of the Bauhaus involved the student band. Although it was ostensibly a jazz band, the art student musicians also drew on a range of influences and musical references. Contemporary descriptions of the band are redolent of a proto-Spike Jones and His City Slickers or Frank Zappa and the Mothers of Invention:

The Bauhaus Band started with the musical improvisations of a group of painters and sculptors on trips around Weimar. Accordion music and the pounding of chairs, the rhythmic smacking of a table and revolver shots in time with fragments of German, Slavic, Jewish and Hungarian folk songs would swing the company into a dance. This dance music soon became known all over Germany and was played at artists' festivals everywhere; but since it could never be successfully transferred to paper, it remained gaily impromptu, even later when the instrumentation was expanded to include two pianos, two saxophones, clarinet, trumpet, trombone, banjos, traps, etc. (Bayer, Gropius and Gropius 1975, 85)

A contemporary journalist, Kole Kokk, wrote of the Bauhaus dances in the *8 Uhr Abendblatt* in February 1924:

All is primitive, there is not the least refinement . . . Everything has been done by the Bauhaus students themselves. First of all, there is the orchestra, the best jazz band that I have ever heard ragging; they are musicians to their fingertips. In invention and glorious colouring the costumes leave far behind anything that can be seen at our performances. (quoted in Bayer, Gropius and Gropius 1975, 94)

The influence of the Bauhaus was felt in art schools in the United States and England in the years following its demise in Germany.

Since the 1950s, pop culture–conscious young art students have continued to be attracted to the idea of focusing their creativity in a musical direction. English art schools in particular have been successful in producing successive generations of popular musicians, from jazz and skiffle to punk and beyond, in the process creating popular styles and sensibilities. Writing about jazz in 1957, for example, Oliver observes that 'those in close contact with Art Schools and student groups in the early days of the so-called Revival Period must have noted the receptivity of Art Students to jazz' (2). He concludes that 'from the art schools at this time came many of the musicians whose position in the jazz world after the war was established at an early date – Humphrey Lyttelton, Wally Fawkes, Monty Sunshine, Eric Silk' (1957, 2). The number of groups since the late 1950s that have had members with art school backgrounds – from the Beatles, the Rolling Stones, the Animals, the Yardbirds, the Pretty Things, the Kinks, the Who and the Bonzo Dog Doo-Dah Band to Queen, Roxy Music, Ian Dury, the Sex Pistols, the Clash, Pulp and Blur – indicates that the process is ongoing. In the United States, ex-art students include Alice Cooper, Chris Stein, David Byrne, Chris Frantz, Tina Weymouth, Chrissie Hynde, Laurie Anderson, Lee Ranaldo, Kim Gordon and Michael Stipe. A symbiotic relationship has developed between popular music and the visual arts, with video, graphic design, photography, fashion and styling projecting its images. The individuals and group members responsible for these images are also, almost invariably, the products of art schools.

Art schools have provided access to further and higher education for creative individuals who may lack the conventional qualifications that educational establishments traditionally require of school-leavers. Students are recruited by means of an assessment of experiential learning evidenced in their practical portfolio. A number of the teaching and learning methodologies traditionally employed in art schools are transferable and mirrored in the process and production of pop – for example, practical studio-based, project-centered work, experimental approaches to media and exploration of self, presented for critique by the peer group.

Moreover, knowledge of the works and activities of nonconformist art movements of the twentieth century has provided a rich and fertile ground for inspiration and appropriation. References to movements such as Futurism, Dada, Surrealism, Pop Art and Situationism, their images, imagery, attitude and stance, abound in a diverse array of examples in pop.

The art school experience has affected aspiring musicians in a variety of ways and has provided an environment where musical activities valuing spontaneity and intuition over technique and technical ability can be explored – from social interaction (meeting like-minded people, forming bands, organizing audiovisual collaborations), through the acquisition of art historical reference points, including the naming of bands, to a meaningful educational experience with a lasting effect on ways of seeing and thinking. These connections are evident in the following statement by John Lennon:

> I'm not interested in good guitarists. I'm in the game of all those things, of concept and philosophy, ways of life, and whole movements in history. Just like Van Gogh was or any other of those fuckin' people – they are no more or less than I am or Yoko is – they were just living in those days. I'm interested in expressing myself like they expressed it, in some way that will mean something to people in any country, in any language, and at any time in history. (Wenner 1973, 162–63)

Throughout their career as a group, the Beatles developed strong associations with the visual arts both socially and through their work. Through John Lennon and Stuart Sutcliffe they were involved in the bohemian community surrounding Liverpool College of Art in the late 1950s. Lennon was a contributor to *Merseybeat* magazine, which was founded and edited by fellow student (and Beatle chronicler) Bill Harry. Lennon, Sutcliffe and art student friends produced the now-restored murals in the basement of the Jacaranda Club where they also played. In Hamburg, their friendship with photographers Astrid Kirchherr, Jürgen Vollmer and artist/musician Klaus Voormann produced some of the archetypal (pre-fame) images of pop. During the Beatles' second trip to Hamburg in 1961, they played at the Top Ten Club, where Astrid Kirchherr observed that

> 50% of the customers . . . were art students, and Stuart became very friendly with them. One night they brought their teacher with them, Eduardo Paolozzi. He and Stuart got on well and Stuart explained his passion for art to him. (quoted in *Get Rhythm* (August 2001))

Artist and bass player Stuart Sutcliffe subsequently left the group to study with Paolozzi at the Hamburg School of Art before dying at a tragically young age.

Art and Popular Music: Crossovers and Collaborations

London in the mid- to late 1960s saw a particularly fruitful period in crossovers between art and pop on both social and creative levels. In the midst of the Beatles' popularity, Paul McCartney was helping to set up Indica Books and Gallery (1966–70) with his future biographer Barry Miles. Indica provided an important point of interaction for artists, dealers and musicians and was the site of the famous meeting of John Lennon and Yoko Ono at an exhibition of her work.

The art dealer and gallery owner Robert Fraser introduced the Beatles to artists Peter Blake and Richard Hamilton, who subsequently created the record sleeves for *Sergeant Pepper's Lonely Hearts Club Band* and the *White Album*, respectively. A newspaper photograph of Robert Fraser handcuffed to Mick Jagger was transformed by Richard Hamilton into *Swingeing London* (1968–69). This, and the portrait of a naked John Lennon and Yoko Ono used for their *Two Virgins* album sleeve, provide two of the lasting images of the 1960s, and they symbolize the close relationship that existed between art and pop at the time.

The marriage and early creative collaborations of John Lennon and Yoko Ono produced the avant-garde tape pieces *Unfinished Music No. 1: Two Virgins* (1968), *Unfinished Music No. 2: Life with the Lions* (1969) and the *Wedding Album* (1969), as well as the track 'Revolution 9' (the *White Album*, 1968), which has been described by Ian MacDonald (1994) as 'the world's most widely distributed avant-garde artefact' (230). The pioneering work of Yoko Ono has become an acknowledged influence on later generations of art-rockers, including the B-52's and Sonic Youth. In the CD-reissue packaging to *Unfinished Music No. 2: Life with the Lions*, Thurston Moore of Sonic Youth states, 'I make sounds to look at. This I know from Yoko. I live in her shadow.'

There have been numerous collaborations between artists and pop musicians since the 1960s, often blurring the boundaries between these terms and involving a convergence of media. The German term 'Gesamtkunstwerk,' used by Wassily Kandinsky to describe a total work of art, is useful in this context. Andy Warhol's creation of the Exploding Plastic Inevitable multimedia events in 1966, involving simultaneous films, slides, lights, effects, dancers and live music by the Velvet Underground, provided an influence for future generations.

The neo-Dada collage approach to music and performance can also be evidenced in the work of Frank Zappa, especially with the Mothers of Invention, which also employed a visual parallel with the Kurt Schwitters–like collage packaging designs of collaborator Cal Schenkel. As Zappa put it:

Dada has remained alive and well in my household since . . . forever. Even though the kids don't have the faintest idea of what it is, they're it. The whole house, and everything connected with what goes on around here, reeks of it.

INTERCONTINENTAL ABSURDITIES (founded 1968) is a company dedicated to *Dada in Action*. In the early days, I didn't even know what to call the stuff my life was made of. You can imagine my delight when I discovered that someone in a distant land had the same idea – AND a nice, short name for it. (quoted in Zappa 1989, 255)

The absurd features of Dada and Surrealism, now commonplace references in pop video, were also referenced to lyrical and musical effect by the Bonzo Dog Doo-Dah Band (originally the Bonzo Dog Dada Band). The band was given its own vignette in the Beatles' 'Magical Mystery Tour' film, and Paul McCartney produced the band's hit single 'I'm the Urban Spaceman.' In an altogether different take on reference to art practise, ex-art student Pete Townshend was able to frame the instrument-smashing theatrics of early performances by the Who with terms like 'Pop Art' and 'auto-destruction' (the latter gleaned from contact with Gustav Metzger, a visiting artist while Townshend was a student at Ealing College of Art). Townshend's experiments with volume, feedback and fuzz, together with the approaches that former art students Jeff Beck, Eric Clapton and Jimmy Page took to their instruments, helped redefine the electric guitar. Townshend's knowledge of the work of British and US Pop Art also had an impact on the projected images of the Who in the 1960s.

Also drawing on art history, and in many ways a product of the British art school system, Malcolm McLaren used the pop process as the material from which to fashion his art. As he said, 'I learnt all my politics and understanding of the world through the history of art' (quoted in Savage 1991, 24).

Malcolm McLaren's idiosyncratic art of management was employed in his various entrepreneurial activities in the 1970s and after, including the clothing stores he established with Vivienne Westwood, the Sex Pistols and Bow Wow Wow. A peculiar operational hybrid was established with reference to the manager/Svengali in the tradition of 1950s pop manager Larry Parnes and the Futurist/Dada/Situationist *agent provocateur*. His works, especially those produced in collaboration with fellow ex-art students Jamie Reid and Bernard Rhodes, often involved the engineering of the *succès de scandale*, usually via media hype/manipulation. Both the form and the content of these strategies invite comparison with those used earlier by the Futurists, Dada and the Situationists. Similar strategies can also be seen later in the activities of ex-art student Bill Drummond in his work with the KLF and the K Foundation.

In the post-punk period, art historical reference can also be found in numerous band names, including Cabaret Voltaire, the Armoury Show, Bauhaus and Art of Noise. The latter also released material on the Zang Tuum Tumb label, named after the phonetic poem by Italian Futurist leader Fillipo Tomasso Marinetti. The ethos of the artist/non-musician can be found in the following passage from *The Art of Noises* (1913) by Italian Futurist Luigi Russolo:

I am not a musician, I have no acoustical predilections, nor any works to defend. I am a Futurist painter using a much loved art to project my determination to renew everything. And so, bolder than a professional musician could be, unconcerned by my apparent incompetence and convinced that all rights and all possibilities open up to daring, I have been able to initiate the great renewal of music by means of the Art of Noises. (Apollonio 1973, 88)

The role of the artist/non-musician in pop, increasing with the accessibility of new recording technologies, is exemplified in the boundary-dissolving work of Brian Eno, from his 'synth-noise' complements to Bryan Ferry's Pop Art imagery through to his recording studio as musical instrument production work. Roxy Music collaborator Bryan Ferry is also a former art student at the University of Newcastle, taught by Richard Hamilton. Hamilton had made his first Pop collage for the catalog and poster for the exhibition *This Is Tomorrow* (1956) at the Whitechapel Gallery, which he co-organized with other members of the Independent Group. At the time he met Ferry, Hamilton was researching the work of Marcel Duchamp alongside the production of his own brand of Pop Art. Duchamp's *The Bride Stripped Bare by Her Bachelors, Even (the Large Glass)* (1915–23) would later supply Ferry with the album title *The Bride Stripped Bare* (1978).

Brian Eno attended Ipswich College of Art, where he was taught by electronic arts pioneer Roy Ascott, and later Winchester School of Art. Since 1995, he has been a Visiting Professor at the Royal College of Art. Eno has worked with a painterly approach to sound as an artist, composer and producer, creating music (with Roxy Music) and audiovisual installations, pioneering 'Ambient Music' and 'Generative Music' (Eno 1996a, 1996b) and collaborating with Robert Fripp, David Bowie, Laurie Anderson, James and U2, as both artist and producer. U2's 'Zoo TV' exemplifies the degree of Eno's influence on the band. This influence is evident in the following statement by Bono:

The Dadaists . . . were powerful in their time because they had the ability to unzip the pants of the starched trousers of the fascists and mock them. And they were outlawed because of that. And I really feel there is a lot to be learned from that. I've certainly learned a lot from that, philosophically and in terms of expressing myself through our art. The potential for subversion in humour is something new to U2. (quoted in *VOX* (August 1993))

In the 1990s, a new generation of art students emerged on the pop scene. Collaborations, in the spirit of previous generations, took place between so-called 'Brit Pop musicians' and 'Young British Artists.' Damien Hirst directed videos for Blur, and Julian Opie produced packaging designs and publicity. Pulp front-man Jarvis Cocker presented his longstanding enthusiasm for Outsider Art in television documentary form.

The technique of collage, used by visual artists and writers from Dada through to William Burroughs, has gone on to influence works by diverse pop musicians, including David Bowie and Paul McCartney. McCartney's *Liverpool Sound Collage* (2000) provides a link to his early tape collage experiments of the 1960s and contemporary practise in this medium.

In the late twentieth century, copyright issues raised by collage and sampling in the pop music industry increased alongside the development of new technologies. The case of Negativland/U2 illustrates the complex nature of the art versus commerce debate in this area. The late twentieth-century/early twenty-first-century debate surrounding collage/sampling and copyright/ownership can be viewed as a collision between a 'traditional' art practise and the commercial pop music industry.

Popular Music as the Subject of Art

Popular music and its images have been made the subject of art (see, for example, Cassidy 1997). In the context of jazz, Henri Matisse created a series of 20 colored-paper cutout and text compositions entitled *Jazz* (1947) that can be seen as a visual analogy to jazz music. On moving to New York, Piet Mondrian painted his *Broadway Boogie Woogie* (1942–43), which is simultaneously analogous to boogie-woogie piano-playing rhythm and the grid-like street structure of New York. Of his painting *Hot Still Scape for Six Colours – 7th Avenue Style* (1940), Stuart Davis wrote that 'six colours were used . . . as the instruments in a musical composition might be, where the tone-colour variety results from the simultaneous juxtaposition of different instrument groups' (quoted in Sidran 1997, 15). Furthermore, in paintings such as *Owh! In San Pao* (1951) and *Rapt at Rappaport's* (1952), 'Davis's hip visual poetry created an iconographic language, composed of hot colours and modern slang, that cap-

tured the harmonic rubs and angular, syncopated grooves of the music he loved. It was as if jazz had come to three-dimensional life through his art' (Sidran 1997, 16). Jazz was also the subject of paintings by artists of the Harlem Renaissance. In her book on Aaron Douglas, for example, Kirschke (1995) describes the way the artist 'employed jazz themes as a background in many of his paintings and often used the cabaret as a source of inspiration' (41).

Popular music, its images and the industry itself have continued to be made the subject of art, from the paintings and prints of the Pop Artists in the mid-twentieth century – for example, Andy Warhol and Peter Blake, through artists such as Guy Peellaert and David Oxtoby – to late twentieth-century works by artists who have recontextualized or refashioned pop artifacts, vinyl records, CDs and pop packaging within gallery spaces, as in the work of Christian Marclay. Elvis Presley, in particular, has provided inspiration for a broad variety of visual artists (see, for example, Biggs 1994).

Art-Pop videos by groups such as the Residents are held in the collection of the Museum of Modern Art in New York. The historical objects and artifacts of popular music, including musical instruments, articles of clothing, posters and tickets, can also be seen presented in the context of art objects in the gallery or museum space. A number of musicians have continued to draw and paint in parallel with making music, notably Miles Davis, Paul McCartney, Charlie Watts, Ronnie Wood, David Bowie, Patti Smith and Mark Mothersbaugh, and a number have given up music in favor of painting, including Paul Simonon (ex-the Clash) and Don Van Vliet (aka Captain Beefheart).

Bibliography

Apollonio, Umbro, ed. 1973. *Futurist Manifestos*. London: Thames and Hudson.

Ball, Hugo. 1996. *Flight Out of Time: A Dada Diary*, ed. John Elderfield, trans. Ann Raimes. Berkeley, CA: University of California Press. (Originally published as *Die Flucht aus der Zeit*. Luzern: J. Stocker, 1946.)

Bayer, Herbert, Gropius, Walter, and Gropius, Ise, eds. 1975. *Bauhaus, 1919–1928*. London: Secker & Warburg.

Biggs, Bryan. 1994. 'Kitsch Elvis Has Surely Come: Elvis in Art.' In *Aspects of Elvis: Tryin' to Get to You*, ed. Alan Clayson and Spencer Leigh. London: Sidgwick & Jackson, 244–58.

Bockris, Victor, and Malanga, Gerard. 1996. *Up-Tight: The Story of the Velvet Underground*. London: Omnibus.

Cassidy, Donna. 1997. *Painting the Musical City: Jazz and Cultural Identity in American Art, 1910–1940*. Washington, DC: Smithsonian Institution Press.

Eno, Brian. 1996a. 'Ambient Music.' In *A Year with Swollen Appendices*. London: Faber & Faber, 293–97.

Eno, Brian. 1996b. 'Generative Music.' In *A Year with Swollen Appendices*. London: Faber & Faber, 330–32.

Frith, Simon, and Horne, Howard. 1987. *Art into Pop*. London: Methuen.

Goldberg, RoseLee. 1988. *Performance Art: From Futurism to the Present*. London: Thames and Hudson.

Huelsenbeck, Richard. 1991 (1974). *Memoirs of a Dada Drummer*. Berkeley, CA: University of California Press.

Kirschke, Amy Helene. 1995. *Aaron Douglas: Art, Race, and the Harlem Renaissance*. Jackson, MS: University Press of Mississippi.

MacDonald, Ian. 1994. *Revolution in the Head: The Beatles' Records and the Sixties*. London: Fourth Estate.

Marcus, Greil. 1989. *Lipstick Traces: A Secret History of the Twentieth Century*. London: Secker & Warburg.

Matisse, Henri. 1947. *Jazz*. Paris: Tériade.

Miles, Barry. 1997. *Paul McCartney: Many Years from Now*. London: Secker & Warburg.

Negativland. 1992. *The Letter U and the Numeral 2* (Booklet/CD package). Oakland, CA: Seeland.

Oliver, Paul. 1957. 'Art Aspiring.' *Jazz Monthly* 2(12): 2–6.

Peellaert, Guy, and Cohn, Nik. 1974. *Rock Dreams*. London: Pan Books.

Richter, Hans. 1978. *Dada Art and Anti-Art*. London: Thames and Hudson.

Savage, Jon. 1991. *England's Dreaming: Sex Pistols and Punk Rock*. London: Faber & Faber.

Sidran, Ben. 1997. 'The Jazz of Stuart Davis.' In *Stuart Davis*, ed. Philip Rylands. Milan/New York: Electa/Solomon R. Guggenheim Foundation, 13–16.

Tzara, Tristan. 1992. *Seven Dada Manifestos and Lampisteries*, trans. Barbara Wright. London: Calder Publications. (Originally published as *Sept manifestes Dada, lampisteries*. Paris: Éditions Jean-Jacques Pauvert, 1963.)

Vyner, Harriet. 1999. *Groovy Bob: The Life and Times of Robert Fraser*. London: Faber & Faber.

Walker, John A. 1987. *Cross-Overs: Art into Pop/Pop into Art*. London: Comedia/Methuen.

Watson, Ben. 1994. *Frank Zappa: The Negative Dialectics of Poodle Play*. London: Quartet.

Wenner, Jann. 1973. *Lennon Remembers: The Rolling Stone Interviews*. Harmondsworth: Penguin.

Willett, John. 1978. *The New Sobriety 1917–1933: Art and Politics in the Weimar Period*. London: Thames and Hudson.

Zappa, Frank, with Occhiogrosso, Peter. 1989. *The Real Frank Zappa Book*. London: Picador.

Discographical References

Armstrong, Louis. 'Heebie Jeebies.' OKeh 8300. 1926: USA. Reissue: Armstrong, Louis. 'Heebie Jeebies.' *Louis Armstrong: Hot Fives and Sevens, Volume 1*. JSP Records JSPCD312. 1999: UK.

Beatles, The. *The Beatles [White Album]*. Apple PMC/PCS 7067-8. 1968: UK.

Beatles, The. 'Revolution 9.' *The Beatles [White Album]*. Apple PMC/PCS 7067-8. 1968: UK.

Beatles, The. *Sergeant Pepper's Lonely Hearts Club Band*. Parlophone PCS 7027. 1967: UK.

Bonzo Dog Doo-Dah Band, The. 'I'm the Urban Spaceman.' Liberty LBF 15144. 1968: UK.

Ferry, Bryan. *The Bride Stripped Bare*. Polydor POLD 5003. 1978: UK.

Lennon, John, and Ono, Yoko. *Unfinished Music No. 1: Two Virgins*. Apple T-5001. 1968: UK. Reissue: Lennon, John, and Ono, Yoko. *Unfinished Music No. 1: Two Virgins*. Rykodisc RCD 10411. 1997: UK.

Lennon, John, and Ono, Yoko. *Unfinished Music No. 2: Life with the Lions*. Zapple ST-3357. 1969: UK. Reissue: Lennon, John, and Ono, Yoko. *Unfinished Music No. 2: Life with the Lions*. Rykodisc RCD 10412. 1997: UK.

Lennon, John, and Ono, Yoko. *Wedding Album*. Apple SMAX-3361. 1969: UK. Reissue: Lennon, John, and Ono, Yoko. *Wedding Album*. Rykodisc RCD 10413. 1997: UK.

McCartney, Paul. *Liverpool Sound Collage*. EMI LSC01. 2000: UK.

Schwitters, Kurt. *Ursonate*. Wergo WER 6304. 1993: Germany.

Tzara, Tristan, Janco, Marcel, and Huelsenbeck, Richard. 'L'Amiral cherche une maison à louer.' *Dada for Now*. ARK Dove 4. 1985: UK.

Discography

Lipstick Traces. Rough Trade R2902. 1993: UK.

Visual Recordings

Beatles, The. 1967. 'Magical Mystery Tour.' Apple Films Ltd. VC3338.

U2. 1994. 'Zoo TV: Live from Sydney.' PolyGram Video 631373.

COLIN FALLOWS

Artifice

Artifice, as a quality of musical performance, is inseparable from ideas of authenticity, to which it is often opposed. Artifice, theatricality and the playing of roles have served as important dimensions of the performance of popular music since at least the nineteenth century. However, ideas of artifice were at their most influential, in the history of Anglo-American popular music after World War II, during the 1970s, within movements such as glitter or glam rock, which sought to achieve an explicit theatricalization of rock musical performance. This sometimes involved the deliberate adoption, by per-

157

formers, of constructed persona who might change from one record or concert tour to another. David Bowie's transformation, during this period, from the eponymous character of the *Ziggy Stardust* album through to the 'Thin White Duke' of the *Station to Station* album is perhaps the best known of such phenomena.

In the 1980s, ideas of artifice became more widely employed to account for the participation of popular music in a broader cultural condition in which the adoption and discarding of personas was seen as a distinctly postmodern form of subjectivity. Thus, while Madonna has played with the imagery of Marilyn Monroe (at the time of her 1984 album, *Like A Virgin*), and her later flirtation with the accoutrements of bondage culture might be traced to her own, idiosyncratic aesthetic strategies, these strategies were also seen as emblematic of a culture in which everyone could change stylistic surfaces and public identities as they saw fit. The ongoing integration of music within the audiovisual industries, and, in particular, the rise of music video, were believed to have made surface imagery central to popular music to an unprecedented extent.

The fact that artifice has been considered a controversial and often transgressive quality of certain performers and performances since the 1960s is evidence of the transformation of aesthetic values that has developed in the period since World War II. In the nineteenth and early twentieth centuries, popular music was intimately bound up with artifice, theatricality and the playing of roles, both in the musical revues and other stage shows through which so much music was popularized, and in the performance styles of minstrelsy and such singers as Al Jolson. Two major developments in the twentieth century would serve to diminish the place of artifice and theatricality in popular music. One was the growing sense that popular music placed listeners in an intimate relationship with the genuine personalities of performers (in particular, vocalists). The introduction, in the 1920s, of electric recording, which magnified the idiosyncrasies of individual voices, and the importance of the closeup, in film and television performances, nourished the sense that audiences had access to the 'real' thoughts and feelings of performers. Over time, this sense of intimacy would enshrine the sincerity and emotional complexity of performances as a key criterion by which they were judged. The other development was the claim, on the part of jazz and rock performers, that their musics were forms of artistic expression and not merely (if at all) entertainment. The disavowal of audience presence within the performance styles of bebop, and the uncontrolled chaos of the rock festival in the late 1960s, both represented a fundamental denial of the theatricality and artifice of musical performance.

The reembracing of artifice and theatricality in popular music since the 1970s has partly involved the assertion that, inasmuch as popular music may be seen to be centrally concerned with issues of gender, sexuality and generation, its social and political significance is based on the ways in which it plays with the codes of social identity. For Hebdige (1979), the artifice of rock music is part of a broader process, whereby popular culture plays with the codes of the dominant culture for its own, subversive purposes.

Bibliography

Hebdige, Dick. 1979. *Subculture: The Meaning of Style*. London: Methuen.

Discographical References

Bowie, David. *The Rise and Fall of Ziggy Stardust and the Spiders from Mars*. RCA-Victor SF 8287. *1972*: UK.

Bowie, David. 'Thin White Duke.' *Station to Station*. RCA-Victor APLI 1327. *1976*: UK.

Madonna. *Like a Virgin*. Sire 925157. *1984*: USA.

WILL STRAW

Audience

Introduction

The term 'audience' refers most generally to the recipients of all forms of communication. However, a distinction is commonly drawn between the concept of the audience on the one hand, and concepts such as those of a 'readership' and of 'spectators' on the other: 'readership,' for example, is used to denote the audience for written and printed communication, and 'spectators' for the audience at sporting events.

The term 'audience' is customarily used in a specific sense to refer to theatergoers, concertgoers, film and television viewers and radio listeners. More broadly, it is also used to designate the collectivity of individuals who may in a dispersed manner consume a particular cultural product or commodity. While this latter sense of the term overlaps with the more specific one in that viewers and listeners can be dispersed and not necessarily located in one place, it can also be understood to cover those who consume a particular piece of music or music by a particular performer, whatever the medium of transmission, or a particular film, whether in the movie theater, on television or by means of a video. This distinction may be captured in the difference between phrases such as 'television audiences' and 'radio audiences' on the one hand, and 'the audience for *Dallas*' or 'the audience for Céline Dion' on the other.

The term 'audience' should be distinguished from that of 'fan,' especially where popular music is concerned. While fans frequently form parts of audiences, fandom involves elements not present in the mere constitution of an audience. Fandom is based in a specific regard for – or psychological attachment to – particular performers or styles that is often thought of by outsiders as being excessive or pathological in character. However, more recent scholarship (for example, Lewis 1992) has taken a more balanced view of fandom, seeing it as being integrally bound up with the formation of social identities in which sexuality frequently plays a prominent role. While fans may stress issues of inclusion, difference and exclusion in the manner in which they consume their chosen kind of music, therefore, the relation of 'ordinary' audience members to the music to which they are listening may be thought of as not rising much above the pleasures of consumption (see Grossberg 1992a). Fans can be distinguished from 'ordinary' audience members in terms of the level of intensity with which they relate to music, their relative degree of activeness in responding to music, and their ability to engage in fandom outside the audience situation through private, individualized listening.

The term 'audience' thereby invokes a notion of a group or mass of people not necessarily invoked by that of 'fan.' Further, while fans may readily and actively identify themselves as such in a wide range of situations, audience members are only likely to do so when, indeed, they are forming part of an actual audience, thinking of themselves otherwise as listeners, viewers or even, indeed, fans. Moreover, there are some situations in which individuals forming part of an audience may not think of themselves as audience members or even listeners. While individuals in shopping malls, offices and elevators may be thought of as constituting an audience for Muzak, many may be unaware that they are hearing music. In the same way that fans may be distinguished from 'ordinary' audience members in terms of the level of intensity with which they relate to music and performers, different kinds of audiences may be distinguished from one another in terms of the level of awareness or of the intensity of their listening, and in terms of whether their listening is intentional and focused, as in a concert, or a matter of happenstance and therefore casual, as in a shopping mall. The term 'audience' is as a consequence more commonly used by cultural analysts and theorists, and in the music industry, and in advertising and marketing agencies, than it is by audience members themselves. When used in the music industry, and in advertising and marketing agencies, the term 'audience' has something in common with that of 'market.' In this sense, reference is sometimes made to artists 'losing their audience.'

Much attention has been given to the study of audiences. While initial studies assumed that audiences were largely homogeneous, more recent studies have acknowledged their complex and variegated constitution. Further, while initial studies assumed that audiences uncritically assimilated the meanings or messages intended by the producers of cultural commodities, later studies understood the effects of the mass media to be indirect, limited and significantly mediated by a range of factors outside the control of cultural producers. The main problem in discussing audiences, therefore, is that they are constantly shifting, being made and remade across time, and their characteristics are seldom the same from region to region, despite processes of mass consumption and globalization. While it is undoubtedly the intention of cultural producers to create audiences (which is to say, markets) for particular commodities, and thereby to influence, if not control, processes of taste formation, processes of taste formation and of audience or market formation appear to be essentially dialectic. The relative degree of determination and agency involved in these processes has continued to be a matter for debate.

Historical Developments

Until the latter part of the nineteenth century in North America and Europe, performers tended to be itinerant and to travel to audiences. In the largely rural United States of the nineteenth century, for example, musicians would move on an almost daily basis from villages to towns to hamlets in circuses, in medicine shows, in minstrel troupes and in groups such as singing families. As the transportation revolution began to take hold in both North America and Europe, its most immediate effect was to enable performers to reach audiences on a much wider geographical basis. The Virginia Minstrels in 1843, and the Hutchinson Family Singers in 1845, for example, both took advantage of transatlantic steamship services to bring their music to Britain. At the same time, and as urbanization became a more prominent factor in people's lives, it became increasingly common for audiences to travel to performances. The final performance of the Hutchinson Family's British tour, at Manchester's Free Trade Hall in May 1846, was attended by over 4,000 people, and, as one historian notes, 'many special trains were put on to accommodate the concert crowd' (Cockrell 1989, 361). This trend was amplified by growing industrialization, the formation of music industries, increasing commercialization, and a greater emphasis on the promotion of performers and performances. Such developments were eventually to give rise to the modern tour, in which musicians of international reputation perform to very large audiences only in major conurbations.

Another fundamental change in the relations between performers and audiences occurred as a consequence of the advent of recording and electronic communication.

Before the advent of the phonograph and, more importantly, of radio and television, audiences experienced music in the presence of performing musicians only. This could be as part of a spectacle or stage show, whether it were a classical oratorio in a concert hall or a brass band at the local village fete. It could also be as a consequence of performances of sheet music in the home. In this latter case, the audience was not bound by the strictures of time and place, as were audiences in vaudeville theaters. In this sense, audiences of a dispersed character for a particular piece of music could be thought of as being created through the sale and dissemination of sheet music, and its performance in domestic situations.

With the advent of radio in particular, audiences for a particular performer or piece of music became significantly larger and more greatly dispersed. Although 'star performers' such as Al Jolson had undoubtedly existed before the age of radio, radio, recording and film created a greater distance between performers and their mass audiences, and thereby gave rise to a space within which it was easier to construct the persona of the star. As a consequence, the power of the music industries to create stars and, through them, audiences for particular cultural commodities increased. The new media of radio, film and, subsequently, television, together with innovations such as the phonograph and the increasing importance of Muzak, meant that taste communities could be created in both public and private spaces (in the bedroom, the workplace or even the supermarket), away from any direct experience of the performance itself. Indeed, by the early 1970s, progressive rock acts such as Pink Floyd were judged not by their performance abilities per se, but by their ability to faithfully reproduce their recorded sound in a live context. The audio event at home, rather than the performance itself, thus became the authentic expression of musical intent for the audience.

The advent of these emblems of mass culture (radio, television, cinema, mass circulation newspapers and magazines) in the 1920s and 1930s was subsequently seen by communication theorists as heralding an era in which processes of mass production, dissemination and consumption created both specific markets and audiences for various cultural projects and linked these taste communities into a national, and sometimes international, whole. The result was that traditional entertainment, whether a sing-along in the front parlor or a night out at the local music hall, was superseded in popularity by these new cultural forms. Audiences that previously, in the nineteenth century, had been quite heterogeneous, being largely community- and family-based, now became much more targeted in terms of class, age,

gender and ethnicity, although distinctions according to ethnicity and race had always been evident.

The arrival of format radio as a direct response to the challenge of television in the 1940s and 1950s was perhaps the single most important development in this respect. Hitherto, radio had been 'broad-casting,' providing family entertainment deemed acceptable and appealing to all. Now, for commercial reasons, various audiences were being targeted and were the recipients of quite specific musical genres and specific commodities through advertising and sponsorship.

By the 1950s, the whole idea of the 'audience' had fundamentally changed. The term increasingly began to take on its current usage, in which it denotes 'the unknown individuals and groups towards whom mass communications are addressed' (O'Sullivan 1994, 19), rather than a collectivity of admirers of a particular cultural form who attend a musical event in person. In the above formulation, the adjective 'unknown' is of central importance, as markets have tried to second-guess, preempt and create successful cultural forms for various audiences. By the 1950s, the audience was seen as alienated, or atomized, its members unknown to one another, experiencing culture not directly but through massmediated forms.

Analysis

In the postwar period, academics, mainly positivistic, empiricist sociologists in the United Kingdom and the United States, began to turn their attention to issues of teenage delinquency, deviance and criminality. A minority of sociologists examined the role of pop music (usually through a reading of its lyrical content) in creating youth audiences (Denzin 1969–70; Hirsch 1971; Robinson and Hirsch 1972). The common thread that linked most of these approaches was the idea, taken from Theodor Adorno, of a passive audience, regressed, childlike, stupefied by the products of mass culture such as the standardized pop of Tin Pan Alley (see, for example, Adorno 1941). Likewise, leftist British writers, such as Richard Hoggart in his influential *The Uses of Literacy* (first published in 1957), bemoaned the perceived herd-like mentality of British youth, which was understood to result from an Americanization of working-class culture viewed as barbaric. Individuals were thought of either as obedient to the dictates of the pack, subsumed into the overall identity of an undifferentiated, uncritical audience, or as loners, disconnected from society due to an addiction to these new cultural forms which made entertainment a solitary and unrewarding experience.

What caused these reactions was the rise to prominence of a new teenage audience, with its own cultural identity and spending power. The postwar baby boom in the United States meant that, by the 1960s, 40 percent of the population was under 20. Moreover, a sizable proportion of this grouping was important in economic terms, fueling the growth of the music business by purchasing its products. Many white teenagers also took an active interest in black musics and culture, thus helping to create greater exposure for African-American music among white audiences. Youth audiences also began to experience stronger bonds with performers, bonds intensified, in some instances, through an emergent drug culture.

Because of a paucity of research into how these new cultural forms affected individuals, it is impossible to determine the exact impact that mass culture had from the 1920s to the 1960s. However, work in the 1960s – for example, that by Hall and Whannel, first published in 1964 – challenged the idea that audiences passively accepted dominant ideologies by showing that the audience was more active in its use of cultural forms. In the 1970s, the work of the Centre for Contemporary Cultural Studies (CCCS) in Birmingham in the United Kingdom, and particularly that of Paul Willis (1978) and Dick Hebdige (1979), theorized a homology or fit between the life style, clothes and musical preferences of various subcultural groupings such as the Teds, Mods and Punks. Although this idea of a proactive audience was later criticized for being flawed in its romanticized view of subcultural groupings, its lack of attention to mainstream audiences, its lack of focus on the role of women and its avoidance of the actual musical texts themselves (see Laing 1985; McRobbie 1990; Clarke 1990), the work of Willis and Hebdige did much to deflate the long-held argument that the audience for pop was merely being duped, or doped, by the bland products of the capitalist entertainment industry.

Subsequent work on audiences and fans has continued to stress the idea of a proactive audience, one that is critical, discerning and able to negotiate meaning (see Jensen 1992). Important in this respect is the work of Morley (1993) and Hall (1980), with regard to the 'encoding' and 'decoding' of television programs, in which a typology of audience response (the 'dominant-hegemonic,' the 'negotiated' and the 'oppositional') was established which corresponded more to the audience's social condition than to the structure of individual television programs as cultural texts. Another important contribution came from Bourdieu (1984), whose idea of cultural capital and taste communities, which provides a theory to explain the unequal distribution of cultural and symbolic power among individuals, directly influenced the later work of sociologist Simon Frith (1996) and others. There has also been an increasing amount of

research on what Grossberg (1992b) has called the 'secondary audience' – those who do not invest directly in the subcultural trappings of youth culture, or those for whom music plays a pivotal role, but who form a less 'spectacular' and more 'mainstream' audience for popular music. The work of Crafts, Cavicchi and Keil (1993), along with that of Lipsitz (1990), has gone some way to deflating the idea of the audience as an unknowable, depersonalized mass, and has emphasized the importance of an 'idioculture,' wherein each person's response to popular music is intricately and uniquely interwoven with that person's own personal biography, history and sense of place.

The old view of a passive/active audience for popular music has been further challenged by ethnographic surveys (see Finnegan 1989; Cohen 1991), which demonstrate that the division between performer and audience is more porous than customarily imagined, with practitioners of pop self-reflexively incorporating musical influences into their music as both consumers and producers simultaneously.

The idea of the audience as productive and proactive has also meant that a brand of populism has developed (particularly in the work of John Fiske – see, for example, Fiske 1989), which problematically ascribes the meanings of cultural forms wholly to the activities of audiences. Audiences are in this way taken to be capable of investing the blandest of cultural forms with radical responses. This kind of approach has, however, been challenged by scholars such as McGuigan (1992). A useful summary of recent scholarship on audiences in popular music is to be found in Negus (1996, 7–35).

Contemporary Developments

The 1980s and 1990s saw both the rise to prominence of a global community for popular music and, at the same time, a fracturing of these audiences. In line with this fracturing, the music industry, through the deployment of strict generic marketing labels, has identified niche audiences for a myriad of musical styles. The relationship between local scenes and audiences and national, international and global cultures has assumed a pivotal significance within popular music studies.

An added feature of contemporary developments has been the advent of a range of more dramatic phenomena associated with audience participation and behavior. Such phenomena may be traced back to the reactions of 'bobby-soxers' as well as older women to the young Frank Sinatra, and continued with what was regarded by some as hysterical reactions on the part of young women to Elvis Presley and the Beatles. Commenting on this behavior and reactions to it in the context of Presley concerts, Doss (1999) observes that 'much of the postwar critique of Elvis's fans was, in fact, a thinly veiled attack on teenage girls' in an era in which 'sexual panic possessed ... Americans' (49). Condescending reporters, comments Doss, 'repeatedly described how "silly" girls squealed, screamed, shrieked, sobbed, and swooned during Elvis's concerts, emphasizing their irrationality and animalism, their sexual heat' (1999, 49).

Increased drama in audience behavior has continued with phenomena such as slam-dancing and moshing. Rather than regarding these activities as irrational, however, scholars have emphasized the conventions (Tsitsos 1999) and ideologies (Roman 1988) that they manifest. Such scholarly treatment has extended to the use of drugs at raves (Reynolds 1998). In addition, it appears that audiences can be structured spatially and according to age in terms of the level of physical activity at musical events. Fonarow (1997), for example, reports that 'at indie gigs, social relationships are enacted through spatial distribution and different modes of participation within a specific participant framework' (360). Three zones of activity can be identified. In zone one, 'audience density is very high and activities such as diving from the stage on to other audience members or being hoisted by friends and rolling on top of the crowd are quite common' (1997, 361). In zone two, where audience members 'tend to range from early to late twenties,' there is 'a modest amount of physical response ... rocking back and forth, gently moving the head, and tapping one's feet in rhythm to the music' (1997, 365). Zone three comprises 'the bar and the most active socializing in the conventional sense of the word,' and is 'where much of the logistical work for those putting on the event occurs' (1997, 366). It is the 'mediational zone between the inside and outside,' the domain of 'the professionals ... booking agents, promoters, press agents, managers, crew, record personnel, product managers, journalists, and musicians from other bands not performing' (1997, 366–67). As Fonarow concludes, 'As individuals age, they move back through space until they are aged out of the venue all together' (1997, 369).

Contemporary audience participation has also become potentially more dangerous. In 1969, for example, an audience member attending a Rolling Stones concert at Altamont Speedway in Livermore, California was stabbed to death by a member of the Hell's Angels, who had been hired by the group to provide security for the show. Deaths through crushing have also not been uncommon. In June 2000, nine audience members were crushed to death at a Pearl Jam performance in Copenhagen, when concertgoers surged forward to the stage during the band's performance. Such incidents have resulted in the passing of legislation and the additional regulation of concerts. The death of a 14-year-old at a

David Cassidy concert in 1974 caused London's local authorities to impose a partial ban on selected rock acts in the mid- to late 1970s. Crowd Management Strategies, which each year since 1992 has published the *Rock Concert Safety Survey Reports* (these reports review popular concert and festival crowd safety incidents, including deaths, on a worldwide basis), offers expert advice on crowd management at musical events.

At the same time that some forms of audience participation and behavior have become more dramatic, there is also evidence that the importance of popular music in everyday life is diminishing, or rather that audiences are using music in different ways than before. A survey conducted by Gallup in 1991 revealed that, although 14- to 16-year-olds listened to pop music up to four hours a day (three times more than in the mid-1970s), it was ranked very low in the list of 'the most important things in life,' below education, home, friends, money, sex, appearance, work, going out, hobbies and football (see Frith 1991, 88). Grossberg and others have shown that music is now more commonly consumed in connection with other leisure or work practises, creating a background ambiance for the primary activity. Sites for the dissemination of music are ever-proliferating, as attested by the conflation of private and public spaces through the Sony Walkman or the proactive ritualized sing-along that is karaoke.

Furthermore, the audience for popular music is aging. The teenagers of the Sinatra era are now retired. The rise of the compact disc and the attendant reissues of selected popular albums on vinyl, together with the emergence of a range of publications and television networks to cater for the 30–55 age group and the continued popularity of artists such as the Rolling Stones and Neil Young, confirm the fact that youth is no longer as important to the consumption of popular music as it once was. Indeed, certain theorists have argued that the whole concept of 'youth' can now be thought of as comparatively free-floating, an attitude of mind rather than an indicator with any fixed biological referent (see Weinstein 1994).

Pop singers themselves have also been keen to help create their own audiences, fashioning taste communities which identify, through either the music, lyrics, stage performance or video, with an image (of rebelliousness, vulnerability, sexuality, occultism, paranoid alienation or whatever) that helps bond people into specific audiences.

Bibliography

Adorno, Theodor W., with Simpson, George. 1941. 'On Popular Music.' *Studies in Philosophy and Social Sciences* 9: 17–48.

Bourdieu, Pierre. 1984 (1979). *Distinction: A Social Critique of the Judgement of Taste.* London: Routledge.

Clarke, Gary. 1990 (1981). 'Defending Ski-Jumpers: A Critique of Theories of Youth Subcultures.' In *On Record: Rock, Pop, and the Written Word*, ed. Simon Frith and Andrew Goodwin. London: Routledge, 81–96. (Originally published by the University of Birmingham Centre for Contemporary Cultural Studies.)

Cockrell, Dale, ed. 1989. *Excelsior: Journals of the Hutchinson Family Singers, 1842–1846.* Stuyvesant, NY: Pendragon Press.

Cohen, Sara. 1991. *Rock Culture in Liverpool: Popular Music in the Making.* Oxford: Oxford University Press.

Crafts, Susan D., Cavicchi, Daniel, and Keil, Charles. 1993. *My Music.* Hanover, NH: Wesleyan University Press.

Denzin, Norman K. 1969–70. 'Problems in Analyzing Elements of Mass Culture: Notes on the Popular Song and Other Artistic Productions.' *American Journal of Sociology* 75(6): 1035–38.

Doss, Erika. 1999. *Elvis Culture: Fans, Faith and Image.* Lawrence, KS: University Press of Kansas.

Finnegan, Ruth. 1989. *The Hidden Musicians: Music-Making in an English Town.* Cambridge: Cambridge University Press.

Fiske, John. 1989. *Reading the Popular.* London: Routledge.

Fonarow, Wendy. 1997. 'The Spatial Organization of the Indie Music Gig.' In *The Subcultures Reader*, ed. Ken Gelder and Sarah Thornton. London: Routledge, 360–69.

Frith, Simon. 1991. 'He's the One.' *Village Voice* (29 October): 88.

Frith, Simon. 1996. *Performing Rites: On the Value of Popular Music.* Cambridge, MA: Harvard University Press.

Frith, Simon, and Savage, Jon. 1993. 'Pearls and Swine: Against Cultural Populism.' *New Left Review* 198: 107–16.

Grossberg, Lawrence. 1992a. 'Is There a Fan in the House?: The Affective Sensibility of Fandom.' In *The Adoring Audience: Fan Culture and Popular Media*, ed. Lisa A. Lewis. London and New York: Routledge, 50–65.

Grossberg, Lawrence. 1992b. 'Rock and Roll in Search of an Audience.' In *Popular Music and Communication*, ed. James Lull. 2nd ed. Newbury Park, CA: Sage Publications, 175–97.

Hall, Stuart. 1980. 'Encoding/Decoding.' In *Culture, Media, Language: Working Papers in Cultural Studies, 1972–79*, ed. Stuart Hall et al. London: Hutchinson, 128–38.

Hall, Stuart, and Whannel, Paddy. 1990 (1964). 'The Young Audience.' In *On Record: Rock, Pop, and the Written Word*, ed. Simon Frith and Andrew Goodwin. London: Routledge, 27–37. (Originally published in *The Popular Arts.* London: Hutchinson, 1964, 269–83.)

Hebdige, Dick. 1979. *Subculture: The Meaning of Style.* London: Methuen.

Hirsch, Paul M. 1971. 'Sociological Approaches to the Pop Music Phenomenon.' *American Behavioral Scientist* 14: 371–88.

Hoggart, Richard. 1992 (1957). *The Uses of Literacy: Aspects of Working-Class Life, with Special Reference to Publications and Entertainments.* Rev. ed. Harmondsworth: Penguin, in association with Chatto and Windus.

Jensen, Joli. 1992. 'Fandom as Pathology: The Consequences of Characterization.' In *The Adoring Audience: Fan Culture and Popular Media*, ed. Lisa A. Lewis. London and New York: Routledge, 9–29.

Laing, Dave. 1985. *One Chord Wonders: Power and Meaning in Punk Rock.* Milton Keynes: Open University Press.

Lewis, Lisa A., ed. 1992. *The Adoring Audience: Fan Culture and Popular Media.* London and New York: Routledge.

Lipsitz, George. 1990. *Time Passages: Collective Memory and American Popular Culture.* Minneapolis, MN: University of Minnesota Press.

McGuigan, Jim. 1992. *Cultural Populism.* London: Routledge.

McRobbie, Angela. 1990 (1980). 'Settling Accounts with Subcultures: A Feminist Critique.' In *On Record: Rock, Pop, and the Written Word*, ed. Simon Frith and Andrew Goodwin. London: Routledge, 66–80. (First published in *Screen Education* 34 (1980): 37–49.)

Morley, David. 1993. 'Active Audience Theory: Pendulums and Pitfalls.' *Journal of Communication* 43(4): 13–19.

Negus, Keith. 1996. *Popular Music in Theory: An Introduction.* Cambridge: Polity Press.

O'Sullivan, Tim. 1994. 'Audience.' In *Key Concepts in Communication and Cultural Studies*, ed. Tim O'Sullivan et al. London and New York: Routledge, 19–20.

Reynolds, Simon. 1998. 'Rave Culture: Living Dream or Living Death?' In *The Clubcultures Reader: Readings in Popular Cultural Studies*, ed. Steve Redhead, with Derek Wynne and Justin O'Connor. Oxford: Blackwell, 84–93.

Robinson, John P., and Hirsch, Paul M. 1972. 'Teenage Response to Rock and Roll Protest Songs.' In *The Sounds of Social Change: Studies in Popular Culture*, ed. R. Serge Denisoff and Richard A. Peterson. Chicago: Rand McNally, 222–31.

Rock Concert Safety Survey Reports. http://www.crowdsafe.com/reports.html

Roman, Leslie G. 1988. 'Intimacy, Labor, and Class: Ideologies of Feminine Sexuality in the Punk Slam Dance.' In *Becoming Feminine: The Politics of Popular Culture*, ed. Leslie G. Roman and Linda K. Christian-Smith. London: Falmer Press, 143–84.

Shuker, Roy. 1994. *Understanding Popular Music*. London: Routledge.

Taylor, Rogan P. 1985. *The Death and Resurrection Show: From Shaman to Superstar*. London: Anthony Blond.

Tsitsos, William. 1999. 'Rules of Rebellion: Slamdancing, Moshing, and the American Alternative Scene.' *Popular Music* 18(3): 397–414.

Weinstein, Deena. 1994. 'Expendable Youth: The Rise and Fall of Youth Culture.' In *Adolescents and Their Music: If It's Too Loud, You're Too Old*, ed. Jonathon S. Epstein. New York: Garland, 67–85.

Willis, Paul. 1978. *Profane Culture*. London: Routledge.

DAVID BUCKLEY and JOHN SHEPHERD

Authenticity

In popular music, the concept of authenticity (from the Latin *authenticus*, meaning 'coming from the author') is generally connected with how certain forms of popular music have typically been regarded as real or genuine while others have not. Notions of authenticity have been positioned around issues related to historical continuity, artistic expression and sincerity, autonomy from commercial imperatives, technology and production, and the expression of and engagement with the cultures of certain audiences, communities or localities. For critics and audiences, authenticity has often underpinned the way in which popular music has been evaluated and understood. Scholarship has largely avoided resting upon or reinforcing polarized notions of authentic and inauthentic popular music, regarding any claim to authenticity as primarily an ideological construction. According to this view, one form of popular music is no more inherently capable of transmitting 'true' emotion or feeling than another. Hence, current debates around the issue concentrate on how notions of authenticity are constructed, in both the practise and the consumption of popular music.

Frith (1986), for instance, deconstructs notions of authenticity in rock culture, focusing on how certain forms of instrumentation and production values are valued more than others. He argues that 'the continuing core of rock ideology is that raw sounds are more authentic than cooked sounds,' but points out that this is a 'paradoxical belief for a technologically sophisticated medium and rests on an old-fashioned model of communication – A plays to B and the less technology lies between them the closer they are' (1986, 266–67). Likewise, in folk cultures music has often been regarded as 'an expression of the feelings and experiences of an everyday reality' (Redhead and Street 1989, 177–78) and has thus been understood within a tradition of 'music of the people.' This form of authenticity has been regarded as problematic in that it is seen to allude to a rural working culture that never really existed and that was actively created by those within the folk revivals (Middleton 1990; Brocken 1997). Furthermore, there has been the suggestion that these notions are constructed within various types of musics in order to reinforce particular ideological standpoints. Folk movements, for instance, have been linked to left-wing politics. Similarly, it has been argued that, in the mid-1980s, white British rock performers appropriated US rhythm and blues styles in order to add authenticity to the political content of their music (Redhead and Street 1989), because the musical forms of these styles were favored as appropriate vehicles for the transmission of political messages.

Constructions of authenticity have often been linked to the relationship between popular music and the culture industries. Stratton (1982), for instance, argues that the creative process has often been mystified by the artist and the music industry in order to conceal the rational workings of capitalism. Here, the construction of artistic autonomy and authentic expression seek to foreground popular music's aesthetic value while playing down its position as a commodity within a commercial framework. This mystification is further articulated in the way in which, within certain genre cultures, to be seen as pandering to capitalism or 'the market' is to be seen as 'selling out.' Such formulations of 'selling out' tend to be modeled on polarizations involving art and commerce, independent and corporate, underground and mainstream, or on particular artists 'losing touch' with their audience by changing style or acceding to 'commercial' production techniques.

Many critics (Frith 1982; Laing 1985; Harron 1988) have pointed out that the art versus commerce debate was central to the formation of a new dominant 'folk art' aesthetic of rock in the late 1960s. Here, the music was understood to possess a direct emotional capacity that transcends its dissemination through the 'commercial' structures of the culture industries. These 'folk art' musics were regarded as more than 'mere entertainment' because they were set up as valid forms of artistic expression. In the late 1960s, rock and pop became ideologically distinct, with rock becoming popularly understood as the more authentic form. Rock was given critical and subcultural credence either because of its apparent 'roots' in earlier music traditions (folk, country, jazz and blues), because of its merit as art music (psychedelic progressive rock) or because it was seen to articulate the feelings and concerns of its core audience. Conversely, 'pop' was generally seen in terms of 'entertainment' and commercialism rather than of seriousness. As Frith (1983) has noted, the use of a folk art aesthetic has been historically important in the understanding of rock.

Because of the embedded nature of authenticity paradigms within certain types of popular music discourse, the concept has become bound up with image production and marketing within the music industry. Here, the aforementioned formulations are actively used in the way in which acts are presented to the public. Coyle and Dolan (1999) argue that authenticity is a socially constructed concept that has become a central tool in the marketing of popular music: 'Authenticity is a sign and not a quality, and like any sign it functions differentially and deferentially. In the world of commerce, authenticity is simply a matter of trademark' (29). Negus (1992) makes a similar point while arguing that audiences are both self-aware and reflexive in their consumption and understanding of artists who are presented as real or authentic. Using Bruce Springsteen as an example, Negus argues that fans are knowing consumers who both see the construction of the artist's mythologized image and accept it.

It has also been pointed out that different conceptions of authenticity develop depending on how, when and where popular music is listened to and consumed. Thornton (1995) argues that, since the advent of recorded sound, notions of 'liveness' have been privileged within Western popular music. As Grossberg (1992) points out, 'the demand for live performance has always expressed the desire for the visual mark (and proof) of authenticity' (208). However, Thornton explores ways in which notions of authenticity can change and gives an historical account of 'disc cultures,' which have meant that recorded music has become enculturated into certain conceptions of authenticity. Thornton argues that, as new technologies become normalized within a culture, they become regarded as authentic in new ways. Likewise, Chambers (1992) sees the history of Western popular music as being 'the story of a continual appropriation of pop's technology and reproductive capacities' (194). Further, notions of authenticity are not fixed historically in relation to genres of music, as such genres are subject to a constant repositioning within the ideologies surrounding popular music. For instance, although music produced by the Motown label in the 1960s was seen at the time as inauthentic commercial pop, it eventually received retrospective critical acclaim. Indeed, even Motown's oft-cited 'production line' aesthetic became part of its critical cachet through the connotations of workmanship and 'pure' pop product.

Authenticity has also been central to debates surrounding race and popular music. Various African-American musics, for instance, have been read as musical forms in which common practises such as signifyin(g) and antiphony are seen as following a direct line from African oral traditions. Indeed, the drawing of diachronic historical lines through black cultural forms and the identification of common formal traits that run through that history have significantly contributed to the way in which certain genres have been understood and classified as black music. Drawing on the work of black cultural critics Gates (1988) and Stuckey (1987), Floyd (1991) traces elements observed in the 'ring shouts' of African Americans in the nineteenth century through to black contemporary and popular music of the twentieth century. Likewise, Brackett's musicological analysis of James Brown's work (1992) identifies formal elements of it that draw on the rhetorical play and troping of the black vernacular.

Gilroy (1993) seeks to counter what he understands as essentialized notions of authenticity, arguing that black cultural forms have been somewhat unproblematically understood as part of an uninterrupted black oral tradition. He maintains that account needs to be taken of developments and mutations that reflect changes in the contexts and lived experiences of black performers. For Gilroy, black musical forms are not necessarily united by a shared history that can be traced through slavery to Africa, but are informed by communication between diasporic groups. He suggests a transformative process in which different musicians utilize these forms, but not in some uninterrupted, 'pure' sense. Likewise, Tagg (1989) attempts to deconstruct what he sees as 'reductionist' accounts of black music in musicological terms, indicating that many musical traits that have often been regarded as typically 'black' can also be found in European music. However, despite such critiques, it is clear that such formal elements are indeed present in a huge variety of black musics and that they constitute an important cultural marker in tracing a black cultural heritage that is historically linked to the African diaspora.

It is clear, then, that the concept of authenticity is not restricted to discussions of music itself, but is active within the discourses surrounding popular music. It is prevalent in issues of identity, audience reception and subculture and in the marketing and mediation of popular music. It is also clear that the term has been used and understood in numerous ways both in popular music's discourses and in its study. In the light of this multiplicity of uses, authenticity, rather than being a static and concrete concept, should be understood as a number of related 'authenticities' and authenticity paradigms. These 'authenticities' are shaped by considerations such as the specificity of their respected genres, cultures and synchronic historical moments, the production of popular music within its industrial context and particular social dynamics such as race, gender and class.

Bibliography

Brackett, David. 1992. 'James Brown's "Superbad" and the Double-Voiced Utterance.' *Popular Music* 11(3): 309–24.

Brocken, Michael. 1997. *The British Folk Revival: An Analysis of Folk/Popular Dichotomies from a Popular Music Studies Perspective.* Unpublished Ph.D. thesis, University of Liverpool.

Chambers, Iain. 1992 (1988). 'Contamination, Coincidence and Collusion: Pop Music, Urban Culture and the Avant-Garde.' In *Modernism/Postmodernism*, ed. Peter Brooker. London and New York: Longman, 190–96.

Coyle, Michael, and Dolan, Jon. 1999. 'Modeling Authenticity, Authenticating Commercial Models.' In *Reading Rock and Roll: Authenticity, Appropriation, Aesthetics*, ed. Kevin J.H. Dettmar and William Richey. New York: Columbia University Press, 17–35.

Floyd, Samuel A., Jr. 1991. 'Ring Shout!: Literary Studies, Historical Studies, and Black Music Inquiry.' *Black Music Research Journal* 11(2): 265–87.

Frith, Simon. 1982. 'The Sociology of Rock: Notes from Britain.' In *Popular Music Perspectives, 1*, ed. David Horn and Philip Tagg. Göteborg and Exeter: IASPM, 142–54.

Frith, Simon. 1983. *Sound Effects: Youth, Leisure, and the Politics of Rock 'n' Roll.* London: Constable.

Frith, Simon. 1986. 'Art Versus Technology: The Strange Case of Popular Music.' *Media, Culture and Society* 8(3): 263–80.

Gates, Henry Louis, Jr. 1988. *The Signifying Monkey: A Theory of Afro-American Literary Criticism.* New York: Oxford University Press.

Gilroy, Paul. 1993. '"Jewels Brought Back from Bondage": Black Music and the Politics of Authenticity.' In *The Black Atlantic: Modernity and Double Consciousness.* London: Verso, 72–110.

Grossberg, Lawrence. 1992. *We Gotta Get Out of This Place: Popular Conservatism and Postmodern Culture.* London: Routledge.

Harron, Mary. 1988. 'McRock: Pop as Commodity.' In *Facing the Music: Essays on Pop, Rock and Culture*, ed. Simon Frith. London: Mandarin, 173–220.

Laing, Dave. 1985. *One Chord Wonders: Power and Meaning in Punk Rock.* Milton Keynes: Open University Press.

Middleton, Richard. 1990. *Studying Popular Music.* Milton Keynes: Open University Press.

Negus, Keith. 1992. *Producing Pop: Culture and Conflict in the Popular Music Industry.* London: Edward Arnold.

Redhead, Steve, and Street, John. 1989. 'Have I the Right?: Legitimacy, Authenticity and Community in Folk's Politics.' *Popular Music* 8(2): 177–84.

Stratton, Jon. 1982. 'Between Two Worlds: Art and Commercialism in the Record Industry.' *The Sociological Review* 30: 267–85.

Stuckey, Sterling. 1987. *Slave Culture: Nationalist Theory and the Foundations of Black America.* New York: Oxford University Press.

Tagg, Philip. 1989. 'Open Letter: "Black Music," "Afro-American Music" and "European Music."' *Popular Music* 8(3): 285–98.

Thornton, Sarah. 1995. *Club Cultures: Music, Media and Subcultural Capital.* London: Polity.

MARION LEONARD and ROBERT STRACHAN

Carnival

Carnival is generally conceived as a period when the world is turned upside down, and merrymakers in masks and fancy dress challenge everyday norms through displays of unrepressed eroticism, gluttony and incisive social criticism. Music, often with a strong rhythmic feel and satirical lyrics, has frequently accompanied the activities of revelers. While carnivalesque behavior is common to many cultures, carnival proper is associated with the Christian world, denoting a festival that begins sometime after Christmas and generally concludes at midnight before Ash Wednesday, when the excesses of carnival give way to the fasting of Lent. Carnival's links to the Christian calendar are evident in the debate over the etymology of the term, the dominant view being that it derives from the Latin *carnem levare* ('to put away or remove meat'). In many parts of Europe, local terms for the day preceding Lent emerged, such as Shrovetide in the British Isles, Mardi Gras (lit. 'Fat Tuesday') in France and *Fastnacht* in Germany, among others.

Although carnival drew on a diversity of local pagan festivals, it is widely held that the main ancestor of the European medieval carnival was the Roman Saturnalia, the festival of Saturn, which was characterized by lasciviousness and social inversions. The transgressions of medieval carnivals are documented in Rabelais' *Gargantua and Pantagruel* (1534), which inspired Bakhtin (1984) to portray carnival as a sphere for experiencing human equality. The communal and festive nature of carnival represents a cyclical moment in which, through laughter and 'grotesque realism,' expressed through the ambivalent and transformational use of costumes and masks, social hierarchies are temporarily eliminated. Contrasting the free speech employed during carnival with the euphemisms of daily interactions, Bakhtin argued that carnival's uninhibited speech permitted people to express their true views, giving it a revolutionary impact.

This view contrasts with the more pervasive 'safety-valve theory,' in which carnival is seen as periodically dispelling social tensions before they reach the point of eruption. While, down the ages, those in power have recognized the usefulness of designating ritual spaces for people to speak their mind and act out their fantasies, it is also true that carnivalesque excesses have frequently been the target of repression, particularly when they have threatened to break out of the ritual framework. Carnival, therefore, might best be viewed as a complex site of contestation and manipulation, transgression and control, in which the terms of negotiation hinge on the specificities of distinct historical circumstances.

As the medieval period came to a close, for example, people in positions of authority began investing heavily in attempts to curtail the licentiousness and violence of carnival. In some places, carnival came under the patronage of powerful families, and the free-for-all ethos of carnival gave way to spectacle, involving pageantry and lavish masks and floats. With the rise of the middle classes, rationalist ideas became dominant, and the popularity of carnival declined, surviving only in a few isolated pockets, such as Venice and Andalusia.

As carnival declined in Europe, it began to flourish in the Americas, particularly in places where a strong Roman Catholic heritage coexisted with large low-income populations. By the early nineteenth century, spontaneous popular street festivals were common in many regions, much to the displeasure of local officials, who frequently employed heavy-handed tactics to repress them. With the emergence of nationalist sentiments in the early twentieth century, however, attitudes changed, and officials began hailing their carnivals as symbols of national identity. The enthusiasm of the participants and the syncretism of carnival aesthetics were viewed as indicators of the felicitous integration of diverse cultural and racial groups achieved in their nations. Once it became an object of state interest, carnival was subjected to bureaucratic control, typically focused on staged competitions to promote cultural patriotism, as well as to serve the tourist industry.

In Rio de Janeiro, for example, carnival was embraced by the state in 1935, leading to a significant domestication of the city's carnival celebrations. Around the turn of the century, informal mobile dance associations called ranchos or blocos had become common. They were made up of blacks, mulattoes and unskilled white laborers, who danced down the streets to the rhythm of percussion instruments, singing responsorially to the short improvised verses of a leader. Their musical style became known as samba, and in 1928 an association named 'Deixa Falar' was formed, which called itself a 'samba school,' a term soon adopted by other associations. Under state patronage, an official competition between samba schools, with cash prizes, was instituted. To participate in Rio's official celebrations, the schools were expected to present costumes, floats and songs that glorified the nation, its natural beauty and its heroes, starting a trend toward increasingly lavish displays. By the end of the twentieth century, the samba schools in Rio were organized into a federation with a top league of 14 official schools, each with its own history rooted in one of the city's 'shantytown' communities. The baterias (percussion groups) have become the trademark of the schools, recognizable by their use of certain instruments, rhythmic patterns and breaks. Each year, new sambas are composed to provide the theme (enrêdo) to be enacted by each school, and intense anticipation precedes the final announcement of the winning school.

Samba school processions have become widespread throughout Brazil, due mainly to the extensive media coverage given to the carnival parades (desfiles) in Rio de Janeiro. More recently, however, the carnivals of the northeast, particularly the Bahian carnivals, have gained in popularity, attracting tourists year-round. Northeastern carnivals are marked by trios elétricos; while the name refers to the electric guitar-based instrumental groups that initiated the tradition, contemporary trios elétricos are large flat-top trucks carrying a band and a large amount of sound equipment. Often, thousands of people follow their favorite ensemble, dancing to the band's performance of 'axé music.' It was also in the northeast that the blocos afro first emerged in the mid-1970s. With a rhythmic accompaniment based almost exclusively on drums, these associations draw on pan-African styles, especially reggae, marking a growing sense of ethnic identity and solidarity among black Brazilians.

In the Caribbean, masquerades, or mas parades, and unique styles of music have developed to accompany carnival celebrations. The largest and best-known Caribbean carnival takes place in Trinidad and Tobago, where a carnival atmosphere begins to take hold soon after Christmas. Across the island, tents for calypso performances are erected, and the best-known calypsonians release their recordings, in which they chronicle the year's main scandals and events; steel-pan bands begin rehearsing, drawing their melodies primarily from the calypso repertoire; and the mas bands prepare their costumes and floats. The festivities culminate just before Lent, with a five-day ritual pageant in the historic capital city of Port-of-Spain, coordinated by the Carnival Development Committee (CDC): on Friday, the King and

Queen contests are held, in which prizes are awarded to the best costumes; the Saturday *Panorama* is a competition among the year's best steel-pan bands; on *Dimanche Gras*, the 'Calypso King' is elected, a title that has been held by prominent calypsonians such as Lord Executor, Attila the Hun and Mighty Sparrow; the *J'Ouvert*, which takes place on Monday, is marked by the *mas* bands competitions; and on Tuesday, the Parade of the Bands occurs, and members of these groups continue 'wining' (or partying) well into the early hours of Ash Wednesday. In recent years, a modern dance-oriented calypso known as *soca* has come to dominate the street festivities. It is blasted out through sound systems on trucks, and threatens to displace the steel bands.

Elements of the Trinidadian carnival, especially the calypso, have been adopted by several neighboring islands, such as Grenada, Carriacou, Dominica and St. Lucia. Steel pans have become popular in Jamaica. In other parts of the Caribbean, distinct traditions mark the festivity. In Haiti, for example, carnival is celebrated to the sound of *rara* bands, in which ditties containing veiled critiques are accompanied by interlocking melodies produced on bamboo trumpets (*vaksin*).

In the United States, the most visible carnival celebrations are the Mardi Gras festivities of New Orleans. While the central areas of the city are dominated by lavish parades, in black neighborhoods associations or 'tribes' of Mardi Gras Indians take to the streets, donning headdresses and face paint, and singing and dancing to the accompaniment of a standard repertoire.

More recently, the carnivals of the Americas have begun to have a transnational impact. Diasporic Caribbean communities have become the primary agents in the dissemination of carnival, hosting major celebrations in London, New York, Toronto and Caracas. For these communities, carnival has become a symbol of ethnic identity, and it is used in their struggles against discrimination and oppression in the host society. Carnival associations that call themselves samba schools have become popular in Western Europe and Australia (particularly Sydney). These groups, however, are made up almost exclusively of local aficionados, who have adapted the Brazilian prototype to their own local experience.

Bibliography

Augras, Monique. 1998. *O Brasil do samba-enredo* [Brazil of the Theme-Samba]. Rio de Janeiro: Fundação Getulio Vargas.

Averill, Gage. 1997a. *A Day for the Hunter, A Day for the Prey: Popular Music and Power in Haiti*. Chicago: University of Chicago Press.

Averill, Gage. 1997b. 'Pan is we ting.' In *Musics of Multicultural America: A Study of Twelve Musical Communities*, ed. Kip Lornell and Anne K. Rasmussen. New York: Schirmer Books, 101–29.

Bakhtin, Mikhail. 1984. *Rabelais and His World*, trans. Hélène Iswolsky. Bloomington, IN: Indiana University Press. (Originally published as *Tvorchestvo Fransua Rable*. Moscow: Khudozhestvennia literatura, 1965.)

Cohen, Abner. 1993. *Masquerade Politics: Explorations in the Structure of Urban Cultural Movements*. Berkeley, CA: University of California Press.

Cowley, John. 1996. *Carnival, Canboulay and Calypso: Traditions in the Making*. Cambridge: Cambridge University Press.

Crook, Larry N. 1993. 'Black Consciousness, Samba Reggae, and the Re-Africanization of Bahian Carnival Music in Brazil.' *The World of Music* 35(2): 90–108.

DaMatta, Roberto A. 1991. *Carnivals, Rogues, and Heroes: An Interpretation of the Brazilian Dilemma*, trans. John Drury. Notre Dame, IN: University of Notre Dame Press. (Originally published as *Carnavais, malandros e heróis: para uma sociologia do dilema brasileiro*. Rio de Janeiro: Editora Guanabara, 1979.)

Eco, Umberto. 1984. 'Frames of Comic Freedom.' In *Carnival!*, ed. Thomas A. Sebeok. Berlin and New York: Mouton, 1–10.

Kertzer, David I. 1988. 'The Politics of Carnival.' In *Ritual, Politics, and Power*. New Haven, CT: Yale University Press, 145–50.

Lipsitz, George. 1990. 'Mardi Gras Indians: Carnival and Counter-Narrative in Black New Orleans.' In *Time Passages: Collective Memory and American Popular Culture*. Minneapolis, MN: University of Minnesota Press, 233–53.

Manuel, Peter. 1995. *Caribbean Currents: Caribbean Music from Rumba to Reggae*. Philadelphia: Temple University Press.

Mintz, Jerome R. 1997. *Carnival Song and Society: Gossip, Sexuality and Creativity in Andalusia*. Oxford: Berg.

Scott, James C. 1990. *Domination and the Arts of Resistance: Hidden Transcripts*. New Haven and London: Yale University Press.

Turner, Victor W. 1969. *The Ritual Process: Structure and Anti-Structure*. Chicago: Aldine Publishing Company.

Discography

Panorama: Steelbands of Trinidad & Tobago. Delos 4015. *1994*: USA.

Sambas de Enredo '99. BMG International 640842. *1999*: USA.

MARTHA TUPINAMBÁ DE ULHÔA and SUZEL ANA REILY

Censorship

Censorship of popular music is as old as popular music itself. Censorship may be thought of as 'an attempt to interfere, either pre- or post-publication, with the artistic expression of popular music artists with a view to stifling, or significantly altering, that expression' (Cloonan 1995b, 75).

Practically all genres of popular music have encountered attempts to stifle its message at some point or other. To cite examples from the West, there were: moral condemnations of jazz in the 1930s; complaints against the swooning of Frank Sinatra in the 1940s; attacks on rock 'n' roll in the 1950s; protests against the prevalence of drug-related lyrics in the 1960s; moves against punk in the 1970s; attempts to silence rap and heavy metal in Reagan's America; clampdowns on raves under Thatcher in Britain; and attempts to stifle the dissident sounds of the rap band Supreme NTM in France in the 1990s.

To these could be added many more examples drawn from authoritarian regimes in the East. These have included restrictions of foreign music by many countries in Eastern Europe under Communist rule and strict control of domestic music (Ramet 1994). There have also been attempts to control music under fascist regimes in Germany (Dümling 1995) and Argentina (Vila 1992) and under the apartheid regime in South Africa (Denselow 1989). Islamic countries have banned non-Islamic music and, on occasion, all forms of music. One of the most horrific parts of the carnage in Algeria in the 1990s was the deliberate targeting of musicians by death squads purporting to uphold Islam.

The latter example is the most extreme, but graphically illustrates one of the most important aspects of the censorship of popular music: music has been held by its opponents to have power. Censorship of popular music, whether formal or informal, takes place under *all* political regimes. It also occurs throughout the creative process and throughout the distribution of music. The real problem is to distinguish between acts of censorship and the reasons for that censorship.

Censoring the Artistic Process

Censorship can occur throughout the artistic process. Under capitalist relations of production where the whims of the market take precedence, there is a sense in which censorship takes place even before an act is signed to a record label. Decisions about which acts labels sign certainly have censorial implications: a failure to be signed effectively censors many musicians by limiting their potential audience to the point where earning a livelihood as a musician becomes extremely difficult.

Once signed, acts may be 'advised' to alter work in order to reach a wider audience. While Negus (1992) has shown that decisions within record companies are the consequence of negotiations among key players, such negotiations can result in the alteration of musical

expression. This is not direct censorship, but certainly has implications for free musical expression. There have been numerous examples of record companies refusing to release artists' material, generally on grounds of lack of commercial viability, but sometimes as a result of more overt censorship. Warner Brothers' decision to take the track 'Cop Killer' off the first Body Count album in 1992 is perhaps the most patent example of the latter. There have also been disputes between label and artist over choice of covers, resulting in censorship. The original cover of the Rolling Stones' *Beggars Banquet* album is one famous example of this: the band's label, Decca, vetoed a plan to feature a toilet wall on it. In more recent years, decisions over what videos to release to accompany singles have also led to censorship disputes. This problem has often been circumnavigated by a decision to record one video for all audiences and one for adults only.

Under the former Communist regimes of Eastern Europe, censorship was often more direct. Recording facilities were limited and often allocated on a roster basis. Moreover, even if a band was given official permission to release a record (generally on the one, state-owned record label in the country), only a certain number of records would be produced, regardless of the demand. Thus, the potential impact of the music was severely restricted. Nevertheless, the fact that there was no reliance on sales meant that performers in the East were often freer to experiment with their music than their peers in the West (Wicke and Shepherd 1993). However, state-organized censorship of popular music was much more prevalent in the East than in the West.

In the West, the next stage in the censorship process occurs in the marketplace itself. It takes the form of retailers who can refuse to stock records for fear of offending customers. Stores that cater to a 'family' clientele often refuse to stock records from artists on the extreme edges of popular music, including performers of rap and heavy metal. This process has been exacerbated in some instances by campaigns from moralist pressure groups, which have organized consumer boycotts of stores whose selling policies they disapprove of.

Once in the market, records can also face the ultimate form of censorship: the law. While most states claim to allow freedom of speech (at least in the West), all have restrictions on that freedom. Popular music has often tested the limits of freedom of speech. There have been attempts to censor musical expression by law in places as far apart as the former Czechoslovakia, the United Kingdom and New Zealand. Examples of this include the banning of 'Cop Killer' in Ireland prior to Warners' withdrawal of it and the successful prosecution of the anarchist band Crass under British obscenity law in 1984–85.

Most states have laws regarding what is considered to be obscene and other laws that forbid the expression of certain political beliefs. This has most obviously been the case under authoritarian regimes, but has also taken place in the West. For example, the German Federal Republic's restriction on expression of Nazi sentiment caused problems for Kiss in the 1970s (although the Nazi rock scene apparently flourishes in the newly united Germany). In France in the 1990s, the rap band Supreme NTM had difficulties with its track 'Police,' which advocated pissing 'on the brainless police machine.' The band narrowly escaped being sent to jail.

In some states, the constitution can affect the way in which the censorship debate is conducted. In the United States in the 1980s, there was much debate centering on rap and its allegedly offensive nature – especially concerning sexist portrayals of women and the glamorization of violence (often against authority figures such as the police). Matters were complicated, however, by the First Amendment to the US Constitution, which guarantees freedom of speech. This resulted in a number of decisions made by courts in individual states being overturned at the federal level. However, artists such as 2 Live Crew, NWA and Ice-T did suffer censorship. The fact that many of the artists who were censored were black was noted by various commentators and taken to demonstrate that, in these instances, censorship had racist undercurrents.

Rap was also brought to court for a reason that was effectively censorship, but that had its origins in artistic rights. This involved sampling, in which parts of one recording were used in another, often without the permission of the original artists. An added complication was the fact that copyright either does not exist or is not enforced in a number of countries. Rap pioneered the use of sampling, although the practise spread throughout popular music. In various countries, there were a number of court cases involving the use of samples without permission, although many were settled out of court. However, some artists objected to any of their music being used for sampling and refused to allow it. Whether this was censorship of one artist by another remained a moot point, but sampling retains a place in the history of censorship and popular music.

The next stage in the censorship of popular music occurs in the live arena. A live performance is generally governed by a set of regulations about who can be admitted (at venues with alcohol licenses, for example), when the event will take place, what time it must finish and so on. Here, the dividing line between regulation and censorship is frequently blurred. Certainly, there is a long history of safety regulations effectively being used as a form of disguised censorship. For example, in early twentieth-century Britain, a set of fire regulations was imposed on the music halls as a means to curb excesses on the stage. Chevigny (1991) has also shown how, in the United States, regulations can be used to censor a form of popular music – in this case, jazz in live performance.

There has also been a history of more overt censorship of live music, often involving bans by local authorities of performances by certain acts at venues within their jurisdiction. Perhaps the most famous example of this occurred in Britain in 1976–77, when a number of punk gigs, especially those featuring the Sex Pistols, were banned by local authorities. Here, the demarcation between regulation and overt censorship was particularly murky. Gigs were often cancelled because of fears of misbehavior by fans, but the net result was the same: censorship of a genre of popular music in live performance.

Under authoritarian regimes, the censorship of music performance has been much more frequent and routine. In the Communist countries of Eastern Europe, this involved licensing systems that allowed only those performers with state licenses to perform; all other performers were banned. Such systems could be supplemented by laws that restricted the number of people who could gather in one place, thus denying performers an audience. An example of this was the way in which the Plastic People of the Universe were harassed by the authorities in Czechoslovakia in the 1970s, arrested while performing at private parties and eventually jailed.

As well as the censorship of live music in various types of indoor venue, there are instances of censorship of popular music when it has tried to go outdoors. There is a long history of censorship of festivals (Clarke 1982; Cloonan 1996), especially those that have tried to use music to make a political point. The battle to establish the right of popular music to leave the concert hall and go into the country was hard fought. In recent years, raves have encountered the most problems in this regard. In Britain, this resulted in new legislation aimed specifically at raves: the *Entertainments (Increased Penalties) Act* of 1990 and parts of the 1994 *Criminal Justice Act* (McKay 1996). Once more, the dividing line between regulation and censorship was unclear, but again popular music was restricted.

In its recorded form, popular music relies on other media to spread its message. Indeed, the development of popular music is inseparable from that of broadcasting, especially radio. In radio, perhaps the most important distinction to emerge has been that between state-owned and commercial stations. Certainly, political decisions about the correct balance between the two could have a profound effect on the type of popular music produced within a country. But censorship has been used by both state and commercial networks. Thus Britain, which had a totally state-owned broadcasting system until 1973, saw many instances of censorship of pop records (Cloonan 1996), but so did the totally commercially owned system of the United States (Martin and Segrave 1988). Those states that allowed commercial ownership of radio stations still imposed regulations on the type of material they could broadcast, thus limiting the exposure more extreme forms of popular music received on the airwaves. However, it appears that stations without commercial restraints had more freedom to experiment with popular music than those tied to audience ratings that could be sold to advertisers.

In television, a similar division between public and commercial stations existed. Television generally struggled to come to terms with popular music. Thus, Elvis Presley was shown only from the waist up on his first appearance on *The Ed Sullivan Show* in the 1950s. Popular music was more often ignored and/or marginalized by television. By the 1990s, video had moved television coverage of popular music on, but instances such as the video accompanying Madonna's *Justify My Love* in 1990, featuring cross-dressing and lesbianism, stretched the medium to its limits. The rise of satellite television (especially MTV) has seen the proportion of popular music on television increase and has posed problems for states in terms of controlling their own airwaves, but censorship of terrestrial television seems set to continue and popular music will continue to be a target.

Motivations for Censorship

It is noteworthy that the censorship of popular music has often been undertaken for reasons other than objections to the music. Censorship of recorded music has centered more on lyrics than on music, although genres such as punk and rap have had problems getting airplay. Political lyrics have been banned by both record companies and political regimes alike. Similarly, popular music has been attacked and censored for allegedly promoting sexual freedom and/or the use of recreational drugs. Live music performances have often been censored because of concerns about the behavior of fans.

A number of motivations for the censorship of popular music have been apparent. The image of a ruthless business exploiting hapless youth has been one frequently posited by would-be censors, and the desire to protect youth and young children has been a frequent reason given for censorship. Often, this has been combined with a desire to restrict sexually explicit material, itself a major motivation for censorship. This was evidenced by the widespread bans on Jane Birkin's and Serge Gainsbourg's 'Je T'Aime' in the 1960s. The desire to stifle political dissent has also been prevalent, especially under authoritarian regimes, which have silenced musical as well as other criticisms.

Although governments are the major forces in censorship, they are often complemented by moralist campaigners, such as the Parents Music Resource Center (PMRC), formed in the United States in 1985. Its inspiration came from a founder who objected to her eight-year-old daughter listening to Prince's 'Darling Nikki,' which features female masturbation – another example of how the desire to protect children can lead to censorship. The PMRC led a successful campaign to get US record companies to place warning labels on records and CDs that contain explicit material. This subtle form of censorship has continued, although some commentators believe that the net effect of labeling is to attract a younger audience through the appeal of 'forbidden fruit.'

The PMRC has links to fundamentalist Christian churches, and another major potential censor of popular music has been organized religion (Cloonan 1996; Martin and Segrave 1988). A number of churches have called for restrictions on popular music and for their congregations to boycott it. This has been most prevalent in the United States, where portrayals of rock as 'the devil's music' and campaigns against it have often had racist undercurrents. In the 1990s, perhaps the most burning issue concerned the relationship of music to Islam. Certainly to Western eyes, the rise of Islam engendered restrictions on freedom of expression that many commentators found pernicious.

At the close of the twentieth century, the battle for control of popular culture, and especially popular music, was growing apace. It has often been suggested that nation-states are losing the censorship battle, as modern technology has made international borders meaningless. The Internet has frequently been cited as an example of this. But this is to ignore the role that the market and record companies have played in censorship and the pressure that can be applied by non-governmental agencies such as pressure groups and religious leaders. Moreover, control of live popular music has remained firmly within the grasp of the state, and the battle for the airwaves is far from over. Under such circumstances, the nature of the censorship of popular music may change, but it is unlikely to disappear.

Bibliography

Baily, John. 2001. *'Can You Stop the Birds Singing?': The Censorship of Music in Afghanistan.* Copenhagen: Freemuse.

Chevigny, Paul. 1991. *Gigs: Jazz and the Cabaret Laws in New York City*. New York: Routledge.

Clarke, Michael. 1982. *The Politics of Pop Festivals*. London: Junction Books.

Cloonan, Martin. 1992. 'Censorship and Popular Music: An Initial Attempt at Identification.' IASPM Occasional Paper No. 1, University of Liverpool.

Cloonan, Martin. 1995a. '"I Fought the Law": Popular Music and British Obscenity Law.' *Popular Music* 14(3) (October): 349–63.

Cloonan, Martin. 1995b. 'Popular Music and Censorship in Britain: An Overview.' *Popular Music and Society* 19(3) (Fall): 75–104.

Cloonan, Martin. 1996. *Banned!: Censorship of Popular Music in Britain, 1967–92*. Aldershot: Arena.

Denselow, Robin. 1989. *When the Music's Over: The Story of Political Pop*. London: Faber & Faber.

Dümling, Albrecht. 1995. *Entartete Musik* [Degenerate Music]. Berlin: City of Berlin.

Goodwin, Andrew. 1990. 'Sharpening the Blue Pencil.' *New Statesman* (8 May): 27–28.

Halassa, Malu. 1990. 'Banned in the USA.' *New Statesman* (10 August): 27–28.

Hill, Trent. 1992. 'The Enemy Within: Censorship in Rock Music in the 1950s.' In *Present Tense: Rock & Roll and Culture*, ed. Anthony DeCurtis. Durham, NC: Duke University Press, 39–71.

Holden, David. 1993. 'Pop Go the Censors.' *Index on Censorship* 22(5/6) (May/June): 11–15.

Martin, Linda, and Segrave, Kerry. 1988. *Anti-Rock*. Hamden, CT: Archon Books.

McDonald, James. 1988. 'Censoring Rock Lyrics: A Historical Analysis of the Debate.' *Youth and Society* 19(3) (March): 294–313.

McKay, George. 1996. *Acts of Senseless Beauty*. London: Verso.

Negus, Keith. 1992. *Producing Pop: Culture and Conflict in the Popular Music Industry*. London: Edward Arnold.

Peterson, Richard A. 1972. 'Market and Moralist Censors of a Black Art Form: Jazz.' In *The Sounds of Social Change: Studies in Popular Culture*, ed. R. Serge Denisoff and Richard A. Peterson. Chicago: Rand McNally, 236–47.

Ramet, Sabrina Petra, ed. 1994. *Rocking the State: Rock Music and Politics in Eastern Europe and Russia*. Boulder, CO: Westview Press.

Sluka, Jeffrey. 1994. 'Censorship and the Politics of Rock.' *Sites* 29 (Spring): 45–70.

Vila, Pablo. 1992. '*Rock Nacional* and Dictatorship in Argentina.' In *Rockin' the Boat: Mass Music and Mass Movements*, ed. Reebee Garofalo. Boston, MA: South End Press, 209–29.

Wicke, Peter, and Shepherd, John. 1993. '"The Cabaret Is Dead": Rock Culture as State Enterprise – The Political Organizations of Rock in East Germany.' In *Rock and Popular Music: Politics, Policies, Institutions*, ed. Tony Bennett et al. London: Routledge, 26–36.

Discographical References

Birkin, Jane, and Gainsbourg, Serge. 'Je T'Aime . . . Moi Non Plus.' Fontana TF 1042. *1969*: UK.

Body Count. 'Cop Killer.' *Body Count*. Warner Brothers 45139. *1992*: USA.

Madonna. *Justify My Love*. Warner Brothers 21820. *1990*: USA.

Prince. 'Darling Nikki.' *Purple Rain*. Warner Brothers 25110. *1984*: USA.

Rolling Stones, The. *Beggars Banquet*. London 539. *1968*: USA.

Supreme NTM. 'Police.' *J'appuie sur la gâchette*. Sony International 473630 2. *1993*: France.

Visual Recording

Madonna. 1990. 'Justify My Love.' Warner Brothers WAR38224 (video).

MARTIN CLOONAN

Charity Events

From activist African-American jazz musicians in the 1920s lending their talents to everything from anti-lynching campaigns to rent parties, to San Francisco rock bands providing free concerts in the city's parks in the 1960s, the connection between popular music and 'good causes' or simply the creation of a sense of community has long been a part of the popular music landscape. The use of popular music to address topical issues on a grand scale has a more recent history.

The events dubbed 'charity rock' in 1985 took place as the music business, jolted by a worldwide recession, was reinventing itself as an international industry, and as advances in satellite transmission facilitated global broadcasts. With Woodstock as its spiritual touchstone, and capitalism as its enabling force, charity rock allowed the music industry to put on a humanitarian face, even as it exploited a gold mine of untapped markets. It also provided activist musicians with a global platform, and they pushed the humanitarian impulse toward more overt political expression.

Charity rock clearly has historical antecedents in such events as George Harrison's Concert for Bangla Desh in 1971 and the No Nukes concert series of 1979. Still, the story of charity rock as a named phenomenon began with Bob Geldof. Inspired by a BBC documentary on Ethiopian famine, he co-wrote (with Midge Ure) 'Do They Know It's Christmas?' and organized the British pop elite into an ensemble, Band Aid, to record the song, with proceeds donated to famine relief.

Geldof went on to organize Live Aid – the largest single event in human history. Staged simultaneously at Wembley Stadium in London and JFK Stadium in Philadelphia on 13 July 1985, the marathon event featured more than 60 acts, was 'attended' by 1.6 billion people in 160 countries and raised US$67 million.

In the United States, charity rock began with the release of 'We Are the World,' co-written by Michael Jackson and Lionel Richie, produced by Quincy Jones and recorded by the biggest names in US popular music under the name USA for Africa. It provided the finale for Live Aid, even though neither Jackson nor Richie participated.

Celebrated for combining popular art and humane politics, Live Aid was also criticized for its paucity of artists of color and its trivialization of pressing issues. Still, it created an international focus on hunger in Africa, and it opened the door for bolder events.

Just as Live Aid begat Farm Aid, a project spearheaded by Willie Nelson, which became an annual event in the United States, 'We Are the World' served as the model for 'Sun City,' a politically charged anti-apartheid anthem organized by Little Steven (Van Zandt) that included cameo performances by more than 50 rock, rap, rhythm and blues, jazz and salsa artists. 'Sun City' broke new political ground by filling its record jacket with facts and figures about apartheid and by issuing a 'Teacher's Guide' for classroom use.

In 1986, U2 headlined the Conspiracy of Hope tour for Amnesty International/USA. Amnesty took the concept around the world with the 1988 Human Rights Now! tour, featuring Bruce Springsteen, Sting, Peter Gabriel, Tracy Chapman, Youssou N'Dour and others. The organization expanded to 420,000 members worldwide, with an average age of 20.

Two other international concerts were staged at Wembley Stadium, this time on behalf of Nelson Mandela: the Nelson Mandela Seventieth Birthday Tribute (1988), broadcast to 600 million people in more than 60 countries; and the International Tribute for a Free South Africa (1990), which provided the recently freed Mandela with a global platform for his first major address outside South Africa.

Charity rock encouraged a politicized popular culture. By the end of the 1980s, there was scarcely a social issue that was not visibly associated with popular music and musicians: John Cougar Mellencamp's 'Rain on the Scarecrow,' about the despair of rural life; Jackson Browne's *Lives in the Balance*, a moving criticism of US intervention in Central America; Sting's 'They Dance Alone,' about the widows of the 'disappeared' in Argentina; Suzanne Vega's 'Luka,' about child abuse; MTV's Rock the Vote; environmental collaborations between Greenpeace and VH-1; the anti-violence rap anthem 'Self-Destruction'; the Cole Porter tribute AIDS benefit, Red Hot and Blue. Throughout, charity rock's humanitarian impulse existed in tension with baser corporate imperatives and unabashed celebrations of technology. Its progressive edge was further blunted by conservative attacks on popular music in the early 1990s.

Bibliography

Breskin, David. 1985. 'Bob Geldof: The Rolling Stone Interview.' *Rolling Stone* (5 December): 26–34, 60–67.
Carothers, Andre. 1989. 'Can Rock 'n' Roll Save the World?' *Greenpeace* 14(6) (November/December): 6–11.
Denselow, Robin. 1989. *When the Music's Over: The Story of Political Pop*. London: Faber.
Garofalo, Reebee, ed. 1992. *Rockin' the Boat: Mass Music and Mass Movements*. Boston, MA: South End Press.
Street, John. 1990. 'If You Care About Our World, You'll Buy This Album: Green Politics and Rock Music.' *OneTwoThreeFour: A Rock 'n' Roll Quarterly* 8 (Winter): 23–36.
Ullestad, Neil. 1987. 'Rock and Rebellion: Subversive Effects of Live Aid and "Sun City."' *Popular Music* 6(1): 67–76.
Vincent, Ted. 1995. *Keep Cool: The Black Activists Who Built the Jazz Age*. Boulder, CO: Pluto Press.

Discographical References

Artists United Against Apartheid. 'Sun City.' Manhattan 50017. *1985*: USA.
Band Aid. 'Do They Know It's Christmas?' Mercury FEED 1. *1984*: UK.
Browne, Jackson. *Lives in the Balance*. Asylum EKT 31. *1986*: USA.
Mellencamp, John Cougar. 'Rain on the Scarecrow.' Riva 884635. *1986*: USA.
Sting. 'They Dance Alone.' *Nothing Like the Sun*. A&M AMA 6402. *1987*: UK.
USA for Africa. 'We Are the World.' Columbia 04839. *1985*: USA.
Vega, Suzanne. 'Luka.' A&M 2937. *1987*: USA.

REEBEE GAROFALO

Children

For many children in the developed world, popular music, disseminated through electronic sources, including television, radio, film, video, CD, audio cassette and, more recently, CD-ROM, is an integral part of their auditory and visual environment. Popular music is piped into sound systems at supermarkets, suburban shopping malls, skating rinks and even toy stores and is played for recreational purposes in children's homes by their parents and older siblings. It can be heard as a background to a variety of activities in the home, in neighborhoods and in child-care centers.

As a result, children's repertoire of known and preferred music often includes both current popular styles and popular music from previous generations. Children may improvise raps in the playground or classroom or may express a preference for country music or popular classics that were recorded 20 or 30 years earlier but that have continued to receive regular radio play (Campbell 1998; Crafts et al. 1993; Harwood 1987). Children are consumers of popular music de facto and, as their age increases, by choice.

The recognition of children as representing a large and lucrative market has resulted in the creation of popular music in forms designed especially for children. Titles such as *Reggae for Kids* (United States) or *ABC for Kids Dance Party* (an Australian recording subtitled 'Get Down and Boogie') abound. Popular songs are commissioned for children's movies, a prominent example being Elton John's music for *The Lion King* (1994), distributed internationally by Disney. The merchandising of videos and tapes associated with the movie ensures that the music remains in circulation within children's domain. Campbell (1998) reports the frequent appearance of songs from this movie in young children's accounts of song preferences and in their spontaneous performances, which may emulate the performance characteristics (for example, vocal slides) found in the recorded soundtrack.

Similarly, the utilization of 'classic' popular songs in the soundtracks of children's movies leads to a revitalization of such songs, with attendant new meanings as part of children's culture in a new generation. One example of this is the 1970s song by Queen, 'We Are the Champions,' which was used as the theme song in the 1990s movie *The Mighty Ducks*. In turn, the popularity of such newly contextualized songs and their removal from the perceived pernicious influences of the original performance contexts can result in their reclassification by adult gatekeepers of children's commodities as appropriate for children's edification. 'We Are the Champions' is now found in anthologies of children's songs published for the school education market.

Many performers of music aimed at an early childhood audience have adopted performance styles characteristic of various genres of popular music. Specialist early childhood performers such as the Australian group the Wiggles, Raffi from Canada and the group Bouskidou from France have popular music performance backgrounds and have maintained this style in their rendition of newly composed and traditional songs for children. Similarly, many popular music performers have recorded material especially for the child market. The eclecticism of such music can be illustrated by the diversity of performers involved. Recordings of music for children have been produced, for example, by Bobby McFerrin, Sweet Honey in the Rock, Taj Mahal, Maria Muldaur, Little Richard, Manhattan Transfer, the Re-Bops and Buckwheat Zydeco in the United States, the folk artist Steve Waring in France and the Ghanaian highlife band Marriot International Band.

Popular music celebrities are also frequently featured on the *Sesame Street* program, which is broadcast internationally. As a consequence, children are presented, from the early years of childhood, with a wide range of popular music models to emulate – a fact that is not lost on the marketers of children's toys. Child-size versions of musical artifacts associated with the popular music industry, including guitars, keyboards, drumkits and even mini–recording studios, are found in toy stores in many places (Campbell 1998). More recently, record companies have entered the CD-ROM market, and have superimposed recordings of popular music on video and computer game soundtracks.

The misconception that mass-mediated popular music represents a negative influence on children's own culture has frequently permeated educational thought. It is evident, however, that the intrusion of popular music into the environment of children results in enrichment rather than destruction of children's performative traditions. Children engage in 'a dialectic with the mass media and appropriate for their own uses its material and forms' (Mechling 1986, cited in Harwood 1994, 191). The result is the creative use by children of textual, musical and movement material derived from popular music, as well as its reproduction in more standard forms.

Children's exposure to popular music is often manipulated by adults in public spaces, but it also becomes a means by which children control their own repertoire and performance practises in the more private spaces occupied by play, inter-child interaction and solitary or joint listening within friendship groups. Thus, while children's interest in particular popular performers is promulgated by adult-produced television programs, MTV video shows and fanzines aimed at teenagers and preteens, children reappropriate aspects of these performers' styles into their musical play for their own purposes. For example, in the clapping game 'Michael Jackson,' recorded in an Australian playground in 1990, the sexually explicit movements of two prominent US performers are simultaneously invoked and ridiculed:

My name is Michael Jackson, girlfriend Madonna
Kissing in the garden (kiss) (kiss) (ugh) (ugh) [*Kissing and pelvic thrusts*]
Out comes the baby, out comes the boy
All the girls 'Boo hoo' sexy! [*Lift up dresses on 'sexy'*]

The interplay between parody and emulation of adult personae in the children's performance of this game seems to illustrate the 'complex interpolation of fear, fantasy, desire, and mutuality' with which cultural groups may deal with culture contact (Roseman 1995, 17). Roseman (citing Lipsitz 1994) characterizes this as the 'capture of the colonizer,' which is 'accomplished through . . . transformative musical structures embodied and "envoiced" by performance participants' (14). In this case, the 'colonizer' is the adult popular performer, particularly as portrayed in the media.

Children may appropriate particular characteristics of popular icons as a form of empowerment within a play context. In the United Kingdom, Grugeon (1998) has observed instances of the Spice Girls' message of 'girl power' being interpreted not only through direct playground imitation of their performances, but also through the development of exuberant and almost aggressive new games by girls in the playground.

The appropriation of musical and textual material from popular music sources is not a new phenomenon. In fact, cycles of appropriation and reappropriation have developed between children's folkloric play and mediated popular music. For example, the clapping game 'See See My Playmate' originated from the 1940s popular song 'Playmates' by Saxie Dowell (Opie and Opie 1988). Children have passed on this game orally over a period of more than 50 years, with the text changed by mechanisms of rationalization, localization and parody. Variants have been found in locations as diverse as The Netherlands, Morocco, Surinam (Doekes 1993), Australia (Marsh 1997), the United Kingdom and the United States (Riddell 1990).

The text of the song 'Playmates,' focusing on the topic of play, may have led to the continuity of its adaptation to a play context. In a similar way, the coincidence of nonsense vocables in the texts of some popular songs and children's playground songs may contribute to cycles of appropriation between these genres of performance. In the case of the clapping game 'Down Down Baby,' it is not entirely clear whether African-American children initially appropriated part of the text from a popular song, 'Shimmy, Shimmy, Ko-Ko-Bop' (Riddell 1990), or whether the text of this song was derived from the game. Multiple versions of the game proliferated in playgrounds across the United States. One version was repeatedly broadcast globally on *Sesame Street*, and this version is constantly reappropriated by children in different parts of the world to create their own new versions of the game. Localized variants of the game have been reported in Australia, France, The Netherlands and Ghana (Marsh 1997).

On a more general level, musical and movement characteristics of popular music have been adopted as part of the formulaic vocabulary of children's play genres. Children's play chants, for example, are now frequently syncopated, partly as a result of exposure to the syncopated styles of delivery in many popular music forms. Videos, CDs and cassette recordings allow repetitive, self-regulated learning of popular songs by children, in the same way as oral–aural transmission operates in play contexts. The visual aspect of videoclips also contributes to the equal valuing of the musical and the kinesthetic aspects of popular performance and their emulation by children (Campbell 1998; Crafts et al. 1993; Harwood 1987). It can be seen, then, that although popular music clearly has an impact on the lives of many children, its influence is not entirely hegemonic but is accommodated by children in a variety of ways.

Bibliography

Campbell, Patricia Shehan. 1998. *Songs in Their Heads: Music and Its Meaning in Children's Lives*. New York: Oxford University Press.

Crafts, Susan D., Cavicchi, Daniel, and Keil, Charles. 1993. *My Music*. Hanover, NH: Wesleyan University Press.

Doekes, Els. 1993. 'Muziek en beweging in de kinderstraatcultuur' [Music and Movement in Children's Street Culture]. *De Pyramide* 47(1): 11–12.

Grugeon, Elizabeth. 1998. 'Girls on the Playground in the 1990s.' Paper presented at The State of Play: Perspectives on Children's Oral Culture Conference, The National Centre for English Cultural Tradition, University of Sheffield, April.

Harwood, Eve E. 1987. *The Memorized Song Repertoire of Children in Grades 4 and 5 in Champaign, Illinois*. Unpublished Ph.D. thesis, University of Illinois.

Harwood, Eve E. 1994. 'Miss Lucy Meets Dr. Pepper: Mass Media and Children's Traditional Playground Song and Chant.' In *Musical Connections: Tradition and Change. Proceedings of the 21st World Conference of the International Society for Music Education*, ed. Heath Lees. Auckland: International Society for Music Education, 187–93.

Lipsitz, George. 1994. *Dangerous Crossroads: Popular Music, Postmodernism and the Poetics of Place*. London: Verso.

Marsh, Kathryn. 1997. *Variation and Transmission Processes in Children's Singing Games in an Australian Playground*. Unpublished Ph.D. thesis, University of Sydney.

Mechling, J. 1986. 'Children's Folklore.' In *Folk Groups and Folklore Genres: An Introduction*, ed. E. Oring. Logan, UT: Utah State University Press.

Opie, Iona, and Opie, Peter. 1988. *The Singing Game*. Oxford: Oxford University Press.

Riddell, Cecilia. 1990. *Traditional Singing Games of Elementary School Children in Los Angeles*. Unpublished Ph.D. thesis, University of California, Los Angeles.

Roseman, Marina. 1995. 'Decolonising Ethnomusicology: When Peripheral Voices Move in from the Margins.' Keynote address presented at the University of Melbourne Faculty of Music Centennial Conference, Melbourne, June.

Sheet Music

Dowell, Saxie, comp. and lyr. 1940. 'Playmates.' Los Angeles: Anne-Rachel Music.

Discographical References

Queen. 'We Are the Champions.' EMI 2708. *1977*: UK.

Reggae for Kids. Music for Little People RAS 3095. *1992*: USA.

Wiggles, The, and Trapaga, Monica, et al. *ABC for Kids Dance Party*. ABC Music/EMI 8145654. *1995*: Australia.

Discography

Bouskidou. *Du rock pour les mômes*. Arc en ciel 121978. *1991*: France.

Bouskidou. *Eh dis donc soleil*. Arc en ciel 122255. *1993*: France.

Buckwheat Zydeco. *Choo Choo Boogaloo*. Music for Little People/Warner Bros. 42556. *1994*: USA.

Kyser, Kay. 'Playmates.' *His Greatest Hits and Sentimental Favorites*. Good Music 113423. *1995*: USA.

Little Anthony and the Imperials. 'Shimmy, Shimmy, Ko-Ko-Bop.' End 1060. *1960*: USA.

Little Richard. *Shake It All About*. Walt Disney Records DIS0060849. *1992*: USA.

Manhattan Transfer. *Manhattan Transfer Meets Tubby the Tuba*. Summit DCD-152. *1994*: USA.

Marriot International Band. *Ozim, zim*. Cardinal Music Stores CD101. *1994*: UK.

McFerrin, Bobby, and Ma, Yo-Yo. *Hush*. Columbia SK-48177. *1991*: USA.

Raffi. *Bananaphone*. Shoreline 11115. *1994*: USA.

Raffi. *Everything Grows*. Shoreline MCA-10039. *1996*: USA.

Re-Bops, The. *Oldies for Kool Kiddies*. A&M 314-540109-4. *1993*: USA.

Spice Girls, The. *Spice*. Virgin 42174. *1996*: UK.

Spice Girls, The. 'Wannabe.' Virgin VSCDX 1588. *1996*: UK.

Sweet Honey in the Rock. *All for Freedom*. Music for Little People/Warner Bros. 42505. *1989*: USA.

Sweet Honey in the Rock, Taj Mahal, Muldaur, Maria, and Seeger, Pete. *Family Folk Festival*. Music for Little People/Warner Bros. 42506. *1994*: USA.

Waring, Steve, and Mason, Roger. *La Baleine Bleue*. Le Chant du Monde LDX 74530. *1973*: France.

Wiggles, The. *Big Red Car*. ABC Music/EMI 8145404. *1995*: Australia.

Wiggles, The. *The Wiggles*. ABC Records 510 082-4. *1991*: Australia.

Filmography

The Lion King, dir. Roger Allers and Rob Minkoff. 1994. USA. 87 mins. Animated Children's Musical. Original music by Elton John, Hans Zimmer.

The Mighty Ducks, dir. Stephen Herek. 1992. USA. 114 mins. Children's Comedy. Original music by David Newman.

The Wiggles Movie, dir. Leanne Halloran. 1998. Australia. 83 mins. Original music by the Wiggles, John Field.

KATHRYN MARSH

Class

The term 'class' (from the Latin *classis*, a division by property of the people of Rome), though basic in the social and human sciences, and common in everyday discourse, has an exceptionally complex history and an equally complex pattern of modern usages (see Williams 1988, 60–69). In the most general sense, it refers to the existence of particular social groupings, but within this, three distinct and often conflicting focuses can be identified: (a) class as rank, or relative social position (higher, lower, middling and so on); (b) class as social or economic category, assessed by observable qualities (such as wealth, life style or status); and (c) class as social formation, defined by economic relationship (for example, working class, capitalist class, bourgeoisie) and, often, by collective consciousness (Williams 1988, 69). The number of cognate and overlapping terms (status, estate, rank, caste), most of which originate in preindustrial societies but which to some extent have continued in use, muddies the analytical waters still further.

Musical practises always stand in a relationship to social groupings, and can therefore be subject to class analysis – obviously so in the case of popular music, since 'popular' is itself a 'classing' term (meaningless except in conjunction with what is defined as non-'popular'); in particular, the 'popular' in 'popular music' always carries some sense of social subordination. However, the question of which conception of social class is appropriate, not to mention the question of how to conceive the relationship between social class on the one hand and musical practise, form and message on the other, have never received universally agreed answers. Broadly speaking, the strongest tendencies have been to work either with models of social status – leading to emphasis on taste distinctions, taste publics and so on – or with models (usually Marxist) of socioeconomic formation – leading to emphasis on the contributions of music to processes of class conflict, class consciousness and ideological effects.

When folklorists in the nineteenth century developed a concept of 'folk music,' distinguishing it from newer vernacular genres, and when, then and subsequently, social historians noted such practises as music hall, brass bands and parlor ballads, issues to do with 'class' were already inescapable. But in the first half of the twentieth century, such formulations were often submerged by discourses of mass culture, which pictured the social structure differently (and whose influence has remained significant). Some work appeared that drew on a Marxist approach to class, however – for example, studies of jazz by Finkelstein (1948) and Newton (1959) – and the continuing strength of such approaches (Kofsky 1970; Maró-thy 1974) was consolidated with the emergence in the 1970s of 'popular music studies' as a distinct area of intellectual work marked by strong Marxist tendencies, particularly among those influenced by the contemporary school of British 'cultural studies.' The effects of this expansionary tendency were equally clear in work on the music industry (for example, Harker 1980; Chapple and Garofalo 1977), on consumption (especially notable in the writings of 'Birmingham School' subcultural theorists such as Dick Hebdige and Paul Willis), and on the music itself (for example, Laing 1969; Shepherd 1982; Wicke 1990). Clear also, however, was the difficulty of maintaining simple Marxist paradigms in this field – for instance, of directly aligning particular musical practises, contents or effects with distinct class interests and positions – and in response to this problem, scholars increasingly looked to more sophisticated Marxist thinkers: Raymond Williams, Louis Althusser, Antonio Gramsci. Gramsci's theory of hegemony was especially influential, for it seemed to offer a way to admit the possibility of 'alliance' and 'negotiation' between classes, and of a 'relatively autonomous' role for the music, while holding to the ultimate importance of class in 'articulating' the repertoire of cultural and ideological materials (see Middleton 1990). Since the 1980s, the collapse of interest among popular music scholars in the dimension of class has been as striking as its previous centrality. The impact of poststructuralist theories – privileging semiotic process rather than political economy in the construction of subjectivity – and of 'postmodernist' celebrations of consumerism, together with the more widely discernible turn from 'grand narratives' such as Marxism, have tended to refocus attention on the axes of gender and ethnicity, on geographical spaces ('scenes') rather than social ones, and on the dimensions of the local ('identity politics') and/or the global rather than the structuring formations that might lie in-between.

Perhaps most inviting for class analysis are cases of clearly bounded, often relatively isolated social groups, identifiably 'low' in positioning, with a distinct musical practise. Dominican *bacháta* (Pacini Hernandez 1995) or South African *marabi* (Coplan 1980) would seem to fit this paradigm – arguably African-American blues also (Keil 1966), at least until taken up by middle-class whites; and US country music, especially variants such as honky-tonk and Tex-Mex *conjunto* (Malone 1982, 1985; Peña 1985), until they too achieved wider dissemination. (However, it is worth noting Manuel's point (1988, 18–19) that very often the inventors and makers of such musics come from the lumpen proletariat rather than the working class.) Even here, though, interaction with other groups and with musics associated with them seems always to have been a factor (see Keil 1994); and in the extensive and fluid mediascapes, dominated by large organizations and featuring socially differentiated audiences, that characterized most popular music activity in the twentieth century, theories of class ownership of, and class expression through, a specific music seem simplistic. In relation to these contexts, ideas of homology between social and musical structures either have to be written on a very coarse scale or have to be modulated by theories of negotiation (Shepherd et al. 1977; Shepherd 1991). An alternative is to focus on practise rather than form (so that, for example, mass-media musical products can be seen as variably used and interpreted by different social classes). This is the approach found in the work of the Birmingham subcultural theorists and, with a very different slant, in the empirical sociology of musical behavior (Finnegan 1989), where 'class' is defined pragmatically and treated as merely one of many variables. Bourdieu, in an influential theory (1984), brings together empirical work on class-linked cultural behavior and perspectives drawn from the Marxist tradition, connecting 'economy' and 'culture' through a diagnosis of class-specific modes of appreciation, grounded in the differentiated distribution of 'cultural capital.' Thornton (1995) extends this into a theory of '*sub*cultural capital' – though here, with 'identity' constructed *in* media texts and subcultural discourse, music is seen as, if anything, functioning to obscure or even escape class.

It is the 'discursive constructionism' of so much 1980s and 1990s theory that might seem to offer the greatest threat to class-oriented analysis. Yet, if signifying practises are treated as themselves thoroughly material (Williams 1977), and hence always imbricated with the range of other material practises, there seems no reason why a 'constructionist' view of music's meanings and effects need rule out the reality, and relevance to analysis, of social class. During the same period, the rising global power of transnational music-industry (and other) capital, restructuring world society once more, and the rising interest among some scholars in mapping the implications of this for musicians and music-consumers, suggest that the importance of 'class' for popular music studies is by no means exhausted.

Bibliography

Bourdieu, Pierre. 1984 (1979). *Distinction: A Social Critique of the Judgement of Taste*. London: Routledge.

Chapple, Steve, and Garofalo, Reebee. 1977. *Rock 'n' Roll Is Here to Pay: The History and Politics of the Music Industry*. Chicago: Nelson-Hall.

Coplan, David. 1980. 'Marabi Culture: Continuity and Transformation in African Music in Johannesburg, 1920–1940.' *African Urban Studies* 6: 49–78.

Finkelstein, Sidney. 1948. *Jazz: A People's Music*. New York: Citadel.

Finnegan, Ruth. 1989. *The Hidden Musicians: Music-Making in an English Town*. Cambridge: Cambridge University Press.

Hall, Stuart, and Jefferson, Tony, eds. 1976. *Resistance Through Rituals: Youth Subcultures in Post-War Britain*. London: Hutchinson.

Harker, Dave. 1980. *One for the Money: Politics and Popular Song*. London: Hutchinson.

Hebdige, Dick. 1979. *Subculture: The Meaning of Style*. London: Methuen.

Keil, Charles. 1966. *Urban Blues*. Chicago: University of Chicago Press.

Keil, Charles. 1994. 'People's Music Comparatively: Style and Stereotype, Class and Hegemony.' In Charles Keil and Steven Feld, *Music Grooves: Essays and Dialogues*. Chicago and London: University of Chicago Press, 197–217. (First published in *Dialectical Anthropology* 10 (1985): 119–30.)

Kofsky, Frank. 1970. *Black Nationalism and the Revolution in Music*. New York: Pathfinder.

Laing, Dave. 1969. *The Sound of Our Time*. London: Sheed and Ward.

Malone, Bill C. 1982. 'Honky-Tonk: The Music of the Southern Working Class.' In *Folk Music and Modern Sound*, ed. William R. Ferris and Mary L. Hart. Jackson, MS: University of Mississippi Press, 119–28.

Malone, Bill C. 1985 (1968). *Country Music U.S.A.* Rev. ed. Austin, TX: University of Texas Press.

Manuel, Peter. 1988. *Popular Musics of the Non-Western World: An Introductory Survey*. New York: Oxford University Press.

Maróthy, János. 1974. *Music and the Bourgeois, Music and the Proletarian*. Budapest: Akademiai Kiado.

Middleton, Richard. 1990. *Studying Popular Music*. Milton Keynes and Philadelphia: Open University Press.

Newton, Francis. 1959. *The Jazz Scene*. London: McGibbon and Kee.

Pacini Hernandez, Deborah. 1995. *Bacháta: A Social History of a Dominican Popular Music*. Philadelphia: Temple University Press.

Peña, Manuel. 1985. *The Texas-Mexican Conjunto: History of a Working-Class Music*. Austin, TX: University of Texas Press.

Shepherd, John. 1982. 'A Theoretical Model for the Sociomusicological Analysis of Popular Musics.' *Popular Music* 2: 145–77.

Shepherd, John. 1991. *Music as Social Text*. Cambridge: Polity Press.

Shepherd, John, et al. 1977. *Whose Music?: A Sociology of Musical Languages*. London: Latimer.

Thornton, Sarah. 1995. *Club Cultures: Music, Media and Subcultural Capital*. Cambridge: Polity Press.

Wicke, Peter. 1990. *Rock Music: Culture, Aesthetics and Sociology*. Cambridge: Cambridge University Press.

Williams, Raymond. 1977. *Marxism and Literature*. Oxford: Oxford University Press.

Williams, Raymond. 1988 (1976). *Keywords: A Vocabulary of Culture and Society*. Rev. ed. London: Fontana.

Willis, Paul. 1978. *Profane Culture*. London: Routledge.

RICHARD MIDDLETON

Club Culture

The debate concerning the origins and definitions of club culture can be summarized in two competing perspectives, one British, the other North American. From a British perspective, it has been argued that disc jockey (DJ) culture had its origins in the mod subculture of London and Manchester and/or in the northern soul scene, both in the early to mid-1960s (Brewster and Broughton 1999). From a North American perspective, club culture emerged in the context of the US-specific sociopolitical changes of the late 1960s, and had its roots in New York City, the location that, in the early 1970s, spawned the first generation of professional club DJs who spearheaded what is now referred to as the disco era.

Whereas the music in the early British and North American scenarios consisted of US R&B and soul records, the term 'club culture' at the turn of the millennium denotes a phenomenon of global character, referring to the sum total of various art worlds in which a program of mediated music is shaped through the interaction between one or several DJs and a dancing audience. Club culture has spread internationally to encompass more or less any location where urbanism, communications technologies, African-American dance styles and the economic, physical and emotional powers of youths can converge in dance venues of various sorts, which are sometimes referred to as discothèques, as dance clubs or simply as clubs. The stylistic variants of DJ-programmed, mediated dance music have multiplied in number accordingly, accompanied by a host of terms, each referring to a particular, at times locally specific, style of club music. These include hi-NRG, Euro-beat, Euro-disco, Italo-disco, Belgian newbeat, trance, hard trance, rave, Detroit techno, German tekkno, British drum&bass, North American electro-funk, European tech-house, deep house, hip-house, acid house, samba house, Latin house, progressive house and IDM (intelligent dance music). As these styles are also often specific with regard to type of audience, visual style (hair, dress, makeup), lingo and audio technologies (vinyl, CD), it may be more sensible to use the plural form and speak of club cultures.

To the degree that club music has been able to become part of the popular culture of a given mediascape, clubbers may position themselves either within a larger 'mainstream' culture or as members of smaller 'underground' scenes rather than within club culture in general. The lines between 'mainstream' and 'underground' may often be blurred, however, within only a few years, as in the case of the disco crossover from underground to mainstream status between 1970 and 1975 in New York City, or the acid house craze in the United Kingdom between 1987 and 1992. In addition to word-of-mouth publicity, locally specific club cultures have been able to exchange with and influence each other through various media, such as traveling DJs and their fans, fanzines, magazines and, subsequently, radio, television and, more recently, the Internet. In this way, club cultures have begun to converge on each other to appear as variants of one global club culture, while many of the local specificities that distinguish dance music cultures have continued to be maintained and cultivated. One example is the continued practise of identifying dance music styles by location (for example, Philadelphia soul, Chicago house, Jersey sound, Detroit techno, Miami bass, Dutch gabba, Future Sound of London), or the association of mixes on 12″ (30 cm) vinyl recordings named after local dance venues, as in the following examples, which all refer to venues in New York City: Sound Factory mix, Garage version, Shelter dub, Twilo Club mix.

Participants in club culture are often part of a scene, defined by a group of peers who meet to go clubbing regularly, to the same location, as followers of the same DJ or type of dance music. This commonality may be expressed through one or several of the following: dance style (generally African-American), fashions, language, connoisseurship of obscure repertoire (as in the case of northern soul, for example) or sexual orientation. Club cultures are often understood by outsiders in terms of

constructs, made up of a mix of anecdotal impressions, journalistic exposés and/or sociological analyses. These analyses may draw on forms of post-Marxist cultural theory (Thornton 1995) as much as on postmodern critical theory (Rietveld 1998). Often discussed in relation to youth culture and DIY (do-it-yourself) culture, club cultures may be understood as forms of 'generation laboratory,' uncertain in content while resistant to the approval of the adult world. It is, then, a flexible, amorphous concept referring to the practises, legal and illegal, that make up the social world of dance clubs in which DJs, dancers and promoters collaborate (often competitively) to build local systems of music production and consumption that, to varying degrees, bypass not only established music industry channels but, often, local laws and ordinances as well (Davoli and Fantuzzi 2000).

As settings where urban youths meet to socialize away from parental control, dance clubs have had a role in shaping youth culture in general, with particular focus on questions of individual and group identity, as explorable through music and dance, with the help of reality-bending elements such as high-volume musical sound, computer-controlled light beams rhythmically illuminating dark expanses, smoke and fog machines, and drugs such as alcohol, marijuana, cocaine, LSD (lysergic acid diethylamide), MDMA (3,4-methylenedioxymethamphetamine) and GHB (gamma hydroxybutyrate), among others.

Bibliography

Brewster, Bill, and Broughton, Frank. 1999. *Last Night a DJ Saved My Life: The History of the Disc Jockey*. New York: Grove Press.

Davoli, Paolo, and Fantuzzi, Gabriele. 2000. *Clubspotting: A Journey into Club Culture*. Modena: Happy Books.

Fikentscher, Kai. 2000. *'You Better Work!': Underground Dance Music in New York City*. Hanover, NH: University Press of New England.

Malbon, Ben. 1999. *Clubbing: Dancing, Ecstasy and Vitality*. London and New York: Routledge.

Redhead, Steve, with Wynne, Derek, and O'Connor, Justin, eds. 1997. *The Clubcultures Reader: Readings in Popular Cultural Studies*. Oxford: Blackwell.

Rietveld, Hillegonda C. 1998. *This Is Our House: House Music, Cultural Spaces, and Technologies*. Aldershot: Ashgate.

Thornton, Sarah. 1995. *Club Cultures: Music, Media, and Subcultural Capital*. Cambridge: Polity Press.

KAI FIKENTSCHER

Commercialism/Commercialization

Introduction

'Commercialism' refers to the general influence of business principles and practises on people's affairs, including leisure activities. The related term 'commercialization' is more specific, referring to the commodification for profit of artifacts and goods, including cultural items and symbolic merchandise. Commodification therefore involves the production, packaging, promotion and marketing of goods for a consumer market economy.

Although evidencing long histories, processes of commercialism and commercialization were given increased prominence with the rise of consumer/mass society, along with urbanization, industrialization and the beginnings of global markets, in the late eighteenth and nineteenth centuries. With increased and more differentiated consumer demand, individual social identity became more closely identified with the consumption (and display) of goods. Associated with these developments was the rise of advertising as part of increasingly sophisticated marketing techniques and the growing significance of brand names (Fowles 1996, ch. 1).

The Mass Culture Debate

Collectively, these dual processes of commercialism and commercialization were implicit in the production of what came to be termed 'mass society' and an associated 'mass culture.' As a consequence, the processes have been a central element in an ongoing debate over the nature and influence of 'mass culture.' At issue are the nature of 'art' (associated with aesthetic notions of taste and quality); the role of conditions of production; the individual or collective nature of the creation of cultural products; and distinctions between 'high culture' (art) and mass (or popular) culture. The surrounding arguments have been dominated by two broad traditions – Romanticism, and the mass culture critique of the Frankfurt School – and the various responses to them.

Romanticism emerged from French and German artistic and intellectual thought of the late eighteenth century, and became internationally influential in writing, painting, architecture and music. Its dominant aesthetic lay in imagination and emotional response, with the artist seen as the creative and visionary individual whose work was accorded authentic status (Swingewood 1977). Linked to Romanticism was the nineteenth-century 'high culture' tradition, essentially a conservative defense of a narrowly defined 'high' or elite culture, in the classic sense of Matthew Arnold's vision of 'the best that is known and thought in the world' (1869, cited in editor's introduction (1986, xviii)). Adherents of this view asserted an artistic conception of culture, arguing that the only real and authentic culture is art, against which everything else is set. They viewed the valued civilized culture of an elite minority as constantly under attack from an unauthentic majority or mass culture. The analytical emphasis here was on evaluation and discrimination, in a search for the true values of civilization, commonly to be found in Renaissance art, the great nineteenth-century novels and so on.

A stance equally critical of mass culture, but from a Marxist standpoint, was subsequently adopted by the Frankfurt School. A group of German intellectuals, who were initially based at the Institute of Social Research in Frankfurt, but who moved to the United States during the 1930s, the Frankfurt School included Adorno, Marcuse, Horkheimer, Fromm and Benjamin. These writers stressed the commodification of popular cultural forms under the conditions of capitalist production and the constant quest for profit. They criticized mass culture in general, arguing that, under the capitalist system of production, culture had become simply another object, that produced by the 'culture industry,' devoid of critical thought and any oppositional political possibilities.

The Romantic/'high culture' tradition and the views of the Frankfurt School have remained essential to discussions of the nature and operation of commercial culture (Cowen 1998). They were reworked, upheld and critiqued in the work of subsequent British and US cultural commentators, most notably F.R. Leavis in the 1930s, Dwight MacDonald in the 1950s, Raymond Williams in the 1960s and Allan Bloom in the 1980s (see Swingewood 1977).

As critics of both traditions have observed, any firm distinctions between art/'high culture' and mass/popular culture are difficult to maintain. 'High culture' is not divorced from the marketplace. Artistic production always has an economic dimension – as illustrated, for example, by the role of patronage in Renaissance art. All forms of culture are subject, in varying degrees, to the mediating effects of commercialism: 'If mass culture is defined not against middle-class culture, against art, but as a way of processing it, then the crucial high/low conflict is not that between social classes but that produced by the commercial process itself at all levels of cultural expression, in pop as well as in classical music' (Frith 1996, 35).

As some advocates of postmodern theory have argued, the traditionally claimed distinctions between 'high' and 'low' culture have become blurred (for example, Jameson 1991; Kaplan 1987). 'High art' has become increasingly commodified and commercialized, while some forms of popular culture have become more 'respectable,' receiving state funding and broader critical acceptance. Aesthetic production has become generally integrated into commodity production.

Popular Music and Mass Culture

The mass culture debate has been reflected in discussions of the aesthetic value of popular music, and has been at the core of considerations of the operation of the popular music industry.

A succession of commentators has regarded much popular music as mindless fodder, cynically manufactured for undiscriminating youthful consumers (see, for example, Bloom 1987). This general view was extensively developed by Adorno, especially in his attacks on Tin Pan Alley and jazz. Adorno was highly critical of the ruthless exploitation of popular music by the culture/music industries. The core of his critique of popular music was the standardization associated with the capitalist system of commodity production: 'A clear judgement concerning the relation of serious to popular music can be arrived at only by strict attention to the fundamental characteristic of popular music: standardization. The whole structure of popular music is standardized even where the attempt is made to circumvent standardization' (Adorno 1941, 17). In this essay and in his subsequent writings on popular music, Adorno continued to equate the form with Tin Pan Alley and jazz-oriented variations of it, ignoring the rise of rock 'n' roll in the early 1950s. This undermined his critique and resulted in the firm rejection of his views on popular music generally by more contemporary analysts (see, for example, Frith 1983, 43–48).

Nevertheless, Adorno's views on popular music have continued to be widely utilized and debated. Paddison (1993) argues that Adorno's defense of the musical avant-garde can be applied to the work of composers and performers of popular music such as Frank Zappa and Henry Cow. Gendron (1986) recognizes Adorno's exaggeration of the presence of industrial standardization in popular music, but suggests that 'Adorno's analysis of popular music is not altogether implausible,' and offers a supportive reconsideration of it (25; see also Gracyk 1996).

In the 1960s, art discourses began to be applied to 'commercial' popular music, with ongoing discussions of 'rock as art' and the founding of *Rolling Stone* magazine (1967). The Romantic emphasis on the creative individual and authenticity was invoked by musicians, critics and fans seeking to legitimate 'rock' as a new art form. This involved a certain ambiguity, given that the ideology of individualism operates structurally in conjunction with capitalism – a point made evident in the music industry's incorporation of the concept of the auteur into its marketing. In popular music aesthetics, a dichotomy emerged between 'rock' and 'pop,' setting art against commerce, creativity against commodification, and authenticity against the cynically manufactured. The core distinction was between music as creative expression and music controlled by the music industry. While the recording companies were oriented toward selling an economic commodity – recorded music – the economic orientation of this was disguised by the emphasis in the music press on the aesthetic qualities of the music (Stratton 1982).

As with the broader discourse surrounding mass culture, such distinctions have proved difficult to maintain, although they have continued to be widely used, not least by the music press. Popular music critics have generally accepted that the opposing of music as personal expression and music as commercial entertainment, art versus the marketplace, is unsustainable. Gracyk (1996) recommends 'navigating between [these] two positions that are often treated as mutually exclusive. First we should avoid the superficial idea that the idiom employed for purposes of entertainment is distinct from that of artistic expression. But we should always be just as wary of the idea that only one idiom is suitable for all musicians working at any given time . . .' (152).

Music as Commodity

There are aspects of popular music as a commodity that distinguish it from other cultural texts, notably its reproducibility, the ubiquity of its formats and its multiple modes of dissemination. While creating and promoting new music (the industry term is 'product') is usually expensive, actually reproducing it is not. Popular music has been increasingly commodified, recorded and reproduced in various formats – vinyl, audiotape, CD, DAT and video – and in variations within these: the dance mix, the cassette single, the limited collector's edition and so on. These are disseminated in a variety of ways – through radio airplay, discos and dance clubs, television music video shows and MTV-style channels, and live performances. Other means of dissemination involve the use of popular music in film soundtracks and television advertising, and the ubiquitous Muzak. The range of these formats allows a multimedia approach to the marketing of popular music – a marketing that can also involve the sale of memorabilia to fans, especially posters and T-shirts – and a maximization of sales potential, as exposure in each of the various forms strengthens the appeal of the others.

Given that the capitalist music industry is central to the process of making and marketing recorded music, there is a spectrum of aesthetic experience that ranges across the artistic to the commercial in all musical genres, including the classical. Early practises, such as the eighteenth-century patronage of composers, commissioning of work and advent of public (but paying) concerts, demonstrated that music was hardly immune from commercial influences and constraints (Cowen 1998). (It is worth noting that the distinction between 'high' and 'low' music cultures did not yet exist.) In the nineteenth century, the sale of home pianos, sheet music and phonographs further demonstrated the considerable commercial potential of forms of music increasingly thought of as 'popular.' Commodification – the process through which music is rendered into a material form capable of being packaged, promoted and marketed for purposes of profit – was accelerated toward the end of the nineteenth century, first through sheet music, and then, more accessibly, through recorded sound. The successful commodification of music in the form of records led at the turn of the twentieth century to the rise of record companies, and, subsequently, to the introduction of licensing and copyright legislation and to the establishment of associations of composers and musicians (Chanan 1995; Millard 1995).

An instructive historical example of how the means of sound reproduction constitute a significant element in the commodification of popular music is provided in Farrell's (1998) account of the early days of the gramophone industry in India. The gramophone arrived in India only a few years after its invention in the West, and recorded sound brought many forms of classical Indian music out of the obscurity of such performance settings as the courtesan's quarter and onto the mass market. Indian musicians were introduced to the world of Western media, as photography and recorded sound turned indigenous musics into salable commodities. Economics underpinned the move of Gramophone and Typewriter Ltd. (GTL) to the Indian subcontinent. As John Watson Hawf, the company's agent in Calcutta, put it: 'The native music is to me worse than Turkish but as long as it suits them and sells well what do we care?' (Farrell 1998, 58). For the emergent Indian middle class, the gramophone was both a technological novelty and a status symbol.

Commodification as a term and a concept was used in late twentieth-century popular music studies to critically analyze the relationship between the music industry, the market and music-making. The term came to be used largely in a negative sense in critiques of the aggressive and calculated marketing of popular music trends, as with the British 'New Pop' performers of the early 1980s, associated with the rise of music video and MTV (Frith 1988; Harron 1988). New musical genres were frequently perceived as beginning with Romantic overtones (essentially valuing creative over commercial considerations), but soon becoming commodified. A familiar historical litany was apparent here, moving through rock 'n' roll in the 1950s, soul in the 1960s, reggae and punk in the 1970s, rap in the 1980s and alternative music in the 1990s.

The debate surrounding commodification has centered on the extent and cultural significance of such co-optation or incorporation and its associated commercialization (with clear parallels to the mass culture debate). For some, it is clear that genres initially couched in the language of rebellion have metamorphosed into those espousing the language of the cash register:

> In light of the music industry's profitable involvement in all facets of the commercial mainstream, the story of rock and roll should be used by the Harvard School of Business as one of its case studies. Far from the threat that social and political critics would have it seem, rock and roll has become the corporate spine of American entertainment. (Eliot 1989, 201)

Others have argued for a balance between commodification and consumer sovereignty:

> My starting point is what is possible for us as consumers – what is available to us, what we can do with it – is a result of decisions made in production, made by musicians, entrepreneurs and corporate bureaucrats, made according to governments' and lawyers' rulings, in response to technological opportunities. The key to 'creative consumption' remains an understanding of these decisions, the constraints under which they are made, and the ideologies that account for them. (Frith 1988, 6–7)

Marketing

Marketing has come to play a crucial role in the circulation of cultural commodities. Central to the process is product positioning and the imbuing of cultural products with social significance to make them attractive to consumers. In popular music, this has centered on the marketing of genre styles and stars, and these have come to function in a similar manner to brand names, 'serving to order demand and stabilize sales patterns' (Ryan 1992, 185). The marketing of popular music includes the use of genre labels as signifiers, radio formatting practises and standardized production processes (for example, the production team of Mike Stock, Matt Aitken and Pete Waterman – known as SAW – and UK dance pop in the 1980s). The deployment of new technologies in electronic data processing, combined with greater concentration of music retailing, has permitted retail, distribution and production 'to be arranged as an interconnected logistic package,' allowing 'music retailers to delineate, construct and monitor the "consumer" of recorded music more intricately than ever before' (du Gay and Negus 1994, 396).

Stars are economic entities who are used to mobilize audiences and promote the products of the music industry. They represent a unique form of commodity that is both a labor process and a product, and audience identification with particular stars is a significant marketing device. Several popular music stars (for example, Elvis

Presley, Jimi Hendrix, Bob Marley and Kurt Cobain) have continued to generate enormous income after their death, which has frozen their appeal in time while allowing their continued marketing through both back catalogs and previously unreleased material.

Popular music has continued to exhibit a marked ambivalence in relation to commercialism/commercialization. There is a tension between the notions of Romanticism frequently attached to particular genres, performers and musical practises, and their commodification. This is especially evident through the contemporary blurring of advertising and programming, epitomized by MTV.

Bibliography

Adorno, Theodor W., with Simpson, George. 1941. 'On Popular Music.' *Studies in Philosophy and Social Sciences* 9: 17–48.

Adorno, Theodor W., with Simpson, George. 1991. *The Culture Industry: Selected Essays on Mass Culture*, ed. J. Bernstein. London: Routledge.

Arnold, Matthew. 1986 (1869). *Culture and Anarchy*. London: Cambridge University Press.

Bloom, Allan. 1987. *The Closing of the American Mind*. New York: Simon & Schuster.

Chanan, Michael. 1995. *Repeated Takes: A Short History of Recording and Its Effects on Music*. London and New York: Verso.

Cowen, Tyler. 1998. *In Praise of Commercial Culture* (esp. Ch. 4). Cambridge, MA and London: Harvard University Press.

du Gay, Paul, and Negus, Keith. 1994. 'The Changing Sites of Sound: Music Retailing and the Composition of Consumers.' *Media, Culture and Society* 16(3): 395–413.

Eliot, Marc. 1989. *Rockonomics: The Money Behind the Music*. New York: Franklin Watts.

Farrell, Gerry. 1998. 'The Early Days of the Gramophone Industry in India: Historical, Social and Musical Perspectives.' In *The Place of Music*, ed. Andrew Leyshon, David Matless and George Revill. New York and London: Guilford Publications, 57–82.

Fowles, Jib. 1996. *Advertising and Popular Culture*. Thousand Oaks, CA: Sage.

Frith, Simon. 1983. *Sound Effects: Youth, Leisure and the Politics of Rock 'n' Roll*. Rev. ed. London: Constable.

Frith, Simon. 1988. 'Video Pop: Picking Up the Pieces.' In *Facing the Music*, ed. Simon Frith. New York: Pantheon, 88–130.

Frith, Simon. 1992. 'The Industrialization of Popular Music.' In *Popular Music and Communication*, ed. James Lull. 2nd ed. Newbury Park, CA: Sage, 49–74.

Frith, Simon. 1996. *Performing Rites: On the Value of Popular Music*. Cambridge, MA: Harvard University Press.

Garofalo, Reebee. 1994. 'Culture Versus Commerce: The Marketing of Black Popular Music.' *Public Culture* 7(1): 275–87.

Gendron, Bernard. 1986. 'Theodor Adorno Meets the Cadillacs.' In *Studies in Entertainment: Critical Approaches to Mass Culture*, ed. Tania Modleski. Bloomington, IN: Indiana University Press, 18–36.

Gracyk, Theodore. 1996. *Rhythm and Noise: An Aesthetics of Rock*. Durham, NC: Duke University Press.

Harron, Mary. 1988. 'McRock: Pop as a Commodity.' In *Facing the Music*, ed. Simon Frith. New York: Pantheon, 173–220.

Hill, Dave. 1986. *Designer Boys and Material Girls: Manufacturing the 80's Pop Dream*. Poole: Blandford Press.

Jameson, Fredric. 1991. *Postmodernism, or, The Cultural Logic of Late Capitalism*. Durham, NC: Duke University Press.

Kaplan, E. Ann. 1987. *Rocking Around the Clock: Music Television, Postmodernism, and Consumer Culture*. New York: Methuen.

Millard, Andre J. 1995. *America on Record: A History of Recorded Sound*. Cambridge: Cambridge University Press.

Negus, Keith. 1996. *Popular Music in Theory: An Introduction*. Cambridge: Polity Press.

Paddison, M. 1993. *Adorno's Aesthetics of Music*. Cambridge: Cambridge University Press.

Rimmer, Dave. 1985. *Like Punk Never Happened: Culture Club and the New Pop*. London: Faber.

Ryan, B. 1992. *Making Capital from Culture*. Berlin and New York: Walter de Gruyter.

Stratton, Jon. 1982. 'Between Two Worlds: Art and Commercialism in the Record Industry.' *The Sociological Review* 30: 267–85.

Swingewood, A. 1977. *The Myth of Mass Culture*. London: Macmillan.

ROY SHUKER

Community

The term 'community' originates from the fourteenth-century word *communitatem*, meaning 'community of relations or feelings,' and it has tended to be associated with human (ethnic) groups that are bounded, rooted and local and involve face-to-face interaction between group members. One of the basic principles of ethnomusicology has been that the chief function of music and song is to express the shared feelings and mold the joint activities of such communities (Lomax 1978), a principle that has also been applied to popular music. The term 'community' has been commonly and loosely used in relation to popular music, however, and a popular music 'community' can take many forms: it might comprise a group of people who share a particular musical activity or taste, occupation or culture, for example. But popular music can also play an important role for nonmusical communities, such as those that share a life style based around kinship, class, religion or ethnicity, or those linked to a particular geographical place.

For example, in most UK cities, those involved with the making of guitar-based 'alternative' rock music form various networks, cliques and factions and are divided by such factors as musical style, social class, feuds and rivalries; at the same time, however, they are united by factors such as age and gender, a collective ideology and mythology, webs of interlinking social networks and a gossip grapevine, and by hurdles and struggles familiar to all of them in their common quest for success. In this sense, perhaps, they could be referred to as a local rock 'community,' and many of them also talk of and perceive themselves as part of such a community (Cohen 1991).

This linking of local alternative rock culture in Britain and North America with notions of community, heritage and local identity is quite common (Straw 1991; Cohen 1994), implying geographical and historical stability, rootedness and an organic relationship between musical sounds and styles and the places in which they are produced and consumed. The participatory nature of much music-making encourages this sense of community, which is why the rock 'n' roll scene in Austin, Texas has been described as an 'embryonic signifying community' – a kinetic entity involving strong sentiments, a sense of excitement or 'buzz,' a context for exploration and performance of new identities, a focus for collective action and a strong sense of belonging (Shank 1994).

However, some popular music-makers, researchers and writers feel that the term 'community' carries too much cultural and intellectual 'baggage' and misrepresents local music-making. Finnegan (1989), in her study of local musical worlds in the English town of Milton Keynes, prefers to use the notion of musical 'pathways' rather than musical 'communities' or 'networks' in an attempt to use a metaphor that will not present those worlds as either too close-knit or too disparate and fragmented, and that conveys a sense of music-making as an active, open and dynamic process. Others, however, prefer to talk of local music 'scenes.' Straw (1991) has studied local popular music scenes in North America and points out that such scenes do not simply correspond to a particular group, class or community, but are created through various 'coalitions' and 'alliances' based on musical preferences and on factors such as class, race, gender and age. The North American dance scene, for example, operates within and across different spaces, forging connections between various urban locations. It

thus has a sense of alliance or connection with dance scenes in other places and a cosmopolitan outlook that makes it more attuned to music activity elsewhere.

Rock musicians and audiences in different places are similarly connected by means of: international music concerts and festivals; fan clubs and internationally distributed fanzines, newsletters and professional music magazines; radio and television broadcasts; music industry conventions and multinational record companies; and computer discussion groups and Web sites. Thus, despite the emphasis in rock culture on community and its rootedness in particular places, local rock music needs to be understood vis-à-vis broader transnational or 'global' relations and processes. However, instead of abandoning the term 'community' in this context, an alternative approach might be to examine how community is created through such global relations and processes.

There exist, for example, numerous large geographically dispersed or international groups of popular music fans, including fans of the Beatles and Bruce Springsteen, which represent a diversity of ages, socioeconomic backgrounds and nationalities, and within which distinctions between different types of fans and fandom are the subject of much discussion and debate (Cohen 1997; Cavicchi 1998). Nevertheless, these fan groups or networks have their own shared social practises and discourse, conventions and rituals; most of their members feel isolated from non-fans and are keen to establish relationships with other fans. Such relationships are developed, maintained and strengthened via correspondence through fanzines and newsletters, letter-writing and computer discussion groups, face-to-face interaction at concerts, tours and other events, and personal visits. A sense of community is important to such fans. Springsteen fans, for example, refer to the 'instant connection and knowing' that occur between fans meeting for the first time, and many Beatles fans use the term 'community' (as well as terms like 'family' and 'congregation') to describe the strong bonds that develop between them and the affinity that they feel. Both sets of fans also create a sense of community through the sharing of familiar stories – for example, accounts of how they became fans, their pilgrimages as fans, their experiences of attending concerts, or the occasions when they met Bruce or a Beatle in person. Such tales often involve the use of religious terms and phrases, and they form an important basis for social interaction and the establishment of bonds between fans, enabling them to understand their experiences as shared and to see themselves as members of a specific community. Beatles fans usually attribute to music the power to unite them, and again the participatory, collective, performative nature of much music-making and listening encourages a sense of community by intensifying the feelings and experiences of those involved; however, some fans also assert their community membership by demonstrating their knowledge of Bruce- or Beatles-related facts and figures. These large international fan groups are thus to some extent 'imagined communities.' Nevertheless, the idea of community influences and shapes the social relations involved in fandom so that fans establish relationships with other fans through their sense of group identity (Cavicchi 1998).

This creation of community through popular music can also be important for nonmusical communities. Jewish immigrants arriving in Britain and the United States from Eastern Europe during the late nineteenth century, for example, used religious and folk music to frame various rituals and events, such as wedding ceremonies and religious festivals, and to heighten their special social and symbolic significance. The music helped bring these immigrant groups together and deepen their sense of collectivity. Yiddish records were often purchased and passed around these groups, stimulating collective memory and reminding the groups of their Eastern European origins and homelands and their experiences of homelessness and emigration. In addition, Jewish immigrants listened to more commercial forms of popular music, gathering around pianos in their neighborhoods to sing popular songs of the day and frequenting local dance halls, music halls and cinemas where many Jewish musicians performed. The modern entertainment industry was just beginning to emerge, and for many enterprising immigrants the music industry provided employment and income. Access to the music industry was relatively easy compared with other industries due to lower financial barriers and less discrimination. It was an area not yet dominated by Gentile talent and capital, partly because it was considered risky and disreputable. Consequently, Jews entered the industry at every level – as performers, agents and managers, as promoters of clubs, cinemas and other venues, and as owners of music instrument and record stores. Popular music was thus important to the immigrants' sense of identity, belonging and place. It helped them to develop, define and distinguish themselves as a community and to symbolize that community, often in situations of considerable uncertainty. It also linked them with Jewish communities elsewhere, marking relations of affinity and alliance.

Many such communities – like the rock communities discussed above – consider certain popular music forms and styles to be their own, associating them with notions of ownership and authenticity. But popular music can also signal internal divisions within such

communities along lines of class, age, gender and so on, and it can divide whole communities. Divisions between 'Irish' and 'British' identities in Northern Ireland, for example, are dramatically emphasized by musicians, such as members of the militaristic marching flute and drum bands of the Protestant Orangemen. Such musical factors 'are as much a part of the violence of the political situation as the shooting and bombs' (Stokes 1994, 10). The marches have also acted as a focus and trigger for Irish sectarian conflict in cities like Liverpool in the United Kingdom, representing an appropriation of public space and a marking of territory (McManus 1994, 5). Also in Liverpool, a so-called 'color bar' used to operate in many of the city's clubs and dance halls, leading to a situation in which black musicians performed in 'white' spaces, and the leisure activities of the city's black 'community' have long been restricted through various means to one particular geographical area of the city. What is significant, therefore, is how music is used in specific situations to mark community boundaries, 'to maintain distinctions between us and them, and how terms such as "authenticity" are used to justify these boundaries' (Stokes 1994, 6).

Popular music thus plays an important role in the creation of community, and this is a political and contested process. These popular music 'communities' are not necessarily bounded and rooted, but shifting and transitory, cosmopolitan and transnational, because popular music is a global culture involving relations of alliance and affinity between geographically dispersed groups and styles, cultural change and interaction, and musical 'routes' as opposed to 'roots.'

Bibliography

Cavicchi, Daniel. 1998. *Tramps Like Us: Music and Meaning Among Springsteen Fans*. New York: Oxford University Press.

Cohen, Sara. 1991. *Rock Culture in Liverpool: Popular Music in the Making*. Oxford: Oxford University Press.

Cohen, Sara. 1994. 'Mapping the Sound: Identity, Place, and the Liverpool Sound.' In *Ethnicity, Identity and Music: The Musical Construction of Place*, ed. Martin Stokes. Oxford: Berg, 117–34.

Cohen, Sara. 1997. '"Welcome to Beatle City": Music Fandom and Urban Tourism.' Unpublished paper presented at the 'Music Fan Cultures' conference, University of Copenhagen, October.

Cohen, Sara. 1998. 'Sounding Out the City: Music and the Sensuous Production of Place.' In *The Place of Music*, ed. Andrew Leyshon, David Matless and George Revill. New York and London: Guilford Publications, 155–76. (First published in *Transactions of the Institute of British Geographers* 20(4) (1995): 434–46.)

Finnegan, Ruth. 1989. *The Hidden Musicians: Music-Making in an English Town.* Cambridge: Cambridge University Press.

Lomax, Alan. 1978. *Folk Song Style and Culture.* New Brunswick, NJ: Transaction. (First published Washington, DC: American Association for the Advancement of Science, 1968.)

McManus, Kevin. 1994. *Ceilies, Jigs and Ballads: Irish Music in Liverpool.* Liverpool: Institute of Popular Music.

Shank, Barry. 1994. *Dissonant Identities: The Rock'n'Roll Scene in Austin, Texas.* Hanover, NH: University Press of New England.

Stokes, Martin, ed. 1994. *Ethnicity, Identity and Music: The Musical Construction of Place.* Oxford: Berg.

Straw, Will. 1991. 'Systems of Articulation, Logics of Change: Communities and Scenes in Popular Music.' *Cultural Studies* 5(3): 368–88.

SARA COHEN

Consumption

The term 'consumption' refers to the manner in which individuals and social groups engage with cultural forms, in particular the social uses they make of these forms in constructing social/personal identities/life styles. At the heart of theoretical debates has been the relative emphasis to be placed on consumption as an active process, and the degree to which it is determined or shaped by cultural production and institutions, as well as social structures.

Social theorists critical of the emergence of mass society/culture in the later nineteenth and early twentieth centuries used the term 'mass' in relation to the audience and 'consumption' to emphasize the determined nature of this process – the dominant market and the manipulated consumer. Later analyses placed progressively greater emphasis on the uses that consumers (the term represents a significant change of focus, with its implication of an active process) made of media: analysis of uses and gratifications (which emerged in the 1960s, largely within US media sociology), reception analysis and subcultural studies all stressed the active nature of consumption.

At the end of the twentieth century, the dominant paradigm of audience studies stressed the active nature of media audiences, while also recognizing that their consumption was, at the same time, shaped by social conditions (Ang 1991; Morley 1992). This was to emphasize consumer sovereignty: the view that the consumers'/audiences' exercise of their 'free' choice in the marketplace was a major determinant of the nature and availability of particular cultural commodities. In a contemporary form of cultural studies, consumer sovereignty was tied to the notion of the active audience, to produce a debated view of semiotic democracy (Fiske 1989). Subsequently, there was an emphasis on the domestic sphere of much media consumption, and the interrelationship of the use of various media forms.

Popular Music Consumption

The consumption of popular music has been regarded as a mix of passive and active processes. Historically, cultural debate about popular music has focused on the nature and significance of its commodification as 'mass culture.' Commercial constraints aside, there exists a tension between musical audiences as collective social groups and, at the same time, as individual consumers.

Following Adorno's negative view of the production and nature of recorded popular music (1991), in the 1950s and 1960s teenagers were often regarded as a new mass market, mindless commercial fodder for the providers of popular music (Abrams 1959; Hall and Whannel 1964). Subsequently, there was a move toward stressing the active nature of music audiences, particularly in the study of youth subcultures, members of which were seen to appropriate musical styles as a basis (subcultural capital) for their identity (Hebdige 1979; Trondman 1990).

Two related factors have usually been seen to underpin the consumption of popular music: pleasure and cultural capital.

Popular Music as a Source of Pleasure

Popular music provides many forms of pleasure, ranging from the cerebral to the physical. These are embraced within the construction of taste and fandom, a complex phenomenon related to the formation of social identities. Fandom offers its participants membership of a community not defined in traditional terms of status, located within an area of sensibility in which the fan's relation to cultural texts 'operates in the domain of affect or mood' (Grossberg 1992, 56).

In relation to consumption practises, a distinction can be made between fans and aficionados, with different affective investments involved (Shuker 1998). Fans will collect the recordings put out by their favored performers, but these are only one aspect of an interest that focuses, rather, on the image and persona of the star. For example, studies of the post-punk British 'new pop' performers of the 1980s (Culture Club, Duran Duran, Wham!, Spandau Ballet, Nik Kershaw and Howard Jones) showed how they drew upon a fanatical female following, with their support, in extreme cases, bordering on the pathological. At the same time, however, such '[p]op fans aren't stupid. They know what they want. And ultimately, all the media manipulation in the world isn't going to sell them something they haven't got any use for' (Rimmer 1985, 108).

As ideological and economical constructs, stars play a significant role in consumption (Buxton 1983). For many fans, a strong identification with stars helps them to get through their lives and provides emotional and even physical comfort, a source of pleasure and empowerment: 'By participating in fandom, fans construct coherent identities for themselves. In the process, they enter a domain of cultural activity of their own making which is, potentially, a source of empowerment in struggles against oppressive ideologies and the unsatisfactory circumstance of everyday life' (Lewis 1992, 3; see also Vermorel and Vermorel 1985).

Aficionados are those who see themselves as 'serious' devotees of particular musical styles or performers, usually those regarded (in some sense) as more 'authentic.' Their emotional and physical investments are different from those of mainstream 'fans,' as are the social consumption situations in which they operate. The aficionados' intense interest is usually at more of an intellectual level and is focused on the music per se rather than on star personae. Aficionados prefer to describe themselves as 'into' particular performers and genres, and often display impressive knowledge of them. They are characterized by 'secondary involvement' in music: the seeking out of rare releases, such as picture discs and bootlegs; the reading of fanzines in addition to commercial music magazines; regular concert going; and an interest in record labels and in producers as well as performers. Aficionados frequently become record collectors on a large scale, supporting an infrastructure of specialist and secondhand record stores (see the contributions to Aizlewood 1994; Smith 1995).

Popular Music as a Form of Cultural Capital

Musical cultural capital is demonstrated through a process whereby individuals, in acquiring a taste for particular artists and genres, both discover the 'history' and assimilate a selective tradition. They can then knowledgeably discuss artists, records, styles, trends, recording companies, music magazines and so on. Cultural capital can be displayed and shaped around recordings. This process occurs with music that is popular among the individuals' peer groups or subcultures. In both cases, it serves a similar function, distancing its adherents from other musical styles and their consumers. In the case of allegiance to non-mainstream genres/performers, cultural capital serves to assert an oppositional stance (as with heavy metal; see Arnett 1996).

Consumption is not simply a matter of 'personal' preference, but is, in part, socially constructed. Bourdieu (1984) shows how 'taste' is both conceived and maintained in the efforts of social groups to differentiate and distance themselves from others, and underpins varying social status positions. Music has traditionally been a crucial dimension of this process. The musical tastes and styles followed or adopted by particular groups of consumers are affected by a number of social factors, including class, gender, ethnicity and age. Particular genres (for example, Christian rock) have become carriers of ideology, creating symbols with which listeners can identify (Reid 1993). Adolescent consumption has been the focus of a number of studies (for example, Roe 1983; Shepherd 1986; Hakanen and Wells 1993), comprehensively brought together by Christenson and Roberts (1998), which demonstrate that consumption patterns reflect the dominant forms of musical cultural capital within peer groups.

At times, specific musical texts are open to quite contradictory readings, reflecting their listeners' social location and the orientation of their values. For example, Meintjes's examination (1990) of South African reaction to Paul Simon's *Graceland* album identifies two main responses: on the one hand, *Graceland* alerted South Africans to the richness of local musics, and opened up market opportunities for blacks; but, on the other hand, it encouraged the appropriation of black music by white South Africans.

Modes of Popular Music Consumption

Historically, popular music has become available in an increasing range of commodity forms, making modes of consumption more and more diverse and complex. They include the purchase of recordings (in various formats), film and video viewing, radio listening and home taping, as well as the various secondary levels of involvement via the music press, the Internet, clubbing, dances and discos, and concert going. These forms frequently interact to construct individual popular music consumption.

Even younger adolescent consumers, who are often seen as relatively undiscriminating and easily swayed by market forces, see their preferences as the product of a more complex set of influences, with the views of their friends paramount (Christenson and Roberts 1998). People's musical consumption, whatever their social background, is often rooted in a substantial and sophisticated body of knowledge about popular music. Most listeners, particularly young people, have a clear understanding of different genres, and an ability to hear and place sounds in terms of their histories, influences and sources. Critics, musicians and consumers constantly make (and justify) judgments about meaning and value (Frith 1996; Willis et al. 1990).

Clubbing, home taping and record collecting constitute three significant forms of consumption. These illustrate the importance of the context of consumption practises. The first takes place primarily in public spaces; the second is a largely domestic practise (except for concert taping, for example by 'Deadheads' – see Sardiello 1994); and the last provides an example of the intersection of public and private consumption practises. During the early 1900s, clubs became a major venue for live music on a regular and continuing basis, often associated with the popularization of particular genres (for instance, jazz). A community network of clubs (or pub) venues can help create a local club scene, at times based around a particular sound (for example, Liverpool/Merseybeat in the early 1960s). While the cohesion of their 'common' musical signatures is frequently exaggerated, such localized developments offer marketing possibilities by providing a 'brand name' with which clubbers can identify. Club cultures are associated with specific locations that continually present and modify sounds and styles. Club cultures are centered on their members' shared taste in music, their consumption of common media and, most importantly, their preference for people with similar tastes to their own (Thornton 1995).

An instructive example is northern soul, a regional cult in northwestern England centered around ballroom/club culture and all-night dancing to 1960s soul records (Shuker 1998). Northern soul became prominent in the early 1970s and has maintained itself with fanzines, continued all-nighters and record compilations. The northern soul scene produces a sense of identity and belonging based on the consumption of 'music as music,' centered around a club scene, where the records have value both as commodities and as bearers of musical meaning. The exchange, buying and selling of records constitute an important part of this, with the use of 'white labels' representing a unique form of fetishization of black musical culture by white consumers (Hollows and Milestone 1998).

Making tape compilations represents a significant aspect of people's engagement with popular music. Home taping, made possible by the development of cassette audiotape and the cassette tape player, is the practise of copying recordings to audio- or videotape from broadcasts or existing recordings. The general practise is frequently criticized by the mainstream music industry, and by many artists, because of the perceived loss of revenue involved. Others regard home taping as a legitimate cultural practise, asserting consumer autonomy. Aside from the convenience of ensuring access to preferred texts, the tape cassette has proved to be 'a practical, flexible and cheap way of consuming and distributing music' (Willis et al. 1990, 62). Home taping is done primarily from the radio, but also from friends' record collections, with 'something of an informal hierarchy of

taste operating here' (Willis et al. 1990, 63). Home taping is also significant as an aspect of consumption that the music industry is largely unable to influence.

Popular music memorabilia collectively represent a significant element of collecting as a broader social phenomenon. Collectible items encompass recordings, including promotional copies and gold discs, musical instruments, autographs, tour programs, posters, tour jackets, concert tickets and T-shirts, plus novelty toys and a whole range of ephemera marketed around major artists like the Beatles.

Record collecting is a major activity, yet a relatively neglected aspect of the consumption of popular music. Record collections can be regarded as

> both public displays of power/knowledge, and private refuges from the sexual or social world; as either structures of control or the by-products of irrational and fetishistic obsession; as material evidence of the homosocial information-mongering which is one underpinning of male power and compensatory undertakings by those unable to wield that power. (Straw 1997, 4; see also Hornby 1995)

Buying recorded music in its various formats 'is a process that involves clear symbolic work: complex and careful exercises of choice from the point of view of initial listening to, seeking out, handling and scrutinizing records' (Willis et al. 1990, 61). This involves gathering information from peers, older siblings and retrospectives in the music press, and systematically searching for items out of back catalogs. This search is carried out through specialist and secondhand record stores, in the bargain bins and at record sales. Record collecting is a male-dominated practise, supported by a network of collector magazines (such as *Goldmine* and *Record Collector*), discographies and price guides, record fairs and secondhand stores.

Bibliography

Abrams, Mark. 1959. *The Teenage Consumer*. London: London Press Exchange.

Adorno, Theodor W., with Simpson, George. 1991. *The Culture Industry: Selected Essays on Mass Culture*, ed. J. Bernstein. London: Routledge.

Aizlewood, John, ed. 1994. *Love Is the Drug*. London: Penguin.

Ang, Ien. 1991. *Desperately Seeking the Audience*. London and New York: Routledge.

Arnett, Jeffrey Jensen. 1996. *Metalheads: Heavy Metal Music and Adolescent Alienation*. Boulder, CO: Westview Press.

Bourdieu, Pierre. 1984. *Distinction: A Social Critique of the Judgement of Taste*, trans. Richard Nice. London: Routledge and Kegan Paul.

Buxton, David. 1983. 'Rock Music, the Star System and the Rise of Consumerism.' *Telos* 57: 93–106.

Christenson, Peter, and Roberts, Donald. 1998. *It's Not Only Rock & Roll: Popular Music in the Lives of Adolescents*. Cresskill, NJ: Hampton Press.

Epstein, Jonathon S., ed. 1994. *Adolescents and Their Music: If It's Too Loud, You're Too Old*. New York and London: Garland Publishing.

Epstein, Jonathon S., ed. 1998. *Youth Culture: Identity in a Postmodern World*. Oxford: Blackwell.

Fiske, John. 1989. *Understanding Popular Culture*. Boston, MA: Unwin Hyman.

Frith, Simon. 1996. *Performing Rites: On the Value of Popular Music*. Cambridge, MA: Harvard University Press.

Grossberg, Lawrence. 1992. *We Gotta Get Out of This Place: Popular Conservatism and Postmodern Culture*. New York: Routledge.

Hakanen, Ernest A., and Wells, Alan. 1993. 'Music Preference and Taste Cultures Among Adolescents.' *Popular Music and Society* 17(1): 55–69.

Hall, Stuart, and Whannel, Paddy. 1964. *The Popular Arts*. London: Hutchinson.

Hebdige, Dick. 1979. *Subculture: The Meaning of Style*. London: Methuen.

Hollows, Joanne, and Milestone, Katie. 1998. 'Welcome to Dreamsville: A History and Geography of Northern Soul.' In *The Place of Music*, ed. Andrew Leyshon, David Matless and George Revill. New York and London: Guilford Publications, 83–103.

Hornby, Nick. 1995. *High Fidelity*. New York: Riverhead Books.

Lewis, Lisa A., ed. 1992. *The Adoring Audience: Fan Culture and Popular Media*. London and New York: Routledge.

Meintjes, Louise. 1990. 'Paul Simon's *Graceland*, South Africa, and the Mediation of Musical Meaning.' *Ethnomusicology* 34(1): 37–73.

Morley, David. 1992. *Television, Audiences, and Cultural Studies*. London: Routledge.

Reid, John Edgar, Jr. 1993. 'The Use of Christian Rock Music by Youth Group Members.' *Popular Music and Society* 17(2): 33–45.

Rimmer, Dave. 1985. *Like Punk Never Happened: Culture Club and the New Pop*. London: Faber.

Roe, Keith. 1983. *Mass Media and Adolescent Schooling*. Stockholm: Almqqvist and Wiksell.

Roe, Keith. 1990. 'Adolescents' Music Use: A Structural-Cultural Approach.' In *Popular Music Research: An Anthology from NORDICOM-Sweden*, ed. Keith Roe and Ulla Carlsson. Göteborg: NORDICOM-Sweden, 41–52.

Roe, Keith, and Carlsson, Ulla, eds. 1990. *Popular Music Research: An Anthology from NORDICOM-Sweden*. Göteborg: NORDICOM-Sweden.

Sardiello, Robert. 1994. 'Secular Rituals in Popular Culture: A Case for Grateful Dead Concerts and Dead Head Identity.' In *Adolescents and Their Music: If It's Too Loud, You're Too Old*, ed. Jonathon S. Epstein. New York and London: Garland Publishing, 115–39.

Shepherd, John. 1986. 'Music Consumption and Cultural Self-Identities: Some Theoretical and Methodological Reflections.' *Media, Culture and Society* 8(3): 305–30.

Shepherd, John. 1991. *Music as Social Text*. Cambridge: Polity Press.

Shepherd, John, et al., eds. 1977. *Whose Music?: A Sociology of Musical Languages*. London: Latimer.

Shuker, Roy. 1998. *Key Concepts in Popular Music*. London and New York: Routledge.

Smith, Giles. 1995. *Lost in Music*. London: Picador.

Straw, Will. 1997. 'Sizing Up Record Collections: Gender and Connoisseurship in Rock Music Culture.' In *Sexing the Groove: Popular Music and Gender*, ed. Sheila Whiteley. London and New York: Routledge, 3–16.

Thornton, Sarah. 1995. *Club Cultures: Music, Media and Subcultural Capital*. Cambridge: Polity Press.

Trondman, Mats. 1990. 'Rock Tastes – On Rock as Symbolic Capital: A Study of Young People's Music Tastes and Music-Making.' In *Popular Music Research: An Anthology from NORDICOM-Sweden*, ed. Keith Roe and Ulla Carlsson. Göteborg: NORDICOM-Sweden, 71–85.

Vermorel, Fred, and Vermorel, Judy. 1985. *Starlust: The Secret Fantasies of Fans*. London: Comedia.

Willis, Paul, et al. 1990. *Common Culture: Symbolic Work at Play in the Everyday Cultures of the Young*. Milton Keynes: Open University Press.

Discographical Reference

Simon, Paul. *Graceland*. Warner Brothers 2-25447. *1986*: USA.

ROY SHUKER

Crime

Throughout the nineteenth and twentieth centuries, crime and popular music were linked in a number of ways: the practise of popular music itself was criminalized in certain instances; popular music was on occasion associated with organized crime; various activities associated with the practise of popular music were subject to criminal investigation and prosecution; penal institutions exercised a degree of influence on the development of popular music; and crime was a prevalent theme in popular song.

The Criminalization of Popular Music

The criminalization of music-making has frequently coincided with the criminalization of poverty. This is apparent in the case of the anti-busking laws of cities such as New York, where it can be argued that municipal governments, in an attempt to 'clean up' cities, have tried to make homelessness invisible. Music-making in the New York City subway system provides an interesting history of conflicts between buskers and officials. In her history of busking in the New York subways, Tanenbaum (1995) outlines the numerous and changing ways in which buskers have been targeted as perpetrators of illegal activities. According to Tanenbaum, busking was illegal in the subway system from its start: 'During the LaGuardia mayoralty (1934–1945), freelance street and subway musicians were equated with beggars, and they shared the status of "undesirables"' (1995, 149). Tanenbaum points out that, although buskers in the United States have had protection under the First Amendment, New York City subway musicians in the late 1970s and early 1980s '. . . were issued summonses for "begging and soliciting" or for "entertaining passengers,"' or they were 'ticketed for such rule violations as "obstructing traffic," "disorderly conduct," and making "unnecessary noise"' (1995, 150).

With the 1985 trial of *People v. Manning*, increased pressure was brought to bear on the Transit Authority to reform its policy against music-making in the subways, which resulted in the ban being lifted. However, musicians were still targeted and ticketed by transit police for 'soliciting donations without prior permission,' playing without an amp, and other violations (Tanenbaum 1995, 151–53). Tanenbaum outlines how the criminalization of busking in the subway system has been inconsistent, and how the lines between criminal, illegal and legal activities have been unclear (1995, 169–84). She argues that one of the main reasons for this inconsistency lies in the way the transit police have enforced rules differently or have invented 'regulations that are far more restrictive than the rules actually in effect' (1995, 174). For example, an Andean music group from Otavalo, Ecuador was fined for playing without a MUNY [Music Under New York] permit, even though this is not illegal.

The criminalization of music-making has also been commonplace under some Communist and military regimes, where it has served the ends of political control. Ramet (1994, 7–8) describes how rock music in Europe's Eastern bloc in the 1970s and 1980s was threatening to authorities because of its Western orientation and the challenges it presented to Communist regimes. The fear that resulted from these challenges, perceived or actual, often led to arrests and the charging of rock musicians. Ramet describes how, in September 1976 in Czechoslovakia, Ivan Jirous and Vratislav Brabenec of Plastic People of the Universe, Pavel Zajicek of DG 307 and the singer Svatopluk Karasek were put on trial. The official indictment charged that '"their texts contain extreme

vulgarity with an anti-socialist and an anti-social impact, most of them extolling nihilism, decadence, and clericalism"' (1994, 63). These musicians were found guilty and given prison sentences of between eight and 18 months.

Authorities also came down hard on some rock musicians in Hungary. Kürti (1994) describes how, in the early 1980s in Hungary, authorities attempted to suppress rock groups whose lyrics and attitudes were becoming more politically radical and overtly oppositional to Communism. Kürti states: 'Hard-core new music bands, namely ETA, CPG, and Mos-oi, were compelled to realize fairly early in their careers that their outspokenness and criticism would not be tolerated. In early 1983, Mos-oi and ETA were banned from public performances, and members faced court trials for their "crimes against the state"' (1994, 89). Members of CPG received both jail sentences and fines.

Participation in rock music in nations under military dictatorships has been similarly criminalized. Vila (1992) describes how, after the 1976 military coup in Argentina, rock concerts acted as autonomous spaces in which young people could distance themselves, if only momentarily, from the violence and fear of day-to-day life. These concerts also played an important role in consolidating youth identity and providing a safe space within which young people could communicate. As with Communist authorities, the Argentinian regime linked rock to political subversion. The police thus took action to shut down rock concerts. Authorities initially attempted to disrupt concerts with tear gas or stink bombs, but later they took more radical action. At concerts at Luna Park, 'hundreds of people were literally "rounded up" and detained for police checks before and after each event.' In addition, 'the owners of concert halls were "advised" not to rent them for rock concerts' (Vila 1992, 215).

Individual musicians have also been targeted in countries with a history of military regimes. In Nigeria in 1985, for example, Fela Kuti was arrested at Lagos airport, as he was preparing to leave for a tour of the United States, for allegedly exporting foreign currency illegally. He served 18 months of a five-year sentence, being freed with the help of Amnesty International. Fela Kuti's most likely 'crime,' however, was opposition to the government. In 1977, over a thousand soldiers had carried out a government-sanctioned attack on the compound in which he lived because of his anti-government activities, causing injuries to his mother from which she died. This led Fela Kuti, among other things, to write a song, 'Coffin for Head of State,' lamenting the death of his mother, which also served as a frequently performed political rant.

In countries thought to be more democratic, popular music, its performance and production can also be criminalized and thereby subject to social control when the activities in question are perceived to contravene established moral codes or social standards. Thus, although the charges leveled against popular musicians in Communist regimes and the sentences handed out to them might seem harsh in comparison to the way in which rock musicians have been treated in more democratic nations, Ramet (1994) suggests that 'the gap between accusations of "political obscenity" [in the Eastern bloc] and charges of sexual obscenity [in the West] is not as great as it might seem at first. The principle at stake is the same in both instances, even if the costs and benefits are dramatically different' (11).

Some performers in countries considered to be more democratic have thus been prosecuted for sexual and other forms of obscenity for reasons of social control. In the United Kingdom, the definition of obscenity contained in the 1959 *Obscene Publications Act* has been used by the government in attempts to limit musical expression (Cloonan 1995). In the United States, the most notable case occurred as a consequence of *As Nasty As They Wanna Be*, the album from Florida rappers 2 Live Crew (*Skyywalker Records v. Navarro* (1990) and *Luke Records Inc. v. Navarro* (1992)). In the case of live performances, Jim Morrison of the Doors was arrested in 1969 in Miami and convicted for 'lewd and lascivious behavior in public' (Martin and Segrave 1993). Where images are concerned, Jello Biafra of the Dead Kennedys was in 1986 charged with violating section 313.1 ('Distribution of Harmful Materials to Minors') of the California state penal code because a poster included in the band's album *Frankenchrist* featured interlocked male and female genitalia.

The notion of obscenity has, however, been lent a distinctly political tinge in less democratic circumstances. It was employed in Germany during World War II, and has been used in various Communist states of Eastern Europe, as well as in Argentina and China (Ramet 1994; Garofalo 1992; Willett 1989). Similar politically motivated prosecutions based on notions of obscenity have also occurred in supposedly democratic nations. The French rappers NTM were, for example, prosecuted in 1996 for anti-police sentiments, escaping with a suspended sentence. More generally during the late twentieth century, numerous musicians were charged under censorship, blasphemy and national security laws in many countries. In Turkey, for example, several singers were convicted of performing songs in the banned Kurdish language (Bastian and Laing, 2003).

The criminalization of music can also be implicit, serving the purposes of social control, for example, to racist ends. Restrictions on where certain musicians can perform in New York City can be understood in these terms. Chevigny (1991) outlines how regulations in New York City clubs from the 1940s until the 1960s influenced the development of jazz by preventing certain musicians from performing in clubs. In 1940, he reports, 'the police began to fingerprint every person who worked in a licensed place, and to issue identification cards, denying the cards to people they thought were not of good character' (1991, 57–58). Clubs could not legally hire a musician without a card. New York state law at this time also 'forbade the employment in a bar of anyone convicted of a felony or certain other offenses, including narcotics crimes' (1991, 59). There are no reported cases of musicians or entertainers being denied cards because of illegal activities in the clubs themselves. Musicians were denied cards most often because of past narcotics charges. This happened to Billie Holiday in 1947, despite her being one of the most popular singers of the time. These regulations 'successfully degraded the status of working in a club' (1991, 60). With the help of lawyers, some artists who were initially refused cards, such as Sonny Stitt and Bud Powell, eventually obtained them. However, a less fortunate Thelonious Monk was denied a card for a six-year period from 1951 to 1957, thus diminishing his influence on jazz at this time. Chevigny argues that, although highly restricting, the card regulations reinforced and encouraged a 'them versus us,' 'square-mainstream' versus 'hip-subcultural' mentality that permeated 1950s New York City bop culture, allowing those musicians denied cards to gain further outsider status. However, Chevigny also suggests that the city's focus on curbing criminal activity in clubs can be read as a seemingly legitimate way to continue racist-inspired attempts to gain control over 'dangerous' black music (1991, 57–61).

Popular Music and Organized Crime

The period in which the practise of popular music was perhaps most visibly connected with organized crime was 1920–33, the era of Prohibition in the United States. Prohibition led directly to an increase in gangsterism: many club owners were forced into buying their bootleg liquor from gangster barons in order to keep open their venues for live music. Performers were offered various inducements (such as liquor, drugs or access to prostitutes) to remain loyal to individual venues and, if this 'loyalty' was betrayed, it was common for the mobster element to threaten or kill the musician concerned.

However, the history of jazz reveals a contrary trend in that gangster-run or -financed clubs were not always a problem for musicians. In Kansas City, for example, organized crime was one significant factor that helped jazz to flourish there despite the Depression (Pearson 1987, xvii). Pearson points out that it was important financially for gangsters to treat musicians well, because musicians constituted a major source of income for clubs. He reports that one musician, Buster Smith, was speaking 'for most of his peers when he [asserted] that gangsters were "the musician's best friend"' (1987, 93).

Organized crime has also played an extensive role in the counterfeiting of popular music recordings. One of the most extreme examples of organized counterfeiting, that carried out by John LaMonte, is outlined by Eliot (1993). A 1977 FBI search of LaMonte's business, House of Sounds, uncovered one of the United States' biggest counterfeit recording operations. In only its third year of operation (1976), House of Sounds grossed approximately $4.5 million. Eliot describes LaMonte's activities as 'a sophisticated buy/reproduce/sell scheme . . . House of Sounds was ostensibly a wholesale operation specializing in previously released recordings, manufacturers' overstocks, and "cut-outs" – records that have not sold well and been returned to the record company for credit' (1993, 216). With James Kennedy, LaMonte also set up James Enterprises to produce counterfeit covers and labels for House of Sounds' counterfeit recordings. LaMonte and Kennedy then sold these finished and seemingly legitimate products to retailers in Europe and the United States.

The illegal activities of LaMonte and his co-conspirators did not play out – and could not have played out – in isolation, but were linked to Capitol Records' selling of 'scrap' recordings. Eliot states that 'Capitol/EMI sold illegal Beatles "scrap" to LaMonte on an ongoing basis for eleven years, at least from the time of the amended and expanded Beatles contract, until [Dennis] White's sworn deposition before the U.S. Department of Justice's Organized Crime Strike Force [in March 1986]' (1993, 217–18). Capitol's illegal treatment of 'scrap' was revealed during a lengthy legal battle in the late 1970s and the 1980s between Capitol and the Beatles' Apple Records primarily over unpaid royalties (Eliot 1993, 212–20). A 1980 audit 'revealed that as early as 1969, Capitol allegedly misclassified an enormous number of Beatles albums as "promotional" including 95,000 promotion (nonroyalty) copies of *Abbey Road*, about ten times the industry norm' (Eliot 1993, 218). Eliot goes on to report that 'documents revealed that Beatles recordings designated for promotion were, in fact, improperly distributed for profit to record wholesalers [such as House of Sounds]' (1993, 218–19).

A similar instance of possible relationships between organized crime and the music industry occurred in the 1980s. Between 1983 and 1989, when it was run by Irving Azoff, MCA was embroiled in allegations of Mafia involvement when alleged criminals were indicted in connection with the purchase of millions of deleted MCA albums (Knoedelseder 1993).

Criminal Investigation and Prosecution

The law makes a distinction between those activities that are illegal and that are subject to criminal investigation and criminal prosecution (such as payola or pay-for-play), and other activities, such as copyright infringement, that are customarily subject to litigation and the dictates of civil law. There is a clear difference between criminal and civil law, but in some instances criminal penalties (such as punitive damages in the United States) can be imposed as a consequence of civil proceedings, thus signaling moral censure and thereby criminalizing certain actions not subject to prosecution under criminal law. For example, although copyright infringements are dealt with in civil lawsuits in federal courts in the United States, a criminal penalty could be imposed. However, there are some jurisdictions in which copyright infringement can be subject to criminal prosecution. Since the late 1980s there has, for example, been an increasing number of criminal prosecutions in Southeast Asia for cassette and CD piracy. The International Federation of the Phonographic Industry (IFPI) reports that, in 2000 alone, 20 CD manufacturing lines with a capacity of 70 million discs were closed down, seven of which were in the Philippines (IFPI 2000).

Together with piracy, the most common forms of copyright infringement in popular music are bootlegging and home taping. Bootlegging tends to take three forms: unauthorized reissuing of deleted or unavailable materials (alternate takes, outtakes, demos and suchlike); live concert recordings; and unauthorized pressings of legally available products. The latter is a form of piracy and defrauds the music industry of a huge amount of revenue. Some estimates put the figure at around 6 percent of total phonograph sales per annum in the mid-1990s (see Shuker 1998, 220).

Criminal law can be used to put a stop to activities that are not criminal per se – ticket touting, for example. The widespread activity of ticket touting (the buying and selling of 'surplus' tickets for sold-out gigs, often at vastly inflated prices), which originated primarily in the United Kingdom in the 1960s and 1970s and which has helped to create a black-market economy around the promotion of popular music (most ticket touts deal in pirated merchandise too), is not illegal. However, touts may be charged by the police for related activities that are criminal – for example, obstructing a public footpath.

The payola scandal in the United States is perhaps the most famous example of criminal investigation into the workings of the music business. The political backdrop of reactionary politics under President Eisenhower and the Establishment's antipathetic view of rock 'n' roll are crucial factors in understanding the issue. In 1955, a US House of Representatives Select Committee made illegal the widespread practise of offering inducements to music executives and disc jockeys to promote individual records. It was found that some record companies were falsifying returns, refusing to pay royalties and failing to credit songwriters, while giving prominent disc jockeys such as Alan Freed co-writing credits on records in return for radio exposure. Freed, who had been rock 'n' roll's most outspoken advocate and who had helped to popularize rhythm and blues music among white audiences in the United States, was convicted of commercial bribery in 1960. The payola investigations were a thinly veiled attack on the emergent style of rock 'n' roll, and an attempt to suppress Broadcast Music Inc. (BMI), whose writers were responsible for most rock music at the time (Morthland 1980; Segrave 1994).

In terms of criminal activity, popular music performers are most often associated with reckless acts of willful alcohol- or drug-induced violence; these acts of violence are directed against themselves, their entourage, their spouses or partners, their fans, or the press and photographers, and frequently occur during tours. Indecency, disorderly or threatening behavior, public intoxication, obstruction, drunken driving, criminal damage (usually linked with the possession of firearms), assault, incitement to riot and possession of illegal substances were just some of the charges brought against popular music performers during the last four decades of the twentieth century. Some performers, such as Jerry Lee Lewis, Chuck Berry and James Brown, have fallen foul of the law many times, their criminal records by now the stuff of rock myth.

Certain popular music performers can also claim to have been treated harshly by the authorities, and their misdemeanors punished perhaps over-severely, in order to set a moral example to youth or to attack groups of color perceived as threatening to the status quo. In the punk era, for example, the Clash's 'Topper' Headon was arrested for the unlikely crime of stealing a bus stop, while the Stranglers' Hugh Cornwell was given an eight-week custodial sentence for his first offense, possession of narcotics. In the 1980s and 1990s, members of the black community in the United States were stereotyped as more likely to be involved in criminal activities, and were subjected to Draconian measures by an overwhelmingly white police force. The videotaped beating of Rodney King in April 1992, an event that led directly to the Los Angeles riots of that year, linked together issues of criminality and race more strongly than ever

before. The sense of injustice at the punishment meted out to black and Hispanic youth was given expression through rap and gangsta rap.

Popular Music and Penal Institutions

The relationship between penal institutions and popular music is not simply that prisoners have created popular music. Prisons as institutions have helped shape music itself, and the criminal pasts of some musicians have influenced the way in which they have been promoted and received.

An interesting example of the relationship between prisons and popular music is provided by the R&B harmony group the Prisonaires. The Prisonaires were formed in the Tennessee State Penitentiary in Nashville by Johnny Bragg, a talented street singer who was sentenced to 99 years in 1943 for six counts of rape. The other members were Ed Thurman and William Stewart, who were serving time for murder, John Drue, who was serving time for larceny, and Marcel Sanders, who was serving time for involuntary manslaughter. The Prisonaires had one hit with 'Just Walkin' in the Rain,' which was recorded by Sam Phillips for Sun Records in 1953 (Dougan 1999, 448–49). This song 'played a small, yet significant role in the history of rock and roll as the song that put Sun Records on the map' (Dougan 1999, 449). Dougan argues that the Prisonaires' music, mediated through the institution of the prison, 'is ultimately the music of unhappy people – men caught in a paradoxical search for personal freedom while fully cognizant of a future assigned to prison' (1999, 464).

Perhaps the best-known musician with a prison past is African-American blues singer/guitarist Huddie Ledbetter (aka Leadbelly). The interesting relationships between Leadbelly, prison and how he was perceived and presented have been outlined by Filene (1991). Leadbelly was 'discovered' by John and Alan Lomax in 1933 while he was serving a term in Angola Prison, Louisiana for murder. Leadbelly's criminal past overly influenced how he was and has continued to be perceived by audiences, something that is due largely to how the Lomaxes marketed and promoted him. The Lomaxes focused on his convict past and depicted him as a 'savage, untamed animal.' John Lomax said of Leadbelly that 'he was the type known as "killer" and had a career of violence the record of which is a black epic of horrifics,' and that he 'was a "natural," who had no idea of money, law, or ethics and who was possessed of virtually no restraint' (quoted in Filene 1991, 610). Filene points out that the Lomaxes probably and intentionally overemphasized Leadbelly's criminal past as a marketing ploy. John Lomax even 'had him perform in his old convict clothes "for exhibition purposes ... though he always hated to wear them'" (Filene 1991, 611).

Crime as a Theme in Popular Music

Crimes and criminals have long constituted the subject matter of ballads, which often raise these events and people to mythical proportions. The most prominent criminal figure in US music is likely Stagger Lee. In his partial discography to 'Stack Lee: The Man, the Music, and the Myth' (1996), Eberhart lists some 158 versions of the Stagger Lee ballad published or recorded since 1897. Performers of this ballad include 'Ma' Rainey ('Stack O'Lee Blues,' 1925), Woody Guthrie ('Stagolee,' 1941), Fats Domino ('Stack & Billy,' 1959), the Journeymen ('Stackolee,' 1963), James Brown ('Stagger Lee,' 1967), the Grateful Dead ('Stagger Lee,' 1978), and Nick Cave and the Bad Seeds ('Stagger Lee,' 1996) (Eberhart 1996, 56–65). The Stagger Lee ballad likely originated in 1896 or 1897, although its authors are unknown. Although the ballad is based on a real man, a real murder and a real criminal prosecution (Lee Shelton's murder of William Lyons in a St. Louis saloon in 1895), 'one hundred years of cultural accretion have mutated the myth of Stagger Lee into an icon much larger than the man' (Eberhart 1996, 43). Interestingly, some versions of the ballad present Stagger Lee as entirely bad, while others are more sympathetic (Eberhart 1996, 33–34).

Violent crime has long formed a part of the subject matter for blues. Some of the best examples of this trend come from the Depression era, from the overcrowded, impoverished and crime-ridden black areas of northern and southern US cities (Oliver 1990, 165). According to Oliver, the weapon of choice for poor urban blacks was the knife, and specifically a clasp knife, which was the choice of prostitutes (1990, 177–78). The clasp knife is the weapon used in the song 'Two By Four Blues,' and was 'the weapon that killed blues singer Charlie Jordan on 9th Street, St. Louis' (Oliver 1990, 178). The razor was also a weapon of choice, not for murder but for its permanent scarring effects. In 'Got Cut All To Pieces' (1928), Bessie Tucker sings of the razor's use:

I got cut all to pieces, aah-aaah ... about a man I love, (*twice*)
I'm gonna get that a-woman, just as sho' as the sky's above. (Oliver 1990, 178)

Urban blues songs of this era also depict the brutal muggings that frequently occurred in poor black areas (Oliver 1990, 179–91). Songs about violent assault include 'Hijack Blues' and 'Gutter Man Blues' (Oliver 1990, 181). The extremely high rate of violent crime in Depression-era Memphis, 'the murder capital of America,' is evident in songs such as Furry Lewis's 'Furry's Blues' (1928) (Oliver 1990, 183–84). Oliver suggests that

'[I]t is probably indicative of one of the functions of blues – to bolster confidence by emphasizing assertiveness and unwillingness to submit to repression – that while aggressive positions are taken by many singers, blues very seldom reflects a violent crime from the victim's point of view' (1990, 185).

Appalachian hillbilly ballads also rarely depict violent crimes from the victim's point of view. Tunnell (1992) suggests that songs told from the murderer's perspective can be explained functionally as a warning to others, and thus serve as a reinforcement of moral values (178). Although crime is not a common subject in the family-oriented genre of bluegrass, nonetheless 'the violent crime of man killing woman dominates crime stories of bluegrass songs' (Tunnell 1992, 177).

Criminal activities of all kinds have continued to prove a popular resource for lyricists over the years, from the Euro-pop of Boney M's 'Ma Baker' in 1977, the country stylings of Johnny Cash's 'Folsom Prison Blues' (1956), the punk call-to-arms of the Clash's 'White Riot' (1977) and reggae star Junior Murvin's 'Police and Thieves' (1980), to the ironic laddism of Madness's 'Shut Up' (1981). Songs about outlaws are exemplified in Woody Guthrie's 'Pretty Boy Floyd' (1939), and Bob Marley and the Wailers' 'I Shot the Sheriff' (1973), while examples of songs about miscarriages of justice are to be found in Bob Dylan's 'George Jackson' (1971) and 'The Lonesome Death of Hattie Carroll' (1964).

The criminal fraternity has also been a focus of attraction for many performers. The post-punk performer Morrissey, for example, was obsessed by those 'mythogenic' criminals Ron and Reggie Kray, as demonstrated by his 'The Last of the Famous International Playboys' (1989). The theme of crime is also to be found in the lyrics of many gangsta raps, most notoriously, perhaps, in NWA's 'Fuck Tha Police' (1989).

Bibliography

Bastian, Vanessa, and Laing, Dave. 2003. 'Twenty Years of Music Censorship: A Global Perspective.' In *Policing Pop*, ed. Reebee Garofalo and Martin Cloonan. Philadelphia: Temple University Press.

Chevigny, Paul. 1991. *Gigs: Jazz and the Cabaret Laws in New York City*. New York: Routledge.

Cloonan, Martin. 1995. '"I Fought the Law": Popular Music and British Obscenity Law.' *Popular Music* 14(3) (October): 349–63.

Cloonan, Martin. 1996. *Banned!: Censorship of Popular Music in Britain, 1967–92*. Aldershot: Arena.

Dougan, John. 1999. 'The Mistakes of Yesterday, the Hopes of Tomorrow: Prison, Pop Music, and the Prisonaires.' *American Music* 17(4): 447–68.

Eberhart, George M. 1996. 'Stack Lee: The Man, the

Music, and the Myth.' *Popular Music and Society* 20(1): 1–70.

Eliot, Marc. 1993. *Rockonomics: The Money Behind the Music*. New York: Citadel Press.

Filene, Benjamin. 1991. '"Our Singing Country": John and Alan Lomax, Leadbelly, and the Construction of an American Past.' *American Quarterly* 43(4): 602–24.

Frith, Simon. 1993. *Music and Copyright*. Edinburgh: Edinburgh University Press.

Garofalo, Reebee, ed. 1992. *Rockin' the Boat: Mass Music and Mass Movements*. Boston, MA: South End Press.

Haskins, Jim. 1994 (1977). *The Cotton Club*. New York: Hippocrene Books, Inc.

Herman, Gary. 1994. *Rock 'n' Roll Babylon*. 3rd rev. ed. London: Plexus.

International Federation of the Phonographic Industry (IFPI). 2000. *Music Piracy Report*. London: IFPI.

Jenks, Chris, and Lorentzen, Justin J. 1997. 'The Kray Fascination.' *Theory, Culture & Society* 14(3): 87–107.

Knoedelseder, William. 1993. *Stiffed!: A True Story of MCA, the Music Business and the Mafia*. New York: Harper Collins.

Kürti, László. 1994. '"How Can I Be a Human Being?": Culture, Youth, and Musical Opposition in Hungary.' In *Rocking the State: Rock Music and Politics in Eastern Europe and Russia*, ed. Sabrina Petra Ramet. Boulder, CO: Westview Press, 73–102.

Martin, Linda, and Segrave, Kerry. 1993. *Anti-Rock: The Opposition to Rock 'n' Roll*. New York: Da Capo.

Morthland, John. 1980. 'Payola.' In *The Rolling Stone Illustrated History of Rock and Roll*, ed. Jim Miller. San Francisco: Rolling Stone Books.

Negus, Keith. 1996. *Popular Music in Theory: An Introduction*. Cambridge: Polity.

Oliver, Paul. 1990. *Blues Fell This Morning: Meaning in the Blues*. 2nd ed. Cambridge: Cambridge University Press.

Pearson, Nathan W. 1987. *Goin' to Kansas City*. Urbana, IL: University of Illinois Press.

Ramet, Sabrina Petra, ed. 1994. *Rocking the State: Rock Music and Politics in Eastern Europe and Russia*. Boulder, CO: Westview Press.

Rose, Tricia. 1994. *Black Noise: Rap Music and Black Culture in Contemporary America*. Hanover and London: Wesleyan University Press.

Salewicz, Chris. 1987. 'See You in Court.' *Q* 10: 46–49.

Segrave, Kerry. 1994. *Payola in the Music Industry: A History, 1880–1991*. Jefferson and London: McFarland.

Sharkey, Alix. 1998. 'This Is Not An Act.' *Dazed & Confused* (November): 66–72.

Shuker, Roy. 1998. *Key Concepts in Popular Music*. London and New York: Routledge.

Tanenbaum, Susie J. 1995. *Underground Harmonies: Music and Politics in the Subways of New York*. Ithaca, NY: Cornell University Press.

Tunnell, Kenneth D. 1992. '99 Years Is Almost for Life: Punishment for Violent Crime in Bluegrass Music.' *Journal of Popular Culture* 26(3): 165–81.

Vila, Pablo. 1992. '*Rock Nacional* and Dictatorship in Argentina.' In *Rockin' the Boat: Mass Music and Mass Movements*, ed. Reebee Garofalo. Boston, MA: South End Press, 209–29.

Willett, Ralph. 1989. 'Hot Swing and the Dissolute Life: Youth, Style and Popular Music in Europe 1939–49.' *Popular Music* 8(2): 157–63.

Discographical References

Boney M. 'Ma Baker.' Atlantic K 10965. *1977*: UK.

Brown, James. 'Stagger Lee.' *Cold Sweat*. King 1020. *1967*: USA.

Cash, Johnny. 'Folsom Prison Blues.' Sun 140. *1956*: USA.

Cave, Nick, and the Bad Seeds. 'Stagger Lee.' *Murder Ballads*. Mute/Reprise 46195. *1996*: USA.

Clash, The. 'White Riot.' CBS 5058. *1977*: UK.

Davis, Walter. 'Hijack Blues.' Victor 23343. 1932: USA.

Dead Kennedys. *Frankenchrist*. Alternative Tentacles 45. *1985*: USA.

Domino, Fats. 'Stack & Billy.' *Let's Play Fats Domino*. Imperial 9065. *1959*: USA.

Dylan, Bob. 'George Jackson.' Columbia 45516. *1971*: USA.

Dylan, Bob. 'The Lonesome Death of Hattie Carroll.' *The Times They Are A-Changin'*. Columbia 8905. *1964*: USA.

Grateful Dead, The. 'Stagger Lee.' *Shakedown Street*. Arista 4198. *1978*: USA.

Guthrie, Woody. 'Pretty Boy Floyd.' *Woody Guthrie: The Early Years*. Legacy 345. 1939; *1964*: USA.

Guthrie, Woody. 'Stagolee.' *Woody Guthrie: The Early Years*. Legacy 345. 1941; *1964*: USA.

Hannah, George. 'Gutter Man Blues.' Paramount 12788-A. 1929: USA.

Johnson, Merline. 'Two By Four Blues.' OKeh 06446. 1941: USA.

Journeymen, The. 'Stackolee.' *New Directions in Folk Music*. Capitol ST-1951. *1963*: USA.

Kuti, Fela. 'Coffin for Head of State.' *Coffin for Head of State/Unknown Soldier*. Universal 547379. *2000*: USA.

Lewis, Furry. 'Furry's Blues.' Victor V-38519. 1928: USA.

Madness. 'Shut Up.' Stiff BUY 126. *1981*: UK.

Marley, Bob, and the Wailers. 'I Shot the Sheriff.' *Burnin'*. Island ILPS 9256. *1973*: UK.

Morrissey. 'The Last of the Famous International Playboys.' HMV POP 1620. *1989*: UK.

Murvin, Junior. 'Police and Thieves.' Island WIP 6539. *1980*: UK.

NWA. 'Fuck Tha Police.' *Straight Outta Compton.*
Fourth & Broadway BRLP 534. *1989*: USA.

Prisonaires, The. 'Just Walkin' in the Rain.' Sun 186.
1953: USA.

Rainey, 'Ma.' 'Stack O'Lee Blues.' Paramount 12357.
1925: USA.

2 Live Crew. *As Nasty As They Wanna Be.* Luke 91651-2.
1989: USA.

Tucker, Bessie. 'Got Cut All To Pieces.' Victor 38018.
1928: USA.

JANET HILTS, DAVID BUCKLEY and JOHN SHEPHERD

Cultural Imperialism

The 'Cultural Imperialism Thesis' and Its Opponents

'Cultural imperialism' is a term that has been widely
used to refer to the way in which the cultures of less
developed countries are affected by the arrival of media
forms and technologies associated with 'the West,'
including Western popular music. The 'cultural imperialism thesis' holds that, as the age of direct political and
economic domination by colonial powers has supposedly come to an end, a new, more indirect form of international domination is under way. This involves, in Herbert Schiller's words, the adoption in economically
peripheral countries of 'the values and structures of the
dominating center of the [modern world] system'
(1976, 9).

As Sreberny-Mohammadi (1997) points out, the concept is an 'evocative metaphor' rather than a 'precise
construct' (49). But there are a number of important
issues to which the term potentially draws attention.
One writer (Lee 1980) has provided a useful categorization of such issues: the flow of Western cultural products to the non-West; the ownership of the means of
cultural production and distribution by Western-based
multinationals; the transfer of metropolitan media systems from the West to the non-West; and infringements
on traditional and indigenous ways of life.

The term was at its most popular during the 1970s and
early 1980s, when concern about such developments
found expression in a series of UNESCO reports, seminars and declarations (most notably, the MacBride
Report (UNESCO 1980)). From the early 1980s onward,
however, a paradigm shift occurred in the way radical
writers understood international mass communications.
Those working within critical social science began to
react against the cultural imperialism thesis (see, for
example, Fejes 1981). Some of the most effective critiques of the concept came from scholars of popular
music (for instance, Laing 1986; Goodwin and Gore
1990; Garofalo 1993). The cultural imperialism thesis
was felt to be inadequate for understanding interna-

tional musical flows in the late twentieth century for a
number of reasons.

Firstly, whereas a previous generation of writers was
deeply concerned that Western cultural exports might
inhibit or destroy indigenous cultural traditions (e.g.,
Lomax 1978 (originally published in 1968)), more recent
writers have tended to stress the value of cross-
fertilization, syncretism and 'hybridity' in popular
music. Cultural studies has come to see all cultures as
'hybrids' of older forms (e.g., Chambers 1994), and to
consider the idea of a pure, uncontaminated tradition as
problematic, and even dangerous, because it might serve
to support racism and reactionary versions of nationalism. A number of recent studies have shown how various
local popular musics are the result of complex reinterpretations of imported styles and technologies (for
example, Hatch 1989 on Indonesia; Waterman 1990 on
Nigeria). Often, the imported music is itself the product
of other groups marginalized within the world economy,
such as the Hawaiian guitar-playing that influenced the
Nigerian palm-wine musicians in Waterman's account.
Indeed, much of the popular music that traverses the
globe is the result of the creativity of the African diaspora. Multinationals may control the circulation of this
music, but, given the oppression suffered by the peoples
of the African diaspora over many centuries, it is difficult
to identify jazz, soul, reggae and other forms as simply
the products of a dominant Western culture.

Secondly, whereas the cultural imperialism thesis
tended to assume the negative impact of Western cultural exports, many writers have stressed the creative
and active uses made by audiences of internationally distributed recordings. The internationalization of rock 'n'
roll in the 1960s is often given as an example of how
some 'Western' popular music has encouraged people to
question dominant forms of power in the societies in
which they live. Laing (1986), for example, stresses how
rock 'n' roll was 'an instance of the use of foreign music
by a generation as a means to distance themselves from
a parental "national" culture' (338), and Wicke (1990)
has written about the positive dimensions of this use in
postwar Stalinist Eastern Europe. Countering this, proponents of the cultural imperialism thesis stress that
much of the most prestigious popular music of the world
is sung in English. While local musicians might eventually synthesize distinctive versions of imported music,
such as rap (see Mitchell, 2001), these local variants are
often denigrated by local audiences, as well as by consumers in the more lucrative Anglophone markets. Arguably, too, the emphasis on English in many genres
excludes non-English-speaking audiences from full identification and engagement with the global popular music
on offer. Critics of the cultural imperialism thesis have

claimed, however, that lyrics are relatively unimportant in many key pop genres (e.g., Frith 1991). What is more, Chinese- and Spanish-language shares of global sales are gradually increasing (see *Financial Times: Music and Copyright*, 22 November 1995).

Thirdly, many writers, both those working specifically on popular music and those concerned with world affairs in general, have come to prefer the term 'globalization' to 'cultural imperialism.' In a nutshell, the globalization approach argues that the different parts of the world are increasingly connected, and that the nation-state is diminishing in importance as transnational 'flows' of people, ideas and information intensify. The cultural imperialism thesis was, according to many recent critics, reliant on a model of international power that attributed too much analytical significance to relations between *national* cultures. In studies of the music industry, moreover, some have claimed that the global spread of ownership of the multinationals beyond their traditional power bases in Europe and the United States to the Far East means that it is no longer possible to talk of the countries of the imperial 'center' imposing their popular music on the countries of the 'periphery' (Frith 1991, 267; Garofalo 1993, 22, 27). On the other hand, this may simply entail a reconfiguration of the notion of the center, rather than its eclipse.

Popular music, then, provides some evidence against the cultural imperialism thesis. But even if one should not talk in functionalist terms of the conscious imposition of one set of cultures on another, the logic of the global market means that access to distribution and committed publicity and promotion still seems to be extremely unequal, and this inequality is geographical and nationally differentiated. This may mean that it is possible to hold on to a modified, more precisely stated version of the cultural imperialism thesis. The continuing currency of issues which the term 'globalization' does not always seem adequate to address can be indicated by reference to recent debates surrounding two controversial musical genres: 'Euro-pop' and 'world music.'

Euro-pop

With rare exceptions, continental European popular musicians have often been held in contempt by British and US audiences. 'Euro-pop' was a scathing term for the pidgin English and perceived lack of authentic musicianship among a breed of 1970s and 1980s European acts. Laing (1992, 139) concluded a survey of national and transnational trends in European popular music by speculating that the next U2 might come from Wrocaw or Bratislava. But there have been few signs of the emergence of such groups. In the history of European acts on the global scene, only ABBA has even come close to

being at the center of pop myth, and even its significance since the 1970s has been primarily based on a kitsch aesthetic. Indeed, the mid-1990s saw the reestablishment of London as the European center for the most fashionable pop sounds, whether in dance music or in indie/alternative pop/rock. The power centers are not shifting as quickly as some critics of cultural imperialism have predicted.

World Music

'World music' (often referred to in the United States as 'world beat') was a term adopted by a number of recording and music press entrepreneurs to allow 'non-Western' popular musics to be promoted more adequately in Britain. (The term is also used sometimes to refer to the work of Western musicians who draw on non-Western sources, most notably Paul Simon's *Graceland* album (1986).) Without doubt, some non-Western musicians have achieved international success and recognition. The most notable examples include Nusrat Fateh Ali Khan (Pakistan) and Youssou N'Dour (Senegal). But the impact of such musicians has been very limited. They are enjoyed by a rather older, middle-class audience. They hardly register as popular, either in terms of total sales or in terms of their centrality to global popular culture. In addition, such musicians are often the subject of discourses that see their music as valuable only to the extent that it conforms to certain Western notions of authenticity and tradition (see Feld 1994). Thus, the notion of 'world music' tends to serve as an all-embracing category for that which is not perceived as Western pop, and this in turn functions to exclude non-Western musicians from global pop markets by defining them as exotic (Born and Hesmondhalgh 2000). In this respect, as Goodwin and Gore (1990) point out, world music can be seen as the product of the effects of cultural imperialism, rather than a significant counter to them.

Conclusion

The situation of continental European and non-Western musicians in the international recording industry suggests, then, that, even if the cultural imperialism model has conceptual flaws, as indicated above, the issues that the term was intended to draw attention to have continued to exist in the world of popular music – in particular, systematic global inequalities in cultural prestige and economic profit.

Bibliography

Born, Georgina, and Hesmondhalgh, David, eds. 2000. *Western Music and Its Others: Difference, Representation and Appropriation in Music.* Berkeley and London: University of California Press.

Chambers, Iain. 1994. *Migrancy, Culture, Identity*. London: Routledge.

Fejes, Fred. 1981. 'Media Imperialism: An Assessment.' *Media, Culture and Society* 3(3): 281–89.

Feld, Steven. 1994. 'From Schizophonia to Schismogenesis: On the Discourses and Commodification Practices of "World Music" and "World Beat."' In Charles Keil and Steven Feld, *Music Grooves: Essays and Dialogues*. Chicago and London: University of Chicago Press, 257–89.

Frith, Simon. 1991. 'Anglo-America and Its Discontents.' *Cultural Studies* 5(3): 263–69.

Garofalo, Reebee. 1993. 'Whose World, What Beat: The Transnational Music Industry, Identity, and Cultural Imperialism.' *The World of Music* 35(2): 16–32.

Goodwin, Andrew, and Gore, Joe. 1990. 'World Beat and the Cultural Imperialism Debate.' *Socialist Review* 20(3): 63–80.

Hatch, Martin. 1989. 'Popular Music in Indonesia.' In *World Music, Politics and Social Change*, ed. Simon Frith. Manchester: Manchester University Press, 47–67.

Laing, Dave. 1986. 'The Music Industry and the "Cultural Imperialism" Thesis.' *Media, Culture and Society* 8(3): 331–41.

Laing, Dave. 1992. '"Sadeness," Scorpions and Single Markets: National and Transnational Trends in European Popular Music.' *Popular Music* 11(2): 127–40.

Lee, Chin-Chuan. 1980. *Media Imperialism Reconsidered: The Homogenizing of Television Culture*. Beverly Hills, CA: Sage.

Lomax, Alan. 1978 (1968). *Folk Song Style and Structure*. New Brunswick, NJ: Transaction Books.

Mitchell, Tony, ed. 2001. *Global Noise: Rap and Hip-Hop Outside the USA*. Middletown, CT: Wesleyan University Press.

Rutten, Paul. 1991. 'Local Popular Music on the National and International Markets.' *Cultural Studies* 5(3): 294–305.

Schiller, Herbert. 1976. *Communication and Cultural Domination*. New York: International Arts and Science Press.

Sreberny-Mohammadi, Annabelle. 1997. 'The Many Cultural Faces of Imperialism.' In *Beyond Cultural Imperialism: Globalization, Communication and the New International Order*, ed. Peter Golding and Phil Harris. London: Sage, 49–68.

Tomlinson, John. 1991. *Cultural Imperialism: A Critical Introduction*. London: Pinter.

UNESCO. 1980. *Many Voices, One World*. Paris: UNESCO.

Waterman, Christopher A. 1990. *Jùjú: A Social History and Ethnography of an African Popular Music*. Chicago: University of Chicago Press.

Wicke, Peter. 1990. *Rock Music: Culture, Aesthetics and Sociology*. Cambridge: Cambridge University Press.

Discographical Reference

Simon, Paul. *Graceland*. Warner Brothers WX 52. *1986*: UK.

DAVID HESMONDHALGH

Cultural Policy/Regulation

'Cultural policy' denotes the ensemble of actions undertaken by governments to foster artistic and media production at a national or local level. According to a committee of experts appointed by the Council of Europe, the primary purpose of cultural policy is 'to preserve the national heritage and to pass it on to future generations, as well as to support artistic creation in all its diversity. It is also about disseminating all forms of culture, from the oldest to the most modern, across as wide an audience as possible, to make art more accessible' (Council of Europe 1997, 230).

The origins of national policies in Europe can be traced to state support for the establishment of museums and public libraries in the mid-nineteenth century. McGuigan (1996, 54) has traced four 'discursive moments' in British cultural policy: social control; national prestige; social access; and value for money. These themes, in varying configurations, can be found in the evolution of cultural policy in many other nation-states.

With the prominent exception of the United States, national governments throughout the world develop and administer cultural policies, usually through a specific Ministry of Culture. The most common policy measure is the provision of state funding for specific institutions or projects.

In the case of music, national, regional and local governments in Western Europe have generally favored institutions such as opera houses and symphony orchestras which reproduce the European art music tradition. The various forms of popular music were, until relatively recently, denied support either because they were seen as aesthetically inferior or because they were tainted by association with 'commercialism' (Malm 1982, 45), or both. The position was different in the USSR and other Communist states. While classical music organizations were strongly supported, funding was also provided for state-sponsored folk music and dance ensembles and even for rock music, notably in the former GDR (Wicke and Shepherd 1993; Maas and Reszel 1998). Folk ensembles and modern dance orchestras were supported by the state in newly independent African countries with socialist ideologies, such as Guinea and Mali, in the 1960s and 1970s.

By the early 1990s, Bennett et al. (1993) could claim

that 'within Europe, North America and Australia the role of government has become a crucial factor in the structural organization of rock music at the local, the national and ultimately at the global level' (9). They stressed four areas where governments had placed rock as part of their agenda: arts budgets; social welfare programs; employment and training programs; and the defense of national identity (1993, 9–10). Wallis and Malm (1984) showed that 'government attitudes towards national styles of popular music began to change in the Seventies' (219) and extended the consideration of music policies to developing countries (see also Wallis and Malm 1993).

In most countries, however, popular music receives a very small amount of the music budget. In the case of the United Kingdom, the proportion given to nonclassical music has been only 2 percent. Additionally, certain types of popular music have been favored in many countries. Again, in Britain, jazz and the musics of ethnic minorities have received subsidies for touring, while rock and pop music have received less funding. Initiatives taken by city governments in Britain in the 1980s to support local recording and performance venues have been analyzed by Frith (1993) and Street (1993).

The position of popular music vis-à-vis cultural policy has been enhanced in recent years in countries where governments have re-branded the arts as 'cultural industries,' 'copyright industries' or 'creative industries.' In these circumstances, popular music has been recognized as a prime site for social inclusion (i.e., the integration of alienated minorities into mainstream society), job creation and the generation of export earnings, including those from tourism. As one of the copyright industries, the music industry has been able, with mixed success, to lobby governments for reforms in intellectual property legislation.

The training and education policies of some national governments have been influenced both by the social inclusion issue and by the recognition of popular music as a valuable industry. A Centre for Aboriginal Studies in Music was set up in 1975 at the University of Adelaide in Australia. In the United Kingdom, as part of a government initiative, a 'New Deal for Musicians' was introduced in 1999 to provide training for young unemployed musicians.

Music export agencies were established with government backing in The Netherlands (Conamus, 1962), Australia (Export Music Australia, 1988), France (Le Bureau Export de la Musique française, 1993) and Sweden (Export Music Sweden, 1993). In other countries, state agencies give financial support for representatives from music publishers and record companies to attend international trade fairs such as MIDEM (Marché d'Industrie de Disque et d'Editions Musicale) in France and PopKomm in Germany.

State support for popular music has also taken the form of 'cultural protectionism' (Wright 1991), usually through a limitation of the amount of foreign-produced music broadcast on radio. Such measures have been introduced, for example, in Australia, Canada and France. In Canada, the CanCon (Canadian content) rules, legislated in 1970 to take effect in January 1971, required stations to broadcast a minimum of 30 percent Canadian music as a condition of license renewal (Wright 1991).

France and Canada have the most complex systems of state support for popular music. The French system dates from the formation of the Centre d'information du rock by the populist-socialist Minister of Culture Jack Lang in 1984 (Looseley 1995). This was a recognition that popular music was worthy of support in its own right as an art form. (A similar institution, SPN (Stichting Popmuziek Nederland – a national institute for rock and pop music), was financed by the Dutch government.) Much subsequent funding for popular music in France and several other European countries has been provided by subventions from the private copying levy paid by distributors of blank media and from a redistributive tax on concert tickets. This funding is typically used to subsidize training schemes, recording projects and small concert venues.

In addition to the CanCon rules, the Canadian government established the Sound Recording Development Program in 1986. The aim of this program was to stimulate the production of Canadian content recordings and the development of the Canadian industry infrastructure. Three of the six components of the program are administered by FACTOR (the Foundation to Assist Canadian Talent on Records), a private, nonprofit organization which, in also administering the contributions of its 16 sponsoring broadcasters, is dedicated to providing assistance toward the growth and development of the Canadian independent recording industry. In 1994, FACTOR distributed over Can\$3 million to 568 projects, ranging from sound recordings to international tours proposed by members of the English-speaking record industry.

As well as receiving financial and other support for its expansion, popular music is subject to various forms of restriction and regulation by different government ministries. Performers and promoters of live music must comply with rules governing crowd safety, noise levels and the sale of alcohol. In many countries, performance venues must also be licensed by local state agencies. There are further rules governing foreign performers, who may need to apply for immigration permits and may be subject to a 'withholding tax' on their fees. In performance and on record, musicians are required to comply with censorship rules in some countries.

Bibliography

Bennett, Tony, et al., eds. 1993. *Rock and Popular Music: Politics, Policies, Institutions*. London: Routledge.

Council of Europe. 1997. *Cultural Policy in the Russian Federation*. Strasbourg: Council of Europe Publishing.

Frith, Simon. 1993. 'Popular Music and the Local State.' In *Rock and Popular Music: Politics, Policies, Institutions*, ed. Tony Bennett et al. London: Routledge, 14–24.

Looseley, David L. 1995. *The Politics of Fun: Cultural Policy and Debate in Contemporary France*. Oxford: Berg.

Maas, Georg, and Reszel, Hartmut. 1998. 'Whatever Happened to . . .: The Decline and Renaissance of Rock in the Former GDR.' *Popular Music* 17(3): 267–77.

Malm, Krister. 1982. 'Phonograms and Cultural Policy in Sweden.' In *The Phonogram in Cultural Communication*, ed. Kurt Blaukopf. Vienna and New York: Springer-Verlag, 43–73.

McGuigan, Jim. 1996. *Culture and the Public Sphere*. London and New York: Routledge.

Street, John. 1993. 'Local Differences?: Popular Music and the Local State.' *Popular Music* 12(1): 43–55.

Wallis, Roger, and Malm, Krister. 1984. *Big Sounds from Small Peoples: The Music Industry in Small Countries*. London: Constable.

Wallis, Roger, and Malm, Krister. 1993. *Media Policy and Music Activity*. London: Routledge.

Wicke, Peter, and Shepherd, John. 1993. '"The Cabaret Is Dead": Rock Culture as State Enterprise – The Political Organization of Rock in East Germany.' In *Rock and Popular Music: Politics, Policies, Institutions*, ed. Tony Bennett et al. London: Routledge, 25–36.

Wright, Robert. 1991 '"Gimme Shelter": Observations on Cultural Protectionism and the Recording Industry in Canada.' *Cultural Studies* 5(3): 306–16.

DAVE LAING

Death

Death has long been a theme of popular song in Western culture, reflecting that society's fascination with and uncertainty about it, as opposed to the stoic realism some other societies display in relation to the topic. English-language nursery rhymes, for example, a genre developed in an age in which child mortality was high, are littered with references to maiming and death ('Three Blind Mice,' 'Jack and Jill,' 'Ring-a-Ring-a-Roses,' 'Oranges and Lemons' and 'Humpty Dumpty' are among the best known). Death, as personified by the scythe-wielding skeleton leveler, or the grim figure of the undertaker or hangman, became part of the collective con-

sciousness of Western thought, and the ever-present threat of pestilence, famine, disease, war and capital punishment ensured that death was a constant motif not only in music, but also in the pictorial arts, literature (in the form of the elegy) and the theater.

Perhaps the first popular songs that dealt directly with death were the eighteenth-century 'murder ballads,' which were further developed in North American popular song in the nineteenth and twentieth centuries and remained popular through to the 1990s (see the work of Australian singer Nick Cave in particular). Throughout the nineteenth century, the War of 1812, the Crimean War, the American Civil War and the Boer War were marked by songs dealing with death on the battlefield, and widowhood. According to journalist Alan Clayson (1992), however, the first 'death discs' (that is, the first popular recorded hits dealing with death) were Theodore F. Morse's and Edward Madden's 1903 song 'Two Little Boys,' recorded by Rolf Harris in 1969, and the 1910 recording 'Don't Go Down in the Mine, Dad.'

The various genres of popular music have tended to have their own distinctive ways of dealing with the topic of death. In light entertainment, death was viewed in a mildly humorous way, such as in Leslie Sarony's 'Ain't It Grand To Be Blooming Well Dead.' In the blues tradition, the songs tended to have a greater realism – for example, Blind Lemon Jefferson's 'Hangman's Blues,' Bukka White's 'Fixin' to Die Blues' (covered by Bob Dylan in 1962) and St. Louis Jimmy's 'Going Down Slow.' Blues performers often led violent lives and met equally violent ends, and nowhere was this outlaw recklessness better expressed than in the work of Leadbelly. His self-styled 'devil's ditties,' written while he was in prison, included 'Black Girl,' which told the tale of a train driver who perished in a crash: 'His head was found on the driving wheel but his body has never been found' (Clayson 1992, 24).

The realism of the blues was, as 'Black Girl' shows, often tempered by a moralizing, almost voyeuristic sense of black humor. The country and western tradition also included a number of songs dealing with death and disaster, often in a more overtly patriarchal tone, with family values well to the fore. Vernon Dalhart's 'The Wreck of the Old '97,' later covered by Johnny Cash, was, in 1924, the first country and western song to become a million-seller.

By the early 1960s, there was a recognizable death cult within popular music, activated by the deaths of a number of the icons of popular culture, in particular James Dean. Again, there were semi-comic songs, sometimes with a necrophiliac overtone, like Jimmy Cross's 'I Want My Baby Back' (1965), which has since become a cult classic. There also existed a tradition of sentimental pop hits about death, such as Bobby Goldsboro's 'Honey' (1968). A more serious and dramatic engagement with the theme can be found in the work of singers such as Jacques Brel (with 'If You Go Away,' 'Seasons in the Sun' and 'My Death') and, through Brel's influence in particular, the Walker Brothers ('Nite Flights' and 'The Electrician'). But perhaps the quintessential death song was 'Leader of the Pack' (1964) from the all-girl group the Shangri-Las.

It was in the period following the mid-1960s that death became a more pervasive theme in the lyrics of popular songs. As Cooper (1991) concludes, 'the death theme became more visible and more broadly explored in popular lyrics after 1965' (82). During the 1970s, certain styles of hard rock, most significantly heavy metal, death metal and goth, were directly dependent on the iconography of death – voodoo (via Screamin' Jay Hawkins) and horror (particularly the figure of the undead Count Dracula). And by the 1970s and 1980s, rock music had also begun to respond to the growing number of rock star fatalities, notably with David Bowie's 'Rock 'n' Roll Suicide' (1972) and Kate Bush's 'Blow Away' (1980).

This vein of songwriting was connected to, although separate from, tributes responding to the deaths of important figures in popular culture, including musicians. Tribute songs go back as far as the early part of the twentieth century. Early examples include 'There's a New Star in Heaven Tonight – Rudolph Valentino,' recorded in 1926 by Vernon Dalhart (Valentino died in 1926), 'Death of Jimmie Rodgers,' recorded in 1934 by Bradley Kincaid (Rodgers died in 1933), and 'Death of Bessie Smith,' recorded in 1939 by Booker T. Washington (Bessie Smith was killed in a car crash in 1937). More recent examples include Elton John's 'Candle in the Wind,' a song written in 1973 as a tribute to Marilyn Monroe (who died in 1962), which became a hit in 1974. In 1997, the lyrics were rewritten by Bernie Taupin (the lyricist of the original song) so that 'Candle in the Wind' could be sung by Elton John as a tribute to Princess Diana at her funeral.

Rock music's detractors, whether they be self-styled consumer watchdog committees or representatives of religious communities, have alleged that hard rock's insistent beat and loud volume, on a song such as the Blue Öyster Cult's '(Don't Fear) The Reaper' (itself a song about a suicide pact), can, through its tribalistic musicality, actually influence the behavior of fans. It has also been claimed that instructions to kill, or other various satanic messages, have been encoded subliminally within popular music texts (a process called 'backmasking'), in the form of backward messages and loops. The link between some Beatles' tracks, such as

'Blackbird,' 'Piggies' and 'Helter Skelter,' and the activities of the Manson family and the Sharon Tate murder provides evidence for this way of thinking. Further evidence is provided through the case of one fan, Richard Dickinson, who, believing himself to be the evil Isis of the Bob Dylan song 'One More Cup of Coffee,' stamped his mother to death and poured coffee granules on her corpse. Hard-rock acts, including Ozzy Osbourne and Judas Priest, have been the subject of unsuccessful lawsuits seeking to connect the suicide of fans to subliminal messages encoded in their music. The live stage shows of hard-rock performers have also been linked to teen suicide. For example, in 1974 a 13-year-old fan hanged himself after watching a fake hanging sequence at an Alice Cooper concert.

At rock concerts, fatalities occasioned by inadequate facilities or unsatisfactory policing are comparatively rare, although one fan was stabbed to death by Hell's Angels entrusted by the band with security duties at the Rolling Stones' Altamont gig in 1969, and 11 fans died after a stampede at a Who concert in 1979. There have also been isolated, but high-profile incidences of fans being crushed to death. The death of a 14-year-old at a David Cassidy concert in 1974 led to London's local authorities imposing a partial ban on selected rock acts in the mid- to late 1970s. The *Rock Concert Safety Survey Reports*, which have been published each year since 1992 by Crowd Management Strategies, review popular concert and festival crowd safety incidents, including deaths, on a worldwide basis.

Certain causes of death are particularly associated with performers: accidental overdose (Keith Moon, Jimi Hendrix, Nick Drake and Janis Joplin), alcoholism (John Bonham, Hank Williams), accidental electrocution (ex-Yardbird Keith Relf, Stone the Crows' Les Harvey), car crashes (Eddie Cochran, Harry Chapin, Falco), airplane crashes (Otis Redding, Glenn Miller, Jim Reeves, John Denver), shootings, either accidental (as in the case of Johnny Ace after a round of Russian roulette) or intentional (John Lennon, Marvin Gaye), and, to a lesser extent, stabbings (Nancy Spungen). Very often, the cause of death is a combination of intoxicants or the presence of high levels of intoxicants leading to death by other means, such as drowning (the Beach Boys' Dennis Wilson) or asphyxiation ('Mama' Cass Elliot). Suicide is comparatively uncommon, with Joy Division's Ian Curtis and Nirvana's Kurt Cobain the best known.

Popular musicians have also died in political circumstances, the case of Víctor Jara in Chile in 1973 being one of the best known. Jara, who was an essential part of the *nueva canción* movement in Latin America associated with socialist, revolutionary activities, was killed with other political prisoners by the military after the coup that ousted Salvador Allende as president of Chile. Another instance of the popular musician as martyr is to be found in 1998, with the murder of the Algerian singer Lounes Matoub by his political enemies. Matoub was a leader of the campaign to rehabilitate the Berber heritage in Algeria. His death resulted in riots, with his funeral being attended by thousands of mourners. Matoub's songs gave expression to a common Berber inheritance and in this way provided a focus for the Berber movement.

Pop writers and aficionados have pointed to some bizarre coincidences with regard to rock star death, thereby adding an important component to the mythology surrounding pop music. For instance, 'Mama' Cass Elliot and Keith Moon died in the same Curzon Place apartment in Mayfair, London, and Otis Redding had recently recorded 'The Dock of the Bay' when his light aircraft crashed into a lake near Madison, Wisconsin in 1967. Likewise, Eddie Cochran had just recorded 'Three Steps to Heaven' before he was killed in 1960. And the most popular song by Lynyrd Skynyrd, half of whom were killed in an airplane crash in 1977, was 'Free Bird.'

The deaths of a number of rock icons, most notably those of Buddy Holly (1959), Jimi Hendrix (1970), Jim Morrison (1971), Elvis Presley (1977), John Lennon (1980), Bob Marley (1981) and Kurt Cobain (1994), have had a huge impact on popular culture. Holly's death was utilized in Don McLean's 'American Pie' (1971) 'to symbolize the end of American innocence' (Cooper 1991, 86). In the case of the politically active Marley, his death was treated as an occasion for national mourning in his home country of Jamaica, and his funeral afforded the same gravitas and ceremony usually reserved for a head of state, a unique phenomenon within popular music. Lennon's and Cobain's deaths not only gave rise to myriad conspiracy theories, but were taken to symbolize cultural endings (to the 1960s' counterculture and the 'Generation X' of the early 1990s' 'slacker' culture, respectively). Presley's death, probably through a self-administered overdose of prescription drugs, has had the greatest impact. An estimated 1.5 million fans visited his grave in the first year after his death. So profound a shock was his death that a number of cults, sects and fan groupings formed, variously claiming that their idol is still alive or worshiping him as a secular deity (see Marcus 1991; Denisoff and Plasketes 1995). A linked phenomenon, and an important part of the mythologization of popular music, is the belief that some living rock performers – for example, Sir Paul McCartney and Bob Dylan – are, in fact, dead, their places taken by impostors. The Beatles' albums *Sergeant Pepper's Lonely Hearts Club Band* (1967) and *Abbey Road* (1969) have been subjected to detailed scrutiny by conspiracy theorists looking for clues to McCartney's alleged 'death.'

New technologies such as sampling have facilitated some macabre and, some would say, inappropriate duets between dead and living artists. The long-dead duo of Patsy Cline and Jim Reeves sang together on 'Have You Ever Been Lonely?' in 1981, while, in 1991, Natalie Cole sang 'with' her dead father, using his 1951 vocal track for the award-winning 'Unforgettable'; Nat 'King' Cole also 'appeared' in the video. Finally, in 1995, the three remaining Beatles took unreleased John Lennon vocal tracks from the late 1970s and constructed two 'new' Beatles' songs for their *Anthology* boxed set.

Indeed, death can be used as an effective promotional tool, and the exploitation of a dead artist's back-catalog product, together with film and media tie-ins, publishing deals, trademarking and other promotional devices, can be very lucrative. As writer George Melly (1970) aptly put it, 'Death is the one certain way to preserve a pop legend, because age, in itself, is considered a compromise' (32).

The variety of contemporary, or near contemporary, songs dealing with death is considerable, ranging, for example, from those concerned with mass murders to those psychotically comedic in character. Songs like 'Dachau Blues' by Captain Beefheart (1969) and the Sex Pistols' 'Belsen Was a Gas' (1978) appropriate, in an apolitical manner, a particular historical moment of mass murder and suffering for its shock content. The Beatles' 'Maxwell's Silver Hammer' (1969) continues the comedic, nursery-rhyme-influenced tradition of songs about death, while 'I Don't Like Mondays' by the Boomtown Rats (1979) alludes to a real-life incident of mass killing. A detailed analysis of the considerable number of more contemporary songs in which death is a theme can be found in Cooper (1991, 82–93).

Musicologist Philip Tagg (1990) has shown that the global phenomenon of death has given rise to a wide variety of music all over the world. In Northern European societies, funeral music is commonly quiet, slow-paced and composed in a minor key. It often deploys what Tagg identifies as 'an aeolian pendulum,' with a B minor to G progression common. However, in other cultures it can be very different indeed, and unrecognizable as funeral music to Western ears. For example, in West African culture, quick, energetic music is played at the funeral of a young person, the tempo of the musical accompaniment reflecting the age of the deceased. Interestingly, Tagg discusses how certain post-1966 Western rock songs, including the Kinks' 'Dead End Street,' David Bowie's '1984' and Bob Dylan's and Jimi Hendrix's 'All Along the Watchtower,' deploy the same aeolian chordal progression associated with classical requiems. Significantly, many of these aeolian rock songs deal with dystopian, gloomy or disquieting themes. Other earlier attempts in popular music to deliberately create an eerie, morbid musical setting, such as the Vaughn Monroe 1949 hit '(Ghost) Riders in the Sky,' also commonly used the aeolian mode. David Bowie's 'Warszawa' (1977), the Stranglers' 'Waltz in Black' (1981), Japan's 'Ghosts' (1982), and Elton John's 'Funeral for a Friend' (1973) and 'Song for Guy' (1978) are more recent examples of the appropriation of these musical symbols of the macabre in mainstream popular music.

Perhaps the best-known association between popular music, death and funerals is to be found in New Orleans' tradition of jazz funerals. When jazz funerals began remains uncertain, but it may be assumed that they emerged from music funerals after the period of Reconstruction in the South (1863–77) and have continued ever since the turn of the century, although their prominence and popularity have waxed and waned over the years. Created to mark the passing of a significant person within the community, jazz funerals have become notable for the singing and dancing of the second line, the musicians and performers who follow the first line of family members and mourners as the funeral processes from the home of the deceased to the church, from the church to the cemetery, and from the cemetery back onto the streets. Jazz funerals are so named because their rules of performance emulate the spirit of jazz: freedom, spontaneity, polyphony and improvisation. However, along with jazz, the music performed at jazz funerals can include blues, gospel, spirituals and hip-hop. Performances by the second line as jazz funerals progress through the streets are characterized by imitation, parody and signifying, all usually reflections on the life and personality of the deceased. Since the 1970s, the second line has gained in importance in comparison with the first line, as jazz funerals have played a greater role in the tourist and heritage industries of New Orleans, and have become increasingly commercialized.

Bibliography

Clayson, Alan. 1992. *Death Discs*. London: Gollancz.

Cooper, B. Lee. 1991. *Popular Music Perspectives: Ideas, Themes, and Patterns in Contemporary Lyrics*. Bowling Green, OH: Bowling Green State University Popular Press.

Denisoff, R. Serge, and Plasketes, George. 1995. *True Disbelievers: The Elvis Contagion*. New Brunswick, NJ: Transaction.

Herman, Gary. 1994. *Rock 'n' Roll Babylon*. London: Plexus.

Kein, Sybil. 1995. 'The Celebration of Life in New Orleans Jazz Funerals.' In *Feasts and Celebrations in North American Ethnic Communities*, ed. Ramón A. Gutiérrez and Geneviève Fabre. Albuquerque, NM: University of New Mexico Press, 101–10.

Lomax, Alan. 1993. *The Land Where the Blues Began*. London: Methuen.

Malone, Bill C. 1985. *Country Music, U.S.A.* Rev. ed. Austin, TX: University of Texas Press.

Marcus, Greil. 1991. *Dead Elvis: A Chronicle of a Cultural Obsession*. New York: Doubleday.

Marcus, Greil. 1993. 'Rock Death in the 1970s: A Sweepstakes.' In Greil Marcus, *In the Fascist Bathroom: Writings on Punk, 1977–1992*. London: Viking, 57–78.

Melly, George. 1970. *Revolt into Style: The Pop Arts in Britain*. London: Allen Lane.

Ostendorf, Berndt. 1996. 'The Cultural Exceptionalism of New Orleans' Music.' In *Demokratie und Kunst in Amerika* [Democracy and Art in the United States], ed. Olaf Hansen and Thomas Liesemann. Trieste: Edizione Parnaso, 93–101.

Ostendorf, Berndt, with Smith, Mike. 2000. 'Jazz Funerals and the Second Line: African American Celebration and Public Space in New Orleans.' In *Ceremonies and Spectacles: Performing American Culture*, ed. Teresa Alves, Teresa Cid and Heinz Ickstadt. Amsterdam: VU University Press, 238–72.

Rock Concert Safety Survey Reports. http://www.crowdsafe.com/reports.html

Shapiro, Harry. 1988. *Waiting for the Man: The Story of Drugs and Popular Music*. London and New York: Quartet.

Smith, Michael P. 1994. 'Behind the Lines: The Black Mardi Gras Indians and the New Orleans Second Line.' *Black Music Research Journal* 14(1): 43–73.

Sutcliffe, Phil. 1994. 'Bloody Hell.' Q 91: 30–31.

Tagg, Philip. 1990. '"Universal" Music and the Case of Death.' In *La musica come linguaggio universale: genesi e storia de un'idea* [Music as Universal Language: The Birth and History of an Idea], ed. Raffaele Pozzi. Firenze: Olschki, 227–65.

Sheet Music

Geddes, Will, comp., and Donnelly, Robert, lyr. 1910. 'Don't Go Down in the Mine, Dad.' London: Wright.

Morse, Theodore F., comp., and Madden, Edward, lyr. 1903. 'Two Little Boys.' London: Herman Darewski Music Publishing Co.

Discographical References

Beatles, The. *Abbey Road*. Apple PCS 7088. *1969*: UK.

Beatles, The. *Anthology 1*. Apple CDPCSP 727. *1995*: UK.

Beatles, The. 'Blackbird.' *The Beatles [White Album]*. Apple PMC/PCS 7067-8. *1968*: UK.

Beatles, The. 'Helter Skelter.' *The Beatles [White Album]*. Apple PMC/PCS 7067-8. *1968*: UK.

Beatles, The. 'Maxwell's Silver Hammer.' *Abbey Road*. Apple PCS 7088. *1969*: UK.

Beatles, The. 'Piggies.' *The Beatles [White Album]*. Apple PMC/PCS 7067-8. *1968*: UK.

Beatles, The. *Sergeant Pepper's Lonely Hearts Club Band*. Parlophone PCS 7027. *1967*: UK.

Blue Öyster Cult. '(Don't Fear) The Reaper.' Columbia 10384. *1976*: USA.

Boomtown Rats, The. 'I Don't Like Mondays.' Ensign ENY 30. *1979*: UK.

Bowie, David. '1984.' *Diamond Dogs*. RCA-Victor APL 1-0576. *1974*: UK.

Bowie, David. 'My Death.' *Ziggy Stardust*. RCA 4862. 1973; *1983*: UK.

Bowie. David. 'Rock 'n' Roll Suicide.' *The Rise and Fall of Ziggy Stardust and the Spiders from Mars*. RCA-Victor SF/PK 8267. *1972*: UK.

Bowie, David. 'Warszawa.' *Low*. RCA-Victor PL 12030. *1977*: UK.

Brel, Jacques. 'La Mort.' *La Valse a Mille Temps*. Barclay 816721-2. *1958*: France.

Brel, Jacques. 'Le Moribond.' *Ne Me Quitte Pas*. Barclay 816729-2. *1972*: France.

Brel, Jacques. 'Ne Me Quitte Pas.' *Ne Me Quitte Pas*. Barclay 816729-2. *1972*: France.

Bush, Kate. 'Blow Away.' *Never for Ever*. EMI EMA 794. *1980*: UK.

Captain Beefheart and His Magic Band. 'Dachau Blues.' *Trout Mask Replica*. Straight RS 2027. *1969*: USA.

Cash, Johnny. 'The Wreck of the Old '97.' *Johnny Cash at San Quentin*. Columbia CS 9827. *1969*: USA.

Cline, Patsy, with Reeves, Jim. 'Have You Ever Been Lonely?' RCA 12346. *1981*: USA.

Cochran, Eddie. 'Three Steps to Heaven.' London HLG 9115. *1960*: UK.

Cole, Natalie, with Cole, Nat 'King.' 'Unforgettable.' Elektra 64875. *1991*: USA.

Cross, Jimmy. 'I Want My Baby Back.' Tollie 9039. *1965*: USA.

Dalhart, Vernon. 'The Prisoner's Song'/'The Wreck of the Old '97.' Victor 19427. 1924: USA.

Dalhart, Vernon. 'There's a New Star in Heaven Tonight – Rudolph Valentino'/'I Lost a Wonderful Pal.' Columbia 718-D. 1926: USA.

Dylan, Bob. 'Fixin' to Die Blues.' *Bob Dylan*. Columbia 8579. *1962*: USA.

Dylan, Bob. 'One More Cup of Coffee.' *Desire*. Columbia 33893. *1976*: USA.

Goldsboro, Bobby. 'Honey.' United Artists 50283. *1968*: USA.

Harris, Rolf. 'Two Little Boys.' Columbia DB 8630. *1969*: UK.

Jacks, Terry. 'If You Go Away.' Bell 1362. *1974*: UK.

Jacks, Terry. 'Seasons in the Sun.' Bell 1344. *1974*: UK.

Japan. 'Ghosts.' Virgin VS 472. *1982*: UK.

Jefferson, Blind Lemon. 'Hangman's Blues.' Paramount 12679. 1928: USA.

Jimi Hendrix Experience, The. 'All Along the Watchtower.' Reprise 0767. *1968*: USA.

John, Elton. 'Candle in the Wind.' *Goodbye Yellow Brick Road*. MCA 10003. *1973*: USA.

John, Elton. 'Funeral for a Friend.' *Goodbye Yellow Brick Road*. MCA 10003. *1973*: USA.

John, Elton. 'Something About the Way You Look Tonight'/'Candle in the Wind 1997.' A&M 568108. *1997*: USA.

John, Elton. 'Song for Guy.' *A Single Man*. MCA 3027. *1978*: USA.

Kincaid, Bradley. 'Death of Jimmie Rodgers'/'Jimmie Rodgers' Life.' Bluebird 5377. 1934: USA.

Kinks, The. 'Dead End Street.' Pye 7N 17222. *1966*: UK.

Ledbetter, Huddie (Leadbelly). 'Black Girl.' *Rock Island Line*. Smithsonian/Folkways 2014. 1951: USA.

Lynyrd Skynyrd. 'Free Bird.' MCA 40328. *1975*: USA.

McLean, Don. 'American Pie – Parts I & II.' United Artists 50856. *1971*: USA.

Monroe, Vaughn. '(Ghost) Riders in the Sky'/'Single Saddle.' Victor 20-3411. 1949: USA.

Redding, Otis. 'The Dock of the Bay.' *The Dock of the Bay*. Volt 419. *1968*: USA.

Sarony, Leslie. 'Ain't It Grand To Be Blooming Well Dead.' Imperial 2688. 1932: UK.

Sex Pistols, The. 'Belsen Was a Gas.' *The Great Rock & Roll Swindle*. Virgin 2510. *1978*: UK.

Shangri-Las, The. 'Leader of the Pack.' Red Bird 014. *1964*: USA.

St. Louis Jimmy. 'Going Down Slow.' Bluebird B8889. 1941: USA.

Stranglers, The. 'Waltz in Black.' *The Men in Black*. Liberty LBG 30313. *1981*: UK.

Walker Brothers, The. 'Nite Flights.' *Nite Flights*. GTO GTLP 033. *1978*: UK.

Walker Brothers, The. 'The Electrician.' *Nite Flights*. GTO GTLP 033. *1978*: UK.

Washington, Booker T. 'Death of Bessie Smith.' Bluebird B8352. 1939: USA.

White, Bukka. 'Fixin' to Die Blues.' Vocalion 05588. 1940: USA.

DAVID BUCKLEY with JOHN SHEPHERD and BERNDT OSTENDORF

Deviance

Deviant behavior may be defined as behavior that deviates from what is considered acceptable within any given society at any given time, and for this reason it is not an absolute, fixed and immutable over time. For example, following the Judeo-Christian tradition, which has tended to consider it a form of pathology, Freud viewed homosexuality as a form of deviant behavior, a notion that subsequent psychoanalytic theory has questioned. By contrast, in upper-class society in the ancient world, homosexuality was seen as normal. Likewise, although transvestism has been regarded as a form of deviant behavior in various cultures, in ancient Greece it was socially acceptable. A classic discussion of this kind of relativistic 'boundary maintenance' with regard to 'normal' and 'deviant' phenomena on a cross-cultural basis is to be found in Mary Douglas's book *Purity and Danger* (1966).

Musicians and performers have been looked upon as constituting deviant groups on a remarkably cross-cultural basis. In a seminal discussion, Merriam (1964) notes the way that, in many 'traditional' societies, musicians customarily engage in behavior that in other individuals would be regarded as deviant. The attitude toward musicians in these societies is, however, often ambivalent, as Merriam notes: '[I]n such cases there is a definite question as to whether the attitude towards musicians is not ambivalent and whether musicians may not in fact occupy a special situation in which behaviour not tolerated in others is considered acceptable, or is at least tolerated for them' (1964, 134). Musicians can in this way be argued to provide an important form of mediation 'between order and disorder, between that which is safe and normal, and that which is dangerous and powerful' (Shepherd 1977, 72). This connection to and mediation of deviant phenomena and behavior on the part of musicians can be regarded as an institutionalization of a society's or culture's capacity to react to the unforeseen, to challenges presented to it both externally and internally. In the latter instance, musical activities often seem to provide a safe forum within which the airing of grievances as well as of challenges to authority can be handled safely, thus ensuring social stability. A detailed discussion of such processes in the case of the Tiv of Nigeria is provided by Keil (1979).

Musicians and performers within a variety of Western cultures over the last two millennia have equally been regarded as deviant, but often with less tolerance for, and appreciation of, the possibly positive social role that deviance can fulfill. The itinerant performer, for instance, was frequently dubbed an 'out-caste,' a symbolic link to those pagan forces of disorder and revelry that the Judeo-Christian tradition has often sought to repress and control. In medieval Europe, for example, traveling players were classified as vagabonds. Many forms of popular entertainment in the early modern period, such as the pantomime, the circus and the traveling play, contained a figure such as Harlequin, a devilish, cross-dressing man/woman figure, and, in turn, an antecedent of the gender-bending tradition in rock. A more contemporary example of behavior defined as deviant and deserving of sanctions within the Judeo-Christian tradition is to be found in the curtailing in 1996 of the careers of US Christian music singers Michael English and Marabeth Jordan, when it emerged that they had had an adulterous affair.

Deviance in music is, indeed, as often as not gendered, and linked to issues of sexuality. This aspect of deviance can be argued to have had a particular effect on the role of women as musicians. As ethnomusicologist Ellen Koskoff (1989) has observed: 'In most societies, a woman's identity is believed to be embedded in her sexuality; that is, she is seen (and may see herself) primarily as a sexual partner, childbearer, and nurturer. Thus, one of the most common associations between women and music ... links women's primary sexual identity and role with music performance.' One way in which sexuality affects music performance, concludes Koskoff, is through the manner in which 'cultural beliefs in women's inherent sexuality may motivate the separation of or restriction upon women's musical activities' (1989, 6). These beliefs are 'often expressed in terms of menstruation taboos or in anxiety about women's insatiable and destructive sexual appetites' (Koskoff 1989, 7). Transgression of this separation or restriction is frequently regarded as deviant behavior that compromises the moral standing of the women in question. In discussing the merengue music of the Dominican Republic, for example, Austerlitz (1997) reports that, in an air of male-dominated sexuality, 'many Dominicans believe that unaccompanied women should not go to discotheques and that performing merengue is no fitting occupation for women.' One woman reported to Austerlitz that '"in Santo Domingo people generally think that [playing] merengue is only for men,"' and that any woman who plays it must be "a crazy girl, a bad girl"' (116).

In more specifically Western contexts, it has equally been the expectation that women's role in music should be similarly circumscribed. In commenting on the symbolism of the early Christian martyr Cecilia as the patron saint of music, Cook and Tsou (1994) observe that 'many ... feminist scholars ... have ... learned that the source of this symbol was stereotypical and patriarchal. Cecilia was in many ways the *patronized* saint of music, limited, by her sex, to a passive role of idealized, even swooning, muse or performer, but not as an active creator. Cecilia thus presented cultural notions of acceptable female practices' (1). As Leppert (1988) notes in the context of eighteenth-century England, 'the music females made, and were expected to make, was either tolerated or valued largely to the degree to which it kept within the bounds of the ideology of domesticity' (147). Much the same observation could be made with respect to the role of middle-class urban women in the United States during the late nineteenth and early twentieth centuries as providers of family entertainment at the piano. Transgression of these expectations and restrictions would be regarded as deviant behavior, as often as not carrying connotations of moral impropriety.

If performers were viewed as moral outlaws, their more avid fans have also tended to be regarded as themselves constituting deviant groups. Particularly during the twentieth century, their responses to the 'bland' products of mass culture – such as pop music – were deemed inappropriately orgiastic, tribal and excessive by many cultural critics. Fans have in these ways been seen as displaying pathological tendencies, as being compliant to forms of mass suggestion encoded within popular music, and as demonstrating an imbalance that was attributed to an emotional or psychological deficiency.

This attitude toward fans comes closer to the more normative and less relativistic understanding of deviance that is to be found within the discipline of developmental psychology. Within developmental psychology, deviant behavior has customarily been divided into three main groupings: psychotic disorders, such as schizophrenia and bipolar disorder (manic-depression); non-psychotic disorders, such as anxiety disorders and phobias; and personality disorders (psychopathy and sociopathy). Examples of all three may be found within the realm of popular music. Severe stage fright, for example, as suffered by XTC's Andy Partridge to such an extent that he has not toured since the early 1980s, could be deemed to be a non-psychotic disorder. Likewise, satyriasis, a 'condition' that manifests itself as extreme promiscuity and that has been attributed by certain rock writers to rock star Brian Jones from the Rolling Stones, is another example of behavior normatively defined as psychologically deviant. It can be argued that the pampered, hedonistic life style experienced by certain rock stars has perhaps fostered the practise of certain forms of sexually deviant behavior. For example, Chuck Berry was prosecuted for using a surveillance camera hidden in a washroom to film female guests at his hotel. However, it is perhaps the case that such individuals would have indulged in such behavior regardless of their rock star status, and that such acts may simply attract more media coverage because of the fame of the perpetrators. It therefore remains to be demonstrated whether there is any inherent link between such forms of deviant behavior and the practise of popular music.

Rather than considering deviance to be the result of some psychological defect in the individual, sociologists, criminologists and cultural theorists have in contrast tended to examine society's power structures and, in particular, its legal and moral codes, in order to define deviant behavior as a social construct. Different societies are characterized by different rules, and hence a wide variety of activities could be considered deviant (see O'Sullivan 1994, 83). A seminal text in assessing the role of deviance within popular music is Howard Becker's *Outsiders* (1963), which examines how a group of semiprofessional jazz musicians gave rise to a 'culture of a deviant group.' Becker argues that, 'although deviant behavior is often proscribed by law – labelled criminal if engaged in by adults or delinquent if engaged in by youths – this need not be the case. Dance musicians . . . are a case in point. Though their activities are formally within the law, their culture and way of life are sufficiently bizarre and unconventional for them to be labelled outsiders' (1997, 55). Becker goes on to give a subtle reading of how jazz musicians defined their world as 'hip' in contrast to the 'square' world inhabited by everyone else (including their audience, who simply did not 'get' pure jazz at all). The musicians' self-conscious taboo-breaking marked them as a deviant group (largely within the law), with their own argot, sexual orientations and so on. Becker's work is also important in that, although it discusses jazz musicians as a deviant group, it helps to open up that definition and to dissociate deviance from dysfunctional or lawless behavior. Significantly, according to more contemporary definitions of deviance, the activities of Becker's jazz musicians would in fact no longer be regarded as deviant.

In the 1970s, British academics, such as Phil Cohen, who were interested in subcultures and their relationship to class, also looked at the role of deviance within this context. Cohen argued that deviance was a 'specific counter-ideology' with delinquency 'serving as a means of recruitment into deviant groups.' Later in the decade, Hebdige (1979) wrote about the punk subculture as characterized by two forms of deviance: social (the exact origin of punk was 'symbolically disfigured by the make-up, masks and aliases' (121)) and sexual (hence punks' use of 'taboo' sexual garments and accessories). This gave the impression of what he called 'multiple warping' (121), which had the effect of covering up punk's class origin and shocking the liberal observer.

Theories of deviance have tended to be an overwhelmingly male preserve, a fact pointed out in the work of McRobbie and Garber (1997). For them, 1970s deviancy theory was 'a celebration rather than an analysis of the deviant form – an identification by powerless intellectuals with deviants who appeared more successful in controlling events' (1997, 114). Hebdige (1997) went on to argue that 'the category "youth" only gets activated . . . in the supposedly disinterested tracts on "deviance" . . . when young people make their presence felt by going out of bounds' (402). In this reading, deviance is a tactic deployed by youth to air grievances and to strike back at processes underlying hegemonic orders.

A common theme in all recent studies of deviance has been the general acceptance of the term's profound relativity. What one individual, group of individuals, 'reference group' (see A.K. Cohen 1997) or even society regards as deviant behavior is constantly in flux and is always ideologically loaded. Such relativity emerges clearly in the manner in which some musicians come to be criticized for engaging in musical practises that for some individuals transgress genre norms. The discursive and ideological character of the processes through which musical genres are formed and maintained thus explains the attitude of fans toward musicians who transgress genre norms. Examples of this phenomenon are to be found when Miles Davis developed fusion, which many jazz aficionados immediately reacted to as being 'not quite jazz' (see, for example, Chambers 1985, 168, 183), and when Bob Dylan 'went electric,' which offended fans of urban folk music.

Bibliography

Austerlitz, Paul. 1997. *Merengue: Dominican Music and Dominican Identity*. Philadelphia: Temple University Press.

Becker, Howard. 1963. *Outsiders: Studies in the Sociology of Deviance*. Chicago: Free Press of Glencoe.

Becker, Howard. 1997 (1963). 'The Culture of a Deviant Group: The "Jazz" Musician.' In *The Subcultures Reader*, ed. Ken Gelder and Sarah Thornton. London and New York: Routledge, 55–65. (First published in *Outsiders: Studies in the Sociology of Deviance*. Chicago: Free Press of Glencoe, 1963.)

Chambers, Jack. 1985. *Milestones II: The Music and Times of Miles Davis Since 1960*. Toronto: University of Toronto Press.

Cohen, Albert K. 1997 (1955). 'A General Theory of Subcultures.' In *The Subcultures Reader*, ed. Ken Gelder and Sarah Thornton. London and New York: Routledge, 44–54. (First published in *Delinquent Boys: The Culture of the Gang*. Glencoe, IL: Free Press, 1955.)

Cohen, Phil. 1997 (1972). 'Subcultural Conflict and Working-Class Community.' In *The Subcultures Reader*, ed. Ken Gelder and Sarah Thornton. London and New York: Routledge, 90–99. (First published in *Working Papers in Cultural Studies* 1 (1972).)

Cook, Susan C., and Tsou, Judy S. 1994. 'Introduction: "Bright Cecilia."' In *Cecilia Reclaimed: Feminist Perspectives on Gender and Music*, ed. Susan C. Cook and Judy S. Tsou. Urbana, IL: University of Illinois Press, 1–14.

Douglas, Mary. 1966. *Purity and Danger: An Analysis of Concepts of Pollution and Taboo*. London: Routledge.

Hebdige, Dick. 1979. *Subculture: The Meaning of Style*. London: Methuen.

Hebdige, Dick. 1997 (1983). 'Posing . . . Threats, Striking . . . Poses: Youth, Surveillance, and Display.' In *The Subcultures Reader*, ed. Ken Gelder and Sarah Thornton. London and New York: Routledge, 393–405. (First published in *SubStance* 37/38 (1983): 68–88.)

Herman, Gary. 1994. *Rock 'n' Roll Babylon*. London: Plexus.

Keil, Charles. 1979. *Tiv Song*. Chicago: University of Chicago Press.

Koskoff, Ellen. 1989. 'An Introduction to Women, Music and Culture.' In *Women and Music in Cross-Cultural Perspective*, ed. Ellen Koskoff. Urbana, IL: University of Illinois Press, 1–23.

Leppert, Richard D. 1988. *Music and Image: Domesticity, Ideology and Socio-Cultural Formation in Eighteenth-Century England*. Cambridge: Cambridge University Press.

McRobbie, Angela, and Garber, Jenny. 1997 (1975). 'Girls and Subcultures.' In *The Subcultures Reader*, ed. Ken Gelder and Sarah Thornton. London and New York: Routledge, 112–20. (First published in *Resistance Through Rituals: Youth Subcultures in Post-War Britain*, ed. Stuart Hall and Tony Jefferson. London: Routledge, 1975.)

Merriam, Alan P. 1964. *The Anthropology of Music*. Evanston, IL: Northwestern University Press.

O'Sullivan, Tim. 1994. 'Deviance.' In *Key Concepts in Communication and Cultural Studies*, ed. Tim O'Sullivan et al. London and New York: Routledge, 83–85.

Shepherd, John. 1977. 'The Musical Coding of Ideologies.' In John Shepherd et al., *Whose Music? A Sociology of Musical Languages*. London: Latimer New Dimensions, 69–124.

Taylor, Rogan P. 1985. *The Death and Resurrection Show: From Shaman to Superstar*. London: Anthony Blond.

DAVID BUCKLEY and JOHN SHEPHERD

Disasters and Accidents

Calamitous unexpected events, whether caused by nature, humanity, technology or combinations of these, have been a frequent subject of song in a great many cultures over a long period of time. In treating such events, song makes a contribution to society's mechanisms for dealing with the stresses and tensions that the events cause by offering a range of specific perspectives, from fear of calamity to actual experience of it, from the means of avoiding calamity (more often moral or religious than practical) to that of attending to its consequences. While many songs explicitly seek to draw lessons or to point fingers, others are content to state what happened and leave conclusions to the listener.

Song's most common approach to the subject of disaster is to concentrate on one specific event, real or imagined. Sometimes, a song's treatment of an event avoids focusing on specific individuals, as, for example, in 'When the "Evening Star" Went Down' by Henry Clay Work (1866). In this case, the avoidance of a focus on individuals is part of Work's message, which is to show that such events are no respecters of rank or profession (Finson 1994, 116).

More often, however, calamitous events narrated in song are centered on the experience of only a few people, sometimes just one individual. The industrial folk song 'Johnny Seddon,' for example, most probably created by immigrant Irish workers in the coalfields of County Durham, England in the mid-nineteenth century, focuses on the death of a collier of that name, as described by his lover. But, as Lloyd (1967) points out, it is 'vague in detail – not even the name of the pit is mentioned – and passive in mood' (357). More specific, and less passive, are the songs of Woody Guthrie. The dust storms that afflicted the American Southwest in the 1930s were the subject of a series of songs written by Guthrie, which he called his 'dust-bowl ballads' and which he recorded for Victor in 1940. Guthrie experienced the dust storms himself in Oklahoma and wrote from personal experience how 'We saw outside our window/Where wheatfields they had grown/Was now a rippling ocean/Of dust the wind had blown' ('The Great Dust Storm'). Several of Guthrie's dust-bowl songs are about the consequences of the disaster. Again, they are often personalized. 'Dust Bowl Refugee' centers on a family whose life is now lived on the highway, while in 'Dust Pneumonia Blues' the singer 'can't yodel for the rattlin' in my lung.'

Guthrie's songs also illustrate the possible role of the commentator in disaster songs. His dust-bowl ballads were, he said, 'liberal as the dickens and as progressive as the angels' (Klein 1980, 159). The deep sense of empathy with the victims of the disaster pointed up society's failings to assist them properly, while the often satirical tone of many of the songs suggested that this 'natural' disaster was not entirely nature's fault.

Some particular major natural disasters have featured very prominently in song. Among the most notable of these was the Mississippi flood of 1927. As with several other disasters in the South, this one, in which well over half a million people were left homeless, had disproportionately severe consequences for the African-American communities, and this was reflected in numerous blues

and also in gospel recordings of the time. In one of the best-known (and bestselling) songs about the flood, Charley Patton's 'High Water Everywhere' (1929), Patton relives the experience, noting that he wanted to make for the hill country 'but they got me barred' – an accurate reference to the fact that the National Guard prevented blacks from leaving the area (Oliver 1990, 219, 222).

References to the Mississippi flood in gospel recordings, such as 'The 1927 Flood' by Elder Edwards (1928), could be imbued with a sense of divine retribution. The people, Edwards sang, '. . . had prayed for a deal/But the Lord didn't have no deal' (Oliver 1984, 195). Similar sentiments appear in gospel recordings that make reference to other natural disasters. Some cast their net of references much more broadly and less specifically to get their message across. Sister Cally Fancy, for example, in 'Everybody Get Your Business Right' (1929), admonishes her listeners that 'God's warning you in tornadoes/Earthquakes and windstorms too' (Oliver 1984, 193).

Probably the single largest category of disaster songs is that involving industry and technology; and, within this category, two specific contexts stand out: the mine and the railroad.

Lloyd (1967) has shown how the mining song cited above, 'Johnny Seddon,' was succeeded by songs that were far more specific about the event they chronicled and, in due course, by songs that were highly outspoken in terms of their interpretation of the event. 'The Donibristle Moss Moran Disaster,' for example, referring to an incident in Fife, Scotland in 1901, asks rhetorically, after describing the disaster, 'Was that not another blunder?' and answers, 'My God, it was a sin' (Lloyd 1967, 358). By 1934, a songwriter, in a song about a mining disaster in Wales, was stating unambiguously that the reason the reports on the disaster had gone missing was that 'the colliery manager had them destroyed/To cover his criminal ways' (Lloyd 1967, 359).

In the United States, songs about both mining and railroad disasters proliferated, especially from the 1890s to the 1920s, and, as Green (1972) and Cohen (1981) have shown, they often had extremely complex histories, moving in and out of the oral/vernacular and commercial traditions. One particular mining song documented by Green, 'The Dream of the Miner's Child,' recorded by Vernon Dalhart for OKeh in 1925, had its textual origins at least partially in an English music hall song – 'Don't Go Down in the Mine, Dad' by Will Geddes and Robert Donnelly – published as sheet music in 1910. The different melody of Dalhart's recording appears to have been the work of Andrew Jenkins, a songwriter who lived near Atlanta. This song in turn gave birth to others, with different locations for their disasters, the most notable being Blind Alfred Reed's 'Explosion in the Fairmount Mines' (1927), which relates an incident in West Virginia in 1907 in which over 300 people died (Green 1972, 115–34).

The equally complex history of a celebrated railroad disaster song, 'The Wreck of the Old '97' (also recorded by Vernon Dalhart, in 1924), adds further dimensions to processes of imitation, appropriation and reinvention that have occurred around disaster songs, suggesting the extent to which their powerful subject matter made a particularly strong impact. As Cohen's meticulous research has shown, the source of key phrases in the lyrics of this song predates the disaster itself (1903), coming from an 1865 song by Henry Clay Work, 'The Ship That Never Return'd' (which included the lines that were to become a lyrical 'hook': 'Did she never return? She never return'd – /Her fate it is yet unlearn'd'). Parodies of this song had appeared by 1888, so that when ideas from the lyrics were used for 'The Wreck of the Old '97' the song had already acquired more than one layer of meaning. Songs about the railroad accident itself were so numerous that legal action was taken in the 1920s (Cohen 1981, 197–226).

As a category of historical events, the phenomenon of disaster also embraces less sudden and dramatic but equally calamitous occurrences such as famine, which often happen on a more widespread geographical basis. Late twentieth-century outbreaks of famine in the developing world occasioned a response in which music played a new role. Band Aid (1984), Live Aid (1985) and Farm Aid (1986) were humanitarian responses to widespread disasters, using music as the key to raise awareness and funds. Such activity was not without controversy, as Street (1997) has shown. In a particularly scathing attack, Marcus (1993), for example, argues that Live Aid embodied the hegemonic ideology of 'Pepsification' and a willful self-aggrandizement and self-promotion on the part of the participants. A strong argument could be made in purely financial terms, if the amount of money raised by Live Aid – £50 million – was set against the increased earnings for the artists featured. But others, such as Hebdige (1988), have also pointed to other, more positive factors, such as a return to neighborliness and a sense of interdependence that had been lost in the politics of the 1980s. Commenting on the apparent gulf between the critics and a general public clearly moved by the disaster and the opportunity to contribute to its relief, Simon Frith suggested that 'grumbling cynicism' risked missing the point (Rijven, Marcus and Straw 1985, 1).

The link between disaster, music and humanitarian response that had evolved in the context of long-running problems such as famine was extended to single calamitous events in September 2001, in the wake of the terrorist attacks on the World Trade Center in New York and the Pentagon in Washington, DC. Television networks in the United States collaborated to air *America: A Tribute to Heroes*, a two-hour commercial-free telethon to raise money for victims of the tragedy. The show was broadcast live from New York and Los Angeles, and among the numerous popular music stars who appeared were Bruce Springsteen, Paul Simon, Neil Young and Willie Nelson.

Bibliography

Cohen, Norm. 1981. *Long Steel Rail: The Railroad in American Folksong*. Urbana, IL: University of Illinois Press.

Finson, Jon W. 1994. *The Voices That Are Gone: Themes in Nineteenth-Century American Popular Song*. New York: Oxford University Press.

Green, Archie. 1972. *Only a Miner: Studies in Recorded Coal-Mining Songs*. Urbana, IL: University of Illinois Press.

Hebdige, Dick. 1988. *Hiding in the Light: On Images and Things*. London: Routledge.

Klein, Joe. 1980. *Woody Guthrie: A Life*. New York: Knopf.

Lloyd, A.L. 1967. *Folk Song in England*. London: Lawrence and Wishart.

Marcus, Greil. 1993 (1985). 'Number One with a Bullet.' In Greil Marcus, *In the Fascist Bathroom: Writings on Punk 1977–1992*. London: Viking, 280–84.

Oliver, Paul. 1984. *Songsters and Saints: Vocal Traditions on Race Records*. Cambridge: Cambridge University Press.

Oliver, Paul. 1990. *Blues Fell This Morning: Meaning in the Blues*. 2nd ed. Cambridge: Cambridge University Press.

Rijven, Stan, Marcus, Greil, and Straw, Will. 1985. *Rock for Ethiopia*. IASPM Working Paper 7. Exeter: IASPM.

Street, John. 1997. *Politics and Popular Culture*. Cambridge: Polity Press.

Sheet Music

Geddes, Will, comp., and Donnelly, Robert, lyr. 1910. 'Don't Go Down in the Mine, Dad.' London: Wright.

Work, Henry Clay, comp. and lyr. 1865. 'The Ship That Never Return'd.' Chicago: Root and Cady.

Work, Henry Clay, comp. and lyr. 1866. 'When the "Evening Star" Went Down.' Chicago: Root and Cady.

Discographical References

Dalhart, Vernon. 'The Dream of the Miner's Child.' OKeh 40498. 1925: USA.

Dalhart, Vernon. 'The Wreck of the Old '97.' Victor 19427. 1924: USA.

Edwards, Elder. 'The 1927 Flood.' OKeh 8647. 1928: USA.

Fancy, Sister Cally. 'Everybody Get Your Business Right.' Brunswick 7110. 1929: USA.

Guthrie, Woody. *Dust Bowl Ballads*. RCA LPV 502. 1940; *1964*: USA.

Lowe, Jez. 'Johnny Seddon.' *Galloways*. Musica Pangaea 10006. *1997*: USA.

McGinn, Matt. 'The Donibristle Moss Moran Disaster.' *The Iron Muse: A Panorama of Industrial Folk Song*. Topic 12T86. *1963*: UK.

Patton, Charley. 'High Water Everywhere, Parts I and II.' Paramount 12909. 1929: USA.

Reed, Blind Alfred. 'Explosion in the Fairmount Mines.' Victor 21191. 1927: USA.

DAVID HORN and DAVID BUCKLEY

Drugs and Addiction

The link between drugs and the performing arts has a long history. Hallucinogens were a staple element in shamanistic cultures, and natural psychoactive drugs, such as the fly agaric mushroom, were in widespread use. The shaman's show, which included music, song, dance and various magic tricks, incorporated the use of such intoxicants by both performer and audience (see Taylor 1985). McKenna (1992) has argued that the use of natural hallucinogens led to an anti-hierarchical orgiastic community, a cultural model that would, in part, be revived by the 1960s counterculture.

Drug-taking, particularly the taking of opium, in the late eighteenth and early nineteenth centuries by artists and writers such as Goethe, Blake, Coleridge, De Quincey, Wordsworth and, later, Baudelaire and Rimbaud, paved the way for twentieth-century Bohemianism: 'They were the first beatniks and hippies of modern times: they had sex, drugs and Beethoven' (Taylor 1985, 186).

But perhaps the first real link between performance, drug use and the rise of popular culture can be found in the popularity of medicine shows in the nineteenth and early twentieth centuries in the United States. Medicine shows promoted the use of drugs by both performer and audience, as cocaine and morphine formed the basis of many of the miracle cures on offer. They also provided an opportunity for amateur musicians, many of them playing in the blues idiom, to escape the conformity of urban life and to learn their trade on the road. The link between itinerancy and racism (a majority of these bluesmen were black) was also established, as was the link between drugs and lawlessness. The black bluesman or singer (called 'Sambo' by whites), carrying his herbs and roots in his mojo bag, became a powerful symbol of outlaw romance – a rejection of, or at least an alternative to, the mundaneness of mainstream North American life.

Likewise, jazz and drugs were so closely connected that 'images of one were used to condemn the other' (Shapiro 1988, 46). The connection between jazz and drugs has been evidenced, for example, in 'Mezz' Mezzrow's autobiography, *Really the Blues*, which is in effect the autobiography of a drug pusher in the jazz world, 'the mezz' being 'the best brand of marihuana; anything unusually good' (1964, 308). From the 1930s onward, the use of heroin was common among jazz musicians. An analgesic/opiate originally introduced by doctors as a cure for morphine addiction, heroin is a highly addictive injectable narcotic. The aura of cool detachment (often called the 'nod') reported by users to follow the initial euphoria after injection matched the sense of icy 'cool' that became associated with bebop and the figure of the hipster. Heroin also had the side effect of drying the mucous membranes, thus keeping many musicians cold- and flu-free. It is so deeply addictive that musicians such as Charlie Parker felt well enough to perform on stage only once they had had a 'hit.' In the 1930s and 1940s, venues such as the Lincoln Gardens, Charlie's, the Cotton Club and the Plantation Club were centers of drug abuse, prostitution and criminal activity, while many other venues in the United States banned bebop on account of its association in the popular imagination with heroin. One of the frankest and least sentimental accounts of the connection between jazz and drugs is to be found in Hampton Hawes's autobiography *Raise Up Off Me*. Hawes was a west-coast jazz pianist, and a contemporary of Miles Davis and Charlie Parker.

The influx of marijuana from Mexico and Puerto Rico into the mainland United States in the first three decades of the twentieth century reinforced the connection in the minds of members of the white mainstream (particularly law enforcers) between the harmful use of intoxicants and drugs and an alien, un-American life style. Marijuana, a weak hallucinogen, was given a Mexican name by North Americans, and the image of the black musician became synonymous with drug use in general.

Legislation was enacted on both sides of the Atlantic to curb drug abuse. In the United States, narcotic drugs were criminalized in 1915 (1920 in the United Kingdom), and marijuana in 1937 (1928 in the United Kingdom). In the United States, the *Boggs Act* (1951) and the *Narcotics Control Act* (1956) introduced punitive custodial sentences, with equal sentences for both 'soft' drugs (like marijuana) and hard drugs. Black musicians were again a prime target.

From the mid-1960s onward, heroin use was also widespread within the rock community. Famous users included Jimi Hendrix, Eric Clapton, Janis Joplin and Sid

Vicious. McKenna (1992) calls heroin 'the perfect drug for anyone who has been damaged by lack of self-esteem or traumatised by historical upheaval' (208), while singer Patti Smith has spoken about a 'heroin consciousness,' a sense of disconnectedness and 'cool' that can be displayed even by those who are not heroin users. A prerequisite of this 'cool' can often be to affect the symptoms of intoxication even where none are actually being felt. Indeed, medical research has shown that an individual's experience of a narcotic is conditioned by this perception of the type of intoxication that is supposed to be experienced.

Cocaine, derived from coca and a powerful appetite suppressant, has a glamor and mystique among certain users that heroin lacks. Whereas heroin users have traditionally been regarded as societal outcasts, cocaine is the drug of high society and particularly popular in the entertainment industry. It has been estimated that, by the mid-1970s, the film and pop industries accounted for 90 percent of the total cocaine consumption in the United States (Wills and Cooper 1988, 40–41). The use of cocaine has often been justified, as was that of marijuana before it, as a creative aid. Just as the effect of 'New Orleans Sweet Leaf' and its ability to remove inhibitions and to enhance ensemble playing might have been lauded by a jazz musician, so cocaine and amphetamines, both stimulants–euphoriants, were sought after as 'working drugs,' to keep the musician awake, boost confidence, create euphoria and unleash hidden creativity. Although potentially lethal when mixed with heroin (a dose known as a speedball) or smoked as freebase (a purer version that is expensive and dangerous to produce), cocaine is considerably less dangerous to the individual using it than heroin and kills far fewer people annually.

Very often, new drugs are tried out by a powerful elite – members of high society, the intelligentsia or the medical profession – before becoming part of the mainstream drug culture. This happened with LSD (lysergic acid diethylamide), a psychoactive drug and potent hallucinogen, first synthesized from lysergic acid in 1938. Its merits were much discussed by intellectuals such as Dr. Timothy Leary before it was taken up by more mainstream users. Although not physiologically addictive, LSD has powerful mind-altering effects, and in the 1950s and 1960s its use was widespread among Western youth. It also had a marked impact on the practise of popular music. In the United States, groups such as the Grateful Dead and Jefferson Airplane were in the vanguard of acid rock, a music that sought to mimic the sensory disturbance and sense of connectedness and special insight into the universe allegedly provided by LSD (or 'acid,' as it was known) through the utilization of dreamlike song structures, volume, surreal lyrics and disorienting visual

iconography in performance. In the United Kingdom, groups such as Pink Floyd used similar elements. In contrast, Velvet Underground and other east-coast US groups favored 'uppers' such as speed and heroin, and were thus closer to the tradition of the detached 'cool' affected by the hipsters.

In the 1980s and 1990s, the most popular 'designer' drug was Ecstasy, otherwise known as 3,4-methylene-dioxymethamphetamine (MDMA) (although the tablets sold at raves are often a cocktail of speed and LSD). Ecstasy became irrevocably linked with rave culture in the United Kingdom around 1987. Although seemingly comparatively safe, it was responsible for a number of deaths and, as a result, its use by teenagers became the focus of a media 'moral panic.' Ecstasy reportedly fostered a form of 'communitas' on the dance floor, and its energizing qualities and disorienting side effects complemented the very quick tempo and deconstructive attitude toward song structure of acid house music. Ecstasy culture was discussed in 'Mis-Shapes/Sorted for E's and Wizz,' which was a number two hit in the United Kingdom for Pulp in 1995.

Peer pressure is a very important factor in drug use among many musicians and their fans, with each style of music traditionally perceived to have its own favorite narcotic. Thus, sulfate, amphetamines (or 'purple hearts') and various other 'uppers' have traditionally been regarded as the drugs of mods, punks and northern soul aficionados, while marijuana and LSD are considered the drugs of hippiedom and the counterculture, Ecstasy the drug of acid house and rave culture, and so on. However, the most common drug used by both musicians and fans is marijuana. Just as many punks smoked pot as the hippies they purportedly despised; and in the United States in the early 1990s, marijuana (and calls for its legalization) was associated with rap artists like Dr Dre and Cypress Hill.

The use of marijuana was also an important feature of the religious practises of many Rastafarians, both in the West Indies and in various West Indian diasporas, most notably the United Kingdom. 'Ganja,' according to Cashmore (1979), was a form of marijuana 'to which many Rastas were to attach religious significance' (26; see also Chevannes 1994, 156–57, 199–200, 219), and which, soaked in white rum, was believed to possess medicinal properties (Chevannes 1994, 31, 198). As such, it became associated with the music of Bob Marley, a figure central to Rastafarianism outside the West Indies. In the opinion of Cashmore, 'it would not be exaggerating to suggest that Bob Marley was to the seventies wave of English Rastas what Marcus Garvey was to the first Jamaican cultists of the 1930s' (1979, 108). More than any other individual, concludes Cashmore,

Marley 'was responsible for introducing Rastafarian themes, concepts and demands to a truly universal audience' (1979, 108). Ganja featured in the activities of Bob Marley and the Wailers. In 1967, Marley moved from the United States to Jamaica and, with Peter McIntosh (later to be called 'Tosh') and Neville 'Bunny' Livingstone (later to be called 'Bunny Wailer'), formed the Wailers. In 1968, they created their own label. However, the venture was short-lived. Exacerbating the situation, reports Cashmore, 'was the arrest and subsequent imprisonment of Livingstone who fell foul of the government's sweeping proposal to cut down on the production, possession and consumption of ganja due to its connection with violence' (1979, 111). In 1976, after leaving the Wailers, Peter Tosh released a solo album, *Legalize It*, the title track of which celebrates and promotes the use of marijuana. There was considerable discussion at the time that Marley's death in 1981 from cancer might have been linked to his use of marijuana.

Many pop performers, and their fans, are multi-drug users, with alcohol, nicotine and marijuana their everyday intoxicants, and other, more expensive and exotic, drugs reserved for special social events and specific social scenes (for example, the Saturday night rave or the northern soul all-nighter). Combinations of prescription drugs, particularly sleeping pills, and other drugs have caused a number of deaths. Elvis Presley died from an overdose of legally acquired drugs, and Keith Moon from an overdose of heminevrin, a drug prescribed to combat alcoholism (see Fletcher 1998).

Drug-related deaths in rock are legion, although it must be pointed out that they are more often the result of a combination of intoxicants. Also, death is more likely to occur when the user mistakes one drug for another, or overdoses after a period of abstinence, when the body has a reduced tolerance to the accustomed level of narcotic in the bloodstream (as was the case with punk star Sid Vicious in 1979). On the other hand, there have been a number of high-profile recoveries from drug addiction in the world of popular music, two of the more recent examples being provided by Eric Clapton and Elton John. In addition, there have been instances of anti-drug songs. One of the most famous examples was the Verve's 'The Drugs Don't Work' (1997), which was a number one hit in the United Kingdom at the height of dance culture's drug use.

Nicotine addiction, although not peculiar to the practise of popular music, has contributed to the deaths of many popular music performers, or has affected musicians' ability to perform to their full potential. Many singers – for example, David Bowie – have reported a loss of vocal range as a direct result of nicotine abuse.

Drug use and abuse have also been gendered in a quite specific way. Female drug addicts, such as Billie Holiday, were regarded as morally corrupt rather than as unfortunate victims of circumstance, due to the ingrained view of the female as nurturer and mother, and hence more morally 'responsible.'

References to drugs are frequently found in popular music. It is estimated that over a hundred songs referring to the drugs scene were recorded for the black or 'race' radio-listening audience in the 1930s alone. They included 'Cocaine Habit Blues' (1930), 'Reefer Man' (1932) and 'Light Up' (1939). Many more from this era incorporated hip slang, such as getting 'high,' in an effort to give them 'street credibility' (Shapiro 1988, 39). Such references have continued and have reflected a variety of standpoints, from direct denunciation (Tin Machine's 'Crack City' (1989)) to glorification (the Shamen's 'Ebeneezer Goode' (1992)). Very often, drugs are used as a metaphor for another favorite universal in popular song, love, as in Roxy Music's 'Love Is the Drug' (1975). Overt references to drugs in pop, as in the Beatles' 'Day in the Life' (1967) or D Mob's 'We Call It Acieed' (1988), have led to instances of radio censorship.

Although the connection between popular music and drugs has received much publicity, and although there is evidence that drug use in the entertainment industry has at times exceeded that among the general population (as with cocaine use in the 1970s), there is also evidence that, at other times, there has been no great difference. In this respect, Wills and Cooper have concluded that, 'compared to young people in the general population, it does not appear that popular musicians as a whole represent a high-risk group with regard to the use of illegal drugs' (1988, 84).

There is also a popular belief that much of the reason for drug-taking among musicians is nothing more than the almost childlike hedonism of the cosseted rock star existence. However, there is as well substantial evidence that the stress of being a popular musician enters the picture. The popular musician, report Wills and Cooper, 'clashes with businessmen, fellow musicians, music journalists, and in his personal relationships, and his health is at risk from a distinctive profile of stress outcomes' (1988, 99). Rather than expressing his feelings regarding various personality clashes, conclude Wills and Cooper, 'he tends not to confide in those close to him and instead withdraws or gives himself confidence with the use of illegal drugs' (1988, 99). Stress related to drug use took another form in the world of jazz in the period after World War II. Due to the unacceptability of the music, say Wills and Cooper, 'the musician suffered from feelings of alienation and found it difficult to make a living . . . he sometimes felt the need to sustain a sense of heightened emotional arousal, created by music, by taking drugs' (1988, 40).

Part of the attraction of drugs lies also in their illegality and anti-establishment connotations. In the period after World War II, report Wills and Cooper, 'heroin was defiantly anti-establishment' (1988, 39). Former drug addict and record boss Alan McGee wrote in 1998: 'Take away the illegality of drugs and you take away their mystery, their sexiness, which in turn is their main allure.' Warnings to both performers and their audiences about the dangers of hard drugs are, however, destined to go unheeded. The reason, according to writer and jazz musician George Melly, is that, in the pop canon, 'temporary exultation is more important ... than a long life tied to the system' (1970, 30).

Bibliography

Cashmore, Ernest. 1979. *Rastaman: The Rastafarian Movement in England.* London: George Allen & Unwin.

Chevannes, Barry. 1994. *Rastafari: Roots and Ideology.* Syracuse, NY: Syracuse University Press.

Daly, Stephen, and Wice, Nathaniel. 1995. *alt.culture: An A-Z of the 90s Underground and Online.* London: Fourth Estate.

Fletcher, Tony. 1998. *Dear Boy: The Life of Keith Moon.* London: Omnibus.

Hawes, Hampton, and Asher, Don. 1979 (1974). *Raise Up Off Me: A Portrait of Hampton Hawes.* New York: Da Capo Press.

Herman, Gary. 1994. *Rock 'n' Roll Babylon.* London: Plexus.

Lomax, Alan. 1993. *The Land Where the Blues Began.* London: Methuen.

MacKay, George. 1996. *Senseless Acts of Beauty: Cultures of Resistance Since the Sixties.* London and New York: Verso.

Malone, Bill C. 1985. *Country Music, U.S.A.* Rev. ed. Austin, TX: University of Texas Press.

McGee, Alan. 1998. 'Cocaine Supernova.' *The Guardian* (14 March): 13–14.

McKenna, Terrence. 1992. *Food of the Gods: The Search for the Original Tree of Knowledge.* New York: Bantam.

Melly, George. 1970. *Revolt into Style: The Pop Arts in Britain.* London: Allen Lane.

Mezzrow, Milton 'Mezz,' and Wolfe, Bernard. 1964. *Really the Blues.* New York: Signet Books. (First published New York: Random House, 1946.)

Shapiro, Harry. 1988. *Waiting for the Man: The Story of Drugs and Popular Music.* London and New York: Quartet.

Taylor, Rogan. 1985. *The Death and Resurrection Show: From Shaman to Superstar.* London: Anthony Blond.

Thornton, Sarah. 1995. *Club Cultures: Music, Media and Subcultural Capital.* Cambridge: Polity.

Wills, Geoff, and Cooper, Cary L. 1988. *Pressure Sensitive: Popular Musicians Under Stress.* London: Sage Publications.

Discographical References

Bailey, Buster. 'Light Up'/'Man with a Horn Goes Berserk.' Vocalion 4564. 1939: USA.

Beatles, The. 'Day in the Life.' *Sergeant Pepper's Lonely Hearts Club Band.* Parlophone PCS 7027. *1967*: UK.

Calloway, Cab. 'Reefer Man'/'You Gotta Hi-De-Ho.' Brunswick 6340. 1932: USA.

D Mob. 'We Call It Acieed.' ffrr FFR 13. *1988*: UK.

Memphis Jug Band, The. 'Cocaine Habit Blues.' Victor V38620. 1930: USA.

Pulp. 'Mis-Shapes/Sorted for E's and Wizz.' Island CID 620. *1995*: UK.

Roxy Music. 'Love Is the Drug.' Island WIP 6248. *1975*: UK.

Shamen, The. 'Ebeneezer Goode.' One Little Indian 78 TP7. *1992*: UK.

Tin Machine. 'Crack City.' *Tin Machine.* EMI 1004. *1989*: UK.

Tosh, Peter. 'Legalize It.' *Legalize It.* Columbia 34253. *1976*: USA. Reissue: Tosh, Peter. 'Legalize It.' *Legalize It.* Columbia 34258. *1990*: USA.

Verve, The. 'The Drugs Don't Work.' Hut HUT C/DG 88. *1997*: UK.

DAVID BUCKLEY and JOHN SHEPHERD

Ethnicity and Race

The Greek term '*ethnos*' was used by classical authors to describe groups of threatening outsiders (both human and nonhuman). More currently, the expressions 'ethnic' and 'ethnic group' are widely used to refer to distinct groups united by common ancestry and culture. The notion of 'ethnic identity' often acts as a discursive foil to the normative forms of identity promoted by the nation-state, and accompanies claims that these differences should, in a liberal context, be acknowledged and cultivated, or, in a totalitarian context, be controlled, if not entirely eradicated. Academic discussions of the term, particularly within the field of social anthropology, have been critical of these usages, while remaining attentive to their political dynamics. Since the late 1960s, anthropologists have consistently stressed that ethnicity is less a category of things (i.e., 'ethnic groups') than a process of categorization and boundary construction. They have also insisted that these processes take place within an ensemble of mutually constitutive social relations, and that they are constrained, if not entirely defined, by the material circumstances and the relative power of the groups doing the defining and being defined. Dominant groups promote the most visible and readily discernible ethnic categories and definitions, while subordinated groups are often 'muted,' drawing on the categories and definitions of the dominant group(s), and inflecting them in ways that are often difficult for outsiders to understand, sometimes intentionally so (for a review, see Stokes 1997).

The concept of race (Spanish *raza*) defined Christian, aristocratic bloodlines during the *Reconquista* in the early modern Iberian Peninsula, and gained some currency across southern Europe. It was, however, transformed by modern European colonialism and the slave trade. By the early eighteenth century, the term implied a permanent zoological type. Darwin's *On the Origin of Species* (1859) challenged the notion of permanence, but introduced the idea that race might be inscribed (and therefore manipulated) within an evolutionary framework. Pseudoscientific uses of the term persist, both in its eighteenth-century taxonomic and in its nineteenth-century evolutionary forms. The emergence of European musicology, underlining Europe's distinct cultural destiny, is thoroughly marked by its engagement with racially conceived 'others' (see Radano and Bohlman 2000); popular musics are no less marked by the colonial encounter and the racial alterities ('othernesses') generated by it. The histories of African and Latin American popular musics are hard to understand without a full comprehension of the legacy of British, French, Spanish and Portuguese constructions of indigenous culture, and their absorption by postcolonial elites (see Collins and Richards 1989, Waterman 1990, Davis 1996 and Erlmann 1991 for discussions of music in western, northern and southern Africa; see Wade 1998, Reily 1997 and Austerlitz 1997 for discussions of music and race in postcolonial Colombia, Brazil and the Dominican Republic, respectively).

'Race' and 'ethnicity' are sometimes opposed in cultural analysis: race is taken to refer to identities imposed from above, while ethnicity is distinguished by its voluntary and elective nature. The distinction is, arguably, misleading. The processes that produce all categories of cultural difference are invariably marked by long colonial or neo-colonial histories; ethnicities may also be intensely naturalized (through notions of genetic stock, psychological disposition and so forth), and may carry enormous, if ambiguous, moral force and disciplinary weight, with complex colonial histories (as in the case of Celticisms on the European fringe). Conversely, both racial and ethnic categories can be deployed strategically for the purposes of self-representation. In both cases, as has often been noted, these 'strategic' identities often homogenize and reduce markers of difference to stereotyped criteria that say more about the dominant multi-

cultural system and minority elite interests within that system than about the groups represented. They also flatten out crucial power relations defined by class and gender, along with more finely tuned ethnic and religious distinctions within these groups. The distinction between 'race' and 'ethnicity' is thus not always useful, nor easy to maintain, and both suffer, as analytical categories, from the same kinds of problem.

The analysis of musical practises defined by race or ethnicity thus requires careful attention to the relations that pertain between those doing the defining and those who are being defined, and an historical view of the material, technological and political conditions surrounding these acts of definition. It also requires careful attention to the ways in which performance mediates notions of belonging. The idea that performance provides a simple and homologous representation of a social group has been heavily criticized (see, for example, Middleton 1990). Musical performance has come to be seen more often as a space in which meanings are generated rather than simply 'reflected'; performance meanings are subject to interpretation, creative misunderstanding and mishearing, debate and dispute. They exist, in other words, on complex social and cultural terrain. 'Ethnic' meanings attaching to music are subject to the same performative forces; they shift rapidly, and can include and exclude in previously unexpected ways.

The use of concepts such as articulation (Guilbault 1997) and mediation (Negus 1997) in more recent popular musical scholarship, drawing heavily on Stuart Hall (see particularly Hall 1986), does much to emphasize the labile, contested and negotiated historicity of ethnic categories in popular music. Essentializing definitions connecting race and cultural style have, however, continued to be promoted from many quarters. Ethno-nationalism in many parts of the world has done much to absolutize cultural differences in 'ethnic' terms, music among them. This may be attributable to the collapse in faith in the universalizing ideals of the Enlightenment project and its modern manifestations ('good' nationalism for Weber, Gellner and Habermas, class struggle for Marxists), and the withdrawal of the state from everyday life for those living in many parts of the industrialized West and the former Soviet bloc. While it remains an 'arguable and murky term' (Chapman, McDonald and Tonkin 1989, 11), ethnicity continues to demand attention, and its critical analysis remains a complex and crucial project in popular music studies and elsewhere.

National Ethnicities

Nation-states shape ethnic identities through defining legitimate and illegitimate forms of belonging, and controlling their public expression. Music and other forms of expressive culture are often significant in the process of nation-building. Media, and the radio in particular, have often allowed for the dissemination of national cultures in situations of wide linguistic diversity, poor communication systems and low literacy rates. The crucial significance of cultures in binding together, and permitting communication within, nation-states has been stressed, both on the part of intellectuals committed to the nation-state (from romantics such as Jean-Jacques Rousseau to liberals such as Ernest Gellner), and on the part of its critics. Hobsbawm and Ranger (1983) defined national cultures influentially as 'invented traditions': a form of false-consciousness necessary to industrial capitalist accumulation at that particular juncture in history. Anderson (1983) stressed the importance of print media in forging national consciousness; significant for Anderson was not whether national traditions were 'invented' or not, but the style and the manner of mediation through which national imagining took place.

National musical styles reflect the agendas of those elites whose fortunes are most bound up with the nation-state. Folklore movements shaped a variety of European national musical styles in the nineteenth and early twentieth centuries, in opposition primarily to the self-proclaimed universalism of Austro-German symphonicism. For critics, this imposed bourgeois musical forms that were quite alien in a regionally based, working-class context (see Harker 1985), and were part of an internal process of colonization by the state's elites. Nation-building in a postcolonial context has been marked by similar hegemonic strategies on the part of postcolonial elites, although full of tensions and ambivalences, as famously elaborated in Fanon's impassioned critique of African postcolonial experience (1967).

Assertions of a unitary national musical culture have been less of an option where the musical practises and ideologies associated with colonial elites were impossible to forget, and, in some instances, had a determining effect on the values of the postcolonial nation's new leaders. Consistent efforts were made, nonetheless, to forge national styles from a variety of other elements, each of which was often clearly evaluated and ethnically 'marked.' Just as creolism was dismissed by colonists, it could be legitimately celebrated in popular musical forms by the postcolonial state. *Jújù* music in Nigeria drew on palm-wine recreational music among urban migrants, on the European popular styles cultivated by the colonists, the musics of repatriated slaves from Brazil, and 'indigenous' forms of Yoruba praise-singing and instrumental music. The genre was heavily cultivated by the Yoruba elites who dominated the oil-rich state after independence, as a metaphor of a benign and deeply traditional hierarchical system (Waterman 1990).

What could and could not participate in the new ethnic mix has invariably been strictly controlled; all nations define themselves with reference to unacceptable 'others,' often perceived as polluting from without (undefined border areas or border disputes with a neighboring nation-state) or within (populations that have reasons for resisting the new national order, and reasons for identifying with a neighboring nation-state). The production of a national musical style through the state's media system often has a great deal to do with the symbolic excision of this problematic 'other,' whether tainted by 'the Orient' in modernizing Eastern European and Middle Eastern states (Buchanan 1996; Stokes 1992) or by 'Africa' in the New World (Austerlitz 1997; Pacini Hernandez 1995; Wade 1998). Merengue in the Dominican Republic took, in addition, a determinedly 'rustic' turn under its dictator Trujillo (stressing, for example, accordion rather than saxophone), who used merengue not only as a means of asserting the country's Hispanic as opposed to its African heritage, but as a means of coercing his rivals, the country's former elites, who regarded merengue as lowbrow (Austerlitz 1997).

'Development' in a new national context has resulted in the accumulation of wealth and power in particular areas; labor migration has been the consequence, in which efforts to plan and control these enormous movements of population have been either inadequate or cynical (poor populations living in squatter towns on the fringes of a capital city are easier to control than poor populations in a remote province). Popular migrant musics have often circulated in the unofficial economy, using cheap and portable technologies; from around the mid-1970s, the audio cassette and cassette recorder have been of fundamental significance (Manuel 1993). These musics have sometimes initially been perceived as hostile or oppositional to the state, but have subsequently been co-opted. Despite the fact that these styles often embrace precisely those excised by nationalist ideologues, many express a desire to reconcile rural traditions and urban modernity in ways that are not ultimately incompatible with elite or bourgeois world-views (on *chicha* and other Peruvian migrant genres, see Turino 1993; on *musica sertaneja* in Brazil, see Reily 1992; on *conjunto* in Mexico and the United States, see Peña 1985; on *bacháta* in the Dominican Republic, see Pacini Hernandez 1995). Migrant musics are, in addition, difficult to prohibit effectively, especially when, as in the case of Algerian *rai*, they are taken up by transnational media systems, beyond any effective national control (Virolle 1995; Langlois 1996).

Control of media systems remains problematic, at least from the point of view of national cultural legislators. All states recognize the importance of coherent media policies, in terms of copyright legislation and quota systems, whether promoting totalitarian or liberal cultural policies. All attempt to put musical meaning-making in more easily controllable, or more democratically acceptable, hands. Many writers (Wallis and Malm 1984; Born 1993) have stressed the significance of liberal states using media policies to promote cultural diversity, often perceived as being threatened by the homogenizing effects of transnational markets. Benign or otherwise, few states exercise complete control over the media domains within their jurisdiction. Any analysis of ethnicity requires attention to the continuing salience of the institutional and ideological power of the nation-state, but this is far from being the whole story.

Transnational and 'Global' Ethnicities

Popular musical styles signify beyond the nation-state, and theories of transnationalism and globalization attempt to account for this fact. Transnationalism may be distinguished from globalization: the latter implies the movement of people, goods, information and capital in spaces that lie entirely beyond the nation-state system, while the former implies movements across borders, but within the nation-state system. Whether modern corporations are indeed becoming truly global, multicentered and placeless, or continue to operate within the nation-state system, older certainties of 'center' and 'periphery' have clearly been radically destabilized. 'Global' identities at play in 'world music' are widely understood in terms of a once excluded periphery speaking its voice defiantly in the old center, asserting its rightful place (see, for example, Broughton et al. 1994; and, for an explicitly Afrocentric version, Collins 1992). For some writers, notably Chambers (1985) and Lipsitz (1994), this moment of radical cultural dislocation offers distinct possibilities for cultural and political transformation.

The cultural imperialism thesis, which posited the eventual 'grey out' of local styles (Lomax 1968) through the importation of dominant technologies and cultures from the centers to the peripheries, clearly requires reformulation. Slobin (1993), also drawing heavily on Appadurai (1990), discusses these new forms of musical belonging in terms of a new set of relations between supercultures, subcultures and intercultures, and the creative possibilities that these allow. Arguing explicitly against the cultural imperialism thesis in a similar vein, Mitchell (1996) suggests that rap and rock styles operate regionally to produce hybrids obeying a creative local dynamic in Italy, the Czech Republic, New Zealand and Australia. The Italianization of rap in the south of Italy is possible through the continuing exclusion of this part of the country as more 'African' than 'European' by northern Italian elites, the consequent appeal of African-American musical forms, and their articulation with local discourses of *rispettu* (respect, honor), an indigenous culture of agonistic verbal jousting, and so forth. Although the electric guitar has been disparaged by nationalist intellectuals for its homogenizing, even imperialist, force, rock has generated a wide variety of nationally phrased variants (Regev 1997). Global dislocation may thus produce rather than erase new kinds of locality and new expressions of belonging, obeying quite varied logics.

For others, however, 'globalization' is big-business rhetoric, obscuring the work of a few big corporations with clear national bases dominating markets that are themselves nationally defined (see, for example, Harker 1997; Negus 1992, 1997; Laing 1992). One might stress, therefore, the continuing hegemony of large media corporations and the perpetuation of conservative, essentially Western, aesthetic criteria in the construction of exemplary 'others' (Feld 1994; Erlmann 1996; Guilbault 1997). Rather than destabilizing musical styles and allowing for creative pluralities and reconnections (of, for example, African-American music with its 'roots'), one might argue that the self-conscious creolizations of 'world music' fetishize borders in the very heart of 'world' musical ethnic styles (the hyphen in Afro-Celt, gypsy-jazz and so forth) – a fetishization that feeds long-established First-World tastes and reproduces metropolitan cultural capital. For some writers, therefore, 'world music' constructs and incorporates its 'others' according to essentially the same logic as that operating in other spheres of late capitalist accumulation, while acknowledging the fact that the center is seldom clearly defined and the historical process occurs unevenly (see, in particular, Erlmann 1996). Ethnic difference, in a scenario that owes much to Baudrillard's nihilistic vision, is condemned to a domain of hyperreal, empty signification and, ultimately, complete meaninglessness (Baudrillard 1983).

Others provide a more nuanced and necessarily less conclusive picture, in which the musical shaping of identities in a global environment emerges from complex and dialectical processes. Any theory of globalization clearly requires attention to the circulation of elite forms and the appropriation of popular forms in a variety of different periods and places. Movements of musical styles between elites and popular classes, and between colonial centers and peripheries have always been multidimensional, a fact that is particularly salient when considering the transformations and indigenizations of the European eighteenth-century *contradanse* in the Caribbean in the nineteenth and twentieth centuries in merengue in the Dominican Republic, Venezuela and Puerto Rico, *compas direk* in Haiti, *danza* in Cuba, *conjunto* in Mexico and so forth (see Austerlitz 1997 for a summary). Guilbault's study of *zouk* (1993) connects the genre with the emergence of a distinct sense of Antillean identity. *Zouk* musicians have attempted to reconcile a variety of local, West African and other Caribbean instruments and popular styles with the dictates of the Parisian world music markets and comply with the 'international sound' (Euro-American tunings and intonation, harmony, electric instruments). The resulting hybrid style 'challenges the traditional way of thinking about "we" as a self-enclosed unit by highlighting its relational character' (1993, 210). But as well as putting into play a creative and open-minded sense of Antillean belonging, *zouk* also makes audible some of the fundamental dilemmas of postcolonial Antillean identity, in particular overdependence on transient metropolitan tastes and markets. Its impact on the different islands has been varied, as has its impact on changing experiences of gender and sexuality. 'Globalization,' however conceived, has clearly operated in complex ways, producing rather than effacing identities ('ethnic' and others) whose long-term effects cannot be easily anticipated.

Diaspora and Race

If terms such as 'globalization' have often directed attention to the ways in which styles and cultural artifacts move around the world, the concepts of migration and diasporas bring attention back to the movements of people. Discussions of popular musics made in situations of migration have tended to focus on movements within nation-states, moves from villages to cities, and some degree of accommodation with hegemonic urban/national musical codes. Discussions of diasporas, on the other hand, have tended to focus on multiple movements and connections, and, often, a more thorny relationship with the 'host' society, expressed in an impassioned imaginary of redemption through return. Recent theoretical writing on diasporas has, however, raised a number of distinct propositions concerning the nature of contemporary 'ethnic' identities. These have been most sharply focused on the African diasporas of the circum-Atlantic world (Gilroy 1993). Other diasporas have been the subject of similar analyses (on *rai*, rap and the French Maghrebi diaspora, see Gross, McMurray and Swedenburg 1996; on rap and the Turkish-German diaspora, see Robins and Morley 1996; on the Asian diaspora in Britain, see Sharma, Hutnyk and Sharma 1996).

Gilroy (1993) directs his 'Black Atlantic' thesis against nationalist claims to black racial exclusivity on the one hand and Enlightenment universalism on the other. The former position suggests that black musics can be defined according to their residual Africanisms and can be authentically experienced and understood only from within communities that have experienced the brutal dislocation of slavery. As Gilroy notes, the claim is exclusive, ignoring the variety of black experience within the diaspora, and ignoring its complicity with white racial exclusivism and apartheid-like schemes for 'separate but equal' coexistence. Enlightenment universalists put forward the idea that race is irrelevant to the building of a just and rational society, and abhor any suggestion that particular groups of people, defined by ethnicity or, indeed, in any other way, should claim exclusive access to particular truths and rights. Gilroy is skeptical of claims to pure truth, seeing the rationalist Enlightenment project and modernity itself as fundamentally tainted by the history of slavery. Black cultural styles are not, then, pure 'construction,' as many on the white North American and European left would like to believe. On the contrary, Gilroy argues, they have shaped and responded to the very specific experiences of African slaves and their descendants. On the other hand, it is impossible to understand them by reference to their African 'retentions,' as though these have been directly transmitted from history to the present untouched. Gilroy suggests attention be paid to the ways in which black cultural styles have crossed and recrossed the Atlantic, establishing hybridizing 'routes' rather than 'roots,' new modalities of 'diasporic intimacy,' and strategies for accommodating rather than resisting change.

In many ways, Gilroy's work develops a process of questioning how the notion of 'culture' might apply to African-American experience initiated by cultural anthropologists such as Melville Herskovits (1958), whose notions of syncretic ('mixed') cultures were developed in opposition to conservative 'culture of poverty theorists' in the United States, and those who, quite simply, believed African Americans to be culturally lacking (see Keil 1966). It also engages with the persistent theme of double-consciousness in black literary theory, '[that] sense of always looking at one's self through the eyes of others,' as Du Bois wrote in 1903 (1969, 45). Literary theory has drawn heavily on African-American musical practises to articulate the peculiarities of black cultural experience, in particular its 'combative spirituality' and 'kinetic orality' (West 1996, 81), and techniques of troping and signifying (destabilizing, critical repetition, often connected with West African trickster mythology) (Gates 1984).

The legacy of black criticism has had complex ramifications for the study of African-American popular musics. This can be traced from the Harlem Renaissance (see Floyd 1990) and the assimilationist struggles of the civil rights movement, to the Afrocentric nationalism of Stokely Carmichael and Malcolm X, to the poststructuralist criticism of Houston Baker and Henry Gates, for whom race is, first and foremost, 'a pernicious act of language' and a problem of warped communication (Gates 1985, 5). On the one hand, there has been a certain stress on affirming their connections with Africa and the ghetto, and their dilution outside. Jones (1963), for example, identifies a 'blues continuum' ranging from its 'folkloric' country forms to its white-assimilated urban forms, and decries the 'ultimate sterility' of black music adapted for white audiences, 'hated by the middle class Negro and not even understood by whites' (169; see also Rose 1994 on rap). Black musics have, however, emerged as a result of sustained interactions with non-black cultures in the New World and elsewhere, and this kind of analysis often relies on vague musical criteria ('call-and-response,' 'blue notes,' 'noise,' heavy involvement of the body in playing and singing styles), which could equally apply to a wide variety of musics with no historical connection to Africa whatsoever (Tagg 1989). As many have also noted, these kinds of 'nativist' approaches are inclined simply to invert, and in the process reproduce, racial hierarchies (see Monson 1996 for a review of the debates over Afrocentrism). On the other hand, black musical signification is seen as mobile and hybridizing, readily available in 'strategically anti-essentialist' oppositional cultural politics the world over (Lipsitz 1994; see also Hebdige 1979). Arguably, this approach is inclined to ignore the historical *longue-durée* (in which, as in the case of merengue, yesterday's emancipatory hybridity becomes today's totalitarianism), and to separate texts from their historically specific moments of production. Between these positions, a number of more empirically driven historical studies have explored the complex relationships between musicians, entrepreneurs and audiences in relation to 'race' records, black radio and television (see, in particular, Dates and Barlow 1993). The movements of African-American popular styles 'back' into Africa have also been the subject of a number of recent studies (Collins 1992; Erlmann 1991; Dibango 1994), all of which are highly attentive to the complex and interconnected ways in which their 'Africanness' is perceived, mediated and used by white, black and other diasporic audiences.

Bibliography

Anderson, Benedict. 1983. *Imagined Communities*. London: Verso.

Appadurai, Arjun. 1990. 'Disjuncture and Difference in the Global Cultural Economy.' *Public Culture* 2(2): 1–24.

Appadurai, Arjun. 1996. *Modernity at Large: Cultural Dimensions of Globalization*. Minneapolis, MN: University of Minnesota Press.

Austerlitz, Paul. 1997. *Merengue: Dominican Music and Dominican Identity*. Philadelphia: Temple University Press.

Baudrillard, Jean. 1983. *Simulations*. New York: Semiotexte.

Born, Georgina. 1993. 'Afterword: Music Policy, Aesthetic and Social Difference.' In *Rock and Popular Music: Politics, Policies, Institutions*, ed. Tony Bennett et al. London: Routledge, 266–91.

Broughton, Simon, et al. 1994. *The Rough Guide to World Music*. London: Penguin.

Buchanan, Donna. 1996. 'Wedding Musicians, Political Transition and National Consciousness in Bulgaria.' In *Retuning Culture: Musical Changes in Central and Eastern Europe*, ed. Mark Slobin. Durham, NC: Duke University Press, 200–38.

Chambers, Iain. 1985. *Urban Rhythms: Pop Music and Popular Culture*. London: Macmillan.

Chapman, Malcolm, McDonald, Maryon, and Tonkin, Elizabeth. 1989. 'Introduction: History and Social Anthropology.' In *History and Ethnicity*, ed. Elizabeth Tonkin, Maryon McDonald and Malcolm Chapman. London: Routledge, 1–21.

Collins, John. 1992. *West African Pop Roots*. Philadelphia: Temple University Press.

Collins, John, and Richards, Paul. 1989. 'Popular Music in West Africa.' In *World Music, Politics, and Social Change*, ed. Simon Frith. Manchester: Manchester University Press, 13–46.

Darwin, Charles. 1950 (1859). *On the Origin of Species by Means of Natural Selection; or, The Preservation of Favoured Races in the Struggle for Life*. London: Watts.

Dates, Jannette, and Barlow, William. 1993. *Split Image: African Americans in the Mass Media*. 2nd ed. Washington, DC: Howard University Press.

Davis, Ruth. 1996. 'The Art/Popular Music Paradigm and the Tunisian Ma'luf.' *Popular Music* 15(3): 313–23.

Dibango, Manu (with Danielle Rouard). 1994. *Three Kilos of Coffee: An Autobiography*. Chicago: University of Chicago Press.

Du Bois, W.E.B. 1969 (1903). *The Souls of Black Folks*. New York: New American Library.

Erlmann, Veit. 1991. *African Stars: Studies in Black South African Performance*. Chicago: University of Chicago Press.

Erlmann, Veit. 1996. 'Aesthetics of the Global Imagination: Reflections on World Music in the 1990s.' *Public Culture* 8(3): 467–88.

Fanon, Frantz. 1967. *Black Skin, White Masks*, trans. Charles Lam Markmann. New York: Grove Press.

Feld, Steven. 1994. 'From Schizophonia to Schismogenesis: On the Discourses and Commodification Practices of "World Music" and "World Beat."' In Charles Keil and Steven Feld, *Music Grooves: Essays and Dialogues*. Chicago and London: University of Chicago Press, 257–89.

Floyd, Samuel A., Jr., ed. 1990. *Black Music in the Harlem Renaissance: A Collection of Essays*. New York: Westport.

Gates, Henry Louis, Jr. 1984. 'The Blackness of Blackness: A Critique of the Sign and the Signifying Monkey.' In *Black Literature and Literary Theory*, ed. Henry Louis Gates, Jr. New York: Methuen, 285–317.

Gates, Henry Louis, Jr. 1985. 'Writing Race and the Difference It Makes.' In *Race, Writing and Difference*, ed. Henry Louis Gates, Jr. Chicago: University of Chicago Press, 1–21.

Gilroy, Paul. 1993. *The Black Atlantic: Modernity and Double Consciousness*. London: Verso.

Gross, Joan, McMurray, David, and Swedenburg, Ted. 1996. 'Arab Noise and Ramadan Nights: *Rai*, Rap, and Franco-Maghrebi Identities.' In *Displacement, Diaspora, and Geographies of Identity*, ed. Smadar Lavie and Ted Swedenburg. Durham, NC: Duke University Press, 119–55.

Guilbault, Jocelyne. 1993. *Zouk: World Music in the West Indies*. Chicago: University of Chicago Press.

Guilbault, Jocelyne. 1997. 'Interpreting World Music: A Challenge in Theory and Practice.' *Popular Music* 16(1): 31–44.

Hall, Stuart. 1986. 'On Postmodernism and Articulation.' *Journal of Communication Inquiry* 10(2): 45–60.

Harker, Dave. 1985. *Fakesong: The Manufacture of British 'Folksong,' 1700 to the Present Day*. Milton Keynes: Open University Press.

Harker, Dave. 1997. 'The Wonderful World of the IFPI: Music Industry Rhetoric, the Critics and the Classical Marxist Critique.' *Popular Music* 16(1): 45–80.

Hebdige, Dick. 1979. *Subculture: The Meaning of Style*. London: Methuen.

Herskovits, Melville J. 1958. *The Myth of the Negro Past*. Boston, MA: Beacon Press.

Hobsbawm, Eric, and Ranger, Terence. 1983. *The Invention of Tradition*. Cambridge: Cambridge University Press.

Jones, LeRoi [Imamu Amiri Baraka]. 1963. *Blues People: Negro Music in White America*. New York: William Morrow.

Keil, Charles. 1966. *Urban Blues*. Chicago: University of Chicago Press.

Laing, Dave. 1992. '"Sadeness," Scorpions and Single Markets: National and Transnational Trends in European Popular Music.' *Popular Music* 11(2): 127–39.

Langlois, Tony. 1996. 'The Local and Global in North African Popular Music.' *Popular Music* 15(3): 259–73.

Lipsitz, George. 1994. *Dangerous Crossroads: Popular Music, Postmodernism and the Poetics of Place*. London: Verso.

Lomax, Alan. 1968. *Folk Song Style and Culture*. Washington, DC: American Association for the Advancement of Science.

Manuel, Peter. 1993. *Cassette Culture: Popular Music and Technology in North India*. Chicago: University of Chicago Press.

Middleton, Richard. 1990. *Studying Popular Music*. Milton Keynes and Philadelphia: Open University Press.

Mitchell, Tony. 1996. *Popular Music and Local Identity: Rock, Pop and Rap in Europe and Oceania*. London: Leicester University Press.

Monson, Ingrid. 1996. *Saying Something: Jazz Music and Interaction*. Chicago: University of Chicago Press.

Negus, Keith. 1992. *Producing Pop: Culture and Conflict in the Popular Music Industry*. London: Edward Arnold.

Negus, Keith. 1997. *Popular Music in Theory: An Introduction*. Hanover, NH: University Press of New England.

Pacini Hernandez, Deborah. 1995. *Bacháta: A Social History of a Dominican Popular Music*. Philadelphia: Temple University Press.

Peña, Manuel. 1985. *The Texas-Mexican Conjunto: History of a Working-Class Music*. Austin, TX: University of Texas Press.

Radano, Ronald, and Bohlman, Philip V. 2000. 'Introduction: Race and Music, Their Past, Their Presence.' In *Music and the Racial Imagination*, ed. Ronald Radano and Philip V. Bohlman. Chicago: University of Chicago Press.

Regev, Motti. 1997. 'Rock Aesthetics and Musics of the World.' *Theory, Culture and Society* 14(3): 125–42.

Reily, Suzel Ana. 1992. '*Musica Sertaneja* and Migrant Identity: The Stylistic Development of a Brazilian Genre.' *Popular Music* 11(3): 337–58.

Reily, Suzel. 1997 (1994). 'Macunaima's Music: National Identity and Ethnomusicological Research in Brazil.' In *Ethnicity, Identity and Music: The Musical Construction of Place*, ed. Martin Stokes. Oxford: Berg, 71–96.

Robins, Kevin, and Morley, David. 1996. 'Almanci, Yabanci.' *Cultural Studies* 10(2): 248–54.

Rose, Tricia. 1994. *Black Noise: Rap Music and Black Culture in Contemporary America*. Hanover, NH: University Press of New England.

Sharma, Sanjay, Hutnyk, John, and Sharma, Ashwani, eds. 1996. *Dis-Orienting Rhythms: The Politics of the New Asian Dance Music*. London: Zed Books.

Slobin, Mark. 1993. *Subcultural Sounds: Micromusics of the West*. Hanover, NH: Wesleyan University Press.

Stokes, Martin. 1992. *The Arabesk Debate: Music and Musicians in Modern Turkey*. Oxford: Clarendon Press.

Stokes, Martin. 1997 (1994). 'Introduction: Ethnicity,

Identity and Music.' In *Ethnicity, Identity and Music: The Musical Construction of Place*. Oxford: Berg, 1–27.

Tagg, Philip. 1989. 'Open Letter: "Black Music," "Afro-American Music" and "European Music."' *Popular Music* 8(3): 285–98.

Turino, Thomas. 1993. *Moving Away from Silence: Music of the Peruvian Altiplano and the Experience of Urban Migration*. Chicago: University of Chicago Press.

Virolle, Marie. 1995. *La Chanson Rai: De l'Algérie profonde à la scène internationale* [Rai: From Deepest Algeria to the International Scene]. Paris: Karthala.

Wade, Peter. 1998. 'Music, Blackness, and National Identity: Three Moments in Colombian History.' *Popular Music* 17(1): 1–19.

Wallis, Roger, and Malm, Krister. 1984. *Big Sounds from Small Peoples: The Music Industry in Small Countries*. London: Constable.

Waterman, Christopher A. 1990. *Jùjú: A Social History and Ethnography of an African Popular Music*. Chicago: University of Chicago Press.

West, Cornel. 1996. 'Black Strivings.' In Henry Louis Gates, Jr. and Cornel West, *The Future of the Race*. New York: Alfred A. Knopf, 65–106.

MARTIN STOKES

Exoticism

The term 'exoticism' refers to a musical phenomenon explored by many composers and musicians who, through the centuries, have employed various musical styles to evoke, romanticize, exorcize and assimilate the unknown, the 'Other.' The phenomenon of exoticism is evident in European music of the eighteenth and nineteenth centuries, as well as in the popular music of the twentieth century more generally. In contrast, the term 'exotica' refers to a popular music genre of the 1950s and 1960s in which a sense of the exotic figures prominently.

Exoticism as a Phenomenon

The character of exoticism in any particular instance depends on an individual's geographic or cultural location. Many of the musical compositions to be discussed below, especially those written in Europe in the nineteenth and twentieth centuries, go hand in hand with colonialist expansion in the Middle East and – together with paintings and literary works of the same period – are generally referred to as Orientalist artworks. As pointed out by Edward Said in his influential book *Orientalism* (1978), they tended to serve Western purposes, coexisting with or lending support to the global enterprises of European and North American empires.

Europe's interest in the Middle East led painters and writers to travel to Egypt, Palestine or Maghreb. In their paintings, artists like Eugène Delacroix, Jean Auguste Dominique Ingres, Alexandre-Gabriel Decamps and Théodore Chassériau cherished a mysterious and exotic idea of the imagined Orient. At the same time, odalisques, Arabic hostesses, exotic heroines (the Queen of Sheba, Cleopatra, Salome, Salammbô) and many other female characters began to inhabit the writings of Gustave Flaubert, Théophile Gautier, Stéphane Mallarmé, Algernon Charles Swinburne, Oscar Wilde and Gabriele d'Annunzio.

Exoticism in European Music of the Eighteenth and Nineteenth Centuries

As compared to painters 'in the field' and writers traveling to the Orient or drawing inspiration from diaries, translations and travelogs, musicians could rely only on a few approximate transcriptions. Thus, their only possibility was to evoke and visually suggest the 'Other,' the distant. The penchant of European musicians for the faraway and for the use of unusual instruments dates back to the eighteenth century. Under Ottoman rule, Europe was confronted with the notion of the exotic in music, experiencing the sound of the Turkish military bands that would soon inspire the so-called *alla Turca* style. The latter represented the first attempt by European musicians to come to terms with the presumed music of a distant land.

As noted by Mary Hunter (1998), the result was an ethnic indeterminacy used to signify general barbarity rather than Turkishness per se. The *alla Turca* style tended to manipulate elements of the prevailing European musical vocabulary to represent threat, barbarism, crudity and, most of all, musical illiteracy. Overtures to such operas as Christoph Willibald Gluck's *La Rencontre Imprévue* and Mozart's *Die Entführung aus dem Serail* incorporated features – repeated thirds, ornaments, repetitive duple rhythms – and instruments – cymbals, bass drum, tambourine – that helped to conjure up a stereotypically sensual (the seraglio women, for instance) and treacherous idea of the Turk and the Orient in general. Many were the artists who were influenced by the *turquerie*, among them Gioacchino Rossini (*La pietra del paragone*; *L'Italiana in Algeri*) and Carl Maria von Weber (*Abu Hassan*; *Oberon*).

The eighteenth and nineteenth centuries would also witness the rise of the *grand opéra*, a genre of musical theater in which composers like Félicien David (*La Perle du Brésil*, 1851) and Giacomo Meyerbeer (*L'Africaine*, 1865) evoked distant lands and cultures through 'local color.' World fairs helped to increase Europe's penchant for the exotic, especially the well-known 1889 Paris *Exposition Universelle*, which featured a variety of ethnic music. For the first time, European composers – especially Ravel and Debussy – could have direct contact with foreign musicians. The *Exposition Universelle* featured a famous gamelan orchestra from Java, which accompanied authentic Javanese dancing and which had a huge impact on the style of Debussy (for instance, in the piano piece 'Pagodes') and Ravel (*Ma mère l'oye*). Ravel's *Boléro*, his most famous work, became a source of inspiration for many composers. *Boléro* celebrated Spanish exoticism, relying on sensual rhythm, repetition and instruments that moved from silence to an orgiastic denouement.

It is important to note that Spain has always been considered to be at the core of European musical and cultural exoticism. Its exoticizing occurred during Napoleon's invasion and occupation of Spain (1808–13). During these years, Spanish stereotypes like the guerrilla fighter, the gypsy guitar-player and the Spanish dancer came to prominence, serving the purposes of the dominant culture. A character such as the female Spanish dancer, infused with sexuality and passion, has, in particular, indelibly influenced popular culture and music. In 'La spagnola,' for example, a song dating back to 1906, Nilla Pizzi, one of Italy's most famous popular singers, praised the character of a gorgeous female Spanish singer resembling an unknown – and therefore more dangerous – flower, the woman being an enchanter of love and voluptuousness. In 'Guitarrera,' another popular Italian song, the Spanish woman becomes a burning flower, dispensing chants and kisses. Even a so-called Spanish style, relying on descending thirds and other melodic formulae, has become conventionalized and continues to be entrenched as a stylistic feature of the exotic in popular music.

Orientalism was also a strong ingredient of the music of the New Russian School (Balakirev, Borodin, Cui, Musorgsky, Rimsky-Korsakov) featured prominently at the 1889 *Exposition Universelle*. The skeptical attitude of these composers toward established European musical traditions, together with their exposure to exotic influences and to popular music, led them to branch out in new compositional directions within established traditions. Japan also provided the basis for a fascination with the exotic on the part of many composers, from Pietro Mascagni (*Iris*, 1898) to Giacomo Puccini (*Madama Butterfly*, 1904). This fascination was also evident in the work of Impressionist painters, infusing European culture even more with evidence of the exotic.

Exoticism in Popular Music of the Twentieth Century

In jazz, especially Afro-Cuban jazz, the works of Duke Ellington and Dizzy Gillespie exhibited a strong fascination with the exotic. Ellington referred to his shows at the Cotton Club as 'jungle music,' referring mainly to the 'urban jungle' of Harlem. In his compositions, he often incorporated birdcalls, animal sounds and ambient noises, suggesting a trite African primitivism. According to Philippe Carles and Jean-Louis Comolli (1972), this superficial introduction of Africa into his work offered black people the exotic vision of a mythical Africa littered with savage landscapes and primeval forests. At the same time, it evoked for the white audience a sensual and mysterious sound imbued with transgression and an antagonism to the civilized world.

Ellington's name is also inextricably linked to 'Caravan,' a composition credited to Ellington and Juan Tizol, which, over the years, became an exotic standard. The motor rhythms of Ellington's marching beat evoked languid Oriental lands with camels walking through the sand. Juan Tizol was also the composer of 'Perdido,' a song whose lyrics (written by Ervin Drake) epitomized well the United States's fascination with the most trite Latin exoticisms: 'Bolero. I glanced as we danced the bolero. He said, taking off his sombrero, "Let's meet for a sweet siesta."'

North American popular music is littered with compositions evoking the faraway. These often rely on many of the exotic formulae mentioned above. Popular musicians produced many Eastern-flavored songs ('In a Persian Market,' 'Calcutta,' 'Istanbul'), Pacific eulogies ('Quiet Village,' 'Hawaiian War Chant,' 'Hawaiian Wedding Song,' 'Moon of Manakoora,' 'Bali Ha'i') and Latin numbers ('Tico Tico,' 'Brazil,' 'Baia,' 'La Cucaracha,' 'The Peanut Vendor,' 'Perfidia,' 'Siboney,' 'Malagueña'). A composition such as 'In a Persian Market,' written by Albert Ketèlbey in 1920, often provided material for pianists and pit orchestras that accompanied silent films containing exotic subjects. In the late 1920s, 'Malagueña,' a song about a Spanish woman from Malaga by Ernesto Lecuona, came to embody – through its ritual and formulaic character – Latin exotica. It was no surprise that it was chosen by composer André Kostelanetz as the lead track for his South Pacific LP venture, *Lure of the Tropics*.

A few years later, this song was also featured on *The Soul of Spain*, 101 Strings' debut album. Over the years, the orchestra has tried to capture the imagined and exoticized 'soul' of countries such as England, Mexico and Italy, employing trite formulae such as flamenco guitar touches to conjure up Mexican music or accordions to evoke Hungarian dances. According to music critic Joseph Lanza (1995), 101 Strings' 'postcard approach' supplied North America with an exact replica of the world it wanted. Their music, as that of 1950s exotica composers (from Les Baxter to Martin Denny), captured the feel for foreign lands as culled and reassembled from Hollywood/Broadway stockpiles of color-treated sunsets. As noted by film critic Bill Feret (1984), Hollywood itself helped to establish many exotic musical stereotypes, resorting, for instance, to samba and tango which lent themselves nicely to swaying palm trees and sensual tropical settings.

Hollywood often resorted to a composer like Xavier Cugat, frequently employed in Latin-tinged musicals. One of his trademarks was to add fake tribal sounds to rumba or, later in the 1950s, to mambo and cha-cha. Cugat, as musicologist John Storm Roberts observed (1972), was the forerunner of many 'gringo-Latino' bands that produced watered-down versions of Cuban music for the US market.

As well as witnessing the rise of the musical genre 'exotica' – a genre that focused on the islands of the South Pacific, especially Hawaii, and featured 'semi-exotic' percussion instruments such as congas and bongos – the late 1950s saw the rise of albums extolling the exotic Middle East. Among them were *I Remember Lebanon* and *Music of the Middle East – Port Said*, two belly-dance records very popular in the United States whose intent was to evoke an oversexualized image of the Orient. On *Port Said*, tenor Mohammed El-Bakkar lured the listener into ancient slave markets – as described in the record's liner notes – populated with sensuous maidens dancing to instruments like drums, bells, cymbals, sticks and oboes. In *Orienta*, a 1959 record by the Markko Polo Adventurers, the musicians' main intent was to combine the 'charm of the Orient' with the 'wit of the Occident.' This was achieved through an array of sensual 'oriental' percussion sounds combined with a touch of 'pop 'n' jazz.' In the end, as the liner notes confirmed, '(Everything) resembles the dreams of an imaginative person who has fallen asleep during a "Dr. Fu Manchu" movie on television.'

To a certain extent, the Adventurers and other 'extollers' of the exotic East such as Tak Skindo, Sondi Sodasi, Anita Darian and Alex Stordahl foreshadowed the 1960s sitar fad triggered by Indian musician and composer Ravi Shankar. The latter inspired many rock groups, especially the Beatles who, in 1965, recorded 'Norwegian Wood (This Bird Has Flown),' the first popular song to feature a sitar. Following the tritest Orientalist principles, the instrument was played in a Western fashion, with a total absence of the drones that typically stem from raga, the modal system of Indian classical music. The song started a trend that has continued within pop and rock music, indelibly associating the sitar with the exotic.

In the following years, so-called raga rock – that is, rock music based on a few raga ingredients (the lowered seventh degree of the major scale, for instance) – came to great prominence. In particular, many groups (such as the Rolling Stones, the Yardbirds, the Kinks and the Who) of the so-called 'British invasion,' as well as

numerous US psychedelic bands, developed a strong infatuation with Indian meditation and yogis, delving deeply into the exotic East, often for drug-related reasons only. As musicologist Jonathan Bellman (1998) observes in describing a Kinks' song ('See My Friends'), many were the exotic formulae and stereotypes shared and adopted by rock composers of the same period: sounds that were jangling, drone-based and unquestionably quasi-Indian – all that was necessary in a pop-exotic context.

Conclusion

The 'exotic' within popular music is the subject of ongoing debate. It frequently comes to prominence in discussions of the works of Western musicians such as Paul Simon, Peter Gabriel and David Byrne – works that reveal a penchant for Third World musics. Suffice it to say that borrowings and reworkings of indigenous sounds have often disguised a subtle but insidious form of artistic colonialism. This is confirmed by the fact that the intention of spreading musical styles and cultures, together with the artistic mores and experiences of other peoples, has seldom resulted in the creation of local cultural and musical facilities aimed at freeing indigenous musicians from the ambit of Western patrons.

Bibliography

Adinolfi, Francesco. 2000. *Mondo Exotica: Suoni, visioni e manie della generazione Cocktail* [Mondo Exotica: Sounds, Visions and Manias of the Cocktail Generation]. Torino: Einaudi.

Bellman, Jonathan, ed. 1998. *The Exotic in Western Music*. Boston, MA: Northeastern University Press.

Carles, Philippe, and Comolli, Jean-Louis. 1972. *Free Jazz, Black Power*. Paris: Union générale d'éditions.

Feret, Bill. 1984. *Lure of the Tropix: A Pictorial History of the Tropic Temptress in Films, Serials and Comics*. London and New York: Proteus Books.

Hunter, Mary. 1998. 'The "Alla Turca" Style in the Late Eighteenth Century: Race and Gender in the Symphony and the Seraglio.' In *The Exotic in Western Music*, ed. Jonathan Bellman. Boston, MA: Northeastern University Press, 43–73.

Lanza, Joseph. 1995. *Elevator Music: A Surreal History of Muzak, Easy-Listening, and Other Moodsong*. New York: Picador.

Roberts, John Storm. 1972. *Black Music of Two Worlds*. New York: Praeger.

Said, Edward W. 1978. *Orientalism*. New York: Pantheon Books.

Smith, R.J. 1995. 'Music Out of the Moon.' *LA Weekly* (14–20 July): 23–32.

Discographical References

101 Strings Orchestra, The. 'Malagueña.' *The Soul of Spain, Vol. 1.* Somerset SF 6600. *1959*: USA.

Apiazu, Don. 'The Peanut Vendor (El Manisero).' *Don Apiazu.* Harlequin HQCD 10. *1991*: UK.

'Bali Ha'i.' *South Pacific.* RCA SB-2011. *1958*: USA.

Beatles, The. 'Norwegian Wood (This Bird Has Flown).' *Rubber Soul.* Parlophone PMC 1267. *1965*: UK.

Boni, Carla. 'Guitarrera.' Columbia DQ-2603. *1971*: Italy.

Cugat, Xavier. 'Perfidia.' *Bim Bam Bum (1935–1940).* Harlequin HQCD 14. *1991*: UK.

Cugat, Xavier, and His Orchestra. 'La Cucaracha.' *Golden Classics.* Collectables COL 5666. *1995*: USA.

Denny, Martin. 'Moon of Manakoora.' *Hypnotique/Exotica, Vol. 3.* Scamp SCP 9714-2. *1997*: USA.

Denny, Martin. 'Quiet Village.' *Exotica.* Scamp SCP 9712-2. *1996*: USA.

El-Bakkar, Mohammed, and His Oriental Ensemble. *Music of the Middle East – Port Said.* Audio Fidelity AFSD 5833. *1958*: USA.

Ellington, Duke. 'Caravan.' *Duke Ellington & Friends.* Verve 833 291-2. *1987*: USA.

El-Safi, Wadih, and Salam, Najah. *I Remember Lebanon.* Fiesta FLP 1290. *1958*: USA.

Four Lads, The. 'Istanbul.' *The Very Best of the Four Lads: Moments to Remember.* Taragon TARCD 1079-2. *2000*: USA.

Kinks, The. 'See My Friends.' *Kinks-Size Kinkdom.* Rhino R21S-75769. *1988*: USA.

Kostelanetz, André. *Lure of the Tropics.* Columbia CL 780. *1950*: USA.

London Promenade Orchestra, The. *Ketèlbey: In a Persian Market.* Philips DDD 81. *1983*: UK.

Lyman, Arthur. 'Hawaiian War Chant.' *Hawaiian Sunset: The Sounds of Arthur Lyman.* Rykodisc/Hifi RCD 50365. *1996*: USA.

Markko Polo Adventurers, The. *Orienta.* RCA-Victor LSP-1919. *1959*: USA.

Pizzi, Nilla. 'La spagnola.' *Personale di Nilla Pizzi.* RCA CD 71334. *1991*: Italy.

Ros, Edmundo. 'Brazil.' *Lounge Music Goes Latin.* Chronicles 314535882-2. *1996*: USA.

Schory, Dick. 'Baia.' *Music for Bang, Baa-Room and Harp.* RCA 7432135742-2. *1996*: USA.

Smith, Ethel. 'Tico Tico.' *Maracas, Marimbas and Mambos: Latin Classics at MGM.* Rhino R2 72722. *1997*: USA.

Valente, Caterina. 'Siboney.' *The Hi-Fi Nightingale.* Decca DL-8203. *1956*: USA.

Vaughan, Sarah. 'Perdido.' *Ultra Lounge, Vol. 15: Wild, Cool & Swingin' Too!* Capitol 53411. *1997*: USA.

Welk, Lawrence, and His Orchestra. 'Calcutta.' *Discoveries Presents Stereo Instrumental Oldies.* Varèse Sarabande VSD 6009. *1999*: USA.

Williams, Andy. 'Hawaiian Wedding Song.' *The Very Best of Andy Williams: 50 Cool Tracks from the Emperor of Easy.* Columbia CDC CB 722. *1999*: USA.

FRANCESCO ADINOLFI

Fans

In popular culture, the term 'fan,' derived from 'fanatic,' was first used in 1889 to describe keen and regular followers of baseball. It then became common to describe enthusiastic followers of film (1915) and theater (1919) as fans. However, the term has since then often been used pejoratively. Just as the fanatic's political, religious or other beliefs greatly exceed what society considers is reasonable and may lead to acts of violence, so the fan is often associated with an unnatural and excessive regard for a particular sport, pastime or performer.

Until the 1990s, theories of fandom conformed to the customary pejorative connotations of the term 'fan,' and were overwhelmingly negative in their assessments. Jensen (1992) states that 'the literature on fandom is haunted by images of deviance' (9). She argues that two caricatures of the pop fan have emerged: the pathological fan who enters into an intense fantasy relationship with a celebrity figure (such as Madonna's stalker or John Lennon's fan/assassin); and the atomized individual who seeks solace in the frenzy of the crowd (hence, presumably, the violence of the soccer fan or of the punk; see Buford 1992).

A change in thinking about fans was signaled by the publication in 1992 of *The Adoring Audience: Fan Culture and Popular Media*, the volume in which Jensen's essay appeared. In the Introduction to this volume, Lisa Lewis observes that fans 'have been overlooked or not taken seriously as research subjects by critics and scholars,' and have been 'maligned and sensationalized by the popular press' (1992, 1). However, she continues, 'If we approach fandom as a serious and complicated arena right from the beginning, perhaps we will be less inclined to trivialize . . . fan behaviors' (1992, 2).

Pejorative and sensationalized accounts of fandom have therefore themselves become the subject of critical comment. Doss (1999), for example, has argued that 'much of the postwar critique of Elvis's fans was, in fact, a thinly veiled attack on teenage girls, steadily maligned throughout 1950s America for profoundly violating social norms' (49). Recent work on fandom has thus replaced the model of blind obsession and sexual infatuation with ones that stress creative, proactive ways in which fans interact with the objects of their desire (see Wise's (1990) discussion of the feminized, anti-macho Presley) – ones in which the fans' relationship with the stars is less unequal. In treating its subject seriously, recent work on fandom has also adopted an ethnographic approach (see, for example, Weinstein 1991; Cavicchi 1998).

In the light of this more balanced approach, the concepts of the fan and fandom have not been easy to define. Fiske (1992) has argued that 'fandom is typically associated with cultural forms that the dominant value system denigrates ... It is thus associated with the cultural tastes of subordinated formations of the people' (30). However, as Shuker (1994) observes, while 'this is plausible ... not all fans ... occupy such social positions' (242). Grossberg (1992) has argued that, while 'the sensibility of the consumer operates by producing structures of pleasure' (55), 'the category of the fan ... can only be understood in relation to a different sensibility ... [that] operates in the domain of affect or mood' (56).

For Grossberg, 'affect is not the same as either emotions or desires' (1992, 56). Rather, affect 'determines how invigorated we feel in particular moments of our lives. It defines the strength of our investment in particular experiences, practices, identities, meanings, and pleasures. In other words, affect privileges volition over meaning' (1992, 57). Shuker observes that, 'even conceding the obvious difficulty of defining affect, and the specificities evident in the operation of sensibility, Grossberg's discussion of these becomes rather too amorphous to be helpful' (1994, 243). Nonetheless, the idea that the fan can be distinguished from the consumer or ordinary audience member not just pejoratively in terms of behavior considered to be excessive or unreasonable, but in a more balanced way in terms of the degree of psychological investment in a particular cultural commodity or persona, seems to be an important one. As Lewis puts it, 'We all know who the fans are. They're the ones who wear the colors of their favorite team, the ones who record their soap operas on VCRs to watch after the work day is over, the ones who tell you every detail about a movie star's life and work, the ones who sit in line for hours for front row tickets to rock concerts' (1992, 1).

As well as making a distinction between consumers or ordinary audience members on the one hand, and fans on the other, an understanding of the term 'fan' also needs to take account of the term and concept of 'aficionado.' Jensen states that 'aficionadohood' – the attachment to elite, prestige-conferring objects – has been regarded by theorists as in some way safer than and superior to the fan's attachment to popular, mass-mediated objects. However, a more balanced and less judgmental approach to this distinction is also desirable and possible. In Shuker's thinking, aficionados remain fans, but their investment is 'usually at more of an intel-lectual level and focused on the music *per se* rather than on the persona of the performer(s)' (1994, 243). For Shuker, 'both categories of fan engage in fandom as an active process, and both often display impressive knowledge of their preferred genres or performers.' However, he concludes, 'their emotional and physical investments are different, as are the social consumption situations in which their fandom operates' (1994, 243).

Aficionados are characterized more by what Straw (1990) has referred to as '"secondary involvement" in music: the hunting down of rare tracks, the reading of music-oriented magazines, the high recognition of record labels or producers,' as well as by the presence in their lives of 'complex hierarchies based on knowledge of the music or possession of obscure records, on relationships to opinion leaders as the determinants of tastes and purchases' (104). It is interesting that the term 'jazz aficionado' was preferred to that of 'jazz fan' or 'jazzfan' in the 1930s and 1940s by those determined to see jazz established as an art form with its own, intrinsic set of values and concerned to distinguish themselves from those perceived as having more plebeian tastes in music (see, for example, Frith 1988, 45–63). Keightley (1996) has examined 'aficionadohood' with reference to the growth of interest in hi-fi in the 1950s. The concept of the aficionado may also be useful in understanding the relation of fans to some popular music genres, including, for example, dance music. Fans of these genres do not generally subscribe to the cult of personality that is so ingrained in Anglo-American popular music. Instead, they are more interested in the style and the genre itself (northern soul, house, ambient, techno, jungle) than in the performers.

If fans and aficionados can be distinguished from consumers and ordinary audience members in terms of the degree of intensity with which they characteristically engage with music and performers, they can be distinguished also in terms of their willingness, if not their desire, to become organized institutionally. Popular performers in the nineteenth century, like the Hutchinson Family and Henry Russell, could count on a partisan audience. However, the twentieth century witnessed the advent of the fan base. The formation of fan bases, such as the one that came into being in the wake of the hysterical response to the death of actor Rudolph Valentino in 1926, was correlated with the success of Hollywood from the 1920s onward. What differentiated the new fan bases of the twentieth century from the audiences for the Hutchinson Family and Henry Russell was the way in which fans were able to create institutional forms through which to appreciate specific performers and genres of popular music. This led to fan clubs, fan mail (letters of appreciation sent to individual performers), fan writing (novels, screenplays and films inspired by fans' devotion) and fanzines. The term 'fanzine,' first used in connection with science-fiction fan magazines in 1941, denoted usually low-budget publications coordinated by and written for fans of a certain author, genre or artist.

In the 1940s and 1950s, record labels began funding official fan clubs and appreciation societies, and the music business started utilizing and targeting specific fan groupings. For example, British big-band leader Ted Heath's principal male singer, Dickie Valentine, had a large fan club, which met every year in the Hammersmith Palais in London. These meetings started an important trend within popular music and were subsequently echoed by fan conventions and gatherings around the world. Some fans, such as 'Deadheads' (followers of psychedelic rock group the Grateful Dead), Elvis freaks and Beatles' fans, have continued to meet regularly, long after the end of the artists' careers. The funerals of musicians can also be an occasion for vast gatherings of fans. Danielson (1997) reports that, when Umm Kulthūm, 'unquestionably the most famous singer in the twentieth-century Arab world,' died in 1975, 'her funeral was described as bigger than that of President Jamāl 'Abd al-Nāsir' (1). Likewise, Edith Piaf's biographer reports that, on the day of her funeral (14 October 1963), 'forty thousand people crowded into the Père Lachaise cemetery . . . Her funeral was like her life – crazy!' (Berteaut 1972, 477).

The first recognizable fan grouping for an individual performer was probably the 'bobby-soxers,' the legion of adolescent female fans of Frank Sinatra in the 1940s. Although, as Kahn (1946) argues, 'the adulation they have been pouring . . . on their idol since early in 1943 is not without precedent' (44) (Kahn refers to Franz Liszt and Rudolph Valentino as precedents), it certainly signaled a qualitative shift in the relations between audiences and popular musicians. Recognition of this shift has been a principal theme in the work on fans carried out by the Vermorels (1985, 1989).

Performers such as Elvis Presley in the 1950s, the Beatles in the 1960s, David Bowie in the 1970s, Madonna in the 1980s and Nirvana in the 1990s all had fiercely partisan fans. Importantly, they consciously cultivated their fan bases and tailored their image to create and bond together a group of supporters, often 'selling' an ideology to their fans to unite them. Bowie, for example, sold sexual ambivalence and alienation, Madonna sexual freedom for women. Certain pop songs, such as the Beatles' 'All You Need Is Love' (1967), David Bowie's 'All the Young Dudes' (recorded by Mott the Hoople in 1972) and Oasis's 'D'You Know What I Mean?' (1997), deliberately target fans, or the type of

fans the performers would like to have, and thus play an important role in creating an audience.

A second level of fandom is more transitory, and is associated overwhelmingly with the teenage or preteenage female. The rise and decline of teeny-bopper and weeny-bopper acts, such as the Monkees, the Osmonds, David Cassidy, the Bay City Rollers, Bros, New Kids on the Block, Take That and the Spice Girls, represent an industry phenomenon, the high levels of fanaticism being sustainable for only short periods of time.

In the 1990s, the discourse of fan literature spread to the Internet, thus arguably breaking down the distance between star performer and fan. In addition to the 150 or so Web sites set up by his fans, David Bowie, for example, has two official sites (*BowieNet* and *Bowieart*), and has even released material exclusively on the Internet. Since the 1990s, the Internet has become of increasing importance in the formation of fan bases.

Bibliography

Berteaut, Simone. 1972. *Piaf: A Biography*. New York: Harper & Row.

Bowieart. http://www.bowieart.com/

BowieNet. http://www.davidbowie.com/

Buford, Bill. 1992. *Among the Thugs*. London: Mandarin.

Cavicchi, Daniel. 1998. *Tramps Like Us: Music and Meaning Among Springsteen Fans*. New York: Oxford University Press.

Danielson, Virginia. 1997. *The Voice of Egypt: Umm Kulthūm, Arabic Song, and Egyptian Society in the Twentieth Century*. Chicago and London: University of Chicago Press.

Doss, Erika. 1999. *Elvis Culture: Fans, Faith and Image*. Lawrence, KS: University Press of Kansas.

Fiske, John. 1992. 'The Cultural Economy of Fandom.' In *The Adoring Audience: Fan Culture and Popular Media*, ed. Lisa A. Lewis. London and New York: Routledge, 30–49.

Frith, Simon. 1988. *Music for Pleasure: Essays in the Sociology of Pop*. New York: Routledge.

Grossberg, Lawrence. 1992. 'Is There a Fan in the House?: The Affective Sensibility of Fandom.' In *The Adoring Audience: Fan Culture and Popular Media*, ed. Lisa A. Lewis. London and New York: Routledge, 50–65.

Jensen, Joli. 1992. 'Fandom as Pathology: The Consequences of Characterization.' In *The Adoring Audience: Fan Culture and Popular Media*, ed. Lisa A. Lewis. London and New York: Routledge, 9–29.

Kahn, E.J., Jr. 1946. *The Voice: The Story of an American Phenomenon*. New York and London: Harper & Brothers.

Keightley, Keir. 1996. '"Turn It Down!" She Shrieked:

Gender, Domestic Space, and High Fidelity, 1948–59.' *Popular Music* 15(2): 149–77.

Lewis, Lisa A., ed. 1992. *The Adoring Audience: Fan Culture and Popular Media*. London and New York: Routledge.

Melly, George. 1989 (1970). *Revolt into Style: The Pop Arts*. Oxford: Oxford University Press.

Shuker, Roy. 1994. *Understanding Popular Music*. London: Routledge.

Straw, Will. 1990 (1983). 'Characterizing Rock Music Culture: The Case of Heavy Metal.' In *On Record: Rock, Pop, and the Written Word*, ed. Simon Frith and Andrew Goodwin. London: Routledge, 97–110.

Vermorel, Fred, and Vermorel, Judy. 1985. *Starlust: The Secret Life of Fans*. London: W.H. Allen.

Vermorel, Fred, and Vermorel, Judy. 1989. *Fandemonium!: The Book of Fan Cults and Dance Crazes*. London: Omnibus.

Weinstein, Deena. 1991. *Heavy Metal: A Cultural Sociology*. New York: Lexington Books.

Wise, Sue. 1990 (1984). 'Sexing Elvis.' In *On Record: Rock, Pop, and the Written Word*, ed. Simon Frith and Andrew Goodwin. London: Routledge, 390–98. (First published in *Women's Studies International Forum* 7 (1984): 13–17.)

Discographical References

Beatles, The. 'All You Need Is Love.' Parlophone R 5620. *1967*: UK.

Mott the Hoople. 'All the Young Dudes.' CBS 8271. *1972*: UK.

Oasis. 'D'You Know What I Mean?' Creation CRE 256. *1997*: UK.

DAVID BUCKLEY and JOHN SHEPHERD

Fanzines

The fanzine is an amateur form of publishing, one that is prompted less by commercial gain than by an enthusiasm for its subject. It is written, edited and produced by fans. To establish a fanzine is to provide an alternative or a counter-discourse to the mainstream; it can also establish a discourse where no substantial discourse has previously existed. Some commentators would locate the roots of fanzine publishing in the amateur journalism of the second half of the 1800s and, in particular, in the establishment in the United States of amateur press associations. Some would go further, citing as antecedents the popular journalism that sprang up around political revolutions and movements as far back as the English Civil War, or the small magazines of the arts that have been in existence since the nineteenth century, or even the anarchist publications of the same time. However, the publications that have come to be known as fanzines have their origins in the amateur science-fiction magazines of the late 1920s. Magazines with titles such

as *Amazing Stories* not only presented short stories in the genre, but also provided space for readers to discuss the science upon which the stories were premised. The term 'fanzine' was first applied to science-fiction fan magazines in 1941 by US science-fiction writer Russ Chauvenet.

The 1930s witnessed the appearance of what were arguably the earliest popular music fanzines. Titles such as *Down Beat*, *Hot Jazz*, *Swing* and *Tempo* served the growing fan base of dedicated listeners to jazz in the United States, listeners who wanted to explore further than the radio or their local music venues allowed. Some of these magazines would go on to become fixtures of the scene and enjoy wider circulation and acknowledgment: *Down Beat*, for example, has continued as a highly respected, professionally produced magazine with a worldwide circulation. Such longevity, although not common among fanzines, speaks to the close relationship such publications have with the music scenes they support and encourage. The fanzine is typically necessary in the evolution of a genre in order to validate music that is generally ignored or reviled by the mainstream critics. In some cases, as in jazz, it existed to provide more detailed and reflective coverage than was available within the confines of the daily newspaper or general-interest magazine. The fanzine heralded the birth of the specialist music magazine.

In the 1950s and 1960s, while publications such as *Melody Maker* and *New Musical Express* in the United Kingdom sought to embrace emerging musical styles and began to take popular music seriously, the need for fanzines remained significant. The British fanzines *Blues Unlimited* (1963) and *Blues and Soul* (1968) appeared at critical moments in popular music; in both cases, the attention of the mainstream music press was drawn by revolutionary syntheses of existing genres. The musicians who provided the raw material – the 'roots music' – tended to be forgotten. Along with folk movement fanzines such as *Sing Out!* (1950), such titles developed and sustained interest in these genres and have kept enthusiasts informed.

For fanzines, there have been few opportunities for external funding (at least in the early days of publication); for many, there may be no desire even to seek such funding, in order to remain 'independent.' Consequently, production values are often very different from those of mainstream magazines. Until the 1970s, it was common for copy to be hammered out on old typewriters, headlines hand-lettered (in some cases, entire issues were hand-written) and illustrations etched onto duplicating stencils. As the photocopier became more widely available, original illustrations and graphics 'borrowed' from album sleeves and the commercial press could easily be incorporated into the text. Although not all fanzines were as resolutely amateurish as these methods suggest, all had at their heart a 'domesticity of production.' The US jazz magazine *Coda* began in 1958 as a 12-page mimeographed fanzine, put together by its editor and a team of volunteers working for beer and pizza. *Mojo Navigator Rock 'n' Roll News*, the predecessor to Greg Shaw's *Who Put the Bomp!*, similarly began as a two-page stapled, mimeographed newsletter. Whether because of financial stringency or ideological purity, fanzine producers were determined to preserve the values of the amateur, either in the unashamed full flood of enthused prose about their heroes and obsessively detailed discographical or other historical documentation, or in the direct, populist approach to production and distribution that sidestepped sterile professionalism and mainstream markets for individualistic creativity in both the content and the promotion of the publication.

The dominant sociological understanding of the fanzine is that its power is drawn from its subcultural location. Consequently, the defining moment of fanzine publishing – identified as the symbolic product of troubled youth, of rebellion, of subcultural struggle – has become the punk fanzine of the latter half of the 1970s. Beginning in the United States with *Punk* (1975) and in the United Kingdom with *Sniffin' Glue* (1976), thousands of fanzines appeared throughout the world. Why the need for so many fanzines? They did not simply celebrate the music: at their core was a very real desire to declare the individual identities and the various communities that made up the scene (in this can be seen the precursor of the 'perzine' of the 1980s and 1990s, concerned above all with the personal life of the fanzine editor). It is not only the content of the fanzine that is important here, but its attitude and position in relation to the dominant culture. Perhaps it is its position in relation to the means of production that gives it its greatest ideological power in this instance.

Such media open themselves up to continual democratization as more readers realize the potential of working from such positions. Fanzine readers are never simply relegated to the letters pages (which are, in most cases, extensive); rather, they contribute reviews, interviews, discographies, histories, analyses and artwork. Readers become writers, editors, designers, publishers, printers and distributors. There occurs a radical realignment of roles and responsibilities, which pertains even where the content is mainstream. There remain hundreds of fanzines that deal with the work and life of such rock stalwarts as Elvis Presley, the Rolling Stones, Bruce Springsteen and Pink Floyd. Fans of rock auteurs such as Bob Dylan have continued to find the *oeuvres* of their favorite artists inexhaustible as sites for criticism, documentation and speculation. Fanzines are created from the available technological resources of the dominant order, resources that tend to be used to create top-down media products that minimize or even discourage participation among their consumers. They offer a space for the creation, development and enacting of a community of interest. In the case of Internet fanzines, the opportunities are further enhanced: freed from the physical limits of the printed publication, contributors post immediate impressions of gigs attended earlier that day or the night before, or requests for information (the address of a record label, a catalog number). Increasingly, the personal Web page is being employed as a fanzine. The Internet has become an extension of fanzine culture, enabling individuals to write and to communicate as often or as rarely as they wish, unconstrained even by the rather flexible notions of frequency, circulation and production values of the printed fanzine.

Fanzines need not concentrate on a single artist or genre: they often cut across genres. At times, this approach has a geographic rationale. In the 1980s, the German fanzine *Gorilla Beat* explored the music of artists as diverse as the Pretty Things, Procol Harum, the Pink Fairies and Joy Division in part because the editor loved these musics, and in part because these musical associations made sense to a particular German audience in a way they would not have done to a British or a North American audience of the same time. Similarly, some Japanese fanzines are sites for heterogeneous musical appreciation, where genres and artists are shorn of their original cultural contexts. Elsewhere, the fanzine is employed to sustain indigenous musical cultures in the face of a mainstream press obsessed with the current North American or British stars. These cultures are not necessarily 'folk' in origin; they might just as easily draw from rock music or jazz, as in the French fanzines *Notes* and *Improjazz*. In other cases, fanzines might have a sociopolitical dimension, as in the numerous fanzines published in Japan and South America that deal with 'extreme' musics (such as industrial music, grindcore and death metal) that are in stark contrast to the dominant mores of the society within which they are produced. Before 1989, the production of a fanzine anywhere in Eastern Europe was a political act even more significant than these. Fanzines in the Eastern bloc have been little researched, but there are examples from Poland, Hungary and the former Czechoslovakia that derive much from the aesthetic and subcultural values of punk and might be considered as forms of dissident publishing, as serious an undertaking as any explicitly political *samizdat*. In common with most *samizdat* publishing, such publications have diminished in number and importance with the liberalization of government and markets in these countries.

The amateur status of the fanzine does not prevent it from making significant inroads into mainstream music culture. Some fanzine editors (Paul Morley and Jon Savage are conspicuous examples in the United Kingdom) have gone on to become established, professional music journalists. Rock fanzines such as Paul Williams's *Crawdaddy!* (1966; not only the first rock fanzine, but arguably the first rock magazine) and Greg Shaw's *Who Put the Bomp!* (1970) became places where rock journalism was significantly developed; later, professional writers such as Lester Bangs, Dave Marsh and Greil Marcus used these titles to experiment with new styles and perspectives. *Folk Roots*, perhaps the premier magazine in its field, was instrumental in conceptualizing its subject matter as 'world music,' and in introducing a multiplicity of rural and urban folk-based genres of the East and South to Western audiences. It has come to enjoy worldwide distribution, yet it began life in the 1970s as *The Southern Rag*, a small-circulation, regional English folk fanzine. Paul Stump (1997) has talked of fanzines keeping certain musics alive 'in much the same way artisanal crafts or endangered wildfowl survive: through the selfless, financially unremunerative toil of devotees' (339). Fanzines dedicated to all types of 'endangered music' (as well as those given over to less threatened species) do so as artisanal media *sans pareil*.

Bibliography

Atton, Chris. 2001a. *Alternative Media* (Ch. 3). London: Sage.

Atton, Chris. 2001b. 'Living in the Past?: Value Discourses in Progressive Rock Fanzines.' *Popular Music* 20(1) (January): 29–46.

Dickinson, Bob. 1997. *Imprinting the Sticks: The Alternative Press Beyond London* (Ch. 6). Aldershot: Arena.

Duncombe, Stephen. 1997. *Notes from Underground: Zines and the Politics of Alternative Culture*. London: Verso.

Perry, Mark. 2000. *Sniffin' Glue: The Essential Punk Accessory*. London: Sanctuary House.

Rau, Michelle. 1994. 'Towards a History of Fanzine Publishing: From APA to Zines.' *Alternative Press Review* (Spring/Summer): 10–13.

Stump, Paul. 1997. *The Music's All That Matters: A History of Progressive Rock*. London: Quartet.

Triggs, Teal. 1995. 'Alphabet Soup: Reading British Fanzines.' *Visible Language* 29(1): 72–87.

The Zine & E-Zine Resource Guide. http://www.zinebook.com/resource.html

CHRIS ATTON

Fascism

'Fascism' was originally the name of a political movement that was founded in Italy in 1919 as the *Fascio di Combattimento* (Combat Group). Under the leadership of Benito Mussolini, the Fascist Party was in power in Italy from 1922 to 1945. Later, 'fascism' became an umbrella term for all extreme nationalistic and dictator-led anti-liberal, anti-Jewish and anti-Marxist movements that opposed parliamentary democracy. Although such movements were fairly widespread in Europe in the 1920s and 1930s as a reaction to the social and political turmoils of the time – for example, the *Falange* under Franco (Spain), the British Union of Fascists, the *Croix-de-Feu* and the *Parti Populaire Français* (France), the *Nationaal-Socialistische Beweging* (The Netherlands), the *Rex* movement (Belgium), the *Nasjonal Samling* (Norway), the *Frontismus* (Switzerland), the *Heimwehren* (Austria), the *Pfeilkreuzler* (Hungary) and the *Ustascha* (Croatia), to name just a few – the most disastrous offshoot was the National-Socialist movement, founded in Germany in 1920. The National-Socialist German Workers' Party came to power under Hitler in 1933 and was responsible for the outbreak of World War II and for the initiation of the Holocaust. The use of 'fascism' as an umbrella term therefore became questionable, since not only did the Holocaust clearly differentiate the German National-Socialist movement from all other extreme right-wing movements of that time and later, but all such movements, despite clear similarities, had their own particular traits.

Among their similarities was fascist groups' distinctive relationship to popular music. Music seemed to provide an ideal means by which such groups could attempt to appeal to the masses and to create groups of followers submissively dependent on their leaders. Songs especially could be used to serve these ends: people could sing them together, march to them in a show of physical uniformity and, through them, receive a clear ideological message promoting the political goals of the movement. Characteristic of this use of song was the transformation of music or musical material with an already established mass appeal into aggressive right-wing combat songs through the substitution of new nationalistic lyrics and slight changes in the musical arrangements. The blatant propagandist use or, better, misuse of already existing music, whether working-class songs, folk songs or military songs from the past, has been characteristic of all fascist movements, and more recently punk or heavy metal rock has frequently been used as the musical platform for nationalistic and fascist propaganda. There is little or no genuine 'fascist music,' and even where music was created under fascist regimes it remained firmly rooted in the appropriate musical traditions.

Another aspect of fascism's purely pragmatic relationship to popular music was the ruthless fight against any music that could not be used to manipulate people into becoming unconditional followers of a movement and its leaders wherever fascism became the dominating form of social power. The suppression of jazz and swing and of the musical avant-garde in Germany in the 1930s is a typical example, and it became widely known through the notorious exhibition *Entartete Musik*, organized during the *Reichsmusiktage* in Düsseldorf in 1938. The exhibition was set up to demonstrate the supposedly degenerate nature of modern, North American and Jewish music, including jazz and big band swing, in order to legitimize the oppression of musicians and their audiences.

Bibliography

Beck, Earl R. 1985. 'The Anti-Nazi "Swing Youth."' *Journal of Popular Culture* 19(3): 45–54.

Kater, Michael H. 1992. *Different Drummers: Jazz in the Culture of Nazi Germany*. New York: Oxford University Press.

Meyer, Michael. 1977. 'The SA Song Industry: A Singing Ideological Posture.' *Journal of Popular Culture* 11(3): 568–80.

Polster, Bernd. 1989. *'Swing Heil': Jazz im Nationalsozialismus* ['Swing Heil': Jazz in the Era of National Socialism]. Berlin: Transit Buchverlag.

Warren, Roland L. 1972. 'The Nazi Use of Music as an Instrument of Social Control.' In *The Sounds of Social Change: Studies in Popular Culture*, ed. R. Serge Denisoff and Richard A. Peterson. Chicago: Rand McNally, 72–78.

Wicke, Peter. 1985. 'Sentimentality and High Pathos: Popular Music in Fascist Germany.' *Popular Music* 5: 149–58.

Zwerin, Michael. 1985. *La Tristesse de Saint Louis: Swing Under the Nazis*. London and New York: Quartet Books.

PETER WICKE

Fashion

Fashion in popular culture is representative of two basic processes. Firstly, and most commonly, fashion is understood to be the wearing of clothes in a specific combination by an individual to create a desired 'look.' Secondly, and in a broader sense, fashion is also a way of comprehending or identifying a particular social or cultural trend within popular culture. In this way, individuals seen to be wearing certain clothes are associated with other kinds of meaningful activity (such as dancing, eating or drug-taking), as well as with other cultural products (such as a particular kind of music or literature, or certain films or television programs). Similarly, one can also describe certain cultural commodities aside from clothes – music, dance crazes, clubs, geographical locations, personalities – as 'fashionable.' Fashion, there-fore, is tied into patterns of consumption, and it is also a way in which individuals themselves can be seen to be active, or to be creative, in the construction of an identity for themselves, as they decide to buy certain clothes and not others, to listen to specific musical genres and to indulge in particular kinds of cultural activity.

The business of fashion is, therefore, to encourage the sale of commodities. Numerous industries, including clothing and shoe manufacturers, book and magazine publishers, and furniture designers, as well as both the film and the music industries, depend on the rapid turnover of various cultural goods that is organized and inspired by the concept of 'fashion' and the 'fashionable.' The annual and/or seasonal change in styles creates an illusion of obsolescence for a series of otherwise broadly similar goods (whether they are CDs, pants, hairstyles or shoes), creating a situation in which individuals are encouraged to buy goods that may be only slightly different from those that they already possess (flared as opposed to tapered pants, for example). Fashion therefore fuels the mass production and consumption of apparently different cultural commodities for profit and thereby may be understood as exploitative (for the classic exposition of this approach, see Adorno and Horkheimer 1979). Fashion as a practise, however, is often understood by individuals as an opportunity for them to express themselves both as uniform (like everyone else) and as individual (defiantly against the mainstream) (for an early exposition of this position, see Hall and Jefferson 1976).

As a cultural commodity and a social practise, popular music presents opportunities for both the mass exploitation of particular styles and trends and the individual creation and organization of personal style and fashion. Indeed, the tension – or overlap – between these two processes often characterizes the numerous instances in which popular music and fashion are seen to interrelate. One of the key arenas in which these processes occur is the 'subculture' (see, for example, Hall and Jefferson 1976; Hebdige 1979). The subculture may be identified with a group of individuals – as in 'teds,' 'rockers,' 'hippies' – or with a specific place – as in 'northern soul' or 'house.' In either case, these nodes of place, music and fashion are inhabited and embodied by individuals who characterize and identify themselves through the clothes they wear and the music they listen to, and by the kind of activities in which they participate (for an elaboration of this concept in relation to popular music, see Straw 1991). As an example, 'teds' in Britain in the 1950s were identified by their dress (long frock coats, drainpipe trousers, elaborately quiffed hair), by their music (rock 'n' roll) and by their style of dancing (jive). In the United States at almost the same time, urban

African Americans created another subculture, adopting the zoot suit and dancing the lindy hop to the accompaniment of rhythm & blues or 'jump and jive' (for a vivid description of this scene, see Haley 1966). In both these subcultures, as in others, issues relating to politics, gender and, in particular, race were always implicit, and, as with the zoot-suit riots in East Los Angeles in the late 1940s, they have at times become explicit. With regard to other musical genres, fashions and their associated subcultures – whether reggae, two-tone or skinhead 'stomp' – the racial and political implications of the music–fashion–community nexus are perhaps more obviously inseparable from one another (for examples of the often complex relationship between black music, fashion and white audiences, see Hebdige 1987 and Gilroy 1987).

The most familiar version of the history of any subcultural style suggests that the generation of fashion and the creation or adoption of a musical genre are seen to have come initially from individuals (the fans and musicians), and that it is this 'authentic' form of cultural production and activity which is then co-opted by the mainstream and represented by fashion manufacturers and multinational music corporations, which in turn promote the style and music in the mass market of fashion magazines, teen boutiques and the charts. In the 1990s, however, this seemingly inevitable process was seen to have undergone revision, with some subcultures understood to be self-consciously negotiating their position vis-à-vis the commercial aspects of their activities (for an example of one such revision, see Thornton 1995). Indeed, one of the most interesting ironies within the various histories of different fashion/music subcultures is the origin and legacy of one defiantly anti-fashion musical subculture – punk – which, with its ripped clothes, safety pins and amateur, deliberately shocking hairstyles, seemed to base itself on an ideology that was 'non-fashion' and even 'anti-commodity.' Yet, not only was one of punk's original locales a clothes store (Sex, owned by Vivienne Westwood and Malcolm McLaren), but different 'looks' inspired by the punk style – Jean Paul Gaultier's use of underwear as outerwear or Gianni Versace's creation of the infamous 'safety-pin dress,' for example – have continued to be incorporated into both mainstream and *haute couture* fashion. Nevertheless, it is also true that the impact of punk and other subcultures has meant that, in the latter part of the twentieth century, the credibility of street fashion (often associated with a particular musical style) effectively destabilized the previous dominance of the fashion house and the chain store as the arbiters and dictators of popular taste.

Fashion and popular music therefore relate to one another in a variety of different ways. Firstly, they can be connected in a direct commercial manner when individual singers or groups exploit their popularity through merchandising. The most common practise is for a group or individual musician to license the sale of T-shirts or more expensive items, such as 'tour jackets,' which are then sold at concerts or through direct marketing within fan associations. Less frequently, groups or individuals may also license the sale of items such as jewelry or cosmetics.

Secondly, the popularity of groups or a certain genre of music can also indirectly encourage a particular style, fashion or fashion accessory. The committed reggae listener (whether white or black) may grow dreadlocks; the country music fan (whether living in Hong Kong or Nashville) may wear cowboy boots. More indirectly still, the short-lived popularity of certain groups may inspire equally short-lived fashion trends or crazes: for example, the popularity of tartan in teenage fashion for a short period in the 1970s in Britain was tied to the equally short-lived success of the Scottish Bay City Rollers, although not all those who wore tartan were likely to be fans (for a lively account of this particular craze, see Garratt 1994).

Thirdly, singers and musicians may simply popularize or 'make meaningful' certain existing fashion items. The wearing of ponchos by Chilean musicians and their fans in exile in the 1970s and early 1980s suggested solidarity with the peasants of the altiplano. The wearing of certain brands of sports and leisure wear by different rap or hip-hop stars may make or indicate a political or personal statement, which fans may then employ within a local rather than an (inter)national arena.

Fourthly, musicians may also patronize a certain designer, who may then be inspired to create a particular 'look' or item of clothing for individuals that can subsequently be worn on concert tours and in music videos. A notable example of this is Jean Paul Gaultier's variations on the 'conical bra,' as worn by Madonna and her dancers, both male and female, in her Blond Ambition tour in 1990.

In contrast to all of the above, however, there is, it should be noted, a strong tradition of musicians and music fans deliberately 'dressing down' and emphasizing the bohemian (and often defiantly uncommercial) aspects of their life style. For some musicians, 'dressing up' or becoming 'fashionable' may imply a loss of credibility and connection to the real world, and many fans and musicians have been and have continued to be wary of musical genres in which the style or look of the performer seems to mean more than the music. Traditional working clothes (such as denim jeans, for example) were adopted and popularized by many musicians precisely because they were not 'fashionable' but uniform, and, crucially, seemed to provide visible evidence of a close association between the performer and the audience.

Unsurprisingly, this kind of style is most frequently adopted by performers from musical genres most often linked to the 'common people' or to the lives of working people; obvious examples would include certain country and folk performers, and even some rock artists, such as Bruce Springsteen. Ironically, however, this non-fashion statement is easily co-opted by manufacturers keen to associate their product with the seeming authenticity of past working practises and 'original' music. The Levi's campaign of the late 1980s and the 1990s employed both music and image to encourage precisely this connection between 'original' music, jeans and working-class culture, emphasizing both the authenticity and the nostalgia inherent in this series of associations (for useful discussions of this campaign, see Goldman 1992 and Corner 1995).

Bibliography

Adorno, Theodor, and Horkheimer, Max. 1979. *Dialectic of Enlightenment*. London: Allen Lane.

Barthes, Roland. 1983. *The Fashion System*. New York: Hill.

Clarke, John. 1976. 'Style.' In *Resistance Through Rituals: Youth Subcultures in Post-War Britain*, ed. Stuart Hall and Tony Jefferson. London: Hutchinson, 175–91.

Corner, John. 1995. 'Adworlds.' In *Television Form and Public Address*. London: Edward Arnold, 105–35.

Garratt, Sheryl. 1994. 'All of Me Loves All of You.' In *Love Is the Drug: Living as a Pop Fan*, ed. John Aizlewood. London: Penguin, 72–86.

Gelder, Ken, and Thornton, Sarah, eds. 1997. *The Subcultures Reader*. London: Routledge.

Gilroy, Paul. 1987. *There Ain't No Black in the Union Jack: The Cultural Politics of Race and Nation*. London: Unwin Hyman.

Goldman, Robert. 1992. *Reading Ads Socially*. London: Routledge.

Haley, Alex (with Malcolm X). 1966. *The Autobiography of Malcolm X*. Harmondsworth: Penguin Books.

Hall, Stuart, and Jefferson, Tony, eds. 1976. *Resistance Through Rituals: Youth Subcultures in Post-War Britain*. London: Hutchinson.

Hebdige, Dick. 1974. 'Aspects of Style in the Deviant Sub-Cultures of the 1960s.' *CCCS Stencilled Papers*. Birmingham: University of Birmingham, 20, 21, 24 and 25.

Hebdige, Dick. 1976. 'The Meaning of Mod.' In *Resistance Through Rituals: Youth Subcultures in Post-War Britain*, ed. Stuart Hall and Tony Jefferson. London: Hutchinson, 87–96.

Hebdige, Dick. 1979. *Subculture: The Meaning of Style*. London: Methuen.

Hebdige, Dick. 1987. *Cut 'n' Mix: Culture, Identity and Caribbean Music*. London and New York: Methuen.

Hebdige, Dick. 1988. *Hiding in the Light: On Images and Things*. London and New York: Routledge.

Lury, Celia. 1996. *Consumer Culture*. Cambridge: Polity Press.

McRobbie, Angela, and Nava, Mica, eds. 1984. *Gender and Generation*. London: Macmillan.

Mercer, Kobena. 1987. 'Black Hair/Style Politics.' *New Formations* 3: 33–54.

Schwichtenberg, Cathy, ed. 1993. *The Madonna Connection: Representational Politics, Subcultural Identities, and Cultural Theory*. Boulder, CO: Westview Press.

Straw, Will. 1991. 'Systems of Articulation, Logics of Change: Communities and Scenes in Popular Music.' *Cultural Studies* 5(3): 368–88.

Thorne, Tony. 1993. *Fads, Fashions and Cults: From Acid House to Zoot Suit*. London: Bloomsbury.

Thornton, Sarah. 1995. *Club Cultures: Music, Media and Subcultural Capital*. Cambridge: Polity Press.

Wilson, Elizabeth. 1990. 'Deviant Dress.' *Feminist Review* 35: 65–73.

KAREN LURY

Gender and Sexuality

Gender and sexuality are two related social phenomena that inform the practise and interpretation of popular music. There exists an important difference between 'gender' on the one hand, and 'sexuality' and 'sex' on the other. While 'sex' indicates biological differences between males and females, 'gender' refers to the socially or culturally constructed categories of masculinity and femininity. 'Sexuality' refers to feelings, activities and identities associated with erotic desire. Studies of gender and popular music have tended to problematize any apparent natural connection between biological sex and social abilities, attributes and aptitudes. Likewise, studies of sexuality and popular music have generally avoided essentialist conceptions of sexuality as a natural and constant phenomenon, focusing instead on its social construction and the way in which it is enacted and embodied or 'performed' (Butler 1990).

Issues concerning gender and sexuality are central to the way in which various forms of popular music have been understood. Indeed, many popular music styles have been regarded as synonymous with sexuality. The possibility that the beat, lyrics or performance styles of popular music might express or incite sexual desire has caused authorities to make periodic attempts to curtail its influence. For example, in Britain during the late Victorian period a number of established 'reformers,' including the Social Purity Branch of the British Women's Temperance Association, representatives from total abstinence federations and Christian groups, spoke out against the songs and performances of London's music halls, linking what occurred on stage to the 'demoralisation' (sexual excitement) of the audience (Davis 1991, 39).

Similar moral panics concerning popular music and sexuality have continued to emerge. From its beginnings, rock 'n' roll (a genre whose name itself has sexual connotations) was commonly perceived as somehow encouraging mass sexual abandon and loss of control among youths and teenagers. This view of rock 'n' roll was perpetrated by the popular media and so-called 'moral guardians,' such as the Church and other established institutions, and it was exemplified by a 1956 television broadcast of a performance by Elvis Presley in which he was filmed only from the waist up in order to hide the swaying hips that had become one of the hallmarks of his performance style.

Popular music's power to threaten and transgress is ultimately grounded in the mores and conventions of the particular societies in which it exists. An extreme example is the case of the singer Hanan Bulu-bulu, who has been referred to as the 'Madonna of Sudanese pop.' Her concerts were banned and she suffered physical assault by Islamic fundamentalists because of the content of her material and her sexually suggestive performance style and image (Verney 1994, 196).

Performance Practise

In contrast, studies of musical practise have highlighted the way in which musical rituals are used as a tool for social cohesion through their reproduction of gender norms. Accounts from the first half of the nineteenth century describing certain African music conventions show how male and female musicians were selected to perform on different social occasions. Southern (1983) details how 'occasions associated with children, adolescent girls, and funerals, in particular, generally called for musical performance by women. On the other hand, warrior songs, hunting songs, fishermen and boating songs, and other kinds of co-operative work songs were the province of the men' (9). Furthermore, music can be central to traditional ritualized social settings when certain gendered behavioral norms are allowed to be transgressed – for instance, during the female drumming rituals of the Sudanese *zar* gatherings, women are allowed to 'smoke and drink and act out rebellious fantasies without having their religious piety called into question' (Verney 1994, 191).

The categorization of musical compositions and sounds according to gender has been common practise

throughout popular music history, and there has also existed a gendered coding of musical instruments. Some critics have even assumed that the design of certain musical instruments echoes particular aspects of the human form and have suggested that these instruments have a natural association with either men or women. For example, Kurt Sachs argued in 1940:

The player's sex and the form of his or her instrument, or at least its interpretation, depend on one another. As the magic task of more or less all primitive instruments is life, procreation, fertility, it is evident that the life-giving roles of either sex are seen or reproduced in their shape or playing motion. (quoted in Koskoff 1989, 4)

While such an unproblematic association between a musician's sex and performance practise would find few supporters in contemporary popular music criticism, some instruments, such as the guitar, have continued to be read as phallic within particular areas of rock discourse. This association between masculinity and particular musical instruments has had a direct impact on female performers. As Homan (1999) notes, the masculine culture of the Australian rock pub has been such that, around 1960, a number of popular female rock vocalists, including Noeleen Batley, Brenda Lee and Dinah Lee, 'were allowed to perform provided they did not attempt to pick up an instrument' (36).

Certain instruments are thus associated with performance by either men or women. In English culture, the flute and the piano have traditionally been regarded as feminine. During the nineteenth century, there was a piano in many English parlors, and it became a symbol of domestic life. Middle- and upper-class women were encouraged to learn how to play the instrument, and their skill as pianists was regarded as a measure of their femininity. Moreover, their performance on the piano was a familiar part of the rituals of courtship. This association of women with piano-playing might help to explain why there have been so many women keyboard players in rock and pop bands in comparison, for example, with women electric guitarists (there are, however, many women acoustic guitarists, and women have played plucked instruments in the home for as long as they have played keyboard instruments). The comparative paucity of women electric guitarists may also have to do with a socially constructed ideology of technology as the proper preserve of men.

It is clear, then, that ideas about gender inform popular music practise and are facilitated and replicated through a set of socially constructed norms. Green's research on music education in the classrooms of English secondary schools (1997) has shown how teachers collude with their pupils in the perpetuation of a gendered understanding of music whereby particular instruments and certain musical practises, such as singing, are regarded as masculine or feminine. As Green argues, 'When boys in schools perform "popular music" or "fast music," play drums and electric instruments, or manipulate technology, they are furthering a symbolic representation of their masculinity' (1997, 185). Dominant gender ideologies are thus reproduced within schools, and children are socialized into typical gender-related musical behavior from an early age.

These gender ideologies are also promoted through forms of mass media such as videos and magazines. For instance, some critics have offered a feminist analysis of promotional music videos (Lewis 1990; Hurley 1994). Where magazines are concerned, Bayton (1997) studied 1980s and 1990s trade publications for guitarists and found that women's presence in such magazines was minimal. All the magazine covers depicted male guitarists; the overwhelming majority of the photographs, features and news within the magazines concerned were of or on male guitarists; 'all the technical advice pages and playing advice were by men'; and the advertisements in the magazines were carefully worded to 'endow their gadgets with masculinity' (1997, 43). Théberge (1997) notes that, in such advertisements, 'photos depicting bikini-clad women lounging across stacks of amplifiers are not uncommon' (124) and points to the 'near-total absence' of women in the world of musicians' magazines in general (122). He writes, for example: 'By the end of 1995, after twenty years of publishing and a total of some 236 issues, *Keyboard* had devoted its cover story to only a handful of select female artists' (122–23).

Unsurprisingly, therefore, music technology has also tended to be categorized as male. Bayton describes how 'young women may be drawn towards the electric guitar but are put off by the multitude of electronic and electrical components, which are a basic requirement for a rock performance,' and how technical language is often used by male musicians 'as a power strategy in a mystifying way in order to exclude women' (1997, 42). Keightley (1996) shows how, during the late 1940s and the 1950s, home audio or high-fidelity sound reproduction technologies came to be conceived as masculine, and were used by male listeners 'to produce a domestic space gendered as masculine' (150).

The social construction of gender through popular music practise takes a specific form within different popular music genres. A major debate within popular music studies has concerned the way in which different musical genres and styles display and/or appeal to particular gendered and sexual identities. There is no doubt that the musical construction of gender and sexuality can be central to the formation and articulation of group identities and cultures. Many teenage girls address ideas about sexuality and sexual relationships through the ways in which they consume and discuss popular music, for example, and particular homosexual and lesbian groups differentiate themselves through their popular music tastes and practises. Where the construction of homosexual identities is concerned, some critics have pointed to a 'homosexual gaze' within MTV (Drukman 1995).

In exploring the relations between music genres and the social construction of gender, some scholars have attempted to account in more detail for the masculinity of rock music. Frith and McRobbie (1990) were the first to do so in a seminal article entitled 'Rock and Sexuality,' first published in 1978. In this article, they rejected biological explanations for rock's masculinity and focused instead on the way in which boys and girls are 'socialized' from an early age by social institutions such as family, school and media into established patterns of male and female behavior, which are then reflected in rock culture. They suggested that girls are encouraged to adopt a passive, subordinate role and a concern with romance, marriage and motherhood, while boys learn to be more active and dominant, and they illustrated the way in which these conventions of male and female behavior are reflected in two contrasting musical styles – 'cock rock' and 'teenybop.'

Frith and McRobbie described 'cock rock' as characterized by male performers who are 'aggressive, dominating, and boastful' (1990, 374), produce loud, rhythmic music and lyrics in which women are treated as subordinate and as sex objects, and perform live concerts to predominantly male audiences. 'Teenybop,' on the other hand, is based on a softer ballad style of music and is generally aimed at audiences of young girls. The performance styles and visual images of boy bands from the Osmonds (United States) to Menudos (Mexico) and Boyzone (Ireland) have much less of the swagger, roughness and 'street' connotations of heavy metal. Instead, these bands sing in a manner that is more gentle, intimate and 'cute'; and the lyrics of their songs revolve around romance and involve expressions of self-pity and vulnerability that encourage girls to fantasize about being the singer's partner. Here, then, according to Frith and McRobbie, are two musical styles that involve contrasting types of masculinity and male sexuality and that reflect or express male culture and control, both produced by a music industry that is dominated by men and that limits and constrains the presentation and participation of women. According to Frith's and McRobbie's argument, therefore, rock culture is not naturally male in the sense of its musicians being born to create music in a particularly male way. Rather, it expresses established social conventions, ideas and values concerning male and female behavior.

Since Frith's and McRobbie's article was published, accounts of the masculinity of rock in popular music studies have become more sophisticated and have drawn attention away from the notion of preexisting male or female cultures into which people are socialized and which their behavior reflects toward a more dynamic process through which masculinity and femininity are actively constructed. Hence, rather than simply reflecting male culture, rock actually influences or produces that culture (Frith 1990; Taylor and Laing 1979; Negus 1996; Walser 1993). Walser (1993), for example, has suggested that the electric guitar, black leather or denim stage clothes, and a rasping, throaty singing voice are recognizable images and stereotypes of male power drawn upon by many heavy metal performers, but he has also highlighted the existence of several masculine types within heavy metal, all of which express different types of control over women. There are bands like AC/DC which create musical fantasy worlds without women; bands like Guns n' Roses which express misogynist attitudes; bands like Bon Jovi whose members appear as romantic heroes; and bands like Poison which adopt more androgynous and 'glam,' 'feminine' or 'camp' styles of performance and dress. These styles do not necessarily reflect any real power on the part of the men involved in making or listening to the music. Rather, they present a spectacle of male power and offer a musical means through which men can articulate certain tropes of masculinity. Thus, heavy metal, according to Walser, does not simply reflect a preexisting male culture but actually plays a role in creating that culture through a deliberate 'forging' of masculinity.

The musical meanings of heavy metal are not fixed, however, but are open to interpretation. Walser states, for example, that male fans of 'harder' styles of heavy metal have often denounced glam metal, with its fusion of male and female images and its suggestions of homosexuality, pointing out that 'real men don't wear make-up.' Yet, other fans, particularly women, have defended glam performers by praising their musical abilities, emphasizing the intensity of the experience they provide, or simply admiring their 'guts' (1993, 130). Hence, there is no simple or straightforward connection between rock music and the lives of rock musicians or audiences, and gender roles and ideologies do not exist prior to rock to be expressed or suppressed by it. Rather, rock influences the ways in which people think about men and women and how they should behave. It is not male in any fixed or essential way, but is actively made male through social practise and ideology, part of a continual process through which a variety of masculine roles and categories are defined, contested and transformed.

The ideologies of gender within popular music have affected the visibility of women musicians in certain musical genres. Women's presence in rock music culture, for example, has been marginalized in histories and canons of the genre. Studies have also concentrated on the visibility of women within the music industry, examining such topics as the gendering of specific occupations within that industry, the industry's masculinist culture and the 'glass ceiling' encountered by women aiming at high-level positions within record companies. Negus (1992) suggests that women in the US and UK music industries have traditionally worked within prescribed 'female roles,' such as those of administrators, personal assistants and secretaries, and although women have come to account for a large percentage of workers within public relations and promotion departments, it has continued to be unusual for women to be employed in positions where they are key decision-makers. The extent to which such issues of gender intersect with those of race has also been the subject of study. For instance, research in Australia has revealed that 'not only has there never been a female Aboriginal artist signed to a major label but there is no record of any Australian music company ever employing an Aboriginal woman in any capacity on a continuing basis' (Langman 1993, 90).

Lyrics and Interpretation

Different popular music genres and styles thus involve specific conventions of male and female behavior and portray specific male and female images or types. Tagg (1989), for example, points to the way in which familiar male and female images or stereotypes are conveyed through Western instrumental music. Furthermore, while topics of love, sexuality and romance are common lyrical themes within popular music, particular genres and styles have their own conventions regarding the way in which these topics are expressed (as indicated by the lyrics of 'cock rock' and 'teenybop'). For example, Bradby (1990) discusses how the lyrics and pronoun structure of girl-group songs from the 1960s relate to teenage sexual relationships. The songs revolve around lyrical themes of courtship or romance, perhaps voicing the lead singer's desire to be in a relationship. Bradby argues that the chorus singers offer an important contribution to the meaning of the song: '[T]he chorus acts in such a way as to restrain, or dampen, the exuberant fantasies and desires of the lead singer. Representing the mother, other girls, or just "everybody," the chorus is often the backdrop against which the lead singer must show her own strength and determination' (1990, 364).

A contrasting example of lyrical convention can be found in the Dominican popular music form *bacháta*. As Pacini Hernandez (1990) points out, while *bacháta* songs are centrally concerned with emotional relationships, these are almost always offered from a male point of view: 'Bachata is essentially men's music – written about women, but by and for men' (351). Pacini Hernandez explains that, while the first recorded *bacháta* songs of the early 1960s were concerned with 'tragic, plaintive laments of love lost or unrequited' (1990, 153), this musical genre has developed into a form 'principally concerned with sexuality and, moreover, a specific kind of sexuality: casual sex with no pretence to longevity, often mediated by money, whose principal social context is the bar/brothel' (1990, 351).

In a number of musical genres, the enactment by a musician of a particular set of gendered codes and behavioral conventions can enhance his/her reputation as an authentic performer. In country music, for example, there are a number of established gender-specific performance roles, modes of display and lyrical reference points. As Jensen (1993) argues, the lyrics to US honky-tonk music often present very prescribed representations of men and women. In such lyrics, 'women are tarnished angels. They can bring light and beauty into your life, but they are tainted and so give pain.' Men, on the other hand, 'are struggling to maintain their self-respect. They do the best they can but are misunderstood and mistreated. They want to find a woman who will be good, kind and true' (1993, 126). The star image of country music performers has frequently been cultivated to echo the gendered characterizations found in their songs. Details of the unhappy personal lives of country stars have often enhanced their public profiles by establishing them as genuine communicators. The summary depiction of Tammy Wynette by Riese (1989) illustrates the way in which the star has been framed within the clichés of her chosen musical genre: 'She had always been the betrayed but valiant trooper; the protective mother, fighting to keep and provide for her children; the long-suffering wife, trying to rehabilitate and hold on to her wayward husband' (95).

However, the establishment of particular gender conventions and codes within musical genres does not exclude or prohibit alternative representations or articulations of identity. As a number of critics have highlighted, the meanings of particular styles and performances are not simply received by music listeners but are actively created by them. Thus, interpretations of gender and sexuality need to consider not only the intention of the performer but also the interpretation of the listener. Ortega (1995), for example, explains that the ultra-masculine image of US country singer Johnny Cash has

become iconic for a number of lesbian fans. In this instance, the figure of Johnny Cash holds meaning for the lesbian fan not despite, but precisely because of, his macho public image. Negus (1996, 131) cites the research of Louise Allen, which shows how the country and western style has been taken and reused in certain lesbian subcultures as a sign of lesbian identity that parodies and subverts the codified gendered tropes of the genre.

Resistance and Play

The gender conventions and codes of musical genres may be well established, but there is also a history of artists who have resisted, altered and interacted with them. Many artists have chosen to explore gender and sexual behaviors, images and identities through popular music performance, and in doing so some of them have challenged or subverted more established or acceptable conventions and ideologies. In 1875, the British music hall artist Vesta Tilley did her first public performance in drag, and throughout her subsequent career she took on various male guises. Maitland (1986) writes: 'The very last song she sang at her farewell performance in 1920 was "Jolly Good Luck to the Girl who Loves a Soldier"; when she reached the last chorus her clear voice sang out "Girls, if you want to love a soldier, you can all love ME"' (10). The 'gender-bending' performances of Vesta Tilley influenced other women performers, such as Marlene Dietrich. Likewise, in the early 1970s male 'glam rock' performers such as David Bowie, Lou Reed and Marc Bolan used camp and androgynous imagery in their theatrical performance styles, images and lyrical concerns, and more recently female pop performers such as Annie Lennox, Madonna and k.d. lang have also generated much discussion and debate by incorporating a variety of masculine and androgynous elements into their performance styles and images.

In most cases, a clear distinction has been made between the real and performed selves of such artists, but sometimes this distinction has been deliberately or unintentionally blurred. Madonna in particular has pushed at the boundaries of acceptability by exploring a broad range of male and female images and stereotypes in her live performances and videos. She has, for example, juxtaposed the familiar stereotypes of virgin and whore and played upon sadomasochistic and homosexual or lesbian imagery in a way that deliberately blurs male and female identities. In the case of k.d. lang, Bruzzi (1997) describes how she collected her first Canadian music industry award in 'ill-fitting bridal wear and white trainers' (197). While lang had not publicly stated that she was a lesbian at this stage in her career, Bruzzi argues that she was clearly critiquing notions of a fixed gender identity and was 'in these early years, using drag as her primary mode of self-identification' (1997, 197). Through their 'gender-bending' performance styles and images, these and other popular music performers have thus questioned established gender-related identities, drawing attention to and manipulating male and female images in a manner that highlights their social constructedness.

Conclusion

Gender and sexuality clearly play a significant part in popular music practise and ideology. Indeed, many scholars would argue that gender and sexuality can be explored in relation to all aspects of popular music culture. The breadth and diversity of the perspectives that have been adopted in the study of gender and sexuality in relation to popular music practise and discourse would seem to support this position.

Bibliography

Bayton, Mavis. 1997. 'Women and the Electric Guitar.' In *Sexing the Groove: Popular Music and Gender*, ed. Sheila Whiteley. London: Routledge, 37–49.

Bradby, Barbara. 1990. 'Do-Talk and Don't Talk: The Division of the Subject in Girl-Group Music.' In *On Record: Rock, Pop and the Written Word*, ed. Simon Frith and Andrew Goodwin. New York: Pantheon Books, 341–68.

Bruzzi, Stella. 1997. 'Mannish Girl: k.d. lang – From Cowpunk to Androgyny.' In *Sexing the Groove: Popular Music and Gender*, ed. Sheila Whiteley. London: Routledge, 191–206.

Butler, Judith. 1990. *Gender Trouble: Feminism and the Subversion of Identity*. London: Routledge.

Davis, Tracy C. 1991. 'The Moral Sense of the Majorities: Indecency and Vigilance in Late-Victorian Music Halls.' *Popular Music* 10(1): 39–52.

Drukman, Steven. 1995. 'The Gay Gaze, or Why I Want My MTV.' In *A Queer Romance: Lesbians, Gay Men and Popular Culture*, ed. Paul Burston and Colin Richardson. London: Routledge, 81–95.

Frith, Simon. 1990. 'Afterthoughts.' In *On Record: Rock, Pop and the Written Word*, ed. Simon Frith and Andrew Goodwin. New York: Pantheon Books, 419–24.

Frith, Simon, and McRobbie, Angela. 1990. 'Rock and Sexuality.' In *On Record: Rock, Pop and the Written Word*, ed. Simon Frith and Andrew Goodwin. New York: Pantheon Books, 371–89. (First published in *Screen Education* 29 (1978).)

Green, Lucy. 1997. *Music, Gender, Education*. Cambridge: Cambridge University Press.

Homan, Shane. 1999. 'Counter-Sites: Mixed Audiences, Prejudices and Performance Within the Australian Rock Pub.' In *Musics and Feminisms*, ed. Sally Macar-thur and Cate Poynton. Sydney: Australian Music Centre, 35–40.

Hurley, Jennifer M. 1994. 'Music Video and the Construction of Gendered Subjectivity (Or How Being a Music Video Junkie Turned Me into a Feminist).' *Popular Music* 13(3): 327–38.

Jensen, Joli. 1993. 'Honky-Tonking: Mass Mediated Culture Made Personal.' In *All That Glitters: Country Music in America*, ed. George H. Lewis. Bowling Green, OH: Bowling Green University Popular Press, 118–30.

Keightley, Keir. 1996. '"Turn It Down!" She Shrieked: Gender, Domestic Space, and High Fidelity, 1948–59.' *Popular Music* 15(2): 149–78.

Koskoff, Ellen, ed. 1989. *Women and Music in Cross-Cultural Perspective*. Urbana and Chicago: University of Illinois Press.

Langman, Diane. 1993. 'Australian Women's Contemporary Music Inc.: The Case for Feminist Intervention into the Music Industry.' *Perfect Beat: The Journal of Research into Contemporary Music and Popular Culture* 1(2): 90–94.

Lewis, Lisa A. 1990. *Gender Politics and MTV: Voicing the Difference*. Philadelphia: Temple University Press.

Maitland, Sara. 1986. *Vesta Tilley*. London: Virago.

Negus, Keith. 1992. *Producing Pop: Culture and Conflict in the Popular Music Industry*. London: Edward Arnold.

Negus, Keith. 1996. *Popular Music in Theory: An Introduction*. Cambridge: Polity Press.

Ortega, Teresa. 1995. '"My Name Is Sue! How Do You Do": Johnny Cash as Lesbian Icon.' In *Readin' Country Music: Steel Guitars, Opry Stars and Honky Tonk Bars*, ed. Cecelia Tichi. Durham, NC: Duke University Press, 259–72.

Pacini Hernandez, Deborah. 1990. 'Cantando la cama vacia: Love, Sexuality and Gender Relationships in Dominican *Bachata*.' *Popular Music* 9(3): 351–67.

Riese, Randall. 1989. *Nashville Babylon: The Uncensored Truth and Private Lives of Country Music's Stars*. London: Guild Publishing.

Southern, Eileen. 1983. *The Music of Black Americans: A History*. New York: W.W. Norton.

Tagg, Philip. 1989. 'An Anthropology of Television Music?' *Svensk tidskrift för musikforskning*: 19–42.

Taylor, Jenny, and Laing, Dave. 1979. 'Disco-Pleasure-Discourse: On "Rock and Sexuality."' *Screen Education* 31: 43–48.

Théberge, Paul. 1997. *Any Sound You Can Imagine: Making Music/Consuming Technology*. Hanover, NH: Wesleyan University Press/University Press of New England.

Verney, Peter. 1994. 'Yearning to Dance: Sudan Is the Bridge of Africa and Arabia.' In *World Music: The Rough*

Guide, ed. Simon Broughton et al. London: Rough Guides Ltd., 190–97.

Walser, Robert. 1993. *Running with the Devil: Power, Gender, and Madness in Heavy Metal Music*. Hanover, NH: Wesleyan University Press/University Press of New England.

SARA COHEN and MARION LEONARD

Groupies

The term 'groupie' was first used around 1967 to describe girls who follow pop stars or members of rock groups, often in the hope of deliberately provoking sexual relations with them. Other names for groupies include 'band chicks,' 'star fuckers,' 'band aids,' 'band rats,' 'band molls' and 'snuff queens' (in country music). The favored form of sexual practise is fellatio, which fits perfectly with the groupie ethos of servility. The infamous Plaster Casters from Chicago made casts of pop star erections (see Burks and Hopkins 1970).

The phenomenon of the groupie existed before the term itself was coined (see, for example, McCarthy 1942). Fame is not necessarily the attraction, 'but the sort of renown associated with those men whose lives carry some sort of risk, threatening to be short and therefore lived at a high pitch of excitement' (Herman 1994, 117). Although essentially abused, some groupies regard themselves as being in a privileged position, as being closer to the seat of power than their fellow fans. Many come from 'respectable' backgrounds.

How groupies see themselves and how others see them does not, therefore, constitute a uniform or easily discernible picture. It may be simplistic to assume that groupies view themselves only in terms of the musicians with whom they have sex. Garratt (1984), for example, suggests that Pat Hartley, a woman who was part of Andy Warhol's New York City scene, 'saw it [being a groupie] as a form of autonomous female activity' (149). Hartley, quoted from the magazine *Spare Rib*, states that a lot of groupie activity and identity had to do with female camaraderie, support and competition. She also stresses that the girls actively chose the guys, and not the other way round. Although Hartley's statements suggest that groupies possess some autonomy and power in groupie–musician relations, this power is arguably quite limited. Garratt suggests that this autonomy is really only about 'the freedom to be used by the consumer of your choice' (1984, 149).

The idea that some form of autonomy is central and important to the activities of groupies does not seem to be shared by male authors who wrote about them in the 1960s. Although somewhat ambiguous about the characteristics of what makes groupies successful, the authors of the *Rolling Stone*'s 1969 special issue, 'Groupies: The Girls of Rock,' seem to rate groupies in terms of how they are perceived by male musicians, an idea that contrasts sharply with the idea that groupie success hinges on freedom or autonomy. Here, 'beauty' is stressed to be a defining characteristic of groupie success: 'Few groupies are truly beautiful girls – though obviously some are. But all the most successful are striking in appearance . . .' (Burks, Hopkins and Nelson 1969, 26). Nolan (1969) also suggests that looks are essential to succeeding as a groupie when he describes top groupie Nico as ' . . . the most awe-inspiring, lonely, ghostly-death's-head-of-a-god-awful-gorgeous-girl in the whole round world' (81).

The *Rolling Stone* authors and Nolan imply that, beyond good looks, groupies of note are those known relatively well by the stars. Nolan describes Sherry Sklar as a notable groupie because stars knew her and she was 'a person in her own right . . . part of pop society, even if only the fringes . . .' (1969, 82). Similarly, the *Rolling Stone* authors argue that 'Catherine Jones is Los Angeles' "top groupie" because she is LA's most desirable groupie.' Jones's success was explained primarily in terms of her good looks and being a 'sought after chick' (Burks, Hopkins and Nelson 1969, 19). The photographs of the groupies taken by Baron Wolman for the *Rolling Stone* special issue also emphasize that groupie prestige does not come from their active (or somewhat autonomous) pursuit of stars, but from their passive desirability to men. These photographs, with the exception of those of the Plaster Casters, mirror fashion photography by presenting the women as extremely sweet, pretty and unthreatening.

The phenomenon of groupies may be understood in terms of the lack of opportunities for women in 1960s rock culture. Reynolds and Press (1995) point out that, 'for the most part, women's medium for rebellion was limited, in the counterculture, to sexuality . . . [and that] the motto for these "sexually liberated" rock chicks might have been: if you can't beat 'em, fuck 'em' (232). Similarly, Garratt suggests that, 'with so few role models to follow, to fantasize about being on stage as a *female* performer may be almost a contradiction in terms. Instead, most of us dream of being a pop star's girlfriend: fame and recognition by proxy' (1984, 148).

Two seminal groupie texts are Mary McCarthy's *The Company She Keeps* (1942), and Jenny Fabian's and Johnny Byrne's *Groupie* (1969). The latter is a largely autobiographical tale of a groupie journalist working with the UK *Daily Telegraph* in the late 1960s. Another document is Frank Zappa's *The Groupie Papers*, which appeared as a sleeve note to a double album by the GTOs, *Permanent Damage*, produced by Zappa (see Gray 1993, 114). The GTOs (which stands for 'Girls Together Outrageously') were a 'groupie group' comprising young women familiar to musicians in the Los Angeles area. One of these young women, Pamela Des Barres, wrote a 'kiss-and-tell' memoir, *I'm with the Band*, which was published in 1987 (see Gray 1993, 215), as well as *Take Another Little Piece of My Heart* (1992) and *Rock Bottom* (1996). According to Reynolds and Press (1995), Zappa 'celebrated groupies as Freedom Fighters of the Sexual Revolution' (232).

Bibliography

Burks, John, and Hopkins, Jerry. 1970. *Groupies and Other Girls*. New York: Bantam.

Burks, John, Hopkins, Jerry, and Nelson, Paul. 1969. 'Groupies: The Girls of Rock.' *Rolling Stone* (15 February): 11–26.

Des Barres, Pamela. 1987. *I'm with the Band: Confessions of a Groupie*. New York: Beech Tree Books.

Des Barres, Pamela. 1992. *Take Another Little Piece of My Heart: A Groupie Grows Up*. New York: William Morrow.

Des Barres, Pamela. 1996. *Rock Bottom: Dark Moments in Music Babylon*. New York: St. Martin's Press.

Fabian, Jenny, and Byrne, Johnny. 1969. *Groupie*. London: New English Library.

Gaar, Gillian G. 1992. *She's a Rebel: The History of Women in Rock & Roll*. Seattle, WA: Seal Press.

Garratt, Sheryl. 1984. 'All of Us Love All of You.' In Sue Steward and Sheryl Garratt, *Signed, Sealed and Delivered: True Life Stories of Women in Pop*. Boston, MA: South End Press, 138–51.

Gray, Michael. 1993. *Mother!: The Frank Zappa Story*. London: Plexus.

Herman, Gary. 1994. *Rock 'n' Roll Babylon*. London: Plexus.

McCarthy, Mary. 1942. *The Company She Keeps*. New York: Simon and Schuster.

Nolan, Tom. 1969. 'Groupies: A Story of Our Times.' In *The Age of Rock, Vol. 1*, ed. Jonathan Eisen. New York: Vintage Books/Random House, 77–93.

Reynolds, Simon, and Press, Joy. 1995. *The Sex Revolts: Gender, Rebellion, and Rock 'n' Roll*. Cambridge, MA: Harvard University Press.

Sullivan, Caroline. 1999. *Bye Bye Baby: My Tragic Love Affair with the Bay City Rollers*. London: Bloomsbury.

Discographical Reference

GTOs, The. *Permanent Damage*. Straight STS 1059. *1969*: USA.

JANET HILTS and JOHN SHEPHERD with DAVID BUCKLEY

Heritage

'Heritage' can be defined as something inherited, passed on or transferred from the past. The notion of heritage is distinct from that of history because it places more emphasis on a sense of ownership of the past than on simply knowledge of it; and it is distinct from the notion of tradition because, in the case of heritage, the past has contemporary significance, whereas this is not necessarily so with tradition (Kong 1998). Different types or categories of heritage are commonly distinguished: for example, built heritage, which includes buildings and monuments; natural heritage, which includes landscape and parks; and cultural heritage, which includes art and literature, cultural artifacts and distinctive ways of life. In certain circumstances, popular music has also been included in the latter category and defined as a heritage.

Finn (1992) does not define or discuss the concept of heritage in his book *The Bluesman: The Musical Heritage of Black Men and Women in the Americas*, but he has clearly used the term in the book's title to emphasize his view that blues music is an inheritance that belongs to, and has specific and contemporary meaning for, African Americans. Finn criticizes white people who try to claim the blues as their own, arguing:

> The blues is part of the white American's heritage, but it is different from the other arts: it is the product of a special kind of inhumanity, one people suffered at the hands of another. The outcome has been an art form so deeply imbued with the stamp of that experience that it is inseparable from the people from whom it springs. The blues is the cultural memory of slavery, a musical memoir commemorating the history of blacks in the United States. Unlike other arts, its intrinsic spirit can only be transmitted by blood or, if you like, psychically. No amount of enthusiasm, no amount of time spent living with black people, will ever endow a non-African American with it. 'Only people who have been down the line,' says James Baldwin, 'know what the music is about.'
>
> Anyone . . . can play a 'blues.' But only a black American can be a bluesperson. He alone was the Man Without A Name, the Nigger, the Sambo. He alone lives the blues. (1992, 230)

In New Orleans, jazz has been officially categorized as the city's heritage. Jazz archives, museums and monuments have been established in the city and well-known jazz venues have been preserved. The first New Orleans Jazz & Heritage Festival took place in 1970, and in 1990 the Heritage School of Music was established in the city 'to educate our young musicians and to help further them in their training of jazz composition, style and repertoire' (http://www.nojhf.org/hsmusic.htm).

This emphasis on the preservation and continuity of 'our' music, and on passing musical traditions on from one generation to another, shows how heritage is commonly linked to collective identity and cultural prestige. As such, heritage has been harnessed by local governments and nation-states to serve their political agendas.

Singapore was established as an independent nation in 1965, at a time when the state was 'adamant in its condemnation of popular music as decadent' (Kong 1998, 458). By 1997, however, popular music had become redefined as part of Singapore's national heritage. The country's National Archives had launched a project entitled Retrospin, which aimed to construct the history of English popular music in Singapore. This project had both political and economic motivations, seeking to construct a sense of national identity, unity and loyalty within a country that was relatively new and socially diverse, and to utilize heritage as a national asset that would attract tourists. Music was chosen as a focus for the project because of its general appeal, and English popular music was chosen because it transcended existing ethnic and language affiliations within the country, and because it was associated with youth and one of the project's aims was to teach young people in Singapore about their past.

During the late 1990s, popular music was also being redefined as a national heritage in the United Kingdom. This can be illustrated with reference to two notoriously conservative institutions which had previously shown little interest in popular culture. The National Trust is a registered charity, founded in 1895 to act as 'a guardian for the nation' in the acquisition and protection of coastline, countryside and buildings threatened 'by the impact of uncontrolled development and industrialisation' (www.nationaltrust.org.uk). In 1997, the Trust purchased Sir Paul McCartney's former home in Liverpool and developed it as a visitor attraction. English Heritage is England's Historic Buildings and Monuments Commission, established in 1983 to offer advice and give grants for the preservation of historically important buildings. It has established a scheme that involves displaying blue plaques in a prominent position on the front of buildings deemed to have a significant cultural heritage, and with regard to music this has tended to involve buildings associated with classical musicians and composers. In 1998, however, English Heritage honored, for the first time, a popular rather than a classical musician by erecting a blue plaque on the former London residence of rock guitarist Jimi Hendrix. In 2001, another blue plaque was unveiled on the former Liverpool home of John Lennon.

The work of organizations like the National Trust illustrates how in certain circumstances heritage has been rather narrowly defined for cultural, economic or political reasons. Heritage has often been closely associated, for example, with established institutions such as museums, galleries and trusts that have chosen specific figures, events or aspects of the past to be officially commemorated and preserved, and have tended to define heritage selectively to refer to so-called 'high culture.' Thus, in the late 1990s, Britain's newly elected Labour government renamed its Department of Culture and Heritage the Department of Culture, Media and Sport, partly in order to distance itself from the more conservative, dated and elitist connotations of the former title. In order to gain cultural prestige and support for popular music, therefore, some have tried to get it included in the category of heritage by presenting it as, or likening it to, high culture. In Liverpool, for example, the directors of the city-based tour operator Cavern City Tours have argued that local Beatles tourism should receive greater acknowledgment and funding from Liverpool City Council because 'The Beatles are to Liverpool what the Pope is to Rome and Shakespeare to Stratford' (Cohen 1997, 97).

Moore (1997), writing about the Rock 'n' Roll Hall of Fame in Cleveland, Ohio, states that the museum 'marks a deliberate attempt to raise rock and roll to high culture' (90). The museum opened in 1995 at a cost of $100 million and is based on an extensive collection of rock memorabilia. Moore refers to a newspaper article that states: 'There's little doubt that the building marks an impressive statement about the artistic credentials of rock 'n' roll. It suggests, by using the architect who designed the Louvre expansion, that the artefacts of rock 'n' roll are every bit as important as the art of Picasso' (Lee 1995, 10).

Selective and official definitions and uses of heritage have been critiqued in some quarters, making 'heritage' a contested term. In November 1999, a conference entitled 'Whose Heritage?' was held in Manchester. The conference was coordinated and funded by the Arts Council of England, with additional support from other national and regional arts and heritage organizations, and one of its aims was to address the rather narrow notion of heritage traditionally promoted by public museums and other established institutions, and to draw attention to different or alternative heritages (in the plural). The conference reflected the turn toward a broader notion of heritage that had taken place in Britain during the 1980s and 1990s, encompassing the notion of heritage as everyday and popular culture. Britain's public museums were also challenged during the 1980s and 1990s by the rise of a so-called 'heritage industry' related to leisure and tourism and to local, regional and national economic development. Here, the notion of heritage was used to promote an increasing number of urban industrial sites, exhibitions and so-called 'heritage centers,' which aimed to bring the past to life in as entertaining a way as possible and to present it as a place to visit and become immersed in (Lowenthal 1985). Many of these centers were run on a commercial basis from the private sector, and their success forced a response from public-sector museums. The latter began to move away from the older notion of museums as collections of objects and as educators, and to place more emphasis on entertainment, on becoming more democratic and inclusive, and on embracing the everyday and the popular.

These trends were evident in the increasing 'heritagization' and 'museumification' of popular music, involving a proliferation of popular music museums and heritage sites. In the Czech Republic, for example, a popular music museum and archive called Popmuseum was established in Prague in 2000 with funding from the municipal authorities of Prague and from the European Union Cultural Capital of Europe program. Popmuseum includes an exhibition detailing the history of Czechoslovak rock between 1956 and 1972. In Sheffield, the ill-fated National Centre for Popular Music opened in 1998. This was a major visitor attraction developed by a registered educational charity entitled Music Heritage Ltd. The Centre was described in its own publicity materials as 'a unique interactive arts and education centre celebrating the diversity and influence of popular music; the only centre of its kind in the world; state of the art technology providing hands-on experience; a celebration of popular music in all its global forms; informing, questioning and challenging.' The Centre was established with money from the Heritage Lottery (which is where individuals seeking funds for cultural projects from the UK National Lottery apply) and from the European Regional Development Fund, but it failed to attract the predicted visitor numbers and closed in 2000.

In Liverpool, the Cavern Club – which had been made famous by the Beatles, who performed there on a regular basis between 1961 and 1963 – was rebuilt in 1984 near the location of the original club and was promoted as 'the place where it all began.' The owners of the new club tried to build it to the same specifications as the original and claimed that thousands of the original bricks had been used. Another replica of the club was later built in the Beatles Story museum, which opened in Liverpool's docklands area in 1995 and attempted to re-create the experience of the early 1960s through the use of smells and sounds as well as visual images. In 1993, a regeneration initiative had also been launched by a group of professional businesspeople based in an area of the city surrounding the Cavern Club. They named the area the Cavern Quarter and aimed to improve it through the development of tourism and heritage, retail and entertainment. They emphasized the importance of creating and marketing a distinctive and cohesive image for the Quarter in order to attract visitors, business and investment, and they based this

image around popular music and, more specifically, around the Beatles (Cohen 2001).

In Memphis, Tennessee, the city's Beale Street, famous for its popular music connections and particularly for its connections with Elvis Presley, was similarly rebuilt and marketed to visitors as the 'birthplace of the blues,' while Graceland, the former house of Elvis Presley, was opened to the public complete with gift shops and theme restaurants.

The global success of the Beatles and Elvis Presley has meant that they are not just perceived as the heritage of two particular cities, but as heritage in a broader sense. In their book *Heritage and Tourism in 'the Global Village'* (1993), Boniface and Fowler describe a tourist visit to Hawaii and entertain serious doubts about the authenticity of the music and dance presented to them as part of '"the" Hawaiian heritage':

> In heritage terms, it was marvellously nostalgic, for what I heard was my heritage, not that of Polynesia or the Pacific, let alone Hawaii ... I suppose that exactly thirty years on from Elvis Presley's film, *Blue Hawaii* (November 1961), this time-warp stuff is now part of Hawaii's heritage too, certainly quite as strong as the more traditional, but actually bogus, guitar-based heritage music associated with the islands in popular perception. This point may seem a diversion, incidental to 'heritage and tourism': it is not, for in the case of Hawaii ... it is precisely the need to entertain the tourist which has created and perpetuated a peculiar but unmistakably 1950s local style of music. (52)

Boniface and Fowler describe this attempt to portray music from an Elvis Presley film as authentic Hawaiian music as 'a heritage conspiracy.' Others, drawing on Hobsbawm's and Ranger's influential book *The Invention of Tradition* (1983), point to the way in which heritage is 'invented.' Kong (1998), for example, describes the Retrospin project in Singapore as part of the invention of national popular music heritage. Kneafsey (1997), writing about traditional music in Ireland, comments on music traditions that would have taken place in people's homes but now take place in pubs in order to make them accessible for tourists. She describes this as not just an invention, but also a commodification of tradition. Stocks (1996), however, has described this shift to music-making in pubs as a necessity and as a positive process, suggesting that the old cottages associated with the traditional life have become empty and derelict and that it is progress that is changing the traditional life rather than heritage and tourism (255). Clearly, the term 'heritage,' like 'tourism,' raises familiar ideological distinctions between representation and the real, and between authenticity and commerce. Hewison (1987), for example, has written an influential critique of the 'heritage industry' which describes it as not just producing a version of the past but as producing politically strategic 'false-history.' He regards the growth of heritage culture in Britain as being determined by a marked industrial decline, describes it as an ugly product of social failure and declares: 'Instead of manufacturing goods, we are manufacturing heritage, a commodity which nobody seems able to define, but which everybody is eager to sell' (9).

However, the examples of popular music heritage mentioned above illustrate that the term 'heritage' can encompass a variety of different types of initiative. These initiatives have implications for the way in which popular music is perceived and valued. For some, for example, the promotion of popular music as heritage sits uneasily with the notion of popular music as contemporary culture associated with a rebellious, anti-Establishment stance, with subcultures and with the authenticity of 'the street,' and with change rather than stasis. The notion of popular music heritage also raises questions about how the popular musical past is being constructed and represented, and about what is included and excluded in this process and what such choices reveal about relations between culture and politics.

Bibliography

Boniface, Priscilla, and Fowler, Peter J. 1993. *Heritage and Tourism in 'the Global Village'*. London and New York: Routledge.

Cohen, Sara. 1997. 'Liverpool and the Beatles: Exploring Relations Between Music and Place, Text and Context.' In *Keeping Score: Music, Disciplinarity, Culture*, ed. David Schwarz, Anahid Kassabian and Lawrence Siegel. Charlottesville, VA: University Press of Virginia, 90–106.

Cohen, Sara. 2001. 'Popular Culture in Liverpool.' In *Liverpool at the Millennium: Living in the City*, ed. R. Meegan and M. Maddon. Liverpool: Liverpool University Press.

Finn, Julio. 1992. *The Bluesman: The Musical Heritage of Black Men and Women in the Americas*. New York: Interlink Books.

Hewison, Robert. 1987. *The Heritage Industry: Britain in a Climate of Decline*. London: Methuen.

Hobsbawm, Eric, and Ranger, Terence, eds. 1983. *The Invention of Tradition*. Cambridge: Cambridge University Press.

Kneafsey, Moya. 1997. *Tourism and Place Identity: Change and Resistance in the European Celtic Periphery*. Ph.D. thesis, University of Liverpool.

Kong, Lily L.L. 1998. 'The Invention of Heritage: Popular Music in Singapore.' In *Popular Music: Intercultural Interpretations*, ed. Tôru Mitsui. Kanazawa: Graduate Program in Music, Kanazawa University, 448–60.

Lee, V. 1995. 'Rolling Back (Some of) the Years.' *The Guardian* (1 September): 10.

Lowenthal, David. 1985. *The Past Is a Foreign Country*. Cambridge: Cambridge University Press.

Moore, Kevin. 1997. *Museums and Popular Culture*. London: Cassell.

Stocks, Jayne. 1996. 'Heritage and Tourism in the Irish Republic: Towards a Giant Theme Park?' In *Tourism and Culture: Image, Identity and Marketing*, ed. Mike Robinson, Nigel Evans and Paul Callaghan. Sunderland: Centre for Travel and Tourism in association with Business Education Publishers Ltd., 251–60.

SARA COHEN

Hybridity and Globalization (Intercultural Exchange, Acculturation)

Etymology and History

A powerful and yet highly problematic metaphor for cultural identity, the term 'hybridity' has been at the center of one of the most vigorous critical debates in recent years, emerging from and, in turn, affecting fields such as cultural studies, postcolonial studies, anthropology, literature and the arts. Derived from the Latin *hybrida* and generally used in the sciences in the more limited sense of the 'offspring of parents that differ in genetically determined traits' (*New Encyclopaedia Britannica* 1998, Vol. 6, 183), the meaning of the broader metaphor has undergone significant shifts over the past 100 years. At the turn of the twentieth century, for instance, 'hybridism' was a key term in the European racial imagination that was reflected in such things as an entry of seven columns in the *Encyclopaedia Britannica* of 1910–11. But the obsession with 'mongrelism,' crossbreeding and fertility was not so much about natural evolution per se as about the supposedly objective linkages the members of the master race perceived between British colonial supremacy, modern class society and nature. Hybridism was, above all, a metaphor for the vicissitudes and perils of cross-racial encounters made possible by colonial expansion. Beyond this, and no doubt because of the biological connection between crossbreeding and sterility, the term almost became a metaphor for death and extinction itself.

Subsequent ideologies of difference and intercultural exchange, both before and after World War II, modified the idea of the inherent incompatibility of different cultural identities, arguing instead for the inevitability of assimilation, acculturation and, still later, syncretism. Basic to these concepts are two interrelated responses to the large-scale cultural changes which occurred in the twentieth century. The first is the tendency to view such changes in mechanistic terms, stressing patterns and models of 'culture contact' rather than agency and unevenness. For instance, where early ethnomusicological studies of African music did take cognizance of the emergent Westernized musics of the cities, they did so either by seeking to isolate Western influences from certain 'traits' considered essential to a style's (and, by implication, a culture's) 'real' identity, or by emphasizing the role of these new musics as agents of adaptation. In both cases, however, some expression of nostalgia for the supposedly untouched traditional forms was common.

The second response is marked by a lack of attention to questions about how such criteria for defining pristine identities came about in the first place, and whether the stakes ethnomusicologists, anthropologists and 'Natives' have in processes of cultural change are embedded in larger networks of power imbalances. Frequently, the legitimacy of the colonial project remained unquestioned. Modernization and development – the integration on differential terms of the colonies and emerging nation-states of the 'Third World' into the capitalist world economy – were the parameters against which all other histories, all other cultural practises were to be weighed.

The failure of the Enlightenment project, the growing disjunctures of global economic networks and the remarkable imperviousness of culture to Western agendas of modernization led many scholars to reexamine the homogenizing claims of universal Reason. Beginning in the 1980s, the term 'hybridity' – as well as a number of parallel concepts such as 'creolization' (Hannerz 1987) and 'carnevalization' – attracted renewed scholarly and somewhat more sympathetic attention, possibly echoing the now accepted scientific view in genetics that 'almost all individuals of sexually reproducing organisms, including man, are hybrids, because their parents usually differ in several genes' (*Encyclopaedia Britannica* 1972, Vol. 11, 921–22). At the broadest level, then, while 'apparently incongruous syntheses ... have in many ways become icons of postmodernism' (Shaw and Stewart 1994), it is equally true to say that intermixtures and juxtapositions of cultures have a long history, even in the very heart of modern Western societies. In fact, it is because of the unsettling specter of miscegenation and the profound hybridity of European society that notions of racial purity and cultural homogeneity have occupied such a prominent place in various forms of nineteenth-century imperial ideology (Young 1995).

As a master trope of postcolonial critical theory, however, 'hybridity' is not an uncontested term, little consensus having been reached as to the political implications of transcultural practises. Although it is often assumed that hybrid cultural forms in and of themselves subvert dominant orders (see Lipsitz 1994; Taylor 1997) and that 'hybridity is the antidote to essentialist notions of identity and essentialism' (Cashmore 1996, 166), there is no reason to assume that 'crossover practices are always liberatory or that articulating an autonomous identity or a national culture is always reactionary' (Clifford 1997, 10). In fact, what matters politically is 'who deploys nationality or transnationality, authenticity or hybridity against whom, with what relative power and ability to sustain a hegemony' (10). Although there can be no doubt that fixed categories such as 'tribe' or 'race' and the taxonomies used to give them meaning are inventions designed to bolster Western dominance, scholars have begun to acknowledge the powerful role played by more conventional notions of immutable racial or national identities, evocations of authenticity and cultural homogeneity in invigorating the struggles of people of color and of religious and sexual minorities. Current debates about hybridity, then, far from ignoring the ambiguities of identity politics in the postcolonial world, grapple with the uneasy balance between unforeseen circulations, uncontrolled eccentricities and unruly intermixtures on the one hand, and the representational hegemony of Western culture and the attempts at resistance fed by more exclusivist and fundamentalist interpretations of cultural identity on the other.

Nation-State and Nationalism

Of all the articulations of identity that hybrid cultural forms contest and are caught up with, the modern nation-state and various types of nationalist discourse are probably the most important. And it is the links between the nation-state, nationalism and various hybrid contestations and entanglements with the nation that have become the object of the most sustained scrutiny to date undertaken by students of popular music. As a rich literature on the new popular musics of the 'Third World' – and to a somewhat lesser degree on the advanced countries of the West (for example, Hebdige (1979) on reggae in Britain) – demonstrates, hybrid musical practises often disrupt the putatively homogeneous times and spaces of the nation-state, but at other times they exist quite comfortably alongside nationalist assertions of unity. In Turkey, peasant and migrant populations have for a long time resisted the state's attempt at imposing a modern, European-style Turkish identity by means of education and the media. The politics and aesthetics of *arabesk* music, to a large degree, are determined by the unresolved antagonism between the homogenizing state and the masses of the urban poor (Stokes 1992). The Miri of southern Sudan, by contrast, have successfully defended their cultural integrity by selectively incorporating from the dominant Arabic culture of the North only the more innocuous musical practises (Baumann 1987).

In some contexts, the nation-state as the sole controlling force of a country's mass media may also come to the rescue of cultural heterogeneity. Thus, while in one sense it might be argued that hybrid cultural forms are rarely supportive of exclusively nationalist ideologies, the state, confronted with an overwhelming influx of Western images, sounds and cultural artifacts, may at times become the guarantor of whatever internal diversity it is capable of tolerating. Tanzania, for instance, is one of several countries that have tried successfully to promote 'national' musics by reserving some 85 percent of the music content on its national broadcasting service for local music products. But here, as in many other cases, the definition of what counted as representative of Tanzanian culture rested in the hands of the Swahili-speaking minority dominating the state apparatus (Malm and Wallis 1992, 113–14).

Diaspora, Travel and Migrancy

Some celebrations of difference and hybridity, while critical of official nationalist discourse, may reproduce the very orientalist stereotypes the state and dominant social forces have created of minorities and, in this case especially, immigrant communities. Thus, Israeli rock influenced by Arabic music celebrates an 'other' quite blatantly at odds with the images of backwardness that the Israeli majority projects of the Palestinian minority, but at the same time it takes a stable 'oriental' identity as its reference point (Shiloah and Cohen 1983; Regev 1986). Similarly, an examination of the new *bhangra* dance music popular among South Asian immigrants in Great Britain has led some observers to guard against a fetishization of marginality and the erosion of numerous idiosyncracies operating within South Asian communities (Sharma, Hutnyk and Sharma 1996).

Although hybrid cultural politics and musical practises may well partake of state-driven nationalist agendas or, alternatively, lead to new exoticisms and articulations of racial or ethnic exclusivism, some musics have also been shown to lend themselves to more pliant, anti-essentialist forms of opposition. This is perhaps more typical of the conflicted relationship between the nation-state, nationalist ideology and hybrid cultural practises in diasporic communities. Thus, as Gilroy's musings on African-American music (1993) suggest, the music of black Americans is a product of the slaves' encounter with the West and at the same time has emerged in opposition to modernity. It may thus serve as a model for what Gilroy calls anti-antiessentialism, a critique of the oppressive history and racial injuries of the 'host' country that refuses to let go of memories of collective identity even where it resists grounding these in a direct and unilineal genealogy rooted in the African past.

Similarly, as a recent study of the music of Maghrebian immigrants in France has shown, *rai* performers and audiences construct complex identities around notions of sexuality, romantic love and adolescence that are inspired by Western liberal ideals of gender equality and at the same time reproduce more traditional images of Arabness (Gross, McMurray and Swedenburg 1996). Thus, while female *rai* singers often advocate more freedom for women, the jackets of their cassettes reproduce clichés of a more subdued kind of femininity and the ideal Arab woman. Many carry no picture of the singer at all. The reasons given for these representations are by no means universally accepted and, as the study also shows, Maghrebi rappers and *rai* musicians deploy a whole range of strategies to fight racism and assert their dignity, brazenly hybrid ones as well as playful, orientalizing ones.

Another important focus that emerged from the current interest in hybridity and diaspora and that promises to yield new insights into the history of popular music is the rather diverse set of practises described as travel, migrancy, immigration or displacement. In the recent past, all these practises have been dealt with to some extent by ethnomusicologists (Turino (1993) on labor migration in Peru; Erlmann (1996) on Zulu migrant laborers in South Africa; Reyes Schramm (1986) on refugees), but students of popular music have been less anxious to explore the profound interchange between music and the shifting boundaries of communities and audiences caused by large-scale movements of people. In some cases, migrancy is taken, rather unspecifically, to be a universal phenomenon which 'we all' share (Chambers 1994, 24). Furthermore, the spaces people traverse as tourists, migrants, refugees or touring musicians are often depicted as though they are bounded sites that are already filled with a sound radiating from some center to a boundary, and much less as multiply overlapping contact zones in which identities and musics are always blurred and defy easy definition.

Globalization and Locality

The concern with displacement, although relatively recent, also entailed a vigorous rethinking of the interrelationship between popular music, locality and the growing globalization of intercultural relations. Much of the discussion has grappled with several of the issues already mentioned, such as nationalism, diaspora and migrancy, but other areas of debate include the power of capitalism and commodification in the transformation of 'traditional' cultures, the capacity of Western mass media and cultural imperialism to dominate the collective imagination of large populations, and the contradictions of modernity (for a good overview of the debate, see Tomlinson 1991). While some critics have tended to think about global cultural flows in polarized terms – either positing late capitalism (Jameson 1991) and a regime of simulations and simulacra (Baudrillard 1985) as an all-embracing and undifferentiated system (the homogenization thesis) or, alternatively, privileging 'Third World' cultural practises with anti-hegemonic agency per se (the heterogenization thesis) (Frith 1989; Robinson, Buck and Cuthbert 1991) – the majority of scholars have taken a more nuanced position toward the role of culture in reflecting and mediating global relations of power (for example, Appadurai 1990; Featherstone 1990; Hall 1991; Hannerz 1996).

The same applies to studies of popular music, numerous theoretical interventions having emerged in recent years that seek to provide new conceptual tools and models with which to grasp the twists and turns of global musical flows (Manuel 1993). Slobin (1993), for instance, in an attempt to account for the impossibility of representing both global generality and local specificity, has depicted the interplay of various 'micromusics' in the West as a kind of 'interculture,' a constant oscillation between the pressures of the 'supraculture' and the contention of various subcultures.

Feld (1994), for his part, takes a more sinister view of global musical production at the end of the twentieth century. He draws on Gregory Bateson's term 'schismogenesis' to think through a set of escalating relationships marking the production and consumption of music on a global scale. Schismogenesis is a process through which the cumulative interplay between essentially dissimilar but mutually appropriative actions may lead to a closer symbiotic interdependence of both sides, to the point that they may even become incapable of self-correction and caught up in closed circuits of repetition. Ultimately, what results from this scenario is a grayout of a new type. As discourses of authenticity and difference assert themselves and activities of commercial appropriation in turn get more overt and outrageous, some kind of 'fusion of the parties for mutual business gain' becomes likely (Feld 1994, 273).

As no single model in the foreseeable future is likely to assert preeminence, the challenge that anthropologists, ethnomusicologists and students of popular music will increasingly have to face is not to refine their intellectual maps, but to produce credible accounts of the embedding of richly described local musical worlds in larger impersonal systems of the global economy (see also Marcus and Fischer 1986, 77). Future studies will have

to follow the lead of groundbreaking work such as Manuel's study of the cassette industry in India (1993) or Guilbault's ethnography of *zouk* and creolity in the West Indies (1993) in trying to account for the intersection between global forces and local cultural choices in ways that are as ethnographically 'real' as the traditional concern with local practise.

While it may be premature at this point to predict in what way such global ethnographies will open up new and experimental venues for popular music studies, one way of redirecting future research activities is to view the making of globally connected identities as a two-way process in which positions of alterity are no longer stable, center and periphery are constantly confused, and the West is just as much an 'other' of Africa or Asia as Africans and Asians have been the 'others' of Europeans (Erlmann 1999). In more concrete terms, greater attention will have to be focused on the agency of those (predominantly Western) 'cultural intermediaries' (Bourdieu 1984) or 'symbolic analysts' (Reich 1991) whose practises and discourses are more than just manifestations of some anonymous capitalist world system or the global music industry. More in-depth analyses are needed of 'global' figures, such as Paul Simon, Peter Gabriel, Quincy Jones and Mickey Hart, and how their work has increasingly become the location of struggles over the shifting meanings attached to floundering Western middle-class identities.

Finally, entrenched notions of place, space and locality will have to be reconsidered. While previous scholarship tended to assume a relatively static fit between place, spatial identity and music, an equation that often enabled scholars to produce richly detailed, empirically grounded narratives of local identity and music-making (Finnegan 1989; Stokes 1994), the spaces that scholars of popular music study and work in are no longer necessarily only such rather abstract entities as cities and countries. Increasingly, other spaces, such as studios, malls, music departments and taxis, are becoming sites of inquiry. But as stimulating as such work undoubtedly is on many levels, the danger is that 'macro' here simply turns into 'micro' and that locality – no matter how much its description entails taking into account wider contexts – is being taken as the very essence of social order rather than a figure of social process.

A more fruitful approach to issues of locality is Barber's and Waterman's (1995) study of Nigerian *fújì* and *oríkì*. Although popular performers of these genres draw on a multiplicity of external sources to imagine densely local worlds, the emergent sense of locality is not seen as stemming from any given body of materials or traditions. Rather, the 'ultimate goal of any performance is to intensify the presence, image and prospects of local actors' (243). Although it cannot be ruled out that Yoruba musical productions of place may be driven by the same agendas that underlie movements of national and ethnic purity, Barber and Waterman, by insisting on the processual nature of what they call *fújì* and *oríkì* performers' use of extension, domestication and intensification, do not romanticize such assertions of local identity.

Bibliography

Appadurai, Arjun. 1990. 'Disjuncture and Difference in the Global Cultural Economy.' In *Global Culture: Nationalism, Globalization, and Modernity*, ed. Mike Featherstone. London and Newbury Park: Sage Publications, 295–310.

Barber, Karin, and Waterman, Christopher. 1995. 'Traversing the Global and the Local: Fuji Music and Praise Poetry in the Production of Contemporary Yoruba Popular Culture.' In *Worlds Apart: Modernity Through the Prism of the Local*, ed. Daniel Miller. London: Routledge, 240–62.

Baudrillard, Jean. 1985. 'The Ecstasy of Communication.' In *Postmodern Culture*, ed. Hal Foster. London: Pluto Press.

Baumann, Gerd. 1987. *National Integration and Local Integrity: The Miri of the Nuba Mountains in the Sudan*. Oxford: Clarendon Press.

Bourdieu, Pierre. 1984 (1979). *Distinction: A Social Critique of the Judgement of Taste*. Cambridge, MA: Harvard University Press.

Cashmore, Ellis, ed. 1996. *Dictionary of Race and Ethnic Relations*. New York: Routledge.

Chambers, Iain. 1994. *Migrancy, Culture, Identity*. London: Routledge.

Clifford, James. 1997. *Routes: Travel and Translation in the Late Twentieth Century*. Cambridge, MA: Harvard University Press.

Encyclopaedia Britannica. 1972. 24 vols. Chicago: William Benton.

Encyclopaedia Britannica; A Dictionary of Arts, Sciences, Literature and General Information. 1910–11. 29 vols. 11th ed. Cambridge and New York: Cambridge University Press.

Erlmann, Veit. 1996. *Nightsong: Performance, Power and Practice in South Africa*. Chicago: University of Chicago Press.

Erlmann, Veit. 1999. *Music, Modernity, and the Global Imagination: South Africa and the West*. New York: Oxford University Press.

Featherstone, Mike. 1990. 'Global Culture: An Introduction.' In *Global Culture: Nationalism, Globalization, and Modernity*, ed. Mike Featherstone. London and Newbury Park: Sage Publications, 1–14.

Feld, Steven. 1994. 'From Schizophonia to Schismogenesis: On the Discourses and Commodification Practices of "World Music" and "World Beat."' In Charles Keil and Steven Feld, *Music Grooves: Essays and Dialogues*. Chicago and London: University of Chicago Press, 257–89.

Finnegan, Ruth. 1989. *The Hidden Musicians: Music-Making in an English Town*. Cambridge: Cambridge University Press.

Frith, Simon, ed. 1989. *World Music, Politics, and Social Change*. Manchester: Manchester University Press.

Gilroy, Paul. 1993. *The Black Atlantic: Modernity and Double Consciousness*. Cambridge, MA: Harvard University Press.

Gross, Joan, McMurray, David, and Swedenburg, Ted. 1996. 'Arab Noise and Ramadan Nights: *Rai*, Rap, and Franco-Maghrebi Identities.' In *Displacement, Diaspora, and Geographies of Identity*, ed. Smadar Lavie and Ted Swedenburg. Durham, NC: Duke University Press, 119–55.

Guilbault, Jocelyne. 1993. *Zouk: World Music in the West Indies*. Chicago: University of Chicago Press.

Hall, Stuart. 1991. 'The Local and the Global: Globalization and Ethnicity.' In *Culture, Globalization and the World-System: Contemporary Conditions for the Representation of Identity*, ed. Anthony D. King. Binghamton, NY: SUNY Binghamton, Department of Art and Art History, 19–39.

Hannerz, Ulf. 1987. 'The World in Creolisation.' *Africa* 57: 546–59.

Hannerz, Ulf. 1996. *Transnational Connections: Culture, People, Places*. New York: Routledge.

Hebdige, Dick. 1979. *Subculture: The Meaning of Style*. London: Methuen.

Jameson, Fredric. 1991. *Postmodernism, or, The Cultural Logic of Late Capitalism*. Durham, NC: Duke University Press.

Lipsitz, George. 1994. *Dangerous Crossroads: Popular Music, Postmodernism and the Poetics of Place*. London: Verso.

Malm, Krister, and Wallis, Roger. 1992. *Media Policy and Music Activity*. London and New York: Routledge.

Manuel, Peter. 1993. *Cassette Culture: Popular Music and Technology in North India*. Chicago: University of Chicago Press.

Marcus, George E., and Fischer, Michael M.J. 1986. *Anthropology as Cultural Critique: An Experimental Moment in the Human Sciences*. Chicago: University of Chicago Press.

New Encyclopaedia Britannica. 1998. 32 vols. 15th ed. Chicago: Encyclopaedia Britannica, Inc.

Regev, Motti. 1986. 'The Musical Soundscape as a Contested Area: "Oriental Music" and Israeli Popular Music.' *Media, Culture and Society* 8: 343–52.

Reich, R.B. 1991. *The Work of Nations*. New York: A.A. Knopf.

Reyes Schramm, Adelaida. 1986. 'Tradition in the Guise of Innovation: Music Among a Refugee Population.' *Yearbook for Traditional Music* 18: 91–102.

Robinson, Deanna Campbell, Buck, Elizabeth B., and Cuthbert, Marlene. 1991. *Music at the Margins: Popular Music and Global Cultural Diversity*. Newbury Park, CA: Sage Publications.

Sharma, Sanjay, Hutnyk, John, and Sharma, Ashwani, eds. 1996. *Dis-Orienting Rhythms: The Politics of the New Asian Dance Music*. London: Zed Books.

Shaw, Rosalind, and Stewart, Charles, eds. 1994. *Syncretism/Anti-Syncretism: The Politics of Religious Synthesis*. London: Routledge.

Shiloah, Amnon, and Cohen, Erik. 1983. 'The Dynamics of Change in Jewish Oriental Ethnic Music in Israel.' *Ethnomusicology* 27: 227–51.

Slobin, Mark. 1993. *Subcultural Sounds: Micromusics of the West*. Hanover, NH: Wesleyan University Press.

Stokes, Martin. 1992. *The Arabesk Debate: Music and Musicians in Modern Turkey*. Oxford: Clarendon Press.

Stokes, Martin, ed. 1994. *Ethnicity, Identity and Music: The Musical Construction of Place*. Oxford: Berg.

Taylor, Timothy. 1997. *Global Pop: World Music, World Markets*. London and New York: Routledge.

Tomlinson, John. 1991. *Cultural Imperialism: A Critical Introduction*. Baltimore, MD: Johns Hopkins University Press.

Turino, Thomas. 1993. *Moving Away from Silence: Music of the Peruvian Altiplano and the Experience of Urban Migration*. Chicago: University of Chicago Press.

Young, Robert J.C. 1995. *Colonial Desire: Hybridity in Theory, Culture and Race*. London: Routledge.

VEIT ERLMANN

Identity

Identity is the cultural mode of imagining belonging, or shared substance, whether this is predicated on race, ethnicity, nationhood, class, gender or sexuality. Primordialists see certain forms of identity as possessing an inherent logic, linking communities in an homologous relationship to the expressive forms they produce. Blues, jazz and rap, for example, are seen as having special meanings rooted in the African-American experience of slavery and the ghetto, while other meanings are understood as being essentially derivative (see, for example, Jones 1963; Rose 1994). Constructivists see identities as plural, context-dependent and performative: acts of identity are understood as underpinning the phenomenon of identity rather than vice versa. Black expressive forms might thus be seen as fluid and manipulable signs in the formation of subaltern identity, eliding racialized political interventions for strategic purposes (see Spivak 1995; see also Sharma, Hutnyk and Sharma 1996 on *bhangra* in the United Kingdom) or drawing attention to their hybrid, fractured nature (Lipsitz's 'strategic anti-essentialism' (1994)).

Constructivist theories of identity have been criticized from many quarters. Freudian and Lacanian theorists stress the ways in which processes of identification disrupt identities (homoerotic mechanisms in reading and looking, for example, underpin, but also disrupt, heterosexual subject formation; see Fuss 1995). The reduction of identities to textual mechanisms has been critiqued for its mimeticism, that is, its assumption that the subject is an inert tabula rasa before engagement with the text (see Rothenberg and Valente 1995). Others argue that even constructivist discussions of identity have failed to move beyond an inherent solipsistic particularism, reducing the scope for an adequate theorization of agency, social transformation and translation (Butler 1995). In popular music studies, discussions of music and identity formation continue to confront the ongoing assumption of the 'universal' Enlightenment subject on which much historical and analytical thinking about music continues to rest. The connection between music-making and identity formation poses many problems, but remains an important and continuing project.

'Ethnic' identities, throughout the modern period, have predominantly been constructed by, or in reaction to, the nation-state. German romantic philosophy posited the nation as a unit of shared destiny, united by blood, territory and shared myths of origin. Media systems, from print to the radio, have been crucial to the construction of the national public sphere. Music, disseminated by print or radio, has been used as an explicit arm of state policy in many new nation-states. Many attempts to use mass-mediated musics have been entirely unsuccessful, at least from the point of view of the ideologues who initially promoted them. The Indian intelligentsia could not come up with anything to rival the enormous popularity of Hindi-language film music in the 1950s (Manuel 1993). Other national styles were successfully cultivated for regional export (such as that of Umm Kulthūm under Nasser in Egypt, or merengue under Trujillo in the Dominican Republic; see, respectively, Danielson 1997 and Austerlitz 1997).

Nationalism and popular national styles flourish outside the nation. Popular musics have been particularly important to migrant and diasporic communities cultivating ties of sentimental attachment to the home country, or creating actively oppositional national spaces.

The Kurdish diaspora in Scandinavia, for example, has been particularly active in shaping a Kurdish popular musical style in opposition to the Iranian, Turkish and Iraqi co-option or proscription of Kurdish culture (Blum and Hassanpour 1996). Some such diasporic genres are taken up by nationally based, but transnationally active, media industries. These either cultivate the oppositional politics that they identify in the music, as in the case of salsa, or with little difficulty reconcile the commercial imperative (captive migrant markets) with the ethos of liberal multiculturalism, as in the case of *conjunto* in North America, or *zouk* and *rai* in France (see, respectively, Peña 1985, Guilbault 1993 and Virolle 1995).

The grip of the nation-state on identity formation was weakened by the transnational flow of labor and commodities in the latter part of the twentieth century. The cultural imperialism thesis suggested that North American popular culture would displace all others as US military and economic power spread across the globe, and local identities would be either displaced or maintained as colorful but emasculated 'heritage' in a global cultural environment (see, for example, Lomax 1968). Many would argue that this has not happened. The circulation of musical technologies and ideas allows for new articulations of, for example, rock and rap with national and regional identities; it has brought sounds from the peripheries into the countercultural spaces of the center, and permitted the emergence of new and more localized subcultural forms outside state control (Manuel 1993; Mitchell 1996; Regev 1997; Slobin 1993). These self-consciously hybrid diasporic cultures undermine essentialist claims to particular musical styles as the authentic cultural property of particular groups (Gilroy 1993). The attendant destabilization of center–periphery relations has, for some writers, enormous emancipatory potential (Chambers 1985; Lipsitz 1994).

Others have pointed to the continued power of nationally based media industries in shaping their transnational markets (Negus 1997; Laing 1992), and to the tendency of dominant groups to shape other musical styles according to their own aesthetic criteria (on world music/world beat, see Erlmann 1996; Feld 1994). Contrary to a certain sociological optimism, neither nationalism nor the state showed signs of disappearing toward the end of the twentieth century. While strong arguments are often made for the continued salience of the state as a redistributive mechanism in a globalized free market, and a means of maintaining diversity, musical and otherwise (see, for example, Wallis and Malm 1984; Born 1993), nationalism has fewer apologists. Many ethnonationalist popular musical genres, such as Serbian turbofolk or German neo-Nazi bands, are clearly a part of the symbolic process of claiming and purifying national

space on the part of those marginalized by, and often seeing themselves in defiant opposition to, the 'new world order.' The explicit link between sexuality, violence and identity in these genres suggests the potential saliency of analytical techniques derived from psychoanalysis, and the limits of structuralist approaches to identity that stress its consensual and ordered quality (for a review and a Kleinian perspective, see Born 1998).

Traumas within the nation-state system at the beginning of the twentieth century pushed other forms of identity to the center of political thought and action, particularly those based on gender and, later, sexuality. Critics of Enlightenment universalism (in both its liberal and its Marxist forms) have stressed its gendered and heteronormative nature, and have attended to the alternative and critical projects, particularly in the domain of culture, that it usually conceals. Popular music scholars have stressed the centrality of popular music in shaping gendered and sexual identities. Frith's and McRobbie's influential theorization of 'cock rock' and 'teenybop' (1979) was subsequently much disputed. Their dualistic distinction between controlling corporations and the resignifying capacities of audiences was criticized by Taylor and Laing (1979). Dyer's 'defence of disco' (1990) emphasized the heterosexual assumptions implicit in Frith's and McRobbie's argument, and Frith himself subsequently reflected on the original article's confusion as to whether sexuality was a social fact (rooted in biology, expressed by music) or a social discourse (actively constructed through music, among other things) (Frith 1990).

The 'construction' of identities through expressive activity, however, remains a messy process. Some would argue that the musical sign operates as a marker of identity in more complex, and often rather arbitrary, ways. Poststructuralism and queer theory, in particular, foreground the playful and reflexive nature of sexual signification and stress the instability and incomplete nature of the musical sign, unable to fully exclude its 'other' or recognize the presence of the 'other' in the self. The textual construction of heteronormative male–female love in many rock lyrics, for example, is marked by the irruption of a decidedly non-heteronormative desire in the musical performance, generated through repetition, 'nonsense' syllables and details of vocal timbre (see, for example, Bradby and Torode 1984). From a more ethnographic perspective, others stress the continuing and equally unstable processes involved in the musical construction of gendered and sexual identities: the constant cultural 'work' involved in the marginalization of women in the worlds of heavy metal (Walser 1993) and rock (Cohen 1991). The utopian possibilities of information and biotechnology in structuring new gendered and sexual identities have been the focus of a more recent body of writing on dance music and rave, drawing heavily on the work of Harraway (1992), and cyborg theory (Bradby 1993). Music certainly provides the means by which people may consider other modes of belonging or coexistence, although in this case there is little to suggest that dominant gendered and sexual identities have, in practise, been fundamentally shaken.

Bibliography

Austerlitz, Paul. 1997. *Merengue: Dominican Music and Dominican Identity*. Philadelphia: Temple University Press.

Blum, Stephen, and Hassanpour, Amir. 1996. '"The Morning of Freedom Rose Up": Kurdish Popular Song and the Exigencies of Cultural Survival.' *Popular Music* 15(3): 325–43.

Born, Georgina. 1993. 'Afterword: Music Policy, Aesthetic and Social Difference.' In *Rock and Popular Music: Politics, Policies, Institutions*, ed. Tony Bennett et al. London: Routledge, 266–91.

Born, Georgina. 1998. 'Anthropology, Kleinian Psychoanalysis, and the Subject in Culture.' *American Anthropologist* 100(2): 373–86.

Bradby, Barbara. 1993. 'Sampling Sexuality: Gender, Technology and the Body in Dance Music.' *Popular Music* 12(2): 155–76.

Bradby, Barbara, and Torode, Brian. 1984. 'Pity Peggy Sue.' *Popular Music* 4: 183–206.

Butler, Judith. 1995. 'Collected and Fractured: Response to Identities.' In *Identities*, ed. Kwame Anthony Appiah and Henry Louis Gates, Jr. Chicago: University of Chicago Press, 439–47.

Chambers, Iain. 1985. *Urban Rhythms: Pop Music and Popular Culture*. London: Macmillan.

Cohen, Sara. 1991. *Rock Culture in Liverpool: Popular Music in the Making*. Oxford: Oxford University Press.

Danielson, Virginia. 1997. *The Voice of Egypt: Umm Kulthūm, Arabic Song, and Egyptian Society in the Twentieth Century*. Chicago: University of Chicago Press.

Dyer, Richard. 1990 (1979). 'In Defence of Disco.' In *On Record: Rock, Pop and the Written Word*, ed. Simon Frith and Andrew Goodwin. London: Routledge, 410–18.

Erlmann, Veit. 1996. 'Aesthetics of the Global Imagination: Reflections on World Music in the 1990s.' *Public Culture* 8(3): 467–88.

Feld, Steven. 1994. 'From Schizophonia to Schismogenesis: On the Discourses and Commodification Practices of "World Music" and "World Beat."' In Charles Keil and Steven Feld, *Music Grooves: Essays and Dialogues*. Chicago and London: University of Chicago Press, 257–89.

Frith, Simon. 1990 (1985). 'Afterthoughts.' In *On Record: Rock, Pop and the Written Word*, ed. Simon Frith and Andrew Goodwin. London: Routledge, 419–24.

Frith, Simon, and McRobbie, Angela. 1979. 'Rock and Sexuality.' *Screen Education* 29: 3–19.

Fuss, Diana. 1995. 'Fashion and the Homospectatorial Look.' In *Identities*, ed. Kwame Anthony Appiah and Henry Louis Gates, Jr. Chicago: University of Chicago Press, 90–114.

Gilroy, Paul. 1993. *The Black Atlantic: Modernity and Double Consciousness*. London: Verso.

Guilbault, Jocelyne. 1993. *Zouk: World Music in the West Indies*. Chicago: University of Chicago Press.

Harraway, Donna. 1992. 'The Promises of Monsters: A Regenerative Politics for Inappropriate/d Others.' In *Cultural Studies*, ed. Lawrence Grossberg, Cary Nelson and Paula A. Treichler. New York: Routledge, 295–337.

Jones, LeRoi [Imamu Amiri Baraka]. 1963. *Blues People: Negro Music in White America*. New York: William Morrow.

Laing, Dave. 1992. '"Sadeness," Scorpions and Single Markets: National and Transnational Trends in European Popular Music.' *Popular Music* 11(2): 127–39.

Lipsitz, George. 1994. *Dangerous Crossroads: Popular Music, Postmodernism and the Poetics of Place*. London: Verso.

Lomax, Alan. 1968. *Folk Song Style and Culture*. Washington, DC: American Association for the Advancement of Science.

Manuel, Peter. 1993. *Cassette Culture: Popular Music and Technology in North India*. Chicago: University of Chicago Press.

Mitchell, Tony. 1996. *Popular Music and Local Identity: Rock, Pop and Rap in Europe and Oceania*. London: Leicester University Press.

Negus, Keith. 1997. *Popular Music in Theory: An Introduction*. Hanover, NH: University Press of New England.

Peña, Manuel. 1985. *The Texas-Mexican Conjunto: History of a Working-Class Music*. Austin, TX: University of Texas Press.

Regev, Motti. 1997. 'Rock Aesthetics and Musics of the World.' *Theory, Culture and Society* 14(3): 125–42.

Rose, Tricia. 1994. *Black Noise: Rap Music and Black Culture in Contemporary America*. Hanover, NH: University Press of New England.

Rothenberg, Molly Ann, and Valente, Joseph. 1995. 'Fashionable Theory and Fashion-able Women: Returning Fuss' Homospectatorial Look.' In *Identities*, ed. Kwame Anthony Appiah and Henry Louis Gates, Jr. Chicago: University of Chicago Press, 413–23.

Sharma, Sanjay, Hutnyk, John, and Sharma, Ashwani, eds. 1996. *Dis-Orienting Rhythms: The Politics of the New Asian Dance Music*. London: Zed Books.

Slobin, Mark. 1993. *Subcultural Sounds: Micromusics of the West*. Hanover, NH: Wesleyan University Press.

Spivak, Gayatri Chakravorty. 1995. 'Acting Bits/Identity Talk.' In *Identities*, ed. Kwame Anthony Appiah and Henry Louis Gates, Jr. Chicago: University of Chicago Press, 147–80.

Taylor, Jenny, and Laing, Dave. 1979. 'Disco-Pleasure-Discourse: On "Rock and Sexuality."' *Screen Education* 31: 43–48.

Virolle, Marie. 1995. *La Chanson Rai: De l'Algérie profonde à la scène internationale*. [*Rai* From Deepest Algeria to the International Scene]. Paris: Karthala.

Wallis, Roger, and Malm, Krister. 1984. *Big Sounds from Small Peoples: The Music Industry in Small Countries*. London: Constable.

Walser, Robert. 1993. *Running with the Devil: Power, Gender and Madness in Heavy Metal Music*. Hanover and London: Wesleyan University Press.

MARTIN STOKES

Illness, Injury and Disease

The influence of illness, injury and disease on popular music takes three principal forms: as part or consequence of musical activity; as subject or theme; and as metaphor.

Certain medical conditions are linked to instrumental performance and can have serious consequences. Drummers often suffer from osteoarthritis in the neck and back. For singers, the most common complaints are sore throats, and the growth of nodules on the vocal cords, a condition that, if untreated, can permanently damage the voice. Woodwind and trumpet players are prone to cancer of the throat (Miles Davis died of this in 1991). Particularly since the advent of high-level amplification, both musicians and audience members have been prone to tinnitus and other hearing impediments (in live appearances, the Who's Pete Townshend is forced to play in a transparent soundproof booth, so acute are his hearing difficulties).

A number of illnesses and injuries are likely to be caused, or worsened, by life on the road. Occupational hazards include electrocution (sometimes fatal) caused by faulty equipment, injury or death suffered by road crews while setting up gigs (for example, accidental deaths as a result of falling from lighting rigging) and automobile accidents. Many rock performers, from Patti Smith to Frank Zappa, have suffered concussion, broken bones, dislocations and strains, caused either by fans or by various antics such as stage-diving.

The most widespread cause of illness in gigging musicians is general fatigue. Colds, influenza and bronchial infections are common reasons for the cancellation of performances. More serious is nervous exhaustion, which can lead to mental or physical breakdown (as it did, for example, in the case of the Beach Boys' Brian Wilson). There have even been cases of paranoid schizophrenia (Pink Floyd's 'Syd' Barrett, for instance), although this cannot necessarily be attributed solely to a rock star's life style. Depression is also common, and has been a factor in the suicide of performers such as Ian Curtis and Michael Hutchence.

Many complaints, both serious and minor, can be attributed to aspects of the particular life styles that have become associated with musicians at different times and in different environments. Gastric problems caused either by overindulgence or by food poisoning are frequent on-the-road hazards. The large amounts of drink and drugs consumed also contribute to ill health. Smoking can lead both to impairment of performance (diminution in vocal range) and to serious illness. In the case of English trumpeter and comedian Roy Castle, lung cancer followed prolonged exposure to cigarette smoke in clubs – he himself was a nonsmoker. In addition, one result of the promiscuous life style of some performers is a high incidence of HIV-related illnesses.

The fact that performers, musical and otherwise, are more prone to some illnesses and complaints than other members of society and that they can require specialist treatment has been recognized in the formation of supporting organizations such as the British Performing Arts Medicine Trust (founded in 1984). Among the problems that the Trust identifies as most frequently encountered are voice nurture, hearing difficulties, stage fright, tendinitis and depression.

Perhaps because of a predictably negative response in the marketplace, songs about specific illnesses and diseases have never been particularly common. One exception within rock and pop is 'Poison Ivy' (1959) by the Coasters, a song about venereal disease. Occasionally, commercially successful singers have sung about their own experience of illness. US country singer Jimmie Rodgers, for example, made two recordings – 'T.B. Blues' (1931) and 'Whippin' That Old T.B.' (1933) – about the disease that was to kill him. Probably the genre with the most extensive references to illness and disease is the blues. As Oliver (1990, 244ff.) has shown, the black experience of illnesses and diseases associated with diet (pellagra rashes), employment conditions (in particular silicosis, common among mine workers), poor sanitation and water quality (typhus), and exposure to cold (pneumonia) was widely reflected in blues songs. In overcrowded tenements, tuberculosis was often particularly rife – 'the dirty T.B.,' Victoria Spivey called it (her record label, OKeh, in turn described Spivey as 'a blues shouter with a turn for sorrowin' talk' (Oliver 1990, 248)).

In contrast to the serious tone of 1920s and 1930s blues concerning life-threatening illness, New Orleans rhythm and blues pianist Huey 'Piano' Smith recorded his novelty dance song, 'Rockin' Pneumonia and the Boogie Woogie Flu,' in 1957. It was his biggest hit. In the musical theater, too, medical issues have sometimes been humorously treated. In Cole Porter's song 'The Physician,' for example (from the musical *Nymph Errant*), the singer is disappointed when a thorough and enthusiastic medical checkup fails to encourage the doctor to make a confession of love ('He went through wild ecstatics/When I showed him my lymphatics/But he never said he loved me'). (A similar theme was explored in the 1960 comic duet by Peter Sellers and Sophia Loren, 'Goodness Gracious Me.')

Within the discourse of popular song, disease or illness is often used metaphorically, most often for being in love. Love is a 'bug,' an affliction, which the unsuspecting victim may catch, rather like the flu (see 'Lovesick Blues' (1962), 'Love Bug' (1977), 'Love Injection' (1980), 'Love Kills' (1984), 'Love Is Contagious' (1988) and so on). In blues singer Sleepy John Estes' 'Milk Cow Blues' (1930), being rejected by a lover and made to feel second best is described as 'a slow contagion killing me by degrees.' There are also numerous songs that deal with alcohol and drugs as metonyms for illness. In a rather different use of metaphor, country singer David McCarn attached to his protest song about cotton mill bosses in North Carolina in 1930, 'Poor Man, Rich Man,' the subtitle 'Cotton Mill Colic No. 2.'

The music industry has responded in a direct way to certain illnesses, particularly HIV and AIDS, to raise money and public awareness. The death of Queen's Freddie Mercury led to the Freddie Mercury Tribute Concert for AIDS Awareness, while many pop performers, such as Madonna, have added their voices to safe-sex campaigns.

Bibliography

Clayson, Alan. 1992. *Death Discs*. London: Gollancz.
Herman, Gary. 1994. *Rock 'n' Roll Babylon*. London: Plexus.
'Nurse! The Screens.' 1993. *Q* 83: 48–53.
Oliver, Paul. 1990. *Blues Fell This Morning: Meaning in the Blues*. 2nd ed. Cambridge: Cambridge University Press.
Wills, Geoff, and Cooper, Cary L. 1988. *Pressure Sensitive: Popular Musicians Under Stress*. London: Sage.

Sheet Music

Porter, Cole, comp. and lyr. 1933. 'The Physician.' New York: Warner Bros.

Discographical References

Charles, Tina. 'Love Bug.' CBS 5680. *1977*: UK.
Coasters, The. 'Poison Ivy.' London HLE 8938. *1959*: UK.
Estes, Sleepy John. 'Milk Cow Blues.' Victor V38614. 1930: USA.
Ifield, Frank. 'Lovesick Blues.' Columbia DB 4913. *1962*: UK.
McCarn, David. 'Poor Man, Rich Man.' Victor 23506. 1930: USA. Reissue: McCarn, David. 'Poor Man, Rich Man.' *Songs of Complaint and Protest* (Folk Music in America, Vol. 7). Library of Congress LBC 7. *1977*: USA.
Mercury, Freddie. 'Love Kills.' CBS A 4735. *1984*: UK.
Rodgers, Jimmie. 'T.B. Blues.' Victor V23535. 1931: USA.
Rodgers, Jimmie. 'Whippin' That Old T.B.' Victor V23751. 1933: USA.
Sellers, Peter, and Loren, Sophia. 'Goodness Gracious Me.' Parlophone R 4702. *1960*: UK.
Sevelle, Taja. 'Love Is Contagious.' Paisley Park W 8257. *1988*: USA.
Smith, Huey 'Piano,' and the Clowns. 'Rockin' Pneumonia and the Boogie Woogie Flu.' Ace 530. *1957*: USA. Reissue: Smith, Huey 'Piano,' and the Clowns. 'Rockin' Pneumonia and the Boogie Woogie Flu.' *Havin' A Good Time*. Ace LP 1004. *1959*: USA.
Spivey, Victoria. 'Dirty T.B. Blues.' Victor V38570. 1929: USA.
Trussel. 'Love Injection.' Elektra K 12412. *1980*: USA.

DAVID BUCKLEY and DAVID HORN

Industrialization

'Industrialization' describes the process of economic transformation whereby a subsistence or craft labor process or entire economy is replaced by one dominated by mechanization, the division of labor, heightened productivity and mass production. Because industrialization typically involves the recruitment of large work forces and settles them in specific locations, it is closely linked to both migration and urbanization. Industrialization has an impact on popular music in two principal ways. Firstly, general processes of industrialization affect the creation, performance and consumption of popular music. Secondly, popular music itself has undergone its own process of industrialization. Indeed, for some scholars, popular music is distinguished from other forms of music by the industrial character of its process of production.

Industrialization and Music

What is generally referred to as the Industrial Revolution was initiated in Britain and elsewhere in Northern Europe during the late eighteenth century. It created new forms of work and new social groups based on the production process. The emerging working classes were often migrants from rural areas moving to the sites of the mills, mines or factories. This process of social upheaval also marked subsequent phases of industrialization, whether in the exploitation of copper in Africa or of gold in Australia, or in the expansion of the factory-based manufacturing industry in the United States, which drew millions of immigrants from Europe and migrants from the rural southern states.

The immediate musical responses to industrialization were often expressed through industrial folk song, which comprised lyrics describing the experience of work set to existing tunes. The folk-song historian A.L. Lloyd wrote of this process: 'As the old lyric of the countryside crumbled away, a new lyric of the industrial towns arose . . . reflecting the life and aspirations of a raw class in the making, of men handling new-fashioned tools, thinking new thoughts, standing in a novel relationship to each other and their masters' (1967, 316).

The English cotton industry had its songs of hand-loom weavers and factory maids (Lloyd 1967, 303); the US railway industry had the ballad of the mythical John Henry (Seeger and Reiser 1985, 32–35). In South Africa, displaced Zulu mine workers created *iscathamiya*, a form of music and dance that conjured up their homeland (Erlmann 1996). In Trinidad, indentured labor, brought by the British from India in the nineteenth century to work on the sugar plantations and in the factories, created a diasporic music culture (Myers 1998).

But industrialization also made obsolete the 'work songs' of older types of labor organization. 'By applying chemical and mechanical techniques to fulling cloth and using steam to power ships, the industrial revolution did away with the need for waulking songs and sea shanties and, indeed, for work-songs of most kinds' (Palmer 1988, 85).

The process of industrialization enforced a relatively strict division between work time and other time, a distinction that had been marked in preindustrial agricultural and manufacturing activities (Thompson 1967). Non-work time was necessary (in Marx's terms) for the reproduction of labor power, and many employers and their allies in religious and philanthropic institutions attempted to guide workers and their families into 'rational recreation' rather than the popular culture of the tavern.

In some cases, the new industrialists organized the musical activities of their workers through the formation of brass bands (notably in Britain), choirs or glee clubs, such as the club formed by the Hawaiian Electric Company in the 1920s. On a more individual level, the more affluent members of the industrial work force were able to purchase musical instruments (above all, pianos) and printed music for domestic entertainment.

Industrial workers, as such, were defined equally as consumers, purchasing their food, clothing and other necessities as commodities and services. The economic importance of such consumption to the equilibrium of modern capitalism has been emphasized by various authors, who have defined this system as a 'consumer society' supported by an ideology of 'consumerism' (Miles 1998). The essential tools of consumerism included advertising, plugging and marketing.

The process of consumption extended to cultural goods and services, including entertainment. In the words of Ewen and Ewen (1982), 'On a narrowly economic level, the origin of mass culture can be seen as an extension of the necessity to generate and maintain an industrial labor force and expand markets' (57). In this way, industrialization precipitated both participants in, and mass audiences for, various types of popular culture.

The Industrialization of Music

The industrial revolution in music can be traced to the latter part of the nineteenth century and the mass production and organized marketing of musical instruments and sheet music copies, plus the organization of professional musical entertainment in the theater, vaudeville show, music hall or dance hall.

In the second half of the nineteenth century, piano manufacture underwent massive expansion in Europe and North America, as the guitar-making industry would in the 1950s. While pianos were still assembled by hand, important components, including the action, were mass-produced and supplied to piano manufacturers by specialist firms, notably in Germany and the United States (Ehrlich 1990; Lieberman 1995).

The industrial history of music publishing and recording to some extent bears out Adorno's comment, made in his essay 'On Popular Music' (first published in 1941), that the production of popular music was '"industrial" only in its promotion and distribution, whereas the act of producing a song-hit still remains in a handicraft stage' (1990, 306). While the factory system was applied to the mass production of printed music from the mid-nineteenth century and to the production of piano rolls and discs from the early twentieth century, songs and original recordings were created in a more old-fashioned manner by self-employed individuals selling their copyrights or their performances to publishers and labels. Nevertheless, the emergence of the Tin Pan Alley publishing matrix in the 1890s brought to the fore the concept of music created for the market. In the words of Irving Berlin, 'I wrote about what people wanted to hear. I packaged their feelings and sold them back . . . I serviced them. I met the market' (quoted in Whitcomb 1987, 12).

Musical performance was transformed into a service industry by the advent of the music hall (UK) and vaudeville (US) systems. Specialist promoters such as Charles

Morton, the 'father' of music hall, and agents like the New York-based William Morris developed the characteristic division of labor that brought skilled musical performances to numerous industrial towns and cities.

The division of labor created by the industrialization of the music industry was complex. The industry provided employment not only for composers, musicians and singers, but also for professional managers, pluggers and copyists in music publishing, booking agents, concert promoters and venue staff in the live music sector, and recording engineers, factory hands and marketing specialists in the area of recorded music. The first fully professional North American songwriter was Stephen Foster in the 1850s. Half a century later, New York publishers elicited songs from dozens of songwriters. The demand for mass entertainment created work for increasing numbers of singers and instrumentalists, who formed trade unions to improve their pay and conditions.

Analytical Perspectives

The industrialization of music itself has been the subject of both theoretical elaboration and empirical historical research. The theoretical dimension has been dominated by the concept of 'culture industry' introduced by Adorno and Horkheimer (1979) in 'The Culture Industry – Enlightenment as Mass Deception,' the fourth chapter of their *Dialectic of Enlightenment*. The emphasis here was on the power of mass culture to mold audiences 'to become whatever the system wants' (1979, 153); but, in 'On Popular Music,' Adorno presented 'standardization' as the essential characteristic of songs created by the culture industry (1990, 305–309).

While few were willing to accept his overwhelmingly negative view of the culture industry, many subsequent authors have portrayed the struggle to create meaningful popular culture and popular music as one undertaken against the institutions and pressures of the industry. Writing in the mid-1960s, the English Marxist Ian Birchall provided a typical formulation when he wrote that pop music was '(like any art-form in a commercial society, only more so) squeezed out between two conflicting pressures. On the one hand the publishers and manufacturers, geared to the obsolescence principle, constantly promote new crazes. On the other, working class youth seeks a medium to express their experience in modern society' (quoted in Laing 1969, 189–90).

Nevertheless, the mainstream of popular music scholarship has generally 'domesticated' the idea of the music industry and deployed it in a critically and morally neutral manner. In an essay devoted to the history of the recording industry, Frith (1987) asserts that 'the "industrialization of music" can't be understood as something that happens *to* music but describes a process in which music itself is made – a process ... which fuses (and confuses) capital, technical, and musical arguments' (54). From a different sociological perspective, Peterson has defined the production of popular culture as subject to a series of industrial 'constraints,' most recently in his study of the country music industry (1997). Other authors, such as Lash and Urry (1994), have discussed the prominent role of the culture industries, including music, in the era of 'post-Fordist' industrial production.

Postindustrialism

A less remarked feature of music history has been the impact of 'deindustrialization.' This term refers to the closure and supersession of industries, usually those that were created during the Industrial Revolution. Lipsitz (1994) discusses the effect of deindustrialization on the musical life of the US city of St. Louis, while the contraction of the coal-mining and shipbuilding industries in Britain inspired the composition of a number of folkstyle songs, including Johnny Handle's 'Farewell to the Monty' and Matt McGinn's 'The Ballad of Q4' (Palmer 1988, 92).

Economic historians have argued that the initial Industrial Revolution has been followed by others based on different forms of production or of service industries. Among the most significant of these for the popular music industry have been international tourism and the revolution in information technology.

Music is involved with tourism through the provision of entertainment for foreign visitors and through the marketing of sites with important musical connotations. In the Bahamas, for example, with over 3 million visitors a year, employment was created in the 1980s for musicians who performed a repertoire of local folk music plus generic Caribbean and North American pop music (Wood 1998). Cohen (1997) has described and analyzed the Liverpool tourist industry, which is linked to Beatles and Merseybeat.

As the first cultural industry to make use of both digital processes and the new forms of communication, exchange and distribution offered by the Internet, music was an important component of the new industrial revolution of the 1990s, based on telecommunications and information technologies (Alderman 2001).

Bibliography

Adorno, Theodor W. 1990 (1941). 'On Popular Music.' In *On Record: Rock, Pop, and the Written Word*, ed. Simon Frith and Andrew Goodwin. London: Routledge, 301–14.

Adorno, Theodor W., and Horkheimer, Max. 1979 (1944). *Dialectic of Enlightenment*, trans. John Cumming. London: Verso.

Alderman, John. 2001. *Sonic Boom: Napster, P2P and the Battle for the Future of Music*. London: Fourth Estate.

Cohen, Sara. 1997. 'Popular Music, Tourism, and Urban Regeneration.' In *Tourists and Tourism: Identifying with People and Places*, ed. Simone Abram, Jacqueline Waldren and Donald V.L. Macleod. Oxford: Berg, 71–90.

Ehrlich, Cyril. 1990. *The Piano: A History*. Rev. ed. Oxford: Oxford University Press.

Erlmann, Veit. 1996. *Nightsong: Performance, Power, and Practice in South Africa*. Chicago: University of Chicago Press.

Ewen, Stuart, and Ewen, Elizabeth. 1982. *Channels of Desire: Mass Images and the Shaping of American Consciousness*. New York: McGraw-Hill.

Frith, Simon. 1987. 'The Industrialization of Popular Music.' In *Popular Music and Communication*, ed. James Lull. Newbury Park, CA: Sage, 53–77.

Laing, Dave. 1969. *The Sound of Our Time*. London: Sheed & Ward.

Lash, Scott, and Urry, John. 1994. *Economies of Signs and Space*. London and Thousand Oaks, CA: Sage.

Lieberman, Richard K. 1995. *Steinway & Sons*. New Haven and London: Yale University Press.

Lipsitz, George. 1994. *Dangerous Crossroads: Popular Music, Postmodernism, and the Poetics of Place*. London and New York: Verso.

Lloyd, A.L. 1967. *Folk Song in England*. London: Lawrence & Wishart.

Miles, Steven. 1998. *Consumerism as a Way of Life*. London: Sage.

Myers, Helen. 1998. *Music of Hindu Trinidad: Songs from the India Diaspora*. Chicago: University of Chicago Press.

Palmer, Roy. 1988. *The Sound of History: Songs and Social Comment*. Oxford: Oxford University Press.

Peterson, Richard A. 1997. *Creating Country Music: Fabricating Authenticity*. Chicago and London: University of Chicago Press.

Seeger, Pete, and Reiser, Bob. 1985. *Carry It On!: A History in Song and Picture of the Working Men and Women of America*. New York: Simon & Schuster.

Thompson, E.P. 1967. 'Time, Work-Discipline and Industrial Capitalism.' *Past and Present* 38: 56–97.

Whitcomb, Ian. 1987. *Irving Berlin and Ragtime America*. London: Century Hutchinson.

Wood, Vivian Nina Michelle. 1998. 'The Bahamas.' In *The Garland Encyclopedia of World Music. Vol. 2: South America, Mexico, Central America, and the Caribbean*, ed. Dale A. Olsen and Daniel E. Sheehy. New York: Garland Publishing, 801–12.

Discographical References

Handle, Johnny. 'Farewell to the Monty.' *Along the Coaly Tyne*. Topic 498. *1999*: UK.

McGinn, Matt. 'The Ballad of Q4.' *The Best of Matt McGinn*. Castle Music America 699. *2001*: USA.

DAVE LAING

Journalistic Practises

Introduction

Music journalism can be defined as the practise of reporting or writing about music for publication in specialist or nonspecialist print media, including the music press, life-style magazines, newspapers, biographies and histories. Music journalism has been important in the negotiation and ascription of popular music meanings, as well as integral to the marketing of popular music. Because the subject of such journalism is music, a distinction can be drawn between music journalism and general journalistic practise. Hence, music journalists generally work within a particular discourse of criticism, adhering to certain stylistic conventions and employing common critical criteria. The music journalist's expertise is in capturing the essence of music, the atmosphere of performance, and building the public image of a star or act. The method of documentation informs the way in which music has been judged and valued.

Early Conventions

Music journalism and specialist music publications have existed in some form since the nineteenth century. Until the 1960s, journalism relating to pop and rock 'n' roll tended to be fairly prosaic. The pieces were largely factual and statistical, and made little use of emotive or atmospheric language or detailed scene-setting. Reviews of live and recorded music were generally dryly descriptive (detailing the songs played, the group members and so on), and judged performance in terms of technical or generic competence and audience reaction. Interviews recounted plainly the factual details of an artist's career or personal life. For example, the tone of a review of a live concert, printed in the weekly UK publication *Melody Maker* in 1957, is straightforward, with an unanimated relaying of facts: 'The Deep River Boys came to Glasgow Empire for the thirteenth time this week and received a well-deserved crescendo of applause' (Innes 1957, 9).

This concentration on entertainment value and proficiency was fairly typical of popular music criticism of the time. However, the critical emphasis in 1950s coverage of other genres, such as folk and jazz, was somewhat different. Journalism that addressed the folk revival, in journals such as *Sing Out!* (United States) and *Sing* (United Kingdom), attempted to contextualize the music within the ideological framework of the movement. As in the case of contemporary jazz journalists, such as the US commentator Nat Hentoff, the writing in these publications was grounded in analysis that reflected on the music's social uses, history and relationship to tradition – all traits that would be repeated in later rock journalism.

The New Journalism

From the mid-1960s onward, music journalism increasingly revealed the profound influence of the emerging New Journalism movement. Spearheaded by color-supplement and magazine writers such as Tom Wolfe and Hunter S. Thompson and novelists such as Norman Mailer and Truman Capote, the New Journalism undertook to take journalism out of the realm of mere 'dry' reporting of facts by utilizing many of the stylistic components of fiction. Its conventions had an important influence on style and content, as well as on the construction of the image of the journalist within music (especially rock) journalism. Stylistic traits pioneered by the new journalists, such as scene-by-scene construction, third-person point of view, recording of everyday detail and the inclusion of the persona of the journalist within the text, were appropriated by US and UK music critics from the end of the 1960s. The fact that many new journalists explicitly created a new cultural agenda that treated popular culture as worthy of serious analysis has also been attributed to the influence of the New Journalism. For example, Tom Wolfe, writing in 1966, makes clear that the subject matter of much of his writing constitutes a definite shift in aesthetic boundaries:

> The educated classes, the people who grow up to control visual and printed communication media, are all plugged into what is ... an ancient, aristocratic aesthetic. The Jerk, the Monkey and rock music still seem beneath serious consideration. Yet all these rancid people are creating new styles all the time and changing the life of the whole country in ways that nobody even seems to bother to record, much less analyse. (Wolfe 1981, 12)

Significantly, this evolution in writing style occurred at the same time as mainstream rock music began to take itself more seriously, with the incorporation of art and folk aesthetics into the genre. Subsequent journalistic criticism began to reflect and reinforce this position.

The Underground Press

Parallel to these developments was the rise of the underground press in the late 1960s. Peck's (1985) history of the underground press in the 1960s situates the rise of magazines catering to a rock audience within the framework of cultural and political debate. Indeed, the editorial raison d'être of many underground periodicals was to provide an audience with published music criticism. Correspondingly, the association of many types of popular music with notions of radicalism, opposition and dissent influenced the style and content of music journalism. For example, in Britain in the late 1970s, journalists writing for the weekly music press sought to mimic the oppositional voice of punk rock by presenting themselves as speaking *for* a new youth culture rather than merely *about* one. Moreover, when writing for an independent or underground publication, journalists often chose to mark themselves off from mainstream discourses. For instance, underground publications such as *Oz* (Australia and United Kingdom) and *International Times* (United Kingdom) reveled in their status as channels for dissent and in their frequent pillory by daily 'Establishment' papers. A 1969 report in the British Sunday tabloid *The People* opined: 'Maybe they are published for ideological reasons. But there's no ideology in teaching kids to take drugs and mutilate their sex organs, as *Oz* does. I implore shop and discotheque owners: Don't help to spread this muck' (quoted in Hutchinson 1992, 104).

The radicalism exhibited in these underground publications was inevitably contextual and a reaction to particular and temporary dominant discourses. For example, in South Africa in the 1970s and 1980s, a proliferation of 'black' magazines (some, like *Pace*, covert products of the apartheid state's propaganda onslaught) recognized and made space for the coverage of black popular music, in English and in some African languages. A counter-critique then developed in the pages of various independent and underground radical publications, and in the covertly imported publications of exiled cultural workers and the Department of Arts and Culture of the African National Congress. While the mainstream magazines merely described and adulated, these more radical journals dealt with popular music as having meaning for South African society and politics. Particularly influential was the *MEDU Newsletter* (Botswana), published by a group of cultural exiles and Botswana citizens, which at one time included both Hugh Masekela and *Cry Freedom* soundtrack composer Jonas Gwangwa. These journalists presented indigenous popular music as a legitimate and culturally important practise, while also providing a documentation of music not valued by the dominant culture.

Underground periodicals and, latterly, fanzines and zines have been particularly tied to popular music criticism because they have served, and have continued to function, as a training ground for many journalists, and have been the impetus for many who have chosen as a career reporting and editing in the mainstream or underground press. Toynbee (1993) cites the ex-underground UK press journalist Charles Shaar Murray as an influential figure in the development of journalistic style from the early 1970s onward. Toynbee argues that Murray, in his close reading of rock texts, mixed post-Leavisite literary criticism with auteurism from film criticism, as well as attempting to draw up a rock canon that encompassed Elvis, blues guitarists and avant-garde musicians. He argues that these elements were central to the 're-establishment of a high/low culture demarcation' within rock ideology (1993, 291). Added to these elements was the development of a 'mid-Atlantic' journalese, which mixed North American slang, regular clusters of short sentences, puns and contemporary metaphor.

The Rock Journalist

Linked to this stylistic evolution was the development of the cult of the rock journalist, in which the figure of the writer took on the romantic attributes of the rock star. Journalists of the 1970s, such as Nick Kent (United Kingdom) and Lester Bangs (United States), carefully cultivated public images of themselves. For instance, at the start of his retrospective review of Van Morrison's *Astral Weeks*, Bangs places the record in relation to his own experiences and to popular cultural myths relating to late-1960s burnout: 'It was particularly important to me because the fall of 1968 was such a terrible time: I was a physical and mental wreck, nerves shredded and ghosts and spiders looming and squatting across the mind' (1991, 20). Kent's writing is peppered with references to his own drug-taking, hedonism and personal relationships with such infamous rock stars as Sid Vicious and Keith Richards. Hill (1991) describes music journalists of this time as a 'fraternity [which] unerringly reflected the culture it documented' (173). The figure of the journalist can thus be linked to the specifically male image of the romantic bohemian figure entrenched within rock mythology.

McDonnell's and Powers's (1995) collection of rock writing by women celebrates the proliferation of women in this field, reflecting that they are rarely celebrated as great or 'legendary' writers or included in the canon of rock criticism. Sullivan's (1995) account of the day-to-day demands of her career further suggests that the romantic image of the journalist is a construction that is directly at odds with the realities of the profession. She outlines the drawbacks of the job: its low pay and unsociable hours; the necessity of traveling alone to get to gigs; and the severe limitations imposed by deadlines on the amount of research a journalist can do on a particular artist.

Journalistic Style and Practise

While the influence of the New Journalism is evident across a wide spectrum of music journalism, there are also differences in journalistic style and practise across publications. Specialist music magazines and newspapers may, for example, use a brash, opinionated tone to establish credibility with their readership. Music reviews and interviews with musicians are often littered with obscure or canonical musical reference points, which serve simultaneously to establish the journalist's authority and to target the publication at an imagined audience of music connoisseurs. As national and local newspapers are not targeted at such niche markets, the content of music articles is inevitably distinct. Music sections in local newspapers generally cover local gigs and events and publicize local musicians. Alternatively, concert and album reviews in national newspapers often comprise part of a popular culture section that offers readers an overview of current music, book and film releases. Thus, the form and content of articles are shaped by considerations of the role and readership of a publication. Caroline Sullivan, music columnist for the British newspaper *The Guardian*, comments that her 'readership is mainly educated and left-of-centre, and I take this into account when deciding what to write about. It's not necessary to be quite so cutting edge as in the music press, but I do have to monitor trends and be adaptable' (1995, 141).

On a more general level, music journalism has its own particular conventions in the way in which music is represented in descriptive terms. It has been widely argued (Stratton 1982; Breen 1987; Frith 1996) that the effusiveness of the criteria by which music is judged and described has led to music journalism being a confused and unstable form. Frith (1996) contends that 'the language of music criticism . . . depends upon the confusion of the subjective and objective' (67). Following Roland Barthes' observation that, in music criticism, musical work and performance are 'invariably translated into the poorest linguistic category: the adjective,' Frith points out that adjectives are used by music journalists to 'relate music to its possible uses' and in the generic classification of a particular piece (67).

Stratton's (1982) research among British music journalists bears out this confusion in that it concludes that their writing is grounded in the use of critical language and assumptions that are in direct opposition to the rationalizing objective needs of capitalism. They are, in a sense, forced into a subjective critical position. Stratton points out that the critical criteria of journalism generally fail to value and discuss elements of work when judging a musical text. Thus, time spent writing, rehearsing or performing (elements of the creative process that are linked to commerce and production) is all but ignored. Instead, value is placed on subjective notions, such as the 'quality of emotion' and the 'quality of the idea' apparent in a piece of music. In this mode, criticism rests on qualities that are grounded in such relative concepts as 'authenticity,' emotional directness and intensity. The ambiguous and uncertain nature of the critical criteria of music journalism is echoed in the answers of Stratton's respondents to questions about how they judge music. For instance, 'it doesn't matter who the guy was who did it; if the end product has some indefinable quality about it then that's great' (1982, 277). This is perhaps illustrative of Jones's comment that authenticity is the most 'invisible and opaque of the ideas that occupy popular music critics, yet it is referred to in almost all popular music criticism' (1992, 101).

Journalistic and academic writing about popular music have often intersected, most notably in the work of Greil Marcus, Jon Savage, Dave Laing, Simon Frith and Robert Christgau. Much of their work was concerned with the exploration and deconstruction of popular music mythologies, along with the location of music with regard to its social uses. Indeed, many of Laing's and Frith's early journalistic work went on to inform debates within popular music studies (reflected in their subsequent involvement and influence in the field). Nehring (1997) argues that the late 1980s and 1990s saw the adaptation of academic postmodern theory by British and North American music journalists. Writers such as Simon Reynolds, Joy Press and David Stubbs incorporated ideas taken from literary criticism, such as psychoanalysis and poststructuralism, to explore the cultural significance of music, including movements such as 'new pop,' 'dreampop' and 'shambling.'

However, although journalists such as Reynolds were celebrated and controversial, such appropriation of academic theory was limited to a small number of writers. They can be regarded as the exception, since many contemporary journalists operated within the stylistic conventions established in the 1960s and 1970s. Arguably, traits associated with postmodernism were more widely apparent in the rise of the life-style magazine in the 1980s. Hebdige (1988) sees the UK music and fashion magazine *The Face* as an exemplar of postmodernism: it 'renounces social realism . . . and promotes consumer aesthetics and multiple style elites,' and 'goes out of its way to blur the line between politics and parody and pastiche' (161). Hebdige argues that the content of *The Face* is decontextualized and that it adds up to an 'empty chain of signifiers' (161). His observations, however, lean heavily on the magazine's layout and juxtaposition of subject matter. The writing itself is still contained within particular reference points and, despite its use of irony and intertextuality, it is nevertheless grounded within the contexts of popular cultural journalism.

Conclusion

Whatever the stylistic developments and changes over the years, most music journalism has been closely linked to the music industry, with journalists themselves deeply involved in its promotional cycle. Due to the very nature of criticism, music journalism has an inherent need to be seen as autonomous. Many journalistic techniques, then, are part of the process that creates an image of critical distance and separation from the promotional arm of the music industry. The music journalist must, at the same time, promote the products released through the industry, and anticipate and reflect the reception of his/her readership. Because of this duality, music writing provides an invaluable temporal index to the fast-moving cycles of the music industry and culture for popular music fans and scholars. As such, music journalism has continued to be an important and influential forum in which popular music discourses are created and mediated.

Bibliography

Bangs, Lester. 1991. *Psychotic Reactions and Carburetor Dung: Literature as Rock and Roll, Rock and Roll as Literature*. London: Minerva.

Breen, Marcus. 1987. 'Rock Journalism: The Betrayal of Impulse.' In *Missing in Action: Australian Popular Music in Perspective*, ed. Marcus Breen. Kensington, Victoria: Verbal Graphics, 202–27.

Frith, Simon. 1996. *Performing Rites: On the Value of Popular Music*. Oxford: Oxford University Press.

Hebdige, Dick. 1988. *Hiding in the Light: On Images and Things*. London: Routledge.

Hill, Dave. 1991. 'Rock Journalists and How to Use Them.' In *The Rock File: Making It in the Music Business*, ed. Norton York. Oxford: Oxford University Press, 173–82.

Hutchinson, Roger. 1992. *High Sixties: The Summers of Riot & Love*. Edinburgh: Mainstream.

Innes, Robert. 1957. 'Deeps Do It Again.' *Melody Maker* (5 October): 9.

Jones, Steve. 1992. 'Reviewing Rock Writing: The Origins of Popular Music Journalism.' *American Journalism* (Winter/Spring): 87–107.

Kent, Nick. 1994. *The Dark Stuff: Selected Writings on Rock Music 1972–1993*. London: Penguin.

McDonnell, Evelyn, and Powers, Ann, eds. 1995. *Rock She Wrote: Women Write About Rock, Pop and Rap*. London: Plexus.

Nehring, Neil. 1997. *Popular Music, Gender and Postmodernism: Anger Is an Energy*. London: Sage.

Peck, Abe. 1985. *Uncovering the Sixties: The Life and Times of the Underground Press*. New York: Pantheon.

Reynolds, Simon, and Press, Joy. 1995. *The Sex Revolts:*

Gender, Rebellion and Rock 'n' Roll. London: Serpent's Tail.

Stratton, John. 1982. 'Between Two Worlds: Art and Commercialism in the Record Industry.' *The Sociological Review* 30: 267–85.

Sullivan, Caroline. 1995. 'The Joy of Hacking: Women Rock Critics.' In *Girls! Girls! Girls!: Essays on Women and Music*. London: Cassell, 138–45.

Toynbee, Jason. 1993. 'Policing Bohemia, Pinning Up Grunge: The Music Press and Generic Change in British Pop and Rock.' *Popular Music* 12(3): 289–300.

Wolfe, Tom. 1981. *The Kandy-Kolored Tangerine-Flake Streamline Baby*. London: Picador.

Discographical References

Cry Freedom (Original soundtrack). MCA 6224. *1987*: USA.

Morrison, Van. *Astral Weeks*. Warner Brothers 1768. *1969*: USA. Reissue: Morrison, Van. *Astral Weeks*. Warner Brothers 2-1768. *1987*: USA.

Filmography

Cry Freedom, dir. Richard Attenborough. 1987. UK/USA. 157 mins. Biography/Political Drama. Original music by George Fenton, Jonas Gwangwa.

MARION LEONARD and ROBERT STRACHAN with GWEN ANSELL (South Africa) and STEVE JONES (United States)

Kinship

'Kinship' is a term generally used to denote relationships between individuals and groups that are defined through blood, and there are many different ways in which commercial and mass-industrialized forms of popular music reflect, address and influence kinship practises, relations and ideologies. Yet popular music, particularly rock and pop, has often been associated with an anti-kinship or anti-family ideology, an ideology reflected in the lack of discussion on kinship in academic and journalistic writing on popular music. Rock ideology, for example, has tended to romanticize rebellion, nonconformism and intergenerational conflict; and rock has been linked with youthful male peer groups, public spaces such as the 'street' and the 'road,' and the more sensational or spectacular aspects of popular music culture. Kinship and the more private, everyday and domestic spheres of family and home have thus been marginalized.

However, well-known popular songwriters such as Lennon and McCartney, who have written lyrics about sex and revolution, have also written songs about their mothers, wives and children (for example, 'Mother' by John Lennon and 'Lovely Linda' by Paul McCartney). And there are many other ways in which popular music relates closely to kinship and to family life. Blood relatives, for example, frequently share music-making as a hobby or profession. Hence, Mike McCartney, like his brother Paul, joined a pop band and had songs in the charts, while sisters Dannii and Kylie Minogue have both enjoyed successful careers as solo pop performers. Other siblings perform in the same musical group – for example, the Gallagher brothers of the British rock band Oasis, and the Wilson brothers who performed with their cousin in the Beach Boys. Some groups are comprised entirely of siblings, including pop groups like the Osmonds and the Jackson 5, and the Beverley, Andrews and Nolan Sisters. Husbands and wives also perform in public together – the pop duo Sonny and Cher is an example – as do blood relatives of different generations – for instance, Naomi Judd and her daughter Wynonna, who performed as the country group the Judds; Frank Sinatra and his daughter Nancy, who performed as a duo; and Wizz Jones and his son Simeon, who have performed as a folk duo.

There are also many musicians who might not perform with their parents, but who nevertheless have chosen similar musical careers. Julian Lennon, Dweezil Zappa, Zak Dylan and Ziggy Marley have all followed in the musical footsteps of their famous fathers. Similarly, the fathers and uncles of the pop band 3T were members of the Jackson 5. Other well-known 'musical families' include country music dynasties such as the Carter and Stoneman Families, and the illustrious musical family of *balafon* player Mory Kanté from eastern Guinea. Family groupings are also commonplace within English concertina bands (Cohen and McManus 1991), New Orleans jazz bands (Barker and Buerkle 1973) and US minstrel groups (Hamm 1979, 142). In some cultures, particular castes, lineages or other kinship groups are categorized as musical and those born within them become musicians through family inheritance. Youssou N'Dour, for example, is a singing *griot* born into a Senegalese *griot* family through his mother's line. In addition, some musical genres and styles, such as country and gospel, promote a strong family ideology in order to sustain notions of tradition and to perpetuate specific values. The Carter Family acted as a powerful emblem of this ideology in country music.

Family members in musical groups do not necessarily experience harmonious relationships, and friction and feuding between musical kin are commonplace. Notorious examples include the reported rivalry between solo artists Julian and Sean Lennon, and the arguments and physical fights between the Gallagher brothers of Oasis and the Davies brothers of the Kinks.

Relatives often take on an organizational or administrative role to help develop the musical careers of their fellow kin. The Osmonds, the Jackson 5 and the Beach Boys, for example, were all managed by their fathers, while Derek Ryder achieved notoriety in the British music press when he took on the job of roadie for the Happy Mondays, his son Shaun's band. Mothers and other female relatives have played similar roles. The Spice Girls and other all-women pop groups, for example, emotionally and tearfully thanked their mothers during their acceptance speeches at a 1998 British awards ceremony, and both mothers and daughters are regularly photographed together. Wilmer (1987), Finnegan (1989) and Cohen (1991) have highlighted the activities of mothers, wives and girlfriends who have worked behind the scenes to support their relatives' musical activities.

More commonly, of course, relatives offer moral support as fans and audience members, and parents encourage their children to learn music in order to broaden their range of opportunities and skills, enrich their leisure time or acquire particular values. Hence, many parents stretch the family budget to allow for the purchase of instruments and lessons, take their children to those lessons and provide space at home for them to rehearse.

Relatives also influence each other's musical tastes and listening practises. Adolescents, for example, may reject musical styles favored by their parents; hence the familiar emphasis on the so-called 'generation gap' in connection with rock and pop music. But the opposite is also true. Many young people, for example, are introduced to certain musicians and musical genres and styles through their parents (Cohen and McManus 1991), and different generations of the same family often share similar musical tastes, are fans of the same performers and attend fan conventions and concerts together (Cavicchi 1998). Popular music can thus be a focus for both family conflict and family cohesion.

Similarly, music recordings may be played by people in such a way as to define their own space or identity within the family or home, and to distance, alienate or exclude other relatives. Family members may also fight for control of domestic music technologies (Crafts et al. 1993). In the nineteenth century, however, collective music-making in the home was an important aspect of family life, with women in particular encouraged to play the piano as a symbol of femininity and domesticity. Such family entertainment was threatened by the growth of commercialized leisure and the mass media, but in many cultures music has remained a focus for family gatherings and celebrations. It has been suggested that collective family participation in musical activities, whether singing, dancing, playing or listening, helps unite families and heighten their sense of belonging and togetherness. It is often musical activities or dances that initially bring couples together (Cohen and McManus 1991; Cohen 1995), and within many families and kinship networks particular popular songs and styles evoke collective memories and convey a sense of family tradition and continuity (Cohen 1998).

For these reasons, kinship is often used as a metaphor to describe popular music groups and their relationships. For example, despite the fact that members of rock bands are not usually blood relations, they often describe their bands as being 'like a family' in order to convey the strength of the ties that exist between the members and their sense of collective identity. The closeness of such bonds can intensify underlying tensions and rifts, which frequently surface and lead to conflicts that cause bands to split up, much like the family feuding and clan rivalries that commonly occur within groups of related kin. New bands often emerge from such breakups, and musicians frequently move from one band to another. In some ways, this mirrors patterns of intermarriage and relations of exchange and alliance between kinship groups. Many musicians thus situate themselves within complex 'family trees' that they construct in order to trace the history and roots of the bands they have performed with (Frame 1983). Some musical groups whose members are not blood relations have adopted kinship-related names, such as the Lighthouse Family, the Mamas and the Papas, Sister Sledge and the Four Brothers.

All of these examples show that kinship is closely bound up with popular music practises, relations and ideologies. People frequently become involved with popular music through their relatives, and kinship networks are an important recruitment channel for musical groups and organizations. Within some popular music genres and styles, such as country and barbershop, family participation in music-making is particularly emphasized, and many popular music genres and styles reflect aspects of family life, such as courtship rituals and patterns of immigration and intermarriage, the sexual division of labor within the household and the organization of the family economy. Kinship thus has an important and often hidden influence on popular music culture, and the family and home are significant contexts for popular music-making, learning and listening.

Bibliography

Barker, D., and Buerkle, J.V., eds. 1973. *Bourbon Street Black: The New Orleans Black Jazzman*. New York: Oxford University Press.

Cavicchi, Daniel. 1998. *Tramps Like Us: Music and Meaning Among Springsteen Fans*. New York: Oxford University Press.

Cohen, Sara. 1991. *Rock Culture in Liverpool: Popular Music in the Making*. Oxford: Oxford University Press.

Cohen, Sara. 1995. 'Popular Music in 20th Century

Liverpool: A Case Study.' In *Popular Music Perspectives III*, ed. Peter Wicke. Berlin: Zyankrise, 289–96.

Cohen, Sara. 1997. 'Men Making a Scene: Popular Music and the Production of Gender.' In *Sexing the Groove: Popular Music and Gender*, ed. Sheila Whiteley. London: Routledge, 17–36.

Cohen, Sara. 1998. 'Sounding Out the City: Music and the Sensuous Production of Place.' In *The Place of Music*, ed. Andrew Leyshon, David Matless and George Revill. New York and London: Guilford Publications, 155–76. (First published in *Transactions of the Institute of British Geographers* 20(4) (1995): 434–46.)

Cohen, Sara, and McManus, Kevin. 1991. *Harmonious Relations: Popular Music and Family Life on Merseyside*. Liverpool: National Museums and Galleries on Merseyside.

Crafts, Susan D., Cavicchi, Daniel, and Keil, Charles. 1993. *My Music*. Hanover, NH: Wesleyan University Press.

Finnegan, Ruth. 1989. *The Hidden Musicians: Music-Making in an English Town*. Cambridge: Cambridge University Press.

Frame, Pete. 1983 (1980). *Rock Family Trees*. London: Omnibus.

Hamm, Charles. 1979. *Yesterdays: Popular Song in America*. New York: Norton.

Wilmer, Valerie. 1987. *As Serious As Your Life: The Story of the New Jazz*. London: Pluto Press.

Discographical References

Lennon, John. 'Mother.' *John Lennon and the Plastic Ono Band*. Apple PCS 3372. *1970*: UK.

McCartney, Paul. 'Lovely Linda.' *McCartney*. Apple STAO-3363. *1970*: UK.

SARA COHEN

Law

Law is the state-sanctioned body of disciplinary regulations and prohibitions that is intended to ensure the undisturbed functioning and reproduction of almost every aspect of a society's mode of life. As such, law has its own institutions, practises, rituals and discourses within which human or corporate subjects are interpellated as, for example, holders of rights or property, defendants, witnesses, plaintiffs, jurors, prosecutors, advocates and judges.

Harris (1979) describes three interlocking dimensions of law: institutional legal systems center on courts of law and include such institutions as legislatures, police, prisons, legal professions, legal departments of governments, corporations and trade unions; historic legal systems such as Common Law or Islamic Shari'a Law are written collections of maxims (sometimes called case law) used to adjudicate by precedent in legal disputes;

and momentary law is the ensemble of rules, laws or codes produced by legislatures and courts. Each of these dimensions has its own efficacy in the complex process of legal practise.

Discussion of the social function of law has been characterized by either 'consensus' or 'conflict' models. The consensus model posits that law represents the value consensus of society – the values and perspectives fundamental to social order, which are in the public interest to protect. It further argues that the state's position in regard to the legal system is value-neutral and that in pluralistic societies the law mediates between competing interest groups (Chambliss 1976, 4).

The best-known source of the conflict model is Marxism. In the Marxist tradition, the legal system is regarded as an essential component of what Althusser (1971) called 'Repressive State Apparatuses,' although he emphasized (following Gramsci (1971)) that the efficacy of the law depended on the hegemonically achieved consent of the governed, as well as on the threat of force and punishment exercised by the state through police, prisons and so on.

Elsewhere, the theorist of power in societies, Michel Foucault, argued that, in Western societies, 'the exercise of power has always been formulated in terms of law' (1979, 87). This formulation stresses the semiotic or ideological importance of legal discourse as a means of maintaining social control.

In its aesthetic, technological, cultural and economic aspects, popular music is articulated with law. In relation to music recording, Gaines (1992) has presented the interdependence of law and other social, cultural and economic practises by stating that a key issue is 'how "extrinsic" changes in the material production of sound are felt "intrinsically" in the internal formal structures of law and culture' (17).

Popular Music in the Law

Only a few pieces of legislation have been drafted specifically to regulate forms of music. The Rome Convention of 1961 is concerned primarily with the 'protection of phonograms,' while Section 63 of the UK *Criminal Justice and Public Order Act* (1994) prohibited outdoor raves, defined as events 'at which amplified music is played during the night,' where '"music" includes sounds wholly or predominantly characterised by the emission of a succession of repetitive beats.' Generally, though, there is no such thing as a body of 'music law.'

Law schools and university music departments may offer courses under the title 'music law,' and books have certainly been written on the subject, but in fact the law seldom concerns itself directly with music. Rather, the law addresses music only as a form of property, as a commodity to be bought or sold, or as a contributory factor, as when it serves some other purpose such as ostensibly inducing undesirable behavior of some kind (teen pregnancy, skinhead violence, noise pollution, political opposition and so on). When music serves such a purpose, or becomes part of a business transaction, the law's concern with fashioning and enforcing rules of conduct in those areas may lead to the regulation of music, but only as a byproduct of some other regulatory purpose. Lawmakers are generally not interested enough in the public's listening habits to institute legislation solely aimed at regulating music.

Nevertheless, the performers, audiences and institutions of popular music have been subjected to, and affected by, three principal areas of legislation: intellectual property law; laws pertaining to commercial and financial practises; and laws designed to preserve social control and public order.

Intellectual Property Law

Intellectual property legislation, dealing with patents, trademarks and copyright, is the area of law with the greatest impact on contemporary popular music. International treaties and national laws protect songs and compositions, music recordings and even performances as intellectual property, together with novels, paintings, software, pharmaceutical products and other types of artistic and scientific creations. These laws also define the owners of intellectual property and their entitlements or 'rights.' Among the rights awarded by intellectual property legislation to authors of music – as owners of copyright in their compositions – are performing, mechanical, copying, distribution and moral rights.

These positive rights are accompanied by laws limiting the operation of the rights and by definitions of actions that infringe on intellectual property rights and damage the interests of owners of those rights. Limitations to the monopoly copyright in compositions and recordings include a time limit for copyright ownership, after which a song or recording becomes part of the 'public domain.'

Under most national laws, songs enter the public domain 70 years after the death of the last surviving composer, and music recordings and performances 50 years after they were made. However, while copyright law does not require the payment of royalties on public-domain works, it does not determine the relative price at which public-domain material is sold. If a music store offers thousands of pages of public-domain sheet music for sale alongside thousands of other pages of music protected by copyright, should the public-domain music not be free? If the law, specifically copyright law, were responsible for turning music into a commodity, the

answer would be 'yes,' and music could easily be rescued from commodification simply by the repeal of the world's copyright laws. In fact, however, public-domain music, allegedly owned by no one, can be as much a commodity as the latest pop hit, as demonstrated by the fact that it can cost just as much at the music store. The truth is that even public-domain music is always owned by someone – namely, in the first instance, the person who buys a blank piece of paper and imprints public-domain notes on it. If a music lover wants that piece of paper, he/she will have to pay the publisher. As long as music is embodied in a tangible form of any kind, it will have an owner, and if that owner chooses to sell it, it will be a commodity.

To counterbalance the monopoly granted to songwriters, copyright law in most countries recognizes limitations on an artist's exclusive rights, to safeguard the public's right to benefit from the dissemination of copyrighted works and the ideas they contain. Accordingly, when strict enforcement of an artist's monopoly in his/her work could inhibit the very creativity that copyright law is intended to promote, users are free to make some limited use of the work without infringing the author's copyright.

One way in which the law accomplishes this is by allowing songwriters to claim protection only for their particular 'expressions' and not for the general ideas underlying those expressions. Thus, any songwriter is free to create a quiet acoustic guitar number in A minor with a heavy metal closing over a repeated Am-G-F progression, but is not free to copy the other, more specific details of 'Stairway to Heaven' (without the songwriters' permission). Another, more expansive form of users' rights permits the use of specific expression as well, when the social benefit of the copying is thought to outweigh the social benefit of enforcing the writer's exclusivity. Under US law, this doctrine is codified as 'fair use' for purposes such as 'criticism, comment, news reporting, teaching (including multiple copies for classroom use), scholarship, or research.' A more indirect form of 'criticism and comment,' and one that has been extensively analyzed in the music context, is parody. Parody is afforded the protection of fair use because it is thought to have a beneficial effect on society's intellectual growth by offering commentary on the arts, literature, politics and other aspects of life.

The principal infringements of copyright punishable by civil damages, fines or imprisonment are plagiarism and piracy. Plagiarism is alleged to have occurred when a composer has copied a 'substantial' part of an existing copyrighted work. A related issue is the sampling of existing recordings, although sampling disputes are now generally settled by a financial agreement between the record companies owning the rights to the sampled and sampling recordings.

In legal terms, piracy is the unauthorized commercial manufacture, distribution and sale of commercially issued recordings or of performances. The phenomenon of piracy highlights the important distinction between the adoption of legislation and its effectiveness in terms of deterrence and enforcement. In many countries where piracy dominates the music business, adequate anti-piracy laws exist, but the penalties for copyright infringement are weak and enforcement of copyright law is not a priority for police, customs officials or the courts.

The existence and operation of intellectual property law have been a topic of criticism and controversy in recent decades. The objections to this law include criticisms of the patenting policies of agribusiness and pharmaceutical industries and of the domination of the copyright-based industries by transnational corporations, and critiques of the concept of the unique creator as the philosophical basis of copyright. The emergence of the Internet has encouraged equally far-reaching rejections of the intellectual property system by those who believe that the Internet is by nature a commodity-free zone (Barlow 1994).

Laws Pertaining to Commercial and Financial Practises

As the public-domain example discussed above shows, the law does not somehow transform music into a commodity in order to regulate it, but merely regulates the circulation of commodities in general, including those that happen to have musical attributes. These musical attributes include the pricing of soundcarriers and certain uses of copyrighted music, the alleged anti-competitive behavior of large record companies to ensure oligopolistic dominance of the soundcarrier market, and the regulation of musical labor markets through such factors as contract law, immigration law and tax laws.

In various countries, governments have at times introduced legislation to set the price of soundcarriers with the aim of protecting smaller retailers from the price-cutting strategies of large supermarket chains. Such laws have gradually been rescinded, with the prominent exception of those in Japan. However, in the area of authors', musicians' and record companies' rights, government agencies are frequently involved in establishing the level of royalties to be paid by music users. In the United States, the mechanical royalty paid by record companies to music publishers and composers is one of the only commercial market prices set by the federal government. In many countries, copyright laws stipulate that monopoly-owning collection societies must be overseen by government agencies and that government-appointed arbitrators must resolve disputes over performing right payments between societies and music users.

The consolidation of power within the international music industry, where five companies have a combined market share of at least 70 percent, has attracted the attention of competition authorities, notably in the United States, the European Union and Australia. Such authorities have been able to prevent corporate mergers, outlaw unfair marketing practises and monitor pricing policies.

As in other industries, musicians and their employers are subject to a range of labor legislation covering aspects such as health and safety, welfare benefits and terms of employment. Contract law is especially important for the music industry, as the multiplicity of economic relationships involving musicians is enshrined in a number of different contracts with personal managers, music publishers, record companies, booking agents and others. Partly as a result of this, there is a rich history of case law involving actions for breach or termination of contract because of unfair behavior by one party.

Like all employers and employees, those involved in the music industry are required to pay income tax. However, musicians can be especially affected by tax regulations in several ways. Composers and songwriters resident in Ireland can gain exemption from tax under the 1969 *Finance Act*. This law applies to royalties or other earnings from sales of the works of writers, composers and artists whose work is recognized as having 'cultural or artistic merit.' In 1999, 59 classical and popular music composers benefited from the exemption out of a total of over 4,000 creators.

Musicians and others involved in international tours are also affected by the tax regimes of foreign countries and their country of origin. Many governments levy so-called 'withholding' taxes on foreign entertainers. Under this system, a relatively high proportion of a musician's performance fee must be paid to the tax authorities and the artist must then make a claim for a rebate based on evidence of professional expenses incurred on the tour. In the 1990s, it was claimed that the 30 percent withholding tax in Germany had caused foreign musicians to avoid performing there. Some governments permit their citizens to avoid paying domestic tax if they work partly or wholly abroad. A change in the UK rules in 1998 caused the cancellation of British concerts on the Rolling Stones' Bridges to Babylon tour because these performances would have caused group members and some of their tour crew to lose their exemption from paying UK levels of income tax.

Laws regulating the admission of immigrant workers have affected musicians, notably in the United States where the American Federation of Musicians successfully campaigned for the Alien Contract Labor Law to be amended in 1932 to exclude all foreign musicians except for 'virtuosos of the first rank' (Kraft 1996, 29). This rule was relaxed in the 1960s, although the cost of visas and the bureaucratic delays in granting them have continued to affect foreign performers wishing to play in the United States.

Commodities and services associated with popular music are subject to sales or value-added tax legislation. In the European Union, the tax on sales of recorded music varies widely, and the music industry has campaigned for a harmonization of such taxes at a level comparable to that set for books and other cultural commodities.

Laws Designed to Preserve Social Control and Public Order

The conflict model of law emphasizes the function of the legal system to preserve the social and political status quo. In many societies, some forms of popular music and some musicians have been associated with deviant behaviors and beliefs. As such, popular music has been subject to censorship legislation through prosecutions for such offenses as obscenity or the expression of banned political or religious views. Such deviant activities as possession of illegal drugs have also led to the arrest of numerous musicians.

At various times, too, some parts of the music industry have been linked to criminal activity. From the Prohibition era, nightclubs in the United States were often controlled by people involved in organized crime, as was the jukebox business in many US cities. The crucial importance of radio airplay for the commercial success or failure of sound recordings led to the practise of 'payola' or the systematic bribery of radio executives. In the United States and elsewhere, those involved in these illegal activities have been prosecuted under anti-corruption and racketeering laws (Dannen 1990, 14).

Bibliography

Althusser, Louis. 1971. *Lenin and Philosophy, and Other Essays*, trans. Ben Brewster. London: New Left Books.

Barlow, John Perry. 1994. 'The Economy of Ideas: A Framework for Patents and Copyrights in the Digital Age (Everything You Know About Intellectual Property Is Wrong).' *Wired* 2.03 (March): 1–13.
http://www.wired.com/wired/archive/2.03/economy.ideas.html

Chambliss, William J. 1976. 'Functional and Conflict Theories of Crime.' In *Whose Law? What Order?: A Conflict Approach to Criminology*, ed. William J. Chambliss and Milton Mankoff. New York: John Wiley, 1–28.

Dannen, Fredric. 1990. *Hit Men: Power Brokers and Fast Money Inside the Music Business*. New York: Times Books.

Foucault, Michel. 1979. *The History of Sexuality. Vol. 1: The Will to Knowledge*. London: Allen Lane.

Gaines, Jane M. 1992. *Contested Culture: The Image, the Voice, and the Law*. London: BFI Publishing.

Gramsci, Antonio. 1971. *Selections from the Prison Notebooks of Antonio Gramsci*, ed. and trans. Quintin Hoare and Geoffrey Nowell Smith. London: Lawrence & Wishart.

Harris, J.W. 1979. *Law and Legal Science: An Inquiry into the Concepts Legal Rule and Legal System*. Oxford: Clarendon Press.

Kraft, James P. 1996. *Stage to Studio: Musicians and the Sound Revolution, 1890–1950*. Baltimore, MD: Johns Hopkins University Press.

Discographical Reference

Led Zeppelin. 'Stairway to Heaven.' *Led Zeppelin 4*. Atlantic K50008. *1971*: UK.

DAVE LAING, ROBERT CLARIDA and JAY FLEMA

Locality

Popular music is linked with 'locality' in many ways. Locality may be defined as a geographical place or a location where events take place, although the term is usually used to refer to sub-national places (cities, neighborhoods and so on). Locality is significant both as a social and material setting for popular music events or activities, and in terms of popular music meaning and ideology. Individual listeners may interpret popular music texts in idiosyncratic ways, with particular songs and sounds evoking personal memories of and attachments to specific localities, but popular music texts can also convey ideas about locality that are collectively understood.

Locality as a Social and Material Setting for Popular Music Activity

Locality provides a distinctive social and economic context or setting for popular music production and consumption, which influences local musical sounds and styles. Attempts have been made, for example, to account for the Beatles and to explain how they and the melodic, guitar-based pop music they produced early on in their career reflected socioeconomic aspects of Liverpool, the city from which they came. Some point to Liverpool's role as a port and to its shipping connections with the United States, which are generally believed to have contributed to the early popularity of country, doo-wop and beat music in the city. The Beatles and other Liverpool musicians were also exposed to North American popular music influences through the mass media and through the military. Between 1943 and 1993, for example, a US air base – the largest military base in Europe during World War II – was in operation a few miles to the west of Liverpool. US servicemen stationed at the air base regularly visited Liverpool clubs and dance halls, where they mixed with local musicians and audiences; conversely, local musicians performed at the base with their own bands or went there to listen to visiting US musicians performing jazz, country, rhythm and blues, soul and rock 'n' roll (McManus 1994).

The influence of Liverpool's immigrant groups on the city's musical culture has also been highlighted, most notably the Irish influence which is often mentioned in relation to the Beatles. The largest influx of immigrants to the port of Liverpool came from Ireland, particularly after the potato famine of the 1840s, and it has been estimated that 296,231 Irish people landed in Liverpool in 1847 alone (Neal 1988, 7). Other immigrant groups, however, have also influenced Liverpool's musical life. During the late nineteenth century, for example, a wave of Jews from Eastern Europe settled in Liverpool, many of whom were fleeing the Crimean War. They increased the city's Jewish population to around 11,000, and many of them became popular performers or dance- and concert-hall owners and patrons, or established the music businesses that helped to promote and support the Beatles and other local bands during the 1960s.

Popular music not only reflects, but also shapes, the everyday social and economic life of a locality and the rituals and routines of which it is comprised. Within a locality, for example, popular music is often a focus or frame for social gatherings, special occasions and celebrations, and it is widely broadcast as 'background music' in public and private spaces, contributing to a local soundscape. Popular music is also a common topic of daily conversation and social interaction within a locality, with people engaging in regular discussion about the latest hit songs or stars or exchanging recordings and other musical artifacts. Local social groupings, such as those distinguished in terms of class, age or ethnicity, can often be identified through their characteristic musical tastes and activities; hence, popular music influences social relationships and experiences within a locality, and can be implicated in a politics of locality involving local struggles for power, prestige and place (Cohen 1998).

In addition, popular music is produced and consumed through what are commonly referred to as local music 'scenes' (Shank 1994; Straw 1991) or 'worlds' (Finnegan 1989), consisting of networks of groups, organizations and businesses based in a particular locality and involved with the production and consumption of specific musical styles and genres; hence the familiar references to a local 'rock scene' or 'folk scene.' These scenes are not necessarily reliant upon or organized around the locality, but may have a geographically dispersed membership involving connections and exchanges between music-makers and audiences based in different localities (Straw 1991). They may also produce sounds influenced by the importation and mixing of musical genres and styles that accompany local histories and experiences of travel and migration, thus reflecting the cosmopolitan or translocal, geographically mobile and globally interconnected nature of popular music, and the way in which it moves across localities and helps to maintain relations of alliance and affinity between them. Hence, localities and local music scenes are not fixed and bounded but in flux, influenced by cultural change and interaction and by musical 'routes' rather than 'roots.'

In some instances, local music scenes have been referred to as local music 'industries' in order to draw attention to their business infrastructures and their impact, or potential impact, on local economies. Cities such as New Orleans and Austin in the United States, for example, and Manchester, Sheffield and Liverpool in the United Kingdom all experienced severe economic decline during the 1980s and lost their traditional industries. During the 1980s and 1990s, the city governments concerned turned to the arts and cultural industries as a component of their local regeneration strategies and developed initiatives or policies aimed at protecting, promoting and developing local popular music activities, businesses and industries. Popular music was increasingly valued in terms of its potential both to promote new and vibrant images of the locality that would help to attract visitors, investment and publicity, and to generate business, jobs and income and thus improve the local economy (see Cohen 1991a; Frith 1993; Street 1993; Shank 1994). Such developments have informed, and have been informed by, a sense of local identity, and by locality as meaning, discourse and ideology.

Locality and the Meaning and Ideology of Popular Music

Straw (1991) has pointed to what he calls the 'musical localism' of alternative North American rock scenes of the late 1980s, where an organic relationship between musical sounds and styles and the places in which they were produced and consumed was emphasized. Local music scenes were linked with notions of community, implying geographical rootedness and historical stability, difference and authenticity. A similar 'rhetoric of the local' has characterized alternative rock culture in the United Kingdom (Street 1995) and is evident in some music journals which associate the musicians and sounds of alternative rock scenes with the localities they come from, and distinguish between the musicians and music of localities in ways that exaggerate local rivalries and differences.

Locality also features in popular music texts. The titles of many popular songs, for instance, refer to particular localities, as do the names of many musical groups and styles. In addition, locality may be visually represented in music videos, on record sleeves and so on, and referred to or implied in popular music lyrics. Examples of the latter include the territorial references to urban US neighborhoods in rap, and the lyrics of songs about leaving and returning written by various migrant populations (for example, the Irish), for whom concepts of 'home' and 'homeland' can evoke strong emotions, reminding them of the places they have left behind, their collective origins and their experiences of homelessness and emigration. Popular music has played an important role for Irish immigrants in the United Kingdom and the United States, for example, helping them to maintain an Irish tradition and a sense of Irish identity and connection with Ireland. Hence, in contexts of change and mobility, uncertainty and unfamiliarity, the connection between popular music and locality may be intensified. Popular music can preserve and transmit local collective memory and help people to locate themselves within and in relation to different imagined places at the same time.

In addition to lyrics, musical instruments, sounds and structures can also signify locality. Irish fiddle playing, for example, like the Irish 'session,' has come to signify Irishness and is often featured on the soundtrack of films depicting Ireland or tourist advertisements for Ireland. However, the styles of fiddle playing and the kinds of session that came to signify Irishness originated in part outside Ireland, created by Irish immigrants in the United States and the United Kingdom. The Beatles and their music have also been used by the media and the tourist industry to represent or signify a locality, in this case the city of Liverpool, but such musical representations are often contested. Some have argued, for example, that representing Liverpool through the Beatles has drawn attention away from the rich diversity of the city's musical culture and presented the city in a fixed and narrow manner that misrepresents it and does it an injustice (Cohen 1997, 2001). These examples emphasize the fact that popular music does not simply reflect a geographical locality but constructs it, associating it with particular ideas, images and meanings and influencing how people think about and imagine it and consequently act toward it.

Locality and local identity have continued to be important to people despite, but also because of, globalization, an emphasis on global culture and the rise of a discourse of the global (Negus 1992; Wallis and Malm 1984). Various writers have suggested that an increased emphasis on popular music and local identity, and on defining the distinctiveness of local music, may reflect a fear of losing cultural identity in the face of globalization. Popular music sounds and styles defined as local and 'authentic' are distinguished from those considered to be commercial and placeless or nonlocal. However, popular music's connections with locality may also be emphasized by the global music industry and the media in an effort to sustain and extend a market for musical commodities. Music offers a specific and powerful means through which locality can be constructed. Stokes (1994b), writing about Irish and Turkish migrants, points out that, for many migrant communities, place or locality is something constructed through music with an intensity not found elsewhere in their social lives (114). The physical and emotional effects of music intensify the experiences it evokes and can help to increase its effectiveness in producing a sense of local identity and belonging. Stokes (1994a) goes so far as to suggest that 'the musical event, from collective dances to the act of putting a cassette or CD into a machine, evokes and organises collective memories and presents experiences of place with an intensity, power and simplicity unmatched by any other social activity' (3).

Bibliography

Cohen, Sara. 1991a. 'Popular Music and Urban Regeneration: The Music Industries of Merseyside.' *Cultural Studies* 5(3): 332–46.

Cohen, Sara. 1991b. *Rock Culture in Liverpool: Popular Music in the Making*. Oxford: Oxford University Press.

Cohen, Sara. 1997. 'Popular Music, Tourism, and Urban Regeneration.' In *Tourists and Tourism: Identifying with People and Places*, ed. Simone Abram, Jacqueline Waldren and Donald V.L. Macleod. Oxford and New York: Berg, 71–90.

Cohen, Sara. 1998. 'Sounding Out the City: Music and the Sensuous Production of Place.' In *The Place of Music*, ed. Andrew Leyshon, David Matless and George Revill. New York and London: Guilford Publications, 155–76. (First published in *Transactions of the Institute of British Geographers* 20(4) (1995): 434–46.)

Cohen, Sara. 2001. 'Popular Culture in Liverpool.' In *Liverpool at the Millennium: Living in the City*, ed. R. Meegan and M. Maddon. Liverpool: Liverpool University Press.

Finnegan, Ruth. 1989. *The Hidden Musicians: Music-Making in an English Town*. Cambridge: Cambridge University Press.

Frith, Simon. 1993. 'Popular Music and the Local State.' In *Rock and Popular Music: Politics, Policies, Institutions*, ed. Tony Bennett et al. London: Routledge, 14–24.

McManus, Kevin. 1994. *Ceilies, Jigs and Ballads: Irish Music in Liverpool*. Liverpool: Institute of Popular Music.

Neal, Frank. 1988. *Sectarian Violence: The Liverpool Experience 1819–1914*. Manchester: Manchester University Press.

Negus, Keith. 1992. *Producing Pop: Culture and Conflict in the Popular Music Industry*. London: Edward Arnold.

Shank, Barry. 1994. *Dissonant Identities: The Rock 'n' Roll Scene in Austin, Texas*. Hanover, NH: Wesleyan University Press/University Press of New England.

Stokes, Martin. 1994a. 'Introduction.' In *Ethnicity, Identity, and Music: The Musical Construction of Place*, ed. Martin Stokes. Oxford: Berg, 1–27.

Stokes, Martin. 1994b. 'Place, Exchange and Meaning: Black Sea Musicians in the West of Ireland.' In *Ethnicity, Identity, and Music: The Musical Construction of Place*, ed. Martin Stokes. Oxford: Berg, 97–116.

Straw, Will. 1991. 'Systems of Articulation, Logics of Change: Communities and Scenes in Popular Music.' *Cultural Studies* 5(3): 368–88.

Street, John. 1993. 'Local Differences?: Popular Music and the Local State.' *Popular Music* 12(1): 43–56.

Street, John. 1995. '(Dis)located?: Rhetoric, Politics, Meaning and the Locality.' In *Popular Music: Style and Identity*, ed. Will Straw et al. Montréal: The Centre for Research on Canadian Cultural Industries and Institutions, 255–63.

Wallis, Roger, and Malm, Krister. 1984. *Big Sounds from Small Peoples: The Music Industry in Small Countries*. London: Constable.

SARA COHEN

Love and Courtship

Music's association with love and courtship is long-standing in popular culture. Popular songs address and represent love from a variety of angles and provide a rich source of data for studies of the social and cultural construction of love, courtship and close relationships.

Historically, love and courtship have been subject to myriad variations (Shepherd 1982), interacting with demographic trends and changes in the structure of work and family life. With mass migration and de-traditionalization during the nineteenth century, intimate relationships were increasingly individualized as the former ties of extended kinship networks, geographical rooting to place and ascribed social statuses and identities were undermined. Increasingly, the concept of 'love' – individuated, romantic love – came to be seen as the primary means of self-actualization. It is in this context that the popular song came to serve as a medium or reference point for the constitution of individual experiences of love. The configurations of love's topoi in popular song have thus served a didactic function in modern society. For this, song lyrics were critical, projecting various images of love and situations of intimacy, and emphasizing the value of 'true' and idyllic love (Goodfellow 1995, 1999; Cooper 1986, 1991).

Content analyses of song lyrics have helped to document the role of songs in representing modes of love in emerging modern societies. Tawa's survey of mid-nineteenth-century North American song lyrics, first published in 1976, identifies four types of love song: songs devoted to a family member (for example, a mother); songs that expressed 'warm regard for friends'; songs that described 'fond attachment' to some kind of object (for example, a family Bible); and songs that extolled the virtues of an amour or a love relationship. Horton (1990) locates individual lyrics from 1955 at various points in a 'drama' of love and courtship, extending from initial attraction to lost love. Songs can be seen to outline the parameters of being a romantic agent and the divisions of these patterns along gendered lines, with the 'reluctant' female ('Handle me with gentleness and say you'll leave me never') and the aggressively wooing male (for example, 'You've been teasin' long enough/Now I'm gonna call your bluff') (see Horton 1990, 16–17).

Broadly surveyed, the repertoires of feeling depicted by song lyrics since World War II range from the lyrical ('The First Time Ever I Saw Your Face') to the upbeat ('I've Got My Love to Keep Me Warm') or the double-entendre ('Come Fly with Me'); from Elvis Presley's 'Love Me Tender' to the Troggs' 'Love Is All Around,' to more overtly sexual content as found in blues, rap and rock 'n' roll, and an emphasis on cheating and loss as found in country music (Fox 1992). Simultaneously, popular song served as an arena for moral contest, perhaps best illustrated by cases of 'scandalous' or notorious songs, either through lyrics or through musical features such as the overtly 'sexualized' rhythms of rock 'n' roll. This repertoire is a vital part of couple culture and adult socialization. It is attested by the widespread notion of 'our song' (Coward 1983) and is a constituent ingredient of film, where the emotional content of courtship and love is (almost always) musically specified (compare, for example, the early music style of the 1968 soundtrack of Franco Zeffirelli's *Romeo and Juliet* ('A time for us, some day there'll be/When chains are torn by courage born of a love that's free') with the 1996 pop music soundtrack of Baz Luhrmann's *Romeo + Juliet* (for example, Des'ree's 'Kissing You,' as the lovers gaze at each other through a tank of tropical fish)).

Particularly in film, it is possible to see music being mapped directly onto particular images and scenarios of romance and vice versa, where the music serves to clarify the action and is active in constituting plot (for example, *Tous les Matins du Monde* (1991)).

Music's role in the constitution of everyday courtship experiences is evident throughout history in the serenade, in the use of the hi-fi in bachelor pads (as depicted in the film *Pillow Talk* (1959)), and in the playing of music on car radios and in dance halls, discos and nightclubs. Toward the end of the twentieth century, record companies began to produce anthologies expressly devoted to 'setting the mood' for love. Subsequently, music's impact on intimate politics in social situations has become subject to investigation.

In recent years, academic discourse has provided concepts and methods with which to analyze the role of popular song as a constitutive medium of emotional states and close relationships. The idea that popular music provides a matrix of 'subject positions' – ways of feeling and being in relation to love – was given considerable impetus and a feminist orientation in the late 1970s, in essays such as that of Frith and McRobbie on rock and sexuality, originally published in 1978. There, the focus turns from popular music lyrics to the more complex matter of musical form and gesture. Contrasting the male genre of 'cock rock' with the emphasis in teenage magazines on pop stars and the music of romance, Frith and McRobbie argue that gender difference and gendered approaches to love, romance and sexuality derive from popular music representations and the forms of socialization associated with music and musical practise. 'Feminine' renditions of love and courtship emphasize emotions, caring, loving and sacrificing, while the rhythmic insistence and vocal styles of heavy metal simulate phallocentric thrusting and a drive toward climax. Elaborating in this analytic vein, Shepherd (1987) considers vocal timbre. His work contrasts timbres associated with cock rock's reliance on the use of constricted vocal cords with those of the 'woman-as-nurturer' sound, with its relaxed use of the voice and 'warmer,' more 'nurturing' tone. Similar points can be made with regard to instrumentation: the saxophone's erotic timbre contrasted with the timbres of the flute, harp or acoustic guitar, characteristic of the *Moods of Love* compilations. The theses advanced by these authors have, however, been challenged by other writers on rock music and sexuality, such as Taylor and Laing (1979) and Tagg (1998).

It has frequently been observed that the gender differences represented by popular music in relation to love and courtship are bound up with generic practises employed in classical music and opera, dating back at least to the era of the Enlightenment (McClary 1991; Wheelock 1993; DeNora 1997). Late twentieth-century work focusing on women's subversion of male aesthetic dominance in popular music highlights stereotypical and male hegemonic discourses of love and courtship as being under challenge. In an analysis of women's rap music, Rose (1994) shows how female rap provides a forum in which to pose alternative depictions of love and courtship in African-American culture. For example, Salt 'N' Pepa's 'Tramp' castigates male promiscuity, a topic otherwise widely celebrated in rap. The lyrics warn listeners that the track is not a 'simple rhyme' but, as Rose observes, a parable about courtship rituals. McClary's treatment of Madonna (1991) also deals with the feminine appropriation of popular music's traditional gendered treatment of love and romance. In an examination of Madonna's subversive musical strategies, such as the use of irony, parody and impersonation, McClary shows how traditional conceptions of the feminine role in scenarios of love, courtship and erotic activity are subject to resistance and change. McClary suggests that, in 'Open Your Heart,' the avoidance of rhythmic pulse and evasion at cadence points generate non-teleological structures of erotic energy.

Studies of the musical representation of love and courtship need also to be viewed in the context of music-producing institutions (Martin 1995). Negus (1992), for example, shows how working practises within the popular music industry are linked to an artistic ideology associated with college-educated white males who came of age in the 'rock generation' of the 1960s and 1970s. The result of this occupational stratification is that women and unfamiliar styles and artists are marginalized. In light of these occupational/structural issues, Martin (1995) observes, the meanings of musical genres – such as musical representations of love and courtship – are linked closely to claims and counterclaims made by interested parties. Studies of women working as popular music artists (Steward and Garratt 1984; Greig 1989) have helped to highlight the impact that employment patterns within popular music have on representations of women's social and psychological place in the love/courtship matrix.

The idea of distinct spheres in which feminine and masculine articulations of love, courtship and sexuality in music exist has been subject to critique by Bradby (1990), whose analysis of 'girl group' music emphasizes the cross-fertilization between gendered genres. Bradby's semiotic approach documents how codes of romance typical in 'girl group' music have permeated and 'feminized' male rock discourses. Her work demonstrates that musical representations of love and courtship can be subject to constant negotiation and renegotiation and can have the potential to foster culturally innovative experiences and emotional forms.

How popular music 'gets into' the conduct and experience of love and courtship has also been a key issue for popular music studies. Music is, of course, a vehicle for bringing couples together (Cohen and McManus 1991; Cohen 1995). Thornton's study of UK club culture (1995) describes music's role in relation to social status, showing how young clubbers seek to accumulate 'subcultural capital' within the club music scene as a courtship strategy and as a means of impressing others.

Harking back to sociological work of the 1960s (such as Denzin 1969–70), Martin (1995) observes that all cultural products provide locations around which social relationships and images of self are created and maintained. The question of how popular music can be understood to compose or trigger particular forms of romantic and intimate action and experience illuminates Frith's more general preoccupation with how popular music provides terms in and through which to build emotional experience (Frith 1988).

One of the earliest discussions of this issue can be found in Dyer's autobiographical essay 'In Defence of Disco,' first published in 1979, which describes some of the ways in which musical materials enable different forms of embodied erotic being: cock rock enables 'thrusting' forms of erotic conduct, while pop, sentimental music and disco enable 'whole body eroticism.' Dyer's essay has continued to be valuable because it offers an account of how, for a particular individual, music not only represents desire and a repertoire of feeling, but actually enters into the enactment and experience of these as they transpire in real time.

Studies of gender and musical taste have also drawn attention to music's link to love and courtship. Shepherd and Giles-Davis (1991) report on the consumption and use of music by a small number of middle-class English-speaking teenage girls in Montréal, showing how music provides a kind of template for sexual and emotional development. Similar work has been undertaken in the psychology of music, with emphasis placed on music's link to modes of feeling and social occasion (Juslin and Sloboda 2001), and within ethnomusicology (Crafts, Cavicchi and Keil 1993). Within sociology, focus has turned to how music is employed during intimate occasions and how it may draw bodies into temporal trajectories (rhythms, pulses, styles of movement, and grammars of feeling and of the body). Here, music is viewed as a nonverbal accomplice in particular intimate forms of action (DeNora 2000), such that the question of 'who puts what on the record player' as a prelude or backdrop to intimacy is overtly conceived as an issue of love's real-time construction and its politics.

Anecdotal information from music fans has helped to illustrate this point. *CUE Magazine* devoted a special section to the 'love' question in its 1994 Valentine's Day issue, examining the burgeoning market devoted to 'music for romance' and printing reports from readers on the music that 'got them in the mood.' The Vermorels' study of popular music fans (1985) shows how, at times, music permeates the very fabric of love and courtship, such that the experience is mediated or made virtual through the imagery of songs and stars.

Bibliography

Bradby, Barbara. 1990. 'Do-Talk and Don't-Talk: The Division of the Subject in Girl-Group Music.' In *On Record: Rock, Pop, and the Written Word*, ed. Simon Frith and Andrew Goodwin. London: Routledge, 341–68.

Carey, James T. 1972. 'Changing Courtship Patterns in the Popular Song.' In *The Sounds of Social Change: Studies in Popular Culture*, ed. R. Serge Denisoff and Richard A. Peterson. Chicago: Rand McNally & Co., 198–212.

Cohen, Sara. 1995. 'Popular Music in 20th Century Liverpool: A Case Study.' In *Popular Music Perspectives III*, ed. Peter Wicke. Berlin: Zyankrise, 289–96.

Cohen, Sara, and McManus, Kevin. 1991. *Harmonious Relations: Popular Music and Family Life on Merseyside*. Liverpool: National Museums and Galleries on Merseyside.

Cooper, B. Lee. 1986. *A Resource Guide to Themes in Contemporary American Song Lyrics, 1950–1985*. New York: Greenwood Press.

Cooper, B. Lee. 1991. *Popular Music Perspectives: Ideas, Themes, and Patterns in Contemporary Lyrics*. Bowling Green, OH: Bowling Green State University Popular Press.

Coward, Rosalind. 1983. 'Our Song.' In *Female Desire: Women's Sexuality Today*. London: Paladin, 143–50.

Crafts, Susan D., Cavicchi, Daniel, and Keil, Charles. 1993. *My Music*. Hanover and London: Wesleyan University Press.

DeNora, Tia. 1997. 'The Biology Lessons of Opera Buffa: Gender, Nature, and Bourgeois Society on Mozart's Buffa Stage.' In *Opera Buffa in Mozart's Vienna*, ed. Mary Hunter and James Webster. Cambridge: Cambridge University Press, 146–64.

DeNora, Tia. 2000. *Music in Everyday Life*. Cambridge: Cambridge University Press.

Denzin, Norman K. 1969–70. 'Problems in Analyzing Elements of Mass Culture: Notes on the Popular Song and Other Artistic Productions.' *American Journal of Sociology* 75(6): 1035–38.

Dyer, Richard. 1990 (1979). 'In Defence of Disco.' In *On Record: Rock, Pop, and the Written Word*, ed. Simon Frith and Andrew Goodwin. London: Routledge, 410–18.

'The Fast Food of Love.' 1994. *CUE Magazine* (February): 68–71.

Fox, Aaron. 1992. 'The Jukebox of History: Narratives of Loss and Desire in the Discourse of Country Music.' *Popular Music* 11(1): 53–72.

Frith, Simon. 1988. 'Why Do Songs Have Words?' In *Music for Pleasure: Essays in the Sociology of Pop*. Cambridge: Polity Press, 105–28. (First published in A.L. White, ed. 1987. *Lost in Music: Culture, Style and the Musical Event*. London: Methuen, 77–106.)

Frith, Simon, and McRobbie, Angela. 1990 (1978). 'Rock and Sexuality.' In *On Record: Rock, Pop, and the Written Word*, ed. Simon Frith and Andrew Goodwin. London: Routledge, 371–89.

Goodfellow, William D. 1995. *SongCite: An Index to Popular Songs*. New York: Garland.

Goodfellow, William D. 1999. *SongCite: An Index to Popular Songs. Supplement I*. New York: Garland.

Greig, Charlotte. 1989. *Will You Still Love Me Tomorrow?: Girl Groups from the 50s On*. London: Virago.

Horton, Donald. 1990 (1956–57). 'The Dialogue of Courtship in Popular Song.' In *On Record: Rock, Pop, and the Written Word*, ed. Simon Frith and Andrew Goodwin. London: Routledge, 14–26.

Juslin, Patrik N., and Sloboda, John A., eds. 2001. *Music and Emotion: Theory and Research*. Oxford: Oxford University Press.

Martin, Peter. 1995. *Sounds and Society: Themes in the Sociology of Music*. Manchester: Manchester University Press.

McClary, Susan. 1991. 'Living to Tell: Madonna's Resurrection of the Fleshly.' In *Feminine Endings: Music, Gender and Sexuality*. Minneapolis, MN: University of Minnesota Press, 148–68.

Moore, John. 1988. '"The Hieroglyphics of Love": The Torch Singers and Interpretation.' *Popular Music* 8(1): 31–58.

Negus, Keith. 1992. *Producing Pop: Culture and Conflict in the Popular Music Industry*. London and New York: Edward Arnold.

Oliver, Paul. 1990. *Blues Fell This Morning: Meaning in the Blues*. 2nd ed. Cambridge: Cambridge University Press. (First published London: Cassell, 1960.)

Pacini Hernandez, Deborah. 1990. 'Cantando la cama vacia: Love, Sexuality and Gender Relationships in Dominican "Bachata."' *Popular Music* 9(3): 351–67.

Peterson, Richard A. 1997. *Creating Country Music: Fabricating Authenticity*. Chicago: University of Chicago Press.

Rose, Tricia. 1994. *Black Noise: Rap Music and Black Culture in Contemporary America*. Hanover and London: Wesleyan University Press.

Russell, Dave. 1987. *Popular Music in England, 1840–1914: A Social History*. Manchester: Manchester University Press.

Shepherd, John. 1982. *Tin Pan Alley*. London: Routledge.

Shepherd, John. 1987. 'Music and Male Hegemony.' In *Music and Society: The Politics of Composition, Performance and Reception*, ed. Richard Leppert and Susan McClary. Cambridge: Cambridge University Press, 151–72.

Shepherd, John, with Giles-Davis, Jennifer. 1991. 'Music, Text and Subjectivity.' In John Shepherd, *Music as Social Text*. Cambridge: Polity Press, 174–85.

Spaeth, Sigmund. 1934. *The Facts of Life in Popular Song*. New York: Whittlesey House.

Steward, Sue, and Garratt, Sheryl. 1984. *Signed, Sealed and Delivered: True Life Stories of Women in Pop*. London: Pluto Press.

Tagg, Philip. 1998. 'Essay Review.' *Popular Music* 17(3): 331–48.

Tawa, Nicholas E. 1989. 'The Ways of Love in the Mid-Nineteenth Century American Song.' In *American Popular Music: Readings from the Popular Press. Vol. 1: The Nineteenth Century and Tin Pan Alley*, ed. Timothy E. Scheurer. Bowling Green, OH: Bowling Green State University Popular Press, 47–62. (First published in *Journal of Popular Culture* 10(2)(1976): 337–51.)

Taylor, Jenny, and Laing, Dave. 1979. 'Disco-Pleasure-Discourse: On "Rock and Sexuality."' *Screen Education* 31: 43–48.

Thornton, Sarah. 1995. *Club Cultures: Music, Media and Subcultural Capital*. Cambridge: Polity Press.

Turino, Thomas. 1983. 'The Charango and the Sirena: Music, Magic, and the Power of Love.' *Latin American Music Review* 4(1): 81–119.

Vermorel, Fred, and Vermorel, Judy. 1985. *Starlust: The Secret Fantasies of Fans*. London: Comedia.

Wheelock, Gretchen. 1993. '*Schwarze Gredel* and the Engendered Minor Mode in Mozart's Operas.' In *Musicology and Difference: Gender and Sexuality in Music Scholarship*, ed. Ruth A. Solie. Berkeley and London: University of California Press, 201–24.

Discographical References

Des'ree. 'Kissing You.' *Romeo + Juliet* (Original soundtrack). Capitol 37715. *1996*: USA.

Fitzgerald, Ella, and Armstrong, Louis. 'I've Got My Love to Keep Me Warm.' *Jazz Masters 24: Ella Fitzgerald and Louis Armstrong*. PolyGram 521851. *1994*: UK.

Flack, Roberta. 'The First Time Ever I Saw Your Face.' *Softly with These Songs: The Best of Roberta Flack*. Atlantic 82498-2. *1993*: USA.

Madonna. 'Open Your Heart.' *True Blue*. Sire 2-25442. *1986*: USA.

Moods of Love. Columbia 492962 2. *1998*: USA.

Presley, Elvis. 'Love Me Tender.' RCA 47-6643. *1956*: USA.

Romeo and Juliet (Original soundtrack). Capitol 400. *1968*: USA.

Romeo + Juliet (Original soundtrack). Capitol 37715. *1996*: USA.

Salt 'N' Pepa. 'Tramp.' *A Blitz of Salt 'N' Pepa Hits*. Poly-Gram 8282692. *1991*: UK.

Sinatra, Frank. 'Come Fly with Me.' *Frank Sinatra: The Collection*, Vol. 1. Hallmark 310102. *1995*: USA.

Tous les Matins du Monde (Original soundtrack). Valois 4640. *1994*: France.

Troggs, The. 'Love Is All Around.' *The First Summer of Love*. PolyGram 533862-2. *1997*: UK.

Filmography

Pillow Talk, dir. Michael Gordon. 1959. USA. 102 mins. Romantic Comedy. Original music by Frank De Vol.

Romeo and Juliet, dir. Franco Zeffirelli. 1968. Italy/UK. 140 mins. Tragedy. Original music by Nino Rota, Eugen Walter.

Romeo + Juliet, dir. Baz Luhrmann. 1996. USA. 120 mins. Tragedy. Original music by Craig Armstrong, Marius de Vries, Nellee Hooper.

Tous les Matins du Monde, dir. Alain Corneau. 1991. France. 114 mins. Musical Drama. Original music by Jordi Savall.

TIA DENORA

Migration and Diffusion

Human movement around the planet has influenced the character and history of popular music in many ways, involving not only transference (for example, of musical instruments, styles and genres) from one place to another, but also dispersal across a wide range of places. Factors characterizing movements of people as voluntary or forced, temporary or permanent have also been influential, as have alliances that have been forged out of shared experiences, sometimes across centuries. Equally important have been the consequences of movement, affecting a range of phenomena from the state of mind of those involved and their use of music to respond to it, to the complex musical encounters that have occurred in the new social and cultural environments which the movement of people has helped to create. Beginning in the early twentieth century, popular music has also been deeply affected by the ability of technology and industry to disseminate it around the planet independently of human movement (though not of human agency).

Migration

Much of the history of human movement, along with many of its features, is contained in the term 'migra-tion.' Migration consists of the mass movements of people, whether by land, sea or air, or these combined. Migration may be distinguished from seasonal human movement, which is regarded as nomadism. By contrast with nomadism, migration is usually seen as being uni- or omni-directional and without intended permanent return.

Migrations may be characterized by the numbers of people who move, the reasons for their departure or the nature of their target destination. Reasons for departure may or may not involve the exercise of free will. Enslavement, for example, is involuntary and enforced, as is transportation, which has been used as a punishment for misdemeanors. Voluntary migration is the outcome of decision, often as a result of weighing the disadvantages – social, economic, religious – of remaining against the perceived benefits of relocating. However, the degree to which this has always been the case is conjectural, for the dispersal of people from Africa and throughout the globe may have been prompted by many factors – climatic and topographic conditions, the exhaustion of natural resources or foods for hunters and foragers, claiming and protecting territory, and other social and environmental issues, among others.

Music and Migration

In its simplest form, the transfer of music via migratory movement has typically involved processes by which sets of musical practises and/or actual instruments have accompanied migrating peoples from one location to another. In all cases, the role of memory has been a highly significant factor, and in some instances, notably that of enslaved African peoples, it was the key to the transfer.

Many problems in establishing and understanding patterns of early migration, such as the settling of the Polynesian islands and the populating of South America, have been the subject of dispute, while remaining unresolved. Yet, in some instances, existing traditions in music can be demonstrated as having been directly influenced by historic migrations. A notable example is the *cante jondo*, or 'deep song,' of flamenco, which is associated with Andalusia. Although the balance of influence is open to debate, Arabic, Hebrew, Romany and Castillean-Spanish elements are present, as the form is an amalgam of vocal and instrumental styles and techniques from these diverse immigrant traditions from the Middle East, by way of North Africa and Central and Southern Europe.

As the above example illustrates, the link between music and migration is often complex and is frequently tied to equally important consequential processes of convergence arising from contiguity. Comparable developments in, or influences on, regional musics can also be traced through the settling of Dutch, Spanish, Portuguese, French and British migrants in colonies in the East Indies, Brazil and South America, the Caribbean, North and West Africa, India, South Africa, Australia and New Zealand, and others. In South and Central America and in the Caribbean, the music of the immigrants was frequently synthesized with rhythms that slaves brought from Africa, which ultimately led to such genres as the habanera, beguine, tango, *son* and rumba. In the Andean states, the meeting of indigenous music with that of the immigrants was less dramatic, but significant nonetheless. In the Dutch and British colonies, localized traditions that were distinguished more by content than by form, such as the 'bush ballads' of Australian settlers, developed among immigrants.

The Australian case provides a profile of the ways in which migration can generate locally distinctive musics which, nonetheless, rely for the meanings and functions that they acquire in their new localities on the recognizable residue of the homeland tradition from which they came. The convicts brought with them songs specifically about enforced transportation. Some were remorseful cautionary tales addressed largely to an English public, but another stream fed an opposing tradition in the Australian mythos. These were songs of defiance, including some from the Irish nationalist revolution of 1798, as in the rebel anthem 'Croppy Boy' which rallied the convict rebels at Castle Hill in New South Wales in 1804. In time, the spirit of these songs was grafted onto local events, their themes and the ballad form becoming the template for colonial 'treason songs,' celebrating such local acts of convict mutiny as the seizing of the brig *Cyprus* in 1828. Although suppressed, the tradition reappeared as bushranger ballads, with their local geography, flora, fauna, characters and slang, and the motif of defiant independence: the transposed political rebel enshrined in the Irish broadside ballad which also provided the musical and metrical model for the Australian genre. Thus, immigrant Irish sentiments modulated into Australian anti-authoritarian stereotypes. Just as the references were transmuted, so the song forms themselves transmigrated from Irish folk to Australian 'bush ballad.'

The Example of North America

Post-agrarian European history is interwoven with industrialization and expansionary capitalism. These have both reflected and resulted in massive increases in demographic mobility in and beyond Europe, including growing urbanization and the establishment of frontier colonies. A focal point of these dynamics is North America, whose complex history of immigration and internal migration illustrates very many of the ways in which

music and migration have interconnected, and where music involved in and affected by migration would have the most profound influence on twentieth-century popular music.

The 'Great Migration' that brought the Puritans to the New World in the first half of the seventeenth century was part of a broad movement of British, Dutch, Swedish, French and other European migrants to the American colonies, encouraged by utopian visions of religious and political emancipation, and material prospects offered by natural resources and, later, industrial development and its infrastructures. During the first half of the eighteenth century, a quarter of a million Scottish-Irish migrants arrived in the colonies from the counties of Ulster. Many settled in the southern part of the Appalachian Mountains, where their musical traditions were adapted to the new environment and laid down at least part of the roots of what would later emerge, via other encounters still to come, as country music. Scottish immigrants also settled in Cape Breton, where their music has survived, and as far south as the Carolinas. Germans migrated in large numbers, as Pennsylvania's policy of religious tolerance encouraged the settling of Moravians, Amish and other religious groups and denominations, many of which, unlike the celibate Shakers, flourished. British controls on emigration were lifted in the 1820s, resulting in a new wave of Irish migrants, which swelled to a flood during the potato-famine years of the 1840s.

Various stages in this wave of immigration corresponded also to shifts in ethnic profiles. The 1840s and 1850s saw considerable growth in the American Jewish population, for example. Following the Civil War, the source of immigrants shifted from the north and west of Europe to the south and east, with increasing numbers of Italian, Portuguese, Bohemian and Jewish skilled and unskilled laborers. During this period, the West was opened up, and large numbers of would-be farmers, ranchers and homesteaders crossed the plains. Internal migration of established groups also contributed to the ethnic mix; for example, Acadians expelled from Nova Scotia by the British in 1755 settled in Louisiana to become the ancestors of the bayou-country Cajuns, in whose culture music was to be especially important. French immigrants generally settled in Canada, where a large proportion of the population was already French-speaking; by the 1950s, this proportion had risen to a third, the majority of which lived in Québec.

By the beginning of the twentieth century, nearly half the population of the 11 Plains and western states were first-generation immigrants, although the proportion of 'second-stage' immigrants from the Midwest was growing fast. Clustered European ethnic groups produced settlements of, for example, Ukrainians in North Dakota, Swedes in Minnesota and Kansas, Finns in Delaware, and Norwegians in Wisconsin and the state of Washington. Many brought with them their European customs – architecture, food, costume, dialects, dances, musical instruments and musical forms – proclaiming their dual allegiance. Central to this duality were the unfolding cultural relationships spawned in the new encounters that migration had enabled.

In 1900, two-thirds of all Irish and Italian immigrants in the United States lived in cities, as did three out of four Jews, most of whom were of German or Russian origin. For unskilled immigrant workers opportunities lay in seasonal agricultural labor. In the southwest, descendants of the Hispanics and Mexican Americans who first settled the region predominated, their numbers increased by legally admitted braceros (migratory laborers) and 'wetbacks' (illegal immigrants). Between 1910 and 1930, one in 10 of the male population of Mexico migrated to the United States and, in spite of large-scale deportation of wetback labor, the numbers continued to grow. By the 1950s, there were a million Mexicans in Texas alone, and 'Tex-Mex' culture, strong in music, was established. By the 1990s, Latinos outnumbered the Anglophone population in California. However, there remained pockets of other groups – for example, Germans in Texas and Chinese in Mississippi – that retained their distinct identity.

The intricate and multilayered fabric of North America bears the imprint of numerous groups whose loyalties and cultural dualities are self-proclaimed in such terms as Swedish Americans, Hispanic Americans, Native Americans or African Americans. This last group, the black community, a tenth of the nation's population, contributed significantly to twentieth-century internal migrations. The patterns of white and black migration between contiguous regions in the period 1870–1950 were further complicated by the decline of the cotton industry, the Great Depression, the 'dust-bowl' years of the late 1930s and wartime industrial labor demands. For African Americans from the South, the principal destinations were the northern cities of Chicago, Detroit and New York; 2 million blacks migrated to the north between 1910 and 1940, and another million during World War II, although few migrated west (even to California) until the defense factories attracted them. The impact of black migration on the popular music of the urban north was immeasurable.

Migration as Subject

Songs recounting and reflecting on the migration experience and its aftermath performed an important role in the process of adjustment. Some appeared in print at the time – as, for example, those of the California gold rush era, by 'internal migrants,' which were published in contemporary 'songster' collections (and have subsequently been anthologized). Others remained within oral tradition, and were later collected by scholars. Theodore C. Blegen, for example, collected a number of items by Danes, Norwegians, Swedes and others, relating to the migration experience (1959). Forty emigrant ballads were collected and classified by Robert L. Wright and published in the original Swedish and in English translation (1965). They included songs of justification, of warning, of nostalgia and farewell, of disaster and disillusion, revealing the ethical dilemmas and emotional turmoil of the emigrants, as expressed in their ballads between 1854 and 1938.

Migration as a theme was evident in the recordings, both field and commercial, of many immigrant groups made in the 1930s. Some, like 'Wujko Politykan' ('Uncle, the Politician') by the Ukrainian singer Ewgen Zukowsky, for example, told of disillusionment, while others, like 'Dzieci w Krateczki' ('Children in Squares') by candystore owner Wladyslaw Polak, were ironic and amusing. An album of *Songs of Migration and Immigration*, edited by Richard K. Spottswood, includes examples of songs of Polish, Mormon, Texan, Oklahoman and African-American origin. Songs about the interstate migration of the 'Okies,' or Oklahoma dust-bowl refugee migrants, were created and performed by Woody Guthrie, and some were recorded from migrating workers in temporary refugee camps. Itinerants and temporary migrants – hobos, railroad 'bums' and migrants seeking work – also created songs; 86 of them, by a variety of what George Milburn called 'gutter jongleurs,' were included by him in his 1930 compilation *The Hobo's Hornbook*.

A major body of songs of internal migration was created by blues singers. Declarations of the intention to migrate were noted in the earliest text collections that included blues, and the theme was prominent in recorded blues, Leroy Carr's 1934 recording of 'Florida Bound Blues' even being advertised as the 'famous migration blues.' A number of blues songs were recorded in the 1940s and 1950s and marked the beginning of the massive postwar migration of blacks from the South (estimated by some to be in the region of 5 million people) that occurred in the decades following the mechanization of the southern plantations and major changes in the economy.

The rise of individualism in the modern era introduced a new element into the migration narrative. Apart from movements that involved and even helped to constitute communities (such as German Lutherans in South Australia, expatriate Finns in Sweden, the Boers in South Africa), a substantial body of migration narratives arose that were underpinned by atomization and alienated individualization. Migration songs thus looked both forward and back, sometimes simultaneously ('California, here I come, right back where I started from').

It is significant that, in the general category of migration songs, songs of utopian destinations – the 'promised land' theme – are countered by a substantial body of narratives of nostalgia. Many such narratives center on the dream of return. The proliferation of 'take me home' songs since the nineteenth century reflects a growing market in all countries affected by the social changes associated with modernity and mass mobilization: 'Carry Me Back to Old Virginny' (US); 'I'm Going Back to Yarrawonga' (Australia). (The most famous early 'take me home' song, 'I'll Take You Home Again, Kathleen' (1876), also illustrates the subtle intertwining of return, nostalgia, ethnicity and commerce that could occur in mainstream popular songs. Written by a German American, Thomas P. Westendorf, for whom it was a huge but solitary hit, it lacks specific references but was widely taken for an Irish song of immigration, even by the Irish 'back home.')

As in the examples considered above, a 'back home' motif could easily modulate into protest, shading into sedition and treason. These 'take me home' songs have played a significant role in the mythologization of place and history, particularly at times of rapid social change. The Australian composition 'On the Road to Gundagai' was composed by Jack O'Hagan in 1922, but its massive popularity dates from 1931, in the depths of the Great Depression, when its wistful 'return' to pastoral innocence reinforced an earlier conservative and anti-modernist bush tradition.

Diaspora

Within the overall phenomenon of human movement, a particular significance has come to be attached to the concept of 'diaspora.' The word (from the Greek for dispersion) originally applied uniquely to the dispersion of the Jews in the Greco-Roman world, where it generally had connotations of voluntary movement (as opposed to exile). Its modern use has tended to draw attention to dispersion as a result of oppression, war, violation of human rights or appropriation of territory. It has also come to mean group migration where assimilation is incomplete and where homeland culture survives in the new context, as has been the case with Chinese and, to a lesser extent, Japanese immigrants in the United States. The term is also used more broadly to refer to the expulsion of some peoples, such as the Armenians, and the forcible transportation of others, such as the movement of people of African origin and descent to the Americas. By extension, it also embraces further movement of such peoples, so that black immigrants to Britain from the Caribbean can be said to be part of a 'black diaspora.'

Building on the work of scholars such as Édouard Glissant and St. Clair Drake in the context of black studies, Gilroy (1993) has seen 'diaspora' – an 'undertheorised idea,' in his view (6) – as a key term with which to discuss the issue of how dispersed black peoples can display both unity with and differentiation from each other. For Gilroy, the term operates as a counterbalance both to arguments that give undue emphasis to a unifying dynamic in the face of 'the conspicuous differentiation and proliferation of black cultural styles and genres,' and to a pluralistic 'orthodoxy' that denies the possibility of any such dynamic (1993, 6). 'Diaspora' can be used rather 'to project the rich diversity of black cultures in different parts of the world in counterpoint to their common sensibilities – both those features residually inherited from Africa and those generated from the special bitterness of New World racial slavery' (1993, 6).

Music demonstrates this counterpoint particularly clearly, not only in its expression of these historical relationships, but, in the modern era, in the 'two-way traffic' that has seen, for example, 'the mutation of jazz and African-American cultural style in the townships of South Africa and the syncretised evolution of Caribbean and British reggae music and Rastafari culture in Zimbabwe' (Gilroy 1993, 199). Such phenomena Gilroy terms 'diaspora conversations' (1993, 199).

Casting analysis more widely, and setting diaspora alongside the global market, Lipsitz (1994) sees dispersed peoples – 'people from colonized countries long connected to global migrations' – taking on roles as 'cross-cultural interpreters and analysts' (7) and using music extensively to do so. Experts in displacement, and therefore in the impact of outside forces on the sense of place, they use music to cement and develop alliances, to set up 'a polylateral dialogue among aggrieved populations' (1994, 7). Lipsitz's insight is well illustrated by the song 'Samba Lando,' written in 1979 by members of the group Inti-illimani and Patricio Manns, all Chilean musicians politically exiled in Europe. The song, which warns of the dangers of 'new slavemasters,' is both a paean to the black people of Africa (the title is Yoruba) and of the Americas, and an expression of solidarity with them.

Diffusion and Dissemination

In addition to its use to denote the movement of people from one place to another, 'migration' is sometimes used metaphorically to account for the spread, assimilation, adoption and influence of instruments, musical forms and songs. For example, the reappearance of the main melody of George F. Root's American Civil War song 'Tramp! Tramp! Tramp!' and of the words and melody of Rodgers' and Hammerstein's 'You'll Never Walk Alone' (from the musical *Carousel*) in singing by English soccer crowds might be described metaphorically as a 'migration' from one cultural context to another.

More accurately, in the case of these two examples, the process involves the diffusion of repertoire (via publishing and by traveling performers), followed by the spatial passing on of the songs between contiguous cultures and social groups. The same process could occur for instruments and styles. But, as the second of these examples suggests, diffusion – leading to metaphorical 'migration' – also takes place via technological-industrial dissemination involving the mass media.

The development of the media through the late nineteenth century, increasing exponentially through the twentieth, overtook physical migration as a means by which popular music was disseminated. Before that point, the first of the media to influence dissemination had been music publishing. Up to the middle of the nineteenth century, the influence of publishing on the dissemination of popular music had been tied in part to migration; the first publishers of popular song in the United States, for example, were European emigrants. As transportation improved and performers traveled more widely – touring, rather than migrating – performance began to have a greater influence on dissemination. The arrival of the Virginia Minstrels in Britain in 1845, for example, enabled the concept of the minstrel show to be disseminated there.

There seems little doubt that the combination of widespread dissemination via relatively cheap published scores and the ability of performers to travel quickly and more widely was a powerful influence on the emergence of an aesthetic of universality around classical music in the latter half of the nineteenth century. Although by the end of the century, with the advent of skillfully and energetically promoted sheet music, popular music was more widely and rapidly disseminated than ever before, the fact that much popular music was still diffused orally via contiguity – whether associated with migration or not – limited its radius of influence. The arrival and establishment of record companies and, later, of film companies changed this situation radically.

The portability of acoustic utterances, once confined to the limits of earshot, and the possibility of their merger with portable visual images, reconfigured the movement and dispersal of music around the planet, and did so beyond the capacity of terms designed for other forms of movement and dispersal to encompass. Apparently impermeable terms like 'instrument' (a means of bringing music into existence) and 'media' (a means of delivering music intact) leaked into each other. Prior to the development of sound recording and film, music was stored in either the performer or the score for delivery to reception spaces. Sound recording and film produced storage and delivery systems enabling music to be disseminated, but these systems are also 'instruments.' When music is disseminated technologically, the media of its dissemination become partners in the composition – the form, the sound, the meaning. The fact that, for so many people, jazz was first heard internationally through sound recordings altered both its forms and its meanings. What was a regional folk music in New Orleans became a marker of urban modernity in other countries. The technological particularities of record production also modified the music. The duration of the recording, for example, produced a model of 'composition' and performance in diasporic sites that has continued to be broadly observed in, for example, jazz styles, which were disseminated on 78 rpm 10" (25 cm) recordings. Subsequent developments in music mediation, such as feedback, tape splicing, sampling and scratching, have even more extravagantly demolished the distinctions that once underpinned the difference between the character of music and the vehicles by means of which it was moved.

Bibliography

American Folklife Center. 1982. *Ethnic Recordings in America: A Neglected Heritage*. Washington, DC: Library of Congress.

Anderson, Hugh. 1975. *The Story of Australian Folksong*. 3rd ed. Melbourne: Hill of Content.

Anderson, Hugh. 2000. *Farewell to Judges and Juries: The Broadside Ballad and Convict Transportation to Australia, 1788–1868*. Hotham Hill, Victoria: Red Rooster Press.

Blegen, Theodore C. 1959. 'Singing Immigrants and Pioneers.' In *Studies in American Culture*, ed. Joseph J. Kwiat and Mary C. Turpie. Minneapolis, MN: University of Minnesota Press, 171–88.

Burma, John H. 1974. *Spanish Speaking Groups in the U.S.* Detroit, MI: Blaine-Etheridge. (First published Durham, NC: Duke University Press, 1954.)

Degler, Carl N. 1962 (1959). *Out of Our Past: The Forces That Shaped Modern America*. New York and Evanston: Harper Collophon.

Dorson, George, ed. 1949. *Pennsylvania Songs and Legends*. Philadelphia: University of Pennsylvania Press.

Dwyer, Richard A., and Lingenfelter, Richard E., eds. 1964. *Songs of the Gold Rush*. Berkeley, CA: University of California Press.

Edwards, Ron. 1991 (1976). *Great Australian Folk Songs*. Willoughby, NSW: Ure Smith Press.

Erlmann, Veit. 1990. 'Migration and Performance: Zulu Migrant Workers' Iscathamiya Performance in South Africa 1890–1950.' *Ethnomusicology* 34(2): 199–219.

Gamble, Clive. 1986. *The Palaeolithic Settlement of Europe*. Cambridge: Cambridge University Press.

Gilroy, Paul. 1991. 'Sounds Authentic: Black Music, Ethnicity, and the Challenge of the Changing Same.' *Black Music Research Journal* 11(2): 111–36.

Gilroy, Paul. 1993. *The Black Atlantic: Modernity and Double Consciousness*. London: Verso.

Greenaway, John. 1970 (1953). 'The Migratory Workers.' In *American Folksongs of Protest*, Ch. 5. New York: Octogon Books, 173–208.

Hughes, Robert. 1987. *The Fatal Shore: A History of the Transportation of Convicts to Australia, 1787–1868*. London: Collins Harvill.

Irwin, Geoffrey. 1992. *The Prehistoric Exploration and Colonisation of the Pacific*. Cambridge: Cambridge University Press.

Johnson, Bruce. 2000. *The Inaudible Music: Jazz, Gender and Australian Modernity*. Sydney: Currency Press.

Jones, Maldwyn Allen. 1960. *American Immigration*. Chicago: University of Chicago Press.

Lipsitz, George. 1994. *Dangerous Crossroads: Popular Music, Postmodernism, and the Poetics of Place*. London: Verso.

Lyman, Stanford M. 1977. *The Asian in North America*. Santa Barbara and Oxford: ABC-Clio Press.

May, Robin. 1977. *The Gold Rushes: From California to the Klondike*. London: William Luscombe/Mitchell Beazley Group.

Meredith, John, and Anderson, Hugh. 1985 (1967). *Folk Songs of Australia and the Men and Women Who Sang Them*, Vol. 1. Kensington, NSW: New South Wales University Press.

Meredith, John, Covell, Roger, and Brown, Patricia. 1987. *Folk Songs of Australia and the Men and Women Who Sang Them*, Vol. 2. Kensington, NSW: New South Wales University Press.

Milburn, George, ed. 1930. *The Hobo's Hornbook: A Repertory for a Gutter Jongleur*. New York: Ives Washburn.

Neidle, Cecyle S. 1972. *The New Americans*. New York: Twayne Publishers Inc.

Noble, Allen G. 1992. *To Build in a New Land: Ethnic Landscapes in North America*. Baltimore, MD: Johns Hopkins University Press.

Oliver, Paul. 1990. *Blues Fell This Morning: Meaning in the Blues*. 2nd ed. Cambridge: Cambridge University Press. (First published London: Cassell, 1960.)

Oliver, Paul, ed. 1997. *Encyclopedia of Vernacular Architecture of the World. Vol. 3: Sect. VI, North America*. Cambridge: Cambridge University Press, 1785–1968.

Reily, Suzel Ana. 1992. '*Musica Sertaneja* and Migrant Identity: The Stylistic Development of a Brazilian Genre.' *Popular Music* 11(3): 337–58.

Shryock, Henry S., Jr. 1964. *Population Mobility Within the United States*. Chicago: University of Chicago Community and Family Study Center.

Smith, Anthony D. 1995 (1986). *The Ethnic Origins of Nations*. Oxford: Blackwell.

White, Sid, and Solberg, S.E. 1989. *Peoples of Washington: Perspectives on Cultural Diversity*. Pullman, WA: Washington State University Press.

Wright, Robert L. 1965. *Swedish Emigrant Ballads*. Lincoln, NE: University of Nebraska Press.

Young, Jan. 1972. *The Migrant Workers and Cesar Chavez*. New York: Julian Messner.

Sheet Music

Bland, James A., comp. and lyr. 1878. 'Carry Me Back to Old Virginny.' New York: John F. Perry.

McBeath, Cpl Neil, AIF, comp. 1919. 'I'm Going Back to Yarrawonga.' Sydney: Alberts Music (published in the United Kingdom by Francis, Day and Hunter).

Meyer, Joseph, Jolson, Al, and DeSylva, Buddy, comps. and lyrs. 1924. 'California, Here I Come.' New York: Witmark & Sons.

O'Hagan, Jack, comp. and lyr. 1922. 'On the Road to Gundagai.' Melbourne: Allans Music (Aust.).

Rodgers, Richard, comp., and Hammerstein II, Oscar, lyr. 1945. 'You'll Never Walk Alone.' New York: Williamson Music.

Root, George F., comp. and lyr. 1864. 'Tramp! Tramp! Tramp! or The Prisoner's Hope.' Chicago: Root & Cady.

Westendorf, Thomas P., comp. and lyr. 1876. 'I'll Take You Home Again, Kathleen.' Cincinnati: Church.

Discographical References

Carr, Leroy. 'Florida Bound Blues.' Vocalion 03233. 1934: USA.

Inti-illimani. 'Samba Lando.' *Sing to Me the Dream*. Redwood Records RR407. *1984*: USA.

Polak, Wladyslaw. 'Dzieci w Krateczki.' *Songs of Migration and Immigration*. Folk Music in America, Vol. 6. Library of Congress LBC 6. *1976*: USA.

Songs of Migration and Immigration (ed. Richard K. Spottswood). Folk Music in America, Vol. 6. Library of Congress LBC 6. *1976*: USA.

Zukowsky, Ewgen. 'Wujko Politykan.' *Songs of Complaint and Protest*. Folk Music in America, Vol. 7. Library of Congress LBC 7. *1987*: USA.

Discography

Corridos & Tragedias de la Frontera: Mexican American Border Music. Folklyric 7019/20. 1928–37; *1994*: USA.

Guthrie, Woody. *Talking Dust Bowl*. Folkways Records FA-2011. 1950: USA.

Marshall, Brian, and His Tex-Slavik Playboys. *Texas Polish Roots*. Arhoolie CD 464. *1997*: USA.

Reed, Wallace 'Cheese,' et al. *Folksongs of the Louisiana Acadians* (rec. Harry Oster). Arhoolie CD 359. 1959; *1994*: USA.

PAUL OLIVER, BRUCE JOHNSON and DAVID HORN

Morality

Popular music's relationship to morality is as complex as the term 'morality' itself. In seeking to distinguish 'good' from 'bad,' 'morality' describes the approved codes of behavior that order human relations in any given society. 'Morality' refers to matters such as bonds of trust and principles of promise-keeping. The practises associated with such matters embody 'good behavior.' Failure to live by the rules embedded in these practises may result in someone being deemed 'immoral.' Equally, though, 'morality' refers to a preferred set of relations, a set that may not obtain in the present, but that may nonetheless be advocated and aspired to in order for some higher social end to be achieved in the future. What counts as 'moral' behavior may vary according to time and place. However, throughout its history, and certainly since the times of classical Greece, music has been linked to these different notions of morality.

Both Christian and Islamic cultures have from time to time viewed musicians as being representatives of immorality, as people associated with itinerant and irresponsible sections of society. At the same time, there has been a rival tradition which associates music with moral improvement. In Europe and the United States during the nineteenth century, music was valued for the lessons it could provide in moral propriety and good behavior. With regard to England, for example, Rainbow (1968) refers to John Turner, who in 1833 noted that a more general diffusion of vocal music would 'contribute largely to the rooting out of dissolute and debasing habits,' and that songs chosen for performance should have texts that were 'simple in character, but conveying sentiments of pure and exalted morality' (quoted in Rainbow 1968, 157). Rainbow refers as well to Joseph Mainzer, who in 1849 argued that 'music must be an integral part of our education; both for its own sake, and for the sake of the public services of the church' (quoted in Rainbow 1968, 133).

The legacy of such arguments has remained strongly entrenched in views concerning popular music's moral implications. On the one hand, popular music has often been celebrated for the ways in which it has served religious ends, as, for example, in both black and white gospel traditions in the United States, as well as in the opposition of black churches to apartheid in South Africa. However, popular music has often been criticized, and harshly so, for its perceived associations with immoral behavior. Typical of such criticisms have been the characterization of the blues as 'the devil's music,' and the opprobrium heaped on the entertainment music of the African-American community at the end of the nineteenth century and the beginning of the twentieth because of its associations with the honky-tonks (bars) and bordellos (brothels) of the sporting belts or red-light districts of southern towns and cities. This view of the moral undesirability of much African-American music – usually linked to questions of sexuality – continued throughout the twentieth century. It has been an attitude adopted also toward many musical forms influenced by African-American music. The early 1920s, for example, witnessed a moral backlash against the perceived excesses – sexual and otherwise – associated with the emergence of white jazz. The year 1919 saw the enactment of Prohibition, 1920 the banning of dancing on Broadway after midnight, and the mid-1920s a fast-growing conservatism in the music programming of the newly established medium of radio, as the kind of energetic, small-band jazz performed by the Original Dixieland Jazz Band was replaced by the more restrained dance music typical of larger organizations such as Paul Whiteman and His Orchestra.

Such views as expressed since World War II have been manifest most often in the phenomenon of the 'moral panic.' The history of popular music is marked by a series of such moral panics: the crisis over Elvis's crotch; the outraged response to John Lennon's claim that the Beatles were a greater phenomenon than Jesus; the reaction to satanic sentiments in heavy metal or to cop-killing attitudes in rap; and, of course, the permanent panic engendered by the link between drugs and music. What each of these moments represents, with its attendant proliferation of editorials and splashy headlines, is the sense that music and musicians encourage or embody a life style that offends against established values and practises. These moral panics are directed against particular songs or performers, or against whole cultures. Such reactions only make sense, however, because of the implied link between morality and music. It is not just social morality that is under attack, but music's own moral virtue.

The immediate object of this animosity is less important than the underlying morality that is being articulated or defended. What music provides, in this context, is a space in which competing moral orders are articulated. Equally, morality is not articulated only through a negative reaction to particular sounds and images; music and musicians may also actively construct a moral vision. This trend was, for example, noticeable in the United Kingdom and the United States from at least the eighteenth century onward. English broadside ballads often conveyed a moral message. This moralizing persisted as such ballads crossed the Atlantic to the United States. 'The Berkshire Tragedy, or the Wottan Miller: With An Account of Murdering His Sweetheart,' for example, became, in the United States, 'The Lexington Murder' (Laws 1957, 104–22), a traditional ballad that admonished young men not to 'let the devil get the upper hand of you.' Equally moralistic were temperance songs, common in the United States during the second half of the nineteenth century and the early part of the twentieth. Typical of this genre was 'Father's a Drunkard and Mother Is Dead' (1866), a tear-jerking ballad almost pathetic in the heights of sentimentality to which it aspired.

Such moralizing continued as the United States witnessed a rapid change from a fundamentally rural to a fundamentally urban economy. As Brooks (1978) has observed, 'in all respects save the abolition of slavery, the Civil War was not an end but a beginning. With it, industry and capital forever gained the upper hand over agrarian gentility' (1). This change did not go uncontested, however, as agrarian and labor interests took aim at what they perceived as the immoral exploitation of ordinary people at the hands of capitalists. Alongside songs such as Henry Russell's 'A Life in the West' (1855), which glorified, if not idealized, the values and virtues of the rural life, were songs such as 'The Farmer Is the Man That Feeds Them All' and 'The Hand That Holds the Bread' (1874), songs that, in strongly implying 'the moral superiority of the agrarian' (Pankake 1977, 3), were openly critical of the evils heaped on farmers by entrepreneurial middlemen.

Yet, at the same time, there were those songs that sought to instruct people in how to lead their lives in the new, emerging social order. As people moved from the land to towns and cities in search of jobs, they experienced a major change of cultures. In particular, the presence and importance of the extended family were considerably weakened as it was replaced in urban environments by the nuclear family. Whereas, previously, it would have been exceptional for the partners in a marriage not to have known one another since childhood, it would now increasingly be the case for marriage partners to have known each other for only a short time before marriage, and to have known each other only within the context of a romantic relationship leading to marriage. In a situation where there was considerable

opposition to industrial capitalism as a new way of life, the concept of romantic love became crucially important as a foundation and raison d'être for the nuclear family. Popular songs in the form of the sentimental ballad became important in promoting and establishing this role for romantic love. 'A Bird in a Gilded Cage,' for example, one of the most popular sentimental ballads of 1900, told the story of a young woman who had chosen to marry an old man for money rather than the young man whom she loved. The moral of the song is clear and didactically so. The woman, says the song's chorus, bedecked in her finery and jewelry, only appears to be happy; in fact, she is not. She has wasted her life, the reason being that 'youth cannot mate with age.' Her beauty 'was sold for an old man's gold,' concludes the song; 'she's a bird in a gilded cage.'

As part of the continuing opposition to the emergence of industrial capitalism, the interests of labor were given expression through songs such as 'The Future America' (1891), which describes a 'land where the wealthy few can make the many do their royal will,' and 'Come All You Coal Miners,' which, in exhorting the audience to join the singer in sinking 'this capitalist system in the darkest pits of hell,' is, as Pankake observes, 'bold and assertive in richly earned anger and righteous outrage' (1977, 3). This last song, written and performed by Sarah Ogan (later, Sarah Ogan Gunning), came out of the Depression years, a time when northern labor organizers, reformers, radicals and the liberal intelligentsia traveled from the North to lend support to spontaneous labor uprisings that were spreading right across the South. As Green (1965) observes, from the Southern Highlands 'came a group of topical songs using old melodies to set off intensely stark and militant texts.' In a sense, he concludes, 'Piedmont mill village and Cumberland mine camps became meeting grounds for the ideologies of Andrew Jackson and Karl Marx, Abraham Lincoln and Mikhail Bakunin' (1).

The radicalism betrayed by such songs was noticeably messianic in its intent of replacing one set of social relations judged to be manifestly unjust with another, more egalitarian in character. From these origins sprang the work and career of Woody Guthrie and, subsequently, the 'urban folk revival,' a movement initially characterized by the songs of Peter, Paul and Mary, the Kingston Trio and Pete Seeger. Through its opposition to the Vietnam war (as exemplified, for example, in the song 'Where Have All the Flowers Gone?' written by Pete Seeger, and a hit for the Kingston Trio in 1962) and its espousing of the civil rights movement (through, for example, 'We Shall Overcome,' a rewritten gospel song that was a hit for Joan Baez in 1965), the urban folk revival provided – in large part through the songs of Bob

Dylan – a link to the 'counterculture' of the 1960s, a culture that itself tended to adopt the moral high ground in its opposition to capital, government and the military. This was not the first time the world of popular music had become entangled with questions to do with the morality of war. At the time of World War I, for example, Al Piantadosi's and Alfred Bryan's 'I Didn't Raise My Boy to Be a Soldier' (1915) was answered approximately a year later by Irving Berlin's 'Let's All Be Americans Now.'

The distinctively moral message about racial inequality expressed in association with the civil rights movement continued with the formation of Rock Against Racism initiatives in the United States and the United Kingdom in the late 1970s. Musicians offered themselves as spokespeople for, and symbols of, the fight against racism in the music industry and in the wider society. Despite suspicions concerning the presumed 'immoral' life style of musicians, their music nonetheless imparted to them a certain moral authority.

Live Aid was a classic example of this phenomenon. In events in the United States and the United Kingdom, and in hundreds of similar events across the world, musicians were engaged in promoting concern for the victims of starvation in Ethiopia. Bob Geldof, the main instigator of Live Aid, came to represent a collective conscience. He wanted to make people feel that they had a duty to give.

Although Live Aid was presented in morally unambiguous terms, its actual morality (the values it represented) was more confused. For some commentators (like Hebdige 1988), it represented a populist challenge to the selfish ethos of the New Right. The ruthless individualism of Thatcherism and Reaganism, in which all relations were reduced to market exchanges and valued only through cost-benefit analysis, was seen to be countered by the collective altruism of Live Aid, and of the events that preceded it and the events, such as Farm Aid, that succeeded it. Other commentators were less persuaded of Live Aid's moral virtues (see, for example, Rijven and Straw 1989). Some of these commentators argued that its apparent humanist concerns were actually the moral equivalent of globalization. Live Aid worked with a rhetoric of 'universal humanism,' which created, on the one hand, an undifferentiated compassionate mass whose differences were lost to view, buried beneath the clouds of superficial sympathy (Marcus 1989), and, on the other hand, a rigid demarcation between 'us,' who cared, and 'them,' who suffered. This moral equation was seen as the product of the commercial interests organized around Live Aid. It was the (im)morality of global capitalism that wanted to create an undifferentiated mass market and to marginalize those who threatened or could not participate in this order.

That music could become part of this moral debate is itself a legacy of its intimate connection to questions of morality. This intimacy with regard to personal affairs is revealed, for example, through the guilt and bitterness of cheating songs, familiar elements of almost all genres, but no more so, perhaps, than in country music, where moral issues have not infrequently been discussed publicly through song. Webb Pierce's 'Back Street Affair' (1952), for example, inspired Kitty Wells's 'Paying for That Back Street Affair' (1953). Kitty Wells's own rise to stardom came as a result of 'It Wasn't God Who Made Honky Tonk Angels' (1952), an answer to Hank Thompson's hit of a few months earlier, 'The Wild Side of Life' (1952). Debates over the morality or otherwise of various attitudes toward different forms of sexual behavior can be perceived also in the songs of male rappers on the one hand, and in the work of women rappers such as Queen Latifah and Salt-N-Pepa on the other. Popular music has thus typically worked with the experiences of moral dilemmas over a long period of time. It has variously explored feelings of anguish, confusion, shame, insecurity, indignation, righteousness and chauvinism.

Morality is also bound up with the daily routines of the musician, although this varies with genre, and serves to qualify the general moral suspicion of musicians. The rhetoric of integrity is certainly crucial to the self-image of musicians. Such integrity may be measured in terms of business relations (not 'selling out'); equally, it may refer to an approach to musical sources (authenticity). Such notions of integrity may be as much the products of marketing as of genuine personal commitment, but the point is how such moral virtues have an integral role in the construction of musical credibility.

Business practise inevitably touches on ethical questions. At one level, such issues may be decided within informal structures: groups may decide to share songwriting credits, and thereby retain parity in the distribution of royalties; alternatively, a single member may claim such rights, with the huge disparities of income that this may entail. At another, more formal level, the routine practises of record company policy, enshrined in the terms of contracts, will contain moral judgments about individual rights and deserts. But the morality of music-making was most powerfully evoked by the dilemmas posed by apartheid in South Africa. First, there was the Sun City campaign in 1985. A group of musicians, organized by Steve Van Zandt and operating under the collective name Artists United Against Apartheid, recorded an album, the proceeds from which were to help the fight against apartheid. Their actions were an immediate response to the decisions of groups like Queen to play in Sun City in South Africa. Secondly, also prompted by the cultural boycott of South Africa, there was Paul Simon's *Graceland* album, recorded with South African musicians, although in this case there was tremendous controversy, because Simon actually recorded in South Africa (see Hamm 1989). What both these examples represent is the moral choice that is implicated in the practise of making music.

Business ethics are not, of course, peculiar to the music industry. What is distinctive, however, is the way in which music may help to construct morality. This aspect of the relationship between music and morality depends, crucially, on the way in which morality is itself conceptualized. If morality is viewed as an established code, preordained or implied by all human action, then music can at best be no more than an expression of (or deviation from) this moral order. Alternatively, if morality is seen as a discursively constituted practise, then music may function as part of the constituting process. Its capacity to articulate moral feelings and sentiments makes it part of the dialog by which moral codes are constructed and revised.

Finally, the aesthetics of popular music can themselves be connected to morality. Frith (1996) has argued for a need to understand aesthetic judgment, people's response to popular music, in ethical terms. Although this move may appear to take the discussion a long way from 'moral panic,' there is actually a connection. The fears that music generates stem from its capacity to conjure up moral orders that both appeal and appall, and it reinforces the tradition that has long bound music and morality together.

Bibliography

Bailey, Peter. 1978. 'The Case of the Victorian Music Halls.' In Peter Bailey, *Leisure and Class in Victorian England: Rational Recreation and the Contest for Control, 1830–1885*. London: Routledge & Kegan Paul, 147–68.

Binder, Amy. 1993. 'Constructing Racial Rhetoric: Media Depiction of Harm in Heavy Metal and Rap Music.' *American Sociological Review* 58 (December): 753–67.

Brooks, William. 1978. Notes to *The Hand That Holds the Bread: Progress and Protest in the Gilded Age – Songs from the Civil War to the Columbian Exposition*. New World Records NW 267.

Charrington, Frederick. 1885. *The Battle of the Music Halls*. London: Dyer Bros.

Frith, Simon. 1996. *Performing Rites: On the Value of Popular Music*. Cambridge, MA: Harvard University Press.

Green, Archie. 1965. Notes to *Girl of Constant Sorrow*, by Sarah Ogan Gunning. Folk-Legacy Records FSA-26.

Hamm, Charles. 1989. 'Graceland Revisited.' *Popular Music* 8(3): 299–304.

Hebdige, Dick. 1988. *Hiding in the Light: On Images and Things*. London and New York: Routledge.

Heeley, John. 1986. 'Leisure and Moral Reform.' *Leisure Studies* 5: 57–67.

Laws, G. Malcolm. 1957. *American Balladry from British Broadsides*. Philadelphia: American Folklore Society.

Marcus, Greil. 1989. 'We Are the World?' In *Zoot-Suits and Second-Hand Dresses: An Anthology of Fashion and Music*, ed. Angela McRobbie. Basingstoke: Macmillan, 276–82.

Pankake, Jon. 1977. Notes to *Oh My Little Darling: Folk Song Types*. New World Records NW 245.

Rainbow, Bernarr, ed. 1968. *Handbook for Music Teachers*. London: Novello.

Rijven, Stan, and Straw, Will. 1989. 'Rock for Ethiopia (1985).' In *World Music, Politics, and Social Change*, ed. Simon Frith. Manchester: Manchester University Press, 198–209.

Storch, Robert D. 1977. 'The Problem of Working Class Leisure: Some Roots of Middle Class Moral Reform in the Industrial North, 1825–1850.' In *Social Control in Nineteenth Century Britain*, ed. A.P. Donajgrodzki. London: Croom Helm, 138–62.

Webb, Sidney, and Webb, Beatrice. 1903. *The History of Liquor Licensing in England, Principally from 1700 to 1830*. London: Longmans.

Sheet Music

Berlin, Irving, comp. and lyr., Meyer, George, comp., and Leslie, Edgar, lyr. 1917. 'Let's All Be Americans Now.' New York: Waterson, Berlin and Snyder.

Dodge, H.C., lyr. 1891. 'The Future America' (to the melody of 'My Country, 'Tis of Thee'). In *The Alliance and Labor Songster*, ed. Leopold Vincent. Indianapolis, IN: Vincent Bros.

Parkhurst, Mrs. E.A., comp., and Stella (of Good Samaritan Division No. 1) (Bradley, Nellie H.), lyr. 1866. 'Father's a Drunkard and Mother Is Dead.' Washington, DC: John F. Ellis.

Piantadosi, Al, comp., and Bryan, Alfred, lyr. 1915. 'I Didn't Raise My Boy to Be a Soldier.' New York: Leo Feist.

Root, George F., comp. and lyr. 1874. 'The Hand That Holds the Bread.' In *The Trumpet of Reform*, ed. George F. Root and Mrs. S.M. Smith. Chicago: Root and Cady.

Russell, Henry, comp., and Morris, G.P., lyr. 1855. 'A Life in the West.' London: Musical Bouquet Office (No. 487).

Seeger, Pete, comp. and lyr. 1961. 'Where Have All the Flowers Gone?' New York: Fall River Music Inc.

Von Tilzer, Harry, comp., and Lamb, Arthur J., lyr. 1900.

'A Bird in a Gilded Cage.' New York: Shapiro, Bernstein and Von Tilzer.

Discographical References

American Quartet. 'Let's All Be Americans Now.' Victor 18256. 1917: USA. Reissue: American Quartet. 'Let's All Be Americans Now.' *Songs of World Wars I & II*. New World Records NWA 222. *1977*: USA.

Artists United Against Apartheid. *Sun City*. Manhattan 50017. *1985*: USA.

Baez, Joan. 'We Shall Overcome.' Fontana TF 564. *1965*: USA. Reissue: Baez, Joan. 'We Shall Overcome.' *Best of Joan Baez*. Vanguard 505. *1997*: USA.

Carson, Fiddlin' John. 'The Farmer Is the Man That Feeds Them All.' OKeh 40071. 1923: USA. Reissue: Carson, Fiddlin' John. 'The Farmer Is the Man That Feeds Them All.' *Oh My Little Darling: Folk Song Types*. New World Records NW 245. *1977*: USA.

Cincinnati's University Singers. 'The Future America.' *The Hand That Holds the Bread: Progress and Protest in the Gilded Age – Songs from the Civil War to the Columbian Exposition*. New World Records NW 267. *1978*: USA.

Cincinnati's University Singers. 'The Hand That Holds the Bread.' *The Hand That Holds the Bread: Progress and Protest in the Gilded Age – Songs from the Civil War to the Columbian Exposition*. New World Records NW 267. *1978*: USA.

Hargis, Wesley. 'The Lexington Murder.' Library of Congress Archive of American Folk Song 90A. 1934: USA. Reissue: Hargis, Wesley. 'The Lexington Murder.' *Oh My Little Darling: Folk Song Types*. New World Records NW 245. *1977*: USA.

Harvey, Morton. 'I Didn't Raise My Boy to Be a Soldier.' Victor 17716. 1915: USA. Reissue: Harvey, Morton. 'I Didn't Raise My Boy to Be a Soldier.' *Songs of World Wars I & II*. New World Records NWA 222. *1977*: USA.

Jackson, Clifford, and Basquin, Peter. 'A Life in the West.' *Where Home Is – Life in Nineteenth-Century Cincinnati: Crossroads of the East and West*. New World Records NW 251. *1977*: USA.

Kingston Trio, The. 'Where Have All the Flowers Gone?' Capitol 4671. *1962*: USA. Reissue: Kingston Trio, The. 'Where Have All the Flowers Gone?' *Back to Back Hits*. Cema Special Markets 19463. *1998*: USA.

Ogan, Sarah (later, Sarah Ogan Gunning). 'Come All You Coal Miners.' Library of Congress Archive of American Folk Song 1944 A. 1937: USA. Reissue: Ogan, Sarah (later, Sarah Ogan Gunning). 'Come All You Coal Miners.' *The Hand That Holds the Bread: Progress and Protest in the Gilded Age – Songs from the Civil War to the Columbian Exposition*. New World Records NW 267. *1978*: USA.

Pierce, Webb. 'Back Street Affair.' Decca 28369. 1952: USA. Reissue: Pierce, Webb. 'Back Street Affair.' *King of Honky Tonk: From the Original Master Tapes*. Country Music Foundation 19. *1994*: USA.

Porter, Steve. 'A Bird in a Gilded Cage.' Columbia 4608. 1900: USA. Rerecording: Bolcom, William, and Morris, Joan. 'A Bird in a Gilded Cage.' *Let's Do It: Bolcom and Morris at Aspen*. Omega OCD-3004. *1989*: USA.

Prince, Faith. 'Father's a Drunkard and Mother Is Dead.' *The Hand That Holds the Bread: Progress and Protest in the Gilded Age – Songs from the Civil War to the Columbian Exposition*. New World Records NW 267. *1978*: USA.

Simon, Paul. *Graceland*. Warner Brothers WX 52. *1986*: USA.

Thompson, Hank. 'The Wild Side of Life.' Capitol 1942. 1952: USA. Reissue: Thompson, Hank. 'The Wild Side of Life.' *Vintage*. Capitol 36901. *1996*: USA.

Wells, Kitty. 'It Wasn't God Who Made Honky Tonk Angels.' Decca 28232. 1952: USA. Reissue: Wells, Kitty. 'It Wasn't God Who Made Honky Tonk Angels.' *Kitty Wells' Greatest Hits*. King Special 1414. *1995*: USA.

Wells, Kitty. 'Paying for That Back Street Affair.' Decca 28578. 1953: USA. Reissue: Wells, Kitty. 'Paying for That Back Street Affair.' *Kitty Wells' Greatest Hits*. King Special 1414. *1995*: USA.

Discography

Queen Latifah. *All Hail the Queen*. Tommy Boy 1022. *1989*: USA.

Salt-N-Pepa. *Blacks' Magic*. London 422-828362-2. *1989*: USA.

USA for Africa: We Are the World. PolyGram 824822. *1985*: USA.

Visual Recording

'We Are the World: The Video Event.' '5. RCA/Columbia Pictures Home Video.

JOHN SHEPHERD and JOHN STREET

Moral Panic

'Moral panic' is a sociological term used to describe the process by which supposedly 'deviant' youth subcultures or musics are labeled, mediated and demonized by the mass media, and are subsequently subject to control and legislation. The term entered the language of critical discourse in the 1970s with Cohen's (1972) study of negative media reactions to British mods and rockers in the 1960s. Cohen puts forward a model in which media labeling of youth subcultures as deviant causes 'amplification' of the perceived problem and ultimately elicits official reaction. In Cohen's model, the process of 'amplification,' in which the dissemination of information about the perceived 'problem' serves to affect its social reality, follows the initial press coverage.

'Moral panic' has been applied retrospectively to discourses surrounding subcultures that stretch back centuries. Pearson (1983) points to sensationalist newspaper coverage of London street gangs in the 1890s, where 'hooligans' were reported as posing a threat to social order and control, at odds with public decency, and symptomatic of a general decline in morality. This type of report has long associations with popular music, from accounts of jazz in the 1920s to reports of 'rock 'n' roll riots' from the 1950s onward. Leonard (1962), for instance, points to the way in which mediated attacks on jazz were grounded in barely concealed racism. Here, the African roots of jazz provided 'fuel for racial fears' (39), which were seen as threatening to white North American society.

Over the years, the tone and content of these media reports have been remarkably limited, displaying similarities across a number of decades and a variety of musical movements. Moreover, it has often been the music itself that has been reported as being central to a process of corruption of its audience. In this context, music is described as 'hypnotic' or 'droning,' and is perceived as destabilizing youth, transporting them out of their senses into 'zombie-like' states. For instance, a 1964 *Seattle Daily Times* review of a concert on the Beatles' first North American tour describes the music as 'loud, primitive, insistent and strongly rhythmic,' which 'releases ... the controlled, newly acquired physical impulses of the teenager' (Saibel 1964, 1).

In the language of moral panic, music is represented as threatening, in that it is perceived to incite behavior and reactions that are outside social norms. The physical descriptions used by the *Seattle Daily Times* reporter (who writes of the audience becoming 'frantic, hostile, uncontrolled, screaming, unrecognizable beings' (Saibel 1964, 1)) are almost identical to portrayals of other audiences and youth cultures, from Elvis fans in the 1950s to acid house in the 1980s. Moreover, the idea of threat implicit in many moral panics is not only physical but also ideological. For example, in Malaysia in the 1980s, the influence of Western music was represented as destabilizing notions of social cohesion and Malay national cultural identity.

It has also been noted that media exposure not only serves to fuel moral panic in the media themselves, but also is active in the creation and development of events. For instance, on the public holidays following media reports of the so-called 'mod riots' of the mid-1960s in the United Kingdom, more young people were attracted to the seaside resorts where the initial disturbances took place, thus greatly increasing the numbers attending and

the amount of 'trouble' (Cohen 1972). Hence, the relationship between subculture and media is one of symbolic interaction in which initial representations serve to influence subsequent events.

This process of 'amplification' can also be seen to influence reaction on an institutional level, affecting the actions of police, courts and government. In 1976, after sensationalist accounts of punk, local councils in the United Kingdom banned concerts by the Sex Pistols. Likewise, sensationalist reporting in the 1990s about trance music and drug culture in Israel led to a severe police crackdown on trance music being played in public places (Regev 1998). Aside from these occasional bans and stopgap measures, there have been instances where reaction to moral panic has involved legislation in which measures specifically targeting popular music have become enshrined in law. The UK government's *Criminal Justice Act* of 1994, for instance, specifically refers to music in its wording. The Act gives police and courts punitive powers to combat not just illegal 'raves,' but 'gathering[s] on land in the open air of 100 or more persons (whether or not trespassers) at which amplified music is played.' Furthermore, the Act attempts to make specific reference to dance music by categorizing music as 'sounds wholly or predominantly characterized by the emission of a succession of repetitive beats.'

However, moral panic should not be understood merely in terms of a linear process of discovery, 'amplification' and restraint. The process has become such a common strain in popular journalism that there is a multidirectional flow of symbolic information between the mass media and music and youth cultures. Thornton (1995) argues that there are no authentic, unmediated layers of subcultures that are exploited by the mass media. Rather, media coverage (both positive and negative) is vital to the life of youth subcultures, and the media participate in their 'assembly, demarcation and development' (1995, 160). Thornton makes the point that a number of people involved in the acid house scene predicted, and indeed actively courted, moral panic before it happened. Hence, 'disapproving tabloid stories [may be seen to] legitimize and authenticate youth cultures' (1995, 132).

Bibliography

Cohen, Stanley. 1972. *Folk Devils and Moral Panics: The Creation of the Mods and Rockers*. London: MacGibbon and Kee.

Leonard, Neil. 1962. *Jazz and the White Americans: The Acceptance of a New Art Form*. Chicago: University of Chicago Press.

Pearson, Geoffrey. 1983. *Hooligan: A History of Respectable Fears*. London: Macmillan.

Regev, Motti. 1998. 'Trance Music in Israel: Subculture into Art.' Paper presented at IASPM UK Conference, Liverpool.

Saibel, Bernard. 1964. 'Beatlemania Analyzed: Frightening Says Child Expert.' *Seattle Daily Times* (Saturday, 22 August): 1. (Reprinted in *Birth of Beatlemania: 1964 Historic Concert Tour of America*. Los Angeles: O'Brien Publishing Company, 1978.)

Thornton, Sarah. 1995. *Club Cultures: Music, Media and Subcultural Capital*. Cambridge: Polity Press.

ROBERT STRACHAN

Music Festivals

The popular music festival is an event of a broadly celebratory nature at which a series of musical performances takes place. It is most often held over several days in one location or at several sites within a town or region. Although a festival may encompass a range of popular musical idioms, sometimes from different parts of the world, the majority are organized around a specific genre or set of genres, or around a specific theme. The phenomenon of the specialized popular music festival was a twentieth-century creation, and thousands are now held annually around the world.

The roots of the popular music festival are diverse. Festivals organized around more traditional styles – of which there are a great many in Europe alone – owe a debt to long-established festival traditions. Usually centered on the religious calendar and with a strong local community orientation and a leading role for music, such festivals declined in number as communities came under pressure from industrialization and urbanization. In the early twentieth century, attempts began to be made to engineer revivals of this ancient tradition. In the United States, for example, Bascom Lamar Lunsford initiated the Mountain Dance and Folk Festival in Asheville, North Carolina in 1928 (Jones 1984). In many cases, these new versions of old traditions dispensed with religious associations, but in some instances they reinvented them. Writing in 1984, Robert Cantwell described the bluegrass festival as 'a camp meeting, a ritual gathering in which the warmth and solidarity of the community closes around the soul stripped and wounded in its effort to be free. Psychologically, its form is precisely that of the Baptist meeting' (253).

By contrast, the roots of the rock festival seem to lie more obviously in the practise of the popular cultural phenomenon of carnival, especially in its anti-bourgeois utopianism and its encouragement of the energies and passions suppressed by modern industrial life. Indeed, the characteristics that usually distinguish pop festivals from traditional festivals – youthful exuberance, excess, appetite and an encompassing social anxiety – could all be described as 'carnivalesque.'

The history of the music festival, however, should act as a warning against oversimplified analysis. The genteel chautauqua of nineteenth-century North America with its educational mission – accompanied by yodelers, whistlers, harmony groups and jubilee singers – might seem an unlikely forerunner of the modern rock festival. Yet, visually, it too was a city of tents, and its religious origins find an echo in its modern counterpart's search for 'earth magic.' Furthermore, even the chautauqua, with imitations springing up throughout the nation, soon became the prey of entrepreneurs. It could also be regarded as a cousin of the many folk or traditional festivals that abound in Europe and elsewhere. Some of these festivals (such as the Festival des Récollets in Privas, France) offer a range of musics from klezmer to Celtic rock, while others have a more specific focus. The annual Khamoro Festival in Prague is the largest Gypsy cultural event on the continent and a showcase for the rich traditions of the Roma. There are, on the other hand, links between a nomadic life style and the counterculture, both British and North American, that has historically animated modern rock festival culture.

At a time when Gypsies, along with Jews and homosexuals, were being demonized and murdered in Europe, the art of jazz was recruited on behalf of tolerance and democracy. After the war, some of those jazz-loving democrats attended the first international music festivals of size and importance. The Nice Jazz Festival in 1948 featured Louis Armstrong and his All Stars, while the Paris Jazz Festival in the following year brought together Sidney Bechet and Charlie Parker. Their rapport during the jam session that closed the four-day event showed how the festival setup could accommodate, even integrate, different styles of music. Later, at the Newport Jazz Festival in 1969, Miles Davis, also present on that Parisian occasion, was encouraged by playing alongside rock musicians to continue the move toward fusion jazz on which he had embarked.

Although the Beaulieu Jazz Festival began on a small scale in 1956, it was the 1958 festival, a two-day event attracting 4,000 people, that can lay claim to being the first real popular music festival in postwar Britain. In 1960, the festival was marred by violent clashes between rival groups of fans ('trads' and modernists). In this respect (riotous behavior), an element of festival culture was established for decades to come. Jazz and folk festivals in the United States likewise gave encouragement to their pop counterparts. In 1967, during the 'Summer of Love,' the Monterey International Pop Festival south of San Francisco attracted 50,000 people. Despite subsequent recriminations, the event was a complete success from a musical point of view, thus creating a demand for bigger and even better festivals. In Britain in 1969, two free concerts in Hyde Park (one featuring the Rolling Stones) were swiftly followed by Bob Dylan's performance at the spectacular Isle of Wight Festival in August, the month that also witnessed the biggest of the North American festivals – the legendary Woodstock Music and Arts Fair in upstate New York. Its sociopolitical ambitions subsumed in Abbie Hoffman's manifesto, 'Woodstock Nation,' the event has regularly been coupled with the Rolling Stones' free concert at Altamont, California as the zenith and nadir of festivals, bringing the idea of the sixties to a premature end. Morthland's (1981) description is representative: 'Altamont turned into a nightmare of drug casualties, stench from toilets and fire and food and vomit, faulty sound, and the brutal violence [inflicted by Hell's Angels acting as "security"]' (337). To set the record straight, Woodstock – three days of rain and mud, with insufficient food and inadequate sanitation – was no joy ride, although the documentary movie of 1970 contributed to Woodstock mythology by concentrating on performances and a vision of the 'love-and-peace' community. The film's huge profits, it could be said, were a melancholy reminder of the ability of promoters and large corporations to co-opt the counterculture. Resolutely white and middle-class, Woodstock's relation to Altamont could be examined more profitably in terms of class constituencies.

Festival culture in Britain, however, followed different and more enduring routes. The Cropredy Festival, predicated upon the commitment of Fairport Convention, has for two decades promoted an English musical tradition, derived from Vaughan Williams, miners' songs, Cecil Sharp's collections and postwar protest song – all supplemented by elements of rock and country music. The more aggressive and political bands of the 'new folk' movement of the 1990s, such as the Levellers, have found their natural home at the celebrated Glastonbury Festival.

Internationalism, expressed in the urge to embrace many indigenous musics, has distinguished the World of Music, Arts and Dance (WOMAD) movement since its first festival in the west of England in 1982. It has retained a countercultural role, resisting the hegemony of technology and the domination of popular music by Anglo-Saxon and African-American interests. Since 1988, its family-oriented events (there are special programs for children) have been staged on every continent and have sought to promote multiculturalism through music.

In other countries and continents, festivals have followed a similar agenda, encouraging contemporary creativity or seeking to safeguard vanishing traditions. The core of the successful MetroPop Song Festival in Manila is a songwriting competition for amateurs and professionals that has become a powerful force for the composition of new pop songs and for the introduction of emerging artists and performers. It has produced one musical and political legend in Freddie Aguilar, a singer-songwriter who appeared at the first Manila festival in the late 1970s. Subsequently, Aguilar and his lyrics became increasingly affected by social turmoil in the Philippines. In response to radio censorship, he used the platform of the festival to call on Filipinos to support peaceful, democratic change. In 1981, Aguilar was given a special achievement award at the Manila festival.

For over two decades, the Los Isleños Heritage and Cultural Fiesta in St. Bernard Parish outside New Orleans has attracted thousands of visitors by celebrating the culture of Spanish-speaking Isleños descended from Canary Islanders. It is focused on folk ballads which, written in the traditional 10-stanza *decima*, tell stories in eighteenth-century Spanish about characters ranging from cruel medieval knights to modern Delacroix Island fishermen. Ethnic food (such as *caldo*, gumbo and *jumbalayo*) is provided, and such ancient arts as shrimp-net making and decoy-duck carving are demonstrated. The music at the festival in 2001 (from Los Sagittarius and others) was predominantly, but not exclusively, Spanish in flavor. In its attention to traditions under threat (some exhibits are devoted to local Houma Indian and French crafts) and in the outreach nature of its interactive workshops, the Los Isleños Fiesta is a model of what a popular music festival could aspire to be.

It is at local festivals that musicians, while not wholly avoiding contemporary sounds, can choose from indigenous and global styles to create their own musical identity. This coexistence and integration of styles can also be achieved at more broadly based events, such as the nomadic Festival of Pacific Arts.

Many epic fiestas (festivals), notably in Asia and Latin America, constitute a rite of religious celebration while welcoming a diversity of musical approach and retaining an element of the spectacular. At the great temple festivals of southern India, trumpets and drums accompany parades of chariots and elephants. Elsewhere in the nation, snake charmers and folk theater groups provide the nonmusical entertainment.

At the World Sacred Music Festival held in Fez, Morocco's holiest city, the nature of the music guarantees the occasion's significance. Patterns of tourism, however, ensure some extramural activities such as visits to shrines and to healing hot springs, as well as seminars on cultures and civilizations. Much of the music is Islamic, with Sufi chants and drumming maintaining a recurrent sound during the festival. Moroccan and Azerbaijani contributions are also featured, although the geographical range extends further: from Pakistani chants to Western spiritual music of the Renaissance and Baroque periods. In the year 2001, the greatest impact was made by the gospel singing of the Edwin Hawkins Choir, a group with considerable festival experience whose enthusiastic, vibrant style swept away all boundaries.

Although fundamentalist Christians have for years denounced the festival at Glastonbury, in southwest England, as the work of the devil, the border between the material and the spiritual at this event has always seemed tenuous. The town's history and associations are mixed and remarkable. Its pre-Christian role was as a center of Druid learning. Later, when the town was allegedly visited by Joseph of Arimathea and by Jesus Christ, it became a place of pilgrimage and healing, but as the mythical Isle of Avalon it was also associated with the tales of King Arthur.

The first Glastonbury Festival (of popular music) at a Somerset dairy farm in 1970 was inspired by the Bath Blues Festival at Shepton Mallet. A more grandiose predecessor emerged, however: in 1914, British composer Rutland Boughton, encouraged by Elgar, Vaughan Williams and playwright George Bernard Shaw, turned his Arthurian visions of a rural semi-pagan Britain into Celtic-Wagnerian operas, and these were performed to piano accompaniment in Glastonbury's cramped Assembly Rooms for nearly a decade.

At least Boughton sought a musical language rooted in English folk song. A folkish and mystical component was evident in the two Glastonbury (or Pilton) festivals of the early 1970s. The second of these (held in 1971), which attracted an audience of 12,000, was known as the Glastonbury Fair, its centerpiece a pyramid-cum-stage built over a 'blind spring' for the absorption and release of energies. Musically, the British hippie establishment was well represented by David Bowie, Hawkwind, Quintessence, Brinsley Schwarz and Melanie.

In a general way, Glastonbury has achieved a balance between acknowledging the growth of consumerism and sustaining a countercultural agenda. The stone circle of the Sacred Space, the marketplace of alternative life styles known as the Green Fields, the circus and theater entertainments – all these testify to the continuing project of supplying a supra-musical experience that celebrates the creative, the spiritual and the humane.

Already in the 1970s, the rock festival was described as 'a thing of the past.' The attempt to revive Woodstock in 1999, it has been claimed, demonstrated a breathtaking insensitivity and greed that led inevitably to disaster. Held on an old army base near the original site, the anniversary event, priced at $150 for three days, scheduled

three hard-core heavy metal bands in succession. The resultant audience frenzy led to rape, looting, arson and, consequentially, the arrival of 700 riot police. Water was sold at $5 a bottle.

Those skeptical of or hostile toward the grand style of festival of the 1960s and 1970s have come to include considerable numbers of politically aware and ecologically concerned young people. However, the *idea* of the festival has remained vigorous, as Gwyneth Jones's science fiction novel *Bold as Love* (2001), which imagines post-devolution England becoming one single rock festival site, demonstrates. The Glastonbury Festival, physically in abeyance, has a presence on the Internet. More genial, accessible popular music festivals abound and flourish, along with newcomers such as the Big Chill in Dorset, England. Bluegrass festivals in the United States, such as the International Bluegrass Music Association's Fan Fest in Louisville, Kentucky, are devoted to musicianship and encourage mixing by old and young, on stage and off – not so much festivals as country fairs or less sanctimonious chautauquas.

Bibliography

Agostinelli, Anthony J., ed. 1977. *The Newport Jazz Festival, Rhode Island, 1954–1971: A Bibliography, Discography, and Filmography*. Providence, RI: Agostinelli.

Anderson, Jack. 1987. *The American Dance Festival*. Durham, NC: Duke University Press.

Barsamian, Jacques, and Jouffa, François. 1986. *L'Âge d'or de la rock music: Blues, Country, Rock 'n' Roll, Soul, San Francisco Sound, Underground, Hippies, Festivals*. Paris: Ramsay.

Bettelheim, Judith, ed. 1993. *Cuban Festivals: An Illustrated Anthology*. New York: Garland.

Cantwell, Robert. 1984. *Bluegrass Breakdown: The Making of the Old Southern Sound*. Urbana, IL: University of Illinois Press.

Cantwell, Robert. 1993. *Ethnomimesis: Folklife and the Representation of Culture*. Chapel Hill, NC: University of North Carolina Press.

Clarke, Michael. 1982. *The Politics of Pop Festivals*. London: Junction Books.

Cobbold, Chryssie Lytton. 1985. *Knebworth Rock Festivals*. London: Omnibus.

Davis, Martha Ellen. 1972. 'The Social Organization of a Musical Event: The Fiesta de Cruz in San Juan, Puerto Rico.' *Ethnomusicology* 16(1): 38–62.

Denselow, Robin. 1990. *When the Music's Over: The Story of Political Pop*. London: Faber.

Goldblatt, Burt. 1977. *Newport Jazz Festival: The Illustrated History*. New York: Dial Press.

Hinton, Brian. 1995. *Message to Love: The Isle of Wight*

Festival, 1968–1969–1970. Chessington: Castle Communications.

Jones, Gwyneth. 2001. *Bold as Love.* London: Victor Gollancz.

Jones, Loyal. 1984. *Minstrel of the Appalachians: The Story of Bascom Lamar Lunsford.* Boone, NC: Appalachian Consortium Press.

Laing, Dave, and Newman, Richard, eds. 1994. *Thirty Years of the Cambridge Folk Festival.* Ely: Music Maker Publications.

Landy, Elliott. 1994. *Woodstock Vision: The Spirit of a Generation.* New York: Continuum.

Makower, Joel. 1989. *Woodstock: The Oral History.* New York: Doubleday.

Monestel, Manuel. 1987. 'A Song for Peace in Central America.' *Popular Music* 6(2): 231–32.

Morthland, John. 1981. 'Rock Festivals.' In *The Rolling Stone Illustrated History of Rock and Roll*, ed. Jim Miller. London: Picador, 337.

Santelli, Robert. 1980. *Aquarius Rising: The Rock Festival Years.* New York: Dell Publishing.

Sia, Joseph J. 1970. *Woodstock '69: Summer Pop Festivals – A Photo Review.* New York: Scholastic Book Services.

Spitz, Bob. 1989. *Barefoot in Babylon: The Creation of the Woodstock Music Festival, 1969.* New York: W.W. Norton.

Von Schmidt, Eric, and Rooney, Jim. 1994 (1979). *Baby, Let Me Follow You Down: The Illustrated Story of the Cambridge Folk Years.* 2nd ed. Amherst, MA: University of Massachusetts Press.

Whisnant, David E. 1979. *Folk Festival Issues: Report from a Seminar, March 2–3, 1978, Sponsored by the National Council for the Traditional Arts.* Los Angeles: John Edwards Memorial Foundation.

Young, Jean, and Lang, Michael. 1979. *Woodstock Festival Remembered.* New York: Ballantine Books.

Filmography

Jazz on a Summer's Day, dir. Bert Stern. 1959. USA. 85 mins. Musical Performance.

Woodstock – 3 Days of Love & Music, dir. Michael Wadleigh. 1970. USA. 230 mins. Documentary. Original music by Larry Johnson, Joni Mitchell.

RALPH W. WILLETT

Myth

'Myth' is one of the most complex terms in the history of ideas, although it was coined as recently as the nineteenth century (see Williams 1983, 210–12). In common parlance, a myth is a popularly held belief that is untrue. In relation to cultural theory, however, a myth is something more complex: a set of processes that can involve speech (including the written or printed word), music, drama and images – and, in the modern world, the capa-

cities of electronic communication and the mass media – through which societies, cultures and groups make sense of the world to themselves. Simply put, a myth is 'a story by which a culture explains or understands some aspect of reality or nature' (Fiske 1990, 88).

Although all myths may in one way or another be taken to contain elements of the fictive, they also constitute a basically important component of the *constructed* realities through which societies and cultures deal with *presented* realities, including the unknown. In this sense, myths may at the same time be both 'true' and 'false.' They can be likened to metaphors in the way in which they link contrasting items (for example, concrete as against abstract, familiar and local as against unfamiliar and remote) to mediate and explain the world. Often, it is the local and familiar that is configured mythically to mediate and explain the remote and unfamiliar.

One of the best-known, if controversial, understandings of myth is provided by Lévi-Strauss in his essay 'The Structural Study of Myth' (1968, 206–31). In this analysis, Lévi-Strauss argues that each individual occurrence in a myth belongs to a particular theme. In the case of the Oedipus myth, says Lévi-Strauss, these occurrences belong to one of four themes: the overrating of blood relations; the underrating of blood relations; the denial of the autochthonous origin of people (that is, a denial of the idea that people are born from the Earth); and the persistence of the autochthonous origin of people. Thus, Oedipus marrying his mother, Jocasta, belongs to theme one, while Oedipus killing his father, Laious, belongs to theme two. As Lévi-Strauss observes, theme four is to theme three as theme one is to theme two. That is, persistence and denial are related oppositionally in the same way as underrating and overrating. In this way, 'the inability to connect two kinds of relationships is overcome (or rather replaced) by the assertion that contradictory relationships are identical inasmuch as they are both self-contradictory in a similar way' (1968, 216). Following from this, concludes Lévi-Strauss, the Oedipus myth 'has to do with the inability, for a culture which holds the belief that mankind is autochthonous ... to find a satisfactory transition between this theory and the knowledge that human beings are actually born from the union of man and woman' (1968, 216).

The term '*bricolage*' is important in understanding Lévi-Strauss's approach to myth. According to Hawkes (1977), *bricolage* 'involves a "science of the concrete" ... which, far from lacking logic, in fact carefully and precisely orders, classifies and arranges into structures the *minutiae* of the physical world ... by means of a "logic"' that is different from the abstract logic of the modern world. The structures thus derived, continues Hawkes, '"improvised" or "made-up" (these are rough translations of the process of *bricoler*) as *ad hoc* responses to an environment, then serve to establish homologies and analogies between the ordering of nature and that of society, and so satisfactorily "explain" the world and make it able to be lived in' (1977, 51). People in a 'traditional' society may think of themselves as bears or as eagles, therefore, because the analogy this evokes 'is not between social groups and natural species but between the differences which manifest themselves on the level of groups on the one hand and on that of species on the other' (Lévi-Strauss 1966, 115). As Lévi-Strauss elsewhere observes, 'to say that clan A is "descended" from the bear and that clan B is "descended" from the eagle is nothing more than a concrete and abbreviated way of stating the relationship between A and B as analogous to a relationship between species' (1969b, 100). In other words, as Hawkes concludes, 'the man does not believe he is a bear, but the bear indicates his standing and role in the community, analogously defined, as part of a pattern of "oppositions," against the standing of someone else' (1977, 53).

Since Lévi-Strauss's understanding of myth rests on the order of *abstract* relations between items that are concrete and 'bundles' of such items (as in the Oedipus myth), there seems to be considerable potential in this understanding for a similar understanding of music. As Middleton (1990) has observed,

To the extent that musical meanings have to do less with the significance of discrete sound-events than with systems of internally validated relationships between events, it seems natural to look for a 'structural semantics,' which would consider the meaning of units and parameters in terms of their relationships with other units and parameters and in terms of their positions on various 'axes' referring to binary oppositions or continua – axes such as repetition/change, quantity of variation, tonal polarity, melodic type . . . timbre . . . and so on. (222)

Middleton goes on to remark that 'there is a striking similarity between this musical model and Lévi-Strauss's theory of myth – which, in the event, Lévi-Strauss has often compared to music' (1990, 222).

Lévi-Strauss was most explicit on this 'special relationship' between myth and music in *The Raw and the Cooked*. 'Since . . . music stands in opposition to articulate speech,' he argues, 'it follows that music, which is a complete language, not reducible to speech, must be able to fulfill the same functions on its own account. Looked at in the round and in its relation to other sign systems, music is close to mythology' (1969a, 29). For Lévi-Strauss, there was a crucial difference between language on the one hand, and myth and music on the other. While language possesses both a diachronic

dimension (*parole*) and a synchronic dimension (*langue*), Lévi-Strauss argues that myth and music are diachronic and synchronic at the same time, thereby constituting a third time referent. That is, while the concrete articulation of language in actual utterances is achieved diachronically, but according to the logic of an unuttered 'deep structure' which is synchronic, the concrete articulation of myth and music involves, simultaneously, principles that are both diachronic and synchronic. In music, sound events clearly follow one another in time diachronically; yet, as Lévi-Strauss observes, 'because of the internal organization of the musical work, the act of listening to it immobilizes passing time; it catches it and enfolds it as one catches and enfolds a cloth flapping in the wind' (1969a, 16). In myth, items or bundles of items have meaning at the level of myth – and over above their meaning at the level of language alone – because of the way in which they resonate thematically with one another. This parallel between myth and music is well captured by Hawkes when he says – in drawing an analogy between myth and an orchestral score – that 'when we hear any myth being told, we only ever encounter the "orchestra score" line by line, diachronically, and we infer (or "hear") the resonances of each "bundle" as we go along, just as, to take another musical analogy, when we listen to a soloist in a jazz group we (and he) infer from his solo performance the original sequence of chords; the "tune" from which it derives, and on which it contributes a tonal commentary' (1977, 45).

However, music is not the same as myth. While it shares with myth this third time referent, it also, like language, supports and underwrites myth. Further, while language supports myth, which is always therefore, at least in part, 'linguistic,' it does not in the same sense 'support' music. For this reason, concludes Lévi-Strauss, mythology 'occupies an intermediary position between two diametrically opposed types of sign systems – musical languages on the one hand and articulate speech on the other' (1969a, 27). As Shepherd and Wicke (1997) conclude, 'through a comparison with the non-denotative medium of music, Lévi-Strauss was striving to grasp myth at a certain level in its specific character as incorporating principles of structuralism which go beyond those of myth *as linguistically manifest*' (45).

Although the sounds of music are rarely as semantically concrete in their functioning as are the sounds of language – indeed, *because* the sounds of music are rarely as semantically concrete in their functioning as are the sounds of language – music, and popular music specifically, would seem to possess enormous potential to act mythically at the abstract level evoked through the metaphoric, concrete relationality described by Lévi-Strauss. Middleton suggests one instance of this in referring to 'Philip Tagg's study of Abba's "Fernando," where an oscillation between "then" and "now," expressed through exotic/familiar, tense/relaxed contrasts, could easily be explored in "mythic" terms' (1990, 224; see Tagg 1982, 1991). However, the capacity of popular music to act in this way, to mythically respond to and deal with reality as presented – with all its contradictions and problems – must be seen as endemic to the various traditions of popular music themselves, especially when it is considered that these traditions stretch considerably beyond the musical use of sounds alone to include the entire range of language, dance, movement and images – more recently electronically mediated – at the disposal of myth. It is interesting to note in this context that Mellers (1973) thinks of the Beatles as creating a modern mythology. The essence of their achievement, he says, 'is that it is a return from literate and visual to aural and oral culture' (190).

The ability of music to act mythically in the kind of all-encompassing sense referred to by Mellers seems to find a resonance in other cultures. Reck (1977), for example, observes that 'in India . . . the universe hangs on sound. Not ordinary sound, but a cosmic vibration so massive and subtle and all-encompassing that everything seen and unseen . . . is filled with it' (7). Equally, 'to the Navaho in the American Southwest, music . . . has been an expression of harmony between man and the forces of nature' (Reck 1977, 8). In some cases, the power of music to act in this all-encompassing manner is assumed to be other-worldly in its origins, thus invoking myths to do with the origins of music. According to Reck, most people of the world say that music 'originated somewhere other than in man. It came some time far in the past from gods or other supernatural beings who, perhaps when man needed it or asked for it, perhaps even at the moment of man's creation, gave music as a gift' (1977, 8). However, this all-encompassing capacity of music is seen in another way by Attali (1985). Observing that 'Lévi-Strauss, for his part, has tried to show that music in our societies has become a substitute for myth,' Attali argues that 'music is not only a modern substitute for myth; it was present in myths in their time.' For Attali, 'music appears in myth as *an affirmation that society is possible* . . . Its order simulates the social order, and its dissonances express marginalities. *The code of music simulates the accepted rules of society*' (1985, 28–29). Whether ascribing worldly or other-worldly origins and functions to music, explanations of music as myth themselves begin to take on an aura of the mythical.

The manner in which music works as myth is likely more concrete and specific and less general than writers such as Mellers, Reck and Attali suggest. For authors such as Barthes, processes of myth are imbued with processes of power in the specific character of their operation (see Barthes 1972). Barthes argues that myths operate to shore up existing structures of power, 'naturalize' history and make the political agendas of the powerful seem unexceptional. The argument could be made that certain types of chauvinistic or nationalistic music such as national anthems can act in this way.

Similar forces can be argued to be at work within popular music history. The importance of a myth in such cases lies in its function as both reflector and determinant of an ideological position. For example, the attribution of natural rhythm to blacks has resulted in a myth that has deep resonance with the cultural and racial orthodoxy of white North America. Likewise, both the widely held belief that the rise of rock 'n' roll was linked to the rise to economic importance of the baby-boom generation and the belief (established by the British rock press) that punk rock was linked to urban, working-class protest are myths that serve the hegemonic, if not ideological, predispositions of certain classes or sections in society.

On occasion, such myths continue to be debated and to take on a life that in this respect is cyclical. In 1989, for example, Hobsbawm argued that, although it is obvious 'that jazz was not simply "born in New Orleans,"' New Orleans could nonetheless 'defend its title as the cradle of jazz against all comers, for there, and there alone, did the jazz band emerge as a mass phenomenon' (12). This version of history did not, however, go uncontested. For example, in 1997 Gioia challenged the conventional wisdom that New Orleans was 'the cradle of jazz.' Observing that 'with the passage of time, and the mythification of the role of jazz in New Orleans bordellos, it has become increasingly difficult to separate fact from fiction,' he argues that close investigation of the facts supporting 'the standard accounts [that] focus on Storyville . . . as the birthplace of jazz' casts 'more than a few doubts on this colorful lineage' (1997, 31). Three years later, in the context of a careful examination of ethnic relations in New Orleans based on criteria of *both* culture and color, Johnson (2000) argued that understanding the roots of jazz 'requires scholarly inquiry into the peculiar urban mix of late nineteenth-century New Orleans, for it was that unique mix that gave rise to the music' (249).

The important point, it can be argued, is not so much who is right and who is wrong, but what such debates reveal about the frequently delicate and complex relations that exist between reality and the fictive in myth's function of assisting people in dealing with and making sense of the world. In the light of the complex historical and cultural forces at play in such shifts of scholarship, therefore, it is pertinent to refer to writers like Lipsitz, who, in being influenced by the work of Mikhail Bakhtin, has argued for a dialogical approach to the understanding of how history functions within popular music. Following this approach, many competing histories comment on and critique the present, rather than viewing history as being either closed off or at an end. Myth plays a central role in this formulation. Lipsitz's view of myth is close to that of Burke (1989), who argues that myth 'has a symbolic meaning made up of stereotyped incidents and involving characters who are larger than life, whether they be heroes or villains' (103).

An early example of such a figure is to be found in the persona of John Henry, an African-American railroad worker who met his death during the construction of the Big Bend Tunnel on the C. & O. railroad in approximately 1873. Henry is reputed to have died after a contest between himself and a steam drill in driving spikes into the ground ('John Henry told his captain,/"A man ain't nothin' but a man,/And before I'd let that steam-drill beat me down,/I'd die with this hammer in my hand"'). However, 'John Henry did not actually die after the contest with the steam-drill. His death came later in familiar Big Bend style when a slab of rock fell from the ceiling and crushed him' (Lomax and Lomax 1975, 314). More recent and more consciously constructed examples of larger-than-life figures are to be found in the Who's *Tommy* (1969) and David Bowie's *Ziggy Stardust* (1972), both of which involve universal themes within the rock business, most importantly the myth of rock superstardom as messianism.

Some popular music performers are more 'mythogenic' than others, not simply in terms of the universal subjects they sing about, but in terms of the manner in which their manipulation of the media has *intentionally* produced falsehoods that have attained mythic proportions (for example, the mythology surrounding Bowie's and Michael Jackson's alien ancestry, or the belief that Paul McCartney is, in fact, dead). These media falsehoods are important in that they not only help to promote the artist through sensationalism, but they also create a mythic stature for him/her that is guaranteed to fascinate the public. As a result, certain mythic themes are associated with particular entertainers. As Frith has noted in his essay on rock biography (1983), most writers try to look behind the myth surrounding a rock persona to find the true essence, but, in the pop world, it is often the myth itself that has more meaning.

Involving complex relations between reality and imagination, therefore, myth and popular music intersect in a number of ways: in the manner in which music displays a special affinity with processes of myth; in the manner in which understandings of music's origins and mythical attributes may themselves take on aspects of the mythical; in the manner in which myth plays a role in popular music history; and in the manner in which various persona in popular music take on mythical dimensions. In all these types of intersection, however, one constant remains: the necessity and ability of myth as manifest through popular music and its history to help people make acceptable and workable sense of the world in which they live.

Bibliography

Attali, Jacques. 1985. *Noise: The Political Economy of Music*, trans. Brian Massumi. Minneapolis, MN: University of Minnesota Press. (Originally published as *Bruits: essai sur l'économie politique de la musique*. Paris: Presses Universitaires de France, 1977.)

Barthes, Roland. 1972. *Mythologies*, trans. Annette Lavers. New York: Hill and Wang. (Originally published as *Mythologies*. Paris: Éditions du Seuil, 1957.)

Burke, Peter. 1989. 'History as Social Memory.' In *Memory: History, Culture and the Mind*, ed. Thomas Butler. Oxford: Basil Blackwell, 97–113.

Fiske, John. 1990. *Introduction to Communication Studies*. 2nd ed. London: Routledge.

Frith, Simon. 1983. 'Essay Review: Rock Biography.' *Popular Music* 3: 271–77.

Gioia, Ted. 1997. *The History of Jazz*. New York: Oxford University Press.

Hawkes, Terence. 1977. *Structuralism and Semiotics*. London: Methuen.

Hobsbawm, Eric J. 1989. *The Jazz Scene*. New York: Pantheon Books.

Jenks, Chris, and Lorentzen, Justin J. 1997. 'The Kray Fascination.' *Theory, Culture & Society* 14(3): 87–107.

Johnson, Jerah. 2000. 'Jim Crow Laws of the 1890s and the Origins of New Orleans Jazz: Correction of an Error.' *Popular Music* 19(2): 243–51.

Lévi-Strauss, Claude. 1966. *The Savage Mind*. London: Weidenfeld & Nicolson. (Originally published as *La Pensée sauvage*. Paris: Plon, 1962.)

Lévi-Strauss, Claude. 1968. 'The Structural Study of Myth.' In Claude Lévi-Strauss, *Structural Anthropology*, trans. Claire Jacobson and Brooke Grundfest Schoepf. Harmondsworth: Penguin, 206–31. (Originally published as *Anthropologie structurale*. Paris: Plon, 1958.)

Lévi-Strauss, Claude. 1969a. *The Raw and the Cooked*, trans. John and Doreen Weightman. New York: Harper & Row. (Originally published as *Le Cru et le cuit*. Paris: Plon, 1964.)

Lévi-Strauss, Claude. 1969b. *Totemism*, trans. Rodney Needham. Harmondsworth: Penguin. (Originally published as *Le Totémisme aujourd'hui*. Paris: Presses Universitaires de France, 1962.)

Lipsitz, George. 1990. *Time Passages: Collective Memory*

and American Popular Culture. Minneapolis and London: University of Minnesota Press.

Lomax, John A., and Lomax, Alan, eds. 1975. *Folk Song: U.S.A.* New York: Plume Books.

Longhurst, Brian. 1996. *Popular Music and Society*. Cambridge: Polity.

Mellers, Wilfrid. 1973. *Twilight of the Gods: The Beatles in Retrospect*. London: Faber & Faber.

Middleton, Richard. 1990. *Studying Popular Music*. Milton Keynes: Open University Press.

Reck, David. 1977. *Music of the Whole Earth*. New York: Scribner.

Shepherd, John, and Wicke, Peter. 1997. *Music and Cultural Theory*. Cambridge: Polity Press.

Small, Christopher. 1987. *Music of the Common Tongue: Survival and Celebration in Afro-American Music*. London: John Calder.

Tagg, Philip. 1982. 'Analysing Popular Music: Theory, Method and Practice.' *Popular Music* 2: 37–67.

Tagg, Philip. 1991. *Fernando the Flute: Analysis of Musical Meaning in an Abba Mega-Hit*. Liverpool: Institute of Popular Music, University of Liverpool.

Williams, Raymond. 1983. *Keywords: A Vocabulary of Culture and Society*. Rev. ed. London: Flamingo.

Sheet Music

Handy, W.C., comp. 1922. 'John Henry Blues.' New York: Handy Brothers Music Co., Inc.

Discographical References

Bowie, David. *The Rise and Fall of Ziggy Stardust and the Spiders from Mars*. RCA-Victor SF 8287. *1972*: UK.

Who, The. *Tommy*. Track 613013/4. *1969*: UK.

Discography

Ledbetter, Huddie (Leadbelly). 'John Henry.' *Leadbelly: Complete Recorded Works, Vol. 2 (1940–1943)*. Document DOCD 5227. *1995*: Austria.

JOHN SHEPHERD and DAVID BUCKLEY

Nationalism

Introduction

The history of popular music's encounters with nationalism is long, complex and fraught. Nation-states have frequently demonstrated an awareness of the kinds of uses to which popular music can be put in the articulation of their particular idea of nation, and have just as frequently found themselves at the receiving end of its subversive, capricious effects. The branding of Britain as 'Cool Britannia' in the late 1990s and the subsequent 'de-cooling' of the Blair government, for example, are testament to the difficulty propagandists have had in appropriating popular musics to national(ist) ends. There have been numerous attempts to articulate what it

is about a certain music that helps mark out its 'national' characteristics. What is it, for example, about so-called 'Britpop' that makes it 'British' (or, rather, 'English,' since it is centered on an English northwest/southeast axis)? Commentators of broadly differing ideological locations and institutional affiliations have often been moved to search for the essential musical characteristic that marks out from the rest the 'Britishness' of, for example, Oasis, or the 'Spanishness' of a band like Mecano. If this *is* feasible – if it is really possible to determine what it is about this music that makes it British or Spanish – then it is thereby also possible to appropriate that music in order to articulate a nation's difference from others. In this view, popular music can thus be constituted as a primary means by which people attempt to mark out and legislate their cultural territory.

Yet, the difficulty many scholars (and other commentators) have had in demonstrating the veracity of these claims to music's territorializing effects is also a marker of how complex the cultural operation of music can be in any given community, from the smallest village to the largest national unit. Some have suggested (Lipsitz 1994) that the dynamics through which popular culture is utilized are framed most powerfully by the global and local dimensions, and that the nation-state has become an emptied-out shell that impacts on musical practises only in the most extreme, highly propagandized situations. Nationalism, in this view, is a loosely determined, atavistic ideological attachment to a dead or dying ideal, and popular music, ever the mudflinger it seems, is invariably a major player in its demise (see, in particular, Maróthy 1974).

Definitions

Broadly speaking, the term 'nationalism' can be said to embrace those ideologies that place particular emphasis on an intense identification with a 'nation' (whether this be a politically extant nation-state or an imagined ideal nation). It is the doctrine according to which a person's nation – and his/her political, social and ideological allegiance to that nation – is the determining agency in the construction of that person's identity. Perhaps one of the most enduring and persuasive characterizations of nationalism is that formulated by Gellner (1983), in which nationalism invariably constitutes an ideological response to a perceived mismatch between the 'reality' of the political state and an 'imagined' ideal nation.

As Anderson (1991) has suggested, a nation, the particular conception of which is inevitably the primary determiner of nationalist ideology, constitutes a kind of 'imagined' community. This community imagines itself in a particular manner: its members engage in a confident imagining of allegiances, which are based on the supposition of a commonality among all compatriots – a commonality that no member can ever test exhaustively. The supposition is based on a kind of 'faith.' Crucial to this conception of the nation is its reliance on the rise of print culture: nationalist appropriations of localized musical traditions, for example, depended heavily on the circulation of the cultural products of these local traditions in print. Folk and urban song collectors like Cecil Sharp in England, František Bartoš in Moravia and Bohemia, and Béla Bartók in Romania and Hungary, articulated this tendency, prevalent in European nationalisms in particular, to want to administer a national culture from a 'gathered-up' central resource and to redistribute localized cultural products in a generalized national idiom to the local communities that fashioned them.

Histories

Nationalism as a political ideology has a long history, especially in Europe. Anderson's emphasis on print culture suggests that the conditions for the incubation of nationalism existed as early as the sixteenth century. However, it seems clear that modern nationalism as a loosely defined cluster of ideologies was nurtured by the Enlightenment, in which an emphasis on the desirability of the general education of the populace set firmly in place the mechanisms for the dissemination of national(ist) literatures and national(ist) cultures. It was in the nineteenth century in particular, then, that nationalism emerged as a dominant ideology and was fostered by the notion that citizens of a nation share an almost mystical adherence to the collective *Volk*, a notion frequently attributed to Johann Gottfried von Herder (1744–1803). Herderian nationalism is founded on this essentially romantic conception of the nation as collective project and has remained a dominant strand of nationalist ideologies.

Many forms of popular music practise have been implicated in Herderian nationalist debates. The rise of urban song in the nineteenth century, for example, was also characterized by its almost immediate absorption into state censorship apparatus in England, France, Germany and the United States. Another example, the formation of the music hall repertoire in the latter half of the nineteenth century in Britain and the United States, serves as a useful illustration of some of the ways in which nation-states use popular musics for their own propagandist purposes. By contrast, the construction of the urban *chanson* in France, and the rise of the *flamenquistas nuevas* in Spain in the first decades of the twentieth century are both indicators of a growing popular fascination with indigenous musics as markers of a shared national tradition. The rise in popularity of *Arabesk* in Turkey in the 1950s, banned from public broadcast, shows how non-indigenous (in this case, Arabic) musics can be appropriated to counter-hegemonic yet nationalist ends (Stokes 1992). In postwar Serbia, the emergence of neofolk and the subsequent popularity of turbofolk among late-urban Serbian nationalists (the 'peasant urbanites,' as sociologist Andrei Simić (1973) famously dubbed them) showed how a 'national' musical style can be formed from a range of musical sources such as Bulgarian turbofolk, dance music, traditional folk song and so on. In recent decades, the rise of *flamencos jóvenes* (also termed *nuevo flamenco*) is an indication of how traditional regional styles (such as flamenco's *cante jondo*, *canto intermedio* and *cante chico*) can be hybridized with other 'world' musics to produce a rich and fluid national musical style, which is nonetheless, unlike turbofolk, preferred by the liberal 'global' youth of Spain.

Drawing on Bourdieu's notion of 'habitus,' 'the history incarnated in bodies, in the form of that system of enduring dispositions' (1990, 190) and the 'correction' of that notion by Lash and Urry (1993), Regev (1997) has shown some of the ways in which national identities are often simultaneously embraced and contested in the 'trans-cultural' practises of popular music. He characterizes this tendency as a core practise of what he terms 'reflexive communities' (127). These communities co-opt the means given to them (the cultural field into which they are 'thrown') in order to construct a proactive stylistic hybridity (Regev cites highlife, pop-*rai*, *bhangra*-rock, *jit* and various forms of rap, among others, as examples) that forms an aesthetic site in which new critical identities are forged in opposition to older more 'conservative' identities. The challenge to the 'traditional' ethnic-national authority that such identities invariably represent, a challenge to the fathers' generation, is nonetheless a challenge that is fundamentally located *within* that community, and forms part of its national 'narrative.' This is particularly true of communities where the 'meanings' of imported rock and pop styles are fiercely contested.

Many of the 'new' musical nationalisms that have emerged in the last 100 years are articulations of a postcolonial predicament. In the developing world, and in parts of post-Soviet Central and Eastern Europe, rapid cultural fragmentation – an increasing tendency toward cultural hybridization – is framed by debates in which pressing (re-)negotiations of national identity after the colonial (or Soviet) predicament dominate. For Spivak (1994), the postcolonial predicament is one in which the colonizing West has already constructed for itself an image of the former colonies as the silent, consumable, available, conquerable Other (the 'subaltern'). The colonized cultures are thereby forced, in the aftermath of (often rapid) withdrawal, to negotiate an identity for themselves, which both rejects the colonization and simultaneously must embrace the trauma of that colonization. Spivak has famously focused this negotiation on a core epistemological question: 'Can the subaltern speak? What must the elite do to watch out for the continuing construction of the subaltern?' It is a predicament '[c]onfronted by the ferocious standardizing benevolence of most US and Western European human-scientific radicalism (recognition by assimilation)' (1994, 90).

Nationalist articulations of popular musics in the developing world are thus often supported by national governments; yet, this kind of 'official' sanctioning of national popular cultures is rarely about saving older (pre-colonial) indigenous traditions. In Ghana and Nigeria in the 1950s, for example, the popular dance form highlife, combining indigenous African forms with black American and other Western forms, became embroiled in the intense national rivalries between the two countries, and highlife became a site of discourse about national allegiance without any recourse to a 'musical' argument: nationalist debates seemed to center on the relative efficacies of the two musical infrastructures, and not on the musical products 'themselves' (Collins 1992; Sackey 1996). In the Morocco of the 1970s, bands like Nass El-Ghiwan and Jil Jilala helped form a national popular style which, because of its fusing of indigenous and Western rock influences, was seen as capable of transcending the tribal and racial differences that had characterized earlier musical traditions – the traditions of the old colonial power utilized to smooth out local difference. In Algeria, the fate of many pop-*rai* singers, such as Cheb Hasni, at the hands of the governing FLN party helped form a radicalized Islamic-nationalist articulation of this Algerian-Western hybrid among expatriate communities in France. Moroccan communities in Spain have also constructed their own expatriate *rai* traditions, especially in the *barrios bajos* of Barcelona. The Palestinian singer Reem Yousef Kelani, famous for her interpretation of the Arab form *maqamaat*, was born in Manchester, educated in Kuwait and now lives in London. Her work as an ethnographer, collecting old Palestinian songs from, and interviewing, older refugees in Lebanon, marks her out as a sophisticated exemplar of a diasporic musical tradition being re-founded or conserved after the trauma of the Palestinian dispersal.

Nationalism and Popular Music Studies

The field of popular music studies in the Anglo-American tradition is dominated by two ideological orientations, neither of which has dealt altogether constructively with nationalism. The first, essentially Marxist in orientation, has tended to view the nation-state as an antiquated bourgeois construction, and scholars of this tradition have found it difficult to track the ideological fluidity of nationalist sentiments and their implication in popular music practises (Lomax 1978; Maróthy 1974; Porter 1993; Krims 2000). The second, essentially a liberal tradition, has tended to view the nation-state as a sovereign but simply pragmatic unit, and scholars of this tradition seek (admittedly often with a critical edge) to reduce national sentiment in popular music to an array of beguiling and seductive differences, available for consumption in the global market (Letts 2000; Wiggins 1996; Aubert 1996).

A third (now minority) tradition, largely 'conservative,' but also drawing on conservationist and green ideologies, seeks to wrench 'national' (and 'regional') musical traditions from the steady advance of a perceived global erosion of difference (Ricros 1993; Matović 1995).

Except in the third tradition, theorizations of national identity and nationalist practise have often been eclipsed by, on the one hand, the ethnographic tendency to study musical practises in the local context and, on the other, by theorizations of globalization and so-called 'late' capitalism that seem to all but obliterate the operational efficacy of national units. This tendency to eclipse debates on nationalism and the nation-state is clearly a symptom of the globalizing tendency of Anglo-American scholarship. Only outside the Anglo-American scholarly hegemony (Castro 1997; Steingress 1997; Otero Garabis 1998; Erlmann 1999) and in a handful of some recent studies within the Anglo-American tradition touched by other traditions (Radano and Bohlman 2000; Askew 1997; Shabazz 1999; Mitchell 1994) have scholars sought to engage constructively with the kinds of cultural practise that characterize nationalist allegiances.

The reasons for this avoidance of nation and national identity in the study of world musics are complex. In seeking to articulate the 'national' dimension in music from, for example, Bosnia and Herzegovina in the late 1960s, scholars are faced with an extraordinarily complex problem. The folk revival saw the emergence of so-called *novokomponovana narodna muzika* (literally, 'newly composed folk music'), which synthesized urban and rural forms and constructed a newly national form quite unlike anything that had come from Bosnia's rural indigenous musical traditions. Similar developments in Bulgaria in the 1970s led to the growing popularity of the hybrid *svatbarska muzika* ('wedding music') and drew on a wide range of popular and folk styles from Macedonia,

Hungary, Serbia and Romania, but it is nonetheless articulated by Bulgarians as authentically 'Bulgarian.' How are both idioms to be linked with a national identity if it so candidly abandons its own musical traditions? What are the political and ideological processes at work that facilitate this kind of rapid appropriation to nationalist ends of non-indigenous musics?

Similar examples abound, demonstrating that the relationship between 'purely musical' characteristics and national sentiment is extraordinarily slippery. Clearly, then, the role of national identity and nationalist ideologies in the formation and articulation of a musical practise is open-ended and, since popular music has long been associated with political dissent, the nation-state has consistently demonstrated its determination to seek out and procure for itself a stake in the management of the possible deployments of 'its' popular musics. Similarly, popular musics have been used 'from the ground up' as sites for populist and popular critiques of the 'mismatch' that often occurs between political state and idealized nation.

Bibliography

Anderson, Benedict. 1991 (1983). *Imagined Communities: Reflections on the Origin and Spread of Nationalism*. Rev. ed. London: Verso.

Askew, Kelly Michelle. 1997. *Performing the Nation: Swahili Musical Performance and the Production of Tanzanian National Culture*. Ph.D. thesis, Harvard University.

Aubert, Laurent, ed. 1996. *Cahiers de musiques traditionnelles 9: Nouveaux Enjeux* [Books of Traditional Musics 9: New Stakes]. Geneva: Ateliers d'ethnomusicologie.

Bourdieu, Pierre. 1990. *The Logic of Practice*, trans. Richard Nice. Stanford, CA: Stanford University Press.

Castro, Paulo Ferreira de. 1997. 'Nacionalismo musical ou os equivocos da portugalidade' [Musical Nationalism, or the Ambiguities of Portugueseness]. In *Portugal e o mundo: O encontro de culturas na música* [Portugal and the World: The Encounter of Cultures in Music], ed. Salwa el-Shawan Castelo-Branco, trans. Ivan Moody. Lisbon: Dom Quixote, 155–62, 163–70.

Collins, John. 1989. 'The Early History of West African Highlife Music.' *Popular Music* 8(3) (October): 221–30.

Collins, John. 1992. *West African Pop Roots*. Rev. ed. Philadelphia: Temple University Press. (First published London: Foulsham, 1985.)

Erlmann, Veit. 1999. *Music, Modernity, and the Global Imagination: South Africa and the West*. New York: Oxford University Press.

Frith, Simon. 1992. 'The Industrialization of Popular Music.' In *Popular Music and Communication*, ed. James Lull. Newbury Park, CA: Sage, 49–74.

Garrido Rodriguez, Manuel. 1996. 'O nacionalismo e a música tradicional [Nationalism and Traditional Music]. *Anuario da gaita* 11: 16–17.

Gellner, Ernest. 1983. *Nations and Nationalism*. Oxford: Blackwell.

Krims, Adam. 2000. *Rap Music and the Poetics of Identity*. Cambridge: Cambridge University Press.

Lash, Scott, and Urry, John. 1993. *Economies of Signs and Space*. London: Sage Publications.

Letts, Richard. 2000. 'Some Effects of Globalisation on Music.' *Resonance* 29: 4–8.

Lipsitz, George. 1994. *Dangerous Crossroads: Popular Music, Postmodernism, and the Poetics of Place*. London: Verso.

Lomax, Alan. 1978. *Folk Song Style and Culture*. New Brunswick, NJ: Transaction Books.

Maróthy, János. 1974. *Music and the Bourgeois, Music and the Proletarian*. Budapest: Akadémiai Kiadó.

Matović, Ana. 1995. 'Uticaj srpskog pozorista na ocuvanje i prenosenje narodnih melodija' [The Role of the Serbian Theater in the Preservation and Transmission of Traditional Melodies]. In *Srpska Akademija Nauka i Umetnosti, Muzikoloski Institut* [Serbian Academy of Arts and Sciences, Musicological Institute: Papers 1995]. Belgrade: Srpska Akademija Nauka i Umetnosti, Muzikoloski Institut, 155–65.

Middleton, Richard. 1990. *Studying Popular Music*. Milton Keynes: Open University Press.

Mitchell, Timothy. 1994. *Flamenco Deep Song*. New Haven, CT: Yale University Press.

Otero Garabis, Juan. 1998. *Naciones rítmicas: La construcción del imaginario nacional en la música popular y la literatura del Caribe Hispano* [Rhythmic Nations: The Construction of the National Imaginary in Popular Music and Literature of the Spanish-Speaking Caribbean]. Ph.D. thesis, Harvard University.

Porter, James. 1993. 'Convergence, Divergence, and Dialectic in Folksong Paradigms.' *The Journal of American Folklore* 106(1): 61–98.

Radano, Ronald, and Bohlman, Philip V., eds. 2000. *Music and the Racial Imagination*. Chicago: University of Chicago Press.

Regev, Motti. 1997. 'Rock Aesthetics and Musics of the World.' *Theory, Culture and Society* 14(3): 125–42.

Ricros, Andre. 1993. 'Estrategias en la Comunidad Europea sobre el estudio y la recuperación del patrimonio musical tradicional y popular' [Strategies in the European Community for the Study and Preservation of Popular and Traditional Musical Heritage]. In *La promoción de los patrimonios musicales populares y tradicionales en Europa* [The Promotion of Europe's Popular and Traditional Musical Heritage]. Madrid: Centro de

Documentación Musical, Instituto Nacional de las Artes Escenicas y de la Música, 31–41.

Sackey, Chrys Kwesi. 1996. *Highlife: Entwicklung und Stilformen ghanäischer Gegenwartsmusik* [Highlife: Development and Stylistic Forms of Present-Day Ghanaian Music]. Münster: Mainzer Beiträge zur Afrikaforschung.

Shabazz, David L. 1999. *Public Enemy Number One: A Research Study of Rap Music, Culture, and Black Nationalism in America*. Clinton, SC: Awesome Records.

Simić, Andrei. 1973. *The Peasant Urbanites: A Study of Rural-Urban Mobility in Serbia*. New York and London: Seminar Press.

Spivak, Gayatri Chakravorty. 1994. 'Can the Subaltern Speak?' In *Colonial Discourse and Post-Colonial Theory: A Reader*, ed. Patrick Williams and Laura Chrisman. New York: Columbia University Press, 66–111.

Steingress, Gerhard. 1997. 'Romantische Wahlverwandtschaften und nationale Glückseligkeiten: Ein Versuch uber musikalische Beruhrungen von spanischer Zarzuela, Wiener Operette und andalusischem Cante flamenco' [Romantic Affinities and National Blessings: The Spanish Zarzuela, Viennese Operetta, Andalusian Flamenco, and Their Musical Interrelationships]. In *Das Land des Glucks: Österreich und seine Operetten* [The Land of Happiness: Austria and Her Operettas]. Klagenfurt: Hermagoras, 180–206.

Stokes, Martin. 1992. *The Arabesk Debate: Music and Musicians in Modern Turkey*. New York and Oxford: Oxford University Press.

Wiggins, Trevor. 1996. 'Globalisation: L'Afrique occidentale dans le monde ou le monde en Afrique occidentale' [Globalization: Western Africa in the World or the World in Western Africa]. In *Cahiers de musiques traditionnelles 9: Nouveaux Enjeux* [Books of Traditional Musics 9: New Stakes], ed. Laurent Aubert. Geneva: Ateliers d'ethnomusicologie, 189–200.

Discography

African Highlife. Fontana MGF-27519. *1967*: UK.

Balkanska duša Valentin Valdes. Payner 9602121. *1996*: Bulgaria.

Jil Jilala. *Chamaa*. BUDA Musique 50586-2. n.d.: France.

Khaled, Cheb. *Khaled*. Barclay 511 815 2. *1992*: France.

Melodija. *Bogat beden*. Payner 9604130. *1996*: Bulgaria.

Nass El-Ghiwan. *Chansons de Nass El-Ghiwan*. BUDA Musique 824672. n.d.: France.

Popular Turkish Folk Songs. ARC 1598. *2000*: UK.

The Young Flamencos/Los Jóvenes Flamencos. Hannibal HNCD-1370. *1991*: USA.

IAN BIDDLE

Nostalgia

Derived from the Greek *nostis*, or 'return,' and *algos*, or 'pain,' nostalgia has been identified since the late seventeenth century as nostomania, philopatridaglia or, more simply, as homesickness – a form of melancholy associated with detachment from one's home or country. An eighteenth-century diagnosis of melancholia among Swiss migrants who had left their Alpine homes in search of work established the recognition of nostalgia as a medical condition. Since then, it has become a more generalized 'passion for return' or, in the words of the Italian poet Niccolo Tommasseo, 'the noble privilege of poor nations.'

Although there has been little research on the subject, it would appear that songs of longing and of regret for the loss of home-life are common to societies of every period and in many parts of the world. The subject of nostalgia played a significant part in the popular song traditions of China, as in the laments of soldiers during the expansionist period of the Han dynasty. Two millennia later, nostalgia remains as an important theme of and motivation for song in the *huaynos* of Peru, the *saudade* of Brazil, the *bhaoaia* of Bengal, the *csángós* of Hungary, the *fados* of Portugal and the complex Arab-Hebraic-Gypsy tradition of *cante jondo* in Spain, the *enka* ballads of Japan and the *iscathamiya* of Zulu migrant workers in South Africa. In Western Europe and the United States, yearning for 'home' in some or all of the associations noted above is frequently to be found in popular song of the nineteenth and twentieth centuries. For instance, it is characteristic of numerous Irish songs, and of much of the country and old-time repertoires.

If there is a common thread binding these song traditions that are expressive of nostalgia, it is that the singers are from cultures far removed from their countries of origin, through either expulsion, exile, migration or diaspora, although it is to be noted that it is not a theme common in blues and African-American song. It is, however, a feature of songs that sentimentalized the African-American condition in the United States, such as Stephen Foster's 'The Old Folks at Home.' Nostalgia in songs may be the product of deeply felt emotions of separation and loss, but it is also frequently sentimental in character. While its persistence in a 'new' nation may appear anomalous, the sense of identity gained from reflection on past experience and the 'old countree,' and the uncertainty and disruption created through continual westward migration may, in part, account for its popularity. Such songs as 'Do They Miss Me at Home?' by Mrs. S.M. Grannis, with words by Carolina A. Mason, were reflective of the emotional pull which found early, and highly successful, expression in Sir Henry Bishop's 'Home, Sweet Home' of 1823, with words by the American lyricist John Howard Payne.

The century-long vogue for nostalgic songs in Anglophone countries was largely inspired by the 10-volume collection of *Irish Melodies* compiled by Thomas Moore and published in London and Dublin, in instalments, between 1808 and 1834, and with only a year's delay, in Philadelphia. The range of songs was considerable, and many reflected the themes of 'nostalgia for youth, home, parents, old friends, lost innocence and happiness' (Hamm 1979, 182). Among the most popular of songs published during the period were the compositions of Henry Russell, including 'Woodman, Spare That Tree' of 1837, with lyrics by George P. Morris, and 'The Old Arm Chair' (1840), for which Eliza Cook wrote the words. Over the years, thousands of songs found a place in what Arthur J. Lamb termed, in his hit song of 1902, 'The Mansion of Aching Hearts.'

Apart from songs that expressed nostalgic sentiments, which continued to flourish in the first half of the twentieth century, there were many that were featured in stage shows, which were themselves nostalgic in their recollection or evocation of a past period, or 'golden age.' Instances from World War II include *For Me and My Gal* (1942), with Gene Kelly and Judy Garland, which, curiously, was based on a story set in World War I. Garland was required to go back to the turn of the century for *Meet Me in St. Louis*, while the show that set the pattern for a new generation of musical plays, *Oklahoma!*, was set in the Territory of four decades before. While the shows depicted in their settings, their costumes and their action an affinity with earlier periods, there was nostalgia, too, for the musical successes of the past, and the manner of their delivery. This was evident in the 1970s with the resuscitation of *The Desert Song* and *No, No, Nanette*, first shown on Broadway in 1925, and groping even further back with a revival of the 1915 show, *Very Good, Eddie*.

If the world of entertainment was nostalgic for its own past, there was also a deep nostalgia in the general public for songs that represented the values associated with a former age, recalled with affection if not accuracy. The sing-along appeal of Harry Dacre's 'Daisy Bell' of 1892, and 'If You Were the Only Girl in the World' by Nat D. Ayer and Clifford Grey, popularized by Rudy Vallee in the 1930s, was matched only by the lilt and key of such songs. Many such sing-along nostalgic songs were set to waltz time, which could bring together Gussie Lord Davis's 1880s song, 'Irene, Goodnight,' popularized half a century later by the black songster Leadbelly, and Eily Beadell's and Neil Tollerton's pastiche hit of the 1940s, 'Cruising Down the River.'

The variety of nostalgic songs and their different genres does not suggest a single common element among them, nor any clear indication of what makes them successful beyond their capacity to inspire an affect in the listener which resonates in memories and emotions, although it is important to note that nostalgia as often as not constitutes the psychological dimension of the 'hook' in sentimental ballads as disparate as 'A Bird in a Gilded Cage' (1900) and 'Yesterday' (1965). Few were as wide-reaching in their appeal as Hoagy Carmichael's 'Star Dust,' composed in 1929 with lyrics by Mitchell Parish. It sold 2 million copies and was 'recorded over five hundred times in forty-six arrangements and translated into forty languages' (Ewen 1977, 270). Apart from songs that express nostalgia, and nostalgic re-creation through the songs of musical shows, there is also a strong vein in popular music of nostalgia for its own earlier phases or distinct genres. So the devotees of jazz seek to re-create it through simulations, such as the 1980s show *One Mo' Time*, or by playing in the idioms of nascent 'Dixieland' or 'traditional jazz.' Similarly, early phases of rock music are recalled in films such as *Grease*, or imitated live to maturing audiences. The appeal of 'look-alike' and 'sound-alike' performers in the style of Elvis Presley is worldwide, and there is considerable nostalgia evident in the identification with artists that inspires karaoke. In spite of its multiplicity of genres and its industry-driven quest for 'new' sounds, popular music thrives on nostalgia, not only for content but also for its own past.

Bibliography

Disher, Maurice Wilson. 1955. *Victorian Song: From Dive to Drawing Room*. London: Phoenix House.

Erlmann, Veit. 1996. *Nightsong: Performance, Power and Practice in South Africa*. Chicago and London: University of Chicago Press.

Ewen, David. 1977. *All the Years of Popular Music*. Englewood Cliffs, NJ: Prentice-Hall.

Hamm, Charles. 1979. *Yesterdays: Popular Song in America*. New York and London: W.W. Norton and Company.

McCann, Willis. 1941. 'Nostalgia: A Review of the Literature.' *Psychological Bulletin* 38: 165–82.

Moore, Thomas, comp. 1808–34. *Irish Melodies*. 10 vols. London and Dublin: J. Power and W. Power.

Spaeth, Sigmund. 1927. *Weep Some More, My Lady*. Garden City, NY: Doubleday, Page and Company.

Turner, Michael R., ed. 1972. *The Parlour Song Book: A Casquet of Musical Gems*. London: Michael Joseph.

Yano, Christine. 1995. *Shaping of Tears of a Nation: An Ethnography of Emotion in Japanese Popular Song*. Hawaii: University of Hawaii Press.

Sheet Music

Ayer, Nat D., comp., and Grey, Clifford, lyr. 1916. 'If You Were the Only Girl in the World.' London: Feldman.

Beadell, Eily, and Tollerton, Neil, comps. and lyrs. 1945.

'Cruising Down the River.' London: Cinephone Music Co.

Bishop, Henry, comp., and Payne, John Howard, lyr. 1823. 'Home, Sweet Home.' London: Goulding, D'Almaine, Potter & Co.

Carmichael, Hoagy, comp., and Parish, Mitchell, lyr. 1929. 'Star Dust.' New York: Mills Music.

Dacre, Harry, comp. and lyr. 1892. 'Daisy Bell.' New York: T.B. Harms.

Davis, Gussie Lord, comp. and lyr. 1886. 'Irene, Goodnight.' Cincinnati: George Propheter.

Foster, Stephen, comp. and lyr. 1851. 'The Old Folks at Home.' New York: Firth, Pond & Co.

Grannis, S.M., comp., and Mason, Carolina A., lyr. 1852. 'Do They Miss Me at Home?' Boston, MA: Ditson.

Russell, Henry, comp., and Cook, Eliza, lyr. 1840. 'The Old Arm Chair.' Boston, MA: Geo P. Reed.

Russell, Henry, comp., and Morris, George P., lyr. 1837. 'Woodman, Spare That Tree.' New York: Firth, Hall.

Von Tilzer, Harry, comp., and Lamb, Arthur J., lyr. 1900. 'A Bird in a Gilded Cage.' New York: Shapiro, Bernstein and Von Tilzer.

Von Tilzer, Harry, comp., and Lamb, Arthur J., lyr. 1902. 'The Mansion of Aching Hearts.' New York: Harry Von Tilzer Pub. Co.

Discographical Reference

Beatles, The. 'Yesterday.' Capitol 5498. *1965*: USA.

Filmography

Grease, dir. Randal Kleiser. 1978. USA. 110 mins. Musical Romance. Original music by Warren Casey, John Farrar, Barry Gibb, Jim Jacobs, Bill Oakes, J. Scott Simon, Louis St. Louis.

PAUL OLIVER

Obscenity

Introduction

Obscenity in popular music – and its surrounding discourses – is less often a concept employed by practitioners than it is a moral judgment used by critics to validate some types of music and devalue others.

Discussions surrounding the issue of obscenity in popular music are rendered problematic by the lack of any clear definition of the concept of 'obscenity.' Nearly all debates concerning obscenity begin with what can loosely be termed a moral outrage – a response from a group of offended individuals. From there, the debates often move into the spheres of politics and the law. Ensuing legal battles often codify what were previously only vague notions. For example, the 1868 British case of *R. v. Hicklin* offered what was to become the first legal definition of the term 'obscene,' one that would influence all later debates, moral, legal and otherwise. Those

items that had a tendency to 'deprave and corrupt those whose minds are open to such immoral influences, and into whose hands a publication of this sort may fall' were classified as 'obscene' by the judge (Cloonan 1995; see also Davis 1991).

This definition has stood as a rough legal precedent in the United Kingdom, as well as in certain other legal and legislative jurisdictions that have attempted to grapple with the issue. However, these other jurisdictions tend to apply the concept in ways appropriate to their own constitutional, legal and legislative cultures. In the United States, for example, account must be taken of the First Amendment of the Constitution, which guarantees absolute freedom of speech, and which has been limited legally only by the necessities of dealing with 'clear and present danger.' While this still has not protected artists from being tried for peddling products considered to be obscene, artistic freedom has typically triumphed in the US courts.

Obscenity and Popular Music

Where popular music is concerned, the UK definition of obscenity was made manifest in the 1959 *Obscene Publications Act*, which has been used by the government in attempts both successful (Anti-Nowhere League) and unsuccessful (NWA) to limit musical expression (Cloonan 1995). Even in the United States, the First Amendment has not entirely prevented musicians from being prosecuted under obscenity laws. Most notable was the case occasioned by *As Nasty As They Wanna Be*, the album from Florida rappers 2 Live Crew (*Skyywalker Records v. Navarro* (1990) and *Luke Records Inc. v. Navarro* (1992)).

However, claims of obscenity in popular music have not been limited to the sphere of recorded sound alone. Artists have been prohibited from performing certain songs live because the songs' lyrics were considered obscene or because the songs themselves were considered likely to 'deprave and corrupt.' Such prohibition has provided a means of taking a public stance against material considered offensive without the necessity of initiating legal action to actually have an album banned. For example, *The Ed Sullivan Show* took such measures, requiring the Rolling Stones to change the lyrics of their hit 'Let's Spend the Night Together' to 'Let's Spend Some Time Together' when they appeared on the television show in 1967. Similar concerns about the possibly obscene character of lyrics had surfaced during the early years of jazz, when lyrics were attacked as 'vulgar and sensual,' as 'very suggestive, thinly veiling immoral ideas' and as 'unspeakable' (Leonard 1962, 35).

The visual representation of certain themes in live performance has also been considered offensive. In 1956, for example, Elvis Presley was shown only from the waist up when he performed on *The Ed Sullivan Show* so that viewers would not be shocked by his pelvic gyrations. Where stage shows are concerned, Jim Morrison of the Doors was arrested in Miami in 1969 and eventually convicted for 'lewd and lascivious behavior in public by exposing his private parts and by simulating masturbation and oral copulation' during a concert there (Martin and Segrave 1993). The British/French rock band Rockbitch, which, in keeping with its free-love ideology, has featured live sex acts along with its music during concerts, has been subject to effective censorship of its live show in Germany and The Netherlands, among other places (Sharkey 1998).

Outside the realm of live performance, bands have been prosecuted for graphic artwork considered to be obscene that has appeared on or within the covers of their albums. In 1986, for example, Jello Biafra of the Dead Kennedys was charged with violating section 313.1 ('Distribution of Harmful Materials to Minors') of the California state penal code for a poster included in the band's album *Frankenchrist*. The poster contained a painting by Swiss artist H.R. Giger featuring a dozen or so sets of interlocked male and female genitalia. The prosecution was abandoned after a court battle. Stores have also refused to stock albums with covers they consider obscene. In 1988, for example, retailers refused to stock Jane's Addiction debut album for Warner Brothers, *Nothing's Shocking*, because of its cover, which depicted naked Siamese twins strapped to an electric chair. In the same year, retailers also refused to stock Prince's album *Lovesexy*, because it featured a nude photograph of the artist. Covers have also been changed because of complaints from retailers. In 1984, PolyGram changed the cover of the Scorpions' album *Love at First Sting*, following a complaint by Wal-Mart. The cover showed a partially nude couple locked in an embrace. However, even changing the cover cannot always offset objections. In 1988, for example, protesters in Santa Cruz, California picketed retailers carrying Guns N' Roses' debut album *Appetite for Destruction*, even though cover art thought to have been offensive had been replaced.

Most material is deemed obscene in the world of popular music as elsewhere by reference to conventional attitudes toward sex, drugs and violence. However, the concept of obscenity has been expanded to include other forms of behavior considered offensive. The idea of 'political obscenity' – that the creation of cultural products solely for the purpose of political opposition is wrong and unacceptable – was employed in Germany during World War II, as well as in various states of the former Eastern bloc, Argentina and China (Ramet 1994; Garofalo 1992; Willett 1989). However, even supposedly democratic nations have attempted to legislate against what amounts to 'political obscenity.' In the United States, law enforcement agencies fought vigorously against NWA for their 'Fuck Tha Police' (1989) and against Ice-T's thrash metal band Body Count for its 'Cop Killer' (1992). Similar anti-police sentiments landed the French rappers NTM in court in 1996, although they escaped with a suspended sentence. In the United Kingdom, the Sex Pistols' 1977 anti-royalist version of 'God Save the Queen' was banned in 'every conceivable outlet,' in the words of their press officer, but it still managed to top the British pop charts.

Like the Sex Pistols, many artists tagged as obscene have used the label to their ultimate benefit, exploiting its presumed link to things 'countercultural.' When Madonna's video accompanying 'Justify My Love' was banned by MTV in 1990, Warner Brothers Records released it as a retail item, selling directly to the public with considerable success. When the Parents Music Resource Center, led by Tipper Gore, carried out its very public campaigns against certain kinds of popular music in the 1980s, the eventual outcome was the 'voluntary' imposition of 'parental advisory' labels on CDs. However, it has been widely believed that such labeling actually enhanced the appeal of such music for young people.

A crucial question is that of the degree to which materials considered obscene in popular music are likely to affect or corrupt young people. Certain highly publicized cases have placed the blame for the actions of fans on the music of particular groups – for example, Judas Priest was blamed for teenage suicide and 2Pac for the murder of a police officer (Walser 1993; see also Fornäs 1998). Yet, many studies have found the impact of lyrics on fans to be negligible (McDonald 1988). Furthermore, much popular music considered obscene has come from genres that have been regarded at various times as existing at the margins of popular culture – for example, rap, metal, punk and reggae. As a consequence, such music has frequently had to be sought out, and could therefore be argued to be diminished in its impact.

Until more coherent connections are established between cultural products considered obscene and potential damage to the fabric of society, charges of obscenity in relation to popular music and other cultural products will remain unsubstantiated. Moreover, even when such charges are made, proponents of free speech will likely raise a political voice as loud as the moral one it argues against.

Bibliography

Cloonan, Martin. 1995. '"I Fought the Law": Popular Music and British Obscenity Law.' *Popular Music* 14(3) (October): 349–63.

Cloonan, Martin. 1996. *Banned!: Censorship of Popular Music in Britain, 1967–92*. Aldershot: Arena.

Davis, Tracy. 1991. 'The Moral Sense of the Majorities: Indecency and Vigilance in Late-Victorian Music Halls.' *Popular Music* 10(1): 39–52.

Fornäs, Johan. 1998. 'Limits of Musical Freedom.' In *Popular Music: Intercultural Interpretations*, ed. Tôru Mitsui. Kanazawa, Japan: Graduate Program in Music, Kanazawa University, 185–90.

Garofalo, Reebee, ed. 1992. *Rockin' the Boat: Mass Music and Mass Movements*. Boston, MA: South End Press.

Leonard, Neil. 1962. *Jazz and the White Americans: The Acceptance of a New Art Form*. Chicago: University of Chicago Press.

Martin, Linda, and Segrave, Kerry. 1993. *Anti-Rock: The Opposition to Rock 'n' Roll*. New York: Da Capo.

McDonald, James. 1988. 'Censoring Rock Lyrics: A Historical Analysis of the Debate.' *Youth and Society* 19(3) (March): 294–313.

The Obscenity Report. 1971. London: Olympia Press.

Parents Music Resource Center. 1990. *Let's Talk About Rock Music*. Arlington, VA: PMRC.

Pattison, Robert. 1987. *The Triumph of Vulgarity: Rock Music in the Mirror of Romanticism*. New York: Oxford University Press.

Ramet, Sabrina Petra, ed. 1994. *Rocking the State: Rock Music and Politics in Eastern Europe and Russia*. Boulder, CO: Westview Press.

Sharkey, Alix. 1998. 'This Is Not An Act.' *Dazed & Confused* (November): 66–72.

Walser, Robert. 1993. *Running with the Devil: Power, Gender and Madness in Heavy Metal Music*. Hanover and London: Wesleyan University Press.

Willett, Ralph. 1989. 'Hot Swing and the Dissolute Life: Youth, Style and Popular Music in Europe 1939–49.' *Popular Music* 8(2): 157–63.

Discographical References

Body Count. 'Cop Killer.' *Body Count*. Warner Brothers 45139. *1992*: USA.

Dead Kennedys. *Frankenchrist*. Alternative Tentacles 45. *1985*: USA.

Guns N' Roses. *Appetite for Destruction*. Geffen 125. *1987*: USA.

Jane's Addiction. *Nothing's Shocking*. Warner Brothers 25727. *1988*: USA.

Madonna. 'Justify My Love.' Sire 19485. *1990*: USA.

NWA. 'Fuck Tha Police.' *Straight Outta Compton*. Fourth & Broadway BRLP 534. *1989*: USA.

Prince. *Lovesexy*. Paisley Park 25720. *1988*: USA.

Rolling Stones, The. 'Let's Spend the Night Together'/'Ruby Tuesday.' Decca F 12546. *1967*: UK.

Scorpions, The. *Love at First Sting*. Harvest 2400071. *1984*: USA.

Sex Pistols, The. 'God Save the Queen.' Virgin VS 181. *1977*: UK.

2 Live Crew. *As Nasty As They Wanna Be*. Luke 91651-2. *1989*: USA.

Visual Recording

Madonna. 1990. 'Justify My Love.' Warner Brothers WAR38224 (video).

JON CARAMANICA

Photography

For more than a century, popular music has been saturated with photographic images of performers and performances. Photographs have been crucial to the fixing of star images and to journalistic profiles, interviews and reviews. Pictures have also played a part in the practise of ethnomusicology, recording the visual dimension of musical practises just as tape-recording captured the audio aspect.

Soon after the invention of photography in 1840, photographs were being used to portray or advertise English music halls, although line drawings were still widely used. Daguerreotypes of singers who were to endorse new songs also began to appear on sheet music on both sides of the Atlantic, although it was felt that this was a less than prestigious way to decorate a sheet music cover. Sometimes, drawings and photographs were combined, as in the 1865 sheet music cover for the song 'Limerick Races,' which shows a full-length photograph of the music hall owner and singer Sam Collins superimposed on a drawing of a racecourse scene (Mander and Mitchenson 1974, 34). However, by the 1890s, Tin Pan Alley ballads were being illustrated by photographs alone. The cover of the million-selling 'After the Ball,' by Charles K. Harris, contained a shot of a society ballroom (Hamm 1979, 286).

Photography has played an important role in the documentation of the early history of various forms of popular music. The illustrations in such works as Oliver's *The Story of the Blues* (1969) – itself the product of an exhibition – and the jazz histories of Ramsey (1960), Keepnews and Grauer (1981), and Rose and Souchon (1984) both support and extend the textual material. Significant collections of historically valuable photographs are held in museums and libraries, including the Library of Congress in Washington, DC.

Phonography and photography have been closely linked since the earliest days of recorded sound, perhaps because of what Corbett (1990) calls 'the direct attempt to disavow the cleavage of image/sound and to restore the visual to the disembodied voice' (85). Photographs of singers appeared on the exterior of boxes containing cylinders produced by the Edison company, and many record companies printed pictures of stars on the paper sleeves of 78 rpm discs. This practise was carried over into the era of 45 rpm and 33 rpm records, with the widespread use of what Edge (1991) has called 'prosaic identification' shots of performers on sleeves (92).

There have also been less predictable uses of photography in sleeve design. The German ECM label and the US Windham Hill label used nature photographs to illustrate sleeves, while more imaginative portrait shots – some posed, some from performances – were taken by Francis Wolff for the US jazz label Blue Note Records in the 1950s and 1960s. In the swinging London of the mid-1960s, the fashionable photographers of the era – including David Bailey (who did six Rolling Stones album cover shots), Robert Freeman (the Beatles), Michael Cooper (who photographed the covers for *Sergeant Pepper's Lonely Hearts Club Band* and *Their Satanic Majesties Request*), society photographer Norman Parkinson and Terence Donovan – composed images of the equally fashionable pop star elite. A similar process occurred in the United States, where *Vogue*'s Richard Avedon took the cover picture for Simon and Garfunkel's *Bookends*, Irving Penn took a studio portrait of Big Brother and the Holding Company with the Grateful Dead, and fashion photographer Herb Ritts directed the video to accompany Madonna's 'Cherish.'

The publicity shot, commissioned by record companies or managers and supplied to magazines and newspapers, is an associated area of music photography. These pictures are generally shot in the photographer's studio, with lighting and composition from the publicity material used by Hollywood film companies. Ochs (1984) contains numerous examples of publicity shots taken in the 1940s and 1950s by New York studio photographer James Kriegsmann.

The first specialist music photographers emerged in the 1950s, notably in the worlds of jazz and folk music. Many sought to embody the essence of an individual's style in a candid performance shot. An analysis of the work of black New York photographer Roy DeCarava claims that, for him, 'jazz represented the audio equivalent to photography. In sets, musicians pushed themselves to improvise, lending an immediacy to the performance' (Rachleff 1997, 16). Other significant photographers of jazz musicians and performances include Herman Leonard and Valerie (Val) Wilmer.

Photographers are key witnesses to the ephemeral world of performance. Despite advances in movie technology, films of concerts are still rare, and pictures such as those by Alfred Wertheimer of the early Elvis, by David Gahr of the North American folk revival or by William Claxton of the west coast jazz scene of the 1950s are vital historical and aesthetic artifacts. The same is true of pictures taken by song collectors, and researchers have used the camera in tandem with their notebooks and tape recorders. Writing in 1976, Steven Feld asserted that 'photographic and film equipment have become a basic part of the toolkit taken to the field by ethnomusicologists' (297). Perhaps surprisingly, few musicians have been photographers, or at least few have published photographs. Among the exceptions are the jazz bassist Milt Hinton, and Andy Summers, guitarist with the Police.

Until the 1960s, specialist popular music photographers were rare. The British photographer Harry Hammond was apprenticed to a society portrait photographer in the 1930s and, for a period in the late 1940s and early 1950s, was the only professional involved in music photography. The growth of the UK music industry and the phenomenal success of the Beatles made music photography a profession; according to Hammond, there were 200 photographers at every Beatles concert (Hogan 1990). These photographers took advantage of advances in technology. While in the 1950s, according to Hammond, 'it was not unusual to cover a two-hour concert with half-a-dozen dark slide glass plates and a few flashbulbs' (Hogan 1990, 8), the advent of lightweight cameras, zoom and telephoto lenses and advances in processing improved the quality of music photography.

The most important outlets for music photographers' work were specialist music magazines. In Britain, by the early 1960s the first staff photographers were being hired by music publications – Barrie Wentzell at *Melody Maker* was among the earliest – although most photographers still operated on a freelance basis. In the rock field, the advent of *Rolling Stone* magazine gave stylish photography a new prominence. The most renowned of rock photographers is Annie Leibovitz, who was for some years the chief photographer of *Rolling Stone* (Draper 1990). Leibovitz's canvas was the front cover of the magazine – a spot much sought after by musicians and their publicists. A selection of early rock photography can be found in Hirsch (1972).

Some rock photographers became especially associated with a particular artist – for example, Robert Freeman and the Beatles (Burn 1997), Gered Mankowitz and the early Rolling Stones (Hammond and Mankowitz 1990 – this book recounts Mankowitz's methods for shooting group portraits of the Rolling Stones, the Yardbirds and Traffic), Adrian Boot and Bob Marley (Boot and Salewicz 1995), David Nutter and Elton John (Nutter and Taupin 1977), and Ray Stevenson and the Sex Pistols (Stevenson 1978).

During the twentieth century, the primary medium for the dissemination of popular music photography was print, occasionally augmented by T-shirts and other media. In the 1990s, images were included on music CD-ROMs and Web sites devoted to popular music, garnering additional audiences and markets for photographers of popular music and its practitioners.

Bibliography

Avedon, Richard. 1994. *Evidence, 1944–1994*. New York: Random House, Eastman Kodak Professional Imaging in association with the Whitney Museum of American Art.

Bailey, David, and Evans, Peter. 1969. *Goodbye Baby & Amen: A Saraband for the Sixties*. London: Condé Nast.

Boot, Adrian, and Salewicz, Chris. 1995. *Bob Marley: Songs of Freedom*. London: Bloomsbury.

Burn, Gordon. 1997. 'Introduction.' In *The End of Innocence: Photographs from the Decades That Defined Pop*. Zurich: Scalo, 6–12.

Claxton, William. 1992. *Jazz West Coast: Artwork of Pacific Jazz Records*. Tokyo: Bijutsu Shuppan-Sha.

Claxton, William. 1996. *Jazz*. San Francisco: Chronicle Books.

Cooper, Michael, and Southern, Terry. 1993. *The Early Stones: Legendary Photographs of a Band in the Making, 1963–1973*. London: Secker & Warburg.

Corbett, John. 1990. 'Free, Single and Disengaged: Listening Pleasure and the Popular Music Object.' *October* 54 (Fall): 79–101.

Draper, Robert. 1990. *The Rolling Stone Story*. Edinburgh: Mainstream.

Edge, Kevin. 1991. *The Art of Selling Songs: Graphics for the Music Business, 1690–1990*. London: Futures Publications.

Feld, Steven. 1976. 'Ethnomusicology and Visual Communication.' *Ethnomusicology* 20(2): 293–325.

Foresta, Merry A., and Stapp, William F. 1990. *Irving Penn Master Images: The Collections of the National Museum of American Art and the National Portrait Gallery*. Washington, DC: Smithsonian Institution Press.

Gahr, David. 1968. *The Face of Folk Music*. New York: Citadel Press.

Hamm, Charles. 1979. *Yesterdays: Popular Song in America*. New York: W.W. Norton.

Hammond, Harry, and Mankowitz, Gered. 1990. *Pop Star Portraits of the 50s, 60s, 70s and 80s*. London: Treasure Press.

Hinton, Milt, and Berger, David G. 1988. *Bass Line: The Stories and Photographs of Milt Hinton*. Philadelphia: Temple University Press.

Hirsch, Abby. 1972. *The Photography of Rock*. Indianapolis, IN: Bobbs-Merrill.

Hogan, Peter. 1990. 'Introduction.' In Harry Hammond and Gered Mankowitz, *Pop Star Portraits of the 50s, 60s, 70s and 80s*. London: Treasure Press, 5–10.

Keepnews, Orrin, and Grauer, Bill, Jr. 1981. *A Pictorial History of Jazz: People and Places from New Orleans to the Sixties*. Rev. ed. New York: Bonanza Books.

Leonard, Herman. 1989. *The Eye of Jazz*. London: Viking.

Mander, Raymond, and Mitchenson, Joe. 1974. *The British Music Hall*. London: Gentry Books.

Nutter, David, and Taupin, Bernie. 1977. *Elton: It's a Little Bit Funny*. London: Penguin.

Ochs, Michael. 1984. *Rock Archives: A Photographic Journey Through the First Two Decades of Rock & Roll*. Poole: Blandford Press.

Oliver, Paul. 1969. *The Story of the Blues*. London: Barrie & Rockliff.

Rachleff, Melissa. 1997. 'The Sounds He Saw: The Photography of Roy DeCarava.' *Afterimage* (January-February): 15–17.

Ramsey, Frederic. 1960. *Been Here and Gone*. New Brunswick, NJ: Rutgers University Press.

Rose, Al, and Souchon, Edmond. 1984. *New Orleans Jazz: A Family Album*. Rev. ed. Baton Rouge, LA: Louisiana State University Press.

Stevenson, Ray. 1978. *The Sex Pistols File*. London: Omnibus.

Stewart, Charles. 1986. *Chuck Stewart's Jazz Files: Photographs*. New York: Graphic Society.

Summers, Andy. 1983. *Throb*. New York: Quill.

Walker, John A. 1987. *Cross-Overs: Art into Pop/Pop into Art*. London: Comedia/Methuen.

Wertheimer, Alfred. 1979. *Elvis '56: In the Beginning*. New York: Collier Books.

Wilmer, Valerie. 1976. *The Face of Black Music: Photographs*. New York: Da Capo Press.

Sheet Music

Grantham, William, comp., and Wilton, J.H., lyr. 1860. 'Limerick Races: Comic Irish Song.' London: n.p.

Harris, Charles K., comp. and lyr. 1892. 'After the Ball.' Milwaukee, WI: Charles K. Harris.

Discographical References

Beatles, The. *Sergeant Pepper's Lonely Hearts Club Band*. Parlophone PCS 7027. *1967*: UK.

Madonna. 'Cherish.' Sire 22883. *1989*: USA.

Rolling Stones, The. *Their Satanic Majesties Request*. Decca TXS 103. *1967*: UK.

Simon and Garfunkel. *Bookends*. CBS 63101. *1968*: USA.

Visual Recording

Madonna. 1989. 'Cherish.' Warner Brothers Records (video).

DAVE LAING

Politics

The relationship between politics and popular music has taken many guises, but there are two that stand out. The first is the way in which states and other authorities have used music in pursuit of their goals. Music has provided a device for engineering particular political ends and, as such, it has been censored out of fear or sponsored as propaganda. The USSR provided a classic example of this (Starr 1983). The second is even more obvious: the way in which popular music has been a vehicle for expressing political ideas and values, most typically to give voice to protest. But while these two forms of popular music's relationship with politics – music as political control, music as political resistance – are the most familiar, they are neither as preeminent nor as important as they seem.

Political Expression

Popular music has long been associated with political dissent. Numerous writers have documented the social satires and political complaints that are scattered through many musical genres (Denselow 1989; Palmer 1988; Pring-Mill 1987; Ramet 1994). In the West, writers and performers like Woody Guthrie and Bob Dylan stand as icons of this tradition (Denisoff 1971). Equally, African-American blues and gospel have been vehicles for social protest. From the songs born of slavery to the soul sounds associated with the civil rights movement to rap, music has given voice to the sense of grievance and injustice resulting from racial discrimination (Ellison 1989; Oliver 1960; Rose 1994; Ward 1998).

The ubiquity of the music of protest and political opinion can be misleading. It should not be mistaken for either a permanent or a natural feature of popular music. It needs, for example, to be understood in relation to the way in which popular music has been used to support established politicians and parties. Presidents Roosevelt (see Russell 1970) and Mobutu, among others, have been praised in popular song. The fact that music can be used in this way, as praise as well as protest, is indicative of the way in which its political role is constructed rather than preordained.

In any genre, the association with politics has a history. The blues, for example, have more than once provided a vehicle for the discussion of conventional politics (Russell 1970), and have also served the ends of aspiring politicians. In 1908, for instance, W.C. Handy was requested to write a campaign song to help elect E.H. 'Boss' Crump mayor of Memphis. Originally entitled 'Mr. Crump,' 'Memphis Blues' was W.C. Handy's first big success as a songwriter. In the case of country music, the association between musicians and politics has been no less intimate. Malone (1985), for example, recounts the way in which Texan Wilbert Lee 'Pappy' O'Daniel 'rode to fame and political success through his association with . . . popular musicians' (161), organizing a group called the Hillbilly Boys to pro-

mote him, and in 1941 winning a seat in the US Senate. Better known is the case of the Louisiana country musician Jimmie Davis, who in 1944 and 1946 won terms as the governor of that state 'by emulating the Texan politician's campaign tactics' (Malone 1985, 162). The theme song for both campaigns was his own composition, 'You Are My Sunshine.'

By contrast, Western pop of the 1950s rarely, if ever, acknowledged a world beyond the intimacies and anxieties of adolescent romance. In the mid- to late 1960s, this changed, as groups on the US west coast and in the United Kingdom (especially the Rolling Stones and the Beatles), taking their lead from Bob Dylan, began to incorporate references to revolution and political protest into their songs. In the case of John Lennon, this was to lead to intimate association with the Left and to records that dealt almost exclusively with politics (for example, *Sometime in New York City*). And just as Dylan, who himself drew on the example of Guthrie and US folk of the 1920s, had established a place for politics in 1960s pop, so this music was to provide, with the politicization of reggae, a platform for punk's politics in the 1970s (as, for instance, with the Clash's 1979 album, *London Calling*).

Within musical genres, then, the place of politics was partly a consequence of influences and examples, but it was also about industries and audiences, about the ways in which stars and markets were constituted to encourage and legitimate political comment. This is revealed in a comparison between genres. It is noticeable that musical genres differ both in the extent to which 'politics' (in the traditional sense of the word) constitutes an acceptable subject matter and in the type of politics that is incorporated. The differences between hip-hop and country offer an example. Who is being addressed and how they are addressed are different. The 'we' in country constructs one collective identity, while in hip-hop it is another. The subject matter too varies: divorce and marriage (and the politics they imply) may be legitimate for country, but not for hip-hop. The modes of address, the subject matter, the market, all of these vary between genres and thereby constrain, enable and shape political discourse.

Reading Politics

The politics of music does not exist only in the explicit expression of values and views. Music may speak politically without any deliberate intention of doing so. Although there are many artists who address sexual politics more or less directly, there is also a sexual politics of the subtext. Reynolds and Press (1995), for instance, offer radical reinterpretations of the music of the Stones and the Clash in terms of their sexual politics: the bid for freedom as the escape from responsibility in relationships. The surface politics of individualist liberalism disguises a more conservative politics of misogyny. Reynolds and Press deconstruct their texts to reveal this other politics.

Much of this reading, and rereading, of the politics of music tends to concentrate on lyrics, and these are, of course, important sources of meaning. But they are not the only source. The formal lyrical content can be rendered ambiguous or transformed by the act of singing. Words that on the page convey one meaning can be given quite another slant when sung. This can be illustrated by the different ways in which the same song is sung (Sid Vicious and Frank Sinatra singing 'My Way'), by the way in which a singer's inflections may be heard to work against the *apparent* logic of the lyrics (Tammy Wynette's rendering of 'Stand By Your Man,' which is marked as much by pained regret as by blissful celebration (see, for example, Frith and McRobbie 1979, 4, and Shuker 1994, 138–40)) or by the way in which context transforms meaning (protesting Soweto schoolchildren singing 'We Don't Want No Education' from Pink Floyd's *The Wall*).

But meaning, and hence politics, need not reside exclusively with voice and lyrics. Sound too can be involved. McClary (1991), for instance, offers a feminist reading of Madonna's music, drawing attention to the way in which the musical structure serves as a critique of the social structure by refusing convention. Dance music, in which the human voice and lyrics play a minimal or even nonexistent role, might appear to be devoid of the capacity to signify politically. Tagg (1994) has, however, argued that the musical structures and conventions of dance can be read as evocative of a collectivist politics.

Social Movements and Political Identity

Just as music's political meaning is not contained only in its lyrics, so its engagement with politics is not confined to its content. Context matters too. Here, music's political power is comprised of its capacity to unite (and differentiate) people. The most dramatic form of this has been the harnessing of music to mass movements. In the case of, for instance, the civil rights or peace movements, music was grafted onto a preexisting political formation. But with later examples, such as Live Aid or Rock Against Racism, musicians (and their industry) were instrumental in constituting the movement itself.

Music has thus been integral to many social movements. Peace, civil rights and anti-racist movements have all depended on music and musicians to articulate, and bond people to, the common goal (Garofalo 1992). One of the more dramatic examples of music fulfilling this role is offered in accounts of the collapse of the Berlin Wall and the reunification of Germany (Wicke 1992). In Northern Ireland, the group U2 played a small, but potentially significant, part in expediting the peace process. Not only did the group help to make it fashionable to care about peace, but its members also used their own celebrity status to insist that politicians from both sides of the divide appear on stage together – something they were notoriously reluctant to do.

In addition, popular music has often been connected to nationalism and nationalist movements (see Regev 1997). Whether or not it is possible to claim 'authenticity' for a music, in the sense that it belongs to a specific, discrete nation or people, music is a powerful component in the constitution of national and collective identity. In 1998, the Algerian singer Lounes Matoub was murdered by his political enemies. His death prompted riots and a funeral attended by thousands. Matoub was a leader of the campaign to rehabilitate the Berber heritage in Algeria. His songs evoked or helped to forge a common inheritance and to provide a focus for the Berber movement. Music has often been used in such a way, to articulate a displaced or lost identity. It has been a constant presence throughout the conflict in Northern Ireland – in the bands of the Orangemen and in the rebel songs of Sinn Fein and the IRA. It has played its part, too, in the recovery of identity following the breakup of the Soviet Union and Eastern Europe (Slobin 1996).

Music's capacity to function in this way is attributable to the potential it provides for collective, active consumption, for the experience of singing and dancing together; but it also works through its capacity to organize memory and imagination, to constitute places and times (Lipsitz 1994). Indeed, some attempts to explain the rise and survival of social movements have drawn attention to the central role played by music (Eyerman and Jamison 1998).

Political Economy

There has been a natural tendency to view music's relationship to politics in terms of its external manifestations – the songs and the social movements. But politics is also a permanent feature of the internal organization of music. Political issues and values arise from the daily practise of making music.

The focus here has typically been on notions of incorporation and selling out (Chapple and Garofalo 1977; Harker 1980). The music industry is seen as predatory and conservative. It commercializes trends and fashions that exist outside the marketplace and, in this process of commercialization, it smooths over the disruptive, awkward originality of the artists, rendering them politically inconsequential. In trying to resist this kind of process, musicians have chosen to make music in ways that stand in opposition to the conventions of commercialism. The Art Ensemble of Chicago, a jazz collective, provides one example of this strategy, the rock band Henry Cow another (Cutler 1985). The politics of commercial resistance is also captured in the distinction between types of record company: the major and the independent. The former represents bureaucratic standardization, the latter democratic difference. The corollary of this industrial divide is the contrast made between the musician who refuses to compromise and the musician who capitulates to the lure of the industry's money. The language of this politics has remained part of the rhetoric that frames the discussion of popular music, especially in the British weekly music publications *New Musical Express* and *Melody Maker*, and in accounts of the rise (and 'fall') of dance culture. A similar logic can be detected in claims about the fate of R&B or pop generally (George 1988).

A revisionist literature has emerged that challenges these assumptions. This focuses on the pervasiveness of commercial considerations throughout the history of popular music (Goodman 1997). As such, there was no 'golden age.' Equally, emphasis on the political distinction between the major and the independent overlooked the extent to which the independents were, in fact, *dependent* on the majors; indeed, it was the majors that could afford to take the risks, while their rivals were forced, by financial exigency, to operate conservatively.

But, while the simple dichotomies between the 'commercial' and the 'artistic,' between the 'authentic' and the 'synthetic,' between the major and the independent, may have become blurred, it does not follow that political questions are irrelevant. Late twentieth-century work on the record industry (Hesmondhalgh 1997; Negus 1992) reveals the ways in which company practise can be understood politically, not simply as calculations of the bottom line, but as the acting out of principles and judgments.

Censorship and Sponsorship

The potential political power of music has been reflected, however distortedly, in the censorship practised by nation- and local states. Regimes vary in the degree to which they have censored and what they have censored, but, whatever form their actions have taken, they have had the effect of politicizing the meaning, performance and consumption of music. They have, insofar as the censorship has worked, denied access to certain forms of expression and the identities and values that may be constituted by them. And, insofar as the censorship has failed and the music has continued to be made and to circulate, the state has invested these acts with a meaning that they might not otherwise articulate. As

Grossberg (1992) suggests, any piece of music or performance does not in and of itself contain a political meaning. Its meaning is acquired by a variety of mediating processes, of which the reaction of the state is but one.

As an example, the Parents Music Resource Center, with its call for the control of records and videos, acted to designate very diverse musics (from that of Kiss to that of John Denver) as equally dangerous to the political order. In the same way, the *Criminal Justice Act* in the United Kingdom was introduced to curb raves, investing events that otherwise evinced a minimal political consciousness with a considerable political significance.

This relationship between censor and the censored helps to establish the political meaning of music. The politics of the music does not exist independently of the state, but through it. Thornton (1995) draws attention to the way in which a similar process works in the constitution of cultural capital in the reaction to 'moral panics.' The identity of musical culture is parasitic on the reaction of the state.

This kind of political involvement, and its impact on music, represents a dramatic form of a more mundane reality: the way in which national and local state policies impact on the creation, distribution and consumption of music. Concern about the 'cultural imperialism' of the global music industry has drawn attention to the ways in which national and local states manage and mediate the activities of musical production. From the imposition of quotas to the generation of subsidies, states may affect whether indigenous music fails or flourishes. These interventions form part of a larger continuum, along which are mapped such issues as copyright law, education curriculum and broadcasting policy, all of which have an impact on popular music. The point is that the mix of policies, the balance of interests and political ideologies are factors that help to shape a country's or a region's music (Malm and Wallis 1992).

Symbolic Politics

The fact that political processes have these consequences does not mean they constitute part of politicians' conscious deliberations. Indeed, one of the variations between states is the degree to which cultural policy includes or excludes popular music (Bennett et al. 1993). But what has become increasingly apparent to politicians is the symbolic potential of popular music. At one level, music is used and exploited to represent countries – either as a measure of their economic achievements or as a symbol of their identity. At another level, music is harnessed to the packaging of politicians. Pop stars are used to convey a sense of fashionableness or hipness to politicians and their parties. While the result may be a series of tacky or ill-judged photo opportunities, the process is revealing of the relationship between popular music and politics. What the music represents for the politician is a 'people.' Both musicians and politicians trade in popularity – the creation of an affective community. And, as traditional forms of political communication are reconstituted within the political economy of the new mass media technologies, so politicians find themselves needing to engage with the repertoire of techniques and gestures of popular culture.

Conclusion

The relationship between politics and popular music is conducted in many ways in many different contexts. It exists in the language and style of musical expression; it is articulated in the form and identity of social and nationalist movements; it is negotiated within the political economy of the industry, and is contained in the policies implemented by nation- and local states; and, finally, it finds expression in political communication. While there are many dimensions to the relationship, they do not exist in discrete realms. The capacity of musicians to act as representatives of political causes is itself dependent on developments in the music industry's political economy.

Bibliography

Bennett, Tony, et al., eds. 1993. *Rock and Popular Music: Politics, Policies, Institutions*. London: Routledge.

Chapple, Steve, and Garofalo, Reebee. 1977. *Rock 'n' Roll Is Here to Pay: The History and Politics of the Music Industry*. Chicago: Nelson-Hall.

Cutler, Chris. 1985. *File Under Popular*. London: November Books.

Denisoff, R. Serge. 1971. *A Great Day Coming: Folk Music and the American Left*. Urbana, IL: University of Illinois Press.

Denselow, Robin. 1989. *When the Music's Over: The Story of Political Pop*. London: Faber & Faber.

Ellison, Mary. 1989. *Lyrical Protest: Black Music's Struggle Against Discrimination*. New York: Praeger.

Eyerman, Ron, and Jamison, Andrew. 1998. *Music and Social Movements*. Cambridge: Cambridge University Press.

Frith, Simon, and McRobbie, Angela. 1979. 'Rock and Sexuality.' *Screen Education* 29: 3–19.

Garofalo, Reebee, ed. 1992. *Rockin' the Boat: Mass Music and Mass Movements*. Boston, MA: South End Press.

George, Nelson. 1988. *The Death of Rhythm and Blues*. New York: Pantheon.

Goodman, Fred. 1997. *The Mansion on the Hill: Dylan, Young, Geffen, Springsteen, and the Head-On Collision of Rock and Commerce*. New York: Times Books.

Grossberg, Lawrence. 1992. *We Gotta Get Out of This Place: Popular Conservatism and Postmodern Culture*. London: Routledge.

Harker, Dave. 1980. *One for the Money: Politics and Popular Song*. London: Hutchinson.

Hesmondhalgh, David. 1997. 'Post-Punk's Attempt to Democratise the Music Industry: The Success and Failure of Rough Trade.' *Popular Music* 16(3): 255–74.

Lipsitz, George. 1994. *Dangerous Crossroads: Popular Music, Postmodernism and the Poetics of Place*. London: Verso.

Malm, Krister, and Wallis, Roger. 1992. *Media Policy and Music Activity*. London and New York: Routledge.

Malone, Bill C. 1985 (1968). *Country Music U.S.A.* Rev. ed. Austin, TX: University of Texas Press.

McClary, Susan. 1991. *Feminine Endings: Music, Gender, and Sexuality*. Minneapolis, MN: University of Minnesota Press.

Negus, Keith. 1992. *Producing Pop: Culture and Conflict in the Popular Music Industry*. London: Edward Arnold.

Oliver, Paul. 1960. *The Meaning of the Blues*. New York: Collier Books.

Orman, John. 1984. *The Politics of Rock Music*. Chicago: Nelson-Hall.

Palmer, Roy. 1988. *The Sound of History: Songs and Social Comment*. New York: Oxford University Press.

Pring-Mill, Robert. 1987. 'The Role of Revolutionary Song: A Nicaraguan Assessment.' *Popular Music* 6(2): 179–89.

Ramet, Sabrina Petra, ed. 1994. *Rocking the State: Rock Music and Politics in Eastern Europe and Russia*. Boulder, CO: Westview Press.

Regev, Motti. 1997. 'Rock Aesthetics and Musics of the World.' *Theory, Culture and Society* 14(3): 125–42.

Reynolds, Simon, and Press, Joy. 1995. *The Sex Revolts: Gender, Rebellion, and Rock 'n' Roll*. Cambridge, MA: Harvard University Press.

Rose, Tricia. 1994. *Black Noise: Rap Music and Black Culture in Contemporary America*. Hanover, NH: University Press of New England.

Russell, Tony. 1970. *Blacks, Whites and Blues*. London: Studio Vista.

Shuker, Roy. 1994. *Understanding Popular Music*. London: Routledge.

Slobin, Mark, ed. 1996. *Retuning Culture: Musical Changes in Central and Eastern Europe*. Durham, NC: Duke University Press.

Starr, Frederick S. 1983. *Red and Hot: The Fate of Jazz in the Soviet Union, 1917–1980*. New York: Oxford University Press.

Tagg, Philip. 1994. 'From Refrain to Rave: The Decline of Figure and the Rise of Ground.' *Popular Music* 13(2): 209–22.

Thornton, Sarah. 1995. *Club Cultures: Music, Media and Subcultural Capital*. Cambridge: Polity Press.

Ward, Brian. 1998. *Just My Soul Responding: Rhythm and Blues, Black Consciousness and Race Relations*. London: UCL Press.

Wicke, Peter. 1992. '"The Times They Are A-Changin'": Rock Music and Political Change in East Germany.' In *Rockin' the Boat: Mass Music and Mass Movements*, ed. Reebee Garofalo. Boston, MA: South End Press, 81–92.

Sheet Music

Davis, Jimmie, and Mitchell, Charles, comps. and lyrs. 1940. 'You Are My Sunshine.' New York: Peer International.

Handy, W.C., comp., and Norton, George A., lyr. 1913. 'Memphis Blues.' New York: Theron C. Bennett Co.

Discographical References

Clash, The. *London Calling*. Epic 36328. *1979*: UK.

Davis, Jimmie. 'You Are My Sunshine.' Decca 5813. 1940: USA. Reissue: Davis, Jimmie. 'You Are My Sunshine.' *You Are My Sunshine: 1937–1946*. Bear Family 16216. *1998*: Germany.

Lennon, John. *Sometime in New York City*. Apple PCSP 716. *1972*: UK.

Pink Floyd. *The Wall*. Harvest SHDW 411. *1979*: UK.

Sex Pistols, The. 'No One Is Innocent'/'My Way.' Virgin VS 220. *1978*: UK.

Sinatra, Frank. 'My Way.' Reprise 0817. *1969*: USA.

W.C. Handy Orchestra, The. 'Memphis Blues.' OKeh 4896. 1923: USA. Reissue: W.C. Handy Orchestra, The. 'Memphis Blues.' *Father of the Blues*. Blues Foundation of Memphis DRG SL-5192. 1923–62: USA.

Wynette, Tammy. 'Stand By Your Man.' Epic 10398. *1968*: USA.

Discography

Dylan, Bob. *The Freewheelin' Bob Dylan*. Columbia 8786. *1963*: USA.

Guthrie, Woody. *This Land Is Your Land: The Asch Recordings, Vol. 1*. Smithsonian/Folkways 40100. *1997*: USA.

JOHN STREET

Popularity

The definition of 'popularity' (Latin *populus* meaning 'the people'; *popularis* meaning 'of, belonging to or involving the whole people or a majority of it') is the quality or fact of being popular, that is, being liked, favored or approved by someone, some people or people in general.

Despite the apparent precision of this definition, the term 'popularity' has a broad spectrum of meanings, depending on the historical and sociocultural contexts in which it is being used. The term can also be employed for purposes of legitimation or denigration. In English usage, a distinction needs to be drawn between popularity and 'the popular.' As a key concept for musical thinking and cultural studies, the latter has been used in opposition to 'art' and 'folk.' Like other labels and oppositions (for example, the ancient Roman trichotomy of *musica mundana*, *humana* and *instrumentalis*, or the dualism of black and white music), these three have been created to defend or establish cultural identity or hegemony rather than to analyze it. As Shepherd (1985) has shown, the combining of 'popular' and 'music' into a single phrase has been widely assumed to result in a label denoting a definable entity, but such a label is actually a 'putative category of music whose existence might only be established with the greatest difficulty' (95). Middleton (1990) makes no attempt to fence in 'popular music' with a rigid definition, instead advocating that it be located as an 'active tendency' within the ever-changing musical field (7).

The concept of popularity is not used to draw the same antitheses. It would be possible, for example, to speak of 'the popularity of folk music' without necessarily invoking or referring to a tension or opposition. Nor is it used to serve as a label, either singly or in tandem with another word. Nevertheless, the term is not unproblematic. Use of 'popularity' is based, broadly, on the assumption that there is a definable social subject that is active in conferring this status upon something. However, it is unclear who, in any one context, 'someone,' 'some people' or 'people in general' are. Mainly for this reason, popularity – in much the same way as authenticity and autonomy – has come to be widely regarded as a contested ideological construction lacking conceptual clarity (Hall 1981; Wicke 1992).

When 'popularity' is applied to fixed social subjects like the masses, ordinary people, the working class, the people, the society or the public, these subjects are often thought of as sharing homogeneous forms of cultural practise. In relating this to music, Middleton (1990) describes it as sociological essentialism. One result of its application is that the term 'popularity' can also denote a set of structural qualities of particular musical texts – qualities that are thought to fit the musical practises of the social subject. The music is then often characterized by terms such as 'light,' 'simple' or 'trivial.' The main function of music in these contexts is considered to be that of entertainment.

Middleton distinguishes between essentialists and positivists. Positivists focus on quantitative aspects and view popularity in terms of measurable degrees of dissemination – as, for example, in airplay statistics or sales figures. It is often believed that record charts, as published weekly since 1949 in the US music magazine *Billboard*, measure popularity. In reality, charts have been developed as a complex instrument to aid the effective organization of sales, and not as a way to represent cultural reality. Thus, charts influence the popularity of artists and records rather than express it.

Positivistic approaches have been criticized for making no distinction between availability and acceptance. In addition, the methods used in quantitative research often lead to reification: music is reduced to records or songs, while, at the same time, people are regarded solely as consumers or listeners rather than participants in multidimensional cultural processes. However reliable sales information might be in statistical terms, the figures can only disclose how many items (be it sheet music, tapes, CDs or audio files) were sold or how many television or radio sets were tuned to a certain station at a particular time. They do not normally reveal whether, to what extent or over what period the music is influential, memorized or reproduced. The figures do not deal in such matters as whether music creates meaning for individuals and groups and, if so, how, nor do they say anything about the context in which signification is produced.

This is not to doubt the potential of critical quantitative studies of reception that use more refined methods, since they can at least be helpful in deconstructing myths of popularity and in illuminating the processes of mystification within the music industry (Hamm 1982; Harker 1995; Parker 1991).

Attempts to achieve a consensus on how both the term and the concept of popularity should be approached have tended to find themselves replaced by the analysis of the respective discursive functions and prerequisites of the term in various contexts. From the point of view of economics, for example, popularity equals (supposed) sales potential; thus, the issue of popularity is a vital criterion for investments. Popular music historians, for their part, have tended to regard popularity as a feature of a certain set of genres and styles, while cultural theorists typically evaluate and explain it as both a product of and a stabilizing element within dominant ideologies.

How both the role and the outcome of the debate about popularity are judged depends on the ways in which the music industry and musical discourse are organized. This role may change, for example because of technological developments in the means of production and dissemination. Whether the term 'popularity' will keep its prominent status as a flexible instrument with which to delineate borders between changing musical spheres or will be consolidated into an historical category itself, however it may be defined, remains to be seen.

Bibliography

Hall, Stuart. 1981. 'Notes on Deconstructing "the Popular."' In *People's History and Socialist Theory*, ed. Raphael Samuel. London: Routledge, 227–40.

Hamm, Charles. 1982. 'Some Thoughts on the Measurement of Popularity in Music.' In *Popular Music Perspectives, 1*, ed. David Horn and Philip Tagg. Göteborg and Exeter: IASPM, 3–15.

Harker, Dave. 1995. 'Popular Music Doesn't Matter.' In *Popular Music Perspectives, 3*, ed. Peter Wicke. Berlin: Zyankrise, 451–66.

Middleton, Richard. 1990. *Studying Popular Music*. Milton Keynes and Philadelphia: Open University Press.

Parker, Martin. 1991. 'Reading the Charts: Making Sense with the Hit Parade.' *Popular Music* 10(2): 205–17.

Shepherd, John. 1985. 'Definition as Mystification: A Consideration of Labels as a Hindrance to Understanding Significance in Music.' In *Popular Music Perspectives, 2*, ed. David Horn. Göteborg and Exeter: IASPM, 84–98.

Wicke, Peter. 1992. 'Populäre Musik als theoretisches Konzept' [Popular Music as a Theoretical Concept]. *PopScriptum* 1: 6–42.

MARKUS HEUGER

Popular Music Criticism

Criticism can be defined as a specific category of writings on popular music which are more ambitious than straight journalism, and less ambitious than conventional scholarship: serious comment that is reflective and may evidence scholarly components. The passing of judgments that are the result of serious reflection in the standard music review can be seen as the prototype of criticism. However, in-depth interviews, the overview, the debate article and the essay could also perpetuate the expressions of taste normally to be found in the standard music review. Since the 1930s, critics have performed a key role in constructing public, as well as academic, discourse on jazz and, later, rock.

Popular music criticism has evolved slowly since the 1930s when jazz was adopted by the educated middle classes (cf. Frith 1988). Jazz criticism was first published in specialist magazines like *Melody Maker* (UK, 1926–2000), *Down Beat* (US, 1934–), *Jazz Hot* (France, 1935–), and *h.o.t.* (Denmark, 1934–35), and it also soon became a subject of books that would prove influential (for example, Panassié's *Le Jazz Hot* (1934)). A main goal was to argue that jazz was 'authentic' ('hot'), could be considered as being different from other popular music ('sweet') and be ranked among the other arts, even though it was judged according to somewhat different criteria. Such claims were sustained, by Panassié and others, through the argument that jazz was a 'primitive' – and therefore superior – art, while other writers, such as R.D. Darrell, sought to overcome prejudice against the music (and against black musicians) by stressing the commitment of musicians like Duke Ellington to accepted artistic ideals and values (Gennari 1991, 469). Still others, most of them of a younger generation, established outlets in contemporary political journals (such as John Hammond in *New Masses*, Otis Ferguson in *New Republic* and B.H. Haggin in *Nation*), where they expressed the need for jazz to be given cultural esteem on its own terms, as part of a wider social and political issue, and stressed the music's political connections as the collective response of African Americans to oppression. It was this group in particular who, as Ron Welburn has stated, 'forged a jazz press of journalistic and aesthetic analysis and established a vocabulary for the critical scrutiny of jazz' (1983; quoted in Gennari 1991, 472).

Within jazz criticism, positions defending the old and the new were soon established: first, New Orleans style versus swing; a little later, swing versus bebop (Gendron 1995, 32). During the 1950s, the jazz-as-art stance became firmly established. Another influential Frenchman, André Hodeir, published his *Hommes et problèmes du jazz* (1954), the first effort in 'scholarly, formalist criticism' (Gennari 1991, 481), and several North American critics took his lead, among them Martin Williams, who also edited several collections of jazz writings (see Williams 1979). The question of race had been central in most jazz writing since the beginning, and most writers (nearly all of them white) took a liberal or left-wing stance against racial oppression. It was only in the 1960s that African-American writers came to make a mark, most notably LeRoi Jones (Imamu Amiri Baraka) with his *Blues People: Negro Music in White America* (1963). Jones praised both John Coltrane and James Brown while relating them to the African-American cause, so central to the 1960s. West-coast critic Ralph Gleason shared Jones's views and became one of the writers central to popular music criticism, transferring free jazz's expressive aesthetics to rock (by becoming co-founder and columnist of *Rolling Stone*). In England, *Melody Maker* critic Max Jones became a similarly pivotal figure, mainly by serving as an example and mentor to young rock critics.

Since its inception, informed jazz criticism has remained a connoisseur's topic. Especially since the 1940s, authors of books, magazine articles and occasional newspaper criticism have contributed to a discourse on jazz, depicting it as an art form placed among other 'high' arts. When blues criticism began to emerge in the late 1950s, it too was directed at a small audience, but its priorities were markedly different. In claiming the music's validity as an art form on its own terms, blues criticism harked back to some earlier schools of jazz writing. Especially significant for later developments in criticism was the emphasis in writers such as Paul Oliver (for example, *Blues Fell This Morning* (1960)) on the particular

social circumstances in which the music was embedded, and the particular social world that it expressed.

When rock criticism evolved from the mid-1960s onward, it owed a particular debt to both jazz and blues criticism (the latter can be seen, for example, in the way rock criticism directed attention at the music's strong social connections, its specific means of expression and its transgression of the divisions between 'high' and 'low' art). But, at the same time, it distinguished itself from them in its emergence as a type of discourse that treated rock/pop music as a mass cultural art form (this discourse would later have a retroactive impact on blues and jazz criticism themselves).

In the 1960s, the readership consisted mainly of the insiders in rock culture; however, since the 1970s rock criticism has been part of the general cultural landscape. A number of sources contributed to the shaping of the public discourse on rock – for example, popular culture journalism, film, jazz and folklore discourses, philosophy of art and contemporary debates on Pop Art, New Journalism, the resistance of youth, technology and US culture. Rock critics of the late 1960s and early 1970s were often part of the ongoing rise of working-class youth into the new middle stratum, and rock music became a way of mediating between their background and 'legitimate' culture.

At the beginning, writing on pop and rock concentrated on sales figures, news, gossip and fan viewpoints. A more critical approach first emerged in *Melody Maker*, in which young writers like Ray Coleman and Chris Welch appropriated some criteria from jazz criticism, shifting their focus from image to craftsmanship, questions of artists' intentions and the authenticity of the British beat and R&B scene. From 1963–64 onward, this development resulted in an increasing number of in-depth interviews, feature articles and critical reviews. At the same time, the success of the Beatles prompted outsiders like art music critic William Mann to praise the group, as he did in a famous article published in *The Times* of London (December 1963, 4). But the spirit of 'Swinging London' found its first congenial interpreter in Nik Cohn's bluntly subjective account of rock 'n' roll culture as a subversive and utopian dream world. Cohn wrote for *The Observer* and *Queen* magazine and produced one of the first books on rock history in 1969 (Cohn 1996).

In the United States, Paul Williams issued the first rock magazine, *Crawdaddy!*, in 1966, featuring his long, personal essays on the US rock scene and, in particular, the achievements of Bob Dylan. The magazine came to include critics who were later to become influential, such as Jon Landau, Peter Guralnick and Richard Meltzer. While Williams's perspective was that of the informed fan, Richard Goldstein's essays for *The Village Voice*, *New York* magazine and *The New York Times* represented the more prestigious connection to New Journalism and writers such as Norman Mailer and Tom Wolfe.

Rolling Stone (1967–) and *Creem* (1969–94) soon established themselves as the leading rock magazines of the United States and the world. Although their perspectives on the subject differed widely, both magazines discussed rock albums and performances at length, both as the most important contemporary art and as social commentary. Landau and Greil Marcus molded and edited the review section of *Rolling Stone*. Dave Marsh and Lester Bangs edited *Creem*. Along with Robert Christgau, who had written about rock since the late 1960s and edited the music section of *The Village Voice* from 1974, these critics became the most respected and influential early rock writers.

These five 'founding fathers' of rock criticism agreed first in understanding rock as authentic, socially relevant and 'bodily,' which is to say 'corporeal,' music. The authenticity argument drew on rock's roots in the music of oppressed peoples, its close ties to contemporary anti-Establishment communities and the minds of gifted individuals. They agreed second in considering the Beatles, the Rolling Stones and Bob Dylan to be central in a shared canon of rock music. Apart from this, these critics represented a range of individual positions. Landau adopted the auteur theory of film criticism, exploring how artistic authenticity is expressed through control of technology, and celebrated black soul in the late 1960s. Marcus excelled in tracing the cultural roots of rock in North American culture, interpreting the music as a more or less unconscious medium for the collective memory of the oppressed (see Marcus 1975). Marsh specialized in crystallizing the narratives of songs, performances and artists' lives, particularly the story of underprivileged boys turning to rock as a salvation and a way to 'get out of this place.' Bangs translated the spirit of rock into a recklessly subjective writing style, which made him the first star of rock criticism. Christgau elaborated the small consumer-guide format, relying on his reflected, embodied taste and his belief that pop could be the object of intelligent consumption.

Dozens of other US critics contributed to the establishment of rock criticism. Ellen Willis was the first to introduce feminist perspectives into a male-dominated branch of criticism; Richard Meltzer provided a dash of Dada; and several others developed a personal profile, not only in the specialist magazines but increasingly in newspapers, weeklies and other media as well. In Britain, *Let It Rock* critics like Simon Frith, Dave Laing and Charlie Gillett were greatly inspired by the US critics, but added a far stronger social perspective, often in Marxist terms. The main strand of popular music criticism, however, was established by a number of *New Musical Express* (*NME*) (1952–) critics such as Nick Kent and Charles Shaar Murray, recruited in 1972 from the underground press and fully conversant with Lester Bangs.

By the mid-1970s, rock critics all over the Western world could draw on a fairly well-defined type of discourse introduced by a few widely disseminated US and British publications, but adapted to national and local discussions and problems. For instance, late-1960s rock critics in Denmark merged the broad cultural perspectives of US critics with indigenous versions of cultural radicalism, while Norwegian, Swedish and Icelandic critics often drew on the work of their British forerunners. In this tradition, playful irreverence was as important as good reporting.

The punk era was a period of transition. In Britain, where it caused most commotion, punk was embraced by old-school critics like *NME* stars Kent and Shaar Murray and new-fashioned fanzine writers alike. As *NME* editor Neil Spencer wrote, 'punk and the music press were made for each other' (1991, xi). Banned from both venues and airplay, punk was dependent on print exposure, while its intricacies, in their turn, called for expert explanations. In practise, much punk criticism stopped at attempts to sort out the posers and point to the real thing. Both 'realist' (the Clash) and 'avant-garde' (the Gang of Four) acts were made to comply with the inherited authenticity paradigm.

Yet punk made a significant difference, in part by vastly increasing the market for writing on rock and in part by opening the doors to unorthodox youngsters like Paul Morley, Ian Penman, Julie Burchill and Tony Parsons. With *'The Boy Looked at Johnny': The Obituary of Rock and Roll* (1978), Burchill and Parsons authored the definitive 'anti-hippie' statement. The standards of the book highlight the continuity mentioned above, even to the point where 'authenticity' becomes a caricature. At the same time, the book's *carnevalesque*, tabloid style communicates the artifice of punk culture, the very 'posing' that the surface text condemns, and so anticipates the criticism of the early 1980s.

'The age of style,' as Jon Savage christened the first half of the 1980s, ushered in the most important change in the history of rock criticism since 1967: the authenticity of rock was abandoned in favor of a celebration of pop artifice and smart consumerism. This change was most apparent in Britain, but it soon spread to other countries as well. *The Face* (1980–) took the lead by publishing monthly, by introducing glossy paper and a magazine format and, most importantly, by creating a new relation between text and image, which privileged the latter. Thus, it ushered rock criticism into a postmodern world where the 'pleasure-seeking bricoleur replaces the truth-and-justice-seeking rational subject of the Enlightenment' (Hebdige 1988, 166).

Intellectually inclined critics like Savage and Frith sought out the critical potential of New Pop for a couple of years. Others, especially Morley and Penman, redefined the critic's role as that of a star. Taking inspiration from, among other things, Pop Art, Situationist happenings and poststructuralist theory, they thought of their task as that of 'destabilizing' the pop process from within. Although the use of literary cutup techniques and arguments with musicians often became only a pretense for the journalists' narcissism, it opened up new ways of writing, pointed toward a more comprehensive approach to new academic theory and, to a large extent, rehabilitated pop as a proper subject for criticism, albeit with a characteristic, ironic slant.

The 1980s and 1990s witnessed a still-growing polarization between consumer guidance and academically informed criticism. Institutionally, these polarities can be exemplified by British magazines like *Q* (1986–) and *The Wire* (1982–), respectively. *Q* focuses on mainstream pop and rock, and its pieces are anonymous in style, stressing information, gossip, puns and so on. The dominance of such magazines thus represents a 'return to a state of pre-criticism' (Lindberg et al. 2000, 472). *The Wire* is anti-mainstream, covering all things considered avant-garde, and the writers deliver aesthetic judgments, distinguishing good music from bad on the basis of such art criteria as originality and artistic vision. The connoisseur stance of *The Wire* can be found among its collaborators as well: the Swedish *Pop*, German *Spex* and Japanese *Marquee*.

Among contributors to *The Wire* are Simon Reynolds, who competently draws on poststructuralist theory in his discussion of dance (see Reynolds 1998), and David Toop, whose writing is informed by an anthropological mindset (see Toop 1995). These and a few other critics (such as Frith, who has been successful both as a critic and as an academic) have introduced contemporary topics from the humanities into rock criticism, thus shrinking the gap between the two, and have reinstated rock criticism as a specific kind of cultural criticism, often using the book as their medium.

In the United States, the polarization has been less obvious, as national publications like *Rolling Stone*, *Spin* (1985–) and *The Source* (1988–) have continued to print qualified criticism on occasion. Although purely journalistic criteria dominate, aesthetic standards have diversified, especially since non-Caucasians and women gained admittance to the market. Critics like Nelson George, who writes on African-American musics, have

continued to rely on the old authenticity paradigm, while others (for example, Ann Powers) have combined the politics of identity with a sense of subculture in a quest for 'the important.' Still others (for instance, Chuck Eddy) have tapped into the renegade tradition of Meltzer and Bangs in order to turn the canon upside down, cruising popular music for the fun of it and dropping any claims to transcendence. Compared to the situation in the Nordic countries, national differences in the United States in the 1990s diminished due to the growth of transnational consumerism.

In general, the aesthetic standards of rock criticism are eclectic and allow for a vast range of critical positions. The tension between a 'rock' approach that situates the music in a context of social and/or aesthetic revolt and a 'pop' approach that regards it as part of a consumerist life style has pervaded critical practise since its beginnings. It was vital to stress this opposition in 1967, but the construction became increasingly problematic during the 1970s and, significantly, it was a self-conscious return to pop that broke up the dominant authenticity paradigm in the early 1980s. It is characteristic of the 'intermediary aesthetic' (Lindberg et al. 2000, xvi) informing the field that many critics value this tension as an asset which contributes to the vitality of the music. Thus, acts and musicians may appear too 'arty' as well as too 'commercial.'

However, it is possible to posit a common platform, one whose basic tenet is, on the one hand, that rock matters, and, on the other hand, that it need not always be 'important' in order to matter, that is, in terms of being 'original' or capable of striking lyrical observations. What is required of rock is, rather, a strong sensuous experience that may temporarily expel the boredom of everyday life or, with more academically inclined critics, may represent a utopian promise of transcendence. Thus, Greil Marcus speaks of 'the recreation of the moment' (1969, 16); Robert Christgau of 'epiphanies' (1973, 2); and Simon Reynolds, following Roland Barthes, of 'bliss' (1990, 13).

Rock critics express and add primarily to the self-understanding of rock culture. This requires from the writer readability, know-how and stylishness, with the effect that penetrating reflections are often introduced in a treacherously light tone. In practise, rock criticism represents a weighty contribution to contemporary cultural criticism. In taking popular culture seriously and stressing that meaning is context-dependent, the early rock critics anticipated the advent of cultural studies as well as postmodernism.

Bibliography

Burchill, Julie, and Parsons, Tony. 1978. *'The Boy Looked at Johnny': The Obituary of Rock and Roll*. London: Pluto Press.

Christgau, Robert. 1973. *Any Old Way You Choose It: Rock and Other Pop Music, 1967–1973*. Baltimore, MD: Penguin Books.

Cohn, Nik. 1996 (1969). *Awopbopaloobop Alopbambloom: The Golden Age of Rock*. New York: Da Capo Press.

Frith, Simon. 1988. 'Playing with Real Feeling – Jazz and Suburbia.' In Simon Frith, *Music for Pleasure: Essays in the Sociology of Pop*. Cambridge: Polity Press, 45–63.

Gendron, Bernhard. 1995. '"Mouldy Figs" and Modernists: Jazz at War (1942–1946).' In *Jazz Among the Discourses*, ed. Krin Gabbard. Durham, NC: Duke University Press, 31–56.

Gennari, John. 1991. 'Jazz Criticism: Its Development and Ideologies.' *Black American Literature Forum* 25(3): 449–523.

Hebdige, Dick. 1988. 'The Bottom Line on Planet One: Squaring Up to *The Face*.' In *Hiding in the Light: On Images and Things*. London and New York: Routledge, 155–76.

Hodeir, André. 1956. *Jazz: Its Evolution and Essence*, trans. David Noakes. New York: Grove. (Originally published as *Hommes et problèmes du jazz*. Paris: Portulan, 1954.)

Jones, LeRoi (Imamu Amiri Baraka). 1963. *Blues People: Negro Music in White America*. New York: William Morrow & Co.

Lindberg, Ulf, et al. 2000. *Amusers, Bruisers & Cool-Headed Cruisers: The Fields of Nordic and Anglo-Saxon Rock Criticism*. Århus: Århus University, Department of Scandinavian Studies.

Marcus, Greil. 1969. 'Who Put the Bomp in the Bomp De-Bomp De-Bomp?' In *Rock and Roll Will Stand*, ed. Greil Marcus. Boston, MA: Beacon Press, 6–27.

Marcus, Greil. 1975. *Mystery Train: Images of America in Rock 'n' Roll Music*. New York: E.P. Dutton.

Oliver, Paul. 1960. *Blues Fell This Morning: The Meaning of the Blues*. London: Cassell.

Panassié, Hugues. 1936. *Hot Jazz: The Guide to Swing Music*, trans. Lyle and Eleanor Dowling. New York: M. Witmark and Sons. (Originally published as *Le Jazz Hot*. Paris: Correa, 1934.)

Reynolds, Simon. 1990. *Blissed Out: The Raptures of Rock*. London: Serpent's Tail.

Reynolds, Simon. 1998. *Energy Flash: A Journey Through Rave Music and Dance Culture*. London: Picador.

Spencer, Neil. 1991. 'Introduction.' In Charles Shaar Murray, *Shots from the Hip*. London and New York: Penguin Books.

Toop, David. 1995. *Ocean of Sound: Aether Talk, Ambient Sound and Imaginary Worlds*. London: Serpent's Tail.

Williams, Martin T., ed. 1979 (1959). *The Art of Jazz: Essays on the Nature and Development of Jazz*. New York: Da Capo Press.

ULF LINDBERG, GESTUR GUDMUNDSSON, MORTEN MICHELSEN and
HANS WEISETHAUNET

Popular Music Education

The term 'popular music education' denotes training, instruction or pedagogy relating to popular music. Popular music education takes place at a wide variety of sites and educational institutions, which often have divergent teaching strategies and objectives. It also covers a variety of educational levels, catering to different ages and demographic groups. The range of education options includes informal training, private instruction and community-led initiatives, as well as music education in schools, conservatories and universities up to postgraduate level. The field can generally be divided into three main areas: practical, theoretical and vocational (although within individual institutions and disciplines there can be significant crossover among these). Practical popular music education is concerned primarily with instrumental tuition and the use of music technology. Theoretical popular music education attempts to develop an understanding of popular music's structures, logics, ideologies and economics. Finally, vocational popular music education involves the provision of courses designed to prepare students for employment within the music business and related industries. This heterogeneity of purpose means that there is no one congruous educational method that can be thought of as a pedagogy of popular music. Rather, teaching practise tends to be shaped and legitimated by the projected use value and disciplinary emphasis of the specific educational program.

Popular Music Education in Schools

School programs in a large number of countries worldwide provide music lessons as part of compulsory education, encompassing performance, composition, listening and appraisal. Music education within schools may also take the form of extracurricular instrumental lessons or work within ensembles, which occurs outside normal school hours. Such teaching occurs across different levels of school education from primary to the final year of high school, and therefore it encompasses a range of educational strategies, from music appreciation to advanced-level instrumental tuition. Mainstream class-based music education has commonly been viewed as forming part of a balanced general education. Learning outcomes have therefore been assessed with regard to a general educational objective that has underlying concerns about the development of analytical skills and the broadening of knowledge and experience. Instrumental tuition has generally been regarded as a more specialist pursuit related to the development of specific skills.

However, the introduction of popular music into schools has been sporadic, with many countries lacking any statutory entitlement to music education at all. Until the 1970s, most systematized school-level music education was based on traditional Western models, which focused on singing and on the appreciation of classical music (a situation that has persisted in countries as disparate as Ghana, Thailand, Korea and Singapore). Since the early 1980s, popular music has been introduced successfully into music textbooks for schools and in state-approved programs in countries such as Bulgaria and Japan (see Koizumi 1998). Such progressive initiatives are, however, lacking in numerous other countries, where the teaching of popular music styles within schools has caused controversy and has often faced resistance. For instance, the introduction of a broad music education (including rock, pop, jazz and non-Western musics) proposed by the United Kingdom's National Curriculum Council in 1991 was met with opposition from traditionalists (for example, O'Hear 1991; Scruton 1991; see Shepherd and Vulliamy 1994). This resistance led to a rejection of the plans, and the final policy document pertaining to music education in schools stated that 'the emphasis was to be on the "special" classical tradition' (Street 1997, 94). Gammon (1999) comments that the final inclusion criteria relating to popular and world musics were 'over-heavy and overly prescriptive.'

The integration of certain types of popular music into national curricula has often been based on appraisals by education authorities as to the importance of certain popular and folk musics to the cultural heritage of a nation or locality. The acceptance of jazz as a valued national art form is reflected in the design of the national music curriculum in the United States, where children are allowed to begin learning the theory and practise of the genre from the start of their music education. Elsewhere, the structure of popular music education can be related to tensions between the local and the global. The teaching of indigenous popular and folk musics to children is often part of a wider protectionist project that aims to balance the effects of globalized culture through the preservation of local cultures. The inclusion of indigenous music in education programs has also been affected by political changes. Hong Kong provides an illustration: education authorities began to incorporate Chinese traditional music into the curriculum before the takeover of Hong Kong by China in 1997.

Aside from music education within primary and secondary schools, training in the performing arts for those under 18 years of age is offered by a number of dedicated institutions. While some of these centers are state-financed and state-run, there is also a long-established private 'stage school' system, in which school-age children are trained in various aspects of the performing

arts. This form of vocational schooling has provided a foundation for a number of successful popular musicians. In the late 1990s, many high-profile UK pop performers (such as Billie Piper, Martine McCutcheon, Emma Bunton of the Spice Girls, Melanie Blatt and Nicole and Natalie Appleton of All Saints, and Scott Robinson of Five) were educated and trained from an early age at the Sylvia Young Theatre School.

Popular music has also made its way into school teaching as part of other educational initiatives. During the 1980s and 1990s, the rise in information technology training meant that music technology often became incorporated into music teaching in schools. In the United Kingdom, for instance, the allocation of funds by the government-led Technical and Vocational Education Initiative enabled many music departments to invest in electronic equipment (Comber, Hargreaves and Colley 1993, 125). Such investment allowed the teaching of techniques central to popular music practise, such as sampling, sequencing, mixing and modeling. Despite these relatively recent advances, the teaching of popular music in schools has remained uneven throughout the world, and there are numerous differences in approach internationally. Some countries have fully integrated popular music into their national music curricula, while others have continued a sole concentration on art musics, and still others lack a cohesive overall policy on music education.

Popular Music Education in Universities

Numerous courses relating to popular music education are now provided within further education, higher education (at both undergraduate and postgraduate levels) and lifelong learning. These can be broadly separated into practical or vocational courses and programs with a purely academic emphasis, although there is some degree of crossover between the two. The content and emphasis of practical or vocational courses vary: some courses provide tuition in musical skills and performance techniques, while others offer vocational qualifications in practical areas such as sound production, lighting and stage design. There are also a number of courses that aim to develop expertise in management and promotion.

Certain types of popular music performance have been integrated into existing classically based conservatories. For instance, the New South Wales State Conservatorium of Music (Australia) inaugurated a diploma in jazz studies in 1973, and in the same period the State Academy of Music in Sofia (Bulgaria) opened a faculty for pop, rock and jazz musicians, vocalists and instrumentalists. However, this incorporation has often been generically specific, with some styles being more readily accepted than others within such institutions. There have also been differences in performance evaluation according to genre. The criteria for the evaluation of jazz performance, for instance, are perhaps more developed than those found in courses dealing with pop or rock forms. The enculturation of jazz within educational institutions over a number of years has led to a largely standardized pedagogy across institutions akin to the more established classical conservatory model. The incorporation of other forms of popular music within the academy has led to a need for new approaches to teaching and learning, approaches that move away from traditional conservatory methods to techniques more suited to popular music styles. As Tagg (1998) points out: 'It is impossible to "freeze" popular music skills into a set of repeatable study packages because changing social and musical practices require by definition changing criteria for how those practices can be assessed' (231). An oft-cited problem here is that the traditional concentration on the study of notation within the study of Western art music cannot simply be transferred to the study of popular music. Björnberg (1993) argues that 'overemphasis on notated structures can . . . act as a preventive factor towards the students' attainment of style-specific musical idioms' (74).

Issues of pedagogy have also been much debated with regard to the analytical study of popular music within universities. It has been argued that the teaching of music within academe has often been value-laden, and as such the academy is an unsuitable framework for the teaching of popular music. Tagg argues that 'the traditional hierarchical aesthetics of music' often underlying university teaching are 'totally counterproductive to the understanding of the real musical practices of most people in most situations in modern society' (1998, 224). The profusion of generic codes within popular music and its rapidly changing styles and aesthetics present certain problems for standardized teaching models. Since the 1970s, institutions of higher education throughout the world have responded to these challenges by developing programs that concentrate on or incorporate the analytical study of popular music. Reflecting the field of popular music studies itself, the content of these courses is variable and may include aspects of musicology, anthropology, history and cultural studies. Popular music studies is widely integrated within many courses in the arts and humanities, taking the form of options and units within degree subjects such as communication studies, cultural studies, sociology, music and anthropology. However, although popular music studies is an interdisciplinary field, educational programs have often been weighted toward particular approaches. For example, instruction in popular

music in departments of sociology and cultural studies has often neglected the rigorous study of musical structures. Conversely, few music departments have included the in-depth study of popular music as a social practise in their programs. The lack of musicological research and teaching concerned with popular music is perhaps facilitated by the overriding hegemony of Western art music traditions within many university music departments. For instance, Wicks's (1998) survey of US universities found that fewer than 3 percent of courses offered by music departments were concerned with music outside the Western art tradition (including 'world musics,' indigenous North American folk musics, and rock and its related genres).

Popular music studies has, however, gained recognition as a distinct subject area, as evidenced by the establishment of specialist teaching and research centers, such as the Institute of Popular Music at the University of Liverpool (United Kingdom) and the Centre for Popular Music Research at The Humboldt University (Germany). There is also a wide range of undergraduate degree courses in popular music at institutions such as the Queensland Conservatorium (Australia), the University of Natal (South Africa) and over 50 institutions of higher education in the United Kingdom. However, popular music education has remained unevenly distributed across the world and has been more readily accepted in some areas than others. For instance, the study of popular music within universities has become strongly established in areas of Western Europe, Scandinavia, the United States, Australasia and Japan while remaining at a nascent level in other parts of the world.

There are a number of universities that offer vocationally oriented courses targeted toward students wishing to attain specific skills related to careers in popular music. For example, there are numerous sound engineering courses such as those offered at the University of Pretoria (South Africa), Luleå University of Technology (Sweden) and various UK universities (including Salford, Surrey and the Liverpool Institute for Performing Arts). In recent years, a number of universities have also developed undergraduate and postgraduate courses concerned with an analysis of the music industry. These include courses with a management emphasis (for example, the Music Business/Management programs at Berklee College of Music in Boston (United States)) and courses aimed at giving practitioners a better knowledge of the workings of the industry. These courses frequently have to negotiate the tension between the academic endeavor to understand the music industry, often from a sociological perspective, and the instructive training and networking experience associated with vocational education. Jones (2002) argues that it is important for such courses to combine a number of approaches to the industry, as 'to teach the music industry either from a strictly management science perspective, or from a skills based "vocational" perspective ... is to miss not only the multi-layered richness of the experience of making, mediating and using popular music but to create partial (and thereby misleading) misunderstandings of how pop works as a "product" and an "industry."'

Vocational Education

As well as the aforementioned university courses, there are various educational channels through which vocational education takes place. These range from commercially run fee-paying courses to government-funded schemes and community arts projects. For instance, private colleges such as the Harris Institute for the Arts in Toronto (Canada) offer music industry management courses, while private sound engineering courses are often run from working recording studios. Examples also exist of partnership agreements bringing together commercial and state bodies in the establishment of teaching institutions. For example, in the United Kingdom the British Phonographic Industry (BPI) was involved in the establishment of the BRIT School, a state-funded secondary school for the performing arts. The British government has also initiated vocational training as part of its employment strategy. In 1998, it introduced the New Deal for Musicians program as part of an existing welfare-to-work scheme aimed at tackling youth unemployment figures. Recognizing the contribution that musicians make to the economy and culture of Britain, the government introduced the 'New Deal' scheme to assist young musicians in their pursuit of a career in the music industry (see Cloonan 2000).

Community education groups have also been involved with programs that fall broadly under the rubric of vocational education. However, despite specific training elements, such courses are usually part of the agenda of the community arts movement. For instance, umbrella community arts organizations such as Kontaktnätet in Sweden, Sound Sense in the United Kingdom and the Federation of Music Collectives in Ireland have used popular music as a mixture of vocational training and a component of a general capacity-building educational agenda. The activities of these groups have encompassed a broad range of educational approaches, including studio technology courses, instrumental tuition, workshops and music industry courses. Such courses have been intended not only to have a direct vocational benefit, but also to facilitate the building of self-esteem, to help combat social exclusion and to assist in the acquisition of transferable skills (Leonard and Strachan, 2002). Community-based groups have also

used music education to preserve the cultural heritage of particular 'ethnic' and national groups. For instance, in 1951 Cumann Ceoltóirí na Éireann (later to become Comhaltas Ceoltóirí Éireann) was founded in Dublin with the express purpose of protecting Irish cultural heritage through the promotion of indigenous Irish cultural forms; this was to be done by establishing educational groups within Irish communities. The Comhaltas movement is made up of community-led groups which run classes and courses in Irish traditional music and song and Irish dancing. By the beginning of the twenty-first century, the movement had groups in the United Kingdom, the United States, Japan, Italy and Australia.

Non-Institutional Education

The role of popular music education (especially with regard to instrumental tuition) is somewhat confused by the way in which musicians become involved in certain genres. In rock and pop forms, for example, musicians are often self-taught or are engaged in differing types of informal training. In a study of how individuals become rock musicians, Bennett (1980) points out that 'rock music is exemplified by the processes of self-recruitment and learning without pedagogy' (18). Bennett's findings suggest that many rock musicians acquire musical skills outside the formal learning environment and that that learning commonly occurs at particular moments in individuals' lives. He suggests that, during adolescence, rock musicians often initially copy from recordings, but that, in order to progress, once a certain level of competence has been achieved, they are likely to form bands in which peer group learning takes place. Many musicians develop practical popular music skills through one-on-one tuition in instrumental playing or in singing, given by experienced musicians. Such tuition usually takes place on a private basis and is often conducted by teachers who may have extensive performance and recording experience, but lack formal teaching qualifications (for further reading on informal learning practises, see Green 2001).

This process of unstructured non-institutional learning can be subject to gender differences, with boys and girls learning particular instruments at different times. Clawson's (1999) research among US rock musicians indicated that, for her male respondents, the median age to begin playing a rock instrument was 13 years and the average age for participation in a first band was 15 1/2 years. In contrast, her female respondents began to play rock instruments at the median age of 21, and just 26 percent of the women in her study had played in a band prior to high-school graduation – unlike the men, for whom this was an almost universal experience (106).

The way in which popular music is learned and practised can have an effect on the performance traditions of particular genres. A lack of formal tuition can encourage musicians to improvise different playing styles or techniques. As Lilliestam (1996) notes, 'it is quite common for self-taught blues and rock musicians to use unorthodox playing techniques, chordings and fingerings' (203). Lilliestam comments that the dominance of notated music as part of a classical music tradition has led to the belief that notation 'contains the final truth about music' and that such thinking neglects the way in which music is learned, passed on and commonly practised (1996, 196). In a related sense, while there has been a tradition of recording traditional folk music in notated form, the value of these notated tunes has been much debated. For example, within Irish traditional music, collections of notated tunes are seldom prioritized as definitive. As Ó Canainn (1993) comments: 'The various collections of Irish music have never been regarded by traditional performers as a standard against which their performance is to be measured or its correctness checked' (8). Commentators have argued that print versions of traditional music fail to capture the 'essence' of the music.

Conclusion

Despite encompassing a wide spectrum of practises, from formal education to learning by ear, study and training related to popular music are relatively recent developments, and consequently the issues that surround them have remained widely debated from a variety of perspectives. Nevertheless, these developments and debates are undoubtedly having an effect on music education as a whole. The prioritization of Western art music within educational institutions, from schools to universities, is being challenged, and the growing incorporation of popular music into educational programs is indicative of how educators are attempting to address the diverse ways in which individuals experience and engage with music in their everyday lives.

Bibliography

Bennett, H. Stith. 1980. *On Becoming a Rock Musician*. Amherst, MA: University of Massachusetts Press.

Björnberg, Alf. 1993. '"Teach You to Rock"?: Popular Music in the University Music Department.' *Popular Music* 12(1): 69–77.

Clawson, Mary Ann. 1999. 'Masculinity and Skill Acquisition in the Adolescent Rock Band.' *Popular Music* 18(1): 99–114.

Cloonan, Martin. 2000. 'Labour's New Deal for Musicians: Turning Rebellion into Money?' In *Changing Sounds: New Directions and Configurations in Popular Music*, ed. Tony Mitchell and Peter Doyle with Bruce Johnson. Sydney: University of Technology, 298–304.

Comber, Chris, Hargreaves, David J., and Colley, Ann. 1993. 'Girls, Boys and Technology in Music Education.' *British Journal of Music Education* 10: 123–34.

Gammon, Vic. 1999. 'National Curricula and the Ethnic in Music.' In *Critical Musicology: A Transdisciplinary Online Journal*. http://www.leeds.ac.uk/music/Info/CMJ/Articles/1999/01/01.html

Green, Lucy. 2001. *How Popular Musicians Learn: A Way Ahead for Music Education*. Aldershot: Ashgate.

Jones, Mike. 2002. 'Learning to Crawl: The Rapid Rise of Music Industry Education.' In *The Business of Music*, ed. Michael Talbot. Liverpool: Liverpool University Press.

Koizumi, Kyôko. 1998. 'Popular Music as Acquired Capital: Some Problems in Japanese Music Education.' In *Popular Music: Intercultural Interpretations*, ed. Tôru Mitsui. Kanazawa: Graduate Program in Music, Kanazawa University, 77–83.

Leonard, Marion, and Strachan, Rob. 2002. 'Collective Responsibilities: The Arts Council, Community Arts and the Music Industry in Ireland.' In *The Business of Music*, ed. Michael Talbot. Liverpool: Liverpool University Press.

Lilliestam, Lars. 1996. 'On Playing by Ear.' *Popular Music* 15(2): 195–216.

Ó Canainn, Tomás. 1993. *Traditional Music in Ireland*. Cork: Ossian.

O'Hear, Anthony. 1991. 'Out of Sync with Bach.' *The Times Educational Supplement* (22 February).

Scruton, Roger. 1991. 'Rock Around the Classroom.' *The Sunday Telegraph* (10 February).

Shepherd, John, and Vulliamy, Graham. 1994. 'The Struggle for Culture: A Sociological Case Study of the Development of a National Music Curriculum.' *British Journal of Sociology of Education* 15(1): 27–40.

Street, John. 1997. *Politics and Popular Culture*. Cambridge: Polity Press.

Tagg, Philip. 1998. 'The Göteborg Connection: Lessons in the History and Politics of Popular Music Education and Research.' *Popular Music* 17(2): 219–42.

Wicks, Sammie Ann. 1998. 'America's Popular Music Traditions as "Canon-Fodder."' *Popular Music and Society* 22(1): 55–89.

MARION LEONARD and ROBERT STRACHAN with LUCY GREEN (United Kingdom) and CLAIRE LEVY (Bulgaria)

Popular Music in Advertising

Introduction

Popular music is used in advertising as part of a system or method of attracting public attention to the desirability of commercial products. Up to the early twentieth century, this took the form of live performance and notated music, but popular music's main contribution has been in recorded or broadcast form (through radio, television and cinema), especially when linked to forms of visual expression. The sponsorship of broadcast popular music shows and the appearance of popular music artists in advertisements to offer product endorsement illustrate the strong links between advertising and popular music.

Popular music is a major component within advertising; for example, 'of the estimated sixty billion broadcast advertising hours encountered by North Americans each year, approximately three-quarters employ music in some manner' (Huron 1989, 560). Music in advertising may take the form either of specially composed music, songs or jingles, or of existing popular music or songs, sometimes with lyrical changes (known as 'parody lyrics') to promote a particular product.

Historical Background

There is an historical link between advertising and popular song. Street cries, which were sales pitches sung to draw attention to the wares of market or street vendors, have been documented for centuries. Julien (1985) points to eleventh-century fruit vendors in Paris whose messages were 'proclaimed in song' (417). In his account of London street life of the mid-nineteenth century, first published in 1851, Henry Mayhew describes the 'musical cries' of costermongers which were used to advertise such diverse products as confectionery and 'dog's meat' (1969, 112). At the same time, North American accounts point to similar uses of song in African-American culture. The African-American novelist William Wells Brown observed that, '[i]n the market . . . the costermongers, or street vendors are the men of music' (quoted in Epstein 1981, 181). Music also played a central role in late nineteenth-century medicine shows, which toured the United States using musical performance and burlesque in order to sell patent medicines.

Contemporary advertising, which may be generally defined as the mass dissemination of information promoting specific items or particular brands of mass-produced products, originated in the early nineteenth century (see Hindley and Hindley 1972). Loeb (1994) argues that Victorian advertising was the first to promote 'materialistic fantasies,' which were central to the emergence of a 'materially defined cultural ideal' (vi). Indeed, Williams (1980) describes advertising as 'the official art of modern capitalist society' (184). This phase of advertising was marked by its encouragement of consumers to seek a definition of self through product choices. Boorstin (1973) contends that social cohesion was found in the 'consumption communities' formed by popular styles and expenditure patterns among consumers (173). Maltby (1989) argues that, in the second half of the

nineteenth century, advertising agencies began to 'advise their clients on the design and appearance of their advertisements; as they did so they created a crucial instrument, by which a mass public could be educated to desire the pleasures of consumption' (34). The rise of modern advertising saw the beginning of the promotion of products on the merits not merely of their practical use, but rather of their symbolic use. It became the medium through which to create or reinforce the image of a product and convey its status.

Throughout the twentieth century, music was used as a central component in the process of associating products and brands with particular life styles and attitudes. By the time of the mass-mediated broadcast of music, consumer culture and sophisticated advertising were already widespread. By 1920, for instance, two-thirds of all US newspaper and magazine revenue was generated from advertising (Leiss, Kline and Jhally 1990). However, with technological developments and the beginnings of mass communication, the use of music to promote commercial products (and, indeed, advertising in general) came to be implemented on a much larger scale. The advent of commercial radio saw the development of a close relationship between advertising agencies and radio programmers. As the raison d'être of these stations was purely commercial, radio output was often tailored to the advertisers' needs: 'In-house creative teams, working in liaison with the agency's sales divisions, devised and developed programme ideas to the client's brief' (Barnard 1989, 19). From the beginnings of US radio in the 1920s, music and advertising were inextricably linked. Hillbilly music, for instance, was used to sell everything from cars to patent medicine. Malone (1985) describes how country music was used to sell foodstuffs, work clothes, politics and religion. He remarks that the sale of pharmacological items was so popular among hillbilly advertisers 'that it almost seemed as if the format of the old-time medicine show had been transferred to the hillbilly radio show' (101).

Broadcast and Live Show Sponsorship

When national radio networks started to appear in the United States in the mid-1920s, major companies began to pursue a policy of single-sponsorship programming in which a show was sponsored entirely by one product. Sponsorship of radio shows proved to be a powerful tool in the promotion of particular products and brands and, by 1927, many advertising agencies in the United States were spending over half their budgets on radio promotion (Eberly 1982). The cigarette manufacturer Lucky Strike saw a rise in sales of over 1.5 million between 1928 and 1929 following campaigns linked to popular music shows in the United States (Maltby 1989). The 1930s saw a preponderance of product-sponsored radio programs, such as *The Joe Loss Show*, sponsored by Meltonian shoe polish, and *The Palmolive Hour*, starring Morton Downey. Perhaps the most famous European product-sponsored show was J. Walter Thompson's *The Ovaltineys*, a children's show broadcast by the English-language commercial station Radio Luxembourg. The broadcasts mixed children's entertainment with a distinctive theme tune promoting the beverage Ovaltine. This close relationship between commerce, advertising and programming has continued throughout the history of commercial radio and can be seen as having a major effect on the way in which popular music is presented and programmed. In a discussion of European pirate radio stations of the 1960s, Chapman (1990) remarks that stations had 'little editorial say in the music policy of these shows as individual responsibilities were delegated to the respective advertising agencies' (174).

The link between sponsorship and popular music can also be found in the corporate backing of live events and tours. Atsuko (1991) points to the emergence in the 1980s of the strategy of 'crowned concerts,' where Japanese corporations used sponsored tours in conjunction with mixed television, radio and billboard advertising campaigns, featuring multinational stars such as Madonna and Michael Jackson. This kind of marketing has not been linked exclusively with major international stars. For instance, Arnold (1997) points to grass-roots sponsorship of relatively unknown US bands by Budweiser beer and Skoal Bandits chewing tobacco, in which acts were given financial support, equipment and stage sets. The 1990s saw the large-scale corporate sponsorship of rock festivals, including Woodstock (United States), Glastonbury (United Kingdom) and Roskilde (Denmark), which received backing from a variety of international corporations. There were also a number of major exclusive sponsorship deals made, where events such as the Virgin (cola) and Tennants (beer) rock festivals and the Ericsson@Homelands (mobile phones) dance music festival actually took the names of their backers.

Popular Music Artists and Styles in Advertising

Aside from broadcast or live show sponsorship, the advertising industry has capitalized on the popularity of particular music artists or styles in advertisements themselves. Apart from the actual appearance of popular music artists in advertisements, this may involve the use of preexisting popular music, or of accompanying music or jingles written in the style of a current hit or currently fashionable genre (known as a 'knock-off' within the advertising industry). Such advertising campaigns – for example, Lucky Strike's use of Woody Guthrie's 'So

Long, It's Been Good to Know You' in the 1940s – tap into both the star potential of an artist and the music's cultural and semiotic associations. Booth (1990) suggests that the main purpose of popular song in advertising is to coerce the consumer into identifying with the position of the advertiser in a parallel process to that of the listener identifying with the emotional/ideological position of the singer.

Within radio and television promotions, product and consumer information and advertising slogans are often conveyed in the form of lyrics (which generally mention a product's name, along with its supposed attributes or uses) sung to a simple melody, referred to as a jingle. Jingles can take the form of specially written music or preexisting material with amended (parody) lyrics. Booth (1990) traces the first broadcast jingle to Minneapolis in 1929, when a barbershop quartet was used to promote Wheaties. In 1939, a jingle for Pepsi-Cola (an adaptation of the English folk tune 'D'ye Ken John Peel') was played 296,426 times on 469 radio stations and was so popular that 'the public were even willing to put nickels into jukeboxes to hear it' (Turner 1953, 321).

There is usually a direct correlation between the notes played in a jingle and the lyrical phrasing. The 1950s slogan for Pepsodent toothpaste provides an example of this mnemonic device: 'You'll won-der where the yellow went when you brush your teeth with Pep-so-dent.' In some television and cinema advertisements, a slogan or tag line for a product will appear on screen while a simple melody is played. Frequently in these instances, although the slogan is not sung, the prosody of the lyrics aligns completely with the rhythm and contour of the melody – a technique that Tagg (1999) refers to as 'transscansion.' An example of such a device can be noted in the 1999 advertisements for the Intel computer microchip, in which a four-note melody plays against the printed tag line 'Intel Inside.' There is some debate over the effectiveness of jingles as a device for conveying detailed product information. However, experimental tests recorded by Yalch (1991) illustrate that jingles aid listeners in recalling advertising slogans. Wells, Burnett and Moriarty (1989) argue that 'finger-snapping, toe-tapping songs have tremendous power because they are so memorable. Jingles are good for product identification and reminder messages, but they do not effectively convey complex thoughts and copy points' (201).

Music especially composed for advertising may also take the form of underscores that work alongside the story line of a particular advertisement. These may utilize the semiotic conventions of a film score or use popular music styles and genres in order to reinforce a narrative. Cook (1994) analyzes the use of music in several UK television advertisements in terms of the way in which their generic and stylistic components are used and the way in which the small snatches of music within the advertisements make coherent sense only within their visual context. He concludes that 'musical styles and genres offer unsurpassed opportunities for communicating complex social or attitudinal messages practically instantaneously' (35).

Likewise, the use of preexisting popular music may be seen as utilizing the existing semiotic and cultural associations of a particular piece and is often central in the process of branding a particular product, product line or company: the 'combination of associations attached to a product (name, package, history, advertising, promotion, and so on) by which consumers differentiate one product from another' (Clark 1999, 26). Mosmans (1995) argues that the focus within advertising has become value creation rather than product creation; that is, the ascription of symbolic and cultural associations to a product is more important than highlighting its usefulness. For instance, the use of music was central to Bartle Bogle Hegarty's highly successful UK campaign for Levi's jeans in the 1980s. This campaign was integral to the branding of Levi's as a 'classic' and 'authentic' product. The series of advertisements matched stylized images of 1950s Americana (laundromats, GIs, Cadillacs) with soul, blues and early rock 'n' roll. The combination of this particular mixture of imagery and music was used to evoke a sense of history. In 1993, a UK marketing manager described the campaign message as 'timeless America but not retro' (Richmond 1993, 37).

Alternatively, musical semiotics can be exploited where a soundtrack is used to set the mood of a particular advertisement. For example, a car manufacturer may use music to convey a message regarding the powerful performance or visual elegance of a vehicle (Cook 1994). Popular music is especially important in campaigns that tap into youth culture in order to target a youth market. 'It is particularly within the issue of products designed for young people that advertising reveals its true procedures: parasitic appropriation and the seductive manipulations of musical practices and modes, along with imaginative cinematography designed for the young' (Ala and Ghezzi 1985, 405).

Branding has a close relationship to life styles and subcultures associated with popular music. Here, music is used to target a particular age group or to fit advertisements into particularly inclusive or exclusive frames of reference. Frank (1995) points to an early 1990s advertisement that appeared in US business papers, promoting the advertising potential of MTV. The advertisement depicted a youth dressed in 'grunge' clothes (associated with US alternative rock culture) and read: 'Buy this 24 year old and get all his friends absolutely free . . . he

knows a lot. More than just what CDs to buy . . . He knows what car to drive and what credit cards to use. And he's no loner. What he eats, his friends eat. What he wears, they wear. What he likes, they like' (112). Even products not immediately associated with youth can often be branded as having a relevance to youth life styles, since the 18–30 age group is regarded by the advertising industry as a taste leader in the general market. The marketing manager of the Ericsson mobile phone company justified a campaign for the company that used dance music and culture by explaining that 'young people, especially clubbers, dictate trends [which are] followed by the rest of the population' (Doward 1999, 5).

The use of popular music in advertising can be linked to debates surrounding the process of globalization, in which the worldwide predominance of multinational corporations and media conglomerates is seen to have an effect on the character of local cultures. As Savan (1994) points out, 'Marketers believe that modern communications have spawned a "global teen," kids who have more in common with kids halfway across the earth than they do with other generations in the next room' (89). In this context, music is used to associate products with cosmopolitan attributes and non-localized (although it may be argued that these are often Western) values. This is borne out in Gillespie's (1995) research among young London Punjabis in which she formulates a hierarchy of desirable values from her respondents' reactions to Levi's and L.A. Gear sportswear advertisements. At the top of this hierarchy lie conceptions of 'coolness,' which are in turn linked to global, cosmopolitan attitudes and success. The non-linguistic nature of music, combined with the predominance of multinational record and entertainment industries, means that it is central in transmitting and denoting these values and associations.

The use of existing popular music in advertising is a useful income generator for artists and publishers and an extremely effective promotional tool. Research has suggested that a popular music track can delay the effect of 'wear-out,' a process whereby the viewer becomes bored by repeated showings of an advertisement, resulting in a reduction of its effectiveness in communicating product information (Yalch 1991, 274). The effectiveness of music in advertising has resulted in the payment of enormous fees to major artists for the use of their music. In 1995, the Rolling Stones were paid US$8 million for the use of 'Start Me Up' in a worldwide campaign for Microsoft's Windows '95. As a consequence of the commercial success of pairing music with advertising, the record industry has cashed in on the popularity of particular radio and television advertisements and a number of records have traded on the success of advertising music. After Lester Flatt and Earl Scruggs signed a sponsorship deal with the Martha White Mills flour company in 1953, the company's theme tune became a popular part of their repertoire. In 1971, the New Seekers produced a hit single, 'I'd Like to Teach the World to Sing,' which was a rewritten version of the Coca-Cola jingle 'I'd Like to Buy the World a Coke.' Similarly, in the late 1970s both David Dundas and John Du Cann had success in the United Kingdom with lyrically amended versions of Brutus and Lee Cooper jeans advertising jingles, respectively.

The 1980s and 1990s saw a rapid rise in marketing synergy between the airing of a particular advertisement and the commercial release of a piece of popular music. It has become commonplace for record companies to pitch their artists' back catalog and forthcoming releases to advertising agencies. In 1999, the track 'Right Here, Right Now' by UK artist Fatboy Slim was used in a pan-European commercial for the sports manufacturer Adidas. Fatboy Slim was already one of the year's most successful artists in the United Kingdom, and the heavy rotation of the advertisement, coinciding with the European release of the track as a single, was used to establish the artist's profile across Europe (Morgan 1999). Thus, the use of a track in an advertisement has been recognized by the record industry as a powerful promotional device, which is often employed to launch a new act or release and which may have the effect of generating sales on back catalog or older material. For instance, the previously unknown acts Babylon Zoo, Freak Power and Stiltskin all enjoyed chart hits after their music was used in European advertisements for Levi's.

Perhaps the most high-profile example of this synergy was the simultaneous release of Madonna's single 'Like a Prayer' and a worldwide Pepsi-Cola campaign in 1989. The advertisement featuring the song was broadcast on the same day in 40 countries and watched by around 300 million people. These tie-in releases may also have product information written on the record and CD sleeves. In the United Kingdom, for instance, the 1999 rerelease of Andy Williams' 'Music to Watch Girls By' was facilitated by its use in a major television advertising campaign for Fiat cars. The sleeve of the release carried a sticker that read 'as featured in the Fiat Punto TV ad' and included a telephone number and Web site address for product information. De Launey (1995) points out that, in the 1990s in Japan, the majority of successful releases were tie-ins in some form (related to advertising, television and film). Hence, tie-ins have come to be regarded as such an essential part of the music industry marketing process that it has become a 'buyers' market, and the buyers are demanding more and more conces-

sions from the artists, including asking record and management companies to waive their rights to songs' (218).

The use of popular music can also be related to discourses surrounding the commodification of subcultural musics (Eliot 1989; Savan 1994; Frank 1995) and has been central to debates about purity, threat and co-optation. When an artist's music is used for the purpose of advertising, it is often seen as a lapse in artistic integrity. Chapple and Garofalo (1977) argue that the use of 1960s US rock in advertising was a central part of the general process of co-optation and commercialization of an 'authentic' musical movement which reflected and addressed the concerns of the counterculture – the implication being that advertising 'integrated the music into the consumer system' and therefore emptied it of its original (supposedly anti-materialistic) social meanings and effects (308).

Similarly, Frank (1995) traces the same process through to early 1990s US alternative rock, citing the use of 'alternative' acts Sonic Youth, Lois and Belly to promote US clothing chain stores. Here, rather than an artist's star persona being used to elicit immediate audience recognition (indeed, the artists involved may not be widely known outside specific taste cultures), a particular artist serves to evoke a sense of 'cool,' thereby implying that the product is associated with a particular attitude, life style and ideology. Frank (1995) argues that, '[e]ver since the 1960s hip has been the native tongue of advertising, "anti-establishment" the vocabulary by which we are taught to cast off our old possessions and buy whatever they have decided to offer this year' (112).

Because of the art versus commerce dichotomy embedded within rock ideology, the use of an artist's material in a campaign may be regarded as detrimental to his/her carefully cultivated public image. Some artists will only sanction advertisements for products that seem to 'fit' with public perceptions of their persona. For instance, a representative of Fatboy Slim's record company makes the link between the artist's profile and products that the company is happy to be associated with: 'The reason we chose to accept this deal [with Adidas sportswear] where we've turned down so many others is that . . . it would not alter people's perceptions of the artist and the product was considered credible enough. Put simply, Adidas is cool' (Morgan 1999, 52).

This phenomenon may vary with circumstances, as an artist may allow the use of a particular song or be involved in product endorsement in one area while vetoing its use in another. This moral right, or the right to preserve the integrity of a work, is granted to composers by the Berne Convention and other copyright legislation. In the 1980s, for instance, the British group Madness allowed its music and image to be used to advertise

Honda in Japan while turning down requests for UK campaigns. However, Eliot (1989) argues that many 'artists have no say in whether or not the music they're identified with in the public's mind becomes part of a commercial campaign' (201). There have been a number of legal battles over the control of music in advertising. In 1993, Tom Waits sued his publishing company Third Story for allowing the use of a cover of his song 'Heartattack and Vine' in a Levi's advertisement aired in 17 countries. In 1990, Waits had won $2,475,000 in punitive damages from Frito-Lay and Tracy Locke after radio advertisements used a 'soundalike' to promote Doritos chips. Likewise, the Beatles sued in 1989 when their publishing company allowed the use of 'Revolution' for an advertisement for Nike training shoes.

Bibliography

Ala, Nemesio, and Ghezzi, Emilio. 1985. 'Music and Advertising on Italian Television.' In *Popular Music Perspectives, 2*, ed. David Horn. Göteborg and Exeter: IASPM, 405–16.

Arnold, Gina. 1997. *Kiss This: Punk in the Present Tense*. New York: St. Martin's Griffin.

Atsuko, Kimura. 1991. 'Japanese Corporations and Popular Music.' *Popular Music* 10(3): 317–26.

Barnard, Stephen. 1989. *On the Radio: Music Radio in Britain*. Milton Keynes: Open University Press.

Boorstin, Daniel J. 1973. *Americans: The Democratic Experience*. New York: Random House.

Booth, Mark W. 1990 (1981). 'Jingle: Pepsi-Cola Hits the Spot.' In *On Record: Rock, Pop and the Written Word*, ed. Simon Frith and Andrew Goodwin. New York: Pantheon Books, 320–25.

Chapman, Robert. 1990. 'The 1960s Pirates: A Comparative Analysis of Radio London and Radio Caroline.' *Popular Music* 9(2): 165–78.

Chapple, Steve, and Garofalo, Reebee. 1977. *Rock 'n' Roll Is Here to Pay: The History and Politics of the Music Industry*. Chicago: Nelson-Hall.

Clark, Harold F., Jr. 1999. 'Brand Ideas and Their Importance: "When Do You Tell the Agency What the Brand Means?"' In *How to Use Advertising to Build Strong Brands*, ed. John Philip Jones. Thousand Oaks, CA: Sage Publications, 25–36.

Cook, Nicholas. 1994. 'Music and Meaning in the Commercials.' *Popular Music* 13(1): 27–40.

De Launey, Guy. 1995. 'Not-So-Big in Japan: Western Pop Music in the Japanese Market.' *Popular Music* 14(2): 203–25.

Doward, Jamie. 1999. 'Music to the Ears in the Quest for Cred.' *The Observer* (2 May): 5 (Business Section).

Eberly, Philip K. 1982. *Music in the Air: America's Changing Tastes in Popular Music, 1920–1980*. New York: Hastings House.

Eliot, Marc. 1989. *Rockonomics: The Money Behind the Music*. London: Omnibus Press.

Epstein, Dena J. 1981. *Sinful Tunes and Spirituals: Black Folk Music to the Civil War*. Urbana, IL: University of Illinois Press.

Frank, Tom. 1995. 'Alternative to What?' In *Sounding Off: Music as Subversion/Resistance/Revolution*, ed. Ron Sakolsky and Fred Wei-han Ho. New York: Autonomedia, 109–20.

Gillespie, Mary. 1995. 'Cool Bodies: TV Ad Talk.' In *Television, Ethnicity and Cultural Change*. London: Routledge, 175.

Hindley, Diana, and Hindley, Geoffrey. 1972. *Advertising in Victorian England, 1837–1901*. London: Wayland.

Huron, David. 1989. 'Music in Advertising: An Analytic Paradigm.' *The Musical Quarterly* 73(4): 557–74.

Julien, Jean-Rémy. 1985. 'The Use of Folklore and Popular Music in Radio Advertising.' In *Popular Music Perspectives, 2*, ed. David Horn. Göteborg and Exeter: IASPM, 417–27.

Leiss, William, Kline, Stephen, and Jhally, Sut. 1990. *Social Communication in Advertising: Persons, Products and Images of Well-Being*. Scarborough, ON: Nelson.

Loeb, Lori Anne. 1994. *Consuming Angels: Advertising and Victorian Women*. Oxford: Oxford University Press.

Malone, Bill C. 1985. *Country Music, U.S.A.* Rev. ed. Austin, TX: University of Texas Press.

Maltby, Richard, ed. 1989. *Dreams for Sale: Popular Culture in the 20th Century*. London: Harrap.

Mayhew, Henry. 1969 (1851). *Mayhew's London. Being Selections from London's Labour and the London Poor*, ed. Peter Quennell. London: Spring Books.

Morgan, Emma. 1999. 'The Bands Who Like to Say . . . Yes!' *Select* (May): 49–52.

Mosmans, A. 1995. 'Brand Strategy: Creating Concepts That Drive the Business.' *Journal of Brand Management* 3(3): 156–65.

Richmond, Susannah. 1993. 'Levi's: The Golden Decade.' *Campaign* 5 (February): 36–37.

Savan, Leslie. 1994. *The Sponsored Life: Ads, TV, and American Culture*. Philadelphia: Temple University Press.

Tagg, Philip. 1999. 'Introductory Notes to the Semiotics of Music.' Version 2 (Unpublished course material used at Griffith University, Brisbane, Australia).

Turner, E.S. 1953. *The Shocking History of Advertising*. New York: E.P. Dutton.

Wells, William, Burnett, John, and Moriarty, Sandra. 1989. *Advertising: Principles and Practice*. Englewood Cliffs, NJ: Prentice-Hall.

Williams, Raymond. 1980. *Problems in Materialism and Culture*. London: Verso and New Left Books.

Yalch, Richard F. 1991. 'Memory in a Jingle Jungle: Music as a Mnemonic Device in Communicating Advertising Slogans.' *Journal of Applied Psychology* 76(2): 268–75.

Discographical References

Babylon Zoo. 'Spaceman.' EMI CDEM 416. *1996*: UK.

Beatles, The. 'Revolution.' Apple 2276. *1968*: UK.

Du Cann, John. 'Don't Be a Dummy.' Vertigo 6059 241. *1979*: UK.

Dundas, David. 'Jeans On.' Air CHS 2094. *1976*: UK.

Fatboy Slim. 'Right Here, Right Now.' *Right Here, Right Now*. Sony International 667149. *1999*: UK.

Freak Power. 'Turn On Tune In Cop Out.' Fourth & Broadway BRCD 317. *1995*: UK.

Guthrie, Woody. 'So Long, It's Been Good to Know You.' *Woody Guthrie: Library of Congress Recordings* (rec. Alan Lomax, 1940). Elektra EKL-271/2. *1964*: USA.

Madonna. 'Like a Prayer.' Sire 27539. *1989*: USA.

New Seekers, The. 'I'd Like to Teach the World to Sing.' Elektra 45762. *1971*: USA.

Rolling Stones, The. 'Start Me Up.' Rolling Stones RSR 108. *1981*: UK.

Stiltskin. 'Inside.' White Water LEV 1CD. *1994*: UK.

Waits, Tom. 'Heartattack and Vine.' *Heartattack and Vine*. Asylum 295. *1980*: USA.

Williams, Andy. 'Music to Watch Girls By.' Columbia 44065. *1967*: USA. Rerelease: Williams, Andy. 'Music to Watch Girls By.' *Born Free/Love Andy*. Collectables 6049. *1999*: USA.

ROBERT STRACHAN and MARION LEONARD

Popular Music in Film

The broad category of films that depict popular music artists, performance or cultures includes documentaries and performance films, 'biopics' (films that depict the life of a popular music artist or act), film dramas based on fictional characters working in the music industry, 'star vehicles' (films created to promote an artist) and films that represent subcultures associated with popular music. These cinematic representations have played an important part in the mediation, creation and reinforcement of popular music's ideologies, images and mythologies.

The relationship between popular music and cinema is almost as old as the medium of film itself. Films were shown at the 1900 Paris World Fair, which featured theater actors performing sketches with synchronized gramophone accompaniment (Wallis and Malm 1988). There were also a number of performance films using this method in the first two decades of the twentieth century, such as those made and shown in Sweden

between 1905 and 1914 (Wallis and Malm 1988). Technological advancements in sound-on-film in the 1920s, such as Movietone and Vitaphone, were perceived by major US film studios as a way of tapping into popular music markets. Albert Warner of Warner Brothers envisaged that 'radio music programs' on film would be a principal use of these new technologies (Chanan 1995). *The Jazz Singer* (1927), the film generally accepted as being the first full-length sound film, acted as a star vehicle for Al Jolson. The film's plot, involving a young singer's conflict between family and the entertainment industry, was used as a way of framing Jolson's performances of songs such as 'Blue Skies' and 'My Mammy.' *The Jazz Singer* was perhaps a logical progression for the film industry, as many US cinemas had already capitalized on the popularity of the genre by offering mixed programs of silent movies and live jazz (Crafton 1996).

Aside from being the first massively successful 'talkie,' *The Jazz Singer* set a precedent for the way in which the film industry has capitalized on the commercial potential of popular music stars. From the Paul Robeson and Bessie Smith films of the 1930s and the Edith Piaf films of the 1940s to the Spice Girls' film of the late 1990s, star vehicles have utilized the fame of popular music artists in order to gain mass appeal. As Thompson (1995) argues, 'Big pop names will ... supply both charisma and crowds' (33). Whereas in film musicals, songs (often mimed by actors to recordings made by uncredited singers) may be used as illustrative of plot or character formation, in the star vehicle the narrative is essentially a framing device for the star and his/her popular music performance. Unlike the traditional musical, where characters may burst into song in any situation or location, performance in these films is generally limited to naturalized performance settings that are consistent with the narrative and setting of the film, such as fictional concerts, nightclubs, television stations, parties or social gatherings. Consequently, in order to naturalize performance within the narrative of these films, popular music performers tended to be restricted to playing either fictional musicians or characters with extracurricular musical talents. Performance is thus legitimated within the film by its contextualization within apparently realistic settings, the 'backstage' theme being predominant in such contextualization. At the same time, the inclusion of popular music performances in films also benefited popular music. By the late 1920s, the inclusion of songs in films helped to promote and sell records.

The precedence of musical performance within the star vehicle format meant that the line between the star and the character being played was often blurred. Indeed, during the late 1950s and 1960s, films such as

The Tommy Steele Story (1957), *A Hard Day's Night* (1964) and *I've Gotta Horse* (1965) took the form to its natural conclusion by presenting performers playing fictionalized versions of themselves. This development attempted to provide an even more 'authentic' representation of performance with a minimum suspension of disbelief. The performers were ostensibly 'themselves' offering a 'real' musical performance. Some filmmakers have combined the formats of star vehicle, drama, biopic, social commentary and documentary. For instance, *Rude Boy* (1980), featuring the Clash, mixes film of live performance with documentary footage (such as scenes from the Notting Hill riots of 1978 and a Margaret Thatcher speech at the Conservative Party Conference) and has a plot involving a roadie and the band acting as 'themselves.' With its mix of fact, fiction and social context, the film is a promotional vehicle for the band, a documentary and a film addressing subcultural concerns.

In addition to increasing their public profile, the casting of musicians in films can also affect a repositioning of their public image. Elvis Presley, perhaps the most prolific star vehicle performer, made over 25 films between *Love Me Tender* in 1956 and *The Trouble with Girls* in 1969. Operating primarily as a medium for Presley's singing talents, the films were commercially successful but critically unacclaimed. Indeed, Elvis's films of the 1960s are central to the way in which the singer has traditionally been historicized and the way in which his career has been periodized. The films (and the music they contain) have been widely interpreted as constituting a loss of artistic integrity in which the 'authentic' Elvis of the mid- to late 1950s becomes co-opted and corrupted by commercial concerns. Frank Sinatra, on the other hand, is an example of how an artist's film career can help to strengthen his/her musical popularity and critical credibility. In the early 1950s, Sinatra's record sales were in decline, despite his appearance in star vehicle movies such as *Meet Danny Wilson* (1952). The turnaround in Sinatra's career has generally been credited to a nonmusical film, *From Here to Eternity* (1953). Although the film gave Sinatra a 'straight' role, its success was instrumental in the revitalization of his career as a singer. The role helped market Sinatra to an adult audience, acting as a platform for his musical transition to a 'serious' album-oriented star. The fact that Sinatra went on to make over 40 (nonmusical and musical) films shows that, along with notable examples such as Kris Kristofferson and Cher, he is an exception, as few popular music 'stars' have enjoyed prolonged careers in the film industry.

Another way in which the film industry has tapped into the public appeal of popular music stars is through biopics: cinematic accounts of the lives of artists or groups. The formula was first used to great commercial success in films set during the swing era, with movies such as *The Glenn Miller Story* (1954) and *The Benny Goodman Story* (1955). These films often offer a highly selective and romanticized version of their subjects' lives, which create, and reflect, mythologies surrounding popular music performers. Biopics work as a space for common themes and mythologies to be repeated and reworked. For instance, many films, from *The Glenn Miller Story* to *Bird* (1988), concentrate on stars who have died 'before their time.' The death of the subject not only provides a neat narrative conclusion but also enables the standard tropes of popular music stardom and mythology ('rags to riches,' 'fatalistic decline,' 'doomed genius' and so on) to be projected onto the star. As Atkinson (1995) points out, the form 'traffics in the culture myth of . . . the musical genius/god courting untimely death by way of his or her extraordinariness' (21).

The representations of these performers can often be understood in gendered terms. Viewers are invited to consider the decline of male musicians in terms of the heroic and female performers in terms of the tragic. *Bird* and *The Doors* (1991), for instance, are highly stylized hagiographies of Charlie Parker and Jim Morrison respectively, which place their subjects' excessive behavior, drink and drug problems within the discourse of the doomed romantic. In contrast, films such as the Edith Piaf biopic *Piaf* (1974), *The Rose* (1979), based on the life of Janis Joplin, and the Patsy Cline film *Sweet Dreams* (1985) present their equally excessive subjects as victims of circumstance who are to be pitied rather than deified.

Since the 1950s, there has been a tradition of films that have made the link between popular music and youth culture without specifically relying on a star to 'carry' the film. *The Blackboard Jungle* (1955) was the first of a number of films that used popular music to signify the generation gap and teenage rebellion. The story of a teacher's relationship with his 'delinquent' pupils, the film used popular music as a blunt illustration of the alienation of youth. In the film's most famous scene, the teacher (Glenn Ford) brings his expensive collection of jazz records into the classroom in an attempt to relate to his pupils. The 78s are subsequently used as frisbees and smashed by the teenagers in an act symbolizing a rejection of adult values and mores. Doherty (1988) comments, 'throughout *Blackboard Jungle* there is a real sense that the terms of the social contract between young and old have changed' (76). Although it was billed as an 'adult' film, *The Blackboard Jungle* found enormous success in the youth market, thereby illustrating the com-

319

mercial potential of the teenage sector to the film industry. The film also promoted Bill Haley's earlier release, 'Rock Around the Clock.' Used as the theme tune, the record sold 2 million copies in the wake of the film's success.

A number of films used rock 'n' roll culture as their central theme to exploit this newfound commercial potential of the teenage market. Following the success of *The Blackboard Jungle*, *Rock Around the Clock* (1956) was the first of a number of films in which rock 'n' roll performance was framed by a dramatic account of its culture. Although the actual content of the film is fairly inoffensive (a standard obscurity-to-success story), widespread media reports of rioting at cinema screenings helped to cement the view of rock 'n' roll as a delinquent form. After the success of *Rock Around the Clock*, many other cash-in movies were quickly produced to the same formula: *Rock, Rock, Rock* (1956), *The Girl Can't Help It* (1956) and *Shake, Rattle and Rock* (1957). The Hollywood film industry played an important role in mirroring, contributing to and exploiting the 'moral panic' surrounding rock 'n' roll in the mid-1950s. Indeed, the success of earlier youth films, such as *The Wild One* (1954) and *Rebel Without a Cause* (1955), had already iconicized the figure of the rebellious youth. Berland (1993) argues that these films created an ideological 'space' for Elvis's success. The relationship between rock and cinema was thus somewhat contradictory, as a leading article in *Variety* magazine illustrates: 'While its money-making potential has made it all but irresistible, its Svengali grip on the teenagers has produced a staggering wave of juvenile violence and mayhem' (quoted in Doherty 1988, 82).

Although the rock 'n' roll film has antecedents in 'social conscience' films such as *Angels with Dirty Faces* (1938) and 'exploitation movies' such as *Reefer Madness* (1936), these early films were the first to cement the perceived interrelationship between rock and teenage delinquency on film. They also mark the beginning of a long line of films that have attempted to portray the life styles and subcultures associated with popular music genres. These texts often glamorize and exaggerate already existing associations between popular music styles and social practise. This is not to say that youth and subculture films involving popular music all used the same strategies or were all of one genre, as representations of youth ranged from melodrama to romantic comedy. For instance, the film *Niewinni Czarodzieje* (Innocent Sorcerers) (1960) looks at the alienation of a group of friends involved in a jazz subculture, exploring its themes using gentle comedy, whereas *Beat Girl* (1960) approaches the same subject from within the tradition of the exploitation movie.

As youth and popular music films evolved, the issues they raised were addressed in an increasingly sophisticated manner, with many aspiring to great levels of 'seriousness' that would have been unthinkable at the start of the movie era. Films such as *Blow-Up* (1966), *One Plus One* (1970) and *Performance* (1970) were closer to the tradition of the European art film than the Hollywood cash-in movie. Antonioni's *Blow-Up* is an acerbic comment on the fashionable world of 'swinging London,' rich in visual and thematic metaphor. The film uses its setting in the worlds of fashion, art and music in an attempt to deal with themes such as the relationship between image and reality. Alternatively, *Performance* uses the uneasy relationship between a rock star and a gangster to explore issues of class, masculinity and sexuality within a distinct historical moment. Likewise, *Megáll Az Idó* (Time Stands Still) (1981) parallels two teenagers' search for identity through US rock 'n' roll with Hungarian national identity under Soviet rule.

The themes and issues within popular music film are generally grounded in the social meanings, contexts and implications of the individual genre or subculture they address. *Easy Rider*'s (1969) tale of two hippies traveling across the United States mixes the road movie form with a rock soundtrack to address countercultural politics and US mythology. Like many popular music films, *Easy Rider* deals with 'escape from the claustrophobia of petit-bourgeois life ... and from an intolerant "normality"' (Eyerman and Löfgren 1995, 62), but its use of music and its thematic concerns are symbiotic with its social and (sub)cultural context. Likewise, *Nashville* (1975), Robert Altman's epic portrait of the Nashville country scene, uses a genre traditionally associated with conservative and socially cohesive cultural values to examine and satirize contemporary issues relating to the crisis of US identity in the wake of the Vietnam war. The portrayal of the disco and punk movements in *Young Soul Rebels* (1992) explores the roles that race, class, gender and sexuality play within subcultures. Likewise, *Fly By Night* (1993) highlights the issues of race, gender and cultural politics within Afro-American culture, through a narrative involving a fictional hip-hop group.

The representation of subcultures on film has not been restricted to the depiction of contemporary music-related movements. Since the 1970s, there have been a number of nostalgic representations of popular music practise and subculture on film. *That Thing You Do!* (1996) and *Die Heartbreakers* (The Heartbreakers) (1982) illustrate how past popular music genres and eras are reevaluated and reinterpreted in contemporary settings. The film *Quadrophenia* (1979) offers the viewer the narrative of a fictitious group of mods who exist in a world of all-night clubs, scooter gangs and heavy amphetamine consumption. Any contradictory elements of 'mod life' are sacrificed or stylized in the pursuit of a hyper-real narrative depiction. Filmic representations of past youth cultures have occasionally influenced contemporary subcultural revivals. The release of *Quadrophenia* is a pertinent example, as it was central to the mod revival of the late 1970s. Thus, popular music shares a complex relationship with film. While filmmakers have capitalized on the popularity of musicians and traded in (and reinforced) the mythologies surrounding popular music, film depictions have also enhanced the popularity of performers and informed musical and subcultural practise.

Bibliography

Atkinson, Michael. 1995. 'Long Black Limousine: Pop Biopics.' In *Celluloid Jukebox: Popular Music and the Movies Since the 50s*, ed. Jonathan Romney and Adrian Wootton. London: British Film Institute, 20–31.

Berland, Jody. 1993. 'Sound, Image and Social Space: Music Video and Media Reconstruction.' In *Sound and Vision: The Music Video Reader*, ed. Simon Frith, Andrew Goodwin and Lawrence Grossberg. London: Routledge, 25–43.

Chanan, Michael. 1995. *Repeated Takes: A Short History of Recording and Its Effects on Music*. London: Verso.

Crafton, Donald. 1996. 'The *Jazz Singer*'s Reception in the Media and at the Box Office.' In *Post-Theory: Reconstructing Film Studies*, ed. David Bordwell and Noel Carroll. Madison, WI: University of Wisconsin Press, 460–80.

Doherty, Thomas. 1988. *Teenagers and Teenpics: The Juvenilization of American Movies in the 1950s*. Winchester, MA: Unwin Hyman.

Eyerman, Ron, and Löfgren, Ovar. 1995. 'Romancing the Road: Road Movies and Images of Mobility.' *Theory, Culture and Society* 12(1) (February): 53–79.

Thompson, Ben. 1995. 'Pop and Film: The Charisma Crossover.' In *Celluloid Jukebox: Popular Music and the Movies Since the 50s*, ed. Jonathan Romney and Adrian Wootton. London: British Film Institute, 32–41.

Wallis, Roger, and Malm, Krister. 1988. 'Push-Pull for the Video Clip: A Systems Approach to the Relationship Between the Phonogram/Videogram Industry and Music Television.' *Popular Music* 7(3): 267–84.

Discographical References

Haley, Bill, and His Comets. '(We're Gonna) Rock Around the Clock.' Decca 29124. 1955: USA.

Jolson, Al. 'Blue Skies.' *Let Me Sing and I'm Happy: Al Jolson at Warner Bros. 1926–1936*. Rhino 72544. 1927; 1996: USA.

Jolson, Al. 'My Mammy.' *Let Me Sing and I'm Happy: Al Jolson at Warner Bros. 1926–1936*. Rhino 72544. 1927; 1996: USA.

Filmography

A Hard Day's Night, dir. Richard Lester. 1964. UK. 90 mins. Rock Musical. Original music by John Lennon, Paul McCartney.

Angels with Dirty Faces, dir. Michael Curtiz. 1938. USA. 97 mins. Crime Drama. Original music by Max Steiner.

Beat Girl, dir. Edmond T. Greville. 1960. UK. 85 mins. Drama. Original music by John Barry, Trevor Peacock.

The Benny Goodman Story, dir. Valentine Davies. 1955. USA. 116 mins. Biography. Original music by Harry Brown, Joseph E. Gershenson, Alan Harding, Henry Mancini, Sol Yaged.

Bird, dir. Clint Eastwood. 1988. USA. 160 mins. Biography. Original music by Lennie Niehaus.

The Blackboard Jungle, dir. Richard Brooks. 1955. USA. 101 mins. Urban Drama. Original music by Charles Wolcott.

Blow-Up, dir. Michelangelo Antonioni. 1966. Italy/UK. 102 mins. Psychological Thriller. Original music by Herbie Hancock, the Yardbirds.

Die Heartbreakers [The Heartbreakers], dir. Peter F. Bringmann. 1982. West Germany. 110 mins. Comedy. Musical direction by Lothar Meid.

The Doors, dir. Oliver Stone. 1991. USA. 138 mins. Musical Drama. Original music by John Densmore, Robby Krieger, Ray Manzarek, Jim Morrison.

Easy Rider, dir. Dennis Hopper. 1969. USA. 94 mins. Adventure. Original music by David A. Axelrod, Hoyt Axton, Antonia Durzen, Bob Dylan, Gerry Goffin, Jimi Hendrix, Jack Keller, Carole King, Roger McGuinn, Larry Waner.

Fly By Night, dir. Steve Gomer. 1993. USA. 100 mins. Urban Drama. Original music by Kris Parker.

From Here to Eternity, dir. Fred Zinnemann. 1953. USA. 118 mins. Romantic Drama. Original music by George Duning, James Jones, Freddy Karger, Morris W. Stoloff, Robert Wells.

The Girl Can't Help It, dir. Frank Tashlin. 1956. USA. 99 mins. Rock Musical. Original music by Lionel Newman, Bobby Troup.

The Glenn Miller Story, dir. Anthony Mann. 1954. USA. 113 mins. Biography. Original music by Joseph E. Gershenson, Henry Mancini, Frank Skinner, Herman Stein.

I've Gotta Horse, dir. Kenneth Hume. 1965. UK. 92 mins. Musical Comedy. Original music by David Heneker, John Taylor.

The Jazz Singer, dir. Alan Crosland. 1927. USA. 89 mins. Drama. Original music by Louis Silvers.

Love Me Tender, dir. Robert Webb. 1956. USA. 89 mins. Rock Musical. Original music by Lionel Newman.

Meet Danny Wilson, dir. Joseph Pevney. 1952. USA. 86

mins. Drama. Musical direction by Joseph E. Gershenson.

Megáll Az Idó [Time Stands Still], dir. Péter Gothár. 1981. Hungary. 99 mins. Drama. Original music by György Selmeczi.

Nashville, dir. Robert Altman. 1975. USA. 157 mins. Musical Drama. Original music by Richard Baskin, Keith Carradine.

Niewinni Czarodzieje [Innocent Sorcerers], dir. Andrzej Wajda. 1960. Poland. 85 mins. Original music by Krzysztof Komeda.

One Plus One, dir. Jean-Luc Godard. 1970. UK. 110 mins. Experimental. Original music by Mick Jagger, Keith Richard, the Rolling Stones.

Performance, dir. Donald Cammell and Nicolas Roeg. 1970. UK. 105 mins. Experimental. Original music by Jack Nitzsche.

Piaf, dir. Guy Casaril. 1974. France/USA. 105 mins. Biography. Original music by Ralph Burns.

Quadrophenia, dir. Franc Roddam. 1979. UK. 115 mins. Rock Musical. Original music by John Entwistle, Pete Townshend, the Who.

Rebel Without a Cause, dir. Nicholas Ray. 1955. USA. 111 mins. Family Drama. Original music by Leonard Rosenman.

Reefer Madness, dir. Louis J. Gasnier. 1936. USA. 67 mins. Addiction Drama. Original music by Abe Meyer.

Rock Around the Clock, dir. Fred Sears. 1956. USA. 77 mins. Rock Musical. Musical direction by Freddy Karger.

Rock, Rock, Rock, dir. Will Price. 1956. USA. 78 mins. Rock Musical. Original music by Chuck Berry, Charles F. Calhoun, Buddy Dufault, George Goldner, Leroy Kirkland, Freddie Mitchell, Glen Moore, Johnny Parker, Aaron Schroeder, Al Sears, Al Weisman, Ben Weisman.

The Rose, dir. Mark Rydell. 1979. USA. 134 mins. Biography. Original music by Paul A. Rothchild.

Rude Boy, dir. Jack Hazan and David Mingay. 1980. UK. 133 mins. Rock Musical. Original music by Mick Jones, Joe Strummer.

Shake, Rattle and Rock, dir. Edward L. Cahn. 1957. USA. 76 mins. Rock Musical. Original music by Alexander Courage.

Sweet Dreams, dir. Karel Reisz. 1985. USA. 115 mins. Biography. Original music by Charles Gross.

That Thing You Do!, dir. Tom Hanks. 1996. USA. 110 mins. Rock Musical. Original music by Howard Shore.

The Tommy Steele Story, dir. Gerard Bryant. 1957. UK. 71 mins. Rock Musical. Original music by Lionel Bart.

The Trouble with Girls, dir. Peter Tewksbury. 1969. USA. 105 mins. Rock Musical. Original music by Scott Davis, Billy Strange.

The Wild One, dir. Laslo Benedek. 1954. USA. 79 mins. Drama. Original music by Leith Stevens.

Young Soul Rebels, dir. Isaac Julien. 1992. UK. 103 mins. Drama. Original music by Simon Boswell.

ROBERT STRACHAN and MARION LEONARD

Pornography

Material and activities that many would judge to be pornographic have featured in the history of popular music. However, providing an account of the pornographic in popular music is complicated by the disagreements and divisions that surround the term 'pornography,' and the political and moral perspectives of those who contribute to these debates. As McNair (1996) points out, the term is, indeed, 'a political one, signifying very different things to different people and groups, at different times and in different places' (viii). The meaning of the term is as a consequence contested, and it is not possible to give a straightforward definition.

Definition: History and Issues

The term derives from the Greek words *porne* and *graphe*, which combine to form *pornographos*. *Pornographos* did not have the contemporary meanings of the term 'pornography,' but referred to 'a specific subcategory of biography – tales of the lives of the courtesans – which may not contain any obscene material at all' (Parker 1992, 91). In ancient Greek culture, *pornographos* meant someone who 'represents [prostitutes] in speech or in pictorial form, [who] admits knowledge of prostitutes and shares it publicly' (Henry 1992, 263).

As McNair observes, 'the circulation of any sexual representation, pornographic or otherwise, was constrained until the eighteenth and nineteenth centuries by the undeveloped state of the media, and the lack of means of mechanical reproduction' (1996, 43). The first instances of modern pornography date back to the sixteenth century, when sexually explicit images began to appear that differentiated themselves from the already established tradition of sexual representation in European art by combining 'the explicit representation of sexual activity . . . and the challenge to moral conventions of the day' (Hunt 1993, 26). While early modern pornography was sexually arousing, therefore, it was also explicitly subversive. By the eighteenth century, however, novels like *Fanny Hill*, which circulated in relatively large quantities due to 'the new possibilities offered by the medium of print . . . signalled the emergence of a more recognizably modern pornography, in so far as it had little or no political agenda, but pursued the aim of sexual arousal alone' (McNair 1996, 43). By the nineteenth century, apolitical pornography had become the norm.

A working definition of the term 'pornography' could

thus be: any material that is sexually explicit and is created with the intention of causing sexual arousal. Difficulties arise immediately, however, in agreeing on what is sexually explicit. This has led to a distinction between 'hard' and 'soft' pornography in which 'soft' pornography is less graphic. Yet, this distinction also varies according to situation. In the United Kingdom, hardcore pornography is that which represents vaginal and oral sex. In contrast, however, US hard-core pornography denotes 'images which show more than vaginal and oral sex, and all other minority-interest material' (Thompson 1994, 2).

A second difficulty arises in relation to the element of intention. Sexually explicit material in a sex education film clearly does not have the intent of arousal, although that may, indeed, be a consequence. Again, sexual arousal may be a consequence of contact with materials such as leather and fur that are neither sexually explicit nor created with the intention of sexual arousal. Pornography, it might be argued, lies as much in the eye of the beholder as it does in the intent of the creator; yet, the element of perception has played a minor role in discussions of what is pornographic.

Reactions to pornography have differed, and have themselves affected what is understood to be pornographic. Further, the increasingly wide dissemination of pornography from the 1960s onward in photographic and filmic form (particularly videos) has contributed to an environment favoring increased tolerance. The liberal view of pornography, probably still dominant at the beginning of the twenty-first century but decreasingly so, is that it is harmless and that it should be more or less freely available. By contrast, feminists have argued that pornography is harmful and, in so doing, have added another dimension to its definition. According to this interpretation, 'pornography represents sex, and seeks to arouse, but it does so in the social context of patriarchy.' Consequently, 'the objectification and fetishization of women present in much pornography is a reflection of male dominance' (McNair 1996, 47). The issue here is the dominance of the male viewer or reader as voyeur, and hence one of male power. Pornography is harmful in being linked to misogyny.

Moral conservatives have also judged pornography pejoratively. According to McNair, moral conservatism is 'founded on adherence to Judaeo-Christian family values, which stress the virtues of the nuclear family, monogamous sexual relationships within marriage, and the reproductive rather than recreational functions of sexual behaviour' (1996, 49). As a consequence, a wide range of materials and activities can be judged pornographic by moral conservatives. McLaughlin (1996), commenting on the activities of Donald Wildmon, a United Methodist minister from Mississippi who 'since 1976 . . . has been involved in a highly visible and successful crusade against pornography and indecency in the United States' (31), observes that Wildmon is not interested in questions of definition or distinction: 'For Wildmon what constitutes pornography is self-evident, a matter of common sense. He knows it, and he claims we all know it, when we see it. His definition of porn is very inclusive. *thirtysomething* is porn because it promotes homosexuality as a valid lifestyle. *The Simpsons* is dangerous because it mocks the nuclear family' (1996, 35).

If a liberal attitude to pornography can be linked to its increasing dissemination from the 1960s onward, this spread is understood by moral conservatives as symptomatic of a wide range of social ills. Thus, for Wildmon, 'pornography is not an aberration in our society; rather, it is an inherent and inevitable feature of modern culture . . . Wildmon sees modern culture as dominated by secular, humanist, rationalist, anti-authoritarian, individualist, relativist thought.' Thus, 'the battle against pornography is a battle against what seems to him the most obviously vile aspect of that worldview' (McLaughlin 1996, 38).

For Wildmon, the problems of modern culture have more to do with a decline in Christian values than with capitalism as such. Yet, for this reason, capitalism divorced from Christian values is seen as highly problematic. 'Divorce capitalism from Christian ethics,' he says, 'and you have an economic system which makes Communism look like a Sunday School picnic' (Wildmon 1985, 15). For many, however, pornography is seen in any case as an intrinsic condition of capitalism. Soble (1986), for example, has argued that 'the use of pornography is an attempt to recoup in the domain of sexual fantasy what is denied to men in production and politics; in this sense the use of pornography in capitalism provides substitute gratification' (81). Marxist-influenced approaches to understanding pornography typical of the Frankfurt School and mass society theorists of communication thus view pornography 'as the mass cultural, commoditized form of sexual representation, implicated in the alienation and anomie which . . . have characterized capitalism in the twentieth century' (McNair 1996, 51).

It is, however, interesting that both feminists and mass society theorists of communication have made a distinction between pornography and erotica, thus allowing for sexually explicit representations that are assumed not to be degrading and harmful. For mass society theorists – in a distinction which resonates partially with that made between pornography and art in the sixteenth century (where pornography had the distinguishing feature of subverting moral conventions) – pornography is a product of mass culture, whereas erotica is art. For Barbara Smith (1988), for example, 'pornography does not describe sexuality, it describes sexual *acts*. It solidifies white, male, heterosexual fantasies, and then commoditizes them.' Consequently, 'erotica is sexualized Art and pornography is sexualized capitalism' (179). However, as McNair comments, 'efforts by cultural commentators to fit pornography into the high culture/low culture dichotomy are as elitist and questionable as similar efforts in other areas of media production' (1996, 57).

For feminists, the distinction between pornography and erotica has to do with power relations. Thus, while erotica can be sexually arousing, it represents sexuality in non-hierarchical and non-subordinating ways. As Gloria Steinem put it, 'erotica is about sexuality, but pornography is about power and sex-as-weapon' (1980, 38). While it can be as explicit as pornography, therefore, erotica lacks 'sexualized and sexually explicit dominance, subordination and violence' (Itzin 1992, 18). The problem with such distinctions is that, while a clear line between pornography and erotica can be drawn in terms of intent and content, there is no guarantee – given the possibility for an equally sexually explicit and arousing content in each case – that male voyeurs will not react in exactly the same way in each instance. Once again, the possibility has to be countenanced that pornography exists as much in the eye of the beholder as it does in the intent of the producer.

A criticism leveled against all these debates has been that they 'rarely distinguish heterosexual pornography from homosexual pornography; the two are lumped together on the basis of their sexual explicitness and representation of sexual desire and the treating of people as sexual objects' (Fejes and Petrich 1993, 406). However, 'gay male pornography ... occupies a very different space in the sexual system of modern patriarchal society.' While the construction of masculinity in gay male pornography draws from a heterosexual masculinity, therefore, 'the object of sexual desire and pleasure is a man; here women are absent' (Fejes and Petrich 1993, 406). In a parallel fashion, 'while lesbian pornography is not as extensive as gay male pornography, it represents as much, if not more of, a challenge to heterosexist, patriarchal notions of sexuality as gay male pornography, since it represents women giving and receiving sexual pleasure in ways not dependent on men' (Fejes and Petrich 1993, 408).

However, the spaces occupied by gay and lesbian pornography are not just sexual in character; they are also social. In the words of Fejes and Petrich, while 'the gay and lesbian community organizes itself around a vision of sexuality and gender that is at odds with the dominant, heterosexist society,' it is at the same time 'uniquely the product of a modern urban technological society which allows individuals to separate themselves from the power of family, religion, and community of birth and define new expressions of identity, sexuality, and sociality' (1993, 397). It is hardly surprising, then, that moral conservatives such as Wildmon find homosexual culture and activity intrinsically objectionable and pornographic.

Despite basic differences in culture and sexual orientation between homosexual and heterosexual society, the debates on the acceptability or otherwise of pornography that occur within gay and lesbian communities are not greatly dissimilar to those that occur in heterosexual society. Thus, 'while some gay males agree with feminist critics that gay and heterosexual pornography are equally destructive for their reliance on subordination and objectification ... the dominant gay male opinion ... defends the positive aspects of gay pornography since it does not explicitly reproduce the gender relations predominant in a patriarchal heterosexual society' (Fejes and Petrich 1993, 406). Equally, 'within the feminist debate on pornography, lesbian pornography is highly controversial ... with some feminists arguing that its sexual objectification renders it no different than male pornography' (Fejes and Petrich 1993, 408). By contrast, others (for example, Dorenkamp 1990) have argued that lesbian pornography constructs images of female sexuality whose control lies outside male sexual hierarchy.

The concept of 'pornography' is thus at best ambiguous and relative in its meanings according to a variety of different interests and motivations. This has made legislation in relation to pornography difficult to determine. Many jurisdictions have thus relied on the concept of 'obscenity' in prosecuting activities perceived as pornographic, but, given the equally ambiguous and relative character of this concept, prosecutions have been limited. It was difficulties with prosecution, censorship and control, together with the impact of the postwar sexual revolution (itself associated with a marked increase in the dissemination of materials perceived as pornographic), that resulted in a dominantly liberal attitude toward pornography during the second half of the twentieth century.

Pornography and Popular Music

The ambiguity and relativism of the term 'pornography' make it in many instances difficult, if not impossible, to determine whether popular music is pornographic. The difficulty can be illustrated by reference to Keil's work on the Tiv of Nigeria (1979). Many Tiv songs are sexually explicit (as well as being very humorous). The performance of these sexually explicit songs is institutionalized, and serves the purpose of mocking and deflating male authority figures, thus curbing possible excesses in the exercise of political power. It seems more than likely that moral conservatives would judge such songs – as well as, possibly, certain parts of Keil's work – to be pornographic. Further, the combination of sexual explicitness and the subversion of authority has something in common with pornographic practises of the early modern period. However, the principal purpose of these kinds of Tiv song is not sexual arousal, and it is unclear whether this is even a secondary consequence. On these grounds, liberals might not find the songs pornographic. And, given the relationship of these songs to possible excesses of male power, it also seems unlikely that feminists would find them pornographic. An added difficulty is whether the term 'pornography' is even appropriate in discussing sexually explicit material on a universal, cross-cultural basis. It seems possible that the albeit contested meanings associated with the term are specific to modern and postmodern capitalist societies and those that have been significantly influenced by them.

By these standards, the term might more appropriately be applied in certain cases to the music of North Indian cassette culture. As Manuel (1993) reports, the sexual content of many songs in this tradition can be traced back to 'Indian folk and elite cultures' which 'have always reflected a healthy and uninhibited fondness for the erotic in art' (172). The terminology used by Manuel with respect to the presence of sexual content in the development of cassette-based songs is, however, that of the 'sensual,' the 'lewd,' the 'ribald,' the 'titillating' and even the 'obscene,' rather than that of the 'pornographic.' Yet, Manuel observes that the 'commodification of ribald folk songs can . . . be argued to have altered the portrayal of gender . . . even in the case of familiar traditional songs' (1993, 175). This, he continues, has certainly been the case with Indian films: 'the spread of video among the upper and middle classes has resulted in feature films being increasingly oriented toward lower-class male audiences, whom producers evidently assume to be . . . fond of depictions of violence and rape.' To some extent, concludes Manuel, 'mass-mediated popular musics like commercial Bhojpuri folk song may reflect or acquire aspects of the same male orientation' (1993, 175).

There is always a danger, however, in attempting to judge the presence or otherwise of pornographic content by a simple, surface reading of texts. This becomes evident in Manuel's (1998) work on the attitudes of Caribbean-American students at a working-class college in New York City to Caribbean popular music. As Manuel observes, 'in Caribbean popular music, there is no shortage of songs whose representations of gender, from a North American liberal or left perspective, would seem controversial, if not overtly patriarchal or misogynist' (1998, 12). Manuel recounts that many students did not listen to the lyrics of this music, which is mostly dance music 'in which the literal meaning of the text may be functionally secondary to purely musical aspects providing rhythmic drive' (1998, 14). Students also devised a number of strategies for discounting the meaning and impact of lyrics that were sexist, misogynist and arguably, in some cases, pornographic. These strategies were important in part because the students enjoyed the music as music. However, there were some for whom a tension between the enjoyment of the music and the objectionable character of the lyrics was evident. Manuel reports one young woman as saying 'It's funny how you can be so disgusted with something and like it so much' (1998, 15).

The notion of pornography has in some cases affected the creation of the historical record where popular music is concerned, especially where attitudes of moral conservatism have prevailed. Such attitudes predominated during the late nineteenth and early twentieth centuries, when song collection was at its height. Cecil Sharp and Charles Marson, for example, routinely excluded or changed references to sexuality in their *Folk Songs from Somerset* in order, in the words of Harker (1985), 'to conform to the bourgeois taste both Sharp and Marson affected to despise' (195): 'In a few instances the sentiment of the song has been softened, because the conventions of our less delicate and more dishonest time demand such treatment' (Sharp and Marson 1904–1909, Vol. 1, xvi). A.L. Lloyd did not prevaricate, however. Pegg (1976) reports Lloyd as having, in *Folk Song in England*,

hard words for what he calls 'pornographic' song, much of which, he says, is 'crude, hateful, gruelling to listen to.' This is in contrast to 'erotic folk song' which has a '. . . clean joy and acceptance to the realities of virginity and desire, passion and pregnancy, [belonging] to a country people living an integrated deeply-communal life, in tune with natural events, with the cycle of the seasons.' (76)

As Pegg states, 'There is a whole side of folk song which, in England at any rate, has received scarcely any scholarly attention. This is the field of obscene or pornographic song' (1976, 76). Pegg goes on to recount the ways in which this situation has, to a degree, been rectified, in the process giving an interesting account of British rugby songs (1976, 76–88).

Material of a sexually explicit, if not pornographic, character has been present in a wide range of popular music from an early time. The tradition of explicit references to sex goes back at least to the time of the blues and songs such as 'Jelly Roll' and 'Sixty Minute Man.' Further, during the early days of recorded blues, raunchy songs were recorded nearly as often as love songs and laments, although lyrics might vary between live and recorded performances. Sexually explicit material, couched in sexual argot, is also to be found in mainstream pop songs such as the Beatles' 'Day Tripper' ('She's a prick teaser') and 'Penny Lane' ('Four of fish and finger pie'), as well as Lou Reed's 'Walk on the Wild Side' ('But she never lost her head, even when she was giving head').

Certain genres of popular music, however, have been predicated on what could be regarded as a soft-core pornographic content. Jane Birkin's and Serge Gainsbourg's international hit 'Je T'aime . . . Moi Non Plus' (1969) is said to have caused an increase in the birthrate nine months after its release. Seventies disco in particular dealt in material that could be regarded as soft-core pornography. Donna Summer's most explicit song, 'Down Deep Inside' (1977), contained the line 'Something warm is sliding inside of me' and a faked mid-song orgasm. The faked orgasm has been one of the main ways of communicating sexually explicit elements in pop, as Yoko Ono's 'Kiss, Kiss, Kiss' (1980), Led Zeppelin's 'Whole Lotta Love' (1971), Lil' Louis' 'French Kiss' (1989) and PJ Harvey's 'The Dancer' (1995) evidence. The male orgasm, as heard on the Led Zeppelin track, is a relative rarity within pop, a fact that adds weight to claims that rock essentially gives expression to a macho credo.

Sexual fetishism, an area that carries with it a potentially pornographic element, can also be found within pop, for example in the Velvet Underground's 'Venus in Furs' (1967) and Roxy Music's 1973 album track 'In Every Dream Home a Heartache' (where the lyrics allude to a sex act with a blowup doll). Right-wing libertarian Frank Zappa's *oeuvre* is full of explicit references to sex, on tracks like 'Penis Dimension,' 'Why Does It Hurt When I Pee?' and 'I Promise Not to Come in Your Mouth.' However, it was punk and post-punk music that brought the sexually taboo to the core of pop music. Punk band names (Buzzcocks, Penetration, the Slits, Throbbing Gristle and the Cunts) were often constructed to shock along sexual lines.

Other genres of popular music, notably rap, grunge, industrial and hard-core, have utilized explicit sexual imagery for shock value. For example, in the early 1980s, the group Plasmatics, whose singer, Wendy O. Williams, took to the stage in leathers and fetishistic clothing, was said by critics to play 'pornographic rock.' The members of the 1980s and 1990s band the Mentors, on the other hand, were self-styled porno-punk rockers who performed a repertoire of lyrically highly provocative and explicit material. Gangsta rap has been notable for its sexually explicit content, perhaps the best-known example being the album *Doggystyle* (1993) by Snoop Doggy Dogg, as has Jamaican dance hall music, as evidenced in Inner Circle's 'Sweat' (1993).

However, dance hall music has also been notable for its flaunting of female sexuality in addition to its promotion of male sexual prowess. According to Chang and Chen (1998), 'one of Jamaica's biggest celebrities throughout the nineties has been Carlene, "the dancehall queen," whose main claim to fame was a superbly rounded shape, a flair for skimpy "dancehall" designs, and outstanding "whining" (dancing) ability' (205). On the one hand, report Chang and Chen, 'some expressed amazement that women should so willingly degrade themselves'; on the other, it seems that 'sex to Jamaican women is not vulnerability, but a source of female power' (1998, 205). Once again, the ambiguity and relativity of pornography as a concept become evident. This notwithstanding, West Indian music as imported into the United Kingdom has definitely been perceived as pornographic. Marks (1990) reports that the size of the market for recordings of West Indian music in the late 1960s was such that, 'despite a ban by the BBC and the resulting lack of airplay, "Wet Dream" by Max Romeo went to no. 10 in the charts' (108).

Visually, images that some people regard as pornographic have been incorporated into the rock mainstream in the form of album cover designs, stage shows and videos. For example, for the cover of John Lennon's and Yoko Ono's *Two Virgins* album the two are shown in full frontal nudity. In 1976, the Rolling Stones took to the stage in the shadow of a huge inflatable penis. David Bowie's video for 'China Girl' (1983) had to be cut for mainstream viewing because of nudity.

Popular culture from the 1970s onward evidenced a mainstreaming of products that could be regarded as pornographic. Cultural critic Leon Hunt, in his revisionist analysis *British Low Culture* (1998), talks of the 'pornification' of British culture during this time, with the popularity of tabloid newspapers such as *The Sun*, films such as *The Confessions of . . .* series and magazines such as *Penthouse*, *Men Only* and *Mayfair*. Movies such as *Groupie Girl* (1970) and *Permissive* (1970) portrayed sexuality in the rock world, particularly the phenomenon of the groupie. By 1984, it was estimated that, in the United States, the porn industry was worth $7 billion, more than the film and the record industries put together (Ross 1993, 223). Madonna, Samantha Fox and the Spice Girls' Geri Halliwell are three examples of porn stars or 'page 3' girls (topless models featured on page 3 of many British tabloids) who made a successful transition to pop.

A certain fascination with soft-core and porn movie soundtracks was evident in the United States and Europe from the mid-1980s onward. Clubs such as Leigh Bowery's Taboo in the 1980s and Smashing in the 1990s featured soundtracks to porn movies on their playlists. In the late 1990s, there was a booming underground market for both rare and new porn music, as evidenced by the success of Italy's Bistro and Germany's Crippled Dick labels. The rehabilitation of porn movie music in the 1990s was part of a general movement to rehabilitate trash culture (that is, degraded, obscure works of popular culture) in general. Easy listening and porn soundtracks were an important part of this movement: 'In the spaces of trash culture, the implicit claim runs, one finds the purest glimpse of a sexual energy or a transgressive anti-conventionalism' (Straw 1997, 12). The rationale behind this was an anti-rock stance with 'collecting refigured as anthropology, an expedition into the natural wilderness of discarded styles and eccentric musical deformations' (Straw 1997, 13).

Moral conservatives have attempted to curb the presence of pornography in popular music, although, given the difficulties with prosecution and censorship, with only mixed success. In the 1980s and 1990s, various organizations were set up in an effort to censor rock music, including Tipper Gore's PMRC (Parents Music Resource Center) in the United States. Prosecutions of rock stars on pornography charges have been rare, with Frank Zappa's arrest in 1963 for involving an underage girl in making porn soundtracks being one of the few instances.

Bibliography

Chang, Kevin O'Brien, and Chen, Wayne. 1998. *Reggae Routes: The Story of Jamaican Music*. Philadelphia: Temple University Press.

Dorenkamp, Monica. 1990. 'Sisters Are Doing It.' *Outweek* (5 September): 373–81.

Fejes, Fred, and Petrich, Kevin. 1993. 'Invisibility, Homophobia and Heterosexism: Lesbians, Gays and the Media.' *Critical Studies in Mass Communication* 10(4): 396–422.

Harker, Dave. 1985. *Fakesong: The Manufacture of British 'Folksong' 1700 to the Present Day*. Milton Keynes: Open University Press.

Henry, Madeleine M. 1992. 'The Edible Woman: Athenaeus' Concept of the Pornographic.' In *Pornography and Representation in Greece and Rome*, ed. Amy Richlin. New York: Oxford University Press, 250–68.

Herman, Gary. 1994. *Rock 'n' Roll Babylon*. London: Plexus.

Hunt, Leon. 1998. *British Low Culture: From Safari Suits to Sexploitation*. London and New York: Routledge.

Hunt, Lynn, ed. 1993. *The Invention of Pornography: Obscenity and the Origins of Modernity, 1500–1800*. New York: Zone Books.

Itzin, Catherine, ed. 1992. *Pornography: Women, Violence, and Civil Liberties*. Oxford: Oxford University Press.

Keil, Charles. 1979. *Tiv Song: The Sociology of Art in a Classless Society*. Chicago: University of Chicago Press.

Lloyd, A.L. 1967. *Folk Song in England*. London: Lawrence & Wishart.

Manuel, Peter. 1993. *Cassette Culture: Popular Music and Technology in North India*. Chicago: University of Chicago Press.

Manuel, Peter. 1998. 'Gender Politics in Caribbean Popular Music: Consumer Perspectives and Academic Interpretation.' *Popular Music and Society* 22(2): 11–29.

Marks, Anthony. 1990. 'Young, Gifted and Black: Afro-American and Afro-Caribbean Music in Britain 1963–88.' In *Black Music in Britain: Essays on the Afro-Asian Contribution to Popular Music*, ed. Paul Oliver. Milton Keynes: Open University Press, 102–17.

McLaughlin, Thomas. 1996. *Street Smarts and Critical Theory: Listening to the Vernacular*. Madison, WI: University of Wisconsin Press.

McNair, Brian. 1996. *Mediated Sex: Pornography and Postmodern Culture*. London: Arnold.

Parker, Holt N. 1992. 'Love's Body Anatomized: The Ancient Erotic Handbooks and the Rhetoric of Sexuality.' In *Pornography and Representation in Greece and Rome*, ed. Amy Richlin. New York: Oxford University Press, 90–111.

Paytress, Mark. 1998a. 'A Soundtrack for the Weekend, Sir?' *Record Collector* 223: 62–68.

Paytress, Mark. 1998b. 'Cum On, Cum On!' *Record Collector* 223: 56–61.

Paytress, Mark. 1998c. 'Pasta Fishy, Oh!' *Record Collector* 223: 69–71.

Pegg, Bob. 1976. *Folk: A Portrait of English Traditional Music, Musicians and Customs*. London: Wildwood House.

Ross, Andrew. 1993 (1989). 'The Popularity of Pornography.' In *The Cultural Studies Reader*, ed. Simon During. London and New York: Routledge, 221–42.

Sharp, Cecil J., and Marson, Charles L. 1904–1909. *Folk Songs from Somerset*. London: Simpkin, Marshall & Co.

Smith, Barbara. 1988. 'Sappho Was a Right-Off Woman.' In *Feminism and Censorship: The Current Debate*, ed. Gail Chester and Julienne Dickey. London: Prism, 178–84.

Soble, Alan. 1986. *Pornography: Marxism, Feminism, and the Future of Sexuality*. New Haven, CT: Yale University Press.

Steinem, Gloria. 1980. 'Erotica and Pornography: A Clear and Present Difference.' In *Take Back the Night*, ed. Laura Lederer. New York: William Morrow and Co., 35–39.

Straw, Will. 1997. 'Sizing Up Record Collections: Gender and Connoisseurship in Rock Music Culture.' In *Sexing the Groove: Popular Music and Gender*, ed. Sheila Whiteley. London and New York: Routledge, 3–16.

Thompson, Bill. 1994. *Soft Core: Moral Crusades Against Pornography in Britain and America*. London: Cassell.

Wildmon, Donald E. 1985. *The Home Invaders*. Wheaton, IL: Victor Books.

Discographical References

Beatles, The. 'Day Tripper'/'We Can Work It Out.' Parlophone R 5389. *1965*: UK.

Beatles, The. 'Penny Lane'/'Strawberry Fields Forever.' Parlophone R 5570. *1967*: UK.

Birkin, Jane, and Gainsbourg, Serge. 'Je T'aime . . . Moi Non Plus.' Fontana TF 1042. *1969*: UK.

Bowie, David. 'China Girl.' EMI America EA 157. *1983*: UK.

Inner Circle. 'Sweat (A La La La Long).' Big Beat 10131. *1993*: Jamaica.

Led Zeppelin. 'Whole Lotta Love.' *Led Zeppelin 4*. Atlantic K 2401012. *1971*: UK.

Lennon, John, and Ono, Yoko. *Two Virgins: Unfinished Music No. 1*. Apple T-5001. *1968*: UK.

Lewis, Furry. 'Jelly Roll.' *Complete Works (1927–1929)*. Document DOCD-5004. *1990*: Austria.

Lewis, Jerry Lee. 'Sixty Minute Man.' *Rare and Rockin': Original Sun Recordings*. Charly 70. *1987*: USA.

Lil' Louis. 'French Kiss.' ffrr FX 115. *1989*: UK.

Ono, Yoko. 'Kiss, Kiss, Kiss.' *Double Fantasy*. Geffen K 99131. *1980*: USA.

PJ Harvey. 'The Dancer.' *To Bring You My Love*. Island CID 8035. *1995*: UK.

Reed, Lou. 'Walk on the Wild Side.' RCA 2303. *1973*: USA.

Romeo, Max. 'Wet Dream.' Unity UN 503. *1969*: Jamaica.

Roxy Music. 'In Every Dream Home a Heartache.' *For Your Pleasure*. Island ILPS 9232. *1973*: UK.

Snoop Doggy Dogg. *Doggystyle*. Priority 50605. *1993*: USA.

Summer, Donna. 'Down Deep Inside' (Theme from *The Deep*). Casablanca CAN 111. *1977*: USA.

Velvet Underground, The. 'Venus in Furs.' *The Velvet Underground & Nico*. Verve V6-5008. *1967*: USA.

Zappa, Frank. 'I Promise Not to Come in Your Mouth.' *Zappa in New York*. Discreet K 69204. *1978*: USA.

Zappa, Frank. 'Penis Dimension.' *200 Motels*. MCA MCA2-4183. *1971*: USA.

Zappa, Frank. 'Why Does It Hurt When I Pee?' *Joe's Garage Act 1*. CBS 86101. *1979*: USA.

Discography

Risqué Blues: Sixty Minute Man. King 1415. *1996*: USA.

Risqué Rhythm: Nasty 50s R&B. Rhino 70570. *1991*: USA.

Filmography

Groupie Girl, dir. Derek Ford. 1970. UK. 86 mins. Original music by John Fiddy, Alan Hawkshaw.

Permissive, dir. Lindsay Shonteff. 1970. UK.

JOHN SHEPHERD and DAVID BUCKLEY

Propaganda

The term 'propaganda' (from the Latin *propagare*, meaning 'to spread out, extend') denotes the systematic, widespread dissemination of particular religious, political or ideological concepts, opinions or doctrines. The term was first used in this sense for a committee of cardinals, the Congregation for the Propagation of the Faith (*Congregatio de Propaganda Fide*), established in 1622 by Pope Gregory XV. The term became known among the general public with the emergence of the mass press and the establishment of the modern bourgeois party state during the nineteenth century. However, it was not until the time of the Russian Revolution that the term changed to a specific concept developed in the service of political action. And, although the ideological functions of popular music were clearly apparent during the nineteenth century – as, for example, in the case of war songs, national songs, union songs and strike ballads – it was not until propaganda became a developed concept that it was applied to the practise of popular music.

After the Russian Revolution of 1917, the concept of propaganda was developed by Lenin, as part of his theory of revolution, into a theoretical category and, under the heading of 'agitation and propaganda' (frequently shortened to 'agit-prop'), it was implemented as a special task in the strategy of the Communist Party. Artists connected with the Russian Revolution expanded Lenin's concept of propaganda into the area of art and culture, where it was transformed into 'agit-prop art' by members of the Russian avant-garde of the early 1920s (Majakowski, Tretjakow, Lissitzky). Its musical equivalent was created in Germany during the same period by the composer Hanns Eisler. While the interrelationship between social and artistic revolution was foregrounded in this context as the basis for the imagined propagandist function of art, under Stalin art was turned into a pure instrument of distribution for the empty formulae of a watered-down version of the so-called 'Marxist-Leninist ideology.' Propaganda, now redefined as the openly manipulative influence of the minds of the masses, became institutionalized in a special department of the Communist Party's organization.

A similar misanthropic definition of propaganda, with even more devastating consequences, emerged at roughly the same time in Germany at the opposite end of the political spectrum, under the overall control of Joseph Goebbels within Hitler's National Socialist German Workers' Party (NSDAP). The manipulative preparation of the German population for the National Socialists' plans of conquest and extermination was an openly declared intention of Goebbels' 'Ministry for People's Enlightenment and Propaganda,' established immediately after Hitler's rise to power, with consequences that are only too well known. Similar processes developed in Italy under Mussolini, in Spain under Franco and in Japan during World War II. Since that time, the term 'propaganda' has been burdened with connotations that have been reinforced by the perpetuation of Stalin's concept of the term and the total subordination of the media in particular under the propaganda doctrine of the Communist Party in all the countries under Soviet rule, including China until the early 1960s. After that time, however, popular music continued to be used in China in the service of propaganda within a Maoist state. This use expanded to include the writing of songs by Communist Party composers to inculcate in the population a high degree of motivation for state-ordained tasks, such as becoming literate or getting the harvest in on time.

Popular music has played an important role in the service of propaganda, either as part of propagandist strategies or as the provider of a supporting milieu. According to a more general definition of the term, most church songs belong in the category of propaganda, since they have clearly been composed and performed to spread religious ideas. But the concepts of propaganda developed in the twentieth century in relation to specific political doctrines and ideologies integrated popular music into strategies for action in a much more indirect way. The most cynical form was developed by Goebbels' Ministry of Propaganda, which worked out detailed strategies for the supportive use of popular music in radio broadcasting. The music selected for this goal, popular hit songs and instrumental dance music mainly in the swing idiom of the time, was not openly propagandist. Rather, its function was to create an atmosphere of day-to-day normality and optimism in which Goebbels' Ministry could introduce its strategies of propagandist rhetoric. In contrast, the Stalinist concept of propaganda used popular music in a much more direct way. So-called 'mass songs,' songs for the masses to sing, used music as a medium of transmission of ideological formulae.

Even if 'propaganda' is a loaded term historically and restricted in a rather narrow sense to the dissemination of political, ideological or religious ideas, the use of music in the context of modern advertising strategies, as the provider of a supportive programming milieu or as an element of commercials, is in every respect analogous to the utilization of music for political goals. Examples of this analogous use of music in the service of ideological or political goals are to be found in the activities of radio stations such as Radio Free Europe and the Voice of America.

PETER WICKE

Radio

Music has been a staple of radio programming since broadcasting began in the 1920s. Radio's social power and cultural reach have profoundly influenced musical culture, yet its influence on music in a given historical and cultural context is determined by a number of factors, including methods of finance, regulation, number of available channels, processes of decision-making and governing ideology. Nevertheless, by the simple act of drawing attention to some musical performances and implicitly ignoring others, all radio systems serve to focus public attention and shape musical culture.

The Nature of Radio and Music

Public attention is critical for the development of popular music. However, this attention is finite. Radio serves as a means to allocate public attention by aggregating individuals into audiences. A radio network system creates the possibility of simultaneous listening by millions of individuals over vast areas. This aggregation, spread over space and compacted in time, accelerates the effects of allocating attention to musical performances. These effects were already apparent in the United States in the 1930s, as both the time required to produce a hit song and the song's period of popularity were decreased with the development of radio networks (MacDougald 1979).

Since radio systems have distinct institutional structures and ideologies, their criteria for selecting music frequently clash with the values of musical communities (Berland 1993; Rothenbuhler 1985, 1996; Rothenbuhler and McCourt 1992). Therefore, radio does not merely accelerate the flow of change in musical culture; rather, it is an active participant in this change. For example, early radio relied heavily on music because it was an inexpensive and convenient source of programming. Performers often volunteered their services, and their performances could be shortened or extended to fit time constraints. Recital music was commonly programmed for its air of genteel respectability rather than for any aesthetic value (Barnouw 1966). Similarly, early stations in the southern United States often programmed country music because of an abundance of local performers, yet these stations did little to develop the music until years later, after entrepreneurs from the record industry had shown the way (Daniel 1990; Peterson 1997).

The effects of allocating attention to a musical performance may be roughly schematized as 'positive' or 'negative.' This allocation may evoke popularity among audiences as they respond to familiar forms of expression and assimilate new forms. It may also exhaust popularity as audiences tire of a particular musical performance or form. Allocation may have a similar dual effect for musicians and other participants in a musical culture. On the one hand, exposing a musical performance to other musicians provides the opportunity for imitation and thus helps to spread musical ideas. On the other hand, exposure may lead to innovation through variation, recombination and invention.

Radio's aggregation of individuals into audiences has two primary effects: a reduction of musical diversity in space; and an increase in musical diversity in time. Radio airplay focuses public attention on a few songs within a short period of time. This focusing is a catalyst for songs and genres to become popular and inspire imitation. Thus, songs and genres will quickly reach, exceed and exhaust their potentials, with the result that musical cultures can both form and change quickly under radio's influence. For example, network radio helped to spread swing music across the United States and define a national moment (Millard 1995; Stowe 1994). Similarly, massive radio play and a hit film (*Saturday Night Fever*) helped to disseminate disco throughout the United States in the mid-1970s.

Radio has had another long-term effect on music: it has helped to make music ubiquitous and, therefore, something that may not require great attention. This process began with recording, which allowed music listening without the presence of musicians. With recording, music became portable, convenient and, of course, commodified (see Chanan 1995; Eisenberg 1987; Millard 1995; Rothenbuhler and Peters 1997). Although the experience of attending a nightclub or symphony performance cannot be recorded, something like the sound of it can; and something like that sound can be reproduced at will, in the private space of the home. Through its constant availability and portability, and the increase in the number of stations available to listeners, radio pushed this convenience to new levels. As recorded music became ubiquitous and easily controlled by listeners, it increasingly assumed the status of an ambient soundtrack for everyday life. Radio has changed the shape of attention to music. As the sheer amount of time spent listening to music has increased, the demands and quality of attention have surely been reduced.

Radio's Institutional Contingencies

The relationship of radio and music is marked by several contingencies. First, radio systems with limited channels will almost inevitably feature less musical diversity. In the late 1920s and early 1930s, the US radio system shifted from programming that originated locally to network programming, with a concomitant decrease in the diversity of music. As the networks shifted their advertising and programming to television in the 1950s, the US radio system shifted back to local programming and began targeting previously overlooked audiences, with a corresponding increase in musical diversity leading to the national breakthrough of rock 'n' roll (Barlow 1999; Fornatale and Mills 1980; Ennis 1992; Kloosterman and Quispel 1990; Peterson 1990). Subsequently, Radio Luxembourg and offshore pirate stations provided programming alternatives to state-operated systems in Europe (Barnard 1989; Chapman 1992).

A second contingency involves the locus of programming decision-making. When local stations air network or syndicated programming, they defer many programming decisions to centralized groups frequently located in national cultural centers. This deferral reduces the overall number of decision-makers within the system, and also reduces the diversity of influences on the decision-makers. Similarly, when station programmers defer to national consultants and base their programming on national charts, their programming becomes highly standardized.

Third, the source of radio funding is crucially important to music programming. From the outset, US commercial radio networks depended on national advertising money, which led them to construct national audiences from individuals in varied geographical, cultural and social situations. They therefore emphasized mainstream musical variety shows and live musical performances from prestigious clubs in major cities. Early examples of programming that targeted ethnic or taste minorities, such as programs featuring African-American musicians in Chicago and other urban centers, were strictly local in nature and depended on local advertising revenues (see, for example, Barlow 1999, 25; Barnouw 1966, 130).

While the British Broadcasting Corporation (BBC) is funded only by license fees (apart from its separate international service), it faces demands to serve national interests. In contrast, the US public radio system depends on a mix of funding from corporations, individuals, institutions and government. This mix of funding requires public stations to serve diverse constituencies, which results in more diverse musical programming than that found on commercial stations (Engelman 1996; McCourt 1999; Rowland 1993; Stavitsky 1994). Public radio stations are the major broadcast outlets for classical, jazz, blues and folk music in the United States. Noncommercial community stations also feature programming that serves ethnic or minority audiences, and student radio stations play a much more important role in the development of popular music than might be guessed from their number, locations and frequently low power.

Broadcasting ideology also figures in the impact of radio on music. Nationalism may be a primary component in broadcasting ideology, and it is manifested in policies favoring the music of the home nation. For example, the government-controlled Mexican radio network of the 1930s featured an explicitly nationalist music policy (Hayes 1996). Countries such as France and Canada require fixed percentages of national music (see, for example, Grenier 1993; Machill 1996). The US system is dominated by marketplace ideology. While many commercial broadcasters boast that they merely reflect audience demands, the reality is a highly conservative system in which broadcasters air only music that attracts substantial numbers of listeners (see, for example, Glasser 1984; Wallis and Malm 1993).

In contrast, systems with a public-service ideology attempt to meet the needs of a larger range of audience members. This may include programming music for both ethnic and taste minorities; more frequently, it includes some version of cultural uplift – either music for the betterment of the people or music for the 'better' people. Nevertheless, massive popularity is less important than quality or diversity for public-service broadcasters (see, for example, Briggs 1985; Scannell and Cardiff 1991). Many noncommercial broadcasters in the United States, pirate broadcasters and, paradoxically, a few commercial broadcasters in countries previously dominated by single national or governmental channels maintain an explicit commitment to serving as alternatives to dominant systems, thus increasing the diversity of music available by radio (see, for example, Barlow 1988; Hochheimer 1993; Lasar 1999; Lewis and Booth 1990; Sakolsky and Dunifer 1998; Soley 1999).

At the station level, two primary programming strategies – flow and block – have important implications for musical culture (see, for example, Berland 1993; Rothenbuhler 1996). Commercial stations tend to emphasize programming flows. Because they make money by attracting and holding audience attention, it is in their interest to have a consistent sound, so that the listening experience can be relatively uninterrupted. Commercial stations therefore adopt formats built around narrowly defined types of music, and program short-lists of the songs within these types. This flow strategy is efficient for managing listeners' time; once attracted, they are not presented with clear breaks in the schedule that would invite them to change channels. Noncommercial stations depend on funding from a variety of constituencies, or may be responsible for serving varied interests. These stations tend to favor block programming, in which discrete segments featuring different types of music are assembled into schedules. Since these segments are designed to attract specialized interests, they tend to delve more deeply into musical genres and play a much greater number of different songs. The block programming strategy, then, results in more musical diversity across a broadcast day.

Both flow and block strategies are based on assumptions about the audience. Programmers who employ a block strategy assume their audience is active, knowledgeable and wants to learn more about new music or the history of a given style. Programmers who favor a flow strategy assume the audience is essentially passive, seeking music for ambient purposes. The block strategy is intended to promote concentrated listening to music, while the flow strategy is designed to maximize commercial income. Block programming tends to be defined by musical and cultural criteria, while flow programming tends to be defined by business, demographic and popularity criteria. The proliferation of flow-formatted radio stations produces a musical culture in which popularity marked by less focused listening is a norm, in which demographics contribute to the definition of identity and taste, and in which business success can be argued to predominate over concerns with musical value.

As bleak as this conclusion appears, it is important to remember that, while many radio programmers do not really care about music, they inadvertently can play key roles in musical revolutions. When regulatory changes or technological innovations challenge existing media, these media are often forced to redefine themselves. In the 1950s, US radio stations lost to television the network programming and national advertising money that had supported them. The US Federal Communications Commission (FCC) also allowed more stations to get on the air, which created a dramatic increase in the number of stations competing for programming material, on-air talent and advertising dollars. In response, stations began targeting overlooked or 'marginal' audiences. This strategy led to the first radio stations programmed by and for African Americans in the United States and a substantial diffusion of music that had been relegated to a small market niche, thus revolutionizing North American popular music. When the FCC ruled in the mid-1960s that major market stations holding AM and FM licenses could no longer merely duplicate their AM programming on FM facilities, these stations scrambled for programming alternatives. This resulted in increased amounts of religious and foreign-language radio programming in the United States. It also inaugurated free-form radio, which promoted progressive rock and helped spread the counterculture across the nation (Krieger 1979; Tankel and Williams 1993).

Toward the end of the twentieth century, new possibilities for delivering 'radio' appeared in the form of satellites, cable and the Internet. As these delivery systems develop, they will open up new possibilities for the allocation of attention to musical performances, thus challenging – if not changing – the established system. Whether musical revolutions will come about will depend on complex interactions among channels, methods of funding, regulation and decision-making processes. If the outcome tends to multiply the number and diversity of decisions, there is a good chance it will open up space for musical diversity and innovation.

Bibliography

Barfield, Ray. 1996. *Listening to Radio, 1920–1950*. Westport, CT: Praeger.

Barlow, William. 1988. 'Community Radio in the US: The Struggle for a Democratic Medium.' *Media, Culture and Society* 10(1): 81–105.

Barlow, William. 1999. *Voice Over: The Making of Black Radio*. Philadelphia: Temple University Press.

Barnard, Stephen. 1989. *On the Radio: Music Radio in Britain*. Philadelphia: Open University Press.

Barnouw, Erik. 1966. *A Tower in Babel: A History of Broadcasting in the United States. Vol. 1, to 1933*. New York: Oxford University Press.

Berland, Jody. 1993. 'Radio Space and Industrial Time: The Case of Music Formats.' In *Rock and Popular Music: Politics, Policies, Institutions*, ed. Tony Bennett et al. London: Routledge, 104–18.

Briggs, Asa. 1985. *The BBC: The First Fifty Years*. New York: Oxford University Press.

Chanan, Michael. 1995. *Repeated Takes: A Short History of Recording and Its Effects on Music*. London and New York: Verso.

Chapman, Robert. 1992. *Selling the Sixties: The Pirates and Pop Music Radio*. New York: Routledge.

Daniel, Wayne W. 1990. *Pickin' on Peachtree: A History of Country Music in Atlanta, Georgia*. Urbana, IL: University of Illinois Press.

DeLong, Thomas A. 1980. *The Mighty Music Box*. Los Angeles: Amber Crest Books.

Eberly, Philip K. 1982. *Music in the Air: America's Changing Tastes in Popular Music, 1920–1980*. New York: Hastings House.

Eisenberg, Evan. 1987. *The Recording Angel: The Experience of Music from Aristotle to Zappa*. New York: Penguin.

Engelman, Ralph. 1996. *Public Radio and Television in America: A Political History*. Thousand Oaks, CA: Sage.

Ennis, Philip H. 1992. *The Seventh Stream: The Emergence of Rocknroll in American Popular Music*. Hanover, NH: Wesleyan University Press.

Fornatale, Peter, and Mills, Joshua E. 1980. *Radio in the Television Age*. Woodstock, NY: Overlook Press.

Glasser, Ted. 1984. 'Competition and Diversity Among Radio Formats: Legal and Structural Issues.' *Journal of Broadcasting* 28(2): 127–42.

Grenier, Line. 1993. 'Policing French-Language Music on Canadian Radio: The Twilight of the Popular Record Era?' In *Rock and Popular Music: Politics, Policies, Institutions*, ed. Tony Bennett et al. London: Routledge, 119–41.

Hayes, Joy E. 1996. '"Touching the Sentiments of Everyone": Nationalism and State Broadcasting in Thirties Mexico.' *The Communication Review* 1(4): 411–39.

Hochheimer, John. 1993. 'Organizing Democratic Radio: Issues in Praxis.' *Media, Culture and Society* 15(3): 473–86.

Kloosterman, Robert C., and Quispel, Chris. 1990. 'Not Just the Same Old Show on My Radio: An Analysis of the Role of Radio in the Diffusion of Black Music Among Whites in the South of the United States of America, 1920 to 1960.' *Popular Music* 9(2): 151–64.

Krieger, Susan. 1979. *Hip Capitalism*. Beverly Hills, CA: Sage.

Lasar, Matthew. 1999. *Pacifica Radio: The Rise of an Alternative Network*. Philadelphia: Temple University Press.

Lewis, Peter, and Booth, Jerry. 1990. *The Invisible Medium: Public, Commercial and Community Radio*. Washington, DC: Howard University Press.

MacDougald, Duncan, Jr. 1979 (1941). 'The Popular Music Industry.' In *Radio Research 1941*, ed. Paul F. Lazarsfeld and Frank N. Stanton. New York: Arno Press, 65–109.

MacFarland, David T. 1993. *The Development of the Top 40 Radio Format*. North Stratford, NH: Ayer.

Machill, Marcel. 1996. 'Musique as Opposed to Music: Background and Impact of Quotas for French Songs on French Radio.' *The Journal of Media Economics* 9(3): 21–36.

McCourt, Tom. 1999. *Conflicting Communication Interests in America: The Case of National Public Radio*. Westport, CT: Praeger.

Millard, Andre J. 1995. *America on Record: A History of Recorded Sound*. Cambridge: Cambridge University Press.

Peterson, Richard A. 1990. 'Why 1955?: Explaining the Advent of Rock Music.' *Popular Music* 9(1): 97–116.

Peterson, Richard A. 1997. *Creating Country Music: Fabric-*

ating Authenticity. Chicago: University of Chicago Press.

Rothenbuhler, Eric W. 1985. 'Programming Decision Making in Popular Music Radio.' *Communication Research* 12: 209–32.

Rothenbuhler, Eric W. 1996. 'Commercial Radio as Communication.' *Journal of Communication* 46(1): 125–43.

Rothenbuhler, Eric W., and McCourt, Tom. 1992. 'Commercial Radio and Popular Music: Processes of Selection and Factors of Influence.' In *Popular Music and Communication*, ed. James Lull. 2nd ed. Newbury Park, CA: Sage, 101–15.

Rothenbuhler, Eric W., and Peters, John Durham. 1997. 'Defining Phonography: An Experiment in Theory.' *Musical Quarterly* 81(2): 242–64.

Rowland, William, Jr. 1993. 'Public Service Broadcasting in the United States: Its Mandate, Institutions and Conflicts.' In *Public Service Broadcasting in a Multichannel Environment: The History and Survival of an Ideal*, ed. Robert Avery. New York: Longman, 157–94.

Sakolsky, Ron, and Dunifer, Stephen. 1998. *Seizing the Airwaves: A Free Radio Handbook*. San Francisco: AK Press.

Scannell, Paddy, and Cardiff, David. 1991. *A Social History of British Broadcasting. Vol. 1, 1922–1939, Serving the Nation*. Oxford: Basil Blackwell.

Soley, Lawrence. 1999. *Free Radio: Electronic Civil Disobedience*. Boulder, CO: Westview Press.

Stavitsky, Alan. 1994. 'The Changing Conception of Localism in U.S. Public Radio.' *Journal of Broadcasting and Electronic Media* 38(1): 19–33.

Stowe, David W. 1994. *Swing Changes: Big-Band Jazz in New Deal America*. Cambridge, MA: Harvard University Press.

Tankel, Jonathan David, and Williams, Wenmouth, Jr. 1993. 'Resource Dependence: Radio Economics and the Shift from AM to FM.' In *Media Economics: Theory and Practice*, ed. Alison Alexander, James Owers and Rod Carveth. Hillsdale, NJ: Lawrence Erlbaum Associates, 157–68.

Wall, Tim. 2000. *Constructing Popular Music Radio: Music and Cultural Identity in Radio Station Discourse*. Ph.D. thesis, Department of Cultural Studies, University of Birmingham, UK.

Wallis, Roger, and Malm, Krister. 1993. 'From State Monopoly to Commercial Oligopoly: European Broadcasting Policies and Popular Music Output Over the Airwaves.' In *Rock and Popular Music: Politics, Policies, Institutions*, ed. Tony Bennett et al. London: Routledge, 156–68.

Filmography

Saturday Night Fever, dir. John Badham. 1977. USA. 119 mins. Rock Musical. Original music by Barry Gibb, Maurice Gibb, Robin Gibb, Barry Robin, David Shire.

ERIC W. ROTHENBUHLER and TOM MCCOURT

Rave Culture

'Rave' has always had numerous definitions. In the Bible, the term 'to rave' means 'to prophesy.' The word 'raving' has roots in Jamaica that allude to 'letting loose on the weekend.' Dictionaries have traditionally defined a raver as an 'uninhibited pleasure-loving person,' while a 'rave-up' was simply a 'lively party.' It was only in the late 1980s in England that the word 'rave' was aligned with a specific subculture, as evidenced in the latest edition of the Canadian Oxford Dictionary (1998), which defines a rave as 'a large often illicit all-night party or event, often held in a warehouse or open field, with dancing to loud fast electronic music.'

Any attempt to define 'rave' needs to reflect the amorphous character of the event itself, which can go on for a few hours, a whole night or an entire weekend. A rave can be an indoor party with 50 people or an outdoor 'happening' with 15,000 people. There may be two DJs or more than 20, spinning any variant of electronica. Some ravers may take Ecstasy, LSD, marijuana; some take nothing at all. Other than DJs, electronic dance music, willing participants and a venue, what can be called a 'rave' defies parameters.

Raving is primarily a weekend event, allowing participants to be whatever they choose during the week and a 'raver' on the weekends. For some, however, rave has become an all-consuming life style. The ambiguity of the definition of 'rave' is evident at rave events themselves. Some parties appear spiritual, liberating and even magical; others, however, demonstrate rave's extremist nature, where drug use seems excessive and abusive, demeaning the culture's more meaningful attributes.

Rave started as an alternative, underground, renegade culture that hid from police and media exposure and rejected the high-profile nature of clubs. The precursor to rave was the acid house scene that developed in London, England in 1988. Its inspiration was the mixing of US acid house and techno music with popular dance music, coupled with Ecstasy or MDMA (3,4-methylenedioxymethamphetamine), that occurred the summer before in the favored English vacation location of Ibiza, off the coast of Spain. One vacationer, Danny Rampling, attempted to re-create his Ibizan holiday bliss by opening a small after-hours club in London called Shoom (see Garratt 1998; Collin and Godfrey 1997; Reynolds 1998). Around the same time, in London's West End, free all-night parties under the name

'Hedonism' were taking place in an empty warehouse. Promoters of these parties were not inspired by Ibiza, but by New York's Paradise Garage, the legendary club that gave its name to garage music (see Garratt 1998). Together, these two UK scenes were the beginning of 'acid house' and the embryonic stage of rave (see Garratt 1998; Collin and Godfrey 1997).

Although it would be unfair to assume that everyone participating in raves indulges in Ecstasy, it would be unrealistic not to acknowledge that the combination of Ecstasy and house music was the inspiring factor in rave's development. MDMA alters the brain's electrical impulses. It is an amphetamine-based drug that creates feelings of empathy, happiness, sensuality and sociability and heightens the sensations related to touch (see Saunders 1993).

Acid house promoters started experimenting with spontaneous outdoor events that came to be known as raves. Promoters started withholding announcements of upcoming raves until a few hours before the event in order to avoid police closures. Events were secretly advertised on pirate radio, on flyers and by word of mouth. Cellphones and advanced messaging systems helped to create a circuit of last-minute directions to either meeting points or the actual location. These massive outdoor gatherings began showcasing a barrage of lasers, strobe lights, massive inflatable 'bouncy castles' and special effects. Promoters attempted to outdo one another by making raves increasingly spectacular. It was not long before the secret, underground world of rave started to be taken to the masses and moved into larger, privately owned and sometimes disued warehouse locations where promoters and ravers could avoid the restrictive hours of licensed clubs.

The first law associated with raves was the *Entertainments (Increased Penalties) Act* (the *Bright Act*), enacted in 1990 in England, which placed fines of up to £20,000 and imposed sentences of six months in jail on the organizers of unlicensed raves. Because of the risk of having an event closed by police and of being charged themselves, promoters started bringing rave to mainstream clubs. By the summer of 1992, British raves were drawing crowds of well over 20,000 people. The *Criminal Justice and Public Order Act* was passed in 1994 and defined raves as outdoor gatherings of over a hundred people, at which amplified music characterized by the emission of a succession of repetitive beats was played (see Brewster and Broughton 2000; Collin and Godfrey 1997).

By the time rave had become passé in some parts of London, similar scenes were emerging not only in other cities but also across oceans. Dissemination to the United States was due in part to North American DJs who had played overseas or to expatriate Britons who had experienced rave or acid house firsthand. As rave spread, it assumed new forms, ensuring its longevity.

Raves are often viewed as utopian and anarchistic by their participants because drug use is welcomed and social barriers are overthrown. PLUR (peace, love, unity and respect) is one of the unofficial rave credos. It is this dogma at raves that has allowed heterosexual males to feel uninhibited enough to hug and massage one another openly without fear of public scrutiny, while for females raves have fostered an environment so unfettered by ritualized gender roles that they can hug males, dance and interact freely without worrying about being objectified and solicited for dates. The 'vibe' at rave parties develops from the mix of people, music and energy that creates a sense of collectivity and community.

Rave has been accused by many of being apolitical, meaningless and hedonistic. No one can argue against the celebratory intent behind raving, but perhaps it is rave's sheer hedonism that is meaningful and political. It marks a refusal to conform to socialized gender roles or to established codes of interaction and personal conduct. Although there are ritualistic and artistic tendencies woven into the rave agenda, it is seen more or less as an arena in which teens and young adults can play.

The style associated with the rave scene started to reflect rave's freedom from socialized barriers by privileging comfort and mobility over body-hugging fashions. The uniforms that developed were androgynous and childlike: baggy clothes, lollipops, teddy bears, baseball caps, visors, beaded necklaces and bracelets, body sparkles, safety chains, baby articles, and paraphernalia related to children's television and cartoon characters (such as Winnie the Pooh and the Teletubbies) all became synonymous with rave. By the mid-1990s, especially in North America, this 'baggy' fashion eventually defined rave 'style' and gave rise to the ubiquitous 'phat' pants. Some ravers started sewing panels into their loose jeans to make the bottoms wider, while others tried to look as 'teddy-like' as possible and made loose-fitting pants out of pastel fun-fur.

Subcultural style not only initiates new trends, but also gives new meaning to old ones (see Hebdige 1979). Some ravers used baby soothers to stop the teeth grinding caused by excessive 'speed' and Ecstasy intake. This trend was soon adopted as rave style because it fitted the dominant childlike look. A similar trend occurred with Vicks VapoRub and Vicks inhalers, used to enhance the Ecstasy 'rush': both were stripped of their intended use as cold remedies to become symbols of rave and, more specifically, of Ecstasy use. Ritual elements developed around the hard-core rave scene: whistles, used as musical accompaniment; glo sticks, held in the hands for visual effect while dancing; and, sometimes, white gloves, worn to draw attention to stylized hand movements.

As the size and number of parties increased, promotion companies started to become more specialized musically and would cater to a particular subgenre of house or techno music. Events would often have multiple stages or rooms, all showcasing various types of electronica. Rave involves more people with each passing season, growing not as a scene but as *scenes*. As the definition of what is considered 'rave' music expands, a much broader cross section of youth is attracted to rave culture. This hybridization of music genres has electronic dance music caught in a maze of semantics and classifications.

Unlike other subcultures that enjoy their burst of popularity and then quietly fade into subcultural archives, rave has endured countless cycles and resurgences and has been disseminated to virtually every corner of the globe. As it grows in one area, it decays in another and becomes another sub-scene, dress code, venue and soundscape. With each cycle, rave's old-timers proclaim its death, as the new recruits rejoice in their discovery. Rave music transcends the limits of words that were evident in the musics of previous cultures, while rave style transcends the parameters dictated by fashion, for each region has created its own style which continually evolves. Rave events themselves circumvent the laws intended to suppress them by finding new locations in fields, cowsheds and even licensed clubs. This is why rave is limited when it is defined by *place*. Perhaps it is simply an environment that allows the experience of certain freedoms, dance and emotions (McCall 2001).

Bibliography

Brewster, Bill, and Broughton, Frank. 2000. *Last Night a DJ Saved My Life: The History of the Disc Jockey*. New York: Grove Press. (First published London: Headline Book Publishing, 1999.)

Cohen, Stanley. 1980. *Folk Devils and Moral Panics: The Creation of the Mods and Rockers*. Oxford: Martin Robertson.

Collin, Matthew, and Godfrey, John. 1997. *Altered State: The Story of Ecstasy Culture and Acid House*. London: Serpent's Tail.

Eisner, Bruce. 1994. *Ecstasy: The MDMA Story*. Berkeley, CA: Ronin Publishing Inc.

Garratt, Sheryl. 1998. *Adventures in Wonderland: A Decade of Club Culture*. London: Headline Book Publishing.

Hebdige, Dick. 1979. *Subculture: The Meaning of Style*. London: Methuen.

Henderson, Sheila. 1997. *Ecstasy: Case Unsolved*. London: Pandora.

McCall, Tara. 2001. *This Is Not a Rave: In the Shadow of a Subculture*. Toronto: Insomniac Press.

Redhead, Steve, ed. 1993. *Rave Off: Politics and Deviance in Contemporary Youth Culture*. Aldershot: Avebury.

Redhead, Steve, with Wynne, Derek, and O'Connor, Justin, eds. 1998. *The Clubcultures Reader: Readings in Popular Cultural Studies*. Oxford: Blackwell.

Reynolds, Simon. 1998. *Energy Flash: A Journey Through Rave Music and Dance Culture*. London: Picador.

Saunders, Nicholas. 1993. *E for Ecstasy*. London: Nicholas Saunders.

Thornton, Sarah. 1995. *Club Cultures: Music, Media, and Subcultural Capital*. Cambridge: Polity Press.

TARA MCCALL

Record Collecting

Belk (1995) estimates that, in the contemporary Western world, approximately one-quarter to one-third of adults are willing to identify themselves as 'collectors' (ch. 2). Obviously, as Pearce (1995) states in her Preface, 'the gathering together of chosen objects for purposes regarded as special is of great importance, as a social phenomenon, as a focus of personal emotion, and as an economic force.' As such, collecting has been the subject of considerable theoretical speculation and empirical study (see Pearce 1998 for a useful overview of the literature).

Record collecting is a major activity, yet a relatively neglected aspect of the consumption of popular music. While fan accounts and a bestselling novel provide some insights (Aizlewood 1994; Smith 1995, 133–45; Hornby 1995), more extended critical discussion is sparse. Drawing on some of the considerable general literature on collecting and collectors, Straw (1997) usefully speculates on the psychology of record collecting as a social practise, especially its largely male character, but his analysis lacks any embedding in the views of collectors themselves. Building on Straw, and the extensive writing of Pearce (1995, 1998) on collecting, Shuker (1999) has interviewed a number of self-identified record collectors to provide more empirical support for speculations about the nature and psychology of the activity.

The term 'record collecting' is shorthand for a variety of related practises. Foremost is the collection by individuals of sound recordings in various formats, although often with a marked preference for vinyl. This is the dimension of record collecting focused on here. Such record collecting serves a variety of purposes:

(a) a means of self-education, as exemplified by the classical and jazz appreciation societies and record clubs of the 1930s and 1940s in Britain (see LeMahieu 1988);

(b) a way to display musical cultural capital to a peer group (and outsiders);

(c) a platform on which to establish the history and scholarship of various genres – for example, Joel Whitburn's personal collection includes all of the 18,000 pop singles to have appeared in *Billboard*'s 'Hot 100,' and it provides the basis for his record research books and supplements (see Whitburn 1988, 173);

(d) a platform for performance, particularly through cover versions, as with the British proto-R&B groups of the early 1960s, most notably the Rolling Stones and the Animals; and

(e) a means of documenting various vernacular and 'native' musics and underpinning associated scholarship, as demonstrated, for example, by the work of ethnomusicologists and field researchers such as Harry Smith (the *Anthology of American Folk Music*) and Charles Keil and Steven Feld (1994).

In addition, there is the collecting undertaken by institutions: many national libraries or archives (for example, the Library of Congress) have important collections of sound recordings and sheet music, while a number of universities have significant music collections, usually serving popular music teaching programs (for example, the University of Liverpool in the United Kingdom, Bowling Green State University in the United States and Brock University in Canada).

Both individual and institutional collecting will frequently embrace the collection of related literature and memorabilia. The involvement of both private collectors and the Hard Rock Café chain has stimulated interest – and prices – in the collecting of popular music memorabilia, and several major auction houses conduct regular sales (see Maycock 1994).

In 'explaining' record collecting as a social activity, there has been a tendency to characterize it in terms of obsession and compulsion, and the frequent valorization of obscure performers and genres. (The latter tendency is also characteristic of the 'best of' lists by reviewers in the 'alternative' music press, many of whom are record collectors.) This approach, while emphasized here, is more applicable to record collecting by individuals in the private sphere of domestic consumption than to collecting activities motivated by scholarship and cultural preservation.

Straw (1997) observes that record collecting can be regarded as 'either structures of control or the by-products of irrational and fetishistic obsession; as material evidence of the homosocial information-mongering which is one underpinning of male power and compensatory undertakings by those unable to wield that power' (4). In common with other forms of

collecting, record collecting can represent a public display of power and knowledge, serving as a form of cultural capital within the peer group. Collecting also provides a private refuge from the wider world and the immediate domestic environment. In Hornby's novel *High Fidelity*, Rob Fleming, a London record store owner who is a committed record collector, recatalogs his album collection in times of stress: 'Is it so wrong, wanting to be at home with your record collection? It's not like collecting records is like collecting stamps, or beer mats, or antique thimbles. There's a whole world in here, a nicer, dirtier, more violent, more colourful, sleazier, more dangerous, more loving world than the world I live in' (1995, 73).

Muensterberger (1994) has theorized that collecting is a way of overcoming childhood anxiety by creating a sense of order and completion. This can border on the obsessional: Eisenberg (1988) describes the case of 'Clarence,' a New York record collector crippled with arthritis and now on welfare, living in an unlit, unheated 14-room house 'so crammed with trash that the door wouldn't open – and with three-quarters of a million (vinyl) records' (2). 'Clarence' had inherited the house from his parents, along with a considerable sum of money, now gone, which enabled him to pursue his dream of owning a complete collection of jazz, pop and rock recordings, along with ethnological field recordings and various recorded ephemera (1988, 1ff.).

Record collecting is a male-dominated practise. Shuker's opportunity sample of 21 collectors included only three women, and none of their collecting was on the scale of that of a number of the men. A Canadian documentary on record collectors, referred to by Straw (1997), included only five women among its 100 subjects. The huge success, especially with male readers, of Hornby's novel *High Fidelity* suggests considerable empathy with the protagonist, Rob Fleming. And Fleming's store, Championship Vinyl, 'for the serious record collector,' gets by 'because of the people who make a special effort to shop here Saturdays – young men – always young men' (1995, 37). For male collectors, the social role of collecting appears to be a significant part of masculinity. Straw (1997) suggests that 'record collections, like sports statistics, provide the raw materials around which the rituals of homosocial interaction take shape. Just as ongoing conversation between men shapes the composition and extension of each man's collection, so each man finds, in the similarity of his points of reference to those of his peers, confirmation of a shared universe of critical judgement' (5).

The process of collecting can take on the nature of a ritual. Frequently, it is the search itself that provides gratification, although the anticipation of a 'find' is central to this. Buying recorded music in its various formats 'is a process that involves clear symbolic work: complex and careful exercises of choice from the point of view of initial listening to seeking out and scrutinizing records' (Willis et al. 1990, 61). This is brought out by Shuker's interviewees, who constantly referred to both the effort and the pleasure involved in systematically gathering information from peers, older siblings, the music press, especially collector magazines, discographies, price guides and back catalogs, and then searching for particular recordings. This search will frequently encompass specialist and secondhand record stores, mail-order and Internet shopping, record fairs, and the bargain bins at mainstream record and general retail stores. Once items are acquired, they must then be ordered and classified – an ongoing process.

Collecting can both stimulate and, possibly, ossify particular musical genres. Small record labels have historically served a collectors' market, since they have been willing to release (or rerelease) material in smaller pressings that larger companies have considered uncommercial. This practise was long evident in the folk, jazz and blues fields, and was part of the advent of rock 'n' roll in the 1950s. The cult status of 1960s garage rock is linked to the Nuggets and Pebbles compilation series, which rescued many recordings from obscurity. Similarly, labels such as Rhino and Charly have established their commercial success through catering to a collectors' market with well-packaged compilations and reissues (see the compilation and reissues listings in the *All Music Guide to Rock* (1995)).

In their obituary of punk rock, Burchill and Parsons (1987, 96) regard the mania for collecting rare punk records as part of the music's demise. On the other hand, the emergence of the new independent labels was partly in response to collector and fan interest in punk music. Chiswick Records owner Ted Carroll ran a record store specializing in oldies, and saw the music of emerging punk performers as ideal material for his customers: 'I knew there wasn't a large market for such groups, but felt sure there would be a small, but large enough collector's market' (cited in Laing 1985, 10).

Record collector magazines are a key part of the infrastructure of record collecting. They include the US-based *Goldmine* (1974–) and *Discoveries* (1986(?)–), and the UK-published *Record Collector* (1979–). Such magazines feature extensively researched artist, label or genre retrospectives with accompanying discographies, and devote considerable space to advertising.

Bibliography

Aizlewood, John, ed. 1994. *Love Is the Drug*. London: Penguin.

Belk, Russell W. 1995. *Collecting in a Consumer Society*. London: Routledge.

Burchill, Julie, and Parsons, Tony. 1987. *'The Boy Looked at Johnny': The Obituary of Rock and Roll*. Boston and London: Faber and Faber.

Discoveries: For Record and CD Collectors. http://www.csmonline.com/discoveries

Eisenberg, Evan. 1988. *The Recording Angel: Music, Records and Culture from Aristotle to Zappa*. London: Picador.

Erlewine, Michael, Bogdanov, Vladimir, and Woodstra, Chris, eds. 1995. *All Music Guide to Rock: The Best CDs, Albums & Tapes: Rock, Pop, Soul, R&B and Rap*. San Francisco: Miller Freeman Books.

Goldmine: The Collectors Record and Compact Disc Marketplace. http://www.krause.com/goldmine

Hornby, Nick. 1995. *High Fidelity*. London: Gollancz.

Keil, Charles, and Feld, Steven. 1994. *Music Grooves: Essays and Dialogues*. Chicago and London: University of Chicago Press.

Laing, Dave. 1985. *One Chord Wonders: Power and Meaning in Punk Rock*. Milton Keynes: Open University Press.

LeMahieu, D.L. 1988. *A Culture for Democracy: Mass Communication and the Cultivated Mind in Britain Between the Wars*. Oxford: Clarendon Press.

Maycock, Stephen. 1994. *Miller's Rock & Pop Memorabilia*. London: Miller's/Reed.

Muensterberger, Werner. 1994. *Collecting: An Unruly Passion. Psychological Perspectives*. Princeton, NJ: Princeton University Press.

Pearce, Susan M. 1995. *On Collecting*. London: Routledge.

Pearce, Susan M. 1998. *Collecting in Contemporary Practice*. London: Sage.

Record Collector: CDs, Records & Pop Memorabilia. London: Diamond Publishing.

Shuker, Roy. 1999. 'A Time to Gather Stones Together: Record Collecting as Social Practice.' Unpublished research paper, School of English & Media Studies, Massey University, New Zealand.

Smith, Giles. 1995. *Lost in Music*. London: Picador.

Straw, Will. 1997. 'Sizing Up Record Collections: Gender and Connoisseurship in Rock Music Culture.' In *Sexing the Groove: Popular Music and Gender*, ed. Sheila Whiteley. London: Routledge, 3–16.

Whitburn, Joel, comp. 1988. *Billboard Top 1000 Singles, 1955–1987*. Milwaukee, WI: Hal Leonard Books and Billboard Publications.

Willis, Paul E., et al. 1990. *Common Culture: Symbolic Work at Play in the Everyday Cultures of the Young.* Milton Keynes: Open University Press.

Discographical Reference

Anthology of American Folk Music, Vols. 1–3 (ed. Harry Smith). Smithsonian/Folkways 40090. 1952; *1997*: USA.

ROY SHUKER

Religion and Spirituality

Introduction

The relationship between popular music and religion has heightened the struggles and accommodations that exist between music and religion in general. Because both music and religion, through performance and ritual, induce experiences of embodied power, they can be either rivals or associates. The global media reach and appeal of popular musics in the twentieth century raised the stakes of competition, in the one case, and elucidated the symbiotic bonds, in the other.

The fundamental historical, musical and social sources of popular music are deeply imbued with religious elements. African, Afro-Caribbean and African-American musical sources are connected with religious practises of spirit possession and spirit communication. South Asian popular forms, such as *qawwālī* and film music, developed from the metaphoric analogy of human love to divine love found in Hindu and Muslim devotional practises. The hymnody of European and North American Protestantism derived from folk tunes that were appropriated to liturgical contexts during the Reformation.

As used here, 'religion' is taken to include institutional expressions of organized religion, charismatic forms of popular religion, and those individual experiences that are characterized by plumbed depths or transcendence within human life – that which is commonly called 'spiritual.'

Religious Proscriptions Against Popular Music

Religious proscriptions against music have been related to codes of purity, morality and anti-somatic mind/body dualisms. Regulations against musical expression have often exhibited a gendered dimension, discouraging music because of its sensual effects and prohibiting women's musical expression more stringently than men's (Jones 1987, 1991; Rycenga 1999). Judaism, Christianity and Islam have adopted the strongest positions against musical expression, reflecting those traditions' ambivalence toward the body; but cultures shaped by these monotheistic traditions also produced a wealth of popular musics in the twentieth century. Thus, proscriptions have rarely been absolute.

Forms of religious opposition to popular music fall into two broad categories: institutional and individual. The first occurs when religious organizations take a public stand against a particular genre, artist or song. Examples of this – such as the boycotts and record-burnings that took place under the auspices of church groups following John Lennon's 1966 declaration that the Beatles were 'more popular than Jesus now' (Martin and Segrave 1988, 178; Schultheiss 1980, 155ff.) – have constituted a kind of explicit cultural contestation. The second form occurs when individual performers (often amidst the battles created by religious opposition to popular music) waver between popular music and religious conviction. Famous examples of this phenomenon (beginning with Franz Liszt in nineteenth-century Europe) have included Thomas A. Dorsey, Yusuf Islam (aka Cat Stevens; see http://catstevens.com for interviews concerning his conversion to Islam), Little Richard and Jimmy Snow, who toured with Elvis Presley before finding a vocation as an evangelical Pentecostal minister, preaching against the evils of rock music (Martin and Segrave 1988, 50, 74; 'Ex-R'n'R Star . . .' 1961). 'Big' Bill Broonzy, however, admitted going in the other direction: having started as 'a preacher – preached in the church. One day I quit and went to music' (Szatmary 1991, 3). Blind Lemon Jefferson gained fame as a blues performer, but simultaneously recorded religious songs under the name Deacon L.J. Bates.

The institutional and individual forms of opposition between religious consciousness and popular music performance share a common strategy: popular music is 'othered' in cosmological terms. The music becomes associated with Satan, with the demonic in general or with sinful activities, such as sex, drugs and drink. This yoking of musical skill with sinister forces has had a long lineage. Its high profile in the blues tradition, where guitarist Robert Johnson was reputed to have struck a bargain and sold his soul to the devil, has been traced to both African and European sources (Walser 1993; Ventura 1985). The legend resurfaced in the persistent rumors that three of the four members of Led Zeppelin had sold their souls to Satan in exchange for instant success and massive popularity (S. Davis 1985).

The 'othering' of popular music by religious authorities is part of a larger structural antinomy. When an institutionalized religion champions cultural conformity, class and race respectability, and the political status quo, popular musicians are made to signify – and they often willingly adopt – a contrary stance. Martin and Segrave (1988) suggest that '[w]ith its black roots, its earthy, sexual or rebellious lyrics, and its exuberant acceptance by youth, rock and roll has long been under attack by the establishment world of adults' (3), a world whose authority has often been instantiated by religious institutions, as highlighted in the early religious opposition to rock music by the US Catholic Youth Organization (18–29).

Religious institutions that represent adult authority and pious decorum have been opposed to popular music on the basis of its association with dance and therefore, by implication, with sexuality. When a religion's primary interaction with the world is through moralism, its opposition to any powerful medium not under its direct control can be assumed. Thus, the presumed suspension of rational control characteristic of bodily activity and ecstasy is labeled morally deviant and dangerous. Upon taking control of Sudan in 1989, the National Islamic Front immediately began 'clamping down on Sudanese musicians with a puritanical zeal that has forced many of the country's best-loved performers into exile or silence' (Verney 1994, 190). This culminated in an attack on Hanan Bulu-bulu, 'the provocative Madonna of Sudanese pop,' whose concerts were banned. Her stage performances drew on suggestive traditional bridal dances and urban women's music; thus, she was condemned for 'immoral behaviour' and branded as '"half-Ethiopian" – a euphemism for sexual licentiousness' (Verney 1994, 196).

The reactionary US critic Carl Raschke (1990) suggests that heavy metal music begets *violence* – often the most irrational and uncontrollable violence engineered by the Archfiend himself,' since rock music wants to 'provoke an upsurge of the irrational' and 'get the listeners to react, not ruminate' (166, 170; emphasis in original). The genre may have changed from one generation to another, but the tone and content of the attacks have remained consistent. Speaking in 1938, Archbishop Beckman felt similarly about jazz: he feared that '"jam sessions," "jitter-bugs," and cannibalistic rhythmic orgies . . . [are] wooing our youth along the primrose path to hell!' (Merriam 1964, 243).

As can be seen from this last example, the tenor of Christian critiques of popular music were, and are, heavily burdened with racism and classism. When a southern segregationist in the United States attacked a 1956 rock concert, he stated in no uncertain terms that 'Christians will not attend this show. Ask your preacher about jungle music' (Martin and Segrave 1988, 42). These racist attacks facilitated the 'othering' of popular music, warranting the ultimate religious insult from the monotheistic traditions: the label of 'pagan.'

Shared Functions of Music and Religion: The 'Pagan' Contexts of Popular Music

The word 'pagan' is, itself, a term of contestation. Originally a term invented by Roman city-dwellers to describe less sophisticated country-dwellers, it was transformed into a scornful obloquy by which Christian and Muslim invaders could dismiss indigenous religions as 'inferior' and 'primitive.' By this definition, all polytheistic systems were deemed pagan. The vital relationship between music, dance and religious ritual in polytheistic traditions was often singled out by missionaries as indicative of moral decay and satanic influence.

Given the preexistence of this discourse against 'pagan' music and religion, it is not surprising that it resurfaced with the advent of popular musics, especially since those musics often had their roots in African, Native American, South Asian Hindu and Pacific Islander polytheistic religious cultures. Resistance to jazz often referred to the use of drums as a form of 'primitivism,' and '[a]nti-jazz groups were formed and banners paraded proclaiming, in a revealing phrase, "Down with Jazz and Paganism"' (Taylor 1985, 165). A Minneapolis Catholic Youth Center newsletter from the mid-1950s 'advised its readers to "Smash the records you possess which represent a pagan culture and a pagan concept of life"' (Martin and Segrave 1988, 25–26).

The connection of pagan traditions to drums, and to a more active form of ritual participation than is common in monotheistic traditions, is not entirely fallacious – only the condemnatory judgment is. Almost all indigenous religious traditions have formal means for maintaining communication with the spirit realm (whether the spirit realm is understood as the realm of deities, ancestors or of secondary types of spirits like demiurges or saints). The most common forms of this communication are shamanism and spirit possession, both of which employ drums, rattles, flutes, whistles, kazoos and other similar instruments (Eliade 1972; Nketia 1962). Even more importantly, both the shaman and the spirit medium function as religious virtuosos, whose success depends on community support, community participation, and their own performative ability to travel, or be possessed, through the vehicle of sound. The fact that such performances are made possible by the attainment of an altered state of consciousness, frequently through the use of hallucinogens, makes the comparison to popular music quite fecund.

It has been argued that voodoo, a syncretic religious tradition built around spirit possession, was one of the origins for the jazz that emerged in New Orleans. Ventura (1985) speculates that the African cosmology of the crossroads resurfaced 'in Congo Square, [where] African metaphysics first became subsumed in music. A secret within the music instead of the object of the music' (124). Cavin (1975) highlights the role of the voodoo queens of New Orleans, who operated as 'charismatic authorities,' creating a context where an 'exchange between European and African culture and music' developed in a predominantly female and thoroughly interracial environment, imbued with creative religious ideas and activities (13, 21–22).

Taylor (1985) develops the comparison of shamanism and popular music. He, too, argues that popular music combines worlds, thus bringing together a variety of spiritual powers. Taylor notes how rock syncretizes the power of black blues, Christian gospel music, Native American traditions and sex (172), so that rock 'succeeded, like nothing before it had done, in *demonstrating* an occult mystery. In so doing it directly reflected its shamanistic heritage, for the shaman seeks to bring to the whole tribe a very special and unusual vision of the world . . . [a] vision that cures human ordinariness' (207; emphasis in original).

The active role of music in religious ritual has provided evocative myths for popular musicians. Cross-cultural explorations of percussion undertaken by Grateful Dead drummer Mickey Hart were inspired by the comparative mythologist Joseph Campbell, and led to the Dead playing a show at the Pyramids (Hart 1990; Sylvan 1998). Likewise, feminist New Age percussionist Layne Redmond (1998) traces her music to ancient goddess-based traditions as described by archeologist Marija Gimbutas. The jazz-band leader Sun Ra was far ahead of these relative newcomers: his flights of religious speculation were based on a study of ancient Egyptian and other African sources, and his ritual leadership of the Arkestra was deliberately based on the religio-political functions of West African master musicians (Szwed 1997; Sun Ra 1988).

The varied neo-pagan movements of Europe and North America are intricately linked to popular music. The 'magickal' explorations of Aleister Crowley (1875–1947) provided a major inspiration for Jimmy Page of Led Zeppelin, who actually purchased Crowley's Loch Ness mansion (S. Davis 1985). The signature song of the band, 'Stairway to Heaven,' draws on a variety of neo-pagan themes, such as the idyll of the rural past, the sacredness of Nature and the contradictions of Christianity. A romanticized Celtic pagan past has been integral to the musical appeal of Enya and Loreena McKennitt. The Lilith Fair, a tour of women rock musicians organized by Sarah McLachlan, took its name from a feminist reclamation of Lilith, the mythical first wife of Adam; Lilith has also been prominently associated with contemporary feminist goddess religions. Tori Amos and PJ Harvey have extended feminist critiques of Christianity into their music (Rycenga 1997).

Music, Religion and Resistance

Religion itself has a dual character: its supernatural authority can be used either to validate existing power structures or to pose an alternative to arbitrary, temporary and unjust structures of human power. Popular music, in its mass dissemination, can create an effective medium for a countercultural stance, which, in turn, is made more powerful by association with religious righteousness. Black churches in South Africa, by nurturing musical groups like Ladysmith Black Mambazo, became visible and audible centers of resistance to apartheid, while also focusing global attention on their struggle (Marre and Charlton 1985, 43–44).

The co-development of Rastafarianism and reggae in Kingston, Jamaica from the 1930s onward exemplified the blending of music and religion into a counter-discourse. The Rastafarian critique of racism and imperialism in religion, and its projection of a Pan-African religious vision, found a worldwide audience through reggae. In the 1970s, the popularity of bands like the Abyssinians, Bob Marley and the Wailers, and Burning Spear imparted a religious logic to political critique and the use of ganja. Marley's description of Rastas and reggae musicians as 'soul rebels' epitomized music's role in this religious resistance.

An earlier example of this role for music can be found in the back-and-forth movement of gospel from black churches to popular music genres (Maultsby 1992). Aretha Franklin is one of many black soul singers who received her training in gospel music, and she has often returned to sing in church. Embodied forms of worship in black North American Christian churches were often criticized by racists as signs of backwardness. But the validation of gospel music by record-buyers and radio listeners created a cultural space for this form of Christianity, so markedly different in style from that of the mainline white Protestant churches. The high profile of gospel music also ensured the survival of musical forms that had sustained black slaves in the struggle against slavery. As Dahl (1984) notes, 'During slavery the church was . . . the place where highly codified (because dangerous) emotions were vented in song and witness . . . The black church, it could almost be said, was the first jam session – and black women . . . mostly poor women, culture bearers and music makers who remained anonymous beyond the black church . . . were always powerhouses in it' (5–6, 152).

But the politics of respectability, and the internal contradictions within Christianity, could make the black church alternatively a source of popular music creativity and a force opposed to popular music. Such a clash occurred over the blues (A. Davis 1998). Davis points out that the blues presented a cosmological vision, one that 'disputed the binary constructions associated with Christianity' and 'blatantly defied the Christian imperative to relegate sexual conduct to the realm of sin' (123). By giving women an autonomous sense of self, and a power based in the body, the blues also revealed fault lines of class and gender in the black community. Thus, a song like Bessie Smith's 'Preachin' the Blues' 'establishes the realm of the blues as spiritually coexistent with and simultaneously antithetical to Christian religious practices' (129). The blues – a popular music form that, while secular, encroached on religious ground, and was therefore condemned from the pulpit – formed a counter-discourse that revealed the tensions within African-American Christianity (Ventura 1985, 133–34).

The religious critique of popular music has created a situation in which the deployment of religious symbols becomes highly charged and bitterly contested. Heavy metal bands choose names that 'invoke the auratic power of blasphemy or mysticism (Judas Priest, Black Sabbath, Blue Öyster Cult),' and the Devil becomes a 'transgressive icon' rather than a worshiped reality (Walser 1993, 2, 151). Similarly, the cultural subtexts evoked by Madonna are often steeped in religious imagery, from her name to her celebrated video for 'Like a Prayer,' to her controversial use of Hindu facial markings in a provocative performance at the MTV awards ceremony in 1988 (McClary 1991; Scott 1993).

There is, as Lewis (1990) notes, an irony in the fact that women were so long excluded from performing religious music, since 'churches are often the first place a musically inclined girl sings before an audience' now that the 'secularization of music and fragmentation of religious power' have opened this venue as a 'safe' place for women to express themselves musically. She notes that both Tina Turner and Pat Benatar have credited their religious upbringing with launching their musical careers (Lewis 1990, 56–57, 74, 81; Post 1994, 42).

Popular Music with Religious Intent

As a result of religious proscriptions against or suspicions about secular music in some cultures, musicians have often wrapped themselves in a cloak of devotion in order to have their music recorded and heard at all. Jones (1987) reports how Tunisian popular singers have felt compelled to highlight their piety, by performing the ''umra, or minor pilgrimage' or by recording 'a spate of devotional songs to be used in religious segments on radio and television and for record releases' (80).

The political movements and countercultural tendencies of the 1960s were marked by an 'eclectic taste for mystic, occult, and magical phenomena,' as well as by extended exploration of Asian religious traditions by Westerners (Roszak 1969, 125). Similarly, a cross-fertilization of Western and Asian forms of music occurred. While Ravi Shankar was trained as a Hindustani classical performer, his worldwide celebrity made him a popular music icon. Shankar's contact with musicians as varied as Dizzy Gillespie, John Coltrane and George Harrison legitimated this religio-musical alternative. Similarly, Indian film music deftly combined its classical religious heritage with the song forms of Western music, prompting singing star Lata Mangeshkar to reiterate traditional formulae while maintaining a hectic, modern schedule: 'I believe that music and God are one. My father always maintained that music has a power that leads to a short cut to God. Yes, I am religious and yes, I do pray, but not four hours a day . . . I pray according to the free time I have, when I'm not recording film music' (Marre and Charlton 1985, 146).

John Coltrane's explorations of religious thought, whether African, Asian or Western Christian, had an influence on jazz and rock musicians of the 1960s. Coltrane said that, in compositions like *Om*, *A Love Supreme* and *Meditations*, he was on a quest for 'something that hasn't been played before.' This 'continual looking which may be described as the spiritual aspects of improvisation . . . was obviously also an ideal metaphor for the spiritual searching of mankind and, in his last years, Coltrane felt the need to make this absolutely explicit' (Priestley 1987, 52–53). The effects of Coltrane's explorations were varied. Roger McGuinn of the Byrds credits a tape of Coltrane's 'India' and of his 'Africa' with inspiring the psychedelic opening of 'Eight Miles High' (Thomas 1975, 198–99). Sonny Rollins reexamined his music and spirituality in the light of Coltrane's influence (Fiofori 1971). But Amiri Baraka was critical of the depoliticization that was fostered when the music 'gets to be ultra-metaphysical where you get a lot of "Om-m-m-m-m" in it' (Priestley 1987, 56).

Popular music's power has led some musicians into a mythologizing replete with religious connotations. Sun Ra's claim to legendary origins on Saturn, John Lennon's challenge to all theologies in 'Imagine,' Maurice White's spiritual mission as the leader of Earth, Wind & Fire, Nusrat Fateh Ali Khan's charge to bring *qawwālī* to the world and the martyrdom of Algerian Berber singer Lounes Matoub, murdered in 1998 by Islamic traditionalists for his political opinions (Barry and Holmes 1998) – all these stand as examples of charismatic spiritual leadership on the part of popular musicians. The music of Yes, exemplified in lengthy songs such as 'Sound Chaser' and 'The Revealing Science of God,' has taken this mythologization into sound itself, imparting a sense of music's immanent sacredness.

The politics of religiously based popular music has often trodden a thin line between aggressive proselytizing and ecumenical harmonizing. Qureshi (1992) charts the development of *qawwālī* under the Indian recording industry's title of 'Muslim devotional' (111). From the time of Partition (1948), 'one can observe a shift away from a more orthodox supralocal Islam to a heterodox Sufism which addresses Indian Islam and Indian saints, and embraces a general humanism extolling all religions' (115).

A genre of rock music called 'Christian rock' has had to overcome both secular suspicion and internal religious criticisms in order to flourish. Contemporary Christian music (CCM) has become a billion-dollar industry in the United States, with its own charts, distribution networks and awards shows. Its highest-grossing artist, singer Amy Grant, became a 'crossover' success in 1991 with her secular single, 'Baby Baby.' But her very success has raised questions within evangelical Protestant circles, as her fame, her lyrics and her behavior (including a divorce and remarriage) have been scrutinized for signs of worldly ensnarement (Howard and Streck 1999; Clark 2000). Conversely, at the beginning of U2's career, the avowed charismatic Christianity of three of its members made them suspect in the eyes of secular critics, especially when songs like 'Gloria' seemed unctuously pious. The fact that their brand of Christianity was inclusive rather than dogmatic eventually placated their detractors, but bands more closely associated with evangelical Christianity, like Stryper, have rarely enjoyed sustained commercial success.

Conclusion

Comparisons between the functions of religion and those of music have multiplied since the advent of popular music. The dedication of fans, the ritual aura of concerts and the near-theological hairsplitting among cognoscenti are all reminiscent of religious enthusiasm (Leonard 1987; Taylor 1985), as are explicit religious communities based on popular music, such as Deadheads, the Church of John Coltrane and the cult of Elvis sightings (Sylvan 1998). The idea that popular music provokes religious experience has been both lauded (Hart 1990) and damned (Pattison 1987), but, as Sylvan suggests, popular music may well provide 'a significant alternative religious choice that bypasses the narrow opposition between traditional religious institutions and secular humanism' (1998, 22). Whether skeptically denouncing religious hypocrisy, as in Jethro Tull's 'My God,' or amplifying religious criticism of a sinful world, as in U2's 'Sunday Bloody Sunday,' there is no doubt that popular music will continue to give expression to the emotionally potent themes of religion.

Bibliography

Baker, Paul. 1979. *Why Should the Devil Have All the Good Music?* Waco, TX: Word Books.

Barrett, Leonard E. 1988. *The Rastafarians: Sounds of Cultural Dissonance.* Rev. ed. Boston, MA: Beacon Press. (First published Boston, MA: Beacon Press, 1977.)

Barry, Kevin, and Holmes, Mary. 1998. 'Algerian Singer Murdered.' *News and Letters* 43(7) (August-September): 12.

Boehm, Uwe, and Buschmann, Gerd. 2000. *Popmusik – Religion – Unterricht. Modelle und Materialien zur Didaktik von Popularkultur* [Pop Music – Religion – Instruction: Models and Materials for Teaching Popular Culture]. Münster: LIT-Verlag.

Cavin, Susan. 1975. 'Missing Women: On the Voodoo Trail to Jazz.' *Journal of Jazz Studies* 3(1): 4–27.

Clark, Kim. 2000. 'Water and Dirt Makes Mud: Amy Grant, Contemporary Christian Music, and Celebrity.' Unpublished paper.

Dahl, Linda. 1984. *Stormy Weather: The Music and Lives of a Century of Jazzwomen.* New York: Pantheon Books.

Davis, Angela Y. 1998. *Blues Legacies and Black Feminism: Gertrude 'Ma' Rainey, Bessie Smith, and Billie Holiday.* New York: Pantheon.

Davis, Stephen. 1985. *Hammer of the Gods: The Led Zeppelin Saga.* New York: Ballantine Books.

Eliade, Mircea. 1972. *Shamanism: Archaic Techniques of Ecstasy,* trans. Willard R. Trask. Princeton, NJ: Princeton University Press.

'Ex-R'n'R Star Turned Evangelist Says Despite Polish, Beat's Still Evil.' 1961. *Variety* 224 (25 October): 69.

Fiofori, Tam. 1971. 'Re-Entry: The New Orbit of Sonny Rollins.' *Downbeat* 38(17): 14–15, 39.

Floyd, Samuel A. 1995. *The Power of Black Music: Interpreting Its History from Africa to the United States.* New York: Oxford University Press.

Gray, J. Patrick. 1980. 'Rock as a Chaos Model Ritual.' *Popular Music and Society* 2(7): 75–83.

Hart, Mickey, with Stevens, Jay. 1990. *Drumming at the Edge of Magic: A Journey into the Spirit of Percussion.* San Francisco: Harper San Francisco.

Howard, Jay R., and Streck, John M. 1999. *Apostles of Rock: The Splintered World of Contemporary Christian Music.* Lexington, KY: University Press of Kentucky.

Jones, L. JaFran. 1987. 'A Sociohistorical Perspective on Tunisian Women as Professional Musicians.' In *Women and Music in Cross-Cultural Perspective,* ed. Ellen Koskoff. Urbana, IL: University of Illinois Press, 69–83.

Jones, L. JaFran. 1991. 'Women in Non-Western Music.' In *Women and Music: A History,* ed. Karin Pendle. Bloomington, IN: Indiana University Press, 314–30.

Leonard, Neil. 1987. *Jazz: Myth and Religion.* New York: Oxford University Press.

Lewis, Lisa A. 1990. *Gender Politics and MTV: Voicing the Difference.* Philadelphia: Temple University Press.

Marre, Jeremy, and Charlton, Hannah. 1985. *Beats of the*

Heart: Popular Music of the World. New York: Pantheon Books.

Martin, Linda, and Segrave, Kerry. 1988. *Anti-Rock: The Opposition to Rock 'n' Roll*. Hamden, CT: Archon Books.

Maultsby, Portia. 1992. 'The Impact of Gospel Music on the Secular Music Industry.' In *We'll Understand It Better By and By: Pioneering African American Gospel Composers*, ed. Bernice Johnson Reagon. Washington, DC: Smithsonian Institution Press, 19–33.

McCarthy, Kate. 2000. *Casing the Promised Land: The Religious Visions of American Rock and Roll*. Berkeley, CA: University of California Press.

McClary, Susan. 1991. *Feminine Endings: Music, Gender, and Sexuality*. Minneapolis, MN: University of Minnesota Press.

Merriam, Alan P. 1964. *The Anthropology of Music*. Evanston, IL: Northwestern University Press.

Nketia, J.H. Kwabena. 1962. *African Gods and Music*. Legon: Institute of African Studies, University of Ghana.

Pattison, Robert. 1987. *The Triumph of Vulgarity: Rock Music in the Mirror of Romanticism*. New York: Oxford University Press.

Plaskow, Judith. 1979. 'The Coming of Lilith: Toward a Feminist Theology.' In *Womanspirit Rising: A Feminist Reader in Religion*, ed. Carol P. Christ and Judith Plaskow. San Francisco: Harper and Row, 198–209.

Post, Jennifer C. 1994. 'Erasing the Boundaries Between Public and Private in Women's Performance Traditions.' In *Cecilia Reclaimed: Feminist Perspectives on Gender and Music*, ed. Susan C. Cook and Judy S. Tsou. Urbana, IL: University of Illinois Press, 35–51.

Priestley, Brian. 1987. *John Coltrane*. London: Apollo Press.

Qureshi, Regula. 1992. '"Muslim Devotional": Popular Religious Music and Muslim Identity Under British, Indian and Pakistani Hegemony.' *Asian Music* XXIV(1): 111–21.

Raschke, Carl A. 1990. *Painted Black: From Drug Killings to Heavy Metal. The Alarming True Story of How Satanism Is Terrorizing Our Communities*. San Francisco: Harper and Row.

Reagon, Bernice Johnson, ed. 1992. *We'll Understand It Better By and By: Pioneering African American Gospel Composers*. Washington, DC: Smithsonian Institution Press.

Reckford, Verona. 1997. 'Reggae, Rastafarianism and Cultural Identity.' In *Reggae, Rasta, Revolution: Jamaican Music from Ska to Dub*, ed. Chris Potash. New York: Schirmer, 3–13.

Redmond, Layne. 1998. *When the Drummers Were Women: A Spiritual History of Rhythm*. New York: Three Rivers Press.

Roszak, Theodore. 1969. *The Making of a Counter Culture: Reflections on the Technocratic Society and Its Youthful Opposition*. Garden City, NY: Doubleday Anchor.

Rycenga, Jennifer. 1997. 'Sisterhood: A Loving Lesbian Ear Listens to Progressive Heterosexual Women's Rock Music.' In *Keeping Score: Music, Disciplinarity, Culture*, ed. David Schwarz, Lawrence Siegel and Anahid Kassabian. Charlottesville, VA: University Press of Virginia, 204–28.

Rycenga, Jennifer. 1999. 'Music: An Overview.' In *The Encyclopedia of Women and World Religions*, Vol. II, ed. Serinity Young. New York: Macmillan Reference USA, 687–90.

Schultheiss, Tom. 1980. *A Day in the Life: The Beatles Day-by-Day, 1960–1970*. Ann Arbor, MI: Pierian Press.

Scott, Ronald B. 1993. 'Images of Race and Religion in Madonna's Video "Like a Prayer": Prayer and Praise.' In *The Madonna Connection: Representational Politics, Subcultural Identities, and Cultural Theory*, ed. Cathy Schwichtenberg. Boulder, CO: Westview Press, 57–77.

Sullivan, Lawrence, ed. 1997. *Enchanting Powers: Music in the World's Religions*. Cambridge, MA: Harvard University Press.

Sun Ra. 1988. *The Immeasurable Equation*. Philadelphia: El Saturn.

Sylvan, Robin. 1998. *Traces of the Spirit: The Religious Dimensions of Popular Music*. Ph.D. thesis, University of California at Santa Barbara.

Szatmary, David P. 1991. *Rockin' in Time: A Social History of Rock-and-Roll*. 2nd ed. Englewood Cliffs, NJ: Prentice-Hall.

Szwed, John. 1997. *Space Is the Place: The Life and Times of Sun Ra*. New York: Pantheon Books.

Taylor, Rogan P. 1985. *The Death and Resurrection Show: From Shaman to Superstar*. London: Anthony Blond.

Thomas, J.C. 1975. *Chasin' the Trane: The Music and Mystique of John Coltrane*. Garden City, NY: Doubleday and Co.

Ventura, Michael. 1985. *Shadow Dancing in the USA*. Los Angeles: Jeremy P. Tarcher.

Verney, Peter. 1994. 'Yearning to Dance: Sudan Is the Bridge of Africa and Arabia.' In *World Music: The Rough Guide*, ed. Simon Broughton et al. London: Rough Guides Ltd., 190–97.

Walser, Robert. 1993. *Running with the Devil: Power, Gender, and Madness in Heavy Metal Music*. Hanover, NH: Wesleyan University Press.

Discographical References

Byrds, The. 'Eight Miles High.' *Fifth Dimension*. Columbia 9349. *1966*: USA. Reissue: Byrds, The. 'Eight Miles High.' *Fifth Dimension*. Sony 64847. *1996*: USA.

Coltrane, John. 'Africa.' *Africa/Brass*. Impulse! 6. *1961*:

USA. Reissue: Coltrane, John. 'Africa.' *Africa/Brass*. GRP 168. *1995*: USA.

Coltrane, John. *A Love Supreme*. Impulse! 155. 1964; *1995*: USA.

Coltrane, John. 'India.' *Impressions*. Impulse! 5887. 1961–63: USA.

Coltrane, John. *Meditations*. Impulse! 39139. 1965; *1992*: USA. Reissue: Coltrane, John. *Meditations*. GRP 199. *1996*: USA.

Coltrane, John. *Om*. Impulse! 39118. 1965: USA.

Grant, Amy. 'Baby Baby.' A&M 1549. *1991*: USA.

Jethro Tull. 'My God.' *Aqualung*. Reprise 2035. *1971*: USA. Reissue: Jethro Tull. 'My God.' *Aqualung: 25th Anniversary Special Edition*. Capitol 52213. *1996*: USA.

Led Zeppelin. 'Stairway to Heaven.' *Led Zeppelin IV*. Atlantic 7208. *1971*: USA. Reissue: Led Zeppelin. 'Stairway to Heaven.' *Led Zeppelin IV*. Atlantic 82638. *1994*: USA.

Lennon, John, and the Plastic Ono Band. 'Imagine.' Apple 1840. *1971*: UK. Reissue: Lennon, John, and the Plastic Ono Band. 'Imagine.' *The John Lennon Collection*. Capitol 91516. *1989*: USA.

Madonna. 'Like a Prayer.' Sire 27539. *1989*: USA.

Smith, Bessie. 'Preachin' the Blues.' Columbia 14195-D. 1927: USA. Reissue: Smith, Bessie. 'Preachin' the Blues.' *Her Best Recordings: 1923–1933*. Best of Jazz 4030. *1996*: USA.

U2. 'Gloria.' *October*. Island 842 297. *1981*: UK.

U2. 'Sunday Bloody Sunday.' *War*. Island 00671. *1983*: UK.

Yes. 'The Revealing Science of God.' *Tales from Topographic Oceans*. Atlantic 2-908. *1974*: USA. Reissue: Yes. 'The Revealing Science of God.' *Tales from Topographic Oceans*. Atlantic 7567826832. *1995*: USA.

Yes. 'Sound Chaser.' *Relayer*. Atlantic 18122. *1974*: USA. Reissue: Yes. 'Sound Chaser.' *Relayer*. Atlantic 7567826642. *1995*: USA.

Discography

Abyssinians, The. *Satta Massagana*. Heartbeat 120. *1993*: Jamaica.

Amos, Tori. 'Crucify.' *Little Earthquakes*. Atlantic 82358-2. *1991*: USA.

Beatles, The. 'Within You, Without You.' *Sergeant Pepper's Lonely Hearts Club Band*. Parlophone 46442. *1967*: UK.

Burning Spear. *Chant Down Babylon: The Island Anthology*. Island 524190. *1996*: UK.

Earth, Wind & Fire. *All 'n All*. Columbia 34905. *1977*: USA.

Enya. *The Memory of Trees*. Reprise 46106. *1995*: USA.

Franklin, Aretha. *Amazing Grace*. Atlantic 906. *1972*: USA.

Harrison, George, Shankar, Ravi, et al. *Concert for Bangla Desh*. Apple 3385. *1971*: UK.

Hart, Mickey. *Mickey Hart's Mystery Box*. Rykodisc 10338. *1996*: USA.

Hart, Mickey, and Planet Drum. *Supralingua*. Rykodisc 10396. *1998*: USA.

Hart, Mickey, with Flora Purim. *Planet Drum*. Rykodisc 10206. *1991*: USA.

Islam, Yusuf (Cat Stevens). *Prayers of the Last Prophet*. Mountain of Light/Resurgence RSG 7006. *1999*: UK.

Johnson, Robert. 'Crossroad Blues.' Vocalion 03475. 1936: USA. Reissue: Johnson, Robert. 'Crossroad Blues.' *The Complete Recordings*. Columbia 46222. *1990*: USA.

Johnson, Robert. 'Preachin' Blues.' Vocalion 04630. 1936: USA. Reissue: Johnson, Robert. 'Preachin' Blues.' *The Complete Recordings*. Columbia 46222. *1990*: USA.

Ladysmith Black Mambazo. *Shaka Zulu*. Warner Brothers 25582. *1987*: USA.

Led Zeppelin. 'Nobody's Fault But Mine.' *Presence*. Swan Song 8416. *1976*: USA.

Little Richard. *King of the Gospel Singers*. Mercury 12288. *1965*: USA.

Little Richard. *Sings the Gospel [Prime Cuts]*. Stateside 10054. *1964*: USA.

Mangeshkar, Lata. *An Era in an Evening*. Sony International 487989. *1999*: USA.

Mangeshkar, Lata. *Hits in the 80's*. EMI India 5347. *1990*: India.

Marley, Bob, and the Wailers. *Catch a Fire*. Island ILPS 9241. *1973*: UK.

Marley, Bob, and the Wailers. *Exodus*. Island ILPS 9498. *1977*: UK.

McKennitt, Loreena. *The Mask and Mirror*. Warner Brothers 45420. *1994*: USA.

McLachlan, Sarah. *Surfacing*. Arista 18970. *1997*: USA.

Nusrat Fateh Ali Khan. *Shahbaaz*. Real World 86239. *1991*: UK.

PJ Harvey. 'Water.' *Dry*. Too Pure/Indigo 5001. *1992*: UK.

Redmond, Layne, and the Mob of Angels. *Since the Beginning*. Redmond RDM11. *1993*: USA.

Stevens, Cat. 'Morning Has Broken.' *Teaser and the Firecat*. A&M 75021-4313. *1971*: USA.

Stryper. *To Hell with the Devil*. Enigma SEAX-73277. *1986*: USA.

Sun Ra. *Space Is the Place* (Original soundtrack). Evidence ECD 22070-2. *1972*: USA. Reissue: Sun Ra. *Space Is the Place* (Original soundtrack). Evidence 22070. *1993*: USA.

Sun Ra. *The Magic City*. Evidence ECD 22069-2. 1965: USA. Reissue: Sun Ra. *The Magic City*. Evidence 22069. *1993*: USA.

Filmography

Space Is the Place (aka *Sun Ra & His Intergalactic Arkestra: Space Is the Place*), dir. John Coney. 1974. USA. 85 mins. Science Fiction. Original music by Sun Ra.

Visual Recordings

Madonna. 1990. 'Like a Prayer.' *The Immaculate Collection*. Warner Reprise Video 38195-3.

Sun Ra. 1974. 'Space Is the Place.' Rhapsody Films (video).

JENNIFER RYCENGA

Resistance and Protest

Both the terms 'resistance' and 'protest' were applied to popular songs in the United States in the 1930s. The composer Charles Seeger wrote that folk music was acceptable if 'it shows clearly a spirit of resentment towards oppression or vigorous resistance' (Cantwell 1996, 93). Meanwhile, the Communist journal *New Masses* gave a collection of black North American music the title *Negro Songs of Protest* (Gellert 1936).

The first academic study of the phenomenon defined protest songs as 'spontaneous outbursts of resentment, composed without the careful artistry that is a requisite of songs that become traditional' (Greenway 1953). The same author traced the Anglophone protest song to the medieval period and such songs as 'The Cutty Wren,' but the term has now come to be used almost solely to describe lyrics created in the twentieth century (and often sung to well-known tunes) either by various social and occupational groups – black North Americans, soldiers, industrial workers, those subject to colonial exploitation – or by professional songwriters. Although such protest was synonymous with left-wing or 'progressive' causes (see, for example, Lieberman 1989), Dunaway (1987) has pointed out that right-wing groups such as the Ku Klux Klan also created protest songs, while the role of Plastic People of the Universe in Communist Czechoslovakia was one example of resistance to left-wing regimes.

Collections of Anglophone protest songs were edited by Alan Lomax and others (Lomax 1999 (originally published in 1967); Hille 1948; Seeger and MacColl 1961) before the term was taken up by the music industry as a descriptor for compositions dealing with nuclear weapons, civil rights, the Vietnam war and other topics by young singer-songwriters such as Bob Dylan, Phil Ochs, Donovan and Country Joe McDonald. The ersatz protest song 'Eve of Destruction' (1965), composed by P.F. Sloan for Barry McGuire, sold a million copies.

An important Spanish-language protest song movement also arose in the 1960s (see, for example, Pring-Mill 1983, 1987, 1993; Stilman 1972; Vettori 1974). The beginnings of the *nueva canción Chilena* (Chilean new song) movement in 1966 were followed in 1967 by the first Latin American festival of *canción protesta*, held in Havana (Ossorio 1967). It was this event that inspired Barbara Dane to establish her Paredon label, which specialized in the issue of protest and revolutionary songs on an international basis between 1969 and 1980. (In 1991, Paredon was acquired by the Smithsonian Institution.)

In Africa, *chimurenga* songs – *chimurenga* is the Shona word for resistance, revolution or struggle – were performed and broadcast in Zimbabwe by Thomas Mapfumo during the anti-colonial struggle of the 1960s. Above all, in the 1970s there was the 'stubborn utopia projected through Bob Marley's music and anti-colonial imaginings' (Gilroy 2000, 133). The pervasive trope of 'protest' in rock culture can, however, lead to the mistaken assumption that other musics necessarily share these characteristics. This has been strongly argued by Schade-Poulsen (1999) in relation to the *rai* genre of Algeria (28–32) and by de Kloet (1998) in a study of Chinese popular music.

The terms 'protest' and 'resistance' are often used interchangeably, but a distinction can be made between protest songs as explicit statements of opposition to the political, economic or social status quo and music of resistance which may be more coded or opaque in its expression of dissidence – what Lipsitz (1994) has called 'immanent resistance.' The flexibility of 'resistance' in this sense, and its connection with the influential Gramscian concepts of hegemony and subordination, have made the concept one of the most widely used explanatory tools in the study of popular musical forms. It informs analyses of Western youth subcultures (Hall and Jefferson 1976) and African migrant workers' dance (Erlmann 1996), as well as numerous studies of African-derived musics in the Americas, recent examples of which include work on Brazilian music (Fryer 2000), Haitian music (Averill 1997) and Duke Ellington's 'jungle' music of the 1920s (Middleton 2000), and on music and the 'black public sphere' (Neal 1999).

Bibliography

Averill, Gage. 1997. *A Day for the Hunter, A Day for the Prey: Popular Music and Power in Haiti*. Chicago: University of Chicago Press.

Cantwell, Robert. 1996. *When We Were Good: The Folk Revival*. Cambridge, MA: Harvard University Press.

de Kloet, Jeroen. 1998. 'Living in Confusion, Remembering Clearly: Rock in China.' In *Popular Music: Intercultural Interpretations*, ed. Tôru Mitsui. Kanazawa: Graduate Program in Music, Kanazawa University, 38–50.

Dunaway, David King. 1987. 'Music as Political Communication in the United States.' In *Popular Music and Communication*, ed. James Lull. Newbury Park, CA: Sage Publications, 36–52.

Erlmann, Veit. 1996. *Nightsong: Performance, Power, and Practice in South Africa*. Chicago: University of Chicago Press.

Fryer, Peter. 2000. *Rhythms of Resistance: African Musical Heritage in Brazil*. London: Pluto Press.

Gellert, Lawrence. 1936. *Negro Songs of Protest*. New York: American Music League.

Gilroy, Paul. 2000. *Between Camps: Nations, Cultures and the Allure of Race*. London: Penguin.

Greenway, John. 1953. *American Folksongs of Protest*. Philadelphia: University of Pennsylvania Press.

Hall, Stuart, and Jefferson, Tony, eds. 1976. *Resistance Through Rituals: Youth Subcultures in Post-War Britain*. London: Hutchinson.

Hille, Waldemar, ed. 1948. *The People's Song Book*. New York: Boni & Gaer.

Lieberman, Robbie. 1989. *My Song Is My Weapon: People's Songs, American Communism, and the Politics of Culture, 1930–1950*. Urbana, IL: University of Illinois Press.

Lipsitz, George. 1994. *Dangerous Crossroads: Popular Music, Postmodernism, and the Poetics of Place*. London and New York: Verso.

Lomax, Alan, ed. 1999 (1967). *Hard Hitting Songs for Hard-Hit People*. Lincoln, NE: University of Nebraska Press.

Middleton, Richard. 2000. 'Musical Belongings: Western Music and Its Low-Others.' In *Western Music and Its Others: Difference, Representation, and Appropriation in Music*, ed. Georgina Born and David Hesmondhalgh. Berkeley, CA: University of California Press, 59–85.

Neal, Mark Anthony. 1999. *What the Music Said: Black Popular Music and Black Public Culture*. New York: Routledge.

Ossorio, José Maria. 1967. 'Encuentro de la Canción Protesta – Crónica' [A *Canción Protesta* Gathering – An Account]. *Revista Casa de las Americas* 45 (November): 138–56.

Pring-Mill, Robert. 1983. 'Cantas – Canto – Cantemos: Las Canciones de Lucha y Esperanza como Signos de Reunion e Identidad' [You Sing – I Sing – We Sing: The Songs of Struggle and Hope as Signs of Reunion and Identity]. *Romantisches Jahrbuch* 34: 318–54.

Pring-Mill, Robert. 1987. 'The Roles of Revolutionary Song – A Nicaraguan Assessment.' *Popular Music* 6(2): 179–89.

Pring-Mill, Robert. 1993. *The Uses of Spanish-American So-Called 'Protest' Song*. IPM Occasional Paper 4. Liverpool: Institute of Popular Music.

Schade-Poulsen, Marc. 1999. *Men and Popular Music in Algeria: The Social Significance of Raï*. Austin, TX: University of Texas Press.

Seeger, Peggy, and MacColl, Ewan, eds. 1961. *Songs for the Sixties*. London: Workers' Music Association.

Stilman, Eduardo, ed. 1972. *Antología Crítica de la Canción de Protesta* [Critical Anthology of the Protest Song]. Buenos Aires: Ediciones Corregidor.

Vettori, Giuseppe, ed. 1974. *Canzoni Italiane di Protesta 1794–1974: Dalla Rivoluzione Francese alla Repressione Chilena* [Italian Songs of Protest, 1794–1974: From the French Revolution to the Chilean Repression]. Rome: Newton Compton.

Discographical References

Ian Campbell Folk Group, The. 'The Cutty Wren.' *Songs of Protest* (EP). Topic TOP 82. *1962*: UK.

McGuire, Barry. 'Eve of Destruction.' Dunhill 4009. *1965*: USA.

DAVE LAING

Revivals

In popular music, a revival is a deliberate, often concerted attempt to revitalize public interest in and knowledge of an area of popular music whose popularity has waned. In some cases, the music being revived has remained broadly familiar; in others – especially those involving a considerable lapse of time between original appearance and revival – public knowledge may have become quite limited; in still others, a music may be revived in a different geographical context, among an audience without any, even distant, memory of it. Revivals may have a narrow focus, such as an individual instrument, or an individual musician or group, but the most common type involves a genre or subgenre. Popular music may also play a part in a broader revival, such as one involving a period or decade.

The motivation behind revivals is often complex, but certain tendencies may be identified. One is a desire to (re-)introduce a music considered by those responsible for the revival to be more 'authentic.' In this, revivals are often linked to a sense of dissatisfaction with contemporary music. In the case of revivals of genres, this is often connected in turn to interest in roots and origins. Viewing these roots and their products from the historically (and, often, socially) remote perspective of the revival may tend to create a historiography of the earlier era as musically and socially continuous and whole, in contrast to the perceived erosive effects of mass production, fad and fashion, and media dissemination in the present. Notions of better times, 'natural' music, and individual and communal creativity unsullied by the march of progress create environments in which revivals prosper. In this way, the word 'revival' suggests not only reenactment, but also rebirth.

Throughout the twentieth century, revivals of pre-existing popular music coexisted with and influenced contemporary music-making. However, because these concepts of revival were frequently linked, historiographically, to notions of authenticity, the governing factors were political as well as musical. Thus, a revival could suggest not only a reaction to and discontent with the contemporary music of the day, but a withdrawal from mainstream cultural activities as well. The US revivalist folk movement of the 1930s, for example, was closely associated with left-wing political thought as well as concerned with harnessing a (somewhat patronizing) musical romanticism. Similarly, UK folklorist Bert Lloyd's small reader *The Singing Englishman* (1944) was a Marxist interpretation of England's performance past. However debatable were these politicized interpretations of the past, the notion has nonetheless persisted that much can be learned from previous popular music traditions.

Although such revivals often take place, broadly, in the same geographical and cultural region as that which nourished the 'original,' that need not always be the case. The blues revival in Europe in the 1950s, for example, constituted a revival of fortunes for the African-American musicians involved, such as 'Big' Bill Broonzy, but for much of the audience it represented a new musical and cultural experience. In this context, while the issue for some was the injection into the contemporary scene, via the revival, of a music more steeped in realism than contemporary popular music was perceived to be, for others it was more a question of new sound worlds and new cultural icons, alongside contemporary ones – sounds and images that could be appropriated and worked with in new contexts.

Because musical styles are vital and pliable, and respond to the desires of the present – even if the needs of those involved appear to be based on conserving the apparent purity of the past – revivals inevitably involve older forms of music in a process of recontextualization. Thus, while the term 'folk music revival' has been used to describe the phenomenon of younger singers and players from outside a 'traditional' culture perpetuating its music, it has also come to include more eclectic musicians who are open to a variety of influences.

If, in some cases, appropriation and recontextualization were opportunities created by revivals, in others they can be identified as the motivation behind them. At the end of the twentieth century, this logic became explicit and, together with the postmodern fashion of appropriation and recontextualization, prompted innumerable revivals of global popular music. From the Japanese affectation of the 1950s look and sound of British rock 'n' roller Cliff Richard to the easy listening revival observable in the United Kingdom during the mid-1990s, revivals with an element of kitsch, irony and bricolage occurred all over the world, to the regret of many 'purists.'

Such revivals typically involve a relearning process, and many previously 'hidden' genres of music have benefited from reevaluation. One such genre was easy listening. But reevaluations can bring losses as well as gains. What the easy listening revival demonstrated was that, in choosing to overlook the original meanings of the genre, as it developed in the United States in the 1950s, in favor of an ironic treatment, and in showing little concern for the historical context that spawned it, the revival risked impoverishing the genre at the same time as it revitalized it.

Few revivals have been without their contradictions and controversies. Folk music has been one of the most heavily 'revived' musics, and folk music revivals occurred all over the world during the twentieth century. At the turn of the century, composers such as Grainger, Bartók, Rimsky-Korsakov and Vaughan Williams resolutely included 'folk' elements in their compositions in order to revive endangered cultures and stimulate a benign nationalism in their respective countries. Collector and composer Cecil Sharp (1859–1924) spearheaded this movement in England, and included English morris dancing as part of his brief. However, it has been argued that Sharp and others merely constructed folk images (Harker 1985). Indeed, it has even been suggested that Sharp's concept of morris dancing (a tradition that had virtually died out by the late nineteenth century) was an invention based on less than 'direct experience.'

Numerous apparent contradictions also characterized the postwar folk revival in the United States, when, in Robert Cantwell's words, 'the carriers of a superannuated ideological minority found themselves celebrated as the leaders of a mass movement; when an esoteric and anti-commercial enthusiasm turned into a commercial bonanza; when an alienated, jazz-driven literary bohemia turned to the simple songs of old rural America' (1996, 18). Rather than emphasizing the contradictions, however, Cantwell sees these examples as evidence of what he terms 'the nocturnal life' of history, where the boundaries between contradictory ideas and forces 'swim about in a kind of cultural ectoplasm where forms change places with one another' (1996, 18), engendering unexpected (and often unintended) transformations.

Similarly unexpected consequences followed the postwar revival of traditional New Orleans jazz in the United Kingdom. British jazz performer Ken Colyer was considered something of a connoisseur for attempting to imitate the sounds of early twentieth-century New Orleans jazz in the London jazz cellars of the 1940s and 1950s.

Colyer's view was that innovation was irresponsible and improper (even a process outside his own musical concerns), and he was highly intransigent; yet, it was from his traditional jazz shows that skiffle emerged, a hybrid of jazz, folk and blues. Less than a decade later, the Liverpool rock groups of the early 1960s were attempting to revive what they felt to be the initial impact of 'authentic' mid-1950s rock in the face of the torrent of media-driven singers. These groups also regarded imitation as a form of 'keeping the faith,' but this essence of purist revivalism did not prevent them from being spirited recontextualizers. The Beatles, for example, were regarded as one of the best – but also the most original – cover bands in Liverpool, a reminder that imitation is as much a part of musical creativity as is originality.

In the United States, the folk revival reached its zenith in the early 1960s and was challenged only by the arrival of the Beatles in 1964. Bob Dylan, unwilling darling of the US folk revival, understood that the Beatles' commercially based songwriting was as potentially enduring as anything traditional. This created divisions within the ranks of the revivalist movement in the United States and Europe concerning musical 'purity' that have yet to be fully resolved (see MacColl 1990).

As popular music began to fragment in the 1970s, it underwent a series of revivals, resulting in the myriad contributions that were manifested as punk. This period also marked the appearance of occasional industry-led revivals, a phenomenon with quite different motivation. One such revival of 1950s rock 'n' roll in the early 1970s in the United Kingdom was a commercial failure, but first attracted Sex Pistols manager Malcolm McLaren into the popular music arena.

A further source of revivals has been the music press. Here, the motivation often appears to be a professional one: a music paper may seek to predict (and encourage) a revival in order to be distinguished from a rival paper. One such revival was that identified by *New Musical Express* in the early 1990s, and named by the paper 'the New Wave of the New Wave.'

From the 1970s, popular music experienced numerous revivals. Early in the decade, a DJ/dance floor interest in obscure 1960s soul in areas of the north of England created the phenomenon of 'northern soul' (which experienced a further revival in the late 1990s). An interest in 1960s US garage music, initiated by New York journalist Lenny Kaye in his liner notes to the renowned album compilation *Nuggets*, created a revivalist movement that has continued unabated. British magazines such as *Nuggets*, *Let It Rock*, *Zig Zag* and *Dark Star* attempted to recall the atmosphere of the 1950s and 1960s, and yearned for music that was 'at its best . . . exhilarating, sexy, fun,'

able to 'capture the spirit of summer, girls, bout of flu, or whatever in 2 1/2 minutes of perfect trivia' (Langley 1977, 11).

In the late 1990s, Brian Setzer (former leader of rockabilly revivalists the Stray Cats) revived interest in 1940s jump blues. At the same time, the Swedish group ABBA experienced a worldwide revival that was almost on a par with its initial popularity. Because the group steadfastly refused to re-form, various sound-alike cover groups and stage shows working with ABBA material experienced widespread popularity.

A major issue concerning popular music revivals, however, has continued to be the apparent acceptance at face value by many of those involved that certain musics were originally constructed in the manner in which they have been revived. This has led to idealized and stylized revivals, such as the 1990s craze for 1970s disco music – which suggested that the 1970s are a place that can be 'visited' – and the simultaneous revival of 'authentic' Irish music. The latter case involved revivalists who determined authenticity by means of the idea of a unitary 'Celtic sound,' and who risked ignoring the degree to which that sound, if it existed, was itself a deliberate musical construction created out of a specific historical rejoinder to certain social and cultural moments. The revival thus became a means of making a link to a past that may never have existed. Once 'revived,' a sound was called upon to act both as a stabilizing center in an otherwise destabilized present, and as a bridge between the present and an idealized past. This frequently raised the question – for example, in the case of the 1990s easy listening revival – of what it was, exactly, that was being revived.

Bibliography

Cantwell, Robert. 1996. *When We Were Good: The Folk Revival*. Cambridge, MA: Harvard University Press.

Groom, Bob. 1971. *The Blues Revival*. London: Studio Vista.

Harker, Dave. 1985. *Fakesong: The Manufacture of British 'Folksong,' 1700 to the Present Day*. Milton Keynes: Open University Press.

Langley, Peter. 1977. 'The Rediscovery of a Pop Aesthetic: Big Star, Dwight Twilley, and the Raspberries.' *Nuggets* 7 (April/May): 11–14.

Lloyd, A.L. (Bert). 1944. *The Singing Englishman: An Introduction to Folksong*. London: Workers' Music Association.

MacColl, Ewan. 1990. *Journeyman: An Autobiography*. London: Sidgwick & Jackson.

Sandberg, Larry, and Weissman, Dick. 1976. *The Folk Music Sourcebook*. New York: Knopf.

Discographical Reference

Nuggets: Original Artyfacts from the First Psychedelic Era 1965–1968. Sire 3716. *1972*: USA. Reissue: *Nuggets: Original Artyfacts from the First Psychedelic Era 1965–1968.* Rhino 75466. *1998*: USA.

MIKE BROCKEN and DAVID HORN

Scene (Location)

The term 'scene' has an ambiguous relationship to ideas of location in music, inasmuch as it both challenges the pertinence of locality in musical analysis and represents an attempt to refine concepts of the local. Although it has been common within discussions of popular music for decades, the term 'scene' has only since the early 1990s begun to receive theoretical consideration within academic work. Indeed, 'scene' has long been one of the most elastic of notions within vernacular discourse on popular music. It has, on occasion, been used to give unity to geographically dispersed activities that have certain genres of music as their focus, as in references to the 'grunge scene.' This use of the term designates sets of presumably interrelated activities unfolding in a variety of locales. With slightly greater frequency, however, it is used in a more strictly geographical sense, though the level of generalization may vary widely in usage, from neighborhoods to large, multinational regions. Thus, one may find works on popular music that refer to the 'Seattle scene,' the 'South London scene' or the 'Soviet rock scene.'

The elasticity of the term 'scene' has become symptomatic of a theoretical problem within popular music studies, as within cultural studies more generally. The term 'scene' has represented one attempt to characterize the informal sorts of social organization that have taken shape around particular cultural practises. Writers typically have recourse to 'scene' when the activities being described encompass cultural roles that extend beyond (or blur the lines between) those of either performer or audience, and when the relationships between individuals involved in cultural practises offer some combination of the formal and informal. A 'South London scene,' for example, would presumably encompass musicians, club-goers, disc jockeys, record-buyers and several classes of entrepreneurs (record-store owners, club-night promoters and so on), as well as a host of markers of local distinctiveness (such as styles of music, dress and dance). If the term 'scene' has seemed particularly pertinent to the analysis of popular music, this has been, in part, because – compared, for example, to the fields of film and television creation – a wide range of musical activities can be found between the purely professional level of the international music industry and the sorts of amateur and quasi-amateur practises that are to be found

in any locale. The term 'scene' is intended, in part, to embrace the totality of these activities.

In this, the term 'scene' has evoked longstanding attempts, within the history and analysis of artistic practise, to delineate the social contexts within which painting, literature and other cultural forms take shape. Since the decline of artistic academies in the nineteenth century, most artistic activity of lasting significance has transpired outside the walls of institutions, in the more loosely organized social settings of urban bohemia and artistic subcultures. One longstanding project of the sociology of art has been to chart the ways in which such subcultures, while apparently unorganized and chaotic, nevertheless constitute economic systems of support, interpersonal relationships of authority and influence, and forms of interaction in which the social and the professional are intertwined. Attention to these systems will normally take the analyst away from such purely sociological categories as 'subculture' and 'bohemia,' and in the direction of concepts more suitable to an analysis of cultural labor and aesthetic cross-fertilization.

The idea of the 'art world,' as developed by Becker (1982) and Crane (1987), offers one attempt to comprehensively map the social contexts in which artistic activities take place. In asking what interpersonal, material and economic conditions are necessary for the production of works of art, Becker invited an analysis of the social systems in which this production is embedded. As well, by stressing the necessary complexity of these systems, Becker and Crane invited a consideration of the broader character of urban life and its importance to artistic production and cultural change.

In an important study of session musicians in the country music field, Peterson and White (1979) drew distinctions between the categories of 'school,' 'circle' and 'simplex.' An artistic school was an academy or similar institution in a strict sense, while a 'circle' designated the more informal social groups in which artists typically congregated and interacted, within urban centers such as New York. A 'simplex,' in contrast, was an unofficially organized group of artistic creators, such as session musicians, who controlled their specific labor market through a set of interactional patterns, informal barriers to entry and typical patterns of career development. While each of these categories represents an attempt to specify the contexts of artistic work, each, as well, presumes relationships that are social as well as professional, and through which aesthetic values come to take shape and be reproduced.

The term 'scene' became central to popular music studies in the late 1990s. Straw (1991) defined a 'scene' in opposition to the idea of musical 'community,' preferring the former's capacity to designate the range of musical activities unfolding within a given geographical space. In doing so, he drew implicitly on the work of Becker (1982), and Peterson and White (1979), and their concern for the unofficial boundaries that take shape around and within spheres of cultural activity and serve to perpetuate larger social divisions.

A scene, for Straw, became 'that cultural space in which a range of musical practices co-exist, interacting with each other within a variety of processes of differentiation, and according to widely varying trajectories of change and cross-fertilization' (373). Straw's rethinking of the notion of 'scene' was devised to intervene against a perceived over-valorization of the sorts of musical localism common within alternative rock scenes in North America in the late 1980s. While the small-scale, artisanal character of musical activity in a multitude of local scenes made this activity seem more firmly grounded than many others in local identities, Straw argued that the culture of alternative rock was a highly cosmopolitan one. From one locale to another, a relatively similar range of styles and practises had been replicated, suggesting that an analysis of this activity might be as full of lessons about musical cosmopolitanism and globalization as it was about the persistence or resurgence of specifically local identities and values. Against studies of musical localism that placed undue emphasis on styles and genres seen to have an organic relationship to the places in which they were practised, Straw proposed an emphasis on the ways in which local scenes have, informally and usually unknowingly, organized their diversity and their relationship to other localities. In particular, as his subsequent analysis of alternative rock and dance music sought to demonstrate, local musical styles would be caught up in the very different sorts of temporalities (rates of change and turnover) that characterize the life of such styles at an international level.

Among those who have criticized these formulations, Olson (1998) has suggested that Straw's scenes are 'empty vessels,' whose effectivity for those participant in them remains undescribed. In his important study of the Austin, Texas music scene, Shank (1994) has offered one way of accounting for this effectivity. A scene, Shank suggests, 'can be defined as an overproductive signifying community; that is, far more semiotic information is produced than can be rationally parsed' (122). This sense of an excess within scenes may be read at one level as acknowledging the diversity and pluralism of local scenes, and as a necessary corrective to attempts to privilege certain individual styles as more locally appropriate than others. Shank's notion of an 'overproductive signifying community' extends beyond this diversity, however, to suggest a radical, transformative quality in locally based live music activity of the sort found in Austin. 'Through this display of more than can be understood,' Shank writes, 'encouraging the radical recombination of elements of the human in new structures of identification, local rock'n'roll scenes produce momentary transformations within dominant cultural meanings' (122). While the pertinence of this account to such cultural forms or musical styles as salsa or house music is uncertain, Shank's rethinking of scene goes furthest in linking subcultural theory's interest in disruption and resistance to the sorts of questions that have accompanied a renewed interest in locality and its pertinence to musical analysis.

There has been an implicit consensus within popular music studies that an analysis of locality is necessarily linked to an analysis of globalization. Inasmuch as all musical commodities and styles 'land' (i.e., are received or produced) somewhere, they necessarily exist and circulate within local scenes whose relationship to the global remained at the end of the twentieth century one of the most compelling and urgent of questions facing popular music scholarship.

Bibliography

Becker, Howard. 1982. *Art Worlds*. Berkeley, CA: University of California Press.

Crane, Diane. 1987. *The Transformation of the Avant-Garde: The New York Art World, 1940–1985*. Chicago and London: University of Chicago Press.

Olson, Mark J.V. 1998. '"Everybody Loves Our Town" – Scenes, Spatiality, Migrancy.' In *Mapping the Beat: Popular Music and Contemporary Theory*, ed. Thomas Swiss, John Sloop and Andrew Herman. Oxford: Blackwell, 269–89.

Peterson, Richard A., and White, Howard G. 1979. 'The Simplex Located in Art Worlds.' *Urban Life* 7(4) (January): 411–39.

Shank, Barry. 1994. *Dissonant Identities: The Rock'n'Roll Scene in Austin, Texas.* Hanover, NH: University Press of New England.

Straw, Will. 1991. 'Systems of Articulation, Logics of Change: Communities and Scenes in Popular Music.' *Cultural Studies* 5(3): 368–88.

WILL STRAW

Slavery

Introduction

Slavery, or the enforced deprivation of the liberty of individuals or groups in order that they may be exploited by a dominant society, has been a feature of otherwise 'civilized' cultures for millennia. The term 'slave' derives from the brutal enforced labor endured by many thousands of Slavic peoples at the hands of their

German captors over some two centuries at the end of the first millennium A.D. The direct and indirect influence of slavery, one of the most ancient of social institutions, on the development of much popular music has been profound.

Antiquity and the Middle Ages

The palaces and temples of the Mesopotamian city-states employed slave labor for 3,000 years, as the new kingdom of Egypt did to some extent. Slaves in ancient Greece were not without rights, but in the classical Greece of the fifth century B.C., 25 percent of the population of Attica were domestic slaves, purchased in the markets of Greek cities. In Roman times, the scale of enslavement increased to unprecedented levels, with slaves chained together in gangs, working in the mines and on the immense latifundia, or agricultural estates, in conditions that anticipated those of South America 2,000 years later (Westermann 1955).

The extent to which the music and songs of the slaves were performed, heard, adopted or suppressed remains an open question. Assyrian reliefs in the British Museum depict players on trumpets and drums accompanying the work of moving massive stone sculptures and felling 'palm trees belonging to a captured city' (Engel 1864). In Egypt, the playing of the harp, flute and drums was common at popular festivals, as Herodotus (b. 484 B.C.) observed, noting that 'a musician is the son of a musician ... Neither may others on account of their fine voice apply themselves to the profession of music, but each adheres to the profession of his father.' Musicians were members of a caste, but it is apparent in some Egyptian murals that Nubians were among their number, while the work song of threshers sung to their oxen exists in hieroglyphic metrical form (Engel 1864).

By the time of the enslavement of the Slavic peoples by Germans, the invasion of North Africa by Arabs had taken place, the indigenous Berber tribes eventually submitting to the relentless Muslim advance. Berbers of the western provinces of the Maghreb had already established trade links with Sub-Saharan Africa and, in the ninth century, were bringing black slaves to North African ports and palaces. A thriving trade ensued, eventually dominated by the successive states of the Western Sudan, Kanem, Bornu and Mali, which operated their own stratified slave-based societies (Davidson 1980; Everett 1978; Fisher and Fisher 1971). Moors and Berbers joined the Arabs in the conquest of Spain, and it is likely that the combination of African, Moor, Arab and Berber traditions in music and song was an important constituent in the formation of the flamenco idioms (Borneman 1958). As Arab influence extended more widely over Europe, the impact of this cultural combination on other

musical traditions may well have been a significant one (Van der Merwe 1989, 11–14).

The Middle Passage

Europeans entered the slave trade with the Portuguese exploration of the African fringe in the mid-fifteenth century. Following successful slave trading in the Senegambia (Upper Guinea) region, they established El Mina, the first of many slave shipping forts on the southern coast of West Africa, in what is now Ghana. With the opening up of the Spanish and Portuguese colonies in the New World following the partition of the Treaty of Tordessillas (1494), measures were taken to enslave the indigenous Native American Indian populations. Their reluctance to submit to working on the plantations and their attempts at resistance were countered with brutal massacres. Because disease and suppression decimated the Indians, the trade in African slaves was deflected to the West Indies. In the ensuing century, competition between European nations seeking to dominate the trade led to the building of additional forts by the Portuguese and Spanish, as well as by the Dutch, French, Danes, and even Swedes and Germans. The British became seriously involved in the slave trade in the mid-seventeenth century, striving to maintain the sugar plantations in the islands of the West Indies and seeking to take over the lucrative traffic in human lives in exchange for weapons, textiles, iron and other metals (Pope-Hennessey 1967).

As transatlantic trade developed and as the labor needs of the colonies increased, the shipping of slaves, an activity that Britain came to dominate, became a key element. Ships carrying manufactured goods sailed from English ports first to Africa, where they exchanged weapons, cotton textiles, liquor and various foodstuffs for cargoes of slaves. The slaves were then transported to the New World (most often the West Indies), where they were sold, the ships usually returning home with produce from the colonies. The shipping of slaves occurred in what was termed the 'Middle Passage,' from the Ivory, Gold and Slave coasts of West Africa to the Bahamas and Jamaica. Tribal kingdoms supplied prisoners of war from raids on the peoples of the hinterlands, the chiefs reputedly being as wily as the European traders in their commerce. The Middle Passage was infamous for the brutality with which the slaves were treated, the insufferable conditions of poor food, stale air and iron shackles, with close packing and little or no sanitation causing loss of life from disease and depression (Pope-Hennessey 1967). On some slave ships, it was the practise to bring the slaves on deck, 'where they were made to exercise, and encouraged, by the music of their beloved banjar, to dancing and cheerfulness,' as George

Pinckard of Jamaica wrote in 1796 (quoted in Epstein 1977, 10). The notebooks and recollections of Africans who endured the passage, and of traders and ships' officers who were engaged in the trade have survived in sufficient numbers to confirm both the privations they experienced and the callousness of their captors (Newton 1764; Canot 1928; Zamba 1847).

Making slaves dance, sing or play music on deck was not prompted by humanitarian sympathy but, rather, by commercial motives: dying slaves meant a loss of profits. And the profits were considerable, making immense fortunes for the merchant adventurers of Liverpool and Bristol. In 1732, some 88 ships sailed from Liverpool for Africa, trading for a total of 25,720 slaves. Seventy-five years later, 185 slave ships left Liverpool in the space of 16 months, gaining 49,213 slaves from the African trade (Dicky Sam 1969). That year, 1807, the antislavery lobby introduced its Abolition bill in the House of Lords and, subsequently, in the House of Commons, where it was passed without a division. But although the trade in slaves was abolished, and the legislation rigorously enforced by the Royal Navy for many years, the institution of slavery on the plantations of the West Indies continued for three decades (Ward 1969).

Slavery in the Caribbean

Estimates of the number of Africans shipped to the Americas vary considerably, a figure as high as 30 million having been seriously propounded. An estimate of some 10 million is thought to be closer to the truth, of which by far the majority were imported to the West Indies and the Spanish and Portuguese possessions in South America. While the African element of the population of some islands remained a relatively small percentage of the whole, in others, such as Jamaica, Haiti and Santo Domingo, the proportion was far greater: Jamaica in the mid-eighteenth century received over 70,000 slaves; with further imports, the island was supporting over 300,000 slaves by 1832, of which 155,000 worked on the sugar plantations and 45,000 on the coffee farms (Appleby 1983). In all, there were nearly a thousand slave-holding properties, some raising livestock or pimentoes, while others were engaged in fishing, lime burning or the 'jobbing' tasks such as road building (Higman 1976). Slavery was abolished in the British West Indies two years later, in 1834, by which time the system was proving ruinous. Of the slaves, approximately a third were Africans, the remainder being 'creoles,' born in the New World of African or part-African descent. After Emancipation, many white planters left, and with natural increase there were 620,000 blacks and a mere 15,000 whites living in Jamaica by 1890. With such a preponderance of blacks,

local traditions, such as the Jonkonnu ('John Canoe') festival, continued, in spite of attempts to suppress them.

Throughout the West Indies, slave music was tolerated, especially at specific times, such as at Christmas or on feast days in the Roman Catholic islands. In Trinidad, which was underdeveloped during three centuries of Spanish rule, the arrival (by invitation) of French planters in the late eighteenth century heralded the celebration of carnival and Shrovetide festivals, and the dancing of the *calinda* and the *jhouba* 'for long hours . . . to the sound of [their] voices and the African drum' (Borde 1883, quoted in Cowley 1996, 14). Black 'chantwells,' or lead singers with a gift for improvisation, were regarded favorably by French planters, but when the British took the island in 1797, dancing and festivities were restricted to pre-curfew hours. In the early 1800s, *convois* or 'regiments' formed for 'the purpose of dancing and innocent amusement' were common in Trinidad (Cowley 1996, 13) (as they were in Grenada, Martinique and elsewhere), where slave drummers and fiddlers performed for both black and white functions.

The tracing of slave culture is made more problematic by the interweaving of the various cultural influences that had a bearing on it. This is evident in Haiti, superficially the most 'African' of West Indian cultures which, however, has Spanish, French and Native American elements. The first slaves were imported as early as 1510 by the Spanish, who relinquished control of the island to the French in 1677. African elements persisted, but escaping slaves, or maroons, made contact with Indian tribes whose influence has also been traced in aspects of Haitian cults (Deren 1975). Melville Herskovits found no direct correlation between specific African tribal sources and retentions presumed to be African that he encountered in Haiti. In spite of the large number of Congolese Africans imported to the island, he found few traces of Congolese, Gold Coast or Ivory Coast elements (Herskovits 1937). Others found Yoruba and Ibo practises, and all authorities credit the Fon of Dahomey, from whom the cult of *vodun* (voodoo) came, with exercising the greatest influence on Haitian religious life (Bastide 1971). Central to the Rada rituals is the rhythm of the drums, which are played for a variety of sacred songs and dances performed for the divinities. Secular practises common to many African cultures were also sustained during slavery, such as communal timing in field labor maintained by group singing to the beat of the hoes (Courlander 1960). Depending on the nations that had dominion over it, the patterns of land ownership and types of crop cultivation, and the scale of dependence on forced and imported labor, each island of the Antilles has its own slavery profile. This, in turn, is reflected in the musical forms and functions that evolved during and after Emancipation, eventually to be manifest in, for instance, the *kaiso* (calypso) of Trinidad or the beguine of Martinique.

Slavery in South America

In the Spanish and Portuguese colonies of South America, the number of imported slaves ran to many millions. However, the multiplicity of the descendants of the slaves, the classification of mulattoes with some white blood and the number of freedmen, coupled with the destruction of the archives of the slave trade by the first Republican government of Brazil (the country with the greatest proportion of slaves on the continent), make accurate figures impossible. The first slaves were introduced into Brazil by the Portuguese in 1538. Slaves were considered necessary to work the huge latifundia for the monocultural production of sugar with, in some cases, several hundred slaves on a single plantation. Each plantation was managed from the *casa grande* – the 'Big House' – in a complex that included the *senzalas*, the extensive but crudely constructed slave quarters. Although slaves were brutally exploited both in their work and sexually, the abilities – including the musical talents – of some slaves were recognized. A planter in the early seventeenth century, Mangue la Bote, kept a 30-piece slave orchestra, establishing a tradition that persisted in some 'Big Houses' for more than two centuries, as sugar gave way to the highly lucrative cultivation of coffee (Freyre 1966). Black musicians played in the churches of the province of São Paulo in the eighteenth century, and Catholic priests supported religious dances and ceremonies that had African associations, such as the *congada*, or the crowning of the 'Queen of Angola,' first performed in Recife in the seventeenth century (Appleby 1983).

At the end of the eighteenth century, two-thirds of the Brazilian population of 3.2 million were slaves or free blacks; 50 years later, their numbers had grown to 4.4 million in a total population of 7.3 million (Franklin 1974). Emancipation of slaves did not take place in Brazil until 1888. The greatest concentration of blacks was, and has remained, in the northeastern and eastern states, with the majority in Bahia, Minas Gerais and Pernambuco. In the rituals of the fetishistic religions of black Brazil, *candomble*, *macumba* and *Xango*, African retentions in music have survived, with chants and *atabaques*, or drums, displaying direct links with the Shango cult of the Nigerian Yoruba (Correa de Azevedo 1981; Verger 1954). When studied by Melville Herskovits, Afro-Bahian music had the highest levels of African retentions in the Brazilian black cultural traditions. There was evidence of similar survivals in other South American countries, but the most remarkable were those in the Guianas, particularly French Guiana and Suriname, where maroons, or fugitives from slavery, escaped to establish their own villages and an essentially African culture. Although reduced in number, the 'bush negroes' of Suriname have retained more of the African inheritance than any other comparable group in the Americas (Herskovits and Herskovits 1936).

Slavery in the Southern United States

Herskovits considered that African elements were less evident in North American black culture than in any of the other major cultural regions in the Americas that had utilized slave labor. It is undisputed that black culture in the United States was essentially syncretic, profoundly shaped by the culture of the dominant white North Americans and deeply ingrained with the values of the Protestant churches (both of whose cultural practises would in turn be influenced by the response of the slaves to the encounter). Compared with Central America and South America, the United States imported a small proportion of the slaves (less than a million) who endured the horrors of the Middle Passage. The Dutch began importations of slaves – they landed 20 black indentured servants at Jamestown in Virginia in 1619 – but 40 years were to pass before Virginia gave slavery statutory recognition. Several of the signatories to the Declaration of Independence were slaveholders, including Thomas Jefferson, who, however, subsequently fought to end slavery.

Historians such as Peter Wood (1974) and Gwendolyn Midlo Hall (1992), while not disputing Herskovits's broad conclusion, have pointed to the need to consider the regional variations in slave culture in North America, especially in the colonial period. In her work on the formation of the Afro-Creole culture of New Orleans, Hall draws attention to the evidence in the French national archives in Paris that, during the peak of the French slave trade from Africa to the French colony of Louisiana in the 1720s, the majority of slaves came from Senegambia, and included a 'strong and influential contingent' from one tribe, the Bambara (Hall 1992, 68). This circumstance, combined with the Senegambian tradition, learned at the crossroads of world trading routes, of 'willingness to add and incorporate useful aspects of new cultures encountered' allowed the growth of a 'coherent, functional, well-integrated slave culture' in the particular environment of eighteenth-century New Orleans (1992, 87). More recent research has revealed that the Senegambia region 'yielded the mix of gender, age and size that planters in the Americas – if the instructions given to slave-ship captains are reliable evidence – wanted first' (Eltis 2000, 165). Perhaps because of their fierce resistance to enslavement, fewer than 5 percent of slaves came from tribes of the Senegambia region. Virginia was the principal market in the Americas for those from the area in the seventeenth century (Eltis 2000, 168–72).

Before and after American independence, most slaves were to be found on southern plantations. These plantations, though seldom as extensive as the latifundia, were large and devoted to a monoculture: formerly to the cultivation of rice and sugar, and later, where conditions were appropriate, to the production of cotton. Production on such a scale demanded a considerable labor force. By 1860, slaves numbered nearly 4 million, at a time when the white population of the South was just double that figure. Of the latter, less than 400,000 owned slaves and half of these owned five slaves or fewer. A mere 12 percent owned more than 20 slaves each, well below the number (approximately 50) considered necessary for efficient productivity (Franklin 1974). But it was the wealthy planters who wielded political and commercial power, and their large plantations that attracted the attention of travelers to the South. Medium or large, the plantations customarily divided the slave work force between the 'field' slaves and the 'house' slaves. Those who worked in the fields led a life of unremitting toil 'from sunup to sundown' year-round, under the direction of white overseers and the lashes of the work-gang 'drivers,' who were frequently slaves themselves. The nature of gang labor required coordinated effort and this was sustained by group singing. Such 'work songs,' though wild and unintelligible to their ears, were often noted by visitors to the South, such as Frederick Law Olmsted. An architect by profession, he wrote an extensive account of his travels in the 'cotton kingdom' in the late 1850s, which revealed much of the attitudes, problems, iniquities and paradoxes of the slavery system, strengthening the case of the Abolitionists (Olmsted 1953).

Following the slave insurrection led by Nat Turner in 1831, the Abolitionist movement was initiated with William Lloyd Garrison's paper, the *Liberator*. Accounts such as that contained in the journal that the English actress Frances Anne Kemble kept in 1838–39 on her husband's Georgian plantation fueled opposition to slavery (Kemble 1961). One of the major spokespersons for Abolition was Frederick Douglass, himself a self-educated ex-slave who had made a courageous escape from bondage. He was one of many former slaves whose autobiographies revealed the iniquities of the system from within; several of them, like Henry 'Box' Brown, who had himself nailed into a box and shipped to the North, had escaped by their own efforts (Douglass 1962). Others had been conducted between the 'stations,' or

secure refuges, of the Underground Railroad. The 'railroad' created a web of covert 'lines,' by which escaping slaves could evade the 'patter-rollers' (patrols) and their hounds. The 'railroad' assisted 3,000 slaves in their bid for freedom (Coffin 1879; Buckmaster 1943).

The slaves who remained in the South were not necessarily passive; a number of revolts took place that were ruthlessly put down (Aptheker 1943; Litwack 1979). Slavery was hierarchical, and the house slaves often benefited from their more privileged position as house servants, cooks, nursemaids, coachmen and musicians. Although drums were forbidden, as they could be used for communication to incite insurrection, instrumental music was customarily provided by black fiddlers and banjo players for dances and functions at the 'Big House.' Their own jigs and capers were a source of amusement, but black musicians were also expected to play tunes from the white traditions, thus extending their range and repertoires. In the 'quarters,' the rows of huts where the field slaves were housed, music was frequently allowed after sundown, and gatherings where ring shouts of an African nature were performed also took place. Although seemingly barbaric to the curious whites who heard them, these gatherings were largely religious in nature. Christianity in its Baptist and Methodist forms was readily adopted by slaves, who rejoiced in the promise of remission from earthly sufferings in the eternal happiness of the afterlife (Raboteau 1978). Their anthems and spiritual songs reflected these expectations and encapsulated the values inculcated by preachers both white and black. But they were also metaphoric, and many spirituals encoded expressions of dissatisfaction, resistance and freedom in their religious sentiments (Fisher 1968; Blassingame 1979). Belief in witchcraft and conjure also flourished in the 'quarters,' especially when the lack of medical attention encouraged dependence on spells and potions to cure disease or depression.

Not all slaves lived on the plantations or farms of the South; there were also slaves in the cities. In 1820, three out of every four Charleston households and two-thirds of those in Richmond had one or more slaves. In Mobile and Savannah, more than half the households had slaves and, until the decline of slavery that began some 20 years later, the percentage of those owning slaves, though, of course, not of slaves in bondage, was higher in the cities than in the rural South (Wade 1964). The cities also attracted 'freedmen of color,' slaves who had earned their freedom or had been liberated. This was especially the case in New Orleans, where at the outbreak of the Civil War in 1861 over 25,000 blacks lived, of whom some 10,000 were free. Both slaves and freedmen were employed as skilled craftsmen and in more menial jobs, and many enjoyed a social life altogether richer than any in the 'Big Houses' of the plantations. While, for white males, the celebrated 'Quadroon Balls' were a significant aspect of New Orleans social life, dances were held by slaves in the city even in their masters' houses. Slaves who gathered on Sundays in Congo Square to dance the *counjaille, calinda* and *bamboula* were a great popular attraction; the architect Benjamin Latrobe witnessed several hundred dancing to a drum and string band in the square in 1819 (Latrobe, quoted in Epstein 1977, 97–98). Accomplished musicians playing conventional Western instruments were numerous too; in the 1830s, there were over a hundred members of the Negro Philharmonic Society of New Orleans, while other free blacks had their own militia companies with brass bands (Blassingame 1973; Kmen 1966). Such a musical tradition prepared the ground for the eventual flowering of New Orleans jazz.

The degree to which slavery was a repressive institution or a protective, even benign one, the extent to which the black family disintegrated or thrived in the 'quarters,' the question of whether slavery was economically successful or fundamentally unsound – these and a score of other assessments, issues and revisions of the evidence have fed a vast literature on the subject (Phillips 1963; Stampp 1956; Genovese 1972; Gutman 1976; Fogel and Engerman 1976, 1989; David et al. 1976). This literature has drawn firsthand material from the many antebellum slave recollections that have been published and critically appraised (Davis and Gates 1985). Of particular importance is the 19-volume 'composite autobiography' that constitutes over 2,000 narratives collected from ex-slaves for the Federal Writers' Project of the Work Projects Administration (WPA), 1936–38 (Botkin 1945; Rawick 1972; Yetman 1970). Although the circumstances of collection, the accuracy of transcription and the relationships between collector and narrator are open to consideration, the narratives provide further information on the role of music and song within the varieties and complexities of slave experience and culture.

That the role of music in slavery was itself varied and complex cannot be doubted, and although it is by no means as vast, a considerable literature has also grown up both to document that role and its consequences and to identify and debate the many issues that the subject raises – issues such as African survivals, the relationship of music to kinetic behavior, connections between diasporic slave peoples, and the particular importance and function of musical practises (including the subtle workings of imitation and parody) in the context of social, economic and would-be cultural domination.

In this catalog of human exploitation, oppression, humiliation, defiance, resistance and enduring spirit there remains a final, but indisputable, irony: had there been no history of enslavement in Africa, nor of the shipment of slaves in their millions to the Americas, there would have been no African-American cultures. And without these there would have been no popular music as it developed in its many directions in the twentieth century.

Bibliography

Appleby, David P. 1983. *The Music of Brazil*. Austin, TX: University of Texas Press.

Aptheker, Herbert. 1943. *American Slave Revolts*. New York: Columbia University Press.

Bastide, Roger. 1971. *African Civilisations in the New World*. London: C. Hurst and Company.

Blassingame, John W. 1973. *Black New Orleans*. Chicago: University of Chicago Press.

Blassingame, John W. 1979. *The Slave Community: Plantation Life in the Antebellum South*. 2nd rev. ed. Oxford: Oxford University Press.

Borneman, Ernest. 1958. 'Creole Echoes.' In *Just Jazz 2*, ed. Sinclair Traill and Gerald Lascelles. London: Peter Davies, 25–52.

Born in Slavery: Slave Narratives from the Federal Writers' Project, 1936–1938. http://memory.loc.gov/ammem/snhtml/

Botkin, B.A., ed. 1945. *Lay My Burden Down: A Folk History of Slavery*. Chicago: University of Chicago Press.

Buckmaster, Henrietta. 1943. *Out of the House of Bondage*. London: Victor Gollancz.

Canot, Capt. Theodore. 1928. *Adventures of an African Slaver. Told in the Year 1854 to Brantz Mayer*. New York: Albert & Charles Boni.

Coffin, Levi. 1879. *Reminiscences of Levi Coffin*. London: Sampson Low, Marston, Searle and Rivington.

Correa de Azevedo, Luis Hector. 1981. 'Music and Musicians of African Origin in Brazil.' *The World of Music* 25(2): 53–63.

Courlander, Harold. 1960. *The Drum and the Hoe: Life and Lore of the Haitian People*. Berkeley, CA: University of California Press.

Cowley, John. 1996. *Carnival, Canboulay and Calypso: Traditions in the Making*. Cambridge: Cambridge University Press.

David, Paul A., et al. 1976. *Reckoning with Slavery*. Oxford: Oxford University Press.

Davidson, Basil. 1980. *The African Slave Trade*. Boston, MA: Little, Brown.

Davis, Charles T., and Gates, Henry Louis, Jr. 1985. *The Slave's Narrative*. Oxford: Oxford University Press.

Deren, Maya. 1975 (1953). *The Voodoo Gods*. London: Paladin.

Dicky Sam, A Genuine. 1969 (1884). *Liverpool and Slavery: An Historical Account of the Liverpool-African Slave Trade*. Newcastle-upon-Tyne: Frank Graham.

Douglass, Frederick. 1962 (1892). *Life and Times of Frederick Douglass*. New York: Collier Books.

Eltis, David. 2000. *The Rise of African Slavery in the Americas*. Cambridge: Cambridge University Press.

Eltis, David, et al. 1999. *The Trans-Atlantic Slave Trade: A Database on CD-ROM*. Cambridge: Cambridge University Press.

Engel, Carl. 1864. *The Music of the Most Ancient Nations*. London: John Murray.

Epstein, Dena J. 1977. *Sinful Tunes and Spirituals: Black Folk Music to the Civil War*. Urbana, IL: University of Illinois Press.

Everett, Suzanne. 1978. *The Slaves: An Illustrated History of the 'Most Monstrous Evil'*. London: Bison Books.

Fisher, Allan G.B., and Fisher, Humphrey J. 1971. *Slavery and Muslim Society in Africa*. London: Doubleday and Company.

Fisher, Miles Mark. 1968 (1953). *Negro Slave Songs in the United States*. New York: Russell & Russell.

Fogel, Robert William, and Engerman, Stanley L. 1976. *Time on the Cross: Evidence and Methods. A Supplement*. London: Wildwood House.

Fogel, Robert William, and Engerman, Stanley L. 1989 (1974). *Time on the Cross: The Economics of American Negro Slavery*. New York: Norton.

Franklin, John Hope. 1974 (1947). *From Slavery to Freedom: A History of Negro Americans*. 4th ed. New York: Alfred A. Knopf.

Freyre, Gilberto. 1966 (1946). *The Masters and the Slaves (Casa-Grande & Senzala)*. New York: Alfred A. Knopf.

Genovese, Eugene D. 1972. *Roll, Jordan Roll: The World the Slaves Made*. New York: Pantheon Books.

Gutman, Herbert G. 1976. *The Black Family in Slavery and Freedom, 1750–1925*. Oxford: Basil Blackwell.

Hall, Gwendolyn Midlo. 1992. 'The Formation of Afro-Creole Culture.' In *Creole New Orleans: Race and Americanization*, ed. Arnold R. Hirsch and Joseph Logsdon. Baton Rouge, LA: Louisiana State University Press.

Herskovits, Melville J. 1937. *Life in a Haitian Valley*. New York: Alfred A. Knopf.

Herskovits, Melville J., and Herskovits, Frances S. 1936. *Suriname Folk-lore*. New York: AMS Press.

Higman, B.W. 1976. *Slave Population and Economy in Jamaica, 1807–1834*. Cambridge: Cambridge University Press.

Kemble, Frances Anne. 1961 (1863). *Journal of a Residence on a Georgian Plantation in 1838–1839*. New York: Knopf.

Kmen, H.A. 1966. *Music in New Orleans: The Formative Years, 1791–1841*. Baton Rouge, LA: Louisiana State University Press.

Litwack, Leon F. 1979. *Been in the Storm So Long: The Aftermath of Slavery*. London: The Athlone Press.

Newton, John. 1764. *An Authentic Narrative of Some Particulars in the Life of John Newton*. 6th ed. London: Johnson.

Olmsted, Frederick Law. 1953 (1861). *The Cotton Kingdom: A Traveller's Observations on Cotton and Slavery in the American Slave States*. New York: Alfred A. Knopf.

Phillips, Ulrich Bonnell. 1963 (1929). *Life and Labor in the Old South*. Boston, MA: Little, Brown and Company.

Pope-Hennessey, James. 1967. *Sins of the Fathers: A Study of the Atlantic Slave Traders, 1441–1807*. London: Weidenfeld and Nicolson.

Raboteau, Albert J. 1978. *Slave Religion: The 'Invisible Institution' in the Antebellum South*. Oxford: Oxford University Press.

Rawick, George P. 1972. *From Sundown to Sunup: The Making of the Black Community*, Vol. 1. Westport, CT: Greenwood Press.

Stampp, Kenneth M. 1956. *The Peculiar Institution: Slavery in the Ante-Bellum South*. New York: Random House.

Van der Merwe, Peter. 1989. *Origins of the Popular Style: The Antecedents of Twentieth-Century Popular Music*. Oxford: Clarendon Press.

Verger, Pierre. 1954. *Dieux d'Afrique: Culte des Orishas et Vodouns* [Gods of Africa: Orisha and Voodoo Cults]. Paris: Paul Hartmann Éditeur.

Wade, Richard C. 1964. *Slavery in the Cities: The South, 1820–1860*. Oxford: Oxford University Press.

Ward, W.E.F. 1969. *The Royal Navy and the Slavers*. London: George Allen & Unwin.

Waterman, Richard A. 1952. 'African Influence on the Music of the Americas.' In *Acculturation in the Americas*, 2, ed. Sol Tax. Chicago: University of Chicago Press, 207–18.

Westermann, W.L. 1955. *The Slave Systems of Greek and Roman Antiquity*. Philadelphia: American Philosophical Society.

Wood, Peter H. 1974. *Black Majority: Negroes in Colonial South Carolina From 1670 Through the Stono Rebellion*. New York: Knopf.

Yetman, Norman R. 1970. *Life Under the 'Peculiar Institution': Selections from the Slave Narrative Collection*. New York: Holt, Rinehart and Winston.

Zamba. 1847. *The Life and Adventures of Zamba, an African Negro King, and His Experience of Slavery in South Carolina*. London.

Discography

Field Recordings, Vols. 10–11 (1933–41). Document DOCD-5600. *1998:* Austria.

PAUL OLIVER

Socialism and Communism

Socialism is a political theory of social organization that was developed in the early nineteenth century as a counter model to capitalism. It was based on the idea of organizing society according to the principles of social equality and social justice. 'Socialism' was also the name of the political movement founded to strive for the realization of these goals.

According to the theory of socialism, private ownership of the means of production – the main source of social inequality – should be replaced by a system of community control. All means of production should therefore remain free from ownership but should be controlled by politically established regulations. Early forms of this theory can be traced to the anonymously published *Code de la nature, ou le véritable esprit de ses loix, de tout tems négligé ou méconnu* (1755) by the French philosopher Morelly. The critique of the concept and of the realities of private ownership was a widespread tendency among members of the eighteenth-century French Enlightenment such as Babeuf and Cabet. In the first half of the nineteenth century, these ideas were developed by social theoreticians like Claude Henri de Saint-Simon, Pierre-Joseph Proudhon and Charles Fourier into a distinct corpus of political and social theories, and it was the criticism of these theories that formed the basis for the enormously influential work of Karl Marx and Friedrich Engels.

It was in its Marxist form that socialism became a working-class movement, merging the rather elitist intellectualism of early French socialism with a broad-based social activism. For Marx, socialism in the form of the socialization of the realm of production was simply the first phase of 'communism,' a term coined in France around 1840 by revolutionist Louis Auguste Blanqui that denoted a stateless and classless society. 'The Communist Manifesto' of Karl Marx and Friedrich Engels (1848), commissioned by the London branch of the Communist League, is considered the foundation of this movement, which eventually led to the foundation of socialist parties throughout Europe during the last third of the nineteenth century.

The Russian Revolution of 1917 and the political course of its leader V.I. Lenin polarized the socialist movement in Europe and resulted in a split between the older, more reformist part of the working-class movement, firmly anchored in bourgeois democracy and represented by social democratic parties, and the newly founded communist parties with the much more radical goal of overthrowing bourgeois society through a proletarian revolution. One of the main reasons why Lenin consolidated this polarization, and institutionalized it in 1919 with the founding of the Comintern (Communist International) as the umbrella organization of the worldwide socialist movement, was the agreement in 1914 by the parliamentary representatives of the German Social Democratic Party to allocate money to World War I, a decision that allied the working-class movement with the nationalist and aggressive elements of the capitalist society.

As early as 1922, the German radical socialist and Marxist theoretician Rosa Luxemburg hinted, in a brilliant analysis of the Russian Revolution, at the danger that the socialist concept of society, with its need to institute social control over the means of production, would deteriorate into an undemocratic form of bureaucratic dictatorship, particularly if forced into existence under unfavorable economic conditions, as in Russia in 1917. Her warning turned out to be apposite: soon after the death of Lenin in 1924, Stalin revised the Marxist political theory into a crude ideology to serve as legitimation for a form of arbitrary party dictatorship with ruthless terrorist traits, later fostered by the need to mobilize the Russian people for one of the biggest campaigns of World War II. Stalinism, although officially condemned after Stalin's death in 1953, left traces wherever communist parties came to power after, and mainly as a consequence of, World War II. So the transformation of Marxist theory into a political ideology was never reversed. As a consequence of this, Marxist political and economic theory essentially ceased to exist under the rule of communist parties, except for vague notions of social and economic development, expressed in authorized formulations and abandoned as soon as pragmatically convenient, fast made obsolete by the dynamics of economic and technological development.

This, and the course of the Cold War, encouraged the emergence of state bureaucratic systems ruled by communist parties and touted as so-called 'real existing socialism,' which, despite all the differences between countries as diverse as the former USSR, the former GDR, Hungary, Poland, China, Cuba and North Vietnam, turned out to be economically highly inefficient. Started by the Russian Revolution at the beginning of the twentieth century, this system ended with the dissolution of the Soviet Union toward the end of the century after Gorbachev introduced the policies of *glasnost* and *perestroika*. With this, socialism and communism became part of history and, in the end, failed to represent the never-ending need of the people for more justice and equality in society.

It was this aspiration – to institute social justice and equality – that made the political doctrines of socialism and communism attractive to artists and popular musicians all over the world. Particularly after the Comintern, in light of the Depression, proclaimed its new policy of the People's Front in 1935 in order to break out of its deviationist isolation, the Left became a strong and visible factor in the area of culture. In the United States, for instance, this led during the 1930s to a song movement that found its most influential and best-known exponents in Woody Guthrie, Pete Seeger and the Almanac Singers. Although the relationship between popular musicians and politics has never been straightforward and free from contradictions, socialism and communism have remained factors within popular music culture, as illustrated by material ranging from John Lennon's song 'Power to the People' as one facet in his broad and contradictory spectrum of political statements to the music of political activists like folk musician Leon Rosselson and the punk band the Redskins, to name only the most famous examples.

The status and development of popular music within those countries that considered themselves socialist constituted a different story. In contrast to folk music, popular music was originally perceived as a form of capitalist mass manipulation and was tolerated only as an unavoidable heritage of the bourgeois past. It took a long time for this attitude to change. Not only did all attempts to create a folk music–based socialist alternative to Western popular music fail, but also the do-it-yourself spirit of early rock music, especially, could not be suppressed in the long run. It either created a broad-based musical underground, as in the former Soviet Union, using audio cassettes as an independent and uncontrollable means of distribution or it forced the political integration of pop and rock music into the culture of these countries. The form that this integration took varied greatly from country to country. Since, in light of the economic and political survival of the power system, not much more remained of the claims to socialism than pragmatic compromises, it was up to the cultural bureaucracy in each country to handle the situation as smoothly as possible. Many very gifted musicians managed to find their way through the bureaucratic and political maze of this system, and the outcome was in most cases a unique, interesting and inspired music that disappeared, together with the so-called 'real existing socialism,' after the events of 1989.

Bibliography

Bright, Terry. 1986. 'Pop Music in the USSR.' *Media, Culture and Society* 8(3): 357–69.

Cushman, Thomas. 1995. *Notes from Underground: Rock Music Counterculture in Russia*. Albany, NY: State University of New York Press.

Denselow, Robin. 1990. *When the Music's Over: The Story of Political Pop*. London and Boston: Faber and Faber.

Lieberman, Robbie. 1989. *My Song Is My Weapon: People's Songs, American Communism, and the Politics of Culture, 1930–1950*. Urbana, IL: University of Illinois Press.

Lipsitz, George. 1981. *Class and Culture in Cold War America: A Rainbow at Midnight*. New York: Praeger.

Luxemburg, Rosa. 1922. *Die Russische Revolution* [The Russian Revolution]. Berlin: Verlag Gesellschaft und Erziehung.

Ramet, Pedro, and Zamascikov, Sergei. 1990. 'The Soviet Rock Scene.' *Journal of Popular Culture* 24(1): 149–74.

Ramet, Sabrina Petra, ed. 1994. *Rocking the State: Rock Music and Politics in Eastern Europe and Russia*. Boulder, CO: Westview Press.

Ryback, Timothy W. 1990. *Rock Around the Bloc: A History of Rock Music in Eastern Europe and the Soviet Union*. New York: Oxford University Press.

Szemere, Anna. 1992. 'The Politics of Marginality: A Rock Musical Subculture in Socialist Hungary in the Early 1980s.' In *Rockin' the Boat: Mass Music and Mass Movements*, ed. Reebee Garofalo. Boston, MA: South End Press, 93–114.

Troitsky, Artemy. 1987. *Back in the USSR: The Story of Rock in Russia*. London and New York: Omnibus.

Wicke, Peter. 1985. 'Young People and Popular Music in East Germany: Focus on a Scene.' *Communication Research* 12(3): 319–25.

Wicke, Peter. 1992a. 'The Role of Rock Music in Processes of Political Change in the GDR.' In *Popular Music and Communication*, ed. James Lull. 2nd ed. London: Sage, 196–206.

Wicke, Peter. 1992b. '"The Times They Are A-Changin'"': Rock Music and Political Change in East Germany.' In *Rockin' the Boat: Mass Music and Mass Movements*, ed. Reebee Garofalo. Boston, MA: South End Press, 81–92.

Wicke, Peter. 1996a. 'Pop Music in the GDR: Between Conformity and Resistance.' In *Changing Identities in East Germany: Selected Papers from the Nineteenth and Twentieth New Hampshire Symposia*, ed. Margy Gerber and Roger Woods. Lanham, MD: University Press of America, 25–37.

Wicke, Peter. 1996b. 'Popular Music and Processes of Social Transformation: The Case of Rock Music in Former East Germany.' In *Socio-Cultural Aspects of Music in Europe*, ed. Paul Rutten. Brussels: European Music Office/Directorate General X, 77–84.

Wicke, Peter, and Shepherd, John. 1993. '"The Cabaret Is Dead"': Rock Culture as State Enterprise – The Political Organization of Rock in East Germany.' In *Rock and*

Popular Music: Politics, Policies, Institutions, ed. Tony Bennett et al. London and New York: Routledge, 25–36.

Discographical Reference

Lennon, John. 'Power to the People.' Apple R 5892. *1971*: UK.

PETER WICKE

Soundcarrier

Introduction

Music is carried by airwaves vibrating at around 50 to 20,000 cycles per second (the full range of hearing in a healthy adult). During the eighteenth and nineteenth centuries, scientists discovered how to detect traces of these vibrations, and in 1877 two inventions contrived the means to transmit these waves electrically (the telephone, invented by Alexander Graham Bell) and mechanically (the phonograph, invented by Thomas Edison). The two technologies are significantly different. The telephone is a simultaneous form, like radio, in which the sound waves are transient. In the phonograph, the sound waves were given durable form by the cylinder, which constituted the soundcarrier proper (later replaced by the disc, or record). Since the record needed a machine for it to be played on, it was thus a linked commodity, like the camera and film, and this linkage helped to determine the pattern of its exploitation. The record was both durable and a commodity of an entirely novel type: it turned the performance of music, which was previously as ephemeral as speech and involved the presence of the musician, into a disembodied material object that could be bought and sold. This factor would completely change the political economy of the music business.

Mechanical Technologies

The record was the first of several types of soundcarrier that would revolutionize the form and reach of music in the course of the twentieth century, but at first its effects were muted. A vivid demonstration of scientific magic, it nevertheless suffered from severe technical limitations – namely, a very limited frequency range and high levels of noise and distortion. For the telephone, such limitations were less serious, for it was found that the human brain needs remarkably little information to understand speech, and the narrower the bandwidth, the easier the design of the equipment. Vocal and instrumental music were more problematic. Thus, while the telephone experienced slow but steady growth, the early phonograph was little more than a novelty, the stuff of entertainment arcades and 'educational' lectures.

Moreover, as long as the soundcarrier took the form of a cylinder, the invention that promised repeatable recording but not its replication was able to capture the imagination but not to satisfy the demand it aroused. The problem with the cylinder was that every recording was in effect an original: there was no means of mass production. At best, it was possible to produce a few recordings at a time or to copy them on a pantograph. Only the disc, patented in 1887 by Emile Berliner, made mass production possible, and thus enabled musicians, as Berliner himself put it, 'to derive an income from the royalties on the sale of their phonautograms' (quoted in Gelatt 1977, 38). Musicians quickly began to experience recording as a new and contradictory form of exploitation, in which other people were always making more from records than they were, although the rewards to be gained with success often outstripped all other sources of musical moneymaking. At the same time, the disc produced a separation of functions through which the figure of the consumer was constituted, since henceforth the cumbersome and more costly disc-cutting apparatus needed for recording was restricted to professional usage, and machines sold to the record buyer were capable only of playback.

The aesthetic effects of the mechanical soundcarrier, which now began to manifest themselves, were several and cumulative, and can hardly be considered apart, as if they were mere byproducts or epiphenomena. They were present from the outset and took multiple forms that conditioned the evolving political economy of the record industry, along with modes of both listening and music-making. In the first place, there was the physical separation of listening and performing, which had various implications. On the one hand, the performance became disembodied, transportable and vendible; this was to alter ways of listening by taking music into new settings, placing it in new surroundings. Indeed, the record, by carrying music into a whole range of new spaces, took it not only beyond the reach of the individual musician, but also beyond the sphere of printed music. This had an explosive effect on popular musics, as singers and players could now be imitated by those who could never hear them in person, and who often had no formal musical training to boot. The result was the rapid development of new styles through imitation and emulation, in which the soundcarrier displayed a double character, promoting both the song and the singer, both the music and the way it was put across. At the same time, musicians were able for the first time to hear themselves as others heard them. This, in the case of classical traditions, would change the nature of interpretation, which, as the musicologist Richard Taruskin has charted, became progressively less subjective and more analytical (Taruskin 1988).

In both cases, mechanical reproduction had effects on

what Roland Barthes (1977), reviving a medieval term, called *musica practica*: the everyday practise of music, as opposed to its theory; music by ear rather than by the book, the practise through which it is transmitted from generation to generation, and which every generation modifies according to its own needs.

Moreover, from the earliest days, the record had a multiplier effect with a dynamic spatial and geographical character. From the moment it achieved success, the record industry, like cinema, was international. A recording could be made anywhere, not only in the place where it was to be manufactured and sold. For example, Italian immigrants in the United States provided a market for records of operatic excerpts recorded in Italy, where opera was a popular art form. This market grew sufficiently large and influential that a record of Enrico Caruso singing 'Vesti la Giubba,' issued by the Victor company in 1907, became the first disc to sell a million copies.

Recordings of operatic excerpts by the leading singers of the day helped to establish the phonograph's credentials as a respectable form of diversion, although classical music already represented only a fraction of the market – according to an advertisement by the Victor Talking Machine Company in 1905, popular artists outsold opera singers by three to one or more, but there was 'good advertising in Grand Opera' (quoted in Gelatt 1977, 30). A double pattern of recording – records for the home market and for export to immigrant communities – meant that, from the very beginning, an enormous range of musics was recorded. By 1900, the catalog of the London-based Gramophone Company already offered 5,000 titles, including recordings in English, Scottish, Irish, Welsh, French, German, Italian, Spanish, Viennese, Hungarian, Russian, Persian, Hindi, Sikh, Urdu, Arabic and Hebrew, and the company had factories making discs in Britain, France, Spain and Austria; it also had plants in Riga, Latvia, serving the Russian market, and in Calcutta, serving the Far East. As a portable mechanical novelty, the phonograph penetrated communities all over the world in advance of electricity. In India, where there were no music publishers but a huge potential market, the Gramophone Company engaged musicians to train suitable singers and to set poems to music for them, thereby generating a supply of 2,000–3,000 new songs every year. The result was not only to secure the company a near-monopoly, but also to create a musical genre that would enter the cinema with the emergence of the Indian film musical in the 1940s.

Electronic Technologies

When electrical recording was introduced in 1925, as a result of research into telephony and the development of radio technology, not only did phonographs with electric motors, amplifiers and loudspeakers bring a huge improvement in quality, but amplification took recorded music into public spaces previously denied to the weak sound of the horn, thus extending its domain and producing new ways of using it. The cinema applied amplification to its own form of soundcarrier, the optical soundtrack. Meanwhile, records were played down telephone lines to be amplified as Muzak in factories, restaurants, hotels, salons and swimming pools. At the same time, the record developed a symbiotic relationship with radio. Radio learned to use records to fill up airtime, while the record industry used radio as an aural showcase. Both roles were facilitated by the appearance in the 1930s of the disc jockey, who would subsequently redefine the character of the record as a cultural object for new generations. The record industry thus lost its independent character, becoming incorporated into a much larger cultural industry, which after the middle of the century became increasingly transnational.

In the mid-twentieth century, postwar reconstruction brought renewed vigor to the market. First came the introduction of two new formats, both using smaller grooves known as 'microgrooves': the long-playing record (LP, revolving at 33 1/3 rpm) for classical music and albums; and the 7" (18 cm) 45 rpm record, which came in two forms – extended play (EP) for classical music and the so-called 'single' for pop music. The single had the same duration as the 78. It therefore preserved the restricted, established form of the commercially successful pop song, rather than developing it in line with the potential for longer recording and playback times made possible by the new format of the soundcarrier (which began only in the late 1960s). When electric recording had been introduced in the mid-1920s, the new equipment had been backward-compatible – the new machines had been able to play the old format. This time, the solution was to incorporate the old format alongside the new, to allow the market a period of transition, and the standard domestic gramophone was equipped to play 78s, 45s and LPs of all sizes. Later, when stereophonic sound was introduced in 1958, there was again backward-compatibility with existing microgroove records, which could be played on the new equipment. But this was not the case with the introduction of the compact disc (CD) in 1977, which was a completely new format.

Aesthetic Effects – I

Initially, the range of forms that the record could carry was restricted by the technical constraints of early recording systems, including the brief duration and limited tonal range of the record. While the extended works of classical music were chopped up into sections without regard to their musical logic, popular musical forms like dance music were truncated so that they could be squeezed into the three minutes that constituted one side of a 78 rpm record. This forced the music to become more concise, terse and economic, often to the detriment of musical content and quality. Thus, as the market expanded and demand increased, music publishers in the major centers of the music business organized the supply of new songs as a production line, with a consequent standardization of form that the philosopher Theodor W. Adorno (1967) would describe as 'always new and always the same' (126). Adorno infamously failed to distinguish between Tin Pan Alley and jazz as a musical art form, where the improvisational nature of the music prevented the publishers from exercising control. Here, creative musicians, including blues singers, often turned the need for discipline to good account, and the disc spurred the development of many new musical genres to fit the format. Moreover, the record played a key role in the international dissemination of jazz beyond the United States, and in the creation of a new musical idiom that became the lingua franca of a popular music which was disseminated on every continent of the globe.

At the same time, while the record industry constructed early paradigms of a new kind of international company with global ambitions, culturally speaking the record only accelerated an age-old characteristic of music. Since music is portable and travels easily, musical cultures were rarely isolated, and for centuries every wave of migration and conquest had had the effect of producing musical cross-fertilization. Mechanical reproduction intensified this process by opening up musics everywhere to new foreign musical influences. Because the industry was based on the commercial aspect of the record and was controlled by advanced industrial capital, the principal effect was the beginning of the Westernization of non-Western musics. Nonetheless, musical influences traversed the world in different directions. By the late 1920s, when Russian musicians were playing jazz in Moscow, recordings of popular music were being made in Southeast Asia that incorporated the Hawaiian guitar. In the 1930s, Eastern European Jewish immigrants to Palestine were composing Argentinian tangos in Hebrew with Hasidic-inflected melodies. In the 1940s and 1950s, records of Caribbean music began to find their way to Africa by means of black intellectuals meeting at universities in England and France, sowing the seeds for new styles of African urban music such as Congo-Latin.

Tape Technologies

The 1930s saw developments in an alternative recording technology, employing a different soundcarrier in the form of the magnetic tape recording, a method pioneered in 1898 by the Danish inventor Valdemar Poulson using wire as the soundcarrier. Originally held back by the lack of amplification, the development of magnetic recording was taken up again in the 1930s, when the BBC tried out machines using a polished metal strip as the soundcarrier (soon discontinued because it was deemed too dangerous), and a plastic-based tape was developed in Nazi Germany under conditions of military secrecy. The latter development was appropriated by US entrepreneurs in the late 1940s when they acquired the patents as part of the spoils of war. Within a few years, magnetic tape completely took over the recording process not only in the record industry and radio broadcasting, but also in film production, and it was soon being sold to the affluent consumer for amateur use. Then, in 1963, serious competition was brought into the popular consumer market with the introduction of the audio cassette, which married tape to the battery-powered transistor radio introduced in the 1950s. Miniaturization and the compact cassette not only gave tape a new cheapness and portability, but, because it reunited the functions of recording and playback, also allowed ease of duplication at the edge of the market and outside it, thus contributing to the growth of new forms and styles before they were recognized by the major record companies. The technology was also applied to the television signal, and the first professional videotape recorders appeared in the mid-1950s, although it was almost 20 years before improvements in video recording technology led to the introduction of domestic videotape machines using a similar format to that of the audio cassette, and rather longer before the equipment became genuinely portable.

The soundcarrier had now taken on multiple forms. On the one hand, it was divided into those dedicated to sound alone, and those that incorporated the soundcarrier into an audiovisual medium. On the other hand, it was divided into formats that only carried and reproduced the sound, and those that also captured and recorded it. The original cylinder phonograph did both. Disc technology separated these functions, marketing the former to the consumer and restricting the latter to professional usage. Tape reunited what the disc system had separated – the functions of recording and playback – thus handing over to the consumer the means of production of recordings, even though the quality did not originally match professional standards. Nevertheless, it promoted recording by amateurs both in the reactive form of copying records and taping from the radio, and in the proactive form of making music and recording it. Rock groups started making demo tapes – amateur recordings intended to attract the attention of talent-spotters. Often, a recording would be made on a high-quality reel-to-reel machine and then distributed on cassette.

Above all, the cassette accelerated and extended the reach of recorded music. In Western countries, it intensified a market that had already penetrated virtually every social class, especially among youth; in the underdeveloped world, it spread through the shantytowns of cities like Lima or Johannesburg, and reached the most isolated villages in the Andes or the Sahara. Everywhere, it created local markets just large enough to sustain minority tastes and new trends by musicians marginal to the international music industry, and often served as a means of disseminating musics suppressed for political reasons. The phenomenon was repeated the world over, in Nigeria and Indonesia, Israel and India, Turkey and China, which all had their own forms of 'cassette music' (see Manuel 1993).

From the point of view of consumption, a proliferation of technically different types of soundcarrier competed for the consumer's attention. On the supply side, however, at the level of production, there was both diversification and convergence. The various media used different forms of soundcarrier (although the content was readily transferable between them), and they dealt in the same double contents, the song and the singer, which they traded among themselves. Here, the soundcarrier was incidental, a technical detail. On the other hand, the ease and cheapness with which the recording could be copied also increased the practise of piracy, which was destined to grow with further technological advances.

Digital Technologies

The record companies fought back against piracy in the same way as they had combated competition from alternative entertainments: they introduced another new format. The CD, like practically all new record formats before it, used the classical market to establish itself and then took over the popular market. Not everyone agreed on the superiority of the new soundcarrier; some insisted that the sound of the new digital form of recording was colder than that of the existing analog systems. But the economics were decisive. While the consumer continued to pay high prices for a soundcarrier that was at the cutting edge of technology, the costs of production rapidly fell, and the producer's profit margins went up – conditions that encouraged diversity and the exploitation of the archives left behind by previous formats.

By the 1980s, the diversification of musical voices promoted by the proliferation of the soundcarrier was reflected in a reversal of flow from advanced to underdeveloped countries, with the rise of the trend known as 'world music.' At the same time, new musical forms like rap spread like wildfire around the world from their individual points of origin. Meanwhile, as the soundcarrier took on digital form, which made it even easier to transfer from one format to another, the physical nature of the carrier ceased to govern the manner in which the music reached the listener, and convergence also meant that music was increasingly able to escape constraints resulting from either technical boundaries or claims of ownership – thus returning to something like the condition of music before the advent of mechanical reproduction, when a good song circulated freely.

A new stage arrived in the 1990s, with advances in computer technology and the growth of the Internet, which affected both the creation and the distribution of music. Back in the 1950s and 1960s, computers and other devices had been used by the pioneers of electronic music, who stored the results on magnetic tape. When keyboard synthesizers first appeared on the market in the late 1960s, they represented a new performing instrument – while samplers and sequencers, with their own built-in storage devices, became studio gizmos. When all these were interfaced with the computer through a protocol called MIDI (musical instrument digital interface), introduced in 1982, the computer started to become a new means of musical creation, a tool of composition not as notes on paper but in sound – a trend that took off when hard disc storage grew large enough for the computer to become a soundcarrier in its own right.

Since the sound signal was now recorded not as an analog waveform but as a digital data stream, it also became capable of streaming over the Internet and being stored on other new types of memory-storage devices produced by the computer industry. The most radical effect of this new technological revolution took shape in the late 1990s through a computer program called MP3, which packaged sound files for dissemination over the Web. Using MP3, millions of people were able to download free music, much of which had been pirated, generally causing the record companies great anxiety on account of falling sales. The result was that the record companies took action against Napster, the company that promoted MP3 on the Web, and it was forced to close down operations in 2001. However, at this time, it seemed unlikely – given the unruly character of the Internet, the resourcefulness of computer programmers and the avidity of the audience – that the free dissemination of music on the Web could be halted.

Aesthetic Effects – II

The aesthetic effects of the mechanical soundcarrier began with the divorce between the location of performance and the site of listening. The reception of music changed radically in the process, often by releasing music from traditional constraints. As a result, musical culture underwent changes and shifts both positive and negative. Classical traditions acquired a larger audience than ever before, but the record congealed performance, the listener was deprived of the physical presence of the performer, and music came to be experienced as an interchangeable series of physical objects rather than a living experience. In popular musics, the huge expansion of the record market promoted, on the one hand, a formulaic production line for new material and, on the other, new forms and styles of performance with varying degrees of authenticity and originality. Often, these were correlated with subcultural social movements, especially with the growth of teenage and youth culture which developed out of postwar reconstruction in the 1950s, a process that intensified the age-old links between musical taste and social identity.

All along, the reception of the record has been mediated by the construction of the figure of the consumer as record collector, as adumbrated in the magazines and reviews that have grown up to promote the record industry. However, while music has been divided into different compartments for the purposes of market management – literally so in the topology of the record store – at home listeners are liable to take over by mixing up the records they listen to, often in blithe disregard for both social expectations and the received hierarchy of taste.

There has been an alteration in modes of listening. On the one hand, records (like radio) induce a new passivity in listeners by relegating music to the background, placing it in situations where it is only half-heard (as, similarly, wallpaper is chosen and then ignored). On the other hand, the record can intensify receptivity, by allowing listeners to match music to mood or simply to listen to it undistracted in the most intimate setting. Indeed, the gamut of social space is reconfigured by means of sound reproduction, from the home to the shopping mall, by way of the jukebox in the café or bar, the cassette player in the automobile and the ghetto blaster on the street. Also, the Walkman allows listeners to wander around freely within their own bubble of music. The results of this ubiquity raise questions about control over the sound environment – from specific noise that precipitates domestic arguments and disputes between neighbors (even the murder of persistent noise-makers) to a general increase in noise that has deleterious effects on psychological and physical health.

But the soundcarrier also lends itself to the creative uses of the imagination in the most unexpected ways. The machine designed to record and reproduce can be made to manipulate the sound, especially in conjunction with ancillary equipment. The tape recorder thus became an inventive tool in the creation of esoteric electronic music in the 1950s, and commercial popular music not long afterward. As mixing, multitracking and remixing became primary techniques, a new technical form of musicality began to emerge, often associated with the creative input of the record producer, who thereby acquired special cultural status. This tendency for the soundcarrier to behave in certain conditions like a musical instrument goes further than the general law whereby technological inventions typically lead to uses that could not previously have been imagined. Thus, even the record player, which only replays old LPs, can be used as an instrument, in the form of record scratching, in which records are manipulated on turntables by being jiggled backward and forward under the pickup to produce not a reproduction of the music, but a series of more or less rhythmic noises. A transgression of intended purpose, not to mention musical norms, nothing symbolizes better than the art of the record scratcher the paradoxical double character of the soundcarrier in its evolution from mechanical novelty to major determinant of the shape of musical culture at the beginning of the twenty-first century.

Bibliography

Adorno, Theodor W. 1967. 'Perennial Fashion – Jazz.' In Theodor W. Adorno, *Prisms*, trans. Samuel and Shierry Weber. London: Neville Spearman, 119–32.

Adorno, Theodor W. 1978. 'On the Fetish Character in Music and the Regression of Listening.' In *The Essential Frankfurt School Reader*, ed. Andrew Arato and Eike Gebhardt. Oxford: Oxford University Press, 270–99.

Barthes, Roland. 1977. 'Musica Practica.' In Roland Barthes, *Image, Music, Text*, trans. Stephen Heath. London: Fontana/Collins, 149–54.

Chanan, Michael. 1995. *Repeated Takes: A Short History of Recording and Its Effects on Music*. London: Verso.

Gelatt, Roland. 1977. *The Fabulous Phonograph, 1877–1977*. 2nd rev. ed. London: Cassell.

Manuel, Peter. 1993. *Cassette Culture: Popular Music and Technology in North India*. Chicago: University of Chicago Press.

Taruskin, Richard. 1988. 'The Pastness of the Present and the Presence of the Past.' In *Authenticity and Early Music: A Symposium*, ed. Nicholas Kenyon. Oxford: Oxford University Press, 137–207.

Wallis, Roger, and Malm, Krister. 1984. *Big Sounds from*

Small Peoples: The Music Industry in Small Countries.
London: Constable.

Discographical Reference

Caruso, Enrico. 'Vesti la Giubba.' Victor 88061. 1907:
USA.

MICHAEL CHANAN

Sport

Sport and popular music are two elements of popular
culture that, worldwide, are possibly the easiest for
people to identify with. Both are able to attract weekly
audiences of hundreds of thousands to live events and
millions to television, yet both can be played and
enjoyed at the most basic level, without necessarily a
common language or culture. As multimillion-dollar
industries with individual and team or group superstars,
they attract many aspiring stars, and both have long
been viewed as a path to riches for the talented underprivileged.

There is an increasing amount of interaction between
popular music and sport, and their consumption and
production have many similarities; yet, at first glance,
the two worlds tend to meet only on a peripheral level.
The few sports that use music as an integral part of competition (such as gymnastics, ballroom dancing, ice
dance and synchronized swimming) tend to use popular
classics (for example, 1983 World Ice Dance champions
Torvill and Dean choreographed their winning routine
to Ravel's 'Bolero') and are themselves, with the possible
exception of gymnastics, sports that are marginalized by
the 'mainstream' sports fans and writers.

It is through the use of popular music as entertainment for sports spectators that the relationship between
sport and popular music has really developed. With the
growth of mass spectator sports such as soccer and US
football in the late nineteenth century, marching bands
were used as a spectacle to amuse crowds before games
and at half time; they introduced the concept of 'community singing' by the crowds and brought the repertoire of the bands and of composers such as Sousa to the
fore. At soccer games in the United Kingdom, spectators
who sang along to the tunes in the pre-match period
subsequently revived the same tunes (such as Sousa's
'Stars and Stripes Forever') during periods of play, often
with spontaneously adapted lyrics, as an expression of
support for their teams. Although the bands have now
largely been replaced by pop records as pre-match entertainment, their songs are still commonly sung by fans in
between adaptations of more modern songs. Many pop
songs have subsequently joined them as part of the tradition, an early UK example being Liverpool soccer club
supporters' adoption of 'You'll Never Walk Alone,' a hit
for Gerry and the Pacemakers in the Merseybeat era

although it was originally from the stage musical *Carousel*. A host of other songs have been adopted by soccer
crowds, some of them unlikely: fans of Italian AC Milan
soccer club frequently sing their version of the Beatles'
'Yellow Submarine'; the Gap Band's chant 'Oops Up Side
Your Head' is a UK soccer favorite years after it was written; and the Pet Shop Boys' revival of the Village People's
'Go West' inspired almost every UK soccer crowd to produce its own version of the song. Italian soccer fans regularly sing adaptations from works such as Verdi's *Aida*,
and an even more unlikely example of a sports crowd's
adoption of a piece of music is found in rugby union,
where the traditional song of the (predominantly white)
English supporters has for many years been the spiritual
'Swing Low Sweet Chariot.'

While the spontaneity of the crowd's singing at such
sporting events has been an integral part of the experience of spectating, there have been attempts by organizers in recent years to set the agenda for the crowd's
songs. There is a precedent for this in baseball, where
traditionally an organist has played popular pieces
during breaks in the play, and musical motifs are often
used to lead the crowd at potentially important points
in the game. Other US sports, such as ice hockey and
football, have also adopted this practise, using extracts
from popular hits such as 'Rock and Roll' by Gary Glitter
and 'Tubthumping' by Chumbawamba. However, the
practise has now been taken a step further: whereas, previously, part of the joy of victory was the crowd's spontaneous eruption into songs of its own choosing, victory
for the home team in important games in such sports as
soccer and rugby league is now almost inevitably followed by the public-address system playing Tina Turner's 'The Best' and/or Queen's 'We Are the Champions'
(the latter particularly unsuited to the vocal range of the
average supporter). The use of such recordings is often
explained as an attempt to control the crowd's celebrations, which might otherwise become provocative and
threatening, but many spectators find the practise
intrusive and distracting.

The traditional singing of national anthems immediately before the start of major sporting events has also
become more structured. Although it has long been customary in the United States for a popular star of the
moment to sing the anthem at the beginning of the
Superbowl, this practise has been adopted by sports in
other countries only comparatively recently. British
singer Paul Young, for example, led the national anthem
at the beginning of the Euro 96 soccer tournament,
where previously the band would have struck up the
tune and the crowd would have joined in. This development has meant that many arrangements of the
anthems by guest singers, designed to highlight the

singer's vocal ability, have deprived the spectators of the opportunity to participate. On the other hand, some organized uses of music – such as theme songs played as the home team enters the arena or the baseball anthem 'Take Me Out to the Ball Game,' written in 1908, which is sung by millions of fans each year – are part of tradition and spectators would feel shortchanged if they did not take place.

While 'Take Me Out to the Ball Game' is unusual in that it is a song written specifically about a sport that has entered the ceremony of the game, sports and sporting challenges have been the inspiration for songs for many years. In the United Kingdom, 'The Hambledon Cricket Song,' a song about a local cricket team, dates back to the late 1760s, and countless others subsequently appeared, mainly in the folk/traditional idiom. They included songs that celebrated the achievements of individual cricketers such as W.G. Grace and Ranjitsinji in 1895, and a work dedicated to a particular touring team (Australia 1899) that predated the late twentieth-century football team songs by some 70 years. Other nineteenth-century ballads addressed sports such as bull-running, bare-knuckle fighting, foot racing and boat racing. In the United States, 'The Baseball Polka' (1858), 'The Red Stockings Schottisch' (1869) and 'Slide Kelly Slide' (1889) are early examples of the same genre.

With the advent of sound recording, popular sports such as baseball continued to provide inspiration either as the subject ('The Baseball Game,' 1916) or through personalities and events ('Did You See Jackie Robinson Hit That Ball?,' 1949). Similarly, in the United Kingdom soccer attracted the attention of early recording artists ('At the Football Match Last Saturday,' 1905; 'Pass! Shoot!! Goal!!!,' 1931). However, recordings of songs concerning particular sports or teams really began to become popular in the early 1970s, when a trend emerged for soccer teams in the United Kingdom to record songs commemorating their participation in major sporting events, such as the FA Cup or the World Cup. Since then, almost every team in the soccer league, even those that attract a relatively small following, has recorded and released a single, and the practise is now not just a UK phenomenon: most teams competing in the 1998 World Cup produced their own records. Although such recordings have historically been little more than novelty records, a number of compilation albums featuring them were issued in the early 1990s on British labels such as Exotica and Richmond. The more recent trend in soccer records has been to attempt to attain some credibility by bringing in established groups (such as New Order with 'World in Motion,' and Lightning Seeds with 'Three Lions') to write material and participate in the recordings. A further development has

been the production of compilation albums to mark sporting events: for example, for the 1998 World Cup, Sony released *Allez! Ola! Ole!*, a compilation of songs written for teams from participating countries, including Brazil, Cameroon and Japan.

While a number of sports figures are known to be musicians and to play as a hobby (tennis players John McEnroe and Pat Cash have performed charity gigs, and Damon Hill regularly played in a Formula 1 drivers' band at post-Grand Prix parties), some have attempted to enter the commercial market as solo artists, with occasional one-off successes (Glenn Hoddle, Kevin Keegan). However, basketball's Shaquille O'Neal is the only sports player to come close to a sustained, internationally successful music career.

At the beginning of the twenty-first century, the worlds of sport and popular music are moving closer, and commercial interests are dominant. In both worlds, television rights, merchandising and sponsorship outrank the drawing of crowds as the primary source of income. Music is playing a greater role in the presentation of sports on television and radio and is regularly cut with action to promote programs and to accompany post-match analysis. Pop and sports stars appear side by side in style magazines, advertisements and gossip columns. The distinction between the two worlds has become blurred, and it is predominantly the marketing and managing of sports and sportspeople, as well as of pop music and pop stars, that is shaping the future of both industries.

Sheet Music

Austin, Mrs. Hettie Shirley, comp. 1869. 'The Red Stockings Schottisch.' New York: J.L. Peters.

Blodgett, J.R., comp. 1858. 'The Baseball Polka.' Buffalo, NY: Blodgett & Bradford.

Kelly, J.W., comp. and lyr. 1889. 'Slide Kelly Slide.' New York: Frank Harding.

Sousa, John Philip, comp. and lyr. 1898. 'Stars and Stripes Forever.' Cincinnati, OH: The John Church Company.

Von Tilzer, Albert, comp., and Norworth, Jack, lyr. 1908. 'Take Me Out to the Ball Game.' New York: York Music Co.

Discographical References

Allez! Ola! Ole! Columbia SONYTV46CD. *1998*: UK.

Baddiel and Skinner and the Lightning Seeds. 'Three Lions.' Epic 6632732. *1996*: UK.

Beatles, The. 'Yellow Submarine.' Parlophone R 5493. *1966*: UK.

China Black. 'Swing Low Sweet Chariot.' PolyGram TV SWLOW 2. *1995*: UK.

Chumbawamba. 'Tubthumping.' EMI/Electrola CDEM 486. *1997*: UK.

'Did You See Jackie Robinson Hit That 'll?' *Baseball's Greatest Hits*. Rhino 70710. *1989*: USA.

Gap Band, The. 'Oops Up Side Your Head.' Mercury MER 22. *1980*: UK.

Gerry and the Pacemakers. 'You'll Never Walk Alone.' Columbia DB 7126. *1963*: UK.

Glitter, Gary. 'Rock and Roll (Parts 1 & 2).' Bell 1216. *1972*: UK.

New Order. 'World in Motion.' Factory/MCA FAC 2937. *1990*: UK.

Pet Shop Boys, The. 'Go West.' Parlophone CDR 6356. *1993*: UK.

Queen. 'We Are the Champions.' EMI 2708. *1977*: UK.

Royal Air Force Band, The. 'Stars and Stripes Forever.' Columbia DB567. 1931: UK.

Sheridan, Mark. 'At the Football Match Last Saturday.' HMV B470. 1905: UK.

'Take Me Out to the Ball Game.' *Baseball's Greatest Hits*. Rhino 70710. *1989*: USA.

Torvill and Dean. 'Bolero.' Safari SKATE1. *1983*: UK.

Turner, Tina. 'The Best.' Capitol CL 543. *1989*: USA.

Weber and Fields. 'The Baseball Game.' Columbia A2092. 1916: USA.

Whelan, Albert. 'Pass! Shoot!! Goal!!!' Imperial 2404. 1931: UK.

Discography

Baseball's Greatest Hits. Rhino 70710. *1989*: USA.

Baseball's Greatest Hits, Let's Play 2. Rhino 70959. *1990*: USA.

Bend It! 91. Exotica PELE1CD. *1991*: UK.

4–2–4. Richmond MONDE15CD. *1993*: UK.

ANDREW LINEHAN

Stardom

The Oxford English Dictionary dates the first usage of the term 'stardom' to the mid-nineteenth century ('The theatres of New York differ from each other in their power of giving lustre to Stardom,' *The Times* (September 1865)). In the nineteenth century, Liszt and Paganini were the objects of a level of attention and adulation that prefigured twentieth-century stardom. However, the beginnings of contemporary stardom are customarily associated with the advent of mass production, mass consumption and new technologies. These innovations resulted in stardom becoming more instantaneous, with audiences created around famous individuals. It was at this time that the epithet 'star' entered contemporary usage in connection with theatrical and sporting heroes.

Although the advent of the contemporary star system is usually associated with Hollywood, its first manifestations are to be found in the world of music. The beginnings of the star system can be traced to the entertainment provided by the music hall and vaudeville. As music halls and vaudeville theaters began operating on an increasingly large scale, promoters, pluggers, impresarios and entrepreneurs all worked to sell stars to target audiences. This led to remarkable increases in the payment of musicians. DiMeglio (1973), for example, reports that 'Lillian Russell, who was paid $35 weekly prior to 1900, was drawing $3,000 a week after the turn of the century. Eva Tanguay drew $3,500 a week. Once he had attained stardom, Al Jolson was assured $2,500 a week whenever he wished to appear. Ken Murray's salary of $2,000 each week during the late 1920's, put him in the same class as the great slugger of the New York Yankees, Babe Ruth . . . Ethel Waters . . . was absolutely awestruck when, during the early 1930's, her weekly rate reached $3,500, with an occasional $4,000 thrown in' (21).

In the first half of the twentieth century, the two institutions that made the largest contribution to the development of stardom were radio and Hollywood. The arrival of radio in the 1920s broadened the demographic base for popular music and created a huge audience for individual performers such as Eddie Cantor and Rudy Vallee, who were followed by figures such as Bing Crosby and Frank Sinatra. Hollywood also created a star system and star-making machinery. Individual appearances, promotional strategies and the selling of a star independently of that individual's screen or stage persona became integral to the industry. Many mainstream popular singers worked in both film and music. Those who worked in music only were often destined to remain a minority attraction. 'There's a New Star in Heaven Tonight' (1926), written by Irving Mills, J. Keirn Brennan and Jimmy McHugh about the death of Rudolph Valentino, was possibly the first popular song to mention the concept of 'the star.'

Stars may be thought of as 'individuals who, as a consequence of their public performances or appearances in the mass media, become widely recognized and acquire symbolic status' (Shuker 1998, 282). The relationship between audiences and fans on the one hand, and stars on the other, is marked by a considerable emotional investment by the former in the latter. This has to do with the formation and maintenance of identities on the part of individuals and groups. Stars are popular, explain O'Sullivan et al. (1994), 'because they are regarded with some form of active esteem and invested with cultural value. They resonate within particular lifestyles and cultures' (207). As Shuker observes, the important question in understanding stardom is 'not so much "what is a star?," but how stars function within the music industry, within textual narratives, and, in particular, at the level of individual fantasy and desire' (1998, 283). There are considerable elements of illusion and fantasy in the creation of a star. Stars 'function as mythic constructs, playing a key role in their fans' ability to construct meaning out of everyday life.' They are also economic entities, marketing devices 'used to mobilize audiences and promote the products of the music industry' (1998, 283). During the 1970s, stars began to be eclipsed by 'superstars,' a term associated with the advent of 'supergroups.' These were groups such as Emerson, Lake and Palmer, and Crosby, Stills, Nash and Young, formed out of performers who had previously attained stardom with other groups.

The character of stars in popular music has changed over the years. In the immediate post-World War II era, most pop stars were clean-cut and non-threatening. Crosby and Frankie Laine conjured up images of 'a responsible sweetheart or dashing young husband. There was certainly nothing antisocial about [them]' (Melly 1989, 29). All this was to change under the twin impact of film star James Dean and singer Elvis Presley. Both exuded an overt, though vulnerable, sexuality that had first been brought to popular culture by Frank Sinatra in the 1940s, occasioning mass adulation on the part of 'bobby-soxers.' In addition, audience reactions to a singer such as 'the Nabob of Sob,' Johnnie Ray, may in the early 1950s have prefigured some of the emotional scenes of excessive adulation that were to accompany the rise to fame of Presley in the mid-1950s. But it was Presley's 'exotic' sexuality, hitherto the preserve of black entertainers, that ushered in a new era of sexual explicitness.

The rock era itself has always been personality-driven. Many rock stars are viewed as auteurs who transcend the banality of the pop process by making a highly individualistic contribution to popular culture, while pop stars are seen as merely the puppets of the music business. Rock idols such as Jimi Hendrix, the Rolling Stones, Bob Dylan, the Beatles, David Bowie, Bob Marley, Bruce Springsteen, Madonna, Prince and Michael Jackson have been brilliantly packaged and sold by what Stokes (1976) has called 'the star-making machinery' – an intricate promotional nexus of music industry personnel selling a myth of stardom through the mass media. Some of the most enduring stars have worked on a cross-generic basis, sold as a brand name across film, music, music videos and television.

A star is therefore not just a singer or performer, but someone whose iconography makes him/her a barometer of the times or a representative of an ideology or idea. Many of the most prominent popular stars embody archetypal ideas and myths. For example, the social construct of 'the boy next door' has been applied to various

performers throughout the history of popular music, from Cliff Richard and Paul Anka to Jason Donovan and the pop group Hanson. Other performers, such as Bruce Springsteen and Eric Clapton, have been sold as 'authentic' rock stars, their 'authenticity' inextricably bound up with a perceived fidelity to the blues, rock music and notions of virtuosity. Conversely, David Bowie, Madonna and Prince have been packaged as 'artificial' – they stress artifice, bricolage, sexual ambivalence and outrage. In the final analysis, both 'authentic' and 'artificial' rock poses are media and promotional constructs that have a complicated relationship with the performer's own personality.

Television tends to produce 'personalities' or 'celebrities' rather than stars, because television personalities seldom break out of their medium or become embodiments of a cultural idea. Correspondingly, 'actors become stars when their off-screen lifestyles and personalities equal or surpass acting ability in performance' (Gledhill 1991, xiv). This also holds true for the world of popular music, in which larger-than-life excess is positively encouraged. Keith Moon became as famous for his hotel-wrecking and substance abuse as for his drumming.

The achievement of stardom is not, however, simply reducible to marketing and hype. Historically, white, good-looking males, born in either the United States or the United Kingdom, have a vastly greater chance of becoming successful rock stars. The only Third World popular music superstar to emerge during the twentieth century was reggae artist Bob Marley. However, stardom has also been an important phenomenon in many non-Western cultures. Gandhy and Thomas (1991) report that 'stardom in India developed in parallel with – and with awareness of – the Hollywood star system' (108). Yet, the position of the star in the Indian film industry is different from that of stars in Hollywood. The position stars command today, say Gandhy and Thomas, ' – both economically and in the popular imagination – is the result of an idiosyncratic economic system that has accorded them more absolute power than even their Hollywood contemporaries.' They are 'the subject of voyeuristic fascination and extraordinary tolerance, and stars accept, on the whole graciously, an adoration close to veneration' (1991, 107).

Such veneration has marked the death of a number of musicians worldwide, suggesting an equal, if not greater, star status for such performers. When Umm Kulthūm, 'unquestionably the most famous singer in the twentieth-century Arab world' died in 1975, for example, 'her funeral was described as bigger than that of President Jamāl 'Abd al-Nāsir' (Danielson 1997, 1). The death in 1935 of tango singer Carlos Gardel, 'the defender of

Argentine culture and . . . the symbol of the Argentine people' (Castro 1990, 133), 'produced in Buenos Aires a great outpouring of . . . public grief and [marked] the end of an era in Argentine popular music.' His death also marked 'the beginning of the man as a symbol of *porteño* creole values' (Castro 1990, 129). And when Edith Piaf died in 1963, 'Paris wept . . . Forty thousand people crowded into the Père Lachaise cemetery . . . Her funeral was like her life – crazy!' (Berteaut 1972, 477). Death has played a significant role in the production of stardom in the West as elsewhere. Death freezes the appeal of the star 'while enabling their continued marketing through both the back catalogue and previously unreleased material' (Shuker 1998, 283).

Stardom is not always comprehensively embraced, however. In certain vastly popular musical genres, such as gospel, new age, ambient and almost all genres of dance music, the cult of celebrity so beloved of rock, pop, soul and jazz has been eschewed. As Spencer (1990) observes, 'gospel music does not encourage individuals to be truly *unique* . . . in order to apply their particular vocations to converting the world for the good of the family of God and humanity; rather individuals are taught to lose their identities in Christ's' (205). Gospel music, says Spencer, 'is basically of the "Christ against Culture" . . . type' (1990, 205). This has created problems for some performers. Boyer (1995) reports that 'Columbia Records made Mahalia Jackson an international star and the "World's Greatest Gospel Singer," but many gospel singers and people from the African American church felt that the singing was not the same' (91). The popular market, continues Boyer, 'wanted "Rusty Old Halo" and "You'll Never Walk Alone," while the African American church audience wanted "When I Wake Up in Glory" and "If We Never Needed the Lord Before."' Jackson solved the problem, concludes Boyer, 'by creating two performance styles: one for the recording studio and the other for live performance' (1995, 91). Songs warning of the evils of the star system, such as Phil Ochs's 'Chords of Fame' (1970) and Joni Mitchell's 'Free Man in Paris' (1974), are also not uncommon.

As Shuker has observed, 'there is a large body of theoretically oriented work on film stars' (1998, 283). Alberoni (1972), for example, has defined the star as a person 'whose institutional power is very limited or nonexistent, but whose doings and way of life arouse a considerable and sometimes even a maximum degree of interest' (75). Dyer (1979) has suggested the idea of 'a total star text,' and argued that, far from being bland reproducers of the dominant creative and cultural conditions of the day, stars could be read as radically reconciling, creating or exposing ideological contradictions (see Gledhill 1991). A helpful overview of the theoretically

informed literature on stardom in film has been provided by Hayward (1996). However, 'the study of stardom in popular music is largely limited to personal biographies of widely varying analytical value' (Shuker 1998, 283). Over the last two decades of the twentieth century, academics tended to shy away from dealing with the lives of mainstream rock icons, leaving journalists to concentrate on the section of the popular music process (the impact of individual stars) that most fascinates the general public.

This trend notwithstanding, Geoffrey Stokes's *Star-Making Machinery* (1976) – one of the first attempts to look at the packaging of a pop band – is a seminal text on stardom in the music industry. In addition, Savage (1996) has stressed the importance of gay culture in the formation of rock ideology and has shown how artists such as Elvis Presley, the Beatles and David Bowie mined the gay subculture for the trappings of their stardom. Savage argues that Britain plays a crucial role in the stylization of popular music, taking forms of popular music as developed in the United States and endowing them with sartorial excess (with the Sex Pistols as the embodiment of this strategy).

Song texts concerning stardom abound within Anglo-American popular music. Particularly significant are those songs that act as self-fulfilling prophecies, such as Bowie's 'Star' (1972), Bros's 'When Will I Be Famous?' (1987) and Oasis's 'Rock 'n' Roll Star' (1994), all by – at the time, would-be – stars about stardom itself.

Bibliography

Alberoni, Francesco. 1972. 'The Powerless "Elite": Theory and Sociological Research on the Phenomenon of the Stars.' In *Sociology of Mass Communications*, ed. Denis McQuail. Harmondsworth: Penguin Books, 75–98.

Berteaut, Simone. 1972. *Piaf: A Biography*. New York: Harper & Row.

Boyer, Horace Clarence. 1995. *How Sweet the Sound: The Golden Age of Gospel*. Washington, DC: Elliott & Clark Publishing.

Buxton, David. 1990 (1983). 'Rock Music, the Star System, and the Rise of Consumerism.' In *On Record: Rock, Pop, and the Written Word*, ed. Simon Frith and Andrew Goodwin. London: Routledge, 427–40.

Castro, Donald S. 1990. *The Argentine Tango as Social History, 1880–1955: The Soul of the People*. San Francisco: Mellen Research University Press.

Danielson, Virginia. 1997. *The Voice of Egypt: Umm Kulthūm, Arabic Song, and Egyptian Society in the Twentieth Century*. Chicago and London: University of Chicago Press.

DiMeglio, John E. 1973. *Vaudeville U.S.A.* Bowling Green, OH: Bowling Green University Popular Press.

Dyer, Richard. 1979. *Stars*. London: BFI Publishing.

Gandhy, Behroze, and Thomas, Rosie. 1991. 'Three Indian Film Stars.' In *Stardom: Industry of Desire*, ed. Christine Gledhill. London: Routledge, 107–31.

Gledhill, Christine, ed. 1991. *Stardom: Industry of Desire*. London and New York: Routledge.

Hayward, Susan. 1996. *Key Concepts in Cinema Studies*. London and New York: Routledge.

Herman, Gary. 1994. *Rock 'n' Roll Babylon*. London: Plexus.

Hill, Dave. 1986. *Designer Boys and Material Girls: Manufacturing the '80s Pop Dream*. Poole: Blandford Press.

James, Clive. 1993. *Fame in the 20th Century*. London: BBC Books.

Melly, George. 1989 (1970). *Revolt into Style: The Pop Arts in the 50s and 60s*. Oxford: Oxford University Press.

O'Sullivan, Tim, et al. 1994. *Key Concepts in Communication and Cultural Studies*. 2nd ed. London and New York: Routledge.

Savage, Jon. 1996. *Time Travel: Pop, Media and Sexuality, 1976–96*. London: Chatto & Windus.

Shuker, Roy. 1998. *Key Concepts in Popular Music*. London and New York: Routledge.

Spencer, Jon Michael. 1990. *Protest and Praise: Sacred Music of Black Religion*. Minneapolis, MN: Fortress Press.

Stokes, Geoffrey. 1976. *Star-Making Machinery: The Odyssey of an Album*. Indianapolis, IN: Bobbs-Merrill.

Wise, Sue. 1990 (1984). 'Sexing Elvis.' In *On Record: Rock, Pop, and the Written Word*, ed. Simon Frith and Andrew Goodwin. London: Routledge, 390–98.

Sheet Music

McHugh, Jimmy, comp., and Mills, Irving, and Brennan, J. Keirn, lyrs. 1926. 'There's a New Star in Heaven Tonight – Rudolph Valentino.' New York: Mills Music.

Discographical References

Bowie, David. 'Star.' *The Rise and Fall of Ziggy Stardust and the Spiders from Mars*. RCA-Victor SF 8287. *1972*: UK.

Bros. 'When Will I Be Famous?' CBS ATOM 2. *1987*: UK.

Mitchell, Joni. 'Free Man in Paris.' Asylum 11041. *1974*: USA.

Oasis. 'Rock 'n' Roll Star.' *Definitely Maybe*. Creation CRECD 169. *1994*: UK.

Ochs, Phil. 'Chords of Fame.' *Phil Ochs Greatest Hits*. A&M 4253. *1970*: USA.

DAVID BUCKLEY and JOHN SHEPHERD

The State

The state is a politically organized system of institutions, rules and regulations that unifies large numbers of people within a particular geographical area under a sovereign governing power. The state has a long and complex history – from the polis, the city-states of ancient Greece, in which the concept of the state and the first establishment of state apparatus emerged, through the legal system of the Roman Empire, the feudal power regimes of aristocracy and monarchy in the Middle Ages, to the modern nation-state, a complex unification of executive, legislative and judicial powers. It was in the sixteenth-century writings of Niccolò Machiavelli (Italy) and Jean Bodin (France) that there emerged the modern concept of the state as a centralizing force to unify and stabilize the whole of society, and this became the foundation for the ideological and cultural formation of the nation.

The history of the relationship between the state and music is equally long. Plato, in his seminal work *Republic*, hinted at the essential role of music in the functioning of any state system. State regulations to control music, particularly if it was considered potentially dangerous, subversive or unruly, were instituted as music developed. From the beginning, folk and popular music, the musical expressions of ruled groups in society and therefore always of potential danger for the ruling forces, were especially targeted for disciplinary measures by all kinds of authorities, religious and secular. Over the course of history, this music frequently became the subject of special state legislation. Most notorious were the regulations against dancing and its accompanying music – they constitute an early example of the conscious exercise of power by the body politic in relation to music (Wicke 1998). In some instances, as in fascist Germany during the 1930s and 1940s or under the Stalinist system of the former Soviet Union, where music was utilized as a means of propaganda, the state even acted as the exclusive organizer of popular music and developed drastic methods for its control.

There have been three main areas of state involvement in popular music: regulation and legislation; policing; and direct or indirect sponsorship.

Regulation and Legislation

The state frames the legal system within which music operates. Regulation and legislation can be targeted directly at popular music or can have indirect consequences for popular music by addressing issues in other areas of society. The Black Codes, a series of statutes passed in 1865–66 in some US states, are an example of legislation that had immense consequences for the development of popular music, although their purpose was to reassert the control over freed slaves that had been removed by the Emancipation Proclamation of 1863 and the Thirteenth Amendment to the Constitution of 1865.

Laws governing trade and industry, tax and immigration are further examples of legislation with more or less immediate consequences for the development of popular music. For instance, in 1935 the British Ministry of Labour decided to bar North Americans from taking jobs in the United Kingdom, with the consequence that, between 1935 and 1953, British audiences had no access to any live performances by US bands. Conversely, the US immigration laws and the issue of temporary work permits for visiting musicians to perform their music had a long-lasting influence on the presence of foreign music in the United States (see Jones 1993). More important, because they are of direct relevance to the economic infrastructure of the music industry, are copyright laws which, since the beginning of the twentieth century, have been one of the main subjects of debates, campaigns and negotiations between state authorities and representative bodies from the popular music industry, such as the Recording Industry Association of America (RIAA) and similar organizations elsewhere (see Frith 1993).

The state interferes directly with popular music through legislation set up to regulate musical practise itself. In all Western industrialized societies, licensing was used as the way to create a freelance musicianship as a basis for the development of popular music. The dissolution of the musicians' guilds, instituted in the fifteenth and sixteenth centuries, and their replacement by licensing systems for musicians did not occur earlier than the first third of the nineteenth century. Such licensing systems, but in different forms, can still be found. Although similar local government regulations existed, and have continued to exist, almost everywhere, the most notorious have been New York City's cabaret laws because of the outstanding importance of this city in the history of popular music (see Chevigny 1991). In 1926, the city council of New York decided to restrict cabarets, a US hybrid of restaurant and theater, to certain forms of music and certain areas of the city. The relevant paragraph of this legislation, in place until 1988, read as follows:

'Cabaret': Any room, place or space in the city in which any musical entertainment, singing, dancing or other form of amusement is permitted in connection with the restaurant business or the business of directly or indirectly selling to the public food or drink, except eating or drinking places, which provide incidental musical entertainment, without dancing, either by mechanical devices, or by not more than three persons playing piano, organ, accordian [sic], guitar or any stringed instrument or by not more than one singer accompanied by himself or a person playing piano, organ, accordian, guitar or any stringed instrument.

(NYC Administrative Code, Section B32-296.0 [1971])

In practise, this meant that, before 1988, any restaurant in New York City that sought to offer live music that involved more than a trio had to have a cabaret license, and any restaurant that sought a cabaret license had to be located in an area of the city that was designated by the authorities for that kind of entertainment. This law was enforced between 1940 and 1957 by the issuance of identity cards for musicians, which could be denied for countless reasons. The case of Billie Holiday, who was refused an identity card in 1947 because of narcotic offenses, was a famous example of such a policy. Club licensing, local regulations for music in restaurants and public places, and the licensing of musicians, bands and orchestras to play at venues in certain districts, at certain locations or at certain times (after-hours shows and so on) have been a hidden and rarely discussed component of the framework of popular music development for a long time.

Another important area of state legislation that directly affects popular music is broadcasting. Guidelines for programming policies and content regulations, such as the domestic content quotas in many European countries, are of great relevance to the music, the musicians and the music industry as well.

Policing

Censorship, although not limited to the state and state authorities (see Cloonan 1996), is one of the main forms of popular music policing. There are innumerable devices for censoring popular music. Many laws have or can have, if applied appropriately, censorial implications. Licenses of any kind and their maintenance are an example: they have been used again and again to censor and police popular music. The reasons for censorship are as diverse as the cases to be found, ranging from supposed political subversion, through attacks on and disparagement of any kind of authority, the violation of moral or religious standards, to indecency or pornographic issues, by far the most common. The fact that popular music is often considered by state authorities as a deviant form of music makes it particularly vulnerable to that kind of attack, since the protection of artistic freedom to be found in many societies is often interpreted as being meant just for 'high' culture.

Direct or Indirect Sponsorship

Even if it is normally not considered the business of the state, direct or indirect sponsorship of popular music and popular music events occurs much more frequently than is apparent. For example, in many societies, music education and instruction in playing a musical instrument, if not free, are heavily subsidized. Such sponsorship is normally done for general cultural and social reasons, but it certainly benefits popular music too. Social programs aimed at getting young people off the streets or alleviating unemployment are often supported by public investment in social-cultural locations, which not only give young people their own space but also provide musicians with performance opportunities. The nonprofessional sector of popular music, often perceived as providing an opportunity for social-work programs, is supported by grants, by the provision of rehearsal space or by access to the media. Indirect sponsorship can also occur through broadcasting regulations. The institution of the CanCon regulations in 1970 in Canada ensured the expansion of the national market for Canadian music, for example (see Shuker 1994, 63).

Direct sponsorship occurs when popular music events are granted tax exemptions. For instance, the Berlin Love Parade, the largest musical event of recent times, which brings together more than 1 million ravers each year, is state-supported because it is licensed as a political demonstration instead of as a musical event; this saves the organizers and commercial sponsors of the event millions of deutsche marks in tax. Direct sponsorship can also occur in relation to the recording of popular music, as when the Sound Development Recording Program was established in Canada in 1986, for example (see Laroche 1988).

Festivals of all kinds are state-sponsored in one way or another. Many countries support performing tours by their musicians as part of their foreign policy. The German Goethe-Institut and the French Maison de la France are typical examples: as part of the broad spectrum of their mandate, they foster the presence of their national musics abroad through the provision of substantial amounts of money to reduce the costs of the organizers of musical events in foreign countries. As states have come to recognize the significance of the local music industries, industrial development programs, job creation schemes and employment campaigns have become an increasingly important means of the state sponsorship of popular music. State schemes such as these are coordinated and conceptualized as part of the broad spectrum of cultural policy, youth policy or industrial policy and, to this extent, are always the subject of political debate.

Bibliography

Chevigny, Paul. 1991. *Gigs: Jazz and the Cabaret Laws in New York City*. New York: Routledge.

Cloonan, Martin. 1996. *Banned!: Censorship of Popular Music in Britain, 1967–92*. Aldershot: Arena.

Cloonan, Martin. 1999. 'Popular Music and the Nation State: Towards a Theorisation.' *Popular Music* 18(2): 193–207.

Frith, Simon, ed. 1993. *Music and Copyright*. Edinburgh: Edinburgh University Press.

Jones, Steve. 1993. 'Who Fought the Law?: The American Music Industry and the Global Popular Music Market.' In *Rock and Popular Music: Politics, Policies, Institutions*, ed. Tony Bennett et al. London and New York: Routledge, 83–98.

Laroche, Karyna. 1988. *The Sound Recording Development Program: Making Music to Maintain Hegemony*. M.A. thesis, School of Canadian Studies, Carleton University, Canada.

Shuker, Roy. 1994. *Understanding Popular Music*. London: Routledge.

Wicke, Peter. 1998. *Von Mozart zu Madonna: Eine Kulturgeschichte der Popmusik* [From Mozart to Madonna: A Cultural History of Pop Music]. Leipzig: Kiepenheuer.

PETER WICKE

Subculture

The term 'subculture' wound its way through twentieth-century cultural and social theory with a number of important twists and turns. According to one of its simplest definitions, 'subculture' simply designates 'a subdivision of a national culture' (Gordon 1997, 41). More commonly, however, the notion of 'subculture' has authorized sociologists to treat parts of their own society as strange and exotic. As Sumner (1994, 92) has noted, subcultural theory helped to encourage the convergence of anthropology and sociology, with Western researchers viewing their own social contexts in much the same way as anthropologists confronted tribal societies they considered primitive or folkloric. In 1915, Robert Park, for example, in his influential call for an analysis of contemporary urban life, suggested that the 'same patient methods of observation which anthropologists like Boas and Lowie have expended on the study of the life and manners of the North American Indian' could be extended to investigations of Greenwich Village or Chicago's North Side (Park 1997, 16).

This sense of subcultures as manifestations of a tribal life within contemporary cities has persisted in the study of the fan cultures that surround popular music genres (see, for example, Epstein 1998), and in analyses of the linguistic peculiarities and behavioral rituals of criminal subcultures (see, for example, Maurer 1964). More commonly, the analysis of 'subcultures' has focused on social groups presumed to be on the margins of mainstream life or occupying positions near the bottom of dominant economic or moral scales. Thus, for many years, the study of subcultures found its richest development within the sociology of deviance, in the study of social groups devoted to criminality or to forms of behavior (such as homosexual sex) deemed illicit by the dominant society. In certain instances, sociological research of this sort examined the subcultural activity surrounding certain kinds of music, such as jazz (see, for example, Becker 1964). By emphasizing the sets of rules, patterns of ritual and processes of reproduction typical of such subcultures, and therefore asserting their internal coherence as cultural systems, deviance theorists contributed to the development of a more broadly relativist view of culture.

Popular music and the social worlds in which it is embedded have figured prominently in two traditions of subcultural analysis. In certain respects, popular music has received attention within subcultural analysis because of its persistent association with other activities, such as drug consumption or sexualized interaction, that have been the focus of the sociology of deviance. Cressey's (1932) analysis of the 'taxi dancer' subculture of early twentieth-century dance halls, while concerned principally with a form of sexual commerce, is an important early study of one social institution in which music and dancing were central. Literary, scholarly and journalistic depictions of bohemia, from the nineteenth century through to the present, have noted the intermingling of musicians, visual artists, petty criminals and sexual 'deviants' within the 'spectacle of heterogeneity' characteristic of bohemian subcultures (Russo 1995, 129). Throughout this tradition, the emphasis has been on the existence of distinct 'moral regions' (Park 1997, 27) within a larger culture, and on the ways in which distinct moral systems challenge dominant social and cultural values.

A second tradition of research has been less preoccupied with noting deviance than with mapping the contours of subcultural life in more detached folkloric or organizational terms. If popular music has figured prominently in this tradition, it has done so in part because of its tendency to serve as one focal aspect of distinctive social groups – ones marked by habits of dress, styles of speech, patterns of congregation and life styles in a broader sense. In this sense, subcultures are studied less in terms of the moral strictures that give them their distinctiveness and more through an emphasis on the institutional, economic and discursive conditions under which they are able to reproduce themselves. For example, Thornton's important study of rave culture in Britain (1995) sets out to delineate the interlocking economies, institutions and forms of social cohesion and division within which raves, as events, unfolded.

In the 1970s, various strands of subcultural research were drawn together into a relatively coherent body of work that would come to be known simply as 'subcultural theory' (for example, Hall and Jefferson 1976). Sub-

cultural theory took from the tradition of deviance theory its emphasis on the ways in which the value systems of subcultures departed from those that were dominant within the larger culture. However, the inflection of this tradition by the Althusserian Marxist theory of ideology, with its emphasis on the role of ideology in offering a 'magical' solution to social contradictions, led to new sorts of claims about the sociopolitical status of subcultural challenges to dominant value systems. In perhaps the most notable of subcultural theory's claims, forms of male public congregation and violence were seen as attempts to resolve, in the realm of cultural practise, contradictions between an economic system that was destroying traditional working-class rituals and an educational system that condemned the male population of working-class neighborhoods to a life of physical labor.

Later developments of subcultural theory, most notably in the work of Hebdige (1979), shifted their emphasis from a perception of subcultural activity as a largely unconscious use of subcultural practises to resolve ideological contradiction to a sense of it as a deliberately transgressive manipulation of signs and symbols. In work that coincided with the rise of punk culture, Hebdige drew attention to the subcultural work through which punks selected and recombined artifacts (such as old ties and garbage bin liners) from the dominant culture. Here, as in many subsequent developments of subcultural theory, the Marxist analysis of resistance to ideological systems was further expanded within an avant-gardist discourse concerned with the transgressive disruption of meaning systems through artistic strategies such as appropriation and collage.

Since the late 1970s, the appeal of the notion of 'subculture' in the analysis of popular music may be seen to have waned. A number of critiques have noted the tendency for subcultural studies to focus on self-consciously collective, publicly visible and frequently spectacular forms of cultural activity, and to privilege these at the expense of less public, less visible and less obviously disruptive forms. The most influential of these critiques have been from feminist scholars, who have noted the ways in which traditional subcultural theory has privileged the masculine domains of the street corner and the soccer stadium over those sites of interaction, such as the bedroom, where young girls are more likely to congregate and interact (McRobbie 1980). Other writers, such as Cagle (1995), have encouraged attention to the sorts of dispersed (and, therefore, less publicly visible) communities of affinity made possible by modern media and, more recently, by the Internet.

At the same time, however, ideas about cultural consumption developed within subcultural theory have become an integral part of broader conceptualizations of popular culture. The idea that consumption will almost inevitably involve the creative (and possibly transgressive) appropriation of objects from the dominant culture and their insertion into new contexts of meaning has become one of the founding assertions of certain strains within cultural studies (see, for example, Fiske 1987). As well, many writers have suggested that the audiences and markets for cultural commodities in general are fragmenting into niche- and sub-markets held together by the circulation of specialized forms of knowledge and new, small-scale forms of communication (such as Internet discussion groups; see Straw 1997). In this context, cultural consumption in general may increasingly come to resemble a form of subcultural activity, with no residual sense of a dominant mass culture against which it may define itself.

Bibliography

Becker, Howard. 1964. *Outsiders: Studies in the Sociology of Deviance*. New York: The Free Press.

Cagle, Van M. 1995. *Reconstructing Pop/Subculture: Art, Rock, and Andy Warhol*. Thousand Oaks, CA: Sage.

Cressey, Paul G. 1932. *The Taxi-Dance Hall*. New York: Greenwood Press.

Epstein, Jonathon, ed. 1998. *Youth Culture: Identity in a Postmodern World*. Malden, MA: Blackwell.

Fiske, John. 1987. *Television Culture*. London: Methuen.

Gelder, Ken, and Thornton, Sarah, eds. 1997. *The Subcultures Reader*. London: Routledge.

Gordon, Milton M. 1997 (1947). 'The Concept of the Sub-Culture and Its Application.' In *The Subcultures Reader*, ed. Ken Gelder and Sarah Thornton. London: Routledge, 40–43.

Hall, Stuart, and Jefferson, Tony, eds. 1976. *Resistance Through Rituals: Youth Subcultures in Post-War Britain*. London: Hutchinson.

Hebdige, Dick. 1979. *Subculture: The Meaning of Style*. London: Methuen.

Lipsitz, George. 1994. *Dangerous Crossroads: Popular Music, Postmodernism and the Poetics of Place*. London: Verso.

Maurer, David. 1964 (1955). *Whiz Mob: A Correlation of the Technical Argot of Pickpockets with Their Behavior Pattern*. New Haven, CT: College and University Press.

McRobbie, Angela. 1980. 'Settling Accounts with Subcultures: A Feminist Critique.' *Screen Education* 34 (Spring): 37–49.

Park, Robert. 1997 (1915). 'The City: Suggestions for the Investigation of Human Behaviour.' In *The Subcultures Reader*, ed. Ken Gelder and Sarah Thornton. London: Routledge, 16–27.

Russo, Mary. 1995. *The Female Grotesque: Risk, Excess and Modernity*. London: Routledge.

Straw, Will. 1997. '"Organized Disorder": The Changing Space of the Record Shop.' In *The Clubcultures Reader: Readings in Popular Cultural Studies*, ed. Steve Redhead, Derek Wynne and Justin O'Connor. Oxford: Blackwell Publishers Ltd., 57–65.

Sumner, Colin. 1994. *The Sociology of Deviance: An Obituary*. New York: Continuum.

Thornton, Sarah. 1995. *Club Cultures: Music, Media and Subcultural Capital*. Cambridge: Polity Press.

WILL STRAW

Taste

'Taste' refers to the ability to make critical judgments about artistic works. Popular music scholarship has explored the premises that underpin distinctions between 'good' and 'bad' music, and has sought to uncover the processes that inform contemporary notions of taste. Critics have argued that, rather than being governed purely by autonomous psychological or biological factors, aesthetic choices are embedded in social relationships. While the selection of particular musical products can be understood as an exercise in 'personal taste,' it has been widely agreed that these choices work symbolically to give expression to the ways in which listeners identify themselves socially.

Since Herbert Gans (1966) coined the term 'taste culture' to describe the correspondence between social strata or class membership and certain cultural items (including music), a number of researchers have attempted to conduct empirical investigations into the factors that inform musical taste. These studies have attempted to test the hypothesis that there exists a correlation between musical preference and social status. Critics have focused on the importance of factors additional to class, such as age and race (Denisoff and Levine 1972), gender (Christenson and Peterson 1988), religious and political persuasion (Orman 1984) and geographical location. These studies suggest that aesthetic judgment is greatly informed by the social identity of the audience. Theorists such as Lewis (1992) have pointed out that, while it is tempting to describe tastes as personal and idiosyncratic, 'we pretty much listen to, and enjoy, the same music that is listened to by other people we like or with whom we identify' (137).

The relationship between taste and social identity is thus not a 'natural' one. Indeed, Bourdieu (1986) proposes a 'cultural economy' in which taste is a construct that is actively re-created in social relations in order to reproduce hegemony. Bourdieu's formulation of 'cultural capital' to describe life-style choices and cultural hierarchies articulated through the consumption of particular cultural forms has been highly influential in the study of popular cultural taste. Here, taste groups such as subcultures (Thornton 1995) and fans (Fiske 1992) are seen to be part of a microcosm of the wider cultural economy, in which status is conferred through the ability to display one's knowledge about particular popular cultural artifacts and practises. Similarly, Becker (1982) suggests that the way in which artistic works are made and understood is closely tied to the institutional practises and socially constructed discourses of the 'art worlds' in which they are produced. Following on from both Becker and Bourdieu, Frith (1996, 36–46) gives the example of the discourses and institutions of 'bourgeois, folk and commercial' musics, which work to concurrently construct differing aesthetic codes through which the shared values of their respective taste groups are created.

Since the work of the Frankfurt School on the culture industries, a central theme within the study of popular music has been that taste is in some way subject to mediation by the music industry and media. It has been argued that the industry attempts to create, react to and cater for taste cultures. Hirsch (1990), for instance, describes the media as 'surrogate consumers' who act as taste leaders, filtering out and selecting cultural products for wider consumption. Toynbee (1993) explores the ways in which the British weekly music press act as cultural gatekeepers. He highlights the manner in which they function as a filter, employing didactic and corrective strategies to suggest which musical products their readership should value, enjoy and admire. These theorists do not suggest, however, that the music industries successfully dictate taste, merely that they are active in trying to chart, shape and predict consumer responses. Other theorists have echoed this approach by positioning taste or fan groups outside any purely prescriptive model of audience reception. Studies of these groups have shown that affiliations to particular performers, musical genres or particular texts are often acted out in creative ways that have not been predicted by the culture industries.

Taste may also be understood to have a bearing on the ways in which the academy selects music for study. Brooks (1982) argues that taste often informs the study of music (particularly art musics), influencing the manner in which people judge and value particular performers, eras and musical texts. He warns against musical analysis that employs seemingly objective criteria but has underlying premises built on value judgments. Brooks argues for a more inclusive approach to the study of music, suggesting that we should 'acquire a taste for tastelessness' (1982, 18), where all music can be analyzed without prejudice. Thus, if all music is treated as worthy of study, a more comprehensive and balanced knowledge of music will result.

Bibliography

Becker, Howard S. 1982. *Art Worlds*. Berkeley, CA: University of California Press.

Bourdieu, Pierre. 1986 (1984). *Distinction: A Social Critique of the Judgement of Taste*, trans. Richard Nice. London: Routledge & Kegan Paul.

Brooks, William. 1982. 'On Being Tasteless.' *Popular Music* 2: 9–18.

Christenson, Peter G., and Peterson, Jon Brian. 1988. 'Genre and Gender in the Structure of Music Preferences.' *Communication Research* 15(3): 282–301.

Denisoff, R. Serge, and Levine, Mark H. 1972. 'Youth and Popular Music: A Test of the Taste Culture Hypothesis.' *Youth and Society* 4(2): 237–55.

Fiske, John. 1992. 'The Cultural Economy of Fandom.' In *The Adoring Audience: Fan Culture and Popular Media*, ed. Lisa A. Lewis. London and New York: Routledge, 30–49.

Frith, Simon. 1996. *Performing Rites: On the Value of Popular Music*. Cambridge, MA: Harvard University Press.

Gans, Herbert. 1966. 'Popular Culture in America: Social Problem in a Mass Society or Social Asset in a Pluralist Society?' In *Social Problems: A Modern Approach*, ed. Howard S. Becker. London: John Wiley and Sons, 549–620.

Hirsch, Paul M. 1990. 'Processing Fads and Fashions: An Organization-Set Analysis of Cultural Industry Systems.' In *On Record: Rock, Pop and the Written Word*, ed. Simon Frith and Andrew Goodwin. New York: Pantheon Books, 127–39. (First published in *American Journal of Sociology* 77 (1972): 639–59.)

Lewis, George H. 1992. 'Who Do You Love?: The Dimensions of Musical Taste.' In *Popular Music and Communication*, ed. James Lull. 2nd ed. London: Sage Publications, 134–51.

Orman, John M. 1984. *The Politics of Rock Music*. Chicago: Nelson-Hall.

Thornton, Sarah. 1995. *Club Cultures: Music, Media and Subcultural Capital*. Cambridge: Polity Press.

Toynbee, Jason. 1993. 'Policing Bohemia, Pinning Up Grunge: The Music Press and Generic Change in British Pop and Rock.' *Popular Music* 12(3): 289–300.

MARION LEONARD and ROBERT STRACHAN

Television

Television has played a very significant part in bringing popular music to the attention of global audiences. Indeed, it is impossible to imagine popular music culture on the scale witnessed at the end of the twentieth century without the intervention of television. Over the years, television has acquired a vast repertoire of popular music–related genres: the straight pop chart shows, such as *Top of the Pops* in Britain and *Solid Gold* in the United States; the rock documentary and live music broadcast, both of which attempt to offer a more direct experience of popular music performance and culture; the Eurovision Song Contest and the variety show, which have offered a more mainstream account of popular music; and the less obvious genres, such as advertising and the television theme tune, which have covertly brought popular songs and artists into the public consciousness.

But the impact of television is not limited to its role as a medium for the dissemination of popular music and the creation of global audiences alone. Indeed, 'television,' as a cultural discourse and a socially situated medium, has had a profound influence on the ways in which popular music has been received by audiences, critics and the 'Establishment' or parent culture.

For the parent culture, popular music on television is, in a sense, doubly deviant. On the one hand, popular music has, since the 1950s, been ascribed by the parent culture a decisive role in producing, rather than simply expressing, teenage delinquency. Yet, on the other hand, concerns, indeed 'moral panics,' over the potentially harmful effects of television on young people have a parallel history. Frequently, research into young people's television consumption is informed by the assumption that the medium is a potential source for their delinquency: whether as a result of the content of television (too much sex, violence, vulgar entertainment and so on), or the context of viewing (the private space of the home, viewers 'slumped' in front of the set uncritically digesting the secondhand experiences offered by television) (Halloran 1970; Oswell 1998). However, these moral panics have since largely disappeared in the wake of concerns over new media and delivery formats such as computer games and video (Barker 1984; Skirrow 1986). Indeed, the late 1980s and 1990s witnessed more positive accounts of the relationship between television and young people (see, for example, Messenger Davies 1989).

Television in the West has also functioned for adults as a window on the world of youth and popular music culture. It is through this medium that the full impact of youth and popular music culture can be experienced: its anger and rage, its dissension and nonconformist ideologies, its subversive ambitions and intimations of sexual and moral abandon have been routinely paraded before parents and guardians through popular music programming. As a result, television has given youth and popular music culture a very public presence and, in the process, left it open to criticism and censure from authority figures. Indeed, from the earliest days of television there was evident the now familiar public clamor and outcry from parents and moral guardians over the presumed excesses of particular programs and performers.

This public exposure and censure of popular music programming is significant for the ways in which discourses form around youth and popular music culture and for the ways in which television is understood by that culture. Public criticism of programs and performers can lead to self-censorship and the toning down of performances. A famous and frequently cited example of this process is Elvis Presley's television performances in the late 1950s. Presley had become a popular figure with young people, yet his suggestive body language, in particular his gyrating hips, provoked moral outrage among parents. As a result, subsequent television performances were censored or subdued: for example, Presley's performance on *The Ed Sullivan Show* was framed from the waist up, while his gyrating during 'Hound Dog' on *The Steve Allen Show* was intercut with images of a real hound dog. Other programs have suffered censure and sometimes cancellation at the hands of outraged parents. In Britain, examples include *The Tube* (Tyne Tees, 1982–87), *The Word* (Planet 24, 1990–95) and *Whatever You Want* (RPM, 1982–83). The upshot of this process is that television's presentation of popular music is often understood by youth audiences to be an expurgated version of the real thing.

However, at the same time, public outcries over the presumed excesses of popular music programs might be reassuring evidence for youth audiences that their culture is transgressive and that it is distinct from, and incomprehensible to, the parent culture. In other words, while public disapproval may threaten the programs and lead to censorship and cancellation, it nevertheless functions to authenticate the performances and to assure youth audiences that their culture is different and transgressive.

During the late 1960s and the 1970s, rock music emerged with a set of ideologies that functioned to move television and popular music even further apart. According to these accounts, television and rock culture sit at opposing ends of a political and ideological spectrum: rock is an active, politicized youth culture, which offers liberation, community and transcendence, while television is a passive, divisive and manipulative medium that perpetrates an insidious form of social control. These accounts, while specific to the 1960s and 1970s, have remained as residual forms. For example, the Disposable Heroes of Hiphoprisy's 'TV: The Drug of the Nation,' with its implications of social control and passive consumption, is testimony to the persistence of the rock–television opposition. Within rock ideologies, then, television and music are incompatible media working to fulfill different and conflicting agendas.

But many of the charges concerning the incompatibility between popular music and television cannot be separated from the aesthetic and formal limitations of the medium. For example, it is commonly noted that television has a weak sound in comparison with the sound systems of clubs and concert venues. Again, the particular ways in which television produces meaning and the ways in which it is consumed militate against the reception of popular music programs as 'authentic' and 'oppositional' texts. To understand this, a return to one of the foundational texts in television studies, Raymond Williams's *Television, Technology and Cultural Form* (1974), is necessary. Williams's notion of television 'flow' recognized the ways in which television programs do not communicate as discrete texts but, rather, interrelate and merge with one another to produce an aggregate meaning. Subsequent accounts of television, informed by this notion of flow, have recognized the difficulty of producing radical or oppositional programs within the constraints of a conservative or mainstream television schedule: the flow of the schedule threatens to overwhelm and flatten out difference and opposition (Caughie 1981). Cubitt has drawn similar conclusions for music videos. He points out that there is a limit to the 'subversive effects' of such videos because of the specific modes of consumption that are involved in television viewing where 'the flow takes precedence over the individual "text," the overall discourse over the utterances of which it is made up' (1991, 53). Furthermore, the context in which television is consumed is understood to militate against a full and authentic experience of popular music and its cultures. This context is provided by the domestic and familial institutions that are at odds with the values and aspirations of youth and popular music culture. Again, Cubitt, discussing one of the last remaining British prime-time pop programs, *Top of the Pops* (BBC, 1964), claims that there is a certain frustration for young people watching this program within the family circle, since this context always threatens to undo or diminish youth fantasies and ideologies of community, independence and mastery. He suggests that *Top of the Pops* can offer entry 'into that wonderful world without parents. But if the camera draws us in, the family pulls us out. Real parents are always likely to burst in on the dream of community and disrupt it' (1986, 48).

However, with changes in television delivery systems and in modes of consumption, it may be that the notion of 'flow' has come to have increasingly less to do with an individual's experience of television. Most homes have videocassette recorders, which can literally halt the flow of television's discourse. Furthermore, consumption of television is just as likely to take place away from the family, perhaps in the bedroom with members of the peer group rather than parents. These developments, along with the rise of specialized channels and niche programming, mean that the idea of radical programs being swept up and diluted by the flow of a mainstream schedule and consumed within the supervisory gaze of the family has come to have less explanatory power for contemporary viewing patterns.

It should be noted that network television has tended to figure quite modestly within academic and journalistic accounts of popular music, and much of the writing that does exist has been prompted by a relatively recent innovation in television broadcasting: MTV. Since its launch in 1981, the channel has been the source of an inordinate amount of debate, much of which has had little to do with music and more to do with concerns over a perceived paradigm shift from modernism to postmodernism. Nevertheless, the channel has raised a number of important issues regarding television's use of popular music. One issue concerns the channel's global presence, which has been viewed by many as a potential site for the incorporation of smaller and indigenous cultures and their music. Indeed, this debate followed MTV as it expanded into more and more territories (Banks 1996). However, while some guardians of national and indigenous cultures may flinch at MTV's 'one way flow of music,' for some of the people of these countries – the actual audiences – it can feel like a connection to the rest of the world's youth culture, bringing with it a sense of freedom and community (Hujic 1996). Another recurrent issue surrounding MTV is the relationship between image and music, and the extent to which the channel has made music a visual experience. The concern voiced by many academics and critics is that the images that accompany music television work against the 'openness' of music to limit and fix its meaning. The assumption here is that music is a purely aural and abstract medium which has been compromised by the arrival of television. This claim, however, has been challenged, most notably by Goodwin (1993), who has argued that images have had an important role in the writing and production of music. Indeed, it is worth noting that until the nineteenth century, before the advent of recording technology, music would have been as much a visual as an aural experience.

It is important to recognize that the relationship between television and popular music is not unvarying and should be viewed in its appropriate historical and cultural context. The quarrel between popular music and television seems to have eased. There may be a number of reasons for this. Certainly, dedicated music channels such as MTV have functioned to normalize the relationship between popular music and television. Furthermore, it may be that television is no longer the unified medium that it once was, transmitting a narrow set of conservative and mainstream values. The medium has fragmented and can now serve smaller, sometimes oppositional, constituencies. Again, MTV, with its promotion of an alternative culture, might be considered a prime example, and perhaps a pioneer, of this process.

Bibliography

Attallah, Paul. 1986. *Music Television.* Working Paper in Communications. Montréal: McGill University.

Banks, Jack. 1996. *Monopoly Television: MTV's Quest to Control the Music.* Boulder, CO: Westview Press.

Barker, Martin, ed. 1984. *The Video Nasties: Freedom and Censorship in the Media.* London: Pluto Press.

Caughie, John. 1981. 'Rhetoric, Pleasure and "Art Television" – Dreams of Leaving.' *Screen* 22(4): 9–31.

Cubitt, Sean. 1986. 'Top of the Pops: The Politics of the Living Room.' In *Television Mythologies: Stars, Shows and Signs,* ed. Len Masterman. London: Comedia, 46–48.

Cubitt, Sean. 1991. *Timeshift: On Video Culture.* London: Routledge.

Frith, Simon. 1988. 'Afterword. Making Sense of Video: Pop into the Nineties.' In Simon Frith, *Music for Pleasure: Essays in the Sociology of Pop.* New York: Routledge, 205–25.

Frith, Simon. 1993. 'Youth/Music/Television.' In *Sound and Vision: The Music Video Reader,* ed. Simon Frith, Andrew Goodwin and Lawrence Grossberg. London: Routledge, 67–84.

Goodwin, Andrew. 1993. *Dancing in the Distraction Factory: Music Television and Popular Culture.* London: Routledge.

Halloran, James. 1970. *Television and Delinquency.* Leicester: Leicester University Press.

Hill, John. 1991. 'Television and Pop: The Case of the 1950s.' In *Popular Television in Britain: Studies in Cultural History,* ed. John Corner. London: BFI, 90–107.

Hujic, Lida. 1996. '"I Hope You're Enjoying Your Party": MTV in Wartorn Bosnia.' *Screen* 37(3) (Autumn): 268–78.

Messenger Davies, Maire. 1989. *Television Is Good for Your Kids.* London: Hilary Shipman.

Oswell, David. 1998. 'A Question of Belonging: Television, Youth and the Domestic.' In *Cool Places: Geographies of Youth Cultures,* ed. Tracey Skelton and Gill Valentine. London: Routledge, 35–49.

Puhovski, Nenad, Skeggs, Beverley, and Wollen, Tana. 1993. 'All Around the World: Televising Live Music.' In *It's Live But Is It Real?,* ed. Nod Miller and Rod Allen. London: John Libbey.

Skirrow, Gillian. 1986. 'Hellivision: An Analysis of Video Games.' In *High Theory/Low Culture: Analysing Popular Television and Film,* ed. Colin McCabe. Manchester: Manchester University Press, 115-42.

Williams, Raymond. 1974. *Television, Technology and Cultural Form.* London: Fontana.

Discographical References

Disposable Heroes of Hiphoprisy, The. 'TV: The Drug of the Nation.' Fourth & Broadway 440541. *1992*: USA.

Presley, Elvis. 'Hound Dog.' RCA 47-6604. *1956*: USA.

PETER MCLUSKIE

The Theater

Popular music and the theater enjoy a close relationship that has its roots deep in both their histories. The most prominent connections in the relationship may be identified as: the functions allocated by the theater to music; the contribution of music to theatrical events and forms; the influence of theatrical practise on musical practise and vice versa; and the influence of attitudes toward the theater on attitudes to music. Less obvious than these but equally significant is the paradigm – popular music as theater. All these connections are evident in the theater's various roles as: public performance venue; site of conflict over notions of reality and artifice; location for the development of theatrical forms and performance practises; and commercial enterprise.

The Theater as Public Performance Venue

As a 'framed public space' (Middleton 1990, 80), the theater has provided a physical environment whose characteristics have significantly influenced the production and reception of popular music. The European idea, which emerged in the sixteenth century, of a specially constructed public building with a raised stage and accompanying galleries, put in place the notion of a distinct, socially designated and (variably) regulated space for live theatrical performance. Here, over the following three to four centuries, theatrical forms and practises developed in response to the opportunities offered by the character of the space, and sets of conventions evolved within the 'frame' – the raised stage at the front and the proscenium arch that acted as a frame inside the frame, the arrangement of audiences in tiers, the employment of winches to 'change the scene' and create the illusion of moving from place to place, and the use of lighting to create mood. In Japan, Kabuki theater emerged in response to a variation on this arrangement: the 'distinctive runway projecting obliquely from the stage into the auditorium and known as the Flower Walk' (Wickham 1985, 27).

The presence of musicians in theaters was commonplace, indeed frequently essential. The orchestra, whether large or small, provided a range of services that, by the nineteenth century, not only included a scene-setting overture, accompaniment for any onstage singing and dancing and entertainment for intermissions, but, in Victorian London, 'covered scene changes as well, cued entrances, sounded character motifs, took actors off stage, reinforced mood and often played *with*, or at least *under*, an actor's voice' (Booth 1991, 123). As two particular strands of popular theatrical entertainment emerged in the nineteenth century – the variety show (music hall, minstrel show, vaudeville, revue) and the musical, both of which gave music a more prominent role – the theater became for many the principal location where popular music was experienced in public, and hence public response was frequently conditioned by – and read through – the framed theatrical space.

With the advent of recording and broadcast media in the twentieth century, the theater gradually conceded to them its leading role in the provision of public performance involving popular music, but theatrically derived conventions centering around the idea of the stage retained an important presence. Although deriving elements from other institutions, such as the concert hall and, especially in the case of African-American music, the church, much live performance of popular music in the twentieth century, on both a small and a large scale, was conceived around the idea of the theatrical stage, with all its accouterments potentially present.

The audiences for live popular music, too, frequently continued to be thought of and to behave in accordance with practises laid down in the theater. While some performance styles expected a contemplative audience response, as had begun to develop for 'straight' drama around the mid-1800s, others encouraged audience participation in the form of interaction, as had been the case throughout much of European and North American theater until that point. This latter type of audience behavior was also characteristic, of course, of some African-American church worship and, viewed over a broad historical span, provides a good illustration of how similar practises, developed in distinct contexts, came together under the broad umbrella of popular music.

As popular music ceased to rely so heavily on the theater for performance, but continued to be theatrically conceived, a significant change occurred. One particular history-within-a-history of the theater had been the inexorable rise to domination of the partnership between words, acting and visual experience. Music had often found itself in a subservient role and, by the early twentieth century, only in the specialist genres involving music drama (opera, operetta, the still-youthful musical comedy) and at certain times in variety shows could music be said to command primary attention. One

consequence of the establishment of recording and radio in daily life in many different countries in the 1920s and 1930s was popular music's move to a more central position in everyday experience, resulting in a change in its status in people's perceptions. In experiencing this move, popular music, in a sense, de-theatricalized itself. The majority of music on record and on radio was received first and foremost as sound, not as part of a theatrical experience, and, although music and theater (and, from the late 1920s, film) continued to come together in the genre of the musical, the explicit music–theater collaboration became something of a separate stream. From the early 1930s, whenever popular music born in a theatrical context became part of the popular mainstream, it tended to do so by being dissociated from its original context – as, for example, in the case of many of Cole Porter's songs for his 1930s musicals. Having attained a position of centrality outside the theater, popular music was able to return gradually to the theater on its own terms, in the form of stage-based live performance, and to use its theatrical history and connotations to assert its own primacy in a theatrically conceived environment.

Reality and Artifice

Of the many conflicts and struggles for which the theater has provided a forum during its history, the one with most relevance to its relationship with popular music has been the argument over reality and artifice. This had its roots in explicitly anti-theatrical attitudes, but its effects were felt beyond those confines.

For many in the theater audience, from one culture to another, the actor's assumption of an identity other than his/her own has been readily accepted. Indeed, in nineteenth-century China, appreciation of the skill with which actors achieved this formed the center of knowledgeable theatergoing (Wickham 1985, 26). But the theater frequently encountered hostility – which faded only with the twentieth century – from those who deplored what they saw as an entire art form based on hypocrisy and deceit: pretending to be someone other than one's 'true' self was, variously, a crime against the social ideal, an undermining of morality or a sin against the divine order (since only God could bestow a person's selfhood) – or all three. Mimicry and impersonation were the chief, but not the only, targets. Also singled out were all forms of exhibition, elaboration and decoration, across the entire range of theatrical activity. The 'whole complex of theater, dance, music, gorgeous attire, luxurious diet, cosmetics, feminine seductiveness, feminine sexuality, transvestism, etc., aroused a painful anxiety in the foes of the stage' (Barish 1981, 115). Underlying this anxiety was not only fear of chaos, but the perception that theatrical ways 'represented a deeply disturbing temptation, which could only be dealt with by being disowned and converted into a passionate moral outrage' (Barish 1981, 115).

Most famously associated with anti-theatricality were the Puritans, among whose diatribes none was quite so ferociously outspoken as William Prynne's *Histriomastix* (1633). Music, in Prynne's text, is guilty by association. The 'amorous Pastoralls, lascivious ribaldrous Songs and Ditties,' the 'effeminate lust-provoking Musicke' are not only 'accomplices in the sinful masquerade,' but their contribution also makes the plays 'inexpedient and unlawfull unto Christians' (Barish 1981, 86).

Although this opinion was far from unanimously shared (and not even all Puritans shared Prynne's attitude), the legacy of anti-theatricality influenced attitudes to all theatrical components for the next 250 years, especially in Protestant countries and especially among those who held or aspired to positions of moral authority. As far as music was concerned, however, this view was counterbalanced by another (which many Puritans also espoused) – that of music's potential moral force. That this produced a profound sense of ambiguity, indeed of ultimately unresolvable paradox, was already evident in the seventeenth century. London publisher John Playford wrote in his *An Introduction to the Skill of Musick* (1655) of music's role as a 'Solace of Men, which as it is agreeable unto Nature so it is allowed by God . . .'; however, he continued: 'I believe it is an helper both to Good and Evil, and will therefore honour it when it moves to Virtue, and shall beware of it when it would flatter into Vice' (Chase 1987, 4).

As popular music developed its commercial base in the nineteenth century and became an important site of discourse concerning the role and nature of music, tensions between these two views of music's function – as encouraging and revealing integrity (the religious dimension had waned in explicit significance), but as prone to be used to display artifice and inauthenticity – were clearly evident, providing a space for performers to offer themselves as reconciliators of the two. One such was songwriter-performer Henry Russell, who toured the United States extensively in the 1830s and 1840s as a one-man show. Russell's approach was to set melodrama in both songs and their performances alongside a choice of 'messages' about social and moral ills. In further extricating popular song performance from the charge of theatrical inauthenticity, the role of a small number of women performers was significant. The success on the popular concert stage (including theater performances) of performers such as Swedish solo singer Jenny Lind or Abby Hutchinson (the one woman in the Hutchinson Family Singers) gave encouragement to those who

wanted to see the power of the domestic equation in which woman + home + music = moral stability extended into the public arena, to establish a place there for authenticity and integrity.

It would be wrong, however, to overemphasize the extent to which this was achieved at the time. The second half of the nineteenth century saw the separation from straight drama of various forms of variety theater, entertaining audiences with a sequence of 'acts,' and those forms used music voraciously. In this context, impersonation renewed itself, taking on a new guise in the form of ethnic and racial stereotyping, and music was crucial to its success. One change that did occur, however, was the emergence by the turn of the century of a sense that the two apparently antagonistic principles of performance – impersonation and authenticity – could coexist and, indeed, might intermingle, albeit ambiguously.

Discourses on theatricality and sincerity continued to characterize popular music in the whole of the twentieth century, in a variety of forms and contexts. Although at times oppositional, the dialectic was more often a subtle one: a song in a film soundtrack could confirm in listeners/viewers a sense of unreality, but still move them to tears. Audiences, too, became highly competent at recognizing this interplay in live performance. While this was going on, the theater itself saw the development of genres dealing in greater 'realism,' in which the objective was to strip away the layers of daily life concealing reality. Although operating at some remove from popular music's own continuing concerns with (in)authenticity, this development made a latter-day contribution to the debate, for it meant that, even in more contrived, less 'realistic' genres involving music, such as the Broadway musical, music's contribution could be seen as one of helping the audience to perceive the reality by means of the artifice.

Popular Music in Theatrical Forms and Performance Practises

A wide variety of types of popular music evolved in a theatrical context, according to the needs and conventions of specific genres. Some involved instrumental music only, ranging from music for entr'actes and entrance cues to dance numbers; others involved mainly vocal music; and still others (perhaps the majority) used both. Of the various forms that developed, accompanied song was the single most important, in terms of both its contribution and its legacy. Accompanied theatrical song, for one or more voices, may be said to perform one of three main functions: the dramaturgical function; the function of enabling and expressing the idea of performance itself; and the function of supporting interpersonal observation (as, for example, in the comic variety song) – in other words, song-as-drama, song-as-spectacle, song-as-commentary.

The dramaturgical role for song is most apparent in the so-called 'integrated' genres. Most frequently associated with Western theater, integration of 'speech, song and dance . . . into a unified dramatic style' is also characteristic of Indian folk theater forms (Manuel 1988, 160). In 'integrated' musicals, song not only supports the interdependence of plot, character and events, but also often assumes the role of preparing for events to come or reflecting on those that have passed. In *Show Boat* (1927), for example, a show often considered the first fully 'integrated' musical, the character Julie's song 'Can't Help Lovin' Dat Man' connects itself to music that has already been associated in the action with African-American stevedores, before the audience knows that Julie is of mixed race and that this status will be a focal point of the story (Swain 1990). Theatrical song of this type is thus involved not merely in expressing particular aspects of character, but in locating people within ongoing situations, referring forward and back.

The role of song in supporting spectacle is found both within drama-centered musicals and in loosely linked variety shows – and in the various types of theater that combine elements of both. Although in musicals spectacle often has a dramatic raison d'être, in essence the underlying rationale in all these cases is the same: the enjoyment of an effective combination of music, performance, costumes, lighting and scenery for its own sake.

Song as interpersonal observation or commentary can and does occur in musicals, but it is more often found in shows that are not dramatically conceived entities. Frequently, it takes the form of comic song, particularly of an ironic or, indeed, self-deprecating nature, as in a song such as 'Hungry Women' from the Broadway show *Whoopee* (1928) ('feed 'em and weep, they never eat cheap'), or English music hall performer George Formby's 'With My Little Stick of Blackpool Rock'; or it plays up to stereotyping tendencies in the society at large, as, for example, in the fashion on the US vaudeville stage for 'Paddy songs' caricaturing Irish immigrants.

Each of these song types has its own legacy within popular music outside the theater. Characteristics of song-as-drama are taken up in two particularly important ways. First, they provide a model, loosely but clearly followed, of how popular song can treat narrative situations. Narrativity, in much popular song, is treated dramatically: listeners find themselves dropped into an ongoing situation, the explanation for which is made only partially available. Typical musical structures (for example, verse–chorus), with their in-built tendencies to repeat and reflect, lend themselves to this approach. In this respect, songs are closer to plays than to poems (Frith 1987). Second, song-as-drama encourages role-playing, the assumption of alternative personae.

The legacy within popular music of song-as-spectacle is most clearly seen in a focus on performance and on the theatricality of performance, involving both performers' kinetic behavior (gesture and so on) and accompanying effects, among which lighting is especially important. Although this is most evident in the exaggerated form – or at least the 'grandeur' – of gesture necessary for visibility in a large-scale venue, it need not be exclusively that. Some more intimate performance styles appear to be deliberately conceived to contrast with more grandiose versions, while not denying that the overall goal is the enjoyment of the performance.

The legacy of theatrical song-as-commentary is less clear-cut, perhaps because of a decline in the explicitly 'comic' song in the second half of the twentieth century. Stereotyping and caricature in song also declined in the twentieth century (some types of rap being a partial exception). The influence of this song type is, however, apparent at a broader level in songs and performances that adopt a confiding, observational stance. Here, however, an increase has been noticeable in the element of ambiguity. Songs that confide often like to use a shifting narrative perspective to introduce an element of uncertainty as to who is observing whom.

In the theater, these three song types may frequently be distinguished, although not always: a song may serve a dramatic function and be 'about performance.' In popular music performance, yet more types are encountered, each with its own lineage (such as 'statement songs,' in which the influence of the church can perhaps be detected), providing performers with a rich array both of song types and, perhaps especially, of performance connotations and possibilities. It is not surprising that, as a result, popular music performance can involve an intermingling of such features in richly meaningful ways.

The Theater as Commercial Enterprise

Until well into the twentieth century, popular music's ability to be its own employer was limited. In the world of increasing commercial – especially urban – leisure, it had few social–physical institutions that were uniquely its own and, with the major exception of the public dance halls that began to appear in the early twentieth century, mainly depended on others requiring its services in some form. Recording changed the situation, turning popular music's lack of a dedicated social space to its advantage. However, before this occurred, the professional theater was one of popular music's major employers.

The theater provided employment both directly and indirectly: directly, in the form of paid work for singers, dancers, instrumentalists, arrangers and musical directors (the last two often the same person) for particular productions; indirectly, by offering songwriters and publishers a channel through which their songs might reach the public ear. In some instances, songwriters were also directly employed and, as the musical increased in importance, they often engaged in a kind of partnership with the theater management in their separate incarnations as composer and lyricist.

Around the end of the nineteenth century, as music publishers were setting up enclaves in cities such as London and New York where professional theater was strong, the theater's role in the marketing and promotion of popular music became crucial. It was part of an integrated, cyclical system, the precursor of more elaborate twentieth-century versions, in which a published song was promoted by a song plugger, taken on by a theater manager or individual performer, included in a show, heard by the public and purchased as sheet music. In the process, all the parties benefited, including the theater itself, especially if the song became popular. Although the system was still in place in the 1930s, the theater's role was increasingly seen as a minor one in a new environment characterized by the commercial integration of publishing, recording, radio and cinema, which, despite rivalry, the uncertainty of corporate takeovers and swings in public favor, set up an enduring domination. In this media-dominated context, the theater came to be associated with a different agenda: the preservation of live music.

The high-pressure environment of the professional theater also provided an ancillary benefit in the form of concentrated opportunities for learning for all involved, whether songwriters, performers, producers or managers. Less advantageous in human terms for the performers in particular, although also important in terms of both earning and learning, was another feature of professional theatrical life: the touring circuit. As railways revolutionized both the means of transportation and its speed, the theater was able to make touring a fundamental element of its financial structure. Some company managers planned their own tours, but more often the organization was in the hands of an alliance of theater owners. Most notorious of these, in US popular music history, was the Theater Owners Booking Agency (TOBA), which booked African-American performers, usually for pitiful rewards. For some musicians, whether well or poorly paid, the touring theater circuit was the root of their success; for others, it was the source of their disillusionment.

Another aspect of theatrical economics involving popular music – that of investment – has its own particular history. Originally regarded as an essential part of the budget, music acquired a reputation for raising the costs of a production and, as the genre of the musical developed between the late 1920s and the 1950s, for increasing the element of risk for investors. Costs were one element in the genre's decline in the 1960s and 1970s. But as, in many of the major cities of the world in the latter part of the twentieth century, theatrical productions as a whole became more and more expensive to stage (and 'serious' drama turned increasingly to subsidy), the cost-intensive, high-investment musical came back into its own, now in the guise of the world-touring, technologically sophisticated 'megamusical' (Burston 1998) – so much so that, in many cities and countries, the overall financial health of the theater, in terms of box office receipts, became crucially dependent on its drawing power.

Conclusion

By the end of the twentieth century, the direct connections between the theater and popular music were less apparent than those involving television and cinema. But in several key aspects of live performance – the configuration of the performance venue, the audience–performer relationship, the ongoing popularity of theatrically conceived performance styles, the role of lighting – enduring features of their historical relationship were still very much in evidence. By this time, too, audiences exposed to a range of presentational styles developed in and for different contexts – from theater to nightclub to television studio – had become increasingly competent at understanding them and the ways in which they interrelated in performance.

Bibliography

Barish, Jonas. 1981. *The Antitheatrical Prejudice*. Berkeley, CA: University of California Press.

Booth, Michael R. 1991. *Theatre in the Victorian Age*. Cambridge: Cambridge University Press.

Burston, Jonathan. 1998. 'Theatre Space as Virtual Space: Audio Technology, the Reconfigured Singing Body, and the Megamusical.' *Popular Music* 17(2): 205–18.

Chase, Gilbert. 1987. *America's Music: From the Pilgrims to the Present*. 3rd ed. Urbana, IL: University of Illinois Press.

Frith, Simon. 1987. 'Why Do Songs Have Words?' In *Lost in Music: Culture, Style and the Musical Event*, ed. Avron Levine White. London: Routledge, 77–106.

Manuel, Peter. 1988. 'Popular Music in India, 1901–86.' *Popular Music* 7(2): 157–76.

Middleton, Richard. 1990. *Studying Popular Music*. Buckingham: Open University Press.

Playford, John. 1655. *An Introduction to the Skill of Musick*.

London: John Playford. (Reprint of the 12th (1694) edition, with introduction, glossary and index by Franklin B. Zimmerman. New York: Da Capo Press, 1972.)

Prynne, William. 1633. *Histriomastix*. London: Michael Sparke. (Reprint, with preface by Arthur Freeman. New York: Garland Publishing, 1974.)

Swain, Joseph P. 1990. *The Broadway Musical: A Critical and Musical Survey*. New York: Oxford University Press.

Wickham, Glynne. 1985. *A History of the Theatre*. Oxford: Phaidon.

Sheet Music

Gifford, Harry, comp., and Cliffe, Fred E., lyr. 1937. 'With My Little Stick of Blackpool Rock.' London: Lawrence Wright.

Kern, Jerome, comp., and Hammerstein II, Oscar, lyr. 1927. 'Can't Help Lovin' Dat Man.' New York: T.B. Harms.

Discographical References

Cantor, Eddie. 'Hungry Women.' Victor 21831. 1928: USA.

Formby, George. 'With My Little Stick of Blackpool Rock.' Regal Zonophone MR-2431. 1937: UK. Reissue: Formby, George. 'With My Little Stick of Blackpool Rock.' *I'm the Ukulele Man*. Empress RAJCD 801. *1998*: USA.

DAVID HORN

Tourism

Those involved with tourism employ numerous different definitions of it, and many academic researchers on tourism find it difficult to define tourism in any analytically useful way (see, for example, Stokes 1999; Abram, Waldren and Macleod 1997). There is some consensus, however, that tourism can be regarded as being undertaken by temporarily leisured people who voluntarily visit a place away from home for the purpose of experiencing a change (Boissevain 1996, 3, quoting Valene Smith).

The relationship between popular music and tourism is complex, and the two can be connected in a variety of different ways. Geographical locations have on many occasions attained special significance through their association with commercial forms of popular music. There are popular songs and musicians, musical genres and styles, for example, that have strong connections with particular places, and this inspires people to visit those places. Quinn (1996, 386) cites statistics from the Irish Tourist Board which suggest that, for 69 percent of visitors in 1993, traditional Irish folk music was either 'a very important' or 'a fairly important' factor in their consideration of Ireland as a holiday destination. Like-

wise, so-called 'world music' has encouraged Western tourists to visit various parts of Africa, Asia and Latin America, with the expectation of seeking out indigenous music. Evidence as to whether Irish rock musicians and pop groups, like players of traditional Irish folk music, have attracted tourists to Ireland is unavailable, but in 1994 Ireland's Department of Tourism and Trade stated that 'many people's first exposure to Irish culture is through musicians (such as U2, the Cranberries, Hot House Flowers, the Chieftains, Clannad, Enya) . . . which in turn inspires them to visit Ireland' (quoted in Quinn 1996, 387).

The increasing recognition that traditional and popular music can attract tourism has encouraged tourist officials and entrepreneurs throughout the world to package and stage musical activities and events for tourist consumption. In Indonesia, there are specific gamelan tours, while visitors to Dublin can follow the 'Rock & Stroll Trail' to buildings and geographical sites of musical significance, such as those connected with the rock band U2, or can participate in the city's 'Musical Pub Crawl.' Other well-known popular music tourist sites include Graceland, the Memphis home of Elvis Presley, Beale Street in Memphis, which has been rebuilt and is marketed to visitors as the 'birthplace of the blues,' and the country music attractions of Nashville and Dollywood in Tennessee. There also exist published tour guides devoted to popular music, such as *Fodor's Rock & Roll Traveler USA: The Ultimate Guide to Juke Joints, Street Corners, Whiskey Bars and Hotel Rooms Where Music History Was Made* (Perry and Glinert 1996), and *Coast to Coast: A Rock Fan's U.S. Tour* (Bull 1993). Music festivals and carnivals also attract tourists, whether they be small-scale and local occasions or large and internationally renowned events, like the Montreux Jazz Festival in Switzerland or the Rio Carnival in Brazil. The economic impact of such events has been increasingly recognized, leading to a proliferation of festivals in some places and to an emphasis on their tourist dimension. Similarly, popular music museums have been developed as tourist attractions, such as the Rock and Roll Hall of Fame and Museum in Cleveland, Ohio and the National Centre for Popular Music in Sheffield, England. In addition, fans who travel to pop concerts may be counted in tourist statistics.

Popular music is, of course, not just a tourist attraction in its own right, but has a significant role to play in tourism more generally. Musical theater, cabaret and summer shows are a familiar feature of English seaside resorts (see Hughes and Benn 1996). Some UK policymakers have also been emphasizing the importance of developing a vibrant nightlife in England's city centers in order to attract and entertain tourists during their stay. Live or recorded, popular music has an important role to play as a central feature of pubs, bars, nightclubs and discothèques, and as part of other social activities in which tourists engage. Black Sea musicians, for example, earn a regular income by playing for tourists in Istanbul nightclubs (Stokes 1994). Popular music may also feature in advertisements and literature aimed at tourists; hence, Ireland has been described as 'a land of music and easy laughter' in a US travel magazine (O'Connor 1993, 70), while the New Orleans tourist board has urged visitors to 'come join the parade' (Atkinson 1996, 154).

Liverpool and New Orleans are two of the best-known cities for popular music tourism. Their popular music scenes have made them perhaps the world's most famous 'music cities,' with Liverpool known for the Beatles and Merseybeat and New Orleans famous for jazz. It was largely because of this shared characteristic that the two cities were officially twinned in 1988.

As the birthplace of and an influence on the Beatles, Liverpool has attained symbolic significance for Beatles fans, many of whom visit the city on what they describe as a music 'pilgrimage.' During the 1970s, this prompted a small group of Liverpool Beatles fans to organize an annual Beatles convention and to produce literature detailing the Beatles' local connections. During the 1980s, a few local businesses and organizations began promoting Beatles-related activities in a more systematic and professional manner for the benefit not only of fans, who represented a rather limited, specialized and thus not very lucrative market, but also of other local and visiting groups. A Beatles store was opened, for example, as was a Beatles museum, and a business was launched that specialized in Beatles tours. Local Beatles-related activities and events thus became more directed toward, and influenced by, the tourist industry, and during the mid-1990s Beatles tourism became officially recognized and supported by Liverpool City Council, which had turned to tourism and the service industries in its efforts to regenerate the city and reverse its economic decline (see Cohen 1997, 2001).

Similarly, New Orleans has attracted visiting jazz fans since the early 1940s, but again it was only in the 1990s that jazz and popular music tourism began to be promoted in a serious way by the city authorities and by newly established organizations such as the Arts Tourism Partnership. Their interest was prompted by the sudden collapse of the local oil industry during the mid-1980s, and by the success of the New Orleans Jazz and Heritage Festival, which started in 1968 and has come to incorporate a diversity of musical genres and styles, thus broadening out from a narrow and obvious focus on jazz. In 1993, the number of national and international visitors to this festival exceeded 350,000. Meanwhile,

the airport in New Orleans plays only the music of New Orleans artists, street musicians perform in Jackson Square, and tourist bars in the French Quarter and on Bourbon Street hire bands to play in a Dixieland style that many traditional jazz fans consider to be hackneyed and clichéd (see Atkinson 1997).

Popular music tourism initiatives in Liverpool and New Orleans have, like other forms of musical and cultural tourism, often been mired in controversy. For example, descriptions of Liverpool as 'the home of the Beatles' and of New Orleans as 'the birthplace of jazz' have been hotly contested and periodically embraced or rejected by various groups and organizations within those cities. There have been debates in each of the cities over whether popular music tourism benefits local residents and musicians as well as city visitors; whether it is a commemoration of and tribute to the local musical past or merely a means of exploiting and cashing in on it; whether the focus on the musical past has a negative influence on each city's contemporary music scene; and whether popular music tourism is an effective or appropriate focus for strategies aimed at improving each city's image and quality of life, generating local employment and attracting investment. Concerns have also been raised in both cities about whether representations of local musical culture staged for tourists are distortions of the truth, and whether commercial tourism is destroying the perceived authenticity of local culture.

Such concerns, issues and debates are commonly raised by tourism and have tended to inform people's understanding of what tourism is. Tourists, for example, have typically been assumed to be mobile, privileged outsiders who 'gaze' upon relatively powerless and less mobile insiders or 'others,' and tensions between visitors and inhabitants are common. Typically, concern is raised over whether the cultural events that these people observe are real or merely a show staged for profit, and the ideological opposition between authenticity and commerce is also commonly introduced. Considerable debate, for example, has surrounded the promotion of tourism based around traditional musics. Many fear that tourism will destroy local music traditions and will end up staging authenticity and inventing tradition, but others welcome tourism as a means of preserving local music traditions, promoting local identity and pride and contributing to local economies.

Tourism has been commonly associated with sun, sea and sand, but it has also involved visits to urban locations and events and sites of cultural interest. For example, tourism based around so-called 'high' culture, including Western classical music, has long been in existence. From the seventeenth to the early nineteenth centuries, the wealthy European elite toured Western

European cities to encounter varied cultural experiences. Clearly, however, tourism can take many different forms and involve many different motives. Some tourists may seek to temporarily escape the constraints and obligations of their everyday domestic and working lives so that they can return home revitalized; hence, some anthropologists (for example, Graburn 1989) have defined tourism as a liminal, inverted realm in that it takes people out of their usual spatial and temporal environments. Other tourists, as MacCannell (1976) has suggested, may seek to escape the superficiality, instability and inauthenticity of modern society in quest of 'authenticity.' There are also those whom Urry (1990) refers to as 'postmodern tourists,' because they seek a contrast with their ordinary, everyday lives but at the same time accept 'that there is no authentic tourist experience' (11). All of these motives, as well as others, are evident among tourists visiting Liverpool because of its connections with the Beatles. For example, between 1961 and 1963 the Beatles performed regularly at the Cavern Club, situated in Liverpool's Mathew Street, but the club was demolished in 1973 and later rebuilt. Some visitors bemoan the inauthenticity of the reconstructed club, and some are unaware that the 'real,' original club no longer exists. Others feel that, if they cannot see the original club, the reconstructions of it erected both in Mathew Street and in the Beatles Story, a museum located in Liverpool's dockland area, are the next-best thing and help them to learn more about the Beatles. There are also those who simply take delight in what they perceive to be the kitschy and inauthentic nature of such copies (Cohen 2001).

The 1980s and 1990s, as shown by the examples of Liverpool and New Orleans, witnessed a growth of cultural tourism in North America and Western Europe. The term 'cultural tourism' covers a broad range of activities and cultural forms, but it generally involves an emphasis on the tourist dimension of arts and cultural events and activities, and it marks a trend toward organized tourism based around more specialist interests, including heritage and nostalgia, rather than around standard, package tours. Popular music has played a part in this development and has increasingly emerged as a subject for tourism. Popular music offers attractions for tourism, and in turn tourism generates audiences for popular music. The growth of popular music tourism can illustrate much about connections between popular music, place and local identity, and can also direct attention away from the familiar tourist 'gaze' (Urry 1990) to demonstrate that tourism is not only about the visual.

Bibliography

Abram, Simone, Waldren, Jacqueline, and Macleod, Donald V.L., eds. 1997. *Tourists and Tourism: Identify-* *ing with People and Places*. Oxford and New York: Berg.

Atkinson, Connie. 1996. "'Shakin' Your Butt for the Tourist'': Music's Role in the Identification and Selling of New Orleans.' In *Dixie Debates: Perspectives on Southern Cultures*, ed. Richard H. King and Helen Taylor. New York: New York University Press, 150–64.

Atkinson, Connie. 1997. 'New Orleans: Popular Music and the Social, Cultural, and Economic Production of Locality.' In *Tourists and Tourism: Identifying with People and Places*, ed. Simone Abram, Jacqueline Waldren and Donald V.L. Macleod. Oxford and New York: Berg, 91–106.

Boissevain, Jeremy, ed. 1996. *Coping with Tourists: European Reactions to Mass Tourism*. Providence, RI: Berghahn Books.

Bull, Andy. 1993. *Coast to Coast: A Rock Fan's U.S. Tour*. London: Black Swan.

Cohen, Sara. 1997. 'Popular Music, Tourism, and Urban Regeneration.' In *Tourists and Tourism: Identifying with People and Places*, ed. Simone Abram, Jacqueline Waldren and Donald V.L. Macleod. Oxford and New York: Berg, 71–90.

Cohen, Sara. 2001. 'Popular Culture in Liverpool.' In *Liverpool at the Millennium: Living in the City*, ed. R. Meegan and M. Maddon. Liverpool: Liverpool University Press.

Graburn, Nelson. 1989. 'Tourism: The Sacred Journey.' In *Hosts and Guests: The Anthropology of Tourism*, ed. Valene L. Smith. 2nd ed. Philadelphia: University of Pennsylvania Press, 21–36.

Hughes, Howard L., and Benn, Danielle. 1996. 'Seaside Entertainment and UK Local Authorities.' In *Managing Cultural Resources for the Tourist*, ed. Mike Robinson, Nigel Evans and Paul Callaghan. Proceedings from a Conference on 'Tourism and Culture: Towards the 21st Century.' Sunderland: Centre for Travel and Tourism in association with Business Education Publishers Ltd., 181–92.

MacCannell, Dean. 1976. *The Tourist: A New Theory of the Leisure Class*. New York: Schocken Books.

O'Connor, Barbara. 1993. 'Myths and Mirrors: Tourist Images and National Identity.' In *Tourism in Ireland: A Critical Analysis*, ed. Barbara O'Connor and Michael Cronin. Cork: Cork University Press, 68–85.

Perry, Tim, and Glinert, Ed. 1996. *Fodor's Rock & Roll Traveler USA: The Ultimate Guide to Juke Joints, Street Corners, Whiskey Bars and Hotel Rooms Where Music History Was Made*. New York: Fodor's Travel Publications.

Quinn, Bernadette. 1996. 'The Sounds of Tourism: Exploring Music as a Tourist Resource with Particular Reference to Music Festivals.' In *Managing Cultural Resources for the Tourist*, ed. Mike Robinson, Nigel Evans and Paul Callaghan. Proceedings from a Conference on 'Tourism and Culture: Towards the 21st Century.' Sunderland: Centre for Travel and Tourism in association with Business Education Publishers Ltd., 383–96.

Stokes, Martin. 1994. 'Exchange and Meaning: Black Sea Musicians in the West of Ireland.' In *Ethnicity, Identity, and Music: The Musical Construction of Place*, ed. Martin Stokes. Oxford: Berg, 97–115.

Stokes, Martin. 1999. 'Music, Travel and Tourism: An Afterword.' *The World of Music* 41(3): 141–56.

Urry, John. 1990. *The Tourist Gaze: Leisure and Travel in Contemporary Societies*. London and Newbury Park: Sage Publications.

SARA COHEN

Urbanization

'Urbanization' is the term used to refer to a complex set of social, economic and technological processes whereby forms of living and organization characteristic of rural communities are replaced by forms associated with the growth of towns, cities and conurbations. Processes of urbanization have occurred differently in various parts of the world. Whereas industrialization was a major force in the development of urbanization in Northern and Western Europe and the United States, for example, urbanization in areas such as Latin America and Africa has tended to be associated more with forces of colonialism and imperialism, linked as these are to forms of capitalist economic development. As a form of expression and communication endemic to human societies, music and its practise have been affected in some fundamental ways by the advent of urbanization.

Urbanization in the Western World

Processes whereby the center of gravity in social and economic affairs shifted from the countryside to urban areas have been instigated since the middle of the eighteenth century by changes in the character of social relationships connected with work. Where Northern and Western Europe and the United States are concerned, for example, relationships typical of rural economies – based on sets of mutual yet often highly inequitable rights and obligations – were gradually replaced by those of a more contractual nature, as cottage industries became established, the circulation of money became less sluggish, mercantile capitalism succeeded feudalism as a way of life, and the mercantile or middle classes became more powerful socially, economically and politically. Through these processes, villages, towns and even small cities ceased to be extensions of rural life, serving as the location of the market and other centralized institutions such as the church, the bank and the hotel. The countryside slowly but surely became an extension of

conurbations, providing them with food, lumber, coal and other materials essential to life.

These changes set the scene for – and were associated with – the dramatic technological developments to emerge from the Industrial Revolution, the establishment of factories and the succession of mercantile capitalism by industrial capitalism. These developments – fundamental to urban life of the twentieth century in the Western world – occurred during the eighteenth and nineteenth centuries in Western and Central Europe, and during the nineteenth and early twentieth centuries in the United States. The advent of machinery in rural occupations such as textiles and agriculture threw many people out of work. The growth of railroads and the introduction of the telegraph during the nineteenth century revolutionized the speed of transportation and communication, a speed and effectiveness further enhanced by the advent of cars, buses, airplanes, telephones, radio, television and, subsequently, information technologies.

A pattern of migration from the countryside to cities thus became established as people sought work in the manufacturing industries and commercial organizations of cities. The migration was as dramatic as the technological and fiscal changes occasioning it. In the United States, an explosion in the urban population was reinforced in the northeastern part of the country in particular by emigration from the countries of Central and Eastern Europe. Whereas the rural population of the United States doubled between 1860 and 1900, that of towns and cities quadrupled. Only one in six people lived in a town with a population of over 8,000 in 1860. By 1900, that figure was one in three. New York, which in 1860 had a population of 800,000, had one in 1900 of 2,500,000. The population of Memphis went from 23,000 to 100,000 in the same period (Shepherd 1982, 23). In England and Wales, in 1831 'only about a quarter of the people lived in towns with over 20,000 inhabitants' (Horn 1987, 10). The 'point of no return was reached in 1851, when the census revealed that the population was equally divided between town dwellers and urban dwellers' (Meller 1976, 2). In 1871, the proportion of urban dwellers had increased to 61.8 percent, in 1891 to 72.05 percent and, in 1911, to 80 percent.

Urbanization and Popular Music in the West

Mass urbanization has had fundamental and profound consequences for popular music in the Western world. Popular music existed before mass urbanization. In the United States, for example, rural populations during the mid-nineteenth century were entertained by traveling troupes and artists: circuses, medicine men, singing families, theatrical groups and minstrel shows. Even those troupes not explicitly associated with music had musicians whose job it was to attract audiences from scattered rural environs. Sheet music was manufactured and was available in the general stores of hamlets, villages and towns, where it might sit on the shelves for a long time before being sold.

However, with mass urbanization, patterns of musical life changed. In England, there were dramatic increases in the number of band contests during the second half of the nineteenth century. In 1913, notes Russell (1987), 'a crowd estimated at between seventy and eighty thousand could be attracted to the Crystal Palace National Band Championships' (1). Whereas in 1840 a piano had been a luxury item, it has been estimated that, by 1910, 'there was one piano for every ten to twenty of the population' (Russell 1987, 1). This increase in the number of pianos was made possible only because of the transportation facilities provided by the railway, which by mid-century had become a commonplace in the life of England (Scott 1989, 46). By the turn of the century, the piano was becoming increasingly common in working-class homes. A similar trend was evident in the United States, where, says Roell (1989), 'the American piano industry set out to establish a democracy of music lovers, in which music would be consequential if not indispensable in *everyone's* life' (31; italics in original). This was made possible by 'the production of inexpensive upright pianos sold increasingly on credit terms' (Roell 1989, 31).

An equally important development during this period in the changing patterns of musical life in England resulted from the influence of music halls. The music hall industry, centered in London, 'began to reach more deeply into the ranks of the middle-class audience and to thrust into the middle-sized provincial communities it had previously ignored' (Russell 1987, 2). Pianos and the music hall created a demand for sheet music that had a profound effect on the technology of the music-printing industry, the dissemination of sheet music from London to the rest of the country by rail, and the kind of music printed, which had to be technically easy enough for the vast majority of the piano-playing public (Scott 1989, 52–58). The number of professional musicians increased. In the period from 1871 to 1911, the number of individuals recorded in the census as 'musicians and music masters' more than doubled, from 19,000 to 47,000 (Russell 1987, 1).

With mass urbanization in the United States, musicians who had previously been traveling artists frequently began to work in the vaudeville theaters of cities. Audiences drawn from the concentrated populations of urban areas now went to the artists, who traveled less frequently, rather than artists traveling on a regular basis to audiences who were considerably dispersed. The practise of popular music as a commercial undertaking intensified. Songs were written at speed and under considerable pressure by composers and lyricists in the cubicles of Tin Pan Alley music publishing houses. They were advertised intensively through vaudeville performances and various forms of plugging. And they were mass-produced in commodity form as sheet music for quick sale.

By 1900, urbanization had created the circumstances within which it took 30 days to create a hit, and 60 days to kill it. The logic of the music industry as but one form of business within industrial capitalism had been established. While forms of the mass commodification and mass dissemination of popular music were to change radically in line with the dramatic technological advances of industrial capitalism, the basic financial logic of the music industry was to remain relatively unchanged.

It is mass urbanization that has been primarily responsible for the establishment of the modern music industry. While popular music clearly predated mass urbanization, most popular music has for this reason been closely associated with it. The term 'urban popular music' is often used, justifiably or not, to connote the range of modern popular music as a whole. As Nettl (1978, 16) has observed, cities have always constituted distinctive and seminal social and musical environments in their concentrations of wealth, power, heterogeneous social groups and institutionalized forms of musical patronage. Cities provide the necessary technological infrastructure for the modern music industry, including facilities for the recording, production and dissemination of popular music. Urban populations, with their density and their participation in cash economies, constitute concentrated, easily accessible markets for music producers and for the mass media in general.

One consequence of this has been an emphasis on conformity and the creation of a homogeneous cultural identity. Mass urbanization in both England and the United States initially favored the creation of a sense of national culture. The period from 1840 to 1870 in England, observes Russell (1987), 'saw an increasing unification of taste and repertoire encouraged above all by the railway, the music-hall industry [and] music publishers . . . music-hall artists toured the country performing virtually the same repertoire at each venue' (3). Despite some local variations, 'by the end of the nineteenth century something very close to a mass culture had emerged in England, a sharing of common taste across a broad social range' (Russell 1987, 6).

The move toward a homogeneous cultural identity in the United States took place later than in England, during the first three decades of the twentieth century.

This move was not an easy one, the transition from a rural to an urban economy causing considerable social disruption. Traditional work habits and patterns of kinship were disrupted, and opposition to industrial capitalism resulted. It is interesting to find, therefore, that in the early years of the twentieth century many popular songs in the United States were concerned with reinforcing didactically the values of romantic love which underpinned the formation of the nuclear, as opposed to the extended, family (for example, 'A Bird in a Gilded Cage' (1900)). The nuclear family – in which the father and mother customarily had not known one another before meeting and marrying, and for which the values of romantic love were as a consequence an essential rationale – became both a cornerstone of urban life and a symbol of the social mobility that facilitated and characterized it.

However, as industrial capitalism became more established as a way of life during the 1920s, didacticism and celebration gave way to an emphasis on the presumed pleasures of domestic life in an urban setting (for example, 'My Blue Heaven' (1927)). One aspect of this domestic life was the way in which the home became more important, both in reality and symbolically, as a pivotal location for the musical experiences of the urban middle classes. As men went out to work and left women at home, or engaged in social reform outside it, one of women's duties became that of providing musical entertainment in the home at the piano.

The attempt to create a homogeneous 'American identity' in the face of opposition to industrial capitalism and, until World War I, emigration from Central and Eastern Europe, was an expression of the power of white, middle-class society, and was an identity made very much in its image. As a consequence, the music of poorer, working-class white people and of African-American communities tended not to play a central role in the music industry until the 1940s, although from the 1920s onward the record industry and radio played important roles in the dissemination of blues and country music, respectively. During the 1940s and into the 1950s, stresses and resulting structural realignments within the music industry, together with social changes instigated as a consequence of World War II, created more central spaces for country music and rhythm and blues in particular within the music industry. In the context of continuing technological advances, which have facilitated the more effective marketing and distribution of different forms of popular music, cultural and musical heterogeneity has received a more forceful expression through the music industry that was its progeny. As, from the 1970s onward, increasingly sophisticated electronic means for the storing and dissemination of popular music have gradually encompassed the non-Western world, the range of music recorded, marketed and distributed by the music industry has grown exponentially. Some have understood this phenomenon to be characteristic of a 'postmodern' culture which typifies what is taken to be 'late capitalist' societies.

Urbanization and Popular Music in the Non-Western World

Those changes that characterized urbanization in the West have affected the non-Western world as well, generally but not exclusively within a more recent time period. In countries such as Brazil, however, urbanization occurred contemporaneously with that in the United States. The city of São Paulo, for example, doubled its population from 31,500 to 65,000 between 1872 and 1890, and then quadrupled it to 240,000 by 1900 as a consequence of its role as the regional center of commerce and credit for the burgeoning coffee industry (Hahner 1986).

In the non-Western world, social and cultural dislocation has been greatly amplified. This has been reflected through the practises of popular music. Popular music has always been an effective vehicle for expressing the tensions of urban life. As Coplan (1982) has stressed, a basic feature of the metropolitan experience is the availability of choice, whether in terms of life style, peer groups, social identity or musical taste. City dwellers generally become exposed to diverse ideologies, music styles and mass-mediated understandings of the world ('media discourses'), whether deriving from abroad or from distinct communities interacting in the urban environment. It is because of these features that conurbations have become centers for the playing out of questions of social identity, social value and social morality through popular music. In Brazil, for example, the development of the *Carnaval* during the second half of the nineteenth and the early part of the twentieth centuries provided a vehicle for the expression of the working-class identities of black and mulatto Brazilians in opposition to elite, upper-class interests. The *Carnaval* evidenced 'the pervasiveness and persistence of lower-class practices which the upper classes sought to repress through police action' (Hahner 1986, 214).

Urbanization in the non-Western world has generally occurred in a much more rapid, uncontrolled and often socially disruptive manner. For rural migrants, unprecedented exposure to alternative music emanating from the Western music industry has often alienated listeners from ancestral rural idioms and stimulated the development of new hybrid forms. Whether the disaffection from tradition has been experienced as disorienting or as liberating, popular music has often played a crucial role in adaptation to new urban environments. Such adaptation comprises not only reactionary adjustment against change, but also the creation of new senses of social identity and correspondingly new forms of metaphorical cultural expression. One example of this is provided by Erlmann (1991, 156–74), who points to the complex ways in which a genre of Zulu male choral music in South Africa, iscathamiya, has mediated processes of urban adaptation for Zulu migrant workers. As Erlmann concludes (1991, 158), 'migrant performers' iscathamiya songs, lyrics, and choreography, like the expressive symbols of migrants elsewhere, are potent resources for action aiming at the definition of social space and at a secure location within [the] multiple, contradicting worlds' of urban existence.

It is by means of these new senses of identity and their cultural expression that artists and communities establish distinctive places for themselves within their socially heterogeneous surroundings. This process invariably involves what has been termed 'syncretic rearticulation.' Through this process of rearticulation, musicians creatively reinterpret and combine in accordance with changing social values and attendant aesthetic sensibilities previously diverse elements of musical structure and content characteristic of different musical genres (Coplan 1982, 119). Popular musicians in both the non-Western and Western worlds have come to serve as cultural brokers who by these means articulate new metaphors for social identity, negotiating new spaces between the opposed tendencies of the traditional and the modern, the rural and the urban, the local and the global, and thereby mediating between them. An interesting example of this with respect to the opposition between the traditional and the modern, and the rural and the urban, was provided in the West through the urban folk music revival of the late 1940s and 1950s.

Many forms of modern popular music, such as Dominican bachata, Turkish arabesk, Thai luktoong and Peruvian chicha, have arisen in connection with rural migrant underclasses (see Pacini Hernandez 1995; Stokes 1992; Siriyuvasak 1990; Turino 1990; Bullen 1993). As disseminated by the mass media and migrant networks, such musics often circulate back to the countryside, narrowing distinctions beween rural and urban cultures. Other genres, such as the early Argentinian tango and Greek rembétika, have evolved in association with what has on occasion been referred to pejoratively as a 'lumpen proletariat,' a homogeneous group of alienated and sometimes degenerate low-wage workers typically forming the lowest social class during the early stages of urbanization. Such musics are distinguished typically by the frank social realism of their song texts, which ambivalently foreground the vicissitudes of bohemian life

and celebrate the figure of the macho and independent, yet emotionally vulnerable, antihero. Several such musical genres have entered the cultural 'mainstream,' as migrant and underclass people are more assimilated into society, their music becomes more sophisticated, and music industries invest in the new cultural forms. Diasporic communities concentrated in metropolitan centers also come to foster syncretic popular idioms, such as Indo-British bhangra, which subsequently return to the music cultures of ancestral homelands.

As rapid urbanization has brought together people of diverse backgrounds, popular music has served variously as a vehicle for social differentiation, mediation or homogenization. In many cases, popular music has served to maintain ethnic, regional or generational distinctions as social subgroups congregate at their own music clubs, form taste cultures around certain genres or performers, and celebrate favored idioms as expressions of their distinct identity. In other cases, music can serve to mediate differences between people of different backgrounds, or even to unite them, especially as music industries seek mass homogeneous markets which transcend the social barriers between urban dwellers. In cities throughout the world, the coexistence of radically diverse communities and media discourses often promotes postmodern sensibilities and multiple social identities which inform popular music cultures in general (Chambers 1990).

Bibliography

Bullen, Margaret. 1993. 'Chicha in the Shantytowns of Arequipa, Peru.' Popular Music 12(3): 229–44.

Chambers, Iain. 1990. Border Dialogues: Journeys in Postmodernity. New York: Routledge.

Coplan, David. 1982. 'The Urbanisation of African Music: Some Theoretical Observations.' Popular Music 2: 112–29.

Erlmann, Veit. 1991. African Stars: Studies in Black South African Performance. Chicago: University of Chicago Press.

Hahner, June E. 1986. Poverty and Politics: The Urban Poor in Brazil, 1870–1920. Albuquerque, NM: University of New Mexico Press.

Horn, Pamela. 1987. Life and Labour in Rural England, 1760–1850. London: Macmillan.

Meller, H.E. 1976. Leisure and the Changing City, 1870–1914. London: Routledge and Kegan Paul.

Nettl, Bruno, ed. 1978. Eight Urban Musical Cultures: Tradition and Change. Urbana and London: University of Illinois Press.

Pacini Hernandez, Deborah. 1995. Bachata: A Social History of a Dominican Popular Music. Philadelphia: Temple University Press.

Roell, Craig H. 1989. *The Piano in America, 1890–1940*. Chapel Hill, NC: University of North Carolina Press.

Russell, Dave. 1987. *Popular Music in England, 1840–1914: A Social History*. Manchester: Manchester University Press.

Scott, Derek B. 1989. *The Singing Bourgeois: Songs of the Victorian Drawing Room and Parlour*. Milton Keynes: Open University Press.

Shepherd, John. 1982. *Tin Pan Alley*. London and Boston: Routledge and Kegan Paul.

Siriyuvasak, Ubonrat. 1990. 'Commercialising the Sound of the People: *Pleng Luktoong* and the Thai Pop Music Industry.' *Popular Music* 9(1): 61–78.

Stokes, Martin. 1992. *The Arabesk Debate: Music and Musicians in Modern Turkey*. Oxford: Oxford University Press.

Turino, Thomas. 1990. 'Somos el Perú: "Cumbia Andina" and the Children of Andean Migrants in Lima.' *Studies in Latin American Popular Culture* 9: 15–37.

Sheet Music

Donaldson, Walter, comp., and Whiting, George, lyr. 1927. 'My Blue Heaven.' New York: Leo Feist Inc.

Von Tilzer, Harry, comp., and Lamb, Arthur J., lyr. 1900. 'A Bird in a Gilded Cage.' New York: Shapiro, Bernstein and Von Tilzer.

JOHN SHEPHERD and PETER MANUEL

War and Armed Conflict

The relationship of popular music to war and armed conflict may be examined from a variety of perspectives. Here, four principal, interconnected headings will be used: function; subject matter; opportunities; and social and cultural consequences. The function of popular music includes the uses of music by those involved in war and armed conflict both within and beyond the actual theater of operation. Subjects drawn from war and featured in popular music (especially, but not uniquely, in song lyrics) range from actual incidents to ideological issues at stake. The opportunities that war and armed conflict present for new musical activity can include artistic, commercial and technological developments, or combinations of these. Popular music's involvement in the social and cultural consequences of war can be seen in a variety of contexts, from phenomena such as population movement to attempts to link music to humanitarian action.

The Function of Popular Music in War and Armed Conflict

In the theater of war and armed conflict, the most common practical function of popular music for a long period of time was to regulate and accompany camp duties. This 'field music' could include providing signals during actual military engagements. (In many wars, up to and including the Gulf War of 1991, musicians also acted as stretcher-bearers and medical assistants.) Music and song also played a part in the circulation of news of events on the battlefield. Frequently, this extended beyond the battlefields themselves. In the eighteenth century, the broadside ballad, for example, developed in England and exported to Australia, Canada and the United States, reported the events of war for the populace. In the Balkans, Russia, Finland and the Middle East, the narrative folk song served a similar function. In the period before the development of mass media, therefore, these song texts acted as important disseminators of news events surrounding war.

Important though both these functions were, music's role in the psychology of warfare was more significant and pervasive, stretching across the history of warfare up to the present day. It was a role played first and foremost in battle itself. As early as the time of the Crusades, minstrels acted as a rallying point in battle, using music both to attempt to strike terror into the enemy and to foster a sense of solidarity within their own forces. In the early modern and modern periods, the wailing sound of the bagpipe was used by British and Canadian military units to unnerve the enemy. In Africa, Zulu tribesmen used chanting, dance (with a distinctive upright posture and high stamping movement) and forms of percussion (the rhythmic beating of spear against shield) for similar purposes.

In more recent times, an unusual instance of music used to put pressure on an enemy occurred in Panama in 1989, when US forces seeking to undermine the unofficial Panamanian leader, General Manuel Noriega (who had taken refuge in the Vatican-owned papal palace, after declaring Panama to be at war with the United States), directed a barrage of loud rock music at him throughout the night. As with the Zulu tribesmen, the pressure was both psychological and physical, but with the additional dimension of modern amplification. The sound from the loudspeakers had the added practical advantage of obscuring voices engaged in actual negotiation.

Music has also regularly played an important role in the maintenance of morale among troops. The physical activity of marching to music is perhaps the most straightforward example of this. Numerous songs relating to fighting in some form found their way into the repertoires of soldiers because of their ability to keep spirits buoyant. Many were unambiguously rousing, while others, such as Broadway composer Frank Loesser's World War II song 'Praise the Lord and Pass the Ammunition' (1942), humorously recognized some inevitable contradictions. Morale among soldiers could also be maintained by negative means, through songs that were severely – often ironically – critical of their superiors. Brand (1962), for example, reported on the decline of patriotic numbers among US troops and the appearance of lyrics such as 'The General got the Croix deGuerre/ The sonofa----- was never there' (190). British soldiers in World War I, faced with the grim awfulness of the trenches, were particularly attracted to an ambiguous type of song, with music hall associations, that appeared on the surface to offer a low-key acceptance of the inevitability of the horror, but at the same time sought to create solidarity from common knowledge, ironically communicated. A good example is 'Pack Up Your Troubles' (1915), with its lines 'What's the use of worrying?/It never was worth while, so/Pack up your troubles in your old kit-bag,/And smile, smile, smile.'

In any armed conflict, music's beneficial psychological effect may be experienced equally by those at home. Music may be turned to by the families and friends of those in the armed forces in an attempt to deal with the stress of separation and uncertainty and, indeed, with the grief of death. Such stress may be reduced by the knowledge that troops at the front and families and friends at home can share the same music, at a time when they can share little else. For their part, military commanders have tended to be suspicious of music of this type if it seems to yield too much to the emotions. In the American Civil War (1861–65), for example, one of the bestselling songs, both at home and among the troops (of both armies, Union and Confederate), Henry Tucker's and Charles Carroll Sawyer's 'Weeping Sad and Lonely, or When This Cruel War Is Over' (1863), was said to have been banned by military commanders for the demoralizing effect it had on men about to fight (Hamm 1979, 240).

The same conflict provides examples of two related functions of song in wartime: to aid recruitment, and to bolster conviction in the justice of the cause. James Sloane Gibbons's poem 'We Are Coming, Father Abra'am,' written in rapid response to President Lincoln's call for volunteers in 1862, was equally rapidly set to music first by Luther O. Emerson and in subsequent months by several others (although, as Hamm wryly notes, 'far more people sang it than responded to its message' (1979, 239)). Probably the most famous example of a rallying song that breathes conviction is Julia Ward Howe's 'Battle Hymn of the Republic' (1862). Written to fit the well-known melody that had been both evangelical hymn and soldier's song, with its rousing chorus 'Glory! glory! hallelujah,' Howe's lyrics merged the figure of divine retribution with that of the

fighter for truth: 'He hath loosed the fateful lightning of His terrible swift sword/His truth is marching on.'

The Subject Matter of Popular Music in War and Armed Conflict

War and the Thematic Content of Popular Song

The song texts produced at various stages of any conflict provide an anatomy of war for public consumption. Although details of specific combat incidents appear in many songs, the creators of song texts have often been more interested in the rich variety of ancillary activity – and its effects on human emotions – that war brings in its wake. As could be expected, reactions to events and situations expressed in song form vary hugely. The issue of recruitment is a good example. As Lloyd (1967, 252) points out, with reference to a collection by Wolfgang Steinitz (1954), in the eighteenth and nineteenth centuries soldiers' and working people's songs in Germany included many that were against recruitment, whereas relatively few such songs were produced in Britain in the same period. In the twentieth century, as the United States entered World War II, 'the draft' was an issue for blues musicians. Some, such as 'Big' Bill Broonzy, confessed that 'when I heard my number called, oooh Lord, I couldn't feel happy to save my soul,' while Arthur 'Big Boy' Crudup remarked with some irony that his country's need for him in war at least meant that 'now if I feel murder, don't have to break the county law' (Oliver 1990, 235–36).

The approach of the blues musician to this and other subjects, such as the moment of separation between loved ones and the lure of fighting (for examples, see Oliver 1990, 237, 239), was almost always to personalize it, putting the singer at the center of the narrative, thus offering a particular individual perspective within a community-centered genre. In other cultures – for example, in the songs to emerge from Latin American revolutionary struggles – the passion with which particular events and activities are recorded is, in the words of Pring-Mill (1987), 'not so much that of a singer's personal response as that of a collective interpretation of events' (179). In the particular context of Nicaragua during the time of the Sandinista revolution, such songs could take on a severely practical purpose. Over half of the tracks on the Frente Sandinista de Liberación Nacional (FSLN) LP *Guitarra Armada* (1979), by the brothers Carlos and Luís Enrique Mejía Godoy, are concerned with passing on information about caring for small arms and making explosives. One particular track, 'Carabina M-1,' describes in detail how to disassemble and reassemble a weapon (Pring-Mill 1987, 180).

War songs also seem to be one of the very few areas of popular song where hatred for others is commonly expressed. In some cases, as, for example, in blues attacking the Japanese after Pearl Harbor, singers are responding to what they perceive as a national mood. In others, the motive involves a hatred that is more parochial. In the sectarian struggles in Northern Ireland, for instance, Protestant loyalist songs celebrate the death of IRA members and sympathizers in songs such as 'The Ballad of Michael Stone' (Stone murdered mourners at an IRA funeral in 1988) (Chapman 2000, 36).

The extensive use of war-related subject matter in popular music is far from limited to a fact-based, literal approach. Progressive rock acts such as Genesis have used depictions of battles for dramatic content ('The Battle of Epping Forest,' 1973), their songs dealing with illusion and fantasy without any direct political content. Many pop songs also deal in a fanciful way with themes such as urban apocalypse and intergalactic warfare, while images of war are very often used as metaphors for emotional conflicts, as in Pat Benatar's 1983 hit, 'Love Is a Battlefield.' In Pink Floyd's *The Wall* (1979) and *The Final Cut* (1983), war and its aftermath appear as subject, as image and as semi-autobiographical rationale (lyricist Roger Waters' father's death in action in 1944 is a constant theme in both). Waters also drew an unusual comparison between war and rock concerts, saying '[p]eople at those big things seem to like being treated badly, to have it so loud and distorted that it really hurts' (quoted in Schaffner 1991, 210).

Ideology, Politics and Song Content

Popular song can serve either to support the dominant ideological rationale of the day behind war and conflict or to oppose it radically. During the 1898 Spanish-American War, highly sentimentalized images of patriotism were deployed within popular song texts as more or less overt pieces of propaganda. In thematic terms, songs such as Paul Dresser's 'Your God Comes First, Your Country Next, Then Mother Dear' (1898) dealt with highly stereotypical images of heroism, mother–son relationships and the honor of serving one's country. Interestingly, the waltz form was used in many of these songs, further reinforcing the link between this form and a backward-looking, sentimentalized view of society (as in 'In the Good Old Summertime' (1902); see Hamm 1979, 296). Stock musical signifiers such as bugle-call figures were commonplace, offering evidence also of the stockpiling of musical information that could be deployed by composers to evince images of war and martiality.

In nineteenth-century Britain, the institution of the music hall tended to support the Tory establishment, providing rousing, jingoistic song texts for performance throughout the Crimean War in the 1850s. In the 1870s, music hall performers backed the party's anti-Russian

stance, and a leading music hall composer of the day, G.W. Hunt, composed a number of songs that implicitly attacked the foreign policy of Liberal prime minister William Gladstone. The song texts of the music hall, as Russell (1987) has shown, became increasingly imperialist and xenophobic, leading to strident anti-German feeling in the early years of the twentieth century. During the early months of the Great War (1914–18), the music hall played an active propagandizing role in recruitment, equating manliness with martiality in many cases. However, as the conflict progressed and the genocide became undeniable, the blithe patriotism of the initial wartime repertoire was toned down (Russell 1987, 123), again evidencing how popular song responds to the circumstances of armed conflict. Those in active combat, however, had a very different repertoire from that found in the bombast of the music hall. Sentimentalized depictions of universals (family, homeland and so on) were commonplace, and among the most popular songs were Jack Judge's and Harry Williams's 'It's a Long, Long Way to Tipperary' (1912) and Haydn Wood's and Frederick Weatherly's 'Roses of Picardy' (1916). Although the horror of the Great War effectively put an end to the worst excesses of patriotic wartime song, the British tabloid press's coverage of the Falklands War between Britain and Argentina in 1982 demonstrated conclusively that the xenophobia of the music hall era continued to play a role four generations later.

During World War II, both the Allied forces and the countries supporting Hitler produced propagandizing, morale-boosting songs. The British 'forces' sweetheart,' Vera Lynn, sang songs such as 'The White Cliffs of Dover' and 'We'll Meet Again,' which again put forward a romanticized, patriotic view of the homeland, while Bud Flanagan and Chesney Allen continued the tradition of comedic wartime song that had developed out of the music hall with their version of Noel Gay's and Ralph Butler's anti-German song 'Run, Rabbit, Run.' On rare occasions, certain songs have such a broad appeal as to be popular with both sides. One such song was 'Lili Marlene' (sometimes 'Lilli Marlene'), Norbert Schultze's setting of a World War I poem that became a hit first with the German Afrikakorps in World War II, in the version by Danish-born singer Lale Andersen. It was adopted by the British 8th Army, and English-language versions were recorded by Anne Shelton for the English market and, most famously, Marlene Dietrich for the North American market. The song was also popular among the Italians and the French (Gammond 1991, 346; Shapiro and Pollock 1985, 1095).

The late 1950s and early 1960s saw the clear emergence of the idea that it was possible to link commercially successful popular music and political opposition to war and the weapons of war. Central to this was the tradition of songs of social comment, in particular that which developed on the political left in the United States in the 1930s. Partly quiescent during the McCarthy era of the late 1940s and early 1950s, this tradition was to reemerge among a younger generation, who acknowledged a debt – in both practical and ideological inspiration – to connecting figures such as Pete Seeger. In subsequent years, songs such as Bob Dylan's 'A Hard Rain's A-Gonna Fall' (1963), UB40's 'The Earth Dies Screaming' (1980) and Billy Bragg's 'Between the Wars' (1985) helped to mobilize support for extramusical campaigns such as the Campaign for Nuclear Disarmament (CND), and demonstrated that popular music can help shape and determine social attitudes.

The counterculture that emerged in the United States in the 1960s, and that was actively critical of the foreign policy of presidents Johnson and Nixon in the Vietnam war, made music central both to its means of expressing opposition and to the alternatives it espoused. The anti-Vietnam movement was pan-generic in terms of musical style, in that rock, soul, folk and a variety of other musical styles all became politicized and critiqued the Establishment line, with Edwin Starr's declamatory soul anthems 'War' (1970) and 'Stop the War Now' (1971) being the most outspoken. Not all music was anti-war, however. 'The Ballad of the Green Berets' (1966), an unashamedly pro-war recording by Staff Sergeant Barry Sadler, for example, was a million-seller.

Images of warfare have also been used metaphorically in support of various social and political causes. The punk group the Clash recorded 'White Riot' in 1977 and 'English Civil War' in 1978, while militant Rastafarian singers such as Bob Marley and Max Romeo (particularly in his *War Ina Babylon*, 1976) have used images of warfare to couch their 'militant' religio-political programs.

The conduct of war has often been accompanied by outbreaks of censorship as a means of regulating the flow of potentially embarrassing, incendiary or indelicate songs. While such censorship has often been government-controlled, in some instances the media have censored themselves. One such occasion occurred at the start of the 1991 Gulf War, when local radio stations in the United Kingdom were issued with a list of 67 songs that were deemed 'inappropriate to play.' These included songs dealing directly with armed conflict, such as Status Quo's 'In the Army Now' (1986), as well as the bizarrely incongruous, such as Rod Stewart's 'Sailing' (1975) and Phil Collins's 'In the Air Tonight' (1981), whose subject matter was somehow seen as likely to offend members of the armed forces and their relatives. The Bristol group Massive Attack was even forced to change its name to

Massive in order to get its single, 'Unfinished Sympathy' (1991), promoted.

One of the more complex recent examples of government involvement in popular music for political purposes, including the conduct of war, occurred in Serbia under the regime of Slobodan Milosevic. To begin with, Milosevic used the nationalist potential of 'neofolk' (folk music forms using rock and pop instruments) to marshal political support among the considerable numbers of the population who were leaving the rural areas for the towns. Neofolk and its audience were deliberately contrasted with urban rock, with its allegiances to the West and Western values. But, as Gordy (1999, 105) notes, in 1994 the regime turned against neofolk and its associations with nationalist mobilization and promoted instead a mixture of techno, dance and folk called 'turbofolk.' In contrast to neofolk, turbofolk, which was Serbia's dominant popular genre during the Balkan conflicts of the 1990s, 'was rarely engaged with national or any other political questions, instead rapturously urging among the ruins the pursuit of leisure, luxury and wholesome happiness' (Gordy 1999, 134). One of the stars of turbofolk, Ceca, was married to the notorious military leader (and later indicted war criminal) Arkan.

Serbia also offers an example of the continued belief in music's role in resistance movements. Although doubts have since been cast on its sources of funding, the Serbian student resistance movement Otpor! has been widely credited with helping to mobilize anti-Milosevic activity. To do so, it integrated a variety of rock-based music into its campaigning.

The Opportunities Presented by War and Armed Conflict

The complexities of wartime have not only provided subject matter for popular music, but have also offered new opportunities for its production, dissemination and consumption. Historically, the first conflict to offer such opportunities on a large scale was the American Civil War, and the first to seize these opportunities were music publishers in the northern states. Firms such as Root and Cady in Chicago were quick to respond to patriotic fervor ('The First Gun Is Fired' (1861) was published three days after the incident that precipitated the outbreak of war between North and South). Root and Cady worked closely with its songwriters, especially George F. Root (brother of the publishing-house partner Ebenezer Root) and Henry Clay Work. Root's 'The Battle Cry of Freedom' (1862) sold at least 350,000 copies (Hamm 1979, 232). Meanwhile, in the southern states, the decline in available music from northern publishers – a byproduct of the war – encouraged new publishers to set up in business. Not all the successful songs of the time were songs of war. Publishers on both sides also responded to an apparent need for songs of love and devotion. (One of these, 'Aura Lee' (1861), would later provide the melody for an Elvis Presley hit, 'Love Me Tender.')

No one at the time of the American Civil War accused publishers or songwriters of exploiting the situation for profit; their efforts were judged according to their ability to maintain morale and inspire patriotism. By the time of World War II, the music industry, by now well established, was nevertheless more circumspect in its response. Music was produced to fit a variety of moods, but production did not actually increase, nor did sales rise. And indeed, in the United States, any efforts to demonstrate the commitment of the music industry to the cause were hampered by the recording ban imposed by the American Federation of Musicians (AFM) in 1942. Even without the ban, however, production was set to fall as a consequence of war: the material from which 78 rpm records were made was imported from Asia and supplies were affected. In this context, the music industry, in the shape of RCA-Victor, willingly fell in with the government initiative to produce recordings (so-called V-discs) especially for US troops overseas.

At the same time, World War II was the first major conflict to provide the music industry with a different kind of opportunity. Radio, by then established in many parts of the world – though by no means all – as the principal medium through which popular music was heard, could use music to cement a relationship with the nation.

In the area of technology, World War II also provided – in part fortuitously – the basis for the postwar growth in importance of magnetic tape, when US troops returned home with German Magnetophon tape machines, manufactured by AEG using iron oxide–coated tape made by I.G. Farben (Millard 1995, 197–98). This was not simply a tale of the lucky spoils of war – scientists and engineers had been working on tape and tape machines in different countries for some time – but the German equipment provided the basis for US manufacturers, such as Ampex, to begin production in the postwar period.

The years after World War II saw a realignment of the global economy. The long period of prosperity between 1945 and 1965 was predicated on US influence. The world market became dominated by multinational corporations, and there was a concomitant development of new technological forms based on electrical rather than electromagnetic modes typical of 'mass culture' (see Middleton 1990, 14). This had a profound effect on the development of the music industry, as new production

methods and new means of sound retrieval facilitated the rise of rock 'n' roll in the mid-1950s.

The Social and Cultural Consequences of War and Armed Conflict

One particular – and particularly frequent – consequence of war and armed conflict has been population displacement. Sometimes in such displacement music can take on the role of sustaining an identity, as it did for many Chilean political exiles, in Europe and elsewhere, following the military coup that overthrew the government of Salvador Allende in 1973. In this case, displacement and political exile as a consequence of armed conflict also brought the music to the attention of people in other lands and from other cultures, who were otherwise unlikely to have discovered it. If, in that example, the process of familiarization that followed displacement did not lead to extensive musical interaction, there have been important instances in which it did. One such case involved the large-scale movement during World War II of African Americans and whites from the southern US states to the cities of the North and the west coast. Engineered to meet the needs of industry, especially the defense industry, this population displacement resulted in new encounters within and between cultural groups. It was on the basis of this movement of people and the subsequent processes of exposure, familiarization and stylistic modification that country music went on to become a nationally popular music (Malone 1985, 178–79). The movement of African Americans to the west coast in the same period (as large, though not as frequently referred to in blues history, as the movement to northern cities such as Chicago) resulted in a rich cross-fertilization of styles both within the blues and between the blues and other idioms (such as crooning) that was to lay the foundation for much music later collected under the term 'rhythm and blues.'

Although not on such a sweeping scale, cultural encounters among members of the armed forces have been another significant consequence of war. Forced together by circumstances, military personnel have brought others from different social and cultural backgrounds into contact with the music that formed their own tastes and practises. If the most immediate cultural consequences of such contacts have been at the level of the individual, in the aftermath of war such individuals have often met and formed alliances on the basis of tastes acquired during active service. Many members of postwar jazz bands in Britain, for example, gained their knowledge and motivation from wartime exposure to the music from enthusiasts in neighboring bunk beds.

A further, rather different role for music in the social and cultural consequences of war can be found in its presence within humanitarian responses to the human suffering that war has caused. Some examples of this concern single, morale-boosting events, as when US singer Paul Robeson sang to a vast open-air crowd in the center of war-damaged Liverpool. Others involve more concerted action. In postwar Bosnia in 1997, for example, a music center was established in the town of Mostar. With funding arranged by the British charity War Child, a network of organizations dedicated to helping children affected by war, and with the active participation of Italian opera singer Luciano Pavarotti and rock musician Brian Eno (among others), the center was set up to provide a range of activity to aid rehabilitation, including music workshops, recording sessions and music therapy. In this particular example, it is noteworthy also that some of the same musical celebrities who were principal supporters of the project played central roles in attempts to resolve difficulties that first emerged in 1999 over accusations of corruption at War Child.

Bibliography

Brand, Oscar. 1962. *The Ballad Mongers: Rise of the Modern Folk Song*. New York: Funk & Wagnalls.

Chapman, Glyn. 2000. *The Political Form and Function of Ulster Loyalist Music*. Unpublished M.A. thesis, Institute of Popular Music, University of Liverpool.

Gammond, Peter. 1991. *The Oxford Companion to Popular Music*. Oxford: Oxford University Press.

Gordy, Eric D. 1999. *The Culture of Power in Serbia: Nationalism and the Destruction of Alternatives*. University Park, PA: Pennsylvania State University Press.

Hamm, Charles. 1979. *Yesterdays: Popular Song in America*. New York: Norton.

Hencke, David. 2001. 'A Charity Caught Up in Chaos.' *The Guardian* (10 January).

Lloyd, A.L. 1967. *Folk Song in England*. London: Lawrence and Wishart.

Malone, Bill C. 1985. *Country Music, U.S.A*. Rev. ed. Austin, TX: University of Texas Press.

Middleton, Richard. 1990. *Studying Popular Music*. Milton Keynes: Open University Press.

Millard, Andre J. 1995. *America on Record: A History of Recorded Sound*. Cambridge: Cambridge University Press.

Oliver, Paul. 1990. *Blues Fell This Morning: Meaning in the Blues*. 2nd ed. Cambridge: Cambridge University Press.

Palmer, Roy. 1990. *'What a Lovely War!': British Soldiers' Songs from the Boer War to the Present Day*. London: Joseph.

Perrone, James E. 2001. *Songs of the Vietnam Conflict*. Westport, CT: Greenwood Press.

Pring-Mill, Robert. 1987. 'The Roles of Revolutionary Song – A Nicaraguan Assessment.' *Popular Music* 6(2): 179–89.

Russell, Dave. 1987. *Popular Music in England, 1840–1914: A Social History*. Manchester: Manchester University Press.

Sample, Duane. 1985. 'The Popular Music of the Spanish-American War: How Popular Was It?' In *Popular Music Perspectives, 2*, ed. David Horn. Göteborg and Exeter: IASPM, 360–66.

Schaffner, Nicholas. 1991. *Saucerful of Secrets: The Pink Floyd Odyssey*. London: Sidgwick & Jackson.

Shapiro, Nat, and Pollock, Bruce, eds. 1985. *Popular Music, 1920–1979: Revised Cumulation*. 3 vols. Detroit, MI: Gale Research.

Steinitz, Wolfgang. 1954. *Deutsche Volkslieder demokratischen Charakters* [German Folk Songs of Democratic Character]. 2 vols. Berlin: Akademie-Verlag.

Sheet Music

Dresser, Paul, comp. and lyr. 1898. 'Your God Comes First, Your Country Next, Then Mother Dear.' New York: Howley, Haviland & Co.

Emerson, Luther O., comp., and (Gibbons, James Sloane), lyr. 1862. 'We Are Coming, Father Abra'am.' Boston, MA: Oliver Ditson & Co.

Evans, George, comp., and Shields, Ron, lyr. 1902. 'In the Good Old Summertime.' New York: Howley, Haviland and Dresser.

Gay, Noel, comp., and Butler, Ralph, lyr. 1939. 'Run, Rabbit, Run.' London: Mills Music.

Howe, Julia Ward, comp. and lyr. 1862. 'Battle Hymn of the Republic, "Glory, Hallelujah."' Boston, MA: Ditson.

Judge, Jack, and Williams, Harry, comps. and lyrs. 1912. 'It's a Long, Long Way to Tipperary.' London: Feldman.

Loesser, Frank, comp. and lyr. 1942. 'Praise the Lord and Pass the Ammunition.' New York: Famous Music.

Poulton, George R., comp., and Fosdick, W.W., lyr. 1861. 'Aura Lee; or, the Maid with the Golden Hair.' Cincinnati: Church.

Powell, Felix, comp., and Asaf, George, lyr. 1915. 'Pack Up Your Troubles in Your Old Kit Bag.' London: Francis, Day & Hunter.

Root, George F., comp. and lyr. 1861. 'The First Gun Is Fired.' Chicago: Root & Cady.

Root, George F., comp. and lyr. 1862. 'The Battle Cry of Freedom.' Chicago: Root & Cady.

Schultze, Norbert, comp., and Leip, Hans, lyr. 1940. 'Lili Marlene.' Berlin: Apollo. (English-language version with words by Tommie Connor. New York: Marks, 1944.)

Tucker, Henry, comp., and Sawyer, Charles Carroll, lyr.

1863. 'Weeping Sad and Lonely, or When This Cruel War Is Over.' Brooklyn, NY: Sawyer & Thompson.

Wood, Haydn, comp., and Weatherly, Frederick E., lyr. 1916. 'Roses of Picardy.' London: Chappell.

Discographical References

Andersen, Lale. 'Lili Marlene.' *Cabaret's Golden Age, Vol. 1.* Pearl 9727. 1939; *1993*: UK.

Benatar, Pat. 'Love Is a Battlefield.' *Live from Earth.* Chrysalis 41444. *1983*: USA.

Bragg, Billy. 'Between the Wars' (EP). Go! Discs AGOEP 1. *1985*: UK.

Broonzy, 'Big' Bill. 'That Old Number of Mine (Number 158).' OKeh 06080. 1940: USA.

Clash, The. 'English Civil War (Johnny Comes Marching Home).' *Give 'Em Enough Rope.* CBS 82431. *1978*: UK.

Clash, The. 'White Riot.' CBS 5058. *1977*: UK.

Collins, Phil. 'In the Air Tonight.' Virgin VSK 102. *1981*: UK.

Crudup, Arthur 'Big Boy.' 'Give Me a 32-20.' Bluebird B-9019. 1942: USA.

Dietrich, Marlene. 'Lili Marlene.' *Some of the Best.* Delta 12651. *1996*: UK.

Dylan, Bob. 'A Hard Rain's A-Gonna Fall.' *The Freewheelin' Bob Dylan.* Columbia PCT-8786. *1963*: USA.

Flanagan and Allen. 'Run, Rabbit, Run.' *We'll Smile Again.* Living Era CDAJA 5194. *1996*: UK.

Genesis. 'The Battle of Epping Forest.' *Selling England by the Pound.* Charisma 6060. *1973*: UK.

Guitarra Armada: Music of the Sandinista Guerrillas. Indica MC-1147. *1979*: Costa Rica.

Lynn, Vera. 'We'll Meet Again.' *We'll Meet Again.* Telstar STAR 2369. *1989*: UK.

Lynn, Vera. 'The White Cliffs of Dover.' *We'll Meet Again.* Telstar STAR 2369. *1989*: UK.

Massive Attack. 'Unfinished Sympathy.' Wild Bunch WBRS 2. *1991*: UK.

Pink Floyd. *The Final Cut.* Harvest SHPF 1983. *1983*: UK.

Pink Floyd. *The Wall.* Harvest SHWD 411. *1979*: UK.

Presley, Elvis. 'Love Me Tender.' RCA 47-6643. *1956*: USA.

Romeo, Max, and the Upsetters. *War Ina Babylon.* Mango 9392. *1976*: UK.

Sadler, Staff Sgt. Barry. 'The Ballad of the Green Berets.' RCA 8739. *1966*: USA.

Shelton, Anne. 'Lili Marlene.' *Here's Anne Shelton.* Hallmark 306282. *1997*: UK.

Starr, Edwin. 'Stop the War Now.' Tamla Motown TMG 764. *1971*: USA.

Starr, Edwin. 'War.' Tamla Motown TMG 754. *1970*: USA.

Status Quo. 'In the Army Now.' Vertigo QUO 22. *1986*: UK.

Stewart, Rod. 'Sailing.' Warner Brothers K 16600. *1975*: USA.

UB40. 'The Earth Dies Screaming.' Graduate GRAD 10. *1980*: UK.

DAVID HORN and DAVID BUCKLEY

Youth

Introduction

The term 'youth' denotes a segment of the population – a sociological and demographic category of people at a variously defined early stage of existence; it also refers to the state of being young, and to the qualities typically associated with that state, including spiritedness, freshness, curiosity and rebelliousness. A substantial amount of scholarship has taken for granted that a special relationship exists between youth and popular music, not least because of the large number of song lyrics dealing with youth-related themes.

Regardless of the veracity of this assumed connection, it has remained a dominant, somewhat commonsensical perspective for the study of popular music: typically, what counts as 'popular music' is a musical form or practise that appears to be primarily expressive of or important to young audiences, consumers, fans, producers and innovators. This is by no means exclusively the case, nor has the music of young people been the only defining feature for popular music scholarship (research on folk and country music has provided important exceptions to this). Nonetheless, connections to youthful audiences or producers have typically conferred a certain mark of legitimacy on a popular musical form or practise, in that such a form or practise can be said to be 'new,' in contrast to associations with 'the old,' and belonging to a constituency, community or historical period, however imagined. Arguably, a reluctance to examine in the same detail the musical predilections of other age categories has been a blind spot for the study of popular music – one that has been made increasingly problematic by the historical instability of the definition of the term 'youth' itself.

The Emergence of Discourses of Youth, Protection and Surveillance

'Youth' is understood as a phase in the process of maturation, overlapping with a number of other terms, including 'adolescent,' 'young adult,' 'minor,' 'teenager' and 'juvenile.' As a denotation of both a segment of the general population and a set of characteristics associated with a stage in life, the term is vicissitudinary. Those considered as 'youth' change historically and contextually, and the description 'youthful' can have a variety of applications. Amply apparent is the fact that youth is not a timeless, natural social grouping or quality, nor is it the result of an essential assortment of biological attributes. Rather, it is the product of historical and cultural forces; and popular music, whether perceived as sound or style, located at clubs, concert halls or home, found in films, magazines, radio or television, is one shifting manifestation of those historical and cultural forces that form affiliations and communities of youth, and that both construct and circulate reigning ideas about youth. The proliferation in the late 1950s and early 1960s of songs addressing their recipients as young or teenaged – for example, 'Only Sixteen,' 'A Teenager in Love' and 'Young Love' – provides one example of this phenomenon.

It is especially important for cultural analysis to treat youth as a discursive construct, mediating understandings of its bracketing categories of 'childhood' and 'adulthood.' For this reason, Hartley (1984) describes youth as a scandalous category: it sullies the boundaries between child and adult, and as such it threatens the stability of those two categories. Given this perspective, any analysis of youth may wish to begin with a discussion of the lines of connection between certain characteristics and a segment of the population in order to inquire how youth, its qualities and culture, *is imagined* as unified and coherent.

The more prevalent connotations associated with youth stem from the impression that its members are not yet fully formed social beings. This theme has been directly addressed in such songs as Eddie Cochrane's 'Summertime Blues,' Felice and Boudleaux Bryant's 'Wake Up Little Susie,' recorded by the Everly Brothers, Nirvana's 'Smells Like Teen Spirit' and Liz Phair's 'Help Me Mary.' Youth indicates a time before complete integration into the world of the adult, and it is frequently treated as somewhat separate from the core operations of a social order. Youth as adult-in-process implies that it holds equal potential for both successful and failed socialization; consequently, there has been abundant discussion of the need for protection of the young in order to guard against insufficient or inappropriate training for adult life. Often, public policy actions are taken in the name of youth; however, as Acland (1995) argues, the concern is, in fact, less with the welfare of youth, and more with the maintenance and reproduction of particular ideas of the adult world. This has led some to suggest that, as Hebdige (1987) puts it, 'youth is present only when its presence is a problem, or is regarded as a problem' (17). The most extreme moments of anxiety with respect to youth result in instances of moral panic (see, for instance, Cohen 1972; and, for a more contemporary critique, McRobbie 1994).

Equally significantly, this position of partial exteriority to the social affords youth some special freedoms.

Typically, youth is a period of life characterized by the practises of 'misrule,' that is, of transgressive and disruptive behavior. Such activities, some of which may be ritualized, are met alternately with degrees of tolerance and disapproval, depending not only on prevailing boundaries for social experimentation but also on the youth community involved. For instance, ideas of femininity dictate a different policing of girls than of boys. Hudson (1984) argues that femininity and adolescence are partially contradictory constructs, with the result that 'young girls' attempts to be accepted as "young women" are always liable to be undermined (subverted) by the perceptions of them as childish [or] immature' (31–32). Similarly, the frequent selective policing of some musical forms (for instance, censorship debates around rap and heavy metal) and of some musical practises (for instance, local restrictions on raves) is, at least in part, motivated by a double impulse of concern for and fear of young audiences. In short, an analysis of the surveillance of the young requires attention to dimensions of class, ethnicity and gender.

Beyond an expectation on the part of the adult world that young people are likely to behave rebelliously, the generally high degree of regulation of youth has resulted in a tendency for young people to actively attempt to carve out spaces specifically for their own activities. This has taken the form of direct challenges to some laws, as in the case of taggers (graffiti artists), or of creative interpretations of public space, as exemplified by skateboarders. Certainly, one consequence of the surveillance of the young – a policing that is intensified for certain, additionally marginal young populations – is, on their part, an active and creative mode of appropriation. Among other outcomes – and, some may say, quite paradoxically – this can spark additional innovation in cultural life. The work of Skelton and Valentine (1998) on the spatial dimensions of youth culture presents documentation of the formation of precisely this kind of cultural identity, with research on British-Chinese youth, disabled youth, 'riot grrrls', youth gangs, ravers and punk squatters. Further, this work highlights the changing determinants of youth culture as indicated by social location, offering analyses of home, school, workplace, street and club.

A dominant approach has suggested that a state between childhood and adulthood did not exist in pre-industrial societies in Europe, and that it was the product of Enlightenment thinking. Indeed, Jean-Jacques Rousseau has often been credited as the first philosopher of 'adolescence,' seeing it as a form of 'second birth.' Prior to this, adulthood appeared rather early and, by many accounts, abruptly, in premodern societies. Often, certain rituals of inclusion, of relatively short duration, marked entrance into the adult world. The idea of an extended period of transition did not arise until the advent of educational institutions, military conscription, wage-labor and lengthening life expectancy. In this respect, many have pointed to the coincidence of industrialization and the 'birth' of the adolescent (see Ariès 1962). This has informed a predominant view that youth is a cultural construct, invented from the ideas of specific historical periods, and, further, that there is a special relationship between youth and modernity (Musgrove 1964). The experience of modernity, with its associated social and cultural upheaval, has thus been perceived as intertwined with the contemporary manifestation of youth; in other words, the complexity of the modern world, its mutating adult roles, its uncertainty of life's expectations and what some would characterize as an abiding anomie demand a lengthy process of development, maturation and training. Such a view has led many to take the cultures of the young as a gauge or metaphor of sorts for the general condition of modern and postmodern life. Often, innovative dances and musics – for instance, swing, rock 'n' roll, hip-hop and techno – have become symbolic of their time. For instance, many studies have argued that the kinds of aural collage used in some hip-hop, via sampling, are a form especially associated with postmodernity (see Hebdige 1987). McRobbie (1994) asserts that a continued, if problematized, study of youth is necessary precisely because 'youth remains a site of cultural innovation' (179). Merely acknowledging the high volume and turnover of cultural forms associated with youth serves as a reminder 'of the extent to which young people tell us a good deal about the scale and the dynamics of social change itself' (McRobbie 1994, 179).

Selective access to schooling – that is, an extended period of training – meant that the modern concept of youth appeared first among upper-class families, while the demands of child labor led to the continuation of the preindustrial precociousness of the young among the working class. By the twentieth century, this notion of youth as a lengthening phase in life and as a denotation of a social group in need of protection had been 'democratized' as it became fixed as a 'natural' stage that deserved special attention and treatment (for instance, compulsory education, juvenile courts, age-of-majority rules and so on) (Gillis 1974). For example, the work of G. Stanley Hall (1904) helped to introduce 'adolescence' into the popular vernacular, describing it as a time of psychological turmoil and stress, hence warranting extraordinary attention. As a seemingly 'natural' category, youth connotatively harbors both the fears and the potentials of that stage of life.

This view of a distinct historical break, in theories about the coincidence of maturation and industrialization, has been challenged. Some research has suggested that the differences between contemporary formations of youth and those associated with preindustrial life are less distinct than previously supposed, and that most of the attributes of youth, including increased instruction for the adult world and the rituals of 'misrule,' were already evident in the centuries before the Enlightenment, if not earlier. It has been argued that the very terms 'modern' and 'traditional' as applied to youth may obfuscate more than they actually explain (Ben-Amos 1995). But it remains apparent that the attributes of youth have less to do with actual behavior or stages of development, and more to do with the myths about the young that circulate in a given era. As Grossberg (1988) writes, 'youth has no meaning except perhaps its lack of meaning, its energy, its commitment to openness and change, its celebratory relation to the present, and its promise of the future' (51).

From Post-World War II Youth Culture to Global Teens

In the study of popular music, youth was first understood in terms of the form it took within the context of the affluence experienced following World War II. As a product of a new and concentrated marketing oriented toward young consumers, as well as a population increase caused by soaring birthrates, particularly in Australia, Canada and the United States, the concept of the 'teenager' was pervasive, especially an internationally disseminated idea of the 'North American teenager.' The connections between musical forms and practises and various commodities ensured that this manifestation of youthfulness held powerful sway, to the point that the distinctions between popular culture and youth culture appeared to vanish. As Lhamon (1990) puts it, youth culture of the 1950s 'became the atmosphere of American life' (8). Further, it became possible to imagine a unity that pertained to the culture of youth, different from that of adults. The burgeoning of rock 'n' roll provided a key site for the formation of the North American teenager (a position argued by, among others, Grossberg (1994)). Most pertinently, rock 'n' roll's relationship to an associated set of other cultural forms, including fashion, dance, food, motion pictures and television, served to construct an imagined coherence for this 'youth culture.' In this respect, the experience of the 1950s, and especially the central features of popular music, provided the necessary elements for the notion of a separate, distinct and unified youth culture to seem to make sense. Under closer scrutiny, however, it is unambiguously clear that there were, and are, many youth cultures, and that other elements, including class, ethnicity and gender, may be greater determinants in the structuring of culture than age. McRobbie (1984) even challenges youth's presumed special connection to music by pointing to the importance of films and images for girls.

Youth culture holds at its nucleus a claim about the coherence of successive generations and the specificity of their ideas and forms of expression that is problematic. Thus, the manner in which a 'baby boomer' generation has been able to appropriate the very idea of youth, and an associated set of musical styles and activities, even as its members have moved well along in the life cycle, is a striking example of the nonessential connection between age, 'youth' and cultural expression, as well as a demonstration of the power of demographic and economic determinants in the formation of specific articulations. By contrast, the notion of Generation X is not especially well correlated to a single segment of the population. The original concept of Generation X (Coupland 1991) was to provide a description of a 'forgotten' youth culture, one that experienced a certain malaise from living with the economic and cultural leftovers of the older baby boomers. Ironically, the application of 'Generation X' to those whom the term initially denoted has become rare; instead, the term has come to be used to capture a general sense of disenfranchisement experienced by people born in both the 1960s and the 1970s.

The powerful connection between 'youth' and the baby boomers has thus been perceived as somewhat disarticulating 'youth' from any special age; it has seemingly become unmoored from 'adolescence.' Redhead (1997) alludes to this development, claiming that the 'lost generation' of the late twentieth century may be better thought of as the 'last generation.' Noting parallel trends across Europe, in England, Germany, Poland, Slovakia and the Czech Republic, he suggests that the increasingly 'permanent' quality of the supposedly transitional stage of youth was partly explained by increasing youth unemployment and a related expansion of periods of education (1997, 100–101). In an earlier work (1990), Redhead interprets the extension of youth well into adulthood as at least a disarticulation of 'youth culture' and 'rock culture,' if not the end of youth culture. Some have seen this as evidence of the powerful role that marketers play in defining the particular characteristics of a generation, suggesting that what is most visible as the youth culture of an era is largely determined by the designations of particularly attractive target markets.

What Lhamon (1990) refers to as the 'atmosphere of American life,' a youth culture seemingly synonymous with the popular culture of the time, did not remain confined to a single continent. Mitterauer (1992) argues that the subsequent history of youth has been one of 'deregionalization,' in which cultural forms and practises have forged a transnational and cosmopolitan youth sphere. Certainly, the decades of vociferous international debate about the 'Americanization' of local and national cultures have had youth culture as their subtext, if not as their primary exemplar. The formation of the 'global teen' has raised concerns about the loss of local and national cultural commitments, as young people have turned to an internationally circulating popular culture in order to construct forms of community and alliance. Thus, 'youth' has frequently appeared, in relation to other trends and concerns about globalization, as, again, the embodiment of fears and potentials – of anxieties about social change in general and the potentials of a global village.

Others, however, have examined the way in which globalization may also result in the creation of diverse peripheral youth musics. For instance, Robinson, Buck and Cuthbert (1991) detail the musical scenes and cultures in several countries, including Greece, Israel, Poland, Hungary, Nigeria, Jamaica and Taiwan. Indeed, one area of substantial research has centered on the national manifestations of youth cultures, often examining the manner in which international musical cultures become the resources from which youth is shaped into nationally defined musical scenes. Examples include Junko's work on popular music in Japan (1991), Mitchell's study of hip-hop in Italy (1995) and research on popular music in Sweden (Fornäs 1990; Fornäs, Lindberg and Sernhede 1995).

Deconstructing Youth

British cultural studies in the 1970s turned toward a close examination of youth culture, reworking within its own context an approach known as 'subcultural theory' (Hebdige 1979; Hall and Jefferson 1976). These primarily structuralist studies helped to challenge the imagined unity of youth by seeking out semiautonomous cultures thriving in the shadow of parent cultures. In these studies, music acted as a central site around which subcultures and their practises emerged and operated. Several groundbreaking studies explored the complexity of youth subcultures, including mods, Rastafarians and punks, by emphasizing the expressive coherence of such communities, although some criticized the studies' implicit assumptions about authenticity. Revisions to this work continued throughout the 1980s and 1990s, pointing out blind spots in the early research and, most importantly, placing issues of gender and ethnicity at the forefront (see Thornton 1995; McRobbie 1980; Rose 1994). In these studies, musical cultures remained of primary importance for the definition and analysis of youth subcultures.

Some have suggested that the study of popular music has moved beyond the presumed special relationship between youth and music. For example, Frith (1994), in a commentary introducing *Young*, a Nordic journal of youth research, notes that the exhaustion of British subcultural theory, the decentering of Anglo-American rock and certain demographic shifts in markets for popular music have 'meant that young people's tastes and activities are no longer central to popular music analysis' (105). Whether or not this is empirically the case, the very idea of the specificity of youth culture as a unit of analysis should be called into question in light of the mobility of 'youth' as the 'other' to adulthood and childhood. Without other determinants, such as gender, sexuality, race, ethnicity and class, any presumptions about age, generation and their related cultures will have no special explanatory power. Hall (1992) asks, 'What is this "black" in black popular culture?,' and thus draws critical attention to the exigencies of rhetorical claims about broad populations. Similarly, one could ask, 'What is this "youth" in youth culture? Who is meant by it? Who is imagined to exist there and who is excluded?' Youth is, in effect, an empty signifier, whose age, connotative associations and related cultural forms shift across time and place.

Bibliography

Acland, Charles R. 1995. *Youth, Murder, Spectacle: The Cultural Politics of 'Youth in Crisis'*. Boulder, CO: Westview Press.

Ariès, Philippe. 1962. *Centuries of Childhood: A Social History of Family Life*, trans. Robert Baldick. New York: Knopf.

Ben-Amos, Ilana Krausman. 1995. 'Adolescence as a Cultural Invention: Philippe Ariès and the Sociology of Youth.' *History of the Human Sciences* 8(2): 69–89.

Cohen, Stanley. 1972. *Folk Devils and Moral Panics: The Creation of the Mods and Rockers*. Oxford: Blackwell.

Coupland, Douglas. 1991. *Generation X: Tales for an Accelerated Culture*. New York: St. Martin's Press.

Fornäs, Johan. 1990. 'Moving Rock: Youth and Pop in Late Modernity.' *Popular Music* 9(3): 291–306.

Fornäs, Johan, Lindberg, Ulf, and Sernhede, Ove. 1995. *In Garageland: Rock, Youth and Modernity*. London: Routledge.

Frith, Simon. 1994. '*Young*. Nordic Journal of Youth Research.' *Popular Music* 13(1): 105.

Gillis, John. 1974. *Youth and History: Tradition and Change in European Age Relations, 1770–Present*. New York: Academic Press.

Grossberg, Lawrence. 1988. *It's a Sin: Essays on Postmodernism, Politics and Culture*. Sydney: Power Publications.

Grossberg, Lawrence. 1994. 'Is Anybody Listening? Does Anybody Care?: On Talking About the State of Rock.' In *Microphone Fiends: Youth Music and Youth Culture*, ed. Andrew Ross and Tricia Rose. New York and London: Routledge, 41–58.

Hall, G. Stanley. 1904. *Adolescence and Its Psychology and Its Relations to Physiology, Anthropology, Sociology, Sex, Crime, Religion, and Education*. New York: D. Appleton.

Hall, Stuart. 1992. 'What Is This "Black" in Black Popular Culture?' In *Black Popular Culture*, ed. Gina Dent. Seattle, WA: Bay Press, 21–33.

Hall, Stuart, and Jefferson, Tony, eds. 1976. *Resistance Through Rituals: Youth Subcultures in Post-War Britain*. London: Hutchinson.

Hartley, John. 1984. 'Encouraging Signs: Television and the Power of Dirt, Speech and Scandalous Categories.' In *Interpreting Television: Current Research Perspectives*, ed. William D. Rowland, Jr. and Bruce Watkins. Beverly Hills, CA: Sage Publications, 119–41.

Hebdige, Dick. 1979. *Subculture: The Meaning of Style*. London: Methuen.

Hebdige, Dick. 1987. *Cut 'n' Mix: Culture, Identity and Caribbean Music*. London and New York: Methuen.

Hebdige, Dick. 1988. *Hiding in the Light: On Images and Things*. London and New York: Routledge.

Hudson, Barbara. 1984. 'Femininity and Adolescence.' In *Gender and Generation*, ed. Angela McRobbie and Mica Nava. London: Macmillan, 31–53.

Junko, Kitagawa. 1991. 'Some Aspects of Japanese Popular Music.' *Popular Music* 10(3): 305–26.

Lhamon, W.T., Jr. 1990. *Deliberate Speed: The Origins of a Cultural Style in the American 1950s*. Washington, DC: Smithsonian Institution Press.

McRobbie, Angela. 1980. 'Settling Accounts with Subcultures: A Feminist Critique.' *Screen Education* 34 (Spring): 37–49.

McRobbie, Angela. 1984. 'Dance and Social Fantasy.' In *Gender and Generation*, ed. Angela McRobbie and Mica Nava. London: Macmillan, 130–61.

McRobbie, Angela. 1994. *Postmodernism and Popular Culture*. London and New York: Routledge.

Mitchell, Tony. 1995. 'Questions of Style: Notes on Italian Hip Hop.' *Popular Music* 14(3): 333–48.

Mitterauer, Michael. 1992. *A History of Youth*, trans. Graeme Dunphy. Cambridge, MA: Blackwell.

Musgrove, Frank. 1964. *Youth and the Social Order*. London: Routledge and Kegan Paul.

Redhead, Steve. 1990. *The End-of-the-Century Party: Youth and Pop Towards 2000*. New York: Manchester University Press/St. Martin's Press.

Redhead, Steve. 1997. *Subculture to Clubcultures: An Intro-*

duction to Popular Cultural Studies. Malden, MA: Blackwell.

Robinson, Deanna Campbell, Buck, Elizabeth B., and Cuthbert, Marlene. 1991. *Music at the Margins: Popular Music and Global Cultural Diversity*. Newbury Park, CA: Sage Publications.

Rose, Tricia. 1994. *Black Noise: Rap Music and Black Culture in Contemporary America*. Hanover, NH: University Press of New England.

Skelton, Tracey, and Valentine, Gill. 1998. *Cool Places: Geographies of Youth Cultures*. New York: Routledge.

Thornton, Sarah. 1995. *Club Cultures: Music, Media and Subcultural Capital*. Cambridge: Polity Press.

Discographical References

Cochrane, Eddie. 'Summertime Blues.' Liberty 55144. *1958*: USA.

Cooke, Sam. 'Only Sixteen.' Keen 2022. *1959*: USA.

Dion and the Belmonts. 'A Teenager in Love.' Laurie 3027. *1959*: USA.

Everly Brothers, The. 'Wake Up Little Susie.' Cadence 1337. *1957*: USA.

James, Sonny. 'Young Love.' Capitol 3602. *1957*: USA.

Nirvana. 'Smells Like Teen Spirit.' Geffen 24425. *1991*: USA.

Phair, Liz. 'Help Me Mary.' Matador OLE 051-2. *1993*: USA.

CHARLES R. ACLAND

4. Stylistic and Textual Dimensions

Genre

In everyday conversations about popular music, as well as in popular music studies, individuals commonly use labels (for example, 'blues,' 'jazz,' 'rock' or 'country') to refer to, and distinguish between, different kinds of music. Implicit in the use of such labels, and subsumed by the labels themselves, are tacit and sometimes disputed agreements on the part of various musical communities (for example, performers, audiences, listeners, fans and scholars) as to the features that customarily constitute the kind of music in question. The term 'genre' (Gr. *genos*; Lat. *genus*) refers to this notion of a similarity of features that characterizes or, in the minds of some people, even defines particular kinds of music, and differentiates them from others. A musical genre can be thought of, then, as a kind of music as customarily recognized by a community according to certain criteria resting variously on stylistic features, performance practises and behavioral norms associated with activities of production and consumption. The term can be defined more specifically as a set of musical events the character of whose articulation is governed by rules of any kind as they are accepted and embodied by a community.

The Provenance of the Term

In common English usage, the term 'genre' – which can be applied to any kind of artistic or cultural event – is more specific than the French word from which it originates. In Latin languages, as well as in Latin itself, the equivalent term for genre means type, kind, class, manner or race, like the ancient Greek word *genos*. As such, the term has been used in philosophical debate throughout the history of Western civilization, and was applied to art and to music at a very early stage. The first clear definition of *genos* was given by Aristotle in Book

I, Chapter 5 of his *Topics*: 'what is predicated in the category of essence of a number of things exhibiting differences in kind.' The function of *genos* in any definition follows from this definition. Two constituents are thus implied: the *genos*, and a specific differentiating factor. For example, in the sentence 'man is a rational animal,' 'animal' is the *genos* and 'rational' the specific differentiating factor.

Since the time of Aristotle and his pupil Theophrastus, the central idea underlying the concept of 'genre' has been that what can be predicated according to the essence of many works of art that differ specifically is the character of their functioning. That is, it is the way in which works function that makes them similar and capable of belonging to the same *genos*. It follows from this that the style of each work of art should be proper to its *genos*, it being clearly understood that, while the concepts of 'genre' and 'style' are related, they are not the same.

Semiologists and cultural theorists in the latter decades of the twentieth century established a framework of theories allowing for a wider view of genres (see, for example, Hawkes 1977, 100–104). As they have developed, these theories have become increasingly media-specific (that is, specific to literature or to cinema or to art), thus avoiding a reductive tendency toward totalizing explanatory models. The raison d'être of these evolving theories has been that of accounting for differences between genres – and their increasing multiplicity – in literature, theater, dance, cinema and music. However, these theories have continued to conform to the philosophical origins of the term 'genre' – a concern with matters of definition. Not surprisingly, many of these modern theories focus on conventions established within communities that relate to performance or to the social use of the genres in question.

Genre and Style in Music

In music, genres emerge as labels for defining similarities and recurrences that members of a community understand as pertinent to identifying and classifying musical events. The process by which naming conventions are established can be explicit, as in the proclamation of an aesthetic manifesto, or in rules, regulations and laws, and marketing campaigns. It can, however, be implicit, 'silent,' never declared (see Lewis 1969). Rules that define a genre can be related to any of the activities involved in a musical event, such as rules of behavior, etiquette, proxemic and kinesic codes, and economic regulations. In this way, the knowledge of 'what kind of music' an individual will be listening to, playing or discussing acts as a compass, helping the individual to choose the proper codes and tools for participation.

Rules that apply to musical features in a stricter sense are often referred to as matters of style rather than matters of genre. However, the concept of 'style' applies also to larger or smaller groupings of music. Such 'groupings' may relate to a period in history, to a period in the life of an artist or even to a single work. Style, therefore, is not a subset of genre. Neither is the reverse the case. Rather, these concepts overlap in a multidimensional realm of meaning dealing with recurring musical features of sets of musical events. In moving to a broader definition of a 'kind of music' in terms of the many activities above and beyond the purely musical that are involved in a musical event, matters of genre are being discussed. In focusing on recurring musical features independently of the other activities involved in musical events, matters of style are being discussed.

It should be pointed out that the use of 'style' as a synonym for 'genre' is more common in English, where 'style' invokes a greater range of meaning than 'genre,' a term that sounds more 'technical,' and thus more specific. In Latin languages, the reverse tends to apply. The term 'style' is also more commonly used in discussions about music than in those about literature or cinema. So, for example, there will typically be discussions concerning the coherence of or changes in Stanley Kubrick's style in film genres such as thrillers, science fiction movies or war movies, it being clearly understood that it is stylistic features, *together with* other elements such as issues of content and economics, that serve to define film genres.

Genre Formation and Maintenance

Categorizing and naming 'kinds,' referring to established genres or inventing new ones constitutes the basic process of all reasoning about music. According to Lakoff (1987) and other cognitivists, such processes form the basis for all human knowledge, and the first level of categorization is that of the genus. The importance of generic terms in discourses about music cannot be underestimated or misunderstood. This is because, in part, there are powerful interests that attempt to impose their own definitions for various reasons and for various purposes. Not least among these have been commercial forces, especially the media, which have been quick to label particular kinds of music, and have therefore played a crucial role in genre formation, actively contributing to the 'recognition' of a 'new' genre and helping to create markets for it. Frequently, the music in question has existed for some time before being labeled in this way and thus being subjected to the discursive processes of genre formation.

Examples of such processes go back at least to the late nineteenth century when, in 1897, a Chicago newspaper promulgated the term 'ragtime,' thus serving to initiate the 'ragtime era' quite some time after the music to which the label referred had been in existence (Blesh and Janis 1950). These kinds of processes led Charles Keil (1966) to argue that 'the blues' did not actually come into existence until the 1930s, the time when the US mass media began common use of the term. The music commonly referred to as 'the blues' can, in fact, be traced back to the period in the nineteenth century immediately following Emancipation, when field hollers began to supplant work songs in African-American communities in the southern United States as a consequence of changes in agrarian economy.

Such is the force of this labeling that, for purposes of commercial gain, labels are often applied very loosely by the media and the marketing wings of the music industry in terms of the characteristics that are accepted by other communities as constituting the genre in question. The label 'ragtime' was thus applied to much music that displayed few of the features of ragtime as understood by other communities in order to help sell other kinds of sheet music when ragtime was very popular.

However, naming musics – categorizing musics – is not just a labeling process, extrinsic to music and its meaning. Rather, it forms the ground on which different actors – for example, musicians, communities or corporations – fight for influence and control. An interesting example of this is provided by Simon Frith (1990), when he gives an account of musicians and sound engineers in conflict over the desired and therefore defining 'sound' of a genre.

Because of their very nature, then, genres can be understood and used as names that 'stand for' complex sets of norms, taking details for granted and leaving much room for ambiguity and conflict. Such conflict is evident in discussions about whether or not a certain piece of popular music is 'really rock,' or 'really jazz,' for example. These discussions often turn into heated arguments, and for two reasons. They become heated, firstly, because what is at stake is discursive control of a particular set of musical practises, control that is centrally important to the ways in which music is implicated in processes of identity formation, both individual and cultural. The second reason is that, by their very nature of engaging different and incommensurable assumptions, such disagreements can never be satisfactorily resolved.

However, genres can also be seen and used as the sets of norms themselves, strict and conservative. Genres generally evolve in the 'lives' they are afforded by the communities that adopt them. Genre formation and maintenance can thus involve processes of 'standing for' as well as constituting 'sets of norms' themselves, with genres perhaps vacillating between the two during their life. There is also a tendency for processes of genre formation and maintenance to move from an initial, diffuse state, to a more rigid and conservative one. Genres, then, can be understood as shortcuts to speed up communication within a musical community (when they 'stand for' sets of norms), as well as standardized codes that allow no margin for deviation (when they themselves constitute sets of norms). In the latter instance, there is no real communication.

The rise and fall of progressive rock in the late 1960s and early 1970s, together with the subsequent explosion of punk rock, provide good examples of a recurring process whereby codes are gradually elaborated, and then become overly strict, allowing for only very predictable texts. At this point, new codes are typically proposed. It should also be pointed out – punk provides an excellent example of this (see Laing 1985) – that rules and codes are made pertinent by the community: what someone sees as the most significant regularity within a certain genre may not be what the community that constituted that genre in the first place saw as its essence (in Aristotelian terms).

A hierarchy of codes always defines the ideology of a genre (Eco 1975; Fabbri 1996), and all discourses about genres are then ideological in the strictest sense of the term, as their intention is that of confirming or criticizing established hierarchies of value. The discursive and ideological processes implicit in genre formation and maintenance go a long way toward explaining the opprobrium heaped on musicians who flout genre norms, such as Miles Davis in developing fusion, which many jazz aficionados immediately categorized as 'not quite jazz' (see, for example, Chambers 1985, 168, 183),

and Bob Dylan in 'going electric,' which outraged aficionados of urban folk music.

Discussions of genre in the context of popular music studies are to be found in Frith (1996), Hamm (2000), Middleton (1990), Moore (1993), Shuker (2001) and Walser (1993).

Bibliography

Blesh, Rudi, and Janis, Harriet. 1950. *They All Played Ragtime: The True Story of an American Music*. New York: Knopf.

Chambers, Jack. 1985. *Milestones II: The Music and Times of Miles Davis Since 1960*. Toronto: University of Toronto Press.

Eco, Umberto. 1975. *Trattato di semiotica generale* [A Theory of Semiotics]. Milano: Bompiani.

Fabbri, Franco. 1982a. 'A Theory of Musical Genres: Two Applications.' In *Popular Music Perspectives, 1*, ed. David Horn and Philip Tagg. Göteborg and Exeter: IASPM, 52–81.

Fabbri, Franco. 1982b. 'What Kind of Music?' *Popular Music* 2: 131–43.

Fabbri, Franco. 1996. *Il suono in cui viviamo* [The Sound We Live In]. Milano: Feltrinelli.

Fabbri, Franco. 1999. *Browsing Music Spaces: Categories and the Musical Mind*. Paper presented at the Third Triennial British Musicological Societies' Conference, University of Surrey, UK.

Frith, Simon. 1990. 'What Is Good Music?' *Canadian University Music Review* 10(2): 92–102.

Frith, Simon. 1996. *Performing Rites: On the Value of Popular Music*. Cambridge, MA: Harvard University Press.

Hamm, Charles. 2000. 'Genre, Performance, and Ideology in the Early Songs of Irving Berlin.' In *Reading Pop: Approaches to Textual Analysis in Popular Music*, ed. Richard Middleton. Oxford: Oxford University Press, 297–306.

Hawkes, Terence. 1977. *Structuralism and Semiotics*. London: Methuen.

Keil, Charles. 1966. *Urban Blues*. Chicago: University of Chicago Press.

Laing, Dave. 1985. *One Chord Wonders: Power and Meaning in Punk Rock*. Milton Keynes: Open University Press.

Lakoff, George. 1987. *Women, Fire, and Dangerous Things: What Categories Reveal About the Mind*. Chicago: University of Chicago Press.

Lewis, David K. 1969. *Convention: A Philosophical Study*. Cambridge, MA: Harvard University Press.

Middleton, Richard. 1990. *Studying Popular Music*. Milton Keynes and Philadelphia: Open University Press.

Moore, Allan. 1993. *Rock, The Primary Text: Developing*

a Musicology of Rock. Milton Keynes and Philadelphia: Open University Press.

Shuker, Roy. 2001. *Understanding Popular Music*. 2nd ed. London and New York: Routledge.

Walser, Robert. 1993. *Running with the Devil: Power, Gender and Madness in Heavy Metal Music*. Hanover and London: Wesleyan University Press.

FRANCO FABBRI and JOHN SHEPHERD

Humor

Introduction

Humor – which may be broadly defined as that which generates laughter – is to be found in some form in the daily life of every human society. It also features centrally in those artistic and cultural practises through which societies reflect upon themselves in a lighter vein, as, for example, in music hall 'sketches.' Although in both daily life and more formal cultural practises humor finds its most frequent expression in verbal and visual forms, ranging from witty jokes and rude drawings to fully developed theatrical comedies of the 'human condition,' music's role in the generation of humor in all these contexts is often a very important one.

Music's contribution to humor in the social interaction of daily life is generally confined to circumstances involving participation in some kind of given, framed activity, as, for example, in songs sung by crowds at soccer matches. The humorous use of music by people conversing over a drink at a bar or waiting at a bus stop is less common than their humorous use of words, and when it does occur it almost invariably becomes theatrical. The use of music to express humor is more commonly found in formal contexts involving musical performance, including those contexts in which it is directed against performance's various formalities.

To participate in the generation of humor, music often forms alliances with verbal and visual media. Here, because its role is typically one of accompaniment, it often functions in a role subservient to those media. However, music is also used because it has features and resources for the production of humor that other media lack. In these situations, music lends added humorous value. In a humorous song in a stage musical, for example, humor can be extracted musically from a character and that character's situation by means not available to words or images. Thus in 'Adelaide's Lament' from *Guys and Dolls*, musical motifs, melodic shape, rhythm, the vocal timbre and intonation of the performer, even the repetition inherent in the song's structure, are used to draw out humor at a subtler, more profound level of humanity, and thus engage audience sympathy at a deeper level also. At the same time, since in daily life people do not normally sing – or at least sing

so much – it is the music that reminds the audience to laugh at the character as a comic stage creation, as well as with her as a person.

In some instances of the alliance between words, images and music, music can be the primary generator of humor. It can, for example, provide a counterpoint to ideas expressed through words or images in ways that suggest the presence of a comic discrepancy which is not evident in the words or images alone. The technique is sometimes adapted in television advertising, where an apparently everyday image (say, a group of people drinking a nameless brand of beer) is made to seem odd through the use of music (a slow, introspective ballad, perhaps, or discordant orchestral sounds), a discrepancy resolved by the introduction of the named brand, and a change to a more appropriate (in this case, more sociable) music.

A further variation of the technique involves a kind of double discrepancy, as, for example, in a 1999 UK tea bag commercial. Here, an initial discrepancy is set up by combining Bill Withers's recording, 'Lovely Day,' with a cartoon image of a weary, unattractive male character getting out of bed in the morning. Viewers who are familiar with the music are likely to expect the discrepancy to be continued, even enhanced, at the line, 'Then I look at you,' by the appearance of an equally unattractive partner, but what appears instead is a friend making tea. That words and images in such contexts would often be taken as the dominant discourse, and music as the subservient, accompanying one, adds further to the humor.

Music is also a major contributor to humor generated in the act of performance, in combinations of movement, gesture, expression and utterance. Here, too, it often works in partnership with words and images and is often used to support them, as in a comic song-and-dance routine on stage or screen; but, because of its simultaneous use of different parameters of expression (rhythm, melody, timbre, inflection and so on), and because of its ability to allow several different voices to talk at once (even when those 'voices' are the sounds produced by accompanying instruments), music can also enormously enrich the possibilities for humor.

An interesting example of this is the use of music by clowns. In most such performances, verbal communication is traditionally abandoned, and the immediate source of humor is activity at the visual level. But without sound and, almost always, music, the humorous effects would often be minimal. The clowns can maximize their humor, and the audience can fully appreciate it, because the various parameters in the accompanying music can handle and enhance any and all aspects of the act, including the exaggerated moments (falling, hitting, colliding) and moments of greater subtlety (sleight-of-hand, sidelong glances).

History

The history of popular music is rich in genres centered on humor and nonsense. Some can be traced back to medieval jesters and folk fairs, where people used music to advertise their wares. The *Commedia dell'Arte* and the *Opéra Comique* helped to establish a language of comedy in music, which was then greatly augmented first by the circus, and later by film cartoons. In the meantime, other major musical traditions centered on humor developed, each taking a different approach. Bawdy songs and students' songs – vast oral repertoires found throughout Europe from the Middle Ages onward – stressed double-entendres and licentious subject matter, and in this way laid the foundations for many subsequent forms of humor in music. British music hall (and its gentler predecessor, the 'pleasure garden'), early US vaudeville, Italian *avanspettacolo* and Neapolitan *macchietta* brought these elements indoors, adding further ingredients of realism, the grotesque and folklore to create a 'total theater' aimed at working-class audiences.

In these forms of popular theater, humor was generated through the use of music to produce what was commonly regarded as a 'lowbrow' and fragmentary type of entertainment with no plot. In seeking to extend the audience for the variety theater into the middle classes and to provide respectable family entertainment in vaudeville, US theatrical entrepreneurs succeeded in expanding the audience for musical humor and engendering forms of it that were less 'lowbrow.'

A more structured form of humor was provided by the tradition that blended the ballad opera, a peculiarly British invention, with operetta. The best-known British comic operas of the nineteenth century, those written by W.S. Gilbert and Arthur Sullivan, were notable for lampooning the manners and mannerisms of figures in authority, and provided an early example of self-referring political satire. These comic operas gave way later in the nineteenth century to musical comedies, for which music was often written by Sidney Jones and which, like the comic operas of Gilbert and Sullivan, attracted mostly middle-class audiences. In contrast to that of the popular theater, aimed primarily at working-class audiences, the humor generated by gags, puns and jokes in musical comedy made sense within a story line. An account of the spread of operetta and musical comedy to the United States and its development there has been given by Gerald Bordman (1981).

The kind of musical humor to be found in operetta and musical comedy also became a vehicle for transcultural satire. Burlesque, for example, in which plots and lyrics had a strong satirical intent, began as a parody of serious opera where Italian conventions became a favorite target. Often, transcultural satire employed ethnic stereotypes. The minstrel show (performed almost exclusively by white people before Emancipation) was devised as a parody of African-American attitudes and behavior as perceived by white people (the attitudes and behavior themselves being parodies of what African Americans regarded as the 'hifalutin' manners of their white masters).

Musical humor directed against ethnic groups from outside was by no means all of a stereotypical nature. Ned Harrigan's songs about different ethnic groups in New York's Lower East Side in the 1880s, for example, were created from close personal knowledge of the behavior and language on the street and combined satire with sympathy. Harrigan's songs (and sketches with Tony Hart) about his Irish-American characters, Dan Mulligan and his 'Mulligan Guard,' also demonstrated that ethnic humor in song could be self-directed, for he himself was of Irish-American extraction.

Whereas many of the music genres involving humor arose and developed mainly in Anglo-Saxon countries, operetta had an international appeal, which gave the upper classes a medium through which to express a more sophisticated kind of humor. At its most successful, this middle-European imitation of opera offered a perfect balance between understatement and open amusement, only rarely evoking hearty laughter. Revue, *variété* and variety were all offshoots of these more organized forms of entertainment. Finally, the French *café-chantant* and the German cabaret developed an intellectual and political type of humor, aimed at a bourgeois audience. The novelty song, usually a three-minute narrative delivered in a dramatic, often clownish, performance, was the last link in a musical chain that started on stage and ended with recording.

With the development of recording technology and the growth of musical culture in the twentieth century, music took on a more specialized role in humor. The possibility of generating humor through music alone was increased by a high level of self-referentialism in music itself. Semioticians refer to this self-referentialism as a 'metalinguistic function,' in which music speaks of itself, but only through music. This approach – which relies heavily on the use of musical quotations (what John Oswald would call 'plunderphonics') – was pioneered by a small number of classical composers playing with 'trivial' materials. It was in this way that Erik Satie, Charles Ives, Kurt Weill, Luciano Berio and Mauricio Kagel helped to bridge the gap between serious and popular music through humor.

In the twentieth century, the art of making people

laugh with music reached its peak with composers such as Carl Stalling, who created a new type of music for the animated cartoons of Disney and Warner Brothers. Their 'Looney Tunes,' 'Merrie Melodies' and 'Silly Symphonies,' as well as their soundtracks for the Bugs Bunny, Mickey Mouse and Donald Duck movies, were the essence of exaggeration through music. The exaggerated performing style of vaudeville found its way into the musical comedy and the musical film in the performances of figures such as Eddie Cantor, Fanny Brice and Al Jolson. Fred Astaire and Jerry Lewis provide examples of other internationally acclaimed performers who contributed to musical humor through the musical comedy and the musical film. Stars with a more domestic appeal in this vein were Karl Valentin, Cab Calloway, Maurice Chevalier and Rodolfo De Angelis. Most of the humor in musical comedy itself tended to be contained within the plot and the opportunities it provided for comic dialog; but it was in the context of the musical that humor expressed in the form of witty, sophisticated lyrics – as in the work of Ira Gershwin, Lorenz Hart, Cole Porter and Noel Coward – came into its own.

A subgenre of musical humor, 'parody records,' has been overtly devoted to humor ('Weird Al' Yankovic, Quartetto Cetra, Renato Carosone, the Barron Knights, the Four Preps, Stan Freberg, the Flying Lizards, the Rutles, the Naples – the last two specializing in Beatles parodies), whereas rock theater has highlighted a kitsch notion of humor (the Incredible String Band, the Tubes, *The Rocky Horror Picture Show*). Rock and pop have themselves supplied many instances of the humorous uses of music, from ephemeral treatments to more thorough explorations of the genre (the Bonzo Dog Band, National Lampoon, the Residents, Frank Zappa, Elio e le Storie Tese). Perhaps the height of parody and satire was reached in the field of rock music with the 'mockumentary' *This Is Spinal Tap*, whereas Quartetto Cetra's television renditions of world-famous historical novels such as *The Count of Monte Cristo*, *The Three Musketeers* and *I Promessi Sposi* (all of them packed into the 'Biblioteca di Studio Uno' VHS series) are among the best examples of musical parodies aimed at a pre-rock television audience. In these mini-operas, no more than 30 minutes long, singers and famous actors from theater and cinema sing well-known melodies. Humor is therefore generated by the clash of historical characters and plots deeply rooted in the collective memory and their musical rendition by means of contemporary 'lowbrow' tunes.

Music was also evident in the growth of political and social satire which took place in the West in the 1950s and 1960s. This music frequently took the form of songs that, though often conceived for club performance, reached wider audiences through recording. The black humor of Harvard college professor turned satirist Tom Lehrer, whether directed against established conventions (as in 'Christmas Carol') or against nuclear devices ('We Will All Go Together When We Go'), found a receptive audience far beyond the confines of club and cabaret, for example.

A touch of (very sophisticated) humor has also been evident in the border zone that includes unorthodox jazz, cabaret, improvised music and avant-garde (the Willem Breuker Kollektief, Misha Mengelberg, Bill Frisell, John Zorn, Mike Westbrook). These performers often speak the same language of the 'absurd' as many progressive bands (Henry Cow, Stormy Six, the early Soft Machine) and various champions of 'pastiche' (Cassiber, the Vienna Art Orchestra, Melody Four, Fred Frith, Steve Beresford).

Analysis

To a greater extent than words and images, music requires a shared cultural background. On an analytical level, humor in music is most likely to emerge from a clash of cultural stereotypes that focuses on the rules of musical communication. The more routinized these rules are, the more successful their comic treatment will be. Clichés of the 'exotic' go hand in hand with the ethnocentrism of humor: a tango 'touch,' for example, is often employed to heighten comic effect.

Humor can be generated by the distortion of a basic tonal rule (e.g., a musician plays deliberately out of tune), the alteration of a piece's duration (e.g., David Bedford's 'Wagner's Ring,' miniaturized in one minute) or the variation of a piece's harmony and rhythm (e.g., the penultimate of the 'Variations on America' by Charles Ives, written in a minor key in a bolero rhythm). These principles were used to great effect by the British actor, comedian and musician Dudley Moore. Humor can also be achieved by playing a piece with instrumentation that is radically different from that of the original (e.g., the Temple City Kazoo Orchestra), or by arranging it in a style that relocates it in an unrelated period (e.g., Big Daddy, Anachronic Jazz Band, UFO Piemontesi). Humor can arise from a gross caricature of a well-known style (Spike Jones) or from moving from one style to another that is as far as possible from the original (e.g., John Belushi's Beethoven transformed into Ray Charles). It can also arise from covering a song in an uncommon language or faking it (e.g., 'Walk on the Wild Side' by Lou Reed, sung in Yiddish by Gefilte Joe and the Fish), or from unexpectedly using quotations that contrast with the mood of the song (e.g., 'Chemical Warfare' by the Dead Kennedys, a punk song brutally interrupted by a Viennese waltz).

Humor can be found in the verbal dimensions of

music alone through the alteration of the lyrics of famous tunes (e.g., the Marx Brothers' treatment of 'The Toreador Song' from *Carmen*). Finally, and this is the most common scenario, humor is the result of the interaction of words, images and music. Nonsense is a subtype of musical humor, which in popular music has taken the form of onomatopoeia, baby talk, magic spells and meaningless syllables. As such, it is widely represented, from Tin Pan Alley ('Ti-Pi-Tin,' 'Zip-A-Dee-Doo-Dah') to Hollywood ('Supercalifragilisticexpialidocioius'), from the Beatles ('Ob-La-Di, Ob-La-Da') to Neapolitan song ('Ndringhete-ndrà'), from rock 'n' roll ('Tutti-Frutti,' 'Papa-Oom-Mow-Mow') to doo-wop ('Get a Job'), from the girl groups ('Da Doo Ron Ron') to Brill Building pop ('Do Wah Diddy Diddy').

Bibliography

Bordman, Gerald. 1981. *American Operetta: From H.M.S. Pinafore to Sweeney Todd*. New York: Oxford University Press.

'Comedy.' 1983. In *The Rolling Stone Encyclopedia of Rock & Roll*, ed. Jon Pareles and Patricia Romanowski. London: Rolling Stone Press/Michael Joseph, 123.

Cooper, B. Lee. 1987. 'Response Recordings as Creative Repetition: Answer Songs and Pop Parodies in Contemporary American Music.' *OneTwoThreeFour: A Rock 'n' Roll Quarterly* 4: 79–87.

Cutler, Chris. 1995. 'Plunderphonics, o saccheggiofonia' [Plunderphonics]. *Musica/Realtà* 48: 53–79.

Finson, Jon. 1997. 'Realism in Late Nineteenth-Century American Musical Theater: The Songs of Edward Harrigan and David Braham.' In *The Collected Songs of Edward Harrigan and David Braham*, ed. Jon Finson. Madison, WI: A-R Editions, xv–xxxvii.

Hosokawa, Shuhei. 1984. 'Gli occhi e il segreto. Il caso dei Residents' [The Eyes and the Secret: The Case of the Residents]. *Musica/Realtà* 13: 77–88.

Mahabir, Cynthia. 1996. 'Wit and Popular Music: The Calypso and the Blues.' *Popular Music* 15(1): 55–81.

Moody, Richard. 1980. *Ned Harrigan: From Corlear's Hook to Herald Square*. Chicago: Nelson Hall.

Oswald, John. 1987. 'Plunderphonics, or Audio Piracy as a Compositional Prerogative.' *Re Records Quarterly* 2(1): 24–29.

Prato, Paolo. 1991. 'Il comico in musica: dalla tradizione colta al rock' [Music and the Comic: From Serious Tradition to Rock]. *Musica/Realtà* 34: 69–79.

Sheet Music

Braham, David, comp., and Harrigan, Ned, lyr. 1873. 'The Mulligan Guard.' New York: William Pond.

Finson, Jon, ed. 1997. *The Collected Songs of Edward Harrigan and David Braham*. Madison, WI: A-R Editions.

Harrigan, Edward (Ned), comp. and lyr. 1872. 'Little Fraud.' Boston, MA: White and Goullard.

Harrigan, Edward (Ned), comp. and lyr. 1883. 'The Controllin' Influence of Drink.' New York: Harding's Music Office.

Loesser, Frank, comp. and lyr. 1950. 'Adelaide's Lament.' New York: Frank Music.

Discographical References

'Adelaide's Lament.' *Guys and Dolls [Broadway Cast]*. Showtime 034. *1997*: USA.

Andrews, Julie, and Van Dyke, Dick. 'Supercalifragilisticexpialidocioius.' HMV CLP 1794. *1965*: USA.

Andrews Sisters, The. 'Ti-Pi-Tin.' Brunswick 02592. *1938*: USA.

Beatles, The. 'Ob-La-Di, Ob-La-Da.' *The Beatles*. Apple PCS 7070. *1968*: UK.

Bedford, David. 'Wagner's Ring.' *Miniatures: A Sequence of Fifty-One Tiny Masterpieces*. Pipe Records. *1980*: UK. Reissue: Bedford, David. 'Wagner's Ring.' *Miniatures: A Sequence of Fifty-One Tiny Masterpieces*. Blueprint BP 159. *1995*: UK.

Crystals, The. 'Da Doo Ron Ron.' Philles 112. *1963*: USA.

Dead Kennedys, The. 'Chemical Warfare.' *Fresh Fruit for Rotting Vegetables*. Cherry Red BRED 10. *1980*: UK.

Exciters, The. 'Do Wah Diddy Diddy.' United Artists. *1963*: USA.

Fisher, Eddie. 'Zip-A-Dee-Doo-Dah.' HMV CLP 1095. *1947*: USA.

Gefilte Joe and the Fish. 'Walk on the Kosher Side.' *Rhino Royale*. Rhino Records RNLP 002. *1978*: USA.

Ives, Charles. 'Variations on America' (see, for example, Nina Deutsch's piano transcription in *Charles Ives: Complete Works for Solo Piano*. Vox Box SVBX 5482. *1976*: USA).

Lehrer, Tom. 'Christmas Carol.' *Songs & More Songs by Tom Lehrer*. Rhino 72776. *1997*: USA.

Lehrer, Tom. 'We Will All Go Together When We Go.' *Songs & More Songs by Tom Lehrer*. Rhino 72776. *1997*: USA.

Little Richard. 'Tutti-Frutti.' Specialty 561. *1956*: USA.

Marx Brothers, The. 'I Want My Shirt.' In *The Cocoanuts* (1929). Sandy Hook Release No. 59. S.H. 2059. *1981*: USA.

'Ndringhete-ndrà' (written by Pasquale Cinquegrana and Giuseppe De Gregorio, 1895; no recording of first performance available). See Miranda Martino in *Neapolitan Songs*. RCA 74321-25854-2. *1995*: Italy.

Rivingtons, The. 'Papa-Oom-Mow-Mow.' Liberty. *1962*: USA.

Silhouettes, The. 'Get a Job.' Ember 1029. *1958*: USA.

Withers, Bill. 'Lovely Day.' *Ain't No Sunshine*. BMG International 50415. *1999*: USA.

Discography

Bonzo Dog Band, The. *Tadpoles*. Liberty LBS 83257. *1969*: UK.

Dr. Demento. *The Greatest Novelty Records of All Time* (6-album set). Rhino Records RNLP 820-1-2-3-4-5. *1985*: USA.

Dr. Demento. *The World's Worst Records!*. Rhino Records RNLP 809. *1983*: USA.

Elio e le Storie Tese. *Italyan, rum casusu cikty*. Sony/Huka-pan 471553. *1992*: Italy.

Jones, Spike. *The Complete Collection*. Kurt Ellenbogen MF 205/4. *1977*: USA.

Miniatures: A Sequence of Fifty-One Tiny Masterpieces (ed. Morgan Fisher). Pipe Records. *1980*: UK.

Murolo, Roberto. *L'umorismo nella canzone napoletana moderna dal 1930 al 1965*. Ricordi ACDOR 29241. *1971*: Italy.

National Lampoon. *Greatest Hits of National Lampoon*. Visa Records 7008. *1978*: USA.

Residents, The. *Third Reich 'n' Roll*. Ralph Records RR1075. *1976*: USA.

25 Years of Recorded Comedy (ed. Marty Wekser). Warner Bros. Records 3BX 3131. *1977*: USA.

Temple City Kazoo Orchestra, The. *Some Kazoos*. Rhino Records RNEP 501. *1978*: USA.

Warner Bros. Symphony Orchestra, The. *Bugs Bunny on Broadway*. Merrie Melodies/Warner Bros. 9-26494-2. *1991*: USA.

Yankovic, 'Weird Al.' *Dare To Be Stupid*. CBS FZ 40033. *1985*: USA.

Zappa, Frank. *We're Only In It For The Money*. Verve 5045. *1968*: USA.

Filmography

The Rocky Horror Picture Show, dir. Jim Sharman. 1975. USA/UK. 100 mins. Musical Comedy. Original music by John Barry, Richard Hartley, Richard O'Brien.

This Is Spinal Tap, dir. Rob Reiner. 1984. USA. 82 mins. Comedy ('Mockumentary'). Original music by Christopher Guest, Michael McKean, Rob Reiner, Harry Shearer.

Visual Recording

Quartetto Cetra. 1993. 'Biblioteca di Studio Uno.' RAI-Nuova ERI (VHS videos).

PAOLO PRATO and DAVID HORN with JOHN SHEPHERD

Iconography

Introduction

The term 'iconography' was originally used in art history to describe sets of visual conventions in the pictorial arts, particularly painting. Rule books giving advice on how best to encode Christian doctrine in art during the Renaissance guided artists in the appropriate use of color, gesture, facial expression and so on (see Branston and Stafford 1997). Iconography is particularly important in religious painting since much of the latter's subject matter works on an allegorical level. Icons are images that represent larger, more important themes and ideas. The depictions of the cross, skulls and candles found in Christian religious artwork form a set of interdependent symbols that stand for universal truths and states of feeling particular to Christian orthodoxy. These icons transcend their literal meaning in becoming symbols of deeper levels of thinking.

Linguistics built on the art history notion of universal or stereotypical imaging which conveyed hidden ideological versions of reality. This notion should be distinguished from more semiotic concepts as evidenced, for example, in the work of Charles S. Peirce. Processes similar to those of universal or stereotypical imaging can be observed at work within popular culture, and particularly within pop performance. However, the relationship between visual iconography and music has remained a largely unexplored area within popular music studies, although one book on the subject did appear in 1995 (Rubin 1995).

Certain genres and styles of popular music, and, more importantly, certain performers, have transcended the status of stardom and become icons. For a visual image to be an icon, it has to have a weight and power that a stereotypical image does not have; pop stars become icons when they represent a particular set of attitudes and beliefs with which they become synonymous. This iconography becomes manifest through painting, photography, posters, album covers, graffiti, T-shirts, video, stage performances, television appearances and so on. Some images within pop function as both iconographic and stereotypical visual signifiers in that, despite being hackneyed and stale through repeated usage, they remain powerful.

Generic Iconography

Although all popular music performers nuance their performances to varying degrees, they are influenced, whether in terms of musical or of visual iconography, by the set of rules and conventions that have become associated with the genre or style of music they choose to perform. For example, some genres of music have dress codes that are inextricably bound up with their visual iconography. Hard rock, and especially heavy metal, has perhaps the greatest number of such iconographic trappings.

Rock and metal are played overwhelmingly by men. They are predicated on virtuoso playing and, especially, on mastery of the electric guitar. The golden age of the male guitar hero was unquestionably the 1960s, with

Jimi Hendrix, Jimmy Page and Eric Clapton in the vanguard, although hard rock, and particularly metal, has always remained extremely popular with both men and women. The stylistic paraphernalia of both lead guitarist and lead vocalist in hard rock and metal acts continued almost unchanged during this period: the lead singer, usually with long hair and tight pants, sang in a declamatory style in which head tones were prominent, while the virtuoso lead guitarist, usually with similar leather sartorial trappings, grasped his guitar as if it were a figurative extension of his body, a technological erection to be played with in front of a voyeuristic audience awaiting vicarious gratification through the symbolic masturbatory act of the musician on stage. The silhouetted image of the guitarist, playing his guitar at crotch level (even when it would have been far more practical and comfortable to play the instrument at chest, or even waist, level), thus became a very powerful icon within popular music, one that adorned magazine covers, posters and videos for decades. By the late 1970s, this 'hypermasculinity' (see Walser 1993) had become a cliché, famously ridiculed by the spoof rock group Spinal Tap, and played with ironically by punk groups such as the Ramones and Peter Hook from New Order. Occultist imagery also became part of metal's visual iconography, from the tongue-in-cheek, though sinister, stage show of Alice Cooper to the deeply disturbing far-right iconography of thrash, speed, snuff and death metal. Throughout, hard rock and metal articulated a masculinity that was based on a technological supremacy over women (gadgetry and aficionadohood are overwhelmingly male preserves). This was also apparent in metal's androgyny and cross-dressing visual elements.

Other genres of popular music also have sets of images, sometimes contradictory, which may be thought of as comprising a visual system – a stockpile of images which both performer and audience expect and with which they feel comfortable. Examples may include: the bare-chested, bejeweled soul singer; the baseball-capped, track-suited b-boy with his shades and gold chains; the country singer with cowboy hat, drapes, jeans and boots; the Vegas crooner in gold lamé, sequins and shades; the bebop musician in beret and shades; and the punk with bondage gear, safety pins and strategically defaced and ripped T-shirt. Indeed, punk had a crucial effect on the visual imagery so prevalent in current youth style. Punk took mundane extramusical artifacts and imbued them with 'magical' symbolic power (the safety pin as earring, the dog collar as necklace, the kettle as purse). Although excessively iconoclastic in the late 1970s, punk helped derail rock iconography from its stereotypical tracks (Hebdige 1979).

Pop Star Iconography

Pop star iconography frequently relies on a relatively unchanging image. Apart from Lou Reed's very brief flirtation with glam extravagance in the 1970s, for example, his wardrobe of black leather and dark shades has remained a permanent part of his visual iconography. Such iconography gains its power through its changelessness. As a result, Reed's look has become forever associated with rock's romantic, visionary, poetic, yet streetwise side, and has become a uniform subsequently adopted by many other singers in a more stereotypical fashion. Little Richard's bouffant hair, pencil-thin mustache and makeup combined to create another static but extremely potent visual image, one that was appropriated wholesale by Prince in the 1970s and 1980s. Another example of unchanging image was Bob Marley, whose denim and dreadlocks remained almost unaltered throughout the 1970s, presenting a powerful iconicity predicated more on a socio-religious look than on a rock star paradigm. Likewise, the 'boy-next-door' image of dependability and exotic ordinariness has underpinned the packaging of a variety of pop stars, from the Osmonds and David Cassidy in the 1970s, to Rick Astley, Kylie Minogue and Jason Donovan in the 1980s, and the pop group Hanson in the 1990s, not to mention the whole career of the evergreen Cliff Richard.

However, for pop performers to become pop icons in themselves (as distinct from portraying a certain iconography), the clichéd nature of pop iconography has to be transcended through change. In the 1960s, this was most evident with the Beatles, and in the 1970s with David Bowie. The Beatles' iconography moved from the leather-clad existentialism of the Hamburg days, through the mop-topped besuited light entertainment of the early Epstein years, to the bearded and beaded hippy mysticism of the late 1960s. Each one of these phases touched upon a variety of strands within popular culture and reflected its *Zeitgeist*.

David Bowie's constantly changing visual iconography was more radical in its scope. He was the first rock artist to fully explore the sartorial outrage of both gender confusion and futurism. A sense of the taboo and the exotic was employed to represent the singer's sense of isolation and cultural dislocation. Bowie used the isolation of the outsider, often enacted thematically through allusions to madness and space-age fantasy (following the tradition established by the likes of Sun Ra, George Clinton and Lee 'Scratch' Perry), to create a variety of different personae. In doing so, he appealed to the emotionally dispossessed fan. He demonstrated that a person's personality is constantly in flux, continually being made and remade. By basing a career on mutability, Bowie helped to change the rules of how pop was packaged. From the mid-1970s onward, it was the constant change of visual iconography, rather than its fixity, that became a much-used tactic.

In Bowie's wake, performers like Boy George, Grace Jones, Annie Lennox, Trent Reznor and Marilyn Manson helped queer pop by presenting images of bisexual outrage for the pop mainstream. But the most discussed and theorized pop icon of the 1980s and 1990s was Madonna. Madonna's image-changing and packaging stressed a relentless eroticism that was new to popular music. Her work dealt almost exclusively with the taboo, although her music was abidingly conformist.

In stark contrast to the tradition of exotica and change, some rock artists have sought direct communion with their audience by mimicking the apparel of the ordinary and the mundane. The apogee of the 'honest Joe' strategy is represented by Bruce Springsteen. The packaging of Springsteen as an authentic rocker, virtuoso performer and demotic spokesperson was couched in a studied visual ordinariness. Springsteen's contrived stage garb of shirt and denims was a resolute attempt to demystify pop iconography and to make the pop superstar–fan relationship even.

Other rock stars have used gimmickry and sartorial excess to forge a distinctive media profile. For example, the wearing of eyeglasses has been used to signify an extravagant, flamboyant iconography (as in the case of Elton John) or a downscale fetishization of ordinariness and a certain awkwardness (such as John Lennon, Elvis Costello and Jarvis Cocker – all performers whose visual iconography was far removed from the flamboyance of an Elton John).

Promotional Packaging

The flow of visual ideas that help to create iconography is integral to how popular music has traditionally been packaged. The history of the development of the album cover reflected the changing status of pop iconography and was crucial in selling pop. Although the first record sleeves date from around 1910, album covers with pictures of artists did not appear until about 1939. On recordings for 'colored' or 'race' labels, geometric designs and abstract patterns took the place of any visual iconography of the star performer, reflecting the racism of the music business at the time. In the 1950s, abstract expressionism was much favored in the cover designs for more abstract music, such as modern jazz. Also in the 1950s, the success of film soundtrack albums led to the use on album covers of poster designs that had originated in connection with film promotions. Indeed, the success of Hollywood, and the symbiosis of film and music evidenced by the careers of Crosby, Sinatra, Presley and Cliff Richard, meant that album cover designs began to reflect

'Hollywood glamor gestalt,' with the image of rockers reduced to a 'wholesome vapidity' (see Hipgnosis and Dean 1977, 10). By the 1960s, in both Britain and the United States, an elite group of style arbiters from the worlds of photography, film and fashion influenced heavily the development of popular music iconography, as well as, in some respects, popular music itself. Sleeve designs drew on everyday objects (particularly from the field of advertising), as well as those of high culture. Pop artists such as Andy Warhol and Richard Hamilton were crucial in this regard, both having a huge impact on pop music (see Frith and Horne 1987). Warhol worked with the Velvet Underground, while Hamilton taught influential art-rocker Bryan Ferry. The sleeve for the Beatles' *Sergeant Pepper's Lonely Hearts Club Band* (1967), designed by Peter Blake and Jann Haworth, perhaps constitutes the apogee of this intersection between art and music. Sleeves 'have their own visual vocabulary – a counterpart to the obsessive themes of rock music. Narcissism, make-up, "style," and instant gratifications for the body and mind are reflected in "mood" portraits of fast cars, fast food, comic strips and violent or fetishistic sexuality' (Hipgnosis and Dean 1977, 83).

Equally crucial to promotional packaging was the development of the logo in the mid-1960s. The first promotional campaigns to adopt a band logo were for US psychedelic rock bands Love and the Doors. The members of Love were not deemed photogenic, while the Doors were initially regarded as an act with only a limited underground appeal, so recognizable logos were designed as mainstream promotional tools. A number of bands adopted such logos in the late 1960s, and even had them registered as trademarks. Some genres of music, such as metal and folk, tended toward a generic logo design, with instantly recognizable components (for example, lightning flashes for metal, Celtic lettering for folk). Logos were also used on T-shirts, album covers and other official merchandise. By the 1980s, it was not unusual for individual artists – Adam Ant, for example – to apply for a trademark for every new aspect of their visual style that might appear on their merchandise, and the legal protection of this visual iconography was an important development (see Rimmer 1985). Pop stars became movable icons that could be 'branded' and sold not only through a variety of official and unofficial merchandise (examples include the Beatles bag, the Donovan jacket, the Bowie pants and Spice Girls pencil cases), but also across generic boundaries through such media as video, film and even art. By the 1980s and 1990s, the meaning of rock star iconography had begun to change, with more and more artists adopting a pan-generic approach to the popular arts. Perhaps a result of the diffused nature of contemporary pop iconography was the fact that the 1990s, with the possible exception of Kurt Cobain, produced no single rock icon that critics and public alike agreed had, to some degree, either defined or represented the age.

Bibliography

Baynton, Mavis. 1997. 'Women and the Electric Guitar.' In *Sexing the Groove: Popular Music and Gender*, ed. Sheila Whiteley. London and New York: Routledge, 37–49.

Black, Johnny. 1996. 'Rock Logos: First Class Stamps.' *Q* 119: 60–67.

Branston, Gill, and Stafford, Roy. 1997. *The Media Student's Book*. London and New York: Routledge.

Frith, Simon, and Horne, Howard. 1987. *Art into Pop*. London: Methuen.

Hebdige, Dick. 1979. *Subculture: The Meaning of Style*. London: Methuen.

Hipgnosis, and Dean, Roger. 1977. *The Album Cover Album*. Limpsfield: Dragon's World Limited.

Montgomery, Martin. 1994. 'Icon/Iconic.' In *Key Concepts in Communication and Cultural Studies*, ed. Tim O'Sullivan et al. London and New York: Routledge, 138–39.

Polhemus, Ted. 1994. *Street Style: From Sidewalk to Catwalk*. London: Thames & Hudson.

Polhemus, Ted, and Procter, Lynn. 1984. *Pop Styles: An A-Z to the World Where Fashion Meets Rock 'n' Roll*. London: Vermilion.

Rimmer, Dave. 1985. *Like Punk Never Happened*. London: Faber & Faber.

Rubin, David S. 1995. *It's Only Rock and Roll: Rock and Roll Currents in Contemporary Art*. New York: Prestel.

Walser, Robert. 1993. *Running with the Devil: Power, Gender, and Madness in Heavy Metal Music*. Hanover and London: Wesleyan University Press.

Discographical References

Beatles, The. *Sergeant Pepper's Lonely Hearts Club Band*. Parlophone PCS 7027. *1967*: UK.

This Is Spinal Tap. Polydor 817846. *1984*: USA.

Filmography

This Is Spinal Tap, dir. Rob Reiner. 1984. USA. 82 mins. Comedy ('Mockumentary'). Original music by Christopher Guest, Michael McKean, Rob Reiner, Harry Shearer.

DAVID BUCKLEY

Signifying

'Signifying' is an African-American vernacular term that has been adopted for use in an academic context to theorize African-American rhetorical practise, including music.

A key figure in identifying and analyzing the term was anthropologist Roger D. Abrahams. Noting its use among black men in the streets of Camingerly, Philadelphia, and elsewhere during the 1960s, Abrahams defined the vernacular meaning of 'to signify' as 'to imply, goad, beg, boast by indirect verbal or gestural means. A language of implication' (1970a, 264). He observed its use as being closely connected with the development of performance technique in verbal competitions (1970b, 39) – contests in which participants attempted to outdo one another with the wit and cleverness of their verbal insults (the best known of these was the 'dirty dozens'); thus, signifying was a key element in a culture where 'words are especially valued as power-devices and men-of-words performers find ready audiences' (1970b, 37).

Although the use of signifying was widespread in African-American society in the twentieth century, those who reported and discussed it rarely arrived at a consensus on its use. Mitchell-Kernan (1973), for example, questioned the stress Abrahams and others placed on verbal dueling. One element all agreed was central, however, was that of playing with meaning (through irony, parody, hyperbole and so on). Abrahams noted the popularity of a toast describing the exploits of a trickster figure from African-American folklore, the Signifying Monkey, 'a well-known cool cat who gains his ends through indirection' (1970b, 88).

In a later work, Abrahams made the important shift of beginning to see signifying as 'not only a term for a way of speaking but for a rhetorical strategy that may be characteristic of a number of designated events' (1976, 51). This view was echoed by Mitchell-Kernan, who wrote of signifying as having many sub-types, which when put together constituted a 'kind of art' (1973, 318). The perception that a rhetorical principle had been uncovered, embracing not only vernacular behavior but all expressive forms, and centered upon a variety of figurative or troping devices, lay behind the seminal academic text on signifying, Henry Louis Gates's *The Signifying Monkey* (1988). In developing his theoretical approach, Gates insisted there was no academically imposed distance between it and vernacular practise; rather, he was identifying 'a theory of criticism that is inscribed within the black vernacular tradition' (xix). Hence, his preferred rendering 'Signifyin(g),' a spelling designed to distinguish the term from standard (white) English usage and retain the flavor of vernacular African-American speech.

Gates sees the Signifying Monkey as a direct descendant of the mythical African figure Esu-Elegbara, who stands among other things as the master of style and interpretation. Signifyin(g), the distinguishing feature of the trickster monkey's behavior, is not the passing on of information, but its manipulation. Hence, 'one does not

411

signify something; rather, one signifies in *some* way' (54; italics in original).

Relating this to the standard English meaning of 'signification' and to the linguistic concept of signifier-signified, Gates proposes that African-American culture has in effect decolonized these usages, replacing the semantic register with the rhetorical, the syntagmatic axis with the paradigmatic: 'everything that must be excluded for meaning to remain coherent and linear comes to bear in the process of Signifyin(g)' (1988, 50). At the same time, the shadow of the other meaning remains: the fact that the act of signifying, in whatever context, could be taken as part of a syntagmatic chain of meaning is part of the ambiguity, introducing a kind of vertigo into North American culture. Borrowing Bakhtin's concept of the double-voiced word and quoting, approvingly, from Gary Saul Morson's elaboration of it as 'a special sort of palimpsest in which the uppermost inscription is a commentary on the one beneath it, which the reader (or the audience) can know only by reading through the commentary that obscures in the very process of evaluating' (Morson, quoted in Gates 1988, 50–51), Gates encapsulates signifying as 'black double-voicedness' (Gates 1988, 51).

As Gates points out, 'signifying' makes several appearances as a vernacular term in African-American musical contexts. The jazz clarinet player Mezz Mezzrow, a great devotee of African-American culture, used the word in his autobiography, first published in 1946, suggesting in a Glossary that it meant 'to hint, put on an act, make a gesture' (Mezzrow and Wolfe 1964, 310). Some recordings included the term in their lyrics (the earliest of these appears to have been Ethel Waters' 1928 recording 'Do What You Did Last Night,' on which she sings 'I ain't signifyin''), and some were made with the word in the title, such as Count Basie's 'Signifying.' Blues singer Mary Johnson was credited on her 1936 recording 'Delmar Avenue' as 'Signifyin' Mary.' Gates's own focus is on African-American literature, not music, but he indicates how relevant he believes his reading of signifying to be to music, drawing attention to what he sees as a type of intertextuality. In jazz in particular, the original piece of music is submitted to a process of 'repetition and revision,' sometimes 'repetition and reversal' (1988, 63–64).

In the wake of Gates's study, other scholars have applied his approach specifically to the goal of developing new understandings of African-American music, particularly jazz. Tomlinson, for example, incorporated Gates's theory in his reassessment of the jazz-rock fusion of Miles Davis, in the context of hostile white and black critics, as a 'complex and eloquent Signifyin(g) on the many musical idioms around him' (1991, 262), a process

that includes a challenge to the traditional verities of jazz itself (1991, 257). Monson acknowledged the influence of Gates in her discussion of the transformative processes at work when, in his 1960 recording of 'My Favorite Things,' John Coltrane takes the Broadway tune, both its musical features and its connotations, 'and inverts the piece on nearly every level,' thus challenging 'the ordinary hegemony of white aesthetic values' (1996, 116).

The most extensive application of Gates's theory to music to appear in the 1990s was in the work of Floyd (1995). Building on Gates's idea of repetition and revision, Floyd defined musical signifying as 'the rhetorical use of preexisting material as a means of demonstrating respect for or poking fun at a musical style, process or practice through parody, pastiche, implication, indirection, humor, tone play or word play . . .' (1995, 8). Signifying occurs in the commentary that musical figures offer 'on other musical figures, on themselves, on performances of other music, on other performance of the same piece' (1995, 95).

If the concept can appear overarching and, indeed, essentialist, Atkinson, in her study of contemporary New Orleans (1997), showed that it also has the ability to reveal the range of creative responses to be found within particular communities. Rather than read the city's African-American musical culture, ranging from the pianist James Booker to second line parades, through models developed elsewhere, she was encouraged by Gates's belief that a community holds within itself a way for it to be studied. Atkinson found in signifying a tool for conceptualizing how, through its own particular mix of transformative performance-centered activity, a culture 'speaks with a difference' (1997, 121).

Among variations in the way signifying theory has been applied to the study of African-American music, one common factor is the perception that signifying techniques create a space between text (whether that text be a specific piece, a pre-given form or a style) and performance, in which each is seen in a new light. Signifying performers establish and exploit a position of duality, placing themselves in the interplay between two expressive statements. This distinguishes African-American musical signifying from Barthes' concept of the 'geno-song,' in which the performing voice 'forms a signifying play having nothing to do with communication' (1990, 295). It also raises problems about the occasional tendency – evident in Gates himself – to equate signifying with intertextuality. This is part of a more general difficulty of transferring to music concepts derived in literary criticism. In the particular instance of musical signifying, it suggests that the tendency of intertextuality – despite all disclaimers – to emphasize

412

language may mean it lacks all the necessary tools to deal with the complexities of musical text-performance relationships. It would be better, Monson implies, to think of music as part of a process in which 'signifying as an aesthetic developed from interactive, participatory, turn-taking games and genres that are multiply authored' and hence as the source of its own signifying practises (1996, 87).

From one perspective, the frequent parallels that have been drawn – by Gates and others – between signifying and other concepts, such as the dialogical theory of Bakhtin, suggest that signifying may not be used to set African-American culture apart. In Tomlinson's words, 'the condition of African-American culture . . . provides a compelling instance of the dialogical condition of all culture' (1991, 262). While not arguing for its uniqueness as an expressive strategy, writers such as Floyd insist on its important contribution to the formation and character of African-American musical culture in particular. There are two reasons for this. The first is that, according to this view, African-American signifying is seen as African in origin, and its continuity suggests that what links African and African-American culture is the centrality of interpretive strategies (Floyd 1995, 5, 94). The second is that because, in the circumstances in which enslaved Africans found themselves, much of the material wherein they did their signifying work of repetition–revision belonged to the culture that denigrated and oppressed them, signifying was a key survival strategy and so attained special significance as a creative response. It was out of this particular experience that African Americans, in Floyd's own words, 'became and continue to be poets in a land that initially denied them the right to become artists of any stripe' (1995, 225).

Bibliography

Abrahams, Roger D. 1970a. *Deep Down in the Jungle: Negro Narrative Folklore from the Streets of Philadelphia.* Rev. ed. Chicago: Aldine.

Abrahams, Roger D. 1970b. *Positively Black.* Englewood Cliffs, NJ: Prentice-Hall.

Abrahams, Roger D. 1976. *Talking Black.* Rowley, MA: Newbury House.

Atkinson, Connie Zeanah. 1997. 'Musicmaking in New Orleans: A Reappraisal.' Unpublished Ph.D. thesis, University of Liverpool.

Barthes, Roland. 1990. 'The Grain of the Voice.' In *On Record: Rock, Pop and the Written Word,* ed. Simon Frith and Andrew Goodwin. New York: Pantheon Books, 293–300.

Floyd, Samuel A. 1995. *The Power of Black Music: Interpreting Its History from Africa to the United States.* New York: Oxford University Press.

Gates, Henry Louis. 1988. *The Signifying Monkey: A Theory of Afro-American Literary Criticism.* New York: Oxford University Press.

Mezzrow, Mezz, and Wolfe, Bernard. 1964. *Really the Blues.* New York: Signet Books. (First published New York: Random House, 1946.)

Mitchell-Kernan, Claudia. 1973. 'Signifying as a Form of Verbal Art.' In *Mother Wit from the Laughing Barrel: Readings in the Interpretation of Afro-American Folklore,* ed. Alan Dundes. Englewood Cliffs, NJ: Prentice-Hall, 310–28.

Monson, Ingrid. 1996. *Saying Something: Jazz Improvisation and Interaction.* Chicago: University of Chicago Press.

Tomlinson, Gary. 1991. 'Cultural Dialogics and Jazz: A White Historian Signifies.' *Black Music Research Journal* 11(2): 229–64.

Discographical References

Basie, Count. 'Signifying.' *Kansas City Shout.* Pablo PACD-2310-859-2. 1980; *1992*: USA.

Coltrane, John. 'My Favorite Things.' Atlantic SD 1361. *1960*: USA.

Johnson, Mary. 'Delmar Avenue.' Decca 7305. 1936: USA.

Waters, Ethel. 'Do What You Did Last Night.' Columbia 14380. 1928: USA.

DAVID HORN

Sound (Local)

The notion of a 'local sound' implies some sort of connection between a geographical locality and a particular musical sound or style. It is commonly assumed, for example, that there exists an organic or natural relationship between popular music sounds and styles and the places in which they are produced and consumed, and that such sounds thus reflect aspects of those places. Hence, certain musical genres are known by the name of the place where they originated, such as 'New Orleans jazz,' 'Mississippi blues,' 'Chicago blues,' 'East Coast rap' and 'West Coast rap.' Specific places do provide a distinctive social, cultural and economic context or setting for popular music production and consumption, and this does have an influence on local musical sounds and styles.

Some local sounds have become quite famous within popular music history. They include the so-called 'Seattle sound,' a combination of punk and heavy metal that was linked with Seattle's grunge music scene of the 1980s and with internationally successful bands such as Nirvana; the so-called 'Philadelphia sound,' a new style of rhythm and blues (R&B) that was characterized by strong melodies and classical-style arrangements using strings, horns and layered background vocals, and linked

413

with performers such as Dusty Springfield, Wilson Pickett, the O'Jays and the Blue Notes, all of whom recorded during the early 1970s at Sigma Sound Studios; the so-called 'Memphis sound,' a distinctive style of soul associated with Stax Records during the 1960s and early 1970s, and linked with Stax artists such as Otis Redding, Johnnie Taylor, and Booker T. and the MGs; and the so-called 'Detroit sound,' a catchy dance-oriented pop with gospel elements, a tight groove and lyrics whose subject matter was typically that of relationships. This latter sound was associated with Detroit's Tamla Motown Record Corporation, established in 1959 by Berry Gordy, and with Tamla Motown artists such as Stevie Wonder, Marvin Gaye, the Four Tops and the Temptations.

Two other examples of 'local sounds' can be discussed in more detail in order to illustrate the processes through which they emerge and endure. The 'Liverpool sound' has been associated with many of the city's rock and pop bands and particularly with the Beatles. The sound is generally guitar- and sometimes keyboard-based, and of medium tempo; it features a strong emphasis on song and melody rather than on rhythm and discord, and relatively high-pitched male vocals characterized by thin, reedy or nasal tones, the distinctiveness of which may be partly attributed to the Liverpool accent and vernacular with their highly recognizable styles of intonation, pronunciation and phrasing. Such sounds might reflect various local factors, such as patterns of immigration and settlement (the Irish immigrants, for example, brought with them an emphasis on song and melody), and trade and military links with the United States which brought to the city such US musical influences as jazz, country, R&B, soul and rock 'n' roll (Cohen 1991).

Similarly, the 'Miami sound' emerged from the specific material and geographical conditions of music production within Miami itself (see Negus 1996, 185–88, and Curtis and Rose 1983). Following the Cuban revolution of 1959, for example, many Cubans migrated to Florida, bringing with them the Spanish language and a range of Afro-Latin musical forms. These interacted with various local rock, soul and disco styles to produce new hybrid musical sounds and styles peculiar to Miami. They involved 'a blend of rock-pop song structure . . . with the repeated rhythmic chordal patterns and matrices of much Latin music' (Negus 1996, 187), a combination of Cuban, rock and disco rhythms, a merging of bongo and conga drums with the electric guitar and piano, and lyrics sung and recorded in both Spanish and English. Many of the Cuban immigrants invested in local music production facilities, which attracted to Miami Latin musicians from elsewhere and produced a creative environment that encouraged the emergence of the new 'Miami sound.' In addition, the growing network of Spanish-language radio stations provided an outlet for the promotion and distribution of the sound.

Local popular music sounds and styles have thus emerged through processes of cultural change and exchange, borrowing and appropriation, blending and imitation – processes that reflect popular music's geographical mobility and widespread commercial availability. It is often difficult, therefore, to distinguish local from nonlocal sounds, and the relationship between the sound and the locality is not a straightforward or homological one; hence, popular music cannot be simply connected to the local as if it directly mirrored it. Furthermore, even if it were possible to point to the existence of a local sound, it would not necessarily mean that those who perform and listen to the music understand it in terms of the local (Street 1995, 259). Nevertheless, the notion of a local sound is important and has continued to attract much discussion and debate. This suggests that a local sound should be considered not only in terms of distinctive structural and political settings for popular music production and consumption, but also in terms of meaning and ideology.

Many Liverpool musicians, for example, believe that there is a distinctive Liverpool rock, dance or country sound, but they tend to define and describe that sound in different ways. Often, the sound is distinguished by contrasting it with the sounds of other places, such as those of nearby Manchester. Popular music sounds are thus used to draw conceptual boundaries between localities, boundaries that reflect rivalries as well as real and perceived differences between places, revolving around issues of class, money and so on. This process often involves the association of local sounds with a romantic ideology familiar to rock and folk culture, involving notions of authenticity, difference, community and local identity, with some musical sounds and styles perceived as more genuine, honest or real with regard to the way in which they represent or express the local (Cohen 1994).

This 'rhetoric of the local' in popular music culture (Street 1995) indicates the way in which the local is imagined through music-related discourse, and how musicians and musical sounds and styles are 'placed' through the way in which people hear and interpret music. The local, national and international music media (especially the music press) strongly influence such definitions and interpretations. Particular music journals, for example, often associate rock musicians and their music with the places they have come from, a practise that varies according to musical style and genre.

Bibliography

Cohen, Sara. 1991. *Rock Culture in Liverpool: Popular Music in the Making*. Oxford: Oxford University Press.

Cohen, Sara. 1994. 'Mapping the Sound: Identity, Place, and the Liverpool Sound.' In *Ethnicity, Identity and Music: The Musical Construction of Place*, ed. Martin Stokes. Oxford: Berg, 117–34.

Curtis, J., and Rose, R. 1983. 'The Miami Sound: A Contemporary Latin Form of Place-Specific Music.' *Journal of Cultural Geography* 4: 110–18.

Negus, Keith. 1996. *Popular Music in Theory: An Introduction*. Cambridge: Polity Press.

Street, John. 1995. '(Dis)located?: Rhetoric, Politics, Meaning and the Locality.' In *Popular Music: Style and Identity*, ed. Will Straw et al. Montréal: The Centre for Research on Canadian Cultural Industries and Institutions, 255–63.

SARA COHEN

Spectacle

A spectacle can be defined as a specially arranged display comprising an impressive entertainment or show. Spectacles therefore involve a fundamental emphasis on the visual.

As a consequence, within popular music the 'spectacular' implies an emphasis on the visual that becomes so predominant as to overshadow, rather than comment upon or complement, the music being performed. Elvis Presley or the Sex Pistols may be said to have had a stage act, in which the visual expression of the music focused on the body, but Jean-Michel Jarre, a solo instrumentalist who has staged huge outdoor shows in urban environments with the help of lasers, projections and state-of-the-art visual interactive sequences, deals in the spectacular. In Jarre's concerts, the attention is firmly on a collage of visual ideas that, for some, threaten to overshadow the musical element of the show and that are disassociated from the site of the performance itself. The performance site – the environment (Jarre has projected images onto skyscrapers and well-known architectural landmarks) – is the rationale behind the show itself.

In some important respects, the emergence in the twentieth century of the Broadway musical, the street carnival and the elaborately staged rock extravaganza resurrected the idea of the spectacle that was common in antiquity. According to Michel Foucault, antiquity had been a civilization of spectacle. The problem facing the temple, the theater and the circus was to render 'accessible to a multitude of men the inspection of a small number of objects' (N.H. Julius, *Leçon sur les prisons* (1831), quoted in Foucault 1998, 478). The modern age, however, was faced with the reverse: how to provide the instantaneous viewing of many people for one individual. Foucault concluded that 'our society is not one of spectacle, but of surveillance' (1998, 478), as the pan-opticon, the security camera and George Orwell's *1984* ('Big Brother is watching you') all suggest.

In contrast, the rock spectacle has developed from a need to solve the same problem that gave rise to the great spectacles of antiquity, but has drawn in addition on possibilities provided by modern technologies. Successful rock groups have been forced by economic logistics to play in ever-larger venues. The main difficulty is how to make the events on stage exciting to huge audiences, nine-tenths of whom are too far away to actually see, and therefore identify with, the intricacies of the performance. By way of a solution, beginning in the 1970s, rock groups adopted an overt theatricality based on grand visual gestures.

Genesis in the Phil Collins era and Pink Floyd pioneered the use of lasers, dry ice, film projections, light shows and, in the case of Pink Floyd, in order to cover up a lack of showmanship and personality on stage, such bold visual spectacles as inflatable flying pigs. Roger Waters, co-founder and ex-member of Pink Floyd, was involved in a similar kind of spectacle when, in 1990, Pink Floyd's *The Wall*, first released in 1979, was performed live in Berlin to celebrate the collapse of the Berlin Wall. As Steve Pond (1990) reports, 'The purpose of the extravagant show [was] to raise money for the Memorial Fund for Disaster Relief, a British charity headed by the decorated World War II flyer Leonard Cheshire' (29). *The Wall* had not been performed live since the Pink Floyd tour of 1980–81. The spectacular character of the 1990 performance, which involved Waters' Bleeding Heart Band (Waters had split acrimoniously with his Pink Floyd colleagues in the mid-1980s), was assured by an array of special guests such as Bryan Adams, Marianne Faithfull, Cyndi Lauper, Joni Mitchell and Sinéad O'Connor, as well as by larger bricks, larger inflatable puppets and a larger audience than for any previous live performance of *The Wall*.

The rock spectacle continued to be developed during the 1970s by even more obviously photogenic and athletic performers such as the Rolling Stones (their 1976 tour included a huge inflatable penis on stage). Very soon the rock spectacle became less about the promotion of an individual artistic vision and more about gadgetry and a certain lighthearted comic-book artifice (for example, Iron Maiden's cadaverous stage monster, Eddie; the entire stage show of the group Kiss; or Alice Cooper's robotic Frankenstein monster). Perhaps the apogee of the pop spectacle was reached by mid-1970s funk, particularly the space-age imagery of George Clinton's Funkadelic and Parliament shows, which saw the band descend to the stage from the mock-up of a huge alien craft hovering above it.

New audiovisual technologies, such as the development of huge 'diamond vision' screens in the 1980s and interactive technologies in the 1990s, have relayed the onstage action via the video screen, thus making the rock spectacle a confusion of television, video and real-time performance.

The rock spectacle forms an important constituent of what, in 1967, Guy Debord famously called 'the society of the spectacle.' He contended that the endless flow of media images was a form of ideological control, which kept the spectator-consumer pacified and isolated. Watson (1994) argues that 'the hypnotism of the spectacle replaces lived life with passive observation of the activities of the famous and the successful' (65). Nowhere, perhaps, was this sense of spectacle better evidenced than in the opening of the 1984 summer Olympic Games in Los Angeles. The suspension of reality involved in the acceptance of such events was nicely pointed out by a *Time* reporter when he asked: 'Why in a world of real troubles should the heart leap up at the spectacle of 125 trumpeters trumpeting, 960 voices choiring, 1,065 high school girls . . . drilling in the sun? . . . Why didn't 84 pianists in blue playing *Rhapsody in Blue* look preposterous?' (Rosenblatt 1984, 10).

Other kinds of events, such as the street carnival, the Mardi Gras and the German tradition of *Karneval/Fasching*, are ones that mix music, revelry and spectacle (often incorporating comedic, cross-dressing elements) rather differently. Writing about the New Orleans Mardi Gras, George Lipsitz has shown how such events not only celebrate a fictive past, 'release tension from the repressions and frustration of everyday life' and uphold the individuals' 'right to be other,' as Mikhail Bahktin wrote (quoted in Lipsitz 1990, 238), but also play a role in voicing the concerns of the disenfranchised and in attacking mainstream society through the spectacle.

Historically, other forms of the spectacular can be found in a variety of different contexts. Minstrelsy, the first indigenous US musical form to win widespread popularity abroad, became increasingly reliant on spectacle. The finale of the minstrel show consisted of dances (breakdowns, double shuffles, heel-and-toe and, later, cakewalks) in which the audience was invited to improvise 'the most ridiculous strutting march' (Clarke 1995, 24). Later in the nineteenth century, the minstrel show included playlets, lampoons of current events and spoofs of popular plays, and developed a repertoire of stock characters and 'ever fancier spectacles' (Clarke 1995, 26).

However, spectacle was more centrally important in musical theater, and from the earliest days. Root (1981) reports that *The Black Crook* (1866) 'is the only popular stage musical of the nineteenth century which is consistently included in histories of American theater or musical theater.' The reason for this, continues Root, 'is

not because it was the first of its genre . . . but because it set a record for the longest continuous run of a Broadway show . . . and attracted more attention in the press and in the pulpit than any other nineteenth-century musical production' (79). *The Black Crook* attracted this attention because it was, indeed, more of a spectacle than a musical. The spectacle took two forms: theatrical, using new stage technology, particularly lighting, to create, in the words of one critic, 'the most magnificent scenic drama ever put before the people of this country' (quoted in Root 1981, 87); and gendered, presenting women as the object of the male gaze. As Root reports, 'there were rumors of costumes approaching nudity for some of the dancers' (1981, 80). The Rev. Charles B. Smythe was as a consequence led to denounce the dancers' 'immodest dress . . . with thin gauze-like material allowing the form of the figure to be discernible,' and 'attitudes [that] were exceedingly indelicate' (quoted in Root 1981, 81).

Women as the object of the male gaze have continued to constitute a prominent dimension of spectacle in popular music. Charters and Kunstadt (1981), for example, refer to a review of the acts at the famous Cotton Club in 1920s Harlem which observed that 'as in the past, the undressed thing goes double.' The review continued: 'The big attraction, of course, are the gals, 10 of 'em, the majority of whom in white company could pass for Caucasians.' The review concluded: 'Possessed of the native jazz heritage, their hotsy-totsy performance of working sans wraps could never be parred by a white gal' (quoted in Charters and Kunstadt 1981, 219).

Such occurrences in music and film attracted the attention of feminist critics in the 1970s. Perhaps the best known of these critics is Laura Mulvey, who in 1975 observed that 'in a world ordered by sexual imbalance, pleasure in looking has been split between active/male and passive/female.' As Mulvey concluded, 'Woman displayed as sexual object is the leitmotif of erotic spectacle: from pin-ups to stripe-tease [*sic*], from Ziegfeld to Busby Berkeley, she holds the look, plays to and signifies male desire' (Mulvey 1990, 33). Gender thus plays an important part in the theorization of spectacle within contemporary culture. More recently, and within the context of popular music specifically, Robert Walser has talked about how 'assertive, spectacular display' is 'problematic in the context of a patriarchal order that is invested in the stability of signs and that seeks to maintain women in the position of object of the male gaze' (1993, 16). The character of this problem was highlighted in the Republic of Ireland in 1986 when singer and topless model Samantha Fox was forced to cut short her show and 'flee to her dressing room after a series of very determined advances by male fans who took the title of her hit song "Touch Me" just a bit too literally' (*Sunday World*, 1 June 1986, quoted in Smith 1989, 24).

Bibliography

Charters, Samuel B., and Kunstadt, Leonard. 1981. *Jazz: A History of the New York Scene*. New York: Da Capo Press.

Clarke, Donald. 1995. *The Rise and Fall of Popular Music*. Harmondsworth: Viking.

Debord, Guy. 1967. *La Société du spectacle* [The Society of the Spectacle]. Paris: Buchet Chastel.

Foucault, Michel. 1998 (1977). 'Discipline and Punish.' In *Literary Theory: An Anthology*, ed. Julie Rivkin and Michael Ryan. Malden and Oxford: Blackwell, 464–87.

Lipsitz, George. 1990. *Time Passages: Collective Memory and American Popular Culture*. Minneapolis and London: University of Minnesota Press.

Marcus, Greil. 1997 (1989). *Lipstick Traces: A Secret History of the Twentieth Century*. London: Macmillan.

Mulvey, Laura. 1990 (1975). 'Visual Pleasure and Narrative Cinema.' In *Issues in Feminist Film Criticism*, ed. Patricia Erens. Bloomington, IN: Indiana University Press, 28–40.

Orwell, George. 1949. *Nineteen Eighty-Four, a Novel*. London: Secker & Warburg.

Pond, Steve. 1990. 'Roger Waters on "The Wall."' *Rolling Stone* (9 August): 29.

Root, Deane L. 1981. *American Popular Stage Music, 1860–1880*. Ann Arbor, MI: UMI Research Press.

Rosenblatt, Roger. 1984. 'A Glorious Ritual.' *Time* (6 August): 10–15.

Smith, Joan. 1989. *Misogynies: Reflections on Myths and Malice*. London: Faber and Faber.

Walser, Robert. 1993. *Running with the Devil: Power, Gender and Madness in Heavy Metal Music*. Hanover and London: Wesleyan University Press.

Watson, Ben. 1994. *Frank Zappa: The Negative Dialectics of Poodle Play*. London: Quartet.

Discographical References

Fox, Samantha. 'Touch Me.' Jive FOXY 1. *1986*: UK.
Pink Floyd. *The Wall*. Columbia 36183. *1979*: USA.
Waters, Roger. *The Wall: Live in Berlin, 1990*. Mercury 846611-1. *1990*: USA.

Visual Recording

Waters, Roger. 1990. 'The Wall Live in Berlin Video.' Mercury 8466111 (video).

DAVID BUCKLEY and JOHN SHEPHERD

Style

'Style' is a term that has a considerable range of meanings. Most generally, style refers (although certainly not exclusively so) to the characteristic manner in which something is done. The term 'style' originates from the Latin word *stilus*, the ancient Roman writing tool, connoting 'a way of writing.'

More specifically, style can refer to: a way of living (as in 'life style'); the distinguishing way in which an action is performed, an operation is carried out, a function fulfilled or a task executed; the mode of expression characteristic of a particular type of writing, painting, architecture or music, or of the artistic or cultural work of a particular individual; and a particular manner of dress, as in fashion.

In all these meanings, there is an implication that style has to do with matters of form and expression rather than with those of substance. Artistic and cultural style, for example, have been thought of by some as little more than vehicles for aesthetic experience (see, for example, Meyer 1956, 65). However, the realms of form and substance are thought of by others as being much more intimately related, with style being indispensable to the essence of what is being executed or expressed.

All these meanings can apply to the world of popular music and in, so doing, frequently overlap and intersect. In the late 1960s, for example, the hippie cultures of cities such as San Francisco could be thought of as evidencing an all-encompassing and distinctive life style, to which particular kinds of social relations, singular fashions of dress and drug use, unusual hairstyles, and a specific type of music all contributed. In its broadest sense, style in popular music therefore typically brings into play a whole range of activities and modes of expression that are not musical in the strictest sense, but without which an appreciation of style in popular music would be incomplete. Popular music is thus one element through which various cultures enact integrated, identifying styles that involve a range of behaviors and modes of expression other than the musical, as well as the appropriation of artifacts and cultural symbols from other times and places. This creation of identity through style has been referred to as a process of 'stylisation' (Hall and Jefferson 1976). A seminal book in understanding such processes is Dick Hebdige's *Subculture: The Meaning of Style* (1979).

Style is a crucial element in the way in which popular musicians are presented, positioned and marketed by the music industry. Through image, dress, performance practises, press releases and media accounts, popular music personae are created and then used by consumers in their own processes of identity formation and maintenance. Central to both sets of processes since the advent of sophisticated recording technologies in the 1960s and afterward has been the notion of the 'sound.' As Jones (1992) has observed, 'the primary impact of recording technology has been to make the sound of a recording its identifying characteristic. One can refer to the "Phil Spector" sound, or the "Motown" sound . . . the overall sound of a record is a means to identify the performer(s)' (12).

The importance of the 'sound' to different styles of popular music raises the issue of style in a more specifically musical context. Where music is concerned, style customarily refers to recurring features of a technical (that is to say, sonic) kind that are taken to be characteristic of a particular set of musical events. Stylistic characteristics in music can thus have to do with, for example, harmonic, melodic, rhythmic, timbral, textural, vocal or instrumental features. In the case of popular music, such features can include sounds produced with the aid of electronic technology, such as fuzz and wah-wah effects in rock guitar playing.

The term has an established history in the academic discipline of musicology, and has been used in relation to the music of an individual composer or performer, of a group of musicians, a place, a period of time or a genre. However, it has equal applicability in relation to popular music. Extended discussions of this more musicological understanding of style in the context of popular music are to be found, for example, in Middleton (1990) and Moore (1993). Reference can therefore be made, on the one hand, to 'the style of Beethoven,' or even to the compositional styles characteristic of different periods of his life (see Grout 1980, 527–48). However, on the other hand, in the case of popular music, such individuality of style can apply not only to composers and performers, but also to producers. An early example is provided by Sam Phillips of Sun Records. Sun, reports Jones, 'had a unique sound, identifiable . . . yet uncharacteristic of other recordings of the mid-1950s' (1992, 61). Like Leonard Chess, observes Guralnick (1971), Phillips 'was one of the first to go for a heavy echo effect, but the overall sound was crisp, clean, and full of life' (174). Other producers with a trademark style have been Trevor Horn in pop music and Mutt Lange in rock.

Where groups of musicians are concerned, reference can be made to the distinctive, a cappella singing style of many doo-wop groups in the 1950s and after. Where places are concerned, reference can be made to the characteristic stylistic features of the choral and instrumental music of Venice in the sixteenth century: 'Venetian music was characteristically of full, rich texture, homophonic rather than contrapuntal, varied and colorful in sonority' (Grout 1980, 288). However, the notion of place in relation to style is just as prevalent, if not more so, in the realm of popular music. Reference is made, for example, to the 'Philadelphia sound,' the 'Memphis sound,' the 'Seattle sound' and the 'Liverpool sound.'

Musicologists talk also of the stylistic characteristics of different periods of music history, such as that of nine-

teenth-century Romanticism. Popular music aficionados talk of 'an 80s production style.' Finally, it is possible to talk of the stylistic features of different genres of music. Hebdige (1987), for example, is clear on the difference between ska and rocksteady. They were, he says, 'mixed differently.' In ska, 'the vocal track had been given prominence.' However, on the new rocksteady records, 'the singers' voices tended to be treated like any other instrument . . . pride of place was given to the bass guitar' (1987, 72).

In referring to codified ways of creating, performing and appreciating music, which must conform also to wider, social conventions, the term 'style' is related to that of 'genre' and is sometimes used as its synonym. However, in a narrower, musicological sense, style implies an emphasis on musical codes, while genre relates to all kinds of other codes that are referred to in the context of a musical event. Thus, in the case of music, discussion of a genre such as heavy metal may have to do with elements such as language, iconography, and conventions governing modes of production and consumption, as in, for example, expected, normative patterns of behavior at heavy metal concerts (see, for example, Weinstein 1991). A discussion of style in the narrower, musicological sense, in the case of heavy metal, would concentrate on the sonic elements of the music, such as virtuoso guitar playing. In this sense, the two terms 'genre' and 'style' cover different sets of phenomena, overlapping only when style is referred to in the discussion of a particular genre – as distinct from the discussion of a composer, performer, group of musicians, place or period. However, the common usage of the term 'style' to indicate a way of living, behaving or dressing also indicates the possibility for very considerable overlap between the two terms.

Nonetheless, as a personal feature, style can be maintained across forms and genres: for example, Ennio Morricone's composing style can be recognized as such in his film music as well as in pop songs, and even in his orchestrations for songs in the singer-songwriter genre. The same can be said of many performers, although a quality that is often demanded from session and backing musicians is exactly the opposite – that is, to be able to perform in a given style, and not to impose their own. On the other hand, parody and stylistic quotation are quite common strategies in popular music, providing composers and performers with straightforward tools to create other 'selves' (and/or to hide their own): well-known examples range from the Beatles' *Sergeant Pepper's Lonely Hearts Club Band* to Bob Dylan's *Nashville Skyline* to a large part of Frank Zappa's work.

The term 'style' can thus carry wider connotations in popular music studies than it has tended to do in established forms of musicology. In the latter, there has been a marked tendency to reduce understandings of music to the perceived conditions of its sounds. This has resulted in a heavily 'stylistic' understanding of music and its significance. With the prominence within popular music studies of different forms of cultural and social theory, the tendency to reduce understandings of music to understandings of its stylistic characteristics has been both strongly resisted and criticized.

Smith (1994) comments on this kind of tendency in discussing styles of Irish traditional music. He observes that 'regional, usually county, categories are often used by musicians and commentators to explain and discuss musical differences between players' (231). In some cases, Smith continues, 'the patterns of differences are elusive and subtle, and research suggests that even the most experienced listeners cannot consistently distinguish stylistic differences.' This does not mean, he concludes, that 'discussion of regional styles of playing is delusion or meaningless, but that more than merely musical sound is being discussed' (1994, 231). Jones has indicated what this 'more' might be in referring to a 'cultural sense.' This sense, he says, 'creates a space within which popular music can operate, and a space within which audience discourse concerning popular music takes on meaning, in terms of sound' (1992, 62). Herein, perhaps, lie both a crucial distinction and a crucial relationship between style and genre.

Bibliography

Grout, Donald Jay. 1980. *A History of Western Music*. 3rd ed. New York: W.W. Norton.

Guralnick, Peter. 1971. *Feel Like Going Home: Portraits in Blues and Rock 'n' Roll*. New York: Outerbridge & Dienstfrey.

Hall, Stuart, and Jefferson, Tony, eds. 1976. *Resistance Through Rituals: Youth Subcultures in Post-War Britain*. London: Hutchinson.

Hebdige, Dick. 1979. *Subculture: The Meaning of Style*. London: Methuen.

Hebdige, Dick. 1987. *Cut 'n' Mix: Culture, Identity, and Caribbean Music*. New York: Methuen.

Jones, Steve. 1992. *Rock Formation: Music, Technology, and Mass Communication*. Newbury Park, CA: Sage Publications.

Meyer, Leonard B. 1956. *Emotion and Meaning in Music*. Chicago: University of Chicago Press.

Middleton, Richard. 1990. *Studying Popular Music*. Milton Keynes and Philadelphia: Open University Press.

Moore, Allan F. 1993. *Rock, the Primary Text: Developing a Musicology of Rock*. Milton Keynes and Philadelphia: Open University Press.

Smith, Graeme. 1994. 'My Love Is in America: Migration and Irish Music.' In *The Irish World Wide: History, Heritage, Identity. Vol. 3: The Creative Migrant*, ed. Patrick O'Sullivan. Leicester: Leicester University Press, 221–36.

Weinstein, Deena. 1991. *Heavy Metal: A Cultural Sociology*. New York: Lexington Books.

Discographical References

Beatles, The. *Sergeant Pepper's Lonely Hearts Club Band*. Parlophone PCS 7027. *1967*: UK.

Dylan, Bob. *Nashville Skyline*. Columbia 09825. *1969*: USA.

JOHN SHEPHERD with FRANCO FABBRI and MARION LEONARD

5. Venues

Venues

Introduction

In terms of the practise of popular music, a 'venue' may be defined as any place where popular music is performed.

Broadly speaking, there are two types of venue. The first is a place where music is performed for an audience, an audience in this instance being defined as listeners gathered primarily to experience the music. In this context, the use of the term 'venue' (derived from the French *venir*, meaning 'to come') implies that venues are places that people come to with the intent of hearing music. This kind of venue (concert halls, stadia) may bear witness to a heightened sense of ritual and territorial power. Indeed, it can be argued that much of the territorial power connected with the term 'venue' comes from the classical music tradition, where the audience and musicians are part of an almost quasi-religious ritual, the venue becoming something of a nonsecular temple and shrine, the musical proceedings directed by the conductor, as personification of the high priest (see Small 1996). However, the venue as a place of intent may not be as imposing or formal, and may bear witness to a less heightened sense of ritual and power. In this vein, ethnographers such as Ruth Finnegan (1989) have written about the complexity of musical practise at the grass-roots level. Library foyers, school halls, churches, public parks and the like all become venues for various amateur and professional musicians within the community. With this first kind of venue, a distinction can be drawn between dedicated spaces such as concert halls, and spaces such as stadia, churches or bars whose primary purpose is usually other than that of musical performance. These latter venues may in this sense be thought of as transitory. Venues of this first kind normally, but not always, require payment for entry.

The second kind of venue is a place where individuals hear music as a consequence of an activity other than that of going to hear a performance of music. People do not normally go to the London Underground specifically to hear their favorite busker, for example. The Underground can thus be thought of as another kind of transitory venue for popular music, one where a public space becomes a venue unintentionally. As a result, these kinds of locations may be said to be venues for popular music. Muzak is ever present in the shopping center, the workplace and even in hotel elevators, for example. Sporting events also constitute venues in which popular music is heard and enjoyed as an adjunct to the main attraction, either in the form of live or recorded music played before the game, or in the form of songs typically sung at a sporting event (for example, the various 'terrace chants' sung and composed by soccer supporters). Venues of this kind do not normally require payment or, if they do (such as in the case of a sporting venue), they do so for the principal activity rather than for the secondary or consequential activity of hearing music. Payment may also be voluntary. There are types of musician, such as buskers, who regularly perform music in subways and shopping malls without any guarantee of financial gain, although financial gain is clearly their intent.

Both kinds of venue may be thought of as being constituted by what Middleton (1990) has referred to as a 'framed public place.' However, in some non-Western cultures, there may not necessarily be any physical space delineated for the performance of music or, if there is, it may not necessarily be a building or structure. In tribal societies, for example, the venue may be the campfire or some other focal point.

Venues for Popular Music in the Nineteenth and Early Twentieth Centuries

Before the advent of significant urbanization in the second half of the nineteenth century, popular music performers would travel to the audience rather than the audience to a venue. The development of vaudeville in the United States and the popularity of public houses (pubs), clubs and the music hall in Great Britain are aspects of urbanization and led to the creation of specific sites where people went to listen to music, thereby marking the end of the near monopoly that itinerant musicians had on the performance of popular music.

One of the earliest venues for the performance of popular music in Britain and Ireland was the pub. The pub had long been a center for various recreational activities such as gaming, gambling and singing. The pub sing-song dates back to the Anglo-Saxon age when people 'wassailed' (made merry) in alehouses. By the mid-nineteenth century, many pubs and music saloons set aside a separate room in which local acts or members of the public could perform 'turns' (see Kelly 1998, 90). Those with power and influence regarded these public spaces as potentially politically subversive, as the working classes sang songs that poked fun at upper-class society.

The concept of the venue as a place to which people went specifically to listen to and to perform music was taken up by the middle and upper classes, as the popularity of London's 'song-and-supper rooms' attests (see Gammond 1993, 585). The ascendancy of the music hall in the mid-1850s was the result of an ever-increasing need to create new venues for the dissemination of popular music. The United States saw the parallel development of the concert saloon – for example, White's Varieties in New York, which opened in 1852 – and the 'variety' repertoire. These saloons 'echoed the London model of a small stage at one end for the entertainers, who had to compete with the eating, drinking, and smoking of the highly vocal customers' (Gammond 1993, 585). By the 1860s, these male-dominated saloons were being superseded by larger halls, such as the Broadway Music Hall, which provided family entertainment. Similar venues were established throughout the major cities of the United States and, by the 1880s, there was a recognizable vaudeville scene. By 1900, according to Gammond, 'it was estimated that the ratio of people patronising vaudeville to those attending other kinds of theatre was ten to one' (1993, 586).

Some historians have suggested that the arrival and development of the music hall in the second half of the nineteenth century retarded an incipient working-class consciousness, as expressed through live entertainment in the pub, that was critical of those with power and influence. During this period, sing-alongs remained popular, but 'amateur performances yielded to the growing numbers of professional entertainers' (Kelly 1998, 91). The music hall was therefore one of the first types of venue to highlight the physical, economic and aesthetic gap between paid performer and paying audience. Whereas in bars and singing saloons the audience members were the performers (and vice versa), the music hall, which soon built up a roster of professional acts and repertoires, and which was often housed in venues that could seat thousands of customers, ensured that the audience became not only 'sedated' in fixed seating, but also more of a 'spectatorate' (Kelly 1998, 92).

Working-men's clubs were originally conceived as an antidote to the 'moral laxitude' of the pub and the music hall, and were initially intended to provide a mixture of entertainment and edification, with readings and lectures part of the evening's entertainment. Soon, however, the emphasis was on the solo 'turn,' where a member of the audience was invited, or cajoled, into performing. Working-men's clubs and clubs with party-political or trade-union affiliations became an important part of working-class entertainment in the United Kingdom, and song and dance were integral to their proper functioning.

In the United States, one particular form of late nineteenth-century drinking and gambling venue played a significant role in the development of popular music. The African-American 'jook joint' emerged after the Civil War as a black-owned, lower-class nightspot catering for both a local and a migratory rural black work force. Particularly during the post-Reconstruction period, after 1877, when the end of government support for black progress in the South turned African Americans back to their own cultural resources, the jooks became crossroad points where ideas and practises from different regions met and cross-fertilized, away from the white gaze. Here, in the words of Hazzard-Gordon (1990), 'dance steps once linked to ritualistic or religious dancing . . . acquired a more firmly rooted secular identity' (81). Providing traveling entertainers both with work and with opportunities to meet each other, the 'smelly shoddy confines' of the jooks, as Zora Neale Hurston described them (quoted in Hazzard-Gordon 1990, 83), became one of the key places where African-American secular music began to take shape.

Further development of African-American music and dance took place in the urban jooks, usually known as honky-tonks – small, noisy bars that also continued the institutionalized link between drinking and music. In due course, the honky-tonk crossed over into working-class white society, becoming a prominent feature of the Texas oil boom during the Depression years of the 1930s. Like the rave warehouse and the festival, the honky-tonk occupied a space outside the geographical limit of both the town and suburb. In the case of the honky-tonk, this was because it was cheaper and safer to set up outside town, and police supervision of such venues tended to be lax. The honky-tonk also had a direct influence on musical practise. As a focal point for a certain disaffection and lawlessness, the lyrical component of the country music performed there, particularly after the Depression of the late 1920s and 1930s, tended to have a more socio-realistic edge, depicting the insecurities of the newly urbanized country dweller in an era of migration and social mobility. There were also topical songs and good-time songs suited to the venue, such as 'Honky Tonk Blues' and 'Stompin' at the Honky Tonk.' The particularly noisy atmosphere prevalent at these venues meant that instrumentation had to change. Since this was primarily music to dance to, the beat became more insistent and the playing of a stock rhythm, utilizing 'closed chords, or the striking of all six strings in unison' (Malone 1985, 154), was a common technique. By the end of the 1930s, the use of the electric guitar was commonplace. Like other small-scale venues such as bars and pubs, honky-tonks were vital in that they gave neophyte performers a chance to cut their teeth. The development of the honky-tonk, therefore, shows how the type of venue in which music is performed can alter an individual style of music over time.

The Relationship Between Venue and Musical Practise

For some genres of popular music, such as those made and enjoyed on a more democratic level in much the same way as folk song, or minstrelsy in the years before urbanization, the venue is the street. Jamaican reggae and ska, LA rap and hip-hop and Latin American calypso are just some examples. Ska emerged in Jamaica's urban slums. Rap and hip-hop incorporate elements of dance and graffiti art, and remain essentially a street phenomenon, forging a 'scene' entirely dependent upon 'face-to-face' social contact and social interaction (Dimitriadis 1996, 179). But almost all styles of music produced on the street migrate to other, more formal venues. The calendric nature of carnival meant that calypso music became part of the colorful street-life parade. However, it was also performed in halls and theaters called 'tents' (see Manuel 1988, 59), analogous to the blues club or 'juke joint' (see Mahabir 1996, 59).

Certain styles of music are overwhelmingly dependent on the site of their production and dissemination. In other words, whereas certain performers and certain styles of music could just as successfully be enjoyed in the smallest club or the largest stadium, other styles depend on a specific environment for their formation. For example, the 1970s 'pub rock' movement was, as Andrew Bennett (1997) points out, 'defined by its venue, not by any musical characteristics.' Pub rock placed the emphasis on accessibility – on making the star–fan relationship more even – and denoted a 'certain sensibility regarding the performance and consumption of popular music in the informal atmosphere of the pub venue' (1997, 98).

Friendly informality is central to pub music throughout Western Europe. The German concept of *Gemütlichkeit* (which roughly translates as 'friendly informality') is central to that country's culture. Likewise, the concept of *hygge*, the Danish equivalent of *Gemütlichkeit*, informs the tradition of pub music in that country (see Björnberg and Stockfelt (1996) and their study of Danish pub music).

Small-scale venues are an essential breeding ground for many genres of popular music throughout the world. For example, cafés, bars, nightclubs, brothels, buses and taxis are just some of the sites that are crucial to the dissemination of the Turkish 'arabesque,' a musical culture highly critical of the state and government (see Stokes 1992). The Latin American musical genre *nueva canción* evolved in the *peñas* (coffeehouses) of Santiago, Chile, in particular, in the early 1960s, before becoming a mass musical movement popular at large-scale festivals. These coffeehouses were frequented by musicians who were also political activists, and the venue, therefore, became part of Latin American oppositional culture. Likewise, in France, the coffee bar was a popular rendezvous in the 1950s and 1960s for intellectuals, artists and musicians critical of those in power.

In his seminal study of grass-roots music-making, Bennett (1980) reveals the internal politics surrounding getting a 'gig.' Bennett identifies three classes of gig: the 'social gig' (such as dances and parties at social clubs, sororities, student events); 'ceremonial gigs' (weddings, parties, bar mitzvahs, graduations and so on); and 'bar gigs.' He not only anatomizes the types of small-scale venue available for the dissemination of popular music, but also shows how the acoustics of any given venue can alter the musical aesthetic of the performers. A 'good room' and, therefore, a 'good venue,' is not simply one in which the band is able to play at its best acoustically with the equipment it has (the correct fit between instruments and space). It is also one that fulfills the band's financial expectations: 'it is rare to hear of a good room which is a small room' (1980, 168). The architectural design of the venue and the materials used in the construction of the building can fundamentally influence both the type of music performed and the cost required to put on a show, as a result of the need to combat the unwanted effects of reverberation using equalization equipment.

The majority of professional artists seldom progress beyond small-scale venues. In the United Kingdom, for example, the majority of auditoria have a seating or standing capacity of less than 4,000. Some of these small venues have become part of rock mythology. The Cavern Club in Liverpool is inexorably associated with the Beatles and Merseybeat, the Marquee in London with the rise of mods and British rhythm and blues, and the 100 Club and the Roxy, also in London, with punk. In the United States, New York's CBGB's was, in the 1970s, the venue par excellence for the emergent new wave scene.

A number of venues have also attained mythical status for one-off events, rather than for any association with a particular style of music. For example, London's Hammersmith Odeon, which was the location for David Bowie's last performance as Ziggy Stardust on 3 July 1973, is the stuff of rock legend, and is something of a shrine for his fans. Other venues are inextricably associated with one performer or one style of music. Certain venues in Las Vegas will forever be associated with late-period Elvis Presley. The Haçienda Club in Manchester is inextricably bound up with the UK indie-dance scene of the 1980s. London's Royal Albert Hall, traditionally associated with classical music, has been used by virtuoso acts such as Eric Clapton, the concert hall's prestige-conferring power bestowed on the serious-minded rock performer. Such venues have undoubtedly acquired a certain kudos over time. For example, there was artistic cachet to be had by jazz musicians if they had recorded at Birdland, a New York nightclub named in honor of saxophonist Charlie Parker.

Large-scale auditoria obviously lack the intimacy of the club and the pub, but compensate for this by highlighting the spectacular elements within popular music through emphasis on visual presentation and increasingly sophisticated production techniques. The term 'stadium rock' was coined in the 1970s to describe the music of performers such as Journey, Foreigner, Kiss and Peter Frampton: a bold, loud, guitar-based music with an often anthem-like musical and lyrical quality, ideal for the dimensions and logic of the stadium gig, where reciprocity has to be established through broad musical and visual gestures. Generally, most outdoor stadia can accommodate anything from 40,000 to 100,000 people. The number of famous stadium concerts are legion, although special mention must be made of the Beatles' gig at Shea Stadium (1965), which helped break the band

in the United States, and Live Aid (1985) at Wembley Stadium, London and the JFK Stadium in Philadelphia, the biggest fund-raising rock gig of all time. With the exception of venues such as Britain's National Exhibition Centre in Birmingham (which can accommodate 25,000) or the National Bowl at Milton Keynes (which has a capacity of 65,000), venues built specifically with the dissemination of the performing arts in mind, almost all stadia are built in order to host sporting events.

Even larger still in terms of audience size (attendances of around 100,000 per day are not unusual) is the festival, or large open-air gig. The rock festival performed an important role in the 1960s, shaping the counterculture, with the Monterey (1967) and Woodstock (1969) festivals the most important. Other landmark open-air concerts include the Rolling Stones' appearance at Hyde Park, London in 1969, and the 1981 gig at Central Park, New York by Simon and Garfunkel. In the 1980s, multicultural festivals such as WOMAD (World of Music, Arts and Dance) provided an important outlet for African and 'world music.' The resurrection of 1960s chic in the 1990s led to a revival of interest in the idea of the rock festival, as the Lollapalooza Festival in the United States and the Glastonbury and Phoenix festivals in the United Kingdom show. Some festivals have been annual events, such as the Montreux Jazz Festival in Switzerland, the rock and pop festival in Bourges, France and Rockpalast in Germany.

Since the rise of urbanization and the establishment of the earliest venues for popular music in the mid-nineteenth century, it has been expected that the audience travel to a venue to watch a performer. Inherent in this relationship was an inequality between the performer – on stage, and therefore physically higher than the audience and more powerful (through the physical properties of electricity as well as through the aura of being a star) – and the audience as dominated spectator. It has been attempted in various types of music and by various performers to break down these barriers, but the inherent inequality of pop performance still remains. Dance music has tried to redefine this star–fan relationship. The dance artist is more curator than originator of new sounds, confusing the distinction between fan (the pop archeologist) and performer by posing as both simultaneously.

Access and the 'Policing' of Venues

The activities of audiences at venues are the subject of both legal regulation and a type of internal ordering that dictates how fans behave at pop concerts. The type of venue chosen by the individual act can structure audience response in a more or less direct way. For example, a hard-core rock group with a young, energetic audience would tend to pick an unseated venue in which dancing, stage-diving and moshing (a more extreme version of slam-dancing) and a more physical star–fan relationship can be accommodated. Other styles of popular music, in which a more considered appreciation of the audiovisual component of the concert is more appropriate, and where dancing is of marginal interest at best (for example, a Pink Floyd or a Mike Oldfield concert), work better in all-seat venues.

Historically, certain classes of individuals have been denied access to certain types of venue. An obvious example would be those jazz clubs in the 1920s and 1930s, such as the Cotton Club in Harlem, where predominantly black performers and exclusively black bar staff, porters and waiters served the needs of a white-only clientele.

Likewise, an insidious form of prejudice has barred women from attending various musical events, events thought of as being overwhelmingly male preserves. In Victorian times, for example, women were dissuaded from attending the theater, their unchaperoned attendance being regarded as a sign of moral decadence. Even now, certain styles of rock music define themselves as so overwhelmingly male in character as to make female attendance exceptional and sometimes even dangerous.

Other venues have always contained an element of the taboo. In the late nineteenth and early twentieth centuries, there was, likewise, a stigma attached to music played in bordellos and honky-tonks. However, the 1980s rave gained much of its attraction because of the act of transgression in attending an illegal gathering.

Some venues have long been associated with dress codes specifically designed to exclude 'unhip' undesirables. In the 1970s, although disco was an institution that afforded an opportunity for the dispossessed (particularly blacks, women and gays) to celebrate a marginalized culture, many venues operated a strict dress code, and would refuse admittance to the unsuitably attired. This form of selection through style was also a feature of the early 1980s New Romantic scene, and is still an effective tool in defining an 'appropriate' clientele for certain clubs.

Venues have been (see Davis 1991; Chevigny 1991) and have continued to be under certain legally defined constraints as regards their proper functioning. In the United Kingdom, they are subject to the control of the local authorities (see Street 1993), which work alongside the police and the local fire services. Venues are covered by a number of regulations concerning licensing, the threat of fire, opening hours, noise levels, capacity and so on. Different styles of music and band have been banned by local authorities, and targeted as undesirable

and a threat to local citizens. For example, in 1971, Slade, then a skinhead band, found it very difficult to get gigs because venues dubbed them, and their fans, as dangerous. Later in the decade, punk and new wave bands such as the Sex Pistols, the Clash and the Stranglers were also banned by a number of venues. The anarchist band Crass, critical of those in authority, has estimated that a third of its planned gigs were censored and never took place (see Cloonan 1996, 160).

Popular Song and the Venue

Popular music is full of lyrical references to venues for the dissemination of popular music. These texts are primarily concerned with boy-meets-girl stories and dancing, such as 'At the Hop' by Danny and the Juniors (1957) or 'Disco Inferno' (1977) by the Trammps. Some songs, such as Pulp's 'Disco 2000' (1995), U2's 'Discothèque' (1997) or XTC's 'Life Begins at the Hop' (1979), have a more knowing irony. In the Smiths' 'Panic' (1986) and in his solo song 'The National Front Disco,' Morrissey has attacked the perceived phoniness of the discothèque (a venue long associated with black music and its culture), but has been accused of racism as a result. A sense of nostalgia is very often involved, as in Elton John's 'Crocodile Rock' (1972).

Bibliography

Bennett, Andrew. 1997. '"Going Down the Pub!": The Pub Rock Scene as a Resource for the Consumption of Popular Music.' *Popular Music* 16(1): 97–108.

Bennett, H. Stith. 1980. *On Becoming a Rock Musician.* Amherst, MA: University of Massachusetts Press.

Björnberg, Alf, and Stockfelt, Ola. 1996. 'Kristen Klatvask fra Vejle: Danish Pub Music, Mythscapes and "Local Camp."' *Popular Music* 15(2): 131–47.

Chevigny, Paul. 1991. *Gigs: Jazz and the Cabaret Laws in New York City.* New York: Routledge.

Cloonan, Martin. 1996. *Banned!: Censorship of Popular Music in Britain, 1967–92.* Aldershot: Avebury.

Davis, Tracy C. 1991. 'The Moral Sense of the Majorities: Indecency and Vigilance in Late-Victorian Music Halls.' *Popular Music* 10(1): 39–52.

Dimitriadis, Greg. 1996. 'Hip Hop: From Live Performance to Mediated Narrative.' *Popular Music* 15(2): 179–94.

Finnegan, Ruth. 1989. *The Hidden Musicians: Music-Making in an English Town.* Cambridge: Cambridge University Press.

Gammond, Peter. 1993. *The Oxford Companion to Popular Music.* Oxford: Oxford University Press.

Haskins, Jim. 1994 (1977). *The Cotton Club.* New York: Hippocrene Books, Inc.

Hazzard-Gordon, Katrina. 1990. *Jookin': The Rise of Social*

Dance Formations in African-American Culture. Philadelphia: Temple University Press.

Kelly, William H. 1998. 'The Adaptability of Karaoke in the United Kingdom.' In *Karaoke Around the World: Global Technology, Local Singing*, ed. Tôru Mitsui and Shuhei Hosokawa. London and New York: Routledge, 83–101.

Mahabir, Cynthia. 1996. 'Wit and Popular Music: The Calypso and the Blues.' *Popular Music* 15(1): 55–81.

Malone, Bill C. 1985. *Country Music, U.S.A.* Rev. ed. Austin, TX: University of Texas Press.

Manuel, Peter. 1988. *Popular Music of the Non-Western World: An Introductory Survey*. New York and Oxford: Oxford University Press.

Middleton, Richard. 1990. *Studying Popular Music*. Milton Keynes: Open University Press.

Small, Christopher. 1996 (1977). *Music, Society, Education*. Hanover, NH: University Press of New England.

Stokes, Martin. 1992. *The Arabesk Debate: Music and Musicians in Modern Turkey*. Oxford: Oxford University Press.

Street, John. 1993. 'Local Differences?: Popular Music and the Local State.' *Popular Music* 12(1): 43–55.

White, Avron Levine. 1987. *Lost in Music: Culture, Style and the Musical Event*. London: Routledge and Kegan Paul.

Discographical References

Bob Dunn's Vagabonds. 'Stompin' at the Honky Tonk.' Decca 5772. 1939: USA.

Danny and the Juniors. 'At the Hop.' ABC-Para 9871. *1957*: USA.

Dexter, Al. 'New Jelly Roll Blues'/'Honky Tonk Blues.' Vocalion 03435. 1937: USA.

John, Elton. 'Crocodile Rock.' DJM DJS 271. *1972*: UK.

Morrissey. 'The National Front Disco.' *Your Arsenal*. HMV CDCSD 3790. *1992*: UK.

Pulp. 'Disco 2000.' Island CID 623. *1995*: UK.

Smiths, The. 'Panic.' Rough Trade RT 193. *1986*: UK.

Trammps, The. 'Disco Inferno.' Atlantic K 10914. *1977*: UK.

U2. 'Discothèque.' Island 854775. *1997*: UK.

XTC. 'Life Begins at the Hop.' Virgin VS 259. *1979*: UK.

DAVID BUCKLEY with JOHN SHEPHERD and DAVID HORN

Part II
The Industry

6. General Terms

Media

Although the term 'medium' has a root meaning of an 'intervening or intermediate agency or substance' (Williams 1976, 169), the most widespread current use of the plural 'media' is to reference the various means and institutions of communication in contemporary societies. More narrowly, the word is often used to describe simply the broadcast media or television and radio.

Following the argument of McLuhan (1966) that media are 'the extensions of man,' it would be plausible to include musical instruments among the means by which popular music has been mediated. However, for the purposes of this entry, the definition of music media will be restricted to those forms, technologies and practises that connect instrumental and vocal music with their audiences or that incorporate music within a multimedia communication practise.

The contemporary music industry interacts with a number of other media industries and institutions. These include film, television, radio, print media, multimedia and computer games and Web-based media. Music is linked with these media in a double process. Firstly, it provides content for the media and consequent income for the music's producers. This can be thought of as a 'business-to-business' relationship, whereby the music business is a supplier of products and services that become integrated components of other cultural products. This use of music in other media is of growing economic importance for the music industry. Brabec and Brabec (1994) provide an example of a US hit single whose earnings from sales ($132,000) are only half that from broadcasting performance royalties ($275,000) and almost equal to the fee for use in a commercial ($125,000). Tracks from *Play*, the bestselling album by

Moby, were featured on six film soundtracks and over a dozen commercials, and as numerous television program themes or trailers (Simpson 2000).

Secondly, music can also receive considerable promotional benefit from its exposure to media audiences, notably on radio and television. Frequent airplay is generally regarded as essential if a record is to become a bestseller.

Sometimes, the interaction between music and other media is described as synergistic, meaning that the association is of mutual economic value. During the 1990s, a decade when mergers and acquisitions created media conglomerates such as Sony and Time-Warner, there was much discussion about the potential benefits to such companies of synergies between their music and film studio divisions. Although such synergies did not occur as widely as analysts expected, there were some dramatic examples, such as the films *The Bodyguard* and *Titanic*. In each case, the success of hit songs from the film performed by well-known artists stimulated cinema attendance, and the success of the film generated further sales of the soundtrack album. The album of *The Bodyguard* eventually sold over 30 million copies and that of *Titanic* over 20 million. Many other soundtrack albums, notably those containing tracks by well-known artists, sold several million copies during that same decade. A more recent example of synergy engineered within one media company was the Universal Mobile project, which provided music from the Universal catalog for cellphones linked to the SFR network in France. SFR was part-owned by Vivendi, Universal's parent company.

Printed Media

The first medium for the transmission of music was writing. The trade in manuscript copies of sacred and secular music was established in Europe, notably in Paris, by the middle of the thirteenth century. The invention and widespread use of printing two centuries later did not immediately change the forms in which written music was circulated. However, by the early seventeenth century a specific popular music business had been established in northern Europe with single-sheet 'broadsides' sold by traveling peddlers like Autolycus in Shakespeare's *The Winter's Tale* (Edge 1991, 12).

In the nineteenth century, specialist music publishers marketed cheap editions of songs with piano accompaniment to a mass audience of the middle and upper working classes in the industrialized countries of Europe and North America. Printed music reached its economic peak at the turn of the twentieth century, when the music departments of chain stores on both sides of the Atlantic could sell millions of songsheets of hits created in Tin Pan Alley (Hamm 1979; Sanjek 1988). These songsheets were often associated with a star vocalist, whose photograph appeared on the cover and who would both feature the song in vaudeville performances and receive a royalty on sales. By the mid-twentieth century, printed music had been surpassed by sound recordings as the principal commodity form. Nevertheless, songbooks containing music by current stars or published for educational use have maintained considerable sales. Krummel's and Sadie's *Music Printing and Publishing* (1990) is the principal authority on the evolution of printing and publishing of all types of music, while Sanjek (1988) and Edge (1991) provide useful accounts of the printed music business in the United States and Great Britain, respectively.

Telegraphy and Telephony

The most important new technology of communication in the second half of the nineteenth century was the telegraph, a form of communication by wire using the Morse code. Some telegraph companies offered a 'singing telegram' service, whereby a messenger would deliver a message by singing a song on the addressee's doorstep. Western Union, the largest US telegraph firm, advertised 'Sing-O-Grams – Telegrams delivered in song for many occasions' (Lubar 1993, 97).

The widespread introduction of telephone technology made telegraphy obsolete, since individuals could now communicate directly by oral means over long distances. In the 1920s, the first 'piped music' programs of the Muzak Corporation were delivered to factories, offices and other premises using telephony. Telephone lines have been used to promote newly issued recordings to potential consumers, and well-known tunes are frequently used in 'on-hold' systems by firms and institutions. The advent of mobile phones in the 1980s brought with it a fashion for choosing musical ring tones. By the start of the twenty-first century, the creation and supply of ring tones had become a niche industry, as many young people frequently changed their ring tone to one based on a current hit tune. Authors' collection societies and music publishers collect fees for the use of music in telephony.

Mechanical Reproduction of Music

Printed music remained the sole mediating form for popular music until the advent of mechanical media in the nineteenth century. This next innovation in music media involved the reproduction not of the work as written but of the sound of a performance of the work.

While sound recording has become by far the most important of these mechanical media, several widely disseminated media, notably barrel organs and player pianos (Pianolas) with piano rolls, preceded it. Music boxes were made and sold to affluent consumers in Europe as early as the eighteenth century. However, they could seldom provide more than a section of one tune and were mainly marketed as children's toys. Barrel organs and barrel pianos had a much larger repertoire. They were ubiquitous features of street life in European and North American cities from the mid-nineteenth century to the early years of the twentieth century. Rosselli (1991) claims that barrel organs 'probably did more to spread elementary knowledge of music than anything else before the coming of gramophone records' (115).

The Pianola was an adaptation of barrel-organ technology for domestic use. It was introduced in the United States in the 1890s by the Aeolian Company and, by the mid-1920s, over 2 million had been sold there (Allen 1985). Pianola owners could purchase new rolls to use on the machine, and many famous composers from Scott Joplin to George Gershwin recorded these rolls. In the sense that it replaced the piano in middle-class homes and that to play it did not require any tuition, the Pianola represented a 'de-skilling' of domestic music-making, a feature it shared with the phonograph and the radio set.

Although sound recording had been developed by Edison as early as 1877, it was not until the beginning of the twentieth century that the recording of musical performances became established alongside the piano roll as a significant form of mediated domestic musical entertainment. The early acoustic recording methods were superseded in the 1920s by electrical recording, which in turn made possible the powerfully amplified jukebox. Further improvements in studio recording were made possible by the use of tape, and playback quality was enhanced by the replacement in the early 1950s of 78 rpm shellac discs by 'unbreakable' 33 rpm and 45 rpm vinyl records. Later innovations included the compact tape cassette, eight-track tape cartridges and digital recordings distributed on compact disc and CD-ROM. Such authors as Gelatt (1977), Chanan (1995), Millard (1995), and Gronow and Saunio (1998) have explored the development of these technologies and of the recorded music industry.

Visual Media: Film and Video

Cinema emerged almost simultaneously with recorded music. Until 1926, film was silent, but music was used to provide an aural dimension to the cinematic experience. Theaters where movies were screened employed musicians to perform improvisations or specially composed scores as accompaniment to the on-screen action. By the 1920s, this was an important source of income for professional musicians (Kraft 1996).

The addition of soundtrack to films abruptly ended this situation. Although sound film continued to employ composers and arrangers, the music was now prerecorded in studios by specialist groups of instrumentalists. While all sound films required theme tunes and background scores, the film musical was a commercially important Hollywood film genre from the 1930s to the 1960s. Many musicals were based on stage shows and were linked to the promotion of recordings and sheet music of specific songs. In later years, many film soundtracks contained previously issued recordings that were compiled onto soundtrack albums whose release dates were coordinated with those of the movies themselves. The impact of soundtrack music was greatly enhanced by improvements in cinema amplification systems, notably those designed by the Dolby company.

The first Ampex videotape recorder was produced in 1957, but video technology did not have a significant impact on popular music until the 1970s, when the music video or promotional video – a short film shot to a recorded music soundtrack using the full range of video editing technologies – became an important marketing tool for the record industry. Collections of music videos and films of concerts were sold on videocassette and subsequently on digital versatile disc (DVD).

During the late 1990s, music became an increasingly important component of video and computer games. As with film soundtracks, bestselling games such as 'Gran Turismo' included previously released tracks as well as specially composed background music.

Broadcast Media: Radio and Television

Music was a major component of radio from its beginnings. One of the first reported amateur broadcasts in the United States involved the placing of a 'wireless telephone' close to a Victrola (Lubar 1993, 214). The rapid growth in the number of radio stations in the country provided employment for many of the musicians laid off by the movie theaters. Small groups and orchestras performed in sponsored shows, and the recognition thus gained brought greater concert attendances and record sales. In Europe, the control of radio by state monopoly broadcasters meant that popular music received less prominence as the national stations prioritized news and 'high' arts programming. Nevertheless, dance orchestras and vocalists established national reputations through radio. By 1941, music took up 75 percent of US airtime, and 50 percent of US radio stations were 'all-music' stations. These numbers increased after television displaced radio as the principal broadcast medium. This phase, from the 1950s onward, also saw the displacement of 'live' performance by disc-based shows on popular music radio and the consequent rise of the personality DJ as a principal hit-maker and target for record company promotional efforts, including payola.

The symbiotic link between radio and popular music has been strengthened by the increasing portability of radio receivers. The first wireless sets were designed as domestic furniture, but they were supplemented by car radios, transistor radios and the Walkman.

Music has been less important as a component of the television medium. Until the 1980s, all television channels were multivalent in their content. Shows presenting primarily musical performances were in the minority, although composers and instrumentalists supplied the demand for title and background music for drama and documentary programs, and were hired to write and perform jingles for television commercials. The advent of cable television in the United States multiplied the number of channels and encouraged the growth of niche music networks, among which MTV has become preeminent (Banks 1996). In turn, the availability of such stations as MTV and the few network popular music shows stimulated the production of music videos (Goodwin 1993).

Zenith Media, a global media services agency, has predicted that, in 2002, the global advertising business will be worth some $360 billion, of which 40 percent will be spent on television advertising and 9 percent on radio advertising. Music has become an increasingly important element of television commercials, as either newly written jingles or background sound, or in the form of previously published and recorded works whose prestige (agencies hope) will enhance the image of the product to be advertised. Advertisers have paid amounts in the millions of dollars for the rights to songs by major artists such as the Rolling Stones and Bob Dylan.

In addition to initial fees or commission fees for original music, composers receive performing right fees each time their music is played in commercials that appear on radio, on television or at the cinema. Such fees are negotiated, collected and distributed by national authors' collection societies, which are important players in the music industry. In many countries, there are similar collection societies representing the economic interests of record companies and recording artists. By the start of the twenty-first century, global payments of performance royalties had reached over $3 billion a year.

The widespread digitization of music through CD technology made it the first of the 'old' media to be widely available on the Internet. Some Internet uses of music, such as the sale of CDs by mail order, were simply transferred from the 'off-line' music business. Others, however, were wholly new. The development of MP3 technology enabled the 'downloading' of music to personal computers. While many individual musicians and listeners welcomed MP3 and used it frequently, the leaders of the off-line music industry were initially hostile because of the widespread copyright infringement involved in the 'peer-to-peer' file-sharing associated with Napster and other Web sites. By 2001, however, the major music companies had reversed their attitude and were attempting to sell subscriptions to their own MP3-based Web sites. With global sales of CDs stagnating, research analysts were predicting that the Internet would be a crucial part of the music business by the end of the twenty-first century's first decade.

Bibliography

Allen, Jeanne. 1985. 'The Industrialization of Culture: The Case of the Player Piano.' In *The Critical Communications Review, Vol. 3: Popular Culture and Media Events*, ed. Vincent Mosco and Janet Wasko. Norwood, NJ: Ablex Publishing Corporation, 93–109.

Banks, Jack. 1996. *Monopoly Television: MTV's Quest to Control the Music*. Boulder, CO: Westview Press.

Brabec, Jeffrey, and Brabec, Todd. 1994. *Music, Money, and Success: The Insider's Guide to the Music Industry*. New York: Schirmer Books.

Chanan, Michael. 1995. *Repeated Takes: A Short History of Recording and Its Effects on Music*. London: Verso.

Edge, Kevin. 1991. *The Art of Selling Songs: Graphics for the Music Business, 1690–1990*. London: Futures Publications.

Gelatt, Roland. 1977. *The Fabulous Phonograph, 1877–1977*. London: Cassell.

Goodwin, Andrew. 1993. *Dancing in the Distraction Factory: Music Television and Popular Culture*. London: Routledge.

Gronow, Pekka, and Saunio, Ilpo. 1998. *An International History of the Recording Industry*, trans. Christopher Moseley. London: Cassell.

Hamm, Charles. 1979. *Yesterdays: Popular Song in America*. New York: W.W. Norton & Company.

Kraft, James P. 1996. *Stage to Studio: Musicians and the Sound Revolution, 1890–1950*. Baltimore, MD: Johns Hopkins University Press.

Krummel, D.W., and Sadie, Stanley, eds. 1990. *Music Printing and Publishing*. New York: W.W. Norton & Company.

Lubar, Steven D. 1993. *InfoCulture: The Smithsonian Book of Information Age Inventions*. Boston, MA: Houghton Mifflin.

McLuhan, Marshall. 1966. *Understanding Media: The Extensions of Man*. 2nd ed. New York: New American Library.

Millard, Andre J. 1995. *America on Record: A History of Recorded Sound*. Cambridge: Cambridge University Press.

Rosselli, John. 1991. *Music and Musicians in Nineteenth-Century Italy*. Portland, OR: Amadeus Press.

Sanjek, Russell. 1988. *American Popular Music and Its Business: The First Four Hundred Years*. 3 vols. New York: Oxford University Press.

Simpson, Dave. 2000. 'Plug and Play.' *The Guardian* (5 May): 14.

Williams, Raymond. 1976. *Keywords: A Vocabulary of Culture and Society*. Oxford and New York: Oxford University Press.

Discographical References

The Bodyguard (Original soundtrack). Arista 18699. *1992*: USA.

Moby. *Play*. Mute 172. *1999*: UK.

Titanic (Original soundtrack). Sony Classical 63212. *1997*: USA.

Filmography

The Bodyguard, dir. Mick Jackson. 1992. USA. 130 mins. Drama. Original music by David Foster, Alan Silvestri.

Titanic, dir. James Cameron. 1997. USA. 195 mins. Historical Film. Original music by James Horner.

DAVE LAING

Music Industry

The term 'music industry' refers to the full range of economic practises necessary to provide performances for audiences and to produce commodities that embody music or that enable music to be created.

The Contemporary Music Industry

The growing awareness among governments and international agencies of music as one of the cultural or creative industries gave rise to a number of official or semiofficial reports on national or regional music industries from the 1980s onward. One of these (Dane, Feist and Laing 1996) identifies five core sectors: concerts, musical theater and other performances; production and sale of sound recordings; administration of copyright in compositions and recordings; manufacture and distribution of musical instruments and of professional recording and amplification equipment; and education and training.

This report lists a further group of media practises and industries that have a 'mutually dependent relationship' with one or more of the core sectors. These are: radio, television, film and advertising films (the audiovisual industries); music press; merchandising; dance (from ballet to discothèques and raves); and manufacture of audio hardware. The music industry derives direct revenues from all of these apart from the music press. It also receives valuable publicity for its products and services from all except the manufacturers of hardware.

A different approach to the structure of the music industry is found in a 1993 report to the Australian government (MIAC 1993). This stresses how the activities of the music industry involve a chain of different professions, each of which adds value to the creative work of musicians and composers. It distinguishes between the 'primary investors,' who supply financial and other resources to exploit the creativity of the 'originators,' and those who are 'secondary investors and facilitators.' The latter include specialist professional advisors such as lawyers and accountants, who provide services to both originators and primary investors.

No generally accepted statistics are available for the world music industry, although some national estimates have been made. The German industry in 1996 was reported to have a market value of $7.2 billion and to have 180,000 employees ('Germany,' 1997). A report on the British industry in 1997 stated that it provided the equivalent of 130,000 full-time jobs, and that domestic spending on music was about $5 billion (Dane, Feist and Manton 1999). On the basis of these and other available figures, a conservative estimate would put the global turnover of the popular music industry at over $60 billion in 2000, and its work force at over 2 billion people. This total is made up of the retail sales of soundcarriers, including pirate goods ($45 billion), the live music and concert business ($8 billion), sales of musical instruments ($4 billion) and the performing rights market ($3 billion).

The total would be considerably higher if sponsorship payments and subsidies given to classical music institutions, such as opera houses and symphony orchestras, were included. The classical music industry's history is usefully summarized by Chanan (1994), and Lebrecht (1996) luridly describes its contemporary crisis.

This version of the music industry is based on a 'Western' model developed in Europe and North America in the nineteenth and twentieth centuries. Transnational corporations and authors' collecting societies have attempted to export it to other regions of the world, with mixed results. While it has been adopted with important national variations in Latin America and large parts of Asia, the music industries of Asian states with Communist regimes and of almost all African countries have remained significantly different from the Western model. In the case of Africa, this is principally because of the very low level of disposable income available to the mass of the population.

History

Several authors have presented a broad periodization of the development of the music industry. In his influential *Noise* (1985), Attali segments the history of musical practise into four networks with corresponding political economies: those of sacrifice, representation, repetition and composition (31–33).

Based on the technologies for communicating music, the Belgian musicologist Sabbe (1998) identifies four stages in the history of the music industry: written music (from the ninth century A.D.); the printing of written music (from the fifteenth century); the recording of sound (from the end of the nineteenth century); and the carrying of music by sound waves (early twentieth century). Sanjek's history of North American popular music and its business (1988) is divided into three parts, with the break points at 1790 and 1900. Sanjek's periodization best captures the key moments of the development of the Western industry, as important concatenations of technological, aesthetic and socioeconomic factors provoked restructuring of the industry near the beginning of both the nineteenth and twentieth centuries. Nevertheless, the European music industry has a prehistory that can be traced to the early medieval period.

The earliest written music is found in manuscripts made by 'music scribes attached to courts and chapels such as those of Mechlin or Ferrara; the music they copied was often widely circulated and much used' (Krummel 1990, 79). In early medieval Europe, musicians were also employed as retainers of rulers and prelates.

While those players were engaged in purveying religious music and polite song and dance, throughout this period there were also traveling entertainers who were often classed as 'vagrants' and subjected to harsh penalties (Clark 1983, 129). These performers provided a plebeian music for the urban and rural lower classes. As Bohlman (1988) has forcefully argued, even those responsible for maintaining and enhancing folk music traditions had some kind of specialized role in their communities, often acknowledged in the form of payment for their performances.

The beginnings of the music industry as an organized provider of products and services for audiences were associated with the advent of merchant capitalism in European cities. Musicians were paid to provide entertainment at festivities and celebrations, while printing provided an economic basis for composers and publishers to sell copies of works to bourgeois amateur music-makers and copies of popular ballads to urban artisans and rural peasantry. The first printed copy of a secular song came from Strasbourg in 1497, although music printing had begun in Japan in 1472. Broadside ballads with musical notation were printed in England in the late seventeenth century. From 1700, hundreds of popular songsheets were published in London.

While the broadsides spread new songs (often set to old tunes) throughout rural areas, more traditional music for dancing and listening survived in most European countries into the twentieth century. Evidence of such music is contained in the thousands of pieces collected by musicians and antiquarians throughout continental Europe and in North America. The exponents of 'folk music' were linked to the music industry through their purchase of instruments, and their own music provided raw material for classical compositions and the performances of folk revivalist singers (many of them professionals) throughout the twentieth century.

The transition from patronage to a market system gathered speed in Europe in the eighteenth century. An important layer of intermediaries between composers and paying audiences emerged. Its members included music publishers, instrument manufacturers, theater managers (or impresarios), and entrepreneurial musicians and composers themselves. The role of publishers in influencing popular taste can be seen in the activity of Breitkopf of Leipzig, which popularized the sentimental German song in the late eighteenth century.

In the early part of the nineteenth century, a specific popular music industry was emerging in Europe and North America. It had three principal elements. The first was a new type of music publishing based on the mass production and dissemination of cheaply priced printed music. The pioneers here included Novello in London and Firth, Pond & Co. in the United States. The most dynamic sector of the popular music business from 1850 to 1920 was undoubtedly the marketing and sale of sheet music. This coincided with the growth of performing right legislation and the realization by publishers that concerts could be a source of income as well as a means of promoting sheet music sales.

The second element was the application of factory production methods to musical instruments. Mass-production methods were applied to demotic instruments like the fiddle, accordion, harmonica and guitar, as well as to ensemble instruments such as horns and woodwind instruments. The latter served the growing number of factory or municipal brass and wind bands. But the most important sector of the musical instrument industry was inaugurated by the introduction of the upright piano in 1827 and its mass production throughout the nineteenth century for sale to the middle classes and skilled working classes. Piano ownership stimulated printed music sales and also led to the demand for player pianos at the start of the twentieth century.

The third element of the new popular music industry was the formation of a performance practise that involved purpose-built venues, entrepreneurs and new types of performers. The venues included the vaudeville halls of the United States, the *bal musettes* of France and the music halls of Britain. The entrepreneurs managed such halls or organized national and international tours by popular performers, making use of innovations in publicity techniques such as poster and newspaper advertising. These techniques helped to establish the status and reputation of the first popular music stars such as the music hall singer Marie Lloyd and vaudeville's Lillian Russell, Eva Tanguay, Al Jolson, Ken Murray and Ethel Waters.

Sabbe's third era, as mentioned above, is associated with the recording technologies developed in the nineteenth century. The earliest of these was the barrel organ, which provided street music in European and US cities throughout the second half of the century. An associated technology was that of the piano roll used in player pianos, millions of which were sold in the United States in the late nineteenth and early twentieth centuries.

The most influential form of recording technology was the sound-recording method developed by Edison, Berliner and others at the end of the nineteenth century. Commercial recordings for use with phonographs and gramophones were made from 1897, but it would be almost 20 years before recordings began to rival sheet music in commercial importance. Sound recording brought with it the most powerful institution of the modern music industry: the record company. Initially, this was the firm that held the patents for sound recording and was mainly concerned with the manufacture of the 'hardware,' the phonographs and gramophones. The production of prerecorded discs or cylinders was a secondary occupation, necessary in order to persuade consumers to purchase the hardware. Few of the earliest record companies had links with publishers or other members of the preexisting music industry.

The global recession of the 1930s caused major

changes in the business structures of the record industry, as major companies were acquired by broadcasters or diversified into other products. In the post-1945 period, the major companies began to buy up music publishers and were again involved in innovations in audio hardware. In the late 1940s, RCA and Columbia launched the new vinyl disc formats; in the 1960s, Philips produced the tape cassette; and in the early 1980s, Philips (as owner of PolyGram) was able to use its ownership of recorded music to launch the compact disc. At the end of the twentieth century, almost all of the largest music companies were themselves subsidiaries of giant media or electronics conglomerates.

Although soundcarriers did not displace sheet music as the principal commodified form of popular music until the 1940s or 1950s, the record industry's pivotal position in the music industry determined many of the ways in which music publishing, performance and the musical instrument business developed in the twentieth century.

Music publishers found their area of initiative drastically curtailed by the vanguard role of record companies in discovering and promoting (through their A&R staff) new vocal and instrumental stars. In other areas of their business, publishers devolved their activities to authors' collection societies, whose royalty administration practises provided the majority of the income for most composers.

In performance, the variety entertainment of vaudeville and music hall was supplanted by social dance, with the introduction of new dance steps, from the tango and the foxtrot to the jitterbug and the twist. Performances by singers and bands came to be described as 'live' shows, an explicit recognition of the hegemonic position assumed by recordings and broadcasts of music, notably when rock and pop acts were required to reproduce on stage the exact sound of highly complex studio productions. The publicity created by recordings enabled the most popular artists to undertake lengthy tours and to perform in large amphitheaters, where sales of merchandise such as T-shirts provided a new source of income.

The popularization of the guitar and synthesizer keyboards through hit records was a leading factor in the development of instrument manufacture. The technological advantages possessed by its electronics industry made Japan the world leader in the musical instrument business.

This new industry structure, overdetermined by the record industry, was established throughout Western Europe, North America and Australasia by the 1960s. In subsequent decades, the major music corporations and collection societies attempted to export this Western type of music industry structure to Latin America, Asia and, less energetically, Africa. In doing so, they were faced with obstacles created by widespread music piracy and by established national regimes of music production and consumption. The results were similar, in many cases, to those of the expansion of the McDonald's fast-food chain. According to a study of its activities in Asia, McDonald's has not 'resisted change or refused to adapt when local customers require flexibility' (Watson 1997, 23). In the case of the major music companies in Asia, the 'flexibility' shown has included a willingness to make ex-pirates into licensees and to invest in local-language music where Anglophone pop has been of interest to a minority of potential consumers (Laing 1998).

Despite this globalizing momentum, the Western model of the music industry has yet to become established in many parts of the world. In Asia, residual economic protectionism and heavy censorship have held up the advance of the major companies in China, Vietnam and elsewhere. It seems likely, however, that China's accession to membership of the World Trade Organization will force the regime to permit foreign companies to operate there. In much of Africa and parts of the Caribbean, preindustrial performance traditions, poverty and piracy have been the principal factors determining the shape of the industry. This combination of factors has acted as a deterrent to the formation of a Western type of music industry, although local artists such as Guyanese-born Eddy Grant (Barbados), Salif Keita (Mali) and Youssou N'Dour (Senegal), who have earned income from their success in the West, have been investing increasingly in studio and label infrastructure in their home countries.

It is tempting to see the increasing importance of the Internet as the catalyst for a new, twenty-first-century phase of development of the music industry. Because of its ease of transmission over low-bandwidth networks, digitized music was the first media commodity to be widely disseminated over the Internet. This was greeted as a triumph of 'disintermediation,' whereby music could be distributed directly from creator to listener, obviating the need for most of the specialist sectors of the music industry – studio producers and retailers as well as record companies. To some degree, this has proved to be accurate, as the economics of on-line delivery or the sale of recordings has dramatically improved the economic position of small niche genres.

The implications of the Internet for the mainstream music industry are more difficult to discern. It was undoubtedly true that this well-entrenched manufacturing and service industry was initially unwilling and unable to recognize the potential importance of the

Internet as a new arena for trading music. By the time industry leaders were persuaded of its importance, their first response was to litigate, and their next was to attempt to buy into the new Internet music business through the acquisition of direct-delivery (MP3) sites and the peer-to-peer file transfer company Napster.

That said, forecasters in the late 1990s and at the beginning of the twenty-first century consistently over-estimated the dollar value of sales through the Internet. The retail value of such sales represented only a small part of the overall industry turnover and seemed likely to remain at less than 10 percent for at least another decade. By that time, however, an unforeseen new Internet music industry may have emerged and may have changed the face of the music industry, as did printing, sound recording and digitization.

Bibliography

Attali, Jacques. 1985. *Noise: The Political Economy of Music*, trans. Brian Massumi. Minneapolis, MN: University of Minnesota Press.

Bohlman, Philip V. 1988. *The Study of Folk Music in the Modern World*. Bloomington, IN: Indiana University Press.

Chanan, Michael. 1994. *Musica Practica: The Social Practice of Western Music from Gregorian Chant to Postmodernism*. London and New York: Verso.

Clark, Peter. 1983. *The English Alehouse: A Social History, 1200–1830*. London: Longman.

Dane, Cliff, Feist, Andy, and Laing, Dave. 1996. *The Value of Music*. London: National Music Council.

Dane, Cliff, Feist, Andy, and Manton, Kate. 1999. *A Sound Performance: The Economic Value of Music to the United Kingdom*. London: National Music Council.

'Germany.' 1997. *Billboard* (19 April): 1, 101.

Krummel, D.W. 1990. 'Music Publishing: Definition and Origins.' In *Music Printing and Publishing*, ed. D.W. Krummel and Stanley Sadie. New York: W.W. Norton, 79–81.

Laing, Dave. 1998. 'Knockin' on China's Door.' In *Popular Music: Intercultural Interpretations*, ed. Tôru Mitsui. Kanazawa: Graduate Program in Music, Kanazawa University, 337–42.

Lebrecht, Norman. 1996. *When the Music Stops . . .: Managers, Maestros and the Corporate Murder of Classical Music*. London: Simon & Schuster.

MIAC. 1993. *Report to Government*. Canberra: Music Industry Advisory Council (Australia).

Sabbe, Herman. 1998. *La Musique et l'Occident – Démocratie et capitalisme (post-)industriel* [Music and the West: (Post)Industrial Democracy and Capitalism]. Hayen, Belgium: Mardaga.

Sanjek, Russell. 1988. *American Popular Music and Its Business: The First Four Hundred Years*. 3 vols. New York and Oxford: Oxford University Press.

Watson, James L., ed. 1997. *Golden Arches East: McDonald's in East Asia*. Stanford, CA: Stanford University Press.

DAVE LAING

Reproduction

In copyright law, 'reproduction' refers to the making of copies in any form, from printed music to phonograms or soundcarriers, and even in non-material form through 'on-line' digital distribution. The production of copies of sound recordings is often called mechanical reproduction.

The reproduction right is one of the principal rights granted to the various categories of right owners in compositions or in sound recordings. Thus, Article 9 of the Berne Convention gives authors 'the exclusive right of authorising the reproduction' of their works, while Article 7(c) of the Rome Convention protects performers from 'the reproduction, without their consent, of a fixation of their performance,' i.e., from bootlegging.

DAVE LAING

7. Audio Technical Terms

Frame

A frame is the smallest temporal unit used in synchronizing audio, film and video equipment. Used as part of a standardized time code scheme of hours, minutes, seconds and frames, the frame usually corresponds to a single unit of the visual medium in question (e.g., a single picture in a strip of film, or one complete traversal of the line scanning beam on a television screen). Typical frame rates include: 30 frames per second (fps), used in synchronizing audio tape recorders and/or black and white video; 25 fps used in European television; 24 fps used in film; and 29.97 fps drop frame, used in color video and US television broadcasting. Drop frame corrects minor inaccuracies between the (North American) color video frame rate and 'real time' (i.e., clock time) that would otherwise cause color video to slowly drift out of sync with real time.

PAUL THÉBERGE

Hi-Fi (FFRR)

'Hi-fi,' the abbreviated form of 'high fidelity,' refers to any sound recording that exhibits extended frequency and dynamic range. Used as early as the 1930s, the term came into widespread use during the late 1940s and was often associated with the introduction of the LP. In its abbreviated form, the term also refers to component-based home audio systems introduced during the 1950s. At the end of World War II, Decca (UK) introduced an improved recording process with the acronym FFRR (full frequency range recording); the process gave 78 rpm discs a frequency range of between 30 Hz and 14,000 Hz and was later applied to LPs.

PAUL THÉBERGE

Mono

An abbreviation of 'monophonic' (or 'monaural'), the term refers to any sound recording made on a single channel and/or reproduced on one loudspeaker. Any number of microphones may be employed during the recording process, but once their signals are mixed to a single channel, the recording becomes monophonic. Until the introduction of stereo records in 1958, all commercial releases were mono; the format was gradually phased out during the late 1960s. When older recordings are reissued, they are often reprocessed to give a quasi-stereo effect. AM radio has continued to be largely monophonic, and care is required during the recording process to ensure that contemporary stereo recordings are compatible with mono reproduction.

PAUL THÉBERGE

Quadraphonic

'Quadraphonic' is a term used to describe a recording and reproduction format using four discrete channels, introduced by the audio industry in 1971, which attempted to offer listeners a greater sense of sonic realism. Quadraphonic (quad) playback required, in addition to the conventional pair of loudspeakers for stereo, a second pair of speakers placed in the rear of the listening area, thus offering an enhanced sense of ambiance (especially in classical music recordings) and the possible reproduction of various spatial effects. Quad recordings were compatible with conventional stereo turntables, although the quad effect could be realized only by passing the signal through a specialized decoder. By 1974, the quad format had largely failed in the marketplace, in part because listeners were unconvinced by its effect on music recording, especially on popular music recording where it had become standard practise to distribute the various vocal and instrumental sounds throughout the listening area. In addition, incompatibilities existed among different methods of encoding the quad signal on records, and the conversion from stereo to quad format required a substantial financial investment on the part of the consumer. Despite the failure of the quad format in the home audio marketplace, some rock groups of the period, such as Pink Floyd, were able to use quadraphonic systems in live concerts to great effect.

Since the rise in popularity of home video during the 1980s, the audio industry has again introduced multichannel reproduction systems, such as Dolby surround sound, for the home. Despite interest in the format on the part of some record producers, the record industry has remained acutely aware of the financial fiasco associated with quad and has been cautious in supporting new recording formats.

PAUL THÉBERGE

Stereo

Stereo is a recording process utilizing two discrete channels of information and reproduced on two (or more) loudspeakers. In addition to directionality of sound, stereo recordings offer the listener a greater sense of depth, clarity and sonic ambiance than is possible in monophonic recordings. Experiments with stereo reproduction date back to the early part of the twentieth century, but the general public was not introduced to the possibilities of stereo until the release of Walt Disney's film *Fantasia* in 1940. Due to technical difficulties, stereo records were not introduced until 1958. Although various multichannel stereo formats were introduced during

the last four decades of the twentieth century, especially in film, two-channel stereo reproduction has remained the record industry standard.

Filmography

Fantasia, dir. James Algar, Samuel Armstrong, Ford I. Beebe, Walt Disney, Jim Handley, Albert Heath, T. Hee, Graham Heid, Wilfred Jackson, Hamilton Luske, Bianca Majolie, Sylvia Moberly-Holland, Bill Roberts, Paul Satterfield, Ben Sharpsteen and Norman Wright. 1940. USA. 116 mins. Animated Musical. Original music by Johann Sebastian Bach, Ludwig van Beethoven, Paul Dukas, Franz Schubert, Igor Stravinsky, Pyotr Tchaikovsky.

PAUL THÉBERGE

White Noise

White noise is a random, electronically produced signal that contains all audible frequencies at equal energy levels. The sound produced by white noise is often compared to that of hissing steam or static. White noise is sometimes used for the purposes of testing audio equipment in sound recording and broadcasting. In electronic music, white noise can be filtered and shaped to produce musically useful sounds or sound effects (such as the sound of surf or wind). So-called 'pink noise' is electronic noise containing an equal amplitude distribution per octave; to the ear, the sound of pink noise has greater emphasis in the lower audio spectrum.

PAUL THÉBERGE

8. Broadcasting

Airplay

The term 'airplay' denotes the broadcast of a commercially released music recording or video on radio or television stations. The music industry uses the term most commonly to describe the actual counting of total plays that a particular release receives in a set time period on a number of stations broadcasting either within a particular radio format, or in a specific city, or in one country or even an entire region of the world.

Resulting airplay charts are published weekly in music trade magazines like *Billboard* and *Radio and Records* (both US), *Music Week* (UK) and *Music and Media* (Europe). While some of these charts do print the total number of plays a track received, the ranking is normally determined by a complex weighting procedure. Airplay on stations with more listeners is made to count for more. The track broadcast the greatest number of times across many stations, large and small, can be beaten to the top of the airplay chart by a track that is played less but aired consistently on those stations with most listeners.

Since airplay in a basic form was first used as an element to help calculate the early radio hit parades in the 1930s, it has become an important measurement of a record release's success for the international music industry, but it is not a straightforward one. It has also been a matter of legal dispute between the radio and record industries for decades. The dispute is no longer over the general principle of broadcasting discs, but over how much should be paid for this copyright, most often calculated as a percentage of a commercial station's total advertising sales revenue.

One problematic application of airplay statistics is when they are combined with record sales in a single chart. The best-known such composite chart is *Billboard*'s Hot 100 in the United States, which combines sales with monitored airplay on 360 Top 40 stations and the results of other surveys of small radio markets and specialist formats. At the end of 1998, the weighting of airplay's influence on the Hot 100 was increased from 40 percent to 80 percent in the complex calculations and, for the first time, songs were allowed in the chart purely on the basis of airplay. Thus, in the United States, a track can be 'released to air' and qualify for airplay and chart listing without having been released as a single in stores. A record company merely needs to decide which track from a new or forthcoming album is the most 'radio-friendly' to be 'released' to radio. In turn, the resulting airplay can influence playlisting decisions on various radio format stations.

The key question about airplay is what ultimately is being measured. With whom is an airplay hit genuinely popular? Record company executives and radio station programmers will argue that heavy airplay for a song means that it is genuinely popular with audiences, even if they do not buy it. But heavy airplay for a record might merely suggest that a record company's radio promotion department is efficient and persuasive; poor airplay does not necessarily mean that the record will not sell. A more exact description might be that songs receiving the most airplay are simply those that radio programmers believe are least likely to cause listeners to switch off their radios.

Bibliography

McCourt, Tom, and Rothenbuhler, Eric W. 1997. 'Sound-Scan and the Consolidation of Control in the Popular Music Industry.' *Media, Culture & Society* 19: 201–18.

KEN GARNER

AM

'AM' is an abbreviation of amplitude modulation, the first generally accepted method of transmitting speech and music electronically through the airwaves, in which the frequency of the wave carrying the broadcast signal remains constant, while its amplitude is varied in sympathy with the amplitude of the signal; hence the term 'AM Radio.'

Technically, the AM band stretches from Europe/Asia's long-wave frequencies between 153 and 279 kilohertz (kHz) to the international shortwave frequencies at 2,000–30,000 kHz, although most local stations are in the middle section, which is known outside the Americas as 'medium wave.' It is this part of the band that is labeled 'AM' on most radio receivers: in the United States, AM stations are found between 535 and 1,705 kHz; in the United Kingdom, between 531 and 1,602 kHz.

Historically, in most countries AM was the standard radio broadcast band of the electromagnetic spectrum – from the pre-World War II European stations like the BBC and Radio Normandie to local Top 40 radio stations across the United States in the 1950s. However, transmissions using the AM band are susceptible to interference and, increasingly in recent years, the band has been used mainly for talk and oldies formats.

KEN GARNER

American Bandstand

American Bandstand was a US television show in the form of a dance party. Originally called *Bandstand*, it began in 1952 as a local Philadelphia broadcast on the ABC network affiliate WFIL-TV. When host Bob Horn was fired in 1956, the station asked Dick Clark, a Syracuse University graduate who had come to WFIL in 1952 as a news announcer, to take his place. In 1957, the show was picked up by ABC-TV for national broadcast and was renamed *American Bandstand*, making Clark a nationally recognized personality. Aired in the after-school, late-afternoon time slot, its simple 'record hop' format – with 'ladies' choices,' 'spotlight dances,' a 'record revue' segment and 'lip-synced' live performances – delighted millions of teenagers, who used the show to learn new dances, and spawned countless local variants in the process. The standout *American Bandstand* 'regulars' were popular enough to become minor celebrities in their own right.

By the end of the decade, *American Bandstand* was being carried by 101 affiliates to 20 million teenagers, bringing in $12 million in annual revenues. Clark was financially involved in 33 music-related corporations, including three record companies, a management firm and a pressing plant. His publishing company held copyright on 162 songs, many of which he helped to popularize on his show.

In rock 'n' roll history, Dick Clark is often positioned opposite DJ Alan Freed as the squeaky-clean advocate of white rock against Freed's preference for African-American sounds. Clark maintains that the characterization is inaccurate. In 1960, both Clark and Freed were summoned before the Congressional committee investigating payola. While Freed was indicted, Clark emerged unscathed. *American Bandstand* moved to California in the mid-1960s and continued broadcasting until 1987, but was never again the cultural force it was in the 1950s and early 1960s.

Bibliography

Clark, Dick. 1997. *Dick Clark's American Bandstand*. New York: Collins Publishers.

Clark, Dick, and Robinson, Richard. 1976. *Rock, Roll and Remember*. New York: Crowell.

Shore, Michael, with Clark, Dick. 1985. *The History of American Bandstand: It's Got a Great Beat and You Can Dance to It*. New York: Ballantine Books.

REEBEE GAROFALO

American Forces Network

What would eventually become the US Armed Forces Radio Service (AFRS) began on Kodiak Island, Alaska in December 1941. US soldiers built a low-power shortwave station, produced their own programs and played donated phonograph records. The station provided a much-needed diversion and boosted morale. From these humble beginnings came the American Forces Network (AFN), which several years later would have 160 transmitters and play specially recorded 'V-discs' (78 rpm records pressed on unbreakable vinylite) by the best-known singers of the day.

In March 1942, the US War Department began producing a variety show for the troops overseas: called *Command Performance*, it featured performances by stars such as Bing Crosby, Eddie Cantor, Spike Jones, Dinah Shore, Ethel Waters and Bob Hope, as well as mailed-in requests from the GIs. All the performers on this extremely popular show volunteered their time. *Command Performance* and *Mail Call*, another celebrity-oriented variety program (with such stars as Ozzie and Harriet and Danny Thomas), were incorporated into the American Forces Network when it officially took to the air on 4 July 1943; popular shows from the CBS and NBC radio networks were also broadcast. Headed by Major Thomas Lewis (a former advertising agency executive), AFN entertained troops all over the world, not only giving them music, news, sports and comedy, but, more importantly, keeping them in contact with US culture and letting them know they were not forgotten.

The first AFN broadcasts originated from London and

used studios at the British Broadcasting Corporation (BBC). Sharing BBC facilities necessitated editing out US commercials from the network shows, and AFRS engineers became adept at creating these special transcriptions (recorded 16″ (40 cm) discs of the programs; audiotape had not yet been perfected).

AFN was a very prolific network: historian Samuel Brylawski notes that,

at the height of its operations during World War II, the Armed Forces Radio Service . . . provided over fifty hours of programming a week to American troops . . . Each month, eighty-three thousand discs were shipped from the States to the AFRS transmitters located throughout the world. In 1945, forty-three programs, comprising fourteen hours of material, were produced weekly for American forces by AFRS. In addition, thirty-six hours a week of American commercial radio (with commercial messages deleted) were distributed to overseas outlets. (Brylawski 1980, 333)

Not only did the AFRS programming boost the morale of the troops and help keep them informed; it also affected the musical tastes of listeners in many of the countries where it was heard by introducing them to US music and US network radio stars. GIs collected the V-discs (which were not sold to the general public in the United States, and which often contained songs not available there), and the songs that the troops requested often became local hits in the countries where they were broadcast. In his contribution to *Pennies from Heaven*, Broadcast Music Inc. (BMI) archivist David Sanjek states that, all over Europe, 'an appetite for American popular music had developed because of the omnipresence of American armed forces radio programs' (Sanjek 1996, 224). Dance music was especially loved. Some of the most popular V-discs featured Benny Goodman, Duke Ellington and Glenn Miller. Miller even took a band to the United Kingdom in 1944 and performed a series of concerts for his British fans. Another genre that US troops introduced to Europe was hillbilly music. Heavy airplay of country and western music on AFN, reports Whitcomb (1972), helped popularize Ferlin Husky and Roy Acuff overseas. When the war ended, there was great resistance in some countries to AFN closing. *Time* magazine noted that, in France, members of the French government and hundreds of distraught fans of 'American hot jazz' pleaded with US military authorities to keep the local AFN station broadcasting even though most of the US troops had left. The station remained in operation for two more years.

The influence of programming from AFN would continue in subsequent conflicts. US troops serving in Korea in the early 1950s or in Saudi Arabia during the Gulf War of the early 1990s still listened eagerly to AFN for news of home and for their favorite hit songs. But they were not the only ones – despite the language barrier, the locals too turned to the shortwave for US jazz or dance music. As Brylawski (1998) has commented: 'I believe that AFRS had . . . a significant influence on the music tastes of their "shadow audience," as AFRTS [Armed Forces Radio and Television Service] terms its inadvertent listeners. Scotsman Harry MacKenzie, co-author of [many] AFRS discographies, is one such listener . . . AFRS supposedly influenced 1950s and later BBC programming by introducing Brits to American pop music and looser radio formats than they were used to.'

Most North Americans were reminded of the existence of the Armed Forces Radio Service (which changed its name to Armed Forces Radio and Television Service in 1954) thanks to the 1987 hit movie *Good Morning, Vietnam*, starring Robin Williams, which was based on a real-life GI and Vietnam veteran named Adrian Cronauer. He and Williams did not meet until after the movie was completed, and Williams has admitted in newspaper interviews that he took considerable license with the character; but the film accurately portrays the importance of the role that AFN has played in the lives of US soldiers.

By 1978, AFRTS was developing a satellite service known as SATNET to feed programming more efficiently to overseas locations. By the early 1990s, the programming was being transmitted in digital audio via a new and improved satellite system known as INMARSAT. While it no longer offers as much live programming or as many celebrities as it did during World War II, AFRTS has continued to provide a number of syndicated format choices (including oldies, country, jazz and rock), and to serve US troops, wherever they are stationed, with news, sports, information, religious programs and, of course, US music 24 hours a day.

Bibliography

Brylawski, Samuel. 1980. 'Armed Forces Radio Service: The Invisible Highway Abroad.' *The Quarterly Journal of the Library of Congress* 37(3–4): 333–43.

Brylawski, Samuel. 1998. Personal communication with author, 24 August.

Sanjek, Russell. 1996. *Pennies from Heaven: The American Popular Music Business in the Twentieth Century* (Updated by David Sanjek). New York: Da Capo.

Simon, George T. 1981. *The Big Bands*. New York: Schirmer. (First published New York: Macmillan, 1967.)

'Vive AFN.' 1946. *Time* 47(14): 72.

Whitcomb, Ian. 1972. *After the Ball: Pop Music from Rag to Rock*. London: Allen Lane.

Filmography
Good Morning, Vietnam, dir. Barry Levinson. 1987. USA. 121 mins. Military Comedy. Original music by Alex North.

DONNA HALPER

Broadcasting

Broadcasting is defined as the act and industry of transmitting messages, programs and programming from one sender to many receivers simultaneously.

Historically, 'broadcast' referred to the practise of scattering or sowing seeds across an area of ground by hand, and acquired a general meaning of 'dispersing widely.' But the term was first used in print to describe one possible use of the new technology of wireless telegraphy and wireless telephony (or radio) by the British engineer Oliver Lodge in 1907: 'It might be advantageous to "shout" the message, speaking broadcast to receivers in all directions' (Briggs 1961, 35).

The first such experimental broadcast combining the human voice and music – rather than just Morse code – had been made a few months earlier by R.A. Fessenden on Christmas Eve 1906 from Brant Rock, Massachusetts (Barnouw 1966; Douglas 1987). But the fact that radio stations designed to broadcast regularly were not established until 1920 shows how this was not at first considered the primary use of radio, with governments and telegraph companies seeing it, rather, as providing a point-to-point system of two-way wireless communication across long distances (this use of radio by private individuals survives only in amateur 'ham' radio, and citizens' band (CB) radio).

Until the late 1970s, almost all broadcasting, whether audio via AM or FM, or television pictures on very high or ultrahigh frequencies, utilized these same fundamental principles of transmitting via freely radiating electromagnetic waves to many receivers. Indeed, at the beginning of the twenty-first century, this continued to be how most people in the world received television and radio output.

This notwithstanding, the term 'broadcasting' has come to be used to cover many technologies and techniques other than the original model of radio and television transmission. Subscription cable and satellite, pay-per-view and video-on-demand programming, cable radio, Internet radio and satellite music services have since been developed and used as substitutes for conventional broadcast radio and television. However, these new forms of broadcasting function differently. The technology of the receiver is an essential element of the electronic communication circuit with conventional radio and television. Radio and television receivers for broadcast signals have become ubiquitous, partially as a consequence of their affordability. Satellite dishes, cable hookups and Internet connections, by contrast, allow for increasingly idiosyncratic patterns of listening and viewing on the part of individual consumers. The patterns of distribution that result from these new forms of broadcasting are as a consequence significantly affected by disparities in the income levels of consumers. In most countries of the world, broadcast signals can be received free or at very low cost compared to subscribing to cable, satellite or Internet. Pay-per-view programming builds an immediate economic decision into the choice of programming and eliminates the 'let's see what's on' attitude of the audience member for broadcasting. This changes the relationship between audience member and programmer. Cable and high-speed Internet connections have become wired services with a high infrastructure cost. This restricts their geography to more affluent and more densely settled areas, as well as requiring audience members to be in homes or offices rather than in vehicles or out-of-doors.

The technical exploitation of cable and satellite from the 1970s on has thus resulted in the definition of broadcasting itself becoming the subject of an economic and cultural debate. Commercial stations financed by the sale of advertising spots argue that a unique aspect of broadcasting is that it is free at the point of reception. Defenders of public-service and national stations use the term 'narrowcasting' to criticize the specialized, market-segmented output of some broadcasters, and the fact that these services are also frequently available only to limited audiences. However, such services persist in describing what they do as broadcasting. Common usage concurs.

Developments in Europe in digital compression, transmission and then decoding of signals by receivers do not rewrite these understood principles of broadcasting: the degree of interaction proposed by such services, offering listeners and viewers the possibility of responding directly to programs and programming, is limited. Similarly, the use of the Internet by established and new broadcasters to transmit live audio streams of data, providing radio programming by wire, may expand listeners' choices vastly, but remains broadcasting by any other name.

The Regulation of Broadcasting

The legal regulation of broadcasting has been deemed a necessity on a universal basis. There are at least three reasons for this. First, broadcast signals transmit in all directions from an antenna, so two signals transmitting on the same frequency (or channel) within each other's geographical area of coverage will interfere with each other – potentially to the extent that neither can be received by any audience member. Second, broadcasting facilities are expensive to build and operate; investors, whether commercial or noncommercial, want to be assured that their attempts to reach an audience will not be interfered with – in both the technical and sociopolitical senses. Third, broadcasting is a powerful medium; for reaching a mass audience, nothing else like it has ever been invented. Governments, whether democratic or authoritarian, have an inherent interest in control over a medium that allows someone to talk to everyone, simultaneously and indiscriminately.

The regulation of broadcasting takes different forms in different countries. However, there is a dominant pattern to this. A periodically renegotiated treaty, in principle worldwide, grants the International Telecommunications Union the power to allocate blocks of the electromagnetic spectrum, including those frequencies useful for radio and television broadcasting, to different countries for different uses. Each country has its own regulating authority, such as the Federal Communications Commission in the United States, which assigns specific frequencies – often called channels – to specific broadcasting facilities for specific uses (as well as assigning other frequencies for other uses, such as cellular telephone, two-way radio and garage-door openers). These licensed facilities then operate with various restrictions on their programming content. Until recent decades in many countries, there were few or no nongovernmental licensed broadcasters. Governments have tended to be conservative broadcasters and thus unintentionally often provide a motive for cultural mavericks and commercial entrepreneurs to collaborate in innovative broadcasting adventures, such as the famous pirate radio stations of Britain in the 1960s.

Broadcasting and Popular Music

Music has played a crucial role in broadcasting from its beginnings. Many of the first broadcasts were of phonograph records. Music made up much of the programming for radio in the pre-television era, and music has dominated radio since television took over as the major mass medium of drama. In the pre-television era, the broadcast of recorded music was rare compared to its ubiquity today. The broadcast of live music had higher status, and the major radio stations and networks with the facilities for their own orchestras, stage or dance bands or for remote broadcasts from concert halls and nightclubs used these opportunities to promote their status. Some of this same attitude of promoting a special event has persisted in, for example, Saturday afternoon broadcasts from the Metropolitan Opera in the United States, as well as in broadcast television and pay-per-view concerts on subscription cable in many countries.

Music also plays an essential, if seemingly secondary, role in television as an element of the soundtrack. In movies, television shows, announcements and commercials, musical soundtracks direct attention and provide emotional cues. In this context, the power of the music operates largely through inattention. Competent television viewers the world over can divide their attention between television and some other activity, looking at the screen when the soundtrack calls their attention, usually without conscious awareness of this essential role of sound in the apparently visual medium. Producers of advertisements, of course, try to manipulate these tendencies, often starting their musical soundtracks at a crescendo and building from there.

Because broadcast signals are ubiquitous, the broadcasting of music has repeatedly resulted in new connections of music and audience, often thwarting attempted regulation and sometimes producing revolutions of popular music style. In the United States in the 1950s, large numbers of white teenagers discovered rhythm and blues by listening to 'Negro-appeal' radio stations. This produced the mass audience through which rock 'n' roll changed the course of popular music. In the countries of the Soviet Union, most forms of jazz and rock 'n' roll were banned as decadent; but radio signals from the West nevertheless allowed them to have a musical influence. In Britain, the BBC's musical programming policy was conservative and restrictive regarding popular music. Pirate radio stations broadcasting from the North Sea during the mid-1960s provided the alternative of rock music. In Canada, broadcasting regulations require radio stations to program a minimum percentage of 'Canadian music,' as defined by CanCon regulations. However, the majority of the Canadian population is within radio signal reach of the huge US market.

Bibliography

Barnouw, Erik. 1966. *A Tower in Babel: A History of Broadcasting in the United States. Vol. I – to 1933.* New York: Oxford University Press.

Briggs, Asa. 1961. *The History of Broadcasting in the United Kingdom. Vol. I: The Birth of Broadcasting.* London: Oxford University Press.

Douglas, George H. 1987. *The Early Days of Radio Broadcasting.* Jefferson, NC: McFarland & Co.

KEN GARNER and ERIC W. ROTHENBUHLER

Eurovision Song Contest

The Eurovision Song Contest is an annual competition for songs and singers representing nations that are members of the European Broadcasting Union. The contest has been televised live across Europe each May since

1956, attracting audiences of many millions. In 1956, seven countries were represented by two songs each, and the winner was Switzerland's Lys Assia with 'Refrain.' By the mid-1990s, some 30 nations were involved, and several had to be excluded each year. From 1962, the winning country became the host for the following year's event.

Votes are cast by national panels, which are not allowed to vote for the song representing their own country. Originally, each panel was required to reflect a cross section of age groups and occupations. In 1997, for the first time, five countries used telephone voting by viewers to compile their votes, which are cast to a maximum of 12 points.

For most of its history, Eurovision has reflected at least some of the main trends in European pop. Among its winners have been Sandie Shaw (UK, with 'Puppet on a String' in 1967), ABBA (Sweden, with 'Waterloo' in 1974) and Céline Dion (representing Switzerland in 1988 with 'Ne Partez Pas Sans Moi'). However, an equally strong pull toward an opportunistic 'Eurovision' style has been apparent. This style has been characterized by a bouncy rhythm complemented by rousing melody and simple lyrics. Its apogee was 'La La La' (Massiel, Spain), the 1968 winner.

By the mid-1990s, when many former Communist countries were joining Eurovision, the contest had lost touch with current trends in European music and was regarded by many in the music and media industries as an insignificant, minor 'camp' entertainment.

Discographical References

ABBA. 'Waterloo.' Epic EPC 2040. *1974*: UK. Reissue: ABBA. 'Waterloo.' *Abbatastic: The Fantastic Songs of ABBA*. Beat Fantastic 8271. *1998*: USA.

Assia, Lys. 'Refrain.' *Eurovision Song Contest Winners 1956–81*. Polydor 2675 221. *1981*: UK.

Dion, Céline. 'Ne Partez Pas Sans Moi.' Carrere 14-454. *1988*: France. Reissue: Dion, Céline. 'Ne Partez Pas Sans Moi.' *Gold, Vol. 1*. Columbia 80287. *1998*: USA.

Massiel. 'La, La, La.' Philips BF 1667. *1968*: UK.

Shaw, Sandie. 'Puppet on a String.' Pye 7N 17272. *1967*: UK. Reissue: Shaw, Sandie. 'Puppet on a String.' *Very Best of Sandie Shaw*. Crimson 202. *1999*: USA.

DAVE LAING

FM

'FM' is an abbreviation of frequency modulation, a method of transmitting signals electronically through the airwaves in which the frequency of the carrier wave is varied in accordance with the amplitude and polarity of the signal; hence the term 'FM Radio.' Invented by the pioneering US engineer Edwin Armstrong, it was first

demonstrated in 1933, and several FM radio stations were in existence by 1940. FM's importance for popular music radio, however, is often dated from 1965, when the US Federal Communications Commission ruled that city stations with both AM and FM licenses could not broadcast the same output on the two frequencies. This led to 'free-form,' 'progressive' or 'FM radio,' with FM stations playing longer tracks from LPs, while AM stations played the singles that dominated the Top 40.

FM became the preferred broadcast band for music radio stations, transmitting at the very high frequencies (it is still sometimes mistakenly called VHF) that facilitate the transmission of stereo broadcasts and are potentially static-free. FM frequencies have been found mostly between 87 and 108 megahertz (MHz), but also between 76 and 90 MHz (Japan only). The old Eastern European FM range of 66 to 72 MHz was being phased out following the collapse of the Soviet Union. Several new Polish and Czech commercial music stations in the late 1990s, for example, had two frequencies, one in 87 to 108 MHz, and one in 66 to 72 Mhz.

FM's offering of high-quality signals over limited distances led FM to be the dominant band for the hundreds of new local commercial pop music stations created by the deregulation of radio across Europe after 1990.

KEN GARNER

Grand Ole Opry

The *Grand Ole Opry* is country music's oldest broadcast variety program, having been aired by station WSM in Nashville, Tennessee since 1925.

The seeds of the *Opry* germinated in November 1925 when the National Life and Accident Insurance Company, owner of the new station (whose call letters represented its slogan 'We Shield Millions'), hired as its director George D. Hay, previously the announcer for the *National Barn Dance*, which WLS in Chicago had inaugurated in April 1924. Alerted by this experience to the listening public's enthusiasm for 'old-time tunes,' which was then being whipped up by anti-jazz propagandists such as the automobile magnate Henry Ford, Hay tested WSM's audience on 28 November 1925 with a two-hour program of fiddling by Uncle Jimmy Thompson. On 26 December, he launched a Saturday-night variety program, largely, but not at that point exclusively, featuring 'old-time' performers.

Initially known as the *WSM Barn Dance*, the program acquired a new name at some point in 1927. One night, the *Music Appreciation Hour* on the NBC network, to which WSM had recently become a subscriber and which preceded Hay's program, discussed the issue of 'musical realism' and closed with a piece depicting a train ride. Hay promptly came on the air saying: 'From here on out for the next three hours we will present nothing but realism.' De Ford Bailey – then, and for many years to come, the show's only African-American performer – played a train imitation on harmonica, 'Pan American Blues,' which Hay followed with these momentous words: 'For the past hour we have been listening to music taken largely from the Grand Opera, but from now on we will present the Grand Ole Opry.' The first identified appearance in print of the new name was on 11 December 1927 but, since the program was otherwise unchanged in style and content, historians have unanimously dated the beginnings of the *Grand Ole Opry* to the events of two years earlier.

The earliest broadcasts were from the WSM studios in the National Life Building, to which audiences were first admitted in 1927. The show later moved to a succession of Nashville theaters and halls, most famously the Ryman Auditorium – its home from 1941 to 1974 – where it attracted a large and faithful audience, some of whom would repeatedly travel great distances to visit what was coming to be recognized as country music's chief place of pilgrimage. Meanwhile, the show's radio audience extended across much of the United States, thanks to the station's powerful transmitter and, as early as 1928, its clear-channel status. In 1939, the relationship between WSM and NBC became two-way, and the *Grand Ole Opry* was nationally networked.

The show typically ran for three or four hours, divided into 15- and 30-minute slots which over the years acquired long-term advertising sponsors such as Prince Albert tobacco. Among the most popular performers of its first five years were De Ford Bailey, the singer and banjoist Uncle Dave Macon and a number of string bands on which Hay conferred such rural titles as the Gully Jumpers, the Fruit Jar Drinkers and the Possum Hunters. During the 1930s, however, the musical bias of the *Grand Ole Opry* began to incline in favor of singing groups like the Vagabonds and of singer-guitarists like the Delmore Brothers or the father-and-son act of Asher Sizemore and Little Jimmie, all of them professional artists rather than the part-timers of earlier days. In both respects the show kept step with national trends in country music.

Artists were supported by the WSM Artists Service Bureau, instituted in 1933, which booked them on tours both individually and as troupes representing the show. During the 1930s and 1940s, the show helped to make the names of Roy Acuff, Bill Monroe, Ernest Tubb, George Morgan and Hank Williams, most of whom remained cast-members until retirement or death. Acuff, Macon and other regulars were featured in the musical film *Grand Ole Opry* (1940). Some of the second-rank artists on the show owed almost everything to its patronage: the pianist Del Wood, who had one unrepeated hit in the early 1950s, remained on the *Opry* for more than 30 years.

The *Grand Ole Opry* maintained its leading role among country music radio shows during the 1940s, 1950s and 1960s, despite challenges from shows such as KWKH's *Louisiana Hayride* in Shreveport or WWVA's *Jamboree* in Wheeling, West Virginia. It was nourished by its symbiotic relationship with the country music recording and publishing industry in Nashville. The first recordings made in the city, by Victor in 1928, were almost all of *Opry* groups, and were probably arranged in collaboration with Hay; the most influential record producer of the postwar era, Owen Bradley, was an ex-member of an *Opry* band; and one of the co-founders of the first significant publishing company in Nashville, Acuff-Rose, established in 1942, was the *Opry*'s most popular artist, Roy Acuff.

To acknowledge the *Grand Ole Opry*'s almost mythic status as the spiritual home of country music, friends (including Acuff) and investors provided it, in 1974, with a purpose-built auditorium in the new Opryland theme park on the outskirts of Nashville, where it continues to be broadcast and televised and where it hosts the annual awards ceremonies of the Country Music Association. But, although new figures in country music occasionally appear on the show, and a few of those with more old-fashioned tastes, such as Tom T. Hall or Ricky Skaggs, have seen it as an honor to be elected members of a company that includes such venerable luminaries as Hank Snow, the *Grand Ole Opry*'s status as a showcase is greatly diminished, and for many younger artists it is an irrelevant antique. The *Grand Ole Opry* is best regarded as a living, if somewhat artificially preserved, memorial of a kind of variety show that has virtually disappeared from country music.

Bibliography

Hurst, Jack. 1975. *Nashville's Grand Ole Opry*. New York: Abrams.

Wolfe, Charles K. 1975. *The Grand Ole Opry: The Early Years, 1925–35*. London: Old Time Music.

Discographical Reference

Bailey, De Ford. 'Pan American Blues.' *Harp Blowers: Complete Recorded Works (1925–1936)*. Document DOCD-5164. *1994*: Austria.

Discography

Nashville, 1928. Document DOCD-8037. *1998*: Austria.

Stars of the Grand Ole Opry 1926–1974. RCA CPK2-0466. *1974*: USA.

Filmography

Grand Ole Opry, dir. Frank McDonald. 1940. USA. 68 mins. Musical Comedy.

TONY RUSSELL

King Biscuit Time

Early in the 1940s, white businesses in the southern United States that catered to a black clientele began to sponsor live music shows on radio oriented toward their customers. At the time, there were no black music shows on the air, and African Americans in the region were beginning to acquire radio receivers in large numbers. One of the first and most influential live music shows was *King Biscuit Time*, which aired on KFFA (AM) in Helena, Arkansas on weekdays from noon to 12:15 p.m. The show was launched in the fall of 1941 as a vehicle to promote King Biscuit Flour (produced and sold by the Interstate Grocery Company, itself based in Helena); it featured a local white announcer named Sonny Payne and the legendary black blues musician Rice Miller, soon to be better known by his radio name, Sonny Boy Williamson. Miller was a superb blues harmonica player and tunesmith, well known throughout the Mississippi Delta region for his witty blues compositions and flamboyant showmanship. He organized a small blues combo that included guitarist Robert Lockwood, pianists Robert 'Dudlow' Taylor and Willie Love, and drummer Peck Curtis; they played on KFFA five days a week at noon, when most of the Delta's field hands were taking their lunch break, and then traveled to evening engagements in the region.

At first, Rice Miller and his band were not paid for their broadcasts; instead, they were allowed to announce their upcoming gigs. Later in the decade, they were paid modestly.

King Biscuit Time became a huge success with black listeners in the mid-South. It developed such a large following that the Interstate Grocery Company began to market a new product called Sonny Boy Corn Meal; each bag had a large picture of a smiling Rice Miller, harmonica in hand, sitting on a giant ear of corn. *King Biscuit Time* enjoyed a lengthy association with KFFA, even though Miller had moved on by the late 1940s. The show pioneered the broadcasting of live blues in the region, and influenced the growth of similar radio programs in the South. In the mid-1960s, Rice Miller returned to Helena from Chicago and rejoined *King Biscuit Time* for a brief period; he died in 1965.

Bibliography

Barlow, William. 1989. *Looking Up at Down: The Emergence of Blues Culture*. Philadelphia: Temple University Press.

Palmer, Robert. 1981. *Deep Blues*. New York: Viking Press.

WILLIAM BARLOW

Make-Believe Ballroom

One of the earliest radio music programs consisting of recorded music rather than live performances, *The World's Largest Make-Believe Ballroom* was launched by Los Angeles air personality Al Jarvis in 1932. The idea was taken up by an early 'record-jockey' Martin Block, who introduced his *Make-Believe Ballroom* on WNEW New York in February 1935. The show was intended to keep listeners tuned to WNEW as they awaited news of the trial of the alleged kidnapper of the child of famous pilot Charles Lindbergh. Block's formula attracted large amounts of sponsorship revenue and was soon imitated by radio stations all over the United States.

Bibliography

Ennis, Philip H. 1992. *The Seventh Stream: The Emergence of Rocknroll in American Popular Music*. Hanover and London: Wesleyan University Press.

Sanjek, Russell. 1988. *American Popular Music and Its Business: The First Four Hundred Years. Vol. III: From 1900 to 1984*. New York and Oxford: Oxford University Press.

DAVE LAING

MTV

Music Television (MTV) was founded in the United States in 1981 and subsequently became the largest international company providing specialist cable and satellite channels featuring popular music, primarily in the form of videoclips.

MTV had been preceded by pioneering attempts at music television shows by Michael Nesmith and others. Its launch came at a time when cable operators in the United States were seeking new formats to attract younger viewers and when record companies were increasingly frustrated by the unwillingness of radio stations to play records by new artists. The channel's first director, Robert Pittman, defined his vision of MTV as 'a visual radio station' (quoted in Shore 1984, 184).

MTV's early programming was dominated by videos of British New Romantic acts such as Duran Duran and A Flock of Seagulls because US labels were slow to produce videos of their artists. By 1983, however, MTV's audience had increased to 15 million viewers and the channel's choice of videos to playlist was having an impact on the sales of singles. The channel's music policy at this point favored white rock and heavy metal bands, and the paucity of black artists featured on MTV led to accusations of racism. As the channel's reach increased to encompass almost all of the United States, it added specialist shows such as *YO! MTV Raps* (1988), *Headbangers' Ball* (1987) and *MTV Unplugged* (1990), and by the start of the 1990s the channel could claim to reflect the spectrum of US pop music.

In 1990, MTV's owners, the Viacom group (which had bought it from Warner Communications and Amex in 1985), added a second music channel, VH-1. This was aimed at the over-25 age group and operated an album-oriented rock (AOR) policy. In 1995, a third channel, M2, was launched, which re-created the 'wall to wall' videoclip format of MTV's origins. In 1998, MTV Networks moved to a further stage in niche programming by offering a multiplex of seven genre-based programs.

The shift from one monolithic channel to a 'bouquet' of alternatives was mirrored in much of MTV's overseas programming activity. In 1987, Viacom launched MTV Europe in partnership with British media owner Robert Maxwell. This English-language channel was distributed throughout Europe by cable and satellite. By 1995, MTV Europe was available in more than 50 million homes in over 30 countries. The channel had been heavily criticized for its emphasis on Anglo-American music, and it had failed to attract large amounts of 'pan-European' advertising. In a major policy change that tacitly acknowledged that its assumption of a unitary global youth culture had been misguided, MTV Europe announced it would provide a range of regional and national services. It subsequently offered national MTV and VH-1 channels in Britain and Germany, and three regional services for South, Central and Northern Europe.

The success of the MTV formula inspired the formation of national competitors such as MuchMusic in Canada and Viva in Germany. Elsewhere, MTV set up Latin American, Australian and Japanese services, each in alliance with local media companies. MTV Asia was launched by an alliance of Viacom and Rupert Murdoch's News Corporation in 1993, but disputes led to the formation of Channel V by Murdoch and four major music companies in opposition to a relaunched MTV Asia owned by Viacom and PolyGram. In line with the European policy, MTV Asia was offered in English- and Hindi-language versions, and its management sought to develop national MTV services in the region.

The cultural and musical significance of MTV and of music video in general has been the subject of much academic attention, notably from Kaplan (1987) and Goodwin (1992), while the network's role in the music and media industries has been analyzed by Denisoff (1988) and Banks (1996).

Bibliography

Banks, Jack. 1996. *Monopoly Television: MTV's Quest to Control the Music*. Boulder, CO: Westview Press.

Denisoff, R. Serge. 1988. *Inside MTV*. New Brunswick and London: Transaction Books.

Goodwin, Andrew. 1992. *Dancing in the Distraction Factory: Music Television and Popular Culture*. Minneapolis, MN: University of Minnesota Press.

Kaplan, E. Ann. 1987. *Rocking Around the Clock: Music Television, Postmodernism and Consumer Culture*. New York and London: Methuen.

Shore, Michael. 1984. *The Rolling Stone Book of Music Video*. New York: Morrow.

DAVE LAING

Pirate Radio

A synonym for illegal radio broadcasting, pirate radio played an important role in the dissemination of popular music in certain European countries in the 1960s. 'Pirate' derived from the fact that many stations were based on ships 'offshore,' outside territorial waters, in order to circumvent legislation. A second generation of land-based, and more covert, operations appeared from the 1970s onward, with different motivation and intentions.

According to Cazenave (1980), the emergence of pirate radio in Britain, and later in Belgium, France and Italy, was a response to the state's broadcasting monopoly. Radio was still the most important vehicle for the integrated industry of domestic entertainment, and the pirates filled a gap in the market left by the conservative state-run channels, which had not reflected changes in entertainment culture, especially in popular music (Miller 1992).

Although there were covert offshore radio broadcasts before the 1960s, for example in the United States in the late 1930s by ships anchored off California, the 'pirate radio era' began with Radio Mercur in 1958, with a light-music format broadcast on VHF to Denmark from a German-registered boat anchored off Copenhagen. It was a commercial success, but it was closed down by armed Danish police in 1962. Radio Mercur's ship was purchased by Radio Syd, a Swedish pirate that operated between 1962 and 1966 but that was closed down when the Swedish Parliament passed a bill outlawing offshore radio (Baron 1975). In The Netherlands, Radio Veronica was the principal offshore pirate station.

Radio Caroline, Radio London and other offshore stations around the coast of Britain appeared in 1964. Radio Luxembourg, a land-based station that had broadcast in English to Britain from the European continent since the 1930s, had pioneered the US model of commercial broadcasting. In collaboration with record companies, the new pirate radio stations capitalized on the popularity of recorded music presented by celebrity DJs. Radio Caroline epitomized this change in the pattern of British

447

sound broadcasting: the first disc played by DJ Chris Moore on its first show was the Beatles' 'Can't Buy Me Love.' The format of the pirate ships' broadcasting was described in *The Guardian* on 22 January 1966 as 'continuous "pop" music and inconsequential chatter . . .' from celebrity DJs. By the end of 1965, an estimated 15 million listeners were tuning in regularly, and a study carried out by National Opinion Polls Ltd. in 1966 established the size of the commercial radio audience, with 45 percent listening to an offshore station and/or Radio Luxembourg during the course of a week (Baron 1975, 42). These developments suggest that pirate radio stations were not an outlet for a subculture, but were a part of the process by which commercial popular music entered the cultural mainstream.

In the summer of 1967, the British government passed the *Marine, &c., Broadcasting (Offences) Act*, and at the same time formulated plans to restructure the BBC. 'Most countries which passed anti-pirate legislation rapidly acknowledged the pirates' programming initiatives, many of which were incorporated into the existing broadcasting system' – such as increasing domestic output in Belgium, opening up a slot on the national network to cater for 'disfranchised lovers of light popular music' in Denmark or, in the case of Sweden, introducing 'Melody Radio' when Radio Syd was outlawed (Chapman 1992).

In 1967, the British era of overt offshore pirate radio ended, and the BBC introduced its new four-channel sound service. In line with the European trend, Radio One was a direct result of the pirate radios and catered for the youth market with a new national pop channel that was largely staffed by former pirate DJs, such as Tony Blackburn and John Peel.

This initiative was followed in 1970 by the introduction in the United Kingdom of privately owned local radio stations, a move that was a direct outcome of the 'action-critique' by the pirate radio stations. The result was that 'British music radio developed and exists within a broadcasting tradition – piratical and populist in flavour, commercial in orientation, with antecedents in American Rock'n'Roll radio – entirely separate from that of the tradition of public service broadcasting established by the BBC' (Barnard 1989, 1).

In the 1970s, the focus of illegal radio broadcasting shifted to France and Italy, where the 'free radio' movements were generally driven by political rather than musical, or commercial, motives. Each government has tried to deal differently with the threat and popularity of its 'pirates,' and Italy has been the most liberal of all. According to Richard Barbrook, who was involved in pirate and community radio broadcasting in the early 1980s, 'the problems of any broadening of independent

radio and community radio are to do with what form the legislation takes, the nature of any new licensing body, how democratic you can make a station, and also the nature of the funding' (quoted in Hind and Mosco 1985, 144).

Britain entered its second significant era of pirate radio (land-based and covert transmissions) in the midst of the worldwide free radio movement in the 1980s. Following the example of US community radio as a voice for minorities, the 'black music pirates' in Britain broadcast reggae and other black music styles that were ignored or censored by the BBC and the licensed commercial stations. As in the 1960s, the perceived popularity of these pirates resulted in the granting of licenses to stations specializing in jazz, dance and hip-hop, notably Kiss FM in London.

The late 1980s also witnessed the rise of unlicensed radio broadcasting in the United States. Historically, pirating frequencies in North America were largely unnecessary due to the structure of the radio industry. The motivation for illegal broadcasting at this point was sparked by the corporate buyouts of local commercial radio stations. Arguing that free speech guaranteed by the First Amendment was at stake, unlicensed broadcasters used low-powered transmitters to create more choice and diversity. One of the first of the so-called microbroadcasters was Black Liberation Radio.

Internet audio broadcasting, or 'webcasting,' has emerged as the successor to the radio pirates. It does not have the limitation of spectrum scarcity and offers great opportunities for unlicensed broadcasters, whether their motivation is musical, cultural or political.

Bibliography
Barnard, Stephen. 1989. *On the Radio: Music Radio in Britain*. Milton Keynes: Open University Press.

Baron, Mike. 1975. *Independent Radio: The Story of Independent Radio in the United Kingdom*. Lavenham: Dalton.

Cazenave, François. 1980. *Les Radios Libres* [Free Radio]. Paris: Presses Universitaires de France.

Chapman, Robert. 1992. *Selling the Sixties: The Pirates and Pop Music Radio*. London: Routledge.

Duchene, Anne. 1967. 'Radio: The Price of Going Pop.' *The Guardian* (11 September). www.guardiancentury. co.uk/

Hind, John, and Mosco, Stephen. 1985. *Rebel Radio: The Full Story of British Pirate Radio*. London: Pluto Press.

Miller, Toby. 1992. 'An Editorial Introduction for Radio.' *Continuum. The Australian Journal of Media and Culture. Special Issue on Radio – Sound* 6(1): 5–13.

Strauss, Neil, ed. 1993. *Radiotext(e)*. New York: Semiotext(e).

Tyler, Bob, and Laing, Dave. 1996. *The European Radio Industry*. London: FT Telecoms & Media.

'What Shall We Tell Caroline?' 1966. *The Guardian* (22 January). www.guardiancentury.co.uk/

Discographical Reference

Beatles, The. 'Can't Buy Me Love.' Parlophone R 5114. *1964*: UK.

VANESSA BASTIAN

Playlist

A playlist is a radio station's or music television channel's selection of a fixed number of music tracks or music videos to form the basis of its programming for a set period of time.

Stations playing current commercial pop singles or videos will normally update their playlists every week, after the previous week's record sales chart is published. However, the United Kingdom's Classic FM, for example, which relies heavily on its 'Hall of Fame,' a list of listeners' 300 favorite classical compositions, updates it via an annual phone-in poll.

Record sales and listener telephone polls are not the only measures of popularity used to compile playlists. Airplay, record company promotion of releases and artists, original listener research (either by telephone call-outs or auditorium testing), magazines and tipsheets, and the enthusiasms of station staff, can all influence the playlist. Music television channels might also consider the visual style of the video.

Playlists are central to programming and radio formats, and their importance and extensive influence over music broadcasting can best be dated to the emergence of these techniques in the early 1950s. In North America, the list will be set by the program director or 'PD,' in Europe more commonly called the head of music. National, state and public-service stations may also convene a weekly playlist committee meeting, bringing together disc jockeys, station producers and even record industry pluggers to advise on the next week's list.

The number of records/videos on a playlist really depends on the format. The figure '40' was set by Todd Storz's and Bill Stewart's celebrated 1953 invention of 'Top 40' radio on their station KOWH-AM in Omaha, Nebraska, inspired by there being 40 records on a bar jukebox. In the 1960s, some radio formats trimmed this to 30 records, or even just 10.

Any contemporary format radio playlist might now feature any number from eight to 25 'A-list' or 'Power' tracks deemed the most popular that week and so played the greatest number of times, and 15 to 30 on the 'B-list' (ex-'A-list' songs on the way down, and new tracks on the way up), played fewer times. In addition to this main weekly published playlist, there might be two further confidential lists, updated less frequently: 30 to 100 'recurrents,' familiar ex-playlist tracks from recent weeks and months; and a 'gold' library of several hundred oldies from recent years.

Bibliography

Fong-Torres, Ben. 1998. *The Hits Just Keep On Coming: The History of Top 40 Radio*. San Francisco: Miller Freeman Books.

Norberg, Eric G. 1996. *Radio Programming: Tactics and Strategy*. Boston, MA: Focal Press.

Rothenbuhler, Eric W., and McCourt, Tom. 1992. 'Commercial Radio and Popular Music: Processes of Selection and Factors of Influence.' In *Popular Music and Communication*, ed. James Lull. 2nd ed. Newbury Park, CA: Sage, 101–15.

KEN GARNER

Programming

'Programming' denotes the total content of what is broadcast on a format radio station. In most formats, except News/Talk, All-Talk or Sport, programming consists mainly of commercially released music on disc. But the term also embraces the news, DJ talk, jingles, commercials, competitions, traffic news, sports bulletins, weather and community announcements between the music items.

'Programming' also refers to the process by which this content, especially the music, is decided upon and then updated on a regular basis, normally weekly.

Before the mid-1950s, the term 'programming' was used to describe the content of the then traditional radio station or network in the United States, consisting of various discrete programs: for example, a sponsored half-hour of country music, followed by a live sports broadcast. But after the introduction of Top 40, the original radio format, and its rapid adoption across the United States between 1954 and 1957, the word 'programming' on its own came increasingly to be associated exclusively with this new way of filling each day's airtime with a consistent, uniform genre of music, while the older style of station program content came to be known as block, segment or sequence programming. This distinction – programming versus programs – has entered commercial format radio usage around the world. Almost the only stations that have continued to broadcast discrete programs with different content are public, public-service or community stations.

The techniques used to manage music programming on a format radio station involve a number of elements that are little understood outside the radio industry, but that have a far-reaching influence on the totality of what music is broadcast.

Elements and Process of Programming

In the process of programming, there is, first, the decision to adopt a particular music radio format or genre; next, there is the creation of a playlist. This in turn involves three further, related elements: codification, rotation and 'clock.'

(a) Codification involves the division of the playlist into sub-lists of records receiving differing numbers of plays (A, B and so on), and the definition of the style of each disc on the list according to a limited set of mainly musical variables, such as tempo, arrangement or genre, gender of performer and date. Each disc is then allocated codes for its combination of these variables at the point at which its details are entered into a computerized music programming system, such as Selector. In November 1992, for example, a Top 40 or Contemporary Hit format radio station might have codified Whitney Houston's 'I Will Always Love You' as A/S/B/F – A-list, slow, ballad, female vocal – and Arrested Development's 'People Everyday' as B/M/R/M – B-list, mid-tempo, rap, male vocal. Limited numerical values can sometimes be used to indicate the depth or sparseness of the arrangement, as well as the mood – such as cheerful, upbeat (4), or sad, downbeat (1) (Keith 1987). Once entered, these codes determine both the number and the location of plays each disc receives while on the playlist, according partly to any general preferences the music programmer may set in the computer (two of the more extreme historical prejudices are 'no two female vocals back-to-back,' and 'never follow a news bulletin with a ballad'), and partly to the remaining two elements of music programming described below.

(b) Rotation denotes the desired frequency with which any record is to be played on the station. Different rotation rates – high, medium and low – are set for A-, B- and C-list discs, respectively. Rotation rate is described by the number of hours that would elapse before a listener might expect to hear the same song again. For example, in the United States, high rotation can mean a repeat pattern as frequent as every 75 minutes (Norberg 1996)! However, a period of 2.5 hours is more common, equating to 70 or more plays per week of each disc. European stations generally operate longer repeat patterns, setting high rotation somewhere between three and six hours, giving each of the A-list discs from 30 to 60 plays per week. Medium rotation might be five (United States) or eight (Europe) hours, and low rotation just one or perhaps two plays of a disc per day. Consequently, rotation rate and playlist length are bound together by mutual implication: the shorter the playlist, the faster the repeat patterns; if slower repeat patterns are wanted, the playlist has to be longer.

(c) 'Clock,' 'Hot Clock,' 'Format Clock,' 'Program Wheel' – or, confusingly, just 'Format' – denotes the fixed sequence of all programming elements in each hour, traditionally planned and represented graphically on a drawn clock face with the hands removed and with pie-slice sectors marked on it, indicating the location and duration of the respective elements. This has come to be accomplished more often by a computerized programming package, which offers the programmer a vertical list sequence on-screen of proposed items from within each category of element. For example:

.00 News
.05 Ad spot (*solus*)
.05.30 Jingle station ident.
.05.35 A-list disc: TEXAS In Our Lifetime A/M/R/F
.08.50 DJ link
.09.05 B-list disc: MANIC STREET PREACHERS You Stole the Sun B/U/R/M

Hour by hour, different discs slot in at the same points on the clock, as determined by their codification, rotation rate and other programming preferences. However, 'day-parting' allocates different 'clocks' to different times of the day, one common practise being the programming of a greater number of up-tempo discs during peak breakfast and afternoon 'drive-time' rush hours on stations in urban areas. But it is unusual for a 24-hour music format station to use more than three, possibly four, such clocks (peak breakfast/late afternoon, weekday daytime/weekend mornings, weekday evenings/weekend afternoons and evenings, for example).

It is entirely possible for a programmer, having set the 'clock' rules and entered the playlist 'adds' into the system, to hit the return key and accept the computer's proposed sequencing of discs for a whole week's programming. The format radio DJ has little, if any, say in what he/she plays.

The Role of Consultants

It is not only the DJ who has little say in the music broadcast on programmed format radio stations. Frequently, the station program director, especially in the United States, will have had no involvement in the choice of format, playlist length and structure, rotation rate, clock and other programming-element preferences. Many US radio stations and groups delegate these decisions to radio consultants.

The first radio consultants were successful format programmers at station groups who simply went freelance in the late 1950s and offered their skills to other stations. The demand for their services arose in the wake of the rapid adoption of Top 40 programming techniques for other musical genres – Beautiful Music or Easy Listening, Country – and the consequent increased intensity of local commercial competition between such differentiated stations. Consultants came to be seen – and chose to promote themselves – as the experts who could fly in, tighten up a station's programming elements and deliver ratings increases, almost overnight.

But it has been historical changes in US radio regulation, and related changing listening habits, that have driven the growth and influence of consultants. In 1965, the Federal Communications Commission (FCC) ruled that owners of both AM and FM station licenses in most markets had to offer different programming on each. At first, this led to the celebrated underground or progressive free-form album rock radio on FM. But as FM listening increased, stations brought in consultants to format their FM output. By 1978, over half of the US radio audience was listening on FM, not AM.

In 1985, the FCC allowed station groups, for the first time, to own more than one FM and one AM license in major cities. After the 1996 *Telecommunications Act*, there were no restrictions on the number of stations a company could own nationally, and companies could have up to eight stations in the largest cities. As groups centralized business control of their burgeoning number of stations, consultants were the obvious way of hiring short-term programming expertise.

Consultants' activities can therefore range from a brief visit to offer advice on an independent station's music programming system, to 'full service': researching a major market for a national group; renaming its station in that market; commissioning or producing new jingles; changing the music format; setting all programming preferences; hiring, training and firing on-air staff; even providing programming – the discs, the DJs, the complete editorial content of airtime – from the consultancy's central syndication service (Keith 1987). On some US music stations, the commercials constitute the only local content.

Effects

The local and creative crisis for the medium of radio in the United States brought about by this centralizing tendency and the growth of consultancy is a separate issue (see Douglas 1999). But, for music, the problematic consequences of programming are more obvious, fundamental and structural, wherever it occurs in the world. Format radio at first divides the audience for music into distinct but commercially driven groups according to taste, and the playlist numerically and stylistically narrows this commercial definition of a particular taste still further (Rothenbuhler and McCourt 1992).

What is less widely understood is the potential for musical exclusion or mistreatment inherent in the details of the programming system. Incorrect codification of a disc can lead to its being played at points on the

clock or at a rotation that it does not merit. Insensitive codification can omit a unique musical characteristic of a disc, which might appeal more widely with proper codification and higher rotation. More seriously, codification itself is both so limited that musical distinctiveness cannot be recognized, and so detailed as to structurally ghettoize certain categories of disc even within those selected – male rap, female ballad, for example – which might be allowed to appear only at certain time points in certain clocks.

Some more experienced programmers in control of their formats are fully aware of these dangers and, consequently, tend to restrict their codification to the barest details necessary to manage rotation – A list or B list? – and program according to their personal 'feel' for a song, and whether each hour-long sequence the computer suggests for the forthcoming week 'sounds right.' However, radio consultants would be as correct as their critics in pointing out that this criterion of musical selection is even more problematic than programming.

Bibliography

Douglas, Susan J. 1999. *Listening In: Radio and the American Imagination*. New York: Times Books/Random House.

Keith, Michael C. 1987. *Radio Programming: Consultancy and Formatics*. Boston, MA: Focal Press.

MacFarland, David T. 1997. *Future Radio Programming Strategies: Cultivating Listenership in the Digital Age*. 2nd ed. Mahwah, NJ: Lawrence Erlbaum Associates.

Norberg, Eric G. 1996. *Radio Programming: Tactics and Strategy*. Boston, MA: Focal Press.

Rothenbuhler, Eric W., and McCourt, Tom. 1992. 'Commercial Radio and Popular Music: Processes of Selection and Factors of Influence.' In *Popular Music and Communication*, ed. James Lull. 2nd ed. Newbury Park, CA: Sage, 101–15.

Discographical References

Arrested Development. 'People Everyday.' Chrysalis 50397. *1992*: USA.

Houston, Whitney. 'I Will Always Love You.' Arista 12490. *1992*: USA.

Manic Street Preachers. 'You Stole the Sun from My Heart.' Epic 6669532. *1999*: UK.

Texas. 'In Our Lifetime.' Mercury MERCD 517. *1999*: UK.

KEN GARNER

Radio

Ever since radio was first harnessed as a technology for broadcasting as opposed to one-to-one communication, in the years following World War I, it has had a major impact on the dissemination, production and consumption of music. How radio became so important to popular music is best examined principally in the context of the two different forces that guided its early growth. In the United States, what was heard on the air was often influenced by corporations and commercial advertisers, while in many other countries – most notably the United Kingdom – the state or the government played a major role in broadcasting, with varying degrees of commercial involvement in radio stations being allowed. As a readily available and relatively inexpensive time filler, music has formed radio's main source of content from its earliest days, and has become one of the principal means through which manufacturers have promoted their products to the public in those countries that have allowed commercial involvement. This has been especially true in the United States, where equipment manufacturers such as Westinghouse, AMRAD and General Electric were the first station owners, and the product name was often part of the station's identity. WGI in Medford Hillside, Massachusetts was often called 'the AMRAD Station.' Other companies used requested call letters to remind listeners of a product: WLS in Chicago was owned by the Sears Roebuck department store, and the initials of the call letters stood for *World's Largest Store*.

Commercial Radio

The Beginnings

The first time that music was played on radio was Christmas Eve 1906. Canadian engineer Reginald Fessenden, who had been experimenting with the 'wireless,' sent out a short program from Brant Rock, Massachusetts. His successful experiment proved that not just Morse code could be broadcast, and it set the stage for much of what followed. Another innovative engineer, Charles 'Doc' Herrold, built what was perhaps the first college station in 1909. He and his wife, Sybil, broadcast a weekly concert of phonograph records to the students. In New York, inventor Lee DeForest had tried on several occasions to broadcast live concerts, including a January 1910 attempt from the Metropolitan Opera House that featured Enrico Caruso, but interference made reception almost impossible.

Meanwhile, amateur radio had become very popular in the United States, and a number of 'hams,' not satisfied with transmitting Morse code messages to friends, had begun sending out their favorite songs as well. There is some evidence that blues legend W.C. Handy did a live show that was broadcast by an amateur station in Memphis in 1914, but for the most part amateurs could not afford studio equipment for broadcasting live orchestras or vocalists, so phonograph music sufficed. These concerts became quite popular with the limited

audience that could receive them – other amateurs, and ships at sea.

The identity of the first commercial radio station to maintain a regular schedule of broadcasting is unclear. A debate on this issue has continued since 1920, the year in which regular commercial broadcasting began. KDKA in Pittsburgh has consistently maintained that it was the first. However, there is evidence that, in the United States, 8MK in Detroit or 1XE in Medford Hillside was on the air before KDKA. Outside the United States, XWA in Canada, as well as stations in Argentina and elsewhere, may also have a claim to be the first (on this issue, consult http://www.ipass.net/~whitetho/). Until February 1922, it was legal for US amateur radio operators to play music or give talks. During commercial radio's first year, some of the amateurs substituted when a local commercial station had equipment problems or could not broadcast on a given night. Some amateurs were not just hobbyists; they also had technological skills, which they put to work improving commercial radio. Hired by major companies like Westinghouse and General Electric, they developed better receivers and made existing equipment easier to use. A number of the early managers and engineers at the commercial stations came from a ham radio background.

Like ham radio, early commercial stations were usually run by volunteers. Even at stations owned by receiver companies, employees were usually not paid extra for taking their turn on the air. Interviews of 'old-timers' suggest that they were perfectly happy to help out and do this work for free, because they felt that they were on the cutting edge of something new and exciting. While some early stations occasionally played phonograph records (in late August 1920, 8MK – which became pioneer station WWJ in Detroit – tested the new station by sending out a classical music concert of recordings by such stars as Enrico Caruso and Amelita Galli-Curci), live talent was generally preferred because the limitations of the early technology made playing phonograph records a difficult procedure that was not always aesthetically pleasing.

The live talent, usually performers affiliated with local music schools, was also expected to volunteer, and at first many performers did. A typical station in the early 1920s broadcast only for a few hours, usually in the evening when reception was supposed to be better. The concept of a 24-hour-a-day station was far in the future. There was not much consistency at this time: listeners might hear anything from a dance orchestra to a preacher to a classical violinist. During these early years, a few major stars (such as comedians Ed Wynn and Eddie Cantor) were heard on the air, a practise decried by magazines such as *Variety*, which feared that free exposure of performers on the air would cause fewer people to attend live vaudeville or stage performances.

As the broadcasting day expanded, the mid-day time slot was often given over to a daily program for housewives, with discussions about cooking, fashion, child-rearing and other topics of interest to the woman at home. Commercials quickly became a major part of the women's shows, as sponsors sought to influence the buying decisions of the female consumer. Herbert Hoover, head of the Department of Commerce's radio division, had already expressed his disapproval of 'direct advertising' – the old name for commercials – and his hope that radio could remain noncommercial was echoed by many educators. But, long before the decision by NBC (National Broadcasting Company) to let advertising defray the cost of broadcasts, local stations had to face the fact that, without some source of revenue, they would have to go off the air. Advertising soon became a 'necessary evil,' preferable to charging the public fees for owning a radio receiver.

Researchers who wonder what early radio sounded like are restricted by the fact that there are few surviving examples from radio's first decade. Several albums that have claimed to be authentic were in fact re-creations, done years later. Because audiotape had not been invented, and what few methods existed to record a program were seldom put to use, researchers must rely mainly on newspaper and magazine accounts of what was on the air. It was not until the late 1920s, when a Chicago advertising executive named Raymond Soat began producing what were called 'electrical transcriptions' – programs already recorded onto a disc, along with commercials, ready to be played by any station – that an actual record of early radio programming was made. Some of these electrical transcriptions have survived, such as a variety show from 1929–30 called *Brunswick Brevities*, which featured a different star each week: Al Jolson, Belle Baker, Ben Bernie and Red Nichols were a few of the performers. It was sponsored by Brunswick-Balke-Collender, which manufactured both phonograph records and record players. However, few stations used transcriptions until the 1930s.

Before the networks brought consistency to radio, there was no policy about what kind of music to play, so some owners insisted on what they liked best, namely, 'good music' (opera or classical). They believed that popular music, whether of the country and western or the jazz variety, was vulgar and should be avoided. There was considerable debate in radio's formative years in the United States as to whether the airwaves should be used for educating the audience, with an emphasis on talks by academics and music from symphony orchestras, or whether it was best to entertain the listeners by taking requests and playing songs that people heard when they went dancing. In a survey by the magazine *The Wireless Age* (1923, 23), it was found that 34 percent of the music on radio was classical or operatic, and 74 percent of that music was performed live. One early Chicago station programmed only opera, an experiment that ended in failure. Other stations assembled their own symphony orchestra and did weekly concerts. Whenever opera stars like Mary Garden and Louise Homer performed on radio, they were well received, but, to the chagrin of the critics, audiences seemed just as happy to hear popular band leaders like Paul Whiteman and Vincent Lopez. As a result, by the late 1920s much less 'good music' was heard, as the majority of the music was of the popular variety. It seemed that every station had its own band leader.

The Formation of Networks

Meanwhile, as more stations came on the air, there was an increasing demand for quality talent. The tastes of radio listeners were becoming more sophisticated and, as the novelty of broadcasting wore off, few famous performers were willing to volunteer more than once – they now expected to be paid for their services. By the mid-1920s, individual stations were seeking ways to sponsor their most popular performers, but, in the smaller cities, it was increasingly difficult to find quality talent. The public's demand to hear the biggest and best stars was one reason why radio networks were established. The networks planned to be fully supported by advertising dollars, making it possible to have a sufficient budget to hire even the big names.

The first of the major networks was NBC, whose November 1926 debut featured a wide range of talent, from opera stars (soprano Mary Garden and baritone Tita Ruffo) to vaudevillians (Weber and Fields), a beloved humorist (Will Rogers) and several major orchestras (including that of popular band leader Vincent Lopez). Twenty-two stations in the eastern United States and the Midwest (the west coast was not hooked up yet) took part in the historic four-hour broadcast. The cost of the program was $50,000, a huge sum in 1926. But the public did not have to pay for any of it, since NBC sold enough advertising to cover such expenses as talent fees for the performers and the leasing of the telephone wires that connected the network stations (Hilliard and Keith 1997, 47–48).

In September 1927, a second network, CBS (Columbia Broadcasting System), made its debut, followed by several regional networks such as the Yankee Network on the east coast and the Don Lee Network on the west coast. These hookups provided big-name talent to small and medium-size stations which would never have had access to so much star power. But even the largest stations saw the benefit of being part of a network, since, once a station was affiliated, it could rely on the network to fill certain hours and no longer had to worry about finding enough high-caliber local talent.

Early Regulation

Although the US government took no official role in what went on the air, politics played a part in early broadcasting. 8MK's first official broadcast on 31 August 1920 was the Michigan election returns; KDKA's first broadcast on 2 November 1920 was the presidential election returns. But, other than the Department of Commerce (the agency that supervised broadcasting in its formative years) making occasional efforts to keep station owners from boosting their transmitting power or changing frequencies illegally, what went on the air was left up to the stations and the growing number of sponsors. In 1927, the Federal Radio Commission (FRC) was created. Because it had more authority than the Department of Commerce, it did a more effective job of policing the airwaves; among its achievements were giving each station an assigned number of watts and a fixed frequency on the AM dial, and punishing stations that deviated from what they had been allotted. But, while the FRC made broadcasting more orderly, it still had limited power over the content on the airwaves.

The FRC was succeeded in 1934 by the Federal Communications Commission (FCC). While the FCC had to decide on a few high-profile license renewal cases, for the most part its regulatory functions were limited to making certain each station aired a sufficient amount of public-service and educational programming (the required amount would gradually diminish over the years), avoided offensive material (certain words, such as 'laxative,' 'syphilis' and 'lynching,' were banned in the early 1930s) and did not advocate any one political group too strongly. One station (WAAB in Boston) almost lost its license for permitting the owner's favorite candidates to speak, while excluding competitors.

Supplying Music to Radio

With the rise of the networks in the late 1920s, radio was no longer in need of volunteers. New and unfamiliar performers now had a more difficult time getting on the air. Since advertisers were now paying for a large number of the programs, they were very selective about which performers were hired. Once chosen, performers became identified not just with the station, but with the sponsor of their show. Radio advertising remained strong even during the Depression, and network programs had no trouble attracting sponsors.

Audience surveys began in 1930 – with demand coming largely from the advertising agencies, which wanted to place their advertisements on the most popular network shows. Archibald Crossley founded the first ratings company, the Cooperative Analysis of Broadcasting. His research determined that the time when most people listened to the radio was from 7:00 p.m. to 11:00 p.m., and the networks began charging more money to sponsor that time period.

Radio and records might have had a competitive and adversarial relationship in the first decade of broadcasting, but by the late 1930s having a hit song on the radio meant that people would want to buy a copy. While most music on the air was still performed live, the technology to make transcriptions had improved, and more shows were being transcribed. But, even in the 1930s and into the early 1940s, the constant demand for music was met by a disciplined core of musicians, arrangers, conductors and copyists (Maltin 1997). Even most local stations still had their own in-house orchestra for those times when they were not airing network programming. Not all performers came to the studios – sometimes, the studios came to them. Since radio's formative years, a number of stations had begun the practise of 'remote' live broadcasting – broadcasting from churches, synagogues, banquet halls and hotels. The hotels were the perfect location because, when a dance orchestra played, the listeners at home could hear applause and audience reaction, giving the show more excitement. Some hotel orchestras even became identified with a radio station and became known as that station's house band. A few local band leaders, such as Joe Rines and Leo Reisman, became so popular thanks to remote broadcasts that each was hired by one of the national networks.

Lack of payment was not the only reason why many performers had not wanted to be on the air in the early days. Most did not feel comfortable alone in a studio, singing into a microphone with nobody to applaud or encourage them. The story goes that, in early 1922, comedian Ed Wynn insisted on an audience before he would perform, so the station managers rounded up passersby, the cleaning crew and whoever else they could find to sit and watch him do his act. Encouraged by the positive reaction this brought, some stations installed a special room where an audience could observe a show. This so-called 'studio audience' would become very important, as it enabled actual fans to interact with the performers while giving the people at home the hope that, one day, they too would be sitting in that audience enjoying a performance by their favorite stars.

Throughout the 1930s, even more stations went on the air, and the demand for more music remained constant. What also remained constant was the increase in fees for the use of music. The American Society of Composers, Authors and Publishers (ASCAP) had originally been founded to collect fees for songwriters. When radio came along, the organization began charging stations for the right to use the songs, and the fees kept escalating. Radio stations had joined together in 1923 to start an advocacy group, the National Association of Broadcasters (NAB), whose initial aim was to fight ASCAP's fees. But ASCAP continued to charge more, and radio continued to protest, culminating in 1940 with the banning of all ASCAP material from the airwaves (see Ryan 1985). While the dispute lasted, US radio listeners were forced back onto a diet of out-of-copyright or traditional songs, plus, crucially, songs licensed by the radio networks' own newly established licensing agency, Broadcast Music Inc. (BMI), often from regional or ethnically based publishers who had been denied membership in ASCAP. Radio audiences became exposed to a greater variety of musical styles than ever before, particularly country music and black rhythm and blues. As Malone (1985) concludes, 'BMI was instrumental . . . in breaking New York's, or Tin Pan Alley's, monopoly on song writing. The American music industry consequently became more decentralized. Songwriters were encouraged all over the United States, and producers of the so-called grassroots material (country and race music) were given a decided boost' (179). The impact of this copyright dispute on the history of popular music cannot be underestimated. BMI proved a major contributing factor to the rise of rock 'n' roll in the 1950s (Whitcomb 1972; Barnard 1989).

The War Years and After

As more US soldiers were sent overseas to fight, radio went along with them. The American Forces Network (AFN) was created by the War Department, and it took to the air in July 1943. Its intent was to keep the fighting forces in touch with home, letting them hear their favorite music by their favorite stars. Among the performers were Bing Crosby, Eddie Cantor, Jack Benny, Count Basie, Dinah Shore, Burns and Allen, Ethel Waters and Bob Hope, all of whom donated their time. AFN exposed US music and US popular culture to a worldwide audience, many of whom had heard about US radio but had never been able to listen to any of the big-name performers until this time. Meanwhile, in the United States, because so many of the male announcers and performers had gone off to war, a number of women found opportunities that they had not been given previously. Many radio stations used newly trained women engineers, and some stations even had an entirely female announcing staff (Halper 2001).

Radio in the United States changed profoundly following World War II. As the networks invested in television,

so the new medium robbed radio of its key personalities, programs, sponsors and advertisers. This provided owners of radio stations with an excuse, sometimes quite justifiable, to cut costs by getting rid of in-house orchestras and moving toward only phonograph records and announcers, who were by now called 'disc jockeys' (DJs).

There is some debate as to exactly who created the format that became known as 'Top 40' (the 40 favorite hits played over and over), but many media historians credit Todd Storz, then station manager of KOWH in Omaha, Nebraska, with this innovation. As early as 1949, Storz noticed that jukebox users tended to select the same discs again and again. Applying this principle to radio, he developed a format in which the most popular (that is, bestselling) records were given the most plays. Although the Top 40 radio format predated rock 'n' roll, it came into its own once the economic power of teenagers was fully appreciated, as it could deliver a ready market for teen-targeted commodities. Rock 'n' roll also boosted sales of another new invention – the portable transistor radio, which allowed young people to hear their favorite songs wherever they went. Rather than dying out, as proponents of television predicted it would, radio became the medium of the youth of the United States. Stations wanting to remain viable had to abandon the older music that had done so well in the 1940s and change over to the Top 40 format.

The change to the Top 40 format did not sit well with many of the musicians who had played in big bands or in-house radio orchestras and, with the encouragement of ASCAP, a number of whose members had been particularly hurt by the change from Tin Pan Alley music to rock (most rock songwriters worked for competitor BMI), Congress launched hearings in 1959 into whether rock radio stations were guilty of 'payola.' The hearings destroyed the careers of several key DJs, most notably Alan Freed, and while the Congressional hearings and the bad publicity did not kill rock 'n' roll, as ASCAP might have hoped, the end result was that DJs lost the considerable control over music policy that they had had prior to the hearings. Radio station managers took over, tightening their stations' music policies. Playlists became tighter too, ostensibly to prevent abuse, although some critics observed later that payola had just moved from the individual DJs to the program directors.

The principle of 'format' radio, or of 'narrow (as opposed to broad) casting' to specifically targeted audiences, was extended through the advent of FM radio to a plethora of new formats, each with a subtly different musical or audience emphasis (Keith 1987; Halper 1991; Scott 1996).

Public-Service Radio

The United States was one of the few countries in which commercial interests came to dominate radio almost completely. In other territories, a more familiar pattern was the development of a state-run system controlled either directly or indirectly by a ruling elite, but with varying degrees of commercial involvement. Australia, for example, had a two-tier broadcasting system from 1936, comprising the national public-service broadcaster, the Australian Broadcasting Corporation (ABC), and a competing, localized commercial sector. Radio's development in Canada was influenced by bilingualism and the proximity and influence of US radio stations. Like Australia, Canada has had a two-tier system, with the Canadian Broadcasting Corporation (CBC), funded by both license fees and advertising, providing national, regional and local public-service broadcasting. However, the influence of the CBC diminished toward the end of the twentieth century as a result of funding cuts.

The most influential broadcasting system on an international scale, however, was the BBC, which began as a cartel operated by wireless manufacturers with the tacit approval of the Postmaster General. The idea of remodeling the British Broadcasting Company as the British Broadcasting *Corporation*, operating under Royal Charter, was that of Director-General John Reith, who shared with his appointees a broad assumption that programming should follow traditional English middle-class notions of culture, entertainment and betterment (Reith 1949; Briggs 1965; McIntyre 1993). It would also be centralized, with limited regional or local input, and run as a monopoly. Crucially, Reith devised a system of funding – a listener's license fee, collected by the government on the BBC's behalf – that obviated the need for advertising or sponsorship and kept government control at arm's length, yet always implicitly present (Crisell 1997).

The BBC's ethos of public-service broadcasting evolved in a decade in which fears of the disintegration of culture in the face of socialism, mass enfranchisement and creeping Americanization were prevalent (Smith 1976). For Reith and his innumerable policy committees – set up to guide broadcasting policy on everything from music to religion and peopled by representatives of the prevailing cultural elite – 'serving the public' meant providing it with access to excellence and knowledge. It also meant defining what constituted excellence – for example, selecting certain musics for broadcasting over others, and framing content according to its educational or entertainment value (Scannell and Cardiff 1991).

The security of fixed financing allowed the BBC to transform itself quickly from a conveyer of information, education and entertainment into a producer of all three. It used its powerful financial position to form new relationships with copyright bodies such as the Performing Right Society (PRS), representing music publishers and composers, the Musicians' Union and variety agencies. By the mid-1930s, the BBC was the largest single employer of musicians in Britain. In areas such as music and drama, the BBC's various programming departments quickly moved to almost complete self-sufficiency in production; this in turn spawned a growing bureaucracy of organization exemplified by policy *diktats* and prioritization of resources for cultural projects (Briggs 1965).

In the 1930s, stations like Radio Normandie and Radio Luxembourg, broadcasting commercially sponsored entertainment programs to the United Kingdom on the US pattern, introduced a major dilemma for the BBC. How could the BBC justify its funding if large numbers of listeners looked elsewhere for entertainment? Reith's departure in 1937 and the coming of World War II prompted a shift in definition for the BBC. The creation of an entertainment-based Forces Programme alongside the National Programme allowed the BBC to move in both directions, boosting its variety and dance music output while maintaining its cultural commitments. During the war, the BBC became consciously concerned with the need to speak to and for (and indeed unify) the whole community of classes, regions and tastes, and it attracted a huge number of personnel from the entertainment world, commercial radio, journalism and advertising in order to do so (Briggs 1965).

World War II was a watershed for the BBC, as it was for broadcasting systems throughout the world. Immediately following the liberation of France, Radiodiffusion de France was assigned a state monopoly of broadcasting. German radio was reconstructed to mirror the domestic systems of the occupying countries. The Italian state broadcaster, RAI, was created in 1946 with the political independence of broadcasts assured by a parliamentary committee; three national networks were instituted three years later. In 1970, the Canadian government introduced restrictive quotas on overseas content, stipulating the amount of domestically produced music that must be broadcast – an initiative that has remained intact (Wallis and Malm 1984). A similar quota was introduced by the Québec government with regard to French-language music.

Shortly after the war in Europe ended, the BBC divided its radio service three ways, the Forces becoming the Light Programme, the National the Home Service and the Third Programme an exclusively arts- and music-based network aimed unequivocally at a minority highbrow audience (Briggs 1965; Carpenter 1996). It provided a generic model of radio broadcasting that even the coming of pop radio and, from 1973 ònward, land-based commercial radio in the United Kingdom could not shake: the three-way division has remained in place, augmented in 1967 by Radio 1, a national pop service introduced in response to the offshore 'pirate' radio stations of 1964–67, which broadcast their version of US Top 40 radio (Harris 1968; Hind and Mosco 1985; Barnard 1989; Chapman 1992).

The BBC's attitude to popular music has profoundly influenced its form, content and commercial direction. From its beginnings, the BBC has maintained a conservative attitude. During the 1930s, a concentration on lightweight, medium-paced and decorous dance music suitable for domestic listening resulted in the marginalization of what was termed 'hot jazz.' This conservatism was to a degree reinforced by the BBC's reliance on live music, and its early adoption of a 'needle time' policy restricting the number of commercially produced records it could play. This left the Corporation unable to counter properly the popularity of the reemerging Radio Luxembourg. The latter inaugurated UK radio's first sales chart-based show after the war and, when the coming of commercial television lured away advertisers and listeners from 1955 onward, it followed the US pattern by switching to record shows aimed at teenagers.

The BBC's Gramophone Department openly favored British artists over North American, while the growth of skiffle was encouraged as a kind of healthy alternative to rock. Its espousal of skiffle on both radio and television steered British teenagers toward making music of their own or toward the AFN, which was easily picked up in pockets of the United Kingdom. British pop music, emerging in the mid-1960s – a development for which the Beatles and the Rolling Stones acted as catalysts – therefore owed its particular shape to a curious mixture of encouragement and benign neglect on the part of the country's primary cultural institution.

With the advent of Radio 1, the BBC's influence on popular music became much more explicit. Radio 1 differentiated itself to a degree from commercial stations through the role it played in promoting new music. When, during the 1980s and 1990s, the BBC faced political pressure to abandon Radio 1 – the argument being that commercial radio stations were now offering such a service without recourse to public funds – it claimed its right to exist by reference not only to its high daytime listening figures but also to its role in promoting new music (Garfield 1998). While there was an element of rewriting history about this, the artists that John Peel and company uncovered over the years certainly included major forces in global music. Unquestionably, the British record industry benefited to an extraordinary

degree from the willingness of certain BBC broadcasters to act as unofficial talent scouts.

Political and Musical Alternativism

The British and US radio systems were left broadly untouched – institutionally at least – by the political mood that, from the early 1970s onward, prompted major structural changes to radio in France, Italy, Canada and Australia in particular. In these and other territories, an unparalleled growth in illegal broadcasting by cooperative groups and radical political organizations had the effect of opening up radio to new voices and interests (Radical Science Collective 1985; Lewis and Booth 1989; Euromedia Research Group 1997). This, coupled with the commercially motivated liberalization of the airwaves that was a hallmark of right-wing political thinking during the 1980s, gave small-scale community radio a legal basis in many territories and led the way to a major commercial expansion of radio at the ground level. Especially in Europe, domestic radio systems began to exhibit a greater diversity of outlook and output – particularly musically – than ever before. However, the degree to which these developments have made an impact on patterns of music production, distribution and sales is debatable: while specialist or niche music stations flourish and occasionally feed records, artists and even styles into the mainstream, European music radio as a whole has become increasingly homogenized thanks to the emergence of transcontinental (and English-language) operators such as Sky Radio and Music Choice Europe. The latter station is perhaps a sign of things to come: part-owned by the Warner Music Group and Sony, it also runs the satellite station Sky Music Choice in collaboration with BSkyB.

Radio in the Rest of the World

Outside Western Europe and North America, the evolution of radio broadcasting was generally determined by state policies rather than by market forces. In the Soviet Union and other Warsaw Pact nations, the Communist authorities strictly controlled the output of national and regional radio stations. Western pop music was generally not permitted to be broadcast, and music policies favored national folk music and classical music. From 1958, the state broadcaster in the German Democratic Republic was instructed that at least 60 percent of its music airplay must be of East German origin (Maas and Reszel 1998, 268). Since 1989, private stations have proliferated in the former Communist states, many of them programming popular music of both local and foreign origin (Tyler and Laing 1996).

The development of radio in Japan was fundamentally affected by Japan's defeat in World War II. The state-owned NHK was founded in 1926 and became a propaganda arm of the state in the 1930s and 1940s. The occupying US forces authorized the setting up of private radio networks in 1950. FEN, the Far East Network of the US army, provided Japanese youth with access to US jazz, pop and rock until the withdrawal of US troops in the 1970s (Hosokawa et al. 1991, 24).

Throughout much of Africa, the Caribbean and Asia, colonial authorities set up national stations modeled on their own metropolitan state networks. The BBC was the model for such networks as All India Radio (AIR) (Baruah 1983), the Jamaica Broadcasting Corporation (Bradley 2000, 88–92) and the Zimbabwean Broadcasting Corporation (Scannell 2001), all of which enjoyed a broadcasting monopoly. Before Zimbabwean independence, the African Service of the Rhodesia Broadcasting Corporation broadcast mbira music, much of it recorded in rural areas (Turino 2000, 77). In the French colony of Congo, the authorities permitted the formation of privately owned stations such as Congolia, which was the first to broadcast performances by local popular musicians in the late 1930s. In 1943, the Free French regime established the powerful transmitter of Radio Brazzaville, which in the late 1950s enabled the station's music broadcasts to be heard throughout much of East and Central Africa, thus disseminating the Congolese rumba sounds of Franco's OK Jazz orchestra and other bands (Waterman 1990, 93).

In many countries of Latin America, state-owned networks are relatively weak, and powerful media conglomerates such as Globo in Brazil and Televisa in Mexico have a dominant position in both television and radio. Mexico has never had national public stations, although from 1937 all private stations were obliged to broadcast *La Hora Nacional*, a government-produced program that included folk and pop music alongside public information messages (Noriega and Leach 1979, 18). In the Caribbean, authoritarian regimes sometimes awarded radio franchises to their own supporters. In the Dominican Republic, La Voz de Dominica, owned by the brother of the dictator Trujillo, had the country's best musicians under exclusive contract in the mid-1950s (Austerlitz 1997, 71).

Wallis and Malm (1984) and Malm and Wallis (1992) discuss the role of state-controlled radio in either supporting or ignoring local musics in a number of Asian, African and Caribbean countries, including the role of the Sri Lankan state broadcaster in disseminating Tamil pop music to South India in the era of the AIR monopoly. Elsewhere, the shift in government policy in the 1970s led to a revival of regional musics within Afghanistan (Slobin 1993, 21–22), and in the 1960s the South African Broadcasting Corporation introduced separate stations with a strong music content for each tribal group in order to preserve the apartheid system (Hamm 1991). Examples of the use of radio to suppress genres considered unacceptable were the banning of *arabesk* in Turkey (Stokes 2000, 227) and the refusal of Algerian state media to program *rai*, which was first given airplay by privately owned stations broadcasting from Algiers (Channel 3) and Tangier in Morocco (Medi 1) (Schade-Poulsen 1999, 20).

After independence, the new governments of most ex-colonies at first maintained the state radio monopoly, although the influence of the neo-liberal economics of international agencies such as the World Bank and the International Monetary Fund eventually led to the emergence of a private radio sector. India was among the last to authorize commercial stations, issuing the first licenses as late as the 1990s. Many of the new Indian city-based stations had pop music formats, in contrast to the Indian classical and folk repertoire performed by the many staff musicians of AIR.

Copyright Issues

The BBC has a unique place in music broadcasting because it is uniquely funded. One of the reasons why Radio 1 has withstood commercial competition so well is that the BBC has been able to absorb the high costs involved in playing records (Barnard 1989). For networks and stations in Britain and many other territories – but not, significantly, in the United States – the payment of performance fees to record companies and recording artists for broadcasting their material is a legal requirement. Well before the 1956 *Copyright Act*, which was ratified internationally by the Rome Convention of 1961, the BBC accepted the principle of payment for recorded music to copyright owners, as represented by Phonographic Performance Ltd. (PPL), a collection agency owned by the record companies.

The absence of a PPL equivalent in the United States helped radio stations keep their budgets down, particularly during the tough television-dominated years of the early 1950s. That copyright reform was never seriously pursued in the US courts by the record companies was a consequence of the close relationship between the labels and the radio networks. The contracting policies of record companies were influenced by the fame already achieved by singers, musicians and especially dance bands on radio. In the United States, the wireless manufacturers, emerging radio networks and record companies enjoyed what has been described as a symbiotic relationship, with a considerable degree of mutual investment – the Victor label, for example, became an adjunct of RCA. This contrasts with the relationship between music publishers and radio in the United States in the years before World War II, which resulted in the dispute between ASCAP and the radio networks that formed the context for the founding of BMI.

Radio and New Technology

Since the 1920s, developments in technology such as transistorization, FM transmission, compact discs, computerization and, latterly, the digital multiplex have opened up new channels of delivery and revolutionized the production of music programming. Such changes have brought new commercial opportunities and a potential reshaping of the balance of power and influence within existing patterns of control and ownership. Since the 1980s – and particularly since the 1996 US *Telecommunications Act* – the US radio industry has become a fierce commercial battleground, with stations and groups changing ownership virtually overnight, and with giant new conglomerates such as Clear Channel Communications emerging to dominate radio at local, national and, potentially, given the latter's aggressive acquisition policy in Australia, New Zealand and the Czech Republic, international levels. However, radio has become not so much a single, clearly delineated industry as one part of a larger multimedia industry in which the music industry is itself a player (Hendy 2000). Technological convergence is accelerating that expansion while also raising a whole raft of financial, legal and copyright issues relating to ownership of the delivered content.

Digital radio – or the broadcasting of digitized signals – is a transmission system promising better sound quality and a more efficient management of the broadcasting spectrum. It was first developed in the 1970s by BBC research engineers, whose system, called digital audio broadcasting (DAB), has since been adopted by Canada, Mexico, South Africa and Australia. The system favored by US interests is in-band on-channel (IBOC).

Digitalized transmission expands the available capacity and so eliminates the problem of scarcity of spectrum that limited radio's growth in its early years and defined its regulatory pattern. Digital broadcasting can also allow text or graphics to be transmitted simultaneously, thus providing additional advertising opportunities. At present, digital radio's growth is inhibited by the high costs involved in launching digital services and by lukewarm consumer interest. Perhaps the most intriguing issue of all, assuming that digital radio becomes accepted, is what will then happen to the old analog spectrum. Especially in the United States and Canada, there remains a hard core of radio operators dedicated to community radio principles, to which low-power, small-scale analog radio is particularly suited. The abandonment of the analog spectrum by radio's major players may open the way – government policies permitting – for these 'microradio' operators to develop it as a genuine, localized alternative to corporately run radio (Barnard 2000).

Potentially even more revolutionary than DAB is Internet radio. Currently, the Internet enables the output of even the smallest, most local station to achieve literally worldwide reach, and without prohibitively high start-up costs or investment in state-of-the-art equipment or transmitters. It breaks down territorial boundaries and disrupts regulatory controls, while also carrying the potential to infringe music copyrights and encourage music piracy. Internet 'stations' do not even need to broadcast by conventional means at all: pirate radio operators have found that they can broadcast freely, without fear of prosecution; in restrictive political regimes, radio stations that are forced off the air can reinvent themselves as Internet stations without having to identify their geographical base. For its advocates, radio on the Web has a democratizing effect on the business of broadcasting, representing a return to the pioneer spirit of unregulated, experimental 1920s radio.

Bibliography

Austerlitz, Paul. 1997. *Merengue: Dominican Music and Dominican Identity*. Philadelphia: Temple University Press.

Barlow, William. 1999. *Voice Over: The Making of Black Radio*. Philadelphia: Temple University Press.

Barnard, Stephen. 1989. *On the Radio: Music Radio in Britain*. Milton Keynes: Open University Press.

Barnard, Stephen. 2000. *Studying Radio*. London: Arnold.

Barnouw, Erik. 1966. *A Tower in Babel: A History of Broadcasting in the United States. Vol. I – to 1933*. New York: Oxford University Press.

Baron, Mike. 1975. *Independent Radio: The Story of Independent Radio in the United Kingdom*. Lavenham: Dalton.

Baruah, U.L. 1983. *This Is All India Radio: A Handbook of Radio Broadcasting in India*. New Delhi: Publications Division, Ministry of Information and Broadcasting.

Bradley, Lloyd. 2000. *Bass Culture: When Reggae Was King*. London: Viking.

Briggs, Asa. 1965. *The History of Broadcasting in the United Kingdom. Vol. II: The Golden Age of Wireless*. London and New York: Oxford University Press.

Carpenter, Humphrey. 1996. *The Envy of the World: Fifty Years of the BBC Third Programme and Radio 3, 1946–1996*. London: Weidenfeld and Nicolson.

Chapman, Robert. 1992. *Selling the Sixties: The Pirates and Pop Music Radio*. London: Routledge.

Crisell, Andrew. 1994. *Understanding Radio*. 2nd ed. London: Routledge.

Crisell, Andrew. 1997. *An Introductory History of British Broadcasting*. London: Routledge.

Denisoff, R. Serge. 1975. *Solid Gold: The Popular Record Industry*. New Brunswick, NJ: Transaction.

Dunning, John. 1998. *On the Air: The Encyclopedia of Old-Time Radio*. New York: Oxford University Press.

Eberly, Philip K. 1982. *Music in the Air: America's Changing Tastes in Popular Music, 1920–1980*. New York: Hastings House.

Engelman, Ralph. 1996. *Public Radio and Television in America: A Political History*. Thousand Oaks, CA: Sage.

Euromedia Research Group. 1997. *The Media in Western Europe: The Euromedia Handbook*. London: Sage.

Fong-Torres, Ben. 1998. *The Hits Just Keep On Coming: The History of Top 40 Radio*. San Francisco: Miller Freeman Books.

Garfield, Simon. 1998. *The Nation's Favourite: The True Adventures of Radio 1*. London: Faber.

Gibian, Peter, ed. 1997. *Mass Culture and Everyday Life*. London: Routledge.

Hale, Julian. 1975. *Radio Power: Propaganda and International Broadcasting*. London: Paul Elek.

Halper, Donna L. 1991. *Radio Music Directing*. Boston, MA: Focal Press.

Halper, Donna L. 2001. *Invisible Stars: A Social History of Women in American Broadcasting*. Armonk, NY: M.E. Sharpe.

Hamm, Charles. 1991. 'The Constant Companion of Man: Separate Development, Radio Bantu and Music.' *Popular Music* 10(2): 147–73.

Harris, Paul A. 1968. *When Pirates Ruled the Waves*. London: Impulse.

Hendy, David. 2000. *Radio in the Global Age*. Malden, MA: Blackwell.

Hilliard, Robert L., and Keith, Michael C. 1997. *The Broadcast Century: A Biography of American Broadcasting*. 2nd ed. Boston, MA: Focal Press.

Hilmes, Michele. 1997. *Radio Voices: American Broadcasting, 1922–1952*. Minneapolis, MN: University of Minnesota Press.

Hind, John, and Mosco, Stephen. 1985. *Rebel Radio: The Full Story of British Pirate Radio*. London: Pluto Press.

Hosokawa, Shuhei, et al. 1991. *A Guide to Popular Music in Japan*. Kanazawa: IASPM Japan.

Keith, Michael C. 1987. *Radio Programming: Consultancy and Formatics*. Boston, MA: Focal Press.

Keith, Michael C. 1997. *Voices in the Purple Haze: Underground Radio and the Sixties*. Westport, CT: Praeger.

Ladd, Jim. 1991. *Radio Waves: Life and Revolution on the FM Dial*. New York: St. Martin's Press.

Lewis, Peter M., and Booth, Jerry. 1989. *The Invisible Medium: Public, Commercial and Community Radio*. London: Macmillan.

Maas, Georg, and Reszel, Hartmut. 1998. 'Whatever Happened to . . .: The Decline and Renaissance of Rock in the Former GDR.' *Popular Music* 17(3): 267–77.

MacDonald, J. Fred. 1979. *Don't Touch That Dial!: Radio Programming in American Life, 1920–1960*. Chicago: Nelson–Hall.

Malm, Krister, and Wallis, Roger. 1992. *Media Policy and Music Activity*. London: Routledge.

Malone, Bill C. 1985. *Country Music, U.S.A.* Rev. ed. Austin, TX: University of Texas Press.

Maltin, Leonard. 1997. *The Great American Broadcast: A Celebration of Radio's Golden Age*. New York: Dutton.

McIntyre, Ian. 1993. *The Expense of Glory: A Life of John Reith*. London: Harper Collins.

Noriega, Luis Antonio de, and Leach, Frances. 1979. *Broadcasting in Mexico*. London: Routledge and International Institute of Communications.

Radical Science Collective. 1985. *Making Waves: The Politics of Communication*. London: Free Association Books.

Reith, J.C.W. 1949. *Into the Wind*. London: Hodder and Stoughton.

Ryan, John. 1985. *The Production of Culture in the Music Industry: The ASCAP–BMI Controversy*. Lanham, MD: University Press of America.

Sakolsky, Ron, and Dunifer, Stephen, eds. 1998. *Seizing the Airwaves: A Free Radio Handbook*. San Francisco: AK Press.

Scannell, Paddy. 1996. *Radio, Television and Modern Life: A Phenomenological Approach*. Oxford: Blackwell.

Scannell, Paddy. 2001. 'Music, Radio and the Record Business in Zimbabwe Today.' *Popular Music* 20(1): 13–26.

Scannell, Paddy, and Cardiff, David. 1991. *A Social History of British Broadcasting. Vol. 1: 1922–1939 – Serving the Nation*. Oxford: Blackwell.

Schade-Poulsen, Marc. 1999. *Men and Popular Music in Algeria: The Social Significance of Raï*. Austin, TX: University of Texas Press.

Scott, Gini Graham. 1996. *Can We Talk?: The Power and Influence of Talk Shows*. New York: Insight.

Shingler, Martin, and Wieringa, Cindy. 1998. *On Air: Methods and Meanings of Radio*. London: Arnold.

Slobin, Mark. 1993. *Subcultural Sounds: Micromusics of the West*. Hanover, NH: University Press of New England.

Smith, Anthony. 1976. *The Shadow in the Cave: A Study of the Relationship Between the Broadcaster, His Audience and the State*. London: Quartet.

Smulyan, Susan. 1994. *Selling Radio: The Commercialization of American Broadcasting, 1920–1934*. Washington, DC: Smithsonian Institution Press.

Stokes, Martin. 2000. 'East, West and Arabesk.' In *Western Music and Its Others: Difference, Representation, and Appropriation in Music*, ed. Georgina Born and David

Hesmondhalgh. Berkeley, CA: University of California Press, 213–33.

Strauss, Neil, ed. 1993. *Radiotext(e)*. New York: Semiotext(e).

Turino, Thomas. 2000. *Nationalists, Cosmopolitans, and Popular Music in Zimbabwe*. Chicago: University of Chicago Press.

Tyler, Bob, and Laing, Dave. 1996. *The European Radio Industry*. 2nd ed. London: Financial Times Management Reports.

Waller, Judith C. 1946. *Radio, the Fifth Estate*. Boston, MA: Houghton Mifflin.

Wallis, Roger, and Malm, Krister. 1984. *Big Sounds from Small Peoples: The Music Industry in Small Countries*. London: Constable.

Waterman, Christopher A. 1990. *Jújù: A Social History and Ethnography of an African Popular Music*. Chicago: University of Chicago Press.

Whitcomb, Ian. 1972. *After the Ball: Pop Music from Rag to Rock*. London: Allen Lane.

STEPHEN BARNARD, DONNA HALPER and DAVE LAING

Radio Format

Introduction

A radio format is a way of organizing the total output of a radio station according to market segmentation of listeners, and targeting a differentiated audience with one particular type of programming all day, day in and day out.

The word 'format' in this context has three different usages: (a) to give a label within the broadcasting industry to the different types of programming content utilized, with Country, Urban, Adult Contemporary and News/Talk all being examples of names of formats; (b) to describe this general approach to organizing radio content and targeting differentiated audiences, via the term 'format radio'; and (c) to describe colloquially the fixed sequence of all programming elements – categories of records, advertisements, jingles, news, travel, competitions – in each hour of any particular format (although this is more precisely called the 'Format Clock').

For music broadcasting, format radio relies heavily on programming elements such as the playlist, charts, airplay and the input of the disc jockey (DJ). But its constituent techniques are inseparable from its market purpose, as demonstrated by its beginnings, in the evolution in the United States of Top 40, the original format.

The Development of Format Radio

On the one hand, 1949–56 were difficult years for US radio: television boomed, the new television networks raided radio for talent, ratings plummeted, critics predicted the death of radio, and hundreds of stations disaffiliated from the national networks. But, on the other hand, thanks largely to the anti-chain broadcasting policies of the Federal Communications Commission (FCC), local, independent AM stations flourished. By 1948, small independent stations were already the most numerous type of station, and between 1946 and 1954 the number of AM stations tripled from 948 to 2,824. These new broadcasters needed programming that would compete economically with that of all the other new stations to win large local audiences, because national advertising had deserted radio for television. Between 1946 and 1958, the local advertising revenue raised by stations quadrupled. The programming device they used to achieve this was what came to be called Top 40 (Keith 1987; Douglas 1999).

There is much disagreement among radio historians about who devised Top 40, as well as about how, where and when it was devised. The central, possibly apocryphal incident involved Todd Storz and Bill Stewart, owner and programmer, respectively, of station KOWH in Omaha, Nebraska, observing one night in a local bar how people not only seemed content to select all their music for the evening from the standard 40 records on the jukebox, but would actually select some of these records many more times than most of the others. Even at the end of the evening, the waitress allegedly put in her own money to hear these most-played songs again.

This incident occurred in 1951, 1953, 1955 or even 1957, depending on the source, but one of the earlier two dates is more likely since, by June 1954, Stewart was working for the other main innovator of Top 40 radio, Gordon McLendon, at KLIF, his station in Dallas. One of McLendon's DJs, Chuck Blore, claimed that McLendon invented the name 'Top 40' as a result of the fact that each DJ was allowed to play only 40 records in his/her four-hour shift. Another event that was claimed to have been responsible for the name was Todd Storz's launching of a show called *Top 40 at 1450* (the station's AM frequency) on his New Orleans station WTIX in 1953, to upstage rival WDSU's *Top 20 at 1280*.

The innovation resulting from the key realization attributed to the Omaha bar incident – that some records on the playlist could be played more times than others – was, in truth, the last in a series of programming innovations that came together to form Top 40. These could be traced back to Al Jarvis's *The World's Largest Make-Believe Ballroom* show, launched on KFWB Los Angeles in 1932, and Martin Block's copying of the idea on New York's WNEW three years later. Each played records as if the live bands were present, and thus they could claim to be the first DJs. The first broadcast on the NBC network of

Your Hit Parade, with live performances of the week's most popular songs, occurred in 1935, and this was followed by the similar *Lucky Lager Dance Time* on Los Angeles's KFAC in 1941. These were the world's first music radio chart shows.

In 1947, McLendon introduced the first sung station-identification jingles on KLIF. In 1949, Storz dropped all KOWH's network and transcription shows, playing popular music records all day, and gradually extending over the next two years the amount of time allotted to the chart-based, playlist shows over the specialist music slots. This introduced the concept of the limited playlist of hit records to fill the entire day. Both KOWH and KLIF were operating such lists by 1953, and soon after changed their schedules from a list of program titles to a list of DJ names. Finally came the jukebox idea – different numbers of plays for various sections of the playlist. Such was the immediate ratings success of these two pioneering stations that, within three or four years, hundreds of small stations across the United States had switched to a Top 40 format (Fong-Torres 1998; Garay 1992; MacFarland 1993; Douglas 1999).

The format techniques of Top 40 were soon applied to different musical styles, in order to differentiate stations and target specific audiences. Some of the earliest to appear, in the late 1950s, were Beautiful Music (lush popular orchestral, vocal and Latin versions of popular tunes), Country, R&B and, on FM, Classical Music. In the 1970s, FM free-form stations were increasingly formatted into Album-Oriented Rock (AOR). Then came Disco formats, Adult Contemporary (hits of recent years), Urban Contemporary (black music) and Contemporary Hit Radio (CHR), the renamed FM reinvention of Top 40 in the 1980s (see Barnes 1988; Keith 1987). In the 1990s, first Adult Contemporary, then Country overtook CHR as the most widely used format in the United States. Examples of newer formats have included Americana (contemporary country-rock, folk-rock, blues and roots), Smooth Jazz (replacing New Age, but still mellow mid-tempo, jazzy-feel instrumental music) and Active (heavy, hard or metal rock designed to be played loud).

The Spread of Format Radio Outside the United States

Outside the United States, format radio's advance depended on the broadcast regulatory context. Local commercial radio did not begin in many Western European countries until the 1970s or 1980s, and was often constrained by public-service requirements. For example, the first commercial stations licensed in the United Kingdom in 1973–74, while adopting a Top 40 format during peak hours, were obliged not only to combine it with more local information during the day than a North American music station might choose, but also

to offer different specialist, sports, community and talk programming in the evening and at weekends. However, a wave of 'deregulation' of broadcasting across Western Europe from the late 1980s to the early 1990s, driven by right-wing and center-right governments, led to a vast expansion of local and national commercial radio free of public-service obligations. These stations are almost all formatted (Wallis and Malm 1993).

But in many countries – including Canada, Sweden and the United Kingdom – regulators, in the interest of widening listener choice, retain some limited say over commercial stations' chosen format. Unlike the United States, where stations can change their format overnight – from All-Talk to Latin, from Adult Contemporary to Country – stations in these other countries have to notify the regulatory authorities of proposed format changes and have them approved (see, for example, Grenier 1990).

The Consequences of Formatting

To the established North American record industry, format radio's role appears largely beneficial, allowing the targeting of artists and releases to stations that are likely to attract listeners who might be interested in buying these recordings. For radio, too, formats enable stations to provide advertisers with detailed research of how their particular format is doing – for example, 'number 1 with 34- to 45-year-old above-average-income homemakers' – even if, overall, they come sixth in the Arbitron ratings. Formatting and market segmentation, introduced to save radio, have become indispensable in the United States, where 10,000 commercial stations compete for a tiny portion (about 7 percent) of the country's $110 billion advertising expenditure (Barnes 1988).

But there the benefits end. The basic problem for music is that format radio is based on what Paul M. Hirsch memorably defined as 'pre-selection': anticipating and making choices for the public (Rothenbuhler and McCourt 1992). This happens at every stage – what discs go on this week's playlist, what format, even which artists a record company chooses to sign and release. How is a record company to get airplay for a new artist whose music does not fit into any format? Format programmers and consultants will claim that they simply play the most popular songs that people want to hear. But most CHR stations in the United States, for example, base their weekly playlist on *Billboard*'s Hot 100, which is calculated largely on what these stations are already playing. In Europe, format radio is seen as contributing to the 'fragmenting' of audiences, which are then segmented; the formats are streamlined to compete for the largest market, leading to formats that are eventually mere musical shades of grey (Wallis and Malm 1993).

Yet, there remains something attractive about the simple commercial populism of Top 40. The founder himself, Todd Storz, summed it up in 1957:

The listener wants to hear his favorite numbers again and again; the programming of music is controlled entirely by the choice of the public – if the public suddenly showed a preference for Chinese music, we would play it; the growing universality of musical taste appears to make possible the application of a single programming standard to many individual markets; the disc jockey is not representative of the public – his own preferences are a dangerous guide. (Barnes 1988, 9–10)

Listeners can still tune in to their favorite station and know that, within an hour or two, their favorite record will be coming on. The station will not, however, necessarily be the favorite station of a neighbor or best friend. Storz was wrong only in assuming that the 'universality of musical taste' of the Top 40 in the 1950s was a permanent condition. At the beginning of the twenty-first century, format radio is perhaps only one manifestation of wider social and economic fragmentation, and it can hardly be blamed for that.

Bibliography

Barnes, Ken. 1988. 'Top 40 Radio: A Fragment of the Imagination.' In *Facing the Music*, ed. Simon Frith. New York: Pantheon Books, 8–50.

Berland, Jody. 1993. 'Radio Space and Industrial Time: The Case of Music Formats.' In *Rock and Popular Music: Politics, Policies, Institutions*, ed. Tony Bennett et al. London: Routledge, 104–18.

Denisoff, R. Serge. 1986. *Tarnished Gold: The Record Industry Revisited*. New Brunswick, NJ: Transaction Books.

Douglas, Susan J. 1999. *Listening In: Radio and the American Imagination*. New York: Times Books/Random House.

Fong-Torres, Ben. 1998. *The Hits Just Keep On Coming: The History of Top 40 Radio*. San Francisco: Miller Freeman Books.

Garay, Ronald. 1992. *Gordon McLendon: The Maverick of Radio*. Westport, CT: Greenwood Press.

Grenier, Line. 1990. 'Radio Broadcasting in Canada: The Case of Transformat Music.' *Popular Music* 9(2) (April): 221–33.

Keith, Michael C. 1987. *Radio Programming: Consultancy and Formatics*. Boston, MA: Focal Press.

MacFarland, David T. 1993. *The Development of the Top 40 Radio Format*. North Stratford, NH: Ayer. (First published New York: Arno Press, 1979.)

Rothenbuhler, Eric W., and McCourt, Tom. 1992. 'Commercial Radio and Popular Music: Processes of Selection and Factors of Influence.' In *Popular Music and Communication*, ed. James Lull. 2nd ed. Newbury Park, CA: Sage, 101–15.

Wallis, Roger, and Malm, Krister. 1993. 'From State Monopoly to Commercial Oligopoly: European Broadcasting Policies and Popular Music Output Over the Airwaves.' In *Rock and Popular Music: Politics, Policies, Institutions*, ed. Tony Bennett et al. London: Routledge, 156–68.

KEN GARNER

Radio France International

Financed by the French state, Radio France International (RFI) is a descendant of the *Poste Colonial* ('Colonial Station'), whose first broadcast was transmitted on shortwave from the studio installed for the *Exposition Coloniale Internationale* ('International Colonial Exhibition') held in Paris in 1931.

Radio France International itself was inaugurated on 6 January 1975. Its mandate is to broadcast daily programs to French-speaking countries. Initially under the direction of Radio France, it became an independent station in 1987. Its partnership with more than 700 radio stations from 143 countries puts it on a par with the three other major international stations – the BBC, Deutsche Welle and Voice of America.

RFI has three stations (or channels): RFI 1, French-language broadcasting; RFI 2, foreign-language broadcasting (18 languages: English, German, Serbian and Croatian, Russian, Romanian, Spanish, Brazilian, Portuguese, Arabic, Persian, Vietnamese, Mandarin, Cambodian, Laotian, Polish, Bulgarian, Creole and Turkish); and RFI 3, music programming transmitted by satellite.

Since 1996, RFI 3 has offered continuous music programming that is divided equally between French music and musics of the world. The record library of RFI maintains a collection of new releases made possible through the cooperation of its partners throughout the world.

Through its Web site (http://www.rfi.fr), RFI has developed a new type of relationship with listeners from all over the world. The sections on its Web site entitled 'Cyber Play-lists' and 'Entrez vos artistes' are testimony to a wealth of cultural exchange.

Bibliography

Brochand, Christian. 1994. *Histoire générale de la radio et de la télévision en France* [A General History of Radio and Television in France]. Vol. 1: 1924–44; Vol. 2: 1944–74. Paris: La Documentation Française.

Brunnquell, Frédéric. 1991. *Fréquence monde: du poste colonial à RFI* [World Frequency: From the Colonial Station to RFI]. Paris: Hachette.

Prot, Robert. 1997. *Dictionnaire de la radio* [Dictionary of the Radio]. Grenoble: Presses Universitaires de Grenoble et INA.

ISABELLE CANNO

Radio Free Europe/Radio Liberty

Radio Free Europe/Radio Liberty (RFE/RL) describes itself as 'a private, international radio service to Central Europe and the former Soviet Union, funded by the U.S. Congress.' In October 1998, the service also began offering programming to Iran and Iraq. RFE/RL broadcasts in 25 languages, offering daily programs of news, as well as analysis and discussion of current events in the regions it serves. In its mission statement, RFE/RL explains that its intent is 'to promote democratic values and institutions by disseminating factual information and ideas.'

Originally, the two services operated separately, although both owe their existence to the Cold War. RFE was the first on the air, on 4 July 1950; its initial broadcasts were to Czechoslovakia, but the service was expanded soon after to include Romania, Poland, Hungary and Bulgaria. The idea behind RFE was to offer an alternative point of view to those Communist countries in the then-Soviet bloc that did not have a free press. While this was a noble goal, controversy arose a few years later when it was revealed that RFE was receiving much of its support from the US Central Intelligence Agency (CIA).

In 1952, RFE moved its broadcast operations from its first European site (an old air base north of Mannheim, Germany) into a newly built broadcast center in Munich. Meanwhile, Radio Liberty (originally known as Radio Liberation) went on the air on 1 March 1953, broadcasting to Russia in the Russian language. As with RFE, it was not long before RL was offering its service in other languages spoken in the region, including Ukrainian, Georgian and Azeri.

In the United States during the Cold War years, RFE was seen as a positive force in fighting Communism; but the governments of the Soviet countries did not always look upon RFE and RL so favorably. The broadcasts were periodically jammed in Russia, while in Hungary RFE was accused of helping to incite the 1956 revolution. One reason for these governments' suspicion of RFE's and RL's broadcasts – the identity of the first broadcasters – is understandable in light of who those broadcasters were. Few of the fledgling RFE and RL announcers were professional journalists – they were often political refugees who had escaped from Soviet bloc countries. It is safe to assume that, as a result, the on-air personnel had few good things to say about the Communist countries they had left, even though the official policy of both RFE and RL was to provide objective news and information. Both RFE and RL became known for providing local news and discussion that frequently contradicted the Communist version of events. The stations did not concentrate on news and talk shows purely by choice, however. In the 1950s, there were signal problems, and constant jamming by Communist countries made music impractical except for certain rare occasions.

As long as there was a Soviet Union, RFE and RL could count on the support of US citizens, who donated money to help keep both services operating. Even after the revelation in 1967 that the CIA was the force behind both RFE and RL, Congress still believed that the two operations served a useful purpose, and it was decided that government funding would continue. By the early 1970s, the two services had been reorganized, with a board of directors (the Board for International Broadcasting (BIB)) overseeing them, and in 1976 RFE and RL were combined. However, when the Soviet Union broke up and the Cold War ended, questions arose in Congress about the future of RFE/RL, and whether it was still necessary to maintain such a service. As a result of this reevaluation process, there were some budget cuts and certain programs were discontinued. At various times since then, politicians have discussed eliminating RFE/RL, or combining it with another service, Voice of America, but such efforts have been rebuffed.

While the role of RFE/RL has been that of teaching journalists in newly democratic countries how to investigate and report the news, and providing objective information to nations in crisis, a changing world has meant changes for the service. For one thing, it ceased operating exclusively on shortwave. At the end of the twentieth century, many affiliates of RFE/RL were broadcasting on AM and FM, as well as using the Internet. And while RFE/RL has in these ways provided over 700 hours a week of programming, the majority of which is news, information and discussion, some affiliates have over the years expanded their programming to include music.

During the early 1950s, Czech composer and classical musician Vaclav Nelhybel supervised the occasional playing of music. Then, during the 1950s, Louis Armstrong was a guest on RL, even performing a song. However, jamming began again, making any music that was broadcast unlistenable. Finally, in the early 1960s, a new transmitter produced a much stronger signal that was more difficult to jam. Inspired by the success of Voice of America's jazz program, *Music-USA*, RL started its own jazz show in January 1963. Guest performers included members of Benny Goodman's band, as well as Zoot Sims and Phil Woods. *This is Jazz* soon became very successful, despite the annoyance of the Soviet government, which labeled jazz decadent and vulgar (Sosin 1999).

Rock music soon became part of a concerted effort to reach the youth of Communist countries. One of RFE's most popular shows in the early 1960s was *Altogether*, and it brought the latest rock hits to Bulgaria, Poland and Romania. Another highly successful show was *Rendez-Vous at 6:10*, hosted by Polish announcer Jan Tyszkiewicz, who not only played the hits for the Polish audience, but also interviewed some of rock's biggest stars, including the Rolling Stones. Shows like these received so much fan mail that they forced government-run stations behind the Iron Curtain to start playing rock music lest they lose their young audience entirely. One audience survey carried out in 1964 showed that, in Czechoslovakia, over 90 percent of young adults listened to RFE and other foreign stations. The reason given was that of hearing the latest dance music (Ryback 1990).

At the end of the twentieth century, listeners could still hear jazz shows on RFE/RL, as well as programs of US dance music. Polish rap singer Liroy (Piotr Marzec) recalled first hearing rap on an RFE station when he was growing up. And singer-songwriters, especially those whose music is political, have been guests on RFE/RL discussion shows.

The center of operations moved in early 1995 to Prague, Czechoslovakia, where a staff of about 400 people continued to produce all the broadcasts of RFE/RL, as well as the services to Iran and Iraq.

Bibliography

Ryback, Timothy. 1990. *Rock Around the Bloc: A History of Rock Music in Eastern Europe and the Soviet Union.* New York: Oxford University Press.

Sosin, Gene. 1999. *Sparks of Liberty: An Insider's Memoir of Radio Liberty.* University Park, PA: Pennsylvania University Press.

Starr, S. Frederick. 1983. *Red and Hot: The Fate of Jazz in the Soviet Union, 1917–1980.* New York: Oxford University Press.

DONNA HALPER

Radio Luxembourg

For over 50 years, Radio Luxembourg was Europe's most famous commercial radio station and, in its day, had an enormous influence on continental European tastes in popular music. Launched in 1933, it broadcast Anglo-American music and entertainment, with announcements mainly in English, during evenings and weekends, for Britain and Western Europe. Initially transmitting on long-wave frequencies, from 1951 it broadcast on 208 meters/1,440 kHz medium wave. For many years it also broadcast to the United States via shortwave.

Founded in 1930 by a group of 'Luxembourgeois,' Belgian and French wireless enthusiasts and entrepreneurs, the *Compagnie Luxembourgeoise de Radiodiffusion* (CLR) posed an instant threat to established state broadcasters in Western Europe, because of its franchise agreement with the Luxembourg government. This agreement permitted CLR to use a frequency that was allocated internationally to the country and, controversially, allowed the operator to use massive power and to broadcast in foreign languages, such as English.

By the mid-1930s, Radio Luxembourg had 4 million listeners in Britain, thanks to its entertaining Sunday schedule, competing only with the BBC's church services and talks. Most programs, like *The Horlicks Hour*, *Palmolive Concert* and *The Ovaltineys*, were sponsored by major brands and presented by musical stars like Gracie Fields and George Formby. Each half-hour show was prerecorded in London on eight 16" (40 cm) transcription discs or on film reels, and then shipped to Luxembourg for broadcast. Some sponsored shows consisted simply of the prerecorded live music, or records, with the announcer in Luxembourg linking the items.

During the 1939–45 war, Radio Luxembourg's transmitter was used to relay Nazi propaganda to Britain. In the late 1940s, the resumed service launched Europe's first chart show, *Top Twenty*, based on sheet music sales. The mix of prerecorded quiz shows, comedy and music continued successfully for a time, but in the early 1960s the station decided to concentrate on the youth pop music market. This led to the station's second period of enormous influence on pop taste, as it played pop hits almost all evening, every evening, while the BBC's light program offered only two pop radio shows a week: *Pick of the Pops*, Sunday's Top 40 chart show with Alan Freeman, and *Saturday Club*, which featured live sessions by performers currently at the top of the charts.

However, even in this successful period, Radio Luxembourg's programs were still sponsored, by record companies like EMI. In response to the North Sea pirate stations (1964–67) and the launch of BBC Radio 1 (1967), from 1968 Radio Luxembourg abandoned sponsored star shows, hiring DJs like Tony Prince, Stuart Henry and Kid Jensen to spin pop records and run spot advertising breaks.

But as local commercial music radio expanded in Britain in the 1980s, the number of listeners dwindled to half a million. The owner of the station, by now renamed CLT (*Compagnie Luxembourgeoise de Telediffusion*), closed down Radio Luxembourg at the end of 1991 in order to concentrate on its major continental radio, television and satellite broadcasting interests. Subsequently, CLT merged with the German film and television production company UFA (Universum Film AG) to form CLT-UFA, one of Europe's biggest commercial broadcasting corporations.

Bibliography

Nichols, Richard. 1983. *Radio Luxembourg: The Station of the Stars*. London: W.H. Allen & Co.

KEN GARNER

Radio Shows

Radio shows are scheduled programs that are generally broadcast regularly at the same time daily or weekly. Shows centered around music, mainly associated initially with specific performers (vocalists, bands or orchestras) and later with individual announcers or disc jockeys (DJs), have played an important role in disseminating popular music of all types.

The earliest radio stations in the United States did not have regular schedules, as they relied on volunteers from local communities to present talks or musical performances on an ad hoc basis. The creation of NBC and CBS, the first national radio networks, in 1926–27 allowed more stations to have regularly scheduled radio shows. Among these were news bulletins, soap operas and drama serials, women's hours, sports commentaries, variety shows and music programs of various kinds. Small-town stations that had previously lacked access to the big names could affiliate with a network and broadcast shows that featured stars like Jessica Dragonette, Duke Ellington and Rudy Vallee. Radio, by this time, was using direct advertising to pay for the network broadcasts. In contrast to the US position, early radio broadcasting in most European countries was conducted as a state monopoly. Nevertheless, the national and regional stations in Europe presented a similar mix of shows to those found in the United States.

There have been various types of radio music shows. These include shows based on live performances by individual singers or bands; live performance shows featuring a variety of musicians; light entertainment variety shows; talent shows; chart shows; listener-request shows; documentaries; shows devoted to particular music genres; and programs of recorded music hosted by DJs or 'air personalities.' The final type has become the most widespread category of music shows on radio.

Live Performances by Individual Singers or Bands

During the mid- to late 1920s, a number of US radio stations moved their studios to hotels, where they could easily assemble a live audience and hire the hotel's 'house band' to broadcast nightly from the hotel ballroom. Local hotel band leaders such as Joe Rines, Jacques Renard and Leo Reisman became so popular that they went on to perform on the national networks.

The national networks were also able to contract nationally recognized band leaders and singers for regular shows. Duke Ellington had been heard locally since 1923 in New York, but his appearances on the networks enhanced his popularity; Benny Goodman had his own show, as did Guy Lombardo, Paul Whiteman and Tommy Dorsey. A popular band that was considered a novelty was Phil Spitalny's All-Girl Orchestra, with its *Hour of Charm* on CBS.

Sponsors purchased entire programs on both national networks and the smallest local stations. Performers who became identified with their sponsor included the A&P Gypsies (sponsored by a chain of grocery stores), the Cliquot Club Eskimos (sponsored by a soft-drink manufacturer) and the Ipana Troubadors (sponsored by a toothpaste company). Local stations in the US South typically programmed live performances by local blues, country or Cajun singers in 15-minute slots sponsored by local businesses. Thus, Bob Wills named his Light Crust Doughboys after the sponsor's product and, from 1948, B.B. King broadcast on WDIA Memphis each day with sponsorship by the makers of Peptikon, a patent medicine (Cantor 1992, 77).

Some sponsors also got the entertainers they hired to sing specialized commercials, or 'jingles,' during the show. The duo of Billy Jones and Ernie Hare was especially adept at singing about their sponsors; they were known first as the 'Happiness Boys' (sponsored by a candy company) and later as the 'Interwoven Pair' (sponsored by a sock manufacturer).

State-owned radio stations in Europe frequently employed their own orchestras and bands. The BBC had its own dance band from 1925, led by Jack Payne and later by Henry Hall, whose *Guest Night* weekly show was broadcast from 1934 until the mid-1950s.

In the Communist era, state-owned monopoly stations were used to promote approved forms of national classical and folk music. In the 1970s, the only station in Tashkent in the USSR transmitted early-morning and late-night programs by the *maqām* or Uzbek national folk ensemble every day (Levin 1996, 51).

But perhaps the most influential and longstanding show of this type was broadcast monthly by Radio Egypt between 1937 and 1973: a concert given by the famous singer Umm Kulthūm, which became an institution throughout the Arab world. 'The broadcasts became occasions for invitations and gatherings around the nearest radio to listen to the evening's program and socialize with friends and relatives . . . Radio became the principal medium through which Umm Kulthūm reached her audience' (Danielson 1997, 87).

Live Performance Shows Featuring a Variety of Musicians

The most outstanding examples of regular US radio programs with a changing cast of bands and singers are the 'barn dance' shows featuring country music. In

Chicago, WLS had begun the *National Barn Dance* in 1924, and it was networked by NBC from 1933; two of its regular performers, Lulu Belle and Skyland Scotty, developed a national following. The legendary *Grand Ole Opry* was launched by WSM in Nashville in 1925, but it was not until the late 1930s that NBC finally gave it a national network slot.

Light Entertainment Variety Shows

The most popular type of program on the US networks in the late 1920s was the variety show, a blend of comedy, instrumental dance music, a vocal soloist or two, and a well-known announcer who served as master of ceremonies. The leading variety shows included Eddie Cantor's show. Among those whose careers received a boost from appearing with Cantor were female vocalists Dinah Shore and Thelma Carpenter. One of the first black entertainers with a starring role on the networks was Jack L. Cooper who, on WSBC in Chicago, hosted a music and comedy program aimed at the black audience that began in 1929.

Elsewhere, the show that was most listened to in Haiti in the 1950s was Radio d'Haiti's *Radio Théâtre*, a variety show broadcast on Sundays between 11:30 a.m. and 2:00 p.m., featuring the Jazz des Jeunes group (Averill 1997, 69).

Talent Shows

Radio shows featuring previously unknown singers, musicians and other entertainers were a feature of broadcasting from the 1930s to the 1950s. The most renowned of US talent shows was *Arthur Godfrey's Talent Scouts*, launched in the mid-1940s. The Canadian-born Carroll Levis hosted similar shows in the United Kingdom for the BBC and for Radio Luxembourg. During the 1950s, Radio Luxembourg recorded a talent show called *When You're Smiling* at Butlin's holiday camps for broadcast to UK audiences.

Chart Shows

Weekly programs listing the most popular songs or bestselling records in a country or city remain a regular part of the schedule at numerous music radio stations. The first show to count down the hits was *Your Hit Parade*, which began in the United States in 1935, and on which singers such as Frank Sinatra performed the most popular songs of the week. The *Jamaican Hit Parade*, hosted by Sonny Bradshaw, began in 1959 on the newly launched Jamaica Broadcasting Corporation (Bradley 2000, 89). In the United Kingdom, the BBC's Light Programme broadcast *Pick of the Pops* in a Sunday afternoon slot from 1962, while the country's commercial radio network broadcast its sponsored *Pepsi Chart Show* in direct competition each Sunday.

Listener-Request Shows

One formula for music shows is to program songs and records requested by listeners. In the 1920s, US listeners expressed their preferences by sending letters and postcards (called 'applause cards') to their favorite stations; the performers who received the most responses began appearing on a regular basis. Among the early fan favorites were the New York band leader Vincent Lopez, Kansas City's Leo Fitzpatrick and his *Nighthawk Frolic*, and the Chicago Civic Opera.

Halloween Martin, the first female to host a morning show in Chicago, played records and took requests as early as 1929. During the 1950s, request shows were among the few places where UK listeners could hear current popular hits. The BBC Light Programme included *Housewives' Choice*, *Two-Way Family Favourites* (for families of service personnel abroad) and *Children's Favourites* in its schedules.

Documentaries

State-owned networks have, for several decades, made space in their evening schedules for documentary shows about aspects of the history of popular music. In the United Kingdom, the BBC's Radio 1 created a 13-part *Story of Pop* in 1973 and, by the 1990s, Radio 1 and Radio 2 had made dozens of documentaries about individual acts, music genres and other music-related topics. In the United States, Public Radio International launched a series of artist profiles in 1988 called *Echoes*, which was eventually broadcast by 143 local non-profit stations.

Shows Devoted to Particular Music Genres

Another aspect of the public-service responsibility of state-financed stations has been a commitment to feature a wide range of musical forms. In the late 1990s, Radio France broadcast some six hours of jazz each week through its various networks. In the same era, the BBC had specialist shows devoted to jazz, blues, folk, country, world music, the cinema organ and brass band music.

The dissemination of non-mainstream North American popular music in Europe and elsewhere was considerably aided by genre-based shows broadcast on the American Forces Network (AFN) and Voice of America (VOA) stations. AFN was aimed at US service personnel stationed in Western Europe after World War II, but its shows were also listened to by teenagers in Germany, Britain and elsewhere who were eager to hear country and western, R&B and rock 'n' roll records not issued in their own countries. VOA was a propaganda station aimed at audiences in the Communist states of Eastern Europe, where Willis Conover's *Jazz Hour* show introduced listeners to current trends in jazz.

Llorens (1991) describes an unusual Peruvian variant on the genre-based show. In the 1980s, Andean migrants living in Lima bought airtime on commercial stations to transmit *programas folklóricas* featuring Andean folk music. Many of the broadcasts could also be heard in the migrants' home provinces.

Programs of Recorded Music Hosted by DJs or 'Air Personalities'

The earliest record-based shows date from the late 1920s. At the BBC, Christopher Stone had a weekly disc night in 1927, while in New York Martin Block's *Make-Believe Ballroom* created the illusion of a 'live' broadcast while consisting entirely of records. Block's show lasted from the mid-1930s until the 1950s.

Ennis (1992, 135) describes three types of DJ, each corresponding to a type of radio show: the air-salesman; the radio station performer; and the musical master of ceremonies. The salesman's boss was the sponsor; the performer used his/her personality to win listener loyalty to the station; and the master of ceremonies was closely linked to the music industry and concerned to create future music hits.

Record-based shows presented by the latter type of DJ played a key role in the rise of R&B and rock 'n' roll in the United States of the 1950s. The pioneering programs of John R (John Richbourg) from the powerful 50,000-watt station WLAC in Nashville could be heard throughout the central United States (Gillett 1983, 39). As rock 'n' roll attracted teenage audiences, numerous stations installed larger-than-life DJs in the post-school afternoon slots. DJs such as Alan Freed on WINS in New York compèred local record hops and became well-known figures on the city's music scene. Freed's show – *Moondog's Rock 'n' Roll Party* – was one of many programs around the United States that included 'Rock 'n' Roll Party' in their titles. Another New York DJ, 'Symphony Sid' Torin, promoted bebop on his Friday evening show on WHOM in the late 1940s.

In Europe, too, stations gradually acknowledged the new teenage audience. Radio Luxembourg scheduled 15-minute shows like Jimmy Savile's *Teen and Twenty Disc Club*, often sponsored by record labels. The French youth audience was targeted from 1959 by *Salut les Copains*, hosted by jazz DJ Daniel Filipacchi on Europe No. 1.

Star DJs are now featured on 'breakfast' or 'morning' shows or on 'drive-time' shows in the late afternoon. Garner (1990) discusses the typical UK breakfast show of the late 1980s. As most stations, especially in North America, have become tightly formatted, with records chosen by computerized playlist systems rather than by individual DJs or producers, the emphasis on the DJ as radio station performer has increased. Often, the non-music elements have aroused attention and controversy, as media watchdog groups debate the effect on young

listeners of certain 'shock jocks' like Howard Stern, whose morning show on New York's WXRK was syndicated throughout the United States and who was known for a crude and very vulgar on-air persona. As radio industry veteran Don Imus had prophetically told a *Billboard* radio seminar in 1971, all an air personality has to do is 'talk dirty and play the hits' (Stark 1994, 98).

Bibliography

Averill, Gage. 1997. *A Day for the Hunter, A Day for the Prey: Popular Music and Power in Haiti*. Chicago: University of Chicago Press.

Bradley, Lloyd. 2000. *Bass Culture: When Reggae Was King*. London: Viking.

Cantor, Louis. 1992. *Wheelin' on Beale: How WDIA-Memphis Became the Nation's First All-Black Radio Station and Created the Sound That Changed America*. New York: Pharos Books.

Danielson, Virginia. 1997. *The Voice of Egypt: Umm Kulthūm, Arabic Song, and Egyptian Society in the Twentieth Century*. Chicago and London: University of Chicago Press.

Ennis, Philip H. 1992. *The Seventh Stream: The Emergence of Rocknroll in American Popular Music*. Hanover and London: Wesleyan University Press.

Garner, Ken. 1990. 'New Gold Dawn: The Traditional English Breakfast Show in 1989.' *Popular Music* 9(2): 193–202.

Gillett, Charlie. 1983. *The Sound of the City: The Rise of Rock and Roll*. Rev. ed. London: Souvenir Press.

Levin, Theodore. 1996. *The Hundred Thousand Fools of God: Musical Travels in Central Asia (and Queens, New York)*. Bloomington, IN: Indiana University Press.

Llorens, J.A. 1991. 'Andean Voices on Lima Airwaves: Highland Migrants and Radio Broadcasting in Peru.' *Studies in Latin American Popular Culture* 10: 177–89.

Stark, Phyllis. 1994. 'Billboard Radio Seminars: A Heritage Act with a Passionate Core.' *Billboard* (17 September): 98–99.

DONNA HALPER and DAVE LAING

Talent Shows

Long before radio existed, there were talent shows. In vaudeville and in theater, hopeful amateurs tried their luck onstage; the prize was sometimes a small amount of money, but more often it was the possibility of being hired. Although few of these amateurs succeeded, occasionally one of them did impress the audience and went on to become a star.

When radio began, the new technology made live broadcasts from a theater or concert hall very difficult; most early broadcasts took place in a studio, often located in a warehouse or factory where radio equipment was manufactured. Early radio lacked glamor, and it also lacked money – few early stations were able to pay performers. Yet there was no shortage of entertainment: amateurs, often from local music schools, were eager to perform. Because radio signals traveled long distances, these performers all hoped that the right people would hear them. Thus, it would be accurate to describe radio programming in its early days in most countries as an ongoing talent show.

This was especially true in the United States. Since broadcasting received no government support, nearly all early performers were volunteers, many of whom had great enthusiasm but minimal talent. However, as radio developed during the 1920s, more selective criteria for getting on the air were established, and that usually meant the performers had to pass an audition. Individual radio shows even made this process into a contest – so-called 'opportunity nights,' when those who envisioned themselves as future radio stars were given an opportunity to perform. By the mid-1920s, many stations had moved to more pleasant surroundings, and a studio audience now provided instant reaction, letting the amateurs know whom they liked best (child performers and players of unusual musical instruments seemed especially popular). And although prizes were small, the thrill of winning seemed to suffice.

It was not until the 1930s that radio talent shows came into their own. With so many people out of work because of the Depression, the idea of 'striking it rich' in radio had great appeal. A program that capitalized on that sentiment was *Major Bowes' Original Amateur Hour*. The concept was developed by Edward Bowes, along with two producers with whom he had worked at station WHN in New York. They had tried what they called an 'amateur hour' during the late 1920s, but without much success; sensing that the time was now right, Bowes and his team created a formula that worked. As broadcast historian John Dunning writes,

> They suddenly saw the amateur hour in terms of a prize fight. The amateurs were the combatants. The more the audience knew about the fighters' personalities, the higher the levels of interest would climb. The bell between rounds might also be utilized – a gong of sorts, to dismiss an amateur who wasn't making it. The gong was like sudden death, like the hook in the rough-and-tumble days of amateur nights in vaudeville. It was rude and crude, but its presence would add another element of suspense. (1998, 426)

Major Bowes' Original Amateur Hour debuted on the NBC radio network in late March 1935, sponsored by Chase & Sanborn coffee. The show was an immediate sensation, in terms of both its ratings and the number of would-be participants. Dunning notes that, at its highest point, the show was receiving over 10,000 applications a week for the 20 available slots on the program (1998, 425). The show's opening lines, 'The wheel of fortune goes round and round, and where she stops, nobody knows,' became a catch phrase in US society. And while few of his contestants ever made large sums of money, Bowes was paid the astronomical sum of $25,000 per show.

However, Major Bowes and his amateur hour attracted controversy. Critics questioned how honest the voting process was (people called in to vote for their favorite amateur, leading to charges that a sponsor or any amateur with a lot of friends could easily manipulate the totals), and whether Bowes decided on the winners in advance. Stories of impoverished hopefuls who had hitchhiked great distances to plead for a tryout, only to be turned away by the major's staff, began to find their way into the media. While the show did achieve high ratings for a while, it led to the discovery of very few future major stars – opera singer Beverly Sills and crooner Frank Sinatra were the best known of the winners.

The most important US show to give amateurs a chance at fame and fortune was *Arthur Godfrey's Talent Scouts*, which started on CBS radio in early July 1946, and went on television in 1948. Godfrey, who was also the host of a successful variety show, *Arthur Godfrey Time*, had a special reason for creating *Talent Scouts*, and it was not simply because the audience enjoyed the rags-to-riches plot line that these shows offered. Unlike other talent shows that had preceded it, Godfrey's show did not offer contestants $100 prizes or dismiss them with a gong. Rather, Godfrey gave them the chance to graduate from *Talent Scouts* and become part of his troupe of regular performers on *Arthur Godfrey Time*. Winning on *Talent Scouts* was not an empty honor – it was a stepping-stone to greater exposure on a highly successful radio show, a show that would become equally successful on television. Although the studio audience helped to decide the winner each week, it was Godfrey himself who decided which few acts would be allowed to audition; he prided himself on having a good ear and a sense of what the public would like. Several of the winners on *Talent Scouts* not only went on to join the 'Little Godfreys' on *Arthur Godfrey Time*, but later had their own hit records on radio. Two of the best examples of this were the McGuire Sisters, whose song 'Sincerely' went to number one on the US pop charts in 1955, and the Chordettes, who had three Top 5 songs during the mid-1950s. It has also been reported (Hardy and Laing 1990) that Guy Mitchell and Johnny Nash were discovered by Arthur Godfrey. On the other hand, Godfrey sometimes got it wrong – among those who failed his audition was Elvis Presley (McNeil 1996, 815).

Many of the radio shows from the United States could easily be received in Canada, and a number of Canadian stations became affiliated with US networks, an arrangement that lasted well into the 1930s. As a result, the US talent shows were very well known in Canada. However, some Canadian stations did produce their own talent shows. Among the first of these to gain a national following was *Ken Sobel's Amateur Hour*, which began in 1931 and was soon heard on stations throughout eastern Canada (legendary jazz pianist Oscar Peterson got his big break on that program). In Halifax, Nova Scotia during the late 1930s, announcer Hugh Mills of CHNS radio began doing a children's show; he was known as Uncle Mel, and on Saturdays he allowed some of his young listeners to try their luck at performing. *Uncle Mel's Talent Show* became an unexpected success, lasting for 15 years. As for network programs, during the 1940s the CBC had two talent shows, one called *Opportunity Knocks* and the other *Singing Stars of Tomorrow*.

Meanwhile, the talent show phenomenon became just as popular in other countries. A Canadian expatriate, Carroll Levis, could certainly be equated with Major Bowes in terms of his celebrity status in his adopted country, England. Starting in October 1937 with a show on Radio Luxembourg, Levis later became the host of a very popular amateur talent show on the BBC, *Carroll Levis Discoveries*. This show, too, produced some well-known phrases, such as 'The new and unknown artists of today are truly the stars of tomorrow.' Countless hopeful contestants tried for their chance at stardom and big cash prizes on Levis' show, which was recorded onstage at various British theaters. As for the genial host, Carroll Levis was able to continue his amateur talent programs well into the television era. In fact, among those who competed on his television show in the late 1950s were Rory Storm and the Hurricanes; three unknowns called John Lennon, Paul McCartney and George Harrison, using the name Johnny and the Moondogs, auditioned, but had to leave to catch the last train home, and never did get on Levis' show. Another popular talent show on British television was *Opportunity Knocks*, with its host Hughie Green, who measured audience response to the contestants on a 'clapometer.' The show ran from 1956 to the late 1970s, and it gave such hit-makers as Mary Hopkin their first big break.

Elsewhere, Australians too embraced the concept of the talent contest (often called a 'talent quest'). Perhaps the best known of the Australian talent shows was *Australia's Amateur Hour*, which began in 1940 and enjoyed 20 years on the air. Sponsored by Lever Brothers, the program was aired all over Australia, and during World War II it was even broadcast to the troops. Listeners could call in and vote for their favorite performer, and the sponsor provided about 15 operators to handle the calls. Among the best known of the winners was Rolf Harris, who later had a Top 5 international hit with 'Tie Me Kangaroo Down Sport.' While *Amateur Hour* was very popular on radio, the program was unable to transfer that success to television.

Another popular Australian talent contest – *Mobil Quest* – went on the air in 1949. It was produced by brother and sister Hector and Dorothy Crawford, and Hector Crawford also conducted the show's studio orchestra. *Mobil Quest* offered large cash prizes and it too was aired all over Australia. Among its winners was operatic soprano Joan Sutherland. There was also a version of the program in New Zealand, where the best-known winner was the outstanding female vocalist Kiri Te Kanawa. In the mid-1960s, Hector Crawford adapted *Mobil Quest* for television, changing its name to *Showcase*.

Television was an excellent medium for talent shows. Whereas on radio it was only sound that mattered, thus restricting performers to singers and instrumentalists, on television much more was possible: now dancers, acrobats and other performers whose act was visual could demonstrate their abilities to the audience. While many of the US radio shows were unable to make the transition to television, several did, among them the previously mentioned *Arthur Godfrey's Talent Scouts* and also *Ted Mack's Original Amateur Hour*, the television version of Major Bowes' radio show. Mack had been an associate of Major Bowes, and he was quite successful with the television show, which began in 1948 and continued for several decades. Locally produced talent shows also did well: in Boston, there was one show, *Community Auditions*, that remained on television for over 37 years!

Programming for young people also benefited from being televised. Walt Disney's show from the late 1950s, *The Mickey Mouse Club*, set aside Fridays for 'Talent Round-Up Day.' The boy or girl who passed Disney's audition process performed on national television, after which the regular cast members of the show made the young performer an 'Honorary Mouseketeer.'

Critics of televised talent shows have pointed out that, on radio, it was a person's skill and personality that counted most, whereas on television physical attraction seemed to be as important as talent. In fact, on one US talent show from the 1980s, contestants could even win on the basis of their appearance. *Star Search*, hosted by Ed McMahon, first went on the air in 1983, and it grouped contestants into a number of categories; there were the usual categories like singing, dancing, acting and comedy, but there was also one for models and spokespersons (performers who hoped to do testimonials for sponsors). The winners were chosen by a panel of judges. The winner in each category returned the following week to face a new set of challengers, and the longest-reigning champion was eligible to become the 'Best New Star of the Year.' This formula has also been adapted by other countries, which have their own version of the show.

While the talent show may not achieve the ratings or command the attention that it once did, in many North American cities it has continued to provide exposure for aspiring performers. In addition, some television channels that play music videos, such as MTV in the United States or MuchMusic in Canada, have had their own version of a talent show: they have offered a prize to an up-and-coming band whose video has been judged the best, and the video and the band itself have then been given airplay on the channel. In an industry where playlists have become tighter and new artists feel they stand little chance against established and successful performers, winning such a competition has afforded a rare opportunity for promising musicians to be heard and seen by millions and perhaps to win a recording contract.

One other type of talent show seems to be unique to the United Kingdom – televised competitions in which participants must create the illusion that they are musical stars by dressing up and performing like them. On the very successful British show *Stars in Their Eyes*, bank clerks, waiters and aerobic instructors suddenly become Marilyn Monroe or Elvis Presley, or even Luciano Pavarotti. Contestants seem to be divided roughly equally between those who impersonate historical figures such as Bobby Darin and Nat 'King' Cole, and those who impersonate more contemporary stars. The contestants may not in 'real life' look like the stars they impersonate. However, they are made up and dressed to look as like them as possible in performance. The judgment on the contestants' performances is, however, usually dependent chiefly on how closely they sound like the stars they are impersonating.

To be chosen to appear on the show, a contestant has to pass a series of intense auditions, and critics, who use adjectives like 'weird' or 'embarrassing' to describe the performances, admit that there is something riveting about watching to see if the imitators will be able to do a credible job. *Stars in Their Eyes* originated in The Netherlands in the late 1980s and came to England in 1990. It has become something of a cultural phenomenon. Annually, as many as 40,000 people contact Granada TV to ask for an application, and the show's consistently high ratings prove that the public remains fascinated by this unusual program. Special shows occasionally allow celebrities to become other celebrities, as

when five cast members of the soap opera *Coronation Street* impersonated the Spice Girls.

A more recent program, *Popstars*, on ITV has also enjoyed some success. This show fed off the fashion in the early twenty-first century for 'reality television' or 'fly-on-the-wall docu-soaps.' In this case, close to 3,000 applicants auditioned for a place in a five-member band. The soap opera component of this program follows the process whereby the five band members are selected and then attempt to secure a recording contract. The concept was first created in Australia, and versions of the show have been televised in Canada, Italy and the United States.

Despite the glamor and excitement of the current talent shows, the reality is that even the winners have very little chance of ever becoming famous. But the thrill of competing and the chance to be on the air continue to motivate people of all ages to come to auditions, hoping that perhaps this time the wheel of fortune will stop for them.

Bibliography

Dunning, John. 1998. *On the Air: The Encyclopedia of Old-Time Radio*. New York: Oxford University Press.

Hardy, Phil, and Laing, Dave. 1990. *The Faber Companion to 20th-Century Popular Music*. London: Faber and Faber.

McNeil, Alex. 1996. *Total Television: The Comprehensive Guide to Programming from 1948 to the Present*. 4th ed. New York: Penguin.

McNeil, Bill, and Wolfe, Morris. 1982. *Signing On: The Birth of Radio in Canada*. Toronto: Doubleday Canada.

Singer, Arthur J. 2000. *Arthur Godfrey: The Adventures of an American Broadcaster*. Jefferson, NC: McFarland.

Discographical References

Chordettes, The. 'Born To Be With You.' Cadence 1291. *1956*: USA.

Chordettes, The. 'Lollipop.' Cadence 1345. *1958*: USA.

Chordettes, The. 'Mr. Sandman.' Cadence 1247. 1954: USA.

Harris, Rolf. 'Tie Me Kangaroo Down Sport.' Columbia DB 4483. *1960*: UK.

McGuire Sisters, The. 'Sincerely.' Coral 61323. 1955: USA.

DONNA HALPER

Television

Since its inception, television has had a profound effect on popular music. Firstly, according to time budget studies carried out in the United States, television occupies one-half of the average person's free time, thus competing with other leisure pursuits, including music-making, concert and club attendance, listening to the radio and listening to records, tapes and compact discs (CDs). At the same time, it brings the audiovisual experience into the home via broadcast, cable, satellite and videocassette. Additionally, music is used for signature tunes, 'idents,' and as background sound in almost all types of television programs and commercials. This is of considerable economic importance for musicians, composers and music publishers.

Television's most fundamental impact on popular music was indirect and occurred in the United States during the 1950s. In the decade following World War II, network radio was the prime means of promoting popular music, and there was a very close relationship, often involving corporate links, between the radio networks, the major record companies, the large publishing houses and Hollywood filmmakers. Through their control of the channels of promotion and distribution of music, the majors effectively sidelined all forms of popular music that did not fit the jazz-tinged dance-band pop music exemplified by artists such as Frank Sinatra, Dinah Shore, Perry Como, the McGuire Sisters and Mitch Miller, and by Broadway musicals.

As television sets appeared in most US homes, the prime radio-network comedy, drama, variety and news programs moved to television, taking the large national advertisers with them, and the radio networks were broken up. At the same time, many new radio stations were licensed, and FM broadcasting was on the horizon. Consequently, radio stations sold at very low prices, many experts reasoning that radio would be abandoned entirely as audiences moved to television, which was seen as radio with pictures. By 1960, live popular, country, middle-of-the-road (MOR) and classical music virtually disappeared from radio, to be replaced by genre-specific recorded music. This genre-specific programming created a huge new demand for a diverse range of musics and stimulated the growth of the large number of small record companies that were being founded in cities and towns across the country. Thus, by making inevitable the transformation of radio, television contributed vitally to the revolution in music that took place between 1950 and 1970 despite programming mostly bland conventional music.

However, some music was broadcast on television in the United States from its earliest days. Music was one of the elements of the hugely popular variety shows, such as *The Ed Sullivan Show*. Late-afternoon programs featuring teen-oriented music were tried in several local markets. By far the most successful of these was *Bandstand* in Philadelphia, which was initiated in 1952. Dick Clark became the master of ceremonies in 1956, and the show went national the following year. Beginning with *The Monkees* in 1966, US television also presented pop

groups in situation comedy or animated cartoon formats.

Similar music shows in which adult presenters took teen music seriously were important in the development of rock in England, Canada and many other countries. In countries outside the Anglo-American axis, television programs devoted to youth music became significant venues for the promotion of national rock music traditions in the 1960s. In Brazil, for example, the program *Jovem Guarda* (1965–68) gave its name to a wave of rock performers (such as Roberto Carlos) who modeled themselves after English-language groups, often performing Portuguese versions of Anglo-American hits. In Québec, similarly, programs such as *Jeunesse d'aujourd'hui* (which premièred in 1962) created a province-wide audience for a myriad of local groups.

Teen pop music was not the only musical form that benefited from regular television exposure. In the United States from 1948 onward, various shows presented country music performers, and from the 1960s soul and R&B also had their specialist shows.

Until the late 1970s, television was notable for the absence of successful, mainstream rock performers from its prime-time programming. Indeed, in the United States, as in many other countries, television remained the refuge of pre-rock vocal music, largely through the success of variety shows featuring performers, such as Dean Martin, whose success on television did not necessarily translate into significant levels of record sales. In many non-English-speaking countries, such as Mexico and Italy, prime-time variety television programs have remained popular, and have served to nourish local celebrities and musical styles. One result of this, noted widely in the music industry press in the late 1990s, has been the tendency for domestic music-buying patterns in several countries to remain distinct from global patterns. In Japan and in some European and Latin American countries, prime-time televisual forms, such as the soap opera or the variety show, have become the principal venues for the maintenance of local star systems. As such, they very often serve to balance the programming of music television networks (such as the regional versions of MTV), which help to promote international musical stars and styles.

The variety show as a format had largely disappeared from US and English-Canadian television in the 1980s. It has returned largely in camouflaged form, in the innumerable awards shows that have proliferated since the 1980s. (Examples of such programs include *The Grammy Awards*, Canada's *The Juno Awards* and *The People's Choice Awards*.) While each program is offered as an annual, special event, the number of such programs has made them a regular feature of television programming.

Within these shows, more musical performances are broadcast than in any other current televisual genre on the general-interest networks (with the exception of the late-night talk show).

Over the years, television has been used to focus people's attention on the turning point in established artists' careers, hoping to bring them greater stature. Early notable examples include the televising of the Beatles' Shea Stadium concert in 1965, and their studio performance with 'friends,' including Mick Jagger, of 'All You Need Is Love' in 1967, which was promoted as being broadcast live to an audience of 200 million people around the world. More than any other single broadcast, this latter event celebrated the newly attained scope of television and showed a rock band's ability to capture attention worldwide. The most successful televised comeback event was Elvis Presley's 1968 special that launched his second Las Vegas–based career. And the 1997 televised Central Park concert of Garth Brooks helped to set him on his way to becoming the bestselling act of all time.

Television is regularly used in the United States to get around the constraints of the in-store merchandising of recorded music. Specially packaged compilations, frequently unavailable in record stores, are advertised for this purpose on television. The marketing of music on television, particularly in the United States, is based on the assumption that the audiences for television programs are typically older than the core audience of those who buy music in recorded form. As such, music is often marketed on television through an appeal to nostalgia, as in the Time-Life compilations of swing or vocal music which are advertised on late-night television. More recently, popular television programs such as *Ally McBeal* have incorporated live musical performances within their own narratives, promoting singer-songwriters and other purveyors of 'adult' popular music to an audience whose purchases of recorded music are thought to be infrequent.

More fatefully for the development of popular music, televised videoclips have become an important medium for exposing new releases, curtailing the hegemony of radio for promotion. Although promotional videoclips had been made years earlier, they became a regular component of the television landscape in 1981 with the launch of MTV. Ironically, the first clip played was the Buggles' 'Video Killed the Radio Star.' Two years later, two country music clip-playing channels, Country Music Television and the Nashville Network, were launched, and Black Music Television began to give wider exposure to African-American recording artists.

Early music videos highlighted the abilities of the most active and flashy performers, including Mick Jagger and Elton John, but film techniques were soon developed that could make any act appear active and dramatic. The tight shots of the music clips gave a clear advantage to young and photogenic performers over older and less visually compelling singers. Madonna, Boy George, Cyndi Lauper and Duran Duran, emerging acts of the mid-1980s, were the first generation to owe their spectacular rise to music television. The special music shows devoted to rap, dance and grunge in the 1990s helped give these genres wider exposure and acceptance.

Subsequently, music television networks have become available in most developed countries of the world, either through the expansion of MTV (through its several 'regional' or multinational versions) or with the development of national networks modeled on it (as with the English-Canadian MuchMusic and French-Canadian MusiquePlus). The extent to which music television has produced a truly global musical culture remains in doubt, as music television networks regularly move back and forth between strategies that favor locally initiated programming and others that presume a relative homogeneity of international tastes.

Music produced especially for television programs has had little broader commercial success over the last half-century. In the late 1950s, musicians associated with the cool, 'west coast' jazz sound often found work performing on the soundtracks of crime-oriented dramatic programs, producing a musical style that connoisseurs have recently embraced and dubbed 'crime jazz.' While composers of television soundtrack music such as Mike Post (*The Rockford Files*, *Hill Street Blues* and so on) have released such music in recorded form, the television soundtrack album has remained a marginal commercial artifact, limited to cult audiences and the buyers of compilation albums. In the United Kingdom, the use of popular recordings in television advertisements has regularly led to their sudden success or rediscovery by record buyers, but this has happened much less frequently in the United States.

Nevertheless, television has continued to use large quantities of specially composed music. Stations and networks need their own brief identifying themes, which are increasingly used in promotional spots for specific programs and for the networks themselves. Oppenheimer (1999) describes how a team of composers wrote 100 variations on the three-note theme of the NBC network in the United States, to be used in 'network IDs, image spots, bumpers and teases' (38).

Additionally, every show needs a signature tune and most include background music, much of which is specially composed. The process of creating music for drama or documentary series with large budgets is similar to that of composing film music: the composer is given a video version of the program and must use special computer technology to synchronize music with pictures. For low-budget productions on specialist cable channels, composers must provide versions of the theme varying in length from 10 seconds to one minute (Davis and Laing 2001, 248–49).

Finally, thousands of advertisements or commercials are made for television each year. Almost all use music in the form of specially composed jingles, background music or new arrangements of well-known works or recordings. Jingles extol a product through the use of brief lyrics set to music, while background music for commercials must enhance the mood desired by the director and advertising agency.

In countries with large television industries and high levels of viewing, some composers are able to earn a living solely or mainly from television. In addition to commission fees, authors of television music receive performance royalties for each broadcast of their work. The music royalties paid by the television industry worldwide are now worth more than $1 billion per year (NMPA 2001).

Alongside these uses of music as a component of its programs, television has profoundly influenced the development of popular music through its impact on other media, its ability to bring the experience of popular music to a wider audience, and its focus on the physical image and actions of performers.

Bibliography

Davis, Sarah, and Laing, Dave. 2001. *The Guerilla Guide to the Music Business*. London: Continuum.

Goodwin, Andrew. 1992. *Dancing in the Distraction Factory: Music Television and Popular Culture*. Minneapolis, MN: University of Minnesota Press.

National Music Publishers Association (NMPA). 2001. *International Survey of Music Publishing Revenues*. New York: NMPA.

Oppenheimer, Jean. 1999. 'Variations on a Theme.' *The Hollywood Reporter: Film and TV Music Special Issue* (January): 38, 52–54.

Peterson, Richard A. 1990. 'Why 1955?: Explaining the Advent of Rock Music.' *Popular Music* 9(1): 97–116.

Sanjek, Russell. 1988. *American Popular Music and Its Business: The First Four Hundred Years. Vol. III: From 1900 to 1984*. New York: Oxford University Press.

Discographical References

Beatles, The. 'All You Need Is Love.' Parlophone R 5620. *1967*: UK.

Buggles, The. 'Video Killed the Radio Star.' Island 49114. *1979*: UK.

RICHARD PETERSON, WILL STRAW and DAVE LAING

Television Shows

Popular music has had strong links with television ever since the launch of the television medium in the United States in the late 1940s. Grossberg (1993) points out that 'television has been, for some fans, their only access to "live" performance' (189) and lists a range of program formats in which this and other televisual portrayals of popular music have occurred.

Perhaps foremost among these has been what Grossberg describes as the presentation of 'occasional acts on variety shows' (1993, 189) – a format whereby television shows can disseminate music to mass audiences together with an instantaneous visual impact. The most dramatic example of this process was the introduction of the previously unknown Elvis Presley on the nationally networked *Milton Berle Show* on 5 June 1956, with a performance that scandalized newspaper critics and delighted millions of young viewers. The largest audiences for such occasional performances are now provided in many countries by national lottery shows, such as Portugal's *Roda Dos Milhoes*.

Early television took over programming ideas from existing entertainment media, including radio. In the 1950s, many local stations in the United States had DJ-style shows that used three-minute clips produced by George Snader, featuring well-known artists performing a single song to camera. Television also provided visual versions of 'live' music shows, such as *Your Hit Parade*, the long-running radio show that was simulcast between 1954 and 1959. British television had its own version of a *Hit Parade* show in 1952.

Singers were soon given their own series, introducing guest vocalists and comics. Some artists made the transition to the small screen more easily than others: Eddie Fisher delighted his sponsor with his performance in the 15-minute *Coke Time* (1953), and the relaxed style of *The Perry Como Show* (1955–63) was later emulated by Andy Williams in the United States and Val Doonican in Britain. However, Frank Sinatra's show for CBS lasted only one season in 1951 after one critic described it as 'a drab mixture of radio, routine vaudeville and pallid pantomime' (Shaw 1968, 88). Some stars were more cautious in dealing with television: Bing Crosby waited until 1955 before making his debut.

Because television was programmed as family entertainment, only a few shows in the United States and elsewhere were devoted solely to popular music. Singers and bands therefore had to perform in talent contests such as *Arthur Godfrey's Talent Scouts* or on variety shows hosted by 'personalities' such as Berle, Steve Allen and Ed Sullivan, on whose show in 1964 the Beatles made their first US public appearance. In Britain, the leading televised variety show for many years was *Sunday Night at the London Palladium*. In Europe, there have been various national singing contests, such as *La Chance aux Chansons* in France, but the major televised talent contests in Europe are Italy's San Remo Festival and the Eurovision Song Contest, which is organized by the European Broadcasting Union (a federation of public broadcasters) and was first transmitted in 1956. The earliest music shows on Japanese television, following its launch in 1953, were *Shirôto Nodojiman Taikai* (Amateur Singing Contests).

The first successful attempt to make teenage pop music televisual was *American Bandstand*, which was networked throughout the United States in the late 1950s and early 1960s. The show introduced a pop television format that was widely emulated on dozens of local stations. On the west coast, British-born producer Jack Good offered an alternative approach by creating in the studio the atmosphere of a live concert with *Shindig* (1964) and *Hullaboloo* (1965) (Whitcomb 1983). A house band (including the cream of Los Angeles's session players) accompanied singers performing live on screen. The live show format was utilized in Europe in the 1960s by such programs as *Ready Steady Go* (UK) and *Rockpalast* (Germany).

By the late 1960s, both these formats had been exhausted, and music television producers in the United States looked to light comedy drama formats such as that of *The Monkees* (1966), *The Partridge Family* and *The Archies*, which was distinguished from its competitors by having animated cartoon characters. The crossover potential of soul music was recognized by the launch of *Soul Train* in 1970, with a format similar to that of *American Bandstand*.

US television responded to the growth of underground music and progressive rock by developing series of filmed concerts, such as NBC's *The Midnight Special*, ABC's *In Concert* and *Rock Concert*, produced by Brill Building and Monkees' mogul Don Kirshner. *In Concert* was simulcast on FM radio stations in larger cities. Unlike the Saturday afternoon teenage shows, these series were broadcast in late-night slots, as was ABC's experimental *Music Scene* (1969) which included comedy as well as rock.

In Western Europe, music television programs followed a similar pattern. Youth audiences in Britain in the 1950s and early 1960s were offered such Jack Good-devised shows as *Six-Five Special* and *Ready Steady Go* and

the BBC's chart show *Top of the Pops*, which began in 1964 and was still in the schedules over 35 years later (Fryer 1998). Another longstanding chart show was *Toppop* in The Netherlands, which ran from 1970 to 1988. The most successful of several British shows to showcase progressive rock was *The Old Grey Whistle Test* (BBC). In Germany, *Beat Club* used the *American Bandstand* formula, as did *Salut Les Copains* in France, *Sabato Sera* in Italy and *Six O'Clock Rock* in Australia.

Important Brazilian music television shows in the 1960s included the São Paulo-produced *Jovem Guarda*, which publicized *ie-ie-ie* (a genre mixing rock and bolero), and *O Fino da Bossa*, a bossa nova show. Mexican television broadcast such shows as *Hulaballoo*, *Yeah yeah* and *Discoteque a go go*, which contained 'lip-synched rock performance . . . that roused the live studio audiences to a screaming, jerking fury' (Zolov 1999, 103).

In the Communist states of Eastern Europe, the single state-controlled television channels presented occasional music shows, such as the monthly *Music Hall* program in Bulgaria in the 1970s.

While public television coverage of popular music is almost indistinguishable from that of private stations in many countries, there has been a distinct contrast between them in France. While shows produced by private channels, such as TF1, have promoted mostly mainstream artists, both national and international, public channels, with programs like music competitions and afternoon broadcasts announced by singing-compères Pascal Sevran (*La Chance aux Chansons*) and Jacques Martin (*Dimanche Martin*), have been more involved in *chanson française* – including the kind of *chanson* that used to be popular decades ago.

There has been only sporadic television coverage of other musical genres. However, jazz and big band music soon found a place on US television. The CBS network's 1957 *The Sound of Jazz* show, featuring leading musicians that included Count Basie, Lester Young and Billie Holiday, was sponsored by Timex, while such band leaders as Tommy and Jimmy Dorsey hosted variety shows. Leonard Feather hosted later US shows, while the series *Jazz 625* ran on BBC television in the United Kingdom in the 1960s.

The premier country music radio show, *Grand Ole Opry*, was simulcast on WSM-TV from 1965, while other country music shows included the comedy-plus-music series *Hee Haw*. *Hootenanny* (1963), videotaped each week at a different college campus, was an attempt by the ABC network to capitalize on the folk revival.

The music television landscape in the United States was altered dramatically in 1981 by the arrival of MTV on cable networks. Founded in Miami, the company eventually reached over 50 million viewers by cable in the United States, Europe, Latin America and Asia. Numerous cable channels specializing in music were launched in Europe in the 1990s. Among these were M6 in France and Viva in Germany. The availability of numerous channels on cable permitted the introduction of 'niche' outlets devoted wholly or mainly to music. These included Black Entertainment Television (BET), The Nashville Network (TNN) and the Box Music Network, the first 'interactive' channel where viewers could phone in to request their favorite music videos. Although videoclips have provided the bulk of program material for all these networks, the stations have also produced documentary and concert shows, of which MTV's *Unplugged* series of the 1990s was perhaps the most renowned.

Notwithstanding the success of the Live Aid event (televised live in 1985 to numerous countries), the lo-fi quality of sound on analog television systems undoubtedly diminished the impact of televised performances: pay-per-view transmissions of concerts have never had the success of televised sporting events. Perhaps because of this, many of the best music television programs have been documentaries illustrating aspects of music history or the contemporary scene. In Britain, BBC television produced Tony Palmer's controversial history of pop, *All You Need Is Love*, in 1976 and several series of its *Rhythms of the World* documentaries on aspects of world music in the late 1980s. An acclaimed US-made series from 1995, *Rock & Roll*, covered rock history, while in 2000 the US producer Ken Burns made the first comprehensive television history of jazz.

Bibliography

Fryer, Paul. 1998. 'Everybody's on Top of the Pops: Popular Music on British Television 1960–1985.' *Popular Music and Society* 21(2): 71–90.

Grossberg, Lawrence. 1993. 'The Media Economy of Rock Culture: Cinema, Post-Modernity and Authenticity.' In *Sound and Vision: The Music Video Reader*, ed. Simon Frith, Andrew Goodwin and Lawrence Grossberg. London: Routledge, 185–209.

Hill, John. 1991. 'Television and Pop: The Case of the 1950s.' In *Popular Television in Britain: Studies in Cultural History*, ed. John Corner. London: British Film Institute, 90–107.

Palmer, Robert. 1995. *Rock & Roll: An Unruly History*. New York: Harmony Books.

Shaw, Arnold. 1968. *Sinatra: Retreat of the Romantic*. London: W.H. Allen.

Shore, Michael, with Clark, Dick. 1985. *The History of American Bandstand: It's Got a Great Beat and You Can Dance to It.* New York: Ballantine Books.

Stocksbridge, Sally. 1989. 'Programming Rock 'n Roll: The Australian Version.' *Cultural Studies* 3(1): 77–88.

Whitcomb, Ian. 1983. *Rock Odyssey: A Musician's Chronicle of the Sixties*. Garden City, NY: Dolphin Books.

Zolov, Eric. 1999. *Refried Elvis: The Rise of the Mexican Counterculture*. Berkeley and Los Angeles: University of California Press.

DAVE LAING with OLIVIER JULIEN (France) and

CATHERINE RUDENT (France)

Transcription Disc

A transcription disc was a shellac or, later, vinyl disc containing a complete recorded radio program or specially recorded musical items for an announcer to introduce. Such discs would be distributed to radio stations for broadcast at a local time of their choosing.

The term 'transcription' was adopted in the early 1930s by the first US transcription syndicates, which marketed prerecorded series to independent or small station groups as a rival method of sharing successful programs; the larger networks insisted that their affiliates broadcast their shows live simultaneously. The term also helped distinguish these discs from what was known as 'mechanical reproduction' – the playing of commercial 78 rpm discs on-air – with its attendant poor sound quality. Most stations did play records on-air. However, until 1940, this practise was the source of a long-running dispute in the United States between the radio, the record industry and the music publishing industry. The sponsored, syndicated musical show on transcription disc thus enabled small stations to sidestep a number of technical and legal problems, as well as to ensure top-quality programs.

The first show to be sold on transcription disc is generally agreed to have been *Amos 'n' Andy*, recorded on either side of a 78 rpm disc in two five-minute segments by Charles J. Correll (Andy) and Freeman Gosden (Amos) at Marsh Studios in Chicago in 1928. The radio station WMAQ had no objection to the recording as long as the show was broadcast live locally. Until it was snapped up by the NBC network in the summer of 1929, the show was syndicated on transcription to about 30 stations by the *Chicago Daily News* for Correll and Gosden.

By 1936, there were four major US transcription companies – the World Broadcasting Service, the Standard Radio Library, the RCA/NBC Thesaurus Library and C.P. MacGregor Services – which, among them, had contracts to supply 350 US stations. Each library had only one station in each major market. By this time, transcription discs were on 16" (40 cm), 33 1/3 rpm discs, allowing 15 minutes per side.

This standard was also used in Europe by Radio Luxembourg, which prerecorded its shows in London, and by the fledgling Transcription Service of the British Broadcasting Corporation (BBC), which was started soon after the launch of the Corporation's Empire Service in 1932.

In the 1950s, microgroove 12" (30 cm), 33 1/3 rpm vinyl discs took over as the normal syndication format, allowing up to two entire 30-minute shows per disc. By this time, and using this method, the BBC's Transcription Service was distributing nearly 700 radio shows per year to stations around the world, in the name of cultural diplomacy or 'the projection of Britain by good radio,' as its chairman R.A. Rendall put it. In 1964, the Service launched its weekly *Top of the Pops* show – not to be confused with the BBC television chart show of the same name – based on unique live BBC radio sessions by the Beatles, the Rolling Stones and other new stars. As a result, the famous green-and-gold-labeled discs have remained, in many cases, the only record of these groups' early live sound.

In the 1980s and 1990s, syndicators gradually switched to compact disc, digital audiotape or satellite transmission for immediate/live or later recorded use of their programs. However, as late as 1987, ABC Watermark was still distributing Casey Kasem's weekly *American Top 40* show to hundreds of stations around the world on sets of four 12" (30 cm) vinyl LPs. As the process of distributing syndicated shows to subscribing stations has become more sophisticated, so the surviving artifacts of the transcription era have become more valued by record collectors.

Bibliography

Barnouw, Erik. 1966. *A Tower in Babel: A History of Broadcasting in the United States. Vol. I – to 1933.* New York: Oxford University Press.

Briggs, Asa. 1979. *The History of Broadcasting in the United Kingdom*, Vol. IV. Oxford: Oxford University Press.

Garner, Ken. 1993. *In Session Tonight: The Complete Radio 1 Recordings*. London: BBC Books.

Millard, Andre J. 1995. *America on Record: A History of Recorded Sound*. Cambridge: Cambridge University Press.

KEN GARNER

Voice of America

Voice of America (VOA) first made its name by broadcasting the US government's viewpoint through newscasts made to Communist countries during the Cold War, but VOA also became known for its broadcasts of US popular music.

The predecessor of VOA was WRUL, an international shortwave radio station founded by inventor and engineer Walter S. Lemmon in 1935. Located near Boston, Massachusetts, WRUL featured educational programming in a number of languages other than English, and by 1939 it was making special news broadcasts to countries under Nazi censorship. During World War II, WRUL (along with all other shortwave stations) was taken over by the US government and, in view of how effective the broadcasts had been in combating Nazi propaganda, the Office of War Information (OWI) decided to create an official government broadcasting service. As a result, Voice of America was born on 24 February 1942. Its initial broadcast to Germany opened with the words, 'The Voice of America speaks – we shall tell the truth.' Its mission was to present the US point of view on political matters, but when it was not providing news and information, VOA began broadcasting popular music.

After the war, there was considerable discussion as to whether the government wanted to maintain VOA, given that a service that presented US propaganda was much more relevant during wartime. Still, VOA managed to marshal enough support to survive, and it was put under the supervision of the US State Department. In 1953, during the Cold War, Congress created a separate agency, the United States Information Agency (USIA), to run VOA and other similar services. The USIA, which during the early 1960s was led by legendary US journalist Edward R. Murrow, gradually expanded the programming that VOA offered – for example, thanks to Murrow's support, regular broadcasts to Africa began in August 1963.

Expanded programming to other parts of the world followed. By the end of the twentieth century, VOA, with offices located in Washington, DC, was broadcasting in 52 languages and providing almost 700 hours of programming on shortwave and medium wave, with an estimated audience of 86 million each week. In addition, VOA provided programming in 46 languages to more than 1,100 AM, FM and cable 'affiliated' stations around the world, which carried certain programs that VOA offered. Although much of the programming was still news-related, most VOA stations offered locally produced shows of popular music; many of these programs took requests from listeners, while broadcasting interviews with well-known local musicians.

Although at times over the years VOA has been seen as far from objective (in its own charter, it states that 'VOA will represent America, not any single segment of American society, and will therefore present a balanced and comprehensive projection of significant American thought and institutions'), it has often provided excellent coverage of issues, and has broadcast a wide range of programs, some educational (such as call-in chat shows during which listeners can ask questions of current newsmakers, or an ongoing series of English lessons by radio) and others entertaining.

A good example of VOA's role in spreading US popular culture occurred from the mid-1950s on, when jazz fans in Eastern Europe discovered a VOA show called *Music-USA*, hosted by a middle-aged New Yorker named Willis Conover. Not only did this show become a huge hit in countries like the USSR and Czechoslovakia, but, to his surprise, Conover himself became an icon, receiving hundreds of fan letters and earning himself a lengthy write-up in both *Time* and *Newsweek*. The success of Conover's show, which remained popular well into the 1980s, inspired Radio Liberty to create its own jazz show in 1963. Conover's devotion to North American jazz, along with VOA's strong signal range, brought this music to an audience of over 30 million avid listeners.

In addition to jazz, during the early 1960s VOA started a successful rock show called *Music Today*. The governments of various Eastern European Communist countries expressed their dislike of both the show and rock music in general. However, the attempts of these governments to keep rock music out of their countries failed. As a consequence, government-run radio stations finally gave in and played rock music rather than risk losing their young audience to VOA and Radio Free Europe (RFE). The institution of *Music Today* thus resulted in numerous imitators, and brought VOA the younger audience it had hoped to reach (Ryback 1990).

At the end of the twentieth century, in addition to programs of local music, many VOA stations aired a weekly look at the US Top 40 hits, courtesy of the *Billboard* charts, as well as offering dance, country and other popular music genres.

VOA has been active on the Internet since 1994. Its Web site allows visitors to hear some of its broadcasts, as well as access news stories from a large number of the countries VOA serves. In addition, VOA has its own television service, which was begun in 1996.

During 1994 and 1995, there was further governmental reorganization, and VOA became part of the International Broadcasting Bureau (IBB), along with Radio Free Europe/Radio Liberty, WORLDNET TV and Film Service, Radio Marti and TV Marti, and Radio Free Asia.

Bibliography

Head, Sydney W. 1985. *World Broadcasting Systems: A Comparative Analysis*. Belmont, CA: Wadsworth Publishing Co.

Hilliard, Robert L., and Keith, Michael C. 1996. *Global Broadcasting Systems*. Boston, MA: Focal Press.

Ryback, Timothy. 1990. *Rock Around the Bloc: A History of Rock Music in Eastern Europe and the Soviet Union*. New York: Oxford University Press.

Sosin, Gene. 1999. *Sparks of Liberty: An Insider's Memoir of Radio Liberty*. University Park, PA: Pennsylvania University Press.

'Soviet Union: The Sound of Music.' 1967. *Newsweek* 69 (5 June): 50.

DONNA HALPER

Your Hit Parade

Your Hit Parade was the name of a US radio and television show that ran from 1935 to 1959.

Sponsored during its entire lifetime by Lucky Strike cigarettes, the weekly show presented live performances of the previous week's top-ranking songs, based on surveys of record and sheet music sales and network radio airplay. Lists that ranked songs in terms of sales and airplay were already being published in *Billboard* and *Variety*. The idea of performing these songs in a special program was conceived either in the advertising agency Lord & Thomas, or in the head office of its clients, the American Tobacco Company, whose president, George Washington Hill, took a personal interest in the music programming in which his company had been involved since 1927.

At the peak of its popularity in the wartime years of the early 1940s, the show attracted listening audiences of between 17 and 19 million. Shows typically employed a featured male and/or female singer such as Snooky Lanson or Dorothy Collins, and an orchestra. Early shows tended to favor loud, up-tempo arrangements, but Frank Sinatra's two lengthy residencies as featured male singer (February 1943 to December 1944 and September 1947 to May 1949) turned the dominant style more toward intimate ballads. His great popularity with a younger age group was evident to listeners in the noisy acclamation he regularly received from the studio audience. During 1950–53, the show ran simultaneously on radio and television, before moving to television alone.

Well before its demise in 1959, *Your Hit Parade* seemed old-fashioned in its adherence to an earlier style of music and its disinclination to bow before the growing supremacy of the record, both in music programming and in the measuring of popularity. Nevertheless, the show ranks as an important precursor of the chart show format. Its exploitation of the hit tune concept allowed it both to familiarize listeners with the pleasures of anticipation and to use the renewable nature of that anticipation to deliver a weekly audience to the sponsors. The show was also a barometer of public taste, although any such assessment must be qualified by the comparative lack of musical choice in US radio for over half of the show's existence, as well as by the lack of candor on the part of the agency as to exactly how its independent surveys were carried out. Also significant was the degree to which, thanks to its recognized ability to draw an audience, the show became a place where the underhand promotional practise of 'pay for play' was evidently widespread.

Bibliography

Eberly, Philip K. 1982. *Music in the Air: America's Changing Tastes in Popular Music, 1920–1980*. New York: Hastings House.

Elrod, Bruce C. 1994. *Your Hit Parade & American Top 10 Hits: A Week-by-Week Guide to the Nation's Favorite Music, 1935–1994*. 4th ed. Ann Arbor, MI: Popular Music Ink.

Hamm, Charles. 1979. *Yesterdays: Popular Song in America*. New York: W.W. Norton.

Williams, John R. 1973. *This Was 'Your Hit Parade.'* Camden, ME: Courier-Gazette Inc.

DAVID HORN

9. Copyright

Author's Right

The longest-established musical copyright is that belonging to the composer or lyricist. This *droit d'auteur* is part of a more general right also granted to creators of literary, dramatic and artistic works and enshrined in the Berne Convention. In states following the so-called Latin philosophy of legislation (principally in continental Europe, Latin America and Francophone Africa), author's rights are synonymous with copyright and are distinguished from the lesser 'neighboring' or related rights granted to performers and record companies. In countries with Anglo-Saxon legal systems (North America, the United Kingdom, Australia and former UK colonies), authors and record companies are regarded equally as owners of copyright.

DAVE LAING

Berne Convention

The Berne Convention for the Protection of Literary and Artistic Works dates back to 1886. As the fundamental international agreement on copyright, it guarantees to composers, songwriters and other types of 'author' control over the use of works created by them. The Convention has been signed by over 100 states, which are obliged to incorporate the terms of the Convention into their national copyright laws.

The original Convention was subsequently revised six times and was augmented by a Copyright Treaty in 1996. The impetus for the revisions was generally the need to provide additional protection when works were created or reproduced by new media technologies. In 1908, for example, photography, sound recording and cinematography were brought within the scope of the Convention, and in 1928 authors were given broadcasting rights. The 1948 revision added television broadcasting to the Convention, and the 1996 Copyright Treaty extended copyright protection to the World Wide Web and the Internet.

In its current form, the Berne Convention provides eight principal rights for authors, including composers and songwriters: public performance right; reproduction right (covering sound and audiovisual recordings); broadcasting right; translation right; adaptation right; moral right; film or cinematographic right; and the *droit de suite*, under which the copyright owner in an artwork can benefit from future sales of the painting or sculpture.

Governments are permitted to exclude certain aspects of the Berne Convention from their national copyright legislation. They can choose to provide either 'national' or 'reciprocal' treatment for foreign authors. While national treatment means that foreign works enjoy the same level of protection as works by authors from within a country, reciprocal treatment means that foreign authors receive only the level of protection they have in their home country.

In the case of broadcasting, governments can substitute a right to 'equitable remuneration' for the stronger right to 'authorise or prohibit' the use of an author's or composer's work on radio and television. Under the equitable remuneration system, broadcasters do not need permission to use music, but they must pay a fair price for the use. In most countries, 'equitable remuneration' is determined by a government-appointed tribunal if the two parties cannot reach agreement.

A third area of discretion concerns the moral rights of an author. When the United States joined the Convention in 1989, pressure from film industry interests ensured that the country excluded moral rights from its domestic legislation, thus protecting film producers from legal action by screenwriters or directors.

The 1996 Copyright Treaty has the status of a 'special agreement' under Article 20 of the Berne Convention. This means that the rights granted under the new treaty are not added directly to the Berne Convention and governments must sign the 1996 Copyright Treaty in addition to remaining members of Berne. The most important additional right granted by the 1996 Copyright Treaty provides protection for authors when their works are used on the Internet, or elsewhere when they are made available 'by wire or wireless means, in such a way that members of the public may access them from a place and at a time individually chosen by them.'

Bibliography

Grosheide, F. Willem. 1994. 'Paradigms in Copyright Law.' In *Of Authors and Origins: Essays on Copyright Law*, ed. Brad Sherman and Alain Strowel. Oxford: Clarendon Press, 203–33.

Porter, Vincent. 1991. *Beyond the Berne Convention: Copyright, Broadcasting and the Single European Market*. London: John Libbey & Co.

Ricketson, Sam. 1987. *The Berne Convention for the Protection of Literary and Artistic Works: 1886–1986*. London: Centre for Commercial Law Studies, Queen Mary College/Kluwer.

DAVE LAING

Bootleg

The term 'bootleg' is borrowed from the Prohibition era in the United States, when illegal alcohol was popularly known as 'bootleg liquor' after the practise of concealing bottles in the leg of a boot, and it denotes a product that is made, carried or sold illegally. For instance, a bootlegged record or cassette contains a recording of a concert, broadcast or unreleased studio production unauthorized by the owner of the copyright in the music or the recorded performance, that is, the composer, singer or record company.

Unlike the market for pirated or counterfeit products – which are inferior but cheaper versions of already published recordings – the market for bootlegs is generally restricted to ardent fans of well-known musicians. In the case of star artists, this market can be substantial and, according to the most comprehensive study of the bootleg phenomenon, the most bootlegged artists are such figures as the Beatles, Bob Dylan and Led Zeppelin (Heylin 1994). The same phenomenon exists in classical music, where the most bootlegged opera singer is Maria Callas.

The earliest bootlegged recordings were made by the librarian of New York's Metropolitan Opera House on cylinders in 1901–1903. Aided by the lack of copyright protection for sound recordings in the United States, albums of numerous opera performances, radio broadcasts and jazz club gigs were distributed on a small scale in the United States up to the 1960s.

The birth of the modern bootleg industry can be traced to 1969 and the first album of unauthorized rock recordings. This was *Great White Wonder*, a double album of Bob Dylan material that included tracks from the unissued *Basement Tapes* of 1967.

The first bootlegged CD was made in the United States in 1987. By the 1990s, a vigorous bootleg CD industry had developed in certain European countries where copyright laws were weak – notably The Netherlands, Italy and Germany. Music industry sources claimed that CD plants in Italy were manufacturing 30,000 copies of individual bootlegged recordings.

Apologists for bootlegging, such as Heylin (1994), argue that it should be distinguished from piracy because most bootleggers pay mechanical royalties and bootlegs do not compete directly with the legitimate products of the record industry. They also note that some artists, notably the Grateful Dead, encourage fans to record their performances, while others are said to collect bootlegged cassettes of their shows. However, a greater number of musicians regard bootlegging as an assault on their right to control which examples of their work should be published.

Music industry bodies have claimed that bootlegging is now the most serious form of piracy in countries such as Britain, where, according to the British Phonographic Industry, sales of bootlegs were worth over £22 million in 1995.

Bibliography

Heylin, Clinton. 1994. *The Great White Wonders: A History of Rock Bootlegs*. London: Viking.

DAVE LAING

Copyright

Copyright is a system of national and international law that empowers certain classes of individuals or corporate entities to control the copying and other uses of artistic products or practises. Copyright is one segment of a broader system of Intellectual Property Rights (IPR) that covers patents, designs and computer software. With regard to popular music, copyright includes a number of specific rights, such as the reproduction right, the performing right and moral rights. In addition to assigning these legal rights, copyright has had a profound impact on the economic and aesthetic dimensions of popular music, to the extent that the music industry is sometimes defined as one of the 'copyright industries.'

Copyright laws affect the uses, performances and recordings of musical works in three principal ways.

First, they assign positions and powers to various legal entities, including the authors of musical works and of sound recordings (the 'copyright owners') and the performers at musical events. Copyright laws also determine the status of the 'non-author,' often – as in US law – by denying employees (of newspapers, film studios or record companies, for instance) the rights accorded to authors, even if an employee is the creator of a work.

Second, copyright laws define limits to these powers, such as the time period within which a work remains under copyright (and after which it becomes part of the 'public domain') and the various types of 'fair use' of a work (that is, those uses that are not subject to the control of the owner of copyright).

Third, the laws define illegal acts that transgress the law of intellectual property and prescribe penalties for the commission of such illegal acts. The range of these acts is quite considerable and includes plagiarism, piracy, bootlegging, parallel importation and passing off (the imitation of a sound, image or design intended to make consumers believe that it is the thing imitated).

History

The history of copyright in Europe (where the concept and system originated) can be divided into two broad periods.

In the first period, beginning in the mid-fifteenth century, the control and assignment of copyright was exercised by absolutist monarchies in feudal and early modern societies as a response to the threat posed by the printing press to the monopoly of ideas enjoyed by church and state. The state awarded an exclusive license to make copies to a limited number of printers, whose output was subject to strict controls. This applied as much to printed music as to other forms of expression. In France, the monarchy gave the family firm of Ballard a monopoly that lasted for over 200 years. In England, only members of the Company of Stationers were permitted to publish. The company was given quasi-judicial powers to punish printers and distributors of unauthorized material.

In the second period, beginning in the eighteenth century, the power to control copyright was determined according to Enlightenment principles and the formal democracy established by the French Revolution. In this period, the concept of the author of a work was given legal status, and authors or their representatives were adjudged to be owners of works and were granted the authority to control the uses of the works. The emergence of this copyright episteme was closely linked both to Romantic ideas of authorship and to the growing importance of the capitalist system of production, particularly in Western and Southern Europe. This system created a 'free market' in cultural products and services

as a replacement for a system based on patronage and guilds (Grosheide 1994).

It is often argued that contemporary copyright laws derive from one or other of two separate legal traditions or paradigms of intellectual property law that emerged in this period. Geller (1994) describes these as the 'marketplace' and 'authorship' paradigms. The former is generally found in jurisdictions rooted in the English common-law tradition and the latter in jurisdictions such as those of continental European nations and their former colonies.

The marketplace paradigm regards a work or recording as the object of legal protection and nominates the copyright owner as the person or company in possession of that work or recording. The authorship paradigm starts from the concept of the author as the owner of his/her artistic creation. This *droit d'auteur* is a narrower but more powerful concept of copyright. It excludes property rights enjoyed by non-authors such as performers and record companies, whose rights are described as *droits de voisins* or neighboring rights. While the economic effects of the two paradigms are generally similar, there are continuing differences – for instance, the greater emphasis on the moral rights of the author in the authorship paradigm.

During the nineteenth century, national copyright laws were enacted in most European and Latin American countries, as well as in the colonies of European countries. The international trade in cultural products led to pressure for national laws to protect foreign works.

Laing (1993) has traced three eras in the internationalization of music copyright. The first, inaugurated in 1886 by the Berne Convention for the Protection of Literary and Artistic Works, was an era of authors' rights based on music's increasing role as an international copyright commodity. In the second, the era of neighboring rights, which occurred between the 1930s and the 1980s, the emphasis switched to the protection of the interests of the film and sound recording industries. This switch was necessitated by the deployment of new technologies of musical production and distribution. The introduction of such technologies, from the phonograph to the Internet and MP3, was a primary motive for copyright law reform in the twentieth century, culminating in the 1996 Copyright and Performers and Phonogram Producers treaties administered by the World Intellectual Property Organization (WIPO).

In the third era, that of economic rights, copyright has been subsumed into international trade agreements alongside manufacturing and other 'service' industries such as banking and insurance. This phase is typified by the unilateral activity of the US government and its 'priority watch list' of foreign countries suspected of intellectual property infringement and the World Trade Organization (WTO) treaty of 1993. This stipulates that any nation-state wishing to become a member of the WTO must, *inter alia*, have in place an IPR system containing minimum standards derived from the Berne Convention. This homogenization process applies even to those countries, notably China, without a tradition of authors' rights.

The Economic Role of Music Copyright

The economic significance of copyright has been measured in a number of countries. The contribution of copyright-related industries to gross national product (GNP) in Finland in 1988 was 2.9 percent, while in Germany it was 3.1 percent of employment and 2.9 percent of gross domestic product (GDP). This contribution is now measured annually in the United States, where the 1997 turnover of copyright industries was over $348 billion, equivalent to 4.3 percent of GDP.

Market mechanisms are needed in order to exploit the powers of copyright ownership. These are generally not specified in copyright law, although their efficacy depends largely on their legally enforceable conditions of existence. One important market mechanism for the music industry is the authors' collection society, which undertakes the 'collective management' of copyright on behalf of a large number of individual owners of copyright. Such societies operate on a national basis and negotiate tariffs with music users such as broadcasters and concert promoters. Similar organizations for the management of neighboring rights exist in many countries. These recognize record companies and recording artists as rights owners, and in Germany the *tonmeister* or record producer also receives royalties from this source.

National societies also represent the musical works administered by all foreign societies, and large amounts of royalties are exchanged between them. With the notable exceptions of the United States and Britain, the 'exports' of national societies are considerably higher than their 'imports.' Although this system gives the societies a monopoly position, national and supranational competition authorities tolerate the position because of the practical convenience of collective management for both authors and music users.

The copyright monopoly enjoyed by the societies is also subject to regulation with regard to the means by which royalty levels are set. While most national copyright systems emphasize the need for a negotiated agreement to be made between owners of copyright and those who wish to use the copyright, there is also a 'backup' mechanism for legally binding arbitration in the event of failed negotiations. Many nations have legislation that also allows for the 'compulsory licensing' of copy-

righted music, which provides the copyright users with a certain countervailing power. Under this mechanism, the owner of copyright is not permitted to prevent a user from broadcasting or recording a musical work; however, the user is committed to paying 'equitable remuneration' to the owner of copyright. The level of that payment is intended to be set by negotiation, although it is frequently referred to an arbitration body.

The cost of copyright is not the only factor in determining the price of musical goods and services. Copyright mechanisms have only an indirect effect on the marketplace of supply and demand, where the exchange between consumers and suppliers of music occurs. In many of its manifestations, the copyright market is a subset of the 'internal' market, where trading occurs between segments of the music industry and those of other media and entertainment industries. For the ultimate supplier of music to the audience (the concert promoter, broadcaster or record retailer, for instance), copyright is a cost to be borne, either as a direct payment to the collecting society or as a fixed component of the price of a musical commodity.

Piracy also plays a significant role in the music copyright economy. By definition, any statistics on the size of pirate markets must be estimations, and there can be great differences between the estimates published by different sources. For example, the International Federation of the Phonographic Industry (IFPI) has stated that the global retail value of pirate soundcarriers in 1999 was $4.1 billion, while the US-based International Intellectual Property Alliance has estimated losses in royalty payments to US music copyright owners alone at $1.7 billion.

While these statistics may be unreliable, some general trends in music piracy can be discerned. Piracy increased dramatically in the 1970s through the widespread use of cassette tapes. Producers of pirate tapes found a large market in Asia, Latin America and Africa, where the majority of the populations could not afford to buy legitimately produced cassettes. Without origination or copyright costs, pirates could make a profit by selling cassettes at a fraction of the retail price of the legitimate products. In the 1990s, CD piracy became more significant, particularly when the plants involved were located in countries such as China and Ukraine where governments were unwilling or unable to enforce national copyright law. In North America and Europe, bootlegging (the trade in unauthorized concert recordings) and the piracy of tour merchandise such as T-shirts are of some significance.

Other forms of copyright infringement are of lesser economic importance. While digital sampling has become a widely used production tool, most samples are now authorized by copyright owners of the sampled work, who share in the royalties received by the musician or producer taking the sample. Cases of plagiarism – in which a composer claims that another has copied his/her work – are dealt with in civil courts, where evidence is taken from academic musicologists acting as expert witnesses. Parallel importation (the import of copyrighted material licensed for sale in foreign countries to compete with the same product domestically) is prohibited in most countries. In the United States and Italy, performers are granted a right of publicity that can be used to prevent others from using their likeness or recordings without permission. This was extended to 'sound-alike' vocals in cases involving Tom Waits and Nancy Sinatra, where their voices had been imitated for use in commercials (Gaines 1992).

However, private copying (the taking of unauthorized copies for domestic use) has become more controversial with the widespread use of MP3 technology and 'peer-to-peer' Web sites, of which Napster was the best known. The earliest forms of private copying ('home taping') made use of tape cassettes. In many countries, this was legalized in return for compensation that took the form of a levy paid on blank media. That levy was later extended to recordable blank CDs.

Peer-to-peer file-sharing involves the exchange of recordings between any number of computer owners logged on to sites with the technology to facilitate such practises. In 2000, the US courts found that Napster was in breach of copyright by enabling people to file-share without first having received the permission of the copyright owners. While Napster itself subsequently agreed to abide by the ruling and entered into licensing agreements with major and independent labels, numerous other unauthorized peer-to-peer Web sites remained. It seemed unlikely that these could be closed down by legal action, and many experts doubted that downloading from these sites was any more damaging to soundcarrier sales than home taping had been in the 1980s.

Critiques of Copyright

The copyright system or aspects of it have come under attack from a range of sources. These include industries that use music in the provision of services (for example, broadcasters, restaurants, bars), governmental antitrust agencies, governments of developing nations, radical academics and some avant-garde musicians.

The academic and theoretical discussions of copyright tend toward a polarization between the apologists for copyright or intellectual property and those who subject it to a critique. Most apologists for copyright rely on justifications drawn from legal or economic discourse, while copyright's critics tend to rely on arguments from economics, aesthetics and politics.

From the viewpoint of conventional legal theory, intellectual property rights are a particular variant of the law of property – but one that is underpinned by a social utility: that giving creators property rights will stimulate the production of scientific knowledge and aesthetic and cultural artifacts.

The preamble to the US *Copyright Act* of 1909 has continued to be used as a touchstone in IPR matters – for example, in the highly influential 1995 report from the US government on Intellectual Property and the National Information Infrastructure (Lehman 1995). Quoting from the 1909 Act, the report states: 'The enactment of copyright legislation [is based upon] the ground that the welfare of the public will be served and the progress of science and useful arts will be promoted by securing to authors for limited periods the exclusive rights to their writings' (Part I, Section A.1).

This brief statement contains the key elements of the pro-copyright orthodoxy by claiming that a copyright monopoly is beneficial to society as a whole and to scientific and artistic 'progress' in particular. It also recognizes the most important limit on copyright – its temporal limit.

While the 1909 Act refers to 'authors' as the beneficiaries of copyright law, an important strand of opposition to the IPR system argues that it is no longer authors (as creative individuals) but media corporations that benefit. Bettig (1996), for example, writes that cultural goods are 'produced within the capitalist social structure of accumulation in order to make a profit. Copyright serves as the mechanism by which this creativity is financed, produced and privately appropriated' (204).

While Bettig is arguing from a proto-Marxist political economy standpoint, some orthodox 'free market' economists are equally critical of the monopoly dimension, which is accused of being inefficient and unable to suitably reward musicians (Taylor and Towse 1998). It has also been pointed out that the dependence of the future of intellectual production on guarantees of economic monopoly has seldom, if ever, been empirically demonstrated, but, rather, has been simply asserted. Indeed, the fact that intellectual production has occurred in societies that lacked a copyright system suggests that copyright protection is not an essential support for such production, but only a contingent one.

A second critique of copyright focuses on its philosophical dependence on the figure of the 'author.' Using poststructuralist ideas, this critique claims that artworks are not produced by sovereign creative individuals, but by a process of 'social authorship' (Toynbee 2001), and that modernist aesthetics have overthrown the concept of the Romantic author (Smiers 2000). A variation on this theme, typified by Barlow (1996), argues that contemporary technologies (in this case, the World Wide Web) make traditional ideas of authorship and ownership obsolete.

The issue of the protection of folklore, including traditional music, introduces a different critique of the author-centered character of the copyright system. Because such music cannot be attributed to a single author, it is often regarded as 'public domain' work, to be used free of charge. Here, though, some governments have modified the intellectual property system to ensure income for the tribal or ethnic group responsible for a folkloric work. Some African and Latin American states have introduced a 'paying public domain,' whereby users of such works pay royalties that are used for the general support of folk arts.

Conclusion

While copyright law is a generally coherent area of jurisprudence, copyright and other intellectual property systems have evolved as the result of pressures from a range of economic, cultural, technological and political factors. Within this complex evolution, music copyright has developed and been adapted in specific ways that cannot easily be regarded as an aspect of a general system.

Notwithstanding the force of the various general critiques of copyright and of the patents system as applied, for example, to plants and drugs (Shiva 1998), it can be argued that the music copyright system is, on balance, of economic benefit to many composers and performers, although it also benefits the transnational corporations that own or administer the majority of profitable copyrighted works and recordings.

Bibliography

Barlow, J.P. 1996 (1994). 'Selling Wine Without Bottles: The Economy of Mind on the Internet.' In *The Future of Copyright in a Digital Environment*, ed. P. Bernt Hugenholtz. The Hague: Kluwer, 169–89.

Bettig, Ronald V. 1996. *Copyrighting Culture: The Political Economy of Intellectual Property*. Boulder, CO: Westview Press.

Gaines, Jane M. 1992. *Contested Culture: The Image, the Voice, and the Law*. London: BFI Publishing.

Geller, Paul Edward. 1994. 'Must Copyright Be Forever Caught Between Marketplace and Authorship Norms?' In *Of Authors and Origins: Essays on Copyright Law*, ed. Brad Sherman and Alain Strowel. Oxford: Clarendon Press, 159–202.

Grosheide, F. Willem. 1994. 'Paradigms in Copyright Law.' In *Of Authors and Origins: Essays on Copyright Law*, ed. Brad Sherman and Alain Strowel. Oxford: Clarendon Press, 203–34.

Laing, Dave. 1993. 'Copyright and the International Music Industry.' In *Music and Copyright*, ed. Simon Frith. Edinburgh: Edinburgh University Press, 22–39.

Lehman, Bruce A., ed. 1995. *Intellectual Property and the National Information Infrastructure: The Report of the Working Group on Intellectual Property Rights*. Washington, DC: US Department of Commerce.

Shiva, Vandana. 1998. *Biopiracy: The Plunder of Nature and Knowledge*. London: Green Books.

Smiers, Joost. 2000. 'The Abolition of Copyright.' *Gazette – The International Journal for Communication Studies* 62(5) (October): 379–406.

Taylor, Millie, and Towse, Ruth. 1998. 'The Value of Performers' Rights: An Economic Approach.' *Media, Culture & Society* 20: 631–52.

Toynbee, Jason. 2001. 'Creating Problems: Social Authorship, Copyright and the Production of Culture.' *Pavis Paper No. 3*. Milton Keynes: Pavis Centre for Social and Cultural Research, The Open University.

DAVE LAING

Copyright Organizations

While copyright owners are granted exclusive rights to control the uses of their works, in most cases it is impractical for a single composer or recording artist to monitor each use by broadcasters, background music companies, concert promoters and others. The main function of copyright organizations is to act on behalf of the owners of copyrights in licensing the use of music and to collect the fees payable by the users to the owners. These organizations generally operate on a national basis, and by the late 1990s there were over 170 such bodies affiliated to the Confédération Internationale des Sociétés d'Auteurs et Compositeurs (CISAC), which was founded in 1926. These copyright organizations administer the rights of composers and music publishers. The collective administration of neighboring rights belonging to performers and producers (for example, recording artists and record companies) is less developed. However, there are more than 20 national bodies performing this function, mostly based in Europe.

History

Although a performing right for playwrights was acknowledged in France in 1777, the oldest national music copyright organization is the Société des Auteurs, Compositeurs et Editeurs de Musique (SACEM), founded in Paris in 1853. Its formation followed the success of a court case brought by several composers against a café whose orchestra performed the composers' works. The court ruled that the composers were entitled to payment when their works were played in public (Attali 1985, 77–81).

After the Berne Convention of 1886 had set an international benchmark for authors' rights, the pace of formation of new national organizations increased. Among those set up at the end of the nineteenth century and in the early years of the twentieth century were: Società Italiana degli Autori ed Editori (SIAE) (Italy, 1882); Sociedad General de Autores y Editores (SGAE) (Spain, 1889); Staatlich Genehmigte Gesellschaft der Autoren, Komponisten und Musikverlager (AKM) (Austria, 1897); Gesellschaft für Musikälische Aufführungs- und Mechanische Vervielfältigungsrechte (GEMA) (Germany, 1903); Het Bureau voor Muziek-Auteursrecht (BUMA) (The Netherlands, 1914); the Performing Right Society (PRS) (United Kingdom, 1914); the American Society of Composers, Authors and Publishers (ASCAP) (United States, 1917); Svenska Tonsättares Internationella Musikbyra (STIM) (Sweden, 1920); Société Belge des Auteurs, Compositeurs et Editeurs (SABAM) (Belgium, 1922); and the Australasian Performing Right Association (APRA) (1926).

The growing importance of piano rolls and gramophone records led to the collection of mechanical royalties from manufacturers of these items. In some countries, a new copyright body was set up to administer the mechanical rights of composers. The first of these were the Copyright Licences Company Ltd. and the Copyright Protection Society of the United Kingdom. Both were established in 1911, and in 1924 they amalgamated to become the Mechanical Copyright Protection Society (MCPS). Other mechanical rights bodies include the Nordisk Copyright Bureau (1915, based in Denmark but serving all Nordic countries), the Harry Fox Agency (United States, 1927), Stichting STEMRA (The Netherlands, 1936) and Austro-Mechana (Austria, 1946).

Although each European country has only one copyright organization, in the United States there are competing performing rights bodies. In 1930, the Society of European Stage Authors and Composers (SESAC) was founded in New York to collect royalties from US productions of European musical shows and operas. In 1941, US radio networks set up a direct competitor to ASCAP (Ryan 1985). Broadcast Music Inc. (BMI) capitalized on the dissatisfaction of country music, blues and jazz composers with ASCAP's restrictive admissions policy and soon established itself as the leading rights body in those fields, although both ASCAP and BMI have since gained members across all genres of music.

Copyright organizations were formed in the major Latin American nations in the early part of the twentieth century. While Sociedad Chilena del Derecho de Autor (SCD) in Chile, Sociedad de Autores y Compositores de Música (SACM) in Mexico and Sociedad Argentina de Autores y Compositores de Música (SADAIC) in Argentina have continued to function as monopolies, Brazil has several competing authors societies, although they operate as members of a federation, Escritório Central de Arrecadação e Distribuição (ECAD). In the smaller nations of Central America, however, copyright organizations were established with the help of CISAC only in the 1990s.

The first music copyright body in Africa was the South African Music Rights Organisation (SAMRO), established in 1962. This was followed in the 1980s and 1990s by many more, including those of Mali (1988), Malawi (1991) and Angola (1993). In Asia, the Japanese Society for Rights of Authors, Composers and Publishers (JASRAC) was set up in 1939, the Copyright Holders' Association (CHA) of Taiwan in 1976, the Composers and Authors Society of Hong Kong (CASH) in 1977, the Composers and Authors Society of Singapore (COMPASS) in 1987 and Yayasan Karya Cipta Indonesia (KCI) in 1990.

In the Soviet Union, Vsesojuznoje Agentstvo po Avtorskim Pravam (VAAP) was set up as a state-controlled agency to administer authors' rights. When Communist regimes were established in Eastern Europe, national authors societies such as Bureau Hongrois pour la Protection des Droits d'Auteur (ARTISJUS) (Hungary, 1907) and Stowarzyszenie Autorow (ZAIKS) (Poland, 1918) were set up. With the collapse of Communist rule, these societies reverted to the control of their members, while VAAP was replaced by the Russian Authors Organization (RAO) in 1993.

The Groupement Européen des Sociétés d'Auteurs et Compositeurs (GESAC) is a lobbying body made up of all authors societies in the European Union. It was formed in 1991.

Neighboring Rights Organizations

The performance rights in sound recordings of record companies and recording artists are enshrined in the Rome Convention of 1961. However, the first national organization to administer these rights – Phonographic Performance Ltd. (PPL) – was set up in Britain in 1934. In France, Administration des Droits des Artistes et Musiciens Interprètes (ADAMI) was set up in 1955 to represent named recording artists and actors, and in 1959 French session musicians created the Société de Perception et de Distribution des Droits des Artistes Interprètes de la Musique et de la Danse (SPEDIDAM). These two bodies, together with the representative associations of record companies, founded the Société civile pour la Perception de la Rémunération Equitable (SPRE) in 1986 to collect royalties on their behalf. The corresponding

Danish body, Gramex, was founded in 1963. A number of countries, notably the United States, have not joined the Rome Convention, and music users in these countries are not required to pay neighboring rights fees for the use of sound recordings. Because of this, a number of European countries operate a reciprocal treatment policy and do not pay performance royalties to US labels and artists, even when US music constitutes a large proportion of airplay.

With the increasing usage of music videos by television stations, the British record industry set up Video Performance Ltd. (VPL) in 1984 to collect fees for these uses. In most countries, however, the existing copyright body carries out this function.

Roles and Functions

The boards of each authors society are composed of publishers and authors elected from each constituency. In general, Anglo-American societies are governed by equal numbers from each category, but societies in continental Europe and Latin America have a majority of authors on their administrative boards. In Spain, SGAE has 36 authors and six publishers on its board. The boards of neighboring rights organizations usually contain both label executives and elected representatives of recording artists.

The organizations operate by issuing licenses to prospective music users. The licenses generally permit the use of the full repertoire of music administered by each organization in return for an agreed payment. A license may be a 'blanket' type, permitting the use of as much music as required, or a 'per-program' type, in which the user pays only for the exact amount of music used. These payments are derived from the tariff negotiated between the society and the music users, which are generally represented by a trade organization – of radio stations or of discothèques, for instance. When copyright organizations and music users cannot reach agreement, the terms of licenses are settled by government-appointed arbitrators. In general, performing right tariffs are settled by each national society, and therefore the rate of payment may vary considerably. For example, radio stations in Europe frequently pay about 5 percent of their advertising revenues in copyright fees, while the rate in the United States is less than 1 percent.

In contrast, the same mechanical royalty is payable by record companies in each country of continental Europe and Latin America. This standard contract has been renegotiated at regular intervals since 1933 by the International Federation of the Phonographic Industry (IFPI) on behalf of the record industry and the International Bureau of Societies Administering the Rights of Mechanical Recording and Reproduction (BIEM). In 1999, the standard rate was reduced from 9.306 percent to 9.009 percent of the 'published price to dealer' (PPD). In the United States, the equivalent phono-mechanical royalty rate is set by a government official, the Register of Copyrights, although the figure itself is initially negotiated between the Harry Fox Agency and the Recording Industry Association of America (RIAA).

Once royalties have been collected, copyright organizations must determine to whom the money should be distributed. To do this, they use either a census or a sample of the music used by the licensee. A census is a complete record of all music use. National public broadcasters and some concert promoters generally supply this. More commonly, copyright organizations take a sample by monitoring a small proportion of the music used by a licensee or category of licensees – for example, one day a month of programming by a local radio station. In cases where it is not possible to take a sample – for instance, where a small retailer uses radio broadcasts to entertain customers – the organization will distribute the royalties by using broadcast censuses, samples or sales chart information.

A key role of copyright organizations is to represent the interests of foreign composers and publishers. Through bilateral contracts and through membership of CISAC, each national society collects royalties for the use of foreign music and forwards these royalties to the relevant foreign societies while receiving payments for the use of its members' works elsewhere in the world. Through national copyright laws, governments may decide that foreign right owners should receive 'national treatment' (that is, all the rights accorded to domestic composers) or should be limited to 'reciprocal treatment' (that is, only those rights that they enjoy in their own country).

To facilitate the bilateral flow of royalties, copyright organizations, through CISAC, have developed a numbering system for musical works, and in 1994 CISAC agreed on a Common Information System program whose goal was to standardize the identification of musical works on a global basis so that music users and CISAC members could deal more efficiently with royalty payments and distributions in an on-line environment. An initial phase was the design of a central Music WorksNet database, which could be accessed by all CISAC members.

An important aspect of the work of copyright organizations is their spending on social security (such as pension schemes for members) and on support for the national music culture through subsidies for performances, recordings or other activities. Under CISAC rules, each organization may spend up to 10 percent of its income for these collective purposes.

Legal Restraints

While more than one copyright organization may operate in the same sphere of copyright collection and administration within one jurisdiction – as in the case of Brazil or the United States – the copyright organization as a form of social institution nonetheless operates as a monopoly: it is the only means by which composers can license their works and the only source of musical repertoire for broadcasters and other users. This situation has generally been accepted by governments and competition authorities, such as anti-monopoly agencies, since the collective administration of rights is of practical benefit to music users as well as to copyright owners (Davies 1989, 82). Nevertheless, many organizations are subject to strict national or international surveillance by competition authorities. The Italian copyright organization is unusual in that its most senior official is actually appointed by the government. In many countries, the power of copyright organizations has been limited by the imposition of a 'compulsory license' whereby an organization cannot deny the use of its repertoire to a music user that has offered payment.

On occasion, the activities of copyright organizations have been the subject of official investigations at the national or international level. A French discothèque operators association complained unsuccessfully to the European Commission that the fees charged by SACEM were high and should be reduced to the level in other European countries. However, broadcaster MTV was more successful in convincing the Commission that VPL was effectively a cartel, since over 50 percent of its videos were owned by only five record companies; consequently, each of these five major companies agreed to license MTV directly and not as part of the VPL-MTV contract.

Copyright organizations faced further challenges in the face of multimedia production and the growing use of music on the Internet. Governments were anxious that problems in clearing rights should not restrain the development of multimedia companies. In response, copyright organizations in several countries set up 'one-stop shops' to assist multimedia producers in situations where several different types of right owners (music, recording, photographic, audiovisual and so on) were involved. In the case of the Internet, most national copyright organizations had started to license Web site operators by the end of the 1990s.

Bibliography

Attali, Jacques. 1985 (1977). *Noise: The Political Economy of Music*. Minneapolis, MN: University of Minnesota Press.

Davies, G. 1989. 'The Public Interest in Collective Administration of Rights.' *Copyright* (March): 81–89.

Ehrlich, Cyril. 1989. *Harmonious Alliance: A History of the Performing Right Society*. Oxford: Oxford University Press.

Ryan, John. 1985. *The Production of Culture in the Music Industry: The ASCAP–BMI Controversy*. Lanham, MD: University Press of America.

World Intellectual Property Organization (WIPO). 1990. *Collective Administration of Copyright and Neighboring Rights*. Geneva: WIPO.

DAVE LAING

Counterfeit

A counterfeit soundcarrier is one made illegally to sound and look exactly like the legitimate product. There have been counterfeits manufactured of all recorded music formats – vinyl albums, music cassettes and compact discs (CDs). Because counterfeiters do not have access to master tapes, the sound quality of a counterfeit cassette or vinyl LP is generally inferior to that of the genuine product, but there is very little loss of quality when a counterfeit CD is digitally reproduced from a legitimately produced CD.

Small-scale counterfeit cassette operations are found in many countries because of the relatively low cost of duplication equipment, but illicit CD production is concentrated in Asian and Eastern European countries where the enforcement of copyright law is weak.

DAVE LAING

Geneva Convention

The Convention for the Protection of Producers of Phonograms Against the Unauthorized Duplication of their Phonograms was adopted at a conference convened in Geneva in 1971 by the United Nations Educational, Scientific and Cultural Organization (UNESCO) and the World Intellectual Property Organization (WIPO). Also known as the Geneva Convention or the Phonograms Convention, it was the result of increasing governmental awareness of the piracy of vinyl discs and cassette tapes. By signing the Convention, governments undertook to protect phonogram producers (i.e., record companies) of other signatory states against the manufacture, importation and distribution to the public of unauthorized copies of works owned by those producers. Signatory governments could take such action through the use of copyright law, unfair competition law or the introduction of penal sanctions.

By the late 1990s, 45 countries were members of the Geneva Convention, but in many ways it had been superseded by new international and bilateral trade agreements. The most notable of these was the World Trade Organization (WTO) treaty of 1993, which emerged from the General Agreement on Tariffs and Trade (GATT) talks. This global free trade agreement included a section on intellectual property (the TRIPS chapter) with an anti-piracy component. Unlike the Geneva Convention, TRIPS provides protection against piracy for recording artists, as well as for record companies.

Bibliography

Masouyé, Claude. 1981. *Guide to the Rome Convention and to the Phonograms Convention*. Geneva: World Intellectual Property Organization (WIPO).

Stewart, Stephen. 1989. *International Copyright and Neighbouring Rights*. 2nd ed. London: Butterworths.

DAVE LAING

Home Taping

'Home taping' refers to the practise of using a tape recorder to copy copyrighted works or recordings from broadcasts or sound or video recordings for domestic, noncommercial use. The legal term 'private copying' emphasizes the difference between this activity and that of piracy, where the purpose of the copying is commercial gain.

Although a small amount of home taping was undertaken by enthusiasts using reel-to-reel tape machines, the practise did not become widespread until the arrival of the compact cassette in the 1960s. Cassette recorders were easy to use and relatively cheap. By the early 1970s, music industry officials were expressing alarm at the scale of home taping, which they claimed was having a negative impact on the sales of discs and prerecorded tapes. This claim was supported by a number of market research surveys in various countries, which generally found that 80–90 percent of blank tape use was for private copying (Davies and Hung 1993). However, the record industry's claim that most acts of home taping represented lost sales was hotly contested by tape manufacturers and consumers' organizations. There followed in the United States and Britain an ineffectual campaign using the slogan 'Home Taping Is Killing Music,' with its misleading use of a skull-and-crossbones image, the symbol of piracy.

After some equally ineffective attempts to develop an inaudible 'spoiler' single for prerecorded products, the music industry's preferred solution to the home taping 'problem' was the imposition of a compensatory levy on the sales of blank cassettes and recording equipment. The levy would be distributed among the copyright owners whose works were presumed to have been copied.

Germany (1965) and Austria (1980) were the first countries to impose such a levy, which was applied in the video as well as in the audio sector. By the late 1990s,

10 other European countries had levies on tapes, machines, or both. However, the European Commission's proposal for a Europe-wide levy was vetoed by three European Union governments, and the falling prices of tapes and recorders caused levy revenues to decline in the 1990s. The division of royalties among the different categories of rights owners and (in some states) a general fund to subsidize music and film production varies from country to country. In Finland, two-thirds of the home taping levies go to a cultural fund, while Germany does not have such a fund. Excluding payments to cultural funds, the proportion of levies received by composers and songwriters is generally around half, with the record industry and recording artists sharing the remainder.

The announcement of the advent of a digital audio tape (DAT) by the consumer electronics industry in 1986 caused the music industry to predict a further escalation in the amount of home taping. When the major record companies refused to license repertoire for prerecorded DAT release, the electronics companies agreed to a scheme to limit digital copying by inserting a chip into their digital tape machines. This Serial Copy Management System (SCMS) invented by Philips permits one copy of a compact disc (CD) to be made, but prevents the 'cloning' of that copy.

The introduction of digital media such as the CD persuaded the US administration to introduce a hardware and software levy for digital-only copying through the *Audio Home Recording Act* of 1992.

By this time, the long shadow of the Internet had persuaded the international record industry to abandon the strategy of the licensing of home taping and to return to prohibition with the aid of new scrambler technologies whose circumvention would be made illegal in the next generation of copyright legislation.

Bibliography

Davies, Gillian, and Hung, Michele. 1993. *Private Copying of Music and Video*. London: Sweet and Maxwell.

Laing, Dave. 1993. 'Copyright and the International Music Industry.' In *Music and Copyright*, ed. Simon Frith. Edinburgh: Edinburgh University Press, 22–39.

DAVE LAING

Mechanical Right

The mechanical right is part of the copyright granted to composers and songwriters. It refers to the incorporation of a musical work into a 'mechanical' device such as a soundcarrier, film, or radio or television program. When copies of recordings of a work are sold, the composer is entitled to receive payment. Similarly, payment must be made when a song or instrumental piece is 'dubbed' or synchronized into a movie, a commercial or a program.

A third type of mechanical right has been recognized in some national copyright laws. This is the right to receive payment in respect of the 'private copying' of musical works.

The mechanical right was internationally recognized in the *Berlin Act* of the Berne Convention of 1908, during a period when the record industry had already established itself as an important new distributor of music. In recognition of the competitive needs of this new industry, the Convention permitted national copyright laws to impose a 'compulsory license' for the recording of musical works. This license prevented music publishers from limiting the recording of a song to one record company only. Typically, such a provision permitted any company to record a work without having to seek permission of the copyright owner as long as a royalty was paid. Germany, the United Kingdom and the United States were the first countries to introduce such a license.

Unlike royalty rates of recording artists (which vary according to the market power of the artist), the mechanical royalty payable on sales of soundcarriers is set by government agencies or by a central agreement between representatives of the record industry and the music publishing industry. The most important of these central agreements was first made in 1927, between the International Bureau of Societies Administering the Rights of Mechanical Recording and Reproduction (BIEM) and the International Federation of the Phonographic Industry (IFPI). The BIEM-IFPI standard contract covers most of continental Europe and Latin America and it has been renegotiated at regular intervals since 1927. In 1998, a new BIEM-IFPI agreement set the standard rate at just under 9.1 percent of the 'published price to dealer' (PPD) or wholesale price. This standard rate is varied by individual national agreements, which cover such matters as television-advertised albums and multitrack compilations.

In certain countries, there is a statutory royalty rate, set by a government agency. This is the case in Japan and Australia. The statutory system in the United Kingdom was abolished in 1988. The subsequent industry agreement set the standard mechanical royalty rate at 8.5 percent of PPD. In the United States, the phonomechanical royalty rate is set by a government official, the Register of Copyrights, although the figure itself is based on a rate negotiated between the record industry and the Harry Fox Agency, a company owned by the National Music Publishers Association. This rate is calculated not on the price of the soundcarrier (as in the United Kingdom and the BIEM-IFPI agreements), but on the quantity of music that a soundcarrier contains. Thus, the 1998 US rate was 6.95 cents per track, with increases every two years until 2006, when the rate will be 9.1 cents per track. Tracks of over five minutes in length are paid at a 'per-minute' rate. The US royalty levels are significantly lower than those set by the BIEM-IFPI contract.

In general, there are no standard rates of payment for the use of music in films, commercials and broadcast programs. In most cases, the fees for synchronization licenses are negotiated between the music user (film producer, advertising agency or broadcaster) and either the music publisher or a royalty collection agency such as the Harry Fox Agency.

Mechanical royalties for private copying take the form of a levy on the price of blank cassettes or minidiscs, recording hardware or both. Private copying is the legal term for home taping or home copying using compact-disc technology. And in the twenty-first century, it is likely that an increasing proportion of the mechanical royalties paid to songwriters will be derived from the digital delivery of recordings – for example, from the Internet to the hard discs of home computers.

DAVE LAING

Moral Right

The Berne Convention and other copyright legislation grant moral rights to a composer or songwriter. These include the right to decide whether or not to publish a work, the right to be credited as the author of a work and the right to preserve the integrity of a work (for example, when it is adapted, arranged or parodied).

These moral rights exist independently of any economic rights enjoyed by publishers and record companies, and the right to integrity has given rise to a number of lawsuits concerning parodies. In *Campbell v. Acuff-Rose Music* (1994), the publisher of Roy Orbison's 'Oh, Pretty Woman' attempted to stop the distribution of a rap version by 2 Live Crew, while the Danish group Diskofil was prevented from releasing a parody of the international hit 'Macarena' in 1996.

Bibliography

Bently, Lionel. 1994. 'Parody and the Difficult Question of Encouraging and Protecting Copyright.' *Music and Copyright* 42 (25 May): 11.

International Association of Entertainment Lawyers. 1993. *Enforcement of Copyright and Related Rights Affecting the Music Industry*. Apeldoorn: Maklu.

Discographical References

Orbison, Roy. 'Oh, Pretty Woman.' Monument 851. *1964*: USA.

2 Live Crew. 'Oh, Pretty Woman.' *As Clean As They Wanna Be*. Luke 91652-2. *1989*: USA.

DAVE LAING

Neighboring Rights

Neighboring rights (from the French *droits de voisins*) are those rights of ownership enjoyed by performers (including musicians) in recordings of their performances, record companies (producers) in sound and audiovisual recordings made by them and broadcasting organizations in their programs. Neighboring rights, which are also referred to as 'related rights,' are so called to distinguish them from the authors' rights codified in the Berne Convention.

The principal neighboring rights are those of reproduction of public performance. The reproduction right gives the owner of the right control over the copying of the recording or broadcast. This right is subject to a time limit, which is customarily 50 years from either the date of recording or the date of first publication. The public performance right concerns the use of recordings by broadcasters, retailers, jukebox operators and others. While the reproduction right gives the owner the power to authorize or prohibit the copying of a recording, the public performance right is generally one of 'equitable remuneration,' whereby a broadcaster or other user can use a recording without permission but must make a reasonable payment for its use.

Minimum international standards of neighboring rights were established by the Rome Convention of 1961, supplemented by the 1994 TRIPS section of the World Trade Organization treaty and the 1996 Treaty on the Rights of Performers and Phonogram Producers. However, varying national levels of protection have been in force since early in the twentieth century. In particular, the performance right was established in the United Kingdom in 1933, but was not introduced in France until 1985 and does not exist in the United States, where broadcasters do not pay royalties to record companies or recording artists.

Bibliography

Porter, Vincent. 1991. *Beyond the Berne Convention: Copyright, Broadcasting and the Single European Market*. London: John Libbey & Co.

Sterling, J.A.L. 1992. *Intellectual Property Rights in Sound Records, Film and Video: Protection of Phonographic and Cinematographic Recordings and Works in National and International Law*. London: Sweet and Maxwell.

DAVE LAING

Performing Right

The performing right is one of the most important aspects of copyright. All owners of copyright in musical works generally enjoy the right to authorize or prohibit the public performance of their work, whether in the form of a concert or through other means (such as broadcasting or background-music systems). A similar right is held by recording artists and their record companies in respect of the broadcasting or public performance of sound and video recordings.

Dramatists enjoy a performing right that has existed in France since the eighteenth century. This enables them to receive royalties when a theater stages their plays. A court case in Paris in 1851 established a similar right for popular songwriters, who would in future be entitled to payment when their works were performed in the presence of an audience (Attali 1985). Subsequent developments such as the player piano, sound recording and sound films, and radio and television broadcasting led to a comprehensive extension of the performing right for authors. By the end of the twentieth century, new legislation had been adopted that established the applicability of the performing right when music is transmitted or downloaded in cyberspace.

The minimum international standards for the performing rights of authors are contained in the Berne Convention, to which over 130 countries are signatories. Under Article 11(1) of the Convention, authors of musical works have 'the exclusive right of authorizing: (i) the public performance of their works, including such performance by any means or process; (ii) any communication to the public of the performance of their works.'

Performing rights for neighboring right owners, such as record companies and performers, were asserted only in 1934, when a British record company successfully won royalties from a restaurant that was entertaining its clientele with gramophone records. This right was eventually codified in the Rome Convention of 1961, and it broadly follows that granted to authors under the Berne Convention.

Pressure from broadcasters, afraid that copyright owners might deny them access to valuable programming material, caused the governments involved in drawing up the conventions to permit the use of 'non-voluntary' licenses by national governments. Such licenses grant broadcasters automatic access to all copyrighted music and sound recordings in return for the payment of 'equitable remuneration' to owners of the right. The amount of this remuneration is to be decided either by agreement between the parties or by an arbitrator appointed by the national government concerned.

The performing right is generally administered by a copyright organization on behalf of all members of each category of right owners. Some national copyright laws specify that such organizations must be licensed by a government agency. The copyright societies issue public performance licenses to many thousands of music users in each country. These users range from radio and television networks to concert promoters, discothèque owners, airlines and providers of music for telephone 'on-hold' services.

Bibliography

Attali, Jacques. 1985 (1977). *Noise: The Political Economy of Music*. Minneapolis, MN: University of Minnesota Press.

Porter, Vincent. 1991. *Beyond the Berne Convention: Copyright, Broadcasting and the Single European Market*. London: John Libbey & Co.

World Intellectual Property Organization (WIPO). 1990. *Collective Administration of Copyright and Neighboring Rights*. Geneva: WIPO.

DAVE LAING

Piracy

The terms 'piracy' and 'pirate' have been used in connection with copyright infringement since the eighteenth century. Within the music industry, there is a long history of piracy of printed music and of the unauthorized performance of operas and other works. In the second half of the twentieth century, this was overshadowed by the widespread piracy of sound recordings through the use of cassettes and compact discs (CDs).

Before recognition was made of the rights of authors to control the use of their work, the sale of printed music without payment to composers was widespread in Europe and elsewhere. During the nineteenth century, however, music publishers joined together to defeat sheet music piracy by bringing prosecutions and by successful lobbying for stricter copyright laws.

In the age of the soundcarrier, three types of pirate product have been defined. These are the counterfeit, which is identical in sound and visually with a legitimate release; the bootleg, which contains a concert recording, radio broadcast or studio outtake that has not been issued by a record company; and the pirate product, which does not resemble a legitimate release and is often a new but unauthorized compilation of previously released tracks.

Although there had been some cases of piracy of vinyl recordings, it was the relative low cost of and ease of copying allowed by cassette recording technology that provided the technological basis for the growth of a pirate music industry in the 1960s and 1970s. Piracy took a stranglehold over the recorded music markets of many countries in Asia, Africa and Latin America. By 1979, the International Federation of the Phonographic Industry (IFPI) was claiming that the music business was losing $1 billion a year to the pirates.

Diplomatic pressure contributed to the strengthening of national copyright laws and their enforcement in many countries during the 1980s and 1990s. But while cassette piracy seemed to have been contained, CD piracy began to flourish in former Communist states (notably Bulgaria and Russia) and in China.

With the growth in importance of the computer and information technology industries, the widespread copying of computer software gave added impetus to international campaigns against the piracy of intellectual property, including music and video. This resulted in the inclusion in the 1993 World Trade Organization (WTO) treaty of the TRIPS chapter dealing specifically with intellectual property protection. States wishing to benefit from the free-trade provisions of the WTO treaty are obliged to ensure their copyright laws reach a minimum international standard.

The threat of a new form of piracy on the Internet, where music files could be downloaded onto computer hard discs, was one motivation for the drafting of two new international copyright treaties in 1996. These treaties, established under the auspices of the World Intellectual Property Organization (WIPO), give copyright owners control over the distribution of their works in digital form, on the Internet and elsewhere.

Although the music industry is reluctant to admit the fact, piracy (like other forms of theft) is unlikely ever to be fully eradicated. In particular, bootlegging has become an aspect of fandom whereby ardent followers of certain artists collect unreleased concert recordings, a practise that has sometimes been condoned or encouraged by the artists themselves (Heylin 1994). Although numerous technical methods to prevent piracy have been proposed, it seems that any of these spoiler signals can be circumvented by a determined and skillful computer programmer. In some countries, record companies have embossed their soundcarriers with holograms to make counterfeiting more difficult. Such tactics, coupled with stronger penalties, can serve to dissuade many criminals from choosing music piracy as a profession and keep the cost of piracy to a manageable level of 5 or 10 percent of the world recorded music market.

Bibliography

Coover, James. 1985. *Music Publishing, Copyright and Piracy in Victorian England*. London and New York: Mansell.

Davies, Gillian. 1986. *Piracy of Phonograms*. London: ESC Publishing.

Gurnsey, John. 1995. *Copyright Theft*. Aldershot and Vermont: ASLIB Gower.

Heylin, Clinton. 1994. *The Great White Wonders: A History of Rock Bootlegs*. London: Viking.

Sanjek, Russell. 1988. *American Popular Music and Its Business: The First Four Hundred Years. Volume II: From 1790 to 1909*. New York and Oxford: Oxford University Press.

DAVE LAING

Public Domain

A composition, sound recording or broadcast enters the public domain once its period of copyright is completed.

At this point, the work is available for use without charge. The public domain system has important commercial implications for the music industry. The international standard copyright period for recordings is 50 years. This means, for example, that the first (1956) recordings of Elvis Presley enter the public domain in the year 2006. At that time, any record company will be able to reissue them without payment of royalties to the current owner of the copyright, BMG, and the Presley estate.

However, such a company will be required to pay a royalty to the composers of Presley songs because the period of copyright protection is much longer for songs and other compositions. In most Western countries, the heirs of composers and songwriters retain the copyright until 70 years after the death of the original creator. At present, the vast majority of works in the public domain are from the classical music sector. Their availability free of charge has greatly influenced the repertoire policies of record companies and promoters.

Problems can be caused when the period of copyright protection varies between nation-states. In Japan, until 1996, foreign recordings entered the public domain after only 25 years, which meant, for example, that for several years the recordings of the Beatles were free of copyright in that country. However, unauthorized Japanese releases of this repertoire would be illegal if exported to a country where Beatles albums remained under copyright.

DAVE LAING

Rental Right
Many national copyright laws include a specific statement that composers, record companies and recording artists can control the rental of their works. Prior to the introduction of such a rental right, significant compact disc (CD) rental businesses developed, notably in Japan and Germany. In the mid-1990s, Japan had over 5,000 stores renting CDs which, surveys showed, were copied by consumers before being returned to the stores. Rental is still permitted in Japan on payment of royalties to copyright owners, although foreign right owners are allowed to delay rental of their CDs for 12 months.

DAVE LAING

Rome Convention
The Rome Convention for the Protection of Performers, Producers of Phonograms and Broadcasting Organizations was the first international agreement to set minimum standards of protection for works created by owners of neighboring or related rights. The Convention was signed in 1961 after almost three decades of lobbying by actors' and musicians' organizations and by representatives of the radio and record industries.

Unlike the Berne Convention, the Rome agreement grants different levels of rights for three distinct interest groups. All three enjoy a minimum period of 20 years' protection for their works and all three can authorize or prohibit the copying of their works. However, this right is qualified for performers: they are unable to control any further uses of an audio or audiovisual recording once they have agreed that a recording can be made. This provision was included to allay the fears of both authors and record companies that performers might gain a veto on the commercial exploitation of recordings.

The rights granted to producers of phonograms under the Rome Convention are also limited. While record companies have full control over the manufacture and distribution of their recordings, they are unable to prevent the broadcasting of a recording once it has been commercially released. Instead, the broadcasting of recordings is subject to the payment of 'equitable remuneration' to record companies and performers, and countries joining the Rome Convention may disregard this provision.

Only about 40 countries had signed the Convention by 1996, when a further international treaty (the Performers and Producers Treaty) concerned with the rights of music performers and record producers was ratified at a conference convened by the World Intellectual Property Organization. This increased the duration of copyright protection to 50 years and began the process of granting protection against Internet piracy.

Bibliography
Alloway, Nicholas, ed. 1984. *50 Years of the International Federation of the Phonographic Industry*. London: IFPI.

DAVE LAING

Royalty
A royalty is a payment made to composers, recording artists and studio producers on the basis of the unit sales of works to which they contribute.

The royalty rate is generally expressed as a percentage of either the wholesale or the retail price of a sheet music, soundcarrier or audiovisual product. In most countries, a standard rate of mechanical royalties to be paid to all composers is set by industry-wide negotiations, although in the United States and Australia this rate is set by a government-appointed body. Other royalties are agreed through contracts between individual parties, such as record companies and recording artists, and between artists and their studio producers.

DAVE LAING

10. Deals and Contracts

Contracts

A contract in the music business, as in general business, is an agreement reached between two or more parties binding them to legally enforceable conduct.

Contracts concerning popular music allocate the various rights recognized under copyright statutes, including: the right to copy the work as in print or mechanical reproduction; the right to issue copies to the public; the right to perform, show or play the work in public; the right to broadcast the work or include it in a cable program service; and the right to make derivative versions, such as arrangements or foreign-language versions.

Examples of standard contractual relationships in music are: an exclusive artist recording services contract; an exclusive songwriter contract with a music publisher; a non-exclusive songwriter contract for one or more specified songs; a record producer contract for production services involved in one or more specific record projects, usually with specified artists; and concert performance contracts between musicians and booking agents or promoters.

The recipient of the services or product (recordings or songs) contracts to pay for them with a specific fee or with royalties based on the number of copies sold or manufactured. (Without this payment – which in contract law is referred to as 'consideration' – such agreements would not be contracts and would not be enforceable in law.) Royalties are payable in either quarterly, semi-annual or annual accounting periods, always with a delay for bookkeeping purposes of 30, 45, 60 or even 90 days before the accounting is completed and paid.

In nearly all music business contracts, there are general basic terms of negotiation that apply, including:

(a) geographic territory;

(b) duration of relationship in days, months, year or years or copyright term and option(s) to extend, if any;

(c) subject matter of contract, such as specified songs or masters and whether they are existent or future productions;

(d) services or functions to be performed by each of the contractual parties in the relationship; for example, songwriter and publisher, manager and artist, or any of the various parties involved in services of record production, manufacture and sale, record distribution, and concert production;

(e) manner of payment inclusive of advances and royalty provisions and time and manner of payment and audit rights.

Special provisions are frequently negotiated, resulting in 35 or more pages of legal provisions for a typical exclusive artist contract. Such extensive contracts will cover the essential basic terms, as well as highly sophisticated provisions such as rights to merchandise name and likeness (such as on souvenir T-shirts), royalties for adjustments for foreign, club, premium and so-called 'free' records distributed for sales promotional purposes and details of computation of royalty after deduction of an agreed 'packaging' allowance for the CD box and liner notes. Most US-origin contracts also treat full recording costs and at least part of video production costs expended by the record company as if they were monetary advances to be recouped from royalty payments. Other special provisions cover approved recording budgets or recording funds for stated minimum recordings; so-called 'controlled composition' provisions relating to reduced mechanical royalty obligations for recorded compositions owned or controlled by the artist; manner of computation of artist royalty, as well as reduction thereof from the agreed rate by whatever is paid to the record producer; special group member provisions, including how to deal with a 'leaving member' and replacement thereof; and specified court jurisdiction or arbitration agreements in the event of disputes, as well as waiver of claims for failure to assert them in a timely manner.

Special provisions for artist engagement contracts for concert appearances are usually set forth in an attached rider to standard printed contracts. Such provisions may include: restrictions on conflicting appearances within a stated geographic area and time period; option for a return engagement; artist requirements for sound and light facilities; and artist control over changes in manner of billing, advertising and accompanying or opening acts, as well as provisions for transportation of the artist to the site of a performance and lodging requirements.

Special provisions for an exclusive songwriter agreement will include: whether the writer is to be deemed an employee for hire or an independent contractor; obligation to participate in demonstration ('demo') recordings and the manner of payment of costs and recovery of all or part thereof as an advance against royalties; manner of promotional assistance, if any, and the charging of all or part thereof as an advance; the right to recapture inactive songs after expiration of the end of term upon repayment of demo costs incurred; approval of the publisher for collaborator assistance, inclusion or exclusion of songs written during the term for motion picture or jingle purposes; and agreed conditions required before proceeding with optional extension of the term, such as a stated monetary earning plateau or achievement of a major record label recording, specification of the minimum number of songs to be delivered during each term and whether such a qualifying song must be in demo form, released record form or major label released record form. Usually, the scheduling of advance royalty payments is tied into fulfillment of such conditions.

Bibliography

Krasilovsky, M. William, and Shemel, Sidney. 1994. *More About This Business of Music*. 5th ed. New York: Billboard Books.

Krasilovsky, M. William, and Shemel, Sidney. 1995. *This Business of Music*. 7th ed. New York: Billboard Books.

M. WILLIAM KRASILOVSKY

Lawsuits

Introduction

Since its inception in the eighteenth and nineteenth centuries, the music industry has expanded enormously, and music has come to be used in numerous ways, many of which were originally unforeseen. As the industry has developed and large amounts of money have become involved, the potential for disputes, and consequent lawsuits, has also increased. This situation has been neatly encapsulated in the business aphorism 'Where there's a hit there's a writ.' Furthermore, technological developments have provided additional areas, such as ownership and the use of copyright material, in which disputes can arise.

Types of Lawsuits

There are different types of lawsuit that may impinge on the music industry. There have been a number of cases, for example, involving the 'cult of celebrity.' These are lawsuits that have been unconnected to the music business itself, but that have gained notoriety and coverage because the litigants were high-profile entertainers. There have also been a number of legal cases involving merchandising and the rights to and of performers. For example, Elvis Presley's estate has been involved in a series of legal disputes regarding ownership of the rights to Elvis's image (see Wall 1996). Rights in personality are not universally recognized, and protection may be limited in those jurisdictions that do not specifically protect this right. Additionally, there has been a series of cases in the United States in which the imitation of a popular musician has led to litigation. The case of *Sinatra v. Goodyear Tire & Rubber Co. (1970)* is a prominent example of this 'sound-alike' phenomenon. Litigation ensued when an advertising agency hired a vocalist to imitate Nancy Sinatra. Although her suit was unsuccessful, the point was forcefully raised in argument that such a ploy could deceive the public and possibly constituted the tort of passing off (see, further, Gaines 1991, 107ff.). Interestingly, Bette Midler was able to prevent such an imitation, for an advertisement for Ford Motor cars, because of the unique nature of her voice (see Stone 1993). There have also been disputes (the number, though, is quite small) that involved other issues such as censorship (Cloonan 1996), backward masking and licensing. The areas that are primarily responsible for legal disputes within the music industry are, however, those of copyright and contracts.

Copyright

Initially, lawsuits involving issues of copyright were focused on plagiarism – the contention that a later artist had copied, in some form, the melody or lyrics of an original composition. This has been effectively dealt with by the copyright law of most countries, with certain acts deemed to be unlawful and protection provided against them. The problems have arisen primarily around the issue of substantiality and the difficulty of proving copying.

Copyright law broadly stipulates that, for the use of a

work to be unlawful, the portion used must be substantial, a measure that is largely subjective and difficult to define. Gauges used to establish this have been instituted, but there has been no one clear test. It is, however, safe to say that it is a matter of fact and degree and that there are some guiding principles that can be used, such as the amount and quality of the original material that has been utilized.

A major US case in this area that is worthy of mention concerned the George Harrison song 'My Sweet Lord.' Bright Tunes Music Corporation brought a copyright action against Harrison in February 1971, alleging that 'My Sweet Lord' infringed the copyright in the song 'He's So Fine,' which was composed by Ronald Mack. After attempts to settle failed, judgment was handed down for the plaintiff, on the basis that 'My Sweet Lord' was 'substantially similar' to 'He's So Fine' (*Bright Tunes Music Corp. v. Harrisongs Music Ltd., 420 F.Supp. 177 (S.D.N.Y.)*; see Biederman et al. 2001). Damages were later assessed at $1,599,987. This dispute continued into a second case: *ABKCO Music Inc. v. Harrisongs Music Ltd. 722 F.2D 990 (2D Cir. 1983)*.

A separate problem is caused by the need to prove that copying has occurred. Such proof is usually established with the guidance of the expert evidence of musicologists. The issue of subconscious copying arose in the United Kingdom in the case of *Francis Day & Hunter v. Bron [1963] Ch 587*, in which the Court of Appeal decreed that subconscious copying was a 'legal' possibility. Copyright law acts only to prevent unauthorized copying of protected material; independent creation of a similar work is not actionable, although if there are strong similarities between two pieces of work, a prima facie case of copying could be brought that might be difficult to disprove. A further debate has concerned the 'fair use' of musical works and, in particular, the use of parody. The rap group 2 Live Crew found that it was the subject of litigation when it utilized Roy Orbison's song 'Oh, Pretty Woman.' The case of *Campbell v. Acuff-Rose Music, Inc. [1994] 114 S.Ct 1164* represented a change of direction by the courts, in that it permitted a commercial parody to qualify as fair use of the copyright material. 2 Live Crew had always been prepared to pay a fee to use the original copyright material, but this had been rejected by the copyright owner, Acuff-Rose.

Issues of copyright have become more problematic as the music industry has begun to develop and utilize new technologies that allow for easier copying and dissemination of works. Sound sampling is a phenomenon that developed rapidly in the 1980s, as the hardware became cheaper and more readily available. At the end of the twentieth century, the law had yet to deal with sound sampling in any coherent fashion. In any event, it

seemed doubtful whether the law could provide any adequate solution that recognizes the conflicting interests at stake.

Copyright law provides excellent examples of the difficulty in applying existing legal principles to new areas of dispute. A prime instance is the copyright infringement involved in the private copying of a sound recording from one format to another – for example, from compact disc to cassette tape. Although a strict legal right, to prevent copying, may exist, it has been generally acknowledged that this is unenforceable and, accordingly, the debate has switched to compensation rather than enforcement. This led, toward the end of the twentieth century, to the introduction, in many European countries, of measures such as tape levies, in order to compensate copyright owners. The debate has been particularly apposite given the particular problems that were emerging with respect to the accessing and downloading of musical works via the Internet.

The use of the Internet to distribute musical works, in compressed MP3 format, has led to litigation to protect the rights of copyright owners. Attempts to limit the sale of MP3 playing hardware failed (*RIAA v. Diamond Multimedia Sys. Inc. 180 F.3d 1079*) and attention switched to Internet companies that were involved in facilitating the swapping of music files. The primary target of the litigation was Napster (*A&M Records Inc. v. Napster Inc. 114 F. Supp. 2d 869*). Behind the action were not only large record companies, but also artists such as Dr. Dre and Metallica. The case raised serious questions concerning the applicability of copyright protection to emerging technologies. The crucial issue went beyond the immediate case to the wider questions of the role and use of the Internet as a means of exchanging information and how the law can satisfactorily resolve the 'unauthorized' use of copyright material. What seems apparent, at least in the short term, is that companies wishing to offer facilities for exchange of copyright material will need to obtain permission in the form of a license. It is doubtful whether this is a suitable long-term solution, and there are problems with attempts to encrypt material. What is being witnessed is the most serious struggle to date between copyright holders and those who wish to use material freely, utilizing a democratizing technology. This battle has been previously fought over the use of 'new' hardware such as photocopiers, cassette players and video recorders. The lessons of the previous disputes suggest that copyright owners will have to accept the situation and adapt their business models accordingly.

Contracts

Initially, contracts within the music industry were fairly short documents encompassing issues of territory, duration and delivery. There were generally separate agreements covering publishing, recording and management issues. The complexity of such agreements has since increased to the point where recording and publishing contracts may be more than 100 pages long. They deal with a number of issues that have arisen as a result of lawsuits brought by disaffected artists attempting to free themselves from restrictive deals or by the industry itself attempting to enforce such agreements. Key litigation has included *Schroeder v. Macaulay [1974] 3 All ER 616* (enforceability of publishing agreements) and *ZTT Records v. Holly Johnson [1993] EMLR 61* (enforceability of recording agreements). The latter case involved the band Frankie Goes to Hollywood and the desire of its lead singer, Holly Johnson, to launch a solo career. Legal action reached its zenith with George Michael's attempt to free himself from his agreement with Sony, *Panayiotou v. Sony Music Entertainment (UK) Limited [1994] EMLR 229* (Greenfield and Osborn 1998). Garfield (1986) provides a useful and interesting history of such contractual disputes in the United Kingdom, and Biederman et al. (2001) provide an analysis of the position in the United States and of the prevailing legal vista. In this context, it is necessary to note the existence of different legal jurisdictions within the United States. The music industry in the United States has centered around New York, Nashville and California, each with a different approach to contractual enforcement.

It is undeniable that the various legal cases have affected music industry practise. Certain contractual conditions have been developed as a result of successful cases: for example, music publishing contracts may allow unused material to revert to the writer, a clear consequence of the decision in *Schroeder v. Macaulay [1974] 3 All ER 616*. Contracts try to anticipate potential legal problems – for example, by requiring artists to guarantee that recordings do not infringe any copyright and by providing an indemnity for the company. There has been a growing trend to try to avoid the courtroom by using methods of alternative dispute resolution (ADR). A good example has been the attempt by the United Kingdom's Music Publishers Association and the Mechanical Copyright Protection Society to set up a Sampling Disputes Panel to deal with problems of unauthorized sampling without recourse to the law. Some record companies have also tried to make the process of bargaining more open and the agreements themselves more transparent in an effort to keep relations between the two sides amicable and less likely to break down. Given wider trends within legal circles, which started toward the end of the twentieth century, it seems likely that this

tendency will continue, resulting in fewer potentially destructive and career-threatening lawsuits.

Bibliography

Biederman, Donald E., et al. 2001. *Law and Business of the Entertainment Industries*. 4th ed. New York: Praeger.

Cloonan, Martin. 1996. *Banned!: Censorship of Popular Music in Britain, 1967–92*. Aldershot: Arena.

Gaines, Jane. 1991. *Contested Culture: The Image, the Voice, and the Law*. Chapel Hill, NC: University of North Carolina Press.

Garfield, Simon. 1986. *Expensive Habits: The Dark Side of the Music Industry*. London: Faber & Faber.

Greenfield, Steve, and Osborn, Guy. 1998. *Contract and Control in the Entertainment Industry: Dancing on the Edge of Heaven*. Aldershot: Dartmouth.

Stone, Reuben. 1993. 'Plagiarism and Originality in Music: A Precarious Balance.' *Media Law and Practice* 14(2): 51.

Wall, David. 1996. 'Reconstructing the Soul of Elvis.' *International Journal of the Sociology of Law* 24: 117–43.

Discographical References

Chiffons, The. 'He's So Fine.' Laurie 3152. *1963*: USA.

Harrison, George. 'My Sweet Lord.' Apple R 5884. *1971*: UK.

Orbison, Roy. 'Oh, Pretty Woman.' Monument 851. *1964*: USA.

2 Live Crew. 'Oh, Pretty Woman.' *As Clean As They Wanna Be*. Luke 91652-2. *1989*: USA.

STEVE GREENFIELD and GUY OSBORN

Licensing

A license is generally a permission to use a musical copyright or master recording as granted by the owner or administrator of the rights to be licensed. It is less than a full assignment of all rights and is frequently for a limited duration, restricted geographic territory and specific media use.

An apt description of licensing as it applies to popular music can be found in Kohn's and Kohn's *The Art of Music Licensing* (1992, 750):

> (A) license is not a right – a right is a claim of ownership that allows you to exclude someone from doing something with respect to the subject of your property; a license is a permission or privilege to do something with respect to another's property that you would not otherwise have the privilege to do without the license.

Licenses can be exclusive or non-exclusive. An exclusive license gives the licensee sole use of a copyright for a particular purpose. In granting a non-exclusive license, the licensor reserves the right to grant a similar license to another licensee – for instance, to use a recording on a compilation album. Types of media use can be: mechanical licenses for recording purposes; master recording licenses; synchronization licenses for film and television purposes; printed media licenses, such as for sheet music, song folios, collections, band music and orchestral music; and, most important of all, performance licenses, as customarily issued by performing right societies such as the Performing Right Society (PRS) in the United Kingdom, and the American Society of Composers, Authors and Publishers (ASCAP) and Broadcast Music Inc. (BMI) in the United States.

License payments take the form of a flat fee or a royalty. A flat fee can be negotiated, as is customarily done for film and for video buyout purposes. A royalty rate can be negotiated either with or without an advance payable at stated times, such as upon execution of the license or, alternatively, upon commercial release of the recording; or a monetary guarantee can be assured, which means that, within a stated time, the royalties will not be less than the guaranteed amount.

Master recording licenses occur when an original owner of the sound recording copyright allows use of the master by another company, such as a record club or foreign label or an issuer of compilation recordings. The level of royalty paid by record clubs for a master recording is usually considerably lower than that of a licensee for foreign manufacture or for compilation issuance. This reduction is due to special circumstances such as unusual advertising costs and membership price incentives, as well as substantial advance monetary payments to the licensor.

Mechanical license royalties are paid by record companies to composers and publishers of songs that have been recorded. These royalties have a maximum rate set either by statutory license rate, as in the United States, or by industry-wide bargaining, as in Europe and Japan. As of 1998, European mechanical rates were 9.306 percent of the 'published price to dealer' (PPD), whereas US rates were up to $0.07 per five minutes or less of song duration (track) per unit.

In most countries, the mechanical license is a 'compulsory' license. This means that the copyright owner may not prevent further recordings of a song being made after the first recording of the song has been issued. This license is, of course, subject to the payment of appropriate mechanical royalties. In the United States, other compulsory licenses occur with regard to cable television, public broadcasting and jukebox performance fees.

Synchronization licenses concern the uses of music in motion picture and television films and in other situations, such as ice skating dance programs, in which the music is used in timed synchronization with visual action. No industry-wide license rate applies for such uses, which have widely varying negotiated rates.

In many countries, the most significant music licensing activity is that of composers' performing rights societies. Collective licensing of musical copyrights for performance rights, mechanical reproduction rights, and frequently synchronization rights as well, is handled by societies in each applicable country. These societies act as a general clearance agency for a large group of songs with a uniform system of collection and distribution of revenues, as well as furnishing an orderly supply of music to radio and television stations and to varied places of live entertainment. In many countries (but not the United States), owners of copyright in sound recordings also have performance rights, which are administered by societies representing recording companies and recording artists.

Merchandising rights represent a relatively new field of activity in the business of popular music. It entails the granting of rights to use the name and likeness of artists, such as on T-shirts, souvenir books, belt buckles, hair clips and numerous other mementos. In the United States, it is based on a recognized 'right of publicity' which, in turn, stems from an earlier recognition of a 'right to privacy' which, in the case of music business celebrities, seems a non sequitur. Right of publicity has been judicially determined to be a valuable right to trade upon the investment of goodwill and to control the manner of exploitation, as well as the financial returns thereof.

Bibliography

Kohn, Al, and Kohn, Bob. 1992. *The Art of Music Licensing*. New York: Aspen Publishers, Inc.

Krasilovsky, M. William, and Shemel, Sidney. 1994. *More About This Business of Music*. 5th ed. New York: Billboard Books.

Krasilovsky, M. William, and Shemel, Sidney. 1995. *This Business of Music*. 7th ed. New York: Billboard Books.

M. WILLIAM KRASILOVSKY

11. The Film Industry and Popular Music

The Film Industry and Popular Music

The US film and music industries were intertwined throughout the twentieth century. Film companies invested in music subsidiaries for several reasons, the most obvious being the control of the copyrights for music that appeared in films and the cross-promotional opportunities offered by a hit song or soundtrack album. Like many other 'synergies' available to the modern entertainment corporation, film and music cross-promotion helps to spread the enormous financial risks of film production across other divisions of a company and creates multiple profit centers from a single intellectual property.

Hollywood and the Music Publishing Business

Between 1910 and 1920, film and music cross-promotion generally operated at the level of exhibition. While, in these days of the silent movie, some theater owners publicized the unique skills of their film accompanists, others included song slides in their programs or employed singers to perform popular songs of the day. Many of these singers were provided by music publishers in the hope that such performances would increase sheet music sales. In exchange for the plug, the exhibitor typically sold copies of sheet music in the theater and retained a small percentage of the earnings. Through this reciprocal relationship, publishers gained greater exposure for their music while exhibitors attracted higher attendance and received the services of top-notch singers for little or no cost (Berg 1976).

The first attempt at coordinated cross-promotion occurred in 1918 when Marshall Neilan commissioned a title song for the film *Mickey* that went on to become an unlikely hit. 'Mickey' was written by Kansas City songwriter Charles N. Daniels, and its sales were boosted by the sheet music's featured photograph of the film's star, Mabel Normand, and advertising copy that highlighted her role in the film (Sanjek 1996). Throughout the second and third decades of the twentieth century, however, hits like 'Mickey' were more the exception than the rule. For years, the American Society of Composers, Authors and Publishers (ASCAP) haggled with theater owners over fees for the music used in silent film accompaniment, a conflict that effectively limited the use of Tin Pan Alley songs in film promotions. Exhibitors countered with lesser-known tunes and original compositions, many of which were provided by production companies and studios. Both factions reached a compromise in 1926 when some 11,000 theater owners became ASCAP licensees and paid more than $500,000 in fees, a figure that comprised about half of the association's income that year.

The coming of sound altered this balance of power, however, as film companies soon realized the need to end their dependence on ASCAP. Although Paramount and Loew's were the first to form their own publishing subsidiaries, it was Warner Brothers' purchase of M. Witmark & Sons that signaled Hollywood's more aggressive stance. Warner quickly added to its newly formed music division by investing in the Harms Music Publishing Company, the Remick Music Corporation and a host of smaller firms. By 1929, Warner's music division alone commanded a major share of the music publishers' vote in ASCAP policy-making. More important, within eight years the 13 houses affiliated with Hollywood were collecting nearly two-thirds of the monies distributed to publishers by ASCAP (Sanjek 1996).

Between 1930 and 1943, Hollywood's control of the music publishing industry gave rise to the film song's greatest period of success. During this period, studios produced dozens of movie musicals, many of them displaying the talents of the industry's top songwriters. Radio-Keith-Orpheum's Astaire-Rogers series alone featured songs by Irving Berlin, Jerome Kern, Cole Porter, and George and Ira Gershwin. Although movie musicals furnished the bulk of such tunes, popular songs also came from westerns, romances and melodramas. Through a combination of radio airplay and record sales, a hit song contributed to a film's popularity, thereby adding up to a million dollars to an individual film's box office gross.

During the 1940s, however, Peatman's surveys for radio indicated that the number of hits coming from Hollywood and Broadway declined from a high of 80 percent to a more modest total of 40 percent (Sanjek 1996). Despite occasional successes from films like *The Third Man* (1949) and *High Noon* (1952), sales and airplay of film songs gradually dwindled after World War II. In 1948, the Supreme Court handed down its decision in the landmark 'Paramount case,' the culmination of a 10-year battle with Hollywood over antitrust issues. To avoid further litigation, several film companies signed consent decrees in which they agreed to sell off their theater holdings, a move that effectively dissolved the studio system's vertically integrated structure. The Paramount decision initiated a trend toward diversification and conglomeration that encouraged studios to look for new cross-promotional outlets, including the burgeoning market for recorded music.

Hollywood and the Record Industry

Hollywood's relationship with the record industry dates back to 1930 when Warner Brothers bought the struggling Brunswick label to press both the discs used in their Vitaphone sound technology and recordings of songs that appeared in their films (Eyman 1997; Millard 1995). Warner's venture was short-lived, however, as the studio sold Brunswick to the American Record Company about a year later. After this initial dalliance, Hollywood had little involvement in the record industry until Metro-Goldwyn-Mayer (MGM) started up its own subsidiary in 1946.

The first albums of motion picture music were collections from musicals, such as *Snow White and the Seven Dwarfs* (1937), *The Wizard of Oz* (1939) and *Gulliver's Travels* (1939). In 1942, RCA-Victor released the first score album, a three-record set of music from *The Jungle Book* that included Miklós Rózsa's music as well as narration by the film's youthful star, Sabu (Karlin 1994). David O. Selznick followed this release with a series of score albums created to promote his films via radio. Selznick's assistant, Ted Wick, produced three such collections for *Since You Went Away* (1944), *Spellbound* (1945)

and *Duel in the Sun* (1946). These albums had small pressings and were mostly sent to disc jockeys, who not only played them but also announced the films' stars and show times (Smith 1998).

The event that most clearly indicated Hollywood's changing relationship with the record industry was Decca Records' acquisition of Universal Pictures in 1952. Throughout the rest of the decade, as the market for recorded music grew, so did Hollywood's interest in it. By 1959, all the major studios had either acquired or created their own record labels. Since most of these companies were start-up ventures, however, they generally lacked the stables of artists and repertoire found at major labels like Decca or RCA-Victor. As film subsidiaries, these new labels not only relied on their parent companies for financial backing, but also pursued different strategies to offset their shortage of talent. Warner Brothers, for example, contracted performers in niche markets and acquired existing labels to build up their A&R rosters. United Artists relied heavily on their film properties for their schedule of releases. Colpix and 20th Century-Fox, on the other hand, floundered throughout the early 1960s, developing only a handful of new artists and soundtrack hits.

Yet, many studios withstood their record subsidiaries' operating losses since they believed that they came out ahead in terms of basic promotion for their films. A theme song or soundtrack circulated the film's title among radio listeners; album covers and retail displays circulated the title among record buyers. Through such channels, film scores provided studios with millions of dollars in 'cuffo [free] promotion.' Moreover, these film-owned labels developed a myriad of new marketing techniques for soundtracks, including radio contests, sales-order screenings for disc jockeys and retailers, and even rack sales within theaters. Film companies employed these techniques to create several hits, such as *Exodus* (1960), *Breakfast at Tiffany's* (1961) and *Doctor Zhivago* (1965) (Smith 1998).

During the 1960s, film soundtracks gradually incorporated elements from rock, funk, soul and country music. In films like *The Graduate* (1967) and *Easy Rider* (1969), the scores themselves took on the form and structure of the typical pop album by packaging several tunes together to create commercially exploitable soundtracks. These compiled scores emerged as a new prototype for film scoring, one that was frequently exploited in youthpics and blaxploitation films, and by several directors in the 'New Hollywood.'

Despite the record industry's emergence as a billion-dollar business, the climate of 'profitless prosperity' and the trend toward market concentration prompted several studios to sell off their recorded music interests.

Dutch PolyGram, for example, bought MGM Records and took over United Artists' distribution system in the early 1970s. Later, Columbia Pictures and 20th Century-Fox sold their respective record subsidiaries to the Bertelsmann and Warner music groups. The only survivors of this shift toward conglomeration were MCA and the Warner Records Group, which by decade's end were among the six majors that accounted for more than 80 percent of the industry's total sales. Not coincidentally, their parent companies were also among a handful of media conglomerates that increasingly dominated the US and global entertainment markets. After Sony purchased CBS Records in January 1988 and Columbia Pictures in September 1989, it joined MCA and Warner Communications as one of only three companies to enjoy major status for both their film and recorded music divisions. Another major, EMI, had significant film interests in the 1970s, although nothing comparable to the six Hollywood majors that dominated film distribution.

Following the success of *Saturday Night Fever* in 1977, the soundtrack album once again surfaced as an important tool of film and music cross-promotion. By the beginning of the 1980s, there was a general industry consensus regarding the necessary ingredients for a hit soundtrack. These included commercially viable music, a hit film, a hit theme song, a 'big-name' recording artist, and advance planning on release schedules for both film and album. With MTV's emergence as a popular cable station, producers also began exploring the use of music videos as cross-promotional tools. Music videos offered certain marketing advantages in that they featured actual footage from the film and gave potential audiences a better idea of its stars, genre and visual style. Paramount innovated the use of 'music trailers' on *Flashdance* (1983) and soon followed with successful campaigns for *Footloose* (1984), *Beverly Hills Cop* (1984) and *Top Gun* (1986).

Between 1987 and 1999, annual sales of soundtrack albums quadrupled, with synchronization and master licensing fees rising at a comparable rate. The remarkable growth of this market made soundtracks increasingly important as both commodities and marketing tools. Indeed, this period featured two of the most successful soundtrack albums of all time, Whitney Houston's *The Bodyguard* and James Horner's *Titanic*. At the same time, however, rising costs forced many filmmakers to sell their soundtrack rights in exchange for monies to cover their music budgets. The combination of these factors encouraged a number of large music conglomerates to start up specialized soundtrack divisions to handle this small, but significant, market. The 1990s also saw the emergence of several new start-up ventures and distribu-

tion arrangements among both large and small film companies, many of them meeting with mixed success. Disney, for example, established its Hollywood Records subsidiary in order to give the company a music arm, but by the end of the 1990s had failed to develop any new recording stars and had had few hits aside from soundtracks like that for *The Lion King* (1994). Similarly, with its own music division faltering, Miramax signed a three-year deal with Capitol Records for distribution of soundtracks for its upcoming films. Finally, some record companies ventured into film production in order to hedge their financial risks and to avoid being engulfed by ever larger entertainment corporations. During the mid-1990s, for example, PolyGram invested about half a billion dollars a year in smaller companies like October Films and Gramercy Pictures. The reasons behind this diversification were simple: as PolyGram chief, Alain Levy, put it, 'If you're complacent you will die or be gobbled up' (Sterngold 1995). PolyGram's film ventures helped the company avert a takeover until it was purchased by Seagram in 1998.

International Perspectives

In addition to Hollywood, popular music has contributed much to the histories and cultures of several other national cinemas. Argentinian tangos, Brazilian sambas and Indonesian *dangdut* have all been popularized by the film musicals of their respective countries. Likewise, soundtracks have also played an important role in both foreign and global markets. During the 1960s, for example, Italy produced hundreds of soundtracks each year, often simply reproducing a film's soundtrack on vinyl, sound effects and all. By 1974, music publishers estimated that film music accounted for about 30 percent of the entire Italian record industry.

By far the most important foreign market for soundtracks, however, is India. India is not only the world's largest film producer in terms of annual output, but its film music is an essential component of the country's mass culture. As the single largest category of popular music in South Asia, Hindi film songs dominate the market in India, accounting for up to 70 percent of the country's total record sales and radio airplay (Arnold 1991). Moreover, film music is also heard in a variety of other contexts. Film songs comprise a large part of courtesans' repertoires in India's urban red-light districts. Puppeteers, snake charmers and regional folk musicians all incorporate film music melodies into their performances. Finally, Hindi film songs are routinely performed at a variety of social gatherings and religious ceremonies, such as festivals, weddings and funerals.

Given the sheer volume of production and the absence of competing popular music traditions, Hindi film song quickly emerged as a staple commodity of the film and music industries. Following the success of India's first 'talkie,' *Alam Ara* (1931), musical interludes became a common feature of the 2,500 sound films made in India before 1945. Moreover, since the average film featured between six and 10 songs, India's film industry was literally churning out several hundred songs each year. Many of these songs were distributed on record by Gramco (the Gramophone Company – His Master's Voice), which exerted a virtual monopoly over the Indian record industry until Polydor entered the scene in the late 1960s.

During the first decade of sound film production, Hindi film songs borrowed melodies from existing stage material or from other light classical music, and employed conventional song structures, such as *ghazal* and *qawwālī* (Arnold 1992). The orchestras for Hindi film songs were generally small and consisted mostly of instruments associated with North Indian classical music, such as the sitar, tabla, harmonium, violin and sarod (Skilman 1986). As time passed, however, music directors at regional studios began to broaden the style of film songs by incorporating Western instrumentation and by absorbing certain regional influences, particularly those associated with Punjabi and Gunerati folk musics.

During the late 1930s, the implementation of a play-back technique brought several changes to Indian film production. The technique involved the prerecording of film songs so that actors could simply mime their performance as the music was 'played back' during shooting. Although actors initially sang their own songs after the technique was introduced, this practise was gradually replaced by the use of specialized playback singers, whose fame sometimes exceeded that of their on-screen counterparts. Playback singer Lata Mangeshkar, for example, became the industry's preeminent female vocalist by making more than 30,000 recordings for some 2,000 films between 1948 and 1984.

After World War II, the Indian Censor Board became concerned with the increasing 'Westernization' of film songs and sought to limit the Western influence by placing restrictions on the amount of broadcast time film songs received on All India Radio. Such regulations proved largely ineffective, however, as audiences simply switched to Radio Ceylon or Radio Goa to hear the latest in film music. Foreign influences continued to color the development of Hindi film song throughout the 1950s, 1960s and 1970s, as Indian composers increasingly utilized elements from Latin American pop, US rock 'n' roll, European classical music and disco. Yet, despite such borrowing, Hindi film song has remained an extremely syncretic form, one that has assimilated elements of many foreign and regional musics, but has continued to be essentially 'Indian' at its core. As a national music, Hindi film songs reflect the dynamism of Indian culture by providing an interface between West and East, villages and cities, modernity and tradition.

Bibliography

Altman, Rick. 1987. *The American Film Musical.* Bloomington, IN: Indiana University Press.

Arnold, Alison E. 1988. 'Popular Film Song in India: A Case of Mass-Market Musical Eclecticism.' *Popular Music* 7(2): 177–88.

Arnold, Alison E. 1991. *Hindi Filmī Gīt: On the History of Commercial Indian Popular Music.* Ph.D. thesis, University of Illinois at Urbana-Champaign.

Arnold, Alison E. 1992. 'Aspects of Production and Consumption in the Popular Hindi Film Song Industry.' *Asian Music* 24(1) (Fall/Winter): 122–34.

Arora, V.N. 1986. 'Popular Songs in Hindi Films.' *Journal of Popular Culture* 20(2): 143–66.

Berg, Charles Merrell. 1976. *An Investigation of the Motives for and the Realization of Music to Accompany the American Silent Film, 1896–1927.* New York: Arno Press.

Burnett, Robert. 1996. *The Global Jukebox: The International Music Industry.* London: Routledge.

Darby, William, and Du Bois, Jack. 1991. *American Film Music: Major Composers, Techniques, Trends, 1915–1990.* Jefferson, NC: McFarland and Company, Inc.

Denisoff, R. Serge, and Romanowski, William D. 1991. *Risky Business: Rock in Film.* New Brunswick, NJ: Transaction Books.

Doty, Alexander. 1988. 'Music Sells Movies: (Re)New(ed) Conservatism in Film Marketing.' *Wide Angle* 10(2): 70–79.

Eyman, Scott. 1997. *The Speed of Sound: Hollywood and the Talkie Revolution, 1926–1930.* New York: Simon and Schuster.

Gomery, Douglas. 1986. *The Hollywood Studio System.* New York: St. Martin's Press.

Gorbman, Claudia. 1987. *Unheard Melodies: Narrative Film Music.* Bloomington, IN: Indiana University Press.

Joshi, G.N. 1988. 'A Concise History of the Phonographic Industry in India.' *Popular Music* 7(2): 147–56.

Kalinak, Kathryn. 1992. *Settling the Score: Music in the Classical Hollywood Film.* Madison, WI: University of Wisconsin Press.

Karlin, Fred. 1994. *Listening to Movies: The Film Lover's Guide to Film Music.* New York: Schirmer Books.

Manuel, Peter. 1988. 'Popular Music in India: 1901–86.' *Popular Music* 7(2): 157–76.

Marks, Martin. 1997. *Music and the Silent Film: Contexts and Case Studies, 1895–1924.* New York: Oxford University Press.

Millard, Andre J. 1995. *America on Record: A History of Recorded Sound*. Cambridge: Cambridge University Press.

Prendergast, Roy. 1992 (1976). *Film Music: A Neglected Art*. New York: W.W. Norton & Company.

Romney, Jonathan, and Wootton, Adrian, eds. 1995. *The Celluloid Jukebox: Popular Music and the Movies Since the 50s*. London: The British Film Institute.

Sanjek, Russell. 1996. *Pennies from Heaven: The American Popular Music Business in the Twentieth Century* (Updated by David Sanjek). New York: Da Capo Press.

Skilman, Teri. 1986. 'The Bombay Film Song Genre: A Historical Survey.' *Yearbook for Traditional Music* 18: 133–44.

Smith, Jeff. 1998. *The Sounds of Commerce: Marketing Popular Film Music*. New York: Columbia University Press.

Sterngold, James. 1995. 'PolyGram Has Eyes for Hollywood.' *New York Times* (10 July): D1, D8.

Thomas, Tony. 1991. *Film Score: The Art and Craft of Movie Music*. Burbank, CA: Riverwood Press.

Wasko, Janet. 1995. *Hollywood in the Information Age*. Austin, TX: University of Texas Press.

Sheet Music

Moret, Neil (aka Daniels, Charles N.), comp. and lyr. 1918. 'Mickey (Pretty Mickey).' Kansas City, KS: Charles N. Daniels.

Discographical References

Bee Gees, The. *Saturday Night Fever*. RSO 2658123. *1977*: USA.

Breakfast at Tiffany's. RCA Lpm-2362. *1961*: USA.

Doctor Zhivago (Original soundtrack). Rhino 71957. *1995*: USA.

Duel in the Sun (Original soundtrack). Unicorn-Kanchana UKCD 2011. 1946: UK.

Easy Rider (Original soundtrack). Alex 3594. *1993*: USA.

Exodus. RCA 1058-2-R. *1986*: USA.

The Film Music of Miklós Rózsa, Spellbound/The Jungle Book. Flapper Records PASTCD 7093. *1996*: UK.

Gulliver's Travels (Original soundtrack). RCA 68475. *1996*: USA.

Houston, Whitney. *The Bodyguard*. Arista-BMG 18699. *1992*: USA.

The Jungle Book, (Original soundtrack). Milan 35711. *1994*: USA.

Karas, Anton. 'The Third Man Theme.' London 536. *1950*: UK. Reissue: Karas, Anton. 'The Third Man Theme.' *Cinema 100: The Official Cinema 100 Album*. EMI Premier PRDFCD1. *1996*: UK.

The Lion King, Disney 60858-2. *1994*: USA.

Ritter, Tex. 'High Noon.' *High Noon*. Bear Family 15634. 1952; *1992*: Germany.

Simon, Paul, and Garfunkel, Art. *The Graduate*. Columbia 3180. *1968*: USA.

Since You Went Away (Original soundtrack). Tsunami Records TSU 0133. 1944: Germany.

Snow White and the Seven Dwarfs (Original soundtrack). Disney 60850. *1993*: USA.

Spellbound and Other Film Music. Varèse Sarabande 47226. 1945: USA.

Titanic (Original soundtrack). Sony Classical 63213. *1997*: USA.

The Wizard of Oz, (Original soundtrack). Rhino 71964. *1995*: USA.

Filmography

Beverly Hills Cop, dir. Martin Brest. 1984. USA. 105 mins. Action Comedy. Original music by Harold Faltermeyer.

The Bodyguard, dir. Mick Jackson. 1992. USA. 130 mins. Melodrama. Original music by David Foster, Jud Friedman, Alan Silvestri.

Breakfast at Tiffany's, dir. Blake Edwards. 1961. USA. 114 mins. Romantic Comedy. Original music by Henry Mancini.

Doctor Zhivago, dir. David Lean. 1965. USA/UK. 197 mins. Romantic Epic. Original music by Maurice Jarre.

Duel in the Sun, dir. King Vidor, Otto Brower, William Dieterle, Sidney Franklin, William Cameron Menzies, and Josef von Sternberg. 1946. USA/UK. 130 mins. Western. Original music by Dimitri Tiomkin.

Easy Rider, dir. Dennis Hopper. 1969. USA. 94 mins. Adventure Drama. Songs written by David A. Axelrod, Hoyt Axton, Antonia Durzen, Bob Dylan, Gerry Goffin, Jimi Hendrix, Jack Keller, Carol King, Roger McGuinn, Larry Waner.

Exodus, dir. Otto Preminger. 1960. USA. 208 mins. War Docudrama. Original music by Ernest Gold.

Flashdance, dir. Adrian Lyne. 1983. USA. 96 mins. Musical Drama. Original music by Dennis Matkosky, Giorgio Moroder, Michael Sembello.

Footloose, dir. Herbert Ross. 1984. USA. 107 mins. Drama. Original music by Miles Goodman, Kenny Loggins, Dean Pitchford, Tom Snow.

The Graduate, dir. Mike Nichols. 1967. USA. 106 mins. Comedy. Original music by Dave Grusin, Paul Simon.

Gulliver's Travels, dir. Dave Fleischer, Willard Bowsky, Orestes Calpini, Roland Crandall, William Henning, Winfield Hoskins, Thomas Johnson, Frank Kelling, Seymour Kneitel, Robert G. Leffingwell, Grim Natwick, and Tom Palmer. 1939. USA. 74 mins. Animated Comedy. Original music by Ralph Rainger, Sammy Timberg, Victor Young.

High Noon, dir. Fred Zinnemann. 1952. USA. 85 mins. Western. Original music by Dimitri Tiomkin.

The Jungle Book, dir. Zoltan Korda. 1942. USA/UK. 109 mins. Adventure. Original music by Miklós Rózsa.

The Lion King, dir. Roger Allers and Robert Minkoff. 1994. USA. 87 mins. Animated Musical. Original music by Elton John, Hans Zimmer.

Mickey, dir. F. Richard Jones, Mack Sennett and James Young. 1918. USA. 105 mins. Comedy.

Saturday Night Fever, dir. John Badham. 1977. USA. 119 mins. Musical Drama. Original music by Barry Gibb, Maurice Gibb, Robin Gibb, Barry Robin, David Shire.

Since You Went Away, dir. John Cromwell. 1944. USA. 172 mins. War Drama. Original music by Louis Forbes, Max Steiner.

Snow White and the Seven Dwarfs, dir. David Hand, Dorothy Ann Blank, William Cottrell, Richard Creedon, Merrill de Maris, Walt Disney, Wilfred Jackson, Larry Morey, Perce Pearce, Dick Richard, Ben Sharpsteen and Webb Smith. 1937. USA. 83 mins. Animated Musical.

Original music by Frank Churchill, Leigh Harline, Larry Morey, Paul J. Smith.

Spellbound, dir. Alfred Hitchcock. 1945. USA. 111 mins. Romantic Mystery. Original music by Miklós Rózsa.

The Third Man, dir. Carol Reed. 1949. UK. 104 mins. Mystery. Original music by Anton Karas.

Titanic, dir. James Cameron. 1997. USA. 195 mins. Romantic Epic. Original music by James Horner.

Top Gun, dir. Tony Scott. 1986. USA. 109 mins. Action Drama. Original music by Harold Faltermeyer, Giorgio Moroder.

The Wizard of Oz, dir. Victor Fleming, George Cukor, Norman Taurog, Richard Thorpe and King Vidor. 1939. USA. 101 mins. Musical Fantasy. Original music by Harold Arlen, George Bassman, George Stoll, Herbert Stothart, Robert W. Stringer; additional music by Felix Mendelssohn-Bartholdy, Modest Moussorgsky, Nikolai Rimsky-Korsakov, Robert Schumann.

JEFF SMITH

12. Hardware

Acetate

An acetate was a disc recording often made at a recording studio directly from master tapes, and was relatively inexpensive and easy to produce. The grooves on an acetate were made on a cutting lathe in a process similar to that used in producing a master lacquer in commercial record production. Acetates were often used by producers, especially during the 1960s, to evaluate how a vinyl pressing would eventually sound, thus allowing recording engineers to make modifications in a mix before submitting it for mastering. Acetates were also used by recording studios for demo purposes; however, because the material is softer than conventional vinyl, it could not withstand the same number of repeated playings. Acetates of tracks by the Beatles and others have become collectors' items and are often sold at auctions of pop memorabilia.

PAUL THÉBERGE

Amplifier

An amplifier is a device that increases the power of an electrical signal. Amplifiers are essential to electronic methods of audio production and reproduction. For example, pre-amps are required to boost the tiny electrical signals produced by microphones, guitar pickups or the stylus of a turntable as they enter an audio system; and large power amps, supplying hundreds and thousands of watts, are necessary to power speaker systems in the home, in the recording studio, on stage and in clubs.

The development of the 'Audion Tube' by Lee DeForest in 1904 laid the basis for amplification, radio broadcasting and other electrical technologies of the early twentieth century. The power-handling capacity of amplifiers was further developed during the late 1920s and early 1930s to meet the needs of public-address systems and cinema exhibitions. But since the 1950s, amplification has become more than a technical necessity; it has become a crucial element in the evolution of the sound of popular music. From the outset, rock 'n' roll established itself as loud, raucous music by virtue of its emphasis on the sound of amplified electric guitars; in the decades that followed, rock became synonymous with both volume and distortion. When an amplifier is pushed beyond its normal capacities, the electronic components become overdriven, resulting in a brighter sound, rich in harmonic content unrelated to the original sound source. Walser has argued that the sound of amplified guitar distortion has become a key aural sign of heavy metal and hard rock genres and an important signifier of power and emotional intensity in the music (1993, 41–45).

Even when tube amplifiers are not overdriven, however, they have a distinct sound, valued by many musicians and engineers, that is difficult to reproduce through other means. Decades after the introduction of solid-state transistors, vacuum tube (or 'valve') amplifiers and other audio devices have continued to be manufactured. Manufacturers of digital technology have even attempted to simulate, in software form, the particular distortion characteristics, buzz and 'warmth' of tube amplifiers in order to cash in on the 'retro' aesthetic prevalent in various genres of pop music.

Since its introduction during the 1950s, however, amplification through transistor circuitry has lent itself to the economies of both power and miniaturization, making it possible to meet the acoustic demands of public venues such as dance clubs and sports stadia, on the one hand, and of the more intimate spaces created by automobiles, portable transistor radios and Sony

Walkmans, on the other. 'Power,' in this instance, is both a description of a physical phenomenon and a cultural value, for it is only through the application of electrical amplification to loudspeakers (or headphones) that both public and private spaces can be invested with a musical intensity unprecedented in cultural history. High-capacity amplifier and loudspeaker systems, in particular, have become part of the technical infrastructure of modern live performance and dance music culture. As such, they must be considered part of a complex social technology, facilitating the coming together of ever-larger crowds for popular music, and thus supporting the needs of both fans and the music industry.

Bibliography

Walser, Robert. 1993. *Running with the Devil: Power, Gender, and Madness in Heavy Metal Music*. Hanover, NH: Wesleyan University Press.

PAUL THÉBERGE

Cassette

'Cassette' is the generic term for any magazine or cartridge holding an audiotape or videotape, but is more specifically applied to the audiotape format introduced by Philips at the 1963 Berlin Radio Show. The sound quality potential of the new compact cassette was underplayed at the launch, and the model EL3300 portable recorder given free to visiting journalists was described as being suitable only for speech recording. However, the medium soon grew in importance and took a leading position in the home entertainment market.

Philips had chosen the slowest tape speed then available, 1 7/8" (4.76 cm) per second, a quarter-track format and a new narrower tape width of 0.15" (3.8 mm). The cassette was much more user-friendly than the open reel-to-reel tapes then in use. The small case (4" × 2.5" × 0.5" (100.4 × 63.8 × 12 mm)) not only protected the tape, but relieved the user of the need to thread the loose end into an empty 'take-up' reel prior to use. A sensible layout of the four tracks, for the two stereo 'sides,' made mono and stereo tapes and machines totally compatible. Unlike the various open-reel media previously available, which interleaved the pairs of stereo tracks, the new left/right tracks were placed side by side, occupying the same space as a half-track mono recording so that any cassette could be played on any machine.

Philips licensed other manufacturers all over the world to build cassette machines and market blank and prerecorded cassettes free of royalty charges. This helped the new medium to spread quickly, but Philips took care to insist on strict compliance with its dimensional, electronic and magnetic specifications to preserve the medium's integrity.

Over the years, many improvements were introduced.

Tape quality greatly improved: the base film and ferric magnetic coating were refined, and better high-performance tapes using chromium dioxide (chrome), then metal particle coatings, raised standards overall. Blank cassettes are sold with a choice of playing times, as indicated by their type numbers: C-60 and C-90 cassettes, for example, run for 30 and 45 minutes per side, respectively. Dolby noise reduction is one improvement that deserves special mention, as it has progressively reduced one of the worst features of a tape: the continuous hiss caused by the granular nature of the magnetic coating. Dolby B (1970) gives about 10 dB noise reduction, while the later Dolby C and Dolby S systems reduce noise almost to inaudibility.

The record industry did not rush to introduce prerecorded 'musicassettes.' But in 1966, when cassette decks and portables had sold in reasonable numbers, and the sound quality had begun to approach acceptable standards for music reproduction, Philips and EMI started to issue stereo cassettes in parallel with their LPs, and the other record labels soon followed.

The popularity of cassettes was given a boost in July 1979 when Sony introduced its 'Walkman' lightweight portable player with plug-in headphones (originally called the 'Stowaway'). Worldwide sales rose rapidly and eventually overtook those of LPs. Philips launched a digital version of the cassette in 1992 with superior sound quality and capabilities, but it was relatively expensive and did not succeed.

Sharing the same universal popularity as the audiocassette, but in the world of video, is the VHS videocassette. This too is relatively inexpensive and, though of lesser quality than the rival video disc media, has been installed in many homes for off-air television recording and for playing rented or 'sell through' commercial videos.

Bibliography

Borwick, John. 1994. *Sound Recording Practice*. 4th ed. Oxford: Oxford University Press.

JOHN BORWICK

Cassette Recorder

The tape cassette recorder has become the most widely used medium for home sound recording and, indeed, for listening to prerecorded music at home, in the car or on the move (rivaled only toward the end of the twentieth century by the compact disc). Philips launched the cassette in 1963, along with a battery-operated portable recorder. This demonstrated the compactness of the medium, but did not fully exploit its potential for high-quality performance.

First developments were in mains-operated models designed to plug into a home hi-fi system, and a series of technical improvements soon followed, such as Dolby noise reduction. The simple numbers 'counter' was replaced in the better machines by a 'real-time' indicator, giving a more helpful cue to tape position. Automatic search of individual recorded items on the tape used a fast-wind system that located gaps of more than four seconds between items and entered directly into the 'Play' mode.

Then came auto-reverse models: they played, or recorded, Side 2 from the end of Side 1 almost instantly, by flipping over either the tape head or the cassette itself before beginning to run in the reverse direction. Another development was the twin-cassette machine with a pair of drives side by side, either to provide almost continuous playback or recording, or to allow straight copying of one cassette to another. High-speed copiers became available, but were resented by the record industry because of the ease with which they could be used to make unauthorized copies of copyright recordings.

At first, there was less interest in portable cassette recorders/players, but this all changed in July 1979 when Sony launched its 'Walkman' portable player with plug-in headphones. Everyone, from joggers to rail travelers, could suddenly enjoy 'music on the move,' and sales of commercial 'musicassettes' rose steeply. In-car cassette players achieved similarly high levels of popularity, with US car manufacturers leading the way by selling new automobiles with cassette/radio tuner units already installed.

Other portables also sold well, but were socially less acceptable since, when they were played loudly, their speakers could cause annoyance to anyone in the vicinity; this was in contrast to the Walkman, whose headphones emitted only faint sounds. When these portables began to be carried around in busy streets and shopping malls, they were given the name 'ghetto blasters' and their owners were often asked to 'turn it down.'

Bibliography

Borwick, John. 1994. *Sound Recording Practice*. 4th ed. Oxford: Oxford University Press.

JOHN BORWICK

Compact Disc

The compact disc (CD) was launched as a joint venture by Sony and Philips at the end of 1982. As the first digitally recorded consumer product to rival the vinyl disc, it took a few years to get established, but it then dominated the prerecorded music market worldwide.

Technology

The CD is only 4.7" (11.5 cm) in diameter and yet it easily matches the LP in frequency spread and dynamic range, and offers a number of user-convenient features.

The digitally encoded signals are pressed into the upper surface of a transparent polycarbonate substrate in the form of a spiraling track of tiny pits. The track begins near the disc center and spirals outward. Instead of a mechanical stylus bearing down onto the record surface, the optical playback head is located beneath the disc and makes no physical contact with it, thus avoiding wear. The traveling head assembly comprises a laser light-beam source, sharply focused through the clear polyvinyl chloride (PVC) substrate onto the underside of the recorded track, and a light-sensitive photo detector which registers the presence or absence of reflected light from the recorded stream of pits to generate an electrical signal that re-creates the original pattern of digital ones and zeros. This in turn is passed through a digital-to-analog converter before being amplified and sent to a pair of loudspeakers (for stereo).

Subcodes keep the laser on track, control the motor speed and provide numerous quick-access and displayed text features, which would be impossible in an analog system. Error correction technology enables the player to ignore the effects of dust, scratches or pinholes, and background noise is virtually nonexistent.

CDs are single-sided but offer a nominal playing time of 74 minutes, which is often exceeded. This requires an astonishing 15 billion bits of digital information, derived from the original analog musical waveform by a process of sampling at a rate of 44.1 kHz and representing each sample by a 16-bit number (word). This provides an audio frequency bandwidth of 20 kHz (the nominal range of human hearing) and a dynamic range of 96 dB, allowing the quietest and loudest musical sounds to be reproduced with very low levels of noise or distortion.

CD players steadily improved in performance after the early days, when keen-eared listeners sometimes complained of a certain hardness of tone compared with that produced by LPs. More effective screening between the digital and analog circuits was introduced, as well as anti-vibration mounting of the disc platform and the optical carriageway, and higher-performance digital/analog (D/A) converters.

In addition, the basic CD format has provided the basis for several other home entertainment and communications media. A recordable version of the CD, called CD-R, has proved popular with professional recording engineers and broadcasters, but too expensive for the average domestic consumer. This non-erasable disc has in turn led to the development of a fully rewritable version, called CD-RW, which should become more affordable in the future. Other applications of the 5" (12.7 cm) silver disc have included CD-I (Interactive), Photo CD and CD-Video.

CD-Video provided only about five minutes of full-motion video plus about 20 minutes of stereo sound and was not a commercial success. A new medium that has the potential to replace all video, audio and computer formats is DVD (digital versatile disc). Introduced in 1997, it has smaller recorded pits and more tracks per inch to give seven times more storage capacity. It was created mainly with video and computer applications in mind, and can accommodate up to 133 minutes of video, as required for feature movies. Quality-conscious hi-fi enthusiasts naturally hope that an audio-only DVD disc format will come along, providing even wider frequency and dynamic ranges, plus up to eight soundtracks for top-quality surround sound.

Sales and Impact on the Music Business

Having been launched in 1982–83 when there was a global slump in the sales of recorded music, the CD was primarily responsible for the considerable prosperity of the international record industry in the late 1980s and the first half of the 1990s. World sales of CD units grew from 5 million in 1983 to 400 million in 1988, when CD sales overtook those of the LP. By 1996, when CD sales reached 2,136 million, the CD had replaced the vinyl LP, whose own sales had reached a peak of 942 million in 1978. By 1996, sales of newly produced vinyl LPs were only 20 million. Sales of the other main format for prerecorded music, the tape cassette, peaked around 1992 at 1,552 million, and in 1996 cassette sales were 1,380 million.

In financial terms, the CD has been a highly successful commodity for those who own its means of manufacture and distribution. It has become a high-priced luxury item with relatively low costs. Global dollar value figures for all recorded music sales showed a quite dramatic shift around 1986 when the CD began to 'take off.' In 1978, the dollar value of world sales grew by 26 percent; in 1979, there was growth of only 5 percent; by 1982, sales had fallen 5 percent; and in 1985 there was growth of only 2 percent. Then, as CD sales gained critical mass, they achieved growth of 23 percent in 1986, 18 percent in 1987 and double-digit (above 10 percent) growth every year through to 1993, when the increase was 6 percent.

CDs have generated large amounts of cash flow and increased profits for the major record companies – Sony, Time Warner, Thorn EMI, Philips-PolyGram and Bertelsmann. Apart from the quantity of CD sales, other contributory factors have included the lower royalties given to artists and composers as part of the CD 'launch' program, the price differential of about 50 percent imposed between cassettes and CDs, and the significant amount of CD sales coming from reissued albums purchased by listeners replacing their obsolete vinyl LPs, where record companies have little or no new recording or marketing costs.

The geographical distribution of CD sales has been extremely uneven. The CD has become the leading format for recorded music in North America, the countries of the European Union and Northern Europe, parts of Latin America, Japan and many nations of the Pacific Rim. Elsewhere – Africa, Central America and the Andean countries, Eastern Europe, parts of Indochina and the Indian subcontinent – the cassette has remained the main vehicle for music. The contrast mirrors the split between, on the one hand, established and emerging capitalist and market economies with high levels of consumption by most or a significant minority of the population and, on the other hand, the rest of the world, the so-called developing nations. The split is also within nations: between the emerging affluent middle classes of China or Brazil and the mass of the population. In many countries, the CD player and a CD collection have become a sign of Westernized 'modern' living, together with McDonald's and Coca-Cola.

By the late 1990s, after Sony's prerecorded minidisc and Philips's digital compact cassette (DCC) failed to replace the analog compact cassette, there were signs in some Western countries that the process of LP replacement was complete and that consumer appetite for the CD was no longer increasing. In addition, record company profits were falling as lower-priced CDs took a greater market share. The industry's strategic planners were considering the potential of Enhanced-CD, DVD or even on-line delivery of music to become a new format to succeed the CD.

Bibliography

Laing, Dave. 1998. 'DDD: Discourse in the Digital Domain.' In *Papers Delivered at the VIIIth International Conference of IASPM, Glasgow, July 1995*, ed. Helmi Järviluoma. Tampere: IASPM.

Pohlmann, Ken C. 1992. *The Compact Disc: A Handbook of Theory and Use*. Rev. ed. Oxford: Oxford University Press.

JOHN BORWICK and DAVE LAING

Cylinders

The cylinder format was used by Thomas Edison in his first experiments in sound recording, and it became the basis of his phonograph invention of 1877. The wax cylinder was the dominant form of sound recording until the first decade of the twentieth century, when the revolving disc emerged as its major competitor. Sales of cylinder records declined through the 1920s, and the demise of the Edison phonograph operation in 1929 brought an end to this format.

Although Edison used several formats in his experiments to inscribe sound on tinfoil, he chose that of a stylus cutting on the surface of a cylinder for his phonograph because of his familiarity with the many lathes in his Menlo Park laboratory. His phonograph had a sheet of tinfoil wrapped around a cylinder, and the mouthpiece/diaphragm assembly vibrated a cutting stylus which inscribed the sound wave onto the tinfoil. Chichester Bell and Charles Tainter had the idea of using a solid wax cylinder instead of the tinfoil, and by the 1880s several companies were marketing wax cylinders to be used on the new talking machines.

Early consumers bought blank cylinders to record their own music. Prerecorded wax cylinders were very expensive until Edison perfected a method of duplicating perfect copies of a cylinder master recording. At the turn of the century, the cost of prerecorded cylinders dropped as Edison began mass production of his 'High Speed Hard Wax' cylinders. A three-minute cylinder recording now cost around $0.50. Millions were sold all over the world as the public embraced this new form of musical entertainment.

Edison's business and his cylinder format were soon experiencing competition from Emile Berliner's gramophone and its disc record. The battle of the two systems was marked by intense technical dispute about the relative advantages of the two formats, but the victory of disc over cylinder was more the result of economic and aesthetic considerations: more music could be recorded on discs, and they were easier to store. The introduction of the double-sided disc was a major blow to the commercial viability of the cylinder record.

Although Edison continued to improve the sound quality and extend the playing time of the cylinder, its sales began to slump. In 1913, Edison effectively conceded victory to the disc format when he introduced his own disc record. Wax cylinders were still manufactured and sold over the next 10 years, but in ever-decreasing numbers. The cylinder was now considered obsolete and little new music was recorded on it. The closure of Edison's phonograph business in 1929 effectively marked the end of the cylinder as a format for prerecorded music. While the audience for recorded music rejected the cylinder format, businesspeople continued to use large, extended-play cylinders on Edison dictating machines in the 1930s. New magnetic media eventually replaced wax cylinders in dictating machines by the end of that decade.

In dominating the world of recorded sound for 20 years, cylinders were the means of introducing the joys of prerecorded music to millions of people. The short time duration of the cylinder's playback limited the amount of classical music that could be recorded, and only a few brief excerpts of well-known pieces were put onto cylinders. A playback time of three minutes was ideal for popular music, and this became the mainstay of cylinder recordings: sentimental ballads, dance music, vaudeville monologs and minstrel songs were reproduced in tens of thousands, bringing the best of popular entertainment to the masses.

Bibliography

Frow, George L., and Sefl, Albert F. 1978. *The Edison Cylinder Phonographs 1877–1929*. Sevenoaks, Kent: Frow.

Gelatt, Roland. 1977. *The Fabulous Phonograph, 1877–1977*. London: Cassell.

Koenigsberg, Allen. 1969. *Edison Cylinder Records, 1889–1912, with an Illustrated History of the Phonograph*. New York: Stellar Productions.

Millard, Andre J. 1995. *America on Record: A History of Recorded Sound*. Cambridge: Cambridge University Press.

Read, Oliver, and Welch, Walter L. 1976. *From Tin Foil to Stereo: The Evolution of the Phonograph*. 2nd ed. Indianapolis/New York: Howard Sams/Bobbs Merrill.

ANDRE MILLARD

DAT

DAT is the popular acronym for digital audio tape recorder, a cassette-based digital recording and playback format first introduced into the Japanese consumer market in 1986. The format uses a smaller version of the rotary-head design commonly found in video cassette recorders (VCRs) and is sometimes designated as R-DAT (rotary head-DAT). The magnetic tape is completely enclosed within a plastic shell and, although smaller in size than a conventional analog cassette, can store up to two hours of CD-quality digital audio.

The entry of DAT into the North American and (some) European markets was delayed during the late 1980s by government lobbyists from the record and music publishing industries and from copyright organizations which feared the medium would spawn a new era in home taping and record piracy. Some of these fears were allayed when representatives of the international record industry and the consumer electronics industries signed an agreement in 1989, recommending a Serial Copy Management System (SCMS) for DAT that would prevent multiple generations of digital copying. Despite this technical fix, the long delays and general uncertainty surrounding DAT effectively prevented the economies of scale typically brought into play following the introduction of most consumer products from ever being achieved. In most Western countries, DAT remained a relatively expensive, professional and semiprofessional recording medium which has never made significant inroads into the consumer market. For semiprofessional musicians, however, DAT's capacity to master demos and other projects in the digital realm has helped narrow the gap between home and professional studios.

PAUL THÉBERGE

Digital Compact Cassette

The digital compact cassette (DCC) was launched in 1992 by Philips in association with Matsushita and others as a deliberate attempt to upgrade the analog compact cassette which they had introduced 30 years earlier. The aim was to give consumers a new digital record/playback medium that would come close to the sound quality standards now provided by the compact disc.

An important requirement for the new DCC was that it should have the same external dimensions, tape width and running speed as the old analog cassette to ensure a degree of 'backward compatibility.' Therefore, DCC machines would also play, but not record on, conventional cassettes, of which many households had large collections. A new type of multitrack record/replay head was needed, with the digital data spread over nine tracks. Even then, a certain amount of bit-rate reduction was necessary to squeeze the CD-type digital signals onto the tape. The resultant sound quality was indeed very close to that of CDs, but the relatively high cost of DCC machines and cassettes prevented the format from persuading many people to give up their analog machines. When the record industry did not issue prerecorded DCC cassettes in any quantity, the system ceased production.

Bibliography

'The Media Maze, Pt. 1.' 1995. *Gramophone Magazine* (April): 176–86.

JOHN BORWICK

Eight-Track Cartridge

The eight-track cartridge was the most successful of a number of ready-threaded tape media developed in the United States from the late 1950s. Issuing prerecorded music on open-reel tapes had not met with much public acceptance, and this was largely blamed on the difficulty of threading the tape onto an empty take-up reel by hand. Early designs were developed by RCA, Bell Sound, Fidelipac and 3M, but Nortronics came forward in 1965 with both an eight-track head and an endless-loop cartridge machine.

This new head enabled RCA and LearJet to finalize a joint 'Stereo 8' design, which was adopted by several large car manufacturers. Ford Motors supplied its 1966 models with a Stereo 8 player built into the dashboard, and RCA produced recorded repertoire. Other companies

joined in and, by 1975, Stereo 8 sales in the United States had reached $583 million, equal to 25 percent of all recorded music sales. This popularity did not spread to other countries to the same extent and, by the mid-1970s, the Philips compact cassette had taken over as the preferred medium for in-car use, as well as for portable cassette players and many home audio systems.

The cartridge used tape with a quarter-inch (6.25 mm) width, wound in an endless loop and carrying four twin-track stereo recordings. All the tracks were recorded in pairs in the same direction for each of the four programs. A metalized foil at the joined ends of the loop marked the start of each program and activated a switching mechanism, which automatically moved the two-track head in line with the next program. The running speed was 3.75" (9.53 cm) per second, the tape being passed between a drive capstan within the player and a pinch-wheel inside the cartridge itself. The tape was withdrawn from the innermost turn of the tape pack on a hub-platform and returned to the outer wind of the stored tape. Back-lubricated tape was needed to allow slippage within the pack, and total playing time was up to 80 minutes.

Bibliography

Kusisto, Oscar P. 1977. 'Magnetic Tape Recording: Reels, Cassettes or Cartridges.' *Journal of the Audio Engineering Society* 25(10/11): 828–35.

JOHN BORWICK

Gramophone

The gramophone and its revolving disc became the pre-eminent form of recorded sound in the twentieth century. It emerged from the shadow of Thomas Edison's phonograph at the end of the nineteenth century to dominate the sales of talking machines and records. Although the gramophone in its original form has long gone and the companies associated with it have merged with others, people have continued to use the term as a generic reference to a record player, and the arrangement of stylus and disc has continued to figure large in the technology of recorded sound.

The gramophone was invented in the 1880s by Emile Berliner, a German immigrant based in Washington, DC. Berliner was a professional inventor who made several important contributions to the technology of sound, including the variable resistance microphone. His first talking machine was demonstrated in 1888. It recorded on a disc rather than the cylinder that had been popularized by Edison in the phonograph. The sound waves were inscribed in spiral form on the surface of the disc, and the stylus followed the spiral groove from the edge to the center of the disc. Initially, the stylus was made of a piece of metal sharpened to a point. Then various other materials were tried, including slivers of wood, pieces of celluloid and small diamonds attached to metal strips. Hardened steel became the preferred material for styli because it was cheap and effective. In contrast to the up-and-down ('hill-and-dale') movement of the stylus in the phonograph, the stylus of the gramophone moved from side to side – laterally – in the groove of the disc record.

Berliner called his invention 'the gramophone,' following the common practise of adding 'phone' to the name of any machine that recorded and played back sound. His first models were powered by a hand crank that was connected to the turntable by a belt. In this very simple machine, the user shouted into the mouthpiece while turning the crank, as the vibrating diaphragm and stylus assembly inscribed the sound signal into the disc.

Edison and other inventors had experimented with the disc or 'plate' format, but most of them had rejected it because of the problem of getting the stylus to maintain a constant speed across the surface of the disc. Another drawback was that, because the grooves in the disc were cut closer and closer together toward the center, there was a greater chance of the stylus jumping from one groove to another as it worked across the disc.

Berliner formed the American Gramophone Company in 1891 and applied himself to improving his invention. He also experimented with many different materials to be used as discs. His first discs were made of an unyielding hard vulcanized rubber. He later tried several soft wax compounds, celluloid and, finally, shellac (a hard natural resin) for the surface of his discs.

A major problem confronting Berliner was the power source of the gramophone. A hand-cranked talking machine had uneven sound reproduction and put too heavy a burden on the user to turn it at an absolutely constant speed. Consequently, sales of the gramophone were low and the future of the Berliner company looked dim. Its prospects brightened with the introduction of critical technical improvements, the work of a mechanic called in as a subcontractor to manufacture parts of the gramophone. Eldridge Johnson solved the difficult problem of a power source by using a spring motor to operate the machine. He also succeeded in improving the sound quality of the gramophone's reproduction by revising the process of recording and finding better wax compounds for the disc record. Johnson's most important experiments were directed at finding a way to duplicate copies of master recordings. He basically copied Edison's approach to this problem and, by 1899, he had managed to make perfect duplicates of master recordings.

By 1900, the gramophone was a cheap, simple machine backed by a growing library of prerecorded discs. It was easier to stamp out duplicate discs than cylinders, and this helped the company to keep its prices low. The industry of recorded sound was now involved in a debate over the relative advantages of disc versus cylinder, as the gramophone proved to be a serious threat to Edison's phonograph and the cylinder format. Berliner had set up manufacturing companies in the United States, Germany and the United Kingdom and, together with numerous other companies producing disc records and players, he challenged the supremacy of the phonograph. Advocates of each system of sound recording claimed technological superiority, but it was difficult to deny the cheapness, ease of storage and longer playing time of the disc.

Like all the other inventors in the field, Berliner formed numerous companies to exploit his talking machine patents. Some were licensed to manufacture his gramophone; others merely had rights to market machines in a designated area. As soon as the technology of the gramophone was perfected, Berliner created business organizations that could both manufacture and market his machines. The Victor Talking Machine Company was formed on the basis of Berliner's and Johnson's patents in 1901. Based in Camden, New Jersey, this company supported the technical development of the gramophone and made millions of machines. The Gramophone Company of London (formed in 1898) had the rights to manufacture and market the machines in Europe. These two companies also sold disc players to Asia, Africa, South America and the Pacific.

There was also a host of other smaller companies making disc-playing machines, many employing technology patented by Berliner and Johnson. Although some companies produced machines and records in both cylinder and disc formats, most had to choose one format or the other. Many decided on the disc format because of the library of recordings built up by Victor and HMV. Unlike Edison, who hated to pay out good money to musicians, the gramophone companies invested heavily in talent, and this paid dividends when highly visible performers, such as Enrico Caruso, recorded on gramophone discs rather than on phonograph cylinders. The prestige that accompanied the recording of classical music stars convinced many music lovers that the gramophone was superior technologically.

The Victor and Gramophone companies each supported a vigorous program of industrial research. They shared technical information, and were responsible for spreading innovations throughout the world. The steady technical improvement of the gramophone, especially in the quality of its sound reproduction, made it the best-selling type of talking machine in the years leading up to World War I. Another great advantage of the disc record was that its diameter could easily be expanded, thus increasing the duration of its playback. Both sides of the disc could be used for recording, effectively doubling the amount of music on the record.

The Victor Company's Victrola model was introduced in 1906 and quickly became the most commercially successful version of the gramophone, establishing a dominant position in the marketplace until the introduction of electronic reproduction in the late 1920s.

The Victrola has rightly been called Eldridge Johnson's masterpiece. It combined technical innovation with a completely new look. Up to this point, every talking machine had been connected to a horn which amplified the sound coming from the record. In the Victrola, the horn was kept totally enclosed within the machine, and was turned out when the machine was in use. The Victrola did not look like a talking machine, but like a fine piece of furniture, and this was the key to its astounding success in the marketplace. Victor produced a whole line of Victrolas, from the budget table model to the beautifully carved free-standing versions in the finest woods. Prices ranged from $25 to $1,500. Millions of people purchased this product, not only because of its sound and the library of Red Seal records, but because it made a statement in middle-class drawing rooms. The Victor Company was well aware that a Victrola gave the impression of refinement and culture, and it exploited this in its advertising.

The Victrola challenged existing ideas about what a gramophone or phonograph should look like and established the basic design of disc players for the next 40 years. Even when the talking machine industry moved from acoustic to electronic reproduction, the casings of the new machines conformed to the Victrola look. The upright, wood-encased mechanism, with all the working parts concealed, became the pattern for the majority of talking machines.

The success of the Victrola virtually decided the contest between cylinder and disc. Although Edison continued to make cylinders, and even introduced his own disc-playing phonograph, he eventually had to concede that Berliner's design had become the standard for the talking machine. In Europe and Asia, people used the term 'gramophone' to refer to all types of talking machine. In the United States, the word 'Victrola' served the same purpose.

The introduction of a radically new sound recording technology in the 1920s did little to change the look of the machine or the disc format. Bell Laboratories' system of electronic amplification and recording naturally brought a different sound quality, but the revolving disc and stylus configuration remained the same. The tech-

nology might be different, but the user still operated the machine in much the same way – by placing a stylus on a revolving disc.

The introduction of reel-to-reel tape recorders in the 1950s did not undermine the dominance of disc record players as the major providers of recorded entertainment. Berliner's basic gramophone was constantly improved in the 1950s and 1960s: unbreakable vinyl discs, microgrooved long-playing records and stereo sound reproduction brought this technology to its peak. After a commercial life of about 100 years, the disc player was gradually replaced by the compact cassette audiotape and the digital compact disc in the 1980s. Nevertheless, the basic concept of recording sound data on a revolving disc remained at the core of the new technologies of compact disc, laser disc, computer hard disc, CD-ROM disc and digital minidisc.

The gramophone was the most popular format of recorded sound in the first half of the twentieth century. The ubiquitous revolving disc brought listeners every conceivable type of music, from folk music of distant places to music created electronically. The gradual increase in the playing time of discs enabled classical works in their entirety to be recorded on albums of discs. The stars of both the opera and the music hall depended on gramophone discs to bring their music to millions.

Bibliography

Baumbach, Robert W. 1981. *Look for the Dog: An Illustrated Guide to Talking Machines*. Woodland Hills, CA: Stationary Press.

Eisenberg, Evan. 1987. *The Recording Angel: The Experience of Music from Aristotle to Zappa*. New York: Penguin.

Gelatt, Roland. 1977. *The Fabulous Phonograph, 1877–1977*. London: Cassell.

Johnson, E.R. Fenimore. 1974. *His Master's Voice Was Eldridge R. Johnson*. Milford, DE: State Media.

Millard, Andre J. 1995. *America on Record: A History of Recorded Sound*. Cambridge: Cambridge University Press.

ANDRE MILLARD

Headphone

The prototype of the headphone was the earpiece of the original telephone (1877) – a simple carbon transducer device that reproduced a transmitted or recorded sound signal at an audible level when held close to the ear. With the advent of wireless telegraphy in the 1890s, the single telephone earpiece was transformed into a pair of earphones connected by a metal headband. These headsets were worn by ships' wireless operators who, alert to the crackling of the dots and dashes of the Morse code, were startled to hear the sounds and voices of the first radio broadcasts in 1906. Similar devices were also in use at fairs and exhibitions during the 1890s and 1900s.

At this time, the phonograph (or gramophone) was an acoustic, as opposed to electronic, device which used a mechanical means of reproduction by passing the playback signal from a mechanical floating stylus to an acoustic horn. However, headphones were in use with the early jukebox type of phonographs. Until the invention of the loudspeaker in the early 1920s, earphones were the only means of listening to the *radio*, and with the popularization of cheap crystal sets the headphone became one of the symbols of modernity.

However, the loudspeaker made the act of listening a collective activity and produced an infinitely richer and fuller sound. It superseded the headphone, which was relegated to a specialized role as a piece of professional equipment used by technicians in recording or broadcasting studios and by radio operators.

Several developments in the 1950s brought headphones back into popular use. Improvements in loudspeaker technology were applied to headphones with spectacular results, and the advent of stereo sound during the 1960s prompted the introduction of studio-quality headphones for private listening. This allowed individuals to listen to music without encroaching on the privacy, or aural space, of others, and reinforced the notion that the experience of art music was an intensely personal one. At the same time, the development of multitrack recording in popular music in particular introduced a change in the image of the musician in the studio: players were often separated by baffles, or recorded individually, and wore headphones to hear each other, because each instrument had to be isolated on its own soundtrack for subsequent mixing.

A new phase began with Sony's introduction of the Walkman in 1979. The Walkman dissolved the physical space between the sound source and the listener's body into a virtual space created by the music's stereo image, making it possible for listeners to carry this virtual space around with them, with consequent effects on both body image and music. One writer (Hosokawa 1984) has likened the Walkman user to 'a latter-day equivalent of the flaneur' described by Walter Benjamin, the figure who strolled through the arcades of mid-nineteenth-century Paris, assimilating the sensory bombardment of objects, people and movements to his own pace and experience as a defense against the shocks of mass urban existence.

Be that as it may, the general external noise level often causes the Walkman wearer to turn up the volume; however, the manufacturers of this equipment give no warning of the physical danger to the ear of extended exposure to very loud sounds at close range, to which users of headphones are especially prone.

Bibliography

Chambers, Iain. 1990. 'A Miniature History of the Walkman.' *New Formations* 11: 1–4.

Chanan, Michael. 1995. *Repeated Takes: A Short History of Recording and Its Effects on Music.* London: Verso.

Hosokawa, Shuhei. 1984. 'The Walkman Effect.' *Popular Music* 4: 165–80.

MICHAEL CHANAN

Jukebox

'Jukebox' is the generic term for coin-operated machines that reproduce music or video recordings, usually in such premises as bars or public houses. The name comes from 'juke joint,' a term applied to bars in black districts of the rural United States in the 1920s ('jooking' meant 'dancing').

The earliest form of the jukebox was also the first commercial form of music reproduction to use the tinfoil phonograph technology developed by Thomas Edison. On 23 November 1889, an entrepreneur called Louis Glass installed a coin-operated phonograph in the Palais Royal, San Francisco. Over the next two years, 16 more licensees of the Edison machine set up some 1,249 booths in various US cities in which paying customers using stethoscope-style earphones could hear music from prerecorded cylinders supplied by Edison's laboratory in Orange, New Jersey.

The popularity of the phonograph soon led companies to sell the machines directly to the public. Although disc-based machines replacing earphones with horns were developed, the public music machines lost their novelty value. The next phase of coin-in-the-slot mechanical music was focused on the player piano, which used perforated paper rolls, and on more elaborate machines like the Seeburg Orchestrion of 1910. This claimed to reproduce the sounds of the mandolin, flute, clarinet, violin and percussion, as well as the piano.

These machines maintained their position of dominance over the phonograph because of the greater volume they could produce in a bar or amusement arcade. It was not until after the introduction of electrical recording in 1925 that the modern jukebox was introduced.

The Birth of the Modern Jukebox

The business in the 1930s was dominated by five manufacturers: Seeburg (which had been founded by a Swedish immigrant, Justus P. Sjoberg); Rock-Ola; AMI; Rudolph Wurlitzer Co. (known also for its theater organs); and Mills Novelty. The most famous individual in the industry was Homer Capehart, who sold his own manufacturing company to Wurlitzer before taking that company 'from worst to first' (Krivine 1976).

The jukeboxes of the early 1930s could take eight 78 rpm discs. By the end of the decade, this had increased to 24. The cost to the customer ranged from $0.05 to $0.25, depending on the location. The repeal of Prohibition in 1933 gave an enormous boost to the jukebox business, as thousands of bars, juke joints and honky-tonks appeared all over the United States. The honky-tonk was the white southern equivalent of the juke joint. It gave its name to a genre of 'hillbilly' music that was often featured on jukeboxes situated in these bars. By 1936, some 150,000 coin machines were taking about half the records manufactured in the United States. By 1940, the number of boxes in operation had risen to 300,000.

The World War II period saw a further expansion of the jukebox industry, providing inexpensive entertainment for service personnel and for the millions of white and black southerners who migrated to the north and west. *Billboard* magazine recognized the importance of the boxes in 1944 by introducing a single jukebox chart that included 'race' and 'hillbilly' records side by side.

New Formats

After 1945, jukebox manufacturers were faced with the need to redesign their machines to accommodate vinyl 45s. Seeburg launched the first 45 rpm jukebox in 1950. Jukeboxes played a vital role in the growth of independent record labels for R&B music, as jukebox operators could guarantee sales of 10,000 singles in the large cities. Some labels were started by jukebox distributors like the Bihari brothers of Modern Records in Los Angeles and Ernie Young of Excello. Morris Levy of Roulette was involved in the New York jukebox scene in his early days.

Manufacturers typically supplied jukeboxes to exclusive distributors in each city or state. These operators placed the boxes in public houses, bars or clubs and split the revenues from the jukeboxes with the location owners. For many years, this was done on a 50-50 basis, although from the 1950s some operators began to demand 60-40 or even 80-20 splits. Operators bought the records increasingly from 'one-stop' regional wholesalers that stocked releases from every label. As the capacity of jukeboxes increased in 1948 to 100 singles and then to 200, specialist programming services were developed to help the operators. The label strips for records were color-coded by genre: red for popular, orange for nostalgia, green for country, blue for R&B and so on.

The profitability of the jukebox business attracted the attention of organized crime. When antitrust pressure from the federal government led Seeburg, the market leader, to agree to end the exclusive distributorships, the 'Mob' moved in as middlemen. In Chicago, criminals boasted that they could launch artists by ordering operators to place certain records in top positions on the city's machines. In Congress, the McLennan hearing on racketeering was told that organized crime ran the jukebox business in at least eight states. In 1957, the FBI identified five members of the Anastasia 'family' in New York as having substantial involvement in jukeboxes. The popular image of gangsterism in the coin machine business was humorously portrayed in the Frank Tashlin film *The Girl Can't Help It*.

With the arrival of teenage rock 'n' roll, jukeboxes moved into ice cream parlors, bowling alleys and skating rinks. In 1959, there were 500,000 boxes in the United States consuming 40 million records a year. By 1965, the industry was turning over some $500 million, and it was dominated by the big three manufacturers, Seeburg, Wurlitzer and Rowe. They sought to adapt their machines to current trends, using specially produced three-track EPs to give over seven minutes of dance music. In 1965, Seeburg advertised its Discotheque model, which came with an 'instant night-club' including modular dance flooring, coasters and table napkins. The first CD jukeboxes were marketed in 1989, and many contemporary models typically include at least 1,000 selections.

Outside the United States

Jukeboxes did not become widespread outside North America until the 1950s. In Britain and Germany, they arrived as part of an 'American invasion' together with US army bases, milk- and coffee-bars and rock 'n' roll. They spread to British public houses as the brewers sought to attract younger drinkers. By the end of the 1970s, there were an estimated 65,000 boxes in Britain, and an EMI Records survey of world record markets stated that in 1975 there were 250,000 jukeboxes in Europe, over 80,000 in Latin America and 44,000 in Japan.

Audiovisual jukeboxes have never rivaled the audio machines in popularity. The first jukeboxes with pictures were built in 1940 by Mills to show 'soundies,' a reel of eight short films featuring performances by music artists of all genres, as well as vaudeville acts and gymnasts. The films were back-projected onto a series of mirrors, which reflected the image onto a 22 1/2″ × 17 1/2″ (57 cm × 44 cm) screen mounted on top of the machine. Although almost 2,000 three-minute films were distributed, the soundie experiment ended in 1947.

In the 1950s, the French Scopitone company and ColorSonics of the United States tried with little success to relaunch the sound-and-picture box with Technicolor films. A third wave of interest in audiovisual boxes was sparked in the 1980s by the arrival of promo-videos or music videos made by record companies for use on television.

In most countries, the use of music in jukeboxes is controlled by copyright law, and jukebox operators are required to pay royalties to organizations representing copyright owners. In the United States, the composers' and publishers' bodies ASCAP and BMI fought a lengthy battle for jukebox fees, which was won only in 1976 when a blanket charge of $8 per machine was voted in as part of a copyright law amendment. In many European nations, fees are also paid to organizations representing the interests of record companies and recording artists.

Jukebox Songs

The importance of the jukebox in the development of US popular music is reflected in the number of well-known songs inspired by the jukebox or mentioning it in their lyrics. In the 1930s, Glenn Miller made 'Juke Box Saturday Night' popular, while Perry Como had a 'Juke Box Baby' and Teresa Brewer urged her listeners to put another nickel in the nickelodeon (an alternative name for the machine) in 'Music Music Music.' The jukebox was even more hymned in country music, though, curiously, not in R&B, which has only 'Juke Box Lil' by Charles Brown. In country music, Kitty Wells sang of the jukebox in the honky-tonk in her famous answer song 'It Wasn't God Who Made Honky Tonk Angels,' while Jim Reeves promised to tell the man to turn the jukebox way down low in 'He'll Have to Go.' In the 1990s, Alan Jackson pleaded, 'Don't Rock the Jukebox.'

In the rock 'n' roll era, Chuck Berry's 'School Day' described how the high-school students would drop the coin right into the slot, and Bill Haley and Carl Perkins sang 'Jukebox Cannonball' and 'Let the Jukebox Keep On Playing,' respectively. In Britain, a leading pop television show used the machine as the focus of a panel game, *Juke Box Jury*, while later the UK rock 'n' roll revivalists, the Rubettes, had a hit with 'Juke Box Jive.'

The baroque design of many jukeboxes from the 1940s and 1950s rivaled that of American automobiles, and there is an intense collectors' market for vintage machines.

Bibliography

Bodoh, A.G. 1977. 'The Jukebox, the Radio and the Record.' *Journal of the Audio Engineering Society* 25(10/11): 836–42.

EMI Records. 1977. *World Record Markets*. London: Henry Melland.

Gelatt, Roland. 1977. *The Fabulous Phonograph, 1877–1977*. London: Cassell.

Hardy, Phil. 1980. 'Drinking Songs.' *Time Out* (25–31 January): 14–15.

Krivine, John. 1976. *Juke Box Saturday Night*. London: New English Library.

Paige, Earl. 1989. ''45s Give Way to CDs on Jukes, Too.' *Billboard* (15 July): 5, 79.

Discographical References

Berry, Chuck. 'School Day.' *Live: Roots of Rock N Roll*. Columbia River 1154. *1998*: USA.

Brewer, Teresa. 'Music Music Music.' London L 604. *1950*: USA.

Brown, Charles. 'Juke Box Lil.' *Race Track Blues*. Route 66 Kix 17. *1987*: Sweden.

Como, Perry. 'Juke Box Baby.' *Yesterday & Today: A Celebration in Song*. RCA 66098-2. *1993*: USA.

Haley, Bill. 'Jukebox Cannonball.' *Boogie with Bill*. Topline TOP 114. *1985*: UK.

Jackson, Alan. 'Don't Rock the Jukebox.' *Greatest Hits Collection*. Arista 18801. *1995*: USA.

Miller, Glenn. 'Juke Box Saturday Night.' RCA RCX 1034. 1945: USA.

Perkins, Carl. 'Let the Jukebox Keep On Playing.' Sun 244. 1955: USA.

Reeves, Jim. 'He'll Have to Go.' *The Best of Jim Reeves*. RCA Camden 46842. *1997*: USA.

Rubettes, The. 'Juke Box Jive.' *Rubettes*. State 2193. *1975*: USA.

Wells, Kitty. 'It Wasn't God Who Made Honky Tonk Angels.' *Kitty Wells Greatest Hits*. King Special 1414. *1995*: USA.

Filmography

The Girl Can't Help It, dir. Frank Tashlin. 1956. USA. 99 mins. Comedy. Original music by Lionel Newman, Bobby Troup.

DAVE LAING

Laser Disc

The laser disc or LD is a well-established disc medium for home cinema, easily surpassing in sound and picture quality the less expensive VHS cassette tape system. The disc is 12″ (30 cm) in diameter and can be single- or double-sided, providing up to 60 minutes of programming per side. The spiraling recorded track is scanned by an optical system resembling that used in a compact disc (CD) player, and indeed an LD machine, which plugs into an ordinary television receiver (and hi-fi system, if required), will also play audio CDs.

The record industry has issued a fair number of music videos on LD, but production costs are much higher than for sound only. There is also the problem of what pictures should accompany the music. Pop concerts, opera and ballet do well, but videos of orchestral or chamber music performances are of limited appeal. LD is therefore used mainly for movies in which surround sound encoding adds an extra dimension to the cinema-like experience.

Bibliography

'The Media Maze, Pt. 2.' 1995. *Gramophone Magazine* (May): 158–67.

JOHN BORWICK

Loudspeaker

A loudspeaker or 'speaker' is an electroacoustic transducer used for transforming electrical signals into sound waves. In other words, it responds to incoming audio frequency electrical signals representing music or speech and, by performing physical vibrations, radiates sound waves that correspond to the original signals.

In practise, it is quite difficult to design a loudspeaker so that the sound reaching a listener matches the original in terms of full frequency range (say 20 Hz to 20 kHz) and full dynamic range (say 100 dB), and spreads the sounds evenly over a wide dispersion angle. For these reasons, the loudspeaker is often described as the weakest link in the whole sound recording and reproduction chain.

Most loudspeakers use the electromagnetic (moving-coil) principle, although electrostatic and ribbon microphones, for example, can produce very high-quality sound at domestic listening levels. The alternating signal current is passed through the 'voice coil.' Interaction between the magnetic field this produces and the fixed field of the powerful permanent magnet in which the coil is immersed produces a force that drives the coil into to-and-fro vibration. The coil is set at the center of a, usually conical, diaphragm of some light but stiff material, which in turn performs piston-like vibrations to set the air in motion.

For efficient radiation of bass frequencies, the diaphragm or cone should be as large as possible, say between 8″ (20 cm) and 15″ (38 cm) in diameter. Unfortunately, a cone of this size tends to focus the higher-frequency sounds along a narrow beam, and to set up unwanted resonances due to the time taken for sound energy to travel out from the coil to the rim. It has therefore become common practise for all but the simplest speakers to divide the frequency range between two or more drive units, each designed to handle a specific band of frequencies. The incoming signal is first passed through a 'crossover' filter network. The 'low-pass' section of the crossover sends only the low frequencies to a relatively large 'woofer,' while the 'high-pass' section feeds the highest frequencies to a smaller 'tweeter.' More elaborate speakers may add to this two-way arrangement one or more 'band-pass' filter sections to feed suitably designed mid-range drivers.

Freed from the need to cover the full frequency range in a single unit, designers can produce real gains in efficiency and sound quality. Best results are obtained with 'active' multiple-unit speakers where the woofer and tweeter have separate amplifiers capable of further fine-tuning to improve performance. A good example of this is the trend toward adding a subwoofer, a unit handling only the lowest band of frequencies from about 200 Hz down to the limits of hearing. This needs a special drive unit and enclosure, but greatly simplifies the design of the basic woofer which can be allowed to roll off at 200 Hz.

The typical cone speaker is actually a doublet radiator emitting sound waves backward as well as forward. At low frequencies in particular, where the wavelength exceeds the cone diameter, the two wavefronts become spherical and bend round the edges. Since they are in antiphase, they tend to cancel and severely limit the low-frequency response.

The answer is to mount the drive units in a baffle or cabinet. A flat baffle will keep the front and back waves apart and so extend the usable frequency range to some degree; but a cut-off frequency is soon reached for any manageable baffle size, below which the output falls steeply. Some form of box or enclosure is a better solution, and several types have evolved:

(a) The *closed box enclosure* is sometimes called an infinite baffle because it really does eliminate the back wave. The enclosed air acts as a restoring force, which has to be tuned to suit the given drive unit and sets a definite cut-off frequency where efficiency drops. It is also necessary to fill the enclosure with glass fiber or other absorbent material to damp internal resonances and 'standing waves.'

(b) The *vented enclosure*, instead of attempting to absorb all the backward-radiated sound energy, redirects the low frequencies in such a way as to reinforce the front wave. It reverses the phase of the back wave by passing it through a carefully dimensioned tunnel or pipe to emerge from a vent or port. Sometimes the port opening has a passive auxiliary bass radiator fitted to give added mass and a smoother extension of bass.

(c) The *transmission line or labyrinth enclosure* takes the vented enclosure principle further by making the sounds travel down a folded pipe containing absorbent material.

(d) The *horn-loaded speaker* achieves high levels of efficiency and is often used, for example, in public-address systems, cinemas and other large auditoria. The effect is something like speaking into a megaphone. Even quite small excursions of the diaphragm or cone can produce high sound pressure levels over a large area.

For outdoor concerts, arrays or stacks of powerful speakers must be erected, together with many watts of amplification and control gear. To provide a well-balanced sound to the entire audience, free of disturbing echoes, special directional speakers are aimed to cover specific areas with minimum overspill. Column speakers, which give a controlled dispersion in the horizontal plane, are mainly used in Europe. Horn speakers are preferred in the United States and can be multicellular, radial or constant-directivity types, giving precise coverage of the chosen audience area and reduced risk of feedback to the onstage microphones.

Bibliography
Borwick, John, ed. 1994. *Loudspeaker and Headphone Handbook*. 2nd ed. Oxford: Focal Press.

JOHN BORWICK

Megaphone
A megaphone is a handheld, usually metal, conical horn. Prior to the development of the microphone in the 1920s, band vocalists performing in large halls or outdoors frequently amplified their voices using such a horn, with the narrow end held close to their mouth. The principle was similar to that of the exponential horn on some pre-electric gramophones, or the small horn attached to the Stroh violin or phonofiddle. In early recording studios, a large fixed horn was likewise used to amplify the voice sufficiently to be recordable. Although obsolete by the 1930s, the megaphone survived into that decade as a gimmick of the US singer and band leader Rudy Vallee, and it has continued to be used for period effect by singers with deliberately old-fashioned dance bands.

TONY RUSSELL

Minidisc
The minidisc (MD) was introduced by Sony in 1992 just 10 years after the compact disc (CD). The MD is only 2.4″ (64 mm) in diameter, yet offers the same playing time and operational features as the CD (74 minutes). In addition, the MD arrived with a recording option already in place, to rival the popular compact cassette as a home recording medium, and has a special buffer system that eliminates the risk of mistracking when jogging or when listening in a car. To get all these features in such a small package, a system of bit-rate reduction was necessary, which marginally restricts sound quality in direct comparison with that of the CD, but still outperforms the tape cassette.

In the event, commercial acceptance of the MD was hindered in most countries outside Japan by the dominance of the CD and the reluctance of the record industry to issue prerecorded MDs in any quantity. It was also affected by the almost simultaneous launch of the digital compact cassette (DCC), which was targeted at much the same market.

Bibliography
'The Media Maze, Pt. 1.' 1995. *Gramophone Magazine* (April): 176–86.

JOHN BORWICK

Phonograph
'Phonograph' was the name originally given by Thomas Edison to the instrument he invented in 1877. The first phonograph recorded sounds on tinfoil. In 1887, wax cylinders replaced tinfoil as the recording medium. The phonograph was originally marketed as a 'talking machine,' but by the late 1880s wax cylinders with prerecorded music were available. From 1900 on, prerecorded cylinders were mass-produced by molding.

After the turn of the century, disc recordings soon replaced cylinders as the medium for marketing recorded music. The production of musical cylinders was eventually discontinued in 1929, but the cylinder phonograph continued to be used as a dictating machine until the 1950s. However, in North American English 'phonograph' became a generic term for any machine used for reproducing sounds, including the disc gramophone which had been introduced by Emile Berliner in 1887, and it remained current to the end of the LP era.

In the United Kingdom and elsewhere in Europe, the word 'gramophone' (originally a trademark of the Gramophone Company) became, by the second decade of the twentieth century, a generic term for disc record players, and the word 'phonograph' was restricted to the cylinder phonograph. In British English, the use of the word became limited to collecting circles, as in 'The City of London Phonograph and Gramophone Society,' an organization for collectors of historical recordings.

Bibliography
Chew, V.K. 1981. *Talking Machines*. London: Science Museum.

Gelatt, Roland. 1956. *The Fabulous Phonograph: The Story of the Gramophone from Tin Foil to High Fidelity*. London: Cassell.

Gronow, Pekka, and Saunio, Ilpo. 1998. *An International History of the Recording Industry*. London: Cassell.

Koenigsberg, Allen. 1990. *Patent History of the Phonograph*. New York: APM Press.

Marty, Daniel. 1981. *The Illustrated History of Talking Machines*. Lausanne: Edita.

Welch, Walter L., and Brodbeck Stenzel Burt, Leah. 1994. *From Tinfoil to Stereo: The Acoustic Years of the Recording Industry, 1877–1929*. Gainesville, FL: University of Florida Press.

PEKKA GRONOW

Radio Receiver

The radio receiver is an apparatus for detecting electromagnetic waves of radio frequency and amplifying them for the listener. With the beginning of radio broadcasting in 1920, the radio receiver created a new form of home entertainment and, in particular, played a key role in the audience experience of popular music for most of the twentieth century.

The history of the radio is foremost a technological one rather than one of design and aesthetics. From the pioneering work of Marconi to the mid-1960s, three main types of circuit were used for listening to sound signals: the crystal, the valve and the transistor detector. Little of the principal scientific knowledge had changed until the advent of new technological means of receiving radio broadcasts at the end of the twentieth century, which challenged the perception and the meaning of the radio receiver.

The early enthusiasts of wireless telegraphy and radio telephony had used the technology to send messages as well as to receive them. But, in 1915, David Sarnoff, an executive of the Marconi Wireless Telegraph Company of America, wrote in a memorandum of a 'plan of development which would make radio a "household utility" in the same way as the piano or phonograph . . . to bring music into the house by wireless' (Lubar 1993, 213).

In its primitive stages, the radio receiver consisted of a set of different components that individually underwent subsequent processes of improvement and design development to overcome technical limitations and to meet the practical needs of users. Early listeners relied on crystal receivers of the 'cat's-whisker' type, which had a habit of becoming maladjusted at crucial points of a broadcast. Although another, more reliable method existed alongside the crystal (the semiconductor), it took about 15 years for it to be supplanted by the three-electrode valve (triode) receiver, first developed in 1906 by Lee De Forest. The reason for favoring a receiver limited to detection and rectification rather than a more reliable receiver able to detect and also amplify signals was mainly the question of cost. The multi-valve receiver sets were battery-operated, very large and housed in upright wooden cabinets called 'consoles,' making them more expensive, stationary and scientific-looking objects. The first attempt at designing a wireless that would fit in with domestic furnishings occurred in the mid-1920s, making Sarnoff's vision a reality.

Westinghouse simultaneously launched and marketed the first commercial radio receiver (the 'Music Box') and the first commercial radio station in Pittsburgh in 1920. Ten years later, more than 50 percent of US homes possessed a radio set. In 1927, the first car radio was manufactured in the United States, and by 1940 over 25 percent of motor vehicles contained a radio receiver, emphasizing the increasing importance of the wireless and the demand for its alternative use outside the home.

The late 1920s also saw the introduction of the electric wireless, which by the early 1930s had become the staple of the wireless industry. 'The simple-to-use "all-enclosed" domestic mains receiver emerged to displace battery sets and dominated the market in console, table and transportable forms' (Hill 1986, 58). This was followed by technical improvements in volume control and the production of receivers with already calibrated wavelengths, which simplified the process of tuning in. In 1931, Ekco produced the first British receiver with the full range of station names printed on the dial. From the early 1930s until the 1970s, it was customary to display the names of stations on the dial. The first remote-control tuning devices and push-button tuning also emerged in the mid-1930s.

In 1947, the transistor (an abbreviation of 'transfer' and 'resistor') was developed at Bell Telephone Laboratories in the United States. Since the transistor was more reliable, much less bulky and consumed less current, it soon began to displace the valve receiver and to open up new ways of using and adapting the radio receiver. In 1947, 'several new "second set" models appeared, incorporating an electric clock which could be arranged to switch the set on or off at a predetermined time, or used as an alternative to a bed-side alarm clock' (Hill 1986, 168).

The third major development in receiving radio signals coincided with the perception of the term 'wireless' as outdated, and by the early 1960s 'transistor' was no longer simply the name of the component, but was becoming the generic term for a portable radio. The United States and Western Europe had been predominant in the field of radio receiver design until this point. Now, pocket-size Japanese transistors from Sony were making an impact on the European market. The appeal of the new product was portrayed in US and British novelty hits by Freddy Cannon and Benny Hill, respectively.

In the United States, the portable receiver's arrival coincided with that of rock 'n' roll. The portable freed white teenagers from having to listen to the family set in the living room. They could now have their own personal receiver for listening to specialist Top 40 stations or to black music stations in their bedrooms or outside the home – on the street or on the beach. Record producers began to mix singles for maximum aural impact via the small and somewhat crude speaker of the portable. Chuck Berry sang of 'cruising and playing the radio' in 'No Particular Place To Go,' while car radio reception of DJ Wolfman Jack's show provided the soundtrack for the film *American Graffiti* (1973).

Stereo and FM (frequency modulation) broadcasting became widespread in the United States in the 1960s, providing improved sound quality, although listeners had to buy new receivers to benefit. FM also allowed the number of stations to be doubled, with the new stations initially serving 'minority' interests such as classical music and 'underground' rock.

Since the 1920s, radio receivers have been packaged with other media. The radiogram (radio plus gramophone) became widely used, and its late-1960s successor was the hi-fi system with its 'tuner,' an integrated radio receiver without the need for a built-in power amplifier. Later hybrid machines included the boombox (aka ghetto blaster), with added bass volume much favored by urban black youth in the 1980s, and the personal stereo pioneered by the Sony Walkman, which enabled users to shut themselves off from their aural environment (Hosokawa 1984). Just as miniaturization offered alternative uses of the radio, so too did different energy sources. Originally developed for parts of the world without access to electricity, the sun-powered or clockwork portables became increasingly popular all over the world.

The traditional art of reception, and hence the science of the receiver (Miller 1992), has lasted almost a century, and at the end of the 1990s it was about to undergo a transformation. As early as 1966, the circuit method of detecting radio frequencies had been challenged by Sony (UK) when it incorporated a silicon chip into a transistor. However, at the beginning of the twenty-first century, other innovations were changing the audio broadcast experience altogether. Following the immense success of digital recording, exemplified by the compact disc, radio engineers developed digital audio broadcasting (DAB), a combination of two digital technologies to produce an even more efficient and more reliable radio broadcast system – although the radio industry in every country now faced the challenge of persuading consumers to purchase a new generation of receivers. Each radio spectrum allocated to the new services would be able to 'carry a mixture of stereo and mono broadcasts and data services ... For years radio has meant words and music but now we can start to think about text, data and even Internet style pages on your radio. Ultimately, Digital Radio displays will have the capability to carry still pictures and graphics' (BBC Online 2000).

Matching the vision of future digital radio has been the use of the personal computer (PC) as a radio receiver for Internet radio or audio 'webcasting.' By using the World Wide Web, existing stations and new ones can transmit music without and beyond the limits of their terrestrial transmitters and reach worldwide audiences. Using the computer as the means for receiving audio programs in real time has changed the notion of the wireless and has challenged the definition of the radio receiver as a detector of waves in the 'ether.'

Bibliography

BBC Online. 2000. *Digital Radio Information: The Future.* http://www.bbc.co.uk/digitalradio/text/information/future/

Hill, Jonathan. 1986. *Radio! Radio!.* Bampton, UK: Sunrise Press.

Hosokawa, Shuhei. 1984. 'The Walkman Effect.' *Popular Music* 4: 165–80.

Lubar, Steven D. 1993. *InfoCulture: The Smithsonian Book of Information Age Inventions.* Boston, MA: Houghton Mifflin.

Miller, Toby. 1992. 'An Editorial Introduction for Radio.' *Continuum. The Australian Journal of Media and Culture. Special Issue on Radio – Sound* 6(1): 5–13.

Wedlake, G.E.C. 1973. *SOS: The Story of Radio-Communication.* Newton Abbot: David & Charles.

Discographical References

Berry, Chuck. 'No Particular Place To Go.' Chess 1898. *1964*: USA.

Cannon, Freddy. 'Transistor Sister.' Swan 4078. *1961*: USA.

Hill, Benny. 'Transistor Radio.' Pye 7N 15359. *1961*: UK.

Discography

American Graffiti (Original soundtrack). MCA 8001. 1973; *1993*: USA.

Filmography

American Graffiti, dir. George Lucas. 1973. USA. 109 mins. Comedy.

VANESSA BASTIAN

Record

A record is strictly speaking any form of storage system for audio or video signals, allowing them to be kept and played back at any future time. However, the term is mainly applied to 'sound only' disc media, such as the phonograph (in US parlance) or gramophone (in Britain). These evolved from the early cylinders and 78 rpm shellac records and, from about 1950, comprised the 12" (30 cm) or 7" (18 cm) discs made of vinyl that became the universal 'music carriers.'

Vinyl discs dominated the music market in this way for nearly half a century (until the arrival of the compact disc (CD)) and are made in two basic formats. The 12″ (30 cm) diameter long-playing (LP) record plays at 33 1/3 rpm and provides about 25 minutes of music per side, well suited to longer musical compositions or recital 'albums.' The 7″ (18 cm) 'single' plays at 45 rpm to provide about seven minutes per side. There are other variants, such as the 12″ (30 cm) single.

From about 1958, the music industry changed over to stereo recording, and issues on both vinyl discs and tape cassettes have been mainly in stereo form ever since. Stereo recording is based on principles established by A.D. Blumlein in 1931. It aims at re-creating from a spaced pair of loudspeakers the same loudness and time of arrival differences at the listener's two ears as would be experienced at a live concert, to produce an apparently natural spread of sound. The procedure is to use microphones in pairs, either spaced apart or close together, but with different directional properties, to record different left and right channel signals.

These signals must be kept separate all the way through to the speakers. Therefore, though stereo recording and playback are relatively easy to achieve on twin-track tapes, they become more difficult on vinyl disc, which was, of course, the principal medium for recorded music in the 1950s. A number of methods were suggested for accommodating two mutually exclusive signals in a single record groove. One idea was to keep the signals at right angles to each other by recording the left channel, say, in the usual lateral manner and the other vertically, i.e., in the 'hill-and-dale' method used on Edison's phonograph cylinders. However, this produced an unbalanced effect, and the industry agreed to adopt one of the configurations originally proposed by Blumlein.

This sends the twin signals to the cutting stylus in such a way that the left channel is cut at +45 degrees to the disc surface and the right channel at −45 degrees. This gives the required separation and can be reproduced using a stereo pickup with twin transducer elements, each responding only to the left or right elements of the recorded waveform. Compatibility with mono discs and pickups was ensured by arranging the phase of the two signals so that movement of the pickup stylus parallel to the record surface (as on a laterally recorded mono record) produced equal and in-phase sound outputs from both the left and right loudspeakers.

There was some consumer resistance to stereo records at first; many people who had bought new LP players less than 10 years earlier were reluctant to invest in a new stereo pickup, with a new stylus size, plus a second amplifier channel and speaker. The standard mono LP pickup stylus had a tip radius of 0.001″ (0.025 mm), compared with the 0.003″ (0.075 mm) used for old 78

rpm records, but it had to be replaced with an even narrower version at 0.0005″ (0.0125 mm) to trace the new stereo grooves cleanly. In time, a compromise 0.0007″ (0.018 mm) stylus, equally effective for mono and stereo records, was used on most record players, while keen audiophiles chose a more expensive biradial elliptical stylus or one of the more exotic 'fine line' styli designed to get even closer to the wedge shape of a cutting stylus.

Around 1970, several record companies issued four-channel 'quadraphonic' records. The idea was to get beyond the limited letter-box sound field that stereo produces in the arc between a pair of speakers, and reproduce the full 360-degree field that surrounds a listener at a concert. They used arrays of four microphones or special mixing circuitry to produce four signals to be fed to four speakers arranged in a square around the listener.

In a commercially disastrous move, different companies chose three incompatible encoding systems to reduce these four channels to two, as required for fitting into the single groove of a stereo record. In the resulting confusion, very few homes bothered to take up any of the systems, and quadraphonic records faded out. Interestingly, surround sound later made a comeback in the cinema and migrated to videos and television programs as an important feature of 'home cinema.'

The next significant record format appeared in 1982 and was an almost immediate success, eventually eclipsing the LP and forming the basis for other media developments in video, computers and communications. This was the CD, and it was made possible by the changeover from analog to digital recording technology.

Bibliography

Audio Engineering Society (AES). 1981. *Disc Recording – An Anthology*, Vols. 1 and 2. New York: AES.

Borwick, John. 1994. *Sound Recording Practice*. 4th ed. Oxford: Oxford University Press.

Eargle, J. 1992. *Handbook of Recording Engineering*. New York: Van Nostrand Reinhold Co.

Gelatt, Roland. 1977. *The Fabulous Phonograph, 1877–1977*. 2nd ed. New York: Macmillan.

Woram, John M. 1982. *Sound Recording Handbook*. New York: Howard W. Sams.

JOHN BORWICK

Shellac

'Shellac' is another name for the type of phonograph record that preceded the vinyl LP. It refers to the hard brittle material then used for making records. Shellac comes from the scales ('shells') of the lac, an insect found in very large numbers in India, Burma and Thailand; 'lac' means 100,000 in the Hindu language. In fact, the discs were comprised of only about 14 percent shellac, to which was added carbon black, scrap and an abrasive limestone filler; the latter was designed to grind the soft steel or fiber replay needle (stylus) tip to the shape of the groove for optimum tracking of the recorded music waveform with minimum noise. Surface was still a serious nuisance, however, as anyone now trying to transfer 78s to a more modern medium will confirm.

Bibliography

Audio Engineering Society (AES). 1981. *Disc Recording – An Anthology*, Vols. 1 and 2. New York: AES.

Borwick, John. 1994. *Sound Recording Practice*. 4th ed. Oxford: Oxford University Press.

Eargle, J. 1992. *Handbook of Recording Engineering*. New York: Van Nostrand Reinhold Co.

Gelatt, Roland. 1977. *The Fabulous Phonograph, 1877–1977*. 2nd ed. New York: Macmillan.

Woram, John M. 1982. *Sound Recording Handbook*. New York: Howard W. Sams.

JOHN BORWICK

Solid State

A solid-state electronic circuit is one consisting chiefly of semiconductor materials or components (transistors). This distinguishes most modern amplifiers, receivers and other devices from the older electronic circuit designs, which relied on thermionic valves or tubes.

Amplifiers using triode or pentode valves, and rectifiers using diodes, were invented at the very beginning of the twentieth century and remained at the heart of practically all electronic equipment until the 1950s. Then solid-state transistor designs quite quickly took over because of their perceived advantages, such as higher power handling, lower inherent noise and reduced bulk, heat, operating voltages and cost. In hi-fi circles, the early transistor amplifiers were felt to lack warmth and fullness of tone. They were also liable to distortion on low-level music signals. Good engineering practise eventually overcame these solid-state problems and the basic benefits ensured an almost total eclipse of the valve.

In recent years, however, audiophiles have renewed their interest in valve designs, and some elaborate models have again become popular. A similar interest in a return to valves is found among some recording engineers, who deliberately seek out older electrostatic (condenser) microphones with built-in valve amplifiers in preference to the newer solid-state equivalents.

Bibliography

Mazda, F., ed. 1983. *Electronics Engineer's Reference Book*. 5th ed. London: Butterworths.

JOHN BORWICK

Stylus

A stylus is a sharply pointed instrument either for cutting a modulated groove on a blank master disc at the recording stage or for retracing the groove on a phonograph record for playback.

The cutting stylus is mounted in an electromagnetic cutterhead which converts the electrical music signals into an alternating force; this causes the stylus to vibrate either from side to side (mono) or, in a more complex manner, effectively in two planes at right angles to each other and at 45 degrees to the disc surface (stereo). The waveform etched into the disc surface has the same frequencies and relative levels as the original sound wave. The diamond or sapphire tip is precisely contoured to a chisel shape for clean cutting into the disc surface. The latter was wax in the early days and then either lacquer or copper. The stylus was sloped at the back for easy removal of the cutaway material (called 'swarf' or 'chip').

The phonograph playback stylus or 'needle' was originally made with a rounded hemispherical tip, whose radius caused it to rest on the walls of the V-shaped groove. In the 78 rpm era (up to around 1950), the 'needle' was made of steel, fiber or thorn, which was rapidly ground to occupy the whole groove by the hard particle-filled shellac disc material. The tip radius had not been standardized, but was about 0.003" (0.075 mm).

After the launch in 1948 of LP records, which had narrower grooves and used a soft vinyl material, hard sapphire or diamond styli were required, with a tip radius of 0.001" (0.025 mm). When stereo records were introduced about 10 years later, styli with a smaller 0.0005" (0.0125 mm) tip radius became necessary. There was still a degree of distortion and loss of high frequencies due to the different shapes of the cutting and playback styli, but hi-fi enthusiasts could obtain more accurate reproduction by paying a little more for elliptical (biradial) or 'fine line' styli that more closely resembled the cutting stylus shape.

Bibliography

Audio Engineering Society (AES). 1981. *Disc Recording – An Anthology*, Vols. 1 and 2. New York: AES.

Borwick, John. 1994. *Sound Recording Practice*. 4th ed. Oxford: Oxford University Press.

Eargle, J. 1992. *Handbook of Recording Engineering*. New York: Van Nostrand Reinhold Co.

Gelatt, Roland. 1977. *The Fabulous Phonograph, 1877–1977*. 2nd ed. New York: Macmillan.

Woram, John M. 1982. *Sound Recording Handbook*. New York: Howard W. Sams.

JOHN BORWICK

Tape

The making of recordings on magnetic tape has a long history and has come to occupy a leading place in every branch of home entertainment, computers and communications. It was the Danish engineer Valdemar Poulsen in 1897 who first demonstrated that sounds could be stored using an electromagnetic head traveling along a steel wire. The head coil carried an alternating current, derived from a telephone mouthpiece and corresponding in frequency and level to the original sound waves, and left the wire in a locally magnetized state. This magnetic 'soundtrack' could then be played back by passing the electromagnet along the wire again so that the recorded field induced a tiny alternating current into the coil, to reproduce the original sounds through a telephone earpiece.

Fifty years later, at the end of World War II, the Allied forces entering Germany found a variety of surprisingly advanced magnetic recorders. The old steel wire or ribbon had been replaced by a flexible plastic base film coated with iron oxide powder, and sound quality had been improved to the point where radio listeners could not detect whether broadcasts, by Hitler and others, were live or recorded. In a very short time, tape recording spread throughout the music industry, as well as radio and television broadcasting.

However, these early tapes were noisy and liable to dropouts or short breaks in the signal, due to the coarse granular nature of the magnetic coating. Short-term speed fluctuations were a serious problem with the first machines, leading to audible 'wow and flutter,' as the pitch changes at low and high frequencies came to be called.

The postwar years saw rapid improvements in every aspect of tape. A tape width of 0.25" (6.25 mm) became standard, with running speeds of 30" (76 cm), 15" (38 cm) and 7.5" (19 cm) per second. The higher speeds used up more tape, but gave higher quality. At first, all recordings used the full width of the tape, but half-track (for stereo, or else to double the available playing time per tape for mono) and then multitrack systems came into use. The record industry began to issue two-track stereo prerecorded tapes on 7" (18 cm) spools running at 7.5" (19 cm) per second, but these were relatively expensive compared with the same music sold on LP records; they were soon replaced by quarter-track tapes on 5" (12.7 cm) spools running at the lower speed of 3.75" (9.53 cm) per second to reduce costs. When cassettes appeared in the mid-1960s, open-reel tapes for domestic users virtually disappeared.

Bibliography

Snel, D.A. 1959. *Magnetic Sound Recording*. Eindhoven: Philips.

JOHN BORWICK

Tape Recorder

A tape recorder is a machine designed for recording and playback of audio and/or video signals using magnetic tape. Its essential features are a constant-speed transport system to move the recording medium from a supply reel to a take-up reel past the recording, erase and playback heads, amplifiers for the record and playback signals, and a high-frequency oscillator to supply bias and erase currents.

Samples of the German Magnetophon tape recorders found by the occupying forces in 1945 were soon brought to the United States and Britain. The development of new, improved recorders and tapes moved quickly in the United States, where ex-servicemen Richard Ranger and John T. Mullin separately demonstrated modified Magnetophons so successfully that Ampex and others were persuaded to begin manufacture of professional tape recorders and the 3M corporation went into production of its 'Scotch' tape. EMI in Britain similarly designed high-quality console recorders and tapes, which recording engineers and broadcasters used in increasing numbers.

The first impact was on professional recording, where the introduction of long-playing records (LPs) made it necessary that a recording medium capable of longer 'takes' than the old four-minute disc-cutting machines be found. In just a couple of years, producers and artists alike had to get used to a change in recording procedures. Tape machines were much easier to transport and set up and offered further benefits, such as almost immediate playback and restart. This was both time-saving and confidence-boosting. It became very easy for artists to repeat a difficult passage, safe in the knowledge that the best take – or even a single note – could be spliced in at a later date.

Mono recording across the full 0.25" (6.25 mm) tape width gave way to half-track stereo in the late 1950s. Then the progressive use of multitrack recorders gave record producers greater freedom in terms of studio layout and the building up of sounds in remix sessions, with separate microphones feeding signals to different tracks. Vocals and other instrumental tracks could be added later, with the artists listening to a premix of the previous tracks on headphones, and each track could be 'panned' anywhere across the stereo stage as required. Larger tape widths became necessary to accommodate the extra tracks, typical examples being eight tracks on 1" (25 mm) tape and 16 or 24 tracks on 2" (50 mm) tape.

Amateur tape recording became a popular hobby, as reduced speeds and smaller reels brought down costs. Commercial prerecorded tapes were first issued in 1954, carrying the same music as was being released on LPs, but these failed to sell in significant numbers. It was the arrival of the compact cassette in 1963 that really made 'tape records' a viable proposition.

Bibliography

Borwick, John. 1994. *Sound Recording Practice*. 4th ed. Oxford: Oxford University Press.

JOHN BORWICK

Video Disc

A video disc is the equivalent of a sound-only LP or CD record, but with the added ability to reproduce pictures as well as sound. This involves the recording of television-standard signals and the decoding of the results on replay for connection to a normal television receiver. Video disc has always had to compete with the popular VHS videocassette recorder system which, besides being cheaper, provides a convenient off-air recording facility.

Early video disc progress in the 1970s was limited because three different systems competed for public acceptance. In the end, the Philips LaserVision system achieved the best results. It used a 12" (30 cm) silver disc based on the same optical technology that would be applied to the development of the CD, and gave one hour's playing time per side with quick access and other user-convenient features.

LaserVision has evolved into the moderately successful laser disc (LD) medium taken up actively by Pioneer and others. However, the 12" (30 cm) LD seems likely to be overtaken in its turn by a more sophisticated 5" (12.7 cm) disc that gives up to 133 minutes of full-motion video, as well as multitrack hi-fi audio. This is the digital versatile disc (DVD), introduced in 1997, which has computer and communications, as well as home entertainment, applications.

Bibliography

'The Media Maze, Pt. 2.' 1995. *Gramophone Magazine* (May): 158–67.

JOHN BORWICK

Video Games

Games employing video imagery and electronically generated sound have transformed the entertainment industries in important ways since the early 1970s. Video games are typically played in one of four ways: in arcades, of the sort that previously housed pinball machines; through a conventional television set, using a game console or other attachment; on portable, handheld devices, such as Nintendo's 'Gameboy'; and, increasingly, on a computer, with CD-ROMs, diskettes or Internet hookups supplying the programming information necessary to run a game.

The origins of the video game are to be found within the subcultures of computer programmers, in particular those working on military applications of computer technology in the postwar period. Indeed, research into flight simulation and weapons guidance systems has spurred the development of the virtual-reality systems that video games have come, over time, to resemble. In the early 1960s, programmers in university laboratories in the United States began exchanging copies of the program for a game called 'Spacewar,' whose graphics were made up of conventional ASCII characters. In 1966, Ralph Baer, an engineer working for military contractors, developed a tennis-like game in which dots crossed the screen of a conventional television set and were bounced back and forth. A further development of this game was purchased in 1971 by Magnavox, which attempted, unsuccessfully, to market a plug-in game console for television sets under the name 'Odyssey.' In 1972, a modified tennis game called 'Pong' was invented by three engineers at the Ampex Corporation, who left that company to found a new firm, Atari, devoted to video games. 'Pong' was hugely popular in arcades, and a home version, marketed in conjunction with the Sears retail chain beginning in 1975, became a phenomenal success.

In the two decades that followed, video games became a billion-dollar industry, through cycles of boom (1980–83) and bust (1984–86). In the late 1980s, Japanese firms such as Nintendo and Sega came to dominate the market, with immensely popular games (such as 'Super Mario') and enhanced display properties that benefited from advances in computer chip technology.

The emergence and popularization of video games have had several implications for the music industries. Firstly, as an entertainment form whose principal appeal is to adolescent males, video games compete directly with popular music for the attention and disposable income of consumers. In the late 1970s and early 1980s, for example, many music industry observers in North America claimed that the decline in record sales observable at that time was a direct result of the ascendant appeal of video console and arcade games. Secondly, video games, like videocassettes and computer software, have come to be sold in stores previously devoted exclusively to musical recordings, as part of the transformation of many record stores into home entertainment retail centers. Finally, as the technologies of video game presentation have improved, the incorporation of popular music within games has become more common. Indeed, as video game companies have come to be integrated within multimedia conglomerates (such as Sony), the release of video games based on musical performers (for example, 'Spice Girls') has become part of campaigns to promote these performers.

Bibliography

Herz, J.C. 1997. *Joystick Nation: How Videogames Ate Our Quarters, Won Our Hearts, and Rewired Our Minds*. New York: Little Brown & Company.

Kent, Steven, Horwitz, Jer, and Fielder, Joe. *History of Video Games.* http://www.videogamespot.com/features/universal/hov/

Sullivan, George. 1983. *Screen Play: The Story of Video Games.* New York: Frederick Warne.

Discography

Buckner and Garcia. *Pac-Man Fever.* Columbia 02673. *1982*: USA.

WILL STRAW

Vinyl

'Vinyl' is the generic term for the vinylite plastic or PVC material chosen by Columbia Records for the new long-playing microgroove records (LPs), which they launched to great acclaim in 1948 to replace the old shellac 78 rpm records. It allowed narrower grooves and the slower 33 1/3 rpm speed to be used, with about a sixfold increase in playing time per side. The new vinyl records, which included 7" (18 cm) singles running at 45 rpm as well as 12" (30 cm) LPs, were almost unbreakable, but the soft surface was easily scratched, causing annoying clicks, and required new lightweight pickups tracking at only a few grams. Consumers also had to buy new turntables with these new speeds, plus 78 rpm if they wanted to keep on playing their collection of 78s. One nuisance not evident on shellac discs was the tendency of vinyl to build up static electrical charges, which caused records to cling to their sleeves and even discharge noisily during play.

Bibliography

Audio Engineering Society (AES). 1981. *Disc Recording – An Anthology*, Vols. 1 and 2. New York: AES.

Borwick, John. 1994. *Sound Recording Practice.* 4th ed. Oxford: Oxford University Press.

Eargle, J. 1992. *Handbook of Recording Engineering.* New York: Van Nostrand Reinhold Co.

Gelatt, Roland. 1977. *The Fabulous Phonograph, 1877–1977.* 2nd ed. New York: Macmillan.

Woram, John M. 1982. *Sound Recording Handbook.* New York: Howard W. Sams.

JOHN BORWICK

Walkman

'Walkman' is the generic term for portable headphone stereo sets that use cassette tapes, compact discs or mini-discs. The name was coined by Akio Morita, the president of Sony, the company that marketed the first model in 1979. The name 'Walkman' was legally registered by Sony, but it has come to be commonly used for any type of headphone stereo (like 'Xerox' for photocopiers in general). Although some Walkmans have recording capabilities, sound reproduction is more fundamental to the apparatus.

Sony has been the target of some lawsuits concerning patents filed by alleged inventors of the Walkman. This is understandable because the basic technological concept – the combination of portable reproduction system and headphones – is not complicated, and it was common to listen to music through headphones (either in a studio or at home) long before the Walkman was introduced. Low-fidelity earphones had been applied to transistor-radio listening since the 1960s, for example, in soccer stadiums. Sony's first model was based on a portable cassette tape *recorder* invented in the mid-1970s and used mainly for outdoor recording and language lessons. Few used it for music listening while walking, although this was technically possible.

Sony shifted the technical emphasis from recording (microphone) to reproduction (headphones) and, to minimize the weight and size, removed the recording device and developed light high-fidelity headphones. Thus, the Walkman was born. This technological transformation allowed the extended use of headphones in public spaces. It is in this new relationship of listening to space that the novelty of the Walkman lies. In fact, an early advertisement by Sony stressed the 'streetwise' nature of its new product by using a photograph of roller skaters and an image of Walkman logos walking like pairs of sneakers. Although, since the 1980s, digital technology has made possible the development and introduction of Walkman models using compact discs (Discman) and minidiscs (MD Walkman), the social characteristics of the Walkman have been basically unaffected.

Some early Sony advertising showed two people with headphone sets listening to the same Walkman. However, this shared experience was soon brushed aside by the image and practise of the solitary listener. Silent youth in commuter trains or on the street, listening to something that cannot be overheard – this has come to be the typical image of Walkman users. Narcissism and autism have been the two characteristics attributed to them. Users have often been accused of indifference to the outside world or of having a preference for a co-cooned life style. They have sometimes been called 'alien' because they have appeared to live in their own world, isolated from others. They have provided a sharp contrast to users of ghetto blasters, who have reproduced their music with loud portable stereos on the street to create a transitory sense of affective, collective identity, and who have often been accused of obtrusiveness. Walkman users have distanced themselves from any sense of collectivity.

The defining characteristic of the customary image of the Walkman is inseparable from the individual use of headphones: the formation of intimate personal aural space. It can provide a musical experience in a public space that is undisturbed by sounds or noises from sources other than the user's own music selection. In this sense, Walkman users arrange, so to speak, a personally designed 'soundtrack' for their mobile space and form singular and autonomous points in the soundscape surrounding them. It is silent from outside, but interactive from inside.

An assessment of the Walkman can thus oscillate between sinister autism and celebratory autonomy. Although initially users of the Walkman were young people, its use has expanded to include people of all ages.

Bibliography

Chambers, Iain. 1994. 'The Aural Walk.' In *Migrancy, Culture, Identity*. London and New York: Routledge, 49–53.

Chow, Rey. 1993. 'Listening Otherwise, Music Miniaturized.' In *Writing Diaspora: Tactics of Intervention in Contemporary Cultural Studies*. Bloomington and Indianapolis: Indiana University Press, 144–64.

du Gay, Paul, et al. 1997. *Doing Cultural Studies: The Story of the Sony Walkman*. London: Sage.

Ferraro, Angelo, and Montagno, Gabriele, eds. 1990. *Estetiche del Walkman* [The Aesthetic of the Walkman]. Naples: Flavio Pagano Editore.

Hosokawa, Shuhei. 1981. *Walkman no Shujigaku* [Rhetoric of the Walkman]. Tokyo: Asahi Shuppan.

Hosokawa, Shuhei. 1984. 'The Walkman Effect.' *Popular Music* 4: 165–80.

SHUHEI HOSOKAWA

13. Instrument Manufacture

Instrument Manufacture

The manufacture and sale of musical instruments constitute an important part of the music industry. While the making of instruments by hand has a long history – and some specialists have continued to make guitars and other instruments in this way for professional musicians and affluent amateurs – mass production has been the dominant feature of the industry since the mid-nineteenth century, with firms supplying the needs of schools, orchestras, military and amateur bands, as well as of hobbyists. In its early stages, the instrument manufacturing trade was strongly interrelated with the music publishing industry; in its contemporary form, it concentrates on the production of instruments, their distribution and retailing. The necessity for maintenance, repair and hire, and the high level of secondhand instrument purchases further characterize this sector of the music industry.

The musical instrument sector has influenced the development of both classical and popular music through innovation in musical instrument design (what Chanan (1994) calls the 'engineering dimension of musical history' (165)), especially when 'the musical idiom is conditioned by the kinds of instruments upon which musicians play' (13).

History

In the Middle Ages, instrument manufacture existed within the institutional framework of church and municipal musicians' guilds. In the sixteenth century, when a new musical public emerged, amateur musicians needed instruments appropriate for use in a domestic context. The violin, which in its modern form emerged around 1550, served this purpose – a product of skilled craftsmanship and engineering, which could be achieved only with the improved precision tools developed at this time.

In the first decade of the eighteenth century, the Prince of Medici commissioned the Florentine craftsman Bartolomeo Cristofori to combine the features of clavichord and harpsichord to create an instrument with a more varied and consistent tone and sound. The result was the pianoforte, which for three centuries has remained one of the most enduring Western musical instruments: most accounts of *musica practica* are based on the history of the piano (see Ehrlich 1990; Loesser 1954; and Weber 1958). During the eighteenth century, the violin and piano became associated with members of the emerging European middle class, eager to practise music in their home using printed sheet music and the first written instruction manuals for playing instruments.

From about 1750, a distinct piano manufacturing industry took shape in association with piano music publishers, piano teachers and piano tuners. The name of the manufacturer was displayed on the instrument, and manufacturers fought to ensure that their products were visible on the concert platform of popular pianist-composers. From the middle of the nineteenth century, demand for pianos spread to the more affluent members of the European and North American working class, many of whom purchased pianos using the newly introduced hire-purchase installment plan (Chanan 1994, 208). Among the leading piano manufacturers were Chappell of London (1840) and the German company Bechstein (1850).

Military wind bands and civilian brass bands in nineteenth-century Europe provided a market for brass and reed instruments. Such innovations as the accordion (first manufactured in Italy in 1863 by Paolo Soprani and others), the concertina (patented by Charles Wheatstone in England in 1829) and the harmonica (mass-produced by Hohner in Germany in 1857) satisfied the demand for instruments for more informal music-making.

The emerging North American instrument manufacturing industry was stimulated by import restrictions, by the impact of German, Irish and Italian immigrant instrument makers, such as C.F. Martin, the guitar maker, and Gretsch, the country's first drum manufacturer, and by the Civil War (1861–65), which encouraged the manufacture of brass instruments and drums for military bands. By the middle of the nineteenth century, North America was also one of the leading centers of piano production in the world. In 1855, the total income of the music trades, including instrument manufacture and sales, in North America was estimated to be $24 million (total national wealth was $4.5 billion), and in 1866 $15 million was spent on pianos alone (Sanjek 1988).

Instrument Manufacture in the Twentieth Century

At the start of the twentieth century, the United States and Europe were equally important in terms of instrument manufacture. The major factors influencing the industry's evolution during the following century were changes in musical taste, significant progress in technology, the impact of two world wars and the entry of Japan as a major competitor in the market.

In the United States, plucked stringed instruments, including the mandolin, the guitar, the ukulele and the banjo, gained in popularity between 1900 and 1930. Demand was stimulated by the formation of clubs and orchestras, and by the popularity of Hawaiian and country (hillbilly) music. The number of guitars produced increased from 78,444 in 1900 to 162,764 in 1929.

The US piano industry enjoyed a boom in the manufacture of player pianos, assisted by the introduction in 1905 of a standard piano roll capable of being used with any manufacturer's instrument. 'Industrial cooperation and standardization thus proved to be essential components in a strategy to both stabilize and stimulate the marketplace' (Théberge 1997, 29). Between 1904 and 1930, 2.5 million player pianos were sold in the United States. The leading firm was Aeolian, which also provided pipe organs for home use, many of them also with automatic playing devices.

During World War I, the supply of woodwind instruments from Europe was interrupted, and band instrument manufacturers in the United States began making their own, often with the help of skilled craftsmen from Europe. The import of instruments from such firms as Selmer (of Paris) resumed in 1918, although US-based manufacturing increased again during World War II.

Encouraged by the popularity of theatrical shows, and especially of jazz bands, the drumset ('trap' set) was developed, with increasing numbers of percussion instruments and such special effects as pedal timpani. The Ludwig Drum Company of Chicago perfected the foot-operated bass drum pedal in 1909. Zildjian, the Turkish cymbal manufacturer, established a US branch in Boston, Massachusetts in 1929. Instruments played with a mallet, such as the vibraphone (invented in 1916 by Leedy), became increasingly popular.

The success of attempts to introduce musical education into public schools in the United States in the mid-1920s led to an increased demand for band instruments. Sales of brass instruments also increased rapidly as a result of the popularity of touring bands. The Conn Company capitalized on the vogue for saxophones.

In the 1930s, the combination of the Depression and the new music media – the gramophone and the radio – 'had a profound effect on the social and economic organization of entertainment so that, for example, the rise of record companies meant the decline of the music publishing and piano-making empires, shifting roles for concert hall owners and live-music promoters' (Frith 1992, 55). During the Depression, instrument sales dropped dramatically, and manufacturers either went out of business or adopted drastic methods of rationalization and diversification to survive. In the keyboard sector, the Aeolian Company and the American Piano Corporation merged in 1932, bringing nearly 20 once-independent piano companies together under the new banner of the Aeolian American Corporation. Guitar manufacturers Martin and Gibson increased investment in product development and added such new features as Martin's 14-fret neck to their product lines.

There were also developments and rapid advances in the field of electronics. A Russian, Leon Termen, invented the theremin, while in 1929 Laurens Hammond invented the first electronic organ, which became the prototype for an affordable electronic instrument ideal for use in commercial popular music. Sales of electronic organs and electric pianos (introduced in the 1950s) in the United States had reached a peak of hundreds of thousands by the end of the 1960s, but these instruments were superseded by more sophisticated instruments in the 1980s.

The most far-reaching application of electronics technology was the electrical amplification of the guitar. After World War II, the electric guitar played a role in contemporary popular music comparable only to that of the piano in the nineteenth century. In 1946, Leo Fender formed the Fender Electric Instrument Company, and by 1948 he was marketing the solid-body Broadcaster; this was followed in 1954 by the Stratocaster, which was to play an important part in the rock 'n' roll revolution.

Further evidence of the close relationship between musical instruments and new musical genres was the fact that, following the first appearance of the Beatles in the United States, 1 million guitars were sold in 1964.

The ownership structure of the industry also changed as established family firms were sold, since '[d]uring the boom years of the 1960s and '70s, large corporations viewed the industry as a potentially lucrative source of additional income' (Théberge 1997, 37). For example, the diversification strategy of CBS (Columbia Broadcasting System) included the purchase not only of the New York Yankees, but also of Steinway & Sons and, in 1965, of the Fender companies for $13 million. In 1960, Bechstein sold shares to the Baldwin Piano and Organ Company of the United States, and Baldwin became full owner of Bechstein in 1973. In the 1960s, the Selmer Company purchased several other manufacturing firms and began to sell brass instruments, saxophones and so on. C.F. Martin also entered a period of acquisition in 1970, incorporating drum, banjo and guitar companies into its business. Later, a reverse trend developed in the mid-1980s, as Fender, Steinway and Bechstein were sold off by their new owners.

Although these developments proved that piano manufacturing could still attract investment, the global production of 750,000 pianos in 1970 was only 20 percent higher than that of 1910. In addition, production in the United States and Europe had fallen as Russia and Japan emerged into the piano manufacturing market. Piano manufacturing in Russia increased tenfold between 1953 and 1970, although this production was mainly for internal sales only. In contrast, Japan quickly overtook both the United States and Germany to become the largest piano manufacturer and exporter in the world. Japanese output of pianos rose from fewer than 10,000 in 1953 to 257,000 instruments in 1969, 35,000 more than were produced in the United States. European production was barely one-fifth of that of Japan. Between 1990 and 1992, global piano production fell to around 600,000 from 1 million instruments, with cheaper models from South Korea and China further squeezing the Western manufacturers of high-cost instruments. In Germany, Bechstein filed for bankruptcy in 1993.

The traditional acoustic piano also faced competition from a new generation of electronic keyboards. Following the invention of the synthesizer (usually attributed to Robert A. Moog in 1965) and its commercial development, electronic instruments developed faster than any other segment of the industry. The first step toward low-cost, portable electronic and digital keyboards for the home market was the synclavier, produced in 1976. This was followed by musical instrument digital interface (MIDI), which would become the standard system for enabling instruments made by different manufacturers to be compatible with each other. Roland's influential TR-808 drum machine appeared in 1980, and in 1983 Yamaha launched the DX7, the bestselling synthesizer of all time. Both machines helped to define the popular music of the 1980s. The possibility of reproducing music was taken a step further in the 1990s when sampling technologies made music recyclable. Sampling of existing prerecorded music made DJs into pop stars and the turntable and mixing desk manufactured by companies such as Technics into instruments.

According to Théberge (1997, 32), quoting from a November 1990 issue of *The Music Trades*, the musical instrument industry 'is . . . composed of a number of product categories that are "in themselves self-contained industries with their own set of customers, trade practices, and challenges."' The fragmented nature of the instrument market has allowed new companies to succeed with a single product line. With little more than one line of electronic keyboards, Casio, for example, became the fifth largest supplier of musical instruments in the United States in less than a decade. One exception has been the Yamaha Corporation of America, which, at the end of the twentieth century, was the top instrument supplier in North America and was capable of supplying instruments in virtually all industry sectors, although its main strength was in digital musical instruments and sound reinforcement equipment. In 1989, 25 percent of total retail sales of musical instruments in the United States was accounted for by the top five companies (Yamaha, Peavey Electronics, Baldwin Piano and Organ Company, Roland Corporation (US) and Casio, Inc.), with Yamaha itself accounting for 10 percent.

National trade associations in several countries provide annual statistics, which indicate how far these new developments have influenced sales of traditional instruments. The two main associations in the United States are the National Association of Music Merchants (NAMM) and the American Music Conference (AMC). The United Kingdom has the Music Industries Association (MIA), while France has the Bureau d'aide à l'Insertion Professionnelle des Étudiants (BIPE), a trade association that is part of the Ministry of Culture. In each country, the education market has remained an important factor. In France, for example, the purchase of specific instruments is a standard requirement for music schools and conservatories, where the piano and the violin have continued to be the most favored instruments. Sales of woodwind, bowed and brass instruments in Europe and the United States stayed at the same level during the 1990s.

A 1995 UK dealer survey commissioned by the MIA showed that, with a total of 381,000 units, the portable keyboard was the bestselling instrument, although this unit figure had fallen from 600,000 in 1991. Guitars were next, with a total of 108,000 units and with slightly more acoustic than electric guitars sold. In comparison to 1991, there had been an increase in guitar sales.

Over the past two centuries, instrument manufacture, like other sectors of the music industry, has experienced mechanization, industrialization, rationalization and democratization. Commentators on this process have been divided as to whether it represents a democratization of music that was welcome or a threat to traditional music-making. Théberge is pragmatic in this regard. Accepting the dialectical nature of the process, he points out that, while new developments in musical practise are driven by technology, the fascination with existing traditional and 'ethnic' instruments has never declined and has helped to bring such instruments and their characteristic sounds back into mainstream popular culture. The Beatles experimented with the sitar, and Jamiroquai and others brought the didjeridu into Western popular cultural consciousness.

Bibliography

Chanan, Michael. 1994. *Musica Practica: The Social Practice of Western Music from Gregorian Chant to Postmodernism*. London: Verso.

Ehrlich, Cyril. 1990 (1976). *The Piano: A History*. Rev. ed. Oxford: Oxford University Press.

Frith, Simon. 1992. 'The Industrialization of Popular Music.' In *Popular Music and Communication*, ed. James Lull. Thousand Oaks, CA and London: Sage, 53–77.

Gammond, Peter. 1991. *The Oxford Companion to Popular Music*. Oxford: Oxford University Press.

Hitchcock, H. Wiley, and Sadie, Stanley, eds. 1986. *The New Grove Dictionary of American Music*. London: Macmillan.

Loesser, Arthur. 1954. *Men, Women and Pianos: A Social History*. New York: Simon and Schuster.

Russell, Dave. 1987. *Popular Music in England, 1840–1914: A Social History*. Manchester: Manchester University Press.

Sadie, Stanley, ed. 1984. *The New Grove Dictionary of Musical Instruments*. London: Macmillan.

Sanjek, Russell. 1988. *American Popular Music and Its Business: The First Four Hundred Years. Vol. II: From 1790 to 1909*. New York: Oxford University Press.

Théberge, Paul. 1997. *Any Sound You Can Imagine: Making Music/Consuming Technology*. Hanover, NH: Wesleyan University Press/University Press of New England.

Trynka, P., ed. 1996. *Rock Hardware*. London: Balafon Books.

Weber, Max. 1958. *The Rational and Social Foundations of Music*, trans. Don Martindale et al. Carbondale, IL: Southern Illinois University Press.

VANESSA BASTIAN

14. Management and Marketing

A&R

'A&R' ('artist and repertoire') is the term used for those who are formally responsible for acquiring new artists and pieces of music for record companies and overseeing the process of song selection, musical arrangement and recording. The term was in widespread use in the United States in the 1940s and probably originated in the 1930s.

In very broad terms, three distinct A&R roles can be identified within the modern music industry: that of talent scout, that of facilitator and that of interventionist. As a talent scout, the A&R person or department is responsible for choosing which artists should be offered a recording contract. As a facilitator, the A&R person's job is to support, encourage and nurture the 'talent,' provide a critical voice and deal with the administrative procedures required for rehearsing, arranging and recording. In contrast, as an interventionist the A&R person is actively involved in all aspects of the creative process, from selecting songs, recruiting musicians and scoring arrangements to producing recordings in the studio. Such an A&R person may also be accorded the role of co-producer or executive producer.

According to Hennion (1981), the French equivalent of the A&R person in the 1970s was the *directeur artistique*.

Bibliography

Frith, Simon. 1976. 'The A&R Men.' In *Rock File 4*, ed. Charlie Gillett and Simon Frith. St. Alban's: Granada, 25–46.

Hennion, Antoine. 1981. *Les Professionnels du disque: une sociologie des variétés* [The Recording Professionals: A Sociology of Entertainment]. Paris: A.-M. Métailié.

Negus, Keith. 1992. *Producing Pop: Culture and Conflict in the Popular Music Industry*. London and New York: Edward Arnold.

KEITH NEGUS and DAVE LAING

Act

Originating in the circus and vaudeville world in the late nineteenth century, the term 'act' referred both to the short performance given and to the performers themselves. Thus, circus managers or vaudeville promoters would include 'high-wire acts' or 'ukulele acts' on their programs. In seventeenth-century English, 'act' had sometimes been used to describe the interval between the main sections of a dramatic performance when a brief entertainment was provided, and it has been suggested that this is the origin of the modern usage.

The second meaning subsequently came into widespread use in the music industry as a simple synonym for any type of vocal or instrumental performer or group. Thus, booking agents would publicize the acts that they represented, and Wale (1972) quotes a promoter's description of his job as 'putting on concerts, booking the acts' (240).

Bibliography

Wale, Michael. 1972. *Vox Pop: Profiles of the Pop Process*. London: Harrap.

DAVE LAING

Advertising of Popular Music

Music publishers, instrument manufacturers, concert promoters and record companies need to inform potential consumers of their products and to stimulate demand for them. Alongside plugging songs and the use of public relations techniques, the music industry has made considerable use of advertising in a wide range of media, from posters and periodicals to radio and television.

Popular music advertising was an essential part of the emergent concert market in the seventeenth century. The first public concerts given in London in the 1670s were advertised through newspapers and handbills 'passed out in coffeehouses and taverns' (Sanjek 1988, Vol. 1, 109).

From the early nineteenth century, the concert poster became a principal means to advertise forthcoming events. The circus manager P.T. Barnum organized large-scale poster and street advertising campaigns, such as that for the 1851 sell-out tour of the United States by Jenny Lind. In Europe, full-color posters for music events and venues were pioneered by Jules Cheret in Paris (Edge 1991, 57).

Popular newspapers were another significant advertising medium, particularly for pianos and other instruments to be used in the home and for concerts. Tawa (1990, 48) gives the example of the Henry Clay Work song 'Kingdom Coming,' whose title was used in local newspaper 'teaser' advertisements in 1862, which preceded the arrival of the touring Christy Minstrels in a stage show of the same name. By the end of the nineteenth century, many newspapers were publishing regular song supplements. New songs could also be advertised by a publisher on the back cover of copies of an already successful song. The early blues recording industry of the 1920s relied heavily on advertising in newspapers such as the *Chicago Defender* that circulated within the black communities of both the South and the North. The records were often offered for sale by mail order.

However, the most favored way of advertising new popular songs and promoting sales of sheet music was plugging, defined by music publisher Edward B. Marks as 'any public performance which is calculated to boost a song.' These performances could be given by singers or organ grinders on the street, by pianists and vocalists in music and department stores that stocked printed music, and in concerts or vaudeville shows. Publishers paid well-known artists to feature a song and the singer would act as an advertising medium as he/she introduced it to new audiences across the United States.

The foundation of the record industry at the beginning of the twentieth century coincided with an exponential growth in the quantity and the technical impact of advertising. While manufacturers of gramophones, discs and cylinders supplied retailers with copies of their catalogs to be given away to consumers, they also took advantage of the new outdoor and print advertising media.

Street advertising reached a peak in the campaigns of the Victor Talking Machine Company, which, in 1906,

erected on Broadway (New York) the world's largest illuminated sign: it measured 40' (12 m) by 50' (15 m) and contained 1,000 electric lights (Hutto 1977). In 1926, Victor advertised Paul Whiteman's 'In a Little Spanish Town' with streetcar posters in big cities aimed at 1.2 million travelers per month; the company was hoping for a 1 percent sales response (Sanjek 1988, Vol. 3, 71).

Other means were occasionally used. In St. Louis, for example, record store owner Jesse Johnson hired planes to shower leaflets advertising new blues records on crowds attending baseball games.

Posters were to remain an indispensable means of advertising concerts and records. Their styles have ranged from the 'boxing bill' designs used to publicize the package tours of the 1950s to the exotic psychedelia of the San Francisco scene in the late 1960s. In many cities, popular music posters are widely and often illegally fly-posted on walls, empty stores and other unauthorized sites, and the fly-posting business is tightly controlled. The dance music scene of the 1990s substituted handbill-size 'flyers' for posters.

In Britain, record and gramophone companies were enthusiastic users of the mass-circulation newspapers that were launched to cater to both the middle class and the skilled working class.

From the 1920s onward, the publication of specialist magazines aimed at music enthusiasts provided a vital advertising medium for record companies, retailers, instrument manufacturers and concert promoters of all types of popular music. Instrument advertisements frequently featured an endorsement by a famous musician, who would usually be supplied with equipment by the manufacturer in return for the endorsement. From the 1960s, pictorial advertisements have been accompanied by the supply of free 'flexi-discs,' cassettes or CDs containing tracks paid for by record companies. The considerable economic dependence of music magazines on industry advertising has given rise to suspicions that editors are inclined to favorably review albums that are advertised in their publications (Jones 1993).

In the rock music era, as popular music aspired to the status of an art form, advertising of new albums often followed the example of the book industry by including quotations from favorable reviews of the product (such as 'I saw rock 'n' roll future and its name is Bruce Springsteen,' taken from a 1974 concert review), or by the invention of 'hip' slogans to attract attention. One of the most notorious of these was the use of the phrase 'The Man Can't Bust Our Music' in Columbia Records' press advertisements for its 'underground' acts. This was one example of a vast amount of advertising placed by record companies in the growing number of alternative and specialist publications that the companies felt provided a link to the unknown youth audience for underground music.

From the 1930s, the broadcasting media offered the possibility of the concert and in-store demonstration with the added advantage of much greater potential audiences. In the early days of US radio, music publishers supplied song-plugger vocalists free of charge to stations. A notable success was that of composer and ukulele player Wendell Hall, whose relentless plugging of 'It Ain't Gonna Rain No Mo'' resulted in over a million sales.

While publishers and record companies continued to plug records to station producers and announcers, they also bought advertising time. Since the 1950s, record companies in many countries have undertaken covert or overt sponsorship of programs that contain only recordings released by themselves. In the 1950s, the English-language service of Radio Luxembourg broadcast 15-minute shows paid for by EMI, Decca and other labels. In 1998, record companies in the United States began a similar practise of paying stations to play and announce their new releases.

Local radio stations have played an increasing role in advertising concerts and festivals, usually through deals with promoters that guarantee the station free tickets or even a proportion of concert profits.

In television, stations in a number of countries regularly transmit programs of videos paid for by individual local labels. A different approach to television advertising was pioneered in the 1960s by K-Tel and other marketing companies. Their campaigns featured specially compiled hits albums, some of which were available only by mail order. The success of these initiatives inspired mainstream record companies to use television campaigns, and television advertising has become a major part of many large labels' marketing budgets. When restrictions on the television advertising of records were lifted in France in 1988, the music industry claimed that within a year it was enjoying a significant increase in sales.

The latest medium for the advertising of popular music is the Internet. Record companies and artists have set up many thousands of Web sites to promote their products, and there are numerous Web sites offering brief sound bites of music that can be ordered for postal delivery and, in a few cases, can be downloaded into the purchaser's computer.

Bibliography

Edge, K. 1991. *The Art of Selling Songs: Graphics for the Music Business 1690–1990*. London: Futures Publications.

Grushkin, P.D. 1987. *The Art of Rock: Posters from Presley to Punk*. New York: Abbeville Press.

Hutto, Edgar. 1977. 'Emile Berliner, Eldridge Johnson and the Victor Talking Machine Company.' *Journal of the Audio Engineering Society* 25(10/11) (October–November): 666–73.

Jones, Steve. 1993. 'Popular Music, Criticism, Advertising and the Music Industry.' *Journal of Popular Music Studies* 5: 79–91.

Sanjek, Russell. 1988. *American Popular Music and Its Business: The First Four Hundred Years*. 3 vols. New York and Oxford: Oxford University Press.

Tawa, Nicholas. 1990. *The Way to Tin Pan Alley*. New York: Schirmer.

Sheet Music

Work, Henry Clay, comp. and lyr. 1862. 'Kingdom Coming.' Chicago: Root & Cady.

Discographical References

Hall, Wendell. 'It Ain't Gonna Rain No Mo''/'Red Headed Music Maker.' Victor 19171. 1923: USA. Reissue: Hall, Wendell. 'It Ain't Gonna Rain No Mo'.' *Howdy! 25 Hillbilly All-Time Greats*. ASV/Living Era 5140. *1995*: USA.

Varner, Tom. 'Kingdom Coming' (comp. Henry Clay Work). *Window Up Above: American Songs 1770–1998*. New World 80552. *1998*: USA.

Whiteman, Paul. 'In a Little Spanish Town'/'Boatman on the Volga.' Victor 20266. 1926: USA. Reissue: Whiteman, Paul. 'In a Little Spanish Town.' *Greatest Hits*. Collectors Choice 61. *1998*: USA.

DAVE LAING

Agent

The job of the booking agent is to arrange performances, concerts and tours for popular music performers. The agent acts as a link between the artist or his/her manager and local promoters. The agent's payment comes from the fee he/she negotiates on behalf of the artist. For many years, it was a standard 10 percent of the fee, although for newer acts it can be more, and for superstars, less.

During the mid-nineteenth century, the agent's function in booking appearances by touring minstrel troupes or vocal groups was often carried out by the manager of the act. With the development of the division of labor in the entertainment industry, the first specialist show business agents represented music hall and vaudeville acts and dramatic actors, as well as music performers. By the end of the nineteenth century, the individual entrepreneurial agent was being displaced in the United States by agencies representing significant numbers of acts. Among the most powerful was the William Morris

Agency, founded in 1898 and, at the end of the twentieth century, still the largest agency in the country.

Such agencies built up close relationships with theater owners, while others, such as the Theater Owners Booking Agency (TOBA), were set up by the owners themselves and thus controlled access to many key performance venues. TOBA, known colloquially as 'tough on black asses,' had the monopoly of bookings on the black entertainment circuit of the 1920s (Vincent 1995).

The first booking agency to specialize in popular music acts was the Music Corporation of America (MCA), founded in 1924 by Billy Stein (who was later joined by his brother Jules). With the advent of dance bands as major entertainment attractions, MCA and other agencies came to exercise considerable power in the US music, theater and radio industries. MCA itself later moved into record, film and television production and was forced to divest itself of its agency business for anti-trust reasons.

In the rock 'n' roll period of the 1950s and 1960s, in Britain and the United States, agents such as Irving Feld of General Artists Corporation (in the United States) and Harold Davison (in Britain) played a key role in setting up 'package tours,' choosing the six or more acts and planning their itineraries.

These agents had little affinity with rock, however, and in 1964 Premier Talent, the first US agency to specialize in rock music, was set up by Frank Barsalona. Beginning with Herman's Hermits and the Who, Barsalona specialized in booking US tours by the leading British acts of the 1960s.

At the end of the 1990s, the US agency scene, like the record industry, was dominated by a handful of companies that booked most of the largest national tours. These companies included William Morris, with over 400 artists; Creative Artists (CAA), with 200; and International Creative Management (ICM), with 250. CAA and ICM each had corporate links with a large British and a European agency, International Talent Booking (ITB) and Fair Warning – Wasted Talent, respectively. Smaller US agencies specializing in particular genres included Erv Woolsey (country) and Fleming, Tamulevich & Associates (roots music).

Outside the Anglophone world, the roles of manager, agent and concert promoter can be blurred. In many countries, there are no specialist agents but, instead, individuals or companies combine management of artists with booking their live shows.

Bibliography

Baskerville, David. 1995. *Music Business Handbook and Career Guide*. 6th ed. Thousand Oaks, CA: Sherwood.

Goodman, Fred. 1997. *The Mansion on the Hill: Dylan, Young, Geffen, Springsteen, and the Head-On Collision of Rock and Commerce*. New York: Random House.

Leighton-Pope, Carl. 1991. 'Booking Agents.' In *The Rock File: Making It in the Music Business*, ed. Norton York. Oxford: Oxford University Press, 194–203.

Vincent, Ted. 1995. *Keep Cool: The Black Activists Who Built the Jazz Age*. London and East Haven: Pluto Press.

Wale, Michael. 1972. *Vox Pop: Profiles of the Pop Process*. London: Harrap.

DAVE LAING

Awards

Perhaps more than any other cultural industry, the music industry worldwide takes every opportunity to present awards to its members. Record industry bodies, authors' societies, composers' organizations and music media all provide annual festivals of self-congratulation for promotional reasons and purposes. Decisions concerning awards are made according to either commercial or artistic criteria. The most financially rewarding of all the awards is Sweden's Polar Music Prize (worth 1 million kronor – $120,000 – to the winner), while the most prestigious are the Grammy awards which, each year since 1958, have been decided on the basis of votes by members of the US National Academy of Recording Arts and Sciences (NARAS).

Awards for Commercial Success

The most common form of award for commercial success is the 'gold disc,' given by national record industry bodies when a single or album achieves a certain level of sales. The quantity of copies that need to be sold for a single or album to qualify for such an award varies greatly according to the size of the national music market. At the end of the twentieth century, an album needed 5,000 unit sales to be awarded a gold disc in Iceland (population 255,000 in 1998), while the equivalent figure in the United States (population 250 million in 1998) was 500,000 (IFPI 1998).

In some cases, the level of sales required for a single or album to qualify for an award is different for different types of music. In Greece, for example, at the close of the twentieth century, a gold award was given to a locally made album that achieved sales of 20,000, but albums of foreign music needed sales of only 15,000. Changes in the relative popularity of different sound-carrier formats have also brought about modifications in the number of sales needed to qualify for an award. In the early 1980s, a single needed 1 million sales in the United States and 500,000 in Britain to be awarded a gold disc. By 1998, when overall sales of singles had fallen, a hit single qualified for gold status with sales of 500,000 in the United States and 400,000 in Britain.

Although many awards ceremonies include categories

that recognize commercial success, only a few are based solely on this criterion. Among these are the Japan Gold Disc awards, the American Music Awards, the so-called World Music Awards, held annually in Monte Carlo, and the IFPI Platinum Europe Awards, first presented in Brussels in 1996.

Awards for Artistic Success

The Mercury Music Prize in the United Kingdom is one of the few awards judged by critics solely on the basis of 'artistic excellence' in the general popular music field. Other awards judged according to such a criterion include the Polar Music Prize (Sweden) and the JAZZPAR jazz award (Denmark). The Polar Music Prize was inaugurated in 1989 by Stig (Stikkan) Anderson, the manager of ABBA, and the Royal Swedish Academy of Music. Annual prizes, presented by the King of Sweden, are awarded for lifetime achievement in the two fields of popular and classical music. Winners in the category of popular music have included Dizzy Gillespie, Joni Mitchell and Paul McCartney. JAZZPAR is worth $30,000 and was inaugurated in 1990. Winners have included Django Bates and Jim Hall. Authors of books on popular music are eligible to receive the Ralph J. Gleason Music Book Award, presented in the United States.

On occasion, the achievements of musicians in the field of popular music have been recognized in a wider context. Malian singer Salif Keita is one of several performers to have been awarded the Chevalier des Arts et des Lettres by the French government, while Joni Mitchell has received a Governor General's award in her native Canada. In Britain, Bob Geldof, Paul McCartney, Elton John and producer George Martin have been knighted.

The Grammy Awards

The Grammy awards have provided a model for many awards ceremonies, and, like the Grammys, the majority of national record industry awards are given to winners chosen by the votes of a specially selected 'electorate.' Grammy voters are drawn from the ranks of industry professionals, as are members of the film industry electorate for the Oscars. The number of those eligible to vote for the Grammys was around 6,000 in 1998. The name 'Grammys' was chosen in a prize competition; the winner was Mrs. Jay Danna of New Orleans, who won 25 vinyl LPs (O'Neil 1993, 12).

The organizers of the Grammys have frequently been criticized for their conservatism – for example, for failing to recognize rock music until the mid-1960s and for not introducing a category for best dance record until 1998, a decade after house and techno had made a significant impact on US popular music. However, by the end of the twentieth century, Grammys were being presented in over 70 categories, including such minority genres as

'best polka album' and 'best musical album for children,' as well as 'best engineered album' and 'best package.' The first winner of the 'record of the year' category was 'Volare,' sung by Domenico Modugno. The only Grammy award to be returned by a recipient was the award for 'best new artist,' presented to Milli Vanilli in 1989; its return followed the revelation that band members did not sing on their hits (O'Neil 1993, 6).

A rapidly growing number of countries outside the United States have 'best recording' ceremonies based on the Grammy model. In the United Kingdom, the Brit Awards show was first staged in 1982, while in France the Victoires de la Musique began in 1986 and Germany's Echo Awards started in 1992. Comparable ceremonies in other parts of the world include: the Junos (founded in 1972) and the Gala de l'ADISQ for Francophone music (1979) in Canada; the Spellemannprisen (1972) in Norway; the Fryderyk Awards (1995) in Poland; the Edisons in The Netherlands; the Porin Music Awards (1994) in Croatia; the South African Music Awards (1995); and the Premios de la Música (1996) in Spain. The Swedish Grammys were held from 1969 to 1972 and then restarted in 1987. Most of these ceremonies are arranged by the national recording industry trade organization, which also determines the composition of the jury of voters.

Other Awards

Awards for songwriters are given by various music business organizations. All three of the United States' performing rights organizations (ASCAP (the American Society of Composers, Authors and Publishers), BMI (Broadcast Music Inc.) and SESAC (originally, the Society of European Stage Authors and Composers)) provide awards for writers in R&B, country music, pop and Latin music. ASCAP and BMI also present awards to the British songwriters affiliated with them. All these awards are based on the amount of radio or television airplay achieved by individual works. In the United Kingdom, the Ivor Novello Awards have been given by the British Academy of Songwriters, Composers and Authors since 1955.

Other performing rights organizations' awards include France's SACEM Grand Prix awards, which are given in eight categories that include jazz, music publishing and best song, the Australasian Performing Right Association Awards, which were inaugurated in 1980, and the COMPASS Awards in Singapore, which date from 1995.

The numerous trade associations that are based on specific genres constitute another important source of music industry awards. In the United States alone, country music has the annual high-profile televised awards show organized by the Country Music Association

(CMA) and the blues community has its W.C. Handy Blues Awards, while gospel and Christian music have the Dove Awards and the Stellar Gospel Music Awards, which date from 1984, and the National Quartet Convention, founded in 1957. Independent record companies and their artists are recognized by the Indie Awards from the National Association of Independent Record Distributors and Manufacturers (NAIRD).

The only awards for record company employees themselves have been those given by the British trade paper *Music Week*, which has offered prizes for such achievements as 'best marketing campaign' and 'best distributor.'

Bibliography

International Federation of the Phonographic Industry (IFPI). 1998. *The Recording Industry in Numbers 1998.* London: IFPI.

O'Neil, Thomas. 1993. *The Grammys: For the Record.* New York and London: Penguin.

Discographical Reference

Modugno, Domenico. 'Volare (Nel Blu Dipinto Di Blu).' Oriole ICB 5000. *1958*: UK.

DAVE LAING

Catalog

The term 'catalog' has come to be used in a metaphorical sense to describe the totality of songs controlled by a music publisher or of recordings owned by a record company (hence 'back catalog' refers to previously issued material); but its origins lie in the issuing of printed lists or catalogs of available recordings by the early record companies in the United States and elsewhere. The first-ever catalog of recordings was issued in 1891 by Columbia (10 pages of cylinder recordings of marches, dance tunes, novelty and sentimental songs, and monologs (Dearling and Dearling 1984, 32)), mainly for coin-in-the-slot jukeboxes at fairgrounds and exhibitions.

These catalogs were provided to the appointed dealers for record companies and, up to about 1920, were generally subdivided into categories of performance, based on instrumental (e.g., 'Banjo,' 'Cornet'), vocal (e.g., 'Soprano'), generic ('Sentimental,' 'Comic,' 'Topical'), ensemble ('Marching Band'), 'ethnic' (e.g., 'Irish,' 'Negro') or other criteria. Gradually, listings based on artist names supplanted most of these categories so that, in the 1920s, companies were using a small number of genre subdivisions, such as 'Opera' and 'Familiar Tunes' (the Columbia company's term for hillbilly or country music).

The introduction of the term 'Race music' for blues and related African-American musical forms is usually credited to Harry H. Pace of OKeh. An issue of the *Chicago Defender* published in March 1922 carried an invitation to its readers to 'ask your neighborhood dealer for a complete list of OKeh race records.' Such segregated lists were to be known as 'Race catalogs,' and some of these became much sought after. They included the Paramount catalog of 1924 and the Victor catalog of 1930; the former was illustrated with line drawings, and the latter (which listed 'Vocal Blues, Religious, Spirituals, Red Hot Dance Tunes, Sermons, Novelties') had vignette photographs of singers and preachers. Portrait photographs were used on the art deco-style covers of the 1938 and 1940 Decca Race records catalogs. Four-page supplements were also issued to keep prospective purchasers up-to-date with releases.

The early catalogs did not necessarily list all the records issued by a company, since it was possible that a record issued after the publication of one edition of a catalog would have been deleted from stock before the next catalog was issued.

After World War II, the segregated 'Race' or 'sepia' catalog all but disappeared – for example, the newly formed Capitol Records had a single roster containing both black and white acts.

By the late 1970s, most of the large record companies had ceased to publish catalogs, although some smaller specialist labels continued to do so. The only comprehensive catalogs of available recordings were published independently and aimed mainly at the retail trade. These catalogs included Schwann in the United States and the popular and classical catalogs of the *Gramophone* magazine in Britain. By the 1990s, leading catalogs were available in CD-ROM format.

Bibliography

Dearling, Robert, and Dearling, Celia. 1984. *The Guinness Book of Recorded Sound.* Enfield: Guinness Books.

DAVE LAING and PAUL OLIVER

Charts

A chart is the numerical ranking of record releases according to retail sales, popularity, radio and television plays or aesthetic criteria within a given geographical location or musical genre. Charts are generally measured over a specific time period, most commonly weekly, but they may be grouped according to months, years or even entire eras. Charts are collated by the collection of statistical data according to such criteria and the placing of the information into an ordered table. Differing categories of charts are understood to have different levels of cultural and economic importance. Retail sales charts are highly valued within the music industry, as they indicate the bestselling singles and so provide vital sales statistics reflecting business performance. Likewise, airplay charts are often informed by retail sales data, but are also reflective of the playlist policies of various broadcasters or of individual radio or television programs. Both these types of charts are central tools in the promotion of popular music, as they provide exposure for current releases as well as acting as useful feedback indicators of the genre preference of different broadcasters to the record industry.

Some charts are based on aesthetic criteria, as evidenced in music magazines that list the 'greatest' or most important records or musicians of all time. Generally, these forms of charts are based on a poll of staff writers or readers, and there is usually a clear fit between those musicians or recordings that have been nominated and those regularly featured in the individual publication. These types of charts are central in demarcating certain canons within popular music genres, and they provide welcome promotion of back catalog material for record companies. These charts tend not to reflect current record sales, but instead to provide an index of acts that are deemed important within the taste cultures of various music genres. The regularity with which such charts are produced indicates the high value placed on them by fans and audiences (see, for example, the special editions of *Mojo*, 1995, 1996, 1997). The demand for such listings is also evident in the proliferation of chart almanacs on the general market (for example, Whitburn 1983; McAleer 1994; Gambaccini, Rice and Rice 1996; O'Brien 1999). Parker (1991) notes that such interest in music charts by audiences indicates a 'consumer obsession with sales figures [which is] almost unique to the record industry' (205).

Early Charts

As early as the second half of the nineteenth century, popularity charts of sheet music sales were produced by music publishers, who circulated lists of their own bestsellers for promotional purposes (Hakanen 1998, 102). The widespread dissemination of popularity charts is linked to their collation and publication by music press and music trade periodicals. From the time it was first published in 1926, the UK magazine *Melody Maker* provided charts of the most popular sheet music of the time, such as 'The Most Popular Dance Orchestrations' and 'This Month's Hits of the Season' (Johnstone 1999, 10). In the mid-1930s, the US magazine *Billboard* produced 'Chart Line,' which listed the most-played songs on the three major US radio networks (Garofalo 1997, 60). In the same period, the US entertainment magazine *Variety* produced charts of jukebox hits (Garofalo 1997, 60), and the UK magazine *Gramophone* produced three separate charts for radio airplay, sheet music and phonogram sales (Parker 1991, 206). In July 1940, *Billboard* introduced its 'Music Popularity Chart,' which listed the

first number one as being 'I'll Never Smile Again' by Tommy Dorsey (with vocals by Frank Sinatra). The numbers of records included on the *Billboard* chart fluctuated from between 10 and 30 until 1955, when the *Billboard* Hot 100 was introduced. The 1950s saw a proliferation of new charts as, for example, the Finnish music press introduced bestseller charts in 1951 (Gronow and Saunio 1998, 129), *New Musical Express* (*NME*) began publishing a UK Top 12 singles chart beginning in 1952 and a UK album chart was established by *Melody Maker* in 1958.

Specialist Charts

Aside from general charts, which attempt to monitor the overall sales patterns or airplay within a given region, there has also been a long history of charts that catalog popularity within specific generic parameters. In addition to its general chart, *Billboard* began a brief listing of the most popular hillbilly and 'race' songs found on jukeboxes in 1944. Malone (1985) points out that, within these charts, it 'was not uncommon to see a song like Floyd Tillman's "They Took the Stars Out of Heaven" included with Ella Fitzgerald's "When My Sugar Walks Down the Street"' (181). In the late 1940s, *Billboard* replaced these lists with new charts for Folk, Country and Western, and Rhythm and Blues songs. These new categorizations have been understood as drawing distinctions not only in generic terms but also with regard to the race of the performer. Chapple and Garofalo (1977) see this differential charting of black and white music as part of the ongoing practise of racial segregation by the music industry, in which the 'black audience was separated as a secondary market with different and inferior promotion budgets' (236). *Billboard* subsequently continued to expand the number of its charts over time. The magazine currently commissions a large number of charts covering numerous genres, while using different indicators of popularity. These charts include Top Gospel, R&B/Hip-Hop Albums and Rap Singles compiled from sales data, Hot Adult Contemporary, Mainstream Rock Tracks, Modern Rock Tracks and Latin compiled from airplay, and Hot Dance Music compiled from a national sample of dance club playlists.

A plethora of charts is highly beneficial for the recording industry, as they open extra channels of promotion. Establishing charts around generic classification helps to promote particular styles of music, giving them a permanence and visibility in the public arena. Charts offer a means of substantiation within the recording industry, as they act as a yardstick by which the success or failure of certain releases can be measured. As Barnes (1988) argues, 'the more charts there are, the more chances the [record] label has to create a success story for a record. Since no record company reveals specific sales figures for a record, trade charts are the industry's report cards' (41). The use of charts as a measure of success within the industry can have real implications for the continuing success of a record or act. For instance, if a recording has achieved high ratings in an individual national chart, it may be more liable to receive priority in terms of marketing budgets and promotion in another market. Chart success for a particular act may also lead to an increase in promotion on subsequent releases, or to attempts to 'cross over' a niche market act to a mainstream audience. The importance of charts for the music industry is borne out by the way in which industry organizations have been instrumental in setting up charts. The trade organization of the British Phonographic Industry (BPI) set up its own official chart in 1969, while the International Federation of the Phonographic Industry (IFPI) sponsors charts in markets such as Austria, Switzerland, Taiwan, Greece and Hong Kong.

The classification of music charts by genre can often be subject to temporal limitations, as genres dip in and out of fashion or as the meanings of particular systems of categorization change over time. The UK independent charts of the 1980s serve as an example, as they were based on a ranking of the bestselling independently distributed records. These indie charts were recognized as responding to the 'fit' between musical style (indie), record company (independent) and nature of distribution (independent). However, this selective definition of independence proved problematic, as the charts were sometimes topped by 'anomalous' acts, such as Kylie Minogue, who performed highly commercial pop music but released and distributed their records independently. The categorization within the charts was further confused by the profusion of distribution deals and buyouts of independent labels by major record companies, along with the direct signing of indie bands to majors. As Hesmondhalgh (1996) points out, 'with the emergence of indie as a genre, rather than as an economic category, many industry insiders began to argue that the Independent Charts should be based on musical style, rather than on the economic status of the distributor' (131).

Systems of Chart Collation

Despite the large variety of charts, and their perceived importance within the music industry, their accuracy and significance are often unclear. Although sales charts are presented as accurate reflections of public taste and buying patterns, there is a wide level of variation in their methods of compilation. The process of collating charts is thus beset by fluctuating levels of accuracy and has historically been open to widespread industry manipulation. In addition to variation in statistical collation, the comparison of different charts can be difficult, as charts can be made up of differing types of information. National charts vary in that some are made up of sales information alone, while others use airplay information or a combination of differing types of data. In many early published charts, it is often difficult to ascertain the criteria for inclusion. Burns (1998), for instance, has pointed out that lists of the 'most popular' tunes for inclusion on the US radio show *Your Hit Parade* in the mid-1930s were determined solely by the advertising agency Lord & Thomas using 'an unspecified methodology' (139). Many subsequent systems that sought to chart the sales of popular music relied on retailers being responsible for manually logging chart returns. The UK singles chart published by *NME* in 1952 was based on information gathered by a telephone poll of just 25 stores and, as such, was liable to be an inaccurate marker and may have been open to unchecked abuse (O'Brien 1999, 12–13). In 1969, the sample was expanded when the British Market Research Bureau (BMRB) took over the collation of the official UK chart and began collecting sales data from 250 record stores. Again, these figures were open to inaccuracy, as sales were logged by hand and submitted to the BMRB by mail. Other systems were even less representative of the individual markets they attempted to log. For instance, in the 1970s *Billboard* polled only 80 US dealers a week and 125 radio stations in its collation of national sales charts (Chapple and Garofalo 1977, 155).

Charts based on the logging of sales data by retailers have been somewhat susceptible to manipulation in various ways. Accuracy may be affected because of the need for retailers to maintain good professional relationships with sales representatives of record companies and distributors. In order to maintain such relationships, stores may have been liable to overrepresent particular products in their chart returns. Chapple and Garofalo point out that US record retailers in the 1970s were 'under constant pressure from distributors and their own good business sense, to emphasize certain heavily backed releases at the expense of others' (1977, 155). Likewise, Wallis and Malm (1984) point out that retailers may have been liable to include records in their chart returns in order to promote existing stock, giving 'false returns reflecting what they would like to sell (phonograms of which they have many on their shelves, or for which they have committed to take a large order from wholesalers)' (250).

The accuracy of charts has been further compromised through attempts by individual record companies to influence their content for their own commercial advantage. Record companies have used tactics such as the use of 'buying teams,' which purchase multiple copies of individual releases from chart return stores, or the use of free products in return for false returns, in order to inflate their chart positions. Likewise, charts that collate airplay as part of their statistical data have been constantly open to abuse through payola, in which record companies have affected radio content through bribes, gifts and financial incentives to radio programmers and DJs. Indeed, the widespread use of such practises has led to some countries abandoning national charts altogether. Wallis and Malm point out that broadcasting organizations in Austria, Trinidad and Tobago, Chile and Sweden all removed chart programs from their schedules, as the major companies were understood to have an unfair advantage and undue influence over the content of charts in these regions (1984, 249–50).

To counteract such manipulation, and to gain a more accurate picture of actual soundcarrier sales and radio plays, chart compilers have constantly sought to update their methods of collation. To this end, the 1980s and 1990s saw a shift toward computerized calculation of sales charts. Advances in technology allowed for computer systems that were able to track record purchases directly at point of sale from an expanded sample of retail outlets. For instance, when the market research organization Gallup took over from the BMRB as the UK chart compiler in 1983, it automated the data collection process and increased the number of chart return stores to 1,500. In 1991, the US *Billboard* charts began using the SoundScan system in order to track the sales section of its figures. By 1997, SoundScan claimed to measure around 85 percent of soundcarrier sales in the United States calculated from point-of-sale information from 3,700 chain record stores, 600 independent retailers and 6,500 general multiples such as discount and department stores (McCourt and Rothenbuhler 1997, 209). In the late 1990s, SoundScan was introduced in Canada and Japan, along with similar computer collation systems in other countries, including the Australian Record Industry Association (ARIA) and Music and Media in Germany. There are also a number of computerized systems designed to give a more exact picture of airplay by radio stations. Broadcast Data Systems (BDS) is used extensively in the United States, Canada and Puerto Rico, while Music Control is used in 17 European countries. Such systems use a digital fingerprint encoded into sound recordings to automatically track individual plays.

Such changes in chart collation can have a direct effect on the types of music that gain media exposure and the way that the recording industry understands the commercial potential of certain genres. For instance, Negus (1999) points out that the number of country albums in the US Top 50 doubled between the week before SoundScan was introduced and the week after, and argues that

the higher proportion and increased level of visibility of country music within the charts meant that artists within the genre became prioritized by record companies (118). The new system also led to the appearance of back catalog material on the chart, along with a higher proportion of independently released material and a higher representation of 'alternative' and hip-hop artists (Peterseil and Grimm 2001). Mike Shalett, the chief executive of SoundScan, claims that 'Independents have flourished, as a group, and represent the second largest constituency after the Warner Music Group since SoundScan started being used for the charts' (Taylor 1997).

Despite the new levels of accuracy and the increased sample base that computer collation allows, there remains evidence to suggest that charts continue to be open to rigging and manipulation by the industry. In 1991, for instance, London Records was fined £50,000 by the BPI for attempted chart hyping after irregular buying patterns were detected in stores in the north of England ('Hypers,' 1991). Similarly, in 2001 allegations of widespread chart corruption were made in the United States, Canada and Costa Rica. The *Los Angeles Times* reported that record companies often employed independent consultants to give away free products in return for retail stores logging extra chart returns on specified products (Philips 2001). Because of their surreptitious nature, it is difficult to ascertain how widespread these abuses are, but it is clear that, despite increased efforts to make the collation process more accurate, inaccuracy and manipulation may still occur.

Impact of Charts on Broadcasting Industries

Charts have had a major effect on the broadcast mediation of popular music, as they often inform the compilation and character of radio and music television playlists. Broadcast programming such as the Top 40 radio format, chart shows, MTV, and individual network television and radio shows concentrates on showcasing and predicting hit songs. Early sponsored chart shows included the *Lucky Strike Hit Parade*, which was broadcast on numerous US radio stations from 1935, and *Lucky Lager Dance Time* (1951), a successful radio show based on *Billboard*'s Honor Roll of Hits. In 1950, *Your Hit Parade* adapted the Lucky Strike format for television: an ensemble cast of singers and musicians interpreted songs from bestseller charts of sheet music and phonograph records, and the most popular songs on radio and jukeboxes.

The genesis of the Top 40 radio format lies in the early 1950s, when radio license owner Todd Storz introduced the concept to his chain of US radio stations. Influenced by University of Omaha research, which suggested that listeners rated music as the major factor in their consumption of radio, Storz abandoned network programming (usually made up of shows led by a 'personality' DJ or band leader) in favor of a much more focused playlist. Storz's policy was to poll local record retail outlets for their bestselling singles and then give the tracks repeated airplay on his stations. The format proved to be financially successful, with dramatically improved audience shares, and Storz's template was quickly copied by large US radio chains such as Bartlett, ABC and Metromedia (Denisoff 1975, 233). The process was further refined in the mid-1960s through the Drake format (instigated by Bill Drake and Gene Chenault across the RKO chain), which narrowed the playlists to a 'tight thirty record playlist plus a few "hit-bound" extras' (Barnes 1988, 12). By the 1970s, Drake-Chenault Enterprises was franchising automated formats to radio stations across the United States, whereby a limited number of 'hit' songs were licensed to individual stations and played in an order formulated by the company (Burns 1996, 5).

This reliance on charts within radio programming has been understood to have had a major impact on the recording and broadcasting industries. For instance, Denisoff argues that the rise of the Top 40 format led to only a very selective group of black artists receiving airplay in the late 1950s and early 1960s, a situation which, he argues, had wider implications for the black music industry in the United States (1975, 235). Joseph Burns argues that, far from fulfilling Storz's original guiding principle that 'the programming of music is controlled by the choice of the public' (Storz, quoted in Barnes 1988, 9), the development of such chart-oriented formats led to a much more prescribed selection of music, which 'was completely in the hands of the programmer and without input from local listeners' (1996, 5). Likewise, Rothenbuhler (1987) points out that, as charts are often made up from radio play as well as sales, neither charts nor radio programming offer a true reflection of public taste, and the curious situation has arisen whereby 'radio airplay in part determines radio airplay' (78).

Global Context

The increasing dominance of globally marketed acts across international territories has meant that US and European charts have assumed significance outside those particular regions. Radio One, the highest-rated FM radio station in Lebanon, has a programming policy based solely on material culled from US, UK and European charts, and has increased its audience share across the Middle East by importing broadcasters from the United Kingdom. This US and European dominance is reflected in the high percentage of globally marketed acts in many domestic charts. In Thailand, for instance,

international repertoire accounted for 72 percent of the total value of album sales and 84 percent of singles in 1999. According to IFPI figures, no domestic artist figured in the Top 10 chart for bestselling singles of the year (MBI 2001, 514). In reaction, many non-Western countries have sought to promote indigenous recording industries and local artists by collating separate charts for domestic and international repertoire. The *Indiatimes*, for instance, publishes a Top 25 chart, which includes international repertoire mainly consisting of US and European artists, along with an Indi Pop Top 10, which tracks retail sales of indigenous Indian popular music, and a Times Sangeet Toppers chart, which includes the most popular music and songs from Bollywood films.

The use of charts as a yardstick for the global consumption of music is further complicated by the fact that, in many countries, true sales figures are difficult to ascertain due to high levels of piracy. According to IFPI figures, in countries such as Russia, Mexico, Brazil, Malaysia and Indonesia pirate copies account for over 50 percent of soundcarrier sales, and in the Chinese and Paraguayan markets this number rises to over 90 percent (IFPI 2001, 10). Hence, in such territories official sales figures and charts often represent under 50 percent of the true market. Such a situation can lead to an underrepresentation of individual genres in charts and sales statistics, as some types of music are more likely than others to be sold through 'unofficial' channels. In the late 1990s, for instance, industry figures indicated that sales of Latin music accounted for less than 1 percent of the US market. However, Negus argues that there is a thriving market for Spanish-language music at flea markets and 'swap meets,' and that the actual percentage of sales could be as high as 7 percent (1999, 141). In a discussion of the explosion of Indian cassette culture in the 1980s, Manuel (1991) estimates that between 40 and 50 percent of cassette sales in northern India were of regional folk and pop styles released by locally based independents, but that true figures were hard to ascertain due to piracy and the absence of data from small labels.

Analysis

A number of scholars have used chart data as the basis for analysis, drawing on the information as a qualitative record of consumer purchasing to examine sociocultural trends and the content of popular music. Anderson et al. (1980), for example, analyze the 628 number one recordings on *Billboard*'s general popularity chart between 1940 and 1977 in order to identify trends in musical genres, types of successful artist, lyrical content and the concentration of major record companies in the market. Alternatively, Fitzgerald (1998) has used the New South Wales Top 40 to consider the impact of British music within Australia from 1963 to 1966, while Bradby (1990) uses UK and US charts to examine the gendered positions of girl-group records. Charts may also be used in the examination of music industry practise and changes in production and dissemination. Phillips and Schlattmann (1990), for example, have used chart statistics from the United States to measure the impact of MTV on record sales, while Sernoe (1998) uses a similar statistical approach to map the changes in popularity of country music in the United States.

Chart statistics may also indicate changing and comparative purchasing patterns among consumers. Readings of the charts may show swift sales from the moment of release (such as singles that immediately achieve a number one position and then quickly fall from the Top 20), or a pattern of 'slow climbers,' which register steadily increasing sales. Analysis may also indicate differences in the rate at which recordings enter and leave the charts, and how this may vary between countries and over time, and may provide a picture of the character of individual markets at particular moments. For instance, the UK singles chart is volatile compared to its US equivalent, which appears to be relatively slow-moving. During 1997 and 1998, 179 singles reached the Top 20 in the United States, compared to the United Kingdom's 757; each of those US entries spent an average of 11 weeks on the chart, a duration that only 6 percent of UK Top 20 entries managed in the same period (O'Brien 1999, 13). Such analysis is useful in comparing industry practise and the contexts of consumption in each country. For example, promotion within the United States often involves breaking local markets catered to by regionally based, genre-specific broadcasters. In comparison, the UK media consist of fewer radio and television stations targeted at nonspecialist audiences, often with a national reach. This results in blanket national promotion and a higher turnover of titles. Rates of chart turnover may also reflect changes in the marketing of singles. In the United Kingdom during the 1990s, it was common to offer discounted products and to implement heavy promotion up to the first week of release. As O'Brien points out, before the 1990s a Top 40 chart entry was a 'good indication that a record was bound for the Top 10. Nowadays, if it does not enter the Top 10 during its first week, it has little chance of ever doing so. Record company marketing strategies are so geared towards the first seven days of release that the odds are stacked against any single climbing higher than its debut position' (1999, 13).

However, such analysis may be complicated by the aforementioned differences in collation between territ-

ories and by inaccuracies within the compilation process. For instance, a comparison between US and UK markets is confused by the fact that, in the United Kingdom, charts are based solely on retail sales, while the United States uses a combination of sales and radio airplay. Hence, any firm conclusions drawn from the analysis of these charts alone offer only a partial representation of the true picture. Indeed, it is clear that charts are a complex configuration of information that offer only partial pictures of popular music's history, value and popularity. Nevertheless, charts remain an important factor in influencing music industry practise and are a central method of ordering information about popular music.

Bibliography

Anderson, Peter, et al. 1980. 'Hit Record Trends, 1940–1977.' *Journal of Communication* 30(2) (Spring): 31–43.

Barnes, Ken. 1988. 'Top 40 Radio: Fragment of the Imagination.' In *Facing the Music: A Pantheon Guide to Popular Culture*, ed. Simon Frith. London: Pantheon Books, 8–50.

Bradby, Barbara. 1990. 'Do-Talk and Don't-Talk: The Division of the Subject in Girl-Group Music.' In *On Record: Rock, Pop, and the Written Word*, ed. Simon Frith and Andrew Goodwin. New York: Pantheon Books, 341–68.

Burns, Gary. 1998. 'Visualising 1950s Hits on *Your Hit Parade*.' *Popular Music* 17(2): 139–52.

Burns, Joseph E. 1996. 'The Creation and Following of Public Opinion: A History of Music Choice in Radio Programming.' Paper presented at the Central States Communication Association Annual Convention, St. Paul, Minnesota.

Chapple, Steve, and Garofalo, Reebee. 1977. *Rock 'n' Roll Is Here to Pay: The History and Politics of the Music Industry*. Chicago: Nelson-Hall.

Denisoff, R. Serge. 1975. *Solid Gold: The Popular Record Industry*. New Brunswick, NJ: Transaction Books.

Fitzgerald, Jon. 1998. '"Brits and Pieces": The 1960s' "British Invasion" Within Australia.' In *Popular Music: Intercultural Interpretations*, ed. Tôru Mitsui. Kanazawa: Graduate Program in Music, Kanazawa University, 513–21.

Gambaccini, Paul, Rice, Tim, and Rice, Jonathan. 1996. *The Guinness Book of British Hit Albums*. 7th ed. Enfield: Guinness Publishing.

Garofalo, Reebee. 1997. *Rockin' Out: Popular Music in the USA*. Boston, MA: Allyn and Bacon.

Gronow, Pekka, and Saunio, Ilpo. 1998. *An International History of the Recording Industry*, trans. Christopher Moseley. London: Cassell.

Hakanen, Ernest A. 1998. 'Counting Down to Number

One: The Evolution of the Meaning of Popular Music Charts.' *Popular Music* 17(1): 95–111.

Hesmondhalgh, David. 1996. *Independent Record Companies and Democratisation in the Popular Music Industry.* Unpublished Ph.D. thesis, Goldsmiths College, London.

'Hypers Face £50,000 Fine.' 1991. *Music Week* (8 June): 1.

International Federation of the Phonographic Industry (IFPI). 2001. *IFPI Music Piracy Report June 2001.* London: IFPI Secretariat.

Johnstone, Nick. 1999. *Melody Maker History of 20th Century Popular Music.* London: Bloomsbury.

Malone, Bill C. 1985. *Country Music, U.S.A.* Rev. ed. Austin, TX: University of Texas Press.

Manuel, Peter. 1991. 'The Cassette Industry and Popular Music in North India.' *Popular Music* 10(2): 189–204.

McAleer, Dave, ed. 1994. *The Warner Guide to UK & US Hit Singles.* London: Little, Brown.

McCourt, Tom, and Rothenbuhler, Eric W. 1997. 'SoundScan and the Consolidation of Control in the Popular Music Industry.' *Media, Culture and Society* 19: 201–18.

Music Business International (MBI). 2001. *Music Business International World Report 2001.* London: United Business Media.

Negus, Keith. 1999. *Music Genres and Corporate Cultures.* London: Routledge.

O'Brien, Karen, ed. 1999. *Guinness British Hit Singles: 12th Edition.* London: Guinness Publishing.

Parker, Martin. 1991. 'Reading the Charts: Making Sense with the Hit Parade.' *Popular Music* 10(2): 205–17.

Peterseil, Yakob, and Grimm, Scott. 2001. *Soundscandal: Rigging the Retail Charts.* http://www.newmediamusic.com/articles/NM01070298.html

Philips, Chuck. 2001. *Music Data Being Altered, Some Say.* http://www.latimes.com/business/la-000057351jul13.story

Phillips, Dennis D., and Schlattmann, Tim. 1990. 'Strip Mining for Gold and Platinum: Record Sales and Chart Performance Pre- and Post-MTV.' *Popular Music and Society* 14(1): 85–96.

Rothenbuhler, Eric W. 1987. 'Commercial Radio and Popular Music: Processes of Selection and Factors of Influence.' In *Popular Music and Communication*, ed. James Lull. Newbury Park, CA: Sage, 78–95.

Sernoe, Jim. 1998. '"Here You Come Again": Country Music's Performance on the Pop Singles Charts from 1955 to 1996.' *Popular Music and Society* 22(1): 17–40.

'Special Edition: The 100 Greatest Albums Ever Made.' 1995. *Mojo* 21 (August).

'Special Edition: The 100 Greatest Guitarists of All Time.' 1996. *Mojo* 31 (June).

'Special Edition: The 100 Greatest Singles of All Time.' 1997. *Mojo* 45 (August).

Taylor, Tess. 1997. 'An Interview with Mike Shalett.' *The Network News* VII(1) (January/February). http://www.narip.com/networknews/archives/shalett.htm

Wallis, Roger, and Malm, Krister. 1984. *Big Sounds from Small Peoples: The Music Industry in Small Countries.* London: Constable.

Whitburn, Joel. 1983. *The Billboard Book of Top 40 Hits.* Enfield: Guinness Publishing.

Discographical References

Dorsey, Tommy. 'I'll Never Smile Again.' Victor 26628. 1940: USA.

Fitzgerald, Ella. 'When My Sugar Walks Down the Street.' *Ella Fitzgerald: 1940–1941.* Melodie Jazz Classics 644. 1941; *1996*: France.

Tillman, Floyd. 'They Took the Stars Out of Heaven.' *Floyd Tillman: Country Music Hall of Fame.* MCA MCAD-10189. 1941; *1991*: USA.

ROBERT STRACHAN and MARION LEONARD

Circuit

Although the term 'circuit' can refer to the circumference of an area or a progression about a district or region, its application to popular music may have arisen from judicial and religious uses. Medieval courts were held by judges in a succession of places according to a prescribed sequence of dates and locations. These 'Courts of Pie Powder' (*pieds poudres*, or dusty feet) settled local disputes. The system was adopted in North America and 'circuit judges' were so identified. In the eighteenth century, the concept of the circuit was also employed by Methodist and other 'nonconformist' denominations, with itinerant lay preachers and 'circuit riders' visiting remote communities to spread the Gospel. When the term was first applied to popular music is uncertain, but it appears to have arisen with the 'theater circuit,' or a number of performance venues linked by a unifying federation or ownership, which offered employment on a regular basis to traveling artists or companies. The theater circuits became significant in Great Britain through the music halls and in the United States with the popularity of vaudeville in the 1890s.

Often comprising a handful of theaters only, the circuit was a response to the post-Reconstruction demand for entertainment in the rapidly growing towns of the prairie and western states. In the Midwest, for example, the Chicagoans George Castle and Charles F. Kohl founded the Kohl & Castle (K&C) Circuit, while Alexander Pantages opened up his chain of 'small-time' theaters, or the Pantages Circuit. The West, however, was largely controlled by Martin Beck, whose Orpheum Circuit linked some 18 theaters. But it was Benjamin Franklin

Keith and E.F. Albee whose theaters dominated vaudeville in the East, and who controlled the United Booking Office. Challengers Marcus Loew and William Morris opened up their chains, with Loew acquiring a dozen theaters of the People's Vaudeville Circuit in 1909, later linking with the circuit of Sullivan and Considine. The circuits of the Shubert brothers, and of Klaw and Erlanger, who had been partners in the United States Amusement Corporation, eventually engaged in commercial conflict. Mergers, takeovers and acrimonious legal disputes were Byzantine in their complexity by the end of the century.

Following the lead of Tony Pastor, whose theater had been one of the first and major venues for popular entertainment, Albee and Keith 'cleaned up' the vaudeville acts to attract a larger, middle-class public. The power of the theater circuit owners was great, but the circuits gave greater assurance to the artists in their employ that their bookings were secure, even over considerable distances. In Great Britain, theaters were frequently independently owned but subject to strict regulations. Distances between them were relatively small, yet the principal circuits, managed by Oswald Stoll, Sir Edward Moss (of Moss Empires) and Frank MacNaughten, controlled a fifth of the investment in British music halls in the first decade of the twentieth century.

Although some African-American entertainers were highly successful vaudeville artists, many felt threatened by the politics of the large concerns, and humiliated by the 'Jim Crow galleries' to which black audiences were confined in the southern circuits. The Barrasso Brothers with S.H. Dudley and the owner-managers of black theaters combined resources to form the Theater Owners' Booking Agency (TOBA) in 1909. Control was assumed by Charles Turpin and Milton Starr from Nashville in 1921 and the 'Toby Time' continued until the Depression closed the theaters.

After World War I, the competition of motion pictures threatened the survival of vaudeville; some circuits went under, while others consolidated, as when, in 1919, the Keith and Orpheum circuits linked up with Pathé and the Radio Corporation of America to create RKO – Radio-Keith-Orpheum – to command a chain of cinemas and a significant slice of the motion picture industry. It was to be consumed, in turn, a score of years later, by Howard Hughes. Though 'legitimate' theater continued, vaudeville declined; many theaters became the venues for musicals, revues and shows and were still host to popular music, while big band jazz dominated the dance halls. Such bands often toured; it was the number of performances, the length of 'runs' (or continuous engagements) and the months of band 'residencies' that became the measure of success.

After World War II, the term 'circuit' returned with the increasing popularity of folk clubs, where solo artists performed before securing a succession of bookings. At this time, when cotton cultivation was being mechanized, thousands of blacks in the South were out of work. Southern pianists could still find work in the sawmill camps and towns of eastern Texas, working the 'barrelhouse circuit' and traveling the southern railroad lines that linked them. Many of those who played 'the box' (guitar) or 'harp' (harmonica) began to tour the rural and city 'joints' or 'jukes,' providing live music until the jukeboxes drove them out. Many played for tips only, and those who were paid to perform earned little – just enough to buy 'chitterlings,' or offal, for their meal. Those who followed such a route between the 'jukes' termed it the 'chittlin' circuit.' But when blues became of interest to an audience beyond the ghettos, what has been called the 'college circuit' developed, as blues singers increasingly performed for students at universities. Soon the 'circuit' was loosely used to identify the movement of entertainers between specialist clubs and venues, and was even applied to lecturers and retired politicians as they appeared at successive academic engagements.

Bibliography

Bailey, Peter, ed. 1986. *Music Hall: The Business of Pleasure*. Milton Keynes: Open University Press.

Green, Abel, and Laurie, Joe Jr. 1951. *Show Biz – From Vaude to Video*. New York: Henry Holt and Company.

Sanjek, Russell. 1988. *American Popular Music and Its Business: The First Four Hundred Years. Vol. II: From 1790 to 1909*. New York: Oxford University Press.

PAUL OLIVER

Concert Promotion

Concert promotion is the business of organizing live shows, from the booking of acts and venues to the arrangement of publicity, security and insurance, and the pricing and sale of tickets. Promotion is possibly the most risky sector of the popular music industry, since the financial success or failure of an event is dependent on the skill of the promoter in negotiating the 'split' of the takings with the artist's agent, in balancing this against ticket prices and actual audience numbers, and in attracting the maximum attendance.

The financial arrangements for a concert can take several forms. The simplest is for a split of the gross box-office takings that typically involves the promoter retaining 15 percent. This arrangement was common in the 1960s, although agents representing very popular acts would bargain for 90/10 splits. More recently, it has become very common for the promoter to guarantee a minimum fee for the act, plus a percentage of either the box-office takings or the 'profits' above a certain amount. Profits are defined as the amount remaining after the promoter's costs have been covered. Thus, the promoter might pay $25,000 plus 85 percent of gross revenues above $30,000. Finally, some deals are based on the net income from a concert. In these cases, the promoter can deduct certain of his/her costs before paying the artist's guaranteed fee or percentage.

The costs of concert promotion are frequently offset by sponsorship arrangements involving local radio stations, the record companies of the artists to be promoted or corporations such as drinks or clothing manufacturers. The sponsorship may take the form of free or subsidized advertising of the concert or a direct subsidy in return for the association of the sponsor's name with the concert or tour.

There are generally different arrangements for performances on campuses and in small clubs, where an agent may negotiate a cash fee that leaves the club manager/promoter to manipulate door prices or drinks tariffs in order to cover costs. In the past, these fees were often subject to deductions for the 'hire' of the club's public-address system and sound engineer, while in the United Kingdom some clubs would ask for a fee from the band, making them 'pay to play.'

Concert promotion originated in the era when professional music-making in Europe was in transition from a dependence on patronage to a nascent market system. The first public concerts were given in London in the late eighteenth century and were promoted by participating musicians. During the nineteenth century, the job of promotion was taken over by theatrical impresarios and music publishers, the latter anxious to promote performances of songs they controlled.

In the early part of the twentieth century, theater or auditorium owners themselves booked acts from agents, often providing touring circuits in the United States where a chain of theaters would be owned by the same company. In the period after 1945, specialist promoters increasingly took over the role of booking halls and presenting concerts.

The concert business grew rapidly in the 1960s as part of the boom in rock music. While many existing venue owners were loath to present this new music, a new generation of young promoters emerged from within the rock scene to set up an informal national network in the United States. When rock audiences increased dramatically in the 1970s, these promoters graduated to presenting concerts in large stadia, and they found themselves pressured by the increasing financial demands of the bands and their booking agents. Promotion now also involved dealing with increasingly complex contract 'riders,' which specified in minute detail the dietary and other requirements of top bands.

Gradually, the promotional sector of the music industry attracted corporate investment as record companies such as Sony, PolyGram and MCA set up venue management and promotion divisions, and amphitheater and hall owners or operators like Ogden Entertainment themselves entered promotion on a large scale. In the 1990s, some US radio broadcasting conglomerates also expanded their role from that of sponsors of local concerts to that of the promotion business itself. Thus, in the late 1990s, SFX (now a subsidiary of media conglomerate Clear Channel Entertainment) purchased a large number of promoters, including Bill Graham Presents in San Francisco and the New York promotion company Delsener-Slater.

Similarly, some major sponsors moved directly into promotion, as when the Labatt beer company of Canada set up CPI, perhaps the most powerful promoter in the world in the late 1980s and early 1990s. CPI's position derived not only from its promotion of local concerts in Toronto and other cities, but also from its role as chief promoter of world tours by such bands as the Rolling Stones and Pink Floyd. In this global role, CPI usurped the position of booking agent and limited the participation of other promoters to arranging parts of the tour in return for an agreed fee. After Labatt was purchased by the Belgian Interbrew conglomerate, CPI was sold to MCA Concerts Canada.

Automated ticketing companies have now entered the concert promotion picture. The largest of these is the US firm Ticketmaster.

Large-scale concert promotion has become an increasingly international business. In Germany, the main promoter, Mama Concerts & Rau, promoted more than 800 concerts in 1992–93 with revenues of $80 million, of which 65 percent was generated by Anglo-American artists, 25 percent by German performers and 10 percent by Italian performers. Industry experts also estimated that, in 1996, the concert business in Europe as a whole was worth $2.66 billion, including the increasingly lucrative sale of merchandise such as T-shirts and baseball caps.

The globalization of popular music has brought further problems of regulation and censorship for the concert promotion business. In Indonesia in the mid-1990s, foreign artists and their representatives were required to appear before a committee of police officers and government officials, who decided whether a concert could go ahead. In 1995, promoters waited eight months for a permit for Swedish group Roxette to appear in China. Many Asian venue owners were also charging higher fees than their Western counterparts (Fitz-Gerald 1996).

Bibliography

Baskerville, David 1995. *Music Business Handbook and Career Guide*. 6th ed. Thousand Oaks, CA: Sherwood.

Fitz-Gerald, Jane. 1996. 'A Question of Performance.' *Music News Asia* (April): 26–28.

DAVE LAING

Distribution

Within the music industry, 'distribution' is the term used to refer to the means by which products such as musical instruments, printed music and soundcarriers reach either retailers or consumers. In recent years, the physical distribution of these products has been supplemented by the digital distribution of sound recordings through cable or via the Internet.

Broadside ballads were distributed in Europe in the early modern period by itinerant traders, who sold them directly to consumers at fairs or markets. In the early nineteenth century, publishers and instrument manufacturers dealt directly with owners of permanent shops or stores that stocked music goods. This process of distribution reached a peak in the United States at the end of the nineteenth century, when general stores and department stores were the prime sites for selling new songs.

The early record industry set up similar systems of distribution but, by the 1950s, more complex systems were in place in the United States, involving the participation of one-stop wholesalers and rack jobbers, who acted as intermediaries between record companies and retailers. The ability of one-stops to alert local stores and jukebox operators to the availability of new records was often crucial to the success of singles on smaller labels, while the speed (or lack of it) with which distributors paid such labels was equally crucial to their financial survival.

Within the contemporary record industry in North America, Australasia and Europe, distribution is split between the networks controlled by vertically integrated major record companies and independent distributors (for example, MNW (Music NetWork) in Sweden and Pinnacle in Britain), which provide access to retailers for smaller, independently owned labels. In many Latin American and Southeast Asian countries, however, the foreign-owned majors are dependent on distribution networks owned either by local record companies or by wholesalers. In Japan, the record companies jointly own a single distribution firm which supplies all recordings to stores.

From the 1950s onward, mail-order distribution of recorded music became increasingly important. Consumers purchased recordings directly from record clubs, television merchandisers or distributors of specialist products that were not often stocked by music retailers. Both retailers and record companies began mail-order

operations on the Internet in the mid-1990s, when a few firms began distributing digitally processed music from independent labels directly to the computers of their Internet customers.

In addition to these national systems, there have been several types of international soundcarrier distribution. In the early years of the industry and at the beginning of the compact disc (CD) era, manufacturing was centered in only a few countries from which discs were exported. More recently, fluctuations in exchange rates have given rise to the phenomenon of parallel imports, whereby some wholesalers or retailers find it cheaper to buy from foreign distributors than from distributors in their own countries.

The trade in pirate cassettes and CDs has also been international in character, with millions of prerecorded tapes shipped from Southeast Asia to Africa in the 1980s and unauthorized CDs leaving China in the 1990s.

DAVE LAING

E-commerce

Electronic commerce, or 'E-commerce,' is defined by the US Department of Commerce as 'business transactions on the [World Wide] Web.' This definition is comparatively versatile (for example, it can be taken to encompass business-to-business transactions as well as standard retail ones), but ultimately it is far too narrow. E-commerce presages not simply a new chapter in commerce but a new chapter in industrialization, with all that this portends for economic, social and cultural change. Not all businesses can simply be relocated to the Web, or combine virtual and 'real world' practises and leave the latter unreconstructed. Even under contemporary conditions, the Department of Commerce definition is deficient. For example, in order for 'business transactions on the Web' to become the predominant form of commercial activity in developed societies, the Web needs to reach vastly more homes and businesses than it does currently. Further, the Web needs to become a more accessible, a far faster and a considerably more secure business environment. Ultimately, though, what is required if E-commerce is to be more than an interesting supplement to conventional retail practises is not only the emergence of a thorough and robust electronic-commercial infrastructure, but a concomitant and concurrent transformation across the entire range of economic practise – from the organization of work to the nature and circumstances of buying. To adapt Marx's terminology, if the *forces* of production are undergoing profound upheaval, then equally the *relations* of production must also experience that same root-and-branch change.

The Context of E-commerce

E-commerce is but one of the dimensions of social and cultural activity that take place in and through the Web. In turn, the Web is only one dimension of the Internet. Thus far, the Internet has grown exponentially through the telephone connection of home personal computers (PCs) by modems to the digital data highways established and maintained by the government and military, by the academic and scientific communities, and by the big business concerns of, predominantly, the developed world. The accelerated rate of innovation in information technology – whether in hardware or in software design – is introducing the possibility of production and consumption taking place electronically on a global scale. As the nature of work changes, so too will patterns and habits of consumption. New types of workers will work on new products in new work environments. Old skills will wither and disappear, and new skills and new forms of income will emerge together with new desires and new needs. For businesses, the cost-benefits of operating in virtual space are potentially enormous, as are those associated with accessing global markets. In essence, E-workers will be supplying goods and services, electronically in digitized forms, to customers throughout the world. In this way, firms will be active 24 hours a day, seven days a week and in a virtual marketplace shorn of many of the overhead costs of conventional business.

Even where products cannot be digitized, there are considerable gains to be made by dealing directly with customers through the Web. For example, an automobile manufacturer might offset production and distribution costs by eliminating costly dependency on the car retailer while simultaneously offering financial and insurance services as 'value-added' dimensions of direct purchase. In this way, work tasks, business practises and customer needs and expectations will be reinvented along the entire length of the supply-and-demand chain. Yet, despite the obvious attractiveness to business of this scenario, it must be tempered with the recognition that new economies are created only through upheaval – they cannot be prefabricated and installed, in toto, on a designated day, with minimum disruption to all concerned. Inevitably, there will be victims – among new as well as old businesses and among new as well as old skill sets. Further, there will be a plethora of interim configurations of economic practise until a comparatively stable and generalized structure emerges. Nowhere is this more apparent than in the music industry, which has become, not entirely willingly, a test bed for the transition to E-commerce.

Although it is often celebrated as, potentially, a great enabling and democratizing force, the current reality of the Web is characterized in and by the phrase 'the digital divide.' Essentially, to access the Web from home on a regular basis requires individual households to have sufficient income, as well as sufficient confidence and expertise, to operate and pay for not simply a PC but for the services of an Internet service provider (ISP) and for those of a telephone company to connect them to the Internet. Until the advent of either a 'broadband,' television-based Web or a multi-platform, wireless version, the PC-driven, modem-connected Web will predominate. Further, even after the demise of the PC-Web, many of the principal methods of doing business over the Internet will have become firmly entrenched. Consequently, the dilemmas facing the major music industry companies – together with the solutions they are pioneering – are likely to act as the template for E-commerce of the future.

E-commerce and the Music Industry

It is fair to argue that popular music is now a cross-generational cultural staple of the developed world. On this basis, the huge numbers of home PC users already represent a market for popular music products and, clearly, record companies, music merchandisers and concert promoters are anxious to tap into this market. The question is, how do they do this? And while record companies large and small, music publishers, music industry associations and collection agencies – to name just some of the many interested parties – seek answers to this question, home PC users are establishing new, and often *non*-commercial, practises with regard to popular music. Basically, the entire commercial culture of E-commerce is being configured *ahead of* its infrastructure. This is not to say that order will never be achieved (the North American 'frontier' of the nineteenth century was eventually 'tamed'), but, in both the types of business models being proposed by major music industry companies, and also in the proposed solutions to real and perceived problems, something of the scale of the qualitative changes facing 'real' businesses in the transition to a virtual world can be glimpsed. The following represent a number of strategic dimensions within the general issue of the transition to E-commerce.

(a) Whether major or independent, conglomerate or micro, *all* record companies face the same challenges where current Web practises are concerned. The existence and persistence of the digital divide mean that record companies can access the mass market for record buyers only through the conventional retail system; however, the Web not only offers the chance to deal directly with customers (thereby lowering prices at a stroke), but also allows companies to know exactly who their customers are. Currently, then, record companies are torn between reassuring retailers on whom they depend that they will remain loyal to the current system and, more or less visibly, searching for Web-based strategies that will maximize the benefit of investment in hardware and in software applications. The justifiable nervousness of the major retailers with regard to the intentions of, especially, the major companies then has an impact on the contemporary decisions they make about what titles they will offer for sale and in what quantities. It may well be the case that, even before it has been instituted, E-commerce is affecting the popularity of (some) records.

(b) Record companies also recognize that digital distribution offers them cost-benefits right along the value chain. For example, if newly signed artists record on digital equipment and their work-in-progress can be accessed and transmitted through the Web, then studio costs (and advances) can be cut while monitoring of production is maximized. The digitization of back catalog means that all recordings owned by a company can be offered for sale without the need for warehousing and physical distribution. Further, marketing and promotional costs can be lowered *and* maximized by the use of databases to target existing customers and by the combination of low-cost, Web-centered promotional strategies with promotion through other routes of data dissemination (E-mail and text messaging, Web-radio broadcasting to global audiences and so on). The downside is that the need for record companies to take charge of promotion and marketing becomes less apparent to their new and existing artists – especially if advances are likely to be reduced while profits soar. It may well be the case that new and existing acts will come to deal directly with their audiences and that, consequently, record companies as such will simply wither away.

(c) While record companies search for ways to maximize the obvious advantages of E-commerce, record buyers have been turning in their millions to 'file-sharing,' or the illegal downloading of copyrighted music. The Recording Industry Association of America (RIAA) won its case against the creators and owners of the Napster software program in 2001, but the key issue of how to prevent Napster 'clones' from perpetuating this form of digital piracy was not resolved. The point here is not so much the loss in royalty income to the owners of the recordings and the songs recorded but, rather, the sea change in the customer's perception of the value of music. Ultimately, it will prove far more difficult (if not impossible) to reverse the expectation that music on the Web is 'free' than it will be to prevent the practise of file-sharing and to configure royalty payment systems.

(d) Further cultural changes in the perception of the value of music derive from the actions of the major com-

panies themselves. The merger of Time Warner with AOL (at the time by far the biggest merger in corporate history) was, and will prove, a watershed in the onset of E-commerce. The merger itself is testimony to the enormous significance of the Web to the global economy. In 1990, AOL did not exist. In a period of five years (1995–2000), it had become the largest ISP in the United States, with a considerable number of subscribers in countries around the world. By 2000, it was strong enough to be considered the dominant partner in a merger with the world's largest publishing group. As a potential 'partner,' Time Warner was doubly attractive to AOL: not only did it enjoy cable television access to millions of subscribers, but it was also home to some of the world's most important media industry brand names – Warner Bros. Pictures, CNN, *Time* magazine and the Warner Music Group (WMG). If the broadband-television model becomes the Web of the future, it will be Time Warner's visual and text-based content that will provide AOL's greatest asset; but, currently, it is access to WMG that affords AOL the opportunity to test new models of E-commerce.

Where the current commercial practises associated with making popular music are concerned, the term 'content' may well sound their death knell. What AOL now owns is an enormous back catalog of songs and recordings, together with a host of contemporary signings and a structure for generating more signings of similar quality. Although it is unlikely, AOL may be tempted to 'give away' all of this music as a 'loss leader' to attract customers to some form of exclusive, Web-based, media subscription service. While incorporation is not a new phenomenon where the 'major' record companies are concerned, until now no merger, no act of incorporation, has so threatened the autonomy and independence of a major company; if WMG should lose the ability to act independently within the borders of an increasingly ill-defined 'record industry,' then the four other majors may well be either tempted or forced to follow suit. Clearly, this would not be 'the end of popular music,' but it would mean that the structures developed over the past century would be revised, perhaps beyond recognition. This, in turn, would at least mean that creators of new music would need to look elsewhere for the financing they require to sustain themselves as music-makers.

(e) The major record companies rely on a steady stream of income from 'catalog sales' to underwrite their search for new talent. If catalog income is lost through a combination of file-sharing piracy and the 'free music,' loss-leading practises of corporate owners, then owners of other forms of music catalog may well be the beneficiaries. For example, the BBC has an enormous archive of radio recordings that it might either broadcast continuously on a subscription service or make available for downloading through a secure payment system. Its popular music concert video and music performance archives, although less extensive, could also be made available in the same ways. In turn, this might tempt commercially autonomous, established artists to participate in new live performance and documentary features exclusively for the BBC or for large networks throughout the world. Similarly, individual music venues could charge subscription rates (or rely on advertising and/or sponsorship) for regular Web broadcasts or, alternatively, agencies could negotiate exclusive deals on entire tours. In these ways, the record company's loss could become the artist's and *the audience's* gain.

Conclusion

The advent of E-commerce cannot be accommodated merely by quantitative or 'technical' adjustments to contemporary business practises; rather, companies must recognize that technological revolutions entail and invoke social and cultural change of similar import and magnitude. In its early years, E-commerce in the music industry has been in a stage of 'phony war' – there has been much posturing and pronouncing, but no large-scale innovation has been attempted, let alone accomplished. In the same period, Napster has come and gone as a free file-sharing service and the Web has experienced a remarkably rapid cycle of 'boom and bust' in the 'dot.com' fiasco. This is exactly as it should be – industrial revolutions do not happen overnight, and there will be many forays into many different versions of commercial and industrial practise until a working model appears. What is certain is that there *will* be E-commerce in popular music products and that the existing patterns of production and consumption of those products will change and change quite considerably, with a consequent effect on the nature and cultural place of popular music itself.

MIKE JONES

Gig

'Gig' is a commonplace colloquial popular music term, used initially by jazz musicians and subsequently adopted widely in popular music in connection with freelance playing activities. The derivation of the term is obscure, although, according to Eubie Blake, it was in use as early as 1905 among leaders of syncopated orchestras such as James Reese Europe (Gold 1975). In common with the word 'jazz' itself, 'gig' may have sexual overtones, being reported by Abrahams (1964) as denoting the vagina or rectum in the context of sexual congress. Other possible origins include 'whirligig,' denoting a

maelstrom of activity, or the French *gigue*, denoting legs or 'shanks' used to move between engagements. Another possibility relates to use of the term to denote a winning combination in the widely prevalent numbers game played in the 1920s in black communities in the United States, since to obtain a playing gig was seen as equivalent to winning money on the numbers.

As a noun, a 'gig' denotes a paying engagement, either a 'one-off' event, or a regular job such as a residency at a club or in a pit orchestra, and the term was in common use among 1920s Chicago jazz players. As a verb, 'to gig' means to play as a freelance and, by extension, 'to be gigging' generally means to be working regularly. However, 'gigging around' is sometimes used to denote musicians' infrequent freelance activities, accepting work wherever it is offered (Gold 1975; Feather 1960). In latter-day musicians' argot, a 'day gig' is a regular non-musical 'day job.'

Bibliography

Abrahams, Roger D. 1964. *Deep Down in the Jungle . . .: Negro Narrative Folklore from the Streets of Philadelphia*. Hatboro, PA: Folklore Associates.

Feather, Leonard. 1960. *The Encyclopedia of Jazz*. New York: Horizon Press.

Gold, Robert S. 1975. *Jazz Talk*. Indianapolis, IN: Bobbs-Merrill.

Levet, Jean-Paul. 1992. *Talkin' That Talk: Le Langage du blues et du jazz* [Talkin' That Talk: The Language of Blues and Jazz]. Paris: Hatier.

ALYN SHIPTON

Hit

The first recorded use of the term 'hit' to mean a show business success was in 1811; the usage was taken from the game of backgammon. In the music industry, 'hit' has been used in conjunction with many kinds of product or activity, from hit shows and hit tunes to hit records and hit parades. Less frequently, a performer is said to be a hit with audiences.

The definition of a hit is almost entirely contextual. The most precise measure of a hit may be that provided by one of the many national or international hit parades or charts listing current songs, shows or records in order of their success in unit sales, ticket sales or amount of radio airplay. Therefore, hit records and songs are those that appear on these lists and are later collected into publications such as those by Whitburn for the United States or by Gambaccini et al. for the United Kingdom. Within these lists, it is possible to have categories of hits – big (Top 10 or Top 20) or small (Top 50, Top 100 or even Top 200).

The term 'hit' can be stretched further to mean any music that finds favor with any segment of the industry or audience. Thus, a turntable hit is one that seems to please radio listeners even though it does not sell many copies.

A record or song that fails to become a hit is a 'miss,' as in the US and British television show *Juke Box Jury*, in which panelists were asked to judge whether a single would be a hit or a miss.

Bibliography

Gambaccini, Paul, et al. 1997. *The Guinness Book of British Hit Singles*. London: Guinness Books.

Whitburn, Joel. 1994. *The Billboard Book of Top 40 Hits*. New York: Billboard Publications.

DAVE LAING

Impresario

A popular music impresario is an entrepreneur who conceives and arranges live performances, often in a series, for musicians and/or companies of musicians. The series can take place at the same venue with changing personnel or can involve a tour of different venues with the same musicians. Particularly in the twentieth century, the distinction between an impresario and the performer of other functions and activities (for example, a manager promoting his/her own 'stable' of performers, an organizer controlling the bookings on a touring circuit) was not always clear, and many music entrepreneurs included the activities traditionally associated with an impresario in a roster of related activities. The designation 'impresario' itself is often ascribed to an individual by others and typically contains connotations of scale and of a willingness to gamble; it is rare as a self-description.

'Impresario' was first used in the context of seventeenth-century Italian theatrical performance, especially opera, to refer to a manager or concessionaire who both arranged and promoted a season of performances for a particular theater. As the practise became widely employed in other parts of Europe by the eighteenth century, Italian impresarios were regularly sought after (if not regularly successful). Most of the impresario's many tasks – assembling companies, commissioning music from composers, determining production details, negotiating deals, organizing publicity, selling blocks of theater seats, paying performers, paying rent and so on – were controlled by contract. The manner in which the tasks were carried out was decided by the impresario – or the impresario's agents – and, in a highly competitive, relatively uncontrolled environment, often involved recourse to unscrupulous practises.

The role of the impresario diversified in the nineteenth century, as commercial popular culture began to establish itself and as the expanding cities and improvements in travel by both land and sea provided larger potential audiences and encouraged the practise of touring. In the wake of these changes, impresarios emerged whose chief function was a judicious mix of promoter, agent and tour organizer. A key figure in this development was P.T. Barnum, whose skillful planning and management of the US tour of Swedish opera singer Jenny Lind in 1850–51 resulted in a 19-city, 95-concert tour and unheard-of proceeds of over $700,000. Originally a circus showman and exhibitor of curiosities (including the 'midget' Tom Thumb), Barnum applied to the Lind project a range of promotional techniques developed in the relatively new world of commercial popular culture. These techniques included selling Jenny Lind merchandise, providing the newspapers with newsworthy anecdotes and sending advance publicity groups to each city to orchestrate a warm welcome for the star. Barnum was already celebrated for his hyperbole ('humbug') and he capitalized on this, but what he also demonstrated was that promotion could be tied to the image of the performer. In Lind's case, this meant emphasizing her goodness and her charitable disposition. It was also significant, both to the public and to Lind herself, that Barnum was known as a reliable, honest dealer with moral standards (one reason for his success had been his ability to make his entertainments 'family' ones).

Following Barnum, a new generation of impresarios emerged in both concert music and popular entertainment (between which, as in the case of Barnum and Lind, the gap was not always huge) – men (invariably) of whom a range of skills was required that extended from a flair for imaginative, competitive publicity to an ability to read ship and railroad timetables and plan intricate touring schedules, whether for opera or for vaudeville companies. One such figure was English opera impresario Colonel James Mapleson, whose achievements included (he himself claimed) organizing a company that gave '48 concerts in 48 cities in 48 days' in 1872. By the late 1870s, he was shifting 'costumes, properties and even singers . . . to and fro across the ocean in accordance with my New York and London requirements' (quoted in Ehrlich 1985, 55).

Although late nineteenth-century vaudeville impresarios such as B.F. Keith and E.F. Albee had much in common with their opera counterparts in terms of promotion and touring, they also differed from them in some key respects. Keith and Albee used their positions as entrepreneurial intermediaries to progress from organizing and touring small-time variety shows to leasing theaters specifically for vaudeville, and then to building their own, in New York, Boston and elsewhere, as part of what became a major show-business empire – an empire that included a touring circuit which dominated vaudeville on the US east coast. In this context, the function of the impresario began to blur, and to become one activity among many interconnected and interdependent ones.

Changes in the scale of operation involving the impresario were apparent on Broadway too, as huge theatrical syndicates began to form, beginning in the last decades of the nineteenth century. The Shubert brothers (Sam, J.J. and Lee) set up in opposition to an existing syndicate in 1900 and began by leasing a theater to stage their own revue. By 1920, they owned or leased a series of theaters in major urban centers and had established a virtual monopoly. Besides running the business side of the empire, the brothers both booked and produced shows (the Shubert organization staged over 500 shows between 1901 and 1954).

Developments such as these connected the idea of the impresario, perhaps irrevocably, with hardheaded, large-scale promotional activities beyond the scope of an organizational intermediary, although the important element of risk and uncertainty remained. This pattern continued well into the rock era, as is shown by the career of a figure such as Bill Graham: he moved from modest beginnings as an organizer of benefit gigs in the San Francisco area in the mid-1960s via a stint as promoter of concerts by seminal west-coast bands to ownership of key venues, the Fillmore West (San Francisco) and the Fillmore East (New York) in 1968, only to close both down three years later. During this time, Graham's notoriously well-developed business sense regularly brought him into conflict with the ostensibly anti-commercial hippy ideals.

But although partial or total control over venues became a major hallmark of the twentieth-century impresario, it has never been a prerequisite. Like Barnum and his successors a century earlier, British impresario Larry Parnes, a central figure in the development of British rock 'n' roll in the 1950s, combined commercial adventurism, astute market sense, the ability to 'package' a performer and a willingness to take risks, culturally and economically, in the cause of introducing new performers to the public (and profiting from the exercise). Parnes's meticulously prepared package tours took nineteenth-century achievements several steps further: '[H]is office resembled a military headquarters with maps on the wall and flags denoting dates and destinations.' Factors beyond the ken of his predecessors informed his planning: 'Demographic surveys of towns, cinema security and even atmospheric conditions were each taken into consideration as Larry plotted his final course' (Rogan 1988, 31).

At the same time as he built on the earlier concept of the role of the popular music impresario, Parnes changed it significantly by also managing the acts he packaged, and, for Parnes, managing included paying close attention to matters such as image and offstage life style. In this, Parnes was mirroring the way in which some operatic impresarios, in both the nineteenth and the twentieth centuries, took a close interest in the personal and stylistic development of their star performers.

In the late twentieth century, two of the figures who best fitted the often larger-than-life image of the impresario were both British. Harvey Goldsmith's dominating role in the rock and pop concert scene included the introduction of the idea of 'stadium rock.' Sir Cameron Mackintosh similarly dominated the musical theater, especially through his promotion and production of shows with music by Andrew Lloyd Webber. The ongoing presence of the risk factor was well illustrated in 1999 by the apparent threat to Goldsmith's empire posed by the failure of a major festival designed (as noted with due irony by some commentators) to mark the eclipse of the sun (Buckingham 1999).

Bibliography

Buckingham, Lisa. 1999. 'Goldsmith Empire Faces Final Curtain: The Eclipse of an Impresario.' *The Guardian* (30 September): 3.

Ehrlich, Cyril. 1985. *The Music Profession in Britain Since the Eighteenth Century: A Social History*. Oxford: Clarendon Press.

Price, Curtis, Milhous, Judith, and Hume, Robert D. 1992. *The Impresario's Ten Commandments: Continental Recruitment for Italian Opera in London 1763–64*. London: Royal Musical Association.

Rogan, Johnny. 1988. *Starmakers and Svengalis: The History of British Pop Management*. London: Macdonald/ Queen Anne Press.

Rosselli, John. 1984. *The Opera Industry in Italy from Cimarosa to Verdi: The Role of the Impresario*. Cambridge: Cambridge University Press.

Toll, Robert C. 1976. *On with the Show: The First Century of Show Business in America*. New York: Oxford University Press.

Ware, W. Porter. 1980. *P.T. Barnum Presents Jenny Lind: The American Tour of the Swedish Nightingale*. Baton Rouge, LA: Louisiana State University Press.

DAVID HORN

Management

In ergonomics and business studies, the term 'management' covers the organization of work practises and of the general activities of a firm or enterprise. Since the publication in 1911 of Frederick Taylor's *The Principles of Scientific Management*, a thriving industry of management theory has developed. Its main trends have included theories of organizational management, which are concerned with the internal structure of the firm (for example, Hammer and Champy 1995); theories of strategic management, dealing with the firm's activities in the marketplace (for example, Porter 1998); theories of corporate cultures, analyzing the manner and style with which the company conducts its business (for example, Peters and Waterman 1984); and theories of knowledge management, focusing on the maximization of the intellectual capital possessed by the firm and its employees (for example, Stewart 1997).

Although much management theory is as relevant to the music business as to other sectors, there has been little direct application of it within the music industry. This can be explained by the preponderance of very small firms within the industry – most management theory is concerned with the manipulation of large organizations and cannot easily be applied to record labels, music publishers or artist management firms with only a handful of staff – and by the conservatism of the industry in its recruitment policies: very few managers are appointed from outside the industry. This conservatism is compounded by a widespread rejection of the idea that music business managers can be trained. This is associated with what Negus (1999) calls a 'mystical' view of management held by many within the industry, which explains success by reference to 'good fortune' or 'being in the right place at the right time' (34).

Nevertheless, the largest companies within the industry have adopted certain management strategies at various stages of their development. One of the earliest examples was the report on CBS Records commissioned from the Harvard Business School in 1964. This resulted in a large-scale restructuring of the company (Davis 1975, 20). However, it is notable that, within a few years, the management of the company regressed to a less sophisticated autocratic style, with successive presidents described as 'aggressive,' 'abrasive' and 'brash' (Negus 1999, 66). EMI and BMG are unusual in that each has pinpointed the need for new approaches and has appointed senior executives from outside the music industry. In the case of EMI, the former flour miller Joseph Lockwood (appointed in 1954) and the food marketing executive Jim Fifield (1988) each made fundamental changes to the company. When the German-born accountant Michael Dornemann was appointed head of BMG after the takeover of RCA Records in 1989, he faced considerable hostility from US record industry executives.

According to Negus, the most common type of strategic management among the major companies is portfolio management, which 'provides a way of viewing the company's labels, genres and artists by dividing them into discrete units (strategic business units)' (1999, 47).

The theory that national variations are a primary influence on corporate cultures (Hampden-Turner and Trompenaars 1994) is supported by the widespread perception, among industry executives, of transnational music companies as being 'Japanese' (Sony), 'German' (BMG) or 'American' (Warner) (Negus 1999, 65–71).

Outside the large companies, the most common management type is entrepreneurial, where an individual dominates a firm through strength of personality or the exercise of exceptional skills. The career of Elvis Presley, for example, can be described as the product of two entrepreneurial managers. First, Sam Phillips, owner of Sun Records, acted as the catalyst for the formation of Presley's vocal style from 1954 to 1956. Second, 'Colonel' Tom Parker managed Presley's professional life in negotiations for record royalties, publishing rights, film appearances and concert performances.

Phillips is a prime example of what Gillett (1975) calls a 'record man' [sic]. Like such figures as Ahmet Ertegun of Atlantic (Gillett 1975) and Leonard Chess of Chess (Cohodas 2000), Phillips has been perceived as combining a spontaneous aesthetic sense with an ear for recognizing future hit styles. The US and UK record industries continued to produce this type of entrepreneur into the 1990s in such figures as rap record company founders Russell Simmons of Def Jam, Sean 'Puffy' Combs of Bad Boy and Alan McGee of Creation Records (Cavanagh 2000).

Parker was the archetype of a kind of personal manager who fought uncompromisingly for his artist and also claimed an exceptionally high proportion of the artist's earnings (O'Neal 1998). Many other managers have shared his unorthodox approach but, in the 1990s, attempts were made to professionalize the role of artist manager, notably through the introduction by the Music Managers Forum (MMF) of training schemes in the United Kingdom and elsewhere. The MMF argued that, since the personal management function takes place at the interface between the artist and every dimension of the industry, successful management demands understanding and knowledge of the record industry, music publishing, touring, merchandising and, sometimes, the procedures of the broadcasting and film industries. Only with such understanding and knowledge can the manager develop an overview of and create a strategy for a musician's career development.

Berry Gordy of Motown represents a different type of entrepreneur, in that he put into practise the 'production line' method of management theorized by Taylor and embodied in the Ford car plant in Detroit. Gordy had briefly worked at Ford before entering the music business, and his Motown 'hit factory' practised a division of labor between specialist songwriters, session musicians, choreographers, engineers and stylists (George 1985).

Attempts in the music industry to combine a corporate management style with that of the entrepreneur have generally been unsuccessful. When PolyGram purchased the independent companies Island and A&M in 1989, it retained the services of their respective founders, Chris Blackwell and Jerry Moss. Within a few years, however, both had left, unable to work within the constraints of the portfolio management system.

Bibliography

Cavanagh, David. 2000. *The Creation Records Story: My Magpie Eyes Are Hungry for the Prize*. London: Virgin.

Cohodas, Nadine. 2000. *Spinning Blues into Gold: Chess Records – The Label That Launched the Blues*. London: Aurum Press.

Davis, Clive, with Willwerth, James K. 1975. *Clive: Inside the Record Business*. New York: Morrow.

George, Nelson. 1985. *Where Did Our Love Go?: The Rise and Fall of the Motown Sound*. New York: St. Martin's Press.

Gillett, Charlie. 1975. *Making Tracks: Atlantic Records and the Growth of a Multi-Billion-Dollar Industry*. St. Alban's: Panther.

Hammer, Michael, and Champy, James. 1995. *Reengineering the Corporation: A Manifesto for Business Revolution*. London: Nicholas Brealey.

Hampden-Turner, Charles, and Trompenaars, Fons. 1994. *The Seven Cultures of Capitalism*. London: Piatkus.

Negus, Keith. 1999. *Music Genres and Corporate Cultures*. London: Routledge.

O'Neal, Sean. 1998. *My Boy Elvis: The Colonel Tom Parker Story*. New York: Barricade Books.

Peters, Thomas J., and Waterman, Robert H. Jr., 1984. *In Search of Excellence: Lessons from America's Best-Run Companies*. New York: Warner Books.

Porter, Michael E. 1998. *Competitive Strategy: Techniques for Analyzing Industries and Competitors*. Rev. ed. New York and London: Free Press.

Stewart, Thomas A. 1997. *Intellectual Capital: The New Wealth of Organizations*. London: Nicholas Brealey.

Taylor, Frederick W. 1911. *The Principles of Scientific Management*. New York: Harper.

DAVE LAING

Manager

The managers of popular music artists have frequently played a major role in the history of the music industry, particularly in the field of post-rock 'n' roll pop music through such figures as 'Colonel' Tom Parker (Elvis Presley's manager), Brian Epstein (the Beatles), Albert Grossman (Bob Dylan) and Frank Dileo (Michael Jackson). While those managers were famous or notorious for masterminding their clients' business affairs, other managers (for example, ABBA's Stig Anderson or Tam Paton of the Bay City Rollers) have been credited with a Svengali-like role in forming the musical style or the visual image of successful artists. The powerful position occupied by the manager has also, on occasion, resulted in cases of malpractise, such as the embezzlement of funds due to the artist.

Personal management crystallized as a specific and separate role within the music business only very slowly. In particular, the present-day notion that a manager should not have any other professional involvement with the act because of a potential conflict of interest was not widely held in the past. In fact, in the period before 1945 in North America, the de facto role of manager was often taken by a music publisher, record company executive or booking agent. In an industry controlled by whites, black musicians needed the assistance of white (often Jewish) managers, such as the pugnacious and unscrupulous Joe Glaser, who controlled the career of Louis Armstrong and founded his Associated Booking Corporation with the proceeds of 40 percent commissions. White band leaders, such as Bob Crosby, paid a band member to take on the role of manager. In Nashville, as late as the 1960s, agents frequently acted as personal managers for the country and western artists whose tours they booked (Shelton 1966).

The issue of conflict of interest came to the fore in Britain and the United States in the 1970s through high-profile disputes involving Gilbert O'Sullivan and the Eagles. O'Sullivan successfully sued Gordon Mills of the MAM organization, who controlled the singer's publishing and record label as well as being his personal manager. Similarly, the Eagles successfully claimed that David Geffen's role as their manager was fatally compromised by his association with the record company and booking agency to which they were contracted (Goodman 1997).

Financial issues are a second principal source of friction. Artists have frequently alleged that managers have taken unreasonably large amounts of the performers' earnings either through the operation of an inequitable contract or by fraudulent behavior. In a smaller number of cases, managers have complained about the termination of a contract by the artist at a moment when the act has 'broken through' to commercial success. Thus, after Guns N' Roses signed a recording deal with Geffen in 1986 and his label (Geffen Records) found them a high-profile manager, the group's previous manager sued for damages in a case that was settled out of court (Sugerman 1992).

The manager's remuneration is tied to the earnings of

the artist. Contracts between artists and manager stipulate the percentage of earnings to which the manager is entitled and how this percentage is to be calculated. In the case of 'Colonel' Tom Parker and Brian Epstein, the figure was 25 percent, while more recent contracts may include different rates for different income sources (Bicknell 1991). Equally significant is whether the manager's fee is 'gross' or 'net.' A gross fee is a percentage of the artist's total earnings before other expenses such as legal fees, payments to backing musicians or booking agents are paid. From the artist's point of view, it is more equitable (and cheaper) to pay the manager a percentage of his/her net earnings which remain after these expenses have been met. Managers may also insure themselves against the severance of their relationship with an artist by claiming a percentage of all future earnings from recording contracts negotiated while they represented the artist. Baskerville (1995, 170–78) provides a useful discussion of the issues at stake in negotiating a typical management contract.

The routes by which individuals become the personal managers of popular music artists have varied historically and geographically. In some famous cases, parents of talented young singers have assumed the managerial role, with generally negative results – for example, Murray Wilson (the Beach Boys), Joe Jackson (the Jackson 5) and George Osmond (the Osmonds). Billy Joel entrusted his management to his brother-in-law, Frank Weber, but ended the relationship in the publicity of a multimillion-dollar lawsuit.

Sometimes, the manager of a young group is a friend who helped them with transportation or bookings in their early days. On other occasions, an industry professional from a booking agency, law firm or record company may leave his/her job to take on the role of full-time manager. Thus, Tom Parker was originally a promoter and publicist, Brian Epstein was a Liverpool record store manager, Albert Grossman was a folk club owner, Sidney Seidenberg was an accountant before he became B.B. King's manager, Peter Grant and Roger Forrester were road managers before guiding the careers of Led Zeppelin and Eric Clapton, respectively, and Stig Anderson was originally an established songwriter and studio owner in Sweden.

Concerted moves to get the management of popular music artists recognized as a legitimate profession within the music industry began in 1991, with the formation in the United Kingdom of the International Managers Forum (IMF). Other chapters of the IMF were subsequently formed in other European countries as well as in North America and Australia. The IMF's main argument was that managers needed training in order to be able to defend their clients' interests in the context of the powerful record industry, but a spate of 'sackings' of managers by artists in 1997 also brought a plea from the IMF that British labels should pay managers' commissions directly to them rather than to the artists. As former Eagles' manager Irving Azoff once cynically remarked: 'Management is a terrible business. Who wants an artist to take 85% of his money?' (Goodman 1997, 247).

Bibliography

Baskerville, David. 1995. *Music Business Handbook and Career Guide*. 6th ed. Thousand Oaks, CA: Sherwood.

Bicknell, Ed. 1991. 'Management.' In *The Rock File: Making It in the Music Business*, ed. Norton York. Oxford: Oxford University Press, 183–93.

Goodman, Fred. 1997. *The Mansion on the Hill: Dylan, Young, Geffen, Springsteen, and the Head-On Collision of Rock and Commerce*. New York: Random House.

Rogan, Johnny. 1988. *Starmakers and Svengalis: The History of British Pop Management*. London: Macdonald Queen Anne Press.

Shelton, Robert, and Goldblatt, Burt. 1966. *The Country Music Story*. Secaucus, NJ: Castle Books.

Sugerman, Danny. 1992. *The Days of Guns N' Roses: Appetite for Destruction*. New York: St. Martin's Press.

DAVE LAING

Market

Markets have played, and continue to play, a crucial role in economic, social and cultural exchange in many societies. Popular music has had a presence at markets for centuries. In England in 1595, a writer complained that, at every market, ballad-singers were 'singing their wares' (Clark 1983, 25), while cassette sellers are found in the markets of most African, Asian and Latin American cities today. Diawara (1998) has provided a powerful evocation and analysis of the continuing importance of such markets in West African life.

Classical economic theory elaborated the term 'market' into a concept denoting the abstract space where supply and demand meet and find equilibrium through the pricing of commodities or services. When demand exceeds supply, prices rise, and where supply is in excess of demand, prices tend to fall. This theory, in its extreme form, claims that distortion by alien forces such as governments or monopolistic practises compromises the operation of a 'free' market in providing equilibrium between supply (the producers) and demand (the consumers).

By the mid-twentieth century, the concept of a free market had become central to much conservative political discourse. It was counterposed to the planned economies of state socialism, where, in the case of popular music, the supply of recorded music was controlled by a state monopoly which, for example, limited the availability of copies of Western pop music to a few compilations pressed in limited numbers.

In recent years, authors such as Miège (1989) and Garnham (2000) have commented on the special characteristics of markets for cultural commodities, in particular the unpredictability of consumer demand for such items as songs, books and films. According to Miège, cultural producers such as record companies and film studios, in order to reduce the risks of failure, bring to the market a 'catalogue' of a large number of different items in the expectation that profits from the small number of hits will compensate for the losses incurred by unsuccessful titles.

Economists have also developed the concept of 'market failure' to describe situations where suppliers are unable or unwilling to provide certain commodities or services. Examples of remedies for market failure in the music industry include subsidies for performances through state funding or private sponsorship in order to make tickets affordable, and the distribution of pirate copies of soundcarriers when legitimate copies are priced too highly for consumers or are simply unavailable because no company holds the rights in a particular country.

In practise, the free market concept developed by the classical economists never becomes a reality, usually because the greater power of the supply side distorts market operations or because the participants do not act as rational economic beings. In the general market for recorded music, the suppliers (the record companies and retailers) determine the recordings to be made available and the prices to be charged. The monopoly status conferred by copyright ownership plays a role here too. In some cases, a small number of large companies operate a de facto cartel that keeps prices high and denies smaller companies the opportunity to compete in the market on equal terms.

There is evidence that cultural workers are prone to behave in ways that contradict their rational economic interests. A study of the British market for classical singers by Towse (1993) found that the market was 'distorted' because the supply of labor was far greater than the demand from opera companies, choirs and so on. She concluded that the participants' behavior was determined by the aesthetic attraction of music even when the likelihood of gaining employment was low. The position of popular musicians is similar. A survey of members of the British Musicians' Union found that only 18 percent had earnings from music that were above the national average wage (York and Laing 2000, 6).

If the free market ideology is ultimately unhelpful for an understanding of the economics of popular music, a less partisan concept of the market is a valuable part of any attempt to describe popular music as one of the cultural industries. The overall market for recorded popular music, for example, can be understood as the sum of a large number of separate but intertwined markets ranging in scope from a global pop market, where transnational companies sell the music of a Céline Dion or a Michael Jackson to an undifferentiated worldwide audience, to the narrowest of niche markets involving musicians who sell copies of their cassettes directly to those attending their performances.

In turn, the distinctions between the various intertwined markets for popular music may be based on various extra-economic factors, as Grenier and Guilbault have pointed out in their discussion of *créolité* and *francophonie* in music (1997). Discussing the musical commodities embodying these specific elements, they write: '. . . record sales, radio airplay and other indicators of the scale of diffusion of these commodities are not necessarily the only criteria used for configuring and defining their respective markets, as linguistic affinities, shared histories, socio-economic and geographic proximities, as well as converging political agendas, also appear to play a significant role' (227).

Bibliography

Clark, Peter. 1983. *The English Alehouse: A Social History, 1200–1830*. London and New York: Longman.

Diawara, Manthia. 1998. *In Search of Africa*. Cambridge, MA: Harvard University Press.

Garnham, Nicholas. 2000. *Emancipation, the Media and Modernity: Arguments About the Media and Social Theory*. Oxford and New York: Oxford University Press.

Grenier, Line, and Guilbault, Jocelyne. 1997. '*Créolité* and *Francophonie* in Music: Socio-Musical Repositioning Where It Matters.' *Cultural Studies* 11(2): 207–34.

Miège, Bernard. 1989. *The Capitalization of Cultural Production*. New York: International General.

Towse, Ruth. 1993. *Singers in the Marketplace: The Economics of the Singing Profession*. Oxford: Clarendon Press.

York, Norton, and Laing, Dave. 2000. *Nice Work – If You Can Get It!: A Survey of Musicians' Employment 1978–98*. London: Rheingold Publishing.

DAVE LAING

Marketing

The term 'marketing' describes the range of methods and practises used to persuade consumers to purchase a product or a service. The marketing of popular music thus includes such activities as television and print advertising, radio plugging and promotion and 'direct marketing' through mailing lists.

The most widely used method of marketing songs is by demonstrating them to potential purchasers. This is now achieved principally through the broadcasting of recordings or by the use of 'listening posts' in stores. Before the advent of radio, songs were performed directly to listeners. Attali (1985) describes how Parisian music publishers used street singers in the mid-nineteenth century as 'door-to-door salesmen' for songbooks, while in Japan similar marketing practises were used into the twentieth century. In Britain, publishers paid well-known singers to feature 'royalty ballads' onstage – so called because the vocalist received a royalty payment on sheet music sales. In the United States, pluggers would arrange for in-store pianists and singers to present songs to shoppers in sheet music departments.

Other forms of popular music marketing include the design and coordination of press advertising and visual displays such as posters and point-of-sale material, the creation of television, radio or cinema commercials, the use of press reviews and interviews, and personal appearances (PAs) by an act either on television and radio or at record stores or clubs. Recent innovations in popular music marketing are music (or 'promotional') videoclips, small leaflets or 'flyers' promoting club nights, the use of Internet Web sites, and the employment of 'street teams' to market R&B and other black music in the United States and the United Kingdom.

The New York publisher Leo Feist was a pioneer of press advertising of sheet music, spending $100,000 annually in newspaper and magazine advertising in the years before World War I (Sanjek 1988, 35). Street posters advertising concerts, festivals and records evolved from the pure typography of music hall posters to vivid images representing the ethos of an event, such as the psychedelic designs of Victor Moscoso and Stanley Mouse for hippie events in San Francisco (Grushkin 1987) and those of John Holder for the annual Cambridge Folk Festival (Laing and Newman 1994).

Major record companies have specialist marketing departments whose task is to design coordinated marketing campaigns for new record releases (Negus 1992; Stokes 1976). The UK record industry spent almost 10 percent of its turnover on advertising in 1999 (British Phonographic Industry 2000), and the cost of a large-scale campaign for an album by a major act could be equivalent to 15–20 percent of the record company's revenue from that title. Marketing textbooks state that successful campaigns often employ a verbal or visual 'hook' that is repeated in various media. Andy Warhol's lips and lolling tongue design for the Rolling Stones' album *Sticky Fingers* and the slogan 'I saw rock 'n' roll's future' for Bruce Springsteen's 'Born To Run' are renowned examples.

Commenting on the marketing of Bruce Springsteen, a US record industry executive said that a new performer must be sold 'to your own record company first, then to the trade and then on to the record buyers' (Goodman 1997, 281). Selling to the trade may include full-page advertisements in the trade magazines read by retailers, promotional gifts sent to retailers and journalists, and, in some countries, special retail discounts such as providing one free single for each copy that is purchased.

Bibliography

Attali, Jacques. 1985. *Noise: The Political Economy of Music*, trans. Brian Massumi. Minneapolis, MN: University of Minnesota Press.

British Phonographic Industry (BPI). 2000. *BPI Statistical Handbook*. London: BPI.

Goodman, Fred. 1997. *The Mansion on the Hill: Dylan, Young, Geffen, Springsteen, and the Head-On Collision of Rock and Commerce*. New York: Times Books.

Grushkin, Paul D. 1987. *The Art of Rock: Posters from Presley to Punk*. New York: Abbeville Press.

Hall, Charles W., and Taylor, Frederick J. 1996. *Marketing in the Music Industry*. Needham Heights, MA: Simon & Schuster Custom Pub.

Laing, Dave, and Newman, Richard, eds. 1994. *Thirty Years of the Cambridge Folk Festival*. Ely: Music Maker Books.

Negus, Keith. 1992. *Producing Pop: Culture and Conflict in the Popular Music Industry*. London: Edward Arnold.

Sanjek, Russell. 1988. *American Popular Music and Its Business: The First Four Hundred Years. Vol. III: From 1900 to 1984*. New York: Oxford University Press.

Stokes, Geoffrey. 1976. *Star-Making Machinery: The Odyssey of an Album*. Indianapolis, IN: Bobbs-Merrill.

Discographical References

Rolling Stones, The. *Sticky Fingers*. Rolling Stones COC 59100. *1971*: UK.

Springsteen, Bruce. 'Born To Run.' Columbia 10209. *1975*: USA.

DAVE LAING

Market Research

Market research is a key practise in initiating a new enterprise or in launching a new product, as well as being essential to sustaining an enterprise of any size or type. For example, an established and powerful business like the Kellogg's company needs to monitor the breakfast cereal (indeed, the 'breakfast') market continuously in order to satisfy itself that it is at least retaining the market share necessary to afford its high levels of capital investment – in grain futures, a bulk-tanker shipping fleet, dockside silos, warehousing and distribution, as well as in manufacturing, packaging and advertising.

Along with other businesses, from car manufacturers to toothpaste suppliers, Kellogg's aims to consolidate and expand its existing customer base. To do this, it needs three vital pieces of information about those customers: who they are, how to maintain their loyalty and how to replace them should they switch to another brand. Additionally, the company wishes to know why some people prefer other breakfast cereals (and breakfasts); how many people who might eat breakfast do not do so (and why); and whether existing and potential customers might purchase other products bearing the Kellogg's brand name whether breakfast-related or not.

To generate and develop knowledge about customers, all consumer goods firms engage in market research. Briefly, this involves determining, firstly, how existing markets are segmented; secondly, what new markets might be emerging; and, thirdly, how existing and emerging markets might be externally realigned in favor of specific products (whether goods or services) through advertising. Market research involves surveying purchase decisions in order to create profiles of consumers. Through the use of a combination of quantitative and qualitative markers, consumers are assigned categories based largely on demographic and psychographic (life style or preference) factors. Market researchers then conduct more intensive and extensive surveys with smaller gatherings of people deemed to be representative of these larger categories. These 'focus groups' are expected to provide the detailed material for the calculated and costly decisions involved in creating the advertising and marketing campaigns that launch new products or 'reposition' existing ones.

Prior to an examination of the use of market research techniques in the music industry, it is necessary to confront common but important discursive errors made when popular music products are discussed. These are, firstly, a colloquial, 'shorthand' use of the term 'music industry' that elides often very different types of firms (and even industries); and, secondly, the frequent use of the terms 'music industry' and 'record industry' interchangeably. It would be better to consider the 'music industry' as an industrial *sector* within which several industries are involved in offering a range of music-related goods and services for public consumption. Each of these industries is, in turn, made up of individual businesses that must all have a clear sense of the market for their products. Further, these firms or enterprises all require methods for gauging existing market share and analyzing market trends, since, without them, there would be no way of estimating efficiency, no capacity for forward planning, no reasonable base from which to innovate, and so on.

Three further defining dimensions of the music-industrial sector bear on how the role and position of market research within the music industry are identified and analyzed.

Firstly, it must be recognized that the core activity of this industrial sector is record-making. What this means is that other areas of music enterprise (among them music publishing and music licensing, live performance, composition for film and television, music broadcasting and merchandising) tend to be reliant on the creation of popular music 'stars' by record companies. For this reason, the way in which record companies select and groom acts for potential stardom is central to the entire business and organizational system of popular music.

Secondly, it must be noted that record-making is dominated by five major, globally active firms. Consequently, not only is the record industry by far the dominant subsector within the music-industrial sector, but five companies within the record industry dominate global production – with the effect that certain techniques and practises of 'star-making' have come to be standardized among and between these companies. On this basis, while it may be the case that, for example, the live performance sector of the music industry will attempt to create databases of customer preferences in order to market forthcoming attractions to them, the creation and/or maintenance of the 'forthcoming attractions' stems directly from the practises of record companies and, notably, from the *standard* practises of the major record companies. It is the ability of the latter to gauge existing and likely markets for popular music acts and their products (and the techniques employed toward this end) that inflects and conditions the market research efforts of what are substantially subordinate subsectors.

Thirdly, this standardization takes place in the context, and against the background, of the essential intangibility of the core product of the music industry, which is music itself, and the consequent intangibility and uncertainty of the myriad cultural and social practises through which music is made use of and made sense of. Put crudely, the music industry knows that music sells, but it does not know, with any great certainty, *which* music will sell. Ultimately, the organizational strategies adopted by companies to survive and prosper in the face of this endemic market uncertainty are what give the record industry, and with it the music industry, its comparative uniqueness within commodity-producing, cultural industries.

For example, while it is true that films can fail to make a profit, that books are remaindered and that television shows are cancelled, each of these sectors can be argued to be both less volatile than popular music and also more susceptible to conventional market research and marketing efforts: film companies can tinker with plot lines and even veto releases, in response to pre-release screenings; publishers can rely on comparatively stable genres for fiction and nonfiction; and television networks can continuously promote new and existing shows. Where pop music is concerned, each week record companies release huge numbers of new records into the marketplace for popular music products in the certain knowledge that almost all of them will fail to attract enough buyers to propel those records into the pop charts. In this way, enormous market wastage is the key operating condition of popular music production. Aspiring pop acts are groomed for stardom in the light of this knowledge. Consequently, how record companies conduct or practise market research is of acute importance for the music industry as a whole.

In terms of the 'standardizing' consequences of the dominance of the record industry subsector of the music industry, then, what must be considered is that the major companies are faced with the continuous need not only for new pop acts, but also for new data on changing patterns of taste and affiliation in existing and emergent popular music-making. If the 'majors' fail in their efforts, then the rest of the music industry also suffers – music publishers will not have the new writers and producers they need to generate royalty income and fees from licenses; music merchandisers will be left with sweat shirts, posters and patches they cannot sell; major venues and public-address and lighting companies will have no big tours to host and service, and so on. With so much resting on their efforts, record companies will seek market information through a strategy that combines consistent and variable market research practises.

Where the consistency of market research practise is concerned, the comparatively stable 'value chain' of record commodification must be considered. From the composition of new material to the distribution of finished records for retail sale, the 'standard' policies of signing, marketing and promotion have characterized the record industry for decades. Given that *all* record company employees are in the business of creating 'stars' (and second-guessing the market for them), it must be recognized that the most fundamental dimension of market research is the employment of individuals who have the ability to gauge the shifting tapestries of taste formation, expression and affiliation. For example, the conventional view of A&R staff is that they are 'talent spotters,' not market researchers; yet, what else is their job but to decide which emergent acts seem, simultaneously, to be making music that might sell as records and to possess the potential to be converted into 'stars' and thus sell enormous numbers of those, and subsequent, records? These emergent acts come to the attention of

A&R staff through a network of trusted informants who, in turn, are close to the 'way stations' of taste formation – local 'scenes' that are articulated not just through changing patterns of public behavior, but also through the less apparent but often decisive changes in patterns of usage of local recording studios, rehearsal rooms and even equipment suppliers (see Toynbee 2000; Negus 1999). At the same time, A&R staff need to be alive to trends in popular culture in general. The myth of A&R is that it represents the continuous search for 'cutting-edge' music; the reality is that it deals in music that will sell, whatever its provenance.

Once contracted by a company to make a record, pop acts (of whatever genre or style) are monitored continuously within the company – but always without their participation (and knowledge). Weekly meetings are held to discuss which of the acts currently making records are to be prioritized in the marketplace. Marketing staff will bring their own expertise to bear in these meetings; however, their sense of the ease or otherwise of marketing a particular act will be based not on conventional market research, but on their sense of the current status of similar acts (and the logistical demands of marketing such acts) in the marketplace as currently constituted.

Further to this, Negus (1999, 53ff.) argues that major record companies now engage in 'portfolio management.' In this account of record-making, major companies invest in a range of popular genres and therefore need to be aware of the distinctively different modes of popularizing music within those genres. As new genres supplant old ones in the public's taste and the fortunes of all genres fluctuate, companies must also vary their data-gathering techniques – from the employment of 'street teams' in rap and R&B to the use of consumer panels and focus groups organized by independent market research groups like Soundata. To these largely US practises can be added the now common UK practise of major label licensing of dance tracks that have already undergone market research through a complex process of white label promotions to DJs and (often) extremely short-run releases on tiny independent labels. All in all, the marketing departments of major record companies are versatile in assessing to whom and how to pitch new and existing acts and their records, but gauging the dynamics of taste remains a constant facet of popularizing music – a facet in evidence in the other, key, departments of record companies.

For example, Negus (1992) has shown how promotions staff will discuss their 'special relationships' with key 'taste-makers' (radio DJs, journalists, television producers and so on) and the likely degree of their receptivity to specific acts at this particular conjuncture. Sales and distribution staff will discuss the current climate in retail in similar terms, while members of the international department will provide a stark assessment of a record's likely reception in other marketplaces given their knowledge of sister A&R and marketing departments (or of licensed affiliates if the company is a smaller 'independent') in other 'territories.' In each area of specialization, the department head will be the apex of his/her own network of intermediaries whose common currency is the volatile one of popular musical taste in its many denominations and forms. On this basis, the pop charts are largely market research devices ex post facto as measures of the shrewdness of an employee in either assembling or accessing and then articulating the sensibility of a particular network – where the proof of the efficacy of past actions lies in chart positions and associated sales figures. The fact that what sells today is not guaranteed to sell tomorrow makes the pop charts unreliable as a market research device; even so, this does not dissuade companies without, say, a boy-band, a 'chill out' artist or a nu-metal act from signing and marketing rivals.

All of this is not to argue that record companies are the beneficiaries only of informal or genre-limited market research. For example, if a member of a promotions team reports back that an influential radio station will not play a particular release, this may well be because that station has carried out its own market research exercise and has changed programming policy accordingly (rather than the decision having flowed from a particular DJ's almost alchemical relationship with a particular style of music). Further, record companies now regularly attempt to create taste-preference and purchasing databases of record buyers through the insertion of data-return cards in CD packaging, and any move of core business to the Web will increase data-collection abilities immeasurably. Further still, analysis of bar-coded retail returns can map at least the geographical and perhaps the social contours of sales of individual records and whole genres (as well as yielding a limited financial profile of consumers), and the same can be true of postal or zip-code sources of ticket purchases, fan-club membership applications and the like.

Ultimately, all record companies are continually faced with the problem of market uncertainty, a condition that ensures that no one can truly predict which records will sell and which will not. To overcome this (or at least to limit its effects), record companies will use any strategy or tactic that promises insight into customer preferences. However, the standard and traditional forms of market research are designed for those companies able to develop, stabilize and maintain brands that are sustained by clear and comparatively incontestable core

products – companies that need to monitor the market performance of those products over often lengthy periods and that are moved to differentiate products and to extend branding only when numbers have been 'crunched' and data thoroughly analyzed. Such is the composition of capital in the record industry that 'non-standard' forms of market research have evolved, but this does not mean that traditional market research techniques play no part in musical-industrial production. At the core of the music industry lies the commodity-producing record industry, which, while it draws on conventional techniques whenever and wherever possible, continues to rely on individual members of staff who are, or declare themselves to be, a physical *embodiment* of market research. While this remains a distinguishing feature of the life and organization of popular music, market research will continue to have a distinctively different cast within the music industry as a whole.

Bibliography

Negus, Keith. 1992. *Producing Pop: Culture and Conflict in the Popular Music Industry*. London and New York: Arnold.

Negus, Keith. 1999. *Music Genres and Corporate Cultures*. London and New York: Routledge.

Toynbee, Jason. 2000. *Making Popular Music: Musicians, Creativity and Institutions*. London: Arnold.

MIKE JONES

Oldie

In radio and record industry patois, an 'oldie' is a hit record or tune from the past with nostalgia value in the present. The word was probably first used with this meaning in 1957 by a Los Angeles disc jockey, Art Laboe.

Laboe noticed that significant numbers of his teenage listeners were requesting songs they remembered from 1955. In response, Laboe introduced a radio feature called 'oldies but goodies,' copyrighted the title and, from 1959, issued compilation albums of old tracks entitled *Oldies But Goodies*. Inspired by Laboe, teenage listener Paul Politi composed the 1961 hit 'Those Oldies But Goodies (Remind Me Of You).'

During the 1970s, some US FM radio stations led by KRTH Los Angeles adopted an 'oldies' format, playing only hits of the past. In the late 1990s, most US radio markets contained one or two oldies stations.

Discographical Reference

Little Caesar and the Romans. 'Those Oldies But Goodies (Remind Me Of You).' Del-Fi 4158. *1961*: USA.

DAVE LAING

One-Hit Wonder

'One-hit wonder' is a mildly derogatory term for a recording artist who managed to achieve only one bestselling single before disappearing into obscurity. Mc-Aleer (1991) includes a list of 24 artists whose sole hit reached number one and a further 50 with just one hit. Many of these hits were 'novelty' records using comedy (Bobby Pickett's combination of horror movie and dance craze), topical events (numerous songs by British soccer teams) or musical gimmicks (B. Bumble's 'rocked-up' Tchaikovsky), or they were occasional recordings by screen or stage personalities, such as Telly Savalas (television's Kojak).

The definition of a one-hit wonder is often relative. In the era when the main pop chart was virtually racially segregated, an R&B artist like Johnny Ace could be a one-hit wonder in *Billboard*'s Top 50 and a regular hitmaker in the black music chart. Similarly, a highly successful British act such as the Rubettes had only one hit in the United States.

Bibliography

Gambaccini, Paul, et al. 1993. *The Guinness Book of British Hit Singles*. 9th ed. London: Guinness Publishing.

McAleer, Dave. 1991. *Chart Beats*. London: Guinness Publishing.

Discographical References

Ace, Johnny. 'Pledging My Love.' Duke 136. 1955: USA.

B. Bumble & the Stingers. 'Nut Rocker.' Rendezvous 166. *1962*: USA.

Pickett, Bobby 'Boris,' and the Crypt-Kickers. 'Monster Mash.' Garpax 44167. *1962*: USA.

Rubettes, The. 'Sugar Baby Love.' Polydor 15089. *1974*: USA.

DAVE LAING

One-Stop

This is a form of record distribution in which a metropolitan or regional distributor or wholesaler offers releases from a large number of record companies to local retailers and jukebox operators, who can therefore order all the records they need from one place instead of from numerous record companies. The term and the practise originated in the United States in the 1930s when one-stops served the jukebox business only. By the 1950s, one-stops were playing a crucial role in the US singles market by providing the link between independent labels and retailers. By the late 1990s, one-stops could be found in most countries with large music markets.

DAVE LAING

On-Line Distribution

On-line distribution of music comprises any way of publishing music in a digital format (for example, on CD), by means of telecommunication networks and computers ('digital telematic environment').

While many radio stations introduced audio compression technology (technology for reducing the amount of storage required for audio computer files) for storing and exchanging audio tracks in the late 1980s, personal computers (Macs and IBM-compatible computers) still required increased computing power and improved schemes (data compression systems) capable of encoding music digitally, in order to be able to receive digitally encoded and transmitted music.

Since 1995, new encoding schemes (for example, MPEG Layer III), public digital networks, personal computers with fast processors, the Web technology, and electronic billing and payment systems have created a potential market for on-line distribution to individual consumers. During 1996, the majority of the world's record companies incorporated the use of Web sites into their marketing strategy. However, this did not involve the on-line dissemination of complete songs. Despite this, several pilot projects for on-line distribution were started in the late 1990s.

What are the benefits and challenges of on-line distribution for the music industry?

(a) Small as well as large record companies have almost equal opportunities to reach the global target market.

(b) A digital recording can reach its market a few minutes after the completion of the mastering process.

(c) Individual artists can bypass the producers and retail outlets in the production chain, and thereby sell fewer copies and still earn more money.

(d) Individual record companies can create their own MoD (music on demand) services, or can collaborate with service providers and other record labels in creating dedicated MoD services that offer not only on-line music, but also multimedia content packed or linked with music tracks.

DAGFINN BACH

Payola

'Payola' refers to the practise of 'paying for play' – that is, offering financial, sexual or other personal inducements in return for record promotion and radio play. Song plugging, as the practise had been called in the late nineteenth century, had long been a cornerstone of Tin Pan Alley marketing. In the World War I era, an estimated $400,000 per year was paid to top singers to promote certain songs. Throughout the first half of the twentieth century, music publishers employed the practise with impunity; but, as the power center of the music industry shifted from publishing houses to record companies in the early 1950s and radio became a pivotal promotional medium for small independent labels promoting rock 'n' roll, the earlier beneficiaries of the time-honored practise did an abrupt about-face. In the

1950s and early 1960s, curtailing payola became the operative strategy for neutralizing rock 'n' roll.

The roots of the so-called payola scandal could be traced to the tension between radio and the American Society of Composers, Authors and Publishers (ASCAP), a 'performing rights' organization that recovers royalty payments for copyrighted songs. By the 1930s, radio had become ASCAP's major source of revenue. In 1939, ASCAP announced plans to double its licensing fee for radio. Radio responded by boycotting ASCAP and forming its own performing rights organization, Broadcast Music Inc. (BMI). While ASCAP represented Tin Pan Alley publishers, BMI recruited its members from among blues and country writers, who would go on to dominate rock 'n' roll in the 1950s.

If rock 'n' roll generated fanaticism among its fans, it also conjured up societal fears of miscegenation, sexuality, violence and juvenile delinquency. Once the music began to displace Tin Pan Alley pop, ASCAP and the other established powers of the music industry exploited such fears to hold the line. *Variety* railed against 'leerics,' referring to the sexual double-entendres found in some rhythm and blues (R&B) crossovers; the major record companies announced campaigns to weed out suggestive lyrics; religious organizations supplied lists of objectionable songs; and police sometimes confiscated offensive records and jukeboxes. These attacks were designed to turn public opinion against rock 'n' roll and to encourage more official interventions, which culminated in the payola hearings of 1959–60.

Throughout the 1950s, ASCAP and the major record companies paraded a succession of Tin Pan Alley stalwarts like Frank Sinatra, Bing Crosby, Steve Allen, Ira Gershwin and Oscar Hammerstein before various government committees to denounce rock 'n' roll and BMI. In 1959, they convinced Congress to investigate payola. Since radio had been the primary vehicle for popularizing rock 'n' roll, DJs became the main targets of these hearings, most notably Alan Freed. Freed had played a major role in promoting R&B to white teenagers, and he also refused 'on principle' to sign a statement that he had never accepted payola. After two indictments ruined his career, he died penniless in 1965.

In the end, the payola hearings unearthed $263,245, less than the estimated annual amount paid out during World War I. The number of DJs who felt compelled to confess their sins resembled the results of a witch hunt. Reams of public testimony and extensive media coverage encouraged more 'acceptable' forms of rock 'n' roll. A bill was passed which finally outlawed payola. Its most immediate effect was to impose on radio a more hierarchical structure that made the flow of popular music easier to control.

Payola, of course, never disappeared. In the late 1960s, the term 'drugola' was added to the lexicon and applied most dramatically in the unceremonious firing of Clive Davis as head of CBS Records. The practise grabbed public attention again in the 1980s in the various scandals associated with the use of independent promoters. Payola probably exists anywhere where there is commercial music; its actual effects remain insufficiently documented.

Bibliography

Dannen, Fredric. 1990. *Hit Men: Power Brokers and Fast Money Inside the Music Business*. New York: Times Books.

Morthland, John. 1980. 'Payola.' In *The Rolling Stone Illustrated History of Rock and Roll*, ed. Jim Miller. San Francisco: Rolling Stone Books.

Segrave, Kerry. 1994. *Payola in the Music Industry: A History, 1880–1991*. Jefferson and London: McFarland.

REEBEE GAROFALO

Plant

A 'plant,' also known as a 'shill,' a 'claque,' a 'stooge' or a 'water boy,' was a person 'planted' in the audience of a variety or vaudeville theater to initiate a positive response to the performance of a song. Before records became the primary commodity of the music industry, the performance of a song in a vaudeville theater was a major marketing event for sheet music publishers. Having persuaded a notable singer to perform one of its songs, a music publisher would plant someone in the theater audience to jump up and applaud and shout vociferously, or to repeat the song's chorus when the song had finished. The members of the audience were meant to think that the plant was one of their own number who had been overwhelmed by the music. The publisher hoped that the actions of the plant would help fix a song in the minds of the audience, and so lead them to buy the sheet music.

Well-known performers and songwriters such as Al Jolson and Harry Von Tilzer worked as plants before they became successful and famous. 'For "Down Where the Wurzburger Flows,"' recounts Russell Sanjek (1988, 413), Harry Von Tilzer 'nightly . . . assisted the young actress who introduced it in remembering supposedly forgotten lines.' The ingenuity of plants is well illustrated in this account, given to Isaac Goldberg (1930, 209), of the plugging of the song 'Please Go 'Way and Let Me Sleep':

I met the girl who did the singing part and fixed the thing up with her . . . I leaned back in my chair with one elbow on the table. As the girl sang, I began to snore. I snored so loud that it disturbed those listening to the singing. They looked around in disgust . . . Just as the policeman and waiter raised me out of my chair

I stretched and yawned like a man dead for slumber and began singing: 'Please go 'way and let me sleep . . .' I kept on singing as I was being led and carried to the elevator. I sang going down and I sang coming up. As the elevator reached the landing the girl on the stage struck up the chorus . . . and the audience tumbled. I never saw an audience go so nearly crazy.

Bibliography

Goldberg, Isaac. 1930. *Tin Pan Alley: A Chronicle of the American Popular Music Racket*. New York: John Day Company. (Reprinted as *Tin Pan Alley: A Chronicle of American Popular Music*. New York: Ungar, 1961.)

Sanjek, Russell. 1988. *American Popular Music and Its Business: The First Four Hundred Years. Vol. II: From 1790 to 1909*. New York: Oxford University Press.

Shepherd, John. 1982. *Tin Pan Alley*. London and Boston: Routledge and Kegan Paul.

Whitcomb, Ian. 1974. *After the Ball: Pop Music from Rag to Rock*. Baltimore, MD: Penguin.

Sheet Music

Von Tilzer, Harry, comp. and lyr. 1902. 'Please Go 'Way and Let Me Sleep.' New York: Harry Von Tilzer Music Pub. Co.

Von Tilzer, Harry, comp., and Bryan, Vincent P., lyr. 1902. 'Down Where the Wurzburger Flows.' New York: Harry Von Tilzer Music Pub. Co.

JOHN SHEPHERD

Plugging

'Plugging' is any action designed to promote the performance for gain of a piece of popular music, or the dissemination or sale of a piece of popular music in the form of a commodity. The term was in use in the early years of the twentieth century, and is to be found in print in the trade magazine *Variety* prior to 1910.

In the late nineteenth century, US music publishers plugged songs to singers and to the general public. They would persuade a well-known singer to sing a song in a vaudeville theater. This was where the white, middle-class women who provided entertainment at home on the piano for their families would hear a song and, as a consequence, might be induced to buy it as sheet music. In the early days of the music business, publishers themselves used to travel round the vaudeville theaters of big cities, attempting to persuade artists to sing their songs. When music publishing houses became well established (certainly no later than 1900 in New York), the larger of them employed professional 'pluggers' to carry out this task. This was a good way to learn the craft of writing a successful song, and many famous songwriters and composers started their careers in this way (for example, Irving Berlin with Harry Von Tilzer's publishing house,

and George Gershwin with the Jerome H. Remick publishing house in 1915).

Plugging could, however, go beyond singing, dancing and other, amusing forms of persuasion to border on bribery, later known as 'payola.' Publishers would buy drinks and meals for artists and their bands in an attempt to induce them to try a song, while artists who agreed to push songs were frequently given royalties as if they were one of the songwriters. That is why the name of a star such as Al Jolson appears on the sheet music of a song as one of its writers when, in fact, the star had not helped to write the song at all. Sometimes, stars were given gifts by publishers; these could range from cars and racehorses to yachts.

Plugging was also aimed at the general public. Pluggers were to be found singing their publisher's songs in music shops, department stores, restaurants and sports arenas, on street corners and on the back of trucks. They were often imaginative and resourceful in thinking up publicity stunts. Thus, Jack Robbins, a 16-year-old plugger, was said to have 'commandeer[ed] a hay wagon, donning farmers' clothes and driving down a busy Chicago street advertising "It's an Old Horse That Knows Its Way Home"' (Whitcomb 1972, 48–49).

With the growing importance of records, publishers employed pluggers to sell songs to A&R executives. The first such plugger was the early recording artist Len Spencer. In the second half of the twentieth century, the record industry invested heavily in plugging, with radio stations as its main target. Record pluggers seek to influence station program directors to add new releases to the playlists. The best pluggers in the United States, such as Dave Clarke, have become key figures in establishing new (especially black) artists (George 1988).

During the rock 'n' roll era in the United States, payola became endemic, and it was used particularly by independent labels which could not otherwise compete with major companies. Music industry payola was the subject of a Congressional inquiry in 1959, and its findings implicated several well-known disc jockeys. By this time, the term 'plugger' had been replaced in the United States by 'promoter,' although the original term has remained current in the United Kingdom.

Within the United States, radio airplay was regarded as the key to success for pop singles, and plugging (or promotion) became a substantial subsector of the music industry, with rival 'tip-sheets' such as the *Gavin Report* and *Monday Morning Quarterback* competing to provide stations with advice on the hot tunes to place on the playlist. A specialist profession of independent promoters also developed, taking over the job of plugging new releases from record company employees. Allegations of payola persisted, and in the early 1990s several major companies brought promotion back in-house (Dannen 1990).

The more genteel approach to the plugger's role in the United Kingdom has been expressed by a former BBC radio producer: 'At worst, a "plugger" merely ensures the delivery of a record to someone's office. At best, the plugger can be a creative link between the artist, management, record company and radio station' (Grundy 1991, 232).

Theodor Adorno argued that plugging was an aspect of the relationship between a song's structure and the listener, rather than an external relation between plugger and disc jockey. Writing in 1941, Adorno spoke of plugging as the means by which the listener 'becomes enraptured with the inescapable' and argued that 'the emphasis on presentation which is provided by plugging must substitute for the lack of genuine individuality in the material' (27).

Bibliography

Adorno, Theodor, with Simpson, George. 1941. 'On Popular Music.' *Studies in Philosophy and Social Sciences* 9: 17–48.

Dannen, Fredric. 1990. *Hit Men: Power Brokers and Fast Money Inside the Music Business*. New York: Times Books.

George, Nelson. 1988. *The Death of Rhythm & Blues*. New York: Pantheon.

Goldberg, Isaac. 1961. *Tin Pan Alley: A Chronicle of American Popular Music*. New York: Ungar.

Grundy, Stuart. 1991. 'Radio.' In *The Rock File: Making It in the Music Business*, ed. Norton York. Oxford: Oxford University Press.

Shepherd, John. 1982. *Tin Pan Alley*. London and Boston: Routledge and Kegan Paul.

Whitcomb, Ian. 1972. *After the Ball: Pop Music from Rag to Rock*. London: Allen Lane.

JOHN SHEPHERD and DAVE LAING

Polls

In contradistinction to the Grammys and other awards given by music industry professionals, polls are the province of music critics and magazine readers. From the 1930s, specialist jazz magazines organized end-of-year contests for many categories of musician or recording. Some polls, notably those of US jazz critics in the 1950s, were regarded as key indicators of the artistic status of performers, but the sheer proliferation of polls in subsequent decades has made them less prestigious. By the late 1990s, Britain alone had over 20 annual music polls for all genres, from dance music to world music and folk.

In jazz, the earliest polls of music critics in the United States were organized by such publications as *Down Beat* and *Esquire*. The first *Esquire* poll in 1943 caused controversy by having black musicians as the winners in many categories. For several years, the winners of the *Esquire* poll gave a concert in New York (Feather 1986). *Down Beat* inaugurated a poll of music critics in 1953, while the Japanese publication *Swing Journal* (founded in 1947) ran its first poll in 1967.

The first jury of rock music critics may have been that of the British monthly *Let It Rock* in 1973. The gap between rock critics and mass taste (even within the music business) was highlighted in 1989 when rock critics polled by *Rolling Stone* voted Milli Vanilli worst new band while the Grammy jury was voting it best new group. In 1998, the UK monthly magazine *Mojo* introduced a different angle by asking leading musicians to vote for their all-time favorite singers.

Popularity polls involving the participation of readers have been a valuable tool in creating brand loyalty for music magazines, and most such publications have organized some form of annual voting. In the United Kingdom, the first readers' poll organized by *Melody Maker* was in 1946; it contained categories for top dance and swing bands and for soloists on 11 instruments. In pop music, *New Musical Express* (NME) organized not only a poll but a pollwinners concert from the early 1950s. The Beatles appeared at several *NME* concerts at Wembley Stadium in London in the mid-1960s. Although *NME* discontinued its concerts in the early 1970s, the tradition was revived in the following decade by the pop paper *Smash Hits*, whose annual awards events were televised.

Bibliography

Feather, Leonard. 1986. *The Jazz Years: Earwitness to an Era*. London: Quartet Books.

DAVE LAING

Promoter

The term 'promoter' is widely used in the music industry to describe the person or company responsible for the physical organization and presentation of a concert or festival. A promoter is often locally based and should be able to use knowledge of local media and audiences to set appropriate ticket prices and to maximize concert attendance by skillful advertising and marketing (Baskerville 2001, 209–24). In the United States, the term 'promoter' also designates a plugger – a person who visits radio stations in order to secure airplay for a recording.

The origins of the contemporary music promoter can be traced to the impresarios of Venetian opera in the seventeenth century who bore the financial risks of theatrical productions (Bianconi 1987). An outstanding nineteenth-century promoter was P.T. Barnum, who organized and marketed the highly profitable US tour by Jenny Lind. A century later, showmanship was also the prime characteristic of figures such as Oscar Davis and 'Colonel' Tom Parker, whose careers linked the worlds of carnival, circus and tent shows to modern country music shows. The rock era of the 1960s and 1970s produced equally colorful promoters, of whom the best known was Bill Graham of San Francisco (Glatt 1993).

By the 1920s, the role of promoter in the US music industry was performed by the managers or owners of ballrooms, theaters and clubs. These promoters formed regional or national circuits of venues and created their own agencies, such as the Theater Owners Booking Agency, to offer artists a series of engagements. By the 1930s, control had shifted to increasingly powerful booking agencies like MCA and William Morris, which would negotiate terms with individual venue owners on behalf of bands or a package of a half-dozen acts.

The period following World War II saw the rise of three other types of promoter: the owners or managers of small clubs that provided a focus for emerging music scenes and were influential in the rise of a number of genres from bebop to rave; the individuals who founded and ran festivals, such as the Newport Jazz (George Wein) and Glastonbury (Michael Eavis) events; and tour promoters who were not linked to specific venues but who organized national or international tours by renting venues or subcontracting work to local promoters.

Until the last decade of the twentieth century, concert promotion was the last sector of the music industry to be dominated by individual entrepreneurs. The corporatization of this sector began when companies such as BCL successfully bid for the right to operate global tours by rock superstars such as the Rolling Stones and U2. This was followed by the vertical integration of the concert sector in the late 1990s as SFX (subsequently a subsidiary of media conglomerate Clear Channel Entertainment), a company that also owned 100 venues in the United States, purchased numerous local rock promoters, including Bill Graham's company. SFX also purchased promotion companies in Europe, where most national music markets are dominated by one or two promoters which generally organize the local portion of world tours. These companies include Mojo Concerts (The Netherlands), Mama Concerts & Rau (Germany) and Herman Schuermans (Belgium).

Bibliography

Baskerville, David. 2001. *Music Business Handbook and Career Guide*. 7th ed. Thousand Oaks, CA: Sage Publications.

Bianconi, Lorenzo. 1987. *Music in the Seventeenth Century*, trans. David Bryant. Cambridge: Cambridge University Press. (Originally published as *Il Seicento*. Turin: Edizioni di Torino, 1982.)

Glatt, John. 1993. *Rage & Roll: Bill Graham and the Selling of Rock*. New York: Birch Lane Press.

DAVE LAING

Rack Jobber

A rack jobber is an individual or company that rents space from retailers to install racks of cassettes or CDs and is responsible for replenishing the stocks. This form of retailing typically occurs in what the record industry calls 'non-traditional' outlets, such as gas stations and grocery stores. Either the rack jobber pays the store a rent and keeps all the proceeds from music sales or the store is paid a percentage of sales. Rack jobbing also occurs in the printed music market, where a rack of music books may be added to a musical instrument store.

In the United States, rack jobbing began with the Music Dealers Service, which from the 1930s operated sheet music racks. In 1952, Elliott Wexler of Philadelphia was the first rack jobber of discs, and rack jobbers played an important role in the 1960s by pioneering the sale of budget-priced LP discs and extending the retail base of the record industry, as they introduced recorded music into supermarkets and discount department stores.

DAVE LAING

Ratings

In the context of broadcasting, 'ratings' are statistically derived figures – usually expressed as percentages – that report the proportion of a potential or actual audience that is listening to or viewing a particular national or local radio or television station or program. Percentages may thus be calculated on the basis of the total potential audience for a station or program, or of only those people actually tuned in to the radio or television.

In the US radio industry (radio has generally been of more importance to popular music than television), the term 'rating' is used in a precise way to mean the percentage of the entire population available in a market that is listening to a station in the average quarter-hour. Because at any one time many people will not have the radio on, this figure can be very small. In other countries, 'ratings' refers more generally to whatever measures of audience are felt to be locally most relevant.

Almost everywhere, however, the term 'share' refers to a station's share of the *total* time spent by all listeners tuned in to all stations. As this excludes those not tuned in, it produces larger figures than the narrow US definition of 'rating.' It is possible for a station to have fewer listeners than a rival but a higher share, because its listeners stay tuned for longer. Thus, share can be a measure of loyalty.

Another, still larger, key measure of radio listening is what is labeled 'reach' in the United Kingdom and 'cumulative' in the United States: counting everyone who listened to a station for at least five minutes during the researched time period. Taking no notice of for how much longer, or how often, listeners tuned in, reach is not so much a measure of loyalty as an acknowledgment that a station has some role to play in individuals' media experiences. In this context, it is not difficult to see why commercial stations tend to value their share (and, in the United States, rating), while public-service national stations point instead to their large reach.

The main systems of gathering and calculating radio ratings in both the United States and the United Kingdom use respondent diaries. Arbitron (United States) and RAJAR/Ipsos-RSL (United Kingdom) distribute printed diaries to individuals, in which they fill in what station they listened to (or none) in every 15-minute period over the course of one week, and where they listened. The fact that much radio listening takes place outside the home – at work, in the car, on a personal stereo – is often cited as the reason for preferring a diary-recall monitoring system rather than an electronic metering device attached to a fixed receiver, despite the obvious risks involved in trusting respondents to remember their listening habits accurately. Systems based on a portable metering device are being developed, but require the sampled listener to wear the meter at all times. 'The willingness of people to do this has still to be proven,' notes RAJAR (1999).

Ratings have their greatest impact on popular music in those countries where radio is dominated by commercial radio format broadcasting. This is especially so in the United States, where a small fall in a station's rating can easily prompt its owners to drop one music format and adopt another overnight. But, more generally, almost everywhere where format radio is dominant, ratings systems contribute significantly to what Hendy (2000) calls the 'clustering' of a few recurring music formats.

'Clustering' occurs because there is a conflict between the nature of ratings research methodologies and the theoretical promise of format radio to offer a variety of music services through market segmentation, catering for 'niches' of particular musical taste as well as for the mainstream. Since they are based on statistical sampling of a total population in any area, audience research methodologies, as described above, will produce only tiny bottom-line 'ratings' for niche music formats. If regulation permits format switching, such stations can be tempted to compete head-on for a slice of the larger mainstream market if this might maximize profits. They might persist in targeting the low-rating niche only if

other research can show that this produces a greater profit from advertising revenue.

Ratings consistently indicate that popular music is more appealing to most radio listeners than speech; they also suggest that formats that play the most familiar, melodic hits are overwhelmingly the most liked (Hendy 2000). But what the dominant methodology does not necessarily do is reveal the intensity of minority-taste listeners' appreciation of their favorite station.

Bibliography

Douglas, Susan J. 1999. *Listening In: Radio and the American Imagination.* New York: Times Books/Random House.

Hendy, David. 2000. *Radio in the Global Age.* Oxford: Polity Press.

Kent, Raymond. 1994. *Measuring Media Audiences.* London: Routledge.

Norberg, Eric G. 1996. *Radio Programming: Tactics and Strategy.* Boston, MA: Focal Press.

RAJAR. 1999. *London: Radio Joint Audience Research Ltd.* London: RAJAR.

KEN GARNER

Record Clubs

Record clubs are mail-order organizations that recruit members through low-price introductory offers. Members must then buy a minimum number of full-price CDs or cassettes from monthly catalogs. The clubs had their origin in the 1930s, when some record companies offered a series of classical music discs on a subscription-only basis.

At the end of the twentieth century, the largest operator of clubs was BMG, whose parent company, Bertelsmann, ran numerous book clubs throughout the world that worked on the same basis. In the United States, the largest record club was Columbia House, founded in 1956 and subsequently owned jointly by Sony Music Entertainment and Warner Music Group. Sony also owned the largest record club in Japan. PolyGram ran the record clubs with most members in France (D.I.A.L.) and the United Kingdom (Britannia).

In many countries, record clubs account for over 10 percent of unit sales of soundcarriers. The clubs, however, are generally unpopular with conventional retailers, record companies, performers and music publishers. The retailers protest at the 'offers' given to potential members as an inducement to join. In the United States, these have included the offer of eight CDs from a range of current hits for $1. Retailers maintain that such offers damage the profitability of record stores, which exist to provide a much wider variety of recorded music. Labels, artists and publishers complain about the reduced royalties they receive from club sales. In the United States and Canada, some labels have refused to supply recordings to clubs.

DAVE LAING

Retailing

Introduction

In contemporary discussions, music retailing has usually been taken to refer to the act of selling recordings to the public, although the retailing of music also encompasses the sale of instruments, sheet music, concert tickets and other merchandise.

Early History

Most of these other forms of retailing predate the selling of recorded music, although their economic significance has greatly decreased. In early modern Europe, selling songsheets or broadsides was an informal business carried out on street corners or at markets and fairs. By the nineteenth century, some major publishers and instrument makers had their own retail stores, although frequently pianos, violins and printed music were sold in general stores alongside bicycles, confectionery and sewing machines. In the Tin Pan Alley era of the early twentieth century, chains of department stores became major suppliers of hit songs, and many featured pluggers singing hits with piano accompaniment. In the United States, the Woolworth chain sold 150 million copies of sheet music in 1913 alone (Sanjek 1988). In many countries at the end of the twentieth century, a significant, if declining, number of specialist stores remained, selling musical instruments, sheet music and, in some cases, a limited stock of CDs.

The Retailing of Recorded Music

The retailing of recorded music has involved a diversity of sales activities in a wide variety of situations. Conventionally, distinctions have been made within the music business between different types of retailers, most notably chain stores, independent specialists, nontraditional outlets such as gasoline stations and supermarkets, and a range of mail-order services and record clubs. In practise, however, the retailing of recordings has involved a much greater diversity than this. Within Britain alone, it might include the selling of *bhangra* music and Indian film soundtracks in corner stores in Leicester, the sale of Latin music in makeshift huts in London's Elephant and Castle shopping center, the selling of bootlegged recordings on the streets of the North London district of Camden, and the sale by amateur and semi-professional musicians and bands of their recordings at concerts, pubs, social clubs, festivals and street parades.

Thus, it would seem that the formally organized music industry provides only a partial perspective on the activities associated with the retailing of recordings. This also has implications for official sales charts, which in many parts of the world are compiled from the monitoring of retail sales in a limited number of outlets that possess technology capable of electronically checking bar codes. That said, however, there have been some significant trends that have shaped the retailing of recordings over the past hundred years.

Music retailers, musicians, record company staff and, of course, the consumer have continually had to respond and adapt to the changing character of the soundcarrier on which recorded music has been circulated. One of the most notable impacts of these changes has been on the physical space of the retail environment. This perhaps became most problematic (for retailers trying to shift products from their shelves) and confusing (for consumers trying to find their way around stores) during the 1980s, when the same recording could be found on cassette tape, vinyl LP and CD. All required retailers to install different types of shelving to allow the best presentation of products to the consumer and to enable the consumer to have access to the information contained on the casing of the cassette, LP or CD. The changes in soundcarriers have also led to a divergence of markets and have influenced the priorities of the major record companies and their decisions about where to locate offices and distribute investment. For example, a country such as Japan, which has circulated most recordings on highly priced CDs (partly because of retail price controls), has been considered a more important global market than India, where more recordings have circulated but on cheaply priced cassettes.

Like other industries, music retailing has been characterized by increased concentration of ownership and the growth of multiple retailers and chain stores at the expense of small, often family-run, independent retailers. The latter have been of historical significance through the role of some independent music stores as proprietors of small record labels – for example, the US jazz label Commodore, the blues and soul label Vee-Jay, and the British punk-era labels Rough Trade and Beggar's Banquet. However, the decline in the number of these stores since the latter part of the 1960s has meant that a considerable number of music recordings are sold by general retailers, such as K Mart and Woolworth's, which place music among a plethora of other merchandise (such as clothing and products for the home), or by large entertainment megastores such as HMV, Tower or FNAC, which stock music as just one item among related entertainment products. This is part of a general trend in which the purchase of musical sounds has become linked to the retailing of associated words and images on related entertainment products (such as videos, books and computer games), and to the retailing of 'life-style' goods for musical consumption (personal cassette players, ghetto blasters, car stereos and so on).

The reason why stores have increasingly stocked other entertainment products has less to do with any natural connections between music and entertainment media and more to do with the issue of pricing. Retail profit margins on T-shirts and greetings cards are usually higher than those on musical recordings. Hence, a store will stock more of those products on which it can make greater profits. For this reason, the major record labels do not ship all recordings at the same trade price. Instead, certain ranges of recordings are regularly shipped at a discount, and special prices are negotiated for bulk shipments. As competition between retailers increased during the 1990s, various stores began selling music as a loss leader – that is, they reduced the price of CDs, and their profit margins, to attract consumers in the hope that, once inside, they would also purchase electronic equipment and other entertainment products with higher profit margins. This placed a further burden on the smaller stores; many could not compete with these discounts and went out of business.

If the chain stores and megastores have been a threat to the small music retailer, then a further challenge has been posed by various mail-order services and attempts to offer recordings via the Internet. As record labels have offered recordings at very cheap prices through various music clubs, so retailers have accused record companies of intruding into the area of distribution. Further, the parent corporations of many major record companies have begun to invest in telecommunications networks in anticipation of the direct transmission and download-ing of music into the home. It is clear that one of the key struggles within the music industry at the beginning of the twenty-first century is over distribution, with tra-ditional retailers and record companies both staking out different claims to this area.

Bibliography

du Gay, Paul, and Negus, Keith. 1994. 'The Changing Sites of Sound: Music Retailing and the Composition of Consumers.' *Media, Culture and Society* 16: 395–413.

Sanjek, Russell. 1988. *American Popular Music and Its Business: The First Four Hundred Years. Vol. III: From 1900 to 1984*. New York: Oxford University Press.

KEITH NEGUS with DAVE LAING

Roadies

Roadies are the contemporary equivalent of the squires of knights-errant – the practical Sancho Panzas, taking care of the equipment of their Quixotic rock musicians on their traveling quests for glory. On rock tours, roadies (the road crew) act as the interface between the musi-cians and their technology. They also form the gateway, often but not always blocked, between the members of the band and their fans.

As rock concerts have become more sonically and visually elaborate, the number and specialization of roadies have increased accordingly. Roadies set up the show, maintain (repair and tune) the musical instru-ments, operate equipment during the show (the lights, sound and special effects), and pack up ('tear down') and transport everything required for each night's concert.

Bands playing at very small venues serve as their own roadies or take good friends on their low-budget every-thing-in-a-van tours. In contrast, arena-sized rock tours employ dozens of roadies, many of whom are well-trained and sometimes well-paid specialists. Each musical instrument has its own 'tech,' and those in charge of the sound and lighting ('engineers') increas-ingly have had formal training. Other roadies are selected solely for their brawn, working as 'grunts' or security staff. All travel together in stacked-bunk buses, get a per diem and often a bonus at the end of the tour in addition to their salary, and eat catered (on lucrative tours, gourmet) backstage meals. Roadies often bask in the reflected glory of the band (including access to its groupies).

Discography

Motorhead. '(We Are) the Road Crew.' *Ace of Spades*. Bronze BRON 531. *1980*: UK.

DEENA WEINSTEIN

Sponsorship

The sponsorship of popular music involves the associ-ation of a specific performer, broadcast or recording with a commercial product. In the case of a performer, this need not entail his/her endorsement of the product. However, sponsorship deals often require the appear-ance of an artist in an advertisement – as when Paul McCartney was featured in television commercials for the VISA credit card company, the sponsor of his 1989 US tour.

Sponsorship became a significant element of the pop-ular music industry in the early years of radio in the United States, when firms were willing to pay stations to link their names with successful musicians and shows. Mail-order company Sears & Roebuck sponsored 'old-time' music on WSB Atlanta as early as 1926, and in the 1930s the network hillbilly show from Chicago was titled the *WLS-NBC Alka-Seltzer National Barn Dance*. Fea-turing blues musicians, the *King Biscuit Time* show on KFFA Helena in 1941 was the forerunner of such pro-grams as B.B. King's *Pepticon* show on WDIA Memphis. One of the most important syndicated shows was *Your Hit Parade*, sponsored by Lucky Strike cigarettes.

Outside the United States, radio sponsorship was limited until the 1980s by the strict regulation of advertising, although Radio Luxembourg broadcast sponsored shows to Britain and France from the 1930s onward. The most lucrative music sponsorship on European radio in the 1990s was the £1 million a year paid by Pepsi-Cola to have its name on a nationally syndicated radio chart show in the United Kingdom.

Live music – concerts, tours and festivals – has now become the most important area for music sponsorship. In particular, the escalating cost of stage lighting, amplification and transportation has made large-scale international tours dependent on financing from sponsors.

The most eager sponsors of popular music have been tobacco and alcohol companies (which are denied other advertising outlets in many countries) and the manufacturers of youth 'life-style' products, such as fashionable clothing, hi-fi equipment such as CD players, convenience foods and soft drinks. Firms such as Coca-Cola, Heineken, Marlboro, Philips and Levi's have spent millions of dollars a year to link their products with various types of music and star artists. For example, in 1987 Benson & Hedges, the cigarette company, became the first major corporation to sponsor a US jazz tour, while in 1995 Coca-Cola spent $1.5 million on its German live music program which included a 'Coca-Cola City Rock' contest for high-school bands. However, the use of rock music events to promote the sale of alcohol to young people was strongly criticized in a report by the US Surgeon General, Everett Koop, in 1989. The large audiences attracted by veteran rock groups and by country stars have brought tour sponsorship from motor manufacturers, including Volkswagen and Ford.

The rock sponsorship trend had begun to accelerate in 1983 when Michael Jackson signed a contract with Pepsi-Cola, which provided a reported $10 million to subsidize Jackson's Bad tour in 1987; this sponsorship increased sales of the drink by 10 percent in the cities where the tour played. Two years later, beer company Anheuser-Busch paid $6 million to sponsor a Rolling Stones tour. However, the close association of an individual artist with a particular product always introduces the risk of negative publicity or controversy, as Pepsi-Cola later discovered, and the company felt it necessary to dissociate itself from such superstars as Jackson and Madonna.

U2 was one of the few groups to refuse commercial sponsorship of its tours in the 1980s, although the group's Zoo TV tour in 1992 involved the participation of MTV.

In Japan, the boundaries between musician, advertiser and sponsor are more blurred: it has become commonplace for the same new track to be used as a commercial recording, a television theme and the soundtrack for an advertisement.

DAVE LAING

Talent Scout

'Talent scout' (or simply 'scout') is an archaic term used to describe an employee or associate of a show business or sports organization whose role, according to the Oxford English Dictionary, is 'to look for suitably talented persons with a view to their employment by that organization.'

In the earliest years of the recording industry, the Gramophone Company's engineer, Fred Gaisberg, would make trips to various countries to record local musicians and singers recruited by the agents appointed by the company to sell its products. Such agents were acting as talent scouts.

In the United States, the early recording industry did not need scouts in order to decide which mainstream popular music artists should be recorded: a hierarchy had already been established by existing systems of show business popularity. However, in some rural or 'ethnic' genres, scouts were needed to seek out talent. Sometimes, these were also the local retail agents of recording companies. Thus, the first hillbilly recording artist, Fiddlin' John Carson, was 'discovered' by Atlanta record dealer Polk Brockman, who suggested to the OKeh company that it should record him. OKeh sent Ralph Peer to make the recording in 1923, and Peer subsequently became the first of the dedicated professional talent scouts whose prime occupation was to seek out 'suitably talented' musicians to be recorded (Porterfield 1979).

Peer and others, notably Frank Walker, Art Satherley and W.R. Calloway, soon made regular 'field trips' throughout the southern and southeastern United States. Walker told an interviewer that he 'rode horses into the woods to find people who were individualistic in their singing' (Shelton and Goldblatt 1966, 211). He made his first field recordings of hillbilly music in 1922 for Columbia in a schoolhouse near Atlanta, Georgia. The English-born Satherley worked for a variety of New York companies and recorded such country artists as Gene Autry and Roy Acuff. Such trips continued throughout the 1930s when, for instance, Eli Oberstein made annual field trips to the South on behalf of Victor's Bluebird label to record music by hillbilly, Cajun, Mexican and black performers.

In the post-World War II era, the major record companies dispensed with field trips as a means of discovering talent, although such figures as Ike Turner and Dave Bartholomew acted as scouts and recording producers for the independent R&B labels Modern and Imperial, respectively. Gradually, the role of the scout was absorbed into that of the artist and repertoire (A&R) executive, to whom aspiring recording artists came or were brought by managers and agents. However, in contemporary pop music the term 'scout' has once again come into use: it describes a junior member of a record company A&R department whose role is to visit clubs to hear new acts or to assess the mountain of demonstration (demo) discs or tapes sent in by aspiring recording artists.

Bibliography

Cohen, Norm. 1972. '"I'm a Record Man": Uncle Art Satherley Reminisces.' *John Edwards Memorial Foundation Quarterly* 8: 18–22.

Porterfield, Nolan. 1979. *Jimmie Rodgers: The Life and Times of America's Blue Yodeler*. Urbana, IL: University of Illinois Press.

Shelton, Robert, and Goldblatt, Burt. 1966. *The Country Music Story: A Picture History of Country and Western Music*. Secaucus, NJ: Castle Books.

DAVE LAING

Tour

While touring by performers has always, in one form or another, been an integral aspect of the practise of popular music, it is only since the 1970s that the 'tour' has developed into a distinctive entity as part of the marketing strategy of major record companies. Before this time, performers and groups would go 'on tour' and in this way serve to promote their records, but touring in itself was regarded as part of the revenue-generating activities of performers. After this time, tours continued, of course, to generate significant revenues, but major record companies viewed them much more explicitly as promotional vehicles for performers and their albums, CDs and singles.

It was for this reason that tours came to be named (for example, the Jacksons' Victory tour of 1984), and to have their identity reinforced by the sale of promotional merchandise such as T-shirts, which customarily had printed on their backs the venues and dates of tour concerts. The role of tours as promotional vehicles for performers and their recordings was considerably enhanced during and after the 1970s by an increased emphasis on the visual drama of staging, which was made possible by the advent of technological devices such as laser beams.

Touring in the United States began in the days preceding mass urbanization, and was a direct consequence of demographics. At this time, the population of the United States was, on the whole, spread thinly throughout rural areas, and there were few cities of notable size. In 1840, for example, only one person in 12 lived in a town with a population of 8,000 or more. In 1860, there were only nine cities with a population of more than 100,000, most of them in the northeast (Baltimore, Boston, Brooklyn, Chicago, Cincinnati, New Orleans, New York, Philadelphia and St. Louis). As a result, it was necessary for performers to travel on an almost daily basis to find and create audiences in small towns, villages and hamlets, rather than for audiences to travel to see performers.

The early practises of popular music in the United States can be understood in light of these demographics. Performers came to audiences mainly in wagons, in showboats, and on the railroads that were springing up all over the Midwest during the mid-nineteenth century. They also came in different kinds of troupes: circuses, medicine shows, singing families, theatrical groups and, perhaps most importantly for the subsequent history of popular music in the United States, minstrel shows. Whatever the kind of troupe, they nearly always included variety acts, which were put on by acrobats, jugglers, dancers, comedians and, of course, singers. In their different ways, all these acts needed music. Many of the musicians who toured the United States at this time were from Europe. The best known of these European musicians were the Swedish soprano Jenny Lind (the 'Swedish Nightingale') and the English baritone Henry Russell.

With the advent of mass urbanization, this kind of touring became much less central to the practise of popular music. The increase in the number of densely populated cities in the United States during the second half of the nineteenth and the early part of the twentieth centuries meant that, in one sense, it was more practicable for audiences to travel to see performers than it was for performers to travel to find audiences. Many musicians who had previously traveled the rural routes of the United States now had more sedentary careers in the vaudeville theaters of cities. However, improvements in transportation at the same time enabled tours on a larger scale to be contemplated. The development of railroads in particular encouraged large-scale touring on the part of minstrel and vaudeville troupes.

Touring remained important for performers in certain other genres. For many jazz musicians such as Duke Ellington, for example, professional life consisted of little else than being 'on the road.' Touring circuits such as the so-called 'chittlin' circuit' also remained an economic necessity until the 1960s for blues and soul artists. Touring thus remained the principal means of earning a living for many musicians. Touring of this sort contrasts vividly with the more modern kind, in which the tour becomes a means of publicizing new material already completed after weeks, and sometimes months, of work in the studio. Ellington, for example, used the time between appearances taken up with traveling to write new music.

Touring also remained in general important to the spread of US popular music and culture, particularly overseas. It was steamships that began to make international touring possible during the nineteenth century. One of the first US ensembles to travel to Europe, and which did so by steamship in 1837, was Francis Johnson's Orchestra, an African-American ensemble from Philadelphia. Other US acts such as the Hutchinson Family Singers and various minstrel troupes toured Europe in the nineteenth century and, in 1918, as part of US involvement in World War I, Lieutenant James (Jim) Reese Europe took his highly talented all-black 369th Infantry ('Hell Fighters') Band across the Atlantic to entertain the troops. The band was a huge success and did much to popularize ragtime music in France. Just after the war, in 1919, the Original Dixieland Jazz Band, which had been instrumental in making jazz popular among white society audiences in the United States, toured Great Britain. From 1935, the number of US jazz tours to Britain was severely limited by a musicians' union restriction, but such artists as Louis Armstrong and Duke Ellington visited Europe. After the relaxation of the ban in 1955, there was a greater two-way flow of acts across the Atlantic, particularly when the Beatles made British music more popular in North America.

With his multi-artist Jazz at the Philharmonic tours of the late 1940s and 1950s, impresario Norman Granz helped to broaden the audience for jazz in North America. In the rock 'n' roll era, national tours of the United States were undertaken by similar 'packages' of up to 10 acts, drawn from current hit-makers. One such tour was the Winter Dance Party of 1958–59, during which Buddy Holly and other singers were killed in an air crash while traveling from one venue to another. The package format was revived in the 1990s by the alternative music Lollapalooza tours and by the all-women Lilith Fair tours. Despite tragedies such as those that killed Buddy Holly in 1959 and Patsy Cline in 1963, air travel during the second half of the twentieth century revolutionized touring in much the same way as had the steamship during the nineteenth century.

By the 1970s, rock bands such as Led Zeppelin were crisscrossing the United States on stadium tours that involved up to 60 concerts. The intensive nature of such tours gave rise to offstage excesses by the bands, chronicled in such books as that by Greenfield (1974). The increasing globalization of pop music led in the 1980s and 1990s to the staging of world tours by such artists as the Rolling Stones, Michael Jackson, U2, Dire Straits and Pink Floyd. Such tours often involved over 100 concerts on five continents and could last for over a year.

U2's PopMart tour of 1998 involved transporting 1,200 tonnes of equipment and 200 personnel in 52 trucks and 15 buses between 62 cities. The Rolling Stones' Bridges to Babylon tour of 1998 grossed $250 million from 108 concerts in 74 cities, and required a tour staff of almost 300.

Bibliography

Badger, Reid. 1995. *A Life in Ragtime: A Biography of James Reese Europe*. New York: Oxford University Press.

Boyer, Richard O. 1990. 'The Hot Bach.' In *The Duke Ellington Reader*, ed. Mark Tucker. Oxford: Oxford University Press, 214–52.

Cockrell, Dale, ed. 1989. *Excelsior: Journals of the Hutchinson Family Singers, 1842–1846* Stuyvesant, NY: Pendragon.

Greenfield, Robert. 1974. *Stones Touring Party*. London: Michael Joseph.

LaBrew, Arthur Randolph. 1994. *Captain Francis Johnson (1792–1844), Great American Bandsman*. Detroit, MI: The author.

Shepherd, John. 1982. *Tin Pan Alley*. London: Routledge & Kegan Paul.

York, Norton, ed. 1991. *The Rock File: Making It in the Music Business*. Oxford: Oxford University Press.

Filmography

On the Road with Duke Ellington, dir. Robert Drew and Mike Jackson. 1974. USA. 58 mins. Documentary.

DAVE LAING and JOHN SHEPHERD

Trade Fairs

Trade fairs are modern marketplaces where members of an industry can meet to offer new products for sale or licensing and to make trading agreements, most often on an international basis. Within the music industry, such fairs generally include showcase concerts, where performers can be displayed to the media and to potential foreign licensees, and also a conference element, where industry members debate issues of common interest. The events are also opportunities for networking or 'schmoozing' in order to make new industry contacts.

The oldest music trade fair is probably the Frankfurt Musikmesse, founded in medieval times, where new musical instruments are exhibited. The largest contemporary music publishing and record industry event is MIDEM (Marché d'Industrie de Disque et d'Editions Musicale). It was first held in Cannes, France in 1967, timed to attract music business executives returning from the San Remo Song Festival in Italy. In its first year, just over 300 people attended; by 1976, there were 5,500 attendees from 40 countries. In 1997, MIDEM attracted almost 11,000 participants from 83 countries and almost 4,000 companies.

The MIDEM organization expanded its activities in the 1990s to include additional annual events for the Asian and Latin American music industries (although MIDEM Latino was held in the United States). Both, however, ran into problems: MIDEM Asia was cancelled in 1998 and the authorities in Miami refused to allow Cuban music industry personnel to attend MIDEM Latino. The Cannes event has also been marred by the seizure by police of alleged pirate CDs from stands of participating companies.

In general, however, MIDEM's success has inspired entrepreneurs in other countries to organize similar events. In the United States, Tom Silverman of Tommy Boy Records was one of the founders of the New Music Seminar, which ran annually in New York from 1981 to 1993 and was intended to feature alternative genres and acts to the pop and rock mainstream. A regional event, South By South West, has been held each year in Austin, Texas since 1987. In Germany, the PopKomm fair was inaugurated in 1989 and In The City became a UK-based event organized by Factory Records chief Tony Wilson.

In Eastern Europe, the first International Records Trade Fair of CMEA (the Comecon bloc) was held in 1977 in Moscow, and in 1989 a trade fair was added to the international song contest, which had been held annually since 1962 at Sopot on the Baltic coast of Poland.

Outside the context of the mainstream record industry, events organized for performers, agents and promoters include WOMEX (Worldwide Music Expo, a European event for world music promoters), BID (Berlin Independents Days, which flourished in the late 1980s), the CINARS (Commerce international des arts de la scène/International Exchange for the Performing Arts) and Ontario Contact in Canada, the US Folk Alliance fair, and the Musicalliance Conference in the United Kingdom, which provides a meeting point for 'minority' genre professionals.

Other trade fairs cater to manufacturers and purchasers of studio, consumer hardware or stage equipment. The best known of these is the biannual show organized by the Audio Engineering Society (AES) in the United States.

Bibliography

Hennessey, M., ed. 1995. *Thirty Years of Music, Thirty Years of MIDEM*. Paris: Reed MIDEM Organisation.

DAVE LAING

Trade Organizations

Like other established industries, the music business monitors the economic and legislative environment in which it has to operate. Such factors as consumer taxes, intellectual property regimes and laws regulating imports can have a significant effect on the commercial health of the industry, both in its 'home' territory and in countries to which music is exported. The lobbying of governmental bodies on these and other issues is a primary function of the industry's trade organizations. Many of these organizations also undertake other functions, such as collecting sales statistics, operating hit parade charts and organizing awards events. These bodies are generally not engaged directly in commercial activities (such as sales of recorded music or the collection of royalties), as these activities are the responsibility of individual firms or copyright organizations. However, some trade organizations are involved in negotiations to set national or international soundcarrier royalty rates or pay rates for session musicians, and many also operate anti-piracy units. These units collect information and bring prosecutions in conjunction with the police and other law enforcement bodies.

Many sectors of the music industry have set up their own national and international trade bodies. There are about 50 national record industry organizations, most of which are affiliated with the International Federation of the Phonographic Industry (IFPI).

Among the most important of these national organizations are the Recording Industry Association of America (RIAA), the Recording Industry Association of Japan (RIAJ), the Syndicat National de l'Edition Phonographique (SNEP) (France) and the British Phonographic Industry (BPI).

Record industry groups that are not affiliated with the IFPI, such as the National Association of Independent Record Distributors and Manufacturers (NAIRD) in the United States, the Canadian Independent Record Production Association (CIRPA) and Verband Unabhängiger Tonträgerprodzenten (VUT) in Germany, consist of smaller record labels that believe they have interests separate from those of the major companies that dominate the IFPI's national groups.

Music publisher associations exist in most countries of Europe, the Americas, Japan and Australasia. They collect data on their members' activities and may issue licenses for such activities as the photocopying of sheet music. Many of these associations belong to the Confédération Internationale des Editeurs de Musique (CIEM). In the United States and a few other countries, smaller publishers have sometimes set up their own organizations in a similar way to the independent record label groups. There are fewer composer and songwriter organizations, although these exist in the United States (the National Academy of Songwriters (NAS)), the United Kingdom (the British Academy of Composers and Songwriters) and elsewhere.

Other segments of the industry that have formed trade

groups include record retailers, artists' managers, concert promoters, recording studio personnel and those concerned with specific music genres.

Recorded music retailer groups can play a significant role in the development of national music markets through their involvement in such matters as the compilation of sales charts and the standardization of sound-carrier packaging. In the United States, the National Association of Recording Merchandisers (NARM) has its own national meetings, and carries out consumer research on behalf of its members. Similar groups exist in Britain (the British Association of Record Dealers (BARD)), Germany (Gesamtverband Deutscher Musikfachgeschäfte (GDM)), The Netherlands (Nederlandse Vereniging van Grammofoonplaten Detailhandelaren (NVGD)) and elsewhere.

The first trade group for managers was the International Managers Forum (IMF), set up in the United Kingdom in 1990. Since the late 1990s, managers' groups have existed in about a dozen other countries. European concert promoters meet regularly to discuss issues of common interest at the International Live Music Conference (ILMC), and have formed national organizations such as the Swiss Music Promoters Association (SMPA) and the Concert Promoters Association (CPA) in Britain. Their transatlantic equivalent is the North American Concert Promoters Association (NACPA).

The recording and audio-science professions constitute another sector with its own set of organizations. Chief among these in the United States is the Audio Engineering Society (AES), which was founded in 1947. The society's conventions, held twice a year, feature the latest developments in audio technology and attract some 20,000 attendees. Recording studios in the United States are represented by the Society of Professional Audio Recording Services (SPARS), while the Music Producers Guild of the Americas (MPGA), a newer organization, campaigns for a separate copyright for record producers.

Among the numerous organizations formed to promote specific music genres, arguably the most powerful is the Country Music Association (CMA), which was founded in Nashville in 1958 as the successor to the Country Music Disk Jockeys Association. The CMA organizes annual awards ceremonies and runs a prestigious museum of country music. Within the United States alone, there are also more than a dozen other genre-based groups serving the interests of gospel, bluegrass, blues and other musical styles. In Europe, one of the most effective bodies is the International Jazz Federation (IJF), which links musicians, promoters, educators and others across the continent.

Music specialists from the legal profession also have their own organizations. These include the International Association of Entertainment Lawyers (IAEL) (which holds seminars annually at the MIDEM trade fair) and the Black Entertainment and Sports Lawyers Association (BESLA) (which was founded in the United States in 1979).

Finally, there are those trade associations from industries that rely on the products of the music business for their own activities. These range from organizations of radio stations to associations of restaurant owners and dance hall managers. Many such groups negotiate industry-wide licenses with collection societies for the use of music, and they are also enthusiastic lobbyists against any national legislation seeking to preserve or extend the rights of members of the music industry.

DAVE LAING

Trade Press

'Trade press' denotes the ensemble of newspapers and magazines devoted solely to events within a particular industry. Its target readership is the members of that industry rather than consumers. Contemporary popular music trade publications such as *Billboard* (US), *Music Week* (UK), *Original Confidence* (Japan) and *Der Musikmarkt* (Germany) provide music industry news, statistics and charts, as well as comments from those inside the record industry. Many also publish national industry directories and organize conferences or awards ceremonies. As trade journals, these publications generally have a selective circulation consisting of workers employed in production, distribution and retail within the music industry. Their importance for those employees is illustrated by the comment of Clive Davis about his time as chief executive of the CBS Records Group:

> It was hard even to devote Sundays to my family. At least part of them had to be devoted to reading the early editions of *Billboard*, *Cash Box* and *Record World*, and the specially delivered reports of Bill Gavin and Kal Rudman, the two most widely read radio advisory services. (Davis 1975, 125)

The purpose of such journals is not to evaluate music in aesthetic terms but, rather, to present news about product launches, sales figures, marketing strategies and media schedules. These publications focus on trading and decision-making and are often biased toward the agenda of the multinational music companies.

During the nineteenth century, the concert music business was served by a number of publications, such as *The Musical World* and *The Musical Times* (founded in London in 1836 and 1844) and *The Musical World and New York Musical Times* (founded in New York in 1852), which exposed the bribing of music critics by foreign opera singers in the 1850s. As music publishers and manufacturers of pianos and other instruments began to serve mass markets, their activities were reported in such journals as *British Bandsman* (1887) for the brass band business, the US-based *Piano Trade*, and *Metronome*, founded in 1885 for North American professionals in popular music. *The Etude* was founded in 1883 as a trade journal for US piano teachers (Sanjek 1988a, 350). The British music hall business was well served by *The Era* (1838), *Music Halls Gazette* (1868), *London Entr'acte* (1869) and other publications (Bailey 1998). The activities of British music publishers, notably in fighting piracy, were reported in *Musical Opinion (and Music Trade Review)* (1877) (Coover 1985).

The commercial exploitation of the phonograph and the gramophone inspired a new generation of the music industry trade press. In the 1890s, *Phonoscope* appeared in the United States, followed by the monthly *Talking Machine World* (1905). Thomas Edison had his own *Edison Phonograph Monthly* (founded in 1893 as *The Phonogram*), addressed mainly to dealers who sold his cylinders and players. The *Phonographische Zeitschrift* was founded in 1900 in Germany, and in Russia *Grammofon-nyi Mir* was demanding action against record pirates as early as 1910. It ceased publication in 1917, shortly before the revolution (Gronow and Saunio 1998, 13, 33). In Britain, there were *Gramophone News* (which was published from 1903 to 1907), *Phono Trader and Recorder* (1904) and *Talking Machine News* (1903), which in 1910 carried news of patent filings, reviews of new models and international reports from Germany, France and the United States.

Some of the early trade journals covered industries adjacent to music. During the 1920s, *Machines Parlantes et Radio* was published in Paris, and competing titles *Music Seller and Small Goods Dealer* (1927) and *Music Dealer & Radio-Gramophone Review* (1927) appeared in London.

The most important current trade publication, *Billboard*, also first reported on music as one of several entertainment industries. As its title indicates, *Billboard* began (in 1894) as a trade journal for the billposting and outdoor advertising industry in North America. It later branched out into coverage of traveling shows, movies and theater, including burlesque and vaudeville. In 1911, song lyrics were reprinted, and the following year the 'Song Reviews' column considered new numbers from a performer's viewpoint. In 1914, *Billboard* published a list of 'Popular Songs Heard in Vaudeville.' By this time its circulation was 38,000 (*Billboard* 1994). In 2001, sales were approximately 50,000.

In 1917, a *Billboard* editorial acknowledged that 'the phonograph has revolutionised the music publishing field' (quoted in *Billboard* 1994, 58), and thereafter the paper's primary focus gradually shifted toward the record industry, with sections added to cover the video and Internet businesses in the 1980s and 1990s, respectively. The record industry has also been *Billboard*'s principal source of advertising revenue. In the 1930s, labels bought space near to the '10 Best Records' charts in order to promote new releases to jukebox operators, while in 1956 RCA-Victor advertised the rollout of its first Elvis Presley campaign in *Billboard*.

From *Billboard*'s earliest years, its editors have spoken out on industry issues. In 1908, *Billboard* supported the controversial efforts of the Motion Picture Patents Company cartel to professionalize the film business. Later, the paper reflected mainstream opinion in the 1950s, when it defended the decision of CBS to force its employees to sign a 'loyalty oath,' and in the 1980s, when it both opposed censorship of song lyrics and attacked racism and sexism in the music business.

Billboard published reports from Europe, such as reviews of London music hall shows, from its earliest years, and it has continued to include regular supplements on the music industries of other countries. *Billboard* also organizes a number of music industry conferences and awards shows for the dance, video and other industry sectors. The magazine has several 'sister' titles, including *Amusement Business*, *Performance* and *Music & Media* (founded in 1984), which reports on the European music and radio industries from London.

The importance of radio airplay for the US record industry was first registered in the trade press in the 1930s, when the general show business magazine *Variety* (founded in 1905) published a weekly list of the 'most plugged' songs (Sanjek 1988b, 199). The increasing value of such airplay in the rock 'n' roll era spawned a number of so-called 'tip-sheets' from the 1950s onward. These weekly publications provide information on current playlists and also 'tip' or predict future airplay hits. In past years, some tip-sheets were accused of involvement in payola by accepting bribes to 'tip' certain records. The most important tip-sheets have included the *Gavin Report* (founded in 1958), *Radio & Records*, *Friday Morning Quarterback* (edited by Kal Rudman) and *Hits* (founded in 1988).

Billboard has had several competitors in the United States. They included *Record World* and *Cash Box* (1937–96), whose title reflected the importance of the jukebox business when the journal was founded. In Canada, *The Record* was published weekly until 1999, when it changed format to become an on-line newsletter.

In Britain, the first trade magazines to cater directly to the music profession were *Rhythm* (1927–39) and the monthly *Melody Maker & British Metronome* (1926–2000), which described itself as 'for all who are directly or indirectly interested in the production of Popular Music.' Both included pieces by well-known band leaders as well as hints for instrumentalists. A US equivalent was *Down Beat*, founded in Chicago in 1934. Although *Melody Maker*, which became a weekly in 1933, was initially aimed at dance band and jazz musicians, by the 1940s it had shifted its focus toward consumers of music. The most important contemporary trade publication in Britain is *Music Week*, which was launched in 1959 as *Record Retailer* and now sells over 12,000 copies. Other, now defunct, British trade publications were: *Music Business Weekly*, which flourished in the 1960s; *Radio & Record News* (1970s); *Record Business*, which championed the new independent record industry of the late 1970s; and two 1990s titles, *RPM* and the *Billboard*-owned *Music Monitor*.

Music Week's owners also published *Music Business International* (*MBI*). Launched in 1988 and closed in 2001, it featured interviews with leading industry executives and articles on national music markets. Originally a monthly publication, *MBI* later appeared six times a year. Another trade paper with a global reach is *Music & Copyright*, a fortnightly newsletter founded by the *Financial Times* newspaper in 1992 and now published by the Informa Group of London. *Music & Copyright* specializes in in-depth statistical analysis of the record and music publishing industries.

In the 1990s, a number of national trade magazines existed in continental Europe. Most shared the format of *Billboard* and *Music Week*, with charts of bestselling discs, lists of new releases, and industry news and opinions. The longest-running trade magazine in continental Europe is the monthly *Musica e Dischi*, founded in Italy in 1945, which claims a circulation of 25,000. In France, the fortnightly publication *Show Magazine* had 6,000 subscribers but ceased publication in 1993. The more modestly produced *La Lettre du Disque* succeeded it. The German market is served by the monthly *Der Musikmarkt*, with a circulation of over 11,000, and the *Billboard*-owned *Musikwoche*. In The Netherlands, *Muziek en Beeld* (with a circulation of 4,000) covers both the music and the video industries. The Spanish monthly publication *Showpress* is principally concerned with the live entertainment industry, while in Sweden the weekly *Topp 40* was published during the mid-1990s. *Tschinn Bumm*, based in Budapest, claimed a circulation of 10,000 within the Hungarian music industry in the early 1990s.

The most important Japanese trade paper is the weekly *Original Confidence* (Oricon), which was founded in Tokyo in 1967. It publishes Top 100 singles and albums and other charts. A Japanese rival, *Music Labo*, owned by the US *Billboard* group, closed in 1994. In India, the trade magazine *Raga to Rock* was founded in 1999. Other Asian trade papers extant in the 1990s included *Music Box* (South Korea) and *Music Week International* (Hong Kong). *Music News Asia* was an attempted 'pan-Asian' journal published in London during the mid-1990s.

In Australia, the weekly *Video & Music Business* had a circulation of 600 in the mid-1990s. *Australian Music Report*, founded in 1974, is primarily a chart publisher but contains some industry news.

Because the largest trade magazines concentrate on the record industry, some trade journals specialize in other sectors of the music industry. *Performance* and *Pollstar* are the principal magazines for the live music scene in the United States, publishing weekly financial data on concerts, news of forthcoming tours and reports from Europe and Australia. *Pollstar*'s Concert Pulse chart lists the Top 50 tours based on ticket sales in the previous three months. European-based counterparts of *Performance* and *Pollstar* have included *Applause* and *Audience*, both based in London. The recording studio sector also has some specialist publications, such as *Pro Sound News* and *Studio Sound*.

In the music publishing sector, *SongLink International* is a UK-based newsletter providing information for songwriters about possible markets for their compositions. The Los Angeles publication *Film Music* is aimed at composers who specialize in film and television scores. There are some trade publications for producers, distributors and retailers of musical instruments. These include *Music Business* (UK) and *Muziekhandel* (The Netherlands). *Webnoize*, the first publication for Internet music news, was, appropriately, available only on-line.

The business aspects of smaller 'niche' genres are sometimes covered in more general publications aimed at consumers. But country music has had its Nashville-based trade papers, such as *Music City News*, founded in 1963 by singing star Faron Young (Malone 1985, 386), and *Music Row*, while *Reggae Report* and *Dub Missive* were small-circulation newsletters of the New York scene in the 1990s (Oumano 1997).

Bibliography

Bailey, Peter. 1998. *Popular Culture and Performance in the Victorian City*. Cambridge: Cambridge University Press.

Billboard. 1994. *100th Anniversary Special Edition, 1894–1994*. 10 November.

Coover, James. 1985. *Music Publishing, Copyright and Piracy in Victorian England*. London and New York: Mansell.

Davis, Clive. 1975. *Clive: Inside the Record Business*. New York: William Morrow & Co.

Gelatt, Roland. 1977. *The Fabulous Phonograph, 1877–1977.* 2nd rev. ed. London: Cassell.

Gronow, Pekka, and Saunio, Ilpo. 1998. *An International History of the Recording Industry.* London: Cassell.

Malone, Bill C. 1985. *Country Music, U.S.A.* Rev. ed. Austin, TX: University of Texas Press.

Oumano, Elena. 1997. 'Reggae: Better Late Than Never.' In *Reggae, Rasta, Revolution*, ed. C. Potash. New York: Schirmer, 110–15.

Sanjek, Russell. 1988a. *American Popular Music and Its Business: The First Four Hundred Years. Vol. II: From 1790 to 1909.* New York and Oxford: Oxford University Press.

Sanjek, Russell. 1988b. *American Popular Music and Its Business: The First Four Hundred Years. Vol. III: From 1900 to 1984.* New York and Oxford: Oxford University Press.

DAVE LAING

15. Publishing

Broadside

Broadsides and Broadsheets

The term 'broadside' originated in England, and referred to a single printed sheet often used for the dissemination of royal proclamations, edicts of the church and other official announcements; 'broadsheets' were printed on both sides. Increasingly from the mid-sixteenth century, broadsides were printed copies of recently written songs, or ballads, sold directly to the public in larger towns, particularly London. 'Ballad' is a derivative of the French *balade*, a verse form established in England in the fourteenth century, and until the early eighteenth century the term referred exclusively to urban songsheets.

Broadside ballads were usually 80–120 lines long so as to fit the folio-size sheets, which usually bore a woodcut illustration and an indication of the tune to which the words should be sung. In the early period, ballads were printed in a heavy gothic type (the 'black-letter' ballads), but by the eighteenth century these had given way to roman type (the 'white-letter' ballads). For a period at the end of the seventeenth century, some broadsides included a representation of musical notation, but this was usually for decoration only rather than a guide to any actual melody. In general, ballads were intended to be performed to tunes already well known to the townspeople.

Development of the Trade

Although few of the earliest ballads have survived, evidence of the broadside trade can be found in the early sixteenth century. It is known, for example, that the Oxford bookseller John Dome worked from a catalog of 120 titles as early as 1520, but the significant development of the ballad form occurred during the second half of the century. Prior to this, printers were mostly concerned with the production of small numbers of books as luxury items for the affluent and educated elite; following the dissolution of the monasteries by Henry VIII in 1536–40, however, new grammar schools were widely established – creating a need for textbooks – and the sixteenth century also saw the gradual spread of elementary schools. The effect of these developments was a general increase in the level of literacy during the period, and a consequent stimulus to the growth and diversification of the printing trade. The authorities' increasing concern over the power of the new medium of broadsides to influence public opinion, and to spread dissent, was apparent in the passage of the *Act for the Advancement of True Religion and the Abolishment of the Contrary* (1543), which referred to the seditious effects of recent 'printed ballads, rhymes, etc' in 'untruly' instructing the king's subjects, and specifically the 'youth of his realm.'

While the king and his privy council were concerned to control the publication of books and broadsides in the interests of imposing political stability and religious orthodoxy, printers sought to protect their growing trade from the effects of competition. The outcome was a successful petition to the king, resulting in the establishment in 1557 of the Company of Stationers with a royal charter, which aimed to restrict all printing and publishing to its members. The titles of all books, plays and broadsides published by members of the Company had to be registered with it, and the Company's agents were authorized to search for, and if necessary destroy, illegal printing presses. In fact, the very first title registered with the Company was a ballad – 'Arise and Wake,' in the name of 'William Perkeryng' – and between 1557 and 1709 (when the *Copyright Act* assigned rights to authors rather than to printers) more than 3,000 broadsides were registered. The actual number in circulation, however, is certain to have been two or three times greater, since the combined effects of the authorities' attempts at censorship and the printers' legal monopoly soon produced a huge illegal trade. The emergence of this genuinely 'underground' press indicates both the strength of demand for the ballads and the profitability of producing them, given the severe penalties handed out to printers who were caught infringing the Company of Stationers' monopoly. Moreover, the persistence of the illegal trade and the seriousness with which the authorities viewed it are demonstrated by the series of legislative moves against it through the seventeenth century.

By the seventeenth century, the religious and moral themes of the early broadsides had been supplemented by more secular concerns – political news and propaganda, satire, crimes, executions, gossip, catastrophes, wars, romantic stories, bawdy tales, freak animals and people, storms, shipwrecks and so on. Thus, in the extent of their influence, their style and their content, the ballads as a medium anticipated the popular journalism of the modern era. Indeed, the general appearance and layout of many broadsides from this period are not dissimilar to those of current tabloid newspapers, although it should be emphasized that the ballads were sold as a primarily oral medium, as songs that were performed by street-sellers in any location where crowds might gather – markets, fairs, taverns, busy corners and so on. Ballad texts often provide a reminder of the way in which ballads were brought to the public, the first lines containing calls to passersby to gather round the seller and listen to the song. Generally, the price was a halfpenny (about the price of a loaf of bread), and there is no doubt that the broadsides sold in sufficient quantities for them to be considered the forerunners of modern mass media.

As the trade developed, the London stationers (so named because of the stalls or 'stations' from which they sold their books, pamphlets and broadsides) came to supply ballads not only to the numerous street-sellers who hawked them around the city, but to the 'chapmen' or peddlers who traveled around rural areas selling all sorts of cheap goods. In this way, the influence of the ballads was extended geographically and socially, and an embryonic distribution network was formed. Eventually, the copyrights of individual printers as a whole were transferred to the Company of Stationers, with printers receiving shares in return. In this way, a common 'ballad stock' was created, with a small number of printers specializing in this market. Legislation abolishing the Star Chamber in 1641 and the expiry of the *Licensing Act* in 1695 did much to relax state controls over the printing trade, and a process of consolidation seems to have been instigated so that, by the eighteenth century, William Dicey and John Marshall had come to dominate production and distribution in London. From their warehouses at Bow Churchyard and Aldermary Churchyard, they supplied both city street-sellers and country chapmen, although in this period there was increasing competition from other printers around the country. In the latter part of the century, too, the appeal of broadsides in London was challenged by the rise of professional singers and of concerts, pleasure gardens and 'singing saloons.' Yet the ballad trade was to revive once more, stimulated partly by the production (from the 1790s) of vast numbers of pamphlets dealing with political and religious issues, and partly by the business acumen of John Pitts (1765–1844) who, as successor to Marshall's son, had gained control of the ballad stock. Against the background of the renewed awareness of street literature, Pitts reprinted many old ballads (some of them dating back more than 200 years), and collected new ones from Irish immigrants and the colorful array of socially marginal characters who clustered in the notorious Seven Dials district of London, where his business was based. After 1813, he was challenged by James Catnach, also of Seven Dials, who specialized in the production of sensationalized (and often fictitious) narratives called 'cocks' or 'catchpennies.' Pitts and Catnach were bitter enemies, but their business successes were sufficient to encourage other printers in London, and many more in the rapidly industrializing cities of the North and Midlands.

Indeed, just as it had in seventeenth-century London, so the broadside ballad flourished again, and for the last time, in the new urban areas of the nineteenth-century city. Just as Catnach had made a small fortune from the trade, so too did Joseph Russell of Birmingham, but these two were hardly typical of the broadside printers, whose activities tended to be small-scale, short-lived and financially unstable. Nonetheless, there was a substantial demand for cheap broadsides in the working-class areas of the new cities, where alternative sources of either news or entertainment were severely limited. This final flourish of the ballad trade reached its peak around mid-century, but from the 1860s there is clear evidence of decline, firstly in London as a result of the prohibition of street musicians, and then – around 20 years later – in the other industrial cities as an effect of the general rise in real incomes, the organization of mass elementary education and the appearance of cheap mass-circulation newspapers, popular music halls and large-scale sporting events.

The rapid eclipse of the broadside ballads in the modern period, however, should not lead to any underestimation of their significance: it can be argued that they were the first, or at least the prototype, mode of mass communication, and one that spanned the entire period from medieval minstrelsy to the emergence of modern mass media. In the present context, too, it is important to note the ways in which the ballad trade anticipated, and in some respects laid the foundations for, the modern music business. This point will be considered further below.

Collectors and Controversies

From their earliest appearance, broadside ballads were the subject of condemnation, not only by political and religious authorities, but by those who regarded their direct language and often bawdy topics as an affront to educated discourse and the standards of polite society. Yet, then as now, there were also those who saw the ballads as rather more than offensive trivia, and collected them as vivid expressions of contemporary popular culture. Most notable among these was the celebrated diarist Samuel Pepys (1633–1703) who, adding to the efforts of earlier collectors, amassed around 1,800 ballads up to the end of the seventeenth century. It is evident that Pepys considered such material, ephemeral as it was, as more representative of his times than the writings of many more educated authors, as illustrated by his quotation of John Selden (whose collection he had acquired): 'As take a Straw, and throw it up into the Air; you may see by that which way the wind is; which you shall not do, by casting up a Stone.' The collection is in the Pepys Library at Magdalen College, Oxford. Another important early collection was that of Robert Harley (1661–1724), the Earl of Oxford, which was eventually purchased by the Duke of Roxburghe in 1788. With some additions, the Roxburghe Collection amounted to 1,500 items when it was obtained by the British Museum in 1845. These are the two largest collections from the first great period of broadsides; from the later period, items from the stock of both Catnach and Pitts are in the Printing Library of the St. Bride Foundation in London, with copies in the British Library. In Cambridge University Library, there are also 25 volumes of ballads collected by Sir Frederic Madden between 1836 and 1873 in England, Scotland and Ireland. In addition, there are significant collections in the British Library and in the municipal libraries of several towns and cities – for example, more than 700 broadsides printed by Thomas Pearson in Manchester in the 1860s and early 1870s, in Manchester Central Library.

In cataloging his collection, Pepys left a clear indication of the range of subjects covered by the early broadsides, dividing his five volumes into 10 categories: '(1) Devotion and Morality; (2) History – True and Fabulous; (3) Tragedy – viz Murders, Executions, Judgements of God; (4) State and Times; (5) Love – Pleasant; (6) Love –

Unfortunate; (7) Marriage, Cuckoldry, etc; (8) Sea – Love, Gallantry, & Actions; (9) Drinking & Good Fellowship; (10) Humour, Frollicks, etc.' The vast majority of broadside ballads, of course, are lost forever, so such classifications provide vital clues to the general themes of the discourse in this period. Since the survival of individual items was a matter of chance, the extent to which those that remain are representative of the ballads as a whole is a matter of conjecture; however, the relatively large number that has been collected is itself some guarantee that the picture is reasonably complete. Moreover, it is apparent that certain of the themes identified by Pepys recurred in various guises – as did many of the ballads themselves, which were widely bought and performed throughout the four centuries of ballad history. So, while individual items may often have been dismissed as trivia, it is clear that the broadside tradition as a whole is far from ephemeral from the point of view of cultural history.

Nevertheless, there has been some debate about the significance of the broadsides. As noted above, early balladeers were persecuted by the authorities for the seditious and irreverent content of their work; by the nineteenth century, however, a more persistent vein of criticism concerned the vulgarity of the ballads from the point of view of the educated middle class. The ballads' affront to polite society, however, was not confined to the iconoclastic tone and often bawdy language of many of them, but – significantly – extended to the actual sounds of the songs and their singers, who were heard as raw and raucous, performing in ways that contrasted strongly with the increasingly standardized expressive conventions of 'educated' music.

Scholars, too, have argued, in ways strikingly similar to those of more recent debates about popular music, over whether the ballads should be regarded as trivia created to entertain the masses (and reconcile them to their lot), or whether the authentic – and otherwise silent – voice of the people can be heard in them. This was the view of Lord Macaulay, who in his *History of England* (1849–61) argued that it was in 'rude rhyme' that the 'common people' expressed their 'love and hatred, their exultation and their distress' (1913, Vol. 1, 410).

On the one hand, then, it can be argued that the ballads, no less than the pop songs of modern times, were trivial fantasies written by individuals (rather than the articulation of communal sentiments), and produced and sold as a commercial enterprise, so are thus unlikely to represent the fundamental concerns of the community. On the other, it has been pointed out that it was indeed the community in general which, by sustaining the ballad trade for so long, and by buying copies of songs that persistently dealt with certain cultural themes, shaped the discourse in which the broadsides were heard. Certain studies have developed this point, arguing that the ballads, far from being escapist or trivial, do provide evidence of a popular world-view concerning important matters such as work, community life and family relationships. For Joyce (1991), this popular morality often judged current events by comparing them to a 'golden age' of 'Old England,' in which notions of individual freedom, justice and fairness (rather than the language of class conflict) occur repeatedly, as does the imagery of rural life. This pattern of myths and symbols could be effective in sustaining a particular view of the social order (and the radical impulse derived from it), as well as providing, in a more mundane sense, important guidance on accepted custom and conduct in the community. Similarly, as Eva (1997) suggests, the performances of street-sellers – rather than just the texts of their songs – were also important elements in this process, their exotic and often marginal characters providing opportunities for arousing empathy, or alternatively the construction of social difference. In such ways, the ballads and their singers could contribute to the affirmation of a popular morality, and the constitution of identities.

Broadsides and the Business of Music

Very little is known about the lives of those who wrote, printed and sang the broadside ballads: precisely because of their socially marginal status, and the perception of them as disreputable and often dangerous people, their works and deeds were ignored by most members of polite society – including historians and social thinkers. Yet, one outstanding account of the street-sellers and their business is presented in Henry Mayhew's *London Labour and the London Poor*, published in parts from 1849, and in a collected edition during 1861–62. As part of his investigation into the social conditions of working people, Mayhew described the ways in which broadside sellers, frequently working in small groups, would appear in the streets, often in the evenings, noisily drawing attention to themselves and their wares. It is clear that Mayhew regarded them as an important element in the popular culture of the period, with the themes of murder and execution particularly popular. Mayhew estimated that the tale of the execution of James Bloomfield Rush in 1849 had sold an astonishing 2.5 million copies, and it is said that James Catnach earned £500 from selling 250,000 copies of a sheet describing the murder of a Mr. Weare by John Thurtell in 1824 (Shepard 1973, 74). On the basis of his investigations, Mayhew also presented details of the wholesale price structure operated by the printers, and the average earnings of the street-sellers.

Despite the general lack of information, it is evident from such accounts that the broadside trade was extensive, was culturally important as a medium of mass communication, and was organized along recognizably modern business lines. The pattern of this business was, moreover, long established: as early as the sixteenth century, printers were buying songs outright from specialist songwriters and distributing them through a network of urban street-sellers and rural chapmen or peddlers. The ballad-singers, moreover, carried out many of the functions that would later be described as marketing – publicizing the songs and performing them in the manner of latter-day song 'pluggers.' Through the ballad trade, the process of large-scale production, distribution, marketing and performance of popular music as a commodity for sale on the market was thus firmly established by the seventeenth century, and by the early nineteenth century the popular music business may be discerned in something like its modern form. As far as popular music is concerned, it may therefore be argued that the 'age of mechanical reproduction' (Benjamin 1992) began in the later Middle Ages, and that the capitalist organization of production predated the Industrial Revolution by around 200 years.

Bibliography

Benjamin, Walter. 1992 (1936). 'The Work of Art in the Age of Mechanical Reproduction.' In *Illuminations*, ed. Hannah Arendt. London: Fontana, 211–44.

Eva, P. 1997. *Popular Song and Social Identity in the Victorian City*. Unpublished Ph.D. thesis, University of Manchester.

Hindley, Charles. 1968 (1878). *The Life and Times of James Catnach (Late of Seven Dials), Ballad Monger*. Detroit, MI: Singing Tree Press.

Joyce, Patrick. 1991. *Visions of the People: Industrial England and the Question of Class, 1848–1914*. Cambridge: Cambridge University Press.

Lee, Edward. 1970. *Music of the People: A Study of Popular Music in Great Britain*. London: Barrie & Jenkins.

Lloyd, A.L. 1975 (1967). *Folk Song in England*. St. Alban's: Paladin.

Macaulay, (Lord) Thomas Babington. 1913 (1849–61). *History of England*. 5 vols. London: Macmillan & Co.

Mackerness, Eric D. 1964. *A Social History of English Music*. London: Routledge and Kegan Paul.

Mayhew, Henry. 1967 (1861–62). *London Labour and the London Poor*. London: Frank Cass & Co.

Middleton, Richard. 1988. 'Popular Music of the Lower Classes.' In *The Romantic Age 1800–1914*, ed. Nicholas Temperley. Oxford: Blackwell, 63–91.

Palmer, Roy, ed. 1974. *A Touch on the Times: Songs of Social Change, 1770–1914*. Harmondsworth: Penguin.

Palmer, Roy. 1979. *A Ballad History of England from 1588 to the Present Day*. London: Batsford.

Palmer, Roy. 1988. *The Sound of History: Songs and Social Comment*. Oxford: Oxford University Press.

Shepard, Leslie. 1962. *The Broadside Ballad: A Study in Origins and Meaning*. London: H. Jenkins.

Shepard, Leslie. 1969. *John Pitts: Ballad Printer of Seven Dials, London, 1765–1844*. London: Private Libraries Association.

Shepard, Leslie. 1973. *The History of Street Literature*. Newton Abbot: David and Charles.

Simpson, Claude M. 1966. *The British Broadside Ballad and Its Music*. New Brunswick, NJ: Rutgers University Press.

Thompson, R.S. 1974. *The Development of the Broadside Ballad Tradition and Its Influence upon the Transmission of Folk Songs*. Unpublished Ph.D. thesis, University of Cambridge.

Vicinus, Martha. 1974. *The Industrial Muse: A Study of Nineteenth Century British Working-Class Literature*. London: Croom Helm.

Würzbach, Natascha. 1990 (1981). *The Rise of the English Street Ballad, 1550–1650*. Cambridge: Cambridge University Press.

PETER MARTIN

Chapbook

A precursor of the songster, the chapbook (the name is a corruption of 'cheap book') was a small publication, suitable for the pocket, often published and sold by ballad printers and broadside sellers. Made of twice- or thrice-folded sheets, chapbooks usually consisted of eight or 16 pages, 2" (5 cm) wide and 3" (7 cm) high, and were often printed as simple songbooks. Some chapbooks had more sensational or more serious intent, with morality stories, brutal murders, dramatic executions or religious experiences being the subject of the publication. Although most catered for a similar audience to that of the broadside ballad, the Cheap Repository tracts of Hannah More, a founder of the Sunday School movement, were directed at a young audience.

Thought to have been first printed in the early sixteenth century, chapbooks were published for some 300 years and were sold in town streets and village lanes by generations of roving chapmen, who also sold laces and ribbons, needles and pins, toys and novelties. A few – including David Lowe of Nottingham (1750–1824) and the lame chapman William 'Hawkie' Cameron from Stirling, noted for his acid wit and street oratory – wrote their memoirs of a hard life on the road. Chapbooks were purchased from the printer at a rate such as 13 (a 'baker's dozen') for ninepence, and were sold by the chapman for a penny each. They were highly popular in the eighteenth century as the reading public increased rapidly, and were often illustrated with woodcuts, some even having a small print on every page. A number were decorated with flowers and were known as 'Garlands,' their contents being love poems and songs. Publishers such as T. Brandard and E. Butler of Birmingham, or James Catnach and John Pitts of Seven Dials, London, produced such chapbooks as 'The Cries of London,' 'Pretty Poems, Songs etc. for the Amusement of Good Little Boys and Girls,' 'The Dover Garland,' 'The Straw Bonnet Garland,' 'The Bee Hive, or The Sips of the Seasons, Being a Choice Collection of the Newest Songs,' 'The Royal Huntsman's Delight' and 'The Lover's Magazine.'

It was the nineteenth-century popularity of cheap and mass-produced books, the flourishing music halls and, because of the railroads, people's greater mobility that together brought about the end of chapbooks and chapmen. But the chapmen's persistent traveling and hawking, often supported by their own singing of the songs from the chapbooks as they sold them in the street, helped lay some of the foundations for the popularization of songs and music through printed media.

Bibliography
Ashton, John. 1966 (1882). *Chap-Books of the Eighteenth Century*. New York: Blom. (First published London: Chatto and Windus, 1882.)

Halliwell-Phillips, James O. 1968 (1849). *A Catalogue of Chap-Books, Garlands, and Popular Histories*. Detroit, MI: Singing Tree Press.

Jones, Trevor. 1970. *Street Literature in Birmingham*. Oxford: Oxford Polytechnic, Book Publishing Course.

Neuburg, Victor E. 1964. *Chapbooks: A Bibliography of References to English and American Chapbook Literature of the Eighteenth and Nineteenth Centuries*. London: Vine Press.

Shepard, Leslie. 1969. *John Pitts: Ballad Printer of Seven Dials, London, 1765–1844*. London: Private Libraries Association.

Shepard, Leslie. 1973. *The History of Street Literature*. Newton Abbot: David and Charles.

PAUL OLIVER

Fake Book

A fake book is a collection of musical scores, in loose-leaf or bound form, used by professional and amateur musicians in performance and also as a learning tool. The scores in a fake book are sketchy, typically conveying only the melody line and basic harmonies (via chord symbols) for various songs; lyrics may or may not be included.

The derivation of the term 'fake book' is unusual, even ironic. To 'fake' music has generally meant to perform 'by ear,' that is, without referring to (or even being able to read) musical notation. In the term 'fake book,' however, the word 'fake' takes on the sense of 'performing from notation pieces which one cannot render by ear' – in other words, to fake (in the sense of 'pretend') intimate familiarity with unfamiliar or only vaguely familiar pieces.

Numerous fake books have been produced, ranging in scope from a few dozen songs to well over a thousand. Until recently, the majority of fake books have been produced without copyright clearance for the songs included in them, and are hence illegal publications having to be marketed surreptitiously; standards of accuracy and legibility have varied widely, and some fake books are notoriously lacking on one or both counts. So-called 'legal' fake books using only formally authorized scores are increasingly the norm (e.g., *The Original, Legal, Musicians' Fake Book*, 1979; Sher 1988, 1997). Some producers of fake books hype the accuracy and authenticity of their wares by incorporating the words 'real book' (as a playful antonym of 'fake book' in the sense of 'fraudulent book') into their publication titles (e.g., Sher 1988, 1997; *The Real Book*, n.d.), or by using the word 'legal' in their publication titles (e.g., *The Original, Legal, Musicians' Fake Book*, 1979).

There is considerable redundancy of repertoire among fake books, owing to the fact that many of them are of the 'all-time favorite songs' variety. Some fake books, however, adopt a more limited mandate by focusing on a particular musical style or time frame (for example, jazz, rock 'n' roll, country, show tunes, Latin American music, Christmas music or the 1970s). Songs in fake books are typically presented in 'lead sheet' notational format, more rarely in 'sheet music' or 'piano-vocal score' format; fake books aimed at jazz enthusiasts may include selections notated in 'master-rhythm part' format, as well as discographical information on recorded sources of the pieces anthologized.

A master index of 64 fake books of the 1970s and 1980s containing altogether over 13,500 different titles has been published (Goodfellow 1990).

Fake books have been an important tool of the commercial musician working in situations where customer requests for particular musical selections are to be expected, and a gratuity for satisfying a request is a possible outcome (and chronic inability to satisfy customer requests an employability liability). While many commercial musicians control a repertoire of several hundred songs, a collection of fake books at the ready is insurance against the possibility that a patron may request a song that the musician knows only vaguely or not at all. It is also the case that fake books are routinely used by many musicians during the course of profes-sional engagements, even in the absence of specific patron requests, as a general-purpose library of performance scores.

Fake books have been an important resource for students and teachers in the numerous jazz and commercial music courses and programs that have arisen in post-secondary institutions and other settings since the 1960s, and also more informally prior to that. A prominent example is *The Real Book*, a well-produced collection of several hundred 'standards' and jazz tunes, published in various iterations since the early 1970s. The potential power of widely used fake books such as *The Real Book* to canonize a particular repertoire and specific details of realization (harmonic practise, in particular) is a matter of concern among some musicians, music scholars and educators.

A close relative of the fake book is the popular music 'song folio' or 'songbook' anthologizing the output of a particular musician or set of musicians. Publications of this type differ from fake books proper in their strict adherence to sheet music or piano-vocal score notational format and also in their relatively circumscribed contents. In recent years, such publications have usually been issued as corollaries of, or follow-ups to, a particular LP/CD (e.g., Harris 1976) or as a music notation analog of a greatest hits recorded anthology (e.g., Kleiner 1981). Professional and amateur musicians alike treat such publications as fake books in their usage.

Another type of songbook publication is the anthology of 'band score' (also 'full score') transcriptions of famous recorded performances. A notable example of the type is *The Beatles Complete Scores* (1993), a 1,136-page volume showing, as far as is possible and practicable in standard musical notation, every sonic event in the Beatles' entire recorded studio output. Publications such as this serve as study scores, but they can also be used as performance scores, in the manner of a fake book: the practise of notating guitar and bass parts in both staff notation and tablature notation underlines the practical performative intentions.

Bibliography

Beatles, The. 1993. *The Beatles Complete Scores*. Milwaukee, WI: Hal Leonard Publishing Corporation and Wise Publications.

Goodfellow, William D. 1990. *Where's That Tune?: An Index to Songs in Fakebooks*. Metuchen, NJ and London: Scarecrow Press, Inc.

Harris, Heather, ed. 1976. *Bob Marley and the Wailers: Rastaman Vibration*. Hialeah, FL: Almo Publications.

Kleiner, Audrey, ed. 1981. *The Bob Marley & the Wailers Songbook*. Hialeah, FL: Almo Publications.

The Original, Legal, Musicians' Fake Book. 1979. Miami Beach, FL: Hansen House.

The Real Book. n.d. Syosset, NY: The RealBook Press.

Sher, Chuck, ed. 1988. *The New Real Book: Jazz Classics, Choice Standards, Pop-Fusion Classics.* Petaluma, CA: Sher Music.

Sher, Chuck, ed. 1997. *The Latin Real Book: Salsa, Brazilian Music, Latin Jazz.* Petaluma, CA: Sher Music.

ROBERT WITMER

Hymnals

Although collections of hymns for use in religious rituals have a long history as a feature of different world religions (for example, Vedic hymns in Sanskrit), they are principally associated with Christian worship.

Before the Protestant Reformation of the sixteenth century, the singing of Latin hymns from manuscripts was the concern of priests and the choir. With the Reformation – and the invention of printing – came a move toward congregational singing, a fundamental transformation that would lead to the hymnal as a symbol of the democratic participation by congregations in their own idiom. Not that the Reformation itself produced a unified view of the kind of hymnals congregations should use. Lutheran tradition encouraged the writing of new hymn texts for use alongside psalms; Luther himself had helped to consolidate a trend begun in Prague in 1501 with a book of eight hymns that he had printed in Wittenberg in 1524. However, the Calvinist approach, developed in exile in Geneva and brought into England after the accession to the throne of Elizabeth I, insisted on the superior character of the psalms and, therefore, on the use of psalters.

In Germany, the Lutheran church accorded hymns and chorale melodies a regular part in services from an early stage, but in England and Scotland psalters were victorious, dominating church music until the eighteenth century (with the aid of a printing monopoly granted to the Stationers' Company in 1603) and also becoming established in the North American colonies. But opinions about the content of psalters were often sharply divided. The *Bay Psalm Book* (*The Whole Booke of Psalmes* (1640)), the first book printed in English in the North American colonies, came into existence because of Puritan dissatisfaction with texts used in England. Psalters sometimes included a few hymns, a notable example being John Playford's *Psalms and Hymns in Solemn Musick* (1671). Nonetheless, their presence contributed little to the growing opposition to the dominant role of psalmody, especially among the dissenting groups that sprang up in the late seventeenth century. This opposition was based on the perception that the texts of metrical psalmody were not conducive to con-gregational singing. The increase in hymn singing within these groups was by no means uncontroversial, however. Some (for example, the Quakers) forbade all hymn singing, while others who were obliged to meet in secret found their singing could betray them.

One consequence of these and other successive disputes was that hymnals and hymn singing were associated from an early stage with divergence from established positions regarding the place, use and type of music appropriate to worship. The ongoing history of the hymnal in the English-speaking world (its major site of influence) was marked by many subsequent arguments, but also by considerable expansion in its use and popularity and, in due course, in its potential as a commercial publishing enterprise.

The first significant development in the establishment of hymnody as the principal form of music used in Protestant worship in English came with the volumes of hymns produced by Isaac Watts in the early eighteenth century. Watts's ideas for the improvement of psalmody (not its abandonment) were based on the belief that 'Congregational Song should represent not God's word to us, but our word to God, and that the thoughts and language of the Psalms could be employed only so far as we could properly make them our own' (Benson 1915, 111). This altering of the focus to personal experience and expression was accompanied by increased attention to the figure of Christ and, especially, to individual personal response to Him. (One of Watts's most famous hymns, 'When I Survey the Wondrous Cross,' first appeared in his *Hymns and Spiritual Songs* (1707).)

Watts's volumes were widely adopted in the independent churches, going through successive editions in the eighteenth century and inspiring an often passionate loyalty. They crossed the Atlantic quite soon after publication in England (Benjamin Franklin printed Watts's *The Psalms of David* in 1729, 10 years after the first London edition), and although enthusiasm for them in North America was slower to develop, their impact there was perhaps even greater than in Europe. The volumes themselves contained no music: Watts wrote in a limited number of meters and anticipated that his hymns would be sung to existing psalm tunes. The influence of his work on music and musical performance would nevertheless be extensive and varied, ranging from Victorian English settings to African-American gospel music.

Important though Watts was to the rise of the hymn and the significance of the hymnal, it was a new denomination, Methodism, that made congregational hymn singing central. John Wesley's first hymnal, *Collection of Psalms and Hymns* (1737), owed its existence to his encounter with Moravian colonists on a voyage to Georgia in 1735. The Moravians opened Wesley's ears to the possibility of greater spirituality expressed through more fervent singing, to replace what Wesley himself later described as the 'miserable, scandalous doggerel' of the old psalters and the droning and bawling of the congregations (Tyerman 1880, 282). The hymnal included five German hymns translated by Wesley himself. As Methodism developed from the late 1730s on, Wesley continued to compile hymnals, with the assistance – and enormous personal contribution as a hymn writer – of his brother Charles. Many small, cheap collections were issued, but because congregations eventually could not afford the numbers of collections being produced, Wesley had his own definitive volume printed in 1780 'for the use of the People called Methodists.' It cost three shillings and contained 525 hymns.

Although the earliest Methodist hymnals contained no tunes, their metrical range was more varied than that of Watts's volumes. Wesley was keenly interested in music and published separate tunebooks, the first in 1742. The 1761 tunebook *Sacred Melody* contained 76 tunes and was designed to be bound with a new book of 149 hymn texts, each of which had a designated tune. With its publication, Wesley became the first all-round hymnbook editor. It was a role he undertook in typical style. In the Preface, he wrote of the difficulties he had encountered in fulfilling his wish to see a 'small and portable volume and one of an easy price' containing both hymns and tunes. The problem was that music masters 'were above following any direction but their own.' Wesley, however, was determined that the envisaged compilation 'should follow my direction – not mending our tunes, but setting them down, neither better nor worse than they were' – to which he added, 'At length I have prevailed.' His advice to congregations was forthright – 'Sing lustily and with a good courage. Beware of singing as if you were half-dead, or half-asleep' (Benson 1915, 241).

As Protestant denominations grew in number, they tended also to subdivide, for a variety of reasons, and the new organizations often saw the production of their own hymnals as essential marks of their identity. Thus, Richard Allen, the leader of one of the first independent African-American churches, the African Methodist Episcopal Church, founded at Bethel in Philadelphia in 1794, compiled and produced *A Collection of Spiritual Songs and Hymns* in 1801 exclusively for the use of black Methodists. The hymnal may well have served as one source of slave spirituals (Southern 1983, 52).

Up to this point, hymnals were generally produced in small print runs. As hymn singing became widely accepted in the Church of England in the first part of the nineteenth century – despite ongoing arguments about appropriate styles and emphases – and as printing techniques improved, both the production and circulation of hymnals increased dramatically. Sales figures rose steadily, bolstered by advertising and by the clergy's frequent recommendation that each member of a congregation should have access to a book in the pew. As they did so, the Established Church took the initiative, a process culminating in the compilation of the most comprehensive hymnal to date, *Hymns Ancient and Modern* (*HA&M*), in 1861. Between then and the second edition of 1875, *HA&M* all but obliterated other Anglican opposition. It was an object lesson in applying the rules of the 'rapidly expanding, unfettered capitalism' of the time (Temperley 1979, 300). *HA&M* 'first "took over" the smaller high-church hymnals, while two large competitors absorbed the low-church and left-of-center markets; it then modified its policies so as to cater for as much of the central and uncommitted market as possible; in the end, it succeeded in capturing the bulk of its rivals' adherents' (Temperley 1979, 300). By 1912, 60 million copies of the book had been sold worldwide.

In terms of content, *HA&M* was eclectic. In adopting this policy, its compilers (including a specialist music editor, W.H. Monk) absorbed another commercial lesson: that of including a sufficiently wide range of styles, from revised-medieval to evangelical, to suit everyone's taste to some degree. In one sense, the widespread acceptance of hymnody and the domination of the Established Church's own hymnal meant that congregational singing was ceasing to have any antithetical status – a situation that was underlined by the increasing tendency to hand over the musical initiative to the choir-and-organist duopoly. In its place came an aspiration to musical excellence, as the presence of rather more harmonically sophisticated settings (by existing hymn standards) encouraged congregations to view their hymnals as scores. Without relinquishing its symbolic power as a sign of both personal and collective religion, the hymnal for many late nineteenth-century Anglican churchgoers was also a way into participation in a musical performance.

Successive editions of *HA&M* acknowledged, albeit in a limited way, another contemporary development: the North American gospel hymn, a key element in the revivalist movement spearheaded by Dwight L. Moody. Both forms of hymnody encouraged participation, but in other ways they were poles apart. Users of *HA&M* belonged, by and large, to an increasingly dominant cultural group in the late nineteenth century. One of revivalism's central aims was to assure the urban poor on the margins of society of the validity of their lives – however apparently degraded – through redemption. Though their hymnody marked them as different, it was not conceived as oppositional: singing from volumes such as

Philip Bliss's and Ira Sankey's *Gospel Hymns and Spiritual Songs* (1875) was an assertion of, and a claim for, a common humanity. Another difference of note was that while, like *HA&M*, gospel hymnals sold in enormous quantities, their authors declined to take royalties (Temperley 1980, 851).

North American revivalist hymnals incorporated elements from contemporary popular idioms such as march rhythms and verse–chorus structures, and may have influenced them in return. In England, a different approach to the popular-secular became apparent with the publication of *The English Hymnal* in 1906, in which music editor Ralph Vaughan Williams had made a conscious effort to include settings derived from European (especially English and Scottish) traditional music. In doing so, he had deliberately set a different course from previous policy, 'which had been to choose familiar, fashionable material . . . Quality, not popularity, was the main criterion for [Vaughan Williams's] selection' (Blezzard 1990, 141). But as a whole, it was the twentieth century's own popular idioms that made the greatest impact on hymnal compilation. In terms of style, these hymnals were often slightly behind the times: the influential 20th Century Church Light Music Group of the 1950s, for example, preferred the idiom of the musical. But mid-century arguments about the appropriateness of popular music, centering on hymnals such as *Thirty 20th Century Hymn Tunes* (1960) by Geoffrey Beaumont, Patrick Appleford and others, tended to concede ground before the proliferation of material, the response of congregations, and an increasingly desperate need to involve the young, evidenced in compilations such as *Youth Praise* (Baughen 1966). Despite increasing secularization, hymnal compilation and production between the 1960s and the 1980s rivaled that of the nineteenth-century heyday.

By no means all these new hymnals were thought of, or referred to, as such by their compilers and users. Particularly influential in the renewed activity of writing and publishing music for group use was the so-called Charismatic Movement, which developed outside the established denominations, beginning in the 1960s. This separation, together with the movement's greater informality and emotionalism, led to the cultivation of a style of music that was consciously differentiated from established hymnody, a difference reflected in a preference for the terms 'worship song' and 'chorus' to replace 'hymn.' Compilations (such as *Sound of Living Waters* (1974)) came to be called 'songbooks.' These songbooks drew together a diversity of folk and popular styles and sources around the guitar, which replaced keyboard instruments in both symbolical and practical terms. The impact of these songbooks on established denominations was considerable, leading to the production of compromise volumes such as *Mission Praise* (1983), in which new worship songs by writers such as Graham Kendrick and long-established hymns were intermingled in one alphabetical sequence.

The hymnal's importance to popular music is many-sided. It began with a combination of song and participatory activity that was conscious of its oppositional status to the dominant church. Although this element often diminished, it never totally disappeared. More consistently present, beginning with hymnals produced during the rise of independent denominations and the evangelical revivals of the eighteenth and nineteenth centuries (especially in England and North America) and enduring into the twentieth century, was an emphasis on personal subjectivity in religious experience and a confidence in the validity of such experience. Thus, for many thousands of people, singing from a hymnal became an activity in which connections were made between music, musical performance, personal significance and emotional depth that would become deep-rooted, both inside and outside the churches. At the same time, hymnal production became a highly successful commercial activity, and remained so in the late twentieth century. While established music publishers such as Novello and Oxford University Press continued to derive revenue from the hymn copyrights, the momentum passed to a new generation of specialist publishers. An example is Thankyou Music, UK-based holders of the copyrights of many contemporary pop hymns.

Bibliography

Adey, Lionel. 1988. *Class and Idol in the English Hymn*. Vancouver: University of British Columbia Press.

Allen, Richard. 1801. *A Collection of Spiritual Songs and Hymns*. Philadelphia: Printed by J. Ormrod.

Baughen, Michael A., ed. 1966. *Youth Praise*. London: Falcon.

Benson, Louis F. 1915. *The English Hymn: Its Development and Use in Worship*. New York: Doran.

Blezzard, Judith. 1990. *Borrowings in English Church Music, 1550–1950*. London: Stainer & Bell.

Bliss, Philip P., and Sankey, Ira D. 1875. *Gospel Hymns and Spiritual Songs*. Cincinnati, OH: Church.

The English Hymnal. 1906. London: Oxford University Press.

Fudge, Roland, Horrobin, Peter, and Leavers, Greg, eds. 1983. *Mission Praise*. Basingstoke: Marshall, Morgan and Scott.

Hymns Ancient and Modern. 1861. London: Novello.

Parry, Simon. 1999. *Twentieth-Century Popular-Style Church Music in England*. Unpublished Ph.D. thesis, University of Liverpool.

Playford, John. 1671. *Psalms and Hymns in Solemn Musick*. London: Printed by W. Godbid.

Pulkingham, Betty, and Harper, Jeanne, eds. 1974. *Sound of Living Waters*. London: Hodder & Stoughton.

Routley, Erik. 1964. *Twentieth Century Church Music*. London: Jenkins.

Southern, Eileen, ed. 1983. *Readings in Black American Music*. 2nd ed. New York: Norton.

Temperley, Nicholas. 1979. *The Music of the English Parish Church*. Cambridge: Cambridge University Press.

Temperley, Nicholas. 1980. 'Hymn, IV: Protestant.' In *The New Grove Dictionary of Music and Musicians*, Vol. 4, ed. Stanley Sadie. London: Macmillan, 846–51.

Thirty 20th Century Hymn Tunes, by Members of the 20th Century Church Light Music Group. 1960. London: Weinberger.

Tyerman, Luke. 1880. *The Life and Times of the Rev. John Wesley*, Vol. 2. 5th ed. London: Hodder & Stoughton.

Watson, J.R. 1997. *The English Hymn: A Critical and Historical Study*. Oxford: Clarendon Press.

Watts, Isaac. 1707. *Hymns and Spiritual Songs*. London: John Lawrence.

Watts, Isaac. 1729. *The Psalms of David*. Philadelphia: Printed by Benjamin Franklin.

Wesley, John. 1737. *Collection of Psalms and Hymns*. Charleston, SC: Printed by Lewis Timothy.

Wesley, John. 1761. *Sacred Melody* [bound as part of *Select Hymns with Tunes Annext*]. London.

Wesley, John. 1780. *A Collection of Hymns for the Use of the People Called Methodists*. London: Printed by J. Paramore.

The Whole Booke of Psalmes . . . [Bay Psalm Book]. 1640. Cambridge, MA: Printed by Stephen Daye.

DAVID HORN

Music Publishers

—Acuff-Rose Music

Founded in Nashville, Tennessee in 1942 by country music star Roy Acuff (1903–92) and veteran songwriter-singer-publisher Fred Rose (1897–1954), Acuff-Rose became the first successful publishing company to specialize in country music. Rose, who had composed hits for Sophie Tucker, the Original Dixieland Jazz Band and Paul Whiteman, moved to Nashville from Chicago in the mid-1930s and hosted a daily radio show on WSM, the home of the *Grand Ole Opry*. The company's most successful songwriter was the legendary Hank Williams, whose hit songs include 'Cold Cold Heart' and 'Hey, Good Lookin'.' Also, 'Tennessee Waltz,' written by Redd Stewart and Pee Wee King and published by Acuff-Rose, became one of the most successful country songs of all time and a crossover phenomenon. The song earned

almost $80,000 in copyright fees during its first year of release. The company's catalog was sold to the Gaylord Corporation, owners of *Opryland*, in 1985 for $22 million.

Bibliography

Jasen, David A. 1988. *Tin Pan Alley*. New York: D. I. Fine.

Sanjek, Russell, and Sanjek, David. 1996. *Pennies from Heaven: The American Popular Music Business in the Twentieth Century*. New York: Da Capo Press.

Discographical References

King, Pee Wee. 'Tennessee Waltz.' Victor 20-2680. 1948: USA. Reissue: King, Pee Wee. 'Tennessee Waltz.' *Pee Wee King & His Golden West Cowboys*. Bear Family BCD 15727. *1995*: Germany.

Page, Patti. 'Tennessee Waltz.' Mercury 5534. 1950: USA. Reissue: Page, Patti. 'Tennessee Waltz.' *A Golden Celebration*. PolyGram 534720. *1997*: USA.

Williams, Hank. 'Cold Cold Heart.' MGM 10904. 1951: USA. Reissue: Williams, Hank. 'Cold Cold Heart.' *The Complete Hank Williams*. PolyGram 536077. *1998*: USA.

Williams, Hank. 'Hey, Good Lookin'.' MGM 11000. 1951: USA. Reissue: Williams, Hank. 'Hey, Good Lookin'.' *The Complete Hank Williams*. PolyGram 536077. *1998*: USA.

DAVID SANJEK

—Campbell Connelly

A British-based music publisher, the firm of Campbell Connelly was formed in London in 1925 by songwriters Jimmy Campbell and Reg Connelly to publish their novelty song, 'Show Me the Way to Go Home.' The duo wrote numerous hit songs for such British singers as Gracie Fields and Flanagan and Allen. Although the firm published work by other British writers, like the band leader Ray Noble ('The Very Thought of You'), its success lay principally in its ability to buy British rights to US hit songs, such as those of De Sylva, Brown and Henderson ('Sonny Boy'), through its Irwin Dash Music Company, and in the formation in 1933 of Cinephonic, a subsidiary that published soundtrack music from pictures made by Gaumont-British Films. In the post-World War II era, Campbell Connelly published the compositions of Eddie Cochran, and set up Ivy Music with the pop music broadcaster Radio Luxembourg.

With a catalog of 60,000 works, the firm was sold to the Music Sales group in the early 1980s.

Sheet Music

Campbell, Jimmy, and Connelly, Reg, comps. and lyrs. 1925. 'Show Me the Way to Go Home.' London: Campbell Connelly.

Henderson, Ray, comp., and De Sylva, Buddy, Brown, Lew & Jolson, Al, lyrs. 1928. 'Sonny Boy.' London: Campbell Connelly.

Noble, Ray, comp. and lyr. 1934. 'The Very Thought of You.' London: Campbell Connelly.

Discography

Jolson, Al. 'Sonny Boy.' Brunswick 4033. 1928: USA. Reissue: Jolson, Al. 'Sonny Boy.' *Let Me Sing & I'm Happy: At Warner Bros. 1926–1936*. Rhino 72544. *1996*: USA.

Noble, Ray. 'The Very Thought of You.' Victor 24657. 1934: USA. Reissue: Noble, Ray. 'The Very Thought of You.' *The Very Thought of You*. Parade/Koch International 2032. *1995*: USA.

DAVE LAING

—Chappell and Company

The music publisher Chappell and Company was founded in London in 1810 by Samuel Chappell, J.B. Cramer and F.T. Latour. The firm passed to Samuel's son William in 1834 when Samuel, the last surviving of the three partners, died.

During the nineteenth century, the firm became one of Britain's leading publishers of popular ballads and light opera. Among its composers and songwriters were Liza Lehmann, Edward German and the partnership of W.S. Gilbert and Arthur Sullivan. The company also manufactured pianos and promoted concerts, including the Promenade Concerts during the period 1915–26. Under the leadership of Leslie Boosey, Chappell and Company was active in the campaign against sheet music piracy and in the formation of the Performing Right Society in 1914. A controlling interest in the firm was purchased in 1929 by Louis Dreyfus, who created a US branch and installed his older brother, Max, as its manager.

Max Dreyfus had begun his musical career as a staff pianist and general utility man at the firm of Howley, Haviland and Dresser, where he had acted principally as the intermediary between the publisher and professional performers by teaching them how to sing material from the company's catalog. He had also arranged music, with considerable success, for other, less technically skilled composers. In his role as head of Chappell, Dreyfus solicited the representation of stage composers and made the firm the preeminent publisher of music for the theater. The company's clients included Rudolf Friml, Jerome Kern, George Gershwin, Vincent Youmans and Richard Rodgers.

Dreyfus believed that nobody could tell if a song might become a hit, but that 'it *would* become one if you worked to sell it.' Chappell bought the T.B. Harms company, which Dreyfus had assisted in making such a prosperous concern with his talent for promotion, and helped Jerome Kern, one of its most successful songwriters, to flourish. In later years, the firm made a considerable amount of money with the success of *My Fair Lady* (1956) and other shows, and formed partnerships with key writers, including Richard Rodgers and Oscar Hammerstein II.

After a long period in the possession of the Dreyfus family, Chappell was sold after the death of Louis in 1966. In 1970, the Harms division was sold to the Lawrence Welk Group for $3.2 million. The North American branch of Philips (Norelco) had owned 49 percent of Chappell and, in 1970, it transferred control of that percentage for a reported $30 million to the Phonogram group. The value of the Chappell material subsequently became a principal asset in this company's market share of the global music economy.

Bibliography

Goldberg, Isaac. 1961 (1930). *Tin Pan Alley: A Chronicle of American Popular Music*. New York: Frederick Ungar.

Jasen, David A. 1988. *Tin Pan Alley*. New York: D. I. Fine.

Krummel, Donald W., and Sadie, Stanley. 1990. *Music Printing and Publishing*. New York: W.W. Norton.

Mair, Carlene. 1961. *The Chappell Story, 1811–1961*. London: Chappell.

Sanjek, Russell, and Sanjek, David. 1996. *Pennies from Heaven: The American Popular Music Business in the Twentieth Century*. New York: Da Capo Press.

DAVID SANJEK with DAVE LAING

—Oliver Ditson and Company

The company that was to become the major music publishing house in the United States by the 1880s was established by Oliver Ditson (1811–88) in a Boston music store in 1835. A year later, Ditson and Samuel H. Parker, a publisher to whom Ditson had earlier been apprenticed, joined forces to form Parker and Ditson, a partnership that ended when Ditson bought Parker out in 1842. The company became Oliver Ditson and Company in 1857.

In the 1840s and 1850s, the company's rapidly expanding catalog ranged from non-copyright music by major European composers (the company brought out the first US edition of Haydn's *Creation* in 1845) to virtually all types of popular song, including some individual songs that would later become world-famous, such as 'Darling Nelly Gray' (1856) and 'Jingle Bells' (1859). One of its greatest successes in publishing original US material was with the Hutchinson Family, most of whose songs bore the Ditson imprint (although Ditson declined to publish the Abolitionist song 'Get Off the Track!' (1844)). In 1858, Oliver Ditson further strengthened his reputation in serious music circles when he purchased

Dwight's Journal of Music, retaining the journal's founder John Sullivan Dwight as editor. As Dwight's tireless advocacy of European musical taste and of the need for more formal music education made the journal known in Europe, Ditson was able to become the US agent for numerous European publishers (Sanjek 1988).

During the American Civil War (1861–65), Oliver Ditson and Company displayed a sensitivity to the publishing opportunities offered by the conflict that was almost on a par with that of Root & Cady, the major Civil War song publisher. The company scored considerable successes with 'We Are Coming, Father Abra'am' (1862), 'Battle Hymn of the Republic' (1862) and 'Tenting on the Old Camp Ground' (1864). Before and, especially, after the war, Ditson expanded its financial base not only by buying out other companies, but by sponsoring the establishment of new ones, such as John Church in Cincinnati and Lyon and Healy in Chicago, in which it then acquired a commercial stake.

The period following Oliver Ditson's death coincided with the rise of New York-based publishers with a narrower concentration on popular music and new, more aggressive promotional techniques based on their connections with professional performance. Oliver Ditson and Company remained in Boston, tied to a wide-ranging, nonspecialist catalog and associated with more old-fashioned ideas of advertising and retail. It fell behind in popular music publishing and moved increasingly into classical and church music, and music education. The company's catalog was purchased by Theodore Presser in 1931.

Bibliography

Fisher, William Arms. 1933. *One Hundred and Fifty Years of Music Publishing in the United States*. Boston, MA: Ditson.

Hamm, Charles. 1979. *Yesterdays: Popular Song in America*. New York: Norton.

Jackson, Richard. 1976. *Popular Songs of Nineteenth-Century America*. New York: Dover Publications.

Sanjek, Russell. 1988. *American Popular Music and Its Business: The First Four Hundred Years. Vol. II: From 1790 to 1909*. New York: Oxford University Press.

Sheet Music

Emerson, Luther O., comp., and Gibbons, James S., lyr. 1862. 'We Are Coming, Father Abra'am.' Boston, MA: Oliver Ditson & Co.

Hanby, Benjamin Russel, comp. and lyr. 1856. 'Darling Nelly Gray.' Boston, MA: Oliver Ditson & Co.

Howe, Julia Ward, lyr. 1862. 'Battle Hymn of the Republic. Adapted to the Favorite Melody of "Glory, Hallelujah."' Boston, MA: Oliver Ditson & Co.

Hutchinson, Jesse, lyr. 1844. 'Get Off the Track! A Song for Emancipation' (to the melody of 'Old Dan Tucker'). Boston, MA: Jesse Hutchinson.

Kittredge, Walter, comp. and lyr. 1864. 'Tenting on the Old Camp Ground.' Boston, MA: Oliver Ditson & Co.

Pierpont, James, comp. and lyr. 1859. 'Jingle Bells (or The One Horse Open Sleigh).' Boston, MA: Oliver Ditson & Co.

DAVID HORN

—Leo Feist Music Publishing Company

Leo Feist (1869–1930) began his career as field manager for a corset company, but he always longed to be a songwriter and publisher. When he sold some of his own songwriting material to Stern and Marks, he attempted to form a partnership with the publisher, but his overtures were rebuffed. Subsequently, he formed his own company with Joe Frankenthaler. Their first hits were by the eminently successful Harry Von Tilzer in 1895 – 'Nobody Cares for Me' and 'Oh, Oh Miss Liberty' – but the firm's foothold in the market was secured only when Feist convinced orchestra leader and composer John Philip Sousa to play 'Smokey Mokes' that same year.

Feist was an energetic marketer. He spent $100,000 annually on advertising and promotion. His well-known motto was 'You Can't Go Wrong with a Feist Song.' Each year, he gathered together his branch managers and key personnel and tried out some 30 to 50 songs on the assembled company. In 1903, he acquired a four-floor office building at West 34th Street in New York City, which included offices for orchestrators, illustrators, educational intermediaries and songwriters.

Feist achieved a major success in 1917 when he bought George M. Cohan's 'Over There' for $25,000 and went on to sell 2 million copies of the sheet music. However, he was less successful in his purchase, that same year, of the rights to the work of the first recorded jazz ensemble, the Original Dixieland Jazz Band. Efforts to sell the ensemble's work, including the popular 'Tiger Rag,' failed – perhaps an indication that the public intuitively recognized that jazz was an improvisational art form and not one to be captured on sheet music.

Feist's greatest success came in 1927 with 'My Blue Heaven,' recorded by Gene Austin and plugged energetically by Eddie Cantor as part of the *Ziegfeld Follies* of that year. Feist went on to sell 5 million copies of the song.

Feist died as the heyday of Tin Pan Alley was coming to an end as a result of the sale of publishing companies to the motion picture industry. In fact, his own company was purchased by MGM in 1934.

Bibliography

Goldberg, Isaac. 1961 (1930). *Tin Pan Alley: A Chronicle of American Popular Music.* New York: Frederick Ungar.

Jasen, David A. 1988. *Tin Pan Alley.* New York: D. I. Fine.

Sanjek, Russell, and Sanjek, David. 1996. *Pennies from Heaven: The American Popular Music Business in the Twentieth Century.* New York: Da Capo Press.

Sheet Music

Cohan, George M., comp. and lyr. 1917. 'Over There.' New York: Leo Feist Music Publishing Co.

Donaldson, Walter, comp., and Whiting, George, lyr. 1927. 'My Blue Heaven.' New York: Leo Feist Music Publishing Co.

Holzman, Abe, comp. and lyr. 1895. 'Smokey Mokes.' New York: Leo Feist Music Publishing Co.

LaRocca, Nick, and Edwards, Eddie, comps. 'Tiger Rag.' 1917. New York: Leo Feist Music Publishing Co.

Von Tilzer, Harry, comp. and lyr. 1895. 'Nobody Cares for Me.' New York: Leo Feist Music Publishing Co.

Von Tilzer, Harry, comp. and lyr. 1895. 'Oh, Oh Miss Liberty.' New York: Leo Feist Music Publishing Co.

Discographical References

Austin, Gene. 'My Blue Heaven.' Victor 20964. 1927: USA. Reissue: Austin, Gene. 'My Blue Heaven.' *Voice of Southland.* ASV/Living Era 5217. *1997*: USA.

Original Dixieland Jazz Band, The. 'Tiger Rag.' Victor 18472. 1918: USA. Reissue: Original Dixieland Jazz Band, The. 'Tiger Rag.' *75th Anniversary.* Bluebird 61098-2. 1917–21; *1992*: USA.

DAVID SANJEK

—T.B. Harms

The preeminent publisher of production music for the Broadway musical theater, T.B. Harms was founded by Thomas B. Harms and his brother Alex T. in 1875. The firm fully emerged when arranger Max Dreyfus (1874–1964) joined in 1898. He soon thereafter purchased a 25 percent interest in the company, and purchased it outright along with songwriter Jerome Kern in 1904. Between then and the sale of the firm to Warner Brothers in 1929, T.B. Harms controlled 90 percent of the music featured on the Broadway stage. Dreyfus served as mentor to some of the most important theatrical composers of the day, including not only Kern but also George Gershwin, Cole Porter, Richard Rodgers and Lorenz Hart, Rudolf Friml and Vincent Youmans. The scope of T.B. Harms's success proved Dreyfus's claim that, although no one could tell if a song would be a hit, 'it *would* become one if you worked to sell it' (Sanjek and Sanjek 1996, 96).

Bibliography

Jasen, David A. 1988. *Tin Pan Alley.* New York: D. I. Fine.

Sanjek, Russell, and Sanjek, David. 1996. *Pennies from Heaven: The American Popular Music Business in the Twentieth Century.* New York: Da Capo Press.

DAVID SANJEK

—Hill & Range

The firm of Hill & Range was founded in 1945 by Julian J. Aberbach and his father Adolph, along with Milton Blink and Gerald King. Julian and his brother Joachim Jean Aberbach had learned publishing in Europe before emigrating to the United States, Jean in 1936, Julian in 1940 (Pugh 1996, 117). The firm made its name by specializing in hillbilly and country and western music, and by co-owning and administering publishing companies with such stars as Eddy Arnold, Bob Wills, Ernest Tubb and Red Foley.

In 1956, Hill & Range made a most notable move: Julian and his brother helped to negotiate the sale of Elvis Presley's contract from Sam Phillips's Sun Records to RCA. It has been reported that the recording company put up $25,000, while the Aberbachs added $15,000 to the deal. However, Guralnick (1994, 520) doubts that the Aberbachs put up this amount, arguing that it was more likely that they might have shared a signing-on fee of $6,000 with RCA. In any event, this transaction led to the establishing of Presley's publishing companies: Hi-Lo Music, Elvis Presley Music Corporation and Gladys Music (the last named after Presley's mother). Hill & Range administered these companies thereafter, and in this way exercised effective control over them.

This arrangement involved the Aberbach brothers in an ongoing relationship with the singer, to whom, over a number of years, they brought material already published and recorded elsewhere for possible recording. An example of this kind of initiative is provided by Otis Blackwell's song 'Don't Be Cruel.' The existing writer and publisher were required to cede part of their copyright to Presley and Hill & Range. In some cases (for example, Presley's recording of Arthur Crudup's 'That's All Right,' with which he made his Sun Records debut in 1954) it appears likely that no royalty agreement was made (Shaw 1978, 33–34).

The success of Hill & Range was such that its owners were able to purchase other catalogs outright or to share in the revenues from their operation. In the mid-1950s, this process led to successful negotiations with the firms owned by Buddy De Sylva and Ernest R. Ball. In 1964, Hill & Range bought Progressive Music, the first publishing company operated by Atlantic Records.

Hill & Range itself sold a major portion of its catalog to Chappell Music, then a subsidiary of the PolyGram organization, in 1975, but retained control of the firms connected to Elvis Presley.

Bibliography

Guralnick, Peter. 1994. *Last Train to Memphis: The Rise of Elvis Presley*. Boston, MA: Little, Brown and Co.

Pugh, Ronnie. 1996. *Ernest Tubb: The Texas Troubadour*. Durham, NC: Duke University Press.

Sanjek, Russell, and Sanjek, David. 1996. *Pennies from Heaven: The American Popular Music Business in the Twentieth Century*. New York: Da Capo Press.

Shaw, Arnold. 1978. *Honkers and Shouters: The Golden Years of Rhythm and Blues*. New York: Macmillan.

Sheet Music

Blackwell, Otis, and Presley, Elvis, comps. and lyrs. 1956. 'Don't Be Cruel.' New York: Shalimar Music/Elvis Presley Music.

Crudup, Arthur, comp. and lyr. 1947. 'That's All Right.' New York: St. Louis Music/Wabash Music.

Discographical References

Crudup, Arthur. 'That's All Right.' Victor 20-2205. 1946: USA. Reissue: Crudup, Arthur. 'That's All Right.' *Complete Recorded Works, Vol. 2 (1946–1949)*. Document DOCD-5202. *1994*: Austria.

Presley, Elvis. 'Don't Be Cruel.' RCA 47-6604. *1956*: USA.

Presley, Elvis. 'That's All Right.' Sun 209. 1954: USA.

DAVID SANJEK

—Howley, Haviland & Company

While not the most enduring of the Tin Pan Alley firms, Howley, Haviland & Company produced a number of successful songs, particularly in the genres of the sentimental song and the 'coon' song. Patrick Howley (1870–1918), manager of the publishing firm of Willis Woodward and Company, and Frederick Benjamin Haviland (1868–1932), New York sales director of the Oliver Ditson Company, founded the company in 1893 because they felt constrained by having to work for others. They aimed to make their work stand out by, among other things, embellishing their sheet music with particularly ornate and colorful art, most often produced by the artists Bert Cobb and Edgar Keller.

Among their 'coon' songs was Paul Dresser's 'I'se Your Nigger If You Wants Me, Lisa Jane,' and it was the work of Dresser (1857–1906) that did most to set the company apart. A Hoosier and the brother of famous novelist Theodore Dreiser, Dresser achieved success in 1897 with his encomium to his home state, 'On the Banks of the Wabash, Far Far Away.' So successful was Dresser and key to the company's success that he was made a partner in 1900, and in 1901 the company's name was changed to Howley, Haviland and Dresser. Public acceptance of the company's work was also facilitated by the plugging of Tin Pan Alley veteran Max Dreyfus.

Haviland left the company in 1903, and it plunged into bankruptcy the following year. Its fortunes revived with Dresser's most famous song, 'My Gal Sal,' published in 1905, but the firm ceased to exist with the songwriter's death the following year.

Bibliography

Goldberg, Isaac. 1961 (1930). *Tin Pan Alley: A Chronicle of American Popular Music*. New York: Frederick Ungar.

Jasen, David A. 1988. *Tin Pan Alley*. New York: D. I. Fine.

Sheet Music

Dresser, Paul, comp. and lyr. 1896. 'I'se Your Nigger If You Wants Me, Lisa Jane.' New York: Howley, Haviland & Co.

Dresser, Paul, comp. and lyr. 1897. 'On the Banks of the Wabash, Far Far Away.' New York: Howley, Haviland & Co.

Dresser, Paul, comp. and lyr. 1905. 'My Gal Sal.' New York: Howley, Haviland and Dresser.

DAVID SANJEK

—Jobete Music

It has long been argued that Berry Gordy's experience on the automobile assembly lines of Detroit during the early 1950s influenced his design of Motown Records. Not only did the company produce and distribute its own recordings, manage its talent, book its artists' appearances and train them in the niceties of professional entertainment, it also had its own publishing company, Jobete Music, founded in 1959.

Gordy began his music business career as a songwriter for Jackie Wilson and others in the mid-1950s. At Motown, he established a stable of house writers and producers, the most notable of whom was the team of Holland-Dozier-Holland, who composed more than 40 Top 10 hits. Gordy routinely pitted his writers against one another, allowing them to vie for the next single by one of his artists. In the process, he assembled a catalog second to few in US popular music.

Gordy sold Motown Records in 1988. He retained ownership of Jobete until 1997, when he sold 50 percent to EMI Music Publishing for $132 million (EMI retained the right to buy the remaining 50 percent for five years). At the time of the sale, there were 15,000 titles in the catalog, with an estimated annual turnover of $50 million. The continued use of the Jobete catalog in films, in commercials and over the airwaves attests to the commercial viability of Gordy's agenda.

Bibliography

George, Nelson. 1985. *Where Did Our Love Go?: The Rise and Fall of the Motown Sound*. New York: St. Martin's Press.

Sanjek, Russell, and Sanjek, David. 1996. *Pennies from*

Heaven: The American Popular Music Business in the Twentieth Century. New York: Da Capo Press.

DAVID SANJEK

—Leeds Music Corporation

The Leeds Music Corporation was founded after the heyday of Tin Pan Alley, at the time when sheet music was beginning to be replaced by recordings as the principal means by which the public consumed music and the publishers earned their profits. Its founder, Lou Levy (b. 1910), became extremely successful in this method of publishing by applying his skills to the marketing of swing jazz, and it was a combination of professional savvy and personal involvement that led to the start of Leeds.

Levy managed the successful Andrews Sisters and was married to one of them, Maxine. He happened to hear the song 'Bei Mir Bist du Schön,' sung in Yiddish, and convinced the songwriters Sammy Cahn and Saul Chaplin to compose a set of English lyrics. He then founded Leeds to promote and profit from the eventually very successful song. Levy believed that 'behind every song is a greater song publisher.' He did not specialize in any one particular genre, but instead sought out whatever kind of song the other publishers were ignoring at the time. 'If your competition is putting out blue dresses, you put out red ones,' he stated.

Levy had particular success with boogie-woogie numbers, including 'Beat Me Daddy (Eight to the Bar)' and 'Boogie Woogie Bugle Boy.' He also had an ear for novelty songs, such as 'Open the Door Richard!' and 'Woody Woodpecker.' Levy's success continued into the period of rock 'n' roll's ascendancy. He acquired the rights to the Beatles' 'I Want to Hold Your Hand' before the song broke on the US charts.

Bibliography

Jasen, David A. 1988. *Tin Pan Alley*. New York: D. I. Fine.

Sheet Music

Lennon, John, and McCartney, Paul, comps. and lyrs. 1963. 'I Want to Hold Your Hand.' London: Northern Songs Ltd.

McVea, Jack, and Howell, Don, comps., and Fletcher, Dusty, and Mason, John, lyrs. 1947. 'Open the Door Richard!' New York: Leeds Music Corporation.

Raye, Don, comp., and Prince, Hughie, lyr. 1941. 'Boogie Woogie Bugle Boy.' New York: Leeds Music Corporation.

Raye, Don, comp., and Prince, Hughie, and Sheehy, Eleanor, lyrs. 1940. 'Beat Me Daddy (Eight to the Bar).' New York: Leeds Music Corporation.

Secunda, Sholum, comp., and Jacobs, Jacob, lyr.; and Cahn, Sammy, and Chaplin, Saul, English lyrs. 1937.

'Bei Mir Bist du Schön.' New York: Leeds Music Corporation.

Tibbles, George, and Idriss, Ramez, comps. and lyrs. 1948. 'Woody Woodpecker.' New York: Leeds Music Corporation.

Discographical References

Andrews Sisters, The. 'Beat Me Daddy (Eight to the Bar).' *The Best of the Andrews Sisters*. DJ Specialist 814557. *1999*: USA.

Andrews Sisters, The. 'Bei Mir Bist du Schön.' *The Best of the Andrews Sisters*. DJ Specialist 814557. *1999*: USA.

Andrews Sisters, The. 'Boogie Woogie Bugle Boy.' *The Best of the Andrews Sisters*. DJ Specialist 814557. *1999*: USA.

Beatles, The. 'I Want to Hold Your Hand.' *Complete BBC Sessions*. Great Dane 9326/9. *1994*: Italy.

Jordan, Louis. 'Open the Door Richard!' *Introduction: His Best Recordings: 1939–1947*. Best of Jazz 4054. *2000*: USA.

Kyser, Kay. 'Woody Woodpecker.' *The V-Disc Recordings*. Collector's Choice Music 4511. *1999*: USA.

DAVID SANJEK

—E.B. Marks

The career of E.B. Marks (1865–1945) is a classic North American success story. Employed as a salesman of household goods, he wrote lyrics on the side as a hobby. In 1893, he approached the publisher Frank Harding, who put him in touch with composer William Loraine. Together, they wrote 'December and May.' Dissatisfied with his royalties, Marks started his own publishing firm in 1894. The firm was successful almost immediately, in part due to Marks's creation of the illustrated song slide, a major marketing tool. In company with his partner, Joseph W. Stern (1870–1934), Marks was also one of the first businessmen to capitalize on the African-American songwriter. They published the work of Bob Cole, and the Johnsons (James Weldon and J. Rosamond, the former a renowned poet and writer, as well as leader of the Harlem Renaissance, and the latter one of the most successful black composers of his day), as well as that of Bert Williams and George Walker. E.B. Marks was also one of the first firms to establish a relationship with BMI, the performance licensing agency, when it opened for business in 1940.

Bibliography

Jasen, David A. 1988. *Tin Pan Alley*. New York: D. I. Fine.

Marks, Edward B. 1934. *They All Sang: From Tony Pastor to Rudy Vallee* (as told to Abbot J. Liebling). New York: Viking Press.

Marks, Edward B. 1972 (1944). *They All Had Glamour: From the Swedish Nightingale to the Naked Lady*. Westport, CT: Greenwood Press. (First published New York: Messner, 1944.)

Sanjek, Russell, and Sanjek, David. 1996. *Pennies from Heaven: The American Popular Music Business in the Twentieth Century*. New York: Da Capo Press.

Sheet Music

Loraine, William, comp., and Marks, E.B., lyr. 1893. 'December and May.' New York: Frank Harding.

DAVID SANJEK

—Mills Music

The music publishing firm Mills Music was founded by Jack Mills in 1919. Formerly, Mills (1891–1979) had been a Tin Pan Alley song plugger, and had also served as the professional manager of the McCarthy & Fisher Company in New York. He first made his mark as a music publisher through the genre of novelty ragtime tunes, a success initiated by his purchase of Zez Confrey's 'Kitten on the Keys' in 1921. This was followed by many popular blues and jazz numbers, including 'Down Hearted Blues,' 'I Just Want A Daddy I Can Call My Own,' 'Graveyard Dream Blues,' 'Farewell Blues' and 'Great White Way Blues.'

The name of the firm was changed to Mills Music, Inc. in 1928. The following year, the company's 10th anniversary, Mills bought the catalogs of Gus Edwards Music, Stark & Cowan, Harold Dixon, McCarthy & Fisher and Fred Fisher Music. Two years later, he added the catalog of Waterson, Berlin & Snyder (minus the music of Irving Berlin, who owned and published his own material). Buying up other firms, some for as little as $300, was a pattern followed by Mills throughout his career as a music publisher. By 1964, when the company was put up for sale, it had gross receipts of $1.4 million and held a catalog of 25,000 copyrights. Wholly owned overseas subsidiaries were purchased over the years in many countries, including Brazil, Great Britain, Canada, Spain and Germany.

The public sale, in 1964, of 277,712 shares of Mills Music stock valued at $4.5 million was fully subscribed, within a few days, at a unit price of $6.50 a share. The balance of approximately $2.5 million was raised through bank loans. Within a week, Mills Music stock was valued at $17 a share. The purchasers were the shareholders of Utilities and Industries (U&I) Corporation and they had bought one of the most valuable catalogs of US standard songs.

In 1969, U&I transferred ownership of its Mills Music stock to the newly formed Belwin-Mills Publishing Corporation. The transaction involved transferring 47 percent of Belwin-Mills's stock to U&I in exchange for its 100 percent interest in Mills Music. The remaining 53 percent of Belwin-Mills was transferred to the Max Winkler family, owners of the Belwin company.

Bibliography

Jasen, David A. 1988. *Tin Pan Alley*. New York: D. I. Fine.

Sanjek, Russell, and Sanjek, David. 1996. *Pennies from Heaven: The American Popular Music Business in the Twentieth Century*. New York: Da Capo Press.

Sheet Music

Confrey, Zez, comp. 1921. 'Kitten on the Keys.' New York: Mills Music.

Cox, Ida, comp. and lyr. 1923. 'Graveyard Dream Blues.' New York: Mills Music.

Dorsey, Thomas A., comp. and lyr. 1923. 'I Just Want A Daddy I Can Call My Own.' Chicago: Thomas A. Dorsey.

Hunter, Alberta, comp. and lyr. 1923. 'Down Hearted Blues.' New York: Mills Music.

Schoebel, Elmer, Mares, Paul, and Rappolo, Leon, comps. and lyrs. 1923. 'Farewell Blues.' New York: Mills Music.

Signorelli, Frank, and Napoleon, Phil, comps. and lyrs. 1922. 'Great White Way Blues.' New York: Mills Music.

Discographical References

Confrey, Zez. 'Kitten on the Keys.' Brunswick 2082. 1921: USA. Reissue: Confrey, Zez. 'Kitten on the Keys.' *Keyboard Wizards of the Gershwin Era, Vol. 4*. Pearl 9204. *1998*: USA.

Confrey, Zez. 'Kitten on the Keys.' Victor 18900. 1921: USA. Reissue: Confrey, Zez. 'Kitten on the Keys.' *Keyboard Wizards of the Gershwin Era, Vol. 4*. Pearl 9204. *1998*: USA.

Cotton Pickers. 'Great White Way Blues.' Brunswick 2380. 1922: USA.

Cox, Ida. 'Graveyard Dream Blues.' Paramount 12044. 1923: USA. Reissue: Cox, Ida. 'Graveyard Dream Blues.' *Complete Recorded Works, Vol. 1 (1923)*. Document DOCD-5322. *1997*: Austria.

Friar's Society Orchestra. 'Farewell Blues.' Gennett 4966. 1923: USA.

Moore, Monette. 'I Just Want A Daddy I Can Call My Own.' Paramount 12028. 1923: USA. Reissue: Moore, Monette. 'I Just Want A Daddy I Can Call My Own.' *Complete Recorded Works, Vol. 1 (1923–1924)*. Document DOCD-5338. *1995*: Austria.

Smith, Bessie. 'Down Hearted Blues.' Columbia A3844. 1923: USA. Reissue: Smith, Bessie. 'Down Hearted Blues.' *1923*. Classics 761. *1996*: USA.

DAVID SANJEK

—Northern Songs

Northern Songs, formed in 1963, was the music publishing company intimately connected with the Beatles' career and the songwriting partnership of John Lennon and Paul McCartney. When the company was formed, Lennon and McCartney each held 20 percent of the firm's assets; their manager, Brian Epstein, through his Nemporer Holdings, held 10 percent; and the British firm Dick James Music held 50 percent. These assets, which were to be held by the shareholders for an initial period of 10 years, consisted of 56 Beatles' copyrights, to which six new Lennon-McCartney songs would be added each year for the 10 years. In reality, however, the pair of songwriters had assigned the rights to their music to another company, Maclen Music, a wholly owned US subsidiary, which turned over all future copyrights to Northern Songs.

In 1965, 1.2 million shares of stock in Northern Songs were offered for public sale. Each share was worth $0.28, but was offered at $1.09. After the offer closed, Lennon and McCartney owned 30 percent of the stock, worth about $640,000; Epstein owned 7.5 percent; and the owners of Dick James Music – James and accountant Charles Silver – owned 37.5 percent. A further 1.6 percent was divided between George Harrison and Ringo Starr, the other two members of the Beatles. The remaining shares were owned by financial institutions.

In 1969, as discord within the group drove the Beatles apart, Northern Songs and Maclen Music were purchased by Associated Television Ltd. (ATV) for $2.5 million. The catalog now contained numerous Lennon-McCartney hits from 'Please Please Me' to 'Yesterday' and 'Strawberry Fields Forever.' ATV lost McCartney's material in 1973 when his contract with the company expired, but became co-publisher of material written by Lennon. ATV went on public sale in 1984 and was purchased by Michael Jackson for an estimated $40 million.

Bibliography

McCabe, Peter, and Schonfeld, Robert D. 1972. *Apple to the Core: The Unmaking of the Beatles*. London: Martin Brian and O'Keefe.

Sanjek, Russell, and Sanjek, David. 1996. *Pennies from Heaven: The American Popular Music Business in the Twentieth Century*. New York: Da Capo Press.

Sheet Music

Lennon, John, and McCartney, Paul, comps. and lyrs. 1963. 'Please Please Me.' London: Northern Songs Ltd.

Lennon, John, and McCartney, Paul, comps. and lyrs. 1965. 'Yesterday.' London: Northern Songs Ltd.

Lennon, John, and McCartney, Paul, comps. and lyrs. 1967. 'Strawberry Fields Forever.' London: Northern Songs Ltd.

Discographical References

Beatles, The. 'Please Please Me.' Parlophone R 4983. *1963*: UK.

Beatles, The. 'Strawberry Fields Forever.' Parlophone R 5570. *1967*: UK.

Beatles, The. 'Yesterday.' Capitol 5498. *1965*: USA.

DAVID SANJEK

—Jerome M. Remick & Company

In 1902, Jerome M. Remick (1869–1931) purchased the Detroit publisher Whitney, Warren Publishing Company. Soon thereafter, Remick bought out Louis Bernstein's half of Shapiro, Bernstein & Company and moved to New York City. In 1904, he bought out Maurice Shapiro from the firm now named Shapiro, Remick & Company, and renamed the firm Jerome H. Remick and Company. So successful was the company that its offices included a 200-seat auditorium that was used as a rehearsal and demonstration hall. The firm's editorial offices remained in Detroit, and more than 50 retail branches were established across the country. Because Remick's was a prolific publisher of songs, the company had to purchase its own printing plant in 1907. Remick's preeminence as a publisher lasted until the end of World War I. The firm specialized in piano rags, printing 1,800 during the first decade of the century. Its first million-copy seller in the genre was Charles L. Johnson's 'Dill Pickle Rag,' published in 1906. Warner Brothers purchased the firm in 1929.

Bibliography

Jasen, David A. 1988. *Tin Pan Alley*. New York: D. I. Fine.

Sanjek, Russell, and Sanjek, David. 1996. *Pennies from Heaven: The American Popular Music Business in the Twentieth Century*. New York: Da Capo Press.

Sheet Music

Johnson, Charles L., comp. 1906. 'Dill Pickle Rag.' New York: Jerome M. Remick & Co.

DAVID SANJEK

—The Richmond Organization

Music publishers have always been willing to adopt new methods to exploit their wares. One of the most prescient in the use of radio was Howard S. Richmond (1918–). He started The Richmond Organization, which became known as TRO, in New York as 1949 drew to a close. During his first full year of operation, he published six hits, including 'Hop Scotch Polka,' 'Music! Music! Music! (Put Another Nickel In),' 'Goodnight, Irene' and 'The Thing.'

The process by which he achieved such a record can be illustrated by his handling of 'Goodnight, Irene.' Richmond purchased several thousand copies of the Weavers' version of this Huddie Ledbetter song and mailed them to 1,500 disc jockeys across the United States. Airplay soon followed and, after only three performances on prime-time network radio, Richmond was able to sell 250,000 copies of sheet music of the song and half a million recordings in a single month. In time, Richmond's ability to use such forms of media exploitation took on an international dimension.

TRO is the publisher of some of Woody Guthrie's best-known songs, such as 'Pastures of Plenty' and 'This Land Is Your Land,' both of which were published under TRO's imprint, Ludlow Music. Over the years, TRO originated and acquired a number of such imprints, such as Hollis Music ('The Thing') and Cromwell Music ('Music! Music! Music! (Put Another Nickel In)' and 'Hop Scotch Polka').

At the end of the twentieth century, TRO was being managed by Richmond's son Larry (1954–).

Bibliography

Jasen, David A. 1988. *Tin Pan Alley.* New York: D. I. Fine.

Sanjek, Russell, and Sanjek, David. 1996. *Pennies from Heaven: The American Popular Music Business in the Twentieth Century.* New York: Da Capo Press.

Shapiro, Nat, and Pollock, Ned, eds. 1985. *Popular Music, 1920–1979: A Revised Cumulation.* 3 vols. Detroit, MI: Gale Research.

Sheet Music

Grean, Charles Randolph, comp. and lyr. 1950. 'The Thing.' New York: Hollis Music.

Guthrie, Woody. 1956. 'This Land Is Your Land.' New York: Ludlow Music.

Guthrie, Woody. 1960. 'Pastures of Plenty.' New York: Ludlow Music.

Ledbetter, Huddie [Leadbelly], and Lomax, John, comps. 1950. 'Goodnight, Irene.' New York: Ludlow Music.

Weiss, Stephan, and Baum, Bernie, comps. and lyrs. 1950. 'Music! Music! Music! (Put Another Nickel In).' New York: Cromwell Music.

Whitlock, Billy, Sigman, Carl, and Rayburn, Gene, comps. 1949. 'Hop Scotch Polka.' New York: Cromwell Music.

Discographical References

Brewer, Teresa. 'Music! Music! Music!' London 30023. 1950: USA. Reissue: Brewer, Teresa. 'Music! Music! Music!' *Music! Music! Music!: The Best of Teresa Brewer.* Varese 5616. *1995*: USA.

Guthrie, Woody. 'Pastures of Plenty.' Smithsonian Acetate 0033. 1947: USA. Reissue: Guthrie, Woody. 'Pastures of Plenty.' *This Land Is Your Land: The Asch Recordings, Vol. 1.* Smithsonian Folkways 40100. *1997*: USA.

Guthrie, Woody. 'This Land Is Your Land' (rec. Moses Asch). Folkways 2481. n.d.: USA. First issue: Guthrie, Woody. 'This Land Is Your Land.' *This Land Is My Land* (10″ LP). Folkways FP 27. *1951*: USA. Reissue: Guthrie, Woody. 'This Land Is Your Land.' *This Land Is Your Land: The Asch Recordings, Vol. 1.* Smithsonian Folkways 40100. *1997*: USA.

Harris, Phil. 'The Thing.' Victor 20-3968. 1950: USA. Reissue: Harris, Phil. 'The Thing.' *The Thing About Phil Harris.* ASV/Living Era 5191. *1996*: USA.

Lombardo, Guy, and His Royal Canadians. 'Hop-Scotch Polka.' Decca 24704. 1949: USA.

Weavers, The. 'Goodnight, Irene.' Decca 27332. 1950: USA. Reissue: Weavers, The. 'Goodnight, Irene.' *The Best of the Decca Years.* MCA 11465. *1996*: USA.

DAVID SANJEK

—Robbins Music Corporation

The Robbins Music Corporation was founded in 1922 when Maurice Richmond created a company to be led by his nephew, John J. 'Jack' Robbins (1894–1959). Robbins was an astute assessor of talent, particularly that of band leaders who could produce and promote music. This attribute helped to jump-start the career of Paul Whiteman, among others, for Robbins encouraged Victor to sign the band leader after he discovered him in 1926. Robbins's understanding of the mechanisms of promotion and production led to the publication by his company of a handbook detailing the ins and outs of the business – *Inside Stuff on How to Write Popular Songs*, written by *Variety*'s music editor, Abel Green.

In the late 1920s, Robbins began a relationship with the film industry that became a success. At first, while film was still silent, he published the work of composers of incidental music, including Erno Rapee and Hugo Reisenfeld. Soon afterward, as sound dominated and then took over the film industry, Robbins began an association with MGM as the publisher of material featured in film musicals. These included the first original such enterprise produced wholly in Hollywood, *The Broadway Melody* (1929).

Robbins's business was bought out by the film studio in 1935, but, before that sale, Robbins had become angered by what he felt to be the studio's inefficient and ill-conceived efforts to promote his music. This resulted in 1932 in a lawsuit against the studio and the American Society of Composers, Authors and Publishers (ASCAP), which Robbins won; as a result, he received more reasonable recompense for his material until the catalog was sold. Subsequently, he devoted his efforts to the jobbing and distribution of music.

Bibliography

Goldberg, Isaac. 1961 (1930). *Tin Pan Alley: A Chronicle of American Popular Music.* New York: Frederick Ungar.

Green, Abel. 1927. *Inside Stuff on How to Write Popular Songs*. New York: Robbins Music Corporation.

Jasen, David A. 1988. *Tin Pan Alley*. New York: D. I. Fine.

Sanjek, Russell, and Sanjek, David. 1996. *Pennies from Heaven: The American Popular Music Business in the Twentieth Century*. New York: Da Capo Press.

Filmography

The Broadway Melody, dir. Harry Beaumont. 1929. USA. 104 mins. Musical. Original music by Nacio Herb Brown, Arthur Freed.

DAVID SANJEK

—Root & Cady

Founding their publishing house in Chicago in 1858, Ebenezer T. Root and Chauncey M. Cady published most of the bestselling popular songs associated with the American Civil War (1861–65). The first of 80 songs and instrumental pieces associated with the war was in print within a few days of the start of hostilities. The company's principal composers were Root's brother, George Frederick Root, and Henry Clay Work. Root composed such songs as 'Tramp, Tramp, Tramp' and 'The Battle Cry of Freedom' (which sold over 350,000 sheet music copies during the war years). Work's bestsellers included 'Marching Through Georgia' and 'Kingdom Coming,' which had sheet music sales of 75,000 and, in addition, were anthologized in several songsters. In 1868, Root & Cady bought the firm of Henry Tolman, and sales exceeded 1 million copies.

The firm closed down after its offices and warehouse were destroyed in the great Chicago fire of 1871. John Church and Company purchased the catalog and also hired Cady as general manager. Cady subsequently moved to New York and set up his own publishing firm of C.M. Cady. This company had one outstanding commercial success with Henry Clay Work's 'Grandfather's Clock' (1876).

Bibliography

Epstein, Dena J. 1969. *Music Publishing in Chicago Before 1871: The Firm of Root and Cady, 1858–1871*. Detroit, MI: Information Coordinators.

Hamm, Charles. 1979. *Yesterdays: Popular Song in America*. New York: W.W. Norton.

Jackson, Richard, ed. 1976. *Popular Songs in Nineteenth-Century America: Complete Original Sheet Music for 64 Songs, Selected and with an Introduction and Notes*. New York: Dover Publications.

Sanjek, Russell. 1988. *American Popular Music and Its Business: The First Four Hundred Years. Vol. II: From 1790 to 1909*. New York: Oxford University Press.

Sheet Music

Root, George Frederick, comp. and lyr. 1862. 'The Battle Cry of Freedom.' Chicago: Root & Cady.

Root, George Frederick, comp. and lyr. 1864. 'Tramp, Tramp, Tramp.' Chicago: Root & Cady.

Work, Henry Clay, comp. and lyr. 1862. 'Kingdom Coming.' Chicago: Root & Cady.

Work, Henry Clay, comp. and lyr. 1865. 'Marching Through Georgia.' Chicago: Root & Cady.

Work, Henry Clay, comp. and lyr. 1876. 'Grandfather's Clock.' New York: C.M. Cady.

DAVE LAING

—Shapiro, Bernstein and Von Tilzer

The denizens of Tin Pan Alley were able and instinctive salesmen, and none were more so than Maurice Shapiro and Louis Bernstein, who mastered the system of persuading star performers to promote their material. Maurice Shapiro (1873–1911) began his publishing career in 1897 at Adelphi Music (which had changed its name to Consolidated Music Publishers by year's end, and changed it again, in 1898, to Universal Music Publishers). Louis Bernstein was Shapiro's brother-in-law and a real-estate dealer in New York City.

Around 1900, they established offices at Broadway and 6th Avenue, near Twenty-Eighth Street, close to what was, at the time, the heart of the theater world, and then relentlessly pursued the singing stars of the day. Bernstein referred to their partner, songwriter Harry Von Tilzer, as 'the greatest [song] plugger in America' for the skill with which he not only crafted material for individual performers but also convinced them to feature it in their acts. The firm's first great hit – 'A Bird in a Gilded Cage,' for which Von Tilzer wrote the music – sold 2 million copies in 1901, and soon afterward Von Tilzer left to set up his own publishing company.

Shapiro and Bernstein became adept at making use of virtually any form of popular expression that came their way in writing and promoting songs. One of the methods adopted by the firm to gain publicity involved allowing William Randolph Hearst in 1916, under a one-year contract, to print their copyrighted material in his newspapers. Songs published in this way sold, on average, 50,000 copies, reconfirming the partners' assumption that songs had to be heard by the people who would buy them. The company was always particularly successful with novelty songs. One of its most lucrative was 'The Prisoner's Song,' written by Guy Massey, which was recorded in 1924 by one of the first successful country performers, Vernon Dalhart, and which remained at the top of the bestseller lists for two years.

Unlike other Tin Pan Alley firms, Shapiro, Bernstein maintained its independence, and in 1947 it formed Mood Music in partnership with Decca Records and Columbia Pictures to publish music from *The Jolson Story*

(1946) and other film musicals. The firm has continued to be controlled by Shapiro's and Bernstein's heirs.

Bibliography

Goldberg, Isaac. 1961 (1930). *Tin Pan Alley: A Chronicle of American Popular Music*. New York: Frederick Ungar.

Sanjek, Russell, and Sanjek, David. 1996. *Pennies from Heaven: The American Popular Music Business in the Twentieth Century*. New York: Da Capo Press.

Sheet Music

Massey, Guy, comp. and lyr. 1924. 'The Prisoner's Song.' New York: Shapiro, Bernstein.

Von Tilzer, Harry, comp., and Lamb, Arthur J., lyr. 1900. 'A Bird in a Gilded Cage.' New York: Shapiro, Bernstein and Von Tilzer.

Discographical Reference

Dalhart, Vernon. 'The Prisoner's Song.' Victor 19427. 1924: USA. Reissue: Dalhart, Vernon. 'The Prisoner's Song.' *Smithsonian Collection of Country Music, Vol. 1*. Smithsonian 42-1. *1991*: USA.

Filmography

The Jolson Story, dir. Alfred E. Green and Alfred W. Green. 1946. USA. 128 mins. Docudrama. Original music by Morris W. Stoloff.

DAVID SANJEK

—Southern Music (including Peermusic)

Southern Music was formed in 1928 by the talent scout/engineer/producer Ralph Peer (1892–1960) and his then employer, Victor Records. Peer had initiated the commercial rise of country (then called 'hillbilly') music with his recording of Fiddlin' John Carson in June 1923, when he was working for the OKeh record label. Peer joined Victor in 1926, and a year later undertook his noteworthy audition and recording sessions in Bristol, Tennessee. There, in 1927, he recorded Jimmie Rodgers and the Carter Family for Victor, and Southern Music became the publisher of both Rodgers's and A.P. Carter's work. In the process of recording these and other individuals, Peer codified much of what later became the standard publishing and contractual relationships between artists and the music industry with regard to session fees and remuneration to writers for 'original' work. In common with many others, Peer bought copyrights from vernacular composers. However, he was more active and successful than most in merchandising such copyrights, thereby promoting commercially music previously in the public domain.

After selling his interest in Southern Music to Victor in 1928, Peer bought the firm back in 1932 when Victor's new owner, RCA, was threatened with an antitrust lawsuit. In the 1930s, he added jazz compositions to the Southern Music catalog, including works by Fats Waller, 'Jelly Roll' Morton and Louis Armstrong. In addition, he obtained the rights to many of the most popular mainstream compositions of the day, such as 'Georgia on My Mind,' 'Rockin' Chair' and 'Lazy River' by Hoagy Carmichael. Soon afterward, the company's roster became more international, particularly through the acquisition of a body of material from Mexico and Central and South America; some of the most popular songs of this genre were published by Peer: 'Tico-Tico,' 'Besamé Mucho' and 'Brazil.' By the mid-1950s, Peer had relinquished control of the business to his son, Ralph Peer II, who renamed the firm Peermusic.

At the end of the twentieth century, the Southern Music catalog, still owned by Peermusic, continued to be one of the broadest and most successful of all popular music catalogs.

Bibliography

Porterfield, Nolan. 1979. *Jimmie Rodgers: The Life and Times of America's Blue Yodeler*. Urbana, IL: University of Illinois Press.

Sheet Music

Abreu, Zequinha, comp., and Drake, Ervin, lyr. 1944. 'Tico-Tico.' New York: Southern Music.

Barroso, Ary, comp., and Russell, S.K., English lyr. 1943. 'Brazil.' New York: Southern Music.

Carmichael, Hoagy, comp. and lyr. 1930. 'Rockin' Chair.' New York: Southern Music.

Carmichael, Hoagy, comp., and Arodin, Sidney, lyr. 1931. 'Lazy River.' New York: Southern Music.

Carmichael, Hoagy, comp., and Gorrell, Stuart, lyr. 1931. 'Georgia on My Mind.' New York: Southern Music.

Velasquez, Consuelo, comp., and Skyler, Sunny, English lyr. 1943. 'Besamé Mucho.' New York: Southern Music.

Discographical References

Carmichael, Hoagy. 'Georgia on My Mind.' Victor 23013. 1930: USA. Reissue: Carmichael, Hoagy. 'Georgia on My Mind.' *Classic Hoagy Carmichael*. Smithsonian Collection 38. *1994*: USA.

Carmichael, Hoagy. 'Rockin' Chair.' Victor 38139. 1930: USA. Reissue: Carmichael, Hoagy. 'Rockin' Chair.' *Classic Hoagy Carmichael*. Smithsonian Collection 38. *1994*: USA.

Cugat, Xavier, and His Waldorf-Astoria Orchestra. 'Brazil.' Columbia 36651. 1943: USA. Reissue: Cugat, Xavier, and His Waldorf-Astoria Orchestra. 'Brazil.' *The Hit Sound of Xavier Cugat*. Charly 631. *1998*: UK.

Cugat, Xavier, and His Waldorf-Astoria Orchestra. 'Tico-Tico.' Columbia 36780. 1944: USA. Reissue: Cugat,

Xavier, and His Waldorf-Astoria Orchestra. 'Tico-Tico.' *The Hit Sound of Xavier Cugat*. Charly 631. *1998*: UK.

Dorsey, Jimmy, and His Orchestra. 'Besamé Mucho.' Decca 18574. 1943: USA. Reissue: Dorsey, Jimmy, and His Orchestra. 'Besamé Mucho.' *Best of Jimmy Dorsey*. Curb 77411. *1992*: USA.

Mills Brothers, The. 'Lazy River.' Decca 28458. 1948: USA. Reissue: Mills Brothers, The. 'Lazy River.' *The Mills Brothers: The Anthology (1931–1968)*. MCA 11279. *1995*: USA.

DAVID SANJEK

—M. Witmark and Company

It is a tribute to both individual enterprise and the energy of the age that M. Witmark and Company was founded in New York in 1886 by a trio of teenage brothers: Isidore (1869–1941), Julius (1870–1929), who was something of a child prodigy in the minstrel show, and Jay (1877–1950). The 'M' in the company's name referred to their father Marcus, who, for legal reasons, signed all the firm's documents. It was the failure of publisher Willis Woodward to give the teenage Julius Witmark a share in the royalties from the 1884 Lindsay/Woodward song 'Always Take Mother's Advice,' in return for performing it on a national tour, that led the Witmark brothers to set up their own publishing company (Sanjek 1988, 315).

M. Witmark broke new ground in the industry by initiating the system of song plugging, hiring an aggressive body of composers and arrangers to demonstrate and promote the company's material. It was, in addition, the first company to house under one roof a complete music organization, comprising songwriters, pluggers, arrangers, and even a 'Minstrel Department,' which produced scores, scripts, costumes and makeup. Isidore also claimed (Witmark and Goldberg 1939) that Witmark pioneered the idea of capitalizing on contemporary subjects in popular song.

The theatrical songwriters published by Witmark included such renowned individuals as George M. Cohan, Victor Herbert and Sigmund Romberg. In addition, Witmark represented the work of many of the writers of the period's notorious 'coon' songs, such as Ernest Hogan's 'All Coons Look Alike to Me' and Theodore Metz's 'A Hot Time in the Old Town.'

M. Witmark's move from 14th Street and Union Square to 28th Street marked the inauguration of the district that came to be known as Tin Pan Alley. The company was sold to Warner Brothers in 1929 for $900,000. According to Jasen (1988, 8), Witmark was the first US music publisher to open a London office.

Bibliography

Jasen, David A. 1988. *Tin Pan Alley*. New York: D. I. Fine.

Sanjek, Russell. 1988. *American Popular Music and Its Business: The First Four Hundred Years. Vol. II: From 1790 to 1909*. New York: Oxford University Press.

Sanjek, Russell, and Sanjek, David. 1996. *Pennies from Heaven: The American Popular Music Business in the Twentieth Century*. New York: Da Capo Press.

Witmark, Isidore, and Goldberg, Isaac. 1939. *From Ragtime to Swingtime: The Story of the House of Witmark*. New York: Furman.

Sheet Music

Hogan, Ernest, comp. and lyr. 1896. 'All Coons Look Alike to Me.' New York: M. Witmark.

Lindsay, Jennie, and Woodward, Willis, comps. and lyrs. 1884. 'Always Take Mother's Advice.' New York: Willis Woodward Co.

Metz, Theodore, comp., and Hayden, Joe, lyr. 1896. 'A Hot Time in the Old Town.' New York: Willis Woodward Co.

DAVID SANJEK

—Lawrence Wright Music Company

Lawrence Wright (1888–1964) began the Lawrence Wright Music Company, a publishing and retail business, in Leicester, England in 1906, to sell music and publish his own songs. His greatest early success was not with one of his own compositions, but with a topical song he heard performed by Will Geddes, a street singer – 'Don't Go Down in the Mine, Dad' (1910). A mining disaster in the northwest of England a few days after the first copies went on sale 'inspired [him] to have printed across the top of every copy, "Half the profits from the first ten thousand sold will go to the relief fund for the Whitehaven pit disaster"' (Wright 1988, 5).

By 1912, Wright had set up business in London's Denmark Street, the area that would later become the city's epicenter of music publishing and promotion. From here, he worked relentlessly to interest music hall artists in performing his published songs, whether written by himself (and now published under the pseudonym 'Horatio Nicholls') or by others, such as William Hargreaves, whose 'Burlington Bertie from Bow' was made famous on the London stage by Hargreaves's US-born wife, Ella Shields. In the 1920s, Wright expanded the company's interests into new areas, presenting a highly successful summer show at the seaside resort of Blackpool in 1924 (it ran until 1956) and, in 1926, launching *Melody Maker* as (the first title page declared) 'a monthly magazine for all who are directly or indirectly interested in the production of popular music.' In all of these ventures, promoting the Wright catalog was the primary aim.

Wright also recognized the increasing importance of the media to the company's fortunes and was very successful in getting company songs broadcast and recorded. When he took the front page of the national newspaper, the *Daily Mail*, for £1,400 to advertise the release of the sheet music and the parts for various arrangements of the song 'Among My Souvenirs' in October 1927, the advertisement included a list of no fewer than 17 already available recordings, on nine different labels, and the exhortation to 'Listen for "Souvenirs" on the wireless tonight,' when it would be performed by four different bands. Wright's sense of the value of publicity also extended to a flair for stunts, as was evident when he engaged camels to ride around Piccadilly Circus in London to promote his song 'Sahara.'

In the 1930s, the company began acquiring the UK publishing rights to the songs of many US songwriters, including Harold Arlen, Hoagy Carmichael and Duke Ellington. After Wright's death, the Lawrence Wright Music Company's catalog was seen as a valuable commercial property and was owned at different times by Northern Songs and Michael Jackson.

Bibliography

White, Mark. 1983. *'You Must Remember This': Popular Songwriters, 1900–1980*. London: Warne.

Wright, Lawrette. 1988. *Lawrence Wright: Souvenirs for a Century*. Chard, Somerset: Matthews Wright Press.

Sheet Music

Geddes, Will, and Donnelly, Robert, comps. and lyrs. 1910. 'Don't Go Down in the Mine, Dad.' Leicester: Lawrence Wright Music Co.

Hargreaves, William, comp. and lyr. 1915. 'Burlington Bertie from Bow.' London: Lawrence Wright Music Co.

Wright, Lawrence, comp., and Frederick, Jean, lyr. 1924. 'Sahara.' London: Lawrence Wright Music Co.

Wright, Lawrence, comp., and Leslie, Edgar, lyr. 1927. 'Among My Souvenirs.' London: Lawrence Wright Music Co.

DAVID HORN

Music Publishing

Music publishing is the complex of activities carried out in order to exploit commercially the work of composers and songwriters. These activities include the acquisition and encouragement of creative talent, the manufacture, sale or hire of printed music, the plugging of musical works to broadcasters, record companies or film producers, and the exploitation and administration of the rights granted to composers and songwriters under copyright law. Those customarily involved in the business of music publishing include specialist music publishers, authors' collection societies and the music creators themselves. During the nineteenth and early twentieth centuries, music publishing was at the center of the music industry as a whole. In the last 50 years or so, however, music publishing has been supplanted by sound recording as the most powerful sector of the industry.

Nevertheless, the global turnover of the music publishing business was calculated to be over $6 billion in 1996. This figure included revenues from printed music, from the use of music in films, television programs and commercials, and from the users of music licensed by the national collection societies. Only 10 percent of the amount came from the sale of sheet music, with 42 percent each coming from payments for performing right usage and mechanical right usage. The remainder came from interest payments and other sources.

The largest national market was the United States ($1.1 billion), followed by Germany ($750 million) and Japan ($626 million). However, the countries where per capita publishing revenues were highest were clustered in continental Europe. They included Austria, Italy and The Netherlands.

History

Books of printed music were among the earliest products of the European printing industry, which developed after movable type was invented by Gutenberg in 1460. In most countries, a single printer or a group of printers was given the monopoly for the printing and distribution of books of all kinds. Where absolute monarchies persisted (as in France and Sweden), such monopolies continued until the latter part of the eighteenth century.

The first specialist music printer was Petrucci of Venice, who produced 61 music publications between 1500 and 1520. Between 1580 and 1600, over 400 books of the then fashionable madrigals were published in Europe. In Germany alone, over 1,000 printers produced music publications in the 200 years after 1500. There was a growing international trade in printed music, with publishers from Venice and elsewhere attending the annual book fair in Frankfurt.

Collections of popular songs were published increasingly in the seventeenth century. These were called *canzonetta* in Italy and *airs à boire* in France, where the monopolist printer Ballard published annual songbooks from 1658 and monthly books from 1696. A few printers, such as Christian Egeholff of Frankfurt, published collections of folk songs. Alongside this there was a persistent market, especially among the artisan and peasant classes, for songsheets (known in England as broadsides) containing only the lyrics of current or traditional ballads.

By 1700, the quality and accuracy of music printing had improved considerably with the spread of engraving techniques, which replaced the original movable type technology. Although the patronage system often gave the royal or aristocratic patron exclusive use of a composer's works, many unauthorized editions appeared throughout Europe. Thus, in the 1760s, Haydn's compositions were republished in Paris, Amsterdam, London and Leipzig without any payment to the composer. Within a decade, Haydn himself had joined forces with Artaria of Vienna to produce fully authorized editions of his works.

The seventeenth and eighteenth centuries also saw the growth of a large middle class devoted to amateur music-making. There was a consequent demand for both domestic instruments (such as harpsichords, lutes and guitars) and printed music, which was increasingly commissioned by publishers to service this new market. This developed earliest in the mercantile centers of The Netherlands and England, where John Playford's musical and dance tutors were bestsellers throughout the second half of the seventeenth century. In Germany, Breitkopf of Leipzig sold large numbers of his editions of the sentimental *Sturm und Drang* genre. Subscription publishing of music, whereby consumers received monthly packages of printed music, was a feature of the eighteenth century, when capitalist economies were taking root in most of Western and Southern Europe and, in the words of one authority, 'accompanied keyboard sonatas were the commercial music of later eighteenth century Europe' (Plantinga 1977, 51).

During the eighteenth century and for much of the nineteenth century, the job of publishing was often combined with that of instrument manufacture, retailing, managing the careers of musicians or even composing itself. At the start of the century, the English composer Purcell would solicit subscriptions for editions of his works through newspaper advertising.

The modern forms of music publishing began to take shape in the early nineteenth century, with the formation of specialist music publishing firms by such figures as Ricordi (1808) in Milan, Boosey (1795), Chappell (1810) and Novello (1811) in London, and Firth, Hall and Pond (1815) in New York. By 1881, Ricordi had published 47,000 works by 2,500 different authors, including the opera composer Verdi. Ricordi remained under family ownership until 1994, when its parent company Dischi Ricordi was purchased by BMG. Novello pioneered the mass production of cheaply priced editions, while Firth, Hall and Pond published the works of North America's first great popular songwriter, Stephen Foster. In 1854, Firth, Hall and Pond was able to boast in an advertisement that it had sold over 130,000 copies of Foster's 'Old Folks At Home' and 90,000 of his 'My Old Kentucky Home' (Austin 1987, 207–208).

Throughout the nineteenth century, the widespread purchase of pianos by middle-class and working-class households in Europe and the Americas stimulated the expansion of the publishing business. In Germany alone, 5,474 works were published in 1885, of which 231 were for symphony orchestra, 1,862 for voice and the majority for piano or other solo instrument.

In the latter part of the nineteenth century, music publishing in the United States began increasingly to reflect the mass marketing and manufacturing practises observable in other enterprises. Prior to this time, US publishers had allowed (expected) the public to come to them; now the roles would be reversed, as publishers actively sought to expand their market (Goldberg 1930). At this time, too, the commercial relationship between the theater and music publishing became more prominent. As vaudeville took over from the minstrel show as the principal form of public theatrical entertainment (expanding its audience in the process to include women and families), it adopted a more aggressive approach to its role in the marketing of newly published material. A major figure in this practise was the New York-based producer Tony Pastor who, as well as 'cleaning up' the stage, introduced one or more new songs to the public every Monday night for 30 years, from 1865 to 1895.

Tin Pan Alley

This was the prelude to an even more dramatic increase in sheet music sales in the early part of the twentieth century. The growth was most evident in the United States, where a new intensity of composition by highly professional songwriters combined with innovative marketing by a new generation of publishers and aggressive retailing, through department stores as well as through the traditional musical instrument emporiums, to expand sales of the biggest hit songs into the millions. A major element of the marketing campaigns was the public performance of material (for example, in department stores) by individuals in the publishers' employ known as 'song pluggers.' Plugging was also aimed at others in the business, especially popular theatrical performers. When a new song was interpolated into a performer's act, the performer's features were regularly added to the cover of the sheet music, and some performers were given a share of the songwriting credits, however minimal their contribution.

The center of the popular music publishing industry was a small section of midtown Manhattan around 28th Street in New York, known as Tin Pan Alley. The highly entrepreneurial publishers included T.B. Harms (founded 1875), M. Witmark and Company (1886), the Leo Feist Music Publishing Company (1895), Shapiro, Bernstein and Von Tilzer (ca. 1900) and Jerome M. Remick & Company (1902). Sheet music sales of popular tunes experienced a similar boom in Western Europe. London had its own Tin Pan Alley in Denmark Street through such publishers as Francis, Day and Hunter (1877) and Lawrence Wright (1906), and the Faubourg St-Martin district of Paris was home to 300 publishers in the 1920s. Other leading European companies founded around this time included Fazer in Finland (1897), Valentim de Carvalho in Portugal (1914) and Hans Sikorski in Germany (1928).

In the 1920s, talking pictures brought a new market for popular songs. In the United States, the newly powerful film studios began to acquire or establish music publishers to control and profit from the supply of songs for the 'talkies.' Paramount Pictures' predecessor, Famous-Lasky Corporation, founded Famous Music in 1928, and in the late 1990s Paramount still controlled the publishing firm as a subsidiary of the Viacom conglomerate. Warner Brothers purchased several companies as the foundation of its modern multinational publishing firm. The MGM studio also bought into the music business through the acquisition of a 51 percent interest in Robbins Music.

During the nineteenth century, some European publishers had set up agencies in the United States and Canada to protect their copyrights. One of the most successful had been the Anglo-Canadian Music Publishers' Association, which flourished from 1885 to 1920. Now, the newly powerful US publishing industry began to seek foreign outlets. In 1906, Witmark of New York opened an office in Paris through which it imported copies of the latest US hits, which were snapped up by Parisian band leaders. In 1929 came the first takeover of a European publisher: Louis Dreyfus bought a controlling interest in the long-established Chappell company of London.

By the 1950s, sales of sound recordings were exceeding those of sheet music and, increasingly, publishers were withdrawing from distributing printed copies of their repertoire. This job was taken on by specialist printed music firms, which devised music book formats as well as retaining the single-song sheets. In the United States these companies were led by Hal Leonard and Cherry Lane, while in Britain by the 1970s the print market was dominated by two companies – Music Sales and IMP.

The most important feature of the publishing industry in this period, however, was the emulation by many record companies in the United States of the earlier example of film studios in forming publishing subsidiaries. In the popular song field it became customary for R&B or rock 'n' roll singer-composers to be signed simultaneously to a record and a publishing deal. Chess Records had Arc Publishing, Atlantic had Duchess and Columbia had April Music.

The major companies that dominated the record industry also bought up publishers, and sometimes sold them to raise cash. In the 1950s, EMI acquired several key British firms, among them Francis, Day and Hunter, Keith Prowse and B. Feldman. EMI next eyed up targets in the United States, buying Columbia Pictures' catalogs for $23.5 million in 1976, the SBK company in 1989 and Filmtrax in 1990. MCA Records set the trend in the United States by purchasing the Leeds Music catalog, and its founder Lou Levy, in 1964.

PolyGram bought the prestigious Chappell catalog in 1968, only to sell it in 1986 to a consortium led by Freddie Bienstock. In turn, Chappell was sold in 1989 to Warner Communications, whose publishing division was renamed Warner Chappell.

Having previously purchased the MGM and UA catalogs, CBS Records was persuaded in 1986 to sell its considerable publishing interests to the buccaneering trio of Stephen Swid, Martin Bandier and Charles Koppelman. Three years later, EMI paid a record price for this catalog, now called SBK. In 1994, EMI pulled off a further coup by purchasing half of Jobete Music, the home of the classic Motown catalog. Through these acquisitions, EMI and Warner Chappell became by far the largest music publishers in the world in the 1990s.

Other major record companies were equally active in the market, although they bought numerous small independent catalogs. After the German media company Bertelsmann purchased RCA Records and its music publishing division in 1986, BMG Music (under former Chappell executive Nicholas Firth) bought or acquired the rights to over 100 smaller catalogs from around the world.

Both PolyGram and CBS Records (now owned by Sony) belatedly realized the folly of selling off their publishing interests and set out to buy their way back into the publishing business. PolyGram rapidly built up an impressive portfolio with the purchase of Dick James Music (early Elton John–Bernie Taupin songs), Island Music and a share of Andrew Lloyd Webber's Really Useful Group. When Seagram-Universal bought the PolyGram group in 1998, PolyGram's publishing catalogs became part of the Universal Music publishing division.

Sony bought the major country music catalog of Tree Music and concluded a lucrative administration deal for ATV Music, a catalog including 250 Lennon-McCartney songs which singer Michael Jackson had bought for $47.5 million in 1984. Another pop star who invested in publishing was Paul McCartney: he had previously sought to buy ATV, but had to be content with building his own publishing firm, MPL, which controlled many of the works of Buddy Holly.

One region that was immune to this trend was Eastern

Europe, where Communist governments had taken music publishers into state ownership. In the USSR all publishing was in the hands of the Muzika firm (founded in 1918), while the Deutscher Verlag für Musik in Leipzig controlled publishing in East Germany. In Czechoslovakia, Supraphon and Opus were combined publishers and record labels.

Music Publishing in Asia and Latin America

During the 1980s and 1990s, the multinational music companies' penetration of the music markets in many parts of Asia and Latin America brought about conflicts over the system of payment to songwriters and composers. In Southeast Asia and India, the custom had been for writers to sell their works outright to record companies or film producers for a small lump sum, or for writers to be employees of such companies. Changes to copyright laws to conform with international standards, and the formation of authors' rights societies and of music publishing companies challenged this customary system and, by the late 1990s, composers in several countries were beginning to receive royalty payments. The situation was made more complex where lyricists produced Chinese-language versions of Western hits and their record company employers claimed that the new lyrics had fully replaced those of the original English-language writer. Another important innovation was the introduction of a collective agreement among multinational publishers and record companies for the payment of mechanical royalties on soundcarrier sales throughout the region.

The position was somewhat different in Latin America, where sheet music publishing had been well established in Argentina and Brazil since the middle of the nineteenth century. By the late 1990s, the Federation of Latin American Publishers (FLADEM) had 4,000 members, mostly small family-owned firms. However, the development of a collecting society system had been slow, and many broadcasters were paying only very low royalties or none at all. Societies were also inefficient, taking one-third of the money they collected in administrative expenses.

Publishers and Composers

The relationship between composers and publishers has never been harmonious. The practise of paying royalties to composers based on the level of financial success of their songs did not become commonplace in Europe and North America until the second half of the twentieth century. Even then, there were other regions of the world and certain sectors of the industry (R&B, film and television music) where a royalty system did not automatically pertain.

The alternative to a royalty agreement was the simple purchase of a song by a publisher for as little as $10 in the Tin Pan Alley era in the United States. The composer then gave up all right to further recompense. 'The simple reason so many composers became publishers,' wrote Hamm (1979, 289–90), 'was to share in the profits of a song that sold well.' In the 1880s, British publishers paid composers between £10 and £100 for each song. Lyrics were usually bought outright, while composers might receive a small royalty of 2d or 3d. In any case, publishers at this time were more concerned with persuading singers to feature their new songs. In both Britain and the United States, singers were given fees for performances and, sometimes, royalties on copies sold.

The buyout system could also be damaging to publishers, since it meant that the composer of a successful song had no reason to bring his/her next composition to the same publisher. One publisher who grasped this point was Ralph Peer, who founded his Southern Music on royalty payments and exclusive contracts with his blues and hillbilly singer-composers.

Another potential source of friction was the attribution of authorship of a song or instrumental piece. In the jazz world, it was commonplace for a publisher or even a band leader to 'have exercised what might be called a sort of droit de seigneur so far as their sidemen's compositions were concerned, either taking over the rights completely or at least sharing them' (Carr 1982, 109). When publishers did consent to authors retaining the copyright in a song, the standard agreement was for the composer to receive 10 percent of the retail price of printed music and 50 percent of other earnings, such as record royalties. However, during the 1960s and 1970s in North America and Britain, this 50/50 split for the life of copyright between publisher and writer was gradually replaced by a more favorable situation for the songwriter. In the competitive pop music market, both new and established artist-composers were often able to negotiate 60 percent or more from mechanical and other earnings for a shorter period of five or 10 years. There was also an increasing trend for the leading specialist pop writers to form their own publishing companies, although these were generally managed by a major publisher.

The Role of Collection Bodies

During the twentieth century, the collection societies established by publishers and composers assumed a major role in the publishing business, as income from the exercise of performing rights and mechanical rights overtook that from sales of printed music and from commissions. The collection societies were responsible for negotiating rates of payment for the myriad uses of music in the entertainment industries and in many other areas of commercial life, such as airliners, retail outlets and telephone 'on-hold' services. With the advent of the Internet and its new technologies for downloading music onto computer hard drives or other playback systems, the societies took on a new role in policing and licensing such activities on behalf of the publishing industry. In this new environment, too, some publishers saw opportunities for themselves to play an active role in marketing the works of songwriters and composers, especially where those writers were also performers. Publishers, they claimed, might now compete with record companies in distributing recordings in this context.

Bibliography

Austin, William W. 1987. *'Susanna,' 'Jeanie,' and 'The Old Folks at Home': The Songs of Stephen C. Foster from His Time to Ours*. 2nd ed. Urbana, IL: University of Illinois Press.

Carr, Ian. 1982. *Miles Davis*. London: Quartet.

Feist, Leonard. 1980. *An Introduction to Popular Music Publishing in America*. New York: National Music Publishers Association.

Goldberg, Isaac. 1930. *Tin Pan Alley: A Chronicle of the American Popular Music Racket*. New York: The John Day Company. (Reprinted as *Tin Pan Alley: A Chronicle of American Popular Music*. New York: Frederick Ungar, 1961.)

Hamm, Charles. 1979. *Yesterdays: Popular Song in America*. New York: Norton.

Krummel, D.W., and Sadie, Stanley, eds. 1990. *Music Printing and Publishing*. New York and London: W.W. Norton.

National Music Publishers Association (NMPA). 1997. *The Global Music Publishing Industry*. New York: NMPA.

Plantinga, Leon. 1977. *Clementi: His Life and Music*. London and New York: Oxford University Press.

Sanjek, Russell. 1988. *American Popular Music and Its Business: The First Four Hundred Years*. 3 vols. New York and Oxford: Oxford University Press.

Sanjek, Russell, and Sanjek, David. 1996. *Pennies from Heaven: The American Popular Music Business in the Twentieth Century*. New York: Da Capo Press.

Sheet Music

[Foster, Stephen C., comp. and lyr.]. 1851. 'Old Folks At Home: Ethiopian Melody, As Sung by the Christy Minstrels. Written and Composed by E.P. Christy.' New York: Firth, Hall and Pond.

Foster, Stephen C., comp. and lyr. 1853. 'My Old Kentucky Home, Good Night.' New York: Firth, Hall and Pond.

DAVE LAING with DAVID SANJEK and DAVID HORN

Sheet Music

Sheet music is a form of music publishing on a single sheet of paper or a small number of sheets, usually folded. Most popular sheet music contains one piece of music, but an edition containing up to three or four items may still be referred to as sheet music. Up to the early decades of the twentieth century, particularly in Europe and North America, sheet music was the dominant form in which popular music was sold and disseminated. The term 'sheet music' itself appears to have become established by the mid-nineteenth century to describe an object that already had a history. Its appearance coincided with the beginnings of an ideological distinction between 'classical' and 'popular,' but it was used to cover music in both spheres. Its currency may initially have been greater in the United States: the 1842 British *Copyright Act* refers to 'Sheets of Music,' but in the 1850s the North American music trade was using 'sheet music' as a useful collective term. *Dwight's Journal of Music*, for example, reported 'a new tariff of retail prices for sheet music, of which the sale is so enormous in this country' ('War,' 1855).

Popular music in sheet music form constitutes an enormous body of material with many typical features and many variations. The piece or pieces contained in an item of popular sheet music are most often songs for solo voice and accompaniment, although some (mainly nineteenth-century) songs are presented in arrangements for solo voice and four-part chorus. Instrumental music is represented chiefly by piano pieces (waltzes, polkas and marches – often available as solos or duets – or piano rags) and by arrangements (such as songs arranged as instrumentals for organ, or piano arrangements of popular orchestral pieces). Accompaniment is usually for solo piano, although in the nineteenth century publishers often published separate editions for piano and guitar accompaniment, reflecting the popularity of both instruments in the middle-class home. Later, tablature for ukulele or banjo was often added, reflecting not so much domestic use as prominence in professional performance. Tablature was revived in the 1960s for the guitar, in an attempt to create a new market among young guitarists. Chord symbols were another added feature.

Many pieces of popular sheet music omit performance indicators altogether, but the most common practise is to provide an initial description of tempo and nothing further, unless there is a marked change in the music.

Tempo indicators are regularly given in Italian, as in classical music (this was even the practise in music hall songs; Ingle's and Chevalier's 'My Old Dutch,' for example, bears the rubric 'andante moderato'). In the Anglophone world, these switched increasingly to English in the twentieth century – so that, for example, 'If I Were a Rich Man' (Bock/Harnick) is recommended to be played with 'a moderate lilt.'

Most published sheet music has a front and back cover containing illustrations and text, but this was not always the case. The earliest 'songsheets' consisted of a single page. In the first sheet music to have 'covers,' the covers were blank, being in effect the non-printed side of a sheet of paper that had been folded in half. Up to the 1820s, some sheet music was accompanied by an illustration, usually at the head of the music, but this involved expensive engraving and it was more common for publishers to present their music without adornment, save perhaps for florid engraving of the title and other information. But the invention of lithography at the end of the eighteenth century heralded a major change in how music was presented. With the advent of the illustrated front cover, produced in black and white at first but from 1837 increasingly in full color, sheet music acquired a major additional selling point, drawing on and reinforcing that of the music. It also created, it could be argued, an art form in its own right, whatever the music inside.

Sheet music covers as a whole show a marked tendency to give prominence to the name of a performer or group particularly associated with the piece in the public mind. This was already happening well before the advent of the illustrated front cover (for example, the songsheet 'Jenny Long Resisted,' published in London by John Walsh around 1700, is headed 'Sung by Mss Campion'; the words 'set by Mr. Leveridge' appear in the middle of the sheet (Smith 1968, 16 and plate 32)), but the marketing potential of the link was more fully exploited by the greater prominence that the full-page cover could offer. On the cover of 'Zip Coon,' for example, a minstrel song published in the early 1830s, no author is given (authorship has remained uncertain to this day), but underneath an illustration of the minstrel dandy character the cover reads 'Sung by Mr. G.W. Dixon' (Jackson 1976, 258). Dixon was one of the leading individual blackface minstrel performers of the day, and attaching his name to the cover was clearly seen as a selling point. Songwriter Stephen Foster recognized so clearly the market value of attaching the name of minstrel troupe leader E.P. Christy to the cover of his song 'Old Folks At Home' that he sold Christy the right to be named as the song's author also (Austin 1987, 202–203).

As it became standard practise to name a song's author(s) on the cover, the performer often retained greater typographical prominence. In an 1881 edition of the satirical music hall song 'Now You're Married I Wish You Joy,' for example, the name of performer Herbert Campbell appears in print almost twice the size of that of authors Hugh Clendon and Harry Nicholls (Locantro 1985, item 9). Many sheet music covers from the first half of the twentieth century combine a lithographic illustration with a photographic insert of featured performers (a practise that allowed local performers to be given prominence on songs published under license outside their country of origin). An equal number of covers from this period are dominated by a large photograph of a performer. In some cases, a specific recording is mentioned. A 1942 edition of 'Jealousy,' published in London by Lawrence Wright, has a photograph of Leslie Hutchinson ('Hutch'), with the caption 'recorded on H.M.V. B.D.1008.' Sometimes, the performer was so well known as to need no clear identification. The cover of the Wright edition of 'When It's Sleepy Time Down South,' published in 1931, is almost entirely taken up by a photograph of band leader Jack Payne, who remains unidentified save for his barely decipherable scrawled dedication across the picture.

The use of the front cover to promote the music inside is complemented on much sheet music by the use of the spare space on the back to advertise other music in the publisher's catalog. Sometimes, this advertising – which can also occur on the inside of the front or back cover if the music itself occupies an odd number of pages – includes short extracts from the music advertised.

Precursors

Sheet music's most immediate predecessor was the 'distinctively English' songsheet (Krummel 1975, 116). In the late seventeenth century, English publishers began issuing what would become a huge number of single-sided folio songsheets, 'in [which] was circulated the vocal music of such popular English musical institutions as the operatic stage and the summer gardens' (Krummel 1975, 116). Many were issued by leading London publishers such as Thomas Cross or John Walsh (who at one time inaugurated a series of 'weekly songs' (Smith 1968, 10)), alongside their editions of flute sonatas or lessons for the harpsichord, but many also appeared bearing names of neither publisher nor printer. Krummel (1980, 267) estimates that a level of several hundred editions per year was reached soon after 1700 and was maintained throughout the eighteenth century. Whether left as single songsheets or gathered together into collections, they provided the foundation of what would become the British commercial music publishing industry.

The broadside ballad, which began life much earlier, was also single-sided, but there were significant differences between it and the songsheet. Whereas the broadside was often topical and informative, the songsheet was generally not. Many broadsides had no notation, and those that did generally used a traditional ballad tune rendered (often inaccurately) without accompaniment. The songsheet, by contrast, had a continuo accompaniment and often an additional part for flute (in Krummel's words, 'the intervention of competent musicians is everywhere evident' (1975, 169)). Broadsides had a wide audience and were intended to be performed and heard in the open air, but songsheets were specifically aimed at the musically literate, amateur and professional, and were increasingly being sold to the emerging urban bourgeoisie for performance at home.

Songsheets were more closely related to songbooks, the anthologies of solo songs with continuo accompaniment and distinctive titles and identities published in a variety of formats, from tall folio to oblong quarto, and in numerous editions, by John Playford and others in the second half of the seventeenth century. Songsheets emerged out of songbooks, as eighteenth-century publishers saw a market for individual items. Their success was such that publishers altered their songbooks accordingly, making them, in effect, little more than collections of available songsheets, with no special identity.

An important development in public leisure in the second half of the eighteenth century, affecting London in particular, provided publishers of songsheets and song collections with a major opportunity to expand their markets. The pleasure gardens of Marylebone, Ranelagh and, most famously, Vauxhall attracted large numbers of visitors and featured regular concerts, often involving the performance of newly written songs. As before, live performance was a key element in creating a market for the music, but the gardens offered opportunity on a new scale. Not only did the output of songs increase to meet the growth in performance (the prolific James Hook, who acted as organist and composer for both Marylebone and Vauxhall in his career, is said to have written over 2,000 songs), but songwriters began to tailor their songs to reflect the greater variety in standards of musical competence among their anticipated purchasers. Publishers for their part responded to the greater numbers of people who had enjoyed the performances, and wished to re-create something of them at home, by increasing their output. No doubt salesmanship in the very popular music stores (often run by the publishers themselves) responded also to those in the audience who had vowed that next day they would buy the music of a particular song, 'if [they] could but remember the tune' (Wroth 1896, 296).

In France, after the Revolution, single songsheets began to be published more often, but the new market that was most significant in terms of future developments was that which began to emerge in the United States in the last decade of the century. Immigrant publishers such as Benjamin Carr, who moved from London to Philadelphia, set up publishing businesses in the growing cities and, in the absence of an international copyright agreement, for many years drew heavily on reprints of European editions (including the songs of Hook) for much of their music. Among the music by native composers, songs were the most frequent, and by the turn of the century Carr, George Gilfert in New York and others were issuing single songs of North American origin, such as Carr's own 'Poor Richard' or Davy's and Lewis's 'Crazy Jane,' as folded sheets. 'Poor Richard' was available for $0.25 separately, or for $0.62 in an eight-page edition with two other songs (Dichter and Shapiro 1941, 12–13).

Before Tin Pan Alley

Of the changes that popular sheet music experienced in the nineteenth century, the most radical concerned its appearance. The development of the illustrated song cover was a landmark, for it not only represented an effective alliance of art and commerce, but also provided popular sheet music for the first time with a clear identity of its own in the publishing world. Each individual item had the potential to establish its own identity also, one that might make a major contribution to sales. Even when, as was often the case, the publisher decided against an illustrated cover, the space available on a printed cover for large bold lettering allowed the song's title in particular to have an impact.

For most of the nineteenth century, publishing popular sheet music was not a specialist activity. Publishers included it as part of their catalogs alongside orchestral scores and songbooks. Many, including those with large catalogs, such as Firth & Pond in New York, were also instrument manufacturers and retailers. The price of popular sheet music was kept comparatively high: in the United States, the average price remained $0.25, rising eventually to $0.60; in Britain, songs sold for three or four shillings. It was in Britain that publisher Alfred Novello introduced the idea of 'cheap music,' not to sell more popular songs but to widen the appreciation and performance of classical music – and to break the hold of trade unions in the process (A Short History, 1887, 32ff.). In the United States, by contrast, a move to discount the price of European classical music in 1855 and reflect the fact that, as it was not yet covered by international copyright agreement, it cost publishers nothing in royalties, was defeated by the formation by a group of publishers of a Board of Music Trade. The Board put in place a system of price control affecting all music which remained in place for 30 years (Sanjek 1983, 5).

Despite the relatively high price of popular sheet music, its sales steadily increased. Some of the reasons were to be found in societal changes: the increase in urban (and suburban) populations; the advent of the railway and the steamship; better postal services. These changes, while proceeding at different speeds in different countries, permitted overall improvement in communication and distribution and overall growth in awareness of popular culture. Other reasons for rising sales lay within musical life itself, in particular the growth of music teaching and the increasing popularity of the piano. The size of the market for popular sheet music by the 1850s was part of a growth in the music trade as a whole. In 1852, the turnover of the North American music industry reached $27 million ('Music Trade,' 1853).

Up to the 1890s, sheet music publishers engaged in little systematic exploitation of their merchandise – by and large, they allowed members of the public to select the music they enjoyed without undue prompting – but they often benefited from the entrepreneurial activity of others. One such entrepreneur was English songwriter-performer Henry Russell. Russell, who toured North America in the 1830s and 1840s, attracted large audiences to his theatrical performances of his own songs. At the same time, he supplied those songs in a steady stream to his publishers. Although the link between performance and sales was common knowledge among publishers, Russell was more prepared to act upon that perception, and in making touring a significant part of the equation he helped to establish an enduring principle.

Russell also recognized that the North American middle classes were, as Hamm has put it, 'with no great history of exposure to classical music, nor to the culture it represented,' but were eager for music to play and hear (1979, 184). Nevertheless, beginning in the 1840s, popular sheet music, its authors, performers and publishers found themselves under attack from a small number of self-appointed arbiters of taste and values. A publication such as *Dwight's Journal of Music* was strident in its distaste for what it saw, embodied in popular sheet music, as an unholy alliance between native inferiority (home-grown authorship), musical tastelessness ('superficial trashy stuff ... the namby-pamby sentimental ballads, the flashy fantasias') and low commerce (the 'sharp-set, speculating Yankee' who peddled the music from town to town) ('War,' 1855; 'Music Trade,' 1853).

If North American publishers felt affected by such dia-

tribes, the Civil War changed that by offering the chance for linking rapid growth in the popular sheet music market – some 10,000 songs were released during the conflict – to a sense of patriotic service. The war had another role in the history of sheet music, for it convinced some newer publishers that popular sheet music could be the foundation of their business. In the short term, the approach was unsuccessful (the Chicago firm of Root & Cady, for example, which published many of the war's most successful songs, concentrated after the war on sheet music and instruction manuals, only for this strategy to prove too narrow), but it hinted at changes to come.

Tin Pan Alley and After

The 1890s in the United States saw the rise of a new breed of publisher, trading uniquely in popular music and plying that trade principally through sheet music. The protection given by the 1891 international copyright agreement to North American and European publishers in each other's territories made it commercially worthwhile for them to operate abroad, usually through licensing alliances with local sub-publishers. As the larger, established publishing houses turned their attention increasingly to international markets and affiliations in the wake of this agreement – and to the cultivated repertoire appropriate to a presence there – they left a space in popular music. This space was filled by young entrepreneurs, many of whom were attracted by popular sheet music's sales potential rather than by any particular musical interest, knowledge or experience. New York became the center of this activity, largely because it was both the base from which the vaudeville theater was run and the place where it gained its largest audiences. (Soon, other countries would have similar concentrations in one major city, while others – notably Germany – maintained a more dispersed structure.) Earlier publishers had recognized the power of the performer's name to sell sheet music, but had exploited it in ways that were fairly low key, according to the customs of the day. Now North American marketing customs were changing fast, involving aggressive sales techniques that entailed relentless processes of product familiarization. Publishers such as Edward B. Marks, the Witmark brothers and Leo Feist adapted the technique to sheet music promotion – or 'plugging' – using vaudeville performers to create first an interest, then a demand. Performers were encouraged (often, that meant paid) to add a new song to their stage act, with additional inducements such as their picture on the sheet music cover, and/or a share in the song's authorship. In the United Kingdom, publishers devised the idea of the 'royalty ballad,' whereby well-known performers often received a royalty on the sheet music sales of the songs they included in their performances.

At the first signs of success, especially in the United States, more copies of the song were printed and pluggers obtained 'every performance possible, in any venue, at any cost, and by every physical and mechanical contrivance available,' until the public's interest in buying the sheet music began to wane. One particular consequence was that the 'shelf-life of a hit grew shorter,' from three years in the 1890s to one year by 1914 (Sanjek 1983, 11). Plugging extended to stores such as Woolworth's, where the buying public not only enjoyed much lower prices for sheet music ($0.10 an item), but also could hear the songs played while making a choice.

In Britain, piracy, which had been a growing problem in the second half of the nineteenth century, became a major one around the turn of the century. The problem had originally been illegal imports from the United States and Canada – steamship personnel were included in those deemed responsible (Coover 1985, 18) – but by the late 1890s, following the international copyright agreement, that problem gradually subsided, to be replaced by a more domestic one. A combination of persistent high pricing, a rapid increase in piano sales and the popularity of the music hall had created unprecedented public demand for sheet music at lower prices, not unlike that in the United States. The first to step into this gap were not younger publishers, however, but an alliance of printers, small storekeepers and the street hawkers who had become a feature of 'the streets and marketplaces of almost every city and town in the British Isles' (Coover 1985, viii), producing, promoting and selling cheap illegal copies. Opposing them was a coalition of the major publishers and the more successful songwriters, who pursued their targets with energy. Pirate sales could be considerable. Songwriter Leslie Stuart informed the government in 1898 that, when he and his publisher closed in on the pirate printer of one of his songs, 100,000 copies had already been sold by hawkers (Coover 1985, 75). Not everyone sympathized with the publishers, who were often judged to be giving both composers and the public a raw deal. Within the trade, enmity between publishers, wholesalers and retailers often came to the surface. Resolution of the situation came eventually with the 1906 *Copyright Act*, following which the US model became established.

In terms of sales, the first two decades of the twentieth century were sheet music's heyday. In 1909 in the United States alone, over 25,000 songs were copyrighted (Sanjek 1983, 8), and in 1910 sheet music sales totaled 30 million copies (Sanjek and Sanjek 1991, 16). If those figures were unprecedented, by the end of the following decade million-selling songs were not uncommon, and

the Whiting-Egan song 'Till We Meet Again' is said to have sold 3.5 million copies in a few months (Sanjek 1983, 12).

These, however, were peaks that would never be reached again. Already in 1909 the sales value of records was comfortably outstripping that of sheet music, but without yet having an adverse effect – indeed, when *Billboard* first began in 1913 to compile information on the comparative sales success of individual songs, it did so on the basis of sheet music sales (Lichtman 1994, 79). During the 1920s, the increasing popularity of records combined with rising sheet music prices, the decline of vaudeville (and of similar genres of music theater elsewhere) and the advent of radio and talking pictures to cause a reduction in sheet music sales. They also reduced its dominance in the industry and helped to put in place an industry that was far more diversified. Cross-sector promotions using recording, radio and, later, Hollywood stars helped maintain a demand for sheet music, and it continued to sell in considerable quantities. When the first chart show, *Your Hit Parade*, was introduced on US radio in 1935, sheet music sales played a major part in the sampling method used to produce the charts (as they had for *Billboard* in 1913). But they did so from a position of declining influence; publishing profit now lay increasingly in getting songs recorded, broadcast and included in films, and in exploiting rights, not in outright sales of printed music.

As one player in a complex and diverse industry, sheet music continued to have a role for some time to come (in 1947 it was still the main yardstick used to compile the British chart, '10 Best Sellers in Britain' (Parker 1991, 206)), but fundamental changes were taking place among consumers also. During much of the history of popular sheet music, success in marketing had depended heavily on selling for amateur performance based on a printed score. Now, as amateur performance declined and the importance of the listener increased – encouraged by records and the radio – another key element was added to sheet music's steady demise as a commercially significant product. Any evidence that amateur performance using printed music might be on the increase (for example, during the latter 1950s) led to attempts to develop a new market for sheet music, sometimes with modest success. In areas where a tradition of amateur performance from notated scores persisted, for example the musical theater, the printed score continued to be an important element, but most often in the form of anthologies (or complete vocal scores) rather than as individual pieces of sheet music.

Conclusion

In legal terms, popular sheet music is an example of a 'fixed form,' one whose embodiment is sufficiently stable to permit repeated reproduction of the same basic entity. This idea is itself predicated on a set of assumptions which privilege those forms of musical activity that can be delineated by formal notation, attributed to an original author, and isolated from each other into differentiable items of property. Sheet music's emergence as the first commodified form of popular music was closely tied to this concept of fixity. It was a merger that would have a continued impact as other forms of 'embodiment,' in particular sound recordings, took over sheet music's role.

While accepting this link between sheet music and sound recordings, historians of popular music have generally gone on to insist on a significant difference in practise between them, involving the role and importance of the performer. One interpretation of the decline in sheet music's presence – commercial and cultural – is to understand it as evidence of a shift, in the twentieth century, toward a more open approach to the production of popular music, less constrained by the ideas of realizing music from a fixed source. Although the case for this argument is strong, the contrast may be too stark. Insufficient attention has yet been paid to how sheet music was used and regarded, but its history also appears to reflect the persistence of a performative tradition (Chanan 1994). The unbroken link, over a long period of time, between music and public performer (rather than author) in the way sheet music was presented suggests that a view of printed music as something that exists to enable performance was at least as important as a view of performance as something that exists to realize printed music. Further, the relative absence of performance guidelines in popular sheet music suggests a wide acceptance of a considerable amount of liberty in that performance. In this view, there may be more of a continuum than has been thought likely, at a level other than the legalistic, between the domain of sheet music and that of its successors.

Bibliography

A Short History of Cheap Music, As Exemplified in the Records of the House of Novello, Ewer & Co. 1887. London: Novello, Ewer & Co.

Austin, William W. 1987. *'Susanna,' 'Jeanie,' and 'The Old Folks At Home': The Songs of Stephen C. Foster from His Time to Ours.* 2nd ed. Urbana, IL: University of Illinois Press.

Chanan, Michael. 1994. *Musica Practica: The Social Practice of Western Music from Gregorian Chant to Postmodernism.* London and New York: Verso.

Coover, James. 1985. *Music Publishing, Copyright and Piracy in Victorian England.* London: Mansell.

Dichter, Harry, and Shapiro, Elliott. 1941. *Early American Sheet Music, Its Lure and Its Lore.* New York: Bowker. (Reprinted as *Handbook of Early American Sheet Music 1768–1889.* New York: Dover Publications, 1977.)

Feist, Leonard. 1980. *An Introduction to Popular Music Publishing in America.* New York: National Music Publishers' Association.

Hamm, Charles. 1979. *Yesterdays: Popular Song in America.* New York: Norton.

Jackson, Richard, ed. 1976. *Popular Songs of Nineteenth-Century America.* New York: Dover Publications.

Krummel, D.W. 1975. *English Music Printing 1553–1700.* London: The Bibliographical Society.

Krummel, D.W. 1980. 'Printing and Publishing, 2.' In *The New Grove Dictionary of Music and Musicians*, Vol. 15, ed. Stanley Sadie. London: Macmillan, 260–74.

Lichtman, Irv. 1994. 'It All Starts with a Song.' *Billboard* (100th Anniversary Issue) (1 November): 79.

Locantro, Tony. 1985. *Some Girls Do and Some Girls Don't: Sheet Music Covers.* London: Quartet Books.

'The Music Trade.' 1853. *Dwight's Journal of Music* 3(10) (11 June): 79.

Parker, Martin. 1991. 'Reading the Charts – Making Sense of the Hit Parade.' *Popular Music* 10(2): 205–57.

Sanjek, Russell. 1983. *From Print to Plastic: Publishing and Promoting America's Popular Music (1900–1980).* Brooklyn, NY: Institute for Studies in American Music.

Sanjek, Russell, and Sanjek, David. 1991. *American Popular Music Business in the 20th Century.* New York: Oxford University Press.

Smith, William C. 1968. *A Bibliography of the Musical Works Published by John Walsh During the Years 1695–1720.* London: The Bibliographical Society.

The Spellman Collection of Victorian Music Covers. http://vads.ahds.ac.uk

'War Among the Music Dealers.' 1855. *Dwight's Journal of Music* 6(15) (13 January): 118.

Wolfe, Richard J. 1980. *Early American Music Engraving and Printing.* Urbana, IL: University of Illinois Press.

Wroth, Warwick. 1896. *The London Pleasure Gardens of the Eighteenth Century.* London: Macmillan.

Sheet Music

Bock, Jerry, comp., and Harnick, Sheldon, lyr. 1964. 'If I Were a Rich Man.' New York: Times Square Music Publications.

Carr, Benjamin, comp. and lyr. ca. 1798–99. 'Poor Richard.' Philadelphia: B. Carr.

Clendon, Hugh, comp., and Nicholls, Harry, lyr. 1881. 'Now You're Married I Wish You Joy. Sung with Immense Success by Herbert Campbell.' London: Francis Bros & Day.

Davy, John, comp., and Lewis, G.M., lyr. 1800. 'Crazy Jane: The Original Ballad.' New York: G. Gilfert.

[Foster, Stephen, comp. and lyr.]. 1851. 'Old Folks At Home: Ethiopian Melody, As Sung by the Christy Minstrels. Written and Composed by E.P. Christy.' New York: Firth, Pond & Co.

Gade, Jacob, comp., and May, Winifred, lyr. 1942. 'Jealousy: Song; Founded on the Famous Tango.' London: Wright.

Ingle, Charles, comp., and Chevalier, Albert, lyr. 1892. 'My Old Dutch.' London: Reynolds.

Leveridge, Richard, comp. and lyr. ca. 1700. 'Jenny Long Resisted. Sung by Mss Campion.' London: John Walsh.

René, Leon, René, Otis, and Muse, Clarence, comps. and lyrs. 1931. 'When It's Sleepy Time Down South.' London: Wright.

Whiting, Richard, comp., and Egan, Raymond B., lyr. 1918. 'Till We Meet Again.' New York: Jerome H. Remick.

'Zip Coon: A Favorite Comic Song, Sung by Mr. G.W. Dixon.' n.d. (183–?). New York: J.H. Hewitt.

DAVID HORN with DAVID SANJEK

Songbook

A songbook is a printed collection of the words and, in most cases, the music of a selection of songs. Although an individual songbook may contain texts of a religious nature, the content of and audience for songbooks have been predominantly secular from the earliest days. The practise of collecting songs into anthologies predated the advent of music printing in Europe. Such anthologies were mostly compiled for the courts and, although printing would gradually allow an extension of the audience, the earliest printed songbooks were also intended largely for courtly use. In some of these collections, however, such as several early sixteenth-century Spanish *cancioneros* containing three- and four-part *villancicos*, texts and tunes with more plebeian origins could be found (Sage 1980, 680).

In the mid-seventeenth century, London publisher John Playford recognized the potential commercial market for secular songbooks, and began to compile them himself. As Krummel (1975, 112) makes clear, Playford, music history's 'first great capitalist,' was able to base his business in part on the existence of an inherited legacy of printing skill from the part-book printers of the madrigal era, but the decline of publishing meant he had to learn that part of the business for himself. In the process, he substantially reinvented it, moving it away from the world of patronage into the marketplace. His songbooks – anthologies of songs for voice/voices and continuo, mostly in tall folio form – constituted one of a range of compilations that also included volumes of dance tunes (tunes that were nearly always also used in songs), collections of catches, and instruction books. However, they were particularly emblematic of his enterprise because of the way their contents deliberately anticipated and responded to a diversity of musical competence among performers using – or hoping to use – them, from highly trained soloists to 'actors barely able to carry a tune,' and to 'casual or ardent amateurs at home' (Krummel 1975, 119).

Playford's policy of continually introducing onto the market 'new' publications that were neither entirely new nor entirely reprinted was copied by other publishers, who sprang up in London and in other British cities in his wake. But, among the songbook titles that shifted to and fro, some became well known in an abbreviated form, serving to suggest a process of continuity across successive editions, even when the contents changed. One of the best examples of this became known as *Pills to Purge Melancholy*. The first publication in this songbook's lineage was issued by John Playford in 1652 as *An Antidote to Melancholy, Made Up into Pills*. It belonged in a category known as 'drolleries,' for the often bawdy humor the songs contained. In 1682, a third edition was published by Playford's son, Henry, under the title *Wit and Mirth: An Antidote Against Melancholy*. In 1699, Henry Playford then produced the first part of a significantly different version, with few of the songs from 1682, entitled *Wit and Mirth; Or Pills to Purge Melancholy*. The book had by now established a reputation, enabling Henry Playford and his business successors to issue four further volumes, the last in 1714. Despite the fact that the market for such songbooks seemed sated, an edition in six volumes was published in 1719–20; now called *Pills to Purge Melancholy*, it contained over a thousand songs (Legman 1959, 97).

With the last edition of *Pills*, two developments that were new to British songbook publishing were evident: (a) the role of editor-compiler, hitherto taken by the publisher himself, had been taken over by a professional musician, in this case songwriter and poet Thomas D'Urfey, who used the opportunity to include many of his own songs; and (b) the established practise of printing tunes to old texts was reversed by D'Urfey, whose approach was to write new words to old tunes (a method that would have one of its most famous English-language applications in another multi-volume songbook enterprise, a little less than a century later: Thomas Moore's *Irish Melodies* (1808–34)).

By the time D'Urfey was engaged in the second of these activities, it was already well established in France as a songwriting technique, and the results of this process – as it had been carried out over a period of years –

were beginning to form the basis of songbook collections. Shortly before D'Urfey's *Pills* revision began to appear in London, with his own newly written texts, there appeared in Paris an anthology of French songs from the previous 100 years, created on the same principle. Compiled and published in 1717 by Jean-Baptiste Christophe Ballard, the latest member of a famous Parisian publishing dynasty, *La Clef des Chansonniers* included 300 'vaudevilles' and other theater songs, which, although often forgotten in their original form, had been given new lyrics – and, not infrequently, new lives.

In this and later collections, the identity of earlier tunes was indicated by printing above the new setting some of the words originally associated with the tune. Later, this means of identification became known as a 'timbre,' and by the early nineteenth century French songbooks collecting together vaudeville songs and other 'airs' were often organized alphabetically by timbre.

A number of significant trends in songbook publishing in eighteenth-century Britain can be identified, some of which would remain a feature of songbook publishing for a long time to come. One was that of making a compilation out of separate, or separable, individual songs. London publishers began publishing collections of this type in the early eighteenth century. The practise continued into the next century, linked to and bolstered by the opportunities for the public to hear the songs in performance at venues such as the pleasure gardens. The increasing popularity of purchasing music in the form of individual items of sheet music tended to reduce the market for such compilations, but the principle of getting a published song to work twice, once as sheet music and once in an anthologized form, without any significant alteration, remained attractive to music publishers (and was still common in the twentieth century).

Another trend involved the publication of a kind of songbook periodical, a magazine containing a small selection of the latest songs. The idea appears to have been pioneered in Paris by the Ballards, with their series of *Airs sérieux et à boire*, which began in 1670 and appeared every month between 1694 and 1724 (Benoit 1992, 10). The best-known London equivalent was John Walsh's monthly collection, entitled *The Monthly Mask of Vocal Music* (subtitled *The Newest Songs Made for the Theatre and Other Occasions*), which he began to issue in 1703. The series ran without a break until 1711, then again from 1717 to 1724, and was regularly collected into annual volumes (Smith 1968, 32).

A further trend was the growing domination of songbooks by 'ballads,' by which was meant a strophic song, intended for the growing amateur domestic market.

With what has been called an 'artful simplicity and a breezy, square-cut tunefulness' (Johnstone 1990, 165), ballads, not theater songs, provided the bulk of the material for the ever more attractively produced multi-volume songbooks, such as *The Musical Miscellany* of 1729–31.

By the late eighteenth century, 'ballad' was increasingly being used to denote something different – older, often anonymous 'heroic' airs and verses – and this more studious, antiquarian interest introduced into the songbook form the presence of the scholar-editor and the concept of a retrospectively conceived 'national' culture. Here, collections of Scottish songs played more than one significant role. David Herd's *Ancient and Modern Scots Songs* (1769) and James Johnson's *Scots Musical Museum* (1787–1803, with many contributions by Robert Burns) were conceived as counterweights to (and, in their way, denials of) England's claims to have a national music. Burns's work, along with that of Englishman Joseph Ritson in both his Scottish and his English songbooks, was also noteworthy for its interest in the song culture of working people. Ritson and, especially, Burns collected material from oral sources, marking another departure for songbooks. All these 'song mediators' (Harker 1985) hoped to see their songbooks result in the preservation – better still, revival – of older song cultures. At the same time, they all had also to deal with the existing structure of the music publishing market and the musical tastes of the mainstay of that market, the middle classes. As Harker points out, the effect of their songbooks 'was to open up workers' song-culture to a predominately bourgeois and petty bourgeois market,' but it was 'on that market's terms: songs were transformed into property, and song-books into commodities' (1985, 37).

During the nineteenth century in Britain, in some industrialized areas, there was some space for working-class songbooks that was less determined by the bourgeois market. Significantly, songbooks such as those featuring the songs of Newcastle-based Ned Corvan, who entertained in the so-called 'concert halls' in the 1850s and 1860s, were compilations of songs also issued as broadsides (Harker 1981). They were produced by broadside printers and they addressed, in characteristically satirical terms, the contemporary concerns of their intended audience, the local seamen and pitmen and their families. As the locally centered working-class concert hall declined (to be replaced by the music hall), some of its repertoire found its way into collections of regional songs (Corvan's, for example, into Thomas and George Allan's *Tyneside Songs and Readings* of 1891), aimed at a wider market (Harker 1980, 162).

In nineteenth-century songbook publishing as a whole, regionalism was an important theme, and the regionally based songbook was a principal means by which nineteenth-century scholar-editors communicated the concept of 'folk song.' In the work of some scholar-editors, such as Cecil Sharp in Britain, particular selection criteria (age, rural origin, anonymity) were strictly adhered to, while in that of others, such as Ludwig Erk (who amassed a vast private collection of German folk songs), more recent music with a known, generally urban genesis was admitted. But regional culture, in most cases, was conceived as a contributor to the idea of national culture, and it was the idea of national song that, once established, was to remain a persistent presence in songbook compiling, in Britain and elsewhere in Europe. Erk's *Deutscher Liederhort* (1856) contains numerous songs of a *volkstümlich* character – folk-like songs that, in his view, were in keeping with national traditions and that had attained a kind of national status.

Many of Erk's various songbook compilations also illustrated another new development: the desire to create a body of national music for use in schools. This was part of a wider move, in both Europe and North America, to improve education and to establish a place for music in that process. The publication (usually by established music publishers) of anthologies of the nation's 'treasury' of songs for specific use in schools persisted in the twentieth century. In some cases, there was a declared link to, and endorsement by, national government policy. *The National Song Book* (1905), for example, edited by Charles V. Stanford, declared in its Preface that it contained 'all the songs recommended for older children by the Board of Education in their Blue Book of Suggestions.' Revising the book in 1938, Geoffrey Shaw remarked that 'to our children [*The National Song Book*] has been a gateway to musical taste and knowledge' (iii). With the exception of some rounds and catches with attributed composers, all the songs in the book are anonymous.

From Germany, too, came another, somewhat different development in educational songbook compilation and publishing: the student songbook. The *Allgemeines deutsches Commersbuch*, first published in 1858, contained a mixture of part songs traditionally associated with student beer-drinking. Later British compilations acknowledged its influence, though they generally played down any suggestion of the revelry it was designed to accompany. But whereas, in the case of children's songbooks, compilers were happy to make decisions on which songs to include without consulting the children themselves, with student songbooks compilers felt unable, as one group put it, to 'follow their own judgement with unrestricted freedom' (*The Scottish Students' Song Book* 1897, vi); instead, they were obliged

to bow to student taste, however hard it was to discern what that might be.

As a distinct potential market for songbooks, students constituted one of a number of social groups targeted by compilers and publishers with their own specially designed songbook. But equally important as a selling point by the late nineteenth century was the idea of 'community.' The image of the 'community singsong' helped to sell many compilations well into the twentieth century (including some with those exact words in the title, as in the *Pocket Sing-Song Book for Schools, Homes and Community Singing* (1927)). Newspapers recognized the ability of the songbook to enhance their image of serving the 'community.' One such songbook, *The News Chronicle Song Book* (Ratcliff 1931), provided African-American singer Paul Robeson with British songs to add to his repertoire during his time in Britain in the 1930s (Harvey 1976). Although many community songbooks retained a nationalistic identity, others were more diverse. *Francis and Day's Popular and Community Song Book for All Occasions* (1935), for example, includes traditional songs from England, Wales, France and the United States alongside hymns, spirituals, minstrel songs, American Civil War songs, music hall songs and other popular commercial numbers.

The practise (begun in the seventeenth century) of issuing periodicals containing several new songs continued in the twentieth century, but by the 1950s the rising sales of records at the expense of sheet music had caused music publishers to rethink their approach to the printed music market. They now began to license to magazine companies the right to print only the lyrics in such US publications of the 1950s as *Hit Parader*, *Song Hits Magazine*, *Country Music Round Up* and *Rhythm and Blues*. Comparable British magazines of a later period included *Number One* and *Smash Hits*.

Songbooks themselves were now closely linked to recordings, so that, for example, in 1956 Robbins Music could publish an 'Album of hit songs from his LP records' by Frank Sinatra, when the songs were composed by a variety of writers (Edge 1991). In the pop sphere, it became increasingly necessary to provide 'added value' to songbook collections of sheet music (such as the LP-size AlbuMusic series of songbook-folios published in the United States by Columbia) through the inclusion of color photographs of the composer/artists, and sometimes interviews with the musicians or introductions to their styles. Particular attention was often paid to design and illustration – for example, in the work of British artist Alan Aldridge, editor of the first book of Beatles lyrics (1969), and in that of graphic designer and pop artist Barney Bubbles, who created the cover for *The Ian Dury Songbook* (1979). The Aldridge volume was one of the first in the rock era to consist solely of song lyrics, but it was followed by those of Bob Dylan (1973), Willie Nelson (Cusic 1995) and Joni Mitchell (1997).

In addition, the fact that many pop musicians compose on their instruments rather than on manuscript paper has meant that sheet music versions of songs can be made only by transcribing from a recorded version. Such transcriptions have been criticized for their inaccuracy (see, for example, Schwartz 1993). One advertised feature of the generic 'Songbooks' edited by Almire Chediak in Brazil since 1988 has been the accuracy of his standardized tablature system.

The folk music revivals in the United States, the United Kingdom and elsewhere during the 1950s and 1960s brought with them a revival of an older genre of songbook: the collections of traditional songs or songsters. The new collections often built on the pioneering achievements of such collectors as John A. Lomax, whose *Cowboy Songs and Other Frontier Ballads* was first published in 1910, John Jacob Niles, whose book of war songs was published in 1927, and Carl Sandburg, whose compilation *The American Songbag* (first published in 1927) brought together 280 items categorized idiosyncratically into such sections as 'Pioneer Memories,' 'Prison and Jail Songs' and 'Blues, Mellows, Ballets.'

Many of the later collections were more tightly thematic, bringing together songs of war (for example, Palmer 1977), songs of industry (MacColl 1954), songs of social comment (Palmer 1974) or cowboy songs (Ohrlin 1973). Collections of songs associated with political struggle, such as that of Seeger and Reiser (1986), harked back to *Socialist Songs with Music* (Industrial Workers of the World), first published in 1901.

Some 'folk song' collections – for example, the *Folk Blues* book published in 1967 by Arc Music – were decidedly opportunistic. *Folk Blues* contained songs by Chuck Berry and Willie Dixon, and informed readers that 'all of the compositions in this collection are recorded on Chess and Checker Records,' the parent company of the publisher.

Songbooks

Ackerman, Paul. 1967. *Folk Blues*. New York: Arc Music.

Airs sérieux et à boire. 1670–1724. Paris: Ballard.

Aldridge, Alan, ed. 1969. *The Beatles Illustrated Lyrics*. London: Macdonald.

Allan, Thomas, and Allan, George, eds. 1891. *Allan's Illustrated Edition of Tyneside Songs and Readings*. Newcastle: T.& G. Allan.

Allgemeines deutsches Commersbuch. 1858. Lahr: Schauenburg.

An Antidote to Melancholy, Made Up into Pills. 1652. London: John Playford.

Ballard, Jean-Baptiste Christophe, ed. 1717. *La Clef des Chansonniers; ou Receuil des Vaudevilles Depuis Cent Ans & Plus*. Paris: Ballard.

Cusic, Don, ed. 1995. *Willie Nelson Lyrics, 1957–1994*. New York: St. Martin's Press.

Dury, Ian. 1979. *The Ian Dury Songbook*. London: Music Sales Ltd.

Dylan, Bob. 1973. *Bob Dylan: Writings and Drawings*. London: Jonathan Cape.

Erk, Ludwig. 1856. *Deutscher Liederhort: Auswahl der vorzüglichern deutschen Volkslieder der Vorzeit unter der Gegenwart*. Berlin: T.C.F. Enslin.

Francis and Day's Popular and Community Song Book for All Occasions. 1935. London: Francis, Day & Hunter.

Herd, David. 1769. *The Ancient and Modern Scots Songs, Heroic Ballads, &c*. Edinburgh: Martin & Wotherspoon.

Industrial Workers of the World (IWW). 1901. *Socialist Songs with Music*. Chicago: IWW.

Johnson, James. 1787–1803. *The Scots Musical Museum*. 6 vols. Edinburgh: J. Johnson.

Lomax, John A. 1938 (1910). *Cowboy Songs and Other Frontier Ballads*. Rev. ed. New York: Macmillan.

MacColl, Ewan, ed. 1954. *The Shuttle and Cage: Industrial Folk-Ballads*. New York: Hargail Music Press.

Mitchell, Joni. 1997. *The Complete Poems and Lyrics*. London: Chatto & Windus.

The Monthly Mask of Vocal Music; or the Newest Songs Made for the Theatre and Other Occasions. 1703–11; 1717–24. London: J. Walsh.

Moore, Thomas. 1808–34. *Irish Melodies*. 10 vols. London: J. Power.

The Musical Miscellany. 1729–31. 6 vols. London: J. Watts.

Niles, John Jacob. 1927. *Singing Soldiers*. New York: Scribners.

Ohrlin, Glenn. 1973. *The Hell-Bound Train: A Cowboy Songbook*. Urbana, IL: University of Illinois Press.

Pills to Purge Melancholy. 1719–20. 6 vols. London: J. Tonson.

Pocket Sing-Song Book for Schools, Homes and Community Singing. 1927. London: Novello.

Ratcliff, T.P., ed. 1931. *The News Chronicle Song Book*. London: News Chronicle.

Ritson, Joseph. 1783. *A Select Collection of English Songs*. 3 vols. London: Printed for J. Johnson.

Ritson, Joseph. 1794. *Scotish Songs* [sic]. 2 vols. London: Printed for J. Johnson.

Sandburg, Carl, comp. 1990 (1927). *The American Songbag*. New York: Harcourt Brace Jovanovich.

The Scottish Students' Song Book. 1897. London: Bayley & Ferguson.

Stanford, Charles Villiers, ed. 1905. *The National Song Book*. London: Boosey.

Stanford, Charles Villiers, and Shaw, Geoffrey, eds. 1938. *The New National Song Book*. London: Boosey.

Wit and Mirth: An Antidote Against Melancholy. 1682. London: Henry Playford.

Wit and Mirth; Or Pills to Purge Melancholy. 1699–1702. 3 vols. London: Henry Playford.

Bibliography

Benoit, Marcelle, ed. 1992. *Dictionnaire de la Musique en France aux XVIIe et XVIIIe siècles* [Dictionary of Music in France in the Seventeenth and Eighteenth Centuries]. Paris: Fayard.

Edge, Kevin. 1991. *The Art of Selling Songs: Graphics for the Music Business, 1690–1990*. London: Futures Publications.

Harker, Dave. 1980. *One for the Money: Politics and Popular Song*. London: Hutchinson.

Harker, Dave. 1981. 'The Making of the Tyneside Concert Hall.' *Popular Music* 1: 27–56.

Harker, Dave. 1985. *Fakesong: The Manufacture of British 'Folksong,' 1700 to the Present Day*. Milton Keynes: Open University Press.

Harvey, Ralph. 1976. Sleeve notes to *A Golden Hour of Paul Robeson*. Golden Hour GH 853.

Johnstone, H. Diack. 1990. 'Music in the Home, 1.' In *Music in Britain: The Eighteenth Century*, ed. H. Diack Johnstone and Roger Fiske. Oxford: Blackwell, 159–201.

Krummel, D.W. 1975. *English Music Printing, 1553–1700*. London: The Bibliographical Society.

Legman, G. 1959. 'Pills to Purge Melancholy: A Bibliographical Note.' *Midwest Folklore* 9(2): 89–102.

Palmer, Roy. 1974. *Touch on the Times: Songs of Social Change*. Harmondsworth: Penguin.

Palmer, Roy, ed. 1977. *The Rambling Soldier: Life in the Lower Ranks, 1750–1900, Through Soldiers' Songs and Writings*. Harmondsworth: Penguin.

Sage, Jack. 1980. 'Cancionero.' In *The New Grove Dictionary of Music and Musicians*, Vol. 2, ed. Stanley Sadie. London: Macmillan, 679–80.

Schwartz, Jeff. 1993. 'Writing Jimi: Rock Guitar Pedagogy as Postmodern Folkloric Practice.' *Popular Music* 12(3): 281–88.

Seeger, P., and Reiser, B. 1986. *Carry It On: A History in Song and Pictures of the Working Men and Women of America*. Poole: Blandford Press.

Smith, William C. 1968. *A Bibliography of the Musical Works Published by John Walsh During the Years 1695–1720*. London: The Bibliographical Society.

DAVID HORN and DAVE LAING

Songsheet Covers

When nineteenth-century ballads, 'heart songs' and dance tunes were published with music for home entertainment, the 14″ x 8″ (35 cm x 20 cm) folded and folioed songsheets became increasingly popular. Songsheets had often followed the lead of concert and chamber music publication, although sometimes with more animated lettering and with ornamental or foliated borders and swags (decorative festoons), but many early songsheets were of a patriotic nature, and the content seemed to dictate symmetrical designs, reminiscent, perhaps, of battle honors. The portrait of a military officer or a politician, or the depiction of a monumental building, the hero of a song, or the performer associated with it, was usually placed centrally – a convention that persisted well into the twentieth century. With the growth in sales and competition among popular-song publishers, more imaginative designs were introduced in order to attract prospective purchasers. These included bucolic scenes with courting couples, idealized 'noble savages,' street scenes and bridges, even industrial buildings and occasional fantasies.

The earliest songsheet illustrations were drawn by professional engravers on copperplate, supplanted by the cheaper steel plate by 1824. The work was exacting, and this undoubtedly exercised restraint on its execution. But in 1793, Aloys Senefelder's (accidental) discovery of the lithographic process greatly increased the potential of songsheet illustration for artists. They could draw on the fine Bavarian stone with a greasy crayon or grease medium, and when the stone was washed with water, which repelled ink, only the grease-drawn areas attracted the ink. A great variety of textures and tones could be achieved when paper was printed using lithography. The process was further developed in Britain by Rudolph Ackerman, but it was the patenting of chromolithography by Engelmann, in 1837, that enabled full-color designs to be achieved, although each color had to be drawn on a separate stone and the printed sheets aligned so that an accurately printed multicolored image resulted. By mid-century, mechanical production was introduced, although hand-printing continued widely until the late 1880s.

The diversity of song themes – from shipwrecks to ice-skating, domesticity to emigration, gypsies to princes, tragic to comic situations, beauty to the grotesque – attracted a great many artists interested in designing songsheets that would exercise their imaginations and skills. A few, such as Henri de Toulouse-Lautrec in France and George Cruikshank in England, were celebrated for their work in other fields, including book illustration and poster design. Songsheet covers, or 'fronts,' also had their own artists who worked exclusively in this vigorous industry. Principal among them was the Galway-born artist Alfred Concanen (1835–86), whose breadth of talent enabled him to design original covers that were full of incident. Some were, admittedly, incongruous, like the 'Red Indians' among tropical palms in the design for Charles Coote's quadrille, 'The Desert Flower.' Others were deceptively simple in their abstract ordering of elements. Concanen was employed by Stannard and Dixon, music sheet printers, before managing his own printing works. Equally well known, despite the fact that he died young, was John Brandard, whose covers were somewhat more elegant, illustrating ballet and opera themes rather than the music hall hits of Concanen's work. Thomas Packer, the master of graduated tints, had a long and successful career. He took a delight in tropical and exotic or colorful scenes, such as for 'Isola Bella,' a quadrille by C.H.R. Marriott. Yet he also produced graphically inventive covers, such as the simulated Victorian collage for G.L.E. Brunn's 'When You Wink the Other Eye,' sung by Marie Lloyd, who was featured in the design.

Such artists took pride in executing their own designs in color lithography; Packer, at the same time, managed a busy works, with many employees. The multitude of entertainers who worked the thousands of music halls – over 500 halls in London alone – kept the artists and the presses very busy. Between 80,000 and 100,000 distinct music sheet fronts are estimated to have been produced by Francis, Day & Hunter, Robert Cocks and Company, Novello, Hapwood and Crew, Metzlet and Company and many others. Some – like Chappell's or Boosey and Co. – continued to publish for more than a century. Though less researched, music sheets were also produced in Germany, Belgium and France, by H. Gray and H. Roet, for example. V. Palyart et Fils lithographed music sheets for the polkas, mazurkas and marches composed by Louis Ganne and published by Enoch Frères. In the United States, music sheet illustration followed a similar trajectory to that in Britain. Symmetrical layouts lasted longer, while the pictorial covers tended to be informative in detail but more conventional in design. Greater prominence was given to the lithographers who carried out the designs than to the artists, such as Joseph Knapp, Henry B. Major and Napoleon Sarony, who lithographed jointly and under their own names. Benjamin Thayer, David Claypoole Johnston and, notably, John H. Bufford, were prolific lithographers. Some publishers were also artists, like the Cincinnati team of Erghot and Forbriger. Winslow Homer was one of the few artists whose name was known to a larger public.

Marches, schottisches, mazurkas, polkas and quick-steps constituted a large proportion of the pre- and post-Civil War music fronts. Fortunately for the artists, these were often titled after new inventions and great exhibitions, as well as military escapades and western adventures. Many, however, were racist caricatures, especially in the 'coon song' era at the close of the nineteenth century. Few were as offensive as Davenport's notorious design for 'The Bully Song,' which May Irwin made popular in 1897. It was during the ragtime era that North American songsheet design took on a character of its own. Mechanical lithography was capable of producing large numbers of covers, although the range of colors was often reduced to one or two tints with black and white. The influence of art nouveau was evident in the designs of Gene Buck (1885–1952) for Ted Snyder, and E.H. Pfeiffer, publishers in New York. He was a talented artist and writer who wrote the lyrics for the *Ziegfeld Follies* of 1915, and became president of the American Society of Composers, Authors and Publishers (ASCAP). He also drew for Jerome H. Remick, whose principal designer was Starmer, who favored a strong foreground motif against a simplified background. Barbelle, who designed and caricatured for Shapiro, Bernstein and Co., was clearly aware of the English prints of William Nicholson and the so-called 'Beggarstaff Brothers,' whose strong outlines were also employed by J. Frew.

By the 1920s, radio and, subsequently, the 'talking picture' industry promoted songs with increasing emphasis on the star artist, such as Duke Ellington or Fats Waller, and less importance placed on the theme. With opportunities consequently reduced for designers, abstraction exerted a measure of influence, but the age of creative sheet music design had passed. Graphic artists had to wait until the advent of the long-playing record before they were given similar opportunities to exercise their ideas and design abilities.

Bibliography

Edge, Kevin. 1991. *The Art of Selling Songs: Graphics for the Music Business, 1690–1990*. London: Futures Publications.

Lawrence, Vera Brodsky. 1975. *Music for Patriots, Politicians and Presidents: Harmonies and Discords of the First Hundred Years*. New York: Macmillan.

Levy, Lester S. 1976. *Picture the Songs: Lithographs from the Sheet Music of Nineteenth-Century America*. Baltimore, MD: Johns Hopkins University Press.

Morgan, Thomas L., and Barlow, William. 1992. *From Cakewalks to Concert Halls: An Illustrated History of African American Popular Music from 1895 to 1930*. Washington, DC: Elliott and Clark Publishing.

Pearsall, Ronald. 1972. *Victorian Sheet Music Covers*. Newton Abbot: David and Charles.

Spellman, Doreen, and Spellman, Sidney. 1969. *Victorian Music Covers*. London: Evelyn, Adams and Mackay.

The Spellman Collection of Victorian Music Covers. http://vads.ahds.ac.uk

Wilk, Max. 1973. *Memory Lane 1890–1925: Ragtime, Jazz,*

Foxtrot and Other Popular Music Covers. London: Studioart.

Sheet Music

Brunn, G.L.E., comp., and Lytton, W.T., lyr. ca. 1894. 'When You Wink the Other Eye' (Cover by T. Packer, lithographed by W.G. Banks). London: Howard & Co.

Coote, C.H., comp. 1865. 'The Desert Flower' (Cover by Concanen, Lee and Siebe, lithographers). London: Chappell & Co.

Marriott, C.H.R., comp. ca. 1871. 'Isola Bella' (Cover by T. Packer). London: J. Williams.

Trevathan, Charles E., comp. and lyr. 1896. 'The Bully Song.' New York: White-Smith Music Publishing Co.

PAUL OLIVER

Songster

Small songbooks of a size suitable for carrying in a coat or hip pocket were produced in the hundreds of thousands in the nineteenth century. Collectively termed 'songsters,' they derived from the earlier chapbooks and were among the most enduring means of disseminating popular songs. Among the earliest were those produced for campfire use, or for entertainment in backwoods and pioneer communities in North America. Some were general collections of songs, such as *The American Mock-Bird* (1760) which, in spite of its title, consisted of British songs. Bound anthologies were produced, such as *The American Songster*, published in two volumes (1788; 1799), each of which contained the words of over 200 songs. Most songsters were simple, unbound and sold for a few cents. Some had as few as 24 pages, others as many as 128. With the rise of minstrel troupes and the widespread popularity of minstrelsy, songsters containing parodies, comic songs and dialect songs were published in large numbers.

Early songsters were not published only in North America, although the collections published in Britain have been inadequately researched. Among the earliest was *The Billington: or, Town and Country Songster* (London, 1790), which had the words of 700 songs. In contrast, *The Sentimental Songster* (Paisley, 1839) and *The Cork Leg Songster* (Glasgow, ca. 1840) each had 24 6" x 3" (15 cm x 8 cm) pages and included the words of 20 songs.

Dime songbooks received a considerable boost with the California gold rush and the opening up of the west to wagon trains, a period when *Put's Golden Songster* (ca. 1848) was most popular. Among the collections were *Grigg's Southern and Western Songster* (Philadelphia, 1835), *Tony Pastor's Comic Songster* (New York, 1872) and *Joe Lang's Aunt Jemima Songster* (New York, 1873). Some 375 separate songsters were published by W.J.A. Lieder of New York, over 300 Dime Song Books by A.J. Fisher and more than 200 of the Favorite Dime Song Books by the Popular Publishing Company, while numerous other songsters were produced by M.M. De Witt, Dick and Fitzgerald, and many other publishers. Few included any music, although they gave some indication of popular tunes to which the songs could be sung.

By the late nineteenth century, songsters had largely been replaced by less ephemeral songbooks in a larger format, with notation included as musical literacy increased. Some were sold by the major surviving minstrel troupes, such as Christy's, and others were distributed by evangelical and social organizations, such as the Salvation Army and the Boy Scouts. The latter's *Hackney Scout Song Book* of the 1930s was, nevertheless, one of the last to be published in the traditional songster format.

Bibliography

Heywood, Charles. 1954. 'Collections – Songsters.' In *A Bibliography of North American Folk Lore and Folk Song, Vol. 1*. New York: Dover Publications, 327–41.

Lowens, Irving. 1976. *A Bibliography of Songsters Printed in America Before 1821*. Worcester, MA: American Antiquarian Society.

PAUL OLIVER

16. Recording

Album

An album is a work of popular music of extended duration, usually a collection of songs. Albums have existed across a range of recording media and may be issued in formats yet to be invented. At one time or another, sets of 78 rpm or 45 rpm singles, individual long-playing records (LPs), open-reel tapes, cassettes, eight-tracks, compact discs (CDs), digital audio tapes (DATs) and minidiscs have all been called 'albums.'

'Album' originally referred to an empty, unmarked container that was purchased for storing assorted 78 rpm singles. The containers often featured blank spaces in which to write the names of songs and performers, reinforcing an early sense of the album as a personal collection (like a photograph album). While albums of 'classical' and operatic works began to appear around 1900, it was not until the 1930s that prepackaged albums of popular music made their debut. These tended to be compilations of previously released singles, such as the commemorative albums issued after the deaths of Bix Beiderbecke and Bessie Smith. Among the first albums of new material were recordings of Broadway musicals, such as the 1931 *Gems from 'The Bandwagon'*, on RCA-Victor's failed 33 1/3 rpm, 10-minute-per-side albums. But it was not until the mid-1940s that 78 rpm album sets of popular music began to be commercially significant; *Billboard* began charting album sales only in 1945. These sets usually featured eight or 12 songs (four or six double-sided singles).

The introduction of the LP in 1948 eventually led to a massive expansion of the market for albums of popular music in the 1950s, so that by the 1960s albums were, in dollar terms, the dominant commodity form of the record industry in the United States and Canada. From 1948 to ca. 1965, LPs were either 10" (25 cm) or 12" (30 cm). Initially, popular songs were restricted to 10" (25 cm) LPs, but by about 1955 they had begun appearing on 12" (30 cm) LPs as well. While the duration of the 12" (30 cm) LP was developed to accommodate the average length of a classical work, pop LPs of the 1950s continued 78 rpm conventions in featuring eight songs (10" (25 cm) LPs) or 12 songs (just as CDs, despite their 80-minute capacity, often feature only 10 short songs, a number established in the mid-1960s). In the 1950s and 1960s, the influence of the 78 model is seen in the fact that albums were often referred to as 'packages,' and songs were said to be 'in' an album. As the individual LP became the standard format for albums, people began to refer to songs as being 'on' an album; this practise has continued, since songs are said to be 'on' a CD. Eventually, albums were released in formats including two or three LP sets (double or triple albums), box sets (of multiple albums, cassettes, CDs), various analog tape formats, and digital media, both tape and disc.

While albums have traditionally been defined by an extended playback length, contemporary CD singles or 12" (30 cm) singles with multiple remixes frequently rival albums in terms of duration. Therefore, 'albums' may be defined by more than a quantity of music. The meaning of 'album' may be structured in opposition to the idea of the single. Where the single is disparaged as commercial, ephemeral and inexpensive, the album can stand for the artistic, the permanent and the valuable in popular music culture. The historical association of albums (both 78 sets and LPs) with symphonic music, along with their higher prices and usually longer commercial lives, contributed to the popular idea that albums were somehow superior cultural commodities. Frequently compared to books, albums may be assembled into personal 'libraries' in a way that singles generally are not. These privileged ideas of the album tend to come into play particularly when discussions are framed in terms of artistic maturity. The expansion of the popular LP market in the 1950s was, in part, due to the LP's emergence as a serious, 'adult' format, in contrast to the 45 rpm single's Top 40, teen constituency.

Subsequently, the advent of a youth market for LPs in the mid-1960s was linked to the development of the album as the vehicle for artistic seriousness and experimentation within rock culture. Albums can be seen to expand the boundaries of popular recordings, whether in terms of the LP's or CD's superior technical fidelity, the greater length of material presented or, especially, an increased sense of artistic possibilities. More than merely a collection of songs, the album here is associated with ideas of complexity. Unlike the single, the album may be conceived as involving a larger totality, with a continuity and coherence of theme, mood, sound or narrative across its duration. Albums have also permitted a movement away from the relatively abbreviated length of the popular song – which had itself been formalized by the limited length of early recording media – into extended pieces, suites and solos. This sense of depth, complexity and artistic ambitiousness is also a reminder that albums have historically involved listening in private, domestic space, where these qualities may most fully be appreciated, although the advent of mobile playback equipment has changed this in recent years.

KEIR KEIGHTLEY

Album Cover

An album cover is the front cover or face of a package of recorded music, whether a bound collection of 78 rpm records, a 10" (25 cm) or 12" (30 cm) long-playing record (LP), a cassette or a compact disc (CD). It usually consists of an image and typography identifying the work/performer(s) (the back cover often contains song titles and/or liner notes describing the work/performer(s); sometimes, however, the back cover is a foldout continuation of the front cover and thus may be considered part of the album cover). From approximately 1950 to 1985, album covers were a primary source of visual imagery for popular music performers. While the reduced size of CD booklets and cassette inserts and the expanded presence of music video may have diminished the importance of the album cover, it has remained a crucial means of advertising and imagining the music contained within.

The album cover performs multiple and interconnected functions. It is a kind of billboard, calling attention to the commodity for sale. This might include not only the recording itself, but also the performer, musical genre, mood and so on. Like illustrated sheet music

covers before it, the album cover also provides an important visual instantiation of the music's or performer's identity and/or potential significance (see Edge 1991). The widespread use of photographs of performers on popular music albums is evidence of the cover's contribution to the creation, maintenance and development of 'star images' (Dyer 1979). As early as 1954, LPs appeared with covers identifying the performer solely with an image (for example, Frank Sinatra's name does not appear on the cover of his *Swing Easy*).

The covers of the first 78 rpm albums of popular music (in the 1930s) tended to be standardized. They resembled hardcover books, with almost no distinct visual elements apart from (usually) embossed gold lettering on a dark-colored background. In the 1940s, Alex Steinweiss, head of Columbia Records' art department in New York, developed numerous distinctive, multicolored covers featuring different designs for each release (see Kohler 1999, which profiles a number of early designers). The emergence of the 12" (30 cm) LP, with its larger cover area, led eventually to an explosion in the variety of design of individual album covers, and certain labels came to be identified by distinctive, in-house design styles (for example, Blue Note in the 1950s, 4AD in the 1980s). However, in the 1970s independent design firms specializing in album graphics for a range of labels and performers, such as Hipgnosis, emerged.

Increasingly, cover design was conceived as a kind of poster art, integrating information and visual experimentation. Beginning in the late 1960s, rock LPs often contained larger foldout posters, lyric sheets and stickers (for instance, Pink Floyd's *Dark Side of the Moon* (1973)). This calls attention to the album cover's status as a form of commercial packaging as well as an artistic statement, and is a reminder of the blurred boundaries between culture and commodity within popular music.

LPs were usually packaged in a protective paper inner sleeve as well as a cardboard outer sleeve and, by the 1970s, it was common to feature extensive design, photographs and liner notes on virtually every surface of the LP package. While these developments (along with deluxe gatefold covers and LP box sets with 12" (30 cm) booklets) provided a great deal of space for visual design and written information, the advent of the cassette and then the CD meant that designers had to work with a reduced cover area (commonly using smaller typefaces within the liner notes and booklets, but in the case of the CD occasionally taking advantage of the plastic CD case or 'jewel box' as a design resource, i.e., using colored plastic or inserting images or items – such as cocktail umbrellas or miniature dice – into a transparent strip of plastic running down the left-hand side of the case between the hinges). However, the CD cover, with its similar square shape, retains many of the design features of the 78 and LP album cover, combining information and image, advertising and adventure.

Bibliography

Dyer, Richard. 1979. *Stars*. London: BFI.

Edge, Kevin. 1991. *The Art of Selling Songs: Graphics for the Music Business, 1690–1990*. London: Futures Publications.

Jones, Steve, and Sorger, Martin. 1999/2000. 'Covering Music: A Brief History and Analysis of Album Cover Design.' *Journal of Popular Music Studies* 11/12: 68–102.

Kohler, Eric. 1999. *In the Groove: Vintage Record Graphics*. San Francisco: Chronicle.

Ochs, Michael. 1996. *1000 Rock Covers*. Cologne: Taschen.

Weinstein, Deena. 1991. *Heavy Metal: A Cultural Sociology*. New York: Lexington Books (see pp. 27–29 for a discussion of heavy metal album covers).

Discographical References

Pink Floyd. *Dark Side of the Moon*. Harvest 11163. *1973*: USA.

Sinatra, Frank. *Swing Easy*. Capitol 528. 1954: USA.

KEIR KEIGHTLEY

A Side

As radio airplay became crucial to the commercial success of singles, record companies began to stamp the side of a disc that contained the more important song with a letter 'A,' indicating that this was the track which disc jockeys should play. On rare occasions, singles would have double A sides to show that both tracks were to be promoted on-air. For example, in the United Kingdom, the Beatles issued 'Day Tripper' and 'We Can Work It Out' as a single with double A sides.

Discographical Reference

Beatles, The. 'Day Tripper'/'We Can Work It Out.' Parlophone R5389. *1965*: UK.

DAVE LAING

B Side

The B side of a two-track single was the less important of the tracks. Each side of promotional copies of singles sent to radio programmers was marked clearly with either 'A' or 'B' to inform disc jockeys which track they should play. Sometimes, however, a DJ would 'flip' a single and play the B side, which might then become a hit. To avoid this, some record companies would send DJs a single-sided record with the B side omitted.

In cases where an outside composer was used to provide the song for an A side, it was commonplace for the B side to be devoted to a track composed by the singer or group featured, thus ensuring they would share in the publishing royalties. In Jamaican music, the B side of singles was often a 'dub' version of the A side with the vocal and lead instrument tracks erased.

DAVE LAING

Concept Album

More than a collection of unrelated songs, the 'concept album' calls attention to its 'conception' as an organic whole, with a deliberate coherence across its component parts. These may include track sequence, cover art and/or liner notes, as well as music, lyrics, performance style and production. Versions from the 1950s include mood music LPs organized by an intended emotional response (relaxation, seduction – for example, the Melachrino Strings' *Music for Daydreaming*, Jackie Gleason's *Music for Lovers Only*), or theme albums that seek to represent or explore a particular idea (loneliness, exotic travel – for example, Frank Sinatra's *Frank Sinatra Sings for Only the Lonely*, Norrie Paramor's *Jet Flight*).

But concept albums are primarily associated with rock culture from around 1966 onward. While the coherence of the first rock concept albums (the Beach Boys' *Pet Sounds*, the Mothers of Invention's *Freak Out*, the Beatles' *Sergeant Pepper's Lonely Hearts Club Band*) lies more in their individual 'sound' than in any clearly discernible unifying idea, later works such as the Who's *Tommy* or Pink Floyd's *The Wall* develop a more explicit form of musical narrative. Through its association with high art forms such as the song cycle, symphony or opera, the concept album is an important part of rock culture's attempts to move beyond the constraints of the romantic pop song. Concept albums foreground the authorial intentions of performers, thereby contributing to their legitimation as serious artists.

Discographical References

Beach Boys, The. *Pet Sounds*. Capitol ST 2458. *1966*: USA.

Beatles, The. *Sergeant Pepper's Lonely Hearts Club Band*. Parlophone PCS 7027. *1967*: UK.

Gleason, Jackie. *Music for Lovers Only*. Capitol 352. 1953: USA.

Melachrino Strings, The. *Music for Daydreaming*. RCA-Victor 1028. 1954: USA.

Mothers of Invention, The. *Freak Out*. Verve 5005. *1966*: USA.

Paramor, Norrie. *Jet Flight*. Capitol T10190. *1958*: USA.

Pink Floyd. *The Wall*. Harvest SHDW 411. *1979*: UK.

Sinatra, Frank. *Frank Sinatra Sings for Only the Lonely*. Capitol W920. *1958*: USA.

Who, The. *Tommy*. Track 613 013/4. *1969*: UK.

KEIR KEIGHTLEY

Cover Version

Introduction

A cover version is, generally, a recording or performance of a song by someone other than either the song's creator or the singer of the first recording of it. The cover version may involve a form of competition, as when several performers on different record labels simultaneously vie for chart success with the same song, or it may be a form of homage, as when one performer uses another's song to invoke that artist or the tradition represented by that song. Thus, the term 'cover version' can denote both industry-driven and aesthetic strategies. In certain popular music traditions where the division of musical labor is common (i.e., where songs are almost always performed by someone other than the songwriter), 'cover version' may not be the most appropriate term. This is because the term calls attention to a distinction between composer and performer that in certain contexts may be unremarkable. Moreover, the meaning of 'cover version' has shifted over time. In contemporary popular music, a number of the term's historical meanings coexist. Thus, it is important to understand in which particular context the term is being employed. It is possible to distinguish five main musical contexts in which the term 'cover version' is used: (a) commercial music before rock; (b) rock 'n' roll; (c) rock; (d) rock homage; and (e) sampled music.

Commercial Music Before Rock

Before about the 1960s, commercial popular music tended to involve a definite division of creative labor: songwriters wrote songs, arrangers arranged, singers sang. Few singers wrote songs and few songwriters sang professionally. Generally, songwriters and music publishers wanted to have as many performers as possible perform their new songs because that would mean more exposure, and thus more sheet music copies sold and more performance royalties earned (although there were occasional 'exclusives' granted to major stars who, it was felt, might promote a song more effectively if they knew that they had sole access to it). Only with the rise of the record, which replaced sheet music as the core commodity of the music industry, did it become important to identify cover versions as such. Because of the close ties within the music industry between record manufacturers and record retailers during the first half of the twentieth century, often only a quite limited range of record companies or 'labels' was available at a particular store. Thus, most record labels sought to have their own version of a hit song recorded and for sale, thereby 'covering' the market for that particular song (as opposed to a particular record).

Into the 1950s, it was not uncommon for a large number of hit songs to appear in recorded versions by different performers in every major label's catalog (for example, in 1956 there were five versions of Weill-Brecht-Blitzstein's 'Mack the Knife' (a theme from The

Threepenny Opera) that made the Top 40). However, because older, long-lasting songs – 'standards' – were also an important part of record industry output, the term 'cover version' did not simply mean a recording of a song that had been previously performed or recorded; rather, the term referred to 'current' performances of songs that had recently become, or were believed to be on their way to becoming, hits (which included revivals of older songs, newly promoted, like 'Mack the Knife'). Thus, temporal connotations of simultaneity or contemporaneity mark the industry-driven use of the term 'cover version' (so that a song may be viewed by the industry in the same way as a news story is viewed by the press: in both cases, a decision is made on whether to 'cover' it). A cover version is an element of industry-wide competition (between multiple versions, performers and labels) – a strategy of making available a performance of a song that is currently being promoted toward (or has already recently achieved) hit status.

Cover versions can also be part of an industry-driven strategy of localization, in which a song popular in a foreign country is adapted for a domestic market. For example, Johnny Hallyday's French-language version of the Chubby Checker hit 'Let's Twist Again' (written by Kal Mann and Dave Appell), 'Viens danser le twist,' offered French audiences the pleasure of a US song in their native language and became Hallyday's first million-seller. In countries with broadcasting policies that demand a minimum amount of domestically produced material, cover versions of foreign (usually US) hits can often become successful, as in the case of the Canadian group Songbird's 1974 hit cover of the Stevie Wonder song 'I Believe.'

Rock 'n' Roll

In the United States during the 1950s, white performers were increasingly covering songs originally recorded by African-American songwriters and/or performers. Because of racial bias, many radio stations would play the white cover versions but not the original African-American versions. While this contributed greatly to the rise of rock 'n' roll within the white mainstream, it also meant that many recordings by African-American performers were pushed aside within the hit parade in favor of versions by white performers. Charges of exploitation and 'rip-off' started to proliferate, and the term 'cover version' began to connote a lack of originality, unfair competition and exploitation rather than a straightforward description of an industry-driven strategy. Paradoxically, white performers were frequently chided for simultaneously 'bleaching' an original (i.e., altering the sound of an original recording to cater to the perceived tastes of white audiences) and 'carbon-copying' it (i.e., stealing every aspect of the arrangement and performance style, and contributing nothing of their own). While the white performer Pat Boone was often singled out as the worst offender – with his versions of songs by Fats Domino, Little Richard and vocal groups such as the Flamingos surpassing their 'originals' in the charts – the triumph of Little Richard's 'Long Tall Sally' over Boone's cover version in 1956 marked a symbolic as well as an economic triumph of original rock 'n' roll over its putatively inferior and commercial 'copy.'

Rock

An important aspect of the development of rock culture in general during the 1960s involved a sustained critique of industry-driven and artistic practises in the mainstream of popular music. The cover version was often singled out as a particularly egregious example of exploitative commercial *and* creative practises. The cover version not only took sales away from the 'original' version, but also denied full artistic expression to the author of the covered song. Thus, the cover version became a symbol of the musical traditions that rock culture sought to reject. Rock culture critiqued the division of musical labor as a form of mediation interfering with the rock artist's authentic self-expression. Rock culture witnessed the rise of the singer-songwriter, who was viewed as a complete artist because of the organic integration of songwriting and performing in a single individual. Thus, songwriting became a key marker of authenticity for rock performers, and the cover version was largely consigned – with a key exception – to the 'alienated' world of commercial pop.

Rock Homage

The key exception was the development of a non-pejorative meaning of 'cover version' within rock, in which the performance of non-performer-originated songs could be seen as a homage or tribute to another artist or tradition (although, occasionally, the audience might not know of the original, and would therefore fail to perceive the cover version as a 'cover'). Rock auteurs, who have established their credentials as 'authentic' musicians by writing the majority of the songs they perform, can perform or record non-original songs without appearing derivative or devious. This is because their motivations are not perceived to be 'commercial,' as in the case of the first two uses of the term 'cover version' considered here, but, rather, are seen to be 'artistic.' In this instance, the cover version may allow rock artists to distinguish their performing skills from their songwriting skills, and use the text of the covered song as a vehicle to highlight the former. 'Tribute albums,' which consist entirely of cover versions of songs created by a single artist or group (such as those of the Beatles or Hüsker Dü), are an explicit and expanded example of the cover as homage. Nonetheless, in singling out a particular song in a live performance or on an album as somehow different from the rest of the performer-written repertoire, the term 'cover version' serves as a reminder that songwriting is key to concepts of authorship and authentic originality in rock culture.

Sampled Music

Another sense of homage emerged during the 1980s and 1990s via the technology of sampling and, although, strictly speaking, it does not involve cover versions, it is worth mentioning. While the use of brief samples of recordings as backgrounds or embellishments for rappers or dance mixes often involves a kind of 'quoting' from other musical works, it is the use of longer samples or entire songs as bed-tracks that is important to a discussion of cover versions. Although Run-D.M.C.'s 'Walk This Way' is clearly a cover version – notwithstanding the participation of the original 'authors,' Aerosmith's Steven Tyler and Joe Perry, in the new version – the numerous rap hits of the 1990s that use extended samples or even entire recordings as their rhythm or backing track may equally be considered a kind of cover version. Puff Daddy's rapping over a new recording of Led Zeppelin's 'Kashmir' on his 'Come with Me' and Will Smith's employment of Grover Washington Jr.'s and Bill Withers's 'Just the Two of Us' for his song of the same title are technically 'adaptations' of preexisting songs. But they can also be considered new performances of those songs (particularly when the track used is not sampled but 're-created' by original members of the group), and are therefore similar to cover versions. These are, in turn, related to the Jamaican practise of 'versioning,' in which a new popular song or rhythm pattern is very quickly copied, adapted or modified in dozens of new permutations or 'versions.'

Conclusion

Contemporary popular music employs each of these inflections of the meaning of 'cover version' in varying degrees. The meaning of the term used in commercial music before rock has returned to the forefront, as the idea of the singer-songwriter has become less prominent than it was in the 1970s. Although the 'cover battles' of the 1950s have faded (despite their occasional recurrence in modified form – for example, the competition between 'Whoomp! (There It Is)' by Tag Team and 'Whoot, There It Is' by 95 South in 1993, or the practise of producing dance-music versions of current pop hits), in contemporary record industry parlance any song recorded by someone other than the author is now called simply a 'cover.' Thus, Aerosmith would be said to have covered Diane Warren's 'I Don't Want to Miss a Thing,' even though it was a specially commissioned song, an 'exclusive' which, at the time, no one else had the opportunity to record (and which was, in fact, subsequently covered for the country market by Mark Chesnutt). At the same time, the growing frequency with which classic rock songs are regularly covered by artists as diverse as Michael Bolton and Pearl Jam suggests that a new term – perhaps 'rock standards' – is needed to describe the corpus of rock songs that are, ironically, increasingly subject to the very performance practise whose rejection defined the emergence of rock culture.

Bibliography

Belz, Carl. 1972. *The Story of Rock*. Oxford: Oxford University Press.

Ennis, Philip H. 1992. *The Seventh Stream: The Emergence of RocknRoll in American Popular Music*. Hanover, NH: Wesleyan University Press.

Kamin, Jonathan. 1972. 'Taking the Roll Out of Rock: Reverse Acculturation.' *Popular Music and Society* 2: 1–17.

Kamin, Jonathan. 1978. 'The White R&B Audience and the Music Industry, 1952–1956.' *Popular Music and Society* 6: 150–67.

Ward, Brian. 1998. *Just My Soul Responding: Rhythm and Blues, Black Consciousness and Race Relations*. London: UCL Press.

Discographical References

Aerosmith. 'I Don't Want to Miss a Thing.' Sony 78952. *1998*: USA.

Aerosmith. 'Walk This Way.' Columbia 10206. *1975*: USA.

Armstrong, Louis, and His All-Stars. 'A Theme from The Threepenny Opera (Mack the Knife).' Columbia 40587. *1956*: USA. Reissue: Armstrong, Louis, and His All-Stars. 'A Theme from The Threepenny Opera (Mack the Knife).' *I Like Jazz: The Essence of Louis Armstrong*. Columbia CK-47916. *1991*: USA.

Boone, Pat. 'Ain't That a Shame.' Dot 15377. 1955: USA. Reissue: Boone, Pat. 'Ain't That a Shame.' *Fifties: Complete*. Bear Family 15884. *1997*: Germany.

Boone, Pat. 'Long Tall Sally.' Dot 15457. *1956*: USA. Reissue: Boone, Pat. 'Long Tall Sally.' *Fifties: Complete*. Bear Family 15884. *1997*: Germany.

Boone, Pat. 'Tutti' Frutti.' Dot 15443. *1956*: USA. Reissue: Boone, Pat. 'Tutti' Frutti.' *Fifties: Complete*. Bear Family 15884. *1997*: Germany.

Checker, Chubby. 'Let's Twist Again.' Parkway 824. *1961*: USA. Reissue: Checker, Chubby. 'Let's Twist Again.' *The Best of Chubby Checker*. Madacy 2395. *1999*: USA.

Chesnutt, Mark. 'I Don't Want to Miss a Thing.' *I Don't Want to Miss a Thing*. MCA 70035. *1999*: USA.

Dick Hyman Trio, The. 'Moritat (A Theme from "The Threepenny Opera").' MGM 12149. *1956*: USA. Reissue: Dick Hyman Trio, The. 'Moritat (A Theme from "The Threepenny Opera").' *Music for a Bachelor's Den*. DCC 79. *1995*: USA.

Domino, Fats. 'Ain't It a Shame.' Imperial 5348. 1955: USA. Reissue: Domino, Fats. 'Ain't It a Shame.' *Out of New Orleans*. Bear Family 15541. *1993*: Germany.

Hallyday, Johnny. 'Viens danser le twist' (EP). Philips 432593. *1961*: France.

Hayman, Richard, and August, Jan. '(A Theme from) The Threepenny Opera (Moritat).' Mercury 70781. *1956*: USA.

'I Don't Want to Miss a Thing' (comp. Diane Warren). *Armageddon [OST]*. Sony 69440. *1998*: USA.

Led Zeppelin. 'Kashmir.' *Physical Graffiti*. Swan Song SSK/SK4 89400. *1975*: UK. Reissue: Led Zeppelin. 'Kashmir.' *Complete Studio Recordings*. Swan Song 82526. *1993*: USA.

Little Richard. 'Long Tall Sally.' Specialty 572. *1956*: USA. Reissue: Little Richard. 'Long Tall Sally.' *The Best of Little Richard*. Madacy 2394. *1999*: USA.

Little Richard. 'Tutti-Frutti.' Specialty 561. *1956*: USA. Reissue: Little Richard. 'Tutti-Frutti.' *The Best of Little Richard*. Madacy 2394. *1999*: USA.

95 South. 'Whoot, There It Is.' Wrap 162. *1993*: USA.

Puff Daddy. *Come with Me [UK]*. Tristar 66242. *1998*: UK.

Puff Daddy. *Come with Me [US#1]*. Sony 78954. *1998*: USA.

Puff Daddy. *Come with Me [US#2]*. Sony 78966. *1998*: USA.

Run-D.M.C. 'Walk This Way.' Profile 5112. *1986*: USA.

Smith, Will. 'Just the Two of Us.' *Big Willie Style*. Columbia 68683. *1997*: USA.

Songbird. 'I Believe.' Mushroom Records M7002. *1974*: Canada.

Tag Team. 'Whoomp! (There It Is).' Life 79500. *1993*: USA.

Vaughn, Billy, and His Orchestra. 'A Theme from (The Threepenny Opera) "Moritat."' Dot 15444. *1956*: USA.

Washington, Grover, Jr., and Withers, Bill. 'Just the Two of Us.' Elektra 47103. *1981*: USA.

Welk, Lawrence, and His Sparkling Sextet. 'Moritat (A Theme from "The Threepenny Opera").' Coral 61574. *1956*: USA.

Wonder, Stevie. 'I Believe (When I Fall in Love It Will Be Forever).' *Talking Book*. Tamla 316. *1973*: USA.

KEIR KEIGHTLEY

Digital Recording

Digital sound processing involves the conversion of conventional alternating current waveforms into a new discontinuous form of signal made up entirely of very short pulses encoded into numbers or digits, and therefore called 'digital.' The sounds that are heard, or picked up through a microphone, arrive as tiny continuous variations in the ambient atmospheric pressure. The electrical signal leaving the microphone reproduces these pressure changes – that is, it is analogous to them; therefore, it is referred to as 'analog' (sometimes spelled 'analogue').

For digital recording or transmission to take place, the analog signals must first be passed through an analog-to-digital converter (ADC). This changes the analog waveform into a stream of constant-amplitude, level pulses. These are individually coded into a digital 'word' in such a way that the receiver or playback device has only to detect the presence or absence of a pulse, not its level, and pass this information through a digital-to-analog converter (DAC) to reproduce the original sound signals. This makes digital signals virtually impervious to interference and capable of operating to any desired order of accuracy.

The ADC operates by sampling the amplitude of the audio waveform at regular intervals and assigning to each sample a binary number of ones and zeros (the digital word) to represent the amplitude at that instant. A higher sampling frequency will reproduce the waveform more accurately, as will an increased number of discrete levels made available by the use of a longer word length (as given by the number of 'bits' per word). As a benchmark, the sampling rate chosen must be at least twice the highest desired audio frequency and the word length should be at least 13-bit.

The British Broadcasting Corporation (BBC) was a pioneer in the use of digital sound processing and introduced the PCM (pulse code modulation) digital system for distributing its radio programs between studios and transmitting stations as early as 1972. The sampling frequency chosen was 32 kHz, to provide the required FM radio bandwidth of 15 kHz, and a 13-bit word length. The results were sufficiently successful to elicit favorable comments on the improved clarity and realism from critical listeners.

By 1975, Nippon Columbia (Denon) in Japan had developed a viable PCM tape recording system, spreading the digital signals over eight tracks on a 2″ (50 mm) video-type helical scan recorder running at 15″ (38 cm) per second and giving a tape/head relative speed of 1,575″ (40 m) per second. When this system was transferred to standard analog LP records, the results were noticeably cleaner than usual, with a complete absence of tape hiss or modulation noise.

Within a few years, all the major record companies had designed or acquired digital tape recorders and were using them almost exclusively for all master recording. However, multitrack pop recording stayed loyal to analog machines, which suited the overdubbing and postproduction techniques developed over many years. The digital tape masters were transferred to analog media – vinyl discs and tape cassettes – and stockpiled in anticipation of some new digital consumer medium in the future. It was acknowledged that the full benefits of digital technology would be experienced only when the music signals were kept in the digital domain all the way from the studio to a DAC in the listener's home.

This was achieved in 1982 when Philips and Sony jointly launched the compact disc. A sampling frequency of 44.1 kHz was chosen, offering an audio response out to 20 kHz, the nominal limit of human hearing, and 16-bit encoding, which gave an unprecedented dynamic range of 96 dB. Other digital consumer media followed, including the digital audio tape (DAT), the digital compact cassette (DCC) and the minidisc (MD).

Professional digital tape recorders have continued to improve, with higher sampling frequencies and bit-rates; optical disc recorders, providing quicker access and other operational advantages, have become increasingly popular. Digital audio broadcasting, and digital video and television, were being demonstrated in late 1997 and seemed destined to take a central position in all methods of communication and home entertainment.

Bibliography

Blesser, B. 1978. 'Digitization of Audio.' *Journal of the Audio Engineering Society* 26(10): 739–71.

Pohlmann, Ken C. 1989. *Principles of Digital Audio*. Indianapolis, IN: Sams.

JOHN BORWICK

EP

Extended play (EP) records use the same formats as singles, but contain more tracks of recorded music. They have served different functions in various phases of record industry history. The first EPs were 7″ (18 cm) vinyl discs containing four or more tracks and produced with picture sleeves. During the 1950s and 1960s, they became a third vinyl format (together with singles and full-length albums), sometimes used by smaller jazz or blues labels, but mainly used for pop music by major record companies, which aimed them at teenagers unable to afford full-length albums. Typically, an EP would reprise hit singles (sometimes by different artists signed to the same label) or four tracks from an LP. For example, the debut album of the Beatles was issued in Britain in March 1963. Between June and November of that year, the 12 tracks of the album were issued on three EPs.

This use of the EP died out in the late 1960s. By then, the Beatles had broken new ground by issuing new material in the format with their *Magical Mystery Tour* double EP. Since the late 1970s, many punk or alternative rock acts have chosen to issue their work as EPs, in both 7″ (18 cm) and 12″ (30 cm) vinyl formats. Ironically, it later became customary for vinyl and CD records issued as singles to contain several tracks of remixes of the same song, while in some countries, such as France and Japan, the 7″ (18 cm) format customarily contained four tracks and the two-track single was unknown.

All the Beatles' EPs were reissued as 3″ (7.5 cm) CDs in 1989, and the British reissue company See For Miles inaugurated an EP reissue series on full-length CDs in the late 1980s.

Discographical References

Beatles, The. *Magical Mystery Tour* (EP). Parlophone MMT-1. *1967*: UK.

Beatles, The. *Please Please Me*. Parlophone PMC 1202. *1963*: UK.

Discography

Beatles, The. *The Beatles (No. 1)* (EP). Parlophone GEP 8883. *1963*: UK.

Beatles, The. *The Beatles' Hits* (EP). Parlophone GEP 8880. *1963*: UK.

Beatles, The. *Twist and Shout* (EP). Parlophone GEP 8882. *1963*: UK.

DAVE LAING

Home Recording

Since the early 1970s, many professional, semiprofessional and amateur musicians have acquired the equipment necessary to establish multitrack recording facilities in their homes. Such facilities allow pop musicians to pursue sound recording as a creative medium without the pressures of paying for commercial studio time at hourly rates.

The home recording movement is the result of a complex interplay among the economic priorities of the record industry, the creative needs of musicians and the marketing strategies of audio and musical instrument manufacturers. Beginning in the 1950s, the increasing volatility of the pop music market created entrepreneurs who, operating out of independent recording facilities, gradually took over the production needs of the record industry. With the rise of multitrack recording in the 1960s, much pop and rock music became a studio product: songs and arrangements were created in the studio through the collaboration of recording artists, entrepreneurial producers and sound engineers. By the early 1970s, many successful artists were investing tens of thousands of dollars in constructing their own studios where they could experiment freely with the new technology and take greater control over aesthetic decision-making.

With the rising costs of studio production and the image of star performers' unconstrained access to the powerful technologies of creation, many semiprofessional and amateur musicians began to look for ways in which they too could construct their own studios and become familiar with the disciplines necessary to work with multitrack equipment. In addition, the growing, do-it-yourself, independent recording movement of the 1970s created a need for recording equipment that was both inexpensive and easy to use. As the demand for consumer audio production equipment grew, a marketing notion of the 'home studio' began to take shape. By 1972, the first four-track tape recorder expressly designed for amateur and semiprofessional use (the TEAC 3340) had been introduced. In an effort to simplify multitracking and make it more affordable for the amateur home market, Tascam (a division of TEAC) introduced the Portastudio concept, which combined inexpensive cassette technology with an integrated mixing console. The idea was copied by a number of other manufacturers. The impetus behind the home recording movement grew stronger during the 1980s with the arrival of inexpensive drum machines, synthesizers and MIDI (musical instrument digital interface), which allowed synthesizers and personal computers to be connected and integrated with sound recording. By the 1990s, digital recording equipment, in tape and hard disc formats, had been introduced; the flexibility and sound quality of these devices, which offered track capability beyond the four- and eight-track configurations typical of analog home recorders, blurred the distinction between home and professional studios.

The home recording phenomenon is testimony to the importance of 'independent' production in popular music, the nature of which is quite different from the organization of production in other entertainment industries. To use multitrack equipment, musicians have had to acquire new forms of technical knowledge and new concepts of musical 'sound' that are quite unlike those associated with conventional music-making. However, as the sound quality of home studio recordings has improved, the record industry has also begun to expect even demo tapes to be of commercial quality. At the same time, the cost of the increasingly diverse set of technologies that make up the home studio has become considerable, giving new meaning to the notion of 'paying your dues' in the music business (Jones 1992).

Bibliography

Durant, Alan. 1990. 'A New Day for Music?: Digital Technologies in Contemporary Music-Making.' In *Culture, *Technology and Creativity*, ed. Philip Hayward. London: John Libbey & Co., 175–96.

Jones, Steve. 1992. *Rock Formation: Music, Technology, and Mass Communication*. Newbury Park, CA: Sage.

Kealy, Edward R. 1979. 'From Craft to Art: The Case of Sound Mixers and Popular Music.' In *On Record: Rock, Pop, and the Written Word*, ed. Simon Frith and Andrew Goodwin. New York: Pantheon, 207–20. (First published in *Sociology of Work and Occupations* 6 (1979): 3–29.)

Théberge, Paul. 1997. *Any Sound You Can Imagine: Making Music/Consuming Technology*. Hanover, NH: Wesleyan University Press/University Press of New England.

PAUL THÉBERGE

Independent

An independent or 'indie' record company, distributor or music publisher is one that is not controlled by a major company in the music industry. Typically, an independent label will focus on talent acquisition and studio production, contracting out the manufacture, marketing or distribution of its recordings to other companies.

Historically, the indies have been identified with small niche markets ('ethnic' or avant-garde, for example) or with influential musical innovation in jazz, rhythm and blues, rock and rap. The historical trend has also been for majors to attempt to control the indie sector through takeovers, the purchase of the contracts of the indies' star acts (for example, Elvis Presley) or the formation of a variety of joint-venture deals with indies.

DAVE LAING

Label

This is the record industry term for the brand name given to a series of commercially issued recordings. The term is metonymic, originating in the fact that the brand name and its distinctive logo appeared on the 'label' stuck to or embossed on the center of 78s and vinyl recordings.

Cylinders had either labels attached to the cylinder box or titles engraved on the cylinder end. The first paper labels for discs appeared in 1901, but many record companies have preferred to stamp paperless labels onto discs. The introduction of vinyl in the late 1940s involved the use of special 'grain-oriented' paper which could stand the much higher temperatures needed in the manufacture of vinyl discs.

A label name may be coterminous with that of the company owning the recordings in the label's catalog. Alternatively, a large record company may own and operate many labels. In the 1990s, for instance, Poly-Gram issued recordings on such labels as Mercury, Island, A&M, Philips, Decca, London, Def Jam, Polydor, Verve, Motown, Barclay and many more.

Historically, licensing agreements sometimes led to two companies using the same label or logo in different parts of the world. Thus, 'Columbia' was a label name used by CBS in the United States and EMI in the United Kingdom until the 1980s, while the famous 'dog and trumpet' logo was used for many years by both EMI and RCA-Victor.

Bibliography

Copeland, Peter. 1991. *Sound Recordings*. London: The British Library.

DAVE LAING

Live Album

A live album is an extended recording that is perceived to be a document of a live performance or performances (with time and place usually indicated). Until the advent of overdubbing in the 1940s, all music was recorded 'live,' although rarely before an audible audience. Thereafter, a finished studio recording might consist of multiple live performances at different times and places, subsequently assembled into a unified piece of music (and, with the advent of computer sequencers, the idea that there is even an originary live-to-multitrack performance is thrown into doubt).

The modern 'live album' is distinguished by its difference from the 'studio album' and its technological tricks, even though both use similar multitrack equipment. The live album is defined by a perceived sense of spontaneous performance, emotional directness and audience interaction. Thus, musical cultures such as, for example, jazz or blues value live albums particularly because of their conviction that instrumental improvisation or emotional expressivity is enhanced by the presence of an audience (and by the absence of the sometimes sterile and uninspiring environment of the recording studio). The live album asserts an idea of sound recording as a transparent mirror that can reveal the undistorted truth of an actual event – a live concert with real, live people – regardless of the subsequent technical improvements that may have been made (remixing, overdubbing, added applause).

KEIR KEIGHTLEY

LP

'LP' is the abbreviation for 'long player' or 'long-playing record.' Since the advent of the compact disc (CD), 'LP' has generally been used to refer to 12″ (30 cm) vinyl albums.

Attempts had been made, almost from the invention

of sound recording, to find a means of recording more than a few minutes of music onto each side of a disc or cylinder. The impetus came primarily from among those involved with the recording of classical music who were unhappy at having to interrupt the flow of a symphonic movement when a disc was changed. According to Copeland (1991), the size, speed and groove-pitch of the disc could be manipulated in order to increase playing time. As early as 1904, the UK-based Neophone company produced a 20″ (50 cm) disc, while the Marathon 12″ (30 cm) disc of 1910 had its grooves closer together and contained eight minutes of music on each side. In 1931, RCA-Victor announced a 12″ (30 cm) disc playing at 33 rpm, its Long-Playing or Program Transcription record, with a playing time of 'up to 30 minutes.'

None of these experiments was commercially successful, and it was not until 1948 that Columbia introduced the now standard 12″ (30 cm) vinyl format long-playing record in the United States. Because the grooves could be closer together on vinyl discs, this LP could hold approximately 20 minutes of music on either side. This enabled jazz musicians to record extended pieces (and to issue unedited concert recordings), although in mainstream popular music the LP typically contained 12 tracks of three or four minutes' duration. This convention persisted into the eras of the tape cassette and of the CD, even though both those formats could accommodate much longer playing times.

To begin with (partly for reasons of price), the LP was associated with music aimed at adults, such as original cast recordings from stage musicals or collections of songs by big bands and crooners. The first million-selling LP in the United States was the cast recording of *Oklahoma!* in 1949. Throughout the 1950s, younger fans generally acquired recorded music on singles (at 45 or 78 rpm) or EPs, although Bill Haley's *Rock Around the Clock* entered the US album charts in 1956.

The size of the LP encouraged label producers, designers and writers to provide visually arresting images and informative notes on the 12″ (30 cm) sleeve in which the disc was sold.

Bibliography

Copeland, Peter. 1991. *Sound Recordings*. London: The British Library.

Millard, Andre J. 1995. *America on Record: A History of Recorded Sound*. Cambridge and New York: Cambridge University Press.

Discographical References

Haley, Bill, and His Comets. *Rock Around the Clock*. Decca DL 8225. *1956*: USA.

Oklahoma! (Original soundtrack). Decca 10046. 1949: USA.

DAVE LAING

Major

A major record company is usually defined as one that owns both manufacturing plants and distribution networks in addition to producing sound recordings. The contrast is with an independent record company, which usually relies on a major or a specialist company for manufacture and distribution.

In the 1990s, the term 'major' came to be defined by a company's global reach. Thus, majors were those companies with branch networks covering the Americas, Europe and the Pacific Rim. In 2002, the companies that were considered 'majors' according to this definition were: BMG, EMI, Sony, Warner Music and Universal (formerly MCA).

DAVE LAING

Matrix

A matrix was, strictly speaking, the 'Mother' from which the negative stamper used to press discs in the 78 rpm era was made, but the term was often applied to the original direct-cut recording from which the stamper derived. The name continued in use for matrices made from tape masters in the early 1950s. Most companies allocated a unique number to each recording, known as a matrix number; it is often to be found impressed in the disc between the grooves and the label and was frequently printed on the label too. This provides a physical means of identifying alternative takes and furnishes information about the origins and date of the recording.

In contrast, LPs and CDs bear 'stamper numbers' whose allocation usually has no relation to the original recording data. As a consequence, the term 'matrix' should be used only in the context of the one-to-one relationship between a recording and a 78 rpm disc. It should be noted that many enthusiasts object to using the term even for later 78s, which were generally not direct-cut.

Bibliography

Barr, Stephen C. 1979. *The (Almost) Complete 78 rpm Record Dating Guide*. Toronto: The author.

Black, Douglas C. [ca. 1946]. *Matrix Numbers: Their Meaning and History*. Melbourne: Australian Jazz Quarterly.

Dixon, Robert M.W., Godrich, John, and Rye, Howard. 1997. *Blues & Gospel Records 1890–1943*. 4th ed. Oxford: Clarendon Press.

Fairchild, Rolph. 1968. 'Decca Master Letter System.' *Matrix* 76: 7–10.

Gelatt, Roland. 1956. *The Fabulous Phonograph: The Story*

of the Gramophone from Tin Foil to High Fidelity. London: Cassell.

Mahony, Dan. 1966. 'Notes on Victor Master Numbers.' *Matrix* 68: 3–5.

Read, Oliver, and Welch, Walter L. 1976. *From Tin Foil to Stereo: The Evolution of the Phonograph.* 2nd ed. Indianapolis/New York: Howard Sams/Bobbs Merrill. (First published Indianapolis, IN: Howard W. Sams, 1959.)

HOWARD RYE

Music Video

The term 'music video' is used in a general sense to designate both the individual videoclip, intended to present a musical performance, and the broader phenomenon of music video programming on television. In addition, it may refer to videocassettes sold in retail stores and containing full-length audiovisual performances or compilations of videoclips. Since the emergence of music video programming services in the 1980s (such as MTV and Canada's MuchMusic), the question of music's relationship to visual accompaniment has been a central one within aesthetic, political and cultural discussions of popular music. The emergence of music video may be seen against the backdrop of broader developments, such as the musical film, which have made the image and personality of performers central components of their meaningfulness and appeal.

Many of the roots of music video lie in longstanding attempts to devise means of presenting short audiovisual clips of musical performances in public contexts. Experiments along these lines were frequently carried out on the fringes of the film industry, and resulted in such devices as the 'Cinematone,' invented in 1938 as a means of projecting short musical films in taverns. The more important event in the early history of such technologies came with the founding of the 'Soundies' corporation in the United States in the early 1940s. Musical shorts, known as 'soundies,' were shown on jukebox-like machines, which consisted of a mirrored screen surrounded by a curtain, onto which were projected three-minute 16 mm short films. Soundies offered the same variety of generic forms that would later characterize the videoclip. On occasion, the performers of songs would be in costume, acting out characters within a thinly sketched fictional narrative or situation. In other instances, mood and tone would be established through particular settings, such as a country meadow or a busy city street. While soundies themselves ceased to be a popular attraction in the 1940s, various attempts at creating audiovisual jukeboxes were marketed in the postwar period, including the 'Scopitone,' which was briefly popular in Europe.

The dissemination of these audiovisual technologies was limited, however, by their use of film. The invention of videotape in the 1950s, and the popularization of the videocassette in the 1970s, would bring about new uses for video in the circulation of popular music. In the late 1970s, the music industry became aware of the marketing potential offered by video playback units installed in retail stores, and began production of short videoclips of musical performances. In many cases, these videoclips were taped at live performances; increasingly, however, they were designed and taped in studios, and involved narrative and graphic elements difficult to produce in concert situations. By the end of the 1970s, the usefulness of short videoclips in promoting artists to audiences, consumers and the press was accepted within the music industry. Nevertheless, the production of promotional videoclips represented a significant added cost to artists and record companies, increasing the levels of investment required to compete for success in the popular music market.

The emergence of the videoclip coincided with a period in which the presence of popular music on television, at least in the United States and Canada, was at an historical low. The variety programming formats which television had inherited from radio, and in which music was prominent, had declined during the 1970s. Rock music was perceived as unattractive to the older, affluent audiences that television programmers desired, and so was banished to late-night concert-format programs such as *Don Kirshner's Rock Concert.* At the same time, the increasingly sophisticated production qualities of popular music were poorly conveyed through the audio playback devices common in television sets manufactured through the 1970s.

In 1981, MTV: The Music Network was launched in the United States by the Warner Amex Satellite Entertainment Company as a 24-hour cable channel devoted primarily to the presentation of short videoclips of musical performances. The purpose of MTV was twofold: on the one hand, it sought to create a form of television programming which targeted the 12–34 age group that other programming was seen to overlook and thus attract television advertisers interested in a teenage market; and, on the other, it was designed to market new musical acts to potential record buyers at a time when the programming of commercial radio stations in the United States was seen as conservative and restrictive. In both respects, MTV succeeded. Music television networks have generally built their appeal to advertisers on their ability to attract precisely defined audiences, even when their target audiences have been outside MTV's original core demographic. (VH-1, launched by MTV in 1985 to target the 25–54 age group, did so through a mixture of light pop, country and soul music.) MTV

622

played a crucial role, as well, in the success of what has sometimes been termed 'the second British invasion' – the popularization, in the United States, of a wave of British performers associated with glamorous, post-punk pop music. As a programming service distributed uniformly across the United States, MTV – like the other national services that have emerged in its wake – had an instantaneous effect on record-buying habits and the broader dissemination of styles and performers. Genre-specific services, such as the US Country Music Television or Black Entertainment Television, have influenced their viewers in a similar fashion, as well as producing new repertoires of images to accompany such musical styles as country and rap (Fenster 1993; Rose 1994).

It is in part because of its early association with style-conscious British pop that MTV sparked popular, critical and academic controversies over the new alliances of music and image which were seen to characterize its programming. The requirement that musical performers present their music with visual accompaniment was seen, by many, as representing the final incorporation of music within a broader culture of image and celebrity. These effects were condemned by those concerned with the formal and aesthetic purity of popular music and embraced by those who, often under the influence of postmodernist theorizing, welcomed evidence of a new culture dominated by surface and stylistic play. (For a consideration of these issues, see Goodwin 1992.)

With time, however, the impact of music television on the culture of popular music has become less clear. The success, in the 1990s, of Nirvana, and of so-called grunge music more generally, depended in large part on the dissemination of this music on MTV, but could not be attributed to an emphasis on style and surface over other, more intrinsically musical values. The important commercial and popular ascendancy of dance club music in the late 1980s and 1990s is striking evidence that significant shifts in musical taste among youth may transpire without the obvious influence of music video as a form or the music video network as a medium. At the same time, the resurgence of national and regional distinctiveness in musical tastes and buying habits since the mid-1990s has led MTV and other music video programmers to move away from uniform, global programming strategies, and has thus reduced the pertinence of claims that music video has produced an international homogeneity of musical tastes. Indeed, the examples of MuchMusic in Canada or Star TV in Asia show that music video networks may play an important role in strengthening regional musical cultures against homogenizing tendencies operative at the global level.

Bibliography

Berland, Jody. 1986. 'Sound, Image, and Social Space: Rock Video and Media Reconstruction.' *Journal of Communication Inquiry* 10(1) (Winter): 34–47.

Denisoff, R. Serge. 1988. *Inside MTV*. New Brunswick, NJ and Oxford: Transaction Books.

Fenster, Mark. 1993. 'Genre and Form: The Development of the Country Music Video.' In *Sound and Vision*, ed. Simon Frith and Andrew Goodwin. London: Routledge, 109–28.

Frith, Simon, and Goodwin, Andrew, eds. 1993. *Sound and Vision*. London: Routledge.

Goodwin, Andrew. 1992. *Dancing in the Distraction Factory: Music Television and Popular Culture*. Minneapolis, MN: University of Minnesota Press.

Kaplan, E. Ann. 1987. *Rocking Around the Clock: Music Television, Postmodernism and Consumer Culture*. New York: Methuen.

Morse, Margaret. 1986. 'Postsynchronizing Rock Music and Television.' *Journal of Communication Inquiry* 10: 15–28.

Rose, Tricia. 1994. *Black Noise: Rap Music and Black Culture in Contemporary America*. Hanover, NH: Wesleyan University Press.

Russell, Deborah. 1993. 'MTV in 2nd Decade: A True Network/Programming Mix Is Full-Service Menu.' *Billboard* 26 (June): 60.

Sanjek, Russell, and Sanjek, David. 1991. *American Popular Music Business in the 20th Century*. New York and Oxford: Oxford University Press.

WILL STRAW

Phonogram

In the music industry, and therefore in popular music, 'phonogram' is a term that denotes any physical medium carrying recorded sound, including analog and compact discs, DVD discs and prerecorded cassettes. The earliest use of 'phonogram' in this sense reported by the Oxford English Dictionary was in 1879. The word is now used almost exclusively in legal discourse and can be found in the titles of the 1961 Rome Convention and the 1996 World Intellectual Property Organization (WIPO) treaty, which refer to 'Producers of Phonograms,' that is, record companies. In general music industry parlance, the term has been superseded by such synonyms as 'soundcarrier,' 'sound recording' and 'phonorecord.' 'Phonogram' was also the name of a record label owned by Philips and later by PolyGram.

DAVE LAING

Picture Disc

Picture discs are records with an image imprinted onto the full face of the record (rather than just the inner label). The earliest picture discs date from the 1920s, when the technique was frequently used to embellish records for children.

Picture discs were reintroduced in the United States and the United Kingdom in the late 1970s as a selling point for 12″ (30 cm) albums and singles and 7″ (18 cm) singles. Examples included 'My Best Friend's Girl' by the Cars, with a picture of an automobile, and the Culture Club album *Colour By Numbers*, with full-color portraits of band members (Edge 1991). The first three-dimensional picture disc (with 3-D spectacles) distributed in Europe was 'I Love You' by the Swiss group Yello, which was released in 1983.

Bibliography

Edge, Kevin. 1991. *The Art of Selling Songs: Graphics for the Music Business, 1690-1990*. London: Futures Publications.

Discographical References

Cars, The. 'My Best Friend's Girl.' Elektra K12301P. *1978*: UK.

Culture Club. *Colour By Numbers*. Virgin V2285. *1983*: UK.

Yello. 'I Love You.' Stiff PBUY 176. *1983*: UK.

DAVE LAING

Production

'Production' is the term used for the process of making a sound recording. In particular, it refers to the contribution made by the producer of the recording, who is usually assisted by a studio engineer. The staging of a musical show or a major tour by a rock band or singer can also be described as a 'production.' In a more general economic sense, 'production' can be used to mean any type of manufacturing, and is the opposite term to 'consumption.'

DAVE LAING

Record Companies

Introduction

Record companies are those firms that issue recorded music to the public. They have played a crucial role in the evolution and growth of the popular music industry worldwide over the last hundred years or so. The variety of sound recording and manufacturing technologies has given rise to an equally varied range of record companies, from vertically integrated multinational enterprises issuing thousands of titles each year to 'back-room' operations run by enthusiasts for a minority music style or by individual musicians concerned only to distribute copies of their own work.

The First Record Companies

In the earliest years of sound recording, cylinders and records were produced and issued to the public by the manufacturers of phonographs and gramophones. The provision of music and speech recordings was at first regarded as a secondary activity designed to encourage consumers to buy the playback hardware. The first record companies were therefore those companies holding the patents that were essential to the manufacture of phonographs and gramophones. In the United States, these were Thomas A. Edison's National Phonograph Company (founded in 1896), the Columbia company (1889), Emile Berliner's Gramophone Company (1893) and Eldridge R. Johnson's Victor company (1901). From a very early stage, each of these four companies established European outlets for its products, and direct successors of three of the four are among the major firms that have continued to dominate the world record industry. The exception is the National Phonograph Company, which lost its leading position in the US market by continuing to manufacture cylinders after that format had been superseded in popularity by the disc format.

The US Columbia company was sold in 1934 to the American Record Company-Brunswick Record Company (ARC-BRC) and in 1938 to the Columbia Broadcasting System (CBS). In turn, CBS sold its record labels to the Sony Corporation of Japan in 1988. Sony has retained Columbia as a label name in many countries. The most successful foreign record companies using Emile Berliner's phonograph patents were in Britain (the Gramophone Company) and in Germany (Deutsche Grammophon). The Gramophone Company merged in 1931 with the UK branch of the Columbia company – which by then had separated from its US parent – to form Electric and Musical Industries Ltd. (EMI) (subsequently EMI Music). In its turn, Deutsche Grammophon, whose corporate links with the Gramophone Company were broken during World War I, became a component part of the Universal Music company. Lastly, Victor was purchased in 1929 by the Radio Corporation of America (RCA) and renamed RCA-Victor. When RCA was purchased in 1985 by General Electric, the RCA-Victor record company was sold off to the German Bertelsmann Music Group (BMG) to become part of the BMG record company.

These early major companies were followed into the phonograph market by dozens of other firms in the first decade of the twentieth century. In the United States, the newcomers generally made both phonographs and cylinders or discs for lower-income groups. In Europe, their counterparts often competed directly with the original firms in the exploitation of international markets, which was a principal feature of the record industry from the beginning.

In 1899, the Gramophone Company of London sent recording engineer Fred Gaisberg on the first of many field trips to make recordings of music in numerous cities of Europe and Asia. The purpose of these recordings was to assist local agents appointed by the manufacturer in the sale of gramophones to the middle and upper classes of each country. Other companies organized similar field trips. The most important of these competitors were Columbia, the French firm Pathé Frères, and the German companies Odeon, Parlophon and Beka, which were all part of the Lindström group by 1910. In India, for example, the Gramophone Company was faced with competition from six other companies.

By the time World War I effectively cut off the Western European companies from their international markets, Britain had 40 gramophone and record companies and the United States over 60. The new entrants to the US market at this time included music publishers (Waterson, Berlin and Snyder with their Little Wonder label), piano and furniture manufacturers (Gennett and Brunswick), and companies in the piano roll business (Aeolian).

The 1920s and 1930s

During the 1920s, the search for new markets led US companies to the music of working-class blacks and whites. Both Columbia and Victor recorded dozens of blues singers for their 'race' series, but Black Swan, the first black-owned company, focused more on concert music (Vincent 1995). Victor also used its European links with the Gramophone Company to issue special recordings for immigrant groups; at one stage, its catalog contained songs in 59 languages (Vernon 1997). Victor and Columbia also made recordings of musicians from immigrant communities in the United States itself (for a discography of immigrant music recorded in the United States during this period, see Spottswood 1990; see also American Folklife Center 1982).

The Depression, which followed the 1929 Wall Street crash, had a devastating impact on record companies in the United States. By the early 1930s, the industry had been reduced to a handful of very small labels and a new 'Big Three' – RCA-Victor, Columbia and ARC. Both RCA-Victor and Columbia were entertainment conglomerates – RCA had film, music publishing and theater interests, as well as radio and records – while ARC was the creation of Herbert Yates, a B-movie magnate whose Republic Pictures specialized in low-budget westerns. Yates had purchased numerous labels that provided cheap ($0.35) records for five-and-dime stores, as well as more prestigious labels. By the time the whole ARC group had been sold to RCA's great rival, CBS, in 1938, a new player had emerged on the US scene. Decca was a

label created in 1934 by Edward Lewis, the head of the Decca (UK) label, and Jack Kapp, formerly with Brunswick. The Decca strategy for survival during the Depression was to provide high-quality entertainers (Bing Crosby, the Andrews Sisters) at lower prices.

In Europe, too, a consolidation occurred in the 1930s. At the end of the 1920s, Columbia (UK) had gained its independence from its US parent and had acquired several of its key rivals, notably Pathé and Lindström. The onset of the Depression was the catalyst for the Columbia–Gramophone Company merger. The new EMI was by far the largest record company in Europe and across most of Asia and Africa. Its only significant competitor in the United Kingdom itself was Decca, which Lewis had founded in 1931. While Decca (UK) had to find new sources of repertoire, EMI continued to benefit from an agreement made in 1907 between the Gramophone Company and Victor whereby each company would have its own trading sphere (the British company had Europe, Africa, Australasia and Southeast Asia) and would license recordings to each other. EMI also had access to music from Columbia in the United States.

The 1940s and 1950s

The US record industry was transformed in the 1940s when the growth in employment provided by the war industries and the immediate postwar boom encouraged the formation of dozens of new companies. Many of the new entrepreneurs had existing links with the music business as retailers, booking agents or jukebox operators. Dance bands and crooners were recorded in Hollywood by Capitol and MGM, an offshoot of the film studio. Mercury was founded in 1947 in Chicago. Folk music recordings were released by Folkways and Elektra, while jazz recordings were issued by Commodore, Blue Note and Norgran. Many more of the new labels, springing up in New York, Chicago, Detroit, Los Angeles and elsewhere, were devoted to various forms of black music. Among the most significant were Atlantic, Savoy, King, Apollo and Aladdin.

When the European record industry restarted after 1945, EMI reestablished its Western European branches, some of which (like HMV in Italy and Germany) had been seized by enemy governments. In Eastern Europe, however, the new USSR-backed Communist regimes included the industry in their programs of nationalization. Any existing labels were amalgamated into state-owned monopoly organizations, such as Amiga in the German Democratic Republic (GDR), Supraphon in Czechoslovakia, Hungaroton in Hungary and Balkanton in Bulgaria. These were vertically integrated firms, which controlled the whole industry from recording to retailing.

During the 1950s, EMI's dominant role in Western Europe was gradually eroded. EMI had suffered from weak management in the 1930s and 1940s, and its US partners (RCA and CBS) were dissatisfied with its efforts to sell US music in European markets, where Hollywood films had begun to create an appreciative audience for US popular culture. The US companies were also under pressure from anti-monopoly agencies, and the global partnerships between EMI and both RCA and CBS/Columbia crumbled as RCA licensed its music through Decca from 1955 and CBS/Columbia gave its European license to the new Philips label, an offshoot of the Dutch electric light bulb and electrical goods firm. In response, EMI guaranteed itself a source of US repertoire through the purchase of Capitol for $8 million in 1955.

The buoyancy of the recorded music market on both sides of the Atlantic brought many more firms into the industry in the 1950s. In France, the Vogue and Barclay labels competed with EMI's Pathé Marconi subsidiary to sign the rising stars of *chanson*. In Italy, the long-established publisher Ricordi set up a record label in 1958; in Sweden, there was Metronome (founded in 1949); and in Spain, there was Hispavox (1952). Deutsche Grammophon (now owned by the industrial giant Siemens) set up branches in the principal European countries, using its Polydor label to sign up local pop talent. In 1962, it merged its music interests with those of the Philips-owned Phonogram group to form Poly-Gram. Another German label, Ariola, backed by the Bertelsmann media group, appeared on the European scene in the late 1950s.

In the United States, the newly discovered teenage pop market encouraged the formation of dozens more labels. Although the major labels (now joined by Capitol and Mercury) retained the contracts of the leading ballad singers and orchestras, the new independents seemed to be more adept at identifying and supporting younger talent from the ghettos, suburbs and rural areas. Many were also able to obtain valuable radio airplay by the judicious use of payola. These labels sprang up all over the country as a result of initiatives by entrepreneurs with an existing interest in the music business as record retailers (for example, Randy Wood of Dot in Tennessee), club owners (the Chess brothers of Chicago with Chess, and Morris Levy in New York with Roulette), jukebox operators (the Bihari brothers, who founded Modern and RPM in Los Angeles), or radio announcers or talent scouts (Sam Phillips of Sun Records in Memphis). The new label owners included the first women to head record companies: Florence Greenberg of pop label Scepter in New York; Vivian Carter of blues and R&B label Vee-Jay in Chicago; and Lillian Shedd McMurry of the Trumpet blues company in Jackson,

Mississippi. Carter and McMurry were also among the few black North American label owners. Another was Berry Gordy, who founded his Motown group of companies in Detroit in 1959.

The new entrants to the US record business also included such major media players as the Warner Brothers film company, the third broadcasting network ABC (the first two being NBC and CBS), and the booking agent and television company MCA, which acquired the Decca (US) label in 1961. MCA was later purchased by the Japanese consumer electronics firm Matsushita, which in turn sold MCA to the drinks conglomerate Seagram of Canada. Seagram changed the corporate name to Universal (after the company's Hollywood film studio). In 1998, it acquired PolyGram, making Universal the largest record company in the world at that stage.

Outside North America and Europe, the larger companies renewed or extended investment in Latin America, where CBS/Columbia set up branches in Mexico and Argentina in the 1940s and in Colombia in 1964. Philips bought CBD in Brazil in 1958.

During the late 1940s and 1950s, a significant number of locally based record companies were established for the first time in Africa and Asia. Prior to this, with the exception of a few labels such as Gallo of Johannesburg, these regions had been served only by local branches or agencies of EMI, Decca or Philips.

The availability of more portable and cheaper tape recording technology and the growth of urban centers assisted the emergence of new companies in Africa. In the Belgian colony of Congo, three studios and labels – Loningisa, Opika and Ngoma – were founded by expatriate Greek traders. In Sierra Leone, the Nugatone label competed with EMI, while Decca and Senafone set up studios in Nigeria.

In Asia, local entrepreneurs set up such companies as PT Musica (Indonesia, 1952) and Jigu (Korea, 1954). In Japan, foreign companies had sold off their labels in the 1930s, but they were now permitted to invest in joint ventures, and several Western record companies joined with local electronics companies to create labels. These included EMI-Toshiba, Warner-Pioneer and CBS-Sony.

The 1960s and 1970s

During the 1960s, the larger US record companies began to replace licensing agreements in Europe with the foundation of wholly owned branches, initially in the larger countries. CBS set up in Britain in 1964 and RCA in Italy in 1962. They were followed by Warner Brothers, A&M and United Artists (UA).

One reason for the US companies' new interest in Europe was the international popularity of British rock. This also triggered the foundation by young British entrepreneurs of a series of new companies, such as Island, Chrysalis, RSO, Charisma and Virgin, between 1966 and 1973. Other new labels were those started by star artists themselves. The most famous of these was the Beatles' Apple (set up in 1967), but others included Brother (the Beach Boys), Rocket (Elton John) and Threshold (the Moody Blues).

In the United States, new genres such as soul and disco brought success to pioneering labels such as Stax, Hi and Casablanca, although most such companies were eventually swallowed up by major companies in a pattern that would be repeated in the following decades.

The boom in record sales and the growth of industrial conglomerates led to a spate of takeovers in the late 1960s and early 1970s in the United States. The most important of these was the creation of Warner Communications by Steve Ross, who built a media empire from an initial holding in his father-in-law's funeral parlor. The resulting amalgamation of the Atlantic, Elektra and Warner labels created one of the two major companies (the other being CBS) that dominated the US record industry for the next 30 years. Less successful record business conglomerates were created by the Transamerica group, which bought the UA and Liberty labels, and by Gulf & Western (G&W), which purchased the Dot and Paramount labels. Transamerica sold out to EMI, while G&W sold its music companies to ABC in 1974; ABC in turn sold its labels to MCA in 1979.

The buoyancy of the US market in this period inspired European companies to attempt to strengthen their position through the purchase of US labels. Philips bought Mercury, EMI bought UA and Liberty in 1978, and in 1980 Bertelsmann's Ariola company formed a joint venture with RCA, finally buying the RCA catalog outright in 1985 when BMG was formed.

The mail-order and record-club sectors had been steadily growing in the United States since 1955, when CBS launched its Columbia House club. A new market for compilation albums sold solely through television advertising was developed in the 1970s by K-Tel, the household goods and brushes marketing company, and a series of imitators, which in Europe included Arcade and Ronco.

A number of gospel and Christian music labels were created in the United States in the late 1970s and early 1980s. These included the first black-owned gospel company, Tyscot of Indianapolis, Reunion and Maranatha!. A very different kind of music inspired a rash of new small companies in Britain and Europe: punk and 'new wave' music were responsible for the creation of such UK labels as 4AD, Rough Trade, Stiff and Beggars Banquet. For a few years, this independent sector, with its own distribution companies like Pinnacle and Spartan, pro-

vided a distinct alternative to the largest UK 'majors,' EMI and PolyGram (which had acquired the ailing Decca company in 1979). Elsewhere in Northern Europe, independent labels and distributors became an established part of the industry. In Sweden, the independents formed their own association, SOM, and were assisted by the MNW distribution and label group.

The 1980s and 1990s

In the mid-1980s, PolyGram spearheaded the launch of the first new recorded music format for almost 20 years, the compact disc (CD), invented by Sony. As the affiliate of Philips, PolyGram initially marketed the new digital software to the classical music market. Despite its early adoption in Japan, other major companies were less enthusiastic about the CD, but by the late 1980s all were issuing albums in three formats. The cost of manufacturing CDs was prohibitive for smaller companies, however, and the introduction of the format cemented the domination of the global record market by the five major companies: in 1992, labels owned by PolyGram, Sony, Warner, EMI and BMG controlled two-thirds of the world market, or 75 percent if labels distributed by them were included in the calculation.

One byproduct of the CD revolution was a brisk trade in defunct companies owning masters from the 1950s to the 1970s, which the purchasers reissued on CD. Thus, in the late 1980s, the Welk Music Group bought the Vanguard catalog, Fantasy bought Pablo and EMI bought Roulette.

The buoyancy of Western record markets in the 1980s encouraged the five major companies to make significant investments in Asia, Latin America and Eastern Europe. While in 1979 only EMI and Warner had set up branches in Southeast Asia, by 1990 all five companies were well established there, with 30 branches or joint ventures between them. Similarly, most of these companies extended their South American branch network to include Ecuador, Peru and Paraguay as well as the larger countries.

After the fall of Communism in Eastern Europe and the Soviet Union, the major companies included these 'emerging' market economies in their plans. Typically, the major company would appoint a licensee from among the new record companies in, for example, Hungary or Poland, convert it into a joint venture and then acquire the whole company.

While classical music sales had benefited from the advent of the CD and from a few isolated megahits (notably PolyGram's 'Three Tenors' recordings), this sector of the record industry became increasingly unprofitable for the major companies and they cut back on new recordings in the 1990s. In contrast, independent companies, such as Bis (Sweden) and Hyperion (UK), filled the gap by providing high-quality recordings of new or relatively obscure works, while the Hong Kong–based Naxos company built up a considerable market for high-quality budget-priced digital recordings of the whole classical repertoire.

There was a similar picture in the recorded jazz and 'world music' sectors. Major companies were halfhearted in their commitment, investing in and then withdrawing from the genres. While companies such as EMI (with Blue Note) and PolyGram (with Verve) owned catalogs of older jazz material, they were reluctant to commit themselves to new recordings and, at a corporate level, combined the management of their classical and jazz divisions. Within the continuing international niche market for jazz, a number of companies continued to thrive. These included Manfred Eicher's German-based ECM, the mainstream jazz label Concord, founded in 1972 by the US millionaire motor dealer Carl Jefferson, and Italy's Black Saint. In the case of 'world music' – the controversial but commercially appropriate name given to traditionally based styles from Africa, Latin America, the Middle East and Asia, presented in concert or on CD for mainly Western and Japanese audiences – major companies such as EMI and PolyGram (through its Island and Barclay subsidiaries) did participate. However, the leading companies were generally those formed by enthusiasts in Europe or the United States, such as Piranha (Germany), Stern's (UK) and Real World (UK), the company associated with singer Peter Gabriel.

The late 1980s and early 1990s saw the demise of the last internationally based, medium-size record companies, as PolyGram purchased Island, A&M and Motown and EMI bought Chrysalis and Virgin. These were just a few of over 200 transactions involving the major companies and independent labels that took place during the 1990s. Some of these were outright acquisitions of independent labels by 'majors,' but most involved the major company taking a minority share of an independent (such as the 49 percent of Creation, home of British rock group Oasis, bought by Sony), forming a joint venture with a smaller company or financing a large number of 'boutique' labels, often operated by former executives from major labels.

Despite these frequent raids on the independent sector, the number of independent labels worldwide remained fairly constant during the 1990s at perhaps 10,000, most of which were extremely small. The growth of house, techno and other dance musics inspired the foundation of dozens of new companies across Europe, among them ARS (Belgium), Mega (Denmark) and Discomagic (Italy), and in Japan, where Avex became a powerful force in the singles and compilations market.

Such innovations ensured that the independents' combined global share of recorded music sales remained constant at between 20 percent and 25 percent, meeting demands for local music or 'minority' genres that the major companies were unable or unwilling to supply or developing new styles of pop music based on a heightened awareness of nascent public taste. It was a commonplace among independent label owners in the United States that the operating systems of major companies made it uneconomic for them to release an album unless they were confident that it would sell 100,000 copies in the United States alone.

These statistics showed that, at some level, the record industry had become an oligopoly, but analysts were not in agreement about the implications of this fact. As early as 1975, Peterson and Berger had used chart analysis to argue in support of the implicit thesis propounded by Gillett (1970) that domination of the US record industry (or of the charts) by a handful of companies restricted musical choice for consumers. This so-called 'four firm thesis' was later disputed by Christianen (1995), who used The Netherlands as his counter-example, while Negus (1999) made the first systematic attempt to describe and analyze the strategic behavior and corporate culture of the major companies.

Bibliography

American Folklife Center. 1982. *Ethnic Recordings in America: A Neglected Heritage*. Washington, DC: Library of Congress.

Christianen, Michael. 1995. 'Cycles in Symbol Production?: A New Model to Explain Concentration, Diversity and Innovation in the Music Industry.' *Popular Music* 14(1): 55–94.

Gillett, Charlie. 1996 (1970). *The Sound of the City: The Rise of Rock 'n' Roll*. London: Souvenir Press.

Gronow, Pekka, and Saunio, Ilpo. 1998. *An International History of the Recording Industry*, trans. Christopher Moseley. London: Cassell.

Negus, Keith. 1999. *Music Genres and Corporate Cultures*. London: Routledge.

Peterson, Richard A., and Berger, David G. 1990 (1975). 'Cycles in Symbol Production: The Case of Popular Music.' In *On Record: Rock, Pop and the Written Word*, ed. Simon Frith and Andrew Goodwin. London: Routledge, 140–59. (First published in *American Sociological Review* 40 (1975): 158–73.)

Sanjek, Russell. 1988. *American Popular Music and Its Business: The First Four Hundred Years. Vol. III: From 1900 to 1984*. New York: Oxford University Press.

Spottswood, Richard K. 1990. *Ethnic Music on Records: A Discography of Ethnic Recordings Produced in the United*

States, 1893–1942. 7 vols. Urbana, IL: University of Illinois Press.

Vernon, Paul. 1997. 'Old World Music.' *Folk Roots* 174 (December): 28–30.

Vincent, Ted. 1995. *Keep Cool: The Black Activists Who Built the Jazz Age.* London and New Haven: Pluto Press.

DAVE LAING

Record Company

Introduction

The modern record company can trace its origins to the businesses that were formed during the 1890s to sell the first phonographs and the cylinders to play on them. At this time, many companies were set up and contributed to the formation of a new business by producing recordings on cylinders, categorizing them with such labels as 'Sentimental,' 'Topical,' 'Irish,' 'Comic' and 'Negro.' This practise drew on the cataloging systems of sheet music publishers, and the music business has continued this practise by using changing genre labels as an integral part of the organization of music for recording, promotion and selling. The phonograph cylinder was gradually replaced by the gramophone disc during the second decade of the twentieth century and, as a recording industry developed, certain key characteristic trends began molding the character and operations of record companies.

These trends persisted throughout the twentieth century, shaping the formation of the modern record company and its business practises. Firstly, connections were established between record companies and the electrical goods and entertainment industries. Secondly, distinctly different major and independent companies constantly appeared and reappeared. Thirdly, a process of concentration and consolidation occurred and, as a result, a few labels accounted for the distribution of most recordings sold in the world. Fourthly, an enduring tension emerged between those parts of the record company oriented to producing the music and those oriented toward selling it.

Connections to the Electrical Goods and Entertainment Industries

The early recording companies were managed by inventors, engineers, advertising personnel and stock market speculators, who had little connection with the impresarios who had been involved in song publishing, theater management and representation of artists. These managers, aware that they were dependent on the technologies of production and reproduction for their existence, developed their recording companies as part of a broader electrical goods industry. Hence, from the earliest days, record companies constituted one part of a business that produced entire systems of recording – not just the discs, but the mastering equipment used for recording in the studio and the storage cabinets and equipment needed for playing recordings in the home. The combination of separate businesses was not peculiar to the music industry; it was part of a broader trend whereby businesses in general were combining and forming multi-divisional corporations.

Such technological connections continued to inform music business strategies throughout the twentieth century. For example, more than 60 years after the formation of Electric and Musical Industries Ltd. (EMI) in 1931, the Japanese Sony Corporation owned the record labels that produced the recordings of Bob Dylan, Bruce Springsteen, the Fugees and Gloria Estefan, manufactured the transistor radios, cassette machines, Walkmans and hi-fi systems used by listeners, and made the tape cassettes and the studio recording technology used by musicians when making their recordings. Thus, the company was vertically integrated through the ownership of manufacturing and distribution systems, technologies of reception, record labels, music publishing and mail-order music clubs; and it had also horizontally integrated a range of record labels within the same corporation and connected these to other entertainment media, such as film and computer games.

These sorts of connections, established by Sony and other major companies, can be traced back to the impetus provided by the introduction of radio broadcasting and the addition of sound to movies in the late 1920s. Realizing the importance of these new media, companies further reorganized to become part of a wider entertainment industry, taking advantage of the obvious connections between the use of music on recordings, in broadcasting and in movies. Bing Crosby, along with his management and staff at Brunswick Records, utilized such connections so that a radio broadcast could be used to promote the sale of his recordings and also to attract audiences to his movies. This early use of multiple media by record companies has continued, and later stars, such as Elvis Presley, the Beatles and Madonna, owed their success not simply to musical recordings, but to movies, radio and television programs, and then videos, as well as to related products such as books, magazines and T-shirts. The circulation of the sounds, words and images of 'recording artists' across various media has been paralleled by the way in which record companies have gradually become integral parts of entertainment companies, which produce and distribute the television programs, films and videos, magazines, books and computer games in which their artists' music and images appear. Whether or not the record companies can be given the credit for actively creating such connections, they have certainly recognized the possibilities and tailored their accounting systems accordingly. Recording contracts have been modified to enable companies to claw back money from an artist's earnings derived from films, books or games to cover any investment lost from musical recordings.

Majors and Independents

Any basic definition of a record company should acknowledge two distinct types of company: majors and independents ('indies'). The term 'majors' is used to refer to those companies integrated into large, heavily capitalized electronic and entertainment corporations that have numerous offices geographically dispersed and investment diversified across a portfolio of musical genres and that are managed according to a bureaucratic, multi-divisional corporate structure. In contrast, the term 'independents' refers to small companies, often run by an entrepreneur or by members of one family, that usually produce one type of music in one specific location. An orthodoxy of twentieth-century popular music history held that the indies have provided the impetus for musical change, being more receptive to new sounds because they are oriented to music alone rather than to a plethora of related products and investment interests.

Hence, various writers (for example, Gillett 1970; Peterson and Berger 1990) have highlighted how independent companies have contributed directly to the growth of folk (Folkways), blues (Chess) and rhythm and blues (R&B) (labels such as Atlantic), the emergence of rock 'n' roll (labels such as Sun Records) and the appearance of salsa (the Fania label), and have provided the impetus for punk rock (Stiff Records) and disco (Casablanca). There has been some debate about this issue, with a key question being whether the term 'independent' refers to a type of music-oriented company, its means of distributing recordings autonomously or its fidelity to an 'alternative' belief system. However, there is much evidence to support the contention that indies have played a key role in finding new genres and popularizing them among audiences that have been neglected by the major corporations.

Over time, however, the distinctions between majors and independents have become blurred as a consequence of a series of interactions and exchanges of staff between these two types of company and, perhaps more significantly, as a consequence of a process of concentration.

Concentration of Record Companies

Since its origins at the end of the nineteenth century, the recording industry has been continually dominated by a few major corporations. Since their formation, these corporations have been increasingly international in their pursuit of markets, and perhaps only partially international in their orientation to sources of repertoire. The recording industry in Europe developed within the context of the imperial competition and expansion of empires. For example, the British company EMI gained access to territories and systems of distribution as a direct result of British colonial administration, which had been established in different parts of the world. In the United States, record companies began developing at a time when the country was making strenuous efforts to become a player on the world political stage and to present itself as a new superpower alongside the older imperial powers. This geopolitical context was not coincidental to the development of the recording industry, and it helped companies from Europe and the United States to dominate the worldwide production and distribution of recordings for much of the twentieth century. It has been estimated that, for most of that time, between five and eight companies accounted for about 70 percent of the recorded music legally distributed and sold (Gronow 1983; Chapple and Garofalo 1977). Although companies have become increasingly multinational and polycentric in their operations since the 1980s, particularly with the involvement of the Japanese Sony Corporation disrupting the North Atlantic dominance, many musicians and fans have continued to be justifiably concerned that such patterns of ownership have limited the potential choice of available music and have restricted the possibilities for musicians who are not from these dominant parts of the world. It is noteworthy that the international marketing of reggae in the 1960s and 1970s and of African and other 'world music' in the 1990s was generally the work of independent rather than major companies.

As subdivisions of large transnational corporations, the major record labels are units within multi-divisional corporations that have a range of income sources and that are able to withstand economic slumps and market changes far better than firms producing only music. It is because of this, it has been argued, that the small independent companies face the continual threat of being forced to 'sell out' to the majors. As the small independents start finding, recording, producing and selling new types of music and as their recordings begin to gain in popularity and generate new audiences, so they are seen to pose a threat to the market dominance and degree of control of music-making enjoyed by the large corporations. At the same time, the successful independents offer an attractive proposition to those majors that may wish to expand their catalogs and increase their share of the market. It is for these reasons that independents have continually been absorbed into the majors via processes of amalgamation, joint venture or complete buyout.

Some of the independents have become fairly large companies themselves before being acquired by a major (as was the case with Virgin Records when it was acquired by EMI in 1992). As the independents are acquired, so the large corporations regain or increase their share of the music market. The former independents may lose their autonomy and may be subject to greater financial control by the majors, but they gain access to the marketing and worldwide distribution networks of the major corporations, an attractive option for many record company personnel and recording artists no matter how 'radical' or 'alternative' their aesthetic ideology. While the plight of small companies has often been romanticized, sometimes according to the notion that they are pursuing 'art' rather than 'commercialism,' there can be little doubt that a key feature of recorded music production has been the constant formation and subsequent integration of independent companies into a bureaucratic corporate music business dominated by a small number of large corporations.

Inside the Record Company

The staff and departments of all sizable record companies are divided, according to their jobs, into three broad categories: (a) those whose job is to find artists and repertoire and record the music; (b) those who are employed to identify the consumers of the music and to promote and sell recordings; and (c) those whose task is to manage, administer and coordinate the overall running of the company, including the manufacture and distribution of its products. The companies also organize their various divisions by using a technique known as portfolio management. This involves separating a company's labels, genres and artists by dividing them into discrete units (sometimes called strategic business units) and thus making visible the performance, profile and contribution of each division. In this way, a company spreads its risks across various musical genres and potential sources of income, and each unit becomes a separate profit center that has to work within its own budget. So, for example, in US record companies, separate rock, R&B, Latin, classical and country divisions all operate in their own way, but compete with each other for resources, extra staff and investment. Similarly, on a wider scale, different national labels are divided from each other and compete for a greater share of corporate finance, personnel and resources.

To attract greater investment and to avoid being closed down and dropped from a corporation's portfolio, an individual unit or label must achieve economic suc-

cess. The first task – that of finding artists and repertoire and recording the music – can involve a whole range of activities and musical practises. It may involve signing a self-contained band whose members write their own songs. In this case, the company would rehearse the band's material and ensure that its music is recorded in the most suitable studio and produced by the most competent producer. Alternatively, a company may acquire a singer and link him/her with various songwriters and then with arrangers, a producer and musicians. Another option is for a record company to subcontract all such tasks to a production unit or independent label and then take the completed package for marketing and distribution. The latter option would involve very little input from the company's A&R division, and the product would be passed directly to the marketing department.

Those involved in marketing make use of various sources of market research data and attempt to match artists with potential audiences. This is usually done by a process of market fragmentation whereby recordings for jazz, techno, classical, country, rock and other genres are promoted in a variety of ways, utilizing different media routes and targeting different consumer groups.

The key challenge for any record company is matching the artist or music with the consumer or purchaser. Here, the division of labor within a company can cause a problem if A&R staff acquire an artist or a recording and the marketing personnel consider that there is no suitable market for the product. The work of administrative staff comes into play in such a case, particularly that of the business affairs division and the distribution staff. Business affairs staff are involved in assessing the economic potential of any acquisition over both the short and long term, and they play a major role in drawing up contracts. They are then involved in continually monitoring an artist's economic performance and will determine at what point an artist, catalog or genre is no longer commercially viable. Staff in the distribution division of a major company, who include market researchers, sales staff and business analysts, work at the interface between record company and retailer. Their task is to coordinate manufacture and monitor stock movements within the company's warehouses and among different retail outlets and to ensure that the company is not pressing too many recordings (and wasting valuable storage space) or making too few recordings (and failing to respond to consumer demand).

Despite these checks and balances, most recordings fail in economic terms. For many years, despite numerous changes in organization and corporate ownership, the same statistic has circulated within the music industry: only one in eight of the artists acquired by a record company sells enough recordings to recoup the initial investment and to be considered a financial success by the label. This is an elusive figure that is as mythical as it is statistical. Yet, it is an indication of how staff within the music industry perceive their daily plight. It is the desire to reduce this rate of failure that has led to the continual buying and selling of companies, the restructuring of departments, the appointment and then dismissal of highly paid senior executives and the sacking of staff. These occur simultaneously with the continual acquisition and then dropping of artists, and the buying and selling of catalogs. This instability and the lack of continuity, for both musicians and recording industry personnel, create a particularly volatile working environment and contribute to the mixture of nervous caution and reckless speculation that has continued to be such a feature of life within record companies.

Bibliography

Chapple, Steve, and Garofalo, Reebee. 1977. *Rock 'n' Roll Is Here to Pay: The History and Politics of the Music Industry*. Chicago: Nelson-Hall.

Frith, Simon. 1988. *Music for Pleasure: Essays in the Sociology of Pop*. New York: Routledge.

Gillett, Charlie. 1996 (1970). *The Sound of the City: The Rise of Rock 'n' Roll*. London: Souvenir Press.

Gray, Herman. 1988. *Producing Jazz: The Experience of an Independent Record Company*. Philadelphia: Temple University Press.

Gronow, Pekka. 1983. 'The Record Industry: The Growth of a Mass Medium.' *Popular Music* 3: 53–76.

Negus, Keith. 1996. *Popular Music in Theory*. Hanover, NH: Wesleyan University Press.

Peterson, Richard A., and Berger, David G. 1990 (1975). 'Cycles in Symbol Production: The Case of Popular Music.' In *On Record: Rock, Pop and the Written Word*, ed. Simon Frith and Andrew Goodwin. London: Routledge, 140–59. (First published in *American Sociological Review* 40 (1975): 158–73.)

Rondón, César M. 1980. *El Libro de la Salsa: Crónica de la Música del Caribe Urbano* [The Book of Salsa: Chronicle of Urban Caribbean Music]. Caracas: Editorial Arte.

KEITH NEGUS

Record Corporations

—BMG

The Bertelsmann Music Group (BMG) is part of the German-owned Bertelsmann company, which is Europe's largest media group, publishing magazines and books and operating radio and television stations. BMG is one of the five leading international music companies through its RCA, Arista and Ariola labels.

Bertelsmann was founded in Gütersloh, Niedersachsen in 1835 as a printer and publisher of hymnbooks. The company entered the music industry in 1958 by launching the Ariola Eurodisc company as an outlet for hit compilations, mostly of German-language pop music. Over the following two decades, Ariola companies were opened in other European countries and in Mexico. To enter the US market, Bertelsmann purchased Arista Records from Columbia Pictures in 1980 and made Arista a joint venture with RCA Records in 1983. The following year, RCA and Bertelsmann formed a global joint-venture music company as a defensive move against the proposed merger of the music companies of Warner and PolyGram. Then, after the RCA Corporation was purchased by General Electric, Bertelsmann bought out the whole of RCA Records in 1986 and named its music division BMG.

RCA can trace its origins to the Victor Talking Machine Company, which was founded in 1901 in Camden, New Jersey by Eldridge R. Johnson, one of the key figures in the development of sound reproduction technology. Victor was a leading manufacturer of phonographs through its Victrola range and was the first record label to issue discs of hillbilly music from Jimmie Rodgers, the Carter Family and others. In 1929, Victor was purchased by the Radio Corporation of America (RCA).

In the 1940s, RCA-Victor engineers perfected the 45 rpm vinyl disc, and the company was one of the largest labels in US popular and classical music. The purchase of Elvis Presley's contract in 1956 from Sun Records brought RCA the biggest pop star of the era, but by the 1980s the company was in decline.

In contrast, Arista was one of the most profitable labels in the United States. Originally known as Bell Records, it was run by the former CBS Records president, Clive Davis. Through such artists as Dionne Warwick, Aretha Franklin and Whitney Houston, Arista became the leading purveyor of soft soul, and it was linked to more contemporary black music through joint-venture deals with LaFace and other companies. Its varied roster also included rock acts Patti Smith and the Grateful Dead, and in the 1990s Arista opened a country music division in Nashville. While the RCA label was less successful, BMG bought out the new-age companies Windham Hill and Private Music. The company also owns the second-largest record club in the United States, BMG Direct.

The company is involved in the concert souvenir and merchandise market through the Nice Man Merchandising company. Its music publishing subsidiary, BMG Songs, is one of the top five companies in the sector. Between 1987 and 1996, BMG Songs purchased over 125 song catalogs in 12 countries, and in 1995 it acquired sub-publishing rights to the important Famous Music catalog for the world outside North America.

Outside the United States, BMG followed its rivals in establishing a large international branch network during the late 1980s and early 1990s. Existing RCA companies in Europe and Latin America were revitalized, and new branches were set up in Scandinavia and Southeast Asia, where six BMG companies were established between 1988 and 1992. In Japan in 1987, BMG formed BMG-Victor, a joint venture with JVC, buying out its partner in 1996. In Australia, the independent label RooArt was purchased in 1996.

Like other European-owned record companies, BMG has a greater market share in its home territories than in North America. In most years, it is the most successful of the majors in the German pop charts, and it became the market leader in Italy when it bought the long-established Ricordi label and publishing company in 1994. In the United Kingdom, BMG bought the independent Rhythm King label, and in 1996 took 20 percent ownership of Jive, a company whose repertoire BMG distributed in the United States and elsewhere. In 2002, BMG took full control of Jive's parent company, Zomba. From 1988, BMG also distributed products from MCA (now Universal) throughout most of the world.

DAVE LAING

—EMI

The UK-based EMI (Electric and Musical Industries Ltd.) was, until the beginning of the twenty-first century, one of the world's five largest international music companies. It shared the leading position in Europe with Universal and remained the global leader of the music publishing industry.

EMI was formed in London in 1931 by the merger of the Gramophone Company and the Columbia Phonograph Company, the two major European record companies. The new firm held exclusive rights for the world outside the Americas and Japan for the repertoire of the two largest US companies, RCA-Victor and Columbia.

The merger was a defensive measure in the face of falling record sales during the onset of the Depression. The merged company's labels included His Master's Voice (HMV), Columbia, Zonophone, Regal, Odeon and Parlophone. EMI owned 50 factories: seven in Asia, two in Australia, three in South America and the remainder in Europe. Within a few years, half of these had been closed, as the company consolidated the activities of the Gramophone Company and Columbia. During the 1930s, the company in the United Kingdom diversified into radio set manufacture and the development of a television broadcast system that was adopted by the BBC shortly before World War II.

Between 1939 and 1945, EMI lost control of its overseas branches and its UK sales were heavily weighted in favor of North American popular music. After 1945, the company recovered its assets in Germany, where it set up the EMI Electrola company. However, EMI was poorly managed until the appointment of Joseph Lockwood as managing director in 1954. Lockwood was faced with a crisis, as both RCA and Columbia were preparing to end their longstanding licensing arrangements. To safeguard access to US repertoire, EMI bought Capitol Records in 1955 for $8.5 million.

The company's fortunes improved during the 1960s, when the Beatles provided 20 percent of EMI's sales in the United Kingdom and the United States, where Capitol had also signed the Beach Boys. However, the resulting strong cash flow and profits were not reinvested in music, but were used by EMI managers to buy into other leisure and technology sectors. During the 1970s, EMI also spent very large sums on developing medical scanning equipment, which lost its potential US market due to recession conditions. By 1979, the company was running at a loss, and after a failed attempt at a merger with the film studio Paramount, EMI was purchased by the UK electrical company Thorn Industries.

In the 1980s, Thorn-EMI's strategy was to focus on three core businesses: Thorn rental, EMI music and HMV retail. A longstanding tradition of promoting EMI-trained managers to top positions was broken in 1988, when US food industry executive James Fifield was brought in to head the music division. He instituted a program of cost-cutting and takeovers that included the SBK Songs music publishing catalog and, in 1992, the Virgin Music Group, for which EMI paid $1 billion.

Virgin added considerably to EMI's turnover and its market share in the United Kingdom, the United States and the larger European countries. In the 1990s, EMI was second only to PolyGram in European market share. The company's top artists included the Pet Shop Boys, Blur and the Spice Girls (UK), Roxette (Sweden), Die Toten Hosen (Germany), Alain Souchon (France) and Canto Gregoriano (Spain). In North America, however, the company's share of sales oscillated between 8 percent and 12 percent, and there were purges of senior management in 1992 and 1996.

Like its rivals, EMI was active in the 'emerging' markets of Latin America and Southeast Asia, acquiring many local companies and opening new EMI branches. By the close of the 1990s, the company had branches in 36 countries and licensees or joint-venture companies in 42 more. In 1996, Thorn and EMI were 'demerged,' and in 1998 EMI announced plans for a further demerger between the music company and the retail division.

During 2000, EMI made two attempts to merge, first with the Warner Music Group, then with BMG. Both attempts failed because of opposition from European competition authorities.

Bibliography

Martland, Peter. 1997. *Since Records Began: EMI, the First 100 Years*. London: Batsford.

Pandit, S.A. 1996. *From Making to Music: The History of Thorn EMI*. London: Hodder & Stoughton.

DAVE LAING

—PolyGram

Until its acquisition by Seagram in 1998, PolyGram was the world's leading record company, with a share of 15–20 percent of the world market. Apart from creating international mega-sellers, PolyGram's policy included investment in local artists and marketing them locally, leaving open the possibility of crossing over to other markets.

The origins of PolyGram can be traced back to the establishing of Philips Phonographische Industrie (PPI) in 1950 by the Dutch firm Philips Electronics NV. One of PPI's first international acquisitions was Mercury Records from Chicago. In 1962, Philips united its record company interests with those of the German electrical group Siemens, which owned the Deutsche Grammophon and Polydor labels. As a consequence of this arrangement, the two electronics firms took a 50 percent share in each other's labels; this was followed by a merger of Phonogram (the new name of PPI) and Polydor to form PolyGram in 1972. In some countries, Phonogram and Polydor remained separate operations, but in most countries they operated as one.

In the following years, the company acquired many additional labels: Verve, Barclay, Decca, RSO and London Records. In conjunction with PolyGram, Philips launched the compact disc (CD) in the early 1980s, a period when the record industry was experiencing its first major drop in sales since the rapid rise of the phonogram market worldwide from the 1960s onward. In a quest for funds to invest in production facilities for CDs, PolyGram sold its publishing arm, Chappell Music, to a consortium of US music publishers, who later sold it to Warner. Siemens decided to withdraw from the music business, selling its PolyGram shares to Philips during the 1980s. Shortly thereafter, PolyGram completed a worldwide public stock offering, with the result that Philips' holding in PolyGram was reduced to 75 percent. PolyGram continued to expand its core recording enterprise, as well as expanding into new areas. Major acquisitions were Island Records in 1988 ($272 million), A&M Records in 1989 ($460 million) and Motown in 1993 ($301 million). Less expensive acquisitions were Def Jam (60 percent share), Rodven Records and Go! Discs.

In the meantime, PolyGram started to build up a new publishing arm, PolyGram Music Publishing, through new signings as well as acquisitions. In 1997, Phonogram Records, in some countries still a separate entity, became Mercury on a worldwide basis. In the same year, the Philips Music Group was created to act as an umbrella organization for four of PolyGram's classical labels: Philips Classics, Point Classics, Gimell and Imaginary Road.

In the mid-1980s, PolyGram decided to start a film unit, on the premise that the film sector was considered a growth market, whereas sales of recorded music were perceived as having reached their ceiling. In the following years, the film venture was developed through a multitude of acquisitions, mainly in the independent sector. A major step in the development of PolyGram Filmed Entertainment (PFE) was the inauguration of a large-scale distribution firm, PolyGram Filmed Entertainment Distribution, in the United States in mid-1997, and the acquisition in December 1997 of the large catalog (over 1,000 titles) of CDR (Consortium de Réalisation SAS), bringing PFE's total catalog of movies to over 1,500.

For 1997, PolyGram reported a 17 percent rise in sales and an 11 percent rise in operating profits. Music accounted for 84 percent of the sales and film for 16 percent. Film was regarded as a source of future profits, as it was still operating at a loss for PolyGram. In 1998, PolyGram employed over 12,000 staff around the world in over 40 offices.

In May 1998, Philips announced the sale of PolyGram to the Canadian company, Seagram. Seagram, originally a wine and spirits company, was already the owner of the Hollywood studio Universal Pictures and the record company Universal Music (formerly MCA). Through the sale of PolyGram, Philips narrowed its focus to future growth in the products and markets of the so-called 'digital revolution.' The aggregate value offered for PolyGram was approximately $10.6 billion. PFE was sold to a third party. Seagram integrated the music divisions of PolyGram and Universal to create the Universal Music Group, a global player with a market share of well over 20 percent. In 2000, Seagram merged with Vivendi, and MCA/Universal was renamed Vivendi-Universal.

PAUL RUTTEN

—Sony Music Entertainment

Sony Music Entertainment (SME) is owned by the leading Japanese consumer electronics company, the Sony Corporation. SME was formed in 1988, after the Sony Corporation purchased the CBS Records Group in January of that year from the US media company CBS Inc. for $2 billion. The Sony Corporation subsequently bought the Hollywood film studio Columbia Pictures in

September 1989. SME and the film company together make up the entertainment division of Sony Corporation, accounting for about 10 percent of Sony's global sales.

The Sony Corporation has its roots in Tokyo Tsushin Kogyo, an electrical repair firm founded by Akio Morita in 1946. Although it is best known for such products as the transistor radio, Walkman and compact disc, Sony entered the music industry in 1964 by forming a joint-venture record label in Japan with CBS. That company, Sony Music Entertainment Japan, has become the leading firm in the Japanese recorded music market.

Worldwide, SME is one of the top three music industry companies, vying for top position with Universal and the Warner Music Group, with much of its success owed to the acquisition of the Columbia (US) roster of artists. SME was by the end of the 1990s a presence in most countries of Europe, Asia and Latin America, where the bulk of its sales were made up of recordings by US artists. An exception to this trend was to be found in France, where Sony/Columbia was a market leader in domestic music, with artists such as Patricia Kaas, Francis Cabrel and Jean-Jacques Goldman. Sony has, since 1990, been the joint owner with the Warner Music Group of Columbia House, which has remained the US market leader in the mail-order sales of music.

Bibliography

Dannen, Fredric. 1990. *Hit Men: Power Brokers and Fast Money Inside the Music Business*. New York: Times Books.

DAVE LAING

—Universal Music Group

The Universal Music Group (UMG) is a division of Vivendi-Universal, the French-owned conglomerate. Universal changed its name from MCA Music Entertainment in 1997 during its ownership by the Canadian Seagram drinks company (80 percent) and the Japanese Matsushita electronics firm (20 percent). After acquiring Poly-Gram from Philips in 1998, Seagram merged in 2000 with Vivendi to form Vivendi-Universal.

UMG's roots lie in the Music Corporation of America (MCA), a booking agency founded in 1929 by Jules Stein. After 1945, MCA diversified into cinema ownership and artist management. In 1962, MCA purchased the Decca (US) record company, which also owned the Universal Studios Hollywood film company. Decca had been set up in 1931 by Jack Kapp, and its catalog included recordings by Bing Crosby, the Andrews Sisters, Louis Armstrong, Bill Haley and Buddy Holly. Decca was also a leading country music company, with such acts as Ernest Tubb and Kitty Wells.

MCA subsequently built up a portfolio of record labels by acquiring ABC-Paramount, Dot, and Dunhill for $30 million in 1979, Chess in 1985 and, in 1990, Geffen, for which MCA paid $465 million. The company also owned a substantial catalog of songs and film scores based on the Leeds Music Company, which it bought in the mid-1960s.

In the 1970s and early 1980s, the MCA group maintained its preeminence in country music through such artists as Barbara Mandrell and the Oak Ridge Boys, but there were fewer successes in pop. These included Tom Petty and Elton John, whose records were issued by MCA's Uni label in the United States.

Between 1983 and 1989, MCA was run by Irving Azoff, and it was embroiled in allegations of Mafia involvement in the music business when alleged criminals were indicted in connection with the purchase of millions of deleted MCA albums (see Knoedelseder 1993).

By this time, the MCA group included the music company, Universal Studios, the Winterland concert venue and merchandising company (purchased in 1988), plus book publishing and theme park interests. In 1990, the group was purchased outright for $6.1 billion by Matsushita, which had seen its great rival Sony buy CBS Records and Columbia Pictures.

Despite gaining the distribution of Motown Records until Motown was sold to PolyGram and achieving some major hits from Boston, Bobby Brown and others, MCA remained one of the less important companies in the record industry in the 1980s.

During the 1990s, the company consolidated its position in both country and black music. The Nashville division, headed by songwriter and producer Jimmy Bowen, had numerous hits with Reba McEntire, Vince Gill, George Strait, Alabama and others. In black music, distribution deals with producer-owned labels Uptown and Silas brought success with Mary J. Blige and Chante Moore, respectively, while MCA's own artists included Gladys Knight. Through Geffen's astute head of A&R, Tom Zuzaut, the company signed top metal and grunge bands Aerosmith, Guns N' Roses and Nirvana.

The change of ownership coincided with a belated decision to establish a large number of MCA companies abroad. Prior to 1994, MCA operated only in Canada, the United Kingdom and Japan, where it had a joint venture with JVC, MCA-Victor. In Britain, MCA's most important recording was the original recording of Tim Rice's and Andrew Lloyd Webber's *Jesus Christ Superstar*. During the following three years, more than 20 MCA branches were set up in Europe, Asia and Latin America. While the primary purpose of the expansion was to increase sales of recordings by US artists, in many countries MCA also began to sign local acts. The acquisition of PolyGram immediately transformed the company's

635

international presence, making it the largest record company, with a global market share, in 2000, of more than 22 percent.

In the United States, Universal revitalized its senior management in the late 1990s, hiring former Warner Music Group executive Doug Morris and signing a distribution agreement with DreamWorks, the media company formed by David Geffen and film producer Steven Spielberg.

Bibliography

Knoedelseder, William. 1993. *Stiffed!: A True Story of MCA, the Music Business and the Mafia*. New York: Harper Collins.

Discographical Reference

Jesus Christ Superstar. MCA MKPS 2011/2. *1972*: UK.

DAVE LAING

—Warner Music Group

A subsidiary of the world's largest media company, AOL-Time Warner, the Warner Music Group (WMG) was, until the beginning of the twenty-first century, one of the five largest international music companies. A $20 billion merger with EMI in January 2000 resulted in the creation of Warner EMI Music, which became one of the world's two largest record companies alongside the Seagram-owned Universal Music Group.

For many years, WMG was the US market leader in recorded music, while its music publishing division, Warner Chappell, was the world's second largest. In the United States, WMG included three main record company divisions: Warner-Reprise, Atlantic Group and Elektra. Its overseas counterpart was Warner Music International (WMI) with headquarters in London. WMI operated in over 60 countries and provided more than half of WMG's recorded music sales.

The group originated with the formation in 1958 of a record label subsidiary of the Warner Brothers film studio, which itself was founded in 1922. Early hits came from the Everly Brothers and Peter, Paul and Mary. In 1964, Warner purchased Reprise, which had been set up by Frank Sinatra in 1960. The Reprise president, Mo Ostin, became a key Warner Brothers executive until his resignation in 1994.

The Californian labels Valiant and Autumn were acquired before the Warner Brothers studio was bought in 1966 by the Seven Arts group. Seven Arts subsequently purchased two important independent labels, Atlantic and Elektra. Founded in 1947 by Ahmet Ertegun and others, Atlantic was primarily a soul and R&B company. Elektra had been formed in 1950 by college student Jac Holzman. Its earliest successes came from folk

song albums by Josh White, Theodore Bikel and Judy Collins.

In 1969, a further takeover occurred when Warner Brothers-Seven Arts was purchased by Kinney, a conglomerate that included car parks and funeral parlors. Kinney chairman Steve Ross became head of the new conglomerate.

From the mid-1960s onward, the Warner group of labels began to dominate the US record market, through Warner's and Elektra's strength in mainstream rock (Neil Young, James Taylor, the Grateful Dead and so on) and Atlantic's position in soul and R&B, plus its acquisition of the US rights to such British bands as Cream, Yes, the Rolling Stones and Led Zeppelin. The group's position was strengthened further when David Geffen sold his Asylum label to Warner in 1972 for $5 million and became head of Asylum and Elektra. In 1975, he left to concentrate on film production and was replaced by Joe Smith.

The group's international activities were coordinated by Atlantic's Nesuhi Ertegun. There were already Warner Brothers Records companies in the United Kingdom (founded in 1961) and Canada (1967) when WEA (Warner-Elektra-Atlantic) International was formed in 1970. New branches in Australia, Japan (a joint venture with consumer electronics group Pioneer), France and Germany soon followed. A manufacturing plant was opened at Alsdorf, Germany in 1975. It has since become the hub of the group's pan-European activities. Later in the decade, the company moved into Latin America and Southeast Asia by opening branches in Brazil, Mexico, Hong Kong, Singapore and Malaysia.

Following the global depression in music sales of the early 1980s, WEA decided to consolidate its position through an agreed merger with PolyGram. But, following opposition from antitrust authorities in Germany and the United States, the merger plan was abandoned. WEA subsequently continued to expand its international activities, often through the acquisition of established labels such as Metronome (Sweden), Teldec (Germany) and CGD (Italy). From the mid-1980s, a 'dual company' structure was established in many countries, with Warner operating through a WEA and an East West label. Despite an overseas roster of over 1,000 artists performing in 25 languages, the great majority of the company's sales have continued to come from its US-based rock, pop and soul acts.

The company became a major force in international music publishing when it paid $275 million for the Chappell catalogs in 1987. Warner already owned the Harms, Witmark and Remick catalogs (purchased by the film company in the 1920s) and Warner Brothers Music, established in various countries during the 1970s.

The names 'Warner Music Group' and 'Warner Music International' were adopted in 1990, the year that Warner Communications chairman Steve Ross became president of the newly merged Time Warner company, which combined the magazine and book business of Time Inc. with Warner's film, music and broadcasting interests. In 1995, Time Warner itself merged with the media empire of Atlanta-based television mogul Ted Turner.

During the second half of the 1990s, WMG saw several changes of senior management and the departure of key executives to other major companies. However, it maintained its leading position in the US record market, although WMI's share of the international market fell.

In 2000, Time Warner merged with Internet company America Online (AOL).

DAVE LAING

Record Industry

The record industry is that part of the overall music industry concerned with the creation of sound recordings and with the manufacture and distribution of soundcarriers (copies of those recordings). The component parts of the industry include: A&R (talent spotting); the negotiation of contracts and administration of royalties; the production and mastering of recordings; the manufacture of copies in tape or disc formats, plus the design and manufacture of packaging; the physical distribution of copies by distributors, mail-order firms, wholesalers, one-stops and rack jobbers; the marketing and promotion of recordings; the production of music videos; and the exploitation and administration of the various rights in recordings, notably in obtaining payment for broadcasting and other uses.

Development of the Industry

The fluctuations in the fortunes of the record industry over the past 100 years have been primarily a function of general economic conditions combined with the successful marketing of innovations in sound-recording technologies. The attractiveness or otherwise of the 'product' offered by the record industry seems to have played a lesser role.

On a global basis, the record industry can be seen to have passed through seven main phases.

1. 1897–1929

Following a period of product development and patent litigation (Gelatt 1977), this was an era of steady expansion as gramophones, phonographs, discs and cylinders fell in price and improved in quality with the introduction of electrical recording in 1925. In addition, recorded music quickly became an international, if not a global, industry. Recordings of local music were made and sold throughout the world, although the principal manufacturing centers were the United States and Germany (of 18 million records made in Germany in 1907, 7 million were exported).

The key contractual relationships between the record industry and both music publishers and recording artists took shape in this period. The 1906 revision of the Berne Convention on authors' rights made it obligatory for record companies to pay a royalty to the composer and publisher of music used on commercially issued soundcarriers. The industry's first royalty agreement with a performer was made in 1902 between the Gramophone Company and the operatic star Enrico Caruso, although in numerous countries for many decades the standard practise was to pay recording artists a single fee for their work.

2. 1929–40

During these years, the industry was devastated by the worldwide economic depression, and annual sales in the United States fell from 140 million units of recorded music in 1929 to 33 million in 1938. Important changes of ownership in the industry took place as the RCA radio firm bought out Victor in 1929, Gramophone and Columbia combined in Europe to form EMI in 1931, and in 1938 the CBS radio network purchased the ARC group which included the US Columbia label.

3. 1940–59

This was an era that began with uncertainty as a consequence of a recording ban instituted by the American Federation of Musicians (AFM) against the major record companies. These companies settled with the AFM during 1943 and 1944. The era was otherwise marked by rapid growth. In the 1940s, this growth was due to the stimulus to the US economy from war-related industries, whose newly affluent workers consumed the products of newly formed pop and R&B labels. This expansion was maintained by the introduction of the new 45 rpm and 33 rpm vinyl disc formats in the United States in 1948–49 and in Europe during the following decade. The structure of the industry in Europe changed in the aftermath of World War II, particularly in Eastern Europe where existing labels were transformed into state-owned monopolies. In Western Europe, entrepreneurs created such labels as Vogue (France), Sonet (Sweden) and CGD (Italy). Similar, but fewer, small companies sprang up in Africa and Asia.

4. 1959–78

During the next era, sales growth was spurred by further technological innovations – stereo recording and the tape cassette, which was introduced by Philips in 1963. There was also an expensive failure when quadraphonic LPs offering four channels of sound did not capture consumer imagination. However, the cassette soon became a close competitor to vinyl records in developed economies, although its greatest impact on the record industry occurred in Asia and Africa, where it crucially lowered the cost of manufacturing and enabled numerous local musicians to issue recordings, as well as facilitating the growth of the pirate music business (Wallis and Malm 1984). In India, the virtual monopoly of EMI's branch company was broken by the advent of 200 regionally based cassette labels (Manuel 1993). This was also a period of decolonization which saw newly independent African countries with socialist ideologies, such as Guinea and Mali, setting up state-owned labels (Charry 2000).

5. 1978–83

Against the background of a general economic crisis associated with a sharp rise in world oil prices that increased the cost of vinyl, a second great decline in sales hit the industry in the late 1970s. In Europe, the Belgian soundcarrier market did not return to its 1979 level until 1987. Referring specifically to the United States, Haring (1996) also attributed this slump to 'home taping; competition from video games, cable TV; youth unemployment; changes in radio formats with a rise in Adult Contemporary and country, which had non-record buying audiences' (16).

6. 1983–95

The sixth era was characterized by a return to technology-led growth. Recovery from the slump of the early 1980s was slow until the growth in popularity of expensively priced CDs led the industry into a new golden decade. As global sales of higher-priced CDs overtook those of both vinyl and cassettes by 1990, the record industry was able to persuade both mechanical rights bodies (representing composers) and recording artists to accept a royalty reduction on CD sales. In Europe alone, these discounts 'saved' the industry $400 million in CD royalties between 1984 and 1992 ('Artists,' 1992). According to one major label executive, the CD enabled the industry 'to restore a reasonableness to the profit margins of record companies' (Terry 1992, C4).

The success of the CD in displacing analog vinyl discs (assisted, critics claimed, by the deliberate phasing out of vinyl by major labels) led the industry to seek a digital replacement for the prerecorded tape cassette. Sony proposed a minidisc, while Philips offered the digital compact cassette. Despite expensive advertising campaigns, both formats failed to establish themselves, although a relaunched minidisc as a simple blank medium had developed a new market by the end of the century, when a recordable version of the standard 5" (12.7 cm) CD was also available to consumers.

In the 1990s, the CD revolution gradually spread outward from North America, Japan and Western Europe. The first CD factories were established in South Africa, Indonesia, Turkey and Brazil, and by 1997 even Vietnam had a CD plant. As with the cassette, pirate manufacturers employed the format, operating plants in China, Taiwan and Eastern Europe.

7. 1995–Present

The current era began with a slowdown in CD player ownership, which had reached saturation point in Western Europe, North America and Japan. The number of manufacturing plants grew dramatically, especially in Asia (the number of CD plants in China rose from three in 1990 to 26 in 1994), but the capacity increased more quickly than demand and factory prices fell to under $1 per unit. Coincidentally, sales in Asia fell after the economic collapse of 1997 in Indonesia, Thailand and elsewhere. Consequently, there was negative growth in the retail value of the global market for recorded music during the late 1990s.

The last few years of the twentieth century found the world record industry facing an uncertain future, as pundits and forecasters argued over the potential for growth in the 'digital delivery' of recorded music using such media as the Internet. The rapidity with which consumers have taken to the Web makes it very probable that the eighth phase of the record industry's development will be defined by the digital delivery of music.

The Contemporary Situation

The Global Market

According to the industry's own trade association, the International Federation of the Phonographic Industry (IFPI), in 2000 over 3.7 billion units of recorded music with a retail value of some $36.9 billion were sold worldwide in over 70 countries. The largest national markets were the United States, Japan, the United Kingdom, Germany and France. The 4 billion units were made up of 2,511 million CDs, 801 million tape cassettes, 376 million singles (mainly on CD) and only 14 million vinyl LPs ('Dollar Value,' 2001). The IFPI also stated that unauthorized (pirate) sales consisted of 640 million CDs and 1.2 billion cassettes with a retail value of $4.2 billion. The principal manufacturing centers were in Eastern Europe and Southeast Asia, and the largest markets for pirated music (by value) were China, Russia, Mexico and Brazil ('Value,' 2001).

Classical music recordings account for less than 10 percent of world sales of recorded music. The remainder is comprised of popular music of all kinds. By country of origin, the highest proportion of global pop music sales in the late 1990s was from the United States (about 35 percent), followed by Japan (13 percent) and the United Kingdom (10 percent).

Despite the trend toward globalization, most evident in the ability of pop and rock superstars such as Michael Jackson, Whitney Houston and U2 to sell millions of albums worldwide, there are still considerable regional variations. In dollar value terms, 40 percent of legitimate world sales in 2000 came from North America, a further 30 percent from the countries of the European Community and 21 percent from the Pacific Rim nations (including Japan). The distribution of unit sales was different, reflecting the contrast in retail prices between different regions. Only 31 percent of units were sold in North America, compared with 34 percent in Europe and 26 percent in the Pacific Rim.

These statistics were derived only from those parts of the world where the international record industry has managed to establish or negotiate the formation of a Western-style market for its products. Throughout most of Africa, for instance, the intertwined problems of mass poverty and endemic cassette piracy have created a very different record industry. With the state unable and the transnational companies unwilling to invest, musicians and studio owners operate African labels on a small-scale basis, and the most successful performers rely on record sales in the world music markets of Europe, Japan and North America to subsidize their activities in the home market (Graham 1992).

The regional differentiation is equally marked in the type of music sold on each continent. The rapid implantation of transnational companies in Southeast Asia during the 1980s and early 1990s caused sales of Western music to increase there, but these have remained relatively low compared with those of indigenous and regional (Chinese-language) music. Similarly, in most Latin American countries, Spanish- or Portuguese-language songs outsell those sung in English. In Europe, the situation is somewhat different, although local-language music increased its share in such countries as Germany and Italy during the 1990s (Laing 1997).

Royalties and the Record Industry

As a general rule, retailing and distribution costs and margins account for half the retail price of a soundcarrier. The remainder is returned to the record company to pay for manufacturing, marketing, administration, origination (recording studio) costs and the royalties payable to the composer and performer of the recorded music.

The royalty rate for payments by record companies to composers and music publishers is set either by statute or by industry-wide agreements. The gross 'mechanical' royalty rate payable ranges from 9.3 percent of the retail price in most of Europe to a smaller amount in Japan and North America, where the rate is based on a certain number of cents per track. In many other countries, notably in Asia and Africa, songs may be 'bought out' by record companies for a flat fee without provision for further royalties, although this practise is under attack from copyright organizations and music publishers in those countries.

Historically, the record industry has had a poor reputation for honoring contracts with artists and for accounting and paying fairly. The ever-growing amount of anecdotal evidence of the cheating of black artists by large and small labels alike indicates that, in the 1940s and 1950s in particular, underpayment was endemic in the United States (Deffaa 1996). Even when payments were made to popular singers or band leaders on a royalty basis, the headline rate was extremely low – in the United Kingdom until the late 1960s, it was standard practise for the artist royalty to be 1.5 pence per side, equivalent to 4 percent of the retail price of a single. All these practises help to explain the super-profits earned by the record industry in boom periods for popular music, such as the 1950s and 1960s. It is reasonable to conclude that the financial success of both majors and independents in the United States and elsewhere in that era was based in large part on the exploitation of many recording artists.

Although the royalty rates have increased since the 1960s, the economic relationships between recording artists and the record industry have remained complex and controversial. Standard recording contracts routinely reduce royalty rates through deductions for studio costs (which are generally paid for by the artist, not the label), for 'free goods' (copies given to reviewers and disc jockeys) and for so-called 'packaging' costs. Since the advent of the record producer as a specialist in the recording process, artists have been expected to pay a producer royalty (often 2 percent) out of their own fees. The practical effect of these deductions is to make the actual amounts paid to artists about half of the 11 percent (for a new act) to 18 percent (superstar rate) written into their recording contracts.

The bargaining power of a few superstar artists has been able to achieve considerably better results than the industry average. In the 1990s, such acts as Madonna, Michael Jackson, Janet Jackson and R.E.M. concluded multi-album deals with major record companies. These included such extras as the funding of an artist-owned label and the signing over of album copyrights to the artist after a certain time period, in addition to payments of advances that could total up to $100 million for each act. The major companies were willing to pay such amounts on the basis of the expectation that global sales for each album by these artists could reach 20 million copies or more.

Corporate Trends

From its earliest years, the corporate structure of the record industry has been influenced by two main trends – extreme volatility and a tendency toward oligopoly. The volatility is signaled by the relatively low cost of entering the recorded music market which has encouraged the formation of many new small firms and by the history of such firms: if successful, they are likely to be acquired by larger firms; if unsuccessful, they close down.

The oligopoly has taken the form of the domination of soundcarrier distribution (and sometimes manufacturing and A&R) by a small number of transnational companies, notably in Western Europe, the Americas and Australasia. During the 1990s, the firms forming the oligopoly were involved in over 200 mergers and acquisitions in all regions of the world apart from Africa. The largest mergers included the purchase of Virgin by EMI in 1992 and the acquisition of Universal first by Seagram and then by Vivendi. Seagram had earlier purchased PolyGram.

At the beginning of the twenty-first century, the oligopoly consisted of Sony, Vivendi-Universal, Bertelsmann, AOL-Time Warner and EMI. All these companies had record company operations in most countries of Europe, the Americas, Asia and Australasia. Despite changes of ownership, the five-firm oligopoly had its roots in the early twentieth-century control of sound-recording patents by the Victor, Columbia, Edison and Gramophone companies. Of the five companies, only AOL-Time Warner was without a direct link to one or more of the founders of the industry. According to independent experts, the combined global market share of the 'big five' in 2000 was 76 percent, although there were regional variations, with the share in Latin America and Europe as high as 84 percent and in Asia only 53 percent. (See Negus (1999) for a discussion of the corporate strategies of major record companies.)

The remaining quarter of the world soundcarrier market consisted of sales by several thousand smaller record companies. A few of these (notably Zomba, edel and Rock) had an international presence, but most were locally based firms issuing only a few titles each year. Nevertheless, independent record companies produced the vast majority of the estimated 20,000 different album titles issued each year worldwide.

The continuing dominance of the record industry by a small number of companies led to charges that they operated as a cartel. In the United States in 1985, the majors settled out of court a price-fixing lawsuit brought by wholesalers, while in 1998 the 'big five' were found guilty of price-fixing in Italy. An investigation in the United Kingdom in 1996 found that, while there was a technical monopoly, it was not against the public interest.

While such hostility from regulators did not pose a serious threat to the majors' position, their power and the central role of the record industry in the evolution of popular music may undergo a significant change in the twenty-first century. This is because of the industry's inability to deal with the challenges of new technologies and the fact that all but one of the majors now form a small part of a much larger conglomerate whose priorities might well run counter to those of the record business.

Bibliography

'Artists Subsidised CD Launch to the Tune of $400m.' 1992. *Financial Times Music & Copyright* 1 (12 September): 5.

Charry, Eric S. 2000. *Mande Music: Traditional and Modern Music of the Maninka and Mandinka of Western Africa*. Chicago: University of Chicago Press.

Deffaa, Chip. 1996. *Blue Rhythms: Six Lives in Rhythm & Blues*. Urbana, IL: University of Illinois Press.

'The Dollar Value of Global Soundcarrier Market Fell by 4.5% in 2000.' 2001. *Music & Copyright* 204 (25 April): 5–11.

Gelatt, Roland. 1977. *The Fabulous Phonograph, 1877–1977*. London: Cassell.

Graham, Ronnie. 1992. *The World of African Music. Stern's Guide to Contemporary African Music, Vol. 2*. London: Pluto Press.

Gronow, Pekka, and Saunio, Ilpo. 1998. *An International History of the Recording Industry*, trans. Christopher Moseley. London: Cassell.

Haring, Bruce. 1996. *Off the Charts: Ruthless Days and Reckless Nights Inside the Music Industry*. New York: Carol Publishing Group.

Laing, Dave. 1997. 'Rock Anxieties and the New Music Networks.' In *Back to Reality: Social Experience in Cultural Studies*, ed. Angela McRobbie. Manchester: Manchester University Press, 116–32.

Manuel, Peter. 1993. *Cassette Culture: Popular Music and Technology in North India*. Chicago and London: University of Chicago Press.

Negus, Keith. 1999. *Music Genres and Corporate Cultures*. London: Routledge.

Terry, Ken. 1992. '1982–1992: Talkin' About a Revolution.' *Billboard* (26 September): C4, 22.

'Value of Pirate Global Soundcarrier Sales Rose 2.4% to

$4.2bn in 2000.' 2001. *Music & Copyright* 207 (20 June): 3–4.

Wallis, Roger, and Malm, Krister. 1984. *Big Sounds from Small Peoples: The Music Industry in Small Countries.* London: Constable.

DAVE LAING

Recording Studio

The recording studio is a technical facility designed for capturing, editing, mixing and/or programming musical performances on a recording medium, such as magnetic tape or a computer hard drive. In its most basic configuration, the studio consists of two adjacent rooms separated by a soundproof window and door. The studio proper, usually the larger of the two rooms and often divided into smaller, acoustically isolated areas, is where the musicians perform and their sounds are picked up by microphones. The control room, containing most of the mixing, recording and processing equipment, is where the engineer and producer record and edit the master recording; electronic instruments, such as synthesizers, samplers and sequencers, are also usually located in the control room. Contemporary studios devoted to recording popular music employ multitrack recording equipment, with 24-track (or greater) recording capability being the professional norm. While the major record companies maintain their own recording facilities, many master tapes are recorded in independently owned studios. The recording studio plays a central role in the production process within the record industry: it is both the technical facility where master tapes are produced and a site where various actors – artists, engineers, producers and A&R personnel – come together to make fundamental aesthetic and commercial decisions concerning the sound and potential marketability of a recording.

Major recording companies have for many years owned and maintained their own recording studios. Often, these are large-scale, multipurpose facilities with a full-time staff of engineers and support personnel. For example, London's well-known Abbey Road Studios, established by EMI in 1931, are reputed to have been one of the first (and largest) purpose-built recording facilities in the world. In the configuration the facility has at the beginning of the twenty-first century, it houses several separate recording studios, the largest of which can hold a full symphony orchestra and chorus; the other studios are suitable for smaller ensembles, and at least one is equipped with a separate vocal booth (a small room, acoustically isolated from the main recording studio), which is essential in most popular music recording. Each of the control rooms is equipped with multitrack tape recorders and is centered around a large recording console outfitted with automated mixing cap-

ability; a large selection of high-quality microphones is available, as are numerous sound-processing devices. Abbey Road Studios are used extensively for recording classical music as well as film soundtracks, and have also been the site of many popular music recordings. Recording facilities such as Abbey Road are renowned for the unusual size and acoustic quality of the studios, the professional quality of the recording equipment, and the highly trained and experienced staff of engineers. The division of labor at such facilities is usually quite strict, the roles of musician, engineer and producer being clearly defined.

The size, structure and organization of a studio such as that found at Abbey Road hark back to a time when most music recording was performed in industry-owned studios. Prior to the 1950s, most recording was done direct to disc, with no possibility of editing or further processing. The acoustics of the studio, the performing skills of the professional big bands and orchestras, and the technical expertise of the engineers were all critical to the success of each recording. With the widespread adoption of magnetic recording in mainstream production during the early 1950s, however, sound-recording technology became available to a wider range of individuals (many of whom had no prior industry experience), and a more flexible approach to sound recording began to develop. Furthermore, the rise of R&B and rock 'n' roll during the same period created a volatility in the marketplace that encouraged entrepreneurial modes of production. Recording studios began to be located in small, makeshift facilities, with a limited (though often specially designed) range of equipment available, and a more experimental attitude toward the recording process being adopted by both producers and engineers.

During the 1950s, a number of small studios, owned and operated by independent producers and engineers, played an influential role in the development of the sound of R&B, soul and early rock 'n' roll music. For example, Cosimo Recording (also known as J&M Studio), owned by Cosimo Matassa, helped to establish New Orleans as a recording center during this period. The acoustics of Matassa's recording studio, his simple, clean recording console and straightforward approach to recording, and his access to a unique group of New Orleans-based session musicians (often under the direction of musician and producer Dave Bartholomew) attracted a number of well-known R&B and early rock 'n' roll artists, including Fats Domino, 'Big' Joe Turner, Ray Charles and Little Richard. His studio came to be known as 'the Nashville of R&B.'

Similarly, Stax Records, operating out of a converted movie theater in Memphis, Tennessee (the front of the theater also served as a record store), was renowned during the early 1960s for its unique sound. The theater was partitioned, homemade curtains were hung to partially reduce the room's natural reverberation and a control room was built onto the former stage area. Together with the musical contributions of a unique group of local musicians and artists, the studio played a significant role in defining the sound of early 1960s soul music. Another influential studio during the early years of soul, Fame Music, was located in even more makeshift facilities: the converted rooms above a drugstore in Muscle Shoals, Alabama. Both studios were used extensively by Atlantic Records' producer Jerry Wexler, and contributed much to the success of that label's roster of soul artists.

At the same time as these studios, and others like them, were making their impact felt on the sound of popular music, other developments were taking place that would reshape the physical characteristics of the recording studio, increase the complexity of the equipment in use and alter the role of the engineer in popular music production. Prior to the 1950s, most recordings were made with no more than one or two microphones, mixing consoles were relatively simple in design, and the ability of the engineer to control the critical musical balances during the recording was relatively limited and it thus remained the responsibility of the musicians themselves. During the 1950s and 1960s, however, engineers began to use additional microphones such that each individual section of the band or orchestra could be given separate attention. With the use of multiple microphones, the acoustics of the studio were altered to reduce the negative effects of sound reflections and to allow for greater separation between individual musical instruments; the use of sound-absorbing materials (rendering the studio acoustics increasingly 'dry') and baffles between instrumental performers became commonplace. To a large extent, the concept of the studio as a room with its own unique acoustic properties became less important while, with the introduction of artificial reverberation systems, the ability of the engineer to design and control the ambient characteristics of the recording increased. The use of additional microphones required mixing consoles with greater input capability (by the early 1960s, consoles with 20 to 24 inputs and two to four outputs could be found in some studios) and an increased reliance on sound-shaping equipment (such as equalizers and compressors). The engineer, in addition to having a technical role in making the recording, began to take on an increasingly important musical role, balancing and altering the sounds of the musical ensemble. Perhaps the most important factor in the creation of the modern studio, however, was the introduction of multitrack tape recording. Each of the develop-

ments outlined above was enhanced and extended by the use of multitrack recording techniques. In addition, the multitrack recorder allowed the engineer to give greater attention to individual instrument sounds when recording, and offered greater freedom in editing, as well as the ability to defer many of the critical decisions concerning the overall balance of the ensemble sound to a later mixdown stage of the recording process.

Among the first to fully exploit the possibilities offered by multiple miking and multitrack recording was Tom Dowd, chief engineer for Atlantic Records during the late 1950s and early 1960s. Dowd paid particular attention to the placement of microphones, especially on bass and drums, and to the creative uses of equalization, bringing out and emphasizing frequencies that favored bass on the low end and cymbals on the high end. In acquiring an early prototype eight-track recorder during the late 1950s (the first was created by Ampex for guitarist Les Paul, to his own specifications), Dowd was able to experiment with multitrack recording in a manner unavailable to most producers and engineers of the period: splitting the rhythm section onto separate tracks and overdubbing and editing vocals freely.

Initially, however, multitrack recording technology and the studio techniques associated with it developed slowly. During the late 1950s and early 1960s, only three- and four-track machines were widely available. Their use required that a number of instrumentalists share a given track (for example, the entire rhythm section might be mixed to a single track during recording), thus greatly restricting the possibility of making alterations at a later time; vocalists and instrumental soloists were often the only musicians virtually guaranteed a separate track but, even then, the possibility of editing between multiple takes of a vocal or solo performance was greatly restricted. By the late 1960s, however, eight-track recorders had become more common and were quickly followed, during the early 1970s, by 16- and 24-track machines.

The increased number of tracks placed a new emphasis on the control room as the focal point of the recording studio. At the center of this development was the expansion and increased complexity of the mixing console – a device that can be considered the engineer's primary 'musical instrument.' During the 1950s and early 1960s, it was not uncommon for engineers to build their own consoles, adapt existing ones to their needs or have them custom-built, by others, to their own specifications. By the time that 16-track tape recorders were introduced at the end of the 1960s, however, the complexity of signal routing, the large-scale implementation of equalization and other factors required that mixing consoles be created by specialized designers and manufacturers. Among the designers who rose to prominence during this period was Rupert Neve. Neve began making custom-designed consoles for the recording, film and broadcast industries in 1961. Operating out of a coach-house in Melbourn, a small village near Cambridge, England from 1964 onward, Neve made innovative transistor-based consoles that established a reputation for flexibility and sound quality virtually unparalleled by any other manufacturer. By the end of the 1960s, he had established a large factory operation in Melbourn, and other manufacturing plants and sales offices soon followed in Scotland, the United States and Canada. Over the years, Neve's company was at the forefront of developments in console design, automation and digitization. In 1997, a Technical Grammy Award was bestowed on Neve, thus highlighting the importance of the development of studio technology within the record industry as a whole.

The creative possibilities offered by multitrack recording, sound processing and mixing began to be increasingly explored by pop and rock artists during the late 1960s. The studio became a compositional environment in which songs evolved through a process of layering and experimentation. Recordings that might have taken a single day to produce earlier in the decade now took weeks to complete: the Beatles' *Sergeant Pepper's Lonely Hearts Club Band* album is among the most notorious, having taken some 700 hours to record. It also signaled the beginning of a period in which the creative roles of artist, producer and engineer would become increasingly blurred within the recording studio.

Recording industry profits were growing rapidly during the same period, and the cost of renting studio time at hourly rates was, at least some of the time, more than offset by the possibility of creating hits. Artists demanded, and received, large recording budgets, which were then poured into independent recording studios, allowing them to grow in both size and number. The five-year period between 1968 and 1973 was one of intense proliferation, with, according to *Billboard* statistics, the number of new studios in the United States increasing to about 70 a year. By the end of this period, the 24-track studio was firmly established as the professional norm, and the need for automatic mixing capabilities was already being felt (the first automated console was introduced by Neve in 1977). The 1970s also gave rise to disco music – the first popular music genre (to be followed by others) that was, for all intents and purposes, created by engineers and producers in the multitrack studio.

By the 1970s, the makeshift studios of the 1950s and 1960s that had given birth to early rock 'n' roll, R&B and soul had largely given way to an increasingly sophisticated and expensive professional studio apparatus: a multitrack mixing console alone could cost over $100,000, and the need to keep up with technical innovations in the audio field made the new recording studios extremely costly to operate and maintain. As record industry sales began to suffer during the late 1970s and early 1980s, the sheer number of independent studios catering to the music industry could not be maintained, and many turned to producing radio and television commercials in order to survive. The shift to digital recording technology during the 1980s and 1990s only exacerbated these problems and forced many studios out of operation. Those that prospered were often able to do so only by diversifying their client base, not only recording popular music but also engaging in film and video post-production and, later, audio for multimedia. By the 1990s, the professional recording studio was often a multipurpose facility, containing some combination of music recording studios, smaller video postproduction suites, and control rooms dedicated to mixing and/or digital editing where little or no actual recording took place.

At the same time as these developments were taking place in the world of professional recording studios, the desire of both professional artists and amateur musicians to learn more about and to participate directly in the recording process was being facilitated by the marketing of low-cost, consumer-oriented multitrack devices. Beginning in the 1970s, a number of manufacturers, led by companies such as Tascam (a division of TEAC, the consumer audio corporation), began designing inexpensive multitrack recorders and consoles, and the idea of a 'home studio' – where musicians could create freely without the pressures of recording schedules and hourly rates – became the focal point of a new market within the audio industry. At first, most home studios, based on four- and eight-track recording technology and possessing inferior microphones and processing devices, could not even begin to rival the sound quality produced by the professional recording studios. During the 1980s, however, the development of inexpensive synthesizers and samplers, MIDI (musical instrument digital interface), sequencing software for personal computers and, by the 1990s, a whole range of digital recording and signal processing devices designed for the home studio allowed home recording enthusiasts to produce professional-sounding recordings.

During the 1990s, many home studio enthusiasts turned to commercial work, giving rise to the so-called 'project studio': a small facility often located in residential neighborhoods, and owned and operated by a single individual functioning simultaneously as composer/arranger, musician, engineer and producer. Unlike semiprofessional and amateur home recording studios, project studios have often come to be seen as being in direct competition with professional studios – 'unfair' competition, because they usually do not pay commercial taxes and do not have the overheads of the professional studios. In large production centers, such as Los Angeles, there has been a concerted effort to use the legal system to close down project studios. In many ways, the recording studio has become a victim of its own success: the technologies that contributed to the rise of the independent recording studio and allowed it to flourish have created the basis of its own competition.

Since the 1950s, the popular music recording studio has demonstrated a distinct evolution that has tended to move away from the large-scale facility, with its rigid hierarchy of production roles, toward a series of smaller, more flexible complexes, with multitrack recording (whether analog or digital) at the center of studio design and practise. While a great deal of recording has continued to be done in larger centers, such as London, New York, Nashville and Los Angeles, the rise of entrepreneurial producers and the widespread availability of multitrack recording technology have made it possible for professional-sounding recordings to be made in virtually any part of the world and on virtually any kind of budget. Some producers have preferred to operate outside urban environments in the comparative calm of rural and/or exotic settings. Chris Blackwell (owner of Island Records), for example, founded Compass Point Studios – a fully professional studio complex, with living accommodation for visiting clients – outside Nassau, the Bahamas, during the late 1970s. And artists themselves have often taken the large advances offered them by the record industry to establish their own personal recording facilities rather than paying out the huge fees demanded by the professional studios; this has become an increasingly important move for many artists associated with genres such as rap and alternative music in order for them to establish creative control over their music. Perhaps most important, the multitrack recording studio, with its associated technologies, has offered popular musicians new ways of making music and has thus been at the center of creative endeavor within the record industry as a whole.

Bibliography

Eargle, John. 1980. *Sound Recording*. 2nd ed. New York: Van Nostrand Reinhold.

Fox, Ted. 1986. *In the Groove: The People Behind the Music*. New York: St. Martin's Press.

Guralnick, Peter. 1986. *Sweet Soul Music: Rhythm and Blues and the Southern Dream of Freedom*. New York: Harper & Row.

Hull, Geoffrey P. 1998. *The Recording Industry*. Boston, MA: Allyn and Bacon.

Ivey, William. 1982. 'Commercialization and Tradition in the Nashville Sound.' In *Folk Music and Modern Sound*, ed. W. Ferris and M.L. Hart. Jackson, MS: University Press of Mississippi, 129–38.

Jones, Steve. 1992. *Rock Formation: Music, Technology, and Mass Communication*. Newbury Park, CA: Sage.

Kealy, Edward R. 1979. 'From Craft to Art: The Case of Sound Mixers and Popular Music.' *Sociology of Work and Occupations* 6(1): 3–29.

Peterson, Richard A., and Berger, David G. 1971. 'Entrepreneurship in Organizations: Evidence from the Popular Music Industry.' *Administrative Quarterly* 16 (March): 97–106.

Shaw, Arnold. 1978. *Honkers and Shouters: The Golden Years of Rhythm & Blues*. New York: Macmillan.

Théberge, Paul. 1997. *Any Sound You Can Imagine: Making Music/Consuming Technology*. Hanover, NH: Wesleyan University Press/University Press of New England.

Discographical Reference

Beatles, The. *Sergeant Pepper's Lonely Hearts Club Band*. Parlophone PCS 7027. *1967*: UK.

PAUL THÉBERGE

Recording Studios

—Abbey Road Studios (UK)

Located at 3 Abbey Road, St. John's Wood in North London, the EMI studios were the first purpose-built recording studios in England. The residential building was converted into three custom-built studios to suit larger recordings of full orchestras and to circumvent the pressures of recording time. Abbey Road Studios were officially opened on 12 November 1931 with a performance (which was recorded) by the London Symphony Orchestra, conducted by the composer Sir Edward Elgar.

Abbey Road Studios were subsequently used to record numerous EMI artists. These included symphony orchestras, music hall celebrities, big band leaders, comedy acts and many visiting international artists. Trumpeter Eddie Calvert's 'Oh Mein Papa' (1953) was the first Abbey Road recording to reach the number one singles spot. Pink Floyd recorded their debut album, *The Piper at the Gates of Dawn*, at Abbey Road, and Cliff Richard achieved a comeback there in the late 1970s with the help of producer Bruce Welch.

During the 1960s, Abbey Road Studios, together with the studios of Decca and Pye, were the most influential record company–owned recording studios in Britain (Cunningham 1998). Often associated with the success of the Beatles, the studios became a household name after the group named its last album to be recorded *Abbey Road* (1969).

Studio 1 is among the largest purpose-built recording studios in the world, offering enough room for a full symphony orchestra and chorus. Because of a drop in the number of classical sessions at the end of the 1980s, it was modified to accommodate movie soundtrack recordings. Many film scores, by such composers as George Fenton, Trevor Jones, John Barry, James Horner and John Williams, have since been recorded at Abbey Road for *Braveheart*, *Star Wars: The Phantom Menace* and other movies.

Studio 2 is associated most closely with the Beatles, and Paul McCartney even had an exact replica built in the basement of his London office. Since the 1960s, the studio has been upgraded, and the control room, located on a separate level overlooking the studio, was rebuilt in 1996 to a Sam Toyoshima design.

In 1976, a Neve console with 36 channels was installed in Studio 3. This was the first piece of studio equipment to be used at Abbey Road that had not been built by EMI's own staff. At the beginning of the twenty-first century, the studio offered a 72-channel SSL 8/ 4000G console and had one of the largest control rooms in London.

The Penthouse Studio was built in 1980 and is situated on the top floor, with a 'window which looked on the outside world; a rare feature for any recording studio' (Southall, Vince and Rouse 1997, 135). It is a self-contained suite that is used primarily as a control room and for DVD authoring.

In addition to the four studios, Abbey Road offers two location recording units, flight-cased for transportation by air, to capture live performances of any genre.

Before 1976, all pieces of equipment were developed in-house by the R&D department and were kept as highly protected EMI trade secrets. In the 1930s, EMI developed its own moving coil microphone system in competition with that of the American Western Electric Company in order to avoid royalty payments. At the end of the twentieth century, Abbey Road had the largest microphone collection in the world. Other inventions and patents, like the magnetic tape and recording machines (BTR-Series) and stereophonic recording and disc cutting, guaranteed that Abbey Road always had a major share of the recording business. With the introduction of CD-Extra in the 1980s and of DVD-authoring facilities in the 1990s, Abbey Road offered advanced multimedia production facilities.

Abbey Road Studios are equally renowned for their cohort of producers and engineers. Many started as tape operators and went on to become well-known producers. Sir George Martin started working at Abbey Road in Nov-ember 1950 and later, as the head of A&R at Parlophone, 'would quickly play an influential part in transferring some of the company's emphasis on classical music into the pop field' (Cunningham 1998, 139). The records produced by Martin at Abbey Road during 1963 for Cilla Black and Gerry and the Pacemakers alone occupied the number one chart position for 32 weeks (Cunningham 1998), but he would leave his biggest imprint as the producer and arranger of the Beatles' material.

Norman Smith engineered Beatles recordings in Studio 2 between 1962 and 1966 before being replaced by Geoff Emerick, who, with Ken Scott, contributed to the experimental nature of the Beatles' music by developing such techniques as artificial double tracking (ADT), flanging and the echo technique STEED (send tape echo echo delay). Dave Harries, who later became Martin's studio manager at AIR Studios, invented the 3M machine, which was first used on George Harrison's song 'While My Guitar Gently Weeps' on *The Beatles* (the White Album) (Cunningham 1998).

In more recent times, Abbey Road Studios have been used for productions such as *The Bends* by Radiohead and *All Change*, Cast's first album with producer John Leckie. Non-EMI-signed band Oasis also recorded some of the songs on its 1997 album *Be Here Now* at Abbey Road. In this album, the band's musical references to the Beatles are as predominant as is the iconography on the album's sleeve.

Bibliography

Abbey Road Studios. http://www.abbeyroad.co.uk/

Cunningham, Mark. 1998 (1996). *Good Vibrations: A History of Record Production*. London: Sanctuary Publishing Ltd.

Southall, Brian, Vince, Peter, and Rouse, Allan. 1997 (1982). *Abbey Road*. London: Omnibus Press.

Discographical References

Beatles, The. *Abbey Road*. Apple PCS 7088. *1969*: UK.

Beatles, The. 'While My Guitar Gently Weeps.' *The Beatles [White Album]*. Apple PMC/PCS 7067-8. *1968*: UK.

Braveheart (Original soundtrack). PolyGram 448295. *1995*: UK.

Calvert, Eddie. 'Oh Mein Papa.' Columbia DB 3337. *1953*: UK.

Cast. *All Change*. Polydor 5293122. *1995*: UK.

Oasis. *Be Here Now*. Epic CRECD219. *1997*: UK.

Pink Floyd. *The Piper at the Gates of Dawn*. Columbia SCX 6157. *1967*: UK.

Radiohead. *The Bends*. Parlophone CDPCS 7372. *1995*: UK.

Star Wars: The Phantom Menace (Original soundtrack). Sony 61816. *1999*: USA.

Filmography

Braveheart, dir. Mel Gibson. 1995. USA. 177 mins. Historical Epic. Original music by James Horner.

Star Wars: The Phantom Menace, dir. George Lucas. 1999. USA. 131 mins. Science Fiction. Original music by John Williams.

VANESSA BASTIAN

—AIR Studios (UK)

After leaving his position at EMI Records, Sir George Martin founded AIR (the acronym for Associated Independent Recordings) with fellow producers John Burgess, Ron Richards and Peter Sullivan in London in 1965. The AIR producers at first rented such studios as Abbey Road, Chappells and Morgan, before acquiring enough capital to build their own facilities. 'Built by producers for producers,' the first AIR studio was built at the end of the 1960s on the fourth floor of the old Peter Robinson department store building in Oxford Circus, London and was officially opened in October 1970. The first album to be recorded there was *A Lot of Bottle* by the Climax Blues Band. It was produced by Chris Thomas, who joined AIR in March 1968 and became 'one of the leading producers of his generation' (Cunningham 1998, 272).

AIR was the first studio to be equipped with a 24-track desk and an early Necam console automation system (Farmer 1993). Younger engineers and producers learned their craft from such AIR staff as Keith Slaughter, Dave Harries, Geoff Emerick and Bill Price. Among the hits produced at AIR were Jeff Beck's *Blow by Blow* (1975) and the first number one hits for T. Rex ('Hot Love') and Roxy Music ('Love Is the Drug' from the *Siren* album). In 1975, Ron Richards and Peter Sullivan left the partnership and John Burgess took over as managing director.

In the early 1970s, George Martin also set up a music production company in Rodmarton Street in London's West End in collaboration with Herman Edel. Known since 1990 as Air-Edel, a sister company of AIR Studios, this is a three-studio complex, which was upgraded in 1999 to full 5.1 monitoring facilities (Sillitoe 2000), the standard surround-sound format at the beginning of the twenty-first century. (This format consists of three speakers across the front and two speakers in the rear; the '.1' signifies a sixth channel called an LFE – low-frequency effects – that is sent to a subwoofer.)

A second AIR studio opened for business in 1979 on the West Indian island of Montserrat. George Martin had been searching for an alternative location away from the noise and distraction of London. Originally wanting to create a relaxing studio atmosphere on a boat, he was inspired by his colleague Geoff Emerick, who had recorded the Wings' album *London Town* in the Virgin Islands. Montserrat, a stable British colony, not only was remote but also offered the necessary communication technology and tax advantages.

Equipped with a desk built to order by Neve (and later duplicated for AIR Studios in London), the Montserrat studio achieved an impressive track record for bestselling albums. The first recording made there was again a Climax Blues Band album, *Flying the Flag*. In 1982, George Martin recorded Ultravox's *Quartet* in both London and Montserrat. The Police recorded *Ghost in the Machine* (1981) and *Synchronicity* (1983) at AIR Montserrat, and Sting used this location to record his first solo album *The Dream of the Blue Turtles* (1985), returning a year later to mix the live recorded material from his first solo tour, *Bring On the Night*. Dire Straits' *Brothers in Arms* (1985), on which the track 'Money for Nothing' was co-written and sung by Sting and Mark Knopfler, was also recorded at AIR Montserrat.

The Oxford Circus and Montserrat studios no longer exist. In 1989, AIR Montserrat was destroyed by Hurricane Hugo, and in 1993 the West End studios were superseded by AIR Lyndhurst, located at Lyndhurst Hall in Hampstead, North London.

Described by Cunningham as 'probably the best studio in the world' (1998, 347), AIR Lyndhurst, created in collaboration with Chrysalis and Pioneer, was able to provide three studios, a television postproduction facility and Lyndhurst Hall (a multipurpose recording complex). The latter, previously a Congregational church built in the 1880s, can accommodate an orchestra of over 100 musicians with chorus and can seat an audience of 500. The first to use the facility was Henry Mancini, who chose Lyndhurst Hall to record the soundtrack for *Son of the Pink Panther*. Among many other film scores recorded there were those for the James Bond movies, *Chocolat*, *Gladiator* and *Hannibal*. The additional three studios were built in the adjoining former missionary school.

Studio 1 was designed according to the specifications of AIR's Oxford Circus Studio 1 and contains AIR's custom-built Neve desk. Studios 2 and 3 have an identical layout, but whereas Studio 2 is equipped with an analog console, Studio 3 is an all-digital mixing room (one of the world's first) (Schoepe 1993). Studio 2 was opened a week after the Lyndhurst Hall studio for the mixing of the Dire Straits live album *On the Night* (Cunningham 1998).

The AIR Lyndhurst studios have subsequently been used by the Manic Street Preachers to mix their number one hit single 'If You Tolerate This Your Children Will Be Next,' and by Elton John, Oasis and Bernard Butler, among many others. At the beginning of 2001, Studio 1 was used by Travis and producer Nigel Godrich for two weeks to record a track for the band's follow-up record to the multi-platinum *The Man Who*, released in June 2001.

The impressive history of AIR has been captured by George Martin on *In My Life* – a compilation of his hits – re-recorded and produced at the AIR Lyndhurst studios shortly before his retirement in 1998.

Bibliography

AIR Studios. http://www.airstudios.com

Cunningham, Mark. 1998 (1996). *Good Vibrations: A History of Record Production*. London: Sanctuary Publishing Ltd.

Farmer, Neville. 1993. 'A New Era at Air.' *Billboard* (6 March): A-3.

Schoepe, Zenon. 1993. 'Air Lyndhurst: The Studio Maintains Its Place in History – and Its Penchant for Making It – in "New" Digs.' *Billboard* (6 March): A-4, A-14/A-15.

Sillitoe, Sue. 2000. 'Air-Edel Gets a Face Lift.' *Audio Media* (January): 36.

Discographical References

Beck, Jeff. *Blow by Blow*. Epic 33409. *1975*: UK.

Chocolat (Original soundtrack). Sony Classical SK 89472. *2001*: USA.

Climax Blues Band, The. *A Lot of Bottle*. Harvest SHSP 4009. *1970*: UK.

Climax Blues Band, The. *Flying the Flag*. Warner Brothers 3493. *1980*: USA.

Dire Straits. *Brothers in Arms*. Vertigo 824 499 2. *1985*: UK.

Dire Straits. *On the Night*. Vertigo 5147662. *1993*: UK.

Gladiator [2000 Original Score]. PolyGram 467094. *2000*: USA.

Hannibal (Original soundtrack). Uptown/Universal 467696. *2001*: USA.

Knopfler, Mark, and Sting. 'Money for Nothing.' *Brothers in Arms*. Vertigo 824 499 2. *1985*: UK.

Mancini, Henry. *Son of the Pink Panther*. Milan 66319-2. *1993*: France.

Manic Street Preachers, The. 'If You Tolerate This Your Children Will Be Next' (CD single). Epic 666345-2 and 666345–5. *1998*: UK.

Martin, George. *In My Life*. Capitol 94866. *1998*: USA.

Police, The. *Ghost in the Machine*. A&M AMLK 63730. *1981*: UK.

Police, The. *Synchronicity*. A&M AMLX 63735. *1983*: UK.

Roxy Music. 'Love Is the Drug.' *Siren*. Island ILPS 9344. *1975*: UK.

Sting. *Bring On the Night*. A&M BRING 1. *1986*: UK.

Sting. *The Dream of the Blue Turtles*. A&M DREAM 1. *1985*: UK.

T. Rex. 'Hot Love.' Fly BUG 6. *1971*: UK.

Travis. *The Invisible Band*. Independiente ISOM25CD. *2001*: UK.

Travis. *The Man Who*. Independiente ISOM9CD. *1999*: UK.

Ultravox. *Quartet*. Chrysalis CDL 1394. *1982*: UK.

Wings. *London Town*. Parlophone PAS 10012. *1978*: UK.

Discography

Butler, Bernard. *People Move On*. Creation/Columbia CRECD221. *1998*: UK.

John, Elton. *Made in England*. Rocket 5261852. *1995*: UK.

Oasis. *Be Here Now*. Epic CRECD219. *1997*: UK.

Filmography

Chocolat, dir. Lasse Hallström. 2000. USA. 121 mins. Romantic Comedy. Original music by Rachel Portman.

Gladiator, dir. Ridley Scott. 2000. USA. 154 mins. Historical Epic. Original music by Lisa Gerrard, Hans Zimmer.

Hannibal, dir. Ridley Scott. 2001. USA. 131 mins. Thriller. Original music by Hans Zimmer.

Son of the Pink Panther, dir. Blake Edwards. 1993. USA. 93 mins. Comedy. Original music by Henry Mancini.

VANESSA BASTIAN

—Atlantic Studios (US)

In 1947, the Atlantic record company established its own studio to record music for release on the Atlantic label. Initially, the studio was based in the label's New York office, where the desks would be piled up in a corner when the room was needed for a recording session with such singers as Joe Turner and Ray Charles (Gillett 1975, 109). With Jesse Stone as arranger, the in-house engineer, Tom Dowd, became known for his meticulous placing of the microphones to balance the sound on one-track recordings. Dowd also ensured that Atlantic adopted new recording technologies, including binaural (stereophonic) sound. A 1952 Atlantic album by Wilbur De Paris and his Dixieland band was claimed to be the first to be made in stereo. The studio was also one of the first to use an Ampex tape machine and to upgrade to eight-track recording.

In 1957, Atlantic moved to a new location, and the original office was converted for use as a permanent studio (Millar 1975, 92). When the company moved to much larger premises on Broadway in the 1960s, purpose-built recording and mixing rooms were included. Here, Dowd engineered and produced albums by Cream, while Atlantic executives Jerry Wexler, Ahmet Ertegun, Nesuhi Ertegun and Arif Mardin produced numerous rock, soul and jazz hits. Songwriters/arrangers Jerry Leiber and Mike Stoller, as well as Phil Spector, produced other sessions.

By the mid-1960s, Atlantic Records was making many of its recordings in Memphis, Muscle Shoals and elsewhere, and the New York studio was less crucial to the label's success. It has remained in use, but has become only one among many state-of-the-art recording operations in New York City.

Bibliography

Cunningham, Mark. 1996. *Good Vibrations: A History of Record Production*. London: Castle Communications.

Gillett, Charlie. 1975. *Making Tracks: Atlantic Records and the Growth of a Multi-Billion-Dollar Industry*. St. Alban's: Panther.

Millar, Bill. 1975. *The Coasters*. London: W.H. Allen.

Picardie, Justine, and Wade, Dorothy. 1993. *Atlantic and the Godfathers of Rock and Roll*. London: Fourth Estate.

Discographical Reference

De Paris, Wilbur. *Wilbur De Paris and His Rampart Street Ramblers*. Atlantic 141. 1952: USA.

Discography

Charles, Ray. 'I've Got a Woman.' Atlantic 1050. 1955: USA.

Cream. *Disraeli Gears*. Reaction 594003. *1967*: UK.

Turner, Joe. 'Shake, Rattle and Roll.' Atlantic 1026. 1954: USA.

DAVE LAING

—Bearsville Studios (US)

Founded by artist-manager Albert B. Grossman in 1970, Bearsville Studios in upstate New York have since been used by many hundreds of artists.

Grossman had been a folk-club promoter and had managed such acts as Bob Dylan, Janis Joplin, and Peter, Paul and Mary. In 1970, he decided to move from management to the formation of a record label and recording studios.

Todd Rundgren was the first resident engineer/producer at Bearsville, working on albums by the Band, Paul Butterfield and Jesse Winchester, as well as recording his own solo and group albums. Others who recorded at the studios in the 1970s were Geoff and Maria Muldaur, Bonnie Raitt and Meat Loaf, whose multimillion-selling *Bat Out of Hell* was recorded with Rundgren and Jim Steinman. In the following decade, Bearsville Studios were host to such acts as Alice Cooper and R.E.M., who cut three albums with producer Scott Litt. Among the albums recorded at Bearsville in the late 1990s were *Post Orgasmic Chill* by British group Skunk Anansie and Branford Marsalis's *Contemporary Jazz*.

By the start of the twenty-first century, there were three separate recording rooms on the site: Studio A, Studio B and Turtle Creek Barn, a self-contained residence/studio. The Bearsville Theater nearby was used for rehearsals and video shoots.

The Bearsville Records label was in operation between 1970 and 1984. Most of its releases were recorded at the studios and were distributed by Warner Brothers. After Grossman's death in 1986, many Bearsville titles were reissued, mainly on the Rhino label.

Discographical References

Marsalis, Branford. *Contemporary Jazz*. Columbia 63850. *2000*: USA.

Meat Loaf. *Bat Out of Hell*. Epic 34974. *1978*: USA.

Skunk Anansie. *Post Orgasmic Chill*. Virgin 47764. *1999*: UK.

Discography

Alice Cooper. *Trash*. Epic 45137. *1989*: USA.

Band, The. *Cahoots*. Capitol EAST 651. *1971*: USA.

Bearsville Box Set (4-CD set). Pony Canyon PCCY-00727. *1996*: Japan.

Butterfield, Paul. *Better Days*. Bearsville BR 2119. *1973*: USA.

Muldaur, Geoff and Maria. *Sweet Potatoes*. Warner Bros. 2073. *1972*: USA.

Raitt, Bonnie. *Give It Up*. Warner Bros. BS 2643. *1972*: USA.

R.E.M. *Green*. Warner Bros. 7599-25795-2. *1988*: USA.

Rundgren, Todd. *Something/Anything*. Bearsville 2066. *1972*: USA.

DAVE LAING

—Black Ark (Jamaica)

Black Ark was a short-lived (1974–80) recording studio owned and operated by legendary Jamaican popular music innovator Lee ('Scratch,' 'the Upsetter') Perry. It was a 'home studio,' operating out of a small, unassuming outbuilding erected for the purpose in the backyard of Perry's suburban residence in Kingston, Jamaica. Perry produced, engineered and mixed the Black Ark recordings.

The establishment of Black Ark (aka 'the Ark') was the capstone of Perry's lengthy involvement in various aspects of the Jamaican popular music industry. It was also a logical follow-up to the success of his Upsetter Records label on which he produced and released a string of local and diasporic Jamaican reggae hits in the late 1960s and early 1970s (including several featuring the Wailers, a group subsequently famous worldwide as Bob Marley and the Wailers).

Artists who were produced and/or recorded at the Black Ark studio included many of the prominent reggae names of the 1970s and after, such as Bob Marley and the Wailers, Max Romeo, Junior Byles, the Mighty Diamonds, the Heptones, Augustus Pablo, Jah Lion and Junior Murvin.

The Black Ark studio was destroyed by fire in 1980 and was not rebuilt. Perry was suspected of arson, but there was insufficient evidence to press charges.

In many ways, the Black Ark studio was technologically at the low end by international music recording industry standards of its day. Its centerpiece was a quarter-inch four-track tape recorder. An Echoplex delay unit and an assortment of other effects units of the period rounded out the Black Ark studio setup. The range of innovative sonic wizardry that Perry coaxed from this basic setup baffled his rival contemporaries and has continued to be a source of bafflement.

Perry and his Black Ark studio were pioneers in the use of tape splicing/sampling and other studio techniques of sound manipulation that have become commonplace in the digital age of Jamaican, African-American and other popular musics.

Perry's status as an icon of Jamaican popular music history – for example, a major reference work on reggae (Larkin 1998) is dedicated to him, and there is a comprehensively informative Lee Perry Web site (http://www.leeperry.com/life/) – has ensured that a representative sample of the Black Ark studio output has continued to be commercially available through various reissues.

Bibliography

Barrow, Steve, and Dalton, Peter. 1997. *Reggae: The Rough Guide*. London: Rough Guides Ltd.

Barrow, Steve, and Katz, David. 1997. Liner notes to *Arkology* (CD set). PolyGram (Island) 524379.

Bradley, Lloyd. 1996. *Reggae on CD: The Essential Guide*. London: Kyle Cathie.

Larkin, Colin, ed. 1998. *The Virgin Encyclopedia of Reggae*. London: Virgin.

Discography

Arkology. PolyGram (Island) 524379. *1997*: UK.

Perry, Lee 'Scratch.' *The Upsetter Shop, Vol. 1: Upsetter in Dub*. Heartbeat 77. *1997*: USA.

Upsetters, The, and Friends. *Build the Ark*. Trojan Duplicate Numbers 3. *1994*: UK.

ROBERT WITMER

—Bokoor Recording Studio (Ghana)

Bokoor (Cool) Studio was opened in 1982 by John Collins, at his father's farm at Ofankor near Accra, Ghana. (The word 'Bokoor,' in Akan, means 'coolness' or 'calmness.') Collins had been managing a Ghanaian guitar band of the same name in the 1970s and, as a result of his recording experiences in Ghana and Nigeria with Bokoor and other bands, he decided to create, for both established and up-and-coming artists, an open-air, mud-built, low-budget studio rather than an expensive air-conditioned one.

Until 1985, Bokoor Studio was one of only two studios operating in Ghana (the other was Ghana Films), and since it opened it has made over 300 demo and professional recordings. The studio released nine records in the mid-1980s (including the 11-band *Guitar and Gun Vol. I and Vol. II* compilations for the British Africagram/Cherry Red label) and over 60 commercial cassettes.

In November 1989, during the 12-hour government-sponsored REVOFEST held at the Accra sports stadium, Bokoor Studio, together with Ghana Films and Sammy Helwani, recorded/mixed many of the country's top musicians and bands, including Wulomei, the African Brothers Band, Bob Cole, Onyina, Ambulley, Papa Yankson, the Kumapim Royals, Onipa Nua, Alhaji Frempong, Lady Talata, Sidiku Buari, Ola Williams and Pozo Hayes. A number of these recordings were featured on the US public radio 'Afro-pop' program (No. 20), which dealt exclusively with this festival.

Although Bokoor Studio has recorded a number of Ghanaian Western-type pop and reggae bands (including, in 1983, the Classique Vibes with Kwadwo Antwi), its main output has been local popular and traditional music, which can be categorized as follows:

(a) Analytical recordings of traditional drumming for Professor J.H.K. Nketia, Dr. Willie Anku and master drummer Michael Ganyoh.

(b) Highlife guitar and concert party bands, including F. Kenya, Kwesi Menu, T.O. Jazz and Yaa Nom (with drummer Okyerema Asante), as well as the country's first 'dialog' concert party cassettes (which include comic interludes between actors) by comedians Waterproof, Super O.D., Ruby Darling and Nkomode.

(c) Highlife dance bands, including King Bruce and the Black Beats, Wofa Rockson (album), Sunsum and the Prisons Band.

(d) Local gospel, including the Genesis Gospel Singers (two albums), the Baptist Disciple Singers (two singles), Compassion Inspiration (with Ray Ellis on keyboards), Reverend Damuah's Africanium Church Choir, the Legon Catholic Charismatic Renewal Band (whose 'Give Us Power' cassette sold 70,000 copies) and the Unipra Church Gospel Singers (album).

(e) Cultural groups (playing a mixture of Western and African instruments), including folk guitarists Koo Nimo and Kwaa Mensah, Abebe and the Bantus, Nii Tetteh's *gome* (or *gombe*) group, Salaam's Cultural Imani Group and the Guna Efee Noko Ga Cultural Troupe.

(f) Fusion music (Afrobeat, Afro-rock, Afro-jazz), including Amartey Hedzolleh, Saka Saka, MauMau

Musiki, Kojo Dadson's Talents and Nokoko and the Pan African Orchestra.

As more and more recording studios began to appear in Accra (by the end of the 1990s there were 12, mainly digital), Bokoor Studio became increasingly mobile and began concentrating on live format recordings. In 1989, it recorded Koo Nimo's 'palm-wine guitar' Adadam group in Kumasi for the background music of John Powell's UNICEF-financed film on intermediate technology, called *The Secret of Wealth*.

In 1994, and at the invitation of the Volta region branch of the Musicians Union of Ghana (Volta has never had a studio), Bokoor Studio began making mobile recordings of Ewe *borborbor*, *akpalu* and *agbadza* drumming groups, as well as a cappella vernacular church choral groups. In 1996 and 1998, the mobile unit made recordings of the Ga master drummer Mustapha Tettey Addy, and in 1997 recorded the traditional *seprewa* (harp-lute) and xylophone player Aaron Bebe Sukutu and the Local Dimension band.

Bokoor Studio recording sessions have appeared in two films, namely, *Repercussions*, featuring Sloopy Mike Gyamfi (BBC, Channel 4, 1993) and *Brass Unbound*, featuring E.T. Mensah's trumpeter son, Edmund (IDTV Holland, 1993).

Bibliography

Collins, John. 1985. *Music Makers of West Africa*. Washington, DC: Three Continents Press.

Collins, John. 1992. *West African Pop Roots*. Rev. ed. Philadelphia: Temple University Press. (First published London: Foulsham, 1985.)

Collins, John. 1994. *Highlife Time*. Accra: Anansesem Press.

Discographical Reference

Guitar and Gun Vol. I and Vol. II. Africagram/Cherry Red A DRY 1 and A DRY 2. *1984*: UK.

Discography

Baptist Disciple Singers/Genesis Gospel Singers, The. 'Awurade Yesu'/'N'tutu.' Africagram/Cherry Red ARID 1. *1984*: UK.

Genesis Gospel Singers, The. *N'tutu*. Africagram/Cherry Red A DRY 5. *1984*: UK.

Genesis Gospel Singers, The. *Onyame Bebe*. Ofori Attah Productions SRT 5KL 482. *1984*: UK.

Uncle Rockson's Dance Band. *Business Women*. Hot Blow Productions Vol. 1. *1985*: Ghana.

Unipra Church Gospel Singers, The. *The Lord's My Shepherd*. Unipra Productions UGS 001. *1985*: UK.

JOHN COLLINS

—Bradley Film and Recording Studios/Bradley's Barn (US)

The Bradley Film and Recording Studios were essential in consolidating the position of Nashville, Tennessee as a recording center during the late 1950s and early 1960s. The enterprise was founded in 1951 by WSM radio's orchestra leader Owen Bradley, who was then producing sessions for Decca country recording chief Paul Cohen, and Bradley's brother Harold, a first-rate studio guitarist and a member of Owen's society dance band. The brothers first concentrated on making industrial films at 2nd Avenue South and Lindsley Avenue, but they also began to hold recording sessions in earnest after moving to the Hillsboro Village area just off Hillsboro Road near Vanderbilt University. Artists who recorded there included Decca country star Kitty Wells and Dot pop star Pat Boone.

In the mid-1950s, Cohen considered shifting his work to Dallas to find better electronics, but the Bradleys persuaded him to stay in Nashville and helped to secure the continuity of recording there. In return for Cohen's guarantee of some 100 sessions a year, in 1955 the Bradleys made him a partner in a new recording facility constructed in a wood-frame house at 804 16th Avenue South. Initially, they installed a basement-level studio, creating a high ceiling by removing the first floor. A second studio, used for both films and commercial recordings, was eventually built inside a military-style Quonset hut. Early equipment included an Ampex 350 mono tape recorder, an Ampex MX-10 mono mixing board and various RCA 44 BX, RCA 77D and Western Electric 639 microphones. In 1961, the Bradleys acquired a three-channel stereo mixing board, custom-built in New York and evidently the first of its type in Nashville. This was used with an Ampex 300 stereo tape recorder. Telefunken microphones and EMT echo chambers further enhanced the studios' capabilities, producing better results than the small rooms previously used for echo effects.

Between 1955 and 1961, the studios were responsible for dozens of hits produced by Cohen, Owen Bradley – who became Decca's country A&R manager in 1958 – Capitol's Ken Nelson, Columbia's Don Law and producers for other labels. These hits included 'El Paso' (Marty Robbins), 'I Ain't Never' (Webb Pierce), 'I'm Sorry' (Brenda Lee), 'I Fall to Pieces' (Patsy Cline) and 'The Battle of New Orleans' (Johnny Horton). Thus, the studios were not only a birthplace of the smooth, pop-influenced 'Nashville sound,' but also a place where hard country sounds were retooled. In these respects, the studios helped country music recover from the commercial inroads made by rock 'n' roll in the mid-1950s, even while giving rock 'n' roll expression in recording sessions by artists such as Buddy Holly and Gene Vincent.

The highly successful facility was purchased in 1962 by Columbia Records, which built new offices around the Quonset hut and kept it in operation until 1982.

For their part, Owen Bradley and his son Jerry opened a new studio, Bradley's Barn, in nearby Mount Juliet, Tennessee in 1965 and rebuilt it after it burned down in 1980. In this studio, Owen recorded stars of the Decca/MCA country roster, including Loretta Lynn and Conway Twitty, and rented the studio to other labels as well. After retiring from Decca/MCA on 1 January 1977, he produced the soundtrack for *Coal Miner's Daughter* (1980), a film recounting Lynn's life; the soundtrack for the Patsy Cline biographical film *Sweet Dreams* (1985), using original Cline vocals; and k.d. lang's top-selling 1988 album *Shadowland: The Owen Bradley Sessions*.

Since Owen Bradley's death in 1998, the studio has continued as a family-run operation.

Bibliography

Daley, Dan. 1996. 'Nashville's Original Engineers: Together Again.' *Mix* 20(7): 92–104, 218–19.

Discographical References

Cline, Patsy. 'I Fall to Pieces.' Decca 31205. *1961*: USA. Reissue: Cline, Patsy. 'I Fall to Pieces.' *The Patsy Cline Collection*. MCA MCAD4-10421. *1991*: USA.

Cline, Patsy. *Sweet Dreams*. MCA MCA D-6149. *1985*: USA.

D'Angelo, Beverly, et al. *Coal Miner's Daughter*. MCA MCSC-1699. *1980*: USA.

Horton, Johnny. 'The Battle of New Orleans.' Columbia 41339. *1959*: USA. Reissue: Horton, Johnny. 'The Battle of New Orleans.' *Honky Tonk Man: The Essential Johnny Horton 1956–1960*. Columbia/Legacy 64761. *1996*: USA.

lang, k.d. *Shadowland: The Owen Bradley Sessions*. Sire 25724-2. *1988*: USA.

Lee, Brenda. 'I'm Sorry.' Decca 31093. *1960*: USA. Reissue: Lee, Brenda. 'I'm Sorry.' *Brenda Lee Anthology, Volume One, 1956–1961*. MCA MCAD2-10384. *1991*: USA.

Pierce, Webb. 'I Ain't Never.' Decca 30923. *1959*: USA. Reissue: Pierce, Webb. 'I Ain't Never.' *From the Vaults: Decca Country Classics, 1946–1961*. MCA MCA CD3-11069. *1994*: USA.

Robbins, Marty. 'El Paso.' Columbia 41511. *1959*: USA. Reissue: Robbins, Marty. 'El Paso.' *The Story of My Life: The Best of Marty Robbins*. Columbia/Legacy 64763. *1996*: USA.

Discography

From the Vaults: Decca Country Classics, 1946–1961. MCA MCA CD3-11069. *1994*: USA.

Filmography

Coal Miner's Daughter, dir. Michael Apted. 1980. USA. 125 mins. Musical Biography. Original music by Owen Bradley, Loretta Lynn, Bob Montgomery, Shel Silverstein.

Sweet Dreams, dir. Karel Reisz. 1985. USA. 115 mins. Musical Biography. Original music by Charles Gross.

JOHN W. RUMBLE

—Brown Radio Productions (US)

Brown Radio Productions was one of the earliest commercial radio and recording enterprises in Nashville, Tennessee. Located downtown at Fourth and Union, the company was established in about 1945 by Charles and William Brown, independent producers of various shows aired via WSM on regional radio networks. One Mutual Network show they handled was *Opry House Matinee* (later called *Checkerboard Jamboree*), staged at the Princess Theater and starring *Grand Ole Opry* kingpins Ernest Tubb and Eddy Arnold. Later, the Browns produced a separate live *Checkerboard Jamboree* program featuring Arnold, which was broadcast from the Maxwell House Hotel, fed to Mutual via WMAK and recorded for sale to radio stations nationwide. Other syndicated, Brown-produced radio programs included *Second Spring*, a soap opera, and *Plantation House Party*, a country show starring the Duke of Paducah. Shows were recorded with a four-input Western Electric 23-C mono console, Magnacorder or Stancil Hoffman tape recorders and a Presto lathe.

By 1950, the Browns were allowing RCA-Victor to bring in RCA engineers and equipment to hold country recording sessions. Hits made in this way included Hank Snow's 'I'm Moving On,' Eddy Arnold's 'Lovebug Itch,' and Johnnie and Jack's 'Poison Love.'

By 1953, the Brown operation had waned. The Browns sold their gear to local engineer Cliff Thomas, who assisted with RCA sessions in a building on Thirteenth Avenue South. Charles Brown moved to Springfield, Missouri in the mid-1950s to produce *The Eddy Arnold Show* for ABC-TV. Eventually, he represented his district in the US House of Representatives.

Discographical References

Arnold, Eddy. 'Lovebug Itch.' Victor 21-0382. 1950: USA. Reissue: Arnold, Eddy. 'Lovebug Itch.' *The Tennessee Plowboy and His Guitar*. Bear Family BCD 15726EI. *1998*: Germany.

Johnnie and Jack. 'Poison Love.' Victor 21-0377. 1951:

USA. Reissue: Johnnie and Jack. 'Poison Love.' *Johnnie and Jack and the Tennessee Mountain Boys.* Bear Family BCD 15553FI. *1992*: Germany.

Snow, Hank. 'I'm Moving On.' Victor 21-0328. 1950: USA. Reissue: Snow, Hank. 'I'm Moving On.' *The Singing Ranger: 1949–1953.* Bear Family BCD 15426(4). *1988*: Germany.

JOHN W. RUMBLE

—Buck Owens Recording Studio (US)

The Buck Owens Recording Studio was a mainstay of the early 1970s ascendancy of the 'Bakersfield sound' school of country music. In 1971, 12 of the United States' top 100 country singles were recorded there. Besides its owner, Alvis Edgar 'Buck' Owens, the other leading exponent of the Bakersfield sound, Merle Haggard, recorded at the facility, as did Owens protégés Susan Raye and Tony Booth, west-coast country star Freddie Hart, folk singer Arlo Guthrie and actress Goldie Hawn.

Founded in 1969, the studio was located in a remodeled 1930s movie theater at 1225 North Chester Avenue in the Oildale section of Bakersfield. It featured a 16-track mixing board and tape recorder, the west coast's second or third modular Moog synthesizer, a room (approximately 170 square meters) able to house a full-size orchestra and an echo chamber. Recording and production supervision was provided by engineers Lee Furr and Terry Gaiser and, eventually, by Owens band member Jim Shaw.

Technical obsolescence and Buck Owens' decreasing emphasis on recording led to the studio's conversion into work space for his broadcasting companies in the mid-1980s.

Bibliography

Scaffidi, Susan. 1993. 'New Life for an Old Studio: Fat Tracks Studio Opens at Hallowed Oildale Site.' *Bakersfield Californian* (10 December): E1, E2.

Shaw, Jim. 1998. Telephone interview with author, 20 November.

Discography

Haggard, Merle, and the Strangers. 'Daddy Frank (The Guitar Man).' Capitol 3198. *1971*: USA.

Owens, Buck, and the Buckaroos. 'Bridge Over Troubled Water.' Capitol 685. *1971*: USA.

Owens, Buck, and the Buckaroos. *Buck Owens' Ruby and Other Bluegrass Specials.* Capitol 795. *1971*: USA.

Raye, Susan. 'L.A. International Airport.' Capitol 3035. *1971*: USA.

ROBERT J. MARLOWE

—Capitol Studios (US)

When songwriters Johnny Mercer and Buddy De Sylva, along with their partner Glenn Wallichs, formed Capitol Records in 1942, they wanted to attract the best musical artists by offering them the most modern audio facilities. A dozen years later, they literally built their company on the excellence of their recorded sound when they erected their now-famous circular Capitol Tower at 1750 Vine Street, Hollywood on top of two basement studios, so ultramodern that their glistening wooden floors floated on a compound that insulated the interior from outside noise. A ramp just off the building's front lobby led directly down to Studio A; attached to it, but separated by a movable wall, was Studio B. Studio A was the larger of the two, but both were designed to accommodate the full orchestras of Billy May, Nelson Riddle, Gordon Jenkins, Stan Kenton and other popular band leaders of the time.

However, no sooner was the Capitol Tower completed in 1955 than a new, stripped-down music, rock 'n' roll, began to emerge. When Capitol first brought its new rockabilly star, Gene Vincent, to Los Angeles in 1957, even the smaller Studio B was too large: Vincent, his four sidemen and two backup singers staked out a corner of the studio, where engineer Ken Nelson placed baffles around them to create, in effect, a smaller, more intimate room. When Johnny Otis's R&B band recorded in Studio A in 1958, Otis took advantage of the extra space to bring in a group of screaming teenagers to liven up the session; their cheering can be heard on 'Ma (He's Making Eyes at Me),' which became a hit for Otis in England.

It was within these studios that Capitol recorded its two major artists: Nat 'King' Cole and Frank Sinatra cut their most popular albums there. Other artists who recorded regularly below the Capitol Tower were Dean Martin, Wanda Jackson, Tennessee Ernie Ford, Stan Freberg and Yma Sumac. Al Jarreau, Natalie Cole, Diane Schur and Brian Setzer have subsequently recorded there.

Capitol has kept the recording technology in both studios on the cutting edge. It includes a fiber-optic network connected with other studios around the world that allows, for instance, a singer at EMI's London studios to record live along with a band in Hollywood. Studios A and B have remained busy partly because they are among the few recording facilities that can accommodate the full orchestras still used on movie (*Forrest Gump*, *Ace Ventura: Pet Detective*) and television (*Home Improvement*, *Murder, She Wrote*) soundtracks. The orchestra for the 1998 Academy Awards, held in March 1999, also rehearsed in Studio A.

Bibliography

Dunn, Lloyd. 1975. *On the Flip Side*. New York: Billboard Publications Inc.

Grein, Paul. 1992. *Capitol Records' 50th Anniversary 1942–1992*. Hollywood, CA: Capitol Records.

Discographical Reference
Otis, Johnny. 'Ma (He's Making Eyes at Me).' Capitol CL 14794. *1958*: UK.

Discography
Cole, Nat 'King.' *The Capitol Collector's Series*. Capitol CPD 7 93590 2. *1990*: USA.

Ford, Tennessee Ernie. *16 Tons of Boogie (The Best of)*. Rhino R2 70975. *1990*: USA.

James, Sonny. *The Capitol Collector's Series*. Capitol CPD 7 91630 2. *1990*: USA.

Otis, Johnny. *The Capitol Years*. Capitol CPD 7 92858 2. *1989*: USA.

Sinatra, Frank. *Come Fly with Me*. Capitol CPD 7 48469 2. *1957*: USA.

Sinatra, Frank. *The Capitol Collector's Series*. Capitol CPD 7 92160 2. *1990*: USA.

Vincent, Gene. *The Capitol Collector's Series*. Capitol CPD 7 94074 2. *1990*: USA.

Filmography
Ace Ventura: Pet Detective, dir. Tom Shadyac. 1994. USA. 85 mins. Comedy. Original music by Ira Newborn.

Forrest Gump, dir. Robert Zemeckis. 1994. USA. 142 mins. Drama. Original music by Joel Sill, Alan Silvestri.

JIM DAWSON

—Castle Recording Laboratory (US)
The Castle Recording Laboratory was the first major professional recording operation in Nashville, Tennessee. By making it easy for visiting producers to record *Grand Ole Opry* talent, as well as visiting artists in country, pop, and rhythm and blues (R&B), the company was crucial to the city's emergence as a recording center during the late 1940s and early 1950s. The company was established in about 1946 by three WSM radio engineers – Aaron Shelton, Carl Jenkins and George Reynolds. Its name was a play on the WSM slogan 'Air Castle of the South,' but it remained an independent enterprise throughout its existence.

Using an eight-input mono mixing board designed by Reynolds, Castle first held sessions in WSM radio studios downtown and piped signals by telephone line to a custom-built lathe at the station's backup transmitter building at Fifteenth Avenue South and Weston. In 1947, operations were moved to rooms on the mezzanine level of the Tulane Hotel on Church Street. Equipment used there included the original mixing board, a Scully lathe and Ampex model 200 tape recorders; most masters were cut direct to disc. A bathroom was remodeled and used as an echo chamber.

In addition to the studio's convenience and technical competence, the helpfulness and engineering talents of its owners – especially Shelton's – attracted many executives and artists. For example, Castle engineers were willing to cut grooves more deeply than most of their competitors in other locales, thus giving Castle-recorded commercial discs a 'hotter' sound that was especially advantageous for jukeboxes, then an important market for recordings.

Although advertising jingles and recorded radio shows comprised important segments of Castle's work, the studio was most famous for commercially released records. With the exception of RCA-Victor, which had an exclusive contract with its engineers' union, all major labels used Castle, as did important independents such as Cincinnati's King Records and the Nashville-based Dot and Bullet labels. In fact, one of the first hits produced with Castle's assistance was 'Near You' (1947), recorded for Bullet by Nashville's Francis Craig Orchestra. Hits by Hank Williams, Red Foley, Ernest Tubb and other leading country acts increased Castle's reputation, as did pop recordings made by the Ray Anthony, Jan Garber and Woody Herman orchestras, all three of which held sessions in Nashville's Ryman Auditorium. By 1953, recording activity at Castle was such that entertainment trade magazines were hailing Nashville as 'the new Music City U.S.A.'

In 1956, various pressures caused the Castle engineers to close their operation. The company's lease was expiring, and the Tulane Hotel's owners were pressing tenants to vacate the premises in anticipation of the razing of the building. Competition from the newer Bradley Film and Recording Studios was increasing, and WSM was beginning to rein in employees with outside business interests. The Castle partners, all with long service records and now absorbed in WSM's expanding television activities, elected to close the company's doors and stay with WSM, but they had already left an indelible mark on the history of recording in Nashville and in country music generally.

Bibliography
Rumble, John W. 1978. 'The Emergence of Nashville as a Recording Center: Logbooks from the Castle Studio, 1952–1953.' *Journal of Country Music* 7(3): 22–41.

Discographical Reference
Francis Craig Orchestra, The. 'Near You.' Bullet 1001. 1947: USA.

Discography
Foley, Red. *Country Music Hall of Fame: Red Foley*. MCA MCAD-10084. *1991*: USA.

Williams, Hank. *The Complete Hank Williams*. Mercury 314-356 077-2. *1998*: USA.

JOHN W. RUMBLE

—Chess Studios (US)

When Chess Records was founded (as Aristocrat in 1947), the company did not have a recording studio, and over the following decade it recorded most of its artists at Universal Recording Studio (at various locales in Chicago). In 1954, Chess moved one block north from its location on Chicago's 49th Street to 48th and Cottage Grove, and there built its first rehearsal studio, but its poor quality forced the company to continue to rely on Universal for most of its recording production. Finally, the company established a first-rate in-house studio – called Chess Studios – in 1957, when it relocated to 2120 S. Michigan Avenue, and it rented the second floor to Sheldon Recording Studios, operated as a Chess subsidiary by engineer Jack Wiener. The studio featured a set of matched echo chambers.

Under Wiener, Sheldon took in considerable outside work, recording sessions for Atlantic and Mercury, for instance. In 1958, Chess took over the studio directly and hired Malcolm Chisholm, who had been the engineer for a considerable number of recordings for Chess when the company was recording at Universal, as sound engineer. When he left, he was replaced in 1960 by Ron Malo, who stayed with the studio until its demise in 1975. Malo upgraded the studio and ran the sound into dual echo chambers in the basement. Almost all the Chess artists were recorded with echo, sometimes to excess. Among the legendary blues and rock 'n' roll artists recorded in this studio were Muddy Waters, Sonny Boy Williamson II, Howlin' Wolf, Chuck Berry and Bo Diddley. The company also built an impressive jazz series, and recorded such artists as the Ramsey Lewis Trio, Ahmad Jamal and Sonny Stitt.

Malo supervised the engineering at recording sessions for most of the company's artists, which by the 1960s meant primarily soul artists: Etta James, the Dells and Billy Stewart, for example. Malo was also the engineer for many sessions with outside artists. In June 1964, for example, the Rolling Stones, seeking to emulate the sound of their legendary blues heroes, came to Chicago to record at the Chess studio; the studio produced half of the tracks on their LP, *12X5*, one of the songs on which was titled in tribute '2120 South Michigan Avenue.' The Rolling Stones subsequently recorded about 20 more tracks at Chess during 1964–65, and in 1965 the Yardbirds recorded 'I'm a Man' there. By 1965, the studio had changed its name to Ter-Mar Recording Studio.

In September 1966, Chess moved all its operations around the corner to 320 E. 21st Street, relocated the Ter-Mar studio there and added a small rehearsal studio. After Leonard Chess died in late 1969, the company went into decline. Malcolm Chisholm rejoined the operation in 1970 but, within two years, the Chess studio was almost inoperative. As a result of its failure to introduce new equipment and to keep up with new trends, the studio had developed a second-rate reputation. When Chess closed its doors in 1975, the studio was dismantled and its equipment sold.

In 1990, the building at 2120 S. Michigan Avenue was dedicated as a Chicago landmark, and hailed as the studio that recorded Chuck Berry, Muddy Waters and other legendary artists. A few years later, the widow of Willie Dixon, Marie Dixon, purchased the building and began a restoration project. In 1997, the building was reopened as a dual-purpose complex: an educational foundation for black artists and a museum of Chess Records and its famous studio.

Bibliography

'Chicago Loses Chess Records.' 1975. *Illinois Entertainer* (December): 25.

Dixon, Willie, with Snowdon, Don. 1989. *I Am the Blues: The Willie Dixon Story*. New York: Da Capo Press.

Gart, Galen. 1993. *First Pressings: The History of Rhythm & Blues, Volume 7: 1957*. Milford, NH: Big Nickel Publications.

Gart, Galen. 1995. *First Pressings: The History of Rhythm & Blues, Volume 8: 1958*. Milford, NH: Big Nickel Publications.

Heatley, Michael. 1992. 'The Yardbirds.' *Goldmine* (12 June): 16.

Pruter, Robert. 1991. 'Chess Records.' In *Chicago Soul*. Urbana, IL: University of Illinois Press, 97–135.

Pruter, Robert. 1996. 'Chess Records.' In *Doowop: The Chicago Scene*. Urbana, IL: University of Illinois Press, 55–83.

Discographical References

Rolling Stones, The. *12X5*. London Ll-3402. *1964*: USA.

Yardbirds, The. 'I'm a Man.' Epic 9857. *1965*: USA.

ROBERT PRUTER

—Companhia dos Técnicos (Brazil)

This studio, which is located in Copacabana, Rio de Janeiro, was established in 1972 by RCA. It was sold in the early 1980s to BMG/Ariola, but the sale was kept quiet, because BMG/Ariola felt that it would be to their disadvantage to dissociate themselves publicly from the prestigious RCA label. In line with many other major record companies, BMG/Ariola sold their studios in Rio in 1993 because of rising maintenance costs and the greater length of time artists took to record 'in-house' as compared to independent studios. It was at this time that the studio became 'Companhia dos Técnicos.'

The studio is among the most important and up-to-date in Rio, boasting two 48-track and one 24-track facilities with both digital and analog technologies, and undertakes work for many major record companies. In 1998, for example, Companhia dos Técnicos was responsible for the live recording of the 'Desfile das Escolas de Samba' ('Parade of the Samba Schools') in the Rio Carnival, which resulted in three CDs released by BMG/Ariola.

Artists of international stature who have recorded at Companhia dos Técnicos include Sarah Vaughan, Dionne Warwick, Nirvana, Tom Jobim, Chico Buarque, Gal Costa and Maria Bathânia.

Discographical References

Escola de Samba Esquenta na Sapucaí. BMG/Ariola 74321580832. *1998*: Brazil.

Escolas de Samba ao Vivo na Sapucaí-Baterias. BMG/Ariola 74321580822. *1998*: Brazil.

Sambas Enredo ao Vivo. BMG/Ariola 74321535932. *1997*: Brazil.

ANNA BOTELHO

—Compass Point Studios (the Bahamas)

Compass Point Studios, located on beachfront property near the city of Nassau on the island of New Providence, the Bahamas, was founded in 1977 by Chris Blackwell, owner of Island Records.

Far from being a facility for local Bahamian musicians, or even musicians from neighboring Caribbean countries, Compass Point has positioned itself as a 'working vacation' studio catering to the needs of established recording artists who are based primarily in North America or Europe. With its combination of excellent recording facilities and an idyllic tropical vacation setting – not to mention the Bahamas' reputation as an international tax haven – Compass Point has attracted numerous high-profile popular music performers and producers for sojourns of several days to several weeks and longer.

Compass Point's heyday was from the late 1970s to the mid-1980s. During the late 1980s and early 1990s, it slid into decline, but then began an upswing in 1993 after undergoing extensive retrofitting and restructuring.

A list of some of the internationally prominent artists who have used the Compass Point facilities, along with detailed information concerning the facilities and surrounding amenities, may be found on-line at Compass Point's home page (http://members.aol.com/compasspnt/index.html).

Bibliography

Boot, Adrian. 1981. 'Laughing Heads.' *Melody Maker* (23 May): 43–44.

ROBERT WITMER

—Davout Studios (France)

Davout Studios was founded in 1965, the first independ-

ent studio to be established in France. As a result, the client list reads like a microcosm of the history of French popular music: Maurice Chevalier, Charles Trenet, Barbara, and Alain Bashung, and composers of film music such as Michel Legrand, who recorded the soundtrack for *Les Demoiselles de Rochefort* at Davout.

Davout's reputation also owes a great deal to the natural acoustics of Studio A, an orchestral room with the largest cubic capacity in Paris, and to the savoir-faire of in-house sound engineer Claude Ermelin, who started his career in the 1960s with a three-track machine and subsequently used almost every existing format before moving to Studer and Sony analog 24- and digital 48-track machines in the early 1990s.

Discography

Bashung, Alain. *Fantaisie Militaire*. Polydor (PolyGram France) 539488. *1998*: France.

Les Demoiselles de Rochefort. United Artists 6662. *1967*: France.

Sanson, Véronique. *Moi le Venin*. WEA (France) 44627. *1988*: France.

Zazie. *Zen*. Mercury (PolyGram France) 532 991. *1995*: France.

Filmography

Les Demoiselles de Rochefort [The Young Girls of Rochefort], dir. Jacques Demy. 1968. France. 124 mins. Musical Romance. Original music by Jacques Demy, Michel Legrand.

OLIVIER JULIEN

—DownTown Studios (South Africa)

DownTown Studios in Johannesburg's city center are the recording facility of the domestic music industry giant, Gallo (Africa). DownTown's history can be traced back to 1932, when Eric Gallo imported a sound engineer from Britain to set up the first studio in Sub-Saharan Africa. As Gallo's company grew, it relocated and improved its studio in 1938; a second studio was added in 1969, and in 1985 Gallo (Africa) acquired RPM Records and its three-studio complex. Revamped in the 1990s, this complex was renamed DownTown Studios.

DownTown is the largest, most active recording studio in southern Africa. Soft front/hard back acoustic design is coupled with state-of-the-art technology. Three 24-track Dolby SR/A studios house an SSL 4000E series console, a Sony and a Harrison console (planned to be replaced by a Neve). The capacity of these analog facilities is enhanced by hard disc and DA8 digital equipment. A 16-track Fostex studio, preproduction programming suite and two editing suites provide additional features. DownTown owns keyboards, drumkits, an array of outboard and MIDI gear, and prized old equipment, including a Manley variable MU stereo compressor and various valve microphones. DownTown's clientele record all local styles (for example, religious musics, soul, *mbaqanga, kwaito, iscathamiya*, rock, jazz and traditional musics). The bulk of the product comprises pop styles geared toward township youth.

As a social institution, DownTown exhibits an apartheid legacy: most executive and technological personnel are white men, most producers are urban black men, and most artists are urban, migrant or rural black men and women.

Until 1996, DownTown employed up to seven in-house engineers, but since then all but one have worked freelance. South African stars such as Ladysmith Black Mambazo record at DownTown. Since the demise of apartheid, international artists such as U2 and Brian Eno have also used the studio, as have producers like G. Bellow, Alan Abrahams, Will Mowat and Phillip Michael Thomas.

Bibliography

Allingham, Rob. 1992. Sleeve notes to *1992 Gallo Gold Awards: 65 Years*. Johannesburg: Gallo (Africa).

Meintjes, Louise. 1997. *Mediating Difference: Producing Mbaqanga in a South African Studio*. Unpublished Ph.D. thesis, University of Texas at Austin.

Discography

From Marabi to Disco: 42 Years of Township Music (compiled by Rob Allingham). African Classics series. Gallo CDZAC61. *1994*: South Africa.

Gospel Spirit of Africa (compiled by Derek Smith). GRC CDRED 615. *1998*: South Africa.

Hits of South Africa, Vol. 2 (compiled by Derek Smith). Gallo CDGMP40568. *1995*: South Africa.

Ladysmith Black Mambazo. *Heavenly*. CDGMP 40715. *1997*: South Africa.

Mahlathini & the Mahotella Queens. *Putting Out the Light*. GMI/Rykodisc HNCD4415. *1984*: South Africa.

Township Swing Jazz, Vol. 1 (compiled by Rob Allingham). African Classics series. Gallo CDZAC53. *1991*: South Africa.

Township Swing Jazz, Vol. 2 (compiled by Rob Allingham). African Classics series. Gallo CDZAC54. *1991*: South Africa.

LOUISE MEINTJES

—The Drive-In (US)

In 1980, Mitch Easter started the Drive-In studio in the garage of his parents' home in Winston-Salem, North Carolina. Easter's goal was to establish a comfortable, low-budget workshop filled with professional equipment, where musicians could make recordings of a relatively high quality. The resulting studio became a pro-duction center for independent rock – and especially independent pop – music in the 1980s and early 1990s.

The garage was initially equipped with a 3M M56 16-track recorder (which has continued to be used by Easter) and a Quantum 20-channel console. In the mid-1980s, Easter upgraded to a 3M M79 24-track recorder and an Amek console. Over the years, the control room was expanded, French doors were installed to create a booth, and numerous instruments and pieces of out-board gear were added. Despite these improvements, the Drive-In was never intended to compete with more pro-fessional studios; Easter merely wanted to provide a venue with recording equipment, a range of instruments and a 'good atmosphere' (Easter 1999).

A measure of attention was drawn to the Drive-In after R.E.M. recorded its debut EP, *Chronic Town*, there in 1982, and then used the studio to record its first album, *Murmur*, in 1983. Other prominent bands of the 1980s based in Athens, Georgia, including Love Tractor and Pylon, also recorded at the Drive-In, as did artists and bands of the 1980s and early 1990s from across the United States, such as Beat Rodeo, Richard Barone, Game Theory, Velvet Crush and Easter's own band, Let's Active. Much of Easter's work as a producer at the Drive-In was carried out in collaboration with fellow North Carolinian Don Dixon. Scott Litt, John Leckie, and dBs Gene Holder and Chris Stamey also worked as producers on projects at the studio.

By 1994, the studio had become too cramped, and Easter moved his recording equipment to a new space: a Victorian house converted into a studio he called Fideli-torium Recordings. Not only was the house able to accommodate more equipment, such as a 'new' 1978 Neve Broadcast console, but it also offered more varied acoustics than the garage studio. Pavement recorded its widely acclaimed 1997 album *Brighten the Corners* at Fid-elitorium, and other indie rock bands that have recorded or mixed at the studio include Son Volt, Helium, Polvo and Archers of Loaf. At the end of the 1990s, Easter began the process of relocating the studio to a new space, one specifically designed for studio use.

Bibliography

Easter, Mitch. 1999. Personal communication with author, 3 March.

Fletcher, Tony. 1990. *Remarks: The Story of R.E.M.* New York: Bantam Books.

Discographical References

Pavement. *Brighten the Corners*. Matador OLE 197. *1997*: USA.

R.E.M. *Chronic Town* (EP). IRS SP 70502. *1982*: USA.

R.E.M. *Murmur*. IRS SP 7064. *1983*: USA.

Discography

Game Theory. *Lolita Nations*. Rational/Enigma STB 73288. *1987*: USA.

Helium. *Magic City*. Matador OLE 195-2. *1997*: USA.

Let's Active. *Afoot* (EP). IRS SP 70505. *1983*: USA.

Love Tractor. *Themes from Venus*. DB Records DB 092. *1989*: USA.

Pylon. *Chomp*. DB Records DB 065. *1983*: USA.

Son Volt. *Wide Swing Tremolo*. Warner Brothers 947059-2. *1998*: USA.

Velvet Crush. *Teenage Symphonies to God*. Sony 550 Music/Creation BK 64442. *1994*: USA.

HOLLY KRUSE

—Dynamic Sounds (Jamaica)

Dynamic Sounds Recording Company Limited is the longest-lived full-service record company in continuous operation in Jamaica. The company was founded by prominent veteran Jamaican band leader and musical entrepreneur Byron Lee (b. 1935). In 1969, Lee purchased West Indies Studios/West Indies Records Limited (WIRL) and renamed the enterprise Dynamic Sounds. The company has remained at the original WIRL premises (established in 1958 at 15 Bell Road, Kingston, Jamaica), and Byron Lee has continued as the president. Dynamic Sounds has been fundamentally a family firm from the beginning, with a number of Lee's relatives (including sons Edward and Byron Jr.) occupying important positions in the company over the years.

Something of a conglomerate (by Jamaican music industry standards, at least), Dynamic Sounds has continually operated according to a policy of covering as many record production and distribution bases as possible. Its well-equipped and highly regarded recording facilities have supplied the releases for the company's in-house labels, including Dynamic, Soul, Jaguar, Tiger and Weed Beat. The facilities have also attracted rental business from numerous independent local producers and the occasional high-profile international act (for example, Paul Simon, Eric Clapton, and the Rolling Stones). Dynamic Sounds has taken on distribution for various local independent producers recording there but releasing on their own labels. The company has also taken on Caribbean representation for various international labels, including US-based Atlantic/Atco, Capitol, Chess/Cadet/Checker and Tamla Motown, and such multinational enterprises as Sony and Warner. Rounding out the 'conglomerate' picture, almost from its inception Dynamic Sounds has been a record company with its own dedicated plating and pressing facilities – a rarity in the Jamaican recording industry.

The heyday of Dynamic Sounds as a preeminent Jamaican recording studio was in the 1970s and early 1980s, when it was one of only a handful of thoroughly up-to-date studios in the country and, according to some commentators, the most consistently professional. During the early 1970s in particular, a substantial portion of the Jamaican records penetrating both local and international hit-parade charts was recorded at Dynamic Sounds.

In 1997, Dynamic Sounds upgraded its recording facilities to 48-track digital capabilities. This was done as a means not so much of remaining competitive in the studio rental business (a number of comparably equipped studios had by then sprung up on the island) as of enhancing the ongoing recording projects of Byron Lee and his perennially popular Dragonaires ensemble.

The manufacturing and distribution arms of Dynamic Sounds have been a mainstay of the company's success over the years and have increasingly become its focus.

Bibliography

Dynamite, Dr. Buster. 1993. Liner notes to *Byron Lee and the Dragonaires Play Dynamite Ska with the Jamaican All-Stars* (CD set). Jamaican Gold 276.

Discography

Lee, Byron, and the Dragonaires and Friends. *Jamaica's Golden Hits, Vol. 3: The Best of Rock Steady and Reggae*. Jamaican Gold 106. *1995*: The Netherlands.

ROBERT WITMER

—EGREM (Cuba)

The record company EGREM (Estudios de Grabaciones y Ediciones Musicales) is the leading Cuban music enterprise. Until the 1990s, this state-operated corporation had a monopoly of the production, manufacturing, licensing, distribution and archiving of Cuban recorded music. While the worldwide dissemination of Cuban music has increased greatly in recent years, limited resources have required that the majority of Cuban CD and cassette manufacturing be done in Canada and Spain. As an umbrella organization, EGREM also operates the management firm PROMUSIC, which coordinates international promotion, performances and tours for EGREM artists. Other EGREM activities include the marketing of musical instruments, the publication of the magazine *Ritmo Cubano* and music retailing through its three stores.

EGREM was formed in 1961, when the revolutionary regime of Fidel Castro nationalized the existing Cuban music industry. EGREM is perhaps best known for its recording facilities, and its main studio – the former Panart recording facility in downtown Havana – has been the studio of choice for generations of Cuban musicians. A permanent aura of spirituality is present there due to decades of legendary and historic recording sessions. In spite of the existence of modern, state-of-the-art digital facilities across town, most Cuban musicians have continued to prefer to record at the old EGREM studios in dusty central Havana.

The building that houses the old EGREM studios is also the site of an impressive and massive archive of recorded Cuban music. Dating from the 1930s to the present, close to 10,000 tapes of all genres, ranging from classical, choral and jazz to folk, popular and traditional, are kept in two climate-controlled vaults – one holding pre-revolution recordings, the other containing material dating from 1958 to the present. An ancient card catalog, created and maintained entirely by hand, keeps track of every recording housed in EGREM's archive. The members of the archive's highly committed, dedicated and experienced staff have an encyclopedic and intimate knowledge of the material and recognize the immeasurable value of Cuban musical history and heritage.

In 1998, a systematic restoration project to preserve the valuable recordings was begun. One by one, in 'real time,' the master tapes are being transferred to digital format. To ensure the integrity of the original recordings, only minor adjustments and repairs are being made, and any unnecessary processing is being avoided.

For over 30 years, all Cuban-based musicians recorded for one or other of EGREM's labels – Areito and Siboney. Among the best known of these musicians are Beny Moré, Orquesta Aragón, Israel 'Cachao' Lopez, Chucho Valdés, Frank Emilio Flynn and Buena Vista Social Club members Ibrahim Ferrer, Rubén González and Compay Segundo. EGREM has issued nonexclusive licenses to issue its repertoire to numerous foreign labels, including the UK-based Tumi and David Byrne's Luaka Bop.

EGREM is much more than a music business empire; it is a cultural institution – a rare case of an institution that inspires love and a great deal of pride not only in its staff and personnel, but also in musicians and artists around the world. As the keeper of one of Cuba's most valuable natural resources – its music – EGREM is a cultural shrine to the Cuban people and a global symbol of artistic integrity.

Discography

Ferrer, Ibrahim. *Tierra Caliente: Ibrahim Ferrer con Los Bocucos*. EGREM 0308. *1998*: Cuba.

Flynn, Frank Emilio. *Frank Emilio Interpreta a Ignacio Cervantes*. EGREM 0228. *1997*: Cuba.

González, Rubén. *Indestructible*. EGREM 0275. *1997*: Cuba.

Lopez, Israel 'Cachao.' *Super Danzónes*. EGREM 0225. *1997*: Cuba.

Moré, Beny. *Canto a Cuba*. EGREM 181. *1996*: Cuba.

Orquesta Aragón. *La Cubanisima*. EGREM 15. *1992*: Cuba.

Raices: Roots of Buena Vista. EGREM 327. *2000*: Cuba.

Segundo, Compay. *Grandes Exitos*. EGREM 0286. *1998*: Cuba.

Valdés, Chucho. *Grandes de La Música Cubana, Vol. 1*. EGREM 0039. *1995*: Cuba.

ALFREDO CRUZ and DAVE LAING

—Eldorado (Brazil)

The owners of the newspapers *Jornal O Estado de São Paulo* and *Jornal da Tarde* and the Eldorado radio station founded the Eldorado recording studio in São Paulo in 1972. For several years, it was the only Brazilian 16-track studio and the most modern in Latin America. Equipped with Ampex recording machines, Dolby processors, 24-input/16-output audio design desk, CBS automatic high-pick controllers, Altec compressors, and EMT and Panasonic echo chambers, it achieved a sound quality comparable to that produced in North American and European studios. The major companies recording in Brazil in the 1970s, such as Philips, Phonogram and Odeon, used the Eldorado studio to record great Brazilian MPB (*música popular brasileira* – Brazilian popular music) artists like Gilberto Gil, Elis Regina, Caetano Veloso and Milton Nascimento. In 1977, the record label Eldorado was created to allow the studio to issue its own products. The first record released was *Revendo com a flauta os bons tempos do chorinho* [The Good Old Times of Choros, with the Flute], a collection of famous *choros* from different periods of Brazilian popular music. It marked the inauguration of a large catalog that includes music from folk, MPB and popular instrumental to classical. In the late 1970s, with the appearance of similarly or even better equipped studios, Eldorado began to lose its share of the market, and it was finally closed down in April 1992.

Bibliography

Castro, Acyr. 1972. 'O som da nossa era: a força do estúdio' [The Sound of Our Era: The Studio's Strength]. *Jornal do Brasil* (11 June): Section B, 4, 5.

'Estúdio Eldorado antecipa o futuro' [Eldorado Studio Foresees the Future]. 1972. *Jornal O Estado de São Paulo* (4 January): 15.

'Imagine o som que pode nascer aqui' [Imagine the Sound That Could Be Born Here]. 1972. *Jornal da Tarde* (4 January): 11.

Discographical Reference

Poyares, Carlos, e Seu Conjunto. *Revendo com a flauta os bons tempos do chorinho*. Eldorado 1.40.404.001-A. *1977*: Brazil.

Discography

Caipira: raízes e frutos (2 discs). Eldorado 35.80.3079/1, 35.80.3079/2. *1980*: Brazil.

Edu da Gaita. *Edu da Gaita*. Eldorado 07.79.0329. *1979*: Brazil.

Klein, Jacques, and Moreira, Ezequiel. *Zequinha de Abreu*. Eldorado 12.79.0325. *1979*: Brazil.

Prado, Almeida (with Fernando Lopes on piano). *Cartas Celestes* (3 discs). Eldorado 66.82.0352/1, 66.82.0352/2, 66.82.0352/3. *1982*: Brazil.

Raíces de America. *Raíces de America*. Eldorado 21.80.0381. *1980*: Brazil.

Sargento, Nelson. *Sonho de um sambista*. Eldorado 07.79.0328. *1979*: Brazil.

JOSÉ ROBERTO ZAN (trans. MARTHA TUPINAMBÁ DE ULHÔA)

—EMI Studios (Powerhouse Studios) (South Africa)

EMI is the only multinational record company to have had direct holdings in a studio in South Africa. Constructed in downtown Johannesburg in 1951, EMI Studios was one of numerous recording facilities active during apartheid. Through the 1970s and into the 1980s, local product was in great demand. This was in part a spinoff from the state-owned broadcasting corporation's policy of programming apolitical black music. In the early 1980s, EMI relocated its recording facility to industrial Johannesburg, expanded it into a state-of-the-art two-studio complex with editing and mastering suites, and renamed the complex Powerhouse Studios. This renaming conveniently obscured the involvement of its mother company at a time when pressure from the anti-apartheid movement to limit foreign investment in South Africa was mounting, and all music multinationals except EMI withdrew their direct holdings from the country. Powerhouse Studios came to rival RPM Studios in size, sophistication and productivity. The full range of local pop, soul, rock, *mbaqanga*, religious and traditional musics was recorded.

The South African music industry met with severe budgetary constraints in the post-apartheid era, at the very time when it was reentering an internationally competitive market. Powerhouse decided to close in 1993 rather than invest in the upgrade that would have enabled it to compete with digital studios worldwide. However, in a move representative of post-apartheid empowerment, the studio was bought by Sizwe Zako, a black South African producer, artist and managing director of a new indie, Zako's Music Productions, which specializes in gospel music and caters to a local black market.

Discography

The Gospel Collection. African Heritage series. CCP Record Company CDCCP(WL) 1144. *1998*: South Africa.

Lord Comforters. *Noyana*. Zako CDZR(WB) 001. n.d.: South Africa.

Only the Poor Man Feel It. EMI 7243 8 322866 2. Remastered at Abbey Road Studios, London. *1995*: South Africa/UK.

The Pop Collection. African Heritage series. CCP Record Company CDCCP(WL) 1142. *1998*: South Africa.

21 Years of SA's Best! EMI Music (SA) CDEMCJ(WB) 5652. *1996*: South Africa.

LOUISE MEINTJES

—Englewood Cliffs Studios (US)

The recording studios at Englewood Cliffs, New Jersey were established by sound engineer Rudy Van Gelder in 1959, replacing an earlier facility he had installed in his home in Hackensack, New Jersey in 1953. Throughout the 1950s and 1960s, Van Gelder's Hackensack and Englewood Cliffs studios served as the location for the vast majority of the hard bop and soul-jazz recordings on the Blue Note and Prestige jazz record labels, including classic sessions by Miles Davis, Art Blakey and Jimmy Smith, among many others. In the early 1960s, the Englewood Cliffs studios were also the site of the significant avant-garde and free-jazz innovations of figures such as John Coltrane and Archie Shepp, captured in a series of celebrated recordings for the Impulse! label.

Originally a practising optometrist, Van Gelder balanced both careers until the move to Englewood Cliffs in 1959, when he turned to sound engineering full time. Since his earliest work for the Blue Note label in 1953, Van Gelder has been the engineer on literally hundreds of jazz sessions for a variety of labels, becoming justifiably famous for the unprecedented clarity and excellent sound balance of his recordings. CD reissues of many of these sessions have confirmed the remarkably high quality of Van Gelder's original analog recordings, firmly establishing his reputation as one of the most successful and highly regarded sound engineers in the history of jazz. Van Gelder was the recipient of *Down Beat* magazine's Lifetime Achievement Award in 1990, and the importance of his contribution to contemporary jazz was further acknowledged in 1999 when, as part of its 60th anniversary celebrations, the Blue Note label introduced the Rudy Van Gelder Edition, a series of classic jazz recordings originally engineered and subsequently digitally remastered by Van Gelder himself. At the beginning of the twenty-first century, Van Gelder was still active at his studios in Englewood Cliffs, engineering sessions by a new generation of jazz performers, including Wallace Roney and T.S. Monk.

Discography

Blakey, Art. *The Best of Art Blakey and the Jazz Messengers: The Blue Note Years*. Blue Note 93205. *1991*: USA.

Coltrane, John. *A Love Supreme*. Impulse! 155. *1964*: USA.

Coltrane, John. *The Classic Quartet: Complete Impulse! Studio Recordings* (8 CDs). GRP 280. *1998*: USA.

Davis, Miles. *Chronicle: The Complete Prestige Recordings (1951–1956)*. Prestige 8PCD-012-2. *1992*: USA.

Monk, T.S. *Monk on Monk*. N2K 10017. *1997*: USA.

Roney, Wallace. *Crunchin'*. Muse 5518. *1993*: USA.

Shepp, Archie. *Four for Trane*. Impulse! 218. *1964*: USA.

Smith, Jimmy. *The Best of Jimmy Smith: The Blue Note Years*. Blue Note 91140. *1988*: USA.

ALAN STANBRIDGE

—Estúdios Centauro (Nicaragua)

Estúdios Centauro were founded by folklorist and music entrepreneur Salvador Cardenal Argüello, their name inspired by the poetry of Pablo Antonio Cuadra. The studios were begun as an adjunct to Radio Centauro, and both the radio station and the studios operated from Cardenal Argüello's home in Managua, the capital of Nicaragua, Central America, for most of their existence. As well as European classical music, Radio Centauro's programming specialized in Nicaraguan folk music and popular music. The Centauro record label released primarily folk-based musics recorded at the studios. However, under the leadership of Cardenal Argüello's son, Lorenzo, the stature of Estúdios Centauro as a central national recording location for musicians performing in a wide range of musical styles increased; some of the first recordings of national popular music, released on various labels, were produced at Centauro in the 1960s.

In the early 1970s, the names of the radio station and label were changed to Güegüense, but the studios retained the name 'Centauro.' The advent of the Sandinista-sponsored government studios eclipsed the national importance of Estúdios Centauro, although Lorenzo Cardenal has remained active in recording projects.

Discography

Carvallo, Jorge Isaac. *Fotografías Musicales*. SISA. *1975*: Nicaragua.

Conjunto Max Blanco, Coro Elia Orozco. *Diciembre en Nicaragua*. Güegüense LD-001. n.d. (mid-1970s): Nicaragua.

Vega, Ramiro, y Orquesta et al. *Salve Azucena Divina*. Andino L.P. 002. n.d. (late 1960s): Nicaragua.

T.M. SCRUGGS

—Estúdios ENIGRAC (Nicaragua)

Estúdios ENIGRAC, the Empresa Nicaragüense de Grabaciones Artísticas y Culturales (the Nicaraguan Company for Artistic and Cultural Recordings), constituted the recording arm of Nicaragua's first Ministry of Culture, founded soon after the Sandinista government came to power in 1979. The studios, located in a renovated build-ing owned by the mistress of the former dictator Somoza, contained only one studio space with control room, and were furnished with donated equipment from Western Europe. Like other projects of the Ministry, throughout the 1980s the studios increasingly felt the effect of the US-initiated war and economic embargo.

The studios, despite technical limitations and the short duration of their existence, recorded an immense variety of musics, almost all of which were released on one of ENIGRAC's labels. The principal engineer at Estúdios ENIGRAC, Román Cerpas Acevedo, creatively adapted the studios' resources to record a wide variety of musical styles and instrumentations. Almost all Nicaraguan popular music released in the 1980s was recorded at Estúdios ENIGRAC's facilities (with the notable exception of the *nueva canción* ('new song') groups of the Mejía Godoy brothers, who were able to utilize better-equipped foreign studios when on tour). Recordings produced at the studios included music by Nicaraguan and exiled Central American *nueva canción* groups, Atlantic coast Creole *palo de mayo* bands and, especially in the studios' last years, various popular music groups. Along with the Ministry of Culture, the studios closed in 1988.

Discography

Dimensión Costeña. *De Que Suda, Suda!*. Chilamate 6004. *1984*: Nicaragua.

Grupo Libertad. *En Broma y en Serio*. Ocarina MC-029. *1983*: Nicaragua.

Grupo Pueblo. *Pueblo*. ENIGRAC NCLP 5015. *1986*: Nicaragua.

Igni Tawanka. *. . . A esas Manos que Prometen . . .* Ocarina MC-008. *1983*: Nicaragua.

Los Girasoles. *Los Girasoles*. Chilamate 006. *1983*: Nicaragua.

Pancasán. *Vamos Haciendo la Historia*. Ocarina MC-011. *1980*: Nicaragua.

1er Festival de la Canción Romántica Nicaragüense, Rafael Gastón Pérez. Chilamate 003. *1983*: Nicaragua.

Zapata, Camilo. *Treinta Temas Escogidos*. ENIGRAC/Discos Pentagrama. n.d. (late 1980s): Mexico.

T.M. SCRUGGS

—Estúdios Mosh (Brazil)

The Brazilian recording studio Estúdios Mosh (Mosh Studios Ltd.) was founded in January 1980 in São Paulo by Oswaldo Malagutti, Jr. and Helio Santisteban, two members of the rock band Pholhas. At first, the studio had one adapted P.A. mixing desk from the band, an MCI eight-track tape recorder and some peripheral equipment. Malagutti bought out his partner and started expanding Mosh. The studio moved to a 2,200 square meter location, where a staff of 30 worked at combining digital technology with 'vintage' equipment in four studios, each with 48 analog tracks, Studer and Otari recording machines, Neve and DDA cabinets, and mastering and digital editing facilities. At Mosh, stars like Chitãozinho & Xororó and Leandro & Leonardo helped to develop the specific sound for *música sertaneja* (Brazilian country music).

CILENE PERES

—Finnvox (Finland)

Finnvox, a recording studio and pressing plant in Helsinki, Finland, was founded in 1965. It was the first studio in Finland designed especially for these purposes. It was originally equipped with a Studer four-track recorder, but soon expanded to eight and 16 tracks. Finnvox was also the first company to offer the complete production process, from the provision of studio facilities to mastering, pressing and cassette duplication, and it was able to attract many new clients when a number of independent record companies started up in Finland in the 1970s. The first head of the studio was the pianist Kalevi Hartti; he was followed by Erkki Ertesuo and Risto Hemmi.

Finnvox became an important force in Finnish popular music after producers started demanding multitrack capabilities from recording studios. The first important album to emerge from Finnvox studios was the debut LP of Blues Section (1967), issued on the Love label. Many other early Love albums, such as Wigwam's *Hard & Horny* (1969), owe their sound to Finnvox.

In the early 1970s, Finnvox enjoyed a virtual monopoly in Finland, as most record companies used at least some of its services. It was also used by radio and television for technically demanding work. By the end of the decade, another pressing plant and a number of competing studios had started operations, but Finnvox was often the first to introduce new recording technologies, such as digital recording, into Finland. After the introduction of the compact disc, Finnvox gradually withdrew from manufacturing and concentrated on recording and mastering. The company began CD mastering in 1987. Since 1995, the studio has used Solid State Logic consoles, with Pro Tools for recording.

Discographical References

Blues Section. *Blues Section*. Love LRLP 3. *1967*: Finland.
Wigwam. *Hard & Horny*. Love LRLP 9. *1969*: Finland.

PEKKA GRONOW

—Gary Paxton Sound Services Inc. (US)

Gary Paxton Sound Services Inc. was probably the most musically eclectic and, for its time, technologically advanced recording facility in Bakersfield, California. Its founder, Gary S. Paxton, was then best known as a Hollywood rock star (half of the duo Skip and Flip, a

member of the Hollywood Argyles) and engineer/producer ('Monster Mash' (1962)). The studio was established in 1967 in an abandoned bank building on North Chester Avenue in the Oildale section of Bakersfield, and later also occupied an adjoining store.

The studio recorded three categories of artists: (a) acts signed to Paxton's Bakersfield International, Countrypolitan, GSP and Garpax labels or acts that had production deals with Paxton – for example, west-coast country rockers Clarence White, Gib Guilbeau and Gene Parsons and Chicano surf duet Doug & Freddie; (b) about 30 western Canadian rock bands, referred by a friend of Paxton's; and (c) local country, rock and gospel performers – for example, country singer Bobby Durham and Chicano rocker Augie Marino. Among the studio's greatest commercial successes was the Gosdin Brothers' 'Hangin' On,' which was on the *Billboard* charts for 11 weeks in 1967; another noteworthy 1967 project was *We're Indian*, a protest album featuring Dennis Payne.

The studio featured over 1,100 square meters of floor space, two echo chambers (one a converted subterranean vault with eight seconds of natural delay), one of the west coast's first eight-track recorders and two of its first synthesizers. The control room was a converted Greyhound bus, giving Paxton mobile recording capabilities.

Paxton abandoned the studio when he moved to Nashville in 1970.

Bibliography

Paxton, Gary S. 1998. Interviews with author, 23 July and 3 September.

Discographical References

Gosdin Brothers, The. 'Hangin' On.' Bakersfield International 1002. *1967*: USA.
Payne, Dennis. *We're Indian*. Red Man LP1492. *1967*: USA.
Pickett, Bobby 'Boris,' and the Crypt-Kickers. 'Monster Mash.' Garpax 44167. *1962*: USA.

ROBERT J. MARLOWE

—Grant Avenue Studio (Canada)

The Grant Avenue Studio was started in 1971 by Canadian producer Daniel Lanois with his brother, Bob, in their parents' basement in Hamilton, Ontario. The studio has functioned for over 25 years as a homely, out-of-the-way, handcrafted recording facility favored by artists as disparate as Brian Eno, the Cowboy Junkies and Gordon Lightfoot.

The original studio was a simple affair, consisting of a quarter-inch, quarter-track Sony tape recorder and two Traynor mixers (which had been designed for use as part of a live public-address system). As rudimentary as this setup was, at the time it was the only recording facility in Hamilton. Over the next few years, the Lanois brothers remodeled their parents' basement and moved first to four-track recording capability, and then to eight-track (in 1974). In 1975, using profits generated from recording rock, folk, children's records and jingle sessions, the Lanois brothers purchased an old two-and-a-half-story house on Grant Avenue.

Bob Lanois spent a year remodeling the first floor of the house, finally opening the studio for business as a 16-track facility in 1976. By the end of the decade, Grant Avenue was outfitted with a 24-track recorder and console. Intrigued by a demo being shopped in New York by Canadian rock group the Time Twins, Brian Eno booked time at the studio and went on to record several of his *Ambient* albums there. When Eno was asked to produce U2's *Unforgettable Fire* sessions, he enlisted the help of Daniel Lanois to record some of the vocals and do some of the mixing at Grant Avenue.

Over the next several years, Lanois became a highly sought-after producer, and he no longer had time to run a studio. Consequently, in 1985, Grant Avenue was sold to session musician Bob Doidge, who has continued to run the studio.

An idiosyncratic facility, the Grant Avenue Studio is noted for its collection of original classic Telefunken tube microphones, tube compression for vocal recording, an irregular floor surface, huge floor-to-ceiling glassed-in drum and vocal booths, wide-open sightlines and a great deal of old brick and glass. In addition, Doidge prides himself on the studio's instrument collection, which includes an array of vintage amplifiers and keyboards, and everything from accordions to cellos, bagpipes and percussion gear.

Many artists are attracted to Grant Avenue for its uniquely casual and informal environment. Located 45 minutes from Toronto, where all Canadian branches of the major record companies have their headquarters, the studio allows sessions to be held in relative privacy, away from recording-company personnel. Reinforcing this sense of privacy, informality and non-pretentiousness is the studio's location on a nondescript, residential street. As well, in contrast to most recording facilities, there is no Studio B, demo studio or rehearsal room. Consequently, at any one time there is only one client in the building whose session is the sole focus of all activity in the studio.

Discographical References

Eno, Brian. *Ambient #2: The Plateaux of Mirror*. Editions EG EGS 202. *1980*: UK.
Eno, Brian. *Ambient #4: On Land*. Editions EG EGED 120. *1982*: UK.
U2. *The Unforgettable Fire*. Island ISI-1011. *1984*: USA.

Discography

Lightfoot, Gordon. *The Painter Passing Through*. Warner Bros. 46949. *1998*: Canada.
Raffi. *Singable Songs for the Very Young*. Shoreline MCA-10037. *1976*: USA.

ROB BOWMAN

—Guillaume Tell Studios (France)

Founded in 1985 in Paris by sound engineer Roland Guillotel, Guillaume Tell rapidly became the most serious rival of Davout Studios (France's first independent studio). Using basically the same recording equipment (Studer and Sony analog 24- and digital 48-track machines, Sony and S.S.L. consoles), it also offers a large orchestral room (Studio A) that is greatly valued by many composers of film music – this is where Claude Petit creates most of his soundtracks – and by French artists such as Charles Aznavour, Mireille Mathieu and Michel Sardou. Finally, it shares with Davout the status of being the favorite recording venue in Paris of international musicians – Prince, INXS, Depeche Mode and Elton John, among others.

Discography

Cyrano de Bergerac (Original soundtrack). DRG 12602. *1990*: France.
Foly, Liane. *Rêve Orange*. Disques Double 30016. *1990*: France.
Paradis, Vanessa. *Variations sur le Même T'Aime*. Polydor (PolyGram France) 843447-2. *1990*: France.
Souchon, Alain. *C'est Déjà Ça*. Virgin (France) 391782. *1995*: France.

OLIVIER JULIEN

—Harry J Studios (Jamaica)

Harry J Studios (also Harry J. Studios) of Kingston, Jamaica was established in 1971 by Jamaican record producer Harry Johnson, mainly on profits from 1969–71 reggae hit singles issued on his Harry J label but recorded in studios owned by others. The most commercially successful was 'The Liquidator' by the Harry J All-Stars, a UK Top 10 hit in 1969. Unlike most other fully equipped Kingston recording studios, Harry J Studios is located in suburban uptown Kingston – in fact, a residential bungalow was retrofitted as a recording studio.

Although there have been some noteworthy releases on Johnson's Harry J label emanating from Harry J Studios, it is mainly from rental business that Harry J Studios has earned a secure place in the history of Jamaican popular music. Through its combination of a sedate uptown setting, a first-rate recording engineer (Sylvan Morris, lured by Johnson from rival Studio One) and an always up-to-date recording console, Harry J Studios has been an attractive recording venue for various independent producers over the years.

Among the many tracks recorded at Harry J Studios, perhaps the most historically significant are those of the mid-1970s output of the Wailers/Bob Marley and the Wailers: the *Burnin'* and *Natty Dread* albums were recorded at Harry J Studios, as were substantial portions of the *Catch A Fire* and *Rastaman Vibration* albums.

Bibliography

Barrow, Steve, and Dalton, Peter. 1997. *Reggae: The Rough Guide*. London: Rough Guides Ltd.

Bradley, Lloyd. 1996. *Reggae on CD: The Essential Guide*. London: Kyle Cathie.

Larkin, Colin, ed. 1998. *The Virgin Encyclopedia of Reggae*. London: Virgin.

Discographical References

Harry J All-Stars, The. 'The Liquidator.' Trojan TR 675. *1969*: UK.

Marley, Bob, and the Wailers. *Catch A Fire*. Island ILPS 9241. *1973*: Jamaica.

Marley, Bob, and the Wailers. *Natty Dread*. Island ILPS 9281. *1974*: Jamaica.

Marley, Bob, and the Wailers. *Rastaman Vibration*. Island ILPS 9383. *1976*: Jamaica.

Wailers, The. *Burnin'*. Island ILPS 9256. *1973*: Jamaica.

ROBERT WITMER

—Keisar Studios (Israel)

For more than a decade, Keisar was the leading studio for Israel's genre of *musica mizrakhit* (oriental music). It was founded in 1978 by Yehouda Keisar, the guitarist for Tsliley ha-Oud, one of the first bands to play and record in this genre. The studio was located in a regular apartment in one of Tel Aviv's poorer neighborhoods. Since it was equipped with only a simple tape recorder, and different rooms of the apartment served as separate 'tracks,' the studio productions were mostly 'live,' one-take recordings, most of which were disseminated as cassettes only.

In 1980, the studio moved to a location at the center of Tel Aviv, and became 16-track. Over the following eight years, Keisar became the recording site for most of the albums by *musica mizrakhit* musicians. Working around the clock and in close association with Reuveni Brothers, the major company of the genre in that period, the studio served as a kind of workshop in which leading *musica mizrakhit* musicians, such as Moshe Ben-Mush and Avihu Medina (at the time still considered 'outsiders' and excluded from mainstream Israeli culture), met and influenced each other, carving out the typical sound of the genre.

Key albums, like Zohar Argov's *Nakhon le-ha-Yom* and Haim Moshe's *Ahavat Hayai*, were recorded in 1982. Other notable musicians who regularly worked at Keisar included Margalit Tsanani, Avner Gedasi and Shimi Tavory. Toward 1988, as new companies established their own studios, Keisar gradually lost its central position despite its upgrade to a 32-track studio, and it eventually closed down.

Bibliography

Halper, Jeff, Seroussi, Edwin, and Squires-Kidron, Pamela. 1989. 'Musica Mizrakhit: Ethnicity and Class Culture in Israel.' *Popular Music* 8: 131–42.

Regev, Motti. 1996. 'Musica Mizrakhit: Israeli Rock and National Culture in Israel.' *Popular Music* 15(3): 275–84.

Discographical References

Argov, Zohar. *Nakhon le-ha-Yom*. Reuveni 859-2. *1982*: Israel.

Moshe, Haim. *Ahavat Hayai*. Reuveni 891-2. *1982*: Israel.

Discography

Argov, Zohar. *Greatest Hits, Vol. 1*. Reuveni 009. *1988*: Israel.

Argov, Zohar. *Greatest Hits, Vol. 2*. Reuveni 010. *1988*: Israel.

Argov, Zohar. *Greatest Hits, Vol. 3*. Reuveni 011. *1988*: Israel.

Moshe, Haim. *Greatest Hits, Vol. 1*. Reuveni 001. *1988*: Israel.

Moshe, Haim. *Greatest Hits, Vol. 2*. Reuveni 002. *1988*: Israel.

Moshe, Haim. *Greatest Hits, Vol. 3*. Reuveni 003. *1988*: Israel.

Tsanani, Margalit. *Greatest Hits, Vol. 1*. Reuveni 008. *1988*: Israel.

Tsanani, Margalit. *Greatest Hits, Vol. 2*. Reuveni 053. *1988*: Israel.

MOTTI REGEV

—Kirios (Spain)

Kirios, a Spanish recording studio, was founded in Madrid in 1967. In its early years, it was called Estudios Celada and was dedicated primarily to recording advertising jingles. Later, it took the name 'Kirios' and focused on the recording of pop and classical music. From its inception, it was a pioneer in adopting new technologies for recording. It was the first Spanish studio to record on four tracks and, later, on eight. For that reason, most record companies used this studio during the 1960s and 1970s. Thus, CBS, for example, once it was established in Spain, used Kirios's facilities. Kirios relied on an important group of musicians, the foremost of whom was the producer, arranger and composer Augusto Algueró, one of the most significant personalities in

Spanish music in the last decades of the twentieth century. Among the most important artists who have recorded at Kirios are Julio Iglesias, Rafael, Joan Manuel Serrat, Massiel and Mari Trini. At the end of the twentieth century, Kirios was the most important recording studio in Spain.

JULIO ARCE

—The Manor (UK)

The Manor was one of the first residential recording studios in Britain. Situated in Shipton-on-Cherwell in Oxfordshire, the 100-acre property was purchased by Richard Branson in 1971. Producer Tom Newman and recording engineer Simon Heyworth started to build a recording studio with a four-track Ampex tape machine and a secondhand valve eight-track mixer in a small stable. Newman and Heyworth worked informally with 19-year-old Mike Oldfield on *Tubular Bells* (1973), which was the first album to be issued on Branson's Virgin Records label. The album unexpectedly sold over 15 million copies and 'established a multi-million pound record company into the bargain' (Newman 1993, 23). The success of *Tubular Bells* provided the start-up capital that Richard Branson needed to build his Virgin empire, and it made The Manor – at a time when the music industry was still in its infancy and dominated by the majors – one of the biggest success stories of the decade (Cunningham 1998).

Much liked by musicians for its communal atmosphere, The Manor always offered up-to-date equipment. *Tubular Bells* was recorded on a new state-of-the-art 16-track Ampex and mixed on a 20-channel console, designed and built for The Manor by Audio Developments of Staffordshire. The studio offered equalization, Dolby noise reduction, quadraphonic monitoring, phasing facilities, echo facilities, a grand piano, and space for 40 musicians and their crew for day and night recording. The equipment was also available for hire from The Manor Mobile.

Among those who recorded at The Manor in its early years were the Bonzo Dog Band, Horslips, and Robert Wyatt. In 1978, John Leckie produced XTC's first album, *White Music*, at The Manor. Hugh Padgham later produced XTC's double album, *English Settlement*, there. According to Cunningham (1998), this was one of the biggest successes of Padgham's fledgling production career. Virgin Records was sold to EMI in 1992 and The Manor was closed three years later. Shortly before its demise, Paul Weller recorded his solo album, *Stanley Road*, at The Manor.

Bibliography

Cunningham, Mark. 1998 (1996). *Good Vibrations: A History of Record Production*. London: Sanctuary Publishing Ltd.

Newman, Richard. 1993. *The Making of Mike Oldfield's Tubular Bells*. Ely, Cambridgeshire: Music Maker Books Ltd.

Discographical References

Oldfield, Mike. *Tubular Bells*. Virgin V2001. *1973*: UK.
Weller, Paul. *Stanley Road*. Go! Discs 828 619-2. *1995*: UK.
XTC. *English Settlement*. Virgin V2223. *1982*: UK.
XTC. *White Music*. Virgin V2095. *1978*: UK.

Discography

Bonzo Dog Band, The. *Let's Make Up and Be Friendly*. United Artists UAS 29288. *1972*: UK.
Horslips. *The Tain*. Atco 7039. *1974*: UK.
Wyatt, Robert. *Rock Bottom*. Virgin 13112. *1977*: UK.

VANESSA BASTIAN

—Mosi Oa Tunya Studios (Zimbabwe)

Mosi Oa Tunya Studios take their name from the original name of the Victoria Falls. The Tonga people of Zimbabwe called them 'Mosi Oa Tunya,' meaning 'the smoke that thunders,' because of the thunderous sound they make. The studios were established in 1989 at the premises of Gramma Records in Southerton, Harare, in the midst of an already thriving recording industry led by Shed Studios. Mosi Oa Tunya, in keeping with their claim, have become the leading generator of popular music recordings in Zimbabwe. With a roster of seasoned musicians possessing the requisite technical, aesthetic and cultural knowledge to work as producers and engineers, Mosi Oa Tunya have managed to adopt and adapt traditional and other music forms into successful music products on the local, regional and international markets. The majority of recordings made at Mosi Oa Tunya fall into three main genres of current Zimbabwean popular music: *sungura*, a Zimbabwean variation of Congolese rumba/*soukous*; *chimurenga* or mbira-based music, a popular music form grounded on the intricate interlocking melodies and rhythms of the mbira, an instrument of the Shona people; and *jiti* or *makwaya*, a genre of choral music mainly performed by young adults and adapted for pop bands.

Of the music recorded at all the recording studios currently in Zimbabwe, that recorded at Mosi Oa Tunya has had the greatest impact locally, regionally and internationally. The music of noted artists such as Thomas Mapfumo, Leonard Dembo and the Khiama Boys has been produced at these studios.

ISAAC KALUMBU

—Muscle Shoals Sound (US)

Since 1969, the name 'Muscle Shoals Sound' has been used to refer to three separate studios in the tri-city area of Muscle Shoals, Sheffield and Florence, in northern

Alabama. While the studios differed in their equipment and acoustical properties, the primary draw in all three cases was the combined playing and production talents of the owners, members of the Muscle Shoals Rhythm Section.

Rhythm guitarist Jimmy Johnson, keyboard player Barry Beckett, bassist David Hood and drummer Roger Hawkins, collectively known as the Muscle Shoals Rhythm Section, came together as a unit in the mid-1960s while playing sessions for producer Rick Hall at Fame Studios in Muscle Shoals. With the help of a loan and a promise of steady work from Atlantic Records vice-president Jerry Wexler, the four musicians incorporated and purchased Bevis Studio in 1969. Located in a former coffin factory at 3614 Jackson Highway in Sheffield, the studio had already been in operation for two years under the aegis of Fred Bevis. The studio was equipped with a four-track recorder at the time of the purchase, and its new owners immediately upgraded the facility to eight-track. Further upgrades to 16- and 24-track were made in 1971 and 1977, respectively. From 1969 to 1978, the studio was the site of recording sessions by an impressive array of rhythm and blues (R&B) and rock 'n' roll artists, including the Rolling Stones, Paul Simon, the Staple Singers, Johnnie Taylor and Bob Seger.

In 1974, the members of the Muscle Shoals Rhythm Section purchased a second property (the former Quinn Ivy Recording Studio), located at 104 East Second Street in Sheffield. This studio was immediately outfitted with 16-track facilities. Neither the Jackson Highway nor the East Second Street studio was acoustically designed for the purpose of recording. Consequently, both studios had numerous acoustic quirks that affected sessions both positively and negatively.

Both studios were closed in 1978, when the Muscle Shoals Rhythm Section purchased what had been a Naval Reserve building at 1000 Alabama Avenue in Sheffield. There, they built from scratch two modern, acoustically designed 24-track recording studios. Initially, one studio had a Neve console while the other had an MCI console, and both used MCI recorders. Eventually, the MCI console in Studio B was upgraded to a Neve, and the two MCI recorders were replaced by Studers. From 1978 to 1985, sessions were cut at these studios by various rock and R&B luminaries, including Bob Dylan, Rod Stewart, Glenn Frey, Bobby Womack, Mavis Staples and Luther Ingram.

In 1985, Malaco Records, based in Jackson, Mississippi, purchased the two Alabama Avenue studios. Since then, the Muscle Shoals Sound facilities have been used primarily to record Malaco's R&B roster, including Bobby 'Blue' Bland, Little Milton, Johnnie Taylor and Denise LaSalle.

Bibliography
Guralnick, Peter. 1986. *Sweet Soul Music*. New York: Harper & Row.

Discography
The Muscle Shoals Sound. Rhino Records R2 71517. 1962–72; *1993*: USA.

ROB BOWMAN

—Nimbus 9 Studio (Canada)

Toronto's Nimbus 9 Studio developed from a production company of the same name, which was originally formed in 1967 by Canadian jingle writers Jack Richardson, Alan Macmillan, Ben McPeek and Peter Clayton. Over the next few years, the production company enjoyed tremendous success, producing a number of hits by such contemporary rock artists as the Guess Who (whose recordings were released on the Nimbus 9 label) and Alice Cooper.

Richardson, along with new employee Bob Ezrin, was responsible for most of the production company's hands-on studio work in New York, Chicago and Los Angeles. Tired of being away from his family for nine months of the year, Richardson suggested that the partnership open its own studio in Toronto. After locating a suitable building at 39 Hazleton Avenue, Richardson and Ezrin built the first acoustically designed recording studio in Canada. In the fall of 1972, the Nimbus 9 Studio opened for business.

Both producers assessed equipment by asking themselves, in Richardson's words, 'with what level of integrity did it process sound?' Consequently, the majority of the recording equipment at Nimbus 9 used tube technology. The initial recording console was a heavily modified Audiotronics board: for example, Richardson and Ezrin removed all the transformers from the board, and also took out the mike pres (preamplifiers) that came with the recording console and replaced them with mike pres made by Jansen. In addition, Nimbus 9 was one of the first studios to have rotating walls that could change from reflective to absorbent surfaces, depending on the project.

Inspired by the work of Sheffield Lab in the United States, Nimbus 9 began to experiment with direct-to-disc recordings in 1974. Over the next five years, 14 direct-to-disc LPs, by Canadian artists such as Rough Trade, FM, Nexus and Rob McConnell and the Boss Brass, were recorded and released on the company's internationally renowned Umbrella label. These direct-to-disc recordings were novel, and involved none of the standard studio recording enhancement features such as reverb and equalization. The result was recordings that included readable information at 24,300 cycles. There was virtually nothing except wire between the music and the master lacquer.

Initially, the studio had 16-track capabilities with 16 inputs, but the producers soon purchased one of the first Mag Link lockup systems and could then piggyback 16- and 24-track recorders. Between 1972 and 1980, Nimbus 9 was very active servicing the then-burgeoning Canadian music industry, recording a wealth of artists that included the Guess Who, David Clayton-Thomas and Copper Penny. In addition, the studio was regularly booked by international artists. All or parts of Pink Floyd's *The Wall*, Peter Gabriel's eponymously titled debut album, Alice Cooper's *Muscle of Love*, Ringo Starr's *Goodnight Vienna* and Lou Reed's *Berlin* were recorded at Nimbus 9.

As a result of tax problems, the studio was sold in 1980. Two years later, its new owners were forced to cease operations.

Discographical References

Alice Cooper. *Muscle of Love*. Warner Bros. K 56018. *1974*: USA.

Gabriel, Peter. *Peter Gabriel*. Atco 147. *1977*: USA.

Pink Floyd. *The Wall*. Columbia 36183. *1979*: USA.

Reed, Lou. *Berlin*. RCA 0207. *1973*: USA.

Starr, Ringo. *Goodnight Vienna*. Apple 3417. *1974*: USA.

Discography

Guess Who. *Road Food*. RCA 0405. *1974*: Canada.

Rough Trade. *Rough Trade Live!*. Umbrella UMB DD1. *1974*: Canada.

ROB BOWMAN

—Norman Petty Recording Studio (US)

The Norman Petty recording studio is best known as the site, in 1957–58, of many of the best recordings of Buddy Holly and the Crickets.

Petty began recording local acts, such as the Stamps-Baxter Gospel Quartet, in the 1940s in a bedroom studio in the small town of Clovis, New Mexico. He was an accomplished organist whose 'Mood Indigo' was a minor hit in 1954. The following year, he opened a permanent studio at 1313 West Seventh Street, an apartment owned by his father. The studio itself was only 10' (3 m) by 22' (6.7 m), and musicians would sometimes have to play in the hallway. It was the only purpose-built recording studio in a large area of West Texas and New Mexico.

When Buddy Holly first recorded at the Petty studio, it had the only live echo chamber in the Southwest, situated in a next-door gas station and with walls with built-in rounded baffles. Petty himself acted as producer, engineer and session musician. He recorded on two mono tape machines, overdubbing by bouncing the sound from one machine to the other.

The first rock 'n' roll hit to be recorded by Petty was 'Party Doll' by Buddy Knox and the Rhythm Orchids. This was followed in 1957–58 by a series of tracks by Buddy Holly and the Crickets. Petty's method of working was less rigid than that in most studios – he charged musicians by the track rather than by the hour. Holly and the Crickets spent long periods developing songs and experimenting with technologies such as overdubbing and echo fading. They recorded over 50 songs at the studio, including 'That'll Be The Day,' 'Peggy Sue' and 'Everyday.'

Among those who recorded at the studio in the late 1950s were Roy Orbison, Peanuts Wilson, Trini Lopez, Waylon Jennings and Carolyn Hester. Petty's later studio band was the Fireballs, led by guitarist George Tomsco. With singer Jimmy Gilmer, it recorded the 1963 hit 'Sugar Shack,' for which Petty employed a Danelectro guitar and a flute sound taken from a Hammond organ. The Fireballs' 1968 Top 10 hit, 'Bottle of Wine,' was the last hit to be recorded at the Petty studio.

After Petty's death in 1984, the studio was managed by Billy Stull.

Discographical References

Crickets, The. 'That'll Be The Day.' Brunswick 55009. *1957*: USA.

Fireballs, The. 'Bottle of Wine.' Atco 6491. *1968*: USA.

Gilmer, Jimmy, and the Fireballs. 'Sugar Shack.' Dot 16487. *1963*: USA.

Holly, Buddy. 'Peggy Sue'/'Everyday.' Coral 61885. *1957*: USA.

Knox, Buddy, and the Rhythm Orchids. 'Party Doll.' Roulette 4002. *1957*: USA.

Norman Petty Trio, The. 'Mood Indigo.' 'X' 0040. 1954: USA.

DAVE LAING

—Paisley Park Studios (US)

Paisley Park Studios, located in a suburb of Minneapolis, Minnesota, were designed by Tom Hidley and The Artist Formerly Known as Prince, and are owned by The Artist. Opened in 1987, the studios have continued to be The Artist's main venue for composing and recording music, as well as for rehearsing prior to going on tour. At one time open to the public, with a recreation center and music video displays, the studios have again been closed to the public and are not booking outside recording sessions.

Virtually all of The Artist's recorded output since his first two albums has been recorded, or partially recorded, at Paisley Park. The studios feature three rooms for recording and a soundstage measuring 1,114 square meters. Studio A, the largest of the three rooms, includes a Solid State Logic 8088 G+ with Ultimation console,

Studer D 820 48-track digital recorder and much outboard equipment. Studio B includes a custom API/DeMedio console with GML moving-fader automation and two Studer A-800 Mark III multitrack machines. Studio C features a Soundcraft TS-24 36-input modified in-line console (used on The Artist's earliest recordings) and a Sony JH-24 multitrack recorder. Studio C was often leased at very low rates to provide a first-rate recording facility for musicians in Minneapolis-St. Paul.

The Paisley Park soundstage is one of the largest in the Midwest, and has been used for a variety of Hollywood films, including *Grumpy Old Men*, *Drop Dead Fred* and The Artist's own *Graffiti Bridge*, and numerous television commercials, music videos and production rehearsals (for the Beastie Boys, Stevie Ray Vaughan, Neil Young and Barry Manilow, among others). The soundstage also includes a hair and makeup salon and production offices. An Avid postproduction room allows for on-line video editing also. The soundstage, like the recording studios, is centrally patched to allow access to all equipment in all areas via 72 audio and four video lines. Finally, Paisley Park includes a full kitchen, with catering facilities, and recreational and lodging areas.

In addition to The Artist's recordings, Paisley Park has been the site of recording sessions by R.E.M., Soul Asylum, The Time, Tevin Campbell and the BoDeans.

Bibliography

Hill, Dave. 1989. *Prince: A Pop Life*. London: Faber and Faber.

Jones, Liz. 1998. *Purple Reign: The Artist Formerly Known As Prince*. Secaucus, NJ: Carol Publishing Group.

Discography

Prince. *Around the World in a Day*. Warner Bros. 92-5286-1. *1985*: USA.

Prince. *Crystal Ball*. BC Concepts BC-0009871. *1998*: USA.

Prince. *Graffiti Bridge*. Paisley Park 27493. *1990*: USA.

R.E.M. *Green*. Warner Bros. WX 234. *1988*: USA.

Filmography

Drop Dead Fred, dir. Ate de Jong. 1991. UK/USA. 103 mins. Comedy. Original music by Randy Edelman.

Graffiti Bridge, dir. Prince. 1990. USA. 90 mins. Musical Drama. Original music by Prince.

Grumpy Old Men, dir. Donald Petrie. 1993. USA. 103 mins. Comedy. Original music by Alan Silvestri.

STEVE JONES

—The Plant (US)

The Plant Recording Studios in Sausalito, California opened their doors in 1972. Located just north of San Francisco, the studios were built by Chris Stone and Gary Kellgren, founders of the Los Angeles/Hollywood counterpart, the Record Plant. Stone and Kellgren wanted studios that would serve as a getaway from the showbiz hubbub that was prevalent in Los Angeles at the time, and chose the bucolic Marin County setting of Sausalito to build studios incorporating redwood interiors, skylights, locally quarried stone and stained glass.

Some of the best-known albums of 1970s rock were recorded at the Plant, including Fleetwood Mac's *Rumours* and Stevie Wonder's *Songs in the Key of Life*, as well as numerous albums by Carlos Santana, Jefferson Starship, Sly and the Family Stone, and Huey Lewis.

Purchased by Arne Frager (a recording engineer at the Plant) in the mid-1990s and refurbished throughout, the Plant's largest room is Studio A, which is 111 square meters. It also has a ceiling height of 28' (8.5 m), three isolation booths and a private lounge. Studio A features a Solid State Logic 4064 G Series console with Total Recall, and the smaller Studio B features a Neve 8068 with GML Automation. A mix room contains a Solid State Logic 4056 G Series with Total Recall.

During Frager's tenure, the Plant has hosted recording sessions for Metallica, Primus and the Dave Matthews Band. Kenny G, Mariah Carey and Michael Bolton are also regular clients. Frager, with associate Paul Marsazalek, has also formed a record label, PopMafia, to showcase San Francisco-based artists.

Bibliography

Sculatti, John. 1985. *San Francisco Nights*. New York: St. Martin's Press.

Discographical References

Fleetwood Mac. *Rumours*. Warner Bros. K 56344. *1977*: USA.

Wonder, Stevie. *Songs in the Key of Life*. Tamla Motown TMSP 6002. *1976*: USA.

Discography

Metallica. *Load*. Warner Bros./Elektra 61923. *1996*: USA.

STEVE JONES

—Polar Studios (Sweden)

Since opening in downtown Stockholm in 1978, Polar Studios have played an important part in the development of both Swedish and international music.

Originally created for and owned by ABBA, Polar Studios are renowned for being the first of Sweden's modern recording studios. Many of the creative sound techniques recorded at Polar and used in the music of ABBA were the result of the work and experimentation of sound engineer and producer Michael B. Tretow.

By the late 1990s, Polar Studios had become a world-class recording facility, often frequented by international artists, including Led Zeppelin, Roxette and the Backstreet Boys.

Polar Studio A consists of four isolated rooms with different acoustics, ranging from the highly ambient stoneroom to totally damped areas. Studio A has a 56-channel Solid State Logic 4056-series mixing console, which is used with Studer A-820 24-track, Studer A-827 24-track and Otari DTR-900 MK II 32-track audio recorders.

Polar Studio B consists of one live room, which has a 48-channel Calrec UA 8000 mixing console that is used with a 3M Digital 32-track audio recorder.

Polar Studios have also gained a reputation for their mixing and mastering facilities, and are often used for music postproduction work.

Discography

ABBA. *Super Trouper*. Polar POLS 322 LP. *1980*: Sweden.

ABBA. *Voulez-vous*. Polar POLS 292 LP. *1979*: Sweden.

Backstreet Boys, The. *Backstreet Boys*. Jive 01241 41598 2 LP. *1996*: Sweden.

Led Zeppelin. *In Through the Out Door*. SSK 59410 LP. *1979*: Sweden.

Roxette. *Have a Nice Day*. EMI 7243 4 9885325 LP. *1999*: Sweden.

ROBERT BURNETT

—Rockfield Studios (UK)

Located near the market town of Monmouth in South Wales, Rockfield was one of the first residential recording studios in the world. In 1962, brothers Charles and Kingsley Ward made their first recordings at what was at the time their farmhouse home. In 1965, the brothers installed two EMI Ferrograph recorders in the attic and began to record local bands. By 1968, the studio at Rockfield was housed in a converted barn, equipped with a 16-track console. The expanded studio initially catered for acts associated with the Welsh and English Midlands rhythm and blues scenes, such as Dave Edmunds' Love Sculpture, Amen Corner and the Doc Thomas Group (one of the bands that eventually formed Mott the Hoople). Indeed, Rockfield has enjoyed a long association with Cardiff-born Edmunds, whose UK number one single 'I Hear You Knocking,' which sold 3 million copies, was recorded at the studio in 1970. Kingsley Ward's short-lived Rockfield record label of the mid-1970s (distributed by RCA) almost exclusively released Dave Edmunds solo records, and Edmunds went on to do production work with artists such as Shakin' Stevens, Hawkwind and the Flamin' Groovies at the studio.

From the 1970s, Rockfield established itself as one of the premier recording locations for British and international rock bands. Throughout the 1970s and 1980s, a number of multimillion-selling and critically acclaimed records were recorded at the studio, including Queen's *A Night at the Opera* (1975), Rush's *Hemispheres* (1978), Robert Plant's *Pictures at Eleven* (1982) and Edie Brickell's *Shooting Rubberbands at the Stars* (1989). In 1993, Rockfield was upgraded to include two 48-track Neve-equipped studios and 16 bedrooms. During the mid-1990s, the studios became associated with the commercial resurgence of rock bands within the UK market, with clients including the Stone Roses, Paul Weller and the Manic Street Preachers. During a 12-month period in 1995–96, five UK number one albums by UK rock acts were recorded there: *It's Great When You're Straight . . . Yeah!* (Black Grape); *Wake Up!* (Boo Radleys); *The Charlatans* (the Charlatans); *(What's the Story) Morning Glory?* (Oasis); and *1977* (Ash).

Its location in rural Wales, 130 miles from the center of the UK recording industry in London, has meant that Rockfield has been a popular location for British bands seeking to escape the distractions of the capital. As Pat Moran, producer and ex-house engineer at Rockfield, explained in an interview: 'Most of the bands . . . seem to like it there too as you can focus on the recording process. Being out in the country means no distractions and it seems to create a relaxing and harmonious atmosphere' (see http://www.sjpdodgy.co.uk/moran/moraninter.html). In addition, its distance from London has meant that Rockfield has been seen as providing an escape from the control of record company staff and management. Indeed, Rockfield has been associated with episodes of immoderate behavior by resident musicians, including a tale of heavy LSD use during an album recording session by the UK band the Teardrop Explodes (Cope 1999) and an incident in which a drunken Liam Gallagher, of multimillion-selling UK act Oasis, attempted to break into the recording area late at night to destroy his brother Noel's guitars (Cavanagh 2000, 469).

Bibliography

Cavanagh, David. 2000. *My Magpie Eyes Are Hungry for the Prize: The Creation Records Story*. London: Virgin.

Cope, Julian. 1999. *Head-On/Repossessed*. London: Thorsons.

Rockfield Studios. http://www.rockfieldstudios.com/

Discographical References

Ash. *1977*. Infectious INFECT 40. *1996*: UK.

Black Grape. *It's Great When You're Straight . . . Yeah!*. Radioactive RAD 11224. *1995*: UK.

Boo Radleys. *Wake Up!*. Creation CRECD 179. *1995*: UK.

Brickell, Edie, and the New Bohemians. *Shooting Rubberbands at the Stars*. Geffen WX 215. *1989*: UK.

Charlatans, The. *The Charlatans*. Beggars Banquet BBQCD 174. *1995*: UK.

Edmunds, Dave. 'I Hear You Knocking.' MAM 1. *1970*: UK.

Oasis. *(What's the Story) Morning Glory?*. Creation CRECD 189. *1995*: UK.

Plant, Robert. *Pictures at Eleven*. Swansong SSK 59418. *1982*: UK.

Queen. *A Night at the Opera*. EMI EMTC 103. *1975*: UK.

Rush. *Hemispheres*. Mercury 9100 059. *1978*: UK.

Discography

Edmunds, Dave. 'Baby I Love You'/'Maybe.' Rockfield ROC 1. *1973*: UK.

Edmunds, Dave. 'Born To Be With You'/'Pick Axe Rag.' Rockfield ROC 2. *1973*: UK.

Edmunds, Dave. 'I Ain't Never'/'Some Other Guy.' Rockfield ROC 6. *1975*: UK.

Edmunds, Dave. 'Needs a Shot of Rhythm and Blues'/'Let It Be Me.' Rockfield ROC 4. *1974*: UK.

ROBERT STRACHAN

—Shed Studios (Zimbabwe)

Shed Studios began their operations in 1976 in the center of Harare, the capital of Zimbabwe, and recorded all the acts signed by Teal Record Company (later Gramma), which was one of only two record companies (the other being the Zimbabwean branch of Gallo, later Zimbabwe Music Corporation) in Zimbabwe in the 1970s through the mid-1980s. The South African parent company of Teal later merged with the South African parent company of Gallo in 1998.

Shed Studios recorded some of the country's most important genres, such as *sungura* (a Zimbabwean variation of Congolese rumba/*soukous*), *chimurenga* or mbira-based music (a popular music form grounded in the intricate interlocking melodies and rhythms of the mbira, an instrument of the Shona people), and *jiti* or *makwaya* (a genre of choral music mainly performed by young adults and adapted for pop bands), as well as some important musical groups during their fledgling stages. The music of groups such as the Devera Ngwena Jazz Band and Thomas Mapfumo and the Blacks Unlimited laid the foundation for Zimbabwean popular music.

Although Shed Studios recorded their music on an eight-track mixing board onto 2″ (5 cm) analog tape, they managed to make some remarkable recordings. They paid due attention to the aesthetic demands of their local and regional audiences, emphasizing the meshing together of drums and the bass, and enhancing the bass and rhythmic components of the music. In 1980, Shed expanded their operations to form a record company, although this development lasted only a few years. The company became regionally visible, all the same, attracting bands from Zambia (for example, The Witch) and recording songs that became hits not only in Zimbabwe but also in South Africa (for example, David Scobbie, the Devera Ngwena Jazz Band). Perhaps the greatest product to come out of Shed Studios was the Bhundu Boys, who became an international success after Shed released the group's music in England.

The dominance of Shed declined with the rise of Mosi Oa Tunya Studios, since Gramma Records began recording its own artists, and Shed began concentrating on jingles, commercials and film soundtracks, although they continued to record groups for some of the new record companies, notably Records and Tape Promotions.

ISAAC KALUMBU

—Shifty Studio (South Africa)

In the early 1980s, South Africa was beginning to feel the weight of a more technological side to its oppression. Truth Commission discoveries in the 1990s illustrated how the state had begun to use more sophisticated propaganda technologies to secure its interests. Technology opened up new fronts for cultural resistance as well, and Shifty Studio was one example of how massive the impact could be. Inspired by the do-it-yourself punk ethic of the 1970s, Shifty began in Johannesburg as an eight-track mobile studio set up inside a caravan. Established by Lloyd Ross and Ivan Kadey in 1981, Shifty quickly built up a reputation for being the kind of studio that would record politically outspoken artists who were kept out of the mainstream.

Shifty Records sprang up as the postproduction arm of the studio to fulfill the need for an independent, politically correct record company and mostly featured the production talents of Lloyd Ross. The very first album released was by a group from Lesotho called Sankomota, who because of their political views had been refused permission to enter South Africa. The studio was driven to Maseru, where the album was recorded.

Warrick Sony joined up with Lloyd Ross and formed an association that has continued to exist. He wrote and produced numerous albums under the name Kalahari Surfers. Warrick Sony brought with him one of the first Fostex B16 tape recorders and the studio became 16-track. Two albums by the activist poet Mzwakhe Mbuli were recorded and released as an underground white-labeled cassette. These albums set a precedent by achieving sales in excess of 25,000 without receiving any airplay. Other artists, such as the late James Phillips, Jennifer Ferguson, Noise Khanyile, Tananas, the Genuines, Johannes Kerkorrel and a whole generation of performers of alternative Afrikaans music, owe their success to Shifty.

By the end of the 1990s, Lloyd Ross had become a filmmaker, and the studio (now 24-track digital with Protools) had relocated to Cape Town and was run by Warrick Sony.

669

Discography

Auld, Robin. *Zen Surfing in the Third World*. Shift 53. *1993*: South Africa.

Cherry Faced Lurcher, The. *Live at Jamesons*. Shift 12. *1984*: South Africa.

Ferguson, Jennifer. *Untimely*. Shift 43. *1990*: South Africa.

Forces Favourites. Shift 10. *1986*: South Africa.

Fosatu Worker Choirs. Shift 6. *1985*: South Africa.

Genuines, The. *Mr Mac & the Genuines*. Shift 22. *1986*: South Africa.

Gereformeerde Blues Band, The. *Eet Kreef*. Shift 32. *1989*: South Africa.

Illegal Gathering/Corporal Punishment. *The Voice of Nooit*. Shift 8. *1985*: South Africa.

Isja. *One for All*. Shift 9. *1986*: South Africa.

Kalahari Surfers, The. *Bigger Than Jesus*. GNP99. *1989*: South Africa.

Kgwanyape Band, The. *Mephato Ya Maloba*. Shift 44. *1986*: South Africa.

Khanyile, Noise. *Itwasa Lika Phuza Shukela*. Tuh2. *1989*: South Africa.

Koos. *Koos*. Shift 31. *1989*: South Africa.

K-Team. *Viva*. Shift 40. *1990*: South Africa.

Letoit, Andre. *Ver Van Die Ou Kalahari*. Shift 21. *1987*: South Africa.

Lurchers, The. *Sunny Skies*. Shift 54. *1993*: South Africa.

Mahlasela, Vusi. *When You Come Back*. Shift 50. *1991*: South Africa.

Mamu Players, The. *Township Boy*. Shift 25. *1988*: South Africa.

Mbuli, Mzwakhe. *Change Is Pain*. Shift 18. *1987*: South Africa.

Morri, Simba. *Wasamata*. Shift 16. *1986*: South Africa.

Radio Rats. *Big Beat*. Shift 46. *1991*: South Africa.

Sankomota. *Sankomota*. Shift 1. *1984*: South Africa.

Tananas. *Tananas*. Shift 26. *1988*: South Africa.

Urban Creep. *Tightroper*. BANGCD21. *1996*: South Africa.

Van der Want/Letcher. *Low Riding*. BANGCD33. *1997*: South Africa.

Voelvry. Shift 29. *1988*: South Africa.

WARRICK SONY

—Sigma Sound Studios (US)

Located in the center of Philadelphia City, Sigma Sound Studios were founded in 1968 by Joseph Tarsia. Sigma's original facility had just one eight-track studio, equipped with a 14-input Electrodyne console that was built in-house, and Scully four- and eight-track recorders. Sigma's early successes have been attributed to a group of young producers and songwriters led by Kenneth Gamble, Leon Huff and Thomas Bell.

During the early 1970s, a string of hits by Sigma recording artists (Jerry Butler, the Intruders, Billy Paul, Dusty Springfield, Wilson Pickett, the O'Jays, the Delfonics, and Harold Melvin and the Blue Notes) gave rise to the 'Philadelphia sound' phenomenon. While not unlike the sound of other rhythm and blues (R&B) records of the time, with their driving rhythms and soulful vocal performances, the Philadelphia sound was characterized by strong melodies and orchestrations that bordered on the classical. Strings, horns and layers of background vocals lent a new dimension to R&B music. A typical production, with its multilayering of sounds, could include as many as 50 players. The challenge that presented itself to the studios was that of spatially controlling all the musical elements so that the sound of the bass drum would retain the power of its tactile impact, and the lyrics would retain their clarity.

With regard to room setup, Sigma tried, whenever possible, to accommodate the musicians' preference for recording together and avoiding the use of headphones. This not only satisfied the musicians, but also contributed to the distinctiveness of the Philadelphia sound. With the players in close proximity, the microphones picked up all the sounds from every instrument in the room, giving the music its own unique ambiance.

By 1974, Sigma's success was attracting artists and producers from all over the world. The studios now had a staff of 24 engineers and support personnel, and had expanded to a four-studio, 24-track recording complex. In 1976, Sigma Sound Studios extended their operations to New York City, where, in February 1977, they opened three state-of-the-art studios at 1697 Broadway. For the next 14 years, Sigma Sound Studios of New York were considered to be among the city's leading recording facilities. As such, they attracted a host of artists that included Billy Joel, Madonna, Paul Simon, the Village People, Steely Dan and Whitney Houston. In 1988, under the pressure of operating studios in two cities and with a 15-year lease about to expire, Sigma sold the New York studios.

In 1971, Sigma Sound Studios became the first to successfully employ mix automation. Then, in 1976, in cooperation with MCI, a Florida-based console manufacturer, and Allison Research, Sigma designed a recording console that employed an Allison Research automation system, a continuous-throw knobless fader, variable Q equalizers, and a buss assign and cue systems of Sigma's design. Two of these custom consoles were built for Sigma's New York studios. The later MCI 600 series console incorporated many of the design features developed by Sigma.

Sigma committed to multitrack digital recording in 1987, adding four 32-track machines to the Philadelphia and New York studios. In 1990, Sigma began to move away from tape-based systems with the purchase of their first digital workstation.

Since their foundation, Sigma Sound Studios have been responsible for over 150 gold and platinum recordings, and have been recognized at the Grammy's for their work on the *Saturday Night Fever* soundtrack and on Patti Labelle's album *Burnin'*. Members of Sigma personnel have been named Best R&B Engineer (*Pro Sound News*), and Engineer (and Studio) of the Year in the dance category (*Billboard* magazine). Sigma's founder was a founding member and first president of the Society of Professional Audio Recording Services (SPARS), and in 1995 Tarsia was inducted into the Philadelphia Music Alliance Walk of Fame. In *The Book of Rock Lists* (Marsh and Stein 1981), he is listed at number five in the category of 'Great Engineers' and, according to the book, 'must be considered the leading engineer in the field of soul and dance' (57).

Bibliography

Marsh, Dave, and Stein, Kevin. 1981. *The Book of Rock Lists*. New York: Dell/Rolling Stone Press.

Discographical References

Labelle, Patti. *Burnin'*. MCA MCAD-10439. *1991*: USA.
Saturday Night Fever. Polydor 800 068. *1977*: USA.

JOSEPH TARSIA

—Smart Studios (US)

The founders of Smart Studios, Wisconsin natives Butch Vig and Steve Marker, began their Madison-based operation as a one-room, four-track studio in 1983. Vig and Marker were musicians in local bands – Spooner and Firetown, respectively, which both had releases on major labels. They soon became involved in production, working with local talent, such as the band Killdozer, which demonstrated the studios' early grunge sound. In 1987, the studios were relocated to an old redbrick industrial building not far from Madison's Capitol Square. With the help of the Russ Berger Design Group, Vig and Marker gutted the building and installed two recording rooms, a lounge and a patio deck. Central to Studio A was the Trident model 80-C 56-input console, while Studio B, designed primarily as a mixdown studio, featured a console previously owned by the Osmond Studios and a vintage Harrison 56-input console that was modified and updated. Smart Studios have also featured a large collection of vintage guitar amps, drums and keyboards that can be made available to clients.

In 1991, the release of Smart Studios' recording of Nirvana's *Nevermind* album brought the company nationwide attention. As a result of the album's success, Vig and Marker have been sought after as producers and engineers, and their subsequent work with the Smashing Pumpkins and L7, among other artists, has further established their reputation for quality work at a cost considerably less than that demanded in studios in Chicago or Los Angeles.

Subsequently, Vig and Marker have returned to performing with Garbage, a band that they helped found and that included another Smart Studios producer, Duke Erikson, as well as Scottish singer Shirley Manson.

Bibliography

Bessman, Jim. 1993. 'Smart Choice Gets Smarter for Alternative Acts.' *Billboard* (13 March): 109.
Kassulke, Natasha. 1994. 'When a Band Gets Smart, Amazing Things Happen.' *Wisconsin State Journal* (18 August): 3.
'Pro Audio Newsline.' 1995. *Billboard* (7 October): 67.
'Smart Studios in Old Gisholt Factory.' 1998. *The Capital Times* (9 May): 1a.

Discographical Reference

Nirvana. *Nevermind*. Geffen DGCD-24425. *1991*: USA.

Discography

Garbage. *Garbage*. Almo Sounds AMSD-80004. *1995*: USA.
Garbage. *Milk*. Almo Sounds AMSD-89007. *1996*: USA.
Garbage. *Version 2.0*. Almo Sounds AMSD-80018. *1998*: USA.
Killdozer. *For Ladies Only*. Touch & Go TG-39. *1989*: USA.
L7. *Bricks Are Heavy*. Slash 2-26784. *1992*: USA.
Smashing Pumpkins. *Gish*. Caroline CAROL-1705-2. *1991*: USA.
Smashing Pumpkins. *Siamese Dream*. Virgin 22252. *1993*: USA.

SUSAN C. COOK

—Stax Studio (US)

What came to be known as the Stax studio was, for all intents and purposes, the recording facility of Memphis, Tennessee's legendary soul label Stax Records. The company's first records, issued in 1957 (under its original name, Satellite Records), were recorded in a garage in north Memphis. In late 1958, owner Jim Stewart relocated the operation to Brunswick, Tennessee, about 48 kilometers outside Memphis. Finding it difficult to get artists to travel to Brunswick to record, Stewart moved his recording operation back to Memphis in the late spring of 1960. He rented an old neighborhood movie theater at 926 East McLemore Avenue, which would remain the primary recording facility of Stax Records (and its Volt, Enterprise, Hip, Chalice, Gospel Truth, Respect and Truth subsidiaries) until Stax was forced into involuntary bankruptcy in December 1975.

The Stax studio was unique in a number of respects. Stewart spent as little money as possible in converting the movie theater into a recording facility. The unleveled floor, combined with the angled walls, meant that there were no parallel surfaces anywhere in the room. The high ceiling (12 meters above the floor at its highest point) gave the studio a very 'live,' reverberant, natural sound.

When the Stax studio opened, it was equipped with an Ampex 350-tube mono tape recorder and two four-channel Ampex portable mixers. As no one but the Stax house band ever recorded in the studio, all eight knobs on the mixers were permanently marked 'echo,' 'bass,' 'horn' and so on. By the end of 1964, Stax, under pressure from its distributor Atlantic Records, had upgraded to a two-track recorder. In the spring of 1965, Atlantic engineer Tom Dowd installed a four-track Scully recorder in the Stax studio. While the studio was now equipped to record overdubs, headphones were not used during Stax sessions until late 1967. Consequently, when an overdub was being recorded, studio speakers were used as monitors. This caused sound from the speakers to bleed into the microphone being used to record the overdub.

In late 1967 or early 1968, Stax upgraded its facilities to eight-track and built what became known as Studio B in the same building. By the summer of 1968, Studio B had also been equipped with an eight-track recorder. The original four-track console was then moved to a newly built small demo studio, commonly referred to as Studio C. By early 1971, Studio A had been upgraded to 16 tracks; Studio B followed suit in June 1971.

Over its 15 years of operation, Studio A was the site of hit recordings by such artists as Otis Redding, Sam and Dave, the Bar-Kays and Isaac Hayes. Stax, as a label, became renowned for its readily identifiable 'sound.' This sound was the result of a number of consistent factors at the studio, including the company's house band, Jim Stewart's engineering aesthetics and the particular idiosyncracies of Studio A.

Bibliography

Bowman, Rob. 1997. *Soulsville U.S.A.: The Story of Stax Records*. New York: Schirmer Books.

Discography

The Complete Stax/Volt Singles: 1959–1968. Atlantic Records 82218-2. *1991*: USA.

The Complete Stax/Volt Soul Singles Volume 2: 1968–1971. Fantasy Records 9SCD-4411-2. *1993*: USA.

The Complete Stax/Volt Soul Singles Volume 3: 1972–1975. Fantasy Records 10SCD-4415-2. *1994*: USA.

ROB BOWMAN

—Strawberry Studios (UK)

Located in Stockport, Greater Manchester, Strawberry was one of the first provincial recording studios in the United Kingdom to gain an international reputation within the recording industry. It was developed by a number of music industry figures whose roots were in the northwest of England. In 1967, Peter Tattersall, the road manager for Billy J. Kramer and the Dakotas, and Eric Stewart, an ex-member of the Mindbenders, bought a small demo studio located above a high-street store. Named after the Beatles' song 'Strawberry Fields Forever,' the original studio that housed the new venture was condemned as a fire risk, and in late 1968 the two founders relocated the enterprise to a disused cinema in the town. With the financial backing and technological expertise of Graham Gouldman (a successful British songwriter who had written numerous hits for the Hollies, the Yardbirds and Herman's Hermits), the new studio was built as a professional-standard eight-track studio, with room to accommodate up to 40 musicians (see Wadsworth 1995).

In the early years of its existence, Strawberry served as both a commercial recording studio and a base for the songwriting team of Stewart, Gouldman and resident session musicians Lol Creme and Kevin Godley. After writing a number of songs for artists such as Freddie and the Dreamers and Ohio Express, the team scored a number two UK hit in 1970 under the name of Hotlegs. In 1972, the group was renamed 10cc and, using Strawberry as a base, it scored a dozen Top 10 UK hits, including three number ones. Owning Strawberry meant that the group was unfettered by the constraints of studio deadlines, and its records became known for their lavish and inventive production values. At the same time, Strawberry became a popular location for artists like the Syd Lawrence Orchestra and the Scaffold, as well as such notable Manchester bands of the 1970s as Sad Cafe and Barclay James Harvest. Strawberry's international reputation was further enhanced when Neil Sedaka recorded his hit comeback album at Strawberry using the in-house musicians and production team (see Tremlett 1976).

In 1976, Strawberry upgraded to 24 tracks with a specially designed control room constructed by Westlake Audio. Subsequently, a number of northern English punk and post-punk records were made at Strawberry, most notably the first Joy Division album *Unknown Pleasures* (1979) and the Sisters of Mercy's 'Temple of Love' (1983). In the late 1980s and early 1990s, Strawberry continued its association with successful bands from northwest England. Early recordings by the Charlatans and Stone Roses were made at the studios, and the successful UK boy-band Take That was formed when, during a recording session, the band's main songwriter, Gary Barlow, met future fellow member Mark Anthony Owen, who was employed as the studio's 'tea boy.'

However, due to decreasing demand, Strawberry's 25

years as a recording studio came to an end in 1992, and the building was converted into a film and video production unit. Nevertheless, Strawberry has remained an important site in the history of music-making in Manchester and the northwest of England, and has been influential in proving that a successful UK studio can be run outside London.

Bibliography

Tremlett, George. 1976. *The 10cc Story*. London: Futura.

Wadsworth, Peter. 1995. *Strawberry Recording Studios, Stockport, 1967–1976*. http://rylibweb.man.ac.uk/data1/sy/pw/pwstrawb.html

Discographical References

Beatles, The. 'Penny Lane'/'Strawberry Fields Forever.' Parlophone R 5570. *1967*: UK.

Joy Division. *Unknown Pleasures*. Factory FACT 10. *1979*: UK.

Sisters of Mercy. 'Temple of Love.' Merciful Release MR 027. *1983*: UK.

Discography

Buzzcocks. 'Everybody's Happy Nowadays.' United Artists UP 36499. *1979*: UK.

Charlatans, The. 'Indian Rope.' Dead Dead Good GOOD ONE SEVEN. *1990*: UK.

Hotlegs. 'Neanderthal Man.' Fontana 6007 019. *1970*: UK.

Sedaka, Neil. *The Tra-La Days Are Over*. MGM 2315 248. *1973*: UK.

10cc. *How Dare You?*. Mercury 9102 501. *1976*: UK.

10cc. *Sheet Music*. UK UKAL 1007. *1974*: UK.

10cc. *10cc*. UK UKAL 1005. *1973*: UK.

10cc. *The Original Soundtrack*. Mercury 9102 50Q. *1975*: UK.

ROBERT STRACHAN

—Studio B Mastering (US)

Studio B Mastering, located inside the Reflection Sound Studios building near uptown Charlotte, North Carolina, is a digital editing, mastering and CD-R (CD-Recordable) duplication facility. Founded in 1990, Studio B was started by producer/engineer David Harris. It began as a computer-based MIDI preproduction suite for use by Reflection's many black gospel and R&B clients, including Kirk Franklin, John P. Kee, the Tri-City Singers and Stephanie Mills. It also offered digital two-track editing as a sideline.

Studio B's focus has changed greatly over the years. The MIDI programming led to work in postproduction for television and film. In 1991, an on-staff composer was hired for this work, which became a large part of Studio B's business. Meanwhile, under the direction of

David Harris, the two-track digital editing business soared, as Studio B was the first facility in the Charlotte area to offer nonlinear editing. This capability was in high demand in the early 1990s, when many engineers and producers began to mix to R-DAT rather than quarter-inch analog, and thus could no longer do razor-blade editing. By 1995, digital editing was clearly Studio B's primary source of income, and mastering capabilities were added to enhance these services.

In 1998, Studio B halted all MIDI programming and composing so that the company could focus on editing and mastering; hence the slight name change to Studio B Mastering. Studio B has provided editing and mastering services for hundreds of local, regional and national artists, such as Hootie and the Blowfish, Southern Culture on the Skids, Guadalcanal Diary and the Spongetones.

As blank CD-R prices dropped between 1996 and 1998, Studio B purchased CD-R duplication equipment and pioneered a whole new medium. CD-R allows little-known musicians to manufacture very small quantities of their recordings and still sell them at a profit.

By the late 1990s, Studio B's equipment included a Digidesign Pro Tools DAW, Apogee analog-to-digital converters, Hafler-powered Tannoy monitors, and numerous pieces of analog outboard gear (including Manley and Tube-Tech).

Discography

ANTiSEEN. *15 Minutes of Fame, 15 Years of Infamy*. Loudsprecher LSD 011. *1999*: Germany.

Apparatus. *Apparatus*. Reconstriction/Cargo Music REC-018. *1995*: USA.

Franklin, Kirk, and Nu Nation. *God's Property*. B-Rite/Interscope 90093. *1997*: USA.

Guadalcanal Diary. *At Your Birthday Party*. Guadco Merch 1. *1999*: USA.

Hootie and the Blowfish. *Kootchypop*. Self-release. *1992*: USA.

Kee, Rev. John P., and the New Life Community Choir. *We Walk by Faith*. Tyscot 4031. *1992*: USA.

Lawrence, Donald, and the Tri-City Singers. *Bible Stories*. Sparrow SPD 51480. *1995*: USA.

Mills, Stephanie. *Something Real*. MCA MCAD-10690. *1992*: USA.

Spongetones, The. *Textural Drone Thing*. Black Vinyl 12246. *1995*: USA.

Trin-I-Tee 5:7. *Trin-I-Tee 5:7*. Interscope 90094. *1998*: USA.

DAVID HARRIS

—Studio 99 (Liberia)

Although two small recording studios existed in Liberia for short periods during the 1970s (ABC and Studio One – both in Monrovia), the country's first multitrack one was Studio 99, which was operated between 1983 and 1985 by Faisal Helwani. Studio 99 recorded over 40 artists during that period, releasing their music in Liberia and West Africa on cassette. In fact, Studio 99 single-handedly recorded most of the top Liberian musical names of the 1980s – prior to the country's disastrous civil war that began in the late 1980s.

Helwani himself is a Ghanaian-Lebanese music producer who promoted Nigeria's Fela Kuti in Ghana during the 1960s and ran Ghana's famous Napoleon Club in Accra during the 1970s, featuring the house bands Hedzolleh (recorded with Hugh Masekela), Basa-Basa, the Bunzus and Edikanfo.

With the technical assistance of Brian Eno, Helwani set up a recording studio in his nightclub in 1980. However, in 1983, due to the economic problems in Ghana at that time, Helwani, together with his recording engineer son, Sammy, and two Ghanaian session musicians, Aweke Glyman (bass) and B.B. Dowuna-Hammond (keyboards), moved his entire studio to the seaside Sinkor district of Monrovia.

The types of music and some of the musicians who recorded at Studio 99 are as follows:

(a) Guitar bands (playing highlife, *maringa*, rumbas, *pachangas* and traditional songs), including Morris Dorley and the Sunset Boys, who sing in the Gola language; the Music Makers band of Sonny Halawanga and Jerome Payne, who play updated Nimba County songs; and 'Kruboy' Emmanuel Koffa, who sings in coastal Kru and pidgin English.

(b) Women artists, including Daisy Moore, who sings in the Voi language, and Fatu Gayflor (ex-Liberian National Cultural Troupe), who sings modern versions of the traditional songs of the Lorma people of northwest Liberia.

(c) Army dance bands, including Robert Toe's band, which performs in pidgin English and Krah, and Jimmy Digg's Lofa Zoes (Lofa Wizards), who perform in the Gbandii language.

(d) Pop bands (playing Afro-rock, *makossa*, *soca* and local disco, reggae and funk), including Willie Dee's group Oxygen, Ox Walker's Humble Rebels, and Donald Cooper and T. Kpan Nimly's Monrovia Brothers. Solo artists (backed by session musicians) include Ciaffa Barclay and O.J. Brown.

(e) Christian choral groups, including only one of Liberia's many a cappella choirs – the 32-strong Lott Carey Baptist Mission Choir, which recorded vernacular hymns.

(f) Non-Liberian artists, including Old Man Pratt from neighboring Sierra Leone, who played guitar with a 'Congo' touch for the Lofa Zoes band; the Africanium Band of neighboring Guinea, whose leader, S.N. Thiam,

plays a guitar style that borrows heavily from the Mandinge *kora* harp-lute; and F. Kenya and his guitar band from the western (Nzima) region of Ghana.

Bibliography

Collins, John. 1985. *Music Makers of West Africa*. Washington, DC: Three Continents Press.

Collins, John. 1992. *West African Pop Roots*. Rev. ed. Philadelphia: Temple University Press. (First published London: Foulsham, 1985.)

Collins, John. 1994. *Highlife Time*. Accra: Anansesem Press.

JOHN COLLINS

—Studio One (Jamaica)

As both a record label and a recording studio, Studio One was a major force in Jamaican popular music of the 1960s, 1970s and early 1980s.

Studio One was one of several in-house labels of Jamaica Recording and Publishing Studio Limited (JRPSL), a Kingston-based enterprise established in 1963 by legendary and pioneering Jamaican sound system operator and record producer Clement 'Coxsone' Dodd. The JRPSL recording studio also came to be referred to as 'Studio One.' Dodd, who began making recordings of Jamaican emulators of North American R&B for the Jamaican record-buying public as a sideline to his sound system business in the late 1950s, was the first of the popular sound system operators to build a personal recording studio for his productions.

One of a small number of record production enterprises active in Jamaica during the heady creative rush of ska, rocksteady and early reggae (from the early 1960s to the early 1970s), Studio One/JRPSL/Clement Dodd had a profound influence on the development and dissemination of these genres. Many of the artists who recorded at Studio One were raw amateurs when they first walked into the studio, but a substantial number survived their 'apprenticeship' and developed into artists of considerable staying power. Indeed, the list of artists produced at Studio One and issued on the Studio One label constitutes a virtual who's who of Jamaican popular music, particularly of the 1960s and 1970s.

Until 1965, all recordings at Studio One were made on a one-track recorder, even though the ska style of the period called for an ensemble of at least three horns and four rhythm instruments, plus one or more singers for the noninstrumental selections. Given these realities, it is not surprising that, by contemporary standards, the early Studio One sound is at times somewhat murky and unevenly balanced (as evident, for example, on *Foundation Ska*, a 1997 CD reissue of 1964 and early to mid-1965 recordings). The sound improved in 1965 when the studio was upgraded to two-track (a number of artists then on the scene have been quick to give equal credit for this improvement to the arrival of recording engineer Sylvan Morris).

By the early 1970s, Studio One/JRPSL was being advertised in the Yellow Pages of the Jamaican telephone directory as the most up-to-date recording facility in the Caribbean, offering eight-track recording, Ampex machines, full echo and equalization facilities, and AKG and Neumann microphones. (The contemporaneous Kingston facilities of Federal Records and Dynamic Sounds were equally well equipped, Dodd's advertisement notwithstanding.)

The prominence of Studio One/JRPSL/Clement Dodd in the Jamaican recording scene lessened during the 1970s with the rise of new studios and new producers. Studio One/JRPSL had effectively ceased regular operations in Jamaica by the mid-1980s with Dodd's semi-permanent relocation to Brooklyn, New York as the proprietor of Coxsone's Music City, a record store and studio catering, according to the storefront signage, to 'Reggae, Salsa, Calypso, Jazz, Gospel and Spanish.'

Through the efforts of Dodd and others, a substantial portion of the Studio One back catalog of 1960s and early 1970s material has been reissued and has continued to be commercially available. Since 1983, Heartbeat Records, a US label specializing in Jamaican popular music reissues, has been particularly assiduous in this regard.

Bibliography

Barrow, Steve, and Dalton, Peter. 1997. *Reggae: The Rough Guide*. London: Rough Guides Ltd.

Bradley, Lloyd. 1996. *Reggae on CD: The Essential Guide*. London: Kyle Cathie.

Chapman, Rob. 1992. *Never Grow Old: Studio One Singles Listing & Rhythm Directory*. 2nd ed. Paignton, UK: The author.

Chapman, Rob. 1996. *Downbeat Special: Studio One Album Discography*. Paignton, UK: The author.

Larkin, Colin, ed. 1998. *The Virgin Encyclopedia of Reggae*. London: Virgin.

Discographical Reference

Skatalites, The. *Foundation Ska*. Heartbeat 185/186. *1997*: USA.

Discography

Best of Studio One. PolyGram/Heartbeat 617507. *1998*: USA.

Downbeat the Ruler – Killer Instrumentals: Best of Studio One, Vol. 3. Heartbeat 38. *1988*: USA.

Respect to Studio One: 33 Dancehall, Reggae and Ska Classics. Heartbeat 181. *1994*: USA.

Solid Gold: Coxsone Style. Heartbeat 80. *1992*: USA.

Studio One Showcase, Vol. 1. PolyGram/Heartbeat 617724. *1999*: USA.

ROBERT WITMER

—Sun Studio (Memphis Recording Service) (US)

The Memphis Recording Service, later Sun Studio, located at 706 Union Avenue, was founded by former WREC radio engineer Sam Phillips in 1950 as one of the first professional recording facilities in Memphis, Tennessee. It achieved legendary status when Phillips discovered Elvis Presley and recorded other famous artists such as Howlin' Wolf, B.B. King, Jerry Lee Lewis, Roy Orbison, Carl Perkins and Johnny Cash.

Sun's success was based on Phillips's skill in developing artists, blurring the division between white and black music and melding country with blues. This, along with his talent for music engineering and production, contributed to the distinctive sound that would mark the birth of rockabilly and rock 'n' roll.

The studio, although built in the confined space of a former radiator shop, offered ideal room acoustics after refurbishment. Recording and mastering facilities were simple, but were used imaginatively 'to create big sounds and vivid atmosphere' (Palmer 1996, 24). Phillips's signature was the use of 'slap-back' tape echo, which involved feeding the original signal from the tape machine through a second machine, with an infinitesimal delay (Palmer 1996, 202). This sound effect was achieved with a console model and a reck-mounted version of the Ampex 350 tape recorder, which Phillips acquired in 1954. Recording and mastering facilities were installed and upgraded gradually and, with equipment primarily from the New Jersey manufacturer Presto, Phillips began by recording on 16" (40 cm) acetate discs before changing to magnetic tape in the winter of 1951. The Presto board was later traded in for an RCA 76-D broadcast console, 'which embellished any passing signal with the warm tube coloration characteristic of the period' (Cunningham 1998, 37). According to Phillips, sparse instrumentation and the right use of microphones were essential to the 'Sun sound.'

The heyday of Sun Studio ended in late 1959 when the studio management changed and the facilities were moved a couple of blocks to 639 Madison Avenue. In 1978, Phillips, together with the heirs of the original owners of 706 Union Avenue, reopened the original site as a tourist attraction, and it was eventually sold to become a museum and Elvis shrine. For a month in 1985, Carl Perkins, Roy Orbison, Johnny Cash and Jerry Lee Lewis returned to the old studio to record the *Class of '55* album. In the late 1980s, the property was leased to Gary Hardy, a local musician, who then founded a label, 706 Records, and a publishing company, Union

Avenue Publishing. Hardy continued to operate 706 Union Avenue as a tourist attraction by day, but began using it as a recording facility again at night. This marked the start of a Sun revival, and many of the original artists returned to use the studio to re-create the Sun sound, as U2 did to record some of *Rattle and Hum* in 1988. With the help of Mark Bell and sole owner Jim Schorr, Sun Studio attracted many artists to record with James Lott, the studio's musical director, chief engineer and musician, throughout the 1990s.

Bibliography

Buskin, Richard. 1999. *Insidetracks: A First-Hand History of Popular Music from the World's Greatest Record Producers and Engineers.* New York: Spike.

Cunningham, Mark. 1998 (1996). *Good Vibrations: A History of Record Production.* London: Sanctuary Publishing Ltd.

'Elvis Presley: The Sun Sessions.' 2000. In *The Mojo Collection: The Ultimate Music Companion,* ed. Jim Irvine. Edinburgh: Mojo Books, 837–38.

Escott, Colin, and Hawkins, Martin. 1980 (1975). *Sun Records: The Brief History of the Legendary Recording Label.* London: Omnibus Press.

Mills, Fetzer. 1999. '706 Union Avenue Reborn: The '90s Revival of Sun Records' Famous Studio.' *Goldmine: The Collectors Record and Compact Disc Marketplace* 25(18)(498) (27 August): 92.

Palmer, Robert. 1996. *Dancing in the Street: A Rock and Roll History.* London: BBC Books.

Discographical References

Class of '55: Memphis Rock & Roll Homecoming. America/Smash/Mercury 830002-1. *1986*: USA.

U2. *Rattle and Hum.* Island 91003. *1988*: USA.

VANESSA BASTIAN

—Tally Recording Studio (US)

Tally Recording Studio was the first recording studio dedicated to country music in Bakersfield, California. As such, it was a crucible for the development of the 'Bakersfield sound,' a highly influential school of country music.

At Tally, co-founders Lewis Talley and Charles Lee 'Fuzzy' Owen gained firsthand session supervision and engineering expertise, and established credentials as recording impresarios. This resulted in Owen reaching a handshake recording and management deal with Merle Haggard, ultimately one of the two leading exponents of the Bakersfield sound. Owen would produce Haggard's first singles on Owen's Tally label and co-produce many of Haggard's albums on the Capitol label. Lewis Talley, too, eventually co-produced Haggard's records.

The other leading exponent of the Bakersfield sound, Alvis Edgar 'Buck' Owens, also recorded at Tally, as did country singer Bonnie Owens and rockabilly singer Wally Lewis, among other local and regional artists. Lewis's 1957 single, 'Kathleen,' was the studio's greatest commercial success.

Founded around 1955, the studio was almost more of a concept than a location. Within two years, it moved twice, from a tiny free-standing structure on East 18th Street, to a storefront on Baker Street, to the back of Talley's house on Hazel Street. Throughout its life span, equipment comprised a used Stencil Hoffman monaural tape machine and an improvised three-channel mixing board. The house band drew from a tightknit group of local nightclub and television performers, many of whom, however, also worked sessions in Los Angeles.

Changes in Talley's personal situation and Owen's professional focus led to the studio's closure by around 1961.

Bibliography

Price, Robert. 1997. '"Fuzzy" Recollections: Owen and His Cousin Lewis Talley Were First to Put It All Down on Vinyl.' *Bakersfield Californian* (29 June): E10.

Discographical Reference

Lewis, Wally. 'Kathleen.' Tally 117/Dot 45-15705. *1957*: USA.

ROBERT J. MARLOWE

—Tambourine Studios (Sweden)

Tambourine Studios in Malmö were started in 1991 as a joint hobby project by local musicians and music enthusiasts. Known locally as the 'pop factory,' the studios are housed in a converted factory building close to the city center.

As the 'Tambourine sound' became known, various bands and musicians began to submit demo tapes to Tambourine Studios. It was among these that Tore Johansson discovered one particular demo by a band called the Cardigans, whose first album, *Emmerdale*, was produced by Johansson and released in 1994.

In 1994, while the Cardigans recorded their second album, *Life*, with Johansson once again as producer, the existing studio was completely rebuilt. In addition to other improvements, a Neve 8068 32-channel mixing desk, previously used at the BBC in London, and MCI, Amex, Foster and Sony tape machines were installed in what would later be called the Green Studio.

Owing to a steady stream of successful artists, plans for a second studio were put into action. The Yellow Studio was completed in 1996 and includes a second (16-channel) Neve mixing desk, also bought in London, this time from the Royal Opera House, and MCI and Sony tape machines.

International artists, such as Hideki Kaji, Tomoyo Harada and St. Etienne, have traveled to Malmö to record in Tambourine Studios.

In 1995, the owners of Tambourine Studios started their own record label, Vibrafon, on which to release Tambourine-produced artists, both domestically and internationally.

Discographical References

Cardigans, The. *Emmerdale*. Trampolene Records TRACD 1501. *1994*: Sweden.

Cardigans, The. *Life*. Trampolene Records TRACD 1503. *1995*: Sweden.

Discography

Cardigans, The. *First Band on the Moon*. Trampolene Records TRACD 1506. *1996*: Sweden.

Tambourine Studios, Volume 1. Vibrafon BIBRCD5. *1995*: Sweden.

Tambourine Studios, Volume 2. Vibrafon BIBRCD39. *1997*: Sweden.

ROBERT BURNETT

—Tamla Motown Studios (US)

The Motown Record Corporation was formed by Berry Gordy in Detroit in 1959, and many of Motown's best-known hits were recorded in a small basement studio at 2648 West Grand Boulevard ('Hitsville USA'). Early recordings were made on a three-track tape machine. Track 1 contained rhythm instruments (piano, bass, drums, guitar), while Track 2 featured 'sweetening' instruments (such as horns and strings) and Track 3 was used for vocals. Three separate playback speakers were used (one for each track), and a simple recording console directed and mixed sounds, with 'effects' patched separately into this console.

By 1964, Motown had built and installed its first eight-track machine, added three more high-powered speakers and established a separate mixing room. It also purchased another studio (Golden World Studios, located a few miles away from 'Hitsville'). Studios and mixing rooms operated 22 hours a day – in three shifts, with two hours scheduled for maintenance. Motown engineers and producers (if they were capable) completed numerous mixes, which were assessed by the 'quality control' department. The engineer or producer with the best mix would be asked for a further set of mixes incorporating suggestions made by the department. As a result, it was common for about 20 mixes to be produced before a final song mix was selected.

Engineers such as Mike McClain, Lawrence Horn and Robert Dennis also oversaw a number of Motown's studio innovations. Guitars and bass were plugged directly into the console, since there was insufficient room for large amplifiers, and direct input eliminated ampli-fier hiss and buzz. Instruments were separated in the studio and the drums placed behind sound baffles. Limiters and punch-ins were used to help Motown's young, untrained vocalists create professional-sounding performances, and extensive equalization was used to produce desired vocal and instrumental tone. A second tape allowed engineers to edit unwanted sounds from song sections, and recordings were assessed on vinyl and via small car-radio-style transistor speakers – the latter process contributing to Motown's treble-oriented, bright-sounding productions.

In the late 1960s, Motown moved its operations to the west coast, where head engineer Guy Costa developed a state-of-the-art multitrack facility in Romaine Street, Los Angeles. For the funk-style pop recordings associated with producer Norman Whitfield and artists such as the Jackson 5 and the Temptations, Motown continued to favor the bright, treble sound that had become a hallmark of its production style. Stevie Wonder (whose Motown contract expired in 1971) pioneered the use of the synthesizer in African-American studio recordings on the self-financed *Music of My Mind*.

Bibliography

Benjamison, P. 1979. *The Story of Motown*. New York: Grove.

Early, Gerald. 1995. *One Nation Under a Groove: Motown and American Culture*. Hopewell, NJ: Ecco.

George, Nelson. 1985. *Where Did Our Love Go?: The Rise and Fall of the Motown Sound*. New York: St. Martin's Press.

Gordy, Berry. 1994. *To Be Loved: The Music, the Magic, the Memories of Motown*. New York: Warner Books.

Licks, Dr. 1989. *Standing in the Shadows of Motown: The Life and Music of Legendary Bassist James Jamerson*. Wynnewood, PA: Dr. Licks Publishing.

The Motown Historical Museum. http://www.recording eq.com/motown.htm

Our Motown Recording Heritage Articles Index. http://www.recordingeq.com/our.htm

Singleton, Raynoma. 1990. *Berry, Me and Motown: The Untold Story*. Chicago: Contemporary Books.

Slutsky, Alan. 1993. 'Motown: The History of a Hit-Making Sound and the Keyboardists Who Made It Happen.' *Keyboard* (May): 84–104.

'Standing in the Shadows of Motown: The Unsung Session Men of Hitsville's Golden Era.' 1983. *Musician* 60: 61–66.

Discographical Reference

Wonder, Stevie. *Music of My Mind*. Tamla TS-314. *1972*: USA.

JON FITZGERALD

—Treasure Isle (Jamaica)

As both a record label and a recording studio, Treasure Isle was a major force in Jamaican popular music of the 1960s and early 1970s.

Treasure Isle was one of several labels of the legendary and pioneering Jamaican sound system operator and record producer Arthur ('Duke,' 'the Trojan') Reid. Reid, like his perennial rival Clement 'Coxsone' Dodd, embarked on record production in the late 1950s as an outgrowth of his sound system business. He gradually became involved in the then-nascent Jamaican popular music recording industry, to the point where he decided to build a personal recording studio for his productions.

The Treasure Isle studio was constructed in 1965 as an upper-story addition to another of Reid's business enterprises, the Treasure Isle Liquor Store in downtown Kingston (hence the music business name, Treasure Isle).

The warm and resonant Treasure Isle recorded sound has been attributed by some commentators to the physical nature of the studio itself – essentially an acoustically undamped, all-wood structure. Other commentators have put equal or more stress on the contributions of Treasure Isle recording engineer Byron 'Smitty' Smith.

The centrality of Treasure Isle in the development and dissemination of Jamaican ska, rocksteady and early reggae (from the early 1960s to the early 1970s) was second only to that of rival studio/label Studio One. The list of artists recorded at the Treasure Isle studio and issued on the Treasure Isle label – and sister labels Duke Reid and Duchess, and concurrently in the United Kingdom on the Trojan label and other imprints – constitutes a virtual who's who of Jamaican popular music of the 1960s and early 1970s. The apex of the Treasure Isle output is generally considered to be the releases spanning the years 1967–69, which practically define the rocksteady idiom, particularly the polish of male vocal group and solo singing.

With Reid's death in 1974, Treasure Isle ceased as a generator of new products, but has continued to be a presence. Treasure Isle productions, particularly those from the heyday of rocksteady, have reappeared through a reissue program that has been intermittently ongoing since the 1970s on the Trojan label (UK) and other non-Jamaican imprints.

Bibliography

Barrow, Steve, and Dalton, Peter. 1997. *Reggae: The Rough Guide*. London: Rough Guides Ltd.

Bradley, Lloyd. 1996. *Reggae on CD: The Essential Guide*. London: Kyle Cathie.

Larkin, Colin, ed. 1998. *The Virgin Encyclopedia of Reggae*. London: Virgin.

Discography

Reid, Duke. *Ba Ba Boom: Classic Rock Steady and Reggae 1967–72*. Trojan CDTRL 265. *1994*: UK.

Reid, Duke. *Soul of Jamaica/Here Comes the Duke*. Trojan 383. *1997*: UK.

Treasure Isle Mood. Heartbeat 195. *1995*: USA.

Treasure Isle Time. Heartbeat 196. *1995*: USA.

ROBERT WITMER

—Triton Studios (Israel)

For many years, Triton was Israel's leading studio, especially for Israeli rock. It was founded in Tel Aviv in 1972 by Tommy Friedman and Frankie Glicksman. Initially an eight-track studio, and considered by Israeli musicians of the period as offering the latest technology, it attracted a young generation of Israeli musicians who were fascinated by recent developments in Anglo-American pop/rock. As a result, the studio became the major creative site for the burgeoning style that came to be known as the 'Israeli rock' of the 1970s.

Highlights of this early period were the first one-man multi-instrumental, self-produced album in Israel, by Mati Caspi (1974), and the three albums of Kaveret – *Sipurey Poogy* (1973), *Poogy be-Pita* (1974) and *Tsafuf ba-Ozen* (1975) – which brought a dramatic change to Israeli music.

In 1976, Triton moved to a new location and became a 16-track studio. Its staff was augmented by Louis Lahav, whose apprenticeship as recording engineer for Bruce Springsteen's first two albums enabled him to become Israel's prime rock producer for several years. At Triton, he recorded Tamuz's *Sof Onat ha-Tapuzim* (1976), a pioneering Hebrew rock album considered by many to be one of the best Israeli albums of all time. After the studio became 24-track in 1978, Lahav produced another influential album there, Shalom Hanoch's *Hatuna Levana* (1981). During the 1980s, major Israeli rock albums, such as Benzeen's *Esrim ve-Arba Shaot* (1982) and T-slam's *Radio Hazak* (1982), were also recorded at Triton, but the studio gradually lost its unique position as new recording sites were established.

Bibliography

Regev, Motti. 1992. 'Israeli Rock or, A Study in the Politics of "Local Authenticity."' *Popular Music* 11: 1–14.

Discographical References

Benzeen. *Esrim ve-Arba Shaot*. NMC 85472-2. *1982*: Israel.

Caspi, Mati. *Mati Caspi*. NMC 80208-2. *1974*: Israel.

Hanoch, Shalom. *Hatuna Levana*. CBS 85125-2. *1981*: Israel.

Kaveret. *Poogy be-Pita*. Hed-Artzi 14419. *1974*: Israel.

Kaveret. *Sipurey Poogy*. Hed-Artzi 14367. *1973*: Israel.

Kaveret. *Tsafuf ba-Ozen.* Hed-Artzi 14541. *1975*: Israel.
Tamuz. *Sof Onat ha-Tapuzim.* CBS 81095-2. *1976*: Israel.
T-slam. *Radio Hazak.* CBS 467055-2. *1982*: Israel.

MOTTI REGEV (with thanks to IZHAR ASHDOT)

—Wally Heider Recording Studio (US)

Recording engineer Wally Heider achieved almost instant success in 1969 when he opened his studio complex in a warehouse at 245 Hyde Street in San Francisco. The facility became the site of the city's burgeoning musical revolution. Jefferson Airplane, Creedence Clearwater Revival, the Grateful Dead, Herbie Hancock, the Pointer Sisters, Santana and many others recorded there. In later years, the Doobie Brothers, the New Riders of the Purple Sage and even jazzman Pharoah Sanders also recorded there.

Heider had originally established his reputation as an on-site producer and engineer. In 1967, with his eight-track Wally Heider Mobile Studio, he recorded the famous Monterey International Pop Festival that introduced Jimi Hendrix and Janis Joplin to the United States. Two years later, he recorded the Rolling Stones live at several venues for their *Gimme Shelter* concert film.

When he opened his San Francisco studio in 1969, Heider made a deal with the locally based Ampex Corporation to test its newest equipment. He was the first to install 16-track Ampex machines and a Quad 8 Board.

His studio complex contained four separate recording rooms: studios A and B on the first floor, and studios C and D upstairs. However, Heider turned Studio B into a games lounge because of sound leakage from Studio A next door. Studio C, which the members of Creedence Clearwater Revival dubbed 'Cosmo's factory' because their drummer Doug 'Cosmo' Clifford spent so much time there, gained a measure of fame when the band named one of its most popular albums, *Cosmo's Factory*, after it. Studio D was one of Heider's first experiments with nonparallel walls and 'wheat chex' – the 'mid-range diffuser/absorber gypsum' devices that covered the walls to control the room's sound. A fifth studio was added in 1980, but it was used mainly as a media room.

In his notes for the 1998 CD reissue of the Jefferson Airplane's *Volunteers* album, Jeff Tamarkin wrote that the '16-track Wally Heider Recording Studio . . . not only met the musicians' artistic needs but made them feel at home. Here they could record at their own pace, surrounded by friends and family, and make the album they truly wanted to make.' The studio became famous for pampering and catering to its clientele. When Grace Slick requested a ring of light around her while she sang, Heider installed a circle of a dozen light canisters in the ceiling.

Engineer Stephen Barncard recalled the studio complex's feverish activity in those early days:

I moved to San Francisco, learned the patch bay and the consoles of the two rooms, and in two weeks I was assisting on [Crosby, Stills, Nash and Young's] *Déjà Vu*. After a month of nights with CSNY, I started assisting on Creedence Clearwater dates in the daytime . . . and CSNY from 8 to 2 a.m. . . . and soon I was engineering my own sessions with artists like . . . Seals and Crofts, Brewer and Shipley, Lovecraft, Steve Miller and Van Morrison. The Grateful Dead were looking for a new sound when they came to Wally Heider's, and we got that with *American Beauty*. (www.barncard.com/barncards/sqb/SQBhtml/sqb__ORIGINAL__bio.html)

Mix magazine's David Schwartz recalled his time there in 1973:

The place was a beehive of recording activity, with four studios and a post-production room. There were 15 albums being produced at one time: David Rubinson and Fred Catero had Studio A locked out, working on five albums . . . Upstairs in C there were a couple of Airplane/Starship projects, Hot Tuna, Crosby/Nash, Pure Prairie League, Commander Cody. Tower of Power had been in there for a year. (www.hydestreet.com/history.html)

Yet, by the summer of 1973, the studio's glory days were over, thanks to the oil crisis, an economic recession, record industry cutbacks and Fantasy Records' new state-of-the-art studio in Berkeley across the bay. But, by then, Heider was also running the successful Wally Heider Sound Studio and Record Plant in Hollywood, located at the corner of Cahuenga Boulevard and Selma Avenue. Bill Withers, T. Rex, Tim Buckley, Quiet Riot, Tom Petty and the Heartbreakers, Frank Zappa and the Mothers of Invention, Rod Stewart and the 1973 Byrds all recorded there.

Hollywood's Filmways Corporation took over Heider's two operations in 1974 and eventually fired him. Tired of the business, Heider moved to Oregon. In 1980, the San Francisco facility was sold and was renamed the Hyde Street Studios. The Hollywood studio closed down in the 1980s.

Bibliography

Biography: Stephen Barncard. http://www.barncard.com/barncards/sqb/SQBhtml/sqb__ORIGINAL__bio.html

San Francisco's Hyde Street Studios: Then and Now. http://www.hydestreet.com/history.html

Tamarkin, Jeff. 1998. Notes to Jefferson Airplane's *Volunteers* album. RCA 67562.

Discographical References

Creedence Clearwater Revival. *Cosmo's Factory*. Fantasy 8402. *1970*: USA.

Crosby, Stills, Nash and Young. *Déjà Vu*. Atlantic 7200. *1970*: USA.

Grateful Dead, The. *American Beauty*. Warner Bros. WS 1893. *1970*: USA.

Jefferson Airplane. *Volunteers*. RCA 4238. *1969*: USA. Reissue: Jefferson Airplane. *Volunteers*. RCA 67562. *1998*: USA.

The Monterey International Pop Festival, June 16–17–18, 1967 (CD boxed set). Rhino Records R2 72825. *1997*: USA.

Rolling Stones, The. *Gimme Shelter*. Decca 5101. *1971*: USA.

Discography

Creedence Clearwater Revival. *Bayou Country*. Fantasy 8387. *1969*: USA.

Creedence Clearwater Revival. *Willy & the Poor Boys*. Fantasy 8397. *1969*: USA.

Crosby, David. *If I Could Only Remember My Name*. Atlantic 7203. *1971*: USA.

Pointer Sisters, The. *The Pointer Sisters*. Blue Thumb BTS-48. *1973*: USA.

Filmography

Gimme Shelter, dir. Al Maysles, David Maysles and Charlotte Mitchell Zwerin. 1970. USA. 91 mins. Documentary. Original music by Mick Jagger, Keith Richards.

JIM DAWSON

—The West Orange Laboratory of Thomas A. Edison (US)

West Orange, New Jersey was the site of Thomas A. Edison's laboratory from 1887 to 1931. It was here that one of the world's first music recording studios was established.

Edison's earlier laboratory had been in Menlo Park, New Jersey. There, in December 1877, utilizing tinfoil as a recording medium, Edison had recorded and reproduced sound for the first time on a simple, hand-cranked mechanism he termed 'the phonograph or speaking machine.' For the next 10 years, Edison's attention was focused elsewhere. In 1887, Edison established a new laboratory complex at West Orange. Aware that others had improved upon his prototype phonograph, he mounted an intensive program to develop a commercially viable recording system.

The initial result of Edison's renewed interest was the 'Perfected' phonograph of June 1888. The new phonograph had an electric motor and governor for precise speed regulation and employed a removable wax cylinder as the recording medium. Unlike the earlier tinfoil medium, this wax cylinder surface could be played repeatedly. Although sufficient for speech, the 'Perfected' phonograph could not adequately reproduce the

tonal qualities and dynamic range needed for musical sound. Edison therefore promoted and marketed the 'Perfected' phonograph as a business tool for office dictation.

Envisioning a future commercial potential for prerecorded music, Edison, in the latter part of 1888, assigned technicians A. Theo E. Wangemann and Walter H. Miller to conduct experimental 'musical tests.' In Room 13 of the West Orange laboratory, they established a recording studio. Maintaining a daily recording log, Wangemann and Miller worked with solo instrumentalists (mainly cornet or clarinet players, often with piano accompaniment), marching bands and small orchestras. The repertoire with which the two experimented included polkas, waltzes, marches and light classical music.

By late 1889, the use of prerecorded musical cylinders in coin-operated phonographs had become a growing trend. The popularity of the 'nickel-in-the-slot' machines in hotel lobbies, saloons and arcades shifted the direction of the fledgling phonograph industry away from business dictation and toward entertainment. Still, during the first half of the 1890s the high prices of phonographs and records precluded any widespread entry into the vast consumer market.

Edison established his National Phonograph Company in January 1896 to produce entertainment products for use in the home. Following the lead of his competitor, the Columbia Phonograph Company, Edison introduced a moderately priced, easy-to-operate cylinder phonograph. Shortly afterward, in March 1897, the production of musical sound recordings on a large scale began with the establishment of a commercial recording studio in the Edison Phonograph Works factory building (adjacent to the West Orange laboratory). Vocal solos, vocal quartets and solo instruments such as the banjo or cornet were often featured, as they could produce the loud, unidirectional sounds needed to drive the recording stylus. The technology could not yet cope effectively with larger ensembles.

In the early years of the twentieth century, the major companies began to move away from the factory-based studio and started to construct purpose-built studios nearer to the entertainment centers, where it was easier to access performing talent. Edison moved his commercial recording studio from West Orange to Manhattan, New York City in 1904. All experimentation and manufacture meanwhile continued at West Orange.

Managed by Walter H. Miller, the New York studio broadened the previously restrictive instrumental formats to include trios and quartets. Accompaniments expanded from piano to small bands and orchestras. Edison record catalogs of this period reflect a cross section of North America's prevailing musical tastes – brass band marches, vaudeville sketches, 'coon' songs, ragtime, Broadway show tunes, classical music and opera.

The new studio and ongoing technical experimentation permitted engineers to have much more influence on the way in which sound was recorded. (Edison himself favored a studio sound without room ambiance, so that each instrument could be clearly heard.) But the acoustic process – as Miller confided to *Talking Machine World* in 1913 – remained unpredictable (Millard 1995, 260ff.). Edison's New York studio was the last major company studio to convert to the electrical recording process, doing so in 1927.

All recording and record manufacture by Edison came to an end in late 1929. The West Orange laboratory continued some experimental work while Edison was still alive, but after his death in 1931 this was gradually brought to a halt. In 1956, the laboratory (including the early experimental studio), together with Edison's home, was donated to the United States Department of the Interior, National Park Service, becoming the Edison National Historic Site.

Bibliography

DeGraaf, Leonard. 1998. 'Thomas Edison and the Origins of the Entertainment Phonograph.' *NARAS Journal* 8(1): 43–69.

Dethlefson, Ronald. 1981. *Edison Blue Amberol Recordings, Volume II, 1915–1929.* Brooklyn, NY: APM Press.

Dethlefson, Ronald. 1997. *Edison Blue Amberol Recordings, 1912–1914.* 2nd ed. Woodland Hills, CA: Stationery X-Press.

Frow, George L. 1982. *The Edison Disc Phonographs and the Diamond Discs: A History with Illustrations.* Sevenoaks, Kent: George L. Frow.

Frow, George L. 1994. *The Edison Cylinder Phonograph Companion.* Sevenoaks, Kent: George L. Frow.

Israel, Paul. 1998. *Edison: A Life of Invention.* New York: John Wiley and Sons, Inc.

Jeffrey, Thomas E., et al., eds. 1993. *Thomas A. Edison Papers: A Selective Microfilm Edition, Part III (1887–1898).* Bethesda, MD: University Publications of America.

Klinger, Bill. 1999. Personal communication with author, April.

Koenigsberg, Allen. 1987. *Edison Cylinder Records, 1889–1912, with an Illustrated History of the Phonograph.* Brooklyn, NY: APM Press.

Marco, Guy A., and Andrews, Frank, eds. 1993. *Encyclopedia of Recorded Sound in the United States.* New York: Garland Publishing, Inc.

Millard, Andre J. 1990. *Edison and the Business of Innovation.* Baltimore, MD: Johns Hopkins University Press.

Millard, Andre J. 1995. *America on Record: A History of Recorded Sound.* Cambridge: Cambridge University Press.

Wile, Raymond. 1978. *Edison Disc Recordings, Books 1 and 2.* Philadelphia: Eastern National Park and Monument Association.

Wile, Raymond, and Dethlefson, Ronald. 1990. *Edison Disc Artists and Records, 1910–1929.* 2nd ed. Brooklyn, NY: APM Press.

JERRY FABRIS and STEPHEN MAMULA with DAVID HORN

—Windmill Lane Recording Studios (Ireland)

Windmill Lane was opened in 1978 by studio engineer Brian Masterson. Situated in an art deco building in an industrial area south of Dublin's city center, the studio has become Ireland's best-known recording studio. Masterson's professional interests as an engineer and producer were focused mainly around Celtic folk music and, from the studio's inception, he began to work with prominent Irish artists such as the Chieftains, Christy Moore, Planxty and Davy Spillane. However, Windmill Lane gained international fame when it became the studio of choice for the Dublin rock band U2. The band's first session in the studio was in mid-1979 for the 'U2: Three' EP. The band went on to record its first three albums at Windmill Lane and has continued to use the facility for various projects. The level of the band's status and its close association with Windmill Lane were such that, during a U2 recording session, future Irish leader Garrett Fitzgerald visited the studio for a photo opportunity during his successful 1982 election campaign (Dunphy 1987, 213).

Indeed, Windmill Lane has since become something of a shrine for U2 devotees, and the outside walls of the studio are decorated with graffiti written by fans from all over the world. The band's decision to record the majority of its work in Dublin constituted a major development in the Irish music industry. Previously, the country's most successful rock acts, Thin Lizzy and the Boomtown Rats, had relocated to England, where they recorded a number of successful albums. U2's subsequent achievements and the band's use of international producers such as Steve Lillywhite and Brian Eno at Windmill Lane proved that it was unnecessary for Irish acts to relocate in order to achieve global success. Indeed, the willingness of such respected producers to use the studio helped to establish its international reputation.

As the country's premier studio, Windmill Lane was used by most of the Irish acts that rose to global prominence during the 1980s and 1990s, and a string of internationally successful albums, such as the Cranberries' *Everybody Else Is Doing It, So Why Can't We?*, Van Morrison's *Days Like This*, Clannad's *Banba* and the Corrs' *In Blue*, were recorded or mixed there. The large recording space at the studio, which can accommodate up to 85 musicians, has also led to its extensive use in the recording of film soundtracks. Windmill Lane has been part of the growing Irish film industry since the late 1980s, with soundtrack music for projects such as *The Field*, *Dancing at Lughnasa*, *Michael Collins* and *The Commitments* having been recorded there. In addition, the producers of the globally successful Irish music and dance revues *Riverdance* and *Lord of the Dance* recorded the commercially released soundtracks at the studio. As a consequence of its success, the studio has undergone constant upgrading and expansion. The studio's postproduction mastering facility, Windmill Lane Masterlabs, opened in 1989, attracting work from many high-profile clients such as the Fugees, Kylie Minogue, Metallica, PJ Harvey and the Rolling Stones, and the main studio has continued to attract artists from around the world.

Bibliography

Dunphy, Eamon. 1987. *Unforgettable Fire: The Story of U2*. London: Viking.

Discographical References

Clannad. *Banba*. RCA 74321139612. *1993*: UK.
The Commitments (Original soundtrack). MCA 10286. *1991*: USA.
Corrs, The. *In Blue*. Atlantic 83352. *2000*: UK.
Cranberries, The. *Everybody Else Is Doing It, So Why Can't We?*. Island CID 8003. *1993*: UK.
Dancing at Lughnasa (Original soundtrack). Sony 60585. *1998*: UK.
The Field (Original soundtrack). Varèse Sarabande 5292. *1990*: USA.
Hardiman, Ronan, and Flatley, Michael. *Lord of the Dance*. PolyGram 533757. *1997*: USA.
Michael Collins (Original soundtrack). Atlantic 82960. *1996*: UK.
Morrison, Van. *Days Like This*. Exile 527 307-2. *1995*: UK.
U2. 'U2: Three' (EP). CBS 7951. *1979*: UK.
Whelan, Bill. *Riverdance*. Atlantic 82816. *1995*: UK.

Discography

Chieftains, The. *Cotton-Eyed Joe*. Claddagh Records CC33. *1981*: Ireland.
Planxty. *After the Break*. Tara 3001. *1979*: Ireland.
Planxty. *The Woman I Loved So Well*. Tara 3005. *1980*: Ireland.
Spillane, Davy. *Shadow Hunter*. Tara 3023. *1990*: Ireland.
U2. *Boy*. Island ILPS 9646. *1980*: UK.
U2. *The Joshua Tree*. Island U 26. *1987*: UK.
U2. *October*. Island ILPS 9680. *1981*: UK.
U2. *War*. Island ILPS 9733. *1983*: UK.

Filmography

The Commitments, dir. Alan Parker. 1991. Ireland/UK/USA. 116 mins. Musical Drama. Original music by Paul Bushnell.
Dancing at Lughnasa, dir. Pat O'Connor. 1998. USA/UK/Ireland. 92 mins. Drama. Original music by Bill Whelan.
The Field, dir. Jim Sheridan. 1990. USA/UK/Ireland. 113 mins. Drama. Original music by Elmer Bernstein.
Michael Collins, dir. Neil Jordan. 1996. USA/UK. 132 mins. Historical Drama. Original music by Elliot Goldenthal.

ROBERT STRACHAN

—WR Studio (Brazil)

WR Studio was founded in 1975 in Salvador, Bahia by ex-salesperson Wesley Rangel. Initially, it produced jingles from one mixing desk and two Akai tape recorders. In 1980, with the addition of an eight-track desk, it started recording local radio artists as well. Some of these recordings, such as the Brazilian version of 'Mrs. Robinson' by the Acordes Verdes band under the leadership of guitarist Luíz Caldas, were an instant success. In 1985, the studio was enlarged and refurbished with 16-track recording equipment. The studio's output increased, and it issued on its own label recordings of what would become a trend – the samba-reggae – by Gerônimo and the Chiclete com Banana band.

By 1988, WR had become a complex of eight studios, the largest of which had a 48-channel facility, a Neve VR Legend cabinet and two Studer A-827 recording machines. The others, apart from two 24-track studios, were used to run small productions and recordings of advertising spots and jingles. By the beginning of the 1990s, the WR label had already issued about 300 LPs and sold approximately 5 million copies. It was responsible for the release of *Axé* music major artists, such as Daniela Mercury, É o Tchan (ex-Gerasamba), Timbalada, Olodum and Companhia do Pagode. Well-known Brazilian MPB (*música popular brasileira* – Brazilian popular music) artists, like Caetano Veloso, Gilberto Gil and Maria Bethânia, as well as guitarist Lee Ritenour, Paul Simon, David Byrne and Israeli singer Ofra Haza, also recorded with WR. Under the 'Estúdios WR' record label, the WR studios also issued Gregorian chant by the Coro dos Monges Beneditinos (São Bento Monastery Choir), as well as music by the Filhos de Gandhi, Dr. Cascadura and Dead Billies bands. WR's output helped to transform Salvador, Bahia into the third most important production center for Brazilian popular music, after Rio de Janeiro and São Paulo.

Bibliography

Garrido, Luís Cláudio. 1991. 'Um estúdio ligado no sucesso' [A Studio Plugged into Success]. *Veja Bahia* (Special issue) (9 January): 4–7.

Mello, André Luiz. 1997. 'WR Studios: tradição e modernidade em Salvador' [WR Studios: Tradition and Modernity in Salvador, Bahia]. *Áudio, Música & Tecnologia* IX(71) (July): 24–26, 28, 30.

Discographical Reference

Caldas, Luíz. *Magia*. PolyGram 826.583-1. *1985*: Brazil.

Discography

Chiclete com Banana. *Sementes*. Continental 1.07.405.298-A. *1984*: Brazil.

Coro dos Monges Beneditinos. *Canto Gregoriano*. WR Discos 970500101. *1997*: Brazil.

Filhos de Gandhi. *Coração de Oxalá*. WR Discos 960100101. *1996*: Brazil.

Gerônimo. *Eu sou negão*. Continental 135.903.001-B. *1987*: Brazil.

Mercury, Daniela. *Daniela Mercury*. Eldorado 225.91.0635. *1991*: Brazil.

Olodum. *Olodum 10 anos*. Continental 1.01.404.383-B. *1989*: Brazil.

Timbalada. *Timbalada*. PolyGram 518.068-1. *1993*: Brazil.

JOSÉ ROBERTO ZAN (trans. MARTHA TUPINAMBÁ DE ULHÔA)

Record Labels/Companies

—A&M (US)

One of the first examples of an artist-owned label, A&M became one of the United States' leading record companies in the 1970s and 1980s. A&M was named after its Los Angeles-based founders, trumpeter Herb Alpert and record industry promotion man Jerry Moss. The label's first release was 'The Lonely Bull' by Alpert and his Tijuana Brass, a million-seller in 1962.

For the next few years, A&M's prosperity was based mainly on a series of easy listening instrumental albums by Alpert, and Latin-flavored music from Sergio Mendes and Brasil '66. There were other pop hits from Chris Montez and the Sandpipers. In the late 1960s, the company opened branches in Canada and the United Kingdom and entered the rock marketplace through such acts as the Flying Burrito Brothers and Joe Cocker. A&M also made successful licensing agreements with Phil Spector (whose classic Ike and Tina Turner track 'River Deep, Mountain High' appeared on A&M), Lou Adler (whose Ode label roster included Carole King (*Tapestry*) and Cheech and Chong) and Leon Russell's Shelter label. In the 1980s, A&M found global success with Janet Jackson and Bryan Adams.

In the first half of the 1970s, the UK branch of A&M developed a strong roster of local artists, including Humble Pie and Supertramp. The company signed the Sex Pistols, but bowed to adverse publicity and canceled the contract almost immediately. The most important British artists signed to A&M in the 1980s were Joan Armatrading and the Police.

The record company was sold in 1989 to PolyGram for $460 million. Alpert and Moss retained control of their music publishing company, Rondor Music, and set up a new record label, Almo Sounds, in 1993.

Discographical References

Alpert, Herb, and the Tijuana Brass. 'The Lonely Bull.' A&M 703. *1962*: USA.

King, Carole. *Tapestry*. A&M AMLS 2025. *1971*: UK.

Turner, Ike and Tina. 'River Deep, Mountain High.' London HLU 10046. *1966*: UK.

DAVE LAING

—Alerce (Chile)

The Chilean record company Alerce was established in 1976 in Santiago by DJ Ricardo García and producer Carlos Necochea. Alerce launched the *canto nuevo* (new song) movement, the direct heir to *nueva canción Chilena* (Chilean new song), which had been prohibited by the military regime in 1973.

Alerce was associated with Filmocentro, a Santiago recording studio, and benefited from the lowered production costs that resulted from the transition in Chile from LPs to cassettes during the early 1980s. The label started the recording, production and distribution of *canto nuevo* groups such as Aquelarre and Santiago del Nuevo Extremo, and of soloists such as Osvaldo Torres, Eduardo Peralta and Isabel Aldunate. In 1982 and 1983, Alerce also organized 'La gran noche del folklore' (The Great Night of Folklore), a folk music festival that reaffirmed *canto nuevo* and earlier traditional folk values and that resulted in censorship by the military regime in 1984.

Initially, Alerce had a more political-cultural than commercial purpose, with an interest in collecting musical material and facilitating its reproduction during a period of heavy censorship and repression. At the same time, it established links with Chilean music production in exile and a connection with the period before the coup d'état by reediting the work of popular singer-songwriter Víctor Jara, as well as that of exiled groups Quilapayún and Inti-illimani, and by making known in Chile the key Cuban singer-songwriters Pablo Milanés and Silvio Rodríguez. These activities provoked the military government to exert strong pressure on Ricardo García.

Alerce's concern about the development of a local music industry resulted in its promotion of the use of

683

local studios for the recording and mastering of its music. Working within a democracy after 1989, Alerce diversified its catalog in the 1990s to encompass all the popular music created and produced in Chile. Since the death of Ricardo García in June 1990, the company has been run by his daughter Viviana Larrea.

Bibliography
Osorio, José, ed. 1996. *Ricardo García: Una obra trascendente* [Ricardo García: A Transcendental Work]. Santiago: Pluma y Pincel.

Discography
Chancho en Piedra. *La Dieta del Lagarto*. Alerce CDAE 317. *1997*: Chile.

Fernández, Tito. *Tito Fernández en el Olympia de París*. Alerce CDAE 111. *1991*: Chile.

Fulano. *Fulano*. Alerce CDAL 199. *1994*: Chile.

Illapu. *Raza Brava*. Alerce CDAE 103. *1992*: Chile.

Los Miserables. *Sin Dios Ni Ley*. Alerce CDAE 253. *1995*: Chile.

Loyola, Margot. *Danzas Tradicionales de Chile*. Alerce CDAE 211. *1994*: Chile.

Manns, Patricio. *Patricio Manns en Chile*. Alerce CDAL 234. *1995*: Chile.

Parra, Isabel. *Como una Historia*. Alerce CDAL 213. *1994*: Chile.

Parra, Roberto, and Parra, Ángel. *Cuecas del Tío Roberto*. Alerce CDAE 283. *1996*: Chile.

Peralta, Eduardo. *Eduardo Peralta*. Alerce ALC 20. *1982*: Chile.

Santiago del Nuevo Extremo. *A Mi Ciudad*. Alerce ALC 80. *1981*: Chile.

Schwenke and Nilo. *Schwenke y Nilo, Vol. 1*. Alerce CDAE 192. *1993*: Chile.

Torres, Osvaldo. *Desde Los Andes a la Ciudad*. Alerce ALC 053. *1985*: Chile.

JUAN PABLO GONZÁLEZ

—Apple (UK)

Apple Records was the only successful segment of Apple Corps Ltd., the company founded by the four Beatles in 1968. The first Apple recordings were by such signings as Welsh folk singer Mary Hopkin, fledgling singer-songwriter James Taylor and beat group Badfinger. Some solo recordings by Beatles members – notably George Harrison's *Wonderwall* soundtrack, and John Lennon's and Yoko Ono's *Two Virgins* and 'Give Peace a Chance' – also appeared on the label. The eclectic catalog (mostly reissued on CD by EMI from 1991 onward) included the Modern Jazz Quartet, classical composer John Tavener and the Radha Krishna Temple.

The label was discontinued in 1975, but Apple Corps has continued to operate as the holding company for the Beatles' business interests.

Bibliography
DiLello, Richard. 1973. *The Longest Cocktail Party*. London: Charisma Books.

Discographical References
Harrison, George. *Wonderwall*. Apple SAPCOR 1. *1968*: UK.

Lennon, John, and Ono, Yoko. *Unfinished Music No. 1: Two Virgins*. Apple SAPCOR 2. *1968*: UK.

Plastic Ono Band, The. 'Give Peace a Chance.' Apple 13. *1969*: UK.

DAVE LAING

—ARC (US)

ARC (*American Record Company*) was formed in August 1929 as the result of a merger between several companies specializing in cheap labels (labels such as Cameo, Oriole and Perfect) and a pressing plant. The following year, as record companies began to feel the effects of the Depression, it was purchased by Consolidated Film Industries, whose owner, Herbert Yates, used his success in the film industry, where he owned a number of studios and produced numerous 'B' movies, as a base for moving into the record industry at a bargain price. In 1931, Yates added the Brunswick labels, purchased from Warner Brothers (who, unlike Yates, were moving out of music). In 1934, through its Brunswick subsidiary, ARC purchased Columbia from Grigsby-Grunow. Four years later, the whole concern was sold to CBS.

Headquartered on Broadway in New York City, ARC's major area of activity was in the market for cheap ($0.35) labels such as Vocalion and so-called 'dime store' ($0.25) labels such as Banner, Perfect and Romeo in the areas of blues, gospel and hillbilly music. At one time, no fewer than nine such labels, each belonging to ARC, were issuing records, with the 'dime store' labels (which retailed in different stores) often duplicating material. The company also produced and manufactured a label, Conqueror, especially for the mail-order catalog of Sears Roebuck, and it was on this label that producer Art Satherley recorded 'singing cowboy' Gene Autry. The top end of the market was not neglected, however, and the company used its Brunswick label to put out its bestselling mainstream artists, such as Bing Crosby.

In the area of blues, ARC recorded a range of material, beginning with piano-guitar duets by 'Georgia Tom' Dorsey and 'Big' Bill Broonzy, such as 'Six Shooter Blues,' solo country blues from 'Big' Bill, such as 'I Can't Be Satisfied,' and good-time blues with titles such as 'Pie-Eating Strut' from the Famous Hokum Boys, a group containing both of these performers. With the acquisition of Brunswick, the company dominated the 'race' record market with leading performers such as Memphis Minnie and Tampa Red, but even cut-price labels had to endure hard times during the worst of the Depression in 1932–33, and for a while no new 'race' records were made (Dixon and Godrich 1970, 73). From 1934 on, as the situation improved, ARC engaged in a series of field trips, recording blues and hillbilly artists in Texas in particular. In November 1936 in San Antonio and in June 1937 in Dallas, ARC recorded the hitherto little-known Robert Johnson, for issue on Vocalion.

Bibliography

Dixon, Robert M.W., and Godrich, John. 1970. *Recording the Blues*. New York: Stein & Day.

Dixon, Robert M.W., Godrich, John, and Rye, Howard. 1997. *Blues & Gospel Records 1890–1943*. 4th ed. Oxford: Clarendon Press.

Millard, Andre J. 1995. *America on Record: A History of Recorded Sound*. Cambridge: Cambridge University Press.

Discographical References

Broonzy, 'Big' Bill. 'I Can't Be Satisfied.' Perfect 157. 1930: USA.

Dorsey, 'Georgia Tom,' and Broonzy, 'Big' Bill. 'Six Shooter Blues.' Oriole 8009. 1930: USA.

Famous Hokum Boys, The. 'Pie-Eating Strut.' Banner 32310. 1930: USA.

Discography

Autry, Gene. *Blues Singer 1929–1931: Booger Rooger Saturday*. Columbia/Legacy 64987. *1996*: USA.

Autry, Gene. *Columbia Historic Edition* (prod. by Art Satherley). Columbia CK-37465. *1982*: USA.

Broonzy, 'Big' Bill. *Complete Recorded Works, Vols. 1–12 (1927–1947)*. Document 5050–5052 (*1991*); 5126–5133 (*1992*); 6047 (*1995*). *1991–92; 1995*: Austria.

Crosby, Bing. *Rare Brunswick Recordings (1930–1931)*. MCA 1502. *1982*: USA.

Famous Hokum Boys, The. *Complete Recorded Works, Vols. 1–2*. Document 5236–5237. *1995*: Austria.

'Georgia Tom' (Thomas A. Dorsey). *Complete Recorded Works, Vols. 1–2 (1928–1934)*. Document 6021–6022. *1992*: Austria.

Johnson, Robert. *King of the Delta Blues*. Sony 65211. *1997*: USA.

Johnson, Robert. *The Complete Recordings*. Columbia/Legacy C2K-46222. *1990*: USA.

Memphis Minnie. *Complete Recorded Works, Vols. 1–5 (1935–1941)*. Document 6008–6012. *1991*: Austria.

Memphis Minnie and Kansas Joe. *Complete Recorded Works, Vols. 1–4 (1929–1934)*. Document 5028–5031. *1991*: Austria.

Tampa Red. *Tampa Red (1928–1942)*. Story of the Blues 3505. *1994*: USA.

Uncle Art Satherley: Country Music's Father. Columbia 46237. *1991*: USA.

DAVID SANJEK and DAVID HORN

—Arcade (The Netherlands)

The Dutch record company Arcade began in the early 1970s as a division of a UK-based company, marketing within The Netherlands compilation albums containing tracks from different artists or the greatest hits of a single group or artist. Arcade licensed this repertoire from other companies solely for this purpose. Releases were heavily promoted by television campaigns.

In 1980, the UK parent company went bankrupt, and the managers of the Dutch branch acquired the worldwide rights to the name. At the end of the 1980s, major companies in The Netherlands stopped licensing repertoire to Arcade and other similar record companies. As a consequence, Arcade relied on independent companies for repertoire. This led to a series of dance compilations using repertoire from indie labels. Arcade was not very successful in building up its in-house, A&R-driven popular music label, Indisc. It did, however, operate its own classical label, Vanguard Music, successfully.

In 1992, Arcade acquired the CNR Music company as the result of a bankruptcy. CNR was one of the oldest Dutch independent record companies, specializing in Dutch-language repertoire among other things. In 1997, Arcade acquired a share in the Dutch dance company IT&T. By the late 1990s, Arcade had become one of the top five companies on the Dutch market. It experienced, however, a slump in sales of compilation albums, partly due to a flourishing trade in illegal compilation CDs, and it underwent reorganization in 1998.

Arcade set up a dual structure in other European countries (Belgium, Germany, Austria, Spain, France, Norway, Sweden and the United Kingdom), combining the Arcade label with local acquisitions focusing on recording and publishing rights. Among its acquisitions in Europe were the Spanish company Divulgacion de Cassettes SA (Divucsa) (*copla* and flamenco) and the French label Flarenasch (which recorded Michel Fugain and Françoise Hardy). At the same time, it tried to promote CNR internationally to exploit its signings in Europe.

At the end of the twentieth century, Arcade was part of the Arcade Entertainment Group, which also owned several radio stations in The Netherlands, the music television station The Music Factory, a film and video label, a CD wholesaler and a CD retail chain. It divested itself of its distribution setup in 1998. The Arcade Entertainment Group was in turn part of the Wegener Arcade

Consortium, which was formed in 1996 from Arcade and Wegener, one of the main Dutch publishers, specializing in regional newspapers, magazines and other printed media. The Wegener Arcade Consortium as a whole had 5,500 employees and a turnover of 1.6 billion guilders in 1997. CD and video accounted for about 25 percent of the turnover.

In 2000, Wegener sold the Arcade division to another Dutch record company, Roadrunner.

PAUL RUTTEN

—Arhoolie (US)

Named after a form of field holler, the Arhoolie label was founded by Chris Strachwitz in 1960, based on recordings made earlier in the year on a field trip in the South. The first issue – by Mance Lipscomb, one of the discoveries of the trip – was *Mance Lipscomb: Texas Songster*. Others by Lightnin' Hopkins, Big Joe Williams and Fred McDowell followed. In the course of his location recording, Strachwitz became interested in, and subsequently developed important catalogs of, Louisiana Cajun and zydeco music, and Mexican and Texas-Mexican (so-called Tex-Mex) music. After developing a mail-order business, he negotiated rights for the releases of many companies (for example, Trumpet Records, of Jackson, Mississippi), which prompted vigorous and varied reissue programs on his Blues Classics and Old Timey labels. A significant acquisition was the Folk-Lyric catalog, and he issued many items under this name. In association with filmmaker Les Blank, Strachwitz produced a number of films, which were later issued on videocassette, featuring such artists as Flaco Jimenez and the Mendoza family. With the advent of the compact disc (CD), he repackaged many of his earlier long-playing records, with additional previously unissued material. Other ventures included Bay Side Record Distributors, the Down Home Music Store in El Cerrito, and a few publications, including his biography of Lydia Mendoza. In existence for 40 years, under the personal direction of Chris Strachwitz, Arhoolie and its related concerns have long been recognized as a major resource for the preservation of US roots music.

Bibliography

Arhoolie Staff. 1997. 'Arhoolie's History.' In *Arhoolie and Folk Lyric Catalogue*. El Cerrito, CA.

Oliver, Paul. 1972. 'Arhoolie and Mister Chris.' *Jazz and Blues* 1(10): 4–6.

Strachwitz, Chris. 1971. *Arhoolie Occasional*. El Cerrito, CA.

Strachwitz, Chris, with Nicolopulos, James. 1993. *Lydia Mendoza: A Family Autobiography*. Houston, TX: Arte Público Press.

Discographical Reference

Lipscomb, Mance. *Mance Lipscomb: Texas Songster*. Arhoolie CD-306. *1960*: USA.

PAUL OLIVER

—Ariola (Germany)

Ariola was the first record label of BMG Entertainment, the major record company privately held by the media giant Bertelsmann AG. BMG Ariola, as it is now known, is BMG's repertoire company for the German-speaking region, with offices in Munich, Hamburg, Switzerland and Austria.

Bertelsmann's move into music was a natural progression from its publishing business. With its existing distribution network and marketing principles, Bertelsmann had a proven infrastructure in place that allowed the company to make music easily available to its loyal *Lesering* (book club) customer base. In 1956, Reinhard Mohn founded the Bertelsmann *Schallplattenring* in Gütersloh and soon realized that the existing music and manufacturing companies were reluctant to license material, fearing serious competition. Therefore, a year later, a manufacturing plant – Sonopress – was set up, which now has subsidiaries all over the world.

With in-house distribution and manufacturing facilities in place, it was then possible for Bertelsmann to launch an autonomous record label. In 1958, Ariola was founded, concentrating its core business on vinyl disc distribution. Initially, only six salespeople were responsible for representing a total of 72 titles. The first release on the Ariola label was Joséphine Baker's 'Die Regenbogenkinder,' and a year later the label had its first number one hit with Dalida's 'Am Tag als der Regen kam,' which stayed at the top of the charts for seven weeks. This success led to quick expansion, and branches of Ariola were opened in Berlin, Düsseldorf, Frankfurt, Hamburg, Stuttgart and Austria. A new label, Athena, was set up to distribute spoken-word recordings, which linked the vinyl disc with the printed word.

In the 1960s, Ariola-Eurodisc Musikproduktion, an independent production company with an emphasis on A&R, was established in Munich to build up national repertoire. Exclusive contracts with artists such as German *schlager* star Peter Alexander in 1965, and the signing of Udo Jürgens, Mireille Mathieu and the Dutch child star Heintje two years later, made Ariola synonymous with German *schlager* music.

The 1960s also marked the start of Ariola's cooperation with other labels. In 1964, the German label made a deal with the label Montana, and the following year with Melodiya, which gave Ariola-Eurodisc the rights to the complete catalog of original recordings of classical music of this Soviet state-run record company. With the aim of expanding into different musical genres, Ariola entered into a licensing agreement with the young label Hansa Musikproduktion, based in Berlin. The Hollies were an important asset for Ariola in its goal of reaching younger consumers, and in the mid-1970s the label would also sign Boney M, the Euro-disco group created by Frank Farian, who was responsible for the act Milli Vanilli. At the end of the decade, Ariola became an international player by taking over two US labels, Liberty and United Artists, with stars such as Shirley Bassey. In 1969, the core of Ariola's business in Gütersloh, the sales and distribution department, was also moved to Munich.

In the 1970s, Ariola pressed ahead with its expansion by opening more subsidiaries and continuing to conquer the international market with further licensing agreements and acquisitions. In 1970, Ariola opened up business in the Benelux countries and Spain. The French office, Arabella France, was opened in 1973 and was later renamed Ariola France. Ariola America, based in Los Angeles, followed in 1975. Two years later, Ariola opened three further offices: Ariola Mexico, Ariola Switzerland and Ariola UK. The year 1977 also marked Bertelsmann AG's first major restructuring process, in which the mother company merged its various entertainment divisions and combined its television, film and music sectors, including UFA-Musikverlag (one of the most significant music publishing groups in the German-speaking region), under its umbrella.

Further expansion through acquisitions had started at the beginning of the decade when Ariola entered a licensing agreement with the record label A&M, acquiring the rights to more US repertoire from stars such as Carole King, Burt Bacharach and the Carpenters. A year later, the British independent label Island was added to Ariola's roster, bringing with it such important rock musicians as Jethro Tull, Cat Stevens and Roxy Music. In 1973, Ariola entered into a collaboration with German label Jupiter Records and, shortly afterward, Bronze Records (to which Manfred Mann's Earth Band was signed) and ABC (home to artists such as Tom Petty, the Crusaders and the extensive back catalog of Bing Crosby and the Mamas & the Papas) joined the company. It was, however, in 1979 that Bertelsmann made the strategic decision to enter the international market more aggressively by acquiring Arista Records from Columbia Pictures, guaranteeing worldwide success with stars such as Aretha Franklin, Barry Manilow and Patti Smith.

Although the 1980s were affected by a music industry recession, Ariola continued its success. In 1981, it entered a distribution deal with CGD, an Italian label that was home to artists like Umberto Tozzi. In 1983, Ariola bought the remainder of Hansa Musikproduktion and negotiated an exclusive deal with another Italian

label, DDD, home to the bestselling star Eros Ramazzotti. In 1985, a further major deal was completed when Ariola entered a joint venture with the US electronics company RCA to form Ariola/RCA Records, only two years after Arista had been partially sold off to RCA Records. In 1987, the privately held company with the reputation of never exceeding its financial resources when investing was strong enough to take over the remaining 75 percent of the Ariola/RCA joint venture. The three record labels – Ariola, Arista and RCA – now belonged to Bertelsmann AG, which reorganized its record companies and labels under one music division, Bertelsmann Music Group (BMG), with headquarters in New York, to form the fifth major record company in the world.

Bibliography

Billboard. http://www.billboard.com

BMG. http://www.bmg.com

BMG Entertainment: Germany/Switzerland/Austria. www.bmgentertainment.de

Southall, Brian. 2000. *The A–Z of Record Labels.* London: Sanctuary Publishing Ltd.

Steinel, Roland. 1992. *Zur Lage und Problematik der Musikwirtschaft* [The Situation and Problems of the Music Business]. München: Edition Roland/Intermedia.

Zeppenfeld, Werner. 1978. *Tonträger in der Bundesrepublik Deutschland: Anatomie eines medialen Massenmarkts* [Recordings in the Federal Republic of Germany: Analysis of a Media Mass Market]. Bochum: Studienverlag Brockmeyer.

Discographical References

Baker, Joséphine. 'Die Regenbogenkinder.' Ariola. *1958*: Germany.

Dalida. 'Am Tag als der Regen kam.' Ariola 35686. *1959*: Germany.

VANESSA BASTIAN

—Arista Records (US)

Arista Records was founded in 1975 as the successor label to Bell Records, a subsidiary of Columbia Pictures Inc. Arista's president between 1975 and 2000 was Clive Davis, the former head of CBS Records. Davis ran the company almost single-handedly, involving himself in its A&R aspects as well as in the business side of the company.

In 1980, Arista was purchased by the German conglomerate Bertelsmann, and RCA Records was appointed as its US distributor. Subsequently, RCA purchased 50 percent of the label and, in 1984, its attempt to acquire the remaining 50 percent led to a merger of RCA and Bertelsmann's record division (BMG). Two years later,

Bertelsmann bought out its partner, becoming the sole owner of Arista.

In the late 1970s, Arista had continued the Bell strategy of middle-of-the-road pop, achieving hits with such artists as Barry Manilow and Melissa Manchester. But the label's most commercially successful artists in the following two decades were soul diva Whitney Houston and saxophonist Kenny G. Whitney Houston was signed to Arista by Davis in 1983 and her first album was the most successful debut ever, selling over 10 million copies worldwide. She was also featured on the soundtrack album of *The Bodyguard*, which became the label's biggest-ever seller with sales of over 30 million. Other soft soul hits came from Dionne Warwick and Aretha Franklin. Kenny G's *Breathless* (1992) sold over 10 million copies. His light jazz style was particularly popular in Japan and Southeast Asia.

Arista was less involved with rock music, although Davis signed the Grateful Dead in 1976 and subsequent albums for the label helped to revive the group's career. He achieved a similar comeback with Carlos Santana's blend of Latin music and rock. Santana's *Supernatural* was a global bestseller in 1999–2000. Davis also formed partnerships with independent labels, the most renowned of which were LaFace, founded by leading US black music songwriters/producers Babyface and L.A. (Kenneth Edmonds and L.A. Reid), and Bad Boy, owned by Sean 'Puffy' Combs (aka P. Diddy).

Although Davis was less interested in foreign markets, BMG set up a UK branch of Arista in 1985 and European hits were occasionally issued in North America. Among these were recordings by the Eurythmics, Milli Vanilli and Ace of Base.

In 2000, Bertelsmann company policy forced Davis's retirement. His successor was L.A. Reid. Davis went on to found J Records with funding from Bertelsmann.

Discographical References

The Bodyguard (Original soundtrack). Arista 18699. *1992*: USA.

Houston, Whitney. *Whitney Houston*. Arista 206978. *1985*: USA.

Kenny G. *Breathless*. Arista 18646-2. *1992*: USA.

Santana. *Supernatural*. Arista 19080. *1999*: USA.

Filmography

The Bodyguard, dir. Mick Jackson. 1992. USA. 130 mins. Drama. Original music by David Foster, Alan Silvestri.

DAVE LAING

—Atlantic (US)

Unique among the independent record companies started in the 1940s that originally concentrated on African-American rhythm and blues (R&B) and jazz,

Atlantic was still, at the end of the twentieth century, an active label, albeit within a corporate umbrella.

Founded in New York City in 1947 by Ahmet Ertegun and Herb Abramson, by the mid-1950s Atlantic had become a leading R&B imprint with a succession of hits by Ruth Brown, Joe Turner, the Clovers, Clyde McPhatter and the Drifters, and Ray Charles. Jerry Wexler, soon to become an important producer and partner, joined the company in 1953. The hit roster was further enhanced by LaVern Baker, the Coasters (brought to the company from Los Angeles by writers/arrangers/producers Jerry Leiber and Mike Stoller) and Chuck Willis. Aside from the R&B core, meanwhile, Ahmet's brother Nesuhi built a formidable jazz catalog (John Coltrane, the Modern Jazz Quartet, Charles Mingus and more) and, with its Atco subsidiary, in 1958 the company successfully launched its first white pop star, Bobby Darin.

After a worrying transition period that extended into the next decade, Atlantic again came to the fore with a realigned group of artists made up of the Drifters, Ben E. King and Solomon Burke. This reemergence was in addition fueled through a pact with Stax Records (Carla and Rufus Thomas, Booker T. and the MGs, the Mar-Keys, Otis Redding, Eddie Floyd, among others). Adding Don Covay, Wilson Pickett, Joe Tex, Sam and Dave, Percy Sledge and Aretha Franklin to its impressive roster, the company became a major player in 1960s soul music. Many of its soul recordings emanated from southern studios.

Unlike similarly rooted 'indies,' however, Atlantic then invested heavily in the burgeoning, post-'British invasion,' white rock market. By the time the company was absorbed by Seven Arts (which, in turn, was quickly acquired by the Kinney Corporation in 1969), Atlantic was more commercially successful with its rock releases, especially in the rapidly expanding album market, than it had been with its R&B/soul artists. The artists of this new-era Atlantic included Sonny and Cher, the Rascals, Buffalo Springfield, Cream, Vanilla Fudge, Iron Butterfly, Led Zeppelin, and Crosby, Stills, Nash and Young. The label continued this trend toward rock music after being taken over, with bands such as King Crimson and Yes. It also distributed the recordings that symbolized the Rolling Stones' newfound independence.

The Kinney Corporation metamorphosed into WEA (Warner-Elektra-Atlantic, subsequently to become the Warner Music Group (WMG)), within which corporations Atlantic has ebbed and flowed as the 'A' constituent. Throughout each decade, the label recorded various genres of music according to market trends and demands, a particularly successful example toward the end of the twentieth century being folk-rock as exemplified through the group, the Corrs. However, it is probably true to say that, throughout the world, the name 'Atlantic' has most commonly been associated with the catalog it built up during the 20 years it was an independent company.

Bibliography

Ertegun, Ahmet, et al. 1998. *What'd I Say: The Atlantic History of Music*. New York: Welcome Rain.

Gillett, Charlie. 1974. *Making Tracks: The Story of Atlantic Records*. London: Souvenir Press.

Ruppli, Michel. 1979. *Atlantic Records: A Discography* (*Discographies*, No. 1). Westport, CT: Greenwood Press.

Wade, Dorothy, and Picardie, Justine. 1990. *Music Man: Ahmet Ertegun, Atlantic Records, and the Triumph of Rock 'n' Roll*. New York: Norton.

Wexler, Jerry, and Ritz, David. 1993. *Rhythm and the Blues: A Life in American Music*. New York: Knopf.

Discography

Atlantic Blues Box. Atlantic 82309. *1986*: USA.

Atlantic Hit 45's '58–77. Atlantic 81909-2. *1988*: USA.

Atlantic Hit 45's '80–88. Atlantic 81910. *1988*: USA.

Atlantic Jazz: 12 Volume Box Set. Atlantic 81712-4. *1986*: USA.

Atlantic Records 50 Years: The Gold Anniversary. Atlantic 83088. *1998*: USA.

Atlantic Rhythm & Blues 1947–1974. Atlantic 7-82305-2. *1991*: USA.

Atlantic Rock & Roll. Atlantic 82306. *1991*: USA.

CLIFF WHITE

—Avex Trax (Japan)

A contemporary Japanese pop and dance music label, headed by Tom Yoda, Avex was set up in 1988 to import CD compilations of dance music from European and US independent labels. By 1990, Avex had started its own Super Eurobeat compilation series and had set up a recording studio near Tokyo to record foreign artists specifically for Japanese dance audiences. By 1995, the company had 7 percent of the national recorded music market and was opening overseas branches in London, New York and Hong Kong. During the late 1990s, Avex also became involved in concert promotion, music publishing and artist management.

DAVE LAING

—Balkanton (Bulgaria)

The national state-owned Radioprom, founded in 1947 and renamed Balkanton in 1953, was at one time the only record company in Bulgaria, holding a monopoly in the record industry for more than 40 years. It inherited the first Bulgarian record label, Simonavia, founded in 1924 by the entrepreneur Simeon Petrov, an ex-military aviator and a pioneer in the field of recording.

Initially, music was recorded at the studio of the national radio station in Sofia, but from 1961 onward it was also recorded in the studio established at Balkanton. At that time, LPs replaced older forms of phonograms. Audio cassettes began to be produced from 1978 onward and, after the introduction of digital recording technology in 1985, CDs also became available in the late 1980s.

From 1953 to 1971, the company was run by Yossif Tzankov, a songwriter and a prominent figure in the history of Bulgarian pop music, and from 1971 to 1986 by Alexander Yossifov, a composer. Balkanton developed a strategy that aimed to produce and promote mostly national music in a variety of genres, predominantly popular. To implement this strategy, it targeted local and Eastern European markets, especially the Soviet Union where Bulgarian pop music was greatly in demand. Prominent in this regard during the 1970s and 1980s were Bulgarian pop singers Lili Ivanova, Emil Dimitrov and Yordanka Hristova, among others. At that time, too, chart-topping Western pop music (by the Beatles, for instance) was reissued on licensed compilation releases, millions of which sold in the Soviet Union.

Two musical ensembles, working full time with the company, were largely responsible for shaping the Balkanton sound: Balkanton's in-house orchestra and the four-member rock-oriented group FSB (Formation Studio Balkanton). Along with the national radio's Estrada Orchestra, the Balkanton orchestra took a leading role in recording activities from 1962 to 1975. From 1976 onward, FSB introduced a more advanced technological approach to recording. The consequent change in the sound recorded was reflected in most of the pop and rock music produced. After 1989, the role of Balkanton declined because of the advent of competitive recording facilities run by many private enterprises. At the close of the twentieth century, Balkanton was a joint-stock company owned by the state.

Bibliography

Krustev, Venelin, ed. 1967. *Enciclopedija na bulgarskata muzikalna kultura* [Encyclopedia of Bulgarian Music Culture]. Sofia: BAN.

Rupchev, Jordan, and Hofman, Heinz Peter. 1987. *ABeVe na popmuzikata* [ABC of Pop Music]. Sofia: Muzika.

Discography

Beatles, The. *Love Songs*. Balkanton BTA 1141/42 (under license to EMI Records Ltd.). *1977*: Bulgaria.

Dimitrov, Emil. *Pee Emil Dimitrov*. Balkanton BTA 1217. *1971*: Bulgaria.

Hristova, Yordanka. *Yordanka Hristova*. Balkanton BTA 10650. *1980*: Bulgaria.

Ivanova, Lili. *Lili Ivanova*. Balkanton BTA 11719. *1986*: Bulgaria.

Ivanova, Lili. *Pee Lili Ivanova*. Balkanton BTA 1180. *1971*: Bulgaria.

CLAIRE LEVY

—Barclay (France)

In February 1945, Nicole and Eddie Barclay established the Blue Star record label in Paris. The musicians recorded were those promoted at the 'Club,' where Eddie Barclay was in charge of musical programming. At first, the firm had little to work with (the offices were in the Barclays' home), but progress was fast, and, as early as 1948, the label's catalog contained 200 titles. The firm then moved to the 8th *arrondissement* and changed its name to Productions Phonographiques Françaises (PPF) (French Phonographic Productions). In January 1953, PPF became the Compagnie Phonographique Française CPF-Barclay (the French Phonographic Company CPF-Barclay), with offices at 20, rue de Madrid, still in the 8th *arrondissement*.

As an established company, Barclay distributed the recordings of important foreign labels: Verve, Prestige, Atlantic, Mercury, Dial, Wax and Gotham. The Blue Star label was temporarily abandoned in favor of the general name of Barclay. A number of labels other than the one carrying its own name were subsequently established by Barclay. The most celebrated remains Riviera, dedicated to performers of French variety or pop music (*variété française*) and to some dance music groups. Barclay's list began to become diversified, but the company continued to specialize in French variety or pop music.

November 1956 saw another move, to Neuilly-sur-Seine, where all the company's activities, including warehousing, were centralized. However, space quickly became inadequate, and the inventory was transferred in 1957 to Colombes. In 1957, Barclay also established its own studio in the 8th *arrondissement*, with equipment that made it one of the best recording studios in Paris.

The great names of *chanson française* figured in Barclay's catalog: Henri Salvador, Charles Aznavour, Jacques Brel, Léo Ferré, Dalida and Mireille Mathieu. Jazz was still present, but less than before. Barclay continued to record Stéphane Grappelli, Chet Baker, René Thomas and Lester Young.

In 1975, the jazz catalog was reactivated and the Blue Star label found new life thanks to reissues, as well as to new recordings. In 1978, CPF-Barclay employed 350 people. In July 1978, Eddie Barclay sold his enterprise to the PolyGram group, but remained as president and managing director until 1983.

With the end of this company, 'a page was turned in the history of recording and, with that, in the history of

an independent company which numbered among the most creative in the production and distribution of *chanson française* as well as jazz' (Ruppli and Lubin 1993, 3).

At the end of the twentieth century, the Barclay label comprised an important division of PolyGram.

Bibliography

Ruppli, Michel, and Lubin, Jacques. 1993. *Blue Star*. Paris: AFAS.

Discography

Aznavour, Charles. *Autobiographie*. Barclay 813 585-2. *1980*: France.

Aznavour, Charles. *Visages de l'Amour*. Barclay 90 010 LP. *1974*: France.

Baker, Chet. *In Paris: Barclay Sessions 1955–1956*. Poly-Gram 5435472. *2000*: France.

Brel, Jacques. *Jacques Brel [J'Arrive]*. Barclay 821 595. *1968*: France.

Brel, Jacques. *Les Marquises*. Barclay 810 537. *1977*: France.

Dalida. *Les Années Barclay* (10-CD set). Barclay 511099-2. *1991*: France.

Ferré, Léo. *Léo Ferré Chante Aragon*. Barclay 899. *1998*: France.

Grappelli, Stéphane, and Smith, Stuff. *Violins No End*. Original Jazz Classics 890. 1957; *1996*: France.

Mathieu, Mireille. *Mireille Mathieu Made in France*. Barclay 80 352. *1985*: France.

Salvador, Henri. *Dans mon île/Ça pince*. Barclay 80090. *1958*: France.

Thomas, René. *Meeting Mr. Thomas*. Barclay 84091. *1963*: France.

GIUSY BASILE (trans. JOHN SHEPHERD)

—Belter (Spain)

The Spanish record company Belter was founded in Barcelona in 1956. For many years, it was a distributor in Spain for the US label Atlantic. In the 1960s and 1970s, Belter experienced significant expansion, but it finally went bankrupt in 1983. Belter had one factory for pressing records, called Fabricsa, and another for producing tapes, called Duplicsa. The former made records for EMI-Odeón and, when this multinational record company stopped using the factory's services, Belter could not cope with its financial problems and it had to close.

During its early years, Belter specialized, above all, in recording singers of *copla* (Spanish song) and of modern Spanish song that incorporated an Andalusian folk influence. The most important singer of this modern Spanish song was Manolo Escobar. Also, soloists like Carmen Sevilla, Conchita Bautista, Emilio José and Víctor Manuel recorded for Belter.

The success of Italian music, and the rapid popularization of the San Remo Song Festival, led the company to focus its commercial interests on Italian singers and Spanish performers who imitated the style of Italian melodic song from the 1960s. In contrast to other Spanish companies, Belter did not pay much attention to the young pop and rock groups that emerged in the 1960s, but it did record some young groups: for example, Los Mismos, Los Tifones and Los Gritos.

A few years before it closed down, Belter produced records that represented the new Spanish pop of the late 1970s: in 1978, it produced a record by the group Burning; in 1982, the first record of PVP; and, in 1983, the first record of Los Burros, a group that later became the highly successful El Ultimo de la Fila.

Bibliography

Irles, Gerardo. 1997. ¡Sólo para fans! La música ye-yé y pop española de los años 60 [Only for Fans: Spanish Ye-Yé and Pop Music of the 1960s]. Madrid: Alianza Editorial.

Jones, Daniel E. 1988. 'La industria fonográfica: cima de las transnacionales' [The Record Industry: The Top Transnationals]. In Las industrias culturales en España [The Cultural Industries of Spain], ed. Enrique Bustamante and Ramón Zallo. Madrid: Akal.

Ordovás, Jesús. 1986. Historia de la música pop española [The History of Spanish Pop Music]. Madrid: Alianza Editorial.

Pardo, José Ramón. 1975. Historia del pop español [The History of Spanish Pop]. Madrid: Guía del ocio.

Discography

Aguilé, Luis. Camarero, champagne. Belter B 12691. *1979*: Spain.

Caracol, Manolo. Manolo Caracol. Belter B 1960. *1980*: Spain.

Escobar, Manolo. El Porompompero. Belter B 4424. *1980*: Spain.

Escobar, Manolo. Las canciones de amor de Manolo Escobar. Belter B 4427. *1980*: Spain.

Historia del cante flamenco. Belter B 38566. *1979*: Spain.

Las grandes canciones del cancionero. Belter B 3359-2. *1979*: Spain.

Pasodobles. Belter B 3854. *1979*: Spain.

Piquer, Conchita. Conchita Piquer. Belter B 1140. *1980*: Spain.

Raimon. Totes les cançons. Belter B 34189. *1981*: Spain.

Reina, Juanita. Juanita Reina. Belter B 41111. *1979*: Spain.

JULIO ARCE

—Black Saint/Soul Note (Italy)

An important contemporary jazz label of the 1980s and 1990s, Black Saint was founded in Milan, Italy in 1975. The label was acquired by distributor IREC three years later and, under the direction of Giovanni Bonandrini, it recorded some of the most innovative US musicians of the period. These included Anthony Braxton, David Murray and the World Saxophone Quartet. Bonandrini also released albums from an older generation of jazz musicians on a sister label, Soul Note, which he launched in 1979. These included work by Belgian harmonica virtuoso Toots Thielemans and duet recordings by pianist Cecil Taylor and drummer Max Roach.

Discography

Braxton, Anthony. Six Compositions (Quartet). Black Saint BSR 0086. *1984*: Italy.

David Murray Octet, The. Home. Black Saint BSR 0055. *1981*: Italy.

Roach, Max, and Taylor, Cecil. Historic Concerts. Soul Note SN 1100/1. *1979*: Italy.

Thielemans, Toots. Autumn Leaves. Soul Note 823442. *1984*: Italy.

World Saxophone Quartet, The. Live in Zurich. Black Saint BSR 0077. *1981*: Italy.

DAVE LAING

—Bluebird (US)

A subsidiary of the Victor company, which itself had been absorbed by RCA in 1929, Bluebird was initiated in 1933 as a budget label, with 78 rpm records retailing at $0.35 each. For a time, the Bluebird catalog largely featured former Victor releases by bestselling artists. A substantial number of 'Jelly Roll' Morton titles were issued, around 20 by Bennie Moten's Kansas City Orchestra and a handful by 'King' Oliver. A single series, the B5000 issues, covered popular music, jazz, gospel and blues, a policy that continued until 1938, when the increasing numbers of popular and dance music issues warranted a separate B10000 series. Blues, gospel and hillbilly music then shared the same series, with some 4,000 releases by 1942, when the catalog was split and the 34-0700 Race series commenced.

In addition to these series, special-interest records for foreign and 'ethnic' communities in the United States were also issued on separate numerical series: Cajun on the B2000s; Bohemian, Italian and French-Canadian on 2500s; Eastern European on 2600s; Scandinavian (14 discs) on 2700s; and Mexican on a number of series, especially those in the 3000s. The great Texas-Mexican singer and guitarist Lydia Mendoza, for example, was extensively recorded on Bluebird.

For the blues audience, Bluebird recordings were particularly welcome, largely because of their excellent sound quality. Among the major blues names, solo guitar-playing artists included 'Blind' Willie McTell, Big Joe Williams, Tommy McClennan, Lonnie Johnson and Bo Carter. Pianists also figured prominently, with the singer Leroy Carr accompanied by 'Scrapper' Blackwell creating a new and highly influential urban sound. Tampa Red (guitar) and Walter Davis (piano) were among the most extensively recorded solo blues singers on the label, with Tampa Red also making many records with the formidable boogie-woogie pianist Big Maceo Merriweather. In the late 1930s and the 1940s, a Chicago-based blues idiom was influential, centered on guitarist 'Big' Bill Broonzy, harmonica players 'Sonny Boy' Williamson and William 'Jazz' Gillum, and percussionist Washboard Sam. Dubbed 'the Bluebird beat' by Samuel Charters, the idiom was strongly promoted by the talent scout and recording manager Lester Melrose, who went to great lengths to locate musicians in Chicago and in the southern states.

A number of field recording sessions, notably between 1935 and 1937, were conducted by Eli Oberstein. Significant blues titles were recorded by Bo Carter and the Chatmons, Little Brother Montgomery and others in New Orleans, the Heavenly Gospel Singers in Charlotte, North Carolina, and Joe Pullum and Andy Boy in San Antonio, Texas. Also recorded in San Antonio was Boots and His Buddies, a western swing band.

Bluebird's issues and reissues of hillbilly and country music were every bit as important as their blues releases: many of Jimmie Rodgers's Victor records were issued posthumously on the label and continued to sell in hundreds of thousands. Likewise, the Carter Family was well represented, while new recordings were being made by the Dixon Brothers, Cliff Carlisle, Milton Brown and His Brownies (western swing), the Monroe Brothers (Bill and Charlie), Carson Robison and His Pioneers, and Mainer's Mountaineers, the latter group alone recording over 170 titles.

Jazz recordings were also issued by Bluebird, although, unlike the recordings of its parent company Victor, those by black bands were in the minority. Between 1936 and 1939, the white bands led by Charlie Barnet, Ocie Stockard, Ziggy Elman, Les Brown and Artie Shaw were recorded, with Shaw, for example, recording over 60 titles before rejoining the Victor label in 1940. In the fall of 1939, Bluebird had a major success with Muggsy Spanier and His Ragtime Band, arguably the first band of the 'trad jazz revival.'

Blues recordings on the Bluebird label continued intermittently during the war years, until Arthur 'Big Boy' Crudup cut 'She's Gone' in October 1945. However, it was on the revived Victor label that Crudup recorded 'That's All Right' the following year, unwittingly sowing the seeds for rock 'n' roll. Victor discontinued Bluebird as a label in 1950 (Dixon and Godrich 1970).

Bibliography

Charters, Samuel B. 1959. 'I Got the Bluebird Beat.' In *The Country Blues*. New York: Rinehart & Company, 182–94.

Dixon, Robert M.W., and Godrich, John. 1970. *Recording the Blues*. London: Studio Vista.

Gronow, Pekka. 1982. 'Ethnic Recordings: An Introduction.' In *Ethnic Recordings in America: A Neglected Heritage*. Washington, DC: American Folklife Center, 1–50.

Melrose, Lester. 1970. 'My Life in Recording.' *American Folk Music Occasional* 1: 59–61.

Discographical References

Crudup, Arthur 'Big Boy.' 'She's Gone.' Bluebird 34-0746. 1945: USA.

Crudup, Arthur 'Big Boy.' 'That's All Right.' Victor 20-2205. 1946: USA.

Discography

Gillum, William 'Jazz.' *The Bluebird Recordings 1934–1938*. RCA 66717. *1997*: USA.

McClennan, Tommy. *Bluebird Recordings 1939–1942*. RCA 67430. *1997*: USA.

Merriweather, Big Maceo. *Bluebird Recordings 1941–1942*. RCA 66715. *1997*: USA.

Williamson, 'Sonny Boy.' *The Bluebird Recordings 1937–1938*. RCA 66723. *1997*: USA.

PAUL OLIVER

—Blue Note Records (US)

The Blue Note jazz record label was established in New York in 1939 by German émigré Alfred Lion, who was joined in partnership in 1941 by his fellow countryman Francis Wolff. Initially, the label focused on boogie-woogie and traditional jazz, recording notable sessions by Albert Ammons, Meade 'Lux' Lewis and Sidney Bechet. Blue Note was one of the first nonclassical labels to employ 12'' (30 cm) 78 rpm records instead of the more common 10'' (25 cm) discs, thereby extending the playing time on each side of a record.

Throughout the 1940s and early 1950s, the label extended its musical policy to include small-group swing and bebop performers. Celebrated sessions from this period included those by Ike Quebec (who later became musical advisor for the label) and a series of now-legendary recordings by several major figures of the bebop movement, including Thelonious Monk, Bud Powell and Fats Navarro.

It was in the period from the mid-1950s to the mid-1960s, however, that Blue Note's reputation became firmly established. Focusing on hard bop and soul jazz, the label developed its own distinctive sound, releasing classic recordings by Jimmy Smith, Horace Silver and Art Blakey, among many others. The funky sound of Jimmy

Smith's Hammond organ typified Blue Note's output in this period, and Smith went on to record more than 30 albums for the label.

Although slow to embrace the LP format, issuing its first 12″ (30 cm) long-playing record only in 1955, Blue Note soon became renowned for the unprecedented quality and sound balance of its recordings. Most of them were engineered by Rudy Van Gelder at his studios in Hackensack and, from 1959 onward, at Englewood Cliffs, New Jersey. The introduction of the LP also offered new opportunities for album cover design, and the Blue Note label became as famous for the high standard of its cover art as for the quality of its music and recording. The innovative design work of photographer Francis Wolff and graphic designer Reid Miles has continued to be highly influential and widely imitated.

In the early 1960s, Blue Note continued to record the hard bop and soul jazz that had become its trademark, releasing bestselling albums by Lee Morgan and Horace Silver, as well as important sessions by younger performers such as Herbie Hancock and Wayne Shorter. During this period, the label's musical policy also expanded to embrace the avant-garde: it released significant recordings by such free-jazz pioneers as Eric Dolphy, Ornette Coleman and Cecil Taylor.

Following the purchase of Blue Note by Liberty Records in 1965, Alfred Lion continued with the company until his retirement in 1967. Francis Wolff remained involved with Blue Note until his death in 1971. In the 1970s, the label began recording the jazz-rock and fusion of the period, releasing a major bestselling album by Donald Byrd in 1972. Although the label's reputation declined somewhat throughout the 1970s, the purchase of Liberty by EMI in 1980 and the subsequent transfer of Blue Note to Manhattan Records (a subsidiary of Capitol) signaled a resurgence of interest in the label. Beginning in 1985, a major program of reissues and new recordings (including those by contemporary artists such as Cassandra Wilson, Joe Lovano and Dianne Reeves) reaffirmed Blue Note's continuing significance in the history and development of jazz, and the classic Blue Note sound went on to become an integral part of the acid jazz scene in the late 1980s and the 1990s.

Bibliography

Cuscuna, Michael, and Ruppli, Michel. 1988. *The Blue Note Label: A Discography (Discographies, No. 29)*. Westport, CT: Greenwood Press.

Cuscuna, Michael, et al. 1995. *The Blue Note Years: The Jazz Photography of Francis Wolff*. New York: Rizzoli.

Marsh, Graham, and Callingham, Glyn, eds. 1997. *Blue Note 2: The Album Cover Art*. San Francisco: Chronicle Books.

Marsh, Graham, Cromey, Felix, and Callingham, Glyn, eds. 1991. *Blue Note: The Album Cover Art*. San Francisco: Chronicle Books.

Discographical Reference

Byrd, Donald. *Black Byrd*. Blue Note 84466. *1972*: USA.

Discography

Ammons, Albert, and Lewis, Meade 'Lux.' *The First Day*. Blue Note 98450. 1939: USA.

Bechet, Sidney. *The Best of Sidney Bechet*. Blue Note 28891. *1994*: USA.

The Best of Blue Note, Vols. 1 and 2. Blue Note 96110/97960. *1991*: USA.

Blakey, Art. *The Best of Art Blakey and the Jazz Messengers: The Blue Note Years*. Blue Note 93205. *1991*: USA.

Blakey, Art. *The History of Art Blakey and the Jazz Messengers* (3 CDs). Blue Note 97190. *1992*: USA.

The Blue Note Years, 1939–1999 (14 CDs). Blue Note 96427B. *1998*: USA.

Coleman, Ornette. *At the Golden Circle, Stockholm, Vols. 1 and 2*. Blue Note 84224/84225. *1965*: USA.

Dolphy, Eric. *Out to Lunch*. Blue Note 46524. *1964*: USA.

Hancock, Herbie. *The Best of Herbie Hancock: The Blue Note Years*. Blue Note 91142. *1988*: USA.

Lovano, Joe. *From the Soul*. Blue Note 98636. *1992*: USA.

Monk, Thelonious. *The Best of Thelonious Monk: The Blue Note Years*. Blue Note 95636. *1991*: USA.

Monk, Thelonious. *The Complete Blue Note Recordings* (4 CDs). Blue Note 30363. *1994*: USA.

Morgan, Lee. *The Sidewinder*. Blue Note 84157. *1963*: USA.

Navarro, Fats, and Dameron, Tadd. *The Complete Blue Note and Capitol Recordings of Fats Navarro and Tadd Dameron* (2 CDs). Blue Note 33373. *1995*: USA.

The New Groove: The Blue Note Remix Project. Blue Note 36594. *1996*: USA.

Powell, Bud. *The Best of Bud Powell: The Blue Note Years*. Blue Note 93204. *1989*: USA.

Powell, Bud. *The Complete Blue Note and Roost Recordings* (4 CDs). Blue Note 30083. *1994*: USA.

Quebec, Ike. *1944–1946*. Jazz Chronological Classics 957. *1997*: USA.

Reeves, Dianne. *I Remember*. Blue Note 90264. *1991*: USA.

Reminiscing at Blue Note: Blue Note's Early Classic Piano Sessions. Blue Note 28893. *1994*: USA.

Shorter, Wayne. *The Best of Wayne Shorter: The Blue Note Years*. Blue Note 91141. *1988*: USA.

Silver, Horace. *Song for My Father*. Blue Note 84185. *1964*: USA.

Silver, Horace. *The Best of Horace Silver: The Blue Note Years, Vols. 1 and 2*. Blue Note 91143/93206. *1989*: USA.

Smith, Jimmy. *Back at the Chicken Shack*. Blue Note 84117. *1960*: USA.

Smith, Jimmy. *The Best of Jimmy Smith: The Blue Note Years*. Blue Note 91140. *1988*: USA.

Straight No Chaser: The Most Popular, Most Sampled Songs from the Vaults of Blue Note (2 CDs). Blue Note 28263. *1995*: USA.

Taylor, Cecil. *Unit Structures*. Blue Note 84237. *1966*: USA.

Wilson, Cassandra. *Blue Light 'Til Dawn*. Blue Note 81357. *1993*: USA.

ALAN STANBRIDGE

—Boucherie Productions (France)

Founded in 1986 by songwriter and performer François Hadji-Lazaro, the label Boucherie Productions is one of the few survivors of the so-called *rock alternatif* in France. The name of the label comes from Les Garçons Bouchers, Hadji-Lazaro's band, and his decision to create Boucherie Productions was prompted by his inability to find a label to produce the band's first album.

Success soon came, and Boucherie Productions signed a variety of artists, including Mano Negra, who produced the label's first gold album in 1988, and Pigalle, also led by Hadji-Lazaro. Very much an independent label, Boucherie Productions quickly understood the necessity of making concessions to market forces, despite criticism from the other independent labels. In 1990, Hadji-Lazaro engaged a manager, but remained the A&R man.

Boucherie became the principal label for *rock alternatif*, although it signed bands that were associated with other styles, such as reggae or *chanson française*. This diversification became more obvious in 1992, when it launched three subsidiary labels: Acousteak (entirely devoted to local folk music); Chantons sous la truie (*chanson française*); and Abatrash (trash-oriented music). However, the Boucherie label has continued to be used for other musical styles. Despite this policy of signing a variety of performers and styles, the label is often associated with popular music of the 1980s. Although not as emblematic of alternative music as it used to be, Boucherie Productions at the end of the twentieth century had a catalog of more than 80 releases and was still one of the most important independent labels in France.

Discography

Les Garçons Bouchers. *La Saga*. Boucherie Productions BP 1121. *1990*: France.

L'Eventail Sonore. Boucherie Productions BP 1046. *1998*: France.

Mano Negra. *Patchanka*. Boucherie Productions 101 402. *1988*: France.

Pigalle. 'Dans la Salle du Bar-Tabac de la Rue des Mar-tyrs.' *Regards affligés*. Boucherie Productions BP 1034. *1990*: France.

AYMERIC PICHEVIN

—Brunswick Records (US)

The Brunswick label was founded in 1916 by the Brunswick-Balke-Collender Company, manufacturers of player pianos and billiard balls. Shortly after its inception, the label began issuing vertical-cut discs in Canada, as opposed to the lateral-cut discs that were subsequently issued in the United States in the 1920s.

Key to the company's success were the energy and expertise of producer Jack Kapp. He joined the firm in 1925 when Brunswick purchased the Vocalion company, and was put in charge of the 'race' record division. His primary legacy, however, is with the popular vocalists and dance bands of the day. Kapp was 'known in the trade as a "man of no taste, so corny he's good"' (Sanjek 1988, 126). He disdained the use of radio airplay and believed instead that the technical quality of a recording, combined with a catchy, memorable melody, captured and held the attention of consumers. Brunswick gained an entry into the mass market when it purchased Al Jolson's contract from Columbia. He was attracted by the offer of $10,000 per usable side, a one-third increase over his previous contract. Jolson's renditions of 'Sonny Boy' and 'There's A Rainbow 'Round My Shoulder' sold over a million copies. Similar success was achieved with the recordings released by Bing Crosby, the Boswell Sisters, the Mills Brothers and a number of popular dance bands, including Ted Lewis, Isham Jones, and Guy Lombardo and His Royal Canadians.

The Depression forced the sale of Brunswick, together with other holdings of the Brunswick-Balke-Collender Company, to Warner Brothers in 1930. The Brunswick label and the Brunswick-Balke-Collender Company were in turn purchased by the American Record Company (ARC) in 1931. Shortly thereafter, Kapp left Brunswick, having been hired by Edward Lewis, the founder of Decca (UK), to set up the US branch of Decca. CBS purchased ARC in 1938 and discontinued the Brunswick line.

The label was subsequently acquired by Decca (US) in 1943. In 1957, Decca's Bob Thiele revived Brunswick as a specialty label for rhythm and blues (R&B) and rock 'n' roll. Among its most popular artists were African-American vocalist Jackie Wilson, and Buddy Holly and the Crickets performing their early work. Wilson's manager, Nat Tarnopol, acquired the label in 1960 as an R&B outlet, and signed Barbara Acklin and the Chi-Lites. Brunswick's subsidiary label Dakar, established in 1967 by former OKeh A&R man Carl Davis, had a major hit in the charts in 1968 with Tyrone Davis's 'Can I Change

My Mind.' Tarnopol's reputation was tarnished by the taint of payola, and the company went out of business in 1976 when he was prosecuted for payola-connected infractions.

In 1984, the Brunswick catalog was sold to MCA, the original purchaser of Decca.

Bibliography

Dixon, Robert M.W., and Godrich, John. 1970. *Recording the Blues*. New York: Stein & Day.

Sanjek, Russell. 1988. *American Popular Music and Its Business: The First Four Hundred Years. Vol. III: From 1900 to 1984*. New York: Oxford University Press.

Sanjek, Russell, and Sanjek, David. 1996. *Pennies from Heaven: The American Popular Music Business in the Twentieth Century*. New York: Da Capo Press.

Discographical References

Davis, Tyrone. 'Can I Change My Mind.' Dakar 602. *1968*: USA. Reissue: Davis, Tyrone. 'Can I Change My Mind.' *The Brunswick Years, Vol. 1*. Brunswick 81009. *1995*: USA.

Jolson, Al. 'Sonny Boy.' Brunswick 4033. 1928: USA. Reissue: Jolson, Al. 'Sonny Boy.' *The Al Jolson Story, Part 3 (Rainbow 'Round My Shoulder)*. MCA 27053. *1987*: USA.

Jolson, Al. 'There's A Rainbow 'Round My Shoulder.' Brunswick 4033. 1928: USA. Reissue: Jolson, Al. 'There's A Rainbow 'Round My Shoulder.' *The Al Jolson Story, Part 3 (Rainbow 'Round My Shoulder)*. MCA 27053. *1987*: USA.

Discography

Acklin, Barbara. *Greatest Hits*. Brunswick 81003. *1995*: USA.

Acklin, Barbara. *Love Makes a Woman*. Brunswick 754137. *1968*: USA. Reissue: Acklin, Barbara. *Love Makes a Woman*. Brunswick 3005. *1998*: USA.

Boswell Sisters, The. *That's How Rhythm Was Born*. Sony 66977. *1995*: USA.

Boswell Sisters, The. *The Boswell Sisters 1932–1934*. Biograph BL/C/3. *1972*: USA.

Boswell Sisters, The. *The Boswell Sisters Collection, Vol. 1: 1931–1932*. Collector's Classics 21. *1996*: Denmark.

Boswell Sisters, The. *The Boswell Sisters, Vol. 2, 1930–35: It Don't Mean A Thing If It Ain't Got That Swing*. Biograph BLP-C16. *1984*: USA.

Chandler, Gene. *The Brunswick Years: 1966–1969*. Westside 227. *1999*: USA.

Chi-Lites, The. *A Lonely Man*. Brunswick 754179. *1972*: USA. Reissue: Chi-Lites, The. *A Lonely Man*. Brunswick 3009. *1998*: USA.

Chi-Lites, The. *Give More Power to the People*. Brunswick BL-754170. *1971*: USA. Reissue: Chi-Lites, The. *Give More Power to the People*. Brunswick 3008. *1998*: USA.

Chi-Lites, The. *Greatest Hits*. Rhino 70532. *1992*: USA.

Crosby, Bing. *Rare Brunswick Recordings (1930–1931)*. MCA 1502. *1982*: USA.

Holly, Buddy. *Best of Buddy Holly: 20th Century Masters*. MCA 11956. *1999*: USA.

Holly, Buddy, and the Crickets. *Buddy Holly* (EP). Brunswick 9456-7. *1959*: USA. Reissue: Holly, Buddy, and the Crickets. *Buddy Holly*. Castle NEM630. *1994*: UK.

Jones, Isham, and His Orchestra. *Swinging Down the Lane: 1923–1930*. Memphis Archives 7014. *1995*: USA.

Jones, Isham, and His Orchestra. *The Panico Period*. Retrieval FG404. *1977*: UK.

Lombardo, Guy, and His Royal Canadians. *Enjoy Yourself: Hits of Guy Lombardo*. MCA 11501. *1996*: USA.

Mills Brothers, The. *Chronological, Vols. 1–6*. JSP 301–304, 320, 345. *1994*: USA.

Ted Lewis Orchestra, The. *Ted Lewis Orchestra, Vols. 1–2 (1926–1933)*. Biograph BLPC7, BLPC8. *1973*: USA.

The Brunswick Years, Vol. 1. Brunswick 81009. *1995*: USA.

Wilson, Jackie. *The Soul Years*. Brunswick 33004. *1999*: USA.

Wilson, Jackie. *The Very Best of Jackie Wilson*. Rhino 71559. *1994*: USA.

DAVID SANJEK

—Capitol Records (US)

The founders of Capitol Records in Los Angeles in 1942 were notable participants in the popular music business: songwriter/performer Johnny Mercer, Paramount Pictures executive (and member of the noted songwriting team De Sylva, Brown and Henderson) Buddy De Sylva and record store owner Glenn Wallichs. Soon after the label's inauguration, the music industry faced a record ban as the result of a strike by members of the American Federation of Musicians, which lasted from 1942 to 1944. However, Capitol quickly thereafter established itself as a leading contender in the marketplace. Its early roster of artists was diverse, with a particularly strong contingent of country stars: Tex Ritter, Tennessee Ernie Ford, the Louvin Brothers and Merle Travis. One of the most successful of the artists was vocalist Tex Williams, whose 1947 comedic monolog 'Smoke! Smoke! Smoke! (That Cigarette),' which he co-wrote with Merle Travis, sold over a million copies. In the 1950s and 1960s, Capitol continued to produce prominent country artists, most notably those connected with the 'Bakersfield sound': Merle Haggard and Buck Owens. Mainstream pop was another strong area in the label's catalog. A number of songs by Frank Sinatra, Dean Martin, Nat 'King' Cole, Peggy Lee and the band leader Stan Kenton rose to the top of the charts. Of special note was Capitol's relationship with Sinatra, a relationship that saw the rebirth of the singer's career with albums such as *Songs for Swingin' Lovers!* (1956), featuring the arrangements of Nelson Riddle.

In 1955, the British company EMI acquired a controlling interest in Capitol. This gave the domestic label access to foreign products, but the relationship did not demonstrate significant commercial viability until the acquisition of the Beatles in 1963 (Capitol in fact refused to issue the first few Beatles records, which were licensed by EMI to Vee-Jay). Before this, Capitol had not had much impact in the rock 'n' roll market, despite releases by Gene Vincent and the Blue Caps. The British quartet and the stream of successful songs by the Beach Boys changed all that. Rock 'n' roll dominated Capitol's catalog during the 1960s. It revived the Tower label in 1964, on which was featured work by the British fad phenomenon Freddie and the Dreamers, the garage band the Standells, and the British psychedelic quartet Pink Floyd. When San Francisco achieved cultural prominence, Capitol signed Quicksilver Messenger Service and the Steve Miller Band. Middle-of-the-road artists were courted as well, most notably Glen Campbell, Helen Reddy and Anne Murray, while one of the most critically acclaimed rock bands of the period, the Band, released all its material on Capitol.

During the 1970s, Capitol signed a number of successful rhythm and blues artists – Tavares, Maze and Natalie Cole – and in the same period also acquired international distribution rights for the work of soul diva Diana Ross. As an age of 'superstars' took over the music industry, Capitol benefited from domestic distribution of the work of Paul McCartney and his band Wings. At the same time, the label faced a series of legal, as well as fiscal, dilemmas. A succession of unsuccessful recordings, as well as the breakup of the Beatles, drove down the value of Capitol stock. Stockholders also took issue with the choice of repertoire, as well as with the handling of record dealer discounts. The resulting lawsuit took more than a few years to settle. In 1979, Thorn Electronics purchased EMI for $348 million. Country singer Garth Brooks was Capitol's biggest-selling artist of the 1990s. The roster also included Bonnie Raitt, Bob Seger and the Beastie Boys, whose Grand Royal label was marketed by Capitol.

Bibliography

Sanjek, Russell, and Sanjek, David. 1996. *Pennies from Heaven: The American Popular Music Business in the Twentieth Century.* New York: Da Capo Press.

Discographical References

Sinatra, Frank. *Songs for Swingin' Lovers!*. Capitol 46570. *1956*: USA. Reissue: Sinatra, Frank. *Songs for Swingin' Lovers!*. Alliance 46570. *1996*: USA.

Williams, Tex. 'Smoke! Smoke! Smoke! (That Cigarette).' Capitol A 40001. *1947*: USA. Reissue: Williams, Tex. 'Smoke! Smoke! Smoke! (That Cigarette).' *Vintage Collections Series*. Capitol 36184. *1996*: USA.

Discography

Band, The. *Anthology*. Capitol 11856. *1978*: USA.

Beach Boys, The. *Greatest Hits, Vol. 1*. Capitol 21860. *1999*: USA.

Beach Boys, The. *Greatest Hits, Vol. 2*. Capitol 20238. *1999*: USA.

Beastie Boys, The. *Check Your Head*. Capitol C2-98938. *1992*: USA. Reissue: Beastie Boys, The. *Check Your Head*. Grand Royal 66. *1998*: USA.

Beastie Boys, The. *Paul's Boutique*. Capitol C2-91743. *1989*: USA. Reissue: Beastie Boys, The. *Paul's Boutique*. Grand Royal 65. *1999*: USA.

Beatles, The. *1962–1966*. Capitol C1-90435. *1973*: USA. Reissue: Beatles, The. *1962–1966*. Capitol 97036. *1994*: USA.

Beatles, The. *1967–1970*. Capitol C1-90438. *1973*: USA. Reissue: Beatles, The. *1967–1970*. Capitol 97039. *1994*: USA.

Beatles, The. *The Beatles Collection [14 LP Box]*. Capitol BC-13. *1978*: USA.

Blue Caps, The. *Legendary Blue Caps*. Magnum 89. *1996*: USA.

Brooks, Garth. *Double Live*. Capitol 97424. *1998*: USA.

Brooks, Garth. *In the Life of Chris Gaines*. Capitol 20051. *1999*: USA.

Brooks, Garth. *Limited Series*. Capitol 94572. *1998*: USA.

Brooks, Garth. *Sevens*. Capitol 56599. *1997*: USA.

Campbell, Glen. *Gentle on My Mind: The Collection (1962–1989)*. Razor & Tie 2129. *1997*: USA.

Cole, Natalie. *The Collection*. Capitol 16310. *1988*: USA.

Cole, Nat 'King.' *Nat King Cole [Capitol]*. Capitol C2-99777. 1943–64; *1992*: USA.

Cole, Nat 'King.' *The Greatest Hits [Capitol]*. Capitol 29687. 1944–63; *1994*: USA. Reissue: Cole, Nat 'King'. *The Greatest Hits [Capitol]*. DCC 1127. *1998*: USA.

Ford, Tennessee Ernie. *The Ultimate Collection (1949–1965)*. Razor & Tie 2134. *1997*: USA.

Ford, Tennessee Ernie. *Vintage Collections Series*. Capitol 54319. *1997*: USA.

Freddie and the Dreamers. *Best of Freddie & the Dreamers [Capitol]*. Capitol 11896. *1977*: USA.

Haggard, Merle. *A&E Biography*. Capitol 20304. *1999*: USA.

Haggard, Merle. *Vintage Collections Series*. Capitol 33838. *1996*: USA.

Kenton, Stan. *Retrospective*. Capitol B2-97350. 1943–68; *1992*: USA.

Lee, Peggy. *Capitol Collectors Series, Vol. 1: The Early*

Years. Capitol C2-93195. *1990*: USA. Reissue: Lee, Peggy. *Capitol Collectors Series, Vol. 1: The Early Years*. Alliance 93195. *1996*: USA.

Lee, Peggy. *The Best of Miss Peggy Lee*. Capitol 97308. *1998*: USA.

Louvin Brothers, The. *When I Stop Dreaming: The Best of the Louvin Brothers*. Razor & Tie 2068. *1995*: USA.

Martin, Dean. *Capitol Collectors Series*. Capitol C2-91633. *1989*: USA.

Maze. *Anthology*. Capitol 35885. *1996*: USA.

McCartney, Paul. *All the Best [US]*. Capitol C2-48287. *1987*: USA.

McCartney, Paul, and Wings. *Band on the Run Radio Interview*. Capitol PRO-2955/56. *1973*: USA.

Murray, Anne. *Snowbird*. Capitol 579. *1970*: USA.

Owens, Buck. *The Best of Buck Owens*. Capitol T-2105. *1964*: USA. Reissue: Owens, Buck. *The Best of Buck Owens*. Rhino 71816. *1994*: USA.

Owens, Buck. *The Best of Buck Owens, Vol. 2*. Capitol ST 2897. *1968*: USA. Reissue: Owens, Buck. *The Best of Buck Owens, Vol. 2*. Rhino 71817. *1994*: USA.

Pink Floyd. *Dark Side of the Moon*. Capitol C2-81479. *1973*: USA. Reissue: Pink Floyd. *Dark Side of the Moon [Twentieth Anniversary Limited Edition]*. Capitol C2-81479. *1993*: USA.

Pink Floyd. *Pink Floyd [Tower]*. Tower ST-5093. *1967*: USA.

Pink Floyd. *The Piper at the Gates of Dawn*. Tower ST-5093. *1967*: USA. Reissue: Pink Floyd. *The Piper at the Gates of Dawn*. EMI 59857. *1999*: USA.

Pink Floyd. *Works*. Capitol C2-46478. *1987*: USA.

Quicksilver Messenger Service. *The Best of Quicksilver Messenger Service [Capitol]*. Capitol 57263. *1990*: USA.

Raitt, Bonnie. *Fundamental*. Capitol 56397. *1998*: USA.

Raitt, Bonnie. *Longing in Their Hearts*. Capitol 81427. *1994*: USA.

Raitt, Bonnie. *Luck of the Draw*. Capitol C2-96111. *1991*: USA. Reissue: Raitt, Bonnie. *Luck of the Draw*. DCC 2031. *1997*: USA.

Raitt, Bonnie. *Nick of Time*. Capitol C2-91268. *1988*: USA. Reissue: Raitt, Bonnie. *Nick of Time*. DCC 2025. *1996*: USA.

Reddy, Helen. *Greatest Hits*. Capitol 46490. *1975*: USA.

Reddy, Helen. *Helen Reddy's Greatest Hits (And More)*. Capitol 746490. *1987*: USA.

Reddy, Helen. *I Am Woman: The Essential Helen Reddy Collection*. Razor & Tie 82180. *1998*: USA.

Ritter, Tex. *Capitol Collectors Series*. Capitol C2-95036. *1992*: USA.

Ritter, Tex. *High Noon*. Bear Family 15634. *1992*: Germany.

Ritter, Tex. *Vintage Collections Series*. Capitol 36903. *1997*: USA.

Seger, Bob. *Greatest Hits*. Capitol 30334. *1994*: USA.

Sinatra, Frank. *The Capitol Collectors Series*. Capitol C2-92160. *1989*: USA. Reissue: Sinatra, Frank. *The Capitol Collectors Series*. Capitol 92160. *1992*: USA.

Sinatra, Frank. *The Capitol Years: The Best of Frank Sinatra*. Capitol C2-94777. *1990*: USA. Reissue: Sinatra, Frank. *The Capitol Years: The Best of Frank Sinatra*. Capitol 99225. *1992*: USA.

Standells, The. *The Best of the Standells*. Rhino R2-70176. *1984*: USA.

Steve Miller Band, The. *Anthology*. Capitol 12. *1972*: USA. Reissue: Steve Miller Band, The. *Anthology*. Alliance 94488. *1996*: USA.

Steve Miller Band, The. *Greatest Hits 1974–1978*. Capitol C2-46101. *1987*: USA. Reissue: Steve Miller Band, The. *Greatest Hits 1974–1978*. DCC 2028. *1997*: USA.

Tavares. *Capitol Gold: The Best of Tavares*. Alliance 89380. *1996*: USA.

Tavares. *The Best of Tavares*. Capitol C2-91640. 1977; *1989*: USA. Reissue: Tavares. *The Best of Tavares*. EMI-Capitol Special Markets 56708. *1995*: USA.

Travis, Merle. *Back Home*. Capitol T-891. *1957*: USA.

Travis, Merle. *Folk Songs of the Hills [expanded]*. Capitol 35810. *1996*: USA.

Travis, Merle. *Songs of the Coal Mines*. Capitol ST-1956. *1963*: USA.

Travis, Merle. *Strictly Guitar*. Capitol ST-2938. *1969*: USA.

Travis, Merle. *The Merle Travis Guitar*. Capitol T-650. *1956*: USA.

Travis, Merle. *Walkin' the Strings*. Capitol T-1391. *1960*: USA. Reissue: Travis, Merle. *Walkin' the Strings*. Capitol 35809. *1996*: USA.

Vincent, Gene. *Capitol Collectors Series*. Capitol C2-94074. *1990*: USA. Reissue: Vincent, Gene. *Capitol Collectors Series*. Alliance 94074. *1996*: USA.

Vincent, Gene. *The Capitol Years 1956–63*. Charly BOX 108. *1987*: UK.

Williams, Tex. *Vintage Collections Series*. Capitol 36184. *1996*: USA.

Wings. *Wings Greatest*. EMI 256. *1978*: UK. Reissues: Wings. *Wings Greatest*. Capitol C2-46056. *1986*: USA; EMI 89317. *1999*: UK.

Visual Recordings

Brooks, Garth. 1991. 'Garth Brooks [Video].' Capitol 40023 (video).

Brooks, Garth. 1996. 'Video Collection, Vol. 2.' Capitol 77820 (video).

Raitt, Bonnie. 1995. 'Road Tested [Video].' Capitol 77786 (video).

DAVID SANJEK

—Capricorn (US)

A record company and label founded in the US state of Georgia in 1969 by Phil Walden, Capricorn specialized in 'Southern boogie' rock music. Walden had been the manager of Otis Redding and, following Redding's death in 1967, he signed the Allman Brothers Band and launched his new label.

Others on the label included rock groups Wet Willie and the Marshall Tucker Band, country music veteran Kitty Wells and singer-songwriter Livingston Taylor. The label's high-living image was epitomized by the annual Capricorn picnic, a major southern music event, and Walden was a leading supporter of Jimmy Carter in his successful presidential campaign of 1976.

The label was declared bankrupt in the late 1970s, a victim of the recession in the music industry. Walden restarted Capricorn in 1988, but could not recapture the label's period of glory.

Discography

Allman Brothers Band, The. *Eat a Peach*. Capricorn CX4-0102. *1972*: USA.

Marshall Tucker Band, The. *Searchin' for a Rainbow*. Capricorn CP 0161. *1975*: USA.

Taylor, Livingston. *Over the Rainbow*. Capricorn CP 0114. *1973*: USA.

Wells, Kitty. *Forever Young*. Capricorn 146. *1974*: USA.

Wet Willie. *Dixie Rock*. Capricorn CP 0149. *1975*: USA.

DAVE LAING

—Carl Lindström AG (Germany)

Carl Lindström AG was a German record and phonograph company, founded in Berlin in 1904 by the Swedish engineer Carl Lindström (1867–1932). Lindström had come to Berlin in 1897 and started a clock repair company. Soon after, he developed his own phonograph machine, the Lyra-Phonograph, which was marketed worldwide under the name 'Puck.' It formed the basis for the Lindström empire. In 1910, Carl Lindström AG took over the German Beka-Rekord AG and, with this, began its involvement in the recording business. By the following year, Carl Lindström AG was already represented in Britain, France, Italy, Spain and Austria as a consequence of an aggressive strategy of takeovers. In the same year, it acquired the International Talking Machine Company – at that time one of the leading European manufacturers of records – which operated the German record label Odeon, among others. Parlophon also began life as a Carl Lindström AG label in the early years of the twentieth century.

Carl Lindström AG went on to cover all areas of early recording and was one of the first genuinely European record companies operating worldwide – forming in 1913, for example, the Discos Nacional company in Argentina, which issued the first recordings of the renowned tango singer Carlos Gardél. Because of its worldwide operations, it was severely affected by the

events of World War I: its assets were confiscated in several countries as being enemy-related, and it had to confront war-related currency upheavals and trade barriers.

The company recovered only slowly after World War I. Early in the century, shares in Carl Lindström AG had been purchased by Otto Heineman, a German businessman. Otto Heineman then went to the United States in 1914 with his brother Adolph to study industrial conditions for the rapidly expanding Lindström organization. Stranded in the United States at the outbreak of German hostilities, the Heineman brothers formed an import company at 45 Broadway, New York. Otto Heineman went on to purchase a string of companies that manufactured phonograph parts and, in the spring of 1918, he established OKeh Records in New York. In October 1919, Heineman reorganized his business interests into the General Phonograph Corporation, of which OKeh became a part. The General Phonograph Corporation was financed by and closely allied with the powerful Carl Lindström organization (Sutton 1998) and, in this way, OKeh became a subsidiary of Lindström. Lindström operated OKeh Records until both were sold to Columbia in 1926. As the producer of the first record by a black artist, 'Crazy Blues' by Mamie Smith, OKeh played an important role in the history of popular music.

In 1920, the Ukrainian-born Dajos Bela became Lindström's musical director and, with his various orchestras, went on to record thousands of popular titles, which were issued throughout Europe and the Americas.

However, despite its attempts to recover from the effects of war-related events, Carl Lindström AG was affected by the German recession in the early 1920s and, as a consequence, was taken over by Columbia (UK) in 1926. As part of Columbia (UK) and, later, EMI, Lindström was operated until World War II as a label that represented the valuable cataloging of the early history of recording in all musical areas.

After Hitler came to power in Germany in 1933, circumstances became increasingly difficult for EMI employees in all its German branches. Several Lindström managers had already been arrested in 1933 for pressing so-called 'subversive' records by Jewish musicians. The beginning of World War II marked the end of foreign business activities in Germany.

The Lindström division was closed down with the restructuring of EMI's interests on the German market under the umbrella of EMI Electrola in the 1950s.

Bibliography

50 Jahre Carl Lindström GmbH: 1904–1954 [50 Years of Carl Lindström GmbH: 1904–1954]. 1954. Köln Braunsfeld: Carl Lindström GmbH.

Gronow, Pekka, and Saunio, Ilpo. 1998. *An International*

History of the Recording Industry. London and New York: Cassell.

Kultur und Schallplatte – Mitteilungen der Carl Lindström Kultur Abteilung [Culture and Records – Publications from the Cultural Division of Carl Lindström AG]. 1929. Berlin: Carl Lindström AG.

Martland, Peter. 1997. *Since Records Began: EMI, the First 100 Years*. London: Batsford.

Sutton, Allan. 1998. 'The Origins of OKeh.' *The Mainspring: A Free Online Journal for Collectors of Vintage Records*. http://www.mainspringpress.com/articles.html

Discographical Reference

Smith, Mamie. 'Crazy Blues'/'It's Right Here for You.' OKeh 4169. 1920: USA.

PETER WICKE

—Casa Edson (Brazil)

Casa Edson, located in Rio de Janeiro, was founded in 1900 by a Czech Jew, Frederico (Fred) Figner, who, since 1897, had been making cylinder recordings of Rio de Janeiro's street serenaders. Between 1902 and 1927, Casa Edson issued more than half of the 7,000 mechanical recordings produced in Brazil. These included records of the first Brazilian professional popular music artists, Bahiano (Manuel Pedro dos Santos), Cadete (Manuel Evêncio da Costa Moreira), Eduardo das Neves and Anacleto de Medeiros, performing *modinhas, cançonetas, lundus* and *maxixes*. Casa Edson also issued 'Pelo Telefone' (1917), which was composed by Ernesto dos Santos (Donga) and recorded by Bahiano – a recording famous as symbolizing the birth of modern *carioca* samba.

From 1902, Casa Edson sold US-imported Berliner gramophones and records from its headquarters in Rio de Janeiro and from its branch offices in the states of São Paulo, Minas Gerais, Bahia, Pará and Rio Grande do Sul. In 1904, Casa Edson released its own first commercial recordings (Fred Figner holding one-third of the rights), with technical support from German Zonophone. The wax cylinders were sent to Berliner's Hanover factory, transformed into copper matrices and reproduced, and then returned to Brazil (for example, the seven in the Zon-O-Phone 10.000 series and the 10 in the X-1.000 series). Also in 1904, Casa Edson started issuing International Talking Machine Odeon label records (like the Brazilian two-sided 10.5 in the 40.000 series).

In 1912, in association with Odeon, Fred Figner set up a record factory in Rio de Janeiro to press the records. From 1921, it issued recordings of successful artists of the new electronic era, like Francisco Alves, Araci Cortes and Patrício Teixeira. After 1927, Casa Edson and other labels were surpassed by Odeon, RCA-Victor and Columbia.

Bibliography

Franceschi, Humberto M. 1984. *Registro sonoro por meios mecânicos no Brasil* [Mechanical Recording in Brazil]. Rio de Janeiro: Studio HMF.

Santos, Alcino, et al., comps. 1982. *Discografia brasileira 78 r.p.m.: 1902–1964* [Discography of Brazilian 78s, 1902–1964]. 5 vols. Rio de Janeiro: Funarte.

Tinhorão, José Ramos. 1981. *Música Popular: do Gramofone ao Rádio e TV* [Popular Music: From the Gramophone to Radio and TV]. São Paulo: Editora Ática.

Discographical Reference

Bahiano. 'Pelo Telefone.' Odeon 121.322. 1917: Brazil.

Discography

Alves, Francisco. 'O que é nosso.' Odeon 123.270. 1927: Brazil.

Anacleto de Medeiros e a Banda do Corpo de Bombeiros do Rio de Janeiro. 'Albertina.' Zon-O-Phone 10.171. ca. 1902–1904: Brazil.

Bahiano. 'Isto é bom.' Zon-O-Phone 10.001. ca. 1902–1904: Brazil.

Cadete. 'A mulher.' Zon-O-Phone 10.101. ca. 1902–1904: Brazil.

Silva, Patápio. 'Zinha.' Odeon 10.011. ca. 1902–1904: Brazil.

JOSÉ ROBERTO ZAN (trans. MARTHA TUPINAMBÁ DE ULHÔA)

—CBS-Sony (Japan)

In 1968, the US record company CBS set up a Japanese subsidiary in partnership with the Sony Corporation. This label issued recordings by both Japanese and foreign artists and became one of the leading record companies in Japan. In 1988, the Sony Corporation purchased the CBS Records Group from the US parent company CBS Inc. for $2 billion. Now wholly owned by Sony, the Japanese branch was renamed Sony Music Entertainment Japan (SMEJ). During the following decade, SMEJ became the largest record company in Japan, with a market share of about 16 percent from its 60 labels. Its top-selling Japanese artists included Dreams Come True, and Judy and Mary.

Discography

Dreams Come True. *Love Unlimited*. Sony JPN-ESZB-1. 1996: Japan.

Judy and Mary. *The Power Source*. Sony JPN-ESCB-1805. 1997: Japan.

DAVE LAING

—CEFA (Democratic Republic of Congo)

CEFA (Compagnie d'Enregistrement du Folklore Africain) was one of several Greek-owned labels operating during the early 1950s in Leopoldville, the capital of the Belgian Congo (later Zaire, and then the Democratic

Republic of Congo). Despite its name, it was a label that recorded popular music. When the Belgian guitarist Bill Alexandre set up the studio in 1953, he provided the impetus to generate the continent's most potent music for the next five decades. Alexandre was a jazz guitarist, used to playing in European dance halls, who knew little about folklore music. He brought the first electric guitar to Leopoldville – in fact, he brought two Gibson Les Pauls, two amplifiers, a double bass, an Ampeg tape recorder and one Electro-Voice microphone. He recruited musicians, including the singer Vicky Longomba (at one time co-president of OK Jazz, the leading Congolese band of the period), bassist Roitelet, guitarist Brazzos and the percussionist Roger Izeidi, who later became label manager. After the closure of Opika Records (another Leopoldville label) in 1955, Joseph Kabasele's African Jazz recorded for the label. Alexandre's artistic influence was vital, but his technical expertise and awareness of the growing market enabled him to run the business almost single-handedly – from tuning guitars to playing on hit records, working the tape recorder and delivering 78 rpm discs in the company station wagon. CEFA masters were sent to Germany for pressing. Alexandre left Congo before independence in 1960, but later Izeidi brought OK Jazz to Paris to record 45 rpm singles for the label. Other artists with releases on the label during the 1960s were the 'Orchestres' Cobantou, Casanova and Jamel. Later, when OK Jazz split up, Vicky Longomba's records continued to come out on CEFA. Along with many other independent labels, CEFA was eventually taken over by the African label, managed by Roger Izeidi and owned by the Belgian company, Fonior.

Bibliography

Bemba, Sylvain. 1984. *50 ans de musique du congo-zaïre* [Fifty Years of Music of Congo-Zaïre]. Paris: Presence Africaine.

Ewens, Graeme. 1994. *Congo Colossus – The Life and Legacy of Franco and OK Jazz*. Norfolk, UK: Buku Press/ Sterns.

GRAEME EWENS

—Celluloïd (France)

The Celluloïd label was established in Paris in 1979 by Gilbert Castro, and went on to become a leading French specialist in African music, selling – through its distribution wing Mélodie – to France's African community and to the broader national market beyond. Its catalog includes recordings made in Paris, African productions released under license, world music titles from other continents, and some rock and jazz material.

Celluloïd has put out albums by many of Africa's big names, including Salif Keita, Mory Kanté, Youssou N'Dour, Johnny Clegg, the Gabon singer and composer Pierre Akendengue, and the 'barefoot diva' of Cape Verde music Cesaria Evora. Perhaps its greatest success has been the Senegalese band Touré Kunda, which broke into the French mainstream with sales of 100,000 each for their double album *Paris-Ziguinchor Live* and for *Toubab Bi* (issued by Trema/RCA).

Celluloïd set up a New York branch in 1981 under Jean Karakos. A split between Karakos and Castro occurred two years later, although the US company continued to use the parent name. The mid-1980s saw New York releases from Manu Dibango, Foday Musa Sosa, Touré Kunda and Fela Kuti, with production by Bill Laswell.

In France, Celluloïd continued to produce new albums throughout the 1990s, featuring artists such as *kora* player Jali Musa Jawara and Akendengue.

Other artists figuring in Celluloïd's catalog include Mbilia Bel, Lambarena, Ray Léma, Bevinda, Juan Carlos Caceres, El Cabrero, Lucky Dube, Sam Mangwana, Tshala Muana, Kanté Manfila, Kolinda, Djeli Moussa Diawara, Vasco Martins, Xalam, Stimela, Sarafina, Ngane and Khamba, and Barungwa.

Discographical References

Touré Kunda. *Paris-Ziguinchor Live*. Celluloïd CEL 6106. *1984*: France.

Touré Kunda. *Toubab Bi*. Trema/RCA 310 233. *1987*: France.

Discography

Bel, Mbilia. *Désolé*. Celluloïd 66887-2. *1991*: France.

Bonga. *Katendu*. Celluloïd 79567-2. *1994*: France.

Damba, Fanta. *Fanta Damba*. Celluloïd CEL 6637. *1982*: France.

Dens, Bibi, and Les Marymbas. *Bibi Dens and Les Marymbas*. Celluloïd 66874-4. *1997*: France.

Kanté, Mory. *N'Diarabi*. Celluloïd 66931-2. *1993*: France.

Keita, Salif. *Soro*. Celluloïd 66883-2. *1987*: France.

Keita, Salif, Manfila, Kanté, and Les Ambassadeurs. *Salif Keita, Kanté Manfila and Les Ambassadeurs*. Celluloïd CEL 6717. *1984*: France.

Kouyaté, Fode. *Djelia*. Celluloïd 66947-2. *1996*: France.

Kuti, Fela. *Army Arrangement*. Celluloïd CEL 6115. *1984*: USA.

Ladysmith Black Mambazo. *Homeless*. Celluloïd 66831-2. *1988*: France.

Léma, Ray. *Kinshasa/Washington D.C./Paris*. Celluloïd CEL 66658. *1997*: France.

Lucky Dube. *Captured Live*. Celluloïd 66889-2. *1991*: France.

Lucky Dube. *House of Exile*. Celluloïd 66899-2. *1991*: France.

Lucky Dube. *Slave*. Celluloïd 66834-2. *1988*: France.

Lucky Dube. *Together as One*. Celluloïd 66857-2. *1989*: France.

Mahlathini and the Mahotella Queens. *Paris-Soweto*. Celluloïd 66829-2. *1988*: France.

Mahlathini and the Mahotella Queens. *Thokozile*. Celluloïd 66818-2. *1987*: France.

Manfila, Kanté. *Tradition*. Celluloïd 66860-2. *1988*: France.

Mangwana, Sam. *Rumba Music*. Celluloïd 66928-2. *1993*: France.

Muana, Tshala. *Biduaya*. Celluloïd 66873-2. *1989*: France.

Munan, Maika. *African Swinger*. Celluloïd 66965-2. *1995*: France.

N'Dour, Youssou. *Djamil (Inédits 84–85)*. Celluloïd 66811-2. *1984*: France.

Shoogar Combo. *Kimbe dom*. Celluloïd 66932-2. *1993*: France.

Touré Kunda. *Amadou-Tilo*. Celluloïd CEL 6104. *1984*: USA.

Touré Kunda. *Casamance au clair de lune*. Celluloïd CEL 6102. *1984*: USA.

Touré Kunda. *Les Frères Griots*. Celluloïd CEL 6129. *1987*: USA.

Touré Kunda. *Natalia*. Celluloïd CEL 6113. *1985*: USA.

Vincent, Francky. *Les meilleurs succès de Francky Vincent*. Celluloïd 66905-2. *1992*: France.

Xalam. *Gorée*. Celluloïd 66656-2. *1983*: France.

CHRIS STAPLETON and GIUSY BASILE (trans. JOHN SHEPHERD)

—CGD (Italy)

CGD (Compagnia Generale del Disco) is an Italian record company that was founded in 1948 by singer Teddy Reno. It was purchased during the 1950s by Hungarian-born publisher Ladislao Sugar. In the early 1960s, it became one of the main record companies in Italy, with bestsellers like Johnny Dorelli's 'Love in Portofino' (1960) and Gigliola Cinquetti's 'Non ho l'età,' winner of the Sanremo Song Festival in 1964 and of the subsequent Eurovision Song Contest.

In 1966, Sugar entered an agreement with CBS and established CBS Italiana. In 1970, CGD and CBS Italiana merged to form CBS Sugar, which existed until 1977. CBS then established its own Italian subsidiary, and Sugar reverted to the original CGD trademark. When Ladislao Sugar died in 1981, his son Piero (husband of sixties pop star Caterina Caselli, one of CGD's top-selling artists) became president.

In 1988, CGD was the first Italian major record company to be sold to a multinational corporation, in this case WEA. Probably as a consequence of the strong position of music publishing within the group, CGD inclined more to mainstream pop than to the *canzone*

d'autore (Italy's singer-songwriter genre): big hits were Caterina Caselli's 'Nessuno mi può giudicare' (1966), a symbol of early hippie protest-pop; Massimo Ranieri's 'Rose rosse' (1969), an example of old-fashioned romantic song, or of very early Pavarotti-style pop; Loredana Berté's 'Sei bellissima' (1975); and Umberto Tozzi's 'Ti amo' (1977), an example of canonic and well-executed international mainstream pop.

Discographical References

Berté, Loredana. 'Sei bellissima.' CGD cgd 81178. *1975*: Italy.

Caselli, Caterina. 'Nessuno mi può giudicare.' CGD cgd n-9608. *1966*: Italy.

Cinquetti, Gigliola. 'Non ho l'età.' CGD cgd n-9486. *1964*: Italy.

Dorelli, Johnny. 'Love in Portofino.' CGD cgd fg-5096. *1960*: Italy.

Ranieri, Massimo. 'Rose rosse.' CGD cgd N-9724. *1969*: Italy.

Tozzi, Umberto. 'Ti amo.' CGD cgd 5272. *1977*: Italy.

FRANCO FABBRI

—Chess (US)

Chess, which was Chicago-based, was one of the principal independent labels in the decades following World War II, and it played a significant role in creating a market for deep blues, rhythm and blues (R&B) and rock 'n' roll. Chess traced its origin to Aristocrat, a label founded in 1947. Phil and Leonard Chess gradually bought out the company from its original owners, and in 1950 changed the label's name to Chess. Subsidiary labels added subsequently were Checker and Argo (later called Cadet).

Chess originally achieved major success with blues artists, notably Muddy Waters, Little Walter and Howlin' Wolf, but in the mid-1950s it became a factor in the exploding rock 'n' roll market when its R&B artists Chuck Berry, Bo Diddley, the Flamingos and the Moonglows crossed over onto the pop charts. The company also successfully expanded into the jazz (Ahmad Jamal, Ramsey Lewis Trio) and gospel (Norfleet Brothers, Meditation Singers) fields.

In the 1960s, Chess adapted to the emerging soul market by bringing in 'Billy' Roquel Davis from Detroit as A&R head and by beefing up its in-house production, arranging and writing staff. Among the company's successes in the soul market were Etta James, the Dells, the Radiants, Fontella Bass, Billy Stewart and Little Milton. Chess went into decline after 'Billy' Davis left in 1968 and Leonard Chess died in 1969. In 1970, the new owners of Chess moved its headquarters to New York, and in 1975 the label was closed down. At the end of the twentieth century, the Chess catalog was owned by the Universal Music Company (formerly known as MCA Records).

Bibliography

Fancourt, Leslie, comp. 1983. *Chess Blues Discography*. Faversham: Fancourt.

Fancourt, Leslie, comp. 1991. *A Discography of the R 'n' B Artists on the Chess Labels, 1947–1975*. Faversham: Fancourt.

Galkin, Peter. 1989a. 'Black, White and Blues: The Story of Chess Records, Part One.' *Living Blues* 88 (September–October): 22–32.

Galkin, Peter. 1989b. 'Black, White and Blues: The Story of Chess Records, Part Two.' *Living Blues* 89 (December): 25–29.

Gray, Michael. 1973. 'Chess at the Top.' *Let It Rock* (September): 30–33.

Guralnick, Peter. 1971. 'Chess Records: Before the Fall.' In *Feel Like Going Home*. New York: Outerbridge & Dienstfrey, 181–202.

Pruter, Robert. 1991. 'Chess Records.' In *Chicago Soul*. Urbana, IL: University of Illinois Press, 97–135.

Pruter, Robert. 1996. 'Chess Records.' In *Doowop: The Chicago Scene*. Urbana, IL: University of Illinois Press, 55–83.

Rowe, Mike. 1973. *Chicago Breakdown*. London: Eddison Press.

Ruppli, Michel. 1983. *The Chess Labels: A Discography* (*Discographies*, No. 7). Westport, CT: Greenwood Press.

Shaw, Arnold. 1978. 'Storefront Record Company.' In *Honkers and Shouters: The Golden Years of Rhythm and Blues*. New York: Macmillan, 289–314.

Discography

The Aristocrat of the Blues: The Best of Aristocrat Records. MCA/Chess CHD2-9387. *1997*: USA.

Chess Blues. MCA/Chess CHD4-9340. *1992*: USA.

Chess Club Rhythm & Soul. Kent CDKEND 134. *1996*: UK.

Chess Radio Soul. Kent CDKEND 133. *1996*: UK.

Chess Rhythm & Roll. MCA/Chess CHD4-9352. *1994*: USA.

Chess Soul: A Decade of Chicago's Finest. MCA/Chess CHD2-9388. *1997*: USA.

Chess Uptown Soul. Kent CDKEND 140. *1997*: UK.

The Golden Age of Rhythm & Blues. Chess 2CH 50030. *1972*: USA.

The History of Chess Jazz. MCA/GRP GRD-2-812. *1996*: USA.

None But The Righteous: Chess Gospel Greats. MCA/Chess CHD-9336. *1992*: USA.

ROBERT PRUTER

—Chrysalis (UK)

A UK label founded in 1969 by group managers Chris Wright and Terry Ellis (Chris-Ellis), Chrysalis became a leading international independent company before its takeover by EMI in 1992.

Chrysalis sold millions of albums around the world through Jethro Tull, Ten Years After, Procol Harum, Steeleye Span, Spandau Ballet and others, and expanded into the studio business in 1974 through buying AIR (co-owned by George Martin). The company later distributed such UK labels as 2-Tone (the Specials), Ensign (Sinead O'Connor) and Cooltempo.

Ellis moved to New York to start a US branch in 1975, where Chrysalis signings included Blondie, Pat Benatar and Huey Lewis and the News. He left the company in 1985 and later set up the Imago label. After selling the Chrysalis label to EMI, Wright invested in the UK broadcasting industry before starting the Echo label in 1993.

DAVE LAING

—Columbia (US)

Columbia was established as the Columbia Phonograph Company in 1888 in Washington, DC (taking its name from the 'District of Columbia') as part of the North American Phonograph Company, whose owner, J.P. Lippincott, had succeeded in merging the rival interests of the Edison phonograph and the Bell and Tainter graphophone. The company was incorporated in 1889.

Columbia issued the first-ever catalog of recordings in 1889 (Sutton 1994, 34). By 1891, the catalog contained 10 pages of cylinder recordings of marches, dance tunes, novelty and sentimental songs, and monologs (Dearling and Dearling 1984, 32), mainly for coin-in-the-slot jukeboxes at fairgrounds and exhibitions. A European office was opened in Paris in the same year, the headquarters moving to London in 1900. The company began issuing single-sided 78 rpm discs for the Globe Record Company in 1901, following this with its own Columbia label in 1902. It remained in cylinder production until 1912 (Dearling and Dearling 1984, 36), but concentrated increasingly on discs. The early days of disc manufacture were marked by numerous lawsuits over patent infringement. Once these were settled, around 1903, Columbia's fortunes steadily improved. Its business ranged from the manufacture of pressings for department store labels to its own double-sided discs, introduced in 1908.

Toward 1920, as record sales increased, Columbia made repeated, and often successful, attempts to prize popular recording artists away from other companies. During the 1920s, it became one of a number of rival companies recording across an expanding range of genres, including the music of mainstream dance bands and vocalists, blues, gospel and country music. It had recorded the music of immigrant groups since around 1908 and continued with this strand now, incorporating it as one of its numerous series (Dixon and Godrich 1970; Gronow 1977, 1979). The company's success in the field of blues recording followed the vision of Frank Walker, the first manager of Columbia's 'race' records list, in spotting and recording Bessie Smith in 1923. In 1925, the company became the first to record an African-American preacher, following which it introduced a number of individual preachers, such as Rev. J.M. Gates and Rev. J.C. Burnett, whose records would sell in significant quantities. The purchase of OKeh from the General Phonograph Corporation in 1926 gave the company access to the jazz, blues and hillbilly catalogs of that label, assembled by figures such as Ralph Peer (who had initiated the first country music recordings in 1923).

In the first half of the twentieth century, the company changed hands several times. Declared bankrupt in 1923, it was run by a consortium of managers before being sold in late 1924 for $2.5 million to British-based general manager Louis Sterling. Sterling had been sent by the company to set up a UK branch in 1909 and had himself purchased the same branch in 1923. This UK branch acquired several rivals, including Lindström of Germany and Odéon of France.

With his acquisition of Columbia (US), Sterling obtained a license to use the new electrical recording process developed by Western Electric in Los Angeles on Columbia records produced in the United Kingdom. In the wake of the stock market crash, Columbia (UK) merged with His Master's Voice to form EMI in 1931, but Sterling kept Columbia (US) out of the merger and shortly afterward sold it back across the Atlantic, evidently wary of possible antitrust action. Columbia (US) was thus no longer linked to Columbia (UK).

The purchaser of Columbia (US), Grigsby-Grunow, the manufacturer of the Majestic brand of radios and refrigerators, in turn sold it in 1934 to the American Record Company (ARC). ARC paid $70,000 for the company, adding it to a roster that included Brunswick and Vocalion. In 1938, ARC was in turn bought out by CBS (Columbia Broadcasting System), the radio network that had originally been created by Columbia in the late 1920s when it saw the increasing power of that medium.

Under CBS ownership, Columbia Records became one of the most powerful companies in the record industry. During the 1930s, 1940s and 1950s, Columbia gained a major share of the market in a variety of musical genres, releasing major work by, among others, Benny Goodman, Billie Holiday and Count Basie, as well as such mainstream performers as Doris Day and Frankie Laine. In 1948, Columbia was responsible for the introduction of the long-playing vinyl microgroove record, entering soon afterward into a damaging 'battle of the speeds' with arch-rival RCA-Victor, which had deliberately developed an alternative format, the 45 rpm 7" (18 cm) disc. Consumer uncertainty regarding the new formats ensured that the move to microgroove records was a slow one (Millard 1995, 207).

The popular music chief, Mitch Miller, dominated the mainstream pop sector with his meticulous productions for Tony Bennett, Doris Day, Frankie Laine, Barbra Streisand and his own *Sing Along* albums. Miller, however, was vehemently opposed to rock 'n' roll, and from the late 1950s Columbia lost ground to such companies as RCA-Victor, Decca, Mercury and MGM.

Goddard Lieberson assumed the direction of the label in 1956 and made his mark with original-cast recordings of Broadway musicals. His most notable achievement was Frederick Loewe's and Alan Jay Lerner's *My Fair Lady*, which eventually sold over 6 million copies. Lieberson was so convinced of the show's chances for success that he invested company money in the production, eventually acquiring the rights from the composers. He then sold the rights for the 1964 film to Warner Brothers for $5.5 million and a 47.5 percent share in whatever profits the film earned over $20 million.

In addition to Lieberson, others helped to assemble Columbia's impressive catalog. The renowned John Hammond brought Goodman, Holiday and Basie, and later Bob Dylan and Bruce Springsteen, to the company. However, even more important to the label's purse strings were the activities of Clive Davis, who became managing director in 1965. Columbia had failed to capitalize on rock 'n' roll, but Davis pursued rock acts relentlessly in the wake of the success of the 1967 Monterey Pop Festival, bringing to the company Janis Joplin, Santana, Moby Grape and Electric Flag, led by Mike Bloomfield. Under his direction, and in the wake of a 1964 report by the Harvard Business School which concluded that the company was strategically weak in the growing soul market, Columbia also reached out – as it had with the OKeh label – to the African-American community, signing a number of artists and producers in the early 1970s. Principal among them were Kenny Gamble and Leon Huff of Philly International Records, who wrote and produced a string of hits throughout the decade that were distributed by Columbia. Despite these and other successes, such as those with Sly and the Family Stone, Columbia never became a serious competitor to Warner and MCA in this sector.

In country music, Columbia had done well with Johnny Cash, and became a major force in the 1970s through the efforts of its Nashville A&R head Billy Sherrill, who produced such artists as Tammy Wynette, George Jones and Charlie Rich.

Last of the notable executives associated with the label was the eminently successful and flamboyant Walter

Yetnikoff. Under his direction, Columbia became one of the two largest companies in the US record industry, breaking such megastars as Bruce Springsteen and Michael Jackson, the latter achieving with *Thriller* (1982) an unbroken international sales record of over 40 million.

Yetnikoff engineered the sale of CBS Records to Sony in 1988 for $2 billion before retiring in 1990. He was succeeded by his former assistant, Thomas D. Mottola. Sony was then renamed Sony Music Entertainment (SME), although 'Columbia' was retained as the name of one of SME's labels.

CBS policy was that its various divisions should diversify, and the record company invested in instrument manufacture by purchasing Fender guitars, Leslie amplifiers and Rogers drums. CBS Records also set up the Columbia House record club in 1955 and added the Epic label when the Columbia roster became too large. Since 1990, Columbia House (which has remained the market leader in mail-order music) has been jointly owned by Sony Music and the Warner Music Group.

Historically, Columbia had regarded Latin America as an extension of its own market, and, starting in 1946 in Mexico, CBS Records opened a series of branch companies in the region. Until the early 1960s, CBS handled European markets through licensing agreements with such firms as EMI and Philips. The company then decided to set up its own branches, beginning with the United Kingdom (1963), France and Germany.

By the end of the 1990s, SME had branches in most countries of Europe, Asia and Latin America. Recordings by US artists made up the bulk of the sales of these branches, although there were exceptions such as France, where Sony was the market leader and included top artists like Patricia Kaas, Francis Cabrel and Jean-Jacques Goldman on its roster.

Bibliography

Brooks, Tim. 1999. *The Columbia Master Book Discography, Volume I: U.S. Matrix Series 1 Through 4999, 1901–1910* (*Discographies*, No. 78). Westport, CT: Greenwood Press.

Davis, Clive. 1975. *Clive: Inside the Record Business*. New York: Morrow.

Dearling, Robert, and Dearling, Celia. 1984. *The Guinness Book of Recorded Sound*. Enfield: Guinness Books.

Dixon, Robert M.W., and Godrich, John. 1970. *Recording the Blues*. London: Studio Vista.

Gronow, Pekka. 1977. *Studies in Scandinavian-American Discography*. Helsinki: Finnish Institute of Recorded Sound.

Gronow, Pekka. 1979. *The Columbia 33010-F Irish Series:*

A Numerical Listing. Los Angeles: John Edwards Memorial Foundation.

Hammond, John. 1977. *On Record*. New York: Ridge Press.

Mahony, Dan. 1966. *The Columbia 13/14000-D Series: A Numerical Listing*. 2nd ed. Stanhope, NJ: Walter C. Allen.

Millard, Andre J. 1995. *America on Record: A History of Recorded Sound*. Cambridge: Cambridge University Press.

Randle, Bill. 1974. *The American Popular Music Discography, 1920–1930*. Vol. 3: *The Columbia 1-D Series, 1923–1929*. Bowling Green, OH: Bowling Green University Popular Press.

Rust, Brian. 1999a. *The Columbia Master Book Discography, Volume II: Principal U.S. Matrix Series, 1910–1924* (*Discographies*, No. 78). Westport, CT: Greenwood Press.

Rust, Brian. 1999b. *The Columbia Master Book Discography, Volume III: Principal U.S. Matrix Series, 1924–1934* (*Discographies*, No. 78). Westport, CT: Greenwood Press.

Rust, Brian, and Brooks, Tim. 1999b. *The Columbia Master Book Discography, Volume IV: U.S. Twelve-Inch Matrix Series, 1906–1931* (*Discographies*, No. 78). Westport, CT: Greenwood Press.

Sanjek, Russell, and Sanjek, David. 1996. *Pennies from Heaven: The American Popular Music Business in the Twentieth Century*. New York: Da Capo Press.

Sutton, Allan. 1994. *Directory of American Disc Record Brands and Manufacturers, 1891–1943*. Westport, CT: Greenwood Press.

Discographical References

Jackson, Michael. *Thriller*. Epic 38112. *1982*: USA.

My Fair Lady [Original Broadway Cast]. CBS 05090. *1956*: USA. Reissue: *My Fair Lady [Original Broadway Cast]*. CBS 5090. *1990*: USA.

Discography

Count Basie. *The Essential Count Basie, Vols. 1–3*. Columbia CK-40061, CK-40835, CK-44150. 1936–41; *1991*: USA.

Day, Doris. *Golden Girl: Columbia Recordings 1944–1966*. Sony 65505. *1999*: USA.

Dylan, Bob. *Bob Dylan's Greatest Hits*. Columbia KCL-2663. *1967*: USA. Reissue: Dylan, Bob. *Bob Dylan's Greatest Hits*. Sony 9463. *1999*: USA.

Dylan, Bob. *Bob Dylan's Greatest Hits, Vol. 2*. Columbia 31120. *1973*: USA. Reissue: Dylan, Bob. *Bob Dylan's Greatest Hits, Vol. 2*. Columbia C2K-31120. *1999*: USA.

Dylan, Bob. *Bootleg Series, Vols. 1–3: Rare & Unreleased, 1961–1991*. Columbia C3K-47382. *1991*: USA.

Dylan, Bob. *Bootleg Series, Vol. 4: Live 1966 – The 'Royal*

Albert Hall' Concert. Columbia/Legacy 65759. *1998*: USA.

Electric Flag. *Old Glory: The Best of Electric Flag.* Columbia/Legacy 57629. *1995*: USA.

Goodman, Benny. *Benny Goodman Carnegie Hall Jazz Concert.* Columbia OSL-160. 1938: USA.

Holiday, Billie. *The Quintessential Billie Holiday, Vols. 1–9.* Columbia CK-40646, CK-40790, CK-44048, CK-44252, CK-44423, CK-45449, CK-46180, CK-47030, CK-47031. 1933–42; *1991*: USA.

Joplin, Janis. *Janis.* Columbia/Legacy C3K-48845. *1993*: USA.

Laine, Frankie. *The Essence of Frankie Laine.* Columbia CK-53573. *1993*: USA.

Moby Grape. *Vintage: The Very Best of Moby Grape.* Columbia/Legacy C2K-53041. *1993*: USA.

Santana. *Greatest Hits.* Columbia PC 33050. *1974*: USA. Reissue: Santana. *Greatest Hits.* Sony 33050. *1992*: USA.

Sly and the Family Stone. *Best of Sly and the Family Stone.* Epic CD 4717582. *1998*: USA.

Springsteen, Bruce. *Born in the U.S.A.* Columbia CK-38653. *1984*: USA. Reissue: Springsteen, Bruce. *Born in the U.S.A.* Sony 38653. *1992*: USA.

Filmography

My Fair Lady, dir. George Cukor. 1964. USA. 170 mins. Musical. Original music by Frederick Loewe, Andre Previn.

DAVID HORN, DAVE LAING and DAVID SANJEK

—Decca (UK)

'Decca' was originally the name of a portable phonograph manufactured in 1928 by the London firm of Barnett Samuels. Decca entered the record business through the foresight of Edward Lewis, a stockbroker who organized the purchase of a pressing plant in 1929. Lewis was to run the Decca company for the rest of its independent existence. During the 1930s, the label had British hits from the dance bands of Ambrose and Billy Cotton but, more significantly, Lewis set up a US Decca label with Jack Kapp, a former executive of Brunswick Records. Kapp signed Bing Crosby, the Andrews Sisters and other leading pop artists.

During World War II, Lewis sold his Decca (US) shares to fund research into radar systems. He set up London Records to distribute Decca products in the United States, and Decca's London American label became the European outlet for such US labels as RCA-Victor, Warner Brothers and Decca (US). After the war, he was the first British record industry leader to be convinced of the potential of the microgroove LP record, and Decca introduced its own hi-fi (FFRR) and stereo technologies in the 1950s. The company was also one of the leading pop and classical record labels in Europe, where Decca had several branches in the 1960s. Among the bestselling Decca acts were band leader Mantovani and vocalists Vera Lynn and Tommy Steele.

Decca's A&R staff turned down the Beatles, but signed such leading British groups as the Rolling Stones and the Moody Blues. Decca had further international success with the ballad-singers Tom Jones and Engelbert Humperdinck. However, the decision by US firms to set up their own UK companies broke the Decca–EMI duopoly and caused Decca to lose its European market share throughout the 1970s. In 1979, Lewis agreed to the sale of the Decca music companies to PolyGram for a fee of between £5 million and £15 million, depending on performance. He died soon afterward.

Bibliography

Lewis, Edward R. 1956. *No C.I.C.* London: Universal Royalties.

Discography

Ambrose and His Orchestra Featuring Vera Lynn. *Recollections.* Decca RFL 10. *1981*: UK.

Cotton, Billy, and His Band. *Melody Maker.* Decca RFL 27. *1983*: UK.

Humperdinck, Engelbert. *The Last Waltz.* Decca SKL 4901. *1967*: UK.

Jones, Tom. *Delilah.* Decca SKL 4946. *1968*: UK.

Lynn, Vera. *Vera Lynn: The Decca Years 1936–1960* (2-CD set). Decca 466-921-2. *1999*: UK.

Mantovani and His Orchestra. 'Charmaine.' Decca F 9696. 1951: UK.

Moody Blues, The. *On the Threshold of a Dream.* Dream SML 1035. *1969*: UK.

Rolling Stones, The. *Aftermath.* Decca LK 4786. *1966*: UK.

Rolling Stones, The. *Let It Bleed.* Decca SKL 5025. *1969*: UK.

Steele, Tommy, and the Steelmen. 'Singing the Blues.' Decca F 10819. *1956*: UK.

DAVE LAING

—Decca (US)

While Decca, led by its stockbroker/founder Edward Lewis, had been a successful recording company in England since 1929, it was only in 1934 that the US branch of the company opened its doors, when Lewis brought the services of Jack Kapp to Decca from Brunswick. In the words of Millard (1995), 'Lewis saw that an American record company could provide the music for an international entertainment conglomerate' (168).

The contracts of several artists were acquired at this time, including those of Bing Crosby and Louis Armstrong. At Decca, Kapp continued to stress memorability as the main selling point of recordings; he is said to have hung a sign, 'Where's the melody?' in company offices.

However, his most imaginative and successful innovation was the pricing of discs for the surging jukebox market, which, in the late 1930s, comprised some 150,000 outlets. Kapp undersold his competition by asking only $0.22 per disc from dealers and $0.35 per disc from the public. The $0.35 price was the first flat rate for records (companies had previously posted variable prices in their catalogs). It has often been reckoned that it was the institution of this low flat rate which pulled many record companies out of the Depression. Kapp's approach led to sales of 12 million discs in 1938, 95 percent of which were lower-priced items, and of 13 million the following year. During this period, Decca came to dominate the jukebox supply market.

Kapp also initiated innovations in recording formats. Under his leadership, Decca was among the first record companies to release an original cast album of a Broadway show – *Oklahoma!* in 1943 – and, with *The Jolson Story*, he helped to inaugurate the release of full-length albums by major popular artists. Kapp died in 1949 and was replaced by Milton Rackmil, who purchased a major shareholding in Universal Pictures for $3.75 million shortly after his appointment. In the 1950s, Decca took advantage of the new taste in musical genres. Through producer Owen Bradley, the label climbed to the top of the country charts with hits by Brenda Lee, Patsy Cline and others. Rock hits released by Decca included discs by Buddy Holly and Johnny Burnette and one of the inaugural songs of the genre, Bill Haley's 'Rock Around the Clock' (1955).

Lewis had sold his shares in Decca (US) during World War II, but his UK company continued to distribute Decca (US) recordings in Europe. Decca (US) and Universal were purchased by MCA in 1961. MCA subsequently used the Decca label mainly for country music by such artists as Loretta Lynn and Conway Twitty.

Bibliography

Ginell, Cary. 1989. *The Decca Hillbilly Discography, 1927–1945* (Discographies, No. 35). Westport, CT: Greenwood Press.

Lewis, Edward R. 1956. *No C.I.C.* London: Universal Royalties.

Millard, Andre J. 1995. *America on Record: A History of Recorded Sound*. Cambridge: Cambridge University Press.

Ruppli, Michel. 1996a. *The Decca Labels: A Discography. Volume 1 – The California Sessions* (Discographies, No. 63). Westport, CT: Greenwood Press.

Ruppli, Michel. 1996b. *The Decca Labels: A Discography. Volume 2 – The Eastern & Southern Sessions (1934–1942)* (Discographies, No. 63). Westport, CT: Greenwood Press.

Ruppli, Michel. 1996c. *The Decca Labels: A Discography. Volume 3 – The Eastern Sessions (1943–1956)* (Discographies, No. 63). Westport, CT: Greenwood Press.

Ruppli, Michel. 1996d. *The Decca Labels: A Discography. Volume 4 – The Eastern Sessions (1956–1973)* (Discographies, No. 63). Westport, CT: Greenwood Press.

Ruppli, Michel. 1996e. *The Decca Labels: A Discography. Volume 5 – Country Recordings, Classical Recordings & Reissues* (Discographies, No. 63). Westport, CT: Greenwood Press.

Ruppli, Michel. 1996f. *The Decca Labels: A Discography. Volume 6 – Record Numerical Listings & General Artist Index* (Discographies, No. 63). Westport, CT: Greenwood Press.

Sanjek, Russell, and Sanjek, David. 1996. *Pennies from Heaven: The American Popular Music Business in the Twentieth Century*. New York: Da Capo Press.

Discographical References

Haley, Bill, and His Comets. '(We're Gonna) Rock Around the Clock.' Decca 29124. 1955: USA.

Jolson, Al. *The Jolson Story* (album of four 78 rpm discs). Decca A-469 (23470, 23612–23614). 1946: USA.

Oklahoma! (Original cast) (album of six 78 rpm discs). Decca A-359 (23282–23287). 1943: USA. Reissue: *Oklahoma!*. MCA MCAD-10046. *1990*: USA.

Oklahoma! (Original cast) (issued as a Volume II; album of two 78 rpm discs containing some numbers not in the original 1943 album). Decca A-383 (23380–23381). 1945: USA.

Discography

Armstrong, Louis. *Best of Louis Armstrong: 20th Century Masters*. MCA 11940. *1999*: USA.

Armstrong, Louis. *Best of the Decca Years, Vol. 1: The Singer*. MCA 31346. *1992*: USA.

Armstrong, Louis. *Best of the Decca Years, Vol. 2: The Composer*. MCA 31346. *1992*: USA.

Armstrong, Louis. *Highlights from His Decca Years*. GRP 638. *1994*: USA.

Burnette, Johnny, and the Rock & Roll Trio. *Rockabilly Boogie*. Bear Family 15474. *1989*: Germany.

Cline, Patsy. *Patsy Cline [Black & Silver Label]*. Decca DL-8611. *1957*: USA.

Cline, Patsy. *That's How a Heartache Begins*. Decca DL-74586. *1964*: USA.

Crosby, Bing. *Bing Crosby's Gold Records*. MCA 11719. *1997*: USA.

Haley, Bill, and His Comets. *The Decca Years & More*. Bear Family 15506. *1991*: Germany.

Holly, Buddy. *Rock 'n' Roll Collection*. Decca 7207. *1972*: USA.

Holly, Buddy. *That'll Be the Day [Decca]*. Decca 8707. *1958*: USA.

Jolson, Al. *The Al Jolson Story, Part 1 (You Made Me Love You)*. MCA MCAC-27051. *1984*: USA.

Jolson, Al. *The Al Jolson Story, Part 2 (Rock-A-Bye Your Baby)*. MCA MCAC-27052. *1987*: USA.

Jolson, Al. *The Al Jolson Story, Part 3 (Rainbow 'Round My Shoulder)*. MCA MCAC-27053. *1987*: USA.

Lee, Brenda. *Anthology, Vols. 1 & 2 (1956–1980)*. MCA 10384. *1991*: USA.

DAVID SANJEK

—Decca (West Africa)

In 1947, the British Decca company decided to set up West Africa's first recording studio, in Accra, Ghana, and to launch its West Africa (WA) series. This was prompted by the prewar financial success of companies like His Master's Voice (HMV), whose West African JZ series sold, for instance, 181,000 78 rpm singles in 1930.

The first Decca studio in Accra started under Major Kinder's management in a rented bungalow near Ridge Hospital. Unlike the HMV/EMI West African recordings, which were done on disc, Decca used a ferrograph reel tape for its mono mastering. Decca's WA series was locally distributed by the Société Commerciale du L'Ouest Afrique and the African Picture Company, and in its first year (1947) 46,000 copies of 23 different West African vernacular records were sold. By 1952, Decca (WA) had recorded and produced about 100 different 78 rpm singles, paying the artists 10 shillings per song and twopence in royalties for each single sold. From 1959, Decca (WA) also began to market long-playing (LP) albums.

From the 1950s to the 1970s, Decca (WA) Ghanaian artists and bands included E.T. Mensah's Tempos (50-plus singles and nine albums), King Bruce's Black Beats (60-plus singles and eight albums), Onyina, Otoo Lartey, E.K. Nyame, the Red Spots, the Rhythm Aces, Joe Kelly's Band, the Stargazers, the Builders Brigade Band, the Broadways, the Modernaires, Dr. Gyasi's Noble Kings and the Ramblers. Nigerian artists included highlife artists and bands E.C. Arinze, the Empire Rhythm Orchestra, the Archibogs, the Oriental Brothers and Dr. Sir Warrior; *jùjú* musicians I.K. Dairo (10 albums) and Ebenezer Obey (29 albums); and the pioneer *apala* musician Haruna Ishola (27 albums). Sierra Leone *maringa* musicians included Ebenezer Calender (eight singles) and Famous Scrubbs.

The success of Decca (WA) during the 1950s led to the construction of a studio in Accra on the Winneba Road in Kanseshie and the regular, twice-yearly dispatch from Britain to Yaba, Lagos of two engineers with portable equipment to record Nigerian artists.

By the early 1960s, Decca (WA) was selling 250,000 records a year, and Nigeria became its largest market. As a result, a recording studio was opened there. During the 1970s, Ghana's economic decline and Nigeria's oil boom resulted in Decca (WA) basing itself in Lagos. By the mid-1970s, Decca (WA) was running a 16-track studio there and, under the management (and part-ownership) of Chief Abiola, the Decca (WA) Afrodisia label was launched in 1976. It was around this time that a famous confrontation between Fela Kuti (who had recorded six Afrobeat albums for Decca in 1976–77) and Chief Abiola occurred, and Fela occupied the Decca studio for a while.

When Decca was taken over in 1979 by PolyGram (which already had a Philips factory in Nigeria), Decca sold its West African rights to Afrodisia, a totally Nigerian company. By the late 1980s, Nigeria was pressing around 20 million albums a year. The Record Manufacturers of Nigeria Ltd., with a production capacity of 20,000 albums per day, was a major manufacturer. Decca (WA)/Afrodisia's share in this was 35 percent.

Bibliography

Collins, John. 1985. *Music Makers of West Africa*. Washington, DC: Three Continents Press.

Collins, John. 1992. *West African Pop Roots*. Rev. ed. Philadelphia: Temple University Press. (First published London: Foulsham, 1985.)

Collins, John. 1994. *Highlife Time*. Accra: Anansesem Press.

JOHN COLLINS

—Def Jam (US)

A New York record company specializing in hip-hop, Def Jam was founded in 1984 by university student Rick Rubin and Rush Artist Management head and tyro (novice) producer Russell Simmons. The first release to feature the Def Jam logo was 'It's Yours,' by T La Rock and Jazzy Jay. This was followed by 'I Need a Beat,' by LL Cool J, who was to become one of the label's most commercially successful acts, along with the Beastie Boys and Public Enemy. In 1986, with distribution by CBS (later Sony), the Beastie Boys' *Licensed to Ill* was a number one album in the United States, while Public Enemy, with their articulate black nationalist rap, sold millions of albums during the late 1980s and early 1990s. The Beastie Boys left the label in 1988.

Rubin and Simmons dissolved their partnership acrimoniously in 1987. In 1988, Rubin founded the Def American label in Los Angeles as the embodiment of his belief in music that challenges the boundaries of censorship. In keeping with this belief, he had previously signed the controversial speed-metal act Slayer to Def Jam, only to discover that the label's distributor, Sony, refused to handle the group's *Reign in Blood* album. The album's rights were subsequently transferred to Def

American. The group itself also moved to the Def American label, which went on to release another four of Slayer's albums.

Simmons, meanwhile, expanded his business interests to include fashion, television and films. By the 1990s, Def Jam was facing competition from labels such as Death Row and Bad Boy, which signed the more extreme proponents of gangsta rap. Def Jam's most successful new signings of the decade were Method Man and Jay-Z. In 1994, Def Jam's turnover was $90 million and, in 1995, PolyGram purchased 60 percent of the company, although Simmons remained as chief executive. In January 1999, Public Enemy left the Def Jam label, ostensibly as a result of a dispute concerning the posting by the band of tracks on the Internet for free downloading, a reason denied by Def Jam management.

The 1985 film *Krush Groove* was loosely based on Simmons' life story, and featured performances by Def Jam acts.

Bibliography

Fernando, S.H., Jr. 1994. *The New Beats: Exploring the Music, Culture and Attitudes of Hip-Hop*. New York: Doubleday.

Discographical References

Beastie Boys. *Licensed to Ill*. Def Jam 40238. *1986*: USA.

LL Cool J. 'I Need a Beat.' Def Jam DJ001. *1985*: USA.

Slayer. *Reign in Blood*. Def Jam/Def American 2-24131. *1986*: USA.

T La Rock and Jazzy Jay. 'It's Yours.' Def Jam/PartyTime (Streetwise) PT 104. *1984*: USA.

Discography

Jay-Z. *In My Lifetime*, Vol 1. Roc-A-Fella/Def Jam 536392. *1997*: USA.

LL Cool J. *Mr. Smith*. Def Jam 314 529 583. *1995*: USA.

Method Man. *Tical*. Def Jam 523839. *1994*: USA.

Public Enemy. *It Takes a Nation of Millions to Hold Us Back*. Def Jam CK-44303. *1988*: USA.

Slayer. *Decade of Aggression: Live*. Def American 2-26748. *1991*: USA.

Slayer. *Divine Intervention*. Def American 45522. *1994*: USA.

Slayer. *Seasons in the Abyss*. Def American 2-24307. *1990*: USA.

Slayer. *South of Heaven*. Def American 2-24203. *1988*: USA.

Filmography

Krush Groove, dir. Michael Schultz. 1985. USA. 95 mins. Musical Drama.

DAVE LAING

—Denon (Japan)

Denon is a jazz, classical and pop record label owned by Nippon Columbia Company, Ltd. of Japan. It was formed in Tokyo in 1968 to issue domestic contemporary folk and pop recordings aimed at a new market of young consumers. It enjoyed success with such recordings as 'Francine-no Baai' by the pacifist singer Noriko Shintani and 'Shiroi Cho-no Samba' by Kayoko Moriyama, which topped the charts in March 1970.

In 1974, Nippon Columbia decided to make classical recordings in Europe to issue on Denon, using its newly developed PCM portable digital recorder (DN-023RA). This was followed in 1976 by the New York Jazz series. As in the case of the PCM digital recordings of classical music in Europe, Nippon Columbia sent a recording team with a set of equipment to New York. The first album on the Denon Jazz label was *One Tuesday in New York* by Takashi Mizuhashi and Herbie Hancock, and it was followed by a long list of recordings produced by Reggie Workman, including performances by such innovative musicians as Archie Shepp, Dollar Brand and Billy Harper, along with those of such traditionalists as Tommy Flanagan and Jo Jones. The label was not, however, very successful, with the number of sales decreasing as a result of changes in the jazz music market itself and the emergence of digital recordings in the early 1980s.

Efforts at revitalization were made in 1986, when Sonny Lester was appointed producer of the renewed Denon Jazz series and recorded the Count Basie Orchestra's *Long Live the Chief* (recorded after Basie's death with Frank Foster as leader) and Carmen McRae's *Any Old Time*, as well as such newer artists as Bob Berg (tenor saxophone and soprano saxophone) and the Ritz (a jazz vocal group). Some of these recordings were also released in the United States and Canada. As of June 1996, nearly 50 albums had been released in the Denon Jazz series. Denon later purchased the Savoy jazz catalog and reissued numerous early recordings by Charlie Parker, Dizzy Gillespie, Erroll Garner, Kenny Clarke and others.

Bibliography

All About Jazz Labels (a special edition of *Swing Journal*). 1987. Tokyo: Swing Journal.

Denon Records. http://www.denon.com/denonrecords/default.htm

Oricon No. 1 Hits 500 (1968–1985). 1994. Tokyo: Club House.

The History of Nippon Columbia: The 80th Anniversary. 1990. Tokyo: Nippon Columbia.

Who's Who in Jazz (a special edition of *Swing Journal*). 1988. Tokyo: Swing Journal.

Discographical References

Count Basie Orchestra, The. *Long Live the Chief*. Denon COCY-7101. *1986*: Japan.

McRae, Carmen. *Any Old Time*. Denon COCY-7190. *1988*: Japan.

Mizuhashi, Takashi, and Hancock, Herbie. *One Tuesday in New York*. Denon YX-7563. *1977*: Japan.

Moriyama, Kayoko. 'Shiroi Cho-no Samba.' Denon CD-48. *1970*: Japan.

Shintani, Noriko. 'Francine-no Baai.' Denon CD-24. *1969*: Japan.

Discography

Berg, Bob (aka Berg, Robert). *Back Roads*. Denon COCY-9042. *1991*: Japan.

Berg, Bob (aka Berg, Robert). *Cycles*. Denon COCY-9518. *1988*: Japan.

Dollar Brand (aka Ibrahim, Abdullah; aka Brand, Adolph Johannes). *Anthems for the New Nations*. Denon YX-7537. *1978*: Japan.

Flanagan, Tommy. *Alone To Long*. Denon YX-7523. *1978*: Japan.

Harper, Billy. *Loverhood*. Denon YX-7522. *1978*: Japan.

Jones, Jo. *Our Man Papa Jo!*. Denon YX-7527. *1978*: Japan.

Ritz, The. *Almost Blue*. Denon COCY-7999. *1991*: Japan.

Ritz, The. *Flying*. Denon COCY-9521. *1989*: Japan.

Shepp, Archie. *Day Dream*. Denon YX-7570. *1977*: Japan.

Shepp, Archie. *Lady Bird*. Denon YX-7543. *1979*: Japan.

TAKUO MORIKAWA

—DICAP (Chile)

DICAP (Discoteca del Cantar Popular) (The Discothèque of Popular Song) was created in Santiago, Chile almost by accident by the Communist Youth of Chile in 1968. The Communist Youth had pressed a record, *Por Viet-Nam* (For Vietnam), to finance the Chilean group Quila-payún's 1968 trip to the International Youth Festival in Sofia, Bulgaria. The 1,000 records pressed sold out, demonstrating that a market existed for politically oriented music.

DICAP thus had from its inception a more political-cultural than commercial purpose. DICAP, initially called Jota-Jota, was the principal supporter of the *nueva canción Chilena* (Chilean new song) movement and, in its five years of operation in the country, achieved prestige through the quality of its recordings as well as the extent of its catalog. DICAP formed part of an alternative music industry developed in Chile between 1964 and 1973 to foster popular music and to facilitate the dissemination of songs with political content. In doing so, DICAP was notable for paying its artists more than the current commercial rate in Chile of 2.5 percent royalties. It paid 5 percent, with singers recording their own material receiving 7 percent.

In line with its political-cultural focus, DICAP recorded and distributed a broad range of music, from that of Eisler to bolero music, and from Andean music to the music of the Soviet Red Army. In 1968, the label pressed 4,000 records, representing two titles. By 1973, the number of records pressed by DICAP had risen to 240,000, representing 17 new titles out of a total of 64. For 1973, DICAP had a quota of 300,000 pressings from the only record manufacturing plant in Chile, which it would have utilized had the military coup against Salvador Allende's government not taken place in September. At the time of the coup, DICAP had 16 unreleased master tapes ready for pressing. As part of this growth, DICAP established two new labels in 1970: Pena de los Parra and Canto Libre. The Jota-Jota label was retained for the occasional Communist Party disc.

DICAP's recordings were given little airtime, since radio in Chile had a commercial orientation. This notwithstanding, DICAP did make half-hour tapes of its music which were sent to the smaller radio stations throughout Chile, and which were played by disc jockeys such as Rene Largo Farias and Ricardo García. However, the dissemination of DICAP recordings depended largely on live concerts given by its artists and on a direct distribution system that delivered discs directly to the public through unions, and student and community organizations. DICAP sales never exceeded 5 percent of the total record market in Chile in the early 1970s. The trend toward avoiding intermediaries was characteristic of the alternative circuit of venues, events and record production that sustained Chilean new song from 1964 to 1973. However, DICAP had by 1973 built up a good distribution network through Chilean record stores.

Through DICAP, an alternative philosophy of graphics and image creation was developed, emerging from the office of Vicente and Antonio Larrea. Their approach was to create an illustration that projected the concept of the record and its musical themes, often with a minimal image to create impact or a design inspired by the name of the group. If an artist's photograph appeared, it was usually on the back cover alongside track listings. Colors varied from the brightest available, often on a white background, to more subdued, earthy tones. DICAP had its own logo, with defining logos for its sub-labels, such as the Pena de los Parra label. Each disc was considered more of a cultural object than a commercial product and bore the message 'ese disco es cultura' (This disc is culture).

A few years after the 1973 coup, DICAP reorganized in exile in Paris, and produced Chilean records by remastering tapes. While some records were distributed through the Communist Party, the bulk were relicensed through independent record companies in France and Italy.

Bibliography

Barraza, Fernando. 1972. *La nueva canción Chilena* [Chilean New Song]. Santiago: Quimantú.

Gavagnin, Stefano. 1986. 'A proposito dei complessi cileni: note sul linguaggio e sulla discografia dei gruppi della "nueva canción Chilena"' [Concerning Chilean Groups: Notes on the Language and Discography of Chilean New Song Bands]. *Revista Italiana di musicologia* 21(2): 300–35.

Larrea, Antonio, and Montealegre, Jorge. 1997. *Rostros y rastros de un canto* [Faces and Trails of a Song]. Santiago: Nunatak.

Discographical Reference

Quilapayún. *Por Viet-Nam.* Jota-Jota JJ-01. *1968*: Chile.

Discography

Illapu. *Música Andina.* DICAP DCP-44. *1973*: Chile.

Inti-illimani. *Autores chilenos.* Jota-Jota JJL-13. *1971*: Chile.

Inti-illimani. *Canto para una semilla.* Jota-Jota JJL-16. *1972*: Chile.

Inti-illimani. *Inti-illimani.* Jota-Jota JJL-05. *1969*: Chile.

Jara, Víctor. *El derecho de vivir en paz.* Jota-Jota JJL-11. *1971*: Chile.

Jara, Víctor. *La población.* Jota-Jota JJL-14. *1972*: Chile.

Jara, Víctor. 'Plegaria a un labrador.' Jota-Jota JJS-01. *1969*: Chile.

Jara, Víctor. *Pongo en tus manos abiertas.* Jota-Jota JJL-03. *1969*: Chile.

Loyola, Margot. *Canciones del 900.* DICAP DCP-42. *1973*: Chile.

Parra, Isabel. *Violeta Parra.* DICAP DCP-7. *1972*: Chile.

Quilapayún. *Basta.* Jota-Jota JJ-04. *1969*: Chile.

Quilapayún. *Cantata Santa María de Iquique.* Jota-Jota JJL-08. *1970*: Chile.

JUAN PABLO GONZÁLEZ and JAN FAIRLEY

—Dischi Ricordi (Italy)

Dischi Ricordi, an Italian record company, was established in 1958 as the record production branch of G. Ricordi & Company, the publishing house founded in 1808. If 'Casa Ricordi' is tied to the memory of the life and work of composers like Rossini, Bellini, Verdi, Puccini and others up until Luigi Nono, Dischi Ricordi was at the heart of changes in Italian popular music in the late 1950s and early 1960s. Among Ricordi's first issues are records like Gino Paoli's 'La gatta' (1959) and 'Sassi' (1960), Umberto Bindi's 'Arrivederci' and 'Il nostro concerto' (1959), and others (by Giorgio Gaber, Sergio Endrigo, Enzo Jannacci, Luigi Tenco) that brought the *cantautori* (singer-songwriters) – pioneers of Italy's 'quality song' – to the public's attention.

As a new label, and with the reputation of its parent company behind it, Dischi Ricordi had more freedom to experiment with this new wave of sophisticated songwriting, which did not necessarily appeal to traditional pop singers. To some extent, this focus on quality continued as a priority, although Ricordi soon expanded to record all genres, from rock ballads like Bobby Solo's 'Una lacrima sul viso' (Italy's big hit of 1964), to groups – like Equipe 84 and Dik Dik – covering North American and British hits, to pop superstars like Lucio Battisti and singer-songwriters like Fabrizio De André or the rock-oriented Gianna Nannini.

During the late 1980s and early 1990s, Dischi Ricordi remained the largest Italian record company, and the only one that seemed to be able to compete with multinationals. The group of companies under the Ricordi name was formidable, and included a chain of very profitable music stores all across Italy. It was, therefore, a surprise when the entire group (except for the stores, which were sold to the book publisher Feltrinelli) was bought by BMG in 1994.

Discographical References

Bindi, Umberto. 'Arrivederci.' Ricordi srl-10774. *1959*: Italy.

Bindi, Umberto. 'Il nostro concerto.' Ricordi srl-10-137. *1959*: Italy.

Paoli, Gino. 'La gatta.' Ricordi srl-10114. *1959*: Italy.

Paoli, Gino. 'Sassi.' Ricordi srl-10161. *1960*: Italy.

Solo, Bobby. 'Una lacrima sul viso.' Ricordi srl-10338. *1964*: Italy.

FRANCO FABBRI

—Discos Andino (Nicaragua)

Discos Andino was a label founded and run by Luis Felipe Andino (1924–87). A Managua resident and trumpet player in popular dance bands, Andino was motivated to become involved in recording by what he felt was the lack of attention paid to local Nicaraguan music in the 1950s. He launched his career in recording in 1961–62 with two LPs of previously unrecorded *marimba de arco* trios. Their successful reception spurred him to further ventures. Over the following two decades, he produced several albums by popular musicians, almost all based in or near Managua, as well as a small catalog of folk-rooted musics from the nearby southwest part of the country. In 1977, he released the first LP of English-speaking Creole *palo de mayo* music from the eastern Atlantic coast – a style that went on to become the most popular dance music in Nicaragua in the 1980s. Andino never opened his own recording studio (he used the Managua-based Centauro studios), but his multifarious activities included working closely with groups in the production of albums, composing several songs for groups he recorded, and running one of the nation's best-known music stores.

Bibliography

Scruggs, T.M. 1994. *The Nicaraguan 'baile de la marimba' and the Empowerment of Identity*. Ph.D. thesis, University of Texas at Austin. Ann Arbor, MI: University Microfilms.

Discography

Los Bárbaros del Ritmo. *Palo de Mayo*. LPA-10. *ca. 1971*: Nicaragua.

Los Hermanos López. *Escuela de Danza Folklórica Nicaragüense*. LPA-12. *ca. 1973–77*: Nicaragua.

Marimba de Arco de Elías Palacio [*sic*]. *Fiestas Agostinas*. LPA-009. *ca. 1970*: Nicaragua.

Salva Azucena Divina. LPA-002. *ca. 1965–69*: Nicaragua.

Viva Santo Domingo. LPA-003. *ca. 1965–69*: Nicaragua.

T.M. SCRUGGS

—Discos Fuentes (Colombia)

Discos Fuentes was the first Colombian record company and has remained one of the three top national labels, alongside Sonolux and Codiscos. It specializes in *música tropical*, including Colombian styles (*porro, cumbia* and *vallenato*), but also records salsa and bolero. The company emerged in Cartagena from the radio station Emisora Fuentes, founded in 1934 by Antonio Fuentes López, a local entrepreneur and musician. Before 1945, when Fuentes purchased his own record presses, records were pressed in the United States and Argentina. In 1954, the company moved to Medellín, by then the center of the national record industry. Antonio Fuentes died in 1985, leaving the company in the hands of his children. In the 1990s, the company accounted for about 10 percent of the national market in recorded music.

Under Antonio Fuentes' hands-on direction, the early company stable comprised mostly artists from the local region. Orquesta Emisora Fuentes, Orquesta A Número Uno (directed by Lucho Bermúdez) and José Barros y los Trovadores de Barú made many early recordings, and the guitar player Guillermo Buitrago was very popular. With accordionists Abel Antonio Villa and Luis E. Martínez, Discos Fuentes first recorded the music later known as *vallenato*. The company was advertising nationally by the late 1940s and was important in the growing popularity of music from the country's Caribbean coastal region. In the 1960s and 1970s, important artists included Pedro Laza y sus Pelayeros and the very successful Los Corraleros de Majagual, whence emerged stars such as Alfredo Gutiérrez and Julio 'Fruko' Estrada, the latter a central influence in the company through the 1980s and 1990s, alongside musical director Isaac

Villanueva. The best-known names of the 1980s and 1990s included Fruko y su Orquesta, the Latin Brothers, Joe Arroyo, La Sonora Dinamita and Los Embajadores Vallenatos.

Discography

Arroyo, Joe. *Grandes Exitos de Joe Arroyo y la Verdad*. Discos Fuentes D10150. *1991*: Colombia.

Buitrago, Guillermo. *16 Exitos de Navidad y Ano Nuevo*. Discos Fuentes D10018. *1992*: Colombia.

Cumbia and *Cumbia 2: La Epoca Dorada de Cumbias Colombianas*. Discos Fuentes/World Circuit WCD 033. *1993*: UK.

14 Canonazos Bailables, Vol. 34. Discos Fuentes D10320. *1994*: Colombia.

Fruko. *Salsa y Salsa: 12 Exitos de Fruko*. Discos Fuentes 201744. *1990*: Colombia.

La Sonora Dinamita. *Imparable . . . La Sonora Dinamita*. Discos Fuentes D10175. *1992*: Colombia.

Latin Brothers, The. 'The Black Girl.' Discos Fuentes/Mango Records CIDM1021 842393-2. *1990*: UK.

Los Corraleros de Majagual. *Album de Los Corraleros de Majagual*. Discos Fuentes E30004. *1994*: Colombia.

Los Embajadores Vallenatos. *Lo Mejor del Vallenato*. Discos Fuentes D10173. *1992*: Colombia.

Pedro Laza y sus Pelayeros. *Exitos Bailables*. Discos Fuentes D10047. *1993*: Colombia.

The Tropical Sounds of Colombia. Discos Fuentes/Mango Records CIDM1058 846756-2. *1990*: UK.

PETER WADE

—Document (Austria)

Throughout Document's history (Document was founded in 1990), its record issues have been the productions of Johnny Parth of Vienna. Johnny Parth's ventures before and since have also been underwritten by other companies and by personal associates. This accounts for the diverse labels on which they have appeared. In accordance with an overall policy of issuing, as far as possible, the complete recordings of all artists in the Dixon/Godrich volume *Blues and Gospel Records* in matrix order, several hundred long-playing records were issued in the 1980s. The majority were released on the Document and Blues Documents labels, with substantial series on RST, Wolf Special Editions, Fantasy Selmerphone (women singers) and B.o.B. (Best of Blues). Most were produced in sleeves with full discographical details only. A select series of country blues reissues with sleeve notes, Matchbox Bluesmasters, was issued by Saydisc; 1930s singers were featured on Old Tramp, and gospel singers and preachers on Eden Records.

With the advent of the compact disc (CD), Parth terminated his release of long-playing records and, with the same objectives, remastered and repackaged his issues on Document CDs. Between August 1990 and December 1997, over 700 CDs were released on Document and a further 60 on other labels. During this period, discoveries were made of single copies of rare items, which were issued in a special series called 'Too Late, Too Late.' Another series covered Library of Congress recordings. This program was only possible with the generous help of collectors in Europe and North America, in particular Roger Misiewicz of Canada. Omitting only those singers whose entire output had been issued on CD by other companies (for example, Bessie Smith, Robert Johnson, Henry Thomas), Parth nominally completed his self-appointed task in 1997. At this time, however, the fourth edition of *Blues and Gospel Records (1890–1943)* not only extended the time frame, but also included previously unlisted artists (such as Joséphine Baker and Bert Williams). A complete reissue program has therefore remained notional. Meanwhile, by 1997, Parth had already issued some 30 CDs of Viennese folk music on his Basilisk label and had commenced a series, parallel to the blues and gospel issues, of early (pre-1943) hillbilly and country music.

Bibliography

Dixon, Robert M.W., Godrich, John, and Rye, Howard. 1997. *Blues and Gospel Records 1890–1943*. 4th ed. Oxford: Clarendon Press.

Macleod, R.R. 1994–. *Document Blues* (Lyric transcriptions of blues and gospel records on Document and related labels). Vols. 1–4 (continuing series). Edinburgh: PAT Publications.

Oliver, Paul. 1997. 'Documenting the Blues' (Series of eight programs). London: BBC, Radio Three.

Parth, Johnny. 1998. *The Essential Blues & Gospel CDs for Serious Research*. Part I: Document Records. Part II: Various Labels. Vienna: Document.

PAUL OLIVER

—Duke/Peacock (US)

Duke/Peacock was originally two companies: Peacock, founded in Houston, Texas in 1949 by Don Robey; and Duke, founded in Memphis, Tennessee in 1952 by David Mattis, who merged his label with Robey's later the same year.

From Texas and California, Robey's earliest rhythm and blues (R&B) stars included Clarence 'Gatemouth' Brown, Floyd Dixon, and Johnny Otis and his protégés (Willie Mae 'Big Mama' Thornton among them). With the Duke connection, Robey brought Memphis 'Beale Streeters' Rosco Gordon, Johnny Ace, 'Little' Junior Parker and Bobby 'Blue' Bland into his orbit. Peacock also had an extraordinarily strong gospel roster, including the original Five Blind Boys, the Sensational Nightin-

gales, the Dixie Hummingbirds and the Rev. Cleophus Robinson, among many major acts.

Throughout the 1960s, Duke/Peacock – with its subsidiary labels Back Beat, Songbird and Sure Shot – remained a potent R&B/gospel 'indie' in the southern United States, but apart from its principal star, Bobby Bland (the 'Blue' was dropped during the 1960s soul era), and some success with Joe Hinton, Roy Head, O.V. Wright and Carl Carlton, the company never quite managed to expand its market base beyond this area.

In 1973, Robey sold his company to ABC/Dunhill, which was subsequently subsumed by MCA Records, a division of Universal Music.

Bibliography

Gart, Galen, and Ames, Roy C. 1990. *Duke/Peacock Records: An Illustrated History with Discography*. Milford, NH: Big Nickel Publications.

Discography

Duke-Peacock's Greatest Hits. MCA MCAD-10666. *1992*: USA.

The Best of Duke-Peacock Blues. MCA MCAD-10667. *1992*: USA.

CLIFF WHITE

—ECM Records (Germany)

ECM, which stands for Edition of Contemporary Music, was formed in Munich in 1969 by Manfred Eicher (b. 1943). Eicher combined an enthusiasm for jazz with professional experience as a classical musician (he had been a bassist with the Berlin Philharmonic Orchestra under conductor Herbert von Karajan) and as a freelance record producer for Deutsche Grammophon Gesellschaft (DGG) and EMI. ECM was set up out of a desire to record jazz with the same kind of attention to detail and awareness of sound quality that was typically accorded to classical music – especially chamber music – by these major labels. Eicher was also motivated by the presence in Europe of US jazz musicians who felt dissatisfied with the opportunities available to them to record freely improvised jazz in the United States. ECM's first recording, made in November 1969, featured Mal Waldron and bore the meaningful title *Free At Last*.

Eicher, as CEO and producer, has run the label more or less as a one-person enterprise, reflecting his personal taste for small-group and solo jazz and his interest in 'a search for new principles of organization . . . its only constraint a rejection of anarchic disorganization' (Cook and Morton 1992, 1106). ECM became associated in particular with the recording of contemporary European jazz and has issued many recordings by musicians such as Jan Garbarek, Eberhard Weber, Kenny Wheeler and Norma Winstone. The label has also continued to record

US musicians, such as John Abercrombie, Keith Jarrett (whose 1975 live solo album *The Köln Concert* became the label's biggest-selling recording), Jack DeJohnette and Pat Metheny.

Many of those recorded by ECM have expressed a preference for ECM's policy of allowing musicians considerable scope, as against what they see as the more commercial imperatives of other jazz labels. ECM also established a reputation for its particular attention to sound engineering and the quality of its overall sound production. ECM frequently recorded in Norway, a reflection of Eicher's interest in certain spatial qualities of sound (for a while ECM advertising carried the slogan 'the most beautiful sound next to silence').

ECM sleeve art has been held in high regard both in its own right (to the extent that several exhibitions have been held) and as a component of what has come to be widely spoken of as an 'ECM aesthetic,' involving recording aims and conditions, attitudes to musicians, product presentation and marketing.

Bibliography

Aiken, Jim. 1979. 'Manfred Eicher, Keith Jarrett's Producer' (Interview). *Contemporary Keyboard* 5(9) (September): 50 and *passim*.

Albertson, Chris. 1975. 'The Eicher Touch.' *Saturday Review* (4 October): 44–46.

Cook, Richard, and Morton, Brian. 1992. *The Penguin Guide to Jazz on CD, LP and Cassette*. Harmondsworth: Penguin Books.

Mathieson, Kenny. 1993. 'Editions of the Cool.' *The Wire* 112 (May): 18–20.

Müller, Lars, Wojirsch, Barbara, and Rehm, Dieter, eds. 1995. *ECM: Sleeves of Desire: A Cover Story*. Baden: Verlag Lars Müller.

Rinzler, Paul. 1990. 'Defining a New Style in Jazz History: The ECM Style.' *IAJE Jazz Research Papers* 10: 99–105.

Tucker, Mark. 1998. *Jan Garbarek: Deep Song*. Hull: University of Hull Press.

Woefle, M.A. 1993. 'Jazz-Produktionen bei ECM' [Jazz Productions at ECM]. *Neue Muzikzeitung* 42: 40–41.

Discographical References

Jarrett, Keith. *The Köln Concert*. ECM 1064. *1975*: Germany.

Waldron, Mal. *Free At Last*. ECM 1001. *1969*: Germany.

Discography

Abercrombie, John. *Timeless*. ECM 1047. *1974*: Germany.

DeJohnette, Jack. *New Directions in Europe*. ECM 1157. *1979*: Germany.

Garbarek, Jan. *Folk Songs*. ECM 1170. *1979*: Germany.

Metheny, Pat. *Watercolours*. ECM 1097. *1977*: Germany.

Weber, Eberhard. *Yellow Fields*. ECM 1066. *1975*: Germany.

Wheeler, Kenny. *Music for Large and Small Ensembles*. ECM 1415/6. *1990*: Germany.

Winstone, Norma. *Somewhere Called Home*. ECM 1336. *1986*: Germany.

DAVID HORN and PETER WICKE

—edel music AG (Germany)

At the beginning of the twenty-first century, edel was Europe's leading and largest independent record company, with 80 subsidiaries in 16 countries. edel Gesellschaft für Produktmarketing mbH was founded by Michael Haentjes in Hamburg in 1986 to sell soundtracks via mail order (Gorny and Stark 1999, 76). The company soon expanded its marketing and distribution network to a full-service record production company with equal emphasis on repertoire and marketing. The edel Music Group eventually included many international repertoire companies, as well as manufacturing, distribution, publishing, and media and entertainment ventures.

The German record company gained an international presence in key markets mainly through partnerships with other labels, licensing agreements and joint ventures. In order to compete with the world's largest independent record company, Zomba, which is particularly strong in A&R, edel continued its aggressive expansion strategy by going public on the Frankfurt Neuer Markt in 1998. The sale of stock allowed edel to increase its acquisition activities; Haentjes, however, continued to be the majority shareholder, owning 71 percent of shares.

The company progressed from being a mail-order company to releasing its first CD in 1988 and building a manufacturing plant three years later in Röbel, Mecklenburg-Vorpommern. With the infrastructure in place, edel then started to build up its edel records Europe division, establishing its first subsidiaries in Austria and Switzerland in 1992. Subsidiaries in Italy, Scandinavia, France, Spain and the United Kingdom followed two years later, at the same time as A&R activities began. Also in 1994, edel strengthened its marketing division with the acquisition of Castle Communications, one of the leading independent marketing firms in the United Kingdom.

The company edel classics GmbH was set up in 1993, when edel – for a reported DM 8 million – bought the classical catalog of the former East German state-owned record company VEB Deutsche Schallplatte, renamed it Berlin Classics, and gained access with this to a worldwide distribution network in the classical sector. Other labels in this division include Eterna, CCC and

ART; in all, the catalog has a repertoire of more than 2,000 titles, which amounts to approximately 80 percent of the common classical market.

After building a strong European network, edel music expanded into the major music market in 1995. Only three years before floating on the stock market, edel started operating in the United States with a small-scale soundtrack and compilation division called edel America Records, Inc., USA, which has become part of edel North America.

Having freed its liquid assets, edel's acquisition strategy in 1999 was to strengthen its A&R base. In one year, edel Records, the company's main record division, acquired Mega (Scandinavia), Eagle Rock (United Kingdom) A 45 (Germany) and K-Tel (Finland), all of which are stand-alone labels. The company also entered into agreements with labels such as Almo Sounds, X-IT, Gang Go and Unsubmissive, covering a number of different genres. Its most important strategic move, however, was the 75 percent acquisition in July 1999 of the Belgian label Play It Again Sam (PIAS), which had a strong pan-European and, since mid-2001, North American presence. The company gained access to the UK market with PIAS acquiring a majority stake in distributor Vital Distribution and the Scandinavian-based company Playground JV, which is also the distributor for labels such as Mute Records and Beggars Banquet.

edel entered the all-important North American music market with the acquisition of 80 percent of RED Distribution, Sony Music's US-based distribution company, which is also the largest independent company in this sector. Covering a broad variety of genres, RED had exclusive distribution agreements for artists such as Tom Waits, Emmylou Harris and the nu-metal band Slipknot. On the basis of this distribution infrastructure, edel has launched edel entertainment, Inc., USA in the United States, and has begun to profit from the synergy of its expanding business.

Recognizing that a continuous flow of publishing revenue is essential for a successful recording company, edel first moved into this territory by signing a licensing agreement with Disney in 1998. This arrangement has given edel the rights to all of Disney's recorded music output, especially the soundtracks to its animated feature films, released through the four labels under the umbrella of the Buena Vista Music Group (BVMG): Hollywood Records, Mammoth Records, Lyric Street Records and Walt Disney Records.

Further to acquiring catalog, edel started to sign songwriters to establish the company in the competitive publishing market. The most revenue-generating agreement for edel is expected from its reported $40 million investment in Deston Songs, the joint venture of Desmond Child and his partners.

The company's bestselling artists include Jennifer Paige, Blümchen, Scooter and Sash!. In 2001, the German independent record company won a Grammy for the Best Dance Recording with its international multi-platinum hit 'Who Let the Dogs Out' by the Baha Men. The act is signed with Steve Greenberg's S-Curve Records in the United States, with which edel signed an agreement in 2000 as part of edel International.

Although an independent company, edel music AG has developed a divisional structure with cross-media access, becoming a major player in the music and entertainment market. Other ventures include the strong compilations and special projects segment, which incorporates 'edelkids,' the children's and youth division. edel's investment in the Internet included a partnership with NewCorp Music Group (NMG), Microsoft and Liquid Audio.

In 2000, the company reported losses, and it sold its share of PIAS to that company's former owners. edel also announced that its own future strategy would be to focus on artist development rather than distribution or manufacturing.

Bibliography

Billboard. http://www.billboard.com

edel. http://www.edel.de

edel Music Group. http://www.edel.com

Gorny, Dieter, and Stark, Jürgen. 1999. 'Diese Aktie ist ein Hit – Die Edel Music AG an der Börse. Ein Interview mit Michael Haentjes' [This Share Is a Hit – Edel Music AG on the Stock Market. An Interview with Michael Haentjes]. In *Pop & Kommunikation: Jahrbuch 1999/2000* [Pop and Communication: Yearbook 1999/ 2000]. München: Econ Verlag, 76.

Southall, Brian. 2000. *The A-Z of Record Labels.* London: Sanctuary Publishing Ltd.

'Special Report: Indies Take on the World.' 2000. *MBI Magazine* (December): x.

Discographical Reference

Baha Men, The. 'Who Let the Dogs Out.' edel 0115425ERE. *2000*: Germany.

VANESSA BASTIAN

—Edison (US) (1910–29)

'Edison' was the name given to the cylinder recordings issued by the North American Phonograph Company and the National Phonograph Company between 1890 and 1910, and to the cylinders and discs issued by Thomas A. Edison Incorporated, the company formed by Edison to merge a number of his business concerns, including the National Phonograph Company, in 1910.

The National Phonograph Company became the phonograph subdivision of the new company.

The inventor of the cylinder phonograph finally entered the disc market in 1913 with the vertically cut, 'hill-and-dale' Edison Diamond Discs. The release of the first recordings followed three years of experimentation and test pressings. The records, which were laminated in a hard plastic material called condensite, were much thicker than the laterally cut discs that dominated the market and were playable only on a Diamond Disc phonograph equipped with a diamond stylus. The price of a Diamond Disc phonograph ranged from $60 to $1,000. By the end of the second decade of the twentieth century, Edison's engineers had largely overcome problems with surface noise, allowing the superior sound quality of the Diamond Disc to come into its own.

While experiments with a high-quality disc recording were proceeding, Edison's continuing commitment to improving the cylinder was evident in the celluloid Blue Amberol cylinder recordings, which first appeared in 1912. Successors to the wax Amberols of 1908 and much more durable, Blue Amberols were claimed to survive 3,000 playings without any signs of wear. At first, Blue Amberols were recorded live, but dubbing from Diamond Discs was introduced in 1914 and remained the usual method from then on. Edison cylinders, especially Blue Amberols, continued to sell well for the rest of the decade, the strongest market being the rural United States, but sales declined in the 1920s. Edison was still advertising Blue Amberols in 1927, and remained in cylinder production until the end of that decade.

Edison's role in the development and dissemination of popular music from 1910 through the 1920s was small compared to that of Columbia and Victor, its main rivals. At home with the diversity of the first decade of the century – marching bands, balladeers, 'ethnic' comedians, vocal quartets – the company often lagged behind changes in public taste in the following two decades. Responsibility for this has been variously ascribed to Thomas Edison's own narrow tastes, his close control over the choice of material recorded, his lack of awareness of (or interest in) current market possibilities, or a combination of all three. Sophie Tucker began her recording career with 10 cylinder recordings for Edison in 1910, including 'Some of These Days,' but never recorded for the company again. Edison's venture into blues was a strictly limited affair: two records in 1923, three in 1925, all by women vaudeville blues performers (the 1925 recordings were issued as a 'race' series, but the series was never continued), and three sessions with Eva Taylor and Clarence Williams in 1929. In hillbilly music, Edison's most notable recordings were of the autoharp player Ernest V. 'Pop' Stoneman. The company had some success in the 1920s with a number of popular vaudeville and radio performers, among them Vaughn De Leath (with, for example, 'Are You Lonesome Tonight'), the Happiness Boys ('Show Me the Way to Go Home') and Johnny Marvin ('Ain't She Sweet'). Each of these performers followed the common practise of the time of recording for different labels. Perhaps Edison's most extensive series of recordings was that made in the area of jazz-influenced dance music with the prolific California Ramblers, between 1924 and 1929.

Content with the quality of its acoustic recordings, Edison was in no haste to move into electrical recording. When the company finally did so in 1927, two years later than most of its rivals, it was the last to make the switch. In July 1929, Edison acknowledged the market success of laterally cut discs by belatedly releasing its own, the Edison Needle Type. In preparation, the company had recorded a number of artists (including Vaughn De Leath) on both vertically and laterally cut masters, beginning in January 1928. A matter of weeks after their release, in the immediate aftermath of the Wall Street crash in late October 1929, the company brought all record production to a halt.

Bibliography

Dethlefson, Ronald. 1980–81. *Edison Blue Amberol Recordings*. 2 vols. Brooklyn, NY: APM Press.

Frow, George L. 1982. *The Edison Disc Phonographs and the Diamond Discs: A History with Illustrations*. Sevenoaks, Kent: George L. Frow.

Marco, Guy A., and Andrews, Frank, eds. 1993. *Encyclopedia of Recorded Sound in the United States*. New York: Garland Publishing, Inc.

Millard, Andre J. 1995. *America on Record: A History of Recorded Sound*. Cambridge: Cambridge University Press.

Rust, Brian, with Debus, Allen G. 1973. *The Complete Entertainment Discography, from the Mid-1890s to 1942*. New Rochelle, NY: Arlington House.

Sutton, Allan. 1994. *Directory of American Disc Record Brands and Manufacturers, 1891–1943*. Westport, CT: Greenwood Press.

Wile, Raymond, and Dethlefson, Ronald. 1990. *Edison Disc Artists and Records, 1910–1929*. 2nd ed. Brooklyn, NY: APM Press.

Discographical References

De Leath, Vaughn. 'Are You Lonesome Tonight.' Edison 52044. 1927: USA.

Happiness Boys, The. 'Show Me the Way to Go Home.' Edison 51660. 1925: USA.

Marvin, Johnny. 'Ain't She Sweet.' Edison 51992. 1927: USA.

Tucker, Sophie. 'Some of These Days.' Edison 4M-691 (cylinder). 1910: USA.

Discography

California Ramblers, The. *Edison Laterals 2*. Diamond Cut DCP-301D. 1928–29; *1994*: USA.

De Leath, Vaughn. *The Original Radio Girl: Edison Laterals 5*. Diamond Cut DCP-304D. 1928–29; *1997*: USA.

Edison Diamond Disc Foxtrots. Diamond Cut DCP-307D. 1920–23; *1999*: USA.

Hot Dance of the Roaring 20's: Edison Laterals 3. Diamond Cut DCP-202D. 1928–29; *1995*: USA.

Rolfe, B.A., and His Lucky Strike Orchestra. *Edison Laterals 6*. Diamond Cut DCP-305D. 1928–29; *1998*: USA.

Stoneman, Ernest V. *Ernest V. Stoneman (and His Dixie Mountaineers)*. Diamond Cut DCP-400D. 1928; *1996*: USA.

Taylor, Eva, and Williams, Clarence. *Edison Laterals 4*. Diamond Cut DCP-303D. 1929, 1976–77; *1997*: USA.

Unreleased Edison Laterals 1. Diamond Cut DCP-201S. 1928; *1992*: USA.

DAVID HORN

—Elektra Records (US)

Jac Holzman (b. 1931) founded Elektra Records in New York City in 1950. Initially, the company was identified with the folk milieu of New York City's Greenwich Village and signed a number of the most popular performers: Phil Ochs, Judy Collins, Tom Paxton, Tom Rush, Koerner, Ray and Glover, and Fred Neil. As the folk revival faltered in the face of rock 'n' roll, Elektra adapted to the electrification of vernacular music, signing the Paul Butterfield Blues Band in 1965. Its roster soon thereafter included some of the more influential and groundbreaking rock groups, such as Los Angeles' Love and the Doors, and Detroit's MC5 and the Stooges. At the same time, Elektra achieved its greatest success with the middle-of-the-road balladry of Bread. Singer-songwriters continued to find a home at the label. They included Tim Buckley, the United Kingdom's Incredible String Band, Harry Chapin, and Carly Simon, the most commercially successful of the group. In 1971, Elektra was bought by the WEA conglomerate for $10 million, and Holzman left the company in 1973 when Elektra was amalgamated with Asylum Records, owned by David Geffen. The label's catalog became more diverse, losing some of its longstanding identity in the process. Nonetheless, successful acts continued to be signed, most notably Queen from the United Kingdom. Elektra played a role in the New York punk scene as well by releasing two albums by Television.

The label's unwillingness to depart completely from its earlier identity was witnessed in 1984–85 by a series of box sets, released under the umbrella title *The Jac Holzman Years*, which focused on the folk and singer-songwriter material. In a similar vein, the label's 40th anniversary was commemorated in 1990 by *Rubaiyat*, which brought together songs from Elektra's 'classic' era. In the 1990s, Elektra's roster broadened to include heavy metal (Metallica) and rap (Busta Rhymes).

A complete discography for Elektra for the years 1951–73 can be found at http://www.followthemusic.com/disco.html; http://www.followthemusic.com/disco2.html; and http://www.followthemusic.com/disco3.html. An interview with Jac Holzman, 'Jac Holzman, the Man, the Music, the Doors,' reprinted from *The Doors Collectors Magazine*, can be found at http://www.cinetropic.com/janeloisemorris/interview/holzman/.

Bibliography

Holzman, Jac, and Daws, Gavan. 1998. *Follow the Music: The Life and High Times of Elektra Records in the Great Years of American Pop Culture*. Santa Monica, CA: FirstMedia Books.

Sanjek, Russell, and Sanjek, David. 1996. *Pennies from Heaven: The American Popular Music Business in the Twentieth Century*. New York: Da Capo Press.

Discographical References

Bleecker and MacDougal: The Folk Scene of the 1960s (The Jac Holzman Years). Elektra 60381. *1984*: USA.

Crossroads: White Blues in the 1960s (The Jac Holzman Years). Elektra 60383. *1984*: USA.

Elektra's 40th Anniversary: Rubaiyat. Elektra 60940. *1990*: USA.

O Love Is Teasin': Anglo-American Balladry (The Jac Holzman Years). Elektra 60402-1. *1985*: USA.

Television. *Adventure*. Elektra 2-133. *1978*: USA.

Television. *Marquee Moon*. Elektra 2-1098. *1977*: USA.

Discography

Busta Rhymes. *The Coming*. Elektra 61742. *1996*: USA.

Metallica. *Garage, Inc.* Elektra/Asylum 62299. *1998*: USA.

Metallica. *Master of Puppets*. Elektra 60439-2. *1986*: USA.

Queen. *Greatest Hits*. Elektra 5E-564. *1981*: USA.

DAVID SANJEK

—Elenco (Brazil)

Elenco, an independent record company located in Rio de Janeiro, was founded in 1962 by Aloysio de Oliveira, who while at Odeon had produced 'Chega de Saudade' with João Gilberto. Between 1963 and 1967, when it was sold to Philips, Elenco used RCA-Victor's studio, factory and distribution system. During this period, Elenco issued more than 60 LPs of bossa nova by Tom (Antonio Carlos) Jobim, Dick Farney, Sílvia Telles, João Donato, Lúcio Alves, Sérgio Ricardo, Baden Powell, Edú Lobo, Roberto Menescal, Quarteto em Cy and Nara Leão, among others.

Elenco's entire staff consisted of Aloysio de Oliveira (artistic director, with responsibility for sleeve notes and press releases), Humberto Catarti (sound technician), José Delphino Filho (A&R) and César Villela (art director). Together with photographer Chico Pereira, Villela created low-budget, high-contrast black-and-white record sleeves which were considered extremely modern by the critics.

Stereo records were made at the Rio Som or RCA recording studios in Rio de Janeiro. Several albums were recorded during the intimate 'pocket shows' produced by Oliveira at the Zum-Zum nightclub and the Au Bon Gourmet restaurant. Some albums, like *Vinícius e Caymmi no Zum-Zum* (1965), recorded live and unedited, maintained the same 'cool' atmosphere as the live shows.

Elenco's catalog became an important point of reference both for Brazilian popular music in the following decades and for international musicians, especially those connected with jazz. Among its LPs are *Vinícius e Odette Lara*, *Caymmi visita Tom* and *Baden Powell à vontade*, which led the Brazilian journalist Sérgio Augusto to describe the record company as being to Brazilian popular music what Verve is to jazz and Deutsche Grammophon is to classical music.

Bibliography

Castro, Ruy. 1990. *Chega de Saudade: a história e as histórias da Bossa Nova* [Enough of Nostalgia: The Stories and History of Bossa Nova]. São Paulo: Companhia das Letras.

Jornal Folha de São Paulo 1991. Special Issue (26 September). 5: 14.

Zan, José Roberto. 1997. *Do fundo do quintal à vanguarda: contribuição para uma história social da música popular brasileira* [From the Backyard to the Vanguard: Contributions for a Social History of Brazilian Popular Music]. Ph.D. thesis, Campinas, UNICAMP/IFCH.

Discographical References

Gilberto, João. 'Chega de Saudade.' Odeon 14.360. *1958*: Brazil.

Jobim, Antonio Carlos, and Caymmi, Dorival. *Caymmi visita Tom*. Elenco 17. *1965*: Brazil.

Moraes, Vinícius de. *Vinícius e Odette Lara*. Elenco ME-24. *1963*: Brazil.

Moraes, Vinícius de, and Caymmi, Dorival. *Vinícius e Caymmi no Zum-Zum*. Fontana/Elenco 648506. 1965; *1978*: Brazil.

Powell, Baden. *Baden Powell à vontade*. Elenco 11. *1964*: Brazil.

Discography

Blanco, Billy. *Músicas de Billy na voz do próprio*. Elenco 29. *1965*: Brazil.

Donato, João. *Bud Shank, Donato, Rosinha de Valença*. Elenco 8. *1965*: Brazil.

Leão, Nara. *Nara*. Elenco ME-10. *1964*: Brazil.

Menescal, Roberto. *Surf Board*. Elenco MEV-9. *1964*: Brazil.

JOSÉ ROBERTO ZAN (trans. MARTHA TUPINAMBÁ DE ULHÔA)

—EMI/HMV (Africa)

EMI/HMV was the single most important record company in Sub-Saharan Africa during the first half of the twentieth century. EMI (Electric and Musical Industries Ltd.) was formed in 1931 through the merger of the Gramophone Company and Columbia International Ltd. HMV (His Master's Voice) was launched as the Gramophone Company's main label in 1910.

By 1910, the Gramophone Company had organized a retail system throughout Sub-Saharan Africa, with sister companies or local trading companies representing individual labels. Imported shellacs and windup gramophones were initially aimed at the expatriate market. With the emergence of an African middle class and an urbanized work force, new markets opened up in the 1920s and 1930s. The first recordings of African music were made in London in the 1920s, with artists shipped in from Nigeria, Ghana and South Africa. In 1928, HMV's agent in Zanzibar sent the first group of East African musicians to record in Bombay. Recording tours were initiated to Nigeria and Uganda in 1929, and in the following years such tours were extended to all principal territories.

After the 1931 merger that led to the formation of EMI, the merged company's labels, including HMV and its French sister company, 'La Voix de son Maître,' Odeon, Pathé, Parlophone, Zonophone and Columbia, held a virtual monopoly in most English and French colonies. African music was issued on the EMI labels with a serial prefix specific to the individual sister company or local agent. The HMV GV series, which started in 1933, was the first to introduce a wider African audience to Cuban and Latin American music.

When activity was resumed after World War II, the EMI labels met with stiff competition in the 1950s from a growing number of local record companies. In West Africa, Decca was a particularly tough challenger. The transition of colonies to independent states coincided with the change to vinyl records. Eventually, EMI continued its companies only in Nigeria and South Africa, relying partly on distribution of international artists. An attempt to reestablish the company on the Kenyan market failed in 1977–78. French EMI Pathé-Marconi was active for a while on the new African LP market in the late 1970s, with a series based on licensed material.

717

Bibliography

Collins, John. 1985. *Music Makers of West Africa*. Washington, DC: Three Continents Press.

Melland, Henry. 1971. *World Record Markets*. London: EMI.

Vernon, Paul. 1993. 'Savannaphone.' *Folk Roots* 122 (August): 21, 23, 25.

Wallis, Roger, and Malm, Krister. 1984. *Big Sounds from Small Peoples: The Music Industry in Small Countries*. London: Constable.

Discography

Clegg, Johnny, and Savuka. *Third World Child*. EMI (South Africa) 24 0733 1. *1987*: South Africa.

Dark City Sisters, The. *Star Time*. HMV JCLP 46. *1962*: South Africa.

Denge, Irewolede. 'Oba Oshemawe' (Yoruba)/'Orin Asape Eko' (Yoruba) (78 rpm). HMV JZ 3. 1936: Nigeria.

E.K.'s Band (conducted by E.K. Nyame). 'Otamfo Ne Bo Be Dwo' (Twi)/'Me Ne Wu To Ho' (Twi) (78 rpm). HMV JZ 5247. 1952: Ghana.

Fela and the Africa 70. *Shakara*. EMI (Nigeria) EMI 008N. *1972*: Nigeria.

Franco & l'O.K. Jazz. *À Paris*. EMI Pathé STX 229. *1967*: Democratic Republic of Congo.

I-Choir Li Ka Chaluza (Double Quartet). 'uBangca (Oxford Bags)' (Zulu)/'Ingoduso' (Zulu) (78 rpm). HMV GU 1. 1930: South Africa.

Kumasi Trio, The. 'Amponsah Pt. 1' (Fanti)/'Amponsah Pt. 2' (Fanti) (78 rpm). Zonophone EZ 1001. 1928: Ghana.

Mensah, E.T. 'Rolling Ball'/'Happy Boy' (78 rpm). HMV GV 237. *1956*: Ghana.

Siti binti Saad. 'Uchungu wa Mwana' (Kiswahili) (78 rpm). Columbia WE 4. 1928: Zanzibar/Tanzania.

FLEMMING HARREV

—ENIGRAC (Nicaragua)

ENIGRAC, the Empresa Nicaragüense de Grabaciones Artísticas y Culturales (the Nicaraguan Company for Artistic and Cultural Recordings), was a government-sponsored label (and studio – Estúdios ENIGRAC) founded on the heels of the 1979 triumph of the Sandinista Popular Revolution. It absorbed the Ocarina label, the initial label of Nicaragua's first Ministry of Culture, and grew to become one of the largest and most successful initiatives of the Ministry. The Sandinista government dedicated substantial resources to the label in the the early 1980s, and ENIGRAC's prolific output during this period has remained unmatched in the Nicaraguan music industry: the label produced over 100 titles on LP and/or cassette, and a few 45s. ENIGRAC's mission was twofold: to distribute politically committed music; and

to document previously unrecorded folk-rooted musics.

The first wave of ENIGRAC releases consisted of recordings by politically oriented bands – Pancasán and Guadabarranco, for example – that had formed during the struggle against the Somoza regime in the early and mid-1970s but that had been forced to disband and join the military insurrection before recording. Although not the first to do so, ENIGRAC became the leading label for English-speaking Creole *palo de mayo* music from the eastern Atlantic coast – the most popular dance music in Nicaragua in the 1980s. As the economy reeled from the effects of war and the US-sponsored economic embargo, ENIGRAC was slow to change to cassette production and recognize the value of recording popular dance groups and political singers outside the general Managua area. ENIGRAC effectively closed with the demise of the Ministry of Culture in 1988, although, beginning in the mid-1990s, several releases were reissued by private labels.

Bibliography

Mattelart, Armand. 1986. *Communicating in Popular Nicaragua*. New York: International General.

Scruggs, T.M. 1994. *The Nicaraguan 'baile de la marimba' and the Empowerment of Identity*. Ph.D. thesis, University of Texas at Austin. Ann Arbor, MI: University Microfilms.

Discography

Dimensión Costeña. *De Que Suda, Suda!*. Chilamate 6004. *1984*: Nicaragua.

Los Girasoles. *Los Girasoles*. Chilamate 006. *1983*: Nicaragua.

Los Guadabarranco. *Un Trago de Horizonte*. Ocarina 020. *1982*: Nicaragua.

Mariachi Internacional. *Música Nicaragüense*. Chilamate 001. *1982*: Nicaragua.

Mejía Godoy, Carlos, y los de Palacagüina. *Firuliche*. NCLP 5022. *1987*: Nicaragua.

Mejía Godoy, Luis Enrique, con Mancotal. *A Pesar de Usted*. NCLP 5009. *1985*: Nicaragua.

Paladino, Jorge. *Soy Campesino*. Chilamate 6007. *1986*: Nicaragua.

Pancasán. *Por la Patria*. Ocarina 017. *1982*: Nicaragua.

1er Festival de la Canción Romántica Nicaragüense: Rafael Gastón Pérez. Chilamate 003. *1983*: Nicaragua.

Urtecho, José Coronel. *No Volverá el Pasado – Poesía*. Ocarina 023. *1983*: Nicaragua.

Zinica. *Zinica*. Ocarina 022. *1983*: Nicaragua.

T.M. SCRUGGS

—Essiebons (Ghana)

The Essiebons label has been operating in Accra, Ghana since 1969. It was founded by Dick Essilfie Bondzie, an accountant and record store owner whose father was part-owner of Ghana's first record-pressing plant, RMGL. Essiebons released the country's first indigenous LP in 1970. The label quickly earned Ghana's first Gold Disc for an album release by Dr. K. Gyasi and his Noble Kings. Essilfie Bondzie produced and recorded a wide range of popular artists, from Koo Nimo, the palm-wine troubadour, to brass bands and choral groups. His major success was with CK Mann who, with the Carousel Seven, rejuvenated highlife in the mid-1970s. He also recorded the Congolese guitarist/composer Henri Bowane, the Zairean guitar heroes Zaiko Langa Langa, and the 'International' Sam Mangwana.

By 1978, vinyl had become virtually unobtainable in Ghana, preventing the production of records, and this, combined with worsening economic conditions, sent the local music industry into serious decline. Stereo album matrices had previously been supplied by Poly-Gram in Nigeria, but when that company was 'indigenized' they were no longer available and plates had to be obtained from Kenya. Essiebons then looked for other ways to promote music. In 1979, many Essiebons artists were featured in an independent film entitled *Roots to Fruits*, which was screened briefly in Ghana in 1982. The company continued to release cassettes and, during the 1990s, Essilfie Bondzie licensed several of his productions to European reissue labels.

Bibliography

Collins, John. 1994. *Highlife Time*. Accra: Anansesem Press.

Discography

Bowane, Henri. *Double Take Tala Kaka*. RetroAfric 6. *1994*: UK.

Zaiko Langa Langa. *Zaire-Ghana*. RetroAfric 5. *1994*: UK.

GRAEME EWENS

—Factory Records (UK)

Founded in Manchester, England in 1978 by television presenter Tony Wilson and record producer Martin Hannett, Factory Records was part of the new wave of independent record labels set up in the wake of the punk music explosion. The initial roster of artists included the Durutti Column and Joy Division. Joy Division later became New Order, whose 1983 12″ (30 cm) single 'Blue Monday' sold over 3 million copies worldwide. Other artists on the label included the Happy Mondays and James. In 1984, Factory established the Hacienda nightclub in Manchester and started a classical music label, for which composer Steve Martland recorded. The label's releases were also noted for the distinctive sleeves designed by Peter Saville. The company got into financial difficulties in 1991 and its catalog was sold to Poly-Gram's London label.

Bibliography

Middles, Mick. 1996. *From Joy Division to New Order: The Factory Story*. London: Virgin Books.

Discographical Reference

New Order. 'Blue Monday.' Factory FAC 7312. *1983*: UK.

Discography

Happy Mondays, The. *Bummed*. Factory FACT 220. *1988*: UK.

James. 'Jim One.' Factory FAC 78. *1983*: UK.

Joy Division. 'Love Will Tear Us Apart.' Factory FAC 23. *1980*: UK.

DAVE LAING

—Fania (US)

Fania is a Latin music record company renowned for the commercial exploitation of salsa music. The label was founded in 1964 in New York by band leader Johnny Pacheco and lawyer Jerry Masucci. Its roster featured numerous Puerto Rican and other Caribbean musicians, who were recorded by in-house producers/band leaders Willie Colón and Ray Barretto. Among its most renowned artists were Celia Cruz, Rubén Blades and the Fania All-Stars.

Fania created the satellite label Vaya and acquired Tico, Alegre and Cotique, other New York labels specializing in Latin music, and the Puerto Rican label Inca, whose roster included the group La Sonora Ponceña.

The rise of disco in the late 1970s affected salsa sales and several of Fania's top acts moved to other labels, including RMM which had been set up by salsa promoter Ralph Mercado. Although Fania was less active in the 1990s, it celebrated its 30th anniversary with concerts and special album releases. Masucci subsequently recorded several Cuban acts for his Nueva Fania label shortly before his death in December 1997.

Discography

Barretto, Ray. *Head Sounds*. Fania 388. *1972*: USA.

Colón, Willie. *Cosa Nuestra*. Fania 384. *1972*: USA.

Colón, Willie, and Blades, Rubén. *Siembra*. Fania 537. *1978*: USA.

Cruz, Celia, with Pacheco, Johnny. *Celia and Johnny*. Vaya 31. *1974*: USA.

Fania All-Stars, The. *Latin Soul Rock*. Fania 470. *1973*: USA.

La Sonora Ponceña. *On the Right Track*. Inca 1084. *1988*: USA.

DAVE LAING

—Fazer (Finland)

Fazer Musiikki was a Finnish company active in music publishing, instrument manufacturing, record production, management, and wholesale and retail sales.

Founded in 1897 as a music store in Helsinki by Konrad Georg Fazer (1864–1940), the company soon expanded into music publishing. Around 1910, Fazer became the Finnish agent for the Gramophone Company and started importing and producing records.

From 1945 to 1993, Fazer was the leading independent record company in Finland. The company acted as the local agent for Decca and PolyGram (Philips, Fontana), and produced records on its own Rytmi, Sävel, Shokki and Finndisc labels. From 1955 to 1976, the head of popular record production was the composer Toivo Kärki. Under his guidance, Fazer became the dominant force in Finnish popular music. Bestselling Fazer artists of his era included Olavi Virta, Henry Theel, Tapio Rautavaara, Eila Pellinen, Irwin Goodman, Fredi, Metro-Tytöt (vocal trio) and the Sounds (beat group).

Fazer also played a significant role as publisher of classical music (including Sibelius) and producer of classical records. In 1979, the company launched the Finlandia label especially for classical music. During the 1970s and 1980s, Fazer acquired several independent Finnish record labels (such as Scandia, Triola, Blue Master and Safir) and music publishers and became the owner of the most significant Finnish music copyrights in the popular music field.

From 1941 to 1971, the managing director of Fazer was Roger Lindberg (b. 1915), K.G. Fazer's grandson. Lindberg was also active internationally in trade organizations and served as chair of IFPI (the International Federation of the Phonographic Industry) from 1968 to 1973. In 1993, the Fazer group of companies was sold to the Warner Music Group. Record production has continued on the Fazer Records label.

Bibliography

Gronow, Pekka. 1981. 'Suomen äänilevyteollisuus vuoteen 1945'. [The Recording Industry in Finland to 1945]. In Rainer Strömmer and Urpo Haapanen, *Suomalaisten äänilevyjen luettelo – Catalogue of Finnish Records 1920–1945*. Helsinki: Suomen äänitearkisto, vii–xxvi.

Gronow, Pekka. 1995. 'The Record Industry in Finland, 1945–1960.' *Popular Music* 14(1): 33–53.

Marvia, Einari. 1947. *Fazerin Musiikkikauppa 1897–1947* [Fazer's Music Store 1897–1947]. Helsinki: Fazer.

PEKKA GRONOW

—Festival (Australia)

Festival was a record company established in 1952 in Sydney by the Mainguard investment company. It released primarily overseas material, although it also recorded local artists, including singer and A&R manager Les Welch. With Festival's takeover by LJ Hooker Investments, Ken Taylor succeeded Welch and pioneered a policy of promoting rock, beginning with the highly successful Bill Haley hit, 'Rock Around the Clock,' licensed from Decca (US). Although personally unsympathetic to the music, Taylor saw its commercial potential and built up Australia's first stable of local rock recording artists, most notably Johnny O'Keefe, Col Joye and Dig Richards; later successes included Lucky Starr, the Delltones, the Bee Gees and Noeleen Batley. In addition to launching its own subsidiaries, such as Rex Records, Festival absorbed other existing labels, including Leedon. Taylor left shortly after Festival was bought by Rupert Murdoch's News Limited in 1962. With other changes occurring during the 1960s, Festival's initial pioneering phase came to an end; however, in 1990, Festival still claimed to handle more Australian material than any other company, much of this licensed from Mushroom, an independent label purchased by Festival later in the 1990s.

While Festival is Australia's only non-multinational major, with operations also in New Zealand, the United States (through Rawkus Records) and the United Kingdom it was central to the dissemination of Australian rock in the region. It fostered a high proportion of original compositions, as well as supporting ad hoc developments in sound technologies devised by studio engineer Robert Iredale, who left in 1964. Taylor's grasp of the potential symbiosis with television, which arrived in Australia in 1956, gave momentum to rock, and contributed to the rebirth of the Australian recording industry.

Bibliography

Byrell, John. 1995. *Bandstand . . . and All That*. Kenthurst, NSW: Kangaroo Press.

Hayton, Jon, and Isackson, Leon. 1990. *Behind the Rock: The Diary of a Rock Band 1956–66*. Milsons Point, NSW: Select Books.

Prices Surveillance Authority. 1990. *Inquiry into the Prices of Sound Recordings*. Australia: Commonwealth Government of Australia.

Rogers, Bob, and O'Brien, Denis. 1975. *Rock 'n' Roll Australia: The Australian Pop Scene 1954–64*. Stanmore, NSW: Cassell Australia.

Sly, Lesley. 1993. *The Power and the Passion: A Guide to the Australian Music Industry*. North Sydney: Warner/Chappell Music Australia.

Sturma, Michael. 1991. *Australian Rock 'n' Roll: The First Wave*. Kenthurst, NSW: Kangaroo Press.

Taylor, Ken. 1970. *Rock Generation: The Inside Exclusive*. Melbourne: Sun Books.

Discographical Reference

Haley, Bill, and His Comets. '(We're Gonna) Rock Around the Clock.' Decca 29124. 1955: USA.

Discography

O'Keefe, Johnny. *20th Anniversary Album* (2 LPs). Festival 45139/8. *1977*: Australia.

BRUCE JOHNSON

—Flying Nun (New Zealand)

The Flying Nun label was begun in 1981, in Christchurch, New Zealand, by Roger Shepherd, and was inspired by punk rock's 'do-it-yourself' ethic. The southern city of Dunedin soon became most strongly associated with the label, and the term 'Dunedin sound' was applied to bands such as the Chills and the Verlaines, who used four- or eight-track recording to produce a distinctive 'homemade' sound. Chris Knox's cartoon graphics became the label's signature on album artwork and advertisements. In 1981, Flying Nun's second single release – the Clean's 'Tally Ho' – reached number 19 in the New Zealand singles charts, despite the label's distribution relying on a network of personal friends. Over the following decade, Flying Nun's roster of New Zealand bands became more diverse and the Flying Nun/Dunedin sound less cohesive (see Mitchell 1996, 215–35).

In common with other indie labels, Flying Nun initially operated in a very relaxed, laissez-faire manner. However, as the company developed a more international presence, it increasingly adopted the business arrangements and practises of the mainstream music industry. In 1987, Flying Nun (UK) was established, along with Flying Nun Europe, a joint venture with the German label, Normal. Several licensing arrangements were also made with independent companies in the United States. In 1987, Shepherd made a 'production and distribution' deal with WEA, and Flying Nun shifted its two-person office operation to Auckland. In 1990, a deal was made with the powerful Australian independent label, Mushroom Records, forming Flying Nun Australia and providing the more substantial recording and promotion budgets that would allow bands such as Straitjacket Fits, the Bats, and Headless Chickens to realize their more global musical ambitions.

Flying Nun has continued to develop an international audience for its music, extending its roster to include foreign artists. Emergent New Zealand artists signed include King Loser, Love's Ugly Children and Garageland, who toured Australia as a Flying Nun package called The Sound Is Out There in 1995.

Recognition for the company's overseas exploits came with a New Zealand government Export Award in 1995. By 1996, when Flying Nun celebrated its 15th anniversary, the label had released 430 recordings. In 1996, Shepherd moved to London to run the label's extensive Northern Hemisphere activities, while in New Zealand the company is managed by Lesley Paris. For many, especially the overseas followers of alternative music, Flying Nun is a metonym for New Zealand music as a whole.

Bibliography

Flying Nun Records. http://www.flyingnun.co.nz/

Mitchell, Tony. 1996. *Popular Music and Local Identity: Rock, Pop and Rap in Europe and Oceania*. Leicester: Leicester University Press.

Discographical Reference

Clean, The. 'Tally Ho.' Flying Nun FN 002. *1981*: New Zealand.

Discography

Abel Tasmans, The. *Songs from the Departure Lounge (Best of the Abel Tasmans)*. Flying Nun FN 404. *1998*: New Zealand.

Chills, The. *Kaleidoscope World*. Flying Nun FN 13; also Creation (UK), Flying Nun Europe/Normal. *1986*: New Zealand.

Chills, The. *Submarine Bells*. Flying Nun/Slash FN 148. *1990*: New Zealand.

In Love with These Times. Flying Nun/WEA FN 677. *1988*: New Zealand.

Knox, Chris. *Songs of You & Me*. Flying Nun FN 313. *1995*: New Zealand.

Love's Ugly Children. *Showered in Gold*. Flying Nun FN 380. *1997*: New Zealand.

Straitjacket Fits. *Melt*. Flying Nun/Arista FN 174. *1990*: New Zealand.

Tall Dwarfs, The. *Stumpy*. Flying Nun FN 384. *1998*: New Zealand.

Tuatara. *A Flying Nun Compilation*. Flying Nun FN 045. *1985*: New Zealand.

ROY SHUKER

—Folkways Records (US)

Folkways Records was founded in 1948 by Moses Asch (1905–86). Over the course of the next 38 years, Asch released 2,168 titles on the label. The Folkways catalog consisted of an extraordinary range of material, not all of it musical, from around the world. Although under Asch's leadership the label never had any major commercial hits and the sales of many of its titles numbered in the hundreds, the overall influence of the Folkways catalog has been extensive.

The label developed a loyal following during the US 'folk song revival' in the 1950s and 1960s through its releases of the music of such key revival figures as Woody Guthrie, Cisco Houston, Huddie Ledbetter (Leadbelly) and Pete Seeger. Folkways also recorded many traditional folk artists whose music had a key role in shaping the conception of US folk music (primarily that of the rural South) among those who were attracted to such music but who did not grow up with it as an aspect of their own culture. These folk artists included African-American performers such as the Rev. Gary Davis, Furry Lewis, 'Big' Bill Broonzy, Sonny Terry and Brownie McGhee, Elizabeth Cotten and Memphis Slim, and white southerners such as Hobart Smith, Doc Watson and the Lilly Brothers, among many others. In 1952, Folkways issued the *Anthology of American Folk Music*, a set of three 2-LP boxes, consisting of reissues of music that had originally been released on 78 rpm recordings made in the 1920s and 1930s. Compiled and edited by Harry Smith, the *Anthology* was widely influential, and was responsible for introducing many urban folk music enthusiasts in the northern United States to the music of rural southerners (both black and white) from the era prior to the Depression. It also paved the way for the cottage industry of reissuing other 78 rpm recordings of blues and hillbilly music which thrived from the 1960s onward.

The Folkways output was by no means confined to US folk music. Harold Courlander, a self-taught ethnographer, oversaw the production of the Ethnic Folkways library, a series of albums consisting of field recordings from around the world. Spoken-word recordings of the work of literary figures such as Langston Hughes, James Joyce, Robert Frost and Allen Ginsberg were included in the Folkways catalog, as was music by contemporary North American composers such as Henry Cowell and John Cage. Folkways also released many recordings aimed at the children's market. The work of Ella Jenkins, an African-American woman from Chicago, has been a staple in this area since 1956.

Most Folkways LP releases were packaged in heavy jackets that had a cardboard divider to accommodate the brochure notes accompanying each disc. The quality and extent of the annotation varied widely, ranging from straightforward transcriptions of the song lyrics on the album to in-depth studies of the music. Asch maintained a policy of keeping every title in print, regardless of how many or how few copies were sold.

Asch occasionally ventured into partnerships with other record labels. In 1964, he formed an arrangement with MGM to create the Verve/Folkways label for the release of titles from the Folkways catalog that were thought to have some commercial potential and that needed wider distribution. The arrangement also called for the issuance of previously unreleased material from Asch's archives. This partnership lasted until 1967. In 1966, Asch entered into a similar agreement with Scholastic, a publisher of educational materials, for the release of less commercially viable titles to the educational market. This arrangement lasted until the end of the decade.

The Smithsonian Institution acquired Folkways, its archive of recordings and all its business files in 1987, following negotiations that had begun prior to Asch's death in 1986. The Smithsonian operates Folkways through its Center for Folklife and Cultural Heritage. The Smithsonian has maintained Asch's longstanding policy of keeping all older Folkways recordings available, through the production of on-demand cassette tapes or compact discs. It has also continued to release new recordings under the Smithsonian/Folkways imprint (see http://www.si.edu/folkways/).

Bibliography

Goldsmith, Peter D. 1998. *Making People's Music: Moe Asch and Folkways Records*. Washington, DC: Smithsonian Institution Press.

Shirk, A.V. 1997. 'Moses Asch and Smithsonian/Folkways Records.' *Old-Time Herald* 6(1) (August–October): 16–19, 28, 56. (Available online at http://www.old-timeherald.org/pages/6-1/6-1asch.htm)

Young, Israel. 1977. 'Moses Asch: Twentieth Century Man.' *Sing Out!* 20(1) (May–June): 2–6; 20(2) (July–August): 25–29.

Discographical Reference

Anthology of American Folk Music (ed. Harry Smith). Folkways FA 2951/2952/2953. 1952: USA. Reissue: *Anthology of American Folk Music* (ed. Harry Smith). Smithsonian/Folkways 40090. *1997*: USA.

PAUL F. WELLS

—Fonovisa (Mexico)

Fonovisa is the record company division of the Mexican media conglomerate Televisa S.A., owned by the Azcarraga family. Televisa's interests include 16 radio stations, four television networks, a film studio, newspapers, magazines and two soccer clubs. The record company division was formed in the early 1980s when Televisa bought two local labels, Melody and Profono, as outlets for music recordings by the stars of its *telenovelas* (soap operas).

In the 1990s, Fonovisa broadened its activity by signing foreign artists, such as the multimillion-selling Enrique Iglesias, and by investing in Mexican pop and rock genres such as *tejano* and *grupera*. Fonovisa has branch companies in the United States, and in Argentina and several other South American countries.

Discography

Iglesias, Enrique. *Vivir*. Fonovisa 80001. *1997*: Mexico.

DAVE LAING

—Gael-Linn (Ireland)

A leading source of traditional Irish music, Gael-Linn is a subsidiary of Comhaltas Ceoltóirí Eireann, an organization founded in 1951 to promote Irish language and culture.

Since the 1960s, the label has released numerous albums by living representatives of Irish instrumental and vocal traditions. In 1968, it recorded Sean O'Raida's pioneering group Ceolteoiri Chaulann, the forerunner of the Chieftains. With regard to soloists, Gael-Linn has recorded piper Declan Masterson, Dublin fiddler Paddy Glackin and traditional singers Joe Heaney and Áine Uí Cheallaigh.

One of the most acclaimed Gael-Linn recordings is an album by concertina player Noel Hill and accordionist Tony McMahon, made in 1986 at a session for dancing at a pub in Knocknagree on the border between counties Cork and Kerry.

Discographical Reference
Hill, Noel, and McMahon, Tony. *I gcNoc na Grai*. Gael-Linn CEF 114. *1986*: Ireland.

Discography
Blasta!: The Irish Traditional Music Special. Gael-Linn CDNCD 7. *1997*: Ireland.

DAVE LAING

—Gallo (South Africa)
The Gallo organization was responsible for a number of crucial developments that were central to the creation and advancement of the recording industry in South Africa, and it has had a longstanding involvement with the development of musical talent throughout the southern African subcontinent.

Gallo began operating in 1926 as Brunswick Gramophone House, a small wholesaling and retailing operation in Johannesburg whose owner, Eric Gallo, had secured the license to import and distribute the Brunswick label recordings of the US Brunswick-Balke-Collender Company. A further commercial alliance with Decca Records in the United Kingdom that began around 1932, coupled with astute and aggressive marketing, guaranteed Gallo a large share of the lucrative South African market for imported music. This position was further enhanced when a subsidiary, the Gramophone Record Company (GRC), founded by Eric Gallo and Arnold Golembo in 1940, secured distribution rights for the Capitol (US) label in 1947. When this arrangement was terminated following EMI's acquisition of Capitol, GRC acquired the rights to the Columbia-CBS label in 1956. For many decades, Gallo was also involved in the importation and local manufacture of musical instruments.

Gallo began sending artists to London to record in 1930. The material was released on the newly created Singer imprint, the first independent record label in Sub-

Saharan Africa. In 1933, the company built a recording studio in Johannesburg – also the first in the Sub-Saharan region, if not the entire continent. This enabled Gallo to develop commercially both African and Afrikaans musical talent on a large scale. (The music of English-speaking South Africans only began to be recorded 20 years later in the early 1950s.) Gallo's first record-pressing plant, constructed in 1949, was the third such facility to be built in South Africa, but was the first to manufacture long-playing vinyl discs (1951). Gallo was also the first company in the country to begin mastering on tape, replacing the old direct-to-disc cutting method in 1949.

Gallo's various operations were reorganized as Gallo Africa (Pty) Ltd. in 1946, and the company remained an independent entity until 1983, when a controlling share was acquired by the Premier Milling Company, a subsidiary of the giant Anglo-American conglomerate. Prior to this, however, Gallo had for many years been buying up other record companies, including USA (1960), Trutone (1962), which in turn had absorbed Record Industries in 1955, Troubadour (1969), Meteor (1974) and Teal (merged in 1978). Later, RPM (1981) and Tusk (1996) were acquired. The result of these acquisitions was that about 85 percent of all the recordings ever made in South Africa prior to the early 1980s originated from Gallo-controlled catalogs.

Two Gallo-originated songs were the first from southern Africa to become worldwide hits. 'Mbube,' written and first recorded by Solomon Linda's Original Evening Birds in 1939, was reworked as 'Wimoweh' by the Weavers in 1952, then later as 'The Lion Sleeps Tonight' by the Tokens in 1961, and has since been covered by countless other artists. It is undoubtedly the most popular melody ever to have come out of Africa. 'Skokiaan,' recorded by the Bulawayo Sweet Rhythms Band in 1950, was successfully covered by a number of artists, including Louis Armstrong in 1954, while the original recording appeared briefly in the charts in both the United States and the United Kingdom.

A number of South African musicians with one-time or ongoing Gallo connections have become internationally popular artists. These include the Manhattan Brothers, Miriam Makeba, Hugh Masekela, Jonas Gwangwa, Dollar Brand (Abdullah Ibrahim), Mahlathini and the Mahotella Queens, Ladysmith Black Mambazo and, more recently, Lucky Dube.

Discographical References
Bulawayo Sweet Rhythms Band, The. 'Skokiaan.' Gallo-tone GE1152T. 1950: South Africa.
Solomon Linda's Original Evening Birds. 'Mbube.' Singer

GE829. 1939: South Africa. (Currently available on *From Marabi to Disco*. Gallo CDZAC61.)

Tokens, The. 'The Lion Sleeps Tonight.' RCA 7954. *1961*: USA.

Weavers, The. 'Wimoweh.' Decca 27928. 1952: USA.

Discography

From Marabi to Disco. Gallo CDZAC61. *1994*: South Africa.

Jazz Epistles. Gallo Continental GALP14. *1960*: South Africa. Reissue: *Jazz Epistles*. Gallo CDZAC56. *1992*: South Africa.

Ladysmith Black Mambazo. *Favourites*. Gallo CDGMP40300. *1992*: South Africa.

Lucky Dube. *Serious Reggae Business*. Gallo CDLUCKY10. *1996*: South Africa.

Mahlathini & the Mahotella Queens. *The Best of Mahlathini & the Mahotella Queens*. Gallo CDHUL40274. *1991*: South Africa.

Township Swing Jazz, Vol. 1. Gallo CDZAC53. *1991*: South Africa.

Township Swing Jazz, Vol. 2. Gallo CDZAC54. *1991*: South Africa.

ROB ALLINGHAM

—Geffen Records (US)

Named after its founder, the media mogul David Geffen (1941–), Geffen Records was established in 1979 with financial backing from WEA. Geffen, originally an agent, had been put in charge of Elektra-Asylum in 1973, but had left the music industry in 1976 because of ill health. As head of Geffen Records, Geffen initially signed established artists, Elton John and Donna Summer among them, and achieved his first commercial triumph with John Lennon's and Yoko Ono's *Double Fantasy* (1980). Further hits came from established performers like Cher, Aerosmith, Joni Mitchell and Don Henley (formerly of the Eagles). Heavy metal proved to be another lucrative genre for Geffen. Not only did Geffen Records sign Whitesnake, but the company also scored one of its most notable triumphs with Guns N' Roses' *Appetite for Destruction* (1987), which sold over 16 million copies. Other successful signings included Edie Brickell and the New Bohemians, and Nelson.

In 1989, Geffen Records was the third most successful label in the US industry, and MCA acquired its catalog for $540 million. David Geffen remained as chairperson, and a new subsidiary, DGC, was established. It had its own meteoric success with the work of Nirvana, whose album *Nevermind* (1991) sold over 10 million copies.

David Geffen also expanded into other media. A film company was established and released the hits *Risky Business* (1983) and *Little Shop of Horrors* (1986). The company also assisted in the production of Broadway musicals: *Cats* (1982) and *Dreamgirls* (1981). In 1996, by which time he had left his position as chair of Geffen Records, Geffen initiated a new multimedia company, DreamWorks, in conjunction with filmmaker Steven Spielberg and former Disney executive Jeffrey Katzenberg.

Bibliography

Dannen, Fredric. 1991. *Hit Men: Power Brokers and Fast Money Inside the Music Business*. New York: Vintage.

Sanjek, Russell, and Sanjek, David. 1996. *Pennies from Heaven: The American Popular Music Business in the Twentieth Century*. New York: Da Capo Press.

Discographical References

Guns N' Roses. *Appetite for Destruction*. Geffen 2-24148. *1987*: USA.

Lennon, John, and Ono, Yoko. *Double Fantasy*. Geffen 2001. *1980*: USA.

Nirvana. *Nevermind*. Geffen DGC-24425. *1991*: USA.

Discography

Aerosmith. *A Little South of Sanity*. Geffen 25221. *1998*: USA.

Aerosmith. *Big Ones*. Geffen 24716. *1994*: USA.

Aerosmith. *Done with Mirrors*. Geffen 26695. *1985*: USA. Reissue: Aerosmith. *Done with Mirrors*. Geffen 24091. *1997*: USA.

Aerosmith. *Get a Grip*. Geffen 24455. *1993*: USA.

Aerosmith. *Permanent Vacation*. Geffen 24162. *1987*: USA.

Aerosmith. *Pump*. Geffen 24254. *1989*: USA.

Brickell, Edie, and the New Bohemians. *Shooting Rubberbands at the Stars*. Geffen 24192. *1987*: USA.

Cher. *If I Could Turn Back Time: Greatest Hits*. Geffen 24509. *1999*: USA.

Henley, Don. *Actual Miles: Henley's Greatest Hits*. Geffen 24834. *1995*: USA.

Mitchell, Joni. *Chalk Mark in a Rain Storm*. Geffen 2-24172. *1988*: USA.

Mitchell, Joni. *Dog Eat Dog*. Geffen 24074. *1985*: USA.

Mitchell, Joni. *Night Ride Home*. Geffen 24302. *1991*: USA.

Mitchell, Joni. *Wild Things Run Fast*. Geffen 2019. *1982*: USA. Reissue: Mitchell, Joni. *Wild Things Run Fast*. Mobile Fidelity 570. *1992*: USA.

Nelson. *Because They Can*. Geffen 24525. *1995*: USA.

Whitesnake. *Whitesnake's Greatest Hits*. Geffen 24620. *1994*: USA.

Filmography

Little Shop of Horrors, dir. Frank Oz. 1986. USA. 94 mins. Black Comedy. Original music by Howard Ashman, Miles Goodman, Alan Menken.

Risky Business, dir. Paul Brickman. 1983. USA. 99 mins.

Teen Comedy. Original music by Christopher Franke, Tangerine Dream.

Visual Recordings

Aerosmith. 1989. 'Video 3x5.' Geffen 38146 (video).

Aerosmith. 1990. 'Things That Go Pump.' Geffen 38172 (video).

Aerosmith. 1994. 'Big Ones You Can Look At.' Geffen 39546 (video).

DAVID SANJEK

—Gennett Records (US)

Owned by the Starr Piano Company based in Richmond, Indiana, the Gennett record label took its name from Henry Gennett and his sons, who had operated the Starr Piano Company, founded in 1872, since 1903. After failing with hill-and-dale cut records between 1915 and 1918, Gennett was sued by Victor Records for patent infringement when it used the lateral-cut system, a legal battle that Gennett won in 1922. That year, Gennett recorded the New Orleans Rhythm Kings and 'King' Oliver's Creole Jazz Band. Bix Beiderbecke with the Wolverines and 'Jelly Roll' Morton piano solos were also recorded and, overnight, Gennett became a major jazz record label. Later recordings were made of the State Street Ramblers, as well as solo items by Hoagy Carmichael, including the first release of his composition 'Star Dust.' This was electronically recorded, and Gennett introduced its Electrobeam issues to mark its adoption of the improved method. A field trip to Birmingham, Alabama in 1926 led to recordings by rural African-American artists 'Jaybird' Coleman, Willie Harris and Daddy Stovepipe. 'Race' records were not separately listed by Gennett, but a label to this effect was pasted on the relevant issues. The company's recordings of hillbilly/country bands were numerous, and included titles by Rutherford and Burnett, and Da Costa Woltz's Southern Serenaders. Recordings of opera singers and symphony orchestras, bird songs and railroad sound effects were also issued, the latter being all too appropriate, as the recording studios were, notoriously, beside a busy railroad line.

Gennett helped launch the short-lived Black Patti label of African-American artists, and also issued blues on its subsidiaries Champion Records, Superior and the Sears Silvertone label. Items by 'Scrapper' Blackwell, 'Big' Bill Broonzy and Sam Collins were among them, all issued under pseudonyms on these cheap outlets. The Depression forced the demise of the Gennett catalog, although the family maintained the Starr Piano Company until 1952. In 1939, the brief Varsity Race series was initiated by Eli Oberstein, which included a number of blues recordings from the Gennett catalog, and in the mid-1940s Joe Davis resuscitated the Gennett label by

arrangement with son Harry Gennett, although he soon changed the name to his own. Fred Gennett, the last of the brothers, died in 1964. The Starr Piano factory buildings were destroyed by fire in 1993, although a wall with the Gennett Records logo has been preserved.

Bibliography

Dixon, Robert M.W., Godrich, John, and Rye, Howard. 1997. 'Gennett and Champion.' In *Blues & Gospel Records 1890–1943*. 4th ed. Oxford: Clarendon Press, xxxv–xxxvi.

Kennedy, Rick. 1993. 'Gennett Records: Capturing America's Musical Grassroots.' *78 Quarterly* 1(8): 35–54.

Kennedy, Rick. 1994. *Jelly Roll, Bix and Hoagy: Gennett Studios and the Birth of Recorded Jazz*. Bloomington, IN: Indiana University Press.

Totsi, Tom. 1988–93. 'Gennett-Champion Blues' (series). *78 Quarterly* 1(3),(4),(5),(6),(8).

Sheet Music

Carmichael, Hoagy, comp., and Parish, Mitchell, lyr. 1929. 'Star Dust.' New York: Mills Music.

Discographical Reference

Carmichael, Hoagy. 'Star Dust'/'One Night in Havana.' Gennett 6311. 1931: USA.

Discography

Gennett-Champion Collection. Harrison B. 1927–34: USA.

Gennett Rarities. Jazz Oracle 8009. 1998: USA.

PAUL OLIVER

—Gramco (India)

'Gramco,' or the Gramophone Company, Ltd., was founded in London in 1898. Gramco has been the single most important producer of recorded music in India. In the decades immediately following its founding, Gramco's commitment to develop 'oriental' markets led to energetic, influential and profitable activities in India in the early decades of the twentieth century. Between 1902 and 1910, Gramco released over 4,000 recordings of local music. Through advertising, entrepreneurship, licensing of regional subsidiaries and the construction of record-pressing plants in Calcutta in 1908, and again in nearby Dum Dum in 1928, Gramco was able to marginalize competitors and dominate the Indian music industry for over 70 years.

In 1900, the Gramophone Company 'adopted its famous trademark of a fox terrier listening to a gramophone – "His Master's Voice" (HMV) – although it did not make any extensive use of the trademark for some years' (Jones 1985, 81). It was after 1915 that Gramco's recordings were issued under the label 'HMV.' In 1931, the Gramophone Company amalgamated with Columbia (UK) to form Electric and Musical Industries Ltd. (EMI). EMI continued to use the names 'Gramco' and 'HMV' in India. Until the mid-1930s, most recordings consisted of classical and light-classical pieces, theater songs, and assorted vernacular-language items aimed primarily at the phonograph-owning urban elite. With the advent of sound film in the 1930s and the spread of cheaper phonographs, film music became the dominant popular music category. In the late 1960s, HMV's near-complete monopoly in South Asia was weakened by the competitive entrance of Polydor. More significantly, the dramatic spread of cassette technology from the later 1970s, while increasing the size of the market, precipitated the emergence of hundreds of local competitors – both pirate and legitimate – effectively ending HMV's dominance. Although its problems have been compounded by somewhat phlegmatic management practises, unwise investments, burdensome regulations and other factors, the Gramophone Company of India, acquired by the local RPG Industries group in the mid-1980s (with EMI retaining 12.5 percent of the company), has continued to be a prestigious and important label in India.

Bibliography

Farrell, Gerry. 1993. 'The Early Days of the Gramophone Industry in India: Historical, Social and Musical Perspectives.' *British Journal of Ethnomusicology* 2: 31–53.

Gaisberg, F.W. 1942. *Music on Record*. London: Robert Hale.

Gronow, Pekka. 1981. 'The Record Industry Comes to the Orient.' *Ethnomusicology* 25 (2 May): 251–84.

Jones, Geoffrey. 1985. 'The Gramophone Company: An Anglo-American Multinational, 1898–1931.' *Business History Review* 59(1): 76–100.

Joshi, G.N. 1988. 'A Concise History of the Phonograph Industry in India.' *Popular Music* 7(2): 147–56.

Kinnear, Michael. 1994. *The Gramophone Company's First Indian Recordings: 1899–1980*. Bombay: Popular Prakashan.

Manuel, Peter. 1993. *Cassette Culture: Popular Music and Technology in North India*. Chicago: University of Chicago Press.

PETER MANUEL

—Gramophone Company (UK)

The Gramophone Company Ltd. was established in London in April 1898 by Trevor Williams and William Barry Owen (Jones 1985, 80). Owen was acting as agent for Emile Berliner, and formed the Gramophone Company to exploit Berliner's disc-recording patents outside the United States. Berliner's assistant, Fred Gaisberg, established their first studios in London in July 1898. In December 1900, the company's official name became the Gramophone & Typewriter Co. (and Sister Companies) Ltd. Branches were soon established in countries across the world, including India, Russia and Persia, as well as most European nations. In the early years, records were manufactured principally in Hanover, Germany, initially using mainly the Berliner and G & T (Gramophone & Typewriter) labels. Artists recorded in 1900–1901 included the Christy Minstrels and the pioneer African-American mandolinist Seth Weeks.

In 1903, the Gramophone Company took over the International Zonophone Company and its Zonophone label. Zonophone became the company's subsidiary label for budget-priced popular material and continued in that role for the remainder of the Gramophone Company's independent existence.

In 1910, the company launched His Master's Voice (HMV), which would henceforth be its main label, using the famous dog-and-gramophone trademark based on a painting by Francis Barraud purchased in 1899. Although HMV was not launched as a label until 1910, the trademark was in fact adopted by the Gramophone Company in 1900 (Jones 1985, 81), and was used extensively by the US Victor Talking Machine Company (with which the Gramophone Company had a special relationship from the beginning of the twentieth century) between 1900 and 1910. Records for non-English-speaking territories initially combined the logo with Gramophone (Grammofono in Italy; Gramofono in Spain) labels, but in later years His Master's Voice or translations were substituted.

During World War I, the company lost control of its German operations, which remained in business as Deutsche Grammophon. Subsequent protracted litigation failed to restore ownership to the British company, which established a German operation, Electrola Gesellschaft M.B.H., using an Electrola label.

In the period 1915–20, significant recordings of ragtime and early syncopated music were made in London by the Savoy Quartet, many featuring the African-American drummer Alec Williams, and by a visiting African-American group, the Versatile Four.

In 1921, the Victor Talking Machine Company acquired a majority of the Gramophone Company's equity, 'making it technically a subsidiary of the American firm' (Jones 1985, 78). After this, the Gramophone Company became the outlet in Britain, Europe and Australia for the jazz recordings of Victor (US), and is remembered for its extensive involvement in documenting the emerging dance band scene in Britain. The recordings of the Savoy Orpheans and Savoy Havana Band and of Jack Hylton appeared on the Gramophone Company's labels. Many highly regarded performances were recorded by the studio house bands directed for Zonophone by Bert Firman (1924–28) or his brother John (from October 1928), and for HMV by Carroll Gibbons (1928–29) and later by Ray Noble (1929 onward). These bands featured some of the most skilled arranging and most highly regarded 'hot' soloists of the era.

The company's US interests were taken over in January 1929 by the Radio Corporation of America (RCA), which became a part-owner of the Gramophone Company as a consequence of its acquisition of the Victor company. In April 1931, the Gramophone Company merged with Columbia International Ltd. to form Electric and Musical Industries Ltd. (EMI). This British-owned multinational corporation became one of the largest and most influential recording organizations. Operation of the Gramophone Company's labels was for a long period little affected by the merger in most territories, though in January 1933 the budget-label Zonophone was merged with Columbia's budget-label Regal to form the Regal-Zonophone label in both Britain and Australia.

Bibliography

Jones, Geoffrey. 1985. 'The Gramophone Company: An Anglo-American Multinational, 1898–1931.' *Business History Review* 59(1): 76–100.

Martland, Peter. 1997. *Since Records Began: EMI, the First 100 Years*. London: Batsford.

Petts, Leonard. 1973. *The Story of 'Nipper' and the 'His Master's Voice' Picture*. London: Talking Machine Review.

Rust, Brian, comp. 1976a. *The HMV Studio House Bands 1912–1939*. Chigwell, Essex: Storyville Publications.

Rust, Brian, comp. 1976b. *The Zonophone Studio House Bands 1912–1932*. Chigwell, Essex: Storyville Publications.

Rust, Brian. 1981a. '(British) Berliner, G & T and Zonophone 7-inch Records.' *Talking Machine Review* 63/64.

Rust, Brian. 1981b. 'In the Beginning – Berliner.' *Sounds Vintage* 1(3): 2–5.

HOWARD RYE

—Hispavox (Spain)

Hispavox is a Spanish record company founded in Madrid on 27 June 1953. During the 1960s and 1970s, it was the most important Spanish record company and represented the US company WEA until the latter's establishment in Spain. In 1985, it was absorbed by EMI, but the label identity was retained. EMI-Hispavox accounted for almost 25 percent of record sales in Spain during the latter half of the 1980s.

Hispavox's record catalog includes Spanish classical music, flamenco, zarzuela and, most of all, pop music written over the last few decades of the twentieth century. In the 1960s, the company began to sign up rock

and pop music groups and young soloists, such as Los Pekenikes, Miguel Ríos, Karina, Los Ángeles, Los Mitos, Mari Trini, Los Payos, María Ostiz and Alberto Cortez. During this period, Hispavox was run by a first-rate artistic team, which included Rafael Trabuchelli as producer and Waldo de los Ríos as arranger. It also had some of the best Spanish session musicians at its disposal. Together, they created a special style that became known as the 'Torrelaguna sound' – due to the fact that the recording studio was located on this Madrid street.

At the end of the 1970s and the beginning of the 1980s, the company released discs by various performers and groups of the so-called *movida madrileña*, such as Alaska, Ejecutivos Agresivos, Nacha Pop and Radio Futura, together with recordings by musicians such as Massiel, Juan Pardo, José Luis Perales and Mari Trini, who belonged to the previous generation. As part of the multinational EMI, the label has achieved an excellent sales record, with artists such as Alejandro Sanz, the flamenco singer Remedios Amaya and the female duo Ella baila sola.

Bibliography

Irles, Gerardo. 1997. *¡Sólo para fans! La música ye-yé y pop española de los años 60* [Only for Fans: Spanish Ye-Yé and Pop Music of the 1960s]. Madrid: Alianza Editorial.

Jones, Daniel E. 1988. 'La industria fonográfica: cima de las transnacionales' [The Record Industry: The Top Transnationals]. In *Las industrias culturales en España* [The Cultural Industries of Spain], ed. Enrique Bustamante and Ramón Zallo. Madrid: Akal.

Ordovás, Jesús. 1986. *Historia de la música pop española* [The History of Spanish Pop Music]. Madrid: Alianza Editorial.

Pardo, José Ramón. 1975. *Historia del pop español* [The History of Spanish Pop]. Madrid: Guía del ocio.

Discography

Antología del folclore musical de España. Hispavox HH10-107/110. *1959*: Spain.

Los Pekenikes. *Lo mejor de Los Pekenikes*. Hispavox HHS 11-258. *1973*: Spain.

Pardo, Juan. *Juan mucho más Juan*. Hispavox S 60.503. *1980*: Spain.

Radio Futura. *Música moderna*. Hispavox 7 96149 2. *1991*: Spain.

Ríos, Miguel. *Despierta*. Hispavox HHS 11-182. *1970*: Spain.

Trini, Mari. *L'automne 'Vals de otoño'*. Hispavox HHS 11-247. *1973*: Spain.

JULIO ARCE

—HMV (UK/US)

HMV was a record label first used by the Gramophone Company in 1910 on records issued in Britain. The name

'His Master's Voice' capitalized on the dog-and-gramophone trademark, which was based on a painting by Francis Barraud purchased by the company in 1899 and previously used by the company's US affiliate on its Victor and Monarch records. HMV labels were soon launched in many other countries, although in some places the logo was initially used in combination with variants of the Gramophone label name. Later, translations of HMV were substituted, such as La Voix de son Maître for France, La Voce del Padrone for Italy and La Voz du su Amo for Spain.

HMV remained the company's flagship label in Europe and Australia up to when and after it merged with Columbia International Ltd. to form EMI in April 1931. It was the label used to issue recordings from Victor (US) and was thus the label on which many major jazz recordings, including classics by 'Jelly Roll' Morton, Fats Waller, Duke Ellington and Benny Goodman, were issued outside North America. At various times in the 1930s and 1940s, the label's roster of dance bands included those of Artie Shaw, Tommy Dorsey and Glenn Miller from the United States, and Jack Hylton and Ray Noble from Britain. Elvis Presley and Ray Charles were notable among later HMV artists. After the licensing arrangement between RCA-Victor and EMI terminated in 1957, the HMV catalog concentrated increasingly on classical music, and in 1967 the remaining HMV popular repertoire was transferred to other EMI labels.

Bibliography

Jones, Geoffrey. 1985. 'The Gramophone Company: An Anglo-American Multinational, 1898–1931.' *Business History Review* 59(1): 76–100.

Kelly, Alan. 1988. *His Master's Voice/La Voce del Padrone: The Italian Catalogue. A Complete Numerical Catalogue of Italian Gramophone Recordings Made from 1898 to 1929 in Italy and Elsewhere by the Gramophone Company Ltd.* (*Discographies*, No. 30). Westport, CT: Greenwood Press.

Kelly, Alan. 1990. *His Master's Voice/La Voix de Son Maître: The French Catalogue. A Complete Numerical Catalogue of French Gramophone Recordings Made from 1898 to 1929 in France and Elsewhere by the Gramophone Company Ltd.* (*Discographies*, No. 37). Westport, CT: Greenwood Press.

Kelly, Alan. 1994. *His Master's Voice/Die Stimme Seines Herrn: The German Catalogue. A Complete Numerical Catalogue of German Gramophone Recordings Made from 1898 to 1929 in Germany, Austria, and Elsewhere by the Gramophone Company Ltd.* (*Discographies*, No. 55). Westport, CT: Greenwood Press.

Kelly, Alan, and Kloters, Jacques. 1997. *His Master's Voice/De Stem van zijn Meester: The Dutch Catalogue. A Complete Numerical Catalogue of Dutch and Belgian Gramophone Recordings Made from 1900 to 1929 in Holland, Belgium, and Elsewhere by the Gramophone Company Ltd.* (*Discographies*, No. 72). Westport, CT: Greenwood Press.

Martland, Peter. 1997. *Since Records Began: EMI, the First 100 Years*. London: Batsford.

Pelletier, Paul, comp. 1986a. *Complete British Directory of Popular 78/45 r.p.m. Singles 1950–1980, Volume One: Columbia, Decca, HMV*. London: Record Information Services.

Pelletier, Paul. 1986b. 'The HMV & M-G-M Labels.' *Record Information* 6: 3–24.

Petts, Leonard. 1973. *The Story of 'Nipper' and the 'His Master's Voice' Picture*. London: Talking Machine Review.

Rust, Brian, comp. 1976. *The HMV Studio House Bands 1912–1939*. Chigwell, Essex: Storyville Publications.

Rust, Brian. 1978. *The American Record Label Book*. New Rochelle, NY: Arlington House.

Smith, Michael. 1992. *H.M.V. Recordings: 'BD' Series: Magenta Label, A Discography*. Hastings, East Sussex: Tamarisk Books.

HOWARD RYE

—Hungaroton (Hungary)

Established in 1951 as Qualiton, and later renamed as *Hungaroton Magyar Hanglemezkiadó Vállalat* ('Hungarian Record Company'), Hungaroton was the country's sole record company during the Communist period in Hungary. Hungaroton has since become just one of many minor enterprises struggling with the international majors that dominate a small but lively market. It released its first microgroove record in 1955, its first stereo record in 1962, its first beat single in 1965 and its first beat album in 1967. As the only outlet for the emerging beat and rock scene, as well as for folk and classical music, Hungaroton embodied the principles of state-owned socialist monopolies, acting simultaneously as entrepreneur, censor and provider of culture. By the time it was privatized amid scandal in 1995, Hungaroton was considerably in debt. Owned by a group of Hungarian investors, it has, however, managed to carry on by rereleasing its impressive back catalog on CD, while cautiously putting out new material on its labels, Hungaroton Gong for pop and Hungaroton Classic.

Bibliography

Sagi, Mária. 1982. 'Music on Records in Hungary.' In *The Phonogram in Cultural Communication*, ed. Kurt Blaukopf. Wien: Springer-Verlag, 111–22.

Sebők, János. 1983, 1984. *MagyaRock 1–2*. Budapest: Zeneműkiadó.

Szemere, Anna. 1983. 'Some Institutional Aspects of Pop and Rock in Hungary.' *Popular Music* 3: 121–42.

Szőnyei, Tamás. 1989, 1992. *Az új hullám évtizede 1–2* [The New Wave Decade I–II]. Budapest: Laude Kiadó; Katalizátor Iroda.

TAMÁS SZŐNYEI

—Ice (Caribbean)

Ice Records was set up by Guyana-born Eddy Grant in London in 1975. A former member of the integrated pop band the Equals, Grant had worked increasingly as a producer and session guitarist. Ice issued Grant's subsequent solo recordings, including the 1981 hit 'I Don't Wanna Dance.'

In 1981, Grant moved his base to Barbados, where he built a recording studio and produced tracks by Mighty Gabby, Calypso Rose and other *soca* and calypso artists. Ice reissued many classic calypso recordings by Mighty Sparrow, Roaring Lion and Lord Kitchener, as well as Grant's own music, which included the anti-apartheid hit 'Gimme Hope Jo'Anna.'

Discographical References

Grant, Eddy. 'Gimme Hope Jo'Anna.' Ice ICE 64. *1988*: UK.

Grant, Eddy. 'I Don't Wanna Dance.' Ice ICE 56. *1981*: UK.

Discography

Lord Kitchener. *Klassic Kitchener, Vol. 2*. Ice 941002. *1994*: UK.

Lord Kitchener. *Klassic Kitchener, Vol. 3*. Ice 941802. *1994*: UK.

Mighty Sparrow. *16 Carnival Hits*. Ice 920902. *1992*: UK.

Roaring Lion. *Viva Le King*. Ice 95100. *1995*: UK.

DAVE LAING

—Impulse! (US)

Impulse! was a record company and label established in 1960 as a subsidiary of ABC-Paramount and devoted to recording new jazz. Under the direction initially of Creed Taylor, who soon left to join Verve, and then of Bob Thiele, Impulse! recorded major work by John Coltrane, whose output appeared on the label from 1961 until his death in 1967, and Archie Shepp. The catalog was soon expanded to include a broader spectrum of jazz artists, including Benny Carter, Coleman Hawkins and Duke Ellington, as well as Gil Evans, Max Roach and McCoy Tyner.

From the late 1960s, the label's output slowly decreased in quantity and became less adventurous in content, although there were many posthumous issues of previously unreleased material by John Coltrane. Impulse! passed with its parent company into the ownership of MCA, which reactivated the label in the later 1980s with a catalog principally devoted to reissues of earlier recordings. After MCA was purchased by Seagram and then became a division of Universal Music Group, the Impulse! label was transferred to another division, GRP Recording Company. Under the direction of Tommy LiPuma, new jazz recordings again appeared on the label in the 1990s from a roster that included McCoy Tyner, Horace Silver and Diana Krall. Reissue of the back catalog has also continued, with the distinctive foldout sleeve format, the label's signature in the 1960s, adapted for CD.

Bibliography

Gardner, Mark. 1988. 'Impulse!' In *The New Grove Dictionary of Jazz*, ed. Barry Kernfeld. London/New York: Macmillan/Grove, 563.

Shera, Michael. 1962. 'A Discography of the Impulse Label.' *Jazz Journal* 15(10): 19, 34.

Thiele, Bob (as told to Bob Golden). 1995. *What a Wonderful World: A Lifetime of Recordings*. New York and Oxford: Oxford University Press.

HOWARD RYE

—Intercord Tonträger GmbH (Germany)

Intercord was founded in 1966 in Stuttgart, south Germany by the German Holtzbrinck media group and was Germany's largest independent record label and distributor (through its distribution arm Intercord Record Service (IRS)) until 1994.

As Germany's largest independent label, Intercord achieved success with its German-language repertoire through artists such as Pe Werner and Reinhard Mey. Its most successful band, however, was PUR, which Intercord signed in 1987 on the basis of the song 'Hab' mich wieder mal an Dir betrunken' from PUR's self-produced eponymous album. Intercord also released dance music through its subsidiary label Blow Up!, whose roster included Dance 2 Trance, E-Rotic, Captain Hollywood and Fool's Garden, which were especially successful in Asia. More hardcore-oriented music, such as rave and techno, was released under Intercord's Mad Dog imprint. Intercord was also the licensee of the UK indie Mute, the Belgium-based Play It Again Sam (PIAS) and the US label Roadrunner, to name but a few.

In July 1994, Thorn-EMI bought Intercord to add a third German repertoire source to EMI Electrola and Virgin. EMI had taken the important strategic decision to become Intercord's parent company at a time when speculation was running high that the Holtzbrinck company was about to divest itself of its music division. According to *Billboard*, Intercord had reported sales of DM 160.1 million ($101.4 million), with pre-tax profits of DM 15.4 million ($9.7 million) in 1993, and was sold

729

to Thorn-EMI for DM 132 million ($83.5 million) (*Billboard*, 16 July 1994).

In the first three years after Intercord's incorporation into EMI, the German label continued to operate separately from EMI Electrola's base in Cologne – a business arrangement that was similar to that of Virgin. In July 1997, however, the first step toward Intercord's total integration into the company was taken with the closure of the warehouse in Stuttgart. For logistical reasons, the warehouse activities were integrated into EMI's distribution center in Cologne, forming a single distribution facility for the three EMI-owned companies. Three years later, Intercord closed its headquarters in south Germany and, by 2000, most of its repertoire had been incorporated into EMI Electrola GmbH & Co KG.

Bibliography

EMI. http://www.emimusic.de

Intercord. http://www.intercord.de

Intercord Dance Site. http://www.dancesite.com/intercord

Musikwoche. http://www.mediabiz.de

PUR. http://www.pur.de

Spahr, Wolfgang. 1994. 'Intercord Lives On Under EMI Ownership.' *Billboard* (12 November).

Spahr, Wolfgang. 1997a. 'Germany's Intercord Label Restructures.' *Billboard* (9 November).

Spahr, Wolfgang. 1997b. 'Intercord Finds Large Audience in Asia.' *Billboard* (1 March).

'Thorn-EMI Deal for Intercord Label Completed.' 1994. *Billboard* (16 July).

Discographical Reference

PUR. 'Hab' mich wieder mal an Dir betrunken.' *PUR*. Intercord 845099. *1987*: Germany.

VANESSA BASTIAN

—Island Records (UK)

Chris Blackwell founded Island Records in Jamaica in 1959 to record local jazz and ska music. Blackwell, whose family was linked to the Crosse & Blackwell food empire, moved to London in 1962 and licensed Jamaican productions for distribution to the expatriate Caribbean population in Britain. He began to produce his own records in the United Kingdom with such artists as Millie ('My Boy Lollipop') and the Spencer Davis Group ('Keep On Running'). These were licensed to Fontana (a subsidiary of Philips), but Blackwell subsequently issued further material by white rock bands on the Island label. Among the acts signed to Island in the late 1960s were Traffic, Jethro Tull, Free and King Crimson. The label also signed folk-influenced acts, including Cat Stevens, John Martyn, Nick Drake and Fairport Convention. From the early 1960s, Island also issued blues and soul material from the United States on its Sue label.

In 1973, Blackwell brought leading reggae band the Wailers to Britain and forged a rock-reggae fusion style with the group's charismatic leader Bob Marley. Over the next five years, Marley became the first international reggae star on the strength of his Island albums. Meanwhile, the label diversified through its satellite companies Mango (African and Jamaican music), Antilles (jazz) and Fourth & Broadway (disco and dance). Island also obtained the European rights to two albums recorded by Bob Dylan for Asylum in the United States.

If Marley was Island's star act of the 1970s, the Irish rock band U2 was the label's new superstar in the following decade. Its international hit album *War* coincided with the success of Frankie Goes to Hollywood, whose records appeared on the licensed label ZTT. Other successful acts in the 1980s were the contrasting male vocalists Robert Palmer and Steve Winwood, while Island also nurtured the career of British saxophonist Courtney Pine.

Despite its artistic successes, Island suffered financial losses when it tried to expand its operations. After losing British distribution rights to Virgin and EG, and after an unsuccessful attempt to use independent distribution in the United States, the company closed its distribution and manufacturing activities in 1975. A decade later, Blackwell's growing involvement with films through the Island Pictures subsidiary caused the virtual closure of Island's Los Angeles branch.

In 1989, Blackwell sold Island Records to PolyGram for $272 million. He joined the PolyGram board, from which he eventually resigned in 1997. During the 1990s, the UK branch of Island continued to operate as a separate A&R center, developing the careers of such artists as PJ Harvey, Pulp and Tricky, plus African artists such as Baaba Maal and Angelique Kidjo. The roster of Island (US) included the Irish group the Cranberries and Melissa Etheridge, while the company's reggae roots were maintained by the opening of a Jamaican branch of Mango, which enjoyed worldwide rights to productions by Sly and Robbie.

In 1997, Island began issuing a series of albums celebrating its 40th anniversary.

Discographical References

Island 40, Vol. 1: 1959–1964 – Ska's the Limit. Island 524393. *1997*: UK.

Island 40, Vol. 2: 1964–1969 – Rhythm and Blues Beat. Island 524394. *1997*: UK.

Island 40, Vol. 3: 1968–1975 – Acoustic Waves. Island 524376. *1998*: UK.

Island 40, Vol. 4: 1967–1975 – Electric Currents. Island 524427. *1998*: UK.

Island 40, Vol. 5: Reggae Roots. Island 572486. *1999*: UK.

Millie. 'My Boy Lollipop.' Fontana TF 449. *1964*: UK.

Spencer Davis Group, The. 'Keep On Running.' Fontana TF 632. *1965*: UK.

U2. *War*. Island CID 112. *1983*: UK.

Discography

Cranberries, The. *Everybody Else Is Doing It, So Why Can't We?*. Island CID 8003. *1993*: USA.

Etheridge, Melissa. *Yes I Am*. Island 48660. *1993*: USA.

Fairport Convention. *Liege and Lief*. Island ILPS 9115. *1970*: UK.

Frankie Goes to Hollywood. *Welcome to the Pleasuredome*. ZTT/Island CID 101. *1984*: UK.

Free. *Fire and Water*. Island ILPS 9120. *1970*: UK.

Jethro Tull. *Stand Up*. Island ILPS 9103. *1969*: UK.

Kidjo, Angelique. *Ayé*. Mango IMCD 244. *1993*: UK.

King Crimson. *In the Court of the Crimson King*. Island ILPS 9111. *1969*: UK.

Maal, Baaba. *Firin' in Fouta*. Mango 1109. *1995*: UK.

Marley, Bob, and the Wailers. *Burnin'*. Island ILPS 9256. *1973*: UK.

Martyn, John. *London Conversation*. Island ILPS 952. *1968*: UK.

Palmer, Robert. *Secrets*. Island ILPS 9544. *1979*: UK.

Pine, Courtney. *Journey to the Urge Within*. Antilles ILPS 9846. *1986*: UK.

PJ Harvey. *Rid of Me*. Island CID 8002. *1993*: UK.

Sly and Robbie. *Silent Assassin*. Island 422-842475-2. *1989*: UK.

Stevens, Cat. *Teaser and the Firecat*. Island ILPS 9154. *1971*: UK.

The Island Story. Island CID 25. *1987*: UK.

Traffic. *Mr. Fantasy*. Island ILPS 9061. *1967*: UK.

Tricky. *Maxinquaye*. Fourth & Broadway BRCD 610. *1995*: UK.

Winwood, Steve. *Back in the High Life*. Island CID 9844. *1986*: UK.

DAVE LAING

—Jambo (East Africa)

The Jambo label was introduced in 1948 by East African Sound Studios Ltd., the first entirely local record company in East Africa. Recordings were made in the company's studio in Nairobi, with additional sessions organized in Dar es Salaam and Kampala. Initially, shellacs were pressed in London and shipped back to East Africa. In 1950, the company was taken over by the Africa Ground Cotton Company (Afcot). By then, the Jambo catalog listed 210 records.

A slow response to market demands and a growing unsold stock caused by long delivery dates from London persuaded Afcot to establish its own pressing plant in Nairobi. In 1952, the company's name was changed to East African Records, Ltd. and the studio closed down when the plant began production by re-pressing the bestselling titles from the existing catalog. Recording for the Jambo label was resumed in a new studio in 1955 and, by 1963, a further 600 records had been released. The pressing plant also made shellacs for many of the independent labels that sprang up in East Africa in the mid-1950s. The company diversified its business further with the operation of 60 jukeboxes in East Africa, mostly in African bars in the Nairobi area. With the introduction of commercial radio in Kenya in 1959, the recording studio enjoyed brisk business for a couple of years, producing sponsored programs and advertisements.

Demands on improved studio facilities and investments in the pressing plant to meet the anticipated change to vinyl records led Afcot to sell the company to Katzler & Company in 1961. The label was initially called New Jambo. When vinyl was introduced in 1963, both the label and the recording studio were separated from the company and renamed Equator Sound. East African Records, Ltd., by now merely a pressing plant, was sold off to the Gallo company, based in South Africa.

Bibliography

Graebner, Werner. 1989. *The First 35 Years of Commercial Recording in East Africa, 1928–1963: Processes of Institutionalization*. Research Paper, Institute of African Studies, University of Nairobi.

Harrev, Flemming. 1989. 'Jambo Records and the Promotion of Popular Music in East Africa: The Story of Otto Larsen and East African Records, Ltd., 1952–1963.' In *Perspectives on African Music*, ed. Wolfgang Bender. Bayreuth: Bayreuth African Studies Series 9, 103–37.

Vernon, Paul. 1995. 'Feast of East.' *Folk Roots* 145 (July): 26–27, 29.

Discography

Coast Social Orchestra, The. 'Jamba Recodi' (Swahili)/ 'Tezameni Sociali' (Swahili) (78 rpm). Jambo EA 127. *1948*: East Africa.

Jambo Boys, The. 'Malaika nakupenda' (Swahili)/'Mapenzi Fanya Haraka' (Swahili) (78 rpm). Jambo WS 111. *1958*: East Africa.

Kamau & Kanyata. 'Mache' (Kikuyo)/'Korachi (1)' (Kikuyo) (78 rpm). Jambo EA 128. *1948*: East Africa.

Kiko Kids, The. 'Mahaba' (Swahili)/'Mali Yangu' (Swahili) (78 rpm). Jambo WS 102. *1958*: East Africa.

Konde, Fundi, and His Guitar. 'Ai Empologoma'/'Mapenzi ya Kwetu Sisi' (78 rpm). Jambo EA 245. *1949*: East Africa.

Maruf, Musa. 'Fungua uso wako' (Swahili)/'Bombay Safari' (Swahili) (78 rpm). Jambo EA 122. *1948*: East Africa.

Nanyoga & Party. 'Eriso' (Luganda)/'Ndikuwa' (Luganda) (78 rpm). Jambo EA 146. *1948*: East Africa.

Omar, Ustad. 'Black Market (Part I)' (Swahili)/'Black Market (Part II)' (Swahili) (78 rpm). Jambo EA 232. 1949: East Africa.

Omolo & Party. 'Lana' (Dholuo)/'Rumba' (Dholuo) (78 rpm). Jambo EA 117. 1947: East Africa.

Sykes, Ally. 'Nakupenda Rucky' (Swahili)/'Tabu' (Swahili) (78 rpm). Jambo EA 106. 1947: East Africa.

FLEMMING HARREV

—Jive (UK)

A leading outlet for both white and black popular music in Britain and the United States, the Jive label is part of the Zomba group of companies established in London in 1975 by South African–born music publishers Clive Calder and Ralph Simon.

Jive was launched in London in 1981 and in New York in 1983. Its earliest UK artists included the new romantic group A Flock of Seagulls and Eurovision pop vocal group Tight Fit. More sustained success came with Billy Ocean, whose theme song from the film *The Jewel of the Nile*, 'When the Going Gets Tough,' was an international hit.

In the mid-1980s, Jive's US head of operations, Barry Weiss, signed hip-hop and rap acts Kool Moe Dee, DJ Jazzy Jeff and the Fresh Prince and Whodini. Among its most important subsequent US signings was writer/singer R. Kelly.

The US company later diversified into gospel music, forming the Verity label and purchasing the Brentwood, Reunion and Benson labels. These labels are part of Zomba's Provident Music Group, which has its own distribution network. Provident artists include Vanessa Bell Armstrong and Richard Smallwood.

In Britain, Zomba also owns a studio complex (Battery), music production library Bruton Music and manages several leading studio producers. In 1997, Zomba purchased a share of UK distribution company Pinnacle, while Jive's distributor BMG bought 20 percent of Zomba. BMG acquired the remainder of Zomba in 2002.

Discographical Reference

Ocean, Billy. 'When the Going Gets Tough, the Tough Get Going.' Jive JIVE 114. *1986*: UK.

Discography

A Flock of Seagulls. *A Flock of Seagulls*. Jive HOP 201. *1982*: UK.

Armstrong, Vanessa Bell. *The Secret Is Out*. Verity 43011. *1995*: USA.

DJ Jazzy Jeff and the Fresh Prince. *He's the D.J., I'm the Rapper*. Jive 1091. *1988*: USA.

Kelly, R. *12 Play*. Jive 41527. *1994*: USA.

Kool Moe Dee. *How Ya Like Me Now*. Jive 1079. *1987*: USA.

Smallwood, Richard, with Vision. *Adoration: Live in Atlanta*. Verity 43105. *1996*: USA.

Tight Fit. 'The Lion Sleeps Tonight.' Jive JIVE 9. *1982*: UK.

Whodini. *Open Sesame*. Jive 8494. *1987*: USA.

Filmography

The Jewel of the Nile, dir. Lewis Teague. 1985. USA. 115 mins. Romantic Adventure. Original music by Jack Nitzsche.

DAVE LAING

—King (US)

Founded in Cincinnati, Ohio in 1943 by Syd Nathan, the King Record Company (with three subsidiary labels – Queen (1945), DeLuxe (bought from the original owners in 1948) and Federal (1950)) became a vibrant, self-contained US 'indie' during the 1950s and into the 1960s. With its own recording studio, pressing plant and network of distributors, it remained the idiosyncratic fiefdom of Nathan until his death on 5 March 1968.

Initially profiting from hillbilly and country music (Moon Mullican, Cowboy Copas, Hawkshaw Hawkins), in the late 1940s the company secured a stronghold in the 'race' market with recordings of Bullmoose Jackson, Wynonie Harris, Roy Brown, Ivory Joe Hunter and Tiny Bradshaw, as well as with a range of gospel recordings.

Throughout the 1950s, King was a formidable source of rhythm and blues (R&B), from jazz-rooted musicians (Earl Bostic, Bill Doggett) and from musicians producing the newly emergent R&B sounds that underlay the rock 'n' roll revolution (the Dominoes, Little Esther, Hank Ballard and the Midnighters, Otis Williams and the Charms, the 5 Royales, Little Willie John and Ike Turner's Kings of Rhythm). King's producers included Ralph Bass, Johnny Otis, Sonny Thompson, Henry Glover, Andy Gibson, Hy Grill and Gene Redd.

Despite some continued success with Ballard and R&B guitar 'slingers' Freddie King and Johnny 'Guitar' Watson, by the mid-1960s King had become predominantly a marketing operation for its most outstanding discovery, James Brown (signed in 1956), and his productions.

After Nathan's death, the company was quickly sold twice to become Starday-King, a division of Lin Broadcasting, a coup organized by Nathan's ex-general manager, Hal Neely.

In 1971, Brown, with his back catalog, signed to Polydor. King limped on as a division of the Tennessee Recording and Publishing Company until the mid-1970s, when the balance of its catalog was acquired by Moe Lytle's Nashville-based Gusto Records, which at the end of the twentieth century was trading worldwide as Nestshare Ltd.

Bibliography

Ruppli, Michel. 1985. *The King Labels: A Discography* (*Discographies*, No. 18). Westport, CT: Greenwood Press.

Discography

Brown, James. *Foundations of Funk*. Polydor 5311652. *1996*: USA.

Brown, James. *Live at the Apollo*. King 826. *1963*: USA. Reissue: Brown, James. *Live at the Apollo*. Polydor 8434792. *1990*: USA.

Brown, James. *Roots of a Revolution*. Polydor 8173042. *1989*: USA.

The King R&B Box Set. King KBSCD-7002. *1995*: USA.

CLIFF WHITE

—K-Tel (US/UK)

A pioneer of the television marketing of compilation albums, K-Tel began as a manufacturer of brushes and other household products in the US Midwest. In the late 1960s, K-Tel moved into the music industry and quickly became a leading company.

K-Tel started an international division in 1972, and its first release, *20 Dynamic Hits*, topped the British album chart. By 1990, over 50 K-Tel compilations had been Top 10 hits in the United Kingdom. At its peak in the late 1970s, the company had branches in more than 10 European countries.

In the United States, K-Tel invested its profits unsuccessfully in real estate and filed for protection from its creditors in 1984. The company underwent several changes of ownership before its entertainment division was sold to a management buyout in 1995. At this stage, K-Tel was operating in the United States, Canada and five European countries and had music and video sales worth $60 million a year.

Discographical Reference

20 Dynamic Hits. K-Tel TE 292. *1972*: UK.

DAVE LAING

—LaFace (US)

A record label founded in 1991 and operated by leading US black music songwriters and producers Babyface and L.A. (Kenneth Edmonds and L.A. Reid), LaFace is based in Atlanta, Georgia and is financed and distributed by Arista, a division of BMG.

The label's most successful acts have included Toni Braxton, the male singer Usher and the female vocal group TLC, whose album *CrazySexyCool* sold over 5 million copies in the United States. In 1995, LaFace signed a new five-year agreement with Arista, reportedly invol-

ving guaranteed payments of $10 million. In the following year, Braxton sued the label for breach of contract.

Discographical Reference

TLC. *CrazySexyCool*. LaFace 26009. *1994*: USA.

Discography

Braxton, Toni. *Toni Braxton*. LaFace 26007. *1993*: USA.

Usher. *My Way*. LaFace 26043. *1997*: USA.

DAVE LAING

—Liberty (US)

Founded in Los Angeles, California in 1955 by Si Waronker, Liberty's earliest successes were with sultry torch singer Julie London, the novelty recordings of David Seville and his tape-sped 'Chipmunks,' and rock 'n' roller Eddie Cochran. Through the acquisition of other labels, Waronker, his president, Al Bennett, and principal producer, Snuff Garrett, moved Liberty from being a middle-of-the-road (MOR) and pop label to being a pop-centered label with a nonetheless increasingly broad spectrum of music. Liberty's first spinoff label was Freedom (1958: Johnny Burnette); subsequent acquisitions included Dolton (1959: pop), Blue Note (1963: jazz), Imperial (1963: R&B/rock 'n' roll), Pacific Jazz (1965) and Minit (1963: R&B/soul). In 1966, Liberty resurrected a Minit imprint as an entirely different label based on the west coast.

During the company's heyday in the 1960s, its successful mainstream pop acts included Johnny Burnette, Bobby Vee, Gene McDaniels, the Crickets, the Ventures, Jan and Dean, Vic Dana, Timi Yuro, Jackie DeShannon, Johnny Rivers, Gary Lewis and the Playboys, and Del Shannon. Many significant R&B, soul and jazz artists appeared on its subsidiary labels, particularly Blue Note, which was already a renowned jazz imprint. A UK branch of Liberty was founded in 1967, registering successes with the Bonzo Dog Band and P.J. Proby.

At the end of the 1960s, Liberty promoted long-term R&B/soul acts Ike and Tina Turner and Bobby Womack to crossover success. Liberty was then bought in 1968 by United Artists as part of TransAmerica Corp. In 1979, EMI acquired the catalog, which was subsequently marketed as a division of Capitol Records.

Liberty's principal artists have been reissued on CDs, which have been marketed in the United States by Capitol Records and in the United Kingdom by EMI Records.

Bibliography

Kelly, Michael. 1993. *Liberty Records: A History of the Recording Company and Its Stars, 1955–1971*. Jefferson and London: McFarland & Company Inc.

CLIFF WHITE

—Library of Congress Recordings (US)

The Library of Congress, the national library of the United States, first issued sound recordings for sale in

1942. Intended mainly for scholars and researchers, the recordings were drawn from the collections in the Archive of American Folk Song, which was established within the Library of Congress in 1928. Two of the best known of those engaged in collecting material for the Archive were John A. Lomax and his son Alan, whose extensive field recordings, made in the southern states of the United States from 1933, were especially important in establishing the Archive as a center for research (Porterfield 1996). In this, they built especially on the work of the first curator of the Archive, Robert Winslow Gordon, who himself made an important series of field recordings in Georgia and North Carolina in 1925–28 (Kodish 1986).

The Library of Congress 78 rpm recordings constitute some of the earliest documentary releases of North American traditional music, with special strengths in the music of the southern United States and of North American Indian communities. The recordings in the series devoted to traditional African-American performance were especially notable for their contribution to the documentation of work song, ranging from the prison gang labor songs of James 'Iron Head' Baker and fellow convicts, recorded at Central State Farm, Sugarland, Texas in 1933–34, to the chants and hollers of a railroad gang led by Henry Truvillion, recorded at Wiergate, Texas in 1940, and to the solo field hollers of Thomas Marshall, recorded at Edwards, Mississippi in 1939.

In 1956, the Library of Congress began issuing an influential series of LP recordings that eventually totaled some 70 titles in all. Again drawing on material in the Archive collections, the series began by dubbing the material first issued on 78s (Cowley 1997). Each title typically focused on a single topic and included a variety of artists. Examples include *Afro-American Spirituals, Work Songs, and Ballads* (AFS L3), recorded by John and Alan Lomax and edited by Alan Lomax, and *Versions and Variants of 'Barbara Allen'* (AFS L54), edited by Charles Seeger.

In 1976, as part of the US bicentennial celebrations, the Library issued a 15-LP set, *Folk Music in America*, edited by Richard Spottswood. The set included both archival material from the Library's collections and material originally released commercially on other labels, and it was organized under themes such as 'Religious Music: Congregational and Ceremonial,' and 'Songs of Complaint and Protest.'

Important historical material from the Archive has been issued on other record labels, some of it more than once. Particularly noteworthy are the releases, by Elektra, Document and others, of oral history recordings made by Alan Lomax featuring 'Jelly Roll' Morton (1938), Woody Guthrie (1940) and Huddie Ledbetter (Leadbelly) (1940), on which the interviewees spoke about their lives and experiences, and illustrated their recollections with performances. In the 1980s, the Library of Congress began a series of partnerships with commercial record labels, including Rounder and Rykodisc, to further disseminate parts of its collections.

The Archive itself was renamed the Archive of Folk Song in 1955 and the Archive of Folk Culture in 1981. In that year, it became part of the Library of Congress American Folklife Center, which had been established in 1976. It is actively involved in the digitization of its resources for the American Memory Project, a multimedia presentation of some of the Library's important collections (available on-line at http://memory.loc.gov/ammem/amhome.html). A catalog of recordings is available on-line at http://lcweb.loc.gov/folklife/afc.html.

Bibliography

Check-List of Recorded Songs in the English Language in the Library of Congress Archive of American Folk Song to July, 1940. 1971 (1942). 3 vols. in 1. New York: Arno Press. (First published Washington, DC: Library of Congress, 1942.)

Cowley, John. 1997. 'Library of Congress Archive of Folk Song Recordings.' In *Blues and Gospel Records 1890–1943*, ed. Robert M.W. Dixon, John Godrich and Howard Rye. 4th ed. Oxford: Clarendon Press, xl–xlii.

Kodish, Debora G. 1986. *Good Friends and Bad Enemies: Robert Winslow Gordon and the Study of American Folksong*. Urbana, IL: University of Illinois Press.

Porterfield, Nolan. 1996. *Last Cavalier: The Life and Times of John A. Lomax, 1867–1948*. Urbana, IL: University of Illinois Press.

Russell, Tony. 1982. 'Essay Review: Folk Music in America.' *Popular Music* 2: 259–68.

Discographical References

Afro-American Spirituals, Work Songs, and Ballads (rec. John and Alan Lomax, 1933–39; ed. Alan Lomax). Library of Congress AFS L3. *1956*: USA.

Baker, James 'Iron Head,' and group. 'Go Down, Old Hannah.' *Negro Work Songs and Calls* (rec. John and Alan Lomax and Herbert Halpert, 1933–40; ed. B.A. Botkin). Library of Congress AFS L8. 1933; *ca. 1956*: USA.

Baker, James 'Iron Head,' and group. 'The Grey Goose.' *Afro-American Spirituals, Work Songs, and Ballads* (rec. John and Alan Lomax, 1933–39; ed. Alan Lomax). Library of Congress AFS L3. 1934; *1956*: USA.

Folk Music in America (ed. Richard K. Spottswood). Library of Congress LBC 1–15. *1976*: USA.

Guthrie, Woody. *Woody Guthrie: Library of Congress Recordings* (rec. Alan Lomax, 1940). Elektra EKL-271/2. *1964*: USA. Reissue: Guthrie, Woody. *Woody Guthrie:*

Library of Congress Recordings (rec. Alan Lomax, 1940). Rounder CD 1041–1043. *1988*: USA.

Ledbetter, Huddie (Leadbelly). *Leadbelly: Library of Congress Recordings* (rec. Alan Lomax, 1940). Elektra EKL-301/2. *1966*: USA. Reissue: Ledbetter, Huddie (Leadbelly). *Leadbelly: Library of Congress Recordings* (rec. Alan Lomax, 1940). Rounder CD 1044–1046. *1991*: USA; Rounder CD 1097–1099. *1994*: USA.

Marshall, Thomas. 'Quittin' Time, Songs I and II'/'Mealtime Call.' *Negro Work Songs and Calls* (rec. John and Alan Lomax and Herbert Halpert, 1933–40; ed. B.A. Botkin). Library of Congress AFS L8. 1939; *ca. 1956*: USA.

Morton, 'Jelly Roll.' *Jelly Roll Morton: Library of Congress Recordings* (rec. Alan Lomax, 1938). Classic Jazz Masters CJM 1–8. *1970*: Sweden. Reissue: Morton, 'Jelly Roll.' *Jelly Roll Morton: Library of Congress Recordings* (rec. Alan Lomax, 1938). Rounder CD 1091–1094. *1993*: USA.

Truvillion, Henry, and group. 'Unloading Rails'/'Tamping Ties.' *Negro Work Songs and Calls* (rec. John and Alan Lomax and Herbert Halpert, 1933–40; ed. B.A. Botkin). Library of Congress AFS L8. 1940; *ca. 1956*: USA.

Versions and Variants of 'Barbara Allen' (rec. 1933–54; ed. Charles Seeger). Library of Congress AFS L54. *1996*: USA.

DAVID HORN

—Loningisa (Democratic Republic of Congo)

The Loningisa studio and record label, founded by the Papadimitriou brothers in 1950, was the second Greek-owned label (Ngoma was the first) to flourish in Leopoldville, Belgian Congo (later Zaire, and then the Democratic Republic of Congo). Its name was Lingala for 'shake it up.' (Lingala is the most widely spoken language in Congo.) Initially, Loningisa recorded folklore artists and troubadours, although a string of *maringa* releases by Paul Dewayon's Watam ('delinquent') band guaranteed the allegiance of the first 'youth audience.' The house band, Bana Loningisa ('Loningisa Boys'), was led by the guitarist and composer Henri Bowane (recruited from Ngoma in 1951), who released many hits and arranged for the recording of stars such as Henri Liengo, Adikwa, Tino Mab, Pierre Kalima and Pauline Lisanga, the first female recording artist in Congo (then the Belgian Congo). Each artist had his/her photograph printed on the distinctive green label. Instrumentation on early recordings included guitars, woodwind, accordion, percussion and tuba. Some cuts also featured a Solovox organ played by a European, Carlos Sarti (possibly a pseudonym for Gilbert Warnant). Masters were sent to Britain for pressing, and 78 rpm records were exported across Africa. In 1953, 15-year-old 'Franco' Luambo Makiadi was signed up as a studio guitarist. His own records were instant successes. Loningisa also owned a clothes store and, during Franco's early career, he was used to promote imported fashions. In 1956, Franco, with Jean Serge Essous, Brazzos and other members of Bana Loningisa, formed OK Jazz (the leading Congolese band of the time); they released more than a dozen records in their first year and went on to become the continent's biggest-selling band. Loningisa closed in 1959, when many Europeans left the country in anticipation of an independence debacle.

Bibliography

Bemba, Sylvain. 1984. *50 ans de musique du congo-zaïre* [Fifty Years of Music of Congo-Zaire]. Paris: Presence Africaine.

Ewens, Graeme. 1991. *Africa O-Ye!: A Celebration of African Music*. London: Guinness.

Ewens, Graeme. 1994. *Congo Colossus – The Life and Legacy of Franco and OK Jazz*. Norfolk, UK: Buku Press/Sterns.

Kennis, Vincent. 1995. Sleeve Notes/CD Booklet for *Roots of Rumba Rock, Vols. 1 and 2*. Belgium: Crammed Discs.

Discography

Franco and OK Jazz. *Originalité* [1956–57]. RetroAfric RETRO2CD. *1992*: UK.

Roots of OK Jazz. Crammed Discs CRAW7. *1993*: Belgium.

Roots of Rumba Rock, Vol. 1. Crammed Discs CRAW4. *1991*: Belgium.

Roots of Rumba Rock, Vol. 2. Crammed Discs CRAW10. *1995*: Belgium.

GRAEME EWENS

—Max Music (Spain)

Max Music is a Spanish record company founded in Barcelona in 1983. Although it began as a very small and independent record company, it has since expanded considerably and has opened branches in the United States, Mexico and Germany. Max Music has concentrated on dance music, and especially compilations, such as *Máquina Total*, *Caribe Mix* and *House Mix*. These compilations contain selections of well-known songs chosen according to particular themes. Max Music has also produced records by singers associated with other styles, like María del Monte, Los Providens and Rebecca. One of its most important commercial successes has been a compilation record of Spanish indie groups.

Discography

Bombazo Mix 1. Max Music NM 1155 CDTV. *1995*: Spain.
Caribe Mix 98. Max Music NM 1864 CDTV. *1998*: Spain.

Dream Team. Max Music NM 1350 CDTV. *1995*: Spain.

Internet Mix. Max Music NM 1477 CDTV. *1996*: Spain.

Lo + duro 5. Max Music NM 1430 CDTV. *1995*: Spain.

Máquina Total 9. Max Music NM 1482 CDTV. *1995*: Spain.

Rambo Total. Max Music NM 1420 CDTV. *1996*: Spain.

JULIO ARCE

—Mega Records (Denmark)

Mega Records is the main label of Mega Scandinavia A/S, a subsidiary of the German edel company with head offices in Copenhagen, Denmark. Its roster is primarily Scandinavian, but since 1997 a few German acts have been signed as well. The company was founded in 1983 by Kjeld Wennick, an experienced artist-manager. Affiliated with Mega are the techno label Smart Records and the music publishing company Megasong Publishing. Mega's primary activities consist of developing the artists signed to the company and licensing non-Scandinavian material for Scandinavia. The company has focused on modern dance music, including dance compilations, but it has signed artists from a wide variety of genres (for example, big band music, soul, musicals, punk rock and world music).

Mega's first major success was the Danish duo Laban, who had hits in most countries, including the United States, in the latter part of the 1980s. A few years later, the Swedish rap vocalist Leila K became the bestselling female artist in Europe after Whitney Houston. By the end of the twentieth century, the most successful Mega act was the Swedish pop-reggae group Ace of Base, which had sold 21 million copies of its debut album, *Happy Nation* (1993). It was the first Scandinavian act to become firmly established in the United States. In Europe outside Scandinavia and in the Far East (except for Japan), Ace of Base is represented on license by the PolyGram group. In the United States, the group is licensed to Arista.

Like other Scandinavian record companies, Mega Records has been able to obtain substantial success in the Far East for some of its artists without first introducing the acts in Europe or the United States. Mega was purchased by edel in 1999.

Discographical Reference

Ace of Base. *Happy Nation.* Mega MRCD3206. *1993*: Denmark.

Discography

Leila K. *Carousel.* Mega MRCD3224. *1993*: Denmark.

MORTEN MICHELSEN

—Melodiya (USSR)

Melodiya, a Soviet state record company, was founded in 1964 in Moscow. Its roots can be traced back to the time of the Russian Revolution. Recordings have existed in Russia since 1899, the year of the establishment of the Russian branch of Deutsche Grammophon AG in St. Petersburg. The manufacture of Russian records began in 1902 with the opening of the first Russian record company in Riga by the British Gramophone Company. After the revolution of 1917, Lenin and his Bolshevik Party made it immediately clear that they were aware of the importance of recording technology as a means of propaganda. This led, on 20 August 1919, to the nationalization of the Russian record industry and the foundation of the 'Soviet Plastinki Propaganda Section,' which started releasing recordings of Lenin's speeches in the same year.

Over the following decades, party-controlled state recording facilities throughout the huge Soviet realm released recordings of classical, folk and popular music under the umbrella and label of a special organization called, from the late 1930s, the 'Committee for Radio Information.' It consisted of representatives of the party and state apparatus, and included members of the composers' union.

In 1964, the Soviet recording industry was reorganized and became the responsibility of the Ministry of Culture. It formed the record company Melodiya as an 'all-union company' (which meant that it covered all the republics in the Union of Soviet Socialist Republics) in order to combine and centralize all recording and manufacturing facilities in the Soviet Union. Melodiya handled the recording, manufacturing and wholesale aspects of the record trade within the former USSR; exports were handled through the Soviet agency for book exports, 'Mezdunarodnaya Kniga.' Until the end of the 1980s, Melodiya issued about 1,200 new releases a year, with an estimated annual total sale of 200–300 million units.

As a consequence of Melodiya's monopolistic position, it was also the sole popular music producer in the former Soviet Union, even though that kind of music was considered to be of rather marginal importance. Sixty percent of the annual new releases were classical music, 25 percent folk and only 15 percent popular music. Therefore, a great deal of popular music, like most Russian rock music, was distributed through the unofficial channels of a very vital cassette culture.

After the dissolution of the Soviet Union, Melodiya became a Russian record label. It has continued to survive mainly through the marketing of its valuable classical catalog. Since 1994, it has been represented outside Russia on the basis of an exclusive license agreement with the German music company BMG.

Bibliography

Bennett, John R. 1981. *Melodiya: A Soviet Russian L.P. Discography* (*Discographies*, No. 6). Westport, CT: Greenwood Press.

Gronow, Pekka. 1996. 'Ethnic Music and the Soviet Record Industry.' In *The Recording Industry: An Ethnomusicological Approach*. Tampere: Acta Universitatis Tamperensis 504 (Ser. A), 164ff. (First published in *Ethnomusicology* 19(1) (1975): 91ff.)

Volkow-Lannit, Leonid F. 1964. *Iskustvo zapetsatlennogo zvuka. Otserki po ostorii grammofona* [The Art of Sound Recording: Contributions to the History of the Gramophone]. Moscow: Iskustva.

PETER WICKE

—Mercury Records (US)

Irving Green, Berle Adams and Art Talmadge formed Mercury Records in 1945. A billboard advertisement for Mercury automobiles at the intersection of Jackson and Peoria in Chicago reportedly gave Mercury Records its name.

The first records on Green's initial label were probably pressed in September 1945, and were by R&B artists. Later that year, Tom Owen & His Cowboys became Mercury's first country music act. The reasons for the initial choice of R&B and country were fairly simple: after the war, major labels concentrated on big band and former big band singers for their popular music offerings, leaving the jukebox operators who wanted R&B and country music with few records for their machines. Since jukebox operators were the major buyers of records and because radio did not promote these two musical genres, there was an opportunity for a start-up label to achieve rapid success by catering to these markets.

However, within a year, Mercury branched out into jazz, Latin, Hawaiian, popular classics, polkas, recitations and children's records. Its first pop hit was 'To Each His Own' by Tony Martin; the company also signed Frankie Laine, another successful artist.

By 1946, Mercury had its executive team in place: Irwin Steinberg was chief financial officer, Morrie Price was sales manager and Art Talmadge was hired to work on promotion and to design advertisements for trade papers. Talmadge later became head of A&R. An early producer was Mitch Miller who, before being hired by Columbia, played a major role in Mercury's development as a prominent popular music label. The company grew quickly that first year, and then purchased the bankrupt Majestic label.

Majestic was a well-recognized brand name on radio during World War II. As a manufacturer of radios and parts, with dealerships across the United States, the company had a built-in distribution system for recordings when it purchased the bankrupt Hit and Classic labels from owner Eli Oberstein (former A&R executive with RCA-Victor) in 1945. Jimmy Walker, a former mayor of New York, was named president of the new label, but the flamboyant politician was soon replaced by Ben Selvin, a former dance-band leader.

Record production had to remain at the 1940 level during World War II because of a shortage of shellac. Irving Green, an industrial engineer who had started a record pressing plant, went to EMI in India and made an agreement with J.W. George, factory manager of the plant, for a supply of shellac. This meant that, in the fall of 1945, his plant was able to press 700,000 records a week. Because Green had designed some of the first automatic presses, thus cutting back on the need for skilled labor, his company had an edge over other labels with regard to record pressing.

The Mercury Radio & Television Corporation was incorporated on 1 March 1947; its first president was Berle Adams, manager of Louis Jordan. The company was formed by combining the record company, the pressing plant and the distribution company.

In August 1947, Mercury appointed Les Hutchens as its Nashville representative, becoming the first 'major' label to have a representative in that city. Hutchens did not stay long, but Murray Nash, hired in March 1948, headed country and R&B from Knoxville until he resigned in April 1951, when the label wanted him to move to New Orleans. In November 1951, Walter 'D' Kilpatrick was hired to work in Nashville and to sign country and R&B acts; this made Kilpatrick the first full-time A&R man in Nashville.

By 1952, Mercury was one of six major record manufacturers in the United States, the others being Columbia, Capitol, RCA-Victor, Decca and MGM. During the 1950s, top Mercury acts included the Platters ('The Great Pretender'), Johnny Preston ('Running Bear') and the Big Bopper ('Chantilly Lace').

By 1960, Mercury was grossing $14 million a year, and had its own pressing facility, an LP sleeve plant, sales offices and a line of record players. That year, Talmadge resigned to go to United Artists; Clyde Otis, one of the first black A&R chiefs in New York, joined Talmadge later that year. Shelby Singleton, who had worked on promotion for Mercury in Louisiana, was offered the job of restarting Mercury in Nashville after a deal with Starday fell through. Singleton opened the Mercury office in Nashville in January 1961 and produced a number of country hits during the first nine months of operation. When Otis left Mercury, Singleton was named head of A&R in New York as well, and he commuted between Nashville and New York until January 1967, when he began his own label. One of the early producers for Mercury was Quincy Jones, who produced the Lesley Gore hit 'It's My Party' in 1963.

Philips, the Dutch electronics company, had an agreement with Columbia to represent the firm in the US market. When Columbia canceled that contract, Philips needed to find another US company; it offered $10 million for Dot Records, but it was turned down. In June 1961, Philips purchased Mercury for $3 million. Irving Green remained president until the end of 1969, when Irwin Steinberg replaced him; Steinberg held the position until 1983. Charlie Fach, who had started the Smash subsidiary, was head of A&R.

During the 1960s, Mercury had hits with Bruce Channel ('Hey! Baby'), Roger Miller ('Dang Me,' 'King of the Road,' 'Chug-A-Lug') and Lesley Gore ('It's My Party,' 'Judy's Turn to Cry'). During the 1970s, Rod Stewart, Bachman-Turner Overdrive, Spirit and 10cc produced hits on the Mercury label.

Philips and the German-based Siemens company had established a joint-venture company in 1962 and the new company was renamed Phonogram; in 1972, Poly-Gram was formed by the merger of Phonogram and Polydor, owned by Siemens. In 1974, the US subsidiaries were Mercury-Phonogram, Philips, MGM and United Artists Records, which was acquired early in the 1970s.

During the 1980s, Mercury-Phonogram had hits with Dexy's Midnight Runners and Tears for Fears. In the 1990s, the Mercury-Phonogram subsidiary was renamed Mercury, and it incorporated the Fontana, Vertigo and Rocket labels. At the end of the 1990s, Shania Twain topped the Mercury roster. The dance imprint Manifesto was also successful.

In 1998, the Music Corporation of America (MCA) purchased PolyGram, and the Mercury label was moved under the new Universal corporate umbrella.

Bibliography

Ruppli, Michel, and Novitsky, Ed. 1993a. *The Mercury Labels: A Discography. Volume I – The 1945–1956 Era* (*Discographies*, No. 51). Westport, CT: Greenwood Press.

Ruppli, Michel, and Novitsky, Ed. 1993b. *The Mercury Labels: A Discography. Volume II – The 1956–1964 Era* (*Discographies*, No. 51). Westport, CT: Greenwood Press.

Ruppli, Michel, and Novitsky, Ed. 1993c. *The Mercury Labels: A Discography. Volume III – The 1964–1969 Era* (*Discographies*, No. 51). Westport, CT: Greenwood Press.

Ruppli, Michel, and Novitsky, Ed. 1993d. *The Mercury Labels: A Discography. Volume IV – The 1969–1991 Era and Classical Recordings* (*Discographies*, No. 51). Westport, CT: Greenwood Press.

Ruppli, Michel, and Novitsky, Ed. 1993e. *The Mercury Labels: A Discography. Volume V – Record and Artist Indexes* (*Discographies*, No. 51). Westport, CT: Greenwood Press.

Discographical References

Big Bopper, The. 'Chantilly Lace.' Mercury 71343. *1958*: USA.

Channel, Bruce. 'Hey! Baby.' Smash 1731. *1962*: USA.

Gore, Lesley. 'It's My Party.' Mercury 72119. *1963*: USA.

Gore, Lesley. 'Judy's Turn to Cry.' Mercury 72143. *1963*: USA.

Martin, Tony. 'To Each His Own.' *The Best of Tony Martin: The Mercury Years*. Mercury 532875. 1946; *1996*: USA.

Miller, Roger. 'Chug-A-Lug.' Smash 1926. *1964*: USA.

Miller, Roger. 'Dang Me.' Smash 1881. *1964*: USA.

Miller, Roger. 'King of the Road.' Smash 1965. *1965*: USA.

Platters, The. 'The Great Pretender.' Mercury 70753. 1955: USA.

Preston, Johnny. 'Running Bear.' Mercury 71474. *1959*: USA.

DON CUSIC

—Metronome (Sweden)

Metronome Records was established in Stockholm in 1949 by brothers Anders and Lars Burman. Together with recording engineer Börje Ekberg, the Burman brothers, themselves musicians, were initially interested in developing Metronome as an independent Swedish jazz label. During the 1950s and 1960s, many Scandinavian jazz artists were recorded and produced in Metronome's studio and released on the Metronome label.

In the latter half of the 1960s and in the 1970s, Metronome's musical focus shifted to music in the singer-songwriter genre. The owners' ambition to keep the label Swedish attracted a substantial number of local artists, and a good deal of progressive music emerged on the Metronome label.

Metronome's business concept was based on a 50/50 local/foreign repertoire, and the company was the Swedish distributor for WEA's international catalog of artists. In 1979, WEA decided to set up a Swedish branch and purchased Metronome, which became the nucleus of Warner Music Sweden. At the time of purchase, WEA indicated that it would continue Metronome's policy of supporting local releases. Metronome's domestic image subsequently faded somewhat, and its operations with domestic recording artists decreased. In 1983, WEA sold the Metronome studio to one of its employees.

Bibliography

Burnett, Robert. 1996. *The Global Jukebox: The International Music Industry*. London and New York: Routledge.

Wallis, Roger, and Malm, Krister. 1984. *Big Sounds from Small Peoples: The Music Industry in Small Countries*. London: Constable.

Discography

Magnell, Ola. *Nya Perspektiv*. Metronome 15.557. *1976*: Sweden.

Norman, Charlie. *Boogie Woogie St. Louis Blues*. Metronome 15.1. 1949: Sweden.

Rogefeldt, Pugh. *Pughish*. Metronome 15.368. *1970*: Sweden.

Wadenius, Georg. *Godda Godda*. Metronome 15.350. *1969*: Sweden.

ROBERT BURNETT

—MGM Records (US)

Founded in 1946, the label was initially conceived as a marketing outlet for the soundtracks of MGM films. Soon, however, it scored chart hits with the work of black artists Billy Eckstine and Ivory Joe Hunter, as well as that of country star Hank Williams. For the most part, MGM shunned rock 'n' roll, but notably capitalized on the 11 million-selling singles by pop vocalist Connie Francis. In the wake of the 'British invasion,' MGM Records established a successful relationship with producer Mickie Most and his bands, the Animals and Herman's Hermits. Its more experimental subsidiary, Verve, signed the Velvet Underground and the Mothers of Invention, while Verve/Forecast featured the Blues Project, Tim Hardin and Richie Havens. At the same time, a misguided effort by veteran arranger Alan Lorber to gain a foothold in the underground movement with the 'Boss Town' campaign of 1968 – a campaign that attempted to make Boston 'a target city for the development of new artists from one geographical location' (Lorber 1995) by creating a 'second San Francisco' through the signing of such groups as Ultimate Spinach, the Beacon Street Union and Orpheus – led to a $4 million loss. The label was purchased in 1972 by PolyGram.

Bibliography

Lorber, Alan. 1995. Liner notes to *Ultimate Spinach*. Big Beat 142.

Ruppli, Michel, and Novitsky, Ed. 1998a. *The MGM Labels: A Discography. Volume 1: 1946–1960* (*Discographies*, No. 75). Westport, CT: Greenwood Press.

Ruppli, Michel, and Novitsky, Ed. 1998b. *The MGM Labels: A Discography. Volume 2: 1961–1982* (*Discographies*, No. 75). Westport, CT: Greenwood Press.

Ruppli, Michel, and Novitsky, Ed. 1998c. *The MGM Labels: A Discography. Volume 3: Additional Recordings/ Record and Artist Indexes* (*Discographies*, No. 75). Westport, CT: Greenwood Press.

Sanjek, Russell, and Sanjek, David. 1996. *Pennies from Heaven: The American Popular Music Business in the Twentieth Century*. New York: Da Capo Press.

Discography

Animals, The. *The Animals on Tour*. MGM 4281. *1965*: USA.

Animals, The. *The Animals [US]*. MGM 4264. *1964*: USA. Reissue: Animals, The. *The Animals [US]*. MGM 25646. *1983*: USA.

Animals, The. *British Go Go*. MGM 4306. *1965*: USA.

Animals, The. *Get Yourself a College Girl*. MGM 4273. *1965*: USA.

Beacon Street Union, The. *The Clown Died in Marvin Gardens*. MGM SE-4568. *1968*: USA.

Beacon Street Union, The. *The Eyes of the Beacon Street Union*. MGM SE-4517. *1968*: USA.

Beacon Street Union, The. *The Eyes of the Beacon Street Union/The Clown Died in Marvin Gardens*. See For Miles 495. *1998*: UK.

Blues Project, The. *The Best of the Blues Project*. Verve/ Forecast 3077. *1969*: USA.

Burdon, Eric, and the Animals. *The Best of Eric Burdon and the Animals, 1966–68*. PolyGram 849388. *1991*: USA.

Eckstine, Billy. *Favorites* (10''). MGM E-548. 1951: USA.

Eckstine, Billy. *I Let a Song Go Out of My Heart* (10''). MGM E-257. 1954: USA.

Eckstine, Billy. *Mister B with a Beat*. MGM 3176. 1955 USA.

Eckstine, Billy. *Rendezvous*. MGM E-3209. 1955: USA.

Eckstine, Billy. *Songs by Billy Eckstine* (10''). MGM E-523. 1951: USA.

Eckstine, Billy. *Tenderly*. MGM 2353071. 1952: USA.

Eckstine, Billy. *That Old Feeling*. MGM E-3275. 1955: USA.

Francis, Connie. *The Very Best of Connie Francis*. MGM 4167. *1963*: USA. Reissue: Francis, Connie. *The Very Best of Connie Francis*. PolyGram 827569. *1986*: USA.

Hardin, Tim. *Hang On to a Dream: The Verve Recordings*. PolyGram 521583. *1994*: USA.

Havens, Richie. *A State of Mind*. Verve 2304050. *1971*: USA.

Havens, Richie. *Mixed Bag*. Verve/Forecast 3006. *1967*: USA. Reissue: Havens, Richie. *Mixed Bag*. Verve 835210. *1988*: USA.

Havens, Richie. *Richard P Havens 1983*. Verve/Forecast 3047. *1983*: USA. Reissue: Havens, Richie. *Richard P Havens 1983*. PolyGram 835212. *1990*: USA.

Havens, Richie. *Somethin' Else Again*. Verve/Forecast 3034. *1968*: USA.

Herman's Hermits. *The Best of Herman's Hermits*. MGM 4315. *1965*: USA.

Herman's Hermits. *The Best of Herman's Hermits, Vol. 2*. MGM 4416. *1966*: USA.

Herman's Hermits. *The Best of Herman's Hermits, Vol. 3*. MGM 4505. *1968*: USA.

Hunter, Ivory Joe. *I Get That Lonesome Feeling*. MGM E-3488. *1957*: USA.

Hunter, Ivory Joe. *Since I Met You Baby: The Best of Ivory Joe Hunter*. Razor & Tie 2052. *1994*: USA.

Orpheus. *Ascending*. MGM 4569. *1968*: USA.

Orpheus. *Joyful*. MGM 4599. *1969*: USA.

Orpheus. *Orpheus*. MGM 4524. *1967*: USA.

Orpheus. *The Best of Orpheus*. Big Beat 2143. *1995*: UK.

Ultimate Spinach. *Behold & See*. MGM SE-4570. *1968*: USA. Reissue: Ultimate Spinach. *Behold & See*. Big Beat 148. *1995*: UK.

Ultimate Spinach. *Ultimate Spinach*. MGM 4518. *1967*: USA. Reissue: Ultimate Spinach. *Ultimate Spinach*. Big Beat 142. *1995*: UK.

Ultimate Spinach. *Ultimate Spinach III*. MGM SE-4600. *1969*: USA. Reissue: Ultimate Spinach. *Ultimate Spinach III*. Big Beat 165. *1996*: UK.

Velvet Underground, The. *The Best of the Velvet Underground*. Verve 841164. *1989*: USA.

Velvet Underground, The. *The Velvet Underground*. MGM 8108. *1969*: USA. Reissue: Velvet Underground, The. *The Velvet Underground*. PolyGram 531252. *1996*: USA.

Velvet Underground, The. *The Velvet Underground & Nico*. Verve V6-5008. *1967*: USA. Reissue: Velvet Underground, The. *The Velvet Underground & Nico*. Mobile Fidelity 695. *1997*: USA.

Velvet Underground, The. *White Light/White Heat*. Verve V6-5046. *1967*: USA. Reissue: Velvet Underground, The. *White Light/White Heat*. Mobile Fidelity 724. *1998*: USA.

Williams, Hank. *40 Greatest Hits*. Polydor 821233. *1978*: The Netherlands. Reissue: Williams, Hank. *40 Greatest Hits*. Polydor 821233. *1988*: The Netherlands.

Zappa, Frank, and the Mothers of Invention. *Mothermania: The Best of the Mothers*. Verve V6-5068. *1969*: USA.

Zappa, Frank, and the Mothers of Invention. *The Mothers of Invention*. MGM GAS-112. *1970*: USA.

Zappa, Frank, and the Mothers of Invention. *The Worst of the Mothers*. MGM SE-4754. *1971*: USA.

Zappa, Frank, and the Mothers of Invention. *The XXXX of the Mothers of Invention*. Verve V6-5074. *1969*: USA.

DAVID SANJEK

—Milan (France)

Founded in 1978 by Emmanuel Chamboredon, the Milan Music label specializes above all in film music. From its establishment, distribution of its products has been in the hands of BMG. In 1988, two subsidiary companies were established in the United States: one in New York, which is concerned essentially with financial and administrative matters; and one in Los Angeles, which is concerned with acquisitions, development, marketing and promotion.

In Europe, these different functions were centralized in Paris. However, in 1998 the label signed a new distribution contract whereby Milan Music productions were integrated into BMG International, which undertakes their distribution, marketing support and publicity on a world basis, with the exception of France and North America where BMG acts only as the distributor.

At the beginning of the twenty-first century, Milan's film music list included the music of such movies as *A River Runs Through It*, *The Elephant Man*, *The General's Daughter*, *Ghost*, *Once Were Warriors*, *Primal Fear*, *Rules of Engagement* and *The Truman Show*. Milan also brought out a collection of Alfred Hitchcock scores in 1999 to mark the centennial celebration of the filmmaker's life, and in 2001 released the soundtrack to the popular US television series *Frasier*.

In parallel with its concentration on film music, Milan developed a list of Latin music from Argentina, Brazil, Cuba and Mexico.

Discographical References

A River Runs Through It (Original soundtrack). Milan 24692. *1993*: France.

The Elephant Man (Original soundtrack). Milan 35665. *1994*: France.

Frasier: Music from the Television Series. Milan 35921. *2001*: France.

The General's Daughter (Original soundtrack). Milan 35885. *1999*: France.

Ghost (Original soundtrack). Milan 35733. *1995*: France.

Hitchcock 100 Years: A Bernard Herrmann Film Score Tribute. Milan 74321 14081-2. *1999*: France.

Once Were Warriors (Original soundtrack). Milan 35708. *1995*: France.

Primal Fear (Original soundtrack). Milan 35716. *1996*: France.

Rules of Engagement [Score] (Original soundtrack). Milan 35906. *2000*: France.

The Truman Show (Original soundtrack). Milan 35850. *1998*: France.

Discography

Borges & Piazzolla: Tangos & Milongas. Milan 59712. *1997*: France.

40 Years of Cuban Music: La Isla del Son. Milan 35868. *1999*: France.

Sandoval, Arturo. *The Best of Arturo Sandoval*. Milan 35812. *1997*: France.

Tangos [Milan]. Milan 35857. *1998*: France.

Filmography

A River Runs Through It, dir. Robert Redford. 1992. USA. 123 mins. Family Drama. Original music by Mark Isham.

The Elephant Man, dir. David Lynch. 1980. UK/USA. 125 mins. Drama/Biography. Original music by Samuel Barber, John Morris.

The General's Daughter, dir. Simon West. 1999. USA. 118 mins. Political Thriller. Original music by Carter Burwell.

Ghost, dir. Jerry Zucker. 1990. USA. 127 mins. Romantic Fantasy. Original music by Maurice Jarre.

Once Were Warriors, dir. Lee Tamahori. 1994. New Zealand. 99 mins. Drama. Original music by Murray Grindlay, Murray McNabb.

Primal Fear, dir. Gregory Hoblit. 1996. USA. 129 mins. Courtroom Drama. Original music by James Newton Howard.

Rules of Engagement, dir. William Friedkin. 2000. USA. 128 mins. Courtroom Drama. Original music by Mark Isham.

The Truman Show, dir. Peter Weir. 1998. USA. 102 mins. Comedy Drama. Original music by Burkhard Dallwitz, Philip Glass.

GIUSY BASILE (trans. JOHN SHEPHERD)

—Minos (Greece)

For many years the most successful Greek-owned record company, Minos was purchased by EMI in the early 1990s.

The company was founded by Minos Matsas, who had been employed in 1925 as an engineer and talent scout by the German-owned Odeon company. A few years later, he established his own label to record Greek traditional and popular music. Many of the early Odeon and Minos recordings of leading popular singers were made by Matsas in the reception areas of Athens hotels. In the 1960s, Minos was the first Greek-owned label to replace the system of giving composers of popular music exclusive contracts with a system that contracted singers to exclusive recording deals.

In addition to recording and distributing Greek popular music, Minos became the licensee for RCA in the 1970s and, by 1984, had achieved a domestic market share of 15 percent. EMI later purchased 50 percent of the company, and completed the takeover in 1992 when the combined domestic market share of the two firms was 30 percent.

DAVE LAING

—MNW Records (Sweden)

MNW (Music NetWork) was one of Sweden's leading locally owned record companies and an important distributor of independent labels from the 1970s to the 1990s.

The cooperatively owned label grew out of a four-track recording studio called Sundman in Vaxholm, near Stockholm. Its first release, in 1969, was by Gunder Hägg, a rock band with politically outspoken Swedish lyrics. In the same year, MNW and Silence Records set up Sam-Distribution and, in 1975, MNW opened a vinyl pressing plant, Ljudpress, in Ostersund. In an attempt to decentralize the Swedish music business, MNW helped to set up new labels for music from Gothenburg (Nacksving), Malmö (Amalthea) and northern Sweden (Manifest).

In the late 1970s, MNW built a new roster of young punk and new wave acts. In 1980, it made its first foreign licensing agreement with Rough Trade of London, and it was soon the Swedish representative of other British labels – Factory, Beggars Banquet and 4AD. Sam now distributed Mistlur, the most successful of the newer Swedish labels. During the 1980s, the Swedish independent sector was consolidated as MNW acquired financially troubled labels such as Manifest, Nacksving and Radium and, in 1993, Mistlur. Sam amalgamated with Plattlangarna, a rival distributor with financial problems. The company was renamed Musikdistribution.

Next, the company established branches in Norway, Denmark and Finland and set up a Beijing office. MNW now owned nine active labels, and its Independent Labels Distribution division was the Scandinavian representative of numerous foreign labels, including Mute, Nettwerk, Rykodisc and Rounder. In 1995, MNW had 50 acts on its roster (Burnett 1996, 123), and in 1998 the MNW act Hjalle & Heavy had a Swedish number one album, *På Rymmen*, on MNW's Start Klart label.

In 1998, the company was sold to a group of Swedish investors and long-serving chairman Jonas Sjoststrom resigned. Two years later, MNW reduced the number of distributed labels from 300 to 100. In that year, its share of the Swedish soundcarrier market fell from 6.8 to 6 percent and its sales fell by 22 percent to $16.5 million.

Bibliography

Burnett, Robert. 1996. *The Global Jukebox: The International Music Industry*. London and New York: Routledge.

Discographical Reference

Hjalle & Heavy. *På Rymmen*. Start Klart Records SKRCD-64. 1998: Sweden.

DAVE LAING

—Monitor-EMI (Czech Republic)

Monitor-EMI is the principal record company of the Czech Republic. The original company, Monitor, was typical of the many new small record producers that sprang up immediately after the political changes in Czechoslovakia in November 1989. At first, the company had great success with local street artists, including punk rock and pub rock bands (Orlík, Tři sestry). The company's policy was to produce recordings of important younger representatives of rock-oriented pop music, such as female singer Lucie Bílá,and later of popular folk singers, such as Jarek Nohavica. Over several years, Monitor became a powerful company and its influence increased, especially after its incorporation into EMI in January 1994.

ALEŠ OPEKAR

—Motown (Tamla Motown) (US)

The Motown (from 'Motor Town') Record Corporation was formed in Detroit in 1959 by Berry Gordy, and it became the first black-owned record company to achieve major success in the US pop charts. Motown 'crossover' hits brought a substantial infusion of gospel elements into the popular mainstream.

The failure of Gordy's previous venture, a jazz record store, had taught him that the public liked simple songs with a story and catchy beat. Influenced by Sam Cooke's pop chart success, he began to write songs for Jackie Wilson. Smokey Robinson encouraged Gordy to become involved in the publishing and recording side of the music industry to maximize financial returns from songwriting.

Motown achieved its first major US hit in 1960 ('Shop Around' by the Miracles), and in 1961 the Marvelettes' 'Please Mr. Postman' became Motown's first number one hit. Releasing records under various labels (e.g., Motown, Tamla, Gordy, Soul), the company quickly established itself as a major force on the pop charts, with hits by artists such as Mary Wells, Martha and the Vandellas, Stevie Wonder, Marvin Gaye, the Four Tops, the Temptations and the Supremes. While many US performers struggled in the wake of the Beatles' 1964 'invasion' of the US charts, Motown artists continued successfully. The Supremes, for example, had five consecutive number one hits in 1964–65.

Various factors contributed to Motown's success. Songwriter/producers Robinson and Holland-Dozier-Holland combined evocative relationship-based lyrics with gospel elements (such as handclaps, tambourines, pentatonic scales, repeated riffs and emphatic backbeats) while avoiding the raw sounds of black rhythm and blues which white audiences were reluctant to embrace. Motown's 'tight' groove was created by a core of session musicians drawn from the Detroit jazz scene, including James Jamerson (bass), Earl Van Dyke (keyboards) and Benny Benjamin (drums). Touring Motown Revues gave performers live exposure, while Motown's Artist Development section provided training in areas such as grooming, interview technique and movement.

During the latter part of the 1960s, some artists began to resent Gordy's autocratic style, and in 1968 Holland-Dozier-Holland left Motown, disputing profit shares.

Norman Whitfield became Motown's dominant writer-producer, creating seminal recordings such as the Temptations' 'Cloud Nine' (1968) which moved Motown toward a more funk-oriented sound. 'Cloud Nine' and songs such as Marvin Gaye's 'What's Going On' (1971) demonstrated a social awareness lacking in earlier Motown material, while the Jackson 5, with four consecutive number one hits, beginning with 'I Want You Back' in 1969, reaffirmed Motown's status as a leading producer of catchy, dance-oriented pop.

During the late 1960s, Berry Gordy became increasingly interested in working from California, and by 1973 Motown's activities were concentrated in Los Angeles. At this time, Motown was North America's leading black-owned corporation, and contained a new film division which produced the award-winning Lady Sings the Blues, based on the life of Billie Holiday. Subsequent films were less successful, however, and the company's record division also entered a period of creative decline in the 1970s as it failed to uncover an adequate roster of new recording artists to replace those (such as the Jackson 5, the Four Tops) who had left the label. During the 1980s, the only new stars discovered by the label were the vocal group Boyz II Men, and Motown relied increasingly on its back catalog. In 1988, Gordy sold out to a consortium of MCA and Boston Ventures. In 1993, the Motown label was acquired by PolyGram.

Bibliography

Davis, S. 1988. *Motown: The History*. Enfield: Guinness.

Early, Gerald. 1995. *One Nation Under a Groove: Motown and American Culture*. Hopewell, NJ: Ecco.

Fitzgerald, Jon. 1995. 'Motown Crossover Hits 1963–66 and the Creative Process.' *Popular Music* 14(1): 1–11.

Fong-Torres, Ben. 1990. *The Motown Album: The Sound of Young America*. London: Virgin.

George, Nelson. 1985. *Where Did Our Love Go?: The Rise and Fall of the Motown Sound*. New York: St. Martin's Press.

Gordy, Berry. 1994. *To Be Loved: The Music, the Magic, the Memories of Motown*. New York: Warner Books.

Hirshey, Gerri. 1984. *Nowhere to Run: The Story of Soul Music*. New York: Penguin.

Licks, Dr. 1989. *Standing in the Shadows of Motown: The Life and Music of Legendary Bassist James Jamerson*. Wynnewood, PA: Dr. Licks Publishing.

Slutsky, Alan. 1993. 'Motown: The History of a Hit-Making Sound and the Keyboardists Who Made It Happen.' *Keyboard* (May): 84–104.

'Standing in the Shadows of Motown: The Unsung Session Men of Hitsville's Golden Era.' 1983. *Musician* 60: 61–66.

Discographical References

Gaye, Marvin. 'What's Going On.' Tamla 54201. *1971*: USA.

Jackson 5, The. 'I Want You Back.' Motown 1157. *1969*: USA.

Marvelettes, The. 'Please Mr. Postman.' Tamla 54046. *1961*: USA.

Miracles, The. 'Shop Around.' Tamla 54034. *1960*: USA.

Temptations, The. 'Cloud Nine.' Gordy 7081. *1968*: USA.

Discography

Hitsville USA: The Motown Singles Collection 1959–1971. Motown CA 90028-USA. *1992*: USA.

Filmography

Lady Sings the Blues, dir. Sidney J. Furie. 1972. USA. 144 mins. Musical Biography. Original music by Gil Askey, Michel Legrand.

JON FITZGERALD

—Mushroom (Australia)

Mushroom was a rock music record company established in Melbourne in 1972 by Michael Gudinski. In a US-dominated market, Mushroom single–mindedly promoted Australian groups with professional marketing instincts that exploited such synchronicities as the advent of the national pop television program *Countdown* (1974) and the rise of a glam-rock movement with strong local connections. The Melbourne band Skyhooks, signed to Mushroom, played on *Countdown*'s first color transmission in 1975, and its phenomenal recording and performance successes signaled a new era in Australian pop.

Gudinski developed integrated publishing, recording, television/film, local and overseas tour management services. He established specialist subsidiary labels and bought into others, including a share of the major New Zealand independent, Flying Nun. Mushroom's acts have included Paul Kelly, Split Enz, Cold Chisel, Jason Donovan, Kylie Minogue and mixed-race group Yothu Yindi, whose work marked a turning point in indigenous access to mainstream popular music.

While unable to establish a presence in the US market, Gudinski sold a half share of Mushroom to Rupert Murdoch's communications conglomerate in 1993, providing resources for the establishment of a UK label that was aided by the success of Mushroom artist Peter Andre, and entered into a new distribution arrangement with Sony. In September 1998, citing disillusionment with the effects on Australian music of government policies, Gudinski announced the sale of the remainder of his share to Murdoch.

Gudinski's power inevitably produced claims of unassailable local monopoly, although, at the end of the twentieth century, there were suggestions of a faltering market share in 'alternative' scenes. Nonetheless, Mushroom Records has been central to the burgeoning of the Australian pop scene and its international successes since the 1970s, and a model of the possibilities of independent local activity.

Bibliography

Bebbington, Warren. 1997. *The Oxford Companion to Australian Music*. Melbourne: Oxford University Press.

Beilby, Peter, and Roberts, Michael. 1981. *Australian Music Directory*. North Melbourne: Australian Music Directory.

Guilliat, Richard. 1997. 'Between Rock and a Hard Place.' *Sydney Morning Herald Good Weekend* (11 October): 14–18.

Mitchell, Tony. 1996. *Popular Music and Local Identity: Rock, Pop and Rap in Europe and Oceania*. London and New York: Leicester University Press.

Prices Surveillance Authority. 1990. *Inquiry into the Prices of Sound Recordings*. Australia: Commonwealth Government of Australia.

Sly, Lesley. 1993. *The Power and the Passion: A Guide to the Australian Music Industry*. North Sydney: Warner/Chappell Music Australia.

Walker, Clinton. 1996. *Stranded: The Secret History of Australian Independent Music 1977–1991*. Sydney: Macmillan.

Wilmoth, Peter. 1993. *Glad All Over: The Countdown Years 1974–1987*. Ringwood, Victoria: McPhee Gribble.

Discography

The Mushroom Story: The Seventies. MUSH 330922. *1998*: Australia.

The Mushroom Story: The Eighties, Volume 1. MUSH 331302. *1998*: Australia.

The Mushroom Story: The Eighties, Volume 2. MUSH 331362. *1998*: Australia.

The Mushroom Story: The Nineties, Volume 1. MUSH 331352. *1998*: Australia.

The Mushroom Story: The Nineties, Volume 2. MUSH 331372. *1998*: Australia.

BRUCE JOHNSON

—Mute (UK)

One of the few surviving institutions of the UK punk movement, Mute is an independently minded record company whose most important acts are Depeche Mode and Erasure. The first releases in 1978 by the Normal and Silicon Teens featured the label's owner Daniel Miller. Miller subsequently issued avant-garde work by Yugoslavian rockers Laibach and Greek-born singer Diamanda Galas, but the label's first impact on the UK pop charts came in 1981 with electro-pop group Depeche Mode. This group has subsequently sold millions of records, as has Erasure, the duo formed by ex-Depeche synthesizer player Vince Clarke. Later signings to Mute included Nick Cave and Inspiral Carpets. Mute's associated labels include Blast First (Sonic Youth) and Rhythm King, a leader in 1980s UK dance music through Beatmasters, Bomb the Bass and S'Express. The company was purchased by EMI in 2002.

DAVE LAING

—The National Phonograph Company (US)

The National Phonograph Company was formed by Thomas Edison in 1896 to manufacture and market his phonograph and its cylinder records in the United States. It was the major producer of machines and records in the cylinder format. In the reorganization of Edison's business empire in 1910, the company became the phonograph division of Thomas A. Edison Incorporated. As such, it continued to produce phonographs and cylinders until 1929.

Several entrepreneurs had attempted to form a national marketing organization for recorded sound products before Edison established the National Phonograph Company. Jesse Lippincott had tried and failed with his North American Phonograph Company (formed in 1888), and it was the demise of this organization that freed Edison to market his phonograph inventions. The only other survivor of the Lippincott organization was the Columbia Phonograph Company, which went on to compete with Edison for the rapidly growing market for talking machines.

The National Phonograph Company was based at Edison's West Orange laboratory in New Jersey. The machines were made in a large factory complex that Edison had built next to his laboratory. The company maintained a recording studio at the laboratory building and another in New York City. The formation of the company coincided with the success of Edison's experiments to duplicate copies of master recordings, which permitted the mass production of prerecorded cylinders. Edison's engineers also redesigned the phonograph to make it smaller, lighter and, most important, cheaper. The company could offer a whole range of machines, from the $10 Gem to the Chippendale and Louis XVI models which retailed for more than $400. In 1913, the company unveiled a line of disc players, but its core business was always the cylinder phonograph.

Edison claimed to be a music lover, but he was no lover of expensive performers and therefore preferred to use little-known musicians to record on cylinders. At this time, there was no label on cylinders, and thus the selection was announced on the record before it began.

'The Edison Orchestra' was probably a group of session players assembled just to record. Edward Issler's Orchestra was often used for National Phonograph Company recordings. Both these groups played dance music and well-loved marching band songs like 'Stars and Stripes Forever.' Comic songs and monologs were very popular in Edison's recording studio, ranging from the misadventures of 'Uncle Josh' to minstrel skits. These were usually recorded by vaudeville players like Len Spencer or members of Edison's staff.

Bibliography

Frow, George L. 1982. *The Edison Disc Phonographs and the Diamond Discs: A History with Illustrations.* Sevenoaks, Kent: Frow.

Frow, George L., and Sefl, Albert F. 1978. *The Edison Cylinder Phonographs 1877–1929.* Sevenoaks, Kent: Frow.

Millard, Andre J. 1990. *Edison and the Business of Innovation.* Baltimore, MD: Johns Hopkins University Press.

Millard, Andre J. 1995. *America on Record: A History of Recorded Sound.* Cambridge: Cambridge University Press.

Read, Oliver, and Welch, Walter L. 1976. *From Tin Foil to Stereo: The Evolution of the Phonograph.* 2nd ed. Indianapolis/New York: Howard Sams/Bobbs Merrill.

ANDRE MILLARD

—Ngoma (Democratic Republic of Congo)

Ngoma Records was founded in 1947 in Leopoldville, Belgian Congo (later Zaire, and then the Democratic Republic of Congo) by Nico and Alexandros Jeronomodis, Greek importers and distributors of consumer goods who recognized the commercial potential of the emerging Congolese popular music. The name 'Ngoma' is a Bantu word for a large drum or drumming, as well as for dancing or rhythm in general, and it occurs as a brand name elsewhere in Africa. Ngoma was not the first studio or label in Leopoldville. Radio Congolia, later Radio Congo Belge, had a recording studio, while the Olympia label (launched in 1946) was short-lived. Ngoma artists included the guitarists/composers Antoine Wendo and Henri Bowane, whose joint composition 'Marie-Louise' was the first Congolese hit song; both artists rerecorded it later in different versions. Leon Bukasa (who led the house orchestra, Beguen Band), Oliveira, Feruzi, Adou Elenga and Albert Luampasi were other popular stars of this first generation who recorded for Ngoma. A European pianist named Pilaeïs was recruited to run the studio. Initially, discs were cut directly onto acetate in the studio and manufactured in Belgium. Later, once tape was introduced, masters were sent to France, where the company opened a pressing plant. In competition with Loningisa, CEFA, Opika and Esengo

(Opika and Esengo were other labels based in Leopoldville), Ngoma's products spread the Congolese sound to West and East Africa. Ngoma was the only local label under foreign ownership to survive Congolese independence in 1960. It continued releasing 45s well into the 1960s, but the pressing business began to take precedence and the label faded.

Bibliography

Bemba, Sylvain. 1984. *50 ans de musique du congo-zaïre* [Fifty Years of Music of Congo-Zaire]. Paris: Presence Africaine.

Bender, Wolfgang. 1996. Sleeve Notes/CD Booklet for *Ngoma – The Early Years*. Frankfurt: Popular African Music.

Bender, Wolfgang. 1997. Sleeve Notes/CD Booklet for *Ngoma – souvenir ya independence*. Frankfurt: Popular African Music.

Ewens, Graeme. 1991. *Africa O-Ye!: A Celebration of African Music*. London: Guinness.

Ewens, Graeme. 1994. *Congo Colossus – The Life and Legacy of Franco and OK Jazz*. Norfolk, UK: Buku Press/ Sterns.

Discography

Ngoma – The Early Years, 1948–1960. Popular African Music PAMAP101. *1996*: Germany.

Ngoma – souvenir ya independence. Popular African Music PAMAP102. *1997*: Germany.

GRAEME EWENS

—Nipponophone (Nippon Columbia) (Japan)

The Nipponophone label was launched in 1910 by the Japan Gramophone Company, a joint venture on the part of Emile Berliner's Gramophone Company and Alexander Graham Bell's Columbia Gramophone Company. The Japan Gramophone Company was the first disc and phonograph manufacturer in Japan. In 1927, the Columbia Gramophone Company became the sole owner, and the company was renamed Nippon Columbia. It began to produce wireless sets, and in 1939 it launched the first electric direct-drive turntable, using 'Denon' as its brand name.

In 1951, it became the first Japanese company to issue vinyl LPs, using imported mastering and pressing equipment. Nippon Columbia developed a master tape recorder in 1972 using pulse code modulation (PCM). In 1994, it was one of the consortia of companies to develop the digital versatile disc (DVD). At the beginning of the twenty-first century, the company's largest shareholder was the Hitachi electronics company.

The Nippon Columbia label has a diverse roster of acts, as does Denon, the jazz, classical and pop record label owned by Nippon Columbia. In 2000–2001, the company's sales were $743 million, of which 40 percent came from soundcarriers and video software.

DAVE LAING

—Odeon (Germany)

Odeon was a German record label, founded in Berlin in 1903 by the former director of the International Zonophone Company, F.M. Prescott, as a subsidiary of his Paris-based International Talking Machine Company. The label was named after the Paris opera theater l'Odéon.

Odeon was among the first record companies to regularly produce double-sided records. The company started with a strong roster of French and German opera singers. In 1911, Odeon was integrated into the recording empire of the German Carl Lindström AG, and it became one of the leading labels for early jazz and mainstream dance music in Germany between the wars. With the takeover of Lindström by London-based Columbia in 1926, the label was used as an outlet for Columbia (US) recordings on the German market. In 1931, with the merger of Columbia (UK) and the Gramophone Company, Odeon became part of the newly formed EMI, where it was used as an outlet for the German market until World War II made this impossible.

After World War II, EMI reorganized its German interests under the umbrella of Electrola. Odeon was operated as a classical label, but lost importance to such a degree that it was closed down in 1954.

Bibliography

Gelatt, Roland. 1977. *The Fabulous Phonograph, 1877– 1977*. New York: Macmillan.

Lerch, Dieter. 1988. *Historische Tonträger im Deutschen Musikarchiv. Bd. 2: Beka, Columbia, Gloria, Homocord, Imperial, Kristall, Odeon, Parlophon, Vox* [Historical Recordings in the German Music Archive]. Berlin: Deutsche Bibliothek, Das Archiv.

Odeon Werke, Gesamtverzeichnis [Odeon Recordings: Complete Catalog]. 1950. Berlin: Odeon.

Wahl, Horst. 1986. *Odeon. Die Geschichte einer Schallplatten-Firma* [Odeon: The History of a Recording Company]. Düsseldorf: Sieben.

PETER WICKE

—OKeh (US)

The OKeh imprint was established in New York in 1918 by Otto Heineman of the General Phonograph Corporation to record many kinds of popular music. Early on, its ethnic European music catalog was particularly prominent. In 1920, OKeh initiated the black-music recording industry with the release of Mamie Smith's 'Crazy Blues,' and in the following decade the label made a name for itself by recording blues and jazz discs, most notably the seminal sides of Louis Armstrong's Hot Five and Hot Seven combos.

OKeh pioneered the recording of country and western music in June 1923, when Ralph Peer recorded performances by country music performer Fiddlin' John Carson in Atlanta, Georgia.

In 1926, Columbia acquired the label, but the Depression affected OKeh's activities and, in 1935, Columbia let the imprint lapse. Following a revival of OKeh in 1940 as Columbia's country and blues subsidiary, the label was retired again in 1942 because of a wartime shellac shortage.

In the postwar years, majors such as Columbia saw their control of the rhythm and blues (R&B) market usurped by a host of new, small independent labels, which in Chicago included Miracle, Chess and Chance. In 1951, Columbia revived OKeh as a specialist R&B label, and put Danny Kessler in charge as both sales manager and A&R director. In late 1952, OKeh's distribution was changed from company branches to independent operators to try to improve penetration of the R&B market. The company had notable success with two New York–based artists, Chuck Willis and Big Maybelle.

By the early 1960s, however, OKeh was almost inoperative. In 1962, Columbia hired Carl Davis, a promotion man from the Chicago office, to serve as producer and A&R director, and most subsequent OKeh recordings came out of Chicago. Davis brought in his own team of musicians and arrangers (principally Johnny Pate and Riley Hampton) and, most importantly, writer Curtis Mayfield. Within a year, Davis had rejuvenated OKeh. The most successful OKeh artist was Major Lance, but other OKeh artists included Billy Butler, Walter Jackson, and the Vibrations. Davis was forced out of the company in late 1965. Columbia closed down its OKeh imprint in 1970. The company (now owned by Sony) revived OKeh in 1994 as a small blues imprint.

Bibliography

Grendysa, Peter, and Marshall, James. 1993. Liner notes to *The OKeh Rhythm & Blues Story 1949–1957*. Epic/ OKeh/Legacy E3K 48912.

Koppel, Martin. 1986. 'The Chicago Sound of OKeh.' *Soul Survivor* 5 (Summer): 24–25.

Pruter, Robert. 1981. 'The Emergence of the Black Music Recording Industry, 1920–1923.' *Classic Wax* 3 (May): 4–6.

Pruter, Robert. 1991. 'OKeh Records.' In *Chicago Soul*. Urbana, IL: University of Illinois Press, 76–92.

Pruter, Robert. 1996. 'OKeh Records.' In *Doowop: The Chicago Scene*. Urbana, IL: University of Illinois Press, 135–38.

Sutton, Allan. 1998. 'The Origins of OKeh.' *The Main-*

spring: A Free Online Journal for Collectors of Vintage Records. http://www.mainspringpress.com/articles.html

Discographical Reference

Smith, Mamie. 'Crazy Blues'/'It's Right Here for You.' OKeh 4169. 1920: USA.

Discography

Curtis Mayfield's Chicago Soul. Legacy/Epic ZK 64770. *1995*: USA.

OKeh: A Northern Soul Obsession. Kent CDKEND 132. *1996*: USA.

OKeh: A Northern Soul Obsession, Volume 2. Kent CDKEND 142. *1997*: USA.

OKeh Chicago Blues. Epic EG 37318. *1982*: USA.

OKeh Jazz. Epic EG 37315. *1982*: USA.

OKeh Rhythm & Blues. Epic EG 37649. *1982*: USA.

The OKeh Rhythm & Blues Story 1949–1957. Epic/OKeh/ Legacy E3K 48912. *1993*: USA.

OKeh Soul. Epic EG 37321. *1982*: USA.

OKeh Western Swing. Epic EG 37324. *1982*: USA.

ROBERT PRUTER

—Pacific Jazz/World Pacific (US)

The Pacific Jazz record company and label were established in Los Angeles in 1952 under the ownership of Richard Bock and Roy Harte. Under the direction of Bock, who became sole owner, the label became a major outlet for jazz performers on the west coast. Its roster included Wes Montgomery, 'Groove' Holmes and Chet Baker. The subsidiary World Pacific label was founded in 1958 to issue recordings by Ravi Shankar. The labels were purchased by Liberty in 1965 and ultimately passed to Capitol (subsequently part of EMI), which has continued to use the Pacific Jazz label for reissues of the back catalog.

Bibliography

Gardner, Mark. 1988. 'Pacific Jazz.' In *The New Grove Dictionary of Jazz*, ed. Barry Kernfeld. London/New York: Macmillan/Grove, 949–50.

HOWARD RYE

—Paramount (US)

Regarded by collectors of early blues music as the record label par excellence as far as the quality of the music it recorded is concerned, Paramount's records made in the 1920s are much sought-after. As no company ledgers are known to exist, the history of the company and the compilation of listings of its records in a number of series have presented many problems to researchers.

Founded by the New York Recording Laboratories, probably in 1916, Paramount was based at Port Washington, Wisconsin, and was a subsidiary of a furniture manufacturer, the Wisconsin Chair Company, which also made phonographs. The name of the New York Recording Laboratories derives from the fact that they had operated initially in New York, where they maintained a studio until 1926. Between 1926 and 1929, the New York Recording Laboratories ran a studio in Chicago, after which they opened one in Grafton, Wisconsin, which is where Charley Patton first recorded.

Initially, Paramount issued 'ethnic' recordings on its Puritan label, and occasional items of dance music, before commencing the Paramount releases in 1918. A record label owned by Harry H. Pace, an African American, and named after the 'Black Swan,' Elizabeth Taylor Greenfield, had been launched in 1921 for the recording and issue of diverse types of black music. The venture was short-lived, with trading ending in 1923. However, in May 1924 Black Swan's recordings were leased to Paramount, with titles by Lucille Hegamin and Katie Crippen, among others, being issued. Paramount's 12000 Race series commenced in 1922 and in the ensuing 10 years over a thousand discs were released. These included many titles by gospel groups, including the Norfolk Jubilee Quartette, vaudeville exchanges by performers such as 'Coot' Grant and 'Kid Sox' Wilson, small group jazz by Jimmy O'Bryant's and Jimmy Blythe's washboard bands, with occasional titles by such groups as Lovie Austin's Blues Serenaders, Freddie Keppard's Jazz Cardinals, and the Wisconsin Roof Orchestra. There were also infrequent issues with other aspirations, such as concert-style spirituals by Madame Magdalene Tartt Lawrence.

However, it was for its blues recordings that Paramount was justly famous, its artists ranging from Gertrude 'Ma' Rainey and Papa Charlie Jackson to Blind Blake and Blind Lemon Jefferson in the mid-1920s, and to the first recordings by Charley Patton in 1929 and Eddie 'Son' House in 1930. Credit for the high recording standards of Paramount's blues issues was largely due to recording manager Mayo 'Ink' Williams, the sole black employee, who was paid by royalties from records issued. The recommendations of rural and southern record salesmen such as Henry C. Speir of Jackson, Mississippi were carefully noted, although it was Paramount policy for artists to be brought to the Wisconsin, Chicago or New York studios, and field recording was not undertaken.

In 1924, Paramount began issuing a few items by such hillbilly artists as Henry Whitter and Vernon Dalhart in its popular/dance series and, three years later, sales manager Arthur C. Laibley secured Doc Roberts for a new 3000 series of 'Old Time Tunes.' Included in the series were issues by the Fruit Jar Guzzlers and the Kentucky Thorobreds, the Carver Boys and the Lone Star Ranger,

Sid Harkreader and Hoke Rice, as well as religious items by Leader Cleveland and His Bible Class or Peck's Male Quartette, and a number of records by Frank Ferrara's Hawaiians. Paramount's success led to the issue of instrumental and band recordings by the Paramount Military Band and the Paramount Symphony Orchestra. Popular and War Songs were among the other categories established.

Subsidiary labels were operated, among them Herwin and Broadway, which both leased material to other companies and leased from such labels as Crown and QRS. At its peak, Paramount had an annual turnover of $100,000 but, like other record companies, it was a victim of the Depression and was forced to close its 12/13000 Race series and its 3000 'Old Time Tunes' series. A number of records were made for the Montgomery Ward chain, but the firm had ceased to issue records by 1933. A dozen years later, John Steiner, a Chicago chemist, purchased the rights to Paramount from the surviving Wisconsin Chair Company and reissued a number of items on a revived label for collectors. Although claims have been made to the authorized rights to reissue Paramount discs, all but a handful of known issued blues and gospel recordings on Paramount have been reissued, principally on Document CDs, while many hillbilly and country items have been reissued by Document (Austria) and jazz recordings by RST (Austria).

Paramount records were often poorly recorded, pressed on inferior material and sometimes produced in small numbers. Often extremely rare, they have remained much in demand by collectors for the high quality of the music in many categories, but especially in blues and gospel. A very detailed discography of the latter has been compiled by Max Vreede (1971). There have also been a great many LP and CD reissues of this material, some of it in anthology form. Although hillbilly music on Paramount has not been so well served, a scholarly compilation, entitled *Paramount Old Time Tunes*, was issued by the John Edwards Memorial Foundation in 1974.

Bibliography
Calt, Stephen. 1988. 'The Anatomy of a "Race" Label – Part 1.' *78 Quarterly* 1(3): 9–23.

Calt, Stephen. 1989. 'The Anatomy of a "Race" Label – Part 2.' *78 Quarterly* 1(4): 9–30.

Calt, Stephen, and Wardlow, Gayle Dean. 1990. 'The Buying and Selling of Paramounts (Part 3).' *78 Quarterly* 1(5): 7–24.

Calt, Stephen, and Wardlow, Gayle Dean. 1991. 'Paramount Part 4 (The Advent of Arthur Laibley).' *78 Quarterly* 1(6): 8–26.

Calt, Stephen, and Wardlow, Gayle Dean. 1992. 'Paramount's Decline and Fall.' *78 Quarterly* 1(7): 7–29.

Cohen, Norm. 1974. 'Introduction.' In *Paramount Old Time Tunes* [Sound recording, JEMF 103]. Los Angeles: John Edwards Memorial Foundation, 1–2 (discography: 28–34).

Dixon, Robert M.W., Godrich, John, and Rye, Howard. 1997. 'Paramount.' In *Blues & Gospel Records 1890–1943*. 4th ed. Oxford: Clarendon Press, xxxvi–xxxvii.

Vreede, Max E. 1971. *Paramount 12000/13000 Series*. London: Storyville Publications (illustrated discography).

Vreede, Max E., and Van Rijn, Guido. 1996. 'The Paramount L-Master Series.' *78 Quarterly* 1(9): 67–87.

Whelan, Pete. 1992. 'The Man Who Bought Paramount.' *78 Quarterly* 1(7): 30–41.

Discography

Paramount Old Time Tunes. JEMF 103. *1974*: USA.

Paramount Piano Blues, Vols. 1–3. Black Swan BSCD 011–013. *1994*: Canada.

Paramount Vol. 1: The Piano Blues, 1929–30 (LP). Magpie PY4401. *1980*: UK.

Paramount Vol. 2: The Piano Blues, 1927–32 (LP). Magpie PY4420. *1982*: UK.

Rare Paramount Blues 1926–1929. Document DOCD-5277. *1994*: Austria.

PAUL OLIVER

—Parlophone (Parlophon) (UK/Germany)

Parlophon began life as a label of the German phonograph and record company, Carl Lindström AG, and was established in the early years of the twentieth century. The company issued recordings in Europe and India, and, within the British Empire, the spelling of the label became that of 'Parlophone' in order to conform to the 'made in Britain' requirements of the time. During World War I, Parlophone was confiscated in Britain as enemy property and ceased to exist.

However, the German label continued during this time and, in 1926, became part of Columbia as a consequence of the takeover of a majority of Lindström stocks by Columbia International. With this, Parlophone came back into existence, this time as a distribution arm of the joint Lindström/Columbia enterprise.

After Columbia and the Gramophone Company merged to form EMI in 1931, Lindström, which was in deep financial trouble, ceased to exist, and the Parlophone label came to be used by EMI in Britain for popular music releases. From 1950, the label was managed by producer George Martin, who in 1962 signed the Beatles. Most of the group's subsequent British releases appeared on Parlophone.

DAVE LAING

—Pathé (France)

In France, Charles Pathé (1863–1957) was the pioneer of the recording industry. From 1894, he engaged in the rental and sale of phonographs, and in 1896 established with his brother Emile the Pathé Frères company. He opened a factory at Chatou, whose 150 workers made the 'Le Coq' cylinder playback machine, 'Le Coq' becoming the company's trademark.

Pathé's first catalog – for the years 1897–98 – contained about 8,900 cylinder recordings. These recordings were made in studios in London, Milan and Moscow, as well as in Paris. From 1905, Pathé also made single-sided, vertical-cut recordings designed to be played with a sapphire ball, rather than with the standard steel needle.

The heyday of the Pathé label, certainly where its contribution to the popular music of France is concerned, is commonly regarded as the 1930s. During this period, most of the great names in French popular music recorded for Pathé: Edith Piaf, Jean Sablon, Tino Rossi, Joséphine Baker and Charles Trenet. However, because neighboring rights did not become established in France until 1985, most of these artists are to be found on the recordings of other labels as well. For this reason, and also because of the very broad character of Pathé's contribution to popular music in France, it makes sense to discuss this contribution in terms of the profiles of Pathé's catalogs.

The Early Catalogs

For the first 25 years or so of Pathé's existence, part of the label's catalog was made up of both urban and rural traditional music (classified as children's songs (*chansons enfantines*), ballads and tunes (*romances* and *grands airs*), hymns (*cantiques*), and songs and comic songs (*chansons* and *chansonnettes*)); part was made up of new material more in step with the music of the times. At first, this came from the various kinds of performers (*pochardes*, *comique-troupiers*, *pierreuses*, *diseuses*, *patriotiques* and *excentriques*) who sprang up in the Parisian café scene (*café-concert*), and was listed variously according to genres (for example, comic duets (*duos comiques*)), as well as from well-known singers such as Yvette Guilbert. Nonvocal music was organized into instrumental and orchestral listings, as well as into military music and barrel-organ music, and the music of different kinds of ensembles. Finally, recordings of the spoken word were organized into monologs, sketches, recitations and theater. In 1912, the Pathé catalogs offered complete operas such as *Faust* and *Carmen*, and plays such as *Le malade imaginaire* and *Le Cid*.

For about 25 years, the listings of the Pathé catalogs, which were similar to those of other record company catalogs, did not evolve much. However, around 1920, the advent of African-American and African-American-influenced music gave rise to recordings listed as American Jazz Bands (*Jazz-Bands américains*), the Special Echo Series for Dance (*Série Echo Spéciale pour la danse*) and Hawaiian Bands (*Orchestres hawaïens*). Music hall also featured importantly in the Pathé catalogs.

Developments in the United States

The inclusion of US popular music on the French label was presaged in 1914 by the opening of a New York office and studio and, a year later, a US pressing plant. The US operation, the Pathé Frères Phonograph Company, made its own domestic recordings, as well as drawing on Pathé's huge European catalogs.

A further development occurred in 1920, when Pathé Frères introduced its Actuelle label in order to market lateral-cut as opposed to vertical-cut discs, which were experiencing a decline in market demand. Most of the material released on the Actuelle label was taken from Pathé's vertical-cut recordings. The Pathé Frères Phonograph Company went into bankruptcy in 1922, and was reorganized as the Pathé Phonograph & Radio Corporation. The company suspended production of vertical-cut discs, and established a new label, Pathé Actuelle, to market its lateral-cut recordings, again drawing extensively on existing Pathé masters, but also using material from the Compo Company, Marsh Laboratories and the Regal Record Company. It was the use of material from the Compo Company that enabled Pathé Actuelle to introduce a short-lived 'race' record series in 1924.

The Pathé Phonograph & Radio Corporation began issuing electronic recordings in 1926, and in 1927 combined operations with the Cameo Record Corporation. Cameo and its Pathé subsidiary merged with the Regal Record Company and the independent pressing plant Scranton Button Company to form the American Record Company (ARC) in 1929. The Pathé label ceased operations in the United States in early 1930.

Further Developments in France

The French Pathé Frères company was bought out by Columbia (UK) in 1928 and took the name of Pathé-Marconi. However, the label 'Pathé' was retained.

A real change to Pathé's catalogs occurred in the 1930s, with the introduction of new media – radio, film musicals and electronic recordings – which allowed for a much greater distribution of recorded music. An examination of the Pathé catalog listings demonstrates the musical diversity of the period: Songs and Melodies (*Chants et Mélodies*), Film Music and Musicals (*Musique et chanson de films*), Dance Music and Instruments. Yet, it is the new category, Film Music and Musicals, that denotes the real change in record production as evidenced in the 1930s catalogs.

This change of direction in the catalogs corresponds also to changes in the record industry: as developments in the history of the US company attest, almost all record companies were subject to mergers in coming under the control of more important conglomerates. In 1931, the EMI conglomerate was established through the merger of Columbia (including Pathé) and the Gramophone Company. Pathé continued to keep its separate label identity, and its production became global in scope. The conglomerate's catalogs, like those of other companies, limited their listings to National Pop (*Variété nationale*), International Pop (*Variété internationale*) (which included all kinds of popular music, from rock to sentimental ballads (*la chanson*)) and Classical. Jazz was included under the heading of *Variété*.

In the 1970s, Pathé and other companies in the EMI conglomerate established listings of rock, pop and folk music, to which were later added world music, rap and techno.

GIUSY BASILE and JOHN SHEPHERD

—Philles Records (US)

Philles Records was the brainchild of record producer Phil Spector (1940–). He originally co-owned the label with Lester Sill (hence 'Phil Les'), but he bought Sill out in 1962. Although Philles Records lasted only from 1961 to 1966, it possessed a unique and unmistakable catalog. Its memorability was due to Spector's trademark 'wall of sound': the lavish, layered and lush profusion of instrumentalists, their number magnified by echo effects, which enveloped the performers in a cushion of music.

Many who worked with Spector both admired his undeniable skills and abhorred his autocratic manner. He supervised all the Philles releases and co-wrote a number as well. His musicians, known collectively as 'The Wrecking Crew,' included Tommy Tedesco (guitar), Larry Knechtel (piano, bass), Harold Battiste, Leon Russell (keyboards) and Hal Blaine (drums). Their efforts were guided on many of the recordings by arranger Jack Nitzsche and engineer Larry Levine. The label's roster included the popular 'girl groups' the Crystals ('He's a Rebel' (1962)) and the Ronettes ('Be My Baby' (1963)), as well as the Righteous Brothers ('You've Lost That Lovin' Feelin'' (1964)). Spector also allied himself with some of the most successful and skilled songwriters of the period, such as Gerry Goffin and Carole King, Barry Mann and Cynthia Weil, Jeff Barry and Ellie Greenwich. Philles was predominantly a singles label, but in 1963 Spector assembled a seasonal album, *A Christmas Gift for You*, which featured the label's stable of singers, arrangers and musicians.

It was the failure of a single recording, Ike and Tina Turner's 'River Deep Mountain High,' in 1966 that led

749

to Philles' demise. Perhaps Spector's most elaborate and eloquent effort to date, it was a Top 3 hit in the United Kingdom, but barely entered the US Top 100.

Bibliography

Ribowsky, Mark. 1989. *He's a Rebel*. New York: Dutton.

Sanjek, Russell, and Sanjek, David. 1996. *Pennies from Heaven: The American Popular Music Business in the Twentieth Century*. New York: Da Capo Press.

Discographical References

Crystals, The. 'He's a Rebel.' Philles 106. *1962*: USA. Reissue: Crystals, The. 'He's a Rebel.' *The Best of the Crystals*. ABKCO 7214. *1992*: USA.

Righteous Brothers, The. 'You've Lost That Lovin' Feelin'.' Philles 124. *1964*: USA. Reissue: Righteous Brothers, The. 'You've Lost That Lovin' Feelin'.' *Anthology 1962–1974*. Rhino 71488. *1989*: USA.

Ronettes, The. 'Be My Baby.' Philles 116. *1963*: USA. Reissue: Ronettes, The. 'Be My Baby.' *The Best of the Ronettes*. ABKCO 7212. *1992*: USA.

Spector, Phil. *A Christmas Gift for You from Phil Spector*. Philles PHLP-4005. *1963*: USA. Reissue: Spector, Phil. *A Christmas Gift for You from Phil Spector*. ABKCO 4005. *1990*: USA.

Turner, Ike and Tina. 'River Deep Mountain High.' Philles 131. *1966*: USA. Reissue: Turner, Ike and Tina. 'River Deep Mountain High.' *Proud Mary: The Best of Ike and Tina Turner*. EMI-America E2-95846. *1991*: USA.

DAVID SANJEK

—Play It Again Sam (Belgium)

The Belgian record company Play It Again Sam (PIAS) began its activities in 1983, as an independent distributor within Belgium of mainly British alternative music. It was founded by Kenny Gates and Michel Lambot.

A distribution agreement with the British 4AD label was an important asset for the company in its initial phase. The first signing to PIAS's own label was the British band the Legendary Pink Dots, followed by acts like Meat Beat Manifesto. In the late 1980s and early 1990s, PIAS became the most important distributor of Belgian new beat and witnessed an international breakthrough with its signing of Front 242, the Belgian godfathers of techno. The startup of a Dutch venture enabled the company to cover the Benelux countries and to close distribution deals for this region of Europe. At the end of the twentieth century, PIAS held licensing or distribution deals for the Benelux countries with many well-known labels, such as 4AD, Mute, Tommy Boy, Epitaph, Wall of Sound, Beggars Banquet, XL Records (the Prodigy) and Ministry of Sound.

As an international company encompassing distribution, publishing (Strictly Confidential) and recording, PIAS, at the end of the twentieth century, maintained offices in Belgium, The Netherlands (since 1990), the United Kingdom (since 1994), Germany (since 1995) and France (since 1995), and had approximately 200 employees. Each of these national offices had set up its own A&R operation in both rock and dance music. The Dutch office had become the most extensive and innovative of these national enterprises.

PIAS held a majority share in the British independent distributor Vital Distribution, which, after its merger with RTM (with British labels Mute and Beggars Banquet as shareholders), was one of the most important independent distributors in the United Kingdom.

In June 1999, the German company edel purchased 75 percent of PIAS, but when edel ran into difficulties in 2001 this was bought back by the founders of PIAS.

PAUL RUTTEN

—Pony Canyon (Japan)

A subsidiary of Japanese media corporation Fujisankei, Pony Canyon has been a leading label for Japanese-language pop music. Fujisankei owns Fuji, the leading commercial television network, and 37 radio stations, as well as newspapers, magazines and a film studio.

The Pony Canyon record company was founded in 1966 and, by the early 1990s, it was one of the leading companies in 'idol' music aimed at Japanese teenagers. Its most popular artists included Kudo and Genji, who in 1992 won awards for the best female and male idol, respectively. Other bestselling acts signed to Pony Canyon in the 1990s included male vocal duo Chage and Aska, and female singer Miyuki Nakashima.

During the 1990s, Pony Canyon expanded its activities throughout Southeast Asia, opening branches in Singapore, Taiwan, Hong Kong and Malaysia. Most of these were joint-venture companies with existing labels in each country.

In the 1970s and 1980s, Pony Canyon held Japanese rights to the output of leading Western labels, such as A&M and Virgin, and was a leading video distributor. In 1989, Fujisankei purchased 25 percent of Richard Branson's Virgin Music Group for $150 million in a deal that involved forming a jointly owned label in Japan. Fujisankei's shares were bought by EMI when Virgin was sold in 1992. Pony Canyon now owns 25 percent of Echo, the UK-based label operated by the Chrysalis media group. The company also contracts directly with individual artists, such as Paul Weller and Todd Rundgren, to distribute their recordings in Japan.

Fujisankei owns the Windswept Pacific music publishing company, which has offices in the United States and the United Kingdom.

DAVE LAING

—Prestige (US)

Prestige was a record company and label established in New York in 1949 by Bob Weinstock. It specialized in contemporary jazz, much of it recorded at Rudy von Gelder's studios in Hackensack and Englewood Cliffs, New Jersey. Some sessions were issued on a subsidiary label, New Jazz. In 1960, the separate labels of Swingville (for mainstream jazz), Moodsville and Bluesville were established. Prestige had a large catalog of soul jazz artists, such as Jimmy McGriff, Brother Jack McDuff and Shirley Scott, directed after 1968 by Bob Porter. Fantasy acquired the label in May 1971 and maintained a similar policy with respect to the artists recorded. Much of the back catalog has been reissued on Fantasy's Original Jazz/Blues Classics labels.

Bibliography

Morgan, Alun. 1967. 'The Prestige-Swingville Series.' *Jazz Monthly* 13(1): 19–21; 13(2): 15–16; 13(3): 17–18; 13(7): 21–22.

Ruppli, Michel, with Porter, Bob. 1980. *The Prestige Label: A Discography* (*Discographies*, No. 3). Westport, CT: Greenwood Press.

Shor, Russ. 1995. 'Silent Partners: Bob Porter (Part 1).' *VJM's Jazz & Blues Mart* 97: 5–7.

HOWARD RYE

—Priority (US)

A leading company in west-coast rap music, Priority Records was formed in Los Angeles in 1985 by Bryan Turner. A former K-Tel executive, Turner's first success was with the novelty group California Raisins, based on animated characters used in a television commercial. Priority's most controversial signing was the group NWA, whose *Straight Outta Compton* became an international hit. After the group split up, Priority continued to release records by former member Ice Cube. In 1993, rapper Ice-T joined Priority after his work had been censored by his former distributor Warner. The company had even greater chart success in 1997–98 with releases on the No Limit label owned by rapper Master P.

In the mid-1990s, the company expanded into alternative rock, and in 1996 its distributor, EMI, bought 50 percent of Priority. EMI later acquired the remainder of the company.

Discographical Reference

NWA. *Straight Outta Compton*. Ruthless/Priority 57102. *1989*: USA.

Discography

Ice Cube. *AmeriKKKa's Most Wanted*. Priority 57120. *1990*: USA.

Ice-T. *Home Invasion*. Rhyme Syndicate/Priority 53858. *1993*: USA.

Master P. *Ghetto D*. No Limit/Priority 50659. *1997*: USA.

DAVE LAING

—Private Music (US)

In 1984, former Tangerine Dream member Peter Baumann decided to set up a record company to issue 'contemporary instrumental' recordings. Operating at the meeting-point of new age, avant-garde and world music, Baumann issued albums by such artists as Ravi Shankar, John Tesh, Andy Summers and Yanni, whose new age synthesizer music has provided many US television themes. Baumann expanded into vocal music with Nona Hendryx and Suzanne Ciani. After using independent distribution, Private Music signed a global licensing agreement with BMG International in 1988. BMG subsequently purchased the company in 1996, merging it with Windham Hill.

Discography

The World of Private Music. Private Music 2009. *1986*: USA.

The World of Private Music, Vol. II. Private Music 2023. *1987*: USA.

DAVE LAING

—Regal-Zonophone (UK/Australia)

Regal-Zonophone was a budget-priced record label launched by EMI in Britain and Australia in 1933 to supersede Columbia's Regal label and the Gramophone Company's Zonophone. Regal dated back to 1914 in Britain and 1926 in Australia. Zonophone was founded as an independent company in the United States in 1899 and was absorbed by the Gramophone Company in 1903; after 1910, the label name was used only in Britain and Australia. New Regal-Zonophone issues continued Regal's numerical series, but some Zonophone issues were also re-pressed with the new label. After 1939, the Regal-Zonophone label was less used and was discontinued in 1949. The label was briefly resurrected by EMI for UK pop releases on several occasions during the 1960s, 1970s and 1980s.

Bibliography

Jewson, Ron, Smith, Derek, and Webb, Ray. 1972/73. 'Arthur Gainsbury's Guide to Junkshoppers: Regal.' *Storyville* 42: 211–12; 43: 8–10; 44: 71–72; 45: 92–96.

Rust, Brian A.L. 1978. *The American Record Label Book*. New Rochelle, NY: Arlington House.

HOWARD RYE

—Reprise Records (US)

Reprise Records was founded in 1961 by Frank Sinatra and managed by the influential executive Mo Ostin. Its initial roster abounded with the era's mainstream artists, among them Sinatra, Bing Crosby and Dean Martin. It was not a financially successful venture, and in 1963 Warner Brothers purchased a majority share of the label. Ostin remained in charge, and Reprise transformed itself into one of the mainstays of progressive music. During the 1960s and 1970s, Reprise signed Joni Mitchell, Fleetwood Mac, Neil Young, Frank Zappa, Randy Newman and Gordon Lightfoot. It also distributed the British recordings of artists such as the Kinks (Pye Records) and Jimi Hendrix (Track Records). Warner Brothers retired the Reprise name in 1982, only to revive it in 1986.

Bibliography

Sanjek, Russell, and Sanjek, David. 1996. *Pennies from Heaven: The American Popular Music Business in the Twentieth Century*. New York: Da Capo Press.

Discography

Crosby, Bing. *Return to Paradise Islands*. Reprise R9-6106. *1964*: USA.

Fleetwood Mac. *Bare Trees*. Reprise 2080. *1972*: USA. Reissue: Fleetwood Mac. *Bare Trees*. Warner Brothers 2278. *1987*: USA.

Fleetwood Mac. *Fleetwood Mac*. Reprise 2225. *1975*: USA. Reissue: Fleetwood Mac. *Fleetwood Mac*. Sony International 477358. *1999*: USA.

Fleetwood Mac. *Greatest Hits*. Reprise 25801. *1988*: USA.

Fleetwood Mac. *Rumours*. Reprise 3010. *1977*: USA. Reissue: Fleetwood Mac. *Rumours*. Warner Brothers 3010. *1990*: USA.

Hendrix, Jimi. *Are You Experienced?*. MCA 11602. *1997*: USA.

Hendrix, Jimi. *Are You Experienced?*. Reprise 6261. *1967*: USA.

Hendrix, Jimi. *Are You Experienced?*. [UK]. Track 612001. *1967*: UK.

Hendrix, Jimi. *Monterey International Pop Festival*. Reprise MS-2029. *1970*: USA.

Hendrix, Jimi. *The Cry of Love*. Reprise MS-2034. *1971*: USA. Reissue: Hendrix, Jimi. *The Cry of Love*. Polydor 899. *1993*: UK.

Kinks, The. *The Kink Kronikles*. Reprise L5-6454. *1972*: USA. Reissue: Kinks, The. *The Kink Kronikles*. Warner Brothers 6454. *1989*: USA.

Lightfoot, Gordon. *Sit Down Young Stranger*. Reprise 6392. *1970*: USA.

Lightfoot, Gordon. *Summertime Dream*. Reprise 2246. *1976*: USA. Reissue: Lightfoot, Gordon. *Summertime Dream*. Warner Brothers 2246. *1987*: USA.

Lightfoot, Gordon. *Sundown*. Reprise 2177. *1974*: USA. Reissue: Lightfoot, Gordon. *Sundown*. Warner Brothers 2177. *1987*: USA.

Martin, Dean. *The Best of Dean Martin 1962–1968*. Charly 106. *1996*: UK.

Mitchell, Joni. *Blue*. Reprise 2038. *1971*: USA. Reissue: Mitchell, Joni. *Blue*. DCC 1132. *1999*: USA.

Mitchell, Joni. *Clouds*. Reprise RS-6341. *1969*: USA. Reissue: Mitchell, Joni. *Clouds*. Reprise 2-6341. *1987*: USA.

Mitchell, Joni. *Hits*. Reprise 46326. *1996*: USA.

Mitchell, Joni. *Joni Mitchell*. Reprise 27199. *1968*: USA. Reissue: Mitchell, Joni. *Joni Mitchell*. Reprise 2-6293. *1987*: USA.

Mitchell, Joni. *Ladies of the Canyon*. Reprise 6376. *1970*: USA. Reissue: Mitchell, Joni. *Ladies of the Canyon*. Reprise 2-6376. *1987*: USA.

Mitchell, Joni. *Song to a Seagull*. Reprise 6293. *1968*: USA.

Newman, Randy. *Good Old Boys*. Reprise MS4-2193. *1974*: USA. Reissue: Newman, Randy. *Good Old Boys*. Warner Brothers 2193. *1990*: USA.

Newman, Randy. *Randy Newman*. Reprise 6286. *1968*: USA. Reissue: Newman, Randy. *Randy Newman*. Reprise 7599 267052. *1995*: USA.

Newman, Randy. *Sail Away*. Reprise MS-2064. *1972*: USA. Reissue: Newman, Randy. *Sail Away*. Warner Brothers 2064. *1990*: USA.

Newman, Randy. *Trouble in Paradise*. Reprise 23755. *1983*: USA.

Newman, Randy. *12 Songs*. Reprise RS-6373. *1970*: USA. Reissue: Newman, Randy. *12 Songs*. Warner Brothers 6373. *1990*: USA.

Sinatra, Frank. *The Reprise Collection*. Reprise 2-26340. *1990*: USA.

Young, Neil. *Decade*. Reprise 3RS-2257. *1977*: USA. Reissue: Young, Neil. *Decade*. Reprise 2-2257. *1988*: USA.

Zappa, Frank. *Waka/Jawaka: Hot Rats*. Reprise 2094. *1972*: USA.

Zappa, Frank, and the Mothers of Invention. *Weasels Ripped My Flesh/Burnt Weenie Sandwich*. Reprise 64024. *1979*: USA.

DAVID SANJEK

—Riverside (US)

Riverside was a record company and label established in New York in 1953 by Bill Grauer and Orrin Keepnews. It initially reissued vintage jazz and blues recordings from Paramount, Gennett and QRS. Subsequently, more recent material was licensed from specialist jazz labels such as Circle and Hot Record Society. In 1954, Riverside began recording contemporary jazz, including important works by Thelonious Monk, Wes Montgomery and Jimmy Smith, among others. The 'Living Legends' series comprised new recordings of older styles, including a major documentation recorded in New Orleans. The company folded in 1964, but its back catalog has been reissued on Fantasy's Milestone and Original Jazz Classics labels.

Bibliography

Furusho, Shinjiro. 1984. *Riverside Jazz Records*. Chiba City, Japan: The author.

Hazeldine, Mike, and Martyn, Barry. 1991. 'An Interview with Herb Friedwald.' *New Orleans Music* 2(5): 6–18; 2(6): 6–14.

Keepnews, Orrin. 1987. *The View from Within*. New York and Oxford: Oxford University Press.

Okajima, Toyoki, ed. 1997. *The Riverside Book: Discography of All Series*. Tokyo: Jazz Hihyo (Jazz Critique Special Edition).

HOWARD RYE

—Rock Records (Taiwan)

The leading Taiwanese pop music label, Rock Records, was founded in Seoul by Sam and Johnny Duann in 1980. Through such artists as Emil Chau and Sarah Chen, Rock developed the Mandarin pop genre in competition with Hong Kong's Cantopop. The Rock Records roster includes rapper Jutoupi and blues guitarist Wu Bei. During the 1980s, the company was the licensee of the Western companies BMG, Virgin and EMI. When these set up their own Taiwan branches, Rock took over distribution of music from numerous Western independent labels, including Rykodisc, Creation and Alligator.

The first overseas Rock Records branch was set up in 1991 in Hong Kong. The following year, the company expanded into Singapore and Malaysia. A South Korea branch was established in 1993. Rock started its Magic Stone label in 1989 to sign and produce pop and rock acts from mainland China. Magic Stone artists include heavy rock band Tang Dynasty and modern rock composer Dou Wei.

In Taiwan, Rock has its own recording studio and monthly magazine, and it owns a number of retail outlets. By 1996, the company's annual sales had reached $100 million, of which 40 percent was from outside Taiwan.

DAVE LAING

—Rodven (Venezuela)

A Venezuelan record company, Rodven has been a market leader in merengue, salsa and Latin popular music. With locally produced music more popular than international popular music in Venezuela, Rodven has had a substantial share of the recorded music market there.

Until its purchase by PolyGram in 1995, Rodven was a subsidiary of the Cisneros group of companies, which also owned the Venevisión radio and television stations, a disc and cassette pressing plant, the Big Show Productions concert promotion firm, and the country's leading music retailer, Discocenter.

In 1985, Rodven acquired another Venezuelan label,

T.H. Records, which had a US branch, and in 1987 it acquired the Mexican record company Peerless, whose catalog included albums by Pedro Infante, Prisma, Mario Pintor and various Mexican regional acts. Rodven established a branch in Colombia in 1988.

Because foreign record companies were not permitted to establish Venezuelan subsidiaries until the mid-1990s, Rodven became the local distributor for EMI in 1987, BMG in 1993 and PolyGram in 1995. In that year, Poly-Gram paid $57 million for the Rodven label. The price included the Venezuelan, Mexican and Colombian artist rosters, as well as the pressing plant, a distribution network, Big Show Productions and Discocenter. At this stage, the leading acts signed to Rodven included Ricardo Montaner, Colombian singer-songwriter Soraya, and male vocalists Wilfrido Vargas and Frankie Ruiz. The label's roster of Mexican acts included vocalist Pedro Fernandez and rock band Grupo Limite.

In 1998, PolyGram was sold to the Seagram conglomerate and was merged with the Universal Music Group.

Discography

Fernandez, Pedro. *Coleccion Mi Historia*. PolyGram 537851. *1997*: Venezuela.

Fernandez, Pedro. *Deseos y Delirios*. PolyGram 534120. *1996*: Venezuela.

Grupo Limite. *Coleccion Mi Historia*. PolyGram 537877. *1997*: Venezuela.

Grupo Limite. *Sentimientos*. T.H. Rodven 539331. *1997*: Venezuela.

Infante, Pedro. *Mi Historia*. T.H. Rodven 7517. *1992*: Venezuela.

Infante, Pedro. *Rancheras*. Peerless 10. *1988*: Mexico.

Montaner, Ricardo. *El Ultimo Lugar de Mundo*. T.H. Rodven 2864. *1991*: Venezuela.

Montaner, Ricardo. *Espectacular*. T.H. Rodven 3245. *1996*: Venezuela.

Montaner, Ricardo. *Los Hijos del Sol*. T.H. Rodven 2995. *1996*: Venezuela.

Pintor, Mario. *Soy Un Romantico*. Peerless 86. Mexico.

Prisma. *Con Banda*. Peerless 388. *1995*: Mexico.

Ruiz, Frankie. *Coleccion Mi Historia*. PolyGram 537712. *1997*: Venezuela.

Soraya. *Torre de Marfil*. PolyGram 539067. *1997*: Venezuela.

Vargas, Wilfrido. *Itinerario*. T.H. Rodven 3005. *1996*: Venezuela.

Vargas, Wilfrido. *Oro Merenguero 20 Exitos*. T.H. Rodven 529795. *1996*: Venezuela.

Visual Recordings

Montaner, Ricardo. 'En Concierto.' T.H. Rodven 2924 (video).

Montaner, Ricardo. 'Exitos y Algo Mas.' T.H. Rodven 3099 (video).

Montaner, Ricardo. 'Video Clips de Montaner.' T.H. Rodven 2923 (video).

DAVE LAING

—Rosebud (France)

Rosebud was founded in 1991 by Alan Gac, a 17-year-old fan of Alan McGee of Creation Records. Originally based in Rennes, Brittany, Gac signed several local artists – Les Freluquets, Katerine, Sloy – and Chelsea, the band of Emmanuel Tellier (of *Les Inrockuptibles* fame, *Les Inrockuptibles* being the major French pop/rock magazine), before moving into PolyGram's building in Paris in 1993. The reasons for this move were a new licensing arrangement with Barclay (a PolyGram subsidiary), and pecuniary difficulties that had led him to sell his assets (i.e., master tapes) to that same company. Even though the label was still considered to be very much involved in the French indie pop scene at the close of the twentieth century – the Little Rabbits joined its roster in 1996 – Gac admits that Rosebud's A&R policy has been guided by PolyGram's overall strategy since 1993.

Discography

Chelsea. *Tramway*. Rosebud/Virgin (Virgin France) 31004. *1992*: France.

Katerine. *Mes Mauvaises Fréquentations*. Rosebud/Polydor (PolyGram France) 529842. *1996*: France.

Les Freluquets. *Discorama*. Rosebud/Danceteria 842263. *1992*: France.

Little Rabbits, The. *Yeah!*. Rosebud 7052. *1998*: France.

OLIVIER JULIEN

—Rough Trade Records (UK)

A leading label of British punk and new wave music, Rough Trade was originally a specialist record store in the Notting Hill district of London. The store was opened in 1976 by Geoff Travis to sell reggae, dub and other rare records, and it soon began to stock 'do-it-yourself' fanzines and recordings by such bands as the Desperate Bicycles and the Buzzcocks.

Rough Trade began to move into distribution of such products to similar stores throughout Britain, and in 1978 the Rough Trade label was launched. Its first album release, by Stiff Little Fingers, became an underground hit. Other artists signed to the label on profit-sharing contracts were Cabaret Voltaire, the Fall and Young Marble Giants.

In the early 1980s, the company expanded by helping to form the Cartel, an alliance of regional distributors that became an effective alternative to the national distribution systems of major UK record companies. Branches of the Rough Trade label were also set up in Germany, The Netherlands, Belgium and the United States, primarily as outlets for British artists.

The Smiths provided the company's first mainstream commercial success in 1984 when the group's debut album led to a series of hit records. At the same time, the distribution company increased its activities by handling numerous independent rock and dance labels (including Mute, 4AD, Rhythm King, Creation and Factory) throughout the 1980s. However, the expansion left the company vulnerable to the failure of several major clients and to recession in the UK economy. In 1991, both the distribution company and the Rough Trade label were closed. By this time, Morrissey of the Smiths had left the label to join EMI.

The German Rough Trade company was sold to the local management, and in the United Kingdom a new sales company – RTM – was formed to handle recordings from labels previously distributed by Rough Trade. The Rough Trade label itself was acquired by the One Little Indian company, but the label's later activities had little subsequent impact.

Discographical References

Smiths, The. *The Smiths*. Rough Trade ROUGH 61. *1983*: UK.

Stiff Little Fingers. *Inflammable Material*. Rough Trade ROUGH 1. *1979*: UK.

Discography

Cabaret Voltaire. 'Headkick (Do the Mussolini)' (EP). Rough Trade RT 003. *1978*: UK.

Fall, The. 'How I Wrote "Elastic Man"'/'City Hobgoblins.' Rough Trade RT 048. *1980*: UK.

Smiths, The. *The Queen Is Dead*. Rough Trade ROUGH 96. *1986*: UK.

Young Marble Giants. *Colossal Youth*. Rough Trade ROUGH 8. *1980*: UK.

DAVE LAING

—Rounder Records (US)

Producer and writer Pete Welding described Rounder as 'a label of roots music and its contemporary offshoots,' and the company has made a major contribution to the promotion of bluegrass music and blues since it was founded by three students in Cambridge, Massachusetts in 1970.

The first release was by old-time banjoist George Pegram, but in the following three decades Rounder built up a catalog of almost 2,000 albums, spanning blues, folk, Cajun, soul, reggae, bluegrass and country music. The most successful artists on the Rounder label have been blues revivalist George Thorogood and the Destroyers, and the bluegrass fiddler and singer Alison Krauss, while the Bullseye blues label launched in 1991 includes Ronnie Earl and Etta James on its roster. The company also operates the Philo label, which has issued albums by Nanci Griffith and Iris Dement.

Discography
Rounder Bluegrass Guitar. Rounder CD 11576. *1997*: USA.
Rounder Folk, Vol. 1. Rounder CD 11511. *1988*: USA.
Rounder Old Time Music. Rounder CD 11510. *1988*: USA.

DAVE LAING

—Rykodisc (US)
Founded in Salem, Massachusetts in 1983 as a specialist CD label when that format was in its infancy, Rykodisc acquired CD rights to the Frank Zappa, David Bowie and Jimi Hendrix catalogs. By 1988, it had added an A&R function, signing new artists for release on vinyl and cassette as well as CD.

In 1992, Rykodisc absorbed veteran producer Joe Boyd's London–based Hannibal label, with Boyd becoming head of the company's European division. In 1994, Rykodisc bought the Zappa pop catalog and Gramavision, a New York-based jazz and funk label founded in 1979. In the same year, the company was restructured into three divisions: the label Rykodisc Inc., REP distribution and Rykomusic, the publishing arm.

Discography
Steal This Disc. Rykodisc RCD 00056. *1987*: USA.
Steal This Disc 2. Rykodisc RCD 00076. *1988*: USA.

DAVE LAING

—Savoy (US)
Savoy, a record company and label, was founded in late 1942 in Newark, New Jersey by Herman Lubinsky. It built up substantial catalogs of jazz, rhythm and blues, and gospel music under the A&R direction of Teddy Reig (1945–52), including sessions by Charlie Parker and Dexter Gordon. Reig's successor, Lee Magid, followed a more commercial policy. Fred Mendelsohn, whose Regent label was purchased by Lubinsky in 1948, was with Savoy from 1952 to 1956, and returned in 1960. Under his direction, Savoy increasingly specialized in gospel music. Herman Lubinsky died in 1974, and the catalog was purchased by Arista the following year. The label name has subsequently been used on several reissue series.

Bibliography
Burns, Joe. 1989. 'Mr. Jelly Belly.' *Living Blues* 20(2): 33.
Ruppli, Michel, with Porter, Bob. 1980. *The Savoy Label: A Discography* (*Discographies*, No. 2). Westport, CT: Greenwood Press.
Shaw, Arnold. 1978. *Honkers and Shouters: The Golden Years of Rhythm & Blues*. New York: Macmillan.
Sheridan, Chris. 1980. 'Savoy Records: The Hidden Treasures.' *Jazz Journal International* 13(10): 17–18; 13(12): 18–19.
Shor, Russ. 1995. 'Silent Partners: Bob Porter (Part 2).' *VJM's Jazz & Blues Mart* 98: 4–6.

HOWARD RYE

—Sire (US)
Founded in New York in 1967 by producer Richard Gottehrer and promotion man Seymour Stein, Sire first licensed European underground and blues recordings by Barclay James Harvest, Climax Blues Band, Focus and others. In the early 1970s, Stein discovered the nascent New York punk scene, signing the Ramones, Talking Heads and Richard Hell to recording deals. Subsequently, Warner Brothers Records took a stake in the company. Stein's most important discovery was Madonna, whom he signed to a recording deal in 1984. Madonna later formed her own label, Maverick, which released albums by Alanis Morissette and which operated in association with Sire.

Discography
Just Say Yo. Sire 9257452. *1988*: USA.
The Sire Machine Turns You Up. Sire SMP1. *1978*: UK.

DAVE LAING

—Smithsonian Institution Recordings (US)
The Smithsonian Institution was established by an Act of the US Congress in 1846 as an institution for the 'increase and diffusion of knowledge.' By the late twentieth century, it had become one of the world's largest museum complexes, with over 6,000 employees working in 16 museums and the National Zoo, and in research centers throughout the United States and in various parts of the world.

Early uses of recordings were for scientific research, although Frances Densmore (1867–1957) recorded approximately 2,500 cylinders of Native American music under the auspices of the Smithsonian Institution's Bureau of American Ethnology. Densmore's association with the Smithsonian began in 1907 and lasted over 50 years. Densmore's recordings are now preserved in the Library of Congress Archive of Folk Culture, cataloged by Densmore during the last 15 years of her life with funds provided by the Library.

The Smithsonian did not begin a systematic institutional effort to diffuse knowledge of and through audio recordings until the late 1970s, when it established the Division of the Performing Arts. A record label, called the Smithsonian Collection of Recordings, was initiated and eventually integrated into the Smithsonian Institution Press; it was discontinued in 1998. Although the Smithsonian Collection of Recordings released many fine recordings of classical music, its most influential releases took the form of boxed sets of LPs (and later cassettes and CDs) that focused on specific topics, such as North American jazz, musical theater, country music, folk or blues, or on a single performer, such as Hoagy Carmichael or Duke Ellington. The boxes included tracks licensed from many different sources, with extensive scholarly commentaries. Many of these were both critical and popular successes, and several became standard components of course curricula at North American universities.

In 1987, the Smithsonian embarked on a different kind of dissemination of recorded sound when it acquired the large (2,168 titles) Folkways Records company from the family of its founder, Moses Asch. The Smithsonian acquired all the rights and assumed the contractual obligations of the record company, and committed itself to keeping every title in print. Ethnomusicologist Anthony Seeger was hired as the first curator and director of the record company, which was based in the Smithsonian's Center for Folklife Programs and Cultural Studies. The organization was split into two parts: the Folkways Collection, which would be kept available to the public through mail order and evolving technologies; and Smithsonian Folkways Recordings, a reissue and new projects label distributed through independent commercial enterprises. Convinced that the many small, independent recording labels had made very significant contributions to the culture of the twentieth century, Seeger established a policy of acquiring independent labels for the Smithsonian. As of 1998, Cook Records, Dyer-Bennet Records, Fast Folk Music Magazine, Monitor Records and Paredon Records had joined Folkways in the Smithsonian family of record labels, with all titles kept available to the public. A complete catalog of these labels is available on-line (http://web2.si.edu/folkways/).

Discographical References

American Musical Theater: Shows, Songs, and Stars (4-CD set). Smithsonian Collection of Recordings RD 036. *1989*: USA.

Carmichael, Hoagy. *Classic Hoagy Carmichael* (4-LP set). Smithsonian Collection of Recordings R 038. 1927–87; *1987*: USA.

Classic Country Music (4-CD set). Smithsonian Collection of Recordings RD 042. *1990*: USA.

Ellington, Duke. *American Songbook Series: Duke Ellington.* Smithsonian Collection of Recordings 23172. *1993*: USA.

Ellington, Duke. *Beyond Category.* Smithsonian/RCA 49000. *1994*: USA.

Ellington, Duke. *Duke Ellington 1938.* Smithsonian Collection of Recordings P2-13367. 1938; *1976*: USA.

Ellington, Duke. *Duke Ellington 1939.* Smithsonian Collection of Recordings P2-14273. 1939; *1977*: USA.

Ellington, Duke. *Duke Ellington 1940.* Smithsonian Collection of Recordings DPM2-0351. 1940; *1978*: USA.

Ellington, Duke. *Duke Ellington 1941.* Smithsonian Collection of Recordings DPM2-0492. 1941; *1981*: USA.

Ellington, Duke. *First Annual Tour of the Pacific Northwest* (2-LP set). Folkways FJ 2968. 1952; *1983*: USA.

Folk Song America: A 20th Century Revival (4-CD set). Smithsonian Collection of Recordings RD 046. *1990*: USA.

The Blues (4-CD set). Smithsonian Collection of Recordings RD 101. *1993*: USA.

The Smithsonian Collection of Classic Jazz (5-CD set). Smithsonian Collection of Recordings RD 033. *1995*: USA.

Discography

Bluegrass

American Banjo: Three-Finger and Scruggs Style. Smithsonian Folkways 40037. *1990*: USA.

Mountain Music Bluegrass Style. Smithsonian Folkways 40038. *1991*: USA.

Blues

Johnson, Lonnie. *The Complete Folkways Recordings.* Smithsonian Folkways 40067. 1967; *1993*: USA.

Ledbetter, Huddie (Leadbelly). *Lead Belly's Last Sessions* (4-CD set). Smithsonian Folkways 40068/71. 1948; *1994*: USA.

Ledbetter, Huddie (Leadbelly). *Where Did You Sleep Last Night: Lead Belly Legacy, Vol. 1.* Smithsonian Folkways 40044. 1941–47; *1996*: USA.

McGhee, Brownie. *The Folkways Years (1945–1959).* Smithsonian Folkways 40034. 1945–59; *1991*: USA.

Terry, Sonny. *The Folkways Years (1944–1963).* Smithsonian Folkways 40033. 1944–63; *1991*: USA.

Folk

Anthology of American Folk Music (ed. Harry Smith) (6-CD set). Smithsonian Folkways 40090. *1997*: USA.

Cajun Social Music. Folkways 2621. *1975*: USA. Reissue: *Cajun Social Music.* Smithsonian Folkways 40006. *1990*: USA.

Close to Home: Old Time Music from Mike Seeger's Collection 1952–1967. Smithsonian Folkways 40097. 1952–67; *1997*: USA.

Cowboy Songs on Folkways. Smithsonian Folkways 40043. *1991*: USA.

Don't Mourn – Organize!: Songs of Labor Songwriter Joe Hill. Smithsonian Folkways 40026. *1990*: USA.

Smithsonian Folkways American Roots Collection. Smithsonian Folkways 40062. *1996*: USA.

Wade in the Water: African American Sacred Music Tradi-

tions (4-CD set). Smithsonian Folkways 40076. *1994*: USA.

THE EDITORS

—Sonet (Sweden)

Sonet was founded in Stockholm in 1955 by Swedish jazz enthusiasts as the successor to Storyville, a Danish jazz label established in 1951, and became the most successful of the wholly Swedish-owned independent record companies during the 1960s and 1970s. The company produced a wide range of local artists, and fed a large percentage of the earnings thus derived back into new music production.

In 1968, Sonet opened a London office, which released a number of hit singles by British and North American artists. The company also controlled the European rights to Bill Haley and the Comets for a number of years. In addition, Sonet (UK) held international rights to the Mute label, whose artists included Depeche Mode and Yazoo.

Until the late 1980s, approximately 30 percent of Sonet's income came from its license to sell records on the Island, Chrysalis and Polar labels. However, PolyGram purchased Polar in 1988 and Island in 1990, and EMI purchased Chrysalis in 1989, and, as a result of these changes in the transnational music industry, Sonet lost its Scandinavian license and distribution rights for Island, Chrysalis and Polar.

Sonet attempted to maintain its strong independent role in Sweden by branching out into film and video production and distribution. The company invested funds in domestic repertoire, for both the home and the international market, but, without a steady flow of income from international repertoire via local licensing deals, Sonet soon ran into financial difficulties. In 1991, Sonet's phonogram and publishing business was sold to PolyGram.

Bibliography

Burnett, Robert. 1996. *The Global Jukebox: The International Music Industry*. London and New York: Routledge.

Wallis, Roger, and Malm, Krister. 1992. *Music Policy and Music Activity*. London: Routledge.

Discography

Persson, Peps. *Sweet Mary Jane*. Sonet SLP-2501. *1969*: Sweden.

Rickfors, Mikael. *Tender Turns Tuff*. Sonet SLP-2676. *1982*: Sweden.

Secret Service. *Oh Susie*. Sonet SLP-2655. *1979*: Sweden.

Sir Douglas Quintet. *Midnight Sun*. Sonet SNTF-897. *1983*: Sweden.

Tolonen, Jukka. *Impressions*. Sonet SLP-3023. *1977*: Sweden.

Williams, Jerry. *Mr. Dynamite Jerry Williams and the Violents*. Sonet SLP-35. *1963*: Sweden.

ROBERT BURNETT

—Sonolux (Colombia)

Sonolux (Industria Electrosonora), a Colombian record company, was founded in Medellín in 1949 by Rafael Acosta, a businessman, and Antonio Botero, a technician and agent of rival Discos Fuentes. Its first label, Lyra, recorded mainly Colombian artists, distributing nationwide. Acosta soon left to found Discos Ondina; Otoniel Cardona, later founder of Discos Victoria, joined; and publishing firm Bedout also became a partner until 1974, when the Ardila Lulles corporation took over the company. Hernán Restrepo Duque, radio DJ and great chronicler of Colombian popular music, was artistic director at the company for some 20 years from the mid-1950s. Sonolux moved to Bogotá in 1991.

Guitar-based music from the Colombian Andes (especially *pasillos* and *bambucos*) was an early mainstay of the company and continued to be so in the 1990s with artists such as Garzón y Collazos and Ecuadorian Julio Jaramillo. Music from the Colombian Caribbean region (*porro, cumbia, merecumbé*) was increasingly popular from the 1950s onward, and stars such as Lucho Bermúdez and Pacho Galán recorded with Sonolux. Luis Uribe Bueno, Lucho Bermúdez's bass player, also worked as artistic director at Sonolux in the early 1950s. Antonio María Peñaloza, an important composer and musician from the Caribbean coastal region, worked as an arranger for the Orquesta Sonolux between 1959 and 1963. In the 1990s, Sonolux still sold a range of styles, including salsa, merengue and *vallenato*. In 1994, Sonolux had a massive hit with Carlos Vives' revival of old *vallenato* numbers (*Clásicos de la Provincia*), which broke all national sales records.

Discographical Reference

Vives, Carlos. *Clásicos de la Provincia*. Sonolux 01013901937. *1994*: Colombia.

Discography

Bermúdez, Lucho. *14 Grandes Exitos*. Sonolux 01 00066. n.d.: Colombia.

El Gran Combo de Puerto Rico. *El Gran Combo: Nuestro Aniversario*. Sonolux 01 02026. n.d.: Colombia.

Fantasia Vallenata. Tamborito (Sonolux) 03 00155. n.d.: Colombia.

Galán, Pacho. *In Memoria*. Sonolux 01 01534. n.d.: Colombia.

Garzón y Collazos. *Veinte Exitos con Garzón y Collazos*. Sonolux 01 00011. n.d.: Colombia.

Gutierrez, Alfredo, and Mendoza, Juan Carlos. *Vallenato Mundial*. Tamborito (Sonolux) 03 00175. n.d.: Colombia.

Jaramillo, Julio. *16 Grandes Exitos de Julio Jaramillo*. Sonolux 01 00032. n.d.: Colombia.

La Fiesta del Ano, Vol. 16. Sonolux 01983902006. *1994*: Colombia.

PETER WADE

—Specialty (US)

Launched in Los Angeles, California in 1946 by Art Rupe (from the seeds of his partnership in Juke Box Records, founded in 1944), Specialty became an important independent source of rhythm and blues (R&B), gospel and rock 'n' roll recordings during the 1950s.

Initially successful with west-coast R&B acts (Roy Milton, Joe and Jimmy Liggins, Percy Mayfield), Rupe broadened his horizons to New Orleans in 1952 (Lloyd Price, Guitar Slim), and in 1953 opened an office in Jackson, Mississippi which was managed by Johnny Vincent, who would go on to form Ace Records. From the outset, Specialty was also a strong gospel label (the Pilgrim Travelers, the Soul Stirrers, Alex Bradford and more).

Via the southern connection, in 1955 Specialty signed its hottest property, rock 'n' roll tornado Little Richard, whose incandescent career was doused within two years when he returned to the church. At the same time, the company's other potential crossover star, Sam Cooke (from the Soul Stirrers), decamped in the opposite direction to a secular career with another company.

Specialty recorded more rock 'n' roll (Larry Williams, Don and Dewey, Jerry Byrne) but, following the brief return of Little Richard in 1963–64, Rupe concentrated on other business interests, retaining his historic catalog for reissue projects and overseas licensing until finally selling to Fantasy in 1990.

All of Specialty's principal R&B, gospel and rock 'n' roll artists have been anthologized on CD, marketed in the United States and other nations, excluding Europe, by Fantasy and in the United Kingdom and other European territories by Ace Records.

Discography

Art Rupe: The Story of Specialty, in His Own Words. Ace CDCH2 542. *1998*: UK.

It's Spelt Specialty. Ace CDSPEC1. *1994*: UK.

Little Richard. *The Specialty Sessions*. Ace ABOXCD1. *1989*: UK.

The Specialty Story. Specialty 5SPCD 4412-2. *1994*: USA.

CLIFF WHITE

—Stax Records (US)

Based in Memphis, Tennessee, Stax Records was from 1960 to 1975 the foremost record company specializing in southern soul music. During its first decade, the majority of recordings issued by Stax and its subsidiaries, such as Volt and Enterprise, tended to be made at the company's own handcrafted studio, using the same basic rhythm section, horn players, songwriters, engineers and producers. Consequently, Stax developed a readily identifiable sound that, in many respects, served as the blueprint for late 1960s and early 1970s soul recordings in Muscle Shoals, Alabama and Jackson, Mississippi by a variety of record labels, including Atlantic, Chess and Malaco.

Stax was started largely under the auspices of a white country fiddler named Jim Stewart. It was initially known as Satellite Records and was located first in Memphis (1957), then in Brunswick, some 30 miles east of Memphis (1959), and then, again, in Memphis (1960). Stewart co-owned Satellite Records with his sister, Estelle Axton. While in Brunswick, Stewart had recorded his first black artists, a vocal group known as the Veltones. While promoting their record, Stewart came into contact with Memphis disc jockey and former Sun Records artist Rufus Thomas. In 1960, Rufus and his daughter Carla recorded with Satellite a duet Thomas had written entitled ''Cause I Love You.' The record proved to be a local hit and was quickly picked up by Atlantic Records for national distribution. Atlantic would distribute the vast majority of Stax releases through 1968.

While Stewart had started the company as a country/pop enterprise, the success of the Carla and Rufus record caused him to concentrate his efforts on the then-nascent soul genre. In the fall of 1961, after achieving a national pop and rhythm and blues (R&B) instrumental hit with 'Last Night,' by an integrated studio ensemble known as the Mar-Keys, Stewart and Axton were forced by California-based Satellite Records to change their company's name. Using the first two letters of *St*ewart and *Ax*ton, they renamed the company Stax. By November 1961, a subsidiary label, Volt Records, had been established. Through 1967, under the Stax and Volt imprints, Stewart engineered/produced hits by Carla and Rufus Thomas together and separately, William Bell, Booker T. and the MGs, Otis Redding, Sam and Dave, Eddie Floyd, Johnnie Taylor, the Bar-Kays and a host of lesser-known artists. All of these artists were supported by an interracial house band, and by 1964 the company's office personnel was also interracial. In Memphis in the 1960s, an integrated company was an extremely radical enterprise.

In the fall of 1965, former R&B disc jockey Al Bell (real name Al Isbell) was hired as Stax's first full-time promotion manager. Bell quickly became involved in marketing and A&R in addition to his promotional duties and began single-handedly to transform Stax from a cottage industry into a national R&B powerhouse. In the summer of 1968, he was given 10 percent equity in the company (making Stax interracially owned) and Stax was sold to Gulf and Western. When Estelle Axton decided to sell out in 1969, Bell and Jim Stewart became equal partners, buying the company back from Gulf and Western in July 1970. Bell eventually bought out Stewart's share in October 1972. A visionary in the best sense of the word, Bell began to expand the scope of the company's activities tremendously, recording rock, pop, jazz, country, gospel and comedy records, in addition to soul. He also expanded Stax's business to include motion pictures while, at the same time, making the company extremely active socially and politically within the black community.

Bell also began to work actively toward changing the label's sound, attempting to fuse its southern soul-based aesthetic with those of northern and west-coast producers, hoping to achieve more across-the-board sales success. While Bell's efforts resulted in the early 1970s' success of Isaac Hayes, the Staple Singers and the Dramatics, he ended up destroying what had been the Stax sound, alienating most of the early session musicians and many of the early artists in the process. While Stax enjoyed new levels of corporate success in the 1970s, it became less distinctive as a company.

In October 1972, Bell entered into a distribution agreement with CBS Records. This proved to be an extremely ill fit. By the summer of 1973, due to a number of factors related to this distribution agreement, Stax began to experience cash-flow problems, forcing Bell to borrow heavily from Union Planters National Bank. When Union Planters began to experience its own problems and the Stax–CBS relationship further deteriorated in 1974, Stax found itself in a critical situation. In 1973, the company was also subjected to a number of investigations by various federal grand juries relating to tax evasion, payola and, eventually, fraud. Neither Stax nor any of its principals were ever found guilty of any crime, but the combined pressures on the company eventually forced Stax into involuntary bankruptcy in December 1975.

After being officially declared bankrupt in the summer of 1976, Stax was sold to Sam Nassi and Associates, which the following year resold the company to Fantasy Records. For a brief period in 1978 and 1979, Fantasy revived the Stax imprint, recording new material and issuing a number of outtakes. Fantasy has continued to own the Stax name, masters and contracts but, as a result of the distribution agreement Stax signed with Atlantic Records in May 1965, Atlantic has the rights in perpetuity to distribute Stax products that were originally distributed by Atlantic through May 1968. In addition,

Atlantic has the rights to distribute a number of Otis Redding masters originally issued through 1970. In all cases, Atlantic pays to Fantasy the royalty on this material that was originally due to Stax. Fantasy has continued to distribute Stax material originally issued from June 1968 until the company's demise.

Bibliography
Bowman, Rob. 1995. 'Stax Records: A Musicological Analysis.' *Popular Music* 4(3): 285–320.
Bowman, Rob. 1996. 'Stax Records: A Lyrical Analysis.' *Popular Music and Society* 20(1): 1–34.
Bowman, Rob. 1997. *Soulsville U.S.A.: The Story of Stax Records*. New York: Schirmer Books.
Guralnick, Peter. 1986. *Sweet Soul Music: Rhythm and Blues and the Southern Dream of Freedom*. New York: Harper & Row.

Discographical References
Mar-Keys, The. 'Last Night.' Satellite 107. *1961*: USA.
Thomas, Rufus, and Thomas, Carla. ''Cause I Love You.' Satellite 102. *1960*: USA.

Discography
The Complete Stax/Volt Singles: 1959–1968. Atlantic Records 82218-2. *1991*: USA.
The Complete Stax/Volt Soul Singles Volume 2: 1968–1971. Fantasy Records 9SCD-4411-2. *1993*: USA.
The Complete Stax/Volt Soul Singles Volume 3: 1972–1975. Fantasy Records 10SCD-4415-2. *1994*: USA.

ROB BOWMAN

—Stiff Records (UK)
Stiff was founded in London in July 1976 by artist-managers Dave Robinson and Jake Riviera (aka Andrew Jakeman). They were leading figures in the 'pub rock' scene of the early 1970s and, with £400 borrowed from the group Dr Feelgood, they issued their first single, 'So It Goes' by Nick Lowe. The label's irreverent and zany approach was symbolized by the catalog number 'BUY 1' and by the slogan 'Today's Sounds Today,' a parody of Phil Spector's 1960s catch phrase 'Tomorrow's Sounds Today.' Stiff was among the first to issue material by London's new punk acts, such as the Damned and Elvis Costello. In 1976, Riviera left Stiff to join Radar Records, and Costello and Lowe went with him. However, Robinson signed replacement new-wave acts Ian Dury and the Blockheads, Lene Lovich and Wreckless Eric. In 1978, Stiff organized its Route 78 tour, during which its leading artists traveled around the United Kingdom in a private train.

Apart from Dury, the label's most successful act commercially was Madness, signed in 1979; the group sold millions of albums in the early 1980s. Other Stiff acts, such as Kirsty MacColl and Tracey Ullman, also produced hits during this period.

In 1984, Island Records bought 50 percent of the company, which continued to be managed by Robinson. However, Stiff's parent company went into liquidation two years later, and the Stiff catalog was sold to the ZTT label for £300,000. At this point, Stiff's roster included the Belle Stars, the Pogues and Dr Feelgood, the group whose loan had launched Stiff. ZTT subsequently closed Stiff, later licensing its catalog for reissue purposes.

Bibliography
Muirhead, Bert. 1983. *Stiff: The Story of a Label*. Poole: Blandford Press.

Discographical Reference
Lowe, Nick. 'So It Goes.' Stiff BUY 1. *1976*: UK.

Discography
Belle Stars, The. *The Belle Stars*. Stiff SEEZ 45. *1982*: UK.

Costello, Elvis. *My Aim Is True*. Stiff SEEZ 3. *1977*: UK.

Damned, The. *Damned Damned Damned*. Stiff SEEZ 1. *1977*: UK.

Dr Feelgood. *Classic*. Stiff SEEZ 67. *1987*: UK.

Dury, Ian, and the Blockheads. *New Boots and Panties!!*. Stiff SEEZ 2. *1977*: UK.

Lovich, Lene. *Flex*. Stiff SEEZ 19. *1980*: UK.

MacColl, Kirsty. 'A New England.' Stiff BUY 216. *1984*: UK.

Madness. *One Step Beyond*. Stiff SEEZ 17. *1979*: UK.

Pogues, The. *Rum Sodomy and the Lash*. Stiff SEEZ 58. *1985*: UK.

Ullman, Tracey. 'They Don't Know.' Stiff BUY 180. *1983*: UK.

Wreckless Eric. 'Whole Wide World.' Stiff BUY 16. *1977*: UK.

DAVE LAING

—Sun Records (US)

Sun Records was a pioneering rock 'n' roll and rockabilly record company based in Memphis, Tennessee. It flourished in the late 1950s when it issued the first recordings of Elvis Presley, Jerry Lee Lewis, Carl Perkins and Johnny Cash. As such, it was one of the key non-metropolitan independent labels, which many authors have credited as playing a vital role in the rock 'n' roll revolution of the fifties.

The label was formed in 1952 by Sam Phillips, a former disc jockey who had established his Memphis Recording Service, the first permanent recording studio in Memphis, two years earlier. There, he recorded numerous blues, rhythm and blues (R&B), and country and western performers, leasing tracks by Howlin' Wolf, B.B. King, Jackie Brenston and others to such labels as Chess in Chicago and Modern in Los Angeles.

The Sun label had R&B hits by 'Little' Junior Parker and the Prisonaires (a group formed by inmates of the Tennessee State Penitentiary) before Presley's 'That's All Right (Mama)' was issued in 1954. Produced by Phillips, it utilized the trademark echo sound of the tiny Sun studio. Presley's success led to the purchase of his contract and his Sun masters by RCA-Victor for $35,000 in 1956. However, Phillips created further hits with Perkins ('Blue Suede Shoes'), Lewis ('Whole Lotta Shakin' Goin' On'), Cash ('I Walk the Line'), Roy Orbison ('Ooby Dooby'), Bill Justis ('Raunchy') and Charlie Rich ('Lonely Weekends'). The Justis and Rich records appeared on the Phillips International label that was started by Sam Phillips in 1957. Other rockabilly singers on the Sun label included Charlie Feathers, Warren Smith and Billy Lee Riley.

Although overshadowed by the success of Sun's white rockers, the label issued early work by such R&B artists as Rufus Thomas, James Cotton, Little Milton and Rosco Gordon. Phillips continued to release material until 1969, when the assets of Sun Records, including the studio and over 5,000 master recordings, were purchased by music publisher and producer Shelby Singleton. In Europe, Sun recordings were licensed in 1975 to Charly Records, which developed a comprehensive reissue program.

Bibliography
Escott, Colin, and Hawkins, Martin. 1991. *Good Rockin' Tonight: Sun Records and the Birth of Rock 'n' Roll*. New York: St. Martin's Press.

Discographical References
Cash, Johnny. 'I Walk the Line.' Sun 241. *1956*: USA.

Justis, Bill. 'Raunchy.' Phillips 3519. *1957*: USA.

Lewis, Jerry Lee. 'It'll Be Me'/'Whole Lotta Shakin' Goin' On.' Sun 267. *1957*: USA.

Orbison, Roy, and the Teen Kings. 'Ooby Dooby.' Sun 242. *1956*: USA.

Perkins, Carl. 'Blue Suede Shoes.' Sun 234. *1956*: USA.

Presley, Elvis. 'That's All Right (Mama)'/'Blue Moon of Kentucky.' Sun 209. 1954: USA.

Rich, Charlie. 'Lonely Weekends.' *Lonely Weekends with Charlie Rich*. Phillips International PLP 1970. *1960*: USA.

Discography
Cash, Johnny. *Johnny Cash with His Hot and Blue Guitar*. Sun LP 1220. *1957*: USA.

Cotton, James. 'Cotton Crop Blues.' Sun 206. 1954: USA.

Feathers, Charlie. 'I've Been Deceived.' Sun 503. *1956*: USA.

Gordon, Rosco. 'Just Love Me Baby.' Sun 227. 1955: USA.

Justis, Bill, and His Orchestra. *Cloud Nine*. Phillips International PLP 1950. *1957*: USA.

Little Junior's Blue Flames. 'Feelin' Good.' Sun 187. 1953: USA.

Little Milton. 'Beggin' My Baby.' Sun 194. 1953: USA.

Perkins, Carl. *Dance Album of Carl Perkins*. Sun LP 1225. *1957*: USA.

Prisonaires, The. 'Just Walkin' in the Rain.' Sun 186. 1953: USA.

Rich, Charlie. *Lonely Weekends with Charlie Rich*. Phillips International PLP 1970. *1960*: USA.

Riley, Billy Lee. 'Red Hot.' Sun 277. *1956*: USA.

Smith, Warren, and the Little Green Men. 'Ubangi Stomp.' Sun 250. *1956*: USA.

Thomas, Rufus, Junior. 'Bear Cat.' Sun 181. 1953: USA.

DAVE LAING

—Supraphon (Czech Republic)

Supraphon is a Czech record label and company belonging to the Bonton holding company.

When the Czech record industry was nationalized in 1946, the former privately owned record companies Esta (founded in 1928) and Ultraphon (founded in 1933 as the Czech branch of the German-Dutch company Küchenmeister Ultraphon Maatschappij, which was established in 1929) were merged into the state-owned *Gramofonové závody* ('Gramophone Works'). *Gramofonové závody* produced records as well as record players and other hardware under Ultraphon's Supraphon label.

By 1961, having left its hardware production to Tesla and its foreign trade to Artia, *Gramofonové závody* combined its record production with the music department of *Státní nakladatelství krásné literatury, hudby a umění* (SNKLHU), the 'State Publishing House for Literature, Music and Fine Arts,' to form a new state enterprise called *Státní hudební vydavatelství* (SHV) (the 'State Music Publishing House'). SNKLHU had previously assimilated *Národní hudební vydavatelství Orbis* (the national publishing house, Orbis) in 1953. Since 1951, Orbis had managed the *Hudební matice* ('Musical League') catalog, which comprised compositions by Bedřich Smetana, Antonín Dvořák and others. SHV continued to use the label Supraphon for records until 1967, when the company was renamed Supraphon. In 1975, the company teamed up with Nippon Columbia to make the first digital recording in Europe.

The Supraphon catalog comprises all Czechoslovak classical as well as popular music and spoken-word recordings up to the end of the 1960s, and principal representative recordings in these areas until 1989. Supraphon's international reputation is based on its large classical repertoire. Supraphon was the only state record company in Czechoslovakia until the end of the 1960s.

A second Czech company, Panton, began to produce records in 1967, and a Slovak company, Opus, was established as the Slovak branch of Supraphon in Bratislava in 1971.

Supraphon's book and sheet music department was established as a separate entity, Editio Supraphon, in 1991. In 1993, with privatization taking place within the new Czech Republic, the company became part of a joint-stock venture owned by the Bonton company. Established in January 1990, Bonton was active in film, video and radio, as well as owning record companies such as Bonton Music, Supraphon and Opus. While Bonton Music produced Czech rock, pop, jazz and folk, Supraphon has focused on classical music and the spoken word since 1994. Supraphon has assumed control of the Opus company and, since January 1998, of the Panton label as well.

Bonton (with a 49 percent share) and Sony Software B.V. from The Netherlands (with a 51 percent share) formed a new joint-venture label, Sony Music/Bonton, in February 1998.

Bibliography

Fukač, Jiří, and Vysloužil, Jiří, eds. 1997. *Slovník české hudební kultury* [The Dictionary of Czech Music Culture]. Praha: Editio Supraphon, 243–44, 594.

Macek, Jiří. 1976. *ABC diskofila* [ABC for Record Fans]. Praha: Editio Supraphon.

Matzner, Antonín, Poledňák, Ivan, and Wasserberger, Igor, eds. 1983. *Encyklopedie jazzu a moderní populární hudby* [Encyclopedia of Jazz and Modern Popular Music]. Praha: Editio Supraphon, 112.

Melville-Mason, Graham. 1996. 'Esta, Ultraphon and Supraphon: A Short History of the Czech Record Industry.' *International Classical Record Collector* (Summer): 34–43.

ALEŠ OPEKAR

—Swaggie (Australia)

Swaggie was established by the Graeme Bell jazz band in 1949, originally to carry the band's own recordings. The first issues carried what became the company's permanent logo: the image of an Australian 'swaggie' (a rural itinerant) and his dog. Following the release of five 78 rpm recordings and the band's second overseas tour, the company was sold to Melbourne jazz enthusiast and musician Nevill Sherburn in 1954. Sherburn continued the policy of issuing Australian jazz material, initially on 45 rpm EPs, and, from about 1960, expanded the catalog to include reissues of lesser-known US jazz groups of the 1920s and 1930s in the Swaggie JCS series, with sleeve notes by historian Bill Haesler. Subsequently, the standard format for recordings became the 12" (30 cm) LP and, eventually, there were a few CD releases. The label has been relatively inactive since 1997.

Swaggie was instrumental in bringing the more recondite early US jazz library to the attention of Australian enthusiasts. More significantly, it was responsible for the international dissemination of what is regarded as the Australian jazz sound that emerged from Australia's postwar traditional movement, the earliest documentation of which was on the limited circulation label Ampersand and, to a lesser extent, on Jazzart. This movement produced what has been regarded as the most distinctive contribution to the jazz tradition outside the United States. Swaggie's enduring and prolific catalog was the most comprehensive documentation of this distinctive style, which gained international recognition through the label's distribution in the United States, the United Kingdom, Europe and Japan.

Bibliography

Haesler, Bill. 1992. 'Swaggie.' *Australian Record and Music Review* 12 (January): 17.

Johnson, Bruce. 1987. *The Oxford Companion to Australian Jazz*. Melbourne: Oxford University Press.

Discography

Dave Dallwitz: The Ern Malley Jazz Suite. Swaggie S-1360. *1975*: Australia.

Dave Dallwitz's Southern Jazz Group. Swaggie 1010. 1951: Australia.

Graeme Bell and His Australian Jazz Band, 1949–52. Swaggie S-1397. *1982*: Australia.

Graeme Bell's Australian Jazz Band. Swaggie S.1. 1949: Australia.

Graeme Bell's Australian Jazz Band/Graeme Bell and His Ragtime Piano. Swaggie S.4. 1950: Australia.

Lazy Ade [Monsbourgh] and His Backroom Boys. Swaggie S.1004. 1950: Australia.

Len Barnard's Jazz Band: Classics of Australian Jazz. Swaggie S-1221. *1967*: Australia.

BRUCE JOHNSON

—Syliphone (Guinea)

The one and only record label in Guinea (Conakry) was created in 1959 soon after the country became independent. The company was originally attached to the Haut Commissariat Information Conakry, and later to the Ministère de la Jeunesse. It first produced 7" (18 cm) singles under the label 'Silly Phone,' which was soon changed to 'Syliphone.' In 1967, the first LPs were compiled from singles: *Orchestre de la Paillotte* (renamed Keletigui et ses Tambourins) and *Orchestre du Jardin de Guinée* (renamed Balla et ses Balladins). In 1980, the last LP produced under the umbrella of the Ministère de la Jeunesse was released: *Objectif perfection*, by Balla et ses Balladins.

Bolibana Distribution (based in France) released three more SLP records between 1983 and 1985 around the first European tour of Les Amazones de Guinée. Other products on the Syliphone label were: audiocassettes SYL C 001–009, 7" (18 cm) singles SYL 501–574, a 12" (30 cm) single SYL 575 and 12" (30 cm) LPs GUI 1 and 2.

Despite poor relations between the new Republique de Guinée and France, most of the records were manufactured in and distributed from the old colonial metropolis (in the sixties, a few SLPs were pressed in Germany and Yugoslavia). Distributors based in France were CEDDI (Centre Européen de Distribution International) – for a short while – and then Sonodisc (green-yellow-red label). In 1980, CEA (Centre Européen d'Achats), also based in France, took over, re-pressed the bestsellers and marketed a series of recordings that had been unavailable before (red label). CEA did not last long, and in 1983 Bolibana started distribution and took the label into the CD era.

Syliphone had been created as an instrument of propaganda. Nationally, it took over the role of the *griot* and of the court announcer – essential in a country with 80 percent illiteracy. Internationally, it documented the creativity and ingenuity of the newly independent nation by presenting its national orchestras and highly talented traditional musicians. Side by side with pure propaganda (Sékou Touré's 1970 speech against colonial aggression), Syliphone produced highlights like Kouyaté Sory Kandia's recordings with Keletigui.

In 1998, the Bureau guinéen des droits d'auteurs signed a 'procuration' that gave Syllart Productions worldwide rights concerning the Syliphone catalog and the associated publishing rights. This provoked a legal response from Bolibana Productions, on which no decision had been reached by the beginning of the new millennium. In the meantime, both Syllart and Bolibana continued to produce CDs from the Syliphone catalog.

A comprehensive discography of Syliphone albums and of reissued CDs has been compiled by Graeme Counsel, and is available at http://home.connexus.net.au/~mimt/Radio%20Africa/Syliphon.htm.

Discographical References

Balla et ses Balladins. *Objectif perfection*. Syliphone SLP 75. *1980*: Guinea.

Kandia, Kouyaté Sory. *Grand prix du disque 1970*. Syliphone SLP 12. *1970*: Guinea.

Les Amazones de Guinée. *Au coeur de Paris*. Syliphone SLP 76. *1983*: France.

M'Mah Sylla. *Le rossignol de Guinée*. Syliphone SLP 78. *1985*: France.

Orchestre de la Paillotte. Syliphone SLP 1. *1967*: Guinea.

Orchestre du Jardin de Guinée. Syliphone SLP 2. *1967*: Guinea.

Sona Diabaté des Amazones. *Sons de la savane.* Syliphone SLP 77. *1984*: France.

Touré, Ahmed Sékou. *Appels au peuple.* Syliphone SLP 26. *1971*: Guinea.

GÜNTER GRETZ

—Syllart (Senegal)

Syllart Productions is the trading name of the Senegalese producer and distributor, Ibrahima Sylla. Most of Syllart's productions have been mixed, if not recorded, in Paris.

Since the mid-1980s, when 'world music' began to interest Western listeners, Sylla's slick, distinctive productions have launched many of the Sahel region's major artists and revitalized the careers of several performers from other parts of Africa. At the same time, he has supplied a booming cassette market in West Africa with some of the region's most enduring music.

The son of an influential *marabou* (holy man), Sylla learned the music trade at the Salsa Musique label in Paris before setting up on his own in the early 1980s. The album that announced his presence in 1987 in Britain and the United States was *Soro* by Salif Keita, a groundbreaking release that has remained one of the top-selling African records of all time. Other artists that Sylla produced before they were signed by Western labels included Youssou N'Dour, Baaba Maal and Ismaël Lô. He also 'packaged' selected Congolese/Zairean artists for the Francophone/pan-African market. In the early 1990s, Sylla launched several female singers from the Malian region of Wassoulou, most notably Oumou Sangaré.

Sylla has been one of the few African producers to successfully balance the demands of the home market with those of the international scene. His business sense has been as astute as his production skills. He has maintained a web of familial contacts to distribute his products in Africa and has had licensing agreements for Britain and the United States. An early love of Cuban music inspired him, in the mid-1990s, to record several albums in New York by Africando, a Senegalese rumba band.

Bibliography

Darlington, Lois. 1994. 'Date with Sylla.' In *The Rough Guide to World Music*, ed. Simon Broughton et al. London: Rough Guides Ltd., 272–73.

Discographical Reference

Keita, Salif. *Soro.* Mango 162-539808-2. *1987*: UK.

Discography

Africando. *Balboa.* Stern's 1082. *1998*: USA.
Africando. *Gombo Salsa.* Stern's 1071. *1996*: USA.
Africando. *Trovador 1.* Stern's 1045. *1994*: USA.
Africando. *Volume Two: Tierra Traditional.* Stern's 1054. *1995*: USA.
Lô, Ismaël. *Diawar.* Syllart CD 38759-2. *1989*: France.
Lô, Ismaël. *Natt.* Syllart CD 38740-2. *1987*: France.
Musiques du Mali Vol. 1 & Vol. 2. Syllart CD 38901-2. n.d. (1960s–1970s): France.
Musiques du Mali Vol. 3 & Vol. 4. Syllart CD 38902-2. n.d. (1960s–1970s): France.

GRAEME EWENS

—Tabansi (Nigeria)

The Nigerian businessman Prince G.A.D. Tabansi became involved in the music business in the late 1950s, eventually founding a studio in Onitsha, East Nigeria and launching the first successful indigenous record label, specializing in the guitar/highlife music of the eastern region. Later, a branch was opened in the financial capital, Lagos. Like many successful independents in Africa, the record company offered a full service, from recording to mastering, pressing, sleeve design, printing and distribution. As well as supporting and developing indigenous musicians, the company's factory also manufactured and distributed albums for licensees of imported music, at a time when Nigerian record sales were measured in hundreds of thousands.

By the 1980s, Tabansi's greatest hits included releases by the Sierra Leonean Bunny Mack, and by Felix Lebarty, a local singer nurtured by Tabansi, who had performed at dozens of sessions for successful indigenous artists such as Chris Okotie and Christy Essien. Lebarty's first album, *Lover Boy*, was a huge seller.

In 1982, a new studio was opened in Onitsha, with one of the first 24-track recording machines in Nigeria and a 32-channel mixing desk. Video facilities were also available. In 1983, a shortage of vinyl reduced Nigeria's record production to 25 percent of previous levels, and Prince Tabansi turned his attention beyond Nigeria, signing distribution and licensing deals in the United Kingdom and Kenya. By the 1990s, he had scaled down his music activities, although the office in Lagos and the studio in Onitsha were still active in 1998.

Bibliography

Africa Music magazine (Lagos and London). 1982. 9, 12.

Discographical Reference

Lebarty, Felix. *Lover Boy.* Tabansi TTL 182. *1982*: Nigeria.

GRAEME EWENS

—Telefunken (Germany)

The name 'Telefunken' was trademarked by Gesellschaft für drahtlose Telegraphie (the Wireless Telegraphy Company) in 1903, the year in which the Telefunken company was founded as a joint venture by the German electronics firms Siemens & Halske and AEG to exploit their broadcasting patents. The Telefunken record company was subsequently founded in 1932 as Telefunkenplatten GmbH as a consequence of Telefunken's takeover of Ultraphon, the recording division of the German Küchenmeister-Konzern.

Küchenmeister, a radio, gramophone and film corporation founded in 1925 by Heinrich J. Küchenmeister, started life as Ultraphon AG, a firm that manufactured gramophones. From 1929, it released recordings under the name of Ultraphon Records, not only in Germany but also in France and the Benelux countries. Takeovers in 1930 added the German record labels Adler, Orchestrola-Vocalion and Musica Sacra. The Küchenmeister enterprise – which, in the meantime, had become a huge and highly complex international holding company located in Amsterdam – failed to survive the world economic crisis of the late 1920s/early 1930s and collapsed in the summer of 1932.

Telefunken stabilized its own interests in the radio and gramophone sectors by acquiring the Küchenmeister labels. Ultraphon, in particular, which held exclusive recording rights for the yearly Wagner festival in Bayreuth and had also released some important jazz recordings by, for example, Billy Barton and Lud Gluskin, was firmly established on the German market. Telefunkenplatten GmbH continued this tradition, gaining a reputation for pioneering advances in sound engineering, and thus for improvements in sound quality. The main emphasis in the development of repertoire was on classical music and opera. In 1950, AEG-Telefunken, now the name of the mother company, and Decca (UK) combined their recording interests in the German market by forming Teldec (Telefunken-Decca-Schallplatten GmbH), a company that replaced the German branch of Decca (UK) and Telefunkenplatten GmbH. Teldec concentrated primarily on the classical market, although it also became synonymous with German *schlager* music.

In 1988, Teldec was sold to Warner Music Germany, becoming eastwest records GmbH. In 1994, eastwest released *3 Tenors with Mehta in Concert 94*, an album that achieved record sales for the classical sector. As part of Warner Music's 'two-company' strategy in Germany, WEA and eastwest carried many other label imprints, and in addition eastwest distributed the *schlager* repertoire from the revived Telefunken label. However, in 2001, the Teldec Classics label was relocated from Hamburg to London, operating within a centralized A&R and marketing arrangement under the Warner Classics International (WCI) umbrella. This relocation formed part of the Warner Music Group's restructuring and downsizing after the merger of Time Warner and AOL. The Teldec Classics studio in Hamburg, however, remained under the control of the company's German operation.

Bibliography

Schulz-Köhn, Dietrich. 1940. *Die Schallplatte auf dem Weltmarkt* [The Gramophone Record on the World Market]. Berlin: Rehrer.

Steinel, Roland. 1992. *Zur Lage und Problematik der Musikwirtschaft* [Situation and Problems of the Music Business]. München: Edition Roland/Intermedia.

Zeppenfeld, Werner. 1979. *Tonträger in der Bundesrepublik Deutschland. Anatomie eines medialen Massenmarkts* [Recordings in the Federal Republic of Germany: Anatomy of a Media Mass Market]. Bochum: Studienverlag Brockmeyer.

Discographical Reference

Carreras/Pavarotti/Domingo. *3 Tenors with Mehta in Concert 94*. eastwest 4509962002. *1994*: Germany.

PETER WICKE and VANESSA BASTIAN

—Tommy Boy (US)

Tommy Boy is a leading US hip-hop record label that has specialized in recording non-mainstream rap artists. It was founded in New York City in 1980 by Tom Silverman. Its earliest releases were all 12″ (30 cm) singles (including the controversial 'No Sell Out,' based on recordings of speeches by 'Malcolm X'), and its first hit was 'Planet Rock' by Afrika Bambaataa (1982), produced by Arthur Baker.

Tommy Boy released the early records of pioneering female rapper Queen Latifah and the psychedelic rock-influenced 'daisy' rap group De La Soul, whose use of an unauthorized sample from a record by the Turtles embroiled Tommy Boy in a major lawsuit. De La Soul's debut album was produced by Prince Paul, a member of another Tommy Boy rap group, Stetsasonic. In 1990, Tommy Boy signed the critically acclaimed California rap group Digital Underground.

The company subsequently developed a broader roster of R&B, rap and dance music artists, including the New Jersey group Naughty By Nature, Irish-American rappers House of Pain and British electro group 808 State.

In 1986, Warner Brothers Records bought 50 percent of the label and later took full control. However, Tommy Boy returned to joint-venture status when Silverman repurchased half of the company in 1996.

Silverman was also a founder of the New Music Seminar, the trade fair and talent show held annually in New York between 1981 and 1993.

Discographical References

Afrika Bambaataa and the Soulsonic Force. 'Planet Rock' (12″ single). Tommy Boy TB 823. *1982*: USA.

'Malcolm X'/Keith LeBlanc. 'No Sell Out' (12" single). Tommy Boy TB 840. *1983*: USA.

Discography

De La Soul. *Three Feet High & Rising*. Tommy Boy 1019. *1989*: USA.

Digital Underground. *Sex Packets*. Tommy Boy 1026. *1990*: USA.

808 State. *Ex:el*. Tommy Boy 1042. *1991*: USA.

House of Pain. *Same as It Ever Was*. Tommy Boy 1089. *1994*: USA.

Naughty By Nature. *Poverty's Paradise*. Tommy Boy 1111. *1995*: USA.

Queen Latifah. *All Hail the Queen*. Tommy Boy 1022. *1989*: USA.

Stetsasonic. *On Fire*. Tommy Boy 1012. *1986*: USA.

DAVE LAING

—2-Tone (UK)

Founded in the English Midlands city of Coventry in 1978, 2-Tone was both a label and a genre, which mixed ska and punk and was performed mainly by racially integrated groups. Its early releases were cover versions of Jamaican songs by the Specials, the Selecter and Madness.

After 'A Message To You, Rudy' by the Specials was a UK hit in 1979, 2-Tone signed a distribution agreement with Chrysalis Records. There were later releases by the Bodysnatchers, the Beat, the Higsons and ska trombonist Rico, but the mainstay of 2-Tone was the Specials. They had big hits with 'Ghost Town' (1981) and 'Nelson Mandela' (1984) before the group and the label disbanded in 1985.

Bibliography

Marshall, George. 1990. *The Two Tone Story*. Glasgow: Zoot Publishing.

Discographical References

Specials, The. 'A Message To You, Rudy.' 2-Tone CHSTT 5. *1979*: UK.

Specials, The. 'Ghost Town.' 2-Tone CHSTT 17. *1981*: UK.

Specials, The. 'Nelson Mandela.' 2-Tone CHSTT 26. *1984*: UK.

DAVE LAING

—ULO (Greenland)

The leading record company in the Danish protectorate of Greenland, ULO has issued a large number of albums of Greenlandic music in a wide variety of genres. Among the acts recorded by ULO are rock group Mariina, rappers Nuuk Posse and the veteran Greenlandic band Sume. ULO has also documented performances of traditional music at summit meetings of Inuit from Canada, Siberia and Greenland.

The label was founded by Karsten Sommer in 1979 (the year Greenland became self-governing) and is based in Nuuk. The ULO rock group Zizaka was the first to be awarded a 'sealskin disc' for sales of 10,000 copies of its album *Miki Goes to Nuussuaq* in a country with a population of only 50,000.

Discographical Reference

Zizaka. *Miki Goes to Nuussuaq*. ULO ULO45. *1985*: Greenland.

Discography

Kalaallit Nunaat: Greenland Calling, Vol. 1. ULOCD-57. *1989*: Greenland.

DAVE LAING

—Vanguard (US)

The Vanguard Recording Society was founded in New York in 1950 by musicologist Maynard Solomon and his brother, Seymour, to issue recordings of classical music principally on its Bach Guild label, using the slogan 'recordings for the connoisseur.' Vanguard began to record jazz in 1954 and produced albums by Larry Coryell, Jimmy Rushing, Elvin Jones and others. The company became involved with the folk revival by signing the Weavers in 1956 and Joan Baez in 1959.

Between 1959 and 1972, Vanguard issued 15 Baez albums, mostly produced by Maynard Solomon. Other folk artists recorded on the company's label included Buffy Sainte-Marie, Odetta, John Hammond, and Ian and Sylvia. There were also albums by Paul Robeson, veteran blues singer Skip James and bluegrass stalwart Doc Watson. The signing in 1967 of Country Joe and the Fish, whose albums were produced by Sam Charters, took Vanguard into psychedelic rock; Charters also brought electric blues artists Buddy Guy and James Cotton to the company in the 1960s. The arrival of Kinky Friedman in 1971 introduced Vanguard to country and western music.

The company's catalog was purchased by the Lawrence Welk organization (the Welk Music Group) in 1986 and has subsequently been extensively reissued. During the 1990s, Vanguard began to sign new artists, mostly in the area of folk.

Discography

Baez, Joan. *Joan Baez*. Vanguard VSD 2077. *1960*: USA.

Coryell, Larry. *Spaces*. Vanguard VSD 6558. *1970*: USA.

Cotton, James. *Cut You Loose!*. Vanguard VSD 79283. *1968*: USA.

Country Joe and the Fish. *Electric Music for the Mind and Body*. Vanguard VSD 79244. *1967*: USA.

Friedman, Kinky. *Sold American*. Vanguard VMD 79333. *1973*: USA.

Guy, Buddy. *A Man and His Blues*. Vanguard VSD 79272. *1968*: USA.

Hammond, John. *Country Blues*. Vanguard VSD 79198. *1966*: USA.

Ian and Sylvia. *Four Strong Winds*. Vanguard VRS 9133. *1964*: USA.

James, Skip. *Devil Got My Woman*. Vanguard VSD 79273. *1968*: USA.

Jones, Elvin. *Summit Meeting*. Vanguard VSD 79390. *1976*: USA.

Odetta. *One Grain of Sand*. Vanguard 2153. *1963*: USA.

Robeson, Paul. *Live at Carnegie Hall: May 9, 1958*. Vanguard VCD 72020. *1958*: USA.

Robeson, Paul. *The Odyssey of Paul Robeson*. Vanguard 3007. *1992*: USA.

Rushing, Jimmy. *Goin' to Chicago*. Vanguard VRS 8518. *1971*: USA.

Sainte-Marie, Buffy. *It's My Way!*. Vanguard VMD 79142. *1964*: USA.

Watson, Doc, and Watson, Merle. *Ballads from Deep Gap*. Vanguard VMD 6576. *1967*: USA.

Weavers, The. *The Weavers at Carnegie Hall*. Vanguard VMD 73101. 1955: USA.

DAVE LAING

—V-Disc (US)

'V-disc' is the name given to records manufactured uniquely for distribution between 1943 and 1949 to US army and navy personnel serving overseas.

The service was provided by the Music Section of the Special Services Division, the body charged with maintaining the morale of the armed forces. Up to 1943, the Music Section had principally been concerned with live, usually military music; provision of recorded and broadcast music was the business of the Radio Section, which supplied each member of the forces with a 'kit' that included a radio, a record player, commercial recordings and transcriptions. Following the American Federation of Musicians' (AFM) July 1942 recording ban, the supply of commercial recordings began to diminish, making it difficult for the Radio Section to meet demands for contemporary material. The idea of establishing a special program to fill this gap is credited to Lieutenant Robert Vincent of the Radio Section. Vincent also secured the necessary financial support, and transferred to the Music Section to run the new venture from premises in New York, aided by a staff with considerable record company experience.

Using the RCA-Victor pressing and distribution plant in Camden, New Jersey, the V-disc program shipped its first batch of records in October 1943. By January 1945, the initial total of around 50,000 discs a month had risen to 300,000. Over 8 million discs are said to have been pressed and distributed during the duration of the program, representing approximately 1,000 separate recordings.

Particularly in its early days, the V-disc program derived a considerable amount of material (including items previously unreleased) from commercial companies and from broadcast transcriptions. From an historical point of view, the most interesting material is considered to be that recorded under the aegis of the V-disc operation itself. Using a variety of venues in New York, and issuing the results on 78 rpm discs with closer-than-average grooves (and, consequently, a longer playing time of 6.5 minutes), V-disc staff recorded a wide range of music: light classical and opera, military items, popular vocalists (including the Andrews Sisters, Bing Crosby and Frank Sinatra), dance music, African-American music ('Big' Bill Broonzy, Louis Jordan) and – perhaps especially – jazz (Louis Armstrong, Count Basie, Benny Goodman, Duke Ellington, Art Tatum and many other established performers). In addition to the quality of many of the performances, a factor that gave added interest to the jazz performances in particular was that V-disc staff were able to bring together musicians who were contracted to different record companies.

As a result of the initial agreement made with the AFM that recordings of its members should be made available only to military personnel, no official commercial reissue of the V-disc program has been attempted in the United States, despite constant interest in its contents; however, many recordings of jazz in particular have appeared on small labels in Europe and Japan. An extensive collection of the recordings is held by the US Library of Congress.

Bibliography

Carr, Roy. 1991. 'Diggin' for Victory.' *Record Hunter* (August): 12.

Sears, Richard S. 1980. *V-Discs: A History and Discography* (*Discographies*, No. 5). Westport, CT: Greenwood Press.

Sears, Richard S. 1986. *V-Discs: First Supplement* (*Discographies*, No. 25). Westport, CT: Greenwood Press.

DAVID HORN

—Vee-Jay (US)

Vee-Jay was one of the major independent labels in the decades following World War II that helped create a market for rhythm and blues (R&B) and rock 'n' roll music. The company was founded by record store owners Jimmy Bracken and Vivian Carter in mid-1953 in Gary, Indiana, but within months it was moved to Chicago, and Bracken and Carter were married. Calvin

Carter, Vivian's brother, served as the company's A&R director and producer. In late 1954, Ewart Abner, Jr. joined Vee-Jay as its chief administrator and owner of one-third of the company. Subsidiary labels added by the company included Abner and Tollie.

During the 1950s, Vee-Jay became a major producer of records in the fields of R&B (the Spaniels, Jimmy Reed, the El Dorados, John Lee Hooker), gospel (the Staple Singers, the Swan Silvertones) and jazz (Wynton Kelly, Eddie Harris), and it emerged as the largest black-owned record label before Motown. During the 1960s, Vee-Jay made its presence felt in the soul market. Indeed, Chicago's first soul record had come out of Vee-Jay – 'For Your Precious Love,' a 1958 hit by Jerry Butler and the Impressions. Other successful Vee-Jay soul recording artists were Dee Clark, Betty Everett and Gene Chandler.

In the 1960s, Vee-Jay became an important disseminator of white pop and rock, releasing records by the Four Seasons and the Beatles. In 1963, Abner was forced out of the company, and the new executive staff moved much of the label's operations to Los Angeles in 1964. In 1965, with the company suffering financially, Abner was called back and the headquarters were moved back to Chicago, but these actions could not prevent Vee-Jay from going out of business the following year.

Bibliography

Callahan, Mike. 1981a. 'Both Sides Now, The Story of Stereo Rock and Roll, Vee Jay Records.' *Goldmine* (May): 170–72.

Callahan, Mike. 1981b. 'The Vee Jay Story, Part 1: Scenes from a Family Owned Company.' *Goldmine* (May): 6–18.

Callahan, Mike. 1981c. 'The Vee Jay Story, Part 2: Vee Jay Is Alive and Living in Burbank.' *Goldmine* (May): 161–63.

Pruter, Robert. 1991. 'Vee Jay Records.' In *Chicago Soul*. Urbana, IL: University of Illinois Press, 24–47.

Pruter, Robert. 1996. 'Vee Jay Records.' In *Doowop: The Chicago Scene*. Urbana, IL: University of Illinois Press, 102–34.

Shaw, Arnold. 1978. 'Chicago's Black-Owned Record Company' and 'Randy Wood.' In *Honkers and Shouters: The Golden Years of Rhythm and Blues*. New York: Macmillan, 313–40.

Discographical Reference

Butler, Jerry, and the Impressions. 'For Your Precious Love.' Abner/Falcon 1013. *1958*: USA.

Discography

A Taste of Doowop, Volume One. Vee-Jay NVD2-709. *1993*: USA.

A Taste of Doowop, Volume Two. Vee-Jay NVD2-715. *1993*: USA.

A Taste of Doowop, Volume Three. Vee-Jay NVD2-717. *1993*: USA.

A Taste of Soul, Volume One. Vee-Jay NVD2-710. *1993*: USA.

A Taste of the Blues, Volume One. Vee-Jay NVD2-711. *1993*: USA.

A Taste of the Blues, Volume Two. Vee-Jay NVD2-718. *1993*: USA.

Celebrating 40 Years of Classic Hits: 1953–1993. Vee-Jay NVS2-3-400. *1993*: USA.

The Vee Jay Story. Charly CD LAB 104. *1996*: USA.

ROBERT PRUTER

—Verve (US)

Verve was a record company and label founded in Los Angeles in 1956 by Norman Granz. Granz's existing Clef and Norgran labels were absorbed into the new venture, which recorded hundreds of sessions by jazz musicians in all current styles. The label was sold to MGM for $2.8 million in 1960, but it continued in operation, with Creed Taylor directing many sessions, until Polydor took it over in 1967. In the mid-1960s, Verve also issued rock and blues albums by such artists as the Mothers of Invention and the Blues Project. After 1968, the label name was used for the reissue of the extensive Verve back catalog, but since the late 1980s new material has again been recorded for Verve.

Bibliography

Morgan, Alan. 1978. 'The Verve History of Jazz.' *Jazz Journal International* 31(4): 18–19.

Ruppli, Michel, with Porter, Bob. 1986. *The Clef/Verve Labels: A Discography* (Discographies, No. 26). Westport, CT: Greenwood Press.

HOWARD RYE

—Victor (Japan)

Victor (Japan), JVC and a number of other record labels are wholly owned music subsidiaries of the Japanese consumer electronics conglomerate JVC (the Japanese Victor Company), which itself is part-owned by the country's largest electronics firm, Matsushita.

The US-owned Victor Talking Machine Company made its first recordings in Japan in 1907. It set up the Japanese Victor Company as a wholly owned subsidiary in Japan in 1927 but, by 1938, JVC was wholly owned by Japanese shareholders.

After World War II, JVC's financial position deteriorated and, in 1953, it was rescued by Matsushita, which took a 50 percent holding. With increased investment, JVC engineers developed early stereo technology, color television and the videotape recorder. The company's VHS videocassette system was launched in 1976.

In 1973, JVC placed its music industry activities in a separate division called Victor Music Industries. Victor became one of the country's leading labels.

In the 1990s, the label's most commercially successful acts included SMAP, Keisuke Kuwata and the Southern All Stars. Victor also acted as the Japanese licensee of the US labels Stax, Kama Sutra and Good Time Jazz. In 1996, Victor was the fifth-largest record company in Japan, with a chart share of 8 percent. The company's labels include the *enka* specialist Teichiku, Rewind Recordings and Aosis.

JVC also formed joint-venture record companies in Japan with the Bertelsmann Music Group (BMG) in 1987 and with the Music Corporation of America (MCA, now Universal Music) in 1991. BMG-Victor's leading artists included B'z and Fukuyama. BMG bought out JVC in 1996, while MCA was owned by Matsushita between 1990 and 1995, when it was sold to Seagram. MCA was renamed Universal Music in 1997.

Outside Japan, the JVC label was set up to market world music and jazz recordings by acts such as Lee Ritenour and Gary Burton. In the late 1990s, JVC artist Bill Holman was nominated for a Grammy award, and the label had 'smooth jazz' hits from Paul Hardcastle and Chieli Minucci.

Bibliography

Inoue, Toshiya. 1977. 'The Recording Industry in Japan.' *Journal of the Audio Engineering Society* 25(10/11) (October–November): 802–808.

Discography

Burton, Gary. *Gary Burton and the Berklee All Stars*. JVC JD-3301. *1991*: Japan.

B'z. *The 7th Blues*. BMG-Victor BMCR-6601. *1994*: Japan.

Fukuyama. *On and On*. BMG-Victor BVCR-666. *1994*: Japan.

Hardcastle, Paul. *Cover to Cover*. JVC 2068. *1997*: USA.

Holman, Bill. *Brilliant Corners: The Music of Thelonious Monk*. JVC 2066. *1997*: USA.

Kuwata, Keisuke. *From Yesterday*. Victor JPN-VICL-300. *1992*: Japan.

Minucci, Chieli. 'Dreams.' *It's Gonna Be Good*. JVC 7007. *1998*: USA.

Ritenour, Lee. *Friendship*. JVC VIDC 3. *1979*: Japan.

SMAP. *007 Gold Singer*. Victor VICL-671. *1995*: Japan.

Southern All Stars, The. *Umi No Yeah!!*. Victor VICL-60227. *1998*: Japan.

DAVE LAING

—Victor (US)

One of the oldest record companies in the United States,

Victor was established in Camden, New Jersey in October 1901 as the Victor Talking Machine Company. Its founder, Eldridge R. Johnson, had developed the first spring-wound motors for disc gramophones in 1896 and had supplied them to the inventor of the flat disc, Emile Berliner. Realizing the commercial advantage of linking disc and gramophone manufacture, Johnson, together with Leon F. Douglass, had founded Victor's immediate predecessor, the Consolidated Talking Machine Company, in 1900. The records issued by this company were the first to be produced using two other Johnson ideas: recording on wax disc masters, and producing discs using a duplicate 'stamper,' which gave a much better quality to the grooves and hence a much improved sound quality. These records also bore the first paper labels, yet another Johnson invention. Included among the releases were discs pressed from recordings made in Europe for the Gramophone Company of London, the company set up with exclusive access in Britain to Berliner's manufacturing patents. By arrangement with Berliner, the Consolidated Talking Machine Company's advertising included the famous dog-and-gramophone logo – later to become the trademark of His Master's Voice – the US patent of which had been recently registered by Berliner.

Early in 1901, Johnson was able to settle some lengthy legal proceedings with an old rival of his and Berliner's, Frank Seaman, president of the National Gram-O-Phone Company, and shortly afterward marked the outcome by registering the name 'Victor' as a trademark. The Victor Talking Machine Company was established as a result of a decision by Johnson and Berliner 'to pool their patent, trademark, and manufacturing interests' (Marco and Andrews 1993, 739). The agreement setting up the company detailed a partnership between Victor and the Gramophone Company, a significant element of which was the first suggestion of a trading arrangement to divide up the world for marketing purposes.

The first Victor records featuring the dog-and-gramophone logo appeared in 1902, in the midst of a series of patent battles and takeover maneuvers. By 1903, Victor and its main rival, Columbia, had reached agreement over patents, and the two companies began to dominate the US market.

Taking Johnson's and Douglass's belief in the powers of advertising as an article of faith, the company was at the forefront of promotional campaigns to persuade more affluent sections of the US public to purchase both discs and gramophones (by now typically called phonographs in the United States). In 1906, the company developed and marketed the Victrola, the first playback machine with an internal horn. It retailed at $200. Victor issued a range of popular songs, dance tunes, comic acts and marches to be played on its machines, but was becoming best known for its opera catalog, issued on the famous Red Seal label, which Victor launched in 1903 with recordings (licensed, together with the Red Seal name, from the Gramophone Company) of the Italian tenor Enrico Caruso. The success of Caruso's records led Victor to sign him to an exclusive contract in 1904 – and led Caruso himself, one of the first internationally known musicians to appreciate the potential of recorded sound, to spend much of the rest of his life in New York.

In the second decade of the twentieth century, Victor issued a number of recordings that have since been seen as significant in popular music history – such as titles by James Reese Europe's Society Orchestra in 1913–14 and the first recordings of the Original Dixieland Jazz Band in 1917 – and began the 1920s with the biggest-selling record to date, Paul Whiteman's 'Whispering'/'The Japanese Sandman,' which in due course achieved total sales of well over a million copies. In 1921, the peak year for record production before the advent of radio, the company grossed $51 million in record sales. Yet it was slow to respond to new trends. In the early 1920s, Victor 'stood aloof from the blues craze' (Dixon and Godrich 1970, 12) for some time, while it tried to persuade the newly discovered African-American audience to buy Red Seal records. Its first venture into the 'race' record market, in 1923, was short-lived, and it neglected the area until 1926 (by which time its overall sales figures had more than halved from their 1921 level). A major change came with the hiring of Ralph Peer, who had developed the 'race' and hillbilly catalogs for OKeh. Peer selected and produced recordings in these areas for Victor, in return for which the copyrights in the songs he recorded were granted to his publishing company (Malone 1985, 80). Much recording was done by field units in centers such as Memphis for blues, Atlanta and Bristol, Tennessee for hillbilly music. In Memphis, for example, Peer recorded the Memphis Jug Band, Tommy Johnson and Ishman Bracey; in Bristol, in early August 1927, during three days that would become legendary in country music, he made the first recordings of the Carter Family and Jimmie Rodgers. Sales of Rodgers's records, though held down by the Depression, would reach a point where they 'exceeded the sales of most pop performers in the Victor catalogue' (Malone 1985, 84).

Beginning around 1926, Victor also established itself as a premier jazz label, recording (*inter alia*) 'Jelly Roll' Morton, Duke Ellington, Fats Waller and McKinney's Cotton Pickers. Shortly before this, the company had entered into an agreement with the Radio Corporation of America (RCA) for the installation of radios in its Victrolas, and in 1929 RCA took over the company. The

record and manufacturing company that was said, in its 28-year life span, to have sold 600 million records (Marco and Andrews 1993, 743) thus became part of a major entertainment empire.

The formation of another conglomerate, EMI, in the United Kingdom in 1931 did not pose a threat to RCA, but rather the reverse. For many years, Victor had had a licensing agreement with the Gramophone Company, under which each company could issue recordings from each other's masters and market them across its half of the globe. This arrangement remained in place when the Gramophone Company was subsumed into EMI, and the strong showing of the new British company was helpful to its US partner during the Depression. (The agreement was terminated in 1957.)

The ability of the radio business to remain profitable was another key factor in enabling Victor to survive the economic downturn in the early 1930s. Within its new parent body, Victor was even able to experiment with the possibility of a long-playing record. The idea was not new, but in 1931 Victor engineers developed a prototype revolving at 33 1/3 rpm, chiefly for use in the radio sector. The quality was poor, however, and the company may have lost its nerve. Few recordings were issued commercially, although some test pressings have survived which indicate that pairs of recordings were sometimes made from the same performance using differently placed microphones, providing, on playback, an early version of stereo sound (Kay 1985).

In 1933, the company withdrew its full-price 'race' series and in the same year moved into the cheap record market with a new $0.35 label, Bluebird. Later in the decade, the company's long commitment to classical music resulted in a major commercial success, thanks to the label's radio connections, when conductor Arturo Toscanini's weekly radio broadcasts on NBC resulted in a significant increase in sales of his recordings. But from the mid-1930s to the early 1940s, it was big band swing that proved most profitable. Victor's roster included several of the key band leaders of the period: Glenn Miller (issued on Bluebird), Benny Goodman, Lionel Hampton and Artie Shaw. The company also continued to put out a steady flow of recordings by Duke Ellington, among them 'Take the "A" Train' (1941) and excerpts from the suite 'Black, Brown and Beige' (1944).

In 1946, the label name for Victor records was changed to RCA-Victor, and in 1949 that label issued the first 45 rpm, 7" (18 cm) vinyl records. The decision to develop this format had been taken in order to rival – and be incompatible with – Columbia's development of the 33 1/3 rpm LP. The company also produced a budget-price player for its product, one that could play only 45 rpm records. Neither the company nor the industry at large foresaw the huge commercial success that the format would have in the singles market. Well before that time, however, patents had been merged.

Like other major labels, RCA-Victor was initially hesitant about recording rock 'n' roll, but in 1955 it purchased the contract of Elvis Presley from Sun Records for $35,000, together with the rights to all his Sun recordings. The success of the venture was phenomenal. Chapple and Garofalo (1977) report that 'from 1956–62 [Presley] was responsible for 31 out of RCA's 39 million-selling singles, and from 1958–60 he accounted for nine of their forty Gold Albums. Industry sources have speculated that he accounted for a quarter of RCA Records' total business for at least a decade' (210). Central though the company was to rock 'n' roll through its Presley recordings, it remained essentially ambivalent about both the music and the culture and had no other major successes. In many ways, the company was more at home with musicals (such as *The Sound of Music*) and the Nashville style of country pop developed under the guidance of Chet Atkins, who became head of RCA's country division in 1957. Among those performers who became prominent RCA-Victor country stars via this route were Jim Reeves and Don Gibson.

In the 1960s, with country pop and Presley's more middle-of-the-road (MOR) records selling well alongside those of other Grammy-winning MOR artists such as Henry Mancini and Harry Belafonte, the company's involvement in rock was slight, although it did have success with Jefferson Airplane, on the one hand, and the Monkees, on the other. The manager of a rock band that left the label subsequently remarked that 'their policies are set up for an older industry ... They have a basic incomprehension of what the music's about' (quoted in Chapple and Garofalo 1977, 211). Nevertheless – and with some changes to A&R personnel in the late 1960s – the company signed a number of major performers, including Lou Reed and David Bowie. In the 1970s and 1980s, John Denver, Hall & Oates, and the Eurythmics were also associated with the label.

By the mid-1970s, the corporation of which the record division was a part, RCA Inc., was one of the world's largest, involved in many industries (defense, oil, television and radio, publishing, car rental). In 1985, the entire corporation was bought by General Electric, which then sold on RCA Records to the German-based Bertelsmann Music Group (BMG) in 1986.

Bibliography

Chapple, Steve, and Garofalo, Reebee. 1977. *Rock 'n' Roll Is Here to Pay: The History and Politics of the Music Industry*. Chicago: Nelson-Hall.

Dixon, Robert M.W., and Godrich, John. 1970. *Recording the Blues*. London: Studio Vista.

Fagan, Ted, and Moran, William R. 1986. *The Encyclopedic Discography of Victor Recordings*. Westport, CT: Greenwood Press.

Kay, B. 1985. Liner notes to Duke Ellington, *Reflections in Ellington*. Everybody's 3005.

Malone, Bill C. 1985. *Country Music, U.S.A.* Rev. ed. Austin, TX: University of Texas Press.

Marco, Guy A., and Andrews, Frank, eds. 1993. *Encyclopedia of Recorded Sound in the United States*. New York: Garland.

Rust, Brian. 1970. *The Victor Master Book, Volume 2 (1925–1936)*. Stanhope, NJ: Walter C. Allen.

Sutton, Allan. 1994. *Directory of American Disc Record Brands and Manufacturers, 1891–1943*. Westport, CT: Greenwood Press.

Discographical References

Ellington, Duke. 'Black, Brown and Beige' (excerpts). Victor 280400–280401. 1944: USA. Reissue: Ellington, Duke. 'Black, Brown and Beige' (excerpts). *Black, Brown and Beige: 1944–46 Band Recordings*. RCA 6641. *1988*: USA.

Ellington, Duke. 'Take the "A" Train'/'Sidewalks of New York.' Victor 27380. 1941: USA. Reissue: Ellington, Duke. 'Take the "A" Train'/'Sidewalks of New York.' *Duke Ellington, 1940–41*. Jazz Chronological Classics 837. *1995*: France.

Whiteman, Paul. 'Whispering'/'The Japanese Sandman.' Victor 18690. 1920: USA. Reissue: Whiteman, Paul. 'Whispering'/'The Japanese Sandman.' *Paul Whiteman: Greatest Hits*. Collector's Choice Music 61. *1999*: USA.

Discography

Belafonte, Harry. *Day-O and Other Hits*. RCA 52082-2. *1990*: USA.

Belafonte, Harry. *Jump Up Calypso*. RCA-Victor LSP 2308. *1961*: USA. Reissue: Belafonte, Harry. *Jump Up Calypso*. RCA 52388. *1994*: USA.

Bowie, David. *Aladdin Sane*. RCA RS1001. *1973*: UK. Reissue: Bowie, David. *Aladdin Sane*. EMI 7947682. *1997*: UK.

Bowie, David. *Scary Monsters*. RCA PL 13647. *1980*: UK. Reissue: Bowie, David. *Scary Monsters*. EMI 7993312. *1992*: UK.

Bracey, Ishman. *Ishman Bracey and Charley Taylor (1928–1929)*. Document DOCD 5049. *1994*: Austria.

Carter Family, The. *Anchored in Love: Their Complete Victor Recordings (1927)*. Rounder CD 661064. *1998*: USA.

Denver, John. *Poems, Prayers and Promises*. RCA AFL1-

4499. *1971*: USA. Reissue: Denver, John. *Poems, Prayers and Promises*. RCA 5189. *1988*: USA.

Ellington, Duke. *The Duke Ellington Centennial Edition: The Complete RCA Victor Recordings, 1927–1973*. RCA 63386. *1999*: USA.

Ellington, Duke. *Greatest Hits (RCA Victor)*. RCA 68488. *1996*: USA.

Ellington, Duke. *Indispensable Duke Ellington, Vol. 1–2 (1927–1929)*. RCA 26192. *1995*: USA.

Europe, James Reese. *Too Much Mustard*. Saydisc SDL 221. *1980*: UK.

Eurythmics. *Sweet Dreams*. RCA LP 6063. *1983*: UK. Reissue: Eurythmics. *Sweet Dreams*. RCA 71471. *1995*: UK.

Gibson, Don. *All-Time Greatest Hits*. RCA 2295-2-R. *1990*: USA.

Goodman, Benny. *Greatest Hits (RCA Victor)*. RCA 68489. *1996*: USA.

Hall & Oates. *Bigger Than Both of Us*. RCA AFL1-1467. *1976*: USA. Reissue: Hall & Oates. *Bigger Than Both of Us*. RCA 1467. *1990*: USA.

Hampton, Lionel. *Classics 1937–1939*. EPM/Jazz Archives 157372. *1994*: France.

Jefferson Airplane. *After Bathing at Baxters*. RCA AFL1-4545. *1967*: USA. Reissue: Jefferson Airplane. *After Bathing at Baxters*. RCA 66798. *1996*: USA.

Jefferson Airplane. *Surrealistic Pillow*. RCA AFL1-3766. *1967*: USA. Reissue: Jefferson Airplane. *Surrealistic Pillow*. RCA 3766. *1988*: USA.

Jefferson Airplane. *Volunteers*. RCA AFL1-4238. *1969*: USA. Reissue: Jefferson Airplane. *Volunteers*. RCA 67562. *1998*: USA.

Johnson, Tommy. *Complete Works in Chronological Order*. Document DOCD 5001. *1994*: Austria.

Mancini, Henry. *Breakfast at Tiffany's*. RCA-Victor 2362. *1961*: USA.

Mancini, Henry. *Days of Wine and Roses*. RCA 666003. *1995*: USA.

McKinney's Cotton Pickers. *McKinney's Cotton Pickers 1928–1930*. EPM/Jazz Archives 157432. *1994*: France.

Memphis Jug Band, The. *Complete Recorded Works, 1–3*. Document DOCD 5021–3. *1990*: Austria.

Morton, 'Jelly Roll.' *The Jelly Roll Morton Centennial: His Complete Victor Recordings*. RCA 2631. *1990*: USA.

Original Dixieland Jazz Band, The. *Original Dixieland Jazz Band: 80 Years of Jazz*. Louisiana Red Hot Records 1103. *1998*: USA.

Presley, Elvis. *Elvis*. RCA AFL1-1382. *1956*: USA. Reissue: Presley, Elvis. *Elvis*. RCA 67736. *1999*: USA.

Presley, Elvis. *Elvis Presley*. RCA AFL1-1254. *1956*: USA. Reissue: Presley, Elvis. *Elvis Presley*. RCA 67735. *1999*: USA.

Presley, Elvis. *G.I. Blues*. RCA AFL1-2256. *1960*: USA. Reissue: Presley, Elvis. *G.I. Blues*. RCA 66960. *1999*: USA.

Reed, Lou. *Berlin*. RCA 10207. *1973*: USA. Reissue: Reed, Lou. *Berlin*. RCA 67489. *1998*: USA.

Reed, Lou. *Transformer*. RCA LSP 4807. *1972*: USA. Reissue: Reed, Lou. *Transformer*. BMG Special Products 44541. *1997*: USA.

Reeves, Jim. *Four Walls: The Legend Begins*. RCA 2493. *1991*: USA.

Rodgers, Jimmie. *First Sessions (1927–28)*. Rounder CD 661056. *1998*: USA.

Shaw, Artie. *Artie Shaw and His Orchestra, 1938*. Jazz Chronological Classics 965. *1998*: France.

Waller, Fats. *His Best Recordings, 1928–1942*. Best of Jazz 4006. *1994*: France.

Waller, Fats. *Indispensable Fats Waller, Vol. 1–2 (1926–1935)*. RCA 26162. *1995*: USA.

DAVID HORN and DAVID SANJEK

—Virgin (UK)

Founded by British entrepreneur Richard Branson in 1973, Virgin Records became the world's largest independently owned record company before its sale to Thorn-EMI in 1992.

As a teenager, Branson had launched a national magazine (*Student*) in 1971, followed by the Virgin mail-order record service, before setting up a recording studio at The Manor in the countryside near Oxford. Among the first products of The Manor was Mike Oldfield's multi-million seller, *Tubular Bells*, which gave the Virgin label and music publishing company a successful start in 1973. For its first few years, Virgin specialized in progressive or avant-garde rock from such artists as Faust, Gong, Tangerine Dream and Henry Cow.

With declining sales in the late 1970s, Branson sought unsuccessfully to sign such acts as the Rolling Stones and David Bowie. Instead, Virgin released singles and albums by the Sex Pistols after other labels had canceled the band's contracts. During the late 1970s, there was also a brief flirtation with Jamaican music when Virgin's Front Line subsidiary issued albums by Peter Tosh and others.

By 1980, losses from an attempt to establish a US branch caused Branson to make one-third of his staff redundant, but Virgin recovered strongly after signing Culture Club, Human League, Phil Collins, Simple Minds and others. During most of the 1980s, the label maintained a reputation as one of the most active contemporary pop and rock companies, not least in continental Europe where Virgin companies signed leading local artists.

Lack of funds for investment led Branson to sell Virgin shares on the London stock exchange in 1986, but poor share prices caused him to make the company private again. From 1980, music profits had been used to invest in venues (notably the London gay club Heaven), book publishing, film production (*The Great Rock 'n' Roll Swindle*, *Nineteen Eighty-Four*), cable television (the Music Box and Superchannel networks) and, above all, aviation – the Virgin Atlantic company was launched in 1984. Further investment funds for the airline were raised by the sale of part of the Virgin UK retail group to W.H. Smith and of a quarter of the record company to Fujisankei of Japan in 1990.

A new US record company was set up in 1985 but, despite a roster including Steve Winwood and Paula Abdul, Virgin found it difficult to compete with the major companies. By the late 1980s, the latter were locked in competition to acquire the remaining medium-size record companies, and Virgin's turn came in 1992 when Branson sold out to EMI for about $1 billion.

Once again, one-third of Virgin employees were made redundant, although the senior Virgin executive, Ken Berry, was eventually appointed to run the whole EMI-Virgin music group worldwide. Within the EMI empire, Virgin kept a label identity in several countries and provided hits from Janet Jackson, Meat Loaf, George Michael, the Spice Girls and others.

In 1996, Richard Branson reentered the music business with a new label, V2.

Bibliography

Brown, Mick. 1988. *Richard Branson, The Inside Story*. London: Michael Joseph.

Southern, Terry. 1993. *Virgin Story*. London: Virgin Books.

Discographical Reference

Oldfield, Mike. *Tubular Bells*. Virgin V2001. *1973*: UK.

Filmography

The Great Rock 'n' Roll Swindle, dir. Julien Temple. 1980. UK. 103 mins. Documentary.

Nineteen Eighty-Four, dir. Michael Radford. 1984. UK. 120 mins. Political Satire/Science Fiction. Original music by Eurythmics, Jonathan Gems, Annie Lennox, Dominic Muldowney, Dave Stewart.

DAVE LAING

—Vocalion Records (US)

Among the many labels that recorded blues, gospel and jazz in the 1920s and 1930s, Vocalion was one of the most notable and released some of the most commercially successful discs. Vocalion recorded the Fletcher Henderson Orchestra between 1923 and 1927 – and again in 1936 – as well as other early proponents of jazz, such as J.C. Cobb and His Grains of Corn (1928–29) and Jimmy Bertrand's Washboard Wizards (1926–29).

The label was set up by the Aeolian company in 1921 as a successor to Aeolian-Vocalion, which had operated from 1916 and whose releases included eight recordings by the Original Dixieland Jazz Band, among them 'At the Jass Band Ball.' Vocalion had a number of early successes with bands such as Henderson's and Ben Selvin's, and also issued a small number of 'race' records by women blues performers. Aeolian sold the recording concern to the Brunswick-Balke-Collender Company of Chicago in 1924. Initially, the latter company did little to continue Vocalion's modest presence in the blues. However, in 1926, Brunswick-Balke-Collender inaugurated a 'race' record division under the leadership of Jack Kapp, who had been Columbia's representative in Chicago. The label's first successes were with singing evangelists such as 'Blind Joe' Taggart. The 1000 blues series benefited in particular from J. Mayo Williams's fine eye for talent; Williams was one of the few African-American record men of his day and the owner of the short-lived Black Patti label. Recruited in 1927, he helped locate and record such prominent musicians as the pianist Leroy Carr, who, along with guitarist Francis Hillman 'Scrapper' Blackwell, inaugurated a new style of urban blues with the recording of the classic 'How Long How Long Blues' in Indianapolis in 1928. However, the label's most successful artist and greatest cause of notoriety was Hudson (Woodbridge) Whittaker, aka Tampa Red. In 1928, along with pianist (and eventual gospel pioneer) Thomas A. 'Georgia Tom' Dorsey, he recorded 'It's Tight Like That.'

The label changed hands three times during the 1930s. In 1930, Brunswick-Balke-Collender sold its radio and record divisions to Warner Brothers, which parted with the record division to the American Record Company (ARC) one year later, but retained control of the radio division, presumably considering it a more stable investment at the bottom of the Depression. Helped by a price reduction to $0.35, Vocalion survived the commercial ravages of the Depression, and in 1936–37 made what would become a celebrated series of recordings in San Antonio and Dallas of blues singer Robert Johnson. Along with other ARC labels, Vocalion was sold to CBS in 1938. CBS discontinued Vocalion in 1940, renaming it OKeh. In doing so, it defaulted on the 1931 agreement between Warner Brothers and Brunswick-Balke-Collender and, as a result, the rights in the name Vocalion reverted to Warner Brothers. In 1941, Warner Brothers sold these rights to Decca, which retained the name for limited releases until the 1960s. For example, in 1969 Vocalion released an LP by Patsy Cline, *Country Great! Patsy Cline*.

Bibliography

Dixon, Robert M.W., and Godrich, John. 1970. *Recording the Blues*. New York: Stein & Day.

Sutton, Allan. 1994. *Directory of American Disc Record Brands and Manufacturers, 1891–1943*. Westport, CT: Greenwood Press.

Discographical References

Carr, Leroy. 'My Own Lonesome Blues'/'How Long How Long Blues.' Vocalion 1191. 1928: USA. Reissue: Carr, Leroy. 'My Own Lonesome Blues'/'How Long How Long Blues.' *Complete Recorded Works, Vol. 1 (1928–1929)*. Document DOCD 5134. *1992*: Austria.

Cline, Patsy. *Country Great! Patsy Cline*. Vocalion VL-73872. *1969*: USA. Reissue: Cline, Patsy. *Country Great! Patsy Cline*. MCAC-736. *1988*: USA.

Original Dixieland Jazz Band, The. 'At the Jass Band Ball.' Aeolian-Vocalion AEO 1205. 1917: USA.

Tampa Red. 'It's Tight Like That.' Vocalion 1216. 1928: USA. Reissue: Tampa Red. 'It's Tight Like That.' *Tampa Red (1928–1942)*. Story of the Blues 3505. *1994*: USA.

Discography

Cobb, J.C., and His Grains of Corn. 'Once or Twice.' Vocalion 1449. 1929: USA. Reissue: Cobb, J.C., and His Grains of Corn. 'Once or Twice.' *The Junie Cobb Collection, 1926–29*. Collector's Classics 14. *1993*: Denmark.

Cobb, J.C., and His Grains of Corn. 'Shake That Jelly Roll.' Vocalion 1263. 1928: USA. Reissue: Cobb, J.C., and His Grains of Corn. 'Shake That Jelly Roll.' *The Junie Cobb Collection, 1926–29*. Collector's Classics 14. *1993*: Denmark.

Fletcher Henderson Orchestra, The. 'Baby, Won't You Please Come Home.' Vocalion 1079. 1927: USA. Reissue: Fletcher Henderson Orchestra, The. 'Baby, Won't You Please Come Home.' *1926–1927*. Melodie Jazz Classics 597. *1996*: France.

Fletcher Henderson Orchestra, The. 'Blue Lou.' Vocalion 3211. 1936: USA. Reissue: Fletcher Henderson Orchestra, The. 'Blue Lou.' *1924–1938*. Giants of Jazz 53179. *1998*: Italy.

Fletcher Henderson Orchestra, The. 'Dicty Blues.' Vocalion 14654. 1923: USA. Reissue: Fletcher Henderson Orchestra, The. 'Dicty Blues.' *1923*. Jazz Chronological Classics 697. *1993*: France.

Fletcher Henderson Orchestra, The. 'Hot Mustard.' Vocalion 1065. 1926: USA. Reissue: Fletcher Henderson Orchestra, The. 'Hot Mustard.' *1926–1927*. Melodie Jazz Classics 597. *1996*: France.

Jimmy Bertrand's Washboard Wizards. '47th Street Stomp.' Vocalion 1060. 1926: USA. Reissue: Jimmy Bertrand's Washboard Wizards. '47th Street Stomp.' *Washboard Story*. EPM Musique JA157412. *1996*: France.

Jimmy Bertrand's Washboard Wizards. 'Idle Hour Special.' Vocalion 1060. 1926: USA. Reissue: Jimmy Bertrand's Washboard Wizards. 'Idle Hour Special.' *Washboard Story*. EPM Musique JA157412. *1996*: France.

Jimmy Bertrand's Washboard Wizards. 'Little Bits.' Vocalion 1035. 1926: USA. Reissue: Jimmy Bertrand's Washboard Wizards. 'Little Bits.' *Washboard Story*. EPM Musique JA157412. *1996*: France.

Johnson, Robert. 'Stones in My Passway.' Vocalion 03723. 1937: USA. Reissue: Johnson, Robert. 'Stones in My Passway.' *The Complete Recordings*. Columbia/Legacy C2K-46222. *1990*: USA.

Taggart, 'Blind Joe.' *Complete Recorded Works, Vol. 1 (1926–1934)*. Document DOCD 5153. *1994*: Austria.

Taggart, 'Blind Joe.' *Complete Recorded Works, Vol. 2 (1929–1934)*. Document DOCD 5154. *1994*: Austria.

DAVID SANJEK and DAVID HORN

—Vogue (France)

Vogue was established by Léon Cabat, Albert Ferreri and Charles Delaunay in 1947. It was one of the first French record companies to centralize all aspects of production: recording, pressing and issuing.

From the beginning, Vogue specialized in jazz, recording under several labels: Pop, Royal Jazz, Swing, Blues Legacy, Blues Today, Jazz Legacy, Jazz Sélection, Jazz Today, Kaleidoscope, Mode and Mondio Music.

Vogue recorded all the great figures of jazz who passed through Paris to perform in concerts: Louis Armstrong, Sidney Bechet, Buck Clayton, Bill Coleman, Duke Ellington, Dizzy Gillespie, Coleman Hawkins, Thelonious Monk and Max Roach. However, the company established its success with the recordings of Sidney Bechet after he settled in France.

French jazz found a place in Vogue's lists with the notable recordings of Django Reinhardt, the Quintet of the Hot Club of France, Alix Combelle, Claude Luter and his Orchestra, and Martial Solal.

Vogue lists subsequently diversified to include all musical genres, from classical to international pop: from Albinoni to Petula Clark, from Frédéric François and Christian Vidal to Françoise Hardy and Marc Ogeret, from the *Musée de l'Homme* collection to Johnny Hallyday, and from Jacques Dutronc to Claude-Michel Schönberg.

Vogue changed ownership in the mid-1980s, when it became insolvent and was rescued by Jean-Louis Detry with the aid of a government loan. At this point, it was the French distributor for such labels as Buddah (US), Sugarhill (US), Sonet (Sweden) and Mute (UK). Vogue was bought out in 1992 by the German group BMG.

Discography

Armstrong, Louis. *Pasadena Concert (Gene Norman Presents)*. Vogue 600007. *1956*: France.

Bechet, Sidney. *Sidney Bechet in Paris, Vol. 1*. Vogue 68357. 1953: France.

Bechet, Sidney, with Luter, Claude, and His Orchestra. 'Buddy Bolden Story.' Vogue V 5014. 1948: France.

Clark, Petula. *C'est Ma Chanson*. Vogue 670042. *1988*: France.

Clayton, Buck. *Buck Clayton in Paris*. Vogue 68358. 1949–53; *1995*: France.

Combelle, Alix, and His Orchestra. 'Ton mariage.' Vogue V 3273. 1953: France.

Disques Vogue in Paris: Highlights. RCA 68217. *1995*: France.

Dutronc, Jacques. *Complètement Dutronc*. Vogue 32482. *1996*: France.

Ellington, Duke. *At the Blue Note in Chicago*. Vogue VG 651. 1958; *1985*: France.

Gillespie, Dizzy. *Dizzy Gillespie in Paris, Vol. 2*. Vogue 68361. 1952–53; *1995*: France.

Gillespie, Dizzy, and Roach, Max. *Dizzy Gillespie & Max Roach in Paris*. Vogue 68213. 1948–49; *1995*: France.

Hardy, Françoise. *L'Intégrale Disques Vogue 1962–1967* (4-CD set). Vogue 7432132377. *1995*: France.

Hawkins, Coleman, and Hodges, Johnny. *Coleman Hawkins and Johnny Hodges in Paris*. Vogue 68215. 1949–50; *1995*: France.

Monk, Thelonious, and Turner, Joe. *Thelonious Monk and Joe Turner in Paris*. Vogue 68210. 1952–54; *1995*: France.

Ogeret, Marc. *Imagine*. Vogue LDA 20230. *1976*: France.

Reinhardt, Django. *Django Reinhardt/Sidney Bechet – Deux Géants du Jazz*. Vogue 655611. *1957*: France.

Reinhardt, Django, and Grappelli, Stéphane. *Nuages*. Vogue 670205. 1936–40: France.

Solal, Martial. *Martial Solal with the Kentonians*. Vogue 65007. *1956*: France.

GIUSY BASILE (trans. JOHN SHEPHERD)

—Windham Hill (US)

Founded in California in 1977 by guitarist Will Ackerman, Windham Hill became virtually synonymous with 'new age' instrumental music. Its first release was an album of Ackerman's acoustic music. Among the most commercially successful Windham Hill releases was a series of albums by pianist George Winston evoking the seasons, Mark Isham's mixture of electronic and acoustic instruments, and recordings by the jazz-influenced group Shadowfax.

During the 1980s, Windham Hill added subsidiary labels, such as Rabbit Ears (audio books for children), Open Air (vocal recordings by Jane Siberry, the Nylons, Ian Matthews, Tuck and Patti, and others), Living Music (devoted to Paul Winter's jazz-fusion music) and contemporary jazz labels Hip Pocket and Magenta. The label was also renowned for the quality of its sleeve art, with many albums using artistic nature photographs.

Windham Hill recordings found a significant international audience, particularly in Japan. In the early 1990s, Ackerman sold 50 percent of Windham Hill to BMG, and in 1996 BMG became sole owner of the company.

DAVE LAING

—Word (US)

The largest record company in the Christian and gospel music sector of the US music industry, Word was founded in 1950. It subsequently signed both white and black artists to the Word label, as well as distributing releases from numerous other labels such as Light, Reunion, Myrrh and Marantha. With a strong presence in distribution through Christian bookstores, Word has also formed distribution agreements with mainstream music distributors such as CBS/Epic in the 1960s and A&M in the 1980s.

In the 1950s and 1960s, the company made its greatest impact with classic gospel singers such as Shirley Caesar and the Rev. Milton Brunson. In 1975, Word signed its most successful crossover artist, the white singer-songwriter Amy Grant, whose albums would appear in the *Billboard* pop charts. Subsequently, Word signed such contemporary Christian acts as Ray Boltz and Petra, Christian music's most enduring rock band. Numerous albums issued by Word or its distributed labels have been nominated for Grammy awards.

The company is owned by Nashville media group Gaylord, which bought Word in 1996 from bible publisher Thomas Nelson, which in turn had purchased the company from the radio group Capital Cities/ABC in 1992 for $72 million. Word's turnover in 1992 reached $100 million.

Word has a children's music and video division, Everland Entertainment, and the company established a country music division in 1995. The company also has a music publishing division, which includes the company founded by the early twentieth-century evangelist Homer Rodeheaver. Word has branches in Canada, Australia and the United Kingdom.

Discography

Boltz, Ray. *Moments for the Heart*. Word 5473. *1992*: USA.

Brunson, Rev. Milton, and the Thompson Community Singers. *Available to You*. Word EK-47761. *1988*: USA.

Caesar, Shirley. *Rejoice*. Word MYR 1104. *1980*: USA.

Grant, Amy. *Age to Age*. Myrrh/Word MYR 1124. *1982*: USA.

Our Hymns. Word EK-47742. *1989*: USA.

Petra. *Beyond Belief*. Dayspring/Word EK-48546. *1990*: USA.

DAVE LAING

—Yazoo (US)

Yazoo was a reissue record label devised and managed by Nick Perls from New York. Its initial five long-playing (LP) discs were issued by Belzona Records, but the similarity of the company's name to that of the early Beltona label necessitated a change of title. Belzona (or Belzoni) in Mississippi was where the archetypal songster-blues singer Charley Patton was imprisoned, and the permanent retention of early blues on record was implicit in the name. The label's new name referred to the Yazoo river, town and railroad, immortalized on the US map as the boundary of the Mississippi Delta, and in the song by W.C. Handy entitled 'Yellow Dog Blues.'

Prior to the appearance of Yazoo, the Origin Jazz and Herwin labels had been devoted to reissues of important blues dubbed from rare 78 rpm records. Such 'collector' labels, compiled by collectors with the intention of sharing the music they valued with other, less fortunate, enthusiasts, had, since the early 1950s, flourished on 78 rpm and, later, on 10″ (25 cm) and 12″ (30 cm) microgroove records. What made Yazoo releases special was the impeccable selection of records for reissue, their high musical value and, when compared to other labels, the remarkable quality of the reproduction of the originals. This was a result of Perls's policy of obtaining only 78s in excellent or, in many cases, mint and virtually unplayed condition, even if this involved offering the highest prices to secure them.

Belzona/Yazoo issues were devoted at first to miscellaneous collections of classic items recorded in, or representative of, states such as Mississippi, Alabama and Georgia, or recorded in locations like Memphis, Jackson and St. Louis. Subsequent issues were committed to specific and suitably prolific artists, such as 'Blind' Willie McTell, Bo Carter, 'Big' Bill Broonzy, Frank Stokes, Mississippi John Hurt, Charley Patton (a two-LP set) and the Rev. Gary Davis, a sacred singer. Perls and his team of collectors also compiled issues based on themes such as guitar ragtime, blues duets, hokum blues, country religious music, string ragtime and blues harmonica. A strong preference for guitarists and a focus on the minutiae of guitar technique tended to color both the selection and the emphasis of the sleeve notes. This interest inspired a subsidiary label, Blue Goose, 'a Division of Yellow Bee Productions, Inc.,' produced by Perls from a King Street, New York address; it was devoted to new recordings by veterans such as Bill Williams, Sam Chatmon and Yank Rachell, and sets by younger players such as Larry Johnson, Graham Hine and John Miller, the latter two guitarists being white.

The premature death of Nick Perls in 1987 brought the series to a halt and raised doubts as to its future. In the early 1990s, however, a reissue program of the original LP compilations, digitally remastered for compact disc release, was introduced by Shanachie Records, a company that also issued a range of ethnic and special-interest discs. Under Shanachie's auspices, a Yazoo Piano Blues series based on the collection of Francis Wilford-Smith appeared, while 'old-time,' cowboy, jazz, Yiddish and African issues were also marketed in separate numerical series under the Yazoo banner.

Sheet Music

Handy, W.C., comp. 1914. 'Yellow Dog Rag.' Memphis, TN: Pace Handy. Reissued as: Handy, W.C., comp. 1918. 'Yellow Dog Blues.' New York: Pace Handy.

Discographical Reference

Handy, W.C. 'Yellow Dog Blues.' *W.C. Handy's Memphis Blues Band*. Memphis Archives 7006. 1917–23; *1994*: USA.

Discography

Broonzy, 'Big' Bill. *Do That Guitar Rag, 1928–35*. Yazoo L1035. *1973*: USA. Reissue: Broonzy, 'Big' Bill. *Do That Guitar Rag, 1928–35*. Yazoo CD 1035. *1992*: USA.

Carter, Bo. *Banana in Your Fruit Basket*. Yazoo L1064. *1979*: USA. Reissue: Carter, Bo. *Banana in Your Fruit Basket*. Yazoo CD 1064. *1991*: USA.

Chatmon, Sam. *The Mississippi Sheik*. Blue Goose 2006. *1971*: USA.

Davis, Rev. Gary. *Reverend Gary Davis, 1935–49*. Yazoo L1023. *1970*: USA.

Davis, Rev. Gary. *The Complete Early Recordings*. Yazoo CD 2011. *1994*: USA.

Hine, Graham. *Bottleneck Blues*. Blue Goose 2002. *1970*: USA.

Hurt, Mississippi John. *1928 Sessions*. Yazoo L1065. *1979*: USA. Reissue: Hurt, Mississippi John. *1928 Sessions*. Yazoo CD 1065. *1990*: USA.

Johnson, Larry. *Fast and Funky*. Blue Goose 2001. *1970*: USA. Reissue: Johnson, Larry. *Fast and Funky*. Baltimore Blues Society BBS 100. *1997*: USA.

McTell, 'Blind' Willie. *The Early Years*. Yazoo 1005. *1968*: USA. Reissue: McTell, 'Blind' Willie. *The Early Years*. Yazoo CD 1005. *1989*: USA.

Miller, John. *First Degree Blues*. Blue Goose 2007. *1972*: USA.

Patton, Charley. *Founder of the Delta Blues*. Yazoo L1020. *1970*: USA. Reissue: Patton, Charley. *Founder of the Delta Blues*. Yazoo CD 2010. *1990*: USA.

Stokes, Frank. *Frank Stokes Dream (Memphis Blues Anthology)*. Yazoo L1008. *1968*: USA. Reissued as Stokes, Frank. *Memphis Blues*. Yazoo CD 1008. *1991*: USA.

Williams, Bill. *Low and Lonesome*. Blue Goose 2004. *1970*: USA.

PAUL OLIVER

—Zafiro (Serdisco) (Spain)

Zafiro (Serdisco), a Spanish record company, was founded in the mid-1960s. It did not have a licensing agreement to release records by foreign singers or groups, so it entered the market with a series of previously unrecorded artists – a strategy that constituted a risk. In a few years, Zafiro, together with Hispavox, became one of the most important record companies for the popular music of young Spanish people during the 1960s and 1970s. Its first major success in terms of sales was an album by Los Llopis, a Cuban group that covered US rock 'n' roll successes. Zafiro, trying to reproduce the success of English groups, promoted Los Brincos, a Spanish group, with more success during the 1970s. It also contracted Marisol, Dyango, Los Pájaros Locos, Rosalía, Micky y Los Tonys and Massiel, among others. In 1967, it obtained an exclusive contract for all the songs in the Spanish language of Joan Manuel Serrat, who until then had recorded only in Catalan.

By the end of the 1970s, sales of Zafiro's original roster of groups were in decline and, at the suggestion of DJ Mariscal Romero, the company founded Chapa Discos in 1978 to release music by a new generation of pop and rock groups. The label enjoyed success with Barón Rojo, Leño and Asfalto, who were later transferred to the main Zafiro label.

During the 1980s, Zafiro contracted performers of the new Spanish pop, such as Paraíso and Los Elegantes, and changed its name to Serdisco. It has been one of the few Spanish record companies to compete successfully with and resist the dominance of the multinational record companies.

Bibliography

Irles, Gerardo. 1997. ¡Sólo para fans! La música ye-yé y pop española de los años 60 [Only for Fans: Spanish Ye-Yé and Pop Music of the 1960s]. Madrid: Alianza Editorial.

Jones, Daniel E. 1988. 'La industria fonográfica: cima de las transnacionales' [The Record Industry: The Top Transnationals]. In Las industrias culturales en España [The Cultural Industries of Spain], ed. Enrique Bustamante and Ramón Zallo. Madrid: Akal.

Ordovás, Jesús. 1986. Historia de la música pop española [The History of Spanish Pop Music]. Madrid: Alianza Editorial.

Pardo, José Ramón. 1975. Historia del pop español [The History of Spanish Pop]. Madrid: Guía del ocio.

Discography

Barón Rojo. Siempre estais allí. Serdisco 30112630. 1991: Spain.

Leño. Leño. Chapa-Zafiro 30112175. 1979: Spain.

Los Brincos. 29 grandes éxitos. Zafiro-Serdisco 50000119. 1992: Spain.

Marisol. Marisol. Zafiro-Novola ZL-237. 1978: Spain.

Micky y Los Tonys. Megatón ye-yé. Zafiro NL-1002. 1965: Spain.

Serrat, Joan Manuel. Álbum de oro. Zafiro-Serdisco EP-002. 1981: Spain.

JULIO ARCE

—ZTT (UK)

Best known for its recordings of Frankie Goes To Hollywood (FGTH), ZTT was a British record label founded in 1983 by producer Trevor Horn and business manager Jill Sinclair; journalist Paul Morley was also involved in the enterprise from the beginning. The name ZTT (Zang Tuum Tuum) came from a work by the Italian futurist poet Marinetti. FGTH was an immediate succès de scandale with its Horn-produced tracks 'Relax' and 'Two Tribes.' The label's roster also included Grace Jones and The Art of Noise, whose personnel included film music composer Anne Dudley.

In 1986, ZTT bought the Stiff label, whose catalog included albums by Ian Dury and Lene Lovich. After FGTH split up in 1987, Warner Music (UK) purchased a 50 percent interest in the label. ZTT's most successful subsequent act was Seal, whose contract was transferred to Warner when ZTT became fully independent again in 1997. In July 1998, ZTT signed a distribution agreement with Universal Music for the United States and Canada.

Discographical References

Frankie Goes To Hollywood. 'Relax.' ZTT ZTAS 1. 1983: UK.

Frankie Goes To Hollywood. 'Two Tribes.' ZTT ZTAS 3. 1984: UK.

Discography

Art of Noise, The. (Who's Afraid of?) The Art of Noise!. ZTT ZTTIQ2. 1984: UK.

Jones, Grace. Slave to the Rhythm. ZTT GRACE 1. 1985: UK.

Seal. Seal. ZTT ZTT 9. 1991: UK.

DAVE LAING

—Zyx Music (Germany)

Zyx Music is a German independent record company with subsidiaries in most European countries (Switzerland, The Netherlands, Poland, Austria, France, Italy, the United Kingdom, Sweden) and the United States. With headquarters in Merenberg, Hesse, the company was founded in 1971 by Bernhard Mikulski. The slogan 'Musik aus Leidenschaft' ('Music for the love of it') motivated Mikulski to start importing and distributing popular music. Named Zyx Music in 1992, the company quickly began to expand through licensing contracts with other independent labels and distributors. After Austria became a member of the European Union in 1995, Zyx bought the majority of Echo (now trading under Echo-Zyx). Since March 1999, Zyx has licensed all activities of Arcade Music Germany, and in April 2001 Zyx took responsibility for the distribution, promotion and marketing of the Swedish jazz label Touche Music in the German-speaking territories. The record company also comprises a manufacturing plant and a successful publishing arm, Musikverlag Bernhard Mikulski, known especially for its techno and dance catalog. The business is now run by Christa Mikulski, who took over the company's direction after the death of its founder (her husband) in 1997.

Described by *Billboard* in 1994 as one of the most successful indie labels, Zyx Music achieved its third number one hit in a row with the single 'Cotton Eye Joe' by the Swedish act Rednex, which sold 1.7 million copies; the group is now signed to Zomba Records. Zyx has also had 10 songs on the German singles charts simultaneously with hits such as Whigfield's 'Saturday Night' and Mo-Do's 'Eins, Zwei, Polizei.' Since the year 2000, Zyx's most successful artist has been Gigi D'Agostino, with his Italo-disco sound. His bestselling double album *L'Amour Toujours* contains all his major hit singles: his first success, 'Bla, Bla, Bla,' his second release, 'The Riddle' (a cover version of the Nik Kershaw song) and 'La Passion.'

Web Sites

Billboard. http://www.billboard.com
Mediabiz. http://www.mediabiz.de
Zyx Music. http://www.zyx.de

Discographical References

D'Agostino, Gigi. 'Bla, Bla, Bla.' Zyx 9030-12. *2000*: Germany.
D'Agostino, Gigi. *L'Amour Toujours.* Zyx 20536-2. *2001*: Germany.
D'Agostino, Gigi. 'La Passion.' Zyx 9245-8. *2001*: Germany.
D'Agostino, Gigi. 'The Riddle.' Zyx 9133-8. *2001*: Germany.
Mo-Do. 'Eins, Zwei, Polizei.' Zyx 9063-8. *1994*: Germany.
Rednex. 'Cotton Eye Joe.' Zyx 7380-8. *1994*: Germany.
Whigfield. 'Saturday Night.' Zyx 7191-8. *1994*: Germany.

VANESSA BASTIAN

Record Manufacture

The stages in the manufacture of vinyl records and compact discs (CDs) are surprisingly similar. Of course, the process begins with the making of a master recording. As the musicians perform, the acoustic energy radiated by their vocal cords or instruments, modified to some extent by the hall or studio acoustics, is converted into electrical signals by one or more microphones. A microphone is like a loudspeaker in reverse, having a lightweight diaphragm which vibrates in accordance with the sound waves and generates a small electrical voltage that can be amplified, mixed and corrected as necessary in a control console.

The signal, now in analog or digital form, can be sent to a sound recorder, which will usually be a magnetic tape machine, though optical disc recorders are also used, for storage and subsequent playback. The usual procedure is to record all 'takes' and subsequent 'overdubs,' and then edit together the final version at a postproduction stage.

For classical music, the aim is to get as close as possible to the balance and spatial spread of a live concert in ideal acoustics. Therefore, simple microphone techniques are used and venues chosen for their acoustic attributes. In popular music, separation between individual voices and instruments is vital, plus sharp 'attack,' and a close multi-microphone technique is preferred, along with multitrack recorders. The mixdown stage then allows each track to be sweetened by filtering, adding artificial reverberation and 'panning' to a chosen position across the stereo stage.

For vinyl LP manufacture, the final edited tape or disc is then copied to a master disc, called a lacquer or acetate, on a lathe whose cutting stylus etches an equivalent (analog) waveform into a spiraling groove. This lacquer disc is first sprayed with silver to make it electrically conductive, and then submitted to a series of nickel electroplating processes that produce successive metal-plated discs as follows:

(a) a 'Father' which, when separated from the lacquer, is a negative with ridges instead of grooves, and which can be used as a mold to press a limited number of records;

(b) a 'Mother,' which is a positive and can be played for checking purposes, before 'growing' the required number of stampers one after the other;

(c) a mold or stamper, which again is a negative to be used for mass-production of records.

The two stampers for Sides A and B are placed in the jaws of a thermoplastic press or injection molding machine, along with the labels, suitably centered, and a precisely weighed 'biscuit' or granules of the vinyl material. The pressing cycle of 20 seconds or less involves preheating, closing under high pressure so that the vinyl flows into the stamper groove cavities, cooling and ejection of the final labeled disc.

For CDs, the production master recording is naturally in digital form, with a stream of pulses replacing the continuous analog waveform, and the lacquer Father is replaced by a glass disc with a photosensitive coating. As the master recording is replayed, a laser beam is focused onto the coating and interrupted in accordance with the bitstream to expose a series of tiny areas along a spiraling track. Then, as in photograph developing, the coating is dissolved away to leave pits in the surface.

As in vinyl disc production, this glass master begins a series of electroplating stages to provide a nickel Father from which the Mother and successive stampers can be produced. A high-speed automated press then stamps out discs of clear polycarbonate with the required spiral of pits onto which a reflective metal layer is deposited, followed by a protective layer of lacquer and label printing.

The manufacture of tape cassette recordings (strictly speaking, 'records') is complicated by the fact that each tape must be run through to be individually recorded along its whole length, rather than molded in a single operation. The production master tape is wound as an endless loop and run at 32 or 64 times normal speed. The output signal is relayed to racks of slave recorders carrying large reels or 'pancakes' of cassette tape. About 20 complete programs are copied in turn, recording both Sides A and B simultaneously. This tape has then to be spliced into cassette housings, called C-zeros, which are finally labeled and packaged into the standard library cases.

Bibliography

Audio Engineering Society (AES). 1981. *Disc Recording – An Anthology*, Vols. 1 and 2. New York: AES.

Borwick, John. 1994. *Sound Recording Practice.* 4th ed. Oxford: Oxford University Press.

Eargle, J. 1992. *Handbook of Recording Engineering.* New York: Van Nostrand Reinhold Co.

Gelatt, Roland. 1977. *The Fabulous Phonograph.* 2nd ed. New York: Macmillan.

Woram, John M. 1982. *Sound Recording Handbook.* New York: Howard W. Sams.

JOHN BORWICK

rpm

'rpm' (revolutions per minute) indicates the rotational speed of any motor-driven disc (or cylinder) record/playback system. In the case of phonographs, gramophones or jukeboxes, where the rotational speed determines the musical pitch of the sounds being reproduced, it is clearly essential that the speed used for playback is precisely the same as that used when making the original recording. Otherwise, the music will sound sharp or flat and, of course, the tempo will be wrong.

Exactly the same situation arises in any linear medium such as tape or film, where running speed is usually

quoted in inches per second (ips). Occasionally, playing at the wrong speed can be used for special effect. The high-pitched voices of the late 1950s novelty recording act, the Chipmunks, for example, were achieved by getting the voices to speak or sing slowly at normal pitch during the recording and then running the tape at double speed.

In the early days of acoustic recording on cylinders or discs (invented respectively by Thomas Edison and Emile Berliner), there was little or no standardization, and speeds between about 60 and 90 rpm were common. Home record players therefore needed motors with a variable speed governor, which the user could set by ear or by reference to the rpm figure printed on the label.

When electrical recording took over from the old acoustic-horn recording method around 1925, the need for standardization soon became apparent, and the industry agreed on 78 rpm, the speed then used by Victor and some other labels. In practise, the use of an electrical motor synchronized to the 60 Hz US mains supply and with a 46:1 toothed gear ratio gave a speed of 78.26 rpm (77.92 rpm in 50 Hz countries like the United Kingdom). This had the effect of making US records exported to Britain sound slightly flat, and it is alleged that Victor deliberately introduced a policy of recording at 76 rpm during the 1920s and 1930s so that its records would have more 'zing' than EMI's British discs.

When Columbia Records launched their long-playing records (LPs) in June 1948, they chose a running speed of 33 1/3 rpm as part of the move toward a sixfold increase in playing time (the rest of the increase coming from packing 240 grooves to the inch instead of the 100 grooves on 78 rpm records). Some die-hards saw the change to 33 1/3 rpm as a retrograde step, since a slower running speed in any analog recording medium has the effect of compressing the recorded waveform and making it difficult to scan the upper frequencies. This explains the 'end of side' distortion noticeable on both 78s and LPs. The constant rotational speed inevitably means that the linear speed of the groove under the needle or stylus progressively slows down toward the center of the record and the upper sound frequencies become weaker.

However, as soon as suitable phono cartridges for LPs came along, their superiority over 78s became apparent. The full frequency bandwidth of 20–20,000 Hz could be reproduced for the first time, as well as something approaching the dynamic range of sound-pressure levels experienced at a concert.

A compromise speed of 45 rpm was introduced for 7" (18 cm) singles by Columbia's rival, RCA-Victor, in February 1949, so that consumers had to buy a three-speed record player (phonograph). Indeed, there was brief interest around 1956 in a fourth speed of 16 2/3 rpm, for which a few extra-long-playing discs were issued of the Talking Book variety, where a frequency range of up to 3,000 Hz (the telephone range) was considered adequate.

Record players became simpler after a few years when both the 16 2/3 and 78 rpm speeds became obsolete: 12" (30 cm) LPs and a few 10" (25 cm) 33 1/3 rpm issues covered most musical repertoire, while 7" (18 cm) 45 rpm singles playing for up to 7.5 minutes suited in particular the popular music and jukebox markets.

The compact disc (CD), launched jointly by Philips and Sony in Japan in 1982, and 1983 elsewhere, was the first digital 'music carrier' available to the record industry. It broke with tradition in using a constant linear speed of around 1.2 meters per second. The rotational speed for CDs therefore had to begin high, about 500 rpm at the center of the disc, and fall steadily to about 200 rpm at the outer edge.

Bibliography

Audio Engineering Society (AES). 1981. *Disc Recording – An Anthology*, Vols. 1 and 2. New York: AES.

Borwick, John. 1994. *Sound Recording Practice*. 4th ed. Oxford: Oxford University Press.

Eargle, J. 1992. *Handbook of Recording Engineering*. New York: Van Nostrand Reinhold Co.

Gelatt, Roland. 1977. *The Fabulous Phonograph*. 2nd ed. New York: Macmillan.

Woram, John M. 1982. *Sound Recording Handbook*. New York: Howard W. Sams.

JOHN BORWICK

78

'78' is an alternative generic term for the type of phonograph record in use from the beginning of the twentieth century until soon after the 1948 launch of the long-playing vinyl records that rendered 78 rpm discs obsolete. It refers to the nominal running speed of the record in revolutions per minute. At first, the term was not strictly accurate, as record manufacturers adopted various nonstandard speeds between about 60 and 90 rpm. However, the industry agreed to standardize at 78 rpm soon after electrical recording was introduced in 1925.

Bibliography

Audio Engineering Society (AES). 1981. *Disc Recording – An Anthology*, Vols. 1 and 2. New York: AES.

Borwick, John. 1994. *Sound Recording Practice*. 4th ed. Oxford: Oxford University Press.

Eargle, J. 1992. *Handbook of Recording Engineering*. New York: Van Nostrand Reinhold Co.

Gelatt, Roland. 1977. *The Fabulous Phonograph*. 2nd ed. New York: Macmillan.

Woram, John M. 1982. *Sound Recording Handbook*. New York: Howard W. Sams.

JOHN BORWICK

Single

The single is a recording format (or configuration) typically marked by its shorter recording time compared to the extended recording time of the album. While the longer period of time available on the modern 12" (30 cm) vinyl or CD single renders this distinction somewhat imprecise, the term 'single' generally refers to the smallest unit of popular music available in the retail marketplace.

For the first half of the twentieth century, the 10" (25 cm) 78 rpm record, with approximately four minutes per side, was the mainstay of the record industry. By the 1940s, individual 78 rpm recordings – that is, those not sold in multiple-disc sets as part of albums – had come to be known as singles. The 7" (18 cm) 45 rpm record, introduced by RCA-Victor in 1949, had supplanted the 78 as the preferred medium of the single by the mid-1950s. Thus, until the early 1980s, 'single' effectively meant a 7" (18 cm) 45 containing one song (approximately four minutes of music) per side. (The 45 rpm extended play (EP), introduced in 1951, contained approximately two to three songs per side.)

Like the 78 before it, the 45 was the core format for jukeboxes. It was also the unit whose popularity the hit parade or Top 40 radio formats were said to measure. The distinction between single and album was at times taken to refer to the difference between the single's more 'commercial' function – as either a short-lived bid for immediate popularity or a kind of advertisement or trailer for an album – and the album's more 'artistic' connotations.

Whereas previously the popular song (as a text embodied in sheet music or live radio performance or on the 78) had been the basic commodity of the music industry, the 45's ascendancy in the last half of the twentieth century helped to consolidate an important transition from the song to the record (or recording) as the foundation of the music industry. By the end of the 1980s, the introduction and popularization of new single formats, such as the 12" (30 cm) vinyl single, the CD single and the so-called 'cassingle' (a cassette tape containing two or three songs), had challenged the primacy of the 45 rpm vinyl record. In this process, the recording as text had become increasingly separated from the medium or format in which it was physically embodied as a commodity.

By the end of the 1990s, the production of singles (in vinyl, cassette or CD form) had declined in most countries, although the rate of this decline varied significantly from one national market to another. As the 7″ (18 cm) vinyl single has virtually disappeared and the CD single has failed to replace it entirely (particularly in such national markets as the United States and Canada), the continued need to focus on one or more songs from an album as the centerpiece of promotional strategy and radio airplay has led the industry to accept that individual tracks may be eligible for popularity charts on the basis of airplay alone.

The 12″ (30 cm) vinyl single was introduced in 1975 by RCA Records as a professional and promotional tool exclusively available to disc jockeys (DJs) working in dance clubs. By extending a single song across a record as large as an album, producers were able to offer the expanded audio ranges appropriate to increasingly sophisticated nightclub sound systems. As well, by lengthening musical tracks to seven or eight (or even 15) minutes, producers could remix that song, not only to foreground its rhythmic elements, but also to ensure that it opened and closed with extended instrumental breaks, allowing nightclub DJs to segue smoothly from one record to another without the interference of vocals.

By 1976, and with the release of 'Ten Percent' by the studio group Double Exposure, 12″ (30 cm) dance singles were being issued to the commercial market. Their popularity among dance music fans led to accusations that 12″ (30 cm) single sales were 'cannibalizing,' or cutting into, the sales of disco albums and threatening the commercial viability of disco music.

By the 1980s, the 12″ (30 cm) single had become the focus of a parallel music industry and a new creative underground. Its function was no longer limited to that of offering remixed versions of songs whose 'real' or original versions were elsewhere (on albums or 7″ (18 cm) singles). Increasingly, dance tracks, released only as 12″ (30 cm) singles and bearing little textual resemblance to traditional song forms, were serving as the basis for new kinds of musical experimentation and live performance (as in scratching by hip-hop DJs). Just as the 12″ (30 cm) single became the focus of parallel structures of production, distribution and review, so it nourished musical genres (such as house) whose viability in album form or mainstream broadcast media has remained doubtful.

Despite the single's decline as a mainstream commercial commodity, most notably in North America, the form has survived by aligning itself with relatively stable subcultures and parallel distribution circuits. One of these is the culture of alternative, punk or indie musicians and fans, who have embraced the 7″ (18 cm) vinyl single as an anti-commercial 'orphan' technology – a format on which the early history of rock 'n' roll is inscribed, but which was abandoned as rock matured into an album-based art form. Like the 12″ (30 cm)

single, which has become the focus for new forms of musical production and consumption, the 7″ (18 cm) single has been newly fetishized for its tactile, artisanal qualities and for the commercial marginality that has come to mark it.

Discographical Reference

Double Exposure. 'Ten Percent.' Salsoul 2008. *1976*: USA.

KEIR KEIGHTLEY and WILL STRAW

Sleeve Notes

Sleeve notes or liner notes were the texts that appeared on the reverse of the cover of LPs from the early 1950s onward. Sometimes, the notes or song lyrics also appeared on an 'insert' or separate sheet of paper or card tucked inside the album cover.

During the 1950s, sleeve-note writing developed into a minor literary form in the United States, notably in the jazz field where critics such as Nat Hentoff and Leonard Feather composed short essays to accompany albums. This approach was later extended in the 1970s by, among others, New World Records (Recorded Anthology of American Music, Inc.), whose albums contained extended essays on the theme of the particular album in question, as well as substantial essays on each track. These essays were typically contributed by leading scholars of US music, such as Charles Hamm.

In other parts of the popular music field, however, sleeve notes were often briefer and more utilitarian, limited to a brief definition of the music to be found on an album and a few superlatives. Thus, *Elvis* (1956), the second album by Elvis Presley, included a single paragraph contributed anonymously by RCA executive Chick Crumpacker, which said in part: 'of commercial folk music Presley is the most original singer since Jimmie Rodgers.'

However, the Beatles' debut album, *Please Please Me* (1963), contained a thousand-word note by Tony Barrow, while the Rolling Stones' *Between the Buttons* (1967) included a text based on the language of Anthony Burgess's bestselling novel *A Clockwork Orange*, written by the group's manager Andrew Loog Oldham.

By the late 1960s and the rise of progressive rock, sleeve notes were often abandoned in favor of psychedelic paintings, which were felt to exemplify the spirit of the music.

The miniaturization of later formats for prerecorded music, such as the tape cassette and the compact disc, hastened the demise of sleeve notes (that is, notes contained on the reverse of the album cover), although many CD reissues of older albums are accompanied by scholarly notes and discographies contained in booklets or concertina-style inserts. Indeed, it is arguable that the flood of reissues that occurred in the 1990s brought about a revival in the fortunes of scholarly album notes.

A Grammy award for Best Album Notes (the 'Annotator's Award') was introduced in 1963 (O'Neil 1993). The first winners were Leonard Feather and Stanley Dance for Duke Ellington's *The Ellington Era*. Among later winners of the award were singer Johnny Cash for the pithy notes to his own live album *At Folsom Prison* (1968) and to Bob Dylan's *Nashville Skyline* (1969). Another Dylan album featured in the 1975 Grammys when journalist Pete Hamill won an award for his notes to *Blood on the Tracks*, which compared the singer to W.B. Yeats and William Blake.

Bibliography

Burgess, Anthony. 1962. *A Clockwork Orange*. London: Heinemann.

Davis, Elizabeth A. 1981. *Index to the New World Recorded Anthology of American Music: A User's Guide to the Initial One Hundred Records*. New York: W.W. Norton.

O'Neil, Thomas. 1993. *The Grammys: For the Record*. New York and London: Penguin.

Discographical References

Beatles, The. *Please Please Me*. Parlophone PMC 1202. *1963*: UK. Reissue: Beatles, The. *Please Please Me*. Capitol C2–46435. *1987*: USA.

Cash, Johnny. *At Folsom Prison*. Columbia CS 9639. *1968*: USA. Reissue: Cash, Johnny. *At Folsom Prison*. Sony 65955. *1999*: USA.

Dylan, Bob. *Blood on the Tracks*. Columbia PC 33235. *1975*: USA. Reissue: Dylan, Bob. *Blood on the Tracks*. Sony 33235. *1993*: USA.

Dylan, Bob. *Nashville Skyline*. Columbia 09825. *1969*: USA. Reissue: Dylan, Bob. *Nashville Skyline/New Morning/John Wesley Harding*. Sony 65373. *1997*: USA.

Ellington, Duke. *The Ellington Era, Vol. 1*. Columbia C3L-27. *1963*: USA.

Presley, Elvis. *Elvis*. RCA-Victor AFL-1 1382. *1956*: USA. Reissue: Presley, Elvis. *Elvis*. RCA 5199. *1990*: USA.

Rolling Stones, The. *Between the Buttons*. Decca SKL 4852. *1967*: UK. Reissue: Rolling Stones, The. *Between the Buttons*. London 844 468-2. *1995*: UK.

DAVE LAING

Soundcarrier

Introduction

The recording industry has provided consumers with numerous formats for storing and reproducing sound since the beginning of the twentieth century. These formats have been made possible by advances in the technological means for transferring sound vibrations into another medium.

Mechanical, Electromagnetic and Optical Recording

In 1877, Thomas Alva Edison demonstrated the phonograph, which captured sound vibrations directly onto solid matter – first on tinfoil, then on wax cylinders. The idea was further developed by Emile Berliner, who introduced the gramophone in 1887. The gramophone used a shellac-based disc rather than a wax cylinder as the playback medium, and it was the disc that was eventually to become the industry norm. However, both the phonograph and the gramophone used a stylus attached to a diaphragm to capture sound vibrations and to cut them onto the recording medium. Mechanical recording became the basis of the recording industry for almost 90 years, but the quality of recordings was considerably improved in 1925, when the acoustic process was replaced by electrical recording, using microphones and amplifiers.

In the development of electromagnetic recording on tape, as opposed to that of electrical recording on discs, Valdemar Poulsen had, in 1898, introduced the 'telegraphone.' As with processes of electrical recording, the 'telegraphone' was based on the idea of transferring sound into vibrations in an electric current; however, instead of using the wire to transmit the vibrations into another location, the instrument recorded them as variations of magnetism on steel wire, to be preserved for future playback. Because of the lack of suitable amplifiers, the 'telegraphone' had very limited use, but by the 1930s the development of amplifiers had made possible wire recorders, which were used in broadcasting studios and as dictating machines. When wire was replaced by paper or plastic tape coated with oxide in the 1930s, the modern tape recorder was born. The principle of electromagnetic recording was subsequently extended to include video and data recording.

Optical recording was originally developed for the purposes of the film industry. In this process, developed by Engl, Massolle and Vogt in Germany in the 1920s, the audio signal is recorded on film as variations in lightness and darkness. During playback, the recording is read by a photoelectric cell and converted back to sound.

The three principal systems of sound recording – mechanical, electromagnetic and optical – had thus been established by the 1920s. Over the next 60 years, these technologies were used for a wide variety of purposes, but it was obvious that each of them was especially suited to particular uses. Optical recording was mainly limited to the film industry. It was occasionally also used for recording sound without pictures, but it did not prove practical for this purpose. Mechanical recording, in the form of the disc, became the dominant consumer format. Discs were easy to mass-produce, and they could endure repeated playings. The weak point of the mechanical disc was the difficulty in making recordings. Disc recorders, simplified versions of the disc cutters used in recording studios that could be used to make home recordings on lacquer-coated metal discs, were available in the 1930s and 1940s, but their cost and technical limitations precluded widespread use. Since the 1940s, the most widely used medium for instantaneous recording has been magnetic tape.

Analog Consumer Formats

The first mechanical recording format was the phonograph cylinder, which was originally intended as a home recording device. When the replication of cylinders by molding was perfected by the beginning of the twentieth century, the technology was used with considerable success for the marketing of prerecorded music, but within a few years it was surpassed by disc records. The sound quality of the cylinder was at least equal to that of the disc, and the cylinder phonograph provided the additional possibility of making one's own recordings. However, discs were more easily adapted for mass production than cylinders, and the mass production of discs began shortly after their patenting in 1887, approximately a decade before cylinders began to be replicated. This, together with the relative ease of shipping flat discs and the more aggressive marketing of the disc record companies, probably proved decisive.

At the beginning of the twentieth century, there were several competing, incompatible disc formats on the market, including the Pathé vertical-cut disc (usually 80–100 rpm), the Edison vertical-cut Diamond Disc (80 rpm) and the Berliner lateral-cut disc (originally ca. 70–80 rpm, standardized to 78 rpm in the 1920s), pressed from different materials and requiring different types of playing apparatus. The Berliner disc, pressed from a shellac-based material, had emerged victorious by the 1920s, and to posterity it has become known as 'the 78' rpm disc, most commonly produced in the 10″ (25 cm) size but actually manufactured in sizes ranging from 5″ to 16″ (12 cm to 40 cm) in diameter.

The weak point of the 78 was short playing time – three to five minutes per side – and there were various attempts to overcome this limitation. At first, larger works were marketed on albums of several 78s. The first 33 rpm discs, with slower playing speed giving a longer playing time, were introduced in 1931 by Victor in the United States, but the depressed economic conditions of the time precluded success. In 1948, Columbia (US) reintroduced the 33 rpm disc, and RCA-Victor followed in 1949 with the 45 rpm record, each requiring a dedicated new record player. After a brief 'war of speeds,' the companies decided to join forces and produce players com-

bining both speeds, and by the end of the 1950s the new speeds had become dominant. However, the 78 rpm disc continued to be widely sold in the USSR, India and South America until the 1960s.

The 33 rpm and 45 rpm records had a 'microgroove' cut, requiring a finer and lighter stylus. They were usually pressed on vinyl. Three formats became standard. The 33 rpm long-playing record (LP) was especially well suited to longer works and collections. These LPs, manufactured with individually designed sleeves, were originally produced in 10″ (25 cm) and 12″ (30 cm) sizes, but the latter gradually prevailed. Originally, 45 rpm records that usually carried four titles were also manufactured with individual sleeves. This so-called extended play (EP) format declined after the 1960s, and the main alternative to the LP became the 45 rpm single, usually with a generic sleeve and with one song per side.

In the 1930s and 1940s, tape recorders were expensive instruments designed for professional use. By the mid-1950s, cheaper models for home use had become available, and there were even attempts to distribute prerecorded music to consumers in the form of open-reel tape. However, although this technology offered excellent sound quality, it was difficult to duplicate on a large scale and impractical for home use. Only when it was encased in a plastic cassette or cartridge did tape become a widely accepted consumer format. The cartridge was sold mainly in the United States. The compact cassette, developed by Philips, became the dominant format, because it was practical for home recording and for the distribution of prerecorded music, and by the 1980s it had become the most popular type of soundcarrier worldwide. Open-reel tape was restricted mainly to professional uses, and new formats were developed for multitrack audio and for video recording. After a brief 'battle of formats,' VHS became the dominant consumer format for videotape, and the Beta tape format was relegated to specialized uses. The video laser disc (LD) fared somewhat better, but still presented no serious threat to VHS on the consumer video market.

Digital Recording

A major change occurred in the 1980s when digital recording technology began to replace existing analog formats. The digital technology was available in both tape and disc formats. The main tape format was digital audio tape (DAT). Although a small selection of music recordings was released in the DAT format in the 1980s, DAT never gained acceptance as a consumer format, in part because of opposition from the recording industry. However, DAT has become widely accepted in professional and semiprofessional contexts. Other digital tape formats especially aimed at the consumer market, such as the digital compact cassette (DCC), have failed to make much impact.

On the consumer market, the compact disc (CD) had become the dominant digital format by the 1990s. Developed by Sony and Philips, the CD uses an optical method to record digital audio signals. By 1996, the CD had become the most widely sold type of soundcarrier worldwide: 52 percent of all soundcarriers sold in the world were in this format, while 36 percent were in the form of cassettes and 12 percent were vinyl discs. Recordable CDs (CD-R) also became available.

Two trends in the development of digital audio were apparent in the late 1990s. Firstly, there were attempts to introduce new digital audio formats to replace the CD. The minidisc (MD) had very limited success, but the digital versatile disc (DVD), with both video and audio recording capacity, was expected to reach a mass audience in the late 1990s and to have more success.

Secondly, digital recordings came to be stored in and distributed through computers. In principle, digital recordings can be stored in and distributed through any type of computer memory, but, for a long time, the large storage capacity required for digital audio had favored dedicated audio formats such as the CD. However, with the increase in computer memory capacity, a merging of audio and computer technology became possible.

In recording studios, computer hard discs, magneto-optical discs and special tape formats such as digital linear tape (DLT) had for some time been used for 'tapeless recording.' However, at the end of the twentieth century, the cost of these technologies had made them infeasible for the consumer market. Also, there was not at this time any widely used external memory device usable on home computers that was suitable for the storage of audio, although recordable CD-ROM discs, which can also be used in conjunction with compressed audio files, did show promise of becoming such a medium. However, by the mid-1990s, digital audio had become widely available over the Internet. At the dawn of the twenty-first century, the scene was set for new systems capable of the distribution and marketing of music on demand over the Internet and other data networks, with the potential to cause a decrease in the demand for specialized soundcarriers.

Bibliography

Gronow, Pekka, and Saunio, Ilpo. 1998. *An International History of the Recording Industry*. London: Cassell.

Korentang, Juliana. 1998. *Music on the Internet*. London: Financial Times.

Marco, Guy A., and Andrews, Frank, eds. 1993. *Encyclopedia of Recorded Sound in the United States*. London and New York: Garland Publishing.

Poyser, Tina, ed. 1996. *The Recording Industry in Numbers*. London: IFPI.

Wallis, Roger, and Choi, Cong Ju. 1996. *The Impact of Multimedia on the Entertainment Business: Implications for TV, Video, Music and Games*. London: Financial Times.

PEKKA GRONOW

Soundie

Soundies were three-minute film shorts produced in the United States in the early 1940s for use on a type of visual jukebox. The films featured performances by artists in all genres of popular music and, by means of a series of mirrors, they were back-projected onto a 22 1/2" x 17 1/2" (57 cm x 44 cm) screen mounted on top of a jukebox.

The Mills Novelty Company of Chicago, an established jukebox manufacturer, launched its visual jukebox, the 'Panoram,' at the end of 1940. To supply films, Mills established the Soundies Distributing Corporation of America. Though 'soundie' applies strictly only to the films the corporation distributed, the term is also applied to similar films made for smaller short-lived competing systems, such as Vis-O-Graph and Talk-A-Vision.

Initially, most soundies were sourced from associated companies. Globe Productions began operations in Hollywood as early as July 1940, though distribution began only in January 1941. In March 1941, Mills established Minoco Productions. Globe ceased operations shortly after but, later in 1941, RCM (for James Roosevelt, Sam Coslow and Gordon Mills) Productions was formed.

The films were assembled into reels of eight subjects. Between January 1941 and early 1947, over 1,800 were released, covering a wide range of popular music and entertainment, including jazz and blues, country and western, Latin American and Hawaiian music, musical comedy, vaudeville acts and gymnastics. Budgets soon fell to as little as $750 per subject. As a consequence, soundies preserve the performances of many who failed to attract the attention of the mainstream recording and film industries.

Soundies were included in the American Federation of Musicians' recording ban, launched on 31 July 1942. As a consequence, RCM ran out of prerecorded soundtracks by December. The gap was filled by independent producers who, among other strategies, synchronized performers to old records and used musical numbers cut from feature films. Two reissues were included in each reel, an economical practise not discontinued until February 1945. Soundies Distributing also began direct production under the supervision of William Forest Crouch, formerly head of publicity. This production arm became Filmcraft Productions, producing many later soundies.

Soundies provide an unrivaled documentation of vernacular and jazz dance. Around 300 soundies were by African Americans. The first, by Cee Pee Johnson, was copyrighted on 5 May 1941. Initially, one was included in every third or fourth release of an eight-subject reel, but this soon rose to one per release. Fritz Pollard, a former All-American football halfback, took charge of the African-American catalog in August 1942 and introduced custom reels for specialized locations. William Forest Crouch undertook a further drive to increase the African-American catalog in mid-1943. It includes major documentation of jazz artists, including Louis Armstrong, Cab Calloway, Duke Ellington, Lucky Millinder, Fats Waller, Louis Jordan, the King Cole Trio and the International Sweethearts of Rhythm, as well as many dancers, including Bill Robinson and Mabel Lee.

Restrictions during World War II hampered marketing and, by May 1946, the 10,000 machines reported in June 1943 had dwindled to fewer than 2,500. The last soundies were copyrighted on 30 December 1946, and by mid-1947 distribution had ceased. Many were later marketed to television, and they were also widely distributed in the home-movie market. In the 1990s, many of the most musically interesting items appeared on commercial videos.

Bibliography

Burke, Tony, and Rye, Howard. 1992. 'Louis Jordan on Film.' *Blues & Rhythm: The Gospel Truth* 71: 4–10.

Reuter, Maynard. 1941. 'Movie Machines.' *Billboard* (18 January): 106–107.

Reuter, Maynard. 1944. 'The Future of Juke-Box Pictures.' In *The Billboard 1944 Music Year Book*. New York: Billboard, 124.

Rye, Howard. 1991. Insert notes for 'The Soundies Collection' (VHS videotapes). London: Charly Records.

Stratemann, Klaus. 1981. *Negro Bands on Film. Volume 1: Big Bands 1928–1950, An Exploratory Filmo-Discography*. Lübbecke: Uhle & Kleimann.

Stratemann, Klaus. 1992. *Duke Ellington Day by Day and Film by Film*. Copenhagen: JazzMedia.

Stratemann, Klaus. 1996. *Louis Armstrong on the Screen*. Copenhagen: JazzMedia.

Terenzio, Maurice, MacGillivray, Scott, and Okuda, Ted. 1991. *The Soundies Distributing Corporation of America: A History and Filmography of Their 'Jukebox' Musical Films of the 1940s*. Jefferson, NC and London: McFarland.

'22 New Shorts for Soundies Are Completed.' 1943. *New York Amsterdam News* (21 August): 15.

HOWARD RYE

Videoclip

A videoclip is created when a visual track is added to a sound recording to make a short film for use on television programs or specialist music television networks. Although clips can be shot on film, their production using video became widespread in the music industry when video as a medium became relatively cheap to use during the 1970s.

Alternate names for the videoclip are 'music video' and 'promo' (promotional) or 'promo video.' The latter name emphasizes the function of the video as a marketing tool for a single or album.

DAVE LAING

17. Unions

Musicians' Unions

Musicians have joined together to protect their employment or to seek higher payment and better working conditions since the medieval period in Europe. Today, there are trade unions of musicians in numerous countries and many of them are affiliated with the International Federation of Musicians (FIM).

Beginning in the sixteenth century, professional musicians formed guilds and fraternities to protect their livelihood and to exclude other performers. In Italian city-states, such bodies were set up under the aegis of St. Cecilia and also provided medical assistance and funeral costs for their members (Bianconi 1987, 89). At the beginning of the seventeenth century, the existing Company of Musicians of London was given sweeping powers to regulate music-making in the city, including the authority to imprison anyone found singing 'lascivious' songs (Sanjek 1988, 102).

The first musicians' organizations with modern characteristics appeared in the mid-nineteenth century. Among them was the Musical Mutual Protective Union, founded in New York in 1863. This body arranged work for its members with local employers, as well as operating an insurance scheme. It was a precursor of the largest and most powerful of present-day musicians' unions, the American Federation of Musicians (AFM), which operates in the United States and Canada. Like its British counterpart, the Musicians' Union (MU), the AFM is a general union rather than a craft union. Eligibility for membership is based on proof of paid employment as a musician rather than on the level of musical skills possessed by an applicant.

The AFM was formed in 1896, and by the start of the twentieth century it had 10,000 members and 114 locals (branches). Faced only with small employers without any organizations of their own, the AFM could 'tighten its grip on musical services by imposing price lists and regulating working conditions' (Kraft 1996, 27). From an early stage, US unions campaigned against 'unfair competition' from military bands and tours by foreign musicians (Seltzer 1989, 6). This was also a feature of European unions, notably the British. The latter persuaded the government to withhold work permits from foreigners and, in so doing, prevented many leading US jazz groups from appearing in Britain. This policy was eventually replaced by one of 'exchanges' between US and UK performers, and in the 1960s US jazz musicians toured in exchange for British beat groups.

With the growth of urbanization and the provision of new forms of popular entertainment, including cinema, demand for musical labor grew in the first quarter of the twentieth century, and AFM membership reached a peak of 150,000 in 1928. Subsequent technological changes in the music industry tended toward the mechanization of musical performance, however. In the 1920s, silent cinema gave way to the 'talkies,' and in the 1930s radio stations tended to air networked performances rather than employing local musicians or, even worse, to substitute recorded music for live performances. Both developments meant a loss of employment for musicians that the AFM attempted unsuccessfully to resist and, by 1934, membership had fallen to 100,000. Some temporary redress was achieved in 1937 when a strike threat by the AFM forced many stations to agree to increase their spending on the employment of musicians. At the same time, the AFM secured a doubling of recording session rates.

The new film and record industries provided some work for musicians, and the AFM was able to negotiate minimum fees for the relatively small numbers of

Hollywood soundtrack players (400–500 in the 1930s) and of session musicians in the main recording centers of New York, Los Angeles and (after 1950) Nashville.

The AFM's fight against technological unemployment took a new turn after 1940 when James C. Petrillo became president. He instituted a successful strategy of withdrawal of labor by leading bands from radio networks when AFM members were in dispute with an affiliated station. In 1942, Petrillo announced a ban on the participation of AFM members in recording sessions because '95% of the music in the United States and Canada is canned music. Only 5% is left for the poor professional musician' (Kraft 1996, 135). The ban lasted for two years, until record companies agreed to pay a royalty to the AFM to be used to create employment at free concerts for which instrumentalists would be paid at union scale rates.

In the post-1945 period, the AFM's traditional ability to control local employment and to act as a labor exchange was gradually weakened: a valuable description of this function can be found in Buerkle and Barker (1973). The union has national agreements covering television, film and radio work, in addition to sound-recording sessions. In 2001, the negotiated rate for a three-hour session was $605.70 for a leader or conductor and $302.85 for side musicians. The AFM's membership levels reached a new peak of 320,000 in 1976 before declining again to 231,000 in 1984.

Musicians' unions were formed in a number of European countries at the end of the nineteenth and the beginning of the twentieth centuries. A union of Parisian musicians was founded in 1901, and in 1956 some 30 local unions combined to form the Syndicat National des Artistes Musiciens de France (SNAM).

In Scandinavia, the Norsk Musiker Forbund (Norway) was founded in 1911 and the Finnish Musicians' Union in 1917. About two-thirds of the Finnish union's membership of 3,200 in 2001 were jazz and popular musicians, including DJs. In some European countries, however, musicians from different genres formed separate unions. Thus, there are three organizations in The Netherlands, representing classical musicians, music teachers and popular musicians, respectively. In Germany, the Deutsche Orchestervereinigung e. V. organizes orchestral players, while the music section of the IG Medien union has separate branches for concert musicians and for jazz, rock and pop instrumentalists.

In the United Kingdom, the Amalgamated Musicians' Union was founded in 1893 to resist management proposals to cut the pay of theater musicians in Manchester. In 1921, this body combined with the National Orchestral Union of Professional Musicians to form the MU.

As in North America, European musicians suffered from the introduction of sound films and radio. Membership of the British union fell to 7,000 in 1940, but recruitment drives, particularly among dance band members, increased this to 28,000 in 1949. Membership in the MU had reached 31,000 by the end of the 1990s.

The Musicians' Union of Japan (MUJ) was established in 1983 through the merger of two unions dating from the 1970s. The MUJ has 6,000 members, of whom 2,500 are classical players, 2,500 work in jazz and popular music, and the remainder are teachers, composers and others. The union is one of the larger members of Geidankyo (the Japanese Council of Performers' Organizations), a group of 59 organizations with a total of 60,000 members.

In countries with Communist governments, musicians' unions were generally under the control of state agencies. The last of these was the Chinese Musicians' Association (CMA), founded in 1949. By 2001, it had 34 provincial branches and 9,000 individual members. Its professional committees include one for 'musicians' rights protection.' The re-formed unions of Hungary, Romania, Poland and Croatia were, at the beginning of the twenty-first century, members of the FIM.

In 1948, on the initiative of the Swiss and British, a number of national unions came together to set up the FIM, with offices in Geneva. The offices later moved to Paris. Relations between the FIM and the AFM were uneasy for many years, and the AFM was not affiliated for some time; however, in the mid-1990s, it reaffiliated, but with only a small number of members. At that time, the FIM had member unions in over 30 countries, with a combined membership of over 330,000. In the 1990s, unions from Latin America, the Caribbean and West Africa joined the FIM. Among these were the Jamaica Federation of Musicians & Affiliated Artistes (JFM), with over 2,000 members, and the Musicians' Union of Ghana.

The FIM holds triennial congresses of its members and represents musicians' interests at meetings of global bodies such as the International Labour Organization (ILO) and the World Intellectual Property Organization (WIPO). With the International Federation of Actors (FIA), it played a major role in the establishment of the Rome Convention in 1961. The FIM also collaborates closely with the record industry body, the International Federation of the Phonographic Industry (IFPI), with which it has a mutually beneficial agreement on the collection and distribution of royalties from the exploitation of performing rights in soundcarriers by broadcasters and other music users.

Bibliography

Bianconi, Lorenzo. 1987. *Music in the Seventeenth Century*, trans. David Bryant. Cambridge and New York: Cambridge University Press.

Buerkle, Jack V., and Barker, Danny. 1973. *Bourbon Street Black: The New Orleans Black Jazzman*. New York: Oxford University Press.

Kraft, James P. 1996. *Stage to Studio: Musicians and the Sound Revolution, 1890–1950*. Baltimore, MD: Johns Hopkins University Press.

Leiter, Robert D. 1953. *The Musicians and Petrillo*. New York: Bookman Associates.

Sanjek, Russell. 1988. *American Popular Music and Its Business: The First Four Hundred Years. Vol. I: The Beginning to 1790*. New York and Oxford: Oxford University Press.

Seltzer, George. 1989. *Music Matters: The Performer and the American Federation of Musicians*. Metuchen, NJ: Scarecrow Press.

DAVE LAING

Unions

In addition to instrumentalists, who have formed their own trade unions, other groups of workers associated with the music industry have become unionized and have attempted to reach agreements concerning their conditions of work and remuneration.

The most significant of these unions represent singers who do not qualify for membership of musicians' unions that admit only instrumentalists. In the United States and Canada, many vocalists are members of the American Federation of Television and Radio Artists (AFTRA) and the Alliance of Canadian Cinema, Television and Radio Artists (ACTRA). Among AFTRA's 75,000 members are radio disc jockeys, actors and dancers. The union sets rates for backing vocalists and royalty payments for recording sessions and also represents musicians and actors appearing in music videos shot on tape. If a video is shot on film, the participants are required to be members of the US Screen Actors Guild (SAG) (Baskerville 2001). The American Guild of Variety Artists (AGVA) represents musicians and singers who play the nightclub circuit. In Britain and Australia, most vocalists belong to the actors' organization, Equity.

The live music business in some countries is also subject to union–management agreements that govern the operation of large concert venues. Many stadium staff in the United States and Canada are members of the International Alliance of Theatrical Stage Employees (IATSE). In the United Kingdom, the Broadcasting, Entertainment, Cinematograph and Theatre Union (BECTU) recruits members in all areas of live entertainment and sound engineering. BECTU traces its origins to the United Kingdom Theatrical and Music Hall Operatives' Union, founded in 1890.

Elsewhere in the music industry, workers in the distribution, retail and instrument manufacturing sectors may be unionized. For many years, those engaged in the distribution of soundcarriers and many other goods in the United States were governed by the Teamsters Union. Employees of large retail groups in various countries may be represented by shopworkers' unions. Workers in piano making and other areas of instrument manufacture in the United States have been represented since the 1930s by the United Furniture Workers of America (Lieberman 1995).

Bibliography

Baskerville, David. 2001. *Music Business Handbook and Career Guide*. 7th ed. Thousand Oaks, CA: Sage Publications.

Lieberman, Richard K. 1995. *Steinway & Sons*. New Haven and London: Yale University Press.

DAVE LAING

Index